2018

Getting Financial Aid

2018

CollegeBoard

Getting
Financial Aid

12th Edition
The College Board, New York

The College Board

The College Board is a mission-driven not-for-profit organization that connects students to college success and opportunity. Founded in 1900, the College Board was created to expand access to higher education. Today, the membership association is made up of over 6,000 of the world's leading educational institutions and is dedicated to promoting excellence and equity in education. Each year, the College Board helps more than seven million students prepare for a successful transition to college through programs and services in college readiness and college success — including the SAT® and the Advanced Placement Program®. The organization also serves the education community through research and advocacy on behalf of students, educators, and schools.

For further information, visit www.collegeboard.org.

Editorial inquiries concerning this book should be directed to Guidance Publications, The College Board, 250 Vesey Street, New York, NY 10281; or telephone 800-323-7155.

Copies of this book are available from your local bookseller or may be ordered from College Board Publications, P.O. Box 7500, London, KY 40742-7500. The book may also be ordered online through the College Board Store at www.collegeboard.org. The price is $23.99.

ISBN: 978-1-4573-0924-3

Printed in the United States of America

Distributed by Macmillan. For information on bulk purchases please contact Macmillan Corporate and Premium Sales Department at (800) 221-7945 x5442.

Contents

List of Figures

List of Tables

List of Worksheets

Preface

Financial aid is a great equalizer. In 2016, almost $241 billion in aid was awarded from government and private sources. Coupled with the wide range of lower-cost college options available, financial aid should make a college education affordable for just about everyone.

Yet, according to the American Council on Education, each year *millions* of students who are eligible for this boon don't even apply for it. We assume these students are either unaware of the possibility of aid, or mistakenly believe financial aid is not for them.

And many parents and students who apply for financial aid find the process to be confusing, even intimidating. Like the tax code, the forms and guidelines appear to be full of exceptions, convolutions and incomprehensible terms.

But it doesn't have to be that way. A central aim of this book is to take the confusion and intimidation out of the process by giving clear and direct explanations and simple, step-by-step directions. By combining these explanations and directions with the costs and financial aid facts for every accredited college that reports this data, we hope this book will achieve our ultimate goal of connecting students to colleges that match both their needs and their means.

Acknowledgments

We gratefully acknowledge the many individuals who contributed to this book, including the financial aid officers who lent us their expertise: Vincent Amoroso, Bonnie Lee Behm, Elizabeth Bickford, Joe Paul Case, Mary San Agustin, Mike Scott, and Forrest Stuart. We hope you will find their insight and advice, quoted throughout Part I, as illuminating as we did.

Our resident experts Sandy Baum, Ami Boshardt, Ted Jamieson and Robin Casanova helped update the information in Parts I and II. The descriptions of colleges presented in Part III, "Financial Aid, College by College," were compiled from the College Board's Annual Survey of Colleges in the spring of 2017. The college data were collected, edited and verified by a team of editors led by Chris Hagan, with the guidance of Joe Williams. Jenny Xie, Randy Peery, Kayla Tompkins, David Christ, Karen Villa, Jessica Shaddy, Ivonne Lester, Kelsey Cross, and Blake Bralley compiled, edited and verified the data. Technical support was provided by Assar Tarazi, Susan Redick, Priyanka Sabapathy, and Srinivas Bachu. The team of programmers and typesetters at DataStream Content Solutions, Inc., converted the database into readable pages.

We wish to give special acknowledgment to Renée Gernand, who recently retired. It is with sincere appreciation that we thank her for the leadership and service she gave to both the College Board and the entire higher education community.

Tom Vanderberg, Senior Editor
Guidance Publications

How to Use This Book

Part I: Financial Aid, Step by Step

The first chapter, "Yes, You Can Afford College," establishes our central point: a college can be found to fit any budget. If you are skeptical about that, please start here — we think we make a strong case.

The chapters that follow (Steps 1 through 11) provide easy-to-follow directions on how to get financial aid, including what you need to know, what you need to do, and when you need to do it.

These steps are presented in a logical sequence. But depending upon your own circumstances — where you are in the college application process, what kinds of colleges you're applying to, and the policies of those colleges — you may need to take the steps in a slightly different order, skip some steps, or do some steps simultaneously. A planning calendar on the inside front cover will help you stay on track.

Financial aid forms often use jargon that can at times seem vague or confusing. Throughout Part I, you'll find key terms defined in "Know the Lingo" sidebars (you'll also find a detailed, comprehensive glossary at the end of this book). Other sidebars emphasize or illustrate the main points of each step.

Throughout Part I, you'll find graphs, charts, and tables that summarize information and let you compare different financial aid options. You'll also find checklists and sample worksheets that will help you plan and keep track of your applications.

Part II: Tables and Worksheets

One of the worksheets that you'll find in Part II will help you compare the financial aid award letters that you'll receive from colleges. To drive home the point that no two award letters are alike, we've included two samples of actual award letters that were sent to the same student by two different universities (the names of which we've changed).

Part II also includes a series of worksheets that you can use to estimate how much the federal government will say you should pay for college out of pocket. These worksheets are designed for dependent students and their parents. If you are an independent student, you can do the same thing with the online tools on collegeboard.org. Finally, in Part II you'll find lists of state aid programs, state-sponsored 529 college savings plans and other useful places to find more information.

Part III: Financial Aid College by College

This is where we help you get the "financial aid picture" at specific colleges, including the scholarships they offer to entering students, and their required forms and deadlines. To place this picture in context, we give you brief facts about the kind of college it is, and its basic costs. This information can help you compare the colleges you are considering and find colleges that look affordable. But keep in mind that the financial aid figures are mostly based on averages, meaning many students will be above or below these benchmarks.

The college descriptions in Part III are arranged alphabetically by state or territory. An alphabetical index of all the colleges in the book appears in Part IV.

Every college described in this book is accredited by an agency recognized by the U.S. Department of Education. That's important because only colleges that are accredited by such agencies may distribute federal financial aid to their students.

Where the College Information Comes From

The information in the college descriptions comes from the College Board's most recent Annual Survey of Colleges, which was conducted in the spring of 2017. The information presented was current at the time this book went to press in May 2017 — but be warned that it may have changed by the time you're reading this. Once you have narrowed down a list of colleges that you're interested in, you should confirm critical information, such as financial aid application deadlines and requirements, by visiting the colleges' websites or contacting their financial aid offices.

What's in the College Descriptions

Each college description begins with a shaded box that contains the name of the college, the city or town where it's located, its website address, and its six-digit "federal code" — the code you will need in order to have the information in your FAFSA (Free Application for Federal Student Aid) sent to the college. If a college requires the College Board's CSS/Financial Aid PROFILE®, its four-digit CSS code also appears in this box. (The CSS code is the same code you use to send SAT® and SAT Subject Tests™ scores and AP® Exam scores to a college; the federal code is only used for the FAFSA.)

Below the college name box you'll find a brief summary of what type of college it is — whether it's a four-year private university, a two-year community college or a four-year culinary school run on a for-profit basis. (Definitions of all the different types of schools you might find here are in the glossary.) You'll also find information about the number of students who were enrolled in the 2016–17 school year, and the relative difficulty of obtaining admission to the college.

BASIC COSTS

"Basic Costs" lists the tuition, fees, room and board charged by the college. The date indicates the school year for which these numbers apply — if the college was unable to report final or projected figures for the upcoming school year, the previous year's figures are given. If the college combines tuition, fees, and room and board expenses, that single figure is given as a comprehensive fee.

It's important to note that these figures do not include other out-of-pocket costs, such as books, supplies, transportation and personal expenses. These costs can be substantial, depending upon where and how you live, and what you study. But since these costs vary widely from student to student, we felt it would be misleading to display average amounts.

FINANCIAL AID PICTURE

The core of each college's description is the information about the financial aid it offers. Again, the date indicates the school year for which the college reported numbers — either the current year or the prior year. Depending on the aid programs offered by the college and the figures they reported, you may see one or several of these elements of the financial aid picture:

- **Students with Need.** This shows how financial aid was given to students who could not afford the full cost of attending the college on their own (a full explanation of how "need" is determined is found in Part I, Step 1). The focus is on the entering freshman class, but if a college was unable to provide that breakdown, the numbers are for all undergraduates. Most colleges disclosed the average percentage of need met by financial aid packages, and the relative proportion of aid given as scholarships and grants as opposed to loans or work-study jobs. Use this data to get a sense of how likely a college is to meet your full need, and how much aid will probably come in the form of loans.

- **Students Without Need.** Even though a student does not need financial aid, it's still possible that a college will provide aid based on merit or other criteria, such as alumni affiliation or minority status. That's what is shown here. If a college has a policy of only awarding aid to students who have need, this is also stated here.

- **Scholarships Offered.** This gives details on merit scholarships offered by the college and their criteria for being awarded. Here you can get a sense of whether your GPA or SAT scores put you in the right ballpark for a merit-based grant. You'll also find information about the number of student-athletes who were given a scholarship by the college, and the average award.

- **Cumulative Student Debt.** This tells you how many students borrowed money to pay for college and how much they owed, on average, when they graduated. This is another way for you to measure how much of a college's aid will be loan based. The numbers here only include student loans taken out through the college — not PLUS loans, private education loans or other borrowing done through a third-party lender.

FINANCIAL AID PROCEDURES

The financial aid application forms required by the college, and the priority date and/or deadlines that the financial aid office has set, appear here. This section also includes information about notification — that is, when you can expect to hear back from the financial aid office after applying, and by when they will need your final answer about whether you'll be attending. Unless otherwise noted, all dates given in this section are for applicants who intend to enroll in the fall of 2018. If you plan to apply for admission to the spring 2019 term or later, contact the college's financial aid office to find out about their policies and deadlines.

CONTACT

The final section of each college description lists the mailing address of the school's financial aid office.

Part IV: Scholarship Lists

If you want to zero in on colleges that offer scholarships for your particular talents and interests, the lists in Part IV will help you do that. Arranged alphabetically by state, these lists will point you to colleges that offer scholarships for a variety of achievements. Please note that, in many cases, merit is not the only criterion used by the college when awarding aid: It may require recipients to also demonstrate financial need by submitting the FAFSA or another financial aid form.

At some colleges, every applicant is automatically considered for merit scholarships. At others, you have to specifically apply for a given scholarship. And in some cases, a scholarship is only open to you if you've been recommended by your principal, school counselor or teacher.

What's in the Scholarship Lists

Each list points to colleges that offer aid for a specific talent or area of interest.

Academics. This list names colleges that offer merit aid for academic achievement. Typical criteria include the classes you've taken, your GPA and your standardized test scores.

Art. This list includes colleges that offer merit aid for artistic ability in the visual arts, as reflected by grades in art classes, teacher recommendations and/or a portfolio you submit to the college.

Athletics. If a college offers scholarships for a certain sport, it will be listed here. The letters "M" and "W" indicate whether the scholarship is available to men, women or both.

Music/Drama. This list includes colleges and conservatories that offer merit aid for talent in the performing arts, as reflected by grades in music, dance or drama classes; teacher recommendations; and/or an audition or a submitted tape.

ROTC. Three lists are included here, one each for the Air Force, Army and Naval Reserve Officers' Training Corps. (Marine Corps ROTC is included in Naval ROTC; the Coast Guard and Merchant Marine do not have ROTC programs.) The schools listed may not necessarily have all their ROTC programs on campus; they may have a sponsorship agreement with a neighboring college or university instead. If you enroll in ROTC, you will need to apply separately for the actual ROTC scholarship from the service branch you've chosen — the money doesn't come automatically. Some colleges offer additional institutional scholarships for ROTC candidates from their own funds, beyond what's awarded by the Department of Defense.

Part I

Financial Aid Step by Step

Yes, You Can Afford College

Yes, you can afford college. How do we know? Because most colleges are not as expensive as you think, and because most students get financial aid. And because there are things you can do on your own to reduce the cost of college.

This is not what everyone will tell you. You may hear discouraging words like, "Most colleges are expensive" and "You won't qualify for financial aid." People may hint that college is not worth all the trouble. The financial aid forms may look complicated and confusing.

We will show you how to get past these doubts. You *can* afford college, and we will show you how. With our step-by-step guide through the process, you'll sidestep confusion and be able to focus on the important decisions in front of you.

Why You Can Afford College

Despite media hype about pricey colleges and the soaring cost of higher education, that's not the whole story. If a college wants you as a student, and if you and your parents don't have enough money, the college will usually offer help so you can attend. That help is financial aid — and because of it, **a college's published tuition and fees are not what most people pay**.

Financial aid is a great equalizer, and most students benefit from it. More than two-thirds of all full-time college students receive grants or scholarships to help them foot the bill. Those grants come either from the government, the college or both, and do not have to be paid back. Many students also receive other forms of help, including federal tax credits and deductions that allow their families to keep more of their money at tax time. Thanks to all this assistance, full-time college students usually pay much less than the advertised "sticker" price. In 2016–17, for example, students at four-year private colleges paid an average net price of $14,220 in tuition and fees instead of the average published price of $33,480. Students at four-year public universities received a proportionally similar discount.

Even expensive colleges are less costly than you might think because they offer more financial aid. Since a high-priced college often awards more aid than a low-priced one, a student might end up paying the same out-of-pocket cost at both, or even less at the college with a higher sticker price. **That's why you shouldn't rule out your "dream college" as too expensive until you find out if it wants you and what kind of financial aid package it will give you.**

That said, there are great deals to be found. At a four-year public college — one supported by a state or local government — the average tuition and fees in 2016–17 were $9,650 a year. That's a 70 percent saving over the $33,480 average charged by private colleges. Another way to save money is to spend your first two years at a community college, which is a public college that specializes in two-year education programs. Published tuition and fees at community colleges averaged just over $3,520 a year — a 63 percent saving over the average at a public four-year college.

Here's one last reason you can afford college: you don't have to pay every penny up front. You can borrow money at a low interest rate and pay it back after your studies are over. There are also ways to reduce the amount you have to pay right now. (*See Step 11 for more on these "out-of-pocket" options.*)

MYTH/FACT

Myth: Most colleges are expensive.

Fact: The most expensive colleges get the most media attention, which creates the illusion that all colleges are expensive. The truth is that colleges vary greatly in price, and most are much more affordable than people think, especially once financial aid is factored in.

Figure 1:
Average Tuition, Fees, Room and Board Charges, 2016–17

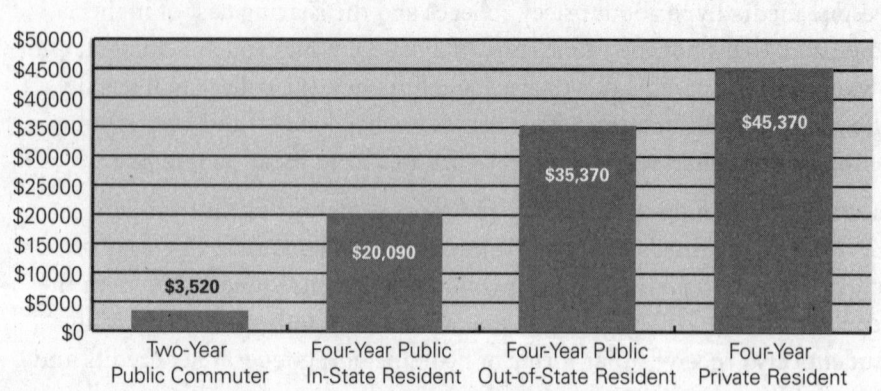

See Step 3 for more about the components of college costs.

Is College Worth It?

Even if you can afford college, is it a good idea? No matter how much financial aid you get, college will still require a sacrifice of money, time, and effort. Kids who go straight to work after high school have more spending money sooner. Does college give enough bang for the buck?

The answer is yes for many reasons including money, job security and personal growth.

In terms of money, college clearly pays. **College graduates earn almost twice as much over their careers than high school graduates.** The difference in earnings between the typical college graduate and the typical high school graduate has increased sharply over the past three decades: from 25 percent to 69 percent for men, and from 43 percent to 70 percent for women.

Figure 2:

Median Annual Earnings by Education Level

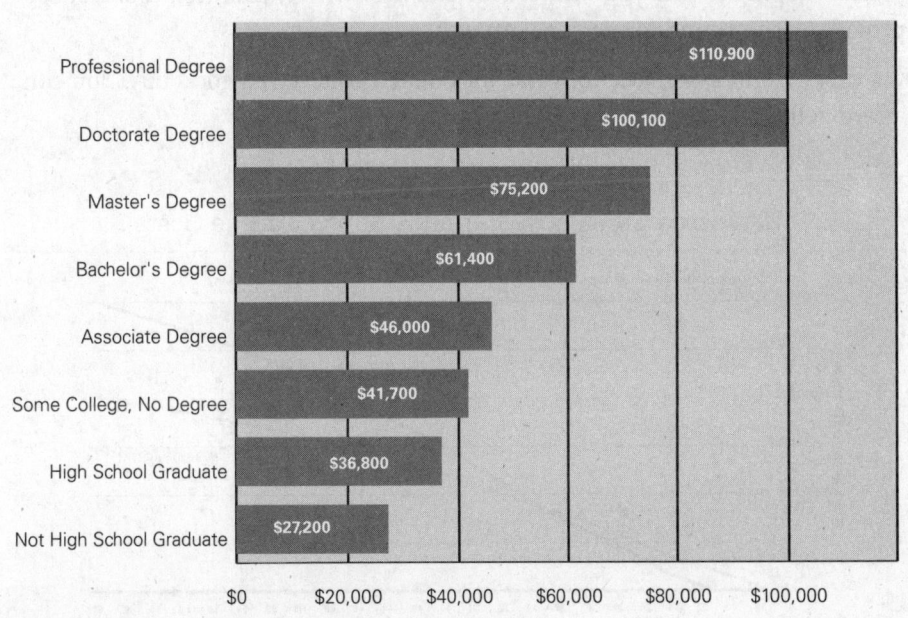

Note: Includes full-time, year-round workers age 25 and older.
Source: Sandy Baum and Kathleen Payea, *Education Pays 2016*, The College Board, New York.

You might think that the increased earnings from your college education won't make up for the total costs and the years that you won't be in the work force. But Figure 3 on the next page shows otherwise. The grey line shows the cumulative earnings at each age for the average high school graduate who enters the workforce full time at the age of 18. The black line shows the average cumulative earnings at each age for a graduate of a four-year public university who enters the workforce at age 22, after subtracting average tuition and fees. As you can see, by age 35 the lines intersect. From that point on, the investment in college pays off.

College also provides better prospects for job security in a world economy that is constantly evolving, with jobs being both destroyed and created by technology and global competition. In such a world you can compete better with a college degree. A college degree teaches you how to acquire knowledge and put it to use no matter what the circumstances. In fact, some higher-education credential — at least an associate degree — is a minimum to stay employed in the "knowledge economy" of the 21st century. **A mere high school diploma is obsolete; college helps to ensure employment**.

But the value of college can't be reduced to dollars alone. It involves intangibles, things you can't touch directly: how you value yourself, your dreams and your ambitions. If you are an artist, a musician, a writer, a builder, a scientist or a thinker, college will help you cultivate your talents. If you are hoping to find yourself, college can help with that search too. College provides rich ground for personal growth.

On every front, as a matter of value for dollars, college is a good buy. You can afford college — and it is worth the price.

Figure 3:
Estimated Cumulative Earnings Minus College Costs

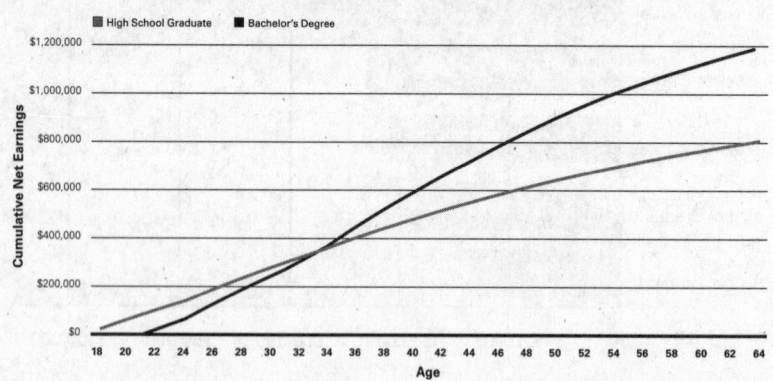

Notes: Based on median 2014 earnings for high school graduates and college graduates at each age and discounted using a 3 percent rate. Earnings for B.A. recipients include only those with no advanced degree.
Source: Sandy Baum and Kathleen Payea, *Education Pays 2016*, The College Board, New York.

How This Book Will Help You

KEEP IN MIND

Don't approach the chronology of this book too rigidly — **not all steps have to come in this order.** For example, Step 9, "Look for Other Sources of Money," can be done at any time. Since many scholarships aren't tied to a particular college, you can start researching and applying for them before you've even begun your college search.

Through this book, you will learn how to make college affordable for you. You'll find out exactly what you need to know so you can apply for financial aid, choose an affordable college and control costs while at college. In Part I, we will walk you step-by-step through the process. There are 11 steps in all:

- **Step 1:** You'll find out the key facts about financial aid.

- **Step 2:** You'll get an idea of how much financial aid you can get.

- **Step 3:** You'll see how and why college costs vary.

- **Step 4:** You'll figure out which forms you need to fill out, and when.

- **Step 5:** You'll learn how to fill out the Free Application for Federal Student Aid (FAFSA).

- **Step 6:** You'll find out how to complete the CSS/Financial Aid PROFILE® application (called the CSS Profile™ for short), if your colleges require it.

- **Step 7:** You'll learn how to fill out any other forms a particular college might require.

- **Step 8:** If your family has special circumstances, you'll find out the best way to explain them to colleges.

- **Step 9:** You'll learn about scholarships and other aid you can get from sources outside of a college.

- **Step 10:** You'll learn how to compare award letters from colleges and decide which offer is best for you.

- **Step 11:** You'll learn how to pay your share of the cost of college through work, loans and other means.

In Part II of the book, tables and worksheets will help you make informed decisions and stay in control of the financial aid process. Part III will paint a clear picture of the financial facts about each college you might want to investigate. That includes its costs and its approach to financial aid.

No one will tell you that paying for college is fun. But what you're getting — a college education — is worth it and is within reach. College is a big-ticket purchase that requires careful thought and preparation, like a house or a car. And it shouldn't be done in the dark. This book will guide you into one of the most important purchases you'll ever make — with your eyes wide open.

Step 1: Let's Go Over the Basics

QUICK OVERVIEW

The first step to getting financial aid is to understand the basic facts about it. Here we will explain what financial aid is (money to help you pay for college), what types there are (the kind that comes free and the kind that doesn't), who gets it and where it comes from.

The most important point: almost everyone qualifies for at least one form of financial aid. As long as you apply, the chances are excellent that you will get some.

Just What Is Financial Aid?

KNOW THE LINGO

Grant — Money that is given away for free, usually on the basis of who needs it

Merit scholarship — Money that is given away for free on the basis of academic qualifications or special talents

Subsidized loan — Money that you have to pay back with interest; however, the federal government pays the interest for you while you are in college

Work-study — A program in which you take a part-time job to earn money for your education; the federal government pays part of your salary

Financial aid package — What a college offers to an accepted student who has applied for aid. Usually a mix of grants, loans and/or work-study.

Financial aid is money given or loaned to you to help you pay for college. Different forms have different rules. The vast majority of aid comes from the federal government, and most of it consists of loans that you must pay back. However, some aid does not require repayment — which makes it the best kind of aid to get.

If you qualify for financial aid, your college will put together an aid "package," usually with different types of aid bundled together. You and your parents will almost certainly still have to pay something, but the aid package will help. Most students qualify for some form of financial aid, so it makes sense to apply for it.

You'll apply for financial aid either at the same time or soon after you apply for admission. You may have to fill out more than one application. At the very least you will fill out the FAFSA, the federal government form. You may also fill out another form, the CSS Profile, which many colleges require. And some colleges and state aid agencies require their own financial aid forms, too. The colleges to which you apply will use the forms to figure out what your family can afford to pay and what your "need" is — that is, the difference between what you can pay and what the college actually costs. If the school wants you as a student but sees that you can't handle the whole bill, it will make you a financial aid offer to help you meet your need. If you accept, that financial aid package is your award.

You will need to apply for financial aid every year that you are in college, mainly because your family's financial situation changes yearly. As a result, your financial aid package will probably be somewhat different from year to year.

Financial aid is a helping hand, not a free pass. In the United States, everyone has a right to a free public school education, but not to a free college education. The federal government and most colleges agree that students and their parents are the ones most responsible for paying for college. "The primary responsibility of paying for the student's education lies with the student and his or her parents," says Forrest M. Stuart, the director of financial aid at Furman University in Greenville, S.C. "Financial aid comes in to fill that gap, if you will, between what they can afford and what the college costs." Even so, financial aid can be the deciding factor in whether or not a student attends college.

Types of Aid

Financial aid may come in many forms. However, all forms can be grouped into two major categories: gift aid and self-help aid.

GIFT AID

Gift aid is free money, money that you don't have to pay back or work for. Naturally, this is the kind of aid most people want. It can take the form of grants or scholarships.

The terms "grant" and "scholarship" are often used interchangeably to mean free money. But here's the difference. A grant is usually given only on the basis of need, or your family's inability to pay the full cost of college. Scholarships are usually awarded only to those who have "merit," such as proven ability in academics, the arts or athletics. Once you're in college, you may have to maintain a minimum GPA or take certain courses to continue receiving a scholarship.

SELF-HELP AID

Self-help aid is money that requires a contribution from you. That can mean paying back the money (if the aid is a loan) or working for the money (if the aid is a work-study job).

The most common form of self-help aid is also the most common of any form of financial aid: the loan. A loan is money that you have to pay back with interest. In light of that, you might not consider this aid at all. But it is — a loan means you don't have to pay the full price of college all at once: You can stretch the payments over time, as you would when buying a house or a car. Furthermore, some student loans (such as Perkins loans and Direct Subsidized Stafford loans) are subsidized by the federal government. These loans are interest free while you are in college, and you don't begin to make any payments until six months after you leave college. The federal government subsidizes, or helps to pay, the loan by keeping the interest rate low and by paying that interest while you're enrolled.

EXPERT ADVICE

"One of the **most important things for students** to understand is what loans are about, and what indebtedness means, so that they don't stumble through four years of college having signed promissory notes blindly, and then come to the end of their senior year and say, I really owe that much money? They should know that they have to pay loans back, and they should **think about their total indebtedness** in relation to what their prospective income is and how it might affect some life choices."

— *Joe Paul Case, dean and director of financial aid, Amherst College, Amherst, Mass.*

Subsidized loans, which are awarded based on need and administered by the college, are the best kind. But you can also take out federal unsubsidized student loans and parent loans, which are also administered by most colleges. However, be careful not to take on more debt than necessary. No matter what kind of loan you take out, you will have to pay it back.

Another form of self-help is work-study. This is financial aid in the form of a job. Since you earn the money through your work, this too may not seem like aid. But it is, because the federal work-study program pays most of your wages. And work-study jobs are usually available right on campus, with limits on your hours so that you won't be unduly distracted from studying.

Aid can also come in the form of tax cuts — income tax deductions and credits for education. But colleges don't award this variety, and you don't apply for it in the same way as you would loans or grants, so we will discuss it separately, in Step 11.

Who Gets Aid?

Grants and loans are not just for the poorest of the poor, nor are scholarships only for the smartest of the smart. The truth about who gets financial aid is somewhat different from what many people think.

Those Who Need It

Most financial aid is based on need, not merit. There is money for merit, but most colleges focus their financial aid packages on meeting financial need.

However, there is a lot of confusion about what need means. Many people think it means a state of dire poverty, so that no working-class or middle-class student need apply. "A lot of people think that they either have to be on welfare or Social Security — really poor — to get financial aid, and that's not correct," says Mary San Agustin, director of financial aid and scholarships at Palomar College in San Marcos, Calif. On the other hand, some rich families mistakenly think they are needy because their high living expenses leave them little money for college. "It's this expectation of, I pay my taxes, so my kid should be entitled to some federal financial aid regardless of how much money I make," says Ms. San Agustin.

Need simply means that your family can't afford to pay the full cost of a particular college. The *amount* of your need will vary from college to college, because it depends on the cost of attending an individual college. Whether your family has need is determined not by whether you think you are rich or poor, but by the financial aid forms you fill out.

Just fill out the forms. If you do have need, you will be considered for financial aid.

Those Who Don't

Despite the overall emphasis on need, many colleges do give away money on the basis of merit. They do this to attract the students they want most, and they may award this money even if it is more than the student needs. However, in many cases, the student both needs the money and has earned it on the basis of merit.

Don't think that only geniuses get merit aid. At many colleges a "B"-average GPA can put you in the running for merit money. Sometimes a separate application for merit aid is required to put you into consideration; sometimes your application for admission is enough. In either case, don't count yourself out by not applying; apply and let the college decide.

Grants are sometimes awarded based on neither need nor merit. For example, you may get a grant if you are in a certain field of study, are a resident of the state or are a student from the same town as the college. (*See Step 9 for more about grants and scholarships.*)

Part-Time Students

Some kinds of aid are only available to students enrolled in college full time — usually 12 or more credit hours of courses per semester. But part-time students are eligible for some financial aid. For example, federal programs such as the Stafford loan require only that students be enrolled at least half-time, whereas others, like the Pell Grant, are available to students enrolled less than half-time. Also, some employers offer tuition reimbursement benefits to students who work full time and go to college part time.

Where the Money Comes From

Financial aid comes from three basic sources: governments (both federal and state), colleges and outside benefactors.

From the Government

The lion's share of total financial aid awarded in this country comes from the federal government. Almost two-thirds of all student aid is sent from Washington. For undergraduates, the largest chunk of that consists of federal loans, which currently total $60 billion a year and represent 32 percent of all student aid. The loans take multiple shapes. Perkins and Stafford loans are for students, while parents may take out a PLUS loan to help pay for their children's educations.

The federal government also funds several grants, including the Pell Grant, the Supplemental Educational Opportunity Grant (SEOG), the Academic Competitiveness Grant and the SMART Grant. The Pell and SEOG are strictly need based, while the last two are based on both need and academic criteria. The government also funds the federal work-study program.

KNOW THE LINGO

Merit aid — Aid awarded on the basis of academics, character or talent

Need-based aid — Aid awarded on the basis of a family's inability to pay the cost of attending a particular college

Non-need-based aid — Aid awarded on some basis other than need or merit, such as grants with eligibility requirements related to field of study or state residence

A much smaller amount of aid (6 percent) is offered by state governments to their residents. Usually this type of aid is for in-state colleges only, but a few states offer "portable" aid that can be used at a college in another state.

From the College

A great deal of financial aid comes from individual colleges, using their own money. In fact, colleges award nearly half of all grants. They may also offer on-campus job opportunities and loans.

Private colleges give more financial aid than public colleges, which can often make a private college just as affordable despite higher tuition.

Outside Grants and Scholarships

Outside grants and scholarships come from sources other than the government or the college. These sources may include corporations like Coca-Cola or community groups like the Elks Club. Some are well known, such as the National Merit Scholarship, but altogether they are a small piece of the financial aid pie: **only 6 percent of all student aid comes from this source**. Pursue them, but don't expect them to outweigh the other aid you will get.

Bear in mind also that your outside scholarship is unlikely to expand the total aid you receive. Most colleges will use an outside scholarship to substitute for some other piece of aid rather than increase the total aid package. Think of your financial aid package as a barrel: when the barrel is full, no more can be added unless something is taken away. The last thing colleges will take away is whatever sum of money your family is expected to contribute. However, at many colleges, the first thing taken away is self-help aid such as loans. Since that could reduce the total amount you will have to pay back later, it is worth applying for outside scholarships. (*See Step 9 for more on these sources of aid.*)

Figure 4:
Undergraduate Student Aid (in billions) by Source, 2015–2016

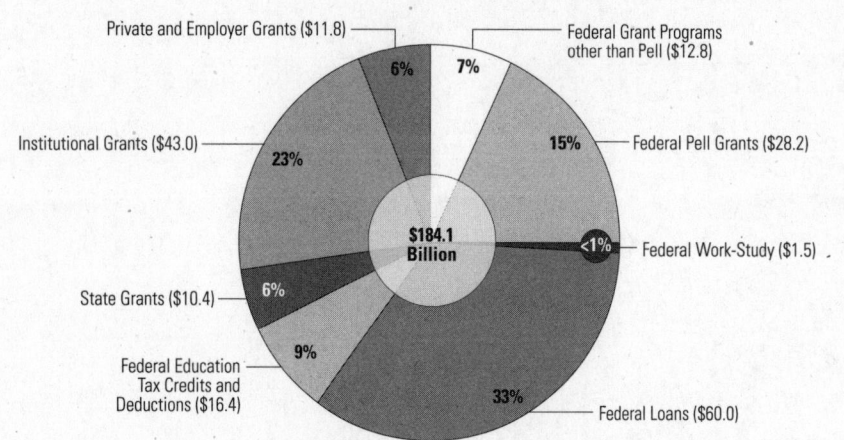

Private and Employer Grants ($11.8) — 6%

Federal Grant Programs other than Pell ($12.8) — 7%

Federal Pell Grants ($28.2) — 15%

Institutional Grants ($43.0) — 23%

$184.1 Billion

Federal Work-Study ($1.5) — <1%

State Grants ($10.4) — 6%

Federal Education Tax Credits and Deductions ($16.4) — 9%

Federal Loans ($60.0) — 33%

These are the main things to know about financial aid:

- It is money to help you pay for college.
- It may come in the form of a gift (grants and scholarships) or in the form of self-help (loans and work-study).
- Most people get it because they need it, though some get it solely because of merit.
- The federal government funds most of it, but states, colleges and outside sources also help.

QUICK RECAP

Step 2: Estimate How Financial Aid Will Work for You

Only rarely does a student get a "free ride" scholarship. You and your parents will be expected to contribute some money to your education — the precise amount will be determined by the college's analysis of financial aid forms you'll fill out. But even before you fill out the forms, you can estimate your share of the cost and how much financial aid you might be offered to cover the rest.

Don't Count Yourself Out

"Probably the question I'm most often asked is, 'Is there a cutoff?'" says Joe Paul Case, the dean and director of financial aid at Amherst College in Amherst, Mass. The simple answer is "no." Colleges also consider such factors as family size, number of children in college, and savings. Many students who would be eligible for financial aid fail to apply because they don't realize this.

"I always tell families, don't cut yourself off from the application process," says Bonnie Lee Behm, the director of financial assistance at Villanova University in Villanova, Pa. "Apply and let it work through the system."

Even if you feel sure that you won't qualify for financial aid, fill out the forms anyway. You have nothing to lose, you probably will be surprised, and you should cover your bases in case your family circumstances might change suddenly.

EXPERT ADVICE

"We always encourage students to **go ahead and apply** for financial aid even though you may not qualify for anything but a student loan. **At least get the paperwork in**, because if something happens in the middle of the year, we already have the financial aid data we need to make adjustments."

— *Forrest M. Stuart, director of financial aid, Furman University, Greenville, S.C.*

What "Expected Family Contribution" Means

Even though you probably will qualify for financial aid, it's unlikely that you will get the fabled "full ride." Almost always, the family is expected to contribute some money. The exact dollar amount will be based on the family's ability to pay. That dollar amount is called the expected family contribution, or EFC.

The EFC is carefully calculated to determine what you can afford to pay based on your financial circumstances — no more and no less. The formulas that the federal government and colleges use to calculate EFC are also calibrated to take into account varying costs of living across the country.

No matter what a college costs, your EFC remains the same. Say your EFC is $8,000. At a college with a total cost of attendance of $11,000, you could get up to $3,000 in financial aid. At a college where the total cost is $25,000, you could get up to $17,000 in aid. **Because of financial aid, any college is at least worth considering; no college should be ruled out in advance as too expensive**.

Costs – EFC = Need

Your expected family contribution is your family's share of college costs. Any cost greater than that is your need. Need varies from college to college because it depends on the cost of the individual college. **It's simple arithmetic: College costs minus your EFC equals the amount of aid you need**. At colleges that award enough financial aid to meet your full need, the aid package will equal the amount of your need. Costs minus aid equals what you pay.

Unmet Need (a.k.a. "Gap")

Unfortunately, not all colleges will award enough aid to meet your full need. Some colleges may "gap" your package — that is, not meet your full need. Economics plays a part here. While some colleges may have enough aid dollars available to meet every student's full need, some colleges lack such funds. If your college cannot meet your full need, costs minus aid will still equal what you pay. But what you pay will be more than your EFC. (*See Step 11 for more information on loans* and other ways to help fill such a gap.)

If you do encounter a "gap" in your award, compare the package with the ones you've gotten from other schools, and consider your priorities. Do you want to go to that college, no matter the cost? Or does cost matter more? (*For more on this topic, see Step 10.*)

It Depends on the College

The amount of aid you get — along with the kind of aid you get, whether gift or self-help — ultimately depends on the college. Formulas and forms are important, but so is the professional judgment of the financial aid officer. And so is the desire of the college to attract you to its campus.

How Colleges Calculate Your Need

As you saw in Step 1, financial aid comes from two main sources: government money (usually in the form of loans and work-study), and the college's own "institutional" money — usually in the form of grants and scholarships. Your financial aid package will probably contain money from both sources.

Just as there are two main sources of aid, there are two main formulas that colleges use to figure out how much aid you should get. One is called the "Federal Methodology," used for aid coming from government money. The Federal Methodology is based on the FAFSA, the federal financial aid form.

For aid coming out of their own money, such as an endowment fund, some colleges use another formula called the "Institutional Methodology." This is based on the College Board's CSS/Financial Aid PROFILE and/or the college's own financial aid application form. (*For more about these forms, see Steps 6 and 7.*) "I just think it does a much better job of measuring ability to pay," says Forrest M. Stuart, whose institution, Furman University, requires the CSS Profile.

So what does all this mean to you? You don't have to know how these formulas work or remember what they are called. The thing to remember is that if you apply to several colleges, because of these different formulas you might end up with a different EFC for one college than you do for another.

Will College Savings Count Against You?

While some families save diligently for their children's college educations, others think this is a mistake. They worry that having a lot of savings will keep colleges from awarding financial aid. **But savings help you more than they hurt you**, and here is why.

When calculating your EFC, colleges subtract what they call an "asset protection allowance" from the amount you have saved. This "allowance" is the amount of money considered reasonable to set aside for educational savings and family emergencies. These savings are clearly worth having, since they aren't included when calculating your EFC. (See Table 11 in Part II to get an estimate of what your parents' asset protection allowance may be.)

Even if your family saves more than the asset protection allowance, those savings will be assessed at a maximum rate of only 5.6 percent. So even if 5.6 percent of your excess savings count "against" you when it comes to federal need determination, 94.4 percent count "for" you. You can use them to meet your expected contribution, whatever it turns out to be.

Essentially, your family will be expected to pay some part of your college costs out of pocket, and if you have savings, you have a pot to draw from. The alternatives are to pay it out of your monthly income or to borrow it — both of which are less appealing choices than using savings. "If I were preparing to send a son or daughter off to school, I would want to have as much savings available to me as I realistically could," says Vincent Amoroso, former director of the Office of Student Financial Services at Johns Hopkins University. "The reason is because, just like in other situations, having money on hand makes it easier for me to make choices that are good for myself and my child."

To be sure, there are other factors your family should consider before saving for college, such as whether they have enough money to save for retirement. But if they can put away any money for college, they should do so without hesitating. (*See Step 11 for information on tax-free college savings plans.*)

Responsibilities Within the Family

Who should pay for college? Your college will expect someone in the family to make a contribution, and you and your parents should figure out who that is before the bill comes due.

"Families should discuss college costs, family budget, financial aid and financing options at the beginning of the college application process, not at the end," says Carlene Riccelli, a college adviser at Amherst Regional High School in Amherst, Mass. Try to reach decisions that are as specific as possible, so that you each know what's expected of you. Don't forget to discuss ways of keeping costs down, such as living at home and taking community college courses.

While it's important to talk about money, your family also needs to talk about other aspects of choosing a college, such as its academic and social environment. Some of the discussion will have nothing to do with money, but others will have financial aspects: for example, going away to an expensive college versus staying home and commuting to a cheaper one. Step 3 will further explore how to think about these issues. But the important thing is to start having the discussions — financial and otherwise — as early as possible.

KNOW THE LINGO

EFC (Expected Family Contribution) — How much money a family is expected to pay for college.

Need — The difference between your EFC and the cost of attending a particular college you've chosen. Financial aid is designed to meet your need, not your EFC.

Unmet need — The difference (if any) between the your need and the financial aid offered by a particular college. Informally, unmet need is also called a **gap**.

Asset protection allowance — The amount of money considered reasonable to set aside for educational savings and emergencies, and is therefore not part of your EFC.

Crunch Some Numbers

If you want a sneak peek at what your expected family contribution will be, Part II of this book contains worksheets and tables that you can use. When you're finished, you will have your estimated EFC.

The figure you come up with will only be an estimate. Your actual EFC may be higher or lower, depending on the exact data you ultimately submit and the particular college's financial aid policies. But at least this exercise will give you a ballpark figure for what you can expect to pay.

Online Calculators

If you'd prefer to estimate your EFC online, there are several websites with special calculators. They include:

- **collegeboard.org** — Our Net Price Calculator lets you "Do the Math" on EFC and to compare your out-of-pocket expenses from one college to another.
- **College and university websites** — These sites also include calculators geared to their individual financial aid policies.

Your Unique Situation Counts Too

Colleges are not just faceless buildings of stone, and your EFC is not fixed in cement. The financial aid officer in charge of distributing a college's financial aid does have some discretion to adjust how the EFC calculations are made based on your individual circumstances.

Step 8 will go into greater detail on how to notify your college about changes in your family's financial situation, such as a lost job. And Step 10 will discuss how to appeal if you think the college hasn't taken all your circumstances into account. Generally, financial aid officers are sympathetic if you are struggling with problems such as caring for an elderly parent or a lost job.

QUICK RECAP

- Your family will be required to pay an expected family contribution, or EFC.
- The costs of the college you attend minus the financial aid you receive equals what you pay.
- College savings will not be held against you.

Step 3: Choosing Colleges, Thinking Costs

QUICK OVERVIEW

This step shows you how to think about cost when choosing a college. You'll see why you shouldn't exclude any college from consideration just because of its price. You'll learn what your different college expenses will be, from tuition to pizza money; how costs can vary from college to college; and how to factor in the financial aid package the college is likely to give.

KNOW THE LINGO

Total cost of attendance — Not just tuition, but also all fees, room and board, transportation, books and supplies, and personal expenses.

Public college — A college or university that is subsidized by taxes and other public revenues and governed by a county, state or federal government agency.

Community college — A two-year public college subsidized by a local government, such as a county or city.

Out-of-state tuition — What public colleges charge students from other states; often more than double the rate for in-state residents.

Reciprocity agreement — A deal between neighboring states that allows residents to attend a public college in either state at the in-state tuition rate.

How to Think About College Costs

When you're thinking about where to apply for college, its "list price" should not be the main consideration. Because financial aid will probably be available to help meet your need, even a college that appears exorbitant may in fact be within reach. A college's published costs are only one part of the equation when it comes to what you'll actually pay. **Until you've applied for and received an offer of financial aid, you won't know the real cost to your family**.

Remember that financial aid works like this: Total cost of attendance *minus* your family's expected family contribution (EFC) *equals* your financial need. As long as the college meets your need, the amount you pay stays the same whatever the price of the college. "I don't think college cost really should be a factor in where students apply for admission," says Vincent Amoroso of Johns Hopkins University. "I say that because your family contribution, in theory, is the same whether you apply to a school that costs $4,000 or to a school that costs $40,000."

In practice, your expected family contribution may actually vary somewhat from college to college. As noted in Step 2, a college using the Federal Methodology to assess your ability to pay might calculate a higher or lower EFC than a college that uses the Institutional Methodology. Even two institutions using the same methodology might calculate slightly different EFCs, depending on how they have treated any special circumstances that may apply to your family. (*See Step 8 for more on special circumstances.*) But in general, the principle holds that your EFC will be constant from college to college, while your need will vary depending on the price of each college.

The main thing to consider when applying for college is whether you and that school will be a good fit. Look for the academic and social aspects that are likely to make you happy and successful there. Are you artistic? Are you mathematical? Do you love to learn for learning's sake? Do you have strong career ambitions in a particular field? Do you long to get away and see the world? Or does it matter more to stay near your family and the place where you grew up? "Students should not just look at a school because it's affordable," says Bonnie Lee Behm of Villanova University. "They should look at a school because it's the right fit for them academically, socially, spiritually and physically. Is cost an important part? Yes. It's a consideration, but only one among many." **And remember — you can find a good fit at more than one college.**

To discover what specific colleges have to offer, research them. You can find a lot of information about majors offered, the composition of the student body, academic policies, and extracurricular and athletic offerings in *The College Board College Handbook*. You can also learn more on the College Search engine on bigfuture.org, and from college guidebooks and websites. If you know people who have gone to the colleges you're considering, talk to them and get their opinions.

So, when deciding which colleges to apply to, don't focus too much on cost. But do be aware of what the costs are; cost may become a factor depending on what financial aid packages you are ultimately offered. Even though your EFC should in principle be the same at all colleges, not all schools always meet full need. And even those that do may meet it with different packages — some with more loans, others with more grants. It makes sense to know what kinds of packages a particular school is likely to give.

By using Part III of this book as a guide, and also by contacting the admissions and financial aid offices of the colleges you're considering, gather as much information as you can about the costs of the school and the type of aid they offer. The rest of Step 3 suggests the kinds of information you should be seeking from each school.

Choosing Colleges

Both you and your parents should be involved in the discussion about where to apply for college. You will share the responsibility for paying for college, so you should all have a voice. Furthermore, your parents can give you good advice about what colleges to consider based on their life experiences, their knowledge of you, and their understanding of the family finances — even if they themselves have never been to college. The deciding vote, however, should be yours. You are the one who will have to start and finish college, and you are more likely to do so successfully if you have chosen the college yourself. "Only the student knows the fit that he or she will have at a particular institution academically, socially and financially as well," says Forrest Stuart of Furman University.

When you begin choosing where to apply, don't exclude any college. Let every college be on the table, even if it seems too difficult academically or financially. Aim high. Shop around. The best colleges for you may not be the ones that occur to you first.

If a college is a good fit for you, there is probably a way to make it work financially. "Apply to those colleges that you think, okay, maybe we could afford these, but also apply above that level, because some schools may be much more manageable than you expect," says Bonnie Lee Behm of Villanova University.

Do Consider a "Financial Safety"

Even though all colleges should be on the drawing board, you should also consider applying to a financial "safety" school — one that is a good academic fit and that you feel fairly confident you can afford. Your financial safety school is one you would be happy attending and that has either low published costs or will almost certainly offer enough grant money to make attendance affordable. A public university in your state, a local community college or a private university where you are highly likely to win a merit scholarship might all be financial safeties.

A financial safety is a good idea because your top choices may not give you as much financial aid as you want. "We know students who are really strong academically, but they're not at the top of their class, and they apply to the college of their dreams," says Elizabeth Bickford, director of the Office of Student Financial Aid and Scholarships at the University of Oregon in Eugene. Despite their hopes for a full merit scholarship, such students may find that they can enroll only if they are willing to take out a large amount in unsubsidized loans — something their family may not be willing to do.

In these and other situations, a financial safety is a good backup. For example, if you accept admission to a far-off university, but find that you can't get used to it and want to come back to the financial safety school near home, it will be easier to transfer if you've already applied and been admitted. Still, Elizabeth Bickford says she encourages students to "dream large, because it's your one opportunity. When you go from high school to that first year in college, that's where most of the scholarships are — for entering freshmen. It's your opportunity to make that big step away from home."

KNOW THE LINGO

Need-blind admission — If a college has a "need-blind admission" policy, this means that it will admit a student solely on the basis of his or her academic merit or other characteristics, regardless of their ability to pay. However, it does not mean the college guarantees to meet full need. You may be admitted, but the college may be unable to offer a financial aid package equal to your need.

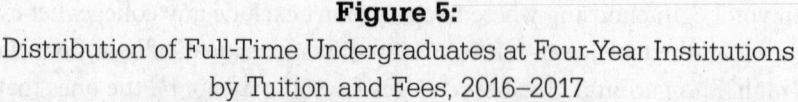

Figure 5:

Distribution of Full-Time Undergraduates at Four-Year Institutions by Tuition and Fees, 2016–2017

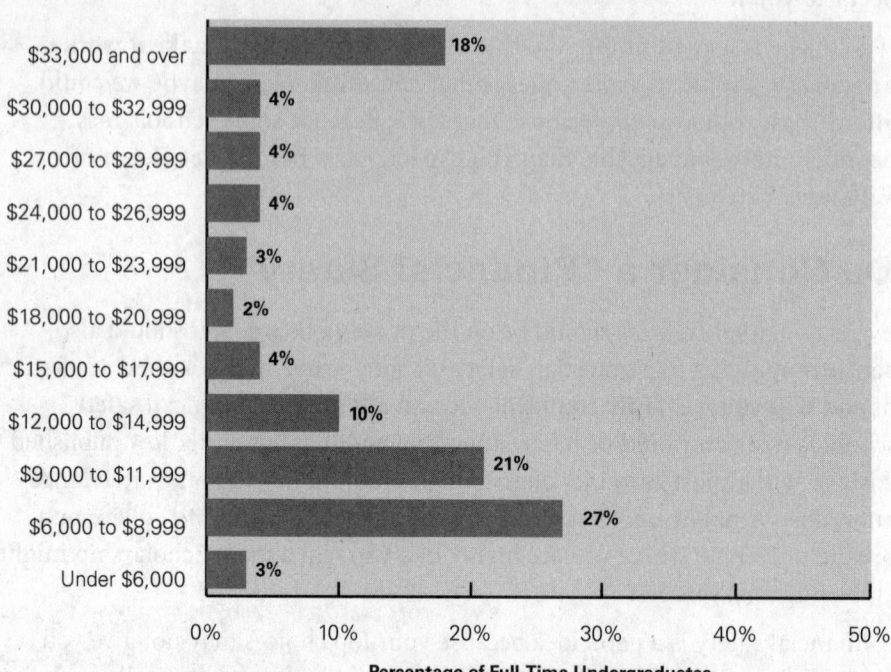

Percentage of Full-Time Undergraduates

Over 60% of full-time undergraduates attend colleges with tuition and fee charges of less than $15,000. After financial aid, many of those students pay an even lower "net price" for tuition.

Source: *Annual Survey of Colleges*, The College Board, New York

Components of College Costs

The price of a college education has several parts. The most obvious is tuition, the cost of taking courses. Tuition varies depending on how many courses you take, but full time students pay a flat rate for a full schedule of courses. If you attend part time, you will likely pay by credit hours, a measure of how long each class is. Most courses are three credit hours apiece, which usually translates to three one-hour classes each week. Most full-time students take an average of four or five courses per semester, for a total of 12 to 15 credit hours per semester for a full load.

Fees are another component of college costs. Fees are usually billed to all students as funding for the college's general expenses, such as the library or student activities. But there may be additional special fees for students enrolled in certain classes or activities. A chemistry student may pay lab fees, for example.

Tuition and fees are just one part of what you'll pay for college, and often not even half. Another large component is room and board. "Room" is the cost of housing you, and "board" is the cost of food. You may live in a dorm on campus, or off campus — in an apartment or a house with other students or at home with your parents. You may be on a meal plan where all your meals are prepared for you for one price, or you may fend for yourself, buying groceries and cooking meals. Either way, these basic living expenses are your room and board.

Taken together, tuition, fees, room and board are the largest chunk of college costs. On average, at four-year public colleges across the nation, these elements together make up 80 percent of what students pay for college. Yet there is still another 20 percent of costs to be accounted for. These include:

- Books and supplies — class expenses that are not covered by tuition and will vary depending on the courses you take.

- Transportation expenses — for on-campus students, this is the cost of trips home during holidays; for commuters, this is the cost of either mass transit or a car. Car costs include parking, gas, insurance and maintenance.

- Computer equipment costs — if required by the college. Some colleges may insist that you buy a certain model of computer, or bring your own computer but have special hardware and software installed to make it work on the campus network.

- Personal expenses — everything from snacks outside the meal plan to newspaper subscriptions to haircuts and toothpaste to membership fees for student groups.

How Costs Can Vary

Each college has different price tags for each of the cost components. For example, books and supplies might cost $1,200 for a typical student at a state university, but $2,500 or more at an art school. Table 1 that follows shows national averages for cost components.

To get specifics for a particular college that you're considering, check its website and look for the school's published estimate of what the average student spends on the different expense categories. The college will use these averages as part of the calculation of your "total cost of attendance," which will partly determine how much aid you're awarded. You can also consult Part III of this book for a school-by-school summary of costs.

However, remember that these average costs are only averages. You are an individual, and you may pay more or less than average, depending on your individual circumstances. For example, if you attend college in California but your family lives in New York, you will pay more for traveling to and from home than if your family is also in California.

Textbook and supply costs can also vary widely depending on your major. If you are an architecture or drafting student, you might have to buy an expensive computer-aided design program that your English major friends won't need. Science students might need to buy a statistical-modeling software package; studio artists a graphic-design suite. At least software like this only has to be bought once and is then used to do work for several classes; furthermore, educational discounts may be available for such purchases. In some programs, students might have to buy supplies that frequently get used up and must be replenished, such as brushes and paints for art students.

Rooming costs will vary a little between different dorm complexes on campus — for example, newer dorms may cost more, and a single room is always more expensive than one shared with a roommate. There will also be differences between various off-campus rooming locations.

Finally, your personal expenses may be higher or lower than average depending on lifestyle factors — but they will almost always be higher than you think. As James Schembari wrote in the *New York Times*, there is always a need for "pizza money" — money to buy pizza, go on a road trip, or hang out at the student union. Books, supplies, travel and everyday expenses "can add $3,000 or more a year, depending on parents' generosity and where their child goes to college," wrote Mr. Schembari.

Table 1:
Average Estimated Undergraduate Budgets, 2016–2017

SECTOR	TUITION AND FEES	BOOKS AND SUPPLIES	ROOM AND BOARD	TRANSPOR-TATION	OTHER EXPENSES	TOTAL EXPENSES*
Public Two-Year						
Resident	$3,520	$1,390	$8,060	$1,160	$2,110	$16,240
Commuter	$3,520	$1,390	—	$1,760	$2,270	$8,940
Public Four-Year						
Resident	$9,650	$1,250	$10,440	$1,160	$2,110	$24,610
Commuter	$9,650	$1,250	—	$1,760	$2,270	$14,930
Out-of-State	$24,930	$1,250	$10,440	$1,160	$2,110	$39,890
Private Four-Year						
Resident	$33,480	$1,230	$11,890	$1,070	$1,650	$49,320
Commuter	$33,480	$1,230	—	$1,760	$2,270	$38,740

Note: Estimates of individual budget items are based on reporting by institutional financial aid offices.
Source: *Annual Survey of Colleges*, The College Board, New York, N.Y.

Ways to Reduce Costs

There are a few time-tested ways of saving money on some of the major cost components of college. To save money on tuition and fees, many students have attended public colleges and community colleges. To save money on room and board, many have commuted rather than roomed on campus. Here are the pros and cons for these money-saving techniques.

Public vs. Private, In-State vs. Out-of-State

Attending a public college in your own state is an excellent way to save money on tuition and fees. Public colleges are subsidized by state taxes, so their tuition and fees for state residents are usually much less than at private colleges — 70 percent less, on average. Depending on the school, the quality of education may be as good or even better than what you would get at a private college.

On the other hand, the true cost picture is more complicated than it looks. Even though private colleges charge more for tuition and fees, most of them also give more scholarships and grants than public colleges do, which helps to even out the costs. "There's an adage that the more expensive the school, the more money they give away," says Mike Scott of Texas Christian University, a private institution.

Cost isn't everything. If a particular private school has some valuable characteristic that you want — smaller classes, professors with whom you want to study — it may be worth the extra tuition money. But cost is a factor to consider. If a certain state school can give you all that you want from college, why not go there and save some money?

If you would like to study at a public college or university in another state, be aware that most public schools charge higher tuition to students from out of state than they do to in-state students. Public colleges currently charge an average of $9,650 in tuition and fees to a state resident, but $24,930 to an out-of-state student. The in- and out-of-state rates for specific public colleges and universities are listed in Part III.

PAYING IN-STATE RATES IN ANOTHER STATE

It is sometimes possible to get the in-state tuition rate, or at least a lowered tuition rate, even if you are an out-of-state student. For example, some state universities have "reciprocity agreements" with neighboring states. South Dakota residents pay tuition rates comparable to state residents at the University of Minnesota and vice versa. There are also discipline-based "consortiums" of public colleges that let you get the in-state tuition rate at another state's public college if your desired major is not available at any public college in your own state.

Your school counselor and state board of education website can give you more information about programs for paying in-state rates in another state.

Community Colleges

Community colleges are another great way of saving money on tuition and fees. A community college is a two-year school subsidized by a state, county or city. Its cost for tuition and fees is usually much lower than that of a four-year institution — 63 percent lower, on average, than a public four-year college. Community colleges often charge tuition in three tiers — in district, in state and out of state — with the lowest price for those who live in the local district. Though most community colleges do not offer a four-year bachelor's degree (though the number that do are on the rise), they do provide courses whose credits can be transferred toward a bachelor's degree at another college. Because those courses cost much less, this can be a way to save money in your first two years of college — money you can use to help pay for the last two years. Four out of 10 college-bound high school graduates start their college education this way.

There are other reasons to attend a community college besides saving money. If you aren't sure whether you want to go to a four-year college, a community college will give you a sense of what the college experience is like. If you don't know what kind of program you want to pursue — science, art, business or something else — you can explore different subject areas at a community college before committing to a four-year program. And if you need to be able to work, you can work out a more flexible schedule at a community college, where many students work full time and attend classes at night and on weekends.

A community college is also a golden opportunity for students who didn't do well enough in high school to win admission to the college of their choice. Community colleges are open to everyone, and some have agreements with four-year colleges that guarantee admission in the third year for students who have maintained good grades. This is the case in California, according to Mary San Agustin of Palomar College, a community college. If students, she says, "have their heart set in going, let's say, to Stanford or U.C. Berkeley, we have an excellent articulation program that allows them to take the two-year required courses and get guaranteed admissions in their junior year at those schools that they prefer to go to." In this way, **a community college can open the door to a four-year college for you**.

Living at Home

An obvious way to save money on room and board is to stay home and commute to a college close by. Instead of paying for campus housing and meals — an average cost of $11,890 a year for private colleges — your housing and meal costs remain what they are.

However, commuting has hidden costs. You will have transportation expenses that you wouldn't have if you lived on campus. If you can use mass transit, these costs will probably be low enough to make economic sense. But if you have to buy a car and pay for gas and insurance, your transportation costs might end up being close to the costs of on-campus room and board. And if you're thinking of relying on family and friends for rides to and from campus, remember that their schedules may not overlap with yours. Your own schedule may change day to day and semester to semester, depending on your classes and activities. You probably will need your own car if mass transit isn't available.

Also, don't forget that you cost money at home, too. You're still eating and using utilities at home, and you'll inevitably add pick-up meals on campus to those costs. Financial aid packages usually offer help in paying for room and board as well as tuition and fees, so your actual cost for living on campus would probably not be as high as the published price.

We're not saying that commuting isn't a bargain — it usually is. (There are other good reasons to live at home, too.) But if you are thinking of commuting just to save money, don't commit to it until you weigh all the costs and assess the financial aid offers from any "live away" colleges to which you may apply.

Living Off-Campus

If you don't want to commute but still want to save money on room and board, you might want to consider living off-campus. By residing near campus in an apartment that you share with classmates, you may be able to live more cheaply than you could in the dorms. **But be sure to check the college's policies** — many do not allow freshmen to live off campus if they're under 21 and not living with their parents.

How to Factor in Financial Aid

Every college publishes an average price for the various cost components, but that published price is probably not the price you will end up paying. Your financial aid package will reduce your actual costs. Yet financial aid packages vary from college to college as much as costs do. In thinking about where you will apply, you need to find out some financial aid basics about each college on your short list. How great a percentage of need does it usually meet? How much aid does it award in grants and how much in loans? Does the college offer any merit scholarships or other forms of aid not based on need?

Part III of this book, "Financial Aid College by College," gives you these financial aid basics, along with a number of other essential facts. These include:

- the school's Web address
- what type of school it is, such as public or private
- how many students are enrolled
- how selective the school is
- basic costs, including tuition, fees, room and board
- financial aid application procedures, including deadlines and required forms
- contact information for the financial aid office

In addition, the "Financial Aid Picture" section of each college's profile tells you how much aid is being distributed to how many students and in what form. This information is useful, but note that it only shows averages. Since few families are "average," the numbers in the financial aid profile shouldn't be considered a guarantee of what you'll get or how much you'll have to pay. For example, in-state students at public colleges usually borrow much less than the average debt per student listed in the profiles, while out-of-state students usually borrow more. You can, however, use the profiles to compare colleges: This college meets a greater percentage of need than most; this college awards a relatively large portion of aid in grants.

Check with the Financial Aid Office Before You Apply

Before you apply for financial aid, check with the financial aid offices of the colleges to which you're planning to apply for admission — by simply visiting their website, or by talking to them on the phone or in person. Confirm which forms you need to complete and the deadlines. Better to get these details right before you get started than to find out after the fact that you filed too late or didn't file the proper form.

Bear in mind also that each college has its own financial aid policies, such as how outside scholarships are treated and whether or not aid awards can be appealed. When you contact the office, whether long distance or in a campus visit, find out as much as you can about these policies, along with facts about costs and the financial aid process. If possible, schedule an interview with a member of the financial aid staff. They'll give you a lot of information, but don't expect them to offer you aid until they've seen your forms.

KEEP IN MIND

The **college profiles in Part III** of this book give the "financial aid picture" for each college, based on averages. Use these profiles to **compare colleges only**; the aid you would get at any college is based on your own individual circumstances, so the amount might be higher or lower than the average for that college.

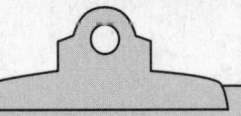

Questions to Ask Colleges

Here are some questions worth asking the aid office:

✔ What are your average costs for the first year for:

- tuition and fees
- room and board
- books and supplies
- transportation
- other personal expenses

✔ What is the range of costs for:

- rooms (single, double)
- board (different meal plans)
- tuition rates (flat rate, per credit, etc.)

✔ By how much will total costs increase each year?

✔ How much have tuition and fees and room and board increased over the past three to five years?

✔ Does financial need have an impact on admission decisions?

✔ Does the school offer both need-based and merit-based financial aid?

✔ Do I need to file a separate application for merit-based scholarships?

✔ If the financial aid package isn't enough, under what conditions, if any, will the aid office reconsider the offer?

✔ How will the aid package change from year to year?

✔ What will happen if my family's financial situation changes?

✔ What are the terms and conditions of your aid programs? For example, what are the academic requirements or other conditions for renewing financial aid from year to year?

✔ When can we expect to receive bills from the college? Is there an option to spread the yearly payment over equal monthly installments?

QUICK RECAP

When deciding where to apply to college, don't exclude any college from consideration because of its "sticker price" — what you will actually pay might be much less. Remember:

- Each school has different costs and financial aid policies.

- When choosing colleges to apply to, consider a "financial safety."

- Your costs might vary from the published averages.

- You might be able to save money at a public college or community college or by commuting — but there are pros and cons to all those strategies.

- Research the colleges you're considering and contact their financial aid offices early.

Step 4: Get Ready for the Forms

Depending on where you'll apply, you may need to file up to three kinds of application forms to get financial aid: the FAFSA, the CSS Profile and forms for individual colleges or states. There are two main things to remember. First, file before the deadlines. The early bird — or at least the timely bird — gets the worm. Second, don't be intimidated. The forms are easier to fill out than they look.

Forms You'll Fill Out

Applying for financial aid is basically a matter of filling out a few financial aid forms on time. The forms may appear complicated, but they are simpler than they look, and millions of people fill them out every year. We will guide you through them so they make sense.

The three steps that follow this one walk you through the application forms you may need to complete: the FAFSA (Step 5), the CSS Profile (Step 6) and whatever forms your individual colleges may require (Step 7). This step will help you create a timeline of which colleges require which forms when.

You may not need to fill out all the forms we describe. Most colleges require only one form, the FAFSA. If you do need to fill out more than one form, take heart. Most of the other forms ask for information similar to what the FAFSA requests. Repeating that information may be annoying, but it isn't hard.

FAFSA: The Federal Form

This is the big one. The FAFSA, or Free Application for Federal Student Aid, must be completed by everyone who wants federal government aid. Just about every college financial aid program requires it, even if they also require other forms. Most schools and states use nothing but the FAFSA to determine eligibility for aid.

There is no charge for completing the FAFSA, and it's easy to do. **Don't pay someone to fill it out for you.**

KEEP IN MIND

Even though this book presents the financial aid forms in order of FAFSA, CSS Profile and institutional forms, **you may need to submit these forms in a different order** depending on the financial aid deadlines of your colleges. In some cases, you may have to file CSS Profile a few weeks before FAFSA, or the institutional form on the same day as FAFSA.

FILING THE FAFSA

The FAFSA can be filled out and submittted online at www.fafsa.ed.gov (FAFSA on the Web). The FAFSA website gives lots of help in completing the form. You don't have to stress about making mistakes because the site checks your information as you go along, and it will find any errors for you to correct before submitting. You can also return to your FAFSA online to update or correct information as needed after you have submitted the form.

The start date for filing the FAFSA has changed. Are you a high school senior graduating in 2018, planning to start college in the fall of 2018? Then you can access and submit your FAFSA on or after **Oct. 1, 2017**. This is new. Under the old rules, you couldn't file the FAFSA before Jan. 1 of the year for which you're seeking aid. This is a great change, because it eliminates the squeeze many students used to face if they were applying to colleges with early deadlines.

Once it's Oct. 1, however, you should aim to file your FAFSA as soon as possible. Don't be fooled by the federal filing deadline (June 30). **Many college deadlines for financial aid are in February or March**, and they need your FAFSA information by then. So, come October, the earlier that you start working on the FAFSA, the better.

IF YOU NEED TO USE A PAPER FAFSA

If you are unable to file the FAFSA online, you can request a paper FAFSA by calling 1-800-433-3243. If you are hearing impaired, contact the TTY line at 1-800-730-8913.

On the paper FAFSA you can only list four colleges to receive your information. You can add up to six more later, but you'll have to wait until your FAFSA is processed and you've received your Student Aid Report.

You'll have to allow at least four weeks for mailing and processing before your earliest deadline. Be sure to make a photocopy for your records before mailing.

CSS PROFILE™

In addition to the FAFSA, some colleges and scholarship programs also require that you fill out the CSS/Financial Aid PROFILE to award their own nonfederal funds. They believe this form gives a more complete picture of students' financial circumstances, allowing them to allocate money as fairly as possible. The CSS Profile service is administered by the College Board, though the College Board itself does not give out any need-based scholarships.

A few colleges require CSS Profile only if you're applying for early decision or early action. Others require it for all applicants. To find out if your colleges require CSS Profile, look them up in Part III of this book or refer to the college's websites.

KEEP IN MIND

File your FAFSA as early as you can. When it comes to financial aid, time really is money. Pay attention to college deadlines! **Those who apply late usually get less** than they are entitled to, because there is less money available in the pool.

KNOW THE LINGO

FAFSA (Free Application for Federal Student Aid) — The form that must be completed by everyone applying for federal government aid.

PROFILE (CSS/Financial Aid PROFILE) — A Web-based form offered by the College Board and used by some colleges and scholarship programs to award their own financial aid.

FSA ID (Federal Student Aid ID) — The username and password used to complete, sign, and submit a FAFSA electronically.

SAR (Student Aid Report) — A report generated after you submit your FAFSA that shows your federally calculated EFC. The SAR is sent to you and to the colleges you listed in your FAFSA.

Priority date — The date by which applications for financial aid must be received in order to be offered the best possible package. After the priority date, applicants are considered on a first-come, first-served basis until the pool of aid money runs out.

The CSS Profile is online only; there are no paper forms. If you don't have a computer at home, use a computer at your school's guidance office or the library. Once you create a College Board account on collegeboard.org, you can start the CSS Profile anytime after October 1st of the year before you intend to start college.

The application will ask about your family and its income and assets. Some colleges also require information from a parent that doesn't live with you, in which case that parent will be asked to complete a separate application.

It's best if you submit the completed CSS Profile at least one week before your earliest college financial aid deadline. You can use the same application for multiple colleges, and you'll receive an online acknowledgment confirming the schools to which you're sending the information.

There is a $25 fee to send your CSS Profile to one college, plus a fee of $16 for each additional institution. However, depending on the information you submit, you may qualify for a fee waiver. Automatically awarded to low-income, first-time applicants, the fee waiver covers the costs of the CSS Profile registration and up to eight school reports.

College Forms

Some colleges — most of them private — require you to complete their own financial aid form as well as the FAFSA. Usually the forms are not complicated, and filling them out is not a big deal. Mike Scott of Texas Christian University says, "We have a very simple online form, where we just ask a couple of extra questions." Some of the questions are about projected enrollment: "Are they going to be full time or part time? When do they think they're going to graduate?" Others are aimed at matching students to outside sources of aid.

Find out if your colleges require you to file their own form, and if they do, file them on time.

State Forms

Most states offer need-based financial aid to their residents, and most colleges will require you to apply for it. Ask your school counselor for information on what form you need to complete to apply for state scholarship or grant programs. In many states, the FAFSA alone is enough to establish eligibility for state aid — but some states require their own form. If your state does, find out the deadline and add it to your master timeline for applying for aid. (*A table showing the deadlines for state aid, and which forms each state requires, appears in Step 7.*)

Know the Deadlines!

Deadlines count. If you're on time, the colleges to which you've applied will have more money to give you; if you're late, they will have less money — or even none. **Late means less money, so be on time!** That means knowing and keeping track of all the financial aid deadlines you have to meet.

This can be tricky, because the deadlines are not all the same. Many schools and states may require you to fill out their own financial aid forms, and those forms may have deadlines that differ from those of the FAFSA or CSS Profile. And **keep in mind that a college's due date for financial aid applications is typically different from its due date for admissions applications**.

Many colleges have no firm deadline or closing date for applying for financial aid; rather, they have a "priority" date. Often falling in February or March, the priority date is the date by which the school needs to receive your application to make its most attractive aid offer. After that date, funds may be limited or used up, and you may not get as much aid as you need. "I urge my students to apply for aid by the priority date," says Lauri Benton, a counselor at Columbia High School in Decatur, Ga. "They are more likely to get the aid they need early in the process, when the colleges have ample money to award."

Some colleges accept financial aid applications on a "rolling" basis. This means that applications are reviewed as they come in on a first-come, first-reviewed basis. Applicants are notified — that is, sent a financial aid award letter — a few weeks after they submit their forms. Most colleges that have a priority date will review late applications on a rolling basis. If you're applying to a rolling-applications college that doesn't have any set deadlines or priority dates, you're best off applying by mid-February or early March, when they will probably still have enough money available to meet your need.

Part III of this book, "Financial Aid College by College," lists deadlines and priority dates for colleges, along with their required forms. But it is worth confirming this information with the schools to which you're applying — at least by visiting their websites in November or December. Remember: Time is money. To get the most aid available, apply by the priority date.

Creating a Timeline for Aid Applications

There are a lot of dates to remember as you apply for financial aid, but they don't have to be overwhelming. You can stay on top of them by making a timeline.

When you've found out the priority dates of the colleges and scholarship programs to which you're applying, as well as those of your state financial aid agency, list them in chronological order. Make that list part of a month-by-month timeline. Don't worry about the past; start the timeline with whatever month you're in now. The chart on the opposite page is an example of the sort of timeline you might construct. (*A blank copy of this chart for you to fill in appears in Part II on page 123.*)

SAMPLE WORKSHEET 1:
Meet Your Application Deadlines

		COLLEGE 1:	COLLEGE 2:	COLLEGE 3:
	College Name	*1st Choice Univ.*	*Private Univ.*	*Financial Safety*
FORMS REQUIRED	FAFSA	*Yes*	*Yes*	*Yes*
	CSS Profile	*For ED (by 11/1)*	*Yes*	*No*
	State form	*Yes*	*No*	*Yes*
	Institutional form	*No*	*Laptop loaner*	*Yes*
	Tax returns	*Verification only*	*Verification only*	*Yes*
	Other			
SCHOOL CODES	Federal code	*999999*	*888888*	*777777*
	CSS code	*999Z*	*999X*	
PRIORITY DATE		*3/1 (FAFSA, State Form)*	*2/1*	*3/15*
CLOSING DATE		*None*	*2/15*	*None*
AFTER APPLYING	Need to send letter?			
	Documentation required?			
COMPARE AWARDS	Notification date	*12/15*	*4/1*	*2 weeks after applying*
	Reply-by date	*Immediately (if accepted ED)*	*5/1*	*4 weeks after notification*

For a blank version of this worksheet that you can photocopy for your own use, see Part II.

Throughout the period that you're applying for aid, keep your timeline where you can see it, check off what you've done, and remind yourself of what to do next. This will put the deadlines in your control. (*See the inside front cover of this book for a calendar of important dates and reminders.*)

Do You Get More Money If You Apply Early?

No. If you apply for financial aid Tuesday and another student applies Wednesday, you don't get more money than that student — so long as both of you apply by the deadline (or the priority date). However, when it comes to the college's own funds, and certain "campus-based" federal student aid programs (such as federal work-study), aid is distributed first-come, first-served once that date has passed. If you apply for aid after the college's deadline or priority date, the pool of funds may be used up. So always apply on time.

WHAT ABOUT EARLY DECISION?

Many schools allow students to apply for admission under early-decision or early-action programs. Whether early acceptance to a school affects the student's financial aid package varies from school to school. Depending on the college, the student accepted early may get more financial aid, less, or the same.

If you are considering early-decision programs, ask each school's financial aid officer: How is financial aid affected if I apply early decision? You may not know exactly what aid you'll get until after you accept. Don't panic: The rules of early decision allow you to turn down the college's acceptance offer if it doesn't offer you enough aid. Just don't put all your eggs into one basket — be sure to apply to a "financial safety school" as well.

KEEP IN MIND

When you fill out the FAFSA, both you and one of your parents need a **FSA ID (Federal Student Aid ID)**. This is important: the FSA ID will allow you to sign your FAFSA electronically, which will cut down your processing time. **You and one of your parents must each obtain a FSA ID** at **the FAFSA website**. You should register for your FSA IDs **before you fill out the FAFSA**. Although you will be prompted to get one if you didn't, it might delay processing time, so it's better to get your FSA ID ahead of time.

Get Your Stuff Together

For maximum efficiency, gather all the records you need to complete the forms before you sit down to work on them. That will save you a lot of time getting up, hunting around and forgetting where you left off. For both you and your parents, you'll probably need tax returns and related documents (such as W-2 forms), as well as end-of-year pay stubs, bank statements and other financial records. If you're filling out the CSS Profile, you will need tax documents from the year that just ended and the previous year. If your parents own their home, you will need current value and mortgage information to fill out the CSS Profile.

The FAFSA and CSS Profile websites provide preapplication worksheets that you can print out as a way to help you gather your information before filling out the actual application. Use them that way. Add a list of all the records you need to assemble. It should be comprehensive and indicate which records are for all forms and which are for the CSS Profile only.

EXPERT ADVICE

If, like many students, you've never filed a tax return, you'll probably find it helpful to **get a blank copy of IRS Form 1040EZ** and the instructions that come with it. This is the simplest tax return form there is, and most high school and college students use it to report their summer and after-school job earnings. If your parents have filed for you in past years, **ask them to walk you through your return** for the last year.

Establish Eligibility

To be eligible for federal financial aid, among other requirements, you'll have to:

- be a U.S. citizen or eligible noncitizen
- have a valid Social Security number
- not have been convicted of sale or possession of drugs
- if male and at least 18 years old, be registered with the Selective Service (in most cases)

Most of these requirements will not require extra work for most students. But two of them may. If you don't have a Social Security number, get one as soon as possible (go to www.ssa.gov to learn how), and certainly before you file your FAFSA. And if you are male, you can register for the Selective Service through the FAFSA application if you haven't already. If you do have a drug conviction, you may still be able to establish eligibility by completing a treatment program.

Income Tax Returns

The CSS Profile asks you for two years of tax information. For example, if you are seeking aid for the 2018–19 academic year you must report income information for both 2016 and 2017. It also asks for estimated income for the next year, which you can base on the prior year's information.

The FAFSA asks you to provide tax information for only one year, the "prior-prior" year. For example, if you are seeking aid for the 2018–19 academic year you only have to provide information from 2016 tax returns. This is another good change because it makes it easier to complete the FAFSA with information imported directly from the IRS, using the IRS Data Retrieval Tool (DRT), rather than with income estimates that may need correcting.

IRS Data Retrieval Tool

Accessible right from your FAFSA online, this tool allows you or your parents to access the IRS tax return information needed to complete the FAFSA and to transfer the data directly onto your FAFSA form. However, it takes a fair amount of time for your tax return information to become available for transfer from the IRS; up to three weeks if you filed your returns electronically and up to eight weeks if you filed by mail. So keep that in mind if you need to file a late tax return for the year you have to provide information.

For many colleges, the IRS Data Retrieval process is the preferred means of completing your FAFSA. If you cannot use this process at the time you initially complete your FAFSA, check with your college(s) to determine how best to update your FAFSA information once your tax returns have been filed.

You'll have to file some forms to get financial aid, but they aren't as difficult as they might look. The main forms are FAFSA and the CSS Profile, plus whatever other forms your colleges or state may require.

- File on time — filing late can cost you money.

- File your FAFSA online. Get a FSA-ID for yourself and for one of your parents early.

- Make a timeline to keep track of your deadlines, including college priority dates.

- As early as possible, check with your colleges to be sure you know what forms they each require and how they want you to provide tax information.

- Gather together the records you need to fill out the forms.

- If you don't have one already, get a Social Security number.

QUICK RECAP

Step 5: Fill Out the FAFSA

The FAFSA may look intimidating, but it's actually pretty easy to fill out. The questions mainly concern your income and assets and those of your parents, but they also touch on other matters, such as your citizenship status and the schools to which you want the FAFSA to be sent. We'll walk you through it, and give you tips about how to avoid delays. Above all: File on time!

General Advice

Nobody likes to fill out forms. And no one enjoys having to share information about family finances. But the potential result — money to help you pay for college — is well worth it. And you will see in this step that the FAFSA is really pretty simple. While the form has six sections, only one requires financial information, and another is, essentially, "sign here." The online FAFSA also has "skip logic" so you don't have to see questions that don't pertain to you.

Again, remember that you don't have to do the steps in this book in exactly the order presented. If the colleges require you to submit the CSS Profile before the FAFSA, then do the CSS Profile first, even though we present the FAFSA first. Since the CSS Profile requires much of the same information needed to fill out the FAFSA, doing the CSS Profile first will make this step much easier.

Help is available by phone and online if you have questions about FAFSA. And don't be afraid to call the financial aid offices of the colleges to which you're applying. If you're confused about this or any other aspect of the financial aid process, these offices can help. "People look at the FAFSA and they find it a bit overwhelming initially," says Vincent Amoroso of Johns Hopkins University. "They come to us seeking guidance and reassurance on how to get through the application process. We show them that it's not as complicated as it looks."

Apply on Time

You can file your FAFSA anytime after Oct. 1 of the year before you'll start college. Most college deadlines for financial aid are in March, and some fall as early as February, so don't let time slip by. You have to leave time for your FAFSA to be processed. Be sure to file your online form at least one week before the earliest deadline. Remember: missing your college's deadline or priority date can cost you money.

Read Instructions Carefully; Fill Out the Form Accurately

With the FAFSA as with all financial aid forms, accuracy is vital. Read the directions. Understand the terms that are being used. Many terms, such as "date of birth," are straightforward, but others, such as "investments," require you to read the instructions carefully so you know what they mean in this context. Even the term "parent," as discussed below, has a special meaning on the FAFSA.

Be as complete and accurate as you can about your financial circumstances. If you submit incorrect data, you might create delays that could endanger your aid. By avoiding errors, you will increase your chances of getting all the aid for which you are eligible.

Keep Track of Your "Save Key" and FSA ID

You don't have to complete the FAFSA on the Web in one sitting. At the start, you'll create a "Save Key" password that will allow you to leave the application before completing it and to return later.

Get FSA IDs ahead of time for both yourself and for one of your parents so you can sign the form electronically. The FSA IDs can be obtained at StudentAid.gov/fsaid.

Give Yourself Time

Even though the FAFSA has been made easier, it is still an important form and requires concentration. Take it seriously; don't try to do it on your phone or while multi-tasking. Use a PC or laptop in a quiet place where you won't be distracted, and give yourself a good hour or so to do it right.

KNOW THE LINGO

If you've never filed an income tax return before — or if your parents file for you — you may not be familiar with these IRS forms:

1040 — The main form of your tax return, this is a summary of all the taxable income you or your parents made last year, possible deductions from that income, the tax owed on that income, and credits that give some of that tax back.

W-2 — A tax form prepared by the employer stating how much taxable income they paid you last year, as well as untaxed benefits you or your parents received from them. Information on this form is used on both the 1040 and the FAFSA.

1099 — A form similar to the W-2 that shows income you received from anyone other than an employer. For example, if one of your parents is an independent contractor, he or she may receive a 1099-MISC showing the nonemployee compensation a client paid them.

1098 — A tax form showing payments for which you can take a deduction or credit. For example, if you take out a student loan, once you begin repaying it you will receive a 1098-E from your lender every year showing how much interest you paid on the loan.

Figure 6:
FAFSA on the Web

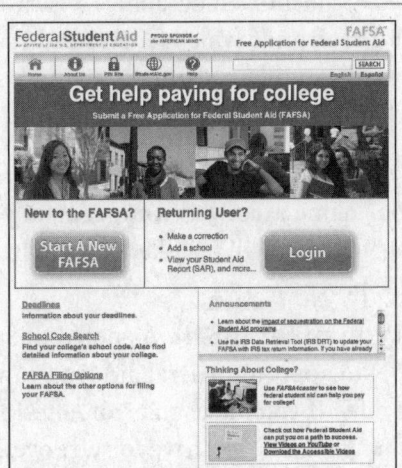

Let's Walk Through It

The FAFSA has five sections that ask questions, each with a common theme. The exact order or wording of these questions may change from year to year, but the substance remains more or less the same. And the purpose never changes: to provide information about yourself and your family that colleges will use to figure out how much federal student aid you qualify for.

There are a few general tips to keep in mind while filling out the FAFSA:

- The word "you" always means you, the student.

- The word "college" means a college, university, community college or any other school beyond high school.

- The phrase "net worth" means the current value of an asset (such as a business) minus the amount of debt owed on it.

- Questions about income are for the previous year; questions about assets ask for their value as of the day you fill out the form.

- When entering dollar figures, round to the nearest dollar and don't use commas or decimal points.

- If you have special financial circumstances that you need to explain, you can't do it on the FAFSA. Instead, write to your colleges directly. (*See Step 8 of this book, "Make Your Special Circumstances Known."*)

Here is a step-by-step walk–through of the key questions on the FAFSA. Since the online form is interactive, it will automatically skip over some questions or sections depending on how you answer. For example, if you say that you're not married, you won't be asked questions about your spouse. For that reason, you might not see all the questions described here.

Step One: Questions About Yourself

These questions (labeled "Student Demographics") gather basic information used to identify you and determine which federal and state programs you may qualify for. For example, the question about your citizenship is there because only U.S. citizens (or eligible noncitizens) can get federal student aid.

Here's the main information this section will ask for:

Your name. Enter your name exactly as it appears on your Social Security card. If the two don't match, you will be asked a few days later to fix it, slowing down the whole process.

Your Social Security number (SSN). As noted in Step 4 of this book, you need to have an SSN to apply for federal aid (you can't even open the online FAFSA without one). If you make an error entering this number on the login page, you can't change it and you have to start over. More delay.

Whether you're male or female. This question is only used to determine if you need to register with the Selective Service System. If you are male between the ages of 18 and 25, you must be registered with the Selective Service (the draft) in order to be eligible for federal aid. This requirement applies to any person assigned the sex of male at birth. If you're not registered, you can do it now on the FAFSA.

Where you live. Use a permanent home mailing address here, not a school or office address.

The state in which you legally reside. You will be asked this question if you have lived in your state for less than five years. Your answer will determine whether you're eligible for scholarships and grants from your state. In some cases, your state of legal residence might be different from the state where you're actually living at the time you fill out the FAFSA. This might be the case if you've recently moved or one of your parents is in the military.

You don't need to request that your information be sent to a state agency; the government will automatically send your processed information to the agency of your state government that administers financial aid programs for state

residents, whether scholarships, grants or loans. Do be aware, however, that some states require an additional financial aid form, as discussed in Step 7 of this book.

Your permanent telephone number. Use a permanent home or cell phone number, not a school or office number.

Your e-mail address. This is optional, but if you provide it, the government can send your Student Aid Report (SAR) by e-mail instead of snail mail, so it will reach you faster. Supply an e-mail address you check regularly.

Your marital status as of today. That means the day you submit your FAFSA. If your marital status changes later, you cannot update it on your FAFSA. In that instance, contact the financial aid office at the colleges you want to attend.

Whether you are a citizen or an eligible noncitizen. You are a citizen if you were born in this country or became a citizen through the naturalization process. An eligible noncitizen is someone such as a U.S. permanent resident holding a green card (Permanent Resident Card), or someone who has refugee status who is allowed to live permanently in the United States. It is not someone visiting on a student visa. If you're an eligible noncitizen, you'll have to fill in your Alien Registration Number. If you're neither a citizen nor an eligible noncitizen, you can't get federal aid, but you may be eligible for state or college aid — so you should still fill out the FAFSA, unless you don't have a Social Security number. In that case, call your colleges.

Whether you've ever been convicted of possessing or selling illegal drugs. Say "yes" only if the offense occurred while you were receiving federal student aid (unlikely if this is your first FAFSA, in which case you won't even see this question online), it's still on your record, and you were tried as an adult.

Your high school completion status next year. Before you can get federal financial aid, you must have completed high school or its equivalent. Select "High school diploma" if you will graduate from a public or private high school this year; "General Educational Development (GED) if you have the GED diploma or expect to pass the GED exam; or "Home schooled" if you will satisfy your state's requirements for successfully completing home schooling at the high school level. If you must select "None of the above," contact the financial aid office at the colleges you want to attend.

Name, city and state of your high school: This info will enable your high school to be notified of the status of your application. You don't have to enter the exact full name of your school (in fact you can even leave it blank). When you hit "confirm" you'll get a list of schools in your area, and then you can select the right one.

What year of college you'll be in next year. Your answer determines the aid programs for which you qualify.

What degree will you be working on in the next school year. Some aid programs are not available for graduate study, a second bachelor's degree or nondegree study. If you are undecided about what type of degree you will be pursuing (for example, if you're applying to both two-year and four-year colleges), check "undecided," but be sure to follow up with each college you're applying to after you've submitted the FAFSA.

The highest level of education completed by your father and mother. This won't affect your federal aid, but some states use this information to award scholarships to students who are the first in their family to attend college.

Whether you're interested in work-study: The best answer is "yes." Preserve your options. You're not committing to anything, and your answer won't affect the amount of grant money you might get.

Step Two: School Selection

This is where you indicate which colleges should receive your FAFSA information. You list the colleges, and the government will send the processed information to them for free.

You can list up to 10 colleges online; but if you are using the paper FAFSA, you can only list four. In either case you can add additional schools later, when you get your Student Aid Report (SAR).

Identify each college by its name or federal school code. You can find the federal school code in Part III of this book (see Figure 7 below). You can also search for it on the FAFSA Web page. The online FAFSA form also has a good search tool for finding a college by city and state.

Housing Plans. For each college, you have to say whether you plan to live on campus, off campus or with your parents. Your answer will affect the housing costs that the school will estimate for you, and therefore your financial need. If you haven't made a decision yet, assume you'll live on campus.

Figure 7:
Finding a College's Federal Code

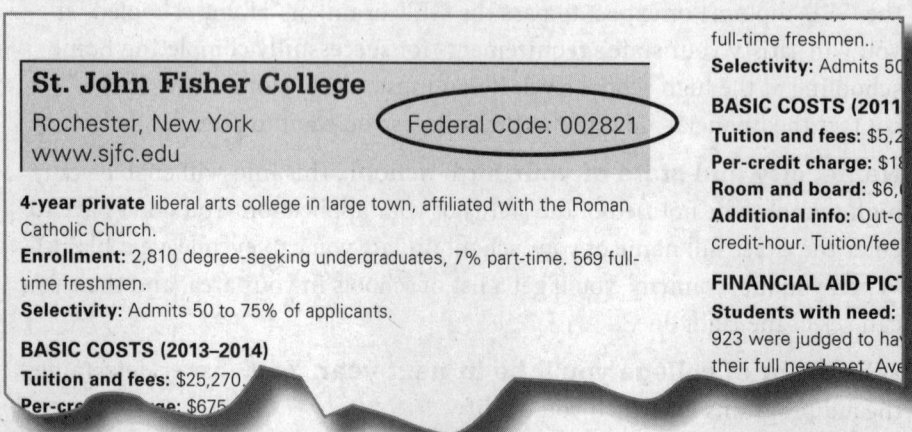

The Federal Code for each college in Part III of this book can be found in its college description.

Step Three: Are You Independent?

The questions in this step determine whether or not you're an independent student. To be considered independent for the purpose of federal student aid eligibility, it doesn't matter if you feel independent, have a job or even live on your own. It also has nothing to do with whether your parents claim you as a dependent on their tax return. But if you can truthfully answer "yes" to at least one of the questions in this step, you will be considered independent.

The things that would classify you as independent are:

• You turn age 24 or older in the year you start college.

- You'll be enrolled in a graduate degree program in the year for which you're seeking aid.

- You're married.

- You have children who get more than half of their support from you.

- You have dependents other than your children or spouse who live with you and get more than half their support from you.

- You're an orphan, or you've been a ward/dependent of the court.

- You're currently serving in, or are a veteran of, the active-duty U.S. armed forces. (If you served only as a reservist and were never activated for reasons other than training, answer "no.")

- You are a homeless, unaccompanied youth (or at risk of being such).

If you are independent, then you can skip the section about your parents' income and assets. But there are certain cases where a college financial aid office will want to know about your parents' finances even if you are an independent. If you do meet one of the criteria on the list above, it's a good idea to ask the colleges to which you're applying whether they'll consider you fully independent for the purpose of awarding their own institutional funds. If one or more of them won't, you should fill out the parent section. The online application will ask you whether you want to fill it out or skip it.

Are you unable to obtain information about your parents? Even if it is determined that you are a dependent, you might be able to show special circumstances that will allow you to submit your FAFSA without parental information. Follow the instructions on the FAFSA carefully, and then follow up immediately with the financial aid office at each college you want to attend.

Step Four: Questions About Your Parents

If you're a dependent student, you have to answer these questions (labeled "Parent Demographics") even if you don't live with your parents. When you're ready to submit the application, you will also need one of your parents to sign it, either on the paper form or by using a PIN on the electronic version.

Modern family life can make the definition of "parent" complicated. But the FAFSA definitions are fairly clear:

- If both your parents are living and married to each other, answer the questions about both of them.

- If only one of your parents is living, answer the questions about him or her.

- If your widowed parent remarried, answer the questions about your stepparent too.

- If you were raised by a single parent, answer the questions about him or her.

- If your parents are divorced or separated, answer the questions about the parent you lived with the most during the past 12 months.

- If that parent remarried, answer the questions about your stepparent, too.

- Don't provide information about grandparents, legal guardians or foster parents. FAFSA doesn't consider them your parents unless they have legally adopted you.

Here's a run-down of the important questions:

Marital status: Indicate the status as it is at the time you submit the form.

Their Social Security numbers: Unlike you, your parents are not required to have Social Security numbers in order for you to file the FAFSA (but in that case you have to enter zeroes). But if they do have Social Security numbers, they must provide them.

Their names: Again, if they have social security cards, their names must exactly match.

The number of people in your parents' household: These include you and your parents. The number who will be in college during the next year is also asked for: that also includes you (but not your parents). These questions affect how much money your parents will be expected to contribute to your education.

Step Five: Your Parents' Financial Information

OK, this is usually the most complicated part of the FAFSA. But this section has been greatly simplified. For the most part, it asks for the same information that your parents must provide on their federal income tax form, and even points out exactly where they can find that information. The main questions are:

If either of your parents is a "dislocated worker." Answer "yes" if one (or both) of your parents has been laid off or has lost their business and is still unemployed. "Dislocated worker" also includes a stay-at-home mom or dad who no longer receives support from a spouse and can't find a job. If you answer "yes" to this question, you should also contact the financial aid office at each college you are applying to. *(See Step 8, "Make Your Special Circumstances Known.")*

Whether anyone in the household received certain federal benefits. A "yes" answer to any of the listed programs, such as free or reduced-price lunch or supplemental nutrition assistance (food stamps), will likely result in a determination that your family should not be expected to contribute any money toward your education.

Whether they're eligible to file the 1040A or 1040EZ tax form. It's to your advantage if they can answer yes, they're eligible to file this form. If they would normally file the 1040A but filed the full 1040 only to take advantage of an education tax benefit relating to a child already in college, they can still check this box.

Their income tax information: The IRS Data Retrieval Process is the preferred means of completing the FAFSA (see description that follows). Check with your college(s) to determine how best to update your FAFSA information if no tax returns have been filed.

What their untaxed income and benefits were. These include items like earned income credits, welfare benefits, Social Security benefits, child support and other money that didn't get taxed. It also includes any contributions your parents made for the previous tax year to deductible Individual Retirement Accounts (IRAs) or employer-sponsored retirement plans such as 401(k)s or 403(b)s. Add this up on worksheets and fill in the totals on the FAFSA. If you're filling out the worksheets online, the information will appear on the confirmation page you'll see after submitting, which you should print out and keep on file in case a financial aid administrator asks about them later.

What their assets are. These include cash, savings and the value of investments, such as stocks and bonds. The amounts to put down are "as of" the day you fill out the FAFSA. Often that is just a best guess, using the most recent bank statements. (Keep in mind that the amount of aid you are entitled to is based much more on family income than on assets.) They do *not* include the home where your parents primarily live (a summer cottage would be included), a family-owned business of less than 100 employees, or a family farm that they live on and operate. However, if your parents own more than one home — a summer cottage, for example, or an investment property — they also should report their equity in that home on the "investments" line. If they own a farm that they don't live on, they also should report the value of that farm as a business. Another thing your parents do not need to include here is any money they have in tax-advantaged retirement accounts, such as IRAs, 401(k)s, 403(b)s and the like.

The IRS Data Retrieval Tool

The IRS Data Retrieval Tool allows students and parents to access the IRS tax return information needed to complete the FAFSA, and transfer the data directly into their FAFSA from the IRS website.

You can use the IRS retrieval tool to transfer your tax return information if:

- You have filed your tax returns
- You have not filed an amended tax return
- Your marital status has not changed since you filed your tax returns
- You are not filing your tax returns as married, filing separately
- You did not file a Puerto Rican or foreign tax return

You might not be able to use the IRS retrieval tool to transfer your tax return information if you **very recently** filed your tax return.

- If you filed your taxes electronically, allow three weeks for the tool to be available.
- If you filed your taxes by mail, allow eight weeks for the tool to be available.

The IRS Retrieval Tool is the preferred means of completing your FAFSA. If you cannot use this process at the time you initially complete your FAFSA, check with your college(s) to determine how best to update your FAFSA information once your tax returns have been filed.

Follow the online instructions to have the IRS data fill in your income data. **Do not change any data once it is transferred to your FAFSA.** Changing any piece of tax data may require follow-up and verification by your college's financial aid office.

Step Six: Your Own Financial Information

These questions ask about *your* income and assets — whether or not you are independent. Income is how much money you made last year; assets are what you own and the savings you have. If you are married, they also want to know about your spouse's income and assets.

These are the main things that this section asks for:

Whether you've completed a tax return for the past year. This means the return that you filed a year ago. If you have, they will ask what form you used, for example, the 1040 or 1040A. If you didn't file any tax return, they will still ask how much you (and, if you have one, your spouse) earned from working.

Whether you're eligible to file the 1040A or 1040EZ tax form. The instructions on the FAFSA explain who can file these forms. Most students can. If you can, say yes.

GOOD TO KNOW

Most students are eligible to file IRS Form 1040EZ or 1040A as their tax return. Some parents can, too. (The rules determining whether you can are explained in the FAFSA instructions.) **If both you and your parents are eligible to file the 1040A or 1040EZ**, it may turn out that only your income (not your assets) will be assessed when calculating your expected family contribution.

What income and tax information you and your spouse reported on your tax returns. Again, these questions are easy to answer if you've already completed your tax return, and if the IRS Data Retrieval tool is available to you. If not, check with your colleges to determine how best to update your FAFSA information.

The number of people in your household: This question refers to the number of people in *your* household, if you have one — not your parents'.

What your untaxed income and benefits were. Once again, these include items like earned income credits, welfare benefits, Social Security benefits, child support and other money that came to you without being taxed. You will be asked about these in a series of questions on screen. (If you are filling out the paper FAFSA, you should use the worksheets that come with the form to add them all up, then fill in the totals on your FAFSA. Don't submit the worksheets, but keep copies of them on file. A financial aid office may want those details later.)

What your assets are. This question is meant to provide a snapshot of your assets, the money or property you currently own. Using current banking statements and investment records, say how much cash and savings you have, as well the total value of any stocks, other investments or investment properties that you might own. If you're still in high school, chances are that you only have a small savings or checking account, which you should report on the line asking for "cash, savings accounts and checking accounts." You may also have some government savings bonds, certificates of deposit (CDs) or a few shares of stock; those should be reported on the line asking about "investments."

Don't include any college savings accounts in this step unless you are independent (you answered "yes" to any question in FAFSA Step Three) and they are owned by you in your own name.

Step Seven: Review Your Answers, Then Sign and Submit

This is easy, but it's still an important step. Take the time to carefully review all your answers for accuracy and spelling — even your name. Be sure to print out your FAFSA if you're filling it out online.

Preparer's information. If you or your family paid a fee to someone to fill out your FAFSA, or to advise you on how to fill it out, that person must provide his or her Social Security number or Employment Identification Number (EIN), and must also sign and date the form. This requirement does not apply to school counselors, financial aid administrators, friends or mentors who helped but did not charge a fee.

Pay heed to this warning from the FAFSA website: "Be wary of organizations that charge a fee to submit your application, or to find you money for school. Some are legitimate and some are scams. Generally, **any help that you pay for can be received free** from your school or Federal Student Aid."

Terms to read before signing. You'll see a list of terms you must agree to by signing. There is nothing onerous here, but there is a scary-sounding penalty for giving "false or misleading information." This does *not* mean honest mistakes or estimates that turn out to be way off; they're talking about intentional fraud.

If your parents provided financial information, one of them also needs to sign. Use your PINs to sign electronically — don't use the "print signature page and mail" option. It just wastes time.

Be sure to keep clicking on "next" until you get to the confirmation page! Your FAFSA is not truly submitted until then.

FAFSA Step Eight: Confirmation

You're done! Be sure to print the confirmation page, and save it to your hard drive as well. If you don't have a printer, write down the confirmation number, date and time. This is your proof that your FAFSA was received.

If you file using the paper form, make a photocopy of it before mailing it, and keep that photocopy together with the worksheets you filled out and all the records you used.

Check Your Student Aid Report!

After you submit your FAFSA, you'll receive your Student Aid Report, or SAR. How long it will take for you to receive it, and in what form, will depend on how you filed the FAFSA. If you filed FAFSA on the Web and signed it with your PIN, you should recieve it immediately, or at most within one to three days. If you filed a paper FAFSA and did not provide an e-mail address, you'll receive a paper SAR within about four weeks.

In whatever form the SAR reaches you, check it over carefully. It will include a summary detailing the information you supplied on the FAFSA. Make sure this information is correct. If not, then you must make corrections. It's easy to do — just go back to www.fafsa.ed.gov, log in and click on "Make FAFSA Corrections." You can also add or remove colleges this way.

Make corrections only if the data on the SAR doesn't accurately represent your family's financial situation at the time the FAFSA was originally filed. For example, if you mistyped a number, or if the federal data-entry clerk misread your handwriting, correct that. But **don't make changes that reflect changes to your income or assets since you filed the FAFSA**. If important changes of that sort have happened — such as a lost job — inform your colleges individually rather than through the FAFSA. (*See Step 8, "Make Your Special Circumstances Known."*)

KEEP IN MIND

You have to leave time for your FAFSA to be processed. If you're filing on paper, allow at least four weeks before your earliest college or state deadline. If you're filing online, leave at least one week before the earliest deadline.

KEEP IN MIND

Eligibility for **federal student aid does not automatically continue** from one year to the next. You have to reapply every year that you're in college. Do that by filling out a **Renewal FAFSA**. This is a partially preformatted version of the FAFSA that you can use so long as you applied for federal aid the previous year.

At the top of the SAR, you should also see an estimate of your EFC: the amount of money your family is expected to contribute toward college costs. You might not see an EFC if there is incorrect or missing information that made it impossible to process your data. If that happens to you, submit the necessary corrections and you'll get your EFC estimate. **The actual EFC calculated by a given college may be different than what you'll see here**, especially if that college uses a different formula, or if its financial aid office has adjusted your EFC based on special circumstances that you brought to the college's attention.

The colleges you requested to receive your FAFSA information will automatically get your SAR. At the corrections stage, you'll have an opportunity to add more colleges to receive your FAFSA information. You can also give a school permission to add itself to the list. Just provide the college with the Data Release Number (DRN) that will be provided on your SAR. The school will use your DRN to access your application record.

The SAR gives you an estimate of how much money your family is expected to pay for college, but not how much financial aid you'll receive. You'll find that out when your individual colleges send you their award letters. Even so, by filing your FAFSA, you've taken a big step toward getting those letters.

If the expected family contribution (EFC) indicated on the SAR looks too high for your family to afford, you should talk to your parents and discuss other financing options with them. (*See Step 11, "Consider Your Out-of-Pocket Options."*) It could also mean that you need to explain some special financial circumstances to the colleges to which you've applied (see Step 8).

QUICK RECAP

The FAFSA is easier than it looks. Most of it is about your income and assets, and that of your parents. Remember:

- File on time. Submit your FAFSA as soon as possible, especially if your colleges have early financial aid deadlines or priority dates.
- Use the IRS data retrieval tool to transfer your tax return information.
- Read instructions.
- Be accurate.
- Reapply every year.

Step 6: Fill Out the CSS Profile™ (If Required)

QUICK OVERVIEW

Whether you have to fill out the CSS/Financial Aid PROFILE depends on the colleges to which you're applying. If you do, you'll find it mainly asks for "more of the same" — information about your family's income, expenses and assets — rather than something completely new. The online form is customized to your situation, so you won't be presented with too many questions that don't apply to you. However, the application does take time to fill out, so leave yourself plenty of time to submit it before your colleges' deadlines.

General Advice

Step 6 is to fill out the CSS Profile — but only if you need to. If the schools to which you're applying don't require this financial aid form, you don't have to complete it. Find out if they require it by checking Part III of this book or the colleges' websites.

The CSS Profile is administered by the College Board, a not-for-profit association of schools and colleges (and the publisher of this book). It is available online only: You can't file on paper. The upside of this is that CSS Profile is available 24 hours a day, seven days a week. Furthermore, its system of online edits alerts you to missing or incorrect information before you submit the application, eliminating a potential source of delays. Firewall protection and data encryption protect the information you submit about your family and their finances. The downside is that if you don't have a computer with Internet access at home, you will have to use one at your school, a library or a parent's workplace.

The CSS Profile doesn't replace the FAFSA: You still need to complete that, too, because that's the form required for federal student aid, which any college will expect you to seek before they give away their own institutional funds. The schools that require the CSS Profile do so because they believe it gives a more complete account of your financial situation to guide them in awarding their own funds. The College Board provides the colleges with your CSS Profile information, and the colleges use it to calculate your expected family contribution and your need.

Since it's designed to give a more complete picture of your finances, it is not surprising that the CSS Profile is longer than the FAFSA. It's the same general concept, but you'll need to gather more records to answer all the questions, and it will take more time to fill out.

Create Your Account and File Early

Because the CSS Profile form is more involved, and because colleges may ask for additional information even after the form is filed, it's important to begin the process well before your colleges' deadlines and leave yourself lots of time to fill out the application. The College Board usually processes your CSS Profile information overnight, but it can take longer when application submissions peak closer to school deadlines. Also, don't assume it can all be completed in one session; you may need to return to the form if a college asks for supplemental information. Fortunately, you can go back and forth to your application online, rather than having to finish it in one sitting.

It's best to submit the CSS Profile at least one week before your earliest financial aid priority date. Remember, colleges use CSS Profile information to determine who gets their limited grant dollars. If you file late, you will have to make do with whatever funds, if any, are left over.

Preparing for the CSS Profile

Get ready for the CSS Profile by collecting important financial documents like tax forms, business and farm statements, and information about other income and assets. Having a PDF copy of your family's tax forms will help speed things along. You can also download and print out the *PROFILE Student Guide* from the CSS Profile site.

The FAFSA and the CSS Profile will both ask you to provide family income information from two years prior to the year you plan to enter college. However, you'll need to gather more records to fill out the CSS Profile than you will for the FAFSA.

For example, expect to answer a few questions about your parents' income for the most recent year or the year just before you enter college and about the anticipated year to come. There are also questions about your projected summer and school-year earnings during your first year in college. The purpose of this is to give financial aid officers a better idea of your family's financial circumstances over time.

EXPERT ADVICE

Most schools that require the CSS Profile use it when they're investing a lot of their own institutional dollars into need-based programs. We use it because **the CSS Profile gives us an added, more in-depth look** at a family's financial strength. Our ultimate goal is to give the right dollars to the right students at the right time, and this CSS Profile application helps us do that."

— Vincent Amoroso, former director, Office of Student Financial Services, Johns Hopkins University

---

GOOD TO KNOW

Help is available to get you through the CSS Profile application. If you're not sure about how to answer any question, **check the online Help Desk** that's built into the online application. If you can't find an answer to your question there, contact the CSS Profile help line, either by e-mail (**help@cssprofile.org**) or by phone (**305-829-9793**).

You can also contact the financial aid office at the college to which you're applying. In addition, your high school counselor may be able to answer your questions.

Documents You'll Need Before You Fill Out Your CSS Profile

It's a good idea to gather the necessary records before you start and have them handy as you work on the CSS Profile. You'll need records for both yourself and your parents.

✔ Federal income tax return from 2 years prior to the year you start college

✔ Federal income tax return for the year before you start college, if completed, or pay stubs and other income-related records

✔ W-2 forms and other records of money earned for those two years

✔ Records of untaxed income for those two years

✔ Current bank statements and mortgage information

✔ Records of stocks, bonds, trusts and other investments

Because the FAFSA and the CSS Profile use the same tax year information to answer a majority of their questions, it may be helpful to complete the CSS Profile soon after you complete the FAFSA while the information is still top of mind. The financial aid deadline dates provided by your colleges are important considerations when making this decision.

Starting the CSS Profile Application

Just like registering ahead of time for a FSA ID, **it's best to begin the CSS Profile well before the first college's deadline.** You can gain access to the CSS Profile application through your College Board account. Creating the username and password for the account is free; you may have done this already if you previously accessed bigfuture.org to search for colleges or register for the SAT. If you don't have Internet access at home, ask your school counselor or librarian if you can use one of the school's computers.

It's important to start collecting documents for the CSS Profile as soon as you're sure about where you'll be applying for aid, but in any case at least one week before the earliest financial aid filing date you need to meet. Accounts can be created at any time and the CSS Profile application can be started beginning Oct. 1 of the year before you intend to start college. Once you begin, you can either complete your application then and there or return to it at a later time. Your CSS Profile application will be customized to your circumstances based on the information you give as you complete the application.

Most families will have to pay a fee of $25 to have their CSS Profile sent to one college, plus $16 for each additional college. The fee can be paid with most major credit cards or bank debit cards. Low-income families applying for the first time may qualify for a fee waiver (see sidebar).

Let's Walk Through It

Your CSS Profile application may contain up to 16 sections; depending on your family's situation, a number of sub-sections may or may not be included. The application includes questions about you and your finances and questions about your parents and their finances. There is a place for you to explain in your own words any special financial circumstances and a place for any supplemental questions that may be required by one or more of the schools to which you're applying. In addition, if your parents are divorced or separated, your noncustodial parent might need to complete an online Noncustodial CSS Profile (be mindful of your college deadlines and allow sufficient time for this.)

To help you fill out the CSS Profile, there are instructions online that you can follow, along with other avenues for help. A few general points to keep in mind:

- If a financial question (such as one about income or assets) doesn't apply to you, enter a zero (0).

- If a nonfinancial question (such as a year or a name) doesn't apply to you, leave it blank. If the field is required, just enter N/A.

GOOD TO KNOW

If you come from a low-income family, and you are applying for financial aid for the first time, **you may be eligible for a fee waiver** covering registration costs and up to eight school reports. Information that you provide on the CSS Profile form determines if you are eligible. **You will automatically get the fee waiver if you qualify** — you don't have to apply for it separately.

- Round all money amounts to the nearest dollar. Don't enter commas or cents.

When you fill out the application, don't be surprised if you don't see all the questions or sections that are mentioned here. The CSS Profile is customized to your situation. That means that when you complete the form, any sections that are known not to apply to you won't even be presented and individual questions that aren't relevant will be greyed out. For example, if your parents are married, you won't be shown any questions that assume you have a noncustodial parent.

Your Basic Information

The CSS Profile begins by asking for some basic information about you, such as your date of birth, where you live, whether you are a U.S. citizen, a veteran, married, etc. These questions usually won't involve looking up documents; just answer them straightforwardly. Some of them (such as the questions about date of birth and being a veteran) are intended to clarify whether you're a dependent or an independent student.

College Information

This section focuses on where you are in school now, and lets you select which colleges should receive your CSS Profile application. When selecting the colleges or scholarship programs where you would like to have your CSS Profile report sent, you will also answer where you expect to live for each school. You can add more colleges or programs to this list after you register, or even after filing your application.

Figure 8:
Finding a College's CSS code

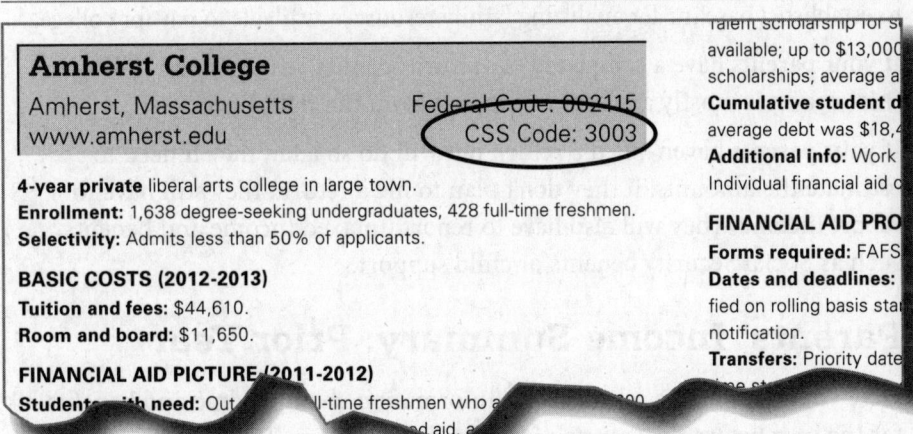

CSS Code for each college in Part III of this book can be found in its college description.

Your Parents' Information

This section asks for some basic information from your parents. The term "parents" as CSS Profile understands it might need some defining. It basically means your custodial parents, the people with whom you live. If both your parents are living, married to each other and have custody of you, answer the questions about both of them. But if that isn't the case, follow these rules:

- If your birth or adoptive parents are divorced, separated or were never married, then you only need to provide information about the parent with whom you live. If you lived with both equally in the past 12 months, answer the questions about the parent who provided most of your financial support.

- If you have a widowed or single parent or a legal guardian, answer the questions only about that person.

- If your parent (as defined above) has married or remarried, include information about your stepparent too.

Your parents should use this section to provide information about themselves, including name, date of birth, employment status, and whether they themselves are in college or graduate school. Some of these questions have to do with clarifying financial strength — for example, the question about what kind of retirement plans your parents have. Some are just matters of housekeeping, such as their preferred daytime telephone number in case they need to be contacted.

Parents' Income and Benefits for the "Prior-Prior" Year

In this section, your parents report their income and benefits from two years before the year you intend to start college. That should be the same tax information you used to complete your FAFSA. Information in this section is used to establish a baseline for analyzing family resources available to pay for college.

If your parents have a completed tax return for that year on hand, filling in this section is mostly a matter of copying from the right lines.

If your parents haven't filed a return but will do so later, they'll need to estimate the amounts. If they don't plan to file a return, they still have to report income. They will also have to report untaxed income and benefits, such as Social Security benefits or child support.

Parents' Income Summary: Prior Year

Here your parents are asked to give information about income and benefits for the year before the year you intend to start college. This is part of a three year set of data that is meant to give the CSS Profile colleges a long-term view of your family's finances. This section asks for that year's earnings from work, other taxable income, and untaxed income. Worksheets are provided to assist you calculate any untaxed income and benefits.

Parents' Income Summary: Anticipated Income

Here your parents have to estimate how much they expect to receive in income and benefits during the year in which you start college. Again, the idea is to establish as clear a picture as possible about your family's finances in the long term, and to show whether the years before you started college was typical or not. Your parents will have to estimate work income, other taxable income, and untaxed income and benefits. In this section they will also be able to, explain any unusual increases or decreases in income and benefits (10 percent or more) from last year.

Parent Income not Reported on Taxes

Some forms of income don't show up on tax forms. This section asks if there are other sources of income that your family is receiving.

Parent Address Information

In this section your parents are asked for some additional information about your family's residence(s) and housing.

Parents' Assets

This section asks about your parents' assets because these are resources that can help them finance college. There are questions about cash and savings and checking accounts (with their value as of the day you fill out the form). If they own their home, there are questions to determine home equity, the difference between the current market value of their home and the outstanding mortgage debt.

There are also questions about the current market value of any other assets they own, including investments and other real estate. They also need to include educational savings accounts, such as 529 prepaid tuition or college savings plans or Coverdell savings accounts that they've opened for you or your siblings.

Business Assets and Farm Assets

These sections will only appear if your parents indicated ownership in a business or farm. There will be questions about value, debt, number of employees, tax form filed and if you live on the farm.

Parents' Expenses

This section asks about certain special expenses your parents might have. These are not just any expenses, such as grocery bills or vacation airfare, but specific costs that might legitimately affect their ability to pay for college. Included here are child support payments, certain educational costs, and medical and dental expenses not covered by insurance.

Information About a Noncustodial Parent

If your parents are divorced or separated, this section asks for information about the parent who doesn't have custody of you. But it should be filled out by your custodial parent. If for any reason you can't get sufficient information about the noncustodial parent, there is an opportunity to explain why. Many colleges want this information because they believe it is the responsibility of both your biological or adoptive parents to pay for your college costs, even if they no longer live together, and even if the parent who does have custody of you has remarried. That's why, after you've filled out this section and submitted your CSS Profile, they may request that your noncustodial parent fill out a supplemental form, the Noncustodial CSS Profile. The section you're filling out here is not that supplemental form; your noncustodial parent will fill out that form if it's required.

Your Own Income and Benefits

This section asks about your own income and benefits, if any, from two years before the year you intend to start college.

If you have a completed tax return for that year, this section is mostly a matter of copying the amounts from the correct lines, such as the adjusted gross income and income tax paid. If you didn't file a return but you did make some money that year, you'll have to report it. Untaxed income also goes in this section. A worksheet is available for you to tally it up.

Your Expected Summer/School-Year Resources for the Coming School Year

Here you're asked to state your expected resources for this coming summer and this coming school year. You're also asked about scholarships you expect to get from sources other than the colleges to which you're applying and how much money your parents think they'll be able to pay for your college expenses.

This may seem like a strange series of questions, especially if you don't know yet where you'll be going to college next year, or where (even if) you'll be working. But colleges that use the CSS Profile want to have as clear a picture as possible of your future resources, not just your past ones. For example, if you currently have an after-school job but will leave that job when you graduate, the financial aid offices need to know that the income from that job won't be available to you anymore once you've started college.

Do the best you can to estimate these figures. If you're not sure how to answer in your particular case, check the CSS Profile help online or contact the financial aid office at the college to which you're applying.

Your Own Assets

This section asks about your assets — the money or property you, the student, currently own. These too affect your ability to pay for college. You need to list any cash you have and any checking or savings accounts in your name. Give their value as of the day you're filling out the application. You should also include any investments, such as certificates of deposit, savings bonds, stocks or real estate that you own. If you have any Individual Retirement Accounts (IRAs) or other tax-advantaged retirement accounts, you should also list them here.

If you're an independent student, then any money you have in 529 prepaid tuition or college savings plans or Coverdell savings accounts should be included here. If you're a dependent, those will be considered your parents' assets, and the information about them should go in the Parent Assets.

This section will also ask you to answer questions about any trust accounts your parents or other relatives may have established for you. A trust account is money that is held for you by somebody else until you reach a certain age, at which point it becomes yours. Colleges want to know about this because if you have a trust, that money will eventually reach your hands, lowering your ultimate financial need. If you have any trust accounts, list their value here and answer the questions about them. But don't include money in Section 529 plans; those aren't the same as trusts.

Your Expenses for the Previous Year

You'll only see these questions if you're an independent student. If you are, you'll be asked about any child support you or your spouse paid to a former spouse and any medical and dental expenses you had last year that weren't covered by insurance. Most colleges will consider these expenses in determining your financial need.

Household Summary

This section asks questions about other dependent members of your household. If you are a dependent student, you will be shown the Parents' Household version. If you are an independent student, you will be asked questions about your household in the Student's Household version, and if required by your school, your parents' household in the Parents' Household section.

The questions in this section ask for more information about these household members: their names, how they're related to you, their ages, and to what extent you or your parents are required to pay for their school or college education last year and next year. The reason for these questions is that if household members other than you are enrolled in college, and your family is paying heavily to fund those educations, the colleges may take this into account when they determine the expected family contribution (EFC) to your own education. If there are younger children in the family, the colleges will assume that a certain portion of the household's income and assets need to be saved for their college educations, which will also affect your EFC.

Explanations/Special Circumstances

This section gives you a chance to explain anything unusual in your application or any special circumstances that affect your family's ability to pay for college. Categories are provided to give examples of when an additional explanation will be helpful to the colleges reviewing your application. You can mention, for example, reasons for unusually high medical or dental expenses, steep rises or falls in income from year to year, or loss of employment. You should also give information about any outside scholarships you've been awarded. This allows the CSS Profile colleges to better understand your financial picture.

In addition to telling the colleges about anything you think it's important that they know about, you should also use this section to expand on your answers to certain questions in previous sections, if there wasn't an explanation box provided per the instructions that you'll find on the CSS Profile website. For example, you can provide details about tuition benefits, gifts from relatives, etc.

You're limited to 2,000 characters (about 300 words) in this section. If you need more space, send the information directly to your colleges, including your name and Social Security number on all correspondence. (**See Step 8 for tips on how to let your college know about your special circumstances.**)

Supplemental Information

You will only see this section if one or more of the colleges to which you're applying requires more information. In that case, you'll see additional questions here. Your answers to these questions will be used only by the colleges that ask for them. Some of the questions colleges ask here are used to determine your eligibility for purely need-based financial aid; others are used to determine if you're eligible for scholarships that have non-need-based criteria.

Here are some examples of the types of questions you might see:

- What is the year, make and model of the family's primary car?

- Do you or either of your parents receive free food or housing as a job benefit?

- What is your family's religious denomination? (This information will be used to determine scholarship eligibility.)

- In what field of study do you plan to major?

After Submitting Your CSS Profile

GOOD TO KNOW

If only one of your birth parents has custody of you, your college may still require information from both parents. If that happens, the main CSS Profile application collects information from one parent, and the **Noncustodial CSS Profile** collects information from the other. After the information is processed, the college will complete the EFC calculation. How to divide up payment of the EFC among you and your parents is a family decision.

After you complete your CSS Profile, you'll receive an online CSS Profile acknowledgment that confirms the colleges to which you're sending the information and gives you the opportunity to review any data you submitted. You should print the acknowledgment, which includes the list of colleges and the data you entered on the form. Once you submit your CSS Profile, you can't revise your information online for the colleges you selected. Use the printed acknowledgment to make changes, if necessary, to the CSS Profile information, and send those corrections directly to your colleges. It is best if the CSS Profile is only sent to colleges only once, so try to have it as complete as possible when you submit. If you do need to make changes, you can re-enter the application to make updates. Some colleges may prefer to receive updates by paper, so check with your colleges for their preference.

The College Board analyzes your data and reports it to the colleges to which you're applying. The schools then apply their own institutional policies to figure out your expected family contribution (EFC). From this analysis, they determine how great your need is and how much institutional financial aid to give you.

SENDING YOUR CSS PROFILE TO ADDITIONAL COLLEGES

You can delete colleges from your list of schools only before you submit the application. After that, all the listed colleges will get your information. But you can add colleges whenever you want, even after you submit the application. Just go to the CSS Profile website and click on "Add Colleges to Submitted Application." The fee is $16 for each additional college or program to which you want your information sent.

When you add additional colleges, you will also be given the opportunity to update or correct any of the information on your original application. Please note, however, that this new information will only be sent to the colleges you're adding. You should directly contact the colleges to which you submitted your original application to update your information with them.

SUPPLEMENTAL FORMS

Some colleges require supplemental information that's not on the CSS Profile application. For example, a college may require a Noncustodial CSS Profile if you don't live with both of your birth parents. When you register for the CSS Profile and indicate that your biological or adoptive parents are not married, you will receive an e-mail with instructions, a temporary password and a link to an application that you should forward to your noncustodial parent to complete. This form can be completed only by the noncustodial parent.

Be aware that these follow-ups take additional time. All the more reason to leave yourself plenty of time to file the CSS Profile before your college financial aid deadlines.

Since the CSS Profile form is customized, the application may not necessarily be the same length as the FAFSA. In some cases the CSS Profile will contain more questions than the FAFSA and in some cases it will contain fewer. The main difference is that it tries to get a more complete picture of your family's finances. A few points to keep in mind:

- File early.
- The CSS Profile is online only, so you have to submit it on a computer.
- There are fees, but students from low-income families may qualify for a fee waiver.
- After you submit your CSS Profile, you'll get an online acknowledgment confirming that you submitted it. You can make corrections, but you should check with your colleges first.
- Depending on your circumstances, you or one of your parents may have to submit supplemental information to one or more of your colleges.

QUICK RECAP

Step 7: Fill Out Any Other Required Forms

QUICK OVERVIEW

The FAFSA and CSS Profile are the big ones, but don't forget to file any other forms that may be required by your state or by the colleges to which you're applying. You don't want to have your application for financial aid marked "incomplete" because you didn't file a one-page form. These forms can vary widely from college to college, and from state to state.

Some Colleges Have Their Own Financial Aid Application

Some colleges have their own forms that you have to submit in addition to the FAFSA and the CSS Profile. A purpose of the form may be to get more information about your finances, or to find out if you're a member of a particular group that is eligible for a special scholarship or grant. If a college requires such a form from all first-time applicants, its description in Part III of the book will say "institutional form required" under the "application procedures" section. Contact the financial aid office at your colleges to find out more.

The good news is that these forms are generally not long or complicated — they are usually just a page or two in length. They manage to stay short because they are intended not to duplicate the FAFSA or CSS Profile forms but to supplement them and help the financial aid office keep track of applications. Such a "one pager" might, for example, ask for basic identifying information, some demographic facts and whether you are interested in loans and work-study. This kind of form is typical at community colleges and most four-year public colleges. "It's almost like an update form," Mary San Agustin says of the institutional form currently in use at her institution, Palomar College. "It's basically just a supplemental form in case any changes occurred since the time the student applied for admission or completed the FAFSA."

Sometimes a college might require a longer form that asks questions about your finances that are about as broad and deep as the FAFSA or CSS Profile. Usually this only happens with colleges that use their own formulas to calculate need, but choose not to use the CSS Profile to help them with it.

Another reason a college might require its own financial aid form is if it requires every student to have a computer on campus. Such schools sometimes have a supplemental form that qualifies needy applicants for a stipend to buy a computer, or places them in a "loaner" program so they can borrow one. The University of Virginia has two forms that deal with computers. One form is for its "laptop loaner" program, and a different form is for a "one-time computer expense" that allows students who want to buy a laptop to add the purchase price to their cost of attendance; that way their aid package may cover the cost.

Still another kind of institutional form is one for early decision applicants. Such a form works as a sort of "pre-read" meant to help students get an early estimate of their expected family contribution and the financial aid package they will receive if they accept an early-decision offer. (The rules of early decision require them to accept the offer if the college offers enough financial aid for them to attend.) Some schools offer a similar pre-read form for student athletes who are being recruited by a coach.

Scholarship and Grant Forms

Some colleges require a separate form for students applying for merit scholarships. This isn't always the case: At many schools, every student who applies for admission is automatically considered for merit scholarships. But at some schools, you must file a separate application for merit scholarships. The rules may even differ from department to department, depending on your major. For example, if you want to major in theater or music performance, you might have to audition. Contact the financial aid office at your colleges for more details, and check with the department in which you're interested in majoring.

Some institutional forms ask questions to find out if you qualify for financial aid funds set aside for students with particular characteristics. For example, the college might offer grants that are only available to children of alumni or descendants of the town's founding families. At most colleges, these grants are part of the need-based aid program, so you have to demonstrate need through the FAFSA along with proving you have the right qualifications for the grant.

Verification of Your Tax Return

Some colleges require you to provide your family's federal or state tax returns for verification. **"Verification" doesn't mean that you did something wrong**. It's not like an IRS audit, where only suspicious tax returns are selected for special scrutiny. Since colleges disburse federal money — in the form of grants, work-study and loans — they are required by law to check the information that a certain percentage of financial aid applicants have submitted.

Not all colleges ask for this information the same way. Some will require you to use the IRS Data Retrieval process; some might require official tax transcripts; others might just want photocopies of the returns. Check directly with the college to verify how you should submit the returns, and if they also require any attached schedules or the W-2s or 1099s you received from employers and banks. Usually you'll also have to fill out a form that allows colleges to confirm details, like how many of your siblings are enrolled in college. The college may ask you to send your documents directly to the financial aid office, or it might ask you to send them to the College Board's Institutional Documentation (IDOC) service.

Some colleges will request verification if the data you submitted on the FAFSA looks unusual. As an extreme example, people who reported that they had no income may be asked how they supported themselves.

State Forms

Most states rely on the FAFSA to award their need-based grants and loans to students. But a few states have their own financial aid forms. For example, New York State has an application for its Tuition Assistance Program (TAP) that is sent to eligible students who submit a FAFSA.

Even though the thought of filling out yet another form may seem burdensome, and you feel sure that you won't qualify for the state aid program, fill it out. If you don't, your application might be marked "incomplete" at your colleges. These state forms are usually short and don't take long to fill out, especially once you do the prep work of filling out the FAFSA. **When you file the FAFSA online, you'll be automatically directed to your state's form.** (If you file the FAFSA paper form, you'll usually have to send away for a paper copy of your state form.)

Table 2:

State Aid Deadlines

Residents of states not listed in this table should contact their state aid office directly.
See "Contact Information for State Aid Programs" in Part II.

STATE	FORM(S) REQUIRED	DEADLINE	NOTES
Alaska	FAFSA	6/30 10/1*	Performance Scholarship Priority date for Alaska Education Grant
Arkansas	FAFSA	6/1	Higher Education Opportunity Grant Academic Challenge awards
California	FAFSA, state form	3/2 9/2	Initial awards Additional community college awards
Connecticut	FAFSA, state form	2/15	Priority date
Delaware	FAFSA	4/15	
District of Columbia	FAFSA, DC form	5/1 5/31	FAFSA DC form
Florida	FAFSA	5/15	
Idaho	FAFSA, state form	3/1	
Illinois	FAFSA	10/1*	Priority date
Indiana	FAFSA	3/10	
Iowa	FAFSA	7/1	
Kansas	FAFSA, state form	4/1	Priority date
Kentucky	FAFSA	10/1*	Priority date
Louisiana	FAFSA	7/1	July 1 of prior year recommended
Maine	FAFSA	5/1	
Maryland	FAFSA	3/1	
Massachusetts	FAFSA	5/1	Priority date
Michigan	FAFSA	3/1	
Minnesota	FAFSA	30 days after start of term	
Missouri	FAFSA	4/1 2/1	Priority date
Mississippi	FAFSA	3/31 9/15	HELP Scholarship MTAG and MESG Grants
Nevada		10/1*	Opportunity Grant
New Jersey	FAFSA	4/15 9/15 2/15	Tuition Aid Grant applicants All other applicants Spring-term applicants only
New York	FAFSA, state form	6/30	
North Carolina		10/1*	Priority date
North Dakota	FAFSA	10/1*	Priority date
Ohio	FAFSA	10/1	
Oklahoma	FAFSA	10/1*	Priority date
Oregon	FAFSA	10/1* 3/1 4/1	Opportunity Grant OSAC Private Scholarships Promise Grant
Pennsylvania	FAFSA, state form	5/1 8/1	4-year degree candidates Other applicants
Rhode Island	FAFSA	3/1	Priority date

* Prior year

STATE	FORM(S) REQUIRED	DEADLINE	NOTES
South Carolina	FAFSA	10/1* 6/30	Priority date for SC Commission on Higher Education Grants Tuition Grants
Tennessee	FAFSA	1/17	
Texas		3/15 10/1*	Priority date
Vermont		10/1*	Priority date
Washington	FAFSA	10/1*	Priority date
West Virginia	FAFSA, state form	3/1 4/15	Promise Scholarship Higher Education Grant

* Prior year

QUICK RECAP

In addition to the FAFSA and CSS Profile, some states and colleges have financial aid forms of their own. Here's what to know about them:

- They're usually short.
- Their questions vary from school to school and from state to state.
- They may determine if you're eligible for special grants.
- They may help verify your financial information, perhaps through questions about your tax returns.
- If state aid is available, apply for it, or your colleges might consider your financial aid application incomplete.
- If one of your colleges requires an institutional application, fill it out, or you'll disqualify yourself from financial aid.

Step 8: Make Your Special Circumstances Known

QUICK
OVERVIEW

If something in your family's financial life can't be explained on the financial aid forms, make sure your colleges know about it. These "special circumstances" may include a lost job, high medical expenses or supporting an extended family. Colleges are willing to listen and, if you make your case, may be able to improve your financial aid package by taking those circumstances into account. This step is about how to prepare your case.

Be a Person, Not Just a Form

Sometimes the financial aid forms you fill out don't tell the whole story. They may not show that your family sends money every month to support relatives in another country. Since the forms are based on the previous year's tax forms, they may not reveal this year's events: how one of your parents just lost a job, or will be shifting from full-time to half-time work. When the forms don't adequately report a special circumstance that affects your family's ability to pay for college, let your college know — it may change how much financial aid you get!

Even if you're not sure your circumstance qualifies as special, speak up. The financial aid office will let you know whether it qualifies. Don't think you're limited to communicating with your college only through the financial aid forms. If there's any doubt in your mind about whether those forms give a true picture of your family's situation, feel free to go beyond the form and contact the financial aid office. **Be a person, not just a form**. There are two reasons to do this: It guarantees that the college knows how much you are able to pay, and it shows that you're interested in the college — which may affect the lengths to which they'll go to help you.

Using the Financial Aid Forms

In some cases, you can inform your colleges of special circumstances through the financial aid forms themselves — the FAFSA, CSS Profile and institutional forms (Steps 5, 6 and 7, respectively, of this book). If you're supporting children, if you've been in the military, or if your parents are divorced, your FAFSA will make that clear. For colleges requiring the CSS Profile, you can use that form to describe special financial circumstances, list special family expenses, such as your family's medical and dental expenses, or any private school tuition that your parents might pay for your younger siblings.

While forms may serve well enough, it may still be a good idea to write a letter or schedule a visit. If there's any doubt in your mind about whether forms convey your situation, definitely contact the college.

Going Beyond the Forms

You may have special circumstances that aren't covered by the forms. Or financially significant events may happen after you submit the forms — events that may be too complicated to explain in a simple correction. If that happens, communicate with the aid office as soon as possible after any financial hardships arise. The sooner you act, the sooner the college can adjust your award — and the more likely they will still have funds available to do so.

Even after you start college, if a financial emergency occurs, let the school know. The financial aid director can often help needy students with unusual expenses, such as medical costs, emergency trips home or funding to allow them to take an unpaid internship in the summer instead of working for money.

How to Contact the College

A letter to the financial aid office explaining your circumstances is often the best way to state your case. Some schools have a form specifically for explaining special circumstances; it's worth asking your colleges what they prefer. The more closely you follow their procedures, the more likely you are to be heard.

No matter how you communicate with your college, be polite, clear and specific. **Remember, you're trying to put a face to the form, so make it a friendly one.** You'll get further by calmly presenting your situation and giving as many relevant specifics as possible. For example, if your parent got laid off, the school might want to know what the prospects for reemployment might be, whether your parent has filed for unemployment benefits and, if so, the amount of the benefit payments awarded. Don't be surprised or offended if the college responds to you with a request for documentation, such as a copy of your most recent tax return or pay stub.

The Special Circumstances Form

Some colleges have a form through which you can let them know about special circumstances. "The purpose of the form is not to make everybody jump through a hoop," says Forrest Stuart, the director of financial aid at Furman. "It's to help the parents and the student put on paper all the information we need to help them out."

Communicating by Letter

With many schools, the best way to contact the aid office is in a letter. Often, it can strengthen your case to enclose photocopies of supporting documentation with the letter — for example, a paper showing your parent was laid off. The aid officer may also ask you for specific documentation.

After sending your letter, follow up with the financial aid office a week or two later to make sure they received it and to see if they have any questions. You can do this by e-mail or telephone. If you live close by, or have scheduled a campus visit, you should also visit the aid office, but call first to make an appointment.

E-Mail

Some colleges prefer to have you contact them by e-mail. At the University of Oregon, applicants can communicate their special financial circumstances through the school's website, where they can find an e-mail address for the financial aid office. "That way, they can do it whenever they think about it," says Elizabeth Bickford, the financial aid director.

Examples of Special Situations

Many circumstances can affect your family's ability to pay for college. They may include a change in your financial situation from what was reported in the financial aid forms, such as a lost job, emergency expenses, health problems or even a windfall that misrepresents your usual level of income.

Family ties can also have financial implications, such as supporting an extended family or going through a divorce. And if you've served in the military, there are some special instructions you need to follow on the financial aid forms.

Change in Financial Situation

Financial aid officers want to know not only that your financial aid situation changed, but why it changed. Certain types of changes are more likely than others to persuade them to give you more financial aid. Generally, aid officers will look more kindly on circumstances that are beyond your control, rather than the result of poor planning. For example, if your father gets laid off because his company has fallen on hard times, that is more likely to get attention than if he retires early to spend more time golfing. And the college is more likely to turn a sympathetic eye to necessary roof repairs than a loan to install a backyard Jacuzzi.

EXPERT ADVICE

"**We must have documentation**, and what we really like too is a nice **letter explaining the situation**. But on top of that, we also like to have a phone call or, if the student's already on campus, to have them come in and talk to us. That way, we can have a **dialogue about the situation** and give them some direction on what to provide to us and how to provide it."

— *Vincent Amoroso, former director, Office of Student Financial Services, Johns Hopkins University*

GOOD TO KNOW

If you're explaining your special financial circumstances by letter, it's best to send it to the financial aid office via mail or fax, so that it can be **easily incorporated into your file**. Write and format it as a standard business letter. **Put your name and Social Security Number** in the first paragraph, so the financial aid office won't have trouble matching the letter to your file.

LOST JOB OR LOST INCOME

If you or your parents had a job when you filled out the FAFSA, and now don't, that will clearly affect your ability to pay. Even if you receive a severance package or collect unemployment benefits, your long-term ability to pay will still be reduced. This is information your financial aid office needs to know. For Palomar College, you would fill out a form that allows the financial aid office to override the FAFSA data with the new data. "You have to still report the previous year's income," according to Palomar's Mary San Agustin, "but we override it with the current-year income."

The FAFSA form asks if you or a parent is a "dislocated worker." But don't think answering "yes" to that question is sufficient to alert colleges to the problem. They will want to know more, and the more information you give them, the more likely they can help you. And given the large number of job losses caused by the current recession, you should try to give them this information as soon as possible. Remember, there is a limit to the amount of financial aid funds available.

Equally important are unusual changes in other sources of income besides wages and salaries. For example, suppose a student's mother became disabled and had to stop working, and her employer's disability insurance plan gave her a large percentage of her salary in the year for which her income was reported on the FAFSA, but a much lower percentage afterward. The FAFSA will show a larger income than she will be receiving once the student arrives in college. This change in disability benefits, like a lost job, needs to be explained to the college.

EMERGENCY SAVINGS DRAWDOWN

An emergency may force your family to spend some of the savings that you reported on the financial aid forms. For example, suppose your house is damaged by a fire the day after you submit the FAFSA. Your family needs to spend a large amount of money to pay for the repairs. Depending on where the money comes from — regular savings, a retirement account, borrowing through a home-equity loan — this will have different effects on your need calculation. But no matter what the emergency or the source of the money you wind up spending is, you should tell the aid office.

Sometimes one crisis will have several different effects. A hurricane might not only destroy an applicant's home, but also put the family breadwinners temporarily out of work. In such a case, make sure the aid office knows about all the different effects on your financial situation.

HEALTH PROBLEMS

A serious health problem in your family can involve both an emergency savings drawdown to pay for medical expenses, and loss of income if the patient is too sick to work. If someone in your family has recently become disabled, developed a chronic illness or had major surgery, this has a clear impact on your family's ability to pay for college. Your college's financial aid office should be able to help.

A letter, or the school's own "special circumstances" form (if they have one), is a good way to let a college know about your family's medical problem. But the financial aid forms provide some paths as well. The CSS Profile form allows you to list medical expenses that weren't covered by insurance last year, and estimate the same for this year. You can also explain high medical expenses in the "Explanations/Special Circumstances" section. The FAFSA, on the other hand, doesn't ask specifically about medical expenses. If your college only uses the FAFSA, and you have unusually high medical expenses, a letter to the college makes sense.

WINDFALL

In financial terms, a windfall is a sum of money you didn't expect to get, which is normally a good thing — but even a windfall can have its downside. On your financial aid forms, if you received a windfall last year, that makes your annual income look higher than it normally is, which will tend to raise your expected family contribution (EFC).

Some windfalls are better than others. A windfall is usually understood as a genuine, one-time boost to your finances. It might be an inheritance from an aunt you never knew or an unusually high year-end bonus from your job. If you get such a windfall, inform the aid office that your reported income was higher than usual, and that they shouldn't expect a repeat performance.

But some windfalls not only make your annual income look bigger than it is, but represent an overall loss to your financial position. Examples include a severance package on losing your job, or an early withdrawal from a retirement plan, such as an IRA, to cover an emergency. In both situations, your records for that year show a boost in income, but that apparent good news conceals bad financial news — that you lost your job in one case, and suffered a massive hit to your retirement savings in the other. If you experience this kind of windfall, explain the reality to your aid office.

Family Ties

Not every family has two parents married to each other. And some families have stronger ties to grandparents, uncles, aunts and cousins than others. Different families live in different ways. The way your family lives may have financial implications that your financial aid office should recognize.

SUPPORTING EXTENDED FAMILY

The financial aid forms tell the colleges about how many people live in your household, including you, your parents and your siblings. But many families give financial support to an extended family of relatives who live outside the household. Immigrant families, for example, often send money regularly to grandparents, aunts or uncles in another country. Since that decreases the amount you have available to pay for college, make sure the financial aid office knows about it.

DIVORCED OR SEPARATED PARENTS

If your parents have divorced or separated, make sure the colleges know how that has affected your ability to pay. To do this, follow the rules on the financial aid forms. For the FAFSA, provide only the information about the parent you lived with more during the past 12 months (your custodial parent) — and, if that parent has remarried, your stepparent. For the CSS Profile, provide not only that data but also information on your other parent, the one who does not have custody of you — your noncustodial parent.

Some colleges that use the CSS Profile will also want your noncustodial parent to submit information separately on the Noncustodial CSS Profile. That information will be confidential; you and your custodial parent won't be able to see the data the other parent provides, nor will that parent see yours. However, the information submitted by your noncustodial parent will affect the college's calculation of your total expected family contribution (EFC). If you don't think it will be possible to get your noncustodial parent to fill out the form, let the college know. However, the school isn't likely to waive its requirement for the form for anything less than a significant reason.

In the parent-income section of either the FAFSA or the CSS Profile, a custodial parent who is receiving alimony or child support payments should report only what he or she received, not what he or she was supposed to receive. In certain circumstances, documented evidence that your noncustodial parent is behind in payments could help support your case if you appeal your award.

Military Service

If you're currently serving in the active-duty military or the reserves, or if you are a veteran, don't assume that your military benefits alone will meet your full financial need. At most institutions, they no longer will. Benefits or not, you should apply for financial aid by submitting the FAFSA and any other required forms.

When filling out these forms, there are a few points to remember. Read the instructions carefully to make sure you qualify as a veteran for purposes of federal student aid. You should report housing allowances, subsistence allowances and untaxed combat pay as income. But don't include veterans' education benefits or ROTC scholarships when answering the questions about your untaxed income. The colleges consider them outside resources to be reported separately. (*See Step 9 for more information on outside resources.*)

Veterans are as liable as anyone to the special situations discussed earlier, from lost jobs to medical crises. That includes windfalls. For example, if you received a lot of combat pay last year but have now been discharged and won't receive it again, you should explain that to the colleges.

QUICK RECAP

If there are special circumstances that affect your ability to pay for college, let your college know.

- Tell the college financial aid office as soon as you know about your special circumstances — either before you get your award or afterward.
- If you have to go beyond the forms, write a letter, e-mail, call or visit.
- Explain your situation clearly, documenting it where appropriate.
- The situations that may affect your ability to pay range from a lost job or high medical bills to status as a veteran or an undocumented immigrant.

Step 9: Look for Scholarships

QUICK OVERVIEW

It's worth it to look for financial aid beyond what you'll get from colleges and federal student aid programs. This "outside money" probably won't amount to a "full ride," but it can help. Begin your search for outside scholarships around the time you start looking for a college because many scholarships have early deadlines.

Scholarships Colleges Give You vs. Scholarships You Get on Your Own

KNOW THE LINGO

Outside money — Grants and scholarships that come from sources other than colleges or the federal government, such as states and private organizations.

Portable money — Grants and scholarships that you can take with you to whichever college you attend.

College-offered money — Grants and scholarships that colleges award from their own funds.

Financial aid doesn't come only from the government and colleges. It also comes in the form of scholarships from outside sources, including states and private donors. This money doesn't come looking for you: You have to find the programs that fit you and apply. You will have to qualify for the scholarship in some way, whether through academic merit, artistic talent or fitting some set of criteria, like being a person of Japanese descent living in New Jersey. **Very few outside scholarships offer anything close to full tuition, fees, room and board.** But they're worth the search because every little bit helps.

The scholarships you can get from outside sources are not exactly like the scholarships you might get from your college. These are the basic facts to know about each type.

College-Offered Scholarships

In most cases, you don't have to apply separately for the scholarships that colleges award. You're automatically considered for them when you apply to the school. If you qualify, the college will include the scholarship in your financial aid package as they see fit. However, some colleges have merit-based scholarships for which you must apply separately.

To find out what the rules are for scholarship aid at your colleges, contact the schools or look at their websites, which usually describe the process for applying for scholarships under "admission" and then under "financial aid." Be sure to do this research *before* you submit your application for admission. At some colleges, you have to indicate on your admissions application that you are applying for a special scholarship; for example, this is true of Boston University's Trustee Scholar Program. At others, you don't have to apply for special scholarships until after you've submitted your application for admission.

Many college merit scholarships have to be renewed from year to year. To make sure yours is renewed, know the school's criteria for keeping it — for example, maintaining a certain GPA. Different scholarships will have different criteria at each college.

Outside Scholarships: State Sources

Almost every state offers scholarships to their residents. These scholarships are usually available only for state residents attending colleges within the state, though a few states offer "portable" aid that a state resident can take to a college in another state.

Take the time to research scholarships and grants in your state. Almost every state has a department of education website that describes state scholarships and how to apply for them. These are usually separate from the state-sponsored, need-based financial aid programs for which you apply through the FAFSA or the state's own financial aid form, such as the Tuition Assistance Program (TAP) in New York State. An example of a state-sponsored, merit-based scholarship program with a separate application process is Florida's Bright Futures Scholarship, for which applicants must show high academic achievement.

Outside Scholarships: Private Sources

Private scholarships are offered by many sources, including foundations, corporations, civic groups, religious organizations, veterans' associations and the military. The Society of Women Engineers offers the Bechtel Corporation Scholarship to high-achieving female students of engineering. United Methodist Scholarships are available to students who belong to that Christian denomination. The Senator George J. Mitchell Scholarship Research Institute offers awards to Maine residents studying in state.

Don't assume you have to be a genius to get a private scholarship. Although many scholarship programs consider academic merit, a range of conditions may qualify you for a scholarship, including interests, ethnic background and community work. The Los Padres Foundation grants scholarships to low-income Latino students. California students pursuing a career in agriculture are eligible for a California Farm Bureau Scholarship.

Most scholarships come with limits. Though a few programs will pay full tuition, the amount of most awards is much smaller, as little as $500 or $1,000.

MYTH/FACT

Myth: "Untold millions" of scholarship dollars are available for use every year.

Fact: Private scholarships are only a small segment of the overall money available for college — **just 6 percent** of all aid to undergraduates. Grants from federal, college and state funds, in that order, are likely to be much more important in your overall financial aid package. It's worth looking for private scholarships, but don't count on them as your sole source of funding.

Many awards are limited to the freshman year of study. Fortunately, other scholarships are only for later years. The Bechtel Corporation Scholarship, for example, is just for women in their sophomore, junior or senior year of study. And once you've declared a major you may find yourself eligible for a scholarship that is aimed only at students in your academic discipline.

Searching for Scholarships

Searching for private scholarships takes effort. But there are a number of Web-based scholarship search engines, like the ones on bigfuture.org and fastweb. com, that can help you zero in on scholarships for which you may qualify. If you like using this book, you might prefer to search for scholarships using the *College Board Scholarship Handbook*. It describes more than 2,400 outside scholarships, internships and loan programs, and is indexed by eligibility requirements — such as minority status, religious affiliation and state of residence — to help you match yourself to the programs.

Beware of commercial scholarship search companies that offer to help you find scholarships for a fee. Some do a responsible job, but many charge exorbitant fees and make fraudulent claims. For example, if they "guarantee" you a scholarship or promise to "do all the work for you," they are probably lying. Getting a scholarship is never guaranteed and, no matter what, you are going to have to do some work to apply.

Your school counselor may be of more help. Many private scholarships send application forms directly to school counselors. Tell your counselor in your junior year or early in your senior year that you are interested in applying for private scholarships.

Searching for scholarships takes time, so start early. You'll need time to find them, request information, gather materials, and complete your application. So look for scholarships as soon as you can — in the summer before your senior year, or by October or November of that year.

Look Locally

When looking for scholarships, it pays to look locally. The fact is, you are more likely to obtain a scholarship from a local organization than from a state or national one.

On the local level, you will be competing with a smaller pool of applicants and are more likely to have characteristics that interest the donors. Again, your school counselor can help. The counseling office will have a file of local scholarships — from banks, the Kiwanis, the local garden club and other groups. Let your counselor know you are looking for scholarships; stop by the counseling office regularly to read the scholarship files or check the scholarship bulletin board. The office may also use Internet announcements, e-mail postings or newsletters to spread the word about scholarship programs to interested students.

Local businesses can also be a source of scholarship money. If you have a part-time job after school or a summer job, check to see if the company that employs you has a scholarship program or offers tuition assistance. For example, Chick-fil-A has a well-known scholarship program for its restaurant employees. Some companies provide their employees with a dependent tuition-assistance benefit. That means one of your parents might be able to get his or her employer to pay some of your tuition.

Military Scholarships and Education Benefits

In return for military service, the armed forces offer a variety of college scholarships and education-assistance plans. For example, in the Reserve Officer Training Corps (ROTC) program offered by the Army, Navy and Air Force, you get scholarship assistance for college while being trained as a military officer. When you graduate, you are commissioned as an officer in the reserves and begin your term of military service.

Educational assistance for veterans is available in most states. If you're a veteran, contact your state veterans' administration for complete information and application forms.

Applying for Scholarships

Once you find the programs for which you qualify, you have to apply. This may mean not only another form to fill out, but compiling supporting documents, such as transcripts, recommendations and an essay. Depending on the program, you may have to provide evidence of leadership, patriotism, depth of character, desire to serve or financial need. Get to know the requirements of each scholarship as early as possible, so you can do any necessary extra work on time.

A few pointers to remember:

Apply early! Apply as early as possible to scholarship programs. If you can, do it in the fall of your senior year, even if the deadlines aren't until February or March. Very often, scholarship programs will have awarded all their funds for the year on a first-come, first-served basis before their stated deadline.

Follow directions. Read instructions carefully and do what they say. Scholarship programs receive hundreds and even thousands of applications. Don't lose out because of failure to submit a school transcript or to provide appropriate recommendations. If you have a question about your eligibility for a particular scholarship or how to complete the application, contact the scholarship sponsors.

Be organized. It's a good idea to create a separate file for each scholarship and sort them by their due dates. Track application deadlines and requirements using Worksheet 2 (**a blank copy of this worksheet appears in Part II**). In one place, store the different supporting documents you may need, such as transcripts, standardized test scores and letters of recommendation.

Check your work. Proofread your applications for spelling or grammatical errors, fill in all blanks, and make sure your handwriting is legible.

Keep copies of everything. If application materials get lost, having copies on file will make it easier to resend the application quickly.

Reapply. Some programs only offer money for the first year of college, but others can be renewed each subsequent year. If your program is one of them, it pays to reapply once you're in college.

SAMPLE WORKSHEET 2:
Scholarship Application Planner

	PROGRAM 1	PROGRAM 2	PROGRAM 3
PROGRAM/SPONSOR	*Wyzant College Scholarship*	*Young Naturalist Awards*	*Town Bank*
ELIGIBILITY REQUIREMENTS	*Competition/talent*	*Competition/talent*	*Need, local residency*
TYPE OF AWARD	*Scholarship*	*Scholarship*	*Internship*
AMOUNT OF AWARD	*$10,000, $3,000, $2,000*	*$50 to $2,500*	*$2,500*
CAN BE USED FOR	*Tuition/fees*	*Any expense*	*Any expense*
CAN BE USED AT	*Any college*	*Any college*	*In-state colleges*
DEADLINE	*May 1*	*Mar. 1*	*April 1*
FORMS REQUIRED	*Application and essay*	*Web form*	*Application (includes need analysis)*
TEST SCORES REQUIRED	*None*	*None*	*SAT*
ESSAY OR ACADEMIC SAMPLE	*Essay*	*Essay, research project*	*None required*
RECOMMENDATIONS	*None*	*None*	*One teacher (Mr. Filmer), Local branch manager*
NOTIFICATION BEGINS	*Not sure*	*Not sure*	*May 15*
REQUIREMENTS TO KEEP AFTER FRESHMAN YEAR	*One-time payment only*	*One-time payment only*	*Based on performance during internship*

For a blank version of this worksheet that you can photocopy for your own use, see Part II.

How a Scholarship Can Affect Your Financial Aid Package

If a college to which you're applying hasn't met your full need — that is, if there's a "gap" in your financial aid award — outside scholarships can be used to fill that gap. That will make the college much more affordable and give you more choices when it comes time to decide which college you want to attend.

If, on the other hand, a college is already meeting your full need, it works a little differently. It would be nice if your outside scholarship were added on top of all your other financial aid to make your total aid package even bigger. But it probably won't be. Following federal policy, your college will most likely count any outside scholarship or tuition assistance you receive as an "outside resource" that decreases your aid package dollar for dollar. So the total amount of your financial aid package will be exactly the same.

You might think this is unfair: This is money you found and, in the case of employer tuition assistance and veteran's benefits, money you earned. On the other hand, it is money that's available to pay for your education without your having to dip into your income and assets. The philosophy behind financial aid is that everyone should pay what they can out of income and assets (your expected family contribution, or EFC), and then financial aid, including any outside resources, makes up the difference. The only way you can pay less than your EFC is if you get so many outside scholarships that they exceed your financial need. This is highly unlikely.

However, **it is still worth getting outside scholarships**. For one thing, it increases your freedom to choose a college regardless of cost. "If I'm a student, the more money that I can bring to the table for myself, the better position I'm going to be in to exercise choices that I might want to make," says Vincent Amoroso of Johns Hopkins University. For another thing, many colleges will use your outside scholarship money to reduce the self-help part of your aid package first — loans and work-study. This can significantly reduce the amount of money you'll owe after college or the time you'll need to spend working during college.

At some colleges, your outside scholarships will not be used to reduce your gift aid (grants and scholarships) unless the amount exceeds your self-help aid. Colleges that don't meet your full financial need may first apply outside scholarships toward filling the gap. Most colleges decide these issues on a case-by-case basis, but a few have stated policies that they publish on their financial aid Web page or will share with you if asked.

In making admission decisions, admission offices are likely to look on outside scholarships favorably. Students who have searched for and found outside scholarships on their own will probably be seen as students with initiative and a sense of responsibility. That makes the student a stronger candidate for admission.

If you win a scholarship after you've already submitted your FAFSA and/or CSS Profile, tell the colleges to which you've applied. Many schools have a special form specifically designed for you to submit this information. If you don't tell the colleges about a scholarship, it could jeopardize your eligibility for federal aid.

Tax Effects

Your outside scholarship may be taxed as income — this depends on the use for which it's designated by the program that awards the scholarship. Generally, scholarship dollars used for costs that are purely educational, such as tuition and fees, will be tax free. But money used for living expenses, transportation or books will be taxed as unearned income. The scholarship program will let you know how much (if any) of your award is taxable, and will send you a copy of the IRS's Form 1098 at the end of each tax year.

If your employer gives you tuition assistance, it's tax free up to $5,250 a year. After that amount, it's taxable. If you get tuition assistance from your parent's employer, that will be included in your parents' taxable income, but they probably will be able to offset some or most of that with an education tax break (see Table 6 in Step 11 for more info.)

It takes work to hunt down and apply for outside scholarships, but it's worth it. Just remember:

- Outside scholarships will probably provide only a small part of the money you need for college, but every little bit helps.
- There are national and statewide scholarships programs, but look locally too.
- Websites, books and your school counselor can help you match outside scholarships to your qualifications.
- Search and apply early, and follow instructions.
- Your outside scholarship may affect the financial aid package awarded by your college, and it may be taxable as income.

QUICK RECAP

Step 10: Weigh the Offers

After you've submitted all the financial aid forms, you'll receive offers of financial aid from the colleges that have accepted you. This step will help you weigh these award letters and make an informed decision based on an "apples to apples" comparison of the packages. If an award leaves you with a larger out-of-pocket share than you think your family can handle, you can appeal.

Comparing Award Letters from Colleges

Soon after a college accepts you for admission, it will send you a financial aid award letter. The letter will detail what you'll get — the financial aid package the college is offering you. It will contain an outline of the expected costs you will incur during a year at the college, your expected family contribution (EFC) toward those costs, and the types and amounts of financial aid the college is offering to make up the difference.

The letter will also contain instructions on how to accept the aid package and how to contact the aid office if you have any questions or want to appeal the award.

It's best to wait until you have the award letters from all the different colleges that have accepted you before deciding which one to accept. If you have questions, wait until you've gotten answers from all the financial aid offices involved before you decide.

The offers in your award letters will differ. The amount and type of aid given will vary, and the letters may also differ in format, especially in how they itemize costs. Since most offers will only describe aid for your first year, an important question to ask is what you should expect to receive after that. Offers that look very similar for year one can be very different for subsequent years.

KNOW THE LINGO

Aid package — The total amount of all financial aid being offered to a student by a college.

Award letter — A document that a college sends to a student detailing the financial aid package. It indicates the type and amount of each scholarship, grant, loan or work-study opportunity being offered.

Appeal — A request that a college reconsider its financial aid package.

SAMPLE WORKSHEET 3:
Compare Your Awards

	COLLEGE 1	COLLEGE 2	COLLEGE 3
Step 1. For each college, list its name, award deadline, and the total cost of attendance (this figure should be in your award letter; if not, refer to the college website or contact the financial aid office).			
Name of college	*Private Univ.*	*Small College*	*Regional State*
Award deadline date	*5/1*	*5/1*	*4 weeks*
Total cost of attendance	*$31,825*	*$33,410*	*$15,566*
Step 2. List the financial aid awards each school is offering. Don't forget that grants, scholarships and work-study do not have to be repaid, while all loans must be repaid.			
Grants and scholarships			
• Pell Grant (federal)			
• SEOG (federal)			
• State	*can't use*	*$2,000*	*$2,000*
• College	*$12,700*	*$13,785*	*$941*
• Other			
Total grants/scholarships	*$12,700*	*$15,785*	*$2,941*
Percentage of package that is grant/scholarship	*60%*	*74%*	*53%*
Work-study opportunities	*$2,000*	*$1,000*	
Subsidized Stafford loan			
Unsubsidized Stafford loan	*$2,625*	*$2,625*	*$2,625*
Perkins loan	*$4,000*	*$2,000*	
Other loan(s)			
Total loans	*$6,625*	*$4,625*	*$2,625*
Percentage of package that is work or loans	*40%*	*26%*	*47%*
Total financial aid award	*$21,325*	*$21,410*	*$5,566*
Step 3. In the rows below, calculate what it will actually cost you to attend each college by subtracting the total financial aid award (row b) from the total cost of attendance (row a) to see the net cost (row c).			
a) Total cost of attendance	*$31,825*	*$33,410*	*$15,566*
b) Total financial aid award	*$21,325*	*$21,410*	*$5,566*
c) Net cost to attend (a minus b)	*$10,500*	*$12,000*	*$10,000*

For a blank version of this worksheet that you can photocopy for your own use, see Part II.

EXPERT ADVICE

"It's **not simply the dollar amount of the grant or scholarship** that families should focus on. They need to **lay out, side by side, the full picture**. What's the cost of attendance, including out-of-pocket expenses? What's the family contribution? What are the elements of aid? What's going to happen with loans, with work?"

— *Joe Paul Case, dean and director of financial aid, Amherst College, Amherst, Mass.*

In weighing the offers, the important thing is to compare apples to apples and not apples to oranges. For example, just because School A offers $10,000 in financial aid while School B only offers $8,000 doesn't necessarily mean School A has the better deal. If School A's aid package has $3,000 in grants and $7,000 in loans, but School B has $6,000 in grants and $2,000 in loans, School B is offering you more free money (grants) than School A.

There is another reason why a financial aid package may not be as big as it seems: higher costs. If one school's costs are higher than another's, you may be left with a higher out-of-pocket expense even after subtracting a "bigger" aid package. **Don't be dazzled by a large award. Instead, look for the bottom line: your net cost to attend the school.**

Here's a true story to illustrate this further. **Two sample award letters appear in Part II.** These were taken from actual letters received by a student. Only the names of the colleges involved have been changed, to "Blue University" and "Green University." The student's first-choice college was Blue U, which cost about $2,000 more than Green U. When she first compared the letters, she was very upset because it looked like Green U was giving her a much bigger scholarship, and much more total aid.

But her school counselor showed her that Blue U was actually offering the better deal. First of all, the grants and scholarship from Green U only looked bigger because they were presented as a total. Secondly, the student loans offered by Blue U (Stafford and Perkins) were subsidized, while the Stafford loan offered by Green U was not. That meant at Green U she would have to pay interest on the loan while she was in college. And third, the $14,810 Green U was "offering" as a parent PLUS loan wasn't really aid at all, but just an option for how her family could pay for their contribution. Bottom line, the true cost to her would be about the same at both colleges, even though Blue U is more expensive.

The College Board has an online "Compare Your Aid Awards" tool on bigfuture.org that lets you do this kind of side-by-side comparison of your awards. You can also use Worksheet 3 in this book to break out the different components of costs and aid packages and compare them side by side (a blank copy of this worksheet appears in Part II). When doing this analysis, keep an eye out for both quantity and quality. On the quantity side, for example, the "Family Share of Costs" figure tells you the amount of money your family will be expected to contribute. Your family will need to decide whether this amount is affordable. Look especially for evidence of "gapping," the practice of leaving a gap between the cost of attendance and the money accounted for by aid and EFC. You will be expected to fill that gap — in effect increasing your EFC.

On the quality side, consider the figures for "% of Award That Is Gift Aid" and "% of Award That Is Loan." The higher the proportion of gift aid (grant or scholarships) to loans, the better the award.

Loans vs. Grants

All other things being equal, it's better to receive a grant or scholarship than a loan. For that reason, a financial aid package with a high percentage of gift aid is more attractive, on the face of it, than one with a high percentage of loans. But you might want to take the award that offers more loans and less gift aid, if that college is a better fit for you overall.

In any event, don't be surprised if your award includes loans. Most aid packages contain them. Loans are optional; you don't have to take them out. But if offered as part of a need-based aid package, they can be an excellent way to help finance your education. The alternative — taking only grant aid and trying to pay the costs that the loans would cover out of pocket — could put your family under much more financial stress than the loan would.

It's usually in your best interest to accept subsidized Stafford and Perkins loans that are part of the aid package. The repayment terms are good and the government pays the interest while you're in school. Unsubsidized loans — such as unsubsidized Stafford, PLUS loan and private loans from a bank — should be studied more carefully to make sure the terms are acceptable. You should understand the specific terms of each loan, including its interest rate, the origination fee, the term of the loan and the grace period before repayment begins. You should also realize that unsubsidized loans are not need based and are typically used to help your families pay their EFC. If a college offers them as part of your aid package, consider them as an option, but don't weigh them equally with subsidized loans in the package.

Work-study jobs are also optional, but if you're offered one and you can manage the time, take it. Having a job on campus brings in income, expands your social networks, allows you to make contacts with professors and administrators, and gives you experience that can improve your résumé.

Appealing Your Award

Even though your award letters are printed in black and white, they aren't necessarily the last word. It is possible to appeal the awards to ask the colleges to reconsider their aid packages. There is no guarantee that they will grant your request, but there are circumstances where it's worth trying.

One reason you might appeal a package is if it has a lot of unsubsidized loans. However, bear in the mind that the college probably offered those loans because there wasn't enough gift aid to go around. Another reason to appeal is if you don't think you can afford the expected family contribution. You will need to have evidence to make that case. The college based its calculation of your EFC on the financial information you submitted. If you think this calculation was wrong, ask the financial aid office how it was made and see if you can find out if a mistake occurred. It will help if you have special circumstances that weren't communicated in your financial aid forms, such as a recent layoff; situations like this will clearly demonstrate why your

---

KEEP IN MIND

Just because you're awarded a loan to pay part of your college costs **doesn't mean you have to accept it**. If your family has funds available in savings or current income, you can use these funds if you prefer. The downside is that you'll have less money available now, which could put your family under financial stress. The upside is that you won't have to pay the money back later with interest.

KNOW THE LINGO

There are three types of federal loans for educational expenses:

Stafford — Loan to students. May be subsidized (if student demonstrates need) or unsubsidized. If subsidized, the government pays the interest on the loan while the student is in college.

PLUS — A federal loan for parents to cover college costs not met by financial aid. Not subsidized.

Perkins — Subsidized loan to students with exceptional need. Perkins-loan debt may be forgiven if the borrower enters a career in the public service.

Questions to Ask About Your Award

These are some questions to ask your college financial aid office if you're awarded gift aid:

✔ What do I have to do to keep my scholarship — do I have to do anything more than maintain satisfactory academic progress?
✔ Is there a minimum GPA or other condition?
✔ Is the scholarship renewable in subsequent years?
✔ If I win an outside scholarship, what happens to my aid?

Questions to ask if you're awarded a loan:

✔ What are the terms of my loan?
✔ What is the interest rate, and when do I start repayment?
✔ How much will I owe by the time I graduate?
✔ What will my monthly repayment be?
✔ By how much will my loan increase after my first year?

Questions to ask if you're awarded work-study:

✔ Do I have a "guaranteed" job, or will I have to find one?
✔ How are jobs assigned?
✔ How many hours per week will I be expected to work?
✔ What is the hourly wage?
✔ How often will I be paid?
✔ Will I be paid directly, or will my student account get credited?

family would have difficulty paying its EFC. (*See Step 8, "Make Your Special Circumstances Known."*)

"I've changed financial aid packages on appeal if somebody can demonstrate why they can't afford it," says Forrest Stuart of Furman University. "It may be the need analysis just didn't take some things into account. If they can show me where there's a real problem, even to the point where they show me their monthly budget, I might say, 'Man, you are right. You've got these medical expenses or you've got this and that. Let me see if I can help you.' I am not perfect, and the need analysis is not perfect, and we'll sometimes overlook something."

Still another reason for appealing an award is if you have better offers from other colleges, and would like to see if this college can match them. Some aid offices will consider matching a better offer from another college. But most will only hear an appeal that's based on your family's financial circumstances. "We don't bargain," says Mike Scott of Texas Christian University. "We just don't want to play that game of, 'Well, we'll give you more money simply because another school gave you more money.'"

You might see the entire appeal process as essentially negotiation or bargaining — trying to get as much as possible from the school you'd like to attend. However, most financial aid officers loathe the term "negotiate." Your appeal will have a better chance of success if it appears not a matter of haggling but of providing information not previously available to the financial aid office.

It will also help your cause if you are obviously doing your part to fund your education. A student who accepts the self-help components of a school's financial aid package will be more likely to get extra help than one who declined them. "If the student is not willing to somehow contribute, either by working or taking out a student loan, then we are very unlikely to give them any extra money," says Mike Scott.

A phone call is a good way to start the appeal process, even though most colleges will want you to put your reasons for an appeal in writing. Some have a specific form for appeals; others would like for you to state your case in a letter. Find out the college's preferred procedure by calling or checking their website. No matter how you file your appeal, your case will be stronger if you can provide data to back it up. A few days after filing your appeal, follow up with a phone call or, if possible, by visiting the aid office. Within a short time, the college will let you know its decision.

If you receive a revised award, take the new award letter and compare it to your other aid packages. **It's best not to decide where to enroll until you've received the final offer from each college**. But keep in mind the deadline set by each college for acceptance of its award. If you miss the deadline, you could lose the package. If you do need more time, try asking the college for an extension.

Follow Up: Accepting an Award

Once you've compared all the awards and any appeals have been ruled upon, you and your family will have to decide on a college. Many factors, including costs and financial aid, will be in play. If your first-choice college has accepted you but not given as much aid as you'd hoped, the choice may be difficult. Do you go to your first-choice college even though it's a financial risk for your family, or to a second-choice college your family can safely afford?

In the end, your own preferences should have the greatest weight. Most of the loan debt, payable after graduation, will be on your shoulders. And your personal happiness at the school will have a major influence on whether you graduate successfully. If your family can put together a sensible financial plan to pay the costs, the best choice is the one that fits you best academically and personally.

Follow whatever instructions came in the award packet. If you're being asked for more information, send it. Complete any forms that came with the award letter. Sign the letter and return it by the due date.

EXPERT ADVICE

"I tell families **not to use the word 'negotiate.'** If an aid package is much lower than what's being offered by similar institutions, families should call and ask if there is additional information that may make a difference."

— *Carlene Riccelli, college adviser, Amherst Regional High School, Amherst, Mass.*

QUICK RECAP

When you receive your award letters from colleges, you'll have to decide which offer to accept.

- Compare apples to apples, analyzing the awards to see what the real costs and financial aid elements are.
- Just because loans are offered, you don't have to accept them. But they're worth considering, especially if they're subsidized loans.
- If you appeal an award, you'll be on stronger ground if you can demonstrate circumstances that weren't previously made clear to the school.
- Your decision about which offer to accept should be based not just on cost but on how well the college fits you academically, socially and personally.

Step 11: Consider Your Out-of-Pocket Options

QUICK OVERVIEW

Financial aid is intended to cover the difference between your expected family contribution (EFC) and the total cost of college. However, you still have to pay your EFC and whatever gap there might be between the aid you received and your financial need. This step is about ways to meet those out-of-pocket costs.

Making Up the Difference

For almost every family, college is going to cost money. Even a generous financial aid package will usually leave you with some bills to pay. Some packages will meet less than your full need and leave you spending more than your EFC.

But you can afford to make up this difference between the total cost of attendance and the aid you're receiving if you take advantage of the various resources available to you. There are a number of programs and strategies that can help you save, pay or borrow for college.

Save for It

You shouldn't spend your entire family savings on college: You need to leave some for other uses, such as retirement and emergency medical costs. But it makes sense to use some of your savings for college.

Don't worry if your family doesn't already have a huge sum of money saved for college. **Every little bit helps, and it's never too late to start saving.** Even while you're applying to college, your family can start saving. Try to save as much as you can from summer and after-school jobs, and encourage your parents to set aside some money from every paycheck. Talk with your parents about how much money you and they already have saved for your college costs, and discuss how your family can afford the rest of the bill.

KNOW THE LINGO

EFC (Expected Family Contribution) — How much money a family is expected to pay for college out of pocket, based on the family's ability to pay.

Need — The difference between your EFC and the cost of attending a particular college you've chosen. Financial aid is designed to meet your need, not your EFC.

Unmet need — The difference (if any) between your need and the financial aid offered by a particular college. Informally, unmet need is also called a **gap**.

Don't believe anyone who says you shouldn't save for college because it will reduce your chances of getting financial aid. As noted in Step 2, savings are worth having so you can pay out-of-pocket costs without having to borrow. Very little, if any, of your parents' savings are counted against you when your financial need is determined. "Parents should not avoid saving because, frankly, a family that has saved has a resource to draw on, whereas a family that hasn't is totally dependent on current income and loans," says Joe Paul Case, dean and director of financial aid at Amherst College in Amherst, Mass.

There are a number of places families can put their savings. The most traditional is a regular bank savings account, which pays a little interest and offers freedom to withdraw and deposit money at any time. A certificate of deposit (CD) has stricter rules about when you can withdraw money, but it usually pays higher interest than a savings account. Both of these options are good for short-term, flexible savings. But neither has any tax incentives — tax breaks that make them especially attractive for college savings.

The following savings vehicles do come with tax breaks:

529 college savings plan. Also known as the QTP (Qualified Tuition Program), these are tax-advantaged accounts sponsored by the various states. Interest earned in these plans is not taxed as income, and some states also offer a state income-tax deduction for contributions their residents make to the state's plan. There are no income restrictions, and contribution limits are high. Grandparents, uncles and aunts are also allowed to contribute to the plan, even if they don't live in the same state as you and your parents — in fact, you don't have to be a resident of a state to contribute to its plan, and you can withdraw funds from a state's plan to pay for expenses at a college in another state. Most plans offer a few different investment types, such as a fund that invests in stocks or one that invests in bonds.

Coverdell Education Savings Account. These tax-free trust or custodial accounts are similar to 529s, but they're sponsored by banks and brokerage houses instead of states, and therefore offer a greater range of investment choices. They can be used to pay private elementary and high school costs as well as college costs, unlike 529s, which can only be used for college costs. Total contributions for the student can't be more than $2,000 in a given year, and your family income has to be less than $110,000 (for single filers) or $220,000 (for joint filers). You can contribute to both a 529 and a Coverdell in the same year for the same student.

529 prepaid tuition plan. Like the 529 college savings plans, these are sponsored by the states, but they work differently. A 529 prepaid tuition plan lets a family make advance tuition payments years before their children will enter college. That allows them to "lock in" today's tuition rates instead of paying the higher rates likely to prevail years from now. Provided the student is admitted, the plans are guaranteed to be honored by public universities and some private colleges in the state that sponsors the plan. However, these plans have drawbacks. They can only be used for tuition and fees, not for room, board or other supplemental costs. When that's combined with the fact that the tuition rates are only locked in for in-state colleges, most parents prefer the more flexible 529 savings plans.

Independent 529 prepaid tuition plan. This is a special 529 prepaid tuition plan sponsored by a group of private colleges and universities and administered by TIAA-CREF. For more information, visit www.independent529plan.org.

U.S. savings bonds. If your parents pay for some of your college costs by cashing in U.S. government savings bonds, the interest that has accumulated on the bond may be tax exempt. That means the interest won't be taxed as income and your tax bill will be smaller. The bond must be issued after 1989 and your parent must have been age 24 or older when the bond was issued. This deduction can't overlap with any other education tax break, and you can't use two different tax breaks to pay for the same expense.

Individual Retirement Account (IRA). Generally, it's not a good idea to raid the family retirement funds, such as IRAs, to pay for college. "We tell parents all the time, you can borrow money to pay for your kid's education. You cannot borrow money to retire with," says Mike Scott of Texas Christian University. It's usually better to take out a PLUS loan than to diminish retirement assets. Still, if your family does need to go into an IRA to pay college expenses, the government doesn't charge the 10 percent additional tax you would ordinarily have to pay for breaking open an IRA before age 59½.

Table 3:

Comparison of Education Savings Options

	COVERDELL EDUCATION SAVINGS ACCOUNT	529 COLLEGE SAVINGS PLAN (QUALIFIED TUITION PROGRAM)	529 PREPAID TUITION PLAN	U.S. GOVERNMENT SAVINGS BONDS	UNIFORM GIFTS TO MINORS ACT ACCOUNT	INDIVIDUAL RETIREMENT ACCOUNT
Tax advantages	Earnings in account not taxed as income	Earnings in account not taxed as income Some states allow residents to deduct contributions for state income tax purposes	Earnings in account not taxed as income Some states allow residents to deduct contributions for state income tax purposes	Interest earned is not taxed if used for qualified expenses	Interest earned is taxed at child's rate	Exception to the 10% early withdrawal penalty rule
Expenses that qualify	• Tuition & fees • Books & supplies • Room & board (if at least half-time) • Expenses for special needs services • K-12 education expenses	• Tuition & fees • Books & supplies • Room & board (if at least half-time) • Computer • Special needs services	Tuition & fees	• Tuition & fees • Contributions to a Coverdell or 529	Any expense (not limited to education)	• Tuition & fees • Books & supplies • Room & board (if at least half-time) • Special needs services
Contribution limits	$2,000 per year	None	None	None	None	$5,500 per year ($6,500 if over 50)
Income phaseout for benefits	$95,000–$110,000 (single filers) $190,000–$220,000 (joint filers)	None	None	Varies by income and filing status	None	Varies by type of account
Other limitations	Assets must be distributed by age 30 Must pay 10% penalty if distributions not used for qualified expenses	Must pay 10% penalty if distributions not used for qualified expenses	Benefits may only be used at colleges that participate in the plan Must pay 10% penalty if distributions not used for qualified expenses	Applies only to Series EE or Series I bonds issued after 1989 and purchased after owner turned 24	Counted as student asset for financial aid purposes	Interest earned will still be taxed at your regular rate

Work for It

Besides a summer job, you might also want to consider working during the school year to help meet expenses. There are two basic approaches. You can go to college full time while working part time, or you can hold a full-time job while attending college part time.

Full-Time Student, Part-Time Job

If you're offered a work-study job as part of your financial aid package, the earnings from that job will go toward your college costs. Even if you're not offered work-study, you may still be able to find a part-time job on or near campus. You can also work during the summer to make money to put toward college.

Work has benefits beyond the extra income it generates. Studies have shown that students who work part time get better grades and are more likely to finish college than those who don't work at all. If the job is on campus, it can enhance your college experience by giving you a chance to meet people beyond your circle of friends and classmates.

On the other hand, don't work so many hours that you jeopardize your ability to get through college. **If you're going to college full time, the recommended workload is about 10 to 15 hours a week**. If you work more than 20 hours a week, you're likely to get overloaded and put yourself at risk of dropping out. If you take fewer courses to make time for work, you may drop below full-time status, which could make you ineligible for many grants and scholarships. If your financial situation makes you feel that you have to work more hours, it might be better to borrow more money so you don't have to work so much.

Part-Time Student, Full-Time Job

A different (and much more difficult) way of approaching work is to be a full-time worker who goes to college part time. This is possible as long as you don't take too many credits in one semester. If you try for more than six to eight credits (two courses) while working full time, you'll probably have trouble getting everything done. On the other hand, if you take fewer than six credits a semester, you won't be eligible for need-based subsidized Stafford or Perkins loans or a Pell Grant.

Working full time while going to school part time is an especially attractive way to pay for an associate degree or a vocational certificate. Most community colleges cater to working students and offer classes at night to meet their needs. If you take six credits per semester, you can probably earn an associate degree in four or five years.

If you're planning on earning a bachelor's degree, however, you should strongly consider attending college full time and borrowing money to replace the income that you won't be earning through a job. Why? If you take only six credits a semester, it will take 10 years to earn a bachelor's! You will probably earn more money in the long run if you get that bachelor's in the usual four or five years, and concentrate on your career after you've earned that degree.

Some employers offer tuition assistance or scholarship money to employees who are attending college. Check to see if your employer is one of them. For a typical educational assistance program, up to $5,250 of those benefits will be tax free each year.

Co-op and Internship Programs

Many colleges sponsor internships or "co-op" (cooperative) programs with local employers. Some interns and almost all co-op participants receive payment from their employers along with academic credit. In co-op programs, you may be able to alternate periods of full-time work and full-time study. Often the business at which you intern hires you after graduation, or at least recommends you to others. Internship and co-op programs can help you make money, get academic credit, gain job experience and make contacts with potential employers. If you are fairly certain about what career you want to pursue, a co-op program in that career can be the best way to earn your degree.

Promising to Work Later

Holding a job during college is not the only way of using work to pay your college costs. There are several programs that allow you to commit to work in public service after graduation in exchange for either a non-need-based scholarship while in college or a stipend that can be used to repay student loans after college. The ROTC program is an example of the former, and AmeriCorps is an example of the latter.

ROTC

In return for military service, the armed forces offer career training and a number of educational benefits to help pay for college, including full college scholarships and education assistance plans. If that deal sounds good to you, check with the Reserve Officers' Training Corps (ROTC) office at your high school or on your college campus. Each branch of the military offers ROTC training. Part IV of this book contains lists of colleges that offer ROTC programs for each service branch.

OTHER SERVICE PROGRAMS

AmeriCorps is a network of national service programs for which you can work as a volunteer, full or part time, for up to a year. After completing a term of service with AmeriCorps, you're eligible for an education award, which can be used either to repay student loans or to pay for college tuition. The amount of the award depends on how long you worked for the program, and for how many hours each week. For more information, go to www.americorps.org.

Another type of program is one that hinges on your financial aid package and the profession you choose after college. If you received a Perkins loan as part of your package, the loan may be forgiven if you enter certain professions serving the public, such as teaching, nursing or law enforcement.

KEEP IN MIND

As noted in Step 2, you will be **expected to contribute** a larger percentage of your **work income to college costs** than your parents will. In general, you will be expected to pay about 50 percent of your earnings toward college.

Borrow It

To borrow money is to spend today what you'll earn in the future. You will have to pay the loan back, with interest, when you start earning money after college. A loan can be intimidating because it assumes you'll have the money for repayment, and you may not feel sure of that.

There are many forms of "bad debt" in our society, such as credit card debt, where you borrow money on unfavorable terms to buy consumer goods that will have little or no value in a year. But an education loan is a "good debt." That's because you are borrowing money on favorable terms to achieve an outcome — higher lifetime earnings — that will more than pay back the loan.

Loans are available that your family can use to borrow money to meet your EFC. The most common types are the unsubsidized Stafford and the PLUS loan, both of which are guaranteed by the federal government, but there are also state and private sources.

How Much Should You Borrow?

If your family decides to borrow money to pay for college, they should consider the total debt that you will carry after graduation. That total debt includes any subsidized, need-meeting loans that you accept as part of the college's aid package as well as any non-need-based loans your family takes out to meet the EFC. When you pay back that debt, you'll do so in the form of monthly payments, and those payments should be affordable based on the income you're likely to have. The total monthly payment will usually be similar to a car payment — $200 to $300 a month. But the amount will vary with the amount borrowed and interest rate offered.

Table 4 that follows will help you determine what your monthly payment will be. It shows monthly repayment over 10 years for a loan of $10,000 at various interest rates. To calculate a monthly payment for a loan amount not listed on the table, multiply the amount borrowed by the repayment factor for your interest rate. For example, if you borrowed $12,500 at 7.5 percent, your monthly payment would be $148.46 ($12,500 × .0118770).

There are some ways to make your repayment burden lighter after college. Many lenders will offer to cut your interest rate a bit if you make your first 12 monthly payments on time. If you borrow from multiple federal loan programs, such as the Perkins, subsidized Stafford and unsubsidized Stafford, you can consolidate these loans after graduation, which will simplify things by allowing you to make only one payment a month. Consolidation also gives you the option of "re-amortizing" your loans — that means stretching your payments over a longer period of time than you would normally have left to repay the debt. If you re-amortize when you consolidate, you will usually have a lower monthly payment, but will pay more interest over the total life of all the loans.

KNOW THE LINGO

Principal — The portion of debt that is left over from the amount you originally borrowed.

Interest — The portion of debt that has been charged to you by the lender as a fee for loaning you the principal.

PART I: FINANCIAL AID STEP BY STEP

Table 4:
Calculating Your Monthly Loan Payment

AMOUNT OF LOAN	INTEREST RATE	REPAYMENT FACTOR	MONTHLY PAYMENT
$10,000	4.00%	.010125	$101.25
	4.50%	.010364	$103.64
	5.00%	.010607	$106.07
	5.50%	.010853	$108.53
	6.00%	.011102	$111.02
	6.50%	.011355	$113.55
	7.00%	.011611	$116.11
	7.50%	.011870	$118.70
	8.00%	.012133	$121.33
	8.50%	.012399	$123.99
	9.00%	.012668	$126.68

GOOD TO KNOW

When you start paying back your educational loan, remember that the **interest may be tax deductible**. To a maximum of $2,500 per year, you can deduct the interest you pay from your income, which will lower your tax bite. In effect, the government will be subsidizing your loan. This is true for every kind of education loan, including PLUS loans.

Types of Non-Need-Based Loans

There are three basic types of loans you can use to pay your out-of-pocket costs: federal, state and private.

FEDERAL LOANS

Federal loans have relatively low interest rates and are guaranteed by the federal government. This means that if you don't pay your loan back to the lender (though, of course, you should), the federal government will. That encourages lenders to lend you money even if you're a student with no credit history and little employment record.

Two basic kinds of federal loans are used for paying an EFC, one for students, one for parents:

Student Loans (Direct Unsubsidized Stafford). While **subsidized** Stafford loans are need-based, meaning they are only awarded to students that demonstrate financial need for aid, an **unsubsidized** Stafford loan is available to anyone who submits the FAFSA, no matter what their financial situation. You don't even have to apply for it.

With a Direct Unsubsidized Stafford loan, you borrow money directly from the federal government, but the loan is provided through your college. You'll be charged only the interest while you're in school, and you can choose to either make monthly interest payments while you're in school, or let the interest accrue (accumulate) until you begin repaying the loan after school. If you let the interest accrue, you won't have to make any monthly payments while you're in college; but the interest will be "capitalized" (added) into the principal of the loan, so your monthly payments after college will be somewhat larger than they would have been if you had paid the interest during college.

Whether or not you let interest accrue, six months after leaving school (your grace period), you have to begin paying back both the principal and the interest. For loans disbursed after July 1, 2016, the interest rate is the same as for subsidized Stafford loans: 3.76%. It's possible that Congress might change the interest rate for new loans disbursed in future years; you can check the current rate on Student Aid on the Web at www.studentaid.ed.gov.

Direct PLUS Loans for parents. With a PLUS loan, your parents borrow money to pay for your education directly from the federal government (but through your college). They can borrow any amount up to your total cost of attendance minus the financial aid you receive. To get a PLUS loan, you must have submitted the FAFSA, and your parents will probably have to fill out an application from the college's financial aid office and pass a credit review.

Your parents will have to start making payments on the entire debt — both the principal and the interest — as soon as the loan money is disbursed to the school; but they can request that payments be deferred until after you leave school, in which case the interest charged while you are in school will be accrued and added to the principal.

The interest rate for Direct PLUS loans is a fixed rate of 6.31% for loans disbursed on or after July 1, 2016. Again, Congress might change the rate for new loans disbursed in future years, so check for the current rate on Student Aid on the Web at www.studentaid.ed.gov.

What if I have trouble repaying the loan? Under certain circumstances, such as economic hardship, you can postpone repayment of a federal student loan by applying for a deferment (during which no interest accumulates) or forbearance (during which it does). Under exceptional circumstances, such as total disability or teaching in a designated low-income school, some borrowers get a loan discharge, or cancellation of the debt. These rules apply to all federal student loans, and may also apply to parent PLUS loans in certain situations.

STATE LOANS

Some states sponsor loan programs for students and parents in their state. These loans are usually neither subsidized nor based on need. Check with your state financial aid agency to find out more.

PRIVATE LOANS

Federal student loans are not available from private lenders. Under the Direct Loan Program, Stafford student loans and PLUS parent loans come directly from the U.S. Department of Education, and loan funds are provided through the college. You or your parents can always take out a loan from a private lender, the same as a car loan for example. But that route is generally the worst way to finance a college education.

HOME-EQUITY LOANS

Many parents consider taking out a loan against their home equity to pay for their children's higher education. While this may be an attractive option for your family, you should keep in mind that, unlike PLUS loans and other education loans, home-equity loans do come with the condition that if you can't pay back the loan, the bank can foreclose on your house.

Table 5:
Comparison of Education Loan Options

	DIRECT SUBSIDIZED STAFFORD	PERKINS	DIRECT UNSUBSIDIZED STAFFORD	DIRECT PLUS	PRIVATE/ ALTERNATIVE EDUCATION LOAN	HOME EQUITY LOAN OR LINE OF CREDIT
BORROWING LIMIT	$3,500 first year $4,500 second year $5,500 third and fourth years Higher limits if parents were denied a PLUS loan	$5,500/year $27,500 undergraduate maximum	$5,500 first year $6,500 second year $7,500 third and fourth years Higher limits if parents were denied a PLUS loan	Maximum is difference between total cost of attendance and financial aid awarded	Depends on lender and credit check	Depends on credit check and home equity
INTEREST RATES	In school: 0% In repayment: 3.76% (fixed) as of July 1, 2016	In school: 0% In repayment: 5% (fixed)	In school: 4.66% (fixed) In repayment: 3.76% (fixed) as of July 1, 2016	6.31% (fixed) as of July 1, 2016	Depends on lender and credit check; may be fixed or variable	Depends on lender and credit check; may be fixed or variable
PROS	Interest that accumulates while you're in college paid by federal government	No fees Interest that accumulates while you're in college paid by federal government Debt may be forgiven if you enter a career in the public service	Option of not making payments during college and "capitalizing" accrued interest into the loan upon graduation Same deferment and forbearance rules as subsidized loans	No collateral required		Can use money for noneducational purposes Repayment term may be longer than for federal loans
CONS	Only available to students with financial need 1% loan fee	Only available to students with financial need Amount of loan you're offered subject to college financial aid office's discretion	1% loan fee	Parents must pass credit check to take out loan Parents must begin paying interest immediately 4.3% origination fee	Borrower must pass credit check Parents may have to cosign May have high origination fees	Home used as collateral for loan Can take several months to secure loan; may need to have house appraised

Cut It

You can cut what you will have to spend on college by reducing the amount of time you have to spend in college. This is an especially smart move if it looks like college won't be affordable even after you contribute all you can from savings, current income and loans. But cutting college time in order to cut college costs is an idea worth considering for other reasons as well.

Getting a Jump on College Credits

Tuition, the cost of taking classes, is usually based on the number of credit-hours required for a degree. But you can cut the cost of tuition by earning some of those credits ahead of time at your own high school or a community college. By doing this, you may also be able to reduce the number of semesters you have to spend in college, which will cut not only your tuition costs but all other costs, such as room and board. Some colleges offer accelerated programs that will help you do that.

AP®/CLEP®

The Advanced Placement Program® (AP®) and the College-Level Examination Program® (CLEP®), which are sponsored by the College Board, help you earn college credit. The programs differ in various ways. For example, students take AP courses as part of their high school curriculum, but they can prepare to take the CLEP examinations by any number of means — in school, on the job or by just reading books in their spare time. These programs are similar, however, in that you earn credit by taking an examination and receiving a score that your college accepts.

Colleges differ as to which programs, courses and scores they accept and how much credit they grant. But every credit you receive means a credit you don't have to pay for in college. Depending on your exam scores and your college's policies, you may be able to graduate a semester or even a year early if you've taken enough CLEP or AP Exams.

To learn more about AP go to apstudent.collegeboard.org

To find out if a college you're interested in grants credit for CLEP, use the CLEP College Search tool at clep.collegeboard.org.

TAKE COMMUNITY COLLEGE CLASSES OVER THE SUMMER

Courses at a community college usually cost much less than at a four-year college. Find out if there are courses you can take at a local community college in the summers and transfer to your four-year college. For example, if you don't have the knowledge of a certain subject that you need to pass a CLEP exam, you may still be able to take that course at a community college over the summer and transfer the credit to your four-year college.

OTHER ACCELERATED PROGRAMS

Some colleges offer an "accelerated program" designed for students who want to graduate in three years. These programs require a lot of work and dedication, but they will cut your college costs substantially by eliminating an entire year of expenses. It's possible to get through these programs if you're determined.

Cutting Other Expenses

Tuition is not the only college cost you can cut. Room, board, books, supplies, transportation — all of these add substantially to your total college bill. (Most people are shocked at what college textbooks cost these days.) Here are some suggestions to reduce these expenses:

BOOKS

- ✔ Buy used textbooks instead of new ones.
- ✔ Comparison shop for textbooks online.
- ✔ Sell your textbooks at the end of the semester.

ROOM AND BOARD

- ✔ Live off campus in a house or apartment that you share with classmates. That can be cheaper than a college dorm. (But check the policy at the college you want to attend — many require freshmen to live on campus.)
- ✔ If you plan to live in a dorm in your sophomore year and beyond, try to get a position as a resident adviser and the free room and board that comes with it.

TRANSPORTATION

- ✔ If you're commuting to school, carpool with a classmate from your area.

Education Tax Breaks

Federal student aid isn't the only way that Uncle Sam can help you pay for college. There are also tax breaks available for higher-education costs. By reducing the amount your family has to pay the government at tax time, these programs amount to federal subsidies for out-of-pocket costs. Some of them take the form of tax credits, which cut your taxes dollar for dollar: That is, a $1 tax credit would make your tax bill $1 smaller. Others take the form of tax deductions, which lower the amount of your income that is subject to tax, indirectly lowering your tax bill.

GOOD TO KNOW

The information about higher-education tax breaks printed here is current as of early 2017. **To make sure you qualify for a deduction or credit** before you file, download IRS Publication 970, "Tax Benefits for Education," from www.irs.gov.

There are two federal income tax credits for college expenses: the **American Opportunity credit** and the **Lifetime Learning credit**. These tax credits let your family reduce the taxes they pay dollar-for dollar, but each credit is for a different amount and has different requirements. And for any one student, a family can only elect to use only one of these credits on the same tax return.

The American Opportunity credit is worth up to $2,500 per year for each eligible student in the family. Unlike most tax credits, if the amount of the credit is more than the amount of tax owed, all or a portion of the excess may be received as a refund. This credit is available for the *first four years* of college. To be eligible, a student must be enrolled at least half-time; and the credit can only be claimed for four tax years for each student in the family. If a family has more than one student in college, it can claim the American Opportunity credit for one student and the Lifetime Learning credit for another student in the same year.

The Lifetime Learning credit is worth up to $2,000 per tax return for educational expenses paid on behalf of all eligible students in the family. You don't get a refund if you can't use all of the credit, but there is *no limit on the number of years* this credit can be claimed for a student. If a family has more than one student in college, it can claim the American Opportunity credit for one student, and the Lifetime Learning credit for another student in the same year.

For each of these tax credits, the amount of the credit depends on your family's income. The American Opportunity credit is gradually reduced if your family's adjusted gross income is more than $180,000 if you have two parents filing a joint return and $90,000 for a parent filing singly. The Lifetime Learning credit phases out after $131,000 for joint returns and $65,000 for single returns.

If your family's income is too high to qualify for either of these tax credits, there's also a tax deduction that may help. With the tuition and fees deduction, you can deduct up to $4,000 of college tuition and fees if your family income isn't more than $65,000 (for single filers) or $130,000 (for joint filers); the deduction is up to $2,000 if your family income isn't more than $80,000 (for single filers) or $160,000 (for joint filers). If you claim this deduction, you can't claim the American Opportunity or Lifetime Learning credits for the same student that year.

KEEP IN MIND

You will need **IRS Form 1098-T** to claim the **American Opportunity** credit, **Lifetime Learning** credit, or a **tuition and fees** deduction. This form shows your educational expenses for the year. Your college should send it to you by Feb. 1 of the year you file your tax return (e.g. Feb. 1, 2018 for expenses incurred in 2017).

Interest paid on student loans is tax deductible up to a maximum of $2,500 per year. This benefit applies to all loans used to pay for college, including PLUS loans. To be eligible for this deduction, your family's income has to be less than $80,000 (for single filers) or $160,000 (for joint filers). The tax break is only for the amount of interest you paid, not the amount you borrowed.

Some states also allow you to take tax credits or deductions from your state income taxes. Find out about yours from your state government.

Table 6:
Federal Income Tax Benefits for Higher Education

	AMERICAN OPPORTUNITY CREDIT	LIFETIME LEARNING CREDIT	TUITION AND FEES DEDUCTION	STUDENT LOAN INTEREST DEDUCTION
AVAILABLE FOR	Tuition, fees, books, supplies and equipment 1st four years of undergraduate study only Associate and bachelor's degree programs only	Tuition and fees only All years of study Any degree program, also nondegree courses to acquire job skills	Tuition and fees only All years of study Attendance at any postsecondary institution participating in a federal student aid program	Any higher education cost All years of study Any degree program
MAXIMUM VALUE	$2,500 credit per student	$2,000 credit per family	Up to $4,000 deduction taken as an adjustment to gross income	$2,500 deduction from taxable income
MAXIMUM INCOME FOR ELIGIBILITY	$80,000–$90,000 (single filers) $160,000–$180,000 (joint filers)	$55,000–$65,000 (single filers) $110,000–$131,000 (joint filers)	$65,000 (single filers) $130,000 (joint filers)	$65,000–$80,000 (single filers) $130,000–$160,000 (joint filers)
CONDITIONS	Student must be enrolled at least half-time Cannot claim the Lifetime Learning credit for the same student in the same year	Cannot claim the American Opportunity credit for the same student in the same year	Cannot claim either the American Opportunity credit or the Lifetime Learning credit for the same student in the same year	Student must have been enrolled at least half-time

QUICK RECAP

To deal with out-of-pocket college costs, you have several options. You can draw on savings or current income to pay, or you can borrow some portion of the total bill. And you can cut the costs.

- Several savings options, including U.S. savings bonds, 529s and Coverdell accounts, have tax benefits that can also help.
- You can work during college or promise to work later through programs like ROTC or AmeriCorps.
- You can borrow through student or parent loans.
- You can reduce your costs by such means as taking college-level courses for credit before you enter college.
- Tax breaks can help you meet college costs.

Once You're in College

QUICK OVERVIEW

Once you're in college, you shouldn't be preoccupied with paying for it. Academics, extracurricular activities and making friends are more important. But there are some things you need to do to stay on target financially. This chapter will tell you what they are.

Reapply for Aid Each Year!

Don't forget to reapply to renew your aid package every year! Check at your financial aid office to make sure you have the right forms and know what the deadlines are. Most colleges have a renewal deadline for financial aid that's a week or two later than the deadline for new applicants.

When you renew, don't expect your aid package to stay exactly the same. It may become more loan heavy each year, with more money in subsidized loans. The borrowing limits on the subsidized Stafford loan are higher for sophomores than for freshmen, and even higher for juniors and seniors. Also, keep in mind that some scholarships and grants are for freshmen only.

While you're reapplying for the financial aid you already have, keep an eye out for new opportunities. As you move on to higher grades and declare a major, you may become eligible for outside scholarships that weren't open to you in the past. Follow the guidelines in Step 9 to look for outside sources of money.

Stay on Track

The next thing to keep in mind is that you have to maintain eligibility for financial aid. For federal student aid, stay in school at least half-time, and avoid illegal drugs. A drug-related conviction can lead to suspension or revocation of your federal-aid eligibility.

You don't have to maintain a particular GPA to maintain federal eligibility (though you do have to meet your individual school's standards for "satisfactory academic progress"). But the financial aid your college gives you, such as

EXPERT ADVICE

"There are students who tell me that the reason they didn't pass their class was they're **too busy working**, because they need the money to support themselves. And I tell them, you need to determine your priorities. There's a limit of how much financial aid I can give you to help offset that."

— *Mary San Agustin, director of financial aid and scholarships, Palomar College, San Marcos, Calif.*

scholarships, may have specific academic requirements. Do your best in all your classes and stay on track academically, not only because it will help you get the most out of college but because it will help you keep your financial aid. To maintain or establish eligibility for academic scholarships, an on-campus job such as a teaching or research assistant, or a "co-op" program between your department and a local employer, you'll need to be in good academic standing.

Maintain Grades

To keep up your grades, you'll have to make decisions about how to spend your time. It's important to build social relationships, pursue extracurricular activities, and earn money through work, but balance those against the need to maintain a good academic record. If you have a job, don't work so hard at it that you jeopardize your aid eligibility.

Don't Stay Too Long

Did you know that only about one-third of all students who enter a four-year college graduate in four years? Most take six or more years to earn a bachelor's degree. Obviously, the longer you stay in college, the more it's going to cost you — not only in tuition, fees, room, board and other expenses, but also in lost earnings from a delayed career.

Make it a goal to graduate on time. Make sure you are on track to complete your college's core requirements, as well as the core requirements for your major.

Speaking of majors, don't feel that you need to rush into choosing one. Except for some very specialized career and technical institutes, most colleges and universities allow you to take time during your first two years to take classes in different fields and make sure you know enough to choose a major that fits your interests and abilities. On the other hand, don't wait so long that you neglect to take the courses that are requirements for a major. You don't want to have to pay for an extra semester to get your biology degree because you didn't take that required organic chemistry course your sophomore year.

Transferring from a Community College

If you're going to a community college, and plan to transfer to a four-year college, **make sure you know all the transfer requirements** — including whatever courses are needed for the major you intend to declare. It helps if your community college has an articulation agreement with the four-year college specifying exactly what courses are required for transfer. Almost all community colleges have a transfer adviser on staff who can help you make sure you're on track. Get to know your adviser and check in with him or her regularly.

MYTH/FACT

Myth: Only certain majors will lead to high earnings after graduation.

Fact: Don't be fooled. If you're not drawn to the major, you probably won't like the work and will leave that field before you ever reach the high earnings. Instead, **choose a major based on your interests and talents**, not on someone else's predictions of industrial trends. And remember that many of today's highest paying fields — such as marketing and software engineering — require critical thinking skills that you will acquire in courses like anthropology and philosophy. To learn more about specific academic fields and what it's like to major in them, read the College Board's *Book of Majors*.

Watch Your Personal Expenses

The purpose of financial aid is to give you the money you need to pay for college costs. But that aid can quickly become too little if you spend too much. To avoid overspending, live within your means and don't run up frivolous debt. That means sticking to a budget and avoiding credit cards.

Student Budgeting

To live within your means, all you have to do is not spend more than you receive in income. The best way to do that is to create a budget at the beginning of each semester and stick to it. Your budget should list the funds you will receive (such as money from parents, savings, work, grants and loans), subtract how much money you plan to spend on given items (such as tuition, fees, room, board, books, clothes and recreation) and calculate the difference — the bottom line. If the bottom line is a negative number — that is, if your expenses exceed your income — you're overspending. Once you have a budget where your income is equal to or greater than your expenses, follow it, and you'll be living within your means.

To create a budget, first examine what you have actually been spending, then **set priorities if you're spending too much**. That alone can help you to spend less, as you realize you can make do with one latte a day instead of two. "You start making conscious decisions about what it is that you want to do," says Elizabeth Bickford of the University of Oregon at Eugene. "You're actually just taking control over your financial spending."

By all means have fun, but don't spend too much money on nonessential items like DVDs, high-end clothes or trips to the beach. Some of your friends at college may have more money than you, but don't let social pressure push you into trying to spend like they do. Learn to suggest ordering pizza from the local hangout instead of driving to an expensive restaurant.

Save money wherever you can — for example, limit your cell phone use to free times. Comparison shop for groceries and supplies. And don't visit the ATM too often: It's too easy to withdraw money and overspend. See collegeboard.org for more advice on budgeting and financial planning.

Credit Card Debt

Be especially careful with your credit cards. They can be convenient for paying for big-ticket items like textbooks and airplane tickets, if you use them sparingly and pay off the entire amount when you get the bill. But if you abuse them, they can land you in a world of trouble.

A credit card is essentially a high-interest loan. Pulling it out at a cash register to make an impulse purchase may give you a feeling of freedom, but you won't feel free once you get the bill — especially when you're still paying interest on that impulse purchase months or years later. If you let the debt accumulate, it may swell so much that you won't be able to pay down the debt. This can affect your future academic career. If you miss payments on your credit cards, or if your credit card debt is high, you can hurt your credit rating. A bad credit rating can harm your chances of getting student loans to pay for graduate school, or a car loan when you start working. It can even prevent you from getting a job with certain security-conscious employers, such as banks or government agencies.

Use credit cards only when you know you can repay the debt promptly. Save them for emergencies. (A spring-break vacation is not an emergency.) Think through each credit card purchase before you spend. If you do get in over your head with credit card use, cut your expenses and talk to your family and financial aid administrator for more guidance.

Saving for Future Needs

While you're trying to live within your means, it's also wise to save for the future. Savings will give you greater freedom to cope with college and personal costs to come. If at all possible, make sure your budget includes money set aside for future needs. Your parents, of course, should do the same.

Try to save what you can from the jobs you have during the school year and in the summer. Think about the following as goals for your savings:

Students should think about …

- ✔ Next year's college expenses
- ✔ Application fees and tuition for graduate school
- ✔ A vacation with friends after you graduate
- ✔ Moving to another city after you graduate
- ✔ The unexpected (such as traveling to a friend's wedding or a family funeral)

Parents should think about …

- ✔ Next year's college expenses
- ✔ College expenses for younger children (if any)
- ✔ Retirement
- ✔ The unexpected (such as making it through a layoff or paying for a child's wedding)

Final Thoughts

Once you're in college, you may sometimes wonder if it's worth it. Can your family afford the expense? Will you be able to repay your student loans? If you've made reasonable choices along the way, the answer is yes. If you ever have doubts, visit your school's career center and do some research into the fields of work you might enter. Find out how much money you're likely to be earning when you first graduate, and how much five years later. A light might go on for you, as Elizabeth Bickford has often observed with other students. "When they see that relationship, many students say, 'Oh, wait a second, I can do that.'"

You will be able to pay back your student loans. College is a sound investment. You can afford college!

QUICK RECAP

Once you're in college, make sure you stay on track financially.

- Reapply for aid every year.
- Maintain your federal eligibility by staying in school the right number of hours and avoiding illegal drugs.
- Keep up your grades. Don't let them get derailed by too much time spent on work or other nonacademic activities.
- Declare a major at a suitable time.
- Make a budget and stick to it.
- Be wary of credit cards.
- Save for future expenses.
- Keep an eye out for new sources of outside scholarships.
- Remember that college is worth it!

Part II

WORKSHEET 1:
Meet Your Application Deadlines

		COLLEGE 1:	COLLEGE 2:	COLLEGE 3:
	College Name	*1st Choice Univ.*	*Private Univ.*	*Financial Safety*
FORMS REQUIRED	FAFSA			
	CSS Profile			
	State form			
	Institutional form			
	Tax returns			
	Other			
SCHOOL CODES	Federal code			
	CSS code			
PRIORITY DATE				
CLOSING DATE				
AFTER APPLYING	Need to send letter?			
	Documentation required?			
COMPARE AWARDS	Notification date			
	Reply-by date			

WORKSHEET 2:
Scholarship Application Planner

	PROGRAM 1	PROGRAM 2	PROGRAM 3
PROGRAM/SPONSOR			
ELIGIBILITY REQUIREMENTS			
TYPE OF AWARD			
AMOUNT OF AWARD			
CAN BE USED FOR			
CAN BE USED AT			
DEADLINE			
FORMS REQUIRED			
TEST SCORES REQUIRED			
ESSAY OR ACADEMIC SAMPLE			
RECOMMENDATIONS			
NOTIFICATION BEGINS			
REQUIREMENTS TO KEEP AFTER FRESHMAN YEAR			

WORKSHEET 3:
Compare Your Awards

	COLLEGE 1	COLLEGE 2	COLLEGE 3
Step 1. For each college, list its name, award deadline and total cost of attendance (this figure should be in your award letter; if not, refer to the college website or contact the financial aid office).			
Name of college			
Award deadline date			
Total cost of attendance			
Step 2. List the financial aid awards each school is offering. Don't forget that grants, scholarships and work-study do not have to be repaid, while all loans must be repaid.			
Grants and scholarships			
• Pell Grant (federal)			
• SEOG (federal)			
• State			
• College			
• Other			
Total grants/scholarships			
Percentage of package that is grant/scholarship			
Work-study opportunities			
Subsidized Stafford loan			
Unsubsidized Stafford loan			
Perkins loan			
Other loan(s)			
Total loans			
Percentage of package that is work or loans			
Total financial aid award			
Step 3. In the rows below, calculate what it will actually cost you to attend each college by subtracting the total financial aid award (row b) from the total cost of attendance (row a) to see the net cost (row c).			
a) Total cost of attendance			
b) Total financial aid award			
c) Net cost to attend (a minus b)			

Figure 9:

Sample Financial Aid Award Letter 1

Blue University   Cost of Attendance: $ 28,706.00

CLASS: 2022

March 22, 2018

TENTATIVE

FINANCIAL AWARD NOTIFICATION FOR 2018–2019

Based on the information that you submitted on your FAFSA and to our office,
Blue University can offer you the following TENTATIVE awards.

This package is based on an award period from 09/10/18 to 06/06/19.

AID AWARD	ACCEPT AWARD		OFFERED AMOUNT
	Yes	NO	
FEDERAL PERKINS LOAN	_____	_____	$1,143
STATE WORK-STUDY	_____	_____	$2,400
BLUE EDUCATIONAL GRANT	_____	_____	$3,538
UNIVERSITY SCHOLARSHIP	_____	_____	$2,000
RESIDENCE HALL GRANT	_____	_____	$2,000
FEDERAL STAFFORD LOAN – SUB.	_____	_____	$2,625

Finalize your financial aid award as soon as possible by forwarding to our office the forms listed on
the Missing Documents Form included with this letter.

Please read the important information pamphlet! Indicate your intent by checking whether or not you
accept each aid award, then sign and return this letter in order to reserve your award(s).

Please refer to the Cost Worksheet to help determine your expenses for the academic year.

If direct loan amounts desired are less than above, please indicate below:

Requested Federal Stafford Loan (Sub.) $ _____
Requested Federal Perkins Loan $ _____

I acknowledge that I have read and will comply with all the supporting information in the Important
Information Pamphlet. Furthermore, if I receive any financial assistance not included in this award
letter, including tuition waivers or employer reimbursement, I will notify your office immediately.

Signature _____   Date _____1

Figure 10:
Sample Financial Aid Award Letter 2

Green University | Office of Student Financial Planning

Cost of Attendance: $ 26,005.00

March 1, 2018

Step 1. Circle A for Accept or D for Decline for each individual award where indicated below:

	Fall 2018	Spring 2019	Total	A / D
Presidential Freshman Scholarship	$3,250	$3,250	$6,500	A / D
Green University Grant	$705	$705	$1,410	A / D
Total Grants and Scholarships			**$7,910**	
Federal Unsubsidized Stafford Loan	$1,313	$1,312	$2,625	A / D
Total Student Loans			**$2,625**	
Federal College Work-Study	$330	$330	$660	A / D
Federal PLUS Loan and/or Green Partnership Loan	$7,405	$7,405	$14,810	

Step 2. Please note the following:

Your awards are based on full-time enrollment for the fall and spring terms and residence hall occupancy for the fall and spring terms (for financial aid purposes, full-time is defined as 12 credits or more per term).

You have been offered loan(s) that require separate loan materials.

The amount of your Green University Grant was based upon residence hall occupancy for the fall and spring terms. A change in housing status may result in a reduction of this award.

Step 3. Please list other financial assistance, scholarships, or loans you will receive not indicated above. List the scholarship/donor name and the expected amount (example: Elks Club $100).

Name	Amount

Step 4. Attention: Your awards are not final until you complete the items on the ACTION REQUESTED page.

Estimate Your EFC
Under Federal Methodology

WORKSHEET 4A:
Estimate a Dependent Student's
Expected Contribution

STUDENT'S INCOME	
1. Taxable income ("adjusted gross income" from IRS Form 1040)	$
2. Untaxed income/benefits	+
3. Taxable student aid	-
4. Total student's income (sum of lines 1 and 2, minus line 3)	=
Allowances	
5. U.S. income tax paid (from IRS Form 1040)	
6. State and other taxes paid (% from Table 7 x line 4)	+
7. F.I.C.A. (Table 8)	+
8. Income protection allowance	$6,420
9. Parents' negative available income offset (line 20 of parents' worksheet, if negative)	+
10. Total allowances (sum of lines 5-9)	=
11. Available income (line 4 minus line 10)	=
12. Available income assessment rate	x 0.50
13. Contribution from income (line 11 x line 12; if negative, enter $0)	=
Student's Assets*	
14. Cash, savings and checking accounts	
15. Other real estate/investment equity	+
16. Business/nonfamily farm equity	+
17. Net worth (sum of lines 14-16)	=
18. Asset assessment rate	x 0.20
19. Contribution from assets (line 17 x line 18; if simple needs test or negative, enter $0)	=
Contribution**	
20. Total Student Contribution (sum of lines 13 and 19)	=

* If you are eligible to file an IRS 1040A or 1040EZ form, or you are not required to file a tax return, and your parents' taxable income is less than $50,000, no assets are included in the methodology.

** If your parents' adjusted gross income is $24,000 or less, and they file or are eligible to file an IRS 1040A or 1040EZ form, no contribution is expected.

WORKSHEET 4B:
Estimate the Parents' Expected Contribution

Parents' Income	
1. Taxable income ("adjusted gross income" from IRS Form 1040)	$
2. Untaxed income/benefits	+
3. Income exclusions (child support paid + education tax credits + taxable combat pay)	-
4. Total parents' income (sum of lines 1 and 2, minus line 3)	=
Allowances	
5. U.S. income tax paid (from IRS Form 1040)	
6. State and other taxes paid (% from Table 7 x line 4)	+
7. F.I.C.A. paid (Table 8)	+
8. Employment allowance (Table 8)	+
9. Income protection allowance (Table 9)	+
10. Total allowances (sum of lines 5-9)	=
11. Available income (line 4 minus line 10; may be negative)	=
Parents' Assets*	
12. Cash, savings and checking accounts	
13. Other real estate/investment equity	+
14. Adjusted business/nonfamily farm equity (Table 10)	+
15. Net worth (sum of lines 12-14)	=
16. Education Savings and Asset protection allowance (Table 11)	-
17. Discretionary net worth (line 15 minus line 16)	=
18. Conversion percentage	x 12%
19. Contribution from assets (line 17 x line 18; if simple needs test or negative, enter $0)	=
20. Adjusted available income (sum of line 11 and line 19; may be negative)	=
Contribution**	
21. Total contribution (calculate using line 20 and Table 12)	=
22. Number of dependent children in college at least half time	÷
23. Parents' contribution for student (line 21 divided by line 22; if negative, enter $0)	=

* If your parents are eligible to file an IRS 1040A or 1040EZ form, or are not required to file a tax return and their taxable income is less than $50,000, no assets are included in the methodology.

** If your parents' adjusted gross income is $24,000 or less, and they are eligible to file an IRS 1040A or 1040EZ form, or are not required to file a tax return, no contribution is expected.

TABLE 7: 2017–2018 Federal EFC Allowances for State Taxes

	Parents TOTAL INCOME		Student TOTAL INCOME		Parents TOTAL INCOME		Student TOTAL INCOME
	$ 0-14,999	$15,000 or more	Any amount		$ 0-14,999	$15,000 or more	Any amount
Alabama (AL)	3%	2%	2%	North Dakota (ND)	2%	1%	1%
Alaska (AK)	2	1	0	Northern Mariana Islands (MP)	2	1	1
American Samoa (AS)	2	1	1	Ohio (OH)	5	4	3
Arizona (AZ)	4	3	2	Oklahoma (OK)	3	2	2
Arkansas (AR)	4	3	3	Oregon (OR)	7	6	5
California (CA)	8	7	6	Palau (PW)	2	1	1
Canada (CN)	2	1	1	Pennsylvania (PA)	5	4	3
Colorado (CO)	4	3	3	Puerto Rico (PR)	2	1	1
Connecticut (CT)	9	8	5	Rhode Island (RI)	7	6	4
Delaware (DE)	5	4	3	South Carolina (SC)	5	4	3
District of Columbia (DC)	8	7	6	South Dakota (SD)	2	1	1
Federated States of Micronesia (FM)	2	1	1	Tennessee (TN)	2	1	1
Florida (FL)	3	2	1	Texas (TX)	3	2	1
Georgia (GA)	5	4	3	Utah (UT)	5	4	3
Guam (GU)	2	1	1	Vermont (VT)	6	5	3
Hawaii (HI)	5	4	4	Virgin Islands (VI)	2	1	1
Idaho (ID)	5	4	3	Virginia (VA)	6	5	4
Illinois (IL)	6	5	3	Washington (WA)	3	2	1
Indiana (IN)	4	3	3	West Virginia (WV)	3	2	2
Iowa (IA)	5	4	3	Wisconsin (WI)	7	6	4
Kansas (KS)	4	3	3	Wyoming (WY)	5	1	1
Kentucky (KY)	5	4	4	Not Reported (NR)	2	1	1
Louisiana (LA)	3	2	2				
Maine (ME)	6	5	4				
Marshall Islands (MH)	2	1	1				
Maryland (MD)	8	7	6				
Massachusetts (MA)	7	6	4				
Mexico (MX)	2	1	1				
Michigan (MI)	5	4	3				
Minnesota (MN)	6	5	5				
Mississippi	3	2	2				
Missouri (MO)	5	4	3				
Montana (MT)	5	4	3				
Nebraska (NE)	5	4	3				
Nevada (NV)	2	1	1				
New Hampshire (NH)	5	4	1				
New Jersey (NJ)	9	8	5				
New Mexico (NM)	3	2	2				
New York (NY)	10	9	7				
North Carolina (NC)	5	4	4				

TABLE 8: Federal EFC Allowances for FICA and Employment

FICA: WAGES

$1 to $118,500	7.65% of income earned by each wage earner (maximum $9,065.25 per person)
$118,501 or more	$9,065.25 + 1.45% of income earned above $118,500 by each wage earner

EMPLOYMENT ALLOWANCE	35% of lesser earned income to a maximum $4,000 (single parent: 35% of earned income to a maximum of $4,000)

TABLE 9: Federal EFC Income Protection Allowance for Parents

Family Size (including student)	Number in College				
	1	2	3	4	5
2	$ 17,910	$ 14,840			
3	22,300	19,250	$ 16,190		
4	27,540	24,480	21,430	$ 18,360	
5	32,490	29,430	26,380	23,320	$ 20,270
6	38,010	34,940	31,900	28,830	25,790

For each additional family member, add $4,290.
For each additional college student, subtract $3,050.

TABLE 10: Federal EFC Adjusted Net Worth of a Business or Farm

NET WORTH	ADJUSTED NET WORTH		
Less than $1	$	0	
$1 to 130,000	$	0	+ 40% of net worth
$130,001 to 385,000	$	52,000	+ 50% of net worth over $130,000
$385,001 to 640,000	$	179,500	+ 60% of net worth over $385,000
$640,001 or more	$	332,500	+ 100% of net worth over $640,000

TABLE 11: Federal EFC Education Savings and Asset Protection Allowance for Parents

AGE OF OLDER PARENT OR STUDENT	COUPLE/ MARRIED	UNMARRIED/ SINGLE
25 or under	$ 0	$ 0
26	1,100	600
27	2,200	1,300
28	3,400	1,900
29	4,500	2,600
30	5,600	3,200
31	6,700	3,800
32	7,800	4,500
33	9,000	5,100
34	10,100	5,800
35	11,200	6,400
36	12,300	7,000
37	13,400	7,700
38	14,600	8,300
39	15,700	9,000
40	16,800	9,600
41	17,100	9,800
42	17,500	10,000
43	17,900	10,200
44	18,400	10,500
45	18,800	10,700
46	19,300	10,900
47	19,800	11,200
48	20,200	11,400
49	20,700	11,700
50	21,200	12,000
51	21,700	12,200
52	22,400	12,500
53	22,900	12,800
54	23,600	13,200
55	24,100	13,500
56	24,800	13,800
57	25,600	14,100
58	26,200	14,500
59	26,900	14,900
60	27,700	15,200
61	28,500	15,600
62	29,300	16,000
63	30,100	16,400
64	31,100	16,900
65 or over	31,900	17,300

TABLE 12: Federal EFC Parents' Contribution from Adjusted Available Income (AAI)

ADJUSTED AVAILABLE INCOME (AAI)	TOTAL CONTRIBUTIONS FROM INCOME		
Less than $ -3,409 (3,409)	$	-750	
$(3,409) to 16,000		22% of AI	
$ 16,001 to 20,100	$	3,520	+ 25% of AAI over $ 16,000
$ 20,101 to 24,200	$	4,545	+ 29% of AAI over $ 20,100
$ 24,201 to 28,300	$	5,734	+ 34% of AAI over $ 24,200
$ 28,301 to 32,300	$	7,128	+ 40% of AAI over $ 28,300
$ 32,301 or more	$	8,728	+ 47% of AAI over $ 32,300

Contact Information for State Aid Programs

ALABAMA
Alabama Commission on
Higher Education
P.O. Box 302000
Montgomery, AL 36130-2000
334-242-1998
www.ache.state.al.us

ALASKA
Alaska Commission on Postsecondary Education
P.O. Box 110505
Juneau, AK 99811-0505
800-441-2962
www.acpe.alaska.gov/

ARIZONA
Arizona Department of Education
1535 West Jefferson Street
Phoenix, AZ 85007
800-352-4558
www.azed.gov/

ARKANSAS
Arkansas Department of Higher Education
423 Main Street, Suite 400
Little Rock, AR 72201
501-371-2000
www.adhe.edu

CALIFORNIA
California Student Aid Commission
P.O. Box 419026
Rancho Cordova, CA 95741-9026
888-224-7268
www.csac.ca.gov

COLORADO
Colorado Department of Education
201 East Colfax Avenue
Denver, CO 80203
303-866-6600
www.cde.state.co.us

CONNECTICUT
Connecticut Office of Higher Education
450 Columbus Boulevard
Hartford, CT 06103-1841
860-947-1800
www.ctohe.org

DELAWARE
Delaware Higher Education Office
The Townsend Building
401 Federal Street, Suite 2
Dover, DE 19901
302-735-4000
www.doe.k12.de.us/dheo

DISTRICT OF COLUMBIA
Office of the State Superintendent
of Education
810 First Street, NE, 9th Floor
Washington, DC 20002
202-727-6436
www.seo.dc.gov

FLORIDA
Florida Department of Education
Office of Student Financial Assistance
325 W. Gaines Street, Suite 1514
Tallahassee, FL 32399-0400
888-827-2004
www.floridastudentfinancialaid.org

GEORGIA
Georgia Student Finance Commission
2082 East Exchange Place
Tucker, GA 30084
800-505-4732
www.gsfc.org

GUAM
University of Guam
Student Financial Aid Office
UOG Station
Mangilao, GU 96923
671-735-2288
www.uog.edu

HAWAII
Hawaii State Department
of Education
1390 Miller Street
Honolulu, HI 96813
808-586-3230
www.hawaiipublicschools.org

IDAHO
Idaho State Department of Education
650 West State Street
P.O. Box 83720
Boise, ID 83720-0027
800-432-4601
www.sde.idaho.gov

ILLINOIS
Illinois Student Assistance Commission
1755 Lake Cook Road
Deerfield, IL 60015-5209
800-899-4722
www.isac.org

INDIANA
State Student Assistance Commission of Indiana
101 West Ohio Street, Suite 300
Indianapolis, IN 46204
888-528-4719
www.in.gov/ssaci

IOWA
Iowa College Student
Aid Commission
430 East Grand Avenue, FL 3
Des Moines, IA 50309
877-272-4456
www.iowacollegeaid.gov

KANSAS
Kansas Board of Regents
1000 SW Jackson Street, Suite 520
Topeka, KS 66612-1368
785-430-4240
www.kansasregents.org

KENTUCKY
KHEAA Student Aid Branch
100 Airport Road
Frankfort, KY 40602
800-928-8926
www.kheaa.com

LOUISIANA
Louisiana Office of Student
Financial Assistance
P.O. Box 91202
Baton Rouge, LA 70821-9202
800-259-5626
www.osfa.la.gov

MAINE
Finance Authority of Maine
Education Assistance Division
5 Community Drive
Augusta, ME 04332-0949
800-228-3734
www.famemaine.com

MARYLAND
Maryland Higher Education Commission
Office of Student Financial Assistance
6 N. Liberty St.
Baltimore, MD 21201
800-974-0203
www.mhec.state.md.us

MASSACHUSETTS
Massachusetts Department of Higher Education
Office of Student Financial Assistance
One Ashburton Place
Boston, MA 02108
617-391-6070
www.osfa.mass.edu

MICHIGAN
Michigan Higher Education Assistance Authority
Office of Scholarships and Grants
P.O. Box 30462
Lansing, MI 48909-7962
888-447-2687
www.michigan.gov/mistudentaid

MINNESOTA
Minnesota Office of Higher Education
1450 Energy Park Drive, Suite 350
St. Paul, MN 55108-5227
800-657-3866
www.ohe.state.mn.us

MISSISSIPPI
Mississippi Office of Student Financial Aid
3825 Ridgewood Road
Jackson, MS 39211-6453
800-327-2980
www.mississippi.edu/riseupms/

MISSOURI
Missouri Department of
Higher Education
205 Jefferson Street
P.O. Box 1469
Jefferson City, MO 65102-1469
800-473-6757
www.dhe.mo.gov

MONTANA
Montana Board of Regents
P.O. Box 203201
2500 Broadway Street
Helena, MT 59620-3201
406-444-6570
http://mus.edu/board/

NEBRASKA
Coordinating Commission for Postsecondary Education
P.O. Box 95005
Lincoln, NE 68509-5005
402-471-2847
www.ccpe.nebraska.gov

NEVADA
Nevada Department of Education
700 East Fifth Street
Carson City, NV 89701
775-687-9220
www.doe.nv.gov

NEW HAMPSHIRE
New Hampshire Postsecondary Education Commission
101 Pleasant Street
Concord, NH 03301-3860
603-271-3494
www.education.nh.gov/highered/

NEW JERSEY
HESAA Grants & Scholarships
P.O. Box 540
Trenton, NJ 08625-0540
800-792-8670
www.hesaa.org

NEW MEXICO
New Mexico Higher Education Department
2044 Galisteo Street
Santa Fe, NM 87505
505-476-8400
www.hed.state.nm.us

NEW YORK
New York State Higher Education Services Corporation
99 Washington Avenue
Albany, NY 12255
888-697-4372
www.hesc.ny.gov

NORTH CAROLINA
North Carolina State Education Assistance Authority
P.O. Box 14103
Research Triangle Park, NC 27709
919-549-8614
www.ncseaa.edu

NORTH DAKOTA
North Dakota University System
10th Floor, State Capitol
600 East Boulevard Ave, Dept. 215
Bismarck, ND 58505-0230
701-328-2960
www.ndus.edu

OHIO
Ohio Board of Regents
25 South Front Street
Columbus, OH 43215
614-466-6000
www.ohiohighered.org/

OKLAHOMA
Oklahoma State Regents for
Higher Education
Tuition Aid Grant Program
655 Research Parkway, Suite 200
Oklahoma City, OK 73104
405-225-9100
www.okhighered.org

OREGON
Oregon Student Assistance Commission
1500 Valley River Drive, Suite 100
Eugene, OR 97401
800-452-8807
www.oregonstudentaid.gov

PENNSYLVANIA
Pennsylvania Higher Education Assistance Agency
P.O. Box 8157
Harrisburg, PA 17105-8157
800-692-7392
www.pheaa.org

PUERTO RICO
Departmento de Educacion
P.O. Box 190759
San Juan, PR 00919-0759
787-759-2000
www.de.gobierno.pr

RHODE ISLAND
Rhode Island Higher Education Assistance Authority
560 Jefferson Boulevard, Suite 100
Warwick, RI 02886-1304
800-922-9855
www.riheaa.org

SOUTH CAROLINA
South Carolina Commission on Higher Education
1122 Lady Street, Suite 300
Columbia, SC 29201
803-737-2260
www.che.sc.gov

SOUTH DAKOTA
South Dakota Department
of Education
Office of Finance and Management
800 Governors Drive
Pierre, SD 57501
605-773-3134
www.doe.sd.gov/

TENNESSEE
Tennessee Student Assistance Corporation
404 James Robertson Parkway,
Suite 1510, Parkway Towers
Nashville, TN 37243-0820
800-342-1663
www.tn.gov.collegepays

TEXAS
Texas Higher Education Coordinating Board
Student Loan Programs
P.O. Box 12788-2788
Austin, TX 78711
800-242-3062
www.hhloans.com

UTAH
Utah Higher Education
Assistance Authority
P.O. Box 145110
Salt Lake City, UT 84114-5110
877-336-7378
www.uheaa.org

VERMONT
Vermont Student Assistance Corporation
P.O. Box 2000
Winooski, VT 05404
800-642-3177
www.vsac.org

VIRGIN ISLANDS
Financial Aid Office, Virgin Islands Board of Education
P.O. Box 11900
St. Thomas, VI 00801
340-774-4546
www.myviboe.com

VIRGINIA
State Council of Higher Education
for Virginia
James Monroe Building
101 North 14th Street, 10th Fl.
Richmond, VA 23219
804-225-2600
www.schev.edu

WASHINGTON
Washington Student Achievement Council
917 Lakeridge Way SW
Olympia, WA 98502
(360) 753-7800
www.wsac.wa.gov

WEST VIRGINIA
West Virginia Higher Education Policy Commission
1018 Kanawha Boulevard East, Suite 700
Charleston, WV 25301
304-558-2101
www.wvhepc.com

WISCONSIN
Wisconsin Higher Educational
Aids Board
P. O. Box 7885
Madison, WI 53707-7885
608-267-2206
www.heab.state.wi.us

WYOMING
Wyoming Department of Education
2300 Capitol Avenue
Hathaway Building, Second Floor
Cheyenne, WY 82002-2060
307-777-7675
www.k12.wy.us

Part III

Financial Aid College
by College

Alabama

Alabama Agricultural and Mechanical University
Huntsville, Alabama
www.aamu.edu   Federal Code: 001002

4-year public university and agricultural college in small city.
Enrollment: 4,616 undergrads, 9% part-time. 1,410 full-time freshmen.
Selectivity: Admits over 75% of applicants.

BASIC COSTS (2016-2017)
Tuition and fees: $9,456; out-of-state residents $17,964.
Per-credit charge: $271; out-of-state residents $542.
Room and board: $7,030.
Additional info: Health Insurance for domestic students: $152; Health Insurance for international students: $1,632. Tuition/fee waivers available for minority students.

FINANCIAL AID PICTURE
Students with need: Need-based aid available for full-time and part-time students. Work study available weekends and for part-time students.
Students without need: No-need awards available for athletics, minority status.
Scholarships offered: Presidential Scholarship: full tuition, course fees, room and board, $1,000 for books and supplies per semester; for students with 3.5 GPA or higher. Provost Scholarship: full tuition, course fees, room and board, $800 for books and supplies per semester; for students with 3.4 GPA or higher. Dean's Scholarship: full tuition, course fees, room and board, $500 for books and supplies per semester; for students with 3.3 GPA or higher.

FINANCIAL AID PROCEDURES
Forms required: FAFSA, institutional form.
Dates and Deadlines: Closing date 3/1. Applicants notified on a rolling basis starting 4/15; must reply within 2 week(s) of notification.

CONTACT
Darryl Jackson, Director of Student Financial Aid
Box 908, Normal, AL 35762
(256) 372-5400

Alabama State University
Montgomery, Alabama
www.alasu.edu   Federal Code: 001005

4-year public university in small city.
Enrollment: 4,703 undergrads, 7% part-time. 1,143 full-time freshmen.
Selectivity: Admits less than 50% of applicants.

BASIC COSTS (2016-2017)
Tuition and fees: $8,720; out-of-state residents $15,656.
Per-credit charge: $289; out-of-state residents $578.
Room and board: $5,422.

FINANCIAL AID PICTURE (2016-2017)
Students with need: 54% of average financial aid package awarded as scholarships/grants, 46% awarded as loans/jobs. Need-based aid available for part-time students. Work study available nights, weekends, and for part-time students.
Students without need: No-need awards available for academics, alumni affiliation, art, athletics, job skills, leadership, minority status, music/drama, religious affiliation, ROTC.

FINANCIAL AID PROCEDURES
Forms required: FAFSA.
Dates and Deadlines: Priority date 4/1; no closing date. Applicants notified on a rolling basis starting 5/1.
Transfers: Applicants notified on a rolling basis starting 5/1.

CONTACT
Marcus Byrd, Director of Financial Aid
PO Box 271, Montgomery, AL 36101-0271
(334) 229-4323

Amridge University
Montgomery, Alabama
www.amridgeuniversity.edu   Federal Code: 016885

4-year private virtual university in small city, affiliated with the Church of Christ.
Enrollment: 292 undergrads, 54% part-time. 12 full-time freshmen.
Selectivity: Open admission; but selective for some programs.

BASIC COSTS (2016-2017)
Tuition and fees: $7,180.
Per-credit charge: $250.

FINANCIAL AID PICTURE (2016-2017)
Students with need: Out of 4 full-time freshmen who applied for aid, 4 were judged to have need. Of these, 4 received aid, and 4 had their full need met. Average financial aid package met 100% of need; average scholarship/grant was $2,188; average loan was $4,016. Need-based aid available for part-time students.
Students without need: No-need awards available for academics, leadership, religious affiliation.

FINANCIAL AID PROCEDURES
Forms required: FAFSA, institutional form.
Dates and Deadlines: Applicants notified on a rolling basis.
Transfers: No deadline. Applicants notified on a rolling basis.

CONTACT
Starr Fain, Financial Aid Director
1200 Taylor Road, Montgomery, AL 36117-3553
(800) 351-4040 ext. 7523

Athens State University
Athens, Alabama
www.athens.edu   Federal Code: 001008

Upper-division public liberal arts and teachers college in large town.
Enrollment: 2,889 undergrads, 58% part-time.

BASIC COSTS (2016-2017)
Tuition and fees: $6,480; out-of-state residents $12,210.

FINANCIAL AID PICTURE (2015-2016)
Students with need: Average financial aid package for all full-time undergraduates was $10,341; for part-time $8,599. 45% awarded as scholarships/grants, 55% awarded as loans/jobs. Work study available nights, weekends, and for part-time students.
Students without need: No-need awards available for academics, alumni affiliation, art, athletics, leadership, minority status.

FINANCIAL AID PROCEDURES
Forms required: FAFSA.
Dates and Deadlines: Applicants notified on a rolling basis starting 6/1; must reply within 3 week(s) of notification.

CONTACT

Mary Chambliss, Director, Student Financial Services
300 North Beaty Street, Athens, AL 35611
(256) 233-8170

Auburn University
Auburn, Alabama
www.auburn.edu   Federal Code: 001009

4-year public university in small city.
Enrollment: 22,095 undergrads, 8% part-time. 4,902 full-time freshmen.
Selectivity: Admits over 75% of applicants.

BASIC COSTS (2016-2017)

Tuition and fees: $10,696; out-of-state residents $28,840.
Per-credit charge: $378; out-of-state residents $1,134.
Room and board: $12,898.

FINANCIAL AID PICTURE (2015-2016)

Students with need: Out of 3,037 full-time freshmen who applied for aid, 1,764 were judged to have need. Of these, 1,764 received aid, and 311 had their full need met. Average financial aid package met 52% of need; average scholarship/grant was $9,078; average loan was $3,670. For part-time students, average financial aid package was $6,167.
Students without need: 1,478 full-time freshmen who did not demonstrate need for aid received scholarships/grants; average award was $7,397.
Scholarships offered: *Merit:* Freshmen and General Scholarships; up to full-tuition; require 28 ACT/1240 SAT and 3.5 GPA. National Achievement Finalists; full-tuition plus additional benefits. *Athletic:* 98 full-time freshmen received athletic scholarships; average amount $37,285.
Additional info: State of Alabama has pre-paid college tuition plan for residents.

FINANCIAL AID PROCEDURES

Forms required: FAFSA.
Dates and Deadlines: Priority date 3/1; no closing date. Applicants notified on a rolling basis starting 10/2; must reply by 5/1.
Transfers: No deadline. Applicants notified on a rolling basis; must reply within 2 week(s) of notification.

CONTACT

Mike Reynolds, Director, Student Financial Services
Quad Center, Auburn, AL 36849-5111
(334) 844-4080

Auburn University at Montgomery
Montgomery, Alabama
www.aum.edu   Federal Code: 008310

4-year public university in small city.
Enrollment: 4,179 undergrads, 26% part-time. 568 full-time freshmen.
Selectivity: Admits over 75% of applicants.

BASIC COSTS (2016-2017)

Tuition and fees: $9,640; out-of-state residents $20,710.
Per-credit charge: $296; out-of-state residents $665.
Room and board: $5,650.

FINANCIAL AID PICTURE (2015-2016)

Students with need: Out of 450 full-time freshmen who applied for aid, 395 were judged to have need. Of these, 395 received aid, and 48 had their full need met. For part-time students, average financial aid package was $5,875.
Students without need: 59 full-time freshmen who did not demonstrate need for aid received scholarships/grants; average award was $4,626.

Scholarships offered: Achievement Scholarship, AUM Freshman Leadership Scholarship, Deichelmann Memorial Scholarship, Freshman Housing Scholarship, Recognition Scholarship, Warhawk Scholarship.

FINANCIAL AID PROCEDURES

Forms required: FAFSA.
Dates and Deadlines: Priority date 3/1; no closing date. Applicants notified on a rolling basis starting 4/15.

CONTACT

Anthony Richey, Director of Financial Aid
PO Box 244023, Montgomery, AL 36124-4023
(334) 244-3571

Bevill State Community College
Jasper, Alabama
www.bscc.edu   Federal Code: 005733

2-year public community college in small town.
Enrollment: 3,215 undergrads.
Selectivity: Open admission; but selective for some programs.

BASIC COSTS (2016-2017)

Tuition and fees: $4,742; out-of-state residents $8,486.
Per-credit charge: $117; out-of-state residents $234.
Room and board: $1,850.
Additional info: Tuition/fee waivers available for unemployed or children of unemployed.

FINANCIAL AID PICTURE

Students with need: Need-based aid available for full-time and part-time students.
Students without need: No-need awards available for academics, leadership, music/drama.

FINANCIAL AID PROCEDURES

Forms required: FAFSA.
Dates and Deadlines: Priority date 5/1; no closing date. Applicants notified on a rolling basis starting 7/1.

CONTACT

Doug Hartley, Financial Aid Director
1411 Indiana Avenue, Jasper, AL 35501
(205) 387-0511

Birmingham-Southern College
Birmingham, Alabama
www.bsc.edu   Federal Code: 001012

4-year private liberal arts college in very large city, affiliated with the United Methodist Church.
Enrollment: 1,290 undergrads, 1% part-time. 328 full-time freshmen.
Selectivity: Admits less than 50% of applicants.

BASIC COSTS (2016-2017)

Tuition and fees: $34,448.
Per-credit charge: $1,383.25.
Room and board: $11,620.

FINANCIAL AID PICTURE

Students with need: Need-based aid available for full-time and part-time students. Work study available nights, weekends, and for part-time students.
Students without need: No-need awards available for academics, alumni affiliation, art, leadership, music/drama, religious affiliation, ROTC, state/district residency.
Scholarships offered: Neal and Anne Berte Scholarship: full tuition; based on academic achievement; 1 awarded. Blount-Monaghan/Vulcan Materials

Company Scholarship: full tuition; based on academic achievement; 1 awarded. William Jones and Elizabeth Perry Rushton Scholarship: full tuition, room and board, fees, books, $2,000 travel stipend; based on academic achievement; 1 awarded. Phi Beta Kappa: full tuition; based on academic achievement. United Methodist Scholarship: $1,000-$2,500; awarded to United Methodist with recommendation from senior United Methodist Minister.

Additional info: Auditions required for music, theatre, dance applicants seeking scholarships. Portfolios required for art applicants seeking scholarships, and essays recommended for all applicants seeking scholarships.

FINANCIAL AID PROCEDURES

Forms required: FAFSA, state aid form.

Dates and Deadlines: Priority date 3/1; no closing date. Applicants notified on a rolling basis starting 3/1; must reply by 5/1.

Transfers: No deadline. Applicants notified on a rolling basis starting 3/1; must reply within 2 week(s) of notification.

CONTACT

Director of Financial Aid Services
900 Arkadelphia Road, Birmingham, AL 35254
(205) 226-4688

Central Alabama Community College

Alexander City, Alabama
www.cacc.edu   Federal Code: 001007

2-year public community college in large town.

Enrollment: 1,497 undergrads, 37% part-time. 340 full-time freshmen.

Selectivity: Open admission; but selective for some programs.

BASIC COSTS (2016-2017)

Tuition and fees: $4,380; out-of-state residents $7,890.

Per-credit charge: $117; out-of-state residents $234.

FINANCIAL AID PICTURE (2015-2016)

Students with need: 75% of average financial aid package awarded as scholarships/grants, 25% awarded as loans/jobs. Need-based aid available for part-time students. Work study available nights.

Students without need: No-need awards available for academics, athletics, music/drama, state/district residency.

FINANCIAL AID PROCEDURES

Forms required: FAFSA.

Dates and Deadlines: Priority date 7/15; no closing date. Applicants notified on a rolling basis.

CONTACT

Cindy Entrekin, Director of Financial Aid
1675 Cherokee Road, Alexander City, AL 35010
(256) 215-4251

Chattahoochee Valley Community College

Phenix City, Alabama
www.cv.edu   Federal Code: 012182

2-year public community college in small city.

Enrollment: 1,529 undergrads.

Selectivity: Open admission; but selective for some programs.

BASIC COSTS (2016-2017)

Tuition and fees: $4,440; out-of-state residents $7,950.

Per-credit charge: $117; out-of-state residents $234.

FINANCIAL AID PICTURE

Students with need: Need-based aid available for full-time and part-time students. Work study available nights, weekends, and for part-time students.

Students without need: No-need awards available for academics, art, athletics, leadership, music/drama.

FINANCIAL AID PROCEDURES

Forms required: FAFSA.

Dates and Deadlines: Priority date 7/1; no closing date. Applicants notified on a rolling basis; must reply within 1 week(s) of notification.

CONTACT

Joan Waters, Director of Financial Aid
2602 College Drive, Phenix City, AL 36869
(334) 291-4915

Columbia Southern University

Orange Beach, Alabama
www.columbiasouthern.edu   Federal Code: 041215

4-year for-profit virtual university in small town.

Enrollment: 24,713 undergrads, 50% part-time. 855 full-time freshmen.

Selectivity: Open admission.

BASIC COSTS (2016-2017)

Tuition and fees: $6,335.

Per-credit charge: $210.

FINANCIAL AID PICTURE (2015-2016)

Students with need: 29% of average financial aid package awarded as scholarships/grants, 71% awarded as loans/jobs. Need-based aid available for part-time students.

FINANCIAL AID PROCEDURES

Forms required: FAFSA, institutional form.

Dates and Deadlines: Applicants notified on a rolling basis.

Transfers: No deadline. Applicants notified on a rolling basis.

CONTACT

Pat Troup, VP Business Affairs
21982 University Lane, Orange Beach, AL 36561
(251) 981-3771 ext. 1226

Concordia College

Selma, Alabama
www.ccal.edu   Federal Code: 010554

4-year private liberal arts college in large town, affiliated with the Lutheran Church - Missouri Synod.

Enrollment: 610 undergrads.

Selectivity: Open admission.

BASIC COSTS (2016-2017)

Tuition and fees: $10,120.

Room and board: $5,700.

Additional info: Additional fees may be applicable. Tuition/fee waivers available for adults.

FINANCIAL AID PICTURE

Students with need: Need-based aid available for full-time and part-time students.

Students without need: This college awards aid only to students with need.

FINANCIAL AID PROCEDURES

Forms required: FAFSA, state aid form, institutional form.

Dates and Deadlines: Priority date 4/1; closing date 4/15. Applicants notified on a rolling basis starting 6/15; must reply within 2 week(s) of notification.

CONTACT

Tharsteen Bridges, Financial Aid Administrator
1712 Broad Street, Selma, AL 36701
(334) 847-5700 ext. 160

Enterprise State Community College

Enterprise, Alabama
www.escc.edu   Federal Code: 001015

2-year public community college in large town.
Enrollment: 1,357 undergrads, 39% part-time. 296 full-time freshmen.
Selectivity: Open admission.

BASIC COSTS (2017-2018)
Tuition and fees: $5,310; out-of-state residents $8,760.

FINANCIAL AID PICTURE (2016-2017)
Students with need: 86% of average financial aid package awarded as scholarships/grants, 14% awarded as loans/jobs.
Students without need: No-need awards available for academics, art, athletics, leadership, music/drama, state/district residency.

FINANCIAL AID PROCEDURES
Forms required: FAFSA.
Dates and Deadlines: Priority date 4/1; no closing date. Applicants notified on a rolling basis starting 3/1.
Transfers: Applicants notified on a rolling basis starting 6/1; must reply within 2 week(s) of notification.

CONTACT
Henry Quisenberry, Director of Financial Aid
Box 1300, Enterprise, AL 36331
(334) 347-2623 ext. 2214

Faulkner State Community College

Bay Minette, Alabama
www.faulknerstate.edu   Federal Code: 001060

2-year public community college in large town.
Enrollment: 1,342 undergrads, 23% part-time. 2,586 full-time freshmen.
Selectivity: Open admission; but selective for some programs.

BASIC COSTS (2016-2017)
Tuition and fees: $4,400; out-of-state residents $7,910.
Per-credit charge: $117; out-of-state residents $234.
Room and board: $5,800.

FINANCIAL AID PICTURE (2016-2017)
Students with need: 75% of average financial aid package awarded as scholarships/grants, 25% awarded as loans/jobs. Work study available nights.
Students without need: No-need awards available for academics, art, athletics, leadership, music/drama.

FINANCIAL AID PROCEDURES
Forms required: FAFSA, institutional form.
Dates and Deadlines: Priority date 7/1; no closing date. Applicants notified on a rolling basis starting 7/1; must reply within 2 week(s) of notification.

CONTACT
James Theeuwes, Director of Financial Aid
1900 Highway 31 South, Bay Minette, AL 36507
(251) 580-2151

Faulkner University

Montgomery, Alabama
www.faulkner.edu   Federal Code: 001003

4-year private university and liberal arts college in large city, affiliated with the Church of Christ.
Enrollment: 2,298 undergrads, 23% part-time. 263 full-time freshmen.
Selectivity: Admits less than 50% of applicants.

BASIC COSTS (2016-2017)
Tuition and fees: $20,130.
Per-credit charge: $620.
Room and board: $7,230.
Additional info: Tuition/fee waivers available for adults, minority students, unemployed or children of unemployed.

FINANCIAL AID PICTURE (2015-2016)
Students with need: Out of 243 full-time freshmen who applied for aid, 227 were judged to have need. Of these, 227 received aid, and 27 had their full need met. Average financial aid package met 62% of need; average scholarship/grant was $11,667; average loan was $3,053. For part-time students, average financial aid package was $6,790.
Students without need: 24 full-time freshmen who did not demonstrate need for aid received scholarships/grants; average award was $6,113. No-need awards available for academics, alumni affiliation, athletics, music/drama, religious affiliation, state/district residency.
Scholarships offered: 32 full-time freshmen received athletic scholarships; average amount $7,178.

FINANCIAL AID PROCEDURES
Forms required: FAFSA, state aid form, institutional form.
Dates and Deadlines: Priority date 3/15; closing date 5/1. Applicants notified on a rolling basis starting 1/1; must reply within 3 week(s) of notification.
Transfers: No deadline. Applicants notified on a rolling basis; must reply within 3 week(s) of notification.

CONTACT
William Jackson, Director of Financial Aid
5345 Atlanta Highway, Montgomery, AL 36109-3398
(334) 386-7195

Gadsden State Community College

Gadsden, Alabama
www.gadsdenstate.edu   Federal Code: 001017

2-year public community and technical college in small city.
Enrollment: 4,548 undergrads.
Selectivity: Open admission; but selective for some programs.

BASIC COSTS (2016-2017)
Tuition and fees: $4,080; out-of-state residents $7,590.
Per-credit charge: $117; out-of-state residents $234.
Room and board: $3,600.
Additional info: Tuition/fee waivers available for minority students, unemployed or children of unemployed.

FINANCIAL AID PICTURE
Students with need: Need-based aid available for full-time and part-time students.
Students without need: No-need awards available for academics, alumni affiliation, art, athletics, job skills, leadership, minority status, music/drama, state/district residency.

FINANCIAL AID PROCEDURES
Forms required: FAFSA, institutional form.
Dates and Deadlines: Priority date 4/15; no closing date. Applicants notified on a rolling basis starting 6/10.

CONTACT
Kelly D'Eath, Director of Financial Aid
1001 George Wallace Drive, Gadsden, AL 35902-0227
(256) 549-8284

George C. Wallace Community College at Dothan
Dothan, Alabama
www.wallace.edu   Federal Code: 001018

2-year public community college in small city.
Enrollment: 3,904 undergrads, 50% part-time. 733 full-time freshmen.
Selectivity: Admits over 75% of applicants.

BASIC COSTS (2016-2017)
Tuition and fees: $4,320; out-of-state residents $7,830.
Per-credit charge: $117; out-of-state residents $234.

FINANCIAL AID PICTURE (2015-2016)
Students with need: 99% of average financial aid package awarded as scholarships/grants, 1% awarded as loans/jobs.
Students without need: No-need awards available for academics, athletics, leadership.

FINANCIAL AID PROCEDURES
Forms required: FAFSA.
Dates and Deadlines: Priority date 5/1; no closing date. Applicants notified on a rolling basis.

CONTACT
Erma Perry, Director of Financial Aid
1141 Wallace Drive, Dothan, AL 36303-0943
(334) 687-3543 ext. 4285

George C. Wallace State Community College at Selma
Selma, Alabama
www.wccs.edu   Federal Code: 005699

2-year public community and technical college in large town.
Enrollment: 1,397 undergrads, 36% part-time. 339 full-time freshmen.
Selectivity: Open admission; but selective for some programs.

BASIC COSTS (2016-2017)
Tuition and fees: $4,080; out-of-state residents $7,590.
Per-credit charge: $117; out-of-state residents $234.

FINANCIAL AID PICTURE (2015-2016)
Students with need: Out of 339 full-time freshmen who applied for aid, 263 were judged to have need. Of these, 227 received aid. Need-based aid available for part-time students.
Students without need: This college awards aid only to students with need.

FINANCIAL AID PROCEDURES
Forms required: FAFSA.
Dates and Deadlines: Priority date 7/11; closing date 6/30. Applicants notified on a rolling basis starting 10/1; must reply within 2 week(s) of notification.
Transfers: No deadline. Applicants notified on a rolling basis starting 7/1; must reply within 2 week(s) of notification.

CONTACT
Anessa Kidd, Director of Financial Aid
PO Box 2530, Selma, AL 36702-2530
(334) 876-9286

Heritage Christian University
Florence, Alabama
www.hcu.edu   Federal Code: 015370

4-year private virtual Bible college in large town, affiliated with the Church of Christ.
Enrollment: 60 undergrads.

FINANCIAL AID PICTURE
Students with need: Need-based aid available for full-time and part-time students.

FINANCIAL AID PROCEDURES
Forms required: FAFSA.
Dates and Deadlines: Priority date 6/1; no closing date. Applicants notified on a rolling basis starting 6/1; must reply by 7/28 or within 2 week(s) of notification.
Transfers: No deadline. Applicants notified on a rolling basis; must reply by 7/28 or within 3 week(s) of notification.

CONTACT
Mechelle Thompson, Financial Aid Director
3625 Helton Drive, Florence, AL 35630
(256) 766-6610 ext. 224

Herzing University: Birmingham
Birmingham, Alabama
www.herzing.edu   Federal Code: 010193

4-year for-profit business and technical college in very large city.
Enrollment: 481 undergrads.

BASIC COSTS (2016-2017)
Additional info: Certificate program tuition for academic year: $12,560 to $13,500. Associate program tuition for academic year: $12,560 to $13,000. Bachelor's program tuition for academic year: $12,560 to $13,000. Additional fees may applicable and costs are subject to change.

FINANCIAL AID PICTURE
Students with need: Need-based aid available for full-time students.
Students without need: This college awards aid only to students with need.

FINANCIAL AID PROCEDURES
Forms required: FAFSA.

CONTACT
Kentray Sims, Director of Financial Services
280 West Valley Avenue, Birmingham, AL 35209
(205) 916-2800

Huntingdon College
Montgomery, Alabama
www.huntingdon.edu   Federal Code: 001019

4-year private liberal arts college in small city, affiliated with the United Methodist Church.
Enrollment: 1,140 undergrads, 23% part-time. 271 full-time freshmen.
Selectivity: Admits 50 to 75% of applicants.

BASIC COSTS (2016-2017)
Tuition and fees: $25,450.
Per-credit charge: $1,020.
Room and board: $9,100.
Additional info: Tuition at time of enrollment locked for 4 years.

FINANCIAL AID PICTURE (2016-2017)

Students with need: Out of 249 full-time freshmen who applied for aid, 222 were judged to have need. Of these, 222 received aid, and 27 had their full need met. Average financial aid package met 68% of need; average scholarship/grant was $16,346; average loan was $3,264. For part-time students, average financial aid package was $6,421.

Students without need: 49 full-time freshmen who did not demonstrate need for aid received scholarships/grants; average award was $12,253. No-need awards available for academics, alumni affiliation, leadership, music/drama, religious affiliation, ROTC, state/district residency.

FINANCIAL AID PROCEDURES

Forms required: FAFSA.

Dates and Deadlines: Priority date 3/1; no closing date. Applicants notified on a rolling basis starting 3/1; must reply by 5/1 or within 2 week(s) of notification.

Transfers: No deadline. Applicants notified on a rolling basis starting 3/1; must reply by 5/1 or within 2 week(s) of notification. Transfer student should be in good academic standing at previous institution and cannot be in default on any previous student loans. While Academic Transfer scholarships are merit-based according to GPA, need-based aid (i.e. FAFSA) contingent upon eligibility and good-standing within Title IV.

CONTACT

Belinda Duett, Director of Student Financial Aid
1500 East Fairview Avenue, Montgomery, AL 36106-2148
(334) 833-4428

Huntsville Bible College

Huntsville, Alabama
www.hbc1.edu
Federal Code: 038943

4-year private Bible college in small city.
Enrollment: 118 undergrads.
Selectivity: Open admission.

BASIC COSTS (2016-2017)

Tuition and fees: $5,390.
Per-credit charge: $175.

FINANCIAL AID PICTURE

Students with need: Need-based aid available for full-time students.
Students without need: This college awards aid only to students with need.

FINANCIAL AID PROCEDURES

Forms required: FAFSA.
Dates and Deadlines: Priority date 4/1; closing date 6/30. Applicants notified by 8/15; must reply by 9/1.
Transfers: Priority date 8/1; closing date 8/15.

CONTACT

Jacqueline Robinson, Financial Officer
906 Oakwood Avenue, Huntsville, AL 35811-1632
(256) 469-7636

Jacksonville State University

Jacksonville, Alabama
www.jsu.edu
Federal Code: 001020

4-year public university in small town.
Enrollment: 6,714 undergrads, 20% part-time. 1,021 full-time freshmen.
Selectivity: Admits 50 to 75% of applicants.

BASIC COSTS (2017-2018)

Tuition and fees: $9,525; out-of-state residents $18,525.
Per-credit charge: $300; out-of-state residents $600.

Room and board: $7,128.

FINANCIAL AID PICTURE (2015-2016)

Students with need: Out of 961 full-time freshmen who applied for aid, 945 were judged to have need. Of these, 945 received aid. For part-time students, average financial aid package was $8,139.

Students without need: No-need awards available for academics, alumni affiliation, art, athletics, leadership, music/drama, ROTC, state/district residency.

Scholarships offered: Four-year tuition scholarship: for entering freshmen from Alabama; 28 ACT or 1230 SAT.

FINANCIAL AID PROCEDURES

Forms required: FAFSA, institutional form.
Dates and Deadlines: Applicants notified on a rolling basis starting 4/16; must reply within 2 week(s) of notification.

CONTACT

Vickie Adams, Director of Financial Aid
700 Pelham Road North, Jacksonville, AL 36265-1602
(256) 782-5006

Jefferson Davis Community College

Brewton, Alabama
www.jdcc.edu
Federal Code: 001021

2-year public nursing and community college in small town.
Enrollment: 1,033 undergrads.
Selectivity: Open admission; but selective for some programs.

BASIC COSTS (2016-2017)

Tuition and fees: $4,080; out-of-state residents $7,590.
Per-credit charge: $117; out-of-state residents $234.
Room only: $3,860.

FINANCIAL AID PICTURE

Students with need: Need-based aid available for full-time and part-time students. Work study available nights.
Students without need: No-need awards available for academics, athletics, leadership.

FINANCIAL AID PROCEDURES

Forms required: FAFSA.
Dates and Deadlines: Applicants notified on a rolling basis; must reply within 2 week(s) of notification.
Transfers: Must reply within 2 week(s) of notification.

CONTACT

Vanessa Kyles, Director of Financial Aid
PO Box 958, Brewton, AL 36427
(251) 809-1516

Jefferson State Community College

Birmingham, Alabama
www.jeffersonstate.edu
Federal Code: 001022

2-year public community college in large city.
Enrollment: 7,256 undergrads, 62% part-time. 1,079 full-time freshmen.
Selectivity: Open admission; but selective for some programs.

BASIC COSTS (2016-2017)

Tuition and fees: $4,440; out-of-state residents $7,950.
Per-credit charge: $117; out-of-state residents $234.

FINANCIAL AID PICTURE

Students with need: Need-based aid available for full-time and part-time students. Work study available nights.

Students without need: No-need awards available for academics, art, leadership, music/drama.
Additional info: Any Alabama resident over age 60 may attend classes tuition free, on a space available basis.

FINANCIAL AID PROCEDURES
Forms required: FAFSA, institutional form.
Dates and Deadlines: Closing date 5/1. Applicants notified on a rolling basis starting 6/1.
Transfers: Transfer students not eligible for academic scholarships until 12 hours have been completed on campus.

CONTACT
Theresa Mays, Financial Aid Director
2601 Carson Road, Birmingham, AL 35215
(205) 856-8509

Judson College
Marion, Alabama
www.judson.edu   Federal Code: 001023

4-year private liberal arts college for women in small town, affiliated with the Baptist faith.
Enrollment: 332 undergrads.
Selectivity: Admits 50 to 75% of applicants.

BASIC COSTS (2016-2017)
Tuition and fees: $17,376.
Per-credit charge: $550.
Room and board: $9,978.

FINANCIAL AID PICTURE (2016-2017)
Students with need: 60% of average financial aid package awarded as scholarships/grants, 40% awarded as loans/jobs. Need-based aid available for part-time students. Work study available nights, weekends, and for part-time students.
Students without need: No-need awards available for academics, art, athletics, music/drama, religious affiliation, ROTC, state/district residency.
Scholarships offered: Full Tuition Scholarship: given to National Merit Finalists or students with 29 ACT and 3.5 GPA; up to 5 awarded. Honor Scholarships: 1 for full-tuition, 2 for $2,500, 3 for $2,000; awarded based on exam scores. Music scholarships: variable amounts awarded based on audition.

FINANCIAL AID PROCEDURES
Forms required: FAFSA, state aid form.
Dates and Deadlines: Priority date 3/1; no closing date. Applicants notified on a rolling basis starting 3/1; must reply within 2 week(s) of notification.
Transfers: No deadline. Applicants notified on a rolling basis starting 3/1; must reply within 2 week(s) of notification.

CONTACT
Melena Verity, Director of Financial Aid
302 Bibb Street, Marion, AL 36756
(334) 683-5157

Lawson State Community College
Birmingham, Alabama
www.lawsonstate.edu   Federal Code: 001059

2-year public community college in small city.
Enrollment: 3,090 undergrads.
Selectivity: Open admission; but selective for some programs.

BASIC COSTS (2016-2017)
Tuition and fees: $4,400; out-of-state residents $7,910.
Per-credit charge: $117; out-of-state residents $234.

Room and board: $4,760.

FINANCIAL AID PICTURE
Students with need: Need-based aid available for full-time and part-time students. Work study available nights.
Students without need: This college awards aid only to students with need.

FINANCIAL AID PROCEDURES
Forms required: FAFSA.
Dates and Deadlines: Closing date 6/1. Applicants notified on a rolling basis starting 8/1; must reply within 2 week(s) of notification.

CONTACT
Cassandra Byrd, Director of Student Financial Services
3060 Wilson Road SW, Birmingham, AL 35221-1717
(205) 929-6380

Lurleen B. Wallace Community College
Andalusia, Alabama
www.lbwcc.edu   Federal Code: 008988

2-year public community college in small town.
Enrollment: 1,419 undergrads, 27% part-time. 414 full-time freshmen.
Selectivity: Open admission.

BASIC COSTS (2016-2017)
Tuition and fees: $4,380; out-of-state residents $7,890.
Per-credit charge: $117; out-of-state residents $234.

FINANCIAL AID PICTURE
Students with need: Need-based aid available for full-time and part-time students.
Students without need: No-need awards available for academics, art, athletics, leadership, music/drama.

FINANCIAL AID PROCEDURES
Forms required: FAFSA.
Dates and Deadlines: Closing date 8/1. Applicants notified on a rolling basis.

CONTACT
Donna Bass, Director of Financial Aid, Andalusia Campus
Box 1418, Andalusia, AL 36420
(334) 881-2272

Miles College
Birmingham, Alabama
www.miles.edu   Federal Code: 001028

4-year private liberal arts college in very large city, affiliated with the Christian Methodist Episcopal Church.
Enrollment: 1,690 undergrads.
Selectivity: Open admission; but selective for some programs.

BASIC COSTS (2016-2017)
Tuition and fees: $11,604.
Per-credit charge: $448.
Room and board: $7,042.
Additional info: Room and Board cost range between $5,882 and $7,042; depending upon the dormitory to which the individual is assigned.

FINANCIAL AID PICTURE
Students with need: Need-based aid available for full-time and part-time students.
Students without need: This college awards aid only to students with need.

FINANCIAL AID PROCEDURES

Forms required: FAFSA, state aid form.
Dates and Deadlines: Priority date 4/15; no closing date. Applicants notified on a rolling basis starting 7/15; must reply within 2 week(s) of notification.

CONTACT

P Lanier, Financial Aid Administrator
5500 Myron Massey Boulevard, Fairfield, AL 35064
(205) 929-1665

Northeast Alabama Community College
Rainsville, Alabama
www.nacc.edu   Federal Code: 001031

2-year public community college in rural community.
Enrollment: 2,008 undergrads, 41% part-time. 488 full-time freshmen.
Selectivity: Open admission.

BASIC COSTS (2016-2017)

Tuition and fees: $4,380; out-of-state residents $7,890.
Per-credit charge: $117; out-of-state residents $234.

FINANCIAL AID PICTURE

Students with need: Need-based aid available for full-time and part-time students.
Students without need: No-need awards available for academics, art, leadership, minority status, music/drama.

FINANCIAL AID PROCEDURES

Forms required: FAFSA.
Dates and Deadlines: Applicants notified on a rolling basis.

CONTACT

Nixon Willmon, Director of Financial Aid
Admissions Office, NACC, Rainsville, AL 35986-0159
(256) 228-6001 ext. 2327

Northwest-Shoals Community College
Muscle Shoals, Alabama
www.nwscc.edu   Federal Code: 005697

2-year public community and technical college in large town.
Enrollment: 2,994 undergrads, 48% part-time. 751 full-time freshmen.
Selectivity: Open admission; but selective for some programs.

BASIC COSTS (2016-2017)

Tuition and fees: $4,351; out-of-state residents $7,861.
Per-credit charge: $117; out-of-state residents $234.
Additional info: Tuition/fee waivers available for minority students, unemployed or children of unemployed.

FINANCIAL AID PICTURE (2015-2016)

Students with need: 53% of average financial aid package awarded as scholarships/grants, 47% awarded as loans/jobs. Need-based aid available for part-time students. Work study available nights.
Students without need: No-need awards available for academics, art, leadership, minority status, music/drama.

FINANCIAL AID PROCEDURES

Forms required: FAFSA.
Dates and Deadlines: Priority date 4/1; closing date 8/1. Applicants notified on a rolling basis starting 6/1; must reply within 2 week(s) of notification.
Transfers: No deadline. Applicants notified on a rolling basis starting 6/1; must reply within 2 week(s) of notification. Students without 1-year Alabama residency before fall term ineligible for state grant.

CONTACT

Meredith Wiley, Director of Student Financial Services
PO Box 2545, Muscle Shoals, AL 35662-2545
(256) 331-6232

Oakwood University
Huntsville, Alabama
www.oakwood.edu   Federal Code: 001033

4-year private liberal arts college in small city, affiliated with the Seventh-day Adventists.
Enrollment: 1,687 undergrads.

BASIC COSTS (2016-2017)

Tuition and fees: $16,720.
Room and board: $9,312.

FINANCIAL AID PICTURE

Students with need: Need-based aid available for full-time students.
Students without need: No-need awards available for academics, leadership, religious affiliation, state/district residency.

FINANCIAL AID PROCEDURES

Forms required: FAFSA, state aid form.
Dates and Deadlines: Closing date 4/15. Applicants notified on a rolling basis starting 4/1.

CONTACT

Lynda Bartholomew, Director of Financial Aid
7000 Adventist Boulevard, NW, Huntsville, AL 35896
(256) 726-7210

Prince Institute of Professional Studies
Montgomery, Alabama
www.princeinstitute.edu   Federal Code: 022960

2-year for-profit technical and career college in large city.
Selectivity: Open admission.

FINANCIAL AID PICTURE

Students with need: Need-based aid available for full-time and part-time students.
Students without need: This college awards aid only to students with need.

FINANCIAL AID PROCEDURES

Forms required: FAFSA.

CONTACT

Emily Lee, Director of Financial Aid
7735 Atlanta Highway, Montgomery, AL 36117-4231
(334) 271-1670

Remington College: Mobile
Mobile, Alabama
http://mobile.remingtoncollege.edu   Federal Code: 026055

2-year private career college in large city.
Enrollment: 881 undergrads.
Selectivity: Open admission.

FINANCIAL AID PICTURE

Students with need: Need-based aid available for full-time students. Work study available nights.

Students without need: This college awards aid only to students with need.

FINANCIAL AID PROCEDURES

Forms required: FAFSA.

CONTACT

James Dunn, National Director of Financial Aid
828 Downtowner Loop West, Mobile, AL 36609-5404
(251) 343-8200

Samford University

Birmingham, Alabama
www.samford.edu   Federal Code: 001036

4-year private university in small city, affiliated with the Baptist faith.
Enrollment: 3,324 undergrads, 4% part-time. 826 full-time freshmen.
Selectivity: Admits over 75% of applicants.

BASIC COSTS (2016-2017)
Tuition and fees: $29,402.
Per-credit charge: $955.
Room and board: $9,830.

FINANCIAL AID PICTURE (2015-2016)
Students with need: Out of 605 full-time freshmen who applied for aid, 381 were judged to have need. Of these, 381 received aid, and 99 had their full need met. Average financial aid package met 72% of need; average scholarship/grant was $14,824; average loan was $3,212. For part-time students, average financial aid package was $7,575.
Students without need: 372 full-time freshmen who did not demonstrate need for aid received scholarships/grants; average award was $10,896. No-need awards available for academics, alumni affiliation, art, athletics, leadership, minority status, music/drama, religious affiliation, ROTC, state/district residency.
Scholarships offered: 26 full-time freshmen received athletic scholarships; average amount $28,396.

FINANCIAL AID PROCEDURES
Forms required: FAFSA, state aid form.
Dates and Deadlines: Priority date 3/1; no closing date. Applicants notified on a rolling basis starting 3/1; must reply by 5/1.
Transfers: Applicants notified on a rolling basis. Student must be fully admitted and all transcripts must be received by admissions office.

CONTACT
Lane Smith, Director of Student Financial Services
800 Lakeshore Drive, Birmingham, AL 35229
(205) 726-2905

Selma University

Selma, Alabama
www.selmauniversity.org   Federal Code: 040673

4-year private university in large town, affiliated with the Baptist faith.
Enrollment: 399 undergrads.
Selectivity: Open admission.

BASIC COSTS (2016-2017)
Tuition and fees: $7,145.
Room and board: $6,000.
Additional info: Tuition/fee waivers available for minority students.

FINANCIAL AID PICTURE
Students with need: Need-based aid available for full-time and part-time students. Work study available weekends and for part-time students.

Students without need: This college awards aid only to students with need.

FINANCIAL AID PROCEDURES

Forms required: FAFSA, institutional form.
Dates and Deadlines: Priority date 5/1; closing date 6/30. Applicants notified on a rolling basis starting 8/23; must reply within 2 week(s) of notification.
Transfers: Closing date 5/1. Applicants notified on a rolling basis; must reply within 2 week(s) of notification.

CONTACT

Nerieko Stephens, Director of Financial Aid
1501 Lapsley Street, Selma, AL 36701

Shelton State Community College

Tuscaloosa, Alabama
www.sheltonstate.edu   Federal Code: 005691

2-year public community and technical college in small city.
Enrollment: 4,647 undergrads.
Selectivity: Open admission.

BASIC COSTS (2016-2017)
Tuition and fees: $4,107; out-of-state residents $7,617.
Per-credit charge: $117; out-of-state residents $234.

FINANCIAL AID PICTURE
Students with need: Need-based aid available for full-time and part-time students. Work study available nights.
Students without need: This college awards aid only to students with need.

FINANCIAL AID PROCEDURES
Forms required: FAFSA.
Dates and Deadlines: Priority date 6/30; no closing date. Applicants notified on a rolling basis starting 7/30.

CONTACT
Rhonda Smith, Director of Fiancial Aid
9500 Old Greensboro Road, Tuscaloosa, AL 35405-8522
(205) 391-2376

Snead State Community College

Boaz, Alabama
www.snead.edu   Federal Code: 001038

2-year public community college in small town.
Enrollment: 1,986 undergrads.
Selectivity: Open admission.

BASIC COSTS (2016-2017)
Tuition and fees: $4,440; out-of-state residents $7,950.
Per-credit charge: $117; out-of-state residents $234.
Room and board: $3,110.

FINANCIAL AID PICTURE
Students with need: Need-based aid available for full-time and part-time students. Work study available nights.
Students without need: No-need awards available for academics, alumni affiliation, art, athletics, leadership, music/drama.

FINANCIAL AID PROCEDURES
Forms required: FAFSA.
Dates and Deadlines: Applicants notified on a rolling basis starting 4/15.

CONTACT
Amanda Childress, Financial Aid Coordinator
PO Box 734, Boaz, AL 35957-0734
(256) 840-4107

Southeastern Bible College

Birmingham, Alabama
www.sebc.edu   Federal Code: 013857

4-year private Bible college in very large city, affiliated with the nondenominational tradition.
Enrollment: 143 undergrads.
Selectivity: Admits over 75% of applicants.

BASIC COSTS (2016-2017)
Tuition and fees: $12,600.
Per-credit charge: $405.
Room and board: $4,975.

FINANCIAL AID PICTURE
Students with need: Need-based aid available for full-time and part-time students.
Students without need: No-need awards available for academics, leadership.

FINANCIAL AID PROCEDURES
Forms required: FAFSA, institutional form.
Dates and Deadlines: Priority date 4/1; no closing date.

CONTACT
Joanne Belin, Director of Financial Aid
2545 Valleydale Road, Birmingham, AL 35244-2083
(205) 970-9215

Southern Union State Community College

Wadley, Alabama
www.suscc.edu   Federal Code: 001040

2-year public community and technical college in small city.
Enrollment: 4,734 undergrads.
Selectivity: Open admission; but selective for some programs.

BASIC COSTS (2016-2017)
Tuition and fees: $4,100; out-of-state residents $7,610.
Per-credit charge: $117; out-of-state residents $234.
Room and board: $3,200.

FINANCIAL AID PICTURE
Students with need: Need-based aid available for full-time and part-time students.
Students without need: No-need awards available for alumni affiliation, art, athletics.

FINANCIAL AID PROCEDURES
Forms required: FAFSA.
Dates and Deadlines: Priority date 4/1; no closing date. Applicants notified on a rolling basis.

CONTACT
Pam Jones, Director of Financial Aid
750 Roberts Street, Wadley, AL 36276
(256) 395-2215

Spring Hill College

Mobile, Alabama
www.shc.edu   Federal Code: 001041

4-year private liberal arts college in large city, affiliated with the Roman Catholic Church.
Enrollment: 1,379 undergrads, 1% part-time. 392 full-time freshmen.

Selectivity: Admits less than 50% of applicants.

BASIC COSTS (2016-2017)
Tuition and fees: $35,798.
Per-credit charge: $1,024.
Room and board: $12,690.

FINANCIAL AID PICTURE (2016-2017)
Students with need: Out of 356 full-time freshmen who applied for aid, 305 were judged to have need. Of these, 305 received aid, and 77 had their full need met. Average financial aid package met 80% of need; average scholarship/grant was $27,459; average loan was $3,428. For part-time students, average financial aid package was $1,506.
Students without need: 85 full-time freshmen who did not demonstrate need for aid received scholarships/grants; average award was $22,880. No-need awards available for academics, alumni affiliation, art, athletics, job skills, leadership, minority status, ROTC, state/district residency.
Scholarships offered: 65 full-time freshmen received athletic scholarships; average amount $7,680.

FINANCIAL AID PROCEDURES
Forms required: FAFSA, state aid form.
Dates and Deadlines: Priority date 3/1; no closing date. Applicants notified on a rolling basis starting 2/15; must reply by 5/1 or within 2 week(s) of notification.
Transfers: No deadline. Applicants notified on a rolling basis starting 3/1; must reply within 2 week(s) of notification.

CONTACT
Melinda McCall, Director of Student Financial Aid
4000 Dauphin Street, Mobile, AL 36608-1791
(800) 548-7886

Stillman College

Tuscaloosa, Alabama
www.stillman.edu   Federal Code: 001044

4-year private liberal arts college in small city, affiliated with the Presbyterian Church (USA).
Enrollment: 1,000 undergrads.

BASIC COSTS (2016-2017)
Tuition and fees: $10,938.
Per-credit charge: $539.
Room and board: $7,180.

FINANCIAL AID PICTURE
Students with need: Need-based aid available for full-time and part-time students. Work study available nights, weekends, and for part-time students.
Students without need: No-need awards available for academics, alumni affiliation, athletics, state/district residency.

FINANCIAL AID PROCEDURES
Forms required: FAFSA, state aid form.
Dates and Deadlines: Priority date 4/15; closing date 8/15. Applicants notified on a rolling basis starting 3/1; must reply by 7/31 or within 4 week(s) of notification.
Transfers: Priority date 3/15; no deadline. Applicants notified on a rolling basis starting 10/15; must reply by 3/15 or within 4 week(s) of notification.

CONTACT
Jacqueline Morris, Director of Financial Aid
3601 Stillman Boulevard, Tuscaloosa, AL 35403
(205) 366-8844

Talladega College
Talladega, Alabama
www.talladega.edu   Federal Code: 001046

4-year private liberal arts college in large town, affiliated with the United Church of Christ.
Enrollment: 1,016 undergrads.
Selectivity: Open admission; but selective for some programs.

BASIC COSTS (2016-2017)
Tuition and fees: $13,828.
Per-credit charge: $466.33.
Room and board: $6,704.
Additional info: Less than 12 or more than 18 credit hours; $466.33 per credit hour.

FINANCIAL AID PICTURE
Students with need: Need-based aid available for full-time and part-time students.
Students without need: This college awards aid only to students with need.

FINANCIAL AID PROCEDURES
Forms required: FAFSA, state aid form, institutional form.
Dates and Deadlines: Closing date 3/1. Applicants notified on a rolling basis starting 2/1; must reply within 2 week(s) of notification.
Transfers: Priority date 3/1; no deadline. Applicants notified on a rolling basis; must reply within 2 week(s) of notification.

CONTACT
627 West Battle Street, Talladega, AL 35160
(256) 761-6256

Troy University
Troy, Alabama
www.troy.edu   Federal Code: 001047

4-year public university in large town.
Enrollment: 14,149 undergrads, 36% part-time. 1,805 full-time freshmen.
Selectivity: Admits over 75% of applicants.

BASIC COSTS (2017-2018)
Tuition and fees: $11,199; out-of-state residents $20,831.
Per-credit charge: $301; out-of-state residents $602.
Room and board: $7,853.

FINANCIAL AID PICTURE (2016-2017)
Students with need: Out of 1,380 full-time freshmen who applied for aid, 1,369 were judged to have need. Of these, 1,369 received aid. For part-time students, average financial aid package was $4,876.
Students without need: 524 full-time freshmen who did not demonstrate need for aid received scholarships/grants; average award was $6,719. No-need awards available for academics, alumni affiliation, art, athletics, leadership, minority status, music/drama, ROTC.
Scholarships offered: 41 full-time freshmen received athletic scholarships; average amount $4,181.

FINANCIAL AID PROCEDURES
Forms required: FAFSA, institutional form.
Dates and Deadlines: Closing date 5/1. Applicants notified on a rolling basis starting 5/1; must reply within 2 week(s) of notification.

CONTACT
Carol Ballard, Vice Chancellor, Financial Aid
University Avenue, Adams Administration 111, Troy, AL 36082
(334) 670-3186

Tuskegee University
Tuskegee, Alabama
www.tuskegee.edu   Federal Code: 001050

4-year private university in small town.
Enrollment: 2,485 undergrads.

BASIC COSTS (2016-2017)
Tuition and fees: $21,470.
Room and board: $9,104.

FINANCIAL AID PICTURE
Students with need: Need-based aid available for full-time and part-time students.
Students without need: No-need awards available for academics, athletics, ROTC, state/district residency.

FINANCIAL AID PROCEDURES
Forms required: FAFSA, institutional form.
Dates and Deadlines: Closing date 2/1. Applicants notified on a rolling basis starting 2/1; must reply within 2 week(s) of notification.
Transfers: Priority date 2/1. Applicants notified on a rolling basis.

CONTACT
Advergus James, Director of Financial Aid Services
Margaret Murray Washington Hall, Tuskegee, AL 36088
(334) 724-4733

United States Sports Academy
Daphne, Alabama
www.ussa.edu   Federal Code: 021706

Upper-division private university in large town.
Enrollment: 270 undergrads.
Selectivity: Open admission; but selective for some programs.

BASIC COSTS (2017-2018)
Tuition and fees: $11,850.
Per-credit charge: $395.
Additional info: Textbooks and examination proctoring fees are covered by the school.

FINANCIAL AID PICTURE (2015-2016)
Students with need: Average financial aid package for all full-time undergraduates was $3,410; for part-time $2,625. 29% awarded as scholarships/grants, 71% awarded as loans/jobs.
Students without need: No-need awards available for academics, state/district residency.

CONTACT
Robin Causey, Financial Aid Counselor
One Academy Drive, Daphne, AL 36526
(251) 626-3303 ext. 7149

University of Alabama
Tuscaloosa, Alabama
www.ua.edu   Federal Code: 001051

4-year public university in small city.
Enrollment: 31,663 undergrads, 8% part-time. 7,176 full-time freshmen.
Selectivity: Admits 50 to 75% of applicants.

BASIC COSTS (2016-2017)
Tuition and fees: $10,470; out-of-state residents $26,950.
Room and board: $9,550.

FINANCIAL AID PICTURE (2015-2016)

Students with need: Out of 4,857 full-time freshmen who applied for aid, 3,520 were judged to have need. Of these, 3,397 received aid, and 944 had their full need met. Average financial aid package met 58% of need; average scholarship/grant was $13,777; average loan was $3,450. For part-time students, average financial aid package was $6,256.

Students without need: 1,855 full-time freshmen who did not demonstrate need for aid received scholarships/grants; average award was $14,821. No-need awards available for academics, alumni affiliation, art, athletics, leadership, minority status, music/drama, ROTC, state/district residency.

Scholarships offered: 112 full-time freshmen received athletic scholarships; average amount $26,680.

FINANCIAL AID PROCEDURES

Forms required: FAFSA.

Dates and Deadlines: Priority date 3/1; no closing date. Applicants notified on a rolling basis starting 4/1; must reply within 3 week(s) of notification.

Transfers: No deadline. Applicants notified on a rolling basis. Scholarship opportunities for transfer students.

CONTACT

Helen Allen, Director, Student Financial Aid
Box 870132, Tuscaloosa, AL 35487-0132
(205) 348-6756

University of Alabama at Birmingham

Birmingham, Alabama
www.uab.edu
Federal Code: 001052

4-year public university in very large city.

Enrollment: 12,092 undergrads, 26% part-time. 1,948 full-time freshmen.

Selectivity: Admits over 75% of applicants.

BASIC COSTS (2016-2017)

Tuition and fees: $9,708; out-of-state residents $22,612.

Per-credit charge: $316; out-of-state residents $746.

Room and board: $9,970.

FINANCIAL AID PICTURE (2016-2017)

Students with need: Out of 1,716 full-time freshmen who applied for aid, 1,277 were judged to have need. Of these, 1,260 received aid, and 177 had their full need met. Average financial aid package met 56% of need; average scholarship/grant was $5,087; average loan was $4,351. For part-time students, average financial aid package was $6,513.

Students without need: 497 full-time freshmen who did not demonstrate need for aid received scholarships/grants; average award was $7,447. No-need awards available for academics, alumni affiliation, art, athletics, leadership, minority status, music/drama, ROTC.

Scholarships offered: *Merit:* Presidential Recognition, Presidential, and Endowed Scholarships: full tuition and required fees for 4 years (up to 15 credit hours per semester for fall and spring only); for in-state students with 33-36 ACT and 3.5 GPA (supplemental application required). Golden Excellence Scholarship: $7,500 per year; for in-state students with 30-32 ACT and 3.5 GPA. Collegiate Honors Scholarship: $5,500 per year; for in-state students with 27-29 ACT and 3.5 GPA or 30-36 ACT and 3.0-3.49 GPA. Breakthrough Scholarship: $3,000 per year; for in-state students with 24-26 ACT and 3.5 GPA. Academic Achievement Scholarship: $2,000 per year; for in-state students with 20-23 ACT and 3.5 GPA or 24-29 ACT and 3.0-3.49 GPA. Blazer Elite Scholarship: $15,000 per year; for out-of-state students with 30-36 ACT and 3.5 GPA. Blazer Gold Scholarship: $12,000 per year; for out-of-state students with 26-29 ACT and 3.5 GPA. Blazer Pride Scholarship: $10,000 per year; for out-of-state students with 24-25 ACT and 3.5 GPA or 26-36 ACT and 3.0-3.49 GPA. Blazer Distinction Scholarship: $7,500 per year, for out-of-state students with 20-23 ACT and 3.5 GPA or 24-25 ACT and 3.0-3.49 GPA. National Merit Finalist/National Achievement Finalist/National Hispanic Recognition Program Scholar Awards: full tuition and required fees for 4 years (up to 15 credit hours per semester for fall and spring only), annual

on-campus housing allotment, and a one-time $2,500 stipend to be used for experiential learning (study away, internships, co-ops, etc.); National Merit Finalists must name UAB as first choice with NMSC. National Achievement Finalists and National Hispanic Recognition Program Scholars must send a copy of their Finalist letter and certificate to the UAB Undergraduate Admissions Office. *Athletic:* 73 full-time freshmen received athletic scholarships; average amount $26,065.

FINANCIAL AID PROCEDURES

Forms required: FAFSA.

Dates and Deadlines: Priority date 3/1; no closing date. Applicants notified on a rolling basis starting 3/15; must reply within 4 week(s) of notification.

Transfers: Applicants notified on a rolling basis; must reply within 4 week(s) of notification.

CONTACT

Helen McIntyre, Director of Financial Aid
1720 2nd Avenue South, Birmingham, AL 35294-4600
(205) 934-8223

University of Alabama in Huntsville

Huntsville, Alabama
www.uah.edu
Federal Code: 001055

4-year public university in small city.

Enrollment: 6,338 undergrads, 17% part-time. 1,203 full-time freshmen.

Selectivity: Admits over 75% of applicants.

BASIC COSTS (2016-2017)

Tuition and fees: $9,842; out-of-state residents $20,612.

Room and board: $9,603.

FINANCIAL AID PICTURE (2016-2017)

Students with need: Out of 1,203 full-time freshmen who applied for aid, 597 were judged to have need. Of these, 596 received aid, and 201 had their full need met. Average financial aid package met 75% of need; average scholarship/grant was $9,402; average loan was $5,682. For part-time students, average financial aid package was $5,259.

Students without need: 451 full-time freshmen who did not demonstrate need for aid received scholarships/grants; average award was $10,118. No-need awards available for academics, art, athletics, leadership, minority status, music/drama, ROTC.

Scholarships offered: 73 full-time freshmen received athletic scholarships; average amount $7,700.

Additional info: Application deadline for institutional scholarships is December 1.

FINANCIAL AID PROCEDURES

Forms required: FAFSA.

Dates and Deadlines: Priority date 4/1; closing date 7/31. Applicants notified on a rolling basis starting 4/1; must reply within 2 week(s) of notification.

Transfers: First-time regularly admitted transfer students who have earned a minimum of 24 transfer credits from an accredited institution of higher learning considered for one-time transfer scholarship award. Super Scholar Transfer Scholarship requires 3.50 college GPA and is currently valued at $3,000 renewable for an additional year. UAH Transfer Merit Scholarship requires 3.00 college GPA and is currently valued at $1,500 renewable for an additional year. Students must be admitted to UAH to be eligible for these awards. Priority consideration is given to students who are admitted to UAH by June 1. Students admitted after the priority deadline may be eligible for awards as funding is available.

CONTACT

Patrick James, Director of Student Financial Services
UAH Office of Undergraduate Admissions, Huntsville, AL 35899
(256) 824-6650

University of Mobile
Mobile, Alabama
www.umobile.edu   Federal Code: 001029

4-year private university and liberal arts college in small city, affiliated with the Baptist faith.
Enrollment: 1,373 undergrads, 10% part-time. 224 full-time freshmen.
Selectivity: Admits 50 to 75% of applicants.

BASIC COSTS (2016-2017)
Tuition and fees: $21,400.
Per-credit charge: $720.
Room and board: $9,600.

FINANCIAL AID PICTURE (2016-2017)
Students with need: Out of 199 full-time freshmen who applied for aid, 180 were judged to have need. Of these, 180 received aid, and 180 had their full need met. Average financial aid package met 67% of need; average scholarship/grant was $5,553; average loan was $3,640. For part-time students, average financial aid package was $9,918.
Students without need: 18 full-time freshmen who did not demonstrate need for aid received scholarships/grants; average award was $8,488. No-need awards available for academics, alumni affiliation, athletics, leadership, music/drama, religious affiliation, state/district residency.
Scholarships offered: 5 full-time freshmen received athletic scholarships; average amount $14,815.

FINANCIAL AID PROCEDURES
Forms required: FAFSA, state aid form, institutional form.
Dates and Deadlines: Applicants notified on a rolling basis starting 2/1.

CONTACT
Marie Batson, Associate Vice President for Enrollment Management
5735 College Parkway, Mobile, AL 36613-2842
(251) 442-2252

University of Montevallo
Montevallo, Alabama
www.montevallo.edu   Federal Code: 001004

4-year public university and liberal arts college in small town.
Enrollment: 2,399 undergrads, 9% part-time. 473 full-time freshmen.

BASIC COSTS (2016-2017)
Tuition and fees: $12,040; out-of-state residents $24,310.
Per-credit charge: $379; out-of-state residents $788.
Room and board: $7,462.

FINANCIAL AID PICTURE (2016-2017)
Students with need: Out of 393 full-time freshmen who applied for aid, 312 were judged to have need. Of these, 310 received aid, and 84 had their full need met. Average financial aid package met 64% of need; average scholarship/grant was $10,078; average loan was $3,155. For part-time students, average financial aid package was $5,992.
Students without need: 126 full-time freshmen who did not demonstrate need for aid received scholarships/grants; average award was $11,053. No-need awards available for academics, art, athletics, leadership, minority status, music/drama, religious affiliation, ROTC.
Scholarships offered: 38 full-time freshmen received athletic scholarships; average amount $9,596.

FINANCIAL AID PROCEDURES
Forms required: FAFSA.
Dates and Deadlines: Priority date 3/1; no closing date. Applicants notified on a rolling basis starting 4/20; must reply within 2 week(s) of notification.

CONTACT
Bob Walker, Director of Financial Aid
Palmer Hall, Station 6030, Montevallo, AL 35115-6000
(205) 665-6050

University of North Alabama
Florence, Alabama
www.una.edu   Federal Code: 001016

4-year public university in large town.
Enrollment: 5,869 undergrads, 13% part-time. 1,159 full-time freshmen.
Selectivity: Admits 50 to 75% of applicants.

BASIC COSTS (2016-2017)
Tuition and fees: $9,920; out-of-state residents $17,840.
Per-credit charge: $264; out-of-state residents $528.
Room and board: $6,696.

FINANCIAL AID PICTURE (2015-2016)
Students with need: Out of 855 full-time freshmen who applied for aid, 751 were judged to have need. Of these, 731 received aid, and 63 had their full need met. Average financial aid package met 53% of need; average scholarship/grant was $4,202; average loan was $2,926. For part-time students, average financial aid package was $5,249.
Students without need: 110 full-time freshmen who did not demonstrate need for aid received scholarships/grants; average award was $5,068. No-need awards available for academics, alumni affiliation, art, athletics, job skills, leadership, minority status, music/drama, religious affiliation, ROTC, state/district residency.
Scholarships offered: 48 full-time freshmen received athletic scholarships; average amount $6,409.

FINANCIAL AID PROCEDURES
Forms required: FAFSA.
Dates and Deadlines: Priority date 6/1; no closing date. Applicants notified on a rolling basis starting 3/30.

CONTACT
Shauna James, Director, Student Financial Services
One Harrison Plaza, UNA Box 5011, Florence, AL 35632-0001
(256) 765-4278

University of South Alabama
Mobile, Alabama
www.southalabama.edu   Federal Code: 001057

4-year public university in small city.
Enrollment: 11,483 undergrads, 16% part-time. 2,083 full-time freshmen.
Selectivity: Admits over 75% of applicants.

BASIC COSTS (2016-2017)
Tuition and fees: $9,060; out-of-state residents $18,120.
Per-credit charge: $302; out-of-state residents $604.
Room and board: $7,340.
Additional info: Tuition/fee waivers available for minority students.

FINANCIAL AID PICTURE (2015-2016)
Students with need: Out of 1,811 full-time freshmen who applied for aid, 1,375 were judged to have need. Of these, 1,375 received aid, and 153 had their full need met. Average financial aid package met 54% of need; average scholarship/grant was $7,184; average loan was $3,464. For part-time students, average financial aid package was $7,601.
Students without need: 395 full-time freshmen who did not demonstrate need for aid received scholarships/grants; average award was $4,923. No-need awards available for academics, alumni affiliation, art, athletics, job

skills, leadership, minority status, music/drama, ROTC, state/district residency.

Scholarships offered: 72 full-time freshmen received athletic scholarships; average amount $15,708.

FINANCIAL AID PROCEDURES

Forms required: FAFSA, institutional form.

CONTACT

Marla Sklopan, Director, Financial Aid
Meisler Hall, Suite 2500, Mobile, AL 36688-0002
(800) 305-6828

University of West Alabama
Livingston, Alabama
www.uwa.edu   Federal Code: 001024

4-year public university in small town.
Enrollment: 1,974 undergrads, 13% part-time. 420 full-time freshmen.
Selectivity: Admits 50 to 75% of applicants.

BASIC COSTS (2016-2017)

Tuition and fees: $8,876; out-of-state residents $16,162.
Per-credit charge: $304; out-of-state residents $608.
Room and board: $6,640.

FINANCIAL AID PICTURE (2015-2016)

Students with need: Out of 378 full-time freshmen who applied for aid, 337 were judged to have need. Of these, 336 received aid, and 3 had their full need met. Average financial aid package met 23% of need; average scholarship/grant was $5,116. For part-time students, average financial aid package was $8,227.

Students without need: 28 full-time freshmen who did not demonstrate need for aid received scholarships/grants; average award was $4,896. No-need awards available for academics, alumni affiliation, art, athletics, leadership, music/drama, state/district residency.

Scholarships offered: *Merit:* Trustee Scholarships: available for students who have qualifying ACT scores; amounts vary depending on the student's composite ACT score. *Athletic:* 59 full-time freshmen received athletic scholarships; average amount $6,150.

FINANCIAL AID PROCEDURES

Forms required: FAFSA.
Dates and Deadlines: Priority date 3/1; no closing date. Applicants notified on a rolling basis starting 4/15; must reply within 2 week(s) of notification.
Transfers: No deadline. Applicants notified on a rolling basis; must reply within 2 week(s) of notification.

CONTACT

Don Rainer, Director of Financial Aid
Station 4, Livingston, AL 35470
(205) 652-3576

Virginia College in Huntsville
Huntsville, Alabama
www.vc.edu   Federal Code: 030106

4-year for-profit business and technical college in small city.
Enrollment: 597 undergrads.
Selectivity: Open admission.

BASIC COSTS (2016-2017)

Additional info: Diploma programs: $14,382-$23,970. Associate programs: $38,352-$49,059. Bachelor programs: $70,200-$75,106. Fees, books supplies range depending on program level and course of study. All costs are subject to change.

FINANCIAL AID PICTURE

Students with need: Need-based aid available for full-time and part-time students. Work study available nights, weekends, and for part-time students.

FINANCIAL AID PROCEDURES

Forms required: FAFSA, institutional form.
Dates and Deadlines: Applicants notified on a rolling basis.

CONTACT

Samantha Williams, Director of Financial Aid
2800 Bob Wallace Avenue, Huntsville, AL 35805
(256) 533-7387

Wallace State Community College at Hanceville
Hanceville, Alabama
www.wallacestate.edu   Federal Code: 007871

2-year public health science and community college in small town.
Enrollment: 4,856 undergrads, 46% part-time. 876 full-time freshmen.
Selectivity: Open admission; but selective for some programs.

BASIC COSTS (2016-2017)

Tuition and fees: $4,380; out-of-state residents $7,890.
Per-credit charge: $117; out-of-state residents $234.
Room and board: $4,600.

FINANCIAL AID PICTURE

Students with need: Need-based aid available for full-time and part-time students. Work study available nights.
Students without need: This college awards aid only to students with need.

FINANCIAL AID PROCEDURES

Forms required: FAFSA.
Dates and Deadlines: Priority date 5/1; no closing date. Applicants notified on a rolling basis starting 7/15; must reply within 2 week(s) of notification.
Transfers: No deadline.

CONTACT

Becky Graves, Director of Student Financial Aid
801 Main Street NW/PO Box 2000, Hanceville, AL 35077-2000
(256) 352-8182

Alaska

Alaska Bible College
Palmer, Alaska
www.akbible.edu   Federal Code: 014325

4-year private Bible college in small town, affiliated with the nondenominational tradition.
Enrollment: 29 undergrads.
Selectivity: Open admission; but selective for some programs.

BASIC COSTS (2016-2017)

Tuition and fees: $9,300.
Room and board: $5,900.

FINANCIAL AID PICTURE (2016-2017)

Students with need: 56% of average financial aid package awarded as scholarships/grants, 44% awarded as loans/jobs. Need-based aid available for part-time students. Work study available nights, weekends, and for part-time students.

Students without need: No-need awards available for academics.

FINANCIAL AID PROCEDURES
Forms required: FAFSA, institutional form.
Dates and Deadlines: Priority date 5/30; no closing date. Must reply within 2 week(s) of notification.
Transfers: Closing date 7/31. Applicants notified by 8/31; must reply within 2 week(s) of notification.

CONTACT
Sandy Anderson, Financial Aid
248 East Elmwood Avenue, Palmer, AK 99645
(907) 745-3201

Alaska Pacific University
Anchorage, Alaska
www.alaskapacific.edu   Federal Code: 001061

4-year private university and liberal arts college in large city, affiliated with the United Methodist Church.
Enrollment: 266 undergrads, 29% part-time. 39 full-time freshmen.
Selectivity: Admits 50 to 75% of applicants.

BASIC COSTS (2017-2018)
Tuition and fees: $20,830.
Per-credit charge: $848.
Room and board: $7,210.

FINANCIAL AID PICTURE
Students with need: Need-based aid available for full-time and part-time students. Work study available nights, weekends, and for part-time students.
Students without need: No-need awards available for academics, alumni affiliation, art, leadership, music/drama, religious affiliation, state/district residency.

FINANCIAL AID PROCEDURES
Forms required: FAFSA.
Dates and Deadlines: Priority date 4/15; no closing date. Applicants notified on a rolling basis starting 2/1; must reply within 4 week(s) of notification.
Transfers: Priority date 6/1; no deadline. Applicants notified on a rolling basis starting 2/1; must reply within 2 week(s) of notification.

CONTACT
Scott Graves, Director, Student Financial Services
4101 University Drive, Anchorage, AK 99508-3051
(907) 564-8341

Charter College
Anchorage, Alaska
www.chartercollege.edu   Federal Code: 017377

4-year for-profit junior and technical college in large city.
Enrollment: 3,256 undergrads.
Selectivity: Open admission.

FINANCIAL AID PICTURE
Students with need: Need-based aid available for full-time and part-time students.

FINANCIAL AID PROCEDURES
Forms required: FAFSA.
Dates and Deadlines: Applicants notified on a rolling basis; must reply within 5 week(s) of notification.

CONTACT
2221 East Northern Lights Boulevard, Suite 120, Anchorage, AK 99508
(907) 777-1314

Ilisagvik College
Barrow, Alaska
www.ilisagvik.edu   Federal Code: 034613

2-year public community college in small town.
Enrollment: 88 undergrads, 72% part-time.
Selectivity: Open admission.

BASIC COSTS (2017-2018)
Tuition and fees: $3,820; out-of-state residents $3,820.
Per-credit charge: $145.
Room and board: $13,000.

FINANCIAL AID PICTURE (2015-2016)
Students with need: 98% of average financial aid package awarded as scholarships/grants, 2% awarded as loans/jobs. Need-based aid available for part-time students. Work study available nights, weekends, and for part-time students.
Students without need: This college awards aid only to students with need.

FINANCIAL AID PROCEDURES
Forms required: FAFSA.
Dates and Deadlines: Closing date 4/15. Applicants notified by 4/15.

CONTACT
Nancy Grant, Financial Aid Manager
100 Stevenson Road, Barrow, AK 99723
(907) 852-1708

University of Alaska Anchorage
Anchorage, Alaska
www.uaa.alaska.edu   Federal Code: 011462

4-year public university in large city.
Enrollment: 11,843 undergrads, 45% part-time. 1,322 full-time freshmen.
Selectivity: Open admission; but selective for some programs.

BASIC COSTS (2016-2017)
Tuition and fees: $7,074; out-of-state residents $21,744.
Per-credit charge: $192; out-of-state residents $681.
Room and board: $10,868.

FINANCIAL AID PICTURE (2016-2017)
Students with need: Out of 1,127 full-time freshmen who applied for aid, 753 were judged to have need. Of these, 727 received aid, and 148 had their full need met. Average financial aid package met 71% of need; average scholarship/grant was $3,330; average loan was $3,298. For part-time students, average financial aid package was $7,087.
Students without need: 109 full-time freshmen who did not demonstrate need for aid received scholarships/grants; average award was $2,606. No-need awards available for academics, art, athletics, leadership, minority status, music/drama, ROTC.
Scholarships offered: 19 full-time freshmen received athletic scholarships; average amount $3,508.

FINANCIAL AID PROCEDURES
Forms required: FAFSA.
Dates and Deadlines: Priority date 4/1; no closing date. Applicants notified on a rolling basis starting 2/1; must reply within 4 week(s) of notification.
Transfers: Closing date 4/15.

CONTACT
Sonya Stein, Director, Student Financial Assistance
PO Box 141629, Anchorage, AK 99514-1629
(907) 786-1480

University of Alaska Fairbanks
Fairbanks, Alaska
www.uaf.edu   Federal Code: 001063

4-year public university in small city.
Enrollment: 5,164 undergrads, 40% part-time. 697 full-time freshmen.
Selectivity: Open admission; but selective for some programs. GED not accepted.

BASIC COSTS (2016-2017)
Tuition and fees: $7,184; out-of-state residents $21,854.
Per-credit charge: $192; out-of-state residents $681.
Room and board: $8,380.

FINANCIAL AID PICTURE (2015-2016)
Students with need: Out of 632 full-time freshmen who applied for aid, 363 were judged to have need. Of these, 346 received aid, and 48 had their full need met. Average financial aid package met 56% of need; average scholarship/grant was $6,898; average loan was $2,943. For part-time students, average financial aid package was $4,462.
Students without need: 125 full-time freshmen who did not demonstrate need for aid received scholarships/grants; average award was $4,569. No-need awards available for academics, art, athletics, music/drama, state/district residency.
Scholarships offered: 10 full-time freshmen received athletic scholarships; average amount $11,800.

FINANCIAL AID PROCEDURES
Forms required: FAFSA, institutional form.
Dates and Deadlines: Priority date 2/15; closing date 7/1. Applicants notified on a rolling basis starting 3/1; must reply within 2 week(s) of notification.
Transfers: Applicants notified on a rolling basis starting 3/1; must reply within 2 week(s) of notification.

CONTACT
Deanna Dieringer, Director of Financial Aid
PO Box 757480, Fairbanks, AK 99775-7480
(888) 474-7256

University of Alaska Southeast
Juneau, Alaska
www.uas.alaska.edu   Federal Code: 001065

4-year public university and liberal arts college in large town.
Enrollment: 1,591 undergrads.

BASIC COSTS (2016-2017)
Tuition and fees: $7,410; out-of-state residents $22,080.
Per-credit charge: $192; out-of-state residents $681.
Room and board: $9,200.

FINANCIAL AID PICTURE
Students with need: Need-based aid available for full-time and part-time students. Work study available nights, weekends, and for part-time students.
Students without need: No-need awards available for academics, job skills, leadership, music/drama, state/district residency.
Additional info: Transfer, continuing, and freshman scholarship deadline March 1.

FINANCIAL AID PROCEDURES
Forms required: FAFSA.
Dates and Deadlines: Priority date 4/15; no closing date. Applicants notified on a rolling basis starting 3/1; must reply within 3 week(s) of notification.

CONTACT
Corinne Soltis, Assistant Director/VA Certifying Official
11120 Glacier Highway, Juneau, AK 99801-8681
(907) 796-6255

Arizona

Arizona Christian University
Phoenix, Arizona
www.arizonachristian.edu   Federal Code: 007113

4-year private Bible and liberal arts college in very large city, affiliated with the nondenominational tradition.
Enrollment: 684 undergrads, 5% part-time. 121 full-time freshmen.
Selectivity: Admits 50 to 75% of applicants.

BASIC COSTS (2017-2018)
Tuition and fees: $24,958.
Room and board: $10,334.

FINANCIAL AID PICTURE (2015-2016)
Students with need: Out of 114 full-time freshmen who applied for aid, 99 were judged to have need. Of these, 99 received aid, and 19 had their full need met. Average financial aid package met 72% of need; average scholarship/grant was $4,530; average loan was $4,329. Need-based aid available for part-time students.
Students without need: 15 full-time freshmen who did not demonstrate need for aid received scholarships/grants; average award was $6,427. No-need awards available for academics, athletics, leadership, music/drama.
Scholarships offered: 12 full-time freshmen received athletic scholarships; average amount $3,583.

FINANCIAL AID PROCEDURES
Forms required: FAFSA.
Dates and Deadlines: Applicants notified on a rolling basis.
Transfers: No deadline. Applicants notified on a rolling basis.

CONTACT
Courtney Rose, Director of Financial Aid
2625 East Cactus Road, Phoenix, AZ 85032-7042
(602) 386-4106

Arizona State University
Tempe, Arizona
www.asu.edu   Federal Code: 001081

4-year public university in small city.
Enrollment: 42,224 undergrads, 8% part-time. 8,278 full-time freshmen.
Selectivity: Admits over 75% of applicants.

BASIC COSTS (2016-2017)
Tuition and fees: $10,370; out-of-state residents $26,470.
Per-credit charge: $692; out-of-state residents $1,074.
Room and board: $11,386.
Additional info: $270 resident surcharge fee is a fee assessed to resident students during the 2016/17 school year.

FINANCIAL AID PICTURE (2015-2016)
Students with need: Out of 6,440 full-time freshmen who applied for aid, 4,785 were judged to have need. Of these, 4,785 received aid, and 1,048 had their full need met. Average financial aid package met 68% of need; average scholarship/grant was $12,360; average loan was $2,953. For part-time students, average financial aid package was $7,567.
Students without need: 2,541 full-time freshmen who did not demonstrate need for aid received scholarships/grants; average award was $8,008. No-need awards available for academics, art, athletics, leadership, music/drama, state/district residency.
Scholarships offered: 45 full-time freshmen received athletic scholarships; average amount $17,734.

Additional info: The Barack Obama Scholars Program assists select Arizona The Barack Obama Scholars Program and College Attainment Grant Program help make college affordable and accessible for students from low income families.

FINANCIAL AID PROCEDURES

Forms required: FAFSA.

Dates and Deadlines: Priority date 3/1; no closing date. Applicants notified on a rolling basis starting 3/1.

Transfers: Applicants notified on a rolling basis starting 4/15.

CONTACT

Melissa Pizzo, Dean, Admissions and Financial Aid Services
PO Box 870112, Tempe, AZ 85287-0112
(855) 278-5080

Arizona Western College

Yuma, Arizona
www.azwestern.edu   Federal Code: 001071

2-year public community college in small city.

Enrollment: 5,996 undergrads, 57% part-time. 662 full-time freshmen.

Selectivity: Open admission; but selective for some programs.

BASIC COSTS (2017-2018)

Tuition and fees: $2,460; out-of-state residents $9,450.

Per-credit charge: $82; out-of-state residents $315.

Room and board: $6,570.

FINANCIAL AID PICTURE

Students with need: Need-based aid available for full-time and part-time students. Work study available nights, weekends, and for part-time students.

Students without need: No-need awards available for academics, art, athletics, leadership, minority status, music/drama.

FINANCIAL AID PROCEDURES

Forms required: FAFSA, institutional form.

Dates and Deadlines: Priority date 4/1; no closing date. Applicants notified on a rolling basis starting 5/1.

CONTACT

Ana English, Director of Financial Aid
PO Box 929, Yuma, AZ 85366-0929
(928) 344-7634

Art Institute of Phoenix

Phoenix, Arizona
www.artinstitutes.edu/phoenix   Federal Code: 040513

3-year for-profit culinary school and visual arts college in very large city.

Enrollment: 1,009 undergrads.

FINANCIAL AID PICTURE

Students with need: Need-based aid available for full-time and part-time students.

FINANCIAL AID PROCEDURES

Forms required: FAFSA.

CONTACT

Abigail Garcia, Director of Administrative and Financial Services
2233 West Dunlap Avenue, Phoenix, AZ 85021-2859

Brookline College: Phoenix

Phoenix, Arizona
www.brooklinecollege.edu   Federal Code: 022188

2-year for-profit nursing and career college in very large city.

Enrollment: 1,429 undergrads.

Selectivity: Open admission.

BASIC COSTS (2016-2017)

Additional info: Diploma programs: $15,225; Associate degree programs: $14,775-$35,000; Bachelor's degree programs: $18,500-$85,000. Fees vary by course and program. All fees are subject to change.

FINANCIAL AID PICTURE

Students with need: Need-based aid available for full-time students.

Students without need: This college awards aid only to students with need.

FINANCIAL AID PROCEDURES

Forms required: FAFSA, institutional form.

CONTACT

Genna Gillary, Corporate Manager of Financial Aid
2445 West Dunlap Avenue, Suite 100, Phoenix, AZ 85021-5820
(602) 644-7110

Brookline College: Tempe

Tempe, Arizona
www.brooklinecollege.edu   Federal Code: 022188

2-year for-profit branch campus and career college in very large city.

Enrollment: 418 undergrads.

Selectivity: Open admission; but selective for some programs.

BASIC COSTS (2016-2017)

Additional info: Diploma programs: $15,225-$28,500; Associate degree programs: $30,000. Fees vary by course and program. All fees are subject to change.

FINANCIAL AID PICTURE

Students with need: Need-based aid available for full-time students.

Students without need: This college awards aid only to students with need.

FINANCIAL AID PROCEDURES

Forms required: FAFSA, institutional form.

CONTACT

Genna Gillary, Corporate Manager of Financial Aid
1140-1150 South Priest Drive, Tempe, AZ 85281-5240
(480) 545-8755

Brookline College: Tucson

Tucson, Arizona
www.brooklinecollege.edu   Federal Code: 022188

2-year for-profit branch campus and career college in very large city.

Enrollment: 507 undergrads.

Selectivity: Open admission.

BASIC COSTS (2016-2017)

Additional info: Diploma programs: $15,225; Associate degree programs: $30,000; Bachelor's degree programs: Criminal Justice: $60,00. Fees vary by course and program. All fees are subject to change.

FINANCIAL AID PICTURE

Students with need: Need-based aid available for full-time and part-time students.

Students without need: This college awards aid only to students with need.

FINANCIAL AID PROCEDURES
Forms required: FAFSA, institutional form.

CONTACT
Genna Gillary, Corporate Manager of Financial Aid
5441 East 22nd Street, Suite 125, Tucson, AZ 85711-5444
(602) 644-7090

Central Arizona College
Coolidge, Arizona
www.centralaz.edu
Federal Code: 007283

2-year public community college in small city.
Enrollment: 4,865 undergrads.
Selectivity: Open admission; but selective for some programs.

BASIC COSTS (2016-2017)
Tuition and fees: $2,520; out-of-state residents $10,980.
Per-credit charge: $84; out-of-state residents $168.
Room and board: $6,900.

FINANCIAL AID PICTURE
Students with need: Need-based aid available for full-time and part-time students. Work study available nights, weekends, and for part-time students.

FINANCIAL AID PROCEDURES
Forms required: FAFSA.
Dates and Deadlines: Priority date 5/1; closing date 7/15. Must reply within 3 week(s) of notification.

CONTACT
Elisa Juarez, Director of Financial Aid
Admissions Office, Coolidge, AZ 85128-9030
(520) 494-5425

Chandler-Gilbert Community College
Chandler, Arizona
www.cgc.maricopa.edu
Federal Code: 030722

2-year public community college in small city.
Enrollment: 14,630 undergrads.
Selectivity: Open admission; but selective for some programs.

BASIC COSTS (2016-2017)
Tuition and fees: $2,610; out-of-state residents $9,840.
Per-credit charge: $86; out-of-state residents $327.

FINANCIAL AID PICTURE
Students with need: Work study available nights, weekends, and for part-time students.

CONTACT
Timothy Wolsey, Director of Financial Aid
2626 East Pecos Road, Chandler, AZ 85225-2499
(855) 622-2332

Cochise College
Douglas, Arizona
www.cochise.edu
Federal Code: 001072

2-year public community college in large town.
Enrollment: 3,719 undergrads, 58% part-time. 453 full-time freshmen.
Selectivity: Open admission; but selective for some programs.

BASIC COSTS (2016-2017)
Tuition and fees: $2,370; out-of-state residents $7,500.
Per-credit charge: $79; out-of-state residents $250.
Room and board: $6,564.

FINANCIAL AID PICTURE (2015-2016)
Students with need: Out of 365 full-time freshmen who applied for aid, 294 were judged to have need. Of these, 283 received aid. For part-time students, average financial aid package was $4,966.
Students without need: 18 full-time freshmen who did not demonstrate need for aid received scholarships/grants; average award was $1,695.
Scholarships offered: 43 full-time freshmen received athletic scholarships; average amount $4,480.

FINANCIAL AID PROCEDURES
Forms required: FAFSA.
Dates and Deadlines: Priority date 5/1; closing date 6/15. Applicants notified on a rolling basis starting 6/1.
Transfers: Applicants notified on a rolling basis starting 6/1. Official college or university transcripts for all institutions previously attended required.

CONTACT
Karen Emmer, Director of Financial Aid
901 North Colombo Avenue, Sierra Vista, AZ 85635-2317
(520) 515-5417

DeVry University: Phoenix
Phoenix, Arizona
www.devry.edu
Federal Code: 008322

4-year for-profit university in large city.
Enrollment: 730 undergrads.

BASIC COSTS (2016-2017)
Tuition and fees: $17,512.
Per-credit charge: $609.

FINANCIAL AID PICTURE
Students with need: Need-based aid available for full-time and part-time students.
Students without need: This college awards aid only to students with need.

FINANCIAL AID PROCEDURES
Forms required: FAFSA.
Dates and Deadlines: Applicants notified on a rolling basis.

CONTACT
2149 West Dunlap Avenue, Phoenix, AZ 85021-2995
(602) 870-9229

Dine College
Tsaile, Arizona
www.dinecollege.edu
Federal Code: 008246

2-year public community college in rural community.
Enrollment: 1,369 undergrads. 69 full-time freshmen.
Selectivity: Open admission.

BASIC COSTS (2017-2018)
Tuition and fees: $1,410; out-of-state residents $1,410.
Per-credit charge: $55.
Room and board: $4,610.

FINANCIAL AID PICTURE (2015-2016)
Students with need: Out of 69 full-time freshmen who applied for aid, 69 were judged to have need. Of these, 69 received aid. For part-time students, average financial aid package was $1,729.

Students without need: This college awards aid only to students with need.

FINANCIAL AID PROCEDURES

Forms required: FAFSA, institutional form.

Dates and Deadlines: Applicants notified on a rolling basis starting 3/1; must reply within 4 week(s) of notification.

Transfers: Priority date 3/17; no deadline. Applicants notified on a rolling basis starting 3/17; must reply within 8 week(s) of notification.

CONTACT

Formon Thompson, Financial Aid Director

PO Box C 04, Tsaile, AZ 86556

(928) 724-6857

Eastern Arizona College

Thatcher, Arizona

www.eac.edu   Federal Code: 001073

2-year public community college in large town.

Enrollment: 5,082 undergrads, 61% part-time. 491 full-time freshmen.

Selectivity: Open admission; but selective for some programs.

BASIC COSTS (2016-2017)

Tuition and fees: $2,400; out-of-state residents $10,800.

Per-credit charge: $80; out-of-state residents $360.

Room and board: $6,280.

FINANCIAL AID PICTURE (2015-2016)

Students with need: Out of 449 full-time freshmen who applied for aid, 381 were judged to have need. Of these, 306 received aid, and 9 had their full need met. Average financial aid package met 36% of need; average scholarship/grant was $6,255. For part-time students, average financial aid package was $3,348.

Students without need: 33 full-time freshmen who did not demonstrate need for aid received scholarships/grants; average award was $1,945. No-need awards available for academics, art, athletics, leadership, music/drama, state/district residency.

Scholarships offered: *Merit:* Departmental Scholarships; in-state tuition; based on 2.5 GPA. Academic Scholarships; in-state tuition; based on 3.0 GPA. Performing Arts Scholarships; amounts vary; based on 2.5 GPA and audition. *Athletic:* 6 full-time freshmen received athletic scholarships; average amount $4,230.

Additional info: Limited number of tuition waivers for New Mexico residents. Unlimited number of waivers for those meeting WUE requirements.

FINANCIAL AID PROCEDURES

Forms required: FAFSA, institutional form.

Dates and Deadlines: Priority date 3/1; no closing date. Applicants notified on a rolling basis starting 3/15.

Transfers: No deadline. Applicants notified on a rolling basis starting 3/15.

CONTACT

Bill Osborn, Director of Financial Aid

615 North Stadium Avenue, Thatcher, AZ 85552-0769

(928) 428-8287

Embry-Riddle Aeronautical University: Prescott Campus

Prescott, Arizona

https://prescott.erau.edu/   Federal Code: 001479

4-year private university in large town.

Enrollment: 2,363 undergrads, 5% part-time. 599 full-time freshmen.

Selectivity: Admits over 75% of applicants.

BASIC COSTS (2017-2018)

Tuition and fees: $34,662.

Per-credit charge: $1,392.

Room and board: $10,468.

FINANCIAL AID PICTURE (2016-2017)

Students with need: Out of 512 full-time freshmen who applied for aid, 424 were judged to have need. Of these, 424 received aid. For part-time students, average financial aid package was $7,085.

Students without need: 91 full-time freshmen who did not demonstrate need for aid received scholarships/grants; average award was $14,063.

Scholarships offered: 36 full-time freshmen received athletic scholarships; average amount $11,265.

FINANCIAL AID PROCEDURES

Forms required: FAFSA.

Dates and Deadlines: Priority date 3/1; no closing date. Applicants notified on a rolling basis; must reply within 4 week(s) of notification.

CONTACT

Debra Hintz, Director, Financial Aid-Prescott Campus

3700 Willow Creek Road, Prescott, AZ 86301-3720

(928) 777-3765

Estrella Mountain Community College

Avondale, Arizona

www.estrellamountain.edu   Federal Code: 031563

2-year public community college in small city.

Enrollment: 7,010 undergrads.

Selectivity: Open admission.

BASIC COSTS (2016-2017)

Tuition and fees: $2,610; out-of-state residents $9,840.

FINANCIAL AID PICTURE (2015-2016)

Students with need: 57% of average financial aid package awarded as scholarships/grants, 43% awarded as loans/jobs. Need-based aid available for part-time students. Work study available nights.

Students without need: No-need awards available for leadership.

FINANCIAL AID PROCEDURES

Dates and Deadlines: Priority date 4/1; no closing date. Applicants notified on a rolling basis starting 4/15.

CONTACT

Rosanna Short, Director, Financial Aid

3000 North Dysart Road, Avondale, AZ 85392

(623) 935-8930

GateWay Community College

Phoenix, Arizona

www.gatewaycc.edu   Federal Code: 008303

2-year public community and technical college in very large city.

Enrollment: 1,306 full-time undergrads.

Selectivity: Open admission; but selective for some programs.

BASIC COSTS (2016-2017)

Tuition and fees: $2,610; out-of-state residents $9,840.

Per-credit charge: $86; out-of-state residents $327.

FINANCIAL AID PICTURE

Students with need: Need-based aid available for full-time and part-time students. Work study available nights, weekends, and for part-time students.

Students without need: No-need awards available for athletics.

FINANCIAL AID PROCEDURES

Forms required: FAFSA, institutional form.

Dates and Deadlines: Closing date 4/15. Applicants notified on a rolling basis; must reply within 4 week(s) of notification.

CONTACT
Suzanne Ringle, Director of Financial Aid
108 North 40th Street, Phoenix, AZ 85034
(602) 286-8115

Glendale Community College
Glendale, Arizona
www.gccaz.edu   Federal Code: 001076

2-year public community college in small city.
Selectivity: Open admission; but selective for some programs.

BASIC COSTS (2016-2017)
Tuition and fees: $2,610; out-of-state residents $9,840.
Per-credit charge: $86; out-of-state residents $327.

FINANCIAL AID PICTURE
Students with need: Need-based aid available for full-time and part-time students. Work study available nights, weekends, and for part-time students.
Students without need: No-need awards available for art, athletics, music/drama.

FINANCIAL AID PROCEDURES
Forms required: FAFSA.
Dates and Deadlines: Priority date 4/30; no closing date. Applicants notified on a rolling basis starting 5/1.
Transfers: No deadline. Applicants notified on a rolling basis.

CONTACT
Ellen Neel, Director of Financial Aid
6000 West Olive Avenue, Glendale, AZ 85302
(623) 845-3366

Grand Canyon University
Phoenix, Arizona
www.gcu.edu   Federal Code: 001074

4-year for-profit university in very large city.
Enrollment: 39,400 undergrads.

BASIC COSTS (2016-2017)
Tuition and fees: $17,170.
Per-credit charge: $688.
Room and board: $15,100.

FINANCIAL AID PICTURE
Students with need: Need-based aid available for full-time and part-time students. Work study available nights, weekends, and for part-time students.
Students without need: No-need awards available for academics, alumni affiliation, art, athletics, leadership, minority status, music/drama, religious affiliation, ROTC, state/district residency.

FINANCIAL AID PROCEDURES
Forms required: FAFSA.
Dates and Deadlines: Applicants notified on a rolling basis.
Transfers: No deadline. Applicants notified on a rolling basis.

CONTACT
Chris Linderson, Vice President of Financial Aid
3300 West Camelback Road, Phoenix, AZ 85017-8562
(800) 800-9776

Mesa Community College
Mesa, Arizona
www.mesacc.edu   Federal Code: 001077

2-year public community college in very large city.
Enrollment: 16,672 undergrads, 65% part-time.
Selectivity: Open admission; but selective for some programs.

BASIC COSTS (2016-2017)
Tuition and fees: $2,595; out-of-state residents $9,825.
Per-credit charge: $86; out-of-state residents $327.

FINANCIAL AID PICTURE (2015-2016)
Students with need: 62% of average financial aid package awarded as scholarships/grants, 38% awarded as loans/jobs. Need-based aid available for part-time students.
Students without need: No-need awards available for academics, athletics.
Additional info: Awards available for Maricopa County residents.

FINANCIAL AID PROCEDURES
Forms required: FAFSA, institutional form.
Dates and Deadlines: Priority date 5/1; no closing date. Applicants notified on a rolling basis starting 7/1.
Transfers: Priority date 7/13. Applicants notified on a rolling basis.

CONTACT
Patricia Peppin, Financial Aid
1833 West Southern Avenue, Mesa, AZ 85202
(480) 471-7401

Mohave Community College
Kingman, Arizona
www.mohave.edu   Federal Code: 011864

2-year public community college in small city.
Enrollment: 2,770 undergrads, 74% part-time. 174 full-time freshmen.
Selectivity: Open admission; but selective for some programs.

BASIC COSTS (2016-2017)
Tuition and fees: $2,640; out-of-state residents $8,715.
Per-credit charge: $81; out-of-state residents $283.5.

FINANCIAL AID PICTURE
Students with need: Need-based aid available for full-time and part-time students. Work study available nights.
Students without need: This college awards aid only to students with need.

FINANCIAL AID PROCEDURES
Forms required: FAFSA, institutional form.
Dates and Deadlines: Priority date 4/15; closing date 7/15. Applicants notified on a rolling basis starting 5/1; must reply within 2 week(s) of notification.

CONTACT
Shannon Sheaff, Director of Financial Aid
1971 Jagerson Avenue, Kingman, AZ 86409
(866) 664-2832

National Paralegal College
Phoenix, Arizona
https://nationalparalegal.edu   Federal Code: 041574

4-year for-profit virtual career college in large city.
Enrollment: 938 undergrads, 5% part-time. 64 full-time freshmen.
Selectivity: Open admission.

BASIC COSTS (2017-2018)
Tuition and fees: $7,995.
Per-credit charge: $325.

FINANCIAL AID PICTURE (2015-2016)
Students with need: 31% of average financial aid package awarded as scholarships/grants, 69% awarded as loans/jobs.

CONTACT
Lisa Pimber, Financial Aid DIrector
717 East Maryland Avenue, Phoenix, AZ 85014-1561
(800) 371-6105 ext. 1

Northern Arizona University
Flagstaff, Arizona
www.nau.edu   Federal Code: 001082

4-year public university in small city.
Enrollment: 26,400 undergrads, 19% part-time. 4,663 full-time freshmen.
Selectivity: Admits over 75% of applicants.

BASIC COSTS (2016-2017)
Tuition and fees: $10,764; out-of-state residents $24,144.
Per-credit charge: $696; out-of-state residents $964.
Room and board: $9,482.
Additional info: Tuition at time of enrollment locked for 4 years.

FINANCIAL AID PICTURE (2015-2016)
Students with need: Out of 4,141 full-time freshmen who applied for aid, 3,225 were judged to have need. Of these, 3,160 received aid, and 419 had their full need met. Average financial aid package met 63% of need; average scholarship/grant was $7,010; average loan was $3,373. For part-time students, average financial aid package was $6,928.
Students without need: 1,043 full-time freshmen who did not demonstrate need for aid received scholarships/grants; average award was $5,897. No-need awards available for academics, alumni affiliation, art, athletics, leadership, minority status, music/drama, ROTC, state/district residency.
Scholarships offered: 60 full-time freshmen received athletic scholarships; average amount $20,219.
Additional info: Guaranteed fixed tuition for 4 years and guaranteed gift aid for 4 years.

FINANCIAL AID PROCEDURES
Forms required: FAFSA.
Dates and Deadlines: Priority date 2/1; no closing date. Applicants notified on a rolling basis starting 2/1.
Transfers: No deadline. Applicants notified on a rolling basis.

CONTACT
Nydia Nittmann, Director of Financial Aid
PO Box 4084, Flagstaff, AZ 86011-4084
(928) 523-4951

Northland Pioneer College
Holbrook, Arizona
www.npc.edu   Federal Code: 011862

2-year public community and technical college in small town.
Enrollment: 3,233 undergrads.
Selectivity: Open admission; but selective for some programs.

BASIC COSTS (2016-2017)
Tuition and fees: $2,170; out-of-state residents $10,120.
Per-credit charge: $70; out-of-state residents $335.

FINANCIAL AID PICTURE
Students with need: Need-based aid available for full-time and part-time students. Work study available nights, weekends, and for part-time students.

Students without need: No-need awards available for academics, art, job skills, leadership, minority status, music/drama, state/district residency.

FINANCIAL AID PROCEDURES
Forms required: FAFSA, institutional form.
Dates and Deadlines: Priority date 6/1; no closing date. Applicants notified on a rolling basis starting 5/15; must reply within 2 week(s) of notification.
Transfers: No deadline. Applicants notified on a rolling basis.

CONTACT
Beaulah Bob-Pennypacker, Financial Aid Coordinator
PO Box 610, Holbrook, AZ 86025-0610
(928) 524-7626

Paradise Valley Community College
Phoenix, Arizona
www.pvc.maricopa.edu   Federal Code: 026236

2-year public community college in very large city.
Enrollment: 2,867 full-time undergrads.
Selectivity: Open admission.

BASIC COSTS (2016-2017)
Tuition and fees: $2,550; out-of-state residents $9,840.
Per-credit charge: $86; out-of-state residents $327.

FINANCIAL AID PICTURE
Students with need: Need-based aid available for full-time and part-time students.

FINANCIAL AID PROCEDURES
Forms required: FAFSA.
Dates and Deadlines: Applicants notified on a rolling basis starting 6/1.

CONTACT
Ken Clarke, Director of Financial Aid
18401 North 32nd Street, Phoenix, AZ 85032
(602) 787-7100

Phoenix College
Phoenix, Arizona
www.phoenixcollege.edu   Federal Code: 001078

2-year public community college in very large city.
Enrollment: 9,745 undergrads.
Selectivity: Open admission; but selective for some programs.

BASIC COSTS (2016-2017)
Tuition and fees: $2,610; out-of-state residents $9,840.

FINANCIAL AID PICTURE
Students with need: Work study available weekends and for part-time students.

FINANCIAL AID PROCEDURES
Forms required: FAFSA.
Dates and Deadlines: Priority date 6/30; no closing date. Applicants notified on a rolling basis.

CONTACT
Cindy Ramos, Director
1202 West Thomas Road, Phoenix, AZ 85013
(602) 285-7425

Prescott College
Prescott, Arizona
www.prescott.edu   Federal Code: 013659

4-year private liberal arts college in small city.
Enrollment: 350 undergrads, 25% part-time. 47 full-time freshmen.
Selectivity: Admits 50 to 75% of applicants.

BASIC COSTS (2016-2017)
Tuition and fees: $28,693.
Room and board: $7,300.

FINANCIAL AID PICTURE (2016-2017)
Students with need: Out of 38 full-time freshmen who applied for aid, 26 were judged to have need. Of these, 26 received aid, and 1 had their full need met. Average financial aid package met 71% of need; average scholarship/grant was $19,534; average loan was $3,262. Need-based aid available for part-time students.
Students without need: 19 full-time freshmen who did not demonstrate need for aid received scholarships/grants; average award was $10,346. No-need awards available for academics, leadership.

FINANCIAL AID PROCEDURES
Forms required: FAFSA.
Dates and Deadlines: Priority date 3/1; no closing date. Applicants notified on a rolling basis starting 3/15.
Transfers: No deadline. Applicants notified on a rolling basis starting 3/15; must reply within 4 week(s) of notification. Dean's 21st Century Global Leader Scholarship: $10,000 per year; 2200 SAT/33 ACT or 3.25 college GPA, proof of volunteering, superior application rating. Merit Scholarship: $8,000 per year; 1550 SAT/23 ACT or 3.0 GPA, proof of volunteering, superior application rating. Phi Theta Kappa Scholarship: $2,000 per year.

CONTACT
Mary Frances Causey, Director of Financial Aid
220 Grove Avenue, Prescott, AZ 86301
(928) 350-1111

Refrigeration School
Phoenix, Arizona
www.refrigerationschool.com   Federal Code: 014127

2-year for-profit technical college in very large city.
Enrollment: 1,185 undergrads.
Selectivity: Open admission; but selective for some programs.

BASIC COSTS (2017-2018)
Additional info: Total program cost varies from $7,970 to $32,930 depending on program.

FINANCIAL AID PICTURE (2015-2016)
Students with need: 39% of average financial aid package awarded as scholarships/grants, 61% awarded as loans/jobs.

CONTACT
Melanie Zuverink, Financial Aid Director
4210 East Washington Street, Phoenix, AZ 85034-1816
(602) 275-7133

Rio Salado College
Tempe, Arizona
www.riosalado.edu   Federal Code: 014483

2-year public community college in very large city.
Enrollment: 18,724 undergrads.
Selectivity: Open admission; but selective for some programs.

BASIC COSTS (2016-2017)
Tuition and fees: $2,620; out-of-state residents $9,850.
Per-credit charge: $86; out-of-state residents $325.

FINANCIAL AID PICTURE
Students with need: Need-based aid available for full-time and part-time students.
Students without need: This college awards aid only to students with need.

FINANCIAL AID PROCEDURES
Forms required: FAFSA, institutional form.
Dates and Deadlines: Priority date 6/30; no closing date. Applicants notified on a rolling basis starting 6/30.

CONTACT
Nanci Regehr, Director of Financial Aid
2323 West 14th Street, Tempe, AZ 85281
(480) 517-8310

Scottsdale Community College
Scottsdale, Arizona
www.scottsdalecc.edu   Federal Code: 008304

2-year public community college in small city.
Enrollment: 3,295 undergrads.
Selectivity: Open admission.

BASIC COSTS (2016-2017)
Tuition and fees: $2,610; out-of-state residents $9,840.
Per-credit charge: $86; out-of-state residents $327.

FINANCIAL AID PICTURE (2015-2016)
Students with need: 72% of average financial aid package awarded as scholarships/grants, 28% awarded as loans/jobs. Need-based aid available for part-time students.
Students without need: No-need awards available for academics, athletics.

FINANCIAL AID PROCEDURES
Forms required: FAFSA.
Dates and Deadlines: Priority date 7/1; no closing date. Applicants notified on a rolling basis starting 7/1; must reply by 7/15 or within 3 week(s) of notification.
Transfers: Priority date 7/1; no deadline. Applicants notified on a rolling basis starting 7/1.

CONTACT
Stacie Beck, Director of Financial Aid
9000 East Chaparral Road, Scottsdale, AZ 85256-2626
(480) 423-6549

South Mountain Community College
Phoenix, Arizona
www.southmountaincc.edu   Federal Code: 015001

2-year public community college in very large city.
Enrollment: 1,340 undergrads.
Selectivity: Open admission.

BASIC COSTS (2016-2017)
Tuition and fees: $2,610; out-of-state residents $9,840.
Per-credit charge: $84; out-of-state residents $325.

FINANCIAL AID PICTURE
Students with need: Need-based aid available for full-time and part-time students. Work study available nights, weekends, and for part-time students.
Students without need: No-need awards available for academics, athletics, minority status, music/drama.

FINANCIAL AID PROCEDURES

Forms required: FAFSA.

Dates and Deadlines: Priority date 5/1; no closing date. Applicants notified on a rolling basis starting 5/15; must reply within 3 week(s) of notification.

CONTACT

Inez Moreno-Weinert, Director of Financial Aid and Placement

7050 South 24th Street, Phoenix, AZ 85042

(602) 243-8300

Southwest University of Visual Arts

Tucson, Arizona

www.suva.edu   Federal Code: 024915

4-year for-profit visual arts college in very large city.

Enrollment: 119 undergrads, 11% part-time. 27 full-time freshmen.

BASIC COSTS (2016-2017)

Tuition and fees: $22,944.

Additional info: Estimated total costs for books and supplies for each program: $3,900-$4,750.

FINANCIAL AID PICTURE

Students with need: Need-based aid available for full-time and part-time students. Work study available nights, weekends, and for part-time students.

Students without need: This college awards aid only to students with need.

Scholarships offered: Board of Trustees Scholarship: Transfer Student Scholarship; Scholarship for Continuing Students.

FINANCIAL AID PROCEDURES

Forms required: FAFSA.

Transfers: No deadline. Applicants notified on a rolling basis.

CONTACT

Julie Mairs

2525 North Country Club Road, Tucson, AZ 85716

(520) 325-0123

Tohono O'odham Community College

Sells, Arizona

www.tocc.edu   Federal Code: 037844

2-year public community college in rural community.

Enrollment: 299 undergrads, 64% part-time. 40 full-time freshmen.

Selectivity: Open admission.

BASIC COSTS (2016-2017)

Tuition and fees: $2,075.

Room and board: $2,400.

FINANCIAL AID PICTURE (2015-2016)

Students with need: 99% of average financial aid package awarded as scholarships/grants, 1% awarded as loans/jobs. Need-based aid available for part-time students.

Students without need: This college awards aid only to students with need.

FINANCIAL AID PROCEDURES

Forms required: FAFSA, institutional form.

Dates and Deadlines: Applicants notified on a rolling basis.

CONTACT

Alvaro Rivera, Financial Aid Director

PO Box 3129, Sells, AZ 85634-3129

(520) 383-8401 ext. 41

University of Arizona

Tucson, Arizona

www.arizona.edu   Federal Code: 001083

4-year public university in very large city.

Enrollment: 33,780 undergrads, 13% part-time. 6,973 full-time freshmen.

Selectivity: Admits over 75% of applicants.

BASIC COSTS (2016-2017)

Tuition and fees: $12,817; out-of-state residents $36,017.

Per-credit charge: $768; out-of-district residents $768; out-of-state residents $1,415.

Room and board: $11,300.

Additional info: Tuition/fee waivers available for minority students.

FINANCIAL AID PICTURE (2015-2016)

Students with need: Out of 4,996 full-time freshmen who applied for aid, 3,620 were judged to have need. Of these, 3,498 received aid, and 470 had their full need met. Average financial aid package met 55% of need; average scholarship/grant was $10,288; average loan was $3,216. For part-time students, average financial aid package was $8,948.

Students without need: 2,036 full-time freshmen who did not demonstrate need for aid received scholarships/grants; average award was $7,703. No-need awards available for academics, art, athletics, leadership, music/drama, state/district residency.

Scholarships offered: *Merit:* Various merit scholarships available. National Merit scholarship: $6,000-$10,000 a year. *Athletic:* 48 full-time freshmen received athletic scholarships; average amount $24,494.

Additional info: Arizona Assurance Program; provides housing, books, and tuition for all new, incoming resident freshmen; must be Pell-eligible with combined family income less than $42,500; funding provided as grants, scholarships, and federal work-study.

FINANCIAL AID PROCEDURES

Forms required: FAFSA. CSS PROFILE required for some; subset of applicants asked to comply based on FAFSA information.

Dates and Deadlines: Priority date 3/1; no closing date. Applicants notified on a rolling basis starting 2/1.

Transfers: Priority date 3/1. Awards based on academic factors for both residents and non-residents and vary in amount each year.

CONTACT

Elizabeth Acree

1428 East University Boulevard, Tucson, AZ 85721-0040

(520) 621-1858

Western International University

Tempe, Arizona

www.west.edu   Federal Code: 014970

4-year for-profit university and business college in very large city.

Enrollment: 1,133 undergrads. 88 full-time freshmen.

Selectivity: Open admission.

BASIC COSTS (2016-2017)

Per-credit charge: $291.

Additional info: $291 per credit hour for undergraduate students regardless of academic level, includes all books for the course.

FINANCIAL AID PICTURE

Students with need: Need-based aid available for full-time students.

Students without need: This college awards aid only to students with need.

FINANCIAL AID PROCEDURES

Forms required: FAFSA, institutional form.

Dates and Deadlines: Applicants notified on a rolling basis.

Transfers: No deadline. Applicants notified on a rolling basis.

CONTACT

Beth Carlisle, Sr Direct of Student Administrative Services

1601 West Fountainhead Parkway, Tempe, AZ 85282

(602) 943-2311

Yavapai College

Prescott, Arizona

www.yc.edu   Federal Code: 001079

2-year public community college in large town.

Enrollment: 8,273 undergrads.

Selectivity: Open admission; but selective for some programs.

BASIC COSTS (2016-2017)

Tuition and fees: $2,370; out-of-state residents $10,980.

Per-credit charge: $79; out-of-state residents $366.

Room and board: $9,212.

FINANCIAL AID PICTURE

Students with need: Need-based aid available for full-time and part-time students.

Students without need: No-need awards available for academics, athletics.

FINANCIAL AID PROCEDURES

Forms required: FAFSA.

Dates and Deadlines: Priority date 4/1; no closing date. Applicants notified on a rolling basis.

CONTACT

Terri Eckel, Financial Aid Operations

1100 East Sheldon Street, Prescott, AZ 86301

(928) 776-2152

Arkansas

Arkansas Baptist College

Little Rock, Arkansas

www.arkansasbaptist.edu   Federal Code: 001087

4-year private liberal arts college in small city, affiliated with the American Baptist Churches in the USA.

Enrollment: 989 undergrads.

Selectivity: Open admission.

BASIC COSTS (2016-2017)

Tuition and fees: $8,760.

Room and board: $8,190.

FINANCIAL AID PICTURE

Students with need: Need-based aid available for full-time and part-time students.

Students without need: This college awards aid only to students with need.

FINANCIAL AID PROCEDURES

Forms required: FAFSA.

Dates and Deadlines: Closing date 4/1. Applicants notified on a rolling basis starting 6/15.

CONTACT

Phillip Rodgers, Director of Financial Aid

1621 Dr. Martin Luther King Drive, Little Rock, AR 72202

(501) 420-1226

Arkansas Northeastern College

Blytheville, Arkansas

www.anc.edu   Federal Code: 012860

2-year public community college in large town.

Enrollment: 1,416 undergrads.

Selectivity: Open admission; but selective for some programs.

BASIC COSTS (2016-2017)

Tuition and fees: $2,180; out-of-district residents $2,480; out-of-state residents $3,980.

Per-credit charge: $67; out-of-district residents $77; out-of-state residents $127.

FINANCIAL AID PICTURE

Students with need: Need-based aid available for full-time and part-time students.

Students without need: No-need awards available for academics, art, minority status, music/drama, state/district residency.

FINANCIAL AID PROCEDURES

Forms required: FAFSA, institutional form.

Dates and Deadlines: Priority date 4/15; no closing date. Applicants notified on a rolling basis starting 3/1; must reply within 2 week(s) of notification.

CONTACT

Mindy Walker, Director of Financial Aid

PO Box 1109, Blytheville, AR 72316-1109

(870) 762-1020 ext. 1160

Arkansas State University

State University, Arkansas

www.astate.edu   Federal Code: 001090

4-year public university in small city.

Enrollment: 8,909 undergrads.

BASIC COSTS (2016-2017)

Tuition and fees: $8,260; out-of-state residents $14,380.

Per-credit charge: $202; out-of-state residents $404.

Room and board: $8,490.

Additional info: There is a College Support Assessment Fee, $22 per-credit hour for undergraduate students and $53 per-credit hour for graduate students, for the Colleges of Business, Engineering, Nursing & Health Professions, and Sciences & Mathematics.

FINANCIAL AID PICTURE

Students with need: Need-based aid available for full-time and part-time students. Work study available nights, weekends, and for part-time students.

Students without need: No-need awards available for academics, alumni affiliation, art, athletics, leadership, minority status, music/drama, ROTC, state/district residency.

FINANCIAL AID PROCEDURES

Forms required: FAFSA, institutional form.

Dates and Deadlines: Priority date 2/15; closing date 7/1. Applicants notified on a rolling basis starting 6/1; must reply within 2 week(s) of notification.

Transfers: Applicants notified on a rolling basis starting 6/1; must reply within 2 week(s) of notification.

CONTACT

Terry Finney, Director of Financial Aid and Scholarships

PO Box 1570, State University, AR 72467-1570

(870) 972-2310

Arkansas State University Mid-South
West Memphis, Arkansas
www.asumidsouth.edu   Federal Code: 015862

2-year public community and technical college in large town.
Enrollment: 1,836 undergrads.
Selectivity: Open admission.

BASIC COSTS (2016-2017)
Tuition and fees: $3,190; out-of-district residents $3,790; out-of-state residents $4,990.
Per-credit charge: $90; out-of-district residents $110; out-of-state residents $150.

FINANCIAL AID PICTURE (2015-2016)
Students with need: 98% of average financial aid package awarded as scholarships/grants, 2% awarded as loans/jobs. Need-based aid available for part-time students. Work study available nights.
Students without need: No-need awards available for academics, state/district residency.

FINANCIAL AID PROCEDURES
Forms required: FAFSA, institutional form.
Dates and Deadlines: Priority date 4/30; no closing date. Applicants notified on a rolling basis starting 6/1; must reply within 2 week(s) of notification.

CONTACT
Crystal Burger, Director of Financial Aid
2000 West Broadway, West Memphis, AR 72301
(870) 733-6741

Arkansas State University: Beebe
Beebe, Arkansas
www.asub.edu   Federal Code: 001091

2-year public community college in small town.
Enrollment: 2,826 undergrads, 28% part-time. 565 full-time freshmen.
Selectivity: Open admission; but selective for some programs.

BASIC COSTS (2016-2017)
Tuition and fees: $3,390; out-of-state residents $5,520.
Per-credit charge: $98; out-of-state residents $169.
Room and board: $5,180.

FINANCIAL AID PICTURE
Students with need: Need-based aid available for full-time and part-time students. Work study available nights, weekends, and for part-time students.
Students without need: No-need awards available for academics, leadership, music/drama.

FINANCIAL AID PROCEDURES
Forms required: FAFSA, institutional form.
Dates and Deadlines: Priority date 6/1; no closing date. Applicants notified on a rolling basis starting 6/1; must reply within 2 week(s) of notification.
Transfers: No deadline. Applicants notified on a rolling basis.

CONTACT
Louise Driver, Director of Financial Aid
PO Box 1000, Beebe, AR 72012-1000
(501) 882-8245

Arkansas State University: Mountain Home
Mountain Home, Arkansas
www.asumh.edu   Federal Code: 901090

2-year public community and technical college in large town.
Enrollment: 1,224 undergrads.

Selectivity: Open admission; but selective for some programs.

BASIC COSTS (2016-2017)
Tuition and fees: $3,480; out-of-state residents $5,460.
Per-credit charge: $94; out-of-state residents $160.

FINANCIAL AID PICTURE
Students with need: Need-based aid available for full-time and part-time students.
Students without need: No-need awards available for academics, alumni affiliation, leadership, state/district residency.
Scholarships offered: Academic Distinction Scholarship: full tuition; for qualified Arkansas residents.
Additional info: Satisfactory academic progress policy for Title IV aid.

FINANCIAL AID PROCEDURES
Forms required: FAFSA, institutional form.
Dates and Deadlines: Priority date 6/1; no closing date. Applicants notified on a rolling basis starting 5/1; must reply within 2 week(s) of notification.
Transfers: No deadline. Applicants notified on a rolling basis starting 7/1; must reply within 2 week(s) of notification. All final academic transcripts required prior to awarding Title IV aid.

CONTACT
Clay Berry, Director of Financial Aid
1600 South College Street, Mountain Home, AR 72653
(870) 508-6100 ext. 195

Arkansas Tech University
Russellville, Arkansas
www.atu.edu   Federal Code: 001089

4-year public university and liberal arts college in large town.
Enrollment: 8,463 undergrads, 20% part-time. 1,937 full-time freshmen.
Selectivity: Admits 50 to 75% of applicants.

BASIC COSTS (2016-2017)
Tuition and fees: $8,280; out-of-state residents $14,850.
Per-credit charge: $219; out-of-state residents $438.
Room and board: $7,036.

FINANCIAL AID PICTURE (2015-2016)
Students with need: Out of 1,867 full-time freshmen who applied for aid, 1,348 were judged to have need. Of these, 1,333 received aid, and 62 had their full need met. Average financial aid package met 59% of need; average scholarship/grant was $4,467; average loan was $2,913. For part-time students, average financial aid package was $5,471.
Students without need: 349 full-time freshmen who did not demonstrate need for aid received scholarships/grants; average award was $6,728. No-need awards available for academics, athletics, leadership, music/drama, ROTC, state/district residency.
Scholarships offered: 58 full-time freshmen received athletic scholarships; average amount $4,697.

FINANCIAL AID PROCEDURES
Forms required: FAFSA, institutional form.
Dates and Deadlines: Priority date 3/15; no closing date. Applicants notified on a rolling basis starting 3/15; must reply within 4 week(s) of notification.
Transfers: No deadline. Applicants notified on a rolling basis starting 5/1; must reply within 2 week(s) of notification.

CONTACT
Niki Schwartz, Director of Student Financial Aid
105 West O Street, Suite 104, Russellville, AR 72801-2222
(479) 968-0399

Black River Technical College

Pocahontas, Arkansas
www.blackrivertech.edu   Federal Code: 011948

2-year public technical college in small town.
Enrollment: 1,560 undergrads.
Selectivity: Open admission; but selective for some programs.

BASIC COSTS (2016-2017)
Tuition and fees: $3,330; out-of-state residents $6,330.
Per-credit charge: $89; out-of-state residents $189.

FINANCIAL AID PICTURE
Students with need: Need-based aid available for full-time and part-time students.
Students without need: No-need awards available for academics, leadership, minority status, music/drama, state/district residency.

FINANCIAL AID PROCEDURES
Forms required: FAFSA, institutional form.
Dates and Deadlines: Priority date 4/1; closing date 6/30. Applicants notified on a rolling basis starting 4/1.
Transfers: No deadline.

CONTACT
Brandi Chester, Financial Aid Director
Highway 304 East, Pocahontas, AR 72455
(870) 248-4000 ext. 4020

Central Baptist College

Conway, Arkansas
www.cbc.edu   Federal Code: 001093

4-year private Bible college in small city, affiliated with the Baptist faith.
Enrollment: 735 undergrads, 11% part-time. 126 full-time freshmen.
Selectivity: Admits 50 to 75% of applicants.

BASIC COSTS (2016-2017)
Tuition and fees: $14,400.
Per-credit charge: $430.
Room and board: $7,500.

FINANCIAL AID PICTURE
Students with need: Need-based aid available for full-time and part-time students. Work study available nights, weekends, and for part-time students.
Students without need: No-need awards available for academics, alumni affiliation, athletics, leadership, music/drama, religious affiliation.

FINANCIAL AID PROCEDURES
Forms required: FAFSA, institutional form.
Dates and Deadlines: Priority date 7/1; closing date 8/1. Applicants notified on a rolling basis starting 4/1.
Transfers: No deadline. Applicants notified on a rolling basis.

CONTACT
Tonya Hammontree, Director of Financial Aid
1501 College Avenue, Conway, AR 72034
(501) 205-8809

College of the Ouachitas

Malvern, Arkansas
www.coto.edu   Federal Code: 009976

2-year public community and technical college in rural community.
Enrollment: 707 undergrads, 39% part-time. 124 full-time freshmen.
Selectivity: Open admission; but selective for some programs.

BASIC COSTS (2016-2017)
Tuition and fees: $3,620; out-of-state residents $6,410.
Per-credit charge: $93; out-of-state residents $186.

FINANCIAL AID PICTURE (2015-2016)
Students with need: Need-based aid available for part-time students.
Students without need: No-need awards available for academics.

FINANCIAL AID PROCEDURES
Forms required: FAFSA.
Dates and Deadlines: Applicants notified on a rolling basis starting 7/1; must reply within 6 week(s) of notification.
Transfers: No deadline. Applicants notified on a rolling basis; must reply within 6 week(s) of notification.

CONTACT
Vickie Young, Director of Financial Aid
One College Circle, Malvern, AR 72104
(501) 337-5000 ext. 1122

Cossatot Community College of the University of Arkansas

De Queen, Arkansas
www.cccua.edu   Federal Code: 012432

2-year public community college in small town.
Enrollment: 916 undergrads.
Selectivity: Open admission; but selective for some programs.

BASIC COSTS (2016-2017)
Tuition and fees: $3,015; out-of-district residents $3,405; out-of-state residents $6,345.
Per-credit charge: $69; out-of-district residents $82; out-of-state residents $180.

FINANCIAL AID PICTURE
Students with need: Need-based aid available for full-time and part-time students. Work study available nights.
Additional info: Active or honorably discharged military and their dependents receive tuition discounts.

FINANCIAL AID PROCEDURES
Forms required: FAFSA, institutional form.
Dates and Deadlines: Priority date 5/1; no closing date. Applicants notified on a rolling basis starting 3/1.
Transfers: Applicants notified on a rolling basis starting 3/1.

CONTACT
Denise Hammond, Director of Financial Aid
183 College Drive, De Queen, AR 71832
(870) 584-4471

Crowley's Ridge College

Paragould, Arkansas
www.crc.edu   Federal Code: 001095

2-year private liberal arts college in large town, affiliated with the Church of Christ.
Enrollment: 193 undergrads.
Selectivity: Open admission.

BASIC COSTS (2017-2018)
Tuition and fees: $12,250.
Room and board: $6,350.

FINANCIAL AID PICTURE
Students with need: Work study available nights, weekends, and for part-time students.

Students without need: No-need awards available for academics, athletics, leadership, music/drama.

FINANCIAL AID PROCEDURES

Forms required: FAFSA.

Dates and Deadlines: Applicants notified on a rolling basis starting 5/30.

Transfers: No deadline. Applicants notified on a rolling basis.

CONTACT

David Goff, Director of Financial Aid
100 College Drive, Paragould, AR 72450
(870) 236-6901 ext. 119

East Arkansas Community College

Forrest City, Arkansas
www.eacc.edu
Federal Code: 012260

2-year public community college in large town.

Enrollment: 1,268 undergrads.

Selectivity: Open admission; but selective for some programs.

BASIC COSTS (2016-2017)

Tuition and fees: $2,850; out-of-district residents $3,150; out-of-state residents $3,660.

Per-credit charge: $84; out-of-district residents $94; out-of-state residents $111.

FINANCIAL AID PICTURE

Students with need: Need-based aid available for full-time and part-time students.

Students without need: This college awards aid only to students with need.

FINANCIAL AID PROCEDURES

Forms required: FAFSA.

Dates and Deadlines: Priority date 3/1; closing date 7/1. Applicants notified on a rolling basis starting 5/15; must reply within 2 week(s) of notification.

CONTACT

Alvin Coleman, Director of Financial Aid
1700 Newcastle Road, Forrest City, AR 72335-2204
(870) 633-4480 ext. 225

Ecclesia College

Springdale, Arkansas
www.ecollege.edu
Federal Code: 038553

4-year private Bible and liberal arts college in large town, affiliated with the interdenominational tradition.

Enrollment: 246 undergrads.

Selectivity: Admits less than 50% of applicants.

BASIC COSTS (2016-2017)

Tuition and fees: $15,140.

Per-credit charge: $475.

Room and board: $5,010.

Additional info: Tuition/fee waivers available for adults.

FINANCIAL AID PICTURE

Students with need: Need-based aid available for full-time and part-time students. Work study available nights, weekends, and for part-time students.

Students without need: No-need awards available for academics, athletics, job skills, leadership, music/drama.

FINANCIAL AID PROCEDURES

Forms required: FAFSA.

Dates and Deadlines: Applicants notified on a rolling basis starting 7/1.

Transfers: No deadline. Applicants notified on a rolling basis starting 2/1; must reply within 4 week(s) of notification.

CONTACT

Linda Sutherland, Director of Financial Aid
9653 Nations Drive, Springdale, AR 72762
(479) 248-7236 ext. 209

Harding University

Searcy, Arkansas
www.harding.edu
Federal Code: 001097

4-year private university in large town, affiliated with the Church of Christ.

Enrollment: 4,411 undergrads, 6% part-time. 988 full-time freshmen.

Selectivity: Admits over 75% of applicants.

BASIC COSTS (2017-2018)

Tuition and fees: $19,190.

Per-credit charge: $598.

Room and board: $6,894.

FINANCIAL AID PICTURE (2015-2016)

Students with need: Out of 873 full-time freshmen who applied for aid, 642 were judged to have need. Of these, 639 received aid, and 261 had their full need met. Average financial aid package met 82% of need; average scholarship/grant was $8,475; average loan was $6,682. For part-time students, average financial aid package was $9,250.

Students without need: 216 full-time freshmen who did not demonstrate need for aid received scholarships/grants; average award was $7,309. No-need awards available for academics, alumni affiliation, art, athletics, leadership, music/drama, religious affiliation, ROTC, state/district residency.

Scholarships offered: 44 full-time freshmen received athletic scholarships; average amount $7,523.

FINANCIAL AID PROCEDURES

Forms required: FAFSA.

Dates and Deadlines: Priority date 4/15; no closing date. Applicants notified on a rolling basis starting 2/15; must reply within 2 week(s) of notification.

Transfers: No deadline.

CONTACT

Jonathan Roberts, Director of Student Financial Services
915 East Market Avenue, Searcy, AR 72149-2255
(501) 279-4257

Henderson State University

Arkadelphia, Arkansas
www.hsu.edu
Federal Code: 001098

4-year public university and liberal arts college in large town.

Enrollment: 3,048 undergrads, 8% part-time. 740 full-time freshmen.

Selectivity: Admits 50 to 75% of applicants.

BASIC COSTS (2016-2017)

Tuition and fees: $8,116; out-of-state residents $14,956.

Per-credit charge: $215; out-of-state residents $443.

Room and board: $6,870.

FINANCIAL AID PICTURE

Students with need: Need-based aid available for full-time and part-time students.

Students without need: No-need awards available for academics, alumni affiliation, art, athletics, job skills, leadership, minority status, music/drama, ROTC, state/district residency.

FINANCIAL AID PROCEDURES

Dates and Deadlines: Priority date 4/15; no closing date. Applicants notified on a rolling basis starting 3/1; must reply within 2 week(s) of notification.

Transfers: No deadline. Applicants notified on a rolling basis starting 3/1; must reply within 2 week(s) of notification.

CONTACT

Vacant at this time
1100 Henderson Street, Arkadelphia, AR 71999-0001
(870) 230-5094

Hendrix College

Conway, Arkansas
www.hendrix.edu   Federal Code: 001099

4-year private liberal arts college in small city, affiliated with the United Methodist Church.
Enrollment: 1,316 undergrads. 350 full-time freshmen.
Selectivity: Admits over 75% of applicants.

BASIC COSTS (2016-2017)

Tuition and fees: $42,440.
Per-credit charge: $1,315.
Room and board: $11,580.

FINANCIAL AID PICTURE (2016-2017)

Students with need: Out of 339 full-time freshmen who applied for aid, 288 were judged to have need. Of these, 288 received aid, and 121 had their full need met. Average financial aid package met 90% of need; average scholarship/grant was $34,350; average loan was $3,331. Need-based aid available for part-time students.
Students without need: 60 full-time freshmen who did not demonstrate need for aid received scholarships/grants; average award was $27,435. No-need awards available for academics, art, leadership, music/drama.

FINANCIAL AID PROCEDURES

Forms required: FAFSA.
Dates and Deadlines: Priority date 3/1; no closing date. Applicants notified on a rolling basis starting 3/1; must reply by 5/1 or within 4 week(s) of notification.
Transfers: Applicants notified on a rolling basis starting 3/1; must reply by 5/1.

CONTACT

Kristina Burford, Director of Financial Aid
1600 Washington Avenue, Conway, AR 72032-3080
(501) 450-1368

John Brown University

Siloam Springs, Arkansas
www.jbu.edu   Federal Code: 001100

4-year private university and liberal arts college in large town, affiliated with the interdenominational tradition.
Enrollment: 1,662 undergrads, 8% part-time. 361 full-time freshmen.
Selectivity: Admits over 75% of applicants.

BASIC COSTS (2016-2017)

Tuition and fees: $25,324.
Per-credit charge: $807.
Room and board: $8,840.
Additional info: Tuition/fee waivers available for adults.

FINANCIAL AID PICTURE (2015-2016)

Students with need: Out of 321 full-time freshmen who applied for aid, 168 were judged to have need. Of these, 168 received aid, and 2 had their full need met. Average financial aid package met 71% of need; average scholarship/grant was $17,775; average loan was $4,750. For part-time students, average financial aid package was $4,416.

Students without need: 189 full-time freshmen who did not demonstrate need for aid received scholarships/grants; average award was $16,142. No-need awards available for academics, alumni affiliation, art, athletics, leadership, music/drama, ROTC.
Scholarships offered: 24 full-time freshmen received athletic scholarships; average amount $12,482.

FINANCIAL AID PROCEDURES

Forms required: FAFSA, state aid form, institutional form.
Dates and Deadlines: Priority date 3/1; no closing date. Applicants notified on a rolling basis starting 3/1; must reply by 5/1.
Transfers: No deadline. Applicants notified on a rolling basis starting 3/1; must reply by 5/1 or within 4 week(s) of notification.

CONTACT

Kim Eldridge, Director of Financial Aid
2000 West University Street, Siloam Springs, AR 72761-2121
(877) 528-4636

Lyon College

Batesville, Arkansas
www.lyon.edu   Federal Code: 001088

4-year private liberal arts college in large town, affiliated with the Presbyterian Church (USA).
Enrollment: 678 undergrads, 1% part-time. 200 full-time freshmen.
Selectivity: Admits 50 to 75% of applicants.

BASIC COSTS (2016-2017)

Tuition and fees: $26,290.
Per-credit charge: $860.
Room and board: $8,440.

FINANCIAL AID PICTURE (2016-2017)

Students with need: Out of 198 full-time freshmen who applied for aid, 168 were judged to have need. Of these, 168 received aid, and 47 had their full need met. Average financial aid package met 69% of need; average scholarship/grant was $16,931; average loan was $2,928. Need-based aid available for part-time students.
Students without need: 32 full-time freshmen who did not demonstrate need for aid received scholarships/grants; average award was $12,680. No-need awards available for academics, alumni affiliation, art, athletics, music/drama, religious affiliation, state/district residency.
Scholarships offered: *Merit:* Brown Scholarship: tuition, room, board, and mandatory fees; based on high school record, standardized test scores; 3 awarded. Anderson Scholarship; tuition and mandatory fees; based on high school record, test scores; 4 awarded. *Athletic:* 29 full-time freshmen received athletic scholarships; average amount $14,980.

FINANCIAL AID PROCEDURES

Forms required: FAFSA, state aid form.
Dates and Deadlines: Applicants notified on a rolling basis starting 12/1; must reply by 8/1.
Transfers: No deadline. Applicants notified on a rolling basis starting 3/1; must reply within 2 week(s) of notification.

CONTACT

Tommy Tucker, Director of Student Financial Assistance
PO Box 2317, Batesville, AR 72501-2317
(870) 307-7257

National Park College

Hot Springs, Arkansas
www.np.edu   Federal Code: 012105

2-year public liberal arts and technical college in large town.
Enrollment: 3,244 undergrads.

Selectivity: Open admission; but selective for some programs.

FINANCIAL AID PICTURE

Students with need: Need-based aid available for full-time and part-time students. Work study available nights, weekends, and for part-time students.
Students without need: No-need awards available for academics, minority status, music/drama, state/district residency.

FINANCIAL AID PROCEDURES

Forms required: FAFSA, institutional form.
Dates and Deadlines: Priority date 7/1; no closing date. Applicants notified on a rolling basis.
Transfers: Transfer applicants must furnish evidence of good standing at previous institution to qualify for financial aid.

CONTACT

101 College Drive, Hot Springs, AR 71913
(501) 760-4235

North Arkansas College

Harrison, Arkansas
www.northark.edu
Federal Code: 012261

2-year public community and technical college in large town.
Enrollment: 2,157 undergrads.
Selectivity: Open admission; but selective for some programs.

BASIC COSTS (2016-2017)

Tuition and fees: $2,610; out-of-district residents $3,330; out-of-state residents $5,460.

FINANCIAL AID PICTURE

Students with need: Need-based aid available for full-time and part-time students. Work study available nights.
Students without need: No-need awards available for academics, athletics, state/district residency.

FINANCIAL AID PROCEDURES

Forms required: FAFSA, institutional form.
Dates and Deadlines: Priority date 5/1; no closing date. Applicants notified on a rolling basis starting 5/1.
Transfers: No deadline. Applicants notified on a rolling basis starting 5/1.

CONTACT

Jennifer Haddock, Director of Financial Aid
1515 Pioneer Drive, Harrison, AR 72601
(870) 391-3266

Northwest Arkansas Community College

Bentonville, Arkansas
www.nwacc.edu
Federal Code: 030633

2-year public community college in small city.
Enrollment: 5,999 undergrads.
Selectivity: Open admission; but selective for some programs.

BASIC COSTS (2016-2017)

Tuition and fees: $3,208; out-of-district residents $4,633; out-of-state residents $4,708.
Per-credit charge: $75; out-of-district residents $123; out-of-state residents $125.

FINANCIAL AID PICTURE

Students with need: Need-based aid available for full-time and part-time students. Work study available nights, weekends, and for part-time students.
Students without need: No-need awards available for academics, leadership, music/drama, state/district residency.

FINANCIAL AID PROCEDURES

Forms required: FAFSA, institutional form.
Dates and Deadlines: Priority date 4/1; no closing date. Applicants notified on a rolling basis starting 4/1; must reply within 2 week(s) of notification.

CONTACT

Michelle Cordell, Director of Financial Aid
One College Drive, Bentonville, AR 72712
(479) 619-4329

Ouachita Baptist University

Arkadelphia, Arkansas
www.obu.edu
Federal Code: 001102

4-year private liberal arts college in large town, affiliated with the Baptist faith.
Enrollment: 1,474 undergrads, 1% part-time. 395 full-time freshmen.
Selectivity: Admits 50 to 75% of applicants.

BASIC COSTS (2017-2018)

Tuition and fees: $25,870.
Per-credit charge: $700.
Room and board: $7,630.

FINANCIAL AID PICTURE (2016-2017)

Students with need: 76% of average financial aid package awarded as scholarships/grants, 24% awarded as loans/jobs. Work study available nights, weekends, and for part-time students.
Students without need: No-need awards available for academics, alumni affiliation, art, athletics, job skills, leadership, minority status, music/drama, religious affiliation, ROTC, state/district residency.

FINANCIAL AID PROCEDURES

Forms required: FAFSA, state aid form.
Dates and Deadlines: Priority date 1/15; closing date 6/1. Applicants notified on a rolling basis starting 11/1.

CONTACT

Susan Hurst, Director of Student Financial Services
OBU Box 3776, Arkadelphia, AR 71998-0001
(870) 245-5570

Ozarka College

Melbourne, Arkansas
www.ozarka.edu
Federal Code: 013217

2-year public community and technical college in rural community.
Enrollment: 1,326 undergrads.
Selectivity: Open admission; but selective for some programs.

BASIC COSTS (2016-2017)

Tuition and fees: $3,445; out-of-state residents $6,385.
Per-credit charge: $88; out-of-state residents $186.

FINANCIAL AID PICTURE

Students with need: Need-based aid available for full-time and part-time students.

FINANCIAL AID PROCEDURES

Forms required: FAFSA.
Dates and Deadlines: Applicants notified on a rolling basis; must reply within 2 week(s) of notification.

CONTACT

Laura Lawrence, Financial Aid Director
218 College Drive, Melbourne, AR 72556-0010
(870) 368-7371 ext. 2010

Philander Smith College

Little Rock, Arkansas
www.philander.edu   Federal Code: 001103

4-year private liberal arts college in small city, affiliated with the United Methodist Church.
Enrollment: 764 undergrads.
Selectivity: Admits less than 50% of applicants.

BASIC COSTS (2016-2017)
Tuition and fees: $12,414.
Per-credit charge: $495.
Room and board: $8,250.

FINANCIAL AID PICTURE
Students with need: Need-based aid available for full-time and part-time students.
Students without need: No-need awards available for academics, athletics, music/drama, religious affiliation.

FINANCIAL AID PROCEDURES
Forms required: FAFSA.
Dates and Deadlines: Priority date 3/1; no closing date. Applicants notified on a rolling basis starting 3/1; must reply within 2 week(s) of notification.
Transfers: Must reply within 2 week(s) of notification.

CONTACT
Kisa Hinton, Director of Financial Aid
900 West Daisy Bates Drive, Little Rock, AR 72202-3718
(501) 370-5350

Phillips Community College of the University of Arkansas

Helena, Arkansas
www.pccua.edu   Federal Code: 001104

2-year public community college in large town.
Enrollment: 683 undergrads, 27% part-time. 114 full-time freshmen.
Selectivity: Open admission; but selective for some programs.

BASIC COSTS (2016-2017)
Tuition and fees: $2,720; out-of-district residents $3,110; out-of-state residents $4,520.
Per-credit charge: $70; out-of-district residents $83; out-of-state residents $130.

FINANCIAL AID PICTURE
Students with need: Need-based aid available for full-time and part-time students. Work study available nights.
Students without need: This college awards aid only to students with need.
Additional info: Tuition waivers given to firefighters and law enforcement officers.

FINANCIAL AID PROCEDURES
Forms required: FAFSA.
Dates and Deadlines: Priority date 4/12; closing date 6/12. Applicants notified on a rolling basis starting 4/12; must reply within 2 week(s) of notification.

CONTACT
Barbra Stevenson, Director of Financial Aid
1000 Campus Drive, Helena, AR 72342
(870) 338-6474 ext. 1160

Pulaski Technical College

North Little Rock, Arkansas
www.pulaskitech.edu   Federal Code: 014167

2-year public community and technical college in small city.
Enrollment: 5,776 undergrads, 52% part-time. 461 full-time freshmen.
Selectivity: Open admission; but selective for some programs.

BASIC COSTS (2016-2017)
Tuition and fees: $5,220; out-of-state residents $6,360.
Per-credit charge: $130; out-of-state residents $168.

FINANCIAL AID PICTURE
Students with need: Need-based aid available for full-time and part-time students.

FINANCIAL AID PROCEDURES
Forms required: FAFSA, institutional form.
Dates and Deadlines: Closing date 5/15. Applicants notified on a rolling basis starting 5/1; must reply within 2 week(s) of notification.

CONTACT
Lavonne Juhl, Director Financial Aid
3000 West Scenic Drive, North Little Rock, AR 72118-3347
(501) 812-2289

Rich Mountain Community College

Mena, Arkansas
www.rmcc.edu   Federal Code: 012435

2-year public community college in small town.
Enrollment: 469 undergrads, 32% part-time. 122 full-time freshmen.
Selectivity: Open admission; but selective for some programs.

BASIC COSTS (2016-2017)
Tuition and fees: $3,210; out-of-district residents $3,630; out-of-state residents $6,900.
Per-credit charge: $77; out-of-district residents $91; out-of-state residents $200.

FINANCIAL AID PICTURE (2015-2016)
Students with need: 99% of average financial aid package awarded as scholarships/grants, 1% awarded as loans/jobs. Need-based aid available for part-time students.
Students without need: No-need awards available for academics.

FINANCIAL AID PROCEDURES
Forms required: FAFSA, institutional form.
Dates and Deadlines: Priority date 7/1; no closing date. Applicants notified on a rolling basis starting 6/1; must reply within 2 week(s) of notification.

CONTACT
Mary Standerfer, Director of Financial Aid
1100 College Drive, Mena, AR 71953
(479) 394-7622 ext. 1420

South Arkansas Community College

El Dorado, Arkansas
www.southark.edu   Federal Code: 013858

2-year public community and junior college in large town.
Enrollment: 1,112 undergrads, 47% part-time. 99 full-time freshmen.
Selectivity: Open admission; but selective for some programs.

BASIC COSTS (2017-2018)
Tuition and fees: $2,748; out-of-district residents $3,138; out-of-state residents $5,418.

Per-credit charge: $83; out-of-district residents $96; out-of-state residents $172.

FINANCIAL AID PICTURE

Students with need: Need-based aid available for full-time and part-time students.

FINANCIAL AID PROCEDURES

Forms required: FAFSA, institutional form.
Dates and Deadlines: Closing date 7/1. Applicants notified on a rolling basis starting 7/1; must reply within 2 week(s) of notification.

CONTACT

Veronda Tatum, Director of Financial Aid
Box 7010, El Dorado, AR 71731-7010
(870) 864-7133

Southeast Arkansas College

Pine Bluff, Arkansas
www.seark.edu   Federal Code: 014893

2-year public community college in small city.
Enrollment: 1,291 undergrads.
Selectivity: Open admission; but selective for some programs.

BASIC COSTS (2016-2017)

Tuition and fees: $3,190; out-of-state residents $5,830.
Per-credit charge: $88; out-of-state residents $176.

FINANCIAL AID PICTURE (2015-2016)

Students with need: 76% of average financial aid package awarded as scholarships/grants, 24% awarded as loans/jobs. Need-based aid available for part-time students. Work study available nights.
Students without need: No-need awards available for academics, leadership, state/district residency.

FINANCIAL AID PROCEDURES

Forms required: FAFSA.
Dates and Deadlines: Priority date 6/1; no closing date. Applicants notified on a rolling basis starting 5/1; must reply within 2 week(s) of notification.
Transfers: Priority date 4/15. Applicants notified on a rolling basis; must reply within 2 week(s) of notification.

CONTACT

Donna Cox, Director of Financial Aid
1900 Hazel Street, Pine Bluff, AR 71603
(870) 543-5909

Southern Arkansas University

Magnolia, Arkansas
www.saumag.edu   Federal Code: 001107

4-year public university in large town.
Enrollment: 3,013 undergrads, 7% part-time. 786 full-time freshmen.
Selectivity: Admits 50 to 75% of applicants.

BASIC COSTS (2016-2017)

Tuition and fees: $8,196; out-of-state residents $11,856.
Per-credit charge: $223; out-of-state residents $345.
Room and board: $5,832.

FINANCIAL AID PICTURE (2015-2016)

Students with need: Out of 756 full-time freshmen who applied for aid, 667 were judged to have need. Of these, 663 received aid, and 225 had their full need met. Average financial aid package met 83% of need; average scholarship/grant was $4,831; average loan was $3,056. For part-time students, average financial aid package was $5,752.

Students without need: 104 full-time freshmen who did not demonstrate need for aid received scholarships/grants; average award was $5,250. No-need awards available for academics, alumni affiliation, art, athletics, leadership, minority status, music/drama, state/district residency.
Scholarships offered: 532 full-time freshmen received athletic scholarships; average amount $4,716.

FINANCIAL AID PROCEDURES

Forms required: FAFSA.
Dates and Deadlines: Priority date 7/1; no closing date. Applicants notified on a rolling basis starting 4/15; must reply within 2 week(s) of notification.

CONTACT

Marcela McRae-Brunson, Director of Financial Aid
Box 9382, Magnolia, AR 71754-9382
(870) 235-4025

Southern Arkansas University Tech

Camden, Arkansas
www.sautech.edu   Federal Code: 007738

2-year public community and technical college in large town.
Enrollment: 715 undergrads.
Selectivity: Open admission; but selective for some programs.

BASIC COSTS (2016-2017)

Tuition and fees: $3,240; out-of-state residents $4,680.
Room only: $2,600.
Additional info: Fees are $900; internet course fee per credit hour: $20.

FINANCIAL AID PICTURE

Students with need: Need-based aid available for full-time and part-time students. Work study available nights, weekends, and for part-time students.
Students without need: No-need awards available for academics, state/district residency.

FINANCIAL AID PROCEDURES

Forms required: FAFSA.
Dates and Deadlines: Priority date 6/1; no closing date. Applicants notified on a rolling basis starting 5/1.
Transfers: Priority date 4/15; closing date 6/1. Applicants notified on a rolling basis starting 5/1.

CONTACT

Jennifer Williams, Director of Financial Aid
PO Box 3499, Camden, AR 71711-1599
(870) 574-4511

University of Arkansas

Fayetteville, Arkansas
www.uark.edu   Federal Code: 001108

4-year public university in small city.
Enrollment: 22,243 undergrads, 11% part-time. 4,938 full-time freshmen.
Selectivity: Admits 50 to 75% of applicants.

BASIC COSTS (2016-2017)

Tuition and fees: $8,820; out-of-state residents $23,168.
Per-credit charge: $240.12; out-of-state residents $718.39.
Room and board: $10,332.

FINANCIAL AID PICTURE (2015-2016)

Students with need: Need-based aid available for full-time and part-time students.
Students without need: No-need awards available for academics, alumni affiliation, art, athletics, leadership, minority status, music/drama, ROTC, state/district residency.

FINANCIAL AID PROCEDURES

Forms required: FAFSA.

Dates and Deadlines: Applicants notified by 4/1.

CONTACT

Wendy Stouffer, Executive Director of Scholarship/Financial Aid

232 Silas H. Hunt Hall, Fayetteville, AR 72701

(479) 575-3806

University of Arkansas at Fort Smith

Fort Smith, Arkansas

www.uafs.edu

Federal Code: 001110

4-year public university in small city.

Enrollment: 5,989 undergrads.

Selectivity: Open admission; but selective for some programs.

BASIC COSTS (2016-2017)

Tuition and fees: $6,701; out-of-state residents $15,011.

Per-credit charge: $160; out-of-state residents $437.

Room and board: $8,242.

FINANCIAL AID PICTURE

Students with need: Need-based aid available for full-time and part-time students. Work study available nights, weekends, and for part-time students.

Students without need: No-need awards available for academics, athletics, job skills, leadership, music/drama.

FINANCIAL AID PROCEDURES

Forms required: FAFSA.

Dates and Deadlines: Priority date 6/15; no closing date. Applicants notified on a rolling basis starting 3/1; must reply within 4 week(s) of notification.

Transfers: No deadline. Applicants notified on a rolling basis starting 3/1; must reply within 4 week(s) of notification.

CONTACT

David Seward, Director of Financial Aid

PO Box 3649, Fort Smith, AR 72913-3649

(479) 788-7090

University of Arkansas at Little Rock

Little Rock, Arkansas

www.ualr.edu

Federal Code: 001161

4-year public university in small city.

Enrollment: 7,573 undergrads.

BASIC COSTS (2016-2017)

Tuition and fees: $8,633; out-of-state residents $20,888.

Per-credit charge: $217; out-of-state residents $625.

Room and board: $8,170.

FINANCIAL AID PICTURE

Students with need: Need-based aid available for full-time and part-time students. Work study available weekends and for part-time students.

Students without need: No-need awards available for academics, art, athletics, leadership, music/drama.

FINANCIAL AID PROCEDURES

Forms required: FAFSA, state aid form.

Dates and Deadlines: Priority date 3/1; no closing date. Applicants notified on a rolling basis starting 5/1.

CONTACT

Carlia Smith, Director of Financial Aid

2801 South University Avenue, Little Rock, AR 72204-1099

(501) 569-3035

University of Arkansas at Monticello

Monticello, Arkansas

www.uamont.edu

Federal Code: 001085

4-year public university and technical college in large town.

Enrollment: 3,733 undergrads.

Selectivity: Open admission; but selective for some programs.

BASIC COSTS (2016-2017)

Tuition and fees: $7,210; out-of-state residents $13,060.

Per-credit charge: $155; out-of-state residents $350.

Room and board: $6,389.

FINANCIAL AID PICTURE

Students with need: Need-based aid available for full-time and part-time students. Work study available nights, weekends, and for part-time students.

Students without need: No-need awards available for academics, athletics, job skills, leadership, music/drama, ROTC, state/district residency.

FINANCIAL AID PROCEDURES

Forms required: FAFSA.

Dates and Deadlines: Priority date 5/1; no closing date. Applicants notified on a rolling basis starting 5/1; must reply within 2 week(s) of notification.

CONTACT

Susan Brewer, Director of Financial Aid

Box 3600, Monticello, AR 71656

(870) 460-1050

University of Arkansas at Pine Bluff

Pine Bluff, Arkansas

www.uapb.edu

Federal Code: 001086

4-year public university in small city.

Enrollment: 2,711 undergrads.

Selectivity: Admits less than 50% of applicants.

BASIC COSTS (2016-2017)

Tuition and fees: $6,676; out-of-state residents $12,706.

Per-credit charge: $157; out-of-state residents $358.

Room and board: $7,418.

Additional info: Tuition/fee waivers available for minority students.

FINANCIAL AID PICTURE

Students with need: Need-based aid available for full-time and part-time students. Work study available weekends and for part-time students.

Students without need: No-need awards available for academics, alumni affiliation, art, athletics, leadership, minority status, music/drama, religious affiliation, ROTC, state/district residency.

FINANCIAL AID PROCEDURES

Forms required: FAFSA.

Dates and Deadlines: Priority date 4/15; no closing date. Applicants notified on a rolling basis starting 3/1.

Transfers: Must supply financial aid transcript from prior college or university.

CONTACT

Janice Kearney, Director, Student Financial Aid

1200 North University Drive, Mail Slot 4981, Pine Bluff, AR 71601-2799

(870) 575-8302

University of Arkansas for Medical Sciences

Little Rock, Arkansas
www.uams.edu   Federal Code: 001109

4-year public university and health science college in large city.
Enrollment: 656 undergrads, 24% part-time.

BASIC COSTS (2016-2017)

Tuition and fees: $9,452; out-of-state residents $19,472.
Per-credit charge: $263; out-of-state residents $597.
Additional info: Tuition shown is for undergraduate College of Health Professions at $245 per hour for resident and $561 for nonresident; College of Nursing UG tuition is $280 per hour for resident and $632 for nonresident. Emergency Medical Sciences/Paramedic students pay $109 per hour. Additional required fees vary by program. Student Housing rates range from $330 to $515 per month depending on housing type and occupancy. Tuition/fee waivers available for minority students.

FINANCIAL AID PICTURE

Students with need: Need-based aid available for full-time and part-time students.
Students without need: No-need awards available for academics, state/district residency.

FINANCIAL AID PROCEDURES

Forms required: FAFSA, institutional form.
Dates and Deadlines: Applicants notified on a rolling basis starting 5/1; must reply within 4 week(s) of notification.
Transfers: Priority date 5/15; no deadline. Applicants notified by 1/15.

CONTACT

Gloria Kemp, Director of Student Financial Services
4301 West Markham Street, Little Rock, AR 72205
(501) 686-6128

University of Arkansas: Community College at Batesville

Batesville, Arkansas
www.uaccb.edu   Federal Code: 014042

2-year public community college in small town.
Enrollment: 1,090 undergrads.
Selectivity: Open admission; but selective for some programs.

BASIC COSTS (2016-2017)

Tuition and fees: $3,000; out-of-district residents $3,375; out-of-state residents $5,100.
Per-credit charge: $70; out-of-district residents $83; out-of-state residents $140.

FINANCIAL AID PICTURE

Students with need: Need-based aid available for full-time students. Work study available nights, weekends, and for part-time students.
Students without need: This college awards aid only to students with need.

FINANCIAL AID PROCEDURES

Forms required: FAFSA.
Dates and Deadlines: Applicants notified on a rolling basis starting 3/1; must reply within 2 week(s) of notification.

CONTACT

Kristen Cross, Director of Financial Aid
Box 3350, Batesville, AR 72503
(870) 612-2036

University of Arkansas: Community College at Hope

Hope, Arkansas
www.uacch.edu   Federal Code: 005732

2-year public community and technical college in small town.
Enrollment: 1,487 undergrads, 52% part-time. 252 full-time freshmen.
Selectivity: Open admission; but selective for some programs.

BASIC COSTS (2016-2017)

Tuition and fees: $2,680; out-of-district residents $2,890; out-of-state residents $5,110.
Per-credit charge: $64; out-of-district residents $71; out-of-state residents $145.

FINANCIAL AID PICTURE

Students with need: Need-based aid available for full-time and part-time students. Work study available nights.
Students without need: No-need awards available for academics.

FINANCIAL AID PROCEDURES

Forms required: FAFSA, institutional form.
Dates and Deadlines: Closing date 7/6. Applicants notified on a rolling basis starting 1/1; must reply within 4 week(s) of notification.
Transfers: No deadline. Applicants notified on a rolling basis.

CONTACT

Becky Wilson, Director of Financial Aid
2500 South Main, Hope, AR 71802-0140
(870) 722-8264

University of Arkansas: Community College at Morrilton

Morrilton, Arkansas
www.uaccm.edu   Federal Code: 005245

2-year public community college in small town.
Enrollment: 1,931 undergrads, 36% part-time. 444 full-time freshmen.
Selectivity: Admits over 75% of applicants.

BASIC COSTS (2016-2017)

Tuition and fees: $3,740; out-of-district residents $3,980; out-of-state residents $4,970.
Per-credit charge: $87; out-of-district residents $95; out-of-state residents $128.

FINANCIAL AID PICTURE

Students with need: Need-based aid available for full-time and part-time students. Work study available nights.
Students without need: No-need awards available for academics, leadership, state/district residency.

FINANCIAL AID PROCEDURES

Forms required: FAFSA, institutional form.
Dates and Deadlines: Priority date 7/1; no closing date.
Transfers: Applicants notified on a rolling basis starting 5/1.

CONTACT

Teresa Cash, Director of Financial Aid
1537 University Boulevard, Morrilton, AR 72110
(501) 977-2055

University of Central Arkansas

Conway, Arkansas
www.uca.edu   Federal Code: 001092

4-year public university in small city.
Enrollment: 9,081 undergrads, 12% part-time. 1,866 full-time freshmen.

Selectivity: Admits over 75% of applicants.

BASIC COSTS (2016-2017)

Tuition and fees: $8,224; out-of-state residents $14,447.

Per-credit charge: $207; out-of-state residents $415.

Room and board: $6,248.

FINANCIAL AID PICTURE

Students with need: Need-based aid available for full-time students. Work study available nights, weekends, and for part-time students.

Students without need: No-need awards available for academics, art, athletics, leadership, minority status, music/drama, ROTC, state/district residency.

Additional info: Room and board may be paid monthly.

FINANCIAL AID PROCEDURES

Forms required: FAFSA.

Dates and Deadlines: Priority date 4/15; closing date 7/1. Applicants notified on a rolling basis starting 5/4.

CONTACT

Cheryl Lyons, Director of Student Financial Aid

201 Donaghey Avenue, Conway, AR 72035

(501) 450-3140

University of the Ozarks

Clarksville, Arkansas

www.ozarks.edu   Federal Code: 001094

4-year private university and liberal arts college in small town, affiliated with the Presbyterian Church (USA).

Enrollment: 640 undergrads.

BASIC COSTS (2016-2017)

Tuition and fees: $23,750.

Room and board: $7,100.

Additional info: Tuition/fee waivers available for minority students.

FINANCIAL AID PICTURE

Students with need: Need-based aid available for full-time and part-time students. Work study available nights, weekends, and for part-time students.

Students without need: No-need awards available for academics, alumni affiliation, art, leadership, minority status, music/drama, religious affiliation, state/district residency.

Additional info: Walton International Scholarship Program provides full scholarships to selected Central American and Mexican residents.

FINANCIAL AID PROCEDURES

Forms required: FAFSA.

Dates and Deadlines: Priority date 2/15; no closing date. Applicants notified on a rolling basis starting 3/1; must reply within 2 week(s) of notification.

CONTACT

Jana Hart, Dean of Admission and Financial Aid

415 North College Avenue, Clarksville, AR 72830-2880

(479) 979-1221

Williams Baptist College

Walnut Ridge, Arkansas

www.wbcoll.edu   Federal Code: 001106

4-year private liberal arts college in small town, affiliated with the Southern Baptist Convention.

Enrollment: 434 undergrads, 3% part-time. 127 full-time freshmen.

Selectivity: Admits 50 to 75% of applicants.

BASIC COSTS (2017-2018)

Tuition and fees: $17,320.

Per-credit charge: $675.

Room and board: $7,850.

FINANCIAL AID PICTURE (2015-2016)

Students with need: Out of 122 full-time freshmen who applied for aid, 88 were judged to have need. Of these, 88 received aid. For part-time students, average financial aid package was $8,944.

Students without need: No-need awards available for academics, art, athletics, leadership, minority status, music/drama, religious affiliation, state/district residency.

Scholarships offered: 89 full-time freshmen received athletic scholarships; average amount $4,891.

Additional info: Art scholarship applicants must submit portfolio.

FINANCIAL AID PROCEDURES

Forms required: FAFSA.

Dates and Deadlines: Priority date 5/1; no closing date. Applicants notified on a rolling basis starting 4/1; must reply within 2 week(s) of notification.

Transfers: Priority date 4/1; no deadline. Applicants notified on a rolling basis starting 4/1; must reply within 2 week(s) of notification.

CONTACT

Barbara Turner, Director of Financial Aid

PO Box 3665, Walnut Ridge, AR 72476

(870) 759-4112

California

Academy of Art University

San Francisco, California

www.academyart.edu   Federal Code: 007531

4-year for-profit university and visual arts college in very large city.

Enrollment: 8,182 undergrads, 41% part-time. 607 full-time freshmen.

Selectivity: Open admission.

BASIC COSTS (2017-2018)

Tuition and fees: $26,490.

Per-credit charge: $873.

Room and board: $15,792.

FINANCIAL AID PICTURE (2015-2016)

Students with need: Out of 315 full-time freshmen who applied for aid, 286 were judged to have need. Of these, 277 received aid, and 8 had their full need met. Average financial aid package met 29% of need; average scholarship/grant was $10,240; average loan was $3,145. For part-time students, average financial aid package was $5,798.

Students without need: 13 full-time freshmen who did not demonstrate need for aid received scholarships/grants; average award was $8,243. No-need awards available for academics, art, athletics.

Scholarships offered: 21 full-time freshmen received athletic scholarships; average amount $18,831.

Additional info: Numerous summer grant programs available.

FINANCIAL AID PROCEDURES

Forms required: FAFSA, institutional form.

Dates and Deadlines: Priority date 3/1; no closing date. Applicants notified on a rolling basis starting 3/15; must reply within 2 week(s) of notification.

Transfers: No deadline. Applicants notified on a rolling basis.

CONTACT

Joe Vollaro, Executive Vice President for Financial Aid/Compliance

79 New Montgomery Street, San Francisco, CA 94105-3410

(415) 618-6273

Allan Hancock College
Santa Maria, California
www.hancockcollege.edu   Federal Code: 001111

2-year public community college in small city.
Enrollment: 8,613 undergrads.
Selectivity: Open admission; but selective for some programs.

BASIC COSTS (2016-2017)
Tuition and fees: $1,418; out-of-state residents $7,358.
Per-credit charge: $46; out-of-state residents $244.

FINANCIAL AID PICTURE
Students with need: Need-based aid available for full-time and part-time students.
Students without need: This college awards aid only to students with need.

FINANCIAL AID PROCEDURES
Forms required: FAFSA.
Dates and Deadlines: Priority date 5/1; no closing date. Applicants notified on a rolling basis starting 6/1.

CONTACT
Robert Parisi, Dean, Student Services
800 South College Drive, Santa Maria, CA 93454-6399
(805) 922-6966 ext. 3200

Alliant International University
San Diego, California
www.alliant.edu   Federal Code: 011117

4-year private university in very large city.
Enrollment: 162 undergrads.
Selectivity: Open admission; but selective for some programs.

BASIC COSTS (2016-2017)
Tuition and fees: $21,340.
Per-credit charge: $700.
Room and board: $8,090.
Additional info: Tuition/fee waivers available for minority students.

FINANCIAL AID PICTURE (2015-2016)
Students with need: 60% of average financial aid package awarded as scholarships/grants, 40% awarded as loans/jobs. Need-based aid available for part-time students. Work study available nights, weekends, and for part-time students.
Students without need: No-need awards available for academics, alumni affiliation, athletics, leadership.
Scholarships offered: Grants and scholarships available based on GPA and SAT/ACT scores.

FINANCIAL AID PROCEDURES
Forms required: FAFSA.
Dates and Deadlines: Priority date 3/2; no closing date. Applicants notified on a rolling basis starting 4/1; must reply within 3 week(s) of notification.
Transfers: Priority date 3/2. Applicants notified on a rolling basis starting 4/1; must reply by 8/1.

CONTACT
Deborah Spindler, Director of Financial Aid
10455 Pomerado Road, San Diego, CA 92131-1799
(858) 635-4559

American Academy of Dramatic Arts: West
Los Angeles, California
www.aada.edu   Federal Code: 014801

2-year private performing arts college in very large city.
Enrollment: 276 undergrads.

BASIC COSTS (2016-2017)
Tuition and fees: $33,190.
Room and board: $12,850.

FINANCIAL AID PICTURE (2016-2017)
Students with need: Average financial aid package for all full-time undergraduates was $19,350. 57% awarded as scholarships/grants, 43% awarded as loans/jobs. Work study available nights, weekends, and for part-time students.
Students without need: This college awards aid only to students with need.
Additional info: The Academy participates in various federal and state financial aid programs and offers a choice of payment plans. The Academy offers a variety of scholarships and assistance opportunities and a choice of payment plans for International Students. The Academy also participates with foreign government aid programs, if available.

FINANCIAL AID PROCEDURES
Forms required: FAFSA, institutional form.
Dates and Deadlines: Priority date 7/1; no closing date. Applicants notified on a rolling basis starting 6/1; must reply within 3 week(s) of notification.
Transfers: Priority date 1/1; no deadline. Applicants notified on a rolling basis.

CONTACT
John Bloch, President
1336 North La Brea Avenue, Los Angeles, CA 90028
(323) 464-2777 ext. 105

American Jewish University
Bel-Air, California
www.college.aju.edu   Federal Code: 002741

4-year private university and liberal arts college in very large city, affiliated with the Jewish faith.
Enrollment: 150 undergrads.

BASIC COSTS (2016-2017)
Tuition and fees: $30,184.
Per-credit charge: $1,208.
Room and board: $15,550.

FINANCIAL AID PICTURE (2016-2017)
Students with need: Need-based aid available for part-time students.
Students without need: No-need awards available for leadership, minority status, music/drama, state/district residency.

FINANCIAL AID PROCEDURES
Forms required: FAFSA, institutional form.
Dates and Deadlines: Priority date 3/2; no closing date. Applicants notified on a rolling basis starting 1/1; must reply by 6/30.
Transfers: Priority date 7/1; no deadline. Applicants notified on a rolling basis; must reply within 3 week(s) of notification.

CONTACT
Larisa Zadoyen, Director of Financial Aid
Office of Undergraduate Admissions, Bel-Air, CA 90077
(310) 476-9777 ext. 222

American River College

Sacramento, California
www.arc.losrios.edu   Federal Code: 001232

2-year public community college in large city.
Enrollment: 23,404 undergrads.
Selectivity: Open admission; but selective for some programs.

BASIC COSTS (2017-2018)
Tuition and fees: $1,518; out-of-state residents $8,846.
Per-credit charge: $46; out-of-state residents $275.
Additional info: Tuition/fee waivers available for minority students.

FINANCIAL AID PICTURE
Students with need: Need-based aid available for full-time and part-time students.
Students without need: This college awards aid only to students with need.

FINANCIAL AID PROCEDURES
Forms required: FAFSA.
Dates and Deadlines: Priority date 3/2; closing date 6/30. Applicants notified on a rolling basis starting 7/1; must reply within 2 week(s) of notification.

CONTACT
Dimitry Proshak, Financial Aid Supervisor
4700 College Oak Drive, Sacramento, CA 95841
(916) 484-8437

Antelope Valley College

Lancaster, California
www.avc.edu   Federal Code: 001113

2-year public liberal arts and technical college in large city.
Enrollment: 10,415 undergrads.
Selectivity: Open admission; but selective for some programs.

BASIC COSTS (2016-2017)
Tuition and fees: $1,420; out-of-state residents $7,750.
Per-credit charge: $46; out-of-state residents $257.

FINANCIAL AID PICTURE (2015-2016)
Students with need: 85% of average financial aid package awarded as scholarships/grants, 15% awarded as loans/jobs. Need-based aid available for part-time students.

FINANCIAL AID PROCEDURES
Forms required: FAFSA, state aid form.
Dates and Deadlines: Applicants notified on a rolling basis starting 7/15; must reply within 2 week(s) of notification.
Transfers: Priority date 3/2; no deadline. Applicants notified on a rolling basis.

CONTACT
Nichelle Williams, Director of Financial Aid
3041 West Avenue K, Lancaster, CA 93536-5426
(661) 722-6337

Antioch University Santa Barbara

Santa Barbara, California
www.antiochsb.edu   Federal Code: 003010

Upper-division private university and liberal arts college in small city.
Enrollment: 117 undergrads.

BASIC COSTS (2016-2017)
Tuition and fees: $22,575.

Per-credit charge: $495.

FINANCIAL AID PICTURE
Students with need: Need-based aid available for full-time and part-time students. Work study available nights, weekends, and for part-time students.

FINANCIAL AID PROCEDURES
Forms required: FAFSA.
Dates and Deadlines: Priority date 4/15; no closing date. Applicants notified on a rolling basis; must reply within 4 week(s) of notification.
Transfers: Priority date 4/1; no deadline.

CONTACT
Heather Nguyen, Assistant Director of Financial Aid
602 Anacapa Street, Santa Barbara, CA 93101
(805) 962-8179 ext. 5108

Art Center College of Design

Pasadena, California
www.artcenter.edu   Federal Code: 001116

4-year private visual arts college in small city.
Enrollment: 1,890 undergrads.

BASIC COSTS (2016-2017)
Tuition and fees: $40,596.
Per-credit charge: $1,669.

FINANCIAL AID PICTURE
Students with need: Need-based aid available for full-time and part-time students.

CONTACT
Victoria Amezcua, Director of Financial Aid
1700 Lida Street, Pasadena, CA 91103
(626) 396-2215

Art Institute of California: Hollywood

North Hollywood, California
www.artinstitutes.edu/hollywood   Federal Code: 031254

4-year for-profit culinary school and visual arts college in very large city.
Enrollment: 1,602 undergrads.

BASIC COSTS (2016-2017)
Additional info: Diploma programs $24,864-$29,960, books and supplies $800-$1,295, room and board $14,920-$18,650. Associate programs $46,620-$48,300, books and supplies $1,400-$2,279, room and board $29,840. Bachelors programs $93,240-$95,445, books and supplies $2,650-$3,629, room and board $55,950.

FINANCIAL AID PICTURE
Students with need: Need-based aid available for full-time and part-time students.

CONTACT
Adis Ceballos, Director of Student Financial Services
5250 Lankershim Boulevard, North Hollywood, CA 91601
(818) 299-5151

Art Institute of California: Los Angeles

Santa Monica, California
www.artinstitutes.edu/losangeles   Federal Code: 007470

2-year for-profit visual arts and career college in large city.
Enrollment: 1,436 undergrads.

BASIC COSTS (2016-2017)

Additional info: Diploma programs $24,864-$29,960, books and supplies $800-$1,366, room and board $15,576-$19,470. Associates programs $46,620-$48,300, books and supplies $1,400-$1,990, room and board $31,152. Bachelors programs $93,240-$95,445, books and supplies $2,750-$3,355, room and board $58,410.

FINANCIAL AID PICTURE (2015-2016)

Students with need: 48% of average financial aid package awarded as scholarships/grants, 52% awarded as loans/jobs. Need-based aid available for part-time students. Work study available nights, weekends, and for part-time students.

Students without need: No-need awards available for academics.

FINANCIAL AID PROCEDURES

Forms required: FAFSA.

Dates and Deadlines: Applicants notified on a rolling basis.

CONTACT

Cynthia Galarza, Director of Student Financial Services
2900 31st Street, Santa Monica, CA 90405-3035
(310) 752-4700

Art Institute of California: Orange County

Santa Ana, California
www.artinstitutes.edu/orangecounty
Federal Code: 007236

3-year for-profit culinary school and visual arts college in very large city.
Enrollment: 1,417 undergrads.

BASIC COSTS (2016-2017)

Additional info: Diploma programs $24,864-$29,960, books and supplies $800-$1,295, room and board $15,588-$19,485. Associates programs $46,620-$48,300, books and supplies $1,400-$1,802, room and board $23,382-31,176. Bachelors programs $93,240-$95,445, books and supplies $2,650-$3,459, room and board $58,455.

FINANCIAL AID PICTURE

Students with need: Need-based aid available for full-time and part-time students. Work study available nights, weekends, and for part-time students.

Students without need: No-need awards available for academics, art, minority status.

FINANCIAL AID PROCEDURES

Forms required: FAFSA, state aid form.

Dates and Deadlines: Applicants notified on a rolling basis; must reply within 2 week(s) of notification.

CONTACT

Silvia Dimas, Director of Student Financial Services
3601 West Sunflower Avenue, Santa Ana, CA 92704-7931
(714) 830-0202

Art Institute of California: San Diego

San Diego, California
www.artinstitutes.edu/sandiego
Federal Code: 016471

3-year for-profit visual arts college in very large city.
Enrollment: 1,634 undergrads.

BASIC COSTS (2016-2017)

Additional info: Diploma programs $24,864-$29,960, books and supplies $800-$1,295, room and board $15,176-$18,970. Associates programs $46,620-$48,300, books and supplies $1,400-$2,279, room and board

$30,352. Bachelors programs $93,240-$95,445, books and supplies $2,650-$3,629, room and board $56,910.

FINANCIAL AID PICTURE

Students with need: Need-based aid available for full-time students.

FINANCIAL AID PROCEDURES

Forms required: FAFSA.

CONTACT

Laverne Arberry-Lamb, Director of Student Financial Services
7650 Mission Valley Road, San Diego, CA 92108-4423

Ashford University

San Diego, California
www.ashford.edu
Federal Code: 001881

4-year for-profit university in very large city.
Enrollment: 35,252 undergrads. 723 full-time freshmen.
Selectivity: Open admission.

BASIC COSTS (2016-2017)

Tuition and fees: $11,032.
Per-credit charge: $443.

FINANCIAL AID PICTURE

Students with need: Need-based aid available for full-time and part-time students. Work study available nights, weekends, and for part-time students.

FINANCIAL AID PROCEDURES

Forms required: FAFSA, institutional form.

Dates and Deadlines: Priority date 3/1; no closing date. Applicants notified on a rolling basis starting 2/15; must reply within 2 week(s) of notification.

CONTACT

Stephanie Stewart, Director, Financial Aid & Policy
8620 Spectrum Center Boulevard, San Diego, CA 92123
(866) 974-5700

Azusa Pacific University

Azusa, California
www.apu.edu
Federal Code: 001117

4-year private university in small city, affiliated with the interdenominational tradition.
Enrollment: 5,762 undergrads, 9% part-time. 1,132 full-time freshmen.
Selectivity: Admits over 75% of applicants.

BASIC COSTS (2016-2017)

Tuition and fees: $36,120.
Per-credit charge: $1,481.
Room and board: $9,492.
Additional info: Tuition/fee waivers available for minority students.

FINANCIAL AID PICTURE (2016-2017)

Students with need: Average financial aid package met 66% of need; average scholarship/grant was $3,501; average loan was $3,592. For part-time students, average financial aid package was $5,645.

Students without need: No-need awards available for academics, athletics, leadership, minority status, music/drama, religious affiliation, ROTC.

FINANCIAL AID PROCEDURES

Forms required: FAFSA, institutional form.

Dates and Deadlines: Priority date 3/2; closing date 7/1. Applicants notified on a rolling basis starting 3/1; must reply within 3 week(s) of notification.

Transfers: Cal Grants not available to first time applicants who are seniors.

CONTACT
Todd Ross, Director of Student Financial Services
901 East Alosta Avenue, Azusa, CA 91702-7000
(626) 812-3009

Barstow Community College
Barstow, California
www.barstow.edu   Federal Code: 001119

2-year public community college in large town.
Enrollment: 2,189 undergrads.
Selectivity: Open admission.

BASIC COSTS (2016-2017)
Tuition and fees: $1,388; out-of-state residents $7,718.
Per-credit charge: $46; out-of-state residents $257.

FINANCIAL AID PICTURE
Students with need: Need-based aid available for full-time and part-time students.
Students without need: This college awards aid only to students with need.

FINANCIAL AID PROCEDURES
Forms required: FAFSA.
Dates and Deadlines: Closing date 6/17. Applicants notified on a rolling basis starting 7/1.

CONTACT
Heather Minehart, Director of Enrollment Services
2700 Barstow Road, Barstow, CA 92311-9984
(760) 252-2411 ext. 7205

Berkeley City College
Berkeley, California
www.berkeleycitycollege.edu   Federal Code: 014311

2-year public community college in small city.
Enrollment: 2,317 undergrads.
Selectivity: Open admission.

BASIC COSTS (2016-2017)
Tuition and fees: $1,432; out-of-state residents $8,332.
Per-credit charge: $46; out-of-state residents $276.
Additional info: Tuition/fee waivers available for adults, minority students, unemployed or children of unemployed.

FINANCIAL AID PICTURE (2015-2016)
Students with need: 84% of average financial aid package awarded as scholarships/grants, 16% awarded as loans/jobs. Need-based aid available for part-time students.
Students without need: This college awards aid only to students with need.

FINANCIAL AID PROCEDURES
Dates and Deadlines: Applicants notified on a rolling basis.

CONTACT
Loan Nguyen, Financial Aid Supervisor
2050 Center Street, Berkeley, CA 94704
(510) 981-2941

Bethesda University of California
Anaheim, California
www.buc.edu   Federal Code: 032663

4-year private university in large city, affiliated with the Christian Church.
Enrollment: 256 undergrads.
Selectivity: GED not accepted.

BASIC COSTS (2016-2017)
Tuition and fees: $7,930.
Per-credit charge: $251.

FINANCIAL AID PICTURE
Students with need: Need-based aid available for full-time and part-time students.
Students without need: This college awards aid only to students with need.

FINANCIAL AID PROCEDURES
Forms required: FAFSA, institutional form.
Dates and Deadlines: Applicants notified on a rolling basis starting 6/30.
Transfers: No deadline.

CONTACT
William Lee, Director of Financial Aid
730 North Euclid Street, Anaheim, CA 92801
(714) 683-1413

Beverly Hills Design Institute
Beverly Hills, California
www.bhdit.edu   Federal Code: 041855

4-year private institute of couture fashion design in very large city.
Enrollment: 25 undergrads.
Selectivity: Open admission; but selective for some programs.

BASIC COSTS (2017-2018)
Tuition and fees: $23,320.
Per-credit charge: $645.
Additional info: Tuition at time of enrollment locked for 4 years.

FINANCIAL AID PICTURE (2015-2016)
Students with need: 33% of average financial aid package awarded as scholarships/grants, 67% awarded as loans/jobs. Need-based aid available for part-time students.
Students without need: This college awards aid only to students with need.

FINANCIAL AID PROCEDURES
Forms required: FAFSA, state aid form.
Dates and Deadlines: Priority date 3/2; no closing date. Applicants notified on a rolling basis starting 3/2.
Transfers: No deadline. Applicants notified on a rolling basis. Maximum college transfer credits cannot exceed 45% of the entire quarter credits hours needed for graduation.

CONTACT
Robert Rice, Director of Financial Aid
8484 Wilshire Boulevard Suite 730, Beverly Hills, CA 90211
(310) 360-8888 ext. 110

Biola University
La Mirada, California
www.biola.edu   Federal Code: 001122

4-year private university and Bible college in large town, affiliated with the interdenominational tradition.

Enrollment: 4,083 undergrads, 3% part-time. 816 full-time freshmen.
Selectivity: Admits 50 to 75% of applicants.

BASIC COSTS (2016-2017)
Tuition and fees: $36,696.
Per-credit charge: $1,529.
Room and board: $9,538.
Additional info: Tuition/fee waivers available for minority students.

FINANCIAL AID PICTURE (2015-2016)
Students with need: Out of 688 full-time freshmen who applied for aid, 582 were judged to have need. Of these, 580 received aid, and 50 had their full need met. Average financial aid package met 55% of need; average scholarship/grant was $16,896; average loan was $3,293. For part-time students, average financial aid package was $10,463.
Students without need: 209 full-time freshmen who did not demonstrate need for aid received scholarships/grants; average award was $8,961. No-need awards available for academics, alumni affiliation, athletics, leadership, music/drama.
Scholarships offered: *Merit:* Scholarships for Underrepresented Groups of Ethnicity: up to $6,500; based on GPA and ethnicity. Community Service Scholarship: $2,700; based on demonstration of outstanding spiritual leadership. Alumni Dependent Scholarship: $500; given to students whose parents completed 30 units of coursework at Biola University. *Athletic:* 19 full-time freshmen received athletic scholarships; average amount $11,965.

FINANCIAL AID PROCEDURES
Forms required: FAFSA.
Dates and Deadlines: Priority date 3/1; no closing date. Applicants notified on a rolling basis starting 1/1.
Transfers: No deadline. Applicants notified on a rolling basis starting 3/1.

CONTACT
Geoff Marsh, Senior Director of Financial Aid
13800 Biola Avenue, La Mirada, CA 90639-0001
(562) 903-4742

Brandman University
Irvine, California
www.brandman.edu   Federal Code: 041618

4-year private virtual university in large city.
Enrollment: 3,382 undergrads, 67% part-time. 28 full-time freshmen.

BASIC COSTS (2016-2017)
Tuition and fees: $15,450.
Additional info: Undergraduate military students who are enrolled in credit hour programs pay a reduced tuition rate of $250 per semester credit hour and are exempt from the technology fee.

FINANCIAL AID PICTURE
Students with need: Need-based aid available for full-time and part-time students.
Students without need: No-need awards available for academics.
Scholarships offered: Disabled Veterans Scholarships.

FINANCIAL AID PROCEDURES
Forms required: FAFSA.
Dates and Deadlines: Applicants notified on a rolling basis starting 5/1.
Transfers: No deadline. Applicants notified on a rolling basis starting 6/1.

CONTACT
Greg Ball, Assistant Vice Chancellor, Financial Aid
16355 Laguna Canyon Road, Irvine, CA 92618

Butte College
Oroville, California
www.butte.edu   Federal Code: 006972

2-year public community college in small city.
Enrollment: 8,072 undergrads.
Selectivity: Open admission; but selective for some programs.

BASIC COSTS (2016-2017)
Tuition and fees: $1,498; out-of-state residents $7,948.
Per-credit charge: $46; out-of-state residents $261.

FINANCIAL AID PICTURE
Students with need: Need-based aid available for full-time and part-time students.
Students without need: This college awards aid only to students with need.

FINANCIAL AID PROCEDURES
Forms required: FAFSA.
Dates and Deadlines: Priority date 5/1; no closing date. Applicants notified on a rolling basis starting 7/9.

CONTACT
Tammera Shinar, Director, Financial Aid & Veteran Services
3536 Butte Campus Drive, Oroville, CA 95965
(530) 895-2311

Cabrillo College
Aptos, California
www.cabrillo.edu   Federal Code: 001124

2-year public community college in large town.
Enrollment: 7,408 undergrads.
Selectivity: Open admission; but selective for some programs.

BASIC COSTS (2016-2017)
Tuition and fees: $1,489; out-of-state residents $7,489.
Per-credit charge: $46; out-of-state residents $246.

FINANCIAL AID PICTURE
Students with need: Need-based aid available for full-time and part-time students.

FINANCIAL AID PROCEDURES
Forms required: FAFSA, institutional form.
Dates and Deadlines: Applicants notified on a rolling basis starting 7/31; must reply within 3 week(s) of notification.
Transfers: Academic transcript required.

CONTACT
Tootie Tzimbal, Director of Financial Aid
6500 Soquel Drive, Aptos, CA 95003
(831) 479-6415

California Baptist University
Riverside, California
www.calbaptist.edu   Federal Code: 001125

4-year private university in large city, affiliated with the Southern Baptist Convention.
Enrollment: 6,904 undergrads, 15% part-time. 1,113 full-time freshmen.
Selectivity: Admits 50 to 75% of applicants.

BASIC COSTS (2017-2018)
Tuition and fees: $32,566.
Per-credit charge: $1,171.

Room and board: $11,540.

FINANCIAL AID PICTURE (2016-2017)

Students with need: Out of 1,034 full-time freshmen who applied for aid, 917 were judged to have need. Of these, 909 received aid, and 196 had their full need met. Average financial aid package met 63% of need; average scholarship/grant was $18,487; average loan was $3,636. For part-time students, average financial aid package was $7,201.

Students without need: 92 full-time freshmen who did not demonstrate need for aid received scholarships/grants; average award was $11,827. No-need awards available for academics, art, athletics, music/drama, religious affiliation, ROTC.

Scholarships offered: *Merit:* Matching room and board scholarship for recipients of the ROTC scholarships. Yellow Ribbon Scholarship for qualified veterans. *Athletic:* 51 full-time freshmen received athletic scholarships; average amount $17,397.

FINANCIAL AID PROCEDURES

Forms required: FAFSA, state aid form.

Dates and Deadlines: Priority date 3/2; no closing date. Applicants notified on a rolling basis starting 3/2; must reply by 6/1.

Transfers: No deadline. Applicants notified on a rolling basis starting 12/15; must reply by 6/1.

CONTACT

Joshua Morey, Director of Financial Aid
8432 Magnolia Avenue, Riverside, CA 92504-3297
(951) 343-4236

California Christian College

Fresno, California
www.calchristiancollege.edu   Federal Code: 014128

4-year private Bible college in large city, affiliated with the Free Will Baptists.

Enrollment: 18 undergrads, 39% part-time. 1 full-time freshmen.

Selectivity: Open admission.

BASIC COSTS (2016-2017)

Tuition and fees: $8,990.

Per-credit charge: $350.

Room only: $4,750.

FINANCIAL AID PICTURE

Students with need: Need-based aid available for full-time and part-time students.

Students without need: This college awards aid only to students with need.

FINANCIAL AID PROCEDURES

Forms required: FAFSA, institutional form.

Dates and Deadlines: Priority date 3/2; no closing date. Applicants notified on a rolling basis starting 5/1.

CONTACT

Melinda Scroggins, Financial Aid Coordinator
5364 East Belmont, Fresno, CA 93727
(559) 251-4215 ext. 1006

California College of the Arts

San Francisco, California
www.cca.edu   Federal Code: 001127

4-year private visual arts college in very large city.

Enrollment: 1,515 undergrads, 5% part-time. 255 full-time freshmen.

Selectivity: Admits over 75% of applicants.

BASIC COSTS (2016-2017)

Tuition and fees: $45,466.

Room only: $9,370.

FINANCIAL AID PICTURE (2016-2017)

Students with need: Out of 131 full-time freshmen who applied for aid, 117 were judged to have need. Of these, 117 received aid, and 9 had their full need met. Average financial aid package met 66% of need; average scholarship/grant was $29,575; average loan was $3,479. For part-time students, average financial aid package was $13,332.

Students without need: 80 full-time freshmen who did not demonstrate need for aid received scholarships/grants; average award was $12,963. No-need awards available for academics, art.

Scholarships offered: Creative Achievement Scholarship: up to $20,000 annually; renewable; based on academic achievement and strength of admissions portfolios.

Additional info: Application deadline for merit scholarships February 1.

FINANCIAL AID PROCEDURES

Forms required: FAFSA, state aid form.

Dates and Deadlines: Priority date 2/1; no closing date. Applicants notified by 4/1.

Transfers: No deadline. Applicants notified on a rolling basis starting 3/1. Scholarships available for community college transfer students.

CONTACT

Dewayne Barnes, Director of Financial Aid
1111 Eighth Street, San Francisco, CA 94107-2247
(415) 703-9528

California College San Diego

San Diego, California
www.cc-sd.edu

4-year private business and health science college in very large city.

Enrollment: 768 undergrads.

Selectivity: Open admission.

BASIC COSTS (2016-2017)

Additional info: 20-month Associate programs: Business Management & Accounting $42,389, Computer Programming $42,273, Computer Technology & Networking $42,408, Medical Specialties $42,411, Respiratory Therapy $49,468. 36-month Bachelor programs: Accounting $74,753, Business Administration $74,620, Computer Science $74,700, Respiratory Therapy $81,719. All fees & books included.

FINANCIAL AID PICTURE

Students with need: Need-based aid available for full-time and part-time students.

FINANCIAL AID PROCEDURES

Forms required: FAFSA, state aid form, institutional form.

CONTACT

Tony Roman, Lean Financial Planner
6602 Convoy Court, Suite 100, San Diego, CA 92111
(619) 680-4430

California Institute of Integral Studies

San Francisco, California
www.ciis.edu   Federal Code: 012154

Upper-division private university in very large city.

Enrollment: 70 undergrads, 14% part-time.

BASIC COSTS (2016-2017)

Tuition and fees: $18,978.

Per-credit charge: $778.

FINANCIAL AID PICTURE

Students with need: Need-based aid available for full-time and part-time students. Work study available nights, weekends, and for part-time students.
Students without need: No-need awards available for academics, alumni affiliation, art, job skills, leadership, minority status, music/drama, ROTC, state/district residency.

FINANCIAL AID PROCEDURES

Dates and Deadlines: Closing date 4/15.
Transfers: No deadline.

CONTACT

Larry Blair, Financial Aid Director
1453 Mission Street, San Francisco, CA 94103
(415) 575-6156

California Institute of Technology

Pasadena, California
www.caltech.edu

Federal Code: 001131
CSS Code: 4034

4-year private university in small city.
Enrollment: 979 undergrads. 235 full-time freshmen.
Selectivity: Admits less than 50% of applicants.

BASIC COSTS (2016-2017)

Tuition and fees: $47,577.
Room and board: $14,100.

FINANCIAL AID PICTURE (2016-2017)

Students with need: Out of 168 full-time freshmen who applied for aid, 122 were judged to have need. Of these, 122 received aid, and 122 had their full need met. Average financial aid package met 100% of need; average scholarship/grant was $44,074; average loan was $2,702.
Students without need: 2 full-time freshmen who did not demonstrate need for aid received scholarships/grants; average award was $5,000.

FINANCIAL AID PROCEDURES

Forms required: FAFSA, CSS PROFILE, state aid form, institutional form.
Dates and Deadlines: Priority date 3/2; no closing date. Applicants notified by 4/15; must reply by 5/1 or within 2 week(s) of notification.
Transfers: Priority date 3/1; no deadline.

CONTACT

Don Crewell, Director of Financial Aid
383 South Hill Avenue, Mail Code 10-90, Pasadena, CA 91125
(626) 395-6280

California Institute of the Arts

Valencia, California
www.calarts.edu

Federal Code: 001132

4-year private visual arts and performing arts college in small city.
Enrollment: 951 undergrads, 2% part-time. 205 full-time freshmen.
Selectivity: Admits less than 50% of applicants.

BASIC COSTS (2016-2017)

Tuition and fees: $45,646.
Room and board: $11,715.

FINANCIAL AID PICTURE (2016-2017)

Students with need: Out of 138 full-time freshmen who applied for aid, 108 were judged to have need. Of these, 108 received aid, and 12 had their full need met. Average financial aid package met 75% of need; average scholarship/grant was $17,500; average loan was $8,500. Need-based aid available for part-time students.

Students without need: 28 full-time freshmen who did not demonstrate need for aid received scholarships/grants; average award was $6,250. No-need awards available for academics, art, minority status, music/drama.

FINANCIAL AID PROCEDURES

Forms required: FAFSA.
Dates and Deadlines: Priority date 2/15; no closing date. Applicants notified on a rolling basis starting 3/1; must reply by 5/1 or within 6 week(s) of notification.
Transfers: Applicants notified by 3/1; must reply by 5/1 or within 6 week(s) of notification.

CONTACT

Robin Bailey-Chen, Director of Financial Aid
24700 McBean Parkway, Valencia, CA 91355
(661) 253-7869

California Lutheran University

Thousand Oaks, California
www.callutheran.edu

Federal Code: 001133

4-year private university and liberal arts college in small city, affiliated with the Evangelical Lutheran Church in America.
Enrollment: 2,887 undergrads, 4% part-time. 638 full-time freshmen.
Selectivity: Admits 50 to 75% of applicants.

BASIC COSTS (2016-2017)

Tuition and fees: $39,760.
Per-credit charge: $1,265.
Room and board: $13,060.

FINANCIAL AID PICTURE (2016-2017)

Students with need: Out of 626 full-time freshmen who applied for aid, 489 were judged to have need. Of these, 489 received aid, and 81 had their full need met. Average financial aid package met 76% of need; average scholarship/grant was $29,971; average loan was $3,612. For part-time students, average financial aid package was $19,003.
Students without need: 149 full-time freshmen who did not demonstrate need for aid received scholarships/grants; average award was $19,445. No-need awards available for academics, alumni affiliation, art, leadership, minority status, music/drama, religious affiliation, state/district residency.
Scholarships offered: Academic Scholarships: range from $3,000 up to $15,000 per year; based on GPA, test scores, and class rank at time of Admission. Presidential Scholarship Program: $17,000 up to full tuition; additional application required. Visual and Performing Arts Scholarships: $1,000-$6,000; application deadline of February 1 and audition with department deadline of February 22.

FINANCIAL AID PROCEDURES

Forms required: FAFSA, state aid form.
Dates and Deadlines: Priority date 3/1; closing date 7/1. Applicants notified on a rolling basis starting 3/15; must reply within 2 week(s) of notification.
Transfers: No deadline. Applicants notified on a rolling basis starting 3/15; must reply within 2 week(s) of notification.

CONTACT

Jerry McKeen, Director of Financial Aid
60 West Olsen Road #1350, Thousand Oaks, CA 91360-2787
(805) 493-3115

California Maritime Academy

Vallejo, California
www.csum.edu

Federal Code: 001134

4-year public university and maritime college in small city.
Enrollment: 1,107 undergrads, 3% part-time. 236 full-time freshmen.

Selectivity: Admits 50 to 75% of applicants.

BASIC COSTS (2016-2017)

Tuition and fees: $6,816; out-of-state residents $17,976.
Room and board: $11,756.

FINANCIAL AID PICTURE (2016-2017)

Students with need: Out of 137 full-time freshmen who applied for aid, 121 were judged to have need. Of these, 121 received aid, and 10 had their full need met. Need-based aid available for part-time students.
Students without need: This college awards aid only to students with need.
Additional info: US Maritime Administration provides annual incentive payment of $3,000 per student, with certain conditions. Tuition waiver for children of deceased or disabled California veterans.

FINANCIAL AID PROCEDURES

Forms required: FAFSA, state aid form.
Dates and Deadlines: Priority date 3/2; no closing date. Applicants notified on a rolling basis starting 4/1.

CONTACT

Priscilla Muha, Director of Financial Aid
200 Maritime Academy Drive, Vallejo, CA 94590
(707) 654-1287

California Miramar University

San Diego, California
www.calmu.edu
Federal Code: 041897

3-year private university and business college in very large city.
Enrollment: 361 undergrads. 14 full-time freshmen.
Selectivity: Open admission.

BASIC COSTS (2016-2017)

Tuition and fees: $9,750.
Per-credit charge: $325.

FINANCIAL AID PICTURE (2015-2016)

Students with need: Out of 14 full-time freshmen who applied for aid, 14 were judged to have need. Of these, 14 received aid, and 7 had their full need met. Average financial aid package met 43.7% of need; average scholarship/grant was $4,199; average loan was $2,768. For part-time students, average financial aid package was $5,948.
Students without need: This college awards aid only to students with need.

FINANCIAL AID PROCEDURES

Forms required: FAFSA, institutional form.
Dates and Deadlines: Applicants notified on a rolling basis; must reply within 4 week(s) of notification.
Transfers: No deadline. Applicants notified on a rolling basis; must reply within 4 week(s) of notification.

CONTACT

Axel Hernandez, Director of Financial Aid
9750 Miramar Road, Suite 180, San Diego, CA 92126
(858) 653-3000 ext. 12

California Polytechnic State University: San Luis Obispo

San Luis Obispo, California
www.calpoly.edu
Federal Code: 001143

4-year public university in large town.
Enrollment: 20,367 undergrads, 4% part-time. 4,928 full-time freshmen.
Selectivity: Admits less than 50% of applicants.

BASIC COSTS (2016-2017)

Tuition and fees: $9,075; out-of-state residents $20,235.
Room and board: $12,507.

FINANCIAL AID PICTURE (2015-2016)

Students with need: Out of 3,866 full-time freshmen who applied for aid, 2,063 were judged to have need. Of these, 1,926 received aid, and 200 had their full need met. Average financial aid package met 56% of need; average scholarship/grant was $3,287; average loan was $3,291. For part-time students, average financial aid package was $6,283.
Students without need: 707 full-time freshmen who did not demonstrate need for aid received scholarships/grants; average award was $2,303. No-need awards available for academics, alumni affiliation, art, athletics, job skills, leadership, music/drama, ROTC, state/district residency.
Scholarships offered: 95 full-time freshmen received athletic scholarships; average amount $3,241.
Additional info: College-administered financial aid is not available for undergraduate international students.

FINANCIAL AID PROCEDURES

Forms required: FAFSA.
Dates and Deadlines: Priority date 3/2; no closing date. Applicants notified on a rolling basis starting 3/15.

CONTACT

Lois Kelly, Director, Financial Aid
Admissions Office, Cal Poly, San Luis Obispo, CA 93407-0031
(805) 756-2927

California State Polytechnic University: Pomona

Pomona, California
www.cpp.edu
Federal Code: 001144

4-year public university in small city.
Enrollment: 23,611 undergrads, 11% part-time. 4,079 full-time freshmen.
Selectivity: Admits 50 to 75% of applicants.

BASIC COSTS (2016-2017)

Tuition and fees: $7,027; out-of-state residents $18,187.
Room and board: $14,514.

FINANCIAL AID PICTURE (2016-2017)

Students with need: Out of 3,458 full-time freshmen who applied for aid, 2,750 were judged to have need. Of these, 2,342 received aid, and 54 had their full need met. Average financial aid package met 56% of need; average scholarship/grant was $9,413; average loan was $3,496. For part-time students, average financial aid package was $7,957.
Students without need: No-need awards available for academics, alumni affiliation, athletics, leadership, state/district residency.
Scholarships offered: 1 full-time freshmen received athletic scholarships; average amount $1,000.

FINANCIAL AID PROCEDURES

Forms required: FAFSA.
Dates and Deadlines: Priority date 3/2; no closing date. Applicants notified on a rolling basis starting 4/1; must reply within 2 week(s) of notification.

CONTACT

Diana Minor, Director of Financial Aid & Scholarships
3801 W Temple Avenue, Pomona, CA 91768-4019
(909) 869-3700

California State University: Bakersfield
Bakersfield, California
www.csub.edu
Federal Code: 007993

4-year public university and liberal arts college in small city.
Enrollment: 8,058 undergrads, 12% part-time. 1,451 full-time freshmen.
Selectivity: Admits over 75% of applicants.

BASIC COSTS (2016-2017)
Tuition and fees: $6,841; out-of-state residents $18,001.
Room and board: $13,968.

FINANCIAL AID PICTURE (2015-2016)
Students with need: Out of 1,372 full-time freshmen who applied for aid, 1,202 were judged to have need. Of these, 1,165 received aid, and 165 had their full need met. Average financial aid package met 15% of need; average scholarship/grant was $3,657; average loan was $1,088. For part-time students, average financial aid package was $3,439.
Students without need: This college awards aid only to students with need.
Scholarships offered: 106 full-time freshmen received athletic scholarships; average amount $1,240.

FINANCIAL AID PROCEDURES
Forms required: FAFSA, state aid form.
Dates and Deadlines: Priority date 3/2; no closing date. Applicants notified on a rolling basis starting 4/1; must reply within 3 week(s) of notification.

CONTACT
Ron Radney, Director of Financial Aid & Scholarships
9001 Stockdale Highway, Bakersfield, CA 93311-1099
(661) 664-2011

California State University: Channel Islands
Camarillo, California
www.csuci.edu
Federal Code: 039803

4-year public university in small city.
Enrollment: 5,625 undergrads.

BASIC COSTS (2016-2017)
Tuition and fees: $6,532; out-of-state residents $17,692.
Room and board: $16,146.

FINANCIAL AID PICTURE
Students with need: Need-based aid available for full-time and part-time students. Work study available nights, weekends, and for part-time students.
Students without need: No-need awards available for academics, leadership, state/district residency.

FINANCIAL AID PROCEDURES
Forms required: FAFSA.
Dates and Deadlines: Priority date 3/2; no closing date. Applicants notified by 4/7.

CONTACT
Sunshine Garcia, Director of Financial Aid
One University Drive, Camarillo, CA 93012
(805) 437-8530

California State University: Chico
Chico, California
www.csuchico.edu
Federal Code: 001146

4-year public university and liberal arts college in small city.
Enrollment: 16,471 undergrads, 10% part-time. 2,313 full-time freshmen.

Selectivity: Admits 50 to 75% of applicants.

BASIC COSTS (2016-2017)
Tuition and fees: $7,044; out-of-state residents $19,776.
Room and board: $12,824.

FINANCIAL AID PICTURE (2015-2016)
Students with need: Out of 2,313 full-time freshmen who applied for aid, 1,871 were judged to have need. Of these, 1,815 received aid, and 274 had their full need met. Average financial aid package met 79% of need; average scholarship/grant was $10,733; average loan was $3,453. For part-time students, average financial aid package was $13,991.
Students without need: 140 full-time freshmen who did not demonstrate need for aid received scholarships/grants; average award was $1,488. No-need awards available for academics, art, athletics, leadership, minority status, music/drama, religious affiliation.
Scholarships offered: *Merit:* President's Scholar Award: 10 awards at $12,000 each; 12 awards at $1,000 each. *Athletic:* 12 full-time freshmen received athletic scholarships; average amount $1,833.

FINANCIAL AID PROCEDURES
Forms required: FAFSA.
Dates and Deadlines: Priority date 3/2; no closing date. Applicants notified on a rolling basis starting 3/2.

CONTACT
Dan Reed, Director of Financial Aid
400 West First Street, Chico, CA 95929-0722
(530) 898-6451

California State University: Dominguez Hills
Carson, California
www.csudh.edu
Federal Code: 001141

4-year public university in small city.
Enrollment: 12,613 undergrads, 26% part-time. 1,255 full-time freshmen.
Selectivity: Admits over 75% of applicants.

BASIC COSTS (2016-2017)
Tuition and fees: $6,418; out-of-state residents $17,578.
Room and board: $12,790.
Additional info: Tuition/fee waivers available for adults.

FINANCIAL AID PICTURE (2015-2016)
Students with need: Out of 1,184 full-time freshmen who applied for aid, 1,107 were judged to have need. Of these, 1,102 received aid, and 17 had their full need met. Average financial aid package met 36% of need; average scholarship/grant was $5,424; average loan was $1,643. For part-time students, average financial aid package was $5,042.
Students without need: 39 full-time freshmen who did not demonstrate need for aid received scholarships/grants; average award was $4,322. No-need awards available for academics, alumni affiliation, art, athletics, leadership, music/drama.
Scholarships offered: 2 full-time freshmen received athletic scholarships; average amount $1,250.

FINANCIAL AID PROCEDURES
Forms required: FAFSA.
Dates and Deadlines: Priority date 3/2; no closing date. Applicants notified on a rolling basis starting 2/28.
Transfers: Applicants notified on a rolling basis starting 4/1; must reply within 3 week(s) of notification.

CONTACT
Delores Lee, Director of Financial Aid
1000 East Victoria Street, Carson, CA 90747
(310) 243-3696

California State University: East Bay

Hayward, California
www.csueastbay.edu   Federal Code: 001138

4-year public university in small city.
Enrollment: 13,289 undergrads, 13% part-time. 1,584 full-time freshmen.
Selectivity: Admits 50 to 75% of applicants.

BASIC COSTS (2016-2017)
Tuition and fees: $6,564; out-of-state residents $17,724.
Room and board: $14,184.

FINANCIAL AID PICTURE (2016-2017)
Students with need: 68% of average financial aid package awarded as scholarships/grants, 32% awarded as loans/jobs. Need-based aid available for part-time students.
Students without need: No-need awards available for academics, athletics, music/drama.

FINANCIAL AID PROCEDURES
Forms required: FAFSA.
Dates and Deadlines: Priority date 3/1; no closing date. Applicants notified on a rolling basis starting 3/30; must reply within 3 week(s) of notification.

CONTACT
Rhonda Johnson, Director of Financial Aid
25800 Carlos Bee Boulevard, Hayward, CA 94542-3095
(510) 885-3018

California State University: Fresno

Fresno, California
www.csufresno.edu   Federal Code: 001147

4-year public university in very large city.
Enrollment: 21,148 undergrads, 14% part-time. 2,468 full-time freshmen.
Selectivity: Admits 50 to 75% of applicants.

BASIC COSTS (2016-2017)
Tuition and fees: $6,311; out-of-state residents $17,471.
Room and board: $9,386.
Additional info: Tuition/fee waivers available for adults, minority students, unemployed or children of unemployed.

FINANCIAL AID PICTURE (2016-2017)
Students with need: Average financial aid package met 69% of need; average scholarship/grant was $10,764; average loan was $3,149. For part-time students, average financial aid package was $7,303.
Students without need: No-need awards available for academics, art, athletics, leadership, music/drama, ROTC, state/district residency.

FINANCIAL AID PROCEDURES
Forms required: FAFSA.
Dates and Deadlines: Priority date 3/2; no closing date. Applicants notified on a rolling basis starting 4/1; must reply within 3 week(s) of notification.
Transfers: No deadline. Applicants notified on a rolling basis starting 4/1; must reply within 3 week(s) of notification.

CONTACT
Denise Tardell, Associate Director of Financial Aid
5150 North Maple Avenue, M/S JA 57, Fresno, CA 93740-8026
(559) 278-2182

California State University: Fullerton

Fullerton, California
www.fullerton.edu   Federal Code: 001137

4-year public university in small city.
Enrollment: 34,416 undergrads, 19% part-time. 4,401 full-time freshmen.
Selectivity: Admits less than 50% of applicants.

BASIC COSTS (2016-2017)
Tuition and fees: $6,436; out-of-state residents $17,596.
Room and board: $15,642.

FINANCIAL AID PICTURE (2015-2016)
Students with need: Out of 3,807 full-time freshmen who applied for aid, 2,966 were judged to have need. Of these, 2,936 received aid, and 2,368 had their full need met. Average financial aid package met 81% of need; average scholarship/grant was $3,615; average loan was $2,640. For part-time students, average financial aid package was $5,578.
Students without need: 55 full-time freshmen who did not demonstrate need for aid received scholarships/grants; average award was $1,287. No-need awards available for academics, art, athletics, leadership, music/drama.
Scholarships offered: 62 full-time freshmen received athletic scholarships; average amount $2,538.
Additional info: Fee waiver for children of veterans killed in action or with service-connected disability whose annual income is $5,000 or less.

FINANCIAL AID PROCEDURES
Forms required: FAFSA.
Dates and Deadlines: Priority date 3/2; closing date 6/6. Applicants notified on a rolling basis; must reply within 4 week(s) of notification.
Transfers: No deadline. Applicants notified on a rolling basis; must reply within 4 week(s) of notification.

CONTACT
Kelly England, Director of Financial Aid
PO Box 6900, Fullerton, CA 92834-6900
(657) 278-3125

California State University: Long Beach

Long Beach, California
www.csulb.edu   Federal Code: 001139

4-year public university in large city.
Enrollment: 32,246 undergrads, 13% part-time. 4,239 full-time freshmen.
Selectivity: Admits less than 50% of applicants.

BASIC COSTS (2016-2017)
Tuition and fees: $6,460; out-of-state residents $17,620.
Room and board: $12,398.

FINANCIAL AID PICTURE (2015-2016)
Students with need: Out of 3,681 full-time freshmen who applied for aid, 2,901 were judged to have need. Of these, 2,800 received aid, and 1,969 had their full need met. Average financial aid package met 82% of need; average scholarship/grant was $7,731; average loan was $3,304. For part-time students, average financial aid package was $10,917.
Students without need: No-need awards available for academics, art, athletics, job skills, leadership, music/drama, state/district residency.
Scholarships offered: Merit: President's Scholar Award: full tuition and fees, campus housing, books. **Athletic:** 64 full-time freshmen received athletic scholarships; average amount $11,865.

FINANCIAL AID PROCEDURES
Forms required: FAFSA.
Dates and Deadlines: Priority date 3/2; no closing date. Applicants notified on a rolling basis starting 3/25; must reply within 3 week(s) of notification.
Transfers: Community college EOP students may be eligible for grant.

CONTACT
Nicolas Valdivia, Director of Financial Aid
1250 Bellflower Boulevard, Long Beach, CA 90840-0106
(562) 985-4641

California State University: Los Angeles

Los Angeles, California
www.calstatela.edu   Federal Code: 001140

4-year public university in very large city.
Enrollment: 24,031 undergrads, 17% part-time. 3,675 full-time freshmen.
Selectivity: Admits 50 to 75% of applicants.

BASIC COSTS (2016-2017)

Tuition and fees: $6,031; out-of-state residents $17,191.
Room and board: $12,860.

FINANCIAL AID PICTURE (2016-2017)

Students with need: Out of 2,207 full-time freshmen who applied for aid, 2,066 were judged to have need. Of these, 2,024 received aid, and 348 had their full need met. Average financial aid package met 65% of need; average scholarship/grant was $8,622; average loan was $3,541. For part-time students, average financial aid package was $9,752.
Students without need: 45 full-time freshmen who did not demonstrate need for aid received scholarships/grants; average award was $2,590.

FINANCIAL AID PROCEDURES

Forms required: FAFSA.
Dates and Deadlines: Priority date 3/3; no closing date. Applicants notified on a rolling basis starting 4/1; must reply within 3 week(s) of notification.

CONTACT

Tamie Nguyen, Director of Center for Student Financial Aid
5151 State University Drive SA101, Los Angeles, CA 90032
(323) 343-6260

California State University: Monterey Bay

Seaside, California
www.csumb.edu   Federal Code: 032603

4-year public liberal arts and teachers college in large town.
Enrollment: 6,923 undergrads, 10% part-time. 799 full-time freshmen.
Selectivity: Admits less than 50% of applicants.

BASIC COSTS (2016-2017)

Tuition and fees: $6,227; out-of-state residents $17,387.
Room and board: $11,930.

FINANCIAL AID PICTURE (2016-2017)

Students with need: Out of 730 full-time freshmen who applied for aid, 640 were judged to have need. Of these, 564 received aid, and 70 had their full need met. Average financial aid package met 65% of need; average scholarship/grant was $10,744; average loan was $3,400. For part-time students, average financial aid package was $7,026.
Students without need: 5 full-time freshmen who did not demonstrate need for aid received scholarships/grants; average award was $700. No-need awards available for athletics.
Scholarships offered: 22 full-time freshmen received athletic scholarships; average amount $3,673.

FINANCIAL AID PROCEDURES

Forms required: FAFSA, state aid form.
Dates and Deadlines: Priority date 3/2; closing date 5/20. Applicants notified by 4/1; must reply by 7/30.

CONTACT

Angeles Fuentes, Director of Financial Aid Services
100 Campus Center, Student Services Building, Seaside, CA 93955-8001
(831) 582-5100

California State University: Northridge

Northridge, California
www.csun.edu   Federal Code: 001153

4-year public university in very large city.
Enrollment: 35,552 undergrads, 19% part-time. 5,517 full-time freshmen.
Selectivity: Admits less than 50% of applicants.

BASIC COSTS (2016-2017)

Tuition and fees: $6,582; out-of-state residents $17,742.
Room and board: $10,272.

FINANCIAL AID PICTURE (2015-2016)

Students with need: Out of 4,920 full-time freshmen who applied for aid, 4,676 were judged to have need. Of these, 4,676 received aid. For part-time students, average financial aid package was $12,419.
Students without need: 670 full-time freshmen who did not demonstrate need for aid received scholarships/grants; average award was $1,466. No-need awards available for academics, athletics, state/district residency.
Scholarships offered: 44 full-time freshmen received athletic scholarships; average amount $12,808.

FINANCIAL AID PROCEDURES

Forms required: FAFSA.
Dates and Deadlines: Priority date 3/2; no closing date. Applicants notified on a rolling basis starting 4/1.

CONTACT

Lili Vidal, Director of Financial Aid
18111 Nordhoff Street, Northridge, CA 91330-8207
(818) 677-4085

California State University: Sacramento

Sacramento, California
www.csus.edu   Federal Code: 001233

4-year public university in very large city.
Enrollment: 27,810 undergrads, 17% part-time. 3,680 full-time freshmen.
Selectivity: Admits 50 to 75% of applicants.

BASIC COSTS (2016-2017)

Tuition and fees: $6,900; out-of-state residents $18,060.
Room and board: $13,916.

FINANCIAL AID PICTURE (2015-2016)

Students with need: Average financial aid package met 62% of need; average scholarship/grant was $8,867; average loan was $3,240. For part-time students, average financial aid package was $7,530.

FINANCIAL AID PROCEDURES

Forms required: FAFSA.
Dates and Deadlines: Priority date 3/2; no closing date. Applicants notified on a rolling basis starting 4/6; must reply within 4 week(s) of notification.

CONTACT

Craig Yamamoto, Financial Aid Director
6000 J Street, Sacramento, CA 95819-6048
(916) 278-6554

California State University: San Bernardino

San Bernardino, California
www.csusb.edu   Federal Code: 001142

4-year public university and liberal arts college in small city.
Enrollment: 18,453 undergrads, 11% part-time. 2,690 full-time freshmen.

Selectivity: Admits 50 to 75% of applicants.

BASIC COSTS (2016-2017)
Tuition and fees: $6,597; out-of-state residents $16,632.
Room and board: $12,966.

FINANCIAL AID PICTURE (2015-2016)
Students with need: Out of 2,553 full-time freshmen who applied for aid, 2,362 were judged to have need. Of these, 2,245 received aid, and 220 had their full need met. Average financial aid package met 62% of need; average scholarship/grant was $10,298; average loan was $3,281. For part-time students, average financial aid package was $6,157.
Students without need: 10 full-time freshmen who did not demonstrate need for aid received scholarships/grants; average award was $3,125.
Scholarships offered: 8 full-time freshmen received athletic scholarships; average amount $3,000.

FINANCIAL AID PROCEDURES
Forms required: FAFSA, state aid form.
Dates and Deadlines: Priority date 3/2; no closing date. Applicants notified on a rolling basis starting 4/1.

CONTACT
Roseanna Ruiz, Director of Financial Aid
5500 University Parkway, San Bernardino, CA 92407-2397
(909) 537-7800

California State University: San Marcos
San Marcos, California
www.csusm.edu   Federal Code: 030113

4-year public university in small city.
Enrollment: 12,470 undergrads, 16% part-time. 2,123 full-time freshmen.
Selectivity: Admits 50 to 75% of applicants.

BASIC COSTS (2016-2017)
Tuition and fees: $7,364; out-of-state residents $18,524.
Room and board: $13,240.

FINANCIAL AID PICTURE (2015-2016)
Students with need: Out of 1,809 full-time freshmen who applied for aid, 1,460 were judged to have need. Of these, 1,394 received aid, and 145 had their full need met. Average financial aid package met 66% of need; average scholarship/grant was $9,343; average loan was $3,246. For part-time students, average financial aid package was $7,175.
Students without need: 1 full-time freshmen who did not demonstrate need for aid received scholarships/grants; average award was $2,250. No-need awards available for academics, athletics, leadership, state/district residency.
Scholarships offered: *Merit:* Fenstermaker scholarships: up to $6,000 a year; awarded to outstanding chemistry, biology, or computer science majors; renewable. *Athletic:* 7 full-time freshmen received athletic scholarships; average amount $4,571.

FINANCIAL AID PROCEDURES
Forms required: FAFSA.
Dates and Deadlines: Priority date 3/2; no closing date. Applicants notified by 4/16; must reply by 3/2 or within 2 week(s) of notification.

CONTACT
Julie Lindenmeier, Director of Financial Aid
333 South Twin Oaks Valley Road, San Marcos, CA 92096-0001
(760) 750-4850

California State University: Stanislaus
Turlock, California
www.csustan.edu   Federal Code: 001157

4-year public business and liberal arts college in small city.
Enrollment: 8,610 undergrads, 16% part-time. 1,330 full-time freshmen.
Selectivity: Admits 50 to 75% of applicants.

BASIC COSTS (2016-2017)
Tuition and fees: $6,728; out-of-state residents $17,888.
Room and board: $10,074.
Additional info: Tuition/fee waivers available for adults.

FINANCIAL AID PICTURE (2016-2017)
Students with need: Need-based aid available for full-time and part-time students. Work study available nights, weekends, and for part-time students.
Students without need: No-need awards available for academics, alumni affiliation, art, athletics, leadership, minority status, music/drama, state/district residency.

FINANCIAL AID PROCEDURES
Forms required: FAFSA, state aid form.
Dates and Deadlines: Priority date 3/2; no closing date. Applicants notified on a rolling basis starting 3/15; must reply within 3 week(s) of notification.
Transfers: No deadline. Applicants notified on a rolling basis starting 3/15; must reply within 3 week(s) of notification.

CONTACT
Noelia Gonzalez, Director of Admissions and Financial Aid
One University Circle, Turlock, CA 95382-0256
(209) 667-3336

California University of Management and Sciences
Anaheim, California
www.calums.edu   Federal Code: 041331

4-year private university and business college in very large city.
Enrollment: 19 undergrads. 8 full-time freshmen.

BASIC COSTS (2016-2017)
Tuition and fees: $9,570.

FINANCIAL AID PICTURE (2015-2016)
Students with need: Average financial aid package for all full-time undergraduates was $20,000.
Students without need: This college awards aid only to students with need.

FINANCIAL AID PROCEDURES
Forms required: FAFSA, institutional form.
Dates and Deadlines: Priority date 5/15; closing date 5/30. Applicants notified on a rolling basis starting 6/15; must reply by 6/30 or within 2 week(s) of notification.
Transfers: No deadline. Applicants notified on a rolling basis starting 6/15; must reply by 6/30 or within 2 week(s) of notification.

CONTACT
Jeffrey Beasca, Chief Compliance Officer
721 North Euclid Streeet, Anaheim, CA 92801-4116
(714) 533-3946

Canada College
Redwood City, California
www.canadacollege.edu   Federal Code: 006973

2-year public community college in small city.
Enrollment: 3,251 undergrads.

Selectivity: Open admission; but selective for some programs.

BASIC COSTS (2016-2017)

Tuition and fees: $1,440; out-of-state residents $8,130.
Per-credit charge: $46; out-of-state residents $265.

FINANCIAL AID PICTURE (2015-2016)

Students with need: 75% of average financial aid package awarded as scholarships/grants, 25% awarded as loans/jobs. Need-based aid available for part-time students.

FINANCIAL AID PROCEDURES

Forms required: FAFSA.
Dates and Deadlines: Priority date 3/2; no closing date. Applicants notified on a rolling basis starting 5/1; must reply within 2 week(s) of notification.

CONTACT

Margie Carrington, Financial Aid Director
4200 Farm Hill Boulevard, Redwood City, CA 94061
(650) 306-3307

Cerro Coso Community College
Ridgecrest, California
www.cerrocoso.edu   Federal Code: 010111

2-year public community college in large town.
Enrollment: 3,675 undergrads.
Selectivity: Open admission.

BASIC COSTS (2016-2017)

Tuition and fees: $1,382; out-of-state residents $8,342.
Per-credit charge: $46; out-of-state residents $278.

FINANCIAL AID PICTURE

Students with need: Need-based aid available for full-time and part-time students. Work study available nights.

FINANCIAL AID PROCEDURES

Forms required: FAFSA.
Dates and Deadlines: Priority date 5/15; no closing date. Applicants notified on a rolling basis starting 6/1; must reply within 2 week(s) of notification.

CONTACT

JoAnn Spiller, Director of Financial Aid and Scholarships
3000 College Heights Boulevard, Ridgecrest, CA 93555-7777
(760) 384-6221

Chabot College
Hayward, California
www.chabotcollege.edu   Federal Code: 001162

2-year public community college in large city.
Enrollment: 9,817 undergrads.
Selectivity: Open admission; but selective for some programs.

BASIC COSTS (2016-2017)

Tuition and fees: $1,414; out-of-state residents $8,704.
Per-credit charge: $46; out-of-state residents $289.

FINANCIAL AID PICTURE

Students with need: Work study available nights, weekends, and for part-time students.
Additional info: Tuition and/or fee waivers for low-income students.

FINANCIAL AID PROCEDURES

Forms required: FAFSA, institutional form.
Dates and Deadlines: Priority date 8/1; no closing date. Applicants notified on a rolling basis.

CONTACT

Kathryn Linzmeyer, Director of Financial Aid
25555 Hesperian Boulevard, Hayward, CA 94545
(510) 723-6746

Chaffey College
Rancho Cucamonga, California
www.chaffey.edu   Federal Code: 001163

2-year public community college in small city.
Enrollment: 16,905 undergrads.
Selectivity: Open admission.

BASIC COSTS (2016-2017)

Tuition and fees: $1,414; out-of-state residents $8,104.
Per-credit charge: $46; out-of-state residents $269.
Additional info: Tuition/fee waivers available for adults.

FINANCIAL AID PICTURE

Students with need: Need-based aid available for full-time and part-time students.
Students without need: No-need awards available for academics.
Additional info: State of California Board of Governors fee waivers to qualified state residents. Criteria for eligibility: households which receive public assistance, meet state's low income guidelines, and demonstrate need as defined by Title IV programs.

FINANCIAL AID PROCEDURES

Forms required: FAFSA.
Dates and Deadlines: Applicants notified on a rolling basis starting 7/15; must reply within 2 week(s) of notification.

CONTACT

Karen Sanders, Financial Aid Supervisor
5885 Haven Avenue, Rancho Cucamonga, CA 91737-3002
(909) 652-6006

Chapman University
Orange, California
www.chapman.edu   Federal Code: 001164

4-year private university and liberal arts college in very large city, affiliated with the Christian Church (Disciples of Christ).
Enrollment: 6,338 undergrads, 3% part-time. 1,419 full-time freshmen.
Selectivity: Admits 50 to 75% of applicants.

BASIC COSTS (2017-2018)

Tuition and fees: $50,594.
Per-credit charge: $1,560.
Room and board: $14,910.

FINANCIAL AID PICTURE (2015-2016)

Students with need: Out of 1,037 full-time freshmen who applied for aid, 832 were judged to have need. Of these, 829 received aid, and 92 had their full need met. Average financial aid package met 72% of need; average scholarship/grant was $16,741; average loan was $3,431. For part-time students, average financial aid package was $13,386.
Students without need: 175 full-time freshmen who did not demonstrate need for aid received scholarships/grants; average award was $17,318. No-need awards available for academics, alumni affiliation, art, music/drama, religious affiliation.

FINANCIAL AID PROCEDURES

Forms required: FAFSA, state aid form.
Dates and Deadlines: Priority date 3/2; no closing date. Applicants notified on a rolling basis starting 3/15; must reply within 3 week(s) of notification.

Transfers: No deadline. Applicants notified on a rolling basis starting 3/15; must reply within 3 week(s) of notification.

CONTACT

Jim Whitaker, Associate Vice Chancellor of Enrollment Management and Chief Financial Aid Officer

Admission Office, Orange, CA 92866

(714) 997-6741

Charles Drew University of Medicine and Science

Los Angeles, California

www.cdrewu.edu   Federal Code: 013653

4-year private university and health science college in very large city.

Enrollment: 88 undergrads, 48% part-time.

Selectivity: Admits less than 50% of applicants.

BASIC COSTS (2016-2017)

Tuition and fees: $16,780.

Per-credit charge: $556.

Additional info: Tuition is based on units taken, and varies by degree level (30 units, BS degree level shown). Fees vary by program.

FINANCIAL AID PICTURE

Students with need: Need-based aid available for full-time and part-time students. Work study available nights, weekends, and for part-time students.

Students without need: No-need awards available for academics, leadership.

FINANCIAL AID PROCEDURES

Forms required: FAFSA.

Dates and Deadlines: Applicants notified on a rolling basis.

Transfers: No deadline. Applicants notified on a rolling basis.

CONTACT

Eulanie Bumagat, Interim Director of Financial Aid

1731 East 120th Street, Los Angeles, CA 90059

(323) 563-4824

Citrus College

Glendora, California

www.citruscollege.edu   Federal Code: 001166

2-year public community college in small city.

Enrollment: 9,875 undergrads.

Selectivity: Open admission.

BASIC COSTS (2016-2017)

Tuition and fees: $1,450; out-of-state residents $8,680.

Per-credit charge: $46; out-of-state residents $287.

FINANCIAL AID PICTURE (2016-2017)

Students with need: 93% of average financial aid package awarded as scholarships/grants, 7% awarded as loans/jobs. Need-based aid available for part-time students. Work study available nights, weekends, and for part-time students.

FINANCIAL AID PROCEDURES

Forms required: FAFSA.

Dates and Deadlines: Closing date 3/1. Applicants notified on a rolling basis; must reply within 2 week(s) of notification.

CONTACT

Carol Thomas, Director of Financial Aid

1000 West Foothill Boulevard, Glendora, CA 91741-1899

(626) 914-8592

City College of San Francisco

San Francisco, California

www.ccsf.edu   Federal Code: 012874

2-year public community college in very large city.

Enrollment: 12,591 undergrads.

Selectivity: Open admission; but selective for some programs.

BASIC COSTS (2016-2017)

Tuition and fees: $1,414; out-of-state residents $8,074.

Per-credit charge: $46; out-of-state residents $268.

Additional info: Tuition/fee waivers available for unemployed or children of unemployed.

FINANCIAL AID PICTURE

Students with need: Work study available nights, weekends, and for part-time students.

Additional info: Board of Governor fee waiver for low income students.

FINANCIAL AID PROCEDURES

Forms required: FAFSA.

Dates and Deadlines: Priority date 3/1; no closing date. Applicants notified on a rolling basis starting 7/1.

CONTACT

Jorge Bell, Dean, Financial Aid

Office of Admissions and Records E-107, San Francisco, CA 94112

(415) 239-3576

Claremont McKenna College

Claremont, California   Federal Code: 001170

www.cmc.edu   CSS Code: 4054

4-year private liberal arts college in large town.

Enrollment: 1,344 undergrads. 321 full-time freshmen.

Selectivity: Admits less than 50% of applicants.

BASIC COSTS (2016-2017)

Tuition and fees: $50,945.

Room and board: $15,740.

FINANCIAL AID PICTURE (2016-2017)

Students with need: Out of 127 full-time freshmen who applied for aid, 118 were judged to have need. Of these, 118 received aid, and 118 had their full need met. Average financial aid package met 100% of need; average scholarship/grant was $44,850; average loan was $3,491. Need-based aid available for part-time students.

Students without need: 14 full-time freshmen who did not demonstrate need for aid received scholarships/grants; average award was $18,590. No-need awards available for academics, leadership, ROTC.

Scholarships offered: McKenna Achievement Award: $10,000 for 4 years; based on strong academic record and outstanding leadership and involvement. Seaver Leadership Scholarship: full tuition for 4 years; awarded to students who demonstrate exceptional promise to become leaders intent on making a positive impact in the world. Interdisciplinary Science Scholarship: full tuition for 4 years; awarded to students who want to major in a science and a non-science and have financial need.

FINANCIAL AID PROCEDURES

Forms required: FAFSA, CSS PROFILE, state aid form.

Dates and Deadlines: Priority date 1/1; closing date 1/1. Applicants notified by 4/1; must reply by 5/1.

Transfers: Closing date 4/1. Applicants notified by 5/15; must reply by 6/1.

CONTACT

Clint Gasaway, Director of Financial Aid

888 Columbia Avenue, Claremont, CA 91711

(909) 621-8356

Coastline Community College
Fountain Valley, California
www.coastline.edu   Federal Code: 013536

2-year public community college in small city.
Enrollment: 8,991 undergrads.
Selectivity: Open admission.

BASIC COSTS (2016-2017)
Tuition and fees: $1,400; out-of-state residents $9,080.
Per-credit charge: $46; out-of-state residents $302.
Additional info: Tuition/fee waivers available for unemployed or children of unemployed.

FINANCIAL AID PICTURE
Students with need: Need-based aid available for full-time and part-time students.
Students without need: This college awards aid only to students with need.
Additional info: Board of Governor's Grant: statewide fee waiver program for students or dependents receiving HFOL/TANF, SSI, General Relief, or whose income meets set standards or who are considered eligible through Federal needs analysis.

FINANCIAL AID PROCEDURES
Forms required: FAFSA, institutional form.
Dates and Deadlines: Priority date 3/2; no closing date. Applicants notified on a rolling basis starting 8/1; must reply within 2 week(s) of notification.

CONTACT
Steve Woodyard, Director of Financial Aid
11460 Warner Avenue, Fountain Valley, CA 92708
(714) 241-6239

Cogswell Polytechnical College
San Jose, California
www.cogswell.edu   Federal Code: 001177

4-year for-profit visual arts and engineering college in small city.
Enrollment: 653 undergrads, 25% part-time. 103 full-time freshmen.
Selectivity: Admits over 75% of applicants.

BASIC COSTS (2016-2017)
Tuition and fees: $19,096.
Room only: $8,500.

FINANCIAL AID PICTURE (2015-2016)
Students with need: 46% of average financial aid package awarded as scholarships/grants, 54% awarded as loans/jobs. Need-based aid available for part-time students.
Students without need: No-need awards available for academics.

FINANCIAL AID PROCEDURES
Forms required: FAFSA.
Dates and Deadlines: Priority date 3/1; no closing date. Applicants notified on a rolling basis starting 4/30; must reply within 4 week(s) of notification.
Transfers: No deadline. Applicants notified by 4/1; must reply within 4 week(s) of notification.

CONTACT
Yariela Perez, Financial Aid Director
191 Baypointe Parkway, San Jose, CA 95134
(800) 264-7955

Coleman University
San Diego, California
www.coleman.edu   Federal Code: 009273

4-year private university and technical college in very large city.
Enrollment: 342 undergrads. 64 full-time freshmen.
Selectivity: Open admission; but selective for some programs.

BASIC COSTS (2016-2017)
Tuition and fees: $20,725.
Per-credit charge: $345.

FINANCIAL AID PICTURE (2015-2016)
Students with need: 99% of average financial aid package awarded as scholarships/grants, 1% awarded as loans/jobs. Need-based aid available for part-time students. Work study available nights.
Students without need: This college awards aid only to students with need.

FINANCIAL AID PROCEDURES
Forms required: FAFSA, institutional form.
Dates and Deadlines: Applicants notified on a rolling basis starting 1/4; must reply within 1 week(s) of notification.
Transfers: No deadline. Applicants notified on a rolling basis starting 1/4; must reply within 1 week(s) of notification.

CONTACT
Axel Hernandez, Director of Financial Aid
8888 Balboa Avenue, San Diego, CA 92123
(858) 499-0202

College of Marin
Kentfield, California
www.marin.edu   Federal Code: 001178

2-year public community college in small town.
Enrollment: 2,780 undergrads.
Selectivity: Open admission; but selective for some programs.

BASIC COSTS (2016-2017)
Tuition and fees: $1,418; out-of-state residents $9,248.
Per-credit charge: $46; out-of-state residents $307.

FINANCIAL AID PICTURE
Students with need: Need-based aid available for full-time and part-time students.
Students without need: This college awards aid only to students with need.

FINANCIAL AID PROCEDURES
Forms required: FAFSA.
Dates and Deadlines: Priority date 3/2; no closing date. Applicants notified on a rolling basis starting 5/15.

CONTACT
David Cook, Director of Financial Aid
835 College Avenue, Kentfield, CA 94904
(415) 457-8811 ext. 7405

College of San Mateo
San Mateo, California
www.collegeofsanmateo.edu   Federal Code: 001181

2-year public community college in small city.
Enrollment: 5,494 undergrads.
Selectivity: Open admission; but selective for some programs.

BASIC COSTS (2016-2017)

Tuition and fees: $1,418; out-of-state residents $8,288.
Per-credit charge: $46; out-of-state residents $275.

FINANCIAL AID PICTURE

Students with need: Need-based aid available for full-time and part-time students.
Students without need: This college awards aid only to students with need.

FINANCIAL AID PROCEDURES

Forms required: FAFSA.
Dates and Deadlines: Applicants notified on a rolling basis starting 6/15.
Transfers: No deadline. Applicants notified on a rolling basis.

CONTACT

Claudia Menjivar, Director of Financial Aid
1700 West Hillsdale Boulevard, San Mateo, CA 94402-3784
(650) 574-6147

College of the Canyons
Santa Clarita, California
www.canyons.edu   Federal Code: 008903

2-year public community college in large city.
Enrollment: 12,258 undergrads.
Selectivity: Open admission; but selective for some programs.

BASIC COSTS (2016-2017)

Tuition and fees: $1,154; out-of-state residents $6,194.
Per-credit charge: $46; out-of-state residents $267.

FINANCIAL AID PICTURE (2016-2017)

Students with need: 83% of average financial aid package awarded as scholarships/grants, 17% awarded as loans/jobs. Need-based aid available for part-time students. Work study available nights, weekends, and for part-time students.
Students without need: No-need awards available for academics, alumni affiliation, art, athletics, job skills, leadership, minority status, music/drama, religious affiliation, ROTC, state/district residency.

FINANCIAL AID PROCEDURES

Forms required: FAFSA, state aid form, institutional form.
Dates and Deadlines: Closing date 3/2. Applicants notified on a rolling basis starting 6/1; must reply within 4 week(s) of notification.
Transfers: No deadline.

CONTACT

Thomas Bilbruck, Director, Financial Aid and Scholarships
26455 Rockwell Canyon Road, Santa Clarita, CA 91355
(661) 362-3242

College of the Desert
Palm Desert, California
www.collegeofthedesert.edu   Federal Code: 001182

2-year public community college in small city.
Enrollment: 7,959 undergrads.
Selectivity: Open admission; but selective for some programs.

BASIC COSTS (2016-2017)

Tuition and fees: $1,420; out-of-state residents $7,600.
Per-credit charge: $46; out-of-state residents $252.
Additional info: Tuition/fee waivers available for adults, minority students, unemployed or children of unemployed.

FINANCIAL AID PICTURE (2015-2016)

Students with need: 99% of average financial aid package awarded as scholarships/grants, 1% awarded as loans/jobs. Need-based aid available for part-time students. Work study available nights, weekends, and for part-time students.
Students without need: No-need awards available for academics, art, minority status, music/drama.

FINANCIAL AID PROCEDURES

Forms required: FAFSA.
Dates and Deadlines: Priority date 3/2; no closing date. Applicants notified on a rolling basis starting 7/1.
Transfers: No deadline. Applicants notified on a rolling basis starting 7/1.

CONTACT

Ken Lira, Director of Financial Aid
43500 Monterey Avenue, Palm Desert, CA 92260
(760) 773-2532

College of the Redwoods
Eureka, California
www.redwoods.edu   Federal Code: 001185

2-year public community college in large town.
Enrollment: 3,684 undergrads.
Selectivity: Open admission; but selective for some programs.

BASIC COSTS (2016-2017)

Tuition and fees: $1,418; out-of-state residents $7,778.
Per-credit charge: $46; out-of-state residents $258.
Room and board: $7,809.

FINANCIAL AID PICTURE

Students with need: Need-based aid available for full-time and part-time students.

FINANCIAL AID PROCEDURES

Forms required: FAFSA, institutional form.
Dates and Deadlines: Priority date 4/15; no closing date. Applicants notified on a rolling basis starting 5/1; must reply within 6 week(s) of notification.

CONTACT

Lynn Thiesen, Director of Financial Aid
7351 Tompkins Hill Road, Eureka, CA 95501-9300
(707) 476-4182

College of the Siskiyous
Weed, California
www.siskiyous.edu   Federal Code: 001187

2-year public community and junior college in small town.
Enrollment: 1,099 undergrads.
Selectivity: Open admission; but selective for some programs.

BASIC COSTS (2016-2017)

Tuition and fees: $1,430; out-of-state residents $7,790.
Per-credit charge: $46; out-of-state residents $258.
Room and board: $8,000.

FINANCIAL AID PICTURE (2015-2016)

Students with need: 63% of average financial aid package awarded as scholarships/grants, 37% awarded as loans/jobs. Need-based aid available for part-time students.
Students without need: This college awards aid only to students with need.

FINANCIAL AID PROCEDURES

Forms required: FAFSA.

Dates and Deadlines: Priority date 5/31; no closing date. Applicants notified by 4/1.
Transfers: No deadline. Applicants notified on a rolling basis.

CONTACT
Janette Harris, Director of Financial Aid
800 College Avenue, Weed, CA 96094-2899
(530) 938-5500

Columbia College
Sonora, California
www.gocolumbia.edu   Federal Code: 007707

2-year public community college in small town.
Enrollment: 1,639 undergrads.
Selectivity: Open admission.

BASIC COSTS (2016-2017)
Tuition and fees: $1,418; out-of-state residents $8,288.
Per-credit charge: $46; out-of-state residents $275.

FINANCIAL AID PICTURE
Students with need: Need-based aid available for full-time and part-time students.
Students without need: No-need awards available for academics.

FINANCIAL AID PROCEDURES
Forms required: FAFSA, state aid form, institutional form.
Dates and Deadlines: Priority date 3/2; closing date 6/1. Applicants notified on a rolling basis starting 6/15; must reply within 2 week(s) of notification.

CONTACT
Marnie Shively, Director of Student Financial Services
11600 Columbia College Drive, Sonora, CA 95370
(209) 588-5105

Columbia College Hollywood
Tarzana, California
www.columbiacollege.edu

4-year private visual arts college in very large city.
Enrollment: 367 undergrads.
Selectivity: Open admission; but selective for some programs.

BASIC COSTS (2016-2017)
Tuition and fees: $21,789.
Room and board: $12,492.

FINANCIAL AID PICTURE
Students with need: Need-based aid available for full-time and part-time students. Work study available nights, weekends, and for part-time students.
Students without need: This college awards aid only to students with need.

FINANCIAL AID PROCEDURES
Forms required: FAFSA, state aid form.
Dates and Deadlines: Priority date 3/2; closing date 5/30. Applicants notified on a rolling basis starting 3/30; must reply within 2 week(s) of notification.
Transfers: No deadline. Applicants notified on a rolling basis starting 3/30; must reply within 2 week(s) of notification.

CONTACT
Maricela Guzman, Associate Manager Financial Aid
18618 Oxnard Street, Tarzana, CA 91356
(818) 345-8414 ext. 110

Concordia University Irvine
Irvine, California
www.cui.edu   Federal Code: 013885

4-year private university and liberal arts college in small city, affiliated with the Lutheran Church - Missouri Synod.
Enrollment: 1,895 undergrads, 6% part-time. 406 full-time freshmen.
Selectivity: Admits 50 to 75% of applicants.

BASIC COSTS (2017-2018)
Tuition and fees: $34,100.
Per-credit charge: $995.
Room and board: $10,760.
Additional info: Tuition/fee waivers available for adults.

FINANCIAL AID PICTURE (2016-2017)
Students with need: Out of 363 full-time freshmen who applied for aid, 294 were judged to have need. Of these, 294 received aid, and 61 had their full need met. Average financial aid package met 74% of need; average scholarship/grant was $21,888; average loan was $3,457. For part-time students, average financial aid package was $6,335.
Students without need: 74 full-time freshmen who did not demonstrate need for aid received scholarships/grants; average award was $13,869. No-need awards available for academics, alumni affiliation, athletics, music/drama, religious affiliation.
Scholarships offered: *Merit:* Presidential Honors (full tuition; 3.9 GPA; 1360 SAT; 29 ACT), Honors ($20,000; 3.7 GPA; 1270 SAT; 27 ACT, Regents ($15,000; 3.7 GPA; 1270 SAT; 27 ACT), Provost ($12,000; 3.5 GPA; 1130 SAT; 23 ACT), Dean ($9,000; 3.3 GPA; 1080 SAT; 21 ACT), Trustee ($7,000; 3.0 GPA; 1080 SAT; 21 ACT). *Athletic:* 33 full-time freshmen received athletic scholarships.

FINANCIAL AID PROCEDURES
Forms required: FAFSA, state aid form.
Dates and Deadlines: Priority date 3/2; closing date 3/2. Applicants notified on a rolling basis starting 1/15; must reply within 4 week(s) of notification.
Transfers: Priority date 3/2; closing date 3/2. Applicants notified on a rolling basis starting 3/15; must reply within 4 week(s) of notification.

CONTACT
Lori McDonald, Director of Financial Aid
1530 Concordia West, Irvine, CA 92612-3203
(949) 214-3066

Copper Mountain College
Joshua Tree, California
www.cmccd.edu   Federal Code: 035424

2-year public community college in small town.
Enrollment: 1,178 undergrads.
Selectivity: Open admission; but selective for some programs.

BASIC COSTS (2016-2017)
Tuition and fees: $1,380; out-of-state residents $10,830.
Per-credit charge: $46; out-of-state residents $361.

FINANCIAL AID PICTURE
Students with need: Need-based aid available for full-time and part-time students.

FINANCIAL AID PROCEDURES
Forms required: FAFSA.
Dates and Deadlines: Priority date 3/2; no closing date.

CONTACT
Brian Heinemann, Director of Financial Aid
6162 Rotary Way, Joshua Tree, CA 92252
(866) 366-3791 ext. 4235

Crafton Hills College
Yucaipa, California
www.craftonhills.edu   Federal Code: 009272

2-year public community college in small city.
Enrollment: 3,225 undergrads.
Selectivity: Open admission.

BASIC COSTS (2016-2017)
Tuition and fees: $1,425; out-of-state residents $7,755.
Per-credit charge: $46; out-of-state residents $257.
Additional info: Tuition/fee waivers available for adults, minority students, unemployed or children of unemployed.

FINANCIAL AID PICTURE (2015-2016)
Students with need: 98% of average financial aid package awarded as scholarships/grants, 2% awarded as loans/jobs. Need-based aid available for part-time students. Work study available nights.
Students without need: This college awards aid only to students with need.

FINANCIAL AID PROCEDURES
Forms required: FAFSA, institutional form.
Dates and Deadlines: Priority date 4/15; closing date 6/2. Applicants notified on a rolling basis starting 7/31; must reply within 2 week(s) of notification.
Transfers: Priority date 1/2; closing date 3/2.

CONTACT
John Muskavitch, Director of Financial Aid
11711 Sand Canyon Road, Yucaipa, CA 92399-1799
(909) 794-2161 ext. 3242

Cuyamaca College
El Cajon, California
www.cuyamaca.edu   Federal Code: 014435

2-year public community college in small city.
Enrollment: 6,753 undergrads.
Selectivity: Open admission.

BASIC COSTS (2016-2017)
Tuition and fees: $1,428; out-of-state residents $7,848.
Per-credit charge: $46; out-of-state residents $260.

FINANCIAL AID PICTURE
Students with need: Work study available nights, weekends, and for part-time students.

FINANCIAL AID PROCEDURES
Forms required: FAFSA.
Dates and Deadlines: Priority date 3/2; no closing date. Applicants notified on a rolling basis; must reply within 2 week(s) of notification.

CONTACT
Ray Reyes, Financial Aid Director
900 Rancho San Diego Parkway, El Cajon, CA 92019-4304
(619) 660-4201

Cypress College
Cypress, California
www.cypresscollege.edu   Federal Code: 001193

2-year public community college in small city.
Enrollment: 11,828 undergrads.
Selectivity: Open admission.

BASIC COSTS (2016-2017)
Tuition and fees: $1,414; out-of-state residents $8,104.
Per-credit charge: $46; out-of-state residents $269.

FINANCIAL AID PICTURE
Students with need: Need-based aid available for full-time and part-time students.

FINANCIAL AID PROCEDURES
Forms required: FAFSA.

CONTACT
Chinh Pham, Director of Financial Aid
9200 Valley View Street, Cypress, CA 90630
(714) 484-7114

De Anza College
Cupertino, California
www.deanza.edu   Federal Code: 004480

2-year public community college in large town.
Enrollment: 17,926 undergrads.
Selectivity: Open admission; but selective for some programs.

BASIC COSTS (2016-2017)
Tuition and fees: $1,515; out-of-state residents $8,400.
Per-credit charge: $31; out-of-state residents $156.

FINANCIAL AID PICTURE
Students with need: Need-based aid available for full-time and part-time students.
Students without need: This college awards aid only to students with need.

FINANCIAL AID PROCEDURES
Forms required: FAFSA.
Dates and Deadlines: Applicants notified on a rolling basis starting 5/15; must reply within 2 week(s) of notification.

CONTACT
Lisa Mandy, Director of Financial Aid
21250 Stevens Creek Boulevard, Cupertino, CA 95014
(408) 864-8718

Deep Springs College
Dyer, Nevada
www.deepsprings.edu   Federal Code: 015483

2-year private liberal arts college for men in rural community.
Enrollment: 26 undergrads. 15 full-time freshmen.

BASIC COSTS (2016-2017)
Tuition and fees: $850.

FINANCIAL AID PICTURE
Students with need: Need-based aid available for full-time students.
Students without need: No-need awards available for academics, job skills, leadership.
Additional info: Every admitted student is awarded a scholarship for the full cost of tuition and room and board. For students in need, additional funds are available for books, travel, and incidental expenses.

FINANCIAL AID PROCEDURES
Forms required: institutional form.
Dates and Deadlines: Applicants notified by 4/15.
Transfers: Transfer students are also eligible for admission and, like all other students, receive a full scholarship for tuition and room and board.

CONTACT
David Neidorf, President
Applications Committee, Dyer, NV 89010-9803
(760) 872-2000 ext. 45

Design Institute of San Diego
San Diego, California
www.disd.edu   Federal Code: 016233

4-year for-profit career college in very large city.
Enrollment: 143 undergrads, 38% part-time. 4 full-time freshmen.

BASIC COSTS (2016-2017)
Tuition and fees: $21,460.

FINANCIAL AID PICTURE (2015-2016)
Students with need: 31% of average financial aid package awarded as scholarships/grants, 69% awarded as loans/jobs. Need-based aid available for part-time students. Work study available nights, weekends, and for part-time students.
Scholarships offered: Building the Legacy Scholarship offered.
Additional info: Financial aid is available for those who qualify. A free Preliminary Financial Aid Profile will be done for anyone who has applied to the college. This profile is an estimate of financial aid eligibility for grants and loans.

FINANCIAL AID PROCEDURES
Forms required: FAFSA.
Dates and Deadlines: Applicants notified on a rolling basis.
Transfers: No deadline. Applicants notified on a rolling basis.

CONTACT
Jackie Gloria, Financial Aid Direcotr
8555 Commerce Avenue, San Diego, CA 92121
(858) 566-1200 ext. 1023

DeVry University: Pomona
Pomona, California
www.devry.edu   Federal Code: 023329

4-year for-profit university in small city.
Enrollment: 1,501 undergrads.

BASIC COSTS (2016-2017)
Tuition and fees: $17,512.
Per-credit charge: $609.

FINANCIAL AID PICTURE
Students with need: Need-based aid available for full-time and part-time students.
Students without need: This college awards aid only to students with need.

FINANCIAL AID PROCEDURES
Forms required: FAFSA.
Dates and Deadlines: Applicants notified on a rolling basis.

CONTACT
901 Corporate Center Drive, Pomona, CA 91768-2642

Diablo Valley College
Pleasant Hill, California
www.dvc.edu   Federal Code: 001191

2-year public community college in large town.
Enrollment: 9,161 undergrads.

Selectivity: Open admission.

BASIC COSTS (2016-2017)
Tuition and fees: $1,390; out-of-state residents $8,500.
Per-credit charge: $46; out-of-state residents $283.

FINANCIAL AID PICTURE
Students with need: Need-based aid available for full-time and part-time students.

FINANCIAL AID PROCEDURES
Forms required: FAFSA, state aid form, institutional form.
Dates and Deadlines: Priority date 3/2; closing date 5/1. Applicants notified on a rolling basis starting 6/1; must reply within 2 week(s) of notification.

CONTACT
Emily Stone, Dean, CalWORKS, EOPS/CARE, Financial Aid and Scholarship
321 Golf Club Road, Pleasant Hill, CA 94523-1529
(925) 696-2009

Dominican University of California
San Rafael, California
www.dominican.edu   Federal Code: 001196

4-year private university in small city.
Enrollment: 1,374 undergrads, 11% part-time. 255 full-time freshmen.
Selectivity: Admits over 75% of applicants.

BASIC COSTS (2016-2017)
Tuition and fees: $43,400.
Per-credit charge: $1,795.
Room and board: $14,220.

FINANCIAL AID PICTURE (2015-2016)
Students with need: Out of 228 full-time freshmen who applied for aid, 208 were judged to have need. Of these, 208 received aid, and 29 had their full need met. Average financial aid package met 70% of need; average scholarship/grant was $26,579; average loan was $3,349. For part-time students, average financial aid package was $10,122.
Students without need: 40 full-time freshmen who did not demonstrate need for aid received scholarships/grants; average award was $18,377. No-need awards available for academics, alumni affiliation, athletics, leadership, minority status, music/drama.
Scholarships offered: 2 full-time freshmen received athletic scholarships; average amount $4,500.
Additional info: 4-year guarantee program.

FINANCIAL AID PROCEDURES
Forms required: FAFSA, institutional form.
Dates and Deadlines: Priority date 3/1; no closing date. Applicants notified on a rolling basis starting 3/15; must reply within 2 week(s) of notification.
Transfers: Must reply within 2 week(s) of notification.

CONTACT
Shanon Little, Director of Financial Aid
50 Acacia Avenue, San Rafael, CA 94901-2298
(415) 257-1350

East Los Angeles College
Monterey Park, California
www.elac.edu   Federal Code: 001222

2-year public community college in very large city.
Enrollment: 19,622 undergrads.
Selectivity: Open admission; but selective for some programs.

BASIC COSTS (2016-2017)
Tuition and fees: $1,404; out-of-state residents $8,064.

PART III: FINANCIAL AID COLLEGE BY COLLEGE

Per-credit charge: $46; out-of-state residents $268.
Additional info: Tuition/fee waivers available for unemployed or children of unemployed.

FINANCIAL AID PICTURE

Students with need: Need-based aid available for full-time and part-time students. Work study available nights, weekends, and for part-time students.
Students without need: This college awards aid only to students with need.
Additional info: Need-based enrollment fee waivers available through a state aid program.

FINANCIAL AID PROCEDURES

Forms required: FAFSA, institutional form.
Dates and Deadlines: Priority date 4/30; no closing date. Applicants notified on a rolling basis; must reply within 4 week(s) of notification.
Transfers: No deadline.

CONTACT

Lindy Fong, Financial Aid Manager
1301 Avenida Cesar Chavez, Monterey Park, CA 91754-6099
(323) 265-8738

El Camino College
Torrance, California
www.elcamino.edu
Federal Code: 001197

2-year public community and junior college in very large city.
Enrollment: 15,407 undergrads.
Selectivity: Open admission; but selective for some programs.

BASIC COSTS (2016-2017)

Tuition and fees: $1,419; out-of-state residents $8,679.
Per-credit charge: $46; out-of-state residents $288.
Additional info: Tuition/fee waivers available for adults.

FINANCIAL AID PICTURE

Students with need: Need-based aid available for full-time and part-time students.
Students without need: No-need awards available for academics, art, athletics, leadership, music/drama.
Additional info: Students may apply for Pell grants until June 30.

FINANCIAL AID PROCEDURES

Forms required: FAFSA, institutional form.
Dates and Deadlines: Priority date 3/2; closing date 6/30. Applicants notified on a rolling basis starting 7/15.
Transfers: Outside scholarships must be reported to financial aid office.

CONTACT

Melissa Guess, Director of Financial Aid
16007 Crenshaw Boulevard, Torrance, CA 90506
(310) 660-3593 ext. 3490

Empire College
Santa Rosa, California
www.empcol.edu
Federal Code: 009032

2-year for-profit business college in large city.
Enrollment: 377 undergrads.
Selectivity: Open admission; but selective for some programs.

FINANCIAL AID PICTURE (2015-2016)

Students with need: Average financial aid package for all full-time undergraduates was $11,415. 36% awarded as scholarships/grants, 64% awarded as loans/jobs. Need-based aid available for part-time students.

Students without need: No-need awards available for academics, leadership.
Scholarships offered: Dean's Scholarship for high school seniors: 10 awarded; $250-$1,500. Dean's Scholarships for Empire College students: 7 awarded; $250-$1,000. Based on academic achievement, letter of intent, extracurricular activities and letter of recommendation.

FINANCIAL AID PROCEDURES

Forms required: FAFSA.
Dates and Deadlines: Applicants notified on a rolling basis.

CONTACT

Mary O'Brien, Financial Aid Officer
3035 Cleveland Avenue, Santa Rosa, CA 95403-2100
(707) 546-4000

Fashion Institute of Design and Merchandising: Los Angeles
Los Angeles, California
www.fidm.edu
Federal Code: 011112

4-year for-profit visual arts and business college in very large city.
Enrollment: 2,624 undergrads, 10% part-time. 392 full-time freshmen.
Selectivity: Admits less than 50% of applicants.

BASIC COSTS (2016-2017)

Tuition and fees: $32,790.
Per-credit charge: $355.

FINANCIAL AID PICTURE (2015-2016)

Students with need: 40% of average financial aid package awarded as scholarships/grants, 60% awarded as loans/jobs.
Students without need: No-need awards available for academics.
Additional info: Tuition/fee expenses may be reduced by applying for admission by December 31 of year before student plans to attend.

FINANCIAL AID PROCEDURES

Forms required: FAFSA, institutional form.
Dates and Deadlines: Priority date 3/1; no closing date. Applicants notified on a rolling basis starting 3/15; must reply within 3 week(s) of notification.

CONTACT

Chris Jennings, Director of Student Financial Aid
919 South Grand Avenue, Los Angeles, CA 90015-1421
(213) 624-1200 ext. 4210

Fashion Institute of Design and Merchandising: San Diego
San Diego, California
www.fidm.edu
Federal Code: 011112

2-year for-profit visual arts and business college in very large city.
Enrollment: 75 undergrads, 8% part-time. 32 full-time freshmen.
Selectivity: Admits less than 50% of applicants.

BASIC COSTS (2016-2017)

Tuition and fees: $32,790.
Per-credit charge: $355.

FINANCIAL AID PICTURE (2015-2016)

Students with need: 47% of average financial aid package awarded as scholarships/grants, 53% awarded as loans/jobs.
Students without need: No-need awards available for academics.
Additional info: Tuition/fee expenses may be reduced by applying for admission by December 31 of year before student plans to attend.

FINANCIAL AID PROCEDURES

Forms required: FAFSA, institutional form.

Dates and Deadlines: Applicants notified on a rolling basis starting 3/15; must reply within 3 week(s) of notification.

CONTACT

Chris Jennings, Director of Student Financial Aid

350 Tenth Avenue, Third Floor, San Diego, CA 92101-7496

(619) 235-2049 ext. 1845

Fashion Institute of Design and Merchandising: San Francisco

San Francisco, California

www.fidm.edu   Federal Code: 011112

2-year for-profit visual arts and business college in very large city.

Enrollment: 332 undergrads, 14% part-time. 51 full-time freshmen.

Selectivity: Admits less than 50% of applicants.

BASIC COSTS (2016-2017)

Tuition and fees: $32,790.

Per-credit charge: $355.

FINANCIAL AID PICTURE (2015-2016)

Students with need: 44% of average financial aid package awarded as scholarships/grants, 56% awarded as loans/jobs.

Students without need: No-need awards available for academics.

Additional info: Tuition/fee expenses may be reduced by applying for admission by December 31 of year before student plans to attend.

FINANCIAL AID PROCEDURES

Forms required: FAFSA, institutional form.

Dates and Deadlines: Priority date 3/1; no closing date. Applicants notified on a rolling basis starting 3/15; must reply within 3 week(s) of notification.

CONTACT

Chris Jennings, Director of Student Financial Aid

55 Stockton Street, San Francisco, CA 94108-5805

(415) 675-5200 ext. 1545

Feather River College

Quincy, California

www.frc.edu   Federal Code: 008597

2-year public community and liberal arts college in small town.

Enrollment: 968 undergrads.

Selectivity: Open admission; but selective for some programs.

BASIC COSTS (2016-2017)

Tuition and fees: $1,461; out-of-state residents $7,821.

Per-credit charge: $46; out-of-state residents $258.

Room only: $5,350.

Additional info: Tuition/fee waivers available for adults, unemployed or children of unemployed.

FINANCIAL AID PICTURE (2015-2016)

Students with need: 70% of average financial aid package awarded as scholarships/grants, 30% awarded as loans/jobs. Need-based aid available for part-time students. Work study available nights, weekends, and for part-time students.

Students without need: This college awards aid only to students with need.

FINANCIAL AID PROCEDURES

Forms required: FAFSA.

Dates and Deadlines: Priority date 3/2; no closing date. Applicants notified on a rolling basis starting 4/1; must reply within 3 week(s) of notification.

CONTACT

Andre Vandervelden, Financial Aid Director

570 Golden Eagle Avenue, Quincy, CA 95971

(530) 283-0202 ext. 283

Foothill College

Los Altos Hills, California

www.foothill.edu   Federal Code: 001199

2-year public community college in large town.

Enrollment: 9,865 undergrads.

Selectivity: Open admission; but selective for some programs.

BASIC COSTS (2016-2017)

Tuition and fees: $1,499; out-of-state residents $8,519.

Per-credit charge: $31; out-of-state residents $187.

FINANCIAL AID PICTURE

Students with need: Need-based aid available for full-time and part-time students. Work study available nights, weekends, and for part-time students.

Scholarships offered: Chancellor's Scholarship: for first-time freshmen who graduate with a 3.5 GPA from Santa Clara or San Mateo County as Chancellor's Scholar; $2,000.

FINANCIAL AID PROCEDURES

Forms required: FAFSA, institutional form.

Dates and Deadlines: Priority date 3/30; no closing date. Applicants notified on a rolling basis starting 5/1; must reply within 3 week(s) of notification.

CONTACT

Kevin Harral, Director, Financial Aid

12345 El Monte Road, Los Altos Hills, CA 94022

(650) 949-7245

Fremont College

Cerritos, California

www.fremont.edu   Federal Code: 030399

2-year for-profit branch campus and career college in very large city.

Enrollment: 276 undergrads.

Selectivity: Open admission; but selective for some programs and for out-of-state students.

BASIC COSTS (2016-2017)

Additional info: Tuition/fee waivers available for unemployed or children of unemployed.

FINANCIAL AID PICTURE

Students with need: Need-based aid available for full-time students.

Students without need: This college awards aid only to students with need.

FINANCIAL AID PROCEDURES

Forms required: FAFSA, institutional form.

CONTACT

Lori Prince, Director of Finance

18000 Studebaker Road, Cerritos, CA 90703

(562) 809-5100

Fresno City College

Fresno, California

www.fresnocitycollege.edu   Federal Code: 001307

2-year public community and liberal arts college in very large city.

Enrollment: 17,180 undergrads.

Selectivity: Open admission; but selective for some programs.

BASIC COSTS (2016-2017)
Tuition and fees: $1,420; out-of-state residents $8,470.
Per-credit charge: $46; out-of-state residents $281.
Additional info: Tuition/fee waivers available for adults, minority students, unemployed or children of unemployed.

FINANCIAL AID PICTURE
Students with need: Need-based aid available for full-time and part-time students.
Students without need: This college awards aid only to students with need.
Additional info: Board of Governors Grant Program to offset enrollment fees based on untaxed income, low income, or calculated need. Students qualifying for program also automatically exempt from health fees. March 2 application deadline for California grants.

FINANCIAL AID PROCEDURES
Forms required: FAFSA, state aid form.
Dates and Deadlines: Priority date 4/15; closing date 6/30. Applicants notified on a rolling basis starting 4/1.

CONTACT
Frank Ramon, Financial Aid Director
1101 East University Avenue, Fresno, CA 93741
(559) 442-8279

Fresno Pacific University
Fresno, California
www.fresno.edu   Federal Code: 001253

4-year private university and liberal arts college in large city, affiliated with the Mennonite Brethren Church.
Enrollment: 2,429 undergrads, 15% part-time. 199 full-time freshmen.
Selectivity: Admits 50 to 75% of applicants.

BASIC COSTS (2016-2017)
Tuition and fees: $29,170.
Per-credit charge: $1,028.
Room and board: $8,060.

FINANCIAL AID PICTURE (2016-2017)
Students with need: Out of 182 full-time freshmen who applied for aid, 172 were judged to have need. Of these, 172 received aid, and 33 had their full need met. Average financial aid package met 49% of need; average scholarship/grant was $11,318; average loan was $5,168. For part-time students, average financial aid package was $12,344.
Students without need: 27 full-time freshmen who did not demonstrate need for aid received scholarships/grants; average award was $13,121.
Scholarships offered: 56 full-time freshmen received athletic scholarships; average amount $9,654.

FINANCIAL AID PROCEDURES
Transfers: No deadline.

CONTACT
Stacie Benedict, Director of Student Financial Services
1717 South Chestnut Avenue, Fresno, CA 93702-4709
(559) 453-2041

Fullerton College
Fullerton, California
www.fullcoll.edu   Federal Code: 001201

2-year public community and technical college in small city.
Enrollment: 18,081 undergrads.

Selectivity: Open admission.

BASIC COSTS (2016-2017)
Tuition and fees: $1,443; out-of-state residents $8,133.
Per-credit charge: $46; out-of-state residents $269.
Additional info: Tuition/fee waivers available for adults, minority students, unemployed or children of unemployed.

FINANCIAL AID PICTURE (2016-2017)
Students with need: 93% of average financial aid package awarded as scholarships/grants, 7% awarded as loans/jobs. Need-based aid available for part-time students.

FINANCIAL AID PROCEDURES
Forms required: FAFSA.
Dates and Deadlines: Applicants notified on a rolling basis.

CONTACT
Greg Ryan, Director of Financial Aid & Veterans Services
321 East Chapman Avenue, Fullerton, CA 92832-2095
(714) 992-7050

Glendale Community College
Glendale, California
www.glendale.edu   Federal Code: 001203

2-year public community college in small city.
Enrollment: 11,549 undergrads.
Selectivity: Open admission; but selective for some programs.

BASIC COSTS (2016-2017)
Tuition and fees: $1,451; out-of-state residents $7,901.
Per-credit charge: $46; out-of-state residents $261.

FINANCIAL AID PICTURE
Students with need: Need-based aid available for full-time and part-time students. Work study available nights, weekends, and for part-time students.
Students without need: This college awards aid only to students with need.

FINANCIAL AID PROCEDURES
Forms required: FAFSA, institutional form.
Dates and Deadlines: Priority date 4/15; no closing date. Applicants notified on a rolling basis starting 6/15; must reply within 2 week(s) of notification.
Transfers: No deadline.

CONTACT
Arda Najarian, Assistant Director of Financial Aid
1500 North Verdugo Road, Glendale, CA 91208-2809
(818) 240-1000 ext. 5916

Golden Gate University
San Francisco, California
www.ggu.edu   Federal Code: 001205

4-year private university in very large city.
Enrollment: 444 undergrads, 67% part-time.

BASIC COSTS (2017-2018)
Tuition and fees: $15,584.
Per-credit charge: $660.

FINANCIAL AID PICTURE (2015-2016)
Students with need: Average financial aid package for all full-time undergraduates was $12,696; for part-time $11,965. 27% awarded as scholarships/grants, 73% awarded as loans/jobs. Work study available nights.
Students without need: This college awards aid only to students with need.

FINANCIAL AID PROCEDURES

Forms required: FAFSA, institutional form.

Dates and Deadlines: Priority date 1/2; no closing date. Applicants notified on a rolling basis; must reply within 3 week(s) of notification.

Transfers: Priority date 6/14; no deadline. Applicants notified on a rolling basis starting 1/2; must reply within 3 week(s) of notification.

CONTACT

Gabriela De la Vega, Director of Financial Aid, Scholarship and Veteran Affairs Benefits

536 Mission Street, San Francisco, CA 94105-2968

(415) 442-7270

Golden West College

Huntington Beach, California
www.goldenwestcollege.edu   Federal Code: 001206

2-year public community college in small city.

Enrollment: 8,922 undergrads.

Selectivity: Open admission; but selective for some programs.

BASIC COSTS (2016-2017)

Tuition and fees: $1,452; out-of-state residents $7,752.

Per-credit charge: $46; out-of-state residents $256.

FINANCIAL AID PICTURE (2015-2016)

Students with need: 87% of average financial aid package awarded as scholarships/grants, 13% awarded as loans/jobs.

Students without need: No-need awards available for academics.

FINANCIAL AID PROCEDURES

Forms required: FAFSA, state aid form, institutional form.

Dates and Deadlines: Closing date 6/30. Applicants notified on a rolling basis starting 7/1; must reply within 3 week(s) of notification.

CONTACT

Adrienne Burton, Financial Aid Director

15744 Golden West Street, Box 2748, Huntington Beach, CA 92647-2748

(714) 892-7711

Grossmont College

El Cajon, California
www.grossmont.edu   Federal Code: 001208

2-year public nursing and community college in small city.

Enrollment: 14,139 undergrads.

Selectivity: Open admission; but selective for some programs.

BASIC COSTS (2016-2017)

Tuition and fees: $1,418; out-of-state residents $7,838.

Per-credit charge: $46; out-of-state residents $260.

FINANCIAL AID PICTURE

Students with need: Need-based aid available for full-time and part-time students. Work study available nights, weekends, and for part-time students.

Students without need: This college awards aid only to students with need.

FINANCIAL AID PROCEDURES

Forms required: FAFSA.

Dates and Deadlines: Priority date 3/2; closing date 6/30. Applicants notified on a rolling basis starting 7/15; must reply within 2 week(s) of notification.

CONTACT

Michael Copenhaver, Director of Financial Aid

8800 Grossmont College Drive, El Cajon, CA 92020

(619) 644-7129

Harvey Mudd College

Claremont, California   Federal Code: 001171
https://www.hmc.edu/   CSS Code: 4341

4-year private engineering and liberal arts college in large town.

Enrollment: 829 undergrads. 214 full-time freshmen.

Selectivity: Admits less than 50% of applicants.

BASIC COSTS (2017-2018)

Tuition and fees: $52,916.

Per-credit charge: $1,637.

Room and board: $17,051.

FINANCIAL AID PICTURE (2015-2016)

Students with need: Out of 152 full-time freshmen who applied for aid, 116 were judged to have need. Of these, 116 received aid, and 116 had their full need met. Average financial aid package met 100% of need; average scholarship/grant was $44,042; average loan was $3,673. Need-based aid available for part-time students.

Students without need: 42 full-time freshmen who did not demonstrate need for aid received scholarships/grants; average award was $10,533. No-need awards available for academics.

Scholarships offered: Harvey S. Mudd Merit Award: for first-time first-year students in science and technology programs; $10,000 annually for 4 years; must maintain minimum 2.75 GPA. Harvey Mudd College-sponsored National Merit Scholarships: from $1,000 to $2,000; based on need.

Additional info: Students can use 100% of their outside awards toward first reducing the need-based portion of their student loans and/or Federal Work Study award. Once need-based student loans and/or Federal Work Study award have been completely eliminated, any additional outside scholarships may reduce need-based Harvey Mudd Scholarship only. However, to maximize financial aid eligibility, students may retain need-based student loans and/or Federal Work Study award up to their federal need.

FINANCIAL AID PROCEDURES

Forms required: FAFSA, CSS PROFILE, state aid form.

Dates and Deadlines: Priority date 2/1; closing date 2/1. Applicants notified by 4/1; must reply by 5/1 or within 1 week(s) of notification.

Transfers: Closing date 3/2. Applicants notified by 5/15; must reply by 6/10 or within 1 week(s) of notification.

CONTACT

Gilma Lopez, Director of Financial Aid

301 Platt Boulevard, Claremont, CA 91711-5901

(909) 621-8055

Holy Names University

Oakland, California
www.hnu.edu   Federal Code: 001183

4-year private university in large city, affiliated with the Roman Catholic Church.

Enrollment: 515 undergrads, 14% part-time. 130 full-time freshmen.

Selectivity: Admits less than 50% of applicants.

BASIC COSTS (2016-2017)

Tuition and fees: $37,074.

Per-credit charge: $1,254.

Room and board: $12,434.

FINANCIAL AID PICTURE (2016-2017)

Students with need: Average financial aid package met 72% of need; average scholarship/grant was $28,705; average loan was $3,858. For part-time students, average financial aid package was $8,416.

Students without need: No-need awards available for academics, athletics, leadership, music/drama, religious affiliation, state/district residency.

Scholarships offered: Aspiring Leadership Grant: $5,500 annually; based on 2.70-2.99 GPA. Honors Scholarship: $8,500 annually; based on 3.00-3.29 GPA. Dean's Scholarship: $9,500 annually; based on 3.30-3.49 GPA. President's Scholarship: $11,000 annually; based on 3.50-3.74 GPA. Regent's Scholarship: $12,000 annually; based on 3.75+ GPA. Durocher Scholarship: full tuition; campus residency required; based on evidence of leadership, contributions to school and/or community and academic achievement, minimum GPA 3.75, minimum SAT 1100 (exclusive of Writing); 1 awarded per year.

FINANCIAL AID PROCEDURES
Forms required: FAFSA.

Dates and Deadlines: Priority date 3/2; no closing date. Applicants notified on a rolling basis starting 9/1; must reply by 8/26 or within 2 week(s) of notification.

Transfers: No deadline. Applicants notified on a rolling basis starting 9/1; must reply by 5/1 or within 2 week(s) of notification.

CONTACT
Tam Lee-Operario, Director of Financial Aid

3500 Mountain Boulevard, Oakland, CA 94619-1699

(510) 436-1327

Hope International University
Fullerton, California

www.hiu.edu   Federal Code: 001252

4-year private university and liberal arts college in small city, affiliated with the Christian Church.

Enrollment: 828 undergrads, 25% part-time. 108 full-time freshmen.

Selectivity: Admits less than 50% of applicants.

BASIC COSTS (2017-2018)
Tuition and fees: $31,800.

Per-credit charge: $1,395.

Room and board: $9,930.

FINANCIAL AID PICTURE (2015-2016)
Students with need: Out of 104 full-time freshmen who applied for aid, 89 were judged to have need. Of these, 89 received aid, and 17 had their full need met. Average financial aid package met 33% of need; average scholarship/grant was $13,194; average loan was $2,582. For part-time students, average financial aid package was $13,008.

Students without need: 6 full-time freshmen who did not demonstrate need for aid received scholarships/grants; average award was $15,250. No-need awards available for academics, athletics, leadership, music/drama.

Scholarships offered: 39 full-time freshmen received athletic scholarships; average amount $12,913.

FINANCIAL AID PROCEDURES
Forms required: FAFSA, institutional form.

Dates and Deadlines: Priority date 3/2; no closing date. Applicants notified on a rolling basis starting 1/1; must reply within 2 week(s) of notification.

Transfers: No deadline. Applicants notified on a rolling basis starting 2/15; must reply within 2 week(s) of notification.

CONTACT
Shannon O'Shields, Director of Student Financial Services

2500 East Nutwood Avenue, Fullerton, CA 92831-3199

(714) 879-3901 ext. 2232

Hult International Business School
San Francisco, California

www.hult.edu/en/undergraduate/bachelor-of-business-administration/

4-year private business college in very large city.

Enrollment: 1,147 undergrads. 144 full-time freshmen.

Selectivity: Admits 50 to 75% of applicants.

BASIC COSTS (2017-2018)
Tuition and fees: $41,550.

Room only: $14,500.

FINANCIAL AID PICTURE (2016-2017)
Students with need: Out of 112 full-time freshmen who applied for aid, 112 were judged to have need. Of these, 112 received aid.

Students without need: 23 full-time freshmen who did not demonstrate need for aid received scholarships/grants; average award was $6,221. No-need awards available for academics, job skills, leadership.

Scholarships offered: Academic Excellence Social Impact Entrepreneurial Impact Global Talent Women in Business Future Global Business Leader DECA.

FINANCIAL AID PROCEDURES
Forms required: institutional form.

Dates and Deadlines: Applicants notified on a rolling basis starting 11/15; must reply by 5/1.

Transfers: No deadline. Applicants notified on a rolling basis starting 11/15; must reply by 5/1 or within 2 week(s) of notification.

CONTACT
Karen Van Dyne, Director of Financial Aid

Humboldt State University
Arcata, California

www.humboldt.edu   Federal Code: 001149

4-year public university and liberal arts college in large town.

Enrollment: 7,942 undergrads, 6% part-time. 1,282 full-time freshmen.

Selectivity: Admits over 75% of applicants.

BASIC COSTS (2016-2017)
Tuition and fees: $7,212; out-of-state residents $18,372.

Room and board: $12,638.

FINANCIAL AID PICTURE (2016-2017)
Students with need: Out of 1,161 full-time freshmen who applied for aid, 934 were judged to have need. Of these, 907 received aid, and 84 had their full need met. Average financial aid package met 69% of need; average scholarship/grant was $9,324; average loan was $6,051. For part-time students, average financial aid package was $10,300.

Students without need: 66 full-time freshmen who did not demonstrate need for aid received scholarships/grants; average award was $623. No-need awards available for academics, alumni affiliation, athletics, minority status, state/district residency.

Scholarships offered: 21 full-time freshmen received athletic scholarships; average amount $2,929.

FINANCIAL AID PROCEDURES
Forms required: FAFSA.

Dates and Deadlines: Priority date 3/1; no closing date. Applicants notified on a rolling basis starting 4/1; must reply within 4 week(s) of notification.

Transfers: Need is most salient factor for some programs.

CONTACT
Peggy Metzger, Director of Financial Aid

One Harpst Street, Arcata, CA 95521-8299

(707) 826-4321

Humphreys College
Stockton, California

www.humphreys.edu   Federal Code: 001212

4-year private liberal arts and teachers college in large city.

Enrollment: 617 undergrads.

BASIC COSTS (2016-2017)
Tuition and fees: $14,004.
Per-credit charge: $389.

FINANCIAL AID PICTURE
Students with need: Need-based aid available for full-time and part-time students. Work study available nights, weekends, and for part-time students.
Students without need: No-need awards available for academics.

FINANCIAL AID PROCEDURES
Forms required: FAFSA.
Dates and Deadlines: Applicants notified on a rolling basis starting 8/15; must reply within 2 week(s) of notification.

CONTACT
Rita Franco, Financial Aid Director
6650 Inglewood Avenue, Stockton, CA 95207-3896
(209) 478-0800 ext. 3903

Imperial Valley College
Imperial, California
www.imperial.edu   Federal Code: 001214

2-year public nursing and community college in large town.
Enrollment: 4,902 undergrads, 51% part-time. 685 full-time freshmen.
Selectivity: Open admission; but selective for some programs.

BASIC COSTS (2016-2017)
Tuition and fees: $1,420; out-of-state residents $7,690.
Per-credit charge: $46; out-of-state residents $255.
Additional info: Tuition/fee waivers available for adults.

FINANCIAL AID PICTURE (2015-2016)
Students with need: 98% of average financial aid package awarded as scholarships/grants, 2% awarded as loans/jobs. Need-based aid available for part-time students. Work study available nights, weekends, and for part-time students.
Students without need: This college awards aid only to students with need.

FINANCIAL AID PROCEDURES
Forms required: FAFSA.
Dates and Deadlines: Priority date 3/2; closing date 6/30. Applicants notified on a rolling basis starting 5/1.
Transfers: No deadline. Applicants notified on a rolling basis.

CONTACT
Lisa Seals, Director of Financial Aid
Box 158, Imperial, CA 92251-0158
(760) 355-6266

Irvine Valley College
Irvine, California
www.ivc.edu   Federal Code: 025395

2-year public community college in small city.
Enrollment: 11,357 undergrads.
Selectivity: Open admission.

BASIC COSTS (2016-2017)
Tuition and fees: $1,418; out-of-state residents $9,698.
Per-credit charge: $46; out-of-state residents $322.
Additional info: Tuition/fee waivers available for minority students.

FINANCIAL AID PICTURE
Students with need: Need-based aid available for full-time and part-time students. Work study available nights.

Students without need: This college awards aid only to students with need.

FINANCIAL AID PROCEDURES
Forms required: FAFSA, state aid form, institutional form.
Dates and Deadlines: Applicants notified on a rolling basis starting 4/30.

CONTACT
Darryl Cox, Director of Financial Aid
5500 Irvine Center Drive, Irvine, CA 92618-4399
(949) 451-5287

John F. Kennedy University
Pleasant Hill, California
www.jfku.edu   Federal Code: 004484

Upper-division private university in large town.
Enrollment: 251 undergrads.
Selectivity: Open admission; but selective for some programs.

BASIC COSTS (2016-2017)
Tuition and fees: $17,469.
Per-credit charge: $478.

FINANCIAL AID PICTURE
Students with need: Need-based aid available for full-time and part-time students.
Students without need: This college awards aid only to students with need.

FINANCIAL AID PROCEDURES
Forms required: FAFSA, institutional form.
Dates and Deadlines: Priority date 3/2; no closing date. Applicants notified on a rolling basis; must reply within 4 week(s) of notification.
Transfers: Priority date 4/1.

CONTACT
Mindy Bergeron, Director of Financial Aid
100 Ellinwood Way, Pleasant Hill, CA 94523-4817
(925) 969-3385

John Paul the Great Catholic University
Escondido, California
https://jpcatholic.edu/   Federal Code: 041937

4-year private university in small city, affiliated with the Roman Catholic Church.
Enrollment: 227 undergrads, 7% part-time. 73 full-time freshmen.
Selectivity: Admits over 75% of applicants.

BASIC COSTS (2016-2017)
Tuition and fees: $24,900.
Per-credit charge: $667.
Room only: $8,100.
Additional info: Tuition at time of enrollment locked for 4 years.

FINANCIAL AID PICTURE
Students with need: Need-based aid available for full-time and part-time students.
Students without need: No-need awards available for academics, leadership.

FINANCIAL AID PROCEDURES
Forms required: FAFSA, institutional form.
Dates and Deadlines: Closing date 4/15. Applicants notified on a rolling basis starting 12/1; must reply by 5/1 or within 2 week(s) of notification.

CONTACT
Lisa Williams, Director of Financial Aid
220 West Grand Avenue, Escondido, CA 92025
(858) 653-6740 ext. 1303

Kaplan College: Riverside
Riverside, California
www.riverside.kaplancollege.com   Federal Code: 030445

2-year for-profit junior and technical college in very large city.
Enrollment: 167 undergrads.
Selectivity: Open admission.

BASIC COSTS (2016-2017)
Additional info: Associate programs: Criminal Justice; $29,292. Diploma programs: Dental Assistant; $17,120; Massage Therapy; Medical Assistant, Medical Billing and Coding Specialist $15,304.

FINANCIAL AID PICTURE
Students with need: Need-based aid available for full-time students. Work study available nights.
Students without need: This college awards aid only to students with need.

FINANCIAL AID PROCEDURES
Forms required: FAFSA, institutional form.
Transfers: No deadline.

CONTACT
Cynthia Arevalo
4040 Vine Street, Riverside, CA 92507
(818) 672-3000

Kaplan College: Sacramento
Sacramento, California
https://www.kaplancollege.com/sacramento-ca
Federal Code: 016720

2-year for-profit technical college in large city.
Enrollment: 429 undergrads.
Selectivity: Open admission; but selective for some programs.

BASIC COSTS (2016-2017)
Additional info: Associate degree program: Criminal Justice; $29,292. Diploma programs: Vocational Nursing; $31,685; Dental Assistant; $17,122; Medical Assistant, Medical Office Specialist $15,727.

FINANCIAL AID PICTURE
Students with need: Need-based aid available for full-time students.
Students without need: This college awards aid only to students with need.

CONTACT
Ryan Smith, Director of Finance
4330 Watt Avenue, Suite 400, Sacramento, CA 95821
(916) 649-8168

La Sierra University
Riverside, California
www.lasierra.edu   Federal Code: 001215

4-year private Bible and liberal arts college in large city, affiliated with the Seventh-day Adventists.
Enrollment: 2,020 undergrads.

BASIC COSTS (2016-2017)
Tuition and fees: $31,590.
Per-credit charge: $850.
Room and board: $8,100.

FINANCIAL AID PICTURE
Students with need: Need-based aid available for full-time and part-time students. Work study available nights, weekends, and for part-time students.
Students without need: No-need awards available for academics, art, athletics, leadership, music/drama, religious affiliation.
Scholarships offered: Sports and Honors Scholarship available for qualified students.

FINANCIAL AID PROCEDURES
Forms required: FAFSA, state aid form.
Dates and Deadlines: Priority date 3/2; closing date 8/15. Applicants notified on a rolling basis starting 4/15; must reply by 8/5 or within 2 week(s) of notification.
Transfers: Closing date 7/1. Applicants notified by 8/15; must reply by 9/1 or within 2 week(s) of notification. Every student whose balance is not completely covered by financial aid must make a payment of at least one-third of the balance due by the published deadline before each quarter. There will continue to be three standard payment options available. Year-in-Advance: Pay the full year's charges minus confirmed aid by the published deadline for Fall and receive a 7% discount. Quarter-in-Advance: Pay each quarter's charges minus confirmed aid by the published deadline for that quarter and receive a 2% discount. Monthly Payment: Pay in three monthly installments for each quarter, with the first payment due by that quarter's published deadline. A $30 fee applies for each quarter that this option is chosen.

CONTACT
Elina Bascom, Director of Student Financial Services
4500 Riverwalk Parkway, Riverside, CA 92515-8247
(951) 785-2175

Laguna College of Art and Design
Laguna Beach, California
www.lcad.edu   Federal Code: 016517

4-year private visual arts college in small city.
Enrollment: 567 undergrads, 13% part-time. 84 full-time freshmen.
Selectivity: Admits less than 50% of applicants.

BASIC COSTS (2017-2018)
Tuition and fees: $29,800.
Per-credit charge: $1,242.
Room only: $9,400.

FINANCIAL AID PICTURE (2015-2016)
Students with need: Out of 80 full-time freshmen who applied for aid, 80 were judged to have need. Of these, 80 received aid. Need-based aid available for part-time students.
Students without need: No-need awards available for art.
Additional info: Need and merit-based scholarship deadline June 1st.

FINANCIAL AID PROCEDURES
Forms required: FAFSA, institutional form.
Dates and Deadlines: Applicants notified on a rolling basis; must reply within 2 week(s) of notification.
Transfers: No deadline. Applicants notified on a rolling basis.

CONTACT
Christopher Brown, Director of Admission and Financial Aid
2222 Laguna Canyon Road, Laguna Beach, CA 92651-1136
(949) 376-6000 ext. 223

Lake Tahoe Community College

South Lake Tahoe, California
www.ltcc.edu   Federal Code: 012907

2-year public community college in large town.
Enrollment: 977 undergrads.
Selectivity: Open admission.

BASIC COSTS (2016-2017)
Tuition and fees: $1,410; out-of-state residents $8,160.
Per-credit charge: $31; out-of-state residents $181.

FINANCIAL AID PICTURE (2015-2016)
Students with need: 97% of average financial aid package awarded as scholarships/grants, 3% awarded as loans/jobs. Need-based aid available for part-time students. Work study available nights.

FINANCIAL AID PROCEDURES
Forms required: FAFSA.
Dates and Deadlines: Closing date 6/30. Applicants notified on a rolling basis starting 7/1; must reply within 2 week(s) of notification.

CONTACT
Julie Cathie, Director of Financial Aid
One College Drive, South Lake Tahoe, CA 96150-4524
(530) 541-4660 ext. 236

Laney College

Oakland, California
www.laney.edu   Federal Code: 001266

2-year public community college in large city.
Enrollment: 3,134 undergrads.
Selectivity: Open admission.

BASIC COSTS (2016-2017)
Tuition and fees: $1,424; out-of-state residents $8,054.
Per-credit charge: $46; out-of-state residents $267.
Additional info: Tuition/fee waivers available for unemployed or children of unemployed.

FINANCIAL AID PICTURE (2015-2016)
Students with need: 91% of average financial aid package awarded as scholarships/grants, 9% awarded as loans/jobs.

FINANCIAL AID PROCEDURES
Forms required: FAFSA, institutional form.
Dates and Deadlines: Priority date 4/1; closing date 6/30. Applicants notified on a rolling basis; must reply within 2 week(s) of notification.

CONTACT
Joseph Koroma, Financial Aid Director
900 Fallon Street, Oakland, CA 94607
(510) 464-3414

Las Positas College

Livermore, California
www.laspositascollege.edu   Federal Code: 030357

2-year public community college in small city.
Enrollment: 6,688 undergrads.
Selectivity: Open admission.

BASIC COSTS (2016-2017)
Tuition and fees: $1,436; out-of-state residents $8,726.
Per-credit charge: $46; out-of-district residents $289; out-of-state residents $289.

Additional info: Tuition/fee waivers available for unemployed or children of unemployed.

FINANCIAL AID PICTURE
Students with need: Need-based aid available for full-time students.

FINANCIAL AID PROCEDURES
Forms required: institutional form.
Dates and Deadlines: Priority date 5/1; no closing date. Applicants notified on a rolling basis starting 7/1; must reply within 2 week(s) of notification.

CONTACT
Andi Schreibman, Financial Aid Officer
3033 Collier Canyon Road, Livermore, CA 94551
(925) 424-1580

Lassen Community College

Susanville, California
www.lassencollege.edu   Federal Code: 001217

2-year public community college in large town.
Enrollment: 1,201 undergrads.
Selectivity: Open admission; but selective for some programs.

BASIC COSTS (2016-2017)
Tuition and fees: $1,403; out-of-state residents $7,433.
Per-credit charge: $46; out-of-state residents $247.
Room only: $3,000.

FINANCIAL AID PICTURE (2015-2016)
Students with need: 79% of average financial aid package awarded as scholarships/grants, 21% awarded as loans/jobs.
Students without need: This college awards aid only to students with need.
Additional info: Board of Governors Grant: low-income California residents can have registration fees waived.

FINANCIAL AID PROCEDURES
Forms required: FAFSA.
Dates and Deadlines: Priority date 7/1; no closing date. Applicants notified on a rolling basis starting 7/1; must reply within 2 week(s) of notification.
Transfers: No deadline.

CONTACT
Matt Levine, Director of Financial Aid
PO Box 3000, Susanville, CA 96130
(530) 251-8849

Le Cordon Bleu College of Culinary Arts: Los Angeles

Pasadena, California
www.chefs.edu/los-angeles   Federal Code: 032103

2-year for-profit culinary school in very large city.
Enrollment: 1,350 undergrads.
Selectivity: Open admission.

FINANCIAL AID PICTURE
Students with need: Need-based aid available for full-time and part-time students. Work study available nights, weekends, and for part-time students.

FINANCIAL AID PROCEDURES
Forms required: FAFSA.
Dates and Deadlines: Applicants notified on a rolling basis.
Transfers: No deadline.

CONTACT

Gabriela Arzate, Director of Student Finance
530 East Colorado Boulevard, Pasadena, CA 91101
(626) 229-1300

Le Cordon Bleu College of Culinary Arts: San Francisco

San Francisco, California
www.chefs.edu/San-Francisco   Federal Code: 015698

2-year for-profit culinary school and career college in very large city.
Enrollment: 442 undergrads.

FINANCIAL AID PICTURE

Students with need: Need-based aid available for full-time students.

FINANCIAL AID PROCEDURES

Forms required: FAFSA, state aid form.
Dates and Deadlines: Applicants notified on a rolling basis; must reply within 1 week(s) of notification.

CONTACT

Director of Financial Aid
350 Rhode Island Street, San Francisco, CA 94103
(415) 771-3500

Life Pacific College

San Dimas, California
www.lifepacific.edu   Federal Code: 016029

4-year private Bible college in large town, affiliated with the Christian Church.
Enrollment: 534 undergrads, 13% part-time. 62 full-time freshmen.

BASIC COSTS (2016-2017)

Tuition and fees: $14,138.
Per-credit charge: $562.
Room and board: $7,608.

FINANCIAL AID PICTURE

Students with need: Need-based aid available for full-time and part-time students.
Students without need: No-need awards available for academics.

FINANCIAL AID PROCEDURES

Forms required: FAFSA.
Dates and Deadlines: Applicants notified on a rolling basis starting 6/1.

CONTACT

Luci Perez, Director of Financial Aid
Attn: Admissions, San Dimas, CA 91773
(909) 599-5433 ext. 326

Lincoln University

Oakland, California
www.lincolnuca.edu   Federal Code: 006975

4-year private university and business college in very large city.
Enrollment: 115 undergrads.

BASIC COSTS (2016-2017)

Tuition and fees: $13,110.
Per-credit charge: $425.

FINANCIAL AID PICTURE

Students with need: Need-based aid available for full-time and part-time students.
Students without need: This college awards aid only to students with need.

FINANCIAL AID PROCEDURES

Forms required: FAFSA.
Dates and Deadlines: Priority date 3/22; closing date 8/22. Applicants notified by 12/1; must reply by 1/2.
Transfers: Applicants notified by 12/1; must reply by 1/1.

CONTACT

James Peterson, Chief Financial Aid Director
401 15th Street, Oakland, CA 94612
(510) 628-8023

Loma Linda University

Loma Linda, California
www.llu.edu   Federal Code: 001218

3-year private university and health science college in large town, affiliated with the Seventh-day Adventists.
Enrollment: 1,061 undergrads.

BASIC COSTS (2016-2017)

Tuition and fees: $32,520.
Room only: $3,960.

FINANCIAL AID PICTURE

Students with need: Need-based aid available for full-time and part-time students.

FINANCIAL AID PROCEDURES

Forms required: FAFSA.
Transfers: Priority date 3/2; no deadline. Applicants notified on a rolling basis starting 4/1; must reply within 4 week(s) of notification.

CONTACT

Verdell Schaefer, Director of Financial Aid
Admissions Processing, Loma Linda, CA 92350
(909) 558-4509

Long Beach City College

Long Beach, California
www.lbcc.edu   Federal Code: 001219

2-year public community college in large city.
Enrollment: 16,381 undergrads.
Selectivity: Open admission.

BASIC COSTS (2016-2017)

Tuition and fees: $1,418; out-of-state residents $9,188.
Per-credit charge: $46; out-of-state residents $305.

FINANCIAL AID PICTURE

Students with need: Need-based aid available for full-time and part-time students.
Students without need: This college awards aid only to students with need.

FINANCIAL AID PROCEDURES

Forms required: FAFSA, institutional form.
Dates and Deadlines: Priority date 5/29; no closing date. Applicants notified on a rolling basis starting 7/6; must reply within 2 week(s) of notification.

CONTACT

Lillian Justice, Director of Financial Aid and Veterans Affairs

4901 East Carson Street, Long Beach, CA 90808

(562) 938-4257

Los Angeles City College

Los Angeles, California

www.lacitycollege.edu   Federal Code: 001223

2-year public community college in very large city.

Enrollment: 10,623 undergrads.

Selectivity: Open admission.

BASIC COSTS (2016-2017)

Tuition and fees: $1,402; out-of-state residents $8,692.

Per-credit charge: $46; out-of-state residents $289.

FINANCIAL AID PICTURE

Students with need: Need-based aid available for full-time and part-time students.

Students without need: This college awards aid only to students with need.

Additional info: Fee waivers available for public assistance and Social Security insurance recipients; fee credits available for low income families.

FINANCIAL AID PROCEDURES

Forms required: FAFSA.

Dates and Deadlines: Priority date 3/2; no closing date. Applicants notified on a rolling basis starting 7/6; must reply within 2 week(s) of notification.

Transfers: No deadline. Applicants notified by 7/1.

CONTACT

Jeremy Villar, Dean of Student Services

855 North Vermont Avenue, Los Angeles, CA 90029-3589

(323) 953-4000 ext. 2025

Los Angeles Harbor College

Wilmington, California

www.lahc.edu   Federal Code: 001224

2-year public community college in small city.

Enrollment: 7,034 undergrads.

Selectivity: Open admission.

BASIC COSTS (2016-2017)

Tuition and fees: $1,404; out-of-state residents $8,064.

Per-credit charge: $46; out-of-state residents $268.

FINANCIAL AID PICTURE

Students with need: Need-based aid available for full-time and part-time students. Work study available nights, weekends, and for part-time students.

Students without need: This college awards aid only to students with need.

FINANCIAL AID PROCEDURES

Forms required: FAFSA, institutional form.

Dates and Deadlines: Priority date 3/2; no closing date. Applicants notified on a rolling basis; must reply within 2 week(s) of notification.

Transfers: Closing date 5/15.

CONTACT

Sheila Millman, Financial Aid Manager

1111 Figueroa Place, Wilmington, CA 90744-2397

(310) 233-4320

Los Angeles Mission College

Sylmar, California

www.lamission.edu   Federal Code: 012550

2-year public community college in large town.

Enrollment: 7,271 undergrads.

Selectivity: Open admission.

BASIC COSTS (2016-2017)

Tuition and fees: $1,404; out-of-state residents $8,694.

Per-credit charge: $46; out-of-state residents $289.

FINANCIAL AID PICTURE (2015-2016)

Students with need: 92% of average financial aid package awarded as scholarships/grants, 8% awarded as loans/jobs. Need-based aid available for part-time students.

Additional info: Board of Governors Fee Waiver available to those in receipt of TANF (CalWORKS), Social Security Insurance, or General Relief. Students may also qualify based on family income.

FINANCIAL AID PROCEDURES

Forms required: FAFSA.

Dates and Deadlines: Priority date 5/1; no closing date. Applicants notified on a rolling basis starting 5/1.

CONTACT

Dennis Schroeder, Financial Aid Director

13356 Eldridge Avenue, Sylmar, CA 91342-3245

(818) 364-7648

Los Angeles Pierce College

Woodland Hills, California

www.piercecollege.edu   Federal Code: 001226

2-year public community college in very large city.

Enrollment: 14,897 undergrads.

Selectivity: Open admission; but selective for some programs.

BASIC COSTS (2016-2017)

Tuition and fees: $1,404; out-of-state residents $8,694.

Per-credit charge: $46; out-of-state residents $289.

FINANCIAL AID PICTURE

Students with need: Need-based aid available for full-time and part-time students. Work study available nights, weekends, and for part-time students.

Students without need: This college awards aid only to students with need.

FINANCIAL AID PROCEDURES

Forms required: FAFSA, institutional form.

Dates and Deadlines: Priority date 3/2; no closing date. Applicants notified on a rolling basis starting 8/1.

CONTACT

Anafe Robinson, Director of Financial Aid, Scholarships & Veterans

6201 Winnetka Avenue, Woodland Hills, CA 91371

(818) 719-6428

Los Angeles Southwest College

Los Angeles, California

www.lasc.edu   Federal Code: 007047

2-year public community college in very large city.

Enrollment: 4,662 undergrads.

Selectivity: Open admission; but selective for some programs.

BASIC COSTS (2016-2017)

Tuition and fees: $1,418; out-of-state residents $8,708.
Per-credit charge: $46; out-of-state residents $289.

FINANCIAL AID PICTURE

Students with need: Need-based aid available for full-time and part-time students.
Additional info: Board of Governors Enrollment Fee Waiver available to students receiving AFDC, SSI/SSP, or General Assistance. May also qualify on basis of income.

FINANCIAL AID PROCEDURES

Forms required: FAFSA.
Dates and Deadlines: Applicants notified on a rolling basis; must reply within 2 week(s) of notification.

CONTACT

Kathaleen Stiger, Financial Aid Director
1600 West Imperial Highway, Los Angeles, CA 90047-4899
(323) 241-5328

Los Angeles Trade and Technical College

Los Angeles, California
www.lattc.edu   Federal Code: 001227

2-year public community and technical college in very large city.
Enrollment: 8,831 undergrads.
Selectivity: Open admission; but selective for some programs.

BASIC COSTS (2016-2017)

Tuition and fees: $1,418; out-of-state residents $7,598.
Per-credit charge: $46; out-of-state residents $252.

FINANCIAL AID PICTURE

Students with need: Need-based aid available for full-time and part-time students. Work study available nights, weekends, and for part-time students.
Students without need: This college awards aid only to students with need.

FINANCIAL AID PROCEDURES

Forms required: FAFSA.
Dates and Deadlines: Priority date 5/1; closing date 6/30. Applicants notified on a rolling basis.
Transfers: No deadline.

CONTACT

Cecilia Kwan, Financial Aid Manager
400 West Washington Boulevard, Los Angeles, CA 90015-4181
(213) 744-9016

Los Angeles Valley College

Valley Glen, California
www.lavc.edu   Federal Code: 001228

2-year public community college in very large city.
Enrollment: 8,831 undergrads.
Selectivity: Open admission; but selective for some programs.

BASIC COSTS (2016-2017)

Tuition and fees: $1,404; out-of-state residents $8,694.
Per-credit charge: $46; out-of-state residents $289.

FINANCIAL AID PICTURE

Students with need: Need-based aid available for full-time and part-time students.
Students without need: This college awards aid only to students with need.

FINANCIAL AID PROCEDURES

Forms required: FAFSA.
Dates and Deadlines: Priority date 5/1; no closing date. Applicants notified on a rolling basis.

CONTACT

Vernon Bridges, Financial Aid Manager
5800 Fulton Avenue, Valley Glen, CA 91401-4096
(818) 947-2412

Los Medanos College

Pittsburg, California
www.losmedanos.edu   Federal Code: 010340

2-year public community college in small city.
Enrollment: 3,704 undergrads.
Selectivity: Open admission.

BASIC COSTS (2016-2017)

Tuition and fees: $1,390; out-of-state residents $8,500.
Per-credit charge: $46; out-of-state residents $283.

FINANCIAL AID PICTURE

Students with need: Need-based aid available for full-time and part-time students.
Students without need: This college awards aid only to students with need.

FINANCIAL AID PROCEDURES

Forms required: FAFSA, state aid form.
Dates and Deadlines: Priority date 3/2; no closing date. Applicants notified on a rolling basis starting 6/1; must reply within 2 week(s) of notification.
Transfers: No deadline. Applicants notified by 6/1.

CONTACT

Loretta Canto-Williams, Director of Financial Aid
2700 East Leland Road, Pittsburg, CA 94565
(925) 439-2181 ext. 3139

Loyola Marymount University

Los Angeles, California
www.lmu.edu   Federal Code: 001234

4-year private university in very large city, affiliated with the Roman Catholic Church.
Enrollment: 6,126 undergrads, 2% part-time. 1,354 full-time freshmen.
Selectivity: Admits 50 to 75% of applicants.

BASIC COSTS (2016-2017)

Tuition and fees: $44,230.
Per-credit charge: $1,816.
Room and board: $14,115.

FINANCIAL AID PICTURE (2015-2016)

Students with need: Out of 1,059 full-time freshmen who applied for aid, 743 were judged to have need. Of these, 733 received aid, and 147 had their full need met. Average financial aid package met 65% of need; average scholarship/grant was $20,509; average loan was $5,109. For part-time students, average financial aid package was $9,550.
Students without need: 414 full-time freshmen who did not demonstrate need for aid received scholarships/grants; average award was $10,832. No-need awards available for academics, alumni affiliation, art, athletics, music/drama, religious affiliation, ROTC.
Scholarships offered: *Merit:* Academic Awards for entering freshmen: range from $1,000 to $15,000. Trustee Scholarship: Full tuition, fees, room and board, selection based on academic accomplishments and interview process; typically 10 awarded each year. Presidential Scholarship: $25,000

and up, based on academic accomplishments and interview process; typically 20 awarded each year. Arrupe Scholarships: Range from $12,500 to full tuition, based on academic accomplishments. LMU Achievement Awards: Range from $1,000 and up, based on academic accomplishments. **Athletic:** 38 full-time freshmen received athletic scholarships; average amount $30,469.

FINANCIAL AID PROCEDURES

Forms required: FAFSA.

Dates and Deadlines: Priority date 2/1; no closing date. Applicants notified on a rolling basis; must reply by 5/1 or within 4 week(s) of notification.

Transfers: Priority date 3/2; no deadline. Applicants notified on a rolling basis starting 6/1; must reply within 3 week(s) of notification.

CONTACT

Michael Keane, Assistant Vice Provost for Financial Aid
1 LMU Drive, Los Angeles, CA 90045-2659
(310) 338-2753

Marymount California University

Rancho Palos Verdes, California
www.marymountcalifornia.edu   Federal Code: 010474

4-year private liberal arts college in large town, affiliated with the Roman Catholic Church.
Enrollment: 942 undergrads, 6% part-time. 219 full-time freshmen.
Selectivity: Admits over 75% of applicants.

BASIC COSTS (2016-2017)

Tuition and fees: $35,834.
Per-credit charge: $1,475.
Room and board: $14,412.

FINANCIAL AID PICTURE (2016-2017)

Students with need: Out of 158 full-time freshmen who applied for aid, 156 were judged to have need. Of these, 156 received aid, and 51 had their full need met. Average financial aid package met 94% of need; average scholarship/grant was $23,201; average loan was $3,500. For part-time students, average financial aid package was $13,572.

Students without need: 25 full-time freshmen who did not demonstrate need for aid received scholarships/grants; average award was $10,959. No-need awards available for academics, art, athletics.

Scholarships offered: **Merit:** President's Scholarship: $8,000; Academic GPA: 3.30 and above; SAT 1530 or ACT 22. Dean's Scholarship: $6,000; Academic GPA 3.00-3.29; SAT 1410 or ACT 20. Achievement Scholarship: $4,500; Academic GPA 2.80-2.99; SAT 1210 or ACT 17. Deadline May 1. All admitted students considered. Renewable for one additional consecutive year. **Athletic:** 4 full-time freshmen received athletic scholarships; average amount $10,750.

FINANCIAL AID PROCEDURES

Forms required: FAFSA.

Dates and Deadlines: Priority date 3/2; closing date 2/15. Applicants notified by 3/1.

CONTACT

Pedro Ladino, Director of Financial Aid
30800 Palos Verdes Drive East, Rancho Palos Verdes, CA 90275-6299
(310) 303-7217

The Master's University

Santa Clarita, California
www.masters.edu   Federal Code: 001220

4-year private liberal arts and seminary college in small city, affiliated with the nondenominational tradition.

Enrollment: 1,154 undergrads, 18% part-time. 199 full-time freshmen.
Selectivity: Admits over 75% of applicants.

BASIC COSTS (2017-2018)

Tuition and fees: $33,020.
Per-credit charge: $1,370.
Room and board: $10,850.

FINANCIAL AID PICTURE (2015-2016)

Students with need: Out of 180 full-time freshmen who applied for aid, 149 were judged to have need. Of these, 145 received aid, and 19 had their full need met. Average financial aid package met 68% of need; average scholarship/grant was $19,411; average loan was $3,318. For part-time students, average financial aid package was $6,461.

Students without need: 37 full-time freshmen who did not demonstrate need for aid received scholarships/grants; average award was $11,255. No-need awards available for academics, alumni affiliation, athletics, job skills, leadership, music/drama, religious affiliation.

Scholarships offered: 14 full-time freshmen received athletic scholarships; average amount $18,253.

FINANCIAL AID PROCEDURES

Forms required: FAFSA, institutional form.

Dates and Deadlines: Priority date 3/2; no closing date. Applicants notified on a rolling basis starting 2/18; must reply by 5/1 or within 2 week(s) of notification.

Transfers: Priority date 3/2; no deadline. Applicants notified on a rolling basis starting 2/18; must reply by 5/1 or within 2 week(s) of notification.

CONTACT

Gary Edwards, Financial Aid Director
Office of Admissions, Santa Clarita, CA 91321-1200
(661) 259-3540 ext. 2290

Mendocino College

Ukiah, California
www.mendocino.edu   Federal Code: 011672

2-year public community college in large town.
Enrollment: 2,586 undergrads.
Selectivity: Open admission.

BASIC COSTS (2016-2017)

Tuition and fees: $1,420; out-of-state residents $7,750.
Per-credit charge: $46; out-of-state residents $257.
Additional info: Tuition/fee waivers available for unemployed or children of unemployed.

FINANCIAL AID PICTURE

Students with need: Need-based aid available for full-time and part-time students. Work study available nights.

Students without need: No-need awards available for academics, leadership, music/drama, state/district residency.

FINANCIAL AID PROCEDURES

Forms required: FAFSA.

Dates and Deadlines: Priority date 5/31; no closing date. Applicants notified on a rolling basis starting 7/1; must reply within 2 week(s) of notification.

Transfers: No deadline. Applicants notified on a rolling basis.

CONTACT

Ulises Velasco, Director of Financial Aid
1000 Hensley Creek/Box 3000, Ukiah, CA 95482
(707) 468-3110

Menlo College
Atherton, California
www.menlo.edu   Federal Code: 001236

4-year private business and liberal arts college in small city.
Enrollment: 774 undergrads, 2% part-time. 158 full-time freshmen.
Selectivity: Admits less than 50% of applicants.

BASIC COSTS (2017-2018)
Tuition and fees: $41,350.
Per-credit charge: $1,693.
Room and board: $13,680.

FINANCIAL AID PICTURE
Students with need: Need-based aid available for full-time and part-time students. Work study available nights, weekends, and for part-time students.
Students without need: No-need awards available for academics, athletics.

FINANCIAL AID PROCEDURES
Forms required: FAFSA.
Dates and Deadlines: Priority date 3/2; closing date 8/1. Applicants notified on a rolling basis starting 12/15; must reply by 5/1 or within 2 week(s) of notification.
Transfers: Closing date 12/15. Applicants notified on a rolling basis starting 12/1; must reply by 5/1 or within 2 week(s) of notification.

CONTACT
Victoria Madrigal, Financial Aid Counselor
1000 El Camino Real, Atherton, CA 94027
(650) 543-3880

Merritt College
Oakland, California
www.merritt.edu   Federal Code: 001267

2-year public community college in large city.
Enrollment: 1,928 undergrads.
Selectivity: Open admission.

BASIC COSTS (2016-2017)
Tuition and fees: $1,420; out-of-state residents $8,320.
Per-credit charge: $46; out-of-state residents $276.
Additional info: Tuition/fee waivers available for unemployed or children of unemployed.

FINANCIAL AID PICTURE
Students with need: Need-based aid available for full-time and part-time students.

FINANCIAL AID PROCEDURES
Forms required: FAFSA, institutional form.
Dates and Deadlines: Priority date 4/1; closing date 6/30. Applicants notified on a rolling basis starting 6/1.

CONTACT
Alice Freeman, Financial Aid Coordinator
12500 Campus Drive, Oakland, CA 94619
(510) 436-2465

Mills College
Oakland, California
www.mills.edu   Federal Code: 001238

4-year private liberal arts college for women in large city.
Enrollment: 806 undergrads, 4% part-time. 169 full-time freshmen.
Selectivity: Admits over 75% of applicants.

BASIC COSTS (2016-2017)
Tuition and fees: $45,620.
Room and board: $12,702.

FINANCIAL AID PICTURE (2016-2017)
Students with need: Out of 162 full-time freshmen who applied for aid, 150 were judged to have need. Of these, 150 received aid, and 27 had their full need met. Average financial aid package met 87% of need; average scholarship/grant was $43,222; average loan was $5,077. For part-time students, average financial aid package was $20,174.
Students without need: 15 full-time freshmen who did not demonstrate need for aid received scholarships/grants; average award was $20,894. No-need awards available for academics, leadership, music/drama.

FINANCIAL AID PROCEDURES
Forms required: FAFSA, state aid form.
Dates and Deadlines: Priority date 2/15; closing date 3/1. Applicants notified on a rolling basis starting 3/1; must reply by 6/30.
Transfers: Priority date 3/2; closing date 7/15. Applicants notified on a rolling basis starting 4/15; must reply by 5/1 or within 2 week(s) of notification.

CONTACT
Dustin Smilth-Salinas, Director of Financial Aid
5000 MacArthur Boulevard, Oakland, CA 94613
(510) 430-2000

MiraCosta College
Oceanside, California
www.miracosta.edu   Federal Code: 001239

2-year public community and junior college in large city.
Enrollment: 12,596 undergrads.
Selectivity: Open admission; but selective for some programs.

BASIC COSTS (2016-2017)
Tuition and fees: $1,428; out-of-state residents $7,758.
Per-credit charge: $46; out-of-state residents $257.

FINANCIAL AID PICTURE (2015-2016)
Students with need: 85% of average financial aid package awarded as scholarships/grants, 15% awarded as loans/jobs. Need-based aid available for part-time students. Work study available nights.
Additional info: Waiver of in-state fees for eligible low-income students.

FINANCIAL AID PROCEDURES
Forms required: FAFSA, state aid form, institutional form.
Dates and Deadlines: Priority date 4/12; no closing date. Applicants notified on a rolling basis; must reply within 1 week(s) of notification.
Transfers: Priority date 4/4; no deadline.

CONTACT
Michael Dear, Director, Financial Aid and Scholarships
One Barnard Drive, Oceanside, CA 92056-3899
(760) 795-6711

Modesto Junior College
Modesto, California
www.mjc.edu   Federal Code: 001240

2-year public community and junior college in large city.
Enrollment: 13,615 undergrads.
Selectivity: Open admission; but selective for some programs.

BASIC COSTS (2016-2017)
Tuition and fees: $1,416; out-of-state residents $8,286.
Per-credit charge: $46; out-of-state residents $275.

FINANCIAL AID PICTURE

Students with need: Need-based aid available for full-time and part-time students. Work study available nights, weekends, and for part-time students.

Students without need: This college awards aid only to students with need.

Additional info: Modesto Junior College scholarship priority deadline 12/15.

FINANCIAL AID PROCEDURES

Forms required: FAFSA, state aid form, institutional form.

Dates and Deadlines: Priority date 3/2; no closing date. Applicants notified on a rolling basis starting 5/1; must reply within 2 week(s) of notification.

CONTACT

Peggy Fikse, Director, Student Financial Services
435 College Avenue, Modesto, CA 95350-5800

Monterey Peninsula College
Monterey, California
www.mpc.edu   Federal Code: 001242

2-year public community college in large town.

Enrollment: 4,449 undergrads.

Selectivity: Open admission; but selective for some programs.

BASIC COSTS (2016-2017)

Tuition and fees: $1,450; out-of-state residents $7,780.

Per-credit charge: $46; out-of-state residents $257.

Additional info: Tuition/fee waivers available for adults, minority students, unemployed or children of unemployed.

FINANCIAL AID PICTURE

Students with need: Need-based aid available for full-time and part-time students.

FINANCIAL AID PROCEDURES

Forms required: FAFSA, institutional form.

Dates and Deadlines: Closing date 6/30. Applicants notified on a rolling basis starting 6/1.

CONTACT

Francisco Tostado, Director of Student Financial Services
980 Fremont Street, Monterey, CA 93940-4799
(831) 646-4000

Moorpark College
Moorpark, California
www.moorparkcollege.edu   Federal Code: 007115

2-year public community college in small city.

Enrollment: 10,680 undergrads.

Selectivity: Open admission; but selective for some programs.

BASIC COSTS (2016-2017)

Tuition and fees: $1,448; out-of-state residents $8,918.

Per-credit charge: $46; out-of-state residents $295.

FINANCIAL AID PICTURE (2015-2016)

Students with need: 86% of average financial aid package awarded as scholarships/grants, 14% awarded as loans/jobs. Need-based aid available for part-time students. Work study available nights.

Students without need: This college awards aid only to students with need.

FINANCIAL AID PROCEDURES

Forms required: FAFSA, state aid form.

Dates and Deadlines: Priority date 5/14; no closing date. Applicants notified on a rolling basis starting 6/15.

Transfers: Priority date 5/16. Applicants notified by 6/16.

CONTACT

Kimberly Korinke, Financial Aid Officer
7075 Campus Road, Moorpark, CA 93021
(805) 378-1463

Mount Saint Mary's University
Los Angeles, California
www.msmu.edu   Federal Code: 001243

4-year private university and liberal arts college for women in very large city, affiliated with the Roman Catholic Church.

Enrollment: 2,789 undergrads, 23% part-time. 541 full-time freshmen.

Selectivity: Admits over 75% of applicants.

BASIC COSTS (2016-2017)

Tuition and fees: $37,722.

Per-credit charge: $1,528.

Room and board: $11,451.

FINANCIAL AID PICTURE (2016-2017)

Students with need: Out of 521 full-time freshmen who applied for aid, 496 were judged to have need. Of these, 494 received aid, and 11 had their full need met. Average financial aid package met 64% of need; average scholarship/grant was $19,743; average loan was $3,504. For part-time students, average financial aid package was $6,247.

Students without need: 16 full-time freshmen who did not demonstrate need for aid received scholarships/grants; average award was $15,605. No-need awards available for academics, alumni affiliation, music/drama.

FINANCIAL AID PROCEDURES

Forms required: FAFSA.

Dates and Deadlines: Priority date 3/1; no closing date. Applicants notified on a rolling basis starting 3/1; must reply by 5/1.

Transfers: No deadline. Applicants notified on a rolling basis starting 3/1; must reply by 5/1 or within 3 week(s) of notification.

CONTACT

La Royce Housely, Director of Student Financing
12001 Chalon Road, Los Angeles, CA 90049
(310) 954-4195

Mount San Antonio College
Walnut, California
www.mtsac.edu   Federal Code: 001245

2-year public community college in small city.

Enrollment: 24,554 undergrads.

Selectivity: Open admission.

BASIC COSTS (2016-2017)

Tuition and fees: $1,441; out-of-state residents $8,671.

Per-credit charge: $46; out-of-state residents $287.

FINANCIAL AID PICTURE (2015-2016)

Students with need: 100% of average financial aid package awarded as scholarships/grants, 0% awarded as loans/jobs. Need-based aid available for part-time students.

Students without need: This college awards aid only to students with need.

FINANCIAL AID PROCEDURES

Forms required: FAFSA.

Dates and Deadlines: Priority date 3/2; no closing date. Applicants notified on a rolling basis starting 7/1.

CONTACT

Chau Dao, Director Financial Aid
1100 North Grand Avenue, Walnut, CA 91789
(909) 274-4450

Mount San Jacinto College

San Jacinto, California
www.msjc.edu
Federal Code: 001246

2-year public community college in small city.
Enrollment: 9,130 undergrads.
Selectivity: Open admission; but selective for some programs.

BASIC COSTS (2016-2017)

Tuition and fees: $1,394; out-of-state residents $8,264.
Per-credit charge: $46; out-of-state residents $275.

FINANCIAL AID PICTURE

Students with need: Need-based aid available for full-time and part-time students. Work study available nights.
Students without need: No-need awards available for academics, music/drama.
Additional info: Board of Governors Grant Program for state residents to defray cost of enrollment fees.

FINANCIAL AID PROCEDURES

Forms required: FAFSA, institutional form.
Dates and Deadlines: Priority date 3/2; no closing date. Applicants notified on a rolling basis starting 5/1; must reply within 3 week(s) of notification.
Transfers: No deadline.

CONTACT

Leisa Navarro, Financial Aid Supervisor
1499 North State Street, San Jacinto, CA 92583
(951) 487-3245

Mt. Sierra College

Monrovia, California
www.mtsierra.edu
Federal Code: 031287

3-year for-profit visual arts and business college in large city.
Enrollment: 530 undergrads.

BASIC COSTS (2016-2017)

Tuition and fees: $15,688.
Per-credit charge: $395.

FINANCIAL AID PICTURE (2015-2016)

Students with need: 46% of average financial aid package awarded as scholarships/grants, 54% awarded as loans/jobs. Need-based aid available for part-time students.

FINANCIAL AID PROCEDURES

Forms required: FAFSA.
Transfers: No deadline. Applicants notified on a rolling basis.

CONTACT

Lida Castillo, Financial Aid Director
101 East Huntington Drive, Monrovia, CA 91016
(626) 873-2100

MTI College

Sacramento, California
www.mticollege.edu
Federal Code: 012912

2-year for-profit business and technical college in large city.
Enrollment: 1,020 undergrads.

FINANCIAL AID PICTURE

Students with need: Need-based aid available for full-time students. Work study available nights.

CONTACT

Paula Perez, Director of Financial Aid
5221 Madison Avenue, Sacramento, CA 95841
(916) 339-1500

National University

La Jolla, California
www.nu.edu
Federal Code: 011460

4-year private university in very large city.
Enrollment: 7,979 undergrads, 62% part-time. 23 full-time freshmen.
Selectivity: Open admission.

BASIC COSTS (2016-2017)

Tuition and fees: $13,092.
Per-credit charge: $362.

FINANCIAL AID PICTURE (2016-2017)

Students with need: 43% of average financial aid package awarded as scholarships/grants, 57% awarded as loans/jobs. Need-based aid available for part-time students.

FINANCIAL AID PROCEDURES

Forms required: FAFSA, state aid form, institutional form.
Dates and Deadlines: Applicants notified on a rolling basis.
Transfers: No deadline.

CONTACT

Valerie Ryan, Director of Financial Aid
11255 North Torrey Pines Road, La Jolla, CA 92037-1011
(858) 642-8500

Northcentral University

San Diego, California
www.ncu.edu
Federal Code: 038133

Upper-division for-profit virtual university in very large city.
Enrollment: 133 undergrads, 91% part-time.

BASIC COSTS (2016-2017)

Tuition and fees: $10,360.
Additional info: One time Learning Management Fee of $450 and Course Materials Fees (CMF) for each course of up to $100.

FINANCIAL AID PICTURE

Students with need: Need-based aid available for full-time and part-time students.

FINANCIAL AID PROCEDURES

Dates and Deadlines: Applicants notified on a rolling basis; must reply within 4 week(s) of notification.
Transfers: No deadline. Applicants notified on a rolling basis.

CONTACT

Ian Cooper, Director Learner Financial Services
8667 East Hartford Drive, Scottsdale, AZ 85255
(888) 327-2877 ext. 8080

Notre Dame de Namur University

Belmont, California
www.ndnu.edu
Federal Code: 001179

4-year private university and liberal arts college in large town, affiliated with the Roman Catholic Church.

Enrollment: 1,097 undergrads.

BASIC COSTS (2016-2017)
Tuition and fees: $33,418.
Per-credit charge: $1,065.
Room and board: $13,398.

FINANCIAL AID PICTURE
Students with need: Need-based aid available for full-time and part-time students. Work study available nights, weekends, and for part-time students.
Students without need: No-need awards available for academics, art, athletics, leadership, music/drama, religious affiliation, ROTC.
Scholarships offered: Presidential Scholarships: up to $26,000 per year; based on academic merit and leadership. Emerging Artist Scholarship: up to $9,500 annually; based on demonstrated talent in the performing and fine arts. Belmont Scholarships: up to $9,000 annually; based on merit. Bay Area Catholic High School: up to $7,500 per year to one student from each of Bay Area Catholic high schools.

FINANCIAL AID PROCEDURES
Forms required: FAFSA. CSS PROFILE accepted but not required.
Dates and Deadlines: Priority date 3/2; no closing date. Applicants notified on a rolling basis starting 2/15; must reply by 5/1 or within 2 week(s) of notification.

CONTACT
Wilbert Lleses, Director of Financial Aid
1500 Ralston Avenue, Belmont, CA 94002-1908
(650) 508-3600

Occidental College
Los Angeles, California   Federal Code: 001249
www.oxy.edu   CSS Code: 4581

4-year private liberal arts college in very large city, affiliated with the nondenominational tradition.
Enrollment: 2,050 undergrads, 1% part-time. 518 full-time freshmen.
Selectivity: Admits less than 50% of applicants.

BASIC COSTS (2016-2017)
Tuition and fees: $51,070.
Room and board: $14,460.

FINANCIAL AID PICTURE (2015-2016)
Students with need: Out of 372 full-time freshmen who applied for aid, 305 were judged to have need. Of these, 305 received aid, and 305 had their full need met. Average financial aid package met 100% of need; average scholarship/grant was $38,734; average loan was $4,592. For part-time students, average financial aid package was $8,349.
Students without need: 54 full-time freshmen who did not demonstrate need for aid received scholarships/grants; average award was $11,808. No-need awards available for academics, leadership, music/drama, state/district residency.
Scholarships offered: Margaret Bundy Scott Scholarship: $25,000. President's Scholarship: $17,500; awarded to top 10-15% of incoming class based on academic achievement, leadership, and citizenship.
Additional info: Work-study programs are available during the day when students are not in class.

FINANCIAL AID PROCEDURES
Forms required: FAFSA, CSS PROFILE, state aid form.
Dates and Deadlines: Priority date 1/15; closing date 1/15. Applicants notified by 3/25; must reply by 5/1.
Transfers: Closing date 4/1. Applicants notified by 6/15; must reply within 2 week(s) of notification. California residents must apply for Cal Grant by completing FAFSA and CSAC's GPA verification form by March 2. For all regular applicants, FAFSA is due Jan. 15; Profile is due April 1.

CONTACT
Gina Becerril, Director of Financial Aid
1600 Campus Road, Los Angeles, CA 90041
(323) 259-2548

Ohlone College
Fremont, California
www.ohlone.edu   Federal Code: 004481

2-year public community college in large city.
Enrollment: 4,586 undergrads.
Selectivity: Open admission; but selective for some programs.

BASIC COSTS (2016-2017)
Tuition and fees: $1,418; out-of-state residents $8,378.
Per-credit charge: $46; out-of-state residents $278.

FINANCIAL AID PICTURE
Students with need: Need-based aid available for full-time and part-time students.

FINANCIAL AID PROCEDURES
Forms required: FAFSA.
Dates and Deadlines: Must reply within 2 week(s) of notification.

CONTACT
Deborah Griffin, Director, Financial Aid
43600 Mission Boulevard, Fremont, CA 94539-0390
(510) 659-6150

Orange Coast College
Costa Mesa, California
www.orangecoastcollege.edu   Federal Code: 001250

2-year public community college in small city.
Enrollment: 17,280 undergrads.
Selectivity: Open admission.

BASIC COSTS (2016-2017)
Tuition and fees: $1,438; out-of-state residents $7,738.
Per-credit charge: $46; out-of-state residents $256.
Additional info: Tuition/fee waivers available for adults, minority students, unemployed or children of unemployed.

FINANCIAL AID PICTURE (2015-2016)
Students with need: 92% of average financial aid package awarded as scholarships/grants, 8% awarded as loans/jobs. Need-based aid available for part-time students.

FINANCIAL AID PROCEDURES
Forms required: FAFSA, state aid form.
Dates and Deadlines: Priority date 3/2; no closing date. Applicants notified on a rolling basis; must reply within 2 week(s) of notification.

CONTACT
Tanisha Bradfield, Financial Aid Director
2701 Fairview Road, Costa Mesa, CA 92628-5005
(714) 432-5508

Otis College of Art and Design
Los Angeles, California
www.otis.edu   Federal Code: 001251

4-year private visual arts college in very large city.
Enrollment: 1,015 undergrads.

BASIC COSTS (2017-2018)
Tuition and fees: $43,270.
Per-credit charge: $1,412.
Room and board: $14,690.
Additional info: The health insurance fee is $2,350/yr but can be waived with proof of insurance.

FINANCIAL AID PICTURE
Students with need: Need-based aid available for full-time and part-time students. Work study available nights, weekends, and for part-time students.
Students without need: No-need awards available for academics, art.

FINANCIAL AID PROCEDURES
Forms required: FAFSA, state aid form.
Dates and Deadlines: Priority date 2/15; no closing date. Applicants notified on a rolling basis starting 3/1; must reply within 2 week(s) of notification.

CONTACT
Jessika Vasquez-Huerta, Director of Financial Aid
9045 Lincoln Boulevard, Los Angeles, CA 90045-9785
(310) 665-6880

Pacific College of Oriental Medicine: San Diego
San Diego, California
www.pacificcollege.edu

2-year for-profit health science and career college in very large city.
Enrollment: 128 undergrads, 46% part-time. 509 full-time freshmen.

FINANCIAL AID PICTURE (2015-2016)
Students with need: Out of 495 full-time freshmen who applied for aid, 495 were judged to have need. Of these, 495 received aid, and 385 had their full need met. Average financial aid package met 95% of need; average scholarship/grant was $5,165; average loan was $4,300. Need-based aid available for part-time students.
Students without need: This college awards aid only to students with need.

FINANCIAL AID PROCEDURES
Forms required: FAFSA, institutional form.
Dates and Deadlines: Priority date 6/30; closing date 8/1. Applicants notified by 9/1; must reply by 9/1.
Transfers: Priority date 9/1. Applicants notified by 9/1; must reply by 9/1.

CONTACT
Beatrice Smith, VP of Financial Aid
7445 Mission Valley Road, Suite 105, San Diego, CA 92108

Pacific Oaks College
Pasadena, California
www.pacificoaks.edu   Federal Code: 001255

Upper-division private teachers college in small city.
Enrollment: 522 undergrads, 100% part-time.

BASIC COSTS (2016-2017)
Tuition and fees: $23,430.
Per-credit charge: $781.

FINANCIAL AID PICTURE (2016-2017)
Students with need: Need-based aid available for full-time and part-time students. Work study available nights, weekends, and for part-time students.
Students without need: This college awards aid only to students with need.

FINANCIAL AID PROCEDURES
Dates and Deadlines: Priority date 4/15; no closing date. Applicants notified on a rolling basis starting 5/1; must reply by 5/15 or within 4 week(s) of notification.
Transfers: Priority date 4/15; no deadline. Applicants notified on a rolling basis.

CONTACT
Lawrence McGhee, Senior Director of Financial Aid
55 Eureka Street, Pasadena, CA 91103
(312) 329-6602

Pacific States University
Los Angeles, California
www.psuca.edu   Federal Code: 031633

4-year private university in very large city.
Enrollment: 32 undergrads.
Selectivity: Open admission; but selective for some programs.

BASIC COSTS (2016-2017)
Tuition and fees: $16,005.
Per-credit charge: $345.
Additional info: Tuition at time of enrollment locked for 4 years.

FINANCIAL AID PICTURE
Students with need: Need-based aid available for full-time students.
Students without need: No-need awards available for academics.

FINANCIAL AID PROCEDURES
Forms required: FAFSA, institutional form.

CONTACT
James Cummings, Director of Financial Aid
3424 Wilshire Boulevard 12th floor, Los Angeles, CA 90010
(323) 731-2383 ext. 209

Pacific Union College
Angwin, California
www.puc.edu   Federal Code: 001258

4-year private liberal arts college in small town, affiliated with the Seventh-day Adventists.
Enrollment: 1,507 undergrads.

BASIC COSTS (2016-2017)
Tuition and fees: $28,329.
Per-credit charge: $810.
Room and board: $7,920.
Additional info: Student Health Plan $750/year.

FINANCIAL AID PICTURE (2016-2017)
Students with need: Need-based aid available for part-time students.
Students without need: No-need awards available for academics, alumni affiliation, art, athletics, leadership, music/drama, religious affiliation, state/district residency.

FINANCIAL AID PROCEDURES
Forms required: FAFSA, institutional form.
Dates and Deadlines: Priority date 3/2; no closing date. Applicants notified on a rolling basis starting 4/1; must reply within 3 week(s) of notification.
Transfers: No deadline. Applicants notified on a rolling basis starting 4/1; must reply within 3 week(s) of notification.

CONTACT
Laurie Wheeler, Director of Student Financial Services
One Angwin Avenue, Angwin, CA 94508-9707
(707) 965-7200

Palo Verde College

Blythe, California
www.paloverde.edu   Federal Code: 001259

2-year public community college in large town.
Enrollment: 1,821 undergrads.
Selectivity: Open admission; but selective for some programs.

BASIC COSTS (2016-2017)
Tuition and fees: $1,380; out-of-state residents $8,340.
Per-credit charge: $46; out-of-state residents $278.

FINANCIAL AID PICTURE
Students with need: Need-based aid available for full-time and part-time students. Work study available nights.
Students without need: This college awards aid only to students with need.

FINANCIAL AID PROCEDURES
Forms required: FAFSA, state aid form, institutional form.
Dates and Deadlines: Applicants notified on a rolling basis starting 7/1; must reply within 4 week(s) of notification.

CONTACT
Diana Mendez, Financial Aid Officer
One College Drive, Blythe, CA 92225
(760) 921-5536

Palomar College

San Marcos, California
www.palomar.edu   Federal Code: 001260

2-year public community college in small city.
Enrollment: 11,907 undergrads.
Selectivity: Open admission; but selective for some programs.

BASIC COSTS (2016-2017)
Tuition and fees: $1,430; out-of-state residents $7,910.
Per-credit charge: $46; out-of-state residents $262.

FINANCIAL AID PICTURE
Students with need: Need-based aid available for full-time and part-time students. Work study available nights.
Students without need: This college awards aid only to students with need.

FINANCIAL AID PROCEDURES
Forms required: FAFSA, institutional form.
Dates and Deadlines: Priority date 4/1; no closing date. Applicants notified on a rolling basis starting 6/1.
Transfers: No deadline.

CONTACT
Patricia Hurley, Interim Director of Financial Aid, Scholarships & Veterans Services
1140 West Mission Road, San Marcos, CA 92069-1487
(760) 891-7510

Patten University

Oakland, California
www.patten.edu   Federal Code: 004490

4-year private university and liberal arts college in large city, affiliated with the interdenominational tradition.
Enrollment: 1,492 undergrads.
Selectivity: Open admission; but selective for some programs.

BASIC COSTS (2016-2017)
Tuition and fees: $3,432.

FINANCIAL AID PICTURE
Students with need: Need-based aid available for full-time and part-time students.

FINANCIAL AID PROCEDURES
Forms required: institutional form.

CONTACT
Denis Clark, Financial Aid Director
2433 Coolidge Avenue, Oakland, CA 94601-2699
(510) 261-8500 ext. 7747

Pepperdine University

Malibu, California
www.pepperdine.edu   Federal Code: 001264

4-year private university and liberal arts college in large town, affiliated with the Church of Christ.
Enrollment: 3,528 undergrads, 9% part-time. 743 full-time freshmen.
Selectivity: Admits less than 50% of applicants.

BASIC COSTS (2016-2017)
Tuition and fees: $50,022.
Per-credit charge: $1,565.
Room and board: $14,330.

FINANCIAL AID PICTURE (2015-2016)
Students with need: Out of 740 full-time freshmen who applied for aid, 436 were judged to have need. Of these, 432 received aid, and 74 had their full need met. Average financial aid package met 75% of need; average scholarship/grant was $35,827; average loan was $4,343. For part-time students, average financial aid package was $25,578.
Students without need: 161 full-time freshmen who did not demonstrate need for aid received scholarships/grants; average award was $21,773. No-need awards available for academics, art, athletics, leadership, music/drama, religious affiliation.
Scholarships offered: 29 full-time freshmen received athletic scholarships; average amount $41,514.

FINANCIAL AID PROCEDURES
Forms required: FAFSA.
Dates and Deadlines: Priority date 2/15; no closing date. Applicants notified by 4/15; must reply by 5/1.

CONTACT
Janet Lockhart, Director of Financial Assistance
24255 Pacific Coast Highway, Malibu, CA 90263-4392
(310) 506-4301

Pitzer College

Claremont, California   Federal Code: 001172
www.pitzer.edu   CSS Code: 4619

4-year private liberal arts college in large town.
Enrollment: 1,062 undergrads, 3% part-time. 268 full-time freshmen.
Selectivity: Admits less than 50% of applicants.

BASIC COSTS (2016-2017)
Tuition and fees: $50,430.
Room and board: $15,762.

FINANCIAL AID PICTURE (2016-2017)
Students with need: Out of 147 full-time freshmen who applied for aid, 110 were judged to have need. Of these, 110 received aid, and 110 had

their full need met. Average financial aid package met 100% of need; average scholarship/grant was $42,956; average loan was $3,242. For part-time students, average financial aid package was $23,952.

Students without need: 4 full-time freshmen who did not demonstrate need for aid received scholarships/grants; average award was $8,561. No-need awards available for academics, leadership.

Scholarships offered: Trustee Community Scholar Award: $5,000 per year; based on extraordinary academic achievement, outstanding leadership or exceptional community service.

FINANCIAL AID PROCEDURES

Forms required: FAFSA, CSS PROFILE, state aid form, institutional form.
Dates and Deadlines: Priority date 2/1; closing date 2/1. Applicants notified by 4/1; must reply by 5/1.
Transfers: Closing date 3/1. Applicants notified by 5/15; must reply by 6/15.

CONTACT

Robin Thompson, Director of Financial Aid
1050 North Mills Avenue, Claremont, CA 91711-6101
(909) 621-8208

Platt College: Los Angeles

Alhambra, California
www.plattcollege.edu   Federal Code: 030627

2-year for-profit visual arts and technical college in very large city.
Enrollment: 661 undergrads.

BASIC COSTS (2016-2017)

Additional info: Diploma programs: $17,925-$22,795; Associate programs: $25,300-$45,550; Bachelor programs: $18,525-$55,080. Fees, books supplies range depending on program level and course of study. All costs are subject to change.

FINANCIAL AID PICTURE

Students with need: Need-based aid available for full-time and part-time students. Work study available nights.

FINANCIAL AID PROCEDURES

Forms required: FAFSA, institutional form.
Dates and Deadlines: Priority date 3/2; no closing date. Applicants notified on a rolling basis starting 1/1.

CONTACT

Nina Martinez, Financial Aid Director
1000 South Fremont Avenue A9W, Alhambra, CA 91803
(626) 300-5444 ext. 230

Platt College: Ontario

Ontario, California
www.plattcollege.edu   Federal Code: 030627

4-year for-profit branch campus and technical college in small city.
Enrollment: 431 undergrads.

BASIC COSTS (2016-2017)

Additional info: Diploma programs: $17,925-$22,795; Associate programs: $25,300-$45,550; Bachelor programs: $18,525-$55,080. Fees, books supplies range depending on program level and course of study. All costs are subject to change.

FINANCIAL AID PICTURE

Students with need: Need-based aid available for full-time and part-time students. Work study available nights.
Scholarships offered: Presidential Scholarship, CAPPS Scholarship, Imagine America Scholarship: $1,000 each; based on application and essay; approximately 100 plus available per calendar year.

FINANCIAL AID PROCEDURES

Forms required: FAFSA, institutional form.
Dates and Deadlines: Priority date 3/2; no closing date. Applicants notified on a rolling basis starting 1/1.
Transfers: No deadline.

CONTACT

Rosemarie Young, Regional Director of Compliance and Civil Rights
3700 Inland Empire Boulevard, Ontario, CA 91764
(909) 941-9410

Platt College: San Diego

San Diego, California
www.platt.edu   Federal Code: 023043

4-year for-profit visual arts and technical college in very large city.
Enrollment: 255 undergrads. 46 full-time freshmen.
Selectivity: Open admission; but selective for some programs and for out-of-state students.

BASIC COSTS (2016-2017)

Additional info: Diploma programs: $17,925-$22,795; Associate programs: $25,300-$45,550; Bachelor programs: $18,525-$55,080. Fees, books supplies range depending on program level and course of study. All costs are subject to change.

FINANCIAL AID PICTURE

Students with need: Need-based aid available for full-time and part-time students.

FINANCIAL AID PROCEDURES

Forms required: FAFSA, state aid form, institutional form.
Dates and Deadlines: Closing date 3/2. Applicants notified on a rolling basis; must reply within 1 week(s) of notification.

CONTACT

Opel Oliver, Director of Financial Aid
6250 El Cajon Boulevard, San Diego, CA 92115
(619) 265-0107

Point Loma Nazarene University

San Diego, California
www.pointloma.edu   Federal Code: 001262

4-year private university and liberal arts college in very large city, affiliated with the Church of the Nazarene.
Enrollment: 3,042 undergrads, 15% part-time. 599 full-time freshmen.
Selectivity: Admits 50 to 75% of applicants.

BASIC COSTS (2017-2018)

Tuition and fees: $34,600.
Per-credit charge: $1,417.
Room and board: $10,150.

FINANCIAL AID PICTURE (2015-2016)

Students with need: Out of 519 full-time freshmen who applied for aid, 405 were judged to have need. Of these, 402 received aid, and 64 had their full need met. Average financial aid package met 65% of need; average scholarship/grant was $18,825; average loan was $3,367. For part-time students, average financial aid package was $10,894.

Students without need: 124 full-time freshmen who did not demonstrate need for aid received scholarships/grants; average award was $11,038. No-need awards available for academics, art, athletics, music/drama, religious affiliation, ROTC.

Scholarships offered: 14 full-time freshmen received athletic scholarships; average amount $15,679.

FINANCIAL AID PROCEDURES

Forms required: FAFSA.

Dates and Deadlines: Priority date 3/2; no closing date. Applicants notified on a rolling basis starting 12/15; must reply by 5/15.

CONTACT

Pam Macias, Director of Financial Aid

3900 Lomaland Drive, San Diego, CA 92106-2899

(619) 849-2068

Pomona College

Claremont, California
www.pomona.edu

Federal Code: 001173
CSS Code: 4607

4-year private liberal arts college in large town.

Enrollment: 1,642 undergrads. 411 full-time freshmen.

Selectivity: Admits less than 50% of applicants.

BASIC COSTS (2016-2017)

Tuition and fees: $49,352.

Room and board: $15,605.

FINANCIAL AID PICTURE

Students with need: Need-based aid available for full-time and part-time students.

Students without need: This college awards aid only to students with need.

Additional info: Financial aid awards loan-free for all eligible students.

FINANCIAL AID PROCEDURES

Forms required: FAFSA, CSS PROFILE, state aid form.

Dates and Deadlines: Priority date 3/1; closing date 3/1. Applicants notified by 4/1; must reply by 5/1.

Transfers: Closing date 3/1. Must reply by 6/1. Candidates required to submit financial aid transcript from previous institution directly to the college.

CONTACT

Pat Coye, Interim Director of Financial Aid

333 North College Way, Claremont, CA 91711-6312

(909) 621-8205

Professional Golfers Career College

Temecula, California
www.golfcollege.edu

Federal Code: 033673

2-year for-profit golf academy in small city.

Enrollment: 311 undergrads.

BASIC COSTS (2016-2017)

Tuition and fees: $15,000.

FINANCIAL AID PICTURE

Students with need: Need-based aid available for full-time students.

FINANCIAL AID PROCEDURES

Transfers: No deadline.

CONTACT

Ann Martin, Financial Aid Director

26109 Ynez Road, Temecula, CA 92591

(800) 877-4380

Providence Christian College

Pasadena, California
www.providencecc.edu

4-year private liberal arts college in large city, affiliated with the nondenominational tradition.

Enrollment: 145 undergrads.

BASIC COSTS (2016-2017)

Tuition and fees: $28,014.

Per-credit charge: $1,132.

Room and board: $8,408.

FINANCIAL AID PICTURE

Students with need: Need-based aid available for full-time and part-time students.

Students without need: No-need awards available for academics, athletics, leadership, music/drama, religious affiliation.

FINANCIAL AID PROCEDURES

Forms required: FAFSA, institutional form.

Dates and Deadlines: Priority date 3/1; closing date 5/1. Applicants notified on a rolling basis starting 3/1; must reply by 5/1 or within 3 week(s) of notification.

Transfers: No deadline. Applicants notified on a rolling basis; must reply by 5/1 or within 3 week(s) of notification.

CONTACT

Tina Bos, Director of Financial Aid

1539 East Howard Street, Pasadena, CA 91104

Reedley College

Reedley, California
www.reedleycollege.edu

Federal Code: 001308

2-year public community college in large town.

Enrollment: 7,804 undergrads.

Selectivity: Open admission.

BASIC COSTS (2016-2017)

Tuition and fees: $1,420; out-of-state residents $8,470.

Per-credit charge: $46; out-of-state residents $281.

Room and board: $6,668.

Additional info: Tuition/fee waivers available for adults, minority students, unemployed or children of unemployed.

FINANCIAL AID PICTURE

Students with need: Need-based aid available for full-time and part-time students.

Students without need: This college awards aid only to students with need.

Additional info: Board of Governors fee waiver available for low-income students. Book voucher available for EOPS students.

FINANCIAL AID PROCEDURES

Forms required: FAFSA, state aid form.

Dates and Deadlines: Priority date 3/2; no closing date. Applicants notified on a rolling basis starting 3/2; must reply within 3 week(s) of notification.

Transfers: Priority date 4/15. March 2 deadline for California grants.

CONTACT

Chris Cortes, Director of Financial Aid

995 North Reed Avenue, Reedley, CA 93654

(559) 638-3641

Rio Hondo College

Whittier, California
www.riohondo.edu

Federal Code: 001269

2-year public community college in small city.

Enrollment: 10,644 undergrads.

Selectivity: Open admission; but selective for some programs.

BASIC COSTS (2016-2017)
Tuition and fees: $1,452; out-of-state residents $7,452.
Per-credit charge: $46; out-of-state residents $246.

FINANCIAL AID PICTURE (2015-2016)
Students with need: 96% of average financial aid package awarded as scholarships/grants, 4% awarded as loans/jobs. Need-based aid available for part-time students.

FINANCIAL AID PROCEDURES
Forms required: FAFSA.
Dates and Deadlines: Priority date 7/15; no closing date. Applicants notified on a rolling basis.

CONTACT
Yvonne Gutierrez-Sandoval, Director Financial Aid
3600 Workman Mill Road, Whittier, CA 90601-1699
(562) 908-3411

Riverside City College
Riverside, California
www.rcc.edu   Federal Code: 001270

2-year public community college in large city.
Enrollment: 15,067 undergrads.
Selectivity: Open admission; but selective for some programs.

BASIC COSTS (2016-2017)
Tuition and fees: $1,416; out-of-state residents $7,746.
Per-credit charge: $46; out-of-state residents $257.
Additional info: Tuition/fee waivers available for adults, unemployed or children of unemployed.

FINANCIAL AID PICTURE
Students with need: Need-based aid available for full-time and part-time students. Work study available nights, weekends, and for part-time students.
Students without need: No-need awards available for academics, alumni affiliation, art, leadership, minority status, music/drama, state/district residency.

FINANCIAL AID PROCEDURES
Forms required: FAFSA, institutional form.
Dates and Deadlines: Priority date 3/1; no closing date. Applicants notified on a rolling basis starting 7/1.
Transfers: Students who received financial aid at another institution and earned less than 2.0 GPA ineligible for aid during first semester. Students must complete 6 units and earn 2.0 GPA to be eligible.

CONTACT
Elizabeth Hilton, Director of Student Financial Services
4800 Magnolia Avenue, Riverside, CA 92506
(951) 222-8710

Sacramento City College
Sacramento, California
www.scc.losrios.edu   Federal Code: 001233

2-year public community college in large city.
Enrollment: 15,921 undergrads.
Selectivity: Open admission.

BASIC COSTS (2016-2017)
Tuition and fees: $1,416; out-of-state residents $8,286.
Per-credit charge: $46; out-of-state residents $275.

FINANCIAL AID PICTURE
Students with need: Need-based aid available for full-time and part-time students. Work study available nights, weekends, and for part-time students.

FINANCIAL AID PROCEDURES
Forms required: FAFSA, state aid form.
Dates and Deadlines: Priority date 3/2; no closing date. Applicants notified on a rolling basis starting 7/1; must reply within 2 week(s) of notification.
Transfers: Priority date 5/30.

CONTACT
Rukiya Bates, Financial Aid Supervisor
3835 Freeport Boulevard, Sacramento, CA 95822
(916) 558-2546

Saddleback College
Mission Viejo, California
www.saddleback.edu   Federal Code: 008918

2-year public community college in small city.
Enrollment: 14,687 undergrads.
Selectivity: Open admission; but selective for some programs.

BASIC COSTS (2016-2017)
Tuition and fees: $1,418; out-of-state residents $9,698.
Per-credit charge: $46; out-of-state residents $322.

FINANCIAL AID PICTURE
Students with need: Need-based aid available for full-time and part-time students.
Students without need: This college awards aid only to students with need.

FINANCIAL AID PROCEDURES
Forms required: FAFSA.
Dates and Deadlines: Closing date 6/30. Applicants notified on a rolling basis starting 4/1.

CONTACT
Ruth Higgins, Interim Director, Financial Aid and Scholarships
28000 Marguerite Parkway, Mission Viejo, CA 92692
(949) 582-4860

St. Mary's College of California
Moraga, California
www.stmarys-ca.edu   Federal Code: 001302

4-year private liberal arts college in large town, affiliated with the Roman Catholic Church.
Enrollment: 2,789 undergrads, 7% part-time. 562 full-time freshmen.
Selectivity: Admits over 75% of applicants.

BASIC COSTS (2016-2017)
Tuition and fees: $44,360.
Per-credit charge: $1,583.
Room and board: $14,880.

FINANCIAL AID PICTURE (2016-2017)
Students with need: Out of 460 full-time freshmen who applied for aid, 385 were judged to have need. Of these, 385 received aid, and 2 had their full need met. Need-based aid available for part-time students.
Students without need: 147 full-time freshmen who did not demonstrate need for aid received scholarships/grants; average award was $17,608. No-need awards available for academics, alumni affiliation, athletics, leadership, music/drama, religious affiliation.
Scholarships offered: *Merit:* Presidential Scholars Scholarships: $25,000 annually based on 3.8 GPA and 1350 SAT. Honors at Entrance Scholarship: $22,000 annually based on 3.7 GPA and 1190-1290 SAT/26-28 ACT. Gael Scholarships: $19,000 annually based on a GPA above 3.26 and SAT over 1000. Lasallian Scholarship: $13,000 annually based on attendance at a U.S.

Lasallian high school. *Athletic:* 58 full-time freshmen received athletic scholarships; average amount $29,578.

FINANCIAL AID PROCEDURES
Forms required: FAFSA.
Dates and Deadlines: Priority date 2/15; no closing date. Applicants notified on a rolling basis starting 12/16; must reply by 5/1.
Transfers: Applicants notified on a rolling basis starting 12/16; must reply by 5/1. Transfer applicants who are accepted will be considered for merit and need based scholarships. Priority for awarding financial aid will be given to transfer students who apply before July 1. After July 1, financial aid consideration will be provided on a rolling basis.

CONTACT
Wilbert Lleses, Dean of Financial Service
1928 Saint Mary's Road, Moraga, CA 94575
(925) 631-4370

Samuel Merritt University
Oakland, California
www.samuelmerritt.edu   Federal Code: 007012

Upper-division private health science and nursing college in large city.
Enrollment: 584 undergrads.
Selectivity: GED not accepted.

BASIC COSTS (2016-2017)
Tuition and fees: $45,491.
Per-credit charge: $1,917.

FINANCIAL AID PICTURE
Students with need: Need-based aid available for full-time and part-time students. Work study available nights, weekends, and for part-time students.
Students without need: No-need awards available for academics, leadership, minority status.
Additional info: Ongoing private scholarships available. Students eligible to work in Medical Center (associated with college).

FINANCIAL AID PROCEDURES
Transfers: Priority date 3/2; no deadline. Applicants notified on a rolling basis; must reply within 3 week(s) of notification.

CONTACT
Mary Robinson, Director of Financial Aid
370 Hawthorne Avenue, Oakland, CA 94609-9954
(510) 869-1550

San Diego Christian College
Santee, California
www.sdcc.edu   Federal Code: 012031

4-year private liberal arts college in small city, affiliated with the nondenominational tradition.
Enrollment: 668 undergrads, 25% part-time. 58 full-time freshmen.
Selectivity: Admits 50 to 75% of applicants.

BASIC COSTS (2016-2017)
Tuition and fees: $29,550.
Per-credit charge: $1,210.
Room and board: $10,974.

FINANCIAL AID PICTURE
Students with need: Need-based aid available for full-time and part-time students. Work study available nights, weekends, and for part-time students.
Students without need: No-need awards available for academics, alumni affiliation, athletics, leadership, music/drama, state/district residency.

Scholarships offered: Early Acceptance Award: $1000: available to applicants who have turned in all admission materials by January 15th.

FINANCIAL AID PROCEDURES
Forms required: FAFSA, state aid form, institutional form.
Dates and Deadlines: Priority date 3/2; closing date 7/15. Applicants notified on a rolling basis starting 4/1; must reply by 5/1 or within 4 week(s) of notification.
Transfers: Applicants notified on a rolling basis starting 4/1; must reply by 5/1 or within 4 week(s) of notification. Transfer students with at least 30 units earned at one institution fall under a different Academic Scholarship awarding grid than first time freshman.

CONTACT
Daniel Reed, Director of Financial Aid
200 Riverview Parkway, Santee, CA 92071-5822
(619) 201-8730

San Diego City College
San Diego, California
www.sdcity.edu   Federal Code: 001273

2-year public community and junior college in very large city.
Enrollment: 11,002 undergrads.
Selectivity: Open admission.

BASIC COSTS (2016-2017)
Tuition and fees: $1,418; out-of-state residents $7,748.
Per-credit charge: $46; out-of-state residents $239.
Additional info: Tuition/fee waivers available for unemployed or children of unemployed.

FINANCIAL AID PICTURE
Students with need: Need-based aid available for full-time and part-time students.
Students without need: This college awards aid only to students with need.

FINANCIAL AID PROCEDURES
Forms required: FAFSA.
Dates and Deadlines: Priority date 4/15; no closing date. Applicants notified on a rolling basis starting 7/1; must reply within 4 week(s) of notification.
Transfers: No deadline. Applicants notified on a rolling basis starting 7/1. Aid is limited to remaining eligibility based on receipt of aid from previous college.

CONTACT
Greg Sanchez, Financial Aid Manager
1313 Park Boulevard, San Diego, CA 92101-4787
(619) 388-3501

San Diego Mesa College
San Diego, California
www.sdmesa.edu   Federal Code: 001275

2-year public community college in very large city.
Enrollment: 15,927 undergrads.
Selectivity: Open admission.

BASIC COSTS (2016-2017)
Tuition and fees: $1,418; out-of-state residents $7,748.
Per-credit charge: $46; out-of-state residents $257.

FINANCIAL AID PICTURE (2016-2017)
Students with need: Need-based aid available for full-time and part-time students.

Students without need: This college awards aid only to students with need.

FINANCIAL AID PROCEDURES

Forms required: FAFSA.

Dates and Deadlines: Priority date 3/2; no closing date. Applicants notified on a rolling basis starting 6/15; must reply within 3 week(s) of notification.

Transfers: No deadline.

CONTACT

Gilda Maldonado, Financial Aid Officer

7250 Mesa College Drive, San Diego, CA 92111

(619) 388-2817

San Diego Miramar College

San Diego, California

www.sdmiramar.edu   Federal Code: 014172

2-year public community college in very large city.

Enrollment: 8,374 undergrads. 6,780 full-time freshmen.

Selectivity: Open admission.

BASIC COSTS (2016-2017)

Tuition and fees: $1,437; out-of-state residents $7,767.

Per-credit charge: $46; out-of-state residents $257.

Additional info: Tuition/fee waivers available for unemployed or children of unemployed.

FINANCIAL AID PICTURE (2015-2016)

Students with need: 91% of average financial aid package awarded as scholarships/grants, 9% awarded as loans/jobs. Need-based aid available for part-time students.

Students without need: 6,780 full-time freshmen who did not demonstrate need for aid received scholarships/grants. No-need awards available for academics, minority status.

Additional info: Private scholarships available.

FINANCIAL AID PROCEDURES

Forms required: FAFSA.

Dates and Deadlines: Priority date 3/2; closing date 6/30. Applicants notified on a rolling basis; must reply by 4/11 or within 3 week(s) of notification.

Transfers: No deadline. Transfers advised to apply early.

CONTACT

Adela Jacobson, Financial Aid Officer

10440 Black Mountain Road, San Diego, CA 92126-2999

(619) 388-7864

San Diego State University

San Diego, California

www.sdsu.edu   Federal Code: 001151

4-year public university in very large city.

Enrollment: 29,853 undergrads, 10% part-time. 4,812 full-time freshmen.

Selectivity: Admits less than 50% of applicants.

BASIC COSTS (2016-2017)

Tuition and fees: $7,084; out-of-state residents $18,244.

Room and board: $14,812.

FINANCIAL AID PICTURE (2016-2017)

Students with need: Out of 3,800 full-time freshmen who applied for aid, 2,700 were judged to have need. Of these, 2,600 received aid, and 200 had their full need met. Average financial aid package met 63% of need; average scholarship/grant was $9,600; average loan was $3,200. For part-time students, average financial aid package was $9,100.

Students without need: 130 full-time freshmen who did not demonstrate need for aid received scholarships/grants; average award was $3,800. No-need awards available for academics, alumni affiliation, art, athletics, leadership, music/drama, ROTC, state/district residency.

Scholarships offered: 90 full-time freshmen received athletic scholarships; average amount $20,500.

FINANCIAL AID PROCEDURES

Forms required: FAFSA, state aid form.

Dates and Deadlines: Priority date 4/1; closing date 3/2. Applicants notified on a rolling basis starting 3/15.

CONTACT

Rose Pasenelli, Director of Financial Aid

5500 Campanile Drive, San Diego, CA 92182-7455

(619) 594-6323

San Francisco Art Institute

San Francisco, California

www.sfai.edu   Federal Code: 003948

4-year private visual arts college in very large city.

Enrollment: 332 undergrads, 7% part-time. 61 full-time freshmen.

Selectivity: Admits over 75% of applicants.

BASIC COSTS (2016-2017)

Tuition and fees: $43,090.

Per-credit charge: $1,849.

Room and board: $15,515.

FINANCIAL AID PICTURE (2016-2017)

Students with need: Out of 40 full-time freshmen who applied for aid, 31 were judged to have need. Of these, 31 received aid, and 2 had their full need met. Average financial aid package met 43% of need; average scholarship/grant was $5,372; average loan was $1,750. For part-time students, average financial aid package was $11,413.

Students without need: 28 full-time freshmen who did not demonstrate need for aid received scholarships/grants; average award was $6,052. No-need awards available for academics, alumni affiliation, art.

Scholarships offered: Several awards based on portfolio reviews during application for admissions process.

FINANCIAL AID PROCEDURES

Forms required: FAFSA.

Dates and Deadlines: Priority date 3/1; no closing date. Applicants notified on a rolling basis starting 3/1; must reply within 2 week(s) of notification.

Transfers: Priority date 3/2; no deadline. Applicants notified on a rolling basis starting 4/1; must reply within 3 week(s) of notification.

CONTACT

Annita Alldredge, Director of Financial Aid

SFAI - Admissions Office, San Francisco, CA 94133

(415) 749-4520

San Francisco Conservatory of Music

San Francisco, California   Federal Code: 001278

www.sfcm.edu   CSS Code: 4744

4-year private music college in very large city.

Enrollment: 187 undergrads, 1% part-time. 54 full-time freshmen.

Selectivity: Admits less than 50% of applicants.

BASIC COSTS (2016-2017)

Tuition and fees: $43,410.

Per-credit charge: $1,868.

Room only: $12,100.

FINANCIAL AID PICTURE (2016-2017)
Students with need: Average financial aid package met 77% of need; average scholarship/grant was $15,220; average loan was $3,750. Need-based aid available for part-time students.
Students without need: No-need awards available for music/drama.

FINANCIAL AID PROCEDURES
Forms required: FAFSA, state aid form, institutional form. CSS/Financial Aid PROFILE required of international applicants for any need-based scholarship funding. The school code for this is: 4744.
Dates and Deadlines: Priority date 2/15; closing date 3/1. Applicants notified on a rolling basis starting 4/1; must reply within 2 week(s) of notification.
Transfers: Priority date 2/15; closing date 7/1. Applicants notified on a rolling basis starting 4/1; must reply within 2 week(s) of notification.

CONTACT
Doris Howard, Director of Financial Aid
50 Oak Street, San Francisco, CA 94102
(415) 503-6235

San Francisco State University
San Francisco, California
www.sfsu.edu   Federal Code: 001154

4-year public university in very large city.
Enrollment: 24,882 undergrads, 15% part-time. 3,531 full-time freshmen.
Selectivity: Admits 50 to 75% of applicants.

BASIC COSTS (2016-2017)
Tuition and fees: $6,484; out-of-state residents $17,644.
Room and board: $12,698.

FINANCIAL AID PICTURE (2016-2017)
Students with need: Average financial aid package met 75% of need; average scholarship/grant was $9,109; average loan was $3,409. For part-time students, average financial aid package was $11,553.
Students without need: This college awards aid only to students with need.
Scholarships offered: Presidential Scholarship: 3.8 GPA and California residency required.

FINANCIAL AID PROCEDURES
Forms required: FAFSA.
Dates and Deadlines: Priority date 3/2; no closing date. Applicants notified on a rolling basis starting 4/15; must reply within 2 week(s) of notification.

CONTACT
Barbara Hubler, Director of Financial Aid
1600 Holloway Avenue, San Francisco, CA 94132
(415) 338-7000

San Joaquin Delta College
Stockton, California
www.deltacollege.edu   Federal Code: 001280

2-year public community college in large city.
Enrollment: 13,681 undergrads.
Selectivity: Open admission; but selective for some programs.

BASIC COSTS (2016-2017)
Tuition and fees: $1,380; out-of-state residents $7,950.
Per-credit charge: $46; out-of-state residents $257.

FINANCIAL AID PICTURE (2015-2016)
Students with need: 92% of average financial aid package awarded as scholarships/grants, 8% awarded as loans/jobs. Need-based aid available for part-time students. Work study available nights, weekends, and for part-time students.
Students without need: No-need awards available for academics, athletics.
Additional info: Enrollment fee waivers available for low-income California residents.

FINANCIAL AID PROCEDURES
Forms required: FAFSA, institutional form.
Dates and Deadlines: Closing date 6/30. Applicants notified on a rolling basis starting 4/1; must reply within 3 week(s) of notification.
Transfers: No deadline.

CONTACT
Tina Lent, Director of Financial Aid, Scholarships & Veterans Services
5151 Pacific Avenue, Stockton, CA 95207-6370
(209) 954-5115

San Joaquin Valley College
Visalia, California
www.sjvc.edu   Federal Code: 021207

2-year for-profit junior college in small city.
Enrollment: 1,892 undergrads.
Selectivity: Open admission; but selective for some programs.

FINANCIAL AID PICTURE
Students with need: Need-based aid available for full-time students.

FINANCIAL AID PROCEDURES
Forms required: FAFSA, state aid form, institutional form.

CONTACT
Kevin Robinson, Vice President of Student Financial Services
8400 West Mineral King Avenue, Visalia, CA 93291-9283
(559) 651-2500

San Jose City College
San Jose, California
www.sjcc.edu   Federal Code: 001282

2-year public community college in very large city.
Enrollment: 4,114 undergrads.
Selectivity: Open admission.

BASIC COSTS (2016-2017)
Tuition and fees: $1,428; out-of-state residents $7,878.
Per-credit charge: $46; out-of-state residents $261.

FINANCIAL AID PICTURE (2015-2016)
Students with need: 97% of average financial aid package awarded as scholarships/grants, 3% awarded as loans/jobs. Need-based aid available for part-time students.
Students without need: This college awards aid only to students with need.
Additional info: Board of Governors Grant (fee waivers) available to all qualified applicants.

FINANCIAL AID PROCEDURES
Forms required: FAFSA.
Dates and Deadlines: Applicants notified on a rolling basis; must reply within 4 week(s) of notification.

CONTACT
Takeo Kubo, Financial Aid Director
2100 Moorpark Avenue, San Jose, CA 95128-2798
(408) 288-3741

San Jose State University

San Jose, California
www.sjsu.edu
Federal Code: 001155

4-year public university and liberal arts college in very large city.
Enrollment: 26,432 undergrads, 18% part-time. 3,065 full-time freshmen.
Selectivity: Admits 50 to 75% of applicants.

BASIC COSTS (2017-2018)
Tuition and fees: $7,418; out-of-state residents $16,346.
Room and board: $13,002.

FINANCIAL AID PICTURE (2016-2017)
Students with need: Out of 2,473 full-time freshmen who applied for aid, 1,939 were judged to have need. Of these, 1,905 received aid, and 1,055 had their full need met. Average financial aid package met 85% of need; average scholarship/grant was $11,596; average loan was $3,366. For part-time students, average financial aid package was $14,634.
Students without need: This college awards aid only to students with need.
Scholarships offered: 77 full-time freshmen received athletic scholarships; average amount $19,780.

FINANCIAL AID PROCEDURES
Forms required: FAFSA.
Dates and Deadlines: Priority date 3/2; no closing date. Applicants notified on a rolling basis starting 3/1.

CONTACT
Coleetta Mcelroy, Director of Financial Aid & Scholarships
One Washington Square, San Jose, CA 95192-0014
(408) 283-7500

Santa Ana College

Santa Ana, California
www.sac.edu
Federal Code: 001284

2-year public community college in large city.
Enrollment: 10,923 undergrads.
Selectivity: Open admission.

BASIC COSTS (2016-2017)
Tuition and fees: $1,418; out-of-state residents $9,068.
Per-credit charge: $46; out-of-state residents $301.

FINANCIAL AID PICTURE (2015-2016)
Students with need: 92% of average financial aid package awarded as scholarships/grants, 8% awarded as loans/jobs.

FINANCIAL AID PROCEDURES
Forms required: FAFSA.
Dates and Deadlines: Priority date 6/30; no closing date. Applicants notified on a rolling basis starting 6/1; must reply within 2 week(s) of notification.

CONTACT
Robert Manson, Associate Dean of Financial Aid
1530 West 17th Street, Santa Ana, CA 92706
(714) 564-6242

Santa Barbara City College

Santa Barbara, California
www.sbcc.edu
Federal Code: 001285

2-year public community college in small city.
Enrollment: 12,867 undergrads.
Selectivity: Open admission; but selective for some programs.

BASIC COSTS (2016-2017)
Tuition and fees: $1,430; out-of-state residents $7,880.
Per-credit charge: $46; out-of-state residents $261.
Additional info: Tuition/fee waivers available for unemployed or children of unemployed.

FINANCIAL AID PICTURE
Students with need: Need-based aid available for full-time and part-time students.
Additional info: California residents may qualify for Board of Governor's Financial Assistance Program, which will allow institutions to waive enrollment fee.

FINANCIAL AID PROCEDURES
Forms required: FAFSA.
Dates and Deadlines: Applicants notified on a rolling basis starting 5/1; must reply within 2 week(s) of notification.

CONTACT
Brad Hardison, Director of Financial Aid
721 Cliff Drive, Santa Barbara, CA 93109-2394
(805) 965-0581 ext. 2716

Santa Clara University

Santa Clara, California
www.scu.edu
Federal Code: 001326
CSS Code: 4851

4-year private university in small city, affiliated with the Roman Catholic Church.
Enrollment: 5,411 undergrads, 1% part-time. 1,317 full-time freshmen.
Selectivity: Admits less than 50% of applicants.

BASIC COSTS (2016-2017)
Tuition and fees: $47,112.
Per-credit charge: $1,309.
Room and board: $13,965.

FINANCIAL AID PICTURE (2016-2017)
Students with need: Out of 778 full-time freshmen who applied for aid, 544 were judged to have need. Of these, 526 received aid, and 242 had their full need met. Average financial aid package met 86% of need; average scholarship/grant was $28,790; average loan was $3,333. Need-based aid available for part-time students.
Students without need: 332 full-time freshmen who did not demonstrate need for aid received scholarships/grants; average award was $11,456. No-need awards available for academics, athletics, music/drama, ROTC.
Scholarships offered: 69 full-time freshmen received athletic scholarships; average amount $34,497.

FINANCIAL AID PROCEDURES
Forms required: FAFSA, CSS PROFILE.
Dates and Deadlines: Priority date 2/1; no closing date. Applicants notified by 4/1; must reply by 5/1 or within 2 week(s) of notification.
Transfers: No deadline. Applicants notified on a rolling basis starting 4/1; must reply by 5/1 or within 2 week(s) of notification.

CONTACT
Nan Merz, Dean of University Financial Services
500 El Camino Real, Santa Clara, CA 95053
(408) 551-1000

Santa Monica College

Santa Monica, California
www.smc.edu
Federal Code: 001286

2-year public community college in small city.
Enrollment: 24,940 undergrads.

Selectivity: Open admission; but selective for some programs.

BASIC COSTS (2016-2017)
Tuition and fees: $1,444; out-of-state residents $10,114.
Per-credit charge: $46; out-of-state residents $335.

FINANCIAL AID PICTURE
Students with need: Need-based aid available for full-time and part-time students.

FINANCIAL AID PROCEDURES
Forms required: FAFSA, institutional form.
Dates and Deadlines: Applicants notified on a rolling basis starting 7/1; must reply within 2 week(s) of notification.
Transfers: No deadline.

CONTACT
Steve Myrow, Director of Financial Aid
1900 Pico Boulevard, Santa Monica, CA 90405-1628
(310) 434-4343

Santa Rosa Junior College
Santa Rosa, California
www.santarosa.edu   Federal Code: 001287

2-year public community college in small city.
Enrollment: 12,017 undergrads.
Selectivity: Open admission; but selective for some programs.

BASIC COSTS (2016-2017)
Tuition and fees: $1,430; out-of-state residents $7,378.
Per-credit charge: $46; out-of-state residents $270.

FINANCIAL AID PICTURE
Students with need: Need-based aid available for full-time and part-time students. Work study available nights.
Students without need: No-need awards available for academics, art, leadership, music/drama, state/district residency.
Additional info: California's Board of Governors Program provides fee waivers for applicants with need.

FINANCIAL AID PROCEDURES
Forms required: FAFSA.
Dates and Deadlines: Priority date 3/1; no closing date. Applicants notified on a rolling basis starting 4/15.

CONTACT
Jana Cox, Director of Student Financial Services
1501 Mendocino Avenue, Santa Rosa, CA 95401-4395
(707) 527-4471

Santiago Canyon College
Orange, California
www.sccollege.edu

2-year public community college in small city.
Enrollment: 4,131 undergrads.
Selectivity: Open admission.

BASIC COSTS (2016-2017)
Tuition and fees: $1,418; out-of-state residents $9,068.
Per-credit charge: $46; out-of-state residents $301.
Additional info: Tuition/fee waivers available for adults, minority students, unemployed or children of unemployed.

FINANCIAL AID PICTURE
Students with need: Need-based aid available for full-time and part-time students.

Students without need: This college awards aid only to students with need.

FINANCIAL AID PROCEDURES
Forms required: FAFSA, state aid form, institutional form.
Dates and Deadlines: Priority date 7/1; no closing date. Applicants notified on a rolling basis starting 6/1.
Transfers: No deadline. Applicants notified by 6/1.

CONTACT
Syed Rizvi, Associate Dean of Student Support Services
8045 East Chapman Avenue, Orange, CA 92869
(714) 628-4876

Scripps College
Claremont, California   Federal Code: 001174
www.scrippscollege.edu   CSS Code: 4693

4-year private liberal arts college for women in large town.
Enrollment: 1,030 undergrads. 277 full-time freshmen.
Selectivity: Admits less than 50% of applicants.

BASIC COSTS (2016-2017)
Tuition and fees: $50,982.
Per-credit charge: $1,587.
Room and board: $15,682.

FINANCIAL AID PICTURE (2015-2016)
Students with need: Out of 154 full-time freshmen who applied for aid, 93 were judged to have need. Of these, 93 received aid, and 93 had their full need met. Average financial aid package met 100% of need; average scholarship/grant was $35,730; average loan was $3,731. Need-based aid available for part-time students.
Students without need: 12 full-time freshmen who did not demonstrate need for aid received scholarships/grants; average award was $16,757. No-need awards available for academics, leadership.
Scholarships offered: James E. Scripps Scholarship: variable amount up to half-tuition; renewable; for distinguished young women whose intellectual and personal promise can be developed with a Scripps education.

FINANCIAL AID PROCEDURES
Forms required: FAFSA, CSS PROFILE, state aid form.
Dates and Deadlines: Closing date 2/1. Applicants notified by 4/1; must reply by 5/1.
Transfers: Priority date 4/1. Applicants notified by 5/1; must reply by 6/1. Students applying for admission as a transfer student should be aware that financial aid may be limited or unavailable.

CONTACT
Patrick Moore, Director of Financial Aid
1030 Columbia Avenue, Claremont, CA 91711-3905
(909) 621-8275

Shasta Bible College and Graduate School
Redding, California
www.shasta.edu   Federal Code: 016802

4-year private Bible and seminary college in small city, affiliated with the Baptist faith.
Enrollment: 44 undergrads.

BASIC COSTS (2016-2017)
Tuition and fees: $11,310.
Per-credit charge: $350.
Room only: $2,800.

FINANCIAL AID PICTURE

Students with need: Need-based aid available for full-time and part-time students.

Students without need: No-need awards available for music/drama.

FINANCIAL AID PROCEDURES

Forms required: FAFSA.

Dates and Deadlines: Closing date 8/1. Applicants notified on a rolling basis.

CONTACT

Linda Iles, Financial Aid Director
2951 Goodwater Avenue, Redding, CA 96002
(530) 221-4275 ext. 32

Shasta College
Redding, California
www.shastacollege.edu   Federal Code: 001289

2-year public community and junior college in small city.

Enrollment: 5,268 undergrads.

Selectivity: Open admission; but selective for some programs.

BASIC COSTS (2016-2017)

Tuition and fees: $1,418; out-of-state residents $7,838.

Per-credit charge: $46; out-of-state residents $260.

FINANCIAL AID PICTURE

Students with need: Need-based aid available for full-time and part-time students.

Students without need: This college awards aid only to students with need.

FINANCIAL AID PROCEDURES

Forms required: FAFSA, institutional form.

Dates and Deadlines: Priority date 3/2; no closing date. Applicants notified on a rolling basis starting 7/1.

CONTACT

Benna Starrett, Director of Financial Aid
Box 496006, Redding, CA 96049-6006
(530) 225-4735

Sierra College
Rocklin, California
www.sierracollege.edu   Federal Code: 001290

2-year public community college in small city.

Enrollment: 13,570 undergrads.

Selectivity: Open admission; but selective for some programs.

BASIC COSTS (2016-2017)

Tuition and fees: $1,428; out-of-state residents $7,998.

Per-credit charge: $46; out-of-state residents $265.

Room and board: $7,400.

FINANCIAL AID PICTURE (2015-2016)

Students with need: 99% of average financial aid package awarded as scholarships/grants, 1% awarded as loans/jobs. Need-based aid available for part-time students. Work study available nights, weekends, and for part-time students.

FINANCIAL AID PROCEDURES

Forms required: FAFSA.

Dates and Deadlines: Priority date 3/2; no closing date. Applicants notified on a rolling basis starting 5/15.

Transfers: No deadline.

CONTACT

Linda Williams, Financial Aid Program Manager
5000 Rocklin Road, Rocklin, CA 95677-3397
(916) 660-7310

Simpson University
Redding, California
www.simpsonu.edu   Federal Code: 001291

4-year private university in small city, affiliated with the Christian and Missionary Alliance.

Enrollment: 788 undergrads, 6% part-time. 117 full-time freshmen.

Selectivity: Admits 50 to 75% of applicants.

BASIC COSTS (2016-2017)

Tuition and fees: $25,950.

Per-credit charge: $1,095.

Room and board: $8,100.

Additional info: Tuition/fee waivers available for minority students.

FINANCIAL AID PICTURE (2016-2017)

Students with need: Out of 114 full-time freshmen who applied for aid, 95 were judged to have need. Of these, 95 received aid, and 13 had their full need met. Average financial aid package met 69% of need; average scholarship/grant was $16,658; average loan was $2,730. For part-time students, average financial aid package was $10,891.

Students without need: 19 full-time freshmen who did not demonstrate need for aid received scholarships/grants; average award was $11,624. No-need awards available for academics, alumni affiliation, athletics, leadership, minority status, music/drama, religious affiliation, state/district residency.

Scholarships offered: 13 full-time freshmen received athletic scholarships; average amount $9,527.

Additional info: Work-study programs available.

FINANCIAL AID PROCEDURES

Forms required: FAFSA, state aid form.

Dates and Deadlines: Priority date 3/2; no closing date. Applicants notified on a rolling basis starting 3/2.

CONTACT

Greg Bailey, Director of Student Financial Services
2211 College View Drive, Redding, CA 96003-8606
(530) 226-4111

Skyline College
San Bruno, California
www.skylinecollege.edu   Federal Code: 007713

2-year public community college in small city.

Enrollment: 5,813 undergrads.

Selectivity: Open admission; but selective for some programs.

BASIC COSTS (2016-2017)

Tuition and fees: $1,446; out-of-state residents $8,136.

Per-credit charge: $46; out-of-state residents $269.

FINANCIAL AID PICTURE (2015-2016)

Students with need: 92% of average financial aid package awarded as scholarships/grants, 8% awarded as loans/jobs. Need-based aid available for part-time students.

FINANCIAL AID PROCEDURES

Forms required: FAFSA, institutional form.

Dates and Deadlines: Priority date 5/2; no closing date. Applicants notified on a rolling basis starting 5/1; must reply within 2 week(s) of notification.

CONTACT

Regina Morrison, Director of Financial Aid
3300 College Drive, San Bruno, CA 94066-1662
(650) 738-4236

Soka University of America

Aliso Viejo, California
www.soka.edu
Federal Code: 038144

4-year private university and liberal arts college in large town.
Enrollment: 419 undergrads. 104 full-time freshmen.
Selectivity: Admits less than 50% of applicants.

BASIC COSTS (2017-2018)

Tuition and fees: $30,106.
Per-credit charge: $1,255.
Room and board: $12,166.

FINANCIAL AID PICTURE (2016-2017)

Students with need: Out of 104 full-time freshmen who applied for aid, 89 were judged to have need. Of these, 89 received aid, and 79 had their full need met. Average financial aid package met 73% of need; average scholarship/grant was $24,472; average loan was $8,584. For part-time students, average financial aid package was $7,500.
Students without need: 7 full-time freshmen who did not demonstrate need for aid received scholarships/grants; average award was $13,785. No-need awards available for academics, athletics, leadership, minority status.
Scholarships offered: *Merit:* Global Merit Scholarship: Full Ride (up to cost of attendance); annually; renewable up to 8 semesters. Soka Merit Scholarship: renewable up to 8 semesters. Makiguchi Scholarship: Full Ride (up to cost of attendance); annually; renewable up to 8 semesters; to one international applicant who has graduated from high school in an African nation. *Athletic:* 3 full-time freshmen received athletic scholarships; average amount $14,000.
Additional info: All admitted students whose annual family income is $60,000 or less qualify for Soka Opportunity Scholarship, which covers full tuition. All admitted students to the BA in Liberal Arts program will be considered for additional scholarship opportunities for higher income levels. 100% of continuing students who were eligible for need-based financial assistance received a need-based scholarship or grant.

FINANCIAL AID PROCEDURES

Forms required: FAFSA, state aid form.
Dates and Deadlines: Priority date 2/15; closing date 3/2. Applicants notified on a rolling basis starting 3/15; must reply by 5/1 or within 2 week(s) of notification.
Transfers: Must reply by 5/1 or within 2 week(s) of notification.

CONTACT

Andrew Woolsey, Director of Enrollment Services
1 University Drive, Aliso Viejo, CA 92656-8081
(949) 480-4342

Sonoma State University

Rohnert Park, California
www.sonoma.edu
Federal Code: 001156

4-year public university and liberal arts college in large town.
Enrollment: 8,550 undergrads.

BASIC COSTS (2016-2017)

Tuition and fees: $7,388; out-of-state residents $18,548.
Room and board: $13,146.

FINANCIAL AID PICTURE

Students with need: Need-based aid available for full-time and part-time students.

Students without need: No-need awards available for academics, alumni affiliation, art, athletics, leadership, minority status, music/drama.
Additional info: Pell Grant recipients see no increase in their fees, students with family incomes of $75,000 or less will pay no fees at all.

FINANCIAL AID PROCEDURES

Forms required: FAFSA.
Dates and Deadlines: Priority date 1/31; no closing date. Applicants notified on a rolling basis starting 3/25; must reply within 2 week(s) of notification.

CONTACT

Susan Gutierrez, Director, Financial Aid
1801 East Cotati Avenue, Rohnert Park, CA 94928-3609
(707) 664-2389

Southern California Institute of Architecture

Los Angeles, California
www.sciarc.edu
Federal Code: 014073

5-year private visual arts and liberal arts college in very large city.
Enrollment: 255 undergrads. 44 full-time freshmen.

BASIC COSTS (2016-2017)

Tuition and fees: $42,900.

FINANCIAL AID PICTURE (2015-2016)

Students with need: Out of 7 full-time freshmen who applied for aid, 7 were judged to have need. Of these, 7 received aid. Need-based aid available for part-time students.
Students without need: 16 full-time freshmen who did not demonstrate need for aid received scholarships/grants; average award was $15,604. No-need awards available for academics, state/district residency.

FINANCIAL AID PROCEDURES

Forms required: FAFSA, institutional form.
Dates and Deadlines: Closing date 3/2. Applicants notified on a rolling basis starting 3/15; must reply within 3 week(s) of notification.
Transfers: Applicants notified on a rolling basis starting 3/15; must reply within 3 week(s) of notification.

CONTACT

Christopher Banks, Finance Director
960 E 3rd Street, Los Angeles, CA 90013
(213) 356-5376

Stanbridge University

Irvine, California
www.stanbridge.edu

4-year for-profit health science and technical college in large city.
Enrollment: 1,073 undergrads.
Selectivity: Open admission; but selective for some programs.

BASIC COSTS (2016-2017)

Additional info: Tuition at time of enrollment locked for 4 years.

FINANCIAL AID PICTURE

Students with need: Need-based aid available for full-time and part-time students.
Students without need: This college awards aid only to students with need.

FINANCIAL AID PROCEDURES

Forms required: FAFSA, institutional form.
Dates and Deadlines: Closing date 3/2. Applicants notified on a rolling basis starting 10/1.

Transfers: Priority date 10/1. Applicants notified on a rolling basis starting 10/1; must reply by 2/15 or within 6 week(s) of notification.

CONTACT
Brian Silvano, Director of HR & Financial Services
2041 Business Center Drive, Suite 107, Irvine, CA 92612

Stanford University

Stanford, California Federal Code: 001305
www.stanford.edu CSS Code: 4704

4-year private university and liberal arts college in small city.
Enrollment: 7,032 undergrads. 1,720 full-time freshmen.
Selectivity: Admits less than 50% of applicants.

BASIC COSTS (2016-2017)
Tuition and fees: $47,940.
Room and board: $14,601.

FINANCIAL AID PICTURE (2015-2016)
Students with need: Out of 960 full-time freshmen who applied for aid, 762 were judged to have need. Of these, 762 received aid, and 719 had their full need met. Average financial aid package met 100% of need; average scholarship/grant was $47,664; average loan was $2,646. Need-based aid available for part-time students.
Students without need: 1 full-time freshmen who did not demonstrate need for aid received scholarships/grants; average award was $6,883. No-need awards available for athletics.
Scholarships offered: *Merit:* SoFi Parent Loan program provides a non-federal education loan option for parents of undergraduate students. *Athletic:* 103 full-time freshmen received athletic scholarships; average amount $46,721.
Additional info: For parents with total annual income below $65,000 and typical assets for this income range, parent contribution toward educational costs not expected. Students will still be expected to contribute from their income and savings. For parents with total annual income below $125,000 and typical assets for this income range, the expected parent contribution will be low enough to ensure that all tuition charges are covered with need-based scholarship, federal and state grants, and/or outside scholarship funds. Families with incomes at higher levels (typically up to $200,000) may also qualify for assistance, especially if more than one family member is enrolled in college.

FINANCIAL AID PROCEDURES
Forms required: FAFSA, CSS PROFILE.
Dates and Deadlines: Priority date 2/16; no closing date. Applicants notified on a rolling basis starting 4/1; must reply by 5/1.
Transfers: Priority date 3/15.

CONTACT
Karen Cooper, Director, Financial Aid
Montag Hall, Stanford, CA 94305-6106
(650) 723-3058

SUM Bible College & Theological Seminary

Oakland, California
www.sum.edu Federal Code: 037524

4-year private Bible and seminary college in very large city, affiliated with the Assemblies of God.
Enrollment: 446 undergrads.
Selectivity: Open admission; but selective for some programs.

BASIC COSTS (2017-2018)
Tuition and fees: $9,125.

Per-credit charge: $277.33.
Room only: $2,500.

FINANCIAL AID PICTURE
Students with need: Need-based aid available for full-time and part-time students.
Students without need: No-need awards available for academics, leadership, religious affiliation.

FINANCIAL AID PROCEDURES
Forms required: FAFSA.
Transfers: No deadline. Applicants notified on a rolling basis.

CONTACT
Rose Stadler, Financial Aid Director
735 105th Avenue, Oakland, CA 94603
(510) 567-6174

Taft College

Taft, California
www.taftcollege.edu Federal Code: 001309

2-year public community college in small town.
Enrollment: 2,650 undergrads.
Selectivity: Open admission.

BASIC COSTS (2016-2017)
Tuition and fees: $1,380; out-of-state residents $7,380.
Per-credit charge: $46; out-of-state residents $246.
Room and board: $4,707.

FINANCIAL AID PICTURE
Students with need: Need-based aid available for full-time and part-time students. Work study available nights.
Students without need: No-need awards available for academics.
Scholarships offered: Taft College Merit Awards: $250; for students from local high schools; available for 2 years; based on GPA of 3.0 or higher. Taft College High School Merit Award: $600; for students from local high schools. Taft College Nonresident Awards: $4,230; applied to nonresident tuition; available for 1 year; based on GPA of 3.0 or higher.

FINANCIAL AID PROCEDURES
Forms required: FAFSA, institutional form.
Dates and Deadlines: Applicants notified on a rolling basis; must reply within 4 week(s) of notification.
Transfers: No deadline.

CONTACT
Barbara Amerio, Director of Financial Aid
29 Cougar Court, Taft, CA 93268
(661) 763-7762

Thomas Aquinas College

Santa Paula, California
www.thomasaquinas.edu Federal Code: 023580

4-year private liberal arts college in rural community, affiliated with the Roman Catholic Church.
Enrollment: 389 undergrads. 89 full-time freshmen.
Selectivity: Admits 50 to 75% of applicants.

BASIC COSTS (2017-2018)
Tuition and fees: $24,500.
Per-credit charge: $681.
Room and board: $7,950.

FINANCIAL AID PICTURE (2016-2017)

Students with need: 59% of average financial aid package awarded as scholarships/grants, 41% awarded as loans/jobs. Work study available nights, weekends, and for part-time students.

Students without need: This college awards aid only to students with need.

FINANCIAL AID PROCEDURES

Forms required: FAFSA, state aid form, institutional form.

Dates and Deadlines: Closing date 3/2. Applicants notified on a rolling basis starting 2/1; must reply by 5/1 or within 2 week(s) of notification.

CONTACT

Gregory Becher, Director of Financial Aid

10000 Ojai Road, Santa Paula, CA 93060-9621

(800) 634-9797

Touro University Worldwide

Los Alamitos, California

www.tuw.edu   Federal Code: 041425

4-year private university and business college in large city.

Enrollment: 405 undergrads, 40% part-time. 8 full-time freshmen.

BASIC COSTS (2016-2017)

Tuition and fees: $9,600.

Per-credit charge: $400.

FINANCIAL AID PICTURE (2016-2017)

Students with need: Average financial aid package met 55% of need; average scholarship/grant was $4,174; average loan was $1,822. For part-time students, average financial aid package was $4,886.

Students without need: No-need awards available for academics, alumni affiliation.

FINANCIAL AID PROCEDURES

Forms required: FAFSA, state aid form, institutional form.

Dates and Deadlines: Priority date 5/15; closing date 8/15. Applicants notified on a rolling basis starting 5/1.

CONTACT

Jayson Capuno, CFO and Bursar

10601 Calle Lee, #179, Los Alamitos, CA 90720

(212) 463-0400 ext. 5736

Trident University International

Cypress, California

www.trident.edu   Federal Code: 041279

4-year for-profit virtual university in very large city.

Enrollment: 4,760 undergrads.

Selectivity: Open admission.

FINANCIAL AID PICTURE

Students with need: Need-based aid available for full-time and part-time students.

FINANCIAL AID PROCEDURES

Forms required: FAFSA, institutional form.

Transfers: No deadline.

CONTACT

Taisha Wright, Director of Financial Aid

Attn: Office of the Registrar, Cypress, CA 90630

(714) 816-0366 ext. 1061

University of California: Berkeley

Berkeley, California

www.berkeley.edu   Federal Code: 001312

4-year public university in small city.

Enrollment: 27,496 undergrads.

BASIC COSTS (2016-2017)

Tuition and fees: $13,485; out-of-state residents $40,167.

Room and board: $15,115.

Additional info: $2612 is the Student Health Insurance Premium. This is a mandatory fee but if a student is covered through private insurance, he or she can waive out.

FINANCIAL AID PICTURE

Students with need: Need-based aid available for full-time and part-time students.

Students without need: No-need awards available for academics, athletics, leadership.

Scholarships offered: University Scholarship, President's Undergraduate Fellowships, Regents and Chancellor's Scholarships, Alumni Scholarships.

Additional info: For resident families whose gross income ranges from $80,000 to $150,000 annually and who have typical assets, parents' contribution capped at maximum of 15% of total income. Tuition and registration fee for low-income California residents covered under the Blue and Gold Opportunity Plan.

FINANCIAL AID PROCEDURES

Forms required: FAFSA, state aid form.

Dates and Deadlines: Closing date 3/2. Applicants notified by 3/31; must reply by 5/1.

Transfers: Applicants notified by 4/15.

CONTACT

Cruz Grimaldo, Director of Financial Aid

110 Sproul Hall, #5800, Berkeley, CA 94720-5800

(510) 642-6000

University of California: Davis

Davis, California

www.ucdavis.edu   Federal Code: 001313

4-year public university in small city.

Enrollment: 29,348 undergrads, 1% part-time. 5,679 full-time freshmen.

Selectivity: Admits less than 50% of applicants.

BASIC COSTS (2016-2017)

Tuition and fees: $14,046; out-of-state residents $40,728.

Room and board: $14,838.

Additional info: $2,292 is the Student Health Insurance Premium. This is a mandatory fee but if a student is covered through private insurance, he or she can waive out.

FINANCIAL AID PICTURE (2016-2017)

Students with need: Out of 4,322 full-time freshmen who applied for aid, 3,377 were judged to have need. Of these, 3,308 received aid, and 644 had their full need met. Average financial aid package met 82% of need; average scholarship/grant was $20,328; average loan was $5,652. For part-time students, average financial aid package was $19,887.

Students without need: 262 full-time freshmen who did not demonstrate need for aid received scholarships/grants; average award was $3,472. No-need awards available for academics, athletics.

Scholarships offered: 49 full-time freshmen received athletic scholarships; average amount $19,202.

FINANCIAL AID PROCEDURES

Forms required: FAFSA, state aid form.

Dates and Deadlines: Priority date 3/2; no closing date. Applicants notified on a rolling basis starting 3/13.

CONTACT
Deborah Agee, Director of Financial Aid
178 Mrak Hall, One Shields Ave, Davis, CA 95616
(530) 752-2390

University of California: Irvine
Irvine, California
www.uci.edu   Federal Code: 001314

4-year public university in small city.
Enrollment: 27,331 undergrads, 2% part-time. 5,746 full-time freshmen.
Selectivity: Admits less than 50% of applicants.

BASIC COSTS (2016-2017)
Tuition and fees: $15,026; out-of-state residents $41,708.
Room and board: $13,661.
Additional info: Required fees include $1,675 for our student health insurance plan. Although this is a mandatory fee, if a student is covered through private insurance, he or she can waive out.

FINANCIAL AID PICTURE (2015-2016)
Students with need: Out of 4,244 full-time freshmen who applied for aid, 3,611 were judged to have need. Of these, 3,505 received aid, and 757 had their full need met. Average financial aid package met 84% of need; average scholarship/grant was $19,675; average loan was $6,874. For part-time students, average financial aid package was $16,739.
Students without need: 107 full-time freshmen who did not demonstrate need for aid received scholarships/grants; average award was $7,501.
Scholarships offered: 22 full-time freshmen received athletic scholarships; average amount $18,472.
Additional info: UC Blue & Gold Opportunity Plan guarantees that in-state students from families earning less than $80,000/yr have system-wide tuition and fees paid through scholarships and grants.

FINANCIAL AID PROCEDURES
Forms required: FAFSA, state aid form.
Dates and Deadlines: Priority date 3/2; closing date 6/26. Applicants notified on a rolling basis starting 4/1.

CONTACT
Rebecca Sanchez, Director, Financial Aid & Scholarships
260 Aldrich Hall, Irvine, CA 92697-1075
(949) 824-8262

University of California: Los Angeles
Los Angeles, California
www.ucla.edu   Federal Code: 001315

4-year public university in very large city.
Enrollment: 30,856 undergrads, 2% part-time. 5,671 full-time freshmen.
Selectivity: Admits less than 50% of applicants.

BASIC COSTS (2016-2017)
Tuition and fees: $13,409; out-of-state residents $40,091.
Room and board: $15,069.

FINANCIAL AID PICTURE (2015-2016)
Students with need: Out of 3,455 full-time freshmen who applied for aid, 3,032 were judged to have need. Of these, 3,032 received aid, and 770 had their full need met. Average financial aid package met 82% of need; average scholarship/grant was $20,537; average loan was $7,302. For part-time students, average financial aid package was $14,728.

Students without need: 163 full-time freshmen who did not demonstrate need for aid received scholarships/grants; average award was $4,240. No-need awards available for academics, alumni affiliation, athletics, ROTC.
Scholarships offered: 63 full-time freshmen received athletic scholarships; average amount $27,381.

FINANCIAL AID PROCEDURES
Forms required: FAFSA, state aid form.
Dates and Deadlines: Priority date 3/2; no closing date. Applicants notified on a rolling basis starting 3/15.

CONTACT
Ronald Johnson, Director, Financial Aid Office
1147 Murphy Hall, Los Angeles, CA 90095-1436
(310) 206-0400

University of California: Merced
Merced, California
www.ucmerced.edu   Federal Code: 041271

4-year public university in small city.
Enrollment: 6,815 undergrads, 1% part-time. 1,782 full-time freshmen.
Selectivity: Admits 50 to 75% of applicants.

BASIC COSTS (2016-2017)
Tuition and fees: $13,262; out-of-state residents $39,944.
Room and board: $15,933.
Additional info: $2,271 is the Student Health Insurance Premium. This is a mandatory fee but if a student is covered through private insurance, he or she can waive out.

FINANCIAL AID PICTURE (2015-2016)
Students with need: Out of 1,716 full-time freshmen who applied for aid, 1,598 were judged to have need. Of these, 1,588 received aid, and 467 had their full need met. Average financial aid package met 87% of need; average scholarship/grant was $22,896; average loan was $4,757. For part-time students, average financial aid package was $14,675.
Students without need: 14 full-time freshmen who did not demonstrate need for aid received scholarships/grants; average award was $10,474. No-need awards available for academics, leadership.
Scholarships offered: *Merit:* Regents' Scholarships: based on strength and breadth of academic program, grades, personal statement, extracurricular activities, community activities, first-generation status, other indicators of academic excellence and promise. *Athletic:* 5 full-time freshmen received athletic scholarships; average amount $500.

FINANCIAL AID PROCEDURES
Forms required: FAFSA.
Dates and Deadlines: Closing date 3/2. Applicants notified on a rolling basis starting 4/1; must reply by 6/1.
Transfers: Applicants notified on a rolling basis starting 3/2.

CONTACT
Ron Radney, Director, Financial Aid & Scholarships
5200 North Lake Road, Merced, CA 95343-5603
(209) 228-7178

University of California: Riverside
Riverside, California
www.ucr.edu   Federal Code: 001316

4-year public university in large city.
Enrollment: 19,788 undergrads, 1% part-time. 5,346 full-time freshmen.
Selectivity: Admits 50 to 75% of applicants.

BASIC COSTS (2016-2017)

Tuition and fees: $13,581; out-of-state residents $40,263.

Room and board: $16,400.

Additional info: $1,629 is the Student Health Insurance Premium. This is a mandatory fee but if a student is covered through private insurance, he or she can waive out.

FINANCIAL AID PICTURE (2016-2017)

Students with need: Out of 4,956 full-time freshmen who applied for aid, 4,387 were judged to have need. Of these, 4,303 received aid, and 1,072 had their full need met. Average financial aid package met 85.3% of need; average scholarship/grant was $22,421; average loan was $6,171. For part-time students, average financial aid package was $15,736.

Students without need: 74 full-time freshmen who did not demonstrate need for aid received scholarships/grants; average award was $7,088. No-need awards available for academics, alumni affiliation, art, athletics, leadership, music/drama, state/district residency.

Scholarships offered: 14 full-time freshmen received athletic scholarships; average amount $32,310.

FINANCIAL AID PROCEDURES

Forms required: FAFSA, state aid form.

Dates and Deadlines: Priority date 3/2; closing date 6/15. Applicants notified on a rolling basis starting 3/1; must reply by 5/1 or within 3 week(s) of notification.

Transfers: Closing date 6/1. Applicants notified on a rolling basis starting 3/1; must reply by 6/1 or within 3 week(s) of notification.

CONTACT

Jose Aguilar, Director of Financial Aid

Undergraduate Admissions, Riverside, CA 92521

(951) 827-3878

University of California: San Diego

La Jolla, California

www.ucsd.edu   Federal Code: 001317

4-year public university in large town.

Enrollment: 23,850 undergrads.

BASIC COSTS (2016-2017)

Tuition and fees: $13,573; out-of-state residents $40,255.

Room and board: $10,976.

Additional info: $2,011 is the Student Health Insurance Premium. This is a mandatory fee but if a student is covered through private insurance, he or she can waive out.

FINANCIAL AID PICTURE

Students with need: Need-based aid available for full-time and part-time students. Work study available nights, weekends, and for part-time students.

Students without need: No-need awards available for academics, art, athletics, leadership, minority status, music/drama.

FINANCIAL AID PROCEDURES

Forms required: FAFSA, state aid form.

Dates and Deadlines: Priority date 3/2; closing date 6/1. Applicants notified on a rolling basis starting 3/15; must reply within 3 week(s) of notification.

Transfers: Applicants notified on a rolling basis; must reply within 3 week(s) of notification.

CONTACT

Ann Klein, Director of Financial Aid

9500 Gilman Drive, 0021, La Jolla, CA 92093-0021

(858) 534-4480

University of California: Santa Barbara

Santa Barbara, California

www.ucsb.edu   Federal Code: 001320

4-year public university in small city.

Enrollment: 21,574 undergrads, 2% part-time. 4,459 full-time freshmen.

Selectivity: Admits less than 50% of applicants.

BASIC COSTS (2016-2017)

Tuition and fees: $14,014; out-of-state residents $40,696.

Room and board: $13,605.

Additional info: $3,150 is the Student Health Insurance Premium. This is a mandatory fee but if a student is covered through private insurance, he or she can waive out.

FINANCIAL AID PICTURE (2015-2016)

Students with need: Out of 3,638 full-time freshmen who applied for aid, 2,831 were judged to have need. Of these, 2,731 received aid, and 411 had their full need met. Average financial aid package met 80% of need; average scholarship/grant was $21,491; average loan was $6,429. For part-time students, average financial aid package was $18,451.

Students without need: 103 full-time freshmen who did not demonstrate need for aid received scholarships/grants; average award was $20,398. No-need awards available for academics, alumni affiliation, athletics, ROTC.

Scholarships offered: 52 full-time freshmen received athletic scholarships; average amount $16,161.

FINANCIAL AID PROCEDURES

Forms required: FAFSA.

Dates and Deadlines: Priority date 3/2; closing date 5/31.

Transfers: California residents must apply for a CAL grant from the California Student Aid Commission; must complete and submit FAFSA by March 2.

CONTACT

Mike Miller, Director of Financial Aid

1210 Cheadle Hall, Santa Barbara, CA 93106-2014

(805) 893-2432

University of California: Santa Cruz

Santa Cruz, California

www.ucsc.edu   Federal Code: 001321

4-year public university in small city.

Enrollment: 16,962 undergrads, 3% part-time. 4,204 full-time freshmen.

Selectivity: Admits 50 to 75% of applicants.

BASIC COSTS (2016-2017)

Tuition and fees: $13,515; out-of-state residents $40,197.

Room and board: $13,874.

Additional info: Campus Health Insurance: $2,877. All undergraduate students are automatically enrolled in and charged for the University of California Student Health Insurance Plan (UC SHIP) unless they choose to submit an on-line insurance waiver confirming they have comparable health insurance coverage. Tuition/fee waivers available for unemployed or children of unemployed.

FINANCIAL AID PICTURE (2015-2016)

Students with need: 79% of average financial aid package awarded as scholarships/grants, 21% awarded as loans/jobs. Need-based aid available for part-time students. Work study available nights, weekends, and for part-time students.

Students without need: No-need awards available for academics, alumni affiliation, art, leadership, music/drama.

Scholarships offered: Regents Scholarships; $4,000-$6,000 per year for 4 years; for outstanding academic achievement.

Additional info: Blue and Gold Opportunity Plan covers the educational and student services fees for CA residents whose family earns less than

$80,000 a year. Blue and Gold students with sufficient financial need can qualify for more grant aid to reduce the cost of attendance.

FINANCIAL AID PROCEDURES

Forms required: FAFSA, state aid form.

Dates and Deadlines: Closing date 3/2. Applicants notified on a rolling basis starting 4/1; must reply within 4 week(s) of notification.

Transfers: The Karl S. Pister Leadership Opportunity Awards Program established by a former chancellor increases opportunities for talented community college students who want to transfer to UCSC. Candidates, nominated by the regional community college presidents, must have overcome adverse socioeconomic circumstances, have a demonstrated commitment to assisting and improving the lives of others and have financial aid eligibility. One recipient is named from each of 13 regional community colleges. Awards are $10,000 per year for 2 years.

CONTACT

Michelle Whittingham, Associate Vice Chancellor, Enrollment Management
Cook House, 1156 High Street, Santa Cruz, CA 95064
(831) 459-2963

University of La Verne
La Verne, California
www.laverne.edu   Federal Code: 001216

4-year private university in large town.
Enrollment: 2,802 undergrads, 3% part-time. 555 full-time freshmen.
Selectivity: Admits less than 50% of applicants.

BASIC COSTS (2017-2018)
Tuition and fees: $41,450.
Per-credit charge: $1,165.
Room and board: $13,140.

FINANCIAL AID PICTURE (2016-2017)
Students with need: Out of 500 full-time freshmen who applied for aid, 476 were judged to have need. Of these, 476 received aid, and 35 had their full need met. Average financial aid package met 48% of need; average scholarship/grant was $16,820; average loan was $3,810. For part-time students, average financial aid package was $20,022.
Students without need: 76 full-time freshmen who did not demonstrate need for aid received scholarships/grants; average award was $19,451. No-need awards available for academics, alumni affiliation, art, leadership, minority status, music/drama, religious affiliation.

FINANCIAL AID PROCEDURES
Forms required: FAFSA, state aid form.
Dates and Deadlines: Priority date 3/2; no closing date. Applicants notified on a rolling basis starting 3/1; must reply by 5/1 or within 2 week(s) of notification.

CONTACT
David Busse, Interim Director, Financial Aid Office
1950 Third Street, La Verne, CA 91750
(800) 649-0160

University of Redlands
Redlands, California
www.redlands.edu   Federal Code: 001322

4-year private university and liberal arts college in small city.
Enrollment: 2,402 undergrads, 1% part-time. 525 full-time freshmen.
Selectivity: Admits 50 to 75% of applicants.

BASIC COSTS (2017-2018)
Tuition and fees: $48,072.

Room and board: $13,862.

FINANCIAL AID PICTURE (2015-2016)
Students with need: Out of 456 full-time freshmen who applied for aid, 393 were judged to have need. Of these, 393 received aid, and 191 had their full need met. Average financial aid package met 84% of need; average scholarship/grant was $29,047; average loan was $5,935. For part-time students, average financial aid package was $9,019.
Students without need: 119 full-time freshmen who did not demonstrate need for aid received scholarships/grants; average award was $18,075. No-need awards available for academics, art, music/drama.

FINANCIAL AID PROCEDURES
Forms required: FAFSA.
Dates and Deadlines: Priority date 11/15; closing date 3/2. Applicants notified on a rolling basis starting 2/17; must reply by 5/1.
Transfers: No deadline.

CONTACT
Emily Baker, Director of Student Financial Services
1200 East Colton Avenue, Redlands, CA 92373-0999
(909) 748-8047

University of San Diego
San Diego, California
www.sandiego.edu   Federal Code: 010395

4-year private university in very large city, affiliated with the Roman Catholic Church.
Enrollment: 5,604 undergrads, 3% part-time. 1,103 full-time freshmen.
Selectivity: Admits 50 to 75% of applicants.

BASIC COSTS (2016-2017)
Tuition and fees: $46,140.
Per-credit charge: $1,570.
Room and board: $12,302.

FINANCIAL AID PICTURE (2015-2016)
Students with need: Out of 788 full-time freshmen who applied for aid, 570 were judged to have need. Of these, 559 received aid, and 77 had their full need met. Average financial aid package met 74% of need; average scholarship/grant was $26,943; average loan was $5,809. For part-time students, average financial aid package was $21,048.
Students without need: 284 full-time freshmen who did not demonstrate need for aid received scholarships/grants; average award was $11,949. No-need awards available for academics, athletics, leadership, music/drama, religious affiliation, ROTC.
Scholarships offered: 27 full-time freshmen received athletic scholarships; average amount $38,759.

FINANCIAL AID PROCEDURES
Forms required: FAFSA.
Dates and Deadlines: Priority date 3/2; no closing date. Applicants notified on a rolling basis starting 3/1; must reply by 5/1 or within 3 week(s) of notification.
Transfers: Entering transfer students are not eligible for institutional merit-based scholarships.

CONTACT
Judith Lewis Logue, Director of Financial Aid Services
5998 Alcala Park, San Diego, CA 92110-2492
(619) 260-4720

University of San Francisco

San Francisco, California
www.usfca.edu

Federal Code: 001325
CSS Code: 4850

4-year private university in very large city, affiliated with the Roman Catholic Church.

Enrollment: 6,664 undergrads, 4% part-time. 1,584 full-time freshmen.

Selectivity: Admits 50 to 75% of applicants.

BASIC COSTS (2016-2017)

Tuition and fees: $44,494.

Per-credit charge: $1,565.

Room and board: $13,990.

FINANCIAL AID PICTURE (2016-2017)

Students with need: Out of 1,178 full-time freshmen who applied for aid, 981 were judged to have need. Of these, 978 received aid, and 160 had their full need met. Average financial aid package met 55% of need; average scholarship/grant was $24,144; average loan was $3,472. For part-time students, average financial aid package was $17,940.

Students without need: 320 full-time freshmen who did not demonstrate need for aid received scholarships/grants; average award was $14,636. No-need awards available for academics, athletics, ROTC.

Scholarships offered: *Merit:* University Scholars Program: up to $20,000 per year for 8 UG Semesters; must have 3.8 weighted GPA as calculated by USF admissions and combined SAT of 1320 on Critical Reading and Math sections or minimum ACT composite test score of 30. Applicants must apply for admission no later than November 15 under the Early Action Plan for the following year. Renewal automatic as long as 3.25 GPA achieved each semester. ***Athletic:*** 23 full-time freshmen received athletic scholarships; average amount $47,292.

Additional info: Most aid to international students is for athletics.

FINANCIAL AID PROCEDURES

Forms required: FAFSA, CSS PROFILE.

Dates and Deadlines: Priority date 12/1; closing date 2/1. Applicants notified on a rolling basis starting 4/1; must reply within 4 week(s) of notification.

Transfers: Closing date 3/1. Applicants notified on a rolling basis starting 4/1; must reply within 4 week(s) of notification.

CONTACT

Mary Booker, Assistant Vice Provost of Student Financial Services
2130 Fulton Street, San Francisco, CA 94117-1080
(415) 422-2020

University of Southern California

Los Angeles, California
www.usc.edu

Federal Code: 001328
CSS Code: 4852

4-year private university in very large city.

Enrollment: 18,557 undergrads, 3% part-time. 2,948 full-time freshmen.

Selectivity: Admits less than 50% of applicants. GED not accepted.

BASIC COSTS (2016-2017)

Tuition and fees: $52,283.

Per-credit charge: $1,733.

Room and board: $14,348.

FINANCIAL AID PICTURE (2015-2016)

Students with need: Out of 1,701 full-time freshmen who applied for aid, 961 were judged to have need. Of these, 960 received aid, and 772 had their full need met. Average financial aid package met 100% of need; average scholarship/grant was $36,995; average loan was $5,058. For part-time students, average financial aid package was $23,857.

Students without need: 703 full-time freshmen who did not demonstrate need for aid received scholarships/grants; average award was $21,761. No-need awards available for academics, alumni affiliation, art, athletics, leadership, music/drama, ROTC.

Scholarships offered: *Merit:* Trustee Scholarship: full tuition; approximately 100 awards annually; finalists invited to mandatory interview. Presidential Scholarship: one-half tuition; approximately 200 awarded annually; finalists invited to a mandatory interview. National Merit Presidential Scholarship: one-half tuition; number of awards varies; admitted Freshmen who are National Merit Finalists and who designate USC as their first-choice college. Deans Scholarship: one-quarter tuition; approximately 50 awards annually; Mork Family Scholarship: full tuition plus $5,000 living stipend; 10 awards annually; Stamps Leadership Scholarship: full tuition plus $5,000 enrichment fund (research, overseas study, etc.); 5 awards annually. ***Athletic:*** 91 full-time freshmen received athletic scholarships; average amount $51,754.

FINANCIAL AID PROCEDURES

Forms required: FAFSA, CSS PROFILE.

Dates and Deadlines: Priority date 2/16; no closing date. Applicants notified by 4/1; must reply by 5/1.

Transfers: Applicants notified by 5/1.

CONTACT

Thomas McWhorter, Dean of Financial Aid
Office of Admission, Los Angeles, CA 90089-0911
(213) 740-4444

University of the Pacific

Stockton, California
www.pacific.edu

Federal Code: 001329

4-year private university in large city.

Enrollment: 3,474 undergrads, 3% part-time. 723 full-time freshmen.

Selectivity: Admits 50 to 75% of applicants.

BASIC COSTS (2016-2017)

Tuition and fees: $44,588.

Per-credit charge: $1,520.

Room and board: $12,858.

FINANCIAL AID PICTURE (2016-2017)

Students with need: Out of 618 full-time freshmen who applied for aid, 541 were judged to have need. Of these, 541 received aid, and 109 had their full need met. Average financial aid package met 65% of need; average scholarship/grant was $27,538; average loan was $6,074. For part-time students, average financial aid package was $19,727.

Students without need: 154 full-time freshmen who did not demonstrate need for aid received scholarships/grants; average award was $12,591. No-need awards available for academics, art, leadership, music/drama, religious affiliation.

Scholarships offered: 28 full-time freshmen received athletic scholarships; average amount $42,678.

FINANCIAL AID PROCEDURES

Forms required: FAFSA.

Dates and Deadlines: Priority date 2/15; no closing date. Applicants notified on a rolling basis starting 3/1.

CONTACT

Lynn Fox, Director of Financial Aid
3601 Pacific Avenue, Stockton, CA 95211-0197
(209) 946-2421

University of the West

Rosemead, California
www.uwest.edu

Federal Code: 036963

4-year private business and liberal arts college in small city, affiliated with the Buddhist faith.

Enrollment: 106 undergrads, 7% part-time. 18 full-time freshmen.

BASIC COSTS (2016-2017)
Tuition and fees: $14,040.
Per-credit charge: $438.
Room and board: $7,156.

FINANCIAL AID PICTURE
Students with need: Need-based aid available for full-time and part-time students. Work study available nights, weekends, and for part-time students.
Students without need: No-need awards available for academics, leadership.
Scholarships offered: Lotus Scholarship: up to $10,000 per year depending on academic merits and financial need. President's Fellowship: full-tuition award. Dean's Fellowship: half-tuition award. Campus Life Leadership Fellowship: full tuition and room and board award plus $1,000 scholarship. Campus Life Assistance Fellowship: full room and board award plus $1,000 scholarship. UWest Scholarship: $1,000 to $2,000 per academic year. Drs. Allen and Lily Huang Student Leadership Award: $2,000, one award each year. Lotus Scholarships: $10,000 or $5,000 per year.

FINANCIAL AID PROCEDURES
Forms required: FAFSA, institutional form.
Transfers: No deadline.

CONTACT
Lezli Fang, Financial Aid Officer
1409 North Walnut Grove Avenue, Rosemead, CA 91770
(626) 571-8811 ext. 138

Vanguard University of Southern California
Costa Mesa, California
www.vanguard.edu   Federal Code: 001293

4-year private university and liberal arts college in small city, affiliated with the Assemblies of God.
Enrollment: 1,765 undergrads, 18% part-time. 408 full-time freshmen.
Selectivity: Admits 50 to 75% of applicants.

BASIC COSTS (2016-2017)
Tuition and fees: $30,980.
Room and board: $9,310.

FINANCIAL AID PICTURE
Students with need: Need-based aid available for full-time students.
Students without need: No-need awards available for academics, athletics, music/drama, religious affiliation.

FINANCIAL AID PROCEDURES
Forms required: FAFSA, state aid form.
Dates and Deadlines: Closing date 3/2. Applicants notified on a rolling basis starting 4/1; must reply within 3 week(s) of notification.
Transfers: Applicants notified on a rolling basis.

CONTACT
Christina Padilla, Director of Financial Aid
55 Fair Drive, Costa Mesa, CA 92626-9601
(714) 955-5490

Ventura College
Ventura, California
www.venturacollege.edu   Federal Code: 001334

2-year public community college in small city.
Enrollment: 8,263 undergrads.
Selectivity: Open admission; but selective for some programs.

BASIC COSTS (2016-2017)
Tuition and fees: $1,418; out-of-state residents $8,888.
Per-credit charge: $46; out-of-state residents $295.

FINANCIAL AID PICTURE
Students with need: Need-based aid available for full-time and part-time students.

FINANCIAL AID PROCEDURES
Forms required: FAFSA, state aid form.
Dates and Deadlines: Priority date 3/2; no closing date. Applicants notified on a rolling basis.

CONTACT
Alma Rodriguez, Director, Financial Aid
4667 Telegraph Road, Ventura, CA 93003
(805) 654-6369

Victor Valley College
Victorville, California
www.vvc.edu   Federal Code: 001335

2-year public community college in small city.
Enrollment: 6,347 undergrads.
Selectivity: Open admission.

BASIC COSTS (2016-2017)
Tuition and fees: $1,402; out-of-state residents $9,172.
Per-credit charge: $46; out-of-state residents $305.

FINANCIAL AID PICTURE
Students with need: Need-based aid available for full-time and part-time students.
Additional info: Board of Governors grant pays enrollment fee in full for low-income students.

FINANCIAL AID PROCEDURES
Forms required: FAFSA, state aid form, institutional form.
Dates and Deadlines: Priority date 3/2; no closing date. Applicants notified on a rolling basis starting 8/1; must reply within 4 week(s) of notification.

CONTACT
Jason Judkins, Director, Financial Aid
18422 Bear Valley Road, Victorville, CA 92392-5850
(760) 245-4271 ext. 2917

West Coast University: Los Angeles
North Hollywood, California
www.westcoastuniversity.edu   Federal Code: 036983

4-year for-profit health science and nursing college in very large city.
Enrollment: 1,435 undergrads.

FINANCIAL AID PICTURE
Students with need: Need-based aid available for full-time and part-time students. Work study available nights, weekends, and for part-time students.
Students without need: No-need awards available for academics.

FINANCIAL AID PROCEDURES
Forms required: FAFSA, state aid form, institutional form.
Dates and Deadlines: Closing date 6/30. Applicants notified on a rolling basis.

CONTACT
Tracy Cabuco, Director of Financial Aid
12215 Victory Boulevard, North Hollywood, CA 91606
(818) 299-5500

West Coast University: Ontario

Ontario, California
www.westcoastuniversity.edu   Federal Code: 036983

4-year for-profit branch campus and nursing college in small city.
Enrollment: 1,061 undergrads.
Selectivity: Open admission; but selective for some programs.

FINANCIAL AID PICTURE
Students with need: Need-based aid available for full-time and part-time students. Work study available nights, weekends, and for part-time students.
Students without need: No-need awards available for academics.

FINANCIAL AID PROCEDURES
Forms required: FAFSA, state aid form, institutional form.
Dates and Deadlines: Closing date 6/30. Applicants notified on a rolling basis.

CONTACT
Raylena Figueroa, Director of Financial Aid
2855 East Guasti Road, Ontario, CA 91761
(909) 467-6100

West Coast University: Orange County

Anaheim, California
www.westcoastuniversity.edu   Federal Code: 036983

4-year for-profit branch campus and nursing college in large city.
Enrollment: 1,477 undergrads.
Selectivity: Open admission; but selective for some programs.

BASIC COSTS (2016-2017)
Tuition and fees: $33,175.
Per-credit charge: $1,377.

FINANCIAL AID PICTURE
Students with need: Need-based aid available for full-time and part-time students. Work study available nights, weekends, and for part-time students.
Students without need: No-need awards available for academics.

FINANCIAL AID PROCEDURES
Forms required: FAFSA, state aid form, institutional form.
Dates and Deadlines: Closing date 6/30. Applicants notified on a rolling basis.

CONTACT
Teresa Salcedo, Director of Financial Aid
1477 South Manchester Avenue, Anaheim, CA 92802
(714) 782-1700

West Hills College: Coalinga

Coalinga, California
www.westhillscollege.com   Federal Code: 001176

2-year public community college in small town.
Enrollment: 2,753 undergrads.
Selectivity: Open admission.

BASIC COSTS (2016-2017)
Tuition and fees: $1,380; out-of-state residents $8,190.
Per-credit charge: $46; out-of-state residents $273.
Room and board: $7,977.
Additional info: Tuition/fee waivers available for unemployed or children of unemployed.

FINANCIAL AID PICTURE
Students with need: Need-based aid available for full-time and part-time students.

FINANCIAL AID PROCEDURES
Forms required: FAFSA.
Dates and Deadlines: Priority date 3/2; no closing date. Applicants notified on a rolling basis starting 6/1.

CONTACT
Mary Mello, Director of Financial Aid
300 Cherry Lane, Coalinga, CA 93210
(559) 934-2310

West Los Angeles College

Culver City, California
www.wlac.edu   Federal Code: 008596

2-year public community college in large town.
Enrollment: 8,545 undergrads.
Selectivity: Open admission.

BASIC COSTS (2016-2017)
Tuition and fees: $1,416; out-of-state residents $8,076.
Per-credit charge: $46; out-of-state residents $268.
Additional info: Tuition at time of enrollment locked for 2 years; tuition/fee waivers available for unemployed or children of unemployed.

FINANCIAL AID PICTURE (2016-2017)
Students with need: 82% of average financial aid package awarded as scholarships/grants, 18% awarded as loans/jobs. Need-based aid available for part-time students.
Students without need: This college awards aid only to students with need.
Additional info: California residents may qualify for Board of Governors Grant Program.

FINANCIAL AID PROCEDURES
Forms required: FAFSA.
Dates and Deadlines: Priority date 5/1; closing date 6/30. Applicants notified on a rolling basis starting 3/1; must reply by 6/30 or within 4 week(s) of notification.
Transfers: Priority date 5/1; closing date 6/30. Applicants notified on a rolling basis starting 5/1; must reply by 6/30 or within 4 week(s) of notification.

CONTACT
Glenn Schenk, Financial Aid Director
9000 Overland Avenue, Culver City, CA 90230
(310) 287-4533

Westmont College

Santa Barbara, California
www.westmont.edu   Federal Code: 001341

4-year private liberal arts college in small city, affiliated with the nondenominational tradition.
Enrollment: 1,275 undergrads. 347 full-time freshmen.
Selectivity: Admits over 75% of applicants.

BASIC COSTS (2017-2018)
Tuition and fees: $44,044.
Per-credit charge: $2,120.
Room and board: $13,886.

FINANCIAL AID PICTURE (2016-2017)
Students with need: Out of 271 full-time freshmen who applied for aid, 246 were judged to have need. Of these, 246 received aid, and 62 had their full need met. Average financial aid package met 83% of need; average scholarship/grant was $28,676; average loan was $3,891.

Students without need: 84 full-time freshmen who did not demonstrate need for aid received scholarships/grants; average award was $17,726. No-need awards available for academics, art, athletics, leadership, music/drama.

Scholarships offered: *Merit:* Scholarships automatically awarded to entering students based on GPA and SAT or ACT scores (first-year students) or college academic GPA (transfers): renewable annually; unlimited number awarded until class is full. First-year scholarships: Presidential, $14,000, must maintain 3.25 GPA; Provost, $12,000, must maintain 3.0 GPA; Dean's, $10,000, must maintain 2.75 GPA. *Athletic:* 16 full-time freshmen received athletic scholarships; average amount $11,059.

FINANCIAL AID PROCEDURES

Forms required: FAFSA. PROFILE accepted but not required.

Dates and Deadlines: Priority date 3/1; no closing date. Applicants notified on a rolling basis starting 12/1; must reply by 5/1 or within 2 week(s) of notification.

Transfers: No deadline. Applicants notified on a rolling basis starting 4/1; must reply by 5/1 or within 2 week(s) of notification. Transfer students may qualify for academic merit scholarships.

CONTACT

Doug Jones, Vice President for Finance
955 La Paz Road, Santa Barbara, CA 93108-1089
(888) 963-4624

Whittier College
Whittier, California
www.whittier.edu
Federal Code: 001342

4-year private liberal arts college in small city.

Enrollment: 1,598 undergrads, 1% part-time. 424 full-time freshmen.

Selectivity: Admits 50 to 75% of applicants.

BASIC COSTS (2016-2017)

Tuition and fees: $44,774.

Per-credit charge: $1,841.

Room and board: $12,902.

FINANCIAL AID PICTURE (2016-2017)

Students with need: Out of 383 full-time freshmen who applied for aid, 355 were judged to have need. Of these, 355 received aid, and 60 had their full need met. Average financial aid package met 78% of need; average scholarship/grant was $34,244; average loan was $5,245. For part-time students, average financial aid package was $34,490.

Students without need: 60 full-time freshmen who did not demonstrate need for aid received scholarships/grants; average award was $20,518. No-need awards available for academics, alumni affiliation, art, minority status, music/drama.

Additional info: Auditions required for talent scholarship applicants in art, music, and theater.

FINANCIAL AID PROCEDURES

Forms required: FAFSA.

Dates and Deadlines: Priority date 3/1; closing date 6/30. Applicants notified on a rolling basis starting 2/15; must reply within 2 week(s) of notification.

Transfers: Priority date 2/1. Applicants notified on a rolling basis starting 3/1; must reply by 6/1 or within 2 week(s) of notification.

CONTACT

Julie Aldama, Director of Financial Aid
13406 East Philadelphia Street, Whittier, CA 90608-0634
(562) 907-4285

William Jessup University
Rocklin, California
www.jessup.edu
Federal Code: 001281

4-year private Bible and liberal arts college in small city, affiliated with the nondenominational tradition.

Enrollment: 1,158 undergrads, 14% part-time. 200 full-time freshmen.

Selectivity: Admits 50 to 75% of applicants.

BASIC COSTS (2017-2018)

Tuition and fees: $29,950.

Room and board: $10,950.

FINANCIAL AID PICTURE (2016-2017)

Students with need: Out of 186 full-time freshmen who applied for aid, 169 were judged to have need. Of these, 169 received aid, and 31 had their full need met. Average financial aid package met 71% of need; average scholarship/grant was $20,936; average loan was $3,366. For part-time students, average financial aid package was $9,250.

Students without need: 24 full-time freshmen who did not demonstrate need for aid received scholarships/grants; average award was $12,098. No-need awards available for academics, art, athletics, leadership, minority status, music/drama, religious affiliation, state/district residency.

Scholarships offered: 9 full-time freshmen received athletic scholarships; average amount $12,563.

FINANCIAL AID PROCEDURES

Forms required: FAFSA.

Dates and Deadlines: Priority date 3/2; no closing date. Applicants notified on a rolling basis starting 3/2; must reply within 3 week(s) of notification.

CONTACT

John Swan, Director of Financial Aid
2121 University Ave, Rocklin, CA 95765
(916) 577-2233

Woodbury University
Burbank, California
www.woodbury.edu
Federal Code: 001343
CSS Code: 4955

4-year private university in very large city.

Enrollment: 1,096 undergrads, 12% part-time. 137 full-time freshmen.

Selectivity: Admits 50 to 75% of applicants.

BASIC COSTS (2016-2017)

Tuition and fees: $37,882.

Per-credit charge: $1,200.

Room and board: $11,133.

FINANCIAL AID PICTURE (2016-2017)

Students with need: Out of 111 full-time freshmen who applied for aid, 104 were judged to have need. Of these, 103 received aid, and 2 had their full need met. Average financial aid package met 56% of need; average scholarship/grant was $22,946; average loan was $2,954. For part-time students, average financial aid package was $10,234.

Students without need: 7 full-time freshmen who did not demonstrate need for aid received scholarships/grants; average award was $13,857. No-need awards available for academics.

FINANCIAL AID PROCEDURES

Forms required: FAFSA, CSS PROFILE, institutional form.

Dates and Deadlines: Priority date 11/15; closing date 2/1. Applicants notified on a rolling basis starting 11/30.

Transfers: No deadline. Applicants notified on a rolling basis starting 4/1; must reply by 5/1 or within 2 week(s) of notification.

CONTACT
Celeastia Williams, Director
7500 Glenoaks Boulevard, Burbank, CA 91504-1052
(818) 767-0888 ext. 273

Yeshiva Ohr Elchonon Chabad/West Coast Talmudical Seminary
Los Angeles, California
yoec@yoec.edu   Federal Code: 015975

4-year private rabbinical and seminary college for men in very large city, affiliated with the Jewish faith.
Enrollment: 161 undergrads.

BASIC COSTS (2016-2017)
Tuition and fees: $13,900.
Room and board: $8,100.
Additional info: Tuition/fee waivers available for minority students.

FINANCIAL AID PICTURE
Students with need: Need-based aid available for full-time students.
Students without need: This college awards aid only to students with need.

FINANCIAL AID PROCEDURES
Forms required: FAFSA, state aid form, institutional form.
Dates and Deadlines: Priority date 1/15; closing date 6/30. Applicants notified by 5/1; must reply by 7/1.

CONTACT
Hendy Tauber, Financial Aid Administrator
7215 Waring Avenue, Los Angeles, CA 90046
(323) 937-3763 ext. 112

Yuba College
Marysville, California
http://yc.yccd.edu   Federal Code: 001344

2-year public community college in small city.
Enrollment: 3,364 undergrads.
Selectivity: Open admission; but selective for some programs.

BASIC COSTS (2016-2017)
Tuition and fees: $1,400; out-of-state residents $7,850.
Per-credit charge: $46; out-of-state residents $261.
Additional info: Tuition/fee waivers available for adults.

FINANCIAL AID PICTURE (2015-2016)
Students with need: Need-based aid available for part-time students.
Students without need: No-need awards available for academics, athletics, job skills, minority status, music/drama.
Additional info: Tuition fee waiver based on Board of Governors Grant.

FINANCIAL AID PROCEDURES
Forms required: FAFSA.
Dates and Deadlines: Priority date 8/7; closing date 3/1. Applicants notified on a rolling basis starting 4/1.

CONTACT
Martin Gutierrez, Dean for EOP&S and Financial Aid
2088 North Beale Road, Marysville, CA 95901
(530) 741-6939

Colorado

Adams State University
Alamosa, Colorado
www.adams.edu   Federal Code: 001345

4-year public liberal arts college in small town.
Enrollment: 1,974 undergrads, 17% part-time. 449 full-time freshmen.
Selectivity: Admits over 75% of applicants.

BASIC COSTS (2016-2017)
Tuition and fees: $9,009; out-of-state residents $19,785.
Per-credit charge: $233; out-of-state residents $682.
Room and board: $7,950.

FINANCIAL AID PICTURE (2016-2017)
Students with need: 53% of average financial aid package awarded as scholarships/grants, 47% awarded as loans/jobs. Need-based aid available for part-time students. Work study available nights, weekends, and for part-time students.
Students without need: No-need awards available for academics, alumni affiliation, art, athletics, leadership, minority status, music/drama, state/district residency.

FINANCIAL AID PROCEDURES
Forms required: FAFSA.
Dates and Deadlines: Applicants notified on a rolling basis starting 4/30.
Transfers: No deadline. Applicants notified on a rolling basis starting 4/30; must reply within 4 week(s) of notification.

CONTACT
Philip Schroeder, Director of Financial Aid
208 Edgemont Boulevard, Alamosa, CO 81101
(719) 587-7306

Aims Community College
Greeley, Colorado
www.aims.edu   Federal Code: 007582

2-year public community college in small city.
Enrollment: 3,672 undergrads, 49% part-time. 451 full-time freshmen.
Selectivity: Open admission; but selective for some programs.

BASIC COSTS (2016-2017)
Tuition and fees: $2,281; out-of-district residents $3,432; out-of-state residents $13,018.
Per-credit charge: $67; out-of-district residents $106; out-of-state residents $425.

FINANCIAL AID PICTURE
Students with need: Need-based aid available for full-time and part-time students. Work study available nights, weekends, and for part-time students.

FINANCIAL AID PROCEDURES
Forms required: FAFSA.
Dates and Deadlines: Priority date 3/15; no closing date. Applicants notified on a rolling basis starting 6/1.

CONTACT
Nancy Gray, Executive Director of Student Financial Assistance
4911 West 20th Street, Greeley, CO 80634
(970) 339-6548

Arapahoe Community College
Littleton, Colorado
www.arapahoe.edu

2-year public community college in large town.
Enrollment: 7,586 undergrads, 78% part-time. 398 full-time freshmen.
Selectivity: Open admission; but selective for some programs.

BASIC COSTS (2016-2017)
Tuition and fees: $4,350; out-of-state residents $17,093.
Per-credit charge: $13; out-of-state residents $562.
Additional info: In-state tuition based upon assumption of Colorado Opportunity Fund waiver of $75 per-credit hour.

FINANCIAL AID PICTURE (2015-2016)
Students with need: 61% of average financial aid package awarded as scholarships/grants, 39% awarded as loans/jobs. Need-based aid available for part-time students.
Students without need: No-need awards available for academics, alumni affiliation, art, leadership, minority status, music/drama, state/district residency.

FINANCIAL AID PROCEDURES
Forms required: FAFSA.
Dates and Deadlines: Priority date 4/1; no closing date. Applicants notified on a rolling basis starting 4/15; must reply by 11/1.

CONTACT
PO Box 9002, Littleton, CO 80160-9002

Bel-Rea Institute of Animal Technology
Denver, Colorado
www.bel-rea.com   Federal Code: 012670

2-year for-profit technical college in very large city.
Enrollment: 489 undergrads.

BASIC COSTS (2016-2017)
Additional info: Tuition is $31,800 for the entire 24 month program. Fees are $100.

FINANCIAL AID PICTURE
Students with need: Need-based aid available for full-time students.
Students without need: This college awards aid only to students with need.

FINANCIAL AID PROCEDURES
Forms required: FAFSA.
Dates and Deadlines: Priority date 8/31; no closing date. Applicants notified on a rolling basis starting 8/15.
Transfers: No deadline.

CONTACT
Stasi Botinelli, Financial Aid Director
1681 South Dayton Street, Denver, CO 80247
(303) 751-8700

CollegeAmerica: Colorado Springs
Colorado Springs, Colorado
www.collegeamerica.edu

4-year private career college in large city.
Enrollment: 430 undergrads.
Selectivity: Open admission.

BASIC COSTS (2016-2017)
Additional info: Tuition varies by program. Associate's programs range from $42,411 to $48,251 for the complete program. Bachelor's programs range from $74,620 to $74,778 for the complete program.

FINANCIAL AID PICTURE
Students with need: Need-based aid available for full-time and part-time students.

FINANCIAL AID PROCEDURES
Forms required: FAFSA, institutional form.

CONTACT
Sonia Martinez, Director of Financial Aid
3645 Citadel Drive South, Colorado Springs, CO 80909

CollegeAmerica: Denver
Denver, Colorado
www.collegeamerica.edu   Federal Code: 025943

2-year private career college in very large city.
Enrollment: 177 undergrads.
Selectivity: Open admission.

BASIC COSTS (2016-2017)
Additional info: Tuition varies by program. Associate's programs range from $42,411 to $48,251 for the complete program. Bachelor's programs range from $74,620 to $74,778 for the complete program.

FINANCIAL AID PICTURE
Students with need: Need-based aid available for full-time students.
Students without need: This college awards aid only to students with need.
Scholarships offered: High School Academic Scholarship: based on outcome of OLSAT exam. Number awarded has no limit. A limited number of Associate Degree and Bachelor Degree Scholarships are available at the Denver campus. Basis for selection: 500 word essay. Reviewed by scholarship committee. Number of awards vary per quarter.

FINANCIAL AID PROCEDURES
Forms required: FAFSA, institutional form.
Dates and Deadlines: Applicants notified on a rolling basis; must reply within 4 week(s) of notification.
Transfers: No deadline. Applicants notified on a rolling basis.

CONTACT
Sonia Martinez, Regional Director of Central Financial Aid
1385 South Colorado Boulevard, 5th Floor, Denver, CO 80222-1912
(303) 300-8740

Colorado Christian University
Lakewood, Colorado
www.ccu.edu   Federal Code: 009401

4-year private university and liberal arts college in large city, affiliated with the nondenominational tradition.
Enrollment: 3,862 undergrads.

BASIC COSTS (2016-2017)
Tuition and fees: $29,360.
Room and board: $11,010.

FINANCIAL AID PICTURE
Students with need: Need-based aid available for full-time and part-time students. Work study available nights, weekends, and for part-time students.
Students without need: No-need awards available for academics, athletics, leadership, music/drama.

FINANCIAL AID PROCEDURES

Forms required: FAFSA.

Dates and Deadlines: Priority date 3/15; no closing date. Applicants notified on a rolling basis starting 4/1; must reply by 5/1 or within 4 week(s) of notification.

Transfers: Priority date 3/1; no deadline. Applicants notified by 3/10; must reply within 4 week(s) of notification.

CONTACT

Steve Woodburn, Director of Student Financial Aid

8787 West Alameda Avenue, Lakewood, CO 80226

(303) 963-3230

Colorado College

Colorado Springs, Colorado

www.coloradocollege.edu

Federal Code: 001347

CSS Code: 4072

4-year private liberal arts college in large city.

Enrollment: 2,084 undergrads. 533 full-time freshmen.

Selectivity: Admits less than 50% of applicants.

BASIC COSTS (2016-2017)

Tuition and fees: $50,892.

Per-credit charge: $2,121.

Room and board: $11,668.

FINANCIAL AID PICTURE (2016-2017)

Students with need: Out of 229 full-time freshmen who applied for aid, 171 were judged to have need. Of these, 171 received aid, and 171 had their full need met. Average financial aid package met 100% of need; average scholarship/grant was $45,278; average loan was $2,999. Need-based aid available for part-time students.

Students without need: 35 full-time freshmen who did not demonstrate need for aid received scholarships/grants; average award was $10,950. No-need awards available for academics, athletics.

Scholarships offered: 12 full-time freshmen received athletic scholarships; average amount $47,858.

FINANCIAL AID PROCEDURES

Forms required: FAFSA, CSS PROFILE.

Dates and Deadlines: Priority date 11/10; closing date 1/15. Applicants notified by 2/15; must reply by 5/1.

Transfers: Closing date 3/1.

CONTACT

Shannon Amundson, Director of Financial Aid

14 East Cache La Poudre Street, Colorado Springs, CO 80903-9854

(800) 260-6458

Colorado Mesa University

Grand Junction, Colorado

www.coloradomesa.edu

Federal Code: 001358

4-year public community and liberal arts college in small city.

Enrollment: 8,734 undergrads, 17% part-time. 2,027 full-time freshmen.

Selectivity: Admits over 75% of applicants.

BASIC COSTS (2016-2017)

Tuition and fees: $8,395; out-of-state residents $20,353.

Per-credit charge: $252.4; out-of-state residents $651.

Room and board: $10,560.

FINANCIAL AID PICTURE (2015-2016)

Students with need: Out of 1,803 full-time freshmen who applied for aid, 1,334 were judged to have need. Of these, 1,316 received aid, and 285 had their full need met. Average financial aid package met 64% of need; average

scholarship/grant was $6,539; average loan was $3,134. For part-time students, average financial aid package was $6,810.

Students without need: 210 full-time freshmen who did not demonstrate need for aid received scholarships/grants; average award was $3,123. No-need awards available for academics, alumni affiliation, art, athletics, leadership, music/drama.

Scholarships offered: 50 full-time freshmen received athletic scholarships; average amount $3,012.

FINANCIAL AID PROCEDURES

Forms required: FAFSA.

Dates and Deadlines: Applicants notified on a rolling basis starting 4/1; must reply within 2 week(s) of notification.

Transfers: No deadline. Applicants notified on a rolling basis starting 4/1.

CONTACT

Curt Martin, Director of Financial Aid

1100 North Avenue, Grand Junction, CO 81501-3122

(970) 248-1396

Colorado Mountain College

Glenwood Springs, Colorado

www.coloradomtn.edu

Federal Code: 004506

2-year public community and liberal arts college in small town.

Enrollment: 5,690 undergrads, 68% part-time. 351 full-time freshmen.

Selectivity: Open admission; but selective for some programs.

BASIC COSTS (2017-2018)

Tuition and fees: $2,160; out-of-district residents $4,110; out-of-state residents $13,170.

Per-credit charge: $62; out-of-district residents $127; out-of-state residents $429.

Room and board: $9,098.

FINANCIAL AID PICTURE (2015-2016)

Students with need: Need-based aid available for full-time and part-time students. Work study available nights, weekends, and for part-time students.

Students without need: This college awards aid only to students with need.

FINANCIAL AID PROCEDURES

Forms required: FAFSA.

Dates and Deadlines: Priority date 3/31; no closing date. Applicants notified on a rolling basis; must reply within 4 week(s) of notification.

Transfers: Transfer scholarships available for Colorado residents with 3.0 GPA and minimum 20 credit hours from previous schools.

CONTACT

Tom Valles, Director of Student Financial Aid

802 Grand Avenue, Glenwood Springs, CO 81601

(970) 947-8277

Colorado Northwestern Community College

Rangely, Colorado

www.cncc.edu

Federal Code: 001359

2-year public community college in rural community.

Enrollment: 957 undergrads, 45% part-time. 153 full-time freshmen.

Selectivity: Open admission; but selective for some programs.

BASIC COSTS (2016-2017)

Tuition and fees: $4,547; out-of-state residents $7,472.

Per-credit charge: $137; out-of-state residents $234.

Room and board: $6,654.

Additional info: In-state tuition based upon assumption of Colorado Opportunity Fund waiver of $75 per-credit hour.

FINANCIAL AID PICTURE (2015-2016)

Students with need: Average financial aid package met 46% of need; average scholarship/grant was $4,497; average loan was $3,194. For part-time students, average financial aid package was $3,646.

Students without need: No-need awards available for academics, athletics, leadership.

Scholarships offered: Academic Scholarships: $200-$1,000; for Colorado residents based on grades, specific talent, area of study; requires application, essay, informal interview, 2.5 GPA.

FINANCIAL AID PROCEDURES

Forms required: FAFSA, institutional form.

Dates and Deadlines: Priority date 5/1; no closing date. Applicants notified on a rolling basis starting 5/15; must reply within 4 week(s) of notification.

Transfers: No deadline.

CONTACT

Merrie Byers, Director, Financial Aid
500 Kennedy Drive, Rangely, CO 81648
(970) 675-3204

Colorado School of Healing Arts
Lakewood, Colorado
www.csha.net   Federal Code: 035844

2-year for-profit career college in small city.
Enrollment: 176 undergrads.
Selectivity: Open admission.

BASIC COSTS (2016-2017)

Additional info: Tuition for advanced training ranges from $950 to $7,111, tuition for certified massage therapy is $9,800, tuition for an AOS degree is $14,403. Fees for books, supplies, and materials vary by program.

FINANCIAL AID PICTURE

Students with need: Need-based aid available for full-time and part-time students.

Students without need: This college awards aid only to students with need.

FINANCIAL AID PROCEDURES

Forms required: FAFSA.

CONTACT

Gina Simpson, Financial Aid Administrator
7655 West Mississippi Avenue, Suite 100, Lakewood, CO 80226
(303) 986-2320 ext. 26

Colorado School of Mines
Golden, Colorado
www.mines.edu   Federal Code: 001348

4-year public university and engineering college in large town.
Enrollment: 4,566 undergrads, 4% part-time. 1,003 full-time freshmen.
Selectivity: Admits less than 50% of applicants.

BASIC COSTS (2016-2017)

Tuition and fees: $17,842; out-of-state residents $36,172.
Per-credit charge: $523; out-of-state residents $1,134.
Room and board: $11,477.

FINANCIAL AID PICTURE (2015-2016)

Students with need: Out of 803 full-time freshmen who applied for aid, 471 were judged to have need. Of these, 471 received aid, and 125 had their full need met. Average financial aid package met 65% of need; average

scholarship/grant was $5,626; average loan was $3,335. For part-time students, average financial aid package was $7,180.

Students without need: 276 full-time freshmen who did not demonstrate need for aid received scholarships/grants; average award was $7,809. No-need awards available for academics, alumni affiliation, athletics, music/drama, ROTC.

Scholarships offered: Merit: E-Days Scholarship, Harvey Scholarship Program, Boettcher Scholarship, Phi Theta Kappa Honor Society Scholarship. **Athletic:** 24 full-time freshmen received athletic scholarships; average amount $5,750.

FINANCIAL AID PROCEDURES

Forms required: FAFSA.

Dates and Deadlines: Priority date 3/1; no closing date. Applicants notified on a rolling basis starting 12/1; must reply by 5/1.

Transfers: Applicants notified on a rolling basis starting 3/15; must reply by 5/1. Federal aid only (Pell grant and Stafford loan). No aid available for second undergraduate degree candidates.

CONTACT

Jill Robertson, Director of Financial Aid
Undergraduate Admissions Office, Golden, CO 80401-6114
(303) 273-3301

Colorado School of Trades
Lakewood, Colorado
www.schooloftrades.edu   Federal Code: 013513

2-year for-profit technical college in small city.
Enrollment: 153 undergrads.
Selectivity: Open admission.

BASIC COSTS (2016-2017)

Additional info: Entire Gunsmithing associate's degree program: $20,681. Books and supplies: $3,500.

FINANCIAL AID PICTURE

Students with need: Need-based aid available for full-time students.

FINANCIAL AID PROCEDURES

Forms required: FAFSA, institutional form.

CONTACT

Robert Martin, President
1575 Hoyt Street, Lakewood, CO 80215-2945
(303) 233-4697 ext. 44

Colorado State University
Fort Collins, Colorado
www.colostate.edu   Federal Code: 001350

4-year public university in small city.
Enrollment: 23,768 undergrads, 7% part-time. 4,463 full-time freshmen.
Selectivity: Admits over 75% of applicants.

BASIC COSTS (2016-2017)

Tuition and fees: $11,052; out-of-state residents $28,346.
Per-credit charge: $396; out-of-state residents $1,301.
Room and board: $11,110.

FINANCIAL AID PICTURE (2015-2016)

Students with need: Out of 3,876 full-time freshmen who applied for aid, 2,431 were judged to have need. Of these, 2,225 received aid, and 789 had their full need met. Average financial aid package met 84% of need; average scholarship/grant was $8,107; average loan was $4,976. For part-time students, average financial aid package was $6,759.

Students without need: 750 full-time freshmen who did not demonstrate need for aid received scholarships/grants; average award was $5,142. No-need awards available for academics, alumni affiliation, art, athletics, leadership, music/drama, state/district residency.

Scholarships offered: 19 full-time freshmen received athletic scholarships; average amount $22,190.

Additional info: Colorado students who have a family Adjusted Gross Income (AGI) on their federal income tax return(s) of $57,000 or less (and who meet other eligibility requirements) given grants to cover at least one-half the cost of tuition. Students who are eligible for a federal Pell Grant receive 100% of base tuition and standard fees.

FINANCIAL AID PROCEDURES

Forms required: FAFSA, institutional form.

Dates and Deadlines: Priority date 3/1; no closing date. Applicants notified on a rolling basis starting 3/1.

CONTACT

Tom Biedscheid, Director of Student Financial Aid
Office of Admissions/Colorado State University, Fort Collins, CO 80523-1062
(970) 491-6321

Colorado State University: Pueblo

Pueblo, Colorado
www.csupueblo.edu   Federal Code: 001365

4-year public university in small city.
Enrollment: 4,227 undergrads.

BASIC COSTS (2016-2017)

Tuition and fees: $9,519; out-of-state residents $24,101.
Per-credit charge: $242.29; out-of-state residents $728.37.
Room and board: $9,910.

FINANCIAL AID PICTURE

Students with need: Need-based aid available for full-time and part-time students. Work study available nights, weekends, and for part-time students.

Students without need: No-need awards available for academics, alumni affiliation, art, athletics, job skills, leadership, minority status, music/drama, ROTC, state/district residency.

Scholarships offered: Merit scholarships of $2,000 or more are awarded to admitted students with a cumulative weighted GPA of 3.5 or higher and either an ACT composite score of 25 or higher or SAT composite (math and verbal) of 1120 or higher. Admitted entering first-year students who have either a 3.8 GPA or 26 ACT Composite or 1200 SAT Composite will be invited to apply for the 25 places available each year in the Honors Program; other interested students may also apply. Tuition awards will be available to students who are accepted to the program.

FINANCIAL AID PROCEDURES

Forms required: FAFSA.

Dates and Deadlines: Closing date 3/1. Applicants notified on a rolling basis starting 3/15; must reply within 3 week(s) of notification.

CONTACT

Sean McGivney, Director of Financial Aid
2200 Bonforte Boulevard, Pueblo, CO 81001-4901
(719) 549-2753

Colorado Technical University

Colorado Springs, Colorado
www.coloradotech.edu   Federal Code: 010148

4-year for-profit university and technical college in large city.
Enrollment: 1,144 undergrads.
Selectivity: Open admission; but selective for some programs.

BASIC COSTS (2016-2017)

Per-credit charge: $325.

Additional info: Associate programs: $30,225-$30,387.50. Bachelor's programs: $58,500-$60,450. Technology fee: $125 per term.

FINANCIAL AID PICTURE

Students with need: Need-based aid available for full-time and part-time students. Work study available nights, weekends, and for part-time students.

Students without need: No-need awards available for academics, ROTC.

FINANCIAL AID PROCEDURES

Forms required: FAFSA.

Dates and Deadlines: Applicants notified on a rolling basis starting 6/30.

Transfers: No deadline.

CONTACT

Cindy Rubek, Director of Student Financial Services
4435 North Chestnut Street, Colorado Springs, CO 80907
(719) 598-0200

Community College of Aurora

Aurora, Colorado
www.ccaurora.edu   Federal Code: 016058

2-year public community college in large city.
Enrollment: 5,831 undergrads, 74% part-time. 333 full-time freshmen.
Selectivity: Open admission.

BASIC COSTS (2016-2017)

Tuition and fees: $4,375; out-of-state residents $17,118.
Per-credit charge: $137; out-of-state residents $562.
Additional info: In-state tuition based upon assumption of Colorado Opportunity Fund waiver of $75 per-credit hour.

FINANCIAL AID PICTURE

Students with need: Need-based aid available for full-time and part-time students.

Students without need: No-need awards available for academics, minority status, music/drama, state/district residency.

FINANCIAL AID PROCEDURES

Forms required: FAFSA.

Dates and Deadlines: Priority date 6/1; no closing date. Applicants notified on a rolling basis starting 7/15.

CONTACT

John Young, Executive Director, Financial Aid
16000 East CentreTech Parkway, Aurora, CO 80011-9036
(303) 360-4709

Community College of Denver

Denver, Colorado
www.ccd.edu   Federal Code: 009542

2-year public community college in very large city.
Enrollment: 8,003 undergrads.
Selectivity: Open admission; but selective for some programs.

BASIC COSTS (2016-2017)

Tuition and fees: $5,174; out-of-state residents $17,917.
Per-credit charge: $137; out-of-state residents $234.
Additional info: In-state tuition based upon assumption of Colorado Opportunity Fund waiver of $75 per-credit hour.

FINANCIAL AID PICTURE

Students with need: Need-based aid available for full-time and part-time students.

Students without need: No-need awards available for academics, leadership, state/district residency.

FINANCIAL AID PROCEDURES

Forms required: FAFSA, institutional form.

Dates and Deadlines: Priority date 4/15; no closing date. Applicants notified on a rolling basis.

CONTACT

Thad Spaulding, Director of Financial Aid

Campus Box 201, PO Box 173363, Denver, CO 80217-3363

(303) 556-5503

Denver School of Nursing

Denver, Colorado

www.denverschoolofnursing.edu

4-year for-profit nursing college in very large city.

Enrollment: 653 full-time undergrads.

BASIC COSTS (2017-2018)

Additional info: Total tuition, fees, books and supplies for the B.S. in Nursing, $55,725. Total tuition, fees, books and supplies for the A.S. in Nursing, $44,756.

FINANCIAL AID PICTURE

Students with need: Need-based aid available for full-time and part-time students.

Students without need: This college awards aid only to students with need.

FINANCIAL AID PROCEDURES

Forms required: FAFSA.

CONTACT

Geri Reichmuth, Director of Financial Aid

1401 19th Street, Denver, CO 80202

DeVry University: Westminster

Westminster, Colorado

www.devry.edu   Federal Code: 014831

4-year for-profit university in very large city.

Enrollment: 237 undergrads, 68% part-time. 7 full-time freshmen.

BASIC COSTS (2016-2017)

Tuition and fees: $17,512.

Per-credit charge: $609.

FINANCIAL AID PICTURE

Students with need: Need-based aid available for full-time and part-time students.

Students without need: This college awards aid only to students with need.

FINANCIAL AID PROCEDURES

Forms required: FAFSA.

Dates and Deadlines: Applicants notified on a rolling basis.

CONTACT

1870 West 122nd Avenue, Westminster, CO 80234-2010

(303) 329-3340

PART III: FINANCIAL AID COLLEGE BY COLLEGE

Fort Lewis College

Durango, Colorado

www.fortlewis.edu   Federal Code: 001353

4-year public business and liberal arts college in large town.

Enrollment: 3,458 undergrads, 9% part-time. 809 full-time freshmen.

Selectivity: Admits over 75% of applicants.

BASIC COSTS (2016-2017)

Tuition and fees: $8,105; out-of-state residents $17,817.

Per-credit charge: $265; out-of-state residents $670.

Room and board: $9,130.

Additional info: Tuition/fee waivers available for minority students.

FINANCIAL AID PICTURE (2015-2016)

Students with need: Out of 684 full-time freshmen who applied for aid, 549 were judged to have need. Of these, 549 received aid, and 90 had their full need met. Average financial aid package met 95% of need; average scholarship/grant was $4,833; average loan was $3,368. For part-time students, average financial aid package was $9,198.

Students without need: 186 full-time freshmen who did not demonstrate need for aid received scholarships/grants; average award was $4,564. No-need awards available for academics; alumni affiliation, art, athletics, leadership, music/drama, state/district residency.

Scholarships offered: *Merit:* Presidential Scholarship: $8,000 out-of-state, $2,000 in-state; 121 admission index required. Provost Scholarship: $7,000 out-of-state, $1,500 in-state; 110-120 admission index required. Dean's Scholarship: $6,000 out-of-state, $1,000 in-state; 101-109 admission index required. Academic Promise Scholarship: $4,000 out-of-state, $750 in-state; 92-100 admission index required. New Mexico Reciprocal Scholarship: New Mexico residents are given in-state tuition rates; based on 3.5 GPA; number of awards limited. *Athletic:* 80 full-time freshmen received athletic scholarships; average amount $5,574.

Additional info: Tuition waived for Native Americans of federally recognized tribes; census number and Certificate of Indian Blood must accompany application.

FINANCIAL AID PROCEDURES

Forms required: FAFSA.

Dates and Deadlines: Priority date 11/15; no closing date. Applicants notified by 3/1; must reply by 9/16.

Transfers: No deadline. Applicants notified on a rolling basis.

CONTACT

Tracey Piccoli, Director of Financial Aid

1000 Rim Drive, Durango, CO 81301-3999

(970) 247-7073

Front Range Community College

Westminster, Colorado

www.frontrange.edu   Federal Code: 007933

2-year public community college in large city.

Enrollment: 14,543 undergrads, 66% part-time. 1,033 full-time freshmen.

Selectivity: Open admission.

BASIC COSTS (2016-2017)

Tuition and fees: $4,479; out-of-state residents $17,222.

Per-credit charge: $137; out-of-state residents $562.

Additional info: In-state tuition based upon assumption of Colorado Opportunity Fund waiver of $75 per-credit hour.

FINANCIAL AID PICTURE

Students with need: Need-based aid available for full-time and part-time students. Work study available nights, weekends, and for part-time students.

Students without need: No-need awards available for academics, job skills, leadership, state/district residency.

FINANCIAL AID PROCEDURES

Forms required: FAFSA, institutional form.

Dates and Deadlines: Priority date 5/1; no closing date. Applicants notified on a rolling basis starting 4/15; must reply within 3 week(s) of notification.

CONTACT

Carolee Goldsmith, Director of Financial Aid

3645 West 112th Avenue, Westminster, CO 80031

(303) 439-9454

IntelliTec College

Colorado Springs, Colorado

http://intelliteccollege.com   Federal Code: 008635

2-year for-profit technical college in large city.

Enrollment: 828 undergrads.

Selectivity: Open admission.

BASIC COSTS (2016-2017)

Additional info: Total tuition, fees, and materials range from $16,543 to $32,921 depending on program.

FINANCIAL AID PICTURE

Students with need: Need-based aid available for full-time and part-time students. Work study available nights.

Students without need: This college awards aid only to students with need.

FINANCIAL AID PROCEDURES

Forms required: FAFSA, state aid form, institutional form.

Dates and Deadlines: Applicants notified on a rolling basis.

Transfers: No deadline.

CONTACT

Candace Valdez, Financial Services Manager

2315 East Pikes Peak Avenue, Colorado Springs, CO 80909

(719) 632-7626

IntelliTec College: Grand Junction

Grand Junction, Colorado

http://intelliteccollege.com   Federal Code: 030669

2-year for-profit technical college in small city.

Enrollment: 94 undergrads.

Selectivity: Open admission.

BASIC COSTS (2017-2018)

Additional info: Total tuition, fees and materials range from $10,200 to $24,750 depending on program.

FINANCIAL AID PICTURE (2015-2016)

Students with need: Need-based aid available for full-time students.

Students without need: This college awards aid only to students with need.

FINANCIAL AID PROCEDURES

Forms required: FAFSA.

Dates and Deadlines: Applicants notified on a rolling basis.

Transfers: No deadline.

CONTACT

Mike Grove, Chief Financial Aid Officer

772 Horizon Drive, Grand Junction, CO 81506

(970) 245-8101

Johnson & Wales University: Denver

Denver, Colorado

www.jwu.edu   Federal Code: 003404

4-year private college in large city.

Enrollment: 1,227 undergrads, 7% part-time. 304 full-time freshmen.

Selectivity: Admits over 75% of applicants.

BASIC COSTS (2016-2017)

Tuition and fees: $31,872.

Room and board: $11,961.

FINANCIAL AID PICTURE

Students with need: Need-based aid available for full-time and part-time students.

Students without need: No-need awards available for academics, alumni affiliation, job skills, leadership, state/district residency.

FINANCIAL AID PROCEDURES

Forms required: FAFSA.

Dates and Deadlines: Applicants notified on a rolling basis starting 3/1; must reply within 2 week(s) of notification.

CONTACT

Lynn Robinson, Chief Financial Aid Officer

7150 Montview Boulevard, Denver, CO 80220

(800) 342-5598 ext. 4648

Lamar Community College

Lamar, Colorado

www.lamarcc.edu   Federal Code: 001355

2-year public community college in small town.

Enrollment: 475 undergrads, 29% part-time. 122 full-time freshmen.

Selectivity: Open admission; but selective for some programs.

BASIC COSTS (2016-2017)

Tuition and fees: $4,539; out-of-state residents $7,464.

Per-credit charge: $137; out-of-state residents $234.

Room and board: $6,200.

Additional info: In-state tuition based upon assumption of Colorado Opportunity Fund waiver of $75 per-credit hour.

FINANCIAL AID PICTURE (2015-2016)

Students with need: 60% of average financial aid package awarded as scholarships/grants, 40% awarded as loans/jobs. Need-based aid available for part-time students.

Students without need: No-need awards available for academics, athletics, minority status, state/district residency.

FINANCIAL AID PROCEDURES

Forms required: FAFSA.

Dates and Deadlines: Priority date 4/1; no closing date. Applicants notified on a rolling basis starting 4/15.

Transfers: No deadline.

CONTACT

Teale Hemphill, Director of Financial Aid

2401 South Main Street, Lamar, CO 81052-3999

Metropolitan State University of Denver

Denver, Colorado

www.msudenver.edu   Federal Code: 001360

4-year public liberal arts college in very large city.

Enrollment: 19,334 undergrads, 36% part-time. 1,609 full-time freshmen.

Selectivity: Admits 50 to 75% of applicants.

BASIC COSTS (2016-2017)
Tuition and fees: $6,930; out-of-state residents $20,096.

FINANCIAL AID PICTURE (2015-2016)
Students with need: Out of 1,368 full-time freshmen who applied for aid, 1,075 were judged to have need. Of these, 926 received aid, and 25 had their full need met. Average financial aid package met 54% of need; average scholarship/grant was $6,129; average loan was $3,182. For part-time students, average financial aid package was $5,897.
Students without need: 265 full-time freshmen who did not demonstrate need for aid received scholarships/grants; average award was $1,921. No-need awards available for academics, state/district residency.
Scholarships offered: 37 full-time freshmen received athletic scholarships; average amount $8,750.

FINANCIAL AID PROCEDURES
Forms required: FAFSA.
Dates and Deadlines: Priority date 3/15; closing date 7/21. Applicants notified by 12/1.
Transfers: No deadline. Applicants notified on a rolling basis starting 12/1.

CONTACT
Cindy Hejl, Director of Financial Aid
Campus Box 16, Denver, CO 80217

Morgan Community College
Fort Morgan, Colorado
www.morgancc.edu
Federal Code: 009981

2-year public community college in large town.
Enrollment: 1,150 undergrads.
Selectivity: Open admission; but selective for some programs.

BASIC COSTS (2016-2017)
Tuition and fees: $4,330; out-of-state residents $17,073.
Per-credit charge: $137; out-of-state residents $562.
Additional info: In-state tuition based upon assumption of Colorado Opportunity Fund waiver of $75 per-credit hour.

FINANCIAL AID PICTURE (2015-2016)
Students with need: Need-based aid available for full-time and part-time students. Work study available nights, weekends, and for part-time students.

FINANCIAL AID PROCEDURES
Forms required: FAFSA.
Dates and Deadlines: Closing date 4/2. Applicants notified on a rolling basis.

CONTACT
Sally Nestor, Director of Financial Aid
920 Barlow Road, Fort Morgan, CO 80701
(970) 542-3100

Naropa University
Boulder, Colorado
www.naropa.edu
Federal Code: 014652

4-year private university and liberal arts college in small city.
Enrollment: 374 undergrads, 7% part-time. 30 full-time freshmen.
Selectivity: Admits over 75% of applicants.

BASIC COSTS (2017-2018)
Tuition and fees: $31,790.
Per-credit charge: $995.
Room and board: $11,880.

FINANCIAL AID PICTURE (2016-2017)
Students with need: Out of 23 full-time freshmen who applied for aid, 22 were judged to have need. Of these, 22 received aid, and 2 had their full need met. Average financial aid package met 83% of need; average scholarship/grant was $25,517; average loan was $3,596. For part-time students, average financial aid package was $13,146.
Students without need: This college awards aid only to students with need.

FINANCIAL AID PROCEDURES
Forms required: FAFSA, state aid form.
Dates and Deadlines: Priority date 3/1; no closing date. Applicants notified on a rolling basis starting 3/1; must reply within 4 week(s) of notification.

CONTACT
Nancy Morrell, Director of Student Financial Aid
2130 Arapahoe Avenue, Boulder, CO 80302-6697
(303) 546-3534

Nazarene Bible College
Colorado Springs, Colorado
www.nbc.edu
Federal Code: 013007

4-year private Bible college in very large city, affiliated with the Church of the Nazarene.
Enrollment: 716 undergrads, 88% part-time. 3 full-time freshmen.
Selectivity: Open admission.

BASIC COSTS (2016-2017)
Tuition and fees: $14,400.
Per-credit charge: $450.

FINANCIAL AID PICTURE
Students with need: Need-based aid available for full-time and part-time students. Work study available nights, weekends, and for part-time students.
Students without need: No-need awards available for academics, minority status, religious affiliation.

FINANCIAL AID PROCEDURES
Forms required: FAFSA.
Dates and Deadlines: Applicants notified on a rolling basis starting 8/1.
Transfers: No deadline. Applicants notified on a rolling basis.

CONTACT
Jenny Madsen, Director of Financial Aid
1111 Academy Park Loop, Colorado Springs, CO 80910-3704
(719) 884-5050

Northeastern Junior College
Sterling, Colorado
www.njc.edu
Federal Code: 001361

2-year public community and junior college in large town.
Enrollment: 1,484 undergrads.
Selectivity: Open admission; but selective for some programs.

BASIC COSTS (2016-2017)
Tuition and fees: $4,710; out-of-state residents $7,635.
Per-credit charge: $212; out-of-state residents $235.
Room and board: $7,874.
Additional info: In-state tuition based upon assumption of Colorado Opportunity Fund waiver of $75 per-credit hour. Tuition/fee waivers available for adults, minority students.

FINANCIAL AID PICTURE (2015-2016)
Students with need: 53% of average financial aid package awarded as scholarships/grants, 47% awarded as loans/jobs. Need-based aid available

for part-time students. Work study available nights, weekends, and for part-time students.

Students without need: No-need awards available for academics, alumni affiliation, art, athletics, job skills, leadership, music/drama, state/district residency.

Additional info: Need-based financial aid available to part-time students taking 6 credits or more per semester.

FINANCIAL AID PROCEDURES
Forms required: FAFSA, institutional form.
Dates and Deadlines: Priority date 3/1; no closing date. Applicants notified on a rolling basis starting 4/15; must reply within 3 week(s) of notification.
Transfers: No deadline. Applicants notified on a rolling basis starting 4/15; must reply within 3 week(s) of notification.

CONTACT
Alice Weingardt, Financial Aid Director
100 College Avenue, Sterling, CO 80751-2399
(970) 521-6751

Otero Junior College
La Junta, Colorado
https://www.ojc.edu   Federal Code: 001362

2-year public community and junior college in small town.
Enrollment: 1,466 undergrads.
Selectivity: Open admission; but selective for some programs.

BASIC COSTS (2016-2017)
Tuition and fees: $4,457; out-of-state residents $7,382.
Per-credit charge: $137; out-of-state residents $234.
Room and board: $6,558.
Additional info: In-state tuition based upon assumption of Colorado Opportunity Fund waiver of $75 per-credit hour.

FINANCIAL AID PICTURE
Students with need: Need-based aid available for full-time and part-time students. Work study available nights, weekends, and for part-time students.
Students without need: No-need awards available for academics, athletics, state/district residency.

FINANCIAL AID PROCEDURES
Forms required: FAFSA.
Dates and Deadlines: Priority date 4/1; no closing date. Applicants notified on a rolling basis starting 4/1; must reply within 2 week(s) of notification.
Transfers: No deadline. Applicants notified on a rolling basis starting 4/1; must reply within 2 week(s) of notification.

CONTACT
Angela Moore, Financial Aid Director
1802 Colorado Avenue, La Junta, CO 81050
(719) 384-6834

Pikes Peak Community College
Colorado Springs, Colorado
www.ppcc.edu   Federal Code: 008896

2-year public community college in large city.
Enrollment: 12,525 undergrads, 61% part-time. 1,210 full-time freshmen.
Selectivity: Open admission.

BASIC COSTS (2016-2017)
Tuition and fees: $4,414; out-of-state residents $17,157.
Per-credit charge: $137; out-of-state residents $562.
Additional info: In-state tuition based upon assumption of Colorado Opportunity Fund waiver of $75 per-credit hour.

FINANCIAL AID PICTURE (2015-2016)
Students with need: Out of 908 full-time freshmen who applied for aid, 681 were judged to have need. Of these, 613 received aid, and 31 had their full need met. Average financial aid package met 40% of need; average scholarship/grant was $4,200; average loan was $3,000. For part-time students, average financial aid package was $7,500.
Students without need: 25 full-time freshmen who did not demonstrate need for aid received scholarships/grants; average award was $500.

FINANCIAL AID PROCEDURES
Forms required: FAFSA.
Dates and Deadlines: Priority date 3/31; closing date 7/1. Applicants notified on a rolling basis; must reply within 2 week(s) of notification.

CONTACT
Ron Swartwood, Director of Financial Aid
5675 South Academy Boulevard, Colorado Springs, CO 80906-5498
(719) 502-3000

Platt College: Aurora
Aurora, Colorado
www.plattcolorado.edu   Federal Code: 030149

4-year for-profit nursing college in very large city.
Enrollment: 215 undergrads.
Selectivity: Open admission; but selective for some programs.

BASIC COSTS (2016-2017)
Additional info: Bachelor programs: $68,265. Fees, books supplies range depending on program level and course of study. All costs are subject to change.

FINANCIAL AID PICTURE
Students with need: Need-based aid available for full-time students.
Students without need: This college awards aid only to students with need.

FINANCIAL AID PROCEDURES
Forms required: FAFSA, institutional form.
Dates and Deadlines: Applicants notified on a rolling basis.

CONTACT
Margie Rose, Director of Financial Aid
3100 South Parker Road, Aurora, CO 80014-3141
(303) 369-5151

Pueblo Community College
Pueblo, Colorado
www.pueblocc.edu   Federal Code: 014829

2-year public community college in small city.
Enrollment: 4,544 undergrads, 64% part-time. 326 full-time freshmen.
Selectivity: Open admission; but selective for some programs.

BASIC COSTS (2016-2017)
Tuition and fees: $4,695; out-of-state residents $17,438.
Per-credit charge: $137; out-of-state residents $562.
Additional info: In-state tuition based upon assumption of Colorado Opportunity Fund waiver of $75 per-credit hour.

FINANCIAL AID PICTURE (2015-2016)
Students with need: Out of 295 full-time freshmen who applied for aid, 247 were judged to have need. Of these, 247 received aid, and 242 had their full need met. Average financial aid package met 95% of need; average scholarship/grant was $5,230; average loan was $981. For part-time students, average financial aid package was $6,756.

Students without need: No-need awards available for academics, art, job skills, leadership, music/drama.

FINANCIAL AID PROCEDURES

Forms required: FAFSA.

Dates and Deadlines: Priority date 3/15; no closing date. Applicants notified on a rolling basis starting 4/1; must reply within 2 week(s) of notification.

Transfers: No deadline. Applicants notified on a rolling basis starting 4/1; must reply within 2 week(s) of notification.

CONTACT

Monica Hardwick, Director of Financial Aid
900 West Orman Avenue, Pueblo, CO 81004-1499
(719) 549-3020

Red Rocks Community College

Lakewood, Colorado
www.rrcc.edu   Federal Code: 009543

2-year public community and career college in small city.
Enrollment: 7,789 undergrads.
Selectivity: Open admission.

BASIC COSTS (2016-2017)
Tuition and fees: $4,695; out-of-state residents $17,438.
Per-credit charge: $137; out-of-state residents $562.
Additional info: In-state tuition based upon assumption of Colorado Opportunity Fund waiver of $75 per-credit hour.

FINANCIAL AID PICTURE

Students with need: Need-based aid available for full-time and part-time students.

Students without need: No-need awards available for academics, leadership, minority status, state/district residency.

FINANCIAL AID PROCEDURES

Forms required: FAFSA.

Dates and Deadlines: Priority date 4/1; no closing date. Applicants notified on a rolling basis starting 5/1.

CONTACT

Linda Crook, Director of Financial Aid
13300 West Sixth Avenue, Lakewood, CO 80228-1255
(303) 914-6256

Redstone College

Broomfield, Colorado
www.redstone.edu   Federal Code: 007297

2-year for-profit technical college in small city.
Enrollment: 552 undergrads.
Selectivity: Open admission.

BASIC COSTS (2016-2017)
Additional info: Tuition and fees for entire Associate degree program $30,960 to $36,875 depending on program. HVAC diploma credential is $18,124.

FINANCIAL AID PICTURE

Students with need: Need-based aid available for full-time students.
Students without need: This college awards aid only to students with need.

FINANCIAL AID PROCEDURES

Forms required: FAFSA, state aid form.

Dates and Deadlines: Applicants notified on a rolling basis; must reply within 2 week(s) of notification.

CONTACT

Alicia Harbin, Financial Aid Director
10851 West 120th Avenue, Broomfield, CO 80021-3401

Regis University

Denver, Colorado
www.regis.edu   Federal Code: 001363

4-year private university and liberal arts college in very large city, affiliated with the Roman Catholic Church.
Enrollment: 3,972 undergrads, 41% part-time. 545 full-time freshmen.
Selectivity: Admits 50 to 75% of applicants.

BASIC COSTS (2017-2018)
Tuition and fees: $34,450.
Per-credit charge: $1,066.
Room and board: $10,420.

FINANCIAL AID PICTURE (2015-2016)
Students with need: Out of 457 full-time freshmen who applied for aid, 379 were judged to have need. Of these, 378 received aid, and 52 had their full need met. Average financial aid package met 82% of need; average scholarship/grant was $21,539; average loan was $3,723. For part-time students, average financial aid package was $10,193.

Students without need: 150 full-time freshmen who did not demonstrate need for aid received scholarships/grants; average award was $13,188. No-need awards available for academics, athletics, leadership, music/drama, religious affiliation, ROTC, state/district residency.

Scholarships offered: 30 full-time freshmen received athletic scholarships; average amount $13,793.

FINANCIAL AID PROCEDURES

Forms required: FAFSA.

Dates and Deadlines: Priority date 5/31; no closing date. Applicants notified on a rolling basis starting 3/15.

Transfers: Applicants notified by 4/1.

CONTACT

Ellie Miller, Director of Financial Aid
3333 Regis Boulevard, Mail Code A12, Denver, CO 80221-1099
(800) 388-2366 ext. 4126

Rocky Mountain College of Art & Design

Denver, Colorado
www.rmcad.edu   Federal Code: 013991

4-year for-profit visual arts college in very large city.
Enrollment: 1,074 undergrads.
Selectivity: Open admission.

BASIC COSTS (2016-2017)
Tuition and fees: $15,870.
Per-credit charge: $594.

FINANCIAL AID PICTURE

Students with need: Need-based aid available for full-time and part-time students. Work study available nights, weekends, and for part-time students.

Students without need: No-need awards available for academics, art, state/district residency.

FINANCIAL AID PROCEDURES

Forms required: FAFSA.

Dates and Deadlines: Priority date 3/15; no closing date. Applicants notified on a rolling basis starting 4/1; must reply within 2 week(s) of notification.

Transfers: Must reply within 2 week(s) of notification.

CONTACT

Michael Dulay, Senior Financial Aid Program Manager
1600 Pierce Street, Denver, CO 80214
(303) 505-6675

Trinidad State Junior College

Trinidad, Colorado
www.trinidadstate.edu   Federal Code: 001368

2-year public community college in small town.
Enrollment: 1,216 undergrads.
Selectivity: Open admission; but selective for some programs.

BASIC COSTS (2016-2017)

Tuition and fees: $4,695; out-of-state residents $7,620.
Per-credit charge: $137; out-of-state residents $234.
Room and board: $6,414.
Additional info: In-state tuition based upon assumption of Colorado Opportunity Fund waiver of $75 per-credit hour.

FINANCIAL AID PICTURE

Students with need: Need-based aid available for full-time and part-time students. Work study available nights.
Students without need: No-need awards available for academics, athletics, state/district residency.

FINANCIAL AID PROCEDURES

Forms required: FAFSA.
Dates and Deadlines: Priority date 5/1; no closing date. Applicants notified on a rolling basis starting 6/15.

CONTACT

Wilma Atencio, Financial Aid Director
600 Prospect Street, Trinidad, CO 81082
(719) 846-5553

United States Air Force Academy

USAF Academy, Colorado
www.academyadmissions.com   Federal Code: 001369

4-year public liberal arts and military college in large city.
Enrollment: 4,237 undergrads. 1,115 full-time freshmen.
Selectivity: Admits less than 50% of applicants.

BASIC COSTS (2017-2018)

Additional info: All cadet expenses, including tuition, room and board and supplies are paid for by the federal government.

CONTACT

HQ USAFA/RR 2304 Cadet Drive, Suite 2400, USAF Academy, CO 80840-5025

University of Colorado Boulder

Boulder, Colorado
www.colorado.edu   Federal Code: 001370

4-year public university in small city.
Enrollment: 27,418 undergrads, 6% part-time. 6,365 full-time freshmen.
Selectivity: Admits over 75% of applicants.

BASIC COSTS (2016-2017)

Tuition and fees: $11,531; out-of-state residents $35,079.
Room and board: $13,590.
Additional info: Tuition at time of enrollment locked for 4 years.

FINANCIAL AID PICTURE (2016-2017)

Students with need: Out of 4,055 full-time freshmen who applied for aid, 2,471 were judged to have need. Of these, 2,412 received aid, and 1,112 had their full need met. Average financial aid package met 82% of need; average scholarship/grant was $11,465; average loan was $5,356. For part-time students, average financial aid package was $13,178.
Students without need: 2,125 full-time freshmen who did not demonstrate need for aid received scholarships/grants; average award was $8,893. No-need awards available for academics, alumni affiliation, art, athletics, leadership, music/drama, ROTC, state/district residency.
Scholarships offered: *Merit:* Presidential Scholars Program: $15,000 per year during freshman and sophomore years, $12,500 per year during junior and senior years; for out-of-state freshmen in top 1 to 3% of admitted out-of-state freshman class, based on GPA and SAT/ACT test scores. Chancellor's Achievement Scholarship: $25,000 over four years; for top 25% of out-of-state admitted new freshmen, based on GPA and SAT/ACT test scores. Norlin Scholars Program; $5,000; based on excellent academic or creative ability; 20-30 annual awards; renewable contingent upon academic progress. President Joseph A. Sewall Award: $5,000 per year; for Colorado residents; based on GPA and SAT/ACT. President Horace M. Hale Award: $3,500 per year; for Colorado residents; based on GPA and SAT/ACT. President James H. Baker Award: $2,500 per year; for Colorado residents; based on GPA and SAT/ACT. Arts and Humanities Achievement Scholarship: awarded to incoming freshmen with a declared Arts & Humanities major; $8,000 ($2,000 per year) for Colorado residents, $12,000 ($3,000 per year) for out-of-state students; based on GPA and SAT/ACT test scores; recipients must remain in one of the eligible Arts and Humanities majors (changes between eligible majors allowed). *Athletic:* 48 full-time freshmen received athletic scholarships; average amount $27,447.
Additional info: Four-year lock on tuition and mandatory fee costs for undergraduate resident students.

FINANCIAL AID PROCEDURES

Forms required: FAFSA. PROFILE accepted but not required.
Dates and Deadlines: Priority date 3/1; no closing date. Applicants notified on a rolling basis starting 3/15; must reply within 3 week(s) of notification.
Transfers: Some financial aid programs available exclusively to transfer students.

CONTACT

Gwen Pomper, Director of Financial Aid
Regent Administrative Center 125, Boulder, CO 80309-0552
(303) 492-5091

University of Colorado Colorado Springs

Colorado Springs, Colorado
www.uccs.edu   Federal Code: 004509

4-year public university in large city.
Enrollment: 10,147 undergrads, 22% part-time. 1,581 full-time freshmen.
Selectivity: Admits over 75% of applicants.

BASIC COSTS (2016-2017)

Tuition and fees: $9,863; out-of-state residents $23,273.
Room and board: $9,800.
Additional info: Students in the Western Undergraduate Exchange program pay 150% of in-state tuition rather than the full out-of-state tuition. Also, most students affiliated with the military are eligible for in-state tuition rates.

FINANCIAL AID PICTURE (2015-2016)

Students with need: Out of 1,466 full-time freshmen who applied for aid, 1,047 were judged to have need. Of these, 954 received aid, and 11 had their full need met. Average financial aid package met 16% of need; average scholarship/grant was $7,255; average loan was $3,342. For part-time students, average financial aid package was $5,885.

Students without need: 170 full-time freshmen who did not demonstrate need for aid received scholarships/grants; average award was $707. No-need awards available for academics, athletics, leadership.

Scholarships offered: 56 full-time freshmen received athletic scholarships; average amount $5,069.

FINANCIAL AID PROCEDURES

Forms required: FAFSA.

Dates and Deadlines: Priority date 3/1; no closing date. Applicants notified on a rolling basis starting 3/15.

CONTACT

Jevita Rogers, Director of Financial Aid
1420 Austin Bluffs Parkway, Colorado Springs, CO 80918
(719) 255-3460

University of Colorado Denver
Denver, Colorado
www.ucdenver.edu   Federal Code: 006740

4-year public university in very large city.
Enrollment: 10,855 undergrads, 26% part-time. 1,278 full-time freshmen.
Selectivity: Admits 50 to 75% of applicants.

BASIC COSTS (2016-2017)

Tuition and fees: $10,741; out-of-state residents $30,361.
Per-credit charge: $303; out-of-state residents $934.
Room and board: $9,693.

FINANCIAL AID PICTURE (2015-2016)

Students with need: Out of 1,128 full-time freshmen who applied for aid, 841 were judged to have need. Of these, 764 received aid, and 24 had their full need met. Average financial aid package met 51% of need; average scholarship/grant was $7,195; average loan was $2,652. For part-time students, average financial aid package was $6,560.

Students without need: 63 full-time freshmen who did not demonstrate need for aid received scholarships/grants; average award was $3,501. No-need awards available for academics, art, leadership, music/drama, state/district residency.

Additional info: Pell eligible, full-time students receive a financial aid package that includes a combination of grants, scholarships, and a work-study award sufficient to fund the student's share of tuition, fees, and estimated book expenses. An eligible student may remain in the program for up to 10 semesters or completion of a bachelor's degree.

FINANCIAL AID PROCEDURES

Forms required: FAFSA.

Dates and Deadlines: Applicants notified on a rolling basis starting 5/1.

Transfers: No deadline. Applicants notified on a rolling basis.

CONTACT

Jessica Luna, Senior Financial Aid Advisor
Box 173364, Campus Box 167, Denver, CO 80217-3364
(303) 556-2886

University of Denver
Denver, Colorado   Federal Code: 001371
www.du.edu   CSS Code: 4842

4-year private university in very large city.
Enrollment: 5,738 undergrads, 5% part-time. 1,377 full-time freshmen.
Selectivity: Admits 50 to 75% of applicants.

BASIC COSTS (2017-2018)

Tuition and fees: $48,669.
Per-credit charge: $1,320.

Room and board: $12,612.

FINANCIAL AID PICTURE (2016-2017)

Students with need: Out of 921 full-time freshmen who applied for aid, 621 were judged to have need. Of these, 616 received aid, and 193 had their full need met. Average financial aid package met 84% of need; average scholarship/grant was $30,469; average loan was $3,347. For part-time students, average financial aid package was $31,718.

Students without need: 524 full-time freshmen who did not demonstrate need for aid received scholarships/grants; average award was $19,861. No-need awards available for academics, art, athletics, music/drama.

Scholarships offered: 49 full-time freshmen received athletic scholarships; average amount $38,835.

FINANCIAL AID PROCEDURES

Forms required: FAFSA, CSS PROFILE.

Dates and Deadlines: Priority date 1/15; no closing date. Applicants notified by 3/1; must reply by 5/1.

CONTACT

Tom Willoughby, Vice Chancellor, Enrollment
2197 South University Boulevard, Denver, CO 80208
(303) 871-4020

University of Northern Colorado
Greeley, Colorado
www.unco.edu   Federal Code: 001349

4-year public university in small city.
Enrollment: 9,095 undergrads, 9% part-time. 1,947 full-time freshmen.
Selectivity: Admits over 75% of applicants.

BASIC COSTS (2016-2017)

Tuition and fees: $8,888; out-of-state residents $20,474.
Per-credit charge: $275.25; out-of-state residents $735.5.
Room and board: $10,566.
Additional info: Costs reflect student share of tuition after the Colorado College Opportunity Fund.

FINANCIAL AID PICTURE (2015-2016)

Students with need: Out of 1,764 full-time freshmen who applied for aid, 1,252 were judged to have need. Of these, 1,218 received aid, and 466 had their full need met. Average financial aid package met 81% of need; average scholarship/grant was $9,348; average loan was $3,216. For part-time students, average financial aid package was $6,103.

Students without need: 269 full-time freshmen who did not demonstrate need for aid received scholarships/grants; average award was $6,381. No-need awards available for academics, athletics, music/drama.

Scholarships offered: 61 full-time freshmen received athletic scholarships; average amount $14,948.

FINANCIAL AID PROCEDURES

Forms required: FAFSA.

Dates and Deadlines: Priority date 3/1; no closing date. Applicants notified on a rolling basis starting 3/1; must reply within 4 week(s) of notification.

CONTACT

Marty Somero, Director of Financial Aid
501 20th Street, Campus Box 10, Greeley, CO 80639
(970) 351-2502

Western State Colorado University
Gunnison, Colorado
www.western.edu   Federal Code: 001372

4-year public university and liberal arts college in small town.
Enrollment: 1,988 undergrads, 4% part-time. 464 full-time freshmen.

Selectivity: Admits over 75% of applicants.

BASIC COSTS (2016-2017)
Tuition and fees: $9,193; out-of-state residents $20,497.
Per-credit charge: $263; out-of-state residents $734.
Room and board: $9,446.
Additional info: Tuition/fee waivers available for unemployed or children of unemployed.

FINANCIAL AID PICTURE (2016-2017)
Students with need: Out of 429 full-time freshmen who applied for aid, 275 were judged to have need. Of these, 275 received aid, and 13 had their full need met. Average financial aid package met 47% of need; average scholarship/grant was $7,549; average loan was $3,324. For part-time students, average financial aid package was $5,284.
Students without need: 125 full-time freshmen who did not demonstrate need for aid received scholarships/grants; average award was $4,528. No-need awards available for academics, alumni affiliation, art, athletics, leadership, music/drama, state/district residency.
Scholarships offered: *Merit:* Academic Excellence Award; $1,000; based on 3.5 GPA and 22 ACT/1010 SAT. Non-resident Leadership Award; $2,500; based on 3.2 GPA, 990 SAT, leadership activities. SAT scores exclusive of Writing. *Athletic:* 23 full-time freshmen received athletic scholarships; average amount $4,657.

FINANCIAL AID PROCEDURES
Forms required: FAFSA.
Dates and Deadlines: Priority date 3/1; no closing date. Applicants notified on a rolling basis starting 3/15.

CONTACT
Carrie Esquibel, Director of Financial Aid
600 North Adams Street, Gunnison, CO 81231
(970) 943-3085

Westwood College: Denver North
Denver, Colorado
www.westwood.edu/locations/colorado/denver-north-campus   Federal Code: 007548

4-year for-profit career college in very large city.
Enrollment: 863 undergrads.

BASIC COSTS (2016-2017)
Additional info: Business Administration: AAS $35,686. Computer Aided Design/Architectural Drafting: AAS $38,367. Construction Management: AAS $35,686. Criminal Justice: AAS $38,717. Dental Assisting: AAS $29,897. Graphic Design: AAS $40,278. Health Information Technology: AAS $38,384. Healthcare Office Administration: AAS $33,586. Medical Assisting: AAS $33,586. Paralegal: AAS $33,250. Automotive Technology: AOS $36,533. Information Technology: AOS $34,825. Business Administration: Major in Management: BS $71,372. Construction Management: BS $71,372. Criminal Justice: Major in Administration: BS $77,434. Information & Network Technologies: Major in CISCO Network Systems: BS $69,650. Medical Assisting: DP $23,990. Additional costs and fees such as books, tool kits, lab fee and online fees may apply.

FINANCIAL AID PICTURE
Students with need: Need-based aid available for full-time and part-time students.
Students without need: No-need awards available for academics, state/district residency.

FINANCIAL AID PROCEDURES
Forms required: FAFSA, state aid form, institutional form.
Dates and Deadlines: Applicants notified on a rolling basis starting 1/1; must reply within 2 week(s) of notification.
Transfers: No deadline.

CONTACT
Armando Guardiola, Director, Financial Aid
7350 North Broadway, Denver, CO 80221
(720) 542-5631

Connecticut

Albertus Magnus College
New Haven, Connecticut
www.albertus.edu   Federal Code: 001374

4-year private liberal arts college in small city, affiliated with the Roman Catholic Church.
Enrollment: 1,218 undergrads, 15% part-time. 129 full-time freshmen.
Selectivity: Admits 50 to 75% of applicants.

BASIC COSTS (2016-2017)
Tuition and fees: $30,526.
Per-credit charge: $1,252.
Room and board: $14,016.

FINANCIAL AID PICTURE (2016-2017)
Students with need: 70% of average financial aid package awarded as scholarships/grants, 30% awarded as loans/jobs. Need-based aid available for part-time students. Work study available nights, weekends, and for part-time students.
Students without need: No-need awards available for academics, state/district residency.

FINANCIAL AID PROCEDURES
Forms required: FAFSA.
Dates and Deadlines: Priority date 3/15; no closing date. Applicants notified on a rolling basis starting 4/15; must reply within 2 week(s) of notification.
Transfers: No deadline. Must reply within 2 week(s) of notification.

CONTACT
Michele Cochran, Director of Financial Aid
700 Prospect Street, New Haven, CT 06511-1189
(203) 773-8508

Asnuntuck Community College
Enfield, Connecticut
www.asnuntuck.edu   Federal Code: 011150

2-year public community and technical college in large town.
Enrollment: 1,658 undergrads, 61% part-time. 222 full-time freshmen.
Selectivity: Open admission.

BASIC COSTS (2016-2017)
Tuition and fees: $4,188; out-of-state residents $12,484.
Per-credit charge: $155; out-of-state residents $465.

FINANCIAL AID PICTURE
Students with need: Need-based aid available for full-time and part-time students. Work study available nights, weekends, and for part-time students.

FINANCIAL AID PROCEDURES
Forms required: FAFSA, institutional form.
Dates and Deadlines: Closing date 6/1. Applicants notified on a rolling basis starting 7/1; must reply within 2 week(s) of notification.
Transfers: Financial aid transcript required.

CONTACT
Beth Egan, Interim Director of Financial Aid
170 Elm Street, Enfield, CT 06082
(860) 253-3000 ext. 3030

Capital Community College

Hartford, Connecticut
www.ccc.commnet.edu   Federal Code: 007635

2-year public community and technical college in small city.
Enrollment: 3,110 undergrads.
Selectivity: Open admission; but selective for some programs.

BASIC COSTS (2016-2017)
Tuition and fees: $4,202; out-of-state residents $11,642.
Per-credit charge: $155; out-of-state residents $465.
Additional info: Tuition/fee waivers available for minority students.

FINANCIAL AID PICTURE
Students with need: Need-based aid available for full-time and part-time students. Work study available nights, weekends, and for part-time students.
Students without need: This college awards aid only to students with need.

FINANCIAL AID PROCEDURES
Forms required: FAFSA.
Dates and Deadlines: Closing date 7/15. Applicants notified on a rolling basis starting 7/15; must reply within 2 week(s) of notification.
Transfers: Closing date 7/1.

CONTACT
Margaret Malaspina, Director of Financial Aid
950 Main Street, Hartford, CT 06103-1207
(860) 906-5127

Central Connecticut State University

New Britain, Connecticut
www.ccsu.edu   Federal Code: 001378

4-year public university in small city.
Enrollment: 9,269 undergrads, 19% part-time. 1,258 full-time freshmen.
Selectivity: Admits 50 to 75% of applicants.

BASIC COSTS (2016-2017)
Tuition and fees: $10,936; out-of-state residents $22,602.
Per-credit charge: $217; out-of-state residents $223.
Room and board: $11,462.

FINANCIAL AID PICTURE (2015-2016)
Students with need: Out of 1,121 full-time freshmen who applied for aid, 1,019 were judged to have need. Of these, 924 received aid, and 111 had their full need met. Average financial aid package met 34% of need; average scholarship/grant was $4,661; average loan was $3,289. For part-time students, average financial aid package was $5,536.
Students without need: 56 full-time freshmen who did not demonstrate need for aid received scholarships/grants; average award was $3,812. No-need awards available for academics, athletics, minority status.
Scholarships offered: 27 full-time freshmen received athletic scholarships; average amount $14,843.

FINANCIAL AID PROCEDURES
Forms required: FAFSA.
Dates and Deadlines: Priority date 2/1; closing date 9/15. Applicants notified on a rolling basis starting 4/1; must reply within 2 week(s) of notification.
Transfers: Priority date 4/15. Applicants notified on a rolling basis.

CONTACT
Richard Bishop, Director of Financial Aid
1615 Stanley Street, New Britain, CT 06050
(860) 832-2200

Charter Oak State College

New Britain, Connecticut
www.charteroak.edu   Federal Code: 032343

4-year public liberal arts and career college in small city.
Enrollment: 1,459 undergrads, 79% part-time.

BASIC COSTS (2016-2017)
Tuition and fees: $9,393; out-of-state residents $12,093.
Per-credit charge: $287; out-of-state residents $377.

FINANCIAL AID PICTURE (2015-2016)
Students with need: Average financial aid package for all full-time undergraduates was $7,454; for part-time $5,012. 35% awarded as scholarships/grants, 65% awarded as loans/jobs.

FINANCIAL AID PROCEDURES
Forms required: FAFSA.
Dates and Deadlines: Priority date 4/15; no closing date. Applicants notified on a rolling basis.
Transfers: No deadline. Applicants notified on a rolling basis.

CONTACT
Ralph Brasure, Director of Financial Aid
55 Paul Manafort Drive, New Britain, CT 06053
(860) 515-3703

Connecticut College

New London, Connecticut   Federal Code: 001379
www.conncoll.edu   CSS Code: 3284

4-year private liberal arts college in large town.
Enrollment: 1,822 undergrads. 472 full-time freshmen.
Selectivity: Admits less than 50% of applicants.

BASIC COSTS (2016-2017)
Tuition and fees: $50,940.
Room and board: $14,060.

FINANCIAL AID PICTURE (2016-2017)
Students with need: Need-based aid available for full-time and part-time students. Work study available nights, weekends, and for part-time students.
Students without need: This college awards aid only to students with need.

FINANCIAL AID PROCEDURES
Forms required: FAFSA, CSS PROFILE.
Dates and Deadlines: Priority date 2/1; no closing date. Applicants notified by 4/1; must reply by 5/1.

CONTACT
Sean Martin, Director of Financial Aid Services
270 Mohegan Avenue, New London, CT 06320
(860) 439-2058

Eastern Connecticut State University

Willimantic, Connecticut
www.easternct.edu   Federal Code: 001425

4-year public university and liberal arts college in large town.
Enrollment: 4,818 undergrads, 11% part-time. 995 full-time freshmen.
Selectivity: Admits 50 to 75% of applicants.

BASIC COSTS (2016-2017)
Tuition and fees: $10,500; out-of-state residents $22,166.
Per-credit charge: $490; out-of-state residents $496.
Room and board: $12,559.

Additional info: New England Regional Program: Tuition: $7822 Fees: $5284.

FINANCIAL AID PICTURE (2015-2016)
Students with need: Need-based aid available for part-time students.

FINANCIAL AID PROCEDURES
Forms required: FAFSA.
Dates and Deadlines: Priority date 3/1; no closing date. Applicants notified on a rolling basis starting 3/1; must reply by 5/1.

CONTACT
Brian Lashley, Assistant Director of Institutional Research
83 Windham Street, Willimantic, CT 06226-2295
(860) 465-5205

Fairfield University
Fairfield, Connecticut
www.fairfield.edu
Federal Code: 001385
CSS Code: 3390

4-year private university in small city, affiliated with the Roman Catholic Church.
Enrollment: 3,955 undergrads, 4% part-time. 1,056 full-time freshmen.
Selectivity: Admits 50 to 75% of applicants.

BASIC COSTS (2016-2017)
Tuition and fees: $46,000.
Per-credit charge: $725.
Room and board: $13,860.
Additional info: Tuition/fee waivers available for minority students.

FINANCIAL AID PICTURE (2016-2017)
Students with need: Out of 817 full-time freshmen who applied for aid, 541 were judged to have need. Of these, 539 received aid, and 158 had their full need met. Average financial aid package met 84% of need; average scholarship/grant was $28,829; average loan was $3,431. For part-time students, average financial aid package was $16,158.
Students without need: 405 full-time freshmen who did not demonstrate need for aid received scholarships/grants; average award was $14,826. No-need awards available for academics, alumni affiliation, art, athletics, leadership, music/drama.
Scholarships offered: Merit: Academic scholarship: $7,000-$25,000; based on high school academic achievement and leadership; renewable for four years; 90% of students received financial aid. **Athletic:** 66 full-time freshmen received athletic scholarships; average amount $21,923.
Additional info: Veteran's Pride Program provides tuition discounts for children of qualified veterans. Bridgeport Tuition Program provides free tuition to qualified students from City of Bridgeport with family income under $50,000.

FINANCIAL AID PROCEDURES
Forms required: FAFSA, CSS PROFILE.
Dates and Deadlines: Closing date 1/15. Applicants notified by 4/1; must reply by 5/1.
Transfers: Closing date 5/1. Applicants notified on a rolling basis starting 4/1; must reply within 3 week(s) of notification.

CONTACT
Diana Draper, Director of Financial Aid
1073 North Benson Road, Fairfield, CT 06824
(203) 254-4125

Gateway Community College
New Haven, Connecticut
www.gatewayct.edu
Federal Code: 008303

2-year public community college in small city.
Enrollment: 6,494 undergrads.

Selectivity: Open admission; but selective for some programs.

BASIC COSTS (2016-2017)
Tuition and fees: $4,188; out-of-state residents $12,524.
Per-credit charge: $155; out-of-state residents $465.

FINANCIAL AID PICTURE
Students with need: Need-based aid available for full-time and part-time students. Work study available nights, weekends, and for part-time students.
Students without need: This college awards aid only to students with need.

FINANCIAL AID PROCEDURES
Forms required: FAFSA, institutional form.
Dates and Deadlines: Applicants notified on a rolling basis; must reply within 2 week(s) of notification.

CONTACT
Raymond Zeek, Director of Financial Aid
20 Church Street, New Haven, CT 06510
(203) 285-2013

Goodwin College
East Hartford, Connecticut
www.goodwin.edu
Federal Code: 015833

2-year private health science and career college in small city.
Enrollment: 3,287 undergrads.
Selectivity: Open admission; but selective for some programs.

BASIC COSTS (2016-2017)
Tuition and fees: $20,400.
Per-credit charge: $690.

FINANCIAL AID PICTURE
Students with need: Need-based aid available for full-time and part-time students. Work study available nights.
Students without need: This college awards aid only to students with need.

FINANCIAL AID PROCEDURES
Forms required: FAFSA, institutional form.
Dates and Deadlines: Applicants notified on a rolling basis starting 7/1.
Transfers: No deadline. Applicants notified on a rolling basis starting 8/1.

CONTACT
Mark Malboeuf, Director of Financial Aid
One Riverside Drive, East Hartford, CT 06118-9980
(860) 727-6723

Holy Apostles College and Seminary
Cromwell, Connecticut
www.holyapostles.edu
Federal Code: 001389

4-year private liberal arts and seminary college in large town, affiliated with the Roman Catholic Church.
Enrollment: 116 undergrads.
Selectivity: Admits over 75% of applicants.

BASIC COSTS (2016-2017)
Tuition and fees: $9,670.
Per-credit charge: $320.

FINANCIAL AID PICTURE
Students with need: Need-based aid available for full-time and part-time students.
Students without need: This college awards aid only to students with need.

FINANCIAL AID PROCEDURES

Forms required: FAFSA.

Dates and Deadlines: Closing date 6/30. Applicants notified on a rolling basis starting 8/25; must reply within 2 week(s) of notification.

Transfers: No deadline. Applicants notified on a rolling basis; must reply within 2 week(s) of notification.

CONTACT

Debora Johnston, Financial Aid Director

33 Prospect Hill Road, Cromwell, CT 06416-2005

(860) 632-3020

Housatonic Community College

Bridgeport, Connecticut

www.hcc.commnet.edu   Federal Code: 004513

2-year public community college in small city.

Enrollment: 4,584 undergrads.

Selectivity: Open admission; but selective for some programs.

BASIC COSTS (2016-2017)

Tuition and fees: $4,178; out-of-state residents $12,514.

Per-credit charge: $155; out-of-state residents $465.

FINANCIAL AID PICTURE (2015-2016)

Students with need: Need-based aid available for full-time and part-time students.

Students without need: This college awards aid only to students with need.

FINANCIAL AID PROCEDURES

Forms required: FAFSA.

Dates and Deadlines: Priority date 11/1; closing date 5/1. Applicants notified on a rolling basis starting 6/1.

CONTACT

Barbara Surowiec, Director of Financial Aid

900 Lafayette Boulevard, Bridgeport, CT 06604-4704

(203) 332-5047

Lincoln College of New England

Southington, Connecticut

www.lincolncollegene.edu

2-year for-profit school of mortuary science and career college in small town.

Enrollment: 536 undergrads.

Selectivity: Open admission.

FINANCIAL AID PICTURE

Students with need: Need-based aid available for full-time and part-time students. Work study available nights, weekends, and for part-time students.

Students without need: No-need awards available for academics.

FINANCIAL AID PROCEDURES

Dates and Deadlines: Applicants notified on a rolling basis starting 1/1.

CONTACT

Gina Swenton, Regional Director of Financial Aid

2279 Mount Vernon Road, Southington, CT 06489-1057

(860) 628-4751

Lyme Academy College of Fine Arts

Old Lyme, Connecticut

www.lymeacademy.edu   Federal Code: 030794

4-year private visual arts college in small town.

Enrollment: 78 undergrads.

BASIC COSTS (2016-2017)

Tuition and fees: $32,222.

Per-credit charge: $1,270.

Room only: $7,300.

FINANCIAL AID PICTURE

Students with need: Need-based aid available for full-time and part-time students. Work study available nights, weekends, and for part-time students.

Students without need: No-need awards available for academics, art, leadership.

FINANCIAL AID PROCEDURES

Forms required: FAFSA.

Dates and Deadlines: Priority date 2/15; closing date 4/15. Applicants notified on a rolling basis starting 3/1; must reply by 5/1 or within 2 week(s) of notification.

Transfers: Closing date 7/31. Applicants notified on a rolling basis starting 2/15; must reply by 5/1 or within 2 week(s) of notification.

CONTACT

Jim Falconer, Director of Financial Aid

84 Lyme Street, Old Lyme, CT 06371

(860) 434-3571 ext. 114

Manchester Community College

Manchester, Connecticut

www.mcc.commnet.edu   Federal Code: 001392

2-year public community college in small city.

Enrollment: 5,952 undergrads.

Selectivity: Open admission; but selective for some programs.

BASIC COSTS (2016-2017)

Tuition and fees: $4,188; out-of-state residents $12,524.

Per-credit charge: $155; out-of-state residents $465.

FINANCIAL AID PICTURE

Students with need: Need-based aid available for full-time and part-time students.

FINANCIAL AID PROCEDURES

Forms required: FAFSA.

Dates and Deadlines: Priority date 5/15; closing date 8/13. Applicants notified on a rolling basis starting 5/1; must reply within 2 week(s) of notification.

CONTACT

Ivette Rivera-Dreyer, Director of Financial Aid

PO Box 1046, MS#12, Manchester, CT 06045-1046

(860) 512-3380

Middlesex Community College

Middletown, Connecticut

www.mxcc.edu   Federal Code: 008038

2-year public community college in large town.

Enrollment: 2,381 undergrads.

Selectivity: Open admission; but selective for some programs.

BASIC COSTS (2016-2017)
Tuition and fees: $4,188; out-of-state residents $12,524.
Per-credit charge: $155; out-of-state residents $465.

FINANCIAL AID PICTURE
Students with need: Need-based aid available for full-time and part-time students.
Students without need: This college awards aid only to students with need.
Additional info: Tuition and/or fee waiver for veterans.

FINANCIAL AID PROCEDURES
Forms required: FAFSA, institutional form.
Dates and Deadlines: Priority date 6/1; no closing date. Applicants notified on a rolling basis starting 7/1; must reply within 2 week(s) of notification.
Transfers: Closing date 9/1.

CONTACT
Irene Martin, Director of Financial Aid
100 Training Hill Road, Middletown, CT 06457-4889
(860) 343-5741

Mitchell College
New London, Connecticut
www.mitchell.edu   Federal Code: 001393

4-year private liberal arts college in small city.
Enrollment: 677 undergrads. 119 full-time freshmen.
Selectivity: Admits over 75% of applicants.

BASIC COSTS (2017-2018)
Tuition and fees: $32,442.
Per-credit charge: $500.
Room and board: $12,750.

FINANCIAL AID PICTURE
Students with need: Need-based aid available for full-time and part-time students. Work study available nights, weekends, and for part-time students.
Students without need: No-need awards available for academics, alumni affiliation, art, leadership.

FINANCIAL AID PROCEDURES
Forms required: FAFSA.
Dates and Deadlines: Priority date 3/1; no closing date. Applicants notified on a rolling basis starting 2/15; must reply within 3 week(s) of notification.

CONTACT
Jacklyn Stoltz, Director of Financial Aid
437 Pequot Avenue, New London, CT 06320-4498
(860) 701-5040

Naugatuck Valley Community College
Waterbury, Connecticut
www.nv.edu   Federal Code: 006982

2-year public community and technical college in small city.
Enrollment: 5,976 undergrads, 63% part-time. 819 full-time freshmen.
Selectivity: Open admission; but selective for some programs.

BASIC COSTS (2016-2017)
Tuition and fees: $4,188; out-of-state residents $12,524.
Per-credit charge: $155; out-of-state residents $465.

FINANCIAL AID PICTURE
Students with need: Need-based aid available for full-time and part-time students.
Students without need: This college awards aid only to students with need.

FINANCIAL AID PROCEDURES
Forms required: FAFSA.
Dates and Deadlines: Priority date 4/1; no closing date. Applicants notified on a rolling basis starting 6/1.
Transfers: Financial aid transcripts required from all previous schools attended.

CONTACT
Catherine Hardy, Director of Financial Aid Services
750 Chase Parkway, Waterbury, CT 06708-3089
(203) 575-8006

Norwalk Community College
Norwalk, Connecticut
http://norwalk.edu/default.asp   Federal Code: 001399

2-year public community college in small city.
Enrollment: 4,598 undergrads, 60% part-time. 607 full-time freshmen.
Selectivity: Open admission; but selective for some programs.

BASIC COSTS (2016-2017)
Tuition and fees: $4,188; out-of-state residents $11,628.
Per-credit charge: $155; out-of-state residents $465.

FINANCIAL AID PICTURE
Students with need: Need-based aid available for full-time and part-time students.
Students without need: No-need awards available for academics, alumni affiliation.

FINANCIAL AID PROCEDURES
Forms required: FAFSA.
Dates and Deadlines: Priority date 7/7; no closing date. Applicants notified on a rolling basis starting 7/1; must reply within 2 week(s) of notification.

CONTACT
Luis Guaman, Director of Financial Aid
188 Richards Avenue, Norwalk, CT 06854-1655
(203) 857-7023

Paier College of Art
Hamden, Connecticut
www.paiercollegeofart.edu   Federal Code: 007459

4-year for-profit visual arts college in small city.
Enrollment: 95 undergrads, 29% part-time. 13 full-time freshmen.
Selectivity: Admits over 75% of applicants.

BASIC COSTS (2016-2017)
Tuition and fees: $15,450.

FINANCIAL AID PICTURE (2015-2016)
Students with need: Out of 10 full-time freshmen who applied for aid, 9 were judged to have need. Of these, 8 received aid. Average financial aid package met 46% of need; average scholarship/grant was $6,003; average loan was $3,500. For part-time students, average financial aid package was $5,856.

FINANCIAL AID PROCEDURES
Forms required: FAFSA.
Dates and Deadlines: Priority date 4/16; closing date 8/1. Applicants notified on a rolling basis starting 3/1; must reply within 3 week(s) of notification.
Transfers: Must reply within 3 week(s) of notification.

CONTACT
John DeRose, Director of Financial Aid
20 Gorham Avenue, Hamden, CT 06514-3902
(203) 287-3034

Post University
Waterbury, Connecticut
www.post.edu   Federal Code: 001401

4-year for-profit university and business college in small city.
Enrollment: 709 undergrads, 6% part-time. 211 full-time freshmen.
Selectivity: Admits less than 50% of applicants.

BASIC COSTS (2016-2017)
Tuition and fees: $29,550.
Per-credit charge: $945.
Room and board: $10,600.
Additional info: Tuition for Online Accelerated Degree Program (ADP) is $570 per credit with no fees.

FINANCIAL AID PICTURE (2015-2016)
Students with need: Need-based aid available for full-time and part-time students. Work study available nights, weekends, and for part-time students.
Scholarships offered: Post University annually awards two full-tuition scholarships to outstanding incoming students pursuing a degree at the Malcolm Baldrige School of Business. The University also offers a full tuition scholarship to one outstanding student from Naugatuck Valley Community College. Eligibility criteria are available on the University website. Academic merit scholarships available based on GPA and test scores; renewable contingent upon maintaining specific GPA.

FINANCIAL AID PROCEDURES
Forms required: FAFSA.
Dates and Deadlines: Priority date 3/15; no closing date. Applicants notified on a rolling basis starting 4/15; must reply by 5/1 or within 3 week(s) of notification.
Transfers: No deadline. Applicants notified on a rolling basis starting 4/15; must reply within 1 week(s) of notification.

CONTACT
Sharon Sweeney, Vice President of Student Finance
800 Country Club Road, Waterbury, CT 06723-2540
(203) 596-4571

Quinebaug Valley Community College
Danielson, Connecticut
www.qvcc.commnet.edu   Federal Code: 010530

2-year public community and technical college in large town.
Enrollment: 1,434 undergrads.
Selectivity: Open admission.

BASIC COSTS (2016-2017)
Tuition and fees: $4,183; out-of-state residents $12,519.
Per-credit charge: $155; out-of-state residents $465.

FINANCIAL AID PICTURE
Students with need: Need-based aid available for full-time and part-time students. Work study available nights.
Students without need: This college awards aid only to students with need.

FINANCIAL AID PROCEDURES
Forms required: FAFSA.
Dates and Deadlines: Closing date 8/1. Applicants notified on a rolling basis starting 5/1.

CONTACT
Kimberly Rich, Financial Aid Director
742 Upper Maple Street, Danielson, CT 06239-1440
(860) 412-7208

Quinnipiac University
Hamden, Connecticut
www.qu.edu   Federal Code: 001402

4-year private university in small city.
Enrollment: 7,042 undergrads, 4% part-time. 1,904 full-time freshmen.
Selectivity: Admits over 75% of applicants.

BASIC COSTS (2016-2017)
Tuition and fees: $43,940.
Per-credit charge: $995.
Room and board: $15,170.

FINANCIAL AID PICTURE (2016-2017)
Students with need: Out of 1,609 full-time freshmen who applied for aid, 1,333 were judged to have need. Of these, 1,330 received aid, and 235 had their full need met. Average financial aid package met 67% of need; average scholarship/grant was $22,466; average loan was $3,453. For part-time students, average financial aid package was $9,669.
Students without need: 452 full-time freshmen who did not demonstrate need for aid received scholarships/grants; average award was $17,609. No-need awards available for academics, athletics.
Scholarships offered: Merit: Academic scholarships; $9,000-$25,000 per year; based on class rank and (if provided) SAT/ACT scores; renewable with full-time status and 3.0 GPA. **Athletic:** 88 full-time freshmen received athletic scholarships; average amount $30,055.

FINANCIAL AID PROCEDURES
Forms required: FAFSA.
Dates and Deadlines: Priority date 3/1; no closing date. Applicants notified on a rolling basis starting 1/15; must reply by 5/1 or within 2 week(s) of notification.
Transfers: No deadline. Applicants notified on a rolling basis starting 3/1; must reply by 5/1 or within 2 week(s) of notification. Students transferring with 2 years of full-time college work and 3.5 GPA may be eligible for transfer scholarship.

CONTACT
Dominic Yoia, Associate Vice President and University Director of Financial Aid
275 Mount Carmel Avenue, Hamden, CT 06518-1908
(203) 582-8750

Sacred Heart University
Fairfield, Connecticut   Federal Code: 001403
www.sacredheart.edu   CSS Code: 3780

4-year private university in large town, affiliated with the Roman Catholic Church.
Enrollment: 5,325 undergrads, 10% part-time. 1,322 full-time freshmen.
Selectivity: Admits 50 to 75% of applicants.

BASIC COSTS (2016-2017)
Tuition and fees: $38,300.
Per-credit charge: $600.
Room and board: $14,450.
Additional info: Tuition/fee waivers available for adults, minority students.

FINANCIAL AID PICTURE (2016-2017)
Students with need: Out of 1,163 full-time freshmen who applied for aid, 941 were judged to have need. Of these, 941 received aid, and 170 had their full need met. Average financial aid package met 56% of need; average scholarship/grant was $15,890; average loan was $4,121. For part-time students, average financial aid package was $6,209.
Students without need: 365 full-time freshmen who did not demonstrate need for aid received scholarships/grants; average award was $12,778. No-need awards available for academics, alumni affiliation, art, athletics, leadership, music/drama, religious affiliation, state/district residency.

Scholarships offered: 59 full-time freshmen received athletic scholarships; average amount $16,129.

FINANCIAL AID PROCEDURES
Forms required: FAFSA, CSS PROFILE.
Dates and Deadlines: Priority date 2/15; no closing date. Applicants notified on a rolling basis starting 3/1; must reply within 2 week(s) of notification.
Transfers: Closing date 2/15. Applicants notified on a rolling basis; must reply within 2 week(s) of notification.

CONTACT
Julie Savino, Executive Director, University Financial Assistance
5151 Park Avenue, Fairfield, CT 06825
(203) 371-7980

St. Vincent's College
Bridgeport, Connecticut
www.stvincentscollege.edu   Federal Code: 006191

2-year private health science college in small city, affiliated with the Roman Catholic Church.
Enrollment: 745 undergrads, 91% part-time. 8 full-time freshmen.
Selectivity: Admits 50 to 75% of applicants.

BASIC COSTS (2016-2017)
Tuition and fees: $18,150.
Per-credit charge: $605.

FINANCIAL AID PICTURE
Students with need: Need-based aid available for full-time and part-time students.
Students without need: No-need awards available for academics.

FINANCIAL AID PROCEDURES
Forms required: FAFSA.
Dates and Deadlines: Priority date 3/15; no closing date. Applicants notified on a rolling basis; must reply within 4 week(s) of notification.

CONTACT
Dorothy Martin-Hatcher, Director of Financial Aid
2800 Main Street, Bridgeport, CT 06606
(203) 576-5513

Southern Connecticut State University
New Haven, Connecticut
www.southernct.edu   Federal Code: 001406

4-year public university in small city.
Enrollment: 7,963 undergrads, 14% part-time. 1,387 full-time freshmen.
Selectivity: Admits 50 to 75% of applicants.

BASIC COSTS (2016-2017)
Tuition and fees: $10,054; out-of-state residents $21,720.
Per-credit charge: $519; out-of-state residents $535.
Room and board: $11,870.

FINANCIAL AID PICTURE (2016-2017)
Students with need: Out of 1,124 full-time freshmen who applied for aid, 938 were judged to have need. Of these, 938 received aid, and 194 had their full need met. Average financial aid package met 68% of need; average scholarship/grant was $6,522; average loan was $3,374. For part-time students, average financial aid package was $9,940.
Students without need: 66 full-time freshmen who did not demonstrate need for aid received scholarships/grants; average award was $3,877. No-need awards available for academics, alumni affiliation, athletics, job skills, ROTC, state/district residency.

Scholarships offered: *Merit:* General Academic Achievement Awards; 90 awarded. Presidential Scholarships, Trustees Scholarships available. *Athletic:* 52 full-time freshmen received athletic scholarships; average amount $7,752.

FINANCIAL AID PROCEDURES
Forms required: FAFSA.
Dates and Deadlines: Priority date 3/5; closing date 3/9. Applicants notified on a rolling basis starting 4/11; must reply within 2 week(s) of notification.
Transfers: Applicants notified on a rolling basis starting 6/15; must reply within 2 week(s) of notification.

CONTACT
Gloria Lee, Director of Financial Aid & Scholarships
131 Farnham Avenue, New Haven, CT 06515-1202
(203) 392-5222

Three Rivers Community College
Norwich, Connecticut
www.threerivers.edu   Federal Code: 009765

2-year public community and technical college in large town.
Enrollment: 3,905 undergrads, 65% part-time. 459 full-time freshmen.
Selectivity: Open admission; but selective for some programs.

BASIC COSTS (2016-2017)
Tuition and fees: $4,188; out-of-state residents $11,628.
Per-credit charge: $155; out-of-state residents $465.

FINANCIAL AID PICTURE
Students with need: Need-based aid available for full-time and part-time students. Work study available nights, weekends, and for part-time students.
Students without need: This college awards aid only to students with need.
Scholarships offered: Various scholarships; $75 to $500.

FINANCIAL AID PROCEDURES
Forms required: FAFSA.
Dates and Deadlines: Priority date 5/1; no closing date. Applicants notified on a rolling basis; must reply within 2 week(s) of notification.
Transfers: No deadline.

CONTACT
Kenneth Briggs, Director of Financial Aid
Admissions Office, Norwich, CT 06360-6598
(860) 215-9040

Trinity College
Hartford, Connecticut   Federal Code: 001414
www.trincoll.edu   CSS Code: 3899

4-year private liberal arts college in large city.
Enrollment: 2,251 undergrads.

BASIC COSTS (2016-2017)
Tuition and fees: $52,760.
Per-credit charge: $1,678.
Room and board: $13,680.
Additional info: Tuition/fee waivers available for adults.

FINANCIAL AID PICTURE
Students with need: Need-based aid available for full-time and part-time students. Work study available nights, weekends, and for part-time students.
Students without need: No-need awards available for academics, leadership.

FINANCIAL AID PROCEDURES
Forms required: FAFSA, CSS PROFILE.

Dates and Deadlines: Priority date 2/1; closing date 3/1. Applicants notified by 4/1; must reply by 5/1 or within 2 week(s) of notification.
Transfers: Closing date 4/1. Applicants notified on a rolling basis starting 5/15; must reply within 2 week(s) of notification.

CONTACT
Kelly O'Brien, Director of Financial Aid
300 Summit Street, Hartford, CT 06106
(860) 297-2046

Tunxis Community College
Farmington, Connecticut
www.tunxis.edu   Federal Code: 009764

2-year public community college in large town.
Enrollment: 3,307 undergrads, 57% part-time. 479 full-time freshmen.
Selectivity: Open admission; but selective for some programs.

BASIC COSTS (2016-2017)
Tuition and fees: $4,188; out-of-state residents $12,524.
Per-credit charge: $155; out-of-state residents $465.

FINANCIAL AID PICTURE
Students with need: Need-based aid available for full-time and part-time students. Work study available nights, weekends, and for part-time students.
Students without need: No-need awards available for academics.
Additional info: Financial aid available to all students showing need. Part-time students encouraged to apply.

FINANCIAL AID PROCEDURES
Forms required: FAFSA.
Dates and Deadlines: Priority date 6/1; no closing date. Applicants notified on a rolling basis starting 3/1.

CONTACT
Sandy Vitale, Director of Financial Aid
271 Scott Swamp Road, Farmington, CT 06032-3187
(860) 773-1422

United States Coast Guard Academy
New London, Connecticut
www.uscga.edu   Federal Code: 001415

4-year public engineering and military college in small city.
Enrollment: 986 undergrads. 298 full-time freshmen.
Selectivity: Admits less than 50% of applicants.

BASIC COSTS (2016-2017)
Tuition and fees: $978.
Additional info: For US Citizens, room, tuition, and board at the Coast Guard Academy are paid for by the government. In addition, all US Cadets receive pay totaling $12,324.00 per year. Cadet pay is furnished by the government for uniforms, equipment, textbooks, and other expenses incidental to training.

CONTACT
Cadet Finance Manager
31 Mohegan Avenue, New London, CT 06320

University of Bridgeport
Bridgeport, Connecticut
www.bridgeport.edu   Federal Code: 001416

4-year private university in small city.
Enrollment: 2,941 undergrads, 27% part-time. 482 full-time freshmen.

Selectivity: Admits 50 to 75% of applicants.

BASIC COSTS (2016-2017)
Tuition and fees: $31,630.
Per-credit charge: $985.
Room and board: $13,320.

FINANCIAL AID PICTURE
Students with need: Need-based aid available for full-time and part-time students. Work study available nights, weekends, and for part-time students.
Students without need: No-need awards available for academics, art, athletics, leadership, music/drama.
Scholarships offered: Academic Excellence and Leadership Scholarship; up to full tuition, room, and board; for students ranking in the top quarter of high school class with 1200 SAT. Academic Scholarship; up to full tuition; for students in the top quarter of class and 1100 SAT. Academic Grant; up to half-tuition; for students in top half of class and 1100 SAT. Challenge Grant; $3,000; for students in the top half of class and 1000 SAT. All SAT scores exclusive of Writing.

FINANCIAL AID PROCEDURES
Forms required: FAFSA.
Dates and Deadlines: Priority date 3/1; no closing date. Applicants notified on a rolling basis starting 4/1; must reply within 4 week(s) of notification.
Transfers: No deadline. Applicants notified on a rolling basis starting 4/1; must reply by 5/1 or within 2 week(s) of notification.

CONTACT
Christine Falzerano, Director of Student Financial Services
126 Park Avenue, Bridgeport, CT 06604
(203) 576-4568

University of Connecticut
Storrs, Connecticut
www.uconn.edu   Federal Code: 007997

4-year public university in large town.
Enrollment: 18,451 undergrads.

BASIC COSTS (2016-2017)
Tuition and fees: $14,066; out-of-state residents $35,858.
Per-credit charge: $469; out-of-state residents $1,377.
Room and board: $12,436.

FINANCIAL AID PICTURE
Students with need: Need-based aid available for full-time and part-time students. Work study available nights, weekends, and for part-time students.
Students without need: No-need awards available for academics, art, athletics, leadership, minority status, music/drama.
Additional info: Institution offers variety of need-based financial aid programs. Financial assistance packages may include grants, loans and work-study awards.

FINANCIAL AID PROCEDURES
Forms required: FAFSA.
Dates and Deadlines: Priority date 3/1; no closing date. Applicants notified on a rolling basis starting 3/1; must reply within 4 week(s) of notification.

CONTACT
Mona Lucas, Director of Student Financial Aid Services
2131 Hillside Road, Unit 3088, Storrs, CT 06269-3088
(860) 486-2819

University of Hartford
West Hartford, Connecticut
www.hartford.edu   Federal Code: 001422

4-year private university in small city.
Enrollment: 4,924 undergrads, 8% part-time. 1,275 full-time freshmen.

Selectivity: Admits 50 to 75% of applicants.

BASIC COSTS (2017-2018)
Tuition and fees: $38,910.
Per-credit charge: $556.
Room and board: $12,346.
Additional info: Tuition/fee waivers available for minority students.

FINANCIAL AID PICTURE (2016-2017)
Students with need: Out of 1,137 full-time freshmen who applied for aid, 1,022 were judged to have need. Of these, 1,022 received aid, and 134 had their full need met. Average financial aid package met 66% of need; average scholarship/grant was $21,397; average loan was $3,568. For part-time students, average financial aid package was $6,599.
Students without need: 206 full-time freshmen who did not demonstrate need for aid received scholarships/grants; average award was $17,147. No-need awards available for academics, alumni affiliation, art, athletics, job skills, leadership, minority status, music/drama.
Scholarships offered: 20 full-time freshmen received athletic scholarships; average amount $35,563.

FINANCIAL AID PROCEDURES
Forms required: FAFSA.
Dates and Deadlines: Priority date 2/1; no closing date. Applicants notified on a rolling basis starting 3/1; must reply by 5/1 or within 2 week(s) of notification.

CONTACT
Victoria Hampton, Director of Student Financial Assistance
Bates House, West Hartford, CT 06117-1599
(860) 768-4296

University of New Haven
West Haven, Connecticut
www.newhaven.edu   Federal Code: 001397

4-year private university in small city.
Enrollment: 4,850 undergrads, 6% part-time. 1,117 full-time freshmen.
Selectivity: Admits over 75% of applicants.

BASIC COSTS (2016-2017)
Tuition and fees: $37,060.
Per-credit charge: $1,190.
Room and board: $15,130.

FINANCIAL AID PICTURE (2016-2017)
Students with need: Out of 971 full-time freshmen who applied for aid, 889 were judged to have need. Of these, 889 received aid, and 125 had their full need met. Average financial aid package met 58% of need; average scholarship/grant was $19,621; average loan was $3,428. For part-time students, average financial aid package was $5,995.
Students without need: 172 full-time freshmen who did not demonstrate need for aid received scholarships/grants; average award was $15,388. No-need awards available for academics, art, athletics.
Scholarships offered: 9 full-time freshmen received athletic scholarships; average amount $28,262.

FINANCIAL AID PROCEDURES
Forms required: FAFSA.
Dates and Deadlines: Priority date 1/1; no closing date. Applicants notified on a rolling basis starting 1/15; must reply by 5/1 or within 2 week(s) of notification.

CONTACT
Karen Flynn, Director of Financial Aid
300 Boston Post Road, West Haven, CT 06516-1916
(203) 932-7315

University of Saint Joseph
West Hartford, Connecticut
www.usj.edu   Federal Code: 001409

4-year private pharmacy and liberal arts college for women in small city, affiliated with the Roman Catholic Church.
Enrollment: 843 undergrads, 14% part-time. 125 full-time freshmen.
Selectivity: Admits over 75% of applicants.

BASIC COSTS (2016-2017)
Tuition and fees: $36,870.
Per-credit charge: $795.
Room and board: $11,095.

FINANCIAL AID PICTURE (2016-2017)
Students with need: 68% of average financial aid package awarded as scholarships/grants, 32% awarded as loans/jobs.
Students without need: No-need awards available for academics, leadership, minority status.

FINANCIAL AID PROCEDURES
Forms required: FAFSA.
Dates and Deadlines: Applicants notified on a rolling basis starting 2/15.
Transfers: No deadline. Applicants notified on a rolling basis starting 2/15.

CONTACT
Ashley Dutton, Director of Student Financial Services
1678 Asylum Avenue, West Hartford, CT 06117
(866) 442-8752

Wesleyan University
Middletown, Connecticut   Federal Code: 001424
www.wesleyan.edu   CSS Code: 3959

4-year private university and liberal arts college in large town.
Enrollment: 2,913 undergrads. 774 full-time freshmen.
Selectivity: Admits less than 50% of applicants.

BASIC COSTS (2016-2017)
Tuition and fees: $50,912.
Room and board: $13,950.
Additional info: Comprehensive residential fee for juniors & seniors is $15,858.

FINANCIAL AID PICTURE (2016-2017)
Students with need: Out of 356 full-time freshmen who applied for aid, 340 were judged to have need. Of these, 340 received aid, and 340 had their full need met. Average financial aid package met 100% of need; average scholarship/grant was $41,149; average loan was $3,020.
Students without need: This college awards aid only to students with need.
Scholarships offered: Freeman Asian Scholars: for international first-year applicants from select East and Southeast Asian countries; 22 awarded.
Additional info: Most families whose income is below $60,000 will not be packaged with loans; grant aid will replace the standard loan in the package. Other students demonstrating significant need will graduate with 4-year packaged loan debt of $10,000 or $14,000 depending on need level. All other students will have their 4-year packaged loan debt reduced by about 30%.

FINANCIAL AID PROCEDURES
Forms required: FAFSA, CSS PROFILE.
Dates and Deadlines: Priority date 2/15; closing date 2/15. Applicants notified by 4/1; must reply by 5/1.
Transfers: Priority date 4/1; closing date 4/1. Applicants notified by 5/15; must reply by 6/1 or within 2 week(s) of notification. No financial aid available for international transfer candidates.

CONTACT
Robert Coughlin, Director of Financial Aid
70 Wyllys Avenue, Middletown, CT 06459-0260
(860) 685-2800

Western Connecticut State University
Danbury, Connecticut
www.wcsu.edu   Federal Code: 001380

4-year public university in small city.
Enrollment: 5,001 undergrads, 18% part-time. 668 full-time freshmen.
Selectivity: Admits 50 to 75% of applicants.

BASIC COSTS (2016-2017)
Tuition and fees: $10,017; out-of-state residents $22,281.
Per-credit charge: $217; out-of-state residents $223.
Room and board: $12,089.

FINANCIAL AID PICTURE (2015-2016)
Students with need: Out of 583 full-time freshmen who applied for aid, 481 were judged to have need. Of these, 471 received aid, and 48 had their full need met. Average financial aid package met 32% of need; average scholarship/grant was $5,810; average loan was $3,150. For part-time students, average financial aid package was $5,587.
Students without need: 5 full-time freshmen who did not demonstrate need for aid received scholarships/grants; average award was $9,546. No-need awards available for academics, art, minority status, music/drama.

FINANCIAL AID PROCEDURES
Forms required: FAFSA, institutional form.
Dates and Deadlines: Priority date 3/15; no closing date. Applicants notified on a rolling basis starting 4/15; must reply by 5/1 or within 2 week(s) of notification.

CONTACT
Melissa Stephens, Director of Student Financial Assistance
181 White Street, Danbury, CT 06810-6826
(203) 837-8581

Yale University
New Haven, Connecticut   Federal Code: 001426
www.yale.edu   CSS Code: 3987

4-year private university in small city.
Enrollment: 5,471 undergrads. 1,367 full-time freshmen.
Selectivity: Admits less than 50% of applicants.

BASIC COSTS (2016-2017)
Tuition and fees: $49,480.
Room and board: $15,170.

FINANCIAL AID PICTURE
Students with need: Need-based aid available for full-time and part-time students. Work study available nights, weekends, and for part-time students.
Students without need: This college awards aid only to students with need.
Additional info: All scholarships based on demonstrated need.

FINANCIAL AID PROCEDURES
Forms required: FAFSA, CSS PROFILE, institutional form.
Dates and Deadlines: Priority date 3/1; closing date 3/1. Applicants notified by 4/1; must reply by 5/1.

CONTACT
Caesar Storlazzi, Director of University Financial Aid
Yale Undergraduate Admissions, New Haven, CT 06520-8234
(203) 432-2700

Delaware

Delaware College of Art and Design
Wilmington, Delaware
www.dcad.edu   Federal Code: 041398

2-year private visual arts college in large city.
Enrollment: 169 undergrads, 5% part-time. 89 full-time freshmen.
Selectivity: Admits over 75% of applicants.

BASIC COSTS (2016-2017)
Tuition and fees: $24,830.
Per-credit charge: $1,005.
Room and board: $12,000.

FINANCIAL AID PICTURE (2016-2017)
Students with need: Average financial aid package met 32% of need; average scholarship/grant was $9,023; average loan was $3,500. For part-time students, average financial aid package was $7,732.
Students without need: 8 full-time freshmen who did not demonstrate need for aid received scholarships/grants; average award was $6,250. No-need awards available for academics, art.

FINANCIAL AID PROCEDURES
Forms required: FAFSA.
Dates and Deadlines: Priority date 4/15; closing date 8/1. Applicants notified on a rolling basis starting 11/1; must reply by 6/1.
Transfers: No deadline. Applicants notified on a rolling basis; must reply within 2 week(s) of notification.

CONTACT
Nicole Little, Director of Financial Aid
600 North Market Street, Wilmington, DE 19801
(302) 622-8000 ext. 105

Delaware State University
Dover, Delaware
www.desu.edu   Federal Code: 001428

4-year public university in large town.
Enrollment: 3,692 undergrads, 6% part-time. 941 full-time freshmen.
Selectivity: Admits less than 50% of applicants.

BASIC COSTS (2016-2017)
Tuition and fees: $7,532; out-of-state residents $16,138.
Per-credit charge: $280; out-of-state residents $638.
Room and board: $11,090.

FINANCIAL AID PICTURE
Students with need: Need-based aid available for full-time and part-time students.
Students without need: This college awards aid only to students with need.
Additional info: Students must file FAFSA by 3/15 every year.

FINANCIAL AID PROCEDURES
Forms required: FAFSA.
Dates and Deadlines: Priority date 3/15; closing date 7/1. Applicants notified on a rolling basis starting 4/1; must reply by 7/10.
Transfers: Closing date 2/15.

CONTACT
Desiree Barns, Assistant Vice President of Student Financial Services
1200 North DuPont Highway, Dover, DE 19901
(302) 857-6250

Delaware Technical Community College: Jack F. Owens Campus

Georgetown, Delaware
https://www.dtcc.edu/our-campuses/georgetown
Federal Code: 007053

2-year public community and technical college in small town.
Enrollment: 3,852 undergrads.
Selectivity: Open admission; but selective for some programs.

BASIC COSTS (2016-2017)
Tuition and fees: $3,664; out-of-state residents $8,698.
Per-credit charge: $139.75; out-of-state residents $350.

FINANCIAL AID PICTURE
Students with need: Need-based aid available for full-time and part-time students.
Students without need: This college awards aid only to students with need.

FINANCIAL AID PROCEDURES
Forms required: FAFSA.
Dates and Deadlines: Priority date 6/1; no closing date. Applicants notified on a rolling basis starting 5/1; must reply within 2 week(s) of notification.

CONTACT
Veronica Oney, Financial Aid Officer
21179 College Drive, Georgetown, DE 19947
(302) 855-5692

Delaware Technical Community College: Stanton/Wilmington Campus

Newark, Delaware
https://www.dtcc.edu/our-campuses/stanton
Federal Code: 021449

2-year public community and technical college in small city.
Enrollment: 6,076 undergrads.
Selectivity: Open admission; but selective for some programs.

BASIC COSTS (2016-2017)
Tuition and fees: $3,664; out-of-state residents $8,698.
Per-credit charge: $139.75; out-of-state residents $350.

FINANCIAL AID PICTURE
Students with need: Need-based aid available for full-time and part-time students.
Students without need: This college awards aid only to students with need.

FINANCIAL AID PROCEDURES
Forms required: FAFSA.
Dates and Deadlines: Priority date 6/1; no closing date. Applicants notified on a rolling basis starting 5/1; must reply within 2 week(s) of notification.

CONTACT
Debra Troxler, Student Financial Aid Officer
400 Stanton-Christiana Road, Newark, DE 19713
(302) 571-5380

Delaware Technical Community College: Terry Campus

Dover, Delaware
https://www.dtcc.edu/our-campuses/dover
Federal Code: 011727

2-year public community and technical college in large town.
Enrollment: 2,732 undergrads.
Selectivity: Open admission; but selective for some programs.

BASIC COSTS (2016-2017)
Tuition and fees: $3,664; out-of-state residents $8,698.
Per-credit charge: $139.75; out-of-state residents $349.5.

FINANCIAL AID PICTURE
Students with need: Need-based aid available for full-time and part-time students.
Students without need: This college awards aid only to students with need.

FINANCIAL AID PROCEDURES
Forms required: FAFSA.
Dates and Deadlines: Priority date 6/1; no closing date. Applicants notified on a rolling basis starting 5/1; must reply within 2 week(s) of notification.

CONTACT
Jennifer Grunden, Financial Aid Director
100 Campus Drive, Dover, DE 19901
(302) 857-1040

Goldey-Beacom College

Wilmington, Delaware
www.gbc.edu
Federal Code: 001429

4-year private business college in small city.
Enrollment: 620 undergrads.

BASIC COSTS (2016-2017)
Tuition and fees: $23,400.
Per-credit charge: $780.
Room only: $5,975.

FINANCIAL AID PICTURE
Students with need: Need-based aid available for full-time and part-time students. Work study available nights, weekends, and for part-time students.
Students without need: No-need awards available for academics, athletics.

FINANCIAL AID PROCEDURES
Forms required: FAFSA.
Dates and Deadlines: Priority date 4/15; closing date 7/15. Applicants notified on a rolling basis starting 3/1; must reply within 2 week(s) of notification.
Transfers: Applicants notified on a rolling basis starting 3/1; must reply within 2 week(s) of notification.

CONTACT
Jane Lysle, Dean of Enrollment Management
4701 Limestone Road, Wilmington, DE 19808
(302) 225-6265

University of Delaware

Newark, Delaware
www.udel.edu
Federal Code: 001431

4-year public university in large town.
Enrollment: 17,669 undergrads, 4% part-time. 4,092 full-time freshmen.

Selectivity: Admits 50 to 75% of applicants.

BASIC COSTS (2016-2017)
Tuition and fees: $12,830; out-of-state residents $32,250.
Per-credit charge: $481; out-of-state residents $1,290.
Room and board: $12,068.

FINANCIAL AID PICTURE (2015-2016)
Students with need: Out of 3,366 full-time freshmen who applied for aid, 2,180 were judged to have need. Of these, 2,147 received aid, and 273 had their full need met. Average financial aid package met 58% of need; average scholarship/grant was $10,142; average loan was $3,674. For part-time students, average financial aid package was $5,208.
Students without need: This college awards aid only to students with need.
Scholarships offered: *Merit:* Scholarships ranging from $1,000 to full cost of education. *Athletic:* 81 full-time freshmen received athletic scholarships; average amount $13,553.
Additional info: 12/15 application deadline to receive scholarship consideration. Sibling/parent tuition credit plan. Senior citizen tuition credit for state residents over 60.

FINANCIAL AID PROCEDURES
Forms required: FAFSA.
Dates and Deadlines: Priority date 1/15; closing date 3/15. Applicants notified on a rolling basis starting 3/15; must reply by 5/1 or within 3 week(s) of notification.
Transfers: No deadline. Aid usually limited to federal and state programs.

CONTACT
Melissa Stone, Director of Student Financial Services
210 South College Avenue, Newark, DE 19716
(302) 831-2126

Wesley College
Dover, Delaware
www.wesley.edu   Federal Code: 001433

4-year private liberal arts college in large town, affiliated with the United Methodist Church.
Enrollment: 1,345 undergrads, 3% part-time. 353 full-time freshmen.
Selectivity: Admits 50 to 75% of applicants.

BASIC COSTS (2016-2017)
Tuition and fees: $25,646.
Room and board: $11,244.

FINANCIAL AID PICTURE
Students with need: Need-based aid available for full-time and part-time students. Work study available nights, weekends, and for part-time students.
Students without need: This college awards aid only to students with need.

FINANCIAL AID PROCEDURES
Forms required: FAFSA, institutional form.
Dates and Deadlines: Priority date 2/1; no closing date. Applicants notified on a rolling basis starting 1/1; must reply within 2 week(s) of notification.
Transfers: No deadline. Applicants notified on a rolling basis; must reply within 2 week(s) of notification.

CONTACT
Michael Hall, Director of Student Financial Aid
120 North State Street, Dover, DE 19901-3875
(302) 736-2494

Wilmington University
New Castle, Delaware
www.wilmu.edu   Federal Code: 007948

4-year private university in large town.
Enrollment: 8,387 undergrads, 57% part-time. 326 full-time freshmen.
Selectivity: Open admission.

BASIC COSTS (2016-2017)
Tuition and fees: $10,670.
Per-credit charge: $354.

FINANCIAL AID PICTURE
Students with need: Need-based aid available for full-time and part-time students. Work study available nights, weekends, and for part-time students.
Students without need: No-need awards available for academics, athletics.

FINANCIAL AID PROCEDURES
Forms required: FAFSA.
Dates and Deadlines: Priority date 4/30; no closing date. Applicants notified on a rolling basis starting 8/5; must reply within 2 week(s) of notification.

CONTACT
Nicole McDaniel-Smith, Director of Financial Aid
320 North Dupont Highway, New Castle, DE 19720
(302) 328-9401 ext. 107

District of Columbia

American University
Washington, District of Columbia   Federal Code: 001434
www.american.edu   CSS Code: 5007

4-year private university in very large city, affiliated with the United Methodist Church.
Enrollment: 7,277 undergrads, 4% part-time. 1,677 full-time freshmen.
Selectivity: Admits less than 50% of applicants.

BASIC COSTS (2016-2017)
Tuition and fees: $44,853.
Per-credit charge: $1,467.
Room and board: $14,526.

FINANCIAL AID PICTURE (2016-2017)
Students with need: Out of 1,235 full-time freshmen who applied for aid, 939 were judged to have need. Of these, 939 received aid, and 458 had their full need met. Average financial aid package met 90% of need; average scholarship/grant was $30,045; average loan was $3,712. For part-time students, average financial aid package was $6,647.
Students without need: This college awards aid only to students with need.
Scholarships offered: 60 full-time freshmen received athletic scholarships; average amount $17,856.

FINANCIAL AID PROCEDURES
Forms required: FAFSA. CSS Profile and FAFSA must be completed by freshmen who are seeking need-based aid.
Dates and Deadlines: Priority date 1/10; closing date 1/10. Applicants notified by 4/1; must reply by 5/1 or within 4 week(s) of notification.
Transfers: Priority date 3/1. Phi Theta Kappa scholarship available.

CONTACT

Brian Lee Sang, Assistant Vice Provost, Undergraduate Financial Aid
4400 Massachusetts Avenue NW, Washington, DC 20016-8001
(202) 885-6500

Catholic University of America

Washington, District of Columbia   Federal Code: 001437
www.cua.edu   CSS Code: 5104

4-year private university in very large city, affiliated with the Roman Catholic Church.

Enrollment: 3,217 undergrads, 4% part-time. 723 full-time freshmen.

Selectivity: Admits over 75% of applicants.

BASIC COSTS (2016-2017)

Tuition and fees: $42,536.

Per-credit charge: $1,655.

Room and board: $13,820.

FINANCIAL AID PICTURE (2016-2017)

Students with need: Out of 579 full-time freshmen who applied for aid, 465 were judged to have need. Of these, 465 received aid, and 220 had their full need met. Average financial aid package met 83% of need; average scholarship/grant was $28,319; average loan was $4,326. For part-time students, average financial aid package was $9,571.

Students without need: 213 full-time freshmen who did not demonstrate need for aid received scholarships/grants; average award was $18,182. No-need awards available for academics, alumni affiliation, music/drama, religious affiliation.

Scholarships offered: Legacy Grant: First-year and transfer students who have a parent, grandparent, or sibling who graduated from Catholic University (undergraduate, graduate, law) are eligible for the Legacy Grant, which is a $1,000 grant renewable for up to four years. Students indicate interest in the program as part of their admission application. Parish Scholarship: Entering freshmen or transfer students who are parishioners of Catholic churches throughout the United States may be nominated by their parish pastor for a $3,000 Parish scholarship, renewable for up to four years. Students indicate interest in the program as part of their admission application. Family Grant: If two or more dependent children of the same family are concurrently registered as full-time students, pursuing their first undergraduate degree, the older sibling(s) is eligible for a Family Grant of $2,000 per year. The Family Grant is only offered in the fall and spring semester, no summer awards are available.

FINANCIAL AID PROCEDURES

Forms required: FAFSA, CSS PROFILE.

Dates and Deadlines: Priority date 2/1; closing date 4/10. Applicants notified on a rolling basis starting 3/10; must reply by 5/1 or within 2 week(s) of notification.

Transfers: No deadline. Applicants notified on a rolling basis starting 4/1; must reply by 5/1 or within 2 week(s) of notification. Transfer students must complete the CSS PROFILE (and Noncustorial PROFILE if applicable) to be considered for institutional need-based aid.

CONTACT

Jo Ann Humphreys, Acting Director of Financial Aid
102 Father O'Connell Hall, Washington, DC 20064
(202) 319-5307

Gallaudet University

Washington, District of Columbia
www.gallaudet.edu   Federal Code: 001443

4-year private university and liberal arts college in very large city.

Enrollment: 1,112 undergrads, 3% part-time. 245 full-time freshmen.

Selectivity: Admits 50 to 75% of applicants.

BASIC COSTS (2016-2017)

Tuition and fees: $16,078.

Per-credit charge: $648.

Room and board: $13,204.

FINANCIAL AID PICTURE

Students with need: Need-based aid available for full-time and part-time students.

Students without need: No-need awards available for leadership.

Additional info: Institution receives substantial aid from state vocational rehabilitation agencies, supplemented by institutional grants when needed.

FINANCIAL AID PROCEDURES

Forms required: FAFSA.

Dates and Deadlines: Applicants notified on a rolling basis starting 3/1.

CONTACT

Shondra Dickson Mitchell, Interim Director of Financial Aid
800 Florida Avenue, NE, Washington, DC 20002
(202) 651-5290

George Washington University

Washington, District of Columbia   Federal Code: 001444
www.gwu.edu/explore   CSS Code: 5246

4-year private university in very large city.

Enrollment: 11,244 undergrads, 8% part-time. 2,578 full-time freshmen.

Selectivity: Admits less than 50% of applicants.

BASIC COSTS (2016-2017)

Tuition and fees: $51,950.

Room and board: $12,500.

Additional info: Tuition at time of enrollment locked for 4 years.

FINANCIAL AID PICTURE (2015-2016)

Students with need: Out of 1,699 full-time freshmen who applied for aid, 1,204 were judged to have need. Of these, 1,188 received aid, and 559 had their full need met. Average financial aid package met 87% of need; average scholarship/grant was $28,416; average loan was $4,674. For part-time students, average financial aid package was $9,573.

Students without need: 903 full-time freshmen who did not demonstrate need for aid received scholarships/grants; average award was $19,477. No-need awards available for academics, art, athletics, music/drama, ROTC.

Scholarships offered: 19 full-time freshmen received athletic scholarships; average amount $28,036.

Additional info: Auditions required for performing arts scholarships.

FINANCIAL AID PROCEDURES

Forms required: FAFSA, CSS PROFILE.

Dates and Deadlines: Priority date 2/1; closing date 2/1. Applicants notified on a rolling basis starting 3/24; must reply by 5/1.

Transfers: Closing date 5/1.

CONTACT

Daniel Small, Director of Student Financial Assistance
2121 I Street NW, Suite 201, Washington, DC 20052
(202) 994-6620

Georgetown University

Washington, District of Columbia   Federal Code: 001445
www.georgetown.edu   CSS Code: 5244

4-year private university in very large city, affiliated with the Roman Catholic Church.

Enrollment: 7,112 undergrads, 3% part-time. 1,573 full-time freshmen.

Selectivity: Admits less than 50% of applicants.

BASIC COSTS (2016-2017)
Tuition and fees: $50,547.
Per-credit charge: $2,082.
Room and board: $15,572.

FINANCIAL AID PICTURE (2016-2017)
Students with need: Out of 1,034 full-time freshmen who applied for aid, 653 were judged to have need. Of these, 653 received aid, and 653 had their full need met. Average financial aid package met 100% of need; average scholarship/grant was $41,492; average loan was $2,723. Need-based aid available for part-time students.
Students without need: No-need awards available for athletics.
Scholarships offered: 74 full-time freshmen received athletic scholarships; average amount $20,133.

FINANCIAL AID PROCEDURES
Forms required: FAFSA, CSS PROFILE.
Dates and Deadlines: Priority date 2/1; no closing date. Must reply by 5/1 or within 2 week(s) of notification.
Transfers: Priority date 3/1. Applicants notified by 5/15; must reply by 5/30 or within 2 week(s) of notification.

CONTACT
Patricia McWade, Dean of Student Financial Services
Room 103 White Gravenor Hall, Washington, DC 20057
(202) 687-4547

Howard University
Washington, District of Columbia
www.howard.edu   Federal Code: 001448

4-year private university in very large city.
Enrollment: 6,796 undergrads.

BASIC COSTS (2016-2017)
Tuition and fees: $24,908.
Per-credit charge: $980.
Room and board: $10,416.

FINANCIAL AID PICTURE
Students with need: Need-based aid available for full-time and part-time students. Work study available nights, weekends, and for part-time students.
Students without need: No-need awards available for academics, alumni affiliation, art, athletics, leadership, music/drama, religious affiliation, ROTC.

FINANCIAL AID PROCEDURES
Forms required: FAFSA.
Dates and Deadlines: Priority date 2/1; closing date 5/1. Applicants notified on a rolling basis starting 2/16; must reply by 2/16 or within 3 week(s) of notification.
Transfers: Priority date 2/1; closing date 5/1. Applicants notified by 6/1; must reply within 3 week(s) of notification.

CONTACT
Dolapo Ogunmakin, Associate Director, Enrollment Analytics
2400 Sixth Street NW, Washington, DC 20059
(202) 806-2820

Trinity Washington University
Washington, District of Columbia
www.trinitydc.edu   Federal Code: 001460

4-year private liberal arts college in very large city, affiliated with the Roman Catholic Church.
Enrollment: 2,129 undergrads.

BASIC COSTS (2016-2017)
Tuition and fees: $23,230.
Room and board: $10,334.

FINANCIAL AID PICTURE
Students with need: Need-based aid available for full-time and part-time students.
Students without need: No-need awards available for academics, alumni affiliation, leadership.

FINANCIAL AID PROCEDURES
Forms required: FAFSA.
Dates and Deadlines: Priority date 3/1; closing date 4/1. Applicants notified on a rolling basis starting 2/1; must reply within 2 week(s) of notification.

CONTACT
Chevaun Whitman, Director of Financial Aid
125 Michigan Avenue, NE, Washington, DC 20017
(202) 884-9530

University of the District of Columbia
Washington, District of Columbia
www.udc.edu   Federal Code: 007015

4-year public university and liberal arts college in very large city.
Enrollment: 4,463 undergrads.

BASIC COSTS (2016-2017)
Tuition and fees: $7,844; out-of-state residents $15,500.
Room and board: $15,027.

FINANCIAL AID PICTURE
Students with need: Need-based aid available for full-time and part-time students. Work study available nights, weekends, and for part-time students.
Students without need: This college awards aid only to students with need.

FINANCIAL AID PROCEDURES
Forms required: FAFSA.
Dates and Deadlines: Applicants notified on a rolling basis starting 6/1; must reply by 8/28 or within 2 week(s) of notification.
Transfers: No deadline. Applicants notified on a rolling basis starting 6/1; must reply by 8/28 or within 2 week(s) of notification.

CONTACT
Steve Schissler, AVP Financial Aid and Enrollment Services
4200 Connecticut Avenue NW, Washington, DC 20008
(419) 530-8700

University of the Potomac
Washington, District of Columbia
www.potomac.edu   Federal Code: 032183

3-year for-profit business college in very large city.
Enrollment: 145 undergrads.
Selectivity: Open admission.

BASIC COSTS (2016-2017)
Additional info: Bachelor degree program: $541 per credit; Associate degree programs: $541 per credit; certificates: $250 per credit. Registration fee $100, technology fee $37.50 per credit hour. Books and supplies range depending on program level and course of study. All costs are subject to change.

FINANCIAL AID PICTURE
Students with need: Need-based aid available for full-time and part-time students.

FINANCIAL AID PROCEDURES
Forms required: FAFSA, institutional form.
Dates and Deadlines: Applicants notified on a rolling basis; must reply within 4 week(s) of notification.

CONTACT
Andrea Ford, Director of Financial Aid
4000 Chesapeake Street NW, Washington, DC 20016
(202) 274-2327

Florida

Adventist University of Health Sciences
Orlando, Florida
www.adu.edu   Federal Code: 031155

4-year private University of Health Sciences in large city, affiliated with the Seventh-day Adventists.
Enrollment: 1,529 undergrads, 64% part-time. 67 full-time freshmen.
Selectivity: Admits over 75% of applicants.

BASIC COSTS (2017-2018)
Tuition and fees: $14,250.
Per-credit charge: $455.
Room and board: $4,200.

FINANCIAL AID PICTURE (2015-2016)
Students with need: Out of 60 full-time freshmen who applied for aid, 51 were judged to have need. Of these, 49 received aid, and 2 had their full need met. Average financial aid package met 27% of need; average scholarship/grant was $6,122; average loan was $2,788. For part-time students, average financial aid package was $4,978.
Students without need: 4 full-time freshmen who did not demonstrate need for aid received scholarships/grants; average award was $950. No-need awards available for state/district residency.

FINANCIAL AID PROCEDURES
Forms required: FAFSA, institutional form.
Dates and Deadlines: Priority date 4/10; no closing date. Applicants notified on a rolling basis starting 3/1.

CONTACT
Daisy Tabachow, Director of Financial Aid
671 Winyah Drive, Orlando, FL 32803
(407) 303-9203

Art Institute of Fort Lauderdale
Fort Lauderdale, Florida
www.aifl.edu   Federal Code: 010195

4-year for-profit visual arts and technical college in large city.
Enrollment: 1,514 undergrads.

BASIC COSTS (2016-2017)
Tuition and fees: $22,105.
Per-credit charge: $489.
Room only: $4,377.

FINANCIAL AID PICTURE
Students with need: Need-based aid available for full-time and part-time students. Work study available nights, weekends, and for part-time students.
Students without need: No-need awards available for academics.
Scholarships offered: Art Institute Merit Awards; $200-300 per quarter; based on GPA.

Additional info: Internal scholarships available. Financial planning program allows personalized service to budget and meet college costs through individualized payment plans.

FINANCIAL AID PROCEDURES
Forms required: FAFSA.

CONTACT
Joy Cummings, Director of Student Financial Service
1799 SE 17th Street, Fort Lauderdale, FL 33316
(954) 308-2165

Ave Maria University
Ave Maria, Florida
www.avemaria.edu   Federal Code: 039413

4-year private university and liberal arts college in small town, affiliated with the Roman Catholic Church.
Enrollment: 1,050 undergrads, 2% part-time. 266 full-time freshmen.
Selectivity: Admits less than 50% of applicants.

BASIC COSTS (2017-2018)
Tuition and fees: $19,970.
Room and board: $10,865.

FINANCIAL AID PICTURE (2016-2017)
Students with need: Out of 221 full-time freshmen who applied for aid, 186 were judged to have need. Of these, 186 received aid, and 48 had their full need met. Average financial aid package met 75% of need; average scholarship/grant was $13,394; average loan was $3,155. For part-time students, average financial aid package was $12,771.
Students without need: 76 full-time freshmen who did not demonstrate need for aid received scholarships/grants; average award was $7,843. No-need awards available for academics, athletics, leadership, music/drama, religious affiliation, state/district residency.
Scholarships offered: 39 full-time freshmen received athletic scholarships; average amount $3,979.

FINANCIAL AID PROCEDURES
Forms required: FAFSA, state aid form.
Dates and Deadlines: Priority date 4/1; no closing date. Applicants notified on a rolling basis starting 10/1.

CONTACT
Anne Hart, Director of Financial Aid
5050 Ave Maria Boulevard, Ave Maria, FL 34142-9505

Baptist College of Florida
Graceville, Florida
www.baptistcollege.edu   Federal Code: 013001

4-year private Bible and teachers college in small town, affiliated with the Southern Baptist Convention.
Enrollment: 430 undergrads, 36% part-time. 32 full-time freshmen.
Selectivity: Admits 50 to 75% of applicants.

BASIC COSTS (2017-2018)
Tuition and fees: $11,100.
Per-credit charge: $340.
Room and board: $4,138.

FINANCIAL AID PICTURE (2016-2017)
Students with need: Average financial aid package met 38% of need; average scholarship/grant was $6,822; average loan was $2,730. For part-time students, average financial aid package was $3,640.
Students without need: No-need awards available for academics, minority status, music/drama, religious affiliation.

FINANCIAL AID PROCEDURES

Forms required: FAFSA, state aid form, institutional form.

Dates and Deadlines: Priority date 4/1; closing date 4/15. Applicants notified on a rolling basis starting 6/15; must reply within 4 week(s) of notification.

Transfers: No deadline.

CONTACT

Stephanie Powell, Director of Financial Aid
5400 College Drive, Graceville, FL 32440
(850) 263-3261 ext. 461

Barry University
Miami Shores, Florida
www.barry.edu
Federal Code: 001466

4-year private university in very large city, affiliated with the Roman Catholic Church.

Enrollment: 3,461 undergrads, 17% part-time. 430 full-time freshmen.

Selectivity: Admits 50 to 75% of applicants.

BASIC COSTS (2016-2017)

Tuition and fees: $28,800.

Per-credit charge: $865.

Room and board: $10,600.

FINANCIAL AID PICTURE (2015-2016)

Students with need: Out of 372 full-time freshmen who applied for aid, 355 were judged to have need. Of these, 354 received aid, and 22 had their full need met. Average financial aid package met 66% of need; average scholarship/grant was $11,272; average loan was $3,210. For part-time students, average financial aid package was $5,858.

Students without need: 42 full-time freshmen who did not demonstrate need for aid received scholarships/grants; average award was $10,956. No-need awards available for academics, alumni affiliation, art, athletics, music/drama.

Scholarships offered: 20 full-time freshmen received athletic scholarships; average amount $18,140.

FINANCIAL AID PROCEDURES

Forms required: FAFSA.

Dates and Deadlines: Applicants notified by 10/15; must reply within 1 week(s) of notification.

CONTACT

H. Dart Humeston, Director of Financial Aid
11300 NE Second Avenue, Miami Shores, FL 33161-6695
(305) 899-3673

Beacon College
Leesburg, Florida
www.beaconcollege.edu
Federal Code: 033733

4-year private liberal arts college in large town.

Enrollment: 314 undergrads, 2% part-time. 66 full-time freshmen.

Selectivity: Admits less than 50% of applicants.

BASIC COSTS (2016-2017)

Tuition and fees: $36,172.

Per-credit charge: $866.

Room and board: $10,690.

FINANCIAL AID PICTURE

Students with need: Need-based aid available for full-time and part-time students. Work study available nights, weekends, and for part-time students.

Students without need: No-need awards available for academics, leadership, state/district residency.

Additional info: Work-study programs offered based on financial need.

FINANCIAL AID PROCEDURES

Forms required: FAFSA, state aid form.

Dates and Deadlines: Priority date 4/1; no closing date. Applicants notified on a rolling basis starting 5/1; must reply within 2 week(s) of notification.

Transfers: No deadline. Applicants notified on a rolling basis starting 5/1; must reply within 2 week(s) of notification.

CONTACT

Shawna Wells-Booth, Financial Aid Director
105 East Main Street, Leesburg, FL 34748
(352) 638-9733

Bethune-Cookman University
Daytona Beach, Florida
www.cookman.edu
Federal Code: 001467

4-year private liberal arts college in small city, affiliated with the United Methodist Church.

Enrollment: 3,741 undergrads, 4% part-time. 1,161 full-time freshmen.

Selectivity: Admits less than 50% of applicants.

BASIC COSTS (2016-2017)

Tuition and fees: $14,410.

Room and board: $8,710.

Additional info: Tuition at time of enrollment locked for 4 years.

FINANCIAL AID PICTURE (2016-2017)

Students with need: Average financial aid package met 49% of need; average scholarship/grant was $10,177; average loan was $3,575. For part-time students, average financial aid package was $8,338.

Students without need: This college awards aid only to students with need.

FINANCIAL AID PROCEDURES

Forms required: FAFSA.

Dates and Deadlines: Priority date 4/1; no closing date. Applicants notified on a rolling basis starting 12/1; must reply within 3 week(s) of notification.

CONTACT

Joseph Coleman, Director of Financial Aid
640 Dr. Mary McLeod Bethune Boulevard, Daytona Beach, FL 32114-3099
(800) 553-9369

Broward College
Fort Lauderdale, Florida
www.broward.edu
Federal Code: 001500

2-year public community college in small city.

Enrollment: 38,674 undergrads, 69% part-time. 3,069 full-time freshmen.

Selectivity: Open admission; but selective for some programs.

BASIC COSTS (2016-2017)

Tuition and fees: $3,405; out-of-state residents $11,058.

Per-credit charge: $114; out-of-state residents $369.

Additional info: Bachelor programs charged at higher tuition rates. Tuition/fee waivers available for adults, minority students.

FINANCIAL AID PICTURE (2016-2017)

Students with need: 78% of average financial aid package awarded as scholarships/grants, 22% awarded as loans/jobs. Need-based aid available for part-time students. Work study available nights, weekends, and for part-time students.

Students without need: No-need awards available for academics, athletics, leadership, state/district residency.

FINANCIAL AID PROCEDURES

Forms required: FAFSA, institutional form.

Dates and Deadlines: Priority date 4/15; no closing date. Applicants notified on a rolling basis starting 6/1.
Transfers: No deadline.

CONTACT
Marielena DeSanctis, Vice President of Student Affairs
225 East Las Olas Boulevard, Fort Lauderdale, FL 33301

Brown Mackie College: Miami
Miami, Florida
www.brownmackie.edu   Federal Code: 005127

2-year for-profit business and career college in very large city.
Selectivity: Open admission.

BASIC COSTS (2016-2017)
Additional info: Program costs vary. Certificate program $9,864, books and supplies $650. Diploma programs $20,300-$24,360, books and supplies $650-$950. Associate programs $33,203-$48,720, books and supplies $650-$1,210. Bachelor's programs $73,080,-$82,720, books and supplies $650-$1,550.

FINANCIAL AID PICTURE
Students with need: Work study available nights.
Students without need: No-need awards available for academics, state/district residency.

CONTACT
Ingrid Ayala, Director of Financial Aid
One Herald Plaza, Miami, FL 33132
(305) 341-6600

Carlos Albizu University
Miami, Florida
www.albizu.edu   Federal Code: 010724

4-year private university in very large city.
Enrollment: 262 undergrads.

BASIC COSTS (2016-2017)
Tuition and fees: $10,294.
Per-credit charge: $323.

FINANCIAL AID PICTURE
Students with need: Need-based aid available for full-time and part-time students. Work study available nights.
Students without need: This college awards aid only to students with need.

FINANCIAL AID PROCEDURES
Forms required: FAFSA, institutional form.
Dates and Deadlines: Priority date 6/1; no closing date. Applicants notified on a rolling basis starting 2/1.
Transfers: No deadline. Applicants notified on a rolling basis.

CONTACT
Ramona Morales, Financial Aid Director
2173 NW 99th Avenue, Miami, FL 33172
(305) 593-1223 ext. 153

Chipola College
Marianna, Florida
www.chipola.edu   Federal Code: 001472

2-year public community and junior college in small town.
Enrollment: 1,673 undergrads, 45% part-time. 214 full-time freshmen.

Selectivity: Open admission; but selective for some programs.

BASIC COSTS (2016-2017)
Tuition and fees: $3,060; out-of-state residents $8,891.

FINANCIAL AID PICTURE (2016-2017)
Students with need: 99% of average financial aid package awarded as scholarships/grants, 1% awarded as loans/jobs. Need-based aid available for part-time students. Work study available nights.
Students without need: No-need awards available for academics, alumni affiliation, art, athletics, job skills, leadership, minority status, music/drama.

FINANCIAL AID PROCEDURES
Forms required: FAFSA, institutional form.
Dates and Deadlines: Priority date 5/1; no closing date. Applicants notified on a rolling basis starting 1/2; must reply within 2 week(s) of notification.

CONTACT
Beverly Hambright, Director of Financial Aid
3094 Indian Circle, Marianna, FL 32446
(850) 718-2223

City College: Miami
Miami, Florida
www.citycollege.edu   Federal Code: 025154

2-year private career college in large city.
Enrollment: 228 undergrads.

BASIC COSTS (2016-2017)
Tuition and fees: $14,625.
Per-credit charge: $320.
Additional info: Additional program fees are charged per credit hour or per course depending on program.

FINANCIAL AID PICTURE
Students with need: Need-based aid available for full-time and part-time students.
Students without need: This college awards aid only to students with need.

FINANCIAL AID PROCEDURES
Forms required: FAFSA, institutional form.
Dates and Deadlines: Applicants notified on a rolling basis.

CONTACT
Armando Rios, President
9300 South Dadeland Boulevard, Miami, FL 33156
(305) 666-9242

College of Business and Technology: Cutler Bay
Cutler Bay, Florida
www.cbt.edu   Federal Code: 030716

2-year for-profit technical and career college in large city.
Enrollment: 123 undergrads. 9 full-time freshmen.
Selectivity: Open admission.

BASIC COSTS (2017-2018)
Per-credit charge: $498.
Additional info: Tuition per semester credit: $498; enrollment fee: $150; student services fee: $120; additional fees vary by program.

FINANCIAL AID PICTURE (2015-2016)
Students with need: 62% of average financial aid package awarded as scholarships/grants, 38% awarded as loans/jobs. Need-based aid available for part-time students. Work study available nights.

Students without need: This college awards aid only to students with need.

FINANCIAL AID PROCEDURES

Forms required: FAFSA.

Transfers: No deadline.

CONTACT

Yazmin Palma, Director of Financial Aid

19151 South Dixie Highway, #203, Cutler Bay, FL 33157

College of Business and Technology: Flagler

Miami, Florida

www.cbt.edu   Federal Code: 030716

2-year for-profit technical and career college in large city.

Enrollment: 301 undergrads. 95 full-time freshmen.

Selectivity: Open admission.

BASIC COSTS (2017-2018)

Per-credit charge: $498.

Additional info: Tuition per semester credit: $498; enrollment fee: $150; student services fee: $120. Additional fees vary by program.

FINANCIAL AID PICTURE (2015-2016)

Students with need: 39% of average financial aid package awarded as scholarships/grants, 61% awarded as loans/jobs. Need-based aid available for part-time students. Work study available nights.

Students without need: This college awards aid only to students with need.

FINANCIAL AID PROCEDURES

Forms required: FAFSA.

Transfers: No deadline.

CONTACT

Yazmin Palma, Financial Aid Director

8230 West Flagler Street, Miami, FL 33144

College of Business and Technology: Hialeah

Hialeah, Florida

www.cbt.edu   Federal Code: 030716

2-year for-profit technical and career college in large city.

Enrollment: 248 undergrads. 83 full-time freshmen.

Selectivity: Open admission.

BASIC COSTS (2017-2018)

Per-credit charge: $498.

Additional info: Tuition per semester credit: $498; enrollment fee: $150; student services Fee: $120; additional fees vary by program.

FINANCIAL AID PICTURE (2015-2016)

Students with need: 43% of average financial aid package awarded as scholarships/grants, 57% awarded as loans/jobs. Need-based aid available for part-time students. Work study available nights.

Students without need: This college awards aid only to students with need.

FINANCIAL AID PROCEDURES

Forms required: FAFSA.

Transfers: No deadline.

CONTACT

Yazmin Palma, Financial Aid Director

935 West 49th Street Suite 203, Hialeah, FL 33012-3436

College of Business and Technology: Kendall

Miami, Florida

www.cbt.edu   Federal Code: 030716

2-year for-profit technical and career college in large city.

Enrollment: 10 undergrads. 10 full-time freshmen.

Selectivity: Open admission.

BASIC COSTS (2017-2018)

Per-credit charge: $498.

Additional info: Tuition per semester credit: $498; enrollment fee: $150; student services fee: $120; additional fees vary by program.

FINANCIAL AID PICTURE (2015-2016)

Students with need: 60% of average financial aid package awarded as scholarships/grants, 40% awarded as loans/jobs. Need-based aid available for part-time students. Work study available nights.

Students without need: This college awards aid only to students with need.

FINANCIAL AID PROCEDURES

Forms required: FAFSA.

CONTACT

Yazmin Palma, Financial Aid Director

8700 W Flagler Street, Miami, FL 33174

College of Business and Technology: Miami Gardens

Miami Gardens, Florida

www.cbt.edu   Federal Code: 030716

2-year for-profit technical and career college in small city.

Enrollment: 116 undergrads. 12 full-time freshmen.

Selectivity: Open admission.

BASIC COSTS (2016-2017)

Tuition and fees: $15,210.

Per-credit charge: $498.

FINANCIAL AID PICTURE (2015-2016)

Students with need: 58% of average financial aid package awarded as scholarships/grants, 42% awarded as loans/jobs. Need-based aid available for part-time students. Work study available nights.

Students without need: This college awards aid only to students with need.

FINANCIAL AID PROCEDURES

Forms required: FAFSA.

Transfers: No deadline.

CONTACT

Yazmin Palma, Director of Financial Aid

5190 NW 167th Street, Miami Gardens, FL 33014-6338

College of Central Florida

Ocala, Florida

www.cf.edu   Federal Code: 001471

2-year public community college in small city.

Enrollment: 6,154 undergrads, 55% part-time. 877 full-time freshmen.

Selectivity: Open admission; but selective for some programs.

BASIC COSTS (2016-2017)

Tuition and fees: $3,213; out-of-state residents $12,656.

Per-credit charge: $107; out-of-state residents $422.
Additional info: Bachelor programs charged at higher tuition rates. Tuition/fee waivers available for minority students.

FINANCIAL AID PICTURE

Students with need: Need-based aid available for full-time and part-time students.
Students without need: No-need awards available for academics, athletics, minority status, music/drama, state/district residency.

FINANCIAL AID PROCEDURES

Forms required: FAFSA.

CONTACT

Maureen Anderson, Director, Financial Aid
3001 SW College Road, Ocala, FL 34474-4415
(352) 873-5803 ext. 1340

Daytona State College

Daytona Beach, Florida
www.daytonastate.edu   Federal Code: 001475

2-year public community and technical college in large city.
Enrollment: 12,112 undergrads, 62% part-time. 1,130 full-time freshmen.
Selectivity: Open admission; but selective for some programs.

BASIC COSTS (2016-2017)

Tuition and fees: $3,112; out-of-state residents $12,001.
Per-credit charge: $102.38; out-of-state residents $398.65.

FINANCIAL AID PICTURE (2015-2016)

Students with need: Need-based aid available for part-time students.
Students without need: No-need awards available for academics, athletics, leadership, music/drama, state/district residency.

FINANCIAL AID PROCEDURES

Forms required: FAFSA.
Dates and Deadlines: Priority date 5/15; no closing date. Applicants notified on a rolling basis starting 3/15.

CONTACT

Kevin McCrary, Director of Financial Aid
Admissions Office Daytona State College, Daytona Beach, FL 32114
(386) 506-3000 ext. 3015

DeVry University: Miramar

Miramar, Florida
www.devry.edu

4-year for-profit university in large town.
Enrollment: 245 undergrads, 58% part-time. 5 full-time freshmen.

BASIC COSTS (2016-2017)

Tuition and fees: $17,512.
Per-credit charge: $609.

FINANCIAL AID PICTURE

Students with need: Need-based aid available for full-time and part-time students.
Students without need: This college awards aid only to students with need.

FINANCIAL AID PROCEDURES

Forms required: FAFSA.
Dates and Deadlines: Applicants notified on a rolling basis.

CONTACT

Assistant Director of Student Finance
2300 SW 145th Avenue, Miramar, FL 33027
(954) 499-9700

DeVry University: Orlando

Orlando, Florida
www.devry.edu   Federal Code: 022966

4-year for-profit university in very large city.
Enrollment: 533 undergrads, 60% part-time. 8 full-time freshmen.

BASIC COSTS (2016-2017)

Tuition and fees: $17,512.
Per-credit charge: $609.

FINANCIAL AID PICTURE

Students with need: Need-based aid available for full-time and part-time students.
Students without need: This college awards aid only to students with need.

FINANCIAL AID PROCEDURES

Forms required: FAFSA.
Dates and Deadlines: Applicants notified on a rolling basis.

CONTACT

Director of Student Finance
4000 Millennia Boulevard, Orlando, FL 32839-2426
(407) 345-2800

Digital Media Arts College

Boca Raton, Florida
www.dmac.edu   Federal Code: 041274

3-year for-profit visual arts college in large city.
Enrollment: 300 undergrads.
Selectivity: Open admission.

BASIC COSTS (2016-2017)

Tuition and fees: $17,610.
Per-credit charge: $582.

FINANCIAL AID PICTURE

Students with need: Need-based aid available for full-time and part-time students.
Students without need: No-need awards available for art.

FINANCIAL AID PROCEDURES

Forms required: FAFSA.
Dates and Deadlines: Applicants notified on a rolling basis starting 1/1; must reply within 4 week(s) of notification.
Transfers: No deadline. Applicants notified on a rolling basis starting 1/1.

CONTACT

Sharon Scheible, Director of Financial Aid
5400 Broken Sound Boulevard, Boca Raton, FL 33487

Eastern Florida State College

Cocoa, Florida
www.easternflorida.edu   Federal Code: 001470

2-year public community college in very large city.
Enrollment: 12,321 undergrads.
Selectivity: Open admission; but selective for some programs.

BASIC COSTS (2016-2017)

Tuition and fees: $3,130; out-of-state residents $12,183.
Per-credit charge: $104; out-of-state residents $406.

FINANCIAL AID PICTURE

Students with need: Need-based aid available for full-time and part-time students.

Students without need: No-need awards available for academics, athletics.

FINANCIAL AID PROCEDURES

Forms required: FAFSA.

Dates and Deadlines: Priority date 4/15; closing date 6/30. Applicants notified on a rolling basis starting 6/1; must reply within 2 week(s) of notification.

Transfers: Transfer students must complete at least 15 credit hours with 3.5 GPA to be considered for merit scholarship.

CONTACT

Indira Dzadovsky, Director of Financial Aid/ Veteran Affairs
1519 Clearlake Road, Cocoa, FL 32922-9987
(321) 433-5530

Eckerd College

St. Petersburg, Florida
www.eckerd.edu   Federal Code: 001487

4-year private liberal arts college in large city, affiliated with the Presbyterian Church (USA).

Enrollment: 1,831 undergrads, 2% part-time. 573 full-time freshmen.

Selectivity: Admits 50 to 75% of applicants.

BASIC COSTS (2016-2017)

Tuition and fees: $41,538.

Per-credit charge: $1,412.

Room and board: $11,336.

FINANCIAL AID PICTURE (2016-2017)

Students with need: Out of 461 full-time freshmen who applied for aid, 382 were judged to have need. Of these, 382 received aid, and 177 had their full need met. Average financial aid package met 87% of need; average scholarship/grant was $24,449; average loan was $4,006. For part-time students, average financial aid package was $35,631.

Students without need: 110 full-time freshmen who did not demonstrate need for aid received scholarships/grants; average award was $17,154. No-need awards available for academics, art, athletics, music/drama, state/district residency.

Scholarships offered: *Merit:* Academic scholarships: $11,000 to $21,000 per year; available to entering freshmen with strong scholastic records regardless of financial need. Transfer scholarships: $7,000-14,000. Artistic Achievement Awards: music, theater, visual arts and creative writing; limited number available through separate application process. Freshman Research Associateships also available. *Athletic:* 13 full-time freshmen received athletic scholarships; average amount $26,600.

FINANCIAL AID PROCEDURES

Forms required: FAFSA.

Dates and Deadlines: Priority date 3/1; no closing date. Applicants notified on a rolling basis starting 2/1.

CONTACT

Patricia Watkins, Director of Financial Aid
4200 54th Avenue South, St. Petersburg, FL 33711
(727) 864-8334

Edward Waters College

Jacksonville, Florida
www.ewc.edu   Federal Code: 001478

4-year private liberal arts college in very large city, affiliated with the African Methodist Episcopal Church.

Enrollment: 933 undergrads.

BASIC COSTS (2016-2017)

Tuition and fees: $13,325.

Per-credit charge: $555.

Room and board: $7,282.

FINANCIAL AID PICTURE

Students with need: Need-based aid available for full-time and part-time students. Work study available nights, weekends, and for part-time students.

FINANCIAL AID PROCEDURES

Forms required: FAFSA.

Dates and Deadlines: Closing date 4/15. Applicants notified on a rolling basis starting 5/1; must reply within 2 week(s) of notification.

CONTACT

Janice Nowak, Director of Financial Aid
1658 Kings Road, Jacksonville, FL 32209
(904) 470-8190

Embry-Riddle Aeronautical University

Daytona Beach, Florida
www.embryriddle.edu   Federal Code: 001479

4-year private university in small city.

Enrollment: 5,407 undergrads, 7% part-time. 1,255 full-time freshmen.

Selectivity: Admits 50 to 75% of applicants.

BASIC COSTS (2016-2017)

Tuition and fees: $33,886.

Per-credit charge: $1,358.

Room and board: $10,826.

FINANCIAL AID PICTURE (2016-2017)

Students with need: Out of 1,024 full-time freshmen who applied for aid, 868 were judged to have need. Of these, 868 received aid. For part-time students, average financial aid package was $7,819.

Students without need: 158 full-time freshmen who did not demonstrate need for aid received scholarships/grants; average award was $13,503.

Scholarships offered: 25 full-time freshmen received athletic scholarships; average amount $10,615.

FINANCIAL AID PROCEDURES

Forms required: FAFSA.

Dates and Deadlines: Priority date 3/1; no closing date. Applicants notified on a rolling basis starting 3/1; must reply within 4 week(s) of notification.

CONTACT

Barbara Dryden, Director of Financial Aid
600 South Clyde Morris Boulevard, Daytona Beach, FL 32114-3900
(386) 226-6300

Embry-Riddle Aeronautical University: Worldwide Campus

Daytona Beach, Florida
https://worldwide.erau.edu/   Federal Code: 001479

4-year private virtual university in small city.

Enrollment: 10,932 undergrads, 74% part-time. 2 full-time freshmen.

Selectivity: Admits 50 to 75% of applicants.

BASIC COSTS (2017-2018)

Tuition and fees: $9,076.

Per-credit charge: $375.

Additional info: Discounted tuition rates offered to active duty military personnel.

FINANCIAL AID PICTURE (2016-2017)

Students with need: For part-time students, average financial aid package was $4,181.

FINANCIAL AID PROCEDURES

Forms required: FAFSA.

Dates and Deadlines: Priority date 3/1; no closing date. Applicants notified on a rolling basis starting 3/1; must reply within 4 week(s) of notification.

CONTACT

Dagmar Bowen, Director of Financial Aid, Worldwide Campus
Attn: Worldwide Imaging, Daytona Beach, FL 32114-3900
(866) 567-7202

Flagler College
Saint Augustine, Florida
www.flagler.edu   Federal Code: 007893

4-year private liberal arts college in large town.

Enrollment: 2,611 undergrads, 3% part-time. 600 full-time freshmen.

Selectivity: Admits 50 to 75% of applicants.

BASIC COSTS (2017-2018)

Tuition and fees: $18,200.

Per-credit charge: $620.

Room and board: $10,688.

FINANCIAL AID PICTURE (2016-2017)

Students with need: Out of 516 full-time freshmen who applied for aid, 399 were judged to have need. Of these, 399 received aid, and 60 had their full need met. Average financial aid package met 56% of need; average scholarship/grant was $9,298; average loan was $3,325. For part-time students, average financial aid package was $4,133.

Students without need: 147 full-time freshmen who did not demonstrate need for aid received scholarships/grants; average award was $2,628. No-need awards available for academics, art, athletics, job skills, leadership, minority status, music/drama, religious affiliation, state/district residency.

Scholarships offered: 19 full-time freshmen received athletic scholarships; average amount $7,430.

FINANCIAL AID PROCEDURES

Forms required: FAFSA, state aid form.

Dates and Deadlines: Priority date 3/1; no closing date. Applicants notified on a rolling basis starting 11/1; must reply within 2 week(s) of notification.

Transfers: Priority date 3/1; no deadline. Applicants notified on a rolling basis starting 3/1; must reply within 2 week(s) of notification. Transfer students receiving Florida-sponsored aid must notify Florida Office of Student Financial Assistance of their transfer.

CONTACT

Sheia Pleasant-Doine, Director of Financial Aid
74 King Street, St. Augustine, FL 32084
(800) 304-4208

Florida Agricultural and Mechanical University
Tallahassee, Florida
www.famu.edu   Federal Code: 001480

4-year public university in small city.

Enrollment: 7,365 undergrads, 10% part-time. 1,293 full-time freshmen.

Selectivity: Admits less than 50% of applicants.

BASIC COSTS (2016-2017)

Tuition and fees: $5,785; out-of-state residents $17,730.

Per-credit charge: $188.16; out-of-state residents $586.18.

Room and board: $10,058.

FINANCIAL AID PICTURE

Students with need: Need-based aid available for full-time and part-time students.

Students without need: No-need awards available for academics, art, athletics, leadership, music/drama, ROTC.

FINANCIAL AID PROCEDURES

Forms required: FAFSA.

Dates and Deadlines: Priority date 3/1; no closing date. Applicants notified on a rolling basis starting 4/15.

Transfers: No deadline. Applicants notified on a rolling basis starting 4/15.

CONTACT

Lisa Stewart, Director of Financial Aid
444 Gamble Street Lucy Moten, Room 204, Tallahassee, FL 32307-3200
(850) 599-3730

Florida Atlantic University
Boca Raton, Florida
www.fau.edu   Federal Code: 001481

4-year public university in small city.

Enrollment: 24,221 undergrads, 35% part-time. 3,048 full-time freshmen.

Selectivity: Admits 50 to 75% of applicants.

BASIC COSTS (2016-2017)

Tuition and fees: $6,039; out-of-state residents $21,595.

Per-credit charge: $201.29; out-of-state residents $719.84.

Room and board: $12,006.

FINANCIAL AID PICTURE (2016-2017)

Students with need: Out of 2,516 full-time freshmen who applied for aid, 1,889 were judged to have need. Of these, 1,857 received aid, and 309 had their full need met. Average financial aid package met 68% of need; average scholarship/grant was $8,472; average loan was $5,578. For part-time students, average financial aid package was $12,038.

Students without need: 122 full-time freshmen who did not demonstrate need for aid received scholarships/grants; average award was $4,023. No-need awards available for academics, athletics, leadership, music/drama, state/district residency.

Scholarships offered: 56 full-time freshmen received athletic scholarships; average amount $15,973.

FINANCIAL AID PROCEDURES

Forms required: FAFSA.

Dates and Deadlines: Priority date 3/1; closing date 6/30. Applicants notified on a rolling basis starting 3/15; must reply by 8/23.

Transfers: Applicants notified on a rolling basis starting 3/15; must reply by 8/23.

CONTACT

Tracy Boulukos, Assistant Provost for Enrollment Management
777 Glades Road, Boca Raton, FL 33431
(561) 297-2738

Florida College
Temple Terrace, Florida
www.floridacollege.edu   Federal Code: 001482

4-year private liberal arts college in large town.

Enrollment: 533 undergrads, 3% part-time. 188 full-time freshmen.

Selectivity: Admits over 75% of applicants.

BASIC COSTS (2016-2017)

Tuition and fees: $16,550.

Per-credit charge: $618.

Room and board: $8,230.

FINANCIAL AID PICTURE (2015-2016)

Students with need: Out of 155 full-time freshmen who applied for aid, 124 were judged to have need. Of these, 124 received aid, and 14 had their full need met. Average financial aid package met 49% of need; average scholarship/grant was $5,779; average loan was $3,501. For part-time students, average financial aid package was $3,752.

Students without need: 40 full-time freshmen who did not demonstrate need for aid received scholarships/grants; average award was $3,449. No-need awards available for academics, athletics, music/drama, state/district residency.

Scholarships offered: 5 full-time freshmen received athletic scholarships; average amount $2,000.

FINANCIAL AID PROCEDURES

Forms required: FAFSA, state aid form.

Dates and Deadlines: Closing date 9/30. Applicants notified on a rolling basis starting 11/1; must reply within 2 week(s) of notification.

Transfers: No deadline. Applicants notified on a rolling basis starting 3/30; must reply within 2 week(s) of notification.

CONTACT

Stephen Blaylock, Financial Aid Director

119 North Glen Arven Avenue, Temple Terrace, FL 33617

(813) 988-5131 ext. 131

Florida College of Natural Health: Bradenton

Bradenton, Florida

www.fcnh.com

2-year for-profit health science and career college in small city.

Enrollment: 143 undergrads.

Selectivity: Open admission; but selective for some programs.

BASIC COSTS (2016-2017)

Additional info: Therapeutic Massage; $12,529, books & supplies; $870. Advanced Therapeutic Massage; $16,644, books & supplies $1,040. Advanced Paramedical Skin Care; $17,761, books & supplies; $1,934. A.S. Advanced Therapeutic Massage; $22,189, books & supplies; $1,629. A.S. Therapeutic Massage and Skin Care; $23,414, books & supplies; $2,502. A.S. Advanced Paramedical Skin Care; $23,307, books & supplies; $2,523.

FINANCIAL AID PICTURE

Students with need: Need-based aid available for full-time students.

Students without need: This college awards aid only to students with need.

FINANCIAL AID PROCEDURES

Forms required: FAFSA.

Dates and Deadlines: Applicants notified on a rolling basis.

CONTACT

Lora Miller, Financial Aid Officer

616 67th Street Circle East, Bradenton, FL 34208

Florida College of Natural Health: Maitland

Maitland, Florida

www.fcnh.com   Federal Code: 030086

2-year for-profit health science and junior college in large town.

Enrollment: 418 undergrads.

BASIC COSTS (2016-2017)

Additional info: Therapeutic Massage $12,543, books & supplies $929. Advanced Therapeutic Massage $16,647, books & supplies $1,115. Skin Care and Electrology $10,215, books & supplies $1,447. Advanced Paramedical Skin Care $17,586, books & supplies $1,734. A.S. Advanced Therapeutic Massage $22,154, books & supplies $1,869. A.S. Therapeutic Massage and Skin Care $23,414, books & supplies $2,502. Advanced Paramedical Skin Care $17,586, books & supplies $1,734.

FINANCIAL AID PICTURE

Students with need: Need-based aid available for full-time students.

Students without need: This college awards aid only to students with need.

FINANCIAL AID PROCEDURES

Forms required: FAFSA.

Dates and Deadlines: Applicants notified on a rolling basis.

CONTACT

Lavern Walden, Director of Financial Aid

2600 Lake Lucien Drive; Suite 240, Maitland, FL 32751

(954) 975-6400

Florida College of Natural Health: Miami

Miami, Florida

www.fcnh.com   Federal Code: 030086

2-year for-profit branch campus and community college in very large city.

Enrollment: 202 undergrads.

Selectivity: Open admission; but selective for some programs.

BASIC COSTS (2016-2017)

Additional info: Therapeutic massage $12,543, books & supplies $929. Advanced therapeutic massage $16,647, books & supplies $1,115. Skin care and electrology $10,387, books & supplies $1,755. Advanced paramedical skin care $17,586, books & supplies $1,734. A.S. Advanced therapeutic massage $22,154, books & supplies $1,869. A.S. Therapeutic massage and skin care $23,322, books & supplies $2,460. A.S. Advanced paramedical skin care $23,093 books & supplies $2,488.

FINANCIAL AID PICTURE

Students with need: Need-based aid available for full-time students.

Students without need: This college awards aid only to students with need.

FINANCIAL AID PROCEDURES

Forms required: FAFSA.

Dates and Deadlines: Applicants notified on a rolling basis.

CONTACT

Jorge Villasante, Director of Financial Aid

7925 Northwest 12th Street, Suite 201, Miami, FL 33126

(954) 975-6400

Florida College of Natural Health: Pompano Beach

Pompano Beach, Florida

www.fcnh.com   Federal Code: 030086

2-year for-profit junior college in very large city.

Enrollment: 203 undergrads.

Selectivity: Open admission; but selective for some programs.

BASIC COSTS (2016-2017)

Additional info: Therapeutic Massage $12,543, books & supplies $929. Advanced Therapeutic Massage $16,647, books & supplies $1,115. Skin

Care and Electrology $10,215, books & supplies $1,547. Advanced Paramedical Skin Care $17,586, books & supplies $1,734. A.S. Advanced Therapeutic Massage $22,154, books & supplies $1,869. A.S. Therapeutic Massage and Skin Care $23,322, books & supplies $2,460. A.S. Advanced Paramedical Skin Care $23,093, books & supplies $1,264.

FINANCIAL AID PICTURE
Students with need: Need-based aid available for full-time students.
Students without need: This college awards aid only to students with need.

FINANCIAL AID PROCEDURES
Forms required: FAFSA.
Dates and Deadlines: Applicants notified on a rolling basis.

CONTACT
Helen Wilson, Director of Financial Aid
2001 West Sample Road, Suite 100, Pompano Beach, FL 33064
(954) 975-6400

Florida Gateway College
Lake City, Florida
www.fgc.edu
Federal Code: 001501

2-year public community college in large town.
Enrollment: 2,156 undergrads.
Selectivity: Open admission; but selective for some programs.

BASIC COSTS (2016-2017)
Tuition and fees: $3,100; out-of-state residents $11,747.
Per-credit charge: $103.32; out-of-state residents $391.57.
Additional info: Bachelor programs charged at higher tuition rates. Tuition/fee waivers available for minority students.

FINANCIAL AID PICTURE
Students with need: Need-based aid available for full-time and part-time students.
Students without need: No-need awards available for academics, leadership, minority status, music/drama, state/district residency.
Scholarships offered: Top 20% Scholarship: $1,000/year; top 20% of graduating class; must complete 70% of all attempted classes and maintain 2.0 GPA. Florida Bright Futures Scholarship: must submit completed (error-free) Florida Financial Aid Application during last year of high school (after 12/1 and prior to graduation).

FINANCIAL AID PROCEDURES
Forms required: FAFSA, institutional form.
Dates and Deadlines: Priority date 6/1; no closing date. Applicants notified on a rolling basis starting 6/1; must reply within 2 week(s) of notification.

CONTACT
Anita Westberry, Director of Financial Aid
149 SE College Place, Lake City, FL 32025-2007
(386) 754-4282

Florida Gulf Coast University
Fort Myers, Florida
www.fgcu.edu
Federal Code: 032553

4-year public university in small city.
Enrollment: 13,659 undergrads, 21% part-time. 2,607 full-time freshmen.
Selectivity: Admits 50 to 75% of applicants.

BASIC COSTS (2016-2017)
Tuition and fees: $6,171; out-of-state residents $25,214.
Per-credit charge: $205.69; out-of-state residents $840.48.
Room and board: $9,120.

FINANCIAL AID PICTURE (2015-2016)
Students with need: Out of 1,926 full-time freshmen who applied for aid, 1,340 were judged to have need. Of these, 1,340 received aid, and 77 had their full need met. Average financial aid package met 41% of need; average scholarship/grant was $4,860; average loan was $7,369. For part-time students, average financial aid package was $6,926.
Students without need: 45 full-time freshmen who did not demonstrate need for aid received scholarships/grants; average award was $4,312. No-need awards available for academics, alumni affiliation, athletics, leadership, minority status, music/drama, religious affiliation, state/district residency.
Scholarships offered: 24 full-time freshmen received athletic scholarships; average amount $6,415.

FINANCIAL AID PROCEDURES
Forms required: FAFSA, state aid form, institutional form.
Dates and Deadlines: Priority date 3/1; closing date 6/30. Applicants notified on a rolling basis starting 2/15.
Transfers: Applicants notified on a rolling basis.

CONTACT
Jorge Lopez-Rosado, Director of Student Financial Services
10501 FGCU Boulevard South, Fort Myers, FL 33965-6565
(239) 590-7920

Florida Institute of Technology
Melbourne, Florida
www.fit.edu
Federal Code: 001469

4-year private university in small city.
Enrollment: 3,419 undergrads, 4% part-time. 759 full-time freshmen.
Selectivity: Admits 50 to 75% of applicants.

BASIC COSTS (2016-2017)
Tuition and fees: $40,446.
Per-credit charge: $1,148.
Room and board: $13,610.

FINANCIAL AID PICTURE (2016-2017)
Students with need: Out of 533 full-time freshmen who applied for aid, 458 were judged to have need. Of these, 458 received aid, and 22 had their full need met. Average financial aid package met 89% of need; average scholarship/grant was $25,931; average loan was $3,673. For part-time students, average financial aid package was $19,445.
Students without need: 229 full-time freshmen who did not demonstrate need for aid received scholarships/grants; average award was $16,185. No-need awards available for academics, alumni affiliation, athletics, music/drama, ROTC, state/district residency.
Scholarships offered: 41 full-time freshmen received athletic scholarships; average amount $22,181.

FINANCIAL AID PROCEDURES
Forms required: FAFSA, state aid form.
Dates and Deadlines: Priority date 3/1; no closing date. Applicants notified on a rolling basis starting 11/1; must reply by 5/1 or within 4 week(s) of notification.
Transfers: No deadline. Applicants notified on a rolling basis starting 2/15; must reply by 5/1 or within 4 week(s) of notification.

CONTACT
Jay Lally, Director of Financial Aid
150 West University Boulevard, Melbourne, FL 32901-6975
(321) 674-8070

Florida International University
Miami, Florida
www.fiu.edu   Federal Code: 009635

4-year public university in very large city.
Enrollment: 41,133 undergrads, 37% part-time. 4,551 full-time freshmen.
Selectivity: Admits less than 50% of applicants.

BASIC COSTS (2016-2017)
Tuition and fees: $6,558; out-of-state residents $18,956.
Per-credit charge: $206; out-of-state residents $619.
Room and board: $10,846.

FINANCIAL AID PICTURE (2015-2016)
Students with need: Out of 2,884 full-time freshmen who applied for aid, 2,881 were judged to have need. Of these, 2,718 received aid, and 165 had their full need met. Average financial aid package met 23% of need; average scholarship/grant was $5,293; average loan was $3,225. For part-time students, average financial aid package was $5,680.
Students without need: 562 full-time freshmen who did not demonstrate need for aid received scholarships/grants; average award was $1,771. No-need awards available for academics, art, athletics, minority status, music/drama, state/district residency.
Scholarships offered: 67 full-time freshmen received athletic scholarships; average amount $14,710.

FINANCIAL AID PROCEDURES
Forms required: FAFSA.
Dates and Deadlines: Priority date 3/1; closing date 5/15. Applicants notified on a rolling basis starting 2/1; must reply by 5/1.
Transfers: Applicants notified on a rolling basis; must reply by 5/1.

CONTACT
Francisco Valines, Director of Financial Aid
Modesto Maidique Campus, PC 140, Miami, FL 33199
(305) 348-7000

Florida Keys Community College
Key West, Florida
www.fkcc.edu   Federal Code: 001485

2-year public community college in large town.
Enrollment: 803 undergrads.
Selectivity: Open admission; but selective for some programs.

BASIC COSTS (2016-2017)
Tuition and fees: $3,277; out-of-state residents $13,162.
Per-credit charge: $109.22; out-of-state residents $438.73.
Room only: $10,200.

FINANCIAL AID PICTURE
Students with need: Need-based aid available for full-time and part-time students.
Students without need: No-need awards available for academics, art, leadership, minority status.

FINANCIAL AID PROCEDURES
Forms required: FAFSA, institutional form.
Dates and Deadlines: Priority date 5/1; no closing date. Applicants notified on a rolling basis starting 6/15; must reply within 2 week(s) of notification.
Transfers: Closing date 5/1. Florida Student Assistance Grant available to students paying Florida resident tuition.

CONTACT
Joyce Lubeck-Sonenberg, Director of Financial Aid
5901 College Road, Key West, FL 33040
(305) 809-3523

Florida Memorial University
Miami Gardens, Florida
www.fmuniv.edu   Federal Code: 001486

4-year private liberal arts college in very large city, affiliated with the American Baptist Churches in the USA.
Enrollment: 1,399 undergrads.

BASIC COSTS (2016-2017)
Tuition and fees: $15,536.
Room and board: $6,734.

FINANCIAL AID PICTURE
Students with need: Need-based aid available for full-time and part-time students.
Additional info: Need-based financial aid available to part-time students taking 6 credits or more per semester.

FINANCIAL AID PROCEDURES
Dates and Deadlines: Applicants notified on a rolling basis; must reply within 2 week(s) of notification.
Transfers: Priority date 3/15; closing date 4/15.

CONTACT
Calvin Davis, Director of Financial Aid
15800 NW 42nd Avenue, Miami Gardens, FL 33054
(305) 430-1168

Florida National University
Hialeah, Florida
www.fnu.edu   Federal Code: 017069

2-year for-profit junior college in very large city.
Enrollment: 3,157 undergrads, 21% part-time. 562 full-time freshmen.
Selectivity: Open admission; but selective for some programs.

BASIC COSTS (2016-2017)
Tuition and fees: $13,250.
Per-credit charge: $525.
Additional info: Tuition at time of enrollment locked for 2 years.

FINANCIAL AID PICTURE (2015-2016)
Students with need: 43% of average financial aid package awarded as scholarships/grants, 57% awarded as loans/jobs. Need-based aid available for part-time students.
Students without need: This college awards aid only to students with need.

FINANCIAL AID PROCEDURES
Forms required: FAFSA, institutional form.
Dates and Deadlines: Applicants notified on a rolling basis.

CONTACT
Omar Sanchez, Vice President of Assessment and Reasearch/Director of Financial Aid
4425 West Jose Regueiro (20th) Avenue, Hialeah, FL 33012
(305) 821-3333 ext. 1003

Florida Southern College
Lakeland, Florida
www.flsouthern.edu   Federal Code: 001488

4-year private liberal arts college in small city, affiliated with the United Methodist Church.
Enrollment: 2,370 undergrads, 2% part-time. 643 full-time freshmen.
Selectivity: Admits less than 50% of applicants.

BASIC COSTS (2016-2017)
Tuition and fees: $33,100.
Per-credit charge: $936.
Room and board: $10,680.

FINANCIAL AID PICTURE (2016-2017)
Students with need: Out of 587 full-time freshmen who applied for aid, 482 were judged to have need. Of these, 481 received aid, and 135 had their full need met. Average financial aid package met 76% of need; average scholarship/grant was $22,691; average loan was $4,303. For part-time students, average financial aid package was $18,159.
Students without need: 160 full-time freshmen who did not demonstrate need for aid received scholarships/grants; average award was $20,580. No-need awards available for academics, alumni affiliation, art, athletics, job skills, leadership, minority status, music/drama, religious affiliation, ROTC, state/district residency.
Scholarships offered: *Merit:* McClug Scholarship; based on 1290 SAT (exclusive of Writing) or 29 ACT, rank in top 5% of class, and 3.5 GPA; 3 awarded. Hollingsworth Scholarship; based on 1290 SAT (exclusive of Writing) or 29 ACT and 3.5 GPA. *Athletic:* 28 full-time freshmen received athletic scholarships; average amount $13,783.

FINANCIAL AID PROCEDURES
Forms required: FAFSA, institutional form.
Dates and Deadlines: Priority date 3/1; closing date 7/1. Applicants notified on a rolling basis starting 3/1; must reply within 3 week(s) of notification.
Transfers: No deadline. Applicants notified on a rolling basis; must reply within 2 week(s) of notification.

CONTACT
William Healy, Director of Financial Aid
111 Lake Hollingsworth Drive, Lakeland, FL 33801-5698
(863) 680-4140

Florida SouthWestern State College
Fort Myers, Florida
www.fsw.edu   Federal Code: 001477

2-year public liberal arts college in small city.
Enrollment: 15,887 undergrads, 64% part-time. 2,097 full-time freshmen.
Selectivity: Open admission; but selective for some programs.

BASIC COSTS (2016-2017)
Tuition and fees: $3,401; out-of-state residents $12,979.
Per-credit charge: $81; out-of-state residents $325.
Room and board: $8,860.
Additional info: Bachelor programs charged at higher tuition rates.

FINANCIAL AID PICTURE
Students with need: Need-based aid available for full-time and part-time students. Work study available nights, weekends, and for part-time students.
Students without need: No-need awards available for academics, art, athletics, leadership, music/drama.

FINANCIAL AID PROCEDURES
Forms required: FAFSA, institutional form.
Dates and Deadlines: Priority date 5/1; closing date 9/16. Applicants notified on a rolling basis starting 6/30.

CONTACT
Matthew Sanchez, Director, Student Financial Aid
8099 College Parkway, Fort Myers, FL 33919
(239) 489-9336

Florida State College at Jacksonville
Jacksonville, Florida
www.fscj.edu   Federal Code: 001484

2-year public community and junior college in very large city.
Enrollment: 20,507 undergrads, 68% part-time. 1,110 full-time freshmen.
Selectivity: Open admission; but selective for some programs.

BASIC COSTS (2016-2017)
Tuition and fees: $3,146; out-of-state residents $12,038.
Additional info: Bachelor programs charged at higher tuition rates.

FINANCIAL AID PICTURE
Students with need: Need-based aid available for full-time and part-time students. Work study available nights, weekends, and for part-time students.
Students without need: No-need awards available for academics, alumni affiliation, art, athletics, job skills, leadership, minority status, music/drama.

FINANCIAL AID PROCEDURES
Forms required: FAFSA, institutional form.
Dates and Deadlines: Priority date 8/1; no closing date.

CONTACT
Angie Nickel, Associate Director of Financial Aid
501 West State Street, Jacksonville, FL 32202
(904) 632-3154

Florida State University
Tallahassee, Florida
www.fsu.edu   Federal Code: 001489

4-year public university in small city.
Enrollment: 32,562 undergrads, 10% part-time. 6,209 full-time freshmen.
Selectivity: Admits 50 to 75% of applicants.

BASIC COSTS (2016-2017)
Tuition and fees: $6,507; out-of-state residents $21,673.
Per-credit charge: $215.55; out-of-state residents $721.1.
Room and board: $10,304.

FINANCIAL AID PICTURE (2015-2016)
Students with need: 60% of average financial aid package awarded as scholarships/grants, 40% awarded as loans/jobs. Need-based aid available for part-time students.
Students without need: No-need awards available for academics, art, athletics, leadership, music/drama, ROTC, state/district residency.

FINANCIAL AID PROCEDURES
Forms required: FAFSA, state aid form.
Dates and Deadlines: Applicants notified on a rolling basis starting 4/5.

CONTACT
Darryl Marshall, Director of Financial Aid
PO Box 3062400, Tallahassee, FL 32306-2400
(850) 644-0539

Florida Technical College: Deland
Deland, Florida
www.ftccollege.edu

2-year for-profit junior and technical college in small city.
Selectivity: Open admission.

BASIC COSTS (2016-2017)
Additional info: Diploma programs $15,697-$22,635. Associate degree programs $31,555-$32,645. Bachelor's degree programs $58,985-$59,335. Other fees vary by program.

FINANCIAL AID PICTURE

Students with need: Need-based aid available for full-time and part-time students. Work study available nights.

Students without need: This college awards aid only to students with need.

FINANCIAL AID PROCEDURES

Forms required: FAFSA.

Dates and Deadlines: Applicants notified on a rolling basis.

Transfers: No deadline. Applicants notified on a rolling basis.

CONTACT

Sandra Follmar, Financial Aid Administrator

1199 South Woodland Boulevard, Deland, FL 32720

Florida Technical College: Orlando

Orlando, Florida

www.ftccollege.edu   Federal Code: 015670

2-year for-profit junior and technical college in large city.

Enrollment: 2,977 undergrads.

Selectivity: Open admission.

BASIC COSTS (2016-2017)

Additional info: Diploma programs $17,089-$17,439. Associate degree programs $31,555-$32,645. Bachelor's degree programs $58,985-$59,335. Other fees vary by program.

FINANCIAL AID PICTURE

Students with need: Need-based aid available for full-time and part-time students.

Students without need: This college awards aid only to students with need.

FINANCIAL AID PROCEDURES

Forms required: FAFSA.

Dates and Deadlines: Applicants notified on a rolling basis.

CONTACT

Jennie Gomeztagle, Financial Services

12900 Challenger Parkway, Orlando, FL 32826-2707

(407) 447-7300

Fortis College: Winter Park

Winter Park, Florida

www.fortis.edu   Federal Code: 022455

2-year for-profit technical college in very large city.

Enrollment: 14 undergrads.

Selectivity: Open admission.

BASIC COSTS (2016-2017)

Additional info: Diploma programs: $6950. Fees, books supplies range depending on program level and course of study. All costs are subject to change.

FINANCIAL AID PICTURE

Students with need: Need-based aid available for full-time students.

Students without need: This college awards aid only to students with need.

FINANCIAL AID PROCEDURES

Forms required: FAFSA.

CONTACT

Cathy Lane, Corporate Finance Director

1573 West Fairbanks Avenue, Suite 100, Winter Park, FL 32789

(407) 843-3984

Full Sail University

Winter Park, Florida

www.fullsail.edu   Federal Code: 016812

4-year for-profit visual arts and music college in very large city.

Enrollment: 17,318 undergrads.

Selectivity: Open admission; but selective for some programs.

BASIC COSTS (2016-2017)

Additional info: Tuition ranges from $56,000-$77,500 for the entire degree program, including books, lab fees, and other educational charges. Does not include Project LaunchBox - an Apple computer and software package.

FINANCIAL AID PICTURE

Students with need: Need-based aid available for full-time students. Work study available nights, weekends, and for part-time students.

FINANCIAL AID PROCEDURES

Forms required: FAFSA.

Dates and Deadlines: Applicants notified on a rolling basis; must reply within 2 week(s) of notification.

CONTACT

3300 University Boulevard, Winter Park, FL 32792-7429

(407) 679-0100 ext. 2300

Gulf Coast State College

Panama City, Florida

www.gulfcoast.edu   Federal Code: 001490

2-year public community college in small city.

Enrollment: 4,017 undergrads, 57% part-time. 586 full-time freshmen.

Selectivity: Open admission; but selective for some programs.

BASIC COSTS (2016-2017)

Tuition and fees: $2,963; out-of-state residents $10,791.

Additional info: Bachelor programs charged at higher tuition rates.

FINANCIAL AID PICTURE (2015-2016)

Students with need: 72% of average financial aid package awarded as scholarships/grants, 28% awarded as loans/jobs. Need-based aid available for part-time students. Work study available nights, weekends, and for part-time students.

Students without need: No-need awards available for academics, athletics, job skills, leadership, minority status, music/drama, state/district residency.

FINANCIAL AID PROCEDURES

Forms required: FAFSA.

Dates and Deadlines: Priority date 7/1; closing date 5/15. Applicants notified on a rolling basis starting 7/1.

Transfers: Priority date 7/1; closing date 5/15.

CONTACT

Chris Westlake, Executive Director, Financial Aid

5230 West US Highway 98, Panama City, FL 32401-1041

(850) 872-3845

Hillsborough Community College

Tampa, Florida

www.hccfl.edu   Federal Code: 007870

2-year public community college in large city.

Enrollment: 23,216 undergrads, 55% part-time. 3,338 full-time freshmen.

Selectivity: Open admission; but selective for some programs.

BASIC COSTS (2016-2017)

Tuition and fees: $3,132; out-of-state residents $11,388.

FINANCIAL AID PICTURE (2015-2016)

Students with need: 57% of average financial aid package awarded as scholarships/grants, 43% awarded as loans/jobs. Need-based aid available for part-time students. Work study available nights, weekends, and for part-time students.

Students without need: No-need awards available for academics, art, athletics, minority status, music/drama.

FINANCIAL AID PROCEDURES

Forms required: FAFSA, institutional form.

Dates and Deadlines: Applicants notified on a rolling basis.

CONTACT

Tierra Smith, Director of Financial Aid
Box 31127, Tampa, FL 33631-3127
(877) 736-2575

Hobe Sound Bible College

Hobe Sound, Florida
www.hsbc.edu   Federal Code: 015463

4-year private Bible college in small town, affiliated with the interdenominational tradition.

Enrollment: 59 undergrads.

BASIC COSTS (2016-2017)

Tuition and fees: $6,090.

Per-credit charge: $275.

Room and board: $5,840.

FINANCIAL AID PICTURE

Students with need: Need-based aid available for full-time and part-time students.

Students without need: No-need awards available for academics, leadership.

FINANCIAL AID PROCEDURES

Forms required: FAFSA.

Dates and Deadlines: Closing date 8/1.

CONTACT

Joanna Wetherald, Director of Financial Aid
PO Box 1065, Hobe Sound, FL 33475
(772) 546-5534 ext. 1003

Hodges University

Naples, Florida
www.hodges.edu   Federal Code: 030375

4-year private university in small city.

Enrollment: 1,476 undergrads.

BASIC COSTS (2016-2017)

Tuition and fees: $17,000.

Per-credit charge: $550.

FINANCIAL AID PICTURE

Students with need: Need-based aid available for full-time and part-time students. Work study available nights, weekends, and for part-time students.

Students without need: No-need awards available for academics.

FINANCIAL AID PROCEDURES

Forms required: FAFSA.

Dates and Deadlines: Priority date 8/15; no closing date. Applicants notified on a rolling basis starting 7/7.

Transfers: No deadline. Applicants notified on a rolling basis.

CONTACT

Joe Gilchrist, Vice President of Student Financial Assistance
2655 Northbrooke Drive, Naples, FL 34119
(239) 513-1122

Indian River State College

Fort Pierce, Florida
www.irsc.edu   Federal Code: 001493

2-year public community college in small city.

Enrollment: 14,044 undergrads.

Selectivity: Open admission; but selective for some programs.

BASIC COSTS (2016-2017)

Tuition and fees: $3,115; out-of-state residents $11,715.

Additional info: Bachelor programs charged at higher tuition rates.

FINANCIAL AID PICTURE

Students with need: Need-based aid available for full-time and part-time students.

Students without need: No-need awards available for academics, athletics, minority status, music/drama, state/district residency.

FINANCIAL AID PROCEDURES

Forms required: FAFSA, institutional form.

Dates and Deadlines: Priority date 7/18; no closing date. Applicants notified on a rolling basis starting 5/15.

CONTACT

Mary Lewis, Director of Financial Aid
3209 Virginia Avenue, Fort Pierce, FL 34981-5596
(772) 462-7450

Jacksonville University

Jacksonville, Florida
www.ju.edu   Federal Code: 001495

4-year private university and liberal arts college in very large city.

Enrollment: 2,841 undergrads, 26% part-time. 501 full-time freshmen.

Selectivity: Admits less than 50% of applicants.

BASIC COSTS (2016-2017)

Tuition and fees: $33,930.

Per-credit charge: $1,130.

Room and board: $13,550.

FINANCIAL AID PICTURE (2016-2017)

Students with need: Average financial aid package met 88% of need; average scholarship/grant was $20,431; average loan was $2,468. For part-time students, average financial aid package was $9,893.

Students without need: No-need awards available for academics, art, athletics, leadership, music/drama, ROTC.

FINANCIAL AID PROCEDURES

Forms required: FAFSA, institutional form.

Dates and Deadlines: Priority date 3/31; no closing date. Applicants notified on a rolling basis starting 2/20.

Transfers: No deadline. Applicants notified on a rolling basis.

CONTACT

Karen Laverdiere, Financial Aid Director
2800 University Boulevard North, Jacksonville, FL 32211-3394
(904) 256-7060

Johnson & Wales University: North Miami

North Miami, Florida
www.jwu.edu   Federal Code: 003404

4-year private university in large city.
Enrollment: 1,553 undergrads, 8% part-time. 372 full-time freshmen.
Selectivity: Admits over 75% of applicants.

BASIC COSTS (2016-2017)
Tuition and fees: $30,746.
Room and board: $11,961.

FINANCIAL AID PICTURE
Students with need: Need-based aid available for full-time and part-time students.
Students without need: No-need awards available for academics, alumni affiliation, leadership, state/district residency.

FINANCIAL AID PROCEDURES
Forms required: FAFSA.
Dates and Deadlines: Applicants notified on a rolling basis starting 3/1; must reply within 2 week(s) of notification.

CONTACT
Lynn Robinson, Director, Financial Aid
1701 Northeast 127th Street, North Miami, FL 33181
(800) 342-5598

Johnson University: Florida

Kissimmee, Florida
www.johnsonu.edu/florida   Federal Code: 015192

4-year private university and branch campus college in small city, affiliated with the Christian Church.
Enrollment: 179 undergrads, 11% part-time. 33 full-time freshmen.
Selectivity: Admits 50 to 75% of applicants.

BASIC COSTS (2016-2017)
Tuition and fees: $14,270.
Per-credit charge: $440.
Room only: $3,200.

FINANCIAL AID PICTURE
Students with need: Need-based aid available for full-time and part-time students. Work study available nights, weekends, and for part-time students.
Students without need: No-need awards available for academics, alumni affiliation, leadership, music/drama, religious affiliation, state/district residency.

FINANCIAL AID PROCEDURES
Forms required: FAFSA, institutional form.
Dates and Deadlines: Priority date 5/1; closing date 7/15. Applicants notified on a rolling basis starting 3/1.
Transfers: Available only if funding remains.

CONTACT
Kayla Williams, Director of Financial Aid
1011 Bill Beck Boulevard, Kissimmee, FL 34744-4402
(407) 569-1368

Jones College

Jacksonville, Florida
www.jones.edu   Federal Code: 001497

4-year private business college in very large city.
Enrollment: 445 undergrads.

Selectivity: Open admission.

BASIC COSTS (2016-2017)
Tuition and fees: $9,540.
Per-credit charge: $315.

FINANCIAL AID PICTURE
Students with need: Need-based aid available for full-time and part-time students. Work study available nights.
Students without need: This college awards aid only to students with need.
Additional info: All new students offered Annie Harper Jones Scholarship during their first semester if enrolled in at least 6 hours.

FINANCIAL AID PROCEDURES
Forms required: FAFSA.
Dates and Deadlines: Priority date 8/1; no closing date. Applicants notified on a rolling basis starting 7/1.
Transfers: No deadline. Applicants notified on a rolling basis starting 7/1.

CONTACT
Becky Davis, Financial Assistant Director
5353 Arlington Expressway, Jacksonville, FL 32211
(904) 743-1122 ext. 100

Jose Maria Vargas University

Pembroke Pines, Florida
www.jmvu.edu   Federal Code: 041620

4-year for-profit university in small city.
Enrollment: 154 undergrads.
Selectivity: Open admission.

BASIC COSTS (2016-2017)
Additional info: Total program costs: Associate programs $28,760-$30,260. Bachelor programs $58,420-$63,420.

FINANCIAL AID PICTURE
Students with need: Need-based aid available for full-time and part-time students.
Students without need: No-need awards available for academics.

FINANCIAL AID PROCEDURES
Forms required: FAFSA, state aid form, institutional form.
Dates and Deadlines: Applicants notified on a rolling basis; must reply within 2 week(s) of notification.
Transfers: No deadline. Applicants notified on a rolling basis; must reply within 2 week(s) of notification.

CONTACT
Edith Paredes, Director of Financial Aid
10131 Pines Boulevard, Pembroke Pines, FL 33026
(954) 322-4460

Keiser University

West Palm Beach, Florida
www.keiseruniversity.edu   Federal Code: 015159

4-year private health science and career college in large city.
Enrollment: 17,361 undergrads, 35% part-time. 4,722 full-time freshmen.
Selectivity: Admits over 75% of applicants.

BASIC COSTS (2017-2018)
Tuition and fees: $19,036.

FINANCIAL AID PICTURE (2015-2016)
Students with need: 37% of average financial aid package awarded as scholarships/grants, 63% awarded as loans/jobs. Need-based aid available for part-time students.

Students without need: No-need awards available for academics, alumni affiliation, job skills, leadership.

FINANCIAL AID PROCEDURES

Forms required: FAFSA.

CONTACT

Frederick Pfeffer, Associate Vice Chancellor-Student Financial Services
2600 North Military Trail, West Palm Beach, FL 33409
(954) 776-4476

Key College
Dania Beach, Florida
www.keycollege.edu   Federal Code: 015191

2-year for-profit business and technical college in very large city.
Enrollment: 59 undergrads.

BASIC COSTS (2016-2017)

Additional info: Associate programs: Court Reporting $33,255, books and supplies $1,800. Paralegal Studies $22,170, books and supplies $2,600. Medical Assistant Specialist $22,170, books and supplies $2,300. Tuition at time of enrollment locked for 2 years.

FINANCIAL AID PICTURE

Students with need: Need-based aid available for full-time and part-time students.
Students without need: This college awards aid only to students with need.
Scholarships offered: Key College Scholarships and Employers Scholarships: merit based; approximately 10 scholarships of $1,000 each, awarded during the academic year.
Additional info: Federal Supplemental Educational Opportunities Grant (FSEOG), PELL grant, ACG, FFEL (federal loan program) available; direct loans offered.

FINANCIAL AID PROCEDURES

Forms required: FAFSA, institutional form.

CONTACT

Amber Young, Director of Financial Services
225 East Dania Beach Boulevard, Dania Beach, FL 33004-3046
(954) 923-4440

Lake-Sumter State College
Leesburg, Florida
www.lssc.edu   Federal Code: 001502

2-year public community and junior college in small city.
Enrollment: 1,786 full-time undergrads.
Selectivity: Open admission; but selective for some programs.

BASIC COSTS (2016-2017)

Tuition and fees: $3,172; out-of-state residents $13,276.
Per-credit charge: $105.73; out-of-state residents $442.54.
Additional info: Bachelor programs charged at higher tuition rates.

FINANCIAL AID PICTURE

Students with need: Need-based aid available for full-time and part-time students. Work study available nights.
Students without need: No-need awards available for academics, art, athletics, leadership, minority status, state/district residency.

FINANCIAL AID PROCEDURES

Forms required: FAFSA, institutional form.
Dates and Deadlines: Priority date 5/29; no closing date. Applicants notified on a rolling basis.
Transfers: No deadline. Applicants notified on a rolling basis.

CONTACT

Audrey Williams, Financial Aid Director
9501 US Highway 441, Leesburg, FL 34788-8751
(352) 365-3567

Lincoln College of Technology: West Palm Beach
West Palm Beach, Florida
www.lincolnedu.com   Federal Code: 016095

2-year for-profit technical college in small city.
Enrollment: 713 undergrads.
Selectivity: Open admission.

BASIC COSTS (2016-2017)

Additional info: Diploma programs: $16,281-$28,351. Associate programs: $18,994-$42,053. Bachelor programs: $55,681-$65,674. Costs include total tuition, materials, tool fees, and registration fee.

FINANCIAL AID PICTURE

Students with need: Need-based aid available for full-time students. Work study available nights, weekends, and for part-time students.

FINANCIAL AID PROCEDURES

Forms required: FAFSA, institutional form.
Dates and Deadlines: Applicants notified on a rolling basis.

CONTACT

Elizabeth Layton, Director of Student Financial Services
2410 Metrocentre Boulevard, West Palm Beach, FL 33407
(561) 842-8324

Lynn University
Boca Raton, Florida
www.lynn.edu   Federal Code: 001505

4-year private university in small city.
Enrollment: 2,053 undergrads, 5% part-time. 559 full-time freshmen.
Selectivity: Admits over 75% of applicants.

BASIC COSTS (2017-2018)

Tuition and fees: $37,010.
Room and board: $11,970.

FINANCIAL AID PICTURE (2016-2017)

Students with need: Out of 521 full-time freshmen who applied for aid, 266 were judged to have need. Of these, 266 received aid, and 266 had their full need met. Average financial aid package met 59% of need; average scholarship/grant was $1,150; average loan was $4,068. For part-time students, average financial aid package was $9,054.
Students without need: 199 full-time freshmen who did not demonstrate need for aid received scholarships/grants; average award was $10,022. No-need awards available for academics, alumni affiliation, athletics, leadership, music/drama.
Scholarships offered: *Merit:* National Merit Scholarship for full tuition up to 16 credits each semester (10 available award per academic year). Presidential Scholarship for Full tuition and room and board up to 16 credits each semester (2 available award per academic year); Dean's Scholarship for $12,000 per academic year; Merit Scholarship for $10,000 per academic year; Academic Grant for $6,000 per academic year. All based on high school GPA and/or test scores. *Athletic:* 67 full-time freshmen received athletic scholarships; average amount $8,915.

FINANCIAL AID PROCEDURES

Forms required: FAFSA.

Dates and Deadlines: Priority date 3/1; no closing date. Applicants notified on a rolling basis starting 11/1; must reply within 2 week(s) of notification.
Transfers: Priority date 3/1; no deadline. Applicants notified on a rolling basis starting 11/1; must reply within 2 week(s) of notification. Up to $10,000 of need met to include federal, state and institutional aid.

CONTACT
John Chambers, Director of Student Financial Assistance
3601 North Military Trail, Boca Raton, FL 33431-5598
(561) 237-7185

Miami Dade College
Miami, Florida
www.mdc.edu/　　　　　　　　　　Federal Code: 001506

2-year public community college in very large city.
Enrollment: 50,604 undergrads, 59% part-time. 6,598 full-time freshmen.
Selectivity: Open admission; but selective for some programs.

BASIC COSTS (2016-2017)
Tuition and fees: $3,547; out-of-state residents $12,075.
Per-credit charge: $118; out-of-state residents $403.
Additional info: Bachelor programs charged at a higher tuition rate.

FINANCIAL AID PICTURE (2015-2016)
Students with need: Out of 6,375 full-time freshmen who applied for aid, 6,373 were judged to have need. Of these, 6,373 received aid, and 4,524 had their full need met. Average financial aid package met 65% of need; average scholarship/grant was $5,480; average loan was $7,143. For part-time students, average financial aid package was $4,074.
Students without need: 130 full-time freshmen who did not demonstrate need for aid received scholarships/grants; average award was $1,181. No-need awards available for academics, art, athletics, music/drama, state/district residency.
Scholarships offered: 6 full-time freshmen received athletic scholarships; average amount $1,260.

FINANCIAL AID PROCEDURES
Forms required: FAFSA.
Dates and Deadlines: Priority date 3/15; closing date 6/30. Applicants notified on a rolling basis starting 5/15.
Transfers: No deadline. Applicants notified on a rolling basis.

CONTACT
Mercedes Amaya, Associate V.P. - Student Financial Services
11011 SW 104th Street, Miami, FL 33176-3393
(305) 237-0382

New College of Florida
Sarasota, Florida
www.ncf.edu　　　　　　　　　　Federal Code: 039574

4-year public liberal arts college in small city.
Enrollment: 861 undergrads. 231 full-time freshmen.
Selectivity: Admits 50 to 75% of applicants.

BASIC COSTS (2016-2017)
Tuition and fees: $6,916; out-of-state residents $29,944.
Per-credit charge: $192; out-of-state residents $832.
Room and board: $9,009.

FINANCIAL AID PICTURE (2016-2017)
Students with need: Out of 208 full-time freshmen who applied for aid, 134 were judged to have need. Of these, 134 received aid, and 53 had their full need met. Average financial aid package met 83% of need; average scholarship/grant was $9,728; average loan was $2,754.

Students without need: 82 full-time freshmen who did not demonstrate need for aid received scholarships/grants; average award was $2,286. No-need awards available for academics, state/district residency.

FINANCIAL AID PROCEDURES
Forms required: FAFSA.
Dates and Deadlines: Priority date 11/1; no closing date. Applicants notified on a rolling basis starting 2/1; must reply by 5/1 or within 2 week(s) of notification.
Transfers: No deadline. Applicants notified on a rolling basis starting 2/1; must reply by 5/1 or within 2 week(s) of notification.

CONTACT
Tara Karas, Director of Financial Aid
5800 Bay Shore Road, Sarasota, FL 34243-2109
(941) 487-5000

North Florida Community College
Madison, Florida
www.nfcc.edu　　　　　　　　　　Federal Code: 001508

2-year public community college in rural community.
Enrollment: 1,167 undergrads.
Selectivity: Open admission; but selective for some programs.

BASIC COSTS (2016-2017)
Tuition and fees: $3,179; out-of-state residents $12,095.

FINANCIAL AID PICTURE
Students with need: Need-based aid available for full-time and part-time students. Work study available nights, weekends, and for part-time students.
Students without need: This college awards aid only to students with need.

FINANCIAL AID PROCEDURES
Forms required: FAFSA.
Dates and Deadlines: Priority date 5/15; no closing date. Applicants notified on a rolling basis starting 6/20; must reply within 2 week(s) of notification.

CONTACT
Andy Barnes, Dean of Administrative Services/CBO
325 NW Turner Davis Drive, Madison, FL 32340
(850) 973-1621

Northwest Florida State College
Niceville, Florida
www.nwfsc.edu　　　　　　　　　　Federal Code: 001510

2-year public technical college in large town.
Enrollment: 4,604 undergrads.
Selectivity: Open admission.

BASIC COSTS (2016-2017)
Tuition and fees: $3,120; out-of-state residents $11,941.
Additional info: Bachelor programs charged at higher tuition rate. Certificates and ATD diplomas charted at a lower tuition rate. Tuition/fee waivers available for minority students.

FINANCIAL AID PICTURE
Students with need: Need-based aid available for full-time and part-time students.
Students without need: No-need awards available for academics, leadership, minority status, ROTC, state/district residency.

FINANCIAL AID PROCEDURES
Forms required: FAFSA, institutional form.
Dates and Deadlines: Priority date 4/1; no closing date. Applicants notified on a rolling basis starting 2/1; must reply within 2 week(s) of notification.

Transfers: Academic transcript evaluated to determine student eligibility for financial aid.

CONTACT
Patricia Bennett, Director of Financial Aid/Veterans Affairs
100 College Boulevard, Niceville, FL 32578-1347
(850) 729-5370

Nova Southeastern University
Fort Lauderdale, Florida
www.nova.edu

4-year private university in small city.
Enrollment: 4,230 undergrads, 28% part-time. 647 full-time freshmen.
Selectivity: Admits 50 to 75% of applicants.

BASIC COSTS (2016-2017)
Tuition and fees: $27,660.
Per-credit charge: $897.
Room and board: $11,540.

FINANCIAL AID PICTURE (2016-2017)
Students with need: Out of 583 full-time freshmen who applied for aid, 495 were judged to have need. Of these, 495 received aid, and 96 had their full need met. Average financial aid package met 86% of need; average scholarship/grant was $18,553; average loan was $2,803. For part-time students, average financial aid package was $24,111.
Students without need: This college awards aid only to students with need.
Scholarships offered: *Merit:* President's Scholarship; up to full tuition; based on GPA and SAT/ACT; over 100 awarded. Dean's Scholarship; $1,000-$9,500; based on GPA and SAT/ACT; 825 awarded. Razor's Edge Scholarship; $10,000; based on leadership qualities and academics; 20 awarded. *Athletic:* 20 full-time freshmen received athletic scholarships; average amount $21,266.

FINANCIAL AID PROCEDURES
Forms required: FAFSA, state aid form.
Dates and Deadlines: Priority date 4/15; no closing date. Applicants notified on a rolling basis starting 3/1.

CONTACT
Stephanie Brown, Vice President of Enrollment and Student Services
3301 College Avenue, Fort Lauderdale, FL 33314
(800) 806-3680

Palm Beach Atlantic University
West Palm Beach, Florida
www.pba.edu   Federal Code: 008849

4-year private university and liberal arts college in small city, affiliated with the interdenominational tradition.
Enrollment: 2,474 undergrads, 7% part-time. 501 full-time freshmen.
Selectivity: Admits over 75% of applicants.

BASIC COSTS (2017-2018)
Tuition and fees: $29,950.
Per-credit charge: $675.
Room and board: $9,770.

FINANCIAL AID PICTURE (2016-2017)
Students with need: Out of 447 full-time freshmen who applied for aid, 374 were judged to have need. Of these, 374 received aid, and 85 had their full need met. Average financial aid package met 67% of need; average scholarship/grant was $19,109; average loan was $3,273. For part-time students, average financial aid package was $7,235.

Students without need: 127 full-time freshmen who did not demonstrate need for aid received scholarships/grants; average award was $13,696. No-need awards available for academics, alumni affiliation, art, athletics, leadership, music/drama, ROTC, state/district residency.
Scholarships offered: 25 full-time freshmen received athletic scholarships; average amount $10,085.

FINANCIAL AID PROCEDURES
Forms required: FAFSA, state aid form.
Dates and Deadlines: Priority date 5/1; no closing date. Applicants notified on a rolling basis starting 3/1; must reply by 5/1.
Transfers: No deadline. Applicants notified on a rolling basis starting 3/1; must reply by 5/1. Florida residential undergraduate students eligible for grant from state if enrolled full-time.

CONTACT
Jen McMahon, Director of Financial Aid
901 South Flagler Drive, West Palm Beach, FL 33416-4708
(561) 803-2126

Palm Beach State College
Lake Worth, Florida
www.palmbeachstate.edu   Federal Code: 001512

2-year public community college in large town.
Enrollment: 26,916 undergrads, 71% part-time. 1,748 full-time freshmen.
Selectivity: Open admission; but selective for some programs.

BASIC COSTS (2016-2017)
Tuition and fees: $3,030; out-of-state residents $10,890.
Per-credit charge: $101; out-of-state residents $363.

FINANCIAL AID PICTURE
Students with need: Work study available nights, weekends, and for part-time students.
Students without need: No-need awards available for academics, alumni affiliation, athletics, leadership, state/district residency.

FINANCIAL AID PROCEDURES
Forms required: FAFSA, institutional form.
Dates and Deadlines: Priority date 7/1; no closing date. Applicants notified on a rolling basis; must reply within 2 week(s) of notification.

CONTACT
Eddie Viera, Director of Student Financial Aid
4200 Congress Avenue, Lake Worth, FL 33461
(561) 868-3330

Pasco-Hernando State College
New Port Richey, Florida
www.phsc.edu   Federal Code: 010652

2-year public community college in large town.
Enrollment: 11,207 undergrads.
Selectivity: Open admission; but selective for some programs.

BASIC COSTS (2016-2017)
Tuition and fees: $3,155; out-of-state residents $12,032.
Additional info: Bachelor programs charged at higher tuition rates.

FINANCIAL AID PICTURE
Students with need: Need-based aid available for full-time and part-time students. Work study available nights, weekends, and for part-time students.
Students without need: No-need awards available for academics, athletics, minority status.
Additional info: Childcare assistance grants available to eligible students.

FINANCIAL AID PROCEDURES

Forms required: FAFSA.

Dates and Deadlines: Applicants notified on a rolling basis.

CONTACT

Rebecca Shanafelt, Director of Financial Aid/Veterans Services

10230 Ridge Road, New Port Richey, FL 34654-5199

(727) 816-3463

Pensacola State College

Pensacola, Florida

www.pensacolastate.edu　　　Federal Code: 001513

2-year public community college in small city.

Enrollment: 7,723 undergrads, 58% part-time. 981 full-time freshmen.

Selectivity: Open admission; but selective for some programs.

BASIC COSTS (2016-2017)

Tuition and fees: $3,137; out-of-state residents $12,593.

Per-credit charge: $104.58; out-of-state residents $419.76.

Additional info: Bachelor programs charged at higher tuition rates.

FINANCIAL AID PICTURE

Students with need: Need-based aid available for full-time and part-time students.

Students without need: No-need awards available for academics, athletics, leadership, music/drama, state/district residency.

FINANCIAL AID PROCEDURES

Forms required: FAFSA.

Dates and Deadlines: Priority date 5/1; no closing date. Applicants notified on a rolling basis starting 3/1; must reply within 2 week(s) of notification.

Transfers: All transfers must submit prior college transcripts for evaluation before Federal and State Aid eligibility is determined.

CONTACT

Karen Kessler, Director of Financial Aid

1000 College Boulevard, Pensacola, FL 32504-8998

(850) 484-1680

Polk State College

Winter Haven, Florida

www.polk.edu　　　Federal Code: 001514

2-year public community college in large town.

Enrollment: 8,583 undergrads, 65% part-time. 524 full-time freshmen.

Selectivity: Open admission; but selective for some programs.

BASIC COSTS (2016-2017)

Tuition and fees: $3,367; out-of-state residents $12,272.

Per-credit charge: $112.22; out-of-state residents $409.06.

Additional info: Bachelor programs charged at higher tuition rates.

FINANCIAL AID PICTURE (2015-2016)

Students with need: Out of 445 full-time freshmen who applied for aid, 395 were judged to have need. Of these, 369 received aid, and 87 had their full need met. Average financial aid package met 34% of need; average scholarship/grant was $4,623; average loan was $3,062. For part-time students, average financial aid package was $3,565.

Students without need: 8 full-time freshmen who did not demonstrate need for aid received scholarships/grants; average award was $869. No-need awards available for academics, athletics, leadership, state/district residency.

Scholarships offered: 30 full-time freshmen received athletic scholarships; average amount $1,538.

FINANCIAL AID PROCEDURES

Forms required: FAFSA.

Dates and Deadlines: Priority date 5/15; no closing date. Applicants notified on a rolling basis.

CONTACT

Director of Student Financial Services

999 Avenue H NE, Winter Haven, FL 33881-4299

(863) 298-6850

Rasmussen College: Fort Myers

Fort Myers, Florida

www.rasmussen.edu

4-year for-profit career college in small city.

Enrollment: 423 undergrads, 39% part-time. 36 full-time freshmen.

Selectivity: Open admission; but selective for some programs.

BASIC COSTS (2016-2017)

Tuition and fees: $13,455.

Per-credit charge: $299.

Additional info: Full-time tuition varies according to program of study. Required course materials fee of $150 per course.

FINANCIAL AID PICTURE

Students with need: Need-based aid available for full-time and part-time students.

FINANCIAL AID PROCEDURES

Forms required: FAFSA, institutional form.

Dates and Deadlines: Applicants notified on a rolling basis.

CONTACT

Debora Murray, Director of Financial Aid

9160 Forum Corporate Parkway, Suite 100, Fort Myers, FL 33905-7805

Rasmussen College: New Port Richey

New Port Richey, Florida

www.rasmussen.edu　　　Federal Code: 008501

4-year for-profit career college in small city.

Enrollment: 370 undergrads, 45% part-time. 13 full-time freshmen.

Selectivity: Open admission; but selective for some programs.

BASIC COSTS (2016-2017)

Tuition and fees: $13,455.

Per-credit charge: $299.

Additional info: Full-time tuition varies according to program of study. Required course materials fee of $150 per course.

FINANCIAL AID PICTURE

Students with need: Need-based aid available for full-time and part-time students.

FINANCIAL AID PROCEDURES

Forms required: FAFSA, institutional form.

Dates and Deadlines: Applicants notified on a rolling basis.

CONTACT

Debora Murray, Director of Student Financial Services

8661 Citizens Drive, New Port Richey, FL 34654

(727) 942-0069

Rasmussen College: Ocala

Ocala, Florida

www.rasmussen.edu　　　Federal Code: 008501

4-year for-profit career college in small city.

Enrollment: 5,042 undergrads, 51% part-time. 113 full-time freshmen.

Selectivity: Open admission; but selective for some programs.

BASIC COSTS (2016-2017)
Tuition and fees: $13,455.
Per-credit charge: $299.
Additional info: Full-time tuition varies according to program of study. Required course materials fee of $150 per course.

FINANCIAL AID PICTURE
Students with need: Need-based aid available for full-time and part-time students.

FINANCIAL AID PROCEDURES
Forms required: FAFSA, institutional form.
Dates and Deadlines: Applicants notified on a rolling basis.

CONTACT
Debora Murray, Director of Financial Aid
2221 Southwest 46th Court, Ocala, FL 34474
(352) 629-1941 ext. 130

Rasmussen College: Tampa/Brandon
Tampa, Florida
www.rasmussen.edu

4-year for-profit branch campus and career college in large city.
Enrollment: 358 undergrads, 60% part-time. 13 full-time freshmen.
Selectivity: Open admission; but selective for some programs.

BASIC COSTS (2016-2017)
Tuition and fees: $13,455.
Per-credit charge: $299.
Additional info: Full-time tuition varies according to program of study. Required course materials fee of $150 per course.

FINANCIAL AID PICTURE
Students with need: Need-based aid available for full-time and part-time students.

FINANCIAL AID PROCEDURES
Forms required: FAFSA, institutional form.
Dates and Deadlines: Applicants notified on a rolling basis.

CONTACT
Debora Murray, Financial Aid Director
4042 Park Oak Boulevard, Tampa, FL 33610

Remington College: Tampa
Tampa, Florida
www.tampa.remingtoncollege.edu   Federal Code: 007586

4-year private technical college in very large city.
Enrollment: 350 undergrads.

BASIC COSTS (2016-2017)
Additional info: Diploma programs: $15,995-$19,990. Associate programs, $33,900. Bachelor's program: $24,700.

FINANCIAL AID PICTURE
Students with need: Need-based aid available for full-time students.
Students without need: This college awards aid only to students with need.

FINANCIAL AID PROCEDURES
Forms required: FAFSA, institutional form.

CONTACT
Shavonne Roberts, Director of Student Financial Services
6302 East Dr. Martin Luther King Jr. Boulevard, Tampa, FL 33619
(813) 935-5700 ext. 217

Ringling College of Art and Design
Sarasota, Florida
www.ringling.edu   Federal Code: 012574

4-year private visual arts college in small city.
Enrollment: 1,331 undergrads, 5% part-time. 355 full-time freshmen.
Selectivity: Admits over 75% of applicants.

BASIC COSTS (2016-2017)
Tuition and fees: $42,990.
Per-credit charge: $1,840.
Room and board: $14,390.

FINANCIAL AID PICTURE (2016-2017)
Students with need: Out of 266 full-time freshmen who applied for aid, 237 were judged to have need. Of these, 237 received aid, and 20 had their full need met. Average financial aid package met 49% of need; average scholarship/grant was $16,106; average loan was $7,191. For part-time students, average financial aid package was $16,222.
Students without need: 22 full-time freshmen who did not demonstrate need for aid received scholarships/grants; average award was $8,500. No-need awards available for academics, art.

FINANCIAL AID PROCEDURES
Forms required: FAFSA.
Dates and Deadlines: Priority date 3/1; no closing date. Applicants notified on a rolling basis starting 4/1.
Transfers: No deadline. Applicants notified on a rolling basis starting 3/1.

CONTACT
Lee Harrell, Director of Financial Aid
2700 North Tamiami Trail, Sarasota, FL 34234-5895
(941) 359-7534

Rollins College
Winter Park, Florida
www.rollins.edu   Federal Code: 001515

4-year private liberal arts college in large town.
Enrollment: 1,925 undergrads. 538 full-time freshmen.
Selectivity: Admits 50 to 75% of applicants.

BASIC COSTS (2016-2017)
Tuition and fees: $46,520.
Room and board: $14,450.

FINANCIAL AID PICTURE (2016-2017)
Students with need: Out of 356 full-time freshmen who applied for aid, 311 were judged to have need. Of these, 311 received aid, and 92 had their full need met. Average financial aid package met 80% of need; average scholarship/grant was $32,953; average loan was $3,499. Need-based aid available for part-time students.
Students without need: 146 full-time freshmen who did not demonstrate need for aid received scholarships/grants; average award was $20,948. No-need awards available for academics, art, athletics, leadership, music/drama, state/district residency.
Scholarships offered: *Merit:* Presidential, Alonzo Rollins; $4,000-$15,000 per year; based on academic record; 130 available per year. Donald Cram; $3,000-$5,000 per year; based on academic record, science major; 10 available per year. *Athletic:* 27 full-time freshmen received athletic scholarships; average amount $19,609.
Additional info: Audition required for theater arts and music scholarship applicants. Portfolio required for art scholarships.

FINANCIAL AID PROCEDURES
Forms required: FAFSA.
Dates and Deadlines: Priority date 3/1; no closing date. Applicants notified on a rolling basis starting 3/1; must reply by 5/1.

Transfers: Priority date 4/15; no deadline.

CONTACT
Steve Booker, Director of Financial Aid
1000 Holt Avenue, Campus Box 2720, Winter Park, FL 32789
(407) 646-2395

Saint Johns River State College
Palatka, Florida
www.sjrstate.edu   Federal Code: 001523

2-year public community college in large town.
Enrollment: 4,807 undergrads, 63% part-time. 644 full-time freshmen.
Selectivity: Open admission; but selective for some programs.

BASIC COSTS (2016-2017)
Tuition and fees: $3,240; out-of-state residents $11,668.
Additional info: Bachelor programs charged at higher tuition rates.

FINANCIAL AID PICTURE (2015-2016)
Students with need: 59% of average financial aid package awarded as scholarships/grants, 41% awarded as loans/jobs. Need-based aid available for part-time students.

FINANCIAL AID PROCEDURES
Forms required: FAFSA.
Dates and Deadlines: Priority date 7/1; no closing date. Applicants notified on a rolling basis.

CONTACT
Daniel Barkowitz, Dean of Enrollment Management
5001 St. Johns Avenue, Palatka, FL 32177-3897
(386) 312-4040

Saint Leo University
Saint Leo, Florida
www.saintleo.edu   Federal Code: 001526

4-year private university in rural community, affiliated with the Roman Catholic Church.
Enrollment: 2,262 undergrads, 3% part-time. 610 full-time freshmen.
Selectivity: Admits 50 to 75% of applicants.

BASIC COSTS (2016-2017)
Tuition and fees: $21,440.
Room and board: $10,210.

FINANCIAL AID PICTURE (2016-2017)
Students with need: Out of 514 full-time freshmen who applied for aid, 446 were judged to have need. Of these, 446 received aid, and 59 had their full need met. Average financial aid package met 71% of need; average scholarship/grant was $16,208; average loan was $3,378. For part-time students, average financial aid package was $14,150.
Students without need: 160 full-time freshmen who did not demonstrate need for aid received scholarships/grants; average award was $8,586. No-need awards available for academics, alumni affiliation, athletics, leadership, minority status, religious affiliation, state/district residency.
Scholarships offered: 24 full-time freshmen received athletic scholarships; average amount $15,744.

FINANCIAL AID PROCEDURES
Forms required: FAFSA, state aid form.
Dates and Deadlines: Priority date 3/1; no closing date. Applicants notified on a rolling basis starting 1/1.

CONTACT
Melinda Clark, Associate Vice President of Financial Aid
Box 6665 MC2008, Saint Leo, FL 33574-6665
(800) 240-7658

St. Petersburg College
Saint Petersburg, Florida
www.spcollege.edu   Federal Code: 001528

2-year public community college in large city.
Enrollment: 25,583 undergrads, 71% part-time. 1,316 full-time freshmen.
Selectivity: Open admission; but selective for some programs.

BASIC COSTS (2016-2017)
Tuition and fees: $3,443; out-of-state residents $11,697.
Additional info: Bachelor programs charged at higher tuition rates.

FINANCIAL AID PICTURE
Students with need: Need-based aid available for full-time and part-time students. Work study available nights, weekends, and for part-time students.
Students without need: No-need awards available for academics.

FINANCIAL AID PROCEDURES
Forms required: FAFSA.
Dates and Deadlines: Priority date 5/1; no closing date. Applicants notified on a rolling basis starting 5/15; must reply within 2 week(s) of notification.

CONTACT
Michael Bennett, Associate Vice-President Financial Aid Services
Box 13489, St. Petersburg, FL 33733-3489
(727) 791-2485

Saint Thomas University
Miami Gardens, Florida
www.stu.edu   Federal Code: 001468

4-year private university in very large city, affiliated with the Roman Catholic Church.
Enrollment: 838 undergrads, 5% part-time. 195 full-time freshmen.
Selectivity: Admits 50 to 75% of applicants.

BASIC COSTS (2016-2017)
Tuition and fees: $28,800.
Per-credit charge: $960.
Room and board: $8,200.

FINANCIAL AID PICTURE
Students with need: Need-based aid available for full-time students.
Students without need: No-need awards available for academics, athletics, leadership, state/district residency.

FINANCIAL AID PROCEDURES
Forms required: FAFSA.
Dates and Deadlines: Priority date 4/1; no closing date. Applicants notified on a rolling basis starting 3/1.
Transfers: Priority date 4/15.

CONTACT
Luis Betancourt, Director of Financial Aid
16401 Northwest 37th Avenue, Miami Gardens, FL 33054-6459
(305) 474-6900

Santa Fe College
Gainesville, Florida
www.sfcollege.edu   Federal Code: 001519

2-year public community college in small city.
Enrollment: 13,799 undergrads, 57% part-time. 1,919 full-time freshmen.
Selectivity: Open admission; but selective for some programs.

BASIC COSTS (2016-2017)
Tuition and fees: $3,203; out-of-state residents $11,487.
Additional info: Bachelor programs charged at higher tuition rates. Tuition/fee waivers available for minority students.

FINANCIAL AID PICTURE
Students with need: Need-based aid available for full-time and part-time students.
Students without need: No-need awards available for academics, art, athletics, leadership, minority status, music/drama, state/district residency.

FINANCIAL AID PROCEDURES
Forms required: FAFSA.
Dates and Deadlines: Priority date 3/15; closing date 6/30. Applicants notified by 8/1.
Transfers: Must have minimum 2.0 GPA to be eligible for financial aid.

CONTACT
Kamia Mwango, Director of Financial Aid
3000 NW 83rd Street, R-01, Gainesville, FL 32606-6210
(352) 395-5480

Schiller International University
Largo, Florida
www.schiller.edu   Federal Code: 023141

4-year for-profit university in small city.
Enrollment: 145 undergrads.
Selectivity: Open admission.

BASIC COSTS (2016-2017)
Additional info: Total program costs: associates $35,400-$47,190; bachelor's $35,400-$70,800.

FINANCIAL AID PICTURE
Students with need: Need-based aid available for full-time and part-time students. Work study available nights.
Students without need: No-need awards available for academics, alumni affiliation, leadership, minority status, state/district residency.
Scholarships offered: One-fourth tuition awards; available to students possessing an outstanding academic record and potential; 50 available for one or two semesters. Knowledge Tuition Awards; one-fourth tuition; available to students with good academic records and financial need; 20 available for one or two semesters.
Additional info: Special scholarship program for US students studying abroad at European campuses of Schiller. Work-study available to students taking 2 or more courses.

FINANCIAL AID PROCEDURES
Forms required: FAFSA, state aid form, institutional form.
Dates and Deadlines: Closing date 4/1. Applicants notified on a rolling basis starting 5/1; must reply within 3 week(s) of notification.
Transfers: No deadline. Applicants notified on a rolling basis.

CONTACT
Andre Sergeyev, Financial Aid Advisor
8560 Ulmerton Road, Largo, FL 33771
(727) 736-5082 ext. 253

Seminole State College of Florida
Sanford, Florida
www.seminolestate.edu   Federal Code: 001520

2-year public community college in large town.
Enrollment: 15,602 undergrads.
Selectivity: Open admission; but selective for some programs.

BASIC COSTS (2016-2017)
Tuition and fees: $3,131; out-of-state residents $11,456.

FINANCIAL AID PICTURE
Students with need: Need-based aid available for full-time and part-time students.
Students without need: No-need awards available for academics, art, athletics, leadership, minority status, music/drama, state/district residency.

FINANCIAL AID PROCEDURES
Forms required: FAFSA.
Dates and Deadlines: Priority date 7/1; no closing date. Applicants notified on a rolling basis starting 4/1.
Transfers: Priority date 5/31; no deadline. Applicants notified on a rolling basis starting 4/1.

CONTACT
Roseann Amato, Director of Financial Aid
100 Weldon Boulevard, Sanford, FL 32773-6199
(407) 708-4722 ext. 3422

South Florida State College
Avon Park, Florida
www.southflorida.edu   Federal Code: 001522

2-year public community and technical college in small town.
Enrollment: 2,063 undergrads, 59% part-time. 229 full-time freshmen.
Selectivity: Open admission; but selective for some programs.

BASIC COSTS (2016-2017)
Tuition and fees: $3,136; out-of-state residents $11,829.
Additional info: Bachelor programs charged at higher tuition rates. Tuition/fee waivers available for minority students.

FINANCIAL AID PICTURE (2015-2016)
Students with need: 91% of average financial aid package awarded as scholarships/grants, 9% awarded as loans/jobs. Need-based aid available for part-time students.
Students without need: No-need awards available for academics, athletics, leadership, minority status, music/drama, state/district residency.

FINANCIAL AID PROCEDURES
Forms required: FAFSA.
Dates and Deadlines: Priority date 4/15; no closing date. Applicants notified on a rolling basis starting 4/1.
Transfers: Students must maintain satisfactory academic progress.

CONTACT
Jerry Donna, Director of Financial Aid
600 West College Drive, Avon Park, FL 33825
(863) 453-6661 ext. 7254

Southeastern University
Lakeland, Florida
www.seu.edu   Federal Code: 001521

4-year private liberal arts and teachers college in small city, affiliated with the Assemblies of God.

Enrollment: 4,155 undergrads, 8% part-time. 1,026 full-time freshmen.
Selectivity: Admits less than 50% of applicants.

BASIC COSTS (2016-2017)
Tuition and fees: $24,160.
Per-credit charge: $965.
Room and board: $9,562.

FINANCIAL AID PICTURE (2016-2017)
Students with need: Out of 951 full-time freshmen who applied for aid, 827 were judged to have need. Of these, 827 received aid, and 94 had their full need met. Average financial aid package met 61% of need; average scholarship/grant was $6,106; average loan was $3,159. For part-time students, average financial aid package was $5,310.
Students without need: 182 full-time freshmen who did not demonstrate need for aid received scholarships/grants; average award was $9,816. No-need awards available for academics, alumni affiliation, athletics, job skills, leadership, minority status, music/drama, religious affiliation, state/district residency.
Scholarships offered: 22 full-time freshmen received athletic scholarships; average amount $9,623.

FINANCIAL AID PROCEDURES
Forms required: FAFSA.
Dates and Deadlines: Priority date 2/15; no closing date. Applicants notified on a rolling basis starting 3/15; must reply within 6 week(s) of notification.
Transfers: Must reply within 6 week(s) of notification.

CONTACT
Michael Yohe, Director of Student Financial Services
1000 Longfellow Boulevard, Lakeland, FL 33801-6034
(863) 667-5024

Southern Technical College
Fort Myers, Florida
www.southerntech.edu   Federal Code: 016068

2-year private career college in large city.
Enrollment: 15,389 undergrads.
Selectivity: Open admission; but selective for some programs.

BASIC COSTS (2016-2017)
Additional info: Full program costs: diplomas $14,500-$20,750; associates $34,290-$55,200; bachelor's $74,700-$82,585.

FINANCIAL AID PICTURE
Students with need: Need-based aid available for full-time and part-time students. Work study available nights, weekends, and for part-time students.

FINANCIAL AID PROCEDURES
Forms required: FAFSA.
Dates and Deadlines: Applicants notified on a rolling basis.
Transfers: No deadline. Applicants notified on a rolling basis.

CONTACT
Laura Selvey, Director of Financial Aid
1685 Medical Lane, Ft. Myers, FL 33907-1108
(813) 630-4401

State College of Florida, Manatee-Sarasota
Bradenton, Florida
www.scf.edu   Federal Code: 001504

2-year public nursing and community college in small city.
Enrollment: 8,752 undergrads, 61% part-time. 934 full-time freshmen.
Selectivity: Open admission; but selective for some programs.

BASIC COSTS (2016-2017)
Tuition and fees: $3,074; out-of-state residents $11,596.
Additional info: Bachelor programs charged at higher tuition rates.

FINANCIAL AID PICTURE (2016-2017)
Students with need: Out of 665 full-time freshmen who applied for aid, 634 were judged to have need. Of these, 632 received aid, and 98 had their full need met. Average financial aid package met 59% of need; average scholarship/grant was $2,951; average loan was $1,610. For part-time students, average financial aid package was $2,387.
Students without need: No-need awards available for academics, art, athletics, music/drama, state/district residency.

FINANCIAL AID PROCEDURES
Forms required: FAFSA.
Dates and Deadlines: Priority date 6/1; closing date 7/28. Applicants notified on a rolling basis starting 3/15.

CONTACT
Director of Financial Aid
Box 1849, Bradenton, FL 34206-1849

Stetson University
DeLand, Florida
www.stetson.edu   Federal Code: 001531

4-year private university in large town.
Enrollment: 3,052 undergrads, 1% part-time. 812 full-time freshmen.
Selectivity: Admits 50 to 75% of applicants.

BASIC COSTS (2017-2018)
Tuition and fees: $44,480.
Per-credit charge: $1,144.
Room and board: $12,684.

FINANCIAL AID PICTURE (2016-2017)
Students with need: Out of 704 full-time freshmen who applied for aid, 618 were judged to have need. Of these, 618 received aid, and 133 had their full need met. Average financial aid package met 77% of need; average scholarship/grant was $28,933; average loan was $3,575. For part-time students, average financial aid package was $11,389.
Students without need: 168 full-time freshmen who did not demonstrate need for aid received scholarships/grants; average award was $24,027. No-need awards available for academics, alumni affiliation, art, athletics, leadership, minority status, music/drama, religious affiliation, ROTC, state/district residency.
Scholarships offered: 25 full-time freshmen received athletic scholarships; average amount $24,915.

FINANCIAL AID PROCEDURES
Forms required: FAFSA.
Dates and Deadlines: Priority date 12/1; no closing date. Applicants notified on a rolling basis starting 3/1; must reply within 2 week(s) of notification.
Transfers: Must reply within 2 week(s) of notification.

CONTACT
Beth Kieft, Director of Financial Aid
Campus Box 8378, DeLand, FL 32723
(386) 822-7120

Tallahassee Community College
Tallahassee, Florida
www.tcc.fl.edu   Federal Code: 001533

2-year public community college in small city.
Enrollment: 11,030 undergrads, 50% part-time. 2,059 full-time freshmen.
Selectivity: Open admission; but selective for some programs.

BASIC COSTS (2016-2017)
Tuition and fees: $3,025; out-of-state residents $11,288.

FINANCIAL AID PICTURE (2015-2016)
Students with need: Out of 1,566 full-time freshmen who applied for aid, 1,079 were judged to have need. Of these, 831 received aid. Need-based aid available for part-time students.
Students without need: No-need awards available for academics, art, athletics, leadership, music/drama, state/district residency.

FINANCIAL AID PROCEDURES
Forms required: FAFSA, institutional form.
Dates and Deadlines: Priority date 6/1; no closing date. Applicants notified on a rolling basis starting 6/1; must reply within 2 week(s) of notification.

CONTACT
William Spiers, Director of Financial Aid
444 Appleyard Drive, Tallahassee, FL 32304-2895
(850) 201-8399

Talmudic University
Miami Beach, Florida
www.talmudicu.edu
Federal Code: 013814

4-year private rabbinical college for men in very large city, affiliated with the Jewish faith.
Enrollment: 29 undergrads.

BASIC COSTS (2016-2017)
Tuition and fees: $13,250.
Room and board: $8,000.

FINANCIAL AID PICTURE
Students with need: Need-based aid available for full-time and part-time students. Work study available nights, weekends, and for part-time students.
Students without need: This college awards aid only to students with need.

FINANCIAL AID PROCEDURES
Forms required: FAFSA, institutional form.
Dates and Deadlines: Applicants notified on a rolling basis.

CONTACT
Peggy Loewy Wellisch, Chief Financial Aid Officer
4000 Alton Road, Miami Beach, FL 33140

Trinity Baptist College
Jacksonville, Florida
www.tbc.edu

4-year private Bible and teachers college in very large city.
Enrollment: 314 undergrads, 12% part-time. 94 full-time freshmen.
Selectivity: Admits 50 to 75% of applicants.

BASIC COSTS (2016-2017)
Tuition and fees: $11,040.
Room and board: $6,270.

FINANCIAL AID PICTURE
Students with need: Need-based aid available for full-time and part-time students. Work study available nights, weekends, and for part-time students.
Students without need: No-need awards available for academics, leadership, state/district residency.
Scholarships offered: Dollar-for-dollar matching scholarship for all students who are awarded the Florida Academic Bright Futures Scholarship or the Florida Medallion Bright Futures Scholarship. Students must be admitted for enrollment at Trinity Baptist College to be eligible for a matching scholarship.

FINANCIAL AID PROCEDURES
Dates and Deadlines: Applicants notified on a rolling basis starting 1/1; must reply within 2 week(s) of notification.
Transfers: Applicants notified on a rolling basis starting 1/1; must reply within 2 week(s) of notification. Transfer must provide copies of official transcripts from all previous schools before financial aid at Trinity Baptist College is packaged and offered.

CONTACT
Mark Elkins, Financial Aid Administrator
800 Hammond Boulevard, Jacksonville, FL 32221
(904) 596-2538

Trinity College of Florida
Trinity, Florida
www.trinitycollege.edu
Federal Code: 030282

4-year private Bible college in small city, affiliated with the interdenominational tradition.
Enrollment: 199 undergrads, 16% part-time. 26 full-time freshmen.
Selectivity: Admits 50 to 75% of applicants.

BASIC COSTS (2017-2018)
Tuition and fees: $15,690.
Per-credit charge: $495.
Room and board: $6,450.

FINANCIAL AID PICTURE (2016-2017)
Students with need: Out of 23 full-time freshmen who applied for aid, 22 were judged to have need. Of these, 22 received aid, and 1 had their full need met. Average financial aid package met 82% of need; average scholarship/grant was $7,142; average loan was $7,008. For part-time students, average financial aid package was $8,335.
Students without need: 1 full-time freshmen who did not demonstrate need for aid received scholarships/grants; average award was $3,500. No-need awards available for academics, leadership.

FINANCIAL AID PROCEDURES
Forms required: FAFSA, institutional form.
Dates and Deadlines: Priority date 3/16; closing date 9/16. Applicants notified on a rolling basis starting 1/5; must reply within 2 week(s) of notification.
Transfers: No deadline. Applicants notified on a rolling basis starting 10/1; must reply within 2 week(s) of notification.

CONTACT
Sue Wayne, Financial Aid Director
2430 Welbilt Boulevard, Trinity, FL 34655-4401
(727) 376-6911 ext. 310

University of Central Florida
Orlando, Florida
www.ucf.edu
Federal Code: 003954

4-year public university in very large city.
Enrollment: 55,292 undergrads, 31% part-time. 6,284 full-time freshmen.
Selectivity: Admits less than 50% of applicants.

BASIC COSTS (2016-2017)
Tuition and fees: $6,368; out-of-state residents $22,467.
Room and board: $9,554.

FINANCIAL AID PICTURE (2015-2016)
Students with need: Out of 5,543 full-time freshmen who applied for aid, 3,813 were judged to have need. Of these, 3,642 received aid, and 336 had their full need met. Average financial aid package met 54% of need; average

scholarship/grant was $5,824; average loan was $3,616. For part-time students, average financial aid package was $5,562.

Students without need: 517 full-time freshmen who did not demonstrate need for aid received scholarships/grants; average award was $3,839. No-need awards available for academics, alumni affiliation, athletics, leadership, ROTC, state/district residency.

Scholarships offered: *Merit:* Academic scholarships: $2,000-$24,000 over 4-year period, freshmen automatically considered. *Athletic:* 91 full-time freshmen received athletic scholarships; average amount $9,876.

FINANCIAL AID PROCEDURES

Forms required: FAFSA.

Dates and Deadlines: Priority date 12/1; closing date 6/30. Applicants notified on a rolling basis starting 3/15; must reply within 3 week(s) of notification.

CONTACT

Alicia Keaton, Director of Financial Aid
Box 160111, Orlando, FL 32816-0111
(407) 823-2827

University of Florida
Gainesville, Florida
www.ufl.edu   Federal Code: 001535

4-year public university in small city.
Enrollment: 33,219 undergrads, 8% part-time. 6,801 full-time freshmen.
Selectivity: Admits less than 50% of applicants.

BASIC COSTS (2016-2017)

Tuition and fees: $6,381; out-of-state residents $28,658.
Per-credit charge: $149.24; out-of-state residents $856.45.
Room and board: $9,910.

FINANCIAL AID PICTURE

Students with need: Need-based aid available for full-time and part-time students. Work study available nights, weekends, and for part-time students.
Students without need: No-need awards available for academics, alumni affiliation, art, athletics, leadership, minority status, music/drama, state/district residency.

FINANCIAL AID PROCEDURES

Forms required: FAFSA.
Dates and Deadlines: Priority date 12/15; no closing date. Applicants notified on a rolling basis starting 2/28.
Transfers: Closing date 12/15. Applicants notified on a rolling basis starting 2/28.

CONTACT

Richard Wilder, Director of Student Financial Aid
201 Criser Hall-PO Box 114000, Gainesville, FL 32611-4000
(352) 392-1275

University of Miami
Coral Gables, Florida   Federal Code: 001536
www.miami.edu   CSS Code: 5815

4-year private university in small city.
Enrollment: 10,615 undergrads, 4% part-time. 2,042 full-time freshmen.
Selectivity: Admits less than 50% of applicants.

BASIC COSTS (2016-2017)

Tuition and fees: $47,004.
Per-credit charge: $1,900.
Room and board: $13,310.

FINANCIAL AID PICTURE (2016-2017)

Students with need: Out of 1,275 full-time freshmen who applied for aid, 944 were judged to have need. Of these, 927 received aid, and 904 had their full need met. Average financial aid package met 97% of need; average scholarship/grant was $8,925; average loan was $3,425. For part-time students, average financial aid package was $18,241.

Students without need: 269 full-time freshmen who did not demonstrate need for aid received scholarships/grants; average award was $19,877. No-need awards available for academics, athletics, music/drama, ROTC, state/district residency.

Scholarships offered: *Merit:* About 45% of incoming freshman receive a merit-based scholarship based on academic performance in high school and standardized test scores. Scholarships range from $8,000 annually to full cost of attendance plus an enrichment stipend. *Athletic:* 5 full-time freshmen received athletic scholarships; average amount $27,263.

FINANCIAL AID PROCEDURES

Forms required: FAFSA, CSS PROFILE.

Dates and Deadlines: Priority date 1/1; closing date 4/15. Applicants notified on a rolling basis starting 1/20; must reply by 5/1.

Transfers: Priority date 3/1. Applicants notified by 3/25; must reply by 5/1.

CONTACT

Raymond Hix, Executive Director of Financial Assistance Services
PO Box 248025, Coral Gables, FL 33124-4616
(305) 284-6000

University of North Florida
Jacksonville, Florida
www.unf.edu   Federal Code: 009841

4-year public university in very large city.
Enrollment: 13,585 undergrads, 29% part-time. 1,861 full-time freshmen.
Selectivity: Admits 50 to 75% of applicants.

BASIC COSTS (2016-2017)

Tuition and fees: $6,394; out-of-state residents $20,112.
Per-credit charge: $213.13; out-of-state residents $693.26.
Room and board: $9,602.

FINANCIAL AID PICTURE (2016-2017)

Students with need: Out of 1,522 full-time freshmen who applied for aid, 996 were judged to have need. Of these, 935 received aid, and 165 had their full need met. Average financial aid package met 90% of need; average scholarship/grant was $6,515; average loan was $3,351. For part-time students, average financial aid package was $6,542.

Students without need: 200 full-time freshmen who did not demonstrate need for aid received scholarships/grants; average award was $3,539. No-need awards available for academics, athletics, leadership, minority status, music/drama, state/district residency.

Scholarships offered: 41 full-time freshmen received athletic scholarships; average amount $10,035.

FINANCIAL AID PROCEDURES

Forms required: FAFSA.

Dates and Deadlines: Closing date 4/1. Applicants notified on a rolling basis starting 3/15.

Transfers: Priority date 4/1; no deadline. Applicants notified on a rolling basis; must reply within 2 week(s) of notification. Students must submit financial aid transcripts from previous institutions attended.

CONTACT

Anissa Agne, Director of Financial Aid
1 UNF Drive, Jacksonville, FL 32224-7699
(904) 620-5555

University of South Florida

Tampa, Florida
www.usf.edu   Federal Code: 001537

4-year public university in very large city.
Enrollment: 30,553 undergrads, 23% part-time. 4,121 full-time freshmen.
Selectivity: Admits less than 50% of applicants.

BASIC COSTS (2016-2017)
Tuition and fees: $6,410; out-of-state residents $17,324.
Per-credit charge: $213.66; out-of-state residents $577.48.
Room and board: $9,700.

FINANCIAL AID PICTURE (2015-2016)
Students with need: Out of 3,539 full-time freshmen who applied for aid, 2,672 were judged to have need. Of these, 2,555 received aid, and 401 had their full need met. Average financial aid package met 66% of need; average scholarship/grant was $9,183; average loan was $4,717. For part-time students, average financial aid package was $7,713.
Students without need: 702 full-time freshmen who did not demonstrate need for aid received scholarships/grants; average award was $3,074. No-need awards available for academics, art, athletics, leadership, music/drama, ROTC, state/district residency.
Scholarships offered: 58 full-time freshmen received athletic scholarships; average amount $10,046.
Additional info: Deferred tuition payment plan available for late financial aid recipients.

FINANCIAL AID PROCEDURES
Forms required: FAFSA.
Dates and Deadlines: Priority date 3/1; no closing date. Applicants notified on a rolling basis starting 3/1.
Transfers: Priority date 1/1; no deadline. Applicants notified on a rolling basis starting 4/15.

CONTACT
Billie Hamilton, Associate Vice President
4202 East Fowler Avenue, SVC 1036, Tampa, FL 33620-9951
(813) 974-4700

University of South Florida: Saint Petersburg

St. Petersburg, Florida
www.usfsp.edu

4-year public university in large city.
Enrollment: 4,028 undergrads, 32% part-time. 584 full-time freshmen.
Selectivity: Admits less than 50% of applicants.

BASIC COSTS (2016-2017)
Tuition and fees: $5,851; out-of-state residents $16,766.
Per-credit charge: $194.03; out-of-state residents $557.85.
Room and board: $11,284.

FINANCIAL AID PICTURE (2015-2016)
Students with need: Out of 515 full-time freshmen who applied for aid, 420 were judged to have need. Of these, 391 received aid, and 48 had their full need met. For part-time students, average financial aid package was $7,482.
Students without need: 36 full-time freshmen who did not demonstrate need for aid received scholarships/grants; average award was $2,958. No-need awards available for academics, art, athletics, leadership, ROTC, state/district residency.
Scholarships offered: Merit aid is available.
Additional info: Financial assistance is offered to students from institutional, state and federal sources as students demonstrate eligibility.

FINANCIAL AID PROCEDURES
Forms required: FAFSA.
Dates and Deadlines: Priority date 3/1; no closing date.

CONTACT
Erin Dunn, Director of Financial Aid
140 Seventh Avenue South, St. Petersburg, FL 33701
(727) 873-4128

University of South Florida: Sarasota-Manatee

Sarasota, Florida
www.usfsm.edu   Federal Code: 001537

4-year public university in small city.
Enrollment: 1,800 undergrads, 44% part-time. 87 full-time freshmen.
Selectivity: Admits less than 50% of applicants.

BASIC COSTS (2016-2017)
Tuition and fees: $5,587; out-of-state residents $16,502.
Per-credit charge: $186.25; out-of-state residents $550.07.

FINANCIAL AID PICTURE (2015-2016)
Students with need: Out of 73 full-time freshmen who applied for aid, 60 were judged to have need. Of these, 56 received aid, and 5 had their full need met. Average financial aid package met 55% of need; average scholarship/grant was $8,045; average loan was $3,482. For part-time students, average financial aid package was $7,313.
Students without need: 5 full-time freshmen who did not demonstrate need for aid received scholarships/grants; average award was $3,200. No-need awards available for academics, alumni affiliation, art, athletics, job skills, leadership, minority status, music/drama, religious affiliation, state/district residency.

FINANCIAL AID PROCEDURES
Forms required: FAFSA.
Dates and Deadlines: Priority date 3/1; no closing date. Applicants notified on a rolling basis starting 3/15.

CONTACT
Gabriela Vega, Director of Financial Aid
8350 North Tamiami Trail, Sarasota, FL 34243
(941) 359-4330

University of Tampa

Tampa, Florida
www.ut.edu   Federal Code: 001538

4-year private university and liberal arts college in large city.
Enrollment: 7,363 undergrads, 3% part-time. 1,801 full-time freshmen.
Selectivity: Admits less than 50% of applicants.

BASIC COSTS (2016-2017)
Tuition and fees: $27,740.
Per-credit charge: $550.
Room and board: $10,196.

FINANCIAL AID PICTURE (2015-2016)
Students with need: Out of 1,443 full-time freshmen who applied for aid, 1,136 were judged to have need. Of these, 1,131 received aid, and 104 had their full need met. Average financial aid package met 61% of need; average scholarship/grant was $13,461; average loan was $3,371. For part-time students, average financial aid package was $5,119.
Students without need: 534 full-time freshmen who did not demonstrate need for aid received scholarships/grants; average award was $7,799. No-need awards available for academics, art, athletics, leadership, music/drama, ROTC.

Scholarships offered: *Merit:* Presidential Scholarship: High school applicants; up to $15,000 per year; must be full time; demonstrate leadership or community service; average unweighted GPA 3.8, average SAT 1350 (ACT 29). Dean's Scholarship: High school applicants; up to $12,000 per year; must be enrolled full time; demonstrate leadership or community service; average unweighted GPA 3.8, average SAT 1240 (ACT 26). Minaret Scholarship: High school applicants; up to $9,000 per year; must be enrolled full time; demonstrate leadership or community service; average unweighted GPA 3.33, average SAT 1180 (ACT 24). Spartan Scholarship: High school applicants; up to $6,000 per year; must be enrolled full time; demonstrate leadership or community service. *Athletic:* 60 full-time freshmen received athletic scholarships; average amount $7,667.

FINANCIAL AID PROCEDURES
Forms required: FAFSA.
Dates and Deadlines: Priority date 1/1; no closing date. Applicants notified on a rolling basis starting 3/1; must reply by 5/1 or within 3 week(s) of notification.
Transfers: No deadline. Applicants notified on a rolling basis starting 3/1; must reply within 3 week(s) of notification. Achievement Awards, Transfer Scholarships, and Phi Theta Kappa Scholarships are available.

CONTACT
Jacqueline LaTorella, Director of Financial Aid
401 West Kennedy Boulevard, Tampa, FL 33606-1490
(813) 253-6239

University of West Florida
Pensacola, Florida
www.uwf.edu   Federal Code: 003955

4-year public university in small city.
Enrollment: 9,652 undergrads, 28% part-time. 1,155 full-time freshmen.
Selectivity: Admits less than 50% of applicants.

BASIC COSTS (2016-2017)
Tuition and fees: $6,359; out-of-state residents $19,241.
Per-credit charge: $211.98; out-of-state residents $641.37.
Room and board: $10,062.

FINANCIAL AID PICTURE (2015-2016)
Students with need: Out of 1,001 full-time freshmen who applied for aid, 742 were judged to have need. Of these, 721 received aid, and 96 had their full need met. Average financial aid package met 59% of need; average scholarship/grant was $5,797; average loan was $3,087. For part-time students, average financial aid package was $4,810.
Students without need: 26 full-time freshmen who did not demonstrate need for aid received scholarships/grants; average award was $1,380. No-need awards available for academics, alumni affiliation, art, athletics, minority status, music/drama, ROTC.
Scholarships offered: 32 full-time freshmen received athletic scholarships; average amount $2,539.

FINANCIAL AID PROCEDURES
Forms required: FAFSA.
Dates and Deadlines: Priority date 3/15; no closing date. Applicants notified on a rolling basis starting 3/1.
Transfers: Applicants notified on a rolling basis.

CONTACT
Shana Gore, Director of Financial Aid
11000 University Parkway, Pensacola, FL 32514-5750
(850) 474-2400

Valencia College
Orlando, Florida
www.valenciacollege.edu   Federal Code: 006750

2-year public community college in very large city.
Enrollment: 38,044 undergrads, 61% part-time. 5,250 full-time freshmen.
Selectivity: Open admission; but selective for some programs.

BASIC COSTS (2016-2017)
Tuition and fees: $3,092; out-of-state residents $11,729.
Additional info: Bachelor programs charged at higher tuition rates.

FINANCIAL AID PICTURE
Students with need: Need-based aid available for full-time and part-time students. Work study available nights.

FINANCIAL AID PROCEDURES
Forms required: FAFSA.
Dates and Deadlines: Closing date 3/15. Applicants notified on a rolling basis starting 4/2; must reply within 2 week(s) of notification.
Transfers: No deadline.

CONTACT
Brenda Wright, Interim AVP, Financial Aid
PO Box 3028, Orlando, FL 32802-3028
(407) 299-5000

Warner University
Lake Wales, Florida
www.warner.edu   Federal Code: 008848

4-year private liberal arts college in large town, affiliated with the Church of God.
Enrollment: 1,027 undergrads.

BASIC COSTS (2016-2017)
Tuition and fees: $20,712.
Room and board: $8,104.

FINANCIAL AID PICTURE
Students with need: Need-based aid available for full-time and part-time students.
Students without need: No-need awards available for academics, alumni affiliation, art, athletics, leadership, music/drama, religious affiliation, state/district residency.

FINANCIAL AID PROCEDURES
Forms required: FAFSA, state aid form.
Dates and Deadlines: Priority date 5/1; no closing date. Applicants notified on a rolling basis starting 3/15; must reply within 2 week(s) of notification.
Transfers: Priority date 10/1; closing date 5/15. Applicants notified on a rolling basis; must reply within 2 week(s) of notification.

CONTACT
Lorrie Steedley, Financial Aid Director
13895 Highway 27, Lake Wales, FL 33859
(863) 638-7202

Webber International University
Babson Park, Florida
www.webber.edu   Federal Code: 001540

4-year private university and business college in rural community.
Enrollment: 654 undergrads, 5% part-time. 177 full-time freshmen.
Selectivity: Admits less than 50% of applicants.

BASIC COSTS (2017-2018)
Tuition and fees: $25,358.
Per-credit charge: $356.
Room and board: $8,694.
Additional info: Tuition/fee waivers available for adults.

FINANCIAL AID PICTURE (2016-2017)
Students with need: Out of 148 full-time freshmen who applied for aid, 143 were judged to have need. Of these, 143 received aid, and 12 had their full need met. Average financial aid package met 59% of need; average scholarship/grant was $17,496; average loan was $3,499. For part-time students, average financial aid package was $5,583.
Students without need: 30 full-time freshmen who did not demonstrate need for aid received scholarships/grants; average award was $8,300. No-need awards available for academics, athletics, leadership.
Scholarships offered: 23 full-time freshmen received athletic scholarships; average amount $6,909.

FINANCIAL AID PROCEDURES
Forms required: FAFSA, institutional form.
Dates and Deadlines: Priority date 5/1; closing date 8/1. Applicants notified on a rolling basis starting 4/1; must reply within 4 week(s) of notification.
Transfers: Priority date 5/1. Applicants notified on a rolling basis. Eligibility for academic scholarships predicated on 12 hours of transferable credit.

CONTACT
Kathy Wilson, Registrar
1201 North Scenic Highway, Babson Park, FL 33827-0096
(863) 638-2930

Georgia

Agnes Scott College
Decatur, Georgia
www.agnesscott.edu   Federal Code: 001542

4-year private liberal arts college for women in very large city, affiliated with the Presbyterian Church (USA).
Enrollment: 886 undergrads. 272 full-time freshmen.
Selectivity: Admits 50 to 75% of applicants.

BASIC COSTS (2017-2018)
Tuition and fees: $39,960.
Per-credit charge: $1,655.
Room and board: $11,970.

FINANCIAL AID PICTURE (2016-2017)
Students with need: Out of 233 full-time freshmen who applied for aid, 210 were judged to have need. Of these, 210 received aid, and 62 had their full need met. Average financial aid package met 85% of need; average scholarship/grant was $29,708; average loan was $3,288. Need-based aid available for part-time students.
Students without need: 62 full-time freshmen who did not demonstrate need for aid received scholarships/grants; average award was $26,447. No-need awards available for academics, leadership, minority status, music/drama, religious affiliation.

FINANCIAL AID PROCEDURES
Forms required: FAFSA. PROFILE required for early decision/early action applicants.
Dates and Deadlines: Priority date 2/15; closing date 5/1. Applicants notified on a rolling basis starting 3/1; must reply by 5/1 or within 3 week(s) of notification.
Transfers: Merit scholarships available.

CONTACT
Patrick Bonones, Director of Financial Aid
141 East College Avenue, Decatur, GA 30030-3797
(404) 471-6395

Albany State University
Albany, Georgia
www.asurams.edu   Federal Code: 001544

4-year public university in small city.
Enrollment: 2,576 undergrads, 15% part-time. 431 full-time freshmen.
Selectivity: Admits less than 50% of applicants.

BASIC COSTS (2016-2017)
Tuition and fees: $6,460; out-of-state residents $19,280.
Per-credit charge: $162; out-of-state residents $590.
Room and board: $7,844.

FINANCIAL AID PICTURE
Students with need: Need-based aid available for full-time and part-time students. Work study available nights, weekends, and for part-time students.
Students without need: No-need awards available for academics, alumni affiliation, athletics, music/drama, ROTC, state/district residency.

FINANCIAL AID PROCEDURES
Forms required: FAFSA.
Dates and Deadlines: Priority date 4/15; closing date 6/30. Applicants notified on a rolling basis starting 1/7; must reply within 2 week(s) of notification.
Transfers: Must reply within 2 week(s) of notification.

CONTACT
Stephanie Lawrence, Director of Financial Aid
504 College Drive, Albany, GA 31705-2717
(229) 430-4650

Albany Technical College
Albany, Georgia
www.albanytech.edu   Federal Code: 005601

2-year public technical college in small city.
Enrollment: 3,894 undergrads.
Selectivity: Open admission; but selective for some programs.

BASIC COSTS (2016-2017)
Tuition and fees: $3,192; out-of-state residents $5,862.
Per-credit charge: $89; out-of-state residents $178.

FINANCIAL AID PICTURE
Students with need: Need-based aid available for full-time and part-time students. Work study available nights.
Students without need: No-need awards available for academics, state/district residency.

FINANCIAL AID PROCEDURES
Forms required: FAFSA, state aid form.
Dates and Deadlines: Applicants notified on a rolling basis starting 5/1.

CONTACT
Helen Catt, Financial Aid Director
1704 South Slappy Boulevard, Albany, GA 31701-3514
(229) 430-3506

Andrew College

Cuthbert, Georgia
www.andrewcollege.edu   Federal Code: 001545

2-year private junior and liberal arts college in small town, affiliated with the United Methodist Church.
Enrollment: 274 undergrads, 3% part-time. 219 full-time freshmen.
Selectivity: Admits over 75% of applicants.

BASIC COSTS (2016-2017)
Tuition and fees: $15,770.
Per-credit charge: $460.
Room and board: $9,650.

FINANCIAL AID PICTURE
Students with need: Need-based aid available for full-time and part-time students.
Students without need: No-need awards available for academics, alumni affiliation, art, athletics, leadership, music/drama, religious affiliation, state/district residency.

FINANCIAL AID PROCEDURES
Forms required: FAFSA, state aid form, institutional form.
Dates and Deadlines: Priority date 4/1; closing date 8/1. Applicants notified on a rolling basis starting 4/15.

CONTACT
Andy Geeter, Vice President of Enrollment Management
501 College Street, Cuthbert, GA 39840-1395
(229) 732-5958

Armstrong State University

Savannah, Georgia
www.armstrong.edu   Federal Code: 001546

4-year public university in small city.
Enrollment: 6,367 undergrads, 26% part-time. 578 full-time freshmen.
Selectivity: Admits over 75% of applicants.

BASIC COSTS (2016-2017)
Tuition and fees: $6,332; out-of-state residents $19,152.
Per-credit charge: $162; out-of-state residents $590.
Room and board: $11,352.

FINANCIAL AID PICTURE (2015-2016)
Students with need: Need-based aid available for part-time students.
Students without need: 26 full-time freshmen who did not demonstrate need for aid received scholarships/grants; average award was $688. No-need awards available for academics, alumni affiliation, art, athletics, job skills, leadership, minority status, music/drama, ROTC, state/district residency.
Scholarships offered: 26 full-time freshmen received athletic scholarships; average amount $6,302.
Additional info: Armstrong Commitment Fund provided to students in sophomore, junior or senior year. Students must demonstrate need, complete financial literacy training, and participate in community service activities.

FINANCIAL AID PROCEDURES
Forms required: FAFSA.
Dates and Deadlines: Priority date 3/15; closing date 4/20. Must reply within 2 week(s) of notification.

CONTACT
Kaye O'Neal, Financial Aid Director
11935 Abercorn Street, Savannah, GA 31419-1997
(912) 344-3266

Art Institute of Atlanta

Atlanta, Georgia
www.artinstitutes.edu/atlanta   Federal Code: 009270

4-year for-profit culinary school and visual arts college in very large city.
Enrollment: 2,623 undergrads.

BASIC COSTS (2016-2017)
Additional info: Diploma programs: $19,440-$29,496, books and supplies $500-$1,145, room and board $15,024-$18,780. Associate programs: $43,740-$46,305, books and supplies $1,276-$1,745, room and board $30,048. Bachelor's programs: $87,480-$90,330, books and supplies $2,376-$3,079, room and board $56,340.

FINANCIAL AID PICTURE
Students with need: Need-based aid available for full-time and part-time students. Work study available nights, weekends, and for part-time students.
Students without need: No-need awards available for academics, art, state/district residency.
Scholarships offered: Art Institutes Scholarship Competition awards $2,000-$56,064 depending on program to winning high school seniors selected on merits of written essay, original artwork, resume, letter(s) of recommendation, and high school academic achievement; up to 1 full-tuition, 2 half-tuition, and 24 partial-tuition scholarships available. Art Institutes Culinary Scholarship Competition awards $2,000-$32,704 to winning high school seniors selected through three-part elimination-style competition to prove academic ability, culinary expertise, and commitment to succeed; up to 1 full-tuition or 2 partial-tuition scholarships available. Various other scholarships and awards available.

FINANCIAL AID PROCEDURES
Forms required: FAFSA, state aid form.
Dates and Deadlines: Applicants notified on a rolling basis starting 3/15.

CONTACT
Chris Schwarzer, Director of Administrative and Financial Services
6600 Peachtree Dunwoody Road, NE, Atlanta, GA 30328
(770) 394-8300

Athens Technical College

Athens, Georgia
www.athenstech.edu   Federal Code: 005600

2-year public community and technical college in small city.
Enrollment: 4,563 undergrads.
Selectivity: Open admission; but selective for some programs.

BASIC COSTS (2016-2017)
Tuition and fees: $3,158; out-of-state residents $5,828.
Per-credit charge: $89; out-of-state residents $178.

FINANCIAL AID PICTURE
Students with need: Need-based aid available for full-time and part-time students.
Students without need: No-need awards available for academics, leadership.

FINANCIAL AID PROCEDURES
Forms required: FAFSA.
Dates and Deadlines: Applicants notified on a rolling basis starting 6/15; must reply within 2 week(s) of notification.

CONTACT
Wanda Hicks, Director of Financial Aid
800 US Highway 29 North, Athens, GA 30601-1500
(706) 355-5009

Atlanta Metropolitan State College
Atlanta, Georgia
www.atlm.edu   Federal Code: 012165

2-year public junior college in very large city.
Enrollment: 2,700 undergrads.

BASIC COSTS (2016-2017)
Tuition and fees: $3,950; out-of-state residents $11,872.
Per-credit charge: $97; out-of-state residents $361.

FINANCIAL AID PICTURE
Students with need: Need-based aid available for full-time and part-time students. Work study available nights, weekends, and for part-time students.
Students without need: This college awards aid only to students with need.

FINANCIAL AID PROCEDURES
Forms required: FAFSA, state aid form.
Dates and Deadlines: Closing date 6/1. Applicants notified on a rolling basis; must reply by 6/30.
Transfers: Priority date 6/1; closing date 6/30. Applicants notified on a rolling basis; must reply by 6/30.

CONTACT
Alicia Scott, Director
1630 Metropolitan Parkway, SW, Atlanta, GA 30310-4498
(404) 756-4002

Atlanta Technical College
Atlanta, Georgia
www.atlantatech.edu   Federal Code: 008543

2-year public community and technical college in very large city.
Enrollment: 3,643 undergrads.
Selectivity: Open admission; but selective for some programs.

BASIC COSTS (2016-2017)
Tuition and fees: $3,290; out-of-state residents $5,960.
Per-credit charge: $89; out-of-state residents $178.

FINANCIAL AID PICTURE
Students with need: Need-based aid available for full-time and part-time students. Work study available nights.

FINANCIAL AID PROCEDURES
Forms required: state aid form.
Dates and Deadlines: Priority date 3/1; no closing date. Applicants notified on a rolling basis starting 4/15.

CONTACT
Lamario Primas, Director of Financial Aid
1560 Metropolitan Parkway, SW, Atlanta, GA 30310-4446
(404) 225-4400

Augusta University
Augusta, Georgia
www.augusta.edu   Federal Code: 001579

4-year public university in small city.
Enrollment: 4,860 undergrads, 16% part-time. 774 full-time freshmen.
Selectivity: Admits 50 to 75% of applicants. GED not accepted.

BASIC COSTS (2016-2017)
Tuition and fees: $10,498; out-of-state residents $29,164.
Per-credit charge: $286; out-of-state residents $893.
Room and board: $9,250.

FINANCIAL AID PICTURE (2016-2017)
Students with need: 62% of average financial aid package awarded as scholarships/grants, 38% awarded as loans/jobs. Need-based aid available for part-time students.

FINANCIAL AID PROCEDURES
Forms required: FAFSA.
Dates and Deadlines: Closing date 3/1. Applicants notified on a rolling basis starting 3/1; must reply within 2 week(s) of notification.

CONTACT
Brenda Burney, Director of Financial Aid
Benet House, 1120 15th Street, Augusta, GA 30912
(706) 737-1524

Bainbridge State College
Bainbridge, Georgia
www.bainbridge.edu   Federal Code: 011074

2-year public agricultural and technical college in large town.
Enrollment: 2,450 undergrads, 68% part-time. 242 full-time freshmen.

BASIC COSTS (2016-2017)
Tuition and fees: $3,772; out-of-state residents $11,366.
Per-credit charge: $91; out-of-state residents $344.

FINANCIAL AID PICTURE
Students with need: Need-based aid available for full-time and part-time students.
Students without need: This college awards aid only to students with need.

FINANCIAL AID PROCEDURES
Forms required: FAFSA, institutional form.
Dates and Deadlines: Priority date 6/1; closing date 8/1. Applicants notified on a rolling basis starting 6/1; must reply within 2 week(s) of notification.
Transfers: Priority date 6/11.

CONTACT
Wes Chapman, Asst. Director of Financial Aid
2500 East Shotwell Street, Bainbridge, GA 39818-0990
(229) 243-6920

Bauder College
Atlanta, Georgia
www.bauder.edu   Federal Code: 011574

4-year for-profit career college in very large city.
Enrollment: 751 undergrads.
Selectivity: Open admission; but selective for some programs.

BASIC COSTS (2016-2017)
Additional info: Bachelor's programs: Business Administration $70,125; Business Administration - Accounting $70,452; Business Administration - Fashion Merchandising $72,772; Criminal Justice $73,139. Associate programs: $34,275-$46,723. Certificate program: Medical Assisting $15,568. Diploma program: Practical Nursing $23,395.

FINANCIAL AID PICTURE
Students with need: Need-based aid available for full-time and part-time students. Work study available nights, weekends, and for part-time students.
Students without need: This college awards aid only to students with need.

FINANCIAL AID PROCEDURES
Forms required: FAFSA, institutional form.
Dates and Deadlines: Applicants notified on a rolling basis starting 7/15.

CONTACT

Rhonda King, Director of Financial Aid
384 Northyards Boulevard NW, Ste 190, Atlanta, GA 30313
(404) 237-7573

Berry College
Mount Berry, Georgia
www.berry.edu

Federal Code: 001554
CSS Code: 5059

4-year private liberal arts college in large town.
Enrollment: 2,055 undergrads. 534 full-time freshmen.
Selectivity: Admits 50 to 75% of applicants.

BASIC COSTS (2016-2017)
Tuition and fees: $33,556.
Per-credit charge: $1,111.
Room and board: $11,730.
Additional info: Tuition/fee waivers available for minority students.

FINANCIAL AID PICTURE (2016-2017)
Students with need: Out of 495 full-time freshmen who applied for aid, 389 were judged to have need. Of these, 389 received aid, and 127 had their full need met. Average financial aid package met 84% of need; average scholarship/grant was $23,045; average loan was $4,091. For part-time students, average financial aid package was $13,813.
Students without need: 145 full-time freshmen who did not demonstrate need for aid received scholarships/grants; average award was $14,323. No-need awards available for academics, art, job skills, leadership, minority status, music/drama, religious affiliation, state/district residency.
Scholarships offered: Georgia Tuition Equalization Grant; $700; for Georgia residents who attend in-state private institutions. HOPE Scholarship, $3,936 annually; Zell Miller Scholarship, $4,348 annually; for Georgia residents from eligible high schools with at least B average in college prep coursework.
Additional info: All students encouraged to work on-campus up to 16 hours per week.

FINANCIAL AID PROCEDURES
Forms required: FAFSA, state aid form. CSS Profile not required for domestic applicants.
Dates and Deadlines: Priority date 1/15; no closing date. Applicants notified on a rolling basis starting 11/1; must reply by 5/1.
Transfers: No deadline. Applicants notified on a rolling basis starting 11/1; must reply by 5/1.

CONTACT
Donna Childres, Director of Financial Aid
PO Box 490159, Mount Berry, GA 30149-0159
(706) 236-1714

Beulah Heights University
Atlanta, Georgia
www.beulah.edu

Federal Code: 030763

5-year private Bible and seminary college in very large city, affiliated with the nondenominational tradition.
Enrollment: 405 undergrads.
Selectivity: Open admission.

BASIC COSTS (2016-2017)
Tuition and fees: $9,390.
Per-credit charge: $303.
Room only: $6,000.

FINANCIAL AID PICTURE (2015-2016)
Students with need: Need-based aid available for full-time and part-time students. Work study available nights, weekends, and for part-time students.

FINANCIAL AID PROCEDURES
Forms required: FAFSA.
Dates and Deadlines: Priority date 2/1; closing date 6/30. Applicants notified on a rolling basis.
Transfers: No deadline. Applicants notified on a rolling basis; must reply within 1 week(s) of notification.

CONTACT
Alyssa Takatori, Director of Financial Aid
892 Berne Street SE, Atlanta, GA 30316
(404) 627-2681 ext. 105

Brenau University
Gainesville, Georgia
www.brenau.edu

Federal Code: 001556

4-year private university and liberal arts college in large town.
Enrollment: 1,638 undergrads, 37% part-time. 152 full-time freshmen.
Selectivity: Admits less than 50% of applicants.

BASIC COSTS (2016-2017)
Tuition and fees: $27,152.
Per-credit charge: $892.
Room and board: $12,418.

FINANCIAL AID PICTURE (2016-2017)
Students with need: Out of 140 full-time freshmen who applied for aid, 125 were judged to have need. Of these, 122 received aid, and 19 had their full need met. Average financial aid package met 70% of need; average scholarship/grant was $20,648; average loan was $4,157. For part-time students, average financial aid package was $9,985.
Students without need: 9 full-time freshmen who did not demonstrate need for aid received scholarships/grants; average award was $18,829. No-need awards available for academics, art, athletics, leadership, music/drama.
Scholarships offered: 3 full-time freshmen received athletic scholarships; average amount $8,667.

FINANCIAL AID PROCEDURES
Forms required: FAFSA, state aid form.
Dates and Deadlines: Priority date 3/1; no closing date. Applicants notified on a rolling basis starting 3/1.
Transfers: Priority date 4/1; no deadline. Applicants notified on a rolling basis starting 3/1.

CONTACT
Pam Barrett, Director of Financial Aid
500 Washington Street SE, Gainesville, GA 30501
(770) 534-6152

Brewton-Parker College
Mount Vernon, Georgia
www.bpc.edu

Federal Code: 001557

4-year private liberal arts college in small town, affiliated with the Southern Baptist Convention.
Enrollment: 466 undergrads.
Selectivity: Admits less than 50% of applicants.

BASIC COSTS (2016-2017)
Tuition and fees: $17,410.
Room and board: $7,440.

FINANCIAL AID PICTURE
Students with need: Need-based aid available for full-time and part-time students. Work study available nights, weekends, and for part-time students.
Students without need: No-need awards available for academics, athletics, leadership, religious affiliation, state/district residency.

Scholarships offered: Scholarships available for academic achievement and SAT scores for incoming freshman transfer students, ranging from $1,500-$3,000 per academic year, available for four years.

FINANCIAL AID PROCEDURES

Forms required: FAFSA, state aid form.

Dates and Deadlines: Priority date 3/15; closing date 7/1. Applicants notified on a rolling basis starting 3/15; must reply within 2 week(s) of notification.

CONTACT

Chris Dooley, Director of Financial Aid

Brewton-Parker College # 2011, Mount Vernon, GA 30445

(912) 583-3215

Carver College

Atlanta, Georgia

www.carver.edu   Federal Code: 036353

4-year private Bible and liberal arts college in very large city.

Enrollment: 55 undergrads.

BASIC COSTS (2016-2017)

Tuition and fees: $12,200.

Per-credit charge: $390.

Room and board: $6,600.

FINANCIAL AID PICTURE

Students with need: Need-based aid available for full-time students.

Students without need: This college awards aid only to students with need.

FINANCIAL AID PROCEDURES

Forms required: FAFSA, institutional form.

CONTACT

Loretta Watson, Financial Aid Director

3870 Cascade Road, SW, Atlanta, GA 30331

(404) 527-4520 ext. 205

Central Georgia Technical College

Warner Robins, Georgia

www.centralgatech.edu   Federal Code: 005763

2-year public community and technical college in small city.

Enrollment: 7,762 undergrads, 69% part-time.

Selectivity: Open admission; but selective for some programs.

BASIC COSTS (2017-2018)

Tuition and fees: $3,208; out-of-state residents $5,878.

Per-credit charge: $89; out-of-state residents $178.

FINANCIAL AID PICTURE

Students with need: Need-based aid available for full-time and part-time students.

Students without need: No-need awards available for academics, athletics, state/district residency.

FINANCIAL AID PROCEDURES

Forms required: FAFSA, state aid form, institutional form.

Dates and Deadlines: Closing date 7/15.

CONTACT

Jackie White, Director, Financial Aid

80 Cohen Walker Drive, Warner Robins, GA 31088

(478) 757-3422

Chattahoochee Technical College

Marietta, Georgia

www.chattahoocheetech.edu   Federal Code: 005620

2-year public community and technical college in large city.

Enrollment: 9,997 undergrads.

Selectivity: Open admission; but selective for some programs.

BASIC COSTS (2016-2017)

Tuition and fees: $3,188; out-of-state residents $5,858.

Per-credit charge: $89; out-of-state residents $178.

FINANCIAL AID PICTURE

Students with need: Need-based aid available for full-time and part-time students. Work study available nights, weekends, and for part-time students.

FINANCIAL AID PROCEDURES

Forms required: FAFSA.

Dates and Deadlines: Applicants notified on a rolling basis.

CONTACT

Kristie Teasley, Director of Financial Aid

980 South Cobb Drive, SE, Marietta, GA 30060-3300

(770) 528-4531

Clark Atlanta University

Atlanta, Georgia

www.cau.edu   Federal Code: 001559

4-year private university in very large city, affiliated with the United Methodist Church.

Enrollment: 3,093 undergrads, 3% part-time. 987 full-time freshmen.

Selectivity: Admits 50 to 75% of applicants.

BASIC COSTS (2016-2017)

Tuition and fees: $22,396.

Per-credit charge: $828.

Room and board: $9,256.

FINANCIAL AID PICTURE (2016-2017)

Students with need: Out of 940 full-time freshmen who applied for aid, 906 were judged to have need. Of these, 901 received aid, and 445 had their full need met. Average financial aid package met 48% of need; average scholarship/grant was $5,987; average loan was $2,227. For part-time students, average financial aid package was $4,995.

Students without need: No-need awards available for academics, art, athletics, leadership, minority status, music/drama, religious affiliation, ROTC, state/district residency.

Scholarships offered: 3 full-time freshmen received athletic scholarships; average amount $3,512.

FINANCIAL AID PROCEDURES

Forms required: FAFSA, state aid form.

Dates and Deadlines: Priority date 3/1; no closing date. Applicants notified on a rolling basis starting 4/1.

CONTACT

James Stotts, Director of Financial Aid

223 James P. Brawley Drive, SW, Atlanta, GA 30314-4391

(404) 880-6018

Clayton State University

Morrow, Georgia

www.clayton.edu   Federal Code: 008976

4-year public university in small city.

Enrollment: 5,723 undergrads, 40% part-time. 490 full-time freshmen.

Selectivity: Admits less than 50% of applicants.

BASIC COSTS (2016-2017)
Tuition and fees: $6,312; out-of-state residents $19,132.
Per-credit charge: $162; out-of-state residents $590.
Room and board: $9,742.

FINANCIAL AID PICTURE
Students with need: Need-based aid available for full-time and part-time students. Work study available nights, weekends, and for part-time students.
Students without need: No-need awards available for academics, athletics, music/drama.

FINANCIAL AID PROCEDURES
Forms required: FAFSA, state aid form.
Dates and Deadlines: Priority date 7/15; no closing date. Applicants notified on a rolling basis.
Transfers: No deadline. Applicants notified on a rolling basis.

CONTACT
Patricia Barton, Director of Financial Aid
2000 Clayton State Boulevard, Morrow, GA 30260-0285
(678) 466-4185

College of Coastal Georgia
Brunswick, Georgia
www.ccga.edu   Federal Code: 001558

4-year public liberal arts college in large town.
Enrollment: 3,478 undergrads, 38% part-time. 733 full-time freshmen.
Selectivity: Admits 50 to 75% of applicants.

BASIC COSTS (2016-2017)
Tuition and fees: $4,434; out-of-state residents $12,692.
Per-credit charge: $103; out-of-state residents $378.
Room and board: $9,688.

FINANCIAL AID PICTURE
Students with need: Need-based aid available for full-time and part-time students. Work study available nights.
Students without need: No-need awards available for academics, alumni affiliation, athletics.

FINANCIAL AID PROCEDURES
Forms required: FAFSA, state aid form.
Dates and Deadlines: Priority date 6/1; no closing date. Applicants notified on a rolling basis starting 4/1.
Transfers: No deadline. Applicants notified on a rolling basis.

CONTACT
Terral Harris, Director of Financial Aid
One College Drive, Brunswick, GA 31520
(912) 279-5722

Columbus State University
Columbus, Georgia
www.columbusstate.edu   Federal Code: 001561

4-year public university and liberal arts college in small city.
Enrollment: 6,529 undergrads, 27% part-time. 847 full-time freshmen.
Selectivity: Admits 50 to 75% of applicants. GED not accepted.

BASIC COSTS (2016-2017)
Tuition and fees: $7,076; out-of-state residents $20,294.
Per-credit charge: $175; out-of-state residents $615.
Room and board: $9,124.

FINANCIAL AID PICTURE (2016-2017)
Students with need: Out of 787 full-time freshmen who applied for aid, 636 were judged to have need. Of these, 629 received aid, and 117 had their full need met. Average financial aid package met 68% of need; average scholarship/grant was $5,083; average loan was $3,485. For part-time students, average financial aid package was $7,074.
Students without need: 30 full-time freshmen who did not demonstrate need for aid received scholarships/grants; average award was $1,853. No-need awards available for academics, alumni affiliation, art, athletics, job skills, leadership, minority status, music/drama, ROTC.
Scholarships offered: 40 full-time freshmen received athletic scholarships; average amount $6,616.

FINANCIAL AID PROCEDURES
Forms required: FAFSA.
Dates and Deadlines: Priority date 5/1; no closing date. Applicants notified on a rolling basis starting 5/15.

CONTACT
Russ Romandini, Director of Financial Aid
4225 University Avenue, Columbus, GA 31907-5645
(706) 507-8807

Columbus Technical College
Columbus, Georgia
www.columbustech.edu   Federal Code: 005624

2-year public technical college in small city.
Enrollment: 3,739 undergrads.
Selectivity: Open admission; but selective for some programs.

BASIC COSTS (2016-2017)
Tuition and fees: $3,188; out-of-state residents $5,858.
Per-credit charge: $89; out-of-state residents $178.

FINANCIAL AID PICTURE
Students with need: Need-based aid available for full-time and part-time students.

FINANCIAL AID PROCEDURES
Forms required: FAFSA.
Dates and Deadlines: Applicants notified on a rolling basis.

CONTACT
Debbie Henshaw, Director of Financial Aid
928 Manchester Expressway, Columbus, GA 31904-6572
(706) 649-1859

Covenant College
Lookout Mountain, Georgia
www.covenant.edu   Federal Code: 003484

4-year private liberal arts college in small city, affiliated with the Presbyterian Church (USA).
Enrollment: 981 undergrads, 1% part-time. 258 full-time freshmen.
Selectivity: Admits over 75% of applicants.

BASIC COSTS (2016-2017)
Tuition and fees: $32,230.
Per-credit charge: $1,340.
Room and board: $9,630.

FINANCIAL AID PICTURE (2015-2016)
Students with need: Out of 233 full-time freshmen who applied for aid, 186 were judged to have need. Of these, 186 received aid, and 60 had their full need met. Average financial aid package met 78% of need; average

scholarship/grant was $20,786; average loan was $5,767. For part-time students, average financial aid package was $15,069.

Students without need: 70 full-time freshmen who did not demonstrate need for aid received scholarships/grants; average award was $912,439. No-need awards available for academics, alumni affiliation, art, job skills, leadership, minority status, music/drama, religious affiliation, state/district residency.

Scholarships offered: Maclellan Scholars Program; minimum SAT 1200 (exclusive of Writing) or ACT 27, high school GPA 3.3. Presidential Scholarship; based on GPA, leadership, Christian commitment, extracurricular activities, work experience, references.

FINANCIAL AID PROCEDURES

Forms required: FAFSA, state aid form.

Dates and Deadlines: Applicants notified on a rolling basis starting 2/1; must reply by 5/1 or within 3 week(s) of notification.

Transfers: Some scholarships may be depleted for mid-semester transfers, such as athletic, diversity or music.

CONTACT

Beth Bailey, Director of Financial Aid
14049 Scenic Highway, Lookout Mountain, GA 30750
(706) 419-1126

Dalton State College
Dalton, Georgia
www.daltonstate.edu   Federal Code: 003956

4-year public liberal arts and teachers college in large town.
Enrollment: 4,671 undergrads.

BASIC COSTS (2016-2017)
Tuition and fees: $4,116; out-of-state residents $12,374.
Per-credit charge: $103; out-of-state residents $378.
Room only: $8,446.

FINANCIAL AID PICTURE
Students with need: Need-based aid available for full-time and part-time students.
Students without need: No-need awards available for academics, leadership, minority status, state/district residency.

FINANCIAL AID PROCEDURES
Forms required: FAFSA.
Dates and Deadlines: Applicants notified on a rolling basis starting 4/1.
Transfers: No deadline. Applicants notified on a rolling basis.

CONTACT
Carol Jones, Director of Student Financial Aid
650 College Drive, Dalton, GA 30720
(706) 272-4545

Darton State College
Albany, Georgia
www.darton.edu   Federal Code: 001543

2-year public community college in small city.
Enrollment: 5,990 undergrads.
Selectivity: Open admission; but selective for some programs.

BASIC COSTS (2016-2017)
Tuition and fees: $3,940; out-of-state residents $11,534.
Room and board: $10,070.

FINANCIAL AID PICTURE
Students with need: Need-based aid available for full-time and part-time students. Work study available nights, weekends, and for part-time students.

Students without need: No-need awards available for academics, alumni affiliation, art, athletics, music/drama, state/district residency.

Additional info: Auditions, portfolios, essays, extracurricular activities impact scholarship decisions.

FINANCIAL AID PROCEDURES

Forms required: FAFSA, state aid form, institutional form.

Dates and Deadlines: Applicants notified on a rolling basis; must reply within 3 week(s) of notification.

CONTACT

Haley Hooks, Director of Financial Aid
2400 Gillionville Road, Albany, GA 31707-3098
(229) 317-6746

DeVry University: Decatur
Decatur, Georgia
www.devry.edu   Federal Code: 009224

4-year for-profit university in large town.
Enrollment: 1,684 undergrads.

BASIC COSTS (2016-2017)
Tuition and fees: $17,512.
Per-credit charge: $609.

FINANCIAL AID PICTURE
Students with need: Need-based aid available for full-time and part-time students.
Students without need: This college awards aid only to students with need.

FINANCIAL AID PROCEDURES
Forms required: FAFSA.
Dates and Deadlines: Applicants notified on a rolling basis.

CONTACT
One West Court Square, Suite 100, Decatur, GA 30030-2556
(404) 292-7900

East Georgia State College
Swainsboro, Georgia
www.ega.edu   Federal Code: 010997

2-year public community and junior college in small town.
Enrollment: 2,885 undergrads, 23% part-time. 1,088 full-time freshmen.
Selectivity: Admits less than 50% of applicants.

BASIC COSTS (2016-2017)
Tuition and fees: $3,762; out-of-state residents $11,356.
Per-credit charge: $91; out-of-state residents $344.
Room and board: $8,338.

FINANCIAL AID PICTURE
Students with need: Need-based aid available for full-time and part-time students.
Students without need: No-need awards available for academics, leadership, state/district residency.

FINANCIAL AID PROCEDURES
Forms required: FAFSA, state aid form, institutional form.
Dates and Deadlines: Priority date 6/1; no closing date. Applicants notified on a rolling basis starting 6/1; must reply within 2 week(s) of notification.
Transfers: Students must provide EGSC with final official transcripts from all institutions previously attended prior to aid being awarded.

CONTACT
Karen Jones, Associate VP of Enrollment Management
131 College Circle, Swainsboro, GA 30401-2699
(478) 289-2012

Emmanuel College
Franklin Springs, Georgia
www.ec.edu   Federal Code: 001563

4-year private liberal arts and teachers college in rural community, affiliated with the Pentecostal Holiness Church.
Enrollment: 770 undergrads, 4% part-time. 238 full-time freshmen.
Selectivity: Admits less than 50% of applicants.

BASIC COSTS (2016-2017)
Tuition and fees: $19,330.
Per-credit charge: $795.
Room and board: $7,400.

FINANCIAL AID PICTURE (2016-2017)
Students with need: 60% of average financial aid package awarded as scholarships/grants, 40% awarded as loans/jobs. Need-based aid available for part-time students. Work study available nights, weekends, and for part-time students.
Students without need: No-need awards available for academics, art, athletics, job skills, leadership, music/drama, religious affiliation, state/district residency.

FINANCIAL AID PROCEDURES
Forms required: FAFSA, state aid form, institutional form.
Dates and Deadlines: Priority date 5/1; closing date 6/15. Applicants notified on a rolling basis starting 3/1; must reply within 2 week(s) of notification.
Transfers: Applicants notified on a rolling basis starting 3/1, must reply within 2 week(s) of notification.

CONTACT
Niki Stinson, Director of Financial Aid
181 Spring Street, Franklin Springs, GA 30639-0129
(706) 245-2843

Emory University
Atlanta, Georgia   Federal Code: 001564
www.emory.edu   CSS Code: 5187

4-year private university in very large city, affiliated with the United Methodist Church.
Enrollment: 6,717 undergrads, 1% part-time. 1,358 full-time freshmen.
Selectivity: Admits less than 50% of applicants. GED not accepted.

BASIC COSTS (2016-2017)
Tuition and fees: $47,954.
Per-credit charge: $1,971.
Room and board: $13,486.

FINANCIAL AID PICTURE (2016-2017)
Students with need: Out of 795 full-time freshmen who applied for aid, 630 were judged to have need. Of these, 630 received aid, and 628 had their full need met. Average financial aid package met 100% of need; average scholarship/grant was $38,834; average loan was $3,688. For part-time students, average financial aid package was $13,902.
Students without need: 50 full-time freshmen who did not demonstrate need for aid received scholarships/grants; average award was $23,424. No-need awards available for academics, art, leadership, music/drama, religious affiliation, state/district residency.
Scholarships offered: Emory and Goizueta Scholars programs: two-thirds tuition to full cost; based on academic merit of incoming first-year students,

requires nomination by appropriate high school official by November 1 of senior year; renewable for four years of undergraduate study.
Additional info: Loan replacement grant and loan cap program available to students from families with total annual incomes of $100,000 or less who demonstrate need for financial aid.

FINANCIAL AID PROCEDURES
Forms required: FAFSA, CSS PROFILE.
Dates and Deadlines: Priority date 2/15; closing date 3/1. Applicants notified by 4/1; must reply by 5/1.
Transfers: No deadline. Applicants notified on a rolling basis starting 5/1. Limitations on aid available to transfer students. Financial aid filing deadline for transfers is 30 days following transfer student admission date.

CONTACT
John Leach, Director of Financial Aid
1390 Oxford Road NE, 3rd Floor, Atlanta, GA 30322
(800) 727-6039

Fort Valley State University
Fort Valley, Georgia
www.fvsu.edu   Federal Code: 001566

4-year public liberal arts and teachers college in small town.
Enrollment: 3,250 undergrads.

BASIC COSTS (2016-2017)
Tuition and fees: $6,566; out-of-state residents $19,386.
Per-credit charge: $162; out-of-state residents $590.
Room and board: $8,010.

FINANCIAL AID PICTURE
Students with need: Need-based aid available for full-time and part-time students.
Students without need: No-need awards available for academics, athletics, music/drama.
Additional info: Financial aid transcripts must be received from former institutions before application for aid will be considered complete and reviewed for awards.

FINANCIAL AID PROCEDURES
Forms required: FAFSA.
Dates and Deadlines: Priority date 3/1; no closing date. Applicants notified on a rolling basis starting 3/15; must reply within 1 week(s) of notification.

CONTACT
Eula Solomon, Director of Financial Aid
1005 State University Drive, Fort Valley, GA 31030-4313
(478) 825-6351

Georgia College and State University
Milledgeville, Georgia   Federal Code: 001602
www.gcsu.edu   CSS Code: 5252

4-year public university and liberal arts college in large town.
Enrollment: 5,923 undergrads, 7% part-time. 1,379 full-time freshmen.
Selectivity: Admits over 75% of applicants.

BASIC COSTS (2016-2017)
Tuition and fees: $9,202; out-of-state residents $27,550.
Room and board: $10,626.

FINANCIAL AID PICTURE (2016-2017)
Students with need: 36% of average financial aid package awarded as scholarships/grants, 64% awarded as loans/jobs. Need-based aid available for part-time students. Work study available nights, weekends, and for part-time students.

Students without need: No-need awards available for academics, alumni affiliation, art, athletics, leadership, music/drama, state/district residency.
Scholarships offered: Trustee Scholarships: $6,000 per year for four years. Presidential Scholarships: $4,000 per year for four years. Vincent Scholarship: $3,000 per year. Scholarships based on superior academic accomplishments, include stipends to be used toward study abroad programs.

FINANCIAL AID PROCEDURES
Forms required: FAFSA, CSS PROFILE.
Dates and Deadlines: Priority date 3/1; no closing date. Applicants notified on a rolling basis starting 3/1.
Transfers: Filing priority date of March 1 for programs with limited funding . Priority date of July 31 in order to have aid funds available to meet payment deadline.

CONTACT
Cathy Crawley, Director of Financial Aid
Campus Box 23, Milledgeville, GA 31061-0490
(478) 445-5149

Georgia Gwinnett College
Lawrenceville, Georgia
www.ggc.edu

4-year public liberal arts college in large town.
Enrollment: 11,444 undergrads, 30% part-time. 2,096 full-time freshmen.
Selectivity: Admits over 75% of applicants.

BASIC COSTS (2016-2017)
Tuition and fees: $5,548; out-of-state residents $16,052.
Per-credit charge: $129; out-of-state residents $479.
Room and board: $12,222.

FINANCIAL AID PICTURE
Students with need: Need-based aid available for full-time and part-time students. Work study available nights, weekends, and for part-time students.
Students without need: No-need awards available for academics, athletics.

FINANCIAL AID PROCEDURES
Forms required: FAFSA.
Dates and Deadlines: Priority date 7/1; no closing date. Applicants notified on a rolling basis starting 5/15.
Transfers: No deadline. Applicants notified on a rolling basis.

CONTACT
Kimberly Jordan, Director of Financial Aid
1000 University Center Lane, Lawrenceville, GA 30043
(678) 407-5701

Georgia Highlands College
Rome, Georgia
www.highlands.edu   Federal Code: 009507

2-year public community and liberal arts college in large town.
Enrollment: 6,014 undergrads, 54% part-time. 981 full-time freshmen.

BASIC COSTS (2016-2017)
Tuition and fees: $3,790; out-of-state residents $11,384.
Per-credit charge: $91; out-of-state residents $344.

FINANCIAL AID PICTURE (2015-2016)
Students with need: 58% of average financial aid package awarded as scholarships/grants, 42% awarded as loans/jobs. Need-based aid available for part-time students. Work study available nights.
Students without need: No-need awards available for academics, art.
Additional info: All Federal Work Study students must be Pell eligible and taking a minimum of 6 credit hours.

FINANCIAL AID PROCEDURES
Forms required: FAFSA, state aid form.
Dates and Deadlines: Priority date 7/1; closing date 4/1. Applicants notified on a rolling basis starting 4/1; must reply within 2 week(s) of notification.
Transfers: No deadline. Applicants notified on a rolling basis starting 5/1; must reply within 2 week(s) of notification. Transfer students are only eligible for aid not used at previous institution in the same aid year and/or the maximum eligibility allowed for a given term. Transfer students cannot receive Federal Aid at two institutions during the same term.

CONTACT
Melinda Ewers-King, Director of Financial Aid
3175 Cedartown Highway, Rome, GA 30161
(706) 295-6311

Georgia Institute of Technology
Atlanta, Georgia   Federal Code: 001569
www.gatech.edu   CSS Code: 5248

4-year public university in large city.
Enrollment: 14,766 undergrads, 7% part-time. 3,087 full-time freshmen.
Selectivity: Admits less than 50% of applicants. GED not accepted.

BASIC COSTS (2016-2017)
Tuition and fees: $12,212; out-of-state residents $32,404.
Room and board: $11,088.

FINANCIAL AID PICTURE (2015-2016)
Students with need: Out of 2,459 full-time freshmen who applied for aid, 1,217 were judged to have need. Of these, 1,144 received aid, and 276 had their full need met. Average financial aid package met 58% of need; average scholarship/grant was $12,920; average loan was $3,945. For part-time students, average financial aid package was $7,458.
Students without need: 301 full-time freshmen who did not demonstrate need for aid received scholarships/grants; average award was $8,532. No-need awards available for academics, athletics, leadership, music/drama, ROTC, state/district residency.
Scholarships offered: *Merit:* Stamps President's Scholarship covers all tuition and fees, meals and housing, personal expenses, books, and $15,000 over four years toward enrichment activities such as study abroad and unpaid research or internships. Recipients also receive a $1,100 stipend for the purchase of a laptop. For in-state students, part of this is expected to be the Zell Miller/HOPE Scholarship provided by the State of Georgia. For out-of-state students, this includes a tuition waiver, which reduces the cost of tuition to the same as that of an in-state student. *Athletic:* 30 full-time freshmen received athletic scholarships; average amount $24,861.

FINANCIAL AID PROCEDURES
Forms required: FAFSA, institutional form. CSS PROFILE required for domestic, first-time applicants.
Dates and Deadlines: Priority date 1/31; closing date 1/31. Applicants notified by 4/15; must reply by 5/1.
Transfers: Priority date 1/31; closing date 7/31. Applicants notified by 6/15; must reply by 6/15. All fees are payable by the deadlines published on the Bursar Calendar for each academic term. Registration is not complete until all fees have been paid.

CONTACT
Marie Mons, Director of Student Financial Planning and Services
Office of Undergraduate Admissions, Atlanta, GA 30332-0320
(404) 894-4160

PART III: FINANCIAL AID COLLEGE BY COLLEGE

Georgia Military College

Milledgeville, Georgia
www.gmc.edu   Federal Code: 001571

2-year public community and military college in large town.
Enrollment: 6,519 undergrads, 33% part-time. 1,497 full-time freshmen.
Selectivity: Open admission; but selective for some programs.

BASIC COSTS (2016-2017)
Tuition and fees: $6,128; out-of-state residents $6,128.
Per-credit charge: $121.

FINANCIAL AID PICTURE
Students with need: Need-based aid available for full-time and part-time students. Work study available nights.
Students without need: No-need awards available for athletics, leadership, ROTC, state/district residency.
Additional info: Institutional aid offered to those enrolled in Cadet Corps who reside on campus.

FINANCIAL AID PROCEDURES
Forms required: FAFSA, state aid form.
Dates and Deadlines: Applicants notified on a rolling basis.
Transfers: No deadline. Applicants notified on a rolling basis. Transfer students must submit financial aid transcript from any prior post-secondary institutions.

CONTACT
Alisa Stephens, Director of Financial Aid
201 East Greene Street, Milledgeville, GA 31061
(478) 387-4842

Georgia Perimeter College

Clarkston, Georgia
www.gpc.edu   Federal Code: 001562

2-year public junior and liberal arts college in very large city.
Enrollment: 18,678 undergrads.

BASIC COSTS (2016-2017)
Tuition and fees: $3,806; out-of-state residents $11,400.
Per-credit charge: $91; out-of-state residents $344.

FINANCIAL AID PICTURE
Students with need: Need-based aid available for full-time and part-time students. Work study available nights, weekends, and for part-time students.
Students without need: No-need awards available for academics, alumni affiliation, art, athletics, job skills, leadership, minority status, music/drama, religious affiliation, ROTC, state/district residency.

FINANCIAL AID PROCEDURES
Forms required: FAFSA.
Dates and Deadlines: Closing date 6/1. Applicants notified on a rolling basis; must reply within 3 week(s) of notification.
Transfers: Priority date 6/1; no deadline.

CONTACT
Ron Stark, Executive Vice President for Administrative and Financial Affairs
555 North Indian Creek Drive, Clarkston, GA 30021-2361
(678) 891-3535

Georgia Piedmont Technical College

Clarkston, Georgia
www.gptc.edu   Federal Code: 016582

2-year public technical college in large city.
Enrollment: 4,050 undergrads.

Selectivity: Open admission; but selective for some programs.

BASIC COSTS (2016-2017)
Tuition and fees: $3,184; out-of-state residents $5,854.
Per-credit charge: $89; out-of-state residents $178.

FINANCIAL AID PICTURE
Students with need: Need-based aid available for full-time and part-time students. Work study available nights, weekends, and for part-time students.
Students without need: No-need awards available for academics, minority status.

FINANCIAL AID PROCEDURES
Forms required: FAFSA.
Dates and Deadlines: Closing date 8/20. Applicants notified on a rolling basis.
Transfers: No deadline.

CONTACT
Lakisha Sanders, Assistant Vice President of Financial Aid
495 North Indian Creek Drive, Clarkston, GA 30021-2397
(404) 297-9522 ext. 1160

Georgia Southern University

Statesboro, Georgia
www.georgiasouthern.edu   Federal Code: 001572

4-year public university in large town.
Enrollment: 17,349 undergrads, 8% part-time. 3,463 full-time freshmen.
Selectivity: Admits 50 to 75% of applicants. GED not accepted.

BASIC COSTS (2016-2017)
Tuition and fees: $7,318; out-of-state residents $20,536.
Per-credit charge: $175; out-of-state residents $615.
Room and board: $10,070.

FINANCIAL AID PICTURE (2015-2016)
Students with need: Out of 3,231 full-time freshmen who applied for aid, 2,300 were judged to have need. Of these, 2,244 received aid, and 318 had their full need met. Average financial aid package met 57% of need; average scholarship/grant was $7,559; average loan was $4,291. For part-time students, average financial aid package was $6,966.
Students without need: 119 full-time freshmen who did not demonstrate need for aid received scholarships/grants; average award was $1,652. No-need awards available for academics, alumni affiliation, art, athletics, leadership, minority status, music/drama, ROTC, state/district residency.
Scholarships offered: *Merit:* 1906 Scholars: tuition for 4 years; 10 awards annually. UHP Scholarships: $1,500 for 4 years; 10 awards annually. Foundation Scholars: $1,500 for 4 years; 10 awards annually. Southern Scholars Ward: $2,000 for 2 years, 20 awards annually. Coca-Cola Foundation Scholars Award: $1,500 for 4 years, 5 awards annually. Miscellaneous renewable and non-renewable awards: ranging from $500-$5,000. *Athletic:* 37 full-time freshmen received athletic scholarships; average amount $11,618.
Additional info: Majority of available scholarships are need-blind.

FINANCIAL AID PROCEDURES
Forms required: FAFSA.
Dates and Deadlines: Priority date 4/20; no closing date. Applicants notified on a rolling basis starting 4/20.
Transfers: No deadline. Applicants notified on a rolling basis starting 3/1.

CONTACT
Tracey Mingo, Director of Financial Aid
PO Box 8024, Statesboro, GA 30458
(912) 478-5413

Georgia Southwestern State University
Americus, Georgia
www.gsw.edu   Federal Code: 001573

4-year public university in large town.
Enrollment: 2,413 undergrads, 27% part-time. 475 full-time freshmen.
Selectivity: Admits 50 to 75% of applicants. GED not accepted.

BASIC COSTS (2016-2017)
Tuition and fees: $6,234; out-of-state residents $19,054.
Per-credit charge: $162; out-of-state residents $590.
Room and board: $7,672.

FINANCIAL AID PICTURE (2016-2017)
Students with need: Out of 447 full-time freshmen who applied for aid, 355 were judged to have need. Of these, 355 received aid, and 43 had their full need met. Average financial aid package met 64% of need; average scholarship/grant was $5,092; average loan was $3,429. For part-time students, average financial aid package was $7,135.
Students without need: 41 full-time freshmen who did not demonstrate need for aid received scholarships/grants; average award was $1,807. No-need awards available for academics, alumni affiliation, art, athletics, leadership, music/drama, state/district residency.
Scholarships offered: 21 full-time freshmen received athletic scholarships; average amount $2,281.

FINANCIAL AID PROCEDURES
Forms required: FAFSA.
Dates and Deadlines: Priority date 4/15; closing date 6/15. Applicants notified on a rolling basis starting 5/1; must reply within 8 week(s) of notification.

CONTACT
Angela Bryant, Director of Financial Aid
800 Georgia Southwestern State University Drive, Americus, GA 31709-9957
(229) 928-1378

Georgia State University
Atlanta, Georgia
www.gsu.edu   Federal Code: 001574

4-year public university in very large city.
Enrollment: 24,729 undergrads, 22% part-time. 3,579 full-time freshmen.
Selectivity: Admits 50 to 75% of applicants. GED not accepted.

BASIC COSTS (2016-2017)
Tuition and fees: $10,686; out-of-state residents $28,896.
Per-credit charge: $286; out-of-state residents $893.
Room and board: $10,972.

FINANCIAL AID PICTURE (2015-2016)
Students with need: Out of 3,456 full-time freshmen who applied for aid, 2,933 were judged to have need. Of these, 2,879 received aid, and 266 had their full need met. Average financial aid package met 62% of need; average scholarship/grant was $5,113. For part-time students, average financial aid package was $7,623.
Students without need: No-need awards available for academics, alumni affiliation, art, athletics, job skills, leadership, minority status, music/drama, religious affiliation, ROTC, state/district residency.

FINANCIAL AID PROCEDURES
Forms required: FAFSA.
Dates and Deadlines: Closing date 4/1. Applicants notified on a rolling basis starting 3/1.
Transfers: Applicants notified on a rolling basis starting 3/1; must reply by 11/1.

CONTACT
Louis Scott, Director of Student Financial Aid
Box 4009, Atlanta, GA 30302-4009
(404) 413-2400

Gordon State College
Barnesville, Georgia
www.gordonstate.edu   Federal Code: 001575

2-year public liberal arts college in small town.
Enrollment: 3,890 undergrads.
Selectivity: Admits less than 50% of applicants.

BASIC COSTS (2016-2017)
Tuition and fees: $4,164; out-of-state residents $12,422.
Per-credit charge: $103; out-of-state residents $378.
Room and board: $6,370.

FINANCIAL AID PICTURE (2015-2016)
Students with need: Need-based aid available for part-time students. Work study available nights, weekends, and for part-time students.
Students without need: No-need awards available for academics, athletics, music/drama, state/district residency.

FINANCIAL AID PROCEDURES
Forms required: FAFSA, state aid form.
Dates and Deadlines: Priority date 5/1; closing date 6/1. Applicants notified on a rolling basis starting 4/1.

CONTACT
Jody DeFore, Director of Financial Aid
419 College Drive, Barnesville, GA 30204
(678) 359-5990

Gupton Jones College of Funeral Service
Decatur, Georgia
www.gupton-jones.edu   Federal Code: 010771

2-year private technical and career college in very large city.
Enrollment: 215 undergrads.
Selectivity: Open admission.

BASIC COSTS (2017-2018)
Tuition and fees: $11,150.

FINANCIAL AID PICTURE
Students with need: Need-based aid available for full-time and part-time students.
Students without need: This college awards aid only to students with need.

FINANCIAL AID PROCEDURES
Forms required: FAFSA.
Dates and Deadlines: Applicants notified on a rolling basis.

CONTACT
Gill Adams, Financial Aid Officer
5141 Snapfinger Woods Drive, Decatur, GA 30035
(770) 593-2257

Gwinnett College
Lilburn, Georgia
www.gwinnettcollege.edu   Federal Code: 025830

2-year for-profit nursing and junior college in large city.
Enrollment: 115 undergrads.

Selectivity: Open admission; but selective for some programs.

BASIC COSTS (2016-2017)
Tuition and fees: $9,850.

FINANCIAL AID PICTURE
Students with need: Need-based aid available for full-time and part-time students.

FINANCIAL AID PROCEDURES
Forms required: FAFSA.

Dates and Deadlines: Applicants notified on a rolling basis.

CONTACT
James Davidson, Director of Financial Aid
4230 Highway 29, Lilburn, GA 30047
(770) 381-7200

Gwinnett Technical College
Lawrenceville, Georgia
www.gwinnetttech.edu

2-year public technical college in large town.
Enrollment: 7,234 undergrads.
Selectivity: Open admission; but selective for some programs.

BASIC COSTS (2016-2017)
Tuition and fees: $3,190; out-of-state residents $5,860.
Per-credit charge: $89; out-of-state residents $178.

FINANCIAL AID PICTURE
Students with need: Need-based aid available for full-time and part-time students.

FINANCIAL AID PROCEDURES
Forms required: FAFSA.

Dates and Deadlines: Closing date 7/8.

CONTACT
Karen Laverdiere
5150 Sugarloaf Parkway, Lawrenceville, GA 30043-5702

Herzing University: Atlanta
Atlanta, Georgia
www.herzing.edu
Federal Code: 014030

3-year for-profit business and technical college in very large city.
Enrollment: 599 undergrads.

BASIC COSTS (2016-2017)
Additional info: Diploma programs: $13,000. Associate programs: $13,000. Bachelor's programs: $12,300-$19,900. All costs are subject to change.

FINANCIAL AID PICTURE
Students with need: Need-based aid available for full-time and part-time students. Work study available nights.
Students without need: No-need awards available for academics.

FINANCIAL AID PROCEDURES
Forms required: FAFSA, institutional form.

Dates and Deadlines: Applicants notified on a rolling basis.

CONTACT
Stephanie Gunby, Director of Financial Aid
3393 Peachtree Road NE, Suite 1003, Atlanta, GA 30326
(404) 816-4533

Kennesaw State University
Kennesaw, Georgia
www.kennesaw.edu
Federal Code: 001577

4-year public university in large town.
Enrollment: 31,613 undergrads, 24% part-time. 5,207 full-time freshmen.
Selectivity: Admits 50 to 75% of applicants. GED not accepted.

BASIC COSTS (2016-2017)
Tuition and fees: $7,326; out-of-state residents $20,782.
Per-credit charge: $177; out-of-state residents $626.
Room and board: $10,500.

FINANCIAL AID PICTURE (2016-2017)
Students with need: Out of 4,998 full-time freshmen who applied for aid, 3,995 were judged to have need. Of these, 3,880 received aid, and 242 had their full need met. Average financial aid package met 38% of need; average scholarship/grant was $4,704; average loan was $2,710. For part-time students, average financial aid package was $5,907.
Students without need: 18 full-time freshmen who did not demonstrate need for aid received scholarships/grants; average award was $1,294. No-need awards available for academics, alumni affiliation, art, athletics, job skills, leadership, minority status, music/drama, ROTC, state/district residency.

FINANCIAL AID PROCEDURES
Forms required: FAFSA.

Dates and Deadlines: Priority date 4/1; no closing date. Applicants notified on a rolling basis starting 4/1.
Transfers: No deadline. Applicants notified on a rolling basis starting 4/1.

CONTACT
Ron Day, Director of Financial Aid
3391 Town Point Drive, Kennesaw, GA 30144
(770) 423-6074

LaGrange College
LaGrange, Georgia
www.lagrange.edu
Federal Code: 001578

4-year private liberal arts college in large town, affiliated with the United Methodist Church.
Enrollment: 902 undergrads, 5% part-time. 263 full-time freshmen.
Selectivity: Admits 50 to 75% of applicants.

BASIC COSTS (2016-2017)
Tuition and fees: $28,460.
Per-credit charge: $1,160.
Room and board: $11,440.

FINANCIAL AID PICTURE (2015-2016)
Students with need: Out of 258 full-time freshmen who applied for aid, 232 were judged to have need. Of these, 232 received aid, and 42 had their full need met. Average financial aid package met 73% of need; average scholarship/grant was $6,772; average loan was $3,591. For part-time students, average financial aid package was $7,429.
Students without need: 12 full-time freshmen who did not demonstrate need for aid received scholarships/grants; average award was $10,067. No-need awards available for academics, art, leadership, music/drama, religious affiliation, state/district residency.
Scholarships offered: Presidential: tuition, room and board; competitive. Fellows: $12,500 per year; competitive. Founders: $10,000 per year; competitive. Hilltop: $7,500 per year. Gateway: $5,500 per year.

FINANCIAL AID PROCEDURES
Forms required: FAFSA, state aid form.

Dates and Deadlines: Priority date 3/1; no closing date. Applicants notified on a rolling basis starting 3/15; must reply within 4 week(s) of notification.

Transfers: No deadline. Applicants notified on a rolling basis starting 3/1; must reply within 3 week(s) of notification.

CONTACT
Michelle Reeves, Director of Financial Aid
601 Broad Street, LaGrange, GA 30240-2999
(706) 880-8241

Life University
Marietta, Georgia
www.life.edu   Federal Code: 014170

4-year private university in very large city.
Enrollment: 718 undergrads, 26% part-time. 112 full-time freshmen.
Selectivity: Admits over 75% of applicants.

BASIC COSTS (2016-2017)
Tuition and fees: $11,220.

FINANCIAL AID PICTURE (2016-2017)
Students with need: Out of 95 full-time freshmen who applied for aid, 85 were judged to have need. Of these, 85 received aid. Average financial aid package met 27% of need; average scholarship/grant was $5,300; average loan was $3,700. For part-time students, average financial aid package was $8,100.
Students without need: No-need awards available for academics, alumni affiliation, athletics, leadership, minority status, state/district residency.
Scholarships offered: 3 full-time freshmen received athletic scholarships; average amount $10,500.

FINANCIAL AID PROCEDURES
Forms required: FAFSA.
Dates and Deadlines: Priority date 3/1; no closing date. Applicants notified on a rolling basis starting 3/1.
Transfers: No deadline. Applicants notified on a rolling basis.

CONTACT
Jessica Magazu, Director of Financial Aid
1269 Barclay Circle, Marietta, GA 30060
(770) 426-2944

Luther Rice University
Lithonia, Georgia
www.LutherRice.edu   Federal Code: 031009

4-year private Bible and seminary college in very large city, affiliated with the Baptist faith.
Enrollment: 347 undergrads, 83% part-time. 3 full-time freshmen.
Selectivity: Open admission.

BASIC COSTS (2017-2018)
Tuition and fees: $8,820.

FINANCIAL AID PICTURE (2015-2016)
Students with need: Out of 3 full-time freshmen who applied for aid, 3 were judged to have need. Of these, 3 received aid. For part-time students, average financial aid package was $8,567.
Students without need: 1 full-time freshmen who did not demonstrate need for aid received scholarships/grants; average award was $2,928. No-need awards available for academics.
Scholarships offered: 1 full-time freshmen received athletic scholarships; average amount $2,928.

FINANCIAL AID PROCEDURES
Forms required: FAFSA.
Dates and Deadlines: Applicants notified on a rolling basis.
Transfers: No deadline. Applicants notified on a rolling basis.

CONTACT
Casey Kuffrey, Director of Financial Aid
3038 Evans Mill Road, Lithonia, GA 30038
(770) 484-1204 ext. 5755

Mercer University
Macon, Georgia
www.mercer.edu   Federal Code: 001580

4-year private university in small city.
Enrollment: 3,032 undergrads, 1% part-time. 827 full-time freshmen.
Selectivity: Admits 50 to 75% of applicants.

BASIC COSTS (2016-2017)
Tuition and fees: $35,130.
Per-credit charge: $1,161.
Room and board: $11,106.

FINANCIAL AID PICTURE (2016-2017)
Students with need: Out of 825 full-time freshmen who applied for aid, 591 were judged to have need. Of these, 591 received aid, and 271 had their full need met. Average financial aid package met 91% of need; average scholarship/grant was $25,244; average loan was $9,769. For part-time students, average financial aid package was $14,740.
Students without need: 207 full-time freshmen who did not demonstrate need for aid received scholarships/grants; average award was $19,796. No-need awards available for academics, art, athletics, job skills, leadership, music/drama, religious affiliation, ROTC, state/district residency.
Scholarships offered: *Merit:* Various scholarships; primarily based on GPA, SAT/ACT, and personal interview; early applications given highest consideration. National Merit finalists and semi-finalists guaranteed full-tuition scholarships. *Athletic:* 32 full-time freshmen received athletic scholarships; average amount $21,633.

FINANCIAL AID PROCEDURES
Forms required: FAFSA.
Dates and Deadlines: Priority date 2/1; no closing date. Applicants notified on a rolling basis starting 1/7; must reply within 2 week(s) of notification.
Transfers: No deadline. Applicants notified on a rolling basis starting 1/7; must reply within 2 week(s) of notification.

CONTACT
Maria Hammett, Associate Vice President, Student Financial Planning
1501 Mercer University Drive, Macon, GA 31207-0001
(478) 301-2670

Middle Georgia State University
Macon, Georgia
www.mga.edu   Federal Code: 001581

4-year public liberal arts college in small city.
Enrollment: 7,164 undergrads.

BASIC COSTS (2016-2017)
Tuition and fees: $4,542; out-of-state residents $13,328.
Per-credit charge: $109; out-of-state residents $402.
Room and board: $8,510.

FINANCIAL AID PICTURE
Students with need: Need-based aid available for full-time and part-time students. Work study available nights, weekends, and for part-time students.
Students without need: No-need awards available for academics, alumni affiliation, art, athletics, job skills, leadership, minority status, music/drama, state/district residency.

FINANCIAL AID PROCEDURES
Forms required: FAFSA.

Dates and Deadlines: Closing date 7/16. Applicants notified on a rolling basis starting 5/1.

CONTACT

Lee Ann Kirkland, Director of Financial Aid
100 College Station Drive, Macon, GA 31206
(478) 471-2800

Morehouse College

Atlanta, Georgia
www.morehouse.edu   Federal Code: 001582

4-year private liberal arts college for men in very large city.
Enrollment: 2,104 undergrads, 4% part-time. 608 full-time freshmen.
Selectivity: Admits 50 to 75% of applicants.

BASIC COSTS (2017-2018)
Tuition and fees: $27,278.
Per-credit charge: $1,013.
Room only: $7,510.

FINANCIAL AID PICTURE
Students with need: Need-based aid available for full-time and part-time students.
Students without need: No-need awards available for academics, alumni affiliation, art, athletics, job skills, leadership, music/drama, ROTC, state/district residency.

FINANCIAL AID PROCEDURES
Forms required: FAFSA, state aid form.
Dates and Deadlines: Priority date 2/15; closing date 4/1. Applicants notified on a rolling basis; must reply within 2 week(s) of notification.
Transfers: Priority date 2/15; no deadline. Applicants notified on a rolling basis; must reply within 2 week(s) of notification.

CONTACT

Sheryl Spivey, Director of Financial Aid
830 Westview Drive SW, Atlanta, GA 30314
(470) 639-0999

North Georgia Technical College

Clarkesville, Georgia
www.northgatech.edu   Federal Code: 005619

2-year public community and technical college in small town.
Enrollment: 2,389 undergrads, 62% part-time. 341 full-time freshmen.
Selectivity: Open admission; but selective for some programs.

BASIC COSTS (2016-2017)
Tuition and fees: $3,188; out-of-state residents $5,858.
Per-credit charge: $89; out-of-state residents $178.
Room and board: $4,800.

FINANCIAL AID PICTURE (2015-2016)
Students with need: 60% of average financial aid package awarded as scholarships/grants, 40% awarded as loans/jobs. Need-based aid available for part-time students. Work study available weekends and for part-time students.

FINANCIAL AID PROCEDURES
Forms required: FAFSA.
Dates and Deadlines: Applicants notified on a rolling basis.

CONTACT

Audra Jimenez, Director of Financial Aid
1500 Highway 197 North, Clarkesville, GA 30523
(706) 754-7726

Oglethorpe University

Atlanta, Georgia
www.oglethorpe.edu   Federal Code: 001586

4-year private liberal arts college in very large city.
Enrollment: 1,125 undergrads.

BASIC COSTS (2016-2017)
Tuition and fees: $35,280.
Per-credit charge: $1,467.
Room and board: $12,710.

FINANCIAL AID PICTURE
Students with need: Need-based aid available for full-time students.
Students without need: No-need awards available for academics, art, leadership, music/drama, religious affiliation, state/district residency.

FINANCIAL AID PROCEDURES
Forms required: FAFSA, state aid form.
Dates and Deadlines: Priority date 2/15; no closing date. Applicants notified on a rolling basis starting 3/1; must reply by 5/1 or within 2 week(s) of notification.
Transfers: No deadline.

CONTACT

Chris Summers, Director of Financial Aid
4484 Peachtree Road NE, Atlanta, GA 30319-2797
(404) 364-8356

Oxford College of Emory University

Oxford, Georgia   Federal Code: 001565
www.oxford.emory.edu   CSS Code: 5186

2-year private branch campus and liberal arts college in large town, affiliated with the United Methodist Church.
Enrollment: 978 undergrads. 502 full-time freshmen.
Selectivity: Admits less than 50% of applicants. GED not accepted.

BASIC COSTS (2016-2017)
Tuition and fees: $43,254.
Per-credit charge: $1,775.
Room and board: $12,006.

FINANCIAL AID PICTURE
Students with need: Need-based aid available for full-time and part-time students. Work study available nights, weekends, and for part-time students.
Students without need: No-need awards available for academics, leadership, religious affiliation, state/district residency.
Scholarships offered: Woodruff Scholarships; full tuition, room and board for 4 years. Dean's Scholarship; full tuition for 4 years. Faculty Scholarships; half tuition for 4 years. 2-year scholarships; range from $8,000-$10,000 a year.
Additional info: Loan reduction program for families with annual assessed incomes of $100,000 or less who demonstrate need.

FINANCIAL AID PROCEDURES
Forms required: FAFSA, CSS PROFILE, state aid form.
Dates and Deadlines: Priority date 2/15; closing date 3/1. Applicants notified on a rolling basis starting 4/1; must reply by 5/1.

CONTACT

Jennifer Patil, Associate Dean for Financial Aid and Enrollment
122 Few Circle, Oxford, GA 30054-1418
(770) 784-8303

Paine College

Augusta, Georgia
www.paine.edu   Federal Code: 001587

4-year private liberal arts college in large city, affiliated with the Christian
Methodist Episcopal Church.
Enrollment: 419 undergrads, 7% part-time. 101 full-time freshmen.
Selectivity: Admits less than 50% of applicants.

BASIC COSTS (2016-2017)
Tuition and fees: $14,224.
Per-credit charge: $529.
Room and board: $6,662.

FINANCIAL AID PICTURE
Students with need: Need-based aid available for full-time and part-time students. Work study available nights, weekends, and for part-time students.
Students without need: No-need awards available for academics, alumni
affiliation, athletics, music/drama, religious affiliation, ROTC.

FINANCIAL AID PROCEDURES
Forms required: FAFSA, state aid form.
Dates and Deadlines: Priority date 3/1; no closing date. Applicants notified
on a rolling basis starting 5/1; must reply within 2 week(s) of notification.

CONTACT
Consuelo Quinn, Director of Financial Aid
1235 15th Street, Augusta, GA 30901
(706) 821-8262

Piedmont College

Demorest, Georgia
www.piedmont.edu   Federal Code: 001588

4-year private nursing and teachers college in rural community, affiliated
with the Christian Church.
Enrollment: 1,276 undergrads, 8% part-time. 273 full-time freshmen.
Selectivity: Admits 50 to 75% of applicants.

BASIC COSTS (2016-2017)
Tuition and fees: $23,112.
Per-credit charge: $963.
Room and board: $9,400.
Additional info: Tuition/fee waivers available for adults.

FINANCIAL AID PICTURE (2016-2017)
Students with need: Out of 259 full-time freshmen who applied for aid,
230 were judged to have need. Of these, 230 received aid, and 59 had their
full need met. Average financial aid package met 78% of need; average
scholarship/grant was $16,946; average loan was $3,195. For part-time students, average financial aid package was $8,639.
Students without need: 43 full-time freshmen who did not demonstrate
need for aid received scholarships/grants; average award was $11,899. No-
need awards available for academics, alumni affiliation, art, leadership,
music/drama, religious affiliation, state/district residency.
Scholarships offered: Academic scholarships; based on superior academics,
leadership, and extracurricular activities.

FINANCIAL AID PROCEDURES
Forms required: FAFSA, state aid form, institutional form.
Dates and Deadlines: Priority date 5/1; no closing date. Applicants notified
on a rolling basis; must reply within 2 week(s) of notification.
Transfers: No deadline. Applicants notified on a rolling basis; must reply
within 2 week(s) of notification.

CONTACT
David McMillion, Director of Financial Aid
1021 Central Avenue, Demorest, GA 30535-0010
(706) 776-0114

Point University

West Point, Georgia
www.point.edu   Federal Code: 001547

4-year private Bible and liberal arts college in small town, affiliated with the
Christian Church.
Enrollment: 1,358 undergrads, 10% part-time. 523 full-time freshmen.
Selectivity: Admits 50 to 75% of applicants.

BASIC COSTS (2016-2017)
Tuition and fees: $19,200.
Room and board: $7,700.

FINANCIAL AID PICTURE (2015-2016)
Students with need: Average financial aid package met 27% of need; average scholarship/grant was $5,678; average loan was $3,500. Need-based aid
available for part-time students.
Students without need: 27 full-time freshmen who did not demonstrate
need for aid received scholarships/grants; average award was $3,700. No-
need awards available for academics, athletics, leadership, music/drama,
state/district residency.
Scholarships offered: 422 full-time freshmen received athletic scholarships;
average amount $6,500.

FINANCIAL AID PROCEDURES
Forms required: FAFSA, state aid form.
Dates and Deadlines: Priority date 4/1; closing date 12/31. Applicants notified on a rolling basis starting 4/1; must reply by 8/30 or within 4 week(s) of
notification.
Transfers: No deadline. Applicants notified on a rolling basis starting 4/1;
must reply by 8/31 or within 4 week(s) of notification.

CONTACT
Janifer Morgan, Director of Financial Aid
507 West 10th Street, West Point, GA 31833
(404) 385-1018

Reinhardt University

Waleska, Georgia
www.reinhardt.edu   Federal Code: 001589

4-year private liberal arts and teachers college in rural community, affiliated
with the United Methodist Church.
Enrollment: 1,326 undergrads, 8% part-time. 353 full-time freshmen.
Selectivity: Admits over 75% of applicants.

BASIC COSTS (2016-2017)
Tuition and fees: $21,644.
Per-credit charge: $692.
Room and board: $7,948.

FINANCIAL AID PICTURE
Students with need: Need-based aid available for full-time and part-time students.
Students without need: No-need awards available for academics, art, athletics, music/drama, religious affiliation, state/district residency.

FINANCIAL AID PROCEDURES
Forms required: FAFSA, state aid form.
Dates and Deadlines: Priority date 7/1; no closing date. Applicants notified
on a rolling basis starting 3/1; must reply within 2 week(s) of notification.
Transfers: No deadline.

CONTACT
Angela Harlow, Director of Financial Aid
7300 Reinhardt Circle, Waleska, GA 30183-2981
(770) 720-5667

Savannah College of Art and Design
Savannah, Georgia
www.scad.edu   Federal Code: 015022

4-year private visual arts and performing arts college in small city.
Enrollment: 10,483 undergrads, 16% part-time. 2,210 full-time freshmen.
Selectivity: Admits 50 to 75% of applicants.

BASIC COSTS (2017-2018)
Tuition and fees: $35,190.
Per-credit charge: $782.
Room and board: $13,905.

FINANCIAL AID PICTURE
Students with need: Need-based aid available for full-time and part-time students.

FINANCIAL AID PROCEDURES
Transfers: Transfer students are eligible to apply for academic and portfolio scholarships.

CONTACT
Kim Beveridge, Director of Financial Aid
PO Box 2072, Savannah, GA 31402-2072
(912) 525-5100

Savannah Technical College
Savannah, Georgia
www.savannahtech.edu   Federal Code: 005618

2-year public technical college in large city.
Enrollment: 4,784 undergrads.
Selectivity: Open admission; but selective for some programs.

BASIC COSTS (2016-2017)
Tuition and fees: $3,158; out-of-state residents $5,828.
Per-credit charge: $89; out-of-state residents $178.

FINANCIAL AID PICTURE
Students with need: Need-based aid available for full-time and part-time students.
Students without need: No-need awards available for academics, leadership, minority status, state/district residency.

FINANCIAL AID PROCEDURES
Forms required: FAFSA.
Dates and Deadlines: Applicants notified on a rolling basis.

CONTACT
Faith Anderson, Financial Aid Director
5717 White Bluff Road, Savannah, GA 31401-5521
(912) 443-5776

Shorter University
Rome, Georgia
www.shorter.edu   Federal Code: 001591

4-year private liberal arts college in large town, affiliated with the Southern Baptist Convention.
Enrollment: 1,342 undergrads, 10% part-time. 317 full-time freshmen.
Selectivity: Admits 50 to 75% of applicants.

BASIC COSTS (2016-2017)
Tuition and fees: $21,910.
Room and board: $9,460.
Additional info: Tuition/fee waivers available for adults.

FINANCIAL AID PICTURE
Students with need: Need-based aid available for full-time and part-time students. Work study available nights.
Students without need: No-need awards available for academics, art, athletics, music/drama, religious affiliation, state/district residency.
Additional info: Cost is reduced for all in-state students by state tuition equalization grant program. College matches for out-of-state full-time students.

FINANCIAL AID PROCEDURES
Forms required: FAFSA, state aid form, institutional form.
Dates and Deadlines: Priority date 4/1; no closing date. Applicants notified on a rolling basis starting 3/1; must reply within 2 week(s) of notification.
Transfers: Priority date 4/15; no deadline. Applicants notified on a rolling basis starting 3/31; must reply within 2 week(s) of notification.

CONTACT
Susan Zeird, CFO
315 Shorter Avenue, Rome, GA 30165
(706) 233-7227

South Georgia State College
Douglas, Georgia
www.sgsc.edu   Federal Code: 001592

4-year public liberal arts college in large town.
Enrollment: 2,635 undergrads.

BASIC COSTS (2016-2017)
Tuition and fees: $3,756; out-of-state residents $11,350.
Per-credit charge: $91; out-of-state residents $344.
Room and board: $8,390.

FINANCIAL AID PICTURE
Students with need: Need-based aid available for full-time and part-time students.
Students without need: No-need awards available for academics.

FINANCIAL AID PROCEDURES
Forms required: FAFSA, institutional form.
Dates and Deadlines: Priority date 6/1; no closing date. Applicants notified on a rolling basis starting 7/6; must reply within 2 week(s) of notification.
Transfers: No deadline.

CONTACT
Latoya Curtis, Director of Financial Aid
100 West College Park Drive, Douglas, GA 31533-5098
(912) 260-4282

South University: Savannah
Savannah, Georgia
www.southuniversity.edu   Federal Code: 013039

4-year for-profit university in small city.
Enrollment: 777 undergrads.

FINANCIAL AID PICTURE
Students with need: Need-based aid available for full-time students.

FINANCIAL AID PROCEDURES
Forms required: FAFSA, state aid form.
Dates and Deadlines: Applicants notified on a rolling basis starting 9/1.

CONTACT
Tressa Brush, Director of Financial Aid
709 Mall Boulevard, Savannah, GA 31406
(912) 201-8000

Southeastern Technical College

Vidalia, Georgia
www.southeasterntech.edu   Federal Code: 030665

2-year public technical college in large town.
Enrollment: 1,542 undergrads.
Selectivity: Open admission; but selective for some programs.

BASIC COSTS (2016-2017)
Tuition and fees: $3,318; out-of-state residents $5,988.
Per-credit charge: $89; out-of-state residents $178.

FINANCIAL AID PICTURE
Students with need: Need-based aid available for full-time and part-time students. Work study available nights.
Students without need: No-need awards available for state/district residency.

FINANCIAL AID PROCEDURES
Forms required: FAFSA, state aid form.
Dates and Deadlines: Applicants notified on a rolling basis starting 4/6.

CONTACT
Mitchell Fagler, Executive Director of Student Affairs/Financial Aid
3001 East First Street, Vidalia, GA 30474
(478) 289-2268

Southern Regional Technical College

Thomasville, Georgia
www.southernregional.edu   Federal Code: 005615

2-year public technical college in large town.
Enrollment: 2,337 undergrads, 53% part-time. 299 full-time freshmen.
Selectivity: Open admission; but selective for some programs.

BASIC COSTS (2016-2017)
Tuition and fees: $3,158; out-of-state residents $5,828.
Per-credit charge: $89; out-of-state residents $178.

FINANCIAL AID PICTURE (2015-2016)
Students with need: 98% of average financial aid package awarded as scholarships/grants, 2% awarded as loans/jobs. Need-based aid available for part-time students. Work study available nights.
Students without need: No-need awards available for state/district residency.

FINANCIAL AID PROCEDURES
Forms required: FAFSA.
Dates and Deadlines: Applicants notified on a rolling basis starting 7/1.

CONTACT
Judi Lovvorn, Executive Director of Financial Aid
15689 US Highway 19 North, Thomasville, GA 31792-9960
(229) 217-4163

Spelman College

Atlanta, Georgia
www.spelman.edu   Federal Code: 001594

4-year private liberal arts college for women in very large city.
Enrollment: 2,122 undergrads, 3% part-time. 531 full-time freshmen.
Selectivity: Admits less than 50% of applicants. GED not accepted.

BASIC COSTS (2017-2018)
Tuition and fees: $27,564.
Room and board: $12,795.

FINANCIAL AID PICTURE (2016-2017)
Students with need: Out of 513 full-time freshmen who applied for aid, 458 were judged to have need. Of these, 456 received aid, and 2 had their full need met. Average financial aid package met 33% of need; average scholarship/grant was $12,459; average loan was $3,914. For part-time students, average financial aid package was $10,026.
Students without need: 3 full-time freshmen who did not demonstrate need for aid received scholarships/grants; average award was $42,292. No-need awards available for academics, alumni affiliation, music/drama, state/district residency.

FINANCIAL AID PROCEDURES
Forms required: FAFSA, state aid form.
Dates and Deadlines: Priority date 2/1; no closing date. Applicants notified on a rolling basis starting 2/15; must reply within 2 week(s) of notification.
Transfers: Priority date 2/1; no deadline. Applicants notified on a rolling basis starting 2/15; must reply within 2 week(s) of notification. No special aid for transfer students for the first year.

CONTACT
Lenora Jackson, Associate Vice President, Enrollment Management
350 Spelman Lane SW, Campus Box 277, Atlanta, GA 30314-4395
(404) 681-3643 ext. 5212

Thomas University

Thomasville, Georgia
www.thomasu.edu   Federal Code: 001555

4-year private university and liberal arts college in large town.
Enrollment: 726 undergrads.
Selectivity: Open admission; but selective for some programs.

BASIC COSTS (2016-2017)
Tuition and fees: $16,715.
Per-credit charge: $630.
Room only: $4,800.

FINANCIAL AID PICTURE
Students with need: Need-based aid available for full-time and part-time students.
Students without need: No-need awards available for academics, athletics, leadership, state/district residency.

FINANCIAL AID PROCEDURES
Forms required: FAFSA, state aid form.
Dates and Deadlines: Priority date 5/1; no closing date. Applicants notified on a rolling basis.
Transfers: Student must submit official academic transcripts from all colleges attended. Financial aid received during current academic year from previous school will be verified through the National Student Loan Data System (NSLDS).

CONTACT
Clifton Mitchell, Director of Financial Aid
1501 Millpond Road, Thomasville, GA 31792-7499
(229) 226-1621 ext. 1000

Toccoa Falls College

Toccoa Falls, Georgia
www.tfc.edu   Federal Code: 001596

4-year private Bible and liberal arts college in large town, affiliated with the Christian and Missionary Alliance.
Enrollment: 796 undergrads, 8% part-time. 139 full-time freshmen.
Selectivity: Admits 50 to 75% of applicants.

BASIC COSTS (2016-2017)
Tuition and fees: $21,314.
Per-credit charge: $863.
Room and board: $7,635.

FINANCIAL AID PICTURE (2015-2016)
Students with need: Out of 139 full-time freshmen who applied for aid, 128 were judged to have need. Of these, 128 received aid, and 13 had their full need met. Need-based aid available for part-time students.
Students without need: 9 full-time freshmen who did not demonstrate need for aid received scholarships/grants; average award was $9,066. No-need awards available for academics, state/district residency.

FINANCIAL AID PROCEDURES
Forms required: FAFSA, institutional form.
Dates and Deadlines: Priority date 5/1; closing date 8/1. Applicants notified on a rolling basis starting 3/1; must reply within 2 week(s) of notification.
Transfers: No deadline. Applicants notified on a rolling basis starting 3/1; must reply within 2 week(s) of notification.

CONTACT
Stuart Spires, Director of Student Financial Services
PO Box 899, Toccoa Falls, GA 30598
(706) 886-7299 ext. 5435

Truett McConnell University
Cleveland, Georgia
www.truett.edu
Federal Code: 001597

4-year private university and liberal arts college in small town, affiliated with the Southern Baptist Convention.
Enrollment: 740 undergrads, 6% part-time. 218 full-time freshmen.
Selectivity: Admits over 75% of applicants.

BASIC COSTS (2016-2017)
Tuition and fees: $18,510.
Per-credit charge: $595.
Room and board: $7,220.

FINANCIAL AID PICTURE (2016-2017)
Students with need: Out of 202 full-time freshmen who applied for aid, 181 were judged to have need. Of these, 181 received aid, and 51 had their full need met. Average financial aid package met 71% of need; average scholarship/grant was $12,076; average loan was $4,121. For part-time students, average financial aid package was $5,952.
Students without need: 30 full-time freshmen who did not demonstrate need for aid received scholarships/grants; average award was $6,426. No-need awards available for academics, alumni affiliation, athletics, leadership, minority status, music/drama, religious affiliation, state/district residency.
Scholarships offered: 30 full-time freshmen received athletic scholarships; average amount $6,283.

FINANCIAL AID PROCEDURES
Forms required: FAFSA, state aid form, institutional form.
Dates and Deadlines: Priority date 4/1; no closing date. Applicants notified on a rolling basis starting 1/1; must reply within 2 week(s) of notification.
Transfers: No deadline. Applicants notified on a rolling basis starting 3/1; must reply within 2 week(s) of notification.

CONTACT
Truitt Franklin, Director of Financial Aid
100 Alumni Drive, Cleveland, GA 30528
(800) 226-8621

University of Georgia
Athens, Georgia
www.uga.edu
Federal Code: 001598

4-year public university in small city.
Enrollment: 27,828 undergrads, 6% part-time. 5,401 full-time freshmen.
Selectivity: Admits 50 to 75% of applicants.

BASIC COSTS (2016-2017)
Tuition and fees: $11,634; out-of-state residents $29,844.
Room and board: $9,600.

FINANCIAL AID PICTURE (2016-2017)
Students with need: Out of 4,619 full-time freshmen who applied for aid, 2,569 were judged to have need. Of these, 2,541 received aid, and 727 had their full need met. Average financial aid package met 77% of need; average scholarship/grant was $10,337; average loan was $3,314. For part-time students, average financial aid package was $7,679.
Students without need: 140 full-time freshmen who did not demonstrate need for aid received scholarships/grants; average award was $3,516. No-need awards available for academics, athletics, ROTC, state/district residency.
Scholarships offered: 109 full-time freshmen received athletic scholarships; average amount $19,640.

FINANCIAL AID PROCEDURES
Forms required: FAFSA.
Dates and Deadlines: Priority date 3/1; no closing date. Applicants notified on a rolling basis starting 5/1; must reply within 2 week(s) of notification.

CONTACT
Bonnie Joerschke, Director of Student Financial Aid
Terrell Hall, Athens, GA 30602-1633
(706) 542-6147

University of North Georgia
Dahlonega, Georgia
www.ung.edu
Federal Code: 001585

4-year public university and liberal arts college in large town.
Enrollment: 17,648 undergrads, 29% part-time. 3,664 full-time freshmen.
Selectivity: Admits 50 to 75% of applicants.

BASIC COSTS (2016-2017)
Tuition and fees: $7,228; out-of-state residents $20,770.
Per-credit charge: $179; out-of-state residents $630.
Room and board: $7,812.

FINANCIAL AID PICTURE (2015-2016)
Students with need: Out of 3,334 full-time freshmen who applied for aid, 2,267 were judged to have need. Of these, 2,259 received aid, and 1,402 had their full need met. Average financial aid package met 69% of need; average scholarship/grant was $5,906; average loan was $3,808. For part-time students, average financial aid package was $6,409.
Students without need: 291 full-time freshmen who did not demonstrate need for aid received scholarships/grants; average award was $1,150. No-need awards available for academics, alumni affiliation, art, athletics, leadership, minority status, music/drama, ROTC, state/district residency.
Scholarships offered: 58 full-time freshmen received athletic scholarships; average amount $3,580.

FINANCIAL AID PROCEDURES
Forms required: FAFSA.
Dates and Deadlines: Priority date 2/20; no closing date. Applicants notified on a rolling basis starting 4/1; must reply within 2 week(s) of notification.

CONTACT
Jill Rayner, Director of Financial Aid
82 College Circle, Dahlonega, GA 30597
(706) 864-1412

University of West Georgia
Carrollton, Georgia
www.westga.edu Federal Code: 001601

4-year public university in large town.
Enrollment: 11,155 undergrads, 19% part-time. 2,375 full-time freshmen.
Selectivity: Admits 50 to 75% of applicants.

BASIC COSTS (2016-2017)
Tuition and fees: $7,188; out-of-state residents $20,406.
Per-credit charge: $175; out-of-state residents $615.
Room and board: $10,352.
Additional info: Tuition/fee waivers available for adults, minority students.

FINANCIAL AID PICTURE (2016-2017)
Students with need: Out of 2,296 full-time freshmen who applied for aid, 1,893 were judged to have need. Of these, 1,867 received aid, and 1,113 had their full need met. Average financial aid package met 46% of need; average scholarship/grant was $5,002; average loan was $3,398. For part-time students, average financial aid package was $7,494.
Students without need: 195 full-time freshmen who did not demonstrate need for aid received scholarships/grants; average award was $1,675. No-need awards available for academics, alumni affiliation, art, athletics, job skills, leadership, minority status, music/drama, religious affiliation.
Scholarships offered: 44 full-time freshmen received athletic scholarships; average amount $4,406.

FINANCIAL AID PROCEDURES
Forms required: FAFSA.
Dates and Deadlines: Priority date 4/1; closing date 7/1. Applicants notified on a rolling basis starting 5/1.

CONTACT
Philip Hawkins, Director of Financial Aid
1601 Maple Street, Carrollton, GA 30118
(678) 839-6421

Valdosta State University
Valdosta, Georgia
www.valdosta.edu Federal Code: 1599

4-year public university in small city.
Enrollment: 8,726 undergrads, 18% part-time. 1,358 full-time freshmen.
Selectivity: Admits 50 to 75% of applicants.

BASIC COSTS (2016-2017)
Tuition and fees: $7,342; out-of-state residents $20,560.
Per-credit charge: $175; out-of-state residents $615.
Room and board: $7,840.

FINANCIAL AID PICTURE (2015-2016)
Students with need: Out of 1,320 full-time freshmen who applied for aid, 1,063 were judged to have need. Of these, 1,053 received aid, and 203 had their full need met. Average financial aid package met 97% of need; average scholarship/grant was $6,862; average loan was $3,310. For part-time students, average financial aid package was $13,145.
Students without need: 17 full-time freshmen who did not demonstrate need for aid received scholarships/grants; average award was $2,250. No-need awards available for academics, art, athletics, minority status, music/drama, ROTC, state/district residency.

Scholarships offered: 23 full-time freshmen received athletic scholarships; average amount $5,993.

FINANCIAL AID PROCEDURES
Forms required: FAFSA.
Dates and Deadlines: Applicants notified on a rolling basis starting 5/1.
Transfers: Priority date 1/1; closing date 4/1. Applicants notified on a rolling basis starting 4/15.

CONTACT
Doug Tanner, Director of Financial Aid
1500 North Patterson Street, Valdosta, GA 31698-0170
(229) 333-5935

Wesleyan College
Macon, Georgia
www.wesleyancollege.edu Federal Code: 001600

4-year private nursing and liberal arts college for women in small city, affiliated with the United Methodist Church.
Enrollment: 608 undergrads, 22% part-time. 98 full-time freshmen.
Selectivity: Admits less than 50% of applicants.

BASIC COSTS (2016-2017)
Tuition and fees: $21,750.
Room and board: $9,290.
Additional info: Tuition/fee waivers available for adults.

FINANCIAL AID PICTURE (2016-2017)
Students with need: Out of 94 full-time freshmen who applied for aid, 85 were judged to have need. Of these, 85 received aid, and 16 had their full need met. Average financial aid package met 76% of need; average scholarship/grant was $16,980; average loan was $5,319. For part-time students, average financial aid package was $8,854.
Students without need: 12 full-time freshmen who did not demonstrate need for aid received scholarships/grants; average award was $11,262. No-need awards available for academics, alumni affiliation, art, job skills, leadership, music/drama, religious affiliation, state/district residency.
Scholarships offered: Academic Scholarships; $1,000 up to tuition and standard room/board; based on minimum 1100 SAT (exclusive of Writing) or 25 ACT and 3.75 GPA, or 1200 SAT (exclusive of Writing) or 27 ACT and 3.5 GPA. Leadership Awards and scholarships for music, art, and theater; range from $1,000-$18,500.

FINANCIAL AID PROCEDURES
Forms required: FAFSA, state aid form, institutional form.
Dates and Deadlines: Priority date 3/15; closing date 6/1. Applicants notified on a rolling basis starting 10/1; must reply within 2 week(s) of notification.
Transfers: Priority date 7/15; no deadline. Applicants notified on a rolling basis starting 3/15; must reply within 3 week(s) of notification. Scholarships available based on number of hours and GPA transferred in, with minimum 30 semester or 45 quarter hours and 3.0 GPA required.

CONTACT
Courtney Haynes, Director of Financial Aid
4760 Forsyth Road, Macon, GA 31210-4462
(478) 757-3994

West Georgia Technical College
Waco, Georgia
www.westgatech.edu Federal Code: 005614

2-year public technical college in small city.
Enrollment: 6,744 undergrads.
Selectivity: Open admission; but selective for some programs.

BASIC COSTS (2016-2017)
Tuition and fees: $3,238; out-of-state residents $5,908.
Per-credit charge: $89; out-of-state residents $178.

FINANCIAL AID PICTURE
Students with need: Need-based aid available for full-time and part-time students. Work study available nights.
Students without need: No-need awards available for state/district residency.

FINANCIAL AID PROCEDURES
Forms required: FAFSA, state aid form, institutional form.
Dates and Deadlines: Applicants notified on a rolling basis; must reply within 1 week(s) of notification.
Transfers: Aid must be in order or cash paid at registration for classes.

CONTACT
Anna English, Executive Director of Financial Aid
176 Murphy Campus Boulevard, Waco, GA 30182
(706) 845-4323

Wiregrass Georgia Technical College
Valdosta, Georgia
www.wiregrass.edu   Federal Code: 005256

2-year public technical college in small city.
Enrollment: 826 undergrads, 68% part-time. 55 full-time freshmen.
Selectivity: Open admission; but selective for some programs.

BASIC COSTS (2016-2017)
Tuition and fees: $3,278; out-of-state residents $5,948.
Per-credit charge: $89; out-of-state residents $178.

FINANCIAL AID PICTURE
Students with need: Need-based aid available for full-time and part-time students. Work study available nights.
Students without need: No-need awards available for academics, job skills, state/district residency.

FINANCIAL AID PROCEDURES
Forms required: FAFSA, state aid form, institutional form.
Dates and Deadlines: Applicants notified on a rolling basis starting 6/1.

CONTACT
Shelia Thomas, Financial Aid Director
4089 Val Tech Road, Valdosta, GA 31602
(229) 333-2107

Young Harris College
Young Harris, Georgia
www.yhc.edu   Federal Code: 001604

4-year private liberal arts college in rural community, affiliated with the United Methodist Church.
Enrollment: 1,199 undergrads.

BASIC COSTS (2016-2017)
Tuition and fees: $29,217.
Room and board: $11,576.

FINANCIAL AID PICTURE (2015-2016)
Students with need: 79% of average financial aid package awarded as scholarships/grants, 21% awarded as loans/jobs. Need-based aid available for part-time students. Work study available nights, weekends, and for part-time students.
Students without need: No-need awards available for academics, art, athletics, job skills, leadership, music/drama, state/district residency.

Scholarships offered: Academic Scholarships; $11,000-$14,000; based on index including GPA and SAT/ACT. Additional awards to a percentage of recipients range from $1,000 to full tuition, room and board.

FINANCIAL AID PROCEDURES
Forms required: FAFSA, state aid form.
Dates and Deadlines: Priority date 5/1; no closing date. Applicants notified on a rolling basis starting 2/15; must reply within 2 week(s) of notification.

CONTACT
Linda Adams, Financial Aid Director
PO Box 116, Young Harris, GA 30582-0116
(706) 379-3111

Hawaii

Brigham Young University-Hawaii
Laie, Hawaii
www.byuh.edu   Federal Code: 001606

4-year private university and liberal arts college in small town, affiliated with the Church of Jesus Christ of Latter-day Saints.
Enrollment: 2,681 undergrads.
Selectivity: GED not accepted.

BASIC COSTS (2016-2017)
Tuition and fees: $5,240.
Room and board: $6,050.
Additional info: 100% higher tuition and per-credit-hour charges for students who are not members of The Church of Jesus Christ of Latter-day Saints.

FINANCIAL AID PICTURE
Students with need: Need-based aid available for full-time and part-time students.
Students without need: No-need awards available for academics, art, athletics, leadership, music/drama, state/district residency.

FINANCIAL AID PROCEDURES
Forms required: FAFSA.
Dates and Deadlines: Closing date 3/15. Applicants notified by 5/1; must reply by 8/31.

CONTACT
Michael Tejada, Financial Aid and Student Accounts Manager
55-220 Kulanui Street, #1973, Laie, HI 96762-1294
(808) 675-3539

Chaminade University of Honolulu
Honolulu, Hawaii
www.chaminade.edu   Federal Code: 001605

4-year private university in large city, affiliated with the Roman Catholic Church.
Enrollment: 1,167 undergrads, 2% part-time. 215 full-time freshmen.
Selectivity: Admits over 75% of applicants.

BASIC COSTS (2016-2017)
Tuition and fees: $23,310.
Per-credit charge: $773.
Room and board: $12,690.
Additional info: Nursing tuition: $28,750.

FINANCIAL AID PICTURE (2015-2016)

Students with need: Out of 196 full-time freshmen who applied for aid, 160 were judged to have need. Of these, 160 received aid, and 33 had their full need met. Average financial aid package met 77% of need; average scholarship/grant was $5,138; average loan was $3,249. For part-time students, average financial aid package was $10,856.

Students without need: 51 full-time freshmen who did not demonstrate need for aid received scholarships/grants; average award was $11,378. No-need awards available for academics, athletics, minority status, religious affiliation, ROTC, state/district residency.

Scholarships offered: 9 full-time freshmen received athletic scholarships; average amount $8,306.

FINANCIAL AID PROCEDURES

Forms required: FAFSA.

Dates and Deadlines: Priority date 2/15; no closing date. Must reply within 4 week(s) of notification.

Transfers: No deadline. Applicants notified on a rolling basis.

CONTACT

Amy Takiguchi, Director of Financial Aid
3140 Waialae Avenue, Honolulu, HI 96816
(808) 735-4780

Hawaii Pacific University
Honolulu, Hawaii
www.hpu.edu   Federal Code: 007279

4-year private university and liberal arts college in large city.
Enrollment: 3,384 undergrads, 25% part-time. 465 full-time freshmen.
Selectivity: Admits over 75% of applicants.

BASIC COSTS (2016-2017)
Tuition and fees: $23,440.
Per-credit charge: $775.
Room and board: $13,898.

FINANCIAL AID PICTURE
Students with need: Need-based aid available for full-time and part-time students. Work study available nights, weekends, and for part-time students.
Students without need: No-need awards available for academics, alumni affiliation, athletics, leadership, music/drama, ROTC.

FINANCIAL AID PROCEDURES
Forms required: FAFSA.
Dates and Deadlines: Priority date 3/1; no closing date. Applicants notified on a rolling basis starting 4/1; must reply by 5/1.
Transfers: No deadline. Must reply within 3 week(s) of notification.

CONTACT
James Oshiro, Executive Director of Financial Aid
1 Aloha Tower Drive, Honolulu, HI 96813
(808) 544-0253

University of Hawaii at Hilo
Hilo, Hawaii
www.hilo.hawaii.edu   Federal Code: 001611

4-year public university and liberal arts college in large town.
Enrollment: 3,124 undergrads.

BASIC COSTS (2016-2017)
Tuition and fees: $7,620; out-of-state residents $20,580.
Per-credit charge: $300; out-of-state residents $840.
Room and board: $8,786.

FINANCIAL AID PICTURE
Students with need: Need-based aid available for full-time and part-time students.
Students without need: No-need awards available for academics, art, leadership, music/drama, state/district residency.
Additional info: Hawaii student incentive grants and tuition waivers (merit and need-based) available to Hawaii residents at participating institutions.

FINANCIAL AID PROCEDURES
Forms required: FAFSA.
Dates and Deadlines: Priority date 3/1; no closing date. Applicants notified on a rolling basis starting 3/1; must reply within 3 week(s) of notification.

CONTACT
Lynette Egusa, Director of Financial Aid
200 West Kawili Street, Hilo, HI 96720-4091
(808) 932-7449

University of Hawaii at Manoa
Honolulu, Hawaii
www.manoa.hawaii.edu   Federal Code: 001610

4-year public university in very large city.
Enrollment: 12,767 undergrads, 16% part-time. 1,679 full-time freshmen.
Selectivity: Admits over 75% of applicants.

BASIC COSTS (2016-2017)
Tuition and fees: $11,732; out-of-state residents $33,764.
Per-credit charge: $453; out-of-state residents $1,371.
Room and board: $13,030.
Additional info: Tuition/fee waivers available for minority students.

FINANCIAL AID PICTURE (2015-2016)
Students with need: Out of 1,487 full-time freshmen who applied for aid, 999 were judged to have need. Of these, 982 received aid, and 312 had their full need met. Average financial aid package met 73% of need; average scholarship/grant was $10,562; average loan was $3,639. For part-time students, average financial aid package was $10,051.
Students without need: 362 full-time freshmen who did not demonstrate need for aid received scholarships/grants; average award was $12,885. No-need awards available for academics, alumni affiliation, art, athletics, leadership, music/drama, ROTC, state/district residency.
Scholarships offered: 36 full-time freshmen received athletic scholarships; average amount $26,658.
Additional info: Hawaii student incentive grants and tuition waivers (merit and need-based) available to Hawaii residents at participating institutions.

FINANCIAL AID PROCEDURES
Forms required: FAFSA.
Dates and Deadlines: Priority date 3/1; no closing date. Applicants notified on a rolling basis starting 4/1; must reply by 5/1 or within 4 week(s) of notification.
Transfers: No deadline. Applicants notified on a rolling basis starting 3/15; must reply within 4 week(s) of notification.

CONTACT
Jodie Kuba, Director of Financial Aid
2600 Campus Road, QLCSS 001, Honolulu, HI 96822
(808) 956-7251

University of Hawaii: Hawaii Community College
Hilo, Hawaii
www.hawaii.hawaii.edu   Federal Code: 005258

2-year public community college in small city.
Enrollment: 2,354 undergrads.

Selectivity: Open admission.

BASIC COSTS (2016-2017)
Tuition and fees: $3,840; out-of-state residents $10,260.
Per-credit charge: $126; out-of-state residents $340.

FINANCIAL AID PICTURE
Students with need: Need-based aid available for full-time and part-time students.
Students without need: This college awards aid only to students with need.
Additional info: Hawaii student incentive grants and tuition waivers (merit and need-based) available to Hawaii residents.

FINANCIAL AID PROCEDURES
Forms required: FAFSA.
Dates and Deadlines: Priority date 4/1; no closing date. Applicants notified on a rolling basis starting 2/1; must reply within 2 week(s) of notification.
Transfers: Applicants notified by 2/1; must reply within 2 week(s) of notification. Residents of Guam, Federated States of Micronesia, Palau, Marianas Islands and certain other island nations considered residents for tuition purpose.

CONTACT
Susan Olsen, Financial Aid Officer
1175 Manono Street, Hilo, HI 96720-5096
(808) 934-2712

University of Hawaii: Honolulu Community College
Honolulu, Hawaii
www2.honolulu.hawaii.edu   Federal Code: 001612

2-year public community and technical college in very large city.
Enrollment: 3,261 undergrads.
Selectivity: Open admission; but selective for out-of-state students.

BASIC COSTS (2016-2017)
Tuition and fees: $3,810; out-of-state residents $10,230.
Per-credit charge: $126; out-of-state residents $340.

FINANCIAL AID PICTURE
Students with need: Need-based aid available for full-time and part-time students.
Students without need: No-need awards available for academics, state/district residency.
Additional info: Hawaii student incentive grants and tuition waivers (merit and need-based) available to Hawaii residents at participating institutions.

FINANCIAL AID PROCEDURES
Forms required: FAFSA.
Dates and Deadlines: Priority date 4/1; no closing date. Applicants notified on a rolling basis starting 7/1; must reply within 3 week(s) of notification.

CONTACT
Jannine Oyama, Financial Aid Officer
874 Dillingham Boulevard, Honolulu, HI 96817
(808) 845-9116

University of Hawaii: Kapiolani Community College
Honolulu, Hawaii
www.kcc.hawaii.edu   Federal Code: 001613

2-year public community college in very large city.
Enrollment: 7,994 undergrads.

Selectivity: Open admission; but selective for some programs.

BASIC COSTS (2016-2017)
Tuition and fees: $3,840; out-of-state residents $10,260.
Per-credit charge: $126; out-of-state residents $340.

FINANCIAL AID PICTURE
Students with need: Need-based aid available for full-time and part-time students.
Students without need: This college awards aid only to students with need.

FINANCIAL AID PROCEDURES
Forms required: FAFSA.
Dates and Deadlines: Priority date 4/1; no closing date. Applicants notified on a rolling basis starting 4/1; must reply within 2 week(s) of notification.
Transfers: No deadline. Applicants notified on a rolling basis.

CONTACT
Jennifer Bradley, Financial Aid Manager
4303 Diamond Head Road, Honolulu, HI 96816-4421
(808) 734-9555

University of Hawaii: Kauai Community College
Lihue, Hawaii
www.kauai.hawaii.edu   Federal Code: 001614

2-year public community college in small city.
Enrollment: 1,045 undergrads.
Selectivity: Open admission; but selective for out-of-state students.

BASIC COSTS (2016-2017)
Tuition and fees: $3,888; out-of-state residents $10,308.
Per-credit charge: $126; out-of-state residents $340.

FINANCIAL AID PICTURE
Students with need: Work study available nights.
Additional info: Hawaii student incentive grants and tuition waivers (merit and need-based) available to Hawaii residents.

FINANCIAL AID PROCEDURES
Forms required: FAFSA, institutional form.
Dates and Deadlines: Priority date 3/1; closing date 5/1. Applicants notified on a rolling basis starting 5/1.
Transfers: Academic transcript evaluation by end of first semester is required.

CONTACT
Jeffrey Anderson, Financial Aid Officer
3-1901 Kaumualii Highway, Lihue, HI 96766-9500
(808) 245-8360

University of Hawaii: Leeward Community College
Pearl City, Hawaii
www.lcc.hawaii.edu   Federal Code: 004549

2-year public community college in large town.
Enrollment: 5,789 undergrads.
Selectivity: Open admission.

BASIC COSTS (2016-2017)
Tuition and fees: $3,840; out-of-state residents $10,260.
Per-credit charge: $126; out-of-state residents $340.

FINANCIAL AID PICTURE

Students with need: Need-based aid available for full-time and part-time students.

Additional info: Leveraging Educational Assistance Partnership (LEAP) funds or tuition waivers available to students with financial need.

FINANCIAL AID PROCEDURES

Forms required: FAFSA.

Dates and Deadlines: Priority date 4/15; no closing date. Applicants notified on a rolling basis starting 6/1; must reply within 2 week(s) of notification.

CONTACT

Gregg Yoshimura, Financial Aid Director
96-045 Ala Ike, Pearl City, HI 96782
(808) 455-0607

University of Hawaii: Maui College

Kahului, Hawaii
www.maui.hawaii.edu

2-year public community college in small city.

Enrollment: 2,825 undergrads, 61% part-time. 330 full-time freshmen.

Selectivity: Open admission; but selective for some programs.

BASIC COSTS (2016-2017)

Tuition and fees: $3,906; out-of-state residents $10,326.

Per-credit charge: $126; out-of-state residents $340.

Additional info: Tuition/fee waivers available for minority students.

FINANCIAL AID PICTURE (2015-2016)

Students with need: 68% of average financial aid package awarded as scholarships/grants, 32% awarded as loans/jobs. Need-based aid available for part-time students. Work study available nights.

FINANCIAL AID PROCEDURES

Forms required: FAFSA, institutional form.

Dates and Deadlines: Closing date 4/1. Applicants notified on a rolling basis starting 6/1; must reply within 4 week(s) of notification.

CONTACT

Jacquelyn Naeole, Financial Aid Director
310 West Kaahumanu Avenue, Kahului, HI 96732-1617
(808) 984-3277

University of Hawaii: West Oahu

Kapolei, Hawaii
www.uhwo.hawaii.edu   Federal Code: 014315

4-year public liberal arts and teachers college in large town.

Enrollment: 2,757 undergrads, 44% part-time. 266 full-time freshmen.

Selectivity: Admits 50 to 75% of applicants.

BASIC COSTS (2016-2017)

Tuition and fees: $7,440; out-of-state residents $20,400.

Per-credit charge: $300; out-of-state residents $840.

FINANCIAL AID PICTURE

Students with need: Need-based aid available for full-time and part-time students.

Students without need: No-need awards available for academics.

FINANCIAL AID PROCEDURES

Forms required: FAFSA.

Dates and Deadlines: Priority date 4/1; no closing date. Applicants notified on a rolling basis starting 4/1; must reply within 2 week(s) of notification.

Transfers: No deadline. Applicants notified by 7/1.

CONTACT

Lester Ishimoto, Financial Aid Officer
91-1001 Farrington Highway, Kapolei, HI 96707
(808) 454-4700

University of Hawaii: Windward Community College

Kaneohe, Hawaii
www.wcc.hawaii.edu   Federal Code: 010390

2-year public community college in small city.

Enrollment: 2,460 undergrads.

Selectivity: Open admission.

BASIC COSTS (2016-2017)

Tuition and fees: $3,820; out-of-state residents $10,240.

Per-credit charge: $126; out-of-state residents $340.

Additional info: Tuition/fee waivers available for minority students.

FINANCIAL AID PICTURE

Students with need: Need-based aid available for full-time and part-time students.

Students without need: No-need awards available for academics.

Additional info: Hawaii student incentive grants and tuition waivers (merit and need-based) available to Hawaii residents.

FINANCIAL AID PROCEDURES

Forms required: FAFSA.

Dates and Deadlines: Priority date 4/1; no closing date. Applicants notified on a rolling basis starting 3/15; must reply within 2 week(s) of notification.

CONTACT

Steven Chigawa, Financial Aid Officer
45-720 Kea'ahala Road, Kaneohe, HI 96744
(808) 235-7449

Idaho

Boise Bible College

Boise, Idaho
www.boisebible.edu   Federal Code: 015783

4-year private Bible college in small city, affiliated with the nondenominational tradition.

Enrollment: 135 undergrads, 10% part-time. 32 full-time freshmen.

BASIC COSTS (2016-2017)

Tuition and fees: $11,750.

Per-credit charge: $375.

Room and board: $3,150.

FINANCIAL AID PICTURE

Students with need: Need-based aid available for full-time and part-time students.

Students without need: No-need awards available for academics, leadership, music/drama, religious affiliation.

FINANCIAL AID PROCEDURES

Forms required: FAFSA, institutional form.

Dates and Deadlines: Priority date 5/1; no closing date. Applicants notified on a rolling basis starting 5/2; must reply by 8/1 or within 2 week(s) of notification.

Transfers: Financial aid and academic transcripts must be on file before federal aid is awarded.

CONTACT
Joyce Anderson, Financial Aid Officer
8695 West Marigold Street, Boise, ID 83714-1220
(208) 376-7731

Boise State University
Boise, Idaho
www.boisestate.edu   Federal Code: 001616

4-year public university in small city.
Enrollment: 16,053 undergrads, 23% part-time. 2,525 full-time freshmen.
Selectivity: Admits over 75% of applicants.

BASIC COSTS (2016-2017)
Tuition and fees: $7,080; out-of-state residents $21,530.
Per-credit charge: $297; out-of-state residents $567.
Room and board: $7,566.

FINANCIAL AID PICTURE (2015-2016)
Students with need: Average financial aid package met 60% of need; average scholarship/grant was $5,626; average loan was $3,456. For part-time students, average financial aid package was $5,121.
Students without need: No-need awards available for academics, alumni affiliation, art, athletics, music/drama.

FINANCIAL AID PROCEDURES
Forms required: FAFSA.
Dates and Deadlines: Priority date 2/15; no closing date. Applicants notified on a rolling basis starting 3/15; must reply by 4/12 or within 4 week(s) of notification.
Transfers: No deadline. Applicants notified on a rolling basis; must reply within 2 week(s) of notification. Financial aid transcripts required from all postsecondary schools attended whether or not financial aid was received.

CONTACT
Diana Fairchild, Director of Financial Aid
1910 University Drive, Boise, ID 83725-1320
(800) 824-7017

Brigham Young University-Idaho
Rexburg, Idaho
www.byui.edu   Federal Code: 001625

4-year private university in large town, affiliated with the Church of Jesus Christ of Latter-day Saints.
Enrollment: 32,042 undergrads, 48% part-time. 3,738 full-time freshmen.
Selectivity: Admits over 75% of applicants.

BASIC COSTS (2016-2017)
Tuition and fees: $3,920.
Per-credit charge: $163.
Room and board: $4,000.

FINANCIAL AID PICTURE
Students with need: Need-based aid available for full-time and part-time students.
Students without need: No-need awards available for academics, alumni affiliation, art, leadership, music/drama.
Additional info: Application deadline for merit scholarships 3/1.

FINANCIAL AID PROCEDURES
Forms required: FAFSA.
Dates and Deadlines: Priority date 5/1; no closing date. Applicants notified on a rolling basis starting 2/1.

CONTACT
Aaron Sanns, Financial Aid and Scholarship Director
120 Kimball Building, Rexburg, ID 83460-1615
(208) 496-1600

Broadview University: Boise
Meridian, Idaho
www.broadviewuniversity.edu   Federal Code: 011166

2-year for-profit career college in large town.
Enrollment: 142 undergrads.
Selectivity: Open admission.

BASIC COSTS (2016-2017)
Additional info: Tuition varies by program. Per-credit-hour charges; $325-$550. Fees vary from $100-$650 per course.

FINANCIAL AID PICTURE
Students with need: Need-based aid available for full-time and part-time students.

FINANCIAL AID PROCEDURES
Forms required: FAFSA, institutional form.
Dates and Deadlines: Applicants notified on a rolling basis starting 7/1; must reply within 2 week(s) of notification.

CONTACT
Cynthianna Hamrick, Director of Financial Aid
2750 East Gala Court, Meridian, ID 83642
(208) 577-2900

College of Idaho
Caldwell, Idaho
www.collegeofidaho.edu   Federal Code: 001617

4-year private liberal arts college in large town.
Enrollment: 953 undergrads, 4% part-time. 235 full-time freshmen.
Selectivity: Admits over 75% of applicants.

BASIC COSTS (2017-2018)
Tuition and fees: $28,755.
Per-credit charge: $1,165.
Room and board: $9,334.
Additional info: Tuition/fee waivers available for adults.

FINANCIAL AID PICTURE (2016-2017)
Students with need: Out of 158 full-time freshmen who applied for aid, 158 were judged to have need. Of these, 158 received aid, and 46 had their full need met. Average financial aid package met 59% of need; average scholarship/grant was $5,445; average loan was $3,401. For part-time students, average financial aid package was $14,170.
Students without need: 57 full-time freshmen who did not demonstrate need for aid received scholarships/grants; average award was $15,745. No-need awards available for academics, alumni affiliation, athletics, job skills, ROTC.
Scholarships offered: 105 full-time freshmen received athletic scholarships; average amount $6,498.

FINANCIAL AID PROCEDURES
Forms required: FAFSA, institutional form.
Dates and Deadlines: Priority date 2/1; no closing date. Applicants notified on a rolling basis starting 12/5.
Transfers: No deadline. Applicants notified on a rolling basis starting 1/31; must reply within 3 week(s) of notification.

CONTACT

Jennifer Worden, Director of Student Financial Aid Services
2112 Cleveland Boulevard, Caldwell, ID 83605-4432
(208) 459-5307

College of Southern Idaho

Twin Falls, Idaho
www.csi.edu   Federal Code: 001619

2-year public community college in large town.
Enrollment: 4,159 undergrads, 50% part-time. 458 full-time freshmen.
Selectivity: Open admission; but selective for some programs.

BASIC COSTS (2016-2017)

Tuition and fees: $3,900; out-of-district residents $5,400; out-of-state residents $8,400.
Per-credit charge: $130; out-of-district residents $180; out-of-state residents $280.
Room and board: $5,590.

FINANCIAL AID PICTURE

Students with need: Need-based aid available for full-time and part-time students.
Additional info: Out-of-state tuition waivers based on GPA and activities.

FINANCIAL AID PROCEDURES

Forms required: FAFSA.
Dates and Deadlines: Priority date 3/1; no closing date. Applicants notified on a rolling basis starting 4/30; must reply within 3 week(s) of notification.

CONTACT

Jennifer Zimmers, Director of Student Financial Aid
Box 1238, Twin Falls, ID 83303-1238
(208) 732-6273

College of Western Idaho

Nampa, Idaho
www.cwidaho.cc   Federal Code: 042118

2-year public community and technical college in large city.
Enrollment: 8,777 undergrads, 67% part-time.
Selectivity: Open admission; but selective for some programs.

BASIC COSTS (2017-2018)

Tuition and fees: $4,170; out-of-district residents $5,170; out-of-state residents $9,180.

FINANCIAL AID PICTURE (2015-2016)

Students with need: 56% of average financial aid package awarded as scholarships/grants, 44% awarded as loans/jobs. Need-based aid available for part-time students. Work study available nights, weekends, and for part-time students.
Students without need: No-need awards available for academics, leadership, minority status.

FINANCIAL AID PROCEDURES

Forms required: FAFSA.
Dates and Deadlines: Priority date 7/15; no closing date. Applicants notified on a rolling basis starting 3/1; must reply within 4 week(s) of notification.
Transfers: No deadline. Applicants notified on a rolling basis starting 3/1; must reply within 4 week(s) of notification.

CONTACT

Nicole McMillin, Director of Financial Aid
MS 3000, Nampa, ID 83653
(208) 562-3000

Eastern Idaho Technical College

Idaho Falls, Idaho
www.eitc.edu   Federal Code: 011133

2-year public technical college in small city.
Enrollment: 559 undergrads, 43% part-time. 676 full-time freshmen.
Selectivity: Open admission; but selective for some programs.

BASIC COSTS (2016-2017)

Tuition and fees: $2,449; out-of-state residents $8,851.
Per-credit charge: $105.5; out-of-state residents $211.
Additional info: Other fees determined based on program and course selection.

FINANCIAL AID PICTURE (2016-2017)

Students with need: 30% of average financial aid package awarded as scholarships/grants, 70% awarded as loans/jobs. Need-based aid available for part-time students.
Students without need: No-need awards available for academics, job skills, state/district residency.

FINANCIAL AID PROCEDURES

Forms required: FAFSA, institutional form.
Dates and Deadlines: Priority date 6/1; no closing date. Applicants notified on a rolling basis starting 6/6.

CONTACT

Shayna Sharp, Director of Financial Aid
1600 South 25th East, Idaho Falls, ID 83404-5788
(208) 535-5374

Idaho State University

Pocatello, Idaho
www.isu.edu   Federal Code: 001620

4-year public university in small city.
Enrollment: 8,314 undergrads, 22% part-time. 1,320 full-time freshmen.
Selectivity: Admits over 75% of applicants.

BASIC COSTS (2016-2017)

Tuition and fees: $6,956; out-of-state residents $21,023.
Per-credit charge: $348; out-of-state residents $576.
Room and board: $6,663.

FINANCIAL AID PICTURE (2015-2016)

Students with need: Out of 1,084 full-time freshmen who applied for aid, 863 were judged to have need. Of these, 850 received aid, and 53 had their full need met. Average financial aid package met 46% of need; average scholarship/grant was $4,955; average loan was $3,067. For part-time students, average financial aid package was $5,339.
Students without need: 159 full-time freshmen who did not demonstrate need for aid received scholarships/grants; average award was $2,324. No-need awards available for academics, alumni affiliation, art, athletics, leadership, minority status, music/drama, ROTC, state/district residency.
Scholarships offered: 50 full-time freshmen received athletic scholarships; average amount $9,749.

FINANCIAL AID PROCEDURES

Forms required: FAFSA.
Dates and Deadlines: Priority date 3/1; no closing date. Applicants notified on a rolling basis starting 4/1.
Transfers: Closing date 3/1. Applicants notified on a rolling basis starting 3/1.

CONTACT

James Martin, Director of Financial Aid
921 South Eighth Stop 8270, Pocatello, ID 83209-8270
(208) 282-2756

Lewis-Clark State College
Lewiston, Idaho
www.lcsc.edu   Federal Code: 001621

4-year public liberal arts and technical college in large town.
Enrollment: 3,038 undergrads, 26% part-time. 503 full-time freshmen.
Selectivity: Admits over 75% of applicants.

BASIC COSTS (2016-2017)
Tuition and fees: $6,120; out-of-state residents $17,620.
Per-credit charge: $272.75.
Room and board: $7,392.

FINANCIAL AID PICTURE (2015-2016)
Students with need: Out of 491 full-time freshmen who applied for aid, 371 were judged to have need. Of these, 369 received aid, and 37 had their full need met. Average financial aid package met 69% of need; average scholarship/grant was $4,275; average loan was $2,856. For part-time students, average financial aid package was $4,685.
Students without need: 93 full-time freshmen who did not demonstrate need for aid received scholarships/grants; average award was $3,603. No-need awards available for academics, alumni affiliation, art, athletics, job skills, leadership, minority status, music/drama, religious affiliation.
Scholarships offered: 18 full-time freshmen received athletic scholarships; average amount $9,380.

FINANCIAL AID PROCEDURES
Forms required: FAFSA.
Dates and Deadlines: Priority date 3/1; closing date 4/1. Applicants notified on a rolling basis starting 4/1; must reply within 2 week(s) of notification.

CONTACT
Laura Hughes, Director of Financial Aid
500 Eighth Avenue, Lewiston, ID 83501-2698
(208) 792-2224

New Saint Andrews College
Moscow, Idaho
www.nsa.edu

4-year private liberal arts college in large town, affiliated with the Christian Church.
Enrollment: 136 undergrads, 10% part-time. 39 full-time freshmen.
Selectivity: Admits over 75% of applicants.

BASIC COSTS (2017-2018)
Tuition and fees: $12,350.
Per-credit charge: $475.

FINANCIAL AID PICTURE (2016-2017)
Students with need: Out of 20 full-time freshmen who applied for aid, 20 were judged to have need. Of these, 20 received aid. Average financial aid package met 27% of need; average scholarship/grant was $4,765.
Students without need: 17 full-time freshmen who did not demonstrate need for aid received scholarships/grants; average award was $2,588. No-need awards available for academics, alumni affiliation.
Additional info: For the 2017/2018 academic year, CSS/Finanical Aid PROFILE will be required with need-based financial aid applications. Students are able to lock in tuition for up to five years with an up-front fee payment.

FINANCIAL AID PROCEDURES
Forms required: institutional form.
Dates and Deadlines: Closing date 3/1. Applicants notified on a rolling basis starting 4/1; must reply within 2 week(s) of notification.
Transfers: Closing date 3/1. Applicants notified on a rolling basis starting 4/1; must reply within 2 week(s) of notification.

CONTACT
Brenda Schlect, Bursar
PO Box 9025, Moscow, ID 83843
(208) 882-1566 ext. 113

North Idaho College
Coeur d'Alene, Idaho
www.nic.edu   Federal Code: 001623

2-year public community college in large town.
Enrollment: 5,779 undergrads.

BASIC COSTS (2016-2017)
Tuition and fees: $4,110; out-of-district residents $5,530; out-of-state residents $10,200.
Room and board: $7,500.
Additional info: Tuition/fee waivers available for minority students.

FINANCIAL AID PICTURE
Students with need: Need-based aid available for full-time and part-time students. Work study available weekends and for part-time students.
Students without need: No-need awards available for academics, art, athletics, leadership, minority status, music/drama, state/district residency.

FINANCIAL AID PROCEDURES
Forms required: FAFSA.
Dates and Deadlines: Priority date 3/15; no closing date. Applicants notified on a rolling basis starting 4/1; must reply within 2 week(s) of notification.

CONTACT
Joe Bekken, Director of Financial Aid
1000 West Garden Avenue, Coeur d'Alene, ID 83814-2199
(208) 769-3368

Northwest Nazarene University
Nampa, Idaho
www.nnu.edu   Federal Code: 001624

4-year private university in small city, affiliated with the Church of the Nazarene.
Enrollment: 1,481 undergrads, 11% part-time. 253 full-time freshmen.
Selectivity: Admits over 75% of applicants.

BASIC COSTS (2017-2018)
Tuition and fees: $29,000.
Per-credit charge: $1,200.
Room and board: $7,000.

FINANCIAL AID PICTURE (2016-2017)
Students with need: Out of 201 full-time freshmen who applied for aid, 173 were judged to have need. Of these, 173 received aid, and 32 had their full need met. Average financial aid package met 79% of need; average scholarship/grant was $19,358; average loan was $7,554. For part-time students, average financial aid package was $8,053.
Students without need: 54 full-time freshmen who did not demonstrate need for aid received scholarships/grants; average award was $13,992. No-need awards available for academics, athletics, leadership, music/drama, religious affiliation, ROTC.
Scholarships offered: 15 full-time freshmen received athletic scholarships; average amount $12,170.

FINANCIAL AID PROCEDURES
Forms required: FAFSA.
Dates and Deadlines: Priority date 1/15; no closing date. Must reply by 5/1.

CONTACT

Ann Crabb, Director of Financial Aid

623 South University Boulevard, Nampa, ID 83686-5897

(208) 467-8422

Stevens-Henager College: Boise

Boise, Idaho

www.stevenshenager.edu   Federal Code: 003674

2-year for-profit technical and career college in small city.

Enrollment: 350 undergrads.

Selectivity: Open admission; but selective for some programs.

FINANCIAL AID PICTURE

Students with need: Need-based aid available for full-time students.

Students without need: This college awards aid only to students with need.

FINANCIAL AID PROCEDURES

Forms required: FAFSA.

CONTACT

Ali Earle, Business Officer

1444 S Entertainment Avenue, Boise, ID 83709

(208) 383-4540 ext. 1804

University of Idaho

Moscow, Idaho

www.uidaho.edu   Federal Code: 001626

4-year public university in large town.

Enrollment: 7,735 undergrads, 6% part-time. 1,684 full-time freshmen.

Selectivity: Admits over 75% of applicants.

BASIC COSTS (2016-2017)

Tuition and fees: $7,232; out-of-state residents $22,040.

Per-credit charge: $302; out-of-state residents $1,042.

Room and board: $8,354.

Additional info: Tuition/fee waivers available for minority students.

FINANCIAL AID PICTURE (2015-2016)

Students with need: Out of 1,422 full-time freshmen who applied for aid, 1,069 were judged to have need. Of these, 1,059 received aid. Average financial aid package met 79% of need; average scholarship/grant was $4,727; average loan was $5,286. For part-time students, average financial aid package was $7,945.

Students without need: 452 full-time freshmen who did not demonstrate need for aid received scholarships/grants; average award was $5,027. No-need awards available for academics, alumni affiliation, art, athletics, leadership, minority status, music/drama, ROTC, state/district residency.

Scholarships offered: 74 full-time freshmen received athletic scholarships; average amount $17,527.

FINANCIAL AID PROCEDURES

Forms required: FAFSA.

Dates and Deadlines: Priority date 12/1; no closing date. Applicants notified on a rolling basis starting 12/20; must reply within 4 week(s) of notification.

Transfers: No deadline. Applicants notified on a rolling basis starting 12/20; must reply within 4 week(s) of notification.

CONTACT

Daniel Davenport, Director Student Financial Aid

875 Perimeter Drive MS 4264, Moscow, ID 83844-4264

(208) 885-6312

Illinois

American Academy of Art

Chicago, Illinois

www.aaart.edu   Federal Code: 001628

4-year private visual arts college in very large city.

Enrollment: 297 undergrads, 27% part-time. 55 full-time freshmen.

Selectivity: Open admission.

BASIC COSTS (2016-2017)

Tuition and fees: $32,100.

FINANCIAL AID PICTURE

Students with need: Work study available nights.

Students without need: No-need awards available for art.

FINANCIAL AID PROCEDURES

Forms required: FAFSA, institutional form.

Dates and Deadlines: Applicants notified on a rolling basis.

Transfers: Financial aid transcript from previously attended college required.

CONTACT

Ione Fitzgerald, Financial Aid Director

332 South Michigan Avenue, Suite 300, Chicago, IL 60604-4302

(312) 461-0600

Augustana College

Rock Island, Illinois

www.augustana.edu   Federal Code: 001633

4-year private liberal arts college in large city, affiliated with the Evangelical Lutheran Church in America.

Enrollment: 2,522 undergrads. 681 full-time freshmen.

Selectivity: Admits 50 to 75% of applicants.

BASIC COSTS (2016-2017)

Tuition and fees: $39,621.

Per-credit charge: $1,700.

Room and board: $10,037.

FINANCIAL AID PICTURE (2015-2016)

Students with need: Out of 645 full-time freshmen who applied for aid, 547 were judged to have need. Of these, 547 received aid, and 137 had their full need met. Average financial aid package met 88% of need; average scholarship/grant was $25,473; average loan was $3,709.

Students without need: 133 full-time freshmen who did not demonstrate need for aid received scholarships/grants; average award was $21,640. No-need awards available for academics, alumni affiliation, art, leadership, music/drama, religious affiliation.

Scholarships offered: Presidential Scholarship: $25,000; 30 ACT or 1260 SAT and rank in the top ten percent of high school class. Dean's Scholarship: $23,000; 25 ACT or 1140 SAT and rank in the top 20 percent of high school class. Founders Scholarship: $21,000; must plan to enroll full-time. Transfer Scholarship: $18,000-$23,000; demonstrated outstanding academic performance in previous college studies.

FINANCIAL AID PROCEDURES

Forms required: FAFSA, institutional form.

Dates and Deadlines: Priority date 2/1; no closing date. Applicants notified on a rolling basis starting 3/1; must reply by 5/1.

Transfers: Priority date 5/1; no deadline. Applicants notified on a rolling basis.

CONTACT
Sue Standley, Director of Financial Assistance
639 38th Street, Rock Island, IL 61201-2296
(309) 794-7207

Aurora University

Aurora, Illinois
www.aurora.edu   Federal Code: 001634

4-year private university in large city.
Enrollment: 3,784 undergrads, 13% part-time. 652 full-time freshmen.
Selectivity: Admits over 75% of applicants.

BASIC COSTS (2017-2018)
Tuition and fees: $23,520.
Per-credit charge: $670.
Room and board: $11,470.
Additional info: Tuition/fee waivers available for adults.

FINANCIAL AID PICTURE (2016-2017)
Students with need: Out of 652 full-time freshmen who applied for aid, 558 were judged to have need. Of these, 558 received aid, and 62 had their full need met. Average financial aid package met 81% of need; average scholarship/grant was $17,131; average loan was $2,707. For part-time students, average financial aid package was $7,026.
Students without need: 93 full-time freshmen who did not demonstrate need for aid received scholarships/grants; average award was $11,637. No-need awards available for academics, alumni affiliation, art, music/drama, religious affiliation, ROTC, state/district residency.
Scholarships offered: Board of Trustees scholarships: $14,000. Presidential Scholarships: $13,000. Dean's Scholarships: $12,000. Opportunity Grants: $9,000. Promise Grant: $3,000.
Additional info: Undocumented students may be considered for limited institutional financial aid based on an internal financial aid document.

FINANCIAL AID PROCEDURES
Forms required: FAFSA.
Dates and Deadlines: Priority date 1/1; no closing date. Applicants notified on a rolling basis starting 3/1.
Transfers: No deadline. Applicants notified on a rolling basis; must reply by 5/1 or within 3 week(s) of notification.

CONTACT
Heather Granart, Dean of Student Financial Services
347 South Gladstone Avenue, Aurora, IL 60506-4892
(630) 844-6190

Benedictine University

Lisle, Illinois
www.ben.edu   Federal Code: 001767

4-year private university and liberal arts college in large town, affiliated with the Roman Catholic Church.
Enrollment: 3,132 undergrads, 14% part-time. 552 full-time freshmen.
Selectivity: Admits 50 to 75% of applicants.

BASIC COSTS (2017-2018)
Tuition and fees: $33,900.
Per-credit charge: $1,030.
Room and board: $9,200.
Additional info: Tuition/fee waivers available for adults.

FINANCIAL AID PICTURE (2016-2017)
Students with need: Out of 511 full-time freshmen who applied for aid, 469 were judged to have need. Of these, 469 received aid. For part-time students, average financial aid package was $7,391.

Students without need: 53 full-time freshmen who did not demonstrate need for aid received scholarships/grants; average award was $12,278. No-need awards available for academics, alumni affiliation, athletics, leadership, music/drama, ROTC, state/district residency.

FINANCIAL AID PROCEDURES
Forms required: FAFSA.
Dates and Deadlines: Priority date 2/1; no closing date. Applicants notified on a rolling basis starting 11/1; must reply within 2 week(s) of notification.
Transfers: No deadline. Applicants notified on a rolling basis starting 3/15; must reply within 2 week(s) of notification.

CONTACT
Diane Battistella, Senior Associate Dean
5700 College Road, Lisle, IL 60532
(630) 829-6100

Benedictine University at Springfield

Springfield, Illinois
www.ben.edu/springfield   Federal Code: 001761

2-year private branch campus college in small city, affiliated with the Roman Catholic Church.
Enrollment: 771 undergrads.

BASIC COSTS (2016-2017)
Tuition and fees: $32,170.
Per-credit charge: $1,030.
Room and board: $8,930.

FINANCIAL AID PICTURE
Students with need: Need-based aid available for full-time and part-time students. Work study available nights, weekends, and for part-time students.
Students without need: No-need awards available for academics, art, athletics, leadership, religious affiliation.

FINANCIAL AID PROCEDURES
Forms required: FAFSA.
Dates and Deadlines: Priority date 4/15; no closing date. Applicants notified on a rolling basis starting 4/15; must reply within 2 week(s) of notification.

CONTACT
1500 North Fifth Street, Springfield, IL 62702-2694
(217) 525-1420

Black Hawk College

Moline, Illinois
www.bhc.edu   Federal Code: 001638

2-year public community college in large town.
Enrollment: 3,397 undergrads, 47% part-time. 703 full-time freshmen.
Selectivity: Open admission; but selective for some programs.

BASIC COSTS (2016-2017)
Tuition and fees: $4,410; out-of-district residents $7,500; out-of-state residents $7,650.
Per-credit charge: $147; out-of-district residents $250; out-of-state residents $255.
Additional info: Tuition for five contiguous counties is $180 per credit hour. Online courses are $147 per credit hour.

FINANCIAL AID PICTURE (2015-2016)
Students with need: Out of 459 full-time freshmen who applied for aid, 318 were judged to have need. Of these, 302 received aid, and 51 had their full need met. Average financial aid package met 72% of need; average scholarship/grant was $2,263; average loan was $1,595. For part-time students, average financial aid package was $1,598.

Students without need: 22 full-time freshmen who did not demonstrate need for aid received scholarships/grants; average award was $1,747. No-need awards available for academics, art, athletics, leadership, music/drama, state/district residency.

Scholarships offered: Merit: Scholarship program; based on need and/or merit. Tuition awards; awarded to students who graduate in the top 10% of their class. **Athletic:** 36 full-time freshmen received athletic scholarships; average amount $2,276.

Additional info: 5/15 deadline for scholarships.

FINANCIAL AID PROCEDURES

Forms required: FAFSA.

Dates and Deadlines: Priority date 5/15; no closing date. Applicants notified on a rolling basis starting 5/1.

Transfers: No deadline. Applicants notified on a rolling basis.

CONTACT

Joanna Dye, Director, Financial Aid
6600-34th Avenue, Moline, IL 61265-5899
(309) 796-5400

Blackburn College
Carlinville, Illinois
www.blackburn.edu   Federal Code: 001639

4-year private liberal arts college in small town, affiliated with the Presbyterian Church (USA).

Enrollment: 588 undergrads, 3% part-time. 169 full-time freshmen.

Selectivity: Admits 50 to 75% of applicants.

BASIC COSTS (2016-2017)

Tuition and fees: $21,162.

Per-credit charge: $692.

Room and board: $7,364.

FINANCIAL AID PICTURE

Students with need: Need-based aid available for full-time and part-time students. Work study available nights, weekends, and for part-time students.

Students without need: No-need awards available for academics, state/district residency.

Additional info: Each resident student works 160 hours per semester.

FINANCIAL AID PROCEDURES

Forms required: FAFSA.

Dates and Deadlines: Priority date 3/1; no closing date. Applicants notified on a rolling basis starting 3/1; must reply within 4 week(s) of notification.

Transfers: No deadline. Applicants notified on a rolling basis; must reply within 4 week(s) of notification.

CONTACT

Jane Kelsey, Director of Financial Aid
700 College Avenue, Carlinville, IL 62626
(217) 854-5774

Blessing-Rieman College of Nursing & Health Sciences
Quincy, Illinois
www.brcn.edu   Federal Code: 006214

4-year private health science and nursing college in large town.

Enrollment: 255 undergrads, 11% part-time.

Selectivity: Admits less than 50% of applicants.

BASIC COSTS (2016-2017)

Tuition and fees: $22,900.

Per-credit charge: $763.

FINANCIAL AID PICTURE (2015-2016)

Students with need: 54% of average financial aid package awarded as scholarships/grants, 46% awarded as loans/jobs. Need-based aid available for part-time students.

Students without need: No-need awards available for academics, alumni affiliation, leadership, state/district residency.

Additional info: Financial aid for freshmen and sophomores administered by Culver-Stockton College and Quincy University. Institution does not have first time, full-time students, only junior and senior students.

FINANCIAL AID PROCEDURES

Forms required: FAFSA.

Dates and Deadlines: Priority date 3/1; closing date 4/1.

Transfers: Applicants notified on a rolling basis starting 12/15.

CONTACT

Erin McHargue, Financial Aid Coordinator
PO Box 7005, Quincy, IL 62305-7005
(217) 228-5520 ext. 6993

Bradley University
Peoria, Illinois
www.bradley.edu   Federal Code: 001641

4-year private university in large city.

Enrollment: 4,464 undergrads, 4% part-time. 929 full-time freshmen.

Selectivity: Admits 50 to 75% of applicants.

BASIC COSTS (2016-2017)

Tuition and fees: $32,120.

Per-credit charge: $850.

Room and board: $10,010.

FINANCIAL AID PICTURE (2015-2016)

Students with need: Out of 836 full-time freshmen who applied for aid, 675 were judged to have need. Of these, 674 received aid, and 121 had their full need met. Average financial aid package met 70% of need; average scholarship/grant was $17,808; average loan was $4,554. Need-based aid available for part-time students.

Students without need: 128 full-time freshmen who did not demonstrate need for aid received scholarships/grants; average award was $11,598. No-need awards available for academics, alumni affiliation, art, athletics, leadership, music/drama.

Scholarships offered: 40 full-time freshmen received athletic scholarships; average amount $20,001.

FINANCIAL AID PROCEDURES

Forms required: FAFSA.

Dates and Deadlines: Priority date 2/1; no closing date. Applicants notified on a rolling basis starting 3/1; must reply by 5/1 or within 2 week(s) of notification.

Transfers: Priority date 3/1; no deadline. Applicants notified on a rolling basis starting 3/1; must reply by 5/1 or within 2 week(s) of notification.

CONTACT

Debra Jackson, Director of Financial Assistance
1501 West Bradley Avenue, Peoria, IL 61625
(309) 677-3089

Carl Sandburg College
Galesburg, Illinois
www.sandburg.edu   Federal Code: 007265

2-year public community college in large town.

Enrollment: 1,467 undergrads.

Selectivity: Open admission; but selective for some programs.

BASIC COSTS (2016-2017)

Tuition and fees: $4,800; out-of-district residents $7,230; out-of-state residents $7,950.

Per-credit charge: $155; out-of-district residents $236; out-of-state residents $260.

FINANCIAL AID PICTURE

Students with need: Need-based aid available for full-time students.

Students without need: No-need awards available for academics, art, athletics, music/drama.

FINANCIAL AID PROCEDURES

Forms required: FAFSA, institutional form.

Dates and Deadlines: Priority date 5/1; no closing date. Applicants notified on a rolling basis starting 5/1; must reply by 8/25 or within 2 week(s) of notification.

Transfers: Must reply by 8/25. Tuition guarantee provides no increase in tuition up to three years as long as enrolled full-time.

CONTACT

Lisa Hanson, Director of Financial Aid

2400 Tom L. Wilson Boulevard, Galesburg, IL 61401

(309) 341-5283

City Colleges of Chicago: Harold Washington College

Chicago, Illinois

www.ccc.edu

2-year public community college in very large city.

Enrollment: 7,943 undergrads.

Selectivity: Open admission; but selective for some programs.

BASIC COSTS (2016-2017)

Tuition and fees: $3,506; out-of-district residents $9,206; out-of-state residents $11,906.

FINANCIAL AID PICTURE

Students with need: Need-based aid available for full-time and part-time students. Work study available nights.

Students without need: This college awards aid only to students with need.

FINANCIAL AID PROCEDURES

Forms required: FAFSA.

Dates and Deadlines: Applicants notified on a rolling basis.

CONTACT

Elina Fonseca, Financial Aid Director

30 East Lake Street, Chicago, IL 60601

(312) 553-6041

City Colleges of Chicago: Harry S. Truman College

Chicago, Illinois

www.ccc.edu

2-year public community college in very large city.

Enrollment: 4,135 undergrads.

Selectivity: Open admission; but selective for some programs.

BASIC COSTS (2016-2017)

Tuition and fees: $3,506; out-of-district residents $9,206; out-of-state residents $11,906.

FINANCIAL AID PICTURE

Students with need: Need-based aid available for full-time and part-time students. Work study available nights, weekends, and for part-time students.

Students without need: This college awards aid only to students with need.

FINANCIAL AID PROCEDURES

Forms required: FAFSA.

Dates and Deadlines: Applicants notified on a rolling basis.

CONTACT

Robert Evans, Financial Aid Director

1145 West Wilson Avenue, Chicago, IL 60640

(773) 907-4810

City Colleges of Chicago: Kennedy-King College

Chicago, Illinois

www.ccc.edu

2-year public community college in very large city.

Enrollment: 2,821 undergrads.

Selectivity: Open admission.

BASIC COSTS (2016-2017)

Tuition and fees: $3,506; out-of-district residents $9,206; out-of-state residents $11,906.

FINANCIAL AID PICTURE

Students with need: Need-based aid available for full-time and part-time students.

Students without need: This college awards aid only to students with need.

FINANCIAL AID PROCEDURES

Forms required: FAFSA.

Dates and Deadlines: Applicants notified on a rolling basis; must reply within 2 week(s) of notification.

CONTACT

Tabitha O'Neil, Financial Aid Director

6301 South Halsted Street, Chicago, IL 60621

(773) 602-5133

City Colleges of Chicago: Malcolm X College

Chicago, Illinois

www.ccc.edu

2-year public community college in very large city.

Enrollment: 4,027 undergrads.

Selectivity: Open admission; but selective for some programs.

BASIC COSTS (2016-2017)

Tuition and fees: $3,506; out-of-district residents $9,206; out-of-state residents $11,906.

FINANCIAL AID PICTURE

Students with need: Need-based aid available for full-time and part-time students.

Students without need: This college awards aid only to students with need.

FINANCIAL AID PROCEDURES

Forms required: FAFSA, institutional form.

Dates and Deadlines: Applicants notified on a rolling basis; must reply within 2 week(s) of notification.

CONTACT

Tamika Davenport, Financial Aid Director

1900 West Van Buren Street, Chicago, IL 60612

City Colleges of Chicago: Olive-Harvey College

Chicago, Illinois
www.ccc.edu

2-year public community college in very large city.
Enrollment: 2,149 undergrads.
Selectivity: Open admission; but selective for some programs.

BASIC COSTS (2016-2017)
Tuition and fees: $3,506; out-of-district residents $9,206; out-of-state residents $11,906.

FINANCIAL AID PICTURE
Students with need: Need-based aid available for full-time and part-time students.

FINANCIAL AID PROCEDURES
Forms required: FAFSA.
Dates and Deadlines: Applicants notified on a rolling basis.

CONTACT
Jolander Jeffries, Financial Aid Director
10001 South Woodlawn Avenue, Chicago, IL 60628
(773) 291-6391

City Colleges of Chicago: Richard J. Daley College

Chicago, Illinois
www.ccc.edu

2-year public community college in very large city.
Enrollment: 3,953 undergrads.
Selectivity: Open admission; but selective for some programs.

BASIC COSTS (2016-2017)
Tuition and fees: $3,506; out-of-district residents $9,206; out-of-state residents $11,906.

FINANCIAL AID PICTURE
Students with need: Need-based aid available for full-time students.

FINANCIAL AID PROCEDURES
Forms required: FAFSA.
Dates and Deadlines: Applicants notified on a rolling basis.
Transfers: College work study jobs and Federal Supplemental Educational Opportunity Grant (SEOG) may not be available to transfers.

CONTACT
Loucynda White, Financial Aid Director
7500 South Pulaski Road, Chicago, IL 60652
(773) 838-7581

City Colleges of Chicago: Wilbur Wright College

Chicago, Illinois
www.ccc.edu

2-year public community college in very large city.
Enrollment: 7,691 undergrads.
Selectivity: Open admission.

BASIC COSTS (2016-2017)
Tuition and fees: $3,506; out-of-district residents $9,206; out-of-state residents $11,906.

FINANCIAL AID PICTURE
Students with need: Need-based aid available for full-time and part-time students.

FINANCIAL AID PROCEDURES
Forms required: FAFSA, institutional form.
Dates and Deadlines: Applicants notified on a rolling basis.

CONTACT
Inesha Kelly, Financial Aid Director
4300 North Narragansett Avenue, Chicago, IL 60634-4276
(773) 481-8100

College of DuPage

Glen Ellyn, Illinois
www.cod.edu   Federal Code: 006656

2-year public community college in large town.
Enrollment: 14,442 undergrads, 56% part-time. 2,193 full-time freshmen.
Selectivity: Open admission; but selective for some programs.

BASIC COSTS (2016-2017)
Tuition and fees: $4,050; out-of-district residents $9,660; out-of-state residents $11,760.
Per-credit charge: $135; out-of-district residents $322; out-of-state residents $392.

FINANCIAL AID PICTURE (2015-2016)
Students with need: Out of 1,600 full-time freshmen who applied for aid, 953 were judged to have need. Of these, 856 received aid. For part-time students, average financial aid package was $3,807.
Students without need: 57 full-time freshmen who did not demonstrate need for aid received scholarships/grants; average award was $2,992. No-need awards available for academics, art, leadership, minority status, music/drama, state/district residency.

FINANCIAL AID PROCEDURES
Forms required: FAFSA.
Dates and Deadlines: Priority date 4/30; no closing date. Applicants notified on a rolling basis starting 6/1; must reply within 2 week(s) of notification.
Transfers: No deadline. Applicants notified on a rolling basis; must reply within 2 week(s) of notification. Must have financial aid application on file indicating previous institutions attended.

CONTACT
Janet Pagan-Klehr, Enrollment Manager
425 Fawell Boulevard, Glen Ellyn, IL 60137-6599
(630) 942-2380

College of Lake County

Grayslake, Illinois
www.clcillinois.edu   Federal Code: 007694

2-year public community college in large town.
Enrollment: 11,466 undergrads.
Selectivity: Open admission; but selective for some programs.

BASIC COSTS (2016-2017)
Tuition and fees: $4,050; out-of-district residents $9,360; out-of-state residents $12,390.
Per-credit charge: $112; out-of-district residents $289; out-of-state residents $390.
Additional info: Tuition/fee waivers available for minority students.

FINANCIAL AID PICTURE
Students with need: Need-based aid available for full-time and part-time students. Work study available nights.

Students without need: No-need awards available for academics, alumni affiliation, art, athletics, leadership, minority status, music/drama.

Scholarships offered: Academic Achievement Scholarship: based on GPA and student essay; tuition and fees.

FINANCIAL AID PROCEDURES

Forms required: FAFSA.

Dates and Deadlines: Priority date 6/3; no closing date. Applicants notified on a rolling basis starting 6/15; must reply within 2 week(s) of notification.

CONTACT

Erin Fowles, Director, Financial Aid

19351 West Washington Street, Grayslake, IL 60030-1198

(847) 543-2062

College of Office Technology

Chicago, Illinois

www.cot.edu   Federal Code: 017378

2-year for-profit career college in very large city.

Selectivity: Open admission.

FINANCIAL AID PICTURE

Students with need: Need-based aid available for full-time and part-time students.

Students without need: This college awards aid only to students with need.

FINANCIAL AID PROCEDURES

Forms required: FAFSA.

Dates and Deadlines: Applicants notified on a rolling basis.

CONTACT

Merysol Perez, Financial Aid Director

1520 West Division Street, Chicago, IL 60622-3312

(773) 278-0042

Columbia College Chicago

Chicago, Illinois

www.colum.edu   Federal Code: 001665

4-year private visual arts and performing arts college in very large city.

Enrollment: 7,739 undergrads, 8% part-time. 1,764 full-time freshmen.

Selectivity: Admits over 75% of applicants.

BASIC COSTS (2016-2017)

Tuition and fees: $25,294.

Room and board: $13,298.

FINANCIAL AID PICTURE (2015-2016)

Students with need: Need-based aid available for part-time students.

FINANCIAL AID PROCEDURES

Forms required: FAFSA. Accepted but not required for domestic applicants.

Dates and Deadlines: Applicants notified on a rolling basis starting 11/1.

Transfers: Applicants notified on a rolling basis starting 11/1.

CONTACT

Cynthia Grunden, Assistant VP of Student Financial Services

600 South Michigan Avenue, Chicago, IL 60605-1996

(866) 705-0200

Concordia University Chicago

River Forest, Illinois

www.cuchicago.edu   Federal Code: 001666

4-year private university and liberal arts college in large town, affiliated with the Lutheran Church - Missouri Synod.

Enrollment: 1,458 undergrads, 7% part-time. 350 full-time freshmen.

Selectivity: Admits less than 50% of applicants.

BASIC COSTS (2016-2017)

Tuition and fees: $30,640.

Per-credit charge: $899.

Room and board: $9,172.

FINANCIAL AID PICTURE

Students with need: Need-based aid available for full-time and part-time students. Work study available nights.

Students without need: No-need awards available for academics, alumni affiliation, music/drama, religious affiliation.

Scholarships offered: Presidential Honors: full tuition; selection by essay; 5 per year. Presidential Scholarships: up to $12,000; selection by ACT and GPA. Community Awards: up to $7,000; selection by ACT and GPA. Transfer Honors: up to $10,000; selection by GPA. Music Scholarships: amount varies; selection by audition.

FINANCIAL AID PROCEDURES

Forms required: FAFSA.

Dates and Deadlines: Priority date 2/1; closing date 6/1. Applicants notified on a rolling basis starting 1/24.

Transfers: No deadline. Applicants notified on a rolling basis; must reply within 4 week(s) of notification.

CONTACT

Aida Asencio-Pinto, Director of Financial Aid

7400 Augusta Street, River Forest, IL 60305-1499

(708) 209-3113

Danville Area Community College

Danville, Illinois

www.dacc.edu   Federal Code: 001669

2-year public community college in large town.

Enrollment: 1,668 undergrads, 43% part-time. 353 full-time freshmen.

Selectivity: Open admission.

BASIC COSTS (2016-2017)

Tuition and fees: $4,200; out-of-district residents $7,050; out-of-state residents $7,050.

Per-credit charge: $125; out-of-district residents $220; out-of-state residents $220.

FINANCIAL AID PICTURE (2015-2016)

Students with need: Out of 298 full-time freshmen who applied for aid, 275 were judged to have need. Of these, 275 received aid, and 81 had their full need met. Average financial aid package met 81% of need; average scholarship/grant was $1,200; average loan was $3,500. Need-based aid available for part-time students.

Students without need: 44 full-time freshmen who did not demonstrate need for aid received scholarships/grants; average award was $4,000. No-need awards available for academics, art, athletics, leadership, minority status, music/drama, state/district residency.

Scholarships offered: 27 full-time freshmen received athletic scholarships; average amount $9,000.

FINANCIAL AID PROCEDURES

Forms required: FAFSA, institutional form.

Dates and Deadlines: Priority date 7/1; no closing date. Applicants notified on a rolling basis starting 3/1.

Transfers: No deadline. NSLDS reviewed before aid disbursed.

CONTACT

Janet Ingargiola, Director of Financial Aid

2000 East Main Street, Danville, IL 61832

(217) 443-8891

DePaul University

Chicago, Illinois
www.depaul.edu   Federal Code: 001671

4-year private university in very large city, affiliated with the Roman Catholic Church.
Enrollment: 15,151 undergrads, 13% part-time. 2,453 full-time freshmen.
Selectivity: Admits 50 to 75% of applicants.

BASIC COSTS (2016-2017)
Tuition and fees: $37,020.
Per-credit charge: $600.
Room and board: $14,277.

FINANCIAL AID PICTURE
Students with need: Need-based aid available for full-time and part-time students. Work study available nights, weekends, and for part-time students.
Students without need: No-need awards available for academics, art, athletics, leadership, music/drama, ROTC, state/district residency.

FINANCIAL AID PROCEDURES
Forms required: FAFSA.
Dates and Deadlines: Priority date 3/1; no closing date. Applicants notified on a rolling basis starting 3/15.
Transfers: Priority date 2/28; no deadline. Applicants notified on a rolling basis starting 5/1; must reply by 8/1.

CONTACT
Paula Luff, Director of Financial Aid
1 East Jackson Boulevard Suite 9000, Chicago, IL 60604-2287
(312) 362-8610

DeVry University: Chicago

Chicago, Illinois
www.devry.edu   Federal Code: 010727

4-year for-profit university in very large city.
Enrollment: 1,149 undergrads.

BASIC COSTS (2016-2017)
Tuition and fees: $17,512.
Per-credit charge: $609.

FINANCIAL AID PICTURE
Students with need: Need-based aid available for full-time and part-time students.
Students without need: This college awards aid only to students with need.

FINANCIAL AID PROCEDURES
Forms required: FAFSA.
Dates and Deadlines: Applicants notified on a rolling basis.

CONTACT
Milena Dobrina, Director of Financial Aid
3300 North Campbell Avenue, Chicago, IL 60618-5994
(773) 929-8509

Dominican University

River Forest, Illinois
www.dom.edu   Federal Code: 001750

4-year private university and liberal arts college in large town, affiliated with the Roman Catholic Church.
Enrollment: 2,288 undergrads, 8% part-time. 495 full-time freshmen.
Selectivity: Admits 50 to 75% of applicants.

BASIC COSTS (2017-2018)
Tuition and fees: $32,530.
Per-credit charge: $1,072.
Room and board: $9,942.

FINANCIAL AID PICTURE (2015-2016)
Students with need: Out of 468 full-time freshmen who applied for aid, 444 were judged to have need. Of these, 443 received aid, and 27 had their full need met. Average financial aid package met 72% of need; average scholarship/grant was $20,870; average loan was $3,265. For part-time students, average financial aid package was $8,839.
Students without need: 41 full-time freshmen who did not demonstrate need for aid received scholarships/grants; average award was $9,404. No-need awards available for academics, alumni affiliation, art, minority status, religious affiliation.
Scholarships offered: Presidential Scholarships; $18,000. Dean's Scholarships; $16,000. Founder's Scholarship, $14,000, Achievement Scholarship, $11,000, Recognition Award, $7,000, Opportunity Award, $4,000 . Merit Scholarships; $4,000-$18,000. All based on ACT/SAT, GPA and class rank. Ida Brechtel Scholarships; $10,000; for students majoring in chemistry or biology/chemistry.

FINANCIAL AID PROCEDURES
Forms required: FAFSA.
Dates and Deadlines: Priority date 2/15; no closing date. Applicants notified on a rolling basis starting 11/15; must reply within 2 week(s) of notification.
Transfers: No deadline. Applicants notified on a rolling basis starting 3/15; must reply within 3 week(s) of notification.

CONTACT
Victoria Lamick, Director of Financial Aid
7900 West Division Street, River Forest, IL 60305-1099
(708) 524-6809

East-West University

Chicago, Illinois
www.eastwest.edu   Federal Code: 015310

4-year private university in very large city.
Enrollment: 512 undergrads.
Selectivity: Open admission; but selective for some programs.

BASIC COSTS (2016-2017)
Tuition and fees: $20,820.

FINANCIAL AID PICTURE
Students with need: Need-based aid available for full-time and part-time students.
Students without need: No-need awards available for academics.
Additional info: Foreign students eligible for institutional scholarship.

FINANCIAL AID PROCEDURES
Forms required: FAFSA.
Dates and Deadlines: Closing date 3/31. Applicants notified on a rolling basis starting 1/4; must reply within 4 week(s) of notification.
Transfers: Closing date 4/1.

CONTACT
Cesar Campos, Director of Financial Aid
816 South Michigan Avenue, Chicago, IL 60605-2185
(312) 939-0111

Eastern Illinois University

Charleston, Illinois
www.eiu.edu   Federal Code: 001674

4-year public university in large town.
Enrollment: 5,750 undergrads, 11% part-time. 733 full-time freshmen.

Selectivity: Admits less than 50% of applicants.

BASIC COSTS (2016-2017)
Tuition and fees: $11,580; out-of-state residents $13,740.
Per-credit charge: $289; out-of-state residents $361.
Room and board: $9,546.
Additional info: Tuition at time of enrollment locked for 4 years.

FINANCIAL AID PICTURE (2016-2017)
Students with need: Out of 709 full-time freshmen who applied for aid, 563 were judged to have need. Of these, 560 received aid, and 53 had their full need met. Average financial aid package met 68% of need; average scholarship/grant was $8,743; average loan was $3,731. For part-time students, average financial aid package was $4,020.
Students without need: 78 full-time freshmen who did not demonstrate need for aid received scholarships/grants; average award was $3,222. No-need awards available for academics, art, athletics, leadership, music/drama, ROTC.
Scholarships offered: *Merit:* Commitment to Excellence Scholarship; for entering freshmen who demonstrated high academic achievement based on GPA and ACT; renewable, based on maintaining basic requirements. *Athletic:* 21 full-time freshmen received athletic scholarships; average amount $7,599.

FINANCIAL AID PROCEDURES
Forms required: FAFSA.
Dates and Deadlines: Priority date 3/1; no closing date. Applicants notified on a rolling basis starting 3/1; must reply by 5/1 or within 2 week(s) of notification.

CONTACT
Mandi Starwalt, Senior Associate Director of Financial Aid and Scholarships
600 Lincoln Avenue, Charleston, IL 61920
(217) 581-3713

Elgin Community College
Elgin, Illinois
www.elgin.edu   Federal Code: 001675

2-year public community college in small city.
Enrollment: 8,057 undergrads, 62% part-time. 927 full-time freshmen.
Selectivity: Open admission; but selective for some programs.

BASIC COSTS (2016-2017)
Tuition and fees: $3,762; out-of-district residents $13,032; out-of-state residents $14,952.
Per-credit charge: $125; out-of-district residents $434; out-of-state residents $498.

FINANCIAL AID PICTURE
Students with need: Need-based aid available for full-time and part-time students. Work study available nights, weekends, and for part-time students.
Students without need: No-need awards available for academics, alumni affiliation, art, athletics, job skills, leadership, minority status, music/drama, religious affiliation, ROTC, state/district residency.

FINANCIAL AID PROCEDURES
Forms required: FAFSA, institutional form.
Dates and Deadlines: Priority date 6/1; no closing date. Applicants notified on a rolling basis starting 4/6; must reply within 3 week(s) of notification.

CONTACT
Amy Perrin, Director of Financial Aid & Scholarships
1700 Spartan Drive, Elgin, IL 60123-7193
(847) 214-7520

Elmhurst College
Elmhurst, Illinois
www.elmhurst.edu   Federal Code: 001676

4-year private liberal arts college in large town, affiliated with the United Church of Christ.
Enrollment: 2,763 undergrads, 3% part-time. 477 full-time freshmen.
Selectivity: Admits 50 to 75% of applicants.

BASIC COSTS (2017-2018)
Tuition and fees: $36,295.
Per-credit charge: $1,026.
Room and board: $10,144.

FINANCIAL AID PICTURE (2016-2017)
Students with need: Out of 407 full-time freshmen who applied for aid, 354 were judged to have need. Of these, 354 received aid, and 62 had their full need met. Average financial aid package met 78% of need; average scholarship/grant was $24,218; average loan was $3,429. For part-time students, average financial aid package was $3,175.
Students without need: 92 full-time freshmen who did not demonstrate need for aid received scholarships/grants; average award was $14,008. No-need awards available for academics, alumni affiliation, art, minority status, music/drama, religious affiliation, ROTC, state/district residency.
Scholarships offered: Presidential Scholarship: up to $18,000. Dean's Scholarship: up to $16,000. Founder's Scholarship: up to $12,000. Trustee Scholarship: up to $10,000. Blue & White Award: up to $8,000. Combination test scores and GPA considered.

FINANCIAL AID PROCEDURES
Forms required: FAFSA.
Dates and Deadlines: Priority date 12/1; no closing date. Applicants notified on a rolling basis starting 12/1; must reply within 3 week(s) of notification.
Transfers: No deadline. Applicants notified on a rolling basis; must reply within 3 week(s) of notification.

CONTACT
Ruth Pusich, Director of Student Financial Services
190 South Prospect Avenue, Elmhurst, IL 60126-3296
(630) 617-3075

Eureka College
Eureka, Illinois
www.eureka.edu   Federal Code: 001678

4-year private liberal arts college in small town, affiliated with the Christian Church (Disciples of Christ).
Enrollment: 664 undergrads, 3% part-time. 164 full-time freshmen.
Selectivity: Admits 50 to 75% of applicants.

BASIC COSTS (2017-2018)
Tuition and fees: $25,390.
Per-credit charge: $700.
Room and board: $9,370.
Additional info: Tuition at time of enrollment locked for 4 years.

FINANCIAL AID PICTURE (2015-2016)
Students with need: Out of 157 full-time freshmen who applied for aid, 138 were judged to have need. Of these, 138 received aid, and 20 had their full need met. Average financial aid package met 80% of need; average scholarship/grant was $14,171; average loan was $3,448. For part-time students, average financial aid package was $9,292.
Students without need: 164 full-time freshmen who did not demonstrate need for aid received scholarships/grants; average award was $9,260. No-need awards available for academics, alumni affiliation, art, leadership, music/drama, religious affiliation.

Scholarships offered: Reagan Fellows Program: full tuition; 5 awarded. Sandifer Mentorships: fully paid mentorship anywhere in the world at end of sophomore year; all freshmen eligible. Eureka College Ministry Fellowship: full tuition scholarships; 2 available each year.

FINANCIAL AID PROCEDURES

Forms required: FAFSA.

Dates and Deadlines: Applicants notified on a rolling basis starting 2/1; must reply by 5/1 or within 3 week(s) of notification.

Transfers: No deadline. Applicants notified on a rolling basis; must reply within 2 week(s) of notification.

CONTACT

Erin Bline, Director of Financial Aid

300 East College Avenue, Eureka, IL 61530-1500

(309) 467-6310

Governors State University

University Park, Illinois

www.govst.edu   Federal Code: 009145

4-year public university in large town.

Enrollment: 3,467 undergrads, 45% part-time. 200 full-time freshmen.

Selectivity: Open admission; but selective for some programs.

BASIC COSTS (2016-2017)

Tuition and fees: $10,516; out-of-state residents $18,676.

Per-credit charge: $272; out-of-state residents $544.

Room only: $5,558.

Additional info: Board plans are declining balance, so lower and higher balances are available and can be changed at any time. Tuition at time of enrollment locked for 4 years.

FINANCIAL AID PICTURE

Students with need: Need-based aid available for full-time and part-time students. Work study available nights, weekends, and for part-time students.

Students without need: No-need awards available for academics, athletics.

Scholarships offered: The university offers merit scholarships for freshmen and dual degree program students.

FINANCIAL AID PROCEDURES

Forms required: FAFSA.

Dates and Deadlines: Priority date 5/1; closing date 10/1. Applicants notified on a rolling basis starting 3/1; must reply within 2 week(s) of notification.

Transfers: No deadline. Applicants notified on a rolling basis starting 3/1; must reply within 2 week(s) of notification.

CONTACT

John Perry, Financial Aid Director

One University Parkway, University Park, IL 60484

(708) 534-4480 ext. 4480

Greenville College

Greenville, Illinois

www.greenville.edu   Federal Code: 001684

4-year private liberal arts college in small town, affiliated with the Free Methodist Church of North America.

Enrollment: 961 undergrads, 5% part-time. 265 full-time freshmen.

Selectivity: Admits 50 to 75% of applicants.

BASIC COSTS (2017-2018)

Tuition and fees: $26,356.

Room and board: $8,922.

FINANCIAL AID PICTURE (2015-2016)

Students with need: Out of 247 full-time freshmen who applied for aid, 220 were judged to have need. Of these, 220 received aid, and 32 had their

full need met. Average financial aid package met 77% of need; average scholarship/grant was $18,029; average loan was $3,260. For part-time students, average financial aid package was $7,408.

Students without need: 45 full-time freshmen who did not demonstrate need for aid received scholarships/grants; average award was $10,398. No-need awards available for academics, alumni affiliation, art, minority status, religious affiliation.

Scholarships offered: McAllaster Honors Scholarship; $12,000; 3.5 GPA and 27 ACT/1210 SAT. President's Scholarships; $9,000; 3.0 GPA, 27 ACT/1210 SAT, and leadership qualities. Dean's Scholarship; $8,000; 3.0 GPA, 22 ACT/ 1020 SAT and leadership qualities. Character & Service Scholarship; $500- $5,000, 2.5 GPA.

FINANCIAL AID PROCEDURES

Forms required: FAFSA.

Dates and Deadlines: Priority date 11/1; no closing date. Applicants notified on a rolling basis starting 11/1.

Transfers: No deadline. Applicants notified on a rolling basis; must reply within 3 week(s) of notification.

CONTACT

David Kessinger, Director of Financial Aid

315 East College Avenue, Greenville, IL 62246

(618) 664-7108

Harper College

Palatine, Illinois

www.harpercollege.edu   Federal Code: 003961

2-year public community college in small city.

Enrollment: 10,172 undergrads, 54% part-time. 1,255 full-time freshmen.

Selectivity: Open admission; but selective for some programs.

BASIC COSTS (2016-2017)

Tuition and fees: $4,113; out-of-district residents $11,825; out-of-state residents $14,090.

Per-credit charge: $119.25; out-of-district residents $376.25; out-of-state residents $451.75.

FINANCIAL AID PICTURE (2015-2016)

Students with need: Out of 1,028 full-time freshmen who applied for aid, 798 were judged to have need. Of these, 627 received aid, and 25 had their full need met. Average financial aid package met 46% of need; average scholarship/grant was $5,090; average loan was $2,606. For part-time students, average financial aid package was $3,216.

Students without need: 38 full-time freshmen who did not demonstrate need for aid received scholarships/grants; average award was $2,728.

FINANCIAL AID PROCEDURES

Forms required: FAFSA, institutional form.

CONTACT

Laura McGee, Director, Scholarships and Financial Assistance

1200 West Algonquin Road, Palatine, IL 60067-7398

(847) 925-6248

Heartland Community College

Normal, Illinois

www.heartland.edu   Federal Code: 030838

2-year public community college in small city.

Enrollment: 3,649 undergrads, 45% part-time. 591 full-time freshmen.

Selectivity: Open admission; but selective for some programs.

BASIC COSTS (2016-2017)

Tuition and fees: $4,320; out-of-district residents $8,370; out-of-state residents $12,420.

Per-credit charge: $135; out-of-district residents $270; out-of-state residents $405.

Additional info: Tuition/fee waivers available for unemployed or children of unemployed.

FINANCIAL AID PICTURE (2015-2016)
Students with need: 61% of average financial aid package awarded as scholarships/grants, 39% awarded as loans/jobs. Need-based aid available for part-time students. Work study available nights, weekends, and for part-time students.

Students without need: No-need awards available for academics, alumni affiliation, athletics, job skills, leadership, minority status, state/district residency.

FINANCIAL AID PROCEDURES
Forms required: FAFSA, institutional form.

Dates and Deadlines: Priority date 12/1; no closing date. Applicants notified on a rolling basis starting 5/15; must reply within 2 week(s) of notification.

Transfers: Priority date 7/1; closing date 8/1. Applicants notified on a rolling basis starting 4/1; must reply within 4 week(s) of notification.

CONTACT
Todd Burns, Director of Financial Aid
1500 West Raab Road, Normal, IL 61761
(309) 268-8020

Highland Community College
Freeport, Illinois
www.highland.edu   Federal Code: 001681

2-year public community college in large town.

Enrollment: 1,473 undergrads, 44% part-time. 337 full-time freshmen.

Selectivity: Open admission; but selective for some programs.

BASIC COSTS (2016-2017)
Tuition and fees: $4,590; out-of-district residents $7,080; out-of-state residents $7,200.

Per-credit charge: $129; out-of-district residents $212; out-of-state residents $216.

FINANCIAL AID PICTURE (2015-2016)
Students with need: Out of 291 full-time freshmen who applied for aid, 237 were judged to have need. Of these, 221 received aid. Average financial aid package met 18% of need; average scholarship/grant was $4,947; average loan was $2,559. For part-time students, average financial aid package was $2,904.

Students without need: 27 full-time freshmen who did not demonstrate need for aid received scholarships/grants; average award was $3,370. No-need awards available for academics, athletics.

Scholarships offered: 4 full-time freshmen received athletic scholarships; average amount $556.

FINANCIAL AID PROCEDURES
Forms required: FAFSA, institutional form.

Dates and Deadlines: Applicants notified on a rolling basis starting 8/1.

Transfers: No deadline. Applicants notified on a rolling basis starting 4/1.

CONTACT
Kathy Bangasser, Director of Financial Aid
2998 West Pearl City Road, Freeport, IL 61032-9341
(815) 599-3559

Illinois Central College
East Peoria, Illinois
www.icc.edu   Federal Code: 006753

2-year public community college in large town.

Enrollment: 7,211 undergrads, 57% part-time. 591 full-time freshmen.

Selectivity: Open admission; but selective for some programs.

BASIC COSTS (2016-2017)
Tuition and fees: $4,200; out-of-district residents $9,000; out-of-state residents $10,500.

Per-credit charge: $140; out-of-district residents $300; out-of-state residents $350.

FINANCIAL AID PICTURE
Students with need: Need-based aid available for full-time and part-time students.

Students without need: No-need awards available for academics, athletics, minority status, music/drama, state/district residency.

FINANCIAL AID PROCEDURES
Forms required: FAFSA.

Dates and Deadlines: Priority date 6/1; no closing date. Applicants notified on a rolling basis starting 5/1; must reply within 2 week(s) of notification.

CONTACT
Beth McClain, Dean of Enrollment Management
1 College Drive, East Peoria, IL 61635-0001
(309) 694-5311

Illinois College
Jacksonville, Illinois
www.ic.edu   Federal Code: 001688

4-year private liberal arts college in large town, affiliated with the Presbyterian Church (USA).

Enrollment: 952 undergrads. 240 full-time freshmen.

Selectivity: Admits 50 to 75% of applicants.

BASIC COSTS (2017-2018)
Tuition and fees: $32,140.

Room and board: $9,190.

FINANCIAL AID PICTURE (2015-2016)
Students with need: Out of 220 full-time freshmen who applied for aid, 206 were judged to have need. Of these, 206 received aid, and 31 had their full need met. Average financial aid package met 88% of need; average scholarship/grant was $24,615; average loan was $4,641. For part-time students, average financial aid package was $13,937.

Students without need: 34 full-time freshmen who did not demonstrate need for aid received scholarships/grants; average award was $19,913. No-need awards available for academics, art, music/drama.

Scholarships offered: College transfer scholarship; available with 12 transferable credit hours and minimum 3.0 GPA.

FINANCIAL AID PROCEDURES
Forms required: FAFSA.

Dates and Deadlines: Priority date 1/31; no closing date. Applicants notified on a rolling basis starting 2/15; must reply within 2 week(s) of notification.

Transfers: No deadline. Applicants notified on a rolling basis starting 6/1; must reply within 2 week(s) of notification.

CONTACT
Katherine Taylor, Director of Financial Aid
1101 West College Avenue, Jacksonville, IL 62650
(217) 245-3035

Illinois Eastern Community Colleges: Frontier Community College
Fairfield, Illinois
www.iecc.edu/fcc   Federal Code: 014090

2-year public community college in small town.

Enrollment: 364 undergrads, 29% part-time. 100 full-time freshmen.

Selectivity: Open admission; but selective for some programs.

BASIC COSTS (2016-2017)

Tuition and fees: $3,250; out-of-district residents $8,812; out-of-state residents $10,678.

Per-credit charge: $83; out-of-district residents $268; out-of-state residents $331.

FINANCIAL AID PICTURE

Students with need: Need-based aid available for full-time and part-time students.

Students without need: No-need awards available for academics, athletics, state/district residency.

FINANCIAL AID PROCEDURES

Forms required: FAFSA, institutional form.

Dates and Deadlines: Applicants notified on a rolling basis starting 8/1; must reply within 2 week(s) of notification.

CONTACT

Lori Noe, Financial Aid Coordinator
Two Frontier Drive, Fairfield, IL 62837-9801
(618) 842-3711

Illinois Eastern Community Colleges: Lincoln Trail College

Robinson, Illinois
www.iecc.edu/ltc
Federal Code: 009786

2-year public community college in small town.

Enrollment: 514 undergrads, 25% part-time. 141 full-time freshmen.

Selectivity: Open admission; but selective for some programs.

BASIC COSTS (2016-2017)

Tuition and fees: $3,250; out-of-district residents $8,812; out-of-state residents $10,678.

Per-credit charge: $83; out-of-district residents $268; out-of-state residents $331.

FINANCIAL AID PICTURE

Students with need: Need-based aid available for full-time and part-time students.

Students without need: No-need awards available for academics, athletics, state/district residency.

FINANCIAL AID PROCEDURES

Forms required: FAFSA, institutional form.

Dates and Deadlines: Applicants notified on a rolling basis starting 8/1; must reply within 2 week(s) of notification.

CONTACT

Barbara Webster, Coordinator of Financial Aid
11220 State Highway 1, Robinson, IL 62454-5707
(618) 544-8657

Illinois Eastern Community Colleges: Olney Central College

Olney, Illinois
www.iecc.edu/occ
Federal Code: 001742

2-year public community college in small town.

Enrollment: 735 undergrads, 35% part-time. 138 full-time freshmen.

Selectivity: Open admission; but selective for some programs.

BASIC COSTS (2016-2017)

Tuition and fees: $3,250; out-of-district residents $8,812; out-of-state residents $10,678.

Per-credit charge: $83; out-of-district residents $268; out-of-state residents $331.

FINANCIAL AID PICTURE

Students with need: Need-based aid available for full-time and part-time students.

Students without need: No-need awards available for academics, athletics, state/district residency.

FINANCIAL AID PROCEDURES

Forms required: FAFSA, institutional form.

Dates and Deadlines: Applicants notified on a rolling basis starting 8/1; must reply within 2 week(s) of notification.

CONTACT

Anrea Puckett, Financial Aid Coordinator
305 North West Street, Olney, IL 62450
(618) 395-7777

Illinois Eastern Community Colleges: Wabash Valley College

Mount Carmel, Illinois
www.iecc.edu/wvc
Federal Code: 001779

2-year public community college in small town.

Enrollment: 636 undergrads, 27% part-time. 147 full-time freshmen.

Selectivity: Open admission; but selective for some programs.

BASIC COSTS (2016-2017)

Tuition and fees: $3,250; out-of-district residents $8,812; out-of-state residents $10,678.

Per-credit charge: $83; out-of-district residents $268; out-of-state residents $331.

FINANCIAL AID PICTURE

Students with need: Need-based aid available for full-time and part-time students.

Students without need: No-need awards available for academics, athletics, state/district residency.

FINANCIAL AID PROCEDURES

Forms required: FAFSA, institutional form.

Dates and Deadlines: Applicants notified on a rolling basis starting 8/1; must reply within 2 week(s) of notification.

CONTACT

Mary Johnson, Financial Aid Coordinator
2200 College Drive, Mount Carmel, IL 62863-2657
(618) 262-8641

Illinois Institute of Art: Chicago

Chicago, Illinois
www.ilic.artinstitutes.edu
Federal Code: 012584

4-year for-profit visual arts college in very large city.

Enrollment: 1,807 undergrads.

FINANCIAL AID PICTURE

Students with need: Need-based aid available for full-time and part-time students.

FINANCIAL AID PROCEDURES

Forms required: FAFSA.

Dates and Deadlines: Priority date 5/1; no closing date. Applicants notified on a rolling basis.

CONTACT

350 North Orleans Street, Chicago, IL 60654

Illinois Institute of Art: Schaumburg
Schaumburg, Illinois
www.artinstitutes.edu/schaumburg Federal Code: 012584

3-year for-profit visual arts and career college in small city.
Enrollment: 902 undergrads.
Selectivity: Open admission.

FINANCIAL AID PICTURE
Students with need: Need-based aid available for full-time and part-time students. Work study available nights, weekends, and for part-time students.
Students without need: No-need awards available for academics, art.
Scholarships offered: Scholarships based on GPA and talent-based scholarships available.

FINANCIAL AID PROCEDURES
Forms required: FAFSA.
Dates and Deadlines: Priority date 3/1; no closing date.
Transfers: No deadline. Applicants notified on a rolling basis.

CONTACT
Walter Thompson, Director of Student Financial Services
1000 North Plaza Drive, Schaumburg, IL 60173
(800) 314-3450

Illinois Institute of Technology
Chicago, Illinois
www.iit.edu   Federal Code: 001691

4-year private university and engineering college in very large city.
Enrollment: 2,800 undergrads, 5% part-time. 479 full-time freshmen.
Selectivity: Admits 50 to 75% of applicants.

BASIC COSTS (2016-2017)
Tuition and fees: $44,884.
Per-credit charge: $1,359.
Room and board: $11,612.

FINANCIAL AID PICTURE (2015-2016)
Students with need: Out of 350 full-time freshmen who applied for aid, 322 were judged to have need. Of these, 322 received aid, and 57 had their full need met. Average financial aid package met 82% of need; average scholarship/grant was $33,676; average loan was $3,861. For part-time students, average financial aid package was $14,127.
Students without need: 156 full-time freshmen who did not demonstrate need for aid received scholarships/grants; average award was $25,552. No-need awards available for academics, alumni affiliation, art, leadership, ROTC.
Scholarships offered: Heald Academic Scholarships; $12,000-$25,000. Camras Scholar Program; full tuition and advanced access to research and leadership development; top 5% of applicant pool. Crown Scholarship; full tuition for five years; first-year full-time architecture student; one offered.

FINANCIAL AID PROCEDURES
Forms required: FAFSA.
Dates and Deadlines: Priority date 12/15; no closing date. Applicants notified on a rolling basis starting 2/15.
Transfers: Priority date 1/15; no deadline. Applicants notified on a rolling basis starting 3/1.

CONTACT
Abigail McGrath, Director of Financial Aid
10 West 33rd Street, Chicago, IL 60616-3793
(312) 567-7219

Illinois State University
Normal, Illinois
www.ilstu.edu   Federal Code: 001692

4-year public university in small city.
Enrollment: 18,571 undergrads, 6% part-time. 3,682 full-time freshmen.
Selectivity: Admits over 75% of applicants.

BASIC COSTS (2016-2017)
Tuition and fees: $14,061; out-of-state residents $25,168.
Per-credit charge: $370.25; out-of-state residents $740.5.
Room and board: $9,948.
Additional info: Tuition at time of enrollment locked for 4 years; tuition/fee waivers available for adults.

FINANCIAL AID PICTURE
Students with need: Need-based aid available for full-time and part-time students. Work study available nights, weekends, and for part-time students.
Students without need: No-need awards available for academics, alumni affiliation, art, athletics, job skills, leadership, minority status, music/drama, ROTC, state/district residency.
Scholarships offered: Various non-need based merit scholarships available, including Presidential Scholars' Program, Provost's Scholarship, and Dean's Scholarship.

FINANCIAL AID PROCEDURES
Forms required: FAFSA.
Dates and Deadlines: Priority date 3/1; no closing date. Applicants notified on a rolling basis starting 4/1; must reply within 2 week(s) of notification.

CONTACT
Jana Albrecht, Director of Financial Aid
Campus Box 2200, Normal, IL 61790-2200
(309) 438-2231

Illinois Valley Community College
Oglesby, Illinois
www.ivcc.edu   Federal Code: 001705

2-year public community college in small town.
Enrollment: 2,517 undergrads, 50% part-time. 189 full-time freshmen.
Selectivity: Open admission; but selective for some programs.

BASIC COSTS (2016-2017)
Tuition and fees: $3,730; out-of-district residents $10,518; out-of-state residents $11,326.
Per-credit charge: $116.6; out-of-district residents $342.86; out-of-state residents $369.79.

FINANCIAL AID PICTURE
Students with need: Need-based aid available for full-time and part-time students. Work study available nights.
Students without need: No-need awards available for academics, art, athletics, leadership, music/drama.
Scholarships offered: Foundation scholarships available.

FINANCIAL AID PROCEDURES
Forms required: FAFSA.
Dates and Deadlines: Priority date 3/1; no closing date. Applicants notified on a rolling basis starting 3/1.

CONTACT
Patty Williamson, Director, Financial Aid
815 North Orlando Smith Avenue, Oglesby, IL 61348-9693
(815) 224-0438

Illinois Wesleyan University

Bloomington, Illinois
www.iwu.edu   Federal Code: 001696

4-year private university and liberal arts college in small city.
Enrollment: 1,763 undergrads. 431 full-time freshmen.
Selectivity: Admits 50 to 75% of applicants.

BASIC COSTS (2017-2018)
Tuition and fees: $45,654.
Per-credit charge: $1,427.
Room and board: $10,574.

FINANCIAL AID PICTURE (2016-2017)
Students with need: Out of 373 full-time freshmen who applied for aid, 289 were judged to have need. Of these, 289 received aid, and 152 had their full need met. Average financial aid package met 89% of need; average scholarship/grant was $28,592; average loan was $4,620.
Students without need: 135 full-time freshmen who did not demonstrate need for aid received scholarships/grants; average award was $21,219. No-need awards available for academics, art, music/drama.
Scholarships offered: Academic scholarships based on high school academic performance, recommendations, testing. Talent awards available in music, art, theater, and musical theater. Limited number of full-tuition awards in music.

FINANCIAL AID PROCEDURES
Forms required: FAFSA, institutional form.
Dates and Deadlines: Priority date 3/1; no closing date. Applicants notified on a rolling basis starting 3/1; must reply by 5/1.
Transfers: No deadline. Applicants notified on a rolling basis; must reply by 5/1 or within 3 week(s) of notification.

CONTACT
Scott Seibring, Director of Financial Aid
PO Box 2900, Bloomington, IL 61702-2900
(309) 556-3096

International Academy of Design and Technology: Chicago

Chicago, Illinois
www.iadtchicago.edu   Federal Code: 021603

4-year for-profit visual arts and technical college in very large city.
Enrollment: 229 undergrads.
Selectivity: Open admission.

FINANCIAL AID PICTURE
Students with need: Need-based aid available for full-time and part-time students.
Students without need: This college awards aid only to students with need.
Additional info: College work study programs available to day and evening students.

FINANCIAL AID PROCEDURES
Forms required: FAFSA.
Dates and Deadlines: Applicants notified on a rolling basis.
Transfers: No deadline. Applicants notified on a rolling basis; must reply within 2 week(s) of notification.

CONTACT
Andrea Watkins, Associate Director of Financial Aid
One North State Street, Suite 500, Chicago, IL 60602
(312) 980-9200 ext. 9251

John A. Logan College

Carterville, Illinois
www.jalc.edu   Federal Code: 008076

2-year public community college in small town.
Enrollment: 2,600 undergrads.
Selectivity: Open admission; but selective for some programs.

BASIC COSTS (2016-2017)
Tuition and fees: $3,420; out-of-district residents $5,070; out-of-state residents $5,640.
Per-credit charge: $109; out-of-district residents $164; out-of-state residents $183.
Additional info: Certificate program costs vary: $1,882-$8,420, books and supplies $167-$3,646.

FINANCIAL AID PICTURE
Students with need: Need-based aid available for full-time and part-time students.
Students without need: This college awards aid only to students with need.

FINANCIAL AID PROCEDURES
Forms required: FAFSA, institutional form.
Dates and Deadlines: Priority date 5/1; no closing date. Applicants notified on a rolling basis starting 5/1.

CONTACT
Sherry Summary, Director for Student Financial Assistance
700 Logan College Road, Carterville, IL 62918
(618) 985-3741 ext. 8308

John Wood Community College

Quincy, Illinois
www.jwcc.edu   Federal Code: 012813

2-year public community college in large town.
Enrollment: 1,440 undergrads.
Selectivity: Open admission; but selective for some programs.

BASIC COSTS (2016-2017)
Tuition and fees: $4,710; out-of-state residents $8,010.
Per-credit charge: $157; out-of-state residents $267.

FINANCIAL AID PICTURE
Students with need: Need-based aid available for full-time and part-time students. Work study available nights, weekends, and for part-time students.
Scholarships offered: Non-need based scholarships and awards are available. Interested students must apply and be selected. Area organizations also have scholarships and awards available.

FINANCIAL AID PROCEDURES
Forms required: FAFSA.
Dates and Deadlines: Applicants notified on a rolling basis starting 3/1.

CONTACT
Melanie Lechtenberg, Director of Financial Aid
1301 South 48th Street, Quincy, IL 62305-8736
(217) 641-4336

Joliet Junior College

Joliet, Illinois
www.jjc.edu   Federal Code: 001699

2-year public community and junior college in small city.
Enrollment: 11,945 undergrads.

Selectivity: Open admission; but selective for some programs and for out-of-state students.

BASIC COSTS (2016-2017)

Tuition and fees: $3,750; out-of-district residents $10,508; out-of-state residents $11,187.

Per-credit charge: $84; out-of-district residents $319; out-of-state residents $341.9.

FINANCIAL AID PICTURE

Students with need: Need-based aid available for full-time and part-time students. Work study available nights, weekends, and for part-time students.

Students without need: No-need awards available for academics.

FINANCIAL AID PROCEDURES

Forms required: FAFSA, institutional form.

Dates and Deadlines: Closing date 6/12. Applicants notified on a rolling basis starting 5/15.

CONTACT

David Seward, Director of Financial Aid

1215 Houbolt Road, Joliet, IL 60431-8938

(815) 729-9020 ext. 2701

Judson University

Elgin, Illinois

www.judsonu.edu   Federal Code: 001700

4-year private university and liberal arts college in small city, affiliated with the American Baptist Churches in the USA.

Enrollment: 1,093 undergrads, 29% part-time. 178 full-time freshmen.

Selectivity: Open admission; but selective for some programs.

BASIC COSTS (2017-2018)

Tuition and fees: $29,434.

Per-credit charge: $1,145.

Room and board: $9,840.

FINANCIAL AID PICTURE (2015-2016)

Students with need: 89% of average financial aid package awarded as scholarships/grants, 11% awarded as loans/jobs. Work study available nights, weekends, and for part-time students.

Students without need: No-need awards available for academics, alumni affiliation, art, athletics, leadership, music/drama, religious affiliation.

Scholarships offered: Trustees' Scholarship: $16,000; based on ACT/SAT and GPA. President's Scholarship: $14,000; based on ACT/SAT and GPA. Dean's Scholarship: $12,000; based on ACT/SAT and GPA. Faculty Scholarship: $10,000; based on ACT/SAT and GPA. University Scholarship: $8,000; based on ACT/SAT and GPA.

FINANCIAL AID PROCEDURES

Forms required: FAFSA.

Dates and Deadlines: Priority date 2/15; closing date 5/1. Applicants notified on a rolling basis starting 3/1; must reply by 5/1 or within 4 week(s) of notification.

Transfers: No deadline. Applicants notified on a rolling basis starting 3/1; must reply by 5/1 or within 4 week(s) of notification.

CONTACT

Diana Winton, Director of Financial Aid

1151 North State Street, Elgin, IL 60123-1404

(847) 628-2530

Kankakee Community College

Kankakee, Illinois

www.kcc.edu   Federal Code: 007690

2-year public community college in large town.

Enrollment: 2,457 undergrads, 58% part-time. 240 full-time freshmen.

Selectivity: Open admission; but selective for some programs.

BASIC COSTS (2016-2017)

Tuition and fees: $4,260; out-of-district residents $9,292; out-of-state residents $20,143.

Per-credit charge: $129; out-of-district residents $297; out-of-state residents $648.

FINANCIAL AID PICTURE

Students with need: Need-based aid available for full-time and part-time students. Work study available nights.

Students without need: No-need awards available for athletics.

FINANCIAL AID PROCEDURES

Forms required: FAFSA.

Dates and Deadlines: Closing date 7/13. Applicants notified on a rolling basis; must reply within 4 week(s) of notification.

Transfers: Applicants notified on a rolling basis; must reply within 4 week(s) of notification.

CONTACT

Deanna Thompson, Director of Financial Aid

100 College Drive, Kankakee, IL 60901-6505

(815) 802-8550

Kaskaskia College

Centralia, Illinois

www.kaskaskia.edu   Federal Code: 001701

2-year public community college in large town.

Enrollment: 1,949 undergrads, 37% part-time. 145 full-time freshmen.

Selectivity: Open admission; but selective for some programs.

BASIC COSTS (2016-2017)

Tuition and fees: $4,470; out-of-district residents $7,530; out-of-state residents $12,330.

Per-credit charge: $133; out-of-district residents $235; out-of-state residents $395.

FINANCIAL AID PICTURE (2016-2017)

Students with need: Out of 114 full-time freshmen who applied for aid, 114 were judged to have need. Of these, 106 received aid. Average financial aid package met 67% of need; average scholarship/grant was $1,092. For part-time students, average financial aid package was $1,585.

Students without need: No-need awards available for academics, athletics, state/district residency.

FINANCIAL AID PROCEDURES

Forms required: FAFSA.

Dates and Deadlines: Priority date 5/15; no closing date. Applicants notified on a rolling basis starting 4/1; must reply within 2 week(s) of notification.

Transfers: No deadline. Applicants notified on a rolling basis.

CONTACT

Jill Klosterman, Director of Financial Aid

27210 College Road, Centralia, IL 62801

(618) 545-3080

Kendall College

Chicago, Illinois

www.kendall.edu   Federal Code: 001703

4-year for-profit culinary school and teachers college in very large city.

Enrollment: 1,516 undergrads.

BASIC COSTS (2016-2017)

Tuition and fees: $25,278.

Per-credit charge: $655.

Room only: $10,500.

Additional info: Tuition and fees quoted are for School of Culinary Arts.

FINANCIAL AID PICTURE

Students with need: Need-based aid available for full-time and part-time students. Work study available nights, weekends, and for part-time students.

Students without need: No-need awards available for academics, alumni affiliation, job skills.

FINANCIAL AID PROCEDURES

Forms required: FAFSA.

Dates and Deadlines: Priority date 4/15; no closing date. Applicants notified on a rolling basis starting 1/1; must reply within 2 week(s) of notification.

Transfers: No deadline. Applicants notified on a rolling basis; must reply within 2 week(s) of notification.

CONTACT

Frank Arce, Director of Financial Aid

900 N. North Branch Street, Chicago, IL 60642-4278

(312) 752-2070

Kishwaukee College

Malta, Illinois

www.kishwaukeecollege.edu   Federal Code: 007684

2-year public community college in rural community.

Enrollment: 4,900 undergrads.

Selectivity: Open admission; but selective for some programs.

BASIC COSTS (2016-2017)

Tuition and fees: $4,230; out-of-district residents $8,100; out-of-state residents $11,970.

Per-credit charge: $129; out-of-district residents $258; out-of-state residents $387.

FINANCIAL AID PICTURE

Students with need: Need-based aid available for full-time and part-time students. Work study available nights, weekends, and for part-time students.

Students without need: No-need awards available for academics, athletics, leadership, music/drama, state/district residency.

FINANCIAL AID PROCEDURES

Forms required: FAFSA, institutional form.

Dates and Deadlines: Priority date 5/1; no closing date. Applicants notified on a rolling basis starting 5/1; must reply within 2 week(s) of notification.

Transfers: Must reply within 2 week(s) of notification. Some state programs not available to sophomore status students.

CONTACT

Pamela Wagener, Director, Financial Aid/Veterans Affairs

21193 Malta Road, Malta, IL 60150-9699

(815) 825-2086 ext. 2240

Knox College

Galesburg, Illinois

www.knox.edu   Federal Code: 001704

4-year private liberal arts college in large town.

Enrollment: 1,334 undergrads, 1% part-time. 347 full-time freshmen.

Selectivity: Admits 50 to 75% of applicants.

BASIC COSTS (2017-2018)

Tuition and fees: $44,958.

Per-credit charge: $5,892.

Room and board: $9,696.

FINANCIAL AID PICTURE (2016-2017)

Students with need: Out of 317 full-time freshmen who applied for aid, 287 were judged to have need. Of these, 287 received aid, and 99 had their full need met. Average financial aid package met 91% of need; average scholarship/grant was $33,547; average loan was $4,899. Need-based aid available for part-time students.

Students without need: 58 full-time freshmen who did not demonstrate need for aid received scholarships/grants; average award was $20,991. No-need awards available for academics, art, leadership, music/drama.

Scholarships offered: Scholarships awarded based on academic achievement, visual and performing arts, writing, service and leadership, and math.

FINANCIAL AID PROCEDURES

Forms required: FAFSA, institutional form.

Dates and Deadlines: Priority date 11/1; no closing date. Applicants notified on a rolling basis starting 12/1; must reply by 5/1.

Transfers: Priority date 11/1. Applicants notified on a rolling basis starting 1/15; must reply by 6/1.

CONTACT

Ann Brill, Director of Financial Aid

2 East South Street, Galesburg, IL 61401

(309) 341-7149

Lake Forest College

Lake Forest, Illinois

www.lakeforest.edu   Federal Code: 001706

4-year private liberal arts college in large town.

Enrollment: 1,514 undergrads, 1% part-time. 358 full-time freshmen.

Selectivity: Admits 50 to 75% of applicants.

BASIC COSTS (2016-2017)

Tuition and fees: $44,116.

Room and board: $9,810.

FINANCIAL AID PICTURE

Students with need: Need-based aid available for full-time students.

Students without need: No-need awards available for academics, alumni affiliation, art, leadership, music/drama.

FINANCIAL AID PROCEDURES

Forms required: FAFSA.

Dates and Deadlines: Priority date 2/15; closing date 5/1. Applicants notified on a rolling basis starting 3/1; must reply by 5/1 or within 2 week(s) of notification.

Transfers: Applicants notified on a rolling basis starting 3/15; must reply by 5/1.

CONTACT

Gerard Cebrzynski, Financial Aid Director

555 North Sheridan Road, Lake Forest, IL 60045-2338

(847) 735-5015

Lake Land College

Mattoon, Illinois

www.lakelandcollege.edu   Federal Code: 007644

2-year public community college in large town.

Enrollment: 3,338 undergrads.

Selectivity: Open admission; but selective for some programs.

BASIC COSTS (2016-2017)

Tuition and fees: $3,789; out-of-district residents $7,613; out-of-state residents $13,415.

FINANCIAL AID PICTURE

Students with need: Need-based aid available for full-time and part-time students. Work study available nights, weekends, and for part-time students.
Students without need: No-need awards available for academics, athletics.

FINANCIAL AID PROCEDURES

Forms required: FAFSA.
Dates and Deadlines: Priority date 5/1; no closing date. Applicants notified on a rolling basis starting 6/1.
Transfers: No deadline.

CONTACT

Paula Carpenter, Director of Financial Aid and Veteran Services
5001 Lake Land Boulevard, Mattoon, IL 61938-9366
(217) 234-5231

Lakeview College of Nursing

Danville, Illinois
www.lakeviewcol.edu   Federal Code: 010501

Upper-division private nursing college in large town.
Enrollment: 284 undergrads, 29% part-time.

BASIC COSTS (2016-2017)

Tuition and fees: $15,840.
Per-credit charge: $495.

FINANCIAL AID PICTURE (2015-2016)

Students with need: 53% of average financial aid package awarded as scholarships/grants, 47% awarded as loans/jobs. Need-based aid available for part-time students.
Students without need: This college awards aid only to students with need.

FINANCIAL AID PROCEDURES

Forms required: FAFSA, institutional form.
Transfers: Priority date 4/15; no deadline.

CONTACT

Janet Ingargiola, Director of Financial Aid
903 North Logan Avenue, Danville, IL 61832
(217) 709-0930

Le Cordon Bleu College of Culinary Arts: Chicago

Chicago, Illinois
www.chefs.edu/Chicago   Federal Code: 016758

2-year for-profit culinary school in very large city.
Enrollment: 958 undergrads.
Selectivity: Open admission.

FINANCIAL AID PICTURE

Students with need: Need-based aid available for full-time and part-time students. Work study available nights.

FINANCIAL AID PROCEDURES

Forms required: FAFSA, institutional form.
Dates and Deadlines: Applicants notified on a rolling basis.
Transfers: No deadline. Applicants notified on a rolling basis.

CONTACT

Nathan Nimrick, Director of Student Finance
361 West Chestnut, Chicago, IL 60610-3050
(312) 944-0882

Lewis and Clark Community College

Godfrey, Illinois
www.lc.edu   Federal Code: 010020

2-year public community college in large town.
Enrollment: 3,681 undergrads.
Selectivity: Open admission; but selective for some programs.

BASIC COSTS (2016-2017)

Tuition and fees: $4,080; out-of-district residents $10,860; out-of-state residents $14,250.
Per-credit charge: $113; out-of-district residents $339; out-of-state residents $452.

FINANCIAL AID PICTURE (2015-2016)

Students with need: 77% of average financial aid package awarded as scholarships/grants, 23% awarded as loans/jobs. Need-based aid available for part-time students.

FINANCIAL AID PROCEDURES

Forms required: FAFSA.
Dates and Deadlines: Priority date 6/1; no closing date. Applicants notified on a rolling basis starting 8/1; must reply within 3 week(s) of notification.
Transfers: No deadline. Applicants notified on a rolling basis.

CONTACT

Angela Weaver, Director, Financial Aid
5800 Godfrey Road, Godfrey, IL 62035-2466
(618) 468-2223

Lewis University

Romeoville, Illinois
www.lewisu.edu   Federal Code: 001707

4-year private university in large town, affiliated with the Roman Catholic Church.
Enrollment: 4,433 undergrads, 16% part-time. 642 full-time freshmen.
Selectivity: Admits 50 to 75% of applicants.

BASIC COSTS (2017-2018)

Tuition and fees: $31,250.
Per-credit charge: $913.
Room and board: $10,460.
Additional info: Tuition/fee waivers available for adults.

FINANCIAL AID PICTURE (2016-2017)

Students with need: Out of 605 full-time freshmen who applied for aid, 534 were judged to have need. Of these, 534 received aid, and 112 had their full need met. Average financial aid package met 88% of need; average scholarship/grant was $18,633; average loan was $3,400. For part-time students, average financial aid package was $12,286.
Students without need: 100 full-time freshmen who did not demonstrate need for aid received scholarships/grants; average award was $12,773. No-need awards available for academics, alumni affiliation, art, athletics, music/drama, religious affiliation, ROTC.
Scholarships offered: 23 full-time freshmen received athletic scholarships; average amount $15,982.

FINANCIAL AID PROCEDURES

Forms required: FAFSA.
Dates and Deadlines: Priority date 10/31; closing date 5/1. Applicants notified on a rolling basis starting 11/1; must reply by 5/1 or within 2 week(s) of notification.
Transfers: Priority date 10/31; no deadline. Applicants notified on a rolling basis starting 11/1; must reply by 5/1 or within 2 week(s) of notification.

CONTACT

Janeen Decharinte, Director of Financial Aid Services

Unit #297, Romeoville, IL 60446-2200

(815) 836-5263

Lincoln Christian University

Lincoln, Illinois

www.lincolnchristian.edu   Federal Code: 001708

4-year private university and Bible college in large town, affiliated with the Church of Christ.

Enrollment: 446 undergrads, 20% part-time. 81 full-time freshmen.

Selectivity: Admits 50 to 75% of applicants.

BASIC COSTS (2016-2017)

Tuition and fees: $13,020.

Per-credit charge: $434.

Room and board: $7,564.

FINANCIAL AID PICTURE

Students with need: Need-based aid available for full-time and part-time students. Work study available nights, weekends, and for part-time students.

Students without need: No-need awards available for academics.

FINANCIAL AID PROCEDURES

Forms required: FAFSA.

Dates and Deadlines: Priority date 3/1; no closing date. Applicants notified on a rolling basis starting 3/1; must reply within 4 week(s) of notification.

CONTACT

Nancy Siddens, Director of Student Financial Aid

100 Campus View Drive, Lincoln, IL 62656-2111

(217) 732-3168 ext. 2322

Lincoln College

Lincoln, Illinois

www.lincolncollege.edu   Federal Code: 001709

2-year private junior and liberal arts college in large town.

Enrollment: 995 undergrads, 27% part-time. 289 full-time freshmen.

BASIC COSTS (2016-2017)

Tuition and fees: $17,700.

Room and board: $7,100.

Additional info: Tuition at time of enrollment locked for 2 years.

FINANCIAL AID PICTURE

Students with need: Need-based aid available for full-time and part-time students. Work study available nights, weekends, and for part-time students.

Students without need: No-need awards available for academics, alumni affiliation, art, athletics, leadership, music/drama.

Additional info: Auditions recommended for music, speech, theater, broadcasting, and dance scholarship candidates, portfolios recommended for art and technical theater scholarship candidates.

FINANCIAL AID PROCEDURES

Forms required: FAFSA.

Dates and Deadlines: Priority date 4/1; no closing date. Applicants notified on a rolling basis starting 6/1; must reply within 3 week(s) of notification.

Transfers: No deadline. Applicants notified on a rolling basis.

CONTACT

Chris Steckmann, Director of Financial Aid

300 Keokuk Street, Lincoln, IL 62656

(217) 732-3155 ext. 231

Lincoln Land Community College

Springfield, Illinois

www.llcc.edu   Federal Code: 007170

2-year public community and junior college in small city.

Enrollment: 3,831 undergrads.

Selectivity: Open admission; but selective for some programs.

BASIC COSTS (2016-2017)

Tuition and fees: $3,780; out-of-district residents $7,230; out-of-state residents $10,680.

Per-credit charge: $115; out-of-district residents $230; out-of-state residents $345.

Additional info: Tuition/fee waivers available for minority students.

FINANCIAL AID PICTURE

Students with need: Need-based aid available for full-time and part-time students. Work study available nights.

Students without need: No-need awards available for academics, athletics, minority status, state/district residency.

FINANCIAL AID PROCEDURES

Forms required: FAFSA, institutional form.

Dates and Deadlines: Closing date 6/30. Applicants notified on a rolling basis starting 4/15; must reply within 2 week(s) of notification.

CONTACT

Lisa Collier, Associate Vice President, Enrollment Services

5250 Shepherd Road, Springfield, IL 62794-9256

(217) 786-2237

Loyola University Chicago

Chicago, Illinois

www.luc.edu   Federal Code: 001710

4-year private university in very large city, affiliated with the Roman Catholic Church.

Enrollment: 10,906 undergrads, 6% part-time. 2,621 full-time freshmen.

Selectivity: Admits 50 to 75% of applicants.

BASIC COSTS (2016-2017)

Tuition and fees: $42,032.

Per-credit charge: $751.

Room and board: $13,770.

FINANCIAL AID PICTURE

Students with need: Need-based aid available for full-time and part-time students. Work study available nights, weekends, and for part-time students.

Students without need: No-need awards available for academics, art, athletics, leadership, music/drama, religious affiliation, ROTC.

FINANCIAL AID PROCEDURES

Forms required: FAFSA.

Dates and Deadlines: Priority date 3/1; no closing date. Applicants notified on a rolling basis starting 2/15; must reply within 3 week(s) of notification.

Transfers: FAFSA must be filed by 3/1 to receive Illinois map grant.

CONTACT

Tobyn Friar, Dir., Financial Aid

1032 West Sheridan Road., Chicago, IL 60660

(312) 915-7803

MacCormac College

Chicago, Illinois

www.maccormac.edu   Federal Code: 001716

2-year private community and junior college in very large city.

Enrollment: 198 undergrads.

BASIC COSTS (2016-2017)
Tuition and fees: $12,820.

FINANCIAL AID PICTURE
Students with need: Need-based aid available for full-time and part-time students.

Students without need: No-need awards available for academics, leadership.

Scholarships offered: The MAC Honor is based on ACT and high school class rank. The High School Business Club Scholarship, which awards $1,800, requires an ACT of at least 20, a GPA of at least 3.0, and membership in a high school business club. The Founders Scholarship, which awards $1,200, requires an ACT of at least 20, a GPA of at least 3.0, and participation in school, community, charity organizations or church.

FINANCIAL AID PROCEDURES
Forms required: FAFSA.

Dates and Deadlines: Closing date 8/15. Must reply within 2 week(s) of notification.

CONTACT
Alexandra Grant, Director of Financial Aid
29 East Madison Street, Chicago, IL 60602
(312) 922-1884 ext. 207

MacMurray College
Jacksonville, Illinois
www.mac.edu   Federal Code: 001717

4-year private liberal arts college in large town, affiliated with the United Methodist Church.
Enrollment: 551 undergrads, 3% part-time. 137 full-time freshmen.
Selectivity: Admits 50 to 75% of applicants.

BASIC COSTS (2017-2018)
Additional info: Tuition at time of enrollment locked for 4 years; tuition/fee waivers available for adults.

FINANCIAL AID PICTURE
Students with need: Need-based aid available for full-time and part-time students. Work study available nights, weekends, and for part-time students.
Students without need: No-need awards available for academics, alumni affiliation, leadership, religious affiliation, state/district residency.
Scholarships offered: Academic scholarships: $6,000-$15,000 per year; based on merit; 3 freshman selected for full-tuition scholarships. Transfer scholarships: up to $10,000; based on academic merit. Leadership scholarship: $5,000; based on committee selection; awarded to one incoming female freshman annually. Alumni referral scholarships: up to $1,000 per year. Children of alumni scholarships: $1,000 per year. Church-matching scholarships: up to $1,500 per year.
Additional info: Merit scholarships for accepted, enrolled freshman and transfer students based on academic record and notified upon admission. Frozen tuition offered for full-time degree seeking new students for their first two years. Students residing on campus for four years will get the 8th semester of room and board waived.

FINANCIAL AID PROCEDURES
Forms required: FAFSA.
Dates and Deadlines: Priority date 2/1; no closing date. Applicants notified on a rolling basis starting 3/1; must reply within 2 week(s) of notification.
Transfers: No deadline. Applicants notified on a rolling basis starting 3/1; must reply within 2 week(s) of notification. Phi Theta Kappa members receive $2,500 per year.

CONTACT
Laci Engelbrecht, Director of One-Stop Student Services
447 East College Avenue, Jacksonville, IL 62650-2590
(217) 479-7041

McHenry County College
Crystal Lake, Illinois
www.mchenry.edu   Federal Code: 007691

2-year public community college in large town.
Enrollment: 4,483 undergrads, 57% part-time. 621 full-time freshmen.
Selectivity: Open admission; but selective for some programs.

BASIC COSTS (2017-2018)
Tuition and fees: $3,404; out-of-district residents $11,616; out-of-state residents $14,003.
Per-credit charge: $104; out-of-district residents $378; out-of-state residents $458.

FINANCIAL AID PICTURE
Students with need: Need-based aid available for full-time and part-time students. Work study available nights, weekends, and for part-time students.
Students without need: No-need awards available for academics, athletics, leadership, music/drama, state/district residency.
Scholarships offered: President's Scholarship; full tuition for 2 years; based on talent in academic areas; students must complete portfolio and have 3.0 GPA. Founding Faculty Scholarship; full tuition for 2 years; based on GPA and essay.
Additional info: Students can apply throughout the award year for federal and state aid. Students with physical handicaps or learning disabilities may apply for special needs scholarship.

FINANCIAL AID PROCEDURES
Forms required: FAFSA, institutional form.
Dates and Deadlines: Priority date 6/1; no closing date. Applicants notified on a rolling basis starting 5/1.

CONTACT
Leana Davis, Director of Financial Aid
8900 US Highway 14, Crystal Lake, IL 60012-2738
(815) 455-8761

McKendree University
Lebanon, Illinois
www.mckendree.edu   Federal Code: 001722

4-year private university and liberal arts college in small town, affiliated with the United Methodist Church.
Enrollment: 2,243 undergrads, 19% part-time. 451 full-time freshmen.
Selectivity: Admits 50 to 75% of applicants.

BASIC COSTS (2016-2017)
Tuition and fees: $28,740.
Per-credit charge: $910.
Room and board: $9,200.

FINANCIAL AID PICTURE (2016-2017)
Students with need: Out of 410 full-time freshmen who applied for aid, 369 were judged to have need. Of these, 366 received aid, and 96 had their full need met. Average financial aid package met 77% of need; average scholarship/grant was $19,238; average loan was $3,363. For part-time students, average financial aid package was $5,045.
Students without need: 70 full-time freshmen who did not demonstrate need for aid received scholarships/grants; average award was $14,221. No-need awards available for academics, alumni affiliation, art, athletics, leadership, music/drama, religious affiliation.
Scholarships offered: *Merit:* Dean's Scholarships; $10,000 annually; based on 3.0 GPA or 22 ACT. Presidential Scholarships; $10,000 annually; based on 3.0 GPA and 22 ACT. Honor's Scholarships; $13,000 annually; based on 3.6 GPA and 27 ACT. Leadership Scholarship; up to $5,000 annually; available to students that have been awarded McKendree University Presidential or Honor's Scholarship and attend Leadership Scholarship Event, during which they

complete two personal interviews and submit an essay. Community Service Scholarship; highly competitive; up to $4,000 annually; must be enrolled full-time; have a 2.5 GPA; and a record of volunteering in high school. **Athletic:** 65 full-time freshmen received athletic scholarships; average amount $11,529.

FINANCIAL AID PROCEDURES
Forms required: FAFSA.
Dates and Deadlines: Applicants notified on a rolling basis starting 4/1.
Transfers: No deadline. Applicants notified by 3/1; must reply within 4 week(s) of notification.

CONTACT
Elizabeth Juehne, Director of FInancial Aid
701 College Road, Lebanon, IL 62254-1299
(618) 537-6828

Midstate College
Peoria, Illinois
www.midstate.edu   Federal Code: 004568

4-year for-profit business college in small city.
Enrollment: 521 undergrads.
Selectivity: Open admission; but selective for some programs and for out-of-state students.

BASIC COSTS (2016-2017)
Tuition and fees: $16,230.
Per-credit charge: $381.25.

FINANCIAL AID PICTURE
Students with need: Need-based aid available for full-time and part-time students. Work study available nights, weekends, and for part-time students.
Students without need: No-need awards available for academics.

FINANCIAL AID PROCEDURES
Forms required: FAFSA, institutional form.
Dates and Deadlines: Applicants notified on a rolling basis; must reply within 4 week(s) of notification.

CONTACT
Irene Bimrose, Director of Financial Assistance
411 West Northmoor Road, Peoria, IL 61614-3558
(309) 692-4092 ext. 1210

Millikin University
Decatur, Illinois
www.millikin.edu   Federal Code: 001724

4-year private university in small city, affiliated with the Presbyterian Church (USA).
Enrollment: 1,917 undergrads, 6% part-time. 420 full-time freshmen.
Selectivity: Admits 50 to 75% of applicants.

BASIC COSTS (2016-2017)
Tuition and fees: $31,924.
Per-credit charge: $449.
Room and board: $11,190.

FINANCIAL AID PICTURE (2015-2016)
Students with need: Out of 409 full-time freshmen who applied for aid, 369 were judged to have need. Of these, 369 received aid, and 85 had their full need met. Average financial aid package met 84% of need; average scholarship/grant was $9,359; average loan was $4,387. For part-time students, average financial aid package was $8,862.

Students without need: 40 full-time freshmen who did not demonstrate need for aid received scholarships/grants; average award was $15,575. No-need awards available for academics, alumni affiliation, art, leadership, minority status, music/drama.
Scholarships offered: Scholarships for students who demonstrate significant potential for contributing to campus life; renewable for 4 years of attendance.

FINANCIAL AID PROCEDURES
Forms required: FAFSA.
Dates and Deadlines: Priority date 1/6; no closing date. Applicants notified on a rolling basis starting 1/6; must reply by 5/1 or within 4 week(s) of notification.
Transfers: Priority date 1/6; no deadline. Applicants notified on a rolling basis starting 1/6.

CONTACT
Cheryl Howerton, Director of Financial Aid
1184 West Main Street, Decatur, IL 62522-2084
(217) 424-6317

Monmouth College
Monmouth, Illinois
www.monmouthcollege.edu   Federal Code: 001725

4-year private liberal arts college in small town, affiliated with the Presbyterian Church (USA).
Enrollment: 1,133 undergrads, 1% part-time. 290 full-time freshmen.

BASIC COSTS (2016-2017)
Tuition and fees: $35,300.
Room and board: $8,300.

FINANCIAL AID PICTURE (2016-2017)
Students with need: Out of 263 full-time freshmen who applied for aid, 245 were judged to have need. Of these, 245 received aid, and 64 had their full need met. Average financial aid package met 89% of need; average scholarship/grant was $27,630; average loan was $3,870. For part-time students, average financial aid package was $21,905.
Students without need: 45 full-time freshmen who did not demonstrate need for aid received scholarships/grants; average award was $21,501. No-need awards available for academics, art, leadership, music/drama, religious affiliation.

FINANCIAL AID PROCEDURES
Forms required: FAFSA.
Dates and Deadlines: Priority date 1/1; no closing date. Applicants notified on a rolling basis starting 2/15; must reply by 5/1 or within 2 week(s) of notification.
Transfers: Priority date 2/1; no deadline. Applicants notified on a rolling basis; must reply by 8/15.

CONTACT
Jayne Schreck, Assoc. VP of Financial Aid
700 East Broadway, Monmouth, IL 61462-1998
(309) 457-2129

Moody Bible Institute
Chicago, Illinois
www.moody.edu   Federal Code: 001727

4-year private Bible and seminary college in very large city, affiliated with the interdenominational tradition.
Enrollment: 2,850 undergrads, 20% part-time. 276 full-time freshmen.
Selectivity: Admits over 75% of applicants.

BASIC COSTS (2016-2017)
Tuition and fees: $12,630.
Per-credit charge: $320.
Room and board: $10,180.

FINANCIAL AID PICTURE (2016-2017)
Students with need: 82% of average financial aid package awarded as scholarships/grants, 18% awarded as loans/jobs. Need-based aid available for part-time students.
Students without need: This college awards aid only to students with need.
Additional info: Aid available to upperclassmen is based on private and not federal/state sources.

FINANCIAL AID PROCEDURES
Forms required: institutional form.
Dates and Deadlines: Applicants notified on a rolling basis; must reply by 7/1.
Transfers: No deadline. Applicants notified on a rolling basis; must reply by 7/1.

CONTACT
Heather Shalley, Director of Financial Aid
820 N LaSalle Boulevard, Chicago, IL 60610
(312) 329-4178

Moraine Valley Community College
Palos Hills, Illinois
www.morainevalley.edu   Federal Code: 007692

2-year public community and junior college in large town.
Enrollment: 11,556 undergrads, 46% part-time. 1,775 full-time freshmen.
Selectivity: Open admission; but selective for some programs.

BASIC COSTS (2017-2018)
Tuition and fees: $4,782; out-of-district residents $9,822; out-of-state residents $11,292.
Per-credit charge: $139; out-of-district residents $307; out-of-state residents $356.

FINANCIAL AID PICTURE (2015-2016)
Students with need: 88% of average financial aid package awarded as scholarships/grants, 12% awarded as loans/jobs. Need-based aid available for part-time students. Work study available nights.
Students without need: No-need awards available for academics, alumni affiliation, athletics, leadership, state/district residency.

FINANCIAL AID PROCEDURES
Forms required: FAFSA, institutional form.
Dates and Deadlines: Priority date 5/1; no closing date. Applicants notified on a rolling basis starting 6/15; must reply within 2 week(s) of notification.

CONTACT
Carissa Davis, Director of Financial Aid
9000 West College Parkway, Palos Hills, IL 60465-2478
(708) 974-5726

Morrison Institute of Technology
Morrison, Illinois
www.morrisontech.edu   Federal Code: 008880

2-year private technical college in small town.
Enrollment: 86 undergrads. 49 full-time freshmen.
Selectivity: Open admission.

BASIC COSTS (2016-2017)
Tuition and fees: $15,790.

Room only: $3,900.

FINANCIAL AID PICTURE
Students with need: Need-based aid available for full-time and part-time students. Work study available nights, weekends, and for part-time students.
Students without need: No-need awards available for academics.

FINANCIAL AID PROCEDURES
Forms required: FAFSA, institutional form.
Dates and Deadlines: Applicants notified on a rolling basis; must reply within 2 week(s) of notification.

CONTACT
Lisa Kramer, Financial Aid Director
701 Portland Avenue, Morrison, IL 61270-2959
(815) 772-7218 ext. 203

Morton College
Cicero, Illinois
www.morton.edu   Federal Code: 001728

2-year public community college in small city.
Enrollment: 3,371 undergrads, 63% part-time. 433 full-time freshmen.
Selectivity: Open admission; but selective for some programs and for out-of-state students.

BASIC COSTS (2016-2017)
Tuition and fees: $3,660; out-of-district residents $7,500; out-of-state residents $9,420.
Per-credit charge: $88; out-of-district residents $216; out-of-state residents $280.

FINANCIAL AID PICTURE (2015-2016)
Students with need: Average financial aid package for all full-time undergraduates was $4,578. Need-based aid available for part-time students. Work study available nights, weekends, and for part-time students.

FINANCIAL AID PROCEDURES
Forms required: FAFSA, institutional form.
Dates and Deadlines: Priority date 6/1; no closing date. Applicants notified on a rolling basis starting 8/3.

CONTACT
Yolanda Freemon, Director of Financial Aid
3801 South Central Avenue, Cicero, IL 60804-4398
(708) 656-8000 ext. 2426

National University of Health Sciences
Lombard, Illinois
www.nuhs.edu   Federal Code: 001732

4-year private university and health science college in large town.
Enrollment: 130 undergrads.

BASIC COSTS (2016-2017)
Tuition and fees: $11,820.
Per-credit charge: $364.
Additional info: Tuition and fees quoted are for Bachelor's program: Biomedical Science. Associate program: Massage Therapy $13,038, technology fee $132, books and supplies $400.

FINANCIAL AID PICTURE
Students with need: Need-based aid available for full-time and part-time students.

FINANCIAL AID PROCEDURES
Transfers: No deadline.

CONTACT
Robert Dame, Director of Financial Aid
200 East Roosevelt Road, Lombard, IL 60148-4583
(630) 889-6700

North Central College
Naperville, Illinois
www.northcentralcollege.edu   Federal Code: 001734

4-year private liberal arts college in small city, affiliated with the United Methodist Church.
Enrollment: 2,626 undergrads, 4% part-time. 589 full-time freshmen.
Selectivity: Admits 50 to 75% of applicants.

BASIC COSTS (2016-2017)
Tuition and fees: $36,654.
Per-credit charge: $1,013.
Room and board: $10,356.

FINANCIAL AID PICTURE
Students with need: Need-based aid available for full-time and part-time students. Work study available nights, weekends, and for part-time students.
Students without need: No-need awards available for academics, art, leadership, minority status, music/drama, religious affiliation, ROTC, state/district residency.
Scholarships offered: Numerous merit and talent scholarship opportunities available.

FINANCIAL AID PROCEDURES
Forms required: FAFSA.
Dates and Deadlines: Applicants notified on a rolling basis starting 3/1; must reply within 4 week(s) of notification.
Transfers: No deadline. Applicants notified on a rolling basis starting 3/1; must reply within 4 week(s) of notification.

CONTACT
Martin Sauer, Vice President for Enrollment Management and Athletics
30 North Brainard Street, Naperville, IL 60566-7063
(630) 637-5600

North Park University
Chicago, Illinois
www.northpark.edu   Federal Code: 001735

4-year private university and liberal arts college in very large city, affiliated with the Evangelical Covenant Church of America.
Enrollment: 2,140 undergrads.

BASIC COSTS (2016-2017)
Tuition and fees: $26,840.
Per-credit charge: $850.
Room and board: $9,310.

FINANCIAL AID PICTURE
Students with need: Need-based aid available for full-time students. Work study available nights.
Students without need: No-need awards available for academics, art, music/drama, religious affiliation.

FINANCIAL AID PROCEDURES
Forms required: FAFSA.
Dates and Deadlines: Priority date 5/1; closing date 8/1. Applicants notified on a rolling basis starting 10/1; must reply by 5/1 or within 3 week(s) of notification.
Transfers: Priority date 6/1. Applicants notified on a rolling basis starting 10/1; must reply within 3 week(s) of notification.

CONTACT
Carolyn Lach, Director of Financial Aid
3225 West Foster Avenue Box 19, Chicago, IL 60625-4895
(773) 244-5560

Northeastern Illinois University
Chicago, Illinois
www.neiu.edu   Federal Code: 001693

4-year public university in very large city.
Enrollment: 7,570 undergrads, 44% part-time. 767 full-time freshmen.
Selectivity: Admits 50 to 75% of applicants.

BASIC COSTS (2016-2017)
Tuition and fees: $12,428; out-of-state residents $22,928.
Per-credit charge: $349; out-of-state residents $699.
Additional info: Tuition at time of enrollment locked for 4 years.

FINANCIAL AID PICTURE (2016-2017)
Students with need: Out of 694 full-time freshmen who applied for aid, 535 were judged to have need. Of these, 457 received aid, and 19 had their full need met. Average financial aid package met 18% of need; average scholarship/grant was $7,774; average loan was $3,314. For part-time students, average financial aid package was $5,832.
Students without need: 9 full-time freshmen who did not demonstrate need for aid received scholarships/grants; average award was $11,524. No-need awards available for academics, alumni affiliation, art, leadership, music/drama, ROTC.

FINANCIAL AID PROCEDURES
Forms required: FAFSA.
Dates and Deadlines: Priority date 2/28; no closing date. Applicants notified on a rolling basis starting 3/15; must reply within 2 week(s) of notification.

CONTACT
Maureen Amos, Director of Financial Aid
5500 North St. Louis Avenue, Chicago, IL 60625
(773) 442-5010

Northern Illinois University
DeKalb, Illinois
www.niu.edu   Federal Code: 001737

4-year public university in large town.
Enrollment: 14,036 undergrads, 12% part-time. 2,289 full-time freshmen.
Selectivity: Admits 50 to 75% of applicants.

BASIC COSTS (2016-2017)
Tuition and fees: $12,212; out-of-district residents $15,998; out-of-state residents $21,677.
Per-credit charge: $315.52; out-of-district residents $441.73; out-of-state residents $697.
Room and board: $9,690.
Additional info: Midwest Out-of-State (Indiana, Iowa, Michigan, Missouri, Ohio, and Wisconsin) Tuition: 13,252. Tuition at time of enrollment locked for 4 years.

FINANCIAL AID PICTURE (2015-2016)
Students with need: Out of 2,084 full-time freshmen who applied for aid, 1,766 were judged to have need. Of these, 1,758 received aid, and 162 had their full need met. Average financial aid package met 65% of need; average scholarship/grant was $9,519; average loan was $3,417. For part-time students, average financial aid package was $6,688.
Students without need: 352 full-time freshmen who did not demonstrate need for aid received scholarships/grants; average award was $4,512. No-need awards available for academics, alumni affiliation, art, athletics, leadership, music/drama, ROTC.

Scholarships offered: 45 full-time freshmen received athletic scholarships; average amount $22,966.

FINANCIAL AID PROCEDURES

Forms required: FAFSA.

Dates and Deadlines: Applicants notified on a rolling basis starting 3/1.

Transfers: No deadline. Applicants notified on a rolling basis starting 3/1. Two year, $1000 - $2,000/year (depending on GPA) transfer scholarship available with 3.0 cumulative transfer GPA and 30 transferable hours completed at time of admission.

CONTACT

Rebecca Babel, Director of Student Financial Aid
1425 West Lincoln Highway, DeKalb, IL 60115-2854
(815) 753-1395

Northwestern College

Chicago, Illinois
www.nc.edu   Federal Code: 012362

2-year for-profit technical and career college in very large city.

Enrollment: 671 undergrads, 63% part-time. 11 full-time freshmen.

Selectivity: Open admission; but selective for some programs.

BASIC COSTS (2016-2017)

Additional info: Full program costs for Medical assisting diploma: $22,820, books and supplies $2,455.

FINANCIAL AID PICTURE

Students with need: Need-based aid available for full-time and part-time students. Work study available nights.

Students without need: No-need awards available for academics, alumni affiliation.

Scholarships offered: Academic Scholarship: $600 per quarter up to six quarters. Board of Directors: $800 per quarter up to six quarters. Centennial: amount varies. Educational Achievement Scholarship: $600 per quarter up to six quarters. Community Scholarship: $800 per quarter up to six quarters. Early Acceptance Scholarship: amount varies. Scholastic Scholarship: $667 per quarter up to six quarters. Presidential Scholarship: $800 per quarter up to six quarters. Excellence Scholarship: $1,200 per quarter up to six quarters. Transfer Student Scholarship: $400 per quarter up to four quarters. Student Success Scholarship: Summer quarter only up to $1,000. American Hero Tuition and First Responders Tuition Discount: 15%. Legacy Tuition Discount: 10%.

Additional info: State grant programs for Illinois residents and alternative loans offered.

FINANCIAL AID PROCEDURES

Forms required: FAFSA, institutional form.

Dates and Deadlines: Priority date 2/15; closing date 6/30. Applicants notified on a rolling basis starting 1/2; must reply within 4 week(s) of notification.

CONTACT

Patricia Kilian, Director of Financial Aid
4811 N. Milwaukee Avenue, STE 203, Chicago, IL 60630
(847) 233-7700 ext. 2103

Northwestern University

Evanston, Illinois   Federal Code: 001739
www.northwestern.edu   CSS Code: 1565

4-year private university in small city.

Enrollment: 8,351 undergrads, 2% part-time. 1,985 full-time freshmen.

Selectivity: Admits less than 50% of applicants.

BASIC COSTS (2016-2017)

Tuition and fees: $50,855.

Room and board: $15,489.

FINANCIAL AID PICTURE (2016-2017)

Students with need: Out of 1,064 full-time freshmen who applied for aid, 905 were judged to have need. Of these, 905 received aid, and 905 had their full need met. Average financial aid package met 100% of need; average scholarship/grant was $42,976; average loan was $2,983.

Students without need: 72 full-time freshmen who did not demonstrate need for aid received scholarships/grants; average award was $8,034. No-need awards available for athletics, music/drama.

Scholarships offered: 77 full-time freshmen received athletic scholarships; average amount $44,745.

FINANCIAL AID PROCEDURES

Forms required: FAFSA, CSS PROFILE.

Dates and Deadlines: Must reply by 5/1 or within 2 week(s) of notification.

Transfers: Closing date 6/1. Transfer student aid limited for first year.

CONTACT

1801 Hinman Avenue, Evanston, IL 60208-3060
(847) 491-7400

Oakton Community College

Des Plaines, Illinois
www.oakton.edu   Federal Code: 009896

2-year public community college in small city.

Enrollment: 2,788 full-time undergrads.

Selectivity: Open admission; but selective for some programs.

BASIC COSTS (2016-2017)

Tuition and fees: $4,053; out-of-district residents $10,465; out-of-state residents $12,655.

Per-credit charge: $123.25; out-of-district residents $342; out-of-state residents $415.

FINANCIAL AID PICTURE (2015-2016)

Students with need: 96% of average financial aid package awarded as scholarships/grants, 4% awarded as loans/jobs. Need-based aid available for part-time students. Work study available nights, weekends, and for part-time students.

Students without need: No-need awards available for academics, art, athletics, leadership, minority status, music/drama, state/district residency.

Scholarships offered: Oakton Merit Scholarship Program; tuition and related fees; first-time, in-district, freshmen in top 10% of high school class.

FINANCIAL AID PROCEDURES

Forms required: FAFSA, institutional form.

Dates and Deadlines: Priority date 3/1; no closing date. Applicants notified on a rolling basis starting 3/1; must reply within 2 week(s) of notification.

Transfers: Applicants notified on a rolling basis starting 5/1.

CONTACT

Jamie Petersen, Director of Financial Aid
Enrollment Center, Des Plaines, IL 60016
(847) 635-1708

Olivet Nazarene University

Bourbonnais, Illinois
www.olivet.edu   Federal Code: 001741

4-year private university and liberal arts college in small city, affiliated with the Church of the Nazarene.

Enrollment: 3,348 undergrads, 10% part-time. 733 full-time freshmen.

Selectivity: Admits over 75% of applicants.

BASIC COSTS (2016-2017)
Tuition and fees: $33,940.
Per-credit charge: $1,373.
Room and board: $7,900.

FINANCIAL AID PICTURE (2015-2016)
Students with need: Out of 700 full-time freshmen who applied for aid, 631 were judged to have need. Of these, 631 received aid, and 167 had their full need met. Average financial aid package met 80% of need; average scholarship/grant was $21,424; average loan was $2,465. Need-based aid available for part-time students.
Students without need: 102 full-time freshmen who did not demonstrate need for aid received scholarships/grants; average award was $15,790. No-need awards available for academics, alumni affiliation, art, athletics, leadership, music/drama, religious affiliation, ROTC, state/district residency.
Scholarships offered: 27 full-time freshmen received athletic scholarships; average amount $9,820.

FINANCIAL AID PROCEDURES
Dates and Deadlines: Priority date 11/4; no closing date. Applicants notified on a rolling basis starting 11/1; must reply within 2 week(s) of notification.
Transfers: Priority date 11/1; no deadline. Applicants notified on a rolling basis starting 11/1; must reply within 2 week(s) of notification.

CONTACT
Greg Bruner, Director of Financial Aid
One University Avenue, Bourbonnais, IL 60914
(815) 939-5249

Parkland College
Champaign, Illinois
www.parkland.edu   Federal Code: 007118

2-year public community college in small city.
Enrollment: 6,990 undergrads, 57% part-time. 948 full-time freshmen.
Selectivity: Open admission; but selective for some programs.

BASIC COSTS (2016-2017)
Tuition and fees: $4,710; out-of-district residents $11,100; out-of-state residents $15,870.
Per-credit charge: $136.5; out-of-district residents $349.5; out-of-state residents $508.5.

FINANCIAL AID PICTURE (2015-2016)
Students with need: 48% of average financial aid package awarded as scholarships/grants, 52% awarded as loans/jobs. Need-based aid available for part-time students. Work study available nights.
Students without need: No-need awards available for academics, athletics, leadership, minority status, music/drama.

FINANCIAL AID PROCEDURES
Forms required: FAFSA.
Dates and Deadlines: Priority date 11/1; no closing date. Applicants notified on a rolling basis; must reply by 3/1.
Transfers: Priority date 11/1; no deadline. Applicants notified on a rolling basis; must reply by 3/1.

CONTACT
Tim Wendt, Director of Enrollment Services
2400 West Bradley Avenue, Champaign, IL 61821-1899
(217) 351-2222

Prairie State College
Chicago Heights, Illinois
www.prairiestate.edu   Federal Code: 001640

2-year public community college in large town.
Enrollment: 4,571 undergrads.

Selectivity: Open admission; but selective for some programs.

BASIC COSTS (2016-2017)
Tuition and fees: $4,755; out-of-district residents $10,755; out-of-state residents $12,735.
Per-credit charge: $133; out-of-district residents $333; out-of-state residents $399.

FINANCIAL AID PICTURE
Students with need: Need-based aid available for full-time and part-time students. Work study available nights, weekends, and for part-time students.

FINANCIAL AID PROCEDURES
Forms required: FAFSA, institutional form.
Dates and Deadlines: Closing date 7/1. Applicants notified on a rolling basis; must reply within 2 week(s) of notification.

CONTACT
Alice Garcia, Director of Financial Aid
202 South Halsted Street, Chicago Heights, IL 60411
(708) 709-3523

Principia College
Elsah, Illinois   Federal Code: 001744
www.principiacollege.edu   CSS Code: 1630

4-year private liberal arts college in rural community, affiliated with the First Church of Christ, Scientist (Christian Science).
Enrollment: 475 undergrads, 3% part-time. 113 full-time freshmen.
Selectivity: Admits over 75% of applicants.

BASIC COSTS (2017-2018)
Tuition and fees: $28,920.
Per-credit charge: $916.
Room and board: $11,430.

FINANCIAL AID PICTURE (2015-2016)
Students with need: Out of 73 full-time freshmen who applied for aid, 72 were judged to have need. Of these, 72 received aid, and 40 had their full need met. Average financial aid package met 96% of need; average scholarship/grant was $26,806; average loan was $5,762. Need-based aid available for part-time students.
Students without need: 38 full-time freshmen who did not demonstrate need for aid received scholarships/grants; average award was $23,648. No-need awards available for academics, alumni affiliation, leadership.
Scholarships offered: Trustee Scholarship; full-tuition; based on GPA and SAT/ACT. Chairman's Scholarship; 3/4 tuition; based on GPA and SAT/ACT. President's Scholarship; 1/2 tuition; based on GPA and SAT/ACT. Dean's Scholarship; 1/4 tuition; based on GPA and SAT/ACT. Arthur Schulz, Jr. Alumni Scholarship; $4,500; based on GPA and SAT/ACT. Children and grandchildren of alumni scholarships; based on GPA. Founders' Scholarships; 1/4 to full-tuition; awarded to students who demonstrate deep commitment to Christian Science, character, and citizenship as evidenced by active participation in these areas.

FINANCIAL AID PROCEDURES
Forms required: CSS PROFILE, institutional form.
Dates and Deadlines: Closing date 3/1. Applicants notified by 4/1.
Transfers: Priority date 3/1.

CONTACT
Tamara Gavaletz, Director of Admissions and Financial Aid
1 Maybeck Place, Elsah, IL 62028-9799
(800) 277-4648 ext. 2813

Quincy University

Quincy, Illinois
www.quincy.edu   Federal Code: 001745

4-year private university and liberal arts college in large town, affiliated with the Roman Catholic Church.
Enrollment: 1,081 undergrads.

BASIC COSTS (2016-2017)
Tuition and fees: $27,128.
Per-credit charge: $710.
Room and board: $10,500.

FINANCIAL AID PICTURE
Students with need: Need-based aid available for full-time students. Work study available nights, weekends, and for part-time students.
Students without need: No-need awards available for academics, alumni affiliation, art, athletics, leadership, music/drama.
Scholarships offered: Academic scholarships: $8,000-$15,000 per year; based on ACT and high school GPA; unlimited number awarded.

FINANCIAL AID PROCEDURES
Forms required: FAFSA.
Dates and Deadlines: Priority date 3/21; no closing date. Applicants notified on a rolling basis starting 3/1; must reply by 5/1 or within 2 week(s) of notification.

CONTACT
Lisa Flack, Director of Financial Aid
1800 College Avenue, Quincy, IL 62301-2699
(217) 228-5260

Rasmussen College: Aurora

Aurora, Illinois
www.rasmussen.edu

2-year for-profit branch campus and career college in small city.
Enrollment: 410 undergrads, 33% part-time. 18 full-time freshmen.
Selectivity: Open admission; but selective for some programs.

BASIC COSTS (2016-2017)
Tuition and fees: $13,455.
Per-credit charge: $299.
Additional info: Full-time tuition varies according to program of study. Required course materials fee of $150 per course.

FINANCIAL AID PICTURE
Students with need: Need-based aid available for full-time and part-time students.

FINANCIAL AID PROCEDURES
Forms required: FAFSA, institutional form.
Dates and Deadlines: Applicants notified on a rolling basis.

CONTACT
Debora Murray, Director of Financial Services
2363 Sequoia Drive, Suite 131, Aurora, IL 60506

Rasmussen College: Mokena/Tinley Park

Mokena, Illinois
www.rasmussen.edu

4-year for-profit career college in large town.
Enrollment: 396 undergrads, 51% part-time. 15 full-time freshmen.
Selectivity: Admits over 75% of applicants.

BASIC COSTS (2016-2017)
Tuition and fees: $13,455.
Per-credit charge: $299.
Additional info: Full-time tuition varies according to program of study. Required course materials fee of $150 per course.

FINANCIAL AID PICTURE
Students with need: Need-based aid available for full-time and part-time students.

FINANCIAL AID PROCEDURES
Forms required: FAFSA, institutional form.
Dates and Deadlines: Applicants notified on a rolling basis.

CONTACT
Debora Murray, Director of Financial Services
8650 West Spring Lake Road, Mokena, IL 60448

Rasmussen College: Rockford

Rockford, Illinois
www.rasmussen.edu

2-year for-profit career college in small city.
Enrollment: 429 undergrads, 48% part-time. 16 full-time freshmen.
Selectivity: Open admission; but selective for some programs.

BASIC COSTS (2016-2017)
Tuition and fees: $13,455.
Per-credit charge: $299.
Additional info: Full-time tuition varies according to program of study. Required course materials fee of $150 per course.

FINANCIAL AID PICTURE
Students with need: Need-based aid available for full-time and part-time students.

FINANCIAL AID PROCEDURES
Forms required: FAFSA, institutional form.
Dates and Deadlines: Applicants notified on a rolling basis.

CONTACT
Debora Murray, Director of Financial Services
6000 East State Street, Fourth Floor, Rockford, IL 61108-2513

Rasmussen College: Romeoville/Joliet

Romeoville, Illinois
www.rasmussen.edu

2-year for-profit career college in large town.
Enrollment: 542 undergrads, 52% part-time. 25 full-time freshmen.
Selectivity: Open admission; but selective for some programs.

BASIC COSTS (2016-2017)
Tuition and fees: $13,455.
Per-credit charge: $299.
Additional info: Full-time tuition varies according to program of study. Required course materials fee of $150 per course.

FINANCIAL AID PICTURE
Students with need: Need-based aid available for full-time and part-time students.

FINANCIAL AID PROCEDURES
Forms required: FAFSA, institutional form.
Dates and Deadlines: Applicants notified on a rolling basis.

CONTACT
Debora Murray, Director of Financial Services
400 West Normantown Road, Romeoville, IL 60446

Rend Lake College

Ina, Illinois
www.rlc.edu   Federal Code: 007119

2-year public community college in rural community.
Enrollment: 1,647 undergrads, 31% part-time. 460 full-time freshmen.
Selectivity: Open admission; but selective for some programs.

BASIC COSTS (2016-2017)
Tuition and fees: $3,750; out-of-district residents $5,700; out-of-state residents $6,450.
Per-credit charge: $110; out-of-district residents $175; out-of-state residents $200.

FINANCIAL AID PICTURE (2015-2016)
Students with need: Out of 424 full-time freshmen who applied for aid, 392 were judged to have need. Of these, 380 received aid, and 81 had their full need met. Average financial aid package met 59% of need; average scholarship/grant was $1,232. For part-time students, average financial aid package was $1,116.

FINANCIAL AID PROCEDURES
Forms required: FAFSA.
Dates and Deadlines: Applicants notified on a rolling basis starting 3/15; must reply within 4 week(s) of notification.
Transfers: No deadline. Applicants notified on a rolling basis starting 3/15; must reply within 4 week(s) of notification.

CONTACT
Cheri Rushing, Director of Financial Aid
468 North Ken Gray Parkway, Ina, IL 62846
(618) 437-5321 ext. 1385

Resurrection University

Chicago, Illinois
www.resu.edu   Federal Code: 022141

Upper-division private health science and nursing college in very large city, affiliated with the Roman Catholic Church.
Enrollment: 603 undergrads.

BASIC COSTS (2016-2017)
Tuition and fees: $25,632.
Per-credit charge: $849.

FINANCIAL AID PICTURE
Students with need: Need-based aid available for full-time and part-time students. Work study available nights, weekends, and for part-time students.
Students without need: No-need awards available for academics, alumni affiliation.

FINANCIAL AID PROCEDURES
Forms required: FAFSA.
Transfers: Priority date 4/1; no deadline. Applicants notified on a rolling basis starting 4/1; must reply within 3 week(s) of notification.

CONTACT
Shirley Howell, Financial Aid Officer
1431 North Claremont Avenue, Chicago, IL 60622
(773) 252-6446

Richland Community College

Decatur, Illinois
www.richland.edu   Federal Code: 010879

2-year public community college in small city.
Enrollment: 2,606 undergrads. 2,606 full-time freshmen.

Selectivity: Open admission; but selective for some programs.

BASIC COSTS (2017-2018)
Tuition and fees: $4,230; out-of-district residents $6,420; out-of-state residents $14,640.

FINANCIAL AID PICTURE
Students with need: Need-based aid available for full-time and part-time students. Work study available nights.
Students without need: No-need awards available for academics, art, leadership, music/drama.

FINANCIAL AID PROCEDURES
Forms required: FAFSA.
Dates and Deadlines: Priority date 7/25; no closing date. Applicants notified on a rolling basis starting 3/20.
Transfers: No deadline. Applicants notified on a rolling basis.

CONTACT
Carmin Ross, Director of Financial Aid
One College Park, Decatur, IL 62521
(217) 875-7200 ext. 271

Robert Morris University: Chicago

Chicago, Illinois
www.robertmorris.edu   Federal Code: 001746

4-year private university in very large city.
Enrollment: 2,345 undergrads, 4% part-time. 819 full-time freshmen.
Selectivity: Admits less than 50% of applicants.

BASIC COSTS (2017-2018)
Tuition and fees: $27,180.
Per-credit charge: $742.
Room and board: $13,200.

FINANCIAL AID PICTURE (2015-2016)
Students with need: Out of 804 full-time freshmen who applied for aid, 756 were judged to have need. Of these, 728 received aid, and 39 had their full need met. Average financial aid package met 52% of need; average scholarship/grant was $12,809; average loan was $3,879. For part-time students, average financial aid package was $8,723.
Students without need: 43 full-time freshmen who did not demonstrate need for aid received scholarships/grants; average award was $12,444. No-need awards available for academics, art, athletics, leadership, music/drama, ROTC, state/district residency.
Scholarships offered: 576 full-time freshmen received athletic scholarships; average amount $8,921.

FINANCIAL AID PROCEDURES
Forms required: FAFSA.
Dates and Deadlines: Applicants notified on a rolling basis.
Transfers: No deadline. Applicants notified on a rolling basis.

CONTACT
Leigh Brinson, Vice President of Financial Services
401 South State Street, Chicago, IL 60605
(312) 935-4077

Rock Valley College

Rockford, Illinois
www.rockvalleycollege.edu   Federal Code: 1747

2-year public community college in small city.
Enrollment: 6,516 undergrads, 54% part-time. 898 full-time freshmen.
Selectivity: Open admission; but selective for some programs.

BASIC COSTS (2017-2018)

Tuition and fees: $3,764; out-of-district residents $8,624; out-of-state residents $15,584.

Per-credit charge: $115; out-of-district residents $277; out-of-state residents $509.

FINANCIAL AID PICTURE (2015-2016)

Students with need: Need-based aid available for part-time students. Work study available nights.

FINANCIAL AID PROCEDURES

Forms required: FAFSA, institutional form.

Dates and Deadlines: Priority date 5/1; no closing date. Applicants notified on a rolling basis; must reply within 4 week(s) of notification.

CONTACT

James Heller, Director of Financial Aid
3301 North Mulford Road, Rockford, IL 61114-5699
(815) 921-4150

Rockford Career College

Rockford, Illinois
www.rockfordcareercollege.edu   Federal Code: 008545

2-year for-profit career college in small city.

Enrollment: 484 undergrads.

Selectivity: Open admission.

BASIC COSTS (2016-2017)

Additional info: Costs vary by program. Certificate programs $5,600-$12,000, books and supplies $75-$200. Associate programs $10,500-$21,000, books and supplies $75-$100.

FINANCIAL AID PICTURE

Students with need: Need-based aid available for full-time and part-time students. Work study available nights.

Students without need: This college awards aid only to students with need.

FINANCIAL AID PROCEDURES

Forms required: FAFSA.

Dates and Deadlines: Applicants notified on a rolling basis.

CONTACT

Lisa Ruch, Director of Financial Aid
1130 South Alpine Road, Rockford, IL 61108
(815) 967-7314

Rockford University

Rockford, Illinois
www.rockford.edu   Federal Code: 001748

4-year private liberal arts college in small city.

Enrollment: 1,039 undergrads, 12% part-time. 168 full-time freshmen.

Selectivity: Admits 50 to 75% of applicants.

BASIC COSTS (2017-2018)

Tuition and fees: $30,050.

Per-credit charge: $785.

Room and board: $8,420.

FINANCIAL AID PICTURE (2015-2016)

Students with need: Out of 163 full-time freshmen who applied for aid, 151 were judged to have need. Of these, 151 received aid, and 19 had their full need met. Average financial aid package met 68% of need; average scholarship/grant was $15,643; average loan was $3,680. For part-time students, average financial aid package was $8,245.

Students without need: 17 full-time freshmen who did not demonstrate need for aid received scholarships/grants; average award was $12,246. No-need awards available for academics, alumni affiliation, leadership, minority status, music/drama, state/district residency.

FINANCIAL AID PROCEDURES

Forms required: FAFSA.

Dates and Deadlines: Priority date 3/1; no closing date. Applicants notified on a rolling basis starting 3/1; must reply within 4 week(s) of notification.

CONTACT

Todd Fischer-Free, Assistant Vice President of Student Administrative Services
5050 East State Street, Rockford, IL 61108-2311
(815) 226-3383

Roosevelt University

Chicago, Illinois
www.roosevelt.edu   Federal Code: 001749

4-year private university in very large city.

Enrollment: 2,710 undergrads, 17% part-time. 336 full-time freshmen.

Selectivity: Admits 50 to 75% of applicants.

BASIC COSTS (2016-2017)

Tuition and fees: $28,119.

Per-credit charge: $759.

Room and board: $12,927.

FINANCIAL AID PICTURE

Students with need: Need-based aid available for full-time and part-time students. Work study available nights, weekends, and for part-time students.

Students without need: No-need awards available for academics, alumni affiliation, art, job skills, minority status.

FINANCIAL AID PROCEDURES

Forms required: FAFSA, institutional form.

Dates and Deadlines: Priority date 3/1; no closing date. Applicants notified on a rolling basis starting 2/1; must reply within 2 week(s) of notification.

Transfers: Applicants notified on a rolling basis starting 3/1; must reply within 2 week(s) of notification.

CONTACT

Barry Paine, Interim Dir Financial Aid
430 S Michigan Ave, Chicago, IL 60605-1394
(866) 421-0935

Rush University

Chicago, Illinois
www.rushu.rush.edu   Federal Code: 009800

Upper-division private health science and nursing college in very large city.

Enrollment: 122 undergrads, 32% part-time.

BASIC COSTS (2016-2017)

Additional info: Tuition/fee waivers available for minority students.

FINANCIAL AID PICTURE

Students with need: Need-based aid available for full-time and part-time students.

Students without need: No-need awards available for academics, minority status.

FINANCIAL AID PROCEDURES

Transfers: Priority date 3/1.

CONTACT

Michael Frechette, Director of Student Financial Aid
College Admissions, Chicago, IL 60612
(312) 942-6256

Saint Anthony College of Nursing

Rockford, Illinois
www.sacn.edu   Federal Code: 009987

Upper-division private nursing college in small city, affiliated with the
Roman Catholic Church.
Enrollment: 230 undergrads, 27% part-time. 1 full-time freshmen.

BASIC COSTS (2016-2017)
Tuition and fees: $24,302.
Per-credit charge: $735.

FINANCIAL AID PICTURE (2015-2016)
Students with need: Out of 1 full-time freshmen who applied for aid, 1
were judged to have need. Of these, 1 received aid, and 1 had their full
need met. Average financial aid package met 100% of need; average scholar-
ship/grant was $10,191. For part-time students, average financial aid pack-
age was $7,151.
Students without need: No-need awards available for academics, leadership.

FINANCIAL AID PROCEDURES
Forms required: FAFSA.
Dates and Deadlines: Priority date 4/15; no closing date. Applicants notified
on a rolling basis starting 4/17.
Transfers: Priority date 4/15. Applicants notified on a rolling basis starting
4/17.

CONTACT
Serrita Woods, Financial Aid Officer
5658 East State Street, Rockford, IL 61108-2468
(815) 395-5089

St. Francis Medical Center College of Nursing

Peoria, Illinois
www.sfmccon.edu   Federal Code: 006240

Upper-division private nursing college in small city, affiliated with the
Roman Catholic Church.
Enrollment: 384 undergrads, 22% part-time.

BASIC COSTS (2017-2018)
Tuition and fees: $20,954.
Per-credit charge: $598.
Room only: $3,600.

FINANCIAL AID PICTURE (2015-2016)
Students with need: Average financial aid package for all full-time undergraduates was $10,035; for part-time $6,152. 34% awarded as scholarships/
grants, 66% awarded as loans/jobs.
Students without need: No-need awards available for academics, alumni
affiliation.
Additional info: OSF Saint Francis Medical Center Education student loan
available to full-time students on a limited basis. Tuition waiver program for
hospital employees available.

FINANCIAL AID PROCEDURES
Forms required: FAFSA, institutional form.
Dates and Deadlines: Priority date 6/1; no closing date. Must reply within 4
week(s) of notification.

Transfers: No deadline. Applicants notified on a rolling basis starting 5/15;
must reply within 4 week(s) of notification.

CONTACT
Nancy Perryman, Coordinator of Student Finance, Financial Assistance
511 NE Greenleaf Street, Peoria, IL 61603-3783
(309) 655-4119

St. John's College

Springfield, Illinois
www.stjohnscollegespringfield.edu   Federal Code: 030980

Upper-division private nursing college in small city, affiliated with the
Roman Catholic Church.
Enrollment: 136 undergrads, 7% part-time.
Selectivity: Open admission; but selective for some programs.

BASIC COSTS (2016-2017)
Tuition and fees: $19,807.
Per-credit charge: $776.
Additional info: Tuition at time of enrollment locked for 2 years.

FINANCIAL AID PICTURE (2015-2016)
Students with need: Average financial aid package for all full-time undergraduates was $18,030; for part-time $1,000. 38% awarded as scholarships/
grants, 62% awarded as loans/jobs. Work study available nights, weekends,
and for part-time students.
Students without need: No-need awards available for alumni affiliation,
minority status.

FINANCIAL AID PROCEDURES
Forms required: FAFSA.
Dates and Deadlines: Applicants notified on a rolling basis.
Transfers: Priority date 2/15; no deadline. Applicants notified on a rolling
basis starting 4/1; must reply within 12 week(s) of notification.

CONTACT
Timothy Marten, Financial Aid Officer
729 East Carpenter Street, Springfield, IL 62702-5321
(217) 814-4705

Saint Xavier University

Chicago, Illinois
www.sxu.edu   Federal Code: 001768

4-year private university in very large city, affiliated with the Roman Catholic
Church.
Enrollment: 2,940 undergrads.

BASIC COSTS (2016-2017)
Tuition and fees: $32,250.
Per-credit charge: $680.
Room and board: $11,060.

FINANCIAL AID PICTURE
Students with need: Need-based aid available for full-time and part-time students.
Students without need: No-need awards available for academics, athletics,
music/drama.

FINANCIAL AID PROCEDURES
Forms required: FAFSA.
Dates and Deadlines: Priority date 2/15; no closing date. Applicants notified
on a rolling basis starting 2/1; must reply by 5/1 or within 2 week(s) of notification.
Transfers: Applicants notified on a rolling basis starting 2/15; must reply by
5/1 or within 2 week(s) of notification.

CONTACT
Susan Swisher, Director of Financial aid
3700 West 103rd Street, Chicago, IL 60655
(773) 298-3073

Sauk Valley Community College
Dixon, Illinois
www.svcc.edu   Federal Code: 001752

2-year public community college in large town.
Enrollment: 1,491 undergrads, 47% part-time. 317 full-time freshmen.
Selectivity: Open admission; but selective for some programs.

BASIC COSTS (2017-2018)
Tuition and fees: $3,586; out-of-district residents $9,438; out-of-state residents $10,194.

FINANCIAL AID PICTURE (2015-2016)
Students with need: Out of 146 full-time freshmen who applied for aid, 116 were judged to have need. Of these, 106 received aid, and 4 had their full need met. Average financial aid package met 44% of need; average scholarship/grant was $4,814; average loan was $1,908. For part-time students, average financial aid package was $5,354.
Students without need: 19 full-time freshmen who did not demonstrate need for aid received scholarships/grants; average award was $2,739. No-need awards available for academics, athletics, minority status, state/district residency.
Scholarships offered: 13 full-time freshmen received athletic scholarships; average amount $2,594.

FINANCIAL AID PROCEDURES
Forms required: FAFSA, institutional form.
Dates and Deadlines: Priority date 8/5; no closing date. Applicants notified on a rolling basis starting 3/20; must reply within 4 week(s) of notification.
Transfers: No deadline. Applicants notified on a rolling basis starting 3/20; must reply within 4 week(s) of notification.

CONTACT
Jennifer Schultz, Director of Financial Assistance
173 Illinois Route 2, Dixon, IL 61021-9112
(815) 288-5511 ext. 339

School of the Art Institute of Chicago
Chicago, Illinois
www.saic.edu   Federal Code: 001753

4-year private visual arts college in very large city.
Enrollment: 2,842 undergrads, 6% part-time. 573 full-time freshmen.

BASIC COSTS (2016-2017)
Tuition and fees: $45,750.
Room and board: $13,100.

FINANCIAL AID PICTURE (2015-2016)
Students with need: Out of 325 full-time freshmen who applied for aid, 277 were judged to have need. Of these, 276 received aid, and 27 had their full need met. Average financial aid package met 63.3% of need; average scholarship/grant was $20,318; average loan was $4,116. For part-time students, average financial aid package was $19,452.
Students without need: 208 full-time freshmen who did not demonstrate need for aid received scholarships/grants; average award was $11,499. No-need awards available for academics, art.
Scholarships offered: Merit scholarships; $2,000 to full tuition; renewable.

FINANCIAL AID PROCEDURES
Forms required: FAFSA.

Dates and Deadlines: Priority date 3/15; no closing date. Applicants notified on a rolling basis starting 3/1.
Transfers: No deadline. Applicants notified on a rolling basis.

CONTACT
Patrick James, Director of Financial Aid
36 South Wabash Avenue, Chicago, IL 60603
(312) 629-6600

Shawnee Community College
Ullin, Illinois
www.shawneecc.edu   Federal Code: 007693

2-year public community college in rural community.
Enrollment: 1,824 undergrads.
Selectivity: Open admission; but selective for some programs.

BASIC COSTS (2016-2017)
Tuition and fees: $3,270; out-of-district residents $5,100; out-of-state residents $5,400.
Per-credit charge: $99; out-of-district residents $164; out-of-state residents $166.

FINANCIAL AID PICTURE
Students with need: Need-based aid available for full-time and part-time students.
Students without need: This college awards aid only to students with need.

FINANCIAL AID PROCEDURES
Forms required: FAFSA.
Dates and Deadlines: Priority date 9/1; no closing date. Applicants notified on a rolling basis; must reply within 2 week(s) of notification.

CONTACT
Tammy Capps, Director of Financial Aid
8364 Shawnee College Road, Ullin, IL 62992
(618) 634-3280 ext. 3280

Shimer College
Chicago, Illinois
www.shimer.edu   Federal Code: 001756

4-year private liberal arts college in very large city.
Enrollment: 61 undergrads.

BASIC COSTS (2016-2017)
Tuition and fees: $33,790.
Per-credit charge: $1,130.
Room and board: $11,516.
Additional info: Tuition/fee waivers available for adults.

FINANCIAL AID PICTURE
Students with need: Need-based aid available for full-time and part-time students. Work study available nights, weekends, and for part-time students.
Students without need: No-need awards available for academics, alumni affiliation.
Scholarships offered: Michel de Montaigne Scholarship: half or full tuition; awarded to new students on the basis of merit in writing and discussion; 2 full and 2 half tuition scholarships awarded each year.

FINANCIAL AID PROCEDURES
Forms required: FAFSA.
Dates and Deadlines: Applicants notified on a rolling basis starting 3/15; must reply by 5/1.
Transfers: Closing date 8/1. Applicants notified on a rolling basis; must reply by 5/1 or within 3 week(s) of notification.

CONTACT
Janet Henthorn, Financial Aid Officer
3424 South State Street, Chicago, IL 60616
(312) 235-3507

South Suburban College of Cook County

South Holland, Illinois
www.ssc.edu   Federal Code: 001769

2-year public community college in large town.
Enrollment: 3,867 undergrads. 508 full-time freshmen.
Selectivity: Open admission; but selective for some programs.

BASIC COSTS (2016-2017)

Tuition and fees: $4,583; out-of-district residents $10,523; out-of-state residents $12,173.
Per-credit charge: $135; out-of-district residents $333; out-of-state residents $358.
Additional info: Tuition/fee waivers available for adults.

FINANCIAL AID PICTURE (2015-2016)

Students with need: Out of 491 full-time freshmen who applied for aid, 448 were judged to have need. Of these, 448 received aid. Average financial aid package met 60% of need. Need-based aid available for part-time students.
Students without need: No-need awards available for academics, art, athletics, music/drama, state/district residency.

FINANCIAL AID PROCEDURES

Forms required: FAFSA.
Dates and Deadlines: Priority date 6/30; no closing date. Applicants notified on a rolling basis starting 5/1.
Transfers: No deadline. Applicants notified on a rolling basis starting 5/11; must reply by 7/15 or within 2 week(s) of notification.

CONTACT

John Semple, Director
15800 South State Street, South Holland, IL 60473
(708) 596-2000 ext. 2438

Southeastern Illinois College

Harrisburg, Illinois
www.sic.edu   Federal Code: 001757

2-year public community college in small town.
Enrollment: 964 undergrads, 34% part-time. 94 full-time freshmen.
Selectivity: Open admission; but selective for some programs.

BASIC COSTS (2016-2017)

Tuition and fees: $3,270; out-of-district residents $5,220; out-of-state residents $5,460.
Per-credit charge: $99; out-of-district residents $164; out-of-state residents $172.

FINANCIAL AID PICTURE

Students with need: Need-based aid available for full-time and part-time students.
Students without need: No-need awards available for academics, alumni affiliation, art, athletics, music/drama.

FINANCIAL AID PROCEDURES

Forms required: FAFSA.
Dates and Deadlines: Priority date 2/15; no closing date. Applicants notified on a rolling basis starting 3/1; must reply within 2 week(s) of notification.
Transfers: Priority date 2/28; no deadline. Applicants notified on a rolling basis starting 4/1; must reply within 2 week(s) of notification.

CONTACT
Michelle Metten, Director of Financial Aid
3575 College Road, Harrisburg, IL 62946
(618) 252-5400 ext. 2450

Southern Illinois University Carbondale

Carbondale, Illinois
www.siu.edu   Federal Code: 001758

4-year public university in large town.
Enrollment: 12,056 undergrads, 13% part-time. 1,588 full-time freshmen.
Selectivity: Admits over 75% of applicants.

BASIC COSTS (2016-2017)

Tuition and fees: $12,231; out-of-state residents $25,880.
Per-credit charge: $303; out-of-state residents $758.
Room and board: $10,186.
Additional info: Required fees do not include the refundable health insurance of $1,250. Tuition at time of enrollment locked for 4 years.

FINANCIAL AID PICTURE (2016-2017)

Students with need: Out of 1,469 full-time freshmen who applied for aid, 1,248 were judged to have need. Of these, 1,239 received aid, and 122 had their full need met. Average financial aid package met 63% of need; average scholarship/grant was $8,605; average loan was $3,373. For part-time students, average financial aid package was $9,349.
Students without need: 110 full-time freshmen who did not demonstrate need for aid received scholarships/grants; average award was $7,224. No-need awards available for academics, alumni affiliation, art, athletics, leadership, minority status, music/drama, ROTC, state/district residency.
Scholarships offered: 59 full-time freshmen received athletic scholarships; average amount $19,840.
Additional info: Need-based financial aid available to part-time students enrolled in minimum of 6 semester hours.

FINANCIAL AID PROCEDURES

Forms required: FAFSA.
Dates and Deadlines: Priority date 3/1; no closing date. Applicants notified on a rolling basis starting 3/15.
Transfers: Must reply within 4 week(s) of notification.

CONTACT

Terri Harfst, Director
Undergraduate Admissions, Mailcode 4710, Carbondale, IL 62901
(618) 453-4334

Southern Illinois University Edwardsville

Edwardsville, Illinois
www.siue.edu   Federal Code: 001759

4-year public university in large town.
Enrollment: 11,652 undergrads, 15% part-time. 1,919 full-time freshmen.
Selectivity: Admits over 75% of applicants.

BASIC COSTS (2016-2017)

Tuition and fees: $11,008; out-of-state residents $23,536.
Per-credit charge: $278; out-of-state residents $696.
Room and board: $10,491.
Additional info: Tuition at time of enrollment locked for 4 years.

FINANCIAL AID PICTURE (2016-2017)

Students with need: Out of 1,732 full-time freshmen who applied for aid, 1,288 were judged to have need. Of these, 1,277 received aid, and 588 had their full need met. Average financial aid package met 71% of need; average

scholarship/grant was $8,608; average loan was $3,316. For part-time students, average financial aid package was $8,177.

Students without need: This college awards aid only to students with need.

Scholarships offered: 25 full-time freshmen received athletic scholarships; average amount $19,142.

FINANCIAL AID PROCEDURES

Forms required: FAFSA.

Dates and Deadlines: Priority date 3/1; closing date 6/1. Applicants notified on a rolling basis starting 3/15; must reply within 4 week(s) of notification.

CONTACT

Sally Mullen, Director of Student Financial Aid
Rendleman Hall, Rm 2120, Edwardsville, IL 62026-1600
(618) 650-3880

Southwestern Illinois College
Belleville, Illinois
www.swic.edu   Federal Code: 001636

2-year public community college in small city.
Enrollment: 9,028 undergrads.
Selectivity: Open admission; but selective for some programs.

BASIC COSTS (2016-2017)

Tuition and fees: $3,420; out-of-district residents $12,120; out-of-state residents $15,750.

Per-credit charge: $109; out-of-district residents $399; out-of-state residents $520.

Additional info: Tuition/fee waivers available for adults.

FINANCIAL AID PICTURE

Students with need: Need-based aid available for full-time and part-time students. Work study available nights.

Students without need: No-need awards available for academics, art, athletics, leadership, minority status, music/drama, ROTC.

FINANCIAL AID PROCEDURES

Forms required: FAFSA, institutional form.

Dates and Deadlines: Priority date 8/1; closing date 5/31. Applicants notified on a rolling basis starting 4/1; must reply within 2 week(s) of notification.

CONTACT

Robert Tebbe, Director of Financial Aid
2500 Carlyle Avenue, Belleville, IL 62221-5899
(618) 235-2700 ext. 5288

Spoon River College
Canton, Illinois
www.src.edu   Federal Code: 001643

2-year public community college in large town.
Enrollment: 1,133 undergrads, 36% part-time. 209 full-time freshmen.
Selectivity: Open admission; but selective for some programs.

BASIC COSTS (2016-2017)

Tuition and fees: $4,500; out-of-district residents $9,390; out-of-state residents $10,470.

Per-credit charge: $125; out-of-district residents $288; out-of-state residents $324.

FINANCIAL AID PICTURE (2015-2016)

Students with need: 67% of average financial aid package awarded as scholarships/grants, 33% awarded as loans/jobs. Need-based aid available for part-time students. Work study available nights.

Students without need: No-need awards available for academics, art, athletics, music/drama, state/district residency.

Scholarships offered: SRC's Foundation offers many scholarships. The application deadline is March 15. Students are required to complete an application and a FAFSA for the upcoming year.

Additional info: Students who have submitted all required forms by the processing deadline are guaranteed to have aid eligibility established by the tuition deadline. All forms submitted after the processing deadline are processed in the order received on a continuing basis.

FINANCIAL AID PROCEDURES

Forms required: FAFSA.

Dates and Deadlines: Priority date 6/21; closing date 7/1. Applicants notified on a rolling basis starting 5/15.

CONTACT

Jo Branson, Director of Financial Aid
23235 North County Road 22, Canton, IL 61520
(309) 649-7030

Taylor Business Institute
Chicago, Illinois
www.tbiil.edu   Federal Code: 011810

2-year for-profit business college in very large city.
Enrollment: 257 undergrads.

BASIC COSTS (2016-2017)

Additional info: Program cost for computerized accounting technician: $29,735; book and supplies: $900. Criminal justice and security administration: $29,401; books and supplies: $900.

FINANCIAL AID PICTURE

Students with need: Need-based aid available for full-time students. Work study available nights.

FINANCIAL AID PROCEDURES

Forms required: FAFSA, state aid form, institutional form.

CONTACT

Florence Davis, Financial Aid Director
318 West Adams Street, 5th Floor, Chicago, IL 60606
(312) 658-5100

Trinity Christian College
Palos Heights, Illinois
www.trnty.edu   Federal Code: 001771

4-year private liberal arts college in very large city.
Enrollment: 1,085 undergrads, 17% part-time. 160 full-time freshmen.
Selectivity: Admits 50 to 75% of applicants.

BASIC COSTS (2016-2017)

Tuition and fees: $27,675.
Per-credit charge: $908.
Room and board: $9,580.

FINANCIAL AID PICTURE (2016-2017)

Students with need: Out of 137 full-time freshmen who applied for aid, 126 were judged to have need. Of these, 126 received aid, and 21 had their full need met. Average financial aid package met 76% of need; average scholarship/grant was $19,405; average loan was $3,712. For part-time students, average financial aid package was $6,990.

Students without need: 17 full-time freshmen who did not demonstrate need for aid received scholarships/grants; average award was $10,462. No-need awards available for academics, alumni affiliation, art, athletics, leadership, minority status, music/drama, religious affiliation.

Scholarships offered: 13 full-time freshmen received athletic scholarships; average amount $4,712.

Additional info: High school transcripts and ACT/SAT required for merit scholarships.

FINANCIAL AID PROCEDURES

Forms required: FAFSA.

Dates and Deadlines: Priority date 12/1; no closing date. Applicants notified on a rolling basis starting 12/15; must reply by 5/1 or within 2 week(s) of notification.

Transfers: Applicants notified on a rolling basis starting 3/1; must reply by 5/1 or within 2 week(s) of notification.

CONTACT

Ryan Zantingh, Director of Financial Aid
6601 West College Drive, Palos Heights, IL 60463
(708) 239-4706

Trinity College of Nursing & Health Sciences

Rock Island, Illinois
www.trinitycollegeqc.edu   Federal Code: 006225

4-year private health science and nursing college in large city.
Enrollment: 222 undergrads, 41% part-time.

BASIC COSTS (2016-2017)

Tuition and fees: $23,307.
Per-credit charge: $687.
Additional info: Tuition and fees vary by program. The amounts reported for this survey are for the Bachelor of Science in Nursing - Basic program which is a two-year program that has a per-credit-hour tuition cost of $687. Associate degree programs are $527 per credit hour.

FINANCIAL AID PICTURE (2016-2017)

Students with need: Average financial aid package for all full-time undergraduates was $5,149; for part-time $4,211. 48% awarded as scholarships/grants, 52% awarded as loans/jobs.

Students without need: This college awards aid only to students with need.

FINANCIAL AID PROCEDURES

Forms required: FAFSA, institutional form.
Dates and Deadlines: Applicants notified on a rolling basis starting 1/1.
Transfers: No deadline.

CONTACT

Travis Lopez, Financial Aid Specialist
2122 25th Avenue, Rock Island, IL 61201-5317
(309) 779-7740

Trinity International University

Deerfield, Illinois
www.tiu.edu   Federal Code: 001772

4-year private university and liberal arts college in large town, affiliated with the Evangelical Free Church of America.
Enrollment: 947 undergrads, 27% part-time. 145 full-time freshmen.
Selectivity: Admits 50 to 75% of applicants.

BASIC COSTS (2017-2018)

Tuition and fees: $30,750.
Per-credit charge: $1,260.
Room and board: $9,240.
Additional info: Tuition/fee waivers available for minority students.

FINANCIAL AID PICTURE (2015-2016)

Students with need: Out of 138 full-time freshmen who applied for aid, 131 were judged to have need. Of these, 131 received aid, and 18 had their full need met. Average financial aid package met 75% of need; average scholarship/grant was $8,303; average loan was $3,932. For part-time students, average financial aid package was $9,304.

Students without need: 5 full-time freshmen who did not demonstrate need for aid received scholarships/grants; average award was $11,000. No-need awards available for academics, alumni affiliation, athletics, leadership, minority status, music/drama, religious affiliation.

Scholarships offered: 5 full-time freshmen received athletic scholarships; average amount $6,410.

FINANCIAL AID PROCEDURES

Forms required: FAFSA.

Dates and Deadlines: Priority date 4/1; no closing date. Applicants notified on a rolling basis starting 11/15; must reply within 4 week(s) of notification.

Transfers: No deadline. Applicants notified on a rolling basis starting 11/15; must reply within 4 week(s) of notification.

CONTACT

Rachael Russiaky, Executive Director for Student Services
2065 Half Day Road, Deerfield, IL 60015
(847) 317-4200

Triton College

River Grove, Illinois
www.triton.edu   Federal Code: 001773

2-year public community and junior college in large town.
Enrollment: 9,880 undergrads, 68% part-time. 629 full-time freshmen.
Selectivity: Open admission; but selective for some programs.

BASIC COSTS (2016-2017)

Tuition and fees: $3,870; out-of-district residents $9,370; out-of-state residents $11,629.
Per-credit charge: $113; out-of-district residents $296; out-of-state residents $371.

FINANCIAL AID PICTURE

Students with need: Need-based aid available for full-time and part-time students. Work study available nights, weekends, and for part-time students.

Students without need: No-need awards available for academics, athletics.

Scholarships offered: Board of Trustees Honor Scholarship: covers tuition and fees; for in-district high school students in top 10% of graduating class.

FINANCIAL AID PROCEDURES

Forms required: FAFSA, institutional form.
Dates and Deadlines: Priority date 4/15; no closing date. Applicants notified on a rolling basis starting 4/1; must reply within 2 week(s) of notification.

CONTACT

Patricia Zinga, Director of Financial Aid
2000 North Fifth Avenue, River Grove, IL 60171
(708) 456-0300 ext. 3441

University of Chicago

Chicago, Illinois   Federal Code: 001774
www.uchicago.edu   CSS Code: 1832

4-year private university and liberal arts college in very large city.
Enrollment: 5,930 undergrads. 1,591 full-time freshmen.
Selectivity: Admits less than 50% of applicants.

BASIC COSTS (2016-2017)

Tuition and fees: $52,491.
Room and board: $15,093.

FINANCIAL AID PICTURE (2016-2017)

Students with need: Out of 893 full-time freshmen who applied for aid, 653 were judged to have need. Of these, 653 received aid, and 653 had their full need met. Average financial aid package met 100% of need; average scholarship/grant was $47,321.

Students without need: No-need awards available for academics, leadership.

Additional info: No Barriers program replaces student loans with grants in all need-based financial aid packages. Grants offered instead of loans in all need based financial aid packages. Families who apply for financial aid do not have to pay a college application fee. Funding available for summer and school-year internships, research positions, study abroad, and career exploration treks for all majors and interests.

FINANCIAL AID PROCEDURES

Forms required: FAFSA, CSS PROFILE, institutional form.

Dates and Deadlines: Priority date 2/15; no closing date. Applicants notified by 4/1; must reply by 5/1.

Transfers: Priority date 4/1. Applicants notified on a rolling basis starting 5/1; must reply by 6/1.

CONTACT

Amanda Fijal, Executive Director, University Financial Aid & ESA Technologies
1101 East 58th Street, Chicago, IL 60637
(773) 702-8666

University of Illinois at Chicago

Chicago, Illinois
www.uic.edu
Federal Code: 001776

4-year public university in very large city.

Enrollment: 17,804 undergrads, 8% part-time. 3,445 full-time freshmen.

Selectivity: Admits 50 to 75% of applicants.

BASIC COSTS (2016-2017)

Tuition and fees: $13,664; out-of-state residents $26,520.

Room and board: $10,960.

Additional info: Health Insurance $1140, Refundable Fees $12. Tuition at time of enrollment locked for 4 years; tuition/fee waivers available for minority students.

FINANCIAL AID PICTURE (2015-2016)

Students with need: Out of 3,150 full-time freshmen who applied for aid, 2,747 were judged to have need. Of these, 2,613 received aid, and 281 had their full need met. Average financial aid package met 62% of need; average scholarship/grant was $13,899; average loan was $3,258. For part-time students, average financial aid package was $10,154.

Students without need: 140 full-time freshmen who did not demonstrate need for aid received scholarships/grants; average award was $5,926. No-need awards available for academics, art, athletics, music/drama, ROTC.

Scholarships offered: 29 full-time freshmen received athletic scholarships; average amount $22,030.

FINANCIAL AID PROCEDURES

Forms required: FAFSA.

Dates and Deadlines: Priority date 2/15; no closing date. Applicants notified on a rolling basis starting 3/15; must reply by 5/1.

CONTACT

Shirley Vega, Interim Director of the Office of Student Financial Aid
Office of Admissions and Records, UIC, PO Box 5220, Chicago, IL 60607-5220
(312) 996-3126

University of Illinois at Urbana-Champaign

Champaign, Illinois
http://illinois.edu
Federal Code: 001775

4-year public university in small city.

Enrollment: 32,752 undergrads, 2% part-time. 7,556 full-time freshmen.

Selectivity: Admits 50 to 75% of applicants.

BASIC COSTS (2017-2018)

Tuition and fees: $15,868; out-of-state residents $31,988.

Room and board: $11,308.

Additional info: Tuition at time of enrollment locked for 4 years.

FINANCIAL AID PICTURE (2015-2016)

Students with need: Out of 5,483 full-time freshmen who applied for aid, 3,770 were judged to have need. Of these, 3,505 received aid, and 496 had their full need met. Average financial aid package met 67% of need; average scholarship/grant was $14,652; average loan was $4,405. For part-time students, average financial aid package was $8,123.

Students without need: 840 full-time freshmen who did not demonstrate need for aid received scholarships/grants; average award was $5,013. No-need awards available for academics, alumni affiliation, art, athletics, leadership, minority status, music/drama, ROTC, state/district residency.

Scholarships offered: *Merit:* President's Award Program: $1,000-$4,000 for 4 years; for members of historically underrepresented group, with ACT score of 22-23 and in the top quarter of their class, or who have an ACT score of 24 or higher and are in the top half of their class. University Achievement Scholarship: $8,000; criteria set by each college, renewable with 3.0 GPA; 50 available. Matthews Scholars: $2,000 per year, renewable for 4 years if GPA of 3.3 is maintained; criteria includes academic achievement, leadership skills, commitment to campus and community efforts, good sponsor relations, diversity of college gender and ethnicity; approximately 150 available. FMC Award of Excellence: $1,000 a year, non-renewable; criteria set by individual colleges; 20 available. Provost Scholarship: full tuition, renewable with 3.0 GPA; National Achievement, National Hispanic Scholar finalists, or National Merit finalists who have indicated the University of Illinois at Urbana-Champaign as their top choice. Campus Merit: $3,000; students in historically underrepresented groups who are in the top 10 percent of their graduating class. National Merit: $500; National Merit finalists who indicated the University of Illinois as their top choice, renewable with 3.0 GPA. James Hunter Anthony and Gerald Blackshear Scholarship: 1 year of tuition and fees, renewable with 3.0 GPA; incoming freshmen who are graduates of an Illinois high school, with superior academic and leadership qualities; need may be considered. *Athletic:* 35 full-time freshmen received athletic scholarships; average amount $35,621.

FINANCIAL AID PROCEDURES

Forms required: FAFSA.

Dates and Deadlines: Priority date 3/15; no closing date. Applicants notified on a rolling basis starting 3/1; must reply by 5/1 or within 3 week(s) of notification.

CONTACT

Daniel Mann, Director of Student Financial Aid
901 West Illinois, Urbana, IL 61801-3028
(217) 333-0100

University of Illinois: Springfield

Springfield, Illinois
www.uis.edu
Federal Code: 009333

4-year public university and liberal arts college in small city.

Enrollment: 2,877 undergrads, 34% part-time. 264 full-time freshmen.

Selectivity: Admits 50 to 75% of applicants.

BASIC COSTS (2016-2017)

Tuition and fees: $11,413; out-of-state residents $20,938.

Per-credit charge: $313.5; out-of-state residents $631.

Room and board: $11,600.

Additional info: Health Insurance $1196, Refundable Fees $8. Tuition at time of enrollment locked for 4 years.

FINANCIAL AID PICTURE (2015-2016)

Students with need: Out of 244 full-time freshmen who applied for aid, 204 were judged to have need. Of these, 197 received aid, and 45 had their full need met. Average financial aid package met 79% of need; average scholarship/grant was $13,815; average loan was $3,108. For part-time students, average financial aid package was $6,975.

Students without need: 51 full-time freshmen who did not demonstrate need for aid received scholarships/grants; average award was $7,615. No-need awards available for academics, alumni affiliation, art, athletics, job skills, leadership, minority status, music/drama, state/district residency.

Scholarships offered: 20 full-time freshmen received athletic scholarships; average amount $6,117.

FINANCIAL AID PROCEDURES

Forms required: FAFSA.

Dates and Deadlines: Priority date 3/1; closing date 11/15. Applicants notified on a rolling basis starting 1/1; must reply within 3 week(s) of notification.

Transfers: No deadline. Applicants notified on a rolling basis.

CONTACT

Carolyn Schloemann, Acting Director, Financial Assistance
One University Plaza, MS UHB 1080, Springfield, IL 62703-5407
(217) 206-6724

University of St. Francis

Joliet, Illinois
www.stfrancis.edu   Federal Code: 001664

4-year private university and liberal arts college in small city, affiliated with the Roman Catholic Church.

Enrollment: 1,343 undergrads, 4% part-time. 215 full-time freshmen.

Selectivity: Admits less than 50% of applicants.

BASIC COSTS (2016-2017)

Tuition and fees: $30,840.

Per-credit charge: $825.

Room and board: $9,084.

FINANCIAL AID PICTURE (2016-2017)

Students with need: Out of 203 full-time freshmen who applied for aid, 186 were judged to have need. Of these, 186 received aid, and 66 had their full need met. Average financial aid package met 86% of need; average scholarship/grant was $20,660; average loan was $3,514. For part-time students, average financial aid package was $8,894.

Students without need: 11 full-time freshmen who did not demonstrate need for aid received scholarships/grants; average award was $12,745. No-need awards available for academics, alumni affiliation, art, athletics, leadership, minority status, music/drama, religious affiliation, state/district residency.

Scholarships offered: 11 full-time freshmen received athletic scholarships; average amount $19,731.

FINANCIAL AID PROCEDURES

Forms required: FAFSA, institutional form.

Dates and Deadlines: Priority date 2/15; no closing date. Applicants notified on a rolling basis starting 2/15.

CONTACT

Bruce Foote, Assistant Director for Institutional Research
500 Wilcox Street, Joliet, IL 60435-6169
(866) 890-8331

VanderCook College of Music

Chicago, Illinois
www.vandercook.edu   Federal Code: 177800

4-year private music and teachers college in very large city.

Enrollment: 103 undergrads, 2% part-time. 21 full-time freshmen.

Selectivity: Admits over 75% of applicants.

BASIC COSTS (2016-2017)

Tuition and fees: $27,180.

Per-credit charge: $1,075.

Room and board: $11,898.

FINANCIAL AID PICTURE (2015-2016)

Students with need: For part-time students, average financial aid package was $5,779.

Students without need: No-need awards available for academics, music/drama.

Additional info: Musical talent considered for partial tuition waiver.

FINANCIAL AID PROCEDURES

Forms required: FAFSA.

Dates and Deadlines: Priority date 3/1; no closing date. Applicants notified on a rolling basis starting 5/1; must reply within 2 week(s) of notification.

Transfers: Priority date 4/1. Must reply by 5/1.

CONTACT

Sirena Covington, Director of Financial Aid
3140 South Federal Street, Chicago, IL 60616-3731
(312) 225-6288 ext. 253

Waubonsee Community College

Sugar Grove, Illinois
www.waubonsee.edu   Federal Code: 006931

2-year public community and junior college in small town.

Enrollment: 8,055 undergrads.

Selectivity: Open admission; but selective for some programs.

BASIC COSTS (2016-2017)

Tuition and fees: $3,780; out-of-district residents $9,038; out-of-state residents $9,768.

FINANCIAL AID PICTURE

Students with need: Need-based aid available for full-time and part-time students. Work study available nights.

Students without need: No-need awards available for academics, art, athletics, leadership, minority status, music/drama, state/district residency.

Scholarships offered: Gustafson Scholarship; provides tuition for 64 semester hours; selected graduates from each in-district school.

FINANCIAL AID PROCEDURES

Forms required: FAFSA.

Dates and Deadlines: Priority date 3/1; no closing date. Applicants notified on a rolling basis starting 4/1.

Transfers: Priority date 3/13; no deadline. Applicants notified on a rolling basis starting 4/13.

CONTACT

Charles Boudreau, Director of Student Financial Aid Services
Route 47 at Waubonsee Drive, Sugar Grove, IL 60554-9454
(630) 466-7900 ext. 5774

Western Illinois University

Macomb, Illinois
www.wiu.edu   Federal Code: 001780

4-year public university in large town.
Enrollment: 8,543 undergrads, 12% part-time. 1,465 full-time freshmen.
Selectivity: Admits 50 to 75% of applicants.

BASIC COSTS (2016-2017)
Tuition and fees: $11,245; out-of-state residents $15,515.
Per-credit charge: $285; out-of-state residents $427.
Room and board: $9,580.
Additional info: Student health insurance $705/semester or $1410 for full academic year. Tuition at time of enrollment locked for 4 years.

FINANCIAL AID PICTURE (2016-2017)
Students with need: Out of 1,367 full-time freshmen who applied for aid, 1,198 were judged to have need. Of these, 1,182 received aid, and 297 had their full need met. Average financial aid package met 63% of need; average scholarship/grant was $104,459; average loan was $3,382. For part-time students, average financial aid package was $6,455.
Students without need: 67 full-time freshmen who did not demonstrate need for aid received scholarships/grants; average award was $2,024. No-need awards available for academics, alumni affiliation, art, athletics, leadership, minority status, music/drama, ROTC.
Scholarships offered: _Merit:_ Western Commitment Scholarships-Merit: based on high school GPA and ACT/SAT score; 4-year scholarships towards the cost of attendance; award levels of $1,000, $2,000, $3,000, and $10,000 for highest ability; renewable for up to 4 years if maintain eligibility. New freshmen who submit all application materials by May 15 are automatically considered. **_Athletic:_** 41 full-time freshmen received athletic scholarships; average amount $10,581.
Additional info: University funded need-based grant and work program continued for student's undergraduate career with emphasis on graduating in 4 years and maintaining an average of 15 hours/semester and satisfactory academic performance.

FINANCIAL AID PROCEDURES
Forms required: FAFSA.
Dates and Deadlines: Applicants notified on a rolling basis starting 1/15.
Transfers: No deadline. Applicants notified on a rolling basis starting 1/15. Transfer students with confirmed Associates degree receive transfer scholarship or book award based on GPA. If they do not qualify for a scholarship, they receive a book award.

CONTACT
Terri Hare, Director of Financial Aid
1 University Circle, Macomb, IL 61455-1390
(309) 298-2446

Wheaton College

Wheaton, Illinois
www.wheaton.edu   Federal Code: 001781

4-year private liberal arts college in small city, affiliated with the nondenominational tradition.
Enrollment: 2,432 undergrads, 1% part-time. 588 full-time freshmen.
Selectivity: Admits over 75% of applicants.

BASIC COSTS (2016-2017)
Tuition and fees: $34,050.
Per-credit charge: $1,419.
Room and board: $9,560.

FINANCIAL AID PICTURE (2016-2017)
Students with need: Out of 415 full-time freshmen who applied for aid, 341 were judged to have need. Of these, 341 received aid, and 78 had their full need met. Average financial aid package met 86% of need; average scholarship/grant was $20,671; average loan was $4,389. For part-time students, average financial aid package was $85,111.
Students without need: 154 full-time freshmen who did not demonstrate need for aid received scholarships/grants; average award was $6,247. No-need awards available for academics, alumni affiliation, art, minority status, music/drama, ROTC.
Scholarships offered: Charles Blanchard President's Award: $5,000 per year for up to 4 years; U.S. citizens with 3.7 GPA on 4.0 scale, plus 1400 SAT/32 ACT; unlimited number available; also available to transfer students. Arthur Holmes Award: $2,500 per year for up to 4 years; U.S. citizens not qualifying for Blanchard Award with 3.6 GPA on 4.0 scale, plus 1330 SAT/30 ACT; unlimited number available; also available to transfer students.

FINANCIAL AID PROCEDURES
Forms required: FAFSA, institutional form.
Dates and Deadlines: Priority date 12/1; no closing date. Applicants notified on a rolling basis starting 1/15.
Transfers: Priority date 2/15; no deadline. Applicants notified on a rolling basis starting 3/1; must reply by 5/1.

CONTACT
Karen Belling, Director of Financial Aid
501 College Avenue, Wheaton, IL 60187-5593
(630) 752-5021

Indiana

Ancilla College

Donaldson, Indiana
www.ancilla.edu   Federal Code: 001784

2-year private junior and liberal arts college in rural community, affiliated with the Roman Catholic Church.
Enrollment: 558 undergrads, 16% part-time. 264 full-time freshmen.
Selectivity: Open admission; but selective for some programs.

BASIC COSTS (2017-2018)
Tuition and fees: $15,830.
Room and board: $9,200.

FINANCIAL AID PICTURE
Students with need: Need-based aid available for full-time and part-time students.
Students without need: No-need awards available for academics, athletics, job skills, leadership.

FINANCIAL AID PROCEDURES
Forms required: FAFSA.
Dates and Deadlines: Closing date 3/10. Applicants notified on a rolling basis starting 3/10; must reply within 2 week(s) of notification.
Transfers: No deadline. Applicants notified on a rolling basis; must reply by 8/1.

CONTACT
Diana Kerrigan, Director of Financial Aid
9601 Union Road, Donaldson, IN 46513
(574) 936-8898 ext. 307

Anderson University

Anderson, Indiana
www.anderson.edu   Federal Code: 001785

4-year private liberal arts college in small city, affiliated with the Church of God.

Enrollment: 1,702 undergrads, 7% part-time. 423 full-time freshmen.
Selectivity: Admits 50 to 75% of applicants.

BASIC COSTS (2016-2017)
Tuition and fees: $28,650.
Per-credit charge: $1,188.
Room and board: $9,550.
Additional info: Tuition/fee waivers available for adults.

FINANCIAL AID PICTURE
Students with need: Need-based aid available for full-time and part-time students. Work study available nights, weekends, and for part-time students.
Students without need: No-need awards available for academics, alumni affiliation, art, leadership, minority status, music/drama, religious affiliation.

FINANCIAL AID PROCEDURES
Forms required: FAFSA.
Dates and Deadlines: Priority date 3/1; no closing date. Applicants notified on a rolling basis starting 3/1.
Transfers: No deadline. Applicants notified on a rolling basis.

CONTACT
Gayla Roberts, Director of Student Financial Services
1100 East Fifth Street, Anderson, IN 46012-3495
(765) 641-4182

Ball State University
Muncie, Indiana
www.bsu.edu   Federal Code: 001786

4-year public university in small city.
Enrollment: 16,095 undergrads, 7% part-time. 3,866 full-time freshmen.
Selectivity: Admits 50 to 75% of applicants.

BASIC COSTS (2016-2017)
Tuition and fees: $9,654; out-of-state residents $25,428.
Per-credit charge: $296; out-of-state residents $980.
Room and board: $9,936.

FINANCIAL AID PICTURE (2016-2017)
Students with need: 44% of average financial aid package awarded as scholarships/grants, 56% awarded as loans/jobs. Need-based aid available for part-time students. Work study available nights, weekends, and for part-time students.
Students without need: No-need awards available for academics, athletics, leadership, minority status, music/drama, ROTC, state/district residency.

FINANCIAL AID PROCEDURES
Forms required: FAFSA.
Dates and Deadlines: Priority date 3/15; no closing date. Applicants notified on a rolling basis starting 4/1.
Transfers: No deadline. Applicants notified on a rolling basis starting 6/1.

CONTACT
John McPherson, Assistant Vice President of Enrollment Services
Office of Admissions, Ball State University, Muncie, IN 47306-0855
(765) 285-5600

Bethel College
Mishawaka, Indiana
www.bethelcollege.edu   Federal Code: 001787

4-year private liberal arts college in small city, affiliated with the Missionary Church.
Enrollment: 1,335 undergrads, 16% part-time. 241 full-time freshmen.
Selectivity: Admits over 75% of applicants.

BASIC COSTS (2017-2018)
Tuition and fees: $27,930.
Room and board: $8,800.
Additional info: Tuition/fee waivers available for adults, minority students.

FINANCIAL AID PICTURE (2016-2017)
Students with need: Need-based aid available for full-time and part-time students. Work study available nights, weekends, and for part-time students.
Students without need: 16 full-time freshmen who did not demonstrate need for aid received scholarships/grants; average award was $11,141. No-need awards available for academics, athletics, leadership, minority status, music/drama, religious affiliation.
Scholarships offered: 4 full-time freshmen received athletic scholarships; average amount $16,625.

FINANCIAL AID PROCEDURES
Forms required: FAFSA.
Dates and Deadlines: Priority date 3/1; closing date 3/10. Applicants notified on a rolling basis starting 12/1.
Transfers: No deadline. Applicants notified on a rolling basis starting 1/1.

CONTACT
Cindi Pedersen, Director of Financial Aid
1001 Bethel Circle, Mishawaka, IN 46545-5591
(574) 807-7415

Brown Mackie College: South Bend
South Bend, Indiana
www.brownmackie.edu   Federal Code: 004583

2-year for-profit community and technical college in small city.
Selectivity: Open admission.

BASIC COSTS (2016-2017)
Additional info: Costs vary by program. Certificate programs $16,896-$18,304, books and supplies $650. Diploma program Practical Nursing $31,236, books and supplies $650. Associate programs $33,312-$40,100, books and supplies $650-$1,130. Bachelor's programs $62,460-$82,720, books and supplies $650-$1,550.

FINANCIAL AID PICTURE
Students with need: Need-based aid available for full-time and part-time students.
Students without need: This college awards aid only to students with need.

FINANCIAL AID PROCEDURES
Forms required: FAFSA.
Dates and Deadlines: Applicants notified on a rolling basis; must reply within 1 week(s) of notification.

CONTACT
Sue Kempt, Senior Financial Aid Officer
3454 Douglas Road, South Bend, IN 46635

Butler University
Indianapolis, Indiana
www.butler.edu   Federal Code: 001788

4-year private university in very large city.
Enrollment: 4,235 undergrads, 2% part-time. 1,255 full-time freshmen.
Selectivity: Admits 50 to 75% of applicants.

BASIC COSTS (2017-2018)
Tuition and fees: $40,175.
Per-credit charge: $1,558.
Room and board: $13,030.

FINANCIAL AID PICTURE (2016-2017)
Students with need: Out of 1,229 full-time freshmen who applied for aid, 789 were judged to have need. Of these, 769 received aid, and 99 had their full need met. Average financial aid package met 63% of need; average scholarship/grant was $19,085; average loan was $4,030. For part-time students, average financial aid package was $8,148.

Students without need: 449 full-time freshmen who did not demonstrate need for aid received scholarships/grants; average award was $14,998. No-need awards available for academics, alumni affiliation, athletics, leadership, music/drama.

Scholarships offered: 19 full-time freshmen received athletic scholarships; average amount $27,386.

FINANCIAL AID PROCEDURES
Forms required: FAFSA.

Dates and Deadlines: Priority date 12/1; no closing date. Applicants notified on a rolling basis starting 1/15; must reply within 3 week(s) of notification.

CONTACT
Melissa Smurdon, Director of Financial Aid
4600 Sunset Avenue, Indianapolis, IN 46208
(317) 940-8200

Calumet College of St. Joseph
Whiting, Indiana
www.ccsj.edu   Federal Code: 001834

4-year private liberal arts college in small city, affiliated with the Roman Catholic Church.
Enrollment: 744 undergrads, 34% part-time. 108 full-time freshmen.
Selectivity: Admits less than 50% of applicants.

BASIC COSTS (2016-2017)
Tuition and fees: $17,570.
Per-credit charge: $550.
Additional info: Tuition at time of enrollment locked for 4 years.

FINANCIAL AID PICTURE
Students with need: Need-based aid available for full-time and part-time students.

Students without need: No-need awards available for academics, alumni affiliation, art, athletics, leadership, music/drama.

Additional info: Immediate computerized estimate of financial aid eligibility available to students applying in person. Students with a zero EFC who are state aid and Pell Grant recipients receive institutional aid to cover tuition.

FINANCIAL AID PROCEDURES
Forms required: FAFSA.

Dates and Deadlines: Priority date 3/10; no closing date. Applicants notified on a rolling basis starting 4/30; must reply within 2 week(s) of notification.

Transfers: No deadline. Applicants notified on a rolling basis. Academic Scholarship for transfer students.

CONTACT
Lynn Miskus, Vice-President of Business & Finance
2400 New York Avenue, Whiting, IN 46394-2195
(219) 473-4296

Crossroads Bible College
Indianapolis, Indiana
www.crossroads.edu   Federal Code: 034567

4-year private Bible college in very large city.
Enrollment: 249 undergrads.

BASIC COSTS (2016-2017)
Tuition and fees: $12,400.

Per-credit charge: $395.

FINANCIAL AID PICTURE
Students with need: Need-based aid available for full-time and part-time students.

Students without need: This college awards aid only to students with need.

FINANCIAL AID PROCEDURES
Forms required: FAFSA, institutional form.

Dates and Deadlines: Priority date 3/1; closing date 3/10. Applicants notified on a rolling basis; must reply within 2 week(s) of notification.

Transfers: No deadline. Applicants notified on a rolling basis; must reply within 2 week(s) of notification.

CONTACT
Phyllis Dodson, Senior Director of Financial Aid
601 North Shortridge Road, Indianapolis, IN 46219
(317) 789-8250

DePauw University
Greencastle, Indiana
www.depauw.edu   Federal Code: 001792

4-year private music and liberal arts college in large town, affiliated with the United Methodist Church.
Enrollment: 2,181 undergrads. 559 full-time freshmen.
Selectivity: Admits 50 to 75% of applicants.

BASIC COSTS (2016-2017)
Tuition and fees: $46,448.
Per-credit charge: $1,427.
Room and board: $12,240.

FINANCIAL AID PICTURE (2016-2017)
Students with need: Out of 468 full-time freshmen who applied for aid, 397 were judged to have need. Of these, 397 received aid, and 108 had their full need met. Average financial aid package met 90% of need; average scholarship/grant was $36,721; average loan was $4,173. For part-time students, average financial aid package was $12,362.

Students without need: 169 full-time freshmen who did not demonstrate need for aid received scholarships/grants; average award was $18,481. No-need awards available for academics, alumni affiliation, leadership, music/drama.

Scholarships offered: Holton Scholarships; $1,000 to full tuition; based on exceptional leadership and/or service; 50 awarded.

FINANCIAL AID PROCEDURES
Forms required: FAFSA, institutional form.

Dates and Deadlines: Priority date 12/16; closing date 2/1. Applicants notified on a rolling basis starting 2/1; must reply by 5/1.

Transfers: Applicants notified by 3/27; must reply by 5/1.

CONTACT
Craig Slaughter, Director of Financial Aid
204 East Seminary Street, Greencastle, IN 46135-1611
(765) 658-4030

Earlham College
Richmond, Indiana
www.earlham.edu   Federal Code: 001793

4-year private liberal arts and seminary college in large town, affiliated with the Society of Friends (Quaker).
Enrollment: 994 undergrads. 355 full-time freshmen.
Selectivity: Admits 50 to 75% of applicants.

BASIC COSTS (2016-2017)

Tuition and fees: $45,300.
Per-credit charge: $1,479.
Room and board: $9,570.

FINANCIAL AID PICTURE (2015-2016)

Students with need: 80% of average financial aid package awarded as scholarships/grants, 20% awarded as loans/jobs. Need-based aid available for part-time students. Work study available nights, weekends, and for part-time students.

Students without need: No-need awards available for academics, leadership, minority status, religious affiliation.

FINANCIAL AID PROCEDURES

Forms required: FAFSA.

Dates and Deadlines: Closing date 3/1. Applicants notified on a rolling basis starting 3/15; must reply by 5/1.

Transfers: Priority date 3/1; no deadline. Applicants notified on a rolling basis starting 3/1; must reply by 5/1 or within 3 week(s) of notification. Deadline for State of Indiana Grants, 3/1 (FAFSA date).

CONTACT

Kathy Gottschalk, Director of Financial Aid
801 National Road West, Richmond, IN 47374-4095
(765) 983-1217

Fortis College: Indianapolis

Indianapolis, Indiana
www.fortis.edu   Federal Code: E01820

2-year for-profit career college in very large city.
Enrollment: 218 undergrads.
Selectivity: Open admission.

BASIC COSTS (2016-2017)

Additional info: Tuition and fees vary by program. Associate's Degree in Nursing; $47,851. Diploma/certificate programs range $15,343-$18,915. Books and supplies vary depending on program and level. All costs are subject to change. Tuition at time of enrollment locked for 2 years.

FINANCIAL AID PICTURE

Students with need: Need-based aid available for full-time and part-time students.

FINANCIAL AID PROCEDURES

Forms required: FAFSA, institutional form.

CONTACT

Jordan Leicher, Director of Administration
9001 North Wesleyan Road, Suite 101, Indianapolis, IN 46268
(317) 808-4800

Franklin College

Franklin, Indiana
www.franklincollege.edu   Federal Code: 001798

4-year private liberal arts college in large town, affiliated with the American Baptist Churches in the USA.
Enrollment: 977 undergrads, 2% part-time. 238 full-time freshmen.
Selectivity: Admits over 75% of applicants.

BASIC COSTS (2016-2017)

Tuition and fees: $30,025.
Per-credit charge: $1,100.
Room and board: $9,355.
Additional info: Tuition/fee waivers available for minority students.

FINANCIAL AID PICTURE (2016-2017)

Students with need: Out of 232 full-time freshmen who applied for aid, 211 were judged to have need. Of these, 211 received aid, and 36 had their full need met. Average financial aid package met 78% of need; average scholarship/grant was $20,533; average loan was $3,242. For part-time students, average financial aid package was $8,338.

Students without need: 27 full-time freshmen who did not demonstrate need for aid received scholarships/grants; average award was $13,111. No-need awards available for academics, alumni affiliation, art, leadership, minority status, music/drama, religious affiliation, state/district residency.

FINANCIAL AID PROCEDURES

Forms required: FAFSA, institutional form.

Dates and Deadlines: Priority date 12/1; closing date 3/10. Applicants notified on a rolling basis starting 11/1; must reply by 5/1 or within 4 week(s) of notification.

Transfers: Must reply by 5/1 or within 2 week(s) of notification.

CONTACT

James Vincent-Dunn, Director of Financial Aid
101 Branigin Boulevard, Franklin, IN 46131-2623
(317) 738-8075

Goshen College

Goshen, Indiana
www.goshen.edu   Federal Code: 001799

4-year private liberal arts college in large town, affiliated with the Mennonite Church.
Enrollment: 793 undergrads, 7% part-time. 185 full-time freshmen.
Selectivity: Admits 50 to 75% of applicants.

BASIC COSTS (2017-2018)

Tuition and fees: $33,200.
Per-credit charge: $1,380.
Room and board: $10,500.

FINANCIAL AID PICTURE (2016-2017)

Students with need: Out of 167 full-time freshmen who applied for aid, 154 were judged to have need. Of these, 154 received aid, and 31 had their full need met. Average financial aid package met 84% of need; average scholarship/grant was $24,235; average loan was $3,730. For part-time students, average financial aid package was $8,363.

Students without need: 31 full-time freshmen who did not demonstrate need for aid received scholarships/grants; average award was $18,370. No-need awards available for academics, art, athletics, leadership, minority status, music/drama.

Scholarships offered: *Merit:* President's Leadership Award: $20,000; must meet two of the following criteria and submit separate application: 3.85 GPA, 1290 SAT (exclusive of Writing) or 29 ACT. National Merit semifinalist: 10 awards offered each year; renews annually with 3.2 GPA. Intercultural Leadership scholarship for first-generation students of color: must have 3.0 GPA and 860 SAT or 18 ACT and complete separate application; 20 awards offered each year. Merit scholarship: levels of $15,000, $13,000, $11,000, $8,000, $6,000 awarded based on combination of ACT or SAT score and high school GPA available to all applicants who qualify. *Athletic:* 11 full-time freshmen received athletic scholarships; average amount $7,408.

FINANCIAL AID PROCEDURES

Forms required: FAFSA.

Dates and Deadlines: Priority date 3/1; no closing date. Applicants notified on a rolling basis starting 1/10.

Transfers: No deadline. Applicants notified on a rolling basis starting 3/1.

CONTACT

Joel Short, Director of Financial Aid
1700 South Main Street, Goshen, IN 46526-4724
(574) 535-7525

Grace College
Winona Lake, Indiana
www.grace.edu   Federal Code: 001800

4-year private liberal arts college in small town, affiliated with the Brethren Church.
Enrollment: 1,614 undergrads, 6% part-time. 398 full-time freshmen.
Selectivity: Admits over 75% of applicants.

BASIC COSTS (2016-2017)
Tuition and fees: $23,120.
Per-credit charge: $824.
Room and board: $8,404.
Additional info: Tuition/fee waivers available for minority students.

FINANCIAL AID PICTURE
Students with need: Need-based aid available for full-time and part-time students. Work study available nights, weekends, and for part-time students.
Students without need: No-need awards available for academics, art, athletics, leadership, minority status, music/drama, religious affiliation, state/district residency.

FINANCIAL AID PROCEDURES
Forms required: FAFSA.
Dates and Deadlines: Closing date 3/1. Applicants notified on a rolling basis starting 3/1; must reply by 5/1.
Transfers: Applicants notified by 3/15; must reply by 5/1. Applicants who miss dates for admission and financial aid are notified on rolling basis until class is full.

CONTACT
Charlette Sauders, Director of Financial Aid Services
200 Seminary Drive, Winona Lake, IN 46590
(574) 372-5100 ext. 6162

Hanover College
Hanover, Indiana
www.hanover.edu   Federal Code: 001801

4-year private liberal arts college in rural community, affiliated with the Presbyterian Church (USA).
Enrollment: 1,083 undergrads. 304 full-time freshmen.
Selectivity: Admits 50 to 75% of applicants. GED not accepted.

BASIC COSTS (2016-2017)
Tuition and fees: $35,514.
Per-credit charge: $965.
Room and board: $10,850.

FINANCIAL AID PICTURE (2015-2016)
Students with need: Out of 302 full-time freshmen who applied for aid, 194 were judged to have need. Of these, 194 received aid, and 54 had their full need met. Average financial aid package met 82% of need; average scholarship/grant was $25,651; average loan was $3,548. For part-time students, average financial aid package was $5,348.
Students without need: 52 full-time freshmen who did not demonstrate need for aid received scholarships/grants; average award was $20,772. No-need awards available for academics, alumni affiliation, leadership, minority status, state/district residency.

FINANCIAL AID PROCEDURES
Forms required: FAFSA.
Dates and Deadlines: Priority date 3/1; no closing date. Applicants notified by 3/1.
Transfers: No deadline. Applicants notified on a rolling basis starting 3/1; must reply by 5/1 or within 2 week(s) of notification.

CONTACT
Richard Nash, Director of Financial Aid
517 Ball Drive, Hanover, IN 47243-0108
(812) 866-7029

Holy Cross College
Notre Dame, Indiana
www.hcc-nd.edu   Federal Code: 007263

4-year private liberal arts college in small city, affiliated with the Roman Catholic Church.
Enrollment: 546 undergrads.

BASIC COSTS (2016-2017)
Tuition and fees: $28,760.
Room and board: $10,500.
Additional info: Tuition at time of enrollment locked for 4 years.

FINANCIAL AID PICTURE
Students with need: Need-based aid available for full-time and part-time students. Work study available nights, weekends, and for part-time students.
Students without need: No-need awards available for academics, athletics, state/district residency.

FINANCIAL AID PROCEDURES
Forms required: FAFSA.
Dates and Deadlines: Priority date 3/1; no closing date. Applicants notified on a rolling basis starting 5/1; must reply within 2 week(s) of notification.
Transfers: No deadline. Applicants notified on a rolling basis starting 9/1; must reply within 3 week(s) of notification. Merit-based transfer scholarships and need-based assistance grants available.

CONTACT
Michael Schmaltz, Director of Financial Aid
54515 State Road 933 North, Notre Dame, IN 46556-0308
(574) 239-8400

Huntington University
Huntington, Indiana
www.huntington.edu   Federal Code: 001803

4-year private university and liberal arts college in large town, affiliated with the United Brethren in Christ.
Enrollment: 924 undergrads, 6% part-time. 196 full-time freshmen.
Selectivity: Admits over 75% of applicants.

BASIC COSTS (2017-2018)
Tuition and fees: $25,540.
Room and board: $8,456.
Additional info: Tuition/fee waivers available for minority students.

FINANCIAL AID PICTURE (2016-2017)
Students with need: Out of 172 full-time freshmen who applied for aid, 155 were judged to have need. Of these, 155 received aid, and 3 had their full need met. Average financial aid package met 85% of need; average scholarship/grant was $8,834; average loan was $3,318. For part-time students, average financial aid package was $1,810.
Students without need: 41 full-time freshmen who did not demonstrate need for aid received scholarships/grants; average award was $3,553. No-need awards available for academics, alumni affiliation, art, athletics, leadership, minority status, music/drama, religious affiliation.
Scholarships offered: *Merit:* Horizon Leader Scholarship: covers all fees associated with tuition and housing costs for up to 8 semesters. *Athletic:* 41 full-time freshmen received athletic scholarships; average amount $11,321.

Additional info: Loan repayment program offered to qualifying students. This program helps students payback their loans after graduation based on their income.

FINANCIAL AID PROCEDURES

Forms required: FAFSA.

Dates and Deadlines: Priority date 3/10; no closing date. Applicants notified on a rolling basis starting 3/15; must reply by 5/1.

Transfers: No deadline. Applicants notified on a rolling basis starting 3/15; must reply by 5/1.

CONTACT

Jerry Davis, Director of Financial Aid

2303 College Avenue, Huntington, IN 46750-1237

(260) 359-4015

Indiana Institute of Technology

Fort Wayne, Indiana

www.indianatech.edu

4-year private business and engineering college in large city.

Enrollment: 8,685 undergrads. 1,077 full-time freshmen.

Selectivity: Admits less than 50% of applicants.

BASIC COSTS (2016-2017)

Tuition and fees: $26,370.

Room and board: $9,580.

Additional info: Academic program fees: Computer Studies; $1,160, Education majors; $620, Engineering; $1,670, Exercise Science; $800. Tuition at time of enrollment locked for 4 years.

FINANCIAL AID PICTURE (2015-2016)

Students with need: Out of 975 full-time freshmen who applied for aid, 936 were judged to have need. Of these, 933 received aid, and 274 had their full need met. For part-time students, average financial aid package was $11,318.

Students without need: 16 full-time freshmen who did not demonstrate need for aid received scholarships/grants; average award was $8,968. No-need awards available for academics, athletics, minority status.

Scholarships offered: 201 full-time freshmen received athletic scholarships; average amount $7,895.

FINANCIAL AID PROCEDURES

Forms required: FAFSA.

Dates and Deadlines: Priority date 3/10; no closing date. Applicants notified on a rolling basis starting 10/1; must reply within 2 week(s) of notification.

Transfers: No deadline. Applicants notified on a rolling basis starting 10/1; must reply within 2 week(s) of notification.

CONTACT

1600 East Washington Boulevard, Fort Wayne, IN 46803

Indiana State University

Terre Haute, Indiana

www.indstate.edu   Federal Code: 001807

4-year public university in small city.

Enrollment: 10,601 undergrads, 12% part-time. 2,772 full-time freshmen.

Selectivity: Admits over 75% of applicants.

BASIC COSTS (2016-2017)

Tuition and fees: $8,746; out-of-state residents $19,076.

Per-credit charge: $310; out-of-state residents $669.

Room and board: $9,785.

FINANCIAL AID PICTURE (2015-2016)

Students with need: Out of 2,636 full-time freshmen who applied for aid, 2,263 were judged to have need. Of these, 2,177 received aid, and 401 had

their full need met. Average financial aid package met 83% of need; average scholarship/grant was $5,817; average loan was $3,069. For part-time students, average financial aid package was $5,016.

Students without need: This college awards aid only to students with need.

Scholarships offered: 82 full-time freshmen received athletic scholarships; average amount $13,342.

Additional info: Financial aid application deadline March 1 for Indiana residents applying for state grant.

FINANCIAL AID PROCEDURES

Forms required: FAFSA.

Dates and Deadlines: Priority date 3/1; closing date 7/1. Applicants notified on a rolling basis starting 3/15.

CONTACT

Crystal Baker, Director of Student Financial Aid

Office of Admissions, John W. Moore Welcome Center, Terre Haute, IN 47809-9989

(800) 841-4744

Indiana University Bloomington

Bloomington, Indiana

www.iub.edu   Federal Code: 001809

4-year public university in small city.

Enrollment: 32,924 undergrads, 3% part-time. 7,846 full-time freshmen.

Selectivity: Admits over 75% of applicants.

BASIC COSTS (2016-2017)

Tuition and fees: $10,388; out-of-state residents $34,246.

Per-credit charge: $284; out-of-state residents $1,030.

Room and board: $10,040.

FINANCIAL AID PICTURE (2015-2016)

Students with need: Out of 5,624 full-time freshmen who applied for aid, 3,601 were judged to have need. Of these, 3,403 received aid, and 1,027 had their full need met. Average financial aid package met 69% of need; average scholarship/grant was $12,495; average loan was $3,029. For part-time students, average financial aid package was $6,635.

Students without need: 1,951 full-time freshmen who did not demonstrate need for aid received scholarships/grants; average award was $7,182. No-need awards available for academics, art, athletics, leadership, minority status, music/drama, religious affiliation, ROTC.

Scholarships offered: *Merit:* Honors College Scholarship; $1,000-$6,000. Hudson & Holland; $6,000; 1100 SAT (23 ACT), top 20% class rank, 3.2 GPA, strong consideration given to students from underrepresented minority backgrounds and those who demonstrate commitment to working with underrepresented/disadvantaged populations. Cox Research Scholarship; Indiana residents; awarded to incoming freshmen of exemplary achievement who are interested in working under the direction of a faculty mentor on research and scholarly activities; total value of more than $63,000 over four years, provides funds for tuition, fees, room and board; includes stipend for research work; 1360 SAT (31 ACT), rank in the top 5% of class. Kelley Scholars Program; tuition and fees, room and board, books (overseas study funding, if requested); business major, 1350 SAT (32 ACT), 3.8 GPA, recipients must display excellence in academics, leadership, and extracurricular involvement. School of Music Dean's Award; amounts vary; exceptional talent displayed in audition. 21st Century Scholars Award; in-state instructional fees; Indiana residence, fulfilled terms pledged in eighth grade, filed FAFSA before 3/1 of senior year. Army and Air Force ROTC Scholarships; tuition, fees, books, monthly stipend. All SAT scores listed exclusive of writing. *Athletic:* 61 full-time freshmen received athletic scholarships; average amount $25,708.

Additional info: Majority of institutional gift aid merit-based. Some need-based grants go to merit winners with financial need.

FINANCIAL AID PROCEDURES

Forms required: FAFSA.

Dates and Deadlines: Priority date 3/10; no closing date. Applicants notified on a rolling basis starting 4/1.

CONTACT

Jackie Kennedy-Fletcher, Director, Office of Student Financial Assistance
300 North Jordan Avenue, Bloomington, IN 47405-1106
(812) 855-6500

Indiana University East

Richmond, Indiana
www.iue.edu   Federal Code: 001811

4-year public university in large town.

Enrollment: 3,082 undergrads, 40% part-time. 341 full-time freshmen.

Selectivity: Admits 50 to 75% of applicants.

BASIC COSTS (2016-2017)

Tuition and fees: $7,073; out-of-state residents $18,683.

Per-credit charge: $216; out-of-state residents $603.

FINANCIAL AID PICTURE (2015-2016)

Students with need: Out of 324 full-time freshmen who applied for aid, 281 were judged to have need. Of these, 270 received aid, and 68 had their full need met. Average financial aid package met 70% of need; average scholarship/grant was $7,627; average loan was $2,568. For part-time students, average financial aid package was $4,888.

Students without need: 22 full-time freshmen who did not demonstrate need for aid received scholarships/grants; average award was $1,611. No-need awards available for academics, alumni affiliation, leadership.

Scholarships offered: *Merit:* IU East Distinguished Scholars; $24,000 ($6,000 annually for 4 years); rank in top 10% of HS class; exceptional SAT or ACT scores; scholars are also expected to apply and remain eligible for the Honors Program; must attend full time and maintain at least a 3.0 GPA. IU East Valedictorian and Salutatorian Scholarships; $16,000 ($4,000 annually for 4 years); rank 1st or 2nd in HS class; must attend full time and maintain at least a 3.0 GPA. Lingle Scholars; $8,000 ($2,000 annually for 4 years); Wayne County students who apply for and are accepted to the IUE Honors Program are eligible. *Athletic:* 16 full-time freshmen received athletic scholarships; average amount $1,195.

FINANCIAL AID PROCEDURES

Forms required: FAFSA, institutional form.

Dates and Deadlines: Priority date 3/10; no closing date. Applicants notified on a rolling basis starting 5/1; must reply within 2 week(s) of notification.

CONTACT

Sarah Soper, Director, Financial Aid & Scholarships
2325 Chester Boulevard, Richmond, IN 47374-1289
(765) 973-8206

Indiana University Kokomo

Kokomo, Indiana
www.iuk.edu   Federal Code: 001814

4-year public university in large town.

Enrollment: 2,771 undergrads, 25% part-time. 553 full-time freshmen.

Selectivity: Admits 50 to 75% of applicants.

BASIC COSTS (2016-2017)

Tuition and fees: $7,073; out-of-state residents $18,683.

Per-credit charge: $216; out-of-state residents $603.

FINANCIAL AID PICTURE (2015-2016)

Students with need: Out of 517 full-time freshmen who applied for aid, 413 were judged to have need. Of these, 399 received aid, and 61 had their full need met. Average financial aid package met 67% of need; average scholarship/grant was $7,762; average loan was $2,619. For part-time students, average financial aid package was $5,364.

Students without need: 43 full-time freshmen who did not demonstrate need for aid received scholarships/grants; average award was $1,807. No-need awards available for academics, athletics, leadership.

Scholarships offered: *Merit:* Herbert Scholarship; incoming freshman with SAT score of 1300 and is in the top 10% of their graduating class, renewable for additional 3 years where cumulative 3.3 GPA is maintained. IU Kokomo Pre-Professional Scholarship Program; $2,500, laptop computer, $1,000 stipend for international travel, faculty mentor, undergraduate research opportunity, tutoring assistance, GRE prep, textbook credit, free software. ESP and STAR Scholarships; any more available. *Athletic:* 3 full-time freshmen received athletic scholarships; average amount $367.

FINANCIAL AID PROCEDURES

Forms required: FAFSA.

Dates and Deadlines: Priority date 3/10; no closing date. Applicants notified on a rolling basis starting 3/30.

CONTACT

Karen Shaw, Director of Office of Scholarships and Financial Aid
Kelley Student Center, Room 230, Kokomo, IN 46902-9003
(765) 455-9216

Indiana University Northwest

Gary, Indiana
www.iun.edu   Federal Code: 001815

4-year public university in small city.

Enrollment: 3,727 undergrads, 27% part-time. 587 full-time freshmen.

Selectivity: Admits over 75% of applicants.

BASIC COSTS (2016-2017)

Tuition and fees: $7,073; out-of-state residents $18,683.

Per-credit charge: $216; out-of-state residents $603.

FINANCIAL AID PICTURE (2015-2016)

Students with need: Out of 542 full-time freshmen who applied for aid, 402 were judged to have need. Of these, 370 received aid, and 53 had their full need met. Average financial aid package met 67% of need; average scholarship/grant was $6,759; average loan was $2,793. For part-time students, average financial aid package was $4,999.

Students without need: 50 full-time freshmen who did not demonstrate need for aid received scholarships/grants; average award was $4,511. No-need awards available for academics, athletics.

Scholarships offered: *Merit:* Valedictorian Scholarship; incoming freshmen ranked first in their high school graduating class. Special Academic Scholarship Tier One; $5,000; incoming full-time freshman who has a 3.5 GPA and a minimum SAT score of 1100 (ACT 24); renewable for 4 years with 3.5 cumulative GPA. Special Academic Scholarship Tier Two; incoming full-time freshman with minimum 3.5 cumulative GPA and a minimum SAT score of 1150 (ACT 25); full tuition waiver for a maximum of 126 credit hours; renewable with a 3.5 cumulative GPA. *Athletic:* 3 full-time freshmen received athletic scholarships; average amount $1,333.

FINANCIAL AID PROCEDURES

Forms required: FAFSA.

Dates and Deadlines: Priority date 3/10; no closing date. Applicants notified on a rolling basis starting 4/15; must reply by 6/30.

CONTACT

Harold Burtley, Director, Scholarships and Financial Aid
3400 Broadway, Gary, IN 46408-1197
(219) 980-6778

Indiana University South Bend

South Bend, Indiana
www.iusb.edu   Federal Code: 001816

4-year public university in small city.
Enrollment: 4,981 undergrads, 24% part-time. 845 full-time freshmen.
Selectivity: Admits over 75% of applicants.

BASIC COSTS (2016-2017)

Tuition and fees: $7,073; out-of-state residents $18,683.
Per-credit charge: $216; out-of-state residents $603.
Room only: $7,222.

FINANCIAL AID PICTURE (2015-2016)

Students with need: Out of 771 full-time freshmen who applied for aid, 623 were judged to have need. Of these, 584 received aid, and 56 had their full need met. Average financial aid package met 62% of need; average scholarship/grant was $7,206; average loan was $2,787. For part-time students, average financial aid package was $4,914.
Students without need: 84 full-time freshmen who did not demonstrate need for aid received scholarships/grants; average award was $1,427. No-need awards available for academics, athletics.
Scholarships offered: Merit: Central Indiana Chapter of the Indiana University Alumni Association: $1,000, four scholarships, student be a resident of Hamilton, Hancock, Hendricks or Marion County, and attending any campus of Indiana University full time in the fall. Pilot Club: $1,000, medical scholarship offered to a current junior who will return to IU South Bend for their senior year; money is for tuition, fees, and/or books. Distinguished Alumni Service Award: $1,000, minimum GPA of 3.5, resident of Indiana, two scholarships for graduating seniors that have a proven record of excellence both in and out of the classroom as demonstrated by both GPA and leadership and service work. **Athletic:** 54 full-time freshmen received athletic scholarships; average amount $846.

FINANCIAL AID PROCEDURES

Forms required: FAFSA, institutional form.
Dates and Deadlines: Priority date 3/10; no closing date. Applicants notified on a rolling basis starting 5/1.

CONTACT

Jill Bertrand, Director of Financial Aid and Scholarships
1700 Mishawaka Avenue, South Bend, IN 46634-7111
(574) 520-4357

Indiana University Southeast

New Albany, Indiana
www.ius.edu   Federal Code: 001817

4-year public university in large town.
Enrollment: 4,964 undergrads, 33% part-time. 835 full-time freshmen.
Selectivity: Admits over 75% of applicants.

BASIC COSTS (2016-2017)

Tuition and fees: $7,073; out-of-state residents $18,683.
Per-credit charge: $216; out-of-state residents $603.
Room only: $6,520.

FINANCIAL AID PICTURE (2015-2016)

Students with need: Out of 757 full-time freshmen who applied for aid, 593 were judged to have need. Of these, 558 received aid, and 52 had their full need met. Average financial aid package met 59% of need; average scholarship/grant was $6,775; average loan was $2,789. For part-time students, average financial aid package was $4,546.
Students without need: 67 full-time freshmen who did not demonstrate need for aid received scholarships/grants; average award was $1,234. No-need awards available for academics, art, athletics, leadership, minority status, music/drama.

Scholarships offered: Merit: Presidential Scholars Award; up to $12,000/year; $6,000 renewable scholarship also provides an additional $6,000 for students living on campus; $1,500 towards a study abroad program, and a laptop; must be an entering first-year student, GPA 3.5+, SAT 1150+ (ACT 25), resident of Indiana. Balfour Scholarship; up to $2,000; for incoming freshman with 1300+ SAT or equivalent ACT, rank in upper 10% of class; renewable for four years with 3.5 GPA. Dr. Sharon Waggoner Scholarship; up to $1,000; for outstanding foreign language student who has completed 2 semesters of foreign language study at IUS. **Athletic:** 9 full-time freshmen received athletic scholarships; average amount $1,611.

FINANCIAL AID PROCEDURES

Forms required: FAFSA.
Dates and Deadlines: Priority date 7/1; no closing date. Applicants notified on a rolling basis starting 5/1.

CONTACT

Traci Armes, Director of Financial Aid
4201 Grant Line Road, New Albany, IN 47150-6405
(812) 941-2246

Indiana University-Purdue University Fort Wayne

Fort Wayne, Indiana
www.ipfw.edu   Federal Code: 001828

4-year public university and branch campus college in large city.
Enrollment: 8,302 undergrads, 24% part-time. 1,517 full-time freshmen.
Selectivity: Admits over 75% of applicants.

BASIC COSTS (2016-2017)

Tuition and fees: $8,213; out-of-state residents $19,727.
Per-credit charge: $238.95; out-of-state residents $622.75.
Room only: $5,962.

FINANCIAL AID PICTURE (2015-2016)

Students with need: 47% of average financial aid package awarded as scholarships/grants, 53% awarded as loans/jobs. Need-based aid available for part-time students. Work study available nights, weekends, and for part-time students.
Students without need: No-need awards available for academics, alumni affiliation, art, athletics, leadership, minority status, music/drama, ROTC, state/district residency.

FINANCIAL AID PROCEDURES

Forms required: FAFSA.
Dates and Deadlines: Priority date 3/10; no closing date. Applicants notified on a rolling basis starting 4/1; must reply within 3 week(s) of notification.

CONTACT

David Peterson, Director of Financial Aid
2101 East Coliseum Boulevard, Fort Wayne, IN 46805-1499
(260) 481-6820

Indiana University-Purdue University Indianapolis

Indianapolis, Indiana
www.iupui.edu   Federal Code: 001813

4-year public university in very large city.
Enrollment: 21,001 undergrads, 18% part-time. 3,725 full-time freshmen.
Selectivity: Admits 50 to 75% of applicants.

BASIC COSTS (2016-2017)

Tuition and fees: $9,205; out-of-state residents $29,791.
Per-credit charge: $271; out-of-state residents $958.

Room and board: $8,462.

FINANCIAL AID PICTURE (2015-2016)

Students with need: Out of 3,393 full-time freshmen who applied for aid, 2,619 were judged to have need. Of these, 2,499 received aid, and 616 had their full need met. Average financial aid package met 69% of need; average scholarship/grant was $9,706; average loan was $3,209. For part-time students, average financial aid package was $5,183.

Students without need: 391 full-time freshmen who did not demonstrate need for aid received scholarships/grants; average award was $5,702. No-need awards available for academics, alumni affiliation, art, athletics, leadership, ROTC, state/district residency.

Scholarships offered: Merit: Dean's Recognition Scholarship; $11,000 annually for 4 years; minimum HS GPA of 3.5 and score 1200+ SAT (26 ACT); students must attend full time and maintain a 3.0 GPA. IUPUI Service Award; $7,000 annually for 4 years; minimum HS GPA; students must attend full time and maintain a 3.0 GPA and must volunteer for 20 hours of service at IUPUI events annually. IUPUI Undergraduate Research Opportunities Program; offers research project and travel grants and conference travel funds; formal research credits may be earned toward graduation. IUPUI Chancellor's Scholarship; $12,000 annually for 4 years; minimum HS GPA of 3.75 with a minimum 1250 SAT (28 ACT); automatically admitted to the IUPUI Honors College to be considered for renewal, students must attend full time, be an active participant in the Honors College and maintain a 3.3 GPA. **Athletic:** 17 full-time freshmen received athletic scholarships; average amount $12,423.

FINANCIAL AID PROCEDURES

Forms required: FAFSA.

Dates and Deadlines: Priority date 3/10; no closing date. Applicants notified on a rolling basis starting 4/1.

CONTACT

Marvin Smith, Director of Student Financial Services
420 University Boulevard, CE 255, Indianapolis, IN 46202-5143
(317) 274-4162

Indiana Wesleyan University

Marion, Indiana
www.indwes.edu   Federal Code: 001822

4-year private university and liberal arts college in large town, affiliated with the Wesleyan Church.

Enrollment: 2,679 undergrads, 2% part-time. 684 full-time freshmen.

Selectivity: Admits 50 to 75% of applicants.

BASIC COSTS (2016-2017)

Tuition and fees: $25,346.

Room and board: $8,148.

FINANCIAL AID PICTURE (2016-2017)

Students with need: Out of 638 full-time freshmen who applied for aid, 541 were judged to have need. Of these, 541 received aid, and 284 had their full need met. Average financial aid package met 91% of need; average scholarship/grant was $3,915; average loan was $3,209. For part-time students, average financial aid package was $18,937.

Students without need: 97 full-time freshmen who did not demonstrate need for aid received scholarships/grants; average award was $9,196. No-need awards available for academics, alumni affiliation, art, athletics, music/drama, ROTC.

Scholarships offered: Merit: Academic Scholarships; $750-$6,000; 3.2 GPA and 1050 SAT (exclusive of Writing) or 23 ACT required. **Athletic:** 68 full-time freshmen received athletic scholarships; average amount $6,479.

FINANCIAL AID PROCEDURES

Forms required: FAFSA, institutional form.

Dates and Deadlines: Closing date 3/10. Applicants notified on a rolling basis starting 3/10.

Transfers: Applicants notified on a rolling basis.

CONTACT

Lisa Montany, Director of Financial Aid
4201 South Washington Street, Marion, IN 46953-4999
(765) 677-2116

Ivy Tech Community College: Bloomington

Bloomington, Indiana
www.ivytech.edu   Federal Code: 035213

2-year public community college in small city.

Enrollment: 3,940 undergrads, 54% part-time. 556 full-time freshmen.

Selectivity: Open admission; but selective for some programs.

BASIC COSTS (2016-2017)

Tuition and fees: $4,175; out-of-state residents $8,052.

Per-credit charge: $135.15; out-of-state residents $264.

FINANCIAL AID PICTURE

Students with need: Need-based aid available for full-time and part-time students. Work study available nights.

FINANCIAL AID PROCEDURES

Forms required: FAFSA.

Dates and Deadlines: Closing date 3/1. Applicants notified on a rolling basis starting 7/1.

CONTACT

Patt McCafferty, Director of Financial Aid
200 Daniels Way, Bloomington, IN 47404-1511
(812) 332-1559

Ivy Tech Community College: Central Indiana

Indianapolis, Indiana
www.ivytech.edu   Federal Code: 009917

2-year public community college in very large city.

Enrollment: 16,060 undergrads, 70% part-time. 1,391 full-time freshmen.

Selectivity: Open admission; but selective for some programs.

BASIC COSTS (2016-2017)

Tuition and fees: $4,175; out-of-state residents $8,052.

Per-credit charge: $135.15; out-of-state residents $264.

FINANCIAL AID PICTURE

Students with need: Need-based aid available for full-time and part-time students. Work study available nights.

FINANCIAL AID PROCEDURES

Forms required: FAFSA.

Dates and Deadlines: Closing date 3/1. Applicants notified on a rolling basis starting 7/1.

CONTACT

Director of Financial Aid
50 West Fall Creek Parkway North Drive, Indianapolis, IN 46208-5752
(317) 921-4882

Ivy Tech Community College: Columbus

Columbus, Indiana
www.ivytech.edu   Federal Code: 010038

2-year public community college in large town.

Enrollment: 2,095 undergrads, 67% part-time. 197 full-time freshmen.

Selectivity: Open admission; but selective for some programs.

BASIC COSTS (2016-2017)
Tuition and fees: $4,175; out-of-state residents $8,052.
Per-credit charge: $135.15; out-of-state residents $264.

FINANCIAL AID PICTURE
Students with need: Need-based aid available for full-time and part-time students. Work study available nights.

FINANCIAL AID PROCEDURES
Forms required: FAFSA.
Dates and Deadlines: Closing date 3/1. Applicants notified on a rolling basis starting 7/1.

CONTACT
Paul Johnston, Director of Financial Aid
4475 Central Avenue, Columbus, IN 47203-1868
(812) 372-9925

Ivy Tech Community College: East Central
Muncie, Indiana
www.ivytech.edu/eastcentral   Federal Code: 009924

2-year public community college in small city.
Enrollment: 4,941 undergrads, 55% part-time. 671 full-time freshmen.
Selectivity: Open admission; but selective for some programs.

BASIC COSTS (2016-2017)
Tuition and fees: $4,175; out-of-state residents $8,052.
Per-credit charge: $135.15; out-of-state residents $264.

FINANCIAL AID PICTURE
Students with need: Need-based aid available for full-time and part-time students. Work study available nights.
Additional info: Higher Education Aid (HEA), Child of Disabled/Deceased Veterans (CDV), Ivy Tech Scholarships (IVTC) and grants, vocational rehabilitation and veteran's assistance available. None require repayment.

FINANCIAL AID PROCEDURES
Forms required: FAFSA.
Dates and Deadlines: Closing date 3/1. Applicants notified on a rolling basis starting 7/1.

CONTACT
Debra Swimm, Director of Financial Aid
4301 South Cowan Road, Muncie, IN 47302-9448
(765) 643-7133 ext. 2309

Ivy Tech Community College: Kokomo
Kokomo, Indiana
www.ivytech.edu   Federal Code: 010041

2-year public community college in large town.
Enrollment: 2,075 undergrads, 61% part-time. 198 full-time freshmen.
Selectivity: Open admission; but selective for some programs.

BASIC COSTS (2016-2017)
Tuition and fees: $4,175; out-of-state residents $8,052.
Per-credit charge: $135.15; out-of-state residents $264.

FINANCIAL AID PICTURE
Students with need: Need-based aid available for full-time and part-time students. Work study available nights.

FINANCIAL AID PROCEDURES
Forms required: FAFSA.

Dates and Deadlines: Closing date 3/1. Applicants notified on a rolling basis starting 7/1.
Transfers: Applicants notified on a rolling basis starting 7/1.

CONTACT
Anjanetta Polk, Director of Financial Aid
1815 East Morgan Street, Kokomo, IN 46903-1373
(765) 459-0561

Ivy Tech Community College: Lafayette
Lafayette, Indiana
www.ivytech.edu   Federal Code: 010039

2-year public community college in large town.
Enrollment: 3,804 undergrads, 52% part-time. 529 full-time freshmen.
Selectivity: Open admission; but selective for some programs.

BASIC COSTS (2016-2017)
Tuition and fees: $4,175; out-of-state residents $8,052.
Per-credit charge: $135.15; out-of-state residents $264.

FINANCIAL AID PICTURE
Students with need: Need-based aid available for full-time and part-time students. Work study available nights.

FINANCIAL AID PROCEDURES
Forms required: FAFSA.
Dates and Deadlines: Closing date 3/1. Applicants notified on a rolling basis starting 7/1.

CONTACT
Beverly Cooper, Director of Financial Aid
3101 South Creasy Lane, Lafayette, IN 47905-6299
(765) 772-9100

Ivy Tech Community College: North Central
South Bend, Indiana
www.ivytech.edu   Federal Code: 008423

2-year public community college in small city.
Enrollment: 4,555 undergrads, 68% part-time. 323 full-time freshmen.
Selectivity: Open admission; but selective for some programs.

BASIC COSTS (2016-2017)
Tuition and fees: $4,175; out-of-state residents $8,052.
Per-credit charge: $135.15; out-of-state residents $264.

FINANCIAL AID PICTURE
Students with need: Need-based aid available for full-time and part-time students. Work study available nights.

FINANCIAL AID PROCEDURES
Forms required: FAFSA.
Dates and Deadlines: Closing date 3/1. Applicants notified on a rolling basis starting 7/1.

CONTACT
Ron Herrell, Director of Financial Aid
220 Dean Johnson Boulevard, South Bend, IN 46601-3415
(219) 289-7001

Ivy Tech Community College: Northeast
Fort Wayne, Indiana
www.ivytech.edu   Federal Code: 009926

2-year public community college in small city.
Enrollment: 6,858 undergrads, 71% part-time. 599 full-time freshmen.
Selectivity: Open admission; but selective for some programs.

BASIC COSTS (2016-2017)
Tuition and fees: $4,175; out-of-state residents $8,052.
Per-credit charge: $135.15; out-of-state residents $264.

FINANCIAL AID PICTURE
Students with need: Need-based aid available for full-time and part-time students. Work study available nights.

FINANCIAL AID PROCEDURES
Forms required: FAFSA.
Dates and Deadlines: Closing date 3/1. Applicants notified on a rolling basis starting 7/1.

CONTACT
Norman Newman, Director of Financial Aid
3800 North Anthony Boulevard, Fort Wayne, IN 46805-1489
(260) 482-9171

Ivy Tech Community College: Northwest
Gary, Indiana
www.ivytech.edu   Federal Code: 010040

2-year public community college in small city.
Enrollment: 7,222 undergrads, 63% part-time. 700 full-time freshmen.
Selectivity: Open admission; but selective for some programs.

BASIC COSTS (2016-2017)
Tuition and fees: $4,175; out-of-state residents $8,052.
Per-credit charge: $135.15; out-of-state residents $264.

FINANCIAL AID PICTURE
Students with need: Need-based aid available for full-time and part-time students. Work study available nights.

FINANCIAL AID PROCEDURES
Forms required: FAFSA.
Dates and Deadlines: Closing date 3/1. Applicants notified on a rolling basis starting 7/1.

CONTACT
Ron Herrell, Director of Financial Aid
1440 East 35th Avenue, Gary, IN 46409-1499
(219) 981-1111

Ivy Tech Community College: Richmond
Richmond, Indiana
www.ivytech.edu   Federal Code: 010037

2-year public community college in large town.
Enrollment: 1,613 undergrads, 72% part-time. 107 full-time freshmen.
Selectivity: Open admission; but selective for some programs.

BASIC COSTS (2016-2017)
Tuition and fees: $4,175; out-of-state residents $8,052.
Per-credit charge: $135.15; out-of-state residents $264.

FINANCIAL AID PICTURE
Students with need: Need-based aid available for full-time and part-time students. Work study available nights.

FINANCIAL AID PROCEDURES
Forms required: FAFSA.
Dates and Deadlines: Closing date 3/1. Applicants notified on a rolling basis starting 7/1.

CONTACT
Director of Financial Aid
2357 Chester Boulevard, Richmond, IN 47374-1298
(765) 966-2656

Ivy Tech Community College: South Central
Sellersburg, Indiana
www.ivytech.edu   Federal Code: 010109

2-year public community college in small town.
Enrollment: 3,616 undergrads, 78% part-time. 175 full-time freshmen.
Selectivity: Open admission; but selective for some programs.

BASIC COSTS (2016-2017)
Tuition and fees: $4,175; out-of-state residents $8,052.
Per-credit charge: $135.15; out-of-state residents $264.

FINANCIAL AID PICTURE
Students with need: Need-based aid available for full-time and part-time students. Work study available nights.

FINANCIAL AID PROCEDURES
Forms required: FAFSA.
Dates and Deadlines: Closing date 3/1. Applicants notified on a rolling basis starting 7/1.

CONTACT
Gary Cottrill, Director of Financial Aid
8204 Highway 311, Sellersburg, IN 47172-1897
(812) 246-3301

Ivy Tech Community College: Southeast
Madison, Indiana
www.ivytech.edu   Federal Code: 009923

2-year public community college in large town.
Enrollment: 1,794 undergrads, 62% part-time. 211 full-time freshmen.
Selectivity: Open admission; but selective for some programs.

BASIC COSTS (2016-2017)
Tuition and fees: $4,175; out-of-state residents $8,052.
Per-credit charge: $135.15; out-of-state residents $264.

FINANCIAL AID PICTURE
Students with need: Need-based aid available for full-time and part-time students. Work study available nights.

FINANCIAL AID PROCEDURES
Forms required: FAFSA.
Dates and Deadlines: Closing date 3/1. Applicants notified on a rolling basis starting 7/1.

CONTACT
Beth Kemper, Director of Financial Aid
590 Ivy Tech Drive, Madison, IN 47250-1881
(812) 265-2580 ext. 4148

Ivy Tech Community College: Southwest

Evansville, Indiana
www.ivytech.edu   Federal Code: 009925

2-year public community college in small city.
Enrollment: 3,428 undergrads, 67% part-time. 270 full-time freshmen.
Selectivity: Open admission; but selective for some programs.

BASIC COSTS (2016-2017)
Tuition and fees: $4,175; out-of-state residents $8,052.
Per-credit charge: $135.15; out-of-state residents $264.

FINANCIAL AID PICTURE
Students with need: Need-based aid available for full-time and part-time students. Work study available nights.

FINANCIAL AID PROCEDURES
Forms required: FAFSA.
Dates and Deadlines: Closing date 3/1. Applicants notified on a rolling basis starting 7/1.

CONTACT
Casey Trela, Director of Financial Aid
3501 First Avenue, Evansville, IN 47710-3398
(812) 426-2865

Ivy Tech Community College: Wabash Valley

Terre Haute, Indiana
www.ivytech.edu   Federal Code: 008547

2-year public community college in small city.
Enrollment: 3,127 undergrads, 57% part-time. 355 full-time freshmen.
Selectivity: Open admission; but selective for some programs.

BASIC COSTS (2016-2017)
Tuition and fees: $4,175; out-of-state residents $8,052.
Per-credit charge: $135.15; out-of-state residents $264.

FINANCIAL AID PICTURE
Students with need: Need-based aid available for full-time and part-time students. Work study available nights.

FINANCIAL AID PROCEDURES
Forms required: FAFSA.
Dates and Deadlines: Closing date 3/1. Applicants notified on a rolling basis starting 7/1.
Transfers: Applicants notified on a rolling basis starting 7/1.

CONTACT
Julie Wonderlin, Director of Financial Aid
8000 South Education Drive, Terre Haute, IN 47802-4898
(812) 299-1121

Kaplan College: Indianapolis

Indianapolis, Indiana
www.kaplancollege.com   Federal Code: 009777

2-year for-profit health science and nursing college in very large city.
Enrollment: 501 undergrads.
Selectivity: Open admission; but selective for some programs.

BASIC COSTS (2016-2017)
Additional info: Criminal Justice: $31,365. Dental Assistant: $16,450. Electrical Technician: $21,904. Medical Assistant: $16,465. Medical Office Specialist: $16,735. Practical Nursing: $23,340. Spanish for Healthcare Workers: $510.

FINANCIAL AID PICTURE
Students with need: Need-based aid available for full-time students.
Students without need: This college awards aid only to students with need.

CONTACT
Vincent O'Neal, Financial Aid Director
7302 Woodland Drive, Indianapolis, IN 46278-1736
(317) 293-6503

Manchester University

North Manchester, Indiana
www.manchester.edu   Federal Code: 001820

4-year private pharmacy and liberal arts college in small town, affiliated with the Church of the Brethren.
Enrollment: 1,254 undergrads. 389 full-time freshmen.
Selectivity: Admits 50 to 75% of applicants.

BASIC COSTS (2017-2018)
Tuition and fees: $31,660.
Per-credit charge: $700.
Room and board: $9,880.

FINANCIAL AID PICTURE (2016-2017)
Students with need: Out of 352 full-time freshmen who applied for aid, 332 were judged to have need. Of these, 332 received aid, and 80 had their full need met. Average financial aid package met 86% of need; average scholarship/grant was $24,878; average loan was $3,403. Need-based aid available for part-time students.
Students without need: 44 full-time freshmen who did not demonstrate need for aid received scholarships/grants; average award was $18,616. No-need awards available for academics, alumni affiliation, music/drama, religious affiliation, state/district residency.
Scholarships offered: Honors Fellowship; full tuition; based on academics; 2 awarded. Presidential Leadership Award; $2,500 travel grant; 3 awarded. Trustee Scholarships; $12,000; based on merit; 40 awarded to each incoming class. Presidential Scholarships; $9,000; based on merit. Arts, service, modern language scholarships; $9,000; based on merit/ability.
Additional info: Students automatically considered for all scholarship programs.

FINANCIAL AID PROCEDURES
Forms required: FAFSA.
Dates and Deadlines: Priority date 3/1; no closing date. Applicants notified on a rolling basis starting 3/18; must reply by 5/1 or within 3 week(s) of notification.
Transfers: Aid eligibility remaining determined by reviewing total credit hours transferred and financial aid transcripts.

CONTACT
Sherri Shockey, Director of Student Financial Services
604 East College Avenue, North Manchester, IN 46962-0365
(260) 982-5066

Marian University

Indianapolis, Indiana
www.marian.edu   Federal Code: 001821

4-year private university and liberal arts college in very large city, affiliated with the Roman Catholic Church.
Enrollment: 2,019 undergrads, 13% part-time. 390 full-time freshmen.
Selectivity: Admits 50 to 75% of applicants.

BASIC COSTS (2017-2018)
Tuition and fees: $33,000.

Per-credit charge: $1,450.
Room and board: $10,206.

FINANCIAL AID PICTURE

Students with need: Need-based aid available for full-time and part-time students. Work study available nights, weekends, and for part-time students.
Students without need: No-need awards available for academics, alumni affiliation, art, athletics, leadership, music/drama, religious affiliation.

FINANCIAL AID PROCEDURES

Forms required: FAFSA, institutional form.
Dates and Deadlines: Closing date 3/10. Applicants notified on a rolling basis starting 3/15; must reply within 2 week(s) of notification.
Transfers: No deadline. Applicants notified on a rolling basis starting 3/15; must reply within 2 week(s) of notification.

CONTACT

Chad Bir, Director of Financial Aid
3200 Cold Spring Road, Indianapolis, IN 46222-1997
(317) 955-6040

Oakland City University

Oakland City, Indiana
www.oak.edu   Federal Code: 001824

4-year private university and liberal arts college in small town, affiliated with the Converge Worldwide.
Enrollment: 496 undergrads, 9% part-time. 84 full-time freshmen.
Selectivity: Admits less than 50% of applicants.

BASIC COSTS (2016-2017)

Tuition and fees: $23,400.
Per-credit charge: $780.
Room and board: $9,180.
Additional info: Tuition/fee waivers available for minority students, unemployed or children of unemployed.

FINANCIAL AID PICTURE (2015-2016)

Students with need: Out of 81 full-time freshmen who applied for aid, 81 were judged to have need. Of these, 81 received aid. Need-based aid available for part-time students.
Students without need: No-need awards available for academics, athletics, minority status, religious affiliation.

FINANCIAL AID PROCEDURES

Forms required: FAFSA.
Dates and Deadlines: Priority date 3/10; no closing date. Applicants notified on a rolling basis starting 5/1.

CONTACT

Nicole Sharp, Director of Financial Aid
138 North Lucretia Street, Oakland City, IN 47660
(812) 749-1224

Purdue University

West Lafayette, Indiana
www.purdue.edu   Federal Code: 001825

4-year public university in small city.
Enrollment: 29,866 undergrads, 4% part-time. 7,227 full-time freshmen.
Selectivity: Admits 50 to 75% of applicants.

BASIC COSTS (2016-2017)

Tuition and fees: $10,002; out-of-state residents $28,804.
Per-credit charge: $348; out-of-state residents $948.
Room and board: $10,030.

Additional info: Differential general service fees: Engineering and new beginning Computer Science undergraduate students pay an additional $2,050 per academic year. Management undergraduate students pay an additional $1,436 per academic year. School of Technology undergraduate students pay an additional $572 per academic year.

FINANCIAL AID PICTURE (2016-2017)

Students with need: Out of 5,339 full-time freshmen who applied for aid, 3,638 were judged to have need. Of these, 3,638 received aid, and 1,892 had their full need met. Average financial aid package met 82% of need; average scholarship/grant was $14,008; average loan was $4,318. For part-time students, average financial aid package was $10,984.
Students without need: 1,000 full-time freshmen who did not demonstrate need for aid received scholarships/grants; average award was $4,966. No-need awards available for academics, athletics, leadership, music/drama, ROTC, state/district residency.
Scholarships offered: *Merit:* Trustees Scholarship; $12,000-$16,000 per year to non-Indiana residents; $10,000 per year to Indiana residents; renewable for up to 4 years of continuous full-time enrollment; for exceptional academic achievement, leadership and service. Presidential Scholarship; $5,000-$10,000 per year to non-Indiana residents; $2,000-$8,000 per year to Indiana residents; renewable for up to four years of continuous full-time enrollment; exceptional academic achievement in leadership and service. *Athletic:* 44 full-time freshmen received athletic scholarships; average amount $25,804.
Additional info: Cooperative work for credit available in many programs. Purdue Promise replaces need based loans with institutional funds after and in conjunction with federal and state eligibility for high-need students; maximum allowable family income is $50,000.

FINANCIAL AID PROCEDURES

Forms required: FAFSA.
Dates and Deadlines: Priority date 3/1; no closing date. Applicants notified by 4/15.

CONTACT

Theodore Malone, Executive Director of Financial Aid
475 Stadium Mall Drive, West Lafayette, IN 47907-2050
(765) 494-0998

Purdue University North Central

Westville, Indiana
www.pnc.edu   Federal Code: 001826

4-year public university in rural community.
Enrollment: 9,619 undergrads, 35% part-time. 1,204 full-time freshmen.
Selectivity: Admits less than 50% of applicants.

FINANCIAL AID PICTURE (2015-2016)

Students with need: Need-based aid available for full-time and part-time students.
Students without need: No-need awards available for academics, athletics, leadership.

FINANCIAL AID PROCEDURES

Forms required: FAFSA.
Dates and Deadlines: Priority date 3/10; closing date 6/30. Applicants notified on a rolling basis starting 4/15; must reply by 8/1 or within 2 week(s) of notification.
Transfers: Priority date 3/1; no deadline.

CONTACT

Brad Remmenga, Director, Financial Aid and Compliance
1401 South US Highway 421, Westville, IN 46391-9542
(219) 785-5460

Purdue University Northwest

Hammond, Indiana
https://www.pnw.edu Federal Code: 001827

4-year public university and branch campus college in small city.
Enrollment: 9,619 undergrads, 35% part-time. 1,204 full-time freshmen.
Selectivity: Admits less than 50% of applicants.

BASIC COSTS (2016-2017)
Tuition and fees: $7,478; out-of-state residents $16,895.
Room and board: $7,560.

FINANCIAL AID PICTURE
Students with need: Need-based aid available for full-time and part-time students. Work study available nights.
Students without need: No-need awards available for academics, athletics, state/district residency.

FINANCIAL AID PROCEDURES
Forms required: FAFSA.
Dates and Deadlines: Priority date 3/10; closing date 6/30. Applicants notified on a rolling basis starting 4/15; must reply within 2 week(s) of notification.

CONTACT
Kevin Popa, Financial Aid and Student Accounts
2200 169th Street, Hammond, IN 46323-2094
(219) 989-2301

Rose-Hulman Institute of Technology

Terre Haute, Indiana
www.rose-hulman.edu Federal Code: 001830

4-year private engineering college in small city.
Enrollment: 2,186 undergrads, 1% part-time. 543 full-time freshmen.
Selectivity: Admits 50 to 75% of applicants. GED not accepted.

BASIC COSTS (2016-2017)
Tuition and fees: $46,210.
Per-credit charge: $1,259.
Room and board: $13,293.
Additional info: Required fees includes student laptop.

FINANCIAL AID PICTURE (2016-2017)
Students with need: Out of 421 full-time freshmen who applied for aid, 340 were judged to have need. Of these, 340 received aid, and 70 had their full need met. Average financial aid package met 75% of need; average scholarship/grant was $27,812; average loan was $3,571. For part-time students, average financial aid package was $31,684.
Students without need: 196 full-time freshmen who did not demonstrate need for aid received scholarships/grants; average award was $11,758. No-need awards available for academics, minority status, ROTC.

FINANCIAL AID PROCEDURES
Forms required: FAFSA.
Dates and Deadlines: Priority date 3/1; no closing date. Applicants notified on a rolling basis starting 3/10; must reply by 5/1.
Transfers: No deadline. Applicants notified on a rolling basis; must reply by 6/1.

CONTACT
Melinda Middleton, Director of Financial Aid
Office of Admissions, Terre Haute, IN 47803-3999
(800) 248-7448

Saint Joseph's College

Rensselaer, Indiana
www.saintjoe.edu Federal Code: 001833

4-year private liberal arts college in small town, affiliated with the Roman Catholic Church.
Enrollment: 948 undergrads, 5% part-time. 259 full-time freshmen.
Selectivity: Admits over 75% of applicants.

BASIC COSTS (2016-2017)
Tuition and fees: $30,080.
Per-credit charge: $990.
Room and board: $9,480.

FINANCIAL AID PICTURE (2015-2016)
Students with need: Out of 249 full-time freshmen who applied for aid, 209 were judged to have need. Of these, 209 received aid, and 39 had their full need met. Average financial aid package met 79% of need; average scholarship/grant was $21,001; average loan was $4,378. For part-time students, average financial aid package was $3,379.
Students without need: 39 full-time freshmen who did not demonstrate need for aid received scholarships/grants; average award was $16,993. No-need awards available for academics, alumni affiliation, art, athletics.
Scholarships offered: 23 full-time freshmen received athletic scholarships; average amount $9,421.

FINANCIAL AID PROCEDURES
Forms required: FAFSA.
Dates and Deadlines: Priority date 3/1; no closing date. Applicants notified on a rolling basis starting 3/1; must reply by 5/1 or within 2 week(s) of notification.
Transfers: No deadline. Applicants notified on a rolling basis starting 9/1; must reply by 5/1 or within 2 week(s) of notification.

CONTACT
Debra Sizemore, Director of Student Financial Services
Box 890, Rensselaer, IN 47978-0890
(219) 866-6163

St. Mary-of-the-Woods College

Saint Mary of the Woods, Indiana
www.smwc.edu Federal Code: 001835

4-year private liberal arts college in rural community, affiliated with the Roman Catholic Church.
Enrollment: 569 undergrads, 28% part-time. 79 full-time freshmen.
Selectivity: Admits 50 to 75% of applicants.

BASIC COSTS (2017-2018)
Tuition and fees: $29,510.
Per-credit charge: $496.
Room and board: $10,914.
Additional info: Tuition at time of enrollment locked for 4 years; tuition/fee waivers available for minority students.

FINANCIAL AID PICTURE (2016-2017)
Students with need: Out of 77 full-time freshmen who applied for aid, 77 were judged to have need. Of these, 77 received aid. For part-time students, average financial aid package was $4,781.
Students without need: No-need awards available for academics, alumni affiliation, art, athletics, job skills.
Scholarships offered: Saint Mother Theodore Guerin Scholarships; 2 per year at $20,000 a year for 4 years, 8 per year at $13,000 a year for 4 years; based on academics, service and leadership. Top Ten on 10 Scholarships; 2 per year at $20,000 a year for 4 years, 8 per year at $13,000 a year for four years; for local students based on academics, service and leadership. Trustees Scholarships; up to $11,000 a year for 4 years; based on academics.

Presidential Scholarships; up to $9,000 a year for 4 years; based on academics. Dean's Scholarships; up to $6,000 a year for 4 years; based on academics. Woods Scholarships; up to $4,000 per year for 4 years; based on academics.

Additional info: Portfolio or audition required of applicants who wish to be considered for Creative Arts Scholarship.

FINANCIAL AID PROCEDURES

Forms required: FAFSA.

Dates and Deadlines: Closing date 3/10. Applicants notified on a rolling basis starting 12/1; must reply within 2 week(s) of notification.

Transfers: Priority date 7/1; no deadline. Applicants notified on a rolling basis starting 12/1; must reply within 8 week(s) of notification. Transfer grants available for students graduating or transferring from Ivy Tech Community College.

CONTACT

Darla Hopper, Director of Financial Aid
1 St Mary of Woods Coll, Saint Mary of the Woods, IN 47876-1099
(812) 535-5100

Saint Mary's College

Notre Dame, Indiana
www.saintmarys.edu
Federal Code: 001836

4-year private liberal arts college for women in small city, affiliated with the Roman Catholic Church.

Enrollment: 1,576 undergrads, 1% part-time. 427 full-time freshmen.

Selectivity: Admits over 75% of applicants.

BASIC COSTS (2017-2018)

Tuition and fees: $40,800.

Per-credit charge: $1,580.

Room and board: $12,100.

FINANCIAL AID PICTURE (2016-2017)

Students with need: Out of 382 full-time freshmen who applied for aid, 316 were judged to have need. Of these, 316 received aid, and 70 had their full need met. Average financial aid package met 87% of need; average scholarship/grant was $29,989; average loan was $3,287. For part-time students, average financial aid package was $9,740.

Students without need: 110 full-time freshmen who did not demonstrate need for aid received scholarships/grants; average award was $15,766. No-need awards available for academics, art, music/drama.

Scholarships offered: Credentials of all admitted candidates automatically reviewed for merit scholarship consideration. Amounts vary depending on academic qualifications, renewable provided minimum GPA requirements are maintained. Grant for the cost of a double room on-campus awarded to any admitted student with a full tuition ROTC scholarship.

Additional info: Saint Mary's also accepts veteran benefits and participates in the Yellow Ribbon Program, through which 100% of a student's tuition and fees can be paid.

FINANCIAL AID PROCEDURES

Forms required: FAFSA.

Dates and Deadlines: Closing date 3/1. Applicants notified on a rolling basis starting 12/15.

Transfers: Priority date 5/15; no deadline. Applicants notified on a rolling basis; must reply by 4/15. To meet Indiana grant deadlines, Indiana residents must submit FAFSA by March 1.

CONTACT

Kathleen Brown, Director of Financial Aid
122 Le Mans Hall, Notre Dame, IN 46556-5001
(574) 284-4557

Taylor University

Upland, Indiana
www.taylor.edu
Federal Code: 001838

4-year private university and liberal arts college in small town, affiliated with the interdenominational tradition.

Enrollment: 1,845 undergrads, 2% part-time. 472 full-time freshmen.

Selectivity: Admits over 75% of applicants.

BASIC COSTS (2016-2017)

Tuition and fees: $31,472.

Per-credit charge: $1,100.

Room and board: $8,845.

FINANCIAL AID PICTURE (2016-2017)

Students with need: Out of 380 full-time freshmen who applied for aid, 291 were judged to have need. Of these, 291 received aid, and 84 had their full need met. Average financial aid package met 78% of need; average scholarship/grant was $18,748; average loan was $4,226. For part-time students, average financial aid package was $11,612.

Students without need: 144 full-time freshmen who did not demonstrate need for aid received scholarships/grants; average award was $13,079. No-need awards available for academics, alumni affiliation, art, athletics, leadership, minority status, music/drama, religious affiliation, state/district residency.

Scholarships offered: 27 full-time freshmen received athletic scholarships; average amount $6,907.

FINANCIAL AID PROCEDURES

Forms required: FAFSA.

Dates and Deadlines: Closing date 3/10. Applicants notified on a rolling basis starting 3/1; must reply by 5/1.

Transfers: Applicants notified on a rolling basis starting 3/1; must reply by 5/1.

CONTACT

Tim Nace, Associate Dean, Enrollment Management and Director of Financial Aid
236 West Reade Avenue, Upland, IN 46989-1001
(765) 998-5358

Trine University

Angola, Indiana
www.trine.edu
Federal Code: 001839

4-year private university and engineering college in small town.

Enrollment: 1,780 undergrads, 4% part-time. 524 full-time freshmen.

Selectivity: Admits over 75% of applicants.

BASIC COSTS (2016-2017)

Tuition and fees: $30,960.

Per-credit charge: $950.

Room and board: $10,350.

Additional info: Tuition for engineering students: $32,950.

FINANCIAL AID PICTURE (2015-2016)

Students with need: Out of 485 full-time freshmen who applied for aid, 442 were judged to have need. Of these, 442 received aid, and 50 had their full need met. Average financial aid package met 80% of need; average scholarship/grant was $5,796; average loan was $4,533.

Students without need: 73 full-time freshmen who did not demonstrate need for aid received scholarships/grants; average award was $11,230. No-need awards available for academics, alumni affiliation, minority status, music/drama.

FINANCIAL AID PROCEDURES

Forms required: FAFSA.

Dates and Deadlines: Priority date 3/1; no closing date. Applicants notified on a rolling basis starting 3/10; must reply by 5/1 or within 2 week(s) of notification.

Transfers: Must reply by 5/1 or within 2 week(s) of notification.

CONTACT

Kim Bennett, Executive Director of Admission and Financial Aid

One University Avenue, Angola, IN 46703

(260) 665-4158

University of Evansville

Evansville, Indiana
www.evansville.edu   Federal Code: 001795

4-year private university and liberal arts college in small city, affiliated with the United Methodist Church.

Enrollment: 2,164 undergrads, 3% part-time. 537 full-time freshmen.

Selectivity: Admits 50 to 75% of applicants.

BASIC COSTS (2016-2017)

Tuition and fees: $33,966.

Per-credit charge: $920.

Room and board: $11,690.

FINANCIAL AID PICTURE (2016-2017)

Students with need: Out of 441 full-time freshmen who applied for aid, 383 were judged to have need. Of these, 383 received aid, and 116 had their full need met. Average financial aid package met 85% of need; average scholarship/grant was $26,378; average loan was $3,825. For part-time students, average financial aid package was $12,737.

Students without need: 138 full-time freshmen who did not demonstrate need for aid received scholarships/grants; average award was $22,868. No-need awards available for academics, alumni affiliation, art, athletics, job skills, music/drama, religious affiliation, state/district residency.

Scholarships offered: 25 full-time freshmen received athletic scholarships; average amount $20,407.

FINANCIAL AID PROCEDURES

Forms required: FAFSA.

Dates and Deadlines: Priority date 12/1; no closing date. Applicants notified on a rolling basis starting 12/15; must reply by 5/1 or within 4 week(s) of notification.

Transfers: No deadline. Applicants notified on a rolling basis starting 12/15; must reply by 5/1 or within 3 week(s) of notification. Indiana state aid is available for a total of 8 semesters at all schools attended.

CONTACT

Cathleen Wright, Director of Financial Aid

1800 Lincoln Avenue, Evansville, IN 47722

(812) 488-2364

University of Indianapolis

Indianapolis, Indiana
www.uindy.edu   Federal Code: 001804

4-year private university and liberal arts college in very large city, affiliated with the United Methodist Church.

Enrollment: 4,242 undergrads, 15% part-time. 967 full-time freshmen.

Selectivity: Admits over 75% of applicants.

BASIC COSTS (2016-2017)

Tuition and fees: $27,420.

Per-credit charge: $1,120.

Room and board: $9,648.

FINANCIAL AID PICTURE (2015-2016)

Students with need: Out of 881 full-time freshmen who applied for aid, 777 were judged to have need. Of these, 776 received aid, and 114 had their full need met. Average financial aid package met 69% of need; average scholarship/grant was $9,558; average loan was $3,270. For part-time students, average financial aid package was $2,349.

Students without need: 122 full-time freshmen who did not demonstrate need for aid received scholarships/grants; average award was $12,232. No-need awards available for academics, alumni affiliation, art, athletics, music/drama, religious affiliation, state/district residency.

Scholarships offered: *Merit:* Presidential Scholarship; full tuition; upper 5% of class, 1270 SAT/29 ACT, strong college prep required. Dean's Scholarship; 50% tuition; upper 7% of class, 1270 SAT/29 ACT, demonstrated leadership, strong college prep required. Alumni Scholarship; 30% tuition; upper 15% of class, 1100 SAT/24 ACT, alumnus connection to school required. Service Award; $2,500; based on demonstrated commitment to community volunteerism. United Methodist Award; $2,500; based on demonstrated commitment to church, activities. SAT scores listed are exclusive of writing portion. *Athletic:* 100 full-time freshmen received athletic scholarships; average amount $14,189.

FINANCIAL AID PROCEDURES

Dates and Deadlines: Applicants notified on a rolling basis.

Transfers: No deadline. Applicants notified on a rolling basis starting 3/1.

CONTACT

Linda Handy, Director of Financial Aid

1400 East Hanna Avenue, Indianapolis, IN 46227-3697

(317) 788-3217

University of Notre Dame

Notre Dame, Indiana   Federal Code: 001840
www.nd.edu   CSS Code: 1841

4-year private university in small city, affiliated with the Roman Catholic Church.

Enrollment: 8,496 undergrads. 2,046 full-time freshmen.

Selectivity: Admits less than 50% of applicants. GED not accepted.

BASIC COSTS (2016-2017)

Tuition and fees: $49,685.

Per-credit charge: $2,049.

Room and board: $14,358.

FINANCIAL AID PICTURE (2016-2017)

Students with need: Out of 1,446 full-time freshmen who applied for aid, 1,056 were judged to have need. Of these, 1,056 received aid, and 1,044 had their full need met. Average financial aid package met 100% of need; average scholarship/grant was $39,044; average loan was $3,821. Need-based aid available for part-time students.

Students without need: 39 full-time freshmen who did not demonstrate need for aid received scholarships/grants; average award was $27,589. No-need awards available for academics, athletics, ROTC.

Scholarships offered: 102 full-time freshmen received athletic scholarships; average amount $34,427.

FINANCIAL AID PROCEDURES

Forms required: FAFSA, CSS PROFILE.

Dates and Deadlines: Priority date 2/15; no closing date. Applicants notified on a rolling basis starting 2/15; must reply by 5/1.

Transfers: Closing date 3/31. Applicants notified on a rolling basis; must reply within 2 week(s) of notification. Require signed and completed federal tax returns, including all schedules and W-2 forms from both the applicant and the parents of the applicant.

CONTACT

Thomas Bear, Executive Director of Student Financial Strategies

220 Main Building, Notre Dame, IN 46556

(574) 631-6436

University of Saint Francis

Fort Wayne, Indiana
www.sf.edu   Federal Code: 001832

4-year private university in large city, affiliated with the Roman Catholic Church.

Enrollment: 1,758 undergrads, 16% part-time. 339 full-time freshmen.

Selectivity: Admits over 75% of applicants.

BASIC COSTS (2017-2018)

Tuition and fees: $29,430.

Per-credit charge: $900.

Room and board: $9,090.

FINANCIAL AID PICTURE (2016-2017)

Students with need: Out of 333 full-time freshmen who applied for aid, 303 were judged to have need. Of these, 303 received aid, and 60 had their full need met. Average financial aid package met 78% of need; average scholarship/grant was $18,899; average loan was $3,350. For part-time students, average financial aid package was $6,409.

Students without need: 35 full-time freshmen who did not demonstrate need for aid received scholarships/grants; average award was $9,821. No-need awards available for academics, art, athletics, music/drama, state/district residency.

Scholarships offered: *Merit:* Academic scholarships may be awarded: up to $12,000 annually. Athletic scholarships. Visual and performing arts scholarships. ***Athletic:*** 42 full-time freshmen received athletic scholarships; average amount $7,147.

FINANCIAL AID PROCEDURES

Forms required: FAFSA.

Dates and Deadlines: Priority date 3/10; no closing date. Applicants notified on a rolling basis starting 12/1; must reply by 8/1.

Transfers: No deadline. Applicants notified on a rolling basis starting 12/1; must reply by 8/1. USF offers academic scholarships to transfer students based on their cumulative college GPA.

CONTACT

Michelle Nisun, Director of Financial Aid
2701 Spring Street, Fort Wayne, IN 46808
(260) 399-8003

University of Southern Indiana

Evansville, Indiana
www.usi.edu   Federal Code: 001808

4-year public university and liberal arts college in small city.

Enrollment: 7,894 undergrads, 15% part-time. 1,661 full-time freshmen.

Selectivity: Admits over 75% of applicants.

BASIC COSTS (2017-2018)

Tuition and fees: $7,605; out-of-state residents $17,848.

Per-credit charge: $236; out-of-state residents $578.

Room and board: $8,896.

FINANCIAL AID PICTURE (2016-2017)

Students with need: Out of 1,545 full-time freshmen who applied for aid, 1,107 were judged to have need. Of these, 1,107 received aid, and 123 had their full need met. Average financial aid package met 81% of need; average scholarship/grant was $7,997; average loan was $3,238. For part-time students, average financial aid package was $6,071.

Students without need: 445 full-time freshmen who did not demonstrate need for aid received scholarships/grants; average award was $3,847. No-need awards available for academics, art, athletics, leadership, music/drama, state/district residency.

Scholarships offered: *Merit:* David L. Rice Merit Scholarship: Minimum 3.0 cumulative high school GPA & a combined Critical Reading & Math SAT

score of 940, RSAT score of 1020, or ACT composite score of 20; award amounts vary. Presidential Scholarship: Students ranked 1st or 2nd in senior class (or students who achieve 4.0 GPA at non-ranking school); Covers full tuition, room/board & provides book stipends. Must attend an accredited high school & earn combined critical reading & math SAT score of 1200, composite RSAT score of 1290 or an ACT composite score of 27. Baccalaureate/Doctor of Medicine Scholarship (B/MD): Competitive; Indiana residents who plan to pursue medical school; interview process; full tuition for 4 years of undergrad study & provisional acceptance into the IU School of Medicine; Must have minimum 3.5/4.0 cumulative high school GPA & combined critical reading & math SAT score of 1200, composite RSAT score of 1290 or ACT composite score of 27. Multicultural Leadership Scholarship: Competitive; $5,000; renewable for 4 years; 3.0/4.0 cumulative high school GPA & demonstrated leadership in multicultural school/community activities/organizations Out-of-State Top Scholar Award: Pays the difference between non-resident & Indiana resident tuition; Must meet 1 of the following criteria & live on campus first year: Achieve min 3.5/4.0 cumulative high school GPA, rank in top 25% of class or attain minimum ACT composite score of 24, combined critical reading & math SAT score of 1090 or composite RSAT score of 1160. Out-Of-State Scholarship: Tuition discount for out-of-state students equal to 120% of in-state tuition rate; Must meet 1 of the following criteria & live on campus first year: Achieve cumulative high school GPA in range of 2.75-3.49/4.0, rank in top 26-50%, or attain ACT composite score of 21-23, combined critical reading & math SAT score of 990-1080 or composite RSAT score of 1070-1150. ***Athletic:*** 29 full-time freshmen received athletic scholarships; average amount $4,627.

Additional info: Merit-based scholarships that require full-time attendance and eligibility for renewal typically requires a designated grade point average. The awards range from $500-$7,500 in value.

FINANCIAL AID PROCEDURES

Forms required: FAFSA.

Dates and Deadlines: Priority date 3/10; no closing date. Applicants notified on a rolling basis starting 4/1; must reply by 4/1.

CONTACT

Mary Harper, Director of Student Financial Assistance
8600 University Boulevard, Evansville, IN 47712
(812) 464-1767

Valparaiso University

Valparaiso, Indiana
www.valpo.edu   Federal Code: 001842

4-year private university in large town, affiliated with the Lutheran Church.

Enrollment: 3,255 undergrads, 1% part-time. 742 full-time freshmen.

Selectivity: Admits over 75% of applicants.

BASIC COSTS (2016-2017)

Tuition and fees: $37,450.

Per-credit charge: $1,615.

Room and board: $10,920.

Additional info: Engineering students pay an additional $740 fee.

FINANCIAL AID PICTURE (2015-2016)

Students with need: Out of 695 full-time freshmen who applied for aid, 619 were judged to have need. Of these, 619 received aid, and 365 had their full need met. Average financial aid package met 94% of need; average scholarship/grant was $28,968; average loan was $4,210. For part-time students, average financial aid package was $9,470.

Students without need: 115 full-time freshmen who did not demonstrate need for aid received scholarships/grants; average award was $17,669. No-need awards available for academics, alumni affiliation, art, athletics, leadership, music/drama, religious affiliation, ROTC, state/district residency.

Scholarships offered: *Merit:* Academic Scholarships; $15,000-full tuition. Departmental and Lutheran Scholarships; amounts vary. ***Athletic:*** 18 full-time freshmen received athletic scholarships; average amount $25,897.

Additional info: Financial assistance based on need, academic record, talent available through university.

FINANCIAL AID PROCEDURES

Forms required: FAFSA.

Dates and Deadlines: Priority date 3/1; no closing date. Applicants notified on a rolling basis starting 3/1.

Transfers: Transfer students eligible for scholarships based on previous college work. Scholarship amounts vary depending on the GPA at previous institutions.

CONTACT

Karen Klimczyk, Director of Financial Aid

Kretzmann Hall, 1700 Chapel Drive, Valparaiso, IN 46383-6493

(219) 464-5015

Vincennes University

Vincennes, Indiana

www.vinu.edu   Federal Code: 001843

2-year public junior college in large town.

Enrollment: 7,563 undergrads, 38% part-time. 1,876 full-time freshmen.

Selectivity: Open admission; but selective for some programs.

BASIC COSTS (2016-2017)

Tuition and fees: $5,574; out-of-state residents $13,184.

Per-credit charge: $177.54; out-of-state residents $431.18.

Room and board: $9,332.

FINANCIAL AID PICTURE

Students with need: Need-based aid available for full-time and part-time students. Work study available nights, weekends, and for part-time students.

Students without need: No-need awards available for academics, art, athletics, job skills, leadership, music/drama, state/district residency.

Scholarships offered: Presidential Scholarship: $2,500 per year for 4 semesters; SAT score and rank in upper 10% of class; limited in number. Blue & Gold Scholarship: $1,750 per year for 4 semesters; SAT score and rank in upper 50% of class; limited number of awards. Indiana Academic Honors/ Technical Honors Diploma: $1,250 per year for 4 semesters. Walters Scholarship: tuition, room and board; for candidates in good standing. Education Scholarship: for education majors, based on SAT scores and rank in upper 10% of class; 1 awarded. Valedictorian/Salutatorian scholarship: tuition and housing or tuition and a stipend for commuters.

FINANCIAL AID PROCEDURES

Forms required: FAFSA.

Dates and Deadlines: Priority date 3/1; no closing date. Applicants notified on a rolling basis starting 5/1; must reply by 8/24.

Transfers: No deadline. Applicants notified on a rolling basis starting 4/1. Transfer students must notify the State Student Assistance Commission within 30 days of the start of term.

CONTACT

Stanley Werne, Director of Financial Aid

1002 North First Street, Vincennes, IN 47591

(812) 888-4361

Wabash College

Crawfordsville, Indiana

www.wabash.edu   Federal Code: 001844

4-year private liberal arts college for men in large town.

Enrollment: 843 undergrads. 215 full-time freshmen.

Selectivity: Admits 50 to 75% of applicants.

BASIC COSTS (2017-2018)

Tuition and fees: $42,250.

Per-credit charge: $1,733.

Room and board: $9,850.

FINANCIAL AID PICTURE (2016-2017)

Students with need: Out of 190 full-time freshmen who applied for aid, 170 were judged to have need. Of these, 170 received aid, and 130 had their full need met. Average financial aid package met 94% of need; average scholarship/grant was $30,243; average loan was $3,190. Need-based aid available for part-time students.

Students without need: 43 full-time freshmen who did not demonstrate need for aid received scholarships/grants; average award was $21,990. No-need awards available for academics, art, leadership, music/drama.

Scholarships offered: Lilly Awards Program: full tuition, on-campus room and board, fees; recognizes outstanding personal achievement and potential for leadership. Fine Arts Scholarship: up to $15,000; based on creativity/ability; approximately 16 awarded. Honor Scholarships: up to full tuition; competitive-based on attendance and performance at Scarlet Honors Weekend; approximately 90 awarded. President's Scholarships, Dean's Scholarships, and Alumni Awards: based on class rank, SAT scores; unlimited number awarded. Awards range from $15,000 to $30,000 per year.

FINANCIAL AID PROCEDURES

Forms required: FAFSA.

Dates and Deadlines: Priority date 1/15; no closing date. Applicants notified on a rolling basis starting 12/15; must reply by 5/1.

Transfers: Closing date 2/15. Applicants notified on a rolling basis starting 12/15; must reply by 5/1 or within 2 week(s) of notification.

CONTACT

Heidi Carl, Director of Financial Aid

PO Box 352, Crawfordsville, IN 47933

(800) 718-9746

Iowa

Allen College

Waterloo, Iowa

www.allencollege.edu   Federal Code: 030691

4-year private health science and nursing college in small city.

Enrollment: 358 undergrads, 25% part-time.

BASIC COSTS (2016-2017)

Tuition and fees: $20,010.

Per-credit charge: $588.

Room and board: $7,281.

FINANCIAL AID PICTURE (2015-2016)

Students with need: 63% of average financial aid package awarded as scholarships/grants, 37% awarded as loans/jobs. Need-based aid available for part-time students.

Students without need: No-need awards available for academics, leadership, minority status, ROTC.

FINANCIAL AID PROCEDURES

Forms required: FAFSA, institutional form.

Dates and Deadlines: Priority date 5/1; no closing date. Applicants notified on a rolling basis starting 5/1; must reply within 2 week(s) of notification.

Transfers: No deadline. Applicants notified on a rolling basis starting 4/1; must reply within 2 week(s) of notification.

CONTACT

Jobyna Johnston, Director of Financial Aid

1825 Logan Avenue, Waterloo, IA 50703

(319) 226-2000

Briar Cliff University

Sioux City, Iowa
www.briarcliff.edu   Federal Code: 001846

4-year private university and liberal arts college in small city, affiliated with the Roman Catholic Church.
Enrollment: 972 undergrads, 19% part-time. 185 full-time freshmen.
Selectivity: Admits 50 to 75% of applicants.

BASIC COSTS (2016-2017)
Tuition and fees: $28,788.
Per-credit charge: $910.
Room and board: $8,782.

FINANCIAL AID PICTURE (2015-2016)
Students with need: Out of 184 full-time freshmen who applied for aid, 158 were judged to have need. Of these, 158 received aid, and 45 had their full need met. Average financial aid package met 30% of need; average scholarship/grant was $16,633; average loan was $4,669. For part-time students, average financial aid package was $9,694.
Students without need: 25 full-time freshmen who did not demonstrate need for aid received scholarships/grants; average award was $1,324. No-need awards available for academics, alumni affiliation, art, athletics, minority status, music/drama, religious affiliation.
Scholarships offered: *Merit:* Presidential Scholarships; awarded each year for achievement and demonstrated leadership, based on application and on-campus interview; 2-5 awarded. *Athletic:* 138 full-time freshmen received athletic scholarships; average amount $7,678.

FINANCIAL AID PROCEDURES
Forms required: FAFSA, state aid form.
Dates and Deadlines: Priority date 3/15; no closing date. Applicants notified on a rolling basis starting 2/1; must reply by 5/1 or within 4 week(s) of notification.
Transfers: Closing date 3/15.

CONTACT
Brian Eben, Assistant Vice President for Enrollment Management
3303 Rebecca Street, Sioux City, IA 51104-2324
(712) 279-5200

Buena Vista University

Storm Lake, Iowa
www.bvu.edu   Federal Code: 001847

4-year private liberal arts college in large town, affiliated with the Presbyterian Church (USA).
Enrollment: 781 undergrads, 1% part-time. 183 full-time freshmen.
Selectivity: Admits 50 to 75% of applicants.

BASIC COSTS (2016-2017)
Tuition and fees: $32,210.
Per-credit charge: $1,083.
Room and board: $9,304.

FINANCIAL AID PICTURE (2016-2017)
Students with need: Out of 171 full-time freshmen who applied for aid, 153 were judged to have need. Of these, 153 received aid, and 33 had their full need met. Average financial aid package met 86% of need; average scholarship/grant was $25,253; average loan was $4,435. For part-time students, average financial aid package was $4,665.
Students without need: 30 full-time freshmen who did not demonstrate need for aid received scholarships/grants; average award was $18,668. No-need awards available for academics, art, minority status, music/drama.
Additional info: Portfolio required of art scholarship applicants, audition required of music and drama scholarship applicants.

FINANCIAL AID PROCEDURES
Forms required: FAFSA.
Dates and Deadlines: Priority date 4/1; no closing date. Applicants notified on a rolling basis starting 2/15.

CONTACT
Leanne Valentine, Director of Financial Assistance
610 West Fourth Street, Storm Lake, IA 50588
(714) 749-2164

Central College

Pella, Iowa
www.central.edu   Federal Code: 001850

4-year private liberal arts college in large town, affiliated with the Reformed Church in America.
Enrollment: 1,184 undergrads, 1% part-time. 323 full-time freshmen.
Selectivity: Admits 50 to 75% of applicants.

BASIC COSTS (2016-2017)
Tuition and fees: $34,612.
Per-credit charge: $1,442.
Room and board: $9,980.

FINANCIAL AID PICTURE (2016-2017)
Students with need: Out of 311 full-time freshmen who applied for aid, 279 were judged to have need. Of these, 279 received aid, and 64 had their full need met. Average financial aid package met 87% of need; average scholarship/grant was $25,511; average loan was $2,352. For part-time students, average financial aid package was $13,043.
Students without need: 44 full-time freshmen who did not demonstrate need for aid received scholarships/grants; average award was $12,893. No-need awards available for academics, alumni affiliation, art, minority status, music/drama, religious affiliation, state/district residency.
Scholarships offered: Students may qualify for academic scholarships up to and including three full-tuition scholarships. Funds are also awarded to students who demonstrate skills and talents in a variety of academic areas.
Additional info: Funds are awarded to students who qualify as National Merit Finalists.

FINANCIAL AID PROCEDURES
Forms required: FAFSA.
Dates and Deadlines: Priority date 1/15; no closing date. Applicants notified on a rolling basis starting 11/15; must reply by 5/1 or within 2 week(s) of notification.
Transfers: No deadline. Applicants notified on a rolling basis starting 3/15; must reply by 5/1 or within 2 week(s) of notification. Transfers only eligible for total of 4 years of state funds.

CONTACT
Wayne Dille, Director of Financial Aid
812 University Street, Pella, IA 50219-1999
(641) 628-5336

Clarke University

Dubuque, Iowa
www.clarke.edu   Federal Code: 001852

4-year private university and liberal arts college in small city, affiliated with the Roman Catholic Church.
Enrollment: 788 undergrads, 7% part-time. 151 full-time freshmen.
Selectivity: Admits 50 to 75% of applicants.

BASIC COSTS (2016-2017)
Tuition and fees: $30,900.
Per-credit charge: $700.

Room and board: $9,200.

FINANCIAL AID PICTURE (2016-2017)

Students with need: Out of 146 full-time freshmen who applied for aid, 132 were judged to have need. Of these, 132 received aid, and 33 had their full need met. Average financial aid package met 78% of need; average scholarship/grant was $23,381; average loan was $3,105. For part-time students, average financial aid package was $10,842.

Students without need: 19 full-time freshmen who did not demonstrate need for aid received scholarships/grants; average award was $24,955. No-need awards available for academics, alumni affiliation, art, athletics, leadership, music/drama.

Scholarships offered: 76 full-time freshmen received athletic scholarships; average amount $4,449.

Additional info: Reduced tuition for family members of BVMs.

FINANCIAL AID PROCEDURES

Forms required: FAFSA.

Dates and Deadlines: Priority date 4/15; no closing date. Applicants notified on a rolling basis starting 3/15; must reply within 2 week(s) of notification.

Transfers: Applicants notified on a rolling basis starting 3/15; must reply within 2 week(s) of notification.

CONTACT

Amy Norton, Director of Financial Aid
1550 Clarke Drive, Dubuque, IA 52001-3198
(563) 588-6327

Clinton Community College

Clinton, Iowa
www.eicc.edu Federal Code: 001853

2-year public community college in large town.

Enrollment: 1,909 undergrads.

Selectivity: Open admission; but selective for some programs.

BASIC COSTS (2016-2017)

Tuition and fees: $4,470; out-of-state residents $6,480.

Per-credit charge: $149; out-of-state residents $216.

FINANCIAL AID PICTURE

Students with need: Work study available nights.

FINANCIAL AID PROCEDURES

Forms required: FAFSA, institutional form.

Dates and Deadlines: Priority date 4/1; no closing date. Applicants notified on a rolling basis starting 5/15; must reply within 2 week(s) of notification.

CONTACT

Teresa Thiede, Financial Aid Officer
1000 Lincoln Boulevard, Clinton, IA 52732
(563) 244-7070

Coe College

Cedar Rapids, Iowa
www.coe.edu Federal Code: 001854

4-year private nursing and liberal arts college in small city, affiliated with the Presbyterian Church (USA).

Enrollment: 1,323 undergrads, 1% part-time. 374 full-time freshmen.

Selectivity: Admits less than 50% of applicants.

BASIC COSTS (2017-2018)

Tuition and fees: $42,430.

Per-credit charge: $1,315.

Room and board: $9,140.

Additional info: Tuition/fee waivers available for adults.

FINANCIAL AID PICTURE (2016-2017)

Students with need: Out of 351 full-time freshmen who applied for aid, 325 were judged to have need. Of these, 325 received aid, and 64 had their full need met. Average financial aid package met 85% of need; average scholarship/grant was $31,524; average loan was $3,808. Need-based aid available for part-time students.

Students without need: 46 full-time freshmen who did not demonstrate need for aid received scholarships/grants; average award was $25,905. No-need awards available for academics, alumni affiliation, art, minority status, music/drama.

Scholarships offered: Scholarships for business/economics, music, art, theater, writing, foreign language, science: based on portfolio or audition; available for non-majors except in science and business/economics. Academic Awards: $6,000-$19,000; based on high school achievement.

FINANCIAL AID PROCEDURES

Forms required: FAFSA.

Dates and Deadlines: Priority date 3/1; no closing date. Applicants notified on a rolling basis starting 12/15; must reply by 5/1 or within 2 week(s) of notification.

CONTACT

Barbara Hoffman, Director of Financial Aid
1220 First Avenue NE, Cedar Rapids, IA 52402
(319) 399-8540

Cornell College

Mount Vernon, Iowa
www.cornellcollege.edu Federal Code: 001856

4-year private liberal arts college in small town, affiliated with the United Methodist Church.

Enrollment: 974 undergrads. 287 full-time freshmen.

Selectivity: Admits 50 to 75% of applicants.

BASIC COSTS (2017-2018)

Tuition and fees: $39,900.

Per-credit charge: $1,240.

Room and board: $8,900.

FINANCIAL AID PICTURE (2016-2017)

Students with need: 78% of average financial aid package awarded as scholarships/grants, 22% awarded as loans/jobs. Need-based aid available for part-time students. Work study available nights, weekends, and for part-time students.

Students without need: No-need awards available for academics, alumni affiliation, art, leadership, minority status, music/drama, religious affiliation.

FINANCIAL AID PROCEDURES

Forms required: FAFSA.

Dates and Deadlines: Priority date 3/1; no closing date. Applicants notified on a rolling basis starting 3/1; must reply by 5/1 or within 2 week(s) of notification.

Transfers: No deadline. Applicants notified on a rolling basis starting 3/1; must reply by 5/1 or within 2 week(s) of notification.

CONTACT

Pam Perry, Director of Financial Assistance
600 First Street SW, Mount Vernon, IA 52314-1098
(319) 895-4216

Des Moines Area Community College

Ankeny, Iowa
www.dmacc.edu Federal Code: 004589

2-year public community college in large town.

Enrollment: 12,814 undergrads, 50% part-time. 1,867 full-time freshmen.

Selectivity: Open admission; but selective for some programs.

BASIC COSTS (2016-2017)
Tuition and fees: $4,410; out-of-state residents $8,820.
Per-credit charge: $147; out-of-state residents $294.

FINANCIAL AID PICTURE
Students with need: Need-based aid available for full-time and part-time students. Work study available nights, weekends, and for part-time students.
Students without need: No-need awards available for academics, athletics, state/district residency.
Scholarships offered: Foundation Freshmen Scholar Award; full tuition, fees and books for maximum of 15 credit hours per semester based on available funds; open to all high school seniors in top 10% of graduating class.

FINANCIAL AID PROCEDURES
Forms required: FAFSA.
Dates and Deadlines: Priority date 4/1; no closing date. Applicants notified on a rolling basis starting 4/1; must reply within 2 week(s) of notification.

CONTACT
Ean Freels, Director of Financial Aid
2006 South Ankeny Boulevard, Ankeny, IA 50023-3993
(515) 964-6282

Dordt College
Sioux Center, Iowa
www.dordt.edu   Federal Code: 001859

4-year private liberal arts college in small town, affiliated with the Christian Reformed Church.
Enrollment: 1,379 undergrads, 1% part-time. 391 full-time freshmen.
Selectivity: Admits over 75% of applicants.

BASIC COSTS (2017-2018)
Tuition and fees: $30,000.
Per-credit charge: $1,190.
Room and board: $9,140.
Additional info: Tuition/fee waivers available for adults.

FINANCIAL AID PICTURE (2016-2017)
Students with need: Out of 336 full-time freshmen who applied for aid, 272 were judged to have need. Of these, 272 received aid, and 137 had their full need met. Average financial aid package met 85% of need; average scholarship/grant was $19,053; average loan was $4,616. For part-time students, average financial aid package was $14,574.
Students without need: 96 full-time freshmen who did not demonstrate need for aid received scholarships/grants; average award was $20,957. No-need awards available for academics, alumni affiliation, art, athletics, leadership, music/drama, religious affiliation.
Scholarships offered: 48 full-time freshmen received athletic scholarships; average amount $2,131.

FINANCIAL AID PROCEDURES
Forms required: FAFSA, institutional form.
Dates and Deadlines: Priority date 4/1; no closing date. Applicants notified on a rolling basis starting 3/1; must reply within 3 week(s) of notification.
Transfers: Closing date 6/1. Applicants notified on a rolling basis starting 10/1.

CONTACT
Harlan Harmelink, Director of Financial Aid
498 Fourth Avenue, NE, Sioux Center, IA 51250
(712) 722-6087

Drake University
Des Moines, Iowa
www.drake.edu   Federal Code: 001860

4-year private university in large city.
Enrollment: 3,196 undergrads, 3% part-time. 765 full-time freshmen.
Selectivity: Admits 50 to 75% of applicants.

BASIC COSTS (2016-2017)
Tuition and fees: $35,206.
Room and board: $9,850.

FINANCIAL AID PICTURE (2016-2017)
Students with need: Out of 657 full-time freshmen who applied for aid, 522 were judged to have need. Of these, 522 received aid, and 152 had their full need met. Average financial aid package met 76% of need; average scholarship/grant was $20,124; average loan was $3,094. For part-time students, average financial aid package was $12,068.
Students without need: 199 full-time freshmen who did not demonstrate need for aid received scholarships/grants; average award was $16,178. No-need awards available for academics, alumni affiliation, art, athletics, minority status, music/drama, ROTC, state/district residency.
Scholarships offered: *Merit:* Drake University Presidential Scholarship; $7,000-$12,000; based on academic merit and awards; unlimited available. National Alumni Scholarship Competition; 6 full-time tuition with room and board and 10 full-time tuition; available to top students. *Athletic:* 26 full-time freshmen received athletic scholarships; average amount $21,525.

FINANCIAL AID PROCEDURES
Forms required: FAFSA.
Dates and Deadlines: Applicants notified on a rolling basis starting 1/1; must reply by 5/1 or within 3 week(s) of notification.
Transfers: No deadline. Applicants notified on a rolling basis starting 3/1; must reply by 5/1 or within 2 week(s) of notification. FAFSA must be filed by 7/1 for Iowa Tuition Grant deadline.

CONTACT
Christine Marchard, Institutional Research and Academic Compliance Assistant
2507 University Avenue, Des Moines, IA 50311-4505
(515) 271-1865

Ellsworth Community College
Iowa Falls, Iowa
www.iavalley.cc.ia.us/ecc   Federal Code: 001862

2-year public community college in small town.
Enrollment: 709 full-time undergrads.
Selectivity: Open admission; but selective for some programs.

BASIC COSTS (2016-2017)
Tuition and fees: $5,670; out-of-state residents $6,780.
Per-credit charge: $163; out-of-state residents $200.
Room and board: $7,300.
Additional info: Tuition/fee waivers available for adults.

FINANCIAL AID PICTURE
Students with need: Need-based aid available for full-time and part-time students. Work study available nights, weekends, and for part-time students.
Students without need: No-need awards available for academics, art, athletics, leadership, minority status, music/drama.
Scholarships offered: Academic scholarships; $500-$1,800; based on ACT and GPA; unlimited number offered. Directors Scholarship; $2,300; for those who are 1st or 2nd in class; unlimited number offered.

FINANCIAL AID PROCEDURES
Forms required: FAFSA, institutional form.

Dates and Deadlines: Closing date 4/1. Applicants notified on a rolling basis starting 2/15; must reply within 4 week(s) of notification.

Transfers: Priority date 4/15.

CONTACT

Tara Miller, Financial Aid Administrator
1100 College Avenue, Iowa Falls, IA 50126
(641) 648-4611 ext. 432

Emmaus Bible College

Dubuque, Iowa
www.emmaus.edu   Federal Code: 016487

4-year private Bible college in small city, affiliated with the Brethren Church.

Enrollment: 251 undergrads, 8% part-time. 65 full-time freshmen.

Selectivity: Admits less than 50% of applicants.

BASIC COSTS (2017-2018)

Tuition and fees: $17,520.

Per-credit charge: $730.

Room and board: $8,100.

FINANCIAL AID PICTURE

Students with need: Need-based aid available for full-time and part-time students. Work study available nights, weekends, and for part-time students.

Students without need: No-need awards available for academics.

FINANCIAL AID PROCEDURES

Forms required: FAFSA.

Dates and Deadlines: Applicants notified on a rolling basis starting 3/1; must reply within 2 week(s) of notification.

CONTACT

Steve Seeman, Financial Aid Director
2570 Asbury Road, Dubuque, IA 52001
(563) 588-8000 ext. 1309

Faith Baptist Bible College and Theological Seminary

Ankeny, Iowa
www.faith.edu   Federal Code: 007121

4-year private Bible and seminary college in large town, affiliated with the General Association of Regular Baptist Churches.

Enrollment: 222 undergrads.

Selectivity: Admits less than 50% of applicants.

BASIC COSTS (2016-2017)

Tuition and fees: $16,766.

Per-credit charge: $595.

Room and board: $6,800.

FINANCIAL AID PICTURE

Students with need: Need-based aid available for full-time and part-time students.

Students without need: No-need awards available for academics, leadership, music/drama.

FINANCIAL AID PROCEDURES

Forms required: FAFSA.

Dates and Deadlines: Priority date 4/1; no closing date. Applicants notified on a rolling basis starting 3/15.

CONTACT

Jordan Sauser, Financial Assistance Director
1900 NW Fourth Street, Ankeny, IA 50023
(515) 964-0601 ext. 206

Graceland University

Lamoni, Iowa
www.graceland.edu   Federal Code: 001866

4-year private university and liberal arts college in rural community, affiliated with the Church of Christ.

Enrollment: 1,261 undergrads, 10% part-time. 256 full-time freshmen.

Selectivity: Admits less than 50% of applicants.

BASIC COSTS (2017-2018)

Tuition and fees: $28,110.

Per-credit charge: $800.

Room and board: $8,480.

FINANCIAL AID PICTURE (2016-2017)

Students with need: Out of 240 full-time freshmen who applied for aid, 216 were judged to have need. Of these, 216 received aid, and 41 had their full need met. Average financial aid package met 78% of need; average scholarship/grant was $20,199; average loan was $3,337. For part-time students, average financial aid package was $5,751.

Students without need: 32 full-time freshmen who did not demonstrate need for aid received scholarships/grants; average award was $14,327. No-need awards available for academics, alumni affiliation, art, athletics, job skills, leadership, music/drama, religious affiliation.

Scholarships offered: *Merit:* Study and Faith Scholarship; 50% tuition; for Community of Christ members. Congregational Matching Grants; up to $500 for other faiths. Merit scholarships; up to $14,000; for incoming freshmen based on GPA and ACT/SAT. Fine Arts, Athletic and Computer Science scholarships available. *Athletic:* 43 full-time freshmen received athletic scholarships; average amount $3,588.

Additional info: Founders Scholarship will supplement other gift aid until percentage of calculated need has been met.

FINANCIAL AID PROCEDURES

Forms required: FAFSA.

Dates and Deadlines: Applicants notified on a rolling basis starting 2/1; must reply within 2 week(s) of notification.

Transfers: No deadline. Applicants notified on a rolling basis; must reply within 2 week(s) of notification.

CONTACT

Talia Brown, Director of Enrollment Operations
1 University Place, Lamoni, IA 50140
(866) 472-2352 ext. 2

Grand View University

Des Moines, Iowa
www.admissions.grandview.edu   Federal Code: 001867

4-year private university and liberal arts college in large city, affiliated with the Evangelical Lutheran Church in America.

Enrollment: 1,876 undergrads, 12% part-time. 335 full-time freshmen.

Selectivity: Admits over 75% of applicants.

BASIC COSTS (2017-2018)

Tuition and fees: $26,516.

Per-credit charge: $642.

Room and board: $8,834.

FINANCIAL AID PICTURE (2016-2017)

Students with need: Out of 306 full-time freshmen who applied for aid, 269 were judged to have need. Of these, 269 received aid, and 96 had their full need met. Average financial aid package met 88% of need; average scholarship/grant was $21,768; average loan was $3,894. For part-time students, average financial aid package was $8,087.

Students without need: 62 full-time freshmen who did not demonstrate need for aid received scholarships/grants; average award was $10,470. No-need awards available for academics, alumni affiliation, art, athletics, music/drama, religious affiliation, ROTC.

Scholarships offered: *Merit:* Presidential Scholarship: up to $16,000. Dean's Scholarship: up to $11,000. Director's Award: up to $9,500. *Athletic:* 191 full-time freshmen received athletic scholarships; average amount $5,192.

FINANCIAL AID PROCEDURES

Dates and Deadlines: Priority date 1/15; no closing date. Applicants notified on a rolling basis starting 12/1; must reply by 5/1 or within 3 week(s) of notification.

Transfers: Priority date 1/15; no deadline. Applicants notified on a rolling basis starting 12/1; must reply by 5/1 or within 3 week(s) of notification.

CONTACT

Michele Dunne, Director of Financial Aid
1200 Grandview Avenue, Des Moines, IA 50316-1599
(515) 263-2963

Grinnell College

Grinnell, Iowa
www.grinnell.edu

Federal Code: 001868
CSS Code: 6252

4-year private liberal arts college in small town.
Enrollment: 1,657 undergrads. 414 full-time freshmen.
Selectivity: Admits less than 50% of applicants.

BASIC COSTS (2016-2017)

Tuition and fees: $48,758.
Per-credit charge: $1,510.
Room and board: $11,980.

FINANCIAL AID PICTURE (2016-2017)

Students with need: Out of 324 full-time freshmen who applied for aid, 273 were judged to have need. Of these, 273 received aid, and 273 had their full need met. Average financial aid package met 100% of need; average scholarship/grant was $41,090; average loan was $2,924. For part-time students, average financial aid package was $11,910.

Students without need: 67 full-time freshmen who did not demonstrate need for aid received scholarships/grants; average award was $17,329. No-need awards available for academics, state/district residency.

Additional info: Need-blind admission policy, 100% of demonstrated institutional need met for all domestic students, with loan cap programs. Students may apply financial aid to off-campus study programs.

FINANCIAL AID PROCEDURES

Forms required: FAFSA, CSS PROFILE.
Dates and Deadlines: Priority date 1/15; closing date 1/15. Applicants notified by 4/1; must reply by 5/1.
Transfers: Closing date 4/1. Applicants notified by 5/20; must reply by 6/1.

CONTACT

Brad Lindberg, Director of Student Financial Aid
1103 Park Street, 2nd Floor, Grinnell, IA 50112-1690
(641) 269-3250

Hawkeye Community College

Waterloo, Iowa
www.hawkeyecollege.edu

Federal Code: 004595

2-year public community and technical college in small city.
Enrollment: 3,648 undergrads.
Selectivity: Open admission; but selective for some programs.

BASIC COSTS (2016-2017)

Tuition and fees: $5,055; out-of-state residents $5,805.
Per-credit charge: $161; out-of-state residents $186.

FINANCIAL AID PICTURE

Students with need: Need-based aid available for full-time students. Work study available nights, weekends, and for part-time students.
Students without need: No-need awards available for academics, state/district residency.

FINANCIAL AID PROCEDURES

Forms required: FAFSA.
Dates and Deadlines: Priority date 7/1; no closing date. Applicants notified on a rolling basis starting 5/1; must reply within 2 week(s) of notification.

CONTACT

Gisella Baker, Director of Financial Aid
Box 8015, Waterloo, IA 50704-8015
(319) 296-4020

Iowa Central Community College

Fort Dodge, Iowa
www.iowacentral.edu

Federal Code: 004597

2-year public community college in large town.
Enrollment: 3,437 undergrads, 21% part-time. 1,157 full-time freshmen.
Selectivity: Open admission; but selective for some programs.

BASIC COSTS (2016-2017)

Tuition and fees: $5,160; out-of-state residents $7,395.
Per-credit charge: $158; out-of-state residents $232.5.
Room and board: $6,600.

FINANCIAL AID PICTURE (2016-2017)

Students with need: Average financial aid package met 67% of need; average scholarship/grant was $1,068; average loan was $1,574. For part-time students, average financial aid package was $1,352.
Students without need: No-need awards available for academics, art, athletics, leadership, music/drama.
Scholarships offered: 90 full-time freshmen received athletic scholarships; average amount $1,389.

FINANCIAL AID PROCEDURES

Forms required: FAFSA.
Dates and Deadlines: Priority date 3/1; no closing date. Applicants notified on a rolling basis starting 4/1.

CONTACT

Linsey Christie, Director of Financial Aid
One Triton Circle, Fort Dodge, IA 50501
(515) 574-5020

Iowa Lakes Community College

Estherville, Iowa
www.iowalakes.edu

Federal Code: 001864

2-year public community college in small town.
Enrollment: 1,200 undergrads, 18% part-time. 318 full-time freshmen.
Selectivity: Open admission; but selective for some programs.

BASIC COSTS (2016-2017)

Tuition and fees: $5,505; out-of-state residents $5,655.
Per-credit charge: $167; out-of-district residents $172; out-of-state residents $178.
Room and board: $6,030.

FINANCIAL AID PICTURE

Students with need: Need-based aid available for full-time and part-time students. Work study available nights, weekends, and for part-time students.

Students without need: This college awards aid only to students with need.

FINANCIAL AID PROCEDURES

Forms required: FAFSA, institutional form.

Dates and Deadlines: Priority date 4/22; no closing date. Applicants notified on a rolling basis starting 4/15.

CONTACT

Steve Pelzer, Director of Financial Aid
300 South 18th Street, Estherville, IA 51334-2725
(712) 362-7917

Iowa State University
Ames, Iowa
www.iastate.edu   Federal Code: 001869

4-year public university in small city.

Enrollment: 30,224 undergrads, 5% part-time. 6,028 full-time freshmen.

Selectivity: Admits over 75% of applicants.

BASIC COSTS (2016-2017)

Tuition and fees: $8,219; out-of-state residents $21,583.

Per-credit charge: $296; out-of-state residents $853.

Room and board: $8,356.

FINANCIAL AID PICTURE (2015-2016)

Students with need: Out of 5,122 full-time freshmen who applied for aid, 3,112 were judged to have need. Of these, 3,068 received aid, and 1,130 had their full need met. Average financial aid package met 82% of need; average scholarship/grant was $8,333; average loan was $3,385. For part-time students, average financial aid package was $9,249.

Students without need: 2,292 full-time freshmen who did not demonstrate need for aid received scholarships/grants; average award was $4,261. No-need awards available for academics, alumni affiliation, art, athletics, leadership, minority status, music/drama, ROTC, state/district residency.

Scholarships offered: 64 full-time freshmen received athletic scholarships; average amount $20,303.

Additional info: Short-term loan program available to meet unplanned needs. Financial counseling clinic provides budget and credit education assistance.

FINANCIAL AID PROCEDURES

Forms required: FAFSA.

Dates and Deadlines: Priority date 3/1; no closing date. Applicants notified on a rolling basis starting 4/1; must reply by 5/1.

Transfers: Priority date 2/15.

CONTACT

Roberta Johnson, Director of Student Financial Aid
100 Enrollment Services Center, Ames, IA 50011-2011
(515) 294-0109

Iowa Wesleyan College
Mount Pleasant, Iowa
www.iwc.edu   Federal Code: 001871

4-year private liberal arts college in small town, affiliated with the United Methodist Church.

Enrollment: 578 undergrads.

BASIC COSTS (2016-2017)

Tuition and fees: $28,646.

Per-credit charge: $710.

Room and board: $10,054.

FINANCIAL AID PICTURE

Students with need: Need-based aid available for full-time students. Work study available nights, weekends, and for part-time students.

Students without need: No-need awards available for academics, alumni affiliation, art, music/drama.

Scholarships offered: Unlimited merit based scholarships; based on ACT/SAT and GPA.

FINANCIAL AID PROCEDURES

Forms required: FAFSA.

Dates and Deadlines: Priority date 4/1; no closing date. Applicants notified on a rolling basis starting 1/1; must reply within 2 week(s) of notification.

Transfers: Applicants notified on a rolling basis.

CONTACT

Phyllis Whitney, Chief Financial Officer
601 North Main Street, Mount Pleasant, IA 52641-1398
(319) 385-6242

Iowa Western Community College
Council Bluffs, Iowa
www.iwcc.edu   Federal Code: 004598

2-year public community and technical college in small city.

Enrollment: 4,208 undergrads, 28% part-time. 1,364 full-time freshmen.

Selectivity: Open admission; but selective for some programs.

BASIC COSTS (2016-2017)

Tuition and fees: $5,255; out-of-state residents $5,405.

Per-credit charge: $157; out-of-state residents $162.

Room and board: $6,200.

FINANCIAL AID PICTURE

Students with need: Need-based aid available for full-time and part-time students.

Students without need: No-need awards available for athletics, music/drama.

FINANCIAL AID PROCEDURES

Forms required: FAFSA.

Dates and Deadlines: Applicants notified on a rolling basis starting 3/1; must reply within 3 week(s) of notification.

CONTACT

Keri Zimmer, Dean of Advising and Academic Success
2700 College Road, Council Bluffs, IA 51502-3004
(800) 432-5852 ext. 3277

Kaplan University: Cedar Falls
Cedar Falls, Iowa
www.kaplanuniversity.edu/cedar-falls-iowa.aspx
Federal Code: 004586

4-year for-profit university and branch campus college in small city.

Enrollment: 306 undergrads, 38% part-time. 7 full-time freshmen.

Selectivity: Open admission; but selective for some programs.

BASIC COSTS (2016-2017)

Additional info: Diploma programs: $9364-$10,540; Associate programs: $10,218; Bachelor programs: $10,218. Fees, books supplies range depending on program level and course of study. All costs are subject to change.

FINANCIAL AID PICTURE

Students with need: Need-based aid available for full-time and part-time students. Work study available nights, weekends, and for part-time students.

Students without need: This college awards aid only to students with need.

FINANCIAL AID PROCEDURES
Forms required: FAFSA, institutional form.
Dates and Deadlines: Applicants notified on a rolling basis.
Transfers: No deadline. Applicants notified on a rolling basis.

CONTACT
Amy Kramer, Director of Financial Aid
7009 Nordic Drive, Cedar Falls, IA 50613

Kaplan University: Cedar Rapids
Cedar Rapids, Iowa
www.kaplanuniversity.edu/cedar-rapids-iowa.aspx
Federal Code: 004220

2-year for-profit liberal arts college in small city.
Enrollment: 454 undergrads, 35% part-time. 4 full-time freshmen.
Selectivity: Open admission; but selective for some programs.

BASIC COSTS (2016-2017)
Additional info: Diploma programs: $9364-$10,540; Associate programs: $10,218; Bachelor programs: $10,218. Fees, books supplies range depending on program level and course of study. All costs are subject to change.

FINANCIAL AID PICTURE
Students with need: Need-based aid available for full-time and part-time students. Work study available nights, weekends, and for part-time students.
Students without need: No-need awards available for academics.

FINANCIAL AID PROCEDURES
Forms required: FAFSA, institutional form.
Dates and Deadlines: Priority date 6/30; no closing date. Applicants notified on a rolling basis.
Transfers: Priority date of 07/08 for filing Iowa Tuition Grant application.

CONTACT
Robert Brooks, Director of Financial Aid Operations
3165 Edgewood Parkway, SW, Cedar Rapids, IA 52404

Kaplan University: Davenport
Davenport, Iowa
www.kaplanuniversity.edu/davenport-iowa.aspx
Federal Code: 004586

4-year for-profit university in large city.
Enrollment: 35,040 undergrads, 88% part-time. 14 full-time freshmen.
Selectivity: Open admission; but selective for some programs.

BASIC COSTS (2016-2017)
Additional info: Diploma programs: $9364-$10,540; Associate programs: $10,218; Bachelor programs: $10,218. Fees, books supplies range depending on program level and course of study. All costs are subject to change.

FINANCIAL AID PICTURE
Students with need: Need-based aid available for full-time and part-time students. Work study available nights.
Students without need: No-need awards available for academics.

FINANCIAL AID PROCEDURES
Forms required: FAFSA, institutional form.
Dates and Deadlines: Applicants notified on a rolling basis starting 3/4; must reply by 6/15 or within 2 week(s) of notification.

CONTACT
Chris Christopherson, Director of Financial Aid
1801 East Kimberly Road, Suite 1, Davenport, IA 52807-2095

Kaplan University: Des Moines
Urbandale, Iowa
www.kaplanuniversity.edu/des-moines-iowa.aspx
Federal Code: 004220

4-year for-profit university in large city.
Enrollment: 780 undergrads.
Selectivity: Open admission; but selective for some programs.

BASIC COSTS (2016-2017)
Additional info: Diploma programs: $9364-$10,540; Associate programs: $10,218; Bachelor programs: $10,218. Fees, books supplies range depending on program level and course of study. All costs are subject to change.

FINANCIAL AID PICTURE
Students with need: Need-based aid available for full-time and part-time students. Work study available nights, weekends, and for part-time students.
Students without need: This college awards aid only to students with need.

FINANCIAL AID PROCEDURES
Forms required: FAFSA, institutional form.
Dates and Deadlines: Priority date 6/30; no closing date.

CONTACT
Summer Vaselaar, Director of Financial Aid
4655 121st Street, Urbandale, IA 50323
(515) 727-2100

Kirkwood Community College
Cedar Rapids, Iowa
www.kirkwood.edu
Federal Code: 004076

2-year public community college in small city.
Enrollment: 9,276 undergrads, 39% part-time. 2,040 full-time freshmen.
Selectivity: Open admission; but selective for some programs.

BASIC COSTS (2016-2017)
Tuition and fees: $4,670; out-of-state residents $5,570.
Per-credit charge: $154; out-of-state residents $184.

FINANCIAL AID PICTURE
Students with need: Need-based aid available for full-time and part-time students. Work study available nights, weekends, and for part-time students.
Students without need: No-need awards available for art, athletics, leadership, music/drama.

FINANCIAL AID PROCEDURES
Forms required: FAFSA.
Dates and Deadlines: Closing date 6/30. Applicants notified on a rolling basis starting 4/1.

CONTACT
Jennifer Hughes, Compliance Reporting Manager
6301 Kirkwood Boulevard SW, Cedar Rapids, IA 52404-2068
(319) 398-1274

Loras College
Dubuque, Iowa
www.loras.edu
Federal Code: 001873

4-year private liberal arts college in small city, affiliated with the Roman Catholic Church.
Enrollment: 1,422 undergrads, 2% part-time. 328 full-time freshmen.
Selectivity: Admits over 75% of applicants.

BASIC COSTS (2016-2017)

Tuition and fees: $31,525.

Per-credit charge: $610.

Room and board: $7,700.

Additional info: Tuition/fee waivers available for minority students.

FINANCIAL AID PICTURE (2016-2017)

Students with need: Out of 305 full-time freshmen who applied for aid, 255 were judged to have need. Of these, 255 received aid, and 87 had their full need met. Average financial aid package met 90% of need; average scholarship/grant was $21,464; average loan was $4,528. For part-time students, average financial aid package was $7,564.

Students without need: 73 full-time freshmen who did not demonstrate need for aid received scholarships/grants; average award was $18,877. No-need awards available for academics, art.

Scholarships offered: Honors and Leadership scholarships: ranging from $1,000 to three full-tuition Presidential Scholarships. Breitbach Catholic Thinkers and Leaders Program: selected applicants receive awards of up to $17,000 per year. Music Scholarship open to all majors. Loras academic scholarships and awards based on high school GPA and ACT scores.

Additional info: Audition or portfolio recommended for music and art financial aid applicants.

FINANCIAL AID PROCEDURES

Forms required: FAFSA.

Dates and Deadlines: Priority date 3/1; no closing date. Applicants notified on a rolling basis starting 3/1; must reply within 3 week(s) of notification.

Transfers: Priority date 3/1; no deadline. Applicants notified on a rolling basis starting 3/1; must reply within 3 week(s) of notification.

CONTACT

Julie Dunn, Director of Financial Planning

1450 Alta Vista Street, Dubuque, IA 52001-0178

(563) 588-7136

Luther College

Decorah, Iowa

www.luther.edu

Federal Code: 001874

4-year private liberal arts college in small town, affiliated with the Evangelical Lutheran Church in America.

Enrollment: 2,121 undergrads, 1% part-time. 520 full-time freshmen.

Selectivity: Admits 50 to 75% of applicants.

BASIC COSTS (2016-2017)

Tuition and fees: $40,040.

Per-credit charge: $1,420.

Room and board: $8,500.

FINANCIAL AID PICTURE (2016-2017)

Students with need: Out of 488 full-time freshmen who applied for aid, 432 were judged to have need. Of these, 432 received aid, and 190 had their full need met. Average financial aid package met 92% of need; average scholarship/grant was $26,547; average loan was $5,436. For part-time students, average financial aid package was $5,435.

Students without need: 85 full-time freshmen who did not demonstrate need for aid received scholarships/grants; average award was $20,486. No-need awards available for academics, alumni affiliation, art, minority status, music/drama.

FINANCIAL AID PROCEDURES

Forms required: FAFSA, institutional form.

Dates and Deadlines: Priority date 3/1; no closing date. Applicants notified on a rolling basis starting 3/15; must reply by 5/1 or within 4 week(s) of notification.

CONTACT

Janice Cordell, Director of Student Financial Planning

700 College Drive, Decorah, IA 52101-1042

(563) 387-1018

Maharishi University of Management

Fairfield, Iowa

www.mum.edu

Federal Code: 011113

4-year private university and liberal arts college in small town.

Enrollment: 320 undergrads, 4% part-time. 20 full-time freshmen.

Selectivity: Admits over 75% of applicants.

BASIC COSTS (2016-2017)

Tuition and fees: $26,530.

Room and board: $7,400.

FINANCIAL AID PICTURE

Students with need: Need-based aid available for full-time and part-time students. Work study available nights, weekends, and for part-time students.

Scholarships offered: Shelley Hoffman Scholarship; $500-$900; applicant must have cerebral palsy, with preference given to students majoring in creative writing; 7 awarded. National Merit Scholarship; full tuition; for NMS finalists; 4 awarded. Ray Prat Scholarship; $500-$1,750; for musically-talented undergraduates; 4 awarded. Girl Scout Gold Award Scholarship; $1,500 renewable; for GS Gold Award recipients; 5 awarded. DeRoy D. Thomas Scholarship; $3,000 each; open to outstanding African American; 1 awarded.

Additional info: Students may earn scholarships through volunteer staff program.

FINANCIAL AID PROCEDURES

Forms required: FAFSA.

Dates and Deadlines: Priority date 7/15; closing date 7/30. Applicants notified on a rolling basis starting 3/1; must reply within 4 week(s) of notification.

Transfers: No deadline. Applicants notified on a rolling basis starting 3/15; must reply within 4 week(s) of notification.

CONTACT

Dan Wasielewski, Director of Financial Aid

Office of Admissions, Fairfield, IA 52557

(641) 472-1156

Mercy College of Health Sciences

Des Moines, Iowa

www.mchs.edu

Federal Code: 006273

4-year private health science college in large city, affiliated with the Roman Catholic Church.

Enrollment: 771 undergrads, 39% part-time. 39 full-time freshmen.

BASIC COSTS (2016-2017)

Tuition and fees: $16,920.

FINANCIAL AID PICTURE (2015-2016)

Students with need: Out of 32 full-time freshmen who applied for aid, 29 were judged to have need. Of these, 27 received aid. Average financial aid package met 64% of need; average scholarship/grant was $6,907; average loan was $3,219. For part-time students, average financial aid package was $8,866.

Students without need: No-need awards available for academics, leadership, minority status.

FINANCIAL AID PROCEDURES

Forms required: FAFSA.

Dates and Deadlines: Priority date 7/1; no closing date. Applicants notified on a rolling basis starting 3/1; must reply within 3 week(s) of notification.

Transfers: Priority date 4/15; closing date 7/1. Applicants notified on a rolling basis starting 3/1; must reply within 3 week(s) of notification.

CONTACT
Joseph Brookover, Financial Aid Director
921 6th Avenue, Des Moines, IA 50309-1200
(515) 643-6611

Morningside College
Sioux City, Iowa
www.morningside.edu   Federal Code: 001879

4-year private liberal arts college in small city, affiliated with the United Methodist Church.
Enrollment: 1,278 undergrads, 2% part-time. 340 full-time freshmen.
Selectivity: Admits 50 to 75% of applicants.

BASIC COSTS (2016-2017)
Tuition and fees: $29,094.
Per-credit charge: $850.
Room and board: $9,210.
Additional info: Tuition/fee waivers available for adults.

FINANCIAL AID PICTURE (2016-2017)
Students with need: Out of 307 full-time freshmen who applied for aid, 281 were judged to have need. Of these, 281 received aid, and 108 had their full need met. Average financial aid package met 79% of need; average scholarship/grant was $6,193; average loan was $4,072. For part-time students, average financial aid package was $6,204.
Students without need: 58 full-time freshmen who did not demonstrate need for aid received scholarships/grants; average award was $16,908. No-need awards available for academics, art, athletics, music/drama, religious affiliation.
Scholarships offered: *Merit:* Trustee Scholarship: $20,000; based on ACT score of 31 and High School GPA of 3.9. President's Scholarship: $15,000; based on ACT score of 27 and High School GPA of 3.9. Dean's Scholarship: $13,000; based on ACT score of 25 and High School GPA of 3.3. Founder Scholarship: $10,000; all other full time Freshmen eligible. Talent Awards: up to $5,000; based on talents in the areas of art, music, and/or theater. Athletic Grants. *Athletic:* 187 full-time freshmen received athletic scholarships; average amount $4,156.

FINANCIAL AID PROCEDURES
Forms required: FAFSA.
Dates and Deadlines: Priority date 3/1; no closing date. Applicants notified on a rolling basis starting 3/15.
Transfers: No deadline. Applicants notified on a rolling basis starting 12/1.

CONTACT
Karen Gagnon, Director Student Financial Planning
1501 Morningside Avenue, Sioux City, IA 51106
(712) 274-5159

Mount Mercy University
Cedar Rapids, Iowa
www.mtmercy.edu   Federal Code: 001880

4-year private liberal arts college in small city, affiliated with the Roman Catholic Church.
Enrollment: 1,570 undergrads, 33% part-time. 243 full-time freshmen.
Selectivity: Admits 50 to 75% of applicants.

BASIC COSTS (2017-2018)
Tuition and fees: $30,582.
Per-credit charge: $920.
Room and board: $9,166.

FINANCIAL AID PICTURE (2016-2017)
Students with need: Out of 222 full-time freshmen who applied for aid, 206 were judged to have need. Of these, 203 received aid, and 49 had their full need met. Average financial aid package met 78% of need; average scholarship/grant was $22,203; average loan was $3,047. For part-time students, average financial aid package was $9,087.
Students without need: 35 full-time freshmen who did not demonstrate need for aid received scholarships/grants; average award was $15,040. No-need awards available for academics, alumni affiliation, art, athletics, leadership, music/drama, religious affiliation.
Scholarships offered: 40 full-time freshmen received athletic scholarships; average amount $5,098.

FINANCIAL AID PROCEDURES
Forms required: FAFSA.
Dates and Deadlines: Priority date 3/1; no closing date. Applicants notified on a rolling basis starting 3/15; must reply by 5/1 or within 3 week(s) of notification.
Transfers: No deadline. Applicants notified on a rolling basis starting 3/1; must reply within 3 week(s) of notification.

CONTACT
Bethany Rinderknecht, Director of Financial Aid
1330 Elmhurst Drive NE, Cedar Rapids, IA 52402-4797
(319) 368-6467

Muscatine Community College
Muscatine, Iowa
www.eicc.edu   Federal Code: 001882

2-year public community college in large town.
Enrollment: 1,600 undergrads.
Selectivity: Open admission; but selective for some programs.

BASIC COSTS (2016-2017)
Tuition and fees: $4,470; out-of-state residents $6,480.
Per-credit charge: $149; out-of-state residents $216.

FINANCIAL AID PICTURE
Students with need: Work study available nights.

FINANCIAL AID PROCEDURES
Forms required: FAFSA.
Dates and Deadlines: Priority date 4/20; no closing date. Applicants notified on a rolling basis starting 5/15; must reply within 2 week(s) of notification.

CONTACT
Robin Jennings, Financial Aid Officer
152 Colorado Street, Muscatine, IA 52761-5396
(563) 288-6060

North Iowa Area Community College
Mason City, Iowa
www.niacc.edu   Federal Code: 001877

2-year public community college in large town.
Enrollment: 1,745 undergrads, 26% part-time. 617 full-time freshmen.
Selectivity: Open admission; but selective for some programs.

BASIC COSTS (2016-2017)
Tuition and fees: $5,002; out-of-state residents $7,113.
Room and board: $6,718.

FINANCIAL AID PICTURE (2015-2016)
Students with need: Out of 500 full-time freshmen who applied for aid, 378 were judged to have need. Of these, 371 received aid, and 69 had their full need met. Average financial aid package met 30% of need; average

scholarship/grant was $2,334; average loan was $1,706. For part-time students, average financial aid package was $2,512.
Students without need: No-need awards available for academics, art, athletics, leadership, music/drama.

FINANCIAL AID PROCEDURES
Forms required: FAFSA, institutional form.
Dates and Deadlines: Priority date 3/1; no closing date. Applicants notified on a rolling basis starting 4/1; must reply within 2 week(s) of notification.

CONTACT
Mary Bloomingdale, Director of Financial Aid
500 College Drive, Mason City, IA 50401
(641) 422-4351

Northeast Iowa Community College
Calmar, Iowa
www.nicc.edu   Federal Code: 004587

2-year public community and technical college in rural community.
Enrollment: 2,262 undergrads, 45% part-time. 392 full-time freshmen.
Selectivity: Open admission; but selective for some programs.

BASIC COSTS (2016-2017)
Tuition and fees: $4,676; out-of-state residents $4,676.
Per-credit charge: $160; out-of-state residents $165.

FINANCIAL AID PICTURE
Students with need: Need-based aid available for full-time and part-time students. Work study available nights, weekends, and for part-time students.
Students without need: No-need awards available for academics, leadership, state/district residency.

FINANCIAL AID PROCEDURES
Forms required: FAFSA.
Dates and Deadlines: Priority date 7/1; no closing date. Applicants notified on a rolling basis starting 4/1.
Transfers: No deadline. Applicants notified on a rolling basis; must reply within 2 week(s) of notification.

CONTACT
Randy Mashek, Director of Financial Aid
PO Box 400, Calmar, IA 52132
(563) 526-3263 ext. 447

Northwest Iowa Community College
Sheldon, Iowa
www.nwicc.edu   Federal Code: 004600

2-year public community college in small town.
Enrollment: 770 undergrads.
Selectivity: Open admission; but selective for some programs.

BASIC COSTS (2016-2017)
Tuition and fees: $5,760; out-of-state residents $6,060.
Per-credit charge: $157; out-of-state residents $167.
Room and board: $4,942.

FINANCIAL AID PICTURE
Students with need: Need-based aid available for full-time and part-time students.

FINANCIAL AID PROCEDURES
Forms required: FAFSA, institutional form.
Dates and Deadlines: Priority date 4/1; no closing date. Applicants notified on a rolling basis starting 5/1.

CONTACT
Karna Hofmeyer, Financial Aid Director
603 West Park Street, Sheldon, IA 51201
(712) 324-5061 ext. 138

Northwestern College
Orange City, Iowa
www.nwciowa.edu   Federal Code: 001883

4-year private liberal arts college in small town, affiliated with the Reformed Church in America.
Enrollment: 1,076 undergrads, 3% part-time. 260 full-time freshmen.
Selectivity: Admits 50 to 75% of applicants.

BASIC COSTS (2016-2017)
Tuition and fees: $29,500.
Room and board: $8,900.
Additional info: Tuition/fee waivers available for adults.

FINANCIAL AID PICTURE (2015-2016)
Students with need: Out of 231 full-time freshmen who applied for aid, 181 were judged to have need. Of these, 181 received aid, and 113 had their full need met. Average financial aid package met 93% of need; average scholarship/grant was $6,370; average loan was $4,322. Need-based aid available for part-time students.
Students without need: 77 full-time freshmen who did not demonstrate need for aid received scholarships/grants; average award was $12,514. No-need awards available for academics, alumni affiliation, art, athletics, music/drama, religious affiliation, state/district residency.
Scholarships offered: 53 full-time freshmen received athletic scholarships; average amount $5,141.

FINANCIAL AID PROCEDURES
Forms required: FAFSA.
Dates and Deadlines: Priority date 2/1; closing date 6/30. Applicants notified on a rolling basis starting 1/1; must reply within 3 week(s) of notification.
Transfers: No deadline. Applicants notified on a rolling basis starting 3/1. Financial aid transcript required for aid.

CONTACT
Eric Anderson, Director of Financial Aid
101 Seventh Street SW, Orange City, IA 51041
(712) 707-7131

St. Ambrose University
Davenport, Iowa
www.sau.edu   Federal Code: 001889

4-year private university in small city, affiliated with the Roman Catholic Church.
Enrollment: 2,381 undergrads, 8% part-time. 453 full-time freshmen.
Selectivity: Admits 50 to 75% of applicants.

BASIC COSTS (2017-2018)
Tuition and fees: $30,016.
Per-credit charge: $915.
Room and board: $10,164.
Additional info: Tuition/fee waivers available for adults.

FINANCIAL AID PICTURE (2016-2017)
Students with need: Average financial aid package met 70% of need; average scholarship/grant was $16,618; average loan was $3,544. For part-time students, average financial aid package was $7,453.
Students without need: No-need awards available for academics, alumni affiliation, art, athletics, minority status, music/drama, religious affiliation.

Scholarships offered: Ambrose Scholarship; 4.0 GPA and 30 ACT or 1320 SAT required. Presidential Scholarship; 3.8 GPA and ACT 26-29 or SAT 1170-1319 required. SAT scores listed are exclusive of Writing.

Additional info: Iowa applicants must apply for financial aid by July 1. Audition required for music, drama scholarship applicants.

FINANCIAL AID PROCEDURES
Forms required: FAFSA.

Dates and Deadlines: Priority date 3/16; no closing date. Applicants notified on a rolling basis starting 2/1; must reply within 2 week(s) of notification.

Transfers: No deadline. Must reply within 2 week(s) of notification.

CONTACT
Julie Haack, Director of Financial Aid
518 West Locust Street, Davenport, IA 52803-2898
(563) 333-6000

St. Luke's College
Sioux City, Iowa
www.stlukescollege.edu   Federal Code: 007291

2-year private health science and nursing college in small city.

Enrollment: 267 undergrads, 57% part-time. 4 full-time freshmen.

Selectivity: Admits less than 50% of applicants.

BASIC COSTS (2017-2018)
Tuition and fees: $20,460.

Per-credit charge: $525.

FINANCIAL AID PICTURE (2015-2016)
Students with need: Out of 4 full-time freshmen who applied for aid, 4 were judged to have need. Of these, 4 received aid. Average financial aid package met 75% of need; average scholarship/grant was $5,356; average loan was $4,000. For part-time students, average financial aid package was $6,825.

Students without need: No-need awards available for academics, job skills, leadership.

FINANCIAL AID PROCEDURES
Forms required: FAFSA.

Dates and Deadlines: Priority date 3/1; no closing date. Applicants notified on a rolling basis starting 2/15; must reply within 2 week(s) of notification.

CONTACT
Danelle Johannsen, Department Chair, Student and Administrative Services
2800 Pierce Street Suite 410, Sioux City, IA 51104
(712) 279-3377

Shiloh University
Kalona, Iowa
www.shilohuniversity.edu   Federal Code: 042596

4-year private virtual seminary college in small town, affiliated with the Christian Church.

Enrollment: 13 undergrads, 92% part-time.

BASIC COSTS (2017-2018)
Tuition and fees: $4,510.

Per-credit charge: $150.

FINANCIAL AID PICTURE (2015-2016)
Students with need: Need-based aid available for full-time and part-time students.

Students without need: No-need awards available for academics.

FINANCIAL AID PROCEDURES
Forms required: FAFSA.

CONTACT
Andrew Thompson, Financial Aid Administrator
100 Shiloh Drive, Kalona, IA 52247
(319) 656-2447

Simpson College
Indianola, Iowa
www.simpson.edu   Federal Code: 001887

4-year private liberal arts college in large town, affiliated with the United Methodist Church.

Enrollment: 1,525 undergrads, 10% part-time. 348 full-time freshmen.

Selectivity: Admits over 75% of applicants.

BASIC COSTS (2017-2018)
Tuition and fees: $37,663.

Per-credit charge: $415.

Room and board: $7,963.

Additional info: Tuition/fee waivers available for adults, minority students.

FINANCIAL AID PICTURE (2016-2017)
Students with need: Out of 348 full-time freshmen who applied for aid, 295 were judged to have need. Of these, 295 received aid, and 83 had their full need met. Average financial aid package met 86% of need; average scholarship/grant was $26,776; average loan was $4,947. For part-time students, average financial aid package was $6,367.

Students without need: 52 full-time freshmen who did not demonstrate need for aid received scholarships/grants; average award was $22,431. No-need awards available for academics, alumni affiliation, art, leadership, minority status, music/drama, religious affiliation, state/district residency.

Scholarships offered: Wesley Service Scholarship; $500 per year; students commit to serve 80 hours of community service a year, keep service journal, read assigned readings, and attend monthly service reflection meetings; number of awards varies. George Washington Carver Scholarship; $15,000 to three-quarters tuition per year; for outstanding freshmen from distinctive and broadly diverse backgrounds who bring in a multicultural perspective; number of awards varies. George Washington Carver Fellowship; 3/4 to full tuition; awarded to outstanding freshmen from distinctive and broadly diverse backgrounds who exhibit potential for leadership and service. John C. Culver Fellowship; range from $16,000 - $20,000 per year, awarded to students who show interest in politics, history, or public service; number of awards varies. Iowa History Center Distinguished Scholarship; range from $16,000 - $20,000 per year, awarded to students who have an interest in Iowa history and the work needed to preserve and promote the history of both the Midwest and the state of Iowa; up to five awarded annually.

Additional info: Music and theater scholarships based on audition. Art scholarships based on portfolio.

FINANCIAL AID PROCEDURES
Forms required: FAFSA.

Dates and Deadlines: Priority date 2/1; no closing date. Applicants notified on a rolling basis starting 12/1; must reply by 5/1 or within 3 week(s) of notification.

Transfers: No deadline. Applicants notified on a rolling basis.

CONTACT
Tracie Pavon, Assistant Vice President for Enrollment and Financial Assistance
701 North C Street, Indianola, IA 50125
(515) 961-1630

Southeastern Community College
West Burlington, Iowa
www.scciowa.edu   Federal Code: 004603

2-year public community and junior college in large town.

Enrollment: 1,762 undergrads, 29% part-time. 346 full-time freshmen.

Selectivity: Open admission; but selective for some programs.

BASIC COSTS (2016-2017)
Tuition and fees: $5,274; out-of-state residents $5,424.
Room and board: $7,400.

FINANCIAL AID PICTURE (2015-2016)
Students with need: Out of 286 full-time freshmen who applied for aid, 219 were judged to have need. Of these, 219 received aid. For part-time students, average financial aid package was $3,850.
Students without need: 13 full-time freshmen who did not demonstrate need for aid received scholarships/grants; average award was $2,812. No-need awards available for academics, art, athletics, minority status.
Scholarships offered: 17 full-time freshmen received athletic scholarships; average amount $5,484.

FINANCIAL AID PROCEDURES
Forms required: FAFSA.
Dates and Deadlines: Priority date 7/1; no closing date. Applicants notified on a rolling basis starting 3/1.

CONTACT
Renae Armentrout, Financial Aid Director
1500 West Agency Road, West Burlington, IA 52655-0605
(319) 752-2731 ext. 5014

Southwestern Community College
Creston, Iowa
www.swcciowa.edu   Federal Code: 001857

2-year public community college in small town.
Enrollment: 893 undergrads.
Selectivity: Open admission; but selective for some programs.

BASIC COSTS (2016-2017)
Tuition and fees: $5,100; out-of-state residents $5,310.
Per-credit charge: $158; out-of-state residents $165.
Room and board: $6,960.

FINANCIAL AID PICTURE (2015-2016)
Students with need: 62% of average financial aid package awarded as scholarships/grants, 38% awarded as loans/jobs. Need-based aid available for part-time students. Work study available nights, weekends, and for part-time students.
Students without need: No-need awards available for academics, athletics, leadership, music/drama, state/district residency.

FINANCIAL AID PROCEDURES
Forms required: FAFSA.
Dates and Deadlines: Closing date 7/1. Applicants notified on a rolling basis starting 6/1; must reply within 2 week(s) of notification.
Transfers: Applicants notified on a rolling basis starting 6/1; must reply within 2 week(s) of notification.

CONTACT
Sarah Freestone, Financial Aid Officer
1501 West Townline Street, Creston, IA 50801
(641) 782-7081 ext. 333

University of Dubuque
Dubuque, Iowa
www.dbq.edu   Federal Code: 001891

4-year private university and seminary college in small city, affiliated with the Presbyterian Church (USA).
Enrollment: 1,921 undergrads, 13% part-time. 435 full-time freshmen.
Selectivity: Admits over 75% of applicants.

BASIC COSTS (2016-2017)
Tuition and fees: $28,700; out-of-state residents $28,700.
Per-credit charge: $775.
Room and board: $9,350.

FINANCIAL AID PICTURE (2016-2017)
Students with need: Average financial aid package met 43% of need; average scholarship/grant was $17,198; average loan was $7,897. For part-time students, average financial aid package was $8,842.
Students without need: No-need awards available for academics, alumni affiliation, leadership, music/drama, religious affiliation, ROTC.

FINANCIAL AID PROCEDURES
Forms required: FAFSA.
Dates and Deadlines: Priority date 4/1; no closing date. Applicants notified on a rolling basis starting 3/1; must reply within 3 week(s) of notification.
Transfers: No deadline. Applicants notified on a rolling basis starting 3/1; must reply within 3 week(s) of notification. Iowa Tuition Grant available to Iowa residents.

CONTACT
Teresa Brahm, Associate Director of Financial Planning, Financial Aid
2000 University Avenue, Dubuque, IA 52001-5099
(563) 589-3396

University of Iowa
Iowa City, Iowa
www.uiowa.edu   Federal Code: 001892

4-year public university in small city.
Enrollment: 22,990 undergrads, 10% part-time. 4,845 full-time freshmen.
Selectivity: Admits over 75% of applicants.

BASIC COSTS (2016-2017)
Tuition and fees: $8,325; out-of-state residents $28,413.
Per-credit charge: $287; out-of-state residents $1,124.
Room and board: $10,108.

FINANCIAL AID PICTURE (2015-2016)
Students with need: Out of 3,705 full-time freshmen who applied for aid, 2,457 were judged to have need. Of these, 2,457 received aid, and 883 had their full need met. Average financial aid package met 70% of need; average scholarship/grant was $8,225; average loan was $4,139. For part-time students, average financial aid package was $10,184.
Students without need: 1,481 full-time freshmen who did not demonstrate need for aid received scholarships/grants; average award was $5,529. No-need awards available for academics, alumni affiliation, art, athletics, leadership, music/drama, ROTC, state/district residency.
Scholarships offered: *Merit:* Presidential Scholarship; $13,000 per year for 4 years; based on ACT/SAT, GPA, essay; 20 awarded each year. Old Gold Scholarship; $3,000 per year for 4 years; 30 ACT/1330 SAT and 3.8 GPA required. National Scholars Award; $4,490 per year for 4 years; for nonresidents who are U.S residents or permanent residents with a Regent Admission Index score of 290. Iowa Scholars Award; $1,000 one-time award; for first-year Iowa residents with 27 ACT/1210 SAT and 3.8 GPA or 30 ACT/1330 SAT and 3.7 GPA. Iowa Heritage Award; $1,500 per year for up to four years; for nonresident students who have a parent, step-parent, legal guardian, or grandparent who graduated from UI. Advantage Iowa Award; from $2,000 to full resident tuition; for first-year students who are U.S. citizens or permanent residents whose enrollment will contribute to a diverse learning environment; eligibility criteria vary, but may include race/ethnicity, socioeconomic factors, first-generation college student, participation in federal Upward Bound program. *Athletic:* 116 full-time freshmen received athletic scholarships; average amount $22,665.

FINANCIAL AID PROCEDURES
Forms required: FAFSA, institutional form.

Dates and Deadlines: Priority date 3/1; no closing date. Applicants notified on a rolling basis starting 3/15.

Transfers: No deadline. Applicants notified on a rolling basis starting 3/15; must reply by 5/1 or within 2 week(s) of notification.

CONTACT

Mark Warner, Director of Student Financial Aid
107 Calvin Hall, Iowa City, IA 52242-1396
(319) 335-1450

University of Northern Iowa

Cedar Falls, Iowa
www.uni.edu
Federal Code: 001890

4-year public university in small city.
Enrollment: 9,943 undergrads, 8% part-time. 1,874 full-time freshmen.
Selectivity: Admits over 75% of applicants.

BASIC COSTS (2016-2017)

Tuition and fees: $8,309; out-of-state residents $18,851.
Per-credit charge: $296; out-of-state residents $735.
Room and board: $8,629.

FINANCIAL AID PICTURE (2015-2016)

Students with need: Out of 1,612 full-time freshmen who applied for aid, 1,152 were judged to have need. Of these, 1,118 received aid, and 209 had their full need met. Average financial aid package met 69% of need; average scholarship/grant was $4,928; average loan was $3,681. For part-time students, average financial aid package was $7,202.
Students without need: 379 full-time freshmen who did not demonstrate need for aid received scholarships/grants; average award was $3,342. No-need awards available for academics, alumni affiliation, art, athletics, leadership, minority status, music/drama, ROTC, state/district residency.
Scholarships offered: *Merit:* Presidential Scholarship Award; $8,000/year for up to 4 years; must be in upper 10% of high school class with 29 ACT or Regent Admission Index of 335 and involved in leadership and service activities; 20 available. Distinguished Scholar Award for Iowans; $1,000-$2,500/year, renewable for a 2nd year; for Iowa residents with 28 ACT or Regent Admission Index of 300. *Athletic:* 42 full-time freshmen received athletic scholarships; average amount $10,069.

FINANCIAL AID PROCEDURES

Forms required: FAFSA.
Dates and Deadlines: Applicants notified on a rolling basis starting 3/15.

CONTACT

Joyce Morrow, Director Financial Aid and Student Employment
1227 West 27th Street, Cedar Falls, IA 50614-0018
(319) 273-2700

Upper Iowa University

Fayette, Iowa
www.uiu.edu
Federal Code: 001893

4-year private university and liberal arts college in rural community.
Enrollment: 3,859 undergrads, 42% part-time. 238 full-time freshmen.
Selectivity: Admits over 75% of applicants.

BASIC COSTS (2017-2018)

Tuition and fees: $29,600.
Per-credit charge: $1,200.
Room and board: $8,370.

FINANCIAL AID PICTURE (2015-2016)

Students with need: Out of 159 full-time freshmen who applied for aid, 153 were judged to have need. Of these, 152 received aid, and 9 had their

full need met. Average financial aid package met 66% of need; average scholarship/grant was $18,591; average loan was $3,208. For part-time students, average financial aid package was $6,961.
Students without need: 78 full-time freshmen who did not demonstrate need for aid received scholarships/grants; average award was $16,320. No-need awards available for academics, alumni affiliation, athletics.

FINANCIAL AID PROCEDURES

Forms required: FAFSA.
Dates and Deadlines: Priority date 3/1; no closing date. Applicants notified on a rolling basis starting 3/1; must reply within 9 week(s) of notification.
Transfers: No deadline. Applicants notified on a rolling basis starting 7/1; must reply within 8 week(s) of notification.

CONTACT

Linda Gebel, Controller
Parker Fox Hall, Fayette, IA 52142
(800) 553-4150 ext. 3

Vatterott College: Des Moines

Des Moines, Iowa
www.vatterott-college.edu
Federal Code: 026092

2-year for-profit health science and technical college in large city.
Enrollment: 239 undergrads.
Selectivity: Open admission.

BASIC COSTS (2016-2017)

Additional info: Certificate program: (5 weeks) $4,250. Diploma programs: (40 weeks) $20,384-$21,500; (50 weeks) $24,440. Associate programs: (70 weeks) $31,260-$39,090; (80 weeks) $38,280. Costs include fees, books and supplies.

FINANCIAL AID PICTURE

Students with need: Need-based aid available for full-time students.
Students without need: This college awards aid only to students with need.
Scholarships offered: Make the Grade Scholarship; up to $1,000; based on final semester grades; available for 1 year after high school graduation.

FINANCIAL AID PROCEDURES

Forms required: FAFSA.
Dates and Deadlines: Applicants notified on a rolling basis.

CONTACT

Afton Erdmann, Financial Aid Administrator
7000 Fleur Drive, Des Moines, IA 50321
(515) 309-9000

Waldorf University

Forest City, Iowa
www.waldorf.edu
Federal Code: 001895

4-year private liberal arts college in small town, affiliated with the Evangelical Lutheran Church in America.
Enrollment: 1,983 undergrads, 24% part-time. 192 full-time freshmen.
Selectivity: Admits 50 to 75% of applicants.

BASIC COSTS (2017-2018)

Tuition and fees: $21,674.
Per-credit charge: $558.
Room and board: $7,384.

FINANCIAL AID PICTURE (2015-2016)

Students with need: Out of 174 full-time freshmen who applied for aid, 162 were judged to have need. Of these, 162 received aid, and 26 had their full need met. Average financial aid package met 72% of need; average

scholarship/grant was $14,566; average loan was $3,978. For part-time students, average financial aid package was $6,715.

Students without need: 29 full-time freshmen who did not demonstrate need for aid received scholarships/grants; average award was $6,798. No-need awards available for academics, alumni affiliation, athletics, job skills, leadership, music/drama, religious affiliation, state/district residency.
Scholarships offered: 34 full-time freshmen received athletic scholarships; average amount $6,211.

FINANCIAL AID PROCEDURES

Forms required: FAFSA, institutional form.
Dates and Deadlines: Priority date 3/1; no closing date. Applicants notified on a rolling basis starting 3/1; must reply within 2 week(s) of notification.
Transfers: Applicants notified on a rolling basis starting 3/1; must reply within 2 week(s) of notification.

CONTACT

Duane Polsdofer, Director of Student Financial Aid
106 South Sixth Street, Forest City, IA 50436-1713
(641) 585-8120

Wartburg College
Waverly, Iowa
www.wartburg.edu   Federal Code: 001896

4-year private liberal arts college in small town, affiliated with the Evangelical Lutheran Church in America.
Enrollment: 1,448 undergrads, 1% part-time. 445 full-time freshmen.
Selectivity: Admits 50 to 75% of applicants.

BASIC COSTS (2016-2017)
Tuition and fees: $38,380.
Room and board: $9,460.

FINANCIAL AID PICTURE
Students with need: Need-based aid available for full-time and part-time students.
Students without need: No-need awards available for academics, alumni affiliation, leadership, music/drama, religious affiliation.
Scholarships offered: Regents scholarship; up to full tuition, fees, room and board; based on 28 ACT (1240 SAT, exclusive of Writing) or rank in top 10% of class; renewable for 4 years with 3.0 GPA. Presidential Scholarship; up to $6,000 per year; based on 25 ACT (1140 SAT, exclusive of Writing) or rank in top 20% of class or 3.5 GPA; renewable for 4 years with 2.7 GPA. Students who participate in Regents Scholarship competition not eligible for Presidential Scholarship.

FINANCIAL AID PROCEDURES
Forms required: FAFSA.
Dates and Deadlines: Priority date 3/1; no closing date. Applicants notified on a rolling basis starting 3/1; must reply within 2 week(s) of notification.

CONTACT
Jennifer Sassman, Director of Financial Aid
100 Wartburg Boulevard, PO Box 1003, Waverly, IA 50677-0903
(319) 352-8262

Western Iowa Tech Community College
Sioux City, Iowa
www.witcc.edu   Federal Code: 004590

2-year public community college in small city.
Enrollment: 2,894 undergrads.
Selectivity: Open admission; but selective for some programs.

BASIC COSTS (2016-2017)
Tuition and fees: $5,250; out-of-state residents $5,280.
Per-credit charge: $143; out-of-state residents $144.
Room and board: $5,355.

FINANCIAL AID PICTURE
Students with need: Need-based aid available for full-time and part-time students. Work study available nights, weekends, and for part-time students.
Students without need: No-need awards available for academics, art, leadership, minority status, music/drama.

FINANCIAL AID PROCEDURES
Forms required: FAFSA.
Dates and Deadlines: Applicants notified on a rolling basis starting 4/1.

CONTACT
Merlyn Kathol, Director of Financial Aid
Box 5199, Sioux City, IA 51102-5199
(712) 274-6402

William Penn University
Oskaloosa, Iowa
www.wmpenn.edu   Federal Code: 001900

4-year private university and liberal arts college in large town, affiliated with the Society of Friends (Quaker).
Enrollment: 1,307 undergrads, 10% part-time. 239 full-time freshmen.
Selectivity: Admits 50 to 75% of applicants.

BASIC COSTS (2017-2018)
Tuition and fees: $25,000.
Room and board: $6,850.

FINANCIAL AID PICTURE
Students with need: Need-based aid available for full-time and part-time students. Work study available nights, weekends, and for part-time students.
Students without need: No-need awards available for academics, alumni affiliation, athletics, leadership, music/drama, religious affiliation.
Scholarships offered: Participation awards for music, drama, media, cheerleading, dance, religious leadership. Academic scholarships; based on high school GPA and ACT/SAT.

FINANCIAL AID PROCEDURES
Forms required: FAFSA.
Dates and Deadlines: Priority date 7/1; no closing date. Applicants notified on a rolling basis starting 1/1; must reply within 3 week(s) of notification.
Transfers: No deadline. Applicants notified on a rolling basis starting 1/1.

CONTACT
Cyndi Peiffer, Director of Financial Aid
201 Trueblood Avenue, Oskaloosa, IA 52577
(641) 673-1060

Kansas

Allen County Community College
Iola, Kansas
www.allencc.edu   Federal Code: 001901

2-year public community college in small town.
Enrollment: 2,377 undergrads.
Selectivity: Open admission.

BASIC COSTS (2016-2017)

Tuition and fees: $2,550; out-of-district residents $2,550; out-of-state residents $2,550.

Per-credit charge: $60; out-of-district residents $60; out-of-state residents $60.

Room and board: $4,830.

FINANCIAL AID PICTURE

Students with need: Need-based aid available for full-time and part-time students. Work study available nights, weekends, and for part-time students.

Students without need: No-need awards available for academics, art, athletics, music/drama, state/district residency.

Additional info: Scholarships for livestock judging, cheerleading, choir, dance, drama, art, academic challenge, and student ambassadors.

FINANCIAL AID PROCEDURES

Forms required: FAFSA.

Dates and Deadlines: Closing date 6/1. Applicants notified on a rolling basis starting 6/1; must reply within 2 week(s) of notification.

Transfers: Priority date 4/1. Applicants notified on a rolling basis starting 3/1.

CONTACT

Kim Murry, Director of Financial Aid
1801 North Cottonwood, Iola, KS 66749
(620) 365-5116 ext. 221

Baker University
Baldwin City, Kansas
www.bakeru.edu   Federal Code: 001903

4-year private liberal arts and teachers college in small town, affiliated with the United Methodist Church.

Enrollment: 858 undergrads, 1% part-time. 238 full-time freshmen.

Selectivity: Admits over 75% of applicants.

BASIC COSTS (2016-2017)

Tuition and fees: $28,030.

Per-credit charge: $830.

Room and board: $8,270.

Additional info: Tuition/fee waivers available for minority students.

FINANCIAL AID PICTURE (2015-2016)

Students with need: 56% of average financial aid package awarded as scholarships/grants, 44% awarded as loans/jobs. Need-based aid available for part-time students. Work study available nights, weekends, and for part-time students.

Students without need: No-need awards available for academics, alumni affiliation, art, athletics, music/drama, religious affiliation.

FINANCIAL AID PROCEDURES

Forms required: FAFSA.

Dates and Deadlines: Priority date 3/1; no closing date. Applicants notified on a rolling basis starting 3/1; must reply within 6 week(s) of notification.

Transfers: No deadline. Applicants notified on a rolling basis starting 3/1; must reply within 6 week(s) of notification.

CONTACT

Jeanne Mott, Senior Director of Financial Aid
618 Eighth Street, Baldwin City, KS 66006-0065
(785) 594-4595

Barclay College
Haviland, Kansas
www.barclaycollege.edu   Federal Code: 001917

4-year private Bible college in rural community, affiliated with the Society of Friends (Quaker).

Enrollment: 250 undergrads, 20% part-time. 36 full-time freshmen.

Selectivity: Admits 50 to 75% of applicants.

BASIC COSTS (2016-2017)

Tuition and fees: $15,990.

Per-credit charge: $295.

Room and board: $8,400.

FINANCIAL AID PICTURE

Students with need: Need-based aid available for full-time and part-time students. Work study available nights, weekends, and for part-time students.

Students without need: No-need awards available for academics, alumni affiliation, leadership, music/drama, state/district residency.

FINANCIAL AID PROCEDURES

Forms required: FAFSA, institutional form.

Dates and Deadlines: Priority date 5/31; closing date 7/15. Applicants notified on a rolling basis starting 1/1; must reply within 4 week(s) of notification.

CONTACT

Ryan Haase, Director of Student Financial Services
607 North Kingman, Haviland, KS 67059
(620) 862-5252 ext. 41

Barton County Community College
Great Bend, Kansas
www.bartonccc.edu   Federal Code: 004608

2-year public community college in large town.

Enrollment: 1,788 undergrads.

Selectivity: Open admission; but selective for some programs.

BASIC COSTS (2016-2017)

Tuition and fees: $3,120; out-of-state residents $4,050.

Per-credit charge: $72; out-of-district residents $72; out-of-state residents $103.

Room and board: $5,624.

FINANCIAL AID PICTURE (2016-2017)

Students with need: Need-based aid available for full-time and part-time students.

Students without need: No-need awards available for academics, athletics.

FINANCIAL AID PROCEDURES

Forms required: FAFSA, state aid form.

Dates and Deadlines: Priority date 3/1; no closing date. Applicants notified on a rolling basis starting 6/1; must reply within 4 week(s) of notification.

CONTACT

Myrna Perkins, Assistant Dean of Student Services/Director of Financial Aid
245 NE 30 Road, Great Bend, KS 67530-9283
(620) 792-2701

Benedictine College
Atchison, Kansas
www.benedictine.edu   Federal Code: 010256

4-year private liberal arts college in large town, affiliated with the Roman Catholic Church.

Enrollment: 1,936 undergrads, 1% part-time. 517 full-time freshmen.

Selectivity: Admits over 75% of applicants.

BASIC COSTS (2016-2017)

Tuition and fees: $27,480.

Per-credit charge: $775.

Room and board: $9,670.

FINANCIAL AID PICTURE (2016-2017)

Students with need: Out of 421 full-time freshmen who applied for aid, 349 were judged to have need. Of these, 349 received aid, and 84 had their full need met. Average financial aid package met 80% of need; average scholarship/grant was $18,227; average loan was $3,086. For part-time students, average financial aid package was $13,108.

Students without need: 163 full-time freshmen who did not demonstrate need for aid received scholarships/grants; average award was $13,295. No-need awards available for academics, alumni affiliation, art, athletics, job skills, leadership, minority status, music/drama, religious affiliation, state/district residency.

Scholarships offered: *Merit:* Presidential Scholarship: full tuition; maintain 3.5 GPA; 5 awarded. Dean's Scholarship: partial tuition; maintain 3.5 GPA; 5 awarded. ***Athletic:*** 46 full-time freshmen received athletic scholarships; average amount $7,019.

FINANCIAL AID PROCEDURES

Forms required: FAFSA.

Dates and Deadlines: Priority date 4/1; no closing date. Applicants notified on a rolling basis; must reply by 2/1 or within 2 week(s) of notification.

Transfers: No deadline. Applicants notified on a rolling basis. Scholarship available for students transferring 2.0 cumulative GPA.

CONTACT

Tony Tanking, Director Financial Aid
1020 North Second Street, Atchison, KS 66002-1499
(913) 360-7484

Bethany College

Lindsborg, Kansas
https://www.bethanylb.edu/   Federal Code: 001904

4-year private liberal arts college in small town, affiliated with the Evangelical Lutheran Church in America.

Enrollment: 650 undergrads, 2% part-time. 207 full-time freshmen.

Selectivity: Admits 50 to 75% of applicants.

BASIC COSTS (2017-2018)

Tuition and fees: $27,472.

Per-credit charge: $545.

Room and board: $10,075.

Additional info: Books are included in the required fees.

FINANCIAL AID PICTURE (2015-2016)

Students with need: Need-based aid available for full-time and part-time students. Work study available nights.

Students without need: No-need awards available for academics, art, athletics, music/drama.

Scholarships offered: Bethany's Merit Scholarships: $7,500 to $16,000; Kansas resident, grade point average and standardized test scores.

Additional info: Tuition-free scholarships worth more than $110,000 offered to all students graduating from a McPherson or Saline County high school for the next five years.

FINANCIAL AID PROCEDURES

Forms required: FAFSA.

Dates and Deadlines: Priority date 4/17; no closing date. Applicants notified on a rolling basis.

Transfers: No deadline. Applicants notified on a rolling basis starting 10/1.

CONTACT

Amy Hoss, Director of Financial Aid
335 East Swensson, Lindsborg, KS 67456-1897
(785) 227-3311 ext. 8248

Bethel College

North Newton, Kansas
www.bethelks.edu   Federal Code: 001905

4-year private liberal arts college in large town, affiliated with the Mennonite Church.

Enrollment: 460 undergrads, 4% part-time. 99 full-time freshmen.

Selectivity: Admits 50 to 75% of applicants.

BASIC COSTS (2017-2018)

Tuition and fees: $27,720.

Room and board: $9,270.

FINANCIAL AID PICTURE (2016-2017)

Students with need: Average financial aid package met 75% of need; average scholarship/grant was $5,027; average loan was $5,755. For part-time students, average financial aid package was $8,337.

Students without need: No-need awards available for academics, alumni affiliation, art, athletics, job skills, leadership, minority status, music/drama, religious affiliation.

Scholarships offered: Scholarships for academically talented students, ranging from 16% to 50% of tuition.

FINANCIAL AID PROCEDURES

Forms required: FAFSA.

Dates and Deadlines: Priority date 4/1; no closing date. Applicants notified on a rolling basis starting 10/1.

Transfers: No deadline. Applicants notified on a rolling basis starting 2/1; must reply within 2 week(s) of notification.

CONTACT

Tony Graber, Director of Financial Aid
300 East 27th Street, North Newton, KS 67117-8061
(800) 522-1887 ext. 232

Butler Community College

El Dorado, Kansas
www.butlercc.edu   Federal Code: 001906

2-year public community college in large town.

Enrollment: 9,363 undergrads.

Selectivity: Open admission; but selective for some programs.

BASIC COSTS (2016-2017)

Tuition and fees: $2,730; out-of-district residents $3,060; out-of-state residents $4,860.

Room and board: $5,800.

Additional info: The required fees for online classes per credit hour are $71.00 ($24.00 required fee + $47.00 online fee). Tuition/fee waivers available for unemployed or children of unemployed.

FINANCIAL AID PICTURE

Students with need: Need-based aid available for full-time and part-time students. Work study available nights, weekends, and for part-time students.

Students without need: No-need awards available for academics, art, athletics, music/drama.

FINANCIAL AID PROCEDURES

Forms required: FAFSA, institutional form.

Dates and Deadlines: Priority date 4/1; no closing date. Applicants notified on a rolling basis starting 5/1; must reply within 2 week(s) of notification.

Transfers: Students with 90 hours or more must have classes validated by degree-granting 4-year institution.

CONTACT

Susie Edwards, Director of Financial Aid
901 South Haverhill Road, El Dorado, KS 67042-3280
(316) 322-3121

Central Christian College of Kansas
McPherson, Kansas
www.centralchristian.edu   Federal Code: 001908

4-year private liberal arts college in large town, affiliated with the Free Methodist Church of North America.
Enrollment: 827 undergrads, 4% part-time. 105 full-time freshmen.
Selectivity: Admits over 75% of applicants.

BASIC COSTS (2016-2017)
Tuition and fees: $25,040.
Per-credit charge: $751.
Room and board: $7,951.

FINANCIAL AID PICTURE
Students with need: Need-based aid available for full-time and part-time students. Work study available nights, weekends, and for part-time students.
Students without need: No-need awards available for academics, alumni affiliation, athletics, leadership, music/drama, religious affiliation.

FINANCIAL AID PROCEDURES
Forms required: FAFSA.
Dates and Deadlines: Priority date 3/1; no closing date. Applicants notified on a rolling basis starting 3/1; must reply within 4 week(s) of notification.
Transfers: No deadline. Applicants notified on a rolling basis; must reply within 4 week(s) of notification.

CONTACT
Nichole Carver, Assistant Director of Financial Aid
1200 South Main, McPherson, KS 67460-5740
(620) 241-0723 ext. 7135

Cloud County Community College
Concordia, Kansas
www.cloud.edu   Federal Code: 001909

2-year public community college in small town.
Enrollment: 1,110 undergrads, 30% part-time. 287 full-time freshmen.
Selectivity: Open admission.

BASIC COSTS (2016-2017)
Tuition and fees: $2,970; out-of-district residents $3,120; out-of-state residents $3,270.
Per-credit charge: $69; out-of-district residents $74; out-of-state residents $79.
Room and board: $5,800.
Additional info: Online tuition is $74.00 per credit hour. The required fees for online classes per credit hour are $55.00 ($30.00 required fees plus $25.00 online course fees). The room and board charge is the highest priced option. Housing units are available from $2500, $2850, and $3350.

FINANCIAL AID PICTURE (2015-2016)
Students with need: 60% of average financial aid package awarded as scholarships/grants, 40% awarded as loans/jobs. Need-based aid available for part-time students. Work study available nights, weekends, and for part-time students.

FINANCIAL AID PROCEDURES
Forms required: FAFSA.
Dates and Deadlines: Priority date 4/1; no closing date. Applicants notified on a rolling basis starting 5/1; must reply within 4 week(s) of notification.

CONTACT
Suzi Knoettgen, Director of Student Financial Aid
2221 Campus Drive, Concordia, KS 66901-1002
(785) 243-1435 ext. 280

Coffeyville Community College
Coffeyville, Kansas
www.coffeyville.edu   Federal Code: 001910

2-year public community and technical college in large town.
Enrollment: 984 undergrads.
Selectivity: Open admission.

BASIC COSTS (2016-2017)
Tuition and fees: $2,160; out-of-state residents $3,630.
Per-credit charge: $37; out-of-state residents $84.
Room and board: $5,900.

FINANCIAL AID PICTURE
Students with need: Need-based aid available for full-time and part-time students. Work study available nights, weekends, and for part-time students.
Students without need: No-need awards available for academics, alumni affiliation, art, athletics, leadership, music/drama, state/district residency.

FINANCIAL AID PROCEDURES
Forms required: FAFSA.
Dates and Deadlines: Priority date 7/1; no closing date. Applicants notified on a rolling basis starting 6/20.

CONTACT
Pam Feerer, Director of Financial Aid
400 West 11th Street, Coffeyville, KS 67337-5064
(620) 252-7357

Colby Community College
Colby, Kansas
www.colbycc.edu   Federal Code: 001911

2-year public community college in small town.
Enrollment: 1,311 undergrads.
Selectivity: Open admission; but selective for some programs.

BASIC COSTS (2016-2017)
Tuition and fees: $3,150; out-of-district residents $3,300; out-of-state residents $4,470.
Per-credit charge: $65; out-of-district residents $70; out-of-state residents $124.
Room and board: $5,640.
Additional info: Online tuition is $79.00 per credit hour. The required fees for online courses are the $40.00 general required fees.

FINANCIAL AID PICTURE
Students with need: Need-based aid available for full-time and part-time students. Work study available nights, weekends, and for part-time students.
Students without need: No-need awards available for academics, athletics, leadership, music/drama.

FINANCIAL AID PROCEDURES
Forms required: FAFSA, state aid form.
Dates and Deadlines: Priority date 6/1; no closing date. Applicants notified on a rolling basis starting 5/1.

CONTACT
Paula Halvorson, Director of Financial Aid
1255 South Range Avenue, Colby, KS 67701
(785) 460-4695

Cowley County Community College
Arkansas City, Kansas
www.cowley.edu   Federal Code: 001902

2-year public community and technical college in large town.
Enrollment: 3,569 undergrads.

Selectivity: Open admission; but selective for some programs.

BASIC COSTS (2016-2017)
Tuition and fees: $2,670; out-of-district residents $2,970; out-of-state residents $4,380.
Per-credit charge: $55; out-of-district residents $65; out-of-state residents $112.
Room and board: $4,900.
Additional info: Online tuition is the same as listed for face-to-face classes in all categories. The required fees for online classes per credit hour are $59.00 ($34.00 required fees plus $25 online course fees).

FINANCIAL AID PICTURE
Students with need: Need-based aid available for full-time and part-time students.
Students without need: No-need awards available for academics, alumni affiliation, art, athletics, leadership, music/drama, state/district residency.

FINANCIAL AID PROCEDURES
Forms required: FAFSA.
Dates and Deadlines: Priority date 4/15; no closing date. Applicants notified on a rolling basis starting 1/15; must reply within 2 week(s) of notification.

CONTACT
Sally Palmer, Director of Financial Aid
PO Box 1147, Arkansas City, KS 67005-1147
(620) 442-0430

Dodge City Community College
Dodge City, Kansas
www.dc3.edu   Federal Code: 001913

2-year public community and technical college in large town.
Enrollment: 1,215 undergrads.
Selectivity: Open admission; but selective for some programs.

BASIC COSTS (2016-2017)
Tuition and fees: $2,100; out-of-district residents $2,610; out-of-state residents $2,850.
Per-credit charge: $30; out-of-district residents $47; out-of-state residents $55.
Room and board: $6,400.

FINANCIAL AID PICTURE
Students with need: Need-based aid available for full-time and part-time students. Work study available nights, weekends, and for part-time students.
Students without need: No-need awards available for academics, athletics, music/drama, state/district residency.

FINANCIAL AID PROCEDURES
Forms required: FAFSA, institutional form.
Dates and Deadlines: Priority date 3/15; no closing date. Applicants notified on a rolling basis; must reply within 2 week(s) of notification.

CONTACT
Russ McBee, Director of Financial Aid
2501 North 14th Avenue, Dodge City, KS 67801-2399
(620) 227-9336

Donnelly College
Kansas City, Kansas
www.donnelly.edu   Federal Code: 001914

2-year private junior and liberal arts college in small city, affiliated with the Roman Catholic Church.
Enrollment: 318 undergrads, 26% part-time. 65 full-time freshmen.
Selectivity: Open admission.

BASIC COSTS (2016-2017)
Tuition and fees: $8,400.
Room and board: $7,650.

FINANCIAL AID PICTURE (2015-2016)
Students with need: Out of 63 full-time freshmen who applied for aid, 63 were judged to have need. Of these, 63 received aid. For part-time students, average financial aid package was $4,342.
Students without need: No-need awards available for academics, religious affiliation.

FINANCIAL AID PROCEDURES
Forms required: FAFSA, institutional form.
Dates and Deadlines: Priority date 4/1; no closing date. Applicants notified on a rolling basis starting 7/1.
Transfers: No deadline. Applicants notified on a rolling basis starting 4/1; must reply within 2 week(s) of notification.

CONTACT
Michael Pepple, Director of Financial Aid
608 North 18th Street, Kansas City, KS 66102-4210
(913) 621-8740

Emporia State University
Emporia, Kansas
www.emporia.edu   Federal Code: 001927

4-year public university in large town.
Enrollment: 3,578 undergrads, 6% part-time. 731 full-time freshmen.
Selectivity: Admits over 75% of applicants.

BASIC COSTS (2016-2017)
Tuition and fees: $6,179; out-of-state residents $19,392.
Per-credit charge: $163; out-of-state residents $603.5.
Room and board: $8,391.

FINANCIAL AID PICTURE (2015-2016)
Students with need: Out of 632 full-time freshmen who applied for aid, 460 were judged to have need. Of these, 457 received aid, and 94 had their full need met. Average financial aid package met 63% of need; average scholarship/grant was $5,670; average loan was $5,203. For part-time students, average financial aid package was $5,063.
Students without need: 170 full-time freshmen who did not demonstrate need for aid received scholarships/grants; average award was $2,370. No-need awards available for academics, alumni affiliation, art, athletics, job skills, leadership, minority status, music/drama, religious affiliation, state/district residency.
Scholarships offered: *Merit:* Hornet Scholars: Based on High School GPA and ACT ($1,000 to $1,800). Foundation Scholars: Based on High School GPA and ACT ($1,900 to $2,700). Presidential Scholars: Based on High School GPA and ACT ($2,500 to $3,600). Valedictorian/Salutatorian Scholarships for students ranked 1 ($500) or 2 ($250) in their class. *Athletic:* 47 full-time freshmen received athletic scholarships; average amount $3,137.
Additional info: Institution's own payment plan is available.

FINANCIAL AID PROCEDURES
Forms required: FAFSA, state aid form.
Dates and Deadlines: Priority date 3/15; no closing date. Applicants notified on a rolling basis starting 2/2; must reply within 2 week(s) of notification.
Transfers: No deadline. Applicants notified on a rolling basis; must reply within 2 week(s) of notification.

CONTACT
Elaine Henrie, Director of Financial Aid
One Kellogg Circle, Campus Box 4034, Emporia, KS 66801-5415
(620) 341-5457

Fort Hays State University

Hays, Kansas
www.fhsu.edu   Federal Code: 001915

4-year public university in large town.
Enrollment: 11,698 undergrads, 52% part-time. 931 full-time freshmen.
Selectivity: Admits over 75% of applicants.

BASIC COSTS (2016-2017)
Tuition and fees: $4,884; out-of-state residents $14,426.
Per-credit charge: $126.3; out-of-state residents $444.4.
Room and board: $7,669.

FINANCIAL AID PICTURE (2015-2016)
Students with need: 38% of average financial aid package awarded as scholarships/grants, 62% awarded as loans/jobs. Need-based aid available for part-time students. Work study available nights, weekends, and for part-time students.
Students without need: No-need awards available for academics, alumni affiliation, art, job skills, leadership, minority status, music/drama, state/district residency.

FINANCIAL AID PROCEDURES
Forms required: FAFSA, institutional form.
Dates and Deadlines: Priority date 3/1; no closing date. Applicants notified on a rolling basis starting 3/15; must reply within 2 week(s) of notification.
Transfers: No deadline. Applicants notified on a rolling basis starting 3/15; must reply within 3 week(s) of notification.

CONTACT
Wendy Rohleder-Sook, Director of Financial Aid
600 Park Street, Hays, KS 67601
(785) 628-4408

Fort Scott Community College

Fort Scott, Kansas
www.fortscott.edu   Federal Code: 001916

2-year public community college in small town.
Enrollment: 1,174 undergrads.
Selectivity: Open admission.

BASIC COSTS (2016-2017)
Tuition and fees: $2,820; out-of-district residents $2,910; out-of-state residents $4,590.
Per-credit charge: $47; out-of-district residents $50; out-of-state residents $106.
Room and board: $5,670.

FINANCIAL AID PICTURE (2015-2016)
Students with need: 54% of average financial aid package awarded as scholarships/grants, 46% awarded as loans/jobs. Need-based aid available for part-time students.

FINANCIAL AID PROCEDURES
Forms required: FAFSA.
Dates and Deadlines: Priority date 7/1; no closing date. Applicants notified on a rolling basis starting 10/1.

CONTACT
Lillie Grubb, Financial Aid Director
2108 S Horton Street, Fort Scott, KS 66701
(620) 223-2700 ext. 3522

Friends University

Wichita, Kansas
www.friends.edu   Federal Code: 001918

4-year private university and liberal arts college in large city, affiliated with the nondenominational tradition.
Enrollment: 1,164 undergrads, 21% part-time. 164 full-time freshmen.
Selectivity: Admits 50 to 75% of applicants.

BASIC COSTS (2017-2018)
Tuition and fees: $27,465.
Per-credit charge: $905.
Room and board: $7,740.

FINANCIAL AID PICTURE (2015-2016)
Students with need: Out of 153 full-time freshmen who applied for aid, 147 were judged to have need. Of these, 147 received aid, and 80 had their full need met. Average financial aid package met 91% of need; average scholarship/grant was $7,100; average loan was $2,969. For part-time students, average financial aid package was $5,565.
Students without need: 17 full-time freshmen who did not demonstrate need for aid received scholarships/grants; average award was $11,635. No-need awards available for academics, alumni affiliation, art, athletics, leadership, music/drama, religious affiliation.
Scholarships offered: 90 full-time freshmen received athletic scholarships; average amount $4,771.

FINANCIAL AID PROCEDURES
Forms required: FAFSA.
Dates and Deadlines: Priority date 3/15; no closing date. Applicants notified on a rolling basis starting 3/1.
Transfers: No deadline. Applicants notified on a rolling basis starting 3/1; must reply within 3 week(s) of notification.

CONTACT
Tony Lubbers, Director of Financial Aid
2100 West University Avenue, Wichita, KS 67213
(800) 794-6945

Garden City Community College

Garden City, Kansas
www.gcccks.edu   Federal Code: 001919

2-year public community college in large town.
Enrollment: 1,887 undergrads.
Selectivity: Open admission; but selective for some programs.

BASIC COSTS (2016-2017)
Tuition and fees: $2,848; out-of-state residents $3,456.
Room and board: $5,250.

FINANCIAL AID PICTURE
Students with need: Need-based aid available for full-time and part-time students. Work study available nights, weekends, and for part-time students.
Students without need: No-need awards available for academics, art, athletics, job skills, leadership, minority status, music/drama, state/district residency.

FINANCIAL AID PROCEDURES
Forms required: FAFSA, institutional form.
Dates and Deadlines: Priority date 3/1; no closing date. Applicants notified on a rolling basis starting 4/15; must reply within 2 week(s) of notification.

CONTACT
Melinda Harrington, Director of Financial Aid
801 Campus Drive, Garden City, KS 67846-6333
(620) 276-9519

Grantham University

Lenexa, Kansas
www.grantham.edu   Federal Code: 041223

4-year for-profit virtual university in large city.
Enrollment: 9,215 undergrads.
Selectivity: Open admission; but selective for some programs.

BASIC COSTS (2017-2018)
Tuition and fees: $6,540.
Per-credit charge: $265.

FINANCIAL AID PICTURE
Students with need: Need-based aid available for full-time and part-time students.

FINANCIAL AID PROCEDURES
Forms required: FAFSA.
Transfers: No deadline. Applicants notified on a rolling basis.

CONTACT
Lindsay Bridgeman, Director Financial Aid
16025 W 113th Street, Lenexa, KS 66219
(866) 850-2980

Haskell Indian Nations University

Lawrence, Kansas
www.haskell.edu   Federal Code: 010438

4-year public university in small city.
Enrollment: 821 undergrads, 4% part-time. 177 full-time freshmen.
Selectivity: Admits 50 to 75% of applicants.

BASIC COSTS (2016-2017)
Tuition and fees: $2,010.
Room and board: $850.

FINANCIAL AID PICTURE (2016-2017)
Students with need: 98% of average financial aid package awarded as scholarships/grants, 2% awarded as loans/jobs. Need-based aid available for part-time students. Work study available nights, weekends, and for part-time students.
Additional info: Some personal expenses may be offset by Bureau of Indian Affairs grants. Most students qualify for only minimum Pell grant.

FINANCIAL AID PROCEDURES
Forms required: FAFSA.
Dates and Deadlines: Priority date 5/15; no closing date. Applicants notified on a rolling basis starting 3/15; must reply within 9 week(s) of notification.
Transfers: Priority date 11/8; closing date 4/15.

CONTACT
Carlene Morris, Financial Aid Officer
155 Indian Avenue, Box #5031, Lawrence, KS 66046-4800
(785) 830-2468

Hesston College

Hesston, Kansas
www.hesston.edu   Federal Code: 001920

2-year private junior and liberal arts college in small town, affiliated with the Mennonite Church.
Enrollment: 398 undergrads, 4% part-time. 142 full-time freshmen.
Selectivity: Open admission; but selective for some programs.

BASIC COSTS (2017-2018)
Tuition and fees: $26,318.

Room and board: $8,578.

FINANCIAL AID PICTURE (2016-2017)
Students with need: Out of 117 full-time freshmen who applied for aid, 104 were judged to have need. Of these, 104 received aid, and 20 had their full need met. Average financial aid package met 77% of need. For part-time students, average financial aid package was $16,000.
Students without need: 13 full-time freshmen who did not demonstrate need for aid received scholarships/grants; average award was $11,980. No-need awards available for academics, alumni affiliation, art, athletics, job skills, music/drama.
Scholarships offered: 11 full-time freshmen received athletic scholarships; average amount $4,913.

FINANCIAL AID PROCEDURES
Forms required: FAFSA.
Dates and Deadlines: Closing date 4/1. Applicants notified on a rolling basis starting 11/1; must reply within 4 week(s) of notification.
Transfers: No deadline. Applicants notified on a rolling basis starting 11/1.

CONTACT
Marcia Mendez, Financial Aid Director
Box 3000, Hesston, KS 67062-2093
(800) 995-2757

Highland Community College

Highland, Kansas
www.highlandcc.edu   Federal Code: 001921

2-year public community college in rural community.
Enrollment: 1,813 undergrads, 40% part-time. 468 full-time freshmen.
Selectivity: Open admission; but selective for out-of-state students.

BASIC COSTS (2017-2018)
Tuition and fees: $2,970; out-of-district residents $3,390; out-of-state residents $3,390.
Per-credit charge: $56; out-of-district residents $70; out-of-state residents $70.
Room and board: $6,176.

FINANCIAL AID PICTURE (2015-2016)
Students with need: 60% of average financial aid package awarded as scholarships/grants, 40% awarded as loans/jobs. Need-based aid available for part-time students. Work study available nights, weekends, and for part-time students.
Students without need: No-need awards available for academics, alumni affiliation, art, athletics, job skills, leadership, music/drama.
Additional info: Auditions and portfolios important for certain scholarship candidates.

FINANCIAL AID PROCEDURES
Forms required: FAFSA.
Dates and Deadlines: Priority date 4/1; no closing date. Applicants notified on a rolling basis starting 4/15; must reply within 4 week(s) of notification.
Transfers: No deadline. Applicants notified on a rolling basis starting 4/1; must reply within 4 week(s) of notification.

CONTACT
Joshua North, Director of Student Financial Aid
606 West Main Street, Highland, KS 66035
(785) 442-6023

Hutchinson Community College

Hutchinson, Kansas
www.hutchcc.edu   Federal Code: 001923

2-year public community college in large town.
Enrollment: 5,527 undergrads, 58% part-time. 846 full-time freshmen.

Selectivity: Open admission; but selective for some programs.

BASIC COSTS (2016-2017)

Tuition and fees: $2,790; out-of-district residents $3,090; out-of-state residents $4,020.

Per-credit charge: $74; out-of-district residents $84; out-of-state residents $115.

Room and board: $5,600.

Additional info: Residence Hall students pay a $50 social fee.

FINANCIAL AID PICTURE (2015-2016)

Students with need: Out of 679 full-time freshmen who applied for aid, 519 were judged to have need. Of these, 502 received aid, and 101 had their full need met. Average financial aid package met 55% of need; average scholarship/grant was $3,935; average loan was $2,904. For part-time students, average financial aid package was $6,537.

Students without need: 183 full-time freshmen who did not demonstrate need for aid received scholarships/grants; average award was $1,821. No-need awards available for academics, art, athletics, leadership, minority status, music/drama, state/district residency.

Scholarships offered: 63 full-time freshmen received athletic scholarships; average amount $3,192.

FINANCIAL AID PROCEDURES

Forms required: FAFSA, institutional form.

Dates and Deadlines: Priority date 2/1; no closing date. Applicants notified on a rolling basis starting 4/1; must reply within 2 week(s) of notification.

CONTACT

Nathan Buche, Financial Aid Director
1300 North Plum, Hutchinson, KS 67501
(620) 665-3568

Independence Community College

Independence, Kansas
www.indycc.edu   Federal Code: 001924

2-year public community college in large town.

Enrollment: 669 undergrads, 23% part-time. 257 full-time freshmen.

Selectivity: Open admission.

BASIC COSTS (2016-2017)

Tuition and fees: $2,805; out-of-district residents $2,985; out-of-state residents $4,185.

Per-credit charge: $53.5; out-of-district residents $59.5; out-of-state residents $99.5.

Room and board: $5,014.

Additional info: Online tuition is the same as listed for face-to-face classes in all categories. The required fees for online classes per credit hour are $70.00 ($40.00 per credit hour required fees plus $30.00 per credit hour online course fees).

FINANCIAL AID PICTURE

Students with need: Need-based aid available for full-time and part-time students. Work study available nights, weekends, and for part-time students.

Students without need: No-need awards available for academics, art, athletics, music/drama, state/district residency.

Additional info: Student labor grants awarded to students not eligible for Federal Work-Study. Students may apply by completing Student Employment Application. Student Support Services (SSS) grants available to eligible participants of the SSS program. Tuition waiver to all persons residing in college's taxing district.

FINANCIAL AID PROCEDURES

Forms required: FAFSA.

Dates and Deadlines: Priority date 4/1; no closing date. Applicants notified on a rolling basis.

CONTACT

Wendy Isle, Chief Fiscal Officer
1057 West College Avenue, Independence, KS 67301
(620) 332-5412

Johnson County Community College

Overland Park, Kansas
www.jccc.edu   Federal Code: 008244

2-year public community college in very large city.

Enrollment: 11,608 undergrads.

Selectivity: Open admission; but selective for some programs.

BASIC COSTS (2016-2017)

Tuition and fees: $2,790; out-of-district residents $3,300; out-of-state residents $6,600.

Per-credit charge: $93; out-of-district residents $110; out-of-state residents $220.

FINANCIAL AID PICTURE

Students with need: Need-based aid available for full-time and part-time students.

Students without need: No-need awards available for academics.

FINANCIAL AID PROCEDURES

Forms required: FAFSA, state aid form.

Dates and Deadlines: Priority date 4/1; no closing date. Applicants notified on a rolling basis starting 4/15; must reply within 2 week(s) of notification.

CONTACT

Christal Williams, Program Director for Student Financial Aid
12345 College Boulevard, Overland Park, KS 66210-1299
(913) 469-3840

Kansas City Kansas Community College

Kansas City, Kansas
www.kckcc.edu   Federal Code: 001925

2-year public community and career college in very large city.

Enrollment: 4,790 undergrads, 62% part-time. 537 full-time freshmen.

Selectivity: Open admission; but selective for some programs.

BASIC COSTS (2016-2017)

Tuition and fees: $3,030; out-of-state residents $7,830.

Per-credit charge: $86; out-of-state residents $246.

FINANCIAL AID PICTURE (2015-2016)

Students with need: 76% of average financial aid package awarded as scholarships/grants, 24% awarded as loans/jobs. Need-based aid available for part-time students. Work study available nights, weekends, and for part-time students.

Students without need: No-need awards available for academics, art, athletics, music/drama.

FINANCIAL AID PROCEDURES

Forms required: FAFSA.

Dates and Deadlines: Applicants notified on a rolling basis starting 5/1; must reply within 4 week(s) of notification.

CONTACT

Mary Dorr, Director of Financial Aid
7250 State Avenue, Kansas City, KS 66112
(913) 288-7697

Kansas State University
Manhattan, Kansas
www.k-state.edu   Federal Code: 001928

4-year public university in small city.
Enrollment: 19,151 undergrads, 8% part-time. 3,559 full-time freshmen.
Selectivity: Admits over 75% of applicants.

BASIC COSTS (2016-2017)
Tuition and fees: $9,874; out-of-state residents $24,775.
Per-credit charge: $300; out-of-state residents $797.
Room and board: $9,150.

FINANCIAL AID PICTURE (2015-2016)
Students with need: Out of 2,774 full-time freshmen who applied for aid, 1,910 were judged to have need. Of these, 1,873 received aid, and 424 had their full need met. Average financial aid package met 80% of need; average scholarship/grant was $4,468; average loan was $3,694. For part-time students, average financial aid package was $9,118.
Students without need: 624 full-time freshmen who did not demonstrate need for aid received scholarships/grants; average award was $5,152. No-need awards available for academics, alumni affiliation, art, athletics, leadership, music/drama, ROTC, state/district residency.
Scholarships offered: 85 full-time freshmen received athletic scholarships; average amount $16,456.

FINANCIAL AID PROCEDURES
Forms required: FAFSA.
Dates and Deadlines: Priority date 3/1; no closing date. Applicants notified on a rolling basis starting 2/15; must reply within 2 week(s) of notification.

CONTACT
Larry Moeder, Assistant Vice President for Student Financial Assistance and Admissions
119 Anderson Hall, Manhattan, KS 66506
(785) 532-6420

Kansas Wesleyan University
Salina, Kansas
www.kwu.edu   Federal Code: 001929

4-year private university and liberal arts college in large town, affiliated with the United Methodist Church.
Enrollment: 678 undergrads, 6% part-time. 161 full-time freshmen.
Selectivity: Admits 50 to 75% of applicants.

BASIC COSTS (2016-2017)
Tuition and fees: $28,000.
Per-credit charge: $280.
Room and board: $8,600.

FINANCIAL AID PICTURE
Students with need: Need-based aid available for full-time and part-time students.
Students without need: No-need awards available for academics, alumni affiliation, art, athletics, job skills, music/drama, religious affiliation.
Additional info: Awards available for residence hall students: minimum $7,000 for 3.0 GPA plus ACT score of 22 or SAT of 950 (exclusive of Writing); minimum $8,000 for 3.5 GPA plus ACT score of 22 or SAT score of 1030 (exclusive of Writing); minimum $9,000 for 3.75 GPA plus ACT score of 25 or SAT score of 1140 (exclusive of Writing). Application deadline March 15.

FINANCIAL AID PROCEDURES
Forms required: FAFSA.
Dates and Deadlines: Closing date 3/15. Applicants notified on a rolling basis starting 2/1; must reply by 8/1 or within 3 week(s) of notification.

Transfers: No deadline. Applicants notified on a rolling basis starting 8/1. Academic scholarships based upon cumulative GPA of transferring credit hours.

CONTACT
Lois Madsen, Director of Student Financial Planning
100 East Claflin Avenue, Salina, KS 67401-6196
(785) 833-4319

Labette Community College
Parsons, Kansas
www.labette.edu   Federal Code: 001930

2-year public community college in large town.
Enrollment: 1,574 undergrads.
Selectivity: Open admission; but selective for some programs.

BASIC COSTS (2016-2017)
Tuition and fees: $2,760; out-of-state residents $3,510.
Per-credit charge: $49; out-of-state residents $74.
Additional info: Tuition/fee waivers available for adults, minority students, unemployed or children of unemployed.

FINANCIAL AID PICTURE
Students with need: Need-based aid available for full-time and part-time students. Work study available nights.
Students without need: No-need awards available for academics, leadership.

FINANCIAL AID PROCEDURES
Forms required: FAFSA.
Dates and Deadlines: Applicants notified on a rolling basis starting 4/4; must reply within 2 week(s) of notification.

CONTACT
Kathy Johnston, Director of Financial Aid
200 South 14th Street, Parsons, KS 67357
(620) 820-1219

Manhattan Area Technical College
Manhattan, Kansas
www.manhattantech.edu   Federal Code: 005500

2-year public technical college in large town.
Enrollment: 417 undergrads, 24% part-time. 55 full-time freshmen.
Selectivity: Open admission; but selective for some programs.

BASIC COSTS (2016-2017)
Tuition and fees: $4,080; out-of-state residents $4,080.
Per-credit charge: $100.

FINANCIAL AID PICTURE
Students with need: Need-based aid available for full-time and part-time students.
Students without need: No-need awards available for academics, leadership.

FINANCIAL AID PROCEDURES
Forms required: FAFSA, institutional form.
Dates and Deadlines: Priority date 7/1; no closing date. Applicants notified on a rolling basis.
Transfers: Priority date 7/1. Applicants notified on a rolling basis.

CONTACT
Laura Weiss-Cook, Director of Financial Aid
3136 Dickens Avenue, Manhattan, KS 66503-2499
(785) 320-4541

Manhattan Christian College

Manhattan, Kansas
www.mccks.edu   Federal Code: 001931

4-year private Bible college in small city, affiliated with the Christian Church.
Enrollment: 294 undergrads.

BASIC COSTS (2016-2017)
Tuition and fees: $14,986.
Per-credit charge: $604.
Room and board: $8,522.

FINANCIAL AID PICTURE
Students with need: Need-based aid available for full-time and part-time students.
Students without need: No-need awards available for academics, leadership, music/drama.

FINANCIAL AID PROCEDURES
Forms required: FAFSA, state aid form.
Dates and Deadlines: Priority date 4/1; no closing date. Applicants notified on a rolling basis starting 4/1; must reply within 2 week(s) of notification.
Transfers: Priority date 4/1; no deadline. Applicants notified on a rolling basis; must reply within 2 week(s) of notification.

CONTACT
Brandon Winter, Financial Aid Counselor
1415 Anderson Avenue, Manhattan, KS 66502

McPherson College

McPherson, Kansas
www.mcpherson.edu   Federal Code: 001933

4-year private liberal arts college in large town, affiliated with the Church of the Brethren.
Enrollment: 643 undergrads, 4% part-time. 199 full-time freshmen.
Selectivity: Admits less than 50% of applicants.

BASIC COSTS (2016-2017)
Tuition and fees: $26,498.
Per-credit charge: $716.
Room and board: $8,411.

FINANCIAL AID PICTURE (2016-2017)
Students with need: Average financial aid package met 86% of need; average scholarship/grant was $5,842; average loan was $7,740. For part-time students, average financial aid package was $6,706.
Students without need: No-need awards available for academics, alumni affiliation, art, athletics, job skills, music/drama, religious affiliation.
Scholarships offered: Presidential Scholarship; $10,000 each year of attendance for four years; competition in fall and spring; 10 awards given per year.

FINANCIAL AID PROCEDURES
Forms required: FAFSA.
Dates and Deadlines: Priority date 3/1; no closing date. Applicants notified on a rolling basis starting 2/1; must reply within 3 week(s) of notification.
Transfers: No deadline. Applicants notified on a rolling basis; must reply within 3 week(s) of notification.

CONTACT
Sara Brubaker, Director of Financial Aid & Admissions Operations
1600 East Euclid Street, McPherson, KS 67460-1402
(620) 242-0400

MidAmerica Nazarene University

Olathe, Kansas
www.mnu.edu   Federal Code: 007032

4-year private university and liberal arts college in small city, affiliated with the Church of the Nazarene.
Enrollment: 1,224 undergrads, 19% part-time. 169 full-time freshmen.
Selectivity: Admits 50 to 75% of applicants.

BASIC COSTS (2017-2018)
Tuition and fees: $29,670.
Per-credit charge: $1,050.
Room and board: $8,138.

FINANCIAL AID PICTURE
Students with need: Need-based aid available for full-time and part-time students.
Students without need: No-need awards available for academics, athletics, music/drama, religious affiliation, ROTC.

FINANCIAL AID PROCEDURES
Forms required: FAFSA.
Dates and Deadlines: Priority date 3/1; no closing date. Applicants notified on a rolling basis starting 11/1; must reply within 2 week(s) of notification.
Transfers: Applicants notified on a rolling basis starting 3/1; must reply within 2 week(s) of notification.

CONTACT
Cathy Colapietro, Director of Student Financial Services
2030 East College Way, Olathe, KS 66062-1899
(913) 917-3298

Neosho County Community College

Chanute, Kansas
www.neosho.edu   Federal Code: 001936

2-year public community college in small town.
Enrollment: 2,151 undergrads.
Selectivity: Open admission; but selective for some programs.

BASIC COSTS (2016-2017)
Tuition and fees: $2,940; out-of-district residents $2,940; out-of-state residents $2,940.
Per-credit charge: $67; out-of-district residents $67; out-of-state residents $67.
Room and board: $6,000.
Additional info: Online tuition is the same as listed for face-to-face classes in all categories. The required fees for online classes per credit hour are $56.00 if the student is in-district, Required fees vary by campus and residency.

FINANCIAL AID PICTURE
Students with need: Need-based aid available for full-time and part-time students. Work study available nights, weekends, and for part-time students.
Students without need: No-need awards available for academics, art, athletics, job skills, leadership, music/drama, state/district residency.
Scholarships offered: Visual and performing arts, Academic Challenge stipends, industrial engineering and business scholarship.

FINANCIAL AID PROCEDURES
Forms required: FAFSA.
Dates and Deadlines: Priority date 4/1; no closing date. Applicants notified on a rolling basis; must reply within 6 week(s) of notification.
Transfers: All academic transcripts and financial aid transcripts must be on file before aid will be awarded.

CONTACT
Jennifer Daisy, Director of Financial Aid
800 West 14th Street, Chanute, KS 66720
(785) 242-2067

Newman University
Wichita, Kansas
www.newmanu.edu   Federal Code: 001939

4-year private university and liberal arts college in large city, affiliated with the Roman Catholic Church.
Enrollment: 1,095 undergrads, 12% part-time. 162 full-time freshmen.
Selectivity: Admits 50 to 75% of applicants.

BASIC COSTS (2016-2017)
Tuition and fees: $27,716.
Per-credit charge: $881.
Room and board: $7,674.
Additional info: Tuition/fee waivers available for adults, unemployed or children of unemployed.

FINANCIAL AID PICTURE (2015-2016)
Students with need: Out of 142 full-time freshmen who applied for aid, 96 were judged to have need. Of these, 96 received aid, and 17 had their full need met. Average financial aid package met 39% of need; average scholarship/grant was $3,740. For part-time students, average financial aid package was $3,756.
Students without need: 155 full-time freshmen who did not demonstrate need for aid received scholarships/grants; average award was $6,026. No-need awards available for academics, art, athletics, music/drama.
Scholarships offered: 49 full-time freshmen received athletic scholarships; average amount $5,699.

FINANCIAL AID PROCEDURES
Forms required: FAFSA.
Dates and Deadlines: Priority date 12/15; no closing date. Applicants notified on a rolling basis starting 12/15; must reply within 4 week(s) of notification.

CONTACT
Myra Pfannenstiel, Director of Financial Aid
3100 McCormick, Wichita, KS 67213-2097
(316) 942-4291 ext. 2103

North Central Kansas Technical College
Beloit, Kansas
www.ncktc.edu   Federal Code: 005265

2-year public technical college in small town.
Enrollment: 785 undergrads.
Selectivity: Open admission.

BASIC COSTS (2016-2017)
Tuition and fees: $3,557; out-of-state residents $3,557.
Per-credit charge: $112.
Room and board: $5,274.

FINANCIAL AID PICTURE
Students with need: Need-based aid available for full-time and part-time students. Work study available nights.
Students without need: No-need awards available for academics, state/district residency.

FINANCIAL AID PROCEDURES
Forms required: FAFSA, state aid form.

CONTACT
Gary Odle, Financial Aid Director
PO Box 507, Beloit, KS 67420
(785) 738-9028

Northwest Kansas Technical College
Goodland, Kansas
www.nwktc.edu

2-year public technical college in small town.
Enrollment: 626 undergrads.
Selectivity: Open admission; but selective for some programs.

BASIC COSTS (2016-2017)
Tuition and fees: $8,300.
Per-credit charge: $140.
Room and board: $4,425.

FINANCIAL AID PICTURE
Students with need: Need-based aid available for full-time and part-time students.
Students without need: This college awards aid only to students with need.

FINANCIAL AID PROCEDURES
Dates and Deadlines: Closing date 8/1.

CONTACT
Penny Nemechek, Financial Aid Coordinator
1209 Harrison, Goodland, KS 67735

Ottawa University
Ottawa, Kansas
www.ottawa.edu   Federal Code: 001937

4-year private university and liberal arts college in large town, affiliated with the American Baptist Churches in the USA.
Enrollment: 533 undergrads.

BASIC COSTS (2016-2017)
Tuition and fees: $27,096.
Per-credit charge: $1,079.
Room and board: $9,550.

FINANCIAL AID PICTURE
Students with need: Need-based aid available for full-time and part-time students. Work study available nights, weekends, and for part-time students.
Students without need: No-need awards available for academics, alumni affiliation, athletics, music/drama, religious affiliation.

FINANCIAL AID PROCEDURES
Forms required: FAFSA.
Dates and Deadlines: Priority date 3/15; no closing date. Applicants notified on a rolling basis starting 2/1; must reply within 4 week(s) of notification.
Transfers: No deadline. Applicants notified on a rolling basis starting 2/1; must reply within 4 week(s) of notification.

CONTACT
Howard Fischer, Financial Aid Director
1001 South Cedar Street, #17, Ottawa, KS 66067-3399
(785) 242-5200 ext. 5571

Pittsburg State University
Pittsburg, Kansas
www.pittstate.edu   Federal Code: 001926

4-year public university in large town.
Enrollment: 5,636 undergrads, 5% part-time. 1,045 full-time freshmen.
Selectivity: Admits over 75% of applicants.

BASIC COSTS (2016-2017)
Tuition and fees: $6,910; out-of-state residents $17,662.
Per-credit charge: $180; out-of-state residents $538.
Room and board: $7,572.

FINANCIAL AID PICTURE (2015-2016)
Students with need: For part-time students, average financial aid package was $4,895.
Students without need: No-need awards available for academics, alumni affiliation, art, athletics, leadership, minority status, music/drama, ROTC.

FINANCIAL AID PROCEDURES
Forms required: FAFSA, state aid form.
Dates and Deadlines: Priority date 3/1; no closing date. Applicants notified on a rolling basis starting 3/1; must reply within 2 week(s) of notification.
Transfers: No deadline. Applicants notified on a rolling basis. Transfer student scholarships available.

CONTACT
Tammy Higgins, Director of Student Financial Assistance
1701 South Broadway, Pittsburg, KS 66762
(620) 235-4240

Pratt Community College
Pratt, Kansas
www.prattcc.edu   Federal Code: 001938

2-year public community and technical college in small town.
Enrollment: 660 undergrads.
Selectivity: Open admission; but selective for some programs.

BASIC COSTS (2016-2017)
Tuition and fees: $3,030; out-of-district residents $3,030; out-of-state residents $3,300.
Room and board: $5,530.
Additional info: Online tuition is $106.00 per credit hour. The required fees for online classes per credit hour are $41.00. There are additional required fees based on residency. In-state, out of district students pay $50.00 per semester, out-of-state students pay $100 per semester, and international students pay $150 per semester.

FINANCIAL AID PICTURE
Students with need: Need-based aid available for full-time and part-time students.
Students without need: No-need awards available for academics, art, athletics, leadership, minority status, music/drama, state/district residency.

FINANCIAL AID PROCEDURES
Forms required: FAFSA, institutional form.
Dates and Deadlines: Priority date 5/1; closing date 8/1. Applicants notified on a rolling basis starting 2/1; must reply within 2 week(s) of notification.

CONTACT
Nikki Powell, Director of Financial Aid
348 Northeast State Route 61, Pratt, KS 67124-8317
(620) 450-2248

Seward County Community College
Liberal, Kansas
www.sccc.edu   Federal Code: 008228

2-year public community and technical college in large town.
Enrollment: 1,700 undergrads, 51% part-time. 372 full-time freshmen.
Selectivity: Open admission.

BASIC COSTS (2016-2017)
Tuition and fees: $2,670; out-of-district residents $2,790; out-of-state residents $3,810.
Per-credit charge: $55; out-of-district residents $59; out-of-state residents $93.
Room and board: $4,800.

FINANCIAL AID PICTURE (2015-2016)
Students with need: 82% of average financial aid package awarded as scholarships/grants, 18% awarded as loans/jobs. Need-based aid available for part-time students.
Students without need: No-need awards available for academics, athletics.

FINANCIAL AID PROCEDURES
Forms required: FAFSA, institutional form.
Dates and Deadlines: Priority date 4/1; no closing date. Applicants notified on a rolling basis starting 4/15; must reply within 4 week(s) of notification.

CONTACT
Donna Fisher, Financial Aid Director
1801 North Kansas Avenue, Liberal, KS 67905-1137
(620) 417-1110

Southwestern College
Winfield, Kansas
www.sckans.edu   Federal Code: 001940

4-year private liberal arts college in large town, affiliated with the United Methodist Church.
Enrollment: 1,157 undergrads, 56% part-time. 90 full-time freshmen.
Selectivity: Admits over 75% of applicants.

BASIC COSTS (2016-2017)
Tuition and fees: $27,250.
Per-credit charge: $1,129.
Room and board: $7,250.

FINANCIAL AID PICTURE (2015-2016)
Students with need: Out of 79 full-time freshmen who applied for aid, 70 were judged to have need. Of these, 70 received aid, and 11 had their full need met. Average financial aid package met 81% of need; average scholarship/grant was $17,958; average loan was $4,933. For part-time students, average financial aid package was $5,903.
Students without need: 11 full-time freshmen who did not demonstrate need for aid received scholarships/grants; average award was $7,273. No-need awards available for academics, athletics, leadership, music/drama.
Scholarships offered: *Merit:* Presidential Scholarship; based on GPA, SAT/ACT, essay, resume, leadership, community service. Scholarships for major; based on GPA, SAT, essay, interview; 3 awarded. *Athletic:* 8 full-time freshmen received athletic scholarships; average amount $4,375.

FINANCIAL AID PROCEDURES
Forms required: FAFSA, institutional form.
Dates and Deadlines: Priority date 4/1; no closing date. Applicants notified on a rolling basis starting 2/1; must reply within 2 week(s) of notification.
Transfers: Priority date 4/1. Applicants notified on a rolling basis starting 2/1; must reply within 2 week(s) of notification. Activity grants and scholarships, except for presidential scholarship and premier scholarships, available to transfer students. Phi Theta Kappa scholarship available for transfer students who are members.

CONTACT

Brenda Hicks, Director of Financial Aid
100 College Street, Winfield, KS 67156
(620) 229-6215

Sterling College

Sterling, Kansas
www.sterling.edu   Federal Code: 001945

4-year private liberal arts college in small town, affiliated with the Presbyterian Church (USA).
Enrollment: 587 undergrads, 7% part-time. 128 full-time freshmen.
Selectivity: Admits less than 50% of applicants.

BASIC COSTS (2017-2018)
Tuition and fees: $24,835.
Room and board: $8,280.

FINANCIAL AID PICTURE (2015-2016)
Students with need: Average financial aid package met 83% of need; average scholarship/grant was $10,743; average loan was $4,520. For part-time students, average financial aid package was $11,279.
Students without need: No-need awards available for academics, alumni affiliation, art, athletics, leadership, music/drama.

FINANCIAL AID PROCEDURES
Forms required: FAFSA.
Dates and Deadlines: Priority date 3/15; no closing date. Applicants notified on a rolling basis starting 2/1; must reply within 2 week(s) of notification.
Transfers: No deadline. Applicants notified on a rolling basis starting 2/1; must reply within 2 week(s) of notification.

CONTACT
Mitzi Suhler, Financial Aid Director
125 West Cooper, Sterling, KS 67579
(620) 278-4407

Tabor College

Hillsboro, Kansas
www.tabor.edu   Federal Code: 001946

4-year private liberal arts college in small town, affiliated with the Mennonite Brethren Church.
Enrollment: 637 undergrads, 18% part-time. 147 full-time freshmen.
Selectivity: Admits 50 to 75% of applicants.

BASIC COSTS (2016-2017)
Tuition and fees: $26,590.
Per-credit charge: $535.
Room and board: $9,280.
Additional info: Tuition/fee waivers available for adults.

FINANCIAL AID PICTURE (2015-2016)
Students with need: Out of 146 full-time freshmen who applied for aid, 117 were judged to have need. Of these, 117 received aid, and 15 had their full need met. Average financial aid package met 69% of need; average scholarship/grant was $5,390; average loan was $3,272. For part-time students, average financial aid package was $9,342.
Students without need: 30 full-time freshmen who did not demonstrate need for aid received scholarships/grants; average award was $10,898. No-need awards available for academics, alumni affiliation, art, athletics, leadership, music/drama, religious affiliation.
Scholarships offered: 108 full-time freshmen received athletic scholarships; average amount $5,273.

FINANCIAL AID PROCEDURES
Forms required: FAFSA.

Dates and Deadlines: Priority date 3/1; no closing date. Applicants notified on a rolling basis starting 3/1; must reply within 5 week(s) of notification.
Transfers: No deadline. Applicants notified on a rolling basis starting 2/20; must reply within 5 week(s) of notification. Transfer students with over 20 transferable credit hours are not eligible for Presidential, National Merit or Dean's scholarships.

CONTACT
Tricia Brothers, Director of Financial Aid
400 South Jefferson, Hillsboro, KS 67063-7135
(620) 947-3121 ext. 1726

University of Kansas

Lawrence, Kansas
www.ku.edu   Federal Code: 001948

4-year public university in small city.
Enrollment: 18,337 undergrads, 9% part-time. 4,032 full-time freshmen.
Selectivity: Admits over 75% of applicants.

BASIC COSTS (2016-2017)
Tuition and fees: $11,455; out-of-state residents $28,239.
Per-credit charge: $349.5; out-of-state residents $909.
Room and board: $10,436.
Additional info: Tuition at time of enrollment locked for 4 years.

FINANCIAL AID PICTURE (2015-2016)
Students with need: Out of 3,152 full-time freshmen who applied for aid, 2,108 were judged to have need. Of these, 2,035 received aid, and 876 had their full need met. Average financial aid package met 78% of need; average scholarship/grant was $7,545; average loan was $3,270. For part-time students, average financial aid package was $9,421.
Students without need: 956 full-time freshmen who did not demonstrate need for aid received scholarships/grants; average award was $5,444. No-need awards available for academics, alumni affiliation, art, athletics, leadership, minority status, music/drama, ROTC, state/district residency.
Scholarships offered: 85 full-time freshmen received athletic scholarships; average amount $18,548.

FINANCIAL AID PROCEDURES
Forms required: FAFSA.
Dates and Deadlines: Priority date 3/1; no closing date. Applicants notified on a rolling basis starting 4/1; must reply within 4 week(s) of notification.

CONTACT
Brenda Maigaard, Director
1502 Iowa Street, Lawrence, KS 66045-7576
(785) 864-4700

University of Kansas Medical Center

Kansas City, Kansas
www.kumc.edu   Federal Code: 001948

Upper-division public university and health science college in very large city.
Enrollment: 506 undergrads, 35% part-time.

BASIC COSTS (2016-2017)
Tuition and fees: $10,416; out-of-state residents $25,794.
Per-credit charge: $319; out-of-state residents $832.
Additional info: Tuition at time of enrollment locked for 2 years.

FINANCIAL AID PICTURE (2015-2016)
Students with need: Average financial aid package for all full-time undergraduates was $15,645; for part-time $9,421. 33% awarded as scholarships/

grants, 67% awarded as loans/jobs. Work study available nights, weekends, and for part-time students.

Students without need: No-need awards available for academics, leadership, state/district residency.

CONTACT

Sara Honeck, Director of Student Financial Aid

KUMC Office of Admissions, Mail Stop 4005, Kansas City, KS 66160

(913) 588-5170

University of St. Mary

Leavenworth, Kansas

www.stmary.edu   Federal Code: 001943

4-year private university in large town, affiliated with the Roman Catholic Church.

Enrollment: 765 undergrads, 16% part-time. 134 full-time freshmen.

Selectivity: Admits less than 50% of applicants.

BASIC COSTS (2017-2018)

Tuition and fees: $27,720.

Per-credit charge: $875.

Room and board: $8,140.

FINANCIAL AID PICTURE (2015-2016)

Students with need: Out of 126 full-time freshmen who applied for aid, 119 were judged to have need. Of these, 119 received aid, and 68 had their full need met. Average financial aid package met 87% of need; average scholarship/grant was $5,880; average loan was $3,161. For part-time students, average financial aid package was $9,601.

Students without need: 5 full-time freshmen who did not demonstrate need for aid received scholarships/grants; average award was $12,500. No-need awards available for academics, alumni affiliation, art, athletics, leadership, music/drama, religious affiliation, ROTC.

Scholarships offered: *Merit:* Essays may be required for scholarship applicants. Auditions recommended for music and drama scholarship applicants. Portfolio reviews for art award applicants. *Athletic:* 97 full-time freshmen received athletic scholarships; average amount $1,351.

FINANCIAL AID PROCEDURES

Forms required: FAFSA, state aid form.

Dates and Deadlines: Priority date 4/1; no closing date. Applicants notified on a rolling basis starting 2/15; must reply within 2 week(s) of notification.

Transfers: No deadline. Applicants notified on a rolling basis starting 2/1; must reply within 2 week(s) of notification.

CONTACT

Annissa Epperson, Director of Financial Aid

4100 South Fourth Street Trafficway, Leavenworth, KS 66048

(913) 758-6172

Washburn University

Topeka, Kansas

www.washburn.edu   Federal Code: 001949

4-year public university in small city.

Enrollment: 4,967 undergrads, 24% part-time. 849 full-time freshmen.

Selectivity: Open admission; but selective for some programs.

BASIC COSTS (2016-2017)

Tuition and fees: $8,300; out-of-state residents $18,620.

Per-credit charge: $273; out-of-state residents $617.

Room and board: $7,527.

FINANCIAL AID PICTURE (2016-2017)

Students with need: Out of 785 full-time freshmen who applied for aid, 539 were judged to have need. Of these, 537 received aid, and 83 had their

full need met. Average financial aid package met 38% of need; average scholarship/grant was $5,623; average loan was $3,251: For part-time students, average financial aid package was $7,442.

Students without need: 145 full-time freshmen who did not demonstrate need for aid received scholarships/grants; average award was $3,184. No-need awards available for academics, alumni affiliation, art, athletics, leadership, minority status, music/drama, state/district residency.

Scholarships offered: 38 full-time freshmen received athletic scholarships; average amount $6,921.

FINANCIAL AID PROCEDURES

Forms required: FAFSA.

Dates and Deadlines: Priority date 2/15; no closing date. Applicants notified on a rolling basis starting 4/1; must reply within 4 week(s) of notification.

Transfers: Must reply within 4 week(s) of notification.

CONTACT

Kandace Mars, Director of Financial Aid

1700 SW College Avenue, Morgan 100, Topeka, KS 66621

(785) 670-1151

Wichita Area Technical College

Wichita, Kansas

www.watc.edu   Federal Code: 005498

2-year public technical college in large city.

Enrollment: 1,482 undergrads.

Selectivity: Open admission; but selective for some programs.

BASIC COSTS (2016-2017)

Tuition and fees: $3,030; out-of-state residents $3,444.

Per-credit charge: $69; out-of-state residents $82.8.

FINANCIAL AID PICTURE

Students with need: Need-based aid available for full-time and part-time students. Work study available nights.

Students without need: This college awards aid only to students with need.

FINANCIAL AID PROCEDURES

Forms required: FAFSA, CSS PROFILE, institutional form.

Dates and Deadlines: Applicants notified on a rolling basis starting 1/1.

Transfers: No deadline. Applicants notified on a rolling basis starting 1/1.

CONTACT

Lacey Ledwich, Director of Financial Aid

4004 North Webb Road, Suite 100, Wichita, KS 67226

(316) 677-9400

Wichita State University

Wichita, Kansas

www.wichita.edu   Federal Code: 001950

4-year public university in large city.

Enrollment: 11,037 undergrads, 22% part-time. 1,270 full-time freshmen.

Selectivity: Admits over 75% of applicants.

BASIC COSTS (2016-2017)

Tuition and fees: $7,895; out-of-state residents $16,634.

Per-credit charge: $212.84; out-of-state residents $504.16.

Room and board: $6,712.

Additional info: On-line only students are charged an on-line area fee of 94.50 per credit hour.

FINANCIAL AID PICTURE (2015-2016)

Students with need: Out of 1,244 full-time freshmen who applied for aid, 480 were judged to have need. Of these, 476 received aid, and 334 had

their full need met. Average financial aid package met 52% of need; average scholarship/grant was $4,340; average loan was $2,044. For part-time students, average financial aid package was $3,773.

Students without need: 547 full-time freshmen who did not demonstrate need for aid received scholarships/grants; average award was $1,349. No-need awards available for academics, alumni affiliation, art, athletics, leadership, minority status, music/drama.

Scholarships offered: 61 full-time freshmen received athletic scholarships; average amount $4,924.

FINANCIAL AID PROCEDURES

Forms required: FAFSA.

Dates and Deadlines: Priority date 10/1; no closing date. Applicants notified on a rolling basis starting 10/15; must reply by 5/1 or within 2 week(s) of notification.

Transfers: Applicants notified on a rolling basis.

CONTACT

Sheelu Surender, Director of Financial Aid
1845 Fairmount, Box 124, Wichita, KS 67260-0124
(316) 978-5337

Kentucky

Alice Lloyd College

Pippa Passes, Kentucky
www.alc.edu   Federal Code: 001951

4-year private liberal arts college in rural community.
Enrollment: 431 undergrads, 6% part-time. 168 full-time freshmen.

BASIC COSTS (2016-2017)

Tuition and fees: $11,550.
Per-credit charge: $212.
Room and board: $6,240.
Additional info: Students from 108 Appalachian counties served by Alice Lloyd College do not pay tuition. Tuition/fee waivers available for minority students.

FINANCIAL AID PICTURE

Students with need: Need-based aid available for full-time and part-time students. Work study available nights, weekends, and for part-time students.
Students without need: No-need awards available for academics, athletics, minority status, state/district residency.
Scholarships offered: Alice Lloyd Scholars Program; tuition, room, board, fees, and books.
Additional info: All students receive financial aid through student work program. No student denied admission because of inability to pay. All full-time students required to work minimum of 10 hours per week.

FINANCIAL AID PROCEDURES

Forms required: FAFSA.
Dates and Deadlines: Closing date 7/1. Applicants notified on a rolling basis starting 3/1; must reply by 7/1 or within 4 week(s) of notification.
Transfers: Priority date 7/1. Applicants notified on a rolling basis starting 3/1; must reply by 7/1 or within 4 week(s) of notification.

CONTACT

Jacqueline Stewart, Director of Financial Aid
100 Purpose Road, Pippa Passes, KY 41844
(606) 368-6058

Asbury University

Wilmore, Kentucky
www.asbury.edu   Federal Code: 001952

4-year private university and liberal arts college in small town, affiliated with the interdenominational tradition.
Enrollment: 1,493 undergrads, 13% part-time. 309 full-time freshmen.
Selectivity: Admits 50 to 75% of applicants.

BASIC COSTS (2017-2018)

Tuition and fees: $29,500.
Per-credit charge: $1,127.
Room and board: $6,950.

FINANCIAL AID PICTURE (2015-2016)

Students with need: Out of 286 full-time freshmen who applied for aid, 253 were judged to have need. Of these, 253 received aid, and 61 had their full need met. Average financial aid package met 81% of need; average scholarship/grant was $12,115; average loan was $2,816. For part-time students, average financial aid package was $7,500.
Students without need: 33 full-time freshmen who did not demonstrate need for aid received scholarships/grants; average award was $12,022. No-need awards available for academics, alumni affiliation, art, athletics, leadership, minority status, music/drama, religious affiliation, ROTC, state/district residency.
Scholarships offered: 12 full-time freshmen received athletic scholarships; average amount $5,864.

FINANCIAL AID PROCEDURES

Forms required: FAFSA.
Dates and Deadlines: Priority date 12/1; no closing date. Applicants notified on a rolling basis starting 11/1; must reply within 4 week(s) of notification.

CONTACT

Ronald Anderson, Director of Financial Aid
One Macklem Drive, Wilmore, KY 40390-1198
(859) 858-3511 ext. 2195

Beckfield College

Florence, Kentucky
www.beckfield.edu   Federal Code: 016726

4-year for-profit nursing and career college in large town.
Enrollment: 808 undergrads.
Selectivity: Open admission; but selective for some programs.

FINANCIAL AID PICTURE

Students with need: Need-based aid available for full-time and part-time students.
Students without need: This college awards aid only to students with need.
Scholarships offered: High School scholarship; tuition for one course per quarter for maximum of 8 quarters; must achieve and maintain 3.0 GPA, be enrolled full-time, and enter college in July or October following graduation from high school. Merit scholarship; $100 per quarter; must maintain 4.0 GPA, perfect attendance, and carry at least 8 quarter credit hours.
Additional info: Deadline for filing of financial aid forms is end of first week of classes.

FINANCIAL AID PROCEDURES

Forms required: FAFSA.
Dates and Deadlines: Applicants notified on a rolling basis.

CONTACT

Kim Villaverde, Corporate Director of Student Financial
16 Spiral Drive, Florence, KY 41042
(859) 371-9393 ext. 1134

Bellarmine University

Louisville, Kentucky
www.bellarmine.edu
Federal Code: 001954

4-year private university and liberal arts college in very large city, affiliated with the Roman Catholic Church.
Enrollment: 2,571 undergrads, 4% part-time. 635 full-time freshmen.
Selectivity: Admits over 75% of applicants.

BASIC COSTS (2017-2018)
Tuition and fees: $40,350.
Per-credit charge: $905.
Room and board: $11,750.
Additional info: Tuition/fee waivers available for adults.

FINANCIAL AID PICTURE (2016-2017)
Students with need: Out of 610 full-time freshmen who applied for aid, 536 were judged to have need. Of these, 535 received aid, and 95 had their full need met. Average financial aid package met 72% of need; average scholarship/grant was $24,796; average loan was $3,468. For part-time students, average financial aid package was $8,774.
Students without need: 95 full-time freshmen who did not demonstrate need for aid received scholarships/grants; average award was $25,298. No-need awards available for academics, alumni affiliation, art, athletics, leadership, minority status, music/drama, religious affiliation, ROTC, state/district residency.
Scholarships offered: *Merit:* Academic awards range from $7,000 to full tuition. *Athletic:* 36 full-time freshmen received athletic scholarships; average amount $6,733.

FINANCIAL AID PROCEDURES
Forms required: FAFSA.
Dates and Deadlines: Priority date 11/1; no closing date. Applicants notified on a rolling basis starting 12/15; must reply by 5/1.
Transfers: Applicants notified on a rolling basis starting 4/15; must reply within 3 week(s) of notification.

CONTACT
Heather Boutell, Director of Financial Aid
2001 Newburg Road, Louisville, KY 40205
(502) 272-8124

Berea College

Berea, Kentucky
www.berea.edu
Federal Code: 001955

4-year private liberal arts college in small town.
Enrollment: 1,612 undergrads. 418 full-time freshmen.
Selectivity: Admits less than 50% of applicants.

BASIC COSTS (2016-2017)
Tuition and fees: $25,470.
Room and board: $6,472.

FINANCIAL AID PICTURE (2016-2017)
Students with need: Out of 418 full-time freshmen who applied for aid, 418 were judged to have need. Of these, 418 received aid. Average financial aid package met 98% of need; average scholarship/grant was $31,803; average loan was $755. Need-based aid available for part-time students.
Students without need: This college awards aid only to students with need.

FINANCIAL AID PROCEDURES
Forms required: FAFSA.
Dates and Deadlines: Priority date 2/1; closing date 5/1. Applicants notified on a rolling basis starting 3/1; must reply by 5/1.
Transfers: Financial aid transcript from previous school(s) must be received before awarding aid.

CONTACT
Theresa Lowder, Director of Student Financial Aid Services
CPO 2220, Berea, KY 40404
(859) 985-3310

Big Sandy Community and Technical College

Prestonsburg, Kentucky
www.bigsandy.kctcs.edu
Federal Code: 001996

2-year public community and technical college in small town.
Enrollment: 3,157 undergrads.
Selectivity: Open admission; but selective for some programs.

BASIC COSTS (2016-2017)
Tuition and fees: $4,920; out-of-state residents $16,620.
Per-credit charge: $156; out-of-state residents $546.
Additional info: Nonresident students living in contiguous counties are charged a discounted non-resident rate of $312 per credit hour.

FINANCIAL AID PICTURE
Students with need: Need-based aid available for full-time and part-time students. Work study available nights, weekends, and for part-time students.
Students without need: No-need awards available for academics.

FINANCIAL AID PROCEDURES
Forms required: FAFSA.
Dates and Deadlines: Priority date 4/1; no closing date. Applicants notified on a rolling basis; must reply within 2 week(s) of notification.
Transfers: Kentucky State Grant must be transferred by August 1 for fall semester, December 1 for spring semester.

CONTACT
Cathy Hurd, Director of Financial Aid
One Bert T. Combs Drive, Prestonsburg, KY 41653
(606) 886-3863

Bluegrass Community and Technical College

Lexington, Kentucky
www.bluegrass.kctcs.edu
Federal Code: 009707

2-year public community and technical college in large city.
Enrollment: 10,392 undergrads.
Selectivity: Open admission; but selective for some programs.

BASIC COSTS (2016-2017)
Tuition and fees: $4,920; out-of-state residents $16,620.
Per-credit charge: $156; out-of-state residents $546.
Additional info: Nonresident students living in contiguous counties are charged a discounted non-resident rate of $312 per credit hour.

FINANCIAL AID PICTURE
Students with need: Need-based aid available for full-time and part-time students. Work study available nights, weekends, and for part-time students.
Students without need: No-need awards available for academics, minority status, state/district residency.

FINANCIAL AID PROCEDURES
Forms required: FAFSA, institutional form.
Dates and Deadlines: Priority date 4/15; no closing date. Applicants notified on a rolling basis starting 6/5; must reply within 3 week(s) of notification.
Transfers: No deadline. Applicants notified on a rolling basis.

CONTACT

Runan Pendergrast, Director of Financial Aid

200 Oswald Building, Cooper Drive, Lexington, KY 40506-0235

(859) 246-6216

Brescia University

Owensboro, Kentucky

www.brescia.edu   Federal Code: 001958

4-year private university and liberal arts college in small city, affiliated with the Roman Catholic Church.

Enrollment: 953 undergrads, 26% part-time. 126 full-time freshmen.

Selectivity: Admits less than 50% of applicants.

BASIC COSTS (2017-2018)

Tuition and fees: $21,850.

Per-credit charge: $590.

Room and board: $9,150.

FINANCIAL AID PICTURE (2015-2016)

Students with need: 56% of average financial aid package awarded as scholarships/grants, 44% awarded as loans/jobs. Need-based aid available for part-time students. Work study available nights, weekends, and for part-time students.

Students without need: No-need awards available for academics, alumni affiliation, art, athletics, minority status, music/drama, religious affiliation, state/district residency.

FINANCIAL AID PROCEDURES

Forms required: FAFSA.

Dates and Deadlines: Priority date 8/1; closing date 8/23. Applicants notified on a rolling basis starting 3/1; must reply within 3 week(s) of notification.

CONTACT

Kristi Eidson, Director of Financial Aid

717 Frederica Street, Owensboro, KY 42301-3023

(270) 685-3131 ext. 4216

Campbellsville University

Campbellsville, Kentucky

www.campbellsville.edu   Federal Code: 001959

4-year private university in large town, affiliated with the Baptist faith.

Enrollment: 2,215 undergrads, 11% part-time. 472 full-time freshmen.

Selectivity: Admits 50 to 75% of applicants.

BASIC COSTS (2016-2017)

Tuition and fees: $24,596.

Per-credit charge: $972.

Room and board: $7,896.

Additional info: Tuition/fee waivers available for adults, minority students, unemployed or children of unemployed.

FINANCIAL AID PICTURE (2015-2016)

Students with need: Out of 456 full-time freshmen who applied for aid, 435 were judged to have need. Of these, 429 received aid, and 70 had their full need met. Average financial aid package met 74% of need; average scholarship/grant was $19,265; average loan was $2,955. For part-time students, average financial aid package was $5,595.

Students without need: 23 full-time freshmen who did not demonstrate need for aid received scholarships/grants; average award was $12,954. No-need awards available for academics, art, athletics, leadership, minority status, music/drama, religious affiliation, state/district residency.

Scholarships offered: 30 full-time freshmen received athletic scholarships; average amount $9,276.

Additional info: Matching scholarships available for students whose church contributes $200 annually. Performance grants available to members of marching band.

FINANCIAL AID PROCEDURES

Forms required: FAFSA.

Dates and Deadlines: Priority date 2/15; no closing date. Applicants notified on a rolling basis starting 3/15.

Transfers: No deadline. Applicants notified on a rolling basis.

CONTACT

Chris Mapes, Director of Financial Aid

1 University Drive, Campbellsville, KY 42718-2799

(270) 789-5013

Centre College

Danville, Kentucky

www.centre.edu   Federal Code: 001961

4-year private liberal arts college in large town, affiliated with the Presbyterian Church (USA).

Enrollment: 1,422 undergrads. 400 full-time freshmen.

Selectivity: Admits 50 to 75% of applicants.

BASIC COSTS (2016-2017)

Tuition and fees: $39,300.

Room and board: $9,950.

FINANCIAL AID PICTURE (2016-2017)

Students with need: Out of 332 full-time freshmen who applied for aid, 243 were judged to have need. Of these, 243 received aid, and 94 had their full need met. Average financial aid package met 90% of need; average scholarship/grant was $31,508; average loan was $3,368.

Students without need: 146 full-time freshmen who did not demonstrate need for aid received scholarships/grants; average award was $21,908. No-need awards available for academics, alumni affiliation, art, leadership, music/drama, ROTC.

Scholarships offered: Institutional Merit Award: $9,500 to full tuition; applications must be on file by February 1; renewable. Music and Drama Scholarships: up to $7,500. Guaranteed minimum award available to admitted Centre Fellows and Kentucky Governor's Scholars. Grissom Scholars Program: Full-tuition scholarship and $5,000 in educational enrichment funds; available to first-year, first-generation applicants, based on academic achievement, 10 awards available.

FINANCIAL AID PROCEDURES

Forms required: FAFSA, institutional form.

Dates and Deadlines: Priority date 1/31; closing date 1/31. Applicants notified on a rolling basis starting 3/19; must reply by 5/1.

Transfers: No deadline. Applicants notified on a rolling basis starting 3/1; must reply within 2 week(s) of notification. Financial aid transcript required.

CONTACT

Brian Hutzley, Vice President for Finance, Treasurer

600 West Walnut Street, Danville, KY 40422-1394

(859) 238-5367

Clear Creek Baptist Bible College

Pineville, Kentucky

www.ccbbc.edu   Federal Code: 017044

4-year private Bible college in small town, affiliated with the Southern Baptist Convention.

Enrollment: 114 undergrads.

Selectivity: Open admission; but selective for some programs.

BASIC COSTS (2016-2017)
Tuition and fees: $8,840.
Per-credit charge: $270.
Room and board: $4,160.

FINANCIAL AID PICTURE (2016-2017)
Students with need: Need-based aid available for part-time students.
Students without need: No-need awards available for academics, alumni affiliation, religious affiliation.

FINANCIAL AID PROCEDURES
Forms required: FAFSA, institutional form.
Dates and Deadlines: Priority date 6/30; no closing date. Applicants notified on a rolling basis starting 6/1; must reply by 8/1.
Transfers: Priority date 5/5; no deadline. Applicants notified on a rolling basis starting 5/5; must reply by 8/1.

CONTACT
Sam Risner, Director of Financial Aid
300 Clear Creek Road, Pineville, KY 40977-9754
(606) 337-3196 ext. 142

Daymar College: Bowling Green
Bowling Green, Kentucky
www.daymarcollege.edu   Federal Code: 004934

2-year for-profit branch campus and career college in small city.
Enrollment: 225 undergrads.
Selectivity: Open admission.

BASIC COSTS (2016-2017)
Additional info: Diploma programs: $22,000-$26,500; Associate programs: $33,000. Fees, books supplies range depending on program level and course of study. All costs are subject to change. Tuition/fee waivers available for adults.

FINANCIAL AID PICTURE
Students with need: Need-based aid available for full-time and part-time students. Work study available nights.
Students without need: This college awards aid only to students with need.

FINANCIAL AID PROCEDURES
Forms required: FAFSA.

CONTACT
Janice Cutliff, Director of Financial Services
2421 Fitzgerald Industrial Drive, Bowling Green, KY 42101
(270) 843-6750

Daymar College: Owensboro
Owensboro, Kentucky
www.daymarcollege.edu   Federal Code: 009313

2-year for-profit business and junior college in small city.
Enrollment: 94 undergrads.
Selectivity: Open admission.

BASIC COSTS (2016-2017)
Additional info: Diploma programs: $22,000-$26,500; Associate programs: $33,000; Bachelor programs: $48,000. Fees, books supplies range depending on program level and course of study. All costs are subject to change.

FINANCIAL AID PICTURE
Students with need: Need-based aid available for full-time and part-time students.
Students without need: This college awards aid only to students with need.

FINANCIAL AID PROCEDURES
Forms required: FAFSA.
Dates and Deadlines: Applicants notified on a rolling basis.

CONTACT
Denise Jernigan, Director of Financial Services
3361 Buckland Square, Owensboro, KY 42301
(270) 926-4040

Daymar College: Paducah
Paducah, Kentucky   Federal Code: 013661
www.daymarcollege.edu   CSS Code: 0669

2-year for-profit technical college in small city.
Enrollment: 47 undergrads.
Selectivity: Open admission.

BASIC COSTS (2016-2017)
Additional info: Diploma programs: $22,000-$26,500; Associate programs: $33,000. Fees, books supplies range depending on program level and course of study. All costs are subject to change.

FINANCIAL AID PICTURE
Students with need: Need-based aid available for full-time students.

FINANCIAL AID PROCEDURES
Forms required: FAFSA, CSS PROFILE.
Dates and Deadlines: Applicants notified on a rolling basis; must reply within 3 week(s) of notification.

CONTACT
JoAnn Price, Financial Aid Officer
509 South 30th Street, Paducah, KY 42001

Eastern Kentucky University
Richmond, Kentucky
www.eku.edu   Federal Code: 001963

4-year public university in large town.
Enrollment: 13,131 undergrads.

BASIC COSTS (2016-2017)
Tuition and fees: $8,868; out-of-state residents $18,180.
Per-credit charge: $357; out-of-state residents $745.
Room and board: $8,666.

FINANCIAL AID PICTURE
Students with need: Need-based aid available for full-time and part-time students. Work study available nights, weekends, and for part-time students.
Students without need: No-need awards available for academics, alumni affiliation, art, athletics, job skills, leadership, minority status, music/drama, ROTC, state/district residency.

FINANCIAL AID PROCEDURES
Forms required: FAFSA.
Dates and Deadlines: Applicants notified on a rolling basis starting 4/1.

CONTACT
Shelley Park, Director of Student Financial Assistance, Scholarship and Veteran Affairs
SSB CPO 54, 521 Lancaster Avenue, Richmond, KY 40475-3102

Elizabethtown Community and Technical College

Elizabethtown, Kentucky
www.elizabethtown.kctcs.edu   Federal Code: 001991

2-year public community and technical college in large town.
Enrollment: 4,524 undergrads.
Selectivity: Open admission; but selective for some programs.

BASIC COSTS (2016-2017)
Tuition and fees: $4,920; out-of-state residents $16,620.
Per-credit charge: $156; out-of-state residents $546.
Additional info: Nonresident students living in contiguous counties are charged a discounted non-resident rate of $312 per credit hour.

FINANCIAL AID PICTURE (2015-2016)
Students with need: 62% of average financial aid package awarded as scholarships/grants, 38% awarded as loans/jobs. Need-based aid available for part-time students. Work study available nights, weekends, and for part-time students.
Students without need: This college awards aid only to students with need.

FINANCIAL AID PROCEDURES
Forms required: FAFSA.
Dates and Deadlines: Priority date 8/1; no closing date. Applicants notified on a rolling basis starting 6/1; must reply within 2 week(s) of notification.
Transfers: Priority date 7/11; no deadline. Applicants notified on a rolling basis; must reply within 2 week(s) of notification.

CONTACT
Michael Barlow, Director of Financial Aid
600 College Street Road, Elizabethtown, KY 42701
(270) 769-2371 ext. 68614

Georgetown College

Georgetown, Kentucky
www.georgetowncollege.edu   Federal Code: 001964

4-year private liberal arts college in large town, affiliated with the Baptist faith.
Enrollment: 982 undergrads, 7% part-time. 296 full-time freshmen.
Selectivity: Admits 50 to 75% of applicants.

BASIC COSTS (2016-2017)
Tuition and fees: $35,850.
Per-credit charge: $1,470.
Room and board: $9,050.
Additional info: Continuing students fee is $50 per semester. The Carte Blanche meal plan provides flexible continuous dining not limited to a fixed number of meals per week.

FINANCIAL AID PICTURE
Students with need: Need-based aid available for full-time and part-time students.
Students without need: No-need awards available for academics, alumni affiliation, art, athletics, leadership, music/drama, religious affiliation, ROTC, state/district residency.

FINANCIAL AID PROCEDURES
Forms required: FAFSA.
Dates and Deadlines: Priority date 2/1; no closing date. Applicants notified on a rolling basis starting 3/1; must reply by 5/1.

CONTACT
Bob Fultz, Director of Student Financial Planning
400 East College Street, Georgetown, KY 40324-1696
(502) 863-8027

Hazard Community and Technical College

Hazard, Kentucky
www.hazard.kctcs.edu   Federal Code: 006962

2-year public community and technical college in small town.
Enrollment: 1,887 undergrads.
Selectivity: Open admission; but selective for some programs and for out-of-state students.

BASIC COSTS (2016-2017)
Tuition and fees: $4,920; out-of-state residents $16,620.
Per-credit charge: $156; out-of-state residents $546.
Additional info: Nonresident students living in contiguous counties are charged a discounted non-resident rate of $312 per credit hour.

FINANCIAL AID PICTURE
Students with need: Need-based aid available for full-time and part-time students.
Students without need: This college awards aid only to students with need.

FINANCIAL AID PROCEDURES
Forms required: FAFSA.
Dates and Deadlines: Priority date 4/1; no closing date. Applicants notified on a rolling basis starting 6/15; must reply within 2 week(s) of notification.

CONTACT
Chuck Anderson, Financial Aid Director
One Community College Drive, Hazard, KY 41701
(606) 487-3061

Henderson Community College

Henderson, Kentucky
www.henderson.kctcs.edu   Federal Code: 001993

2-year public community college in large town.
Enrollment: 1,117 undergrads.
Selectivity: Open admission; but selective for some programs.

BASIC COSTS (2016-2017)
Tuition and fees: $4,920; out-of-state residents $16,620.
Per-credit charge: $156; out-of-state residents $546.
Additional info: Nonresident students living in contiguous counties are charged a discounted non-resident rate of $312 per credit hour.

FINANCIAL AID PICTURE (2015-2016)
Students with need: 58% of average financial aid package awarded as scholarships/grants, 42% awarded as loans/jobs.

FINANCIAL AID PROCEDURES
Forms required: FAFSA.
Dates and Deadlines: Closing date 7/15. Applicants notified on a rolling basis starting 5/1.

CONTACT
Andrew Zellers, Director Of Financial Aid
2660 South Green Street, Henderson, KY 42420
(800) 464-2244

Hopkinsville Community College

Hopkinsville, Kentucky
www.hopkinsville.kctcs.edu   Federal Code: 001994

2-year public community college in large town.
Enrollment: 2,406 undergrads.

Selectivity: Open admission; but selective for some programs.

BASIC COSTS (2016-2017)
Tuition and fees: $4,920; out-of-state residents $16,620.
Per-credit charge: $156; out-of-state residents $546.
Additional info: Nonresident students living in contiguous counties are charged a discounted non-resident rate of $312 per credit hour.

FINANCIAL AID PICTURE
Students with need: Need-based aid available for full-time and part-time students. Work study available nights.
Students without need: No-need awards available for academics, leadership, minority status, state/district residency.
Scholarships offered: The Rotary Scholars Program: two years of full-time study; any graduate of a Christian County high school (beginning with the Class of 2012); 2.5 high school GPA and 95% attendance required.
Additional info: ACT required for academic scholarships.

FINANCIAL AID PROCEDURES
Forms required: FAFSA.
Dates and Deadlines: Priority date 7/15; no closing date. Applicants notified on a rolling basis starting 7/1.
Transfers: No deadline. Applicants notified on a rolling basis.

CONTACT
Jeff Horton, Chief Financial Officer
PO Box 2100, Hopkinsville, KY 42241-2100
(270) 707-3830

Jefferson Community and Technical College
Louisville, Kentucky
www.jefferson.kctcs.edu   Federal Code: 006961

2-year public community and technical college in large city.
Enrollment: 9,279 undergrads.
Selectivity: Open admission; but selective for some programs.

BASIC COSTS (2016-2017)
Tuition and fees: $4,920; out-of-state residents $16,620.
Per-credit charge: $156; out-of-state residents $546.
Additional info: Nonresident students living in contiguous counties are charged a discounted non-resident rate of $312 per credit hour.

FINANCIAL AID PICTURE
Students with need: Need-based aid available for full-time and part-time students.
Students without need: No-need awards available for academics, art, minority status.

FINANCIAL AID PROCEDURES
Forms required: FAFSA, institutional form.
Dates and Deadlines: Priority date 3/15; no closing date. Applicants notified on a rolling basis starting 6/15; must reply within 3 week(s) of notification.

CONTACT
Lisa Schrenger, Financial Aid Officer
109 East Broadway, Louisville, KY 40202
(502) 213-2137

Kentucky Christian University
Grayson, Kentucky
www.kcu.edu   Federal Code: 001965

4-year private university and Bible college in small town.
Enrollment: 564 undergrads.

BASIC COSTS (2016-2017)
Tuition and fees: $18,560.
Per-credit charge: $605.
Room and board: $8,000.

FINANCIAL AID PICTURE
Students with need: Need-based aid available for full-time and part-time students. Work study available nights, weekends, and for part-time students.
Students without need: No-need awards available for academics, alumni affiliation, leadership, minority status, music/drama, religious affiliation.

FINANCIAL AID PROCEDURES
Forms required: FAFSA.
Dates and Deadlines: Priority date 3/1; no closing date. Applicants notified on a rolling basis starting 3/15; must reply within 2 week(s) of notification.

CONTACT
Jennie Bender, Director of Financial Aid
100 Academic Parkway, Grayson, KY 41143-2205
(606) 474-3226

Kentucky Mountain Bible College
Jackson, Kentucky
www.kmbc.edu   Federal Code: 030021

4-year private Bible college in rural community, affiliated with the Christian Church.
Enrollment: 79 undergrads, 23% part-time. 23 full-time freshmen.
Selectivity: Admits 50 to 75% of applicants.

BASIC COSTS (2016-2017)
Tuition and fees: $7,610.
Per-credit charge: $230.
Room and board: $4,850.

FINANCIAL AID PICTURE
Students with need: Need-based aid available for full-time and part-time students. Work study available nights, weekends, and for part-time students.
Students without need: No-need awards available for academics, job skills, leadership, music/drama.

FINANCIAL AID PROCEDURES
Forms required: FAFSA, institutional form.
Dates and Deadlines: Priority date 5/1; no closing date. Applicants notified on a rolling basis starting 3/15.
Transfers: No deadline. Applicants notified on a rolling basis starting 8/30; must reply within 6 week(s) of notification.

CONTACT
Adelle Semrow, Director of Financial Aid
855 Highway 541, Jackson, KY 41339
(606) 693-5000 ext. 175

Kentucky State University
Frankfort, Kentucky
www.kysu.edu   Federal Code: 001968

4-year public university and liberal arts college in large town.
Enrollment: 1,287 undergrads, 19% part-time. 194 full-time freshmen.
Selectivity: Admits less than 50% of applicants.

BASIC COSTS (2016-2017)
Tuition and fees: $7,796; out-of-state residents $18,704.
Per-credit charge: $309; out-of-state residents $763.
Room and board: $6,690.

FINANCIAL AID PICTURE (2015-2016)

Students with need: Out of 186 full-time freshmen who applied for aid, 99 were judged to have need. Of these, 99 received aid, and 3 had their full need met. Average financial aid package met 73% of need; average scholarship/grant was $8,967; average loan was $3,384. For part-time students, average financial aid package was $6,479.

Students without need: 13 full-time freshmen who did not demonstrate need for aid received scholarships/grants; average award was $4,880. No-need awards available for academics, alumni affiliation, art, athletics, leadership, music/drama.

Scholarships offered: 6 full-time freshmen received athletic scholarships; average amount $7,200.

FINANCIAL AID PROCEDURES

Forms required: FAFSA.

Dates and Deadlines: Priority date 4/15; no closing date. Applicants notified on a rolling basis starting 3/15; must reply within 4 week(s) of notification.

Transfers: Priority date 4/15. Applicants notified on a rolling basis; must reply within 4 week(s) of notification.

CONTACT

Qiana Hall, Director of Financial Aid
400 East Main Street, ASB 312, Frankfort, KY 40601
(502) 597-5960

Kentucky Wesleyan College
Owensboro, Kentucky
www.kwc.edu   Federal Code: 001969

4-year private liberal arts college in small city, affiliated with the United Methodist Church.
Enrollment: 691 undergrads.

BASIC COSTS (2016-2017)
Tuition and fees: $24,300.
Per-credit charge: $670.
Room and board: $8,480.

FINANCIAL AID PICTURE
Students with need: Need-based aid available for full-time and part-time students. Work study available nights, weekends, and for part-time students.
Students without need: No-need awards available for academics, alumni affiliation, art, athletics, leadership, music/drama, religious affiliation, state/district residency.
Scholarships offered: Scholarships range from $1,000 to full tuition. Students compete in on-campus scholarship competitions.

FINANCIAL AID PROCEDURES
Forms required: FAFSA.
Dates and Deadlines: Priority date 1/1; no closing date. Applicants notified on a rolling basis starting 2/15; must reply within 2 week(s) of notification.
Transfers: No deadline. Applicants notified on a rolling basis starting 11/15; must reply within 2 week(s) of notification.

CONTACT
Samantha Hays, Director of Financial Aid
3000 Frederica Street, Owensboro, KY 42301
(270) 852-3130

Lindsey Wilson College
Columbia, Kentucky
www.lindsey.edu   Federal Code: 001972

4-year private liberal arts college in small town, affiliated with the United Methodist Church.
Enrollment: 2,038 undergrads, 3% part-time. 484 full-time freshmen.

Selectivity: Open admission; but selective for some programs.

BASIC COSTS (2017-2018)
Tuition and fees: $24,246.
Per-credit charge: $1,000.
Room and board: $9,300.

FINANCIAL AID PICTURE (2016-2017)
Students with need: Out of 484 full-time freshmen who applied for aid, 458 were judged to have need. Of these, 457 received aid, and 112 had their full need met. Need-based aid available for part-time students.
Students without need: This college awards aid only to students with need.

FINANCIAL AID PROCEDURES
Forms required: FAFSA, institutional form.
Dates and Deadlines: Priority date 3/1; no closing date. Applicants notified on a rolling basis starting 5/1; must reply within 2 week(s) of notification.
Transfers: Applicants notified on a rolling basis.

CONTACT
Marilyn Radford, Director of Financial Aid
210 Lindsey Wilson Street, Columbia, KY 42728
(270) 384-8022

Madisonville Community College
Madisonville, Kentucky
www.madisonville.kctcs.edu   Federal Code: 009010

2-year public community college in large town.
Enrollment: 2,265 undergrads.
Selectivity: Open admission; but selective for some programs.

BASIC COSTS (2016-2017)
Tuition and fees: $4,920; out-of-state residents $16,620.
Per-credit charge: $156; out-of-state residents $546.
Additional info: Nonresident students living in contiguous counties are charged a discounted non-resident rate of $312 per credit hour. Tuition/fee waivers available for minority students, unemployed or children of unemployed.

FINANCIAL AID PICTURE
Students with need: Need-based aid available for full-time and part-time students. Work study available nights, weekends, and for part-time students.
Students without need: No-need awards available for minority status.

FINANCIAL AID PROCEDURES
Forms required: FAFSA, institutional form.
Dates and Deadlines: Priority date 7/1; no closing date. Applicants notified on a rolling basis; must reply within 3 week(s) of notification.

CONTACT
Martha Phelps, Director of Financial Aid
2000 College Drive, Madisonville, KY 42431
(270) 824-8693

Maysville Community and Technical College
Maysville, Kentucky
www.maysville.kctcs.edu   Federal Code: 006960

2-year public community and technical college in small town.
Enrollment: 3,525 undergrads.
Selectivity: Open admission; but selective for some programs.

BASIC COSTS (2016-2017)
Tuition and fees: $4,920; out-of-state residents $16,620.

Per-credit charge: $156; out-of-state residents $546.
Additional info: Nonresident students living in contiguous counties are charged a discounted non-resident rate of $312 per credit hour.

FINANCIAL AID PICTURE

Students with need: Need-based aid available for full-time and part-time students. Work study available nights.
Students without need: No-need awards available for academics.

FINANCIAL AID PROCEDURES

Forms required: FAFSA, institutional form.
Dates and Deadlines: Priority date 4/1; no closing date. Applicants notified on a rolling basis starting 3/1; must reply within 3 week(s) of notification.

CONTACT

Sandy Power, Financial Aid Director
1755 US HIghway 68, Maysville, KY 41056
(606) 759-7141 ext. 66404

Midway College

Midway, Kentucky
www.midway.edu
Federal Code: 001975

4-year private liberal arts college in small town, affiliated with the Christian Church (Disciples of Christ).
Enrollment: 989 undergrads.

BASIC COSTS (2016-2017)

Tuition and fees: $23,250.
Per-credit charge: $860.
Room and board: $8,400.

FINANCIAL AID PICTURE

Students with need: Need-based aid available for full-time and part-time students. Work study available nights, weekends, and for part-time students.
Students without need: No-need awards available for academics, alumni affiliation, art, athletics, leadership, minority status, religious affiliation.
Additional info: Audition required of applicants for music scholarships.

FINANCIAL AID PROCEDURES

Forms required: FAFSA, institutional form.
Dates and Deadlines: Applicants notified on a rolling basis; must reply within 4 week(s) of notification.

CONTACT

Kate Ware, Director of Financial Aid
512 East Stephens Street, Midway, KY 40347-1120
(859) 846-5410

Morehead State University

Morehead, Kentucky
www.moreheadstate.edu
Federal Code: 001976

4-year public university in large town.
Enrollment: 6,647 undergrads, 13% part-time. 1,282 full-time freshmen.
Selectivity: Admits over 75% of applicants.

BASIC COSTS (2016-2017)

Tuition and fees: $8,530; out-of-state residents $12,796.
Per-credit charge: $351; out-of-state residents $529.
Room and board: $8,560.
Additional info: Tuition/fee waivers available for minority students.

FINANCIAL AID PICTURE

Students with need: Need-based aid available for full-time and part-time students. Work study available nights, weekends, and for part-time students.

Students without need: No-need awards available for academics, alumni affiliation, art, athletics, leadership, minority status, music/drama, ROTC, state/district residency.

FINANCIAL AID PROCEDURES

Forms required: FAFSA.
Dates and Deadlines: Priority date 3/15; no closing date. Applicants notified on a rolling basis.
Transfers: No deadline. Applicants notified on a rolling basis. Transfer scholarships available.

CONTACT

Donna King, Director of Financial Aid
121 E Second Street, Morehead, KY 40351
(606) 783-2000

Murray State University

Murray, Kentucky
www.murraystate.edu
Federal Code: 001977

4-year public university in large town.
Enrollment: 7,655 undergrads, 10% part-time. 1,459 full-time freshmen.
Selectivity: Admits over 75% of applicants.

BASIC COSTS (2016-2017)

Tuition and fees: $7,944; out-of-state residents $21,648.
Per-credit charge: $331; out-of-state residents $902.
Room and board: $8,588.
Additional info: Tuition/fee waivers available for minority students.

FINANCIAL AID PICTURE (2015-2016)

Students with need: Out of 1,252 full-time freshmen who applied for aid, 992 were judged to have need. Of these, 991 received aid, and 253 had their full need met. Average financial aid package met 35% of need; average scholarship/grant was $6,658; average loan was $4,954. For part-time students, average financial aid package was $5,978.
Students without need: 154 full-time freshmen who did not demonstrate need for aid received scholarships/grants; average award was $5,927. No-need awards available for academics, alumni affiliation, art, athletics, job skills, leadership, minority status, music/drama, ROTC, state/district residency.
Scholarships offered: *Merit:* Excellence Award provides additional $1,000 in scholarship and $500 in housing to one Valedictorian and one Salutatorian at each public high school in our 18 county service region. *Athletic:* 42 full-time freshmen received athletic scholarships; average amount $11,148.
Additional info: Racer Promise grant, for first-time freshman from our 18-county service region who demonstrate financial need, covers up to 8 semesters of mandatory tuition and fees.

FINANCIAL AID PROCEDURES

Forms required: FAFSA.
Dates and Deadlines: Priority date 10/1; no closing date. Applicants notified on a rolling basis starting 12/15; must reply by 5/1.
Transfers: Priority date 10/1; no deadline. Applicants notified on a rolling basis starting 12/15; must reply by 5/1. Transfer Scholarship; students eligible to apply before entering when transferring 36 or more credit hours with 3.25 GPA.

CONTACT

Janet Balok, Director of Financial Aid
102 Curris Center, Murray, KY 42071
(270) 809-2546

National College: Danville

Danville, Kentucky
www.national-college.edu   Federal Code: 010489

2-year for-profit business college in large town.
Enrollment: 81 undergrads.
Selectivity: Open admission.

BASIC COSTS (2016-2017)
Tuition and fees: $14,460.
Per-credit charge: $317.

FINANCIAL AID PICTURE
Students with need: Need-based aid available for full-time and part-time students.
Students without need: This college awards aid only to students with need.

FINANCIAL AID PROCEDURES
Forms required: FAFSA.
Dates and Deadlines: Applicants notified on a rolling basis.

CONTACT
Pam Cotton, Director of Financial Aid and Auditing
115 East Lexington Avenue, Danville, KY 40422
(540) 986-1800

National College: Florence

Florence, Kentucky
www.national-college.edu   Federal Code: 010489

2-year for-profit business college in large town.
Enrollment: 40 undergrads.
Selectivity: Open admission.

BASIC COSTS (2016-2017)
Tuition and fees: $14,460.
Per-credit charge: $317.

FINANCIAL AID PICTURE
Students with need: Need-based aid available for full-time and part-time students.
Students without need: This college awards aid only to students with need.

FINANCIAL AID PROCEDURES
Forms required: FAFSA.
Dates and Deadlines: Applicants notified on a rolling basis.

CONTACT
Pam Cotton, Director of Financial Aid and Auditing
8095 Connector Drive, Florence, KY 41042
(540) 986-1800

National College: Lexington

Lexington, Kentucky
www.national-college.edu   Federal Code: 010489

2-year for-profit business and junior college in small city.
Enrollment: 98 undergrads.
Selectivity: Open admission; but selective for some programs.

BASIC COSTS (2016-2017)
Tuition and fees: $14,460.
Per-credit charge: $317.

FINANCIAL AID PICTURE
Students with need: Need-based aid available for full-time and part-time students.
Students without need: This college awards aid only to students with need.

FINANCIAL AID PROCEDURES
Forms required: FAFSA.
Dates and Deadlines: Applicants notified on a rolling basis.

CONTACT
Pam Cotton, Director of Financial Aid and Auditing
2376 Sir Barton Way, Lexington, KY 40509
(859) 255-0621

National College: Louisville

Louisville, Kentucky
www.national-college.edu   Federal Code: 010489

2-year for-profit business college in large city.
Enrollment: 158 undergrads.
Selectivity: Open admission; but selective for some programs.

BASIC COSTS (2016-2017)
Tuition and fees: $14,460.
Per-credit charge: $317.

FINANCIAL AID PICTURE
Students with need: Need-based aid available for full-time and part-time students.
Students without need: This college awards aid only to students with need.

FINANCIAL AID PROCEDURES
Forms required: FAFSA.
Dates and Deadlines: Applicants notified on a rolling basis.

CONTACT
Pamela Cotton, Director of Financial Aid and Compliance Officer
4205 Dixie Highway, Louisville, KY 40216
(540) 986-1800

National College: Pikeville

Pikeville, Kentucky
www.national-college.edu   Federal Code: 010489

2-year for-profit business college in large town.
Enrollment: 137 undergrads.
Selectivity: Open admission; but selective for some programs.

BASIC COSTS (2016-2017)
Tuition and fees: $14,460.
Per-credit charge: $317.

FINANCIAL AID PICTURE
Students with need: Need-based aid available for full-time and part-time students.
Students without need: This college awards aid only to students with need.

FINANCIAL AID PROCEDURES
Forms required: FAFSA.

CONTACT
Pam Cotton, Director of Financial Aid and Auditing
50 National Collge Boulevard, Pikeville, KY 41501
(540) 986-1800

National College: Richmond
Richmond, Kentucky
www.national-college.edu   Federal Code: 010489

2-year for-profit business college in large town.
Enrollment: 61 undergrads.
Selectivity: Open admission.

BASIC COSTS (2016-2017)
Tuition and fees: $14,460.
Per-credit charge: $317.

FINANCIAL AID PICTURE
Students with need: Need-based aid available for full-time and part-time students.
Students without need: This college awards aid only to students with need.

FINANCIAL AID PROCEDURES
Forms required: FAFSA.
Dates and Deadlines: Applicants notified on a rolling basis.

CONTACT
Pam Cotton, Director of Financial Aid and Auditing
125 South Killarney Lane, Richmond, KY 40475
(540) 986-1800

Northern Kentucky University
Highland Heights, Kentucky
www.nku.edu   Federal Code: 009275

4-year public university in small town.
Enrollment: 11,042 undergrads, 17% part-time. 2,130 full-time freshmen.
Selectivity: Admits over 75% of applicants.

BASIC COSTS (2016-2017)
Tuition and fees: $9,384; out-of-district residents $13,992; out-of-state residents $18,384.
Per-credit charge: $375; out-of-district residents $567; out-of-state residents $750.
Room and board: $8,768.
Additional info: NKU offers a reduced nonresident rate for students from selected Ohio counties.

FINANCIAL AID PICTURE (2015-2016)
Students with need: Out of 1,877 full-time freshmen who applied for aid, 1,492 were judged to have need. Of these, 1,487 received aid, and 397 had their full need met. Average financial aid package met 70% of need; average scholarship/grant was $6,141; average loan was $3,548. For part-time students, average financial aid package was $7,957.
Students without need: 352 full-time freshmen who did not demonstrate need for aid received scholarships/grants; average award was $5,607. No-need awards available for academics, alumni affiliation, art, athletics, leadership, music/drama, ROTC, state/district residency.
Scholarships offered: 46 full-time freshmen received athletic scholarships; average amount $14,942.

FINANCIAL AID PROCEDURES
Forms required: FAFSA.
Dates and Deadlines: Priority date 2/1; no closing date. Applicants notified on a rolling basis starting 3/15.
Transfers: No deadline. Applicants notified on a rolling basis starting 5/30.

CONTACT
Leah Stewart, Director of Financial Assistance
Administrative Center 400, Northern Kentucky University, Highland Heights, KY 41099
(859) 572-5143

Owensboro Community and Technical College
Owensboro, Kentucky
www.owensboro.kctcs.edu   Federal Code: 030345

2-year public community and technical college in small city.
Enrollment: 2,647 undergrads, 44% part-time. 210 full-time freshmen.
Selectivity: Open admission; but selective for some programs.

BASIC COSTS (2016-2017)
Tuition and fees: $4,920; out-of-state residents $16,620.
Per-credit charge: $156; out-of-state residents $546.
Additional info: Nonresident students living in contiguous counties are charged a discounted non-resident rate of $312 per credit hour.

FINANCIAL AID PICTURE (2015-2016)
Students with need: 70% of average financial aid package awarded as scholarships/grants, 30% awarded as loans/jobs. Need-based aid available for part-time students.
Students without need: No-need awards available for academics, art, minority status, music/drama, state/district residency.

FINANCIAL AID PROCEDURES
Forms required: FAFSA.
Dates and Deadlines: Priority date 4/1; no closing date. Must reply within 2 week(s) of notification.
Transfers: Financial aid transcripts from previous institutions may be required.

CONTACT
Andrea Borregard, Interim Director of Financial Aid
4800 New Hartford Road, Owensboro, KY 42303-1899
(270) 686-4521

St. Catharine College
St. Catharine, Kentucky
www.sccky.edu   Federal Code: 001983

4-year private health science and liberal arts college in small town, affiliated with the Roman Catholic Church.
Enrollment: 539 undergrads.
Selectivity: Open admission; but selective for some programs.

BASIC COSTS (2016-2017)
Tuition and fees: $22,100.
Per-credit charge: $730.
Room and board: $9,500.

FINANCIAL AID PICTURE
Students with need: Need-based aid available for full-time and part-time students.
Students without need: This college awards aid only to students with need.

FINANCIAL AID PROCEDURES
Forms required: FAFSA, institutional form.
Dates and Deadlines: Priority date 3/15; no closing date. Applicants notified on a rolling basis.
Transfers: Priority date 2/1; no deadline. Applicants notified on a rolling basis.

CONTACT
Jeremy Pittman, Director of Financial Aid
2735 Bardstown Road, St. Catharine, KY 40061
(859) 336-5082 ext. 1287

Somerset Community College
Somerset, Kentucky
www.somerset.kctcs.edu   Federal Code: 001997

2-year public community and technical college in large town.
Enrollment: 6,639 undergrads.
Selectivity: Open admission; but selective for some programs.

BASIC COSTS (2016-2017)
Tuition and fees: $4,920; out-of-state residents $16,620.
Per-credit charge: $156; out-of-state residents $546.
Additional info: Nonresident students living in contiguous counties are charged a discounted non-resident rate of $312 per credit hour.

FINANCIAL AID PICTURE (2015-2016)
Students with need: Need-based aid available for full-time and part-time students.
Students without need: This college awards aid only to students with need.

FINANCIAL AID PROCEDURES
Forms required: FAFSA.
Dates and Deadlines: Priority date 3/1; no closing date. Applicants notified on a rolling basis starting 5/1; must reply within 2 week(s) of notification.
Transfers: Priority date 3/15; closing date 8/15. Applicants notified on a rolling basis starting 5/1; must reply within 2 week(s) of notification.

CONTACT
Patrick Mayer, Interin Director of Financial Aid
808 Monticello Street, Somerset, KY 42501
(606) 679-8501 ext. 16640

Southeast Kentucky Community and Technical College
Cumberland, Kentucky
www.southeast.kctcs.edu   Federal Code: 001998

2-year public community and technical college in small town.
Enrollment: 1,496 undergrads.
Selectivity: Open admission; but selective for some programs.

BASIC COSTS (2016-2017)
Tuition and fees: $4,920; out-of-state residents $16,620.
Per-credit charge: $156; out-of-state residents $546.
Additional info: Nonresident students living in contiguous counties are charged a discounted non-resident rate of $312 per credit hour.

FINANCIAL AID PICTURE
Students with need: Need-based aid available for full-time and part-time students.
Students without need: This college awards aid only to students with need.
Additional info: March 15 deadline for state financial aid.

FINANCIAL AID PROCEDURES
Forms required: FAFSA.
Dates and Deadlines: Priority date 3/15; no closing date. Must reply within 2 week(s) of notification.

CONTACT
Rebecca Parrott, Vice President for Student Affairs
700 College Road, Cumberland, KY 40823
(606) 589-2145

Spalding University
Louisville, Kentucky
www.spalding.edu   Federal Code: 001960

4-year private university in very large city, affiliated with the Roman Catholic Church.
Enrollment: 1,141 undergrads, 19% part-time. 151 full-time freshmen.
Selectivity: Admits 50 to 75% of applicants.

BASIC COSTS (2016-2017)
Tuition and fees: $24,000.
Per-credit charge: $800.
Room and board: $7,600.

FINANCIAL AID PICTURE
Students with need: Need-based aid available for full-time and part-time students.
Students without need: No-need awards available for academics, alumni affiliation, art, leadership.
Scholarships offered: Egan Service Learning Program: covers the cost of a double room on campus; awarded to students who demonstrate leadership in campus activities and agree to complete service hours within the community. Catherine Spalding Grant: a need based award with a maximum dollar amount of $6,500, opportunity for renewal for eight semesters; requires a minimum GPA of 2.0 and completion of FAFSA.

FINANCIAL AID PROCEDURES
Forms required: FAFSA.
Dates and Deadlines: Priority date 1/1; no closing date. Applicants notified on a rolling basis starting 3/31.
Transfers: Applicants notified on a rolling basis; must reply within 2 week(s) of notification.

CONTACT
Michelle Standridge, Director Financial Aid
845 S Third Street, Louisville, KY 40203
(502) 873-4329

Spencerian College
Louisville, Kentucky
www.spencerian.edu   Federal Code: 004618

2-year for-profit career college in large city.
Enrollment: 392 undergrads, 41% part-time. 74 full-time freshmen.
Selectivity: Open admission; but selective for some programs.

BASIC COSTS (2016-2017)
Tuition and fees: $20,905; out-of-state residents $20,905.
Room and board: $8,925; room only: $5,940.
Additional info: Specific programs have higher comprehensive fees than others which can increase the required fees costs. Books and supplies vary by programs.Bachelor degree and nursing degree programs are at a different per credit hour rate.

FINANCIAL AID PICTURE
Students with need: Need-based aid available for full-time and part-time students.
Students without need: No-need awards available for academics.

FINANCIAL AID PROCEDURES
Forms required: FAFSA, institutional form.

CONTACT
Jill Schuler, Director of Financial Aid
4627 Dixie Highway, Louisville, KY 40216

Spencerian College: Lexington

Lexington, Kentucky
www.spencerian.edu   Federal Code: 004618

2-year for-profit branch campus college in small city.
Enrollment: 73 undergrads.
Selectivity: Open admission; but selective for some programs.

BASIC COSTS (2016-2017)
Tuition and fees: $19,260.
Per-credit charge: $299.
Room only: $5,940.

FINANCIAL AID PICTURE
Students with need: Need-based aid available for full-time and part-time students.
Students without need: This college awards aid only to students with need.

FINANCIAL AID PROCEDURES
Forms required: FAFSA, state aid form, institutional form.
Dates and Deadlines: Applicants notified on a rolling basis starting 1/1.
Transfers: No deadline. Applicants notified on a rolling basis.

CONTACT
Brian Highley, Director of Financial Aid/Compliance Officer
2355 Harrodsburg Rd, Lexington, KY 40504
(859) 223-9608 ext. 5441

Sullivan College of Technology and Design

Louisville, Kentucky
www.sctd.edu   Federal Code: 012088

2-year for-profit technical and career college in very large city.
Enrollment: 379 undergrads.

BASIC COSTS (2016-2017)
Additional info: Full-program tuition cost ranges from $38,160-$44,520 depending on the program of study. The per-credit-hour tuition rate is $420. The approximate cost of books and supplies per academic year varies by program of study. Required fees are a $200 general fee per quarter plus a fee of $240 for online courses. Tech fees range from $150-360 per quarter depending on the program. Rent for a semi-private room is $660 per month or $5,940 for the academic year (9 months/3 quarters). The required meal plan for all housing students includes three meals a day Mon-Fri and brunch and dinner on Sat-Sun (19 meals) and costs $2,985 per academic year. Total room and board for an academic year is $8,925. Tuition at time of enrollment locked for 2 years; tuition/fee waivers available for unemployed or children of unemployed.

FINANCIAL AID PICTURE (2015-2016)
Students with need: 70% of average financial aid package awarded as scholarships/grants, 30% awarded as loans/jobs. Need-based aid available for part-time students.
Students without need: No-need awards available for academics, alumni affiliation, art, job skills.
Scholarships offered: Academic Scholarships; up to $3,000; based on class rank, GPA, essay. Scholarship Day Competition; up to $1,500 based upon testing scores. Scholarship Fair Competition; up to $3,000; based upon open competition in electronics, drafting, interior design, computer networking and art skills. Kentucky Skills USA Scholarships; up to $1,500; based upon state championship competitions in such fields as drafting, electronics, etc.

FINANCIAL AID PROCEDURES
Forms required: FAFSA.
Dates and Deadlines: Applicants notified on a rolling basis; must reply within 2 week(s) of notification.

Transfers: No deadline. Applicants notified on a rolling basis.

CONTACT
Michelle Smith, Financial Planning Director
3901 Atkinson Square Drive, Louisville, KY 40218-4524
(502) 456-6509 ext. 8240

Sullivan University

Louisville, Kentucky
www.sullivan.edu   Federal Code: 004619

4-year for-profit university in large city.
Enrollment: 2,386 undergrads, 34% part-time. 243 full-time freshmen.

BASIC COSTS (2017-2018)
Additional info: Program and housing costs vary by program.

FINANCIAL AID PICTURE
Students with need: Need-based aid available for full-time and part-time students. Work study available nights.
Students without need: This college awards aid only to students with need.

FINANCIAL AID PROCEDURES
Forms required: FAFSA.
Dates and Deadlines: Applicants notified on a rolling basis starting 1/2.

CONTACT
Angela Miller, Director of Financial Planning
3101 Bardstown Road, Louisville, KY 40205
(502) 456-6771

Thomas More College

Crestview Hills, Kentucky
www.thomasmore.edu   Federal Code: 002001

4-year private liberal arts college in small town, affiliated with the Roman Catholic Church.
Enrollment: 1,401 undergrads, 2% part-time. 414 full-time freshmen.
Selectivity: Admits over 75% of applicants.

BASIC COSTS (2016-2017)
Tuition and fees: $29,450.
Per-credit charge: $620.
Room and board: $7,304.

FINANCIAL AID PICTURE (2016-2017)
Students with need: Out of 395 full-time freshmen who applied for aid, 351 were judged to have need. Of these, 351 received aid, and 90 had their full need met. Average financial aid package met 74% of need; average scholarship/grant was $17,412; average loan was $2,997. For part-time students, average financial aid package was $3,339.
Students without need: 58 full-time freshmen who did not demonstrate need for aid received scholarships/grants; average award was $15,759. No-need awards available for academics, alumni affiliation, art, leadership, minority status, music/drama, religious affiliation, ROTC, state/district residency.

FINANCIAL AID PROCEDURES
Forms required: FAFSA.
Dates and Deadlines: Closing date 3/15. Applicants notified on a rolling basis starting 3/1; must reply by 5/1.
Transfers: No deadline. Applicants notified on a rolling basis; must reply by 5/1.

CONTACT
Mark Messingschlager, Director of Financial Aid
333 Thomas More Parkway, Crestview Hills, KY 41017-3495
(859) 344-4043

Transylvania University
Lexington, Kentucky
www.transy.edu   Federal Code: 001987

4-year private liberal arts college in large city, affiliated with the Christian Church (Disciples of Christ).
Enrollment: 960 undergrads, 1% part-time. 242 full-time freshmen.
Selectivity: Admits over 75% of applicants.

BASIC COSTS (2017-2018)
Tuition and fees: $37,290.
Per-credit charge: $995.
Room and board: $10,160.

FINANCIAL AID PICTURE (2016-2017)
Students with need: Out of 217 full-time freshmen who applied for aid, 174 were judged to have need. Of these, 174 received aid, and 44 had their full need met. Average financial aid package met 78% of need; average scholarship/grant was $24,019; average loan was $3,278. For part-time students, average financial aid package was $10,535.
Students without need: 67 full-time freshmen who did not demonstrate need for aid received scholarships/grants; average award was $15,197. No-need awards available for academics, art, leadership, minority status, music/drama, religious affiliation, state/district residency.
Additional info: Auditions and portfolios required for music and art scholarships respectively. Essays required for other scholarship programs.

FINANCIAL AID PROCEDURES
Forms required: FAFSA.
Dates and Deadlines: Priority date 10/15; no closing date. Applicants notified on a rolling basis starting 12/1; must reply by 5/1 or within 2 week(s) of notification.
Transfers: Priority date 10/15; no deadline. Applicants notified on a rolling basis starting 12/1; must reply by 8/1.

CONTACT
Jennifer Priest, Director of Financial Aid
300 North Broadway, Lexington, KY 40508-1797
(859) 233-8239

Union College
Barbourville, Kentucky
www.unionky.edu   Federal Code: 001988

4-year private liberal arts and teachers college in small town, affiliated with the United Methodist Church.
Enrollment: 912 undergrads, 6% part-time. 170 full-time freshmen.
Selectivity: Admits 50 to 75% of applicants.

BASIC COSTS (2016-2017)
Tuition and fees: $25,135.
Per-credit charge: $345.
Room and board: $7,250.

FINANCIAL AID PICTURE (2015-2016)
Students with need: Out of 143 full-time freshmen who applied for aid, 135 were judged to have need. Of these, 132 received aid, and 10 had their full need met. Average financial aid package met 68% of need; average scholarship/grant was $18,423; average loan was $3,538. For part-time students, average financial aid package was $11,689.
Students without need: 32 full-time freshmen who did not demonstrate need for aid received scholarships/grants; average award was $14,777. No-need awards available for academics, alumni affiliation, athletics, leadership, music/drama, religious affiliation.

FINANCIAL AID PROCEDURES
Forms required: FAFSA.

Dates and Deadlines: Priority date 11/1; no closing date. Applicants notified on a rolling basis starting 11/15; must reply within 2 week(s) of notification.
Transfers: No deadline. Applicants notified on a rolling basis starting 2/15; must reply within 2 week(s) of notification.

CONTACT
Andra Butler, Director of Financial Aid
310 College Street, Box 005, Barbourville, KY 40906
(606) 546-1618

University of Kentucky
Lexington, Kentucky
www.uky.edu   Federal Code: 001989

4-year public university in large city.
Enrollment: 21,725 undergrads. 5,167 full-time freshmen.

BASIC COSTS (2016-2017)
Tuition and fees: $11,320; out-of-state residents $26,156.
Per-credit charge: $458; out-of-state residents $1,075.
Room and board: $9,230.
Additional info: UK has separate rates for lower division and upper division undergradute students. The above are the "lower division" costs for a UK undergraduate. Tuition/fee waivers available for adults, minority students.

FINANCIAL AID PICTURE (2015-2016)
Students with need: Out of 4,123 full-time freshmen who applied for aid, 3,024 were judged to have need. Of these, 3,006 received aid. Need-based aid available for part-time students.
Students without need: No-need awards available for academics, alumni affiliation, art, athletics, leadership, minority status, music/drama, ROTC, state/district residency.
Scholarships offered: 108 full-time freshmen received athletic scholarships; average amount $18,519.

FINANCIAL AID PROCEDURES
Forms required: FAFSA.
Dates and Deadlines: Priority date 2/15; no closing date. Applicants notified on a rolling basis; must reply within 3 week(s) of notification.
Transfers: Priority date 4/1.

CONTACT
Nimmi Wiggins, Director of Student Financial Aid
100 Funkhouser Building, Lexington, KY 40506-0054
(859) 257-3172

University of Louisville
Louisville, Kentucky
www.louisville.edu   Federal Code: 001999

4-year public university in very large city.
Enrollment: 15,033 undergrads, 18% part-time. 2,746 full-time freshmen.
Selectivity: Admits 50 to 75% of applicants.

BASIC COSTS (2016-2017)
Tuition and fees: $11,264; out-of-state residents $26,286.
Per-credit charge: $462; out-of-state residents $1,088.
Room and board: $8,130.

FINANCIAL AID PICTURE (2016-2017)
Students with need: Out of 2,419 full-time freshmen who applied for aid, 1,811 were judged to have need. Of these, 1,796 received aid, and 437 had their full need met. Average financial aid package met 61% of need; average scholarship/grant was $9,768; average loan was $3,350. For part-time students, average financial aid package was $6,892.

Students without need: 477 full-time freshmen who did not demonstrate need for aid received scholarships/grants; average award was $7,751. No-need awards available for academics, art, athletics, leadership, minority status, music/drama, ROTC, state/district residency.
Scholarships offered: 103 full-time freshmen received athletic scholarships; average amount $24,134.

FINANCIAL AID PROCEDURES
Forms required: FAFSA.
Dates and Deadlines: Priority date 2/15; no closing date. Applicants notified on a rolling basis starting 4/1.
Transfers: Priority date 3/1.

CONTACT
Sandy Neel, Director of Student Financial Aid
2211 South Brook Street, Louisville, KY 40292
(502) 852-5511

University of Pikeville
Pikeville, Kentucky
www.upike.edu   Federal Code: 001980

4-year private university and liberal arts college in small town, affiliated with the Presbyterian Church (USA).
Enrollment: 1,150 undergrads, 2% part-time. 328 full-time freshmen.
Selectivity: Open admission; but selective for some programs.

BASIC COSTS (2017-2018)
Tuition and fees: $20,200.
Per-credit charge: $842.
Room and board: $7,500.

FINANCIAL AID PICTURE (2015-2016)
Students with need: Out of 323 full-time freshmen who applied for aid, 322 were judged to have need. Of these, 322 received aid, and 186 had their full need met. Average financial aid package met 88% of need; average scholarship/grant was $18,882; average loan was $3,468. For part-time students, average financial aid package was $7,452.
Students without need: This college awards aid only to students with need.
Scholarships offered: University of Pikeville Promise: full-tuition, four-year scholarship that places emphasis on academics and financial need; applicants must submit ACT and HSGPA, file FAFSA by February 15 of senior year in high school, be a Kentucky resident, display full eligibility for Pell Grant and receive CAP and KTG state grants.

FINANCIAL AID PROCEDURES
Forms required: FAFSA.
Dates and Deadlines: Priority date 2/15; no closing date. Applicants notified on a rolling basis starting 2/1; must reply by 5/1.
Transfers: No deadline. Must reply by 5/1 or within 2 week(s) of notification.

CONTACT
Kristen Gast, Financial Aid Director
147 Sycamore Street, Pikeville, KY 41501-1194
(606) 218-5251

University of the Cumberlands
Williamsburg, Kentucky
www.ucumberlands.edu   Federal Code: 001962

4-year private university and liberal arts college in small town, affiliated with the Baptist faith.
Enrollment: 1,938 undergrads, 10% part-time. 409 full-time freshmen.
Selectivity: Admits 50 to 75% of applicants.

BASIC COSTS (2016-2017)
Tuition and fees: $23,000.
Per-credit charge: $690.
Room and board: $9,000.

FINANCIAL AID PICTURE
Students with need: Need-based aid available for full-time and part-time students. Work study available nights, weekends, and for part-time students.
Students without need: No-need awards available for academics, athletics, job skills, leadership, music/drama, religious affiliation, state/district residency.
Scholarships offered: Presidential: up to $22,000; based on outstanding academic credentials; no limit. Dean's: up to $15,000; based on ACT/SAT score and high school GPA; no limit. Kentucky Rogers Scholar: up to full-tuition. Rogers Scholar Graduate: based on ACT/SAT score and GPA; up to 3 per year. Kentucky Governor's Scholar: up to $15,000; GSP graduate; no limit. Christian Leadership: $1,000-$5,000; based on involvement/leadership in church or other religious organizations; no limit. Trustee Scholarship: based upon outstanding academic credentials, letters of recommendations, essays and interview process; full tuition, room and board: up to 5 awarded. Lewis Appalachian Scholarship: based on academic performance and community involvement; available to students from select regions of KY; $1,000; 1 awarded each year.

FINANCIAL AID PROCEDURES
Forms required: FAFSA.
Dates and Deadlines: Priority date 2/1; no closing date. Applicants notified on a rolling basis starting 3/1; must reply within 2 week(s) of notification.
Transfers: Applicants notified on a rolling basis starting 3/1; must reply within 2 week(s) of notification.

CONTACT
Steve Allen, Director of Financial Planning
6178 College Station Drive, Williamsburg, KY 40769
(800) 343-1609

West Kentucky Community and Technical College
Paducah, Kentucky
www.westkentucky.kctcs.edu   Federal Code: 001979

2-year public community and technical college in large town.
Enrollment: 3,787 undergrads, 42% part-time. 712 full-time freshmen.
Selectivity: Open admission; but selective for some programs.

BASIC COSTS (2016-2017)
Tuition and fees: $4,920; out-of-state residents $16,620.
Per-credit charge: $156; out-of-state residents $546.
Additional info: Nonresident students living in contiguous counties are charged a discounted non-resident rate of $312 per credit hour.

FINANCIAL AID PICTURE (2015-2016)
Students with need: 74% of average financial aid package awarded as scholarships/grants, 26% awarded as loans/jobs. Need-based aid available for part-time students.
Students without need: No-need awards available for academics, minority status, state/district residency.

FINANCIAL AID PROCEDURES
Forms required: FAFSA.
Dates and Deadlines: Priority date 4/1; no closing date. Applicants notified on a rolling basis starting 4/15.

CONTACT
Angel Rhodes, Director of Financial Aid
4810 Alben Barkley Drive, Paducah, KY 42002-7380
(270) 534-3248

Western Kentucky University

Bowling Green, Kentucky
www.wku.edu   Federal Code: 002002

4-year public university in small city.
Enrollment: 14,956 undergrads, 13% part-time. 3,068 full-time freshmen.
Selectivity: Admits over 75% of applicants.

BASIC COSTS (2016-2017)
Tuition and fees: $9,912; out-of-state residents $24,792.
Per-credit charge: $413; out-of-state residents $1,033.
Room and board: $7,713.
Additional info: WKU offers a reduced nonresident rate for students from selected counties in TN, IN, IL, OH, MO, FL, and GA.

FINANCIAL AID PICTURE (2015-2016)
Students with need: Out of 2,703 full-time freshmen who applied for aid, 2,037 were judged to have need. Of these, 2,007 received aid, and 717 had their full need met. Average financial aid package met 36% of need; average scholarship/grant was $5,387; average loan was $3,058. For part-time students, average financial aid package was $9,445.
Students without need: 441 full-time freshmen who did not demonstrate need for aid received scholarships/grants; average award was $6,769. No-need awards available for academics, alumni affiliation, art, athletics, job skills, leadership, minority status, music/drama, religious affiliation, ROTC, state/district residency.
Scholarships offered: *Merit:* Academic scholarships; $200 to full tuition; number awarded varies. *Athletic:* 61 full-time freshmen received athletic scholarships; average amount $16,166.

FINANCIAL AID PROCEDURES
Forms required: FAFSA.
Dates and Deadlines: Priority date 2/15; no closing date. Applicants notified on a rolling basis starting 3/1.
Transfers: Transfer students receiving CAP Grant must notify the state agency by December 1 of each year.

CONTACT
Cynthia Burnette, Director of Financial Assistance
1906 College Heights Boulevard #11020, Bowling Green, KY 42101
(270) 745-2755

Louisiana

Baton Rouge Community College

Baton Rouge, Louisiana
www.mybrcc.edu   Federal Code: 037303

2-year public community college in large city.
Enrollment: 7,843 undergrads.
Selectivity: Open admission.

BASIC COSTS (2016-2017)
Tuition and fees: $4,221; out-of-state residents $8,299.

FINANCIAL AID PICTURE
Students with need: Need-based aid available for full-time and part-time students. Work study available weekends and for part-time students.
Students without need: No-need awards available for academics, athletics, leadership, minority status, state/district residency.

FINANCIAL AID PROCEDURES
Forms required: FAFSA, institutional form.
Dates and Deadlines: Priority date 4/15; closing date 6/30. Applicants notified on a rolling basis.

Transfers: No deadline. Applicants notified on a rolling basis.

CONTACT
Rosey Toney, Director of Financial Aid
201 Community College Drive, Baton Rouge, LA 70806
(225) 216-8640

Bossier Parish Community College

Bossier City, Louisiana
www.bpcc.edu/index.html   Federal Code: 012033

2-year public community college in small city.
Enrollment: 5,198 undergrads, 36% part-time. 945 full-time freshmen.
Selectivity: Open admission.

BASIC COSTS (2016-2017)
Tuition and fees: $4,139; out-of-state residents $8,816.

FINANCIAL AID PICTURE (2016-2017)
Students with need: Out of 851 full-time freshmen who applied for aid, 778 were judged to have need. Of these, 699 received aid, and 13 had their full need met. Average financial aid package met 27% of need; average scholarship/grant was $2,077; average loan was $2,443. For part-time students, average financial aid package was $9,094.
Students without need: 2 full-time freshmen who did not demonstrate need for aid received scholarships/grants; average award was $500. No-need awards available for academics, athletics, leadership, minority status, music/drama.
Scholarships offered: 10 full-time freshmen received athletic scholarships; average amount $1,741.

FINANCIAL AID PROCEDURES
Forms required: FAFSA.
Dates and Deadlines: Priority date 6/1; no closing date. Applicants notified on a rolling basis starting 4/1; must reply within 3 week(s) of notification.
Transfers: No deadline.

CONTACT
Vickie Temple, Financial Aid Director
6220 East Texas Street, Bossier City, LA 71111-6922
(318) 678-6026

Centenary College of Louisiana

Shreveport, Louisiana
www.centenary.edu   Federal Code: 002003

4-year private liberal arts college in large city, affiliated with the United Methodist Church.
Enrollment: 473 undergrads, 1% part-time. 130 full-time freshmen.
Selectivity: Admits 50 to 75% of applicants.

BASIC COSTS (2016-2017)
Tuition and fees: $35,430.
Room and board: $12,980.

FINANCIAL AID PICTURE (2016-2017)
Students with need: 87% of average financial aid package awarded as scholarships/grants, 13% awarded as loans/jobs. Need-based aid available for part-time students. Work study available nights, weekends, and for part-time students.
Students without need: No-need awards available for academics, alumni affiliation, art, music/drama, religious affiliation, state/district residency.

FINANCIAL AID PROCEDURES
Forms required: FAFSA.
Dates and Deadlines: Priority date 2/15; no closing date. Applicants notified on a rolling basis starting 3/15; must reply by 5/1.

Transfers: No deadline. Applicants notified on a rolling basis starting 2/15; must reply within 4 week(s) of notification.

CONTACT

Lynette Viskozki, Director of Financial Aid

Office of Admission, Shreveport, LA 71104

(318) 869-5137

Delgado Community College

New Orleans, Louisiana

www.dcc.edu   Federal Code: 004625

2-year public community college in large city.

Enrollment: 14,347 undergrads.

Selectivity: Open admission; but selective for some programs.

BASIC COSTS (2016-2017)

Tuition and fees: $3,911; out-of-state residents $8,200.

FINANCIAL AID PICTURE

Students with need: Need-based aid available for full-time and part-time students. Work study available nights.

Students without need: No-need awards available for academics, athletics, leadership, music/drama, state/district residency.

FINANCIAL AID PROCEDURES

Forms required: FAFSA, institutional form.

Dates and Deadlines: Priority date 5/1; closing date 7/15. Applicants notified on a rolling basis starting 4/1; must reply within 2 week(s) of notification.

CONTACT

Rhonda King, Director of Financial Aid

615 City Park Avenue, New Orleans, LA 70119

(855) 215-8247

Dillard University

New Orleans, Louisiana

www.dillard.edu   Federal Code: 002004

4-year private university and liberal arts college in large city, affiliated with the United Church of Christ.

Enrollment: 1,200 undergrads.

BASIC COSTS (2016-2017)

Tuition and fees: $17,004.

Room and board: $9,874.

FINANCIAL AID PICTURE

Students with need: Need-based aid available for full-time and part-time students. Work study available nights, weekends, and for part-time students.

Students without need: This college awards aid only to students with need.

FINANCIAL AID PROCEDURES

Forms required: FAFSA, institutional form.

Dates and Deadlines: Priority date 12/1; closing date 3/1. Applicants notified on a rolling basis starting 3/1; must reply by 5/1 or within 2 week(s) of notification.

CONTACT

Theodis Wright, Director of Financial Aid

2601 Gentilly Boulevard, New Orleans, LA 70122-3097

(800) 216-8094

Grambling State University

Grambling, Louisiana

www.gram.edu   Federal Code: 002006

4-year public university in small town.

Enrollment: 4,153 undergrads.

BASIC COSTS (2016-2017)

Tuition and fees: $7,379; out-of-state residents $16,394.

Room and board: $6,594.

FINANCIAL AID PICTURE

Students with need: Need-based aid available for full-time and part-time students. Work study available nights, weekends, and for part-time students.

Students without need: No-need awards available for academics, alumni affiliation, art, athletics, job skills, leadership, minority status, music/drama, religious affiliation, ROTC, state/district residency.

FINANCIAL AID PROCEDURES

Forms required: FAFSA.

Dates and Deadlines: Priority date 4/1; closing date 6/1. Applicants notified on a rolling basis starting 3/1; must reply within 2 week(s) of notification.

Transfers: Applicants notified on a rolling basis starting 3/1; must reply within 2 week(s) of notification.

CONTACT

Albert Tezno, Director of Student Financial Aid

403 Main Street, GSU Box 4200, Grambling, LA 71245

(318) 274-6190

Herzing University: Kenner

Kenner, Louisiana

www.herzing.edu   Federal Code: 020897

4-year for-profit branch campus and technical college in very large city.

Enrollment: 466 undergrads.

BASIC COSTS (2016-2017)

Additional info: Associate programs: $12,560- $13,000. Bachelor's programs $12,560- $13,000. All costs are subject to change.

FINANCIAL AID PICTURE

Students with need: Work study available nights, weekends, and for part-time students.

CONTACT

Ava Gomez, Financial Aid Director

2500 Williams Boulevard, Kenner, LA 70062

ITI Technical College

Baton Rouge, Louisiana

www.iticollege.edu   Federal Code: 015270

2-year for-profit technical and career college in large city.

Enrollment: 575 undergrads. 133 full-time freshmen.

Selectivity: Open admission; but selective for some programs.

FINANCIAL AID PICTURE

Students with need: Need-based aid available for full-time students.

Students without need: This college awards aid only to students with need.

FINANCIAL AID PROCEDURES

Forms required: FAFSA.

CONTACT

Connie Roubique, Financial Aid Director

13944 Airline Highway, Baton Rouge, LA 70817

(225) 752-4233 ext. 233

Louisiana College

Pineville, Louisiana
www.lacollege.edu   Federal Code: 002007

4-year private liberal arts college in small city, affiliated with the Southern Baptist Convention.
Enrollment: 868 undergrads, 4% part-time. 248 full-time freshmen.
Selectivity: Admits 50 to 75% of applicants.

BASIC COSTS (2017-2018)

Tuition and fees: $13,838.
Room and board: $5,224.
Additional info: Fees vary by major.

FINANCIAL AID PICTURE

Students with need: Need-based aid available for full-time and part-time students. Work study available nights, weekends, and for part-time students.
Students without need: No-need awards available for academics, art, leadership, music/drama, ROTC.

FINANCIAL AID PROCEDURES

Forms required: FAFSA, institutional form.
Dates and Deadlines: Priority date 3/31; no closing date. Applicants notified on a rolling basis starting 3/1; must reply by 5/1 or within 2 week(s) of notification.
Transfers: No deadline. Applicants notified on a rolling basis; must reply within 4 week(s) of notification. Scholarships available.

CONTACT

Jeremy Treme, Director of Financial Aid
LC Box 566, Pineville, LA 71359
(318) 487-7000 ext. 7386

Louisiana State University and Agricultural and Mechanical College

Baton Rouge, Louisiana
www.lsu.edu   Federal Code: 002010

4-year public university and agricultural college in small city.
Enrollment: 24,365 undergrads.

BASIC COSTS (2016-2017)

Tuition and fees: $10,814; out-of-state residents $27,491.
Room and board: $11,540.

FINANCIAL AID PICTURE

Students with need: Need-based aid available for full-time and part-time students. Work study available nights, weekends, and for part-time students.
Students without need: No-need awards available for academics, athletics, music/drama, ROTC.

FINANCIAL AID PROCEDURES

Forms required: FAFSA, institutional form.
Dates and Deadlines: Priority date 4/1; no closing date. Applicants notified on a rolling basis starting 12/15; must reply by 5/1.
Transfers: No deadline. Applicants notified on a rolling basis starting 10/1; must reply by 5/1 or within 3 week(s) of notification.

CONTACT

Amy Marix
1146 Pleasant Hall, Baton Rouge, LA 70803-2750
(225) 578-3103

Louisiana State University at Alexandria

Alexandria, Louisiana
www.lsua.edu   Federal Code: 002011

4-year public university in small city.
Enrollment: 2,528 undergrads, 32% part-time. 464 full-time freshmen.
Selectivity: Admits less than 50% of applicants. GED not accepted.

BASIC COSTS (2016-2017)

Tuition and fees: $6,707; out-of-state residents $13,973.

FINANCIAL AID PICTURE (2015-2016)

Students with need: Average financial aid package met 99% of need; average scholarship/grant was $8,514; average loan was $5,360. For part-time students, average financial aid package was $2,817.
Students without need: 51 full-time freshmen who did not demonstrate need for aid received scholarships/grants; average award was $9,706. No-need awards available for academics, athletics, ROTC.
Scholarships offered: 7 full-time freshmen received athletic scholarships; average amount $366.

FINANCIAL AID PROCEDURES

Forms required: FAFSA.
Dates and Deadlines: Applicants notified on a rolling basis starting 3/1; must reply within 3 week(s) of notification.
Transfers: No deadline. Applicants notified on a rolling basis starting 3/1; must reply within 3 week(s) of notification.

CONTACT

Deron Thaxton, Director of Financial Aid & Scholarships
8100 Highway 71 South, Alexandria, LA 71302-9121
(318) 473-6423

Louisiana State University at Eunice

Eunice, Louisiana
www.lsue.edu   Federal Code: 002012

2-year public nursing and junior college in large town.
Enrollment: 2,397 undergrads, 42% part-time. 625 full-time freshmen.
Selectivity: Open admission; but selective for some programs.

BASIC COSTS (2016-2017)

Tuition and fees: $4,306; out-of-state residents $9,670.

FINANCIAL AID PICTURE (2015-2016)

Students with need: Average financial aid package met 54% of need; average scholarship/grant was $2,368; average loan was $1,826. For part-time students, average financial aid package was $1,716.
Students without need: 270 full-time freshmen who did not demonstrate need for aid received scholarships/grants; average award was $995. No-need awards available for academics.
Scholarships offered: 33 full-time freshmen received athletic scholarships; average amount $2,271.

FINANCIAL AID PROCEDURES

Forms required: FAFSA, institutional form.
Dates and Deadlines: Priority date 6/1; no closing date. Applicants notified on a rolling basis starting 4/1; must reply within 2 week(s) of notification.
Transfers: No deadline. Applicants notified on a rolling basis starting 4/1; must reply within 2 week(s) of notification.

CONTACT

Jacqueline LaChapelle, Director of Financial Aid
PO Box 1129, Eunice, LA 70535
(337) 550-1282

Louisiana State University Health Sciences Center
New Orleans, Louisiana
www.lsuhsc.edu
Federal Code: 002014

Upper-division public health science and nursing college in large city.
Enrollment: 873 undergrads, 25% part-time.

BASIC COSTS (2016-2017)
Tuition and fees: $6,923; out-of-state residents $13,705.
Room only: $5,370.

FINANCIAL AID PICTURE
Students with need: Need-based aid available for full-time and part-time students. Work study available nights, weekends, and for part-time students.
Students without need: No-need awards available for academics.

FINANCIAL AID PROCEDURES
Forms required: FAFSA, institutional form.
Dates and Deadlines: Priority date 4/15; no closing date. Applicants notified on a rolling basis starting 7/1.

CONTACT
Patrick Gorman, Director of Financial Aid
433 Bolivar Street, New Orleans, LA 70112-7021
(504) 568-4820

Louisiana State University in Shreveport
Shreveport, Louisiana
www.lsus.edu
Federal Code: 002013

4-year public university and teachers college in large city.
Enrollment: 2,233 undergrads, 25% part-time. 251 full-time freshmen.
Selectivity: Admits over 75% of applicants.

BASIC COSTS (2016-2017)
Tuition and fees: $7,264; out-of-state residents $20,418.

FINANCIAL AID PICTURE
Students with need: Need-based aid available for full-time and part-time students. Work study available nights, weekends, and for part-time students.
Students without need: No-need awards available for academics, athletics.

FINANCIAL AID PROCEDURES
Dates and Deadlines: Applicants notified on a rolling basis.

CONTACT
One University Place, Shreveport, LA 71115-2399

Louisiana Tech University
Ruston, Louisiana
www.latech.edu
Federal Code: 002008

4-year public university in large town.
Enrollment: 8,009 undergrads.
Selectivity: GED not accepted.

BASIC COSTS (2016-2017)
Tuition and fees: $8,847; out-of-state residents $29,370.
Room and board: $6,330.

FINANCIAL AID PICTURE
Students with need: Need-based aid available for full-time and part-time students.
Students without need: No-need awards available for academics, alumni affiliation, art, athletics, job skills, leadership, music/drama, ROTC, state/district residency.

FINANCIAL AID PROCEDURES
Forms required: FAFSA, institutional form.
Dates and Deadlines: Priority date 4/15; no closing date. Applicants notified on a rolling basis starting 4/1; must reply within 3 week(s) of notification.
Transfers: Priority date 8/1; no deadline. Applicants notified on a rolling basis starting 8/20; must reply within 2 week(s) of notification.

CONTACT
Aimee Baxter, Director of Student Financial Aid
Box 3178, Ruston, LA 71272
(318) 257-2641

Loyola University New Orleans
New Orleans, Louisiana
www.loyno.edu
Federal Code: 002016

4-year private university and liberal arts college in large city, affiliated with the Roman Catholic Church.
Enrollment: 2,399 undergrads, 5% part-time. 614 full-time freshmen.
Selectivity: Admits 50 to 75% of applicants.

BASIC COSTS (2017-2018)
Tuition and fees: $39,242.
Per-credit charge: $1,073.
Room and board: $13,214.

FINANCIAL AID PICTURE (2015-2016)
Students with need: Out of 575 full-time freshmen who applied for aid, 490 were judged to have need. Of these, 490 received aid, and 70 had their full need met. Average financial aid package met 82% of need; average scholarship/grant was $30,311; average loan was $3,308. For part-time students, average financial aid package was $8,017.
Students without need: 114 full-time freshmen who did not demonstrate need for aid received scholarships/grants; average award was $17,357. No-need awards available for academics, alumni affiliation, art, athletics, music/drama, ROTC.
Scholarships offered: 20 full-time freshmen received athletic scholarships; average amount $8,599.

FINANCIAL AID PROCEDURES
Forms required: FAFSA.
Dates and Deadlines: Priority date 3/1; no closing date. Applicants notified by 3/30; must reply within 2 week(s) of notification.
Transfers: Priority date 3/1; no deadline. Applicants notified on a rolling basis starting 3/1; must reply within 2 week(s) of notification. Transfer scholarship deadline June 1.

CONTACT
Carrie Glass, Director of Scholarships and Financial Aid
6363 St. Charles Avenue, New Orleans, LA 70118-6195
(504) 865-3231

McNeese State University
Lake Charles, Louisiana
www.mcneese.edu
Federal Code: 002017

4-year public university in small city.
Enrollment: 6,155 undergrads, 12% part-time. 1,339 full-time freshmen.
Selectivity: Admits 50 to 75% of applicants.

BASIC COSTS (2016-2017)
Tuition and fees: $7,324; out-of-state residents $18,399.
Room and board: $5,810.

FINANCIAL AID PICTURE (2015-2016)

Students with need: Out of 1,189 full-time freshmen who applied for aid, 850 were judged to have need. Of these, 835 received aid. Need-based aid available for part-time students.

Students without need: No-need awards available for academics, alumni affiliation, art, athletics, leadership, minority status, music/drama, state/district residency.

Additional info: Books may be charged and paid in 2 installments during semester.

FINANCIAL AID PROCEDURES

Forms required: FAFSA, institutional form.

Dates and Deadlines: Priority date 5/1; no closing date. Applicants notified on a rolling basis.

Transfers: Transfer students must exhibit satisfactory academic progress at school most recently attended to be eligible for financial aid.

CONTACT

Taina Savoit, Director of Financial Aid
MSU Box 91740, Lake Charles, LA 70609-1740
(337) 475-5065

Nicholls State University

Thibodaux, Louisiana
www.nicholls.edu   Federal Code: 002005

4-year public university in large town.
Enrollment: 5,280 undergrads, 13% part-time. 1,078 full-time freshmen.
Selectivity: Admits over 75% of applicants.

BASIC COSTS (2016-2017)
Tuition and fees: $7,671; out-of-state residents $18,602.
Room and board: $7,692.

FINANCIAL AID PICTURE

Students with need: Need-based aid available for full-time and part-time students. Work study available nights, weekends, and for part-time students.

Students without need: No-need awards available for academics, athletics, leadership, minority status, music/drama, state/district residency.

FINANCIAL AID PROCEDURES

Forms required: FAFSA, institutional form.

Dates and Deadlines: Priority date 4/15; closing date 6/30. Applicants notified on a rolling basis.

Transfers: Priority date 5/1; no deadline. Applicants notified on a rolling basis.

CONTACT

Casie Triche, Director of Financial Aid
PO Box 2004-NSU, Thibodaux, LA 70310
(985) 448-4048

Northwestern State University

Natchitoches, Louisiana
www.nsula.edu   Federal Code: 002021

4-year public university in large town.
Enrollment: 7,401 undergrads, 30% part-time. 1,306 full-time freshmen.
Selectivity: Admits 50 to 75% of applicants.

BASIC COSTS (2016-2017)
Tuition and fees: $7,102; out-of-state residents $17,890.
Room and board: $8,914.

FINANCIAL AID PICTURE (2015-2016)

Students with need: Need-based aid available for full-time and part-time students. Work study available nights, weekends, and for part-time students.

Students without need: No-need awards available for academics, alumni affiliation, art, athletics, job skills, leadership, minority status, music/drama, religious affiliation, ROTC, state/district residency.

FINANCIAL AID PROCEDURES

Forms required: FAFSA, institutional form.

Dates and Deadlines: Priority date 5/1; no closing date. Applicants notified on a rolling basis starting 5/1; must reply within 4 week(s) of notification.

Transfers: No deadline. Applicants notified on a rolling basis starting 5/1; must reply within 4 week(s) of notification.

CONTACT

Lauren Jackson, Director of Financial Aid
175 Sam Sibley Drive, Student Services Center, Suite 235, Natchitoches, LA 71497
(800) 823-3008

Nunez Community College

Chalmette, Louisiana
www.nunez.edu   Federal Code: 015130

2-year public community and technical college in large town.
Enrollment: 1,454 undergrads, 47% part-time. 137 full-time freshmen.
Selectivity: Open admission; but selective for some programs.

BASIC COSTS (2016-2017)
Tuition and fees: $4,103; out-of-state residents $7,602.
Additional info: Tuition/fee waivers available for minority students.

FINANCIAL AID PICTURE (2015-2016)

Students with need: 92% of average financial aid package awarded as scholarships/grants, 8% awarded as loans/jobs. Need-based aid available for part-time students. Work study available nights.

Additional info: Pell Grants, Stafford Loans, campus work-study, and tuition waiver scholarships available. Louisiana National Guard tuition exemption, teacher tuition exemption, dependents of injured fire-police tuition waivers available.

FINANCIAL AID PROCEDURES

Forms required: FAFSA.

Dates and Deadlines: Priority date 6/1; closing date 8/1.

Transfers: Applicant must supply academic transcripts from every post-secondary school attended before aid is awarded.

CONTACT

John Whisnant, Financial Aid Officer
3710 Paris Road, Chalmette, LA 70043
(504) 278-6478

Our Lady of the Lake College

Baton Rouge, Louisiana
www.ololcollege.edu   Federal Code: 031062

4-year private health science and nursing college in large city, affiliated with the Roman Catholic Church.
Enrollment: 1,254 undergrads.

BASIC COSTS (2016-2017)
Tuition and fees: $15,396.

FINANCIAL AID PICTURE (2015-2016)

Students with need: 35% of average financial aid package awarded as scholarships/grants, 65% awarded as loans/jobs.

Students without need: No-need awards available for academics.

FINANCIAL AID PROCEDURES

Forms required: FAFSA, institutional form.

Dates and Deadlines: Priority date 3/1; no closing date.

CONTACT
Terry Martin, Director of Financial Aid
5414 Brittany Drive, Baton Rouge, LA 70808
(225) 768-1714

Remington College: Baton Rouge
Baton Rouge, Louisiana
http://baton-rouge.remingtoncollege.edu
Federal Code: E00907

2-year private technical college in large city.
Enrollment: 547 undergrads.
Selectivity: Open admission; but selective for some programs.

BASIC COSTS (2016-2017)
Additional info: Total program tuition: Associates $33,900.

FINANCIAL AID PICTURE
Students with need: Need-based aid available for full-time students. Work study available nights.
Students without need: This college awards aid only to students with need.

FINANCIAL AID PROCEDURES
Forms required: FAFSA.
Dates and Deadlines: Applicants notified on a rolling basis; must reply within 1 week(s) of notification.

CONTACT
James Dunn, National Director of Financial Aid
10551 Coursey Boulevard, Baton Rouge, LA 70816
(225) 236-3200

Remington College: Lafayette
Lafayette, Louisiana
http://lafayette.remingtoncollege.edu
Federal Code: 005203

2-year private junior college in small city.
Enrollment: 585 undergrads.
Selectivity: Open admission; but selective for some programs.

BASIC COSTS (2016-2017)
Additional info: Total program tuition: diplomas $15,995-$21,700; associates $27,360- $33,900.

FINANCIAL AID PICTURE
Students with need: Need-based aid available for full-time students. Work study available nights.
Students without need: This college awards aid only to students with need.

FINANCIAL AID PROCEDURES
Forms required: FAFSA, institutional form.

CONTACT
James Dunn, National Director of Financial Aid
303 Rue Louis XIV, Lafayette, LA 70508

River Parishes Community College
Gonzales, Louisiana
www.rpcc.edu
Federal Code: 037894

2-year public community college in rural community.
Enrollment: 3,576 undergrads.

Selectivity: Open admission; but selective for some programs.

BASIC COSTS (2016-2017)
Tuition and fees: $4,079; out-of-state residents $8,123.

FINANCIAL AID PICTURE (2015-2016)
Students with need: 65% of average financial aid package awarded as scholarships/grants, 35% awarded as loans/jobs.

FINANCIAL AID PROCEDURES
Forms required: FAFSA.
Dates and Deadlines: Priority date 4/15; no closing date. Applicants notified on a rolling basis starting 3/1.

CONTACT
Director of Financial Aid
PO Box 2367, Gonzales, LA 70737
(225) 743-8500

St. Joseph Seminary College
St. Benedict, Louisiana
www.sjasc.edu
Federal Code: 002027

4-year private liberal arts and seminary college for men in rural community, affiliated with the Roman Catholic Church.
Enrollment: 137 undergrads.

BASIC COSTS (2016-2017)
Tuition and fees: $16,550.
Per-credit charge: $260.
Room and board: $14,120.

FINANCIAL AID PICTURE
Students with need: Need-based aid available for full-time and part-time students.
Students without need: No-need awards available for academics, leadership.

FINANCIAL AID PROCEDURES
Forms required: FAFSA.
Dates and Deadlines: Priority date 3/15; no closing date. Applicants notified on a rolling basis starting 7/1; must reply within 4 week(s) of notification.
Transfers: Closing date 5/1. Applicants notified on a rolling basis starting 7/1; must reply within 4 week(s) of notification.

CONTACT
Caroline Bizot, Director of Student Financial Aid
75376 River Road, St. Benedict, LA 70457-9990
(985) 867-2248

South Louisiana Community College
Lafayette, Louisiana
www.solacc.edu
Federal Code: 039563

2-year public community college in small city.
Enrollment: 5,640 undergrads.
Selectivity: Open admission; but selective for some programs.

BASIC COSTS (2016-2017)
Tuition and fees: $4,205; out-of-state residents $7,810.

FINANCIAL AID PICTURE
Students with need: Need-based aid available for full-time and part-time students.
Students without need: No-need awards available for academics, leadership, state/district residency.

FINANCIAL AID PROCEDURES
Forms required: FAFSA, institutional form.

Dates and Deadlines: Priority date 5/15; no closing date.

CONTACT
Director of Financial Aid
1101 Bertrand Dr., Lafayette, LA 70506-4124
(337) 521-8910

Southeastern Louisiana University
Hammond, Louisiana
www.southeastern.edu   Federal Code: 002024

4-year public university in large town.
Enrollment: 10,836 undergrads, 17% part-time. 2,157 full-time freshmen.
Selectivity: Admits over 75% of applicants.

BASIC COSTS (2016-2017)
Tuition and fees: $8,042; out-of-state residents $20,521.
Room and board: $6,460.

FINANCIAL AID PICTURE (2015-2016)
Students with need: Out of 2,074 full-time freshmen who applied for aid, 1,639 were judged to have need. Of these, 1,614 received aid, and 221 had their full need met. For part-time students, average financial aid package was $5,584.
Students without need: 213 full-time freshmen who did not demonstrate need for aid received scholarships/grants; average award was $1,720. No-need awards available for academics, athletics, job skills, leadership, music/drama, state/district residency.
Scholarships offered: Merit: Various scholarships: $1,000-$3,500; any student admitted with 24 ACT and 3.0 GPA on a seven-semester transcript qualifies for scholarship. On-campus housing scholarships: range from half-room award to full-room award; based on ACT and GPA. Presidential Honors Scholarship: $2,500-$3,500 plus on-campus housing and meals; based on 30 ACT, 3.0 GPA. **Athletic:** 54 full-time freshmen received athletic scholarships; average amount $9,845.

FINANCIAL AID PROCEDURES
Forms required: FAFSA.
Dates and Deadlines: Priority date 5/1; no closing date. Applicants notified on a rolling basis starting 4/1; must reply within 2 week(s) of notification.
Transfers: Applicants notified on a rolling basis starting 3/1; must reply within 2 week(s) of notification. Financial aid is available for transfer students, including those admitted on probation.

CONTACT
Charles Cambre, Director of Financial Aid
SLU 10752, Hammond, LA 70402
(985) 549-2244

Southern University and Agricultural and Mechanical College
Baton Rouge, Louisiana
www.subr.edu   Federal Code: 002025

4-year public university in large city.
Enrollment: 5,181 undergrads, 12% part-time. 1,061 full-time freshmen.

BASIC COSTS (2016-2017)
Tuition and fees: $8,094; out-of-state residents $15,444.
Room and board: $14,862.

FINANCIAL AID PICTURE (2016-2017)
Students with need: 59% of average financial aid package awarded as scholarships/grants, 41% awarded as loans/jobs.
Students without need: No-need awards available for academics, athletics, ROTC, state/district residency.

Scholarships offered: College of Education, Arts and Humanities Scholarship: full-tuition; based on 22 ACT (or comparable SAT), 3.2 GPA, evidence of community involvement/extracurricular activities; two letters of recommendation. College of Education, Arts and Humanities Scholarship: tuition only; based on 20 ACT (or comparable SAT), 3.0 GPA, evidence of community involvement/extracurricular activities; two letters of recommendation.

FINANCIAL AID PROCEDURES
Forms required: FAFSA.
Dates and Deadlines: Priority date 1/31; closing date 3/30. Applicants notified on a rolling basis starting 5/1; must reply within 3 week(s) of notification.
Transfers: Closing date 5/31. Applicants notified on a rolling basis starting 5/31; must reply within 3 week(s) of notification.

CONTACT
Ursula Shorty, Director of Student Fianacial Aid
T.H. Harris Hall, Baton Rouge, LA 70813
(225) 771-2790 ext. 2790

Southern University at New Orleans
New Orleans, Louisiana
www.suno.edu   Federal Code: 002026

4-year public university in large city.
Enrollment: 1,745 undergrads.
Selectivity: Admits less than 50% of applicants.

BASIC COSTS (2016-2017)
Tuition and fees: $6,421; out-of-state residents $15,322.
Room and board: $8,780.

FINANCIAL AID PICTURE
Students with need: Need-based aid available for full-time and part-time students.
Students without need: This college awards aid only to students with need.

FINANCIAL AID PROCEDURES
Forms required: FAFSA.
Dates and Deadlines: Closing date 4/15. Applicants notified by 5/15; must reply within 1 week(s) of notification.

CONTACT
La'Charlotte' Garrett, Director of Financial Aid
6400 Press Drive, New Orleans, LA 70126
(504) 286-5263

Tulane University
New Orleans, Louisiana   Federal Code: 002029
www.tulane.edu   CSS Code: 6832

4-year private university in very large city.
Enrollment: 6,821 undergrads. 1,856 full-time freshmen.
Selectivity: Admits less than 50% of applicants.

BASIC COSTS (2016-2017)
Tuition and fees: $51,010.
Per-credit charge: $1,964.
Room and board: $13,844.

FINANCIAL AID PICTURE (2016-2017)
Students with need: Out of 1,045 full-time freshmen who applied for aid, 614 were judged to have need. Of these, 614 received aid, and 410 had their full need met. Average financial aid package met 98% of need; average scholarship/grant was $32,702; average loan was $7,005. For part-time students, average financial aid package was $18,149.

Students without need: 674 full-time freshmen who did not demonstrate need for aid received scholarships/grants; average award was $27,266. No-need awards available for academics, athletics, leadership, music/drama, ROTC, state/district residency.

Scholarships offered: *Merit:* Dean's Honor Scholarship: full-tuition. Distinguished Scholars Award: partial tuition. Founders Scholarship: partial tuition. Urban Scholars Award: full-tuition. *Athletic:* 41 full-time freshmen received athletic scholarships; average amount $48,169.

FINANCIAL AID PROCEDURES

Forms required: FAFSA, CSS PROFILE.

Dates and Deadlines: Priority date 2/15; no closing date. Applicants notified on a rolling basis starting 3/15; must reply by 5/1.

Transfers: Applicants notified on a rolling basis starting 2/1; must reply by 5/1 or within 2 week(s) of notification.

CONTACT

Michael Goodman, Associate Vice President for Financial Aid

6823 St. Charles Avenue, New Orleans, LA 70118-5680

(504) 865-5723

University of Holy Cross

New Orleans, Louisiana

www.olhcc.edu   Federal Code: 002023

4-year private liberal arts college in very large city, affiliated with the Roman Catholic Church.

Enrollment: 940 undergrads.

BASIC COSTS (2016-2017)

Tuition and fees: $14,242.

Per-credit charge: $435.

FINANCIAL AID PICTURE

Students with need: Need-based aid available for full-time and part-time students. Work study available nights, weekends, and for part-time students.

Students without need: No-need awards available for academics, state/district residency.

FINANCIAL AID PROCEDURES

Forms required: FAFSA.

Dates and Deadlines: Priority date 7/1; no closing date. Applicants notified on a rolling basis starting 5/15; must reply within 4 week(s) of notification.

Transfers: Must reply within 2 week(s) of notification.

CONTACT

Anna Vaughan, Financial Aid Coordinator

4123 Woodland Drive, New Orleans, LA 70131-7399

(504) 394-7744

University of Louisiana at Lafayette

Lafayette, Louisiana

www.louisiana.edu   Federal Code: 002031

4-year public university in small city.

Enrollment: 15,091 undergrads.

BASIC COSTS (2016-2017)

Tuition and fees: $10,050; out-of-state residents $23,778.

Room and board: $8,112.

FINANCIAL AID PICTURE

Students with need: Need-based aid available for full-time and part-time students. Work study available nights, weekends, and for part-time students.

Students without need: This college awards aid only to students with need.

FINANCIAL AID PROCEDURES

Forms required: FAFSA.

Dates and Deadlines: Priority date 5/1; no closing date. Applicants notified on a rolling basis starting 4/1; must reply within 2 week(s) of notification.

Transfers: Applicants notified on a rolling basis starting 5/1; must reply within 2 week(s) of notification.

CONTACT

Cindy Perez, Director, Student Financial Aid

Box 41210, Lafayette, LA 70504-1210

(337) 482-6506

University of Louisiana at Monroe

Monroe, Louisiana

www.ulm.edu   Federal Code: 002020

4-year public university in small city.

Enrollment: 7,778 undergrads, 33% part-time. 713 full-time freshmen.

Selectivity: Admits over 75% of applicants.

BASIC COSTS (2016-2017)

Tuition and fees: $7,658; out-of-state residents $19,758.

Room and board: $7,400.

FINANCIAL AID PICTURE (2016-2017)

Students with need: Need-based aid available for part-time students.

Students without need: No-need awards available for academics, athletics, ROTC.

FINANCIAL AID PROCEDURES

Forms required: FAFSA.

Dates and Deadlines: Closing date 6/30. Applicants notified on a rolling basis starting 6/1; must reply within 2 week(s) of notification.

CONTACT

Frankie Everett, Director of Financial Aid

700 University Avenue, Monroe, LA 71209-1160

(318) 342-5320

University of New Orleans

New Orleans, Louisiana

www.uno.edu   Federal Code: 002015

4-year public university in very large city.

Enrollment: 5,987 undergrads, 22% part-time. 850 full-time freshmen.

Selectivity: Admits 50 to 75% of applicants.

BASIC COSTS (2016-2017)

Tuition and fees: $8,694; out-of-state residents $22,511.

Per-credit charge: $203; out-of-state residents $663.

Room and board: $9,730.

FINANCIAL AID PICTURE (2016-2017)

Students with need: Out of 816 full-time freshmen who applied for aid, 679 were judged to have need. Of these, 654 received aid, and 52 had their full need met. Average financial aid package met 62% of need; average scholarship/grant was $5,838; average loan was $3,422. For part-time students, average financial aid package was $5,109.

Students without need: 97 full-time freshmen who did not demonstrate need for aid received scholarships/grants; average award was $2,271. No-need awards available for academics, athletics, music/drama.

Scholarships offered: 22 full-time freshmen received athletic scholarships; average amount $4,804.

Additional info: Students in good academic and financial standing eligible to participate in Extended Payment Plan option.

FINANCIAL AID PROCEDURES

Forms required: FAFSA.

Transfers: Mid-year transfers must submit financial aid transcript from all post-secondary schools attended. Others submit NSLDS.

CONTACT

Ann Lockridge, Director Financial Aid and Scholarships

University of New Orleans, 105 Earl K. Long Library, New Orleans, LA 70148

(504) 280-6603

Xavier University of Louisiana

New Orleans, Louisiana

www.xula.edu   Federal Code: 002032

4-year private university in large city, affiliated with the Roman Catholic Church.

Enrollment: 2,293 undergrads, 4% part-time. 684 full-time freshmen.

Selectivity: Admits 50 to 75% of applicants.

BASIC COSTS (2016-2017)

Tuition and fees: $23,046.

Per-credit charge: $858.

Room and board: $8,523.

FINANCIAL AID PICTURE (2015-2016)

Students with need: Out of 669 full-time freshmen who applied for aid, 592 were judged to have need. Of these, 592 received aid, and 2 had their full need met. Average financial aid package met 13% of need; average scholarship/grant was $5,773; average loan was $4,698. For part-time students, average financial aid package was $12,261.

Students without need: 51 full-time freshmen who did not demonstrate need for aid received scholarships/grants; average award was $12,833. No-need awards available for academics, art, athletics, music/drama, ROTC, state/district residency.

Scholarships offered: 20 full-time freshmen received athletic scholarships; average amount $14,963.

FINANCIAL AID PROCEDURES

Forms required: FAFSA.

Dates and Deadlines: Applicants notified on a rolling basis.

CONTACT

Emily Jones, Director of Financial Aid

One Drexel Drive, New Orleans, LA 70125-1098

(504) 520-7517

Maine

Bates College

Lewiston, Maine   Federal Code: 002036

www.bates.edu   CSS Code: 3076

4-year private liberal arts college in small city.

Enrollment: 1,780 undergrads. 498 full-time freshmen.

Selectivity: Admits less than 50% of applicants. GED not accepted.

BASIC COSTS (2016-2017)

Tuition and fees: $50,310.

Room and board: $14,190.

FINANCIAL AID PICTURE (2016-2017)

Students with need: Out of 245 full-time freshmen who applied for aid, 210 were judged to have need. Of these, 210 received aid, and 210 had

---

their full need met. Average financial aid package met 100% of need; average scholarship/grant was $43,506; average loan was $2,235.

Students without need: This college awards aid only to students with need.

Additional info: Priority date for filing required financial aid forms for early decision students is 11/15.

FINANCIAL AID PROCEDURES

Forms required: FAFSA, CSS PROFILE.

Dates and Deadlines: Closing date 1/1. Applicants notified by 4/1; must reply by 5/1.

Transfers: Closing date 3/1. Applicants notified by 6/1; must reply by 6/15.

CONTACT

Geoffrey Swift, Director of Student Financial Services

23 Campus Avenue, Lindholm House, Lewiston, ME 04240

(207) 786-6096

Bowdoin College

Brunswick, Maine   Federal Code: 002038

www.bowdoin.edu   CSS Code: 3089

4-year private liberal arts college in large town.

Enrollment: 1,799 undergrads. 503 full-time freshmen.

Selectivity: Admits less than 50% of applicants. GED not accepted.

BASIC COSTS (2016-2017)

Tuition and fees: $49,900.

Per-credit charge: $965.

Room and board: $13,600.

FINANCIAL AID PICTURE (2016-2017)

Students with need: Out of 290 full-time freshmen who applied for aid, 235 were judged to have need. Of these, 235 received aid, and 235 had their full need met. Average financial aid package met 100% of need; average scholarship/grant was $42,254.

Students without need: 6 full-time freshmen who did not demonstrate need for aid received scholarships/grants; average award was $1,000. No-need awards available for academics, leadership.

Additional info: Regardless of financial circumstances, students admitted will receive the money they need to attend. International students for regular admission must submit their financial aid applications by January 1st.

FINANCIAL AID PROCEDURES

Forms required: FAFSA, CSS PROFILE.

Dates and Deadlines: Closing date 2/15. Applicants notified by 3/20; must reply by 5/1 or within 1 week(s) of notification.

Transfers: Closing date 3/1. Applicants notified by 5/1; must reply by 6/1 or within 1 week(s) of notification. Financial aid usually not available for transfer students. Early Decision applicants must submit financial aid applications by November 15 (ED I) and January 1 (ED II).

CONTACT

Michael Bartini, Director of Student Aid

5000 College Station, Brunswick, ME 04011-8441

(207) 725-3144

Central Maine Community College

Auburn, Maine

www.cmcc.edu   Federal Code: 005276

2-year public community and technical college in small city.

Enrollment: 2,404 undergrads, 44% part-time. 998 full-time freshmen.

Selectivity: Open admission; but selective for some programs.

BASIC COSTS (2016-2017)

Tuition and fees: $3,570; out-of-state residents $6,330.

Per-credit charge: $92; out-of-state residents $184.

Room and board: $8,770.

FINANCIAL AID PICTURE (2015-2016)

Students with need: Out of 937 full-time freshmen who applied for aid, 849 were judged to have need. Of these, 832 received aid, and 144 had their full need met. Average financial aid package met 63% of need; average scholarship/grant was $5,354; average loan was $5,310. For part-time students, average financial aid package was $5,761.

Additional info: Tuition and/or fee waivers may be available to orphans, Native Americans, fire fighters, police, disabled veterans, dependents or survivors of veterans killed in line of duty.

FINANCIAL AID PROCEDURES

Forms required: FAFSA.

Dates and Deadlines: Priority date 5/1; no closing date. Applicants notified on a rolling basis starting 11/1.

Transfers: No deadline. Applicants notified on a rolling basis starting 11/1.

CONTACT

John Bowie, Director of Financial Aid

1250 Turner Street, Auburn, ME 04210-6498

(207) 755-5273

Colby College

Waterville, Maine
www.colby.edu

Federal Code: 002039
CSS Code: 3280

4-year private liberal arts college in large town.

Enrollment: 1,879 undergrads. 510 full-time freshmen.

Selectivity: Admits less than 50% of applicants.

BASIC COSTS (2016-2017)

Tuition and fees: $50,960.

Per-credit charge: $1,880.

Room and board: $13,100.

FINANCIAL AID PICTURE (2016-2017)

Students with need: Out of 293 full-time freshmen who applied for aid, 237 were judged to have need. Of these, 237 received aid, and 237 had their full need met. Average financial aid package met 100% of need; average scholarship/grant was $46,261; average loan was $2,838.

Additional info: Packaged loans have been replaced with institutional grants.

FINANCIAL AID PROCEDURES

Forms required: FAFSA. Required if they want to be eligible for any aid beyond federal aid.

Dates and Deadlines: Closing date 2/1. Applicants notified by 4/1; must reply by 5/1.

Transfers: Closing date 3/1. Applicants notified by 5/30; must reply within 2 week(s) of notification. Students admitted as other than first semester freshmen are eligible for Colby aid for the number of semesters required for graduation as determined by the College at the time of entry.

CONTACT

Elreo Campbell, Director of Financial Aid and Associate Dean of Admissions and Financial Aid

4800 Mayflower Hill, Waterville, ME 04901-8848

(800) 723-3032

College of the Atlantic

Bar Harbor, Maine
www.coa.edu

Federal Code: 011385

4-year private liberal arts college in small town.

Enrollment: 333 undergrads, 7% part-time. 79 full-time freshmen.

Selectivity: Admits 50 to 75% of applicants.

BASIC COSTS (2016-2017)

Tuition and fees: $43,542.

Per-credit charge: $1,433.

Room and board: $9,747.

FINANCIAL AID PICTURE (2016-2017)

Students with need: Out of 75 full-time freshmen who applied for aid, 71 were judged to have need. Of these, 71 received aid, and 37 had their full need met. Average financial aid package met 97% of need; average scholarship/grant was $39,592; average loan was $4,183. For part-time students, average financial aid package was $31,187.

Students without need: 5 full-time freshmen who did not demonstrate need for aid received scholarships/grants; average award was $16,279. No-need awards available for academics, leadership.

Scholarships offered: Students from selected secondary schools, special programs such as robotics, selected summer programs, may receive $10,000 a year in scholarships; graduates of community colleges with a 3.0 average may be eligible for $15,000 per year scholarship.

Additional info: Low-cost classes available for local residents; some business courses covered by grant to the college.

FINANCIAL AID PROCEDURES

Forms required: FAFSA, institutional form.

Dates and Deadlines: Priority date 2/1; closing date 2/1. Applicants notified by 4/1; must reply by 5/1.

Transfers: Closing date 2/1. Applicants notified by 4/1; must reply by 5/1. FAFSA must be filed by 5/1 for Maine residents to be eligible for Maine state grant.

CONTACT

Bruce Hazam, Director of Financial Aid

105 Eden Street, Bar Harbor, ME 04609

(207) 288-5015

Eastern Maine Community College

Bangor, Maine
www.emcc.edu

Federal Code: 005277

2-year public community and technical college in large town.

Enrollment: 2,620 undergrads.

Selectivity: Open admission; but selective for some programs.

BASIC COSTS (2016-2017)

Tuition and fees: $3,676; out-of-state residents $6,436.

Per-credit charge: $92; out-of-state residents $184.

Room and board: $8,130.

FINANCIAL AID PICTURE

Students with need: Need-based aid available for full-time and part-time students. Work study available nights, weekends, and for part-time students.

Students without need: This college awards aid only to students with need.

FINANCIAL AID PROCEDURES

Forms required: FAFSA.

Dates and Deadlines: Priority date 5/1; no closing date. Applicants notified on a rolling basis starting 5/1; must reply within 3 week(s) of notification.

CONTACT
Candace Ward, Registrar/Financial Aid Director
354 Hogan Road, Bangor, ME 04401
(207) 974-4625

Husson University
Bangor, Maine
www.husson.edu   Federal Code: 002043

4-year private business and health science college in large town.
Enrollment: 2,724 undergrads, 14% part-time. 613 full-time freshmen.
Selectivity: Admits over 75% of applicants.

BASIC COSTS (2016-2017)
Tuition and fees: $17,037.
Per-credit charge: $535.
Room and board: $9,220.
Additional info: Some programs have additional lab fees, $820 per year for programs within the New England School of Communications.

FINANCIAL AID PICTURE (2016-2017)
Students with need: Out of 576 full-time freshmen who applied for aid, 497 were judged to have need. Of these, 497 received aid, and 135 had their full need met. Average financial aid package met 72% of need; average scholarship/grant was $9,452; average loan was $3,300. For part-time students, average financial aid package was $5,980.
Students without need: 68 full-time freshmen who did not demonstrate need for aid received scholarships/grants; average award was $3,346. No-need awards available for academics, alumni affiliation, leadership.
Scholarships offered: President's Academic Scholarship: $16,000 over 4 years; min SAT score of 1500 or 22 on the ACT; A average; ranked at the top of class. Provost's Leadership Scholarship: $8,000-$12,000 over 4 years; min SAT score of 1500 or 22 on the ACT; B average or better; ranked near the top of class; nonathletic activities. Dean's Leadership Scholarship: $4,000-$6,000 over 4 years; min SAT score of 1500 or 22 on the ACT; B average or better; history of strong academic performance; nonathletic activities. Future Educator Scholarship: $8,000 over 4 years; for students accepted in the Teacher Education Pine Tree Scholarship: $8,000 over 4 years; out-of-state recognition scholarship based on SAT scores, class rank, and GPA; awarded to first-year entering students only. Scholarships with an Admissions Application Deadline of April 1 or Open-Ended (applications must be complete to be considered). Legacy Scholarship: $4,000 over 4 years; student must have had a parent, grandparent, or great grandparent, who graduated from Husson to receive this scholarship. President's Global Scholarship: $4,000-$20,000 over 4 years; based on merit; the student must provide proof of financial responsibility and be eligible for an I-20 student visa for consideration. Transfer Scholarship: $1,000 for a 2.5 GPA per year; $2,000 for a 3.0 GPA per year. Business CEO Scholarship: $2,000 over 4 years; for select business and criminal justice students; based on SAT scores, class rank, and GPA; completed admissions applications must be received no later than April 1, 2015. AHEAD Scholarship (Affirming Husson's Educational Access and Diversity): $8,000 over 4 years; eligible students must come from a multicultural background to be considered for this limited award; completed admissions applications must be received no later than April 1.

FINANCIAL AID PROCEDURES
Forms required: FAFSA.
Dates and Deadlines: Priority date 4/15; no closing date. Applicants notified on a rolling basis starting 12/1; must reply by 5/1 or within 2 week(s) of notification.
Transfers: No deadline. Applicants notified on a rolling basis starting 2/20; must reply within 2 week(s) of notification.

CONTACT
Anne Tabor, Director of Financial Aid
1 College Circle, Bangor, ME 04401-2999
(207) 941-7156

Kennebec Valley Community College
Fairfield, Maine
www.kvcc.me.edu   Federal Code: 009826

2-year public community and technical college in small town.
Enrollment: 1,613 undergrads, 61% part-time. 790 full-time freshmen.
Selectivity: Open admission; but selective for some programs.

BASIC COSTS (2016-2017)
Tuition and fees: $3,425; out-of-state residents $6,185.
Per-credit charge: $92; out-of-state residents $138.

FINANCIAL AID PICTURE (2015-2016)
Students with need: Out of 786 full-time freshmen who applied for aid, 655 were judged to have need. Of these, 150 received aid, and 5 had their full need met. Average financial aid package met 12% of need; average scholarship/grant was $6,438; average loan was $3,144. For part-time students, average financial aid package was $5,204.
Students without need: This college awards aid only to students with need.

FINANCIAL AID PROCEDURES
Forms required: FAFSA, institutional form.
Dates and Deadlines: Priority date 4/1; no closing date. Applicants notified on a rolling basis starting 5/1.
Transfers: No deadline. Applicants notified on a rolling basis.

CONTACT
Anne Connors, Director of Financial Aid
92 Western Avenue, Fairfield, ME 04937-1367
(207) 453-5121

Landing School of Boatbuilding and Design
Arundel, Maine
www.landingschool.edu   Federal Code: 016778

2-year private technical and career college in small town.
Enrollment: 37 undergrads. 19 full-time freshmen.
Selectivity: Open admission; but selective for some programs.

BASIC COSTS (2016-2017)
Tuition and fees: $22,296.
Additional info: Program fees vary by program.

FINANCIAL AID PICTURE (2015-2016)
Students with need: 47% of average financial aid package awarded as scholarships/grants, 53% awarded as loans/jobs.
Students without need: This college awards aid only to students with need.

FINANCIAL AID PROCEDURES
Forms required: FAFSA.
Dates and Deadlines: Priority date 4/1; no closing date. Applicants notified on a rolling basis starting 3/1; must reply within 3 week(s) of notification.
Transfers: No deadline. Applicants notified on a rolling basis; must reply within 3 week(s) of notification.

CONTACT
Kristy Lank, Director of Admin & Finance
286 River Road, Arundel, ME 04046
(207) 985-7976 ext. 428

Maine College of Art
Portland, Maine
www.meca.edu   Federal Code: 011673

4-year private visual arts college in small city.
Enrollment: 430 undergrads.
Selectivity: Admits over 75% of applicants.

BASIC COSTS (2016-2017)
Tuition and fees: $33,522.
Per-credit charge: $1,340.
Room and board: $11,086.

FINANCIAL AID PICTURE
Students with need: Need-based aid available for full-time and part-time students. Work study available nights, weekends, and for part-time students.
Students without need: No-need awards available for academics, art.

FINANCIAL AID PROCEDURES
Forms required: FAFSA.
Dates and Deadlines: Priority date 3/1; no closing date. Applicants notified on a rolling basis starting 2/15; must reply within 2 week(s) of notification.
Transfers: Closing date 4/15. Applicants notified on a rolling basis starting 2/15; must reply within 2 week(s) of notification.

CONTACT
Carri Frechette, Director of Financial Aid
522 Congress Street, Portland, ME 04101
(207) 699-5073

Maine College of Health Professions
Lewiston, Maine
www.mchp.edu   Federal Code: 006305

2-year private health science and nursing college in large town.
Enrollment: 154 undergrads, 64% part-time. 6 full-time freshmen.
Selectivity: Admits less than 50% of applicants.

BASIC COSTS (2016-2017)
Tuition and fees: $7,600.
Per-credit charge: $236.
Room only: $1,900.

FINANCIAL AID PICTURE (2016-2017)
Students with need: Out of 5 full-time freshmen who applied for aid, 5 were judged to have need. Of these, 5 received aid. Need-based aid available for part-time students.
Students without need: This college awards aid only to students with need.

FINANCIAL AID PROCEDURES
Forms required: FAFSA.
Dates and Deadlines: Applicants notified on a rolling basis starting 4/1; must reply within 2 week(s) of notification.
Transfers: No deadline. Applicants notified on a rolling basis; must reply within 2 week(s) of notification.

CONTACT
Nicole DeBlois, Financial Aid Specialist
70 Middle Street, Lewiston, ME 04240
(207) 795-2270

Maine Maritime Academy
Castine, Maine
www.mainemaritime.edu   Federal Code: 002044

4-year public maritime college in rural community.
Enrollment: 1,014 undergrads, 3% part-time. 247 full-time freshmen.

Selectivity: Admits 50 to 75% of applicants.

BASIC COSTS (2016-2017)
Tuition and fees: $13,078; out-of-district residents $18,108; out-of-state residents $26,158.
Room and board: $10,030.

FINANCIAL AID PICTURE
Students with need: Need-based aid available for full-time and part-time students. Work study available nights, weekends, and for part-time students.
Students without need: No-need awards available for academics, leadership, religious affiliation, state/district residency.

FINANCIAL AID PROCEDURES
Forms required: FAFSA.
Dates and Deadlines: Closing date 4/15. Applicants notified on a rolling basis starting 4/1; must reply within 4 week(s) of notification.

CONTACT
Kathy Heath, Director of Financial Aid
Pleasant Street, Castine, ME 04420
(207) 326-2339

Northern Maine Community College
Presque Isle, Maine
www.nmcc.edu   Federal Code: 005760

2-year public community and technical college in small town.
Enrollment: 637 undergrads, 34% part-time. 117 full-time freshmen.

BASIC COSTS (2016-2017)
Tuition and fees: $3,458; out-of-state residents $6,218.
Per-credit charge: $92; out-of-state residents $184.
Room and board: $7,818.
Additional info: Tuition/fee waivers available for minority students.

FINANCIAL AID PICTURE (2015-2016)
Students with need: Out of 115 full-time freshmen who applied for aid, 106 were judged to have need. Of these, 105 received aid, and 3 had their full need met. Average financial aid package met 50% of need; average scholarship/grant was $6,116; average loan was $2,731. For part-time students, average financial aid package was $5,089.
Students without need: 4 full-time freshmen who did not demonstrate need for aid received scholarships/grants; average award was $1,250.

FINANCIAL AID PROCEDURES
Forms required: FAFSA, institutional form.
Dates and Deadlines: Priority date 5/1; no closing date. Applicants notified on a rolling basis starting 4/15; must reply within 2 week(s) of notification.
Transfers: Priority date 5/1; no deadline. Applicants notified on a rolling basis.

CONTACT
Norma Smith, Financial Aid Coordinator
33 Edgemont Drive, Presque Isle, ME 04769
(207) 768-2790

Saint Joseph's College of Maine
Standish, Maine
www.sjcme.edu   Federal Code: 002051

4-year private liberal arts college in small town, affiliated with the Roman Catholic Church.
Enrollment: 960 undergrads.

BASIC COSTS (2016-2017)
Tuition and fees: $34,800.
Per-credit charge: $1,120.

Room and board: $12,885.

FINANCIAL AID PICTURE

Students with need: Need-based aid available for full-time and part-time students. Work study available nights, weekends, and for part-time students.

Students without need: No-need awards available for academics, alumni affiliation, leadership.

FINANCIAL AID PROCEDURES

Forms required: FAFSA, institutional form.

Dates and Deadlines: Priority date 3/1; no closing date. Applicants notified on a rolling basis starting 3/1; must reply within 3 week(s) of notification.

CONTACT

Jill Golike, Financial Aid Director
278 Whites Bridge Road, Standish, ME 04084-5236
(800) 752-1266

Southern Maine Community College
South Portland, Maine
www.smccme.edu   Federal Code: 005525

2-year public community and technical college in large town.

Enrollment: 5,051 undergrads, 51% part-time. 878 full-time freshmen.

Selectivity: Open admission; but selective for some programs.

BASIC COSTS (2016-2017)

Tuition and fees: $3,760; out-of-state residents $6,520.

Per-credit charge: $92; out-of-state residents $184.

Room and board: $9,238.

FINANCIAL AID PICTURE (2015-2016)

Students with need: 86% of average financial aid package awarded as scholarships/grants, 14% awarded as loans/jobs. Need-based aid available for part-time students. Work study available nights, weekends, and for part-time students.

Students without need: This college awards aid only to students with need.

FINANCIAL AID PROCEDURES

Forms required: FAFSA.

Dates and Deadlines: Priority date 5/1; no closing date. Applicants notified on a rolling basis.

CONTACT

Shaun Gray, Director of Financial Services
2 Fort Road, South Portland, ME 04106-1611
(207) 741-5518

Thomas College
Waterville, Maine
www.thomas.edu   Federal Code: 002052

4-year private liberal arts and teachers college in large town.

Enrollment: 892 undergrads, 5% part-time. 269 full-time freshmen.

Selectivity: Admits over 75% of applicants.

BASIC COSTS (2016-2017)

Tuition and fees: $25,150.

Room and board: $11,482.

FINANCIAL AID PICTURE (2016-2017)

Students with need: Out of 264 full-time freshmen who applied for aid, 248 were judged to have need. Of these, 248 received aid, and 27 had their full need met. Average financial aid package met 85% of need; average scholarship/grant was $16,849; average loan was $4,040. For part-time students, average financial aid package was $11,233.

Students without need: 17 full-time freshmen who did not demonstrate need for aid received scholarships/grants; average award was $11,144. No-need awards available for academics, alumni affiliation, leadership, state/district residency.

FINANCIAL AID PROCEDURES

Forms required: FAFSA.

Dates and Deadlines: Priority date 2/15; no closing date. Applicants notified on a rolling basis starting 1/15; must reply within 2 week(s) of notification.

CONTACT

Jeannine Bosse, Director of Student Financial Services
180 West River Road, Waterville, ME 04901
(207) 859-1105

Unity College
Unity, Maine
www.unity.edu   Federal Code: 006858

4-year private liberal arts college in rural community.

Enrollment: 729 undergrads, 1% part-time. 215 full-time freshmen.

Selectivity: Admits over 75% of applicants.

BASIC COSTS (2016-2017)

Tuition and fees: $27,570.

Per-credit charge: $950.

Room and board: $10,100.

Additional info: Tuition/fee waivers available for minority students.

FINANCIAL AID PICTURE (2016-2017)

Students with need: Out of 210 full-time freshmen who applied for aid, 185 were judged to have need. Of these, 185 received aid, and 21 had their full need met. Average financial aid package met 70% of need; average scholarship/grant was $15,064; average loan was $6,013. For part-time students, average financial aid package was $8,527.

Students without need: 30 full-time freshmen who did not demonstrate need for aid received scholarships/grants; average award was $9,800. No-need awards available for academics, leadership, minority status.

FINANCIAL AID PROCEDURES

Forms required: FAFSA.

Dates and Deadlines: Applicants notified on a rolling basis starting 12/10.

Transfers: No deadline. Applicants notified on a rolling basis starting 12/10.

CONTACT

Rand Newell, Director of Financial Aid
PO 532, Unity, ME 04988-0532
(207) 509-7235

University of Maine
Orono, Maine
www.umaine.edu   Federal Code: 002053

4-year public university in large town.

Enrollment: 8,757 undergrads, 8% part-time. 2,199 full-time freshmen.

Selectivity: Admits over 75% of applicants.

BASIC COSTS (2016-2017)

Tuition and fees: $10,628; out-of-state residents $29,498.

Per-credit charge: $279; out-of-state residents $908.

Room and board: $10,164.

Additional info: New England Regional Student Program tuition is $12960.

FINANCIAL AID PICTURE (2016-2017)

Students with need: Out of 1,987 full-time freshmen who applied for aid, 1,537 were judged to have need. Of these, 1,534 received aid, and 301 had their full need met. Average financial aid package met 85% of need; average

scholarship/grant was $9,199; average loan was $3,727. For part-time students, average financial aid package was $11,806.

Students without need: 632 full-time freshmen who did not demonstrate need for aid received scholarships/grants; average award was $6,073. No-need awards available for academics, alumni affiliation, art, athletics, job skills, leadership, minority status, music/drama, religious affiliation, ROTC, state/district residency.

Scholarships offered: Merit: Academic merit scholarships: range in value from $1,000 to $15,000; most awards are renewable for up to eight (8) consecutive semesters; based upon academic performance and full-time enrollment. **Athletic:** 52 full-time freshmen received athletic scholarships; average amount $22,297.

Additional info: Financial aid is available for students entering in the spring.

FINANCIAL AID PROCEDURES

Forms required: FAFSA.

Dates and Deadlines: Priority date 3/1; closing date 4/15. Applicants notified on a rolling basis starting 1/1.

Transfers: Priority date 3/1; closing date 5/15.

CONTACT

Sarah Doheny, Director of Student Financial Aid
5713 Chadbourne Hall, Orono, ME 04469-5713
(207) 581-1324

University of Maine at Augusta

Augusta, Maine
www.uma.edu   Federal Code: 006760

4-year public university in large town.

Enrollment: 3,632 undergrads.

Selectivity: Open admission; but selective for some programs.

BASIC COSTS (2016-2017)

Tuition and fees: $7,448; out-of-state residents $17,048.

Per-credit charge: $217; out-of-state residents $537.

Additional info: New England Regional Student Program tuition is $10,080.

FINANCIAL AID PICTURE (2016-2017)

Students with need: Average financial aid package met 53% of need; average scholarship/grant was $5,718; average loan was $5,711. For part-time students, average financial aid package was $5,863.

Students without need: No-need awards available for academics, athletics, leadership, music/drama, state/district residency.

FINANCIAL AID PROCEDURES

Forms required: FAFSA.

Dates and Deadlines: Priority date 3/1; no closing date. Applicants notified on a rolling basis starting 3/15; must reply within 2 week(s) of notification.

CONTACT

Sherry McCollett, Director of Student Financial Services
46 University Drive, Augusta, ME 04330
(207) 621-3455

University of Maine at Farmington

Farmington, Maine
www.umf.maine.edu   Federal Code: 002040

4-year public liberal arts and teachers college in small town.

Enrollment: 1,753 undergrads, 6% part-time. 432 full-time freshmen.

Selectivity: Admits over 75% of applicants.

BASIC COSTS (2017-2018)

Tuition and fees: $9,458; out-of-state residents $19,026.

Per-credit charge: $268; out-of-state residents $567.

Room and board: $9,334.

Additional info: Out-of-state dependents of UMF alumni are now eligible for tuition equivalent to the in-state rate. Tuition/fee waivers available for minority students.

FINANCIAL AID PICTURE (2016-2017)

Students with need: Out of 420 full-time freshmen who applied for aid, 359 were judged to have need. Of these, 359 received aid, and 166 had their full need met. Average financial aid package met 87% of need; average scholarship/grant was $8,594; average loan was $5,517. For part-time students, average financial aid package was $9,855.

Students without need: 37 full-time freshmen who did not demonstrate need for aid received scholarships/grants; average award was $2,959. No-need awards available for academics, alumni affiliation, leadership, minority status, music/drama, state/district residency.

Scholarships offered: Academic Excellence Scholarship: for students ranking in the top 10% of their graduating class. Distinction Scholarship: for students ranking in the top 20% of their graduating class. Academic Achievement Scholarship: for students ranking in the top 30% of their graduating class. Students from schools that do not report rank will be considered for these scholarships based on their high school academic courses and grades. The amount awarded varies depending on the scholarship awarded and the residency of the applicant.

Additional info: Freshman students from Franklin County, Maine, offered free on-campus housing for their first year at UMF. FAFSA must be submitted by 3/1 in order for applicant to receive priority consideration from campus.

FINANCIAL AID PROCEDURES

Forms required: FAFSA.

Dates and Deadlines: Priority date 3/1; no closing date. Applicants notified on a rolling basis starting 2/1.

Transfers: Applicants notified on a rolling basis starting 3/15.

CONTACT

Ronald Milliken, Director of Financial Aid
246 Main Street, Farmington, ME 04938
(207) 778-7100

University of Maine at Fort Kent

Fort Kent, Maine   Federal Code: 002041
www.umfk.maine.edu   CSS Code: 3393

4-year public university and branch campus college in small town.

Enrollment: 1,076 undergrads, 38% part-time. 120 full-time freshmen.

Selectivity: Admits over 75% of applicants.

BASIC COSTS (2016-2017)

Tuition and fees: $7,575; out-of-state residents $11,205.

Per-credit charge: $220; out-of-state residents $341.

Room and board: $7,910.

Additional info: New England Regional Student Program tuition is $10,230.

FINANCIAL AID PICTURE (2015-2016)

Students with need: Average financial aid package met 82% of need; average scholarship/grant was $6,068; average loan was $5,709. For part-time students, average financial aid package was $6,724.

Students without need: 4 full-time freshmen who did not demonstrate need for aid received scholarships/grants; average award was $2,500. No-need awards available for academics, leadership.

FINANCIAL AID PROCEDURES

Forms required: FAFSA, CSS PROFILE, state aid form, institutional form.

Dates and Deadlines: Priority date 3/1; no closing date. Applicants notified on a rolling basis starting 3/15.

PART III: FINANCIAL AID COLLEGE BY COLLEGE

CONTACT
Lisa Fournier, Assoc. Director of Financial Aid
23 University Drive, Fort Kent, ME 04743
(207) 834-7606

University of Maine at Machias
Machias, Maine
www.umm.maine.edu   Federal Code: 002055

4-year public university and liberal arts college in rural community.
Enrollment: 560 undergrads, 25% part-time. 116 full-time freshmen.
Selectivity: Admits over 75% of applicants.

BASIC COSTS (2016-2017)
Tuition and fees: $7,480; out-of-state residents $19,300.
Per-credit charge: $222; out-of-state residents $616.
Room and board: $8,486.
Additional info: New England Regional Student Program tuition is $10,320.

FINANCIAL AID PICTURE (2015-2016)
Students with need: Out of 114 full-time freshmen who applied for aid, 107 were judged to have need. Of these, 107 received aid, and 61 had their full need met. Average financial aid package met 77% of need; average scholarship/grant was $9,051; average loan was $4,826. For part-time students, average financial aid package was $9,441.
Students without need: No-need awards available for academics, athletics.

FINANCIAL AID PROCEDURES
Forms required: FAFSA.
Dates and Deadlines: Priority date 3/1; no closing date. Applicants notified on a rolling basis starting 3/1.
Transfers: Applicants notified on a rolling basis starting 3/1.

CONTACT
Stephanie Larrabee, Director of Financial Aid
116 O'Brien Avenue, Machias, ME 04654-1397
(207) 255-1203

University of Maine at Presque Isle
Presque Isle, Maine
www.umpi.edu   Federal Code: 002033

4-year public university in small town.
Enrollment: 790 undergrads, 18% part-time. 171 full-time freshmen.
Selectivity: Admits over 75% of applicants.

BASIC COSTS (2017-2018)
Tuition and fees: $7,884; out-of-state residents $11,634.
Per-credit charge: $228; out-of-state residents $353.
Room and board: $8,264.
Additional info: Tuition/fee waivers available for minority students.

FINANCIAL AID PICTURE (2016-2017)
Students with need: Out of 159 full-time freshmen who applied for aid, 139 were judged to have need. Of these, 139 received aid, and 73 had their full need met. Average financial aid package met 82% of need; average scholarship/grant was $7,523; average loan was $4,438. For part-time students, average financial aid package was $7,336.
Students without need: 9 full-time freshmen who did not demonstrate need for aid received scholarships/grants; average award was $2,222. No-need awards available for academics.

FINANCIAL AID PROCEDURES
Forms required: FAFSA.
Dates and Deadlines: Priority date 4/1; no closing date. Applicants notified on a rolling basis starting 1/10; must reply within 2 week(s) of notification.

CONTACT
Christopher Bell, Director of Student Financial Services
181 Main Street, Presque Isle, ME 04769
(207) 768-9510

University of New England
Biddeford, Maine
www.une.edu   Federal Code: 002050

4-year private university in small city.
Enrollment: 2,374 undergrads, 1% part-time. 719 full-time freshmen.
Selectivity: Admits over 75% of applicants.

BASIC COSTS (2016-2017)
Tuition and fees: $35,598.
Per-credit charge: $1,210.
Room and board: $13,250.

FINANCIAL AID PICTURE (2016-2017)
Students with need: Need-based aid available for full-time and part-time students. Work study available nights, weekends, and for part-time students.
Students without need: No-need awards available for academics.
Scholarships offered: UNE Scholarships and UNE Departmental Award: non-need; based on academic qualifications as determined from GPA and SAT/ACT scores; must be a full-time undergraduate student and maintain a 2.5 GPA.

FINANCIAL AID PROCEDURES
Forms required: FAFSA.
Dates and Deadlines: Priority date 5/1; no closing date. Applicants notified on a rolling basis starting 2/1.
Transfers: No deadline. Applicants notified on a rolling basis.

CONTACT
Paul Henderson, Assistant Vice President of Student Financial Services
11 Hills Beach Road, Biddeford, ME 04005
(207) 602-2404

University of Southern Maine
Portland, Maine
www.usm.maine.edu   Federal Code: 009762

4-year public university in small city.
Enrollment: 5,233 undergrads, 29% part-time. 662 full-time freshmen.
Selectivity: Admits over 75% of applicants.

BASIC COSTS (2016-2017)
Tuition and fees: $8,920; out-of-state residents $21,280.
Per-credit charge: $253; out-of-state residents $665.
Room and board: $9,200.
Additional info: New England Regional Student Program tuition is $11,760.

FINANCIAL AID PICTURE (2015-2016)
Students with need: Out of 623 full-time freshmen who applied for aid, 535 were judged to have need. Of these, 534 received aid, and 250 had their full need met. Average financial aid package met 80% of need; average scholarship/grant was $8,477; average loan was $5,718. For part-time students, average financial aid package was $9,047.
Students without need: 60 full-time freshmen who did not demonstrate need for aid received scholarships/grants; average award was $2,865. No-need awards available for academics, music/drama, state/district residency.

FINANCIAL AID PROCEDURES
Forms required: FAFSA.
Dates and Deadlines: Priority date 2/15; no closing date. Applicants notified on a rolling basis starting 3/15; must reply by 5/1 or within 2 week(s) of notification.

Transfers: Applicants notified on a rolling basis; must reply by 5/1 or within 2 week(s) of notification.

CONTACT
Keith Dubois, Director of Financial Aid Office
PO Box 9300, Portland, ME 04104
(207) 780-5250

Washington County Community College
Calais, Maine
www.wccc.me.edu   Federal Code: 009231

2-year public community and technical college in small town.
Enrollment: 309 undergrads.
Selectivity: Open admission; but selective for some programs.

BASIC COSTS (2016-2017)
Tuition and fees: $3,440; out-of-state residents $6,200.
Per-credit charge: $92; out-of-state residents $184.
Room and board: $5,490.

FINANCIAL AID PICTURE
Students with need: Need-based aid available for full-time and part-time students. Work study available nights.
Students without need: No-need awards available for academics.

FINANCIAL AID PROCEDURES
Forms required: FAFSA, institutional form.
Dates and Deadlines: Applicants notified on a rolling basis starting 11/1.
Transfers: No deadline. Applicants notified on a rolling basis.

CONTACT
Linda Winchester, Financial Aid Director
One College Drive, Calais, ME 04619
(207) 454-1033

York County Community College
Wells, Maine
www.yccc.edu   Federal Code: 031229

2-year public community and technical college in small town.
Enrollment: 1,277 undergrads, 67% part-time. 166 full-time freshmen.
Selectivity: Open admission.

BASIC COSTS (2016-2017)
Tuition and fees: $3,540; out-of-state residents $6,300.
Per-credit charge: $92; out-of-state residents $184.
Additional info: Tuition/fee waivers available for minority students.

FINANCIAL AID PICTURE (2015-2016)
Students with need: Out of 141 full-time freshmen who applied for aid, 111 were judged to have need. Of these, 99 received aid, and 6 had their full need met. Average financial aid package met 47% of need; average scholarship/grant was $5,161; average loan was $2,700. For part-time students, average financial aid package was $3,654.
Students without need: 19 full-time freshmen who did not demonstrate need for aid received scholarships/grants; average award was $711. No-need awards available for academics, alumni affiliation, art, job skills, leadership, state/district residency.

FINANCIAL AID PROCEDURES
Forms required: FAFSA.
Dates and Deadlines: Priority date 5/1; no closing date. Must reply within 2 week(s) of notification.

CONTACT
David Daigle, Director of Financial Aid
112 College Drive, Wells, ME 04090
(207) 216-4410

Maryland

Allegany College of Maryland
Cumberland, Maryland
www.allegany.edu   Federal Code: 002057

2-year public community college in large town.
Enrollment: 2,343 undergrads.
Selectivity: Open admission; but selective for some programs.

BASIC COSTS (2016-2017)
Tuition and fees: $3,755; out-of-district residents $6,995; out-of-state residents $8,345.
Per-credit charge: $117; out-of-district residents $225; out-of-state residents $270.

FINANCIAL AID PICTURE
Students with need: Need-based aid available for full-time and part-time students. Work study available nights.
Students without need: No-need awards available for academics, athletics, leadership, state/district residency.

FINANCIAL AID PROCEDURES
Forms required: FAFSA, institutional form.
Dates and Deadlines: Priority date 3/1; no closing date. Applicants notified on a rolling basis starting 4/15; must reply within 2 week(s) of notification.

CONTACT
Vicki Smith, Director of Financial Aid
12401 Willowbrook Road, SE, Cumberland, MD 21502
(301) 784-5213

Anne Arundel Community College
Arnold, Maryland
www.aacc.edu   Federal Code: 002058

2-year public community college in large town.
Enrollment: 11,821 undergrads, 67% part-time. 1,397 full-time freshmen.
Selectivity: Open admission; but selective for some programs.

BASIC COSTS (2016-2017)
Tuition and fees: $4,010; out-of-district residents $7,010; out-of-state residents $11,780.
Per-credit charge: $108; out-of-district residents $208; out-of-state residents $367.

FINANCIAL AID PICTURE (2015-2016)
Students with need: 74% of average financial aid package awarded as scholarships/grants, 26% awarded as loans/jobs. Need-based aid available for part-time students. Work study available nights, weekends, and for part-time students.

FINANCIAL AID PROCEDURES
Forms required: FAFSA, institutional form.
Dates and Deadlines: Priority date 5/15; no closing date. Applicants notified on a rolling basis starting 7/1; must reply within 2 week(s) of notification.

CONTACT
Richard Heath, Director of Student Financial Services
101 College Parkway, Arnold, MD 21012-1895
(410) 777-2203

Baltimore City Community College
Baltimore, Maryland
www.bccc.edu   Federal Code: 002061

2-year public community college in very large city.
Enrollment: 4,857 undergrads.
Selectivity: Open admission; but selective for some programs.

BASIC COSTS (2016-2017)
Tuition and fees: $3,482; out-of-state residents $7,952.
Per-credit charge: $96; out-of-state residents $245.

FINANCIAL AID PICTURE
Students with need: Need-based aid available for full-time and part-time students. Work study available nights, weekends, and for part-time students.
Students without need: This college awards aid only to students with need.

FINANCIAL AID PROCEDURES
Forms required: FAFSA, state aid form, institutional form.
Dates and Deadlines: Priority date 6/1; no closing date. Applicants notified on a rolling basis starting 7/1; must reply within 2 week(s) of notification.

CONTACT
Vera Brooks, Director of Financial Aid
2901 Liberty Heights Avenue, Baltimore, MD 21215-7893
(410) 462-8348

Bowie State University
Bowie, Maryland
www.bowiestate.edu   Federal Code: 002062

4-year public university in small city.
Enrollment: 4,711 undergrads.
Selectivity: Admits less than 50% of applicants.

BASIC COSTS (2016-2017)
Tuition and fees: $7,880; out-of-state residents $18,416.
Per-credit charge: $234; out-of-state residents $667.
Room and board: $10,200.

FINANCIAL AID PICTURE
Students with need: Need-based aid available for full-time and part-time students. Work study available weekends and for part-time students.
Students without need: No-need awards available for academics, alumni affiliation, art, athletics, music/drama, state/district residency.

FINANCIAL AID PROCEDURES
Forms required: FAFSA.
Dates and Deadlines: Closing date 3/1. Applicants notified on a rolling basis starting 4/1; must reply within 2 week(s) of notification.
Transfers: Applicants notified on a rolling basis starting 4/1; must reply within 2 week(s) of notification.

CONTACT
Deboarh Stanley, Director of Financial Aid
14000 Jericho Park Road, Bowie, MD 20715
(301) 860-3540

Capitol Technology University
Laurel, Maryland
www.capitol-college.edu   Federal Code: 001436

4-year private business and engineering college in large town.
Enrollment: 441 undergrads.

BASIC COSTS (2016-2017)
Tuition and fees: $24,362.
Per-credit charge: $772.
Room only: $5,536.
Additional info: Tuition at time of enrollment locked for 4 years.

FINANCIAL AID PICTURE
Students with need: Need-based aid available for full-time and part-time students. Work study available nights, weekends, and for part-time students.
Students without need: No-need awards available for academics, alumni affiliation, leadership, minority status.

FINANCIAL AID PROCEDURES
Forms required: FAFSA, institutional form.
Dates and Deadlines: Priority date 3/1; no closing date. Applicants notified on a rolling basis starting 4/1; must reply by 5/1 or within 3 week(s) of notification.

CONTACT
Sue Thompson, Director of Financial Aid
11301 Springfield Road, Laurel, MD 20708
(301) 369-2800 ext. 3039

Carroll Community College
Westminster, Maryland
www.carrollcc.edu   Federal Code: 031007

2-year public community college in large town.
Enrollment: 2,942 undergrads, 61% part-time. 474 full-time freshmen.
Selectivity: Open admission; but selective for some programs.

BASIC COSTS (2016-2017)
Tuition and fees: $4,812; out-of-district residents $6,972; out-of-state residents $9,744.
Per-credit charge: $160; out-of-district residents $232; out-of-state residents $324.

FINANCIAL AID PICTURE (2015-2016)
Students with need: 57% of average financial aid package awarded as scholarships/grants, 43% awarded as loans/jobs. Need-based aid available for part-time students. Work study available nights, weekends, and for part-time students.
Students without need: No-need awards available for academics, art, job skills, leadership, state/district residency.

FINANCIAL AID PROCEDURES
Forms required: FAFSA.
Dates and Deadlines: Priority date 3/1; no closing date. Must reply within 2 week(s) of notification.

CONTACT
John Gay, Director of Financial Aid
1601 Washington Road, Westminster, MD 21157
(410) 386-8437

Cecil College
North East, Maryland
www.my.cecil.edu   Federal Code: 008308

2-year public community college in large town.
Enrollment: 2,410 undergrads, 61% part-time. 259 full-time freshmen.
Selectivity: Open admission; but selective for some programs.

BASIC COSTS (2016-2017)
Tuition and fees: $3,840; out-of-district residents $6,540; out-of-state residents $7,890.

Per-credit charge: $107; out-of-district residents $197; out-of-state residents $242.
Additional info: Tuition at time of enrollment locked for 2 years.

FINANCIAL AID PICTURE (2015-2016)
Students with need: 55% of average financial aid package awarded as scholarships/grants, 45% awarded as loans/jobs. Work study available nights, weekends, and for part-time students.
Students without need: No-need awards available for academics, alumni affiliation, athletics, job skills, state/district residency.

FINANCIAL AID PROCEDURES
Forms required: FAFSA.
Dates and Deadlines: Priority date 8/1; no closing date. Applicants notified on a rolling basis; must reply within 2 week(s) of notification.

CONTACT
Amanda Solecki, Director of Financial Aid
One Seahawk Drive, North East, MD 21901
(443) 674-1891

Chesapeake College
Wye Mills, Maryland
www.chesapeake.edu   Federal Code: 004650

2-year public community college in rural community.
Enrollment: 1,807 undergrads, 64% part-time. 277 full-time freshmen.
Selectivity: Open admission; but selective for some programs.

BASIC COSTS (2016-2017)
Tuition and fees: $4,700; out-of-district residents $6,740; out-of-state residents $9,050.
Per-credit charge: $120; out-of-district residents $188; out-of-state residents $265.

FINANCIAL AID PICTURE (2016-2017)
Students with need: Average financial aid package met 40% of need; average scholarship/grant was $1,696. For part-time students, average financial aid package was $2,624.
Students without need: 39 full-time freshmen who did not demonstrate need for aid received scholarships/grants; average award was $1,245. No-need awards available for academics, art, athletics, state/district residency.
Scholarships offered: 8 full-time freshmen received athletic scholarships; average amount $546.

FINANCIAL AID PROCEDURES
Forms required: FAFSA, institutional form.
Dates and Deadlines: Priority date 5/1; no closing date. Applicants notified on a rolling basis starting 5/5; must reply within 2 week(s) of notification.

CONTACT
Mindy Schaffer, Director of Financial Aid
Box 8, Wye Mills, MD 21679-0008
(410) 827-5803

College of Southern Maryland
La Plata, Maryland
www.csmd.edu   Federal Code: 002064

2-year public community college in large town.
Enrollment: 8,358 undergrads.
Selectivity: Open admission; but selective for some programs.

BASIC COSTS (2016-2017)
Tuition and fees: $4,539; out-of-district residents $7,860; out-of-state residents $10,148.

Per-credit charge: $123; out-of-district residents $213; out-of-state residents $275.

FINANCIAL AID PICTURE
Students with need: Need-based aid available for full-time and part-time students. Work study available nights, weekends, and for part-time students.
Students without need: No-need awards available for academics, athletics, leadership.

FINANCIAL AID PROCEDURES
Forms required: FAFSA.
Dates and Deadlines: Priority date 3/1; no closing date. Applicants notified on a rolling basis starting 6/15.

CONTACT
Christian Zimmermann, Director of Financial Assistance
College of Southern Maryland-AOD, La Plata, MD 20646-0910
(301) 934-7531

Community College of Baltimore County
Baltimore, Maryland
www.ccbcmd.edu   Federal Code: 002063

2-year public community college in very large city.
Enrollment: 19,390 undergrads, 69% part-time. 1,862 full-time freshmen.
Selectivity: Open admission; but selective for some programs.

BASIC COSTS (2016-2017)
Tuition and fees: $4,432; out-of-district residents $7,852; out-of-state residents $11,602.
Per-credit charge: $118; out-of-district residents $222; out-of-state residents $337.

FINANCIAL AID PICTURE
Students with need: Need-based aid available for full-time and part-time students. Work study available nights, weekends, and for part-time students.
Students without need: No-need awards available for academics, athletics, state/district residency.
Additional info: On-campus employment typically available.

FINANCIAL AID PROCEDURES
Forms required: FAFSA.
Dates and Deadlines: Priority date 1/9; no closing date. Applicants notified on a rolling basis starting 2/27; must reply within 2 week(s) of notification.

CONTACT
Virginia Zawodny, Director of Financial Aid
800 South Rolling Road, Baltimore, MD 21228-5317
(443) 840-2222

Coppin State University
Baltimore, Maryland
www.coppin.edu   Federal Code: 002068

4-year public liberal arts college in very large city.
Enrollment: 2,885 undergrads.

BASIC COSTS (2016-2017)
Tuition and fees: $6,448; out-of-state residents $12,178.
Per-credit charge: $187; out-of-state residents $563.
Room and board: $9,753.

FINANCIAL AID PICTURE
Students with need: Need-based aid available for full-time and part-time students.
Students without need: No-need awards available for academics, alumni affiliation, athletics, ROTC, state/district residency.

Scholarships offered: Gold Freshman Merit Award: $2,000 per year; awarded to freshmen with 950 SAT and 2.5 GPA. Gold Transfer Merit Award: $1,500 per year; awarded to Maryland Community College transfer students with 2.8 GPA and successful completion of 56 credits. Blue Freshman Merit Award: $1,000 per year; awarded to freshman with 900 SAT and 2.5 GPA. Blue Transfer Merit Award: $800 per year; awarded to Maryland Community College transfer students with 2.5 GPA and successful completion of 25 credits. SAT scores exclusive of Writing.

Additional info: Funds allocated by State of Maryland for minority students enrolled for at least 6 credits who are Maryland residents and US citizens (Minority Grant).

FINANCIAL AID PROCEDURES

Forms required: FAFSA.

Dates and Deadlines: Priority date 3/1; no closing date. Applicants notified on a rolling basis starting 4/15; must reply within 2 week(s) of notification.

CONTACT

Mose Cartier, Director of Financial Aid
2500 West North Avenue, Baltimore, MD 21216
(410) 951-3636

Frederick Community College

Frederick, Maryland
www.frederick.edu   Federal Code: 002071

2-year public community college in small city.
Enrollment: 4,860 undergrads. 813 full-time freshmen.
Selectivity: Open admission; but selective for some programs.

BASIC COSTS (2016-2017)

Tuition and fees: $4,255; out-of-district residents $8,455; out-of-state residents $11,215.
Per-credit charge: $119; out-of-district residents $259; out-of-state residents $351.

FINANCIAL AID PICTURE (2015-2016)

Students with need: 77% of average financial aid package awarded as scholarships/grants, 23% awarded as loans/jobs. Need-based aid available for part-time students.
Students without need: No-need awards available for academics, athletics, state/district residency.
Scholarships offered: Scholarships available for Frederick County Public Schools students with high GPA who will participate in student ambassador program. Other general scholarships available.

FINANCIAL AID PROCEDURES

Forms required: FAFSA, institutional form.
Dates and Deadlines: Priority date 6/1; no closing date. Applicants notified on a rolling basis starting 5/15; must reply within 2 week(s) of notification.
Transfers: Applicants notified on a rolling basis starting 6/1. Financial aid transcripts from prior institutions must be submitted before awards are made.

CONTACT

Brenda Dayhoff, Executive Director, Financial Aid
7932 Opossumtown Pike, Frederick, MD 21702
(301) 846-2480

Frostburg State University

Frostburg, Maryland
www.frostburg.edu   Federal Code: 002072

4-year public university and teachers college in small town.
Enrollment: 4,779 undergrads, 14% part-time. 851 full-time freshmen.
Selectivity: Admits 50 to 75% of applicants.

BASIC COSTS (2016-2017)

Tuition and fees: $8,702; out-of-state residents $21,226.
Per-credit charge: $262; out-of-state residents $530.
Room and board: $9,312.

FINANCIAL AID PICTURE (2016-2017)

Students with need: Out of 759 full-time freshmen who applied for aid, 580 were judged to have need. Of these, 580 received aid, and 100 had their full need met. Average financial aid package met 60% of need; average scholarship/grant was $8,469; average loan was $3,356. For part-time students, average financial aid package was $4,499.
Students without need: 192 full-time freshmen who did not demonstrate need for aid received scholarships/grants; average award was $3,590. No-need awards available for academics, leadership, minority status.

FINANCIAL AID PROCEDURES

Forms required: FAFSA.
Dates and Deadlines: Priority date 3/1; no closing date. Applicants notified on a rolling basis starting 3/15; must reply within 3 week(s) of notification.

CONTACT

Angela Hovatter, Director of Financial Aid
101 Braddock Road, Frostburg, MD 21532-1099
(301) 687-4201

Garrett College

McHenry, Maryland
www.garrettcollege.edu   Federal Code: 010014

2-year public community college in rural community.
Enrollment: 506 undergrads, 12% part-time. 227 full-time freshmen.
Selectivity: Open admission.

BASIC COSTS (2016-2017)

Tuition and fees: $4,100; out-of-district residents $7,760; out-of-state residents $8,960.
Per-credit charge: $103; out-of-district residents $225; out-of-state residents $265.
Room and board: $5,910.

FINANCIAL AID PICTURE (2015-2016)

Students with need: Out of 212 full-time freshmen who applied for aid, 187 were judged to have need. Of these, 187 received aid, and 16 had their full need met. Average financial aid package met 51% of need; average scholarship/grant was $5,140; average loan was $2,870. For part-time students, average financial aid package was $4,950.
Students without need: 32 full-time freshmen who did not demonstrate need for aid received scholarships/grants; average award was $2,451. No-need awards available for academics, athletics, leadership.
Additional info: Many merit and need-based local scholarships available.

FINANCIAL AID PROCEDURES

Forms required: FAFSA.
Dates and Deadlines: Priority date 3/1; no closing date. Applicants notified on a rolling basis starting 6/1; must reply within 2 week(s) of notification.

CONTACT

Cissy Vansickle, Director of Financial Aid
687 Mosser Road, McHenry, MD 21541
(301) 387-3012

Goucher College

Baltimore, Maryland   Federal Code: 002073
www.goucher.edu   CSS Code: 5257

4-year private liberal arts college in small city.
Enrollment: 1,461 undergrads, 2% part-time. 440 full-time freshmen.

Selectivity: Admits over 75% of applicants.

BASIC COSTS (2016-2017)
Tuition and fees: $43,416.
Room and board: $12,300.

FINANCIAL AID PICTURE (2016-2017)
Students with need: Out of 381 full-time freshmen who applied for aid, 329 were judged to have need. Of these, 329 received aid, and 83 had their full need met. Average financial aid package met 84% of need; average scholarship/grant was $33,643; average loan was $2,794. For part-time students, average financial aid package was $13,408.
Students without need: 110 full-time freshmen who did not demonstrate need for aid received scholarships/grants; average award was $17,258. No-need awards available for academics, art, music/drama.

FINANCIAL AID PROCEDURES
Forms required: FAFSA, CSS PROFILE.
Dates and Deadlines: Priority date 2/1; closing date 4/1. Applicants notified on a rolling basis starting 3/1; must reply by 5/1 or within 2 week(s) of notification.
Transfers: Priority date 4/15; no deadline. Applicants notified on a rolling basis starting 4/15; must reply within 2 week(s) of notification.

CONTACT
Stephanie Bender, Director of Financial Aid
1021 Dulaney Valley Road, Baltimore, MD 21204-2753
(410) 337-6141

Hagerstown Community College
Hagerstown, Maryland
www.hagerstowncc.edu   Federal Code: 002074

2-year public community college in small city.
Enrollment: 3,205 undergrads.
Selectivity: Open admission; but selective for some programs.

BASIC COSTS (2016-2017)
Tuition and fees: $3,930; out-of-district residents $5,910; out-of-state residents $7,650.
Per-credit charge: $117; out-of-district residents $183; out-of-state residents $241.

FINANCIAL AID PICTURE
Students with need: Need-based aid available for full-time and part-time students. Work study available nights, weekends, and for part-time students.
Students without need: This college awards aid only to students with need.

FINANCIAL AID PROCEDURES
Forms required: FAFSA.
Dates and Deadlines: Priority date 5/30; no closing date. Applicants notified on a rolling basis starting 4/15.
Transfers: No deadline.

CONTACT
Carolyn Cox, Director, Student Financial Aid and Records
11400 Robinwood Drive, Hagerstown, MD 21742-6514
(240) 500-2473

Harford Community College
Bel Air, Maryland
www.harford.edu   Federal Code: 002075

2-year public community college in small city.
Enrollment: 5,155 undergrads, 60% part-time. 891 full-time freshmen.
Selectivity: Open admission; but selective for some programs.

BASIC COSTS (2016-2017)
Tuition and fees: $4,464; out-of-district residents $7,074; out-of-state residents $9,684.
Per-credit charge: $124; out-of-district residents $211; out-of-state residents $298.

FINANCIAL AID PICTURE (2015-2016)
Students with need: Out of 601 full-time freshmen who applied for aid, 359 were judged to have need. Of these, 320 received aid. Need-based aid available for part-time students.
Scholarships offered: Alfred C. O'Connell Homes Scholarship; full tuition and fees for 2 years; based on 3.25 GPA; 25 awards.

FINANCIAL AID PROCEDURES
Forms required: FAFSA, institutional form.
Dates and Deadlines: Priority date 3/15; no closing date. Applicants notified on a rolling basis starting 4/1; must reply within 2 week(s) of notification.

CONTACT
Amy Spinnato, Director of Financial Aid
401 Thomas Run Road, Bel Air, MD 21015
(443) 443-2257

Hood College
Frederick, Maryland
www.hood.edu   Federal Code: 002076

4-year private liberal arts college in small city, affiliated with the United Church of Christ.
Enrollment: 1,151 undergrads, 6% part-time. 219 full-time freshmen.
Selectivity: Admits 50 to 75% of applicants.

BASIC COSTS (2017-2018)
Tuition and fees: $37,960.
Per-credit charge: $1,090.
Room and board: $12,580.

FINANCIAL AID PICTURE (2016-2017)
Students with need: Out of 210 full-time freshmen who applied for aid, 193 were judged to have need. Of these, 193 received aid, and 30 had their full need met. Average financial aid package met 80% of need; average scholarship/grant was $28,791; average loan was $4,406. For part-time students, average financial aid package was $8,765.
Students without need: 25 full-time freshmen who did not demonstrate need for aid received scholarships/grants; average award was $20,903. No-need awards available for academics, alumni affiliation, leadership, minority status, music/drama, ROTC, state/district residency.

FINANCIAL AID PROCEDURES
Forms required: FAFSA, institutional form.
Dates and Deadlines: Priority date 2/15; no closing date. Applicants notified on a rolling basis starting 3/1; must reply by 5/1 or within 2 week(s) of notification.
Transfers: No deadline. Applicants notified on a rolling basis starting 10/15; must reply within 2 week(s) of notification.

CONTACT
Brenda DiSorbo, Director of Financial Aid
401 Rosemont Avenue, Frederick, MD 21701-8575
(301) 696-3411

Howard Community College
Columbia, Maryland
www.howardcc.edu   Federal Code: 008175

2-year public community college in small city.
Enrollment: 9,114 undergrads, 61% part-time. 1,176 full-time freshmen.

Selectivity: Open admission; but selective for some programs.

BASIC COSTS (2016-2017)
Tuition and fees: $4,693; out-of-district residents $7,183; out-of-state residents $8,533.
Per-credit charge: $134; out-of-district residents $217; out-of-state residents $262.

FINANCIAL AID PICTURE (2015-2016)
Students with need: 77% of average financial aid package awarded as scholarships/grants, 23% awarded as loans/jobs. Need-based aid available for part-time students. Work study available nights, weekends, and for part-time students.

FINANCIAL AID PROCEDURES
Forms required: FAFSA.
Dates and Deadlines: Priority date 3/1; no closing date. Applicants notified on a rolling basis starting 5/1.

CONTACT
Dawn Lowe, Director of Financial Aid Services
10901 Little Patuxent Parkway, Columbia, MD 21044-3197
(443) 518-1260

Johns Hopkins University
Baltimore, Maryland   Federal Code: 002077
www.jhu.edu   CSS Code: 5332

4-year private university in very large city.
Enrollment: 5,691 undergrads. 1,369 full-time freshmen.
Selectivity: Admits less than 50% of applicants.

BASIC COSTS (2016-2017)
Tuition and fees: $50,910.
Per-credit charge: $1,680.
Room and board: $14,976.

FINANCIAL AID PICTURE
Students with need: Need-based aid available for full-time students. Work study available nights, weekends, and for part-time students.
Students without need: No-need awards available for academics, athletics, leadership, ROTC, state/district residency.
Scholarships offered: Hodson Trust Scholarship: $35,000; annually for 4 years; 20 awards. Westgate Scholarship for engineering freshmen: tuition plus $1,000 for 4 years; academic excellence, leadership, demonstrated research experience required; 2 offered per year per class. Wilson Research grants: $10,000. Baltimore Scholars Program: full tuition scholarship for US citizens or permanent residents who have attended a Baltimore City public school for at least 10th, 11th, and 12th grades and meet a residency requirement and a financial need requirement.
Additional info: Selected students receive aid packages without loan expectation, including grants to full need. Private merit aid does not reduce Hopkins grant.

FINANCIAL AID PROCEDURES
Forms required: FAFSA, CSS PROFILE.
Dates and Deadlines: Closing date 3/1. Applicants notified by 4/1; must reply by 5/1.
Transfers: Closing date 3/15. Must reply within 2 week(s) of notification. Aid on funds-available basis.

CONTACT
Tom McDermott, Director of Student Financial Services
3400 North Charles Street, Mason Hall, Baltimore, MD 21218-2683
(410) 516-8028

Johns Hopkins University: Peabody Conservatory of Music
Baltimore, Maryland
www.peabody.jhu.edu   Federal Code: E00233

4-year private music college in very large city.
Enrollment: 265 undergrads.

BASIC COSTS (2016-2017)
Tuition and fees: $45,632.
Per-credit charge: $1,258.
Room and board: $15,122.

FINANCIAL AID PICTURE
Students with need: Need-based aid available for full-time and part-time students. Work study available nights, weekends, and for part-time students.
Students without need: No-need awards available for academics, music/drama.

FINANCIAL AID PROCEDURES
Forms required: FAFSA, institutional form.
Dates and Deadlines: Closing date 2/1. Applicants notified by 4/1; must reply by 5/1.
Transfers: Applicants notified by 4/1; must reply by 5/1.

CONTACT
Rebecca Polgar, Director Financial Aid
One East Mount Vernon Place, Baltimore, MD 21202
(410) 234-4900

Kaplan University: Hagerstown
Hagerstown, Maryland
www.hagerstown.kaplanuniversity.edu
                             Federal Code: 007946

2-year for-profit business and junior college in large town.
Enrollment: 672 undergrads, 77% part-time.
Selectivity: Open admission; but selective for some programs.

BASIC COSTS (2016-2017)
Additional info: Tuition varies by program. Per-credit-hour charges; $371-$460. Fees, books supplies range depending on program level and course of study. All costs are subject to change.

FINANCIAL AID PICTURE
Students with need: Need-based aid available for full-time and part-time students.

FINANCIAL AID PROCEDURES
Forms required: FAFSA, institutional form.
Dates and Deadlines: Applicants notified on a rolling basis starting 6/1; must reply within 2 week(s) of notification.

CONTACT
Kristen Brezler, Director of Financial Aid
18618 Crestwood Drive, Hagerstown, MD 21742
(301) 739-2670

Loyola University Maryland
Baltimore, Maryland   Federal Code: 002078
www.loyola.edu   CSS Code: 5370

4-year private university in very large city, affiliated with the Roman Catholic Church.
Enrollment: 4,067 undergrads, 1% part-time. 1,032 full-time freshmen.
Selectivity: Admits 50 to 75% of applicants.

BASIC COSTS (2016-2017)
Tuition and fees: $46,430.
Room and board: $13,870.

FINANCIAL AID PICTURE (2015-2016)
Students with need: Out of 817 full-time freshmen who applied for aid, 657 were judged to have need. Of these, 657 received aid, and 604 had their full need met. Average financial aid package met 89% of need; average scholarship/grant was $25,990; average loan was $6,010. For part-time students, average financial aid package was $5,500.
Students without need: 218 full-time freshmen who did not demonstrate need for aid received scholarships/grants; average award was $17,165. No-need awards available for academics, athletics, ROTC.
Scholarships offered: 29 full-time freshmen received athletic scholarships; average amount $29,045.

FINANCIAL AID PROCEDURES
Forms required: FAFSA, CSS PROFILE.
Dates and Deadlines: Closing date 1/15. Applicants notified by 3/15; must reply by 5/1.
Transfers: No deadline. Applicants notified on a rolling basis starting 5/1; must reply by 8/1.

CONTACT
Mark Lindenmeyer, Director of Financial Aid / Assistant Vice President for Enrollment
4501 North Charles Street, Baltimore, MD 21210-2699
(410) 617-2576

Maryland Institute College of Art
Baltimore, Maryland
www.mica.edu   Federal Code: 002080

4-year private visual arts college in very large city.
Enrollment: 1,673 undergrads, 1% part-time. 351 full-time freshmen.
Selectivity: Admits 50 to 75% of applicants.

BASIC COSTS (2016-2017)
Tuition and fees: $45,400.
Per-credit charge: $1,820.
Room and board: $12,450.

FINANCIAL AID PICTURE
Students with need: Need-based aid available for full-time and part-time students. Work study available nights, weekends, and for part-time students.
Students without need: No-need awards available for academics, art.

FINANCIAL AID PROCEDURES
Forms required: FAFSA, institutional form.
Dates and Deadlines: Closing date 2/15. Applicants notified by 4/1; must reply by 5/1.
Transfers: Closing date 3/1. Applicants notified by 4/25; must reply by 5/1.

CONTACT
Diane Prengaman, Associate Vice President for Financial Aid
1300 Mount Royal Avenue, Baltimore, MD 21217-4134
(410) 225-2285

McDaniel College
Westminster, Maryland
www.mcdaniel.edu   Federal Code: 002109

4-year private liberal arts college in large town.
Enrollment: 1,528 undergrads. 388 full-time freshmen.
Selectivity: Admits over 75% of applicants.

BASIC COSTS (2017-2018)
Tuition and fees: $41,800.
Per-credit charge: $1,306.
Room and board: $11,110.

FINANCIAL AID PICTURE (2016-2017)
Students with need: Out of 347 full-time freshmen who applied for aid, 315 were judged to have need. Of these, 314 received aid, and 94 had their full need met. Average financial aid package met 90% of need; average scholarship/grant was $35,159; average loan was $4,025. Need-based aid available for part-time students.
Students without need: 68 full-time freshmen who did not demonstrate need for aid received scholarships/grants; average award was $23,009. No-need awards available for academics, ROTC, state/district residency.
Scholarships offered: Academic scholarships: $5,000-$21,000. Honors Scholarship Program: $23,000-full tuition; separate competitive process with application due 1/2; interview required. Dorsey Scholars Program: full tuition, room and board; based on 1400 SAT, 3.8 GPA in rigorous curriculum, discussion-based sessions, interviews, essay. Educator's Legacy Scholarship: $25,000 per year; students with parents/guardians employed full-time in K-12 education.

FINANCIAL AID PROCEDURES
Forms required: FAFSA.
Dates and Deadlines: Priority date 3/1; no closing date. Applicants notified on a rolling basis starting 3/15; must reply by 5/1 or within 2 week(s) of notification.
Transfers: No deadline. Applicants notified on a rolling basis starting 2/15; must reply by 8/1 or within 2 week(s) of notification.

CONTACT
Zhanna Goltser, Director of Financial Aid
2 College Hill, Westminster, MD 21157-4390
(410) 857-2233

Montgomery College
Rockville, Maryland
www.montgomerycollege.edu   Federal Code: 006911

2-year public community college in very large city.
Enrollment: 19,096 undergrads.
Selectivity: Open admission; but selective for some programs.

BASIC COSTS (2016-2017)
Tuition and fees: $4,902; out-of-district residents $9,474; out-of-state residents $12,894.
Per-credit charge: $122; out-of-district residents $249; out-of-state residents $344.

FINANCIAL AID PICTURE
Students with need: Need-based aid available for full-time and part-time students. Work study available nights, weekends, and for part-time students.
Students without need: No-need awards available for academics, alumni affiliation, art, athletics, leadership, minority status, music/drama, state/district residency.
Scholarships offered: Board of Trustees Academic Potential Scholarship: first year of tuition; based on GPA and high school nominations; 125 awards available.

FINANCIAL AID PROCEDURES
Forms required: FAFSA, institutional form.
Dates and Deadlines: Priority date 5/15; no closing date. Applicants notified on a rolling basis starting 5/30.
Transfers: No deadline. Applicants notified on a rolling basis starting 1/1; must reply within 4 week(s) of notification.

CONTACT

Melissa Gregory, Director of Financial Aid

51 Mannakee Street, Rockville, MD 20850

(240) 567-5100

Morgan State University

Baltimore, Maryland

www.morgan.edu   Federal Code: 002083

4-year public university in large city.

Enrollment: 6,333 undergrads, 9% part-time. 1,159 full-time freshmen.

Selectivity: Admits 50 to 75% of applicants.

BASIC COSTS (2016-2017)

Tuition and fees: $7,636; out-of-state residents $17,504.

Per-credit charge: $235; out-of-state residents $592.

Room and board: $9,910.

Additional info: Tuition/fee waivers available for minority students.

FINANCIAL AID PICTURE (2015-2016)

Students with need: Out of 1,019 full-time freshmen who applied for aid, 1,019 were judged to have need. Of these, 1,019 received aid, and 112 had their full need met. Average financial aid package met 37% of need; average scholarship/grant was $6,798; average loan was $3,394. For part-time students, average financial aid package was $5,592.

Students without need: 82 full-time freshmen who did not demonstrate need for aid received scholarships/grants; average award was $7,514. No-need awards available for academics, alumni affiliation, athletics.

Scholarships offered: 47 full-time freshmen received athletic scholarships; average amount $15,225.

FINANCIAL AID PROCEDURES

Forms required: FAFSA.

Dates and Deadlines: Priority date 4/1; no closing date. Applicants notified on a rolling basis; must reply within 2 week(s) of notification.

CONTACT

Tanya Wilkerson, Director of Financial Aid

1700 East Cold Spring Lane, Baltimore, MD 21251

(443) 885-3170

Mount St. Mary's University

Emmitsburg, Maryland

www.msmary.edu   Federal Code: 002086

4-year private university and liberal arts college in rural community, affiliated with the Roman Catholic Church.

Enrollment: 1,717 undergrads, 5% part-time. 417 full-time freshmen.

Selectivity: Admits 50 to 75% of applicants.

BASIC COSTS (2016-2017)

Tuition and fees: $39,000.

Per-credit charge: $1,250.

Room and board: $12,610.

Additional info: Tuition/fee waivers available for minority students.

FINANCIAL AID PICTURE (2016-2017)

Students with need: Out of 372 full-time freshmen who applied for aid, 324 were judged to have need. Of these, 323 received aid, and 85 had their full need met. Average financial aid package met 75% of need; average scholarship/grant was $24,533; average loan was $4,248. For part-time students, average financial aid package was $3,576.

Students without need: 86 full-time freshmen who did not demonstrate need for aid received scholarships/grants; average award was $19,615. No-need awards available for academics, alumni affiliation, athletics, leadership, minority status, ROTC.

Scholarships offered: *Merit:* Founder's Scholarship: full-tuition; student must be accepted into Honors Program, 3.5 GPA, and minimum SAT score of 1220 or higher (exclusive of writing) or ACT score of 25 or higher; 2 awards. *Athletic:* 42 full-time freshmen received athletic scholarships; average amount $17,578.

FINANCIAL AID PROCEDURES

Forms required: FAFSA.

Dates and Deadlines: Priority date 12/1; closing date 3/1. Applicants notified on a rolling basis starting 1/15; must reply by 5/1.

Transfers: Scholarships available based on GPA at previous institution.

CONTACT

David Reeder, Director of Financial Aid

16300 Old Emmitsburg Road, Emmitsburg, MD 21727

(800) 448-4347

Notre Dame of Maryland University

Baltimore, Maryland

www.ndm.edu   Federal Code: 002065

4-year private liberal arts college for women in very large city, affiliated with the Roman Catholic Church.

Enrollment: 869 undergrads, 41% part-time. 93 full-time freshmen.

Selectivity: Admits 50 to 75% of applicants.

BASIC COSTS (2016-2017)

Tuition and fees: $35,019.

Per-credit charge: $1,126.

Room and board: $11,446.

FINANCIAL AID PICTURE

Students with need: Need-based aid available for full-time and part-time students.

Students without need: No-need awards available for academics, alumni affiliation, art, leadership, music/drama, ROTC.

Scholarships offered: Academic/achievement awards: $6,000 to full tuition. Endowed scholarships: $1,000 to $8,000; variable criteria; usually 20-35 awards.

Additional info: Maximum consideration for financial aid if application received by February 15. Auditions and portfolios in areas of art, music and writing considered for scholarships.

FINANCIAL AID PROCEDURES

Forms required: FAFSA.

Dates and Deadlines: Priority date 2/15; no closing date. Applicants notified on a rolling basis starting 3/15; must reply by 5/1 or within 2 week(s) of notification.

Transfers: Applicants notified by 3/15; must reply by 5/1 or within 2 week(s) of notification. Specific non-need based merit scholarships available for transfer students. Transfer scholarships: range from $7000 to full tuition.

CONTACT

Audrey Brooks, Director of Financial Aid

4701 North Charles Street, Baltimore, MD 21210

(410) 532-5369

Prince George's Community College

Largo, Maryland

www.pgcc.edu   Federal Code: 002089

2-year public community college in very large city.

Enrollment: 12,617 undergrads.

Selectivity: Open admission; but selective for some programs.

BASIC COSTS (2016-2017)

Tuition and fees: $4,550; out-of-district residents $7,190; out-of-state residents $10,100.

Per-credit charge: $105; out-of-district residents $193; out-of-state residents $290.

FINANCIAL AID PICTURE

Students with need: Need-based aid available for full-time and part-time students.

Students without need: This college awards aid only to students with need.

FINANCIAL AID PROCEDURES

Forms required: FAFSA, institutional form.

Dates and Deadlines: Priority date 6/1; no closing date. Applicants notified on a rolling basis starting 6/1; must reply within 2 week(s) of notification.

CONTACT

Sharon Hasson, Director of Financial Aid

301 Largo Road, Largo, MD 20774

(301) 322-0866

St. John's College

Annapolis, Maryland

www.sjc.edu   Federal Code: 002092

4-year private liberal arts college in large town.

Enrollment: 434 undergrads. 127 full-time freshmen.

Selectivity: Admits 50 to 75% of applicants.

BASIC COSTS (2017-2018)

Tuition and fees: $51,670.

Room and board: $12,233.

FINANCIAL AID PICTURE (2015-2016)

Students with need: Need-based aid available for full-time and part-time students. Work study available nights, weekends, and for part-time students.

Students without need: No-need awards available for academics.

Scholarships offered: Academic scholarships range up to $20,000 for the academic year; students encouraged to apply under Early Action I or II.

Additional info: All applicants automatically considered for merit scholarships, and all students completing the FAFSA are considered for need-based financial aid.

FINANCIAL AID PROCEDURES

Forms required: FAFSA, state aid form. International students must complete CSS PROFILE.

Dates and Deadlines: Priority date 2/15; no closing date. Applicants notified on a rolling basis starting 12/15; must reply by 5/1 or within 2 week(s) of notification.

Transfers: Must reply by 5/1 or within 2 week(s) of notification.

CONTACT

Steven Bell, Director of Financial Aid

60 College Avenue, Annapolis, MD 21401

(410) 626-2502

St. Mary's College of Maryland

St. Mary's City, Maryland

www.smcm.edu   Federal Code: 002095

4-year public liberal arts college in small town.

Enrollment: 1,618 undergrads, 2% part-time. 394 full-time freshmen.

Selectivity: Admits over 75% of applicants.

BASIC COSTS (2016-2017)

Tuition and fees: $14,192; out-of-state residents $29,340.

Room and board: $12,442.

FINANCIAL AID PICTURE (2015-2016)

Students with need: Out of 327 full-time freshmen who applied for aid, 213 were judged to have need. Of these, 210 received aid, and 14 had their full need met. Average financial aid package met 72% of need; average scholarship/grant was $10,408; average loan was $3,222. Need-based aid available for part-time students.

Students without need: 123 full-time freshmen who did not demonstrate need for aid received scholarships/grants; average award was $3,807. No-need awards available for academics.

FINANCIAL AID PROCEDURES

Forms required: FAFSA.

Dates and Deadlines: Priority date 2/15; no closing date. Applicants notified by 3/15; must reply by 7/1.

Transfers: Applicants notified by 4/15; must reply within 2 week(s) of notification. All financial aid recipients must have GED or high school diploma. Financial aid transcript required from previous colleges attended.

CONTACT

Rob Maddox, Associate Director of Financial Aid

47645 College Drive, St. Mary's City, MD 20686-3001

(240) 895-3000

Salisbury University

Salisbury, Maryland

www.salisbury.edu   Federal Code: 002091

4-year public university and liberal arts college in large town.

Enrollment: 7,657 undergrads, 5% part-time. 1,186 full-time freshmen.

Selectivity: Admits 50 to 75% of applicants.

BASIC COSTS (2016-2017)

Tuition and fees: $9,364; out-of-state residents $17,776.

Per-credit charge: $281; out-of-state residents $631.

Room and board: $11,350.

FINANCIAL AID PICTURE (2015-2016)

Students with need: Out of 938 full-time freshmen who applied for aid, 617 were judged to have need. Of these, 615 received aid, and 103 had their full need met. Average financial aid package met 51% of need; average scholarship/grant was $7,197; average loan was $3,212. For part-time students, average financial aid package was $5,300.

Students without need: 244 full-time freshmen who did not demonstrate need for aid received scholarships/grants; average award was $2,824. No-need awards available for academics, alumni affiliation, art, leadership, music/drama, ROTC, state/district residency.

FINANCIAL AID PROCEDURES

Forms required: FAFSA.

Dates and Deadlines: Priority date 3/1; no closing date. Applicants notified by 3/15; must reply by 5/1.

Transfers: No deadline.

CONTACT

Elizabeth Zimmerman, Director of Financial Aid

1101 Camden Avenue, Salisbury, MD 21801

(410) 543-6165

Stevenson University

Stevenson, Maryland

www.stevenson.edu   Federal Code: 002107

4-year private university in very large city.

Enrollment: 3,598 undergrads, 15% part-time. 783 full-time freshmen.

Selectivity: Admits 50 to 75% of applicants.

BASIC COSTS (2016-2017)
Tuition and fees: $33,168.
Per-credit charge: $780.
Room and board: $12,702.

FINANCIAL AID PICTURE (2016-2017)
Students with need: Out of 740 full-time freshmen who applied for aid, 711 were judged to have need. Of these, 711 received aid, and 117 had their full need met. Average financial aid package met 61% of need; average scholarship/grant was $20,230; average loan was $3,308. For part-time students, average financial aid package was $4,119.
Students without need: 114 full-time freshmen who did not demonstrate need for aid received scholarships/grants; average award was $16,010. No-need awards available for academics, art.
Additional info: Cooperative Education Program allows students to work in their field of study with area corporations.

FINANCIAL AID PROCEDURES
Forms required: FAFSA.
Dates and Deadlines: Priority date 2/15; no closing date. Applicants notified on a rolling basis starting 3/15; must reply by 5/1 or within 2 week(s) of notification.
Transfers: Closing date 3/1. Applicants notified on a rolling basis starting 3/1.

CONTACT
Barbara Miller, Assistant Vice President of Financial Aid
1525 Greenspring Valley Road, Stevenson, MD 21153-0641
(443) 334-3500

Towson University
Towson, Maryland
www.towson.edu   Federal Code: 002099

4-year public university in small city.
Enrollment: 18,968 undergrads, 11% part-time. 2,750 full-time freshmen.
Selectivity: Admits 50 to 75% of applicants.

BASIC COSTS (2016-2017)
Tuition and fees: $9,408; out-of-state residents $21,076.
Per-credit charge: $283; out-of-state residents $768.
Room and board: $11,754.

FINANCIAL AID PICTURE (2016-2017)
Students with need: Out of 2,331 full-time freshmen who applied for aid, 1,615 were judged to have need. Of these, 1,518 received aid, and 153 had their full need met. Average financial aid package met 55% of need; average scholarship/grant was $9,832; average loan was $3,117. For part-time students, average financial aid package was $5,544.
Students without need: 202 full-time freshmen who did not demonstrate need for aid received scholarships/grants; average award was $4,948. No-need awards available for academics, alumni affiliation, art, athletics, leadership, music/drama, ROTC, state/district residency.
Scholarships offered: *Merit:* Wide variety of merit-based scholarships including several scholarships for students in specific majors. *Athletic:* 60 full-time freshmen received athletic scholarships; average amount $9,272.

FINANCIAL AID PROCEDURES
Forms required: FAFSA, state aid form.
Dates and Deadlines: Priority date 1/20; no closing date. Applicants notified on a rolling basis starting 3/21; must reply by 3/15 or within 2 week(s) of notification.
Transfers: Must reply by 5/15 or within 2 week(s) of notification.

CONTACT
David Horne, Director of Financial Aid
8000 York Road, Towson, MD 21252-0001
(410) 704-4236

United States Naval Academy
Annapolis, Maryland
www.usna.edu

4-year public military college in large town.
Enrollment: 4,526 undergrads. 1,178 full-time freshmen.
Selectivity: Admits less than 50% of applicants.

BASIC COSTS (2016-2017)
Additional info: The academy does not charge tuition, room, board, or any other fees. Medical and dental care is provided by the United States Government. Each midshipman receives a monthly salary to cover costs of books, supplies, uniform, laundry, and equipment including a computer and a printer.

FINANCIAL AID PICTURE
Students without need: 1,178 full-time freshmen who did not demonstrate need for aid received scholarships/grants.

CONTACT
52 King George Street, Annapolis, MD 21402-1318

University of Baltimore
Baltimore, Maryland
www.ubalt.edu   Federal Code: 002102

4-year public university and liberal arts college in very large city.
Enrollment: 3,307 undergrads.

BASIC COSTS (2016-2017)
Tuition and fees: $8,596; out-of-state residents $20,242.
Per-credit charge: $302; out-of-state residents $954.

FINANCIAL AID PICTURE
Students with need: Need-based aid available for full-time and part-time students.

FINANCIAL AID PROCEDURES
Forms required: FAFSA, institutional form.
Dates and Deadlines: Applicants notified on a rolling basis.
Transfers: Closing date 5/1. Applicants notified on a rolling basis; must reply within 2 week(s) of notification. Scholarship application deadline 3/1.

CONTACT
Joseph Blevins, Director, Financial Aid
1420 North Charles Street, Baltimore, MD 21201-5779
(410) 837-4763

University of Maryland: Baltimore
Baltimore, Maryland
www.umaryland.edu   Federal Code: 002104

Upper-division public university and health science college in very large city.
Enrollment: 904 undergrads, 22% part-time.

BASIC COSTS (2016-2017)
Tuition and fees: $10,317; out-of-state residents $34,780.
Per-credit charge: $372; out-of-state residents $1,179.
Additional info: Tuition and fees vary by program.

FINANCIAL AID PICTURE
Students with need: Need-based aid available for full-time and part-time students. Work study available nights, weekends, and for part-time students.
Additional info: Maryland state deadline 3/1.

FINANCIAL AID PROCEDURES
Forms required: FAFSA, state aid form.

Dates and Deadlines: Priority date 3/15; no closing date. Applicants notified on a rolling basis starting 4/15; must reply within 2 week(s) of notification.

CONTACT
Patricia Scott, Associate Director of Financial Aid
220 Arch Street, Baltimore, MD 21201
(410) 706-7347

University of Maryland: Baltimore County
Baltimore, Maryland
www.umbc.edu   Federal Code: 002105

4-year public university in large city.
Enrollment: 11,025 undergrads, 14% part-time. 1,543 full-time freshmen.
Selectivity: Admits 50 to 75% of applicants.

BASIC COSTS (2016-2017)
Tuition and fees: $11,264; out-of-state residents $24,492.
Per-credit charge: $341; out-of-state residents $890.
Room and board: $11,218.

FINANCIAL AID PICTURE (2015-2016)
Students with need: Out of 1,220 full-time freshmen who applied for aid, 819 were judged to have need. Of these, 737 received aid, and 119 had their full need met. Average financial aid package met 57% of need; average scholarship/grant was $9,300; average loan was $3,248. For part-time students, average financial aid package was $5,791.
Students without need: 293 full-time freshmen who did not demonstrate need for aid received scholarships/grants; average award was $10,180. No-need awards available for academics, alumni affiliation, art, athletics, music/drama.
Scholarships offered: _Merit:_ UMBC General Merit Awards: $500-$22,000 per year. Scholars Programs Awards: $5,000-$22,000 per year; includes Center for Women and Information Technology Scholars Program, Humanities Scholars Program, Linehan Artist Scholars Program, Meyerhoff Scholars Program (Sciences and Engineering), and Sondheim Public Affairs Scholars Program, tuition, fees, room and board. **_Athletic:_** 44 full-time freshmen received athletic scholarships; average amount $10,016.

FINANCIAL AID PROCEDURES
Forms required: FAFSA.
Dates and Deadlines: Priority date 2/14; no closing date. Applicants notified on a rolling basis starting 3/25; must reply within 2 week(s) of notification.
Transfers: 2-year merit scholarships available for transfer students from community colleges.

CONTACT
Jane Hickey, Director of Financial Aid & Scholarships
1000 Hilltop Circle, Baltimore, MD 21250
(410) 455-2387

University of Maryland: College Park
College Park, Maryland
www.maryland.edu   Federal Code: 002103

4-year public university in large town.
Enrollment: 27,864 undergrads, 6% part-time. 4,543 full-time freshmen.
Selectivity: Admits less than 50% of applicants.

BASIC COSTS (2016-2017)
Tuition and fees: $10,182; out-of-state residents $32,045.
Per-credit charge: $346; out-of-state residents $1,258.
Room and board: $11,758.

Additional info: Tuition figure for junior and senior undergraduate students in business, engineering, and computer science majors is $1400 higher, regardless of residency.

FINANCIAL AID PICTURE
Students with need: Need-based aid available for full-time and part-time students. Work study available nights, weekends, and for part-time students.
Students without need: No-need awards available for academics, art, athletics, leadership, music/drama, ROTC, state/district residency.
Additional info: Prepaid tuition plans available through state.

FINANCIAL AID PROCEDURES
Forms required: FAFSA.
Dates and Deadlines: Priority date 2/15; no closing date. Applicants notified on a rolling basis starting 4/1; must reply by 5/1.

CONTACT
Monique Boyd, Director of Financial Aid
Mitchell Building, College Park, MD 20742-5235
(301) 314-9000

University of Maryland: Eastern Shore
Princess Anne, Maryland
www.umes.edu   Federal Code: 002106

4-year public university in rural community.
Enrollment: 3,163 undergrads, 8% part-time. 1,011 full-time freshmen.
Selectivity: Admits less than 50% of applicants.

BASIC COSTS (2016-2017)
Tuition and fees: $7,804; out-of-state residents $17,188.
Per-credit charge: $212; out-of-state residents $534.
Room and board: $9,388.

FINANCIAL AID PICTURE (2015-2016)
Students with need: Out of 975 full-time freshmen who applied for aid, 866 were judged to have need. Of these, 820 received aid. Average financial aid package met 47% of need; average scholarship/grant was $3,673; average loan was $3,107. For part-time students, average financial aid package was $2,883.
Students without need: 17 full-time freshmen who did not demonstrate need for aid received scholarships/grants; average award was $3,368. No-need awards available for academics, alumni affiliation, art, athletics, leadership, music/drama, ROTC, state/district residency.
Scholarships offered: _Merit:_ STEAM Scholarship: For incoming and transfer students considering one of the STEAM (Science, Technology, Engineering, Agriculture, and Mathematics) majors. **_Athletic:_** 26 full-time freshmen received athletic scholarships; average amount $16,534.

FINANCIAL AID PROCEDURES
Forms required: FAFSA.
Dates and Deadlines: Priority date 3/1; closing date 4/1. Applicants notified on a rolling basis starting 4/16.
Transfers: Priority date 3/16; no deadline. Applicants notified on a rolling basis starting 2/17; must reply within 4 week(s) of notification.

CONTACT
Director of Financial Aid
Student Development Center, Suite 1140, Princess Anne, MD 21853
(410) 651-6172

University of Maryland: University College
Adelphi, Maryland
www.umuc.edu   Federal Code: 011644

4-year public virtual university in large town.
Enrollment: 41,068 undergrads, 77% part-time. 296 full-time freshmen.

Selectivity: Open admission.

BASIC COSTS (2016-2017)
Tuition and fees: $7,266; out-of-state residents $12,426.
Per-credit charge: $284; out-of-state residents $499.

FINANCIAL AID PICTURE (2015-2016)
Students with need: Out of 193 full-time freshmen who applied for aid, 178 were judged to have need. Of these, 142 received aid, and 1 had their full need met. Average financial aid package met 27% of need; average scholarship/grant was $3,686; average loan was $3,003. For part-time students, average financial aid package was $4,430.
Students without need: No-need awards available for academics, leadership.

FINANCIAL AID PROCEDURES
Forms required: FAFSA.
Dates and Deadlines: Priority date 6/1; no closing date. Applicants notified on a rolling basis starting 5/1; must reply within 2 week(s) of notification.

CONTACT
Eugene Lockett, Vice President and Chief Financial Officer
1616 McCormick Drive, Largo, MD 20774
(301) 985-7510

Washington Adventist University
Takoma Park, Maryland
www.wau.edu   Federal Code: 002067

4-year private liberal arts college in large town, affiliated with the Seventh-day Adventists.
Enrollment: 807 undergrads.

BASIC COSTS (2016-2017)
Tuition and fees: $23,400.
Room and board: $8,930.

FINANCIAL AID PICTURE (2015-2016)
Students with need: 70% of average financial aid package awarded as scholarships/grants, 30% awarded as loans/jobs. Need-based aid available for part-time students.
Students without need: No-need awards available for academics, alumni affiliation, athletics, religious affiliation.

FINANCIAL AID PROCEDURES
Forms required: FAFSA.
Dates and Deadlines: Priority date 3/1; closing date 3/31. Applicants notified on a rolling basis starting 5/31; must reply within 4 week(s) of notification.

CONTACT
Sharon Conway, Director of Financial Aid
7600 Flower Avenue, Takoma Park, MD 20912
(301) 891-4005

Washington College
Chestertown, Maryland
www.washcoll.edu   Federal Code: 002108

4-year private liberal arts college in small town.
Enrollment: 1,446 undergrads, 1% part-time. 391 full-time freshmen.
Selectivity: Admits less than 50% of applicants.

BASIC COSTS (2016-2017)
Tuition and fees: $43,842.
Room and board: $10,824.

FINANCIAL AID PICTURE (2015-2016)
Students with need: Out of 308 full-time freshmen who applied for aid, 266 were judged to have need. Of these, 266 received aid, and 74 had their

full need met. Average financial aid package met 91% of need; average scholarship/grant was $29,630; average loan was $3,429. Need-based aid available for part-time students.
Students without need: 106 full-time freshmen who did not demonstrate need for aid received scholarships/grants; average award was $17,710. No-need awards available for academics, art, music/drama.
Scholarships offered: National Honor Society Scholarship: $50,000 over 4 years; applicant must be member of National Honor Society, National Society of High School Scholars, or Cum Laude Society.

FINANCIAL AID PROCEDURES
Forms required: FAFSA.
Dates and Deadlines: Priority date 3/1; no closing date. Applicants notified on a rolling basis starting 1/5; must reply by 5/1 or within 2 week(s) of notification.

CONTACT
Dorryann Barnhardt, Director of Financial Aid
300 Washington Avenue, Chestertown, MD 21620-1197
(410) 778-7214

Wor-Wic Community College
Salisbury, Maryland
www.worwic.edu   Federal Code: 013842

2-year public community college in large town.
Enrollment: 2,654 undergrads, 69% part-time. 360 full-time freshmen.
Selectivity: Open admission; but selective for some programs.

BASIC COSTS (2016-2017)
Tuition and fees: $3,690; out-of-district residents $7,620; out-of-state residents $9,270.
Per-credit charge: $106; out-of-district residents $237; out-of-state residents $292.

FINANCIAL AID PICTURE
Students with need: Need-based aid available for full-time and part-time students. Work study available nights, weekends, and for part-time students.
Students without need: No-need awards available for academics, state/district residency.

FINANCIAL AID PROCEDURES
Forms required: FAFSA, institutional form.
Dates and Deadlines: Priority date 6/1; no closing date. Applicants notified on a rolling basis starting 4/1.

CONTACT
Deborah Jenkins, Director of Financial Aid
32000 Campus Drive, Salisbury, MD 21804
(410) 334-2905

Massachusetts

American International College
Springfield, Massachusetts
www.aic.edu   Federal Code: 002114

4-year private health science and liberal arts college in small city.
Enrollment: 1,408 undergrads, 4% part-time. 346 full-time freshmen.
Selectivity: Admits 50 to 75% of applicants.

BASIC COSTS (2016-2017)
Tuition and fees: $33,200.
Per-credit charge: $685.

Room and board: $13,490.

FINANCIAL AID PICTURE (2015-2016)

Students with need: Out of 322 full-time freshmen who applied for aid, 316 were judged to have need. Of these, 316 received aid, and 29 had their full need met. Average financial aid package met 70% of need; average scholarship/grant was $24,346; average loan was $3,230. For part-time students, average financial aid package was $7,455.

Students without need: 28 full-time freshmen who did not demonstrate need for aid received scholarships/grants; average award was $13,482. No-need awards available for academics, athletics.

Scholarships offered: *Merit:* Presidential, Provost, Opportunity Scholarships: $5,000 to $11,000; based on class rank, SAT, GPA. *Athletic:* 38 full-time freshmen received athletic scholarships; average amount $16,679.

FINANCIAL AID PROCEDURES

Forms required: FAFSA.

Dates and Deadlines: Priority date 10/1; no closing date. Applicants notified on a rolling basis starting 10/20; must reply within 4 week(s) of notification.

CONTACT

Sage Stachowiak, Director of Financial Aid
1000 State Street, Springfield, MA 01109
(413) 205-3259

Amherst College

Amherst, Massachusetts
www.amherst.edu

Federal Code: 002115
CSS Code: 3003

4-year private liberal arts college in large town.
Enrollment: 1,849 undergrads. 471 full-time freshmen.
Selectivity: Admits less than 50% of applicants.

BASIC COSTS (2016-2017)

Tuition and fees: $52,476.
Room and board: $13,710.

FINANCIAL AID PICTURE (2016-2017)

Students with need: Out of 318 full-time freshmen who applied for aid, 246 were judged to have need. Of these, 246 received aid, and 246 had their full need met. Average financial aid package met 100% of need; average scholarship/grant was $51,513; average loan was $352.

Students without need: This college awards aid only to students with need.

FINANCIAL AID PROCEDURES

Forms required: FAFSA, CSS PROFILE.

Dates and Deadlines: Priority date 2/15; no closing date. Applicants notified by 4/1; must reply by 5/1.

CONTACT

Gail Holt, Dean of Financial Aid
PO Box 5000, Amherst, MA 01002-5000
(413) 542-2296

Anna Maria College

Paxton, Massachusetts
www.annamaria.edu

Federal Code: 002117

4-year private liberal arts college in small town, affiliated with the Roman Catholic Church.
Enrollment: 1,057 undergrads, 26% part-time. 218 full-time freshmen.
Selectivity: Admits over 75% of applicants.

BASIC COSTS (2016-2017)

Tuition and fees: $36,110.
Per-credit charge: $1,410.

Room and board: $13,510.

FINANCIAL AID PICTURE (2015-2016)

Students with need: 62% of average financial aid package awarded as scholarships/grants, 38% awarded as loans/jobs. Need-based aid available for part-time students. Work study available nights, weekends, and for part-time students.

Students without need: No-need awards available for academics, music/drama.

FINANCIAL AID PROCEDURES

Forms required: FAFSA.

Dates and Deadlines: Priority date 3/1; no closing date. Applicants notified on a rolling basis starting 4/1.

Transfers: No deadline. Applicants notified on a rolling basis starting 4/1; must reply within 4 week(s) of notification. Deadline May 1 for state aid.

CONTACT

Sandra Pereira, Director of Financial Aid
50 Sunset Lane, Box O, Paxton, MA 01612-1198
(508) 849-3363

Assumption College

Worcester, Massachusetts
www.assumption.edu

Federal Code: 002118

4-year private liberal arts college in small city, affiliated with the Roman Catholic Church.
Enrollment: 1,976 undergrads, 1% part-time. 578 full-time freshmen.
Selectivity: Admits over 75% of applicants.

BASIC COSTS (2016-2017)

Tuition and fees: $36,260.
Per-credit charge: $1,184.
Room and board: $11,660.
Additional info: Tuition at time of enrollment locked for 4 years.

FINANCIAL AID PICTURE (2016-2017)

Students with need: Out of 512 full-time freshmen who applied for aid, 457 were judged to have need. Of these, 457 received aid, and 121 had their full need met. Average financial aid package met 74% of need; average scholarship/grant was $21,789; average loan was $3,361. Need-based aid available for part-time students.

Students without need: 110 full-time freshmen who did not demonstrate need for aid received scholarships/grants; average award was $15,148. No-need awards available for academics, athletics, music/drama.

Scholarships offered: *Merit:* Academic scholarships: $2,500-$22,000 per year; based on academic achievement and leadership talents. *Athletic:* 19 full-time freshmen received athletic scholarships; average amount $12,909.

FINANCIAL AID PROCEDURES

Forms required: FAFSA.

Dates and Deadlines: Closing date 2/15. Applicants notified on a rolling basis starting 2/16; must reply by 5/1.

Transfers: Closing date 3/31. Applicants notified on a rolling basis starting 3/15.

CONTACT

William Smith, Director of Financial Aid
500 Salisbury Street, Worcester, MA 01609-1296
(508) 767-7158

Babson College

Babson Park, Massachusetts
www.babson.edu

Federal Code: 002121
CSS Code: 3075

4-year private business college in large town.
Enrollment: 2,283 undergrads. 588 full-time freshmen.

Selectivity: Admits less than 50% of applicants.

BASIC COSTS (2016-2017)
Tuition and fees: $48,288.
Room and board: $15,376.

FINANCIAL AID PICTURE (2016-2017)
Students with need: Out of 308 full-time freshmen who applied for aid, 236 were judged to have need. Of these, 236 received aid, and 131 had their full need met. Average financial aid package met 97% of need; average scholarship/grant was $37,126; average loan was $3,557.
Students without need: This college awards aid only to students with need.
Scholarships offered: Presidential Scholarship: half tuition; based on high school record, co-curricular achievements, demonstrated leadership, writing skills, standardized test scores; approximately 40 awarded each year. Woman's Leadership Award: one quarter tuition; based on demonstrated leadership experience, future leadership potential, and academic achievement. Diversity Leadership Award: either full or half tuition; awarded to students with the greatest potential for leadership in creating a diverse Babson community. Weissmann Scholarship: full tuition. Global Scholars, full tuition for international students with financial need.

FINANCIAL AID PROCEDURES
Forms required: FAFSA, CSS PROFILE.
Dates and Deadlines: Closing date 2/15. Applicants notified by 4/1; must reply by 5/1.
Transfers: Closing date 4/15. Applicants notified by 5/1; must reply by 6/1.

CONTACT
Melissa Shaak, Director, Student Financial Services
231 Forest Street, Babson Park, MA 02457-0310
(781) 239-4219

Bard College at Simon's Rock
Great Barrington, Massachusetts   Federal Code: 009645
www.simons-rock.edu   CSS Code: 3795

4-year private liberal arts college in small town.
Enrollment: 362 undergrads, 1% part-time. 148 full-time freshmen.
Selectivity: Admits 50 to 75% of applicants.

BASIC COSTS (2016-2017)
Tuition and fees: $52,385.
Room and board: $14,060.
Additional info: Tuition/fee waivers available for minority students.

FINANCIAL AID PICTURE
Students with need: Need-based aid available for full-time students. Work study available nights, weekends, and for part-time students.
Students without need: No-need awards available for academics, alumni affiliation, minority status, state/district residency.
Scholarships offered: Acceleration to Excellence Program: up to full-tuition; for outstanding students who apply during 10th or 11th grade; based on academic excellence, extracurricular distinction, personal motivation, and character.

FINANCIAL AID PROCEDURES
Forms required: FAFSA, CSS PROFILE, state aid form.
Dates and Deadlines: Priority date 2/15; no closing date. Applicants notified on a rolling basis starting 3/15; must reply within 2 week(s) of notification.
Transfers: Priority date 2/1; closing date 5/1.

CONTACT
Denise Ackerman, Director of Financial Aid
Office of Admission, Great Barrington, MA 01230-1990
(413) 528-7297

Bay Path University
Longmeadow, Massachusetts
www.baypath.edu   Federal Code: 002122

4-year private liberal arts college for women in small town.
Enrollment: 1,886 undergrads, 25% part-time. 153 full-time freshmen.
Selectivity: Admits 50 to 75% of applicants.

BASIC COSTS (2016-2017)
Tuition and fees: $32,739.
Room and board: $12,610.

FINANCIAL AID PICTURE (2016-2017)
Students with need: Out of 148 full-time freshmen who applied for aid, 142 were judged to have need. Of these, 142 received aid, and 6 had their full need met. Average financial aid package met 74% of need; average scholarship/grant was $25,036; average loan was $4,238. For part-time students, average financial aid package was $6,037.
Students without need: 12 full-time freshmen who did not demonstrate need for aid received scholarships/grants; average award was $18,843. No-need awards available for academics.
Scholarships offered: 1897 Founders Scholarship: $17,000/year for residents, $12,000/year for commuters. Provost's Scholarship: $15,000/year for residents, $11,000/year for commuters. Dean's Scholarship: $14,000/year for residents, $10,000/year for commuters. Seize the Day Award: $8,000/year for residents, $7,000/year for commuters. Pathways Award: $5,000/year for residents, $5,000/year for commuters.

FINANCIAL AID PROCEDURES
Forms required: FAFSA.
Dates and Deadlines: Priority date 3/1; no closing date. Applicants notified on a rolling basis starting 3/1; must reply within 2 week(s) of notification.
Transfers: No deadline. Applicants notified on a rolling basis starting 3/1; must reply within 2 week(s) of notification.

CONTACT
Stephanie King, Director of Student Financial Services
588 Longmeadow Street, Longmeadow, MA 01106
(413) 565-1000 ext. 1345

Bay State College
Boston, Massachusetts
www.baystate.edu   Federal Code: 003965

2-year for-profit business and nursing college in very large city.
Enrollment: 884 undergrads, 41% part-time. 105 full-time freshmen.

BASIC COSTS (2016-2017)
Tuition and fees: $27,750.
Per-credit charge: $905.
Room and board: $13,000.

FINANCIAL AID PICTURE
Students with need: Need-based aid available for full-time and part-time students. Work study available nights, weekends, and for part-time students.
Students without need: No-need awards available for academics, alumni affiliation, job skills, leadership.

FINANCIAL AID PROCEDURES
Forms required: FAFSA.
Dates and Deadlines: Priority date 3/15; closing date 6/30. Applicants notified on a rolling basis starting 2/1.

CONTACT
Jeanne Stella-Devani, Director of Student Financial Services
122 Commonwealth Avenue, Boston, MA 02116
(617) 217-9066

Becker College

Worcester, Massachusetts
www.becker.edu   Federal Code: 002123

4-year private liberal arts college in small city.
Enrollment: 1,951 undergrads, 20% part-time. 407 full-time freshmen.
Selectivity: Admits 50 to 75% of applicants.

BASIC COSTS (2017-2018)
Tuition and fees: $38,250.
Per-credit charge: $1,444.
Room and board: $13,300.

FINANCIAL AID PICTURE (2015-2016)
Students with need: Out of 379 full-time freshmen who applied for aid, 354 were judged to have need. Of these, 354 received aid, and 35 had their full need met. Average financial aid package met 65% of need; average scholarship/grant was $10,211; average loan was $3,335. For part-time students, average financial aid package was $9,874.
Students without need: 49 full-time freshmen who did not demonstrate need for aid received scholarships/grants; average award was $14,070. No-need awards available for academics, state/district residency.

FINANCIAL AID PROCEDURES
Forms required: FAFSA.
Dates and Deadlines: Priority date 3/15; no closing date. Applicants notified on a rolling basis starting 2/1.
Transfers: No deadline. Applicants notified on a rolling basis starting 2/1.

CONTACT
Heather Ruland, Director of Finacial Aid
Office of Admissions, Worcester, MA 01609
(508) 373-9433

Benjamin Franklin Institute of Technology

Boston, Massachusetts
www.bfit.edu   Federal Code: 002151

2-year private technical college in very large city.
Enrollment: 485 undergrads.

BASIC COSTS (2016-2017)
Tuition and fees: $16,950.
Per-credit charge: $707.
Room and board: $15,050.

FINANCIAL AID PICTURE
Students with need: Need-based aid available for full-time and part-time students.
Students without need: No-need awards available for academics, leadership, state/district residency.

FINANCIAL AID PROCEDURES
Forms required: FAFSA.
Dates and Deadlines: Priority date 3/1; no closing date. Applicants notified on a rolling basis starting 3/1; must reply within 3 week(s) of notification.

CONTACT
Jamie Santiago, Director of Student Financial Services
41 Berkeley Street, Boston, MA 02116
(617) 588-1358

Bentley University

Waltham, Massachusetts
www.bentley.edu   Federal Code: 002124
                                  CSS Code: 3096

4-year private university and business college in small city.
Enrollment: 4,152 undergrads, 2% part-time. 915 full-time freshmen.
Selectivity: Admits less than 50% of applicants.

BASIC COSTS (2016-2017)
Tuition and fees: $45,760.
Room and board: $15,130.

FINANCIAL AID PICTURE (2015-2016)
Students with need: Out of 618 full-time freshmen who applied for aid, 419 were judged to have need. Of these, 419 received aid, and 171 had their full need met. Average financial aid package met 94% of need; average scholarship/grant was $30,336; average loan was $3,767. For part-time students, average financial aid package was $12,012.
Students without need: 185 full-time freshmen who did not demonstrate need for aid received scholarships/grants; average award was $18,101. No-need awards available for academics, athletics, leadership, minority status.
Scholarships offered: 18 full-time freshmen received athletic scholarships; average amount $3,510.

FINANCIAL AID PROCEDURES
Forms required: FAFSA. Deadlines for receipt of CSS Profile for Early Decision candidates is November 15. Regular Decision applicants need to complete the CSS Profile by January 7.
Dates and Deadlines: Closing date 1/7.
Transfers: Closing date 4/15. Applicants notified on a rolling basis starting 4/15. Transfer students are eligible for need-based institutional grants but not academic scholarships.

CONTACT
Donna Kendall, Executive Director of Financial Assistance and Enrollment Management
175 Forest Street, Waltham, MA 02452
(781) 891-3441

Berklee College of Music

Boston, Massachusetts
www.berklee.edu   Federal Code: 002126
                                  CSS Code: 3107

4-year private music and performing arts college in very large city.
Enrollment: 5,972 undergrads, 18% part-time. 1,136 full-time freshmen.
Selectivity: Admits less than 50% of applicants.

BASIC COSTS (2016-2017)
Tuition and fees: $41,398.
Per-credit charge: $1,461.
Room and board: $18,000.

FINANCIAL AID PICTURE (2016-2017)
Students with need: Out of 657 full-time freshmen who applied for aid, 538 were judged to have need. Of these, 501 received aid, and 56 had their full need met. Average financial aid package met 35% of need; average loan was $3,418. For part-time students, average financial aid package was $8,882.
Students without need: 266 full-time freshmen who did not demonstrate need for aid received scholarships/grants; average award was $19,354. No-need awards available for academics, music/drama.

FINANCIAL AID PROCEDURES
Forms required: FAFSA, CSS PROFILE.
Dates and Deadlines: Priority date 12/1; no closing date. Must reply within 2 week(s) of notification.

CONTACT

Tod Oliviere, Assistant Vice President for Student Financial Services
1140 Boylston Street, Boston, MA 02215
(617) 747-2274

Berkshire Community College

Pittsfield, Massachusetts
www.berkshirecc.edu   Federal Code: 002167

2-year public community college in large town.
Enrollment: 1,666 undergrads, 63% part-time. 185 full-time freshmen.
Selectivity: Open admission; but selective for some programs.

BASIC COSTS (2016-2017)
Tuition and fees: $6,240; out-of-state residents $13,260.
Per-credit charge: $26; out-of-state residents $260.

FINANCIAL AID PICTURE
Students with need: Need-based aid available for full-time and part-time students. Work study available nights, weekends, and for part-time students.
Students without need: No-need awards available for academics, job skills, leadership, minority status, state/district residency.

FINANCIAL AID PROCEDURES
Forms required: FAFSA.
Dates and Deadlines: Applicants notified on a rolling basis starting 6/1.
Transfers: No deadline. Applicants notified on a rolling basis.

CONTACT
Anne Moore, Director of Financial Aid
1350 West Street, Pittsfield, MA 01201-5786
(413) 236-1644

Boston Architectural College

Boston, Massachusetts
www.the-bac.edu   Federal Code: 003966

6-year private architecture and design college in very large city.
Enrollment: 308 undergrads, 2% part-time. 22 full-time freshmen.
Selectivity: Open admission; but selective for some programs.

BASIC COSTS (2016-2017)
Tuition and fees: $20,666.
Per-credit charge: $1,688.
Room and board: $13,280.

FINANCIAL AID PICTURE
Students with need: Need-based aid available for full-time and part-time students. Work study available nights, weekends, and for part-time students.
Students without need: No-need awards available for academics, art, leadership.

FINANCIAL AID PROCEDURES
Forms required: FAFSA.
Dates and Deadlines: Priority date 4/15; no closing date. Applicants notified on a rolling basis starting 3/30; must reply within 2 week(s) of notification.
Transfers: No deadline. Applicants notified on a rolling basis starting 3/1; must reply within 2 week(s) of notification.

CONTACT
Janice Wilkos-Greenberg, Director of Financial Aid
320 Newbury Street, Boston, MA 02115-2795
(617) 585-0125

Boston Baptist College

Boston, Massachusetts
www.boston.edu

4-year private Bible college in very large city, affiliated with the Baptist faith.
Enrollment: 89 undergrads.

BASIC COSTS (2016-2017)
Tuition and fees: $15,040.
Per-credit charge: $475.
Room and board: $8,102.

FINANCIAL AID PICTURE
Students with need: Need-based aid available for full-time and part-time students. Work study available nights, weekends, and for part-time students.
Students without need: No-need awards available for academics, alumni affiliation, job skills, leadership, religious affiliation.

FINANCIAL AID PROCEDURES
Forms required: FAFSA, state aid form, institutional form.

CONTACT
Jillian Phillips, Financial Aid Officer
950 Metropolitan Avenue, Boston, MA 02136
(617) 364-3510 ext. 244

Boston College

Chestnut Hill, Massachusetts   Federal Code: 002128
www.bc.edu   CSS Code: 3083

4-year private university in small city, affiliated with the Roman Catholic Church.
Enrollment: 9,309 undergrads. 2,162 full-time freshmen.
Selectivity: Admits less than 50% of applicants.

BASIC COSTS (2016-2017)
Tuition and fees: $51,296.
Room and board: $13,818.

FINANCIAL AID PICTURE (2015-2016)
Students with need: Out of 1,008 full-time freshmen who applied for aid, 861 were judged to have need. Of these, 861 received aid, and 861 had their full need met. Average financial aid package met 100% of need; average scholarship/grant was $35,519; average loan was $3,503. Need-based aid available for part-time students.
Students without need: 26 full-time freshmen who did not demonstrate need for aid received scholarships/grants; average award was $21,093. No-need awards available for academics, athletics, leadership, ROTC.
Scholarships offered: 66 full-time freshmen received athletic scholarships; average amount $49,353.

FINANCIAL AID PROCEDURES
Forms required: FAFSA, CSS PROFILE.
Dates and Deadlines: Priority date 2/1; no closing date. Applicants notified on a rolling basis starting 4/1.
Transfers: Priority date 3/15. Must reply within 2 week(s) of notification.

CONTACT
Mary McGranahan, Director of Financial Aid
140 Commonwealth Avenue, Devlin Hall 208, Chestnut Hill, MA 02467-3809
(617) 552-3300

Boston Conservatory

Boston, Massachusetts
www.bostonconservatory.edu   Federal Code: 002129

4-year private music and performing arts college in very large city.
Enrollment: 565 undergrads.

BASIC COSTS (2016-2017)

Tuition and fees: $43,860.

Per-credit charge: $1,670.

Room and board: $18,000.

FINANCIAL AID PICTURE

Students with need: Need-based aid available for full-time and part-time students. Work study available nights, weekends, and for part-time students.

Students without need: No-need awards available for music/drama.

FINANCIAL AID PROCEDURES

Forms required: FAFSA.

Dates and Deadlines: Priority date 3/1; no closing date. Applicants notified by 4/1; must reply by 5/1.

Transfers: Applicants notified on a rolling basis starting 4/1; must reply within 4 week(s) of notification.

CONTACT

Nicole Brennan, Director of Financial Aid

8 The Fenway, Boston, MA 02215

(617) 912-9147

Boston University

Boston, Massachusetts
www.bu.edu

Federal Code: 002130
CSS Code: 3087

4-year private university in very large city.

Enrollment: 16,511 undergrads, 2% part-time. 3,550 full-time freshmen.

Selectivity: Admits less than 50% of applicants.

BASIC COSTS (2016-2017)

Tuition and fees: $50,240.

Per-credit charge: $1,537.

Room and board: $14,870.

FINANCIAL AID PICTURE (2016-2017)

Students with need: Out of 1,675 full-time freshmen who applied for aid, 1,325 were judged to have need. Of these, 1,320 received aid, and 299 had their full need met. Average financial aid package met 88% of need; average scholarship/grant was $35,861; average loan was $4,034. For part-time students, average financial aid package was $16,692.

Students without need: 249 full-time freshmen who did not demonstrate need for aid received scholarships/grants; average award was $23,169. No-need awards available for academics, alumni affiliation, art, athletics, leadership, music/drama, religious affiliation, ROTC, state/district residency.

Scholarships offered: *Merit:* Trustee Scholar Program: full-tuition and fees (renewable); candidates nominated by high school principals, headmasters, or counselors. Presidential Scholarship: $20,000 (renewable); based on exceptionally strong high school academic record. *Athletic:* 67 full-time freshmen received athletic scholarships; average amount $45,881.

Additional info: Financial aid deadline for early decision applicants: 11/1; Financial Aid deadline for early decision 2 applicants: 1/3. Graduates of Boston's public high schools who complete financial aid application and demonstrate need will be awarded financial aid packages that contain no loans and meet full demonstrated need.

FINANCIAL AID PROCEDURES

Forms required: FAFSA, CSS PROFILE.

Dates and Deadlines: Closing date 2/1. Applicants notified on a rolling basis starting 4/1; must reply by 5/1 or within 2 week(s) of notification.

Transfers: Closing date 3/1. Applicants notified on a rolling basis; must reply by 6/1. Transfer students cannot receive duplicate disbursements simultaneously from different institutions.

CONTACT

Christine McGuire, Vice President for Enrollment and Student Affairs

233 Bay State Road, Boston, MA 02215

(617) 353-2965

Brandeis University

Waltham, Massachusetts
www.brandeis.edu

Federal Code: 002133
CSS Code: 3092

4-year private university in small city.

Enrollment: 3,597 undergrads. 802 full-time freshmen.

Selectivity: Admits less than 50% of applicants.

BASIC COSTS (2016-2017)

Tuition and fees: $51,548.

Per-credit charge: $1,549.

Room and board: $14,380.

FINANCIAL AID PICTURE (2015-2016)

Students with need: Out of 478 full-time freshmen who applied for aid, 373 were judged to have need. Of these, 369 received aid, and 333 had their full need met. Average financial aid package met 95% of need; average scholarship/grant was $40,150; average loan was $3,335. For part-time students, average financial aid package was $40,598.

Students without need: 102 full-time freshmen who did not demonstrate need for aid received scholarships/grants; average award was $14,805. No-need awards available for academics.

Scholarships offered: Justice Brandeis Scholarships; full tuition. Martin Luther King scholarships; tuition and room and board. Presidential scholarships; $25,000. Dean's Awards; $15,000. Waltham High School scholarships; full tuition.

FINANCIAL AID PROCEDURES

Forms required: FAFSA, CSS PROFILE.

Dates and Deadlines: Priority date 2/1; no closing date. Must reply by 5/1.

Transfers: Priority date 4/1. International transfer students seeking scholarship or need-based financial assistance must apply by 2/1.

CONTACT

Sherri Avery, Executive Director of Student Financial Services

415 South Street, MS003, Waltham, MA 02453

(781) 736-3700

Bridgewater State University

Bridgewater, Massachusetts
www.bridgew.edu

Federal Code: 002183

4-year public university in large town.

Enrollment: 9,387 undergrads, 17% part-time. 1,495 full-time freshmen.

Selectivity: Admits over 75% of applicants.

BASIC COSTS (2016-2017)

Tuition and fees: $9,610; out-of-state residents $15,750.

Per-credit charge: $38; out-of-state residents $294.

Room and board: $12,200.

Additional info: Tuition/fee waivers available for minority students, unemployed or children of unemployed.

FINANCIAL AID PICTURE (2015-2016)

Students with need: Out of 1,389 full-time freshmen who applied for aid, 1,041 were judged to have need. Of these, 1,039 received aid, and 95 had their full need met. For part-time students, average financial aid package was $4,029.

Students without need: 14 full-time freshmen who did not demonstrate need for aid received scholarships/grants; average award was $2,195. No-need awards available for academics, alumni affiliation, minority status, ROTC, state/district residency.

Additional info: Tuition and/or fee waivers for Native Americans. Work-study programs available to half-time and full-time students.

FINANCIAL AID PROCEDURES

Forms required: FAFSA.

Dates and Deadlines: Priority date 3/1; no closing date. Applicants notified on a rolling basis starting 4/1; must reply within 3 week(s) of notification.

CONTACT

Janet Gumbris, Director of Financial Aid

Office of Admission-Welcome Center, Bridgewater, MA 02325

(508) 531-1341

Bristol Community College

Fall River, Massachusetts

www.bristolcc.edu   Federal Code: 002176

2-year public community college in small city.

Enrollment: 7,816 undergrads.

Selectivity: Open admission; but selective for some programs.

BASIC COSTS (2016-2017)

Tuition and fees: $5,715; out-of-state residents $11,895.

Per-credit charge: $24; out-of-state residents $230.

Additional info: Tuition/fee waivers available for unemployed or children of unemployed.

FINANCIAL AID PICTURE

Students with need: Need-based aid available for full-time and part-time students. Work study available nights, weekends, and for part-time students.

Students without need: No-need awards available for academics, art, leadership, minority status, music/drama.

FINANCIAL AID PROCEDURES

Forms required: FAFSA, institutional form.

Dates and Deadlines: Priority date 5/1; no closing date. Applicants notified on a rolling basis starting 5/1; must reply within 2 week(s) of notification.

Transfers: No deadline. Applicants notified on a rolling basis starting 3/1.

CONTACT

David Allen, Dean of Financial Aid and Technology

777 Elsbree Street, Fall River, MA 02720-7395

(508) 678-2811 ext. 2515

Bunker Hill Community College

Boston, Massachusetts

www.bhcc.edu   Federal Code: 011210

2-year public community college in very large city.

Enrollment: 12,004 undergrads, 65% part-time. 1,045 full-time freshmen.

Selectivity: Open admission; but selective for some programs.

BASIC COSTS (2016-2017)

Tuition and fees: $4,560; out-of-state residents $10,740.

Per-credit charge: $24; out-of-state residents $230.

Additional info: Tuition/fee waivers available for minority students.

FINANCIAL AID PICTURE

Students with need: Need-based aid available for full-time and part-time students.

Students without need: No-need awards available for academics.

FINANCIAL AID PROCEDURES

Forms required: FAFSA.

Dates and Deadlines: Priority date 5/1; no closing date. Applicants notified on a rolling basis starting 5/1; must reply within 2 week(s) of notification.

Transfers: No deadline. Applicants notified on a rolling basis; must reply within 2 week(s) of notification.

CONTACT

Melissa Holster, Executive Director of Student Financial Services

250 New Rutherford Avenue, Boston, MA 02129-2925

(617) 228-2275

Cambridge College

Cambridge, Massachusetts

www.cambridgecollege.edu   Federal Code: 021829

4-year private liberal arts and teachers college in small city.

Enrollment: 997 undergrads.

Selectivity: Open admission.

BASIC COSTS (2016-2017)

Tuition and fees: $13,760; out-of-state residents $13,760.

Per-credit charge: $401.

FINANCIAL AID PICTURE

Students with need: Need-based aid available for full-time and part-time students. Work study available nights, weekends, and for part-time students.

Students without need: This college awards aid only to students with need.

FINANCIAL AID PROCEDURES

Forms required: FAFSA.

Dates and Deadlines: Priority date 7/15; closing date 10/1. Applicants notified on a rolling basis starting 7/1.

CONTACT

Francis Lauder, Director of Financial Aid

1000 Massachusetts Avenue, Cambridge, MA 02138-5304

(800) 877-4723 ext. 1440

Cape Cod Community College

West Barnstable, Massachusetts

www.capecod.edu   Federal Code: 002168

2-year public community college in small town.

Enrollment: 2,764 undergrads, 66% part-time. 322 full-time freshmen.

Selectivity: Open admission; but selective for some programs.

BASIC COSTS (2016-2017)

Tuition and fees: $6,936; out-of-state residents $13,116.

Per-credit charge: $180; out-of-state residents $386.

Additional info: Tuition/fee waivers available for minority students.

FINANCIAL AID PICTURE

Students with need: Need-based aid available for full-time and part-time students.

Students without need: No-need awards available for academics, art, job skills, leadership, music/drama, state/district residency.

FINANCIAL AID PROCEDURES

Forms required: FAFSA.

Dates and Deadlines: Priority date 5/1; no closing date. Applicants notified on a rolling basis starting 5/1.

Transfers: No deadline. Applicants notified on a rolling basis starting 6/1.

CONTACT

Sherry Andersen, Director of Financial Aid

2240 Iyannough Road, West Barnstable, MA 02668-1599

(508) 362-2131 ext. 4393

Clark University

Worcester, Massachusetts   Federal Code: 002139

www.clarku.edu   CSS Code: 3279

4-year private university and liberal arts college in small city.

Enrollment: 2,247 undergrads, 1% part-time. 543 full-time freshmen.

Selectivity: Admits 50 to 75% of applicants.

BASIC COSTS (2016-2017)

Tuition and fees: $43,150.
Per-credit charge: $1,337.5.
Room and board: $8,450.

FINANCIAL AID PICTURE (2016-2017)

Students with need: Out of 433 full-time freshmen who applied for aid, 343 were judged to have need. Of these, 338 received aid, and 206 had their full need met. Average financial aid package met 91% of need; average scholarship/grant was $26,277; average loan was $4,033. For part-time students, average financial aid package was $15,061.

Students without need: 135 full-time freshmen who did not demonstrate need for aid received scholarships/grants; average award was $18,978. No-need awards available for academics, leadership.

Scholarships offered: Scholarships: $12,000-$18,000 per year; for academic excellence or community service. Presidential LEEP scholarship: full tuition, room and board for four years; awarded to 5 outstanding first year students.

FINANCIAL AID PROCEDURES

Forms required: FAFSA, CSS PROFILE.
Dates and Deadlines: Closing date 2/1. Applicants notified by 3/31; must reply by 5/1 or within 2 week(s) of notification.
Transfers: Closing date 4/1. Applicants notified on a rolling basis starting 6/1; must reply by 7/1 or within 2 week(s) of notification. Financial aid transcript from previous institution(s) attended required.

CONTACT

Mary Ellen Severance, Director of Financial Aid and Student Employment
950 Main Street, Worcester, MA 01610-1477
(508) 793-7478

College of the Holy Cross

Worcester, Massachusetts   Federal Code: 002141
www.holycross.edu   CSS Code: 3282

4-year private liberal arts college in small city, affiliated with the Roman Catholic Church.
Enrollment: 2,910 undergrads. 764 full-time freshmen.
Selectivity: Admits less than 50% of applicants.

BASIC COSTS (2016-2017)

Tuition and fees: $48,940.
Room and board: $13,225.

FINANCIAL AID PICTURE (2016-2017)

Students with need: Out of 546 full-time freshmen who applied for aid, 421 were judged to have need. Of these, 421 received aid, and 421 had their full need met. Average financial aid package met 100% of need; average scholarship/grant was $38,039; average loan was $4,850.

Students without need: 9 full-time freshmen who did not demonstrate need for aid received scholarships/grants; average award was $30,908. No-need awards available for academics, athletics, minority status, state/district residency.

Scholarships offered: 61 full-time freshmen received athletic scholarships; average amount $28,502.

Additional info: Cost of tuition above amount of Pell Grant waived for Worcester residents whose families earn less than $50,000.

FINANCIAL AID PROCEDURES

Forms required: FAFSA. CSS PROFILE required of all students applying for institutional aid.
Dates and Deadlines: Closing date 1/15. Applicants notified by 4/1; must reply by 5/1.
Transfers: Closing date 4/1. Applicants notified by 6/30. Financial aid is limited for transfer students.

CONTACT

Lynne Myers, Director of Financial Aid
One College Street, Worcester, MA 01610-2395
(508) 793-2265

Curry College

Milton, Massachusetts
www.curry.edu   Federal Code: 002143

4-year private liberal arts college in large town.
Enrollment: 2,653 undergrads, 21% part-time. 676 full-time freshmen.
Selectivity: Admits over 75% of applicants.

BASIC COSTS (2017-2018)

Tuition and fees: $38,596.
Per-credit charge: $1,226.
Room and board: $15,415.

FINANCIAL AID PICTURE (2016-2017)

Students with need: Out of 656 full-time freshmen who applied for aid, 545 were judged to have need. Of these, 545 received aid, and 72 had their full need met. Average financial aid package met 71% of need; average scholarship/grant was $9,343; average loan was $3,559. For part-time students, average financial aid package was $5,625.

Students without need: 126 full-time freshmen who did not demonstrate need for aid received scholarships/grants; average award was $17,433. No-need awards available for academics, alumni affiliation, leadership.

Scholarships offered: Trustees Scholarship, Academic Achievement Scholarships, Excellence in Education and Curry Success Scholarships: varying amounts ranging from $3,000-$22,000; based on past academic achievement, promising academic ability, demonstrated leadership skills, character and citizenship, community service and talent.

FINANCIAL AID PROCEDURES

Forms required: FAFSA.
Dates and Deadlines: Priority date 3/1; no closing date. Applicants notified on a rolling basis starting 12/1; must reply by 5/1 or within 2 week(s) of notification.
Transfers: No deadline. Applicants notified on a rolling basis starting 12/1; must reply by 5/1 or within 2 week(s) of notification.

CONTACT

Stephanny Elias, Associate VP of Finance for Student Financial Services
1071 Blue Hill Avenue, Milton, MA 02186-9984
(617) 333-2354

Dean College

Franklin, Massachusetts
www.dean.edu   Federal Code: 002144

2-year private liberal arts and performing arts college in large town.
Enrollment: 1,300 undergrads, 13% part-time. 497 full-time freshmen.
Selectivity: Admits over 75% of applicants.

BASIC COSTS (2016-2017)

Tuition and fees: $36,960.
Room and board: $15,732.

FINANCIAL AID PICTURE (2015-2016)

Students with need: Average financial aid package met 67% of need; average scholarship/grant was $7,216; average loan was $3,319. For part-time students, average financial aid package was $7,815.

Students without need: No-need awards available for academics, music/drama.

Scholarships offered: Trustee's Scholarship: $10,000-$12,000 per year; based on outstanding academic accomplishments or potential. President's

Leadership Scholarship: $8,000-$12,000 per year; given to students with leadership positions during their high school careers. Performing Arts Scholarship: $5,000-$11,000 per year; based on achievement in dance or theater.

FINANCIAL AID PROCEDURES

Forms required: FAFSA.

Dates and Deadlines: Priority date 3/1; no closing date. Applicants notified on a rolling basis starting 3/1; must reply by 5/1 or within 2 week(s) of notification.

Transfers: No deadline. Applicants notified on a rolling basis starting 3/1.

CONTACT

Frank Mullen, Dean of Student Financial Planning and Services
99 Main Street, Franklin, MA 02038-1994
(508) 541-1518

Eastern Nazarene College
Quincy, Massachusetts
www.enc.edu   Federal Code: 002145

4-year private liberal arts college in small city, affiliated with the Church of the Nazarene.

Enrollment: 780 undergrads, 16% part-time. 166 full-time freshmen.

Selectivity: Admits over 75% of applicants.

BASIC COSTS (2017-2018)

Tuition and fees: $31,780.

Per-credit charge: $1,260.

Room and board: $9,334.

FINANCIAL AID PICTURE (2016-2017)

Students with need: Out of 162 full-time freshmen who applied for aid, 162 were judged to have need. Of these, 162 received aid, and 16 had their full need met. Average financial aid package met 68% of need; average scholarship/grant was $23,000; average loan was $3,250. For part-time students, average financial aid package was $4,254.

Students without need: 3 full-time freshmen who did not demonstrate need for aid received scholarships/grants; average award was $12,320. No-need awards available for academics, alumni affiliation, leadership, religious affiliation, ROTC.

Additional info: Participant in Massachusetts University pre-payment plan.

FINANCIAL AID PROCEDURES

Forms required: FAFSA, institutional form.

Dates and Deadlines: Priority date 3/1; closing date 8/1. Applicants notified on a rolling basis starting 12/15; must reply by 8/1 or within 2 week(s) of notification.

Transfers: Applicants notified on a rolling basis starting 12/15; must reply by 8/1.

CONTACT

Delinda Hall, Director of Financial Aid
23 East Elm Avenue, Quincy, MA 02170
(617) 745-3712

Elms College
Chicopee, Massachusetts
www.elms.edu   Federal Code: 002140

4-year private liberal arts college in small city, affiliated with the Roman Catholic Church.

Enrollment: 1,155 undergrads, 17% part-time. 163 full-time freshmen.

Selectivity: Admits over 75% of applicants.

BASIC COSTS (2016-2017)

Tuition and fees: $33,470.

Room and board: $12,236.

FINANCIAL AID PICTURE (2016-2017)

Students with need: Out of 158 full-time freshmen who applied for aid, 150 were judged to have need. Of these, 150 received aid, and 19 had their full need met. Average financial aid package met 75% of need; average scholarship/grant was $24,376; average loan was $3,484. For part-time students, average financial aid package was $7,457.

Students without need: 13 full-time freshmen who did not demonstrate need for aid received scholarships/grants; average award was $14,730. No-need awards available for academics, alumni affiliation, leadership, religious affiliation, state/district residency.

FINANCIAL AID PROCEDURES

Forms required: FAFSA.

Dates and Deadlines: Priority date 3/1; no closing date. Applicants notified on a rolling basis starting 3/15; must reply by 5/1 or within 2 week(s) of notification.

Transfers: No deadline. Applicants notified on a rolling basis starting 3/15.

CONTACT

Kristin Hmieleski, Director of Financial Aid
291 Springfield Street, Chicopee, MA 01013-2839
(413) 265-2249

Emerson College
Boston, Massachusetts   Federal Code: 002146
www.emerson.edu   CSS Code: 3367

4-year private college of communication and the arts in very large city.

Enrollment: 3,782 undergrads, 1% part-time. 881 full-time freshmen.

Selectivity: Admits less than 50% of applicants.

BASIC COSTS (2016-2017)

Tuition and fees: $42,908.

Per-credit charge: $1,317.

Room and board: $16,320.

FINANCIAL AID PICTURE

Students with need: Need-based aid available for full-time and part-time students. Work study available nights, weekends, and for part-time students.

Students without need: No-need awards available for academics, leadership, music/drama, state/district residency.

Scholarships offered: Trustees Scholarships: half-tuition; honors program students may apply. Dean's Scholarships: $14,000. Emerson Stage Scholarships: amounts vary; based on performing arts audition and academic merit.

Additional info: Massachusetts Loan Plan available for parents of dependent undergraduates.

FINANCIAL AID PROCEDURES

Forms required: FAFSA, CSS PROFILE.

Dates and Deadlines: Closing date 3/1. Applicants notified by 4/1; must reply by 5/1 or within 3 week(s) of notification.

Transfers: Priority date 4/1.

CONTACT

Ruthanne Madsen, Vice President for Enrollment, Student Financial Services
120 Boylston Street, Boston, MA 02116-4624
(617) 824-8655

Emmanuel College
Boston, Massachusetts
www.emmanuel.edu   Federal Code: 002147

4-year private liberal arts college in very large city, affiliated with the Roman Catholic Church.

Enrollment: 1,907 undergrads, 4% part-time. 596 full-time freshmen.

Selectivity: Admits 50 to 75% of applicants.

BASIC COSTS (2017-2018)

Tuition and fees: $39,144.

Per-credit charge: $1,205.75.

Room and board: $14,628.

FINANCIAL AID PICTURE (2016-2017)

Students with need: Out of 546 full-time freshmen who applied for aid, 500 were judged to have need. Of these, 500 received aid, and 157 had their full need met. Average financial aid package met 75% of need; average scholarship/grant was $23,727; average loan was $3,634. For part-time students, average financial aid package was $6,207.

Students without need: 94 full-time freshmen who did not demonstrate need for aid received scholarships/grants; average award was $15,973. No-need awards available for academics, leadership.

FINANCIAL AID PROCEDURES

Forms required: FAFSA.

Dates and Deadlines: Priority date 2/15; no closing date. Applicants notified on a rolling basis starting 1/1.

CONTACT

Jennifer Porter, Associate Vice President for Student Financial Services
400 The Fenway, Boston, MA 02115
(617) 735-9938

Endicott College

Beverly, Massachusetts
www.endicott.edu   Federal Code: 002148

4-year private liberal arts college in large town.

Enrollment: 3,081 undergrads, 9% part-time. 713 full-time freshmen.

Selectivity: Admits over 75% of applicants.

BASIC COSTS (2016-2017)

Tuition and fees: $31,312.

Room and board: $14,500.

FINANCIAL AID PICTURE (2016-2017)

Students with need: Out of 688 full-time freshmen who applied for aid, 478 were judged to have need. Of these, 477 received aid, and 50 had their full need met. Average financial aid package met 62% of need; average scholarship/grant was $10,549; average loan was $3,645. For part-time students, average financial aid package was $7,557.

Students without need: 183 full-time freshmen who did not demonstrate need for aid received scholarships/grants; average award was $9,359. No-need awards available for academics, alumni affiliation, art, job skills, leadership, music/drama, religious affiliation, ROTC, state/district residency.

FINANCIAL AID PROCEDURES

Forms required: FAFSA, institutional form.

Dates and Deadlines: Priority date 3/15; no closing date. Applicants notified on a rolling basis starting 3/15; must reply within 2 week(s) of notification.

CONTACT

Marcia Toomey, Director of Financial Aid
376 Hale Street, Beverly, MA 01915-9985
(978) 232-2060

Fisher College

Boston, Massachusetts
www.fisher.edu   Federal Code: 002150

4-year private business and liberal arts college in very large city.

Enrollment: 1,556 undergrads, 28% part-time. 272 full-time freshmen.

Selectivity: Admits 50 to 75% of applicants.

BASIC COSTS (2017-2018)

Tuition and fees: $30,499.

Per-credit charge: $984.

Room and board: $15,768.

FINANCIAL AID PICTURE (2015-2016)

Students with need: Out of 254 full-time freshmen who applied for aid, 214 were judged to have need. Of these, 214 received aid. For part-time students, average financial aid package was $3,822.

Students without need: 58 full-time freshmen who did not demonstrate need for aid received scholarships/grants; average award was $8,110. No-need awards available for academics.

Scholarships offered: Fisher Honor Scholarship: $5,000; based on outstanding academic and personal achievement, contribution to school and community; renewable with 3.0 GPA. Presidential Scholarship: $8,000. Achievement Scholarship: $6,000. Opportunity Award: $5,000. Charles River Award: $3,000.

FINANCIAL AID PROCEDURES

Forms required: FAFSA.

Dates and Deadlines: Priority date 3/15; closing date 3/15. Applicants notified on a rolling basis starting 3/1.

Transfers: Transfer Student Scholarship; $2,500.

CONTACT

Pam Walker, Director of Financial Aid
Office of Admissions, Boston, MA 02116
(617) 236-8821

Fitchburg State University

Fitchburg, Massachusetts
www.fitchburgstate.edu   Federal Code: 002184

4-year public liberal arts and teachers college in small city.

Enrollment: 3,985 undergrads, 14% part-time. 781 full-time freshmen.

Selectivity: Admits 50 to 75% of applicants.

BASIC COSTS (2016-2017)

Tuition and fees: $10,169; out-of-state residents $16,249.

Per-credit charge: $40; out-of-state residents $294.

Room and board: $10,170.

FINANCIAL AID PICTURE (2015-2016)

Students with need: Out of 733 full-time freshmen who applied for aid, 530 were judged to have need. Of these, 516 received aid. For part-time students, average financial aid package was $5,962.

Students without need: 59 full-time freshmen who did not demonstrate need for aid received scholarships/grants; average award was $903. No-need awards available for academics, alumni affiliation, leadership, state/district residency.

FINANCIAL AID PROCEDURES

Forms required: FAFSA.

Dates and Deadlines: Priority date 3/1; no closing date. Applicants notified on a rolling basis starting 2/1; must reply within 2 week(s) of notification.

CONTACT

Brindle Denise, Director, Financial Aid
160 Pearl Street, Fitchburg, MA 01420-2697
(978) 665-3156

Framingham State University

Framingham, Massachusetts
www.framingham.edu   Federal Code: 002185

4-year public university in small city.

Enrollment: 4,100 undergrads, 10% part-time. 739 full-time freshmen.

Selectivity: Admits 50 to 75% of applicants.

BASIC COSTS (2016-2017)
Tuition and fees: $9,340; out-of-state residents $15,420.
Per-credit charge: $41; out-of-state residents $294.
Room and board: $11,250.

FINANCIAL AID PICTURE
Students with need: Need-based aid available for full-time and part-time students. Work study available nights, weekends, and for part-time students.
Students without need: No-need awards available for academics.
Scholarships offered: Senator Paul E. Tsongas Scholarship: full-tuition and fees; available to Massachusetts residents based on 3.75 GPA and test scores; 5 awarded. Merit scholarships: available to students majoring in education, natural or physical sciences based on GPA and test scores.

FINANCIAL AID PROCEDURES
Forms required: FAFSA.
Dates and Deadlines: Priority date 3/1; no closing date. Applicants notified on a rolling basis starting 3/15; must reply by 5/1 or within 2 week(s) of notification.
Transfers: Priority date 11/1; no deadline. Applicants notified on a rolling basis starting 11/1; must reply within 2 week(s) of notification.

CONTACT
Deborah Altsher, Director of Financial Aid
PO Box 9101, Framingham, MA 01701-9101
(508) 626-4534

Franklin W. Olin College of Engineering
Needham, Massachusetts
www.olin.edu   Federal Code: 039463

4-year private engineering college in large town.
Enrollment: 331 undergrads. 79 full-time freshmen.
Selectivity: Admits less than 50% of applicants.

BASIC COSTS (2016-2017)
Tuition and fees: $49,986.
Per-credit charge: $1,560.
Room and board: $15,800.

FINANCIAL AID PICTURE (2016-2017)
Students with need: Out of 59 full-time freshmen who applied for aid, 42 were judged to have need. Of these, 42 received aid, and 42 had their full need met. Average financial aid package met 100% of need; average scholarship/grant was $42,683; average loan was $2,981.
Students without need: 37 full-time freshmen who did not demonstrate need for aid received scholarships/grants; average award was $24,911. No-need awards available for academics, leadership.
Scholarships offered: The Olin Tuition Scholarship: 50% of tuition for up to 8 semesters; awarded to all matriculated students.
Additional info: Financial aid forms not needed for the Olin Tuition Scholarship, which all students receive. FAFSA is required to apply for need-based aid. The Olin Tuition Scholarship covers 50% of tuition for up to eight semesters. Olin meets full demonstrated need for students who qualify.

FINANCIAL AID PROCEDURES
Forms required: FAFSA.
Dates and Deadlines: Closing date 2/15. Applicants notified by 3/24; must reply by 5/1 or within 2 week(s) of notification.
Transfers: Closing date 2/15. Applicants notified by 3/24; must reply by 5/1 or within 2 week(s) of notification.

CONTACT
Jean Ricker, Director of Financial Aid
1000 Olin Way, Needham, MA 02492
(781) 292-2215

Gordon College
Wenham, Massachusetts
www.gordon.edu   Federal Code: 002153

4-year private liberal arts college in small town, affiliated with the nondenominational tradition.
Enrollment: 1,631 undergrads, 4% part-time. 426 full-time freshmen.
Selectivity: Admits over 75% of applicants.

BASIC COSTS (2017-2018)
Tuition and fees: $36,740.
Per-credit charge: $879.
Room and board: $11,000.

FINANCIAL AID PICTURE (2016-2017)
Students with need: Out of 356 full-time freshmen who applied for aid, 296 were judged to have need. Of these, 296 received aid, and 42 had their full need met. Average financial aid package met 70% of need; average scholarship/grant was $20,550; average loan was $3,734. For part-time students, average financial aid package was $15,084.
Students without need: 122 full-time freshmen who did not demonstrate need for aid received scholarships/grants; average award was $15,187. No-need awards available for academics, alumni affiliation, art, leadership, minority status, music/drama, ROTC, state/district residency.
Scholarships offered: Founder's Scholarship; $18,000-$16,000; based on academic achievement. Harold John Ockenga Scholarship; $14,000 to $16,000; based on academic record.T. Leonard Lewis Scholarship; $11,000 to $13,000; based on academic record. Isabel Warwick Wood Scholarship; $9,000; based on academic record. Choral Scholars Program; $5,000; for students with excellent ability/academic performance seeking career in vocal music field. National Merit Finalists and National Achievement Finalist Scholars; $24,000. All scholarships renewable annually.

FINANCIAL AID PROCEDURES
Forms required: FAFSA.
Dates and Deadlines: Priority date 3/1; no closing date. Applicants notified on a rolling basis starting 12/1; must reply by 5/1.
Transfers: Applicants notified on a rolling basis starting 12/1; must reply by 5/1 or within 2 week(s) of notification.

CONTACT
Daniel O'Connell, Senior Director of Student Financial Services
255 Grapevine Road, Wenham, MA 01984-1899
(800) 343-1379

Greenfield Community College
Greenfield, Massachusetts
www.gcc.mass.edu   Federal Code: 002169

2-year public community college in large town.
Enrollment: 1,649 undergrads, 62% part-time. 155 full-time freshmen.
Selectivity: Open admission; but selective for some programs.

BASIC COSTS (2017-2018)
Tuition and fees: $6,632; out-of-state residents $14,282.
Additional info: Tuition/fee waivers available for adults.

FINANCIAL AID PICTURE
Students with need: Need-based aid available for full-time and part-time students. Work study available nights, weekends, and for part-time students.
Students without need: This college awards aid only to students with need.

FINANCIAL AID PROCEDURES
Forms required: FAFSA, institutional form.
Dates and Deadlines: Priority date 4/15; no closing date. Applicants notified on a rolling basis starting 5/1; must reply within 2 week(s) of notification.

CONTACT
Linda Dejardins, Director of Financial Aid
One College Drive, Greenfield, MA 01301
(413) 775-1109

Hampshire College

Amherst, Massachusetts
www.hampshire.edu

Federal Code: 004661
CSS Code: 3447

4-year private liberal arts college in large town.
Enrollment: 1,396 undergrads. 370 full-time freshmen.
Selectivity: Admits 50 to 75% of applicants.

BASIC COSTS (2016-2017)
Tuition and fees: $50,550.
Room and board: $13,274.

FINANCIAL AID PICTURE
Students with need: Need-based aid available for full-time students. Work study available nights, weekends, and for part-time students.
Students without need: No-need awards available for academics, art, leadership, music/drama.

FINANCIAL AID PROCEDURES
Forms required: FAFSA, CSS PROFILE.
Dates and Deadlines: Closing date 1/15. Applicants notified by 4/1; must reply by 5/1 or within 4 week(s) of notification.
Transfers: Closing date 3/15. Applicants notified by 4/15; must reply by 6/1. Phi Theta Kappa Scholarship offered in amounts up to $15,000 per year.

CONTACT
Jennifer Lawton, Director of Financial Aid
893 West Street, Amherst, MA 01002-3359
(413) 559-5484

Harvard College

Cambridge, Massachusetts
www.college.harvard.edu

Federal Code: 002155
CSS Code: 3434

4-year private university and liberal arts college in small city.
Enrollment: 6,648 undergrads. 1,660 full-time freshmen.
Selectivity: Admits less than 50% of applicants.

BASIC COSTS (2016-2017)
Tuition and fees: $47,074.
Room and board: $15,951.

FINANCIAL AID PICTURE (2015-2016)
Students with need: Out of 1,058 full-time freshmen who applied for aid, 908 were judged to have need. Of these, 908 received aid, and 908 had their full need met. Average financial aid package met 100% of need; average scholarship/grant was $51,314; average loan was $2,617. Need-based aid available for part-time students.
Students without need: This college awards aid only to students with need.
Additional info: First year students with family income below $65,000 have a zero expected contribution. A $2,000 "start up grant" helps students to help with initial college expenses.

FINANCIAL AID PROCEDURES
Forms required: FAFSA, CSS PROFILE.
Dates and Deadlines: Closing date 3/1. Applicants notified by 4/1; must reply by 5/1 or within 2 week(s) of notification.
Transfers: Closing date 2/15. Applicants notified by 5/30; must reply within 2 week(s) of notification.

CONTACT
Sally Donahue, Director of Financial Aid
86 Brattle Street, Cambridge, MA 02138
(617) 495-1581

Hellenic College/Holy Cross

Brookline, Massachusetts
www.hchc.edu

Federal Code: 002154

4-year private liberal arts and seminary college in large town, affiliated with the Eastern Orthodox Church.
Enrollment: 119 undergrads, 1% part-time. 42 full-time freshmen.
Selectivity: Admits 50 to 75% of applicants.

BASIC COSTS (2016-2017)
Tuition and fees: $22,490.
Per-credit charge: $950.
Room and board: $16,192.

FINANCIAL AID PICTURE (2015-2016)
Students with need: Out of 42 full-time freshmen who applied for aid, 42 were judged to have need. Of these, 42 received aid. Average financial aid package met 27% of need; average scholarship/grant was $16,200; average loan was $3,612.
Students without need: This college awards aid only to students with need.

FINANCIAL AID PROCEDURES
Forms required: FAFSA, institutional form.
Transfers: No deadline. Applicants notified on a rolling basis; must reply within 2 week(s) of notification.

CONTACT
Kevin Derrivan, CFO
50 Goddard Avenue, Brookline, MA 02445
(617) 850-1239

Holyoke Community College

Holyoke, Massachusetts
www.hcc.edu

Federal Code: 002170

2-year public community college in large town.
Enrollment: 5,364 undergrads, 53% part-time. 929 full-time freshmen.
Selectivity: Open admission; but selective for some programs.

BASIC COSTS (2016-2017)
Tuition and fees: $5,570; out-of-state residents $11,750.
Per-credit charge: $24; out-of-state residents $230.

FINANCIAL AID PICTURE (2015-2016)
Students with need: 78% of average financial aid package awarded as scholarships/grants, 22% awarded as loans/jobs. Need-based aid available for part-time students. Work study available nights.
Students without need: No-need awards available for academics, art, leadership, music/drama.

FINANCIAL AID PROCEDURES
Forms required: FAFSA.
Dates and Deadlines: Priority date 5/1; no closing date. Applicants notified on a rolling basis starting 5/1; must reply within 2 week(s) of notification.

CONTACT
Karen Derouin, Director of Financial Aid
303 Homestead Avenue, Holyoke, MA 01040
(413) 552-2150

Laboure College
Milton, Massachusetts
www.laboure.edu   Federal Code: 006324

2-year private health science and nursing college in large town, affiliated with the Roman Catholic Church.
Enrollment: 751 undergrads, 95% part-time. 1 full-time freshmen.
Selectivity: Admits less than 50% of applicants.

BASIC COSTS (2016-2017)
Tuition and fees: $36,848.
Per-credit charge: $955.

FINANCIAL AID PICTURE (2015-2016)
Students with need: Out of 1 full-time freshmen who applied for aid, 1 were judged to have need. Of these, 1 received aid. Average financial aid package met 80% of need; average loan was $3,500. For part-time students, average financial aid package was $5,000.
Students without need: No-need awards available for academics, alumni affiliation, leadership, religious affiliation.

FINANCIAL AID PROCEDURES
Forms required: FAFSA.
Dates and Deadlines: Priority date 5/1; no closing date. Applicants notified on a rolling basis starting 1/15; must reply within 2 week(s) of notification.
Transfers: Priority date 12/1. Applicants notified on a rolling basis starting 12/1; must reply within 2 week(s) of notification.

CONTACT
Erin Hanlon, Director of Financial Aid
303 Adams Street, Milton, MA 02186
(617) 322-3531

Lasell College
Newton, Massachusetts
www.lasell.edu   Federal Code: 002158

4-year private business and liberal arts college in small city.
Enrollment: 1,778 undergrads, 2% part-time. 437 full-time freshmen.
Selectivity: Admits over 75% of applicants.

BASIC COSTS (2016-2017)
Tuition and fees: $33,600.
Room and board: $13,900.

FINANCIAL AID PICTURE (2016-2017)
Students with need: Out of 406 full-time freshmen who applied for aid, 376 were judged to have need. Of these, 376 received aid, and 58 had their full need met. Average financial aid package met 76% of need; average scholarship/grant was $23,983; average loan was $3,230. For part-time students, average financial aid package was $12,484.
Students without need: 58 full-time freshmen who did not demonstrate need for aid received scholarships/grants; average award was $10,365. No-need awards available for academics, alumni affiliation, leadership.

FINANCIAL AID PROCEDURES
Forms required: FAFSA.
Dates and Deadlines: Priority date 11/20; no closing date. Applicants notified on a rolling basis starting 11/30; must reply by 5/1 or within 2 week(s) of notification.
Transfers: Priority date 11/20; no deadline. Applicants notified on a rolling basis starting 11/30; must reply by 5/1 or within 2 week(s) of notification.

CONTACT
Michele Kosboth, Director of Student Financial Planning
1844 Commonwealth Avenue, Newton, MA 02466-2709
(617) 243-2227

Lesley University
Cambridge, Massachusetts
www.lesley.edu   Federal Code: 002160

4-year private liberal arts and teachers college in very large city.
Enrollment: 1,418 undergrads.

BASIC COSTS (2016-2017)
Tuition and fees: $26,250.
Room and board: $15,300.

FINANCIAL AID PICTURE
Students with need: Need-based aid available for full-time and part-time students. Work study available nights, weekends, and for part-time students.
Students without need: No-need awards available for academics, art, leadership, minority status, state/district residency.
Scholarships offered: Freshmen scholarships: $5,000-full tuition; for students with strong academic backgrounds who have shown a commitment to community service and making a difference in the lives of others.

FINANCIAL AID PROCEDURES
Forms required: FAFSA.
Dates and Deadlines: Priority date 2/15; no closing date. Applicants notified on a rolling basis starting 2/1.
Transfers: Priority date 3/15.

CONTACT
Scott Jewell, Director of Financial Aid
29 Everett Street, Cambridge, MA 02140-2790
(617) 349-8667

Massachusetts Bay Community College
Wellesley Hills, Massachusetts
www.massbay.edu   Federal Code: 002171

2-year public community college in large town.
Enrollment: 3,850 undergrads, 60% part-time. 567 full-time freshmen.
Selectivity: Open admission; but selective for some programs.

BASIC COSTS (2016-2017)
Tuition and fees: $5,910; out-of-state residents $12,090.
Per-credit charge: $24; out-of-state residents $230.
Additional info: Tuition/fee waivers available for unemployed or children of unemployed.

FINANCIAL AID PICTURE
Students with need: Need-based aid available for full-time and part-time students.

FINANCIAL AID PROCEDURES
Forms required: FAFSA.
Dates and Deadlines: Priority date 5/1; no closing date. Applicants notified on a rolling basis starting 4/1.
Transfers: No deadline. Applicants notified on a rolling basis.

CONTACT
Roxanne Dumas, Director of Financial Aid
50 Oakland Street, Wellesley Hills, MA 02481
(781) 239-2600

Massachusetts College of Art and Design
Boston, Massachusetts
www.massart.edu   Federal Code: 002180

4-year public visual arts college in very large city.
Enrollment: 1,722 undergrads, 9% part-time. 292 full-time freshmen.

Selectivity: Admits 50 to 75% of applicants.

BASIC COSTS (2016-2017)
Tuition and fees: $12,200; out-of-state residents $32,800.
Room and board: $13,100.
Additional info: Tuition/fee waivers available for unemployed or children of unemployed.

FINANCIAL AID PICTURE (2015-2016)
Students with need: Out of 254 full-time freshmen who applied for aid, 198 were judged to have need. Of these, 198 received aid. For part-time students, average financial aid package was $6,859.
Students without need: 39 full-time freshmen who did not demonstrate need for aid received scholarships/grants; average award was $8,066. No-need awards available for academics, art, leadership, state/district residency.
Additional info: Tuition waiver available to Vietnam veterans.

FINANCIAL AID PROCEDURES
Forms required: FAFSA.
Dates and Deadlines: Priority date 3/1; no closing date. Applicants notified on a rolling basis starting 3/15; must reply within 3 week(s) of notification.
Transfers: Financial aid transcripts required.

CONTACT
Aurelio Ramirez, Director of Financial Aid
621 Huntington Avenue, Boston, MA 02115-5882
(617) 879-7850

Massachusetts College of Liberal Arts
North Adams, Massachusetts
www.mcla.edu   Federal Code: 002187

4-year public liberal arts college in large town.
Enrollment: 1,408 undergrads, 11% part-time. 325 full-time freshmen.
Selectivity: Admits over 75% of applicants.

BASIC COSTS (2016-2017)
Tuition and fees: $9,875; out-of-state residents $18,820.
Per-credit charge: $43; out-of-state residents $416.
Room and board: $10,078.
Additional info: Tuition/fee waivers available for unemployed or children of unemployed.

FINANCIAL AID PICTURE (2016-2017)
Students with need: Out of 318 full-time freshmen who applied for aid, 257 were judged to have need. Of these, 256 received aid, and 202 had their full need met. Average financial aid package met 79% of need; average scholarship/grant was $6,942; average loan was $3,188. For part-time students, average financial aid package was $9,867.
Students without need: 37 full-time freshmen who did not demonstrate need for aid received scholarships/grants; average award was $3,455. No-need awards available for academics, art, leadership, minority status, music/drama.

FINANCIAL AID PROCEDURES
Forms required: FAFSA.
Dates and Deadlines: Priority date 3/1; no closing date. Applicants notified on a rolling basis starting 3/1; must reply by 5/1 or within 2 week(s) of notification.

CONTACT
Elizabeth Petri, Director of Financial Aid
375 Church Street, North Adams, MA 01247
(413) 662-5219

Massachusetts Institute of Technology
Cambridge, Massachusetts   Federal Code: 002178
web.mit.edu   CSS Code: 3514

4-year private university in small city.
Enrollment: 4,489 undergrads, 1% part-time. 1,113 full-time freshmen.
Selectivity: Admits less than 50% of applicants.

BASIC COSTS (2017-2018)
Tuition and fees: $49,892.
Room and board: $14,720.

FINANCIAL AID PICTURE (2015-2016)
Students with need: Out of 850 full-time freshmen who applied for aid, 633 were judged to have need. Of these, 633 received aid, and 633 had their full need met. Average financial aid package met 100% of need; average scholarship/grant was $42,351; average loan was $2,608. For part-time students, average financial aid package was $38,709.
Students without need: This college awards aid only to students with need.
Additional info: Filing deadline 2/15 for CSS PROFILE.

FINANCIAL AID PROCEDURES
Forms required: FAFSA. If any student wishes to apply for scholarship assistance from MIT, they must submit a CSS profile.
Dates and Deadlines: Priority date 2/15; closing date 2/15. Applicants notified by 3/14; must reply by 5/1.
Transfers: Priority date 4/15; closing date 4/15. Applicants notified on a rolling basis starting 5/15. Access to MIT funds may be limited to fewer than 8 terms.

CONTACT
Stuart Schmill, Dean of Admissions and Student Financial Services
77 Massachusetts Avenue, Room 3-108, Cambridge, MA 02139-4307
(617) 258-8600

Massachusetts Maritime Academy
Buzzards Bay, Massachusetts
www.maritime.edu   Federal Code: 002181

4-year public engineering and maritime college in small town.
Enrollment: 1,641 undergrads, 2% part-time. 402 full-time freshmen.
Selectivity: Admits over 75% of applicants.

BASIC COSTS (2016-2017)
Tuition and fees: $8,004; out-of-state residents $24,600.
Per-credit charge: $322.38; out-of-state residents $1,013.88.
Room and board: $11,978.

FINANCIAL AID PICTURE (2016-2017)
Students with need: Out of 364 full-time freshmen who applied for aid, 250 were judged to have need. Of these, 250 received aid, and 67 had their full need met. Average financial aid package met 66% of need; average scholarship/grant was $12,373; average loan was $3,363. Need-based aid available for part-time students.
Students without need: 31 full-time freshmen who did not demonstrate need for aid received scholarships/grants; average award was $3,586. No-need awards available for academics, alumni affiliation, leadership.

FINANCIAL AID PROCEDURES
Forms required: FAFSA.
Dates and Deadlines: Priority date 3/1; no closing date. Applicants notified on a rolling basis starting 3/20.

CONTACT
Catherine Kedski, Financial Aid Director
101 Academy Drive, Buzzards Bay, MA 02532
(508) 830-5087

Massasoit Community College

Brockton, Massachusetts
www.massasoit.mass.edu   Federal Code: 002177

2-year public community college in small city.
Enrollment: 6,738 undergrads.
Selectivity: Open admission; but selective for some programs.

BASIC COSTS (2016-2017)
Tuition and fees: $5,850; out-of-state residents $12,030.
Per-credit charge: $24; out-of-state residents $230.
Additional info: Tuition/fee waivers available for unemployed or children of unemployed.

FINANCIAL AID PICTURE
Students with need: Need-based aid available for full-time and part-time students.
Students without need: This college awards aid only to students with need.

FINANCIAL AID PROCEDURES
Forms required: FAFSA.
Dates and Deadlines: Priority date 4/15; no closing date. Applicants notified on a rolling basis starting 6/1.

CONTACT
Todd Hughes, Director of Financial Aid
One Massasoit Boulevard, Brockton, MA 02302-3996
(508) 588-9100 ext. 1479

MCPHS University

Boston, Massachusetts
www.mcphs.edu   Federal Code: 002165

4-year private health science and pharmacy college in very large city.
Enrollment: 3,791 undergrads, 5% part-time. 795 full-time freshmen.
Selectivity: Admits over 75% of applicants.

BASIC COSTS (2017-2018)
Tuition and fees: $31,670.
Per-credit charge: $1,125.
Room and board: $15,834.

FINANCIAL AID PICTURE (2016-2017)
Students with need: 38% of average financial aid package awarded as scholarships/grants, 62% awarded as loans/jobs. Need-based aid available for part-time students. Work study available weekends and for part-time students.
Students without need: No-need awards available for academics.

FINANCIAL AID PROCEDURES
Forms required: FAFSA.
Dates and Deadlines: Priority date 3/15; no closing date. Applicants notified on a rolling basis starting 3/15.
Transfers: Massachusetts State Grant deadline May 1.

CONTACT
Elizabeth Goreham, Executive Director of Enrollment Services
179 Longwood Avenue, Boston, MA 02115-5896
(617) 732-2864

Merrimack College

North Andover, Massachusetts
www.merrimack.edu   Federal Code: 002120

4-year private college in large town, affiliated with the Roman Catholic Church.

Enrollment: 3,416 undergrads, 3% part-time. 1,004 full-time freshmen.
Selectivity: Admits over 75% of applicants.

BASIC COSTS (2016-2017)
Tuition and fees: $38,825.
Per-credit charge: $1,310.
Room and board: $14,345.

FINANCIAL AID PICTURE (2016-2017)
Students with need: Out of 870 full-time freshmen who applied for aid, 775 were judged to have need. Of these, 775 received aid, and 92 had their full need met. Average financial aid package met 66% of need; average scholarship/grant was $20,834; average loan was $3,401. For part-time students, average financial aid package was $7,136.
Students without need: 184 full-time freshmen who did not demonstrate need for aid received scholarships/grants; average award was $12,715. No-need awards available for academics, alumni affiliation, athletics, leadership, music/drama, religious affiliation.
Scholarships offered: 58 full-time freshmen received athletic scholarships; average amount $23,278.

FINANCIAL AID PROCEDURES
Forms required: FAFSA.
Dates and Deadlines: Priority date 2/15; no closing date. Applicants notified by 3/15.
Transfers: Priority date 3/15; closing date 8/15. Applicants notified on a rolling basis; must reply within 2 week(s) of notification.

CONTACT
Adrienne Montgomery, Director of Financial Aid
510 Turnpike Street, Suite 201, North Andover, MA 01845
(978) 837-5186

Middlesex Community College

Bedford, Massachusetts
www.middlesex.mass.edu   Federal Code: 009936

2-year public community college in small city.
Enrollment: 7,709 undergrads, 61% part-time. 930 full-time freshmen.
Selectivity: Open admission; but selective for some programs.

BASIC COSTS (2016-2017)
Tuition and fees: $5,900; out-of-state residents $12,080.
Per-credit charge: $195; out-of-state residents $401.
Additional info: Tuition/fee waivers available for adults.

FINANCIAL AID PICTURE
Students with need: Need-based aid available for full-time and part-time students.
Students without need: This college awards aid only to students with need.
Additional info: Application priority date 5/1 for Massachusetts state funds.

FINANCIAL AID PROCEDURES
Forms required: FAFSA.
Dates and Deadlines: Priority date 5/1; no closing date. Applicants notified on a rolling basis starting 7/1.

CONTACT
Robert Baumel, Financial Aid Director
33 Kearney Square, Lowell, MA 01852-1987
(978) 656-3242

Montserrat College of Art

Beverly, Massachusetts
www.montserrat.edu   Federal Code: 013774

4-year private visual arts college in large town.
Enrollment: 378 undergrads.

BASIC COSTS (2016-2017)

Tuition and fees: $29,550.
Room only: $8,600.

FINANCIAL AID PICTURE

Students with need: Need-based aid available for full-time and part-time students. Work study available nights, weekends, and for part-time students.
Students without need: No-need awards available for academics, art.
Scholarships offered: Talent Awards: $5,000-$10,000; based on artistic and academic ability.

FINANCIAL AID PROCEDURES

Forms required: FAFSA, institutional form.
Dates and Deadlines: Priority date 3/1; no closing date. Applicants notified on a rolling basis starting 3/1; must reply by 5/1 or within 2 week(s) of notification.
Transfers: No deadline. Applicants notified on a rolling basis starting 12/20; must reply within 2 week(s) of notification.

CONTACT

Anne McDermott, Director of Financial Aid
23 Essex Street, Beverly, MA 01915
(978) 921-4242 ext. 1155

Mount Holyoke College

South Hadley, Massachusetts   Federal Code: 002192
www.mtholyoke.edu   CSS Code: 3529

4-year private liberal arts college for women in large town.
Enrollment: 2,179 undergrads, 1% part-time. 569 full-time freshmen.
Selectivity: Admits 50 to 75% of applicants.

BASIC COSTS (2016-2017)

Tuition and fees: $45,866.
Per-credit charge: $1,430.
Room and board: $13,440.

FINANCIAL AID PICTURE (2016-2017)

Students with need: Out of 429 full-time freshmen who applied for aid, 334 were judged to have need. Of these, 334 received aid, and 334 had their full need met. Average financial aid package met 100% of need; average scholarship/grant was $33,647; average loan was $2,898. For part-time students, average financial aid package was $32,004.
Students without need: 81 full-time freshmen who did not demonstrate need for aid received scholarships/grants; average award was $17,926. No-need awards available for academics, leadership.
Scholarships offered: Scholarships awarded competitively to first-year candidates and are renewable for up to eight (8) semesters with full-time status and good academic standing; amounts range from $10,000 to full tuition; scholarships are not transferrable to other institutions; number awarded each year varies; approximately 25% of entering first year students are awarded merit-based awards.

FINANCIAL AID PROCEDURES

Forms required: FAFSA, CSS PROFILE.
Dates and Deadlines: Priority date 2/1; closing date 2/1. Applicants notified by 4/1; must reply by 5/1.
Transfers: Closing date 5/15. Applicants notified on a rolling basis starting 4/1; must reply within 4 week(s) of notification.

CONTACT

Kathy Blaisdell, Director of Student Financial Services
Newhall Center, South Hadley, MA 01075-1488
(413) 538-2291

Mount Ida College

Newton, Massachusetts
www.mountida.edu   Federal Code: 002193

4-year private business and liberal arts college in small city.
Enrollment: 1,317 undergrads, 6% part-time. 430 full-time freshmen.

BASIC COSTS (2017-2018)

Tuition and fees: $35,720.
Room and board: $13,680.

FINANCIAL AID PICTURE

Students with need: Need-based aid available for full-time and part-time students. Work study available nights.

FINANCIAL AID PROCEDURES

Forms required: FAFSA, institutional form.
Dates and Deadlines: Priority date 4/15; no closing date. Applicants notified on a rolling basis starting 3/1; must reply within 3 week(s) of notification.

CONTACT

Dyan Teehan, Director of Student Financial Servics
777 Dedham Street, Newton, MA 02459
(617) 928-4785

Mount Wachusett Community College

Gardner, Massachusetts
www.mwcc.edu   Federal Code: 002172

2-year public community college in large town.
Enrollment: 3,570 undergrads, 60% part-time. 485 full-time freshmen.
Selectivity: Open admission; but selective for some programs.

BASIC COSTS (2016-2017)

Tuition and fees: $6,550; out-of-state residents $12,700.

FINANCIAL AID PICTURE (2015-2016)

Students with need: Out of 447 full-time freshmen who applied for aid, 353 were judged to have need. Of these, 338 received aid, and 36 had their full need met. Average financial aid package met 95% of need; average scholarship/grant was $5,136; average loan was $1,524. For part-time students, average financial aid package was $3,987.
Students without need: This college awards aid only to students with need.

FINANCIAL AID PROCEDURES

Forms required: FAFSA.
Dates and Deadlines: Priority date 5/1; no closing date. Applicants notified on a rolling basis starting 3/15; must reply within 2 week(s) of notification.

CONTACT

Kelly Morrissey, Director, FInancial Aid
444 Green Street, Gardner, MA 01440-1000
(978) 632-9169

New England Conservatory of Music

Boston, Massachusetts
www.necmusic.edu   Federal Code: 002194

4-year private music college in very large city.
Enrollment: 382 undergrads, 1% part-time. 86 full-time freshmen.
Selectivity: Admits less than 50% of applicants.

BASIC COSTS (2016-2017)

Tuition and fees: $44,755.
Per-credit charge: $1,420.
Room and board: $13,900.

FINANCIAL AID PICTURE (2015-2016)

Students with need: Out of 52 full-time freshmen who applied for aid, 39 were judged to have need. Of these, 39 received aid, and 10 had their full need met. Average financial aid package met 73% of need; average scholarship/grant was $24,149; average loan was $6,194. For part-time students, average financial aid package was $4,593.

Students without need: 43 full-time freshmen who did not demonstrate need for aid received scholarships/grants; average award was $15,501. No-need awards available for academics, music/drama.

FINANCIAL AID PROCEDURES

Forms required: FAFSA, institutional form.

Dates and Deadlines: Closing date 12/1. Applicants notified by 4/1; must reply by 5/1 or within 2 week(s) of notification.

CONTACT

Lauren Urbanek, Director of Financial Aid
290 Huntington Avenue, Boston, MA 02115-5018
(617) 585-1110

Newbury College

Brookline, Massachusetts
www.newbury.edu   Federal Code: 007484

4-year private business and liberal arts college in large city.
Enrollment: 747 undergrads.

BASIC COSTS (2016-2017)

Tuition and fees: $33,685.
Per-credit charge: $1,020.
Room and board: $14,200.

FINANCIAL AID PICTURE

Students with need: Need-based aid available for full-time and part-time students.
Students without need: This college awards aid only to students with need.

FINANCIAL AID PROCEDURES

Forms required: FAFSA.

Dates and Deadlines: Priority date 3/1; closing date 5/1. Applicants notified on a rolling basis starting 3/1; must reply by 5/1 or within 2 week(s) of notification.

Transfers: No deadline. Applicants notified on a rolling basis starting 3/1; must reply by 5/1 or within 2 week(s) of notification.

CONTACT

Jenny Aguiar, Director of Financial Aid
129 Fisher Avenue, Brookline, MA 02445
(617) 730-7100

Nichols College

Dudley, Massachusetts
www.nichols.edu   Federal Code: 002197

4-year private business and liberal arts college in small town.
Enrollment: 1,259 undergrads, 8% part-time. 351 full-time freshmen.
Selectivity: Admits over 75% of applicants.

BASIC COSTS (2017-2018)

Tuition and fees: $34,000.
Per-credit charge: $350.
Room and board: $13,800.

FINANCIAL AID PICTURE (2016-2017)

Students with need: Out of 326 full-time freshmen who applied for aid, 294 were judged to have need. Of these, 294 received aid, and 61 had their

full need met. Average financial aid package met 81% of need; average scholarship/grant was $21,521; average loan was $3,332. Need-based aid available for part-time students.

Students without need: 53 full-time freshmen who did not demonstrate need for aid received scholarships/grants; average award was $17,221. No-need awards available for academics, alumni affiliation, leadership, ROTC.

FINANCIAL AID PROCEDURES

Forms required: FAFSA.

Dates and Deadlines: Priority date 3/1; closing date 6/1. Applicants notified on a rolling basis starting 12/1; must reply within 4 week(s) of notification.
Transfers: Applicants notified by 3/1; must reply within 4 week(s) of notification.

CONTACT

Jennifer Bianco, Director of Financial Aid
PO Box 5000, Dudley, MA 01571-5000
(508) 213-2372

North Shore Community College

Danvers, Massachusetts
www.northshore.edu   Federal Code: 002173

2-year public community college in small city.
Enrollment: 5,893 undergrads, 64% part-time. 656 full-time freshmen.
Selectivity: Open admission; but selective for some programs.

BASIC COSTS (2016-2017)

Tuition and fees: $6,060; out-of-state residents $13,020.
Per-credit charge: $25; out-of-state residents $257.

FINANCIAL AID PICTURE

Students with need: Need-based aid available for full-time and part-time students.
Students without need: This college awards aid only to students with need.

FINANCIAL AID PROCEDURES

Forms required: FAFSA.

Dates and Deadlines: Priority date 4/15; no closing date. Applicants notified on a rolling basis starting 4/1; must reply within 2 week(s) of notification.

CONTACT

Susan Sullivan, Director of Student Financial Services
One Ferncroft Road, Danvers, MA 01923-0840
(978) 762-4000

Northeastern University

Boston, Massachusetts   Federal Code: 002199
www.northeastern.edu   CSS Code: 3667

4-year private university in very large city.
Enrollment: 17,795 undergrads. 2,676 full-time freshmen.
Selectivity: Admits less than 50% of applicants.

BASIC COSTS (2016-2017)

Tuition and fees: $47,655.
Room and board: $15,600.
Additional info: Tuition/fee waivers available for unemployed or children of unemployed.

FINANCIAL AID PICTURE (2016-2017)

Students with need: Out of 1,832 full-time freshmen who applied for aid, 1,273 were judged to have need. Of these, 1,273 received aid, and 1,273 had their full need met. Average financial aid package met 100% of need; average scholarship/grant was $34,803; average loan was $4,281.

Students without need: 586 full-time freshmen who did not demonstrate need for aid received scholarships/grants; average award was $19,869. No-need awards available for academics, athletics, leadership, ROTC.
Scholarships offered: 57 full-time freshmen received athletic scholarships; average amount $37,703.
Additional info: We meet the full demonstrated institutional need for all full-time incoming undergraduate freshman and transfer.

FINANCIAL AID PROCEDURES
Forms required: FAFSA, CSS PROFILE.
Dates and Deadlines: Priority date 2/15; no closing date. Applicants notified by 4/1; must reply by 5/11.
Transfers: Priority date 5/1; no deadline. Applicants notified on a rolling basis.

CONTACT
Anthony Erwin, Associate Vice-President and Dean of Student Financial Services
200 Kerr Hall, Boston, MA 02115
(617) 373-3190

Northern Essex Community College
Haverhill, Massachusetts
www.necc.mass.edu   Federal Code: 002174

2-year public community and junior college in small city.
Enrollment: 5,530 undergrads, 63% part-time. 712 full-time freshmen.
Selectivity: Open admission; but selective for some programs.

BASIC COSTS (2016-2017)
Tuition and fees: $6,310; out-of-state residents $13,540.
Per-credit charge: $25; out-of-state residents $266.

FINANCIAL AID PICTURE
Students with need: Need-based aid available for full-time and part-time students.
Students without need: No-need awards available for academics.

FINANCIAL AID PROCEDURES
Forms required: FAFSA, institutional form.
Dates and Deadlines: Priority date 5/1; no closing date. Must reply within 2 week(s) of notification.

CONTACT
Alexis Fishbone, Director of Financial Aid
100 Elliott Street, Haverhill, MA 01830-2399
(978) 556-3600

Northpoint Bible College
Haverhill, Massachusetts
www.northpoint.edu   Federal Code: 035705

4-year private Bible college in small city, affiliated with the Assemblies of God.
Enrollment: 227 undergrads.

BASIC COSTS (2016-2017)
Tuition and fees: $11,510.
Per-credit charge: $345.
Room and board: $8,600.

FINANCIAL AID PICTURE
Students with need: Need-based aid available for full-time and part-time students.
Students without need: No-need awards available for academics, leadership, minority status, music/drama, state/district residency.

FINANCIAL AID PROCEDURES
Forms required: FAFSA.
Dates and Deadlines: Priority date 6/1; no closing date. Applicants notified on a rolling basis; must reply within 4 week(s) of notification.

CONTACT
Patricia Stauffer, Financial Aid Director
320 South Main Street, Haverhill, MA 01835
(978) 478-3470

Pine Manor College
Chestnut Hill, Massachusetts
www.pmc.edu   Federal Code: 002201

4-year private liberal arts college in very large city.
Enrollment: 287 undergrads, 2% part-time. 101 full-time freshmen.
Selectivity: Admits over 75% of applicants.

BASIC COSTS (2016-2017)
Tuition and fees: $28,620.
Room and board: $13,280.

FINANCIAL AID PICTURE
Students with need: Need-based aid available for full-time and part-time students. Work study available nights, weekends, and for part-time students.
Students without need: No-need awards available for academics, alumni affiliation, leadership.

FINANCIAL AID PROCEDURES
Forms required: FAFSA.
Dates and Deadlines: Priority date 5/1; no closing date. Applicants notified on a rolling basis starting 4/1; must reply by 5/1 or within 2 week(s) of notification.
Transfers: No deadline. Applicants notified on a rolling basis starting 3/1; must reply by 5/1 or within 2 week(s) of notification.

CONTACT
Debroah Gravel
400 Heath Street, Chestnut Hill, MA 02467
(617) 731-7000

Quinsigamond Community College
Worcester, Massachusetts
www.qcc.edu   Federal Code: 002175

2-year public community college in small city.
Enrollment: 6,917 undergrads, 59% part-time. 896 full-time freshmen.
Selectivity: Open admission; but selective for some programs.

BASIC COSTS (2016-2017)
Tuition and fees: $6,540; out-of-state residents $12,720.
Per-credit charge: $24; out-of-state residents $230.
Additional info: Some programs may require additional fees to support the needs of that program.

FINANCIAL AID PICTURE (2016-2017)
Students with need: 63% of average financial aid package awarded as scholarships/grants, 37% awarded as loans/jobs. Need-based aid available for part-time students. Work study available nights, weekends, and for part-time students.
Students without need: No-need awards available for academics, leadership, minority status.
Additional info: Pell Grant eligible students applying by April 1st generally receive enough grant aid to cover tuition, fees, and books.

FINANCIAL AID PROCEDURES
Forms required: FAFSA.

Dates and Deadlines: Priority date 4/1; no closing date. Applicants notified on a rolling basis starting 4/1.

CONTACT
Karen Grant, Director of Financial Aid
670 West Boylston Street, Worcester, MA 01606
(508) 854-4261

Regis College
Weston, Massachusetts
www.regiscollege.edu   Federal Code: 002206

4-year private health science and liberal arts college in large town, affiliated with the Roman Catholic Church.
Enrollment: 1,235 undergrads, 22% part-time. 269 full-time freshmen.
Selectivity: Admits over 75% of applicants.

BASIC COSTS (2016-2017)
Tuition and fees: $39,040.
Per-credit charge: $1,301.33.
Room and board: $14,740.

FINANCIAL AID PICTURE (2016-2017)
Students with need: Out of 257 full-time freshmen who applied for aid, 240 were judged to have need. Of these, 240 received aid, and 43 had their full need met. Average financial aid package met 60% of need; average scholarship/grant was $21,525; average loan was $3,361. For part-time students, average financial aid package was $6,454.
Students without need: 26 full-time freshmen who did not demonstrate need for aid received scholarships/grants; average award was $11,367. No-need awards available for academics, alumni affiliation.
Additional info: Family tuition discount scholarship offered during any semester in which 2 or more unmarried, dependent siblings attend as full-time undergraduates.

FINANCIAL AID PROCEDURES
Forms required: FAFSA.
Dates and Deadlines: Priority date 2/15; no closing date. Applicants notified on a rolling basis starting 3/15.
Transfers: No deadline. Applicants notified on a rolling basis.

CONTACT
Bonnie Quinn, Director of Financial Aid
235 Wellesley Street, Weston, MA 02493-1571
(781) 768-7180

Roxbury Community College
Roxbury Crossing, Massachusetts
www.rcc.mass.edu   Federal Code: 011930

2-year public community college in very large city.
Enrollment: 2,216 undergrads.
Selectivity: Open admission; but selective for some programs.

BASIC COSTS (2016-2017)
Tuition and fees: $4,980; out-of-state residents $11,610.
Per-credit charge: $26; out-of-state residents $247.

FINANCIAL AID PICTURE
Students with need: Need-based aid available for full-time and part-time students.
Students without need: This college awards aid only to students with need.

FINANCIAL AID PROCEDURES
Forms required: FAFSA, institutional form.

Dates and Deadlines: Closing date 5/1. Applicants notified on a rolling basis starting 6/15; must reply within 2 week(s) of notification.

CONTACT
Ray O'Rourke, Director of Financial Aid
1234 Columbus Avenue, Roxbury Crossing, MA 02120-3400
(617) 541-5322

Salem State University
Salem, Massachusetts
www.salemstate.edu   Federal Code: 002188

4-year public university in large town.
Enrollment: 7,016 undergrads.
Selectivity: Admits 50 to 75% of applicants.

BASIC COSTS (2016-2017)
Tuition and fees: $9,326; out-of-state residents $15,466.
Per-credit charge: $37.92; out-of-state residents $293.75.
Room and board: $13,110.

FINANCIAL AID PICTURE
Students with need: Need-based aid available for full-time and part-time students. Work study available nights, weekends, and for part-time students.
Students without need: No-need awards available for academics.

FINANCIAL AID PROCEDURES
Forms required: FAFSA.
Dates and Deadlines: Priority date 3/1; closing date 9/1. Applicants notified on a rolling basis starting 3/15; must reply within 2 week(s) of notification.

CONTACT
Judy Cramer, Director of Financial Aid
352 Lafayette Street, Salem, MA 01970-5353
(978) 542-6112

School of the Museum of Fine Arts
Boston, Massachusetts
www.smfa.edu   Federal Code: 004667

4-year private visual arts college in very large city.
Enrollment: 278 undergrads.

BASIC COSTS (2016-2017)
Tuition and fees: $52,430.
Room only: $13,566.

FINANCIAL AID PICTURE
Students with need: Need-based aid available for full-time and part-time students. Work study available nights, weekends, and for part-time students.
Students without need: No-need awards available for academics, art.

FINANCIAL AID PROCEDURES
Forms required: FAFSA.
Dates and Deadlines: Closing date 3/15. Applicants notified on a rolling basis starting 4/1; must reply by 5/1 or within 2 week(s) of notification.

CONTACT
Shaun Thomas, Director of Financial Aid
230 The Fenway, Boston, MA 02115
(800) 776-0135

Simmons College
Boston, Massachusetts
www.simmons.edu   Federal Code: 002208

4-year private health science and liberal arts college for women in very large city.

Enrollment: 1,772 undergrads, 10% part-time. 454 full-time freshmen.
Selectivity: Admits 50 to 75% of applicants.

BASIC COSTS (2016-2017)
Tuition and fees: $38,590.
Room and board: $14,500.

FINANCIAL AID PICTURE (2016-2017)
Students with need: Out of 405 full-time freshmen who applied for aid, 353 were judged to have need. Of these, 353 received aid, and 60 had their full need met. Average financial aid package met 80% of need; average scholarship/grant was $28,570; average loan was $3,095. For part-time students, average financial aid package was $15,772.
Students without need: 94 full-time freshmen who did not demonstrate need for aid received scholarships/grants; average award was $19,216. No-need awards available for academics, alumni affiliation.

FINANCIAL AID PROCEDURES
Forms required: FAFSA, institutional form.
Dates and Deadlines: Priority date 3/1; no closing date. Applicants notified on a rolling basis starting 3/15.
Transfers: No deadline. Applicants notified on a rolling basis starting 3/15.

CONTACT
Heather Patenaude, Director of Student Financial Services
300 The Fenway, Boston, MA 02115-5898
(617) 521-2001

Smith College
Northampton, Massachusetts   Federal Code: 002209
www.smith.edu   CSS Code: 3762

4-year private liberal arts college for women in large town.
Enrollment: 2,501 undergrads. 654 full-time freshmen.
Selectivity: Admits less than 50% of applicants.

BASIC COSTS (2016-2017)
Tuition and fees: $47,904.
Room and board: $16,010.

FINANCIAL AID PICTURE (2016-2017)
Students with need: Out of 487 full-time freshmen who applied for aid, 407 were judged to have need. Of these, 407 received aid, and 407 had their full need met. Average financial aid package met 100% of need; average scholarship/grant was $43,839; average loan was $3,011. For part-time students, average financial aid package was $7,386.
Students without need: 60 full-time freshmen who did not demonstrate need for aid received scholarships/grants; average award was $15,484. No-need awards available for academics, state/district residency.
Scholarships offered: Zollman Scholarships: $20,000; for academic excellence; about 15 awarded. STRIDE scholarship: $15,000; about 50 awarded. Springfield/Holyoke Partnership: full-tuition; for academic excellence in Springfield or Holyoke public high schools; up to 4 awarded.
Additional info: Financial aid policy guarantees to meet full financial need, as calculated by college, of all admitted students who have met application deadlines.

FINANCIAL AID PROCEDURES
Forms required: FAFSA, CSS PROFILE, institutional form.
Dates and Deadlines: Closing date 2/15. Applicants notified by 4/1; must reply by 5/1.
Transfers: Priority date 2/15; closing date 4/1. Applicants notified by 4/1; must reply by 5/1. Applicants who apply after admission decision is made cannot receive college aid until they complete at least 32 credits at Smith.

CONTACT
David Belanger, Director of Student Financial Services
7 College Lane, Northampton, MA 01063
(413) 585-2530

Springfield College
Springfield, Massachusetts
www.springfieldcollege.edu   Federal Code: 002211

4-year private health science and liberal arts college in small city.
Enrollment: 2,138 undergrads.

BASIC COSTS (2016-2017)
Tuition and fees: $35,475.
Room and board: $11,890.

FINANCIAL AID PICTURE
Students with need: Need-based aid available for full-time students. Work study available nights, weekends, and for part-time students.
Students without need: No-need awards available for academics, alumni affiliation, art, leadership, minority status, music/drama, state/district residency.

FINANCIAL AID PROCEDURES
Forms required: FAFSA, institutional form.
Dates and Deadlines: Priority date 3/15; no closing date. Applicants notified on a rolling basis starting 2/7; must reply within 2 week(s) of notification.
Transfers: Priority date 5/1. Applicants notified on a rolling basis starting 5/1; must reply by 6/1 or within 2 week(s) of notification.

CONTACT
Edward Ciosek, Director of Financial Aid
263 Alden Street, Springfield, MA 01109
(413) 748-3108

Springfield Technical Community College
Springfield, Massachusetts
www.stcc.edu   Federal Code: 005549

2-year public community and technical college in small city.
Enrollment: 5,124 undergrads.
Selectivity: Open admission; but selective for some programs.

BASIC COSTS (2016-2017)
Tuition and fees: $5,736; out-of-state residents $12,246.
Per-credit charge: $25; out-of-state residents $242.
Additional info: New England Regional Student Program annual tuition and fees $6111.

FINANCIAL AID PICTURE (2015-2016)
Students with need: 79% of average financial aid package awarded as scholarships/grants, 21% awarded as loans/jobs. Need-based aid available for part-time students.

FINANCIAL AID PROCEDURES
Forms required: FAFSA.
Dates and Deadlines: Priority date 5/1; no closing date. Applicants notified on a rolling basis starting 4/1.

CONTACT
Jeremy Greenhouse, Dean of Student Financial Services
One Armory Square, Springfield, MA 01102-9000
(413) 755-4214

Stonehill College
Easton, Massachusetts   Federal Code: 002217
www.stonehill.edu   CSS Code: 3770

4-year private business and liberal arts college in large town, affiliated with the Roman Catholic Church.

Enrollment: 2,472 undergrads, 1% part-time. 732 full-time freshmen.
Selectivity: Admits 50 to 75% of applicants.

BASIC COSTS (2016-2017)
Tuition and fees: $39,900.
Per-credit charge: $1,330.
Room and board: $15,130.
Additional info: Tuition/fee waivers available for minority students, unemployed or children of unemployed.

FINANCIAL AID PICTURE (2016-2017)
Students with need: 80% of average financial aid package awarded as scholarships/grants, 20% awarded as loans/jobs. Need-based aid available for part-time students. Work study available nights, weekends, and for part-time students.
Students without need: No-need awards available for academics, athletics, leadership, ROTC.
Scholarships offered: Moreau Honors Scholarship: $25,000. Shields Merit Scholars Program: $8,000-$10,000. Novak/Sakmar/Templeton Scholarship: $2,500-$10,000. Presidential Scholarship: $16,000-$20,000. Dean's Scholarship: $12,000-$14,000. Stonehill Scholarship: $5,000-$10,000.

FINANCIAL AID PROCEDURES
Forms required: FAFSA, CSS PROFILE.
Dates and Deadlines: Priority date 12/1; closing date 2/1. Applicants notified by 4/1; must reply by 5/1.
Transfers: Closing date 4/1. Applicants notified by 5/25. For transfer students who qualify, merit scholarships and need based aid are provided as aid availability allows.

CONTACT
Eileen O'Leary, Assistant Vice President for Finance/Director of Student Aid and Finance
320 Washington Street, Easton, MA 02357-0100
(508) 565-1088

Suffolk University
Boston, Massachusetts
www.suffolk.edu   Federal Code: 002218

4-year private university in very large city.
Enrollment: 5,185 undergrads, 4% part-time. 1,198 full-time freshmen.
Selectivity: Admits over 75% of applicants.

BASIC COSTS (2016-2017)
Tuition and fees: $35,798.
Per-credit charge: $1,042.
Room and board: $14,730.

FINANCIAL AID PICTURE (2016-2017)
Students with need: Out of 905 full-time freshmen who applied for aid, 823 were judged to have need. Of these, 823 received aid, and 207 had their full need met. Average financial aid package met 78% of need; average scholarship/grant was $12,505; average loan was $4,689. For part-time students, average financial aid package was $19,183.
Students without need: 290 full-time freshmen who did not demonstrate need for aid received scholarships/grants; average award was $14,735. No-need awards available for academics, alumni affiliation.
Scholarships offered: Various scholarships; amounts vary; based on academic achievement, talent, and contribution to applicant's school and community.
Additional info: Foreign students may apply for institutional employment awards.

FINANCIAL AID PROCEDURES
Forms required: FAFSA.
Dates and Deadlines: Closing date 3/1. Applicants notified on a rolling basis starting 2/5; must reply by 5/1 or within 2 week(s) of notification.

CONTACT
Christine Perry, Director of Financial Aid
8 Ashburton Place, Boston, MA 02108
(617) 573-8470

Tufts University
Medford, Massachusetts   Federal Code: 002219
www.tufts.edu   CSS Code: 3901

4-year private university in small city.
Enrollment: 5,459 undergrads, 1% part-time. 1,338 full-time freshmen.
Selectivity: Admits less than 50% of applicants.

BASIC COSTS (2016-2017)
Tuition and fees: $52,430.
Room and board: $13,566.

FINANCIAL AID PICTURE (2016-2017)
Students with need: Out of 664 full-time freshmen who applied for aid, 526 were judged to have need. Of these, 515 received aid, and 515 had their full need met. Average financial aid package met 100% of need; average scholarship/grant was $42,971; average loan was $2,116. For part-time students, average financial aid package was $4,592.
Students without need: This college awards aid only to students with need.
Scholarships offered: National Merit Scholarships: $500 for non-need; $2,000 for need.
Additional info: Students from families with incomes less than $60,000 receive aid awards in which student loans are replaced by grants.

FINANCIAL AID PROCEDURES
Forms required: FAFSA, CSS PROFILE.
Dates and Deadlines: Closing date 2/15. Applicants notified by 4/1; must reply by 5/1.
Transfers: Closing date 3/15. Applicants notified by 6/1; must reply within 2 week(s) of notification.

CONTACT
Patricia Reilly, Director of Financial Aid
Bendetson Hall, Medford, MA 02155
(617) 627-2000

University of Massachusetts Amherst
Amherst, Massachusetts
www.umass.edu   Federal Code: 002221

4-year public university in large town.
Enrollment: 22,958 undergrads, 7% part-time. 4,701 full-time freshmen.
Selectivity: Admits 50 to 75% of applicants.

BASIC COSTS (2016-2017)
Tuition and fees: $15,156; out-of-state residents $32,389.
Per-credit charge: $575; out-of-state residents $1,255.
Room and board: $12,441.

FINANCIAL AID PICTURE (2015-2016)
Students with need: Out of 3,972 full-time freshmen who applied for aid, 2,551 were judged to have need. Of these, 2,533 received aid, and 362 had their full need met. Average financial aid package met 86% of need; average scholarship/grant was $10,748; average loan was $3,397. For part-time students, average financial aid package was $11,268.
Students without need: 891 full-time freshmen who did not demonstrate need for aid received scholarships/grants; average award was $6,130. No-need awards available for academics, art, music/drama, state/district residency.

Scholarships offered: *Merit:* Merit scholarships: all applicants automatically considered. *Athletic:* 50 full-time freshmen received athletic scholarships; average amount $23,900.

FINANCIAL AID PROCEDURES
Forms required: FAFSA.
Dates and Deadlines: Priority date 3/1; no closing date. Applicants notified on a rolling basis starting 4/1; must reply by 5/1 or within 2 week(s) of notification.

CONTACT
Suzanne Peters, Director of Financial Aid
University Admissions Center, Amherst, MA 01003-9291
(413) 545-0801

University of Massachusetts Boston
Boston, Massachusetts
www.umb.edu   Federal Code: 002222

4-year public university in very large city.
Enrollment: 12,210 undergrads, 25% part-time. 1,538 full-time freshmen.
Selectivity: Admits 50 to 75% of applicants.

BASIC COSTS (2016-2017)
Tuition and fees: $13,435; out-of-state residents $32,023.

FINANCIAL AID PICTURE (2015-2016)
Students with need: Out of 1,212 full-time freshmen who applied for aid, 1,035 were judged to have need. Of these, 1,035 received aid, and 403 had their full need met. Average financial aid package met 89% of need; average scholarship/grant was $10,463; average loan was $5,013. For part-time students, average financial aid package was $11,440.
Students without need: 128 full-time freshmen who did not demonstrate need for aid received scholarships/grants; average award was $6,830. No-need awards available for academics, state/district residency.
Additional info: Some Massachusetts state employees and Massachusetts Vietnam veterans eligible for tuition waiver. Some waivers available based on talent and academic excellence.

FINANCIAL AID PROCEDURES
Forms required: FAFSA.
Dates and Deadlines: Priority date 3/1; no closing date.

CONTACT
Judy Keyes, Director of Financial Aid Services
100 Morrissey Boulevard, Boston, MA 02125-3393
(617) 287-6300

University of Massachusetts Dartmouth
Dartmouth, Massachusetts
www.umassd.edu   Federal Code: 002210

4-year public university in large town.
Enrollment: 6,758 undergrads, 12% part-time. 1,358 full-time freshmen.
Selectivity: Admits over 75% of applicants.

BASIC COSTS (2016-2017)
Tuition and fees: $13,188; out-of-state residents $27,473.
Per-credit charge: $532.63; out-of-state residents $1,127.83.
Room and board: $12,470.

FINANCIAL AID PICTURE (2016-2017)
Students with need: Out of 1,235 full-time freshmen who applied for aid, 1,009 were judged to have need. Of these, 1,009 received aid, and 423 had their full need met. Average financial aid package met 85% of need; average scholarship/grant was $10,070; average loan was $7,915. For part-time students, average financial aid package was $10,559.

Students without need: 174 full-time freshmen who did not demonstrate need for aid received scholarships/grants; average award was $4,396. No-need awards available for academics, minority status, ROTC, state/district residency.
Scholarships offered: Chancellor's Merit Scholarship: approximately $2,000; for Massachusetts high school seniors with 1100 SAT (exclusive of Writing) and minimum 3.00 High School GPA; 50 awarded. Solveig E.J. Balestracci Scholarship: $1,000; for academic achievement in marine-related area for residents of New Bedford, Dartmouth, Acushnet, Westport, Mattapoisett, Marion, Rochester or Lakeville; 1 awarded. Boivon Scholarship: $1,000; based on academic involvement in French language and culture. A.J. Carvalho Memorial Scholarship: approximately $5,000; for New Bedford High School graduates of Portuguese descent with 3.0 GPA. Cranston Foundation Scholarship: $500; for entering or current students in the Bioengineering Department.

FINANCIAL AID PROCEDURES
Forms required: FAFSA.
Dates and Deadlines: Priority date 3/1; no closing date. Applicants notified on a rolling basis.
Transfers: Applicants notified on a rolling basis.

CONTACT
Korinne Peterson, Director of Financial Aid
285 Old Westport Road, Dartmouth, MA 02747-2300
(508) 999-8643

University of Massachusetts Lowell
Lowell, Massachusetts
www.uml.edu   Federal Code: 002161

4-year public university in small city.
Enrollment: 12,914 undergrads, 23% part-time. 1,676 full-time freshmen.
Selectivity: Admits 50 to 75% of applicants.

BASIC COSTS (2016-2017)
Tuition and fees: $14,307; out-of-state residents $30,875.
Per-credit charge: $596; out-of-state residents $1,286.
Room and board: $12,073.
Additional info: Starting in fall 2016, UMass Lowell consolidated some mandatory fees into a single tuition charge. Other campus-wide fees; such as student activity, technology fee, housing and dining services have been listed separately.

FINANCIAL AID PICTURE
Students with need: Need-based aid available for full-time and part-time students.
Students without need: No-need awards available for academics, alumni affiliation, art, athletics, leadership, minority status, music/drama, ROTC, state/district residency.

FINANCIAL AID PROCEDURES
Forms required: FAFSA.
Dates and Deadlines: Priority date 3/1; no closing date. Applicants notified on a rolling basis starting 3/21.
Transfers: Applicants notified on a rolling basis starting 3/20.

CONTACT
Joyce McLaughlin, Director of Financial Aid
University Crossing, Suite 420, 220 Pawtucket Street, Lowell, MA 01854-2874
(978) 934-4220

Urban College of Boston
Boston, Massachusetts
www.urbancollege.edu   Federal Code: 031305

2-year private community college in very large city.
Enrollment: 456 undergrads.

Selectivity: Open admission.

BASIC COSTS (2016-2017)
Tuition and fees: $8,910.

FINANCIAL AID PICTURE
Students with need: Need-based aid available for full-time and part-time students.
Students without need: This college awards aid only to students with need.

FINANCIAL AID PROCEDURES
Forms required: FAFSA.
Dates and Deadlines: Priority date 12/10; no closing date. Applicants notified on a rolling basis starting 4/15.

CONTACT
Mia Taylor, Director of Financial Aid
178 Tremont Street, Seventh Floor, Boston, MA 02111
(617) 348-6220

Wellesley College

Wellesley, Massachusetts
www.wellesley.edu

Federal Code: 002224
CSS Code: 3957

4-year private liberal arts college for women in large town.
Enrollment: 2,188 undergrads. 593 full-time freshmen.
Selectivity: Admits less than 50% of applicants.

BASIC COSTS (2016-2017)
Tuition and fees: $48,802.
Room and board: $15,114.

FINANCIAL AID PICTURE (2015-2016)
Students with need: Out of 426 full-time freshmen who applied for aid, 352 were judged to have need. Of these, 352 received aid, and 352 had their full need met. Average financial aid package met 100% of need; average scholarship/grant was $43,423; average loan was $2,678. Need-based aid available for part-time students.
Students without need: This college awards aid only to students with need.

FINANCIAL AID PROCEDURES
Forms required: FAFSA, CSS PROFILE.
Dates and Deadlines: Priority date 2/15; no closing date. Must reply by 5/1.
Transfers: Closing date 3/1. Applicants notified by 5/1; must reply by 6/1. Financial aid for transfer students is calculated using the same formulae used for incoming first-year students. Admission is also still need blind for U.S. Citizens and Permanent Residents.

CONTACT
Scott Juedes, Director of Student Financial Services
106 Central Street, Wellesley, MA 02481-8203
(781) 283-2360

Wentworth Institute of Technology

Boston, Massachusetts
www.wit.edu

Federal Code: 002225

4-year private engineering and technical college in very large city.
Enrollment: 3,931 undergrads, 1% part-time. 959 full-time freshmen.
Selectivity: Admits 50 to 75% of applicants.

BASIC COSTS (2017-2018)
Tuition and fees: $31,840.
Per-credit charge: $995.
Room and board: $12,570.

FINANCIAL AID PICTURE (2016-2017)
Students with need: Out of 843 full-time freshmen who applied for aid, 747 were judged to have need. Of these, 747 received aid, and 57 had their full need met. For part-time students, average financial aid package was $2,497.
Students without need: 204 full-time freshmen who did not demonstrate need for aid received scholarships/grants; average award was $4,716. No-need awards available for academics, leadership, ROTC, state/district residency.
Scholarships offered: Applicants for admission automatically considered for merit scholarships.

FINANCIAL AID PROCEDURES
Forms required: FAFSA.
Dates and Deadlines: Priority date 3/1; closing date 3/1. Applicants notified on a rolling basis starting 3/15; must reply by 5/1 or within 2 week(s) of notification.
Transfers: Review of NSLDS history within 30 days of beginning of enrollment required.

CONTACT
Anne-Marie Caruso, Director of Financial Aid
550 Huntington Avenue, Boston, MA 02115
(617) 989-4020

Western New England University

Springfield, Massachusetts
www.wne.edu

Federal Code: 002226

4-year private university in small city.
Enrollment: 2,717 undergrads, 5% part-time. 722 full-time freshmen.
Selectivity: Admits over 75% of applicants.

BASIC COSTS (2016-2017)
Tuition and fees: $34,874.
Per-credit charge: $613.
Room and board: $13,214.

FINANCIAL AID PICTURE (2016-2017)
Students with need: Out of 677 full-time freshmen who applied for aid, 606 were judged to have need. Of these, 606 received aid, and 87 had their full need met. Average financial aid package met 75% of need; average scholarship/grant was $21,486; average loan was $3,654. For part-time students, average financial aid package was $9,103.
Students without need: 113 full-time freshmen who did not demonstrate need for aid received scholarships/grants; average award was $13,535. No-need awards available for academics, music/drama, ROTC.

FINANCIAL AID PROCEDURES
Forms required: FAFSA.
Dates and Deadlines: Priority date 4/15; no closing date. Applicants notified on a rolling basis starting 3/1; must reply by 5/1 or within 2 week(s) of notification.
Transfers: No deadline. Applicants notified on a rolling basis starting 3/1; must reply by 5/1 or within 2 week(s) of notification.

CONTACT
Kathy Chambers, Director of Financial Aid
1215 Wilbraham Road, Springfield, MA 01119-2684
(800) 325-1122 ext. 2080

Westfield State University

Westfield, Massachusetts
www.westfield.ma.edu

Federal Code: 002189

4-year public university in large town.
Enrollment: 5,474 undergrads, 9% part-time. 1,292 full-time freshmen.

Selectivity: Admits over 75% of applicants.

BASIC COSTS (2016-2017)
Tuition and fees: $9,275; out-of-state residents $15,355.
Per-credit charge: $297.
Room and board: $11,865.
Additional info: Tuition for New England Regional Program: $1,455.

FINANCIAL AID PICTURE (2015-2016)
Students with need: Out of 1,205 full-time freshmen who applied for aid, 929 were judged to have need. Of these, 905 received aid, and 71 had their full need met. Average financial aid package met 58% of need; average scholarship/grant was $6,242; average loan was $3,205. Need-based aid available for part-time students.
Students without need: 14 full-time freshmen who did not demonstrate need for aid received scholarships/grants; average award was $4,585. No-need awards available for academics.

FINANCIAL AID PROCEDURES
Forms required: FAFSA.
Dates and Deadlines: Priority date 3/1; no closing date. Applicants notified on a rolling basis starting 4/1; must reply within 2 week(s) of notification.
Transfers: Priority date 3/1; no deadline. Applicants notified on a rolling basis starting 4/1.

CONTACT
Catherine Ryan, Director of Financial Aid
577 Western Avenue, Westfield, MA 01086-1630
(413) 572-5218

Wheaton College
Norton, Massachusetts
www.wheatoncollege.edu
Federal Code: 002227
CSS Code: 3963

4-year private liberal arts college in large town.
Enrollment: 1,637 undergrads. 528 full-time freshmen.
Selectivity: Admits 50 to 75% of applicants.

BASIC COSTS (2016-2017)
Tuition and fees: $49,012.
Per-credit charge: $1,522.
Room and board: $12,500.

FINANCIAL AID PICTURE (2016-2017)
Students with need: Out of 411 full-time freshmen who applied for aid, 341 were judged to have need. Of these, 341 received aid, and 209 had their full need met. Average financial aid package met 95% of need; average scholarship/grant was $32,620; average loan was $2,806. Need-based aid available for part-time students.
Students without need: 157 full-time freshmen who did not demonstrate need for aid received scholarships/grants; average award was $19,162. No-need awards available for academics.
Scholarships offered: Balfour Scholarship, Trustee Scholarship, and Community Scholarship: award amounts vary (up to $25,000) and are renewable annually throughout a student's academic career; available to applicants selected from the top 30% of the applicant pool in recognition of high academic achievement, regardless of financial need.

FINANCIAL AID PROCEDURES
Forms required: FAFSA, CSS PROFILE.
Dates and Deadlines: Closing date 2/1. Applicants notified by 4/1; must reply by 5/1.
Transfers: Closing date 4/1. Applicants notified on a rolling basis starting 4/15; must reply by 6/1. Financial aid for admitted (transfer) students is determined based on a combined assessment of financial eligibility and the overall academic strength of the candidate.

CONTACT
Robin Randall, Assistant Vice President for Enrollment and Student Financial Services
26 East Main Street, Norton, MA 02766
(508) 286-8232

Wheelock College
Boston, Massachusetts
www.wheelock.edu
Federal Code: 002228

4-year private liberal arts and teachers college in very large city.
Enrollment: 721 undergrads, 1% part-time. 157 full-time freshmen.
Selectivity: Admits over 75% of applicants.

BASIC COSTS (2017-2018)
Tuition and fees: $36,200.
Per-credit charge: $1,090.
Room and board: $14,975.

FINANCIAL AID PICTURE (2016-2017)
Students with need: Need-based aid available for full-time and part-time students. Work study available nights, weekends, and for part-time students.
Students without need: No-need awards available for academics, leadership, state/district residency.
Scholarships offered: Dean's and Merit Scholarships: $13,000-$17,000; granted to all first-year students based on GPA and SAT/ACT scores.

FINANCIAL AID PROCEDURES
Forms required: FAFSA.
Dates and Deadlines: Priority date 2/15; no closing date. Applicants notified on a rolling basis starting 3/1; must reply by 5/1.
Transfers: Priority date 4/15. Applicants notified on a rolling basis starting 4/1.

CONTACT
Elizabeth Gorra, Director of Financial Aid
200 The Riverway, Boston, MA 02215-4104
(617) 879-2443

Williams College
Williamstown, Massachusetts
www.williams.edu
Federal Code: 002229
CSS Code: 3965

4-year private liberal arts college in small town.
Enrollment: 2,042 undergrads. 553 full-time freshmen.
Selectivity: Admits less than 50% of applicants.

BASIC COSTS (2016-2017)
Tuition and fees: $51,790.
Room and board: $13,690.

FINANCIAL AID PICTURE (2016-2017)
Students with need: Out of 358 full-time freshmen who applied for aid, 282 were judged to have need. Of these, 282 received aid, and 282 had their full need met. Average financial aid package met 100% of need; average scholarship/grant was $50,286; average loan was $2,608.

FINANCIAL AID PROCEDURES
Forms required: FAFSA, CSS PROFILE.
Dates and Deadlines: Priority date 2/1; no closing date. Applicants notified by 4/1; must reply by 5/1.
Transfers: Closing date 4/1. Applicants notified by 5/15; must reply within 2 week(s) of notification.

CONTACT
Paul Boyer, Director of Financial Aid
995 Main Street, Williamstown, MA 01267
(413) 597-3131

Worcester Polytechnic Institute
Worcester, Massachusetts   Federal Code: 002233
www.wpi.edu   CSS Code: 3969

4-year private university in small city.
Enrollment: 4,320 undergrads, 2% part-time. 1,093 full-time freshmen.
Selectivity: Admits less than 50% of applicants.

BASIC COSTS (2016-2017)
Tuition and fees: $46,994.
Per-credit charge: $1,288.
Room and board: $13,745.

FINANCIAL AID PICTURE (2015-2016)
Students with need: Out of 910 full-time freshmen who applied for aid, 746 were judged to have need. Of these, 746 received aid, and 396 had their full need met. Average financial aid package met 80% of need; average scholarship/grant was $23,865; average loan was $2,866. For part-time students, average financial aid package was $11,286.
Students without need: 327 full-time freshmen who did not demonstrate need for aid received scholarships/grants; average award was $13,832. No-need awards available for academics, leadership, minority status, ROTC.
Scholarships offered: Merit scholarships: typically $10,000-$25,000; renewable for 4 years.

FINANCIAL AID PROCEDURES
Forms required: FAFSA, CSS PROFILE.
Dates and Deadlines: Priority date 2/1; no closing date. Applicants notified by 4/1; must reply by 5/1.
Transfers: Closing date 2/1. Applicants notified by 4/1; must reply by 5/1.

CONTACT
Monica Blondin, Director, Student Aid and Financial Literacy
100 Institute Road, Worcester, MA 01609-2280
(508) 831-5469

Worcester State University
Worcester, Massachusetts
www.worcester.edu   Federal Code: 002190

4-year public liberal arts and teachers college in small city.
Enrollment: 4,891 undergrads, 18% part-time. 808 full-time freshmen.
Selectivity: Admits 50 to 75% of applicants.

BASIC COSTS (2016-2017)
Tuition and fees: $9,202; out-of-state residents $15,282.
Per-credit charge: $40.42; out-of-state residents $293.75.
Room and board: $11,775.

FINANCIAL AID PICTURE (2015-2016)
Students with need: Out of 757 full-time freshmen who applied for aid, 536 were judged to have need. Of these, 524 received aid, and 192 had their full need met. Average financial aid package met 76% of need; average scholarship/grant was $4,934; average loan was $2,480. For part-time students, average financial aid package was $7,128.
Students without need: No-need awards available for academics, ROTC.
Scholarships offered: Presidential Scholarship: full in-state tuition and fees; 3.75 GPA and 1200 SAT required; 15 awarded. Tsongas Scholarship: full in-state tuition and fees to Massachusetts residents; 3.75 GPA and 1200 SAT required; 5 awarded. Access Scholarship: $1,000 per year; for under-served groups with 2.5 GPA and 920 SAT; 15 awarded.
Additional info: Veterans, Native Americans and those certified by Massachusetts Rehabilitation Commission and Massachusetts Commission for the Blind considered for tuition waivers while funds available. Tuition also waived for needy Massachusetts residents and in-state National Guard members.

FINANCIAL AID PROCEDURES
Forms required: FAFSA.

Dates and Deadlines: Priority date 3/1; closing date 5/1. Applicants notified on a rolling basis starting 12/15; must reply within 3 week(s) of notification.

CONTACT
Jayne McGinn, Director of Financial Aid
Office of Undergraduate Admission, Worcester, MA 01602-2597
(508) 929-8056

Michigan

Adrian College
Adrian, Michigan
www.adrian.edu   Federal Code: 002234

4-year private liberal arts college in large town, affiliated with the United Methodist Church.
Enrollment: 1,622 undergrads, 1% part-time. 490 full-time freshmen.
Selectivity: Admits 50 to 75% of applicants.

BASIC COSTS (2017-2018)
Tuition and fees: $36,010.
Per-credit charge: $890.
Room and board: $10,988.

FINANCIAL AID PICTURE (2015-2016)
Students with need: 71% of average financial aid package awarded as scholarships/grants, 29% awarded as loans/jobs. Need-based aid available for part-time students. Work study available nights, weekends, and for part-time students.
Students without need: No-need awards available for academics, alumni affiliation, art, leadership, music/drama, religious affiliation, ROTC, state/district residency.
Scholarships offered: Academic scholarships: based on 20 ACT and 3.0 GPA.

FINANCIAL AID PROCEDURES
Forms required: FAFSA.
Dates and Deadlines: Priority date 3/1; no closing date. Applicants notified on a rolling basis starting 3/15; must reply by 5/1 or within 2 week(s) of notification.
Transfers: No deadline. Applicants notified on a rolling basis starting 3/15; must reply by 5/1 or within 2 week(s) of notification.

CONTACT
Matthew Rheinecker, Director of Financial Aid
110 South Madison Street, Adrian, MI 49221-2575
(888) 876-0194

Albion College
Albion, Michigan
www.albion.edu   Federal Code: 002235

4-year private liberal arts college in small town, affiliated with the United Methodist Church.
Enrollment: 1,393 undergrads, 1% part-time. 402 full-time freshmen.
Selectivity: Admits 50 to 75% of applicants.

BASIC COSTS (2016-2017)
Tuition and fees: $41,040.
Per-credit charge: $1,720.
Room and board: $11,610.

FINANCIAL AID PICTURE (2016-2017)

Students with need: Out of 374 full-time freshmen who applied for aid, 335 were judged to have need. Of these, 335 received aid, and 69 had their full need met. Average financial aid package met 92% of need; average scholarship/grant was $35,581; average loan was $4,604.

Students without need: 67 full-time freshmen who did not demonstrate need for aid received scholarships/grants; average award was $24,351. No-need awards available for academics, alumni affiliation, art, leadership, music/drama, state/district residency.

Scholarships offered: Academic scholarships: $17,000-$27,000 per year; renewable; subject to satisfactory progress; awarded to students with outstanding academic records or unique skills, talents, or abilities.

FINANCIAL AID PROCEDURES

Forms required: FAFSA.

Dates and Deadlines: Priority date 12/1; no closing date. Applicants notified on a rolling basis starting 12/1.

Transfers: No deadline. Applicants notified on a rolling basis starting 3/15.

CONTACT

Ann Whitmer, Director of Financial Aid
611 East Porter Street, Albion, MI 49224-1831
(517) 629-0440

Alma College
Alma, Michigan
www.alma.edu
Federal Code: 002236

4-year private liberal arts college in large town, affiliated with the Presbyterian Church (USA).

Enrollment: 1,414 undergrads, 3% part-time. 447 full-time freshmen.

Selectivity: Admits 50 to 75% of applicants.

BASIC COSTS (2016-2017)

Tuition and fees: $37,310.

Per-credit charge: $1,150.

Room and board: $10,238.

FINANCIAL AID PICTURE (2016-2017)

Students with need: Out of 432 full-time freshmen who applied for aid, 392 were judged to have need. Of these, 392 received aid, and 48 had their full need met. Average financial aid package met 72% of need; average scholarship/grant was $28,254; average loan was $3,552. For part-time students, average financial aid package was $18,669.

Students without need: 40 full-time freshmen who did not demonstrate need for aid received scholarships/grants; average award was $21,225. No-need awards available for academics, alumni affiliation, art, minority status, music/drama, religious affiliation.

Scholarships offered: Freshman merit awards: up to $21,500; are based on high school GPA, ACT/SAT scores; awarded annually. Transfer student merit awards: up to $19,000; based on college GPA; awarded annually. Top scholars are invited to interview for additional scholarship funds. National Achievement and National Hispanic scholars also are invited to interview for additional scholarship funds that range up to full tuition.

Additional info: Auditions required for music, drama, dance scholarship candidates. Portfolios required for art scholarship candidates.

FINANCIAL AID PROCEDURES

Forms required: FAFSA.

Dates and Deadlines: Priority date 3/1; no closing date. Applicants notified on a rolling basis starting 3/1.

Transfers: No deadline. Applicants notified on a rolling basis starting 3/1; must reply within 3 week(s) of notification.

CONTACT

Michelle McNier, Director of Financial Aid
614 West Superior Street, Alma, MI 48801-1599
(989) 463-7347

Alpena Community College
Alpena, Michigan
www.alpenacc.edu
Federal Code: 002237

2-year public community college in large town.

Enrollment: 1,534 undergrads.

Selectivity: Open admission; but selective for some programs.

BASIC COSTS (2016-2017)

Tuition and fees: $4,290; out-of-district residents $6,450; out-of-state residents $6,450.

Per-credit charge: $125; out-of-district residents $197; out-of-state residents $197.

FINANCIAL AID PICTURE

Students with need: Need-based aid available for full-time and part-time students.

Students without need: No-need awards available for academics, art, athletics, job skills, leadership, music/drama.

FINANCIAL AID PROCEDURES

Forms required: FAFSA.

Dates and Deadlines: Priority date 8/1; no closing date. Applicants notified on a rolling basis starting 5/15; must reply within 3 week(s) of notification.

CONTACT

Rob Roose, Director of Financial Aid
665 Johnson Street, Alpena, MI 49707
(989) 358-7205

Andrews University
Berrien Springs, Michigan
www.andrews.edu
Federal Code: 002238
CSS Code: 1030

4-year private university in small town, affiliated with the Seventh-day Adventists.

Enrollment: 1,467 undergrads, 8% part-time. 294 full-time freshmen.

Selectivity: Admits less than 50% of applicants.

BASIC COSTS (2016-2017)

Tuition and fees: $27,684.

Per-credit charge: $1,116.

Room and board: $8,742.

FINANCIAL AID PICTURE (2016-2017)

Students with need: Out of 294 full-time freshmen who applied for aid, 206 were judged to have need. Of these, 206 received aid, and 47 had their full need met. Average financial aid package met 86% of need; average scholarship/grant was $5,273; average loan was $3,323. For part-time students, average financial aid package was $18,011.

Students without need: 94 full-time freshmen who did not demonstrate need for aid received scholarships/grants; average award was $13,634. No-need awards available for academics, job skills, leadership, music/drama.

FINANCIAL AID PROCEDURES

Forms required: FAFSA, CSS PROFILE, institutional form.

Dates and Deadlines: Priority date 3/31; no closing date. Applicants notified on a rolling basis starting 3/15.

CONTACT

Elynda Bedney, Director of Student Financial Services
100 US Highway 31, Berrien Springs, MI 49104

Aquinas College

Grand Rapids, Michigan
www.aquinas.edu

Federal Code: 002239

4-year private liberal arts college in small city, affiliated with the Roman Catholic Church.

Enrollment: 1,549 undergrads, 9% part-time. 370 full-time freshmen.

Selectivity: Admits over 75% of applicants. GED not accepted.

BASIC COSTS (2017-2018)

Tuition and fees: $31,244.

Per-credit charge: $498.

Room and board: $9,070.

Additional info: Tuition/fee waivers available for adults.

FINANCIAL AID PICTURE (2015-2016)

Students with need: Out of 337 full-time freshmen who applied for aid, 309 were judged to have need. Of these, 309 received aid, and 57 had their full need met. Average financial aid package met 81% of need; average scholarship/grant was $21,588; average loan was $1,984. For part-time students, average financial aid package was $4,288.

Students without need: 46 full-time freshmen who did not demonstrate need for aid received scholarships/grants; average award was $16,026. No-need awards available for academics, alumni affiliation, art, athletics, leadership, minority status, music/drama.

Scholarships offered: *Merit:* Spectrum Scholarship: $3,000, full tuition; awarded to students who have excelled in academics, leadership or community service; renewable. *Athletic:* 16 full-time freshmen received athletic scholarships; average amount $2,906.

FINANCIAL AID PROCEDURES

Forms required: FAFSA.

Dates and Deadlines: Priority date 3/1; no closing date. Applicants notified on a rolling basis starting 3/1; must reply within 2 week(s) of notification.

Transfers: Priority date 4/15; closing date 7/1. Must reply within 2 week(s) of notification.

CONTACT

Darcy Kampfschulte, Director of Financial Aid
1700 Fulton Street E, Grand Rapids, MI 49506-1801
(616) 632-2893

Baker College of Auburn Hills

Auburn Hills, Michigan
www.baker.edu

Federal Code: E00466

4-year private business and technical college in small city.

Enrollment: 3,400 undergrads.

Selectivity: Open admission; but selective for some programs.

BASIC COSTS (2016-2017)

Tuition and fees: $11,250.

Per-credit charge: $250.

FINANCIAL AID PICTURE

Students with need: Work study available nights, weekends, and for part-time students.

Students without need: No-need awards available for academics, alumni affiliation.

FINANCIAL AID PROCEDURES

Forms required: FAFSA, institutional form.

Dates and Deadlines: Priority date 2/21; closing date 9/1. Applicants notified on a rolling basis starting 4/1.

Transfers: Must have been deemed financial aid-eligible at previous school.

CONTACT

Greg Little, Financial Aid Director
1500 University Drive, Auburn Hills, MI 48326
(248) 340-0600

Baker College of Cadillac

Cadillac, Michigan
www.baker.edu

Federal Code: E00461

4-year private business and health science college in large town.

Enrollment: 1,800 undergrads.

Selectivity: Open admission.

BASIC COSTS (2016-2017)

Tuition and fees: $11,250.

Per-credit charge: $250.

Additional info: Off-campus apartments available.

FINANCIAL AID PICTURE

Students with need: Need-based aid available for full-time and part-time students. Work study available nights, weekends, and for part-time students.

Students without need: No-need awards available for academics.

Scholarships offered: Baker College Career Scholarships: $400 per term for 4 years; based on 2.5 GPA after junior year of high school. Board of Regents Scholarships: half tuition for 4 years; based on 3.5 GPA through grade 11.

FINANCIAL AID PROCEDURES

Forms required: FAFSA, institutional form.

Dates and Deadlines: Priority date 2/21; no closing date. Applicants notified on a rolling basis starting 5/1.

Transfers: Priority date 3/20; closing date 9/1.

CONTACT

Kristin Bonney, Financial Aid Officer
9600 East 13th Street, Cadillac, MI 49601
(231) 876-3118

Baker College of Clinton Township

Clinton Township, Michigan
www.baker.edu

Federal Code: E00462

4-year private business and technical college in very large city.

Enrollment: 3,618 undergrads.

Selectivity: Open admission; but selective for some programs.

BASIC COSTS (2016-2017)

Tuition and fees: $11,250.

Per-credit charge: $250.

FINANCIAL AID PICTURE

Students with need: Need-based aid available for full-time and part-time students. Work study available nights, weekends, and for part-time students.

Students without need: No-need awards available for academics, minority status.

FINANCIAL AID PROCEDURES

Forms required: FAFSA, institutional form.

Dates and Deadlines: Priority date 2/21; closing date 9/1. Applicants notified on a rolling basis starting 4/1.

CONTACT

Lisa Harvener, Vice President of Student Services
34950 Little Mack Avenue, Clinton Township, MI 48035
(586) 790-9589

Baker College of Muskegon
Muskegon, Michigan
www.baker.edu   Federal Code: E00463

4-year private business and technical college in small city.
Enrollment: 4,500 undergrads.
Selectivity: Open admission; but selective for some programs.

BASIC COSTS (2016-2017)
Tuition and fees: $11,250.
Per-credit charge: $250.
Additional info: On-Campus Halls/Apartments: $900/person/quarter. Baker Townhouses: $1,000/person/quarter.

FINANCIAL AID PICTURE
Students with need: Need-based aid available for full-time and part-time students. Work study available nights, weekends, and for part-time students.
Students without need: No-need awards available for academics, minority status.
Scholarships offered: Career Scholarship: $4,800 over 4 years; based on GPA over 3.0. Board Regents Scholarship: one-half tuition for 4 years; based on GPA over 3.5. Alternative Scholarship: one-half tuition for 2 years; based on academic success in alternative high school education program.

FINANCIAL AID PROCEDURES
Forms required: FAFSA, institutional form.
Dates and Deadlines: Priority date 2/21; no closing date. Applicants notified on a rolling basis starting 4/1.
Transfers: Priority date 3/21.

CONTACT
Jody Zerlant, Director of Financial Aid
1903 Marquette Avenue, Muskegon, MI 49442
(231) 777-5231

Baker College of Owosso
Owosso, Michigan
www.baker.edu   Federal Code: E00464

4-year private business and technical college in large town.
Enrollment: 3,000 undergrads.
Selectivity: Open admission; but selective for some programs.

BASIC COSTS (2016-2017)
Tuition and fees: $11,250.
Per-credit charge: $250.
Additional info: On-Campus Residence Hall: $1,000-$1,050/person/quarter. Woodard Station Lofts: $950/person/quarter.

FINANCIAL AID PICTURE
Students with need: Need-based aid available for full-time and part-time students. Work study available nights, weekends, and for part-time students.
Students without need: No-need awards available for academics, minority status.

FINANCIAL AID PROCEDURES
Forms required: FAFSA, institutional form.
Dates and Deadlines: Priority date 2/21; closing date 9/1. Applicants notified on a rolling basis starting 4/1.
Transfers: Priority date 3/21.

CONTACT
Nicole Patterson, Financial Aid Director
1020 South Washington Street, Owosso, MI 48867
(989) 720-3430

Baker College of Port Huron
Port Huron, Michigan
www.baker.edu   Federal Code: E00465

4-year private business and technical college in large town.
Enrollment: 1,200 undergrads.
Selectivity: Open admission; but selective for some programs.

BASIC COSTS (2016-2017)
Tuition and fees: $11,250.
Per-credit charge: $250.
Additional info: On-Campus Apartments: 2-person rooms: $1,200/person/quarter. 4-person rooms: $1,000/person/quarter.

FINANCIAL AID PICTURE
Students with need: Need-based aid available for full-time and part-time students. Work study available nights.
Students without need: This college awards aid only to students with need.

FINANCIAL AID PROCEDURES
Forms required: FAFSA, institutional form.
Dates and Deadlines: Priority date 2/21; no closing date. Applicants notified on a rolling basis starting 4/1.
Transfers: Priority date 3/21; closing date 9/1.

CONTACT
Barbara Fosgard, Financial Aid Director
3403 Lapeer Road, Port Huron, MI 48060-2597
(810) 985-7000

Bay College
Escanaba, Michigan
www.baycollege.edu   Federal Code: 002240

2-year public community college in large town.
Enrollment: 1,422 undergrads, 51% part-time. 199 full-time freshmen.
Selectivity: Open admission; but selective for some programs.

BASIC COSTS (2016-2017)
Tuition and fees: $4,548; out-of-district residents $7,038; out-of-state residents $11,928.
Per-credit charge: $116; out-of-district residents $199; out-of-state residents $362.
Room only: $3,000.

FINANCIAL AID PICTURE
Students with need: Need-based aid available for full-time and part-time students. Work study available nights, weekends, and for part-time students.
Students without need: No-need awards available for academics.

FINANCIAL AID PROCEDURES
Forms required: FAFSA.
Dates and Deadlines: Priority date 4/1; no closing date. Applicants notified on a rolling basis starting 2/1; must reply within 2 week(s) of notification.

CONTACT
Laurie Spangenberg, Financial Aid Director
2001 North Lincoln Road, Escanaba, MI 49829-2511
(906) 217-4032

Bay Mills Community College
Brimley, Michigan
www.bmcc.edu   Federal Code: 030666

2-year public community college in rural community.
Enrollment: 461 undergrads.

Selectivity: Open admission.

BASIC COSTS (2016-2017)
Tuition and fees: $3,250; out-of-state residents $3,250.
Per-credit charge: $95.

FINANCIAL AID PICTURE
Students with need: Work study available nights.

FINANCIAL AID PROCEDURES
Forms required: FAFSA.
Dates and Deadlines: Priority date 6/30; no closing date.

CONTACT
Tina Miller, Financial Aid Director
12214 West Lakeshore Drive, Brimley, MI 49715
(906) 248-3354 ext. 8437

Calvin College
Grand Rapids, Michigan
www.calvin.edu   Federal Code: 002241

4-year private liberal arts college in large city, affiliated with the Christian Reformed Church.
Enrollment: 3,722 undergrads, 4% part-time. 944 full-time freshmen.
Selectivity: Admits 50 to 75% of applicants.

BASIC COSTS (2016-2017)
Tuition and fees: $31,730.
Per-credit charge: $760.
Room and board: $9,840.

FINANCIAL AID PICTURE (2015-2016)
Students with need: Out of 855 full-time freshmen who applied for aid, 655 were judged to have need. Of these, 655 received aid, and 129 had their full need met. Average financial aid package met 77% of need; average scholarship/grant was $18,804; average loan was $4,069. For part-time students, average financial aid package was $8,945.
Students without need: 276 full-time freshmen who did not demonstrate need for aid received scholarships/grants; average award was $10,575. No-need awards available for academics, alumni affiliation, art, leadership, minority status, music/drama, religious affiliation, state/district residency.
Scholarships offered: Honors Fellows award: for high-achieving and service-oriented students. Perkins Fellows leadership awards: for high-achieving and service-oriented students. Legacy awards for alumni children. Denominational awards. First generation awards. Various departmental scholarships.

FINANCIAL AID PROCEDURES
Forms required: FAFSA.
Dates and Deadlines: Priority date 2/15; no closing date. Applicants notified on a rolling basis starting 3/15.
Transfers: Priority date 3/15; closing date 8/15. Applicants notified on a rolling basis starting 3/15; must reply by 6/1.

CONTACT
Paul Witte, Director of Financial Aid
3201 Burton Street Southeast, Grand Rapids, MI 49546
(616) 526-6134

Central Michigan University
Mount Pleasant, Michigan
www.cmich.edu   Federal Code: 002243

4-year public university in large town.
Enrollment: 19,551 undergrads, 13% part-time. 3,448 full-time freshmen.
Selectivity: Admits 50 to 75% of applicants.

BASIC COSTS (2016-2017)
Tuition and fees: $12,150; out-of-state residents $23,670.
Per-credit charge: $405; out-of-state residents $789.
Room and board: $9,406.

FINANCIAL AID PICTURE (2015-2016)
Students with need: Out of 3,062 full-time freshmen who applied for aid, 2,285 were judged to have need. Of these, 2,220 received aid, and 1,251 had their full need met. Average financial aid package met 84% of need; average scholarship/grant was $8,560; average loan was $5,859. For part-time students, average financial aid package was $9,377.
Students without need: 748 full-time freshmen who did not demonstrate need for aid received scholarships/grants; average award was $5,127. No-need awards available for academics, alumni affiliation, art, athletics, leadership, minority status, music/drama, ROTC, state/district residency.
Scholarships offered: 50 full-time freshmen received athletic scholarships; average amount $14,688.
Additional info: Tuition waiver for Native American students qualifying under state program criteria.

FINANCIAL AID PROCEDURES
Forms required: FAFSA.
Dates and Deadlines: Priority date 3/1; no closing date. Applicants notified on a rolling basis starting 4/1.

CONTACT
Kirk Yats, Director, Scholarships and Financial Aid
Admissions Office, Mount Pleasant, MI 48859
(989) 774-3674

Cleary University
Howell, Michigan
www.cleary.edu   Federal Code: 002246

4-year private university and business college in small city.
Enrollment: 206 full-time undergrads.
Selectivity: Open admission; but selective for some programs.

BASIC COSTS (2016-2017)
Tuition and fees: $17,500.
Per-credit charge: $625.
Room and board: $9,600.
Additional info: Tuition at time of enrollment locked for 4 years.

FINANCIAL AID PICTURE
Students with need: Need-based aid available for full-time and part-time students. Work study available nights.
Students without need: This college awards aid only to students with need.
Scholarships offered: Oren Beutler Endowed Scholarship: $750; new or continuing full-time student maintaining 3.0 GPA, demonstrated leadership and service to community; one awarded annually; renewable for 4 years. Scholarship for veteran/military students (honorable discharge only).
Additional info: Filing electronically preferred; paper applications available. Tuition guarantee based on continuous enrollment. Essay and recommendations required for scholarship consideration.

FINANCIAL AID PROCEDURES
Forms required: FAFSA.
Dates and Deadlines: Priority date 3/1; no closing date. Applicants notified on a rolling basis starting 3/1; must reply within 2 week(s) of notification.
Transfers: No deadline. Applicants notified on a rolling basis starting 4/1; must reply within 2 week(s) of notification. Aid eligibility for transfer students is determined using aid already received from the other school.

CONTACT
Vesta Smith-Campbell, Director of Financial Aid
3750 Cleary Drive, Howell, MI 48843
(517) 338-3015

College for Creative Studies
Detroit, Michigan
www.collegeforcreativestudies.edu   Federal Code: 006771

4-year private visual arts college in very large city.
Enrollment: 1,377 undergrads, 18% part-time. 256 full-time freshmen.
Selectivity: Admits less than 50% of applicants.

BASIC COSTS (2017-2018)
Tuition and fees: $42,460.
Per-credit charge: $1,368.
Room and board: $8,650.

FINANCIAL AID PICTURE
Students with need: Need-based aid available for full-time and part-time students. Work study available nights, weekends, and for part-time students.
Students without need: No-need awards available for academics, art.

FINANCIAL AID PROCEDURES
Forms required: FAFSA.
Dates and Deadlines: Priority date 7/1; no closing date. Applicants notified on a rolling basis starting 2/15; must reply within 3 week(s) of notification.
Transfers: Priority date 3/21.

CONTACT
Kristin Moskovitz, Director of Financial Aid
201 East Kirby, Detroit, MI 48202-4034
(313) 664-7495

Concordia University
Ann Arbor, Michigan
www.cuaa.edu   Federal Code: 002247

4-year private liberal arts and teachers college in small city, affiliated with the Lutheran Church - Missouri Synod.
Enrollment: 562 full-time undergrads.

BASIC COSTS (2016-2017)
Tuition and fees: $27,710.
Room and board: $9,680.

FINANCIAL AID PICTURE
Students with need: Need-based aid available for full-time and part-time students. Work study available nights, weekends, and for part-time students.
Students without need: No-need awards available for academics, alumni affiliation, art, athletics, leadership, music/drama, religious affiliation.

FINANCIAL AID PROCEDURES
Forms required: FAFSA.
Dates and Deadlines: Closing date 3/1. Applicants notified on a rolling basis starting 3/1; must reply within 3 week(s) of notification.
Transfers: Priority date 5/1. Applicants notified on a rolling basis; must reply within 3 week(s) of notification.

CONTACT
Steven Taylor, Director of Financial Aid
4090 Geddes Road, Ann Arbor, MI 48105
(734) 995-7408

Cornerstone University
Grand Rapids, Michigan
www.cornerstone.edu   Federal Code: 002266

4-year private university and liberal arts college in small city, affiliated with the interdenominational tradition.
Enrollment: 1,856 undergrads, 27% part-time. 274 full-time freshmen.

Selectivity: Admits 50 to 75% of applicants.

BASIC COSTS (2017-2018)
Tuition and fees: $27,520.
Per-credit charge: $1,030.
Room and board: $9,030.
Additional info: Tuition/fee waivers available for minority students.

FINANCIAL AID PICTURE (2016-2017)
Students with need: Out of 252 full-time freshmen who applied for aid, 227 were judged to have need. Of these, 227 received aid, and 35 had their full need met. Average financial aid package met 72% of need; average scholarship/grant was $18,283; average loan was $3,687. For part-time students, average financial aid package was $7,873.
Students without need: 45 full-time freshmen who did not demonstrate need for aid received scholarships/grants; average award was $10,355. No-need awards available for academics, athletics, music/drama.
Scholarships offered: *Merit:* Academic scholarships: based on high school GPA and ACT. ***Athletic:*** 22 full-time freshmen received athletic scholarships; average amount $4,871.
Additional info: Audition required for music scholarship applicants.

FINANCIAL AID PROCEDURES
Forms required: FAFSA.
Dates and Deadlines: Priority date 3/1; no closing date. Applicants notified on a rolling basis starting 12/1.
Transfers: No deadline. Applicants notified by 3/15.

CONTACT
Carol Carpenter, Student Financial Services
1001 East Beltline NE, Grand Rapids, MI 49525-5897
(616) 222-1424

Davenport University
Grand Rapids, Michigan
www.davenport.edu   Federal Code: 015260

4-year private university in small city.
Enrollment: 5,398 undergrads, 53% part-time. 552 full-time freshmen.
Selectivity: Admits over 75% of applicants.

BASIC COSTS (2016-2017)
Tuition and fees: $20,680.
Per-credit charge: $664.
Room and board: $9,358.

FINANCIAL AID PICTURE
Students with need: Need-based aid available for full-time and part-time students. Work study available nights, weekends, and for part-time students.
Students without need: No-need awards available for academics, alumni affiliation, athletics, leadership.

FINANCIAL AID PROCEDURES
Forms required: FAFSA.
Dates and Deadlines: Priority date 3/1; no closing date. Applicants notified on a rolling basis starting 3/1; must reply within 2 week(s) of notification.
Transfers: No deadline. Applicants notified on a rolling basis.

CONTACT
David De Boer, Executive Director of Financial Aid
6191 Kraft Avenue SE, Grand Rapids, MI 49512-9396
(866) 925-3884

Delta College
University Center, Michigan
www.delta.edu   Federal Code: 002251

2-year public community college in small city.
Enrollment: 9,291 undergrads.

Selectivity: Open admission.

BASIC COSTS (2016-2017)
Tuition and fees: $3,065; out-of-district residents $5,180; out-of-state residents $9,680.
Per-credit charge: $99.5; out-of-district residents $170; out-of-state residents $320.

FINANCIAL AID PICTURE
Students with need: Need-based aid available for full-time and part-time students. Work study available nights.
Students without need: No-need awards available for academics, athletics.

FINANCIAL AID PROCEDURES
Forms required: FAFSA.
Dates and Deadlines: Applicants notified on a rolling basis; must reply within 2 week(s) of notification.
Transfers: No deadline. Applicants notified on a rolling basis.

CONTACT
Lisa Martens, Financial Aid Director
1961 Delta Road D101, University Center, MI 48710
(989) 686-9080

Eastern Michigan University
Ypsilanti, Michigan
www.emich.edu
Federal Code: 002259

4-year public university in small city.
Enrollment: 17,256 undergrads, 26% part-time. 2,837 full-time freshmen.
Selectivity: Admits 50 to 75% of applicants.

BASIC COSTS (2016-2017)
Tuition and fees: $11,219; out-of-state residents $27,712.
Per-credit charge: $323; out-of-state residents $873.
Room and board: $9,344.

FINANCIAL AID PICTURE (2015-2016)
Students with need: Out of 2,616 full-time freshmen who applied for aid, 2,090 were judged to have need. Of these, 2,069 received aid, and 143 had their full need met. Average financial aid package met 46% of need; average scholarship/grant was $6,857; average loan was $1,390. For part-time students, average financial aid package was $2,271.
Students without need: 682 full-time freshmen who did not demonstrate need for aid received scholarships/grants; average award was $5,434. No-need awards available for academics, alumni affiliation, art, athletics, leadership, minority status, music/drama, ROTC, state/district residency.
Scholarships offered: 104 full-time freshmen received athletic scholarships; average amount $16,914.

FINANCIAL AID PROCEDURES
Forms required: FAFSA.
Dates and Deadlines: Applicants notified on a rolling basis starting 3/1.
Transfers: No deadline. Applicants notified on a rolling basis starting 3/1.

CONTACT
Mike Valdes, Director
400 Pierce Hall, Ypsilanti, MI 48197
(734) 487-0455

Ferris State University
Big Rapids, Michigan
www.ferris.edu
Federal Code: 002260

4-year public university in large town.
Enrollment: 12,006 undergrads, 27% part-time. 1,788 full-time freshmen.
Selectivity: Admits over 75% of applicants.

BASIC COSTS (2016-2017)
Tuition and fees: $11,760; out-of-state residents $17,640.
Per-credit charge: $392; out-of-state residents $588.
Room and board: $9,651.

FINANCIAL AID PICTURE (2016-2017)
Students with need: Out of 1,678 full-time freshmen who applied for aid, 1,342 were judged to have need. Of these, 1,337 received aid, and 234 had their full need met. Average financial aid package met 72% of need; average scholarship/grant was $4,770; average loan was $3,630. For part-time students, average financial aid package was $6,410.
Students without need: 293 full-time freshmen who did not demonstrate need for aid received scholarships/grants; average award was $5,140. No-need awards available for academics, alumni affiliation, art, athletics, job skills, leadership, minority status, music/drama, ROTC, state/district residency.
Scholarships offered: 64 full-time freshmen received athletic scholarships; average amount $7,690.

FINANCIAL AID PROCEDURES
Forms required: FAFSA.
Dates and Deadlines: Priority date 12/1; no closing date. Applicants notified on a rolling basis starting 12/9; must reply within 3 week(s) of notification.
Transfers: Applicants notified on a rolling basis; must reply within 3 week(s) of notification.

CONTACT
Heidi Wisby, Director of Financial Aid
1201 South State Street, CSS 201, Big Rapids, MI 49307-2714
(231) 591-2110

Finlandia University
Hancock, Michigan
www.finlandia.edu
Federal Code: 002322

4-year private university and liberal arts college in small town, affiliated with the Evangelical Lutheran Church in America.
Enrollment: 600 undergrads.
Selectivity: Open admission; but selective for some programs.

BASIC COSTS (2016-2017)
Tuition and fees: $22,758.
Room and board: $8,800.

FINANCIAL AID PICTURE
Students with need: Need-based aid available for full-time and part-time students. Work study available nights, weekends, and for part-time students.
Students without need: No-need awards available for academics, leadership, religious affiliation, state/district residency.
Additional info: Work/study program; up to $2,800 per year.

FINANCIAL AID PROCEDURES
Forms required: FAFSA, institutional form.
Dates and Deadlines: Priority date 3/1; no closing date. Applicants notified on a rolling basis starting 3/1; must reply within 2 week(s) of notification.
Transfers: Priority date 3/10; no deadline. Applicants notified on a rolling basis starting 2/1; must reply within 2 week(s) of notification.

CONTACT
Sandra Turnquist, Director of Financial Aid
601 Quincy Street, Hancock, MI 49930-1882
(906) 487-7261

Glen Oaks Community College

Centreville, Michigan
www.glenoaks.edu   Federal Code: 002263

2-year public community college in rural community.
Enrollment: 680 undergrads.
Selectivity: Open admission; but selective for some programs.

BASIC COSTS (2016-2017)

Tuition and fees: $4,140; out-of-district residents $6,030; out-of-state residents $7,050.
Per-credit charge: $109; out-of-district residents $172; out-of-state residents $206.

FINANCIAL AID PICTURE

Students with need: Need-based aid available for full-time and part-time students. Work study available nights.
Students without need: No-need awards available for academics, art, athletics, leadership.

FINANCIAL AID PROCEDURES

Forms required: FAFSA, institutional form.
Dates and Deadlines: Applicants notified on a rolling basis.

CONTACT

Jean Zimmerman, Director of Financial Aid and Scholarship
62249 Shimmel Road, Centreville, MI 49032-9719
(269) 467-9945 ext. 260

Gogebic Community College

Ironwood, Michigan
www.gogebic.edu   Federal Code: 002264

2-year public community college in small town.
Enrollment: 793 undergrads, 33% part-time. 218 full-time freshmen.
Selectivity: Open admission; but selective for some programs.

BASIC COSTS (2016-2017)

Tuition and fees: $4,492; out-of-district residents $5,918; out-of-state residents $6,817.
Per-credit charge: $110; out-of-district residents $156; out-of-state residents $185.
Room and board: $5,804.

FINANCIAL AID PICTURE

Students with need: Need-based aid available for full-time and part-time students. Work study available nights, weekends, and for part-time students.
Students without need: No-need awards available for academics, art, athletics, job skills, leadership, music/drama, state/district residency.

FINANCIAL AID PROCEDURES

Forms required: FAFSA.
Dates and Deadlines: Priority date 5/1; no closing date. Applicants notified on a rolling basis starting 3/15; must reply within 2 week(s) of notification.

CONTACT

Sue Forbes, Director of Financial Aid
E4946 Jackson Road, Ironwood, MI 49938
(906) 932-4231 ext. 206

Grace Bible College

Grand Rapids, Michigan
www.gbcol.edu   Federal Code: 002265

4-year private Bible and liberal arts college in small city, affiliated with the Christian Church.

Enrollment: 286 undergrads, 4% part-time. 85 full-time freshmen.
Selectivity: Admits over 75% of applicants.

BASIC COSTS (2017-2018)

Tuition and fees: $19,650.
Per-credit charge: $655.
Room and board: $7,600.

FINANCIAL AID PICTURE (2015-2016)

Students with need: Out of 81 full-time freshmen who applied for aid, 76 were judged to have need. Of these, 76 received aid, and 1 had their full need met. Average financial aid package met 60% of need; average scholarship/grant was $9,607; average loan was $3,236. For part-time students, average financial aid package was $4,856.
Students without need: 9 full-time freshmen who did not demonstrate need for aid received scholarships/grants; average award was $4,694. No-need awards available for academics, music/drama, religious affiliation.

FINANCIAL AID PROCEDURES

Forms required: FAFSA.
Dates and Deadlines: Priority date 3/1; no closing date. Applicants notified on a rolling basis starting 5/15; must reply within 2 week(s) of notification.
Transfers: No deadline. Applicants notified on a rolling basis starting 5/15; must reply within 2 week(s) of notification.

CONTACT

Kurt Postma, Director of Financial Aid
1011 Aldon Street SW, PO Box 910, Grand Rapids, MI 49509
(616) 261-8557

Grand Rapids Community College

Grand Rapids, Michigan
www.grcc.edu   Federal Code: 002267

2-year public community college in small city.
Enrollment: 13,244 undergrads, 68% part-time. 1,499 full-time freshmen.
Selectivity: Open admission; but selective for some programs.

BASIC COSTS (2016-2017)

Tuition and fees: $3,789; out-of-district residents $7,599; out-of-state residents $11,049.
Per-credit charge: $111; out-of-district residents $238; out-of-state residents $353.

FINANCIAL AID PICTURE

Students with need: Need-based aid available for full-time and part-time students. Work study available nights, weekends, and for part-time students.
Students without need: No-need awards available for academics.
Scholarships offered: Michigan Merit Award: $2,500; based on Michigan Educational Assessment Program scores.
Additional info: Tuition reimbursement and/or child-care services for single parents and displaced homemakers who meet Perkins guidelines.

FINANCIAL AID PROCEDURES

Forms required: FAFSA.
Dates and Deadlines: Priority date 4/1; no closing date. Applicants notified on a rolling basis starting 5/1; must reply within 3 week(s) of notification.

CONTACT

Ann Isaackson, Director of Financial Aid
143 Bostwick Avenue NE, Grand Rapids, MI 49503-3295
(616) 234-4030

Grand Valley State University

Allendale, Michigan
www.gvsu.edu   Federal Code: 002268

4-year public university in large town.
Enrollment: 22,081 undergrads, 11% part-time. 4,285 full-time freshmen.

Selectivity: Admits over 75% of applicants.

BASIC COSTS (2016-2017)
Tuition and fees: $11,520; out-of-state residents $16,392.
Per-credit charge: $480; out-of-state residents $683.
Room and board: $8,400.

FINANCIAL AID PICTURE (2016-2017)
Students with need: Out of 3,783 full-time freshmen who applied for aid, 2,605 were judged to have need. Of these, 2,585 received aid, and 397 had their full need met. Average financial aid package met 69% of need; average scholarship/grant was $8,060; average loan was $3,755. For part-time students, average financial aid package was $5,816.
Students without need: 773 full-time freshmen who did not demonstrate need for aid received scholarships/grants; average award was $3,476. No-need awards available for academics, alumni affiliation, art, athletics, music/drama, state/district residency.
Scholarships offered: 32 full-time freshmen received athletic scholarships; average amount $7,943.

FINANCIAL AID PROCEDURES
Forms required: FAFSA.
Dates and Deadlines: Priority date 3/1; no closing date. Applicants notified on a rolling basis starting 3/3; must reply by 5/1 or within 4 week(s) of notification.
Transfers: No deadline. Applicants notified on a rolling basis starting 3/20; must reply within 4 week(s) of notification.

CONTACT
Michelle Rhodes, Director of Financial Aid
1 Campus Drive, Allendale, MI 49401-9403
(616) 331-3234

Great Lakes Christian College
Lansing, Michigan
www.glcc.edu   Federal Code: 002269

4-year private Bible college in small city, affiliated with the Christian Church.
Enrollment: 174 undergrads.

BASIC COSTS (2016-2017)
Tuition and fees: $13,075.
Per-credit charge: $495.
Room and board: $8,500.

FINANCIAL AID PICTURE
Students with need: Need-based aid available for full-time and part-time students. Work study available nights, weekends, and for part-time students.
Students without need: No-need awards available for academics, alumni affiliation, music/drama.

FINANCIAL AID PROCEDURES
Forms required: FAFSA, state aid form, institutional form.
Dates and Deadlines: Closing date 8/1. Applicants notified on a rolling basis starting 5/1; must reply within 3 week(s) of notification.
Transfers: Priority date 3/31; closing date 8/31. Applicants notified on a rolling basis; must reply within 3 week(s) of notification. FAFSA due 6/30.

CONTACT
Ryan Apple, Financial Aid Director
6211 West Willow Highway, Lansing, MI 48917-1231
(517) 321-0242 ext. 227

Henry Ford College
Dearborn, Michigan
www.hfcc.edu

2-year public community college in small city.
Enrollment: 10,958 undergrads, 61% part-time. 1,436 full-time freshmen.

Selectivity: Open admission; but selective for some programs.

BASIC COSTS (2016-2017)
Tuition and fees: $3,482; out-of-district residents $5,522; out-of-state residents $7,592.
Per-credit charge: $93; out-of-district residents $161; out-of-state residents $230.

FINANCIAL AID PICTURE
Students with need: Work study available nights, weekends, and for part-time students.
Students without need: No-need awards available for academics, athletics.

FINANCIAL AID PROCEDURES
Forms required: FAFSA.
Dates and Deadlines: Priority date 6/5; no closing date. Applicants notified on a rolling basis starting 5/15.

CONTACT
Kevin Culler, Director, Financial Aid
5101 Evergreen Road, Dearborn, MI 48128
(313) 845-9616

Hillsdale College
Hillsdale, Michigan
www.hillsdale.edu   Federal Code: 002272

4-year private liberal arts college in small town, affiliated with the Christian Church.
Enrollment: 1,482 undergrads, 3% part-time. 364 full-time freshmen.
Selectivity: Admits less than 50% of applicants.

BASIC COSTS (2016-2017)
Tuition and fees: $25,522.
Per-credit charge: $985.
Room and board: $10,200.

FINANCIAL AID PICTURE (2016-2017)
Students with need: Out of 219 full-time freshmen who applied for aid, 194 were judged to have need. Of these, 188 received aid, and 75 had their full need met. Average financial aid package met 60% of need; average scholarship/grant was $6,969; average loan was $5,214. For part-time students, average financial aid package was $11,105.
Students without need: 162 full-time freshmen who did not demonstrate need for aid received scholarships/grants; average award was $15,192. No-need awards available for academics, alumni affiliation, art, athletics, leadership, music/drama.
Scholarships offered: 75 full-time freshmen received athletic scholarships; average amount $10,594.

FINANCIAL AID PROCEDURES
Forms required: institutional form. CSS PROFILE required for returning students only.
Dates and Deadlines: Priority date 5/1; no closing date. Applicants notified on a rolling basis starting 12/1; must reply within 4 week(s) of notification.

CONTACT
Richard Moeggenberg, Director of Financial Aid
33 East College Street, Hillsdale, MI 49242
(517) 607-2350

Hope College
Holland, Michigan
www.hope.edu

4-year private liberal arts college in small city, affiliated with the Reformed Church in America.

Enrollment: 2,915 undergrads, 2% part-time. 700 full-time freshmen.

Selectivity: Admits over 75% of applicants.

BASIC COSTS (2016-2017)

Tuition and fees: $31,560.

Room and board: $9,690.

Additional info: Tuition/fee waivers available for minority students.

FINANCIAL AID PICTURE (2016-2017)

Students with need: Out of 600 full-time freshmen who applied for aid, 459 were judged to have need. Of these, 458 received aid, and 117 had their full need met. Average financial aid package met 81% of need; average scholarship/grant was $21,105; average loan was $4,085. For part-time students, average financial aid package was $7,303.

Students without need: 190 full-time freshmen who did not demonstrate need for aid received scholarships/grants; average award was $8,714. No-need awards available for academics, art, minority status, music/drama, religious affiliation.

FINANCIAL AID PROCEDURES

Forms required: FAFSA, institutional form.

Dates and Deadlines: Priority date 3/1; no closing date. Applicants notified on a rolling basis starting 3/15.

Transfers: No deadline. Applicants notified on a rolling basis starting 3/25.

CONTACT

Thomas Bylsma, Chief Financial Officer

69 East 10th Street, Holland, MI 49422-9000

(616) 395-7765

Jackson College

Jackson, Michigan

www.jccmi.edu

Federal Code: 002274

2-year public community college in small city.

Enrollment: 5,180 undergrads.

Selectivity: Open admission; but selective for some programs.

BASIC COSTS (2016-2017)

Tuition and fees: $5,250; out-of-district residents $7,050; out-of-state residents $9,300.

Per-credit charge: $135; out-of-district residents $195; out-of-state residents $270.

FINANCIAL AID PICTURE

Students with need: Need-based aid available for full-time and part-time students. Work study available nights, weekends, and for part-time students.

Students without need: No-need awards available for academics, art, athletics, leadership.

FINANCIAL AID PROCEDURES

Forms required: FAFSA, institutional form.

Dates and Deadlines: Priority date 6/15; no closing date. Applicants notified on a rolling basis starting 3/1.

CONTACT

Kim Cvitkovic, Director of Financial Aid

2111 Emmons Road, Jackson, MI 49201-8399

(517) 796-8410

Kalamazoo College

Kalamazoo, Michigan

www.kzoo.edu

Federal Code: 002275

4-year private liberal arts college in small city.

Enrollment: 1,417 undergrads. 347 full-time freshmen.

Selectivity: Admits 50 to 75% of applicants.

BASIC COSTS (2016-2017)

Tuition and fees: $44,857.

Room and board: $9,174.

FINANCIAL AID PICTURE (2016-2017)

Students with need: Out of 310 full-time freshmen who applied for aid, 265 were judged to have need. Of these, 265 received aid, and 132 had their full need met. Average financial aid package met 95% of need; average scholarship/grant was $31,667; average loan was $5,409.

Students without need: 76 full-time freshmen who did not demonstrate need for aid received scholarships/grants; average award was $20,728. No-need awards available for academics, alumni affiliation, art, music/drama.

Scholarships offered: Honors Scholarship: $10,000-24,000 annually; based on academic and co-curricular record and accomplishments; varied number awarded. Enlightened Leadership Awards: $5,000; based on written application and/or creative expression portfolio.

Additional info: Paid career development internship and senior project experiences available on campus.

FINANCIAL AID PROCEDURES

Forms required: FAFSA.

Dates and Deadlines: Priority date 11/15; no closing date. Must reply by 5/1.

Transfers: Closing date 3/1. Must reply by 5/1.

CONTACT

Marian Stowers, Director of Financial Aid

1200 Academy Street, Kalamazoo, MI 49006

(269) 337-7192

Kalamazoo Valley Community College

Kalamazoo, Michigan

www.kvcc.edu

Federal Code: 006949

2-year public community college in small city.

Enrollment: 7,148 undergrads, 64% part-time. 783 full-time freshmen.

Selectivity: Open admission.

BASIC COSTS (2016-2017)

Tuition and fees: $3,220; out-of-district residents $5,380; out-of-state residents $7,150.

Per-credit charge: $100; out-of-district residents $172; out-of-state residents $231.

FINANCIAL AID PICTURE

Students with need: Need-based aid available for full-time and part-time students. Work study available nights, weekends, and for part-time students.

Students without need: No-need awards available for academics, athletics.

FINANCIAL AID PROCEDURES

Forms required: FAFSA, institutional form.

Dates and Deadlines: Priority date 6/1; no closing date. Applicants notified on a rolling basis starting 5/1; must reply within 2 week(s) of notification.

CONTACT

Alisha Cederbreg, Director of Financial Aid

6767 West O Avenue, Kalamazoo, MI 49003-4070

(269) 488-4340

Kellogg Community College

Battle Creek, Michigan

www.kellogg.edu

Federal Code: 002276

2-year public community college in small city.

Enrollment: 3,627 undergrads, 68% part-time. 233 full-time freshmen.

Selectivity: Open admission; but selective for some programs.

BASIC COSTS (2016-2017)

Tuition and fees: $3,585; out-of-district residents $5,561; out-of-state residents $7,721.

Additional info: Current Military Service members pay in-district rates regardless of residency status. Health programs charged at higher rates.

FINANCIAL AID PICTURE

Students with need: Need-based aid available for full-time and part-time students. Work study available nights.

Students without need: No-need awards available for academics, art, athletics, music/drama, state/district residency.

FINANCIAL AID PROCEDURES

Forms required: FAFSA, institutional form.

Dates and Deadlines: Priority date 4/1; no closing date. Applicants notified on a rolling basis starting 3/13.

Transfers: No deadline. Applicants notified on a rolling basis.

CONTACT

Nikki Jewell, Director, Financial Aid
450 North Avenue, Battle Creek, MI 49017-3397
(269) 965-4123

Kettering University

Flint, Michigan
www.kettering.edu   Federal Code: 002262

4-year private university and engineering college in small city.
Enrollment: 1,866 undergrads, 5% part-time. 363 full-time freshmen.
Selectivity: Admits 50 to 75% of applicants.

BASIC COSTS (2016-2017)

Tuition and fees: $39,790.
Per-credit charge: $1,327.
Room and board: $7,780.

FINANCIAL AID PICTURE (2015-2016)

Students with need: Average financial aid package met 59% of need; average scholarship/grant was $19,330; average loan was $3,484. Need-based aid available for part-time students.

Students without need: No-need awards available for academics.

Scholarships offered: Various scholarships: $20,000-$40,000 for 4 years; based on merit. Renewable scholarships: $250-$5,000 per year.

FINANCIAL AID PROCEDURES

Forms required: FAFSA.

Dates and Deadlines: Priority date 3/1; no closing date. Applicants notified on a rolling basis starting 3/17.

Transfers: No deadline. Applicants notified on a rolling basis starting 1/31.

CONTACT

Diane Bice, Director of Financial Aid
1700 University Avenue, Flint, MI 48504-6214
(810) 762-7859

Kirtland Community College

Roscommon, Michigan
www.kirtland.edu   Federal Code: 007171

2-year public community college in rural community.
Enrollment: 1,114 undergrads, 58% part-time. 130 full-time freshmen.
Selectivity: Open admission; but selective for some programs.

BASIC COSTS (2016-2017)

Tuition and fees: $3,900; out-of-district residents $5,370; out-of-state residents $7,980.

Per-credit charge: $109; out-of-district residents $179; out-of-state residents $266.

Additional info: Tuition/fee waivers available for minority students.

FINANCIAL AID PICTURE (2015-2016)

Students with need: Out of 130 full-time freshmen who applied for aid, 111 were judged to have need. Of these, 100 received aid, and 1 had their full need met. Average financial aid package met 45% of need; average scholarship/grant was $5,847; average loan was $2,017. For part-time students, average financial aid package was $4,020.

Students without need: 10 full-time freshmen who did not demonstrate need for aid received scholarships/grants; average award was $1,400. No-need awards available for academics, athletics, leadership, minority status.

Additional info: Federal and institutional work-study programs available.

FINANCIAL AID PROCEDURES

Forms required: FAFSA.

Dates and Deadlines: Priority date 5/1; no closing date. Applicants notified on a rolling basis.

Transfers: No deadline.

CONTACT

Christin Bates, Director of Financial Aid
10775 North Saint Helen Road, Roscommon, MI 48653
(989) 275-5000 ext. 310

Kuyper College

Grand Rapids, Michigan
www.kuyper.edu   Federal Code: 002311

4-year private Bible and liberal arts college in large city, affiliated with the Christian Reformed Church.
Enrollment: 201 undergrads, 16% part-time. 34 full-time freshmen.
Selectivity: Admits 50 to 75% of applicants.

BASIC COSTS (2016-2017)

Tuition and fees: $20,342.
Per-credit charge: $945.
Room and board: $7,280.

FINANCIAL AID PICTURE (2016-2017)

Students with need: Out of 34 full-time freshmen who applied for aid, 33 were judged to have need. Of these, 33 received aid, and 4 had their full need met. Average financial aid package met 73% of need; average scholarship/grant was $14,639; average loan was $4,956. For part-time students, average financial aid package was $9,368.

Students without need: 1 full-time freshmen who did not demonstrate need for aid received scholarships/grants; average award was $8,500. No-need awards available for academics, alumni affiliation, leadership, minority status, music/drama.

Scholarships offered: Achievement Awards: $1,000-$8,000; based on GPA and ACT. Christian Leadership Scholarship: $2,000; renewable annually; based on Christian service activities; 3.2 GPA. Christian Ministry Scholarship: up to $2,000; renewable annually; based on family's primary source of income. Multicultural Scholarships: $500-$5,000; based on 2.5 GPA, academic record, leadership involvement, essays, cross-cultural experiences, and student's ethnic, cultural and socioeconomic background.

FINANCIAL AID PROCEDURES

Forms required: FAFSA.

Dates and Deadlines: Priority date 3/1; no closing date. Applicants notified on a rolling basis starting 3/20; must reply within 2 week(s) of notification.

Transfers: No deadline. Applicants notified on a rolling basis starting 3/15; must reply within 2 week(s) of notification.

CONTACT

Agnes Russell, Director of Financial Aid
3333 East Beltline Avenue NE, Grand Rapids, MI 49525-9781
(616) 988-3656

Lake Michigan College
Benton Harbor, Michigan
www.lakemichigancollege.edu　　　Federal Code: 002277

2-year public community college in large town.
Enrollment: 2,820 undergrads, 63% part-time. 420 full-time freshmen.
Selectivity: Open admission; but selective for some programs.

BASIC COSTS (2016-2017)
Tuition and fees: $4,230; out-of-district residents $5,820; out-of-state residents $5,820.
Per-credit charge: $97; out-of-district residents $150; out-of-state residents $150.
Room only: $7,000.
Additional info: Tuition/fee waivers available for adults.

FINANCIAL AID PICTURE
Students with need: Need-based aid available for full-time and part-time students.
Scholarships offered: Presidential Scholarship: full tuition and fees; at least 10 scholarships available to new high school graduates each year.

FINANCIAL AID PROCEDURES
Forms required: FAFSA.
Dates and Deadlines: Priority date 3/1; no closing date. Applicants notified on a rolling basis starting 4/1; must reply within 2 week(s) of notification.
Transfers: No deadline. Must reply within 2 week(s) of notification.

CONTACT
Susan Fintze, Director, Financial Aid
2755 East Napier Avenue, Benton Harbor, MI 49022-1899
(269) 927-8112

Lake Superior State University
Sault Ste. Marie, Michigan
www.lssu.edu　　　Federal Code: 002293

4-year public university and engineering college in large town.
Enrollment: 2,063 undergrads, 12% part-time. 370 full-time freshmen.

BASIC COSTS (2016-2017)
Tuition and fees: $11,089; out-of-state residents $11,089.
Per-credit charge: $451.
Room and board: $9,442.

FINANCIAL AID PICTURE
Students with need: Need-based aid available for full-time and part-time students. Work study available nights, weekends, and for part-time students.
Students without need: No-need awards available for academics, athletics, state/district residency.

FINANCIAL AID PROCEDURES
Forms required: FAFSA.
Dates and Deadlines: Priority date 3/1; no closing date. Applicants notified on a rolling basis starting 10/1; must reply by 5/1 or within 3 week(s) of notification.
Transfers: Closing date 3/1. Applicants notified on a rolling basis starting 3/1.

CONTACT
Deborah Faust, Director of Financial Aid
650 West Easterday Avenue, Sault Sainte Marie, MI 49783-1699
(906) 635-2678

Lansing Community College
Lansing, Michigan
www.lcc.edu　　　Federal Code: 002278

2-year public community college in small city.
Enrollment: 12,673 undergrads, 61% part-time. 1,458 full-time freshmen.
Selectivity: Open admission; but selective for some programs.

BASIC COSTS (2017-2018)
Tuition and fees: $3,020; out-of-district residents $5,660; out-of-state residents $8,300.

FINANCIAL AID PICTURE
Students with need: Need-based aid available for full-time and part-time students. Work study available nights, weekends, and for part-time students.
Students without need: No-need awards available for academics, job skills.

FINANCIAL AID PROCEDURES
Forms required: FAFSA.
Dates and Deadlines: Closing date 7/19. Applicants notified on a rolling basis starting 2/11.
Transfers: Closing date 7/1. Applicants notified on a rolling basis starting 4/3.

CONTACT
Stephanie Bogard Trapp, Director of Financial Aid
1121 Enrollment Services, Lansing, MI 48901-7210
(517) 483-1200

Lawrence Technological University
Southfield, Michigan
www.ltu.edu　　　Federal Code: 002279

4-year private university in small city.
Enrollment: 2,004 undergrads, 15% part-time. 340 full-time freshmen.
Selectivity: Admits 50 to 75% of applicants.

BASIC COSTS (2016-2017)
Tuition and fees: $31,140.
Per-credit charge: $1,014.
Room and board: $10,107.
Additional info: Tuition/fee waivers available for unemployed or children of unemployed.

FINANCIAL AID PICTURE (2015-2016)
Students with need: Out of 324 full-time freshmen who applied for aid, 256 were judged to have need. Of these, 255 received aid, and 59 had their full need met. Average financial aid package met 73% of need; average scholarship/grant was $15,820; average loan was $5,891. For part-time students, average financial aid package was $12,817.
Students without need: 59 full-time freshmen who did not demonstrate need for aid received scholarships/grants; average award was $15,755. No-need awards available for academics, alumni affiliation, minority status, ROTC, state/district residency.
Scholarships offered: 50 full-time freshmen received athletic scholarships; average amount $9,846.
Additional info: March 1 state deadline for Michigan Competitive Scholarship and Michigan Tuition Grant.

FINANCIAL AID PROCEDURES
Forms required: FAFSA.
Dates and Deadlines: Priority date 4/1; no closing date. Applicants notified on a rolling basis starting 4/1; must reply within 2 week(s) of notification.
Transfers: Applicants notified on a rolling basis starting 4/1; must reply within 2 week(s) of notification.

CONTACT

Susie Poli-Smith, Director of Student Financial Aid

21000 West Ten Mile Road, Southfield, MI 48075-1058

(248) 204-2121

Macomb Community College

Warren, Michigan

www.macomb.edu   Federal Code: 008906

2-year public community college in small city.

Enrollment: 16,543 undergrads, 69% part-time. 1,472 full-time freshmen.

Selectivity: Open admission; but selective for some programs.

BASIC COSTS (2016-2017)

Tuition and fees: $3,180; out-of-district residents $5,670; out-of-state residents $7,170.

Per-credit charge: $97; out-of-district residents $180; out-of-state residents $230.

FINANCIAL AID PICTURE

Students with need: Need-based aid available for full-time and part-time students. Work study available nights, weekends, and for part-time students.

Students without need: No-need awards available for academics, athletics, leadership, music/drama, state/district residency.

FINANCIAL AID PROCEDURES

Forms required: FAFSA, institutional form.

Dates and Deadlines: Priority date 4/15; no closing date. Applicants notified on a rolling basis starting 5/15; must reply within 2 week(s) of notification.

Transfers: Must submit financial aid transcripts from all institutions attended.

CONTACT

Doug Levy, Director of Financial Aid

14500 East Twelve Mile Road, Warren, MI 48088-3896

(586) 445-7228

Madonna University

Livonia, Michigan

www.madonna.edu   Federal Code: 002282

4-year private university and liberal arts college in small city, affiliated with the Roman Catholic Church.

Enrollment: 2,445 undergrads, 45% part-time. 178 full-time freshmen.

Selectivity: Admits over 75% of applicants.

BASIC COSTS (2016-2017)

Tuition and fees: $19,640.

Per-credit charge: $650.

Room and board: $9,550.

FINANCIAL AID PICTURE (2015-2016)

Students with need: Out of 151 full-time freshmen who applied for aid, 124 were judged to have need. Of these, 124 received aid, and 39 had their full need met. Average financial aid package met 74% of need; average scholarship/grant was $12,371; average loan was $2,968. For part-time students, average financial aid package was $6,975.

Students without need: 50 full-time freshmen who did not demonstrate need for aid received scholarships/grants; average award was $7,758. No-need awards available for academics, alumni affiliation, art, athletics, leadership, minority status, music/drama, religious affiliation, state/district residency.

Scholarships offered: 11 full-time freshmen received athletic scholarships; average amount $6,786.

FINANCIAL AID PROCEDURES

Forms required: FAFSA.

Dates and Deadlines: Priority date 12/1; no closing date. Applicants notified on a rolling basis starting 12/15; must reply by 5/1 or within 2 week(s) of notification.

Transfers: No deadline. Applicants notified on a rolling basis starting 1/15; must reply by 7/1 or within 2 week(s) of notification. Deadline for state aid is March 1.

CONTACT

Chris Ziegler, Director of Financial Aid

36600 Schoolcraft Road, Livonia, MI 48150-1176

(734) 432-5664

Marygrove College

Detroit, Michigan

www.marygrove.edu   Federal Code: 002284

4-year private liberal arts college in very large city, affiliated with the Roman Catholic Church.

Enrollment: 481 undergrads.

Selectivity: Admits less than 50% of applicants.

BASIC COSTS (2016-2017)

Tuition and fees: $22,064.

Per-credit charge: $718.

Room and board: $7,125.

FINANCIAL AID PICTURE

Students with need: Need-based aid available for full-time and part-time students.

Students without need: This college awards aid only to students with need.

FINANCIAL AID PROCEDURES

Forms required: FAFSA, institutional form.

Dates and Deadlines: Priority date 3/15; no closing date. Applicants notified on a rolling basis starting 5/15; must reply within 2 week(s) of notification.

CONTACT

Kimberly Gooden, Director, Enrollment Center

8425 West McNichols Road, Detroit, MI 48221-2599

(313) 927-1692

Michigan Jewish Institute

West Bloomfield, Michigan

www.mji.edu   Federal Code: 032843

4-year private liberal arts college in very large city, affiliated with the Jewish faith.

Enrollment: 2,204 undergrads.

Selectivity: Open admission; but selective for some programs.

BASIC COSTS (2016-2017)

Tuition and fees: $10,600.

Per-credit charge: $350.

FINANCIAL AID PICTURE

Students with need: Need-based aid available for full-time and part-time students. Work study available nights, weekends, and for part-time students.

Students without need: This college awards aid only to students with need.

FINANCIAL AID PROCEDURES

Forms required: FAFSA.

Dates and Deadlines: Applicants notified on a rolling basis starting 1/1.

Transfers: Priority date 1/1; no deadline. Applicants notified on a rolling basis starting 1/1.

CONTACT

Sandra Kittle, Financial Aid Administrator
6888 West Maple Road, West Bloomfield, MI 48322
(248) 414-6900 ext. 2104

Michigan State University
East Lansing, Michigan
www.msu.edu   Federal Code: 002290

4-year public university in small city.
Enrollment: 38,851 undergrads, 9% part-time. 8,005 full-time freshmen.
Selectivity: Admits 50 to 75% of applicants.

BASIC COSTS (2016-2017)
Tuition and fees: $14,063; out-of-state residents $37,890.
Per-credit charge: $468.75; out-of-state residents $1,263.
Room and board: $9,734.

FINANCIAL AID PICTURE (2016-2017)
Students with need: Out of 5,525 full-time freshmen who applied for aid, 3,779 were judged to have need. Of these, 3,609 received aid, and 646 had their full need met. Average financial aid package met 60% of need; average scholarship/grant was $10,138; average loan was $3,080. For part-time students, average financial aid package was $9,320.
Students without need: 815 full-time freshmen who did not demonstrate need for aid received scholarships/grants; average award was $9,915. No-need awards available for academics, alumni affiliation, art, athletics, leadership, music/drama, ROTC, state/district residency.
Scholarships offered: 46 full-time freshmen received athletic scholarships; average amount $28,376.

FINANCIAL AID PROCEDURES
Forms required: FAFSA.
Dates and Deadlines: Applicants notified on a rolling basis starting 3/15; must reply within 4 week(s) of notification.

CONTACT
Richard Shipman, Director of Financial Aid
250 Administration Building, East Lansing, MI 48824
(517) 353-5940

Michigan Technological University
Houghton, Michigan
www.mtu.edu   Federal Code: 002292

4-year public university in small town.
Enrollment: 5,753 undergrads, 5% part-time. 1,379 full-time freshmen.
Selectivity: Admits over 75% of applicants.

BASIC COSTS (2016-2017)
Tuition and fees: $14,634; out-of-state residents $30,968.
Per-credit charge: $542; out-of-state residents $1,136.
Room and board: $10,105.

FINANCIAL AID PICTURE (2016-2017)
Students with need: Out of 1,239 full-time freshmen who applied for aid, 881 were judged to have need. Of these, 880 received aid, and 204 had their full need met. Average financial aid package met 81% of need; average scholarship/grant was $9,425; average loan was $3,256. For part-time students, average financial aid package was $8,070.
Students without need: 418 full-time freshmen who did not demonstrate need for aid received scholarships/grants; average award was $5,437. No-need awards available for academics, alumni affiliation, athletics, job skills, leadership, ROTC, state/district residency.
Scholarships offered: 65 full-time freshmen received athletic scholarships; average amount $12,706.

FINANCIAL AID PROCEDURES
Forms required: FAFSA.
Dates and Deadlines: Priority date 3/1; no closing date. Applicants notified on a rolling basis starting 2/1; must reply by 5/1.

CONTACT
Joe Cooper, Director, Student Financial Services Center
1400 Townsend Drive, Houghton, MI 49931-1295
(906) 487-2622

Mid Michigan Community College
Harrison, Michigan
www.midmich.edu   Federal Code: 006768

2-year public community college in small town.
Enrollment: 2,992 undergrads.
Selectivity: Open admission; but selective for some programs.

BASIC COSTS (2016-2017)
Tuition and fees: $3,786; out-of-district residents $6,676; out-of-state residents $6,676.
Per-credit charge: $139; out-of-district residents $251; out-of-state residents $251.
Additional info: Tuition/fee waivers available for adults.

FINANCIAL AID PICTURE
Students with need: Need-based aid available for full-time and part-time students. Work study available nights.
Students without need: No-need awards available for academics, art.

FINANCIAL AID PROCEDURES
Forms required: FAFSA, institutional form.
Dates and Deadlines: Priority date 5/1; no closing date. Applicants notified on a rolling basis starting 4/1; must reply within 2 week(s) of notification.

CONTACT
Gale Crandell, Financial Aid Director
1375 South Clare Avenue, Harrison, MI 48625-9442
(989) 386-6622

Monroe County Community College
Monroe, Michigan
www.monroeccc.edu   Federal Code: 002294

2-year public community college in large town.
Enrollment: 954 full-time undergrads.
Selectivity: Open admission; but selective for some programs.

BASIC COSTS (2016-2017)
Tuition and fees: $3,880; out-of-district residents $6,250; out-of-state residents $6,880.
Per-credit charge: $127; out-of-district residents $206; out-of-state residents $227.
Additional info: Tuition/fee waivers available for minority students.

FINANCIAL AID PICTURE
Students with need: Need-based aid available for full-time and part-time students. Work study available nights, weekends, and for part-time students.
Students without need: No-need awards available for academics, alumni affiliation, art, leadership, music/drama, state/district residency.

FINANCIAL AID PROCEDURES
Forms required: FAFSA, institutional form.
Dates and Deadlines: Priority date 4/1; no closing date. Applicants notified on a rolling basis starting 4/1; must reply within 2 week(s) of notification.

CONTACT

Valerie Culler, Director of Financial Aid/Placement

1555 South Raisinville Road, Monroe, MI 48161-9746

(734) 384-4135

Montcalm Community College

Sidney, Michigan

www.montcalm.edu   Federal Code: 002295

2-year public community and liberal arts college in rural community.

Enrollment: 1,496 undergrads.

Selectivity: Open admission; but selective for some programs.

BASIC COSTS (2016-2017)

Tuition and fees: $3,552; out-of-district residents $5,808; out-of-state residents $8,832.

Per-credit charge: $105; out-of-district residents $199; out-of-state residents $325.

FINANCIAL AID PICTURE

Students with need: Need-based aid available for full-time and part-time students.

Students without need: No-need awards available for academics, state/district residency.

FINANCIAL AID PROCEDURES

Forms required: FAFSA, institutional form.

Dates and Deadlines: Priority date 2/15; no closing date. Applicants notified on a rolling basis starting 4/15; must reply within 2 week(s) of notification.

Transfers: Priority date 3/1; no deadline. Applicants notified on a rolling basis starting 4/15.

CONTACT

Traci Nichols, Director of Financial Aid

2800 College Drive, Sidney, MI 48885

(989) 328-1285

Mott Community College

Flint, Michigan

www.mcc.edu   Federal Code: 002261

2-year public community college in small city.

Enrollment: 6,817 undergrads, 69% part-time. 657 full-time freshmen.

Selectivity: Open admission; but selective for some programs.

BASIC COSTS (2016-2017)

Tuition and fees: $4,666; out-of-district residents $6,260; out-of-state residents $8,598.

Per-credit charge: $130; out-of-district residents $183; out-of-state residents $261.

FINANCIAL AID PICTURE (2015-2016)

Students with need: 48% of average financial aid package awarded as scholarships/grants, 52% awarded as loans/jobs. Need-based aid available for part-time students. Work study available nights.

Students without need: No-need awards available for academics, alumni affiliation, art, athletics, leadership, minority status, music/drama, state/district residency.

FINANCIAL AID PROCEDURES

Forms required: FAFSA.

Dates and Deadlines: Priority date 6/1; no closing date. Applicants notified on a rolling basis starting 5/1.

Transfers: Pell Grants adjusted for amount used at another institution.

CONTACT

Emily Varney, Director - Student Financial Services

1401 East Court Street, Flint, MI 48503-2089

(810) 762-0144

Muskegon Community College

Muskegon, Michigan

www.muskegoncc.edu   Federal Code: 002297

2-year public community college in small city.

Enrollment: 3,441 undergrads, 63% part-time. 466 full-time freshmen.

Selectivity: Open admission; but selective for some programs.

BASIC COSTS (2016-2017)

Tuition and fees: $4,030; out-of-district residents $6,670; out-of-state residents $8,920.

FINANCIAL AID PICTURE

Students with need: Need-based aid available for full-time and part-time students. Work study available nights, weekends, and for part-time students.

FINANCIAL AID PROCEDURES

Forms required: FAFSA.

Dates and Deadlines: Priority date 5/1; no closing date. Applicants notified on a rolling basis starting 6/1; must reply within 2 week(s) of notification.

CONTACT

Bruce Wierda, Director of Financial Aid

221 South Quarterline Road, Muskegon, MI 49442

(231) 777-0221

North Central Michigan College

Petoskey, Michigan

www.ncmich.edu   Federal Code: 002299

2-year public community college in small town.

Enrollment: 2,581 undergrads.

Selectivity: Open admission; but selective for some programs.

BASIC COSTS (2016-2017)

Tuition and fees: $3,730; out-of-district residents $6,094; out-of-state residents $7,684.

Per-credit charge: $103; out-of-district residents $179; out-of-state residents $232.

Room and board: $6,300.

FINANCIAL AID PICTURE

Students with need: Need-based aid available for full-time and part-time students. Work study available nights, weekends, and for part-time students.

FINANCIAL AID PROCEDURES

Forms required: FAFSA, institutional form.

Dates and Deadlines: Applicants notified on a rolling basis starting 4/30.

CONTACT

Virginia Panoff, Director of Financial Aid

1515 Howard Street, Petoskey, MI 49770

(231) 348-6627

Northern Michigan University

Marquette, Michigan

www.nmu.edu   Federal Code: 002301

4-year public university in large town.

Enrollment: 7,989 undergrads.

BASIC COSTS (2016-2017)

Tuition and fees: $10,012; out-of-state residents $15,508.

Per-credit charge: $378; out-of-state residents $607.

Room and board: $9,604.

Additional info: Tuition/fee waivers available for minority students.

FINANCIAL AID PICTURE

Students with need: Need-based aid available for full-time and part-time students. Work study available nights, weekends, and for part-time students.

Students without need: No-need awards available for academics, art, athletics, leadership, music/drama, ROTC, state/district residency.

Scholarships offered: Talent recognition awards: available in art and design, music, theater. Freshman Fellowship: $1,000 in student employment; 3.5 GPA and 24 ACT. Dr. Edgar L. Harden Scholarship: full scholarship; 3.5 GPA and 24 ACT. National Academic Award: $3,500; minimum 3.0 GPA and 19 ACT; awarded to non-Michigan residents. Merit Excellence Award: $2,750-$3,500; based on 3.0 GPA and 33 ACT. Merit Award: $2,250-$3,000; 3.0 GPA and 30-32 ACT. Scholars Award: $1,250-$2,000; 3.0 GPA and 27-29 ACT. Outstanding Achievement: $750-$1,500; 3.0 GPA and 25-26 ACT.

Additional info: Audition or portfolio required for music, drama, and art scholarship applicants. Alumni Dependent Tuition Program gives resident tuition rates to nonresident dependents of NMU alumni who received master's, baccalaureate, or associate degree; renewable.

FINANCIAL AID PROCEDURES

Forms required: FAFSA.

Dates and Deadlines: Priority date 3/1; no closing date. Applicants notified on a rolling basis starting 4/1; must reply within 2 week(s) of notification.

Transfers: No deadline. Applicants notified on a rolling basis starting 4/1; must reply within 2 week(s) of notification. Merit-based transfer scholarships available.

CONTACT

Michael Rotundo, Director of Financial Aid

1401 Presque Isle Avenue, Marquette, MI 49855

(906) 227-2327

Northwestern Michigan College

Traverse City, Michigan

www.nmc.edu   Federal Code: 002302

2-year public community and maritime college in large town.

Enrollment: 3,724 undergrads, 59% part-time. 420 full-time freshmen.

Selectivity: Open admission; but selective for some programs.

BASIC COSTS (2016-2017)

Tuition and fees: $4,015; out-of-district residents $7,063; out-of-state residents $8,934.

Per-credit charge: $104; out-of-district residents $205; out-of-state residents $267.65.

Room and board: $8,750.

FINANCIAL AID PICTURE (2015-2016)

Students with need: 46% of average financial aid package awarded as scholarships/grants, 54% awarded as loans/jobs. Need-based aid available for part-time students. Work study available nights, weekends, and for part-time students.

Students without need: No-need awards available for academics, state/district residency.

FINANCIAL AID PROCEDURES

Forms required: FAFSA.

Dates and Deadlines: Priority date 4/1; no closing date. Applicants notified on a rolling basis starting 5/1; must reply within 3 week(s) of notification.

Transfers: No deadline. Applicants notified on a rolling basis starting 4/1; must reply within 3 week(s) of notification.

CONTACT

Pam Palermo, Director for Financial Aid

1701 East Front Street, Traverse City, MI 49686

(231) 995-1035

Northwood University: Michigan

Midland, Michigan

www.northwood.edu   Federal Code: 004072

4-year private university and business college in large town.

Enrollment: 1,422 undergrads, 2% part-time. 320 full-time freshmen.

Selectivity: Admits 50 to 75% of applicants.

BASIC COSTS (2016-2017)

Tuition and fees: $25,130.

Room and board: $9,880.

FINANCIAL AID PICTURE (2016-2017)

Students with need: Out of 291 full-time freshmen who applied for aid, 232 were judged to have need. Of these, 232 received aid, and 43 had their full need met. Average financial aid package met 67% of need; average scholarship/grant was $5,698; average loan was $3,404. For part-time students, average financial aid package was $10,066.

Students without need: 47 full-time freshmen who did not demonstrate need for aid received scholarships/grants; average award was $10,974. No-need awards available for academics, alumni affiliation, athletics, leadership, minority status.

Scholarships offered: *Merit:* Academic scholarships based on test scores and GPA; unlimited number awarded. *Athletic:* 39 full-time freshmen received athletic scholarships; average amount $11,472.

FINANCIAL AID PROCEDURES

Forms required: FAFSA.

Dates and Deadlines: Priority date 3/1; no closing date. Applicants notified on a rolling basis starting 3/1.

Transfers: No deadline. Applicants notified on a rolling basis.

CONTACT

Mark Martin, Financial Aid Director

4000 Whiting Drive, Midland, MI 48640

(989) 837-4230

Oakland Community College

Bloomfield Hills, Michigan

www.oaklandcc.edu   Federal Code: 002303

2-year public community college in very large city.

Enrollment: 12,202 undergrads.

Selectivity: Open admission.

BASIC COSTS (2016-2017)

Tuition and fees: $2,740; out-of-district residents $5,230; out-of-state residents $5,230.

Per-credit charge: $88; out-of-district residents $171; out-of-state residents $171.

FINANCIAL AID PICTURE

Students with need: Need-based aid available for full-time and part-time students.

Students without need: No-need awards available for academics, athletics, job skills.

FINANCIAL AID PROCEDURES

Forms required: FAFSA.

Dates and Deadlines: Priority date 4/15; no closing date. Applicants notified on a rolling basis starting 4/15.

Transfers: Closing date 6/30. Applicants notified on a rolling basis starting 6/30. Michigan residency required for aid to transfer students.

CONTACT
Wilma Porter, Director of Financial Assistance and Scholarships
2480 Opdyke Road, Bloomfield Hills, MI 48304-2266
(248) 341-2000

Oakland University
Rochester, Michigan
www.oakland.edu   Federal Code: 002307

4-year public university in small city.
Enrollment: 16,233 undergrads, 20% part-time. 2,540 full-time freshmen.

BASIC COSTS (2016-2017)
Tuition and fees: $12,064; out-of-state residents $24,540.
Per-credit charge: $399; out-of-state residents $795.75.
Room and board: $9,620.

FINANCIAL AID PICTURE
Students with need: Need-based aid available for full-time and part-time students.
Students without need: No-need awards available for academics, alumni affiliation, art, athletics, leadership, music/drama.
Scholarships offered: Wide range of scholarships; awarded on basis of accomplishment.

FINANCIAL AID PROCEDURES
Forms required: FAFSA.
Dates and Deadlines: Priority date 2/15; no closing date. Applicants notified on a rolling basis starting 3/8.

CONTACT
Cindy Hermsen, Director of Financial Aid
318 Meadow Brook Road, Rochester, MI 48309-4454
(248) 370-2550

Olivet College
Olivet, Michigan
www.olivetcollege.edu   Federal Code: 002308

4-year private liberal arts college in rural community, affiliated with the United Church of Christ.
Enrollment: 983 undergrads. 246 full-time freshmen.
Selectivity: Admits less than 50% of applicants. GED not accepted.

BASIC COSTS (2017-2018)
Tuition and fees: $26,695.
Room and board: $9,310.

FINANCIAL AID PICTURE (2015-2016)
Students with need: Out of 212 full-time freshmen who applied for aid, 202 were judged to have need. Of these, 202 received aid, and 115 had their full need met. Average financial aid package met 68% of need; average scholarship/grant was $11,555; average loan was $3,420. For part-time students, average financial aid package was $8,910.
Students without need: This college awards aid only to students with need.
Scholarships offered: Scholarships: up to $2,000; for students who demonstrate history of community service and civic responsibility during high school or college. Academic merit scholarships: up to full tuition. All scholarships renewable for 4 years.

FINANCIAL AID PROCEDURES
Forms required: FAFSA.

Dates and Deadlines: Applicants notified on a rolling basis starting 2/1; must reply within 3 week(s) of notification.

CONTACT
Libby Jean, Director of Student Services
320 South Main Street, Olivet, MI 49076
(269) 749-7645

Robert B. Miller College
Battle Creek, Michigan
www.millercollege.edu   Federal Code: 040943

4-year private liberal arts college in small city.
Enrollment: 327 undergrads.

BASIC COSTS (2016-2017)
Tuition and fees: $11,970.

FINANCIAL AID PICTURE
Students with need: Need-based aid available for full-time and part-time students.
Students without need: No-need awards available for academics, leadership.

FINANCIAL AID PROCEDURES
Transfers: No deadline. Applicants notified on a rolling basis starting 4/1.

CONTACT
Kim Cvitkovic, Director of Financial Aid
450 North Avenue, Battle Creek, MI 49017
(269) 660-8021 ext. 2720

Rochester College
Rochester Hills, Michigan
www.rc.edu   Federal Code: 002288

4-year private liberal arts college in small city, affiliated with the Church of Christ.
Enrollment: 960 undergrads.

BASIC COSTS (2016-2017)
Tuition and fees: $22,544.
Room and board: $6,952.
Additional info: Tuition/fee waivers available for minority students.

FINANCIAL AID PICTURE
Students with need: Need-based aid available for full-time and part-time students. Work study available nights, weekends, and for part-time students.
Students without need: No-need awards available for academics, alumni affiliation, athletics, leadership, music/drama, religious affiliation, state/district residency.

FINANCIAL AID PROCEDURES
Forms required: FAFSA.
Dates and Deadlines: Priority date 8/1; no closing date. Applicants notified on a rolling basis starting 1/1; must reply within 2 week(s) of notification.

CONTACT
Jessica Bristow, Director of Financial Aid
800 West Avon Road, Rochester Hills, MI 48307
(248) 218-2029

Sacred Heart Major Seminary
Detroit, Michigan
www.shms.edu   Federal Code: 002313

4-year private seminary college in very large city, affiliated with the Roman Catholic Church.

Enrollment: 260 undergrads.

BASIC COSTS (2016-2017)
Tuition and fees: $18,706.
Per-credit charge: $434.
Room and board: $10,062.
Additional info: Tuition/fee waivers available for adults.

FINANCIAL AID PICTURE
Students with need: Work study available nights, weekends, and for part-time students.
Students without need: No-need awards available for academics, religious affiliation.

FINANCIAL AID PROCEDURES
Forms required: FAFSA, institutional form.
Dates and Deadlines: Applicants notified on a rolling basis; must reply within 2 week(s) of notification.
Transfers: No deadline. Applicants notified on a rolling basis. Must submit certified high school transcript, copy of high school diploma, copy of GED certificate showing passing score, or college transcript showing associate degree as certification of eligibility; must submit financial aid transcripts from all previous post-secondary institutions attended.

CONTACT
Kathy Liberski, Director of Financial Aid
2701 Chicago Boulevard, Detroit, MI 48206-1799

Saginaw Valley State University
University Center, Michigan
www.svsu.edu   Federal Code: 002314

4-year public university in small city.
Enrollment: 7,913 undergrads, 15% part-time. 1,342 full-time freshmen.
Selectivity: Admits over 75% of applicants.

BASIC COSTS (2016-2017)
Tuition and fees: $9,345; out-of-state residents $21,947.
Room and board: $9,185.

FINANCIAL AID PICTURE
Students with need: Need-based aid available for full-time and part-time students. Work study available nights, weekends, and for part-time students.
Students without need: No-need awards available for academics, art, athletics, leadership, minority status, music/drama.
Scholarships offered: Presidential Scholarships: tuition and selective fees up to 136 credit hours; granted to students who are first or second in high school class with 24 ACT or 3.7 GPA and 28 ACT. Dean's Scholarship: $3,000 per year for four years; 3.0 GPA and 24 ACT. University Foundation Scholarship: tuition and selective fees for four courses and $1,000 to apply toward study abroad or a research project; 3.5 GPA and 24 ACT. University Scholarship: $1,000 per year for four years; 3.5 GPA. Various private scholarships also available.

FINANCIAL AID PROCEDURES
Forms required: FAFSA.
Dates and Deadlines: Priority date 1/1; no closing date. Applicants notified on a rolling basis starting 3/1.
Transfers: No deadline. Applicants notified on a rolling basis; must reply within 10 week(s) of notification. Community college scholarship, private scholarships, and Transfer Dean's scholarships available.

CONTACT
Robert Lemuel, Director of Scholarships and Financial Aid
7400 Bay Road, University Center, MI 48710
(989) 964-4900

St. Clair County Community College
Port Huron, Michigan
www.sc4.edu   Federal Code: 002310

2-year public community college in large town.
Enrollment: 2,522 undergrads.
Selectivity: Open admission; but selective for some programs.

BASIC COSTS (2016-2017)
Tuition and fees: $3,724; out-of-district residents $6,694; out-of-state residents $9,514.
Per-credit charge: $105; out-of-district residents $204; out-of-state residents $298.

FINANCIAL AID PICTURE
Students with need: Work study available nights.

FINANCIAL AID PROCEDURES
Forms required: FAFSA.
Dates and Deadlines: Priority date 3/1; no closing date. Applicants notified on a rolling basis starting 5/15; must reply within 2 week(s) of notification.
Transfers: No deadline. Applicants notified on a rolling basis.

CONTACT
Josephine Cassar, Executive Director, Financial Assistance
323 Erie Street, Port Huron, MI 48061-5015
(810) 989-5530

Schoolcraft College
Livonia, Michigan
www.schoolcraft.edu   Federal Code: 002315

2-year public culinary school and community college in small city.
Enrollment: 10,145 undergrads, 70% part-time. 898 full-time freshmen.
Selectivity: Open admission; but selective for some programs.

BASIC COSTS (2016-2017)
Tuition and fees: $3,836; out-of-district residents $5,216; out-of-state residents $7,316.
Per-credit charge: $102; out-of-district residents $148; out-of-state residents $218.

FINANCIAL AID PICTURE
Students with need: Need-based aid available for full-time and part-time students. Work study available nights, weekends, and for part-time students.
Students without need: No-need awards available for academics, athletics, leadership, music/drama, state/district residency.
Scholarships offered: Trustee Scholarships: $750 per semester (fall and winter); renewable for 2nd year; based on essay, GPA, ACT score trustee application, graduation from local high school.

FINANCIAL AID PROCEDURES
Forms required: FAFSA.
Dates and Deadlines: Applicants notified on a rolling basis starting 3/6.
Transfers: No deadline.

CONTACT
Regina Mosley, Executive Director of Student Financial Services
18600 Haggerty Road, Livonia, MI 48152-2696
(734) 462-4433

Siena Heights University
Adrian, Michigan
www.sienaheights.edu   Federal Code: 002316

4-year private university and liberal arts college in large town, affiliated with the Roman Catholic Church.

Enrollment: 2,289 undergrads, 42% part-time. 293 full-time freshmen.
Selectivity: Admits 50 to 75% of applicants.

BASIC COSTS (2016-2017)
Tuition and fees: $24,856.
Room and board: $10,040.

FINANCIAL AID PICTURE
Students with need: Need-based aid available for full-time students. Work study available nights, weekends, and for part-time students.

FINANCIAL AID PROCEDURES
Dates and Deadlines: Priority date 3/15; closing date 8/15.
Transfers: Priority date 3/1; no deadline.

CONTACT
Lori Kosarue, Director of Financial Aid
1247 East Siena Heights Drive, Adrian, MI 49221-1796
(517) 264-7110

Southwestern Michigan College
Dowagiac, Michigan
www.swmich.edu   Federal Code: 002317

2-year public community college in small town.
Enrollment: 1,807 undergrads, 42% part-time. 482 full-time freshmen.
Selectivity: Open admission; but selective for some programs.

BASIC COSTS (2016-2017)
Tuition and fees: $4,891; out-of-district residents $5,941; out-of-state residents $6,353.
Per-credit charge: $115; out-of-district residents $150; out-of-state residents $164.
Room only: $6,160.

FINANCIAL AID PICTURE
Students with need: Need-based aid available for full-time and part-time students. Work study available nights, weekends, and for part-time students.
Students without need: No-need awards available for academics, art, leadership, music/drama.

FINANCIAL AID PROCEDURES
Forms required: FAFSA, institutional form.
Dates and Deadlines: Priority date 7/1; no closing date. Applicants notified on a rolling basis starting 4/1; must reply within 2 week(s) of notification.

CONTACT
Christine Passer, Associate V.P. of Financial Aid/Records
58900 Cherry Grove Road, Dowagiac, MI 49047-9793
(800) 456-8675 ext. 2143

Spring Arbor University
Spring Arbor, Michigan
www.arbor.edu   Federal Code: 002318

4-year private university and liberal arts college in rural community, affiliated with the Free Methodist Church of North America.
Enrollment: 2,100 undergrads, 26% part-time. 305 full-time freshmen.
Selectivity: Admits 50 to 75% of applicants.

BASIC COSTS (2016-2017)
Tuition and fees: $26,730.
Per-credit charge: $635.
Room and board: $9,270.

FINANCIAL AID PICTURE
Students with need: Need-based aid available for full-time and part-time students. Work study available nights, weekends, and for part-time students.

Students without need: No-need awards available for academics, art, athletics, minority status, music/drama, religious affiliation.
Scholarships offered: Trustee Scholarship: $12,000. President Scholarship: $10,000. Provost Scholarship: $7,500. Faculty Scholarship: $4,000. Partnership Scholarship: $1,000. All based on GPA, class rank, and ACT. National Merit Finalist/Semifinalist: 60% tuition.

FINANCIAL AID PROCEDURES
Forms required: FAFSA.
Dates and Deadlines: Priority date 3/1; no closing date. Applicants notified on a rolling basis starting 3/1; must reply within 2 week(s) of notification.
Transfers: No deadline. Applicants notified on a rolling basis starting 5/1; must reply within 2 week(s) of notification. Financial aid transcript required from each college previously attended.

CONTACT
Herbert Rotich, Director of Financial Aid
106 East Main Street, Spring Arbor, MI 49283-9799
(517) 750-6468

University of Detroit Mercy
Detroit, Michigan
www.udmercy.edu   Federal Code: 002323

4-year private university in very large city, affiliated with the Roman Catholic Church.
Enrollment: 2,530 undergrads, 15% part-time. 521 full-time freshmen.
Selectivity: Admits over 75% of applicants.

BASIC COSTS (2017-2018)
Tuition and fees: $41,158.
Per-credit charge: $1,049.
Room and board: $9,220.

FINANCIAL AID PICTURE (2016-2017)
Students with need: Out of 460 full-time freshmen who applied for aid, 359 were judged to have need. Of these, 358 received aid, and 42 had their full need met. Average financial aid package met 84% of need; average scholarship/grant was $30,565; average loan was $4,424. For part-time students, average financial aid package was $8,470.
Students without need: 159 full-time freshmen who did not demonstrate need for aid received scholarships/grants; average award was $22,176. No-need awards available for academics, alumni affiliation, athletics, religious affiliation, state/district residency.
Scholarships offered: *Merit:* Scholarships: $10,000-$21,000 per year; awarded to every full-time freshman student that attends directly out of high school. *Athletic:* 35 full-time freshmen received athletic scholarships; average amount $19,254.

FINANCIAL AID PROCEDURES
Forms required: FAFSA.
Dates and Deadlines: Priority date 4/1; no closing date. Applicants notified on a rolling basis starting 3/1.
Transfers: No deadline. Applicants notified on a rolling basis starting 3/1.

CONTACT
Jenny McAlonan, Director of Scholarship and Financial Aid
4001 West McNichols Road, Detroit, MI 48221-3038
(313) 993-3350

University of Michigan
Ann Arbor, Michigan   Federal Code: 002325
http://umich.edu/   CSS Code: 1839

4-year public university in small city.
Enrollment: 28,761 undergrads, 3% part-time. 6,050 full-time freshmen.

Selectivity: Admits less than 50% of applicants.

BASIC COSTS (2016-2017)
Tuition and fees: $14,402; out-of-state residents $45,410.
Per-credit charge: $556; out-of-state residents $1,848.
Room and board: $10,872.

FINANCIAL AID PICTURE (2015-2016)
Students with need: Out of 4,123 full-time freshmen who applied for aid, 2,446 were judged to have need. Of these, 2,338 received aid, and 1,891 had their full need met. Average financial aid package met 89% of need; average scholarship/grant was $17,410; average loan was $4,365. For part-time students, average financial aid package was $12,479.
Students without need: 1,200 full-time freshmen who did not demonstrate need for aid received scholarships/grants; average award was $5,177. No-need awards available for academics, alumni affiliation, art, athletics, leadership, music/drama, religious affiliation, ROTC, state/district residency.
Scholarships offered: 141 full-time freshmen received athletic scholarships; average amount $26,931.

FINANCIAL AID PROCEDURES
Forms required: FAFSA. Dependent Undergraduate students seeking institutional need-based gift aid must submit a CSS PROFILE. The CSS PROFILE is not required of independent undergraduates, graduate students, and professional degree-seeking students.
Dates and Deadlines: Closing date 4/30. Applicants notified on a rolling basis starting 3/15.

CONTACT
Pamela Fowler, Executive Director, Office of Financial Aid
1220 Student Activities Building, Ann Arbor, MI 48109-1316
(734) 763-6600

University of Michigan: Flint
Flint, Michigan
www.umflint.edu   Federal Code: 002327

4-year public university and branch campus college in small city.
Enrollment: 5,827 undergrads, 34% part-time. 588 full-time freshmen.
Selectivity: Admits 50 to 75% of applicants.

BASIC COSTS (2016-2017)
Tuition and fees: $10,884; out-of-state residents $20,802.
Per-credit charge: $413; out-of-state residents $823.
Room and board: $8,178.

FINANCIAL AID PICTURE (2015-2016)
Students with need: Out of 504 full-time freshmen who applied for aid, 432 were judged to have need. Of these, 407 received aid, and 6 had their full need met. Average financial aid package met 70% of need; average scholarship/grant was $6,781; average loan was $3,194. For part-time students, average financial aid package was $9,481.
Students without need: 25 full-time freshmen who did not demonstrate need for aid received scholarships/grants; average award was $2,711. No-need awards available for academics, art, leadership, music/drama.
Scholarships offered: High school students applying as first-time freshmen have access to more scholarship funds to help pay for their respected UM-Flint education.

FINANCIAL AID PROCEDURES
Forms required: FAFSA.
Dates and Deadlines: Priority date 2/14; no closing date. Applicants notified on a rolling basis starting 2/15.
Transfers: Priority date 2/1; no deadline. Applicants notified on a rolling basis starting 2/15.

CONTACT
Lori Vedder, Financial Aid Director
303 East Kearsley Street, Flint, MI 48502-1950
(810) 762-3444

Walsh College of Accountancy and Business Administration
Troy, Michigan
www.walshcollege.edu   Federal Code: 004071

Upper-division private business college in large city.
Enrollment: 912 undergrads, 92% part-time.

BASIC COSTS (2016-2017)
Tuition and fees: $13,450.
Per-credit charge: $440.

FINANCIAL AID PICTURE (2015-2016)
Students with need: 29% of average financial aid package awarded as scholarships/grants, 71% awarded as loans/jobs. Need-based aid available for part-time students.
Students without need: No-need awards available for academics.

FINANCIAL AID PROCEDURES
Transfers: Priority date 3/1; no deadline. Applicants notified on a rolling basis.

CONTACT
Catherine Berrahou, Director, Financial Aid & Scholarships
PO Box 7006, Troy, MI 48007-7006
(248) 823-1665

Wayne County Community College
Detroit, Michigan
www.wcccd.edu   Federal Code: 009230

2-year public community college in very large city.
Enrollment: 11,747 undergrads, 79% part-time. 713 full-time freshmen.
Selectivity: Open admission; but selective for some programs.

BASIC COSTS (2016-2017)
Tuition and fees: $3,523; out-of-district residents $3,859; out-of-state residents $4,777.
Per-credit charge: $107; out-of-district residents $118; out-of-state residents $149.

FINANCIAL AID PICTURE
Students with need: Need-based aid available for full-time and part-time students.

FINANCIAL AID PROCEDURES
Forms required: FAFSA.
Dates and Deadlines: Priority date 5/1; no closing date. Applicants notified on a rolling basis starting 5/1.

CONTACT
Myra Hawkins, District Associate Vice Chancellor of Student Services
801 West Fort Street, Detroit, MI 48226
(313) 496-2865

Wayne State University
Detroit, Michigan
www.wayne.edu   Federal Code: 002329

4-year public university in very large city.
Enrollment: 16,671 undergrads, 28% part-time. 2,320 full-time freshmen.
Selectivity: Admits over 75% of applicants.

BASIC COSTS (2016-2017)
Tuition and fees: $12,269; out-of-state residents $26,220.
Per-credit charge: $360.39; out-of-state residents $825.42.
Room and board: $9,747.

FINANCIAL AID PICTURE (2015-2016)

Students with need: Out of 1,994 full-time freshmen who applied for aid, 1,644 were judged to have need. Of these, 1,625 received aid, and 217 had their full need met. Average financial aid package met 71% of need; average scholarship/grant was $9,352; average loan was $3,792. For part-time students, average financial aid package was $6,477.

Students without need: 521 full-time freshmen who did not demonstrate need for aid received scholarships/grants; average award was $6,167. No-need awards available for academics, art, athletics, leadership, minority status, music/drama.

Scholarships offered: 38 full-time freshmen received athletic scholarships; average amount $11,371.

Additional info: Need-based institutional grants cover tuition and fees with grants and EFC (no loans).

FINANCIAL AID PROCEDURES

Forms required: FAFSA.

Dates and Deadlines: Priority date 1/1; closing date 6/30. Applicants notified on a rolling basis starting 3/31.

Transfers: Applicants notified on a rolling basis starting 3/31; must reply within 2 week(s) of notification.

CONTACT

Cathy Zajac Kay, Director, Financial Aid
PO Box 02759, Detroit, MI 48202-0759
(313) 577-2100

West Shore Community College

Scottville, Michigan
www.westshore.edu   Federal Code: 007950

2-year public community college in rural community.
Enrollment: 1,269 undergrads.
Selectivity: Open admission; but selective for some programs.

BASIC COSTS (2016-2017)
Tuition and fees: $3,266; out-of-district residents $5,186; out-of-state residents $6,986.

FINANCIAL AID PICTURE (2015-2016)
Students with need: Need-based aid available for full-time and part-time students. Work study available nights, weekends, and for part-time students.

FINANCIAL AID PROCEDURES
Forms required: FAFSA, institutional form.
Dates and Deadlines: Priority date 6/1; no closing date. Applicants notified on a rolling basis starting 5/15; must reply within 2 week(s) of notification.

CONTACT
Rebekah Schaub, Director of Financial Aid
3000 North Stiles Road, Scottville, MI 49454-0277
(231) 845-5518

Western Michigan University

Kalamazoo, Michigan
https://wmich.edu/   Federal Code: 002330

4-year public university in small city.
Enrollment: 17,984 undergrads, 17% part-time. 2,891 full-time freshmen.
Selectivity: Admits over 75% of applicants.

BASIC COSTS (2016-2017)
Tuition and fees: $11,493; out-of-state residents $26,851.
Per-credit charge: $384; out-of-state residents $943.
Room and board: $9,561.

FINANCIAL AID PICTURE (2016-2017)

Students with need: Out of 2,547 full-time freshmen who applied for aid, 2,010 were judged to have need. Of these, 1,960 received aid, and 581 had their full need met. Average financial aid package met 80% of need; average scholarship/grant was $7,104; average loan was $3,375. Need-based aid available for part-time students.

Students without need: 323 full-time freshmen who did not demonstrate need for aid received scholarships/grants; average award was $6,060. No-need awards available for academics, alumni affiliation, art, athletics, music/drama, ROTC, state/district residency.

Scholarships offered: 24 full-time freshmen received athletic scholarships; average amount $33,112.

FINANCIAL AID PROCEDURES

Forms required: FAFSA.

Dates and Deadlines: Priority date 3/1; no closing date. Applicants notified on a rolling basis starting 12/10.

Transfers: No deadline. Applicants notified on a rolling basis starting 5/15.

CONTACT

Terrell Hodge, Interim Director of Financial Aid
1903 West Michigan Avenue, Kalamazoo, MI 49008-5211
(269) 387-6000

Minnesota

Academy College

Bloomington, Minnesota
www.academycollege.edu   Federal Code: 013505

2-year for-profit technical and career college in large city.
Enrollment: 105 undergrads, 56% part-time. 1 full-time freshmen.
Selectivity: Open admission.

FINANCIAL AID PICTURE (2015-2016)
Students with need: 28% of average financial aid package awarded as scholarships/grants, 72% awarded as loans/jobs. Need-based aid available for part-time students. Work study available nights, weekends, and for part-time students.

FINANCIAL AID PROCEDURES
Forms required: FAFSA, institutional form.
Dates and Deadlines: Applicants notified on a rolling basis.

CONTACT
Kellye MacLeod, Director of Financial Aid/Regulatory Complicance
1600 West 82nd Street, Bloomington, MN 55431
(952) 851-0066

Alexandria Technical and Community College

Alexandria, Minnesota
www.alextech.edu   Federal Code: 005544

2-year public community and technical college in large town.
Enrollment: 1,611 undergrads.
Selectivity: Open admission; but selective for some programs.

BASIC COSTS (2016-2017)
Tuition and fees: $5,358; out-of-state residents $5,358.
Per-credit charge: $158.94.

FINANCIAL AID PICTURE (2015-2016)

Students with need: 81% of average financial aid package awarded as scholarships/grants, 19% awarded as loans/jobs. Need-based aid available for part-time students.

Students without need: This college awards aid only to students with need.

FINANCIAL AID PROCEDURES

Forms required: FAFSA.

Dates and Deadlines: Priority date 5/1; no closing date. Applicants notified on a rolling basis starting 6/30; must reply within 2 week(s) of notification.

Transfers: No deadline. Applicants notified on a rolling basis; must reply within 2 week(s) of notification.

CONTACT

Steve Richards, Dean of Technology & Student Financial Services
1601 Jefferson Street, Alexandria, MN 56308-3799
(320) 762-4540

Anoka Technical College
Anoka, Minnesota
www.anokatech.edu   Federal Code: 007350

2-year public technical college in large town.
Enrollment: 1,814 undergrads.
Selectivity: Open admission; but selective for some programs.

BASIC COSTS (2016-2017)

Tuition and fees: $5,535; out-of-state residents $5,535.
Per-credit charge: $165.33.

FINANCIAL AID PICTURE

Students with need: Need-based aid available for full-time and part-time students. Work study available nights.

Students without need: This college awards aid only to students with need.

FINANCIAL AID PROCEDURES

Forms required: FAFSA.

Dates and Deadlines: Applicants notified on a rolling basis starting 7/1.

CONTACT

Brittany Tweed, Director of Financial Aid
1355 West Highway 10, Anoka, MN 55303
(763) 576-7730

Anoka-Ramsey Community College
Coon Rapids, Minnesota
www.anokaramsey.edu   Federal Code: 002332

2-year public community college in small city.
Enrollment: 9,015 undergrads.
Selectivity: Open admission; but selective for some programs.

BASIC COSTS (2016-2017)

Tuition and fees: $4,976; out-of-state residents $4,976.
Per-credit charge: $143.52.

FINANCIAL AID PICTURE

Students with need: Need-based aid available for full-time and part-time students. Work study available nights, weekends, and for part-time students.

Students without need: This college awards aid only to students with need.

FINANCIAL AID PROCEDURES

Forms required: FAFSA, institutional form.

Dates and Deadlines: Priority date 4/1; no closing date. Applicants notified on a rolling basis; must reply within 2 week(s) of notification.

CONTACT

Brittany Tweed, Interum Director of Financial Aid Officer
11200 Mississippi Boulevard NW, Coon Rapids, MN 55433
(763) 433-1500

Art Institutes International Minnesota
Minneapolis, Minnesota
www.artinstitutes.edu/minneapolis   Federal Code: 010248

4-year for-profit culinary school and visual arts college in large city.
Enrollment: 820 undergrads.
Selectivity: Open admission.

FINANCIAL AID PICTURE

Students with need: Need-based aid available for full-time and part-time students.

Students without need: No-need awards available for academics.

FINANCIAL AID PROCEDURES

Forms required: FAFSA.

CONTACT

Greg Woodard, Director of Administrative and Financial Services
15 South Ninth Street, Minneapolis, MN 55402
(800) 777-3643

Augsburg College
Minneapolis, Minnesota
www.augsburg.edu   Federal Code: 002334

4-year private liberal arts college in large city, affiliated with the Evangelical Lutheran Church in America.
Enrollment: 2,530 undergrads, 18% part-time. 478 full-time freshmen.
Selectivity: Admits less than 50% of applicants.

BASIC COSTS (2017-2018)

Tuition and fees: $37,615.
Per-credit charge: $1,155.
Room and board: $9,939.

FINANCIAL AID PICTURE (2015-2016)

Students with need: Out of 426 full-time freshmen who applied for aid, 390 were judged to have need. Of these, 387 received aid, and 65 had their full need met. Average financial aid package met 81% of need; average scholarship/grant was $26,314; average loan was $3,804. For part-time students, average financial aid package was $5,786.

Students without need: 85 full-time freshmen who did not demonstrate need for aid received scholarships/grants; average award was $15,834. No-need awards available for academics, alumni affiliation, art, leadership, music/drama, religious affiliation.

Scholarships offered: President's Scholarships: up to full tuition annually; 3.7 GPA and ACT/SAT score 27 or higher; number awarded determined annually. Regents Scholarships: $4,000-$10,000; top 30% of class rank or test scores. Must apply before 5/1 for both scholarships.

FINANCIAL AID PROCEDURES

Forms required: FAFSA.

Dates and Deadlines: Priority date 3/15; closing date 8/1. Applicants notified on a rolling basis starting 3/1.

Transfers: Priority date 7/1; closing date 8/15. Applicants notified on a rolling basis starting 3/1; must reply by 9/1.

CONTACT

Gina Jones, Director of Financial Aid
2211 Riverside Avenue, Minneapolis, MN 55454
(612) 330-1046

Bemidji State University

Bemidji, Minnesota
www.bemidjistate.edu

Federal Code: 002336

4-year public university in large town.
Enrollment: 4,421 undergrads, 23% part-time. 799 full-time freshmen.
Selectivity: Admits 50 to 75% of applicants.

BASIC COSTS (2016-2017)
Tuition and fees: $8,393; out-of-state residents $8,393.
Per-credit charge: $257; out-of-state residents $257.
Room and board: $7,924.
Additional info: Tuition/fee waivers available for minority students.

FINANCIAL AID PICTURE
Students with need: Need-based aid available for full-time and part-time students. Work study available nights, weekends, and for part-time students.
Students without need: No-need awards available for academics, alumni affiliation, art, athletics, job skills, leadership, minority status, music/drama, ROTC.

FINANCIAL AID PROCEDURES
Forms required: FAFSA, institutional form.
Dates and Deadlines: Closing date 3/31. Applicants notified on a rolling basis starting 3/15.

CONTACT
Lesa Lawrence, Director of Financial Aid
102 Deputy Hall #13, Bemidji, MN 56601-2699
(218) 755-2034

Bethany Lutheran College

Mankato, Minnesota
www.blc.edu

Federal Code: 002337

4-year private liberal arts college in small city, affiliated with the Evangelical Lutheran Synod.
Enrollment: 513 undergrads, 2% part-time. 134 full-time freshmen.
Selectivity: Admits over 75% of applicants.

BASIC COSTS (2016-2017)
Tuition and fees: $26,020.
Per-credit charge: $1,080.
Room and board: $7,960.

FINANCIAL AID PICTURE (2015-2016)
Students with need: Out of 122 full-time freshmen who applied for aid, 110 were judged to have need. Of these, 110 received aid, and 20 had their full need met. Average financial aid package met 86% of need; average scholarship/grant was $17,927; average loan was $4,377. For part-time students, average financial aid package was $10,512.
Students without need: 17 full-time freshmen who did not demonstrate need for aid received scholarships/grants; average award was $10,707. No-need awards available for academics, alumni affiliation, art, music/drama, ROTC.

FINANCIAL AID PROCEDURES
Forms required: FAFSA, institutional form.
Dates and Deadlines: Priority date 4/15; no closing date. Applicants notified on a rolling basis starting 1/1; must reply within 4 week(s) of notification.
Transfers: No deadline. Applicants notified on a rolling basis starting 1/1; must reply within 4 week(s) of notification.

CONTACT
Jeffrey Younge, Director of Financial Aid
700 Luther Drive, Mankato, MN 56001-4490
(507) 344-7328

Bethel University

St. Paul, Minnesota
www.bethel.edu

Federal Code: 002338

4-year private university and liberal arts college in large city, affiliated with the Converge Worldwide.
Enrollment: 2,846 undergrads, 16% part-time. 557 full-time freshmen.
Selectivity: Admits over 75% of applicants.

BASIC COSTS (2017-2018)
Tuition and fees: $36,210.
Per-credit charge: $1,510.
Room and board: $10,340.

FINANCIAL AID PICTURE (2016-2017)
Students with need: Out of 502 full-time freshmen who applied for aid, 433 were judged to have need. Of these, 433 received aid, and 79 had their full need met. Average financial aid package met 81% of need; average scholarship/grant was $21,689; average loan was $3,151. For part-time students, average financial aid package was $15,760.
Students without need: 120 full-time freshmen who did not demonstrate need for aid received scholarships/grants; average award was $12,687. No-need awards available for academics, alumni affiliation, art, leadership, music/drama, state/district residency.

FINANCIAL AID PROCEDURES
Forms required: FAFSA.
Dates and Deadlines: Priority date 4/15; no closing date. Applicants notified on a rolling basis starting 3/1.

CONTACT
Jeffrey Olson, Director of Financial Aid
3900 Bethel Drive, St. Paul, MN 55112-6999
(651) 638-6241

Capella University

Minneapolis, Minnesota
www.capella.edu

Federal Code: 032673

4-year for-profit virtual university in very large city.
Enrollment: 8,750 undergrads.
Selectivity: Open admission; but selective for some programs.

FINANCIAL AID PICTURE
Students with need: Need-based aid available for full-time and part-time students.

CONTACT
Tonia Teasley, VP Learner Services and Operations
225 South Sixth Street, Minneapolis, MN 55402
(888) 227-3552

Carleton College

Northfield, Minnesota
www.carleton.edu

Federal Code: 002340
CSS Code: 6081

4-year private liberal arts college in large town.
Enrollment: 2,045 undergrads. 568 full-time freshmen.
Selectivity: Admits less than 50% of applicants.

BASIC COSTS (2016-2017)
Tuition and fees: $50,874.
Room and board: $13,197.

FINANCIAL AID PICTURE (2015-2016)
Students with need: Out of 438 full-time freshmen who applied for aid, 312 were judged to have need. Of these, 312 received aid, and 312 had

their full need met. Average financial aid package met 100% of need; average scholarship/grant was $42,019; average loan was $4,089.

Students without need: This college awards aid only to students with need.

Scholarships offered: National Merit, National Achievement, National Hispanic Scholars Awards: $2,000 per year; based on outstanding academic achievement and promise.

Additional info: Full financial need of all admitted applicants met through combination of work, loans, grants.

FINANCIAL AID PROCEDURES

Forms required: FAFSA, CSS PROFILE.

Dates and Deadlines: Closing date 2/15. Applicants notified by 3/31; must reply by 5/1 or within 2 week(s) of notification.

Transfers: Closing date 3/15. Applicants notified by 5/15; must reply by 6/1 or within 2 week(s) of notification.

CONTACT

Rodney Oto, Director of Student Financial Services
100 South College Street, Northfield, MN 55057
(507) 222-4138

Central Lakes College
Brainerd, Minnesota
www.clcmn.edu   Federal Code: 002339

2-year public community and technical college in large town.
Enrollment: 2,403 undergrads.
Selectivity: Open admission; but selective for some programs.

BASIC COSTS (2016-2017)
Tuition and fees: $5,348; out-of-state residents $5,348.
Per-credit charge: $157.51.

FINANCIAL AID PICTURE
Students with need: Need-based aid available for full-time and part-time students.

FINANCIAL AID PROCEDURES
Forms required: FAFSA.
Dates and Deadlines: Priority date 6/1; no closing date. Applicants notified on a rolling basis starting 6/10; must reply within 2 week(s) of notification.

CONTACT
Mike Barnaby, Director of Financial Aid
501 West College Drive, Brainerd, MN 56401
(218) 855-8039

Century College
White Bear Lake, Minnesota
www.century.edu   Federal Code: 010546

2-year public community and technical college in large town.
Enrollment: 7,743 undergrads, 57% part-time. 759 full-time freshmen.
Selectivity: Open admission; but selective for some programs.

BASIC COSTS (2016-2017)
Tuition and fees: $5,393; out-of-state residents $5,393.
Per-credit charge: $159.

FINANCIAL AID PICTURE (2015-2016)
Students with need: 45% of average financial aid package awarded as scholarships/grants, 55% awarded as loans/jobs. Need-based aid available for part-time students.
Students without need: This college awards aid only to students with need.

FINANCIAL AID PROCEDURES
Forms required: FAFSA.
Dates and Deadlines: Priority date 5/1; no closing date. Applicants notified on a rolling basis starting 4/1.
Transfers: Priority date 7/1; no deadline. Applicants notified on a rolling basis starting 4/1.

CONTACT
Pam Engebretson, Financial Aid Director
3300 Century Avenue North, White Bear Lake, MN 55110
(651) 779-3305

College of St. Benedict
St. Joseph, Minnesota
www.csbsju.edu   Federal Code: 002341

4-year private liberal arts college in small town, affiliated with the Roman Catholic Church.
Enrollment: 1,958 undergrads, 1% part-time. 503 full-time freshmen.
Selectivity: Admits over 75% of applicants.

BASIC COSTS (2016-2017)
Tuition and fees: $42,271.
Per-credit charge: $1,719.
Room and board: $10,535.

FINANCIAL AID PICTURE (2016-2017)
Students with need: Out of 451 full-time freshmen who applied for aid, 395 were judged to have need. Of these, 395 received aid, and 155 had their full need met. Average financial aid package met 92% of need; average scholarship/grant was $30,440; average loan was $4,604. For part-time students, average financial aid package was $15,855.
Students without need: 96 full-time freshmen who did not demonstrate need for aid received scholarships/grants; average award was $19,922. No-need awards available for academics, alumni affiliation, art, leadership, music/drama, ROTC.
Scholarships offered: Trustees' Scholarships: $23,000 renewable; based on 3.6 GPA, 30 ACT or equivalent SAT, demonstrated leadership and service, faculty interview. President's Scholarships: $16,500-$20,000 renewable; based on GPA, high school rank, ACT/SAT, leadership and service. Dean's Scholarships: $8,000-$16,000 renewable; based on GPA, high school rank, ACT/SAT, leadership and service. Art, music and theater scholarships: $1,000-$4,000 renewable. Intercultural LEAD fellowship: $10,000 renewable; based on GPA, leadership, financial need, first generation college students, commitment to intercultural issues and action, from diverse urban high schools; on campus interview required. Army ROTC and ROTC Nursing Scholarships: based on demonstrated leadership potential, GPA, class standing, ACT/SAT, high achievement with broad interests and willingness to take on challenges. Catholic High School Scholarship: $4,000 renewable; for students attending Catholic high schools outside Minnesota. Saints Scholarship: 4,000 renewable; for students attending public high schools outside Minnesota. FoCuS Scholarship: $23,000 renewable; for students majoring in chemistry. Bonner Leader Scholarship: $2,500 renewable; for students with strong interest in doing service work while at CSB/SJU, preference for students with financial need. Legacy Scholarship: $1,000 renewable; mother, father or grandparent obtained degree from Saint John's or St. Ben's. Benedictine Scholarship: $5,000 renewable; for students from low income families who have completed a college access program such as Upward Bound.
Additional info: Scholarship letters will be mailed on a rolling basis approximately two weeks from the time the admission acceptance letter is sent.

FINANCIAL AID PROCEDURES
Forms required: FAFSA.
Dates and Deadlines: Priority date 3/15; no closing date. Applicants notified on a rolling basis starting 3/15; must reply by 5/1.

Transfers: No deadline. Applicants notified on a rolling basis starting 3/15; must reply by 5/1. Phi Theta Kappa Scholarship: $1,500 renewable; for members of Phi Theta Kappa; only for transfer students.

CONTACT
Stuart Perry, Executive Director of Financial Aid
College of Saint Benedict/Saint John's University, Collegeville, MN 56321-7155
(320) 363-5388

College of St. Scholastica
Duluth, Minnesota
www.css.edu   Federal Code: 002343

4-year private liberal arts college in small city, affiliated with the Roman Catholic Church.
Enrollment: 2,792 undergrads, 19% part-time. 448 full-time freshmen.
Selectivity: Admits 50 to 75% of applicants.

BASIC COSTS (2016-2017)
Tuition and fees: $35,326.
Per-credit charge: $1,088.
Room and board: $9,314.
Additional info: Tuition/fee waivers available for minority students.

FINANCIAL AID PICTURE (2016-2017)
Students with need: Out of 406 full-time freshmen who applied for aid, 365 were judged to have need. Of these, 365 received aid, and 89 had their full need met. Average financial aid package met 83% of need; average scholarship/grant was $7,000; average loan was $3,623. For part-time students, average financial aid package was $7,361.
Students without need: 40 full-time freshmen who did not demonstrate need for aid received scholarships/grants; average award was $20,080. No-need awards available for academics, alumni affiliation, music/drama, religious affiliation, ROTC, state/district residency.
Scholarships offered: Benedictine Scholarship: $5,000-$15,000 per year for up to 4 years. Access Scholarship: $8,500. Both based on GPA, SAT/ACT score; unlimited number awarded. Summit Scholarship: an additional $1,500 for those who qualify for the Benedictine Scholarship and who graduate at the top of their high school class or ACT score greater than 30. Divisional Merit Awards: $4,000; available to transfer students; based on major; unlimited number awarded.

FINANCIAL AID PROCEDURES
Forms required: FAFSA.
Dates and Deadlines: Priority date 3/1; no closing date. Applicants notified on a rolling basis starting 3/1; must reply by 5/1 or within 2 week(s) of notification.

CONTACT
Jon Erickson, Director of Financial Aid
1200 Kenwood Avenue, Duluth, MN 55811-4199
(218) 723-6570

Concordia College: Moorhead
Moorhead, Minnesota
www.concordiacollege.edu   Federal Code: 002346

4-year private liberal arts college in large town, affiliated with the Evangelical Lutheran Church in America.
Enrollment: 2,035 undergrads, 1% part-time. 520 full-time freshmen.
Selectivity: Admits 50 to 75% of applicants.

BASIC COSTS (2016-2017)
Tuition and fees: $36,878.
Per-credit charge: $1,380.

Room and board: $7,810.

FINANCIAL AID PICTURE (2015-2016)
Students with need: Out of 492 full-time freshmen who applied for aid, 391 were judged to have need. Of these, 391 received aid, and 103 had their full need met. Average financial aid package met 91% of need; average scholarship/grant was $23,282; average loan was $4,556. For part-time students, average financial aid package was $15,187.
Students without need: 127 full-time freshmen who did not demonstrate need for aid received scholarships/grants; average award was $16,329. No-need awards available for academics, art, leadership, minority status, music/drama.
Scholarships offered: Concordia College Regents Scholarship: tuition for 4 years; based on 4.13 GPA and 33 ACT. Presidential Distinction Scholarships: $17,000 per year up to 4 years; eligibility based on 4.04 GPA and 30 ACT/1770 SAT; approximately 80 awarded. Faculty Scholarships: $16,000 per year up to 4 years; eligibility based on 3.9 GPA and 27 ACT/1770 SAT; approximately 160 awarded. National Merit Scholars; finalists who name Concordia as their first choice receive minimum of $17,000 per year. Excellence Scholarships: $13,000 to $15,000 per year; based on academic achievement. Concordia College Scholarships: $7,000 to $11,000 per year; for students who show strong potential for success and contribution to the Concordia community. Performance Scholarships: $2,500 per year for up to 4 years; for excellence in music performance, theater performance, speech and debate, and visual arts.

FINANCIAL AID PROCEDURES
Forms required: FAFSA.
Dates and Deadlines: Applicants notified on a rolling basis starting 12/1.
Transfers: No deadline. Applicants notified on a rolling basis starting 4/1. Eligible transfer students are offered merit aid limited to the number of semesters needed to complete their degree as determined through the transfer credit evaluation.

CONTACT
Eric Addington, Associate Vice President of Enrollment and Financial Aid
901 Eighth Street South, Moorhead, MN 56562
(218) 299-3010

Concordia University St. Paul
Saint Paul, Minnesota
www.csp.edu   Federal Code: 002347

4-year private university in large city, affiliated with the Lutheran Church - Missouri Synod.
Enrollment: 2,356 undergrads, 44% part-time. 248 full-time freshmen.
Selectivity: Admits 50 to 75% of applicants.

BASIC COSTS (2017-2018)
Tuition and fees: $21,750.
Room and board: $8,750.

FINANCIAL AID PICTURE (2016-2017)
Students with need: Out of 232 full-time freshmen who applied for aid, 189 were judged to have need. Of these, 187 received aid, and 20 had their full need met. Average financial aid package met 66% of need; average scholarship/grant was $12,077; average loan was $3,461. For part-time students, average financial aid package was $7,296.
Students without need: 34 full-time freshmen who did not demonstrate need for aid received scholarships/grants; average award was $4,593. No-need awards available for academics, art, athletics, minority status, music/drama, religious affiliation.
Scholarships offered: 23 full-time freshmen received athletic scholarships.
Additional info: Church districts and local congregations are major sources of aid for church-vocation students.

FINANCIAL AID PROCEDURES
Forms required: FAFSA, state aid form.

Dates and Deadlines: Priority date 5/1; no closing date. Applicants notified on a rolling basis starting 3/1.

Transfers: No deadline. Applicants notified on a rolling basis. Adult learners in degree completion programs are typically not eligible for most types of institutional scholarships/grants because of discounted tuition rates.

CONTACT

Jeanie Peck, Director of Financial Aid

1282 Concordia Avenue, Saint Paul, MN 55104-5494

(651) 603-6300

Crossroads College
Rochester, Minnesota
www.crossroadscollege.edu   Federal Code: 002366

4-year private Bible college in small city, affiliated with the Christian Church.
Enrollment: 96 undergrads.

BASIC COSTS (2016-2017)
Tuition and fees: $16,500.
Room only: $4,200.

FINANCIAL AID PICTURE
Students with need: Need-based aid available for full-time and part-time students. Work study available nights.
Students without need: No-need awards available for academics, leadership, music/drama, religious affiliation.
Scholarships offered: Home-Educated Grant: $500 per semester if home-schooled for two years during high school. Travel Grant: $500 per semester for student who resides in states other than Minnesota, Iowa, Wisconsin. Crossroads Matching Grant: church funds matched up to $500 per semester; awarded to first year students.

FINANCIAL AID PROCEDURES
Forms required: FAFSA, institutional form.
Dates and Deadlines: Priority date 4/1; closing date 4/15. Applicants notified on a rolling basis starting 2/1; must reply within 4 week(s) of notification.
Transfers: Mid-year transfer students will have financial aid calculated with the prior school term award in mind.

CONTACT

Jason Vagt, Director of Financial Aid

920 Mayowood Road SW, Rochester, MN 55902

(507) 288-4563

Crown College
Saint Bonifacius, Minnesota
www.crown.edu   Federal Code: 002383

4-year private liberal arts college in small town, affiliated with the Christian and Missionary Alliance.
Enrollment: 885 full-time undergrads.

BASIC COSTS (2016-2017)
Tuition and fees: $24,700.
Room and board: $8,160.
Additional info: Tuition/fee waivers available for minority students.

FINANCIAL AID PICTURE
Students with need: Need-based aid available for full-time and part-time students. Work study available nights, weekends, and for part-time students.
Students without need: No-need awards available for academics, alumni affiliation, leadership, minority status, music/drama, religious affiliation.

FINANCIAL AID PROCEDURES
Forms required: FAFSA.

Dates and Deadlines: Priority date 4/1; no closing date. Applicants notified on a rolling basis starting 4/1; must reply within 3 week(s) of notification.

Transfers: No deadline. Applicants notified on a rolling basis; must reply within 3 week(s) of notification. Cannot have attended more than 4 years of college to receive state grant.

CONTACT

Shannon Schaaf, Director of Financial Aid

8700 College View Drive, Saint Bonifacius, MN 55375-9001

(952) 446-4177

Dakota County Technical College
Rosemount, Minnesota
www.dctc.edu   Federal Code: 010402

2-year public technical college in large town.
Enrollment: 2,067 undergrads, 39% part-time. 301 full-time freshmen.
Selectivity: Open admission; but selective for some programs.

BASIC COSTS (2016-2017)
Tuition and fees: $5,662; out-of-state residents $5,662.
Per-credit charge: $167.27.

FINANCIAL AID PICTURE (2015-2016)
Students with need: 39% of average financial aid package awarded as scholarships/grants, 61% awarded as loans/jobs. Need-based aid available for part-time students. Work study available nights.
Students without need: No-need awards available for academics, athletics, leadership.

FINANCIAL AID PROCEDURES
Forms required: FAFSA.
Dates and Deadlines: Applicants notified on a rolling basis starting 3/15.
Transfers: No deadline. FAFSA must be processed within 14 days of the first day of the semester to be considered for Minnesota State Grant for the semester.

CONTACT

Scott Roelke, Director of Scholarships and Financial Aid

1300 145th Street East, Rosemount, MN 55068

(651) 423-8299

Dunwoody College of Technology
Minneapolis, Minnesota
www.dunwoody.edu   Federal Code: 004641

2-year private technical college in very large city.
Enrollment: 1,216 undergrads, 15% part-time. 201 full-time freshmen.
Selectivity: Admits 50 to 75% of applicants.

BASIC COSTS (2016-2017)
Tuition and fees: $24,230.
Additional info: Certificate programs $12,350-$32,517.

FINANCIAL AID PICTURE (2015-2016)
Students with need: Out of 187 full-time freshmen who applied for aid, 156 were judged to have need. Of these, 148 received aid, and 15 had their full need met. Average financial aid package met 40% of need; average scholarship/grant was $7,519; average loan was $3,197. For part-time students, average financial aid package was $5,728.
Students without need: 27 full-time freshmen who did not demonstrate need for aid received scholarships/grants; average award was $2,218.

FINANCIAL AID PROCEDURES
Forms required: FAFSA, state aid form.
Dates and Deadlines: Priority date 6/1; no closing date. Applicants notified on a rolling basis starting 3/1.

Transfers: No deadline. Applicants notified on a rolling basis starting 7/1; must reply within 4 week(s) of notification.

CONTACT
Barbara Charboneau, Director of Financial Aid
818 Dunwoody Boulevard, Minneapolis, MN 55403-1192
(612) 374-5800

Fond du Lac Tribal and Community College
Cloquet, Minnesota
www.fdltcc.edu   Federal Code: E00482

2-year public community college in small town.
Enrollment: 895 undergrads.
Selectivity: Open admission.

BASIC COSTS (2016-2017)
Tuition and fees: $5,210; out-of-state residents $5,210.
Per-credit charge: $157.32.
Room only: $3,598.

FINANCIAL AID PICTURE
Students with need: Need-based aid available for full-time and part-time students.
Students without need: No-need awards available for academics.

FINANCIAL AID PROCEDURES
Forms required: FAFSA.
Dates and Deadlines: Priority date 3/16; no closing date. Applicants notified on a rolling basis starting 4/16.
Transfers: Applicants notified on a rolling basis.

CONTACT
David Sutherland, Director of Financial Aid
2101 14th Street, Cloquet, MN 55720
(218) 879-0816

Globe University: Minneapolis
Minneapolis, Minnesota
www.globeuniversity.edu   Federal Code: 004642

4-year for-profit university and career college in large city.
Enrollment: 164 undergrads.
Selectivity: Open admission; but selective for some programs.

BASIC COSTS (2016-2017)
Additional info: Tuition varies by program. Per-credit-hour charges; $325-$550. Fees vary from $100-$650 per course.

FINANCIAL AID PICTURE
Students with need: Need-based aid available for full-time and part-time students.

FINANCIAL AID PROCEDURES
Forms required: FAFSA, state aid form, institutional form.
Dates and Deadlines: Applicants notified on a rolling basis starting 7/1; must reply within 2 week(s) of notification.

CONTACT
Katie Bergstrom, Financial Aid Manager
80 South Eighth Street, Minneapolis, MN 55402
(612) 455-3000

Globe University: Moorhead
Moorhead, Minnesota
www.globeuniversity.edu   Federal Code: 017145

4-year for-profit university and career college in large town.
Enrollment: 220 undergrads.
Selectivity: Open admission.

BASIC COSTS (2016-2017)
Additional info: Tuition varies by program. Per-credit-hour charges; $325-$550. Fees vary from $100-$650 per course.

FINANCIAL AID PICTURE
Students with need: Need-based aid available for full-time and part-time students.

FINANCIAL AID PROCEDURES
Forms required: FAFSA, state aid form, institutional form.
Dates and Deadlines: Applicants notified on a rolling basis starting 7/1; must reply within 2 week(s) of notification.

CONTACT
Trevor Pearson, Financial Aid Manager
2777 34th Street South, Moorhead, MN 56560
(218) 422-1000

Globe University: Woodbury
Woodbury, Minnesota
www.globeuniversity.edu   Federal Code: 004642

4-year for-profit health science and career college in small city.
Enrollment: 717 undergrads.
Selectivity: Open admission; but selective for some programs.

BASIC COSTS (2016-2017)
Additional info: Tuition varies by program. Per-credit-hour charges; $325-$550. Fees vary from $100-$650 per course.

FINANCIAL AID PICTURE
Students with need: Need-based aid available for full-time and part-time students.

FINANCIAL AID PROCEDURES
Forms required: FAFSA, state aid form, institutional form.
Dates and Deadlines: Applicants notified on a rolling basis starting 7/1; must reply within 2 week(s) of notification.

CONTACT
Jill Garcia, Director of Financial Aid
8089 Globe Drive, Woodbury, MN 55125
(651) 730-5100

Gustavus Adolphus College
St. Peter, Minnesota
www.gustavus.edu   Federal Code: 002353

4-year private liberal arts college in large town, affiliated with the Evangelical Lutheran Church in America.
Enrollment: 2,229 undergrads, 1% part-time. 622 full-time freshmen.
Selectivity: Admits 50 to 75% of applicants.

BASIC COSTS (2016-2017)
Tuition and fees: $42,840.
Room and board: $9,400.

FINANCIAL AID PICTURE (2015-2016)
Students with need: Out of 530 full-time freshmen who applied for aid, 460 were judged to have need. Of these, 460 received aid, and 174 had

their full need met. Average financial aid package met 93% of need; average scholarship/grant was $32,194; average loan was $3,176.

Students without need: 158 full-time freshmen who did not demonstrate need for aid received scholarships/grants; average award was $23,279. No-need awards available for academics, alumni affiliation, art, minority status, music/drama, religious affiliation, ROTC.

Scholarships offered: Presidential Scholarship: $10,000-$14,000. National Merit finalist: $7,500; academic. Legacy Scholarship: $2,500; academic for children or siblings of alumni. Jussi Bjorling Scholarship: $1,000-$4,000; for music; 40 awarded. Anderson Theatre and Dance Scholarship: $2,000; 15 awarded. Dean's Scholarship: $1,000-$10,000; Forensic $500-$2,000.

FINANCIAL AID PROCEDURES

Forms required: FAFSA. CSS PROFILE required of students applying for need-based assistance.

Dates and Deadlines: Priority date 3/15; closing date 4/15. Applicants notified on a rolling basis starting 12/15; must reply by 5/1 or within 2 week(s) of notification.

Transfers: Applicants notified on a rolling basis starting 12/20; must reply by 5/1 or within 2 week(s) of notification.

CONTACT

Doug Minter, Director of Student Financial Assistance
800 West College Avenue, St. Peter, MN 56082
(507) 933-7527

Hamline University

St. Paul, Minnesota
www.hamline.edu
Federal Code: 002354

4-year private university and liberal arts college in very large city, affiliated with the United Methodist Church.
Enrollment: 2,117 undergrads, 2% part-time. 512 full-time freshmen.
Selectivity: Admits 50 to 75% of applicants.

BASIC COSTS (2017-2018)

Tuition and fees: $40,822.
Per-credit charge: $1,225.
Room and board: $10,156.

FINANCIAL AID PICTURE (2015-2016)

Students with need: Out of 492 full-time freshmen who applied for aid, 458 were judged to have need. Of these, 458 received aid, and 96 had their full need met. Average financial aid package met 84% of need; average scholarship/grant was $25,131; average loan was $3,433. For part-time students, average financial aid package was $7,710.

Students without need: 53 full-time freshmen who did not demonstrate need for aid received scholarships/grants; average award was $15,898. No-need awards available for academics, alumni affiliation, art, leadership, minority status, music/drama, religious affiliation.

Scholarships offered: Academic scholarships: ranging from $10,000 to $24,000. Departmental scholarships: $3,000-$5,000 depending on department. National Merit Finalist Scholarship: $24,000. Bishop Hamline Scholarship: $3,000. Hamline Heritage Award (legacy scholarship): $2,000. Hamline Firsts Award: (for first-generation students) range up to $2,500.

FINANCIAL AID PROCEDURES

Forms required: FAFSA.
Dates and Deadlines: Priority date 3/15; no closing date. Applicants notified on a rolling basis starting 3/15; must reply by 5/1 or within 2 week(s) of notification.

Transfers: Priority date 4/1; no deadline. Applicants notified on a rolling basis starting 4/1; must reply within 2 week(s) of notification.

CONTACT

Lynette Wahl, Director of Financial Aid
1536 Hewitt Avenue, St. Paul, MN 55104-1284
(651) 523-3000

Hennepin Technical College

Brooklyn Park, Minnesota
www.hennepintech.edu
Federal Code: 010491

2-year public technical college in small city.
Enrollment: 5,272 undergrads, 64% part-time. 694 full-time freshmen.
Selectivity: Open admission; but selective for some programs.

BASIC COSTS (2016-2017)

Tuition and fees: $5,156; out-of-state residents $5,156.
Per-credit charge: $155.14.

FINANCIAL AID PICTURE (2015-2016)

Students with need: 58% of average financial aid package awarded as scholarships/grants, 42% awarded as loans/jobs. Need-based aid available for part-time students. Work study available nights, weekends, and for part-time students.

Students without need: This college awards aid only to students with need.

FINANCIAL AID PROCEDURES

Forms required: FAFSA, state aid form, institutional form.
Dates and Deadlines: Applicants notified on a rolling basis starting 3/1.
Transfers: No deadline. Applicants notified on a rolling basis.

CONTACT

Tim Jacobson, Director
9000 Brooklyn Boulevard, Brooklyn Park, MN 55445
(952) 995-1418

Institute of Production and Recording

Minneapolis, Minnesota
www.ipr.edu
Federal Code: 041302

2-year for-profit career college in large city.
Enrollment: 243 undergrads.
Selectivity: Open admission.

BASIC COSTS (2016-2017)

Additional info: Tuition varies by program. Per-credit-hour charges; $390. Fees vary from $100-$500 per course.

FINANCIAL AID PICTURE

Students with need: Need-based aid available for full-time and part-time students.

FINANCIAL AID PROCEDURES

Forms required: FAFSA, state aid form, institutional form.
Dates and Deadlines: Applicants notified on a rolling basis starting 7/1; must reply within 2 week(s) of notification.

CONTACT

JR Hunte, Financial Aid Manager
300 North First Avenue, Suite 500, Minneapolis, MN 55401
(612) 244-2800

Inver Hills Community College

Inver Grove Heights, Minnesota
www.inverhills.edu
Federal Code: 006935

2-year public community college in large town.
Enrollment: 3,759 undergrads, 58% part-time. 421 full-time freshmen.
Selectivity: Open admission; but selective for some programs.

BASIC COSTS (2016-2017)

Tuition and fees: $5,285; out-of-state residents $5,285.
Per-credit charge: $157.41.

FINANCIAL AID PICTURE (2015-2016)

Students with need: 44% of average financial aid package awarded as scholarships/grants, 56% awarded as loans/jobs. Need-based aid available for part-time students. Work study available nights, weekends, and for part-time students.

Students without need: This college awards aid only to students with need.

FINANCIAL AID PROCEDURES

Forms required: FAFSA.

Dates and Deadlines: Applicants notified on a rolling basis starting 4/1.

Transfers: Priority date 4/1; no deadline. Applicants notified on a rolling basis.

CONTACT

Scott Roelke, Director of Financial Aid

2500 80th Street East, Inver Grove Heights, MN 55076-3224

(651) 450-3495

Itasca Community College

Grand Rapids, Minnesota

www.itascacc.edu   Federal Code: 002356

2-year public community college in large town.

Enrollment: 894 undergrads.

Selectivity: Open admission; but selective for some programs.

BASIC COSTS (2016-2017)

Tuition and fees: $5,277; out-of-state residents $6,448.

Per-credit charge: $156.05; out-of-state residents $195.05.

Room and board: $5,460.

FINANCIAL AID PICTURE (2015-2016)

Students with need: 64% of average financial aid package awarded as scholarships/grants, 36% awarded as loans/jobs. Need-based aid available for part-time students. Work study available nights, weekends, and for part-time students.

Students without need: No-need awards available for academics, leadership, state/district residency.

FINANCIAL AID PROCEDURES

Forms required: FAFSA.

Dates and Deadlines: Priority date 3/1; no closing date. Applicants notified on a rolling basis starting 4/20.

Transfers: Priority date 3/1; no deadline. Applicants notified on a rolling basis starting 4/20.

CONTACT

Nathan Wright, Financial Aid Director

1851 Highway 169 East, Grand Rapids, MN 55744

(218) 322-2320

Lake Superior College

Duluth, Minnesota

www.lsc.edu   Federal Code: 005757

2-year public community and technical college in small city.

Enrollment: 3,240 undergrads, 50% part-time. 405 full-time freshmen.

Selectivity: Open admission; but selective for some programs.

BASIC COSTS (2016-2017)

Tuition and fees: $5,109; out-of-state residents $9,483.

Per-credit charge: $145.78; out-of-state residents $291.56.

FINANCIAL AID PICTURE

Students with need: Need-based aid available for full-time and part-time students. Work study available nights, weekends, and for part-time students.

Students without need: No-need awards available for academics.

FINANCIAL AID PROCEDURES

Forms required: FAFSA.

Dates and Deadlines: Applicants notified on a rolling basis.

Transfers: No deadline.

CONTACT

LaNita Robinson, Director of Financial Aid

2101 Trinity Road, Duluth, MN 55811

(218) 733-7616

Leech Lake Tribal College

Cass Lake, Minnesota

www.lltc.edu   Federal Code: 030964

2-year public community college in small town.

Enrollment: 275 undergrads.

Selectivity: Open admission.

BASIC COSTS (2016-2017)

Tuition and fees: $4,920; out-of-state residents $4,920.

Per-credit charge: $154.

FINANCIAL AID PICTURE

Students with need: Need-based aid available for full-time and part-time students.

FINANCIAL AID PROCEDURES

Forms required: FAFSA, state aid form, institutional form.

Dates and Deadlines: Applicants notified on a rolling basis; must reply within 4 week(s) of notification.

Transfers: No deadline. Applicants notified on a rolling basis; must reply within 4 week(s) of notification.

CONTACT

Kim Gourneau, Director of Financial Aid

6945 Little Wolf Road NW, Cass Lake, MN 56633

(218) 335-4270

Macalester College

St. Paul, Minnesota   Federal Code: 002358

www.macalester.edu   CSS Code: 6390

4-year private liberal arts college in very large city, affiliated with the Presbyterian Church (USA).

Enrollment: 2,122 undergrads, 1% part-time. 506 full-time freshmen.

Selectivity: Admits less than 50% of applicants.

BASIC COSTS (2017-2018)

Tuition and fees: $52,464.

Per-credit charge: $1,632.

Room and board: $11,672.

FINANCIAL AID PICTURE (2016-2017)

Students with need: Out of 392 full-time freshmen who applied for aid, 350 were judged to have need. Of these, 350 received aid, and 350 had their full need met. Average financial aid package met 100% of need; average scholarship/grant was $38,178; average loan was $3,947. Need-based aid available for part-time students.

Students without need: 74 full-time freshmen who did not demonstrate need for aid received scholarships/grants; average award was $14,973. No-need awards available for academics, minority status.

Scholarships offered: Merit scholarship: $1,000-$18,000; renewable for four years; based on admission application; over 40% of first-year students were awarded merit-based scholarship in 2015-16.

Additional info: College constructs a financial aid package that meets full demonstrated need for all admitted students.

FINANCIAL AID PROCEDURES

Forms required: FAFSA, CSS PROFILE.

Dates and Deadlines: Priority date 2/1; closing date 3/1. Applicants notified by 4/1; must reply by 5/1.

Transfers: Priority date 4/15. Applicants notified by 5/15; must reply within 2 week(s) of notification.

CONTACT

David Wheaton, Vice President for Administration & Finance

1600 Grand Avenue, St. Paul, MN 55105-1899

(651) 696-6214

Martin Luther College

New Ulm, Minnesota

www.mlc-wels.edu   Federal Code: 002361

4-year private college in large town, affiliated with the Wisconsin Evangelical Lutheran Synod.

Enrollment: 783 undergrads, 8% part-time. 161 full-time freshmen.

Selectivity: Admits over 75% of applicants.

BASIC COSTS (2017-2018)

Tuition and fees: $14,680.

Room and board: $5,790.

FINANCIAL AID PICTURE (2015-2016)

Students with need: Out of 149 full-time freshmen who applied for aid, 130 were judged to have need. Of these, 130 received aid, and 13 had their full need met. Average financial aid package met 70% of need; average scholarship/grant was $7,906; average loan was $3,836. For part-time students, average financial aid package was $5,977.

Students without need: 21 full-time freshmen who did not demonstrate need for aid received scholarships/grants; average award was $2,928. No-need awards available for academics, leadership.

Scholarships offered: Academic Scholarship: $500; 3.75 GPA after 6 semesters of high school or 27 ACT. Presidential Scholarship: $1,000; to student selected as high school valedictorian or ranked first in class after 7 semesters.

FINANCIAL AID PROCEDURES

Forms required: FAFSA, institutional form.

Dates and Deadlines: Priority date 4/15; closing date 4/15. Applicants notified on a rolling basis starting 1/29; must reply by 9/1.

CONTACT

Mark Bauer, Director of Financial Aid

1995 Luther Court, New Ulm, MN 56073-3965

(507) 354-8221

McNally Smith College of Music

St. Paul, Minnesota

www.mcnallysmith.edu   Federal Code: 030012

4-year private music and performing arts college in large city.

Enrollment: 408 undergrads, 12% part-time. 95 full-time freshmen.

Selectivity: Admits 50 to 75% of applicants.

BASIC COSTS (2016-2017)

Tuition and fees: $27,940.

Per-credit charge: $1,040.

Room and board: $5,100.

Additional info: Tuition at time of enrollment locked for 4 years.

FINANCIAL AID PICTURE (2015-2016)

Students with need: Out of 93 full-time freshmen who applied for aid, 88 were judged to have need. Of these, 87 received aid, and 25 had their full need met. Average financial aid package met 43% of need; average scholarship/grant was $12,056; average loan was $12,500. For part-time students, average financial aid package was $16,028.

Students without need: No-need awards available for academics, music/drama.

Scholarships offered: Merit-based Premier Scholarships are awarded to incoming and returning students who show outstanding promise in their chosen area of study. The merit-based Conclave Music Business Scholarship is presented to an outstanding McNally Smith College of Music Business student each academic year, and includes tuition and a stipend to attend the Conclave Learning Conference in July. Academic Achievement Scholarships are given in recognition of outstanding academic performance. These scholarships are only available to returning students who are not already receiving a Premier Scholarship. Academic Achievement Scholarships do not require an application, and awards for the upcoming fall semester are determined after previous spring semester grades are posted. Students are issued awards automatically based on GPA.

FINANCIAL AID PROCEDURES

Forms required: FAFSA.

Dates and Deadlines: Priority date 5/1; closing date 8/1. Applicants notified on a rolling basis starting 3/1; must reply within 3 week(s) of notification.

Transfers: Applicants notified on a rolling basis starting 3/1; must reply within 3 week(s) of notification.

CONTACT

Jeffrey Aalbers, Senior Director of Administrative Services

19 Exchange Street East, St. Paul, MN 55101

(800) 594-9500

Mesabi Range College

Virginia, Minnesota

www.mesabirange.edu   Federal Code: 004009

2-year public community and technical college in large town.

Enrollment: 1,373 undergrads.

Selectivity: Open admission.

BASIC COSTS (2016-2017)

Tuition and fees: $5,281; out-of-state residents $6,451.

Per-credit charge: $156.05; out-of-state residents $195.05.

Room only: $3,754.

FINANCIAL AID PICTURE

Students with need: Need-based aid available for full-time and part-time students. Work study available nights, weekends, and for part-time students.

Students without need: No-need awards available for state/district residency.

FINANCIAL AID PROCEDURES

Forms required: FAFSA, institutional form.

Dates and Deadlines: Priority date 4/22; no closing date. Applicants notified on a rolling basis starting 5/1; must reply within 2 week(s) of notification.

Transfers: No deadline.

CONTACT

Jodi Pontinen, Director of Financial Aid

1001 Chestnut Street West, Virginia, MN 55792-3448

(218) 749-7753

PART III: FINANCIAL AID COLLEGE BY COLLEGE

Metropolitan State University

St. Paul, Minnesota
www.metrostate.edu Federal Code: 010374

4-year public university in very large city.
Enrollment: 7,290 undergrads, 61% part-time. 80 full-time freshmen.

BASIC COSTS (2016-2017)
Tuition and fees: $7,566; out-of-state residents $14,394.
Per-credit charge: $218.78.

FINANCIAL AID PICTURE
Students with need: Need-based aid available for full-time and part-time students. Work study available nights, weekends, and for part-time students.
Students without need: No-need awards available for academics, leadership, minority status, state/district residency.

FINANCIAL AID PROCEDURES
Forms required: FAFSA.
Dates and Deadlines: Priority date 3/1; no closing date. Applicants notified on a rolling basis starting 5/1; must reply within 2 week(s) of notification.

CONTACT
Lois Larson, Director of Financial Aid
700 East Seventh Street, St. Paul, MN 55106-5000
(651) 793-1414

Minneapolis Business College

Roseville, Minnesota
www.minneapolisbusinesscollege.edu
Federal Code: 004645

2-year for-profit business and technical college in very large city.
Enrollment: 235 undergrads.
Selectivity: Open admission.

FINANCIAL AID PICTURE
Students with need: Need-based aid available for full-time students.
Students without need: This college awards aid only to students with need.
Additional info: Individual financial planning available for all students to meet the cost of education.

FINANCIAL AID PROCEDURES
Forms required: FAFSA.
Dates and Deadlines: Applicants notified on a rolling basis.

CONTACT
Marie Martin, Director of Student Services
1711 West County Road B, Roseville, MN 55113
(651) 636-7406

Minneapolis College of Art and Design

Minneapolis, Minnesota
www.mcad.edu Federal Code: 002365

4-year private visual arts college in very large city.
Enrollment: 690 undergrads, 2% part-time. 154 full-time freshmen.
Selectivity: Admits 50 to 75% of applicants.

BASIC COSTS (2016-2017)
Tuition and fees: $36,548.
Per-credit charge: $1,505.
Room only: $5,290.

FINANCIAL AID PICTURE (2015-2016)
Students with need: Out of 143 full-time freshmen who applied for aid, 128 were judged to have need. Of these, 125 received aid, and 17 had their full need met. Average financial aid package met 68% of need; average scholarship/grant was $20,760; average loan was $4,190. For part-time students, average financial aid package was $4,128.
Students without need: 26 full-time freshmen who did not demonstrate need for aid received scholarships/grants; average award was $13,692. No-need awards available for academics, alumni affiliation, art.
Scholarships offered: Admissions Merit Scholarships: $6,000-$15,000; based on admissions file. Students admitted to the college automatically entered into scholarship competition.

FINANCIAL AID PROCEDURES
Forms required: FAFSA.
Dates and Deadlines: Priority date 12/1; closing date 3/1. Applicants notified on a rolling basis starting 12/19; must reply by 5/1 or within 2 week(s) of notification.
Transfers: Priority date 4/1; closing date 7/1. Applicants notified on a rolling basis starting 3/1; must reply by 5/1 or within 2 week(s) of notification. Transfer students may apply for admission by the priority deadline of Feb. 15. Only students accepted will receive an award letter. Complete the FAFSA by March 1. Be sure to include MCAD on the list of schools to receive your FAFSA analysis.

CONTACT
Laura Link, Director of Financial Aid
2501 Stevens Avenue, Minneapolis, MN 55404
(612) 874-8782

Minneapolis Community and Technical College

Minneapolis, Minnesota
www.minneapolis.edu Federal Code: 002362

2-year public community and technical college in large city.
Enrollment: 8,187 undergrads.
Selectivity: Open admission; but selective for some programs.

BASIC COSTS (2016-2017)
Tuition and fees: $5,349; out-of-state residents $5,349.
Per-credit charge: $154.

FINANCIAL AID PICTURE
Students with need: Need-based aid available for full-time and part-time students. Work study available nights, weekends, and for part-time students.
Students without need: This college awards aid only to students with need.

FINANCIAL AID PROCEDURES
Forms required: FAFSA.
Dates and Deadlines: Priority date 7/12; no closing date. Applicants notified on a rolling basis starting 7/1.
Transfers: Priority date 7/22; no deadline. Applicants notified on a rolling basis starting 7/1.

CONTACT
Angela Christensen, Director of Financial Aid
1501 Hennepin Avenue, Minneapolis, MN 55403-1710
(612) 659-6240

Minnesota School of Business: Blaine

Blaine, Minnesota
www.msbcollege.edu Federal Code: 017145

4-year for-profit career college in small city.
Enrollment: 239 undergrads.

Selectivity: Open admission.

BASIC COSTS (2016-2017)

Additional info: Tuition varies by program. Per-credit-hour charges; $325-$550. Fees vary from $100-$650 per course.

FINANCIAL AID PICTURE

Students with need: Need-based aid available for full-time and part-time students.

FINANCIAL AID PROCEDURES

Forms required: FAFSA, institutional form.

Dates and Deadlines: Applicants notified on a rolling basis starting 7/1; must reply within 2 week(s) of notification.

CONTACT

Paul Huber, Financial Aid Manager
3680 Pheasant Ridge Dr. NE, Blaine, MN 55449
(763) 225-8000

Minnesota School of Business: Brooklyn Center

Brooklyn Center, Minnesota
www.msbcollege.edu   Federal Code: 017145

2-year for-profit career college in large town.

Enrollment: 109 undergrads.

Selectivity: Open admission.

BASIC COSTS (2016-2017)

Additional info: Tuition varies by program. Per-credit-hour charges; $325-$550. Fees vary from $100-$650 per course.

FINANCIAL AID PICTURE

Students with need: Need-based aid available for full-time and part-time students.

FINANCIAL AID PROCEDURES

Forms required: FAFSA, state aid form, institutional form.

Dates and Deadlines: Applicants notified on a rolling basis starting 7/1; must reply within 2 week(s) of notification.

CONTACT

Tyuon Harris, Financial Aid Manager
5910 Shingle Creek Parkway, Brooklyn Center, MN 55430
(763) 566-7777

Minnesota School of Business: Elk River

Elk River, Minnesota
www.msbcollege.edu   Federal Code: 017145

4-year for-profit university and career college in large town.

Enrollment: 236 undergrads.

Selectivity: Open admission.

BASIC COSTS (2016-2017)

Additional info: Tuition varies by program. Per-credit-hour charges; $325-$550. Fees vary from $100-$650 per course.

FINANCIAL AID PICTURE

Students with need: Need-based aid available for full-time and part-time students.

FINANCIAL AID PROCEDURES

Forms required: FAFSA, state aid form, institutional form.

Dates and Deadlines: Applicants notified on a rolling basis starting 7/1; must reply within 2 week(s) of notification.

CONTACT

Breanna Persons, Financial Aid Manager
11500 193rd Avenue NW, Elk River, MN 55330
(763) 367-7000

Minnesota School of Business: Lakeville

Lakeville, Minnesota
www.msbcollege.edu   Federal Code: 017145

4-year for-profit university and career college in small city.

Enrollment: 195 undergrads.

Selectivity: Open admission.

BASIC COSTS (2016-2017)

Additional info: Tuition varies by program. Per-credit-hour charges; $325-$550. Fees vary from $100-$650 per course.

FINANCIAL AID PICTURE

Students with need: Need-based aid available for full-time and part-time students.

FINANCIAL AID PROCEDURES

Forms required: FAFSA, state aid form, institutional form.

Dates and Deadlines: Applicants notified on a rolling basis starting 7/1; must reply within 2 week(s) of notification.

CONTACT

Jaclyn Oscarson, Financial Aid Manager
17685 Juniper Path, Lakeville, MN 55044
(952) 892-9000

Minnesota School of Business: Plymouth

Plymouth, Minnesota
www.msbcollege.edu   Federal Code: 017145

4-year for-profit university and career college in small city.

Enrollment: 130 undergrads.

Selectivity: Open admission.

BASIC COSTS (2016-2017)

Additional info: Tuition varies by program. Per-credit-hour charges; $325-$550. Fees vary from $100-$650 per course.

FINANCIAL AID PICTURE

Students with need: Need-based aid available for full-time and part-time students.

FINANCIAL AID PROCEDURES

Forms required: FAFSA, state aid form, institutional form.

Dates and Deadlines: Applicants notified on a rolling basis starting 7/1; must reply within 2 week(s) of notification.

CONTACT

Holly Weberg, Financial Aid Manager
1455 County Road 101 North, Plymouth, MN 55447
(763) 476-2000

Minnesota School of Business: Richfield

Richfield, Minnesota
www.msbcollege.edu   Federal Code: 017145

4-year for-profit university and career college in large town.

Enrollment: 693 undergrads.

Selectivity: Open admission; but selective for some programs.

BASIC COSTS (2016-2017)

Additional info: Tuition varies by program. Per-credit-hour charges; $325-$550. Fees vary from $100-$650 per course.

FINANCIAL AID PICTURE

Students with need: Need-based aid available for full-time and part-time students.

FINANCIAL AID PROCEDURES

Forms required: FAFSA, state aid form, institutional form.

Dates and Deadlines: Applicants notified on a rolling basis starting 7/1; must reply within 2 week(s) of notification.

CONTACT

Andrea Howie, Financial Aid Manager

1401 West 76 Street, Suite 500, Richfield, MN 55423

(612) 861-2000

Minnesota School of Business: Rochester

Rochester, Minnesota

www.msbcollege.edu   Federal Code: 017145

4-year for-profit university and career college in small city.

Enrollment: 183 undergrads.

Selectivity: Open admission.

BASIC COSTS (2016-2017)

Additional info: Tuition varies by program. Per-credit-hour charges; $325-$550. Fees vary from $100-$650 per course.

FINANCIAL AID PICTURE

Students with need: Need-based aid available for full-time and part-time students.

FINANCIAL AID PROCEDURES

Forms required: FAFSA, state aid form, institutional form.

Dates and Deadlines: Applicants notified on a rolling basis starting 7/1; must reply within 2 week(s) of notification.

CONTACT

Chris Cook, Financial Aid Manager

2521 Pennington Drive NW, Rochester, MN 55901

(507) 536-9500

Minnesota School of Business: St. Cloud

Waite Park, Minnesota

www.msbcollege.edu   Federal Code: 017145

4-year for-profit university and career college in small city.

Enrollment: 218 undergrads.

Selectivity: Open admission.

BASIC COSTS (2016-2017)

Additional info: Tuition varies by program. Per-credit-hour charges; $325-$550. Fees vary from $100-$650 per course.

FINANCIAL AID PICTURE

Students with need: Need-based aid available for full-time and part-time students.

FINANCIAL AID PROCEDURES

Forms required: FAFSA, state aid form, institutional form.

Dates and Deadlines: Applicants notified on a rolling basis starting 7/1; must reply within 2 week(s) of notification.

CONTACT

Eric Hanson, Financial Aid Manager

1201 Second Street South, Waite Park, MN 56387

(866) 403-3333

Minnesota School of Business: Shakopee

Shakopee, Minnesota

www.msbcollege.edu   Federal Code: 017145

4-year for-profit university and career college in large town.

Enrollment: 210 undergrads.

Selectivity: Open admission.

BASIC COSTS (2016-2017)

Additional info: Tuition varies by program. Per-credit-hour charges; $325-$550. Fees vary from $100-$650 per course.

FINANCIAL AID PICTURE

Students with need: Need-based aid available for full-time and part-time students.

FINANCIAL AID PROCEDURES

Forms required: FAFSA, state aid form, institutional form.

Dates and Deadlines: Applicants notified on a rolling basis starting 7/1; must reply within 2 week(s) of notification.

CONTACT

Laurie Dresow, Financial Aid Manager

1200 Shakopee Town Square, Shakopee, MN 55379

(952) 345-1200

Minnesota State College - Southeast Technical

Winona, Minnesota

www.southeastmn.edu   Federal Code: 002393

2-year public community and technical college in large town.

Enrollment: 1,473 undergrads, 47% part-time. 185 full-time freshmen.

Selectivity: Open admission; but selective for some programs.

BASIC COSTS (2016-2017)

Tuition and fees: $5,553; out-of-state residents $5,553.

Per-credit charge: $165.64.

FINANCIAL AID PICTURE (2015-2016)

Students with need: Out of 155 full-time freshmen who applied for aid, 134 were judged to have need. Of these, 129 received aid, and 2 had their full need met. Average financial aid package met 34% of need; average scholarship/grant was $4,500; average loan was $3,031. For part-time students, average financial aid package was $5,078.

Students without need: 7 full-time freshmen who did not demonstrate need for aid received scholarships/grants; average award was $1,897. No-need awards available for academics, leadership.

Scholarships offered: 8 full-time freshmen received athletic scholarships; average amount $1,723.

FINANCIAL AID PROCEDURES

Forms required: FAFSA, state aid form, institutional form.

Dates and Deadlines: Applicants notified on a rolling basis; must reply within 3 week(s) of notification.

Transfers: Applicants notified on a rolling basis; must reply within 3 week(s) of notification. Mid-year transfer application forms must be accompanied by financial aid transcript.

CONTACT

Tammy Vondrasek, Director of Financial Aid

1250 Homer Road, Winona, MN 55987-0409

(507) 453-2639

Minnesota State Community and Technical College

Fergus Falls, Minnesota
www.minnesota.edu   Federal Code: 005541

2-year public community and technical college in large town.
Enrollment: 4,299 undergrads, 45% part-time. 719 full-time freshmen.
Selectivity: Open admission.

BASIC COSTS (2016-2017)
Tuition and fees: $5,313; out-of-state residents $5,313.
Per-credit charge: $159.15; out-of-state residents $159.15.
Room only: $3,000.

FINANCIAL AID PICTURE
Students with need: Need-based aid available for full-time and part-time students. Work study available nights, weekends, and for part-time students.
Students without need: No-need awards available for academics, art, leadership, minority status, music/drama, state/district residency.
Scholarships offered: Academic and leadership scholarships: $400-$1,000 each; available to 1st and 2nd year students; over 150 awarded annually.

FINANCIAL AID PROCEDURES
Forms required: FAFSA.
Dates and Deadlines: Priority date 6/1; no closing date. Applicants notified on a rolling basis starting 7/1.
Transfers: Priority date 7/1; no deadline. Applicants notified on a rolling basis.

CONTACT
Wendy Olds, Director of Financial Aid
405 Colfax Avenue SW, Wadena, MN 56482-1447
(218) 846-3810

Minnesota State University Mankato

Mankato, Minnesota
www.mnsu.edu   Federal Code: 002360

4-year public university in small city.
Enrollment: 12,292 undergrads.

BASIC COSTS (2016-2017)
Tuition and fees: $7,859; out-of-state residents $15,602.
Per-credit charge: $272; out-of-state residents $584.
Room and board: $8,758.

FINANCIAL AID PICTURE
Students with need: Need-based aid available for full-time and part-time students.
Students without need: No-need awards available for academics, art, athletics, leadership, minority status, music/drama.

FINANCIAL AID PROCEDURES
Forms required: FAFSA.
Dates and Deadlines: Priority date 3/15; no closing date. Applicants notified on a rolling basis starting 3/30; must reply within 2 week(s) of notification.

CONTACT
Sandra Loerts, Director of Financial Aid
122 Taylor Center, Mankato, MN 56001
(507) 389-1185

Minnesota State University Moorhead

Moorhead, Minnesota
www.mnstate.edu   Federal Code: 002367

4-year public university in small city.
Enrollment: 4,966 undergrads, 15% part-time. 857 full-time freshmen.

Selectivity: Admits 50 to 75% of applicants. GED not accepted.

BASIC COSTS (2016-2017)
Tuition and fees: $8,117; out-of-state residents $15,251.
Per-credit charge: $230.25; out-of-state residents $460.5.
Room and board: $8,076.
Additional info: Tuition/fee waivers available for minority students.

FINANCIAL AID PICTURE (2016-2017)
Students with need: Out of 720 full-time freshmen who applied for aid, 510 were judged to have need. Of these, 507 received aid. Need-based aid available for part-time students.
Students without need: No-need awards available for academics, alumni affiliation, art, athletics, leadership, minority status, music/drama, state/district residency.
Additional info: The financial aid application process consists of several steps. At each step institution may ask for information or additional documentation. The entire process can take 6-12 weeks.

FINANCIAL AID PROCEDURES
Forms required: FAFSA.
Dates and Deadlines: Priority date 2/15; no closing date.
Transfers: Closing date 6/30.

CONTACT
Carolyn Zehren, Director of Financial Aid and Scholarships
MSUM Office of Admissions, Box 67, Moorhead, MN 56563
(218) 477-2251

Minnesota West Community and Technical College

Pipestone, Minnesota
www.mnwest.edu   Federal Code: 005263

2-year public community and technical college in large town.
Enrollment: 1,977 undergrads.
Selectivity: Open admission; but selective for some programs.

BASIC COSTS (2016-2017)
Tuition and fees: $5,637; out-of-state residents $5,637.
Per-credit charge: $169.83; out-of-state residents $339.67.
Room only: $2,500.

FINANCIAL AID PICTURE
Students with need: Need-based aid available for full-time and part-time students. Work study available nights, weekends, and for part-time students.

FINANCIAL AID PROCEDURES
Forms required: FAFSA.
Dates and Deadlines: Priority date 6/9; no closing date. Applicants notified on a rolling basis starting 4/9; must reply within 2 week(s) of notification.

CONTACT
Jodi Landgaard, Financial Aid Director
1314 North Hiawatha Avenue, Pipestone, MN 56164
(507) 372-3403

National American University: Bloomington

Bloomington, Minnesota
www.national.edu   Federal Code: E00640

4-year for-profit business and health science college in very large city.
Enrollment: 422 undergrads.
Selectivity: Open admission.

BASIC COSTS (2016-2017)

Tuition and fees: $17,685.
Per-credit charge: $373.
Additional info: Additional fees may apply.

FINANCIAL AID PICTURE

Students with need: Need-based aid available for full-time and part-time students. Work study available nights, weekends, and for part-time students.
Students without need: No-need awards available for academics.

FINANCIAL AID PROCEDURES

Forms required: FAFSA.
Dates and Deadlines: Priority date 8/21; no closing date. Applicants notified on a rolling basis.

CONTACT

Lindsey Regel, Lead Financial Services Representative
7801 Metro Parkway Suite 200, Bloomington, MN 55425

Normandale Community College

Bloomington, Minnesota
www.normandale.edu   Federal Code: 007954

2-year public community college in very large city.
Enrollment: 8,516 undergrads.
Selectivity: Open admission; but selective for some programs.

BASIC COSTS (2016-2017)

Tuition and fees: $5,714; out-of-state residents $5,714.
Per-credit charge: $159.88; out-of-state residents $159.88.

FINANCIAL AID PICTURE

Students with need: Need-based aid available for full-time and part-time students. Work study available nights, weekends, and for part-time students.
Students without need: No-need awards available for academics, art, leadership, music/drama, state/district residency.

FINANCIAL AID PROCEDURES

Forms required: FAFSA, state aid form.
Dates and Deadlines: Priority date 4/1; no closing date. Applicants notified on a rolling basis starting 4/15.

CONTACT

Susan Ant, Director, Financial Aid and Scholarships
9700 France Avenue South, Bloomington, MN 55431
(952) 358-8250

North Central University

Minneapolis, Minnesota
www.northcentral.edu   Federal Code: 002369

4-year private university in large city, affiliated with the Assemblies of God.
Enrollment: 1,301 undergrads.

BASIC COSTS (2016-2017)

Tuition and fees: $22,240.
Room and board: $6,670.

FINANCIAL AID PICTURE

Students with need: Need-based aid available for full-time and part-time students. Work study available nights, weekends, and for part-time students.
Students without need: No-need awards available for academics, leadership, music/drama.
Scholarships offered: President's Scholarship: $2,500 per year; renewable; based on academic performance. Dean's Scholarship: $1,500 per year; renewable; based on academic performance. First Choice Scholarship awarded to those who submit their application early and meet academic criteria.

FINANCIAL AID PROCEDURES

Forms required: FAFSA.
Dates and Deadlines: Applicants notified on a rolling basis starting 3/1; must reply within 2 week(s) of notification.
Transfers: Priority date 4/15; no deadline. Applicants notified on a rolling basis starting 3/1.

CONTACT

Donna Jager, Director of Financial Aid
910 Elliot Avenue, Minneapolis, MN 55404
(800) 289-4488 ext. 289

North Hennepin Community College

Brooklyn Park, Minnesota
www.nhcc.edu   Federal Code: 002370

2-year public community college in small city.
Enrollment: 5,494 undergrads, 69% part-time. 385 full-time freshmen.
Selectivity: Open admission; but selective for some programs.

BASIC COSTS (2016-2017)

Tuition and fees: $5,460; out-of-state residents $5,460.
Per-credit charge: $163.43.

FINANCIAL AID PICTURE

Students with need: Need-based aid available for full-time and part-time students. Work study available nights, weekends, and for part-time students.
Students without need: No-need awards available for academics, art, leadership.
Additional info: Computerized financial aid application.

FINANCIAL AID PROCEDURES

Forms required: FAFSA.
Dates and Deadlines: Priority date 4/15; no closing date. Applicants notified on a rolling basis starting 6/1.
Transfers: No deadline. Applicants notified on a rolling basis.

CONTACT

Steve Yang, Director of Financial Aid and Scholarships
7411 85th Avenue North, Brooklyn Park, MN 55445
(763) 424-0728

Northland Community & Technical College

Thief River Falls, Minnesota
www.northlandcollege.edu   Federal Code: 002385

2-year public community and technical college in small town.
Enrollment: 2,386 undergrads, 47% part-time. 402 full-time freshmen.
Selectivity: Open admission; but selective for some programs.

BASIC COSTS (2016-2017)

Tuition and fees: $5,485; out-of-state residents $5,485.
Per-credit charge: $163.35; out-of-state residents $163.35.

FINANCIAL AID PICTURE (2015-2016)

Students with need: 35% of average financial aid package awarded as scholarships/grants, 65% awarded as loans/jobs. Need-based aid available for part-time students. Work study available nights, weekends, and for part-time students.
Students without need: This college awards aid only to students with need.

FINANCIAL AID PROCEDURES

Forms required: FAFSA.
Dates and Deadlines: Priority date 5/1; no closing date. Applicants notified on a rolling basis starting 5/15.

Transfers: No deadline. Applicants notified on a rolling basis starting 5/1; must reply within 2 week(s) of notification.

CONTACT
Gerald Schulte, Director of Financial Aid
2022 Central Avenue NE, East Grand Forks, MN 56721
(218) 683-8557

Northwest Technical College
Bemidji, Minnesota
www.ntcmn.edu   Federal Code: 005759

2-year public technical college in large town.
Enrollment: 712 undergrads.
Selectivity: Open admission; but selective for some programs.

BASIC COSTS (2016-2017)
Tuition and fees: $5,428; out-of-state residents $5,428.
Per-credit charge: $171.27; out-of-state residents $171.27.
Room and board: $7,924.

FINANCIAL AID PICTURE
Students with need: Need-based aid available for full-time and part-time students. Work study available nights.
Students without need: This college awards aid only to students with need.

FINANCIAL AID PROCEDURES
Forms required: FAFSA.
Dates and Deadlines: Priority date 6/1; no closing date. Applicants notified on a rolling basis starting 3/1.

CONTACT
Lesa Lawrence, Director of Financial Aid
905 Grant Avenue Southeast, Bemidji, MN 56601-4907
(218) 333-6600

Northwestern Health Sciences University
Bloomington, Minnesota
www.nwhealth.edu   Federal Code: 012328

Upper-division private university and health science college in very large city.
Enrollment: 163 undergrads.
Selectivity: Open admission; but selective for some programs.

BASIC COSTS (2016-2017)
Tuition and fees: $12,618.
Per-credit charge: $404.
Additional info: Required fees are based on the university fee and student activity fee. Depending on program, additional fees may be applicable.

FINANCIAL AID PICTURE
Students with need: Need-based aid available for full-time and part-time students.
Students without need: This college awards aid only to students with need.

FINANCIAL AID PROCEDURES
Forms required: FAFSA.
Dates and Deadlines: Priority date 6/1; no closing date. Applicants notified on a rolling basis.

CONTACT
Karen Samstad, Director of Financial Aid
2501 West 84th Street, Bloomington, MN 55431

Oak Hills Christian College
Bemidji, Minnesota
www.oakhills.edu   Federal Code: 016116

4-year private Bible college in large town, affiliated with the interdenominational tradition.
Enrollment: 114 undergrads.

BASIC COSTS (2016-2017)
Tuition and fees: $16,980.
Room and board: $6,506.

FINANCIAL AID PICTURE
Students with need: Need-based aid available for full-time and part-time students. Work study available nights, weekends, and for part-time students.
Students without need: No-need awards available for academics, alumni affiliation.

FINANCIAL AID PROCEDURES
Forms required: FAFSA, institutional form.
Dates and Deadlines: Applicants notified on a rolling basis starting 3/1.
Transfers: No deadline. Applicants notified on a rolling basis starting 3/1.

CONTACT
Matt Myrick, Director of Financial Aid
1600 Oak Hills Road SW, Bemidji, MN 56601-8826
(218) 751-8670 ext. 1284

Pine Technical & Community College
Pine City, Minnesota
www.pine.edu   Federal Code: 005535

2-year public community and technical college in small town.
Enrollment: 1,083 undergrads.
Selectivity: Open admission; but selective for some programs.

BASIC COSTS (2016-2017)
Tuition and fees: $5,037; out-of-state residents $9,586.
Per-credit charge: $151.63; out-of-state residents $303.26.

FINANCIAL AID PICTURE
Students with need: Need-based aid available for full-time and part-time students.
Students without need: No-need awards available for academics, state/district residency.

FINANCIAL AID PROCEDURES
Forms required: FAFSA.
Dates and Deadlines: Priority date 5/5; no closing date. Applicants notified on a rolling basis starting 6/5.

CONTACT
Shawn Reynolds, Financial Aid Director
900 Fourth Street SE, Pine City, MN 55063
(320) 629-5100 ext. 161

Rainy River Community College
International Falls, Minnesota
www.rainyriver.edu   Federal Code: 006775

2-year public community and technical college in small town.
Enrollment: 268 undergrads, 20% part-time.
Selectivity: Open admission.

BASIC COSTS (2016-2017)
Tuition and fees: $5,277; out-of-state residents $6,448.
Per-credit charge: $156.04; out-of-state residents $195.05.

Room and board: $3,930.

Additional info: Tuition/fee waivers available for unemployed or children of unemployed.

FINANCIAL AID PICTURE (2016-2017)

Students with need: Need-based aid available for full-time and part-time students. Work study available nights, weekends, and for part-time students.

Students without need: No-need awards available for academics, alumni affiliation, leadership, minority status, state/district residency.

Additional info: Many scholarship and employment opportunities for applicants showing little or no need.

FINANCIAL AID PROCEDURES

Forms required: FAFSA, institutional form.

Dates and Deadlines: Priority date 6/1; no closing date. Applicants notified on a rolling basis starting 5/1; must reply within 3 week(s) of notification.

CONTACT

Scott Riley, Director of Financial Aid

1501 Highway 71, International Falls, MN 56649

(218) 285-7722

Rasmussen College: Blaine

Blaine, Minnesota

www.rasmussen.edu

4-year for-profit branch campus and career college in small city.

Enrollment: 403 undergrads, 41% part-time. 23 full-time freshmen.

Selectivity: Open admission; but selective for some programs.

BASIC COSTS (2016-2017)

Tuition and fees: $13,455.

Per-credit charge: $299.

Additional info: Full-time tuition varies according to program of study. Required course materials fee of $150 per course.

FINANCIAL AID PICTURE

Students with need: Need-based aid available for full-time and part-time students.

FINANCIAL AID PROCEDURES

Forms required: FAFSA, institutional form.

Dates and Deadlines: Applicants notified on a rolling basis.

CONTACT

Debora Murray, Director of Financial Services

3629 95th Avenue NE, Blaine, MN 55014

Rasmussen College: Bloomington

Bloomington, Minnesota

www.rasmussen.edu   Federal Code: 011686

2-year for-profit branch campus and career college in small city.

Enrollment: 429 undergrads, 49% part-time. 15 full-time freshmen.

Selectivity: Open admission; but selective for some programs.

BASIC COSTS (2016-2017)

Tuition and fees: $13,455.

Per-credit charge: $299.

Additional info: Full-time tuition varies according to program of study. Required course materials fee of $150 per course.

FINANCIAL AID PICTURE

Students with need: Need-based aid available for full-time and part-time students.

FINANCIAL AID PROCEDURES

Forms required: FAFSA, institutional form.

Dates and Deadlines: Applicants notified on a rolling basis.

CONTACT

Debora Murray, Director of Financial Services

4400 West 78th Street, Bloomington, MN 55435

(952) 545-2000

Rasmussen College: Brooklyn Park

Brooklyn Park, Minnesota

www.rasmussen.edu

2-year for-profit branch campus and career college in small city.

Enrollment: 529 undergrads, 52% part-time. 12 full-time freshmen.

Selectivity: Open admission; but selective for some programs.

BASIC COSTS (2016-2017)

Tuition and fees: $13,455.

Per-credit charge: $299.

Additional info: Full-time tuition varies according to program of study. Required course materials fee of $150 per course.

FINANCIAL AID PICTURE

Students with need: Need-based aid available for full-time and part-time students.

FINANCIAL AID PROCEDURES

Forms required: FAFSA, institutional form.

Dates and Deadlines: Applicants notified on a rolling basis.

CONTACT

Debora Murray, Director of Financial Services

8301 93rd Avenue North, Brooklyn Park, MN 55445

Rasmussen College: Eagan

Eagan, Minnesota

www.rasmussen.edu   Federal Code: 004648

2-year for-profit career college in small city.

Enrollment: 499 undergrads, 49% part-time. 23 full-time freshmen.

Selectivity: Open admission; but selective for some programs.

BASIC COSTS (2016-2017)

Tuition and fees: $13,455.

Per-credit charge: $299.

Additional info: Full-time tuition varies according to program of study. Required course materials fee of $150 per course.

FINANCIAL AID PICTURE

Students with need: Need-based aid available for full-time and part-time students.

FINANCIAL AID PROCEDURES

Forms required: FAFSA, institutional form.

Dates and Deadlines: Applicants notified on a rolling basis.

CONTACT

Debora Murray, Director of Financial Services

3500 Federal Drive, Eagan, MN 55122

(651) 687-9000

Rasmussen College: Lake Elmo/ Woodbury

Lake Elmo, Minnesota

www.rasmussen.edu

4-year for-profit career college in small city.

Enrollment: 1,343 undergrads, 80% part-time. 19 full-time freshmen.

Selectivity: Open admission; but selective for some programs.

BASIC COSTS (2016-2017)
Tuition and fees: $13,455.
Per-credit charge: $299.
Additional info: Full-time tuition varies according to program of study. Required course materials fee of $150 per course.

FINANCIAL AID PICTURE
Students with need: Need-based aid available for full-time and part-time students.

FINANCIAL AID PROCEDURES
Forms required: FAFSA, institutional form.
Dates and Deadlines: Applicants notified on a rolling basis.

CONTACT
Debora Murray, Director of Financial Services
8565 Eagle Point Circle, Lake Elmo, MN 55042-8637

Rasmussen College: Mankato
Mankato, Minnesota
www.rasmussen.edu   Federal Code: 016845

2-year for-profit career college in large town.
Enrollment: 381 undergrads, 45% part-time. 12 full-time freshmen.
Selectivity: Open admission; but selective for some programs.

BASIC COSTS (2016-2017)
Tuition and fees: $13,455.
Per-credit charge: $299.
Additional info: Full-time tuition varies according to program of study. Required course materials fee of $150 per course.

FINANCIAL AID PICTURE
Students with need: Need-based aid available for full-time and part-time students.

FINANCIAL AID PROCEDURES
Forms required: FAFSA, institutional form.
Dates and Deadlines: Applicants notified on a rolling basis.

CONTACT
Debora Murray, Director of Financial Services
130 Saint Andrews Drive, Mankato, MN 56001
(507) 625-6556

Rasmussen College: Moorhead
Moorhead, Minnesota
www.rasmussen.edu

4-year for-profit career college in small city.
Enrollment: 190 undergrads, 40% part-time. 8 full-time freshmen.
Selectivity: Open admission; but selective for some programs.

BASIC COSTS (2016-2017)
Tuition and fees: $13,455.
Per-credit charge: $299.
Additional info: Full-time tuition varies according to program of study. Required course materials fee of $150 per course.

FINANCIAL AID PICTURE
Students with need: Need-based aid available for full-time and part-time students.

FINANCIAL AID PROCEDURES
Forms required: FAFSA, institutional form.
Dates and Deadlines: Applicants notified on a rolling basis.

CONTACT
Debora Murray, Director of Financial Services
1250 29th Avenue South, Moorhead, MN 56560

Rasmussen College: St. Cloud
St. Cloud, Minnesota
www.rasmussen.edu   Federal Code: 008694

2-year for-profit career college in small city.
Enrollment: 542 undergrads, 43% part-time. 34 full-time freshmen.
Selectivity: Open admission; but selective for some programs.

BASIC COSTS (2016-2017)
Tuition and fees: $13,455.
Per-credit charge: $299.
Additional info: Full-time tuition varies according to program of study. Required course materials fee of $150 per course.

FINANCIAL AID PICTURE
Students with need: Need-based aid available for full-time and part-time students.

FINANCIAL AID PROCEDURES
Forms required: FAFSA, institutional form.
Dates and Deadlines: Applicants notified on a rolling basis.

CONTACT
Debora Murray, Director of Financial Services
226 Park Avenue South, St. Cloud, MN 56301-3713
(320) 251-5600

Ridgewater College
Willmar, Minnesota
www.ridgewater.edu   Federal Code: 005252

2-year public community and technical college in large town.
Enrollment: 3,580 undergrads.
Selectivity: Open admission; but selective for some programs.

BASIC COSTS (2016-2017)
Tuition and fees: $5,370; out-of-state residents $5,370.
Per-credit charge: $159.69.
Additional info: Tuition/fee waivers available for adults.

FINANCIAL AID PICTURE
Students with need: Need-based aid available for full-time and part-time students. Work study available nights, weekends, and for part-time students.
Additional info: Special funds are available for adult transfer students returning or continuing education after a 7-year absence from academic training. ALLISS grants provide reimbursement for one class, up to five credits for one semester.

FINANCIAL AID PROCEDURES
Forms required: FAFSA, institutional form.
Dates and Deadlines: Applicants notified on a rolling basis.

CONTACT
Jim Rice, Director of Financial Aid
2101 15th Avenue Northwest, Willmar, MN 56201
(320) 222-7474

Riverland Community College
Austin, Minnesota
www.riverland.edu   Federal Code: 002335

2-year public community and technical college in large town.
Enrollment: 2,173 undergrads.

Selectivity: Open admission; but selective for some programs.

BASIC COSTS (2016-2017)
Tuition and fees: $5,508; out-of-state residents $5,508.
Per-credit charge: $162.96.
Room only: $3,000.

FINANCIAL AID PICTURE
Students with need: Need-based aid available for full-time and part-time students. Work study available nights, weekends, and for part-time students.
Additional info: One class tuition-free for Minnesota residents over 25 who have not attended college for at least 7 years.

FINANCIAL AID PROCEDURES
Forms required: FAFSA.
Dates and Deadlines: Priority date 5/15; no closing date. Applicants notified on a rolling basis; must reply within 5 week(s) of notification.
Transfers: No deadline. Applicants notified on a rolling basis.

CONTACT
Gary Schindler, Financial Aid Director
1900 Eighth Avenue, NW, Austin, MN 55912-1407
(507) 433-0511

Rochester Community and Technical College
Rochester, Minnesota
www.rctc.edu   Federal Code: 002373

2-year public community and technical college in small city.
Enrollment: 4,717 undergrads.
Selectivity: Open admission; but selective for some programs.

BASIC COSTS (2016-2017)
Tuition and fees: $5,579; out-of-state residents $5,579.
Per-credit charge: $162.46.

FINANCIAL AID PICTURE
Students with need: Need-based aid available for full-time and part-time students. Work study available nights, weekends, and for part-time students.

FINANCIAL AID PROCEDURES
Forms required: FAFSA.
Dates and Deadlines: Priority date 4/15; no closing date. Applicants notified on a rolling basis.

CONTACT
Beth Diekmann, Director of Financial Aid
Admissions and Records Office (Box 7), Rochester, MN 55904-4999
(507) 285-7271

St. Catherine University
Saint Paul, Minnesota
www.stkate.edu   Federal Code: 002342

4-year private health science and liberal arts college for women in large city, affiliated with the Roman Catholic Church.
Enrollment: 3,086 undergrads, 34% part-time. 420 full-time freshmen.
Selectivity: Admits 50 to 75% of applicants.

BASIC COSTS (2016-2017)
Tuition and fees: $36,999.
Per-credit charge: $1,208.
Room and board: $9,010.

FINANCIAL AID PICTURE
Students with need: Need-based aid available for full-time and part-time students. Work study available nights, weekends, and for part-time students.

Students without need: No-need awards available for academics, alumni affiliation, leadership, state/district residency.
Scholarships offered: St. Catherine of Alexandria Merit Scholarships: $2,000-$6,000; high school seniors in top 15% of class, evidence of academic preparation, outstanding leadership abilities, involvement in extracurricular activities and community service; renewable for 3 years.
Additional info: Audition required for music scholarships.

FINANCIAL AID PROCEDURES
Forms required: FAFSA, institutional form.
Dates and Deadlines: Priority date 4/15; no closing date. Applicants notified on a rolling basis starting 3/30; must reply within 2 week(s) of notification.
Transfers: Applicants notified on a rolling basis; must reply within 2 week(s) of notification.

CONTACT
Elizabeth Stevens, Director of Financial Aid
2004 Randolph Avenue #F-02, St. Paul, MN 55105
(651) 690-6540

Saint Cloud State University
St. Cloud, Minnesota
www.stcloudstate.edu   Federal Code: 002377

4-year public university in small city.
Enrollment: 10,620 undergrads.

BASIC COSTS (2016-2017)
Tuition and fees: $7,800; out-of-state residents $15,718.
Per-credit charge: $227; out-of-state residents $491.
Room and board: $8,230.

FINANCIAL AID PICTURE
Students with need: Need-based aid available for full-time and part-time students. Work study available nights, weekends, and for part-time students.
Students without need: No-need awards available for academics, art, athletics, minority status, music/drama, ROTC.

FINANCIAL AID PROCEDURES
Forms required: FAFSA.
Dates and Deadlines: Priority date 4/15; no closing date. Applicants notified on a rolling basis starting 6/15.
Transfers: No deadline. Applicants notified on a rolling basis starting 6/15.

CONTACT
Michael Uran, Director of Financial Aid
720 Fourth Avenue South, AS 115, St. Cloud, MN 56301
(320) 308-2047

St. Cloud Technical and Community College
St Cloud, Minnesota
www.sctcc.edu   Federal Code: 005534

2-year public community and technical college in small city.
Enrollment: 3,975 undergrads.
Selectivity: Open admission; but selective for some programs.

BASIC COSTS (2016-2017)
Tuition and fees: $5,295; out-of-state residents $5,295.
Per-credit charge: $157.33.

FINANCIAL AID PICTURE (2015-2016)
Students with need: 61% of average financial aid package awarded as scholarships/grants, 39% awarded as loans/jobs. Need-based aid available for part-time students. Work study available nights, weekends, and for part-time students.

Students without need: No-need awards available for academics, leadership, state/district residency.

FINANCIAL AID PROCEDURES

Forms required: FAFSA.

Dates and Deadlines: Applicants notified on a rolling basis starting 6/1.

CONTACT

Anita Baugh, Director of Financial Aid

1540 Northway Drive, St. Cloud, MN 56303

(320) 308-5961

St. John's University

Collegeville, Minnesota

www.csbsju.edu   Federal Code: 002379

4-year private university and liberal arts college in rural community, affiliated with the Roman Catholic Church.

Enrollment: 1,754 undergrads, 1% part-time. 461 full-time freshmen.

Selectivity: Admits over 75% of applicants.

BASIC COSTS (2016-2017)

Tuition and fees: $41,732.

Per-credit charge: $1,709.

Room and board: $9,892.

FINANCIAL AID PICTURE (2016-2017)

Students with need: Out of 399 full-time freshmen who applied for aid, 350 were judged to have need. Of these, 350 received aid, and 140 had their full need met. Average financial aid package met 93% of need; average scholarship/grant was $29,853; average loan was $2,295. For part-time students, average financial aid package was $9,331.

Students without need: 93 full-time freshmen who did not demonstrate need for aid received scholarships/grants; average award was $17,609. No-need awards available for academics, alumni affiliation, art, leadership, music/drama, ROTC.

Scholarships offered: Trustees' Scholarships: $23,000 renewable; based on 3.6 GPA, 30 ACT or equivalent SAT; demonstrated leadership and service; faculty interview. President's Scholarships: $16,500-$20,000 renewable; based on GPA, high school rank, ACT/SAT, leadership and service. Dean's Scholarships: $8,000-$16,000 renewable; based on GPA, high school rank, ACT/SAT, leadership and service. Art, music and theater scholarships: $1,000- $4,000 renewable. Intercultural LEAD fellowship: $10,000 renewable; based on GPA, leadership, financial need; first generation college students; commitment to intercultural issues and action; from diverse urban high schools; on campus interview required. Army ROTC and ROTC Nursing Scholarships: based on demonstrated leadership potential, GPA, class standing, ACT/SAT, high achievement with broad interests and willingness to take on challenges. Catholic High School Scholarship: $4,000 renewable; for students attending Catholic high schools outside Minnesota. Saints Scholarship: 4,000 renewable; for students attending public high schools outside Minnesota. FoCuS Scholarship: $23,000 renewable; for students majoring in chemistry. Bonner Leader Scholarship: $2,500 renewable; for students with strong interest in doing service work, preference for students with financial need. Legacy Scholarship: $1,000 renewable; mother, father or grandparent obtained degree from Saint John's or St. Ben's. Benedictine Scholarship: $5,000 renewable; for students from low income families who have completed a college access program such as Upward Bound.

Additional info: Scholarship letters will be mailed on rolling basis approximately 2 weeks from the time admission acceptance letter is sent.

FINANCIAL AID PROCEDURES

Forms required: FAFSA.

Dates and Deadlines: Priority date 3/15; no closing date. Applicants notified on a rolling basis starting 3/15; must reply by 5/1.

Transfers: Applicants notified on a rolling basis starting 3/15; must reply by 5/1. Phi Theta Kappa Scholarship: $1,500 renewable; for members of Phi Theta Kappa; only for transfer students.

CONTACT

Robert Piechota, Director of Financial Aid

College of St Benedict/St John's University, Collegeville, MN 56321-7155

(320) 363-3664

St. Mary's University of Minnesota

Winona, Minnesota

www.smumn.edu   Federal Code: 002380

4-year private university in large town, affiliated with the Roman Catholic Church.

Enrollment: 1,552 undergrads, 26% part-time. 283 full-time freshmen.

Selectivity: Admits over 75% of applicants.

BASIC COSTS (2016-2017)

Tuition and fees: $32,575.

Per-credit charge: $1,070.

Room and board: $8,635.

FINANCIAL AID PICTURE (2016-2017)

Students with need: Out of 276 full-time freshmen who applied for aid, 242 were judged to have need. Of these, 206 received aid, and 56 had their full need met. Average financial aid package met 82% of need; average scholarship/grant was $23,582; average loan was $3,675. Need-based aid available for part-time students.

Students without need: 74 full-time freshmen who did not demonstrate need for aid received scholarships/grants; average award was $16,821. No-need awards available for academics, alumni affiliation, art, leadership, minority status, music/drama.

FINANCIAL AID PROCEDURES

Forms required: FAFSA.

Dates and Deadlines: Priority date 3/15; no closing date. Applicants notified on a rolling basis starting 2/1; must reply within 3 week(s) of notification.

Transfers: No deadline. Applicants notified on a rolling basis starting 2/1.

CONTACT

Paul Terrio, Director of Financial Aid

700 Terrace Heights #2, Winona, MN 55987-1399

(507) 457-1437

St. Olaf College

Northfield, Minnesota   Federal Code: 002382

www.stolaf.edu   CSS Code: 6638

4-year private liberal arts college in large town, affiliated with the Evangelical Lutheran Church in America.

Enrollment: 2,991 undergrads. 824 full-time freshmen.

Selectivity: Admits less than 50% of applicants.

BASIC COSTS (2016-2017)

Tuition and fees: $44,180.

Per-credit charge: $1,381.

Room and board: $10,080.

FINANCIAL AID PICTURE (2016-2017)

Students with need: Out of 669 full-time freshmen who applied for aid, 569 were judged to have need. Of these, 569 received aid, and 552 had their full need met. Average financial aid package met 99% of need; average scholarship/grant was $32,991; average loan was $2,254. For part-time students, average financial aid package was $6,354.

Students without need: 194 full-time freshmen who did not demonstrate need for aid received scholarships/grants; average award was $15,496. No-need awards available for academics, art, leadership, music/drama.

FINANCIAL AID PROCEDURES

Forms required: FAFSA, state aid form. CSS PROFILE due February 1.

Dates and Deadlines: Closing date 1/15. Applicants notified by 4/1; must reply by 5/1.

CONTACT
Carly Eichhorst, Director of Student Financial Aid
1520 St. Olaf Avenue, Northfield, MN 55057
(507) 786-3019

St. Paul College
Saint Paul, Minnesota
www.saintpaul.edu   Federal Code: 005533

2-year public community and technical college in large city.
Enrollment: 6,410 undergrads.
Selectivity: Open admission; but selective for some programs.

BASIC COSTS (2016-2017)
Tuition and fees: $5,459; out-of-state residents $5,459.
Per-credit charge: $160.

FINANCIAL AID PICTURE
Students with need: Need-based aid available for full-time and part-time students. Work study available nights.
Students without need: No-need awards available for leadership.

FINANCIAL AID PROCEDURES
Forms required: FAFSA.
Dates and Deadlines: Applicants notified on a rolling basis starting 6/1.
Transfers: Priority date 5/1; no deadline. Applicants notified on a rolling basis starting 6/1.

CONTACT
Adam Johnson, Financial Aid Director
235 Marshall Avenue, Saint Paul, MN 55102-1800
(651) 846-1386

South Central College
North Mankato, Minnesota
www.southcentral.edu   Federal Code: 005537

2-year public community and technical college in large town.
Enrollment: 2,823 undergrads.
Selectivity: Open admission.

BASIC COSTS (2016-2017)
Tuition and fees: $5,369; out-of-state residents $5,369.
Per-credit charge: $159.59.

FINANCIAL AID PICTURE (2015-2016)
Students with need: 43% of average financial aid package awarded as scholarships/grants, 57% awarded as loans/jobs. Need-based aid available for part-time students. Work study available nights.

FINANCIAL AID PROCEDURES
Forms required: FAFSA.
Dates and Deadlines: Priority date 5/1; no closing date. Applicants notified on a rolling basis starting 6/1.
Transfers: No deadline. Applicants notified on a rolling basis starting 6/1.

CONTACT
Jayne Dinse, Financial Aid Director
1920 Lee Boulevard, North Mankato, MN 56003
(507) 389-7220

Southwest Minnesota State University
Marshall, Minnesota
www.smsu.edu   Federal Code: 002375

4-year public university and liberal arts college in large town.
Enrollment: 2,285 undergrads, 20% part-time. 472 full-time freshmen.
Selectivity: Admits 50 to 75% of applicants.

BASIC COSTS (2016-2017)
Tuition and fees: $8,344; out-of-state residents $8,344.
Per-credit charge: $234.
Room and board: $7,386.

FINANCIAL AID PICTURE (2016-2017)
Students with need: Out of 394 full-time freshmen who applied for aid, 302 were judged to have need. Of these, 300 received aid, and 33 had their full need met. Average financial aid package met 53% of need; average scholarship/grant was $6,018; average loan was $3,471. For part-time students, average financial aid package was $5,498.
Students without need: 95 full-time freshmen who did not demonstrate need for aid received scholarships/grants; average award was $2,307. No-need awards available for academics, alumni affiliation, art, athletics, leadership, minority status, music/drama, state/district residency.
Scholarships offered: 92 full-time freshmen received athletic scholarships; average amount $2,362.

FINANCIAL AID PROCEDURES
Forms required: FAFSA.
Dates and Deadlines: Applicants notified on a rolling basis starting 5/1.

CONTACT
David Vikander, Director of Financial Aid
1501 State Street, Marshall, MN 56258-1598
(507) 537-6281

University of Minnesota: Crookston
Crookston, Minnesota
www.crk.umn.edu   Federal Code: 004069

4-year public branch campus college in small town.
Enrollment: 1,821 undergrads, 37% part-time. 201 full-time freshmen.
Selectivity: Admits 50 to 75% of applicants.

BASIC COSTS (2016-2017)
Tuition and fees: $11,700; out-of-state residents $11,700.
Per-credit charge: $392; out-of-state residents $392.
Room and board: $8,418.

FINANCIAL AID PICTURE (2016-2017)
Students with need: Out of 177 full-time freshmen who applied for aid, 139 were judged to have need. Of these, 135 received aid, and 32 had their full need met. Average financial aid package met 79% of need; average scholarship/grant was $10,221; average loan was $3,450. For part-time students, average financial aid package was $6,046.
Students without need: 25 full-time freshmen who did not demonstrate need for aid received scholarships/grants; average award was $2,746. No-need awards available for academics, alumni affiliation, athletics, leadership, minority status, music/drama, ROTC, state/district residency.
Scholarships offered: *Merit:* Merit Scholarship: based on a minimum GPA of 3.25 and a minimum ACT score of 21. Presidential Scholarship: $20,000 total ($5,000 annually for four years); based on ACT score of 30 and GPA of 3.25. Chancellor Scholarship: $8,000 total ($4,000 annually for two years); based on ACT score of 27-29 and GPA of 3.25. Distinguished Scholarship: $6,000 total ($3,000 annually for two years); based on ACT score of 25-26 and 3.25 GPA. Merriam Legacy Scholarship: $4,000 total ($2,000 annually for two years); based on ACT score of 23-24 and a 3.25 GPA. Achievement Scholarship: $2,000; based on ACT score of 21-22 and 3.25 GPA. Students

must have earned a cumulative GPA of 3.3 at the end of Spring Semester in order to renew for the following year. *Athletic:* 19 full-time freshmen received athletic scholarships; average amount $4,326.

Additional info: Under the University of Minnesota Promise Scholarship (U Promise), eligible new Minnesota resident undergraduates with a family income of up to $100,000 will be guaranteed a U Promise Scholarship. Eligible new freshman and transfer students enrolling for the first time will receive a guaranteed, multi-year, U Promise Scholarship. Eligible new freshmen will receive a guaranteed need-based scholarship, ranging from $500 to $3,500 each year, for four years. Eligible new transfer students will receive a guaranteed, need-based scholarship, ranging from $500 to $1,500 each year, for two years.

FINANCIAL AID PROCEDURES

Forms required: FAFSA.

Dates and Deadlines: Priority date 3/1; no closing date. Applicants notified on a rolling basis starting 3/1; must reply within 8 week(s) of notification.

Transfers: No deadline. Applicants notified on a rolling basis starting 3/1; must reply within 8 week(s) of notification.

CONTACT

Melissa Dingmann, Director of Financial Aid
2900 University Avenue, Crookston, MN 56716-5001
(218) 281-8563

University of Minnesota: Duluth

Duluth, Minnesota
www.d.umn.edu   Federal Code: 002388

4-year public university in small city.

Enrollment: 9,051 undergrads, 5% part-time. 1,987 full-time freshmen.

Selectivity: Admits over 75% of applicants.

BASIC COSTS (2016-2017)

Tuition and fees: $13,139; out-of-state residents $17,485.

Per-credit charge: $458; out-of-state residents $625.

Room and board: $7,460.

FINANCIAL AID PICTURE (2015-2016)

Students with need: Out of 1,794 full-time freshmen who applied for aid, 1,209 were judged to have need. Of these, 1,181 received aid, and 316 had their full need met. Average financial aid package met 71% of need; average scholarship/grant was $8,648; average loan was $5,593. For part-time students, average financial aid package was $5,744.

Students without need: 301 full-time freshmen who did not demonstrate need for aid received scholarships/grants; average award was $2,070. No-need awards available for academics, alumni affiliation, art, athletics, music/drama, ROTC, state/district residency.

Scholarships offered: 32 full-time freshmen received athletic scholarships; average amount $7,007.

FINANCIAL AID PROCEDURES

Forms required: FAFSA.

Dates and Deadlines: Priority date 3/1; no closing date. Applicants notified on a rolling basis starting 2/1.

Transfers: No deadline. Applicants notified on a rolling basis starting 2/1.

CONTACT

Brenda Herzig, Director of Financial Aid
Solon Campus Center 25, Duluth, MN 55812-3000
(218) 726-8000

University of Minnesota: Morris

Morris, Minnesota
www.morris.umn.edu   Federal Code: 002389

4-year public university and liberal arts college in small town.

Enrollment: 1,680 undergrads, 4% part-time. 375 full-time freshmen.

Selectivity: Admits 50 to 75% of applicants.

BASIC COSTS (2017-2018)

Tuition and fees: $12,846; out-of-state residents $14,846.

Room and board: $7,981.

FINANCIAL AID PICTURE (2016-2017)

Students with need: Out of 345 full-time freshmen who applied for aid, 269 were judged to have need. Of these, 268 received aid, and 77 had their full need met. Average financial aid package met 77% of need; average scholarship/grant was $10,266; average loan was $3,045. For part-time students, average financial aid package was $5,700.

Students without need: 64 full-time freshmen who did not demonstrate need for aid received scholarships/grants; average award was $3,483. No-need awards available for academics.

Scholarships offered: Chancellor's Scholarship: $3,500/year for 4 years; top 5%. Dean's Scholarship: $2,500/year for 4 years; top 10%. Founder's Scholarship: $1,000/year for 4 years; top 20%. National Merit Scholarship: full tuition scholarship for 4 years. Prairie Scholars Award: full tuition/year for 4 years; Morris Scholars Award: $5,000/year for 4 years plus one-time $2,500 research or creative project stipend. President's Distinguished Scholar Award: $1,000 to $3,000/year for four years.

Additional info: Land-grant program waiving tuition for Native Americans.

FINANCIAL AID PROCEDURES

Forms required: FAFSA.

Dates and Deadlines: Applicants notified on a rolling basis starting 4/1.

Transfers: No deadline. Applicants notified on a rolling basis starting 4/1.

CONTACT

Jill Beauregard, Director of Financial Aid
600 East Fourth Street, Morris, MN 56267
(800) 992-8863

University of Minnesota: Rochester

Rochester, Minnesota
http://r.umn.edu

4-year public branch campus and health science college in small city.

Enrollment: 424 undergrads, 4% part-time. 145 full-time freshmen.

Selectivity: Admits 50 to 75% of applicants.

BASIC COSTS (2016-2017)

Tuition and fees: $13,232; out-of-state residents $13,232.

Per-credit charge: $458; out-of-state residents $458.

Room and board: $9,420.

FINANCIAL AID PICTURE (2016-2017)

Students with need: Out of 140 full-time freshmen who applied for aid, 113 were judged to have need. Of these, 111 received aid, and 29 had their full need met. Average financial aid package met 80% of need; average scholarship/grant was $10,546; average loan was $3,716. For part-time students, average financial aid package was $7,062.

Students without need: 10 full-time freshmen who did not demonstrate need for aid received scholarships/grants; average award was $6,006. No-need awards available for academics, leadership.

FINANCIAL AID PROCEDURES

Forms required: FAFSA.

Dates and Deadlines: Priority date 3/1; no closing date. Applicants notified on a rolling basis starting 3/20.

Transfers: Applicants notified by 7/1.

CONTACT

111 South Broadway, Suite 300, Rochester, MN 55904
(507) 258-8069

University of Minnesota: Twin Cities
Minneapolis, Minnesota
http://twin-cities.umn.edu/ Federal Code: 003969

4-year public university in very large city.
Enrollment: 30,975 undergrads, 7% part-time. 5,860 full-time freshmen.
Selectivity: Admits less than 50% of applicants.

BASIC COSTS (2016-2017)
Tuition and fees: $14,142; out-of-state residents $23,806.
Per-credit charge: $483; out-of-state residents $854.
Room and board: $9,377.

FINANCIAL AID PICTURE (2016-2017)
Students with need: Out of 4,720 full-time freshmen who applied for aid, 2,942 were judged to have need. Of these, 2,912 received aid, and 815 had their full need met. Average financial aid package met 77% of need; average scholarship/grant was $10,456; average loan was $3,569. For part-time students, average financial aid package was $7,531.
Students without need: This college awards aid only to students with need.
Scholarships offered: 16 full-time freshmen received athletic scholarships; average amount $7,986.

FINANCIAL AID PROCEDURES
Forms required: FAFSA, institutional form.
Dates and Deadlines: Priority date 3/1; no closing date. Applicants notified on a rolling basis starting 2/15.

CONTACT
240 Williamson Hall, Minneapolis, MN 55455-0213
(612) 624-1111

University of Northwestern - St. Paul
Saint Paul, Minnesota
www.unwsp.edu Federal Code: 002371

4-year private university and liberal arts college in very large city, affiliated with the nondenominational tradition.
Enrollment: 1,952 undergrads.

BASIC COSTS (2016-2017)
Tuition and fees: $29,510.
Room and board: $9,060.
Additional info: Tuition/fee waivers available for minority students.

FINANCIAL AID PICTURE
Students with need: Need-based aid available for full-time and part-time students. Work study available nights, weekends, and for part-time students.
Students without need: No-need awards available for academics, alumni affiliation, leadership, music/drama.
Scholarships offered: Eagle Scholars Program: $12,000-$15,000 per year; ACT score of 30 or SAT score of 1320; up to 15 awarded yearly to incoming freshmen; renewable annually with successful involvement in program, including a cumulative GPA of 3.65 or higher.
Additional info: Students enrolled at least half-time in the FOCUS or Distance Education degree programs may apply for financial aid from the same Federal and state sources as traditional undergraduates. However, their expense budgets and aid are less due to lower tuition.

FINANCIAL AID PROCEDURES
Forms required: FAFSA, institutional form.
Dates and Deadlines: Priority date 3/1; closing date 8/1. Applicants notified on a rolling basis starting 3/1; must reply within 2 week(s) of notification.

CONTACT
Richard Blatchley, Director of Financial Aid
3003 Snelling Avenue North, Saint Paul, MN 55113-1598
(651) 631-5212

University of St. Thomas
Saint Paul, Minnesota
www.stthomas.edu Federal Code: 002345

4-year private university and liberal arts college in very large city, affiliated with the Roman Catholic Church.
Enrollment: 6,111 undergrads, 4% part-time. 1,348 full-time freshmen.
Selectivity: Admits over 75% of applicants.

BASIC COSTS (2016-2017)
Tuition and fees: $39,594.
Per-credit charge: $1,210.
Room and board: $9,760.

FINANCIAL AID PICTURE (2016-2017)
Students with need: Out of 1,069 full-time freshmen who applied for aid, 814 were judged to have need. Of these, 814 received aid, and 166 had their full need met. Average financial aid package met 87% of need; average scholarship/grant was $22,127; average loan was $7,860. For part-time students, average financial aid package was $11,995.
Students without need: 246 full-time freshmen who did not demonstrate need for aid received scholarships/grants; average award was $18,888. No-need awards available for academics, music/drama, ROTC.

FINANCIAL AID PROCEDURES
Forms required: FAFSA.
Dates and Deadlines: Priority date 12/1; no closing date. Applicants notified on a rolling basis starting 1/15; must reply within 3 week(s) of notification.
Transfers: Closing date 2/15.

CONTACT
Kris Roach, Executive Director of Admissions & Financial Aid
2115 Summit Avenue, Mail 5017, Saint Paul, MN 55105

Vermilion Community College
Ely, Minnesota
www.vcc.edu Federal Code: 002350

2-year public community and technical college in small town.
Enrollment: 696 undergrads.
Selectivity: Open admission.

BASIC COSTS (2016-2017)
Tuition and fees: $5,277; out-of-state residents $6,447.
Per-credit charge: $156.05; out-of-state residents $195.05.
Room and board: $5,810.

FINANCIAL AID PICTURE
Students with need: Need-based aid available for full-time and part-time students. Work study available nights, weekends, and for part-time students.

FINANCIAL AID PROCEDURES
Forms required: FAFSA, institutional form.
Dates and Deadlines: Priority date 4/15; no closing date. Applicants notified on a rolling basis starting 4/1.

CONTACT
1900 East Camp Street, Ely, MN 55731-9989
(218) 235-2153

Walden University
Minneapolis, Minnesota
www.waldenu.edu Federal Code: 025402

4-year for-profit virtual university in large city.
Enrollment: 7,329 undergrads, 91% part-time.

Selectivity: Open admission; but selective for some programs.

BASIC COSTS (2016-2017)
Tuition and fees: $15,105.
Per-credit charge: $325.

FINANCIAL AID PICTURE
Students with need: Need-based aid available for full-time and part-time students.
Students without need: This college awards aid only to students with need.

FINANCIAL AID PROCEDURES
Forms required: FAFSA.
Dates and Deadlines: Applicants notified on a rolling basis.
Transfers: No deadline. Applicants notified on a rolling basis.

CONTACT
Teresa Drzewiecki, Exec Director of Financial Aid
100 Washington Avenue South, Suite 900, Minneapolis, MN 55401
(410) 843-8506

White Earth Tribal and Community College
Mahnomen, Minnesota
www.wetcc.edu

2-year private community college in rural community.
Enrollment: 71 undergrads, 31% part-time. 13 full-time freshmen.
Selectivity: Open admission.

BASIC COSTS (2016-2017)
Tuition and fees: $3,518.
Per-credit charge: $130.

FINANCIAL AID PICTURE (2015-2016)
Students with need: Average financial aid package for all full-time undergraduates was $13,000. 99% awarded as scholarships/grants, 1% awarded as loans/jobs. Need-based aid available for part-time students.
Students without need: This college awards aid only to students with need.

FINANCIAL AID PROCEDURES
Forms required: FAFSA, state aid form, institutional form.
Dates and Deadlines: Applicants notified on a rolling basis.

CONTACT
Peggie Chisolm, Financial Aid Coordinator
PO Box 478, Mahnomen, MN 56557
(218) 935-0417 ext. 335

Winona State University
Winona, Minnesota
www.winona.edu   Federal Code: 002394

4-year public university in large town.
Enrollment: 7,486 undergrads, 12% part-time. 1,630 full-time freshmen.
Selectivity: Admits 50 to 75% of applicants.

BASIC COSTS (2016-2017)
Tuition and fees: $9,075; out-of-state residents $14,772.
Per-credit charge: $235; out-of-state residents $426.
Room and board: $8,460.

FINANCIAL AID PICTURE (2015-2016)
Students with need: Out of 1,432 full-time freshmen who applied for aid, 995 were judged to have need. Of these, 971 received aid, and 96 had their full need met. Average financial aid package met 49% of need; average

scholarship/grant was $5,112; average loan was $3,164. For part-time students, average financial aid package was $4,988.
Students without need: 360 full-time freshmen who did not demonstrate need for aid received scholarships/grants; average award was $2,485. No-need awards available for academics, alumni affiliation, art, athletics, leadership, music/drama, ROTC, state/district residency.
Scholarships offered: _Merit:_ Outstanding Academics Honors Award: $3,500; for applicants with ACT 32+ and top 5% of class or 3.9+ HS GPA. WSU Foundation Board Scholarship: $4,000 for ACT 28+ and top 5% of class or HS GPA 3.9+ with essay/interview. Presidential Honor Scholarships: $1,000-$1,500. _**Athletic:**_ 530 full-time freshmen received athletic scholarships; average amount $2,417.

FINANCIAL AID PROCEDURES
Forms required: FAFSA.
Dates and Deadlines: Priority date 5/15; no closing date. Applicants notified on a rolling basis starting 12/1; must reply within 3 week(s) of notification.

CONTACT
Mari Livingston, Associate Director of Financial Aid
Office of Admissions, Winona, MN 55987
(800) 342-5978

Mississippi

Alcorn State University
Lorman, Mississippi
www.alcorn.edu   Federal Code: 002396

4-year public university and agricultural college in rural community.
Enrollment: 2,812 undergrads, 8% part-time. 525 full-time freshmen.
Selectivity: Admits over 75% of applicants.

BASIC COSTS (2016-2017)
Tuition and fees: $6,546.
Per-credit charge: $273.
Room and board: $8,667.

FINANCIAL AID PICTURE (2016-2017)
Students with need: Average financial aid package met 97% of need; average scholarship/grant was $3,070; average loan was $1,714. For part-time students, average financial aid package was $5,627.
Students without need: No-need awards available for academics, athletics, leadership, ROTC.

FINANCIAL AID PROCEDURES
Forms required: FAFSA, institutional form.
Dates and Deadlines: Priority date 3/15; no closing date. Applicants notified on a rolling basis starting 4/1; must reply within 4 week(s) of notification.

CONTACT
Juanita Edwards, Director of Financial Aid
1000 ASU Drive #300, Lorman, MS 39096-7500
(601) 877-6190

Belhaven University
Jackson, Mississippi
www.belhaven.edu   Federal Code: 002397

4-year private university and liberal arts college in large city, affiliated with the Presbyterian Church (USA).
Enrollment: 2,566 undergrads, 48% part-time. 239 full-time freshmen.
Selectivity: Admits less than 50% of applicants.

BASIC COSTS (2016-2017)

Tuition and fees: $23,016.

Per-credit charge: $425.

Room and board: $8,000.

FINANCIAL AID PICTURE (2015-2016)

Students with need: Out of 215 full-time freshmen who applied for aid, 192 were judged to have need. Of these, 192 received aid, and 10 had their full need met. Average financial aid package met 68% of need; average scholarship/grant was $16,268; average loan was $3,313. Need-based aid available for part-time students.

Students without need: 45 full-time freshmen who did not demonstrate need for aid received scholarships/grants; average award was $13,765. No-need awards available for academics, alumni affiliation, art, athletics, job skills, leadership, music/drama.

FINANCIAL AID PROCEDURES

Forms required: FAFSA.

Dates and Deadlines: Priority date 1/31; no closing date. Applicants notified on a rolling basis starting 2/1.

Transfers: No deadline. Applicants notified on a rolling basis.

CONTACT

Debbi Braswell, Director of Financial Aid

1500 Peachtree Street, Jackson, MS 39202

(601) 968-5933

Blue Cliff College: Gulfport

Gulfport, Mississippi

www.bluecliffcollege.edu   Federal Code: 035253

2-year for-profit career college in small city.

Enrollment: 274 undergrads.

BASIC COSTS (2016-2017)

Additional info: Diploma programs: Cosmetology $16,995. Massage therapy $13,144; books and supplies $1,550. Dialysis technician $19,008; books and supplies $1,850. Medical/clinical assistant $13,621; books and supplies $1,850. Associate program: Massage therapy $25,075; books and supplies $1,550.

FINANCIAL AID PICTURE

Students with need: Need-based aid available for full-time and part-time students.

Students without need: This college awards aid only to students with need.

FINANCIAL AID PROCEDURES

Forms required: FAFSA.

CONTACT

Judy May, Financial Planner

12251 Bernard Parkway, Gulfport, MS 39503

Blue Mountain College

Blue Mountain, Mississippi

www.bmc.edu   Federal Code: 002398

4-year private liberal arts college in rural community, affiliated with the Southern Baptist Convention.

Enrollment: 541 undergrads, 9% part-time. 109 full-time freshmen.

Selectivity: Admits less than 50% of applicants.

BASIC COSTS (2016-2017)

Tuition and fees: $11,212.

Per-credit charge: $317.

Room and board: $5,839.

FINANCIAL AID PICTURE (2016-2017)

Students with need: Out of 106 full-time freshmen who applied for aid, 86 were judged to have need. Of these, 86 received aid, and 19 had their full need met. Average financial aid package met 68% of need; average scholarship/grant was $7,783; average loan was $2,946. For part-time students, average financial aid package was $4,225.

Students without need: 7 full-time freshmen who did not demonstrate need for aid received scholarships/grants; average award was $6,369. No-need awards available for academics, alumni affiliation, art, athletics, leadership, music/drama, religious affiliation, state/district residency.

Scholarships offered: *Merit:* ACT/SAT Scholarships: varies from $1,000 to $7,000 per year; based on ACT/SAT score; number varies depending on number of applicants. Valedictorian/Salutatorian Scholarships: $1,000 to $5,000 first year; based on rank in class; unlimited number available. Child of Alumnae/Alumni: $500 first year; must be dependent of graduate; unlimited number available. *Athletic:* 71 full-time freshmen received athletic scholarships; average amount $4,907.

FINANCIAL AID PROCEDURES

Forms required: FAFSA.

Dates and Deadlines: Priority date 3/1; closing date 7/31. Applicants notified on a rolling basis starting 4/1; must reply within 4 week(s) of notification.

Transfers: No deadline.

CONTACT

Beverly Hickey, Director of Financial Aid

PO Box 160, Blue Mountain, MS 38610-0160

(662) 685-4771 ext. 141

Coahoma Community College

Clarksdale, Mississippi

www.coahomacc.edu   Federal Code: 002401

2-year public community college in large town.

Enrollment: 1,759 undergrads, 11% part-time. 494 full-time freshmen.

Selectivity: Open admission; but selective for some programs.

BASIC COSTS (2016-2017)

Tuition and fees: $2,610; out-of-state residents $3,260.

Per-credit charge: $125; out-of-state residents $235.

Room and board: $4,320.

FINANCIAL AID PICTURE (2015-2016)

Students with need: Need-based aid available for part-time students.

Students without need: This college awards aid only to students with need.

FINANCIAL AID PROCEDURES

Forms required: FAFSA, institutional form.

Dates and Deadlines: Priority date 4/1; no closing date. Applicants notified on a rolling basis starting 7/1.

Transfers: Priority date 3/1.

CONTACT

Luke Howard, Director of Financial Aid

3240 Friars Point Road, Clarksdale, MS 38614-9799

(662) 627-2571

Copiah-Lincoln Community College

Wesson, Mississippi

www.colin.edu   Federal Code: 002402

2-year public community college in small town.

Enrollment: 2,490 undergrads.

Selectivity: Open admission; but selective for some programs.

BASIC COSTS (2016-2017)
Tuition and fees: $2,730; out-of-state residents $4,730.
Room and board: $3,400.

FINANCIAL AID PICTURE (2015-2016)
Students with need: 82% of average financial aid package awarded as scholarships/grants, 18% awarded as loans/jobs. Need-based aid available for part-time students. Work study available nights, weekends, and for part-time students.
Students without need: No-need awards available for academics, art, athletics, job skills, leadership, minority status, music/drama, state/district residency.

FINANCIAL AID PROCEDURES
Forms required: FAFSA.
Dates and Deadlines: Closing date 4/1. Applicants notified on a rolling basis starting 4/1; must reply within 2 week(s) of notification.
Transfers: Priority date 4/1; no deadline.

CONTACT
Leslie Smith, Director of Financial Aid
PO Box 649, Wesson, MS 39191
(601) 643-8340

Delta State University
Cleveland, Mississippi
www.deltastate.edu　　　　　Federal Code: 002403

4-year public university in large town.
Enrollment: 2,429 undergrads.

BASIC COSTS (2016-2017)
Tuition and fees: $6,418.
Per-credit charge: $263; out-of-state residents $263.
Room and board: $7,374.

FINANCIAL AID PICTURE
Students with need: Need-based aid available for full-time and part-time students. Work study available nights, weekends, and for part-time students.
Students without need: No-need awards available for academics, alumni affiliation, art, athletics, leadership, music/drama, state/district residency.

FINANCIAL AID PROCEDURES
Forms required: FAFSA, institutional form.
Dates and Deadlines: Priority date 3/1; no closing date. Applicants notified on a rolling basis starting 5/1.
Transfers: Closing date 3/1. Applicants notified on a rolling basis starting 5/1.

CONTACT
Christie Rocconi, Director of Student Financial Assistance
117 Kent Wyatt Hall, Cleveland, MS 38733
(662) 846-4670

East Central Community College
Decatur, Mississippi
www.eccc.edu　　　　　Federal Code: 002404

2-year public community college in rural community.
Enrollment: 2,172 undergrads.
Selectivity: Open admission; but selective for some programs.

BASIC COSTS (2016-2017)
Tuition and fees: $2,290; out-of-state residents $4,370.
Room and board: $3,340.

FINANCIAL AID PICTURE
Students with need: Need-based aid available for full-time and part-time students. Work study available nights.
Students without need: No-need awards available for academics, art, athletics, leadership, music/drama, state/district residency.

FINANCIAL AID PROCEDURES
Forms required: FAFSA, state aid form.
Dates and Deadlines: Priority date 4/1; no closing date. Applicants notified on a rolling basis starting 7/31; must reply within 2 week(s) of notification.

CONTACT
Brenda Carson, Director of Financial Aid
Box 129, Decatur, MS 39327
(601) 635-2111 ext. 378

East Mississippi Community College
Scooba, Mississippi
www.eastms.edu　　　　　Federal Code: 002405

2-year public community college in rural community.
Enrollment: 3,902 undergrads, 36% part-time. 838 full-time freshmen.
Selectivity: Open admission; but selective for some programs.

BASIC COSTS (2016-2017)
Tuition and fees: $2,840; out-of-state residents $5,240.
Room and board: $4,600.
Additional info: Tuition at time of enrollment locked for 2 years; tuition/fee waivers available for adults, minority students.

FINANCIAL AID PICTURE (2016-2017)
Students with need: 60% of average financial aid package awarded as scholarships/grants, 40% awarded as loans/jobs. Need-based aid available for part-time students.
Students without need: No-need awards available for academics, alumni affiliation, art, athletics, leadership, music/drama, state/district residency.

FINANCIAL AID PROCEDURES
Forms required: FAFSA, state aid form, institutional form.
Dates and Deadlines: Priority date 4/1; no closing date. Applicants notified on a rolling basis starting 4/1; must reply within 2 week(s) of notification.
Transfers: Applicants notified on a rolling basis starting 4/1.

CONTACT
Melissa Mosley, Chief Financial Officer
Admissions Office, Scooba, MS 39358
(662) 476-5076

Hinds Community College
Raymond, Mississippi
www.hindscc.edu　　　　　Federal Code: 002407

2-year public branch campus and community college in small town.
Enrollment: 10,042 undergrads, 30% part-time. 2,276 full-time freshmen.
Selectivity: Open admission; but selective for some programs.

BASIC COSTS (2016-2017)
Tuition and fees: $2,840; out-of-state residents $5,640.
Per-credit charge: $110; out-of-state residents $220.
Room and board: $4,000.

FINANCIAL AID PICTURE (2015-2016)
Students with need: 53% of average financial aid package awarded as scholarships/grants, 47% awarded as loans/jobs. Need-based aid available for part-time students. Work study available nights, weekends, and for part-time students.

Students without need: No-need awards available for academics, art, athletics, job skills, leadership, minority status, music/drama, state/district residency.

FINANCIAL AID PROCEDURES

Forms required: FAFSA.

Dates and Deadlines: Priority date 3/15; no closing date. Applicants notified on a rolling basis.

Transfers: Financial aid transcripts from all previous colleges must be on file prior to award letter being released.

CONTACT

Louanne Langston, District Director of Financial Aid & Student Success
HCC Office of Admissions and Records, Raymond, MS 39154-1100
(601) 857-3223

Itawamba Community College
Fulton, Mississippi
www.iccms.edu   Federal Code: 002409

2-year public community and technical college in small town.
Enrollment: 5,037 undergrads.
Selectivity: Open admission; but selective for some programs.

BASIC COSTS (2016-2017)
Tuition and fees: $2,620; out-of-state residents $4,820.
Room and board: $3,150.

FINANCIAL AID PICTURE
Students with need: Need-based aid available for full-time and part-time students.
Students without need: No-need awards available for academics, art, athletics, leadership, music/drama, state/district residency.

FINANCIAL AID PROCEDURES
Forms required: FAFSA, institutional form.
Dates and Deadlines: Applicants notified on a rolling basis starting 4/15.

CONTACT
Terry Bland, Director of Financial Aid
602 West Hill Street, Fulton, MS 38843-1099
(662) 862-8220

Jackson State University
Jackson, Mississippi
www.jsums.edu   Federal Code: 002410

4-year public university in small city.
Enrollment: 7,492 undergrads, 13% part-time. 1,281 full-time freshmen.
Selectivity: Admits 50 to 75% of applicants.

BASIC COSTS (2016-2017)
Tuition and fees: $7,261; out-of-state residents $17,614.
Per-credit charge: $298; out-of-state residents $729.
Room and board: $8,788.
Additional info: Tuition/fee waivers available for minority students.

FINANCIAL AID PICTURE (2016-2017)
Students with need: Need-based aid available for full-time and part-time students. Work study available nights, weekends, and for part-time students.
Students without need: No-need awards available for academics, alumni affiliation, athletics, leadership, minority status, music/drama, ROTC.

FINANCIAL AID PROCEDURES
Forms required: FAFSA.
Dates and Deadlines: Priority date 4/15; no closing date. Applicants notified on a rolling basis starting 3/1.
Transfers: Priority date 4/15. Applicants notified by 3/1.

CONTACT
Betty Moncure, Director, Financial Aid
1400 John R. Lynch Street, Jackson, MS 39217
(601) 979-2227

Jones County Junior College
Ellisville, Mississippi
www.jcjc.edu   Federal Code: 002411

2-year public community and junior college in small town.
Enrollment: 4,066 undergrads.
Selectivity: Open admission; but selective for some programs.

FINANCIAL AID PICTURE (2016-2017)
Students with need: Need-based aid available for full-time and part-time students.
Students without need: No-need awards available for academics, alumni affiliation, art, athletics, leadership, music/drama, state/district residency.

FINANCIAL AID PROCEDURES
Forms required: FAFSA, state aid form, institutional form.
Dates and Deadlines: Priority date 4/1; no closing date. Applicants notified on a rolling basis starting 6/1; must reply within 2 week(s) of notification.
Transfers: Priority date 4/1; no deadline. Applicants notified by 4/1.

CONTACT
Jennifer Suber, Director of Student Financial Aid
900 South Court Street, Ellisville, MS 39437
(601) 477-4040

Meridian Community College
Meridian, Mississippi
www.meridiancc.edu   Federal Code: 002413

2-year public community college in large town.
Enrollment: 3,188 undergrads.
Selectivity: Open admission; but selective for some programs.

BASIC COSTS (2016-2017)
Tuition and fees: $2,550; out-of-state residents $3,630.
Per-credit charge: $150; out-of-state residents $157.

FINANCIAL AID PICTURE
Students with need: Need-based aid available for full-time and part-time students.
Students without need: No-need awards available for academics, art, athletics, leadership, music/drama, state/district residency.
Scholarships offered: Incoming freshmen graduating from a school in Lauderdale County can attend tuition-free.

FINANCIAL AID PROCEDURES
Forms required: FAFSA, institutional form.
Dates and Deadlines: Priority date 6/1; no closing date. Applicants notified on a rolling basis starting 5/15; must reply within 2 week(s) of notification.

CONTACT
Nedra Bradley, Director of Financial Aid
910 Highway 19 North, Meridian, MS 39307-5890
(601) 484-8628

Millsaps College
Jackson, Mississippi
www.millsaps.edu   Federal Code: 002414

4-year private business and liberal arts college in large city, affiliated with the United Methodist Church.

Enrollment: 797 undergrads, 1% part-time. 259 full-time freshmen.
Selectivity: Admits 50 to 75% of applicants.

BASIC COSTS (2016-2017)
Tuition and fees: $37,110.
Per-credit charge: $1,072.
Room and board: $14,303.

FINANCIAL AID PICTURE (2015-2016)
Students with need: Out of 224 full-time freshmen who applied for aid, 192 were judged to have need. Of these, 192 received aid, and 39 had their full need met. Average financial aid package met 81% of need; average scholarship/grant was $29,331; average loan was $3,841. For part-time students, average financial aid package was $3,918.
Students without need: 66 full-time freshmen who did not demonstrate need for aid received scholarships/grants; average award was $24,326. No-need awards available for academics, art, leadership, music/drama, religious affiliation.

FINANCIAL AID PROCEDURES
Forms required: FAFSA.
Dates and Deadlines: Priority date 3/1; no closing date. Applicants notified on a rolling basis starting 3/15; must reply by 5/1 or within 2 week(s) of notification.
Transfers: No deadline. Applicants notified on a rolling basis; must reply within 2 week(s) of notification.

CONTACT
Isabelle Higbee, Director of Financial Aid
1701 North State Street, Jackson, MS 39210-0001
(601) 974-1220

Mississippi College
Clinton, Mississippi
www.mc.edu
Federal Code: 002415

4-year private university in large town, affiliated with the Southern Baptist Convention.
Enrollment: 2,898 undergrads.

BASIC COSTS (2016-2017)
Tuition and fees: $16,740.
Per-credit charge: $495.
Room and board: $9,190.

FINANCIAL AID PICTURE
Students with need: Need-based aid available for full-time and part-time students.
Students without need: No-need awards available for academics, alumni affiliation, art, athletics, leadership, music/drama, religious affiliation, ROTC.
Scholarships offered: Scholarships up to $1,500 based on various criteria including leadership, academics, church and community involvement; extensive number awarded.
Additional info: Student reply date for institutional scholarships: May 1.

FINANCIAL AID PROCEDURES
Forms required: FAFSA, state aid form.
Dates and Deadlines: Priority date 3/1; no closing date. Applicants notified on a rolling basis starting 3/1; must reply by 5/1.
Transfers: No deadline. Applicants notified on a rolling basis starting 3/1; must reply by 5/1.

CONTACT
Cassandra Sessoms, Coordinator of Institutional Research
Box 4026, Clinton, MS 39058-0001
(601) 925-3464

Mississippi Delta Community College
Moorhead, Mississippi
www.msdelta.edu
Federal Code: 002416

2-year public community college in rural community.
Enrollment: 2,305 undergrads.
Selectivity: Open admission; but selective for some programs.

BASIC COSTS (2016-2017)
Tuition and fees: $2,590; out-of-state residents $4,198.
Room and board: $2,880.

FINANCIAL AID PICTURE
Students with need: Need-based aid available for full-time students.
Students without need: No-need awards available for academics, athletics, state/district residency.

FINANCIAL AID PROCEDURES
Forms required: FAFSA, institutional form.
Dates and Deadlines: Closing date 8/1. Applicants notified on a rolling basis; must reply within 2 week(s) of notification.

CONTACT
Amber Kelly, Director of Financial Aid
Box 668, Moorhead, MS 38761
(662) 246-6263

Mississippi Gulf Coast Community College
Perkinston, Mississippi
www.mgccc.edu
Federal Code: 002419

2-year public community college in large city.
Enrollment: 8,975 undergrads.
Selectivity: Open admission; but selective for some programs.

BASIC COSTS (2016-2017)
Tuition and fees: $2,860; out-of-state residents $5,660.
Room and board: $4,100.

FINANCIAL AID PICTURE
Students with need: Need-based aid available for full-time students.
Students without need: This college awards aid only to students with need.

FINANCIAL AID PROCEDURES
Forms required: FAFSA, institutional form.
Dates and Deadlines: Priority date 6/1; no closing date. Applicants notified on a rolling basis starting 7/1.

CONTACT
LaShanda Chamberlain, Director of Financial Aid
PO Box 548, Perkinston, MS 39573
(228) 497-7687

Mississippi State University
Mississippi State, Mississippi
www.msstate.edu
Federal Code: 002423

4-year public university and agricultural college in large town.
Enrollment: 17,371 undergrads, 7% part-time. 3,464 full-time freshmen.
Selectivity: Admits 50 to 75% of applicants.

BASIC COSTS (2016-2017)
Tuition and fees: $7,780; out-of-state residents $20,900.
Per-credit charge: $320; out-of-state residents $866.
Room and board: $9,570.

Additional info: Tuition/fee waivers available for minority students.

FINANCIAL AID PICTURE (2015-2016)
Students with need: Out of 2,880 full-time freshmen who applied for aid, 2,422 were judged to have need. Of these, 2,401 received aid, and 709 had their full need met. Average financial aid package met 61% of need; average scholarship/grant was $6,319; average loan was $3,293. For part-time students, average financial aid package was $8,514.

Students without need: 998 full-time freshmen who did not demonstrate need for aid received scholarships/grants; average award was $3,872. No-need awards available for academics, alumni affiliation, art, athletics, job skills, leadership, minority status, music/drama, ROTC, state/district residency.

Scholarships offered: 94 full-time freshmen received athletic scholarships; average amount $20,949.

FINANCIAL AID PROCEDURES
Forms required: FAFSA, state aid form.
Dates and Deadlines: Priority date 3/1; no closing date. Applicants notified on a rolling basis starting 12/1; must reply by 5/1.
Transfers: No deadline. Applicants notified on a rolling basis.

CONTACT
Paul McKinney, Director
Box 6334, Mississippi State, MS 39762
(662) 325-2450

Mississippi University for Women
Columbus, Mississippi
www.muw.edu   Federal Code: 002422

4-year public university and liberal arts college in large town.
Enrollment: 2,308 undergrads.

BASIC COSTS (2016-2017)
Tuition and fees: $6,065; out-of-state residents $16,634.
Per-credit charge: $249; out-of-state residents $689.
Room and board: $6,902.
Additional info: Tuition/fee waivers available for adults, minority students.

FINANCIAL AID PICTURE
Students with need: Need-based aid available for full-time and part-time students. Work study available nights, weekends, and for part-time students.
Students without need: No-need awards available for academics, alumni affiliation, leadership, minority status, music/drama, ROTC, state/district residency.

FINANCIAL AID PROCEDURES
Forms required: FAFSA, state aid form.
Dates and Deadlines: Priority date 3/1; no closing date. Applicants notified on a rolling basis starting 3/15; must reply within 2 week(s) of notification.
Transfers: Closing date 4/1.

CONTACT
Nicole Patrick, Director of Financial Aid
1100 College St. MUW-1613, Columbus, MS 39701
(662) 329-7114

Northeast Mississippi Community College
Booneville, Mississippi
www.nemcc.edu   Federal Code: 002426

2-year public community college in small town.
Enrollment: 3,047 undergrads.
Selectivity: Open admission; but selective for some programs.

BASIC COSTS (2016-2017)
Tuition and fees: $2,630; out-of-state residents $4,880.
Room and board: $3,850.

FINANCIAL AID PICTURE (2015-2016)
Students with need: 71% of average financial aid package awarded as scholarships/grants, 29% awarded as loans/jobs. Need-based aid available for part-time students.
Students without need: No-need awards available for academics, alumni affiliation, athletics, leadership, music/drama.

FINANCIAL AID PROCEDURES
Forms required: FAFSA, institutional form.
Dates and Deadlines: Priority date 4/1; no closing date. Applicants notified on a rolling basis.
Transfers: No deadline.

CONTACT
Greg Windham, Director of Financial Aid
101 Cunningham Boulevard, Booneville, MS 38829

Northwest Mississippi Community College
Senatobia, Mississippi
www.northwestms.edu   Federal Code: 002427

2-year public community college in small town.
Enrollment: 8,220 undergrads.
Selectivity: Open admission; but selective for some programs.

BASIC COSTS (2016-2017)
Tuition and fees: $2,800; out-of-state residents $5,200.
Per-credit charge: $120; out-of-state residents $220.
Room and board: $3,550.

FINANCIAL AID PICTURE
Students with need: Need-based aid available for full-time students.

FINANCIAL AID PROCEDURES
Forms required: FAFSA.
Dates and Deadlines: Priority date 4/1; no closing date. Applicants notified by 8/16.

CONTACT
Director of Financial Aid
4975 Highway 51 North, Senatobia, MS 38668
(662) 562-3271

Pearl River Community College
Poplarville, Mississippi
www.prcc.edu   Federal Code: 002430

2-year public community college in small town.
Enrollment: 4,350 undergrads.
Selectivity: Open admission; but selective for some programs.

BASIC COSTS (2017-2018)
Tuition and fees: $3,100; out-of-state residents $5,498.
Room and board: $4,800.

FINANCIAL AID PICTURE
Students with need: Need-based aid available for full-time and part-time students.
Students without need: No-need awards available for academics, alumni affiliation, athletics, leadership, music/drama, state/district residency.

FINANCIAL AID PROCEDURES
Forms required: FAFSA, institutional form.

Dates and Deadlines: Priority date 4/17; no closing date. Applicants notified on a rolling basis.

CONTACT
Valerie Horne, Director of Financial Aid
101 Highway 11 North, Poplarville, MS 39470
(601) 403-1212

Rust College
Holly Springs, Mississippi
www.rustcollege.edu   Federal Code: 002433

4-year private liberal arts and teachers college in small town, affiliated with the United Methodist Church.
Enrollment: 1,004 undergrads, 13% part-time. 242 full-time freshmen.
Selectivity: Admits less than 50% of applicants.

BASIC COSTS (2016-2017)
Tuition and fees: $9,500.
Per-credit charge: $396.
Room and board: $4,100.
Additional info: Tuition at time of enrollment locked for 4 years.

FINANCIAL AID PICTURE (2015-2016)
Students with need: Out of 242 full-time freshmen who applied for aid, 242 were judged to have need. Of these, 231 received aid, and 11 had their full need met. Average financial aid package met 75% of need; average scholarship/grant was $5,699; average loan was $3,500. For part-time students, average financial aid package was $8,376.
Students without need: 15 full-time freshmen who did not demonstrate need for aid received scholarships/grants; average award was $3,434. No-need awards available for academics, leadership, music/drama, religious affiliation, state/district residency.

FINANCIAL AID PROCEDURES
Forms required: FAFSA, institutional form.
Dates and Deadlines: Priority date 3/15; closing date 6/30. Applicants notified on a rolling basis starting 4/1; must reply within 2 week(s) of notification.
Transfers: No deadline. Applicants notified on a rolling basis starting 4/1; must reply within 2 week(s) of notification. Transfer students cannot apply for the Honor Track Scholarship Program.

CONTACT
Helen Street, Director of Financial Aid
150 Rust Avenue, Holly Springs, MS 38635-2328
(662) 252-8000 ext. 4062

Southwest Mississippi Community College
Summit, Mississippi
www.smcc.edu   Federal Code: 002436

2-year public community college in rural community.
Enrollment: 1,742 undergrads.
Selectivity: Open admission; but selective for some programs.

BASIC COSTS (2016-2017)
Tuition and fees: $2,800; out-of-state residents $5,500.
Per-credit charge: $115; out-of-state residents $120.
Room and board: $3,670.

FINANCIAL AID PICTURE
Students with need: Need-based aid available for full-time and part-time students.

FINANCIAL AID PROCEDURES
Forms required: FAFSA.
Dates and Deadlines: Applicants notified on a rolling basis.

CONTACT
Joni Wilkinson, Director of Financial Aid
1156 College Drive, Summit, MS 39666
(601) 276-3708

Tougaloo College
Tougaloo, Mississippi
www.tougaloo.edu   Federal Code: 002439

4-year private liberal arts college in large city, affiliated with the United Church of Christ.
Enrollment: 839 undergrads, 3% part-time. 201 full-time freshmen.
Selectivity: Admits less than 50% of applicants.

BASIC COSTS (2016-2017)
Tuition and fees: $10,607.
Per-credit charge: $423.
Room and board: $6,400.
Additional info: Tuition/fee waivers available for adults.

FINANCIAL AID PICTURE
Students with need: Need-based aid available for full-time and part-time students.
Students without need: No-need awards available for academics, art, athletics, leadership, music/drama.

FINANCIAL AID PROCEDURES
Forms required: FAFSA, state aid form, institutional form.
Dates and Deadlines: Priority date 4/15; no closing date. Applicants notified on a rolling basis starting 5/1; must reply within 2 week(s) of notification.
Transfers: No deadline. Applicants notified on a rolling basis starting 2/1; must reply within 2 week(s) of notification.

CONTACT
Maria Thomas, Director of Financial Aid
500 West County Line Road, Tougaloo, MS 39174
(601) 977-7766

University of Mississippi
University, Mississippi
www.olemiss.edu   Federal Code: 002440

4-year public university in large town.
Enrollment: 18,975 undergrads, 7% part-time. 3,904 full-time freshmen.
Selectivity: Admits over 75% of applicants.

BASIC COSTS (2016-2017)
Tuition and fees: $7,754; out-of-state residents $22,022.
Per-credit charge: $319; out-of-state residents $913.
Room and board: $9,099.

FINANCIAL AID PICTURE (2015-2016)
Students with need: Out of 2,790 full-time freshmen who applied for aid, 1,859 were judged to have need. Of these, 1,810 received aid, and 329 had their full need met. Average financial aid package met 76% of need; average scholarship/grant was $9,519; average loan was $3,404. For part-time students, average financial aid package was $2,021.
Students without need: 1,314 full-time freshmen who did not demonstrate need for aid received scholarships/grants; average award was $8,036. No-need awards available for academics, alumni affiliation, art, athletics, leadership, music/drama, ROTC, state/district residency.
Scholarships offered: 52 full-time freshmen received athletic scholarships; average amount $16,687.

FINANCIAL AID PROCEDURES

Forms required: FAFSA.

Dates and Deadlines: Priority date 3/1; no closing date. Applicants notified on a rolling basis starting 4/1; must reply within 4 week(s) of notification.

Transfers: No deadline. Applicants notified on a rolling basis starting 4/1; must reply within 4 week(s) of notification.

CONTACT

Laura Diven-Brown, Director of Financial Aid
145 Martindale, University, MS 38677-1848
(800) 891-4596

University of Mississippi Medical Center

Jackson, Mississippi
www.umc.edu   Federal Code: 004688

Upper-division public health science college in large city.

Enrollment: 701 undergrads.

Selectivity: Open admission; but selective for some programs. GED not accepted.

BASIC COSTS (2016-2017)

Tuition and fees: $7,644; out-of-state residents $21,912.

Per-credit charge: $319; out-of-state residents $913.

FINANCIAL AID PICTURE

Students with need: Need-based aid available for full-time and part-time students.

Students without need: This college awards aid only to students with need.

FINANCIAL AID PROCEDURES

Forms required: FAFSA, state aid form, institutional form.

Dates and Deadlines: Closing date 4/1. Applicants notified by 7/15; must reply within 2 week(s) of notification.

CONTACT

Stacey Mathews, Director of Student Financial Aid
2500 North State Street, Jackson, MS 39216
(601) 984-1117

University of Southern Mississippi

Hattiesburg, Mississippi
www.usm.edu   Federal Code: 002441

4-year public university in small city.

Enrollment: 11,689 undergrads, 13% part-time. 1,513 full-time freshmen.

Selectivity: Admits less than 50% of applicants.

BASIC COSTS (2016-2017)

Tuition and fees: $7,334; out-of-state residents $16,204.

Per-credit charge: $306; out-of-state residents $675.

Room and board: $8,610.

FINANCIAL AID PICTURE (2015-2016)

Students with need: Out of 1,388 full-time freshmen who applied for aid, 1,159 were judged to have need. Of these, 1,150 received aid, and 392 had their full need met. Average financial aid package met 74% of need; average scholarship/grant was $4,999; average loan was $3,245. For part-time students, average financial aid package was $8,829.

Students without need: 159 full-time freshmen who did not demonstrate need for aid received scholarships/grants; average award was $6,732. No-need awards available for academics, alumni affiliation, art, athletics, music/drama, ROTC, state/district residency.

Scholarships offered: 86 full-time freshmen received athletic scholarships; average amount $9,936.

FINANCIAL AID PROCEDURES

Forms required: FAFSA.

Dates and Deadlines: Priority date 12/1; no closing date. Applicants notified on a rolling basis starting 12/15.

Transfers: Merit scholarships available to community college transfer students based on college GPA.

CONTACT

David Williamson, Director of Financial Aid
118 College Drive #5166, Hattiesburg, MS 39406-0001
(601) 266-4774

William Carey University

Hattiesburg, Mississippi
www.wmcarey.edu   Federal Code: 002447

4-year private university and liberal arts college in small city, affiliated with the Baptist faith.

Enrollment: 2,047 undergrads.

Selectivity: Open admission; but selective for some programs.

BASIC COSTS (2016-2017)

Tuition and fees: $11,700.

Per-credit charge: $360.

Room and board: $5,900.

FINANCIAL AID PICTURE

Students with need: Need-based aid available for full-time and part-time students. Work study available nights, weekends, and for part-time students.

Students without need: No-need awards available for academics, alumni affiliation, art, athletics, music/drama, religious affiliation.

FINANCIAL AID PROCEDURES

Forms required: FAFSA.

Dates and Deadlines: Priority date 4/1; closing date 9/1. Applicants notified on a rolling basis starting 6/1; must reply within 2 week(s) of notification.

CONTACT

William Curry, Director of Financial Aid
498 Tuscan Avenue, Hattiesburg, MS 39401
(601) 318-6153

Missouri

Avila University

Kansas City, Missouri
www.avila.edu   Federal Code: 002449

4-year private university and liberal arts college in very large city, affiliated with the Roman Catholic Church.

Enrollment: 1,279 undergrads, 14% part-time. 440 full-time freshmen.

Selectivity: Admits 50 to 75% of applicants.

BASIC COSTS (2016-2017)

Tuition and fees: $27,980.

Per-credit charge: $758.

Room and board: $6,900.

Additional info: Tuition/fee waivers available for adults.

FINANCIAL AID PICTURE (2015-2016)

Students with need: Out of 435 full-time freshmen who applied for aid, 407 were judged to have need. Of these, 405 received aid, and 60 had their full need met. Average financial aid package met 70% of need; average

scholarship/grant was $17,160; average loan was $3,463. For part-time students, average financial aid package was $5,286.

Students without need: 33 full-time freshmen who did not demonstrate need for aid received scholarships/grants; average award was $11,736. No-need awards available for academics, alumni affiliation, art, athletics, music/drama, religious affiliation.

Scholarships offered: 33 full-time freshmen received athletic scholarships; average amount $3,395.

Additional info: Financial aid adjusted based on need for increases in tuition.

FINANCIAL AID PROCEDURES

Forms required: FAFSA, institutional form.

Dates and Deadlines: Closing date 4/1. Applicants notified on a rolling basis starting 2/1; must reply within 2 week(s) of notification.

Transfers: No deadline. Applicants notified on a rolling basis starting 2/1; must reply within 2 week(s) of notification. Non-need-based academic scholarship available for transfer students.

CONTACT

Crystal Bruntz, Director of Financial Aid
11901 Wornall Road, Kansas City, MO 64145-1007
(816) 501-3600

Baptist Bible College
Springfield, Missouri
www.gobbc.edu   Federal Code: 013208

4-year private Bible and seminary college in small city, affiliated with the Baptist faith.

Enrollment: 321 undergrads.

Selectivity: Open admission.

BASIC COSTS (2016-2017)

Tuition and fees: $13,350.

Per-credit charge: $425.

Room and board: $7,280.

FINANCIAL AID PICTURE

Students with need: Need-based aid available for full-time and part-time students.

FINANCIAL AID PROCEDURES

Forms required: FAFSA, institutional form.

Dates and Deadlines: Closing date 5/1. Applicants notified on a rolling basis; must reply within 2 week(s) of notification.

CONTACT

Bob Kotulski, Financial Aid Director
628 East Kearney Street, Springfield, MO 65803
(417) 268-6036

Bolivar Technical College
Bolivar, Missouri
www.bolivarcollege.org   Federal Code: 035793

2-year private branch campus and technical college in small town.

Enrollment: 134 undergrads. 5 full-time freshmen.

Selectivity: Open admission; but selective for some programs.

BASIC COSTS (2016-2017)

Tuition and fees: $13,301.

Additional info: Tuition and fees quoted are for Professional Nursing program. Costs vary by program. Tuition/fee waivers available for adults.

FINANCIAL AID PICTURE (2016-2017)

Students with need: 42% of average financial aid package awarded as scholarships/grants, 58% awarded as loans/jobs. Need-based aid available for part-time students.

Students without need: This college awards aid only to students with need.

FINANCIAL AID PROCEDURES

Forms required: FAFSA, institutional form.

Dates and Deadlines: Priority date 4/1; no closing date.

Transfers: Priority date 4/1; no deadline. Applicants notified on a rolling basis.

CONTACT

Wendy McGowin, Financial Aid
PO Box 592, Bolivar, MO 65613
(417) 777-5062

Calvary Bible College and Theological Seminary
Kansas City, Missouri
www.calvary.edu   Federal Code: 002450

4-year private Bible and seminary college in large city, affiliated with the nondenominational tradition.

Enrollment: 194 undergrads, 32% part-time. 26 full-time freshmen.

Selectivity: Admits over 75% of applicants.

BASIC COSTS (2016-2017)

Tuition and fees: $12,370.

Per-credit charge: $375.

Room and board: $5,630.

Additional info: Tuition/fee waivers available for minority students.

FINANCIAL AID PICTURE (2015-2016)

Students with need: Need-based aid available for full-time and part-time students. Work study available nights, weekends, and for part-time students.

Students without need: No-need awards available for academics, alumni affiliation, music/drama, religious affiliation, ROTC.

FINANCIAL AID PROCEDURES

Forms required: FAFSA.

Dates and Deadlines: Closing date 4/1. Applicants notified on a rolling basis starting 5/1; must reply within 2 week(s) of notification.

Transfers: No deadline. Applicants notified on a rolling basis starting 6/1; must reply within 2 week(s) of notification.

CONTACT

Bob Crank, Financial Aid Director
15800 Calvary Road, Kansas City, MO 64147-1341
(816) 425-6136

Central Christian College of the Bible
Moberly, Missouri
www.cccb.edu   Federal Code: 014619

4-year private Bible college in large town, affiliated with the Christian Church.

Enrollment: 238 undergrads, 15% part-time. 58 full-time freshmen.

FINANCIAL AID PICTURE

Students with need: Need-based aid available for full-time and part-time students.

Scholarships offered: Each semester, 100 open Full-Tuition Scholarships are made available to new or transferring students who have been admitted into a degree or certificate program and attend classes on Moberly campus.

FINANCIAL AID PROCEDURES

Dates and Deadlines: Priority date 4/1; no closing date. Applicants notified on a rolling basis starting 3/1; must reply within 4 week(s) of notification.

Transfers: No deadline.

CONTACT

Rhonda Dunham, Financial Aid Director

911 East Urbandale Drive, Moberly, MO 65270-1997

(888) 263-3900 ext. 121

Central Methodist University

Fayette, Missouri

www.centralmethodist.edu   Federal Code: E00605

4-year private university and liberal arts college in small town, affiliated with the United Methodist Church.

Enrollment: 1,090 undergrads, 3% part-time. 263 full-time freshmen.

Selectivity: Admits 50 to 75% of applicants.

BASIC COSTS (2017-2018)

Tuition and fees: $23,770.

Per-credit charge: $210.

Room and board: $7,730.

FINANCIAL AID PICTURE (2016-2017)

Students with need: Out of 246 full-time freshmen who applied for aid, 229 were judged to have need. Of these, 229 received aid. Average financial aid package met 71% of need; average scholarship/grant was $5,325; average loan was $3,462. For part-time students, average financial aid package was $3,422.

Students without need: 22 full-time freshmen who did not demonstrate need for aid received scholarships/grants; average award was $11,470. No-need awards available for academics, alumni affiliation, athletics, leadership, music/drama, religious affiliation, ROTC.

Scholarships offered: 170 full-time freshmen received athletic scholarships; average amount $5,464.

FINANCIAL AID PROCEDURES

Forms required: FAFSA.

Dates and Deadlines: Applicants notified on a rolling basis starting 11/1; must reply by 8/5.

Transfers: No deadline. Applicants notified on a rolling basis. Merit based institutional financial aid is determined by college transfer GPA.

CONTACT

Kristen Gibbs, Director of Financial Assistance

411 Central Methodist Square, Fayette, MO 65248-1198

(660) 248-6245

Chamberlain College of Nursing: St. Louis

St Louis, Missouri

www.chamberlain.edu   Federal Code: 006385

4-year for-profit nursing college in very large city.

Enrollment: 510 undergrads.

BASIC COSTS (2016-2017)

Tuition and fees: $19,500.

Per-credit charge: $675.

FINANCIAL AID PICTURE

Students with need: Need-based aid available for full-time and part-time students.

Students without need: No-need awards available for academics.

Scholarships offered: Tenet Nurse Citizen Award: full tuition; based on application, essay, interview, renewable with 3.25 GPA, 1 awarded. Chancellor's Award: half tuition; for students with 24 ACT, 3.5 GPA; number awarded subject to fund availability. Merit Scholarships: up to $3,000; based on academic achievement; number awarded subject to fund availability.

FINANCIAL AID PROCEDURES

Forms required: FAFSA, institutional form.

Dates and Deadlines: Applicants notified on a rolling basis starting 4/1; must reply within 2 week(s) of notification.

Transfers: No deadline.

CONTACT

Michelle Mohn, Financial Counselor

11830 Westline Industrial Drive, Suite 106, St. Louis, MO 63146

(314) 768-5604

College of the Ozarks

Point Lookout, Missouri

www.cofo.edu   Federal Code: 002500

4-year private liberal arts college in small town, affiliated with the interdenominational tradition.

Enrollment: 1,512 undergrads, 1% part-time. 345 full-time freshmen.

Selectivity: Admits less than 50% of applicants.

BASIC COSTS (2017-2018)

Tuition and fees: $19,130.

Room and board: $7,100.

FINANCIAL AID PICTURE (2015-2016)

Students with need: Out of 345 full-time freshmen who applied for aid, 333 were judged to have need. Of these, 333 received aid, and 57 had their full need met. Average financial aid package met 78% of need; average scholarship/grant was $15,086. For part-time students, average financial aid package was $15,273.

Students without need: 12 full-time freshmen who did not demonstrate need for aid received scholarships/grants; average award was $14,492. No-need awards available for academics, art, athletics, leadership, minority status, music/drama, ROTC, state/district residency.

Scholarships offered: 7 full-time freshmen received athletic scholarships; average amount $3,142.

Additional info: The College guarantees to meet 100% of total cost for each full-time student without loans of any kind. All full-time students work on campus in exchange for full financial assistance for tuition.

FINANCIAL AID PROCEDURES

Forms required: FAFSA.

Dates and Deadlines: Priority date 2/15; no closing date. Applicants notified on a rolling basis starting 7/1.

Transfers: Applicants notified by 7/1.

CONTACT

Jeff Ford, Financial Aid Director

PO Box 17, Point Lookout, MO 65726-0017

(417) 690-3290

Columbia College

Columbia, Missouri

www.ccis.edu   Federal Code: 002456

4-year private liberal arts college in small city, affiliated with the Christian Church (Disciples of Christ).

Enrollment: 924 undergrads, 13% part-time. 124 full-time freshmen.

Selectivity: Admits 50 to 75% of applicants.

BASIC COSTS (2016-2017)

Tuition and fees: $20,936.
Per-credit charge: $450.
Room and board: $6,440.
Additional info: Entering students will pay a fixed rate that is good for five consecutive years. Lab fees may apply to some classes, all other fees are covered by cost of tuition. Tuition at time of enrollment locked for 4 years.

FINANCIAL AID PICTURE (2015-2016)

Students with need: Out of 98 full-time freshmen who applied for aid, 86 were judged to have need. Of these, 86 received aid, and 16 had their full need met. Average financial aid package met 69% of need; average scholarship/grant was $6,050; average loan was $3,007. For part-time students, average financial aid package was $7,219.
Students without need: 22 full-time freshmen who did not demonstrate need for aid received scholarships/grants; average award was $7,559. No-need awards available for academics, alumni affiliation, art, athletics, leadership, minority status, music/drama, religious affiliation, ROTC, state/district residency.
Scholarships offered: *Merit:* Columbia College Scholarship: full tuition, room/board; requires 3.5 GPA, 26 ACT/SAT equivalent, campus visit, interview, essay, 2 letters of recommendation, resume; renewable with 30 semester hours and 3.6 GPA. Presidential Scholarship: full tuition; requires 3.5 GPA, 26 ACT/SAT equivalent, campus visit, interview, essay, 2 letters of recommendation, resume; renewable with 30 semester hours and 3.6 GPA. Capstone scholarship: 60% of tuition; requires 28 ACT/SAT equivalent and 3.6 GPA; renewable with 3.6 GPA and 27 credits earned annually. Keystone Scholarship: 3.4 GPA or GED equivalent; 26 ACT/SAT equivalent; renewable with 27 credits per year and 3.4 GPA for up to 3 years. *Athletic:* 30 full-time freshmen received athletic scholarships; average amount $11,633.

FINANCIAL AID PROCEDURES

Forms required: FAFSA.
Dates and Deadlines: Priority date 3/1; no closing date. Applicants notified on a rolling basis starting 5/1.
Transfers: No deadline. Applicants notified by 5/1.

CONTACT

Nathan Miller, Senior Director of Student Success and Financial Aid
1001 Rogers Street, Columbia, MO 65216
(573) 875-7390

Conception Seminary College
Conception, Missouri
www.conception.edu
Federal Code: 002467

4-year private seminary college for men in rural community, affiliated with the Roman Catholic Church.
Enrollment: 95 undergrads. 11 full-time freshmen.

BASIC COSTS (2016-2017)

Tuition and fees: $20,706.
Room and board: $12,316.

FINANCIAL AID PICTURE

Students with need: Need-based aid available for full-time and part-time students. Work study available nights, weekends, and for part-time students.
Students without need: No-need awards available for academics.

FINANCIAL AID PROCEDURES

Forms required: FAFSA.
Dates and Deadlines: Applicants notified on a rolling basis starting 8/1; must reply by 8/20.

CONTACT

Justin Hernandez, Financial Aid Officer
Box 502, Conception, MO 64433-0502
(660) 944-2851

Cottey College
Nevada, Missouri
www.cottey.edu
Federal Code: 002458

4-year private liberal arts college for women in small town.
Enrollment: 283 undergrads, 1% part-time. 147 full-time freshmen.
Selectivity: Admits 50 to 75% of applicants.

BASIC COSTS (2017-2018)

Tuition and fees: $20,200.
Per-credit charge: $125.
Room and board: $7,400.

FINANCIAL AID PICTURE (2015-2016)

Students with need: Out of 123 full-time freshmen who applied for aid, 110 were judged to have need. Of these, 110 received aid, and 44 had their full need met. Average financial aid package met 86% of need; average scholarship/grant was $16,895; average loan was $2,827. For part-time students, average financial aid package was $6,191.
Students without need: 34 full-time freshmen who did not demonstrate need for aid received scholarships/grants; average award was $11,723. No-need awards available for academics, alumni affiliation, art, athletics, leadership, music/drama.
Scholarships offered: 7 full-time freshmen received athletic scholarships; average amount $4,326.

FINANCIAL AID PROCEDURES

Forms required: FAFSA.
Dates and Deadlines: Priority date 2/1; no closing date. Applicants notified on a rolling basis starting 4/1; must reply within 2 week(s) of notification.
Transfers: Applicants notified on a rolling basis starting 4/1; must reply within 2 week(s) of notification.

CONTACT

Sherry Pennington, Director of Financial Aid
1000 West Austin Boulevard, Nevada, MO 64772
(417) 667-8181 ext. 2190

Crowder College
Neosho, Missouri
www.crowder.edu
Federal Code: 002459

2-year public community and liberal arts college in small town.
Enrollment: 3,629 undergrads, 41% part-time. 855 full-time freshmen.
Selectivity: Open admission; but selective for some programs.

BASIC COSTS (2016-2017)

Tuition and fees: $3,060; out-of-district residents $4,260; out-of-state residents $4,260.
Per-credit charge: $82; out-of-district residents $122; out-of-state residents $122.
Room and board: $5,002.

FINANCIAL AID PICTURE

Students with need: Need-based aid available for full-time and part-time students. Work study available nights, weekends, and for part-time students.
Students without need: No-need awards available for academics, art, athletics, leadership, minority status, music/drama, state/district residency.

FINANCIAL AID PROCEDURES

Forms required: FAFSA, institutional form.
Dates and Deadlines: Priority date 7/1; no closing date. Applicants notified on a rolling basis starting 5/15; must reply within 4 week(s) of notification.

CONTACT

Stephanie Ferguson, Director of Financial Aid
601 Laclede Avenue, Neosho, MO 64850
(417) 451-3223 ext. 5434

Culver-Stockton College

Canton, Missouri
www.culver.edu   Federal Code: 002460

4-year private liberal arts college in small town, affiliated with the Christian Church (Disciples of Christ).
Enrollment: 998 undergrads, 5% part-time. 268 full-time freshmen.
Selectivity: Admits 50 to 75% of applicants.

BASIC COSTS (2017-2018)
Tuition and fees: $26,040.
Per-credit charge: $590.
Room and board: $8,310.

FINANCIAL AID PICTURE (2016-2017)
Students with need: Out of 250 full-time freshmen who applied for aid, 234 were judged to have need. Of these, 234 received aid, and 41 had their full need met. Average financial aid package met 71% of need; average scholarship/grant was $16,041; average loan was $3,212. For part-time students, average financial aid package was $6,520.
Students without need: 31 full-time freshmen who did not demonstrate need for aid received scholarships/grants; average award was $9,787. No-need awards available for academics, alumni affiliation, art, athletics, leadership, music/drama, religious affiliation.
Scholarships offered: 40 full-time freshmen received athletic scholarships; average amount $5,726.

FINANCIAL AID PROCEDURES
Forms required: FAFSA.
Dates and Deadlines: Priority date 3/1; closing date 6/1. Applicants notified on a rolling basis starting 2/15; must reply within 2 week(s) of notification.
Transfers: Must reply within 2 week(s) of notification.

CONTACT
Tina Wiseman, Director of Financial Aid
One College Hill, Canton, MO 63435-1299
(573) 288-6307

DeVry University: Kansas City

Kansas City, Missouri
www.devry.edu

4-year for-profit university in large city.
Enrollment: 423 undergrads.

BASIC COSTS (2016-2017)
Tuition and fees: $17,512.
Per-credit charge: $609.

FINANCIAL AID PICTURE
Students with need: Need-based aid available for full-time and part-time students.
Students without need: This college awards aid only to students with need.

FINANCIAL AID PROCEDURES
Forms required: FAFSA.
Dates and Deadlines: Applicants notified on a rolling basis.

CONTACT
11224 Holmes Street, Kansas City, MO 64131
(816) 941-0439

Drury University

Springfield, Missouri
www.drury.edu   Federal Code: 002461

4-year private university and liberal arts college in large city, affiliated with the United Church of Christ.
Enrollment: 1,367 undergrads, 2% part-time. 301 full-time freshmen.
Selectivity: Admits 50 to 75% of applicants.

BASIC COSTS (2017-2018)
Tuition and fees: $27,005.
Per-credit charge: $862.
Room and board: $8,036.

FINANCIAL AID PICTURE (2015-2016)
Students with need: Out of 249 full-time freshmen who applied for aid, 205 were judged to have need. Of these, 205 received aid, and 43 had their full need met. Average financial aid package met 73% of need; average scholarship/grant was $15,353; average loan was $4,176. For part-time students, average financial aid package was $10,211.
Students without need: 83 full-time freshmen who did not demonstrate need for aid received scholarships/grants; average award was $7,325. No-need awards available for academics, alumni affiliation, art, athletics, music/drama, religious affiliation.
Scholarships offered: *Merit:* Phi Theta Kappa Scholarship: $1,000. **Athletic:** 38 full-time freshmen received athletic scholarships; average amount $15,936.

FINANCIAL AID PROCEDURES
Dates and Deadlines: Priority date 1/10; no closing date. Applicants notified on a rolling basis starting 12/15; must reply by 5/1.
Transfers: No deadline.

CONTACT
Becky Ahrens, Director of Financial Aid
900 North Benton Avenue, Springfield, MO 65802-3712
(417) 873-7523

East Central College

Union, Missouri
www.eastcentral.edu   Federal Code: 008862

2-year public community college in large town.
Enrollment: 2,338 undergrads, 42% part-time. 525 full-time freshmen.
Selectivity: Open admission; but selective for some programs.

BASIC COSTS (2017-2018)
Tuition and fees: $2,970; out-of-district residents $4,020; out-of-state residents $5,730.
Per-credit charge: $76; out-of-district residents $111; out-of-state residents $168.

FINANCIAL AID PICTURE
Students with need: Need-based aid available for full-time and part-time students.
Students without need: No-need awards available for academics, alumni affiliation, art, athletics, music/drama, state/district residency.

FINANCIAL AID PROCEDURES
Forms required: FAFSA.
Dates and Deadlines: Priority date 3/15; no closing date. Applicants notified on a rolling basis starting 4/1.
Transfers: No deadline. Applicants notified on a rolling basis starting 4/1.

CONTACT
Karen Griffin, Director of Financial Aid
1964 Prairie Dell Road, Union, MO 63084-0529
(636) 584-6588

Evangel University
Springfield, Missouri
www.evangel.edu   Federal Code: 002463

4-year private liberal arts college in small city, affiliated with the Assemblies of God.
Enrollment: 1,619 undergrads, 9% part-time. 362 full-time freshmen.
Selectivity: Admits over 75% of applicants.

BASIC COSTS (2016-2017)
Tuition and fees: $22,081.
Room and board: $7,882.

FINANCIAL AID PICTURE (2015-2016)
Students with need: Out of 357 full-time freshmen who applied for aid, 309 were judged to have need. Of these, 309 received aid, and 38 had their full need met. Average financial aid package met 69% of need; average scholarship/grant was $12,992; average loan was $3,518. For part-time students, average financial aid package was $6,573.
Students without need: This college awards aid only to students with need.
Scholarships offered: 17 full-time freshmen received athletic scholarships; average amount $7,949.

FINANCIAL AID PROCEDURES
Forms required: FAFSA.
Dates and Deadlines: Applicants notified on a rolling basis starting 3/15.

CONTACT
Valerie Sharp, Director of Student Financial Services
1111 North Glenstone, Springfield, MO 65802
(417) 865-2811 ext. 7300

Fontbonne University
St. Louis, Missouri
www.fontbonne.edu   Federal Code: 002464

4-year private university and liberal arts college in large city, affiliated with the Roman Catholic Church.
Enrollment: 953 undergrads, 14% part-time. 141 full-time freshmen.

BASIC COSTS (2016-2017)
Tuition and fees: $24,610.
Per-credit charge: $648.
Room and board: $9,107.

FINANCIAL AID PICTURE (2016-2017)
Students with need: 64% of average financial aid package awarded as scholarships/grants, 36% awarded as loans/jobs. Need-based aid available for part-time students. Work study available nights, weekends, and for part-time students.
Students without need: No-need awards available for academics, alumni affiliation, art, leadership, minority status, music/drama, religious affiliation, state/district residency.

FINANCIAL AID PROCEDURES
Forms required: FAFSA, institutional form.
Dates and Deadlines: Priority date 3/15; no closing date. Applicants notified on a rolling basis starting 2/1; must reply within 2 week(s) of notification.
Transfers: Priority date 2/1; closing date 4/1. Applicants notified on a rolling basis starting 3/1; must reply within 2 week(s) of notification.

CONTACT
Matthew Kearney, Director of Financial Aid
6800 Wydown Boulevard, Saint Louis, MO 63105-3098
(314) 889-1414

Goldfarb School of Nursing at Barnes-Jewish College
St. Louis, Missouri
www.barnesjewishcollege.edu   Federal Code: 003689

Upper-division private nursing college in very large city.
Enrollment: 616 undergrads, 11% part-time.

BASIC COSTS (2017-2018)
Tuition and fees: $20,188.
Per-credit charge: $733.

FINANCIAL AID PICTURE (2015-2016)
Students with need: Average financial aid package for all full-time undergraduates was $3,617; for part-time $3,913. 15% awarded as scholarships/grants, 85% awarded as loans/jobs.
Students without need: No-need awards available for academics, leadership, minority status.

FINANCIAL AID PROCEDURES
Forms required: FAFSA.
Dates and Deadlines: Priority date 2/1; no closing date. Applicants notified on a rolling basis.
Transfers: No deadline. Applicants notified on a rolling basis.

CONTACT
Jason Crowe, Enrollment Manager
4483 Duncan Avenue, St. Louis, MO 63110-1091
(314) 362-9250

Hannibal-LaGrange University
Hannibal, Missouri
www.hlg.edu   Federal Code: 009089

4-year private university and liberal arts college in large town, affiliated with the Southern Baptist Convention.
Enrollment: 1,291 undergrads.

BASIC COSTS (2016-2017)
Tuition and fees: $21,710.
Room and board: $7,608.

FINANCIAL AID PICTURE
Students with need: Need-based aid available for full-time and part-time students.
Students without need: No-need awards available for academics, art, athletics, music/drama, religious affiliation.
Additional info: Work-study opportunities vary according to on-and off-campus needs.

FINANCIAL AID PROCEDURES
Dates and Deadlines: Applicants notified on a rolling basis; must reply by 8/31.
Transfers: No deadline.

CONTACT
Brice Baumgardner, Financial Aid Director
2800 Palmyra Road, Hannibal, MO 63401
(573) 629-3280

Harris-Stowe State University
St. Louis, Missouri
www.hssu.edu   Federal Code: 002466

4-year public business and teachers college in very large city.
Enrollment: 1,445 undergrads, 20% part-time. 265 full-time freshmen.

Selectivity: Open admission.

BASIC COSTS (2016-2017)

Tuition and fees: $5,220; out-of-state residents $9,853.

Per-credit charge: $199; out-of-state residents $392.

Room and board: $9,250.

Additional info: Book Fee $300 projected cost (opt-out-option).

FINANCIAL AID PICTURE (2015-2016)

Students with need: Out of 261 full-time freshmen who applied for aid, 242 were judged to have need. Of these, 242 received aid, and 186 had their full need met. Average financial aid package met 83% of need; average scholarship/grant was $6,956; average loan was $2,701. For part-time students, average financial aid package was $7,502.

Students without need: 23 full-time freshmen who did not demonstrate need for aid received scholarships/grants; average award was $2,532. No-need awards available for academics, alumni affiliation, art, athletics, leadership, music/drama, state/district residency.

Scholarships offered: 5 full-time freshmen received athletic scholarships; average amount $1,068.

FINANCIAL AID PROCEDURES

Forms required: FAFSA, institutional form.

Dates and Deadlines: Closing date 4/1. Applicants notified on a rolling basis starting 4/1; must reply within 3 week(s) of notification.

Transfers: Priority date 4/1. Applicants notified on a rolling basis starting 4/1; must reply within 3 week(s) of notification.

CONTACT

James Green, Director of Financial Assistance

3026 Laclede Avenue, St. Louis, MO 63103-2199

(314) 340-3500

Hickey College

St. Louis, Missouri

www.hickeycollege.edu   Federal Code: 014209

4-year for-profit business and technical college in very large city.

Enrollment: 372 undergrads.

Selectivity: Open admission; but selective for some programs.

BASIC COSTS (2016-2017)

Additional info: Diploma programs: $13,930-$21,800, books and supplies $2,070-$2,785, room and board $5,960-$8,940. Associate programs: $27,810-$31,710, books and supplies $2,610-$3,260, room and board $11,920-$13,410. Bachelor's program: $45,404, books and supplies $4,717, room and board $26,820.

FINANCIAL AID PICTURE

Students with need: Need-based aid available for full-time students.

FINANCIAL AID PROCEDURES

Forms required: FAFSA.

Dates and Deadlines: Applicants notified on a rolling basis.

CONTACT

Deana Pecoroni, Director, Student Services

940 West Port Plaza, St. Louis, MO 63146

(314) 434-2212 ext. 128

Jefferson College

Hillsboro, Missouri

www.jeffco.edu   Federal Code: 002468

2-year public community and technical college in rural community.

Enrollment: 4,496 undergrads, 51% part-time. 817 full-time freshmen.

Selectivity: Open admission; but selective for some programs.

BASIC COSTS (2016-2017)

Tuition and fees: $3,000; out-of-district residents $4,470; out-of-state residents $5,910.

Per-credit charge: $97; out-of-district residents $146; out-of-state residents $194.

Room and board: $5,644.

FINANCIAL AID PICTURE (2015-2016)

Students with need: Out of 773 full-time freshmen who applied for aid, 566 were judged to have need. Of these, 546 received aid, and 10 had their full need met. Average financial aid package met 53% of need; average scholarship/grant was $2,441; average loan was $2,716. For part-time students, average financial aid package was $3,458.

Students without need: No-need awards available for academics, art, athletics, leadership, music/drama, state/district residency.

Scholarships offered: 39 full-time freshmen received athletic scholarships; average amount $5,727.

FINANCIAL AID PROCEDURES

Forms required: FAFSA.

Dates and Deadlines: Priority date 6/1; no closing date. Applicants notified on a rolling basis starting 4/15.

CONTACT

Sarah Bright, Director of Student Financial Services

1000 Viking Drive, Hillsboro, MO 63050-2441

(636) 481-3212

Kansas City Art Institute

Kansas City, Missouri

www.kcai.edu   Federal Code: 002473

4-year private visual arts college in large city.

Enrollment: 629 undergrads, 1% part-time. 163 full-time freshmen.

Selectivity: Admits 50 to 75% of applicants.

BASIC COSTS (2017-2018)

Tuition and fees: $37,800.

Per-credit charge: $1,510.

Room and board: $10,400.

FINANCIAL AID PICTURE (2016-2017)

Students with need: Out of 155 full-time freshmen who applied for aid, 143 were judged to have need. Of these, 142 received aid, and 14 had their full need met. Average financial aid package met 61% of need; average scholarship/grant was $23,282; average loan was $3,382. For part-time students, average financial aid package was $8,611.

Students without need: 19 full-time freshmen who did not demonstrate need for aid received scholarships/grants; average award was $18,855. No-need awards available for academics, art.

Scholarships offered: Merit scholarships: priority application dates 2/1 and 3/1; deadline 8/1.

FINANCIAL AID PROCEDURES

Forms required: FAFSA.

Dates and Deadlines: Priority date 3/15; closing date 4/1. Applicants notified on a rolling basis starting 4/1; must reply within 2 week(s) of notification.

Transfers: No deadline. Applicants notified on a rolling basis starting 4/1; must reply within 2 week(s) of notification.

CONTACT

Lori Baer, Director of Financial Aid

4415 Warwick Boulevard, Kansas City, MO 64111

(816) 802-3337

Lincoln University

Jefferson City, Missouri
www.lincolnu.edu   Federal Code: 002479

4-year public university and liberal arts college in large town.
Enrollment: 2,113 undergrads, 14% part-time. 452 full-time freshmen.
Selectivity: Open admission; but selective for some programs and for out-of-state students.

BASIC COSTS (2016-2017)
Tuition and fees: $7,042; out-of-state residents $13,432.
Per-credit charge: $205; out-of-state residents $418.
Room and board: $6,560.

FINANCIAL AID PICTURE (2016-2017)
Students with need: Out of 432 full-time freshmen who applied for aid, 396 were judged to have need. Of these, 387 received aid, and 27 had their full need met. Average financial aid package met 59% of need; average scholarship/grant was $6,340; average loan was $3,440. For part-time students, average financial aid package was $6,400.
Students without need: 1 full-time freshmen who did not demonstrate need for aid received scholarships/grants; average award was $3,000. No-need awards available for academics, art, athletics, job skills, leadership, minority status, music/drama, ROTC, state/district residency.
Scholarships offered: 4 full-time freshmen received athletic scholarships; average amount $4,974.

FINANCIAL AID PROCEDURES
Forms required: FAFSA, institutional form.
Dates and Deadlines: Priority date 3/1; no closing date. Applicants notified on a rolling basis starting 1/15; must reply within 2 week(s) of notification.
Transfers: No deadline. Applicants notified on a rolling basis starting 1/15; must reply within 2 week(s) of notification.

CONTACT
Alfred Robinson, Director of Financial Aid and Student Employment
820 Chestnut Street, B7 Young Hall, Jefferson City, MO 65101
(573) 681-6156

Lindenwood University

St. Charles, Missouri
www.lindenwood.edu   Federal Code: 002480

4-year private university and liberal arts college in small city, affiliated with the Presbyterian Church (USA).
Enrollment: 7,331 undergrads, 8% part-time. 989 full-time freshmen.
Selectivity: Admits 50 to 75% of applicants.

BASIC COSTS (2016-2017)
Tuition and fees: $16,332.
Per-credit charge: $453.
Room and board: $8,800.

FINANCIAL AID PICTURE (2016-2017)
Students with need: Out of 687 full-time freshmen who applied for aid, 516 were judged to have need. Of these, 516 received aid, and 129 had their full need met. Average financial aid package met 80% of need; average scholarship/grant was $7,712; average loan was $3,293. For part-time students, average financial aid package was $5,199.
Students without need: 391 full-time freshmen who did not demonstrate need for aid received scholarships/grants; average award was $6,915. No-need awards available for academics, art, athletics, leadership, music/drama, ROTC.
Scholarships offered: 93 full-time freshmen received athletic scholarships; average amount $10,058.

FINANCIAL AID PROCEDURES
Forms required: FAFSA.

Dates and Deadlines: Priority date 4/1; no closing date. Applicants notified on a rolling basis.

CONTACT
Lori Bode, Director, Financial Aid
209 South Kingshighway, St. Charles, MO 63301
(636) 949-4923

Logan University

Chesterfield, Missouri
www.logan.edu   Federal Code: 004703

3-year private university in small city.
Enrollment: 93 undergrads, 45% part-time.

BASIC COSTS (2016-2017)
Tuition and fees: $8,380.
Per-credit charge: $275.

FINANCIAL AID PICTURE (2015-2016)
Students with need: Average financial aid package for all full-time undergraduates was $9,312; for part-time $5,719. 19% awarded as scholarships/grants, 81% awarded as loans/jobs.

FINANCIAL AID PROCEDURES
Transfers: No deadline. Applicants notified on a rolling basis starting 7/16; must reply by 9/16.

CONTACT
Kerry Hallahan, Director of Financial Aid
1851 Schoettler Road, Chesterfield, MO 63017
(800) 782-3344

Maryville University of Saint Louis

St. Louis, Missouri
www.maryville.edu   Federal Code: 002482

4-year private university in very large city.
Enrollment: 2,892 undergrads, 26% part-time. 554 full-time freshmen.
Selectivity: Admits over 75% of applicants.

BASIC COSTS (2016-2017)
Tuition and fees: $27,958.
Per-credit charge: $766.
Room and board: $10,088.

FINANCIAL AID PICTURE (2016-2017)
Students with need: Out of 446 full-time freshmen who applied for aid, 397 were judged to have need. Of these, 397 received aid, and 63 had their full need met. Average financial aid package met 60% of need; average scholarship/grant was $18,465; average loan was $2,767. For part-time students, average financial aid package was $9,422.
Students without need: 153 full-time freshmen who did not demonstrate need for aid received scholarships/grants; average award was $14,015. No-need awards available for academics, art, athletics, leadership, minority status, music/drama, ROTC, state/district residency.
Scholarships offered: Merit: University Scholars Program: awarded to full-time freshmen with 28 ACT or 1170 SAT (exclusive of Writing), high school GPA 3.5-4.0; interview required. M-PACT Award: awarded to full-time freshmen based on campus activity and impact on student life. **Athletic:** 57 full-time freshmen received athletic scholarships; average amount $11,487.

FINANCIAL AID PROCEDURES
Forms required: FAFSA.
Dates and Deadlines: Priority date 3/1; no closing date. Applicants notified on a rolling basis starting 3/1; must reply by 5/1 or within 2 week(s) of notification.

Transfers: No deadline. Applicants notified on a rolling basis starting 2/1; must reply by 5/1 or within 2 week(s) of notification. Scholarships available for transfer students.

CONTACT
Martha Harbaugh, Director of Financial Aid
650 Maryville University Drive, St. Louis, MO 63141-7299
(314) 529-9361

Metro Business College
Cape Girardeau, Missouri
www.metrobusinesscollege.edu   Federal Code: 021802

2-year for-profit career college in large town.
Enrollment: 118 undergrads. 15 full-time freshmen.
Selectivity: Open admission.

BASIC COSTS (2016-2017)
Additional info: Tuition by program: Medical billing/coding specialist $21,600; business/computer specialist $21,225; medical specialist $18,875; medical assistant $11,675; administrative assistant $10,925; massage therapy $11,325.

FINANCIAL AID PICTURE (2015-2016)
Students with need: Out of 15 full-time freshmen who applied for aid, 15 were judged to have need. Of these, 15 received aid.

FINANCIAL AID PROCEDURES
Transfers: No deadline. Applicants notified on a rolling basis.

CONTACT
Janie Warne, Financial Aid Director
1732 North Kingshighway, Cape Girardeau, MO 63701
(573) 334-9181

Metro Business College: Jefferson City
Jefferson City, Missouri
www.metrobusinesscollege.edu   Federal Code: 014710

2-year for-profit health science and career college in large town.
Enrollment: 32 undergrads, 9% part-time. 5 full-time freshmen.
Selectivity: Open admission; but selective for some programs.

BASIC COSTS (2016-2017)
Additional info: Tuition by program: Medical billing/coding specialist $21,600; business/computer specialist $21,225; medical specialist $18,875; medical assistant $11,675; administrative assistant $10,925; massage therapy $11,325. Tuition at time of enrollment locked for 2 years.

FINANCIAL AID PICTURE
Students with need: Need-based aid available for full-time and part-time students.

FINANCIAL AID PROCEDURES
Forms required: FAFSA, institutional form.
Dates and Deadlines: Applicants notified on a rolling basis.

CONTACT
Debbie Jenkins, Financial Aid Coordinator
210 El Mercado Plaza, Jefferson City, MO 65109
(573) 635-6600

Metropolitan Community College - Kansas City
Kansas City, Missouri
www.mcckc.edu   Federal Code: 002484

2-year public community college in large city.
Enrollment: 15,158 undergrads, 58% part-time. 2,256 full-time freshmen.
Selectivity: Open admission; but selective for some programs.

BASIC COSTS (2016-2017)
Tuition and fees: $2,890; out-of-district residents $5,290; out-of-state residents $6,910.
Per-credit charge: $95; out-of-district residents $175; out-of-state residents $229.

FINANCIAL AID PICTURE
Students with need: Need-based aid available for full-time students. Work study available nights.
Students without need: No-need awards available for academics, athletics, leadership.

FINANCIAL AID PROCEDURES
Forms required: FAFSA, institutional form.
Dates and Deadlines: Priority date 5/30; closing date 6/30. Applicants notified on a rolling basis starting 4/8.

CONTACT
Dena Norris, Director of Student Financial Aid Services
3200 Broadway, Kansas City, MO 64111
(816) 604-1527

Mineral Area College
Park Hills, Missouri
www.mineralarea.edu   Federal Code: 002486

2-year public community college in small town.
Enrollment: 2,157 undergrads.
Selectivity: Open admission; but selective for some programs.

BASIC COSTS (2016-2017)
Tuition and fees: $3,220; out-of-district residents $4,240; out-of-state residents $5,620.
Room and board: $6,994.

FINANCIAL AID PICTURE
Students with need: Need-based aid available for full-time and part-time students.
Students without need: No-need awards available for academics, alumni affiliation, art, athletics, leadership, music/drama, state/district residency.

FINANCIAL AID PROCEDURES
Forms required: FAFSA.
Dates and Deadlines: Closing date 4/1. Applicants notified on a rolling basis starting 2/15; must reply within 4 week(s) of notification.

CONTACT
Denise Sebastian, Financial Aid Director
PO Box 1000, Park Hills, MO 63601-1000
(573) 518-2133

Missouri Baptist University
St. Louis, Missouri
www.mobap.edu   Federal Code: 007540

4-year private university and liberal arts college in very large city, affiliated with the Baptist faith.

Enrollment: 1,846 undergrads, 22% part-time. 280 full-time freshmen.
Selectivity: Admits 50 to 75% of applicants.

BASIC COSTS (2016-2017)
Tuition and fees: $24,924.
Per-credit charge: $821.
Room and board: $9,940.

FINANCIAL AID PICTURE (2015-2016)
Students with need: 46% of average financial aid package awarded as scholarships/grants, 54% awarded as loans/jobs. Need-based aid available for part-time students. Work study available nights, weekends, and for part-time students.
Students without need: No-need awards available for academics, alumni affiliation, athletics, leadership, music/drama, religious affiliation.

FINANCIAL AID PROCEDURES
Forms required: FAFSA, institutional form.
Dates and Deadlines: Priority date 4/1; no closing date. Applicants notified on a rolling basis starting 4/16; must reply within 2 week(s) of notification.
Transfers: No deadline. Applicants notified on a rolling basis; must reply within 2 week(s) of notification. Institutional academic scholarships available.

CONTACT
Zach Greenlee, Acting Director of Student Financial Services
One College Park Drive, St. Louis, MO 63141-8660
(314) 392-2366

Missouri College
Brentwood, Missouri
www.missouricollege.com   Federal Code: 009795

2-year for-profit technical college in large city.
Enrollment: 553 undergrads.
Selectivity: Open admission; but selective for some programs.

FINANCIAL AID PICTURE
Students with need: Need-based aid available for full-time and part-time students. Work study available nights.

FINANCIAL AID PROCEDURES
Forms required: FAFSA.

CONTACT
Jennifer Malotte, Director of Student Finance
1405 South Hanley Road, Brentwood, MO 63144
(314) 821-7700

Missouri Southern State University
Joplin, Missouri
www.mssu.edu   Federal Code: 002488

4-year public university and liberal arts college in small city.
Enrollment: 5,477 undergrads.

BASIC COSTS (2016-2017)
Tuition and fees: $5,877; out-of-state residents $11,283.
Per-credit charge: $177; out-of-state residents $357.
Room and board: $6,627.

FINANCIAL AID PICTURE
Students with need: Need-based aid available for full-time and part-time students.
Students without need: No-need awards available for academics, alumni affiliation, art, athletics, job skills, leadership, minority status, music/drama, religious affiliation, state/district residency.

FINANCIAL AID PROCEDURES
Forms required: FAFSA.
Dates and Deadlines: Applicants notified on a rolling basis starting 3/15; must reply by 5/1.

CONTACT
Rebecca Diskin, Director of Student Financial Aid
3950 East Newman Road, Joplin, MO 64801-1595
(417) 625-9325

Missouri State University
Springfield, Missouri
www.missouristate.edu   Federal Code: 002503

4-year public university in small city.
Enrollment: 17,300 undergrads, 13% part-time. 3,158 full-time freshmen.
Selectivity: Admits over 75% of applicants.

BASIC COSTS (2016-2017)
Tuition and fees: $7,076; out-of-state residents $14,126.
Per-credit charge: $205; out-of-state residents $440.
Room and board: $7,826.

FINANCIAL AID PICTURE (2016-2017)
Students with need: Out of 2,744 full-time freshmen who applied for aid, 1,895 were judged to have need. Of these, 1,864 received aid, and 356 had their full need met. Average financial aid package met 64% of need; average scholarship/grant was $6,452; average loan was $3,440. For part-time students, average financial aid package was $5,994.
Students without need: 608 full-time freshmen who did not demonstrate need for aid received scholarships/grants; average award was $3,039. No-need awards available for academics, alumni affiliation, art, athletics, job skills, leadership, minority status, music/drama, ROTC, state/district residency.
Scholarships offered: *Merit:* Presidential Scholarship: $12,500 per year plus a full waiver of non-resident fees for non-Missouri residents; based on 30 ACT and either top 10% class rank or 3.90 GPA; 30 awarded. Board of Governors Scholarship: $5,000 per year plus a full waiver of non-resident fees; based on 28 ACT and either top 10% class rank or 3.90 GPA; unlimited number of awards. Provost Scholarship: $2,500 per year plus a full waiver of non-resident fees; based on 26 ACT and either top 20% class rank or 3.70 GPA; unlimited number of awards. Multicultural Leadership Scholarship: $6,250 per year for students in top half of class or 3.00 GPA and who have demonstrated leadership in multicultural school or community activities; 50 awarded. Dean's Scholarship: $1,500 per year plus a full waiver of non-resident fees; based on 24 ACT and either top 10% class rank or 3.90 GPA; unlimited number of awards. *Athletic:* 45 full-time freshmen received athletic scholarships; average amount $14,241.
Additional info: Extensive scholarship program offered to freshmen and transfer students. Out-of-state fee stipends available. Student employment service available to assist students in securing employment on campus and in community.

FINANCIAL AID PROCEDURES
Forms required: FAFSA.
Dates and Deadlines: Priority date 3/31; no closing date. Applicants notified on a rolling basis starting 3/31.
Transfers: No deadline. Applicants notified on a rolling basis.

CONTACT
Vicki Mattocks, Director of Financial Aid
901 South National Avenue, Springfield, MO 65897
(417) 836-5262

Missouri State University: West Plains

West Plains, Missouri
www.wp.missouristate.edu   Federal Code: 031060

2-year public branch campus and liberal arts college in large town.
Enrollment: 1,554 undergrads.
Selectivity: Open admission; but selective for some programs.

BASIC COSTS (2016-2017)

Tuition and fees: $3,890; out-of-state residents $7,460.
Per-credit charge: $119; out-of-state residents $238.
Room and board: $5,702.

FINANCIAL AID PICTURE

Students with need: Need-based aid available for full-time and part-time students. Work study available nights, weekends, and for part-time students.
Students without need: No-need awards available for academics, athletics, state/district residency.

FINANCIAL AID PROCEDURES

Forms required: FAFSA, institutional form.
Dates and Deadlines: Priority date 3/31; no closing date. Applicants notified on a rolling basis; must reply by 4/15.

CONTACT

Donna Bassham, Coordinator of Financial Aid
128 Garfield Avenue, West Plains, MO 65775-2715
(417) 255-7243

Missouri University of Science and Technology

Rolla, Missouri
www.mst.edu   Federal Code: 002517

4-year public university in large town.
Enrollment: 6,857 undergrads, 10% part-time. 1,474 full-time freshmen.
Selectivity: Admits over 75% of applicants.

BASIC COSTS (2016-2017)

Tuition and fees: $9,629; out-of-state residents $26,897.
Per-credit charge: $276; out-of-state residents $852.
Room and board: $9,935.
Additional info: Tuition/fee waivers available for minority students.

FINANCIAL AID PICTURE (2015-2016)

Students with need: Out of 836 full-time freshmen who applied for aid, 790 were judged to have need. Of these, 790 received aid, and 153 had their full need met. Average financial aid package met 29% of need; average scholarship/grant was $10,282; average loan was $7,108. For part-time students, average financial aid package was $7,536.
Students without need: 297 full-time freshmen who did not demonstrate need for aid received scholarships/grants; average award was $6,492. No-need awards available for academics, alumni affiliation, athletics, job skills, leadership, minority status, music/drama, religious affiliation, ROTC, state/district residency.
Scholarships offered: 67 full-time freshmen received athletic scholarships; average amount $10,719.

FINANCIAL AID PROCEDURES

Forms required: FAFSA.
Dates and Deadlines: Priority date 3/1; no closing date. Applicants notified on a rolling basis starting 4/1; must reply within 3 week(s) of notification.
Transfers: Special scholarships available to transfer students.

CONTACT

Bridgette Betz, Director of Financial Assistance
106 Parker Hall, Rolla, MO 65409-1060
(573) 341-4282

Missouri Valley College

Marshall, Missouri
www.moval.edu   Federal Code: 002489

4-year private liberal arts college in large town, affiliated with the Presbyterian Church (USA).
Enrollment: 1,380 undergrads.
Selectivity: Admits less than 50% of applicants.

BASIC COSTS (2016-2017)

Tuition and fees: $19,750.
Room and board: $8,400.

FINANCIAL AID PICTURE

Students with need: Need-based aid available for full-time and part-time students. Work study available nights, weekends, and for part-time students.
Students without need: No-need awards available for academics, state/district residency.
Scholarships offered: Talent scholarships: $1,000 to $13,000; for general achievement, 100 awarded.

FINANCIAL AID PROCEDURES

Forms required: FAFSA.
Dates and Deadlines: Priority date 3/15; no closing date. Applicants notified on a rolling basis starting 2/1; must reply within 6 week(s) of notification.
Transfers: No deadline. Applicants notified on a rolling basis starting 3/14; must reply within 3 week(s) of notification.

CONTACT

Paul Gordon, Director of Financial Aid
500 East College Street, Marshall, MO 65340
(660) 831-4176

Missouri Western State University

St Joseph, Missouri
www.missouriwestern.edu   Federal Code: 002490

4-year public university and liberal arts college in small city.
Enrollment: 4,150 undergrads.
Selectivity: Open admission; but selective for some programs.

BASIC COSTS (2016-2017)

Tuition and fees: $6,652; out-of-state residents $13,080.
Per-credit charge: $198; out-of-state residents $412.
Room and board: $8,565.

FINANCIAL AID PICTURE

Students with need: Need-based aid available for full-time and part-time students.
Students without need: No-need awards available for academics, alumni affiliation, art, athletics, job skills, leadership, minority status, music/drama, state/district residency.
Scholarships offered: Golden Griffon Scholarship: up to $10,000 per year for 4 years; 27 ACT, top 10% of class or 3.5 GPA; evidence of involvement in extracurricular activities and community service; 2 essays and personal interview required; application deadline 2/1. President's Academic Scholarship: up to $4,000 per year; 25 ACT and either rank in the top 15% of class or 3.25 GPA required; application deadline 3/1.

FINANCIAL AID PROCEDURES

Forms required: FAFSA, institutional form.
Dates and Deadlines: Priority date 3/1; no closing date. Applicants notified on a rolling basis starting 4/5; must reply within 3 week(s) of notification.
Transfers: No deadline. Applicants notified on a rolling basis starting 4/15; must reply within 2 week(s) of notification.

CONTACT

Marilyn Baker, Director of Financial Aid
4525 Downs Drive, Saint Joseph, MO 64507
(816) 271-4361

Moberly Area Community College

Moberly, Missouri
www.macc.edu   Federal Code: 002491

2-year public community college in large town.
Enrollment: 5,800 undergrads.
Selectivity: Open admission; but selective for some programs.

BASIC COSTS (2016-2017)

Tuition and fees: $3,120; out-of-district residents $4,770; out-of-state residents $6,360.
Per-credit charge: $86; out-of-district residents $141; out-of-state residents $194.
Room and board: $5,200.

FINANCIAL AID PICTURE

Students with need: Need-based aid available for full-time and part-time students. Work study available nights, weekends, and for part-time students.
Students without need: No-need awards available for academics, alumni affiliation, art, athletics, leadership, music/drama.

FINANCIAL AID PROCEDURES

Forms required: FAFSA.
Dates and Deadlines: Priority date 4/1; no closing date. Applicants notified on a rolling basis starting 4/1; must reply by 7/15 or within 2 week(s) of notification.

CONTACT

Amy Hager, Director of Financial Aid
101 College Avenue, Moberly, MO 65270-1304
(660) 263-4110 ext. 301

National American University: Kansas City

Independence, Missouri
www.national.edu

4-year for-profit university in large city.
Enrollment: 646 undergrads.
Selectivity: Open admission.

BASIC COSTS (2016-2017)

Tuition and fees: $16,200.
Per-credit charge: $360.

FINANCIAL AID PICTURE

Students with need: Need-based aid available for full-time and part-time students. Work study available nights, weekends, and for part-time students.
Students without need: This college awards aid only to students with need.

FINANCIAL AID PROCEDURES

Forms required: FAFSA, institutional form.
Dates and Deadlines: Applicants notified on a rolling basis starting 6/4.

CONTACT

Katie Williams, Financial Services Advisor
3620 Arrowhead Avenue, Independence, MO 64057
(816) 412-7736

North Central Missouri College

Trenton, Missouri
www.ncmissouri.edu   Federal Code: 002514

2-year public community college in small town.
Enrollment: 1,059 undergrads.
Selectivity: Open admission; but selective for some programs.

BASIC COSTS (2016-2017)

Tuition and fees: $3,180; out-of-district residents $4,170; out-of-state residents $5,340.
Per-credit charge: $76; out-of-district residents $109; out-of-state residents $148.
Room and board: $5,849.

FINANCIAL AID PICTURE (2015-2016)

Students with need: 69% of average financial aid package awarded as scholarships/grants, 31% awarded as loans/jobs. Need-based aid available for part-time students.
Students without need: No-need awards available for academics, athletics, leadership.

FINANCIAL AID PROCEDURES

Forms required: FAFSA, institutional form.
Dates and Deadlines: Priority date 7/1; no closing date. Applicants notified on a rolling basis starting 3/15.
Transfers: No deadline. Applicants notified on a rolling basis starting 4/1. Transfer students may not receive same awards after transferring since some funds campus-based.

CONTACT

Kimberly Meeker, Financial Aid Director
1301 Main Street, Trenton, MO 64683
(660) 359-3948 ext. 1402

Northwest Missouri State University

Maryville, Missouri
www.nwmissouri.edu   Federal Code: 002496

4-year public university in large town.
Enrollment: 5,240 undergrads, 7% part-time. 1,336 full-time freshmen.
Selectivity: Admits 50 to 75% of applicants.

BASIC COSTS (2016-2017)

Tuition and fees: $9,179; out-of-state residents $15,499.
Per-credit charge: $306; out-of-state residents $517.
Room and board: $9,612.
Additional info: Tuition/fee waivers available for minority students.

FINANCIAL AID PICTURE (2015-2016)

Students with need: Out of 1,266 full-time freshmen who applied for aid, 952 were judged to have need. Of these, 950 received aid, and 574 had their full need met. Average financial aid package met 71% of need; average scholarship/grant was $7,375; average loan was $3,343. For part-time students, average financial aid package was $5,149.
Students without need: 178 full-time freshmen who did not demonstrate need for aid received scholarships/grants; average award was $3,467. No-need awards available for academics, alumni affiliation, art, athletics, job skills, leadership, minority status, music/drama, ROTC, state/district residency.
Scholarships offered: 29 full-time freshmen received athletic scholarships; average amount $6,366.

FINANCIAL AID PROCEDURES

Forms required: FAFSA.
Dates and Deadlines: Priority date 4/1; no closing date. Applicants notified on a rolling basis starting 3/15.

Transfers: No deadline. Applicants notified on a rolling basis starting 5/10; must reply within 4 week(s) of notification. Transfer scholarship based on academic record.

CONTACT
Charles Mayfield, Director of Financial Assistance
800 University Drive, Maryville, MO 64468-6001
(660) 562-1363

Ozark Christian College
Joplin, Missouri
www.occ.edu   Federal Code: 015569

4-year private Bible college in small city, affiliated with the nondenominational tradition.
Enrollment: 624 undergrads, 23% part-time. 115 full-time freshmen.
Selectivity: Admits 50 to 75% of applicants.

BASIC COSTS (2016-2017)
Tuition and fees: $11,430.
Per-credit charge: $355.
Room and board: $5,140.

FINANCIAL AID PICTURE
Students with need: Need-based aid available for full-time and part-time students.
Students without need: No-need awards available for academics, leadership, minority status.

FINANCIAL AID PROCEDURES
Forms required: FAFSA.
Dates and Deadlines: Priority date 4/1; no closing date. Applicants notified on a rolling basis starting 4/15; must reply within 3 week(s) of notification.
Transfers: Academic transcripts required. ACT scores may qualify student for grants or scholarships.

CONTACT
Kim Balentine, Director of Financial Aid
1111 North Main Street, Joplin, MO 64801
(417) 624-2518 ext. 2043

Ozarks Technical Community College
Springfield, Missouri
www.otc.edu   Federal Code: 030830

2-year public community and technical college in small city.
Enrollment: 13,260 undergrads.
Selectivity: Open admission; but selective for some programs.

BASIC COSTS (2016-2017)
Tuition and fees: $3,600; out-of-district residents $5,115; out-of-state residents $6,600.
Per-credit charge: $98; out-of-district residents $148.5; out-of-state residents $198.

FINANCIAL AID PICTURE (2015-2016)
Students with need: 63% of average financial aid package awarded as scholarships/grants, 37% awarded as loans/jobs. Need-based aid available for part-time students.
Students without need: This college awards aid only to students with need.

FINANCIAL AID PROCEDURES
Forms required: FAFSA, institutional form.
Dates and Deadlines: Closing date 3/31. Applicants notified on a rolling basis starting 5/16.

CONTACT
Kim Cary, College Director of Financial Aid
1001 East Chestnut Expressway, Springfield, MO 65802
(417) 447-6930

Park University
Parkville, Missouri
www.park.edu   Federal Code: 002498

4-year private university in small town.
Enrollment: 9,356 undergrads, 58% part-time. 168 full-time freshmen.
Selectivity: Admits over 75% of applicants.

BASIC COSTS (2016-2017)
Tuition and fees: $12,130.
Per-credit charge: $391.
Room and board: $7,260.
Additional info: Active-Duty Military and their dependents; $250 per-credit-hour. Veterans and their dependents; $329 per-credit-hour.

FINANCIAL AID PICTURE (2015-2016)
Students with need: Need-based aid available for full-time and part-time students. Work study available nights, weekends, and for part-time students.
Students without need: No-need awards available for academics, alumni affiliation, art, athletics, music/drama.

FINANCIAL AID PROCEDURES
Forms required: FAFSA.
Dates and Deadlines: Priority date 4/1; closing date 8/1. Applicants notified on a rolling basis starting 4/1; must reply by 8/1 or within 4 week(s) of notification.
Transfers: Priority date 4/1; closing date 8/1. Applicants notified on a rolling basis starting 8/1; must reply within 4 week(s) of notification.

CONTACT
Cathy Colapietro, Executive Director of Student Financial Services
8700 NW River Park Drive, Parkville, MO 64152
(816) 584-6290

Ranken Technical College
St. Louis, Missouri
www.ranken.edu   Federal Code: 012500

2-year private technical college in very large city.
Enrollment: 1,929 undergrads.
Selectivity: Open admission.

BASIC COSTS (2016-2017)
Tuition and fees: $17,790.
Per-credit charge: $593.
Room and board: $5,900.

FINANCIAL AID PICTURE
Students with need: Need-based aid available for full-time and part-time students. Work study available nights.

FINANCIAL AID PROCEDURES
Forms required: FAFSA, institutional form.
Dates and Deadlines: Priority date 4/1; no closing date. Applicants notified on a rolling basis starting 4/1.

CONTACT
Michelle Williams, Financial Aid Director
4431 Finney Avenue, St. Louis, MO 63113
(314) 286-4863

Research College of Nursing

Kansas City, Missouri
www.researchcollege.edu
Federal Code: 006392

4-year for-profit nursing college in very large city.
Enrollment: 294 undergrads, 2% part-time. 64 full-time freshmen.

BASIC COSTS (2016-2017)
Tuition and fees: $35,800.
Room and board: $9,055.

FINANCIAL AID PICTURE
Students with need: Need-based aid available for full-time students.
Students without need: No-need awards available for academics, leadership.
Additional info: Financial aid handled by Rockhurst University for freshmen and sophomores.

FINANCIAL AID PROCEDURES
Forms required: FAFSA, institutional form.
Dates and Deadlines: Priority date 3/15; no closing date. Applicants notified on a rolling basis starting 3/15.
Transfers: Priority date 4/1; no deadline. Applicants notified by 5/1.

CONTACT
Maureen McKinnon, Director of Financial Aid
2525 East Meyer Boulevard, Kansas City, MO 64132-1199
(816) 995-2814

Rockhurst University

Kansas City, Missouri
www.rockhurst.edu
Federal Code: 002499

4-year private business and liberal arts college in very large city, affiliated with the Roman Catholic Church.
Enrollment: 1,495 undergrads, 6% part-time. 318 full-time freshmen.
Selectivity: Admits 50 to 75% of applicants.

BASIC COSTS (2016-2017)
Tuition and fees: $35,670.
Per-credit charge: $1,164.
Room and board: $9,380.

FINANCIAL AID PICTURE (2015-2016)
Students with need: Out of 316 full-time freshmen who applied for aid, 251 were judged to have need. Of these, 251 received aid, and 67 had their full need met. Average financial aid package met 90% of need; average scholarship/grant was $21,393; average loan was $3,679. For part-time students, average financial aid package was $13,391.
Students without need: 64 full-time freshmen who did not demonstrate need for aid received scholarships/grants; average award was $19,356. No-need awards available for academics, alumni affiliation, athletics, leadership, music/drama.
Scholarships offered: 45 full-time freshmen received athletic scholarships; average amount $12,941.
Additional info: Auditions, portfolios required for some scholarships.

FINANCIAL AID PROCEDURES
Forms required: FAFSA.
Dates and Deadlines: Priority date 3/1; no closing date. Applicants notified on a rolling basis starting 3/1.
Transfers: No deadline. Applicants notified on a rolling basis starting 1/30. Scholarships awarded to qualified first-time transfers.

CONTACT
Maureen McKinnon, Director of Financial Aid
1100 Rockhurst Road, Kansas City, MO 64110-2561
(816) 501-4600

St. Charles Community College

Cottleville, Missouri
www.stchas.edu
Federal Code: 017027

2-year public community college in small city.
Enrollment: 6,188 undergrads, 48% part-time. 1,044 full-time freshmen.
Selectivity: Open admission; but selective for some programs.

BASIC COSTS (2016-2017)
Tuition and fees: $3,180; out-of-district residents $4,710; out-of-state residents $6,690.
Per-credit charge: $98; out-of-district residents $149; out-of-state residents $215.

FINANCIAL AID PICTURE (2015-2016)
Students with need: 82% of average financial aid package awarded as scholarships/grants, 18% awarded as loans/jobs. Need-based aid available for part-time students.
Students without need: No-need awards available for academics, art, athletics, leadership, music/drama.

FINANCIAL AID PROCEDURES
Forms required: FAFSA, institutional form.
Dates and Deadlines: Priority date 6/1; no closing date. Applicants notified on a rolling basis starting 2/1; must reply by 8/1.
Transfers: Applicants notified on a rolling basis starting 4/1; must reply by 8/1.

CONTACT
Kathy Brockgreitens-Gober, Dean of Enrollment Services
4601 Mid Rivers Mall Drive, Cottleville, MO 63376
(636) 922-8270

St. Louis Christian College

Florissant, Missouri
www.stlchristian.edu
Federal Code: 012580

4-year private Bible college in small city, affiliated with the Christian Church.
Enrollment: 105 undergrads, 10% part-time. 14 full-time freshmen.
Selectivity: Admits less than 50% of applicants.

BASIC COSTS (2016-2017)
Tuition and fees: $10,695.
Per-credit charge: $350.
Room and board: $4,800.

FINANCIAL AID PICTURE
Students with need: Need-based aid available for full-time and part-time students.

FINANCIAL AID PROCEDURES
Forms required: FAFSA.
Dates and Deadlines: Closing date 8/1. Applicants notified on a rolling basis starting 7/20; must reply within 2 week(s) of notification.

CONTACT
Pam Ralls, Financial Aid Director
1360 Grandview Drive, Florissant, MO 63033
(314) 837-6777 ext. 1101

St. Louis Community College

Saint Louis, Missouri
www.stlcc.edu
Federal Code: 002469

2-year public community and junior college in large city.
Enrollment: 8,820 undergrads.

Selectivity: Open admission.

BASIC COSTS (2016-2017)

Tuition and fees: $3,180; out-of-district residents $4,560; out-of-state residents $6,240.

FINANCIAL AID PICTURE

Students with need: Need-based aid available for full-time and part-time students.

Students without need: No-need awards available for academics, art, athletics, leadership, music/drama.

FINANCIAL AID PROCEDURES

Forms required: FAFSA.

Dates and Deadlines: Priority date 4/15; no closing date. Applicants notified on a rolling basis starting 4/1.

CONTACT

Paulette Johnson, Manager of Student Financial Aid
300 South Broadway, St. Louis, MO 63102-2800
(314) 644-9117

Saint Louis University

Saint Louis, Missouri
www.slu.edu   Federal Code: 002506

4-year private university in very large city, affiliated with the Roman Catholic Church.

Enrollment: 7,354 undergrads, 9% part-time. 1,617 full-time freshmen.

Selectivity: Admits 50 to 75% of applicants.

BASIC COSTS (2016-2017)

Tuition and fees: $40,726.

Per-credit charge: $1,400.

Room and board: $10,640.

Additional info: Tuition/fee waivers available for unemployed or children of unemployed.

FINANCIAL AID PICTURE (2015-2016)

Students with need: Out of 1,341 full-time freshmen who applied for aid, 1,082 were judged to have need. Of these, 1,082 received aid, and 312 had their full need met. Average financial aid package met 78% of need; average scholarship/grant was $24,456; average loan was $3,379. For part-time students, average financial aid package was $7,760.

Students without need: 466 full-time freshmen who did not demonstrate need for aid received scholarships/grants; average award was $17,750. No-need awards available for academics, art, athletics, leadership, music/drama, religious affiliation, ROTC.

Scholarships offered: *Merit:* Scholarships range from $3,000 - $20,000 based on academic achievement, test score, leadership, and community service. *Athletic:* 59 full-time freshmen received athletic scholarships; average amount $17,807.

Additional info: Presidential scholarship applications are due by December 1st. Martin Luther King Jr. (MLK) Scholarship applications have a priority date of February 1st. Emergency Scholarship Fund available to assist students and families with special circumstances. Institutional Loan Program available to assist some students without other financing options. The Go Further initiative will match, dollar for dollar, all qualified scholarship gifts of $100 and more.

FINANCIAL AID PROCEDURES

Forms required: FAFSA.

Dates and Deadlines: Priority date 2/1; no closing date. Applicants notified on a rolling basis starting 2/1; must reply by 5/1 or within 4 week(s) of notification.

Transfers: Priority date 2/1; no deadline. Applicants notified on a rolling basis starting 2/1; must reply by 5/1 or within 4 week(s) of notification. Students should file FAFSA by 2/1 for Missouri State Funds.

CONTACT

Cari Wickliffe, Asst. V.P. and Director of Student Financial Services
One North Grand Boulevard, St. Louis, MO 63103
(314) 977-2350

St. Luke's College

Kansas City, Missouri
www.saintlukescollege.edu   Federal Code: 009782

Upper-division private health science and nursing college in large city, affiliated with the Episcopal Church.

Enrollment: 462 undergrads, 20% part-time.

BASIC COSTS (2017-2018)

Tuition and fees: $15,674.

Per-credit charge: $484.

Additional info: Tuition/fee waivers available for minority students.

FINANCIAL AID PICTURE (2015-2016)

Students with need: Average financial aid package for all full-time undergraduates was $6,500; for part-time $5,500. 43% awarded as scholarships/grants, 57% awarded as loans/jobs.

Students without need: No-need awards available for academics.

FINANCIAL AID PROCEDURES

Forms required: FAFSA.

Dates and Deadlines: Priority date 4/1; no closing date. Applicants notified on a rolling basis.

Transfers: Priority date 2/1; no deadline. Applicants notified on a rolling basis; must reply within 3 week(s) of notification.

CONTACT

Jennifer Wright, Director of Financial Aid
624 Westport Road, Kansas City, MO 64111
(816) 936-8730

Southeast Missouri State University

Cape Girardeau, Missouri
www.semo.edu   Federal Code: 002501

4-year public university in large town.

Enrollment: 9,028 undergrads, 14% part-time. 1,564 full-time freshmen.

Selectivity: Admits over 75% of applicants.

BASIC COSTS (2017-2018)

Tuition and fees: $6,990; out-of-state residents $12,375.

Per-credit charge: $199; out-of-state residents $379.

Room and board: $8,508.

FINANCIAL AID PICTURE (2015-2016)

Students with need: Out of 1,391 full-time freshmen who applied for aid, 1,063 were judged to have need. Of these, 1,050 received aid, and 183 had their full need met. Average financial aid package met 62% of need; average scholarship/grant was $6,967; average loan was $3,535. For part-time students, average financial aid package was $5,438.

Students without need: 349 full-time freshmen who did not demonstrate need for aid received scholarships/grants; average award was $4,221. No-need awards available for academics, alumni affiliation, art, athletics, job skills, leadership, minority status, music/drama, ROTC, state/district residency.

Scholarships offered: 26 full-time freshmen received athletic scholarships; average amount $10,872.

FINANCIAL AID PROCEDURES

Forms required: FAFSA.

Dates and Deadlines: Priority date 3/1; no closing date. Applicants notified on a rolling basis starting 4/1; must reply within 3 week(s) of notification.

Transfers: Must reply by 8/20 or within 3 week(s) of notification.

CONTACT
Karen Walker, Director of Financial Aid Services
One University Plaza MS 3550, Cape Girardeau, MO 63701
(573) 651-2253

Southwest Baptist University
Bolivar, Missouri
www.sbuniv.edu   Federal Code: 002502

4-year private university in large town, affiliated with the Southern Baptist Convention.
Enrollment: 2,973 undergrads.

BASIC COSTS (2017-2018)
Tuition and fees: $23,290.
Room and board: $7,600.

FINANCIAL AID PICTURE
Students with need: Need-based aid available for full-time and part-time students. Work study available nights, weekends, and for part-time students.
Students without need: No-need awards available for academics, alumni affiliation, art, athletics, minority status, music/drama, religious affiliation.

FINANCIAL AID PROCEDURES
Forms required: FAFSA.
Dates and Deadlines: Priority date 3/15; no closing date. Applicants notified on a rolling basis starting 3/1; must reply within 2 week(s) of notification.

CONTACT
Brad Gamble, Director of Financial Aid
1600 University Avenue, Bolivar, MO 65613-2597
(417) 328-1822

State Fair Community College
Sedalia, Missouri
www.sfccmo.edu   Federal Code: 007628

2-year public community college in large town.
Enrollment: 3,886 undergrads, 40% part-time. 796 full-time freshmen.
Selectivity: Open admission; but selective for some programs.

BASIC COSTS (2016-2017)
Tuition and fees: $3,000; out-of-district residents $4,500; out-of-state residents $6,300.
Per-credit charge: $100; out-of-district residents $150; out-of-state residents $210.
Room and board: $5,000.

FINANCIAL AID PICTURE
Students with need: Need-based aid available for full-time and part-time students. Work study available nights, weekends, and for part-time students.
Students without need: No-need awards available for academics, art, athletics, music/drama, state/district residency.

FINANCIAL AID PROCEDURES
Forms required: FAFSA.
Dates and Deadlines: Priority date 7/1; no closing date. Applicants notified on a rolling basis starting 7/15; must reply within 3 week(s) of notification.
Transfers: No deadline. Applicants notified on a rolling basis starting 7/15; must reply within 3 week(s) of notification.

CONTACT
Lana DeJaynes, Director of Financial Aid
3201 West 16th Street, Sedalia, MO 65301-2199
(660) 596-5834

State Technical College of Missouri
Linn, Missouri
www.statetechmo.edu   Federal Code: 004711

2-year public technical college in rural community.
Enrollment: 1,127 undergrads, 9% part-time. 477 full-time freshmen.
Selectivity: Open admission; but selective for some programs.

BASIC COSTS (2016-2017)
Tuition and fees: $5,873; out-of-state residents $10,665.
Per-credit charge: $159.75; out-of-state residents $319.5.
Room and board: $5,300.

FINANCIAL AID PICTURE (2015-2016)
Students with need: Out of 474 full-time freshmen who applied for aid, 363 were judged to have need. Of these, 363 received aid, and 83 had their full need met. Average financial aid package met 11% of need; average scholarship/grant was $5,308; average loan was $3,209. Need-based aid available for part-time students.
Students without need: 6 full-time freshmen who did not demonstrate need for aid received scholarships/grants; average award was $883. No-need awards available for academics, alumni affiliation, state/district residency.
Scholarships offered: 26 full-time freshmen received athletic scholarships; average amount $915.

FINANCIAL AID PROCEDURES
Forms required: FAFSA.
Dates and Deadlines: Priority date 2/1; no closing date. Applicants notified on a rolling basis starting 3/1; must reply within 3 week(s) of notification.

CONTACT
Becky Whithaus, Director of Financial Aid
One Technology Drive, Linn, MO 65051-3203
(573) 897-5143

Stephens College
Columbia, Missouri
www.stephens.edu   Federal Code: 002512

4-year private liberal arts and career college for women in small city.
Enrollment: 724 undergrads, 16% part-time. 269 full-time freshmen.
Selectivity: Admits 50 to 75% of applicants.

BASIC COSTS (2017-2018)
Tuition and fees: $30,344.
Room and board: $10,424.

FINANCIAL AID PICTURE (2015-2016)
Students with need: Out of 227 full-time freshmen who applied for aid, 227 were judged to have need. Of these, 227 received aid. Average financial aid package met 80% of need; average scholarship/grant was $16,000. For part-time students, average financial aid package was $500.
Students without need: 9 full-time freshmen who did not demonstrate need for aid received scholarships/grants; average award was $10,000. No-need awards available for academics, alumni affiliation, athletics, music/drama, state/district residency.
Scholarships offered: *Merit:* Scholarships based on a combination of ACT and GPA, need based scholarships awarded according to EFC. *Athletic:* 4 full-time freshmen received athletic scholarships; average amount $12,000.

FINANCIAL AID PROCEDURES
Forms required: FAFSA.
Dates and Deadlines: Priority date 2/1; no closing date. Applicants notified on a rolling basis starting 10/1.
Transfers: Phi Theta Kappa students transferring from 2-year institutions eligible for scholarship.

CONTACT
Kim Stonecipher-Fisher, Director of Financial Aid
1200 East Broadway, Columbia, MO 65215
(800) 876-7106

Stevens Institute of Business & Arts
St. Louis, Missouri
www.siba.edu   Federal Code: 008552

2-year for-profit business and liberal arts college in very large city.
Enrollment: 131 undergrads, 17% part-time. 21 full-time freshmen.
Selectivity: Open admission; but selective for some programs.

BASIC COSTS (2017-2018)
Tuition and fees: $14,760.
Per-credit charge: $265.
Additional info: Tuition at time of enrollment locked for 2 years.

FINANCIAL AID PICTURE (2015-2016)
Students with need: 30% of average financial aid package awarded as scholarships/grants, 70% awarded as loans/jobs. Need-based aid available for part-time students.
Students without need: This college awards aid only to students with need.

FINANCIAL AID PROCEDURES
Forms required: FAFSA.
Dates and Deadlines: Applicants notified on a rolling basis.

CONTACT
Chrissa Siampos, Financial Aid Director
1521 Washington Avenue, St. Louis, MO 63103
(314) 421-0949 ext. 1405

Texas County Technical College
Houston, Missouri
www.texascountytech.edu   Federal Code: 035793

2-year private nursing and technical college in small town.
Enrollment: 91 undergrads. 91 full-time freshmen.
Selectivity: Open admission.

BASIC COSTS (2016-2017)
Tuition and fees: $15,810.
Per-credit charge: $424.

FINANCIAL AID PICTURE (2015-2016)
Students with need: 45% of average financial aid package awarded as scholarships/grants, 55% awarded as loans/jobs. Need-based aid available for part-time students.
Students without need: This college awards aid only to students with need.

FINANCIAL AID PROCEDURES
Forms required: FAFSA, state aid form, institutional form.
Dates and Deadlines: Applicants notified on a rolling basis.
Transfers: No deadline. Applicants notified on a rolling basis.

CONTACT
Clarice Casebeer, Financial Aid Liasion
6915 South Highway 63, Houston, MO 65483
(417) 967-5466

Three Rivers Community College
Poplar Bluff, Missouri
www.trcc.edu   Federal Code: 004713

2-year public community college in large town.
Enrollment: 3,087 undergrads.
Selectivity: Open admission; but selective for some programs.

BASIC COSTS (2016-2017)
Tuition and fees: $3,540; out-of-district residents $5,190; out-of-state residents $6,330.
Per-credit charge: $85; out-of-district residents $140; out-of-state residents $178.
Room only: $3,440.

FINANCIAL AID PICTURE
Students with need: Need-based aid available for full-time and part-time students.
Students without need: No-need awards available for academics, athletics, state/district residency.

FINANCIAL AID PROCEDURES
Forms required: FAFSA, institutional form.
Dates and Deadlines: Priority date 4/1; no closing date. Applicants notified on a rolling basis starting 6/1; must reply within 2 week(s) of notification.

CONTACT
Laura Milligan
2080 Three Rivers Boulevard, Poplar Bluff, MO 63901-1308
(573) 840-9607

Truman State University
Kirksville, Missouri
www.truman.edu   Federal Code: 002495

4-year public university and liberal arts college in large town.
Enrollment: 5,302 undergrads, 3% part-time. 1,258 full-time freshmen.
Selectivity: Admits 50 to 75% of applicants.

BASIC COSTS (2016-2017)
Tuition and fees: $7,456; out-of-state residents $13,940.
Per-credit charge: $298; out-of-state residents $568.
Room and board: $8,558.

FINANCIAL AID PICTURE (2015-2016)
Students with need: Out of 1,054 full-time freshmen who applied for aid, 709 were judged to have need. Of these, 709 received aid, and 273 had their full need met. Average financial aid package met 87% of need; average scholarship/grant was $8,587; average loan was $3,679. For part-time students, average financial aid package was $5,424.
Students without need: 532 full-time freshmen who did not demonstrate need for aid received scholarships/grants; average award was $5,573. No-need awards available for academics, alumni affiliation, art, athletics, leadership, minority status, music/drama, ROTC, state/district residency.
Scholarships offered: *Merit:* Pershing Scholarship: up to full-tuition, average room and board, up to $4,000 for study-abroad; awarded to outstanding scholars and leaders; 12 awarded. Truman Leadership Award is a $10,000 award for Missouri residents for demonstrated leadership and academic achievement. Non-Resident Tuition Scholarship: $2,000-$5,000; available to non-Missouri resident freshmen who meet specified academic parameters to assist with the non-resident portion of tuition; unlimited number available. President's Combined Ability: $2,000-$3,000; specified academic parameters based on GPA and standardized test scores; unlimited number available. *Athletic:* 75 full-time freshmen received athletic scholarships; average amount $3,829.

FINANCIAL AID PROCEDURES
Forms required: FAFSA.

Dates and Deadlines: Priority date 2/1; no closing date. Applicants notified on a rolling basis starting 1/1.
Transfers: Applicants notified on a rolling basis starting 1/1. Limited number of automatic and competitive awards offered to transfer students.

CONTACT
Kathy Elsea, Financial Aid Director
100 East Normal Avenue, Kirksville, MO 63501
(660) 785-4130

University of Central Missouri
Warrensburg, Missouri
www.ucmo.edu   Federal Code: 02454

4-year public university in large town.
Enrollment: 8,744 undergrads, 11% part-time. 1,641 full-time freshmen.
Selectivity: Admits over 75% of applicants.

BASIC COSTS (2016-2017)
Tuition and fees: $7,322; out-of-state residents $13,767.
Per-credit charge: $214.85; out-of-state residents $429.7.
Room and board: $8,318.

FINANCIAL AID PICTURE (2015-2016)
Students with need: Out of 1,519 full-time freshmen who applied for aid, 1,060 were judged to have need. Of these, 1,060 received aid, and 169 had their full need met. Average financial aid package met 70% of need; average scholarship/grant was $4,382. For part-time students, average financial aid package was $5,458.
Students without need: 415 full-time freshmen who did not demonstrate need for aid received scholarships/grants; average award was $3,513. No-need awards available for academics, alumni affiliation, art, athletics, leadership, minority status, music/drama, religious affiliation, ROTC, state/district residency.
Scholarships offered: 82 full-time freshmen received athletic scholarships; average amount $5,900.

FINANCIAL AID PROCEDURES
Forms required: FAFSA, institutional form.
Dates and Deadlines: Applicants notified on a rolling basis starting 3/1.
Transfers: No deadline. Must reply within 2 week(s) of notification.

CONTACT
Angela Karlin, Director of Student Financial Assistance
WDE 1400, Warrensburg, MO 64093
(660) 543-8080

University of Missouri: Columbia
Columbia, Missouri
www.missouri.edu   Federal Code: 002516

4-year public university in small city.
Enrollment: 25,544 undergrads, 6% part-time. 4,672 full-time freshmen.
Selectivity: Admits 50 to 75% of applicants.

BASIC COSTS (2016-2017)
Tuition and fees: $9,518; out-of-state residents $25,892.
Per-credit charge: $276; out-of-state residents $822.
Room and board: $10,100.

FINANCIAL AID PICTURE
Students with need: Need-based aid available for full-time and part-time students. Work study available nights, weekends, and for part-time students.
Students without need: No-need awards available for academics, alumni affiliation, art, athletics, leadership, minority status, music/drama, ROTC, state/district residency.

Additional info: Scholarship available for international students based on success during 1st semester.

FINANCIAL AID PROCEDURES
Forms required: FAFSA.
Dates and Deadlines: Priority date 3/1; no closing date. Applicants notified on a rolling basis starting 4/1; must reply within 4 week(s) of notification.
Transfers: No deadline. Applicants notified on a rolling basis starting 4/1; must reply within 4 week(s) of notification.

CONTACT
Nicholas Prewett, Director of Student Financial Aid
230 Jesse Hall, Columbia, MO 65211
(573) 882-7506

University of Missouri: Kansas City
Kansas City, Missouri
www.umkc.edu   Federal Code: 002518

4-year public university in large city.
Enrollment: 7,904 undergrads, 17% part-time. 1,195 full-time freshmen.
Selectivity: Admits 50 to 75% of applicants.

BASIC COSTS (2016-2017)
Tuition and fees: $9,563; out-of-state residents $23,363.
Per-credit charge: $272; out-of-state residents $732.
Room and board: $10,257.

FINANCIAL AID PICTURE (2016-2017)
Students with need: Out of 1,057 full-time freshmen who applied for aid, 820 were judged to have need. Of these, 805 received aid, and 112 had their full need met. Average financial aid package met 64.2% of need; average scholarship/grant was $8,378; average loan was $6,272. For part-time students, average financial aid package was $5,849.
Students without need: 236 full-time freshmen who did not demonstrate need for aid received scholarships/grants; average award was $5,131. No-need awards available for academics, alumni affiliation, art, athletics, leadership, minority status, music/drama, state/district residency.
Scholarships offered: *Merit:* Trustees Scholarship available that covers most educational expenses. *Athletic:* 19 full-time freshmen received athletic scholarships; average amount $18,571.
Additional info: Many automatic scholarships and non-resident fee waivers available for students who apply for admission by 2/1. Automatic awards range from $1,000 to a complete non-resident fee differential.

FINANCIAL AID PROCEDURES
Forms required: FAFSA.
Dates and Deadlines: Priority date 2/1; no closing date. Applicants notified on a rolling basis starting 4/15; must reply within 2 week(s) of notification.
Transfers: Applicants notified on a rolling basis; must reply within 2 week(s) of notification.

CONTACT
Scott Young, Director of Student Financial Aid
5100 Rockhill Road, AC120, Kansas City, MO 64110-2499
(816) 235-1154

University of Missouri: St. Louis
St. Louis, Missouri
www.umsl.edu   Federal Code: 002519

4-year public university in very large city.
Enrollment: 7,737 undergrads, 32% part-time. 415 full-time freshmen.
Selectivity: Admits 50 to 75% of applicants.

BASIC COSTS (2016-2017)
Tuition and fees: $10,065; out-of-state residents $26,277.
Per-credit charge: $336; out-of-state residents $876.
Room and board: $9,220.

FINANCIAL AID PICTURE (2016-2017)
Students with need: Out of 359 full-time freshmen who applied for aid, 300 were judged to have need. Of these, 296 received aid, and 86 had their full need met. Average financial aid package met 75% of need; average scholarship/grant was $11,101; average loan was $3,232. For part-time students, average financial aid package was $6,219.
Students without need: 35 full-time freshmen who did not demonstrate need for aid received scholarships/grants; average award was $8,195. No-need awards available for academics, alumni affiliation, art, athletics, music/drama, ROTC, state/district residency.
Scholarships offered: *Merit:* Curators' Scholarship: $7,000; 28 ACT, top 5% of high school class, Missouri resident. Chancellor's Scholarship: $5,000; 26 ACT, top 10% of high school class. *Athletic:* 17 full-time freshmen received athletic scholarships; average amount $14,577.

FINANCIAL AID PROCEDURES
Forms required: FAFSA.
Dates and Deadlines: Priority date 3/1; no closing date. Applicants notified on a rolling basis starting 4/1; must reply within 2 week(s) of notification.
Transfers: Transfer scholarships awarded to new students entering in fall or spring semesters. Must transfer at least 45 credit hours. Students transferring from Missouri 2-year institution must have minimum cumulative GPA of 3.25 for consideration. Students transferring from non-Missouri 2-year institution or any 4-year institution must have minimum cumulative GPA of 3.5 for consideration. Students starting in fall must be admitted by March 15; spring students must be admitted by October 15.

CONTACT
Anthony Georges, Director of Student Financial Aid
One University Boulevard, St. Louis, MO 63121-4400
(314) 516-5526

Vatterott College: St. Joseph
Saint Joseph, Missouri
www.vatterott-college.edu   Federal Code: 026092

2-year for-profit branch campus and technical college in small city.
Enrollment: 231 undergrads.
Selectivity: Open admission.

BASIC COSTS (2016-2017)
Additional info: Diploma programs: (30 weeks) $13,350; (40 weeks) $19,800; (50 weeks) $20,800; (60 weeks) $21,050. Associate programs: (70 weeks) $30,559-$34,900. Costs include fees, books and supplies.

FINANCIAL AID PICTURE
Students with need: Need-based aid available for full-time and part-time students.
Scholarships offered: Make the Grade Scholarship: up to $1,000; based on high school grades.

FINANCIAL AID PROCEDURES
Forms required: FAFSA.

CONTACT
Marcia Hurley, Financial Aid Administrator
3131 Frederick Avenue, St. Joseph, MO 64506
(816) 364-5399

Washington University in St. Louis
St. Louis, Missouri   Federal Code: 002520
https://www.wustl.edu   CSS Code: 6929

4-year private university in large city.
Enrollment: 7,116 undergrads, 4% part-time. 1,766 full-time freshmen.
Selectivity: Admits less than 50% of applicants.

BASIC COSTS (2017-2018)
Tuition and fees: $51,533.
Room and board: $16,006.

FINANCIAL AID PICTURE (2016-2017)
Students with need: Out of 895 full-time freshmen who applied for aid, 741 were judged to have need. Of these, 732 received aid, and 732 had their full need met. Average financial aid package met 100% of need; average scholarship/grant was $43,839; average loan was $3,276. Need-based aid available for part-time students.
Students without need: 189 full-time freshmen who did not demonstrate need for aid received scholarships/grants; average award was $12,824. No-need awards available for academics, art, leadership, ROTC.
Scholarships offered: Scholarships up to full tuition plus stipend; renewable for 4 years; based upon academic merit.
Additional info: Program available that eliminates need-based loans as part of undergraduate financial assistance awards to families of students with incomes of $75,000 or less.

FINANCIAL AID PROCEDURES
Forms required: FAFSA, CSS PROFILE, institutional form.
Dates and Deadlines: Closing date 2/1. Applicants notified by 4/1; must reply by 5/1.
Transfers: Closing date 3/15. Applicants notified by 5/15; must reply by 6/1.

CONTACT
Michael Runiewicz, Director of Student Financial Services
Campus Box 1089, One Brookings Drive, St. Louis, MO 63130-4899
(314) 935-5900

Webster University
St. Louis, Missouri
www.webster.edu   Federal Code: 002521

4-year private university in very large city.
Enrollment: 2,591 undergrads, 14% part-time. 433 full-time freshmen.
Selectivity: Admits less than 50% of applicants.

BASIC COSTS (2016-2017)
Tuition and fees: $26,425.
Per-credit charge: $670.
Room and board: $11,190.

FINANCIAL AID PICTURE (2016-2017)
Students with need: 64% of average financial aid package awarded as scholarships/grants, 36% awarded as loans/jobs. Need-based aid available for part-time students. Work study available nights, weekends, and for part-time students.
Students without need: No-need awards available for academics, art, leadership, music/drama, state/district residency.
Scholarships offered: Presidential Scholarships: full tuition; 3.75 GPA, top 20% class rank, 27 ACT and interview; 5 awarded. Webster Academic Scholarships: $12,000-$18,000; GPA and ACT; no limit. Leadership Scholarships: $2,000; 3.3 GPA and 24 ACT, resume of activities; 12 awarded.

FINANCIAL AID PROCEDURES
Forms required: FAFSA, institutional form.
Dates and Deadlines: Priority date 4/1; no closing date. Applicants notified on a rolling basis starting 2/1; must reply within 2 week(s) of notification.

Transfers: Closing date 4/1. Applicants notified on a rolling basis starting 2/1; must reply within 2 week(s) of notification.

CONTACT

James Myers, Associate Vice President Undergraduate Admission & Financial Aid

470 East Lockwood Avenue, St. Louis, MO 63119-3194

(314) 968-6992

Westminster College

Fulton, Missouri

www.westminster-mo.edu   Federal Code: 002523

4-year private liberal arts college in large town, affiliated with the Presbyterian Church (USA).

Enrollment: 863 undergrads, 1% part-time. 222 full-time freshmen.

Selectivity: Admits 50 to 75% of applicants.

BASIC COSTS (2017-2018)

Tuition and fees: $25,940.

Per-credit charge: $800.

Room and board: $9,810.

Additional info: Tuition/fee waivers available for minority students.

FINANCIAL AID PICTURE

Students with need: Need-based aid available for full-time and part-time students. Work study available nights, weekends, and for part-time students.

Students without need: No-need awards available for academics, alumni affiliation, leadership, minority status, music/drama.

FINANCIAL AID PROCEDURES

Forms required: FAFSA.

Dates and Deadlines: Priority date 2/15; no closing date. Applicants notified on a rolling basis starting 3/15.

Transfers: Applicants notified on a rolling basis starting 3/1; must reply within 3 week(s) of notification.

CONTACT

Aimee Bristow, Senior Director of Enrollment Management/Student Financial Planning

501 Westminster Avenue, Fulton, MO 65251-1299

(573) 592-5365

William Jewell College

Liberty, Missouri

www.jewell.edu   Federal Code: 002524

4-year private liberal arts college in large town.

Enrollment: 992 undergrads, 2% part-time. 241 full-time freshmen.

Selectivity: Admits 50 to 75% of applicants.

BASIC COSTS (2017-2018)

Tuition and fees: $33,620.

Per-credit charge: $960.

Room and board: $9,640.

FINANCIAL AID PICTURE (2016-2017)

Students with need: Out of 226 full-time freshmen who applied for aid, 184 were judged to have need. Of these, 184 received aid, and 74 had their full need met. Average financial aid package met 83% of need; average scholarship/grant was $22,930; average loan was $4,152. For part-time students, average financial aid package was $7,500.

Students without need: 40 full-time freshmen who did not demonstrate need for aid received scholarships/grants; average award was $20,422. No-need awards available for academics, alumni affiliation, athletics, music/drama.

Scholarships offered: Merit: Academic scholarships: $13,000-$18,000 awarded at time of admittance; competitive awards available; $19,000-$26,000 for those applying by 12/15. All academic scholarships available for 8 consecutive semesters with 2.5 GPA. **Athletic:** 17 full-time freshmen received athletic scholarships; average amount $8,430.

FINANCIAL AID PROCEDURES

Forms required: FAFSA.

Dates and Deadlines: Priority date 3/1; no closing date. Applicants notified on a rolling basis starting 11/1; must reply within 2 week(s) of notification.

Transfers: Closing date 9/15. Applicants notified on a rolling basis starting 3/15; must reply within 2 week(s) of notification. Transfer students evaluated individually by financial aid staff to determine number of semesters of aid available.

CONTACT

Daniel Holt, Director, Financial Aid and Scholarship Services

500 College Hill, Liberty, MO 64068

(816) 415-5974

William Woods University

Fulton, Missouri

www.williamwoods.edu   Federal Code: 002525

4-year private university and teachers college in large town, affiliated with the Christian Church (Disciples of Christ).

Enrollment: 943 undergrads, 12% part-time. 198 full-time freshmen.

Selectivity: Admits over 75% of applicants.

BASIC COSTS (2016-2017)

Tuition and fees: $23,040.

Room and board: $9,300.

FINANCIAL AID PICTURE (2016-2017)

Students with need: Out of 198 full-time freshmen who applied for aid, 198 were judged to have need. Of these, 196 received aid, and 48 had their full need met. Average financial aid package met 66% of need; average scholarship/grant was $12,329; average loan was $4,239. For part-time students, average financial aid package was $5,075.

Students without need: 110 full-time freshmen who did not demonstrate need for aid received scholarships/grants; average award was $9,979. No-need awards available for academics, alumni affiliation, art, athletics, leadership, music/drama, religious affiliation.

Scholarships offered: Merit: LEAD (Leading, Educating, Achieving and Developing) Award: $5,000 for campus residents, $2,500 for commuters; based on commitment to campus and community involvement; renewable each year if commitment has been met in previous year. **Athletic:** 20 full-time freshmen received athletic scholarships; average amount $12,925.

FINANCIAL AID PROCEDURES

Forms required: FAFSA.

Dates and Deadlines: Priority date 3/1; no closing date. Applicants notified on a rolling basis starting 3/15; must reply within 2 week(s) of notification.

Transfers: No deadline. Applicants notified on a rolling basis; must reply within 2 week(s) of notification. Transfer students eligible for scholarships based on incoming GPA.

CONTACT

Deana Ready, Director of Financial Aid

One University Avenue, Fulton, MO 65251-2388

(573) 592-1793

Montana

PART III: FINANCIAL AID COLLEGE BY COLLEGE

Blackfeet Community College
Browning, Montana
www.bfcc.edu   Federal Code: 014902

2-year public tribal community college in small town.
Enrollment: 462 undergrads.
Selectivity: Open admission.

BASIC COSTS (2016-2017)
Additional info: Tuition at time of enrollment locked for 2 years; tuition/fee waivers available for adults, minority students, unemployed or children of unemployed.

FINANCIAL AID PICTURE
Students with need: Need-based aid available for full-time and part-time students.
Students without need: No-need awards available for academics, minority status, state/district residency.

FINANCIAL AID PROCEDURES
Forms required: FAFSA, institutional form.
Dates and Deadlines: Applicants notified on a rolling basis starting 8/1; must reply by 3/1.
Transfers: No deadline. Applicants notified on a rolling basis starting 8/1.

CONTACT
Gaylene DuCharme, Director of Financial Aid
504 SE Boundary, Browning, MT 59417
(406) 338-5421 ext. 2245

Carroll College
Helena, Montana
www.carroll.edu   Federal Code: 002526

4-year private liberal arts college in large town, affiliated with the Roman Catholic Church.
Enrollment: 1,342 undergrads, 2% part-time. 387 full-time freshmen.
Selectivity: Admits 50 to 75% of applicants.

BASIC COSTS (2016-2017)
Tuition and fees: $33,192.
Per-credit charge: $1,340.
Room and board: $9,584.

FINANCIAL AID PICTURE (2015-2016)
Students with need: Out of 329 full-time freshmen who applied for aid, 271 were judged to have need. Of these, 271 received aid, and 67 had their full need met. Average financial aid package met 79% of need; average scholarship/grant was $19,474; average loan was $3,041. For part-time students, average financial aid package was $9,341.
Students without need: 112 full-time freshmen who did not demonstrate need for aid received scholarships/grants; average award was $14,929. No-need awards available for academics, art, athletics, leadership, minority status, music/drama, religious affiliation, ROTC.
Scholarships offered: 72 full-time freshmen received athletic scholarships; average amount $10,164.

FINANCIAL AID PROCEDURES
Forms required: FAFSA.
Dates and Deadlines: Priority date 3/1; no closing date. Applicants notified on a rolling basis starting 3/1; must reply by 5/1 or within 2 week(s) of notification.

CONTACT
Janet Riis, Director of Financial Aid
1601 North Benton Avenue, Helena, MT 59625
(406) 447-5425

Chief Dull Knife College
Lame Deer, Montana
www.cdkc.edu   Federal Code: 014878

2-year public junior college in rural community.
Enrollment: 26 undergrads.
Selectivity: Open admission.

BASIC COSTS (2016-2017)
Tuition and fees: $2,260; out-of-state residents $2,260.
Per-credit charge: $70.

FINANCIAL AID PICTURE
Students with need: Need-based aid available for full-time and part-time students. Work study available nights.
Students without need: No-need awards available for academics.

FINANCIAL AID PROCEDURES
Forms required: FAFSA, institutional form.
Dates and Deadlines: Priority date 3/1; no closing date. Applicants notified on a rolling basis; must reply within 2 week(s) of notification.
Transfers: No deadline. Applicants notified on a rolling basis; must reply within 2 week(s) of notification.

CONTACT
Devin Wertman, Director of Financial Aid
Box 98, Lame Deer, MT 59043
(406) 477-6215

Dawson Community College
Glendive, Montana
www.dawson.edu   Federal Code: 002529

2-year public community college in small town.
Enrollment: 193 undergrads, 19% part-time. 120 full-time freshmen.
Selectivity: Open admission.

BASIC COSTS (2017-2018)
Tuition and fees: $3,630; out-of-district residents $5,070; out-of-state residents $7,650.
Per-credit charge: $67; out-of-district residents $115; out-of-state residents $201.
Room and board: $5,775.

FINANCIAL AID PICTURE (2015-2016)
Students with need: Need-based aid available for part-time students.
Students without need: No-need awards available for academics, art, athletics, music/drama.

FINANCIAL AID PROCEDURES
Forms required: FAFSA.
Dates and Deadlines: Applicants notified on a rolling basis starting 5/15; must reply within 2 week(s) of notification.
Transfers: No deadline. Applicants notified on a rolling basis; must reply within 2 week(s) of notification.

CONTACT
Danielle Dinges, Director of Financial Aid
300 College Drive, Glendive, MT 59330
(406) 377-9410

Flathead Valley Community College

Kalispell, Montana
www.fvcc.edu   Federal Code: 006777

2-year public community college in large town.
Enrollment: 2,206 undergrads.
Selectivity: Open admission; but selective for some programs.

BASIC COSTS (2016-2017)
Tuition and fees: $4,114; out-of-district residents $5,486; out-of-state residents $11,254.

FINANCIAL AID PICTURE
Students with need: Need-based aid available for full-time and part-time students.
Students without need: No-need awards available for academics, athletics.

FINANCIAL AID PROCEDURES
Forms required: FAFSA.
Dates and Deadlines: Priority date 3/1; no closing date. Applicants notified on a rolling basis starting 4/15; must reply within 2 week(s) of notification.

CONTACT
Cynthia Kiefer, Director of Financial Aid
777 Grandview Drive, Kalispell, MT 59901
(406) 756-3849

Fort Peck Community College

Poplar, Montana
www.fpcc.edu   Federal Code: 016616

2-year public community college in rural community.
Enrollment: 323 undergrads.
Selectivity: Open admission.

BASIC COSTS (2016-2017)
Tuition and fees: $2,250; out-of-state residents $2,250.
Per-credit charge: $70.
Room only: $1,350.
Additional info: Tuition/fee waivers available for adults, minority students, unemployed or children of unemployed.

FINANCIAL AID PICTURE
Students with need: Need-based aid available for full-time and part-time students.
Students without need: No-need awards available for academics, minority status, state/district residency.

FINANCIAL AID PROCEDURES
Forms required: FAFSA, institutional form.
Dates and Deadlines: Applicants notified on a rolling basis starting 5/1; must reply within 3 week(s) of notification.
Transfers: No deadline. Applicants notified on a rolling basis starting 5/1; must reply within 3 week(s) of notification.

CONTACT
Lanette Clark, Financial Aid Director
Box 398, 605 Indian, Poplar, MT 59255-0398
(406) 768-6327

Great Falls College Montana State University

Great Falls, Montana
www.gfcmsu.edu   Federal Code: 009314

2-year public community college in small city.
Enrollment: 1,321 undergrads, 50% part-time. 141 full-time freshmen.

Selectivity: Open admission; but selective for some programs.

BASIC COSTS (2016-2017)
Tuition and fees: $3,130; out-of-state residents $9,382.
Additional info: Tuition/fee waivers available for minority students.

FINANCIAL AID PICTURE (2015-2016)
Students with need: Out of 126 full-time freshmen who applied for aid, 110 were judged to have need. Of these, 105 received aid, and 18 had their full need met. Average financial aid package met 61% of need; average scholarship/grant was $4,237; average loan was $4,867. For part-time students, average financial aid package was $7,000.
Students without need: 1 full-time freshmen who did not demonstrate need for aid received scholarships/grants; average award was $2,000. No-need awards available for academics, leadership, minority status, music/drama, state/district residency.

FINANCIAL AID PROCEDURES
Forms required: FAFSA, institutional form.
Dates and Deadlines: Priority date 3/1; no closing date. Applicants notified on a rolling basis starting 4/15.
Transfers: No deadline. Applicants notified on a rolling basis; must reply within 3 week(s) of notification.

CONTACT
Leah Habel, Director of Financial Aid
2100 16th Avenue South, Great Falls, MT 59405
(800) 446-2698 ext. 4334

Helena College University of Montana

Helena, Montana
www.umhelena.edu   Federal Code: 007570

2-year public community and technical college in large town.
Enrollment: 1,063 undergrads.
Selectivity: Open admission.

BASIC COSTS (2016-2017)
Tuition and fees: $3,079; out-of-state residents $8,379.
Per-credit charge: $79; out-of-state residents $252.
Additional info: Tuition/fee waivers available for minority students.

FINANCIAL AID PICTURE
Students with need: Need-based aid available for full-time and part-time students.

FINANCIAL AID PROCEDURES
Forms required: FAFSA, institutional form.
Dates and Deadlines: Priority date 3/1; no closing date. Applicants notified on a rolling basis starting 5/1.
Transfers: Applicants notified on a rolling basis starting 5/1.

CONTACT
Valerie Curtin, Director of Financial Aid
1115 North Roberts Street, Helena, MT 59601-3098
(406) 447-6916

Little Big Horn College

Crow Agency, Montana
www.lbhc.edu   Federal Code: 016135

2-year private community college in rural community.
Enrollment: 284 undergrads. 79 full-time freshmen.
Selectivity: Open admission.

BASIC COSTS (2016-2017)
Tuition and fees: $3,200.

FINANCIAL AID PICTURE (2015-2016)

Students with need: Out of 79 full-time freshmen who applied for aid, 79 were judged to have need. Of these, 79 received aid, and 64 had their full need met. Average financial aid package met 81% of need. Need-based aid available for part-time students.

Students without need: This college awards aid only to students with need.

FINANCIAL AID PROCEDURES

Forms required: FAFSA, institutional form.

Dates and Deadlines: Applicants notified on a rolling basis.

Transfers: No deadline. Applicants notified on a rolling basis.

CONTACT

Beverly Snell, Financial Aid Director
Box 370, Crow Agency, MT 59022
(406) 638-3140

Miles Community College

Miles City, Montana
www.milescc.edu   Federal Code: 002528

2-year public community college in small town.

Enrollment: 397 undergrads, 25% part-time. 128 full-time freshmen.

Selectivity: Open admission; but selective for some programs.

BASIC COSTS (2016-2017)

Tuition and fees: $3,990; out-of-district residents $5,220; out-of-state residents $8,310.

Room and board: $6,030.

FINANCIAL AID PICTURE

Students with need: Need-based aid available for full-time and part-time students. Work study available nights, weekends, and for part-time students.

Students without need: No-need awards available for academics, athletics, leadership.

FINANCIAL AID PROCEDURES

Forms required: FAFSA.

Dates and Deadlines: Priority date 3/1; no closing date. Applicants notified on a rolling basis starting 4/15; must reply within 4 week(s) of notification.

CONTACT

Loren Lancaster, Financial Aid Officer
2715 Dickinson Street, Miles City, MT 59301
(406) 874-6208

Montana State University

Bozeman, Montana
www.montana.edu   Federal Code: 002532

4-year public university in large town.

Enrollment: 14,205 undergrads, 14% part-time. 2,240 full-time freshmen.

Selectivity: Admits over 75% of applicants.

BASIC COSTS (2016-2017)

Tuition and fees: $7,031; out-of-state residents $23,042.

Per-credit charge: $222; out-of-state residents $889.

Room and board: $8,900.

Additional info: Required fees is an average between in-state and out-of-state figures. In-state required fees are $1,557 and out-of-state fees are $1,845. Tuition/fee waivers available for minority students.

FINANCIAL AID PICTURE (2015-2016)

Students with need: Out of 1,744 full-time freshmen who applied for aid, 1,079 were judged to have need. Of these, 1,018 received aid, and 406 had their full need met. Average financial aid package met 75% of need; average

scholarship/grant was $5,214; average loan was $6,124. For part-time students, average financial aid package was $10,521.

Students without need: 366 full-time freshmen who did not demonstrate need for aid received scholarships/grants; average award was $1,868. No-need awards available for academics, alumni affiliation, art, athletics, job skills, leadership, minority status, music/drama, ROTC, state/district residency.

Scholarships offered: 16 full-time freshmen received athletic scholarships; average amount $6,088.

Additional info: Tuition waiver for honorably discharged veterans, children of members of the United States armed forces who, at the time of entry into service, had legal residence in Montana and who were killed in action or who died as a result of injury, disease, or other disability incurred while in the service.

FINANCIAL AID PROCEDURES

Forms required: FAFSA.

Dates and Deadlines: Applicants notified on a rolling basis starting 4/1.

Transfers: Priority date 7/1; no deadline.

CONTACT

Brandi Payne, Director of Financial Aid Services
PO Box 172190, 201 Strand Union Building, Bozeman, MT 59717-2190
(406) 994-2845

Montana State University: Billings

Billings, Montana
www.msubillings.edu   Federal Code: 002530

4-year public university and technical college in small city.

Enrollment: 3,570 undergrads, 31% part-time. 593 full-time freshmen.

Selectivity: Admits over 75% of applicants.

BASIC COSTS (2016-2017)

Tuition and fees: $5,827; out-of-state residents $18,093.

Per-credit charge: $147; out-of-state residents $555.

Room and board: $7,690.

Additional info: Out-of-state students pay an additional $125 in fees.

FINANCIAL AID PICTURE (2015-2016)

Students with need: Out of 502 full-time freshmen who applied for aid, 361 were judged to have need. Of these, 354 received aid, and 88 had their full need met. Average financial aid package met 67% of need; average scholarship/grant was $4,492; average loan was $4,987. For part-time students, average financial aid package was $7,857.

Students without need: 55 full-time freshmen who did not demonstrate need for aid received scholarships/grants; average award was $1,752. No-need awards available for academics, alumni affiliation, art, athletics, job skills, leadership, minority status, music/drama, ROTC, state/district residency.

Scholarships offered: 32 full-time freshmen received athletic scholarships; average amount $2,672.

Additional info: Veterans and honors fee waivers offered.

FINANCIAL AID PROCEDURES

Forms required: FAFSA.

Dates and Deadlines: Priority date 3/1; no closing date. Applicants notified on a rolling basis starting 3/1.

Transfers: Applicants notified on a rolling basis.

CONTACT

Emily Williamson, Director of Financial Aid and Scholarships
1500 University Drive, Billings, MT 59101-0298
(406) 657-2188

Montana State University: Northern

Havre, Montana
www.msun.edu
Federal Code: 002533

4-year public university in large town.
Enrollment: 1,218 undergrads.

BASIC COSTS (2016-2017)

Tuition and fees: $4,922; out-of-state residents $17,122.
Per-credit charge: $117; out-of-state residents $523.
Room and board: $6,410.
Additional info: Out-of-state students pay an additional $110 in fees. Tuition/fee waivers available for minority students.

FINANCIAL AID PICTURE

Students with need: Need-based aid available for full-time and part-time students. Work study available nights, weekends, and for part-time students.
Students without need: No-need awards available for academics, athletics.

FINANCIAL AID PROCEDURES

Forms required: FAFSA, institutional form.
Dates and Deadlines: Priority date 4/15; no closing date. Applicants notified on a rolling basis starting 5/1; must reply within 4 week(s) of notification.

CONTACT

Cindy Small, Director of Financial Aid
Box 7751, Havre, MT 59501-7751
(406) 265-3787

Montana Tech of the University of Montana

Butte, Montana
www.mtech.edu
Federal Code: 002531

4-year public engineering and technical college in large town.
Enrollment: 2,277 undergrads, 9% part-time. 408 full-time freshmen.
Selectivity: Admits over 75% of applicants.

BASIC COSTS (2016-2017)

Tuition and fees: $6,623; out-of-state residents $20,046.
Per-credit charge: $205; out-of-state residents $761.
Room and board: $8,932.

FINANCIAL AID PICTURE (2015-2016)

Students with need: Out of 332 full-time freshmen who applied for aid, 217 were judged to have need. Of these, 217 received aid, and 46 had their full need met. Average financial aid package met 67% of need; average scholarship/grant was $5,807; average loan was $3,003. For part-time students, average financial aid package was $8,052.
Students without need: 73 full-time freshmen who did not demonstrate need for aid received scholarships/grants; average award was $3,839. No-need awards available for academics, alumni affiliation, athletics, leadership, minority status, music/drama, religious affiliation, state/district residency.
Scholarships offered: 19 full-time freshmen received athletic scholarships; average amount $5,737.

FINANCIAL AID PROCEDURES

Forms required: FAFSA.
Dates and Deadlines: Priority date 3/1; no closing date. Applicants notified on a rolling basis starting 3/15; must reply within 2 week(s) of notification.
Transfers: No deadline. Applicants notified on a rolling basis; must reply within 2 week(s) of notification.

CONTACT

Mike Richardson, Director of Financial Aid
1300 West Park Street, Butte, MT 59701-8997
(406) 496-4256

Rocky Mountain College

Billings, Montana
www.rocky.edu
Federal Code: 002534

4-year private liberal arts college in small city, affiliated with the Presbyterian Church (USA).
Enrollment: 885 undergrads, 3% part-time. 216 full-time freshmen.
Selectivity: Admits 50 to 75% of applicants.

BASIC COSTS (2017-2018)

Tuition and fees: $27,566.
Per-credit charge: $1,127.
Room and board: $8,210.

FINANCIAL AID PICTURE (2016-2017)

Students with need: Out of 203 full-time freshmen who applied for aid, 186 were judged to have need. Of these, 186 received aid, and 43 had their full need met. Average financial aid package met 76% of need; average scholarship/grant was $18,300; average loan was $3,217. For part-time students, average financial aid package was $14,579.
Students without need: 11 full-time freshmen who did not demonstrate need for aid received scholarships/grants; average award was $13,091. No-need awards available for academics, athletics, music/drama.
Scholarships offered: 6 full-time freshmen received athletic scholarships; average amount $7,356.

FINANCIAL AID PROCEDURES

Forms required: FAFSA.
Dates and Deadlines: Applicants notified on a rolling basis starting 2/15; must reply within 4 week(s) of notification.
Transfers: No deadline. Applicants notified on a rolling basis starting 2/15; must reply within 4 week(s) of notification.

CONTACT

Jessica Francischetti, Director of Financial Assistance
1511 Poly Drive, Billings, MT 59102-1796
(406) 657-1031

Salish Kootenai College

Pablo, Montana
www.skc.edu
Federal Code: 015023

4-year private liberal arts college in rural community.
Enrollment: 818 undergrads.
Selectivity: Open admission; but selective for some programs.

BASIC COSTS (2016-2017)

Tuition and fees: $6,279; out-of-state residents $11,463.
Per-credit charge: $141.
Additional info: Tuition/fee waivers available for minority students.

FINANCIAL AID PICTURE

Students with need: Need-based aid available for full-time and part-time students. Work study available nights, weekends, and for part-time students.

FINANCIAL AID PROCEDURES

Forms required: FAFSA.
Dates and Deadlines: Priority date 3/31; no closing date. Applicants notified on a rolling basis starting 7/15; must reply within 6 week(s) of notification.

CONTACT

Jackie Swain, Financial Aid Director
PO Box 70, Pablo, MT 59855
(406) 275-4855

Stone Child College

Box Elder, Montana
www.stonechild.edu   Federal Code: 026109

2-year public community and junior college in rural community.
Enrollment: 180 undergrads, 18% part-time. 36 full-time freshmen.
Selectivity: Open admission.

BASIC COSTS (2016-2017)

Tuition and fees: $2,645; out-of-state residents $2,775.

FINANCIAL AID PICTURE

Students with need: Need-based aid available for full-time and part-time students.
Additional info: Scholarships available to high school and GED graduates who apply for college admission during the first term after graduation.

FINANCIAL AID PROCEDURES

Forms required: FAFSA.
Dates and Deadlines: Priority date 3/1; no closing date. Applicants notified on a rolling basis.

CONTACT

Dennis Sangrey, Financial Aid Director
8294 Upper Box Elder Road, Box Elder, MT 59521
(406) 395-4313 ext. 267

University of Great Falls

Great Falls, Montana
www.ugf.edu   Federal Code: 002527

4-year private university and liberal arts college in small city, affiliated with the Roman Catholic Church.
Enrollment: 881 undergrads, 45% part-time. 93 full-time freshmen.
Selectivity: Admits over 75% of applicants.

BASIC COSTS (2017-2018)

Tuition and fees: $25,050.
Per-credit charge: $789.
Room and board: $8,500.

FINANCIAL AID PICTURE (2016-2017)

Students with need: Out of 85 full-time freshmen who applied for aid, 72 were judged to have need. Of these, 72 received aid, and 1 had their full need met. Average financial aid package met 67% of need; average scholarship/grant was $11,364; average loan was $2,983. For part-time students, average financial aid package was $9,253.
Students without need: 8 full-time freshmen who did not demonstrate need for aid received scholarships/grants; average award was $3,605. No-need awards available for academics, alumni affiliation, art, athletics, music/drama, religious affiliation, state/district residency.
Scholarships offered: *Merit:* Freshmen scholarships: $1,000-$6,000; based on high school GPA; renewable. *Athletic:* 21 full-time freshmen received athletic scholarships; average amount $13,040.

FINANCIAL AID PROCEDURES

Forms required: FAFSA.
Dates and Deadlines: Priority date 3/1; no closing date. Applicants notified on a rolling basis starting 3/1; must reply within 3 week(s) of notification.
Transfers: Transfer student scholarships; $2,500-$4,000; based on college GPA; renewable.

CONTACT

Kelli Engelhardt, Director of Financial Aid
1301 20th Street South, Great Falls, MT 59405
(406) 791-5235

University of Montana

Missoula, Montana
http://umt.edu   Federal Code: 002536

4-year public health science and liberal arts college in small city.
Enrollment: 9,356 undergrads, 17% part-time. 1,491 full-time freshmen.
Selectivity: Open admission; but selective for some programs.

BASIC COSTS (2016-2017)

Tuition and fees: $6,215; out-of-state residents $23,669.
Per-credit charge: $146; out-of-state residents $728.
Room and board: $8,826.
Additional info: Out-of-state students pay an additional $72 in fees. Tuition/fee waivers available for minority students.

FINANCIAL AID PICTURE (2016-2017)

Students with need: Out of 1,244 full-time freshmen who applied for aid, 904 were judged to have need. Of these, 882 received aid, and 105 had their full need met. Average financial aid package met 67% of need; average scholarship/grant was $5,068; average loan was $3,811. For part-time students, average financial aid package was $9,483.
Students without need: 332 full-time freshmen who did not demonstrate need for aid received scholarships/grants; average award was $4,114. No-need awards available for academics, athletics, leadership, music/drama, ROTC, state/district residency.
Scholarships offered: 34 full-time freshmen received athletic scholarships; average amount $8,633.
Additional info: Fee waivers for minority students available to American Indians with blood quantum eligibility for, or enrolled membership in, a Montana tribe.

FINANCIAL AID PROCEDURES

Forms required: FAFSA.
Dates and Deadlines: Priority date 2/16; no closing date. Applicants notified on a rolling basis starting 3/16; must reply within 4 week(s) of notification.
Transfers: Applicants notified on a rolling basis starting 4/1.

CONTACT

Kent McGowan, Director of Financial Aid
Lommasson Center 101, Missoula, MT 59812
(406) 243-5373

University of Montana: Western

Dillon, Montana
www.umwestern.edu   Federal Code: 002537

4-year public liberal arts and teachers college in small town.
Enrollment: 1,467 undergrads, 16% part-time. 327 full-time freshmen.
Selectivity: Open admission; but selective for some programs.

BASIC COSTS (2016-2017)

Tuition and fees: $4,284; out-of-state residents $16,206.
Per-credit charge: $129; out-of-state residents $626.
Room and board: $7,482.
Additional info: Out-of-state students pay an additional $72 in fees. Tuition/fee waivers available for minority students.

FINANCIAL AID PICTURE (2016-2017)

Students with need: Out of 314 full-time freshmen who applied for aid, 244 were judged to have need. Of these, 221 received aid. Average financial aid package met 14% of need; average scholarship/grant was $3,004; average loan was $3,467. For part-time students, average financial aid package was $2,510.
Students without need: 2 full-time freshmen who did not demonstrate need for aid received scholarships/grants; average award was $1,250. No-need awards available for academics, alumni affiliation, art, athletics, leadership, state/district residency.

Scholarships offered: *Merit:* Chancellor's Leadership Waiver Scholarship, departmental waiver scholarship, Western Undergraduate Exchange. *Athletic:* 26 full-time freshmen received athletic scholarships; average amount $1,817.

Additional info: Tuition waivers available for veterans, war orphans, Native Americans, senior citizens, and dependents of Montana University System employees.

FINANCIAL AID PROCEDURES

Forms required: FAFSA.

Dates and Deadlines: Priority date 12/1; no closing date. Applicants notified on a rolling basis starting 1/31; must reply within 4 week(s) of notification.

Transfers: No deadline. Applicants notified on a rolling basis starting 4/1; must reply within 4 week(s) of notification. Transfer students must have 2.0 GPA to enter in with good academic standing. Students with transfer GPA below 1.8 must appeal to receive financial aid. Students with transfer GPA between 1.8 and 1.99 enter on financial aid warning.

CONTACT

Arlene Williams, Director of Financial Aid
710 South Atlantic Street, Dillon, MT 59725
(406) 683-7511

Nebraska

Bellevue University

Bellevue, Nebraska
www.bellevue.edu   Federal Code: 002538

4-year private university and business college in large city.
Enrollment: 6,224 undergrads.
Selectivity: Open admission; but selective for some programs.

BASIC COSTS (2016-2017)
Tuition and fees: $9,075.
Per-credit charge: $285.
Room and board: $6,649.
Additional info: First year we are offering room and board on campus.

FINANCIAL AID PICTURE
Students with need: Need-based aid available for full-time and part-time students. Work study available nights, weekends, and for part-time students.
Students without need: No-need awards available for academics, athletics, leadership.

FINANCIAL AID PROCEDURES
Forms required: FAFSA, institutional form.
Dates and Deadlines: Applicants notified on a rolling basis starting 4/15; must reply within 2 week(s) of notification.
Transfers: No deadline. Applicants notified on a rolling basis starting 4/15; must reply within 2 week(s) of notification.

CONTACT
Janet Yale, Director, Financial Aid
1000 Galvin Road South, Bellevue, NE 68005-3098
(402) 557-7095

BryanLGH College of Health Sciences

Lincoln, Nebraska
www.bryanhealthcollege.edu   Federal Code: 006399

4-year private health science college in large city, affiliated with the United Methodist Church.

Enrollment: 590 undergrads.

BASIC COSTS (2016-2017)
Tuition and fees: $16,890.
Per-credit charge: $533.

FINANCIAL AID PICTURE
Students with need: Need-based aid available for full-time and part-time students.
Students without need: No-need awards available for academics, leadership.

FINANCIAL AID PROCEDURES
Forms required: FAFSA, institutional form.
Dates and Deadlines: Closing date 5/1. Applicants notified on a rolling basis starting 5/1; must reply within 3 week(s) of notification.

CONTACT
Deborah Wilke, Financial Aid Director
5035 Everett Street, Lincoln, NE 68506
(402) 481-8984

Central Community College

Grand Island, Nebraska
www.cccneb.edu   Federal Code: 014468

2-year public community and technical college in large town.
Enrollment: 4,055 undergrads, 51% part-time. 600 full-time freshmen.
Selectivity: Open admission.

BASIC COSTS (2016-2017)
Tuition and fees: $2,880; out-of-state residents $4,140.
Per-credit charge: $84; out-of-state residents $126.
Room and board: $6,982.

FINANCIAL AID PICTURE (2015-2016)
Students with need: Out of 522 full-time freshmen who applied for aid, 449 were judged to have need. Of these, 438 received aid, and 136 had their full need met. Average financial aid package met 75% of need; average scholarship/grant was $2,414; average loan was $1,479. For part-time students, average financial aid package was $2,927.
Students without need: 27 full-time freshmen who did not demonstrate need for aid received scholarships/grants; average award was $626. No-need awards available for academics, art, athletics, job skills, leadership, music/drama.
Scholarships offered: 32 full-time freshmen received athletic scholarships; average amount $790.
Additional info: All students are eligible to apply for a Pell Grant. Students enrolled for at least six semester hours (half-time) are eligible to apply for grants, loans, work study, and scholarships. To be considered for full-time benefits, students must be enrolled for at least 12 credit hours during the semester.

FINANCIAL AID PROCEDURES
Forms required: FAFSA, institutional form.
Dates and Deadlines: Priority date 3/1; no closing date. Applicants notified on a rolling basis starting 2/1; must reply within 2 week(s) of notification.

CONTACT
Vicki Kucera, Area Director of Financial Aid Services
3134 West Highway 34, Grand Island, NE 68802-4903
(402) 461-2414

Chadron State College

Chadron, Nebraska
www.csc.edu   Federal Code: 002539

4-year public business and liberal arts college in small town.
Enrollment: 2,046 undergrads, 17% part-time. 382 full-time freshmen.

Selectivity: Open admission; but selective for some programs.

BASIC COSTS (2016-2017)
Tuition and fees: $6,656; out-of-state residents $6,686.
Per-credit charge: $160; out-of-state residents $161.
Room and board: $6,352.
Additional info: Additional Special Rates apply for resident of qualifying states.

FINANCIAL AID PICTURE
Students with need: Need-based aid available for full-time and part-time students. Work study available nights, weekends, and for part-time students.
Students without need: No-need awards available for academics, alumni affiliation, art, athletics, leadership, minority status, music/drama, state/district residency.

FINANCIAL AID PROCEDURES
Forms required: FAFSA, institutional form.
Dates and Deadlines: Priority date 6/1; no closing date. Applicants notified on a rolling basis starting 4/1; must reply within 2 week(s) of notification.

CONTACT
Sherry Douglas, Director of Financial Aid
1000 Main Street, Chadron, NE 69337
(308) 432-6230

Clarkson College
Omaha, Nebraska
www.clarksoncollege.edu   Federal Code: 009862

4-year private health science college in large city, affiliated with the Episcopal Church.
Enrollment: 765 undergrads.
Selectivity: Open admission; but selective for some programs.

BASIC COSTS (2016-2017)
Tuition and fees: $15,780.
Per-credit charge: $499.
Room only: $5,230.

FINANCIAL AID PICTURE
Students with need: Need-based aid available for full-time and part-time students. Work study available nights, weekends, and for part-time students.
Students without need: No-need awards available for academics, alumni affiliation, minority status, religious affiliation.

FINANCIAL AID PROCEDURES
Forms required: FAFSA, institutional form.
Dates and Deadlines: Priority date 4/1; no closing date. Applicants notified on a rolling basis starting 4/13; must reply within 3 week(s) of notification.
Transfers: Priority date 3/1; no deadline. Applicants notified on a rolling basis starting 3/30.

CONTACT
Margie Harris, Director of Student Financial Services
101 South 42nd Street, Omaha, NE 68131-2739
(402) 552-2749

College of Saint Mary
Omaha, Nebraska
www.csm.edu   Federal Code: 002540

4-year private university and liberal arts college for women in large city, affiliated with the Roman Catholic Church.
Enrollment: 744 undergrads, 4% part-time. 102 full-time freshmen.

BASIC COSTS (2017-2018)
Tuition and fees: $19,950.

Per-credit charge: $985.
Room and board: $7,550.

FINANCIAL AID PICTURE (2016-2017)
Students with need: Average financial aid package met 81% of need; average scholarship/grant was $20,751; average loan was $4,098. For part-time students, average financial aid package was $5,594.
Students without need: No-need awards available for academics, athletics, music/drama.

FINANCIAL AID PROCEDURES
Forms required: FAFSA.
Dates and Deadlines: Priority date 3/15; no closing date. Applicants notified on a rolling basis starting 12/15; must reply within 2 week(s) of notification.
Transfers: Priority date 3/15; no deadline. Applicants notified on a rolling basis starting 3/15; must reply within 2 week(s) of notification. Scholarships and need based grants available for full-time transfer students.

CONTACT
Beth Sisk, Director of Financial Aid
7000 Mercy Road, Omaha, NE 68106
(402) 399-2362

Concordia University
Seward, Nebraska
www.cune.edu   Federal Code: 002541

4-year private university in small town, affiliated with the Lutheran Church - Missouri Synod.
Enrollment: 1,233 undergrads, 2% part-time. 323 full-time freshmen.
Selectivity: Admits 50 to 75% of applicants.

BASIC COSTS (2017-2018)
Tuition and fees: $31,000.
Per-credit charge: $890.
Room and board: $8,100.

FINANCIAL AID PICTURE (2016-2017)
Students with need: Out of 301 full-time freshmen who applied for aid, 261 were judged to have need. Of these, 261 received aid, and 81 had their full need met. Average financial aid package met 81% of need; average scholarship/grant was $19,343; average loan was $3,739. For part-time students, average financial aid package was $16,512.
Students without need: 22 full-time freshmen who did not demonstrate need for aid received scholarships/grants; average award was $15,082. No-need awards available for academics, alumni affiliation, art, athletics, leadership, music/drama, religious affiliation.
Scholarships offered: *Merit:* President's scholarship: $19,000 per year; based on GPA and SAT/ACT. Regent's scholarship: $14,500-$15,500 per year; based on GPA and SAT/ACT. Dean's Scholarship: $12,500-$13,500 per year; based on GPA and SAT/ACT. Achievement Award: $8,500-$10,500 per year; based on GPA and SAT/ACT. *Athletic:* 44 full-time freshmen received athletic scholarships; average amount $5,527.

FINANCIAL AID PROCEDURES
Forms required: FAFSA.
Dates and Deadlines: Priority date 3/1; no closing date. Applicants notified on a rolling basis starting 3/1; must reply within 4 week(s) of notification.
Transfers: Applicants notified on a rolling basis starting 3/1; must reply within 4 week(s) of notification.

CONTACT
Lori Read, Dir of Student Financial Services & Student Success Center
800 North Columbia Avenue, Seward, NE 68434-1556
(800) 535-5494 ext. 7270

PART III: FINANCIAL AID COLLEGE BY COLLEGE

Creative Center
Omaha, Nebraska
www.creativecenter.edu
Federal Code: 031643

4-year for-profit visual arts and career college in large city.
Enrollment: 58 undergrads, 5% part-time. 22 full-time freshmen.
Selectivity: Admits over 75% of applicants.

BASIC COSTS (2017-2018)
Tuition and fees: $27,700.

FINANCIAL AID PICTURE
Students with need: Need-based aid available for full-time and part-time students.
Students without need: No-need awards available for academics, art.
Scholarships offered: President's Award: $1,000. Founder's Award: $2,000. Both awards based on portfolio and high school academics. Andy Arrants Memorial Scholarship: supply kit (approx. $500); based on submitted artwork and essay.

FINANCIAL AID PROCEDURES
Forms required: FAFSA.
Dates and Deadlines: Closing date 7/15. Applicants notified on a rolling basis starting 1/1.
Transfers: No deadline. Applicants notified on a rolling basis starting 1/1.

CONTACT
Sandy LaRocca, Director of Financial Aid
10850 Emmet Street, Omaha, NE 68164-2911
(402) 898-1000 ext. 203

Creighton University
Omaha, Nebraska
www.creighton.edu
Federal Code: 002542

4-year private university in very large city, affiliated with the Roman Catholic Church.
Enrollment: 4,149 undergrads, 4% part-time. 1,033 full-time freshmen.
Selectivity: Admits 50 to 75% of applicants.

BASIC COSTS (2016-2017)
Tuition and fees: $37,606.
Per-credit charge: $1,125.
Room and board: $10,600.
Additional info: Tuition/fee waivers available for adults, minority students.

FINANCIAL AID PICTURE (2016-2017)
Students with need: 67% of average financial aid package awarded as scholarships/grants, 33% awarded as loans/jobs. Need-based aid available for part-time students. Work study available nights, weekends, and for part-time students.
Students without need: No-need awards available for academics, alumni affiliation, art, athletics, leadership, minority status, music/drama, ROTC.
Scholarships offered: Diversity Scholarship & Native American Merit Scholarship: $30,000; awarded to students who show commitment to diversity; 3.3 GPA or higher on a 4.0 scale required; applicants evaluated on academic merit, community service, school activities, leadership, and financial need. First-generation college bound students are encouraged to apply. Excellence in the Arts: $4,000; awarded to students who intend to major in music, art, dance, theater, and musical theater. Christina M. Hixson Scholarship in Business Administration: $4,500; awarded to freshman business students from high schools in CO, IA, IL, KA, MN, MO, NE, ND, SD, WI or WY with a minimum of 3.0 GPA. Heider College of Business Administration Ethics and Social Responsibility Scholarship: $2,500; awarded to students with exceptional service accomplishments and leadership potential. Presidential Scholarship: $28,000; awarded to selected applicants in the top 10% of applicant pool, based upon academics. Scott Scholarship: full tuition scholarship in the Heider College of Business Administration; awarded to selected students in the top 10% of applicant pool; based on academics. G. Robert Muchemore Foundation Undergraduate Scholarship: $26,000; awarded to graduates of Nebraska high schools entering as freshmen; based upon academics.

FINANCIAL AID PROCEDURES
Forms required: FAFSA, institutional form.
Dates and Deadlines: Priority date 3/1; no closing date. Applicants notified on a rolling basis starting 3/15; must reply by 3/15 or within 4 week(s) of notification.
Transfers: No deadline. Applicants notified on a rolling basis starting 3/10; must reply by 5/1 or within 2 week(s) of notification.

CONTACT
Paula Kohles, Director of Financial Aid
2500 California Plaza, Omaha, NE 68178-0001
(402) 280-2731

Doane University
Crete, Nebraska
www.doane.edu
Federal Code: 002544

4-year private liberal arts college in small town, affiliated with the United Church of Christ.
Enrollment: 1,041 undergrads. 303 full-time freshmen.
Selectivity: Admits over 75% of applicants.

BASIC COSTS (2016-2017)
Tuition and fees: $30,434.
Per-credit charge: $990.
Room and board: $8,750.

FINANCIAL AID PICTURE (2016-2017)
Students with need: Out of 287 full-time freshmen who applied for aid, 248 were judged to have need. Of these, 248 received aid, and 102 had their full need met. Average financial aid package met 95% of need; average scholarship/grant was $21,913; average loan was $3,520. Need-based aid available for part-time students.
Students without need: 22 full-time freshmen who did not demonstrate need for aid received scholarships/grants; average award was $14,390. No-need awards available for academics, alumni affiliation, art, athletics, music/drama, religious affiliation.
Scholarships offered: 34 full-time freshmen received athletic scholarships; average amount $5,517.

FINANCIAL AID PROCEDURES
Forms required: FAFSA.
Dates and Deadlines: Priority date 2/25; no closing date. Applicants notified on a rolling basis starting 3/15; must reply within 4 week(s) of notification.

CONTACT
Peggy Tvrdy, Director of Financial Aid
1014 Boswell Avenue, Crete, NE 68333
(402) 826-8260

Grace University
Omaha, Nebraska
www.graceuniversity.edu
Federal Code: 002547

4-year private university and Bible college in large city, affiliated with the interdenominational tradition.
Enrollment: 238 undergrads. 51 full-time freshmen.

BASIC COSTS (2016-2017)
Tuition and fees: $21,928.
Room and board: $7,558.

Additional info: Tuition/fee waivers available for minority students.

FINANCIAL AID PICTURE

Students with need: Need-based aid available for full-time and part-time students.

Students without need: No-need awards available for academics, alumni affiliation, athletics, leadership, minority status, music/drama.

FINANCIAL AID PROCEDURES

Forms required: FAFSA.

Dates and Deadlines: Priority date 3/1; closing date 4/1. Applicants notified on a rolling basis starting 3/1; must reply within 3 week(s) of notification.

Transfers: No deadline. Applicants notified on a rolling basis starting 3/1; must reply within 3 week(s) of notification.

CONTACT

Ray Miller, Director of Financial Aid
1311 South Ninth Street, Omaha, NE 68108-3629
(402) 449-2810

Hastings College

Hastings, Nebraska
www.hastings.edu   Federal Code: 002548

4-year private liberal arts college in large town, affiliated with the Presbyterian Church (USA).

Enrollment: 1,108 undergrads. 273 full-time freshmen.

BASIC COSTS (2016-2017)

Tuition and fees: $28,250.

Room and board: $8,880.

Additional info: Tuition/fee waivers available for adults.

FINANCIAL AID PICTURE

Students with need: Need-based aid available for full-time and part-time students. Work study available nights, weekends, and for part-time students.

Students without need: No-need awards available for academics, alumni affiliation, art, athletics, leadership, music/drama.

Scholarships offered: Walter Scott Scholarship Competition: full-tuition, for freshman; 3 awarded. Trustees Scholarships: $14,000 per year. President's Scholarships: $13,000 per year. Dean Scholarships: $12,000 per year. Ambassador Scholarships: $10,000 per year. Ringland Scholarships: $8,000 per year. Pro Rege Scholarships: $7,000 per year. Kessler Scholarship: full tuition, for Christian Ministry students; 3 awarded. Christian Ministry scholarships: $5,000 per year; 3 awarded.

FINANCIAL AID PROCEDURES

Forms required: FAFSA, institutional form.

Dates and Deadlines: Closing date 5/1. Applicants notified on a rolling basis starting 2/15; must reply within 2 week(s) of notification.

Transfers: No deadline. Stafford loans based on number of transferable credits.

CONTACT

Traci Boeve, Financial Aid Director
710 North Turner Avenue, Hastings, NE 68901-7621
(402) 461-7789

Kaplan University: Lincoln

Lincoln, Nebraska
www.lincoln.kaplanuniversity.edu   Federal Code: 004721

2-year for-profit branch campus college in small city.

Enrollment: 449 undergrads, 39% part-time. 4 full-time freshmen.

Selectivity: Open admission; but selective for some programs.

BASIC COSTS (2016-2017)

Additional info: Diploma programs: $9364-$10,540; Associate programs: $10,218; Bachelor programs: $10,218. Fees, books supplies range depending on program level and course of study. All costs are subject to change.

FINANCIAL AID PICTURE

Students with need: Need-based aid available for full-time and part-time students. Work study available nights, weekends, and for part-time students.

Students without need: This college awards aid only to students with need.

FINANCIAL AID PROCEDURES

Forms required: FAFSA, institutional form.

Dates and Deadlines: Applicants notified on a rolling basis starting 2/1.

Transfers: No deadline.

CONTACT

Corinne Combs, Director of Financial Aid
1821 K Street, Lincoln, NE 68508
(402) 474-5315

Kaplan University: Omaha

Omaha, Nebraska
www.omaha.kaplanuniversity.edu   Federal Code: 008491

2-year for-profit career college in large city.

Enrollment: 597 undergrads, 34% part-time. 10 full-time freshmen.

Selectivity: Open admission; but selective for some programs.

BASIC COSTS (2016-2017)

Additional info: Diploma programs: $9364-$10,540; Associate programs: $10,218; Bachelor programs: $10,218. Fees, books supplies range depending on program level and course of study. All costs are subject to change.

FINANCIAL AID PICTURE

Students with need: Need-based aid available for full-time and part-time students. Work study available nights, weekends, and for part-time students.

Students without need: This college awards aid only to students with need.

FINANCIAL AID PROCEDURES

Forms required: FAFSA, institutional form.

Dates and Deadlines: Applicants notified on a rolling basis.

CONTACT

Crystal Faxon, Director Of Financial Aid
5425 North 103rd Street, Omaha, NE 68134
(402) 431-6100

Little Priest Tribal College

Winnebago, Nebraska
www.littlepriest.edu   Federal Code: 033233

2-year private community college in rural community.

Enrollment: 116 undergrads, 28% part-time. 28 full-time freshmen.

Selectivity: Open admission.

BASIC COSTS (2016-2017)

Tuition and fees: $4,276.

Room and board: $4,000.

FINANCIAL AID PICTURE

Students with need: Need-based aid available for full-time and part-time students.

FINANCIAL AID PROCEDURES

Forms required: FAFSA, institutional form.

CONTACT
Sabariyatty Mohhammad, Director of Financial Aid
PO Box 270, Winnebago, NE 68071
(402) 878-3331

Metropolitan Community College
Omaha, Nebraska
www.mccneb.edu   Federal Code: 004432

2-year public community and technical college in large city.
Enrollment: 6,899 undergrads, 61% part-time. 849 full-time freshmen.
Selectivity: Open admission; but selective for some programs.

BASIC COSTS (2016-2017)
Tuition and fees: $2,880; out-of-state residents $4,208.
Per-credit charge: $59; out-of-state residents $88.5.
Room and board: $6,255.

FINANCIAL AID PICTURE
Students with need: Need-based aid available for full-time and part-time students.
Students without need: No-need awards available for academics.

FINANCIAL AID PROCEDURES
Forms required: FAFSA, institutional form.
Dates and Deadlines: Priority date 3/15; no closing date. Applicants notified on a rolling basis starting 4/15.

CONTACT
Wilma Hjelum, Director of Financial Aid & Veteran Services
Box 3777, Omaha, NE 68103-0777
(402) 457-2330

Mid-Plains Community College
North Platte, Nebraska
www.mpcc.edu   Federal Code: 002557

2-year public community and technical college in large town.
Enrollment: 1,215 undergrads, 36% part-time. 330 full-time freshmen.
Selectivity: Open admission; but selective for some programs.

BASIC COSTS (2016-2017)
Tuition and fees: $2,970; out-of-state residents $3,720.
Per-credit charge: $84; out-of-state residents $109.
Room and board: $6,100.

FINANCIAL AID PICTURE (2015-2016)
Students with need: Out of 265 full-time freshmen who applied for aid, 194 were judged to have need. Of these, 189 received aid, and 66 had their full need met. Average financial aid package met 81% of need; average scholarship/grant was $4,537; average loan was $2,404. For part-time students, average financial aid package was $4,533.
Students without need: 37 full-time freshmen who did not demonstrate need for aid received scholarships/grants; average award was $1,273. No-need awards available for academics, art, athletics, music/drama.
Scholarships offered: 89 full-time freshmen received athletic scholarships; average amount $4,142.

FINANCIAL AID PROCEDURES
Forms required: FAFSA, institutional form.
Dates and Deadlines: Priority date 5/1; no closing date. Applicants notified on a rolling basis starting 4/1; must reply within 3 week(s) of notification.
Transfers: No deadline. Applicants notified on a rolling basis starting 4/1; must reply within 3 week(s) of notification.

CONTACT
Erinn Brauer, Director of Financial Aid
1101 Halligan Drive, North Platte, NE 69101
(800) 658-4348

Midland University
Fremont, Nebraska
www.midlandu.edu   Federal Code: 002553

4-year private university and liberal arts college in large town, affiliated with the Evangelical Lutheran Church in America.
Enrollment: 1,213 undergrads, 4% part-time. 341 full-time freshmen.

BASIC COSTS (2016-2017)
Tuition and fees: $30,430.
Room and board: $8,038.
Additional info: Tuition/fee waivers available for minority students.

FINANCIAL AID PICTURE
Students with need: Need-based aid available for full-time and part-time students. Work study available nights, weekends, and for part-time students.
Students without need: No-need awards available for academics, alumni affiliation, art, athletics, leadership, minority status, music/drama, religious affiliation.

FINANCIAL AID PROCEDURES
Forms required: FAFSA, institutional form.
Dates and Deadlines: Priority date 4/15; no closing date. Applicants notified on a rolling basis starting 3/1; must reply within 2 week(s) of notification.
Transfers: Priority date 4/1. Applicants notified on a rolling basis starting 4/1; must reply within 2 week(s) of notification.

CONTACT
Doug Watson, Director of Financial Aid
900 North Clarkson Street, Fremont, NE 68025
(402) 721-5480

Nebraska Christian College
Papillion, Nebraska
www.nechristian.edu   Federal Code: 012976

4-year private Bible college in large town, affiliated with the Christian Church.
Enrollment: 111 undergrads, 2% part-time. 16 full-time freshmen.
Selectivity: Admits 50 to 75% of applicants.

BASIC COSTS (2016-2017)
Tuition and fees: $300.
Per-credit charge: $500.
Comprehensive fee: $24,500.

FINANCIAL AID PICTURE
Students with need: Need-based aid available for full-time and part-time students. Work study available nights, weekends, and for part-time students.
Students without need: No-need awards available for academics, leadership, religious affiliation.

FINANCIAL AID PROCEDURES
Forms required: FAFSA, institutional form.
Dates and Deadlines: Priority date 6/1; no closing date. Applicants notified on a rolling basis starting 5/5.

CONTACT
Sarah Nigro, Financial Aid Officer
12550 South 114th Street, Papillion, NE 68046
(402) 935-9400

Nebraska College of Technical Agriculture

Curtis, Nebraska
www.ncta.unl.edu   Federal Code: 007358

2-year public agricultural college in rural community.
Enrollment: 265 undergrads, 8% part-time. 109 full-time freshmen.
Selectivity: Open admission.

BASIC COSTS (2016-2017)
Tuition and fees: $4,842; out-of-state residents $9,450.
Per-credit charge: $121; out-of-state residents $256.5.
Room and board: $7,098.

FINANCIAL AID PICTURE (2015-2016)
Students with need: Average financial aid package met 61% of need; average scholarship/grant was $6,632; average loan was $3,128. Need-based aid available for part-time students.
Students without need: 25 full-time freshmen who did not demonstrate need for aid received scholarships/grants; average award was $3,619. No-need awards available for academics, leadership, state/district residency.

FINANCIAL AID PROCEDURES
Forms required: FAFSA.
Dates and Deadlines: Priority date 4/1; no closing date. Applicants notified on a rolling basis starting 5/1; must reply within 2 week(s) of notification.
Transfers: No deadline. Applicants notified on a rolling basis; must reply within 2 week(s) of notification.

CONTACT
Justin Brown, Director, Scholarships and Financial Aid
404 East 7th Street, Curtis, NE 69025-0069
(308) 367-5207

Nebraska Indian Community College

Macy, Nebraska
www.thenicc.edu   Federal Code: 015339

2-year public community college in rural community.
Enrollment: 135 undergrads, 73% part-time. 16 full-time freshmen.
Selectivity: Open admission.

BASIC COSTS (2017-2018)
Tuition and fees: $5,150.
Per-credit charge: $170.
Additional info: Book charges are included in the tuition. Tuition/fee waivers available for minority students.

FINANCIAL AID PICTURE (2015-2016)
Students with need: 98% of average financial aid package awarded as scholarships/grants, 2% awarded as loans/jobs. Need-based aid available for part-time students. Work study available nights, weekends, and for part-time students.
Students without need: This college awards aid only to students with need.

FINANCIAL AID PROCEDURES
Forms required: FAFSA.
Dates and Deadlines: Priority date 9/1; no closing date.
Transfers: No deadline. Must reply within 2 week(s) of notification.

CONTACT
Dawne Price, Dean of Student Services
PO Box 428, Macy, NE 68039-0428
(402) 241-5908

Nebraska Methodist College of Nursing and Allied Health

Omaha, Nebraska
www.methodistcollege.edu   Federal Code: 009937

4-year private health science and nursing college in large city, affiliated with the United Methodist Church.
Enrollment: 849 undergrads, 43% part-time. 44 full-time freshmen.
Selectivity: Admits less than 50% of applicants.

BASIC COSTS (2016-2017)
Tuition and fees: $17,210.
Per-credit charge: $568.
Room only: $6,750.

FINANCIAL AID PICTURE (2016-2017)
Students with need: Out of 44 full-time freshmen who applied for aid, 27 were judged to have need. Of these, 27 received aid, and 3 had their full need met. Average financial aid package met 48% of need; average scholarship/grant was $5,798; average loan was $3,193. For part-time students, average financial aid package was $7,635.
Students without need: 17 full-time freshmen who did not demonstrate need for aid received scholarships/grants; average award was $3,419. No-need awards available for academics, alumni affiliation, leadership, religious affiliation.

FINANCIAL AID PROCEDURES
Forms required: FAFSA, institutional form.
Dates and Deadlines: Priority date 3/1; no closing date. Applicants notified on a rolling basis starting 3/15; must reply within 3 week(s) of notification.

CONTACT
Penny James, Director of Financial Aid
720 North 87th Street, Omaha, NE 68114-2852
(402) 354-7225

Nebraska Wesleyan University

Lincoln, Nebraska
www.nebrwesleyan.edu   Federal Code: 002555

4-year private liberal arts college in small city, affiliated with the United Methodist Church.
Enrollment: 1,788 undergrads, 12% part-time. 439 full-time freshmen.
Selectivity: Admits 50 to 75% of applicants.

BASIC COSTS (2016-2017)
Tuition and fees: $31,394.
Per-credit charge: $1,120.
Room and board: $8,758.
Additional info: Tuition/fee waivers available for adults, minority students.

FINANCIAL AID PICTURE (2015-2016)
Students with need: Out of 384 full-time freshmen who applied for aid, 329 were judged to have need. Of these, 329 received aid, and 60 had their full need met. Average financial aid package met 79% of need; average scholarship/grant was $18,314; average loan was $4,133. For part-time students, average financial aid package was $4,889.
Students without need: 106 full-time freshmen who did not demonstrate need for aid received scholarships/grants; average award was $16,017. No-need awards available for academics, alumni affiliation, art, leadership, music/drama.
Scholarships offered: NWU Scholarship: tuition, books, fees, and room and board up to $27,000; competitive; 2 awards per year.

FINANCIAL AID PROCEDURES
Forms required: FAFSA.
Dates and Deadlines: Applicants notified on a rolling basis starting 10/15; must reply by 5/1 or within 2 week(s) of notification.

Transfers: No deadline. Applicants notified on a rolling basis starting 10/15; must reply within 3 week(s) of notification.

CONTACT

Thomas Ochsner, Director of Scholarships and Financial Aid

5000 St. Paul Avenue, Lincoln, NE 68504

(402) 465-2212

Northeast Community College

Norfolk, Nebraska

www.northeast.edu   Federal Code: 002556

2-year public community college in large town.

Enrollment: 2,726 undergrads.

Selectivity: Open admission; but selective for some programs.

BASIC COSTS (2016-2017)

Tuition and fees: $3,285; out-of-state residents $4,365.

Per-credit charge: $90; out-of-state residents $126.

Room and board: $7,800.

FINANCIAL AID PICTURE

Students with need: Need-based aid available for full-time and part-time students. Work study available nights, weekends, and for part-time students.

Students without need: No-need awards available for academics, athletics, music/drama.

FINANCIAL AID PROCEDURES

Forms required: FAFSA, institutional form.

Dates and Deadlines: Applicants notified on a rolling basis; must reply within 2 week(s) of notification.

CONTACT

Stacy Dieckman, Director of Financial Aid

801 East Benjamin Avenue, Norfolk, NE 68702-0469

(402) 844-7285

Peru State College

Peru, Nebraska

www.peru.edu   Federal Code: 002559

4-year public liberal arts and teachers college in rural community.

Enrollment: 1,483 undergrads, 20% part-time. 257 full-time freshmen.

Selectivity: Open admission.

BASIC COSTS (2016-2017)

Tuition and fees: $6,791; out-of-state residents $6,821.

Per-credit charge: $160; out-of-state residents $161.

Room and board: $7,214.

Additional info: Additional Special Rates apply for resident of qualifying states.

FINANCIAL AID PICTURE

Students with need: Need-based aid available for full-time and part-time students. Work study available nights, weekends, and for part-time students.

Students without need: No-need awards available for academics, art, athletics, leadership, music/drama, state/district residency.

FINANCIAL AID PROCEDURES

Forms required: FAFSA.

Dates and Deadlines: Priority date 3/1; no closing date. Applicants notified on a rolling basis starting 3/1; must reply within 2 week(s) of notification.

Transfers: Must have financial aid transcripts from all previous schools sent to college.

CONTACT

Cheryl Reid, Director of Financial Aid

P.O. Box 10, Peru, NE 68421-0010

(402) 872-2228

Southeast Community College

Lincoln, Nebraska

www.southeast.edu   Federal Code: 007591

2-year public community college in small city.

Enrollment: 6,291 undergrads, 43% part-time. 977 full-time freshmen.

Selectivity: Open admission.

BASIC COSTS (2016-2017)

Tuition and fees: $2,836; out-of-state residents $3,466.

Per-credit charge: $61.5; out-of-state residents $75.5.

Room and board: $4,647.

FINANCIAL AID PICTURE

Students with need: Need-based aid available for full-time and part-time students. Work study available nights, weekends, and for part-time students.

Students without need: No-need awards available for academics, leadership, minority status, state/district residency.

FINANCIAL AID PROCEDURES

Forms required: FAFSA, institutional form.

Dates and Deadlines: Applicants notified on a rolling basis; must reply within 2 week(s) of notification.

Transfers: No deadline. Applicants notified on a rolling basis.

CONTACT

Melissa Troyer, Administrative Director of Financial Aid

8800 O Street, Lincoln, NE 68520

(402) 437-2610

Union College

Lincoln, Nebraska

www.ucollege.edu   Federal Code: 002563

4-year private liberal arts college in large city, affiliated with the Seventh-day Adventists.

Enrollment: 759 undergrads, 8% part-time. 172 full-time freshmen.

Selectivity: Admits 50 to 75% of applicants.

BASIC COSTS (2017-2018)

Tuition and fees: $23,070.

Per-credit charge: $916.

Room and board: $6,926.

FINANCIAL AID PICTURE (2015-2016)

Students with need: Out of 142 full-time freshmen who applied for aid, 123 were judged to have need. Of these, 123 received aid, and 26 had their full need met. Average financial aid package met 72% of need; average scholarship/grant was $14,632; average loan was $3,924. For part-time students, average financial aid package was $9,717.

Students without need: 49 full-time freshmen who did not demonstrate need for aid received scholarships/grants; average award was $10,443. No-need awards available for academics, state/district residency.

Additional info: Special institutional grants offered to all freshmen and sophomores demonstrating exceptional financial need.

FINANCIAL AID PROCEDURES

Forms required: FAFSA, institutional form.

Dates and Deadlines: Applicants notified on a rolling basis.

CONTACT
Taryn Rouse, Director of Student Financial Services
3800 South 48th Street, Lincoln, NE 68506-4300
(402) 486-2505

University of Nebraska - Kearney
Kearney, Nebraska
www.unk.edu   Federal Code: 002551

4-year public university in large town.
Enrollment: 4,672 undergrads, 10% part-time. 931 full-time freshmen.
Selectivity: Admits over 75% of applicants.

BASIC COSTS (2016-2017)
Tuition and fees: $6,953; out-of-state residents $13,381.
Per-credit charge: $182; out-of-state residents $396.25.
Room and board: $9,594.

FINANCIAL AID PICTURE (2015-2016)
Students with need: Out of 825 full-time freshmen who applied for aid, 664 were judged to have need. Of these, 660 received aid, and 179 had their full need met. Average financial aid package met 73% of need; average scholarship/grant was $8,711; average loan was $3,570. For part-time students, average financial aid package was $5,672.
Students without need: 161 full-time freshmen who did not demonstrate need for aid received scholarships/grants; average award was $3,914. No-need awards available for academics, alumni affiliation, art, athletics, leadership, minority status, music/drama, ROTC, state/district residency.
Scholarships offered: 36 full-time freshmen received athletic scholarships; average amount $4,702.

FINANCIAL AID PROCEDURES
Forms required: FAFSA, institutional form.
Dates and Deadlines: Priority date 4/1; no closing date. Applicants notified on a rolling basis starting 3/15; must reply within 2 week(s) of notification.
Transfers: No deadline. Applicants notified on a rolling basis starting 3/15.

CONTACT
Mary Sommers, Director of Financial Aid
905 West 25th, Kearney, NE 68849
(308) 865-8520

University of Nebraska - Lincoln
Lincoln, Nebraska
www.unl.edu   Federal Code: 002565

4-year public university in large city.
Enrollment: 20,833 undergrads, 7% part-time. 4,603 full-time freshmen.
Selectivity: Admits over 75% of applicants.

BASIC COSTS (2016-2017)
Tuition and fees: $8,538; out-of-state residents $23,058.
Per-credit charge: $225.25; out-of-state residents $709.25.
Room and board: $10,670.

FINANCIAL AID PICTURE (2015-2016)
Students with need: Out of 3,557 full-time freshmen who applied for aid, 2,656 were judged to have need. Of these, 2,508 received aid, and 594 had their full need met. Average financial aid package met 82% of need; average scholarship/grant was $7,875; average loan was $4,009. For part-time students, average financial aid package was $11,158.
Students without need: 572 full-time freshmen who did not demonstrate need for aid received scholarships/grants; average award was $6,708. No-need awards available for academics, alumni affiliation, art, athletics, leadership, music/drama, state/district residency.

Scholarships offered: 142 full-time freshmen received athletic scholarships; average amount $14,146.

FINANCIAL AID PROCEDURES
Forms required: FAFSA.
Dates and Deadlines: Priority date 4/1; no closing date. Applicants notified on a rolling basis starting 4/1.
Transfers: Priority date 4/1; no deadline. Applicants notified on a rolling basis starting 4/1.

CONTACT
Justin Brown, Director of Scholarships and Financial Aid
1410 Q Street, Lincoln, NE 68588-0417
(402) 472-2030

University of Nebraska - Omaha
Omaha, Nebraska
www.unomaha.edu   Federal Code: 002554

4-year public university in large city.
Enrollment: 12,287 undergrads.

BASIC COSTS (2016-2017)
Tuition and fees: $7,822; out-of-state residents $20,939.
Per-credit charge: $205.25; out-of-state residents $642.5.
Room and board: $10,018.

FINANCIAL AID PICTURE
Students with need: Need-based aid available for full-time and part-time students. Work study available nights, weekends, and for part-time students.
Students without need: No-need awards available for academics, alumni affiliation, art, athletics, leadership, minority status, music/drama, ROTC, state/district residency.

FINANCIAL AID PROCEDURES
Forms required: FAFSA.
Dates and Deadlines: Priority date 4/1; no closing date. Applicants notified on a rolling basis starting 4/15; must reply within 2 week(s) of notification.

CONTACT
Marty Habrock, Director of Financial Aid
6001 Dodge Street, Omaha, NE 68182-0005
(402) 554-2327

University of Nebraska Medical Center
Omaha, Nebraska
www.unmc.edu   Federal Code: 006895

Upper-division public health science college in very large city.
Enrollment: 739 undergrads.

BASIC COSTS (2016-2017)
Additional info: College of Medicine: resident $29,200; nonresident $72,620; Mandatory Fees $1,118. College of Dentistry: resident $29,925; nonresident $73,425; Books/Equipment/Mandatory Fees $8874.50. College of Pharmacy: resident $19,110; nonresident $39,380; Mandatory Fees 1,345. Tuition is assessed on per semester not credit hour basis. Tuition/fee waivers available for minority students.

FINANCIAL AID PICTURE
Students with need: Need-based aid available for full-time and part-time students. Work study available nights, weekends, and for part-time students.

FINANCIAL AID PROCEDURES
Forms required: FAFSA, institutional form.
Dates and Deadlines: Closing date 4/1. Applicants notified by 7/1; must reply by 7/30 or within 2 week(s) of notification.

Transfers: No deadline. Applicants notified on a rolling basis starting 5/1; must reply within 2 week(s) of notification.

CONTACT
Judith Walker, Director of Financial Aid
984230 Nebraska Medical Center, Omaha, NE 68198-4230
(402) 559-4199

Wayne State College
Wayne, Nebraska
www.wsc.edu   Federal Code: 002566

4-year public liberal arts and teachers college in small town.
Enrollment: 2,641 undergrads, 7% part-time. 578 full-time freshmen.
Selectivity: Open admission; but selective for some programs.

BASIC COSTS (2016-2017)
Tuition and fees: $6,427; out-of-state residents $6,457.
Per-credit charge: $160; out-of-state residents $161.
Room and board: $7,110.
Additional info: Out-of-state tuition applies to students taking classes on campus. Out-of-state and off campus tuitions fees are higher. Additional Special Rates apply for resident of qualifying states.

FINANCIAL AID PICTURE (2016-2017)
Students with need: Out of 528 full-time freshmen who applied for aid, 418 were judged to have need. Of these, 410 received aid, and 209 had their full need met. Average financial aid package met 52% of need; average scholarship/grant was $4,789; average loan was $3,182. For part-time students, average financial aid package was $6,613.
Students without need: 57 full-time freshmen who did not demonstrate need for aid received scholarships/grants; average award was $2,448. No-need awards available for academics, art, athletics, leadership, minority status, music/drama, religious affiliation, ROTC, state/district residency.
Scholarships offered: 49 full-time freshmen received athletic scholarships; average amount $3,320.

FINANCIAL AID PROCEDURES
Forms required: FAFSA.
Dates and Deadlines: Priority date 4/1; no closing date. Applicants notified on a rolling basis starting 4/1; must reply within 4 week(s) of notification.

CONTACT
Annette Kaus, Director of Financial Aid
1111 Main Street, Wayne, NE 68787
(402) 375-7230

Western Nebraska Community College
Scottsbluff, Nebraska
www.wncc.edu   Federal Code: 002560

2-year public community college in large town.
Enrollment: 1,143 undergrads, 34% part-time. 312 full-time freshmen.
Selectivity: Open admission; but selective for some programs.

BASIC COSTS (2016-2017)
Tuition and fees: $3,375; out-of-state residents $3,660.
Per-credit charge: $95; out-of-state residents $104.5.
Room and board: $7,010.
Additional info: Border state students from Colorado, Wyoming, and South Dakota pay in-state tuition rates.

FINANCIAL AID PICTURE (2016-2017)
Students with need: Out of 228 full-time freshmen who applied for aid, 180 were judged to have need. Of these, 175 received aid. Average financial

aid package met 91% of need; average scholarship/grant was $5,401; average loan was $2,907. For part-time students, average financial aid package was $7,832.
Students without need: 49 full-time freshmen who did not demonstrate need for aid received scholarships/grants; average award was $1,875. No-need awards available for academics, art, athletics, leadership, music/drama, state/district residency.
Scholarships offered: 64 full-time freshmen received athletic scholarships; average amount $6,646.

FINANCIAL AID PROCEDURES
Forms required: FAFSA.
Dates and Deadlines: Priority date 3/1; no closing date. Applicants notified on a rolling basis.
Transfers: State of Nebraska limits the amount of Nebraska State Grant funds a student receives in any one year.

CONTACT
Sheila Johns, Director of Financial Aid
1601 East 27th Street, Scottsbluff, NE 69361
(308) 635-6011

York College
York, Nebraska
www.york.edu   Federal Code: 002567

4-year private liberal arts and teachers college in small town, affiliated with the Church of Christ.
Enrollment: 417 undergrads. 96 full-time freshmen.
Selectivity: Admits 50 to 75% of applicants.

BASIC COSTS (2016-2017)
Tuition and fees: $17,700.
Per-credit charge: $600.
Room and board: $6,600.

FINANCIAL AID PICTURE
Students with need: Need-based aid available for full-time and part-time students. Work study available nights, weekends, and for part-time students.
Students without need: No-need awards available for academics, alumni affiliation, athletics, leadership, music/drama.

FINANCIAL AID PROCEDURES
Forms required: FAFSA.
Dates and Deadlines: Priority date 4/1; no closing date. Applicants notified on a rolling basis starting 3/1; must reply within 4 week(s) of notification.
Transfers: No deadline. Applicants notified on a rolling basis starting 3/1; must reply within 4 week(s) of notification.

CONTACT
Brien Alley, Director of Financial Aid
1125 East 8th Street, York, NE 68467
(402) 363-5624

Nevada

Art Institute of Las Vegas
Henderson, Nevada
www.artinstitutes.edu/lasvegas   Federal Code: 030846

3-year for-profit culinary school and visual arts college in very large city.
Enrollment: 952 undergrads.
Selectivity: Open admission; but selective for some programs.

BASIC COSTS (2016-2017)
Tuition and fees: $22,645.
Per-credit charge: $481.
Room only: $6,377.

FINANCIAL AID PICTURE
Students with need: Need-based aid available for full-time and part-time students. Work study available nights, weekends, and for part-time students.
Students without need: No-need awards available for academics, state/district residency.
Scholarships offered: Academic Competitiveness Grant: up to $750 the first year and up to $1,300 the second year; available to students who are receiving a Pell Grant, are full time in their first or second year of college in a degree program, who graduated from high school in 2005 or later, and who took a program of study in high school that was considered to be rigorous; each eligible student may receive 2 years of ACG; must have a 3.0 GPA at the end of the first year to receive a second year grant. C-CAP Careers Through Culinary Arts Program: approximately $36,000-$72,000; available to students who are enrolled in a C-CAP program. CKYBER National Kitchen and Bath Association VNU Scholarship: provided for students enrolled in a NKBA (National Kitchen and Bath Association) endorsed program; GPA of 2.7 or higher; must be attending full time for the full academic year; Interior Design program students are eligible to apply. Evelyn Keedy Memorial Scholarship: $30,000 tuition; available to high school seniors who show dedication to their education and a desire for a creative career. National Art Honor Society Scholarship: first Place $20,000, second place $10,000, third place $5,000, fourth place $3,000, fifth place $2,000; high school seniors who also belong to the National Art Honor Society may apply; senior class members of the National Art Honor Society are eligible to compete.

FINANCIAL AID PROCEDURES
Dates and Deadlines: Applicants notified on a rolling basis.
Transfers: No deadline. Applicants notified on a rolling basis.

CONTACT
Dana Sirolli, Director of Student Financial Services
2350 Corporate Circle, Henderson, NV 89074-7737
(702) 369-9944

Career College of Northern Nevada
Sparks, Nevada
www.ccnn.edu   Federal Code: 026215

2-year for-profit career college in large city.
Enrollment: 350 undergrads.
Selectivity: Open admission.

BASIC COSTS (2016-2017)
Additional info: Tuition ranges from $11,850 to $27,500 depending on program. Some programs also have additional fees.

FINANCIAL AID PICTURE
Students with need: Need-based aid available for full-time students.
Students without need: This college awards aid only to students with need.

FINANCIAL AID PROCEDURES
Forms required: FAFSA.
Dates and Deadlines: Applicants notified on a rolling basis.

CONTACT
Patricia Shannon, Director of Financial Aid
1421 Pullman Drive, Sparks, NV 89434
(775) 856-2266

College of Southern Nevada
Las Vegas, Nevada
www.csn.edu   Federal Code: 010362

2-year public community college in very large city.
Enrollment: 28,685 undergrads.
Selectivity: Open admission; but selective for some programs.

BASIC COSTS (2016-2017)
Tuition and fees: $2,910; out-of-state residents $9,688.
Per-credit charge: $92.

FINANCIAL AID PICTURE
Students with need: Work study available nights, weekends, and for part-time students.
Students without need: No-need awards available for state/district residency.

FINANCIAL AID PROCEDURES
Forms required: FAFSA.
Dates and Deadlines: Priority date 5/1; closing date 6/30. Applicants notified on a rolling basis starting 7/15; must reply within 2 week(s) of notification.

CONTACT
Director, Student Financial Services
6375 West Charleston Boulevard, Las Vegas, NV 89146-1164
(702) 651-4047

Great Basin College
Elko, Nevada
www.gbcnv.edu   Federal Code: 006977

4-year public community and teachers college in large town.
Enrollment: 2,065 undergrads.
Selectivity: Open admission; but selective for some programs.

BASIC COSTS (2016-2017)
Tuition and fees: $2,910; out-of-state residents $9,688.
Per-credit charge: $92.
Room only: $3,325.

FINANCIAL AID PICTURE
Students with need: Need-based aid available for full-time and part-time students. Work study available nights, weekends, and for part-time students.

FINANCIAL AID PROCEDURES
Forms required: FAFSA.
Dates and Deadlines: Priority date 6/1; no closing date. Applicants notified on a rolling basis starting 7/1.
Transfers: Priority date 4/1.

CONTACT
Scott Neilsen, Director of Financial Aid
1500 College Parkway, Elko, NV 89801
(775) 753-2267

Kaplan College: Las Vegas
Las Vegas, Nevada
www.kaplancollege.com   Federal Code: 030432

2-year for-profit career college in very large city.
Enrollment: 944 undergrads.
Selectivity: Open admission; but selective for some programs.

BASIC COSTS (2016-2017)
Additional info: Criminal Justice: $292.22 quarter unit credit (95 Credit Hours), total $30,805. Health Information Technology: $293.89 quarter unit

credit (94 Credit Hours), total $30,805. Medical Assistant: $297.03 quarter unit credit (51 Credit Hours), total $15,663. Medical Assistant X-Ray Technician: $291.51 quarter unit credit (70 Credit Hours), total $22,045. Medical Billing and Coding Specialist: $289.09 quarter unit credit (51 Credit Hours), total $15,663. Pharmacy Technician: $258.31 quarter unit credit (57 Credit Hours), total $15,663. Phlebotomy Technician: total $995. Practical Nursing: $313.39 quarter unit credit (89 Credit Hours), total $29,731.

FINANCIAL AID PICTURE

Students with need: Need-based aid available for full-time and part-time students. Work study available nights.

FINANCIAL AID PROCEDURES

Forms required: FAFSA, institutional form.
Transfers: No deadline. Applicants notified on a rolling basis.

CONTACT

Carmen Torres, Director of Finance
3535 West Sahara Avenue, Las Vegas, NV 89102
(702) 368-2338

Nevada State College

Henderson, Nevada
www.nsc.edu   Federal Code: 041143

4-year public nursing and liberal arts college in large city.
Enrollment: 3,637 undergrads, 60% part-time. 251 full-time freshmen.
Selectivity: Admits over 75% of applicants.

BASIC COSTS (2016-2017)
Tuition and fees: $5,131; out-of-state residents $16,244.
Per-credit charge: $146.75.

FINANCIAL AID PICTURE

Students with need: Need-based aid available for full-time and part-time students.

FINANCIAL AID PROCEDURES

Forms required: FAFSA, institutional form.
Dates and Deadlines: Priority date 3/1; no closing date. Applicants notified on a rolling basis starting 5/1.
Transfers: Applicants notified on a rolling basis starting 5/1.

CONTACT

Anthony Morrone, Director of Financial Aid
1125 Nevada State Drive, Henderson, NV 89002
(702) 992-2150

Roseman University of Health Sciences

Henderson, Nevada
www.roseman.edu   Federal Code: 040653

Upper-division private university in very large city.
Enrollment: 385 undergrads.

BASIC COSTS (2016-2017)
Tuition and fees: $36,530.
Per-credit charge: $644.

FINANCIAL AID PICTURE (2016-2017)

Students with need: Average financial aid package for all full-time undergraduates was $6,989. 4% awarded as scholarships/grants, 96% awarded as loans/jobs. Need-based aid available for part-time students. Work study available nights, weekends, and for part-time students.
Students without need: No-need awards available for academics, leadership.

FINANCIAL AID PROCEDURES

Forms required: FAFSA.
Dates and Deadlines: Applicants notified on a rolling basis starting 2/15; must reply within 4 week(s) of notification.
Transfers: No deadline. Applicants notified on a rolling basis starting 1/1; must reply within 4 week(s) of notification.

CONTACT

Sally Mickelson, Director of Financial Aid
11 Sunset Way, Henderson, NV 89014-2333
(702) 968-1635

Sierra Nevada College

Incline Village, Nevada
www.sierranevada.edu   Federal Code: 009192

4-year private liberal arts college in small town.
Enrollment: 478 undergrads, 3% part-time. 93 full-time freshmen.
Selectivity: Admits 50 to 75% of applicants.

BASIC COSTS (2017-2018)
Tuition and fees: $32,639.
Per-credit charge: $1,348.
Room and board: $12,764.

FINANCIAL AID PICTURE (2016-2017)

Students with need: Out of 80 full-time freshmen who applied for aid, 62 were judged to have need. Of these, 62 received aid, and 13 had their full need met. Average financial aid package met 59% of need; average scholarship/grant was $23,109; average loan was $4,737. For part-time students, average financial aid package was $10,400.
Students without need: 28 full-time freshmen who did not demonstrate need for aid received scholarships/grants; average award was $12,540. No-need awards available for academics, athletics.
Scholarships offered: *Merit:* Academic scholarships; $2,000-$12,500 per year; renewable. *Athletic:* 6 full-time freshmen received athletic scholarships; average amount $4,266.
Additional info: Institutional need-based grant provided based on remaining need after being awarded all scholarships and Federal Student Aid. First time freshmen awarded 50% of remaining need and 45% for continuing students.

FINANCIAL AID PROCEDURES

Forms required: FAFSA.
Dates and Deadlines: Closing date 8/17. Applicants notified on a rolling basis starting 11/1.

CONTACT

Nicole Ferguson, Director of Financial Aid
999 Tahoe Boulevard, Incline Village, NV 89451-4269
(775) 831-1314 ext. 7440

Truckee Meadows Community College

Reno, Nevada
www.tmcc.edu   Federal Code: 010363

2-year public community and technical college in large city.
Enrollment: 8,538 undergrads, 72% part-time. 752 full-time freshmen.
Selectivity: Open admission; but selective for some programs.

BASIC COSTS (2016-2017)
Tuition and fees: $2,910; out-of-state residents $9,688.
Per-credit charge: $92.

FINANCIAL AID PICTURE

Students with need: Need-based aid available for full-time and part-time students. Work study available nights, weekends, and for part-time students.

Students without need: No-need awards available for academics, art, leadership, minority status, music/drama, state/district residency.

Additional info: Institutional grants to state residents, short-term emergency loans available. Work-study applications must reply within 10 days of notification.

FINANCIAL AID PROCEDURES

Forms required: FAFSA.

Dates and Deadlines: Applicants notified on a rolling basis starting 3/15.

Transfers: No deadline. Applicants notified on a rolling basis. Must provide academic transcript from previous institution.

CONTACT

Sharon Wurm, Director of Financial Aid, Scholarships and Student Employment
7000 Dandini Boulevard, Reno, NV 89512
(775) 673-7072

University of Nevada: Las Vegas

Las Vegas, Nevada
www.unlv.edu   Federal Code: 002569

4-year public university in very large city.

Enrollment: 24,197 undergrads, 25% part-time. 3,756 full-time freshmen.

Selectivity: Admits over 75% of applicants. GED not accepted.

BASIC COSTS (2016-2017)

Tuition and fees: $7,063; out-of-state residents $20,973.

Per-credit charge: $207.25.

Room and board: $10,734.

FINANCIAL AID PICTURE (2016-2017)

Students with need: Out of 3,334 full-time freshmen who applied for aid, 2,637 were judged to have need. Of these, 2,557 received aid, and 215 had their full need met. Average financial aid package met 53% of need; average scholarship/grant was $5,868; average loan was $3,317. For part-time students, average financial aid package was $7,453.

Students without need: 561 full-time freshmen who did not demonstrate need for aid received scholarships/grants; average award was $3,659. No-need awards available for academics, alumni affiliation, athletics, music/drama.

Scholarships offered: 65 full-time freshmen received athletic scholarships; average amount $21,138.

Additional info: Tuition reduction for state residents through consortium programs and for out-of-state students graduating from high schools in designated counties bordering Nevada, for military dependents residing in-state, and for dependents of children of alumni not residing in-state.

FINANCIAL AID PROCEDURES

Forms required: FAFSA.

Dates and Deadlines: Priority date 11/1; no closing date. Applicants notified on a rolling basis starting 4/1; must reply within 6 week(s) of notification.

CONTACT

Norm Bedford, Director of Financial Aid & Scholarships
4505 Maryland Parkway, Box 451021, Las Vegas, NV 89154-1021
(702) 895-3424

University of Nevada: Reno

Reno, Nevada
www.unr.edu   Federal Code: 002568

4-year public university in small city.

Enrollment: 17,794 undergrads, 14% part-time. 3,803 full-time freshmen.

Selectivity: Admits over 75% of applicants. GED not accepted.

BASIC COSTS (2016-2017)

Tuition and fees: $7,143; out-of-state residents $21,053.

Per-credit charge: $207.25.

Room and board: $10,612.

FINANCIAL AID PICTURE (2015-2016)

Students with need: Average financial aid package met 61% of need; average scholarship/grant was $5,039; average loan was $3,342. For part-time students, average financial aid package was $4,842.

Students without need: No-need awards available for academics, alumni affiliation, art, athletics.

Scholarships offered: Presidential scholarship: $5,000 per year; 3.5 unweighted GPA and 1380 SAT (exclusive of writing)/31 ACT required; must be admitted by 2/1 of year prior to enrollment and meet Nevada residency requirements. Additional scholarships: $2,500-$5,000; based on combination of test scores and unweighted GPA.

Additional info: Reduced out-of-state tuition available for participants in WUE program.

FINANCIAL AID PROCEDURES

Forms required: FAFSA.

Dates and Deadlines: Priority date 3/1; no closing date. Applicants notified on a rolling basis starting 4/1; must reply by 6/1.

Transfers: No deadline. Applicants notified on a rolling basis; must reply within 2 week(s) of notification. 2.0 transfer GPA required to be eligible for aid.

CONTACT

Tim Wolfe, Director, Student Financial Services
Mail Stop 120, Reno, NV 89557
(775) 784-4666

Western Nevada College

Carson City, Nevada
www.wnc.edu   Federal Code: 013896

2-year public community college in small city.

Enrollment: 3,005 undergrads, 59% part-time. 364 full-time freshmen.

Selectivity: Open admission; but selective for some programs.

BASIC COSTS (2016-2017)

Tuition and fees: $2,910; out-of-state residents $9,688.

Per-credit charge: $92.

FINANCIAL AID PICTURE

Students with need: Need-based aid available for full-time and part-time students. Work study available nights.

Students without need: No-need awards available for academics, athletics, state/district residency.

FINANCIAL AID PROCEDURES

Forms required: FAFSA.

Dates and Deadlines: Priority date 4/1; no closing date. Applicants notified on a rolling basis; must reply within 3 week(s) of notification.

Transfers: No deadline. Applicants notified on a rolling basis; must reply within 3 week(s) of notification. Loans received at other schools counted toward limit.

CONTACT

JW Lazzari, Associate Director of Financial Assistance
2201 West College Parkway, Carson City, NV 89703-7399
(775) 445-3264

New Hampshire

Colby-Sawyer College
New London, New Hampshire
www.colby-sawyer.edu   Federal Code: 002572

4-year private liberal arts college in small town.
Enrollment: 1,062 undergrads, 5% part-time. 252 full-time freshmen.
Selectivity: Admits 50 to 75% of applicants.

BASIC COSTS (2017-2018)
Tuition and fees: $40,386.
Room and board: $13,650.

FINANCIAL AID PICTURE (2016-2017)
Students with need: 79% of average financial aid package awarded as scholarships/grants, 21% awarded as loans/jobs. Work study available nights, weekends, and for part-time students.
Students without need: No-need awards available for academics, alumni affiliation, minority status.

FINANCIAL AID PROCEDURES
Forms required: FAFSA.
Dates and Deadlines: Priority date 3/1; no closing date. Applicants notified on a rolling basis starting 1/30; must reply by 5/1.
Transfers: Closing date 4/15. Applicants notified on a rolling basis starting 1/30; must reply within 2 week(s) of notification.

CONTACT
Beth Renzulli, Director of Financial Aid
541 Main Street, New London, NH 03257-7835
(603) 526-3717

Dartmouth College
Hanover, New Hampshire   Federal Code: 002573
www.dartmouth.edu   CSS Code: 3351

4-year private university and liberal arts college in large town.
Enrollment: 4,230 undergrads. 1,116 full-time freshmen.
Selectivity: Admits less than 50% of applicants.

BASIC COSTS (2016-2017)
Tuition and fees: $51,438.
Room and board: $15,141.

FINANCIAL AID PICTURE (2016-2017)
Students with need: Out of 651 full-time freshmen who applied for aid, 533 were judged to have need. Of these, 533 received aid, and 533 had their full need met. Average financial aid package met 100% of need; average scholarship/grant was $49,025; average loan was $4,213. Need-based aid available for part-time students.
Students without need: This college awards aid only to students with need.

FINANCIAL AID PROCEDURES
Forms required: FAFSA, CSS PROFILE.
Dates and Deadlines: Closing date 2/1. Applicants notified by 4/2; must reply by 5/1.
Transfers: Closing date 3/1. Applicants notified by 4/2; must reply by 5/1. Grant budget for transfer students is limited. Some admitted transfer students may not have their full needs met.

CONTACT
Gordon Koff, Director of Financial Aid
6016 McNutt Hall, Hanover, NH 03755
(603) 646-2451

Franklin Pierce University
Rindge, New Hampshire
www.franklinpierce.edu   Federal Code: 002575

4-year private university and liberal arts college in small town.
Enrollment: 1,743 undergrads, 9% part-time. 680 full-time freshmen.
Selectivity: Admits over 75% of applicants.

BASIC COSTS (2016-2017)
Tuition and fees: $34,050.
Per-credit charge: $1,050.
Room and board: $12,700.

FINANCIAL AID PICTURE (2016-2017)
Students with need: Out of 628 full-time freshmen who applied for aid, 584 were judged to have need. Of these, 583 received aid, and 129 had their full need met. Average financial aid package met 76% of need; average scholarship/grant was $22,501; average loan was $3,953. For part-time students, average financial aid package was $5,171.
Students without need: 83 full-time freshmen who did not demonstrate need for aid received scholarships/grants; average award was $17,823. No-need awards available for academics, art, athletics, leadership.
Scholarships offered: *Merit:* Trustee, Presidential, Provost, Deans, Transfer, Achieve, Success, Opportunity, Mascenic, Monadonock, International, Academic Ambition, Athletic, and Alumni scholarships range from $1,000 to $25,000. Marlin Fitzwater Mass Communication: $2,000; 6 awarded. Robert Alvin Performing Arts-Theater, Music, Dance; $2,000; 2 awarded in each category. Leadership Scholarship: $2,000; 10 awarded. *Athletic:* 34 full-time freshmen received athletic scholarships; average amount $11,532.

FINANCIAL AID PROCEDURES
Forms required: FAFSA.
Dates and Deadlines: Priority date 10/1; no closing date. Applicants notified on a rolling basis starting 3/1.
Transfers: No deadline. Applicants notified on a rolling basis starting 3/1; must reply within 2 week(s) of notification.

CONTACT
Ken Ferreira, Executive Director of Student Financial Services
40 University Drive, Rindge, NH 03461-0060
(603) 899-4180

Granite State College
Concord, New Hampshire
www.granite.edu   Federal Code: 031013

4-year public liberal arts college in large town.
Enrollment: 1,802 undergrads, 48% part-time. 48 full-time freshmen.
Selectivity: Open admission; but selective for some programs.

BASIC COSTS (2016-2017)
Tuition and fees: $9,150; out-of-state residents $10,200.
Per-credit charge: $300; out-of-state residents $335.

FINANCIAL AID PICTURE (2015-2016)
Students with need: Need-based aid available for full-time and part-time students. Work study available nights.
Students without need: This college awards aid only to students with need.

FINANCIAL AID PROCEDURES
Forms required: FAFSA, institutional form.
Dates and Deadlines: Applicants notified on a rolling basis starting 4/15.
Transfers: No deadline. Applicants notified on a rolling basis starting 4/15.

CONTACT
Mac Broderick, Director of Financial Aid
25 Hall Street, Concord, NH 03301-7317
(603) 228-3000 ext. 324

Great Bay Community College

Portsmouth, New Hampshire
www.greatbay.edu   Federal Code: 002583

2-year public community and technical college in small town.
Enrollment: 1,887 undergrads.
Selectivity: Open admission; but selective for some programs.

BASIC COSTS (2016-2017)
Tuition and fees: $6,660; out-of-state residents $14,310.
Per-credit charge: $200; out-of-state residents $455.
Additional info: New England Regional tuition: $300 per credit hour.

FINANCIAL AID PICTURE
Students with need: Need-based aid available for full-time and part-time students. Work study available nights, weekends, and for part-time students.
Students without need: This college awards aid only to students with need.

FINANCIAL AID PROCEDURES
Forms required: FAFSA, institutional form.
Dates and Deadlines: Applicants notified on a rolling basis; must reply within 2 week(s) of notification.
Transfers: No deadline. Applicants notified on a rolling basis; must reply within 2 week(s) of notification.

CONTACT
Lauren Hughes, Director of Financial Aid
320 Corporate Drive, Portsmouth, NH 03801
(603) 772-1194

Keene State College

Keene, New Hampshire
www.keene.edu   Federal Code: 002590

4-year public liberal arts college in large town.
Enrollment: 4,068 undergrads, 2% part-time. 918 full-time freshmen.
Selectivity: Admits over 75% of applicants.

BASIC COSTS (2016-2017)
Tuition and fees: $13,613; out-of-state residents $21,997.
Per-credit charge: $458; out-of-state residents $806.
Room and board: $10,390.

FINANCIAL AID PICTURE (2015-2016)
Students with need: Out of 837 full-time freshmen who applied for aid, 667 were judged to have need. Of these, 649 received aid, and 68 had their full need met. Average financial aid package met 67% of need; average scholarship/grant was $8,277; average loan was $3,461. For part-time students, average financial aid package was $6,830.
Students without need: 152 full-time freshmen who did not demonstrate need for aid received scholarships/grants; average award was $3,963. No-need awards available for academics, alumni affiliation, art, music/drama.

FINANCIAL AID PROCEDURES
Forms required: FAFSA.
Dates and Deadlines: Closing date 3/1. Applicants notified on a rolling basis; must reply within 4 week(s) of notification.

CONTACT
Steve Goetsch, Interim Director of Financial Aid
229 Main Street, Keene, NH 03435-2604
(603) 358-2280

Lakes Region Community College

Laconia, New Hampshire
www.lrcc.edu   Federal Code: 007555

2-year public community and technical college in small city.
Enrollment: 845 undergrads, 51% part-time. 188 full-time freshmen.
Selectivity: Open admission; but selective for some programs.

BASIC COSTS (2016-2017)
Tuition and fees: $6,180; out-of-state residents $13,830.
Per-credit charge: $200; out-of-state residents $455.
Additional info: New England Regional tuition: $300 per credit hour.

FINANCIAL AID PICTURE
Students with need: Need-based aid available for full-time and part-time students.

FINANCIAL AID PROCEDURES
Forms required: FAFSA, institutional form.
Dates and Deadlines: Priority date 5/1; no closing date.

CONTACT
Kristen Purrington, Financial Aid Officer
379 Belmont Road, Laconia, NH 03246-9204
(603) 524-3207

Manchester Community College

Manchester, New Hampshire
www.mccnh.edu   Federal Code: 002582

2-year public community and technical college in small city.
Enrollment: 3,075 undergrads.
Selectivity: Open admission; but selective for some programs.

BASIC COSTS (2016-2017)
Tuition and fees: $6,480; out-of-state residents $14,130.
Per-credit charge: $200; out-of-state residents $455.
Additional info: New England Regional tuition: $300 per credit hour.

FINANCIAL AID PICTURE
Students with need: Need-based aid available for full-time and part-time students. Work study available nights, weekends, and for part-time students.
Students without need: This college awards aid only to students with need.
Scholarships offered: NH high school valedictorians receive 100% tuition scholarship.

FINANCIAL AID PROCEDURES
Forms required: FAFSA, institutional form.
Dates and Deadlines: Priority date 5/1; no closing date. Applicants notified on a rolling basis starting 4/15; must reply within 2 week(s) of notification.

CONTACT
Stephanie Weldon, Financial Aid Officer
1066 Front Street, Manchester, NH 03102-8518
(603) 668-6706 ext. 352

Nashua Community College

Nashua, New Hampshire
www.nashuacc.edu   Federal Code: 009236

2-year public community and technical college in small city.
Enrollment: 1,562 undergrads, 60% part-time. 203 full-time freshmen.
Selectivity: Open admission; but selective for some programs.

BASIC COSTS (2016-2017)
Tuition and fees: $6,480; out-of-state residents $14,130.

Per-credit charge: $200; out-of-state residents $455.
Additional info: New England Regional tuition: $300 per credit hour.

FINANCIAL AID PICTURE (2015-2016)

Students with need: Out of 159 full-time freshmen who applied for aid, 135 were judged to have need. Of these, 126 received aid, and 2 had their full need met. Average financial aid package met 31% of need; average scholarship/grant was $4,887; average loan was $2,969. For part-time students, average financial aid package was $4,407.

Students without need: This college awards aid only to students with need.

FINANCIAL AID PROCEDURES

Forms required: FAFSA.

Dates and Deadlines: Applicants notified on a rolling basis; must reply within 2 week(s) of notification.

CONTACT

Anne Eule, Director of Financial Aid
505 Amherst Street, Nashua, NH 03063-1026
(603) 578-8903

New England College
Henniker, New Hampshire
www.nec.edu   Federal Code: 002579

4-year private liberal arts and teachers college in small town.
Enrollment: 1,751 undergrads, 1% part-time. 348 full-time freshmen.
Selectivity: Admits over 75% of applicants.

BASIC COSTS (2016-2017)

Tuition and fees: $35,492.
Per-credit charge: $1,625.
Room and board: $13,536.
Additional info: Tuition/fee waivers available for adults.

FINANCIAL AID PICTURE (2016-2017)

Students with need: Out of 319 full-time freshmen who applied for aid, 308 were judged to have need. Of these, 283 received aid, and 34 had their full need met. Average financial aid package met 74% of need; average scholarship/grant was $25,226; average loan was $4,128. For part-time students, average financial aid package was $16,965.

Students without need: 30 full-time freshmen who did not demonstrate need for aid received scholarships/grants; average award was $21,601. No-need awards available for academics, alumni affiliation, art, job skills, leadership, music/drama, state/district residency.

Scholarships offered: Russell Durgin veteran scholarship, up to $16,000. Any veteran is eligible regardless of time of service.

Additional info: Significant scholarship programs for veterans including non-Post 911 eligible veterans.

FINANCIAL AID PROCEDURES

Forms required: FAFSA, institutional form.

Dates and Deadlines: Closing date 9/1. Applicants notified on a rolling basis starting 1/12; must reply within 4 week(s) of notification.

Transfers: No deadline. Applicants notified on a rolling basis starting 1/1; must reply within 4 week(s) of notification. May 1 deadline for state grant consideration.

CONTACT

Kristen Blase, Director of Student Financial Services
15 Main Street, Henniker, NH 03242
(603) 428-2226

New Hampshire Institute of Art
Manchester, New Hampshire
www.nhia.edu   Federal Code: 031823

4-year private visual arts college in small city.
Enrollment: 339 undergrads, 7% part-time. 65 full-time freshmen.
Selectivity: Admits less than 50% of applicants.

BASIC COSTS (2017-2018)

Tuition and fees: $26,880.
Per-credit charge: $1,095.
Room and board: $11,160.

FINANCIAL AID PICTURE (2016-2017)

Students with need: Out of 60 full-time freshmen who applied for aid, 54 were judged to have need. Of these, 54 received aid. Need-based aid available for part-time students.

Students without need: No-need awards available for academics, art.

FINANCIAL AID PROCEDURES

Forms required: FAFSA.

Dates and Deadlines: Priority date 3/1; no closing date. Applicants notified on a rolling basis starting 1/15.

CONTACT

Elayne Peloquin, Director of Financial Aid
148 Concord Street, Manchester, NH 03104
(603) 836-2578

NHTI-Concord's Community College
Concord, New Hampshire
www.nhti.edu   Federal Code: 002581

2-year public community and technical college in large town.
Enrollment: 3,535 undergrads. 628 full-time freshmen.
Selectivity: Open admission; but selective for some programs.

BASIC COSTS (2016-2017)

Tuition and fees: $6,660; out-of-state residents $14,310.
Per-credit charge: $200; out-of-state residents $455.
Room and board: $9,056.
Additional info: New England Regional tuition: $300 per credit hour.

FINANCIAL AID PICTURE (2015-2016)

Students with need: Out of 533 full-time freshmen who applied for aid, 446 were judged to have need. Of these, 420 received aid, and 13 had their full need met. Average financial aid package met 39% of need; average scholarship/grant was $4,686; average loan was $2,939. For part-time students, average financial aid package was $4,729.

Students without need: This college awards aid only to students with need.

Additional info: 60% of students who apply receive some form of financial aid. State school; all financial aid need-based, primarily from federal sources. No scholarships awarded.

FINANCIAL AID PROCEDURES

Forms required: FAFSA.

Dates and Deadlines: Priority date 5/1; no closing date. Applicants notified on a rolling basis starting 2/17; must reply within 2 week(s) of notification.

Transfers: No deadline. Applicants notified on a rolling basis.

CONTACT

Sheri Gonthier, Financial Aid Director
31 College Drive, Concord, NH 03301
(603) 271-6484 ext. 4013

Plymouth State University

Plymouth, New Hampshire
www.plymouth.edu   Federal Code: 002591

4-year public university and teachers college in small town.
Enrollment: 4,073 undergrads, 3% part-time. 1,343 full-time freshmen.
Selectivity: Admits over 75% of applicants.

BASIC COSTS (2016-2017)

Tuition and fees: $13,472; out-of-state residents $21,732.
Per-credit charge: $459; out-of-state residents $803.
Room and board: $11,008.

FINANCIAL AID PICTURE (2015-2016)

Students with need: Out of 1,241 full-time freshmen who applied for aid, 979 were judged to have need. Of these, 978 received aid, and 213 had their full need met. Average financial aid package met 64% of need; average scholarship/grant was $5,054; average loan was $3,394. For part-time students, average financial aid package was $6,179.
Students without need: 337 full-time freshmen who did not demonstrate need for aid received scholarships/grants; average award was $4,266. No-need awards available for academics, art, leadership, music/drama.

FINANCIAL AID PROCEDURES

Forms required: FAFSA.
Dates and Deadlines: Priority date 3/1; no closing date. Applicants notified on a rolling basis starting 3/1; must reply by 5/1.
Transfers: Applicants notified on a rolling basis starting 3/1.

CONTACT

Crystal Gaff, Director of Financial Aid
17 High Street MSC 52, Plymouth, NH 03264-1595
(603) 535-2338

River Valley Community College

Claremont, New Hampshire
www.rivervalley.edu   Federal Code: 007560

2-year public community college in large town.
Enrollment: 719 undergrads.
Selectivity: Open admission; but selective for some programs.

BASIC COSTS (2016-2017)

Tuition and fees: $6,150; out-of-state residents $13,800.
Per-credit charge: $200; out-of-state residents $455.
Additional info: New England Regional tuition: $300 per credit hour.

FINANCIAL AID PICTURE

Students with need: Need-based aid available for full-time and part-time students.
Students without need: This college awards aid only to students with need.

FINANCIAL AID PROCEDURES

Forms required: FAFSA.
Dates and Deadlines: Closing date 4/1. Applicants notified on a rolling basis; must reply within 2 week(s) of notification.

CONTACT

Julia Dower, Director of Financial Aid
One College Drive, Claremont, NH 03743-9707
(603) 542-7744 ext. 5725

Rivier University

Nashua, New Hampshire
www.rivier.edu   Federal Code: 002586

4-year private university and nursing college in small city, affiliated with the Roman Catholic Church.
Enrollment: 1,375 undergrads, 39% part-time. 286 full-time freshmen.
Selectivity: Admits 50 to 75% of applicants.

BASIC COSTS (2016-2017)

Tuition and fees: $29,700.
Per-credit charge: $970.
Room and board: $11,610.
Additional info: Tuition/fee waivers available for unemployed or children of unemployed.

FINANCIAL AID PICTURE

Students with need: Need-based aid available for full-time and part-time students. Work study available nights, weekends, and for part-time students.
Students without need: No-need awards available for academics, alumni affiliation.
Scholarships offered: Dean's Scholarship: $6,000 for residents, $5,000 for commuters; minimum 1000 SAT (exclusive of Writing); 3.0 GPA; renewable with minimum 2.67 GPA. Presidential Scholarship: $7,000 for residents, $6,000 for commuters; minimum 1150 SAT (exclusive of Writing); 3.4 GPA; renewable with minimum 3.0 GPA. Catholic High School Grant: $4,000 for residents, $3,000 for commuters; for students graduating from Catholic high school; renewable with 2.5 GPA. Honors Scholarship: for honors program participants; $10,000 for residents, $2,000 for commuters. Alumni Scholarship: $2,000; for children of Rivier alumni; renewable with minimum 2.0 GPA. Trustee Scholarship: $8,000 for residents, $7,000 for commuters; minimum 1200 SAT (exclusive of Writing); 3.4 GPA; renewable with minimum 3.0 GPA. Founders Scholarship for National Merit Finalists: full tuition; renewable with minimum 3.0 GPA.

FINANCIAL AID PROCEDURES

Forms required: FAFSA.
Dates and Deadlines: Priority date 3/1; no closing date. Applicants notified on a rolling basis starting 3/1; must reply by 5/1 or within 2 week(s) of notification.
Transfers: No deadline. Applicants notified on a rolling basis starting 3/1; must reply by 5/1 or within 2 week(s) of notification. Scholarship for transfer students with minimum 2.5 GPA and 12 transferable credits.

CONTACT

Valerie Patnaude, Director of Financial Aid
420 South Main Street, Nashua, NH 03060-5086
(603) 897-8510

Saint Anselm College

Manchester, New Hampshire   Federal Code: 002587
www.anselm.edu   CSS Code: 3748

4-year private nursing and liberal arts college in small city, affiliated with the Roman Catholic Church.
Enrollment: 1,916 undergrads, 2% part-time. 517 full-time freshmen.
Selectivity: Admits over 75% of applicants.

BASIC COSTS (2016-2017)

Tuition and fees: $38,826.
Room and board: $13,734.
Additional info: Tuition/fee waivers available for minority students.

FINANCIAL AID PICTURE (2016-2017)

Students with need: Out of 467 full-time freshmen who applied for aid, 375 were judged to have need. Of these, 375 received aid, and 114 had their full need met. Average financial aid package met 81% of need; average

scholarship/grant was $23,638; average loan was $2,692. For part-time students, average financial aid package was $5,382.

Students without need: 131 full-time freshmen who did not demonstrate need for aid received scholarships/grants; average award was $16,408. No-need awards available for academics, alumni affiliation, athletics, leadership, music/drama, state/district residency.

Scholarships offered: Scholarships range from $7,000 to $20,000; based on grades, test results (of considered), and extracurricular experience.

FINANCIAL AID PROCEDURES

Forms required: FAFSA, CSS PROFILE.

Dates and Deadlines: Priority date 2/15; closing date 2/15. Applicants notified on a rolling basis starting 2/1; must reply by 5/1 or within 2 week(s) of notification.

Transfers: Merit scholarships are awarded to qualified transfer students.

CONTACT

Elizabeth Keuffel, Director of Financial Aid

100 Saint Anselm Drive, Manchester, NH 03102-1310

(603) 641-7110

Southern New Hampshire University

Manchester, New Hampshire

www.snhu.edu   Federal Code: 002580

4-year private university and culinary school in small city.

Enrollment: 3,002 undergrads, 3% part-time. 769 full-time freshmen.

Selectivity: Admits over 75% of applicants.

BASIC COSTS (2016-2017)

Tuition and fees: $31,136.

Per-credit charge: $1,282.

Room and board: $12,062.

FINANCIAL AID PICTURE (2016-2017)

Students with need: Out of 699 full-time freshmen who applied for aid, 620 were judged to have need. Of these, 620 received aid, and 95 had their full need met. Average financial aid package met 66% of need; average scholarship/grant was $6,178; average loan was $3,434. For part-time students, average financial aid package was $19,917.

Students without need: 134 full-time freshmen who did not demonstrate need for aid received scholarships/grants; average award was $13,028. No-need awards available for academics, alumni affiliation, art, athletics, job skills, leadership, music/drama, state/district residency.

Scholarships offered: *Merit:* Scholarships up to $20,000 are available to students based primarily on high school GPA. *Athletic:* 47 full-time freshmen received athletic scholarships; average amount $12,245.

FINANCIAL AID PROCEDURES

Forms required: FAFSA.

Dates and Deadlines: Priority date 3/15; closing date 6/30. Applicants notified on a rolling basis starting 3/15; must reply within 3 week(s) of notification.

CONTACT

Jodi Abad, Assistant Vice President of Financial Aid & Compliance

2500 North River Road, Manchester, NH 03106-1045

(603) 668-2211

Thomas More College of Liberal Arts

Merrimack, New Hampshire

www.thomasmorecollege.edu   Federal Code: 030431

4-year private liberal arts college in small city, affiliated with the Roman Catholic Church.

Enrollment: 89 undergrads.

BASIC COSTS (2016-2017)

Tuition and fees: $20,400.

Per-credit charge: $850.

Room and board: $9,700.

FINANCIAL AID PICTURE

Students with need: Need-based aid available for full-time students. Work study available nights, weekends, and for part-time students.

Students without need: No-need awards available for academics.

Scholarships offered: Thomas More Scholarship: full or partial tuition (several awarded); based on superior academic achievement, exceptional promise or potential. Faith and Reason Essay Contest: up to $7,500 per year for 4 years; based on essay.

FINANCIAL AID PROCEDURES

Forms required: FAFSA.

Dates and Deadlines: Priority date 5/1; no closing date. Applicants notified on a rolling basis starting 5/15; must reply within 2 week(s) of notification.

Transfers: No deadline. Applicants notified on a rolling basis; must reply within 2 week(s) of notification.

CONTACT

Clint Hanson, Director of Financial Aid

Six Manchester Street, Merrimack, NH 03054-4818

(603) 880-8308 ext. 23

University of New Hampshire

Durham, New Hampshire

www.unh.edu   Federal Code: 002589

4-year public university in small town.

Enrollment: 12,653 undergrads, 2% part-time. 3,065 full-time freshmen.

Selectivity: Admits over 75% of applicants.

BASIC COSTS (2016-2017)

Tuition and fees: $17,624; out-of-state residents $31,424.

Per-credit charge: $600; out-of-state residents $1,175.

Room and board: $10,938.

Additional info: Tuition/fee waivers available for minority students.

FINANCIAL AID PICTURE (2015-2016)

Students with need: Out of 2,758 full-time freshmen who applied for aid, 2,216 were judged to have need. Of these, 2,178 received aid, and 342 had their full need met. Average financial aid package met 78% of need; average scholarship/grant was $6,686; average loan was $2,668. For part-time students, average financial aid package was $13,066.

Students without need: 446 full-time freshmen who did not demonstrate need for aid received scholarships/grants; average award was $6,022. No-need awards available for academics, art, athletics, leadership, music/drama, ROTC.

Scholarships offered: *Merit:* Presidential Scholarship: half tuition. Various other awards recognizing outstanding high school achievement determined during freshmen candidate application review process; no additional application materials required. *Athletic:* 43 full-time freshmen received athletic scholarships; average amount $30,634.

FINANCIAL AID PROCEDURES

Forms required: FAFSA.

Dates and Deadlines: Closing date 3/1. Applicants notified on a rolling basis starting 12/1; must reply by 5/1.

Transfers: Applicants notified on a rolling basis.

CONTACT

Susan Allen, Director of Financial Aid

3 Garrison Avenue, Durham, NH 03824

(603) 862-3600

University of New Hampshire at Manchester

Manchester, New Hampshire
www.manchester.unh.edu   Federal Code: 002589

4-year public branch campus and liberal arts college in small city.
Enrollment: 712 undergrads, 17% part-time.
Selectivity: Admits 50 to 75% of applicants.

BASIC COSTS (2016-2017)

Tuition and fees: $14,493; out-of-state residents $28,293.
Per-credit charge: $585; out-of-state residents $1,160.
Additional info: New England Regional Student Program tuition is 175% of in-state tuition.

FINANCIAL AID PICTURE

Students with need: Work study available nights, weekends, and for part-time students.
Students without need: No-need awards available for academics.

FINANCIAL AID PROCEDURES

Forms required: FAFSA.
Dates and Deadlines: Closing date 3/1. Applicants notified by 4/1; must reply within 2 week(s) of notification.

CONTACT

Sharon Eaton, Associate Director of Financial Aid
88 Commercial Street, Manchester, NH 03101-1113
(603) 641-4189

White Mountains Community College

Berlin, New Hampshire
www.wmcc.edu   Federal Code: 005291

2-year public community college in large town.
Enrollment: 627 undergrads.
Selectivity: Open admission; but selective for some programs.

BASIC COSTS (2016-2017)

Tuition and fees: $6,510; out-of-state residents $14,160.
Per-credit charge: $200; out-of-state residents $455.
Additional info: New England Regional tuition: $300 per credit hour.

FINANCIAL AID PICTURE

Students with need: Need-based aid available for full-time and part-time students.
Students without need: This college awards aid only to students with need.

FINANCIAL AID PROCEDURES

Forms required: FAFSA, institutional form.
Dates and Deadlines: Priority date 5/1; no closing date. Applicants notified on a rolling basis starting 5/1; must reply within 2 week(s) of notification.
Transfers: No deadline. Applicants notified on a rolling basis starting 5/1; must reply within 2 week(s) of notification.

CONTACT

2020 Riverside Drive, Berlin, NH 03570

New Jersey

Atlantic Cape Community College

Mays Landing, New Jersey
www.atlantic.edu   Federal Code: 002596

2-year public culinary school and community college in small town.
Enrollment: 3,675 full-time undergrads.
Selectivity: Open admission; but selective for some programs.

BASIC COSTS (2016-2017)

Tuition and fees: $4,453; out-of-district residents $6,193; out-of-state residents $7,753.
Per-credit charge: $120; out-of-district residents $178; out-of-state residents $230.
Additional info: Tuition/fee waivers available for unemployed or children of unemployed.

FINANCIAL AID PICTURE

Students with need: Need-based aid available for full-time and part-time students.

FINANCIAL AID PROCEDURES

Forms required: FAFSA, institutional form.
Dates and Deadlines: Priority date 5/1; no closing date. Applicants notified on a rolling basis starting 5/1.

CONTACT

Linda Desantis, Director of Financial Aid and Veterans' Affairs
5100 Black Horse Pike, Mays Landing, NJ 08330-2699
(609) 343-5082

Berkeley College

Woodland Park, New Jersey
www.berkeleycollege.edu   Federal Code: 007502

4-year for-profit business college in large town.
Enrollment: 3,806 undergrads.

FINANCIAL AID PICTURE

Students with need: Need-based aid available for full-time students.
Students without need: No-need awards available for academics, alumni affiliation.

FINANCIAL AID PROCEDURES

Forms required: FAFSA.

CONTACT

Howard Leslie, Vice President Financial Aid
44 Rifle Camp Road, Woodland Park, NJ 07424-0440
(973) 278-5400

Bloomfield College

Bloomfield, New Jersey
www.bloomfield.edu   Federal Code: 002597

4-year private nursing and liberal arts college in large town, affiliated with the Presbyterian Church (USA).
Enrollment: 1,941 undergrads, 9% part-time. 503 full-time freshmen.
Selectivity: Admits 50 to 75% of applicants.

BASIC COSTS (2017-2018)

Tuition and fees: $29,300.
Per-credit charge: $918.

Room and board: $11,700.

FINANCIAL AID PICTURE (2016-2017)

Students with need: Out of 503 full-time freshmen who applied for aid, 476 were judged to have need. Of these, 476 received aid, and 64 had their full need met. Average financial aid package met 69% of need; average scholarship/grant was $18,699; average loan was $3,281. For part-time students, average financial aid package was $11,169.

Students without need: 15 full-time freshmen who did not demonstrate need for aid received scholarships/grants; average award was $19,010. No-need awards available for academics, alumni affiliation, athletics, leadership, religious affiliation.

Scholarships offered: *Merit:* Trustee Scholar Award: $8,000-full tuition; 3.6 GPA, 900 SAT required. Presidential Scholarship: $6,000-full tuition; 3.0 GPA and 900 SAT required. *Athletic:* 52 full-time freshmen received athletic scholarships; average amount $11,964.

FINANCIAL AID PROCEDURES

Forms required: FAFSA.

Dates and Deadlines: Priority date 3/15; closing date 4/15. Applicants notified on a rolling basis starting 4/15; must reply within 2 week(s) of notification.

Transfers: Applicants notified on a rolling basis starting 4/15; must reply within 2 week(s) of notification. Transfer Scholarship: $5,000-full tuition; for transfer students from 2-year colleges with 3.0 GPA. Phi Theta Kappa Transfer Scholarships: up to full tuition; for day transfer students from 2-year colleges with 3.5 GPA with a completed AA/AS degree and are members of Phi Theta Kappa.

CONTACT

Director of Financial Aid
One Park Place, Bloomfield, NJ 07003
(973) 748-9000 ext. 1212

Brookdale Community College
Lincroft, New Jersey
www.brookdalecc.edu   Federal Code: 008404

2-year public community college in small city.
Enrollment: 12,077 undergrads.
Selectivity: Open admission; but selective for some programs.

BASIC COSTS (2016-2017)

Tuition and fees: $4,617; out-of-district residents $8,299; out-of-state residents $9,049.

Per-credit charge: $19.75; out-of-district residents $245.5; out-of-state residents $270.5.

Additional info: Tuition/fee waivers available for unemployed or children of unemployed.

FINANCIAL AID PICTURE

Students with need: Need-based aid available for full-time and part-time students.

Students without need: No-need awards available for academics, athletics.

FINANCIAL AID PROCEDURES

Forms required: FAFSA, institutional form.

Dates and Deadlines: Priority date 5/1; no closing date. Applicants notified on a rolling basis starting 5/1; must reply within 2 week(s) of notification.

CONTACT

Stephanie Fitzsimmons, Director of Financial Aid
765 Newman Springs Road, Lincroft, NJ 07738
(732) 224-2362

Caldwell University
Caldwell, New Jersey
www.caldwell.edu   Federal Code: 002598

4-year private university and liberal arts college in large town, affiliated with the Roman Catholic Church.
Enrollment: 1,632 undergrads, 11% part-time. 404 full-time freshmen.
Selectivity: Admits over 75% of applicants.

BASIC COSTS (2016-2017)

Tuition and fees: $32,800.
Room and board: $11,400.
Additional info: Tuition/fee waivers available for adults.

FINANCIAL AID PICTURE (2016-2017)

Students with need: Out of 331 full-time freshmen who applied for aid, 303 were judged to have need. Of these, 303 received aid, and 37 had their full need met. Average financial aid package met 79% of need; average scholarship/grant was $25,655; average loan was $3,269. For part-time students, average financial aid package was $5,959.

Students without need: 92 full-time freshmen who did not demonstrate need for aid received scholarships/grants; average award was $20,796. No-need awards available for academics, alumni affiliation, art, athletics, leadership, music/drama, religious affiliation, ROTC, state/district residency.

Scholarships offered: 30 full-time freshmen received athletic scholarships; average amount $10,772.

FINANCIAL AID PROCEDURES

Forms required: FAFSA.

Dates and Deadlines: Priority date 4/1; no closing date. Applicants notified on a rolling basis starting 11/1; must reply within 4 week(s) of notification.

Transfers: No deadline. Applicants notified on a rolling basis; must reply within 4 week(s) of notification. Students who have filed for aid through the state previously must file FAFSA by 6/1 for succeeding year.

CONTACT

Eileen Felske, Director of Financial Aid
120 Bloomfield Avenue, Caldwell, NJ 07006-6195
(973) 618-3221

Camden County College
Blackwood, New Jersey
www.camdencc.edu   Federal Code: 006865

2-year public community college in large town.
Enrollment: 10,284 undergrads.
Selectivity: Open admission; but selective for some programs.

BASIC COSTS (2016-2017)

Tuition and fees: $4,320; out-of-district residents $4,440; out-of-state residents $4,440.

Per-credit charge: $107; out-of-district residents $111; out-of-state residents $111.

Additional info: Tuition/fee waivers available for unemployed or children of unemployed.

FINANCIAL AID PICTURE

Students with need: Need-based aid available for full-time and part-time students.

Students without need: No-need awards available for academics, state/district residency.

FINANCIAL AID PROCEDURES

Forms required: FAFSA, institutional form.

Dates and Deadlines: Priority date 5/1; no closing date. Applicants notified on a rolling basis starting 7/1.

Transfers: No deadline.

CONTACT

Felicia Bryant, Director of Financial Aid
Box 200, Blackwood, NJ 08012
(856) 227-7200

Centenary University
Hackettstown, New Jersey
www.centenaryuniversity.edu   Federal Code: 002599

4-year private university and liberal arts college in large town, affiliated with the United Methodist Church.
Enrollment: 1,490 undergrads, 17% part-time. 237 full-time freshmen.
Selectivity: Admits over 75% of applicants.

BASIC COSTS (2017-2018)
Tuition and fees: $32,580.
Per-credit charge: $600.
Room and board: $11,110.

FINANCIAL AID PICTURE (2015-2016)
Students with need: 70% of average financial aid package awarded as scholarships/grants, 30% awarded as loans/jobs. Work study available nights, weekends, and for part-time students.
Students without need: No-need awards available for academics, religious affiliation.
Scholarships offered: Leadership awards: based on demonstrated leadership ability and potential. Equine Award. Centenary Resident Grant. Out-of-State Centenary Grant. Skylands Centenary Grant. Centenary United Methodist Scholarship.

FINANCIAL AID PROCEDURES
Forms required: FAFSA.
Dates and Deadlines: Priority date 2/15; closing date 9/1. Applicants notified on a rolling basis starting 3/1.
Transfers: Students from New Jersey colleges who have received tuition aid grants (TAG) must apply by state deadline. Students must submit financial aid transcripts from all previous institutions attended.

CONTACT
Tonya Williams, Office of Financial Aid
400 Jefferson Street, Hackettstown, NJ 07840-9989

The College of New Jersey
Ewing, New Jersey
www.tcnj.edu   Federal Code: 002642

4-year public liberal arts college in large town.
Enrollment: 6,666 undergrads, 4% part-time. 1,451 full-time freshmen.
Selectivity: Admits less than 50% of applicants.

BASIC COSTS (2016-2017)
Tuition and fees: $15,794; out-of-state residents $26,971.
Per-credit charge: $394; out-of-state residents $789.
Room and board: $12,881.
Additional info: Tuition/fee waivers available for unemployed or children of unemployed.

FINANCIAL AID PICTURE (2015-2016)
Students with need: Out of 1,252 full-time freshmen who applied for aid, 798 were judged to have need. Of these, 744 received aid, and 92 had their full need met. Average financial aid package met 42% of need; average scholarship/grant was $13,596; average loan was $3,406. For part-time students, average financial aid package was $5,025.
Students without need: 189 full-time freshmen who did not demonstrate need for aid received scholarships/grants; average award was $4,750. No-need awards available for academics, art, music/drama.

Additional info: Merit scholarships available to New Jersey high school graduates based on academic distinction. Limited number of scholarships available to out-of-state students who demonstrate exceptional academic achievement in high school and on SAT. The EOF Promise Award meets the direct cost of attendance freshman and sophomore years, with merit scholarship awards available in junior and senior years.

FINANCIAL AID PROCEDURES
Forms required: FAFSA.
Dates and Deadlines: Priority date 2/15; closing date 10/1. Applicants notified on a rolling basis starting 3/15; must reply within 2 week(s) of notification.
Transfers: No deadline. Applicants notified on a rolling basis; must reply within 2 week(s) of notification.

CONTACT
Wil Casaine, Executive Director of Financial Aid
Office of Undergraduate Admissions PO Box 7718, Ewing, NJ 08628-0718
(609) 771-2211

College of St. Elizabeth
Morristown, New Jersey
www.cse.edu   Federal Code: 002600

4-year private liberal arts college in large town, affiliated with the Roman Catholic Church.
Enrollment: 740 undergrads, 23% part-time. 101 full-time freshmen.
Selectivity: Admits 50 to 75% of applicants.

BASIC COSTS (2016-2017)
Tuition and fees: $32,282.
Per-credit charge: $843.
Room and board: $12,744.
Additional info: Tuition/fee waivers available for adults.

FINANCIAL AID PICTURE (2015-2016)
Students with need: Out of 100 full-time freshmen who applied for aid, 100 were judged to have need. Of these, 100 received aid. Need-based aid available for part-time students.
Students without need: No-need awards available for academics, alumni affiliation, art, leadership, state/district residency.
Scholarships offered: Presidential Scholarship: full-tuition; for campus residents. Elizabethan Scholarship: $8,000-$10,000. Seton Scholarship: $3,000-$7,000. Awards guaranteed to eligible students who apply by 3/1 and enroll by 5/1. International scholarships: tuition, room and board; awarded annually for fall semester only to first year students enrolled in Women's College; based on academic record, SAT (if submitted) and TOEFL score.

FINANCIAL AID PROCEDURES
Forms required: FAFSA.
Dates and Deadlines: Closing date 10/1. Applicants notified on a rolling basis starting 11/15; must reply by 5/1 or within 2 week(s) of notification.
Transfers: Priority date 4/15; closing date 8/20. Scholarships available for full-time students who enroll immediately following full-time enrollment at another college. Applicants must have completed 32 credits and have 3.0 GPA. Awards range from $3,500-half tuition. Minimum of 5 awarded annually. Preference given to applications received by 6/1. Limited number of partial scholarships awarded to international students.

CONTACT
LaVerne Walker, Director of Financial Aid
2 Convent Road, Morristown, NJ 07960-6989
(973) 290-4445

County College of Morris

Randolph, New Jersey
www.ccm.edu   Federal Code: 007106

2-year public community college in large town.
Enrollment: 7,188 undergrads.
Selectivity: Open admission; but selective for some programs.

BASIC COSTS (2016-2017)
Tuition and fees: $4,690; out-of-district residents $8,380; out-of-state residents $11,530.
Per-credit charge: $123; out-of-district residents $246; out-of-state residents $351.
Additional info: Tuition/fee waivers available for unemployed or children of unemployed.

FINANCIAL AID PICTURE
Students with need: Need-based aid available for full-time and part-time students.
Students without need: No-need awards available for athletics.

FINANCIAL AID PROCEDURES
Forms required: FAFSA.
Dates and Deadlines: Priority date 3/1; no closing date. Applicants notified on a rolling basis starting 5/1.

CONTACT
Harvey Willis, Director, Financial Aid
214 Center Grove Road, Randolph, NJ 07869-2086
(973) 328-5230

Cumberland County College

Vineland, New Jersey
www.cccnj.edu   Federal Code: 002601

2-year public community college in small city.
Enrollment: 3,080 undergrads, 44% part-time. 657 full-time freshmen.
Selectivity: Open admission; but selective for some programs.

BASIC COSTS (2016-2017)
Tuition and fees: $4,440; out-of-district residents $6,690; out-of-state residents $8,580.
Per-credit charge: $118; out-of-district residents $193; out-of-state residents $256.
Additional info: In-state, out-of-district students will be charged $128 per-credit-hour with appropriate chargeback documentation. Tuition/fee waivers available for unemployed or children of unemployed.

FINANCIAL AID PICTURE
Students with need: Need-based aid available for full-time and part-time students.
Students without need: No-need awards available for academics.

FINANCIAL AID PROCEDURES
Forms required: FAFSA.
Dates and Deadlines: Applicants notified on a rolling basis; must reply within 3 week(s) of notification.

CONTACT
Maurice Thomas, Director, Financial Aid
PO Box 1500, Vineland, NJ 08362
(856) 691-8600 ext. 1311

DeVry University: North Brunswick

North Brunswick, New Jersey
www.devry.edu   Federal Code: 009228

4-year for-profit university in small city.
Enrollment: 583 undergrads, 51% part-time. 21 full-time freshmen.

BASIC COSTS (2016-2017)
Tuition and fees: $17,512.
Per-credit charge: $609.

FINANCIAL AID PICTURE
Students with need: Need-based aid available for full-time and part-time students.
Students without need: This college awards aid only to students with need.

FINANCIAL AID PROCEDURES
Forms required: FAFSA.
Dates and Deadlines: Applicants notified on a rolling basis.

CONTACT
630 US Highway One, North Brunswick, NJ 08902-3362
(800) 333-3879

Drew University

Madison, New Jersey
www.drew.edu   Federal Code: 002603

4-year private university and liberal arts college in large town, affiliated with the United Methodist Church.
Enrollment: 1,407 undergrads, 2% part-time. 350 full-time freshmen.
Selectivity: Admits 50 to 75% of applicants.

BASIC COSTS (2016-2017)
Tuition and fees: $47,752.
Per-credit charge: $1,955.
Room and board: $13,296.

FINANCIAL AID PICTURE (2016-2017)
Students with need: Out of 300 full-time freshmen who applied for aid, 273 were judged to have need. Of these, 273 received aid, and 40 had their full need met. Average financial aid package met 86% of need; average scholarship/grant was $37,882; average loan was $3,438. Need-based aid available for part-time students.
Students without need: 77 full-time freshmen who did not demonstrate need for aid received scholarships/grants; average award was $22,159. No-need awards available for academics, art, leadership, minority status, music/drama.
Scholarships offered: Baldwin Honors Scholarship: $25,000; awarded to students who have earned an A average while enrolled in their high school's most rigorous honors/college preparatory program; minimum score of 1260 (Evidence Based Reading and Writing + Mathematics) on the SAT or a total ACT composite score of 26. Presidential Scholarship: $20,000; awarded to students with a high school GPA in the A- range in an honors curriculum; minimum score of 1150 (Evidence Based Reading and Writing + Mathematics) on the SAT or a total ACT composite score of 24. Dean's Scholarship: $15,000; awarded to applicants with a minimum high school GPA in the B+ range in an honors curriculum. Drew Scholarship: $10,000; awarded to applicants with a minimum high school GPA in the B range in an honors curriculum. Civic Engagement Scholarships: $2,500; students who have demonstrated a sustained commitment to community service and civic engagement throughout their high school years. Drew Scholarship in the Arts: $2,500; applicants for admission with a demonstrated talent for and interest in the fine or performing arts.

FINANCIAL AID PROCEDURES
Forms required: FAFSA.

Dates and Deadlines: Closing date 2/1. Applicants notified by 3/25; must reply by 5/1.

CONTACT
Colby McCarthy, Director of Financial Assistance
36 Madison Avenue, Madison, NJ 07940-4063
(973) 408-3112

Eastern International College
Jersey City, New Jersey
www.eicollege.edu   Federal Code: 031226

2-year for-profit health science and nursing college in very large city.
Enrollment: 433 undergrads, 26% part-time. 160 full-time freshmen.
Selectivity: Open admission.

BASIC COSTS (2016-2017)
Additional info: Costs vary by program. Associate programs $28,500-$51,300, books and supplies $1,000-$9,000. Bachelor's program Diagnostic Medical Sonography $90,600, books and supplies $3,600. Tuition at time of enrollment locked for 2 years.

FINANCIAL AID PICTURE (2015-2016)
Students with need: Out of 156 full-time freshmen who applied for aid, 119 were judged to have need. Of these, 119 received aid, and 108 had their full need met. Average financial aid package met 29% of need; average scholarship/grant was $17,811; average loan was $5,250. For part-time students, average financial aid package was $12,360.
Students without need: No-need awards available for academics.

FINANCIAL AID PROCEDURES
Forms required: FAFSA, state aid form.
Dates and Deadlines: Closing date 6/1. Applicants notified on a rolling basis; must reply within 2 week(s) of notification.
Transfers: No deadline. Applicants notified on a rolling basis; must reply within 2 week(s) of notification. Students transferring from another institution during the same award year in which aid was disbursed must ensure withdrawal and acknowledgment to receive no further funds from the transferring school.

CONTACT
Kinga Gizynska, Financial Aid Director
684 Newark Avenue, Jersey City, NJ 07306
(201) 216-9901

Essex County College
Newark, New Jersey
www.essex.edu   Federal Code: 007107

2-year public community college in large city.
Enrollment: 9,828 undergrads.
Selectivity: Open admission; but selective for some programs.

BASIC COSTS (2016-2017)
Tuition and fees: $4,785; out-of-district residents $8,370; out-of-state residents $8,370.
Per-credit charge: $119.5; out-of-district residents $239; out-of-state residents $239.
Additional info: Tuition/fee waivers available for unemployed or children of unemployed.

FINANCIAL AID PICTURE
Students with need: Need-based aid available for full-time and part-time students.

FINANCIAL AID PROCEDURES
Forms required: FAFSA, institutional form.

Dates and Deadlines: Priority date 6/30; no closing date. Applicants notified on a rolling basis starting 6/15; must reply within 3 week(s) of notification.

CONTACT
Mildred Cofer, Director of Financial Aid
303 University Avenue, Newark, NJ 07102
(973) 877-3000

Felician University
Lodi, New Jersey
www.felician.edu   Federal Code: 002610

4-year private nursing and liberal arts college in large town, affiliated with the Roman Catholic Church.
Enrollment: 1,639 undergrads, 13% part-time. 316 full-time freshmen.
Selectivity: Admits over 75% of applicants.

BASIC COSTS (2016-2017)
Tuition and fees: $32,990.
Per-credit charge: $1,015.
Room and board: $12,380.
Additional info: Tuition/fee waivers available for adults.

FINANCIAL AID PICTURE (2016-2017)
Students with need: Out of 290 full-time freshmen who applied for aid, 284 were judged to have need. Of these, 282 received aid, and 25 had their full need met. Average financial aid package met 73% of need; average scholarship/grant was $16,165; average loan was $3,365. For part-time students, average financial aid package was $5,868.
Students without need: 11 full-time freshmen who did not demonstrate need for aid received scholarships/grants; average award was $15,500. No-need awards available for academics, alumni affiliation, athletics.
Scholarships offered: 31 full-time freshmen received athletic scholarships; average amount $8,661.

FINANCIAL AID PROCEDURES
Forms required: FAFSA, state aid form.
Dates and Deadlines: Priority date 2/15; no closing date. Applicants notified on a rolling basis starting 4/1; must reply within 2 week(s) of notification.

CONTACT
Cynthia Montalvo, Director of Financial Aid
262 South Main Street, Lodi, NJ 07644-2198
(201) 559-6000 ext. 6010

Georgian Court University
Lakewood, New Jersey
www.georgian.edu   Federal Code: 002608

4-year private university and liberal arts college in large town, affiliated with the Roman Catholic Church.
Enrollment: 1,409 undergrads, 6% part-time. 221 full-time freshmen.
Selectivity: Admits 50 to 75% of applicants.

BASIC COSTS (2016-2017)
Tuition and fees: $31,618.
Per-credit charge: $690.
Room and board: $10,808.

FINANCIAL AID PICTURE (2016-2017)
Students with need: Out of 215 full-time freshmen who applied for aid, 208 were judged to have need. Of these, 208 received aid, and 57 had their full need met. Average financial aid package met 80% of need; average scholarship/grant was $19,904; average loan was $5,756. For part-time students, average financial aid package was $13,179.

Students without need: 13 full-time freshmen who did not demonstrate need for aid received scholarships/grants; average award was $12,397. No-need awards available for academics, alumni affiliation, art, athletics, leadership, religious affiliation, state/district residency.

Scholarships offered: 5 full-time freshmen received athletic scholarships; average amount $12,100.

FINANCIAL AID PROCEDURES

Forms required: FAFSA.

Dates and Deadlines: Applicants notified on a rolling basis starting 11/1.

Transfers: No deadline. Applicants notified on a rolling basis starting 11/1.

CONTACT

Randy Brown, Director of Financial Aid
900 Lakewood Avenue, Lakewood, NJ 08701-2697
(732) 987-2258

Hudson County Community College
Jersey City, New Jersey
www.hccc.edu   Federal Code: 012954

2-year public community college in small city.

Enrollment: 7,893 undergrads, 35% part-time. 1,612 full-time freshmen.

Selectivity: Open admission; but selective for some programs.

BASIC COSTS (2016-2017)

Tuition and fees: $5,353; out-of-district residents $9,223; out-of-state residents $13,093.

Per-credit charge: $129; out-of-district residents $258; out-of-state residents $387.

FINANCIAL AID PICTURE

Students with need: Need-based aid available for full-time and part-time students.

Students without need: This college awards aid only to students with need.

FINANCIAL AID PROCEDURES

Forms required: FAFSA.

Dates and Deadlines: Priority date 7/15; no closing date. Applicants notified on a rolling basis starting 6/1; must reply within 1 week(s) of notification.

Transfers: No deadline.

CONTACT

Sylvia Mendoza, Director of Student Financial Assistance
70 Sip Avenue, 1st Floor, Jersey City, NJ 07306
(201) 360-4200

Kean University
Union, New Jersey
www.kean.edu   Federal Code: 002622

4-year public university and liberal arts college in small city.

Enrollment: 11,656 undergrads, 21% part-time. 1,494 full-time freshmen.

Selectivity: Admits over 75% of applicants.

BASIC COSTS (2016-2017)

Tuition and fees: $11,870; out-of-state residents $18,637.

Per-credit charge: $302; out-of-state residents $513.

Room and board: $12,780.

Additional info: Tuition/fee waivers available for unemployed or children of unemployed.

FINANCIAL AID PICTURE (2016-2017)

Students with need: Out of 1,373 full-time freshmen who applied for aid, 1,147 were judged to have need. Of these, 1,066 received aid, and 13 had their full need met. Average financial aid package met 77% of need; average

scholarship/grant was $8,910; average loan was $3,438. For part-time students, average financial aid package was $6,868.

Students without need: 43 full-time freshmen who did not demonstrate need for aid received scholarships/grants; average award was $3,798. No-need awards available for academics, art, leadership, music/drama.

Scholarships offered: William Livingston Scholarship: full in-state tuition and fees; 3.5 GPA, 1360 SAT, 29 ACT. Kean Scholarship: $4,000; 3.5 GPA, 1310 SAT, 28 ACT. Trustee Scholarship: $3,000; 3.0 GPA, 1270 SAT, 26 ACT. Presidential Scholarship: $2,000; 3.0 GPA, 1170 SAT, 24 ACT. Academic Scholar: $1,000; 2.8 GPA ,1080 SAT, 21 ACT.

FINANCIAL AID PROCEDURES

Forms required: FAFSA.

Dates and Deadlines: Closing date 4/17. Applicants notified on a rolling basis starting 3/1; must reply by 5/1.

Transfers: No deadline. Applicants notified on a rolling basis starting 10/1; must reply by 5/1. Aid is Awarded to Transfer students based upon number of credits completed/awarded, at time of transfer. Transfer students can apply for Merit Scholarships offered by the University through the Foundation Office/Scholarship office.

CONTACT

Sherrell Watson-Hall, Director Financial Aid
Office of Admissions - Kean Hall, Union, NJ 07083-0411
(908) 737-3190

Mercer County Community College
Trenton, New Jersey
www.mccc.edu   Federal Code: 002641

2-year public community college in small city.

Enrollment: 6,609 undergrads, 60% part-time. 905 full-time freshmen.

Selectivity: Open admission.

BASIC COSTS (2016-2017)

Tuition and fees: $4,710; out-of-district residents $6,165; out-of-state residents $8,835.

Per-credit charge: $118.5; out-of-district residents $166; out-of-state residents $254.

Additional info: Tuition/fee waivers available for unemployed or children of unemployed.

FINANCIAL AID PICTURE

Students with need: Need-based aid available for full-time and part-time students. Work study available nights.

Students without need: No-need awards available for academics, athletics, state/district residency.

Scholarships offered: MCCC Foundation Scholarship: $2,500; top 25% of high school class; 15 total awards. NJ STARS program: for top 20% of high school class.

FINANCIAL AID PROCEDURES

Forms required: FAFSA.

Dates and Deadlines: Closing date 5/1. Applicants notified on a rolling basis.

CONTACT

Jason Taylor, Director, Financial Aid
PO Box B, Trenton, NJ 08690-1099
(609) 570-3210

Middlesex County College
Edison, New Jersey
www.middlesexcc.edu   Federal Code: 002615

2-year public community college in small city.

Enrollment: 11,371 undergrads.

Selectivity: Open admission; but selective for some programs.

BASIC COSTS (2016-2017)
Tuition and fees: $4,361; out-of-state residents $8,636.
Per-credit charge: $108; out-of-state residents $216.

FINANCIAL AID PICTURE
Students with need: Need-based aid available for full-time and part-time students.

FINANCIAL AID PROCEDURES
Forms required: FAFSA, institutional form.
Dates and Deadlines: Priority date 4/1; no closing date. Applicants notified on a rolling basis starting 5/4.

CONTACT
Lujia Zhang, Director Financial Aid
2600 Woodbridge Avenue, Edison, NJ 08818-3050
(732) 906-2520

Monmouth University
West Long Branch, New Jersey
www.monmouth.edu   Federal Code: 002616

4-year private university in small town.
Enrollment: 4,668 undergrads, 4% part-time. 1,089 full-time freshmen.
Selectivity: Admits over 75% of applicants.

BASIC COSTS (2016-2017)
Tuition and fees: $35,364.
Per-credit charge: $1,003.
Room and board: $13,038.

FINANCIAL AID PICTURE (2016-2017)
Students with need: Out of 998 full-time freshmen who applied for aid, 872 were judged to have need. Of these, 872 received aid, and 112 had their full need met. Average financial aid package met 66% of need; average scholarship/grant was $12,513; average loan was $3,703. For part-time students, average financial aid package was $8,398.
Students without need: 200 full-time freshmen who did not demonstrate need for aid received scholarships/grants; average award was $10,146. No-need awards available for academics, alumni affiliation, art, athletics, state/district residency.
Scholarships offered: *Merit:* Academic Excellence Awards: $2,000-$21,000; based on SAT and GPA; renewable annually as long as required GPA is maintained. *Athletic:* 88 full-time freshmen received athletic scholarships; average amount $26,271.

FINANCIAL AID PROCEDURES
Forms required: FAFSA.
Dates and Deadlines: Priority date 2/15; no closing date. Applicants notified on a rolling basis starting 12/15; must reply within 2 week(s) of notification.
Transfers: No deadline. Applicants notified on a rolling basis starting 1/15; must reply within 2 week(s) of notification.

CONTACT
Claire Alasio, Associate Vice President for Enrollment Management
400 Cedar Avenue, West Long Branch, NJ 07764-1898
(732) 571-3463

Montclair State University
Montclair, New Jersey
www.montclair.edu   Federal Code: 002617

4-year public university in large town.
Enrollment: 16,653 undergrads, 11% part-time. 2,964 full-time freshmen.
Selectivity: Admits 50 to 75% of applicants.

BASIC COSTS (2016-2017)
Tuition and fees: $12,116; out-of-state residents $20,007.
Per-credit charge: $292.26; out-of-state residents $555.3.
Room and board: $14,094.
Additional info: Tuition/fee waivers available for unemployed or children of unemployed.

FINANCIAL AID PICTURE (2015-2016)
Students with need: 59% of average financial aid package awarded as scholarships/grants, 41% awarded as loans/jobs. Need-based aid available for part-time students. Work study available nights, weekends, and for part-time students.
Students without need: No-need awards available for academics, alumni affiliation, art.

FINANCIAL AID PROCEDURES
Forms required: FAFSA.
Dates and Deadlines: Priority date 3/15; no closing date. Applicants notified on a rolling basis starting 4/1; must reply within 2 week(s) of notification.
Transfers: Applicants notified on a rolling basis starting 4/1. Students will be eligible for financial aid beginning fall semester of the academic year for which they are admitted.

CONTACT
James Anderson, Director of Financial Aid
One Normal Avenue, Montclair, NJ 07043
(973) 655-4461

New Jersey City University
Jersey City, New Jersey
www.njcu.edu   Federal Code: 002613

4-year public university in small city.
Enrollment: 6,465 undergrads, 21% part-time. 955 full-time freshmen.
Selectivity: Admits over 75% of applicants.

BASIC COSTS (2017-2018)
Tuition and fees: $11,431; out-of-state residents $20,458.
Per-credit charge: $271; out-of-state residents $571.
Room and board: $12,446.

FINANCIAL AID PICTURE
Students with need: Need-based aid available for full-time and part-time students.

FINANCIAL AID PROCEDURES
Forms required: FAFSA.
Dates and Deadlines: Priority date 4/15; no closing date. Applicants notified by 5/15.

CONTACT
Frank Cuozzo, Director, Financial Aid
2039 Kennedy Boulevard, Jersey City, NJ 07305-1597
(201) 200-3173

New Jersey Institute of Technology
Newark, New Jersey
www.njit.edu   Federal Code: 002621

4-year public university in large city.
Enrollment: 7,336 undergrads, 16% part-time. 1,000 full-time freshmen.
Selectivity: Admits 50 to 75% of applicants.

BASIC COSTS (2016-2017)
Tuition and fees: $16,430; out-of-state residents $31,034.
Per-credit charge: $517; out-of-state residents $1,206.
Room and board: $13,420.

FINANCIAL AID PICTURE (2015-2016)

Students with need: Out of 899 full-time freshmen who applied for aid, 727 were judged to have need. Of these, 700 received aid, and 112 had their full need met. Average financial aid package met 58% of need; average scholarship/grant was $13,482; average loan was $3,284. For part-time students, average financial aid package was $6,168.

Students without need: 155 full-time freshmen who did not demonstrate need for aid received scholarships/grants; average award was $18,046. No-need awards available for academics, alumni affiliation, art, athletics, job skills, leadership, minority status, music/drama, religious affiliation, ROTC, state/district residency.

Scholarships offered: 18 full-time freshmen received athletic scholarships; average amount $26,225.

Additional info: Extensive co-op program for all majors.

FINANCIAL AID PROCEDURES

Forms required: FAFSA.

Dates and Deadlines: Priority date 2/15; no closing date. Applicants notified on a rolling basis starting 11/15; must reply by 5/1 or within 2 week(s) of notification.

Transfers: No deadline. Applicants notified on a rolling basis starting 1/1; must reply within 2 week(s) of notification.

CONTACT

Ivon Nunez, Director of Financial Aid
University Heights, Newark, NJ 07102
(973) 596-3479

Ocean County College

Toms River, New Jersey
www.ocean.edu   Federal Code: 002624

2-year public community college in small city.

Enrollment: 7,374 undergrads, 38% part-time. 1,735 full-time freshmen.

Selectivity: Open admission; but selective for some programs.

BASIC COSTS (2016-2017)

Tuition and fees: $4,345; out-of-district residents $5,035; out-of-state residents $7,735.

Per-credit charge: $112; out-of-district residents $135; out-of-state residents $225.

Additional info: Tuition/fee waivers available for unemployed or children of unemployed.

FINANCIAL AID PICTURE (2015-2016)

Students with need: 61% of average financial aid package awarded as scholarships/grants, 39% awarded as loans/jobs. Need-based aid available for part-time students. Work study available nights, weekends, and for part-time students.

Students without need: No-need awards available for academics, state/district residency.

FINANCIAL AID PROCEDURES

Forms required: FAFSA.

Dates and Deadlines: Applicants notified on a rolling basis starting 7/15; must reply within 1 week(s) of notification.

CONTACT

Eileen Buckle, Director of Financial Aid
College Drive, Toms River, NJ 08754-2001
(732) 255-0400

Passaic County Community College

Paterson, New Jersey
www.pccc.edu   Federal Code: 009994

2-year public community college in small city.

Enrollment: 8,389 undergrads.

Selectivity: Open admission; but selective for some programs.

BASIC COSTS (2016-2017)

Tuition and fees: $4,553; out-of-district residents $5,423; out-of-state residents $7,973.

Per-credit charge: $114; out-of-district residents $143; out-of-state residents $228.

Additional info: Tuition/fee waivers available for unemployed or children of unemployed.

FINANCIAL AID PICTURE

Students with need: Need-based aid available for full-time and part-time students.

Students without need: No-need awards available for academics.

Additional info: Limited scholarship funds available for low income students eligible for federal or state aid.

FINANCIAL AID PROCEDURES

Forms required: FAFSA.

Dates and Deadlines: Priority date 8/1; no closing date. Applicants notified on a rolling basis starting 8/1; must reply within 2 week(s) of notification.

Transfers: Priority date 5/15; closing date 6/30.

CONTACT

Linda Gayton, Director of Financial Aid
One College Boulevard, Paterson, NJ 07505-1179
(973) 684-6100

Pillar College

Newark, New Jersey
www.pillar.edu   Federal Code: 036663

4-year private Bible and liberal arts college in large city, affiliated with the Christian Church.

Enrollment: 369 undergrads.

BASIC COSTS (2016-2017)

Tuition and fees: $19,440.

Per-credit charge: $785.

FINANCIAL AID PICTURE

Students with need: Need-based aid available for full-time and part-time students. Work study available nights.

Students without need: This college awards aid only to students with need.

FINANCIAL AID PROCEDURES

Forms required: FAFSA, state aid form.

Dates and Deadlines: Applicants notified on a rolling basis starting 1/31.

CONTACT

Joel Davis, AVP of Finanance
60 Park Place, Suite 701, Newark, NJ 07102
(973) 803-5000 ext. 1030

Princeton University

Princeton, New Jersey
www.princeton.edu   Federal Code: 002627

4-year private university in large town.

Enrollment: 5,236 undergrads. 1,312 full-time freshmen.

Selectivity: Admits less than 50% of applicants.

BASIC COSTS (2017-2018)

Tuition and fees: $47,500.

Room and board: $15,495.

FINANCIAL AID PICTURE (2016-2017)

Students with need: Out of 929 full-time freshmen who applied for aid, 782 were judged to have need. Of these, 782 received aid, and 782 had their full need met. Average financial aid package met 100% of need; average scholarship/grant was $49,870.

Students without need: This college awards aid only to students with need.

Additional info: All aid need-based; all aid grant money (no loans); institution meets full demonstrated need. FAFSA due 4/15; financial aid application due 11/15 for early action applicants.

FINANCIAL AID PROCEDURES

Forms required: FAFSA, institutional form.

Dates and Deadlines: Closing date 2/1. Applicants notified by 3/31; must reply by 5/1.

CONTACT

Robin Moscato, Director of Financial Aid
Princeton University, Princeton, NJ 08542-0430
(609) 258-3330

Ramapo College of New Jersey

Mahwah, New Jersey
www.ramapo.edu   Federal Code: 009344

4-year public liberal arts college in large town.

Enrollment: 5,445 undergrads, 9% part-time. 928 full-time freshmen.

Selectivity: Admits 50 to 75% of applicants.

BASIC COSTS (2016-2017)

Tuition and fees: $13,870; out-of-state residents $22,870.

Per-credit charge: $281; out-of-state residents $562.

Room and board: $12,030.

Additional info: Tuition/fee waivers available for unemployed or children of unemployed.

FINANCIAL AID PICTURE (2015-2016)

Students with need: Out of 835 full-time freshmen who applied for aid, 573 were judged to have need. Of these, 539 received aid, and 74 had their full need met. Average financial aid package met 65% of need; average scholarship/grant was $13,210; average loan was $3,305. For part-time students, average financial aid package was $4,703.

Students without need: 103 full-time freshmen who did not demonstrate need for aid received scholarships/grants; average award was $12,149. No-need awards available for academics, leadership, state/district residency.

FINANCIAL AID PROCEDURES

Forms required: FAFSA, state aid form.

Dates and Deadlines: Priority date 3/1; no closing date. Applicants notified on a rolling basis starting 4/1; must reply by 5/1 or within 2 week(s) of notification.

Transfers: No deadline. Applicants notified on a rolling basis.

CONTACT

Frederick O'Neill, Director of Financial Aid
505 Ramapo Valley Road, Mahwah, NJ 07430-1680
(201) 684-7549

Raritan Valley Community College

Branchburg, New Jersey
www.raritanval.edu   Federal Code: 007731

2-year public community college in large town.

Enrollment: 7,005 undergrads, 53% part-time. 1,293 full-time freshmen.

Selectivity: Open admission; but selective for some programs.

BASIC COSTS (2016-2017)

Tuition and fees: $5,244; out-of-district residents $6,294; out-of-state residents $6,294.

Per-credit charge: $144; out-of-district residents $179; out-of-state residents $179.

Additional info: Tuition/fee waivers available for unemployed or children of unemployed.

FINANCIAL AID PICTURE

Students with need: Need-based aid available for full-time and part-time students.

Students without need: No-need awards available for academics.

FINANCIAL AID PROCEDURES

Forms required: FAFSA.

Dates and Deadlines: Applicants notified on a rolling basis starting 4/1.

CONTACT

Leonard Mesonas, Director of Financial Aid
118 Lamington Road, Branchburg, NJ 08876-1265
(908) 526-1200 ext. 8273

Rider University

Lawrenceville, New Jersey
www.rider.edu   Federal Code: 002628

4-year private university in small town.

Enrollment: 3,978 undergrads, 9% part-time. 870 full-time freshmen.

Selectivity: Admits 50 to 75% of applicants.

BASIC COSTS (2016-2017)

Tuition and fees: $39,820.

Per-credit charge: $1,140.

Room and board: $14,230.

FINANCIAL AID PICTURE (2016-2017)

Students with need: Out of 781 full-time freshmen who applied for aid, 701 were judged to have need. Of these, 701 received aid, and 101 had their full need met. Average financial aid package met 75% of need; average scholarship/grant was $27,328; average loan was $3,147. For part-time students, average financial aid package was $7,501.

Students without need: 152 full-time freshmen who did not demonstrate need for aid received scholarships/grants; average award was $17,423. No-need awards available for academics, leadership.

Scholarships offered: 53 full-time freshmen received athletic scholarships; average amount $19,658.

FINANCIAL AID PROCEDURES

Forms required: FAFSA.

Dates and Deadlines: Priority date 3/1; no closing date. Applicants notified on a rolling basis starting 3/1.

Transfers: No deadline.

CONTACT

Drew Aromando, Executive Director of Student Financial Services
2083 Lawrenceville Road, Lawrenceville, NJ 08648-3099
(609) 896-5000 ext. 5360

Rowan College at Burlington County

Mt. Laurel, New Jersey
www.rcbc.edu   Federal Code: 007730

2-year public community college in small town.

Enrollment: 7,939 undergrads, 49% part-time. 1,550 full-time freshmen.

Selectivity: Open admission; but selective for some programs.

BASIC COSTS (2016-2017)

Tuition and fees: $4,065; out-of-district residents $4,545; out-of-state residents $6,495.

Per-credit charge: $100; out-of-district residents $116; out-of-state residents $181.

Additional info: Tuition/fee waivers available for unemployed or children of unemployed.

FINANCIAL AID PICTURE

Students with need: Need-based aid available for full-time and part-time students. Work study available nights, weekends, and for part-time students.

Students without need: This college awards aid only to students with need.

FINANCIAL AID PROCEDURES

Forms required: FAFSA.

Dates and Deadlines: Applicants notified on a rolling basis.

CONTACT

Jaclyn Angermeier, Chief Financial and Administrative Officer
900 College Circle, Mt. Laurel, NJ 08054
(856) 222-9311 ext. 1575

Rowan College at Gloucester

Sewell, New Jersey
www.rcgc.edu   Federal Code: 006901

2-year public community and liberal arts college in large town.

Enrollment: 6,229 undergrads, 37% part-time. 1,917 full-time freshmen.

Selectivity: Open admission; but selective for some programs.

BASIC COSTS (2017-2018)

Tuition and fees: $4,335; out-of-district residents $5,175; out-of-state residents $9,075.

Additional info: Tuition/fee waivers available for unemployed or children of unemployed.

FINANCIAL AID PICTURE

Students with need: Need-based aid available for full-time and part-time students. Work study available nights.

FINANCIAL AID PROCEDURES

Forms required: FAFSA, institutional form.

Dates and Deadlines: Priority date 5/1; no closing date. Applicants notified on a rolling basis starting 3/20.

CONTACT

Michael Chando, Executive Director, Admissions & Financial Aid
1400 Tanyard Road, Sewell, NJ 08080-4222
(856) 415-2210

Rowan University

Glassboro, New Jersey
www.rowan.edu   Federal Code: 002609

4-year public university in large town.

Enrollment: 14,208 undergrads, 10% part-time. 2,211 full-time freshmen.

Selectivity: Admits 50 to 75% of applicants.

BASIC COSTS (2016-2017)

Tuition and fees: $13,108; out-of-state residents $21,378.

Per-credit charge: $362; out-of-state residents $682.

Room and board: $11,688.

FINANCIAL AID PICTURE (2015-2016)

Students with need: Out of 2,043 full-time freshmen who applied for aid, 1,447 were judged to have need. Of these, 1,356 received aid, and 61 had their full need met. Average financial aid package met 72% of need; average

scholarship/grant was $9,557; average loan was $3,271. For part-time students, average financial aid package was $5,170.

Students without need: 293 full-time freshmen who did not demonstrate need for aid received scholarships/grants; average award was $6,712. No-need awards available for academics, art, music/drama.

FINANCIAL AID PROCEDURES

Forms required: FAFSA.

Dates and Deadlines: Priority date 3/16; no closing date. Applicants notified on a rolling basis starting 3/16.

Transfers: No deadline. Applicants notified on a rolling basis starting 3/1; must reply within 3 week(s) of notification.

CONTACT

Pam Gordy
Savitz Hall, 201 Mullica Hill Road, Glassboro, NJ 08028-1701
(856) 256-4250

Rutgers, The State University of New Jersey: Camden Campus

Camden, New Jersey
www.camden.rutgers.edu   Federal Code: 002629

4-year public university in small city.

Enrollment: 4,978 undergrads, 19% part-time. 422 full-time freshmen.

Selectivity: Admits 50 to 75% of applicants.

BASIC COSTS (2016-2017)

Tuition and fees: $14,238; out-of-state residents $29,381.

Per-credit charge: $367; out-of-state residents $862.

Room and board: $11,908.

Additional info: Tuition/fee waivers available for unemployed or children of unemployed.

FINANCIAL AID PICTURE (2015-2016)

Students with need: Out of 377 full-time freshmen who applied for aid, 344 were judged to have need. Of these, 344 received aid, and 7 had their full need met. Average financial aid package met 52% of need; average scholarship/grant was $11,710; average loan was $3,757. For part-time students, average financial aid package was $4,862.

Students without need: 21 full-time freshmen who did not demonstrate need for aid received scholarships/grants; average award was $5,064. No-need awards available for academics, alumni affiliation, art, athletics, leadership, music/drama, state/district residency.

Scholarships offered: Outstanding Scholarship Recruitment Program: $2,500-$7,500; for selected in-state resident applicants based on SAT and class rank; 2,500 awarded. Carr Scholarship: $10,000; for selected minority applicants; 150 awarded. Class of 1941 Scholarship: $1,941; descendant of 1941 alumni preferred; 1 awarded. National Merit Scholarship for National Merit finalists; $1,000-$2,000; 15 or more awarded. National Achievement Scholarship for National Achievement finalists; $1,000-$2,000; 2 awarded. Rockland County-Herman T. Hopper Scholarship: out-of-state tuition; for Rockland County, New York resident; 1 awarded. Academic Achievement Award: $1,000; for in-state and out-of-state minority students; 20 awarded. Alumni Federation Scholarship: $1,000; for children of Rutgers University alumni; 20 awarded. National Scholarship: $5,000; for out-of-state students; about 100 awarded university-wide.

FINANCIAL AID PROCEDURES

Forms required: FAFSA.

Dates and Deadlines: Priority date 3/15; no closing date. Applicants notified on a rolling basis starting 3/1; must reply within 4 week(s) of notification.

CONTACT

406 Penn Street, Camden, NJ 08102
(856) 225-6039

Rutgers, The State University of New Jersey: New Brunswick/Piscataway Campus

Piscataway, New Jersey
www.newbrunswick.rutgers.edu   Federal Code: 002629

4-year public university in small city.
Enrollment: 35,782 undergrads, 5% part-time. 6,602 full-time freshmen.
Selectivity: Admits 50 to 75% of applicants.

BASIC COSTS (2016-2017)

Tuition and fees: $14,372; out-of-state residents $30,023.
Per-credit charge: $367; out-of-state residents $878.
Room and board: $12,260.
Additional info: Tuition/fee waivers available for unemployed or children of unemployed.

FINANCIAL AID PICTURE (2015-2016)

Students with need: Out of 4,494 full-time freshmen who applied for aid, 3,602 were judged to have need. Of these, 3,602 received aid, and 219 had their full need met. Average financial aid package met 51% of need; average scholarship/grant was $19,765; average loan was $3,866. For part-time students, average financial aid package was $4,399.
Students without need: 446 full-time freshmen who did not demonstrate need for aid received scholarships/grants; average award was $12,865. No-need awards available for academics, alumni affiliation, art, athletics, leadership, music/drama, state/district residency.
Scholarships offered: *Merit:* Outstanding Scholarship Recruitment Program: $2,500-$7,500; for selected in-state resident applicants based on SAT and class rank; 2,500 awarded. Carr Scholarship: $10,000; for selected minority applicants; 150 awarded. Class of 1941 Scholarship: $1,941; descendant of Class of 1941 alumni preferred. National Merit Scholarship: $1,000-$2,000; for National Merit finalists; 15 or more awarded. National Achievement Scholarship: $1,000-$2,000; for National Achievement finalists; 2 awarded. Rockland County-Herman T. Hopper Scholarship: out-of-state tuition; for Rockland County, New York resident; 1 awarded. Academic Achievement Award: $1,000; 20 awarded; for minority students. Alumni Federation Scholarship: $1,000; for children of Rutgers University alumni; 20 awarded. National Scholarship: $5,000; for out-of-state students; about 100 awards university-wide. *Athletic:* 102 full-time freshmen received athletic scholarships; average amount $25,395.

FINANCIAL AID PROCEDURES

Forms required: FAFSA.
Dates and Deadlines: Priority date 3/15; no closing date. Applicants notified on a rolling basis starting 3/1; must reply within 4 week(s) of notification.

CONTACT

65 Davidson Road, Room 202, Piscataway, NJ 08854-8097
(848) 932-7057

Rutgers, The State University of New Jersey: Newark Campus

Newark, New Jersey
www.newark.rutgers.edu   Federal Code: 002629

4-year public university in large city.
Enrollment: 7,691 undergrads, 13% part-time. 1,192 full-time freshmen.
Selectivity: Admits 50 to 75% of applicants.

BASIC COSTS (2016-2017)

Tuition and fees: $13,829; out-of-state residents $29,480.
Per-credit charge: $367; out-of-state residents $878.
Room and board: $13,459.
Additional info: Tuition/fee waivers available for unemployed or children of unemployed.

FINANCIAL AID PICTURE (2015-2016)

Students with need: Out of 945 full-time freshmen who applied for aid, 869 were judged to have need. Of these, 869 received aid, and 17 had their full need met. Average financial aid package met 53% of need; average scholarship/grant was $11,909; average loan was $3,928. For part-time students, average financial aid package was $5,440.
Students without need: 33 full-time freshmen who did not demonstrate need for aid received scholarships/grants; average award was $10,613. No-need awards available for academics, alumni affiliation, art, athletics, leadership, music/drama, state/district residency.
Scholarships offered: Outstanding Scholarship Recruitment Program: $2,500-$7,500; for selected in-state resident applicants; based on SAT and class rank; 2,500 awarded. Carr Scholarship: $10,000; for selected minority applicants; 150 awarded. Class of 1941 Scholarship: $1,941; descendant of Class of 1941 alumni preferred; 1 awarded. National Merit Scholarship: $1,000-$2,000; for National Merit finalists; 15 or more awarded. National Achievement Scholarship: $1,000-$2,000; for National Achievement finalists; 2 awarded. Rockland County-Herman T. Hopper Scholarship: out-of-state tuition; for Rockland County, New York resident; 1 awarded. Academic Achievement Award: $1,000; for in-and out-of-state minority students; 20 awarded. Alumni Federation Scholarship: $1,000; for children of Rutgers University alumni; 20 awarded. James Bryan Scholarship: $400; for selected in-state freshmen; 3 awarded. National Scholarship: $5,000; for out-of-state students; about 100 awards university-wide.

FINANCIAL AID PROCEDURES

Forms required: FAFSA.
Dates and Deadlines: Priority date 3/15; no closing date. Applicants notified on a rolling basis starting 3/1; must reply within 2 week(s) of notification.

CONTACT

249 University Avenue, Newark, NJ 07102-1896
(973) 353-5151

Saint Peter's University

Jersey City, New Jersey
www.saintpeters.edu   Federal Code: 002638

4-year private university in large city, affiliated with the Roman Catholic Church.
Enrollment: 2,589 undergrads, 8% part-time. 626 full-time freshmen.
Selectivity: Admits 50 to 75% of applicants.

BASIC COSTS (2016-2017)

Tuition and fees: $35,192.
Room and board: $14,956.

FINANCIAL AID PICTURE (2016-2017)

Students with need: 79% of average financial aid package awarded as scholarships/grants, 21% awarded as loans/jobs.
Students without need: No-need awards available for academics, athletics.
Scholarships offered: Academic Awards: full tuition; based on 1100 SAT (exclusive of Writing), 3.0 GPA, and top 20% of class; 50 awarded. Incentive Awards: $500-$4,000; for selected applicants with some qualities necessary for academic awards but who are otherwise ineligible. Residential Grants: $500-$2,500 toward housing; based on academics and extracurricular activities.
Additional info: Cooperative education internships available in all majors, with average salaries exceeding $5,200.

FINANCIAL AID PROCEDURES

Forms required: FAFSA, state aid form.
Dates and Deadlines: Priority date 3/15; no closing date. Applicants notified on a rolling basis starting 1/1; must reply by 5/1 or within 2 week(s) of notification.
Transfers: Student and parents (if dependent students) must be New Jersey residents for at least 1 year prior to start date. Students must complete renewal application before 6/1.

CONTACT

Jennifer Ragsdale, Director of Financial Aid
2641 Kennedy Boulevard, Jersey City, NJ 07306
(201) 761-6060

Salem Community College

Carneys Point, New Jersey
www.salemcc.edu   Federal Code: 005461

2-year public community and junior college in small town.
Enrollment: 912 undergrads, 42% part-time. 194 full-time freshmen.
Selectivity: Open admission; but selective for some programs.

BASIC COSTS (2016-2017)
Tuition and fees: $4,104; out-of-district residents $4,794; out-of-state residents $5,544.
Per-credit charge: $102; out-of-district residents $125; out-of-state residents $150.
Additional info: Tuition/fee waivers available for unemployed or children of unemployed.

FINANCIAL AID PICTURE
Students with need: Need-based aid available for full-time and part-time students.
Students without need: No-need awards available for academics, athletics, state/district residency.

FINANCIAL AID PROCEDURES
Forms required: FAFSA, institutional form.
Dates and Deadlines: Priority date 6/1; no closing date. Applicants notified on a rolling basis starting 4/1; must reply within 2 week(s) of notification.

CONTACT
Ron Burkhardt, Director of Financial Aid
460 Hollywood Avenue, Carneys Point, NJ 08069-2799
(856) 351-2699

Seton Hall University

South Orange, New Jersey
www.shu.edu   Federal Code: 002632

4-year private university in large town, affiliated with the Roman Catholic Church.
Enrollment: 5,818 undergrads.

BASIC COSTS (2016-2017)
Tuition and fees: $39,558.
Per-credit charge: $1,130.
Room and board: $14,732.

FINANCIAL AID PICTURE
Students with need: Need-based aid available for full-time and part-time students. Work study available nights, weekends, and for part-time students.
Students without need: No-need awards available for academics, alumni affiliation, athletics, leadership, music/drama, ROTC.

FINANCIAL AID PROCEDURES
Forms required: FAFSA.

CONTACT
Javonda Asante, Director of Financial Aid
400 South Orange Avenue, South Orange, NJ 07079-2680
(800) 222-7183

Stevens Institute of Technology

Hoboken, New Jersey
www.stevens.edu   Federal Code: 002639

4-year private university and engineering college in small city.
Enrollment: 3,109 undergrads. 737 full-time freshmen.
Selectivity: Admits less than 50% of applicants.

BASIC COSTS (2017-2018)
Tuition and fees: $50,554.
Per-credit charge: $1,626.
Room and board: $14,400.

FINANCIAL AID PICTURE
Students with need: Need-based aid available for full-time and part-time students. Work study available nights, weekends, and for part-time students.
Students without need: No-need awards available for academics, leadership, music/drama, ROTC.
Scholarships offered: Neupauer Scholarship: full tuition; for top candidates in freshman class. Edwin A. Stevens Scholarship: $3,000-$20,000; for top candidates in freshman class. Becton Dickinson Scholarship: full tuition; for top student pursuing engineering degree. DeBaun Performing Arts Scholarship: $1,000-$5,000.

FINANCIAL AID PROCEDURES
Forms required: FAFSA.
Dates and Deadlines: Priority date 2/15; no closing date. Applicants notified on a rolling basis starting 3/30; must reply by 5/1 or within 2 week(s) of notification.
Transfers: Transfer merit scholarships, Phi Theta Kappa awards.

CONTACT
Louis Mayer, CFO, VP for Finance and Treasurer
1 Castle Point Terrace, Hoboken, NJ 07030-5991
(201) 216-5215

Stockton University

Galloway, New Jersey
www.stockton.edu   Federal Code: 009345

4-year public liberal arts college in large town.
Enrollment: 7,825 undergrads, 5% part-time. 1,187 full-time freshmen.
Selectivity: Admits over 75% of applicants.

BASIC COSTS (2016-2017)
Tuition and fees: $13,077; out-of-state residents $19,861.
Room and board: $11,982.
Additional info: Tuition/fee waivers available for unemployed or children of unemployed.

FINANCIAL AID PICTURE (2016-2017)
Students with need: Out of 1,132 full-time freshmen who applied for aid, 876 were judged to have need. Of these, 849 received aid, and 289 had their full need met. Average financial aid package met 76% of need; average scholarship/grant was $9,491; average loan was $3,338. For part-time students, average financial aid package was $10,523.
Students without need: 111 full-time freshmen who did not demonstrate need for aid received scholarships/grants; average award was $6,487. No-need awards available for academics, art, job skills.
Scholarships offered: Freshman Scholarship Program: $2,000-$18,000; based on class rank in top 15%, SAT.
Additional info: Institutional grants are provided to the neediest incoming students.

FINANCIAL AID PROCEDURES
Forms required: FAFSA.
Dates and Deadlines: Priority date 3/1; no closing date. Applicants notified by 4/1; must reply within 2 week(s) of notification.

Transfers: Applicants notified on a rolling basis starting 4/1; must reply within 2 week(s) of notification.

CONTACT
Jeanne Lewis, Director of Financial Aid
101 Vera King Farris Drive, Galloway, NJ 08205
(609) 652-4201

Sussex County Community College
Newton, New Jersey
www.sussex.edu   Federal Code: 025688

2-year public community college in small town.
Enrollment: 2,482 undergrads.
Selectivity: Open admission; but selective for some programs.

BASIC COSTS (2016-2017)
Tuition and fees: $6,750; out-of-district residents $8,850; out-of-state residents $10,950.
Additional info: Tuition/fee waivers available for unemployed or children of unemployed.

FINANCIAL AID PICTURE
Students with need: Need-based aid available for full-time and part-time students. Work study available nights, weekends, and for part-time students.
Students without need: This college awards aid only to students with need.

FINANCIAL AID PROCEDURES
Forms required: FAFSA, state aid form.
Dates and Deadlines: Closing date 6/1. Applicants notified on a rolling basis starting 5/1; must reply within 2 week(s) of notification.

CONTACT
Diane Pienta-Lett, Director, Financial Aid
One College Hill Road, Newton, NJ 07860
(973) 300-2225

Thomas Edison State University
Trenton, New Jersey
www.tesu.edu   Federal Code: 011648

4-year public university in small city.
Enrollment: 16,506 undergrads, 99% part-time.
Selectivity: Open admission; but selective for some programs.

BASIC COSTS (2016-2017)
Tuition and fees: $6,350; out-of-state residents $9,352.
Per-credit charge: $385; out-of-state residents $499.
Additional info: The tuition provided represents the University's Comprehensive Tuition Plan, which enables students to take 36 credits over a 12-month period. The University offers several other tuition plans.

FINANCIAL AID PICTURE
Students with need: Need-based aid available for full-time and part-time students.
Students without need: This college awards aid only to students with need.
Additional info: Financial aid applications should be received two months before each new term begins.

FINANCIAL AID PROCEDURES
Forms required: FAFSA, institutional form.
Dates and Deadlines: Applicants notified on a rolling basis starting 3/1; must reply within 4 week(s) of notification.
Transfers: No deadline. Applicants notified on a rolling basis; must reply within 4 week(s) of notification.

CONTACT
James Owens, Director of Financial Aid
111 West State Street, Trenton, NJ 08608-1176
(609) 633-9658

Union County College
Cranford, New Jersey
www.ucc.edu   Federal Code: 002643

2-year public community college in large town.
Enrollment: 9,704 undergrads, 55% part-time. 1,362 full-time freshmen.
Selectivity: Open admission; but selective for some programs.

BASIC COSTS (2016-2017)
Tuition and fees: $4,620; out-of-district residents $9,240; out-of-state residents $9,240.
Per-credit charge: $183.75; out-of-district residents $367.5; out-of-state residents $367.5.
Additional info: Tuition/fee waivers available for minority students, unemployed or children of unemployed.

FINANCIAL AID PICTURE
Students with need: Need-based aid available for full-time and part-time students. Work study available nights, weekends, and for part-time students.
Students without need: No-need awards available for academics, art, athletics, leadership, minority status, religious affiliation, state/district residency.

FINANCIAL AID PROCEDURES
Forms required: FAFSA, institutional form.
Dates and Deadlines: Applicants notified on a rolling basis starting 4/1.
Transfers: No deadline. Applicants notified on a rolling basis.

CONTACT
Dayne Chance, Director of Financial Aid
1033 Springfield Avenue, Cranford, NJ 07016-1528
(908) 709-7000

Warren County Community College
Washington, New Jersey
www.warren.edu   Federal Code: 016857

2-year public community college in small town.
Enrollment: 1,175 undergrads, 51% part-time. 224 full-time freshmen.
Selectivity: Open admission; but selective for some programs.

BASIC COSTS (2016-2017)
Tuition and fees: $4,590; out-of-district residents $4,890; out-of-state residents $5,490.
Per-credit charge: $135; out-of-district residents $145; out-of-state residents $165.
Additional info: Tuition/fee waivers available for unemployed or children of unemployed.

FINANCIAL AID PICTURE (2016-2017)
Students with need: Need-based aid available for part-time students.
Students without need: No-need awards available for academics, state/district residency.

FINANCIAL AID PROCEDURES
Forms required: FAFSA, state aid form, institutional form.
Dates and Deadlines: Closing date 7/1. Applicants notified on a rolling basis; must reply within 2 week(s) of notification.
Transfers: No deadline. Applicants notified on a rolling basis.

CONTACT
Debra Wulff, Director of Financial Aid
475 Route 57 West, Washington, NJ 07882-4343
(908) 835-2456

William Paterson University of New Jersey

Wayne, New Jersey
www.wpunj.edu   Federal Code: 002625

4-year public university and liberal arts college in large town.
Enrollment: 8,972 undergrads, 17% part-time. 1,372 full-time freshmen.
Selectivity: Admits over 75% of applicants.

BASIC COSTS (2016-2017)
Tuition and fees: $12,574; out-of-state residents $20,466.
Per-credit charge: $319; out-of-state residents $579.
Room and board: $11,103.
Additional info: Tuition/fee waivers available for unemployed or children of unemployed.

FINANCIAL AID PICTURE (2016-2017)
Students with need: Out of 1,313 full-time freshmen who applied for aid, 1,052 were judged to have need. Of these, 1,030 received aid, and 345 had their full need met. For part-time students, average financial aid package was $5,630.
Students without need: 114 full-time freshmen who did not demonstrate need for aid received scholarships/grants; average award was $7,886. No-need awards available for academics, art, music/drama.
Scholarships offered: Trustee Scholarships: $2,000-$8,000; for full time freshmen. Honors College Scholarship: $2,000; for full time freshmen enrolled in program. Talent Awards for Music and Art Students: up to $9,000; based on audition.

FINANCIAL AID PROCEDURES
Forms required: FAFSA.
Dates and Deadlines: Priority date 3/1; no closing date. Applicants notified by 1/17.
Transfers: No deadline. Applicants notified on a rolling basis starting 3/1; must reply within 2 week(s) of notification.

CONTACT
Michael Corso, Director of Financial Aid
300 Pompton Road, Wayne, NJ 07470
(973) 720-3945

New Mexico

Brookline College: Albuquerque

Albuquerque, New Mexico
www.brooklinecollege.edu   Federal Code: 022188

2-year for-profit branch campus and career college in large city.
Enrollment: 357 undergrads.
Selectivity: Open admission.

FINANCIAL AID PICTURE
Students with need: Need-based aid available for full-time students.
Students without need: This college awards aid only to students with need.

FINANCIAL AID PROCEDURES
Forms required: FAFSA, institutional form.

CONTACT
Genna Gillary, Corporate Manager of Financial Aid
4201 Central Avenue NW, Suite J, Albuquerque, NM 87105-1649
(505) 880-2877

Central New Mexico Community College

Albuquerque, New Mexico
www.cnm.edu   Federal Code: 004742

2-year public community and technical college in very large city.
Enrollment: 23,385 undergrads, 70% part-time. 1,857 full-time freshmen.
Selectivity: Open admission.

BASIC COSTS (2016-2017)
Tuition and fees: $1,472; out-of-state residents $6,848.
Per-credit charge: $52; out-of-state residents $276.

FINANCIAL AID PICTURE (2015-2016)
Students with need: Out of 1,625 full-time freshmen who applied for aid, 1,369 were judged to have need. Of these, 1,330 received aid. Need-based aid available for part-time students.
Students without need: 30 full-time freshmen who did not demonstrate need for aid received scholarships/grants; average award was $1,173.

FINANCIAL AID PROCEDURES
Forms required: FAFSA.
Dates and Deadlines: Priority date 5/1; no closing date. Applicants notified on a rolling basis starting 5/1.

CONTACT
Lee Carrillo, Director of Financial Aid
525 Buena Vista Drive, SE, Albuquerque, NM 87106
(888) 453-1304

Clovis Community College

Clovis, New Mexico
https://www.clovis.edu   Federal Code: 004743

2-year public community and junior college in large town.
Enrollment: 1,891 undergrads, 62% part-time. 290 full-time freshmen.
Selectivity: Open admission; but selective for some programs.

BASIC COSTS (2016-2017)
Tuition and fees: $1,176; out-of-district residents $1,248; out-of-state residents $2,376.

FINANCIAL AID PICTURE (2015-2016)
Students with need: Out of 236 full-time freshmen who applied for aid, 205 were judged to have need. Of these, 204 received aid, and 5 had their full need met. For part-time students, average financial aid package was $4,214.
Students without need: 12 full-time freshmen who did not demonstrate need for aid received scholarships/grants; average award was $612. No-need awards available for academics, state/district residency.
Additional info: Endowment of over $1,000,000 to assist nursing students.

FINANCIAL AID PROCEDURES
Forms required: FAFSA.
Dates and Deadlines: Priority date 9/1; no closing date. Applicants notified on a rolling basis starting 4/15.
Transfers: No deadline. Applicants notified on a rolling basis starting 4/15.

CONTACT
April Chavez, Director of Financial Aid
417 Schepps Boulevard, Clovis, NM 88101-8381
(575) 769-4060

Dona Ana Community College of New Mexico State University

Las Cruces, New Mexico
www.dacc.nmsu.edu   Federal Code: 002657

2-year public branch campus and community college in small city.
Enrollment: 9,280 undergrads.
Selectivity: Open admission; but selective for some programs.

BASIC COSTS (2016-2017)

Tuition and fees: $1,632; out-of-district residents $1,968; out-of-state residents $5,184.

Per-credit charge: $68; out-of-district residents $82; out-of-state residents $216.

FINANCIAL AID PICTURE

Students with need: Need-based aid available for full-time and part-time students.

FINANCIAL AID PROCEDURES

Forms required: FAFSA.

Dates and Deadlines: Priority date 3/1; no closing date. Applicants notified on a rolling basis starting 5/1.

CONTACT

Gladys Chairez, Financial Aid Director
MSC-3DA, Las Cruces, NM 88003-8001
(505) 527-7510

Eastern New Mexico University

Portales, New Mexico
www.enmu.edu   Federal Code: 002651

4-year public university in large town.
Enrollment: 3,627 undergrads.

BASIC COSTS (2016-2017)

Tuition and fees: $5,510; out-of-state residents $11,258.
Per-credit charge: $229.59; out-of-state residents $470.21.
Room and board: $6,760.
Additional info: Tuition at time of enrollment locked for 4 years.

FINANCIAL AID PICTURE

Students with need: Need-based aid available for full-time and part-time students. Work study available nights, weekends, and for part-time students.
Students without need: No-need awards available for academics, alumni affiliation, art, athletics, leadership, music/drama, state/district residency.
Scholarships offered: Admissions scholarships are available based on SAT or ACT scores.

FINANCIAL AID PROCEDURES

Forms required: FAFSA.
Dates and Deadlines: Applicants notified on a rolling basis starting 5/1.
Transfers: No deadline. Applicants notified on a rolling basis starting 4/1; must reply by 8/31. Child care grants and non-need-based college work study limited to New Mexico residents.

CONTACT

Brent Small, Director of Financial Aid
1500 South Avenue K, Portales, NM 88130
(575) 562-2194

Eastern New Mexico University: Roswell

Roswell, New Mexico
www.roswell.enmu.edu   Federal Code: 002651

2-year public branch campus and community college in large town.
Enrollment: 1,724 undergrads, 39% part-time. 373 full-time freshmen.

Selectivity: Open admission; but selective for some programs.

BASIC COSTS (2016-2017)

Tuition and fees: $1,944; out-of-district residents $2,088; out-of-state residents $4,920.
Room and board: $8,160.

FINANCIAL AID PICTURE

Students with need: Need-based aid available for full-time and part-time students. Work study available nights, weekends, and for part-time students.
Students without need: No-need awards available for academics.

FINANCIAL AID PROCEDURES

Forms required: FAFSA.
Dates and Deadlines: Priority date 4/1; no closing date. Applicants notified on a rolling basis starting 4/1; must reply within 3 week(s) of notification.

CONTACT

Analisa Bhakta, Director of Financial Aid
PO Box 6000, Roswell, NM 88202-6000
(575) 624-7152

Institute of American Indian Arts

Santa Fe, New Mexico
www.iaia.edu   Federal Code: 014152

4-year public visual arts and liberal arts college in small city.
Enrollment: 263 undergrads.

BASIC COSTS (2016-2017)

Tuition and fees: $4,700; out-of-state residents $4,700.
Per-credit charge: $186.
Room and board: $8,612.

FINANCIAL AID PICTURE

Students with need: Need-based aid available for full-time and part-time students.

FINANCIAL AID PROCEDURES

Forms required: FAFSA, institutional form.
Dates and Deadlines: Priority date 3/15; no closing date. Applicants notified on a rolling basis starting 5/1.

CONTACT

Lara Barela, Financial Aid Director
83 Avan Nu Po Road, Santa Fe, NM 87508-1300
(505) 424-5724

Luna Community College

Las Vegas, New Mexico
www.luna.edu   Federal Code: 009962

2-year public community and liberal arts college in large town.
Enrollment: 699 undergrads, 58% part-time. 70 full-time freshmen.
Selectivity: Open admission; but selective for some programs.

BASIC COSTS (2016-2017)

Tuition and fees: $962; out-of-district residents $1,298; out-of-state residents $2,426.
Per-credit charge: $38; out-of-district residents $52; out-of-state residents $99.

FINANCIAL AID PICTURE (2016-2017)

Students with need: Out of 23 full-time freshmen who applied for aid, 23 were judged to have need. Of these, 23 received aid. Need-based aid available for part-time students.
Students without need: No-need awards available for academics, athletics, state/district residency.

FINANCIAL AID PROCEDURES

Dates and Deadlines: Priority date 3/1; no closing date.

CONTACT

Michael Montoya, Financial Aid Director
366 Luna Drive, Las Vegas, NM 87701
(505) 454-2500 ext. 2002

Mesalands Community College

Tucumcari, New Mexico
www.mesalands.edu   Federal Code: 032063

2-year public community and technical college in small town.
Enrollment: 358 undergrads.
Selectivity: Open admission; but selective for some programs.

BASIC COSTS (2016-2017)
Tuition and fees: $2,145; out-of-state residents $3,465.
Per-credit charge: $55; out-of-state residents $99.

FINANCIAL AID PICTURE
Students with need: Need-based aid available for full-time and part-time students. Work study available nights.
Students without need: No-need awards available for academics, athletics, leadership, minority status, state/district residency.

FINANCIAL AID PROCEDURES
Forms required: FAFSA.
Dates and Deadlines: Priority date 3/31; no closing date. Applicants notified on a rolling basis starting 4/1; must reply within 3 week(s) of notification.

CONTACT
Jessica Elebario, Director of Financial Aid
911 South Tenth Street, Tucumcari, NM 88401
(575) 461-4413 ext. 136

Navajo Technical University

Crownpoint, New Mexico
www.navajotech.edu   Federal Code: 016119

2-year public college in rural community.
Enrollment: 1,351 undergrads, 24% part-time. 355 full-time freshmen.
Selectivity: Open admission.

BASIC COSTS (2016-2017)
Tuition and fees: $2,360; out-of-district residents $4,070.
Per-credit charge: $71.25; out-of-district residents $142.5.
Room and board: $6,270.
Additional info: Tuition at time of enrollment locked for 2 years; tuition/fee waivers available for minority students.

FINANCIAL AID PICTURE (2015-2016)
Students with need: Out of 334 full-time freshmen who applied for aid, 333 were judged to have need. Of these, 332 received aid, and 2 had their full need met. Average financial aid package met 46% of need; average scholarship/grant was $5,879. For part-time students, average financial aid package was $4,900.
Students without need: 13 full-time freshmen who did not demonstrate need for aid received scholarships/grants; average award was $462. No-need awards available for academics.
Scholarships offered: Merit: Boeing Scholarship: amount varies; number of recipients varies. Tom Davis Scholarship: $500 award; 10 recipients per semester. **Athletic:** 1 full-time freshmen received athletic scholarships; average amount $10,390.

FINANCIAL AID PROCEDURES
Forms required: FAFSA, institutional form.

Dates and Deadlines: Priority date 6/30; no closing date. Applicants notified on a rolling basis starting 8/5; must reply by 11/30 or within 4 week(s) of notification.
Transfers: Priority date 7/31; no deadline. Applicants notified by 9/30; must reply by 9/30 or within 4 week(s) of notification.

CONTACT
Tyrrell Hardy, Financial Aid Officer
PO Box 849, Crownpoint, NM 87313
(505) 786-4309

New Mexico Highlands University

Las Vegas, New Mexico
www.nmhu.edu   Federal Code: 002653

4-year public university in large town.
Enrollment: 2,123 undergrads, 32% part-time. 298 full-time freshmen.
Selectivity: Open admission.

BASIC COSTS (2016-2017)
Tuition and fees: $5,400; out-of-state residents $8,500.
Per-credit charge: $164.65; out-of-state residents $293.82.
Room and board: $7,836.

FINANCIAL AID PICTURE (2015-2016)
Students with need: Out of 275 full-time freshmen who applied for aid, 230 were judged to have need. Of these, 229 received aid, and 24 had their full need met. Average financial aid package met 19% of need; average scholarship/grant was $1,838; average loan was $2,138. For part-time students, average financial aid package was $1,843.
Students without need: 163 full-time freshmen who did not demonstrate need for aid received scholarships/grants; average award was $1,871. No-need awards available for academics, alumni affiliation, art, athletics, music/drama, state/district residency.
Scholarships offered: 38 full-time freshmen received athletic scholarships; average amount $3,621.
Additional info: Work study funds available on no-need basis to state residents.

FINANCIAL AID PROCEDURES
Forms required: FAFSA.
Dates and Deadlines: Applicants notified on a rolling basis.
Transfers: Closing date 6/30.

CONTACT
Eileen Sedillo, Director of Financial Aid
Box 9000, Las Vegas, NM 87701
(505) 454-3318

New Mexico Institute of Mining and Technology

Socorro, New Mexico
www.nmt.edu   Federal Code: 002654

4-year public engineering and liberal arts college in small town.
Enrollment: 1,460 undergrads, 5% part-time. 301 full-time freshmen.
Selectivity: Admits less than 50% of applicants.

BASIC COSTS (2016-2017)
Tuition and fees: $6,891; out-of-state residents $20,041.
Per-credit charge: $243; out-of-state residents $791.
Room and board: $7,942.

FINANCIAL AID PICTURE (2016-2017)
Students with need: Average financial aid package met 84% of need; average scholarship/grant was $4,635; average loan was $3,350. For part-time students, average financial aid package was $11,831.

Students without need: No-need awards available for academics, alumni affiliation, minority status, state/district residency.
Additional info: Campus research projects offer student employment based on abilities, interest, and merit.

FINANCIAL AID PROCEDURES

Forms required: FAFSA, institutional form.
Dates and Deadlines: Priority date 5/1; no closing date. Applicants notified on a rolling basis starting 5/1; must reply within 2 week(s) of notification.
Transfers: Priority date 3/1; no deadline. Applicants notified on a rolling basis starting 4/1; must reply within 2 week(s) of notification. Financial aid transcripts required from all colleges attended.

CONTACT

vacant
801 Leroy Place, Socorro, NM 87801
(575) 835-5333

New Mexico Junior College

Hobbs, New Mexico
www.nmjc.edu   Federal Code: 002655

2-year public community and technical college in large town.
Enrollment: 2,949 undergrads.
Selectivity: Open admission; but selective for some programs.

BASIC COSTS (2016-2017)

Tuition and fees: $1,248; out-of-district residents $1,704; out-of-state residents $1,896.
Per-credit charge: $35; out-of-district residents $54; out-of-state residents $62.
Room and board: $4,350.

FINANCIAL AID PICTURE

Students with need: Need-based aid available for full-time and part-time students. Work study available nights, weekends, and for part-time students.
Students without need: No-need awards available for academics, art, athletics, leadership, music/drama.

FINANCIAL AID PROCEDURES

Forms required: FAFSA.
Dates and Deadlines: Priority date 6/1; no closing date. Applicants notified on a rolling basis; must reply within 2 week(s) of notification.

CONTACT

Kerrie Mitchell, Director of Financial Aid
5317 Lovington Highway, Hobbs, NM 88240
(575) 392-4510

New Mexico Military Institute

Roswell, New Mexico
www.nmmi.edu   Federal Code: 002656

2-year public junior and military college in small city.
Enrollment: 422 undergrads. 314 full-time freshmen.
Selectivity: Admits less than 50% of applicants.

BASIC COSTS (2016-2017)

Tuition and fees: $7,799; out-of-state residents $13,439.
Room and board: $5,325.

FINANCIAL AID PICTURE

Students with need: Need-based aid available for full-time students.
Students without need: No-need awards available for academics, alumni affiliation, athletics, leadership, minority status, music/drama, ROTC, state/district residency.

FINANCIAL AID PROCEDURES

Forms required: FAFSA.
Dates and Deadlines: Priority date 2/1; no closing date. Applicants notified on a rolling basis starting 2/1; must reply within 3 week(s) of notification.
Transfers: No deadline. Applicants notified on a rolling basis; must reply within 3 week(s) of notification. New Mexico Scholars Program, New Mexico Lottery Success Scholarship programs available.

CONTACT

Sonya Rodriguez, Director of Admissions & Financial Aid
101 West College Boulevard, Roswell, NM 88201-5173
(575) 624-8066

New Mexico State University

Las Cruces, New Mexico
www.nmsu.edu   Federal Code: 002657

4-year public university in small city.
Enrollment: 11,421 undergrads, 14% part-time. 1,978 full-time freshmen.
Selectivity: Admits 50 to 75% of applicants.

BASIC COSTS (2016-2017)

Tuition and fees: $6,729; out-of-state residents $21,234.
Room and board: $7,988.

FINANCIAL AID PICTURE (2015-2016)

Students with need: Out of 1,667 full-time freshmen who applied for aid, 1,371 were judged to have need. Of these, 1,371 received aid, and 165 had their full need met. Average financial aid package met 65% of need; average scholarship/grant was $10,052; average loan was $2,555. For part-time students, average financial aid package was $5,713.
Students without need: 350 full-time freshmen who did not demonstrate need for aid received scholarships/grants; average award was $3,188. No-need awards available for academics, alumni affiliation, art, athletics, leadership, minority status, music/drama, ROTC, state/district residency.
Scholarships offered: 54 full-time freshmen received athletic scholarships; average amount $8,896.

FINANCIAL AID PROCEDURES

Forms required: FAFSA.
Dates and Deadlines: Priority date 3/1; closing date 6/30. Applicants notified on a rolling basis starting 1/1.
Transfers: Priority date 3/1; closing date 6/30. Applicants notified on a rolling basis starting 1/1. Restrictions only apply to institutional aid, such as number of transfer hours and GPA.

CONTACT

Vandeen McKenzie, Director of Financial Aid
Box 30001, MSC 3A, Las Cruces, NM 88003-8001
(575) 646-4105

New Mexico State University at Alamogordo

Alamogordo, New Mexico
www.nmsua.edu   Federal Code: 002658

2-year public branch campus college in large town.
Enrollment: 1,849 undergrads.
Selectivity: Open admission; but selective for some programs.

BASIC COSTS (2016-2017)

Tuition and fees: $1,968; out-of-district residents $2,328; out-of-state residents $5,280.

FINANCIAL AID PICTURE

Students with need: Need-based aid available for full-time and part-time students. Work study available nights.

Students without need: No-need awards available for academics, state/district residency.

FINANCIAL AID PROCEDURES

Forms required: FAFSA, institutional form.

Dates and Deadlines: Priority date 3/1; no closing date.

CONTACT

Vandeen McKenzie, Financial Aid Director
2400 North Scenic Drive, Alamogordo, NM 88310
(575) 439-3600

New Mexico State University at Carlsbad

Carlsbad, New Mexico
www.cavern.nmsu.edu   Federal Code: 002657

2-year public branch campus and community college in large town.
Enrollment: 1,360 undergrads.
Selectivity: Open admission; but selective for some programs.

BASIC COSTS (2016-2017)

Tuition and fees: $1,108; out-of-district residents $1,852; out-of-state residents $3,868.

Per-credit charge: $42; out-of-district residents $73.

FINANCIAL AID PICTURE

Students with need: Need-based aid available for full-time and part-time students. Work study available nights.

Students without need: No-need awards available for academics, state/district residency.

FINANCIAL AID PROCEDURES

Forms required: FAFSA.

Dates and Deadlines: Priority date 3/1; no closing date. Applicants notified on a rolling basis starting 5/1; must reply within 4 week(s) of notification.

CONTACT

Diana Campos, Financial Aid Coordinator
1500 University Drive, Carlsbad, NM 88220
(575) 234-9226

New Mexico State University at Grants

Grants, New Mexico
www.grants.nmsu.edu   Federal Code: 008854

2-year public branch campus and community college in small town.
Enrollment: 821 undergrads.
Selectivity: Open admission.

BASIC COSTS (2016-2017)

Tuition and fees: $1,896; out-of-district residents $2,064; out-of-state residents $3,936.

FINANCIAL AID PICTURE

Students with need: Need-based aid available for full-time and part-time students. Work study available nights, weekends, and for part-time students.

FINANCIAL AID PROCEDURES

Forms required: FAFSA, institutional form.

Dates and Deadlines: Priority date 3/5; no closing date. Applicants notified on a rolling basis starting 6/15; must reply by 8/28.

CONTACT

Beth Armstead, Vice President for Student Services
1500 North Third Street, Grants, NM 87020
(505) 287-6678

Northern New Mexico College

Espanola, New Mexico
www.nnmc.edu   Federal Code: 005286

4-year public business and nursing college in small town.
Enrollment: 1,601 undergrads.
Selectivity: Open admission; but selective for some programs and for out-of-state students.

BASIC COSTS (2016-2017)

Tuition and fees: $4,560.

FINANCIAL AID PICTURE

Students with need: Need-based aid available for full-time students.

Students without need: This college awards aid only to students with need.

FINANCIAL AID PROCEDURES

Forms required: FAFSA.

Dates and Deadlines: Priority date 3/1; no closing date. Applicants notified on a rolling basis starting 6/1; must reply within 2 week(s) of notification.

CONTACT

Jacob Pacheco, Director of Financial Aid
921 Paseo de Onate, Espanola, NM 87532
(505) 747-2128 ext. 128

St. John's College

Santa Fe, New Mexico
www.sjc.edu   Federal Code: 002093

4-year private liberal arts college in small city.
Enrollment: 326 undergrads, 2% part-time. 67 full-time freshmen.
Selectivity: Admits 50 to 75% of applicants.

BASIC COSTS (2017-2018)

Tuition and fees: $52,320.
Per-credit charge: $1,506.
Room and board: $11,486.

FINANCIAL AID PICTURE (2016-2017)

Students with need: Average financial aid package met 86% of need; average scholarship/grant was $31,750; average loan was $4,500. For part-time students, average financial aid package was $26,480.

Students without need: No-need awards available for academics.

Scholarships offered: Merit awards: range from $18,000 to $23,000; awarded on the strength of the admission application.

Additional info: FAFSA is the only application used to apply for financial aid. Priority filing date is 2/15 for entering students and 3/1 for continuing students. CSS profile is optional for domestic students but required for international students.

FINANCIAL AID PROCEDURES

Forms required: FAFSA.

Dates and Deadlines: Priority date 2/15; no closing date. Applicants notified on a rolling basis starting 12/15; must reply by 5/1 or within 2 week(s) of notification.

Transfers: Applicants notified on a rolling basis starting 12/15; must reply by 5/1 or within 2 week(s) of notification. A limited number of full scholarships are available for qualified students who apply Early Action 1 and 2.

CONTACT

Michael Rodriguez, Director of Financial Aid
1160 Camino Cruz Blanca, Santa Fe, NM 87505
(505) 984-6058

San Juan College
Farmington, New Mexico
www.sanjuancollege.edu   Federal Code: 002660

2-year public community and technical college in large town.
Enrollment: 5,581 undergrads, 52% part-time. 652 full-time freshmen.
Selectivity: Open admission.

BASIC COSTS (2016-2017)
Tuition and fees: $1,492; out-of-state residents $3,892.
Per-credit charge: $46; out-of-state residents $146.

FINANCIAL AID PICTURE (2015-2016)
Students with need: 75% of average financial aid package awarded as scholarships/grants, 25% awarded as loans/jobs. Need-based aid available for part-time students. Work study available nights, weekends, and for part-time students.
Students without need: No-need awards available for academics, state/district residency.

FINANCIAL AID PROCEDURES
Forms required: FAFSA, institutional form.
Dates and Deadlines: Applicants notified on a rolling basis starting 7/1; must reply within 2 week(s) of notification.

CONTACT
Mindi-Kim Schrum, Director for Financial Aid
4601 College Boulevard, Farmington, NM 87402-4699
(505) 566-3323

Santa Fe Community College
Santa Fe, New Mexico
www.sfcc.edu   Federal Code: 016065

2-year public community college in small city.
Enrollment: 4,437 undergrads.
Selectivity: Open admission; but selective for some programs.

BASIC COSTS (2016-2017)
Tuition and fees: $1,356; out-of-district residents $1,644; out-of-state residents $2,940.
Room and board: $11,013.

FINANCIAL AID PICTURE
Students with need: Need-based aid available for full-time and part-time students. Work study available nights, weekends, and for part-time students.
Students without need: No-need awards available for academics, state/district residency.

FINANCIAL AID PROCEDURES
Forms required: FAFSA, institutional form.
Dates and Deadlines: Priority date 5/1; no closing date. Applicants notified on a rolling basis starting 6/1; must reply within 4 week(s) of notification.

CONTACT
Scott Whitaker, Financial Aid Director
6401 Richards Avenue, Santa Fe, NM 87508-4887
(505) 428-1268

Santa Fe University of Art and Design
Santa Fe, New Mexico
www.santafeuniversity.edu   Federal Code: 002649

4-year for-profit visual arts and liberal arts college in small city.
Enrollment: 849 undergrads.

BASIC COSTS (2016-2017)
Additional info: Bachelor's degree tuition ranges from $19,424-$30,846, Room and board - $9,866 a year.

FINANCIAL AID PICTURE
Students with need: Need-based aid available for full-time and part-time students. Work study available nights, weekends, and for part-time students.
Students without need: No-need awards available for academics, art, music/drama, state/district residency.

FINANCIAL AID PROCEDURES
Forms required: FAFSA.
Dates and Deadlines: Priority date 3/15; no closing date. Applicants notified on a rolling basis starting 3/1.
Transfers: No deadline. Applicants notified on a rolling basis starting 3/1. Financial Aid is not credited to student accounts until all financial aid transcripts received.

CONTACT
Celeste Franklin, Director of Financial Aid
1600 Saint Michael's Drive, Santa Fe, NM 87505-7634
(505) 473-6454

Southwest University of Visual Arts
Albuquerque, New Mexico
www.suva.edu   Federal Code: 024915

4-year for-profit visual arts college in very large city.
Enrollment: 209 undergrads.

BASIC COSTS (2016-2017)
Tuition and fees: $22,944.
Additional info: Estimated total costs for books and supplies for each program: $3,900-$4,750. Tuition at time of enrollment locked for 4 years.

FINANCIAL AID PICTURE
Students with need: Work study available nights, weekends, and for part-time students.
Students without need: No-need awards available for academics.
Scholarships offered: Board of Trustees Scholarship, Transfer Student Scholarship, Scholarship for Continuing Students.

FINANCIAL AID PROCEDURES
Forms required: FAFSA.
Transfers: No deadline. Applicants notified on a rolling basis.

CONTACT
Registrar, Office of Institutional Effectiveness
5000 Marble Avenue NE, Albuquerque, NM 87119
(520) 325-0123

Southwestern Indian Polytechnic Institute
Albuquerque, New Mexico
www.sipi.edu   Federal Code: 011185

2-year public community and technical college in large city.
Enrollment: 353 undergrads, 12% part-time. 157 full-time freshmen.
Selectivity: Open admission.

BASIC COSTS (2017-2018)
Tuition and fees: $730.
Room and board: $450.
Additional info: Tuition/fee waivers available for minority students.

FINANCIAL AID PICTURE (2015-2016)
Students with need: Out of 157 full-time freshmen who applied for aid, 110 were judged to have need. Of these, 110 received aid, and 3 had their

full need met. Average financial aid package met 60% of need; average scholarship/grant was $1,299. For part-time students, average financial aid package was $1,564.

Students without need: No-need awards available for academics, leadership, minority status.

Additional info: Students with valid membership in recognized Indian tribe attend tuition-free.

FINANCIAL AID PROCEDURES

Forms required: FAFSA, institutional form.

Dates and Deadlines: Closing date 3/1. Applicants notified on a rolling basis starting 9/30.

Transfers: Priority date 9/13; no deadline.

CONTACT

Joseph Carpio, Director Admissions & Financial aid
PO Box 10146, Albuquerque, NM 87184
(505) 346-2361

University of New Mexico
Albuquerque, New Mexico
www.unm.edu   Federal Code: 002663

4-year public university in very large city.

Enrollment: 19,648 undergrads, 20% part-time. 3,289 full-time freshmen.

Selectivity: Admits less than 50% of applicants.

BASIC COSTS (2016-2017)

Tuition and fees: $6,950; out-of-state residents $21,936.

Room and board: $9,472.

FINANCIAL AID PICTURE (2015-2016)

Students with need: Out of 2,869 full-time freshmen who applied for aid, 2,859 were judged to have need. Of these, 2,816 received aid, and 940 had their full need met. Need-based aid available for part-time students.

Students without need: No-need awards available for academics, alumni affiliation, art, athletics, job skills, leadership, minority status, music/drama, religious affiliation, ROTC, state/district residency.

Scholarships offered: Bridge to Success Scholarship and Success Grant: first semester only; requires New Mexico residency; full-time status in degree-granting program; acceptable GED test score and/or requisite high school GPA per sponsor. NM Legislature Lottery Scholarship: second and subsequent semesters; requires New Mexico residency; full-time status in degree-granting program; acceptable GED test score and/or requisite high school GPA; 15 or more credit hours with a 2.5 GPA in the first semester.

FINANCIAL AID PROCEDURES

Forms required: FAFSA.

Dates and Deadlines: Priority date 3/1; no closing date. Applicants notified on a rolling basis starting 3/31.

CONTACT

Brian Malone, Director of Student Financial Aid
Office of Admissions, Albuquerque, NM 87196-4895
(505) 277-8900

University of the Southwest
Hobbs, New Mexico
www.usw.edu   Federal Code: 013935

4-year private liberal arts and teachers college in large town, affiliated with the nondenominational tradition.

Enrollment: 536 undergrads, 42% part-time. 95 full-time freshmen.

Selectivity: Open admission; but selective for some programs.

BASIC COSTS (2016-2017)

Tuition and fees: $16,560.

Per-credit charge: $552.

Room and board: $7,535.

FINANCIAL AID PICTURE

Students with need: Need-based aid available for full-time and part-time students. Work study available nights, weekends, and for part-time students.

Students without need: No-need awards available for academics, athletics, leadership.

FINANCIAL AID PROCEDURES

Forms required: FAFSA.

Dates and Deadlines: Priority date 4/1; closing date 6/1. Applicants notified on a rolling basis starting 4/1; must reply within 2 week(s) of notification.

Transfers: Applicants notified on a rolling basis starting 4/1; must reply within 2 week(s) of notification.

CONTACT

Dawny Kringel, Director of Financial Aid
6610 North Lovington Highway, #506, Hobbs, NM 88240
(575) 492-2114

Western New Mexico University
Silver City, New Mexico
www.wnmu.edu   Federal Code: 002664

4-year public university in large town.

Enrollment: 1,798 undergrads, 29% part-time. 264 full-time freshmen.

Selectivity: Open admission.

BASIC COSTS (2016-2017)

Tuition and fees: $6,644; out-of-state residents $15,261.

Room and board: $8,936.

FINANCIAL AID PICTURE

Students with need: Need-based aid available for full-time and part-time students.

Students without need: No-need awards available for academics, art, athletics, music/drama.

FINANCIAL AID PROCEDURES

Forms required: FAFSA, institutional form.

Dates and Deadlines: Priority date 3/1; no closing date. Applicants notified on a rolling basis starting 3/1; must reply within 2 week(s) of notification.

CONTACT

Cheryl Hain, Director of Financial Aid
Castorena 106, Silver City, NM 88062
(575) 538-6173

New York

Adelphi University
Garden City, New York
www.adelphi.edu   Federal Code: 002666

4-year private university in large town.

Enrollment: 5,135 undergrads, 8% part-time. 1,215 full-time freshmen.

Selectivity: Admits 50 to 75% of applicants.

BASIC COSTS (2016-2017)

Tuition and fees: $35,740.

Per-credit charge: $1,040.

Room and board: $13,930.

FINANCIAL AID PICTURE (2016-2017)

Students with need: Out of 1,080 full-time freshmen who applied for aid, 932 were judged to have need. Of these, 932 received aid, and 161 had their full need met. Average financial aid package met 51% of need; average scholarship/grant was $21,071; average loan was $3,812. Need-based aid available for part-time students.

Students without need: 209 full-time freshmen who did not demonstrate need for aid received scholarships/grants; average award was $18,535. No-need awards available for academics, alumni affiliation, art, athletics, leadership, minority status, music/drama, religious affiliation, state/district residency.

Scholarships offered: *Merit:* Trustee Scholarships: for full-time freshmen with the most outstanding academic achievement and co-curricular activities, minimum 2020 score on SAT and rank in top 10% of high school class; 12 available. Presidential Scholarship: typically have minimum SAT of 1950 and rank in top 10% of high school class; $15,000-$16,000 depending upon the individual's academic profile; 25 available. Provost Scholarship: minimum SAT of 1800 and rank in the top 15% of high school class or have minimum transfer GPA of 3.5; $12,000 to $14,500; 55 available. Dean's Scholarship: for full-time freshmen with very good academic performances. Generally minimum SAT scores 1580 to 1790 and rank in top 25% of high school class. **Athletic:** 19 full-time freshmen received athletic scholarships; average amount $9,132.

FINANCIAL AID PROCEDURES

Forms required: FAFSA, state aid form.

Dates and Deadlines: Priority date 3/1; no closing date. Applicants notified on a rolling basis starting 3/1.

Transfers: No deadline. Applicants notified on a rolling basis. Transfer priority filing deadline for institutional aid is March 1 for Fall admission and November 1 for Spring admission.

CONTACT

Sheryl Mihopulos, Assistant Vice President
One South Avenue, Nexus Building, Rm. 111, Garden City, NY 11530-0701
(516) 877-3080

Adirondack Community College

Queensbury, New York
www.sunyacc.edu   Federal Code: 002860

2-year public community college in large town.
Enrollment: 3,111 undergrads, 31% part-time. 804 full-time freshmen.
Selectivity: Open admission; but selective for some programs.

BASIC COSTS (2016-2017)

Tuition and fees: $4,611; out-of-state residents $8,787.
Per-credit charge: $174; out-of-state residents $348.
Room and board: $11,410.

FINANCIAL AID PICTURE (2015-2016)

Students with need: 69% of average financial aid package awarded as scholarships/grants, 31% awarded as loans/jobs. Need-based aid available for part-time students.

Students without need: No-need awards available for academics, state/district residency.

Scholarships offered: Academic Excellence Scholarship: $750 per semester for up to 4 semesters; for local high school graduates who are 1st or 2nd in class, GPA 3.5. Hill Scholarship: $500 per semester for 4 semesters; for Fort Edward High School graduate.

FINANCIAL AID PROCEDURES

Forms required: FAFSA, state aid form, institutional form.

Dates and Deadlines: Priority date 4/15; no closing date. Applicants notified on a rolling basis starting 5/1.

CONTACT

Colleen Wise, Director of Financial Aid
640 Bay Road, Queensbury, NY 12804
(518) 743-2223

Albany College of Pharmacy and Health Sciences

Albany, New York
www.acphs.edu   Federal Code: 002885

4-year private health science and pharmacy college in small city.
Enrollment: 901 undergrads, 1% part-time. 153 full-time freshmen.
Selectivity: Admits 50 to 75% of applicants.

BASIC COSTS (2016-2017)

Tuition and fees: $31,981.
Per-credit charge: $1,040.
Room and board: $10,700.

FINANCIAL AID PICTURE (2015-2016)

Students with need: Need-based aid available for part-time students. Work study available nights, weekends, and for part-time students.

Students without need: No-need awards available for academics, alumni affiliation, athletics, state/district residency.

FINANCIAL AID PROCEDURES

Forms required: FAFSA.

Dates and Deadlines: Priority date 2/1; closing date 5/1. Applicants notified by 3/1; must reply within 2 week(s) of notification.

Transfers: Applicants notified by 4/1; must reply within 2 week(s) of notification.

CONTACT

Kathleen Montague, Director of Financial Aid
106 New Scotland Avenue, Albany, NY 12208-3492
(518) 694-7256

Alfred University

Alfred, New York
www.alfred.edu   Federal Code: 002668

4-year private university in rural community.
Enrollment: 1,725 undergrads, 1% part-time. 426 full-time freshmen.
Selectivity: Admits 50 to 75% of applicants.

BASIC COSTS (2017-2018)

Tuition and fees: $32,264.
Per-credit charge: $998.
Room and board: $12,272.
Additional info: Tuition for the School of Art & Design and for programs in bio-materials, ceramic engineering, materials science engineering, and glass engineering is $25,320 for non-NYS residents and $18,412 for NYS residents. Tuition for programs in mechanical, renewable Energy, and undecided engineering is $25,320.

FINANCIAL AID PICTURE (2016-2017)

Students with need: Out of 404 full-time freshmen who applied for aid, 364 were judged to have need. Of these, 364 received aid, and 45 had their full need met. Average financial aid package met 87% of need; average scholarship/grant was $22,872; average loan was $5,463. For part-time students, average financial aid package was $4,054.

Students without need: 12 full-time freshmen who did not demonstrate need for aid received scholarships/grants; average award was $11,750. No-need awards available for academics, art, leadership, music/drama.

FINANCIAL AID PROCEDURES

Forms required: FAFSA, state aid form.

Dates and Deadlines: Closing date 3/15. Applicants notified on a rolling basis starting 2/15; must reply by 5/1 or within 2 week(s) of notification.

Transfers: No deadline. Applicants notified on a rolling basis starting 2/15; must reply by 5/1 or within 2 week(s) of notification.

CONTACT

Charles Scheetz, Director of Student Financial Aid
Alumni Hall, Alfred, NY 14802-1205
(607) 871-2159

American Academy McAllister Institute of Funeral Service

New York, New York
www.funeraleducation.org   Federal Code: 010813

2-year private school of mortuary science in very large city.
Enrollment: 486 undergrads, 83% part-time. 16 full-time freshmen.
Selectivity: Admits over 75% of applicants.

BASIC COSTS (2016-2017)
Tuition and fees: $16,548.
Per-credit charge: $475.

FINANCIAL AID PICTURE (2016-2017)
Students with need: 28% of average financial aid package awarded as scholarships/grants, 72% awarded as loans/jobs.
Students without need: This college awards aid only to students with need.
Additional info: Financial aid application due 30 days before start of semester.

FINANCIAL AID PROCEDURES
Forms required: FAFSA, state aid form.
Dates and Deadlines: Applicants notified on a rolling basis starting 7/1; must reply by 9/1 or within 3 week(s) of notification.
Transfers: Priority date 6/1.

CONTACT
Natalie Givan, Financial Aid Administrator
619 West 54th Street, 2nd Floor, New York, NY 10019-3602
(212) 757-1190

American Academy of Dramatic Arts

New York, New York
www.aada.edu   Federal Code: 007465

2-year private junior and performing arts college in very large city.
Enrollment: 288 undergrads. 117 full-time freshmen.

BASIC COSTS (2016-2017)
Tuition and fees: $33,190.

FINANCIAL AID PICTURE
Students with need: Need-based aid available for full-time students.
Scholarships offered: Merit awards: $1,000-$6,000 for first-year students; Scholarships of $500-$4,000 available for second year; Scholarships of $500-$6,000 available for post-degree third year.
Additional info: Need-based incentive grants of $200-$2,000 for first-year students.

FINANCIAL AID PROCEDURES
Forms required: FAFSA, institutional form.
Dates and Deadlines: Applicants notified on a rolling basis.

CONTACT
Roberto Lopez, Financial Aid Director
120 Madison Avenue, New York, NY 10016
(212) 686-9244 ext. 342

ASA College

Brooklyn, New York
www.asa.edu   Federal Code: 030955

2-year for-profit technical and career college in very large city.
Enrollment: 4,641 undergrads, 8% part-time. 1,334 full-time freshmen.
Selectivity: Open admission.

BASIC COSTS (2017-2018)
Tuition and fees: $14,065.
Per-credit charge: $546.
Room and board: $9,500.

FINANCIAL AID PICTURE (2015-2016)
Students with need: 68% of average financial aid package awarded as scholarships/grants, 32% awarded as loans/jobs. Need-based aid available for part-time students. Work study available nights, weekends, and for part-time students.
Students without need: No-need awards available for academics, alumni affiliation, athletics, leadership, state/district residency.

FINANCIAL AID PROCEDURES
Forms required: FAFSA, state aid form.
Dates and Deadlines: Applicants notified on a rolling basis starting 7/13; must reply by 10/13.
Transfers: No deadline. Applicants notified on a rolling basis starting 7/13; must reply by 10/13.

CONTACT
Victoria Shtamler, Vice President of Student Financial Services
81 Willoughby Street, Brooklyn, NY 11201
(718) 522-9073 ext. 2037

Bard College

Annandale-on-Hudson, New York   Federal Code: 002671
www.bard.edu   CSS Code: 2037

4-year private liberal arts college in small town, affiliated with the Episcopal Church.
Enrollment: 1,926 undergrads, 2% part-time. 507 full-time freshmen.
Selectivity: Admits 50 to 75% of applicants.

BASIC COSTS (2016-2017)
Tuition and fees: $51,614.
Per-credit charge: $1,585.
Room and board: $14,540.

FINANCIAL AID PICTURE (2016-2017)
Students with need: Out of 365 full-time freshmen who applied for aid, 349 were judged to have need. Of these, 349 received aid, and 104 had their full need met. Average financial aid package met 88% of need; average scholarship/grant was $42,292; average loan was $5,898. For part-time students, average financial aid package was $15,417.
Students without need: 4 full-time freshmen who did not demonstrate need for aid received scholarships/grants; average award was $16,625. No-need awards available for academics.
Scholarships offered: Distinguished Scientist Scholarship: full tuition; for students intending to major in math or sciences; 10-20 awarded annually.
Additional info: Excellence and Equal Cost Program for students who graduate in top 10 of public high school class lowers fees to levels equivalent to those at home state university or college.

FINANCIAL AID PROCEDURES
Forms required: FAFSA, CSS PROFILE.
Dates and Deadlines: Closing date 2/15. Applicants notified by 4/1; must reply by 5/1.
Transfers: Applicants notified by 4/1; must reply by 5/1.

CONTACT

Denise Ackerman, Director of Financial Aid

30 Campus Road, Annandale-on-Hudson, NY 12504-5000

(845) 758-7526

Barnard College

New York, New York   Federal Code: 002708

www.barnard.edu   CSS Code: 2038

4-year private liberal arts college for women in very large city.

Enrollment: 2,572 undergrads, 2% part-time. 605 full-time freshmen.

Selectivity: Admits less than 50% of applicants.

BASIC COSTS (2016-2017)

Tuition and fees: $50,394.

Room and board: $15,598.

FINANCIAL AID PICTURE (2016-2017)

Students with need: Out of 302 full-time freshmen who applied for aid, 219 were judged to have need. Of these, 219 received aid, and 217 had their full need met. Average financial aid package met 100% of need; average scholarship/grant was $46,876; average loan was $3,323.

Students without need: This college awards aid only to students with need.

FINANCIAL AID PROCEDURES

Forms required: FAFSA, state aid form. CSS Profile required for returning students, except those who had a parent contribution less than $2,000 in the prior academic year. Returning international students also not required to complete the CSS Profile.

Dates and Deadlines: Closing date 2/15. Applicants notified by 3/31; must reply by 5/1.

Transfers: Closing date 4/16. Applicants notified by 5/1. Transfers admitted in the spring are not eligible for institutional grant aid.

CONTACT

Nanette Dilauro, Director of Financial Aid

3009 Broadway, New York, NY 10027-6598

(212) 854-2154

Berkeley College

White Plains, New York

www.berkeleycollege.edu   Federal Code: 007421

4-year for-profit branch campus and business college in small city.

Enrollment: 465 undergrads.

BASIC COSTS (2016-2017)

Tuition and fees: $24,750.

Per-credit charge: $525.

Room only: $9,000.

FINANCIAL AID PICTURE

Students with need: Need-based aid available for full-time students.

Students without need: No-need awards available for academics, alumni affiliation.

FINANCIAL AID PROCEDURES

Forms required: FAFSA.

Dates and Deadlines: Applicants notified on a rolling basis starting 3/1; must reply within 6 week(s) of notification.

CONTACT

Howard Leslie, VP, Financial Aid

99 Church Street, White Plains, NY 10601

(914) 694-1122

Berkeley College of New York City

New York, New York

www.berkeleycollege.edu   Federal Code: 007502

4-year for-profit business college in very large city.

Enrollment: 3,935 undergrads.

BASIC COSTS (2016-2017)

Tuition and fees: $24,750.

Per-credit charge: $810.

FINANCIAL AID PICTURE

Students with need: Need-based aid available for full-time students.

Students without need: No-need awards available for academics, alumni affiliation.

FINANCIAL AID PROCEDURES

Forms required: FAFSA.

Dates and Deadlines: Applicants notified on a rolling basis starting 3/1; must reply within 6 week(s) of notification.

Transfers: New York State TAP Grant eligibility may be affected.

CONTACT

Howard Leslie, Vice President Financial Aid

3 East 43rd Street, New York, NY 10017

(212) 986-4343

Boricua College

New York, New York

www.boricuacollege.edu   Federal Code: 013029

4-year private liberal arts college in very large city.

Enrollment: 899 undergrads. 142 full-time freshmen.

Selectivity: Admits 50 to 75% of applicants.

BASIC COSTS (2016-2017)

Tuition and fees: $10,625.

FINANCIAL AID PICTURE

Students with need: Need-based aid available for full-time students.

FINANCIAL AID PROCEDURES

Forms required: FAFSA, state aid form.

Dates and Deadlines: Priority date 4/30; no closing date. Applicants notified on a rolling basis; must reply within 3 week(s) of notification.

CONTACT

Rosalia Cruz, Director of Financial Aid

3755 Broadway, New York, NY 10032

(212) 694-1000 ext. 611

Briarcliffe College

Bethpage, New York

www.briarcliffe.edu   Federal Code: 020757

4-year for-profit business and career college in large town.

Enrollment: 1,719 undergrads.

BASIC COSTS (2016-2017)

Additional info: Associate programs: $23,280-$37,440. Bachelor's programs: $21,930-$74,880.

FINANCIAL AID PICTURE

Students with need: Need-based aid available for full-time and part-time students.

Students without need: No-need awards available for academics, alumni affiliation.

FINANCIAL AID PROCEDURES
Forms required: FAFSA, state aid form, institutional form.
Dates and Deadlines: Applicants notified on a rolling basis.

CONTACT
Cindy Roys, Director of Financial Aid
1055 Stewart Avenue, Bethpage, NY 11714
(516) 918-3600

Broome Community College
Binghamton, New York
www.sunybroome.edu   Federal Code: 002862

2-year public community college in small city.
Enrollment: 5,343 undergrads, 23% part-time. 1,713 full-time freshmen.
Selectivity: Open admission; but selective for some programs.

BASIC COSTS (2016-2017)
Tuition and fees: $5,023; out-of-state residents $9,441.
Per-credit charge: $184; out-of-state residents $368.
Room and board: $11,078.

FINANCIAL AID PICTURE
Students with need: Need-based aid available for full-time and part-time students. Work study available nights.

FINANCIAL AID PROCEDURES
Forms required: FAFSA.
Dates and Deadlines: Priority date 3/1; no closing date. Applicants notified on a rolling basis starting 3/15; must reply within 2 week(s) of notification.

CONTACT
Laura Hodel, Director of Financial Aid
Box 1017, Binghamton, NY 13902
(607) 778-5028

Bryant & Stratton College: Albany
Albany, New York
www.bryantstratton.edu   Federal Code: 004749

2-year for-profit business and career college in small city.
Enrollment: 481 undergrads.

BASIC COSTS (2016-2017)
Tuition and fees: $17,190.
Per-credit charge: $573.
Additional info: Tuition and fees may vary by program.

FINANCIAL AID PICTURE
Students with need: Need-based aid available for full-time and part-time students. Work study available nights, weekends, and for part-time students.
Students without need: This college awards aid only to students with need.

FINANCIAL AID PROCEDURES
Forms required: FAFSA, state aid form.
Dates and Deadlines: Closing date 9/17. Applicants notified on a rolling basis.

CONTACT
Jackie Rivers, FA Coordinator
1259 Central Avenue, Albany, NY 12205
(518) 437-1802

Bryant & Stratton College: Syracuse
Syracuse, New York
www.bryantstratton.edu   Federal Code: 008276

2-year for-profit business and junior college in small city.
Enrollment: 503 undergrads.
Selectivity: Open admission.

BASIC COSTS (2016-2017)
Tuition and fees: $17,190.
Per-credit charge: $573.
Room and board: $8,880.

FINANCIAL AID PICTURE
Students with need: Work study available nights, weekends, and for part-time students.
Students without need: This college awards aid only to students with need.

FINANCIAL AID PROCEDURES
Forms required: FAFSA.
Dates and Deadlines: Closing date 9/17. Applicants notified on a rolling basis starting 10/1.
Transfers: Priority date 5/1.

CONTACT
Tami Eiklor, Financial Aid Supervisor
953 James Street, Syracuse, NY 13203
(315) 472-6603

Bryant & Stratton College: Syracuse North
Liverpool, New York
www.bryantstratton.edu

2-year for-profit career college in small city.
Enrollment: 466 undergrads.

BASIC COSTS (2016-2017)
Tuition and fees: $17,190.
Per-credit charge: $573.
Room and board: $8,880.

FINANCIAL AID PICTURE
Students with need: Need-based aid available for full-time and part-time students. Work study available nights.
Students without need: This college awards aid only to students with need.

FINANCIAL AID PROCEDURES
Forms required: FAFSA, state aid form, institutional form.
Dates and Deadlines: Closing date 9/17.
Transfers: No deadline.

CONTACT
Stacey McConnell, Financial Services Manager
8687 Carling Road, Liverpool, NY 13090
(315) 652-6500

Canisius College
Buffalo, New York
www.canisius.edu   Federal Code: 002681

4-year private liberal arts and teachers college in large city, affiliated with the Roman Catholic Church.
Enrollment: 2,488 undergrads, 1% part-time. 600 full-time freshmen.

Selectivity: Admits over 75% of applicants.

BASIC COSTS (2016-2017)
Tuition and fees: $35,424.
Per-credit charge: $970.
Room and board: $13,022.
Additional info: Tuition/fee waivers available for minority students.

FINANCIAL AID PICTURE (2016-2017)
Students with need: Out of 566 full-time freshmen who applied for aid, 512 were judged to have need. Of these, 512 received aid, and 129 had their full need met. Average financial aid package met 86% of need; average scholarship/grant was $26,387; average loan was $4,365. Need-based aid available for part-time students.
Students without need: 82 full-time freshmen who did not demonstrate need for aid received scholarships/grants; average award was $20,100. No-need awards available for academics, alumni affiliation, art, athletics, minority status, music/drama, ROTC.
Scholarships offered: *Merit:* Trustee's Scholarship: $18,000. Dean's Scholarship: $13,000-$14,000. Benefactor's Scholarship: $10,000-$11,000. All based on high school average and SAT/ACT; renewable; open to U.S. and Canadian residents. Transfer scholarships: $6,000-$12,000; based on 2.5 GPA. International students scholarships: up to $17,000; based on SAT (if taken) and TOEFL scores. Specialized scholarships: urban leadership, art, music, dance. *Athletic:* 23 full-time freshmen received athletic scholarships; average amount $24,586.

FINANCIAL AID PROCEDURES
Forms required: FAFSA, state aid form.
Dates and Deadlines: Priority date 2/15; no closing date. Applicants notified on a rolling basis starting 12/20.

CONTACT
Mary Koehneke, Director of Student Financial Aid
2001 Main Street, Buffalo, NY 14208-1098
(800) 541-6348

Cayuga Community College
Auburn, New York
www.cayuga-cc.edu   Federal Code: 002861

2-year public community college in large town.
Enrollment: 2,285 undergrads, 30% part-time. 486 full-time freshmen.
Selectivity: Open admission; but selective for some programs.

BASIC COSTS (2016-2017)
Tuition and fees: $5,069; out-of-state residents $9,568.
Per-credit charge: $187; out-of-state residents $374.

FINANCIAL AID PICTURE (2015-2016)
Students with need: 71% of average financial aid package awarded as scholarships/grants, 29% awarded as loans/jobs. Need-based aid available for part-time students. Work study available nights, weekends, and for part-time students.
Students without need: This college awards aid only to students with need.

FINANCIAL AID PROCEDURES
Forms required: FAFSA, state aid form.
Dates and Deadlines: Priority date 5/1; no closing date. Applicants notified on a rolling basis starting 4/1.
Transfers: No deadline.

CONTACT
Cathleen Patella, Director of Student Financial Aid and Compliance
197 Franklin Street, Auburn, NY 13021-3099
(315) 255-1743 ext. 2470

Cazenovia College
Cazenovia, New York
www.cazenovia.edu   Federal Code: 002685

4-year private liberal arts and career college in small town.
Enrollment: 991 undergrads, 13% part-time. 250 full-time freshmen.
Selectivity: Admits over 75% of applicants.

BASIC COSTS (2016-2017)
Tuition and fees: $32,674.
Room and board: $13,198.

FINANCIAL AID PICTURE (2015-2016)
Students with need: Out of 238 full-time freshmen who applied for aid, 227 were judged to have need. Of these, 227 received aid, and 54 had their full need met. Average financial aid package met 83% of need; average scholarship/grant was $30,445; average loan was $3,068. For part-time students, average financial aid package was $5,468.
Students without need: 23 full-time freshmen who did not demonstrate need for aid received scholarships/grants; average award was $19,393. No-need awards available for academics, leadership.

FINANCIAL AID PROCEDURES
Forms required: FAFSA, state aid form.
Dates and Deadlines: Priority date 3/1; no closing date. Applicants notified on a rolling basis starting 3/1; must reply by 5/1 or within 2 week(s) of notification.
Transfers: No deadline. Applicants notified on a rolling basis starting 11/1; must reply by 5/1 or within 2 week(s) of notification.

CONTACT
Christine Mandel, Director of Financial Aid
3 Sullivan Street, Cazenovia, NY 13035
(315) 655-7887

City University of New York: Baruch College
New York, New York
www.baruch.cuny.edu   Federal Code: 007273

4-year public business and liberal arts college in very large city.
Enrollment: 14,858 undergrads, 24% part-time. 1,400 full-time freshmen.
Selectivity: Admits less than 50% of applicants.

BASIC COSTS (2016-2017)
Tuition and fees: $6,861; out-of-state residents $17,331.
Per-credit charge: $275; out-of-state residents $560.
Room only: $13,768.

FINANCIAL AID PICTURE
Students with need: Need-based aid available for full-time and part-time students.
Students without need: No-need awards available for academics, alumni affiliation, art, state/district residency.
Scholarships offered: Honors college scholarships based on SAT scores and high school GPA.

FINANCIAL AID PROCEDURES
Forms required: FAFSA, state aid form.
Dates and Deadlines: Priority date 4/15; no closing date. Applicants notified on a rolling basis starting 4/15; must reply within 2 week(s) of notification.
Transfers: No deadline. Applicants notified on a rolling basis; must reply within 2 week(s) of notification.

CONTACT
Elizabeth Riquez, Director of Financial Aid
One Bernard Baruch Way, New York, NY 10010
(646) 312-1360

City University of New York: Borough of Manhattan Community College

New York, New York
www.bmcc.cuny.edu   Federal Code: 002691

2-year public community college in very large city.
Enrollment: 25,548 undergrads, 29% part-time. 5,532 full-time freshmen.
Selectivity: Open admission; but selective for some programs.

BASIC COSTS (2016-2017)

Tuition and fees: $5,169; out-of-state residents $9,969.
Per-credit charge: $210; out-of-state residents $320.
Additional info: Tuition/fee waivers available for unemployed or children of unemployed.

FINANCIAL AID PICTURE (2015-2016)

Students with need: Out of 5,037 full-time freshmen who applied for aid, 4,668 were judged to have need. Of these, 4,668 received aid. Need-based aid available for part-time students.
Students without need: This college awards aid only to students with need.

FINANCIAL AID PROCEDURES

Forms required: FAFSA, state aid form, institutional form.
Dates and Deadlines: Priority date 5/1; no closing date. Applicants notified on a rolling basis starting 4/15.
Transfers: No deadline. Applicants notified on a rolling basis starting 6/1; must reply within 2 week(s) of notification.

CONTACT

Ralph Buxton, Director of Financial Aid
199 Chambers Street, New York, NY 10007
(212) 220-1432

City University of New York: Bronx Community College

Bronx, New York
www.bcc.cuny.edu   Federal Code: 002692

2-year public community college in very large city.
Enrollment: 10,919 undergrads.
Selectivity: Open admission.

BASIC COSTS (2016-2017)

Tuition and fees: $5,205; out-of-state residents $10,005.
Per-credit charge: $210; out-of-state residents $320.

FINANCIAL AID PICTURE

Students with need: Need-based aid available for full-time and part-time students. Work study available nights, weekends, and for part-time students.
Students without need: This college awards aid only to students with need.

FINANCIAL AID PROCEDURES

Forms required: FAFSA.
Dates and Deadlines: Closing date 6/30. Applicants notified on a rolling basis starting 8/1.

CONTACT

Sinu Jacob, Financial Aid Officer
2155 University Avenue, Bronx, NY 10453
(718) 289-5700

City University of New York: Brooklyn College

Brooklyn, New York
www.brooklyn.cuny.edu   Federal Code: 002687

4-year public liberal arts college in very large city.
Enrollment: 13,380 undergrads, 24% part-time. 1,320 full-time freshmen.
Selectivity: Admits less than 50% of applicants.

BASIC COSTS (2016-2017)

Tuition and fees: $6,838; out-of-state residents $17,308.
Per-credit charge: $275; out-of-state residents $560.

FINANCIAL AID PICTURE (2016-2017)

Students with need: Out of 1,182 full-time freshmen who applied for aid, 1,159 were judged to have need. Of these, 1,073 received aid, and 592 had their full need met. Average financial aid package met 85% of need; average scholarship/grant was $4,179; average loan was $3,098. For part-time students, average financial aid package was $3,723.
Students without need: 91 full-time freshmen who did not demonstrate need for aid received scholarships/grants; average award was $1,211. No-need awards available for academics, state/district residency.
Scholarships offered: Presidential Scholarship: 8 tuition payments totaling $16,000; 25 awarded. Freshman Scholarships: $1,000-$2,000 for the first year of study. Many scholarships are based on degree of study, academic merit, and community service. Scholarships are subject to financial availability.

FINANCIAL AID PROCEDURES

Forms required: FAFSA, state aid form.
Dates and Deadlines: Priority date 5/1; no closing date. Applicants notified on a rolling basis starting 3/1.
Transfers: Priority date 4/1; no deadline. Must reply within 6 week(s) of notification. Transfer-day orientation offered each semester. Students receive instruction on the rules and regulations of all programs with important deadlines. Students are urged to apply for federal, state and scholarship application as soon as possible. If any students do not qualify for grants and or scholarships, they are asked to consider students loan or to make a tuition plan with the bursar's office.

CONTACT

2900 Bedford Avenue, Brooklyn, NY 11210
(718) 951-5051

City University of New York: City College

New York, New York
www.ccny.cuny.edu   Federal Code: 002688

4-year public university and liberal arts college in very large city.
Enrollment: 12,606 undergrads, 21% part-time. 1,805 full-time freshmen.
Selectivity: Admits less than 50% of applicants.

BASIC COSTS (2016-2017)

Tuition and fees: $6,740; out-of-state residents $17,210.
Per-credit charge: $275; out-of-state residents $560.
Room only: $18,124.
Additional info: Tuition/fee waivers available for minority students.

FINANCIAL AID PICTURE (2016-2017)

Students with need: Out of 1,613 full-time freshmen who applied for aid, 1,526 were judged to have need. Of these, 1,523 received aid, and 1,073 had their full need met. Average financial aid package met 85% of need; average scholarship/grant was $8,589; average loan was $3,080. For part-time students, average financial aid package was $9,132.

Students without need: 216 full-time freshmen who did not demonstrate need for aid received scholarships/grants; average award was $3,486. No-need awards available for academics, alumni affiliation, art, leadership, music/drama, state/district residency.

FINANCIAL AID PROCEDURES

Forms required: FAFSA, state aid form.

Dates and Deadlines: Priority date 3/15; no closing date. Applicants notified on a rolling basis starting 4/1.

Transfers: Priority date 3/31; no deadline. Applicants notified on a rolling basis starting 3/31.

CONTACT

Arshaw Ramkaran, Director of Financial Aid

160 Convent Avenue, A100, New York, NY 10031

(212) 650-7000

City University of New York: College of Staten Island

Staten Island, New York

www.csi.cuny.edu   Federal Code: 002698

4-year public liberal arts college in large city.

Enrollment: 12,139 undergrads, 21% part-time. 2,488 full-time freshmen.

Selectivity: Open admission; but selective for some programs.

BASIC COSTS (2016-2017)

Tuition and fees: $6,889; out-of-state residents $17,359.

Per-credit charge: $275; out-of-state residents $560.

Room and board: $17,227.

FINANCIAL AID PICTURE (2016-2017)

Students with need: Out of 2,223 full-time freshmen who applied for aid, 1,986 were judged to have need. Of these, 1,819 received aid, and 84 had their full need met. Average financial aid package met 40% of need; average scholarship/grant was $8,140; average loan was $9,535. For part-time students, average financial aid package was $4,224.

Students without need: 107 full-time freshmen who did not demonstrate need for aid received scholarships/grants; average award was $1,999. No-need awards available for academics, alumni affiliation, art, leadership, minority status, music/drama, state/district residency.

Scholarships offered: 100 full-time freshmen received athletic scholarships; average amount $1,737.

FINANCIAL AID PROCEDURES

Forms required: FAFSA, state aid form.

Dates and Deadlines: Priority date 1/31; no closing date. Applicants notified on a rolling basis starting 2/15.

CONTACT

Philippe Marius, Director of Financial Aid

2800 Victory Boulevard 2A-103, Staten Island, NY 10314

(718) 982-2030

City University of New York: Guttman Community College

New York, New York

www.guttman.cuny.edu   Federal Code: 042101

2-year public community college in very large city.

Enrollment: 691 undergrads.

BASIC COSTS (2016-2017)

Tuition and fees: $5,193; out-of-state residents $9,993.

Per-credit charge: $210; out-of-state residents $320.

FINANCIAL AID PICTURE

Students with need: Need-based aid available for full-time and part-time students.

FINANCIAL AID PROCEDURES

Forms required: FAFSA, state aid form.

Dates and Deadlines: Closing date 6/30. Applicants notified on a rolling basis starting 4/1.

CONTACT

Vera Senese, Director of Financial Aid

50 West 40th Street, New York, NY 10018

(646) 313-8080

City University of New York: Hostos Community College

Bronx, New York

www.hostos.cuny.edu   Federal Code: 008611

2-year public community college in very large city.

Enrollment: 6,427 undergrads.

Selectivity: Open admission; but selective for some programs.

BASIC COSTS (2016-2017)

Tuition and fees: $5,206; out-of-state residents $10,006.

Per-credit charge: $210; out-of-state residents $320.

FINANCIAL AID PICTURE

Students with need: Need-based aid available for full-time and part-time students.

FINANCIAL AID PROCEDURES

Forms required: FAFSA.

Dates and Deadlines: Priority date 7/1; no closing date. Applicants notified on a rolling basis; must reply within 3 week(s) of notification.

CONTACT

Joseph Alicea, Director of Financial Aid

500 Grand Concourse, Bronx, NY 10451

(718) 518-6555

City University of New York: Hunter College

New York, New York

www.hunter.cuny.edu/main/   Federal Code: 002689

4-year public liberal arts college in very large city.

Enrollment: 15,632 undergrads, 22% part-time. 2,193 full-time freshmen.

Selectivity: Admits less than 50% of applicants.

BASIC COSTS (2016-2017)

Tuition and fees: $6,780; out-of-state residents $17,250.

Per-credit charge: $275; out-of-state residents $560.

Room only: $13,400.

FINANCIAL AID PICTURE (2016-2017)

Students with need: Out of 1,966 full-time freshmen who applied for aid, 1,645 were judged to have need. Of these, 1,524 received aid, and 1,051 had their full need met. Average financial aid package met 80% of need; average scholarship/grant was $8,337; average loan was $3,242. For part-time students, average financial aid package was $4,091.

Students without need: 227 full-time freshmen who did not demonstrate need for aid received scholarships/grants; average award was $2,753. No-need awards available for academics.

FINANCIAL AID PROCEDURES

Forms required: FAFSA, state aid form.

Dates and Deadlines: Priority date 5/1; no closing date. Applicants notified on a rolling basis starting 5/15.

CONTACT

Aristalia Cortorreal Diaz, Director of Financial Aid
695 Park Avenue, New York, NY 10065
(212) 772-4820

City University of New York: John Jay College of Criminal Justice

New York, New York
www.jjay.cuny.edu   Federal Code: 002693

4-year public liberal arts college in very large city.
Enrollment: 12,175 undergrads, 19% part-time. 3,782 full-time freshmen.
Selectivity: Admits less than 50% of applicants.

BASIC COSTS (2016-2017)

Tuition and fees: $6,810; out-of-state residents $17,280.
Per-credit charge: $275; out-of-state residents $560.
Room only: $16,350.

FINANCIAL AID PICTURE (2015-2016)

Students with need: Out of 2,931 full-time freshmen who applied for aid, 2,694 were judged to have need. Of these, 2,481 received aid. Average financial aid package met 85% of need; average scholarship/grant was $2,639; average loan was $3,825. For part-time students, average financial aid package was $4,219.

FINANCIAL AID PROCEDURES

Forms required: FAFSA, state aid form.
Dates and Deadlines: Priority date 4/30; no closing date. Applicants notified on a rolling basis starting 4/1; must reply within 2 week(s) of notification.
Transfers: Closing date 4/30. Must reply within 2 week(s) of notification.

CONTACT

Sylvia Lopez-Crespo, Director of Financial Aid
524 West 59th Street, New York, NY 10019
(212) 237-8149

City University of New York: Kingsborough Community College

Brooklyn, New York
www.kbcc.cuny.edu   Federal Code: 002694

2-year public community college in very large city.
Enrollment: 12,847 undergrads.
Selectivity: Open admission.

BASIC COSTS (2016-2017)

Tuition and fees: $5,253; out-of-state residents $10,053.
Per-credit charge: $210; out-of-state residents $320.

FINANCIAL AID PICTURE

Students with need: Need-based aid available for full-time and part-time students.
Students without need: This college awards aid only to students with need.

FINANCIAL AID PROCEDURES

Forms required: FAFSA.
Dates and Deadlines: Closing date 4/30. Applicants notified on a rolling basis; must reply within 2 week(s) of notification.

CONTACT

Wayne Harewood, Director of Financial Aid
2001 Oriental Boulevard, Brooklyn, NY 11235
(718) 368-4644

City University of New York: LaGuardia Community College

Long Island City, New York
www.lagcc.cuny.edu   Federal Code: 010051

2-year public community college in very large city.
Enrollment: 16,141 undergrads, 34% part-time. 2,490 full-time freshmen.
Selectivity: Open admission.

BASIC COSTS (2016-2017)

Tuition and fees: $5,217; out-of-state residents $10,017.
Per-credit charge: $210; out-of-state residents $320.

FINANCIAL AID PICTURE (2015-2016)

Students with need: Out of 2,172 full-time freshmen who applied for aid, 2,169 were judged to have need. Of these, 1,954 received aid, and 2 had their full need met. Average financial aid package met 40% of need; average scholarship/grant was $6,172; average loan was $890. For part-time students, average financial aid package was $2,938.
Students without need: This college awards aid only to students with need.

FINANCIAL AID PROCEDURES

Forms required: FAFSA, state aid form, institutional form.
Dates and Deadlines: Closing date 4/15. Applicants notified on a rolling basis starting 3/1; must reply within 4 week(s) of notification.

CONTACT

Gail Baksh-Jarrett, Executive Director of Student Financial Services
31-10 Thomson Avenue, Long Island City, NY 11101
(718) 482-7218

City University of New York: Lehman College

Bronx, New York
www.lehman.edu   Federal Code: 007022

4-year public liberal arts college in very large city.
Enrollment: 10,992 undergrads, 40% part-time. 690 full-time freshmen.
Selectivity: Admits less than 50% of applicants.

BASIC COSTS (2016-2017)

Tuition and fees: $6,809; out-of-state residents $17,279.
Per-credit charge: $275; out-of-state residents $560.
Room only: $11,478.

FINANCIAL AID PICTURE (2016-2017)

Students with need: Out of 350 full-time freshmen who applied for aid, 350 were judged to have need. Of these, 325 received aid, and 160 had their full need met. Average financial aid package met 80% of need; average scholarship/grant was $4,613; average loan was $4,042. For part-time students, average financial aid package was $1,685.
Students without need: This college awards aid only to students with need.
Scholarships offered: 219 full-time freshmen received athletic scholarships; average amount $917.

FINANCIAL AID PROCEDURES

Forms required: FAFSA, state aid form.
Dates and Deadlines: Applicants notified on a rolling basis starting 3/1.
Transfers: No deadline. Applicants notified on a rolling basis starting 3/1.

CONTACT

David Martinez, Director of Financial Aid
250 Bedford Park Boulevard West, Bronx, NY 10468
(718) 960-8545

City University of New York: Medgar Evers College

Brooklyn, New York
www.mec.cuny.edu   Federal Code: 010097

4-year public liberal arts college in very large city.
Enrollment: 6,405 undergrads, 27% part-time. 1,101 full-time freshmen.
Selectivity: Open admission; but selective for some programs.

BASIC COSTS (2016-2017)
Tuition and fees: $6,743; out-of-state residents $17,213.
Per-credit charge: $275; out-of-state residents $560.

FINANCIAL AID PICTURE (2016-2017)
Students with need: 84% of average financial aid package awarded as scholarships/grants, 16% awarded as loans/jobs. Need-based aid available for part-time students. Work study available weekends and for part-time students.
Students without need: No-need awards available for academics, leadership.

FINANCIAL AID PROCEDURES
Forms required: FAFSA, state aid form.
Dates and Deadlines: Priority date 1/2; closing date 6/1. Applicants notified on a rolling basis; must reply within 3 week(s) of notification.
Transfers: Priority date 3/1. Must reply within 2 week(s) of notification.

CONTACT
Conley James, Director of Financial Aid
1665 Bedford Avenue, Brooklyn, NY 11225-2201
(718) 270-6194

City University of New York: New York City College of Technology

Brooklyn, New York
www.citytech.cuny.edu   Federal Code: 002696

4-year public technical college in very large city.
Enrollment: 16,040 undergrads, 33% part-time. 3,108 full-time freshmen.
Selectivity: Open admission; but selective for some programs.

BASIC COSTS (2016-2017)
Tuition and fees: $6,720; out-of-state residents $17,190.
Per-credit charge: $275; out-of-state residents $560.

FINANCIAL AID PICTURE
Students with need: Need-based aid available for full-time and part-time students.
Students without need: No-need awards available for state/district residency.
Additional info: Foreign students applying for aid must have resided in New York for at least 1 year.

FINANCIAL AID PROCEDURES
Forms required: FAFSA.
Dates and Deadlines: Priority date 3/31; no closing date.

CONTACT
Sandra Higgins, Director of Financial Aid
300 Jay Street Namm G17, Brooklyn, NY 11201
(718) 260-5700

City University of New York: Queens College

Flushing, New York
www.qc.cuny.edu   Federal Code: 002690

4-year public liberal arts college in very large city.
Enrollment: 15,426 undergrads, 24% part-time. 1,453 full-time freshmen.
Selectivity: Admits less than 50% of applicants.

BASIC COSTS (2016-2017)
Tuition and fees: $6,938; out-of-state residents $17,408.
Per-credit charge: $275; out-of-state residents $560.
Room only: $11,670.

FINANCIAL AID PICTURE (2015-2016)
Students with need: Need-based aid available for full-time and part-time students.
Students without need: No-need awards available for academics, athletics, state/district residency.

FINANCIAL AID PROCEDURES
Forms required: FAFSA, state aid form, institutional form.
Dates and Deadlines: Applicants notified on a rolling basis starting 3/1; must reply within 3 week(s) of notification.
Transfers: No deadline. Applicants notified on a rolling basis starting 3/1.

CONTACT
Clifford Couloute, Acting Director of Financial Aid
6530 Kissena Boulevard, Jefferson 117, Flushing, NY 11367-1597
(718) 997-5123

City University of New York: Queensborough Community College

Bayside, New York
www.qcc.cuny.edu   Federal Code: 002697

2-year public community college in very large city.
Enrollment: 13,596 undergrads, 33% part-time. 2,998 full-time freshmen.
Selectivity: Open admission.

BASIC COSTS (2016-2017)
Tuition and fees: $5,209; out-of-state residents $10,009.
Per-credit charge: $210; out-of-state residents $320.

FINANCIAL AID PICTURE
Students with need: Need-based aid available for full-time students.

FINANCIAL AID PROCEDURES
Forms required: FAFSA, institutional form.
Dates and Deadlines: Applicants notified on a rolling basis starting 7/15.

CONTACT
Veronica Lukas, Director of Enrollment Management and Student Financial Services
222-05 56th Avenue, Bayside, NY 11364-1497
(718) 631-6267

City University of New York: York College

Jamaica, New York
www.york.cuny.edu   Federal Code: 004759

4-year public liberal arts college in very large city.
Enrollment: 7,140 undergrads, 30% part-time. 936 full-time freshmen.
Selectivity: Admits 50 to 75% of applicants.

BASIC COSTS (2016-2017)
Tuition and fees: $6,747; out-of-state residents $17,217.
Per-credit charge: $275; out-of-state residents $560.

FINANCIAL AID PICTURE
Students with need: Need-based aid available for full-time and part-time students.
Students without need: No-need awards available for academics.

FINANCIAL AID PROCEDURES
Forms required: FAFSA, state aid form.
Dates and Deadlines: Priority date 4/1; closing date 5/30. Applicants notified on a rolling basis starting 2/15; must reply within 4 week(s) of notification.
Transfers: No deadline. Applicants notified on a rolling basis starting 3/1.

CONTACT
Beverly Brown, Director of Financial Aid
94-20 Guy R. Brewer Boulevard., Room 1B07, Jamaica, NY 11451
(718) 262-2230

Clarkson University
Potsdam, New York
www.clarkson.edu   Federal Code: 002699

4-year private university in small town.
Enrollment: 3,176 undergrads. 797 full-time freshmen.
Selectivity: Admits 50 to 75% of applicants.

BASIC COSTS (2017-2018)
Tuition and fees: $47,950.
Per-credit charge: $1,556.
Room and board: $14,488.
Additional info: Tuition/fee waivers available for minority students.

FINANCIAL AID PICTURE (2016-2017)
Students with need: Out of 724 full-time freshmen who applied for aid, 645 were judged to have need. Of these, 643 received aid, and 126 had their full need met. Average financial aid package met 89% of need; average scholarship/grant was $33,293; average loan was $3,449. For part-time students, average financial aid package was $570.
Students without need: 135 full-time freshmen who did not demonstrate need for aid received scholarships/grants; average award was $23,918. No-need awards available for academics, alumni affiliation, leadership, minority status, ROTC.
Scholarships offered: _Merit:_ Scholarships ranging from $500 to $28,000 in value, including the Clarkson Scholarship, Clarkson Merit Scholarship, CU PLTW Scholarship, CU FIRST Robotics Scholarship, CU WACE National CO-OP, CU SAE Scholarship, Clarkson Adirondack Scholars Award, Spirit of Innovation, Holcroft Alumni Recognition Awards, Alumni Family Award, and the Alumni Legacy Award. Many require high school grades averaging 85 or higher. Some require a recommendation from a Clarkson alumnus. Most are not limited by major or to a specific number of scholarships awarded. _**Athletic:**_ 10 full-time freshmen received athletic scholarships; average amount $35,597.

FINANCIAL AID PROCEDURES
Forms required: FAFSA, state aid form.
Dates and Deadlines: Priority date 2/1; closing date 3/1. Applicants notified on a rolling basis starting 2/17; must reply by 5/1 or within 2 week(s) of notification.
Transfers: Closing date 4/15. Applicants notified on a rolling basis starting 3/1. Transfer Leadership & Achievement scholarships, Phi Theta Kappa scholarships and Alpha Beta Gamma awards available in addition to state and federal programs.

CONTACT
Kara Pitts, Director of New Student Financial Assistance
Holcroft House, Potsdam, NY 13699
(800) 527-6577

Clinton Community College
Plattsburgh, New York
www.clinton.edu   Federal Code: 006787

2-year public community and career college in large town.
Enrollment: 1,023 undergrads, 29% part-time. 337 full-time freshmen.
Selectivity: Open admission; but selective for some programs and for out-of-state students.

BASIC COSTS (2016-2017)
Tuition and fees: $5,447; out-of-state residents $10,347.
Per-credit charge: $179; out-of-state residents $383.
Room and board: $9,310.

FINANCIAL AID PICTURE (2015-2016)
Students with need: For part-time students, average financial aid package was $4,677.

FINANCIAL AID PROCEDURES
Forms required: FAFSA, state aid form.
Dates and Deadlines: Priority date 6/12; no closing date. Applicants notified on a rolling basis starting 4/12.

CONTACT
Mary LaPierre, Director of Financial Aid
136 Clinton Point Drive, Plattsburgh, NY 12901
(518) 562-4125

Cochran School of Nursing
Yonkers, New York
www.cochranschoolofnursing.us   Federal Code: 006443

2-year private nursing college in small city.
Enrollment: 96 undergrads, 86% part-time.

BASIC COSTS (2017-2018)
Tuition and fees: $11,057.
Per-credit charge: $563.

FINANCIAL AID PICTURE (2016-2017)
Students with need: 24% of average financial aid package awarded as scholarships/grants, 76% awarded as loans/jobs. Need-based aid available for part-time students.
Students without need: This college awards aid only to students with need.

FINANCIAL AID PROCEDURES
Forms required: FAFSA.
Dates and Deadlines: Closing date 4/30. Applicants notified on a rolling basis.
Transfers: No deadline.

CONTACT
Maria Goncalves, Financial Aid Officer
967 North Broadway, Yonkers, NY 10701
(914) 964-4316

Colgate University
Hamilton, New York   Federal Code: 002701
www.colgate.edu   CSS Code: 2086

4-year private university and liberal arts college in small town.
Enrollment: 2,868 undergrads. 766 full-time freshmen.
Selectivity: Admits less than 50% of applicants.

BASIC COSTS (2016-2017)
Tuition and fees: $51,955.

Room and board: $13,075.

FINANCIAL AID PICTURE (2016-2017)
Students with need: Out of 284 full-time freshmen who applied for aid, 240 were judged to have need. Of these, 239 received aid, and 239 had their full need met. Average financial aid package met 100% of need; average scholarship/grant was $48,355; average loan was $1,360.
Students without need: No-need awards available for athletics.
Scholarships offered: 78 full-time freshmen received athletic scholarships; average amount $40,721.

FINANCIAL AID PROCEDURES
Forms required: FAFSA, CSS PROFILE.
Dates and Deadlines: Priority date 1/15; closing date 1/15. Applicants notified by 3/20; must reply by 5/1.
Transfers: Closing date 3/15. Applicants notified by 4/15; must reply by 5/15 or within 2 week(s) of notification. Financial aid for transfer students extremely limited.

CONTACT
Gina Soliz, Director of Financial Aid
13 Oak Drive, Hamilton, NY 13346-1383
(315) 228-7431

College of Mount St. Vincent
Riverdale, New York
www.mountsaintvincent.edu   Federal Code: 002703

4-year private liberal arts college in very large city, affiliated with the Roman Catholic Church.
Enrollment: 1,683 undergrads, 6% part-time. 436 full-time freshmen.
Selectivity: Admits over 75% of applicants.

BASIC COSTS (2017-2018)
Tuition and fees: $36,540.
Per-credit charge: $1,020.
Room and board: $9,500.

FINANCIAL AID PICTURE
Students with need: Need-based aid available for full-time students.
Students without need: No-need awards available for academics, alumni affiliation, leadership.
Scholarships offered: Deans Merit Scholarship: $14,500-$29,500; awarded based on GPA and standardized test scores. Catholic Incentive Award: $12,500-$15,000; offered to students based on their attendance of a Catholic high school. Rising Scholar Award: $12,500-$15,000: Offered to students based on their attendance of a non-Catholic high school. Carazon C. Aquino Scholarship: full tuition; four-year, full tuition awarded to high-achieving student of Filipino descent. Seton Service and Leadership Scholarship: full room and board; students with high academic profiles, must fulfill a commitment to a service project of their choice. Fonthill Writing Award; full room and board; must pursue a minor in writing and be an active participant in writing in a campus club or student organization. Mary Ambrose Dunphy, S.C. Scholarship: $5,500; applicant must be a niece or nephew of a Sister of Charity or the child of an employee of the Sisters of Charity. Transfer Merit Scholarship: $14,000-$18,000; must submit an application and have earned a cumulative grade point average of 2.5-4.0 at previous institutions. Phi Theta Kappa Scholarship: $2,000; awarded to community college students who are members of Phi Theta Kappa and who have a cumulative GPA of 3.5. International Student Merit Scholarship: $14,000-$18,000; offered to international students based on their grade point average, class rank, and standardized test scores.

FINANCIAL AID PROCEDURES
Forms required: FAFSA, state aid form.
Dates and Deadlines: Priority date 3/1; no closing date. Applicants notified on a rolling basis starting 3/1; must reply by 5/1 or within 3 week(s) of notification.

Transfers: Priority date 5/15. Applicants notified on a rolling basis starting 3/1; must reply by 5/1 or within 3 week(s) of notification.

CONTACT
Lorena Matos, Director of Financial Aid
6301 Riverdale Avenue, Riverdale, NY 10471-1093
(718) 405-3289

College of New Rochelle
New Rochelle, New York
www.cnr.edu   Federal Code: 002704

4-year private nursing and liberal arts college in small city, affiliated with the Roman Catholic Church.
Enrollment: 672 undergrads, 9% part-time. 79 full-time freshmen.
Selectivity: Admits less than 50% of applicants.

BASIC COSTS (2017-2018)
Tuition and fees: $36,618.
Per-credit charge: $1,170.
Room and board: $14,136.

FINANCIAL AID PICTURE (2015-2016)
Students with need: Out of 79 full-time freshmen who applied for aid, 75 were judged to have need. Of these, 75 received aid, and 2 had their full need met. Average financial aid package met 74% of need; average scholarship/grant was $14,151; average loan was $3,408. For part-time students, average financial aid package was $8,396.
Students without need: 4 full-time freshmen who did not demonstrate need for aid received scholarships/grants; average award was $34,363. No-need awards available for academics, art, leadership, music/drama.

FINANCIAL AID PROCEDURES
Forms required: FAFSA, institutional form.
Dates and Deadlines: Priority date 2/1; no closing date. Applicants notified on a rolling basis starting 1/1; must reply within 2 week(s) of notification.
Transfers: No deadline. Applicants notified on a rolling basis.

CONTACT
Ann Pelak, Director of Financial Aid
29 Castle Place, New Rochelle, NY 10805-2339
(914) 654-5225

College of Saint Rose
Albany, New York
www.strose.edu   Federal Code: 002705

4-year private liberal arts college in small city.
Enrollment: 2,581 undergrads, 3% part-time. 631 full-time freshmen.
Selectivity: Admits over 75% of applicants.

BASIC COSTS (2016-2017)
Tuition and fees: $30,692.
Per-credit charge: $986.
Room and board: $12,356.

FINANCIAL AID PICTURE (2015-2016)
Students with need: Out of 610 full-time freshmen who applied for aid, 573 were judged to have need. Of these, 573 received aid, and 106 had their full need met. Average financial aid package met 82% of need; average scholarship/grant was $7,313; average loan was $3,509. For part-time students, average financial aid package was $5,981.
Students without need: 52 full-time freshmen who did not demonstrate need for aid received scholarships/grants; average award was $14,923. No-need awards available for academics, alumni affiliation, art, athletics, music/drama.

Scholarships offered: *Merit:* Academic, music, art, athletic awards based on talent. *Athletic:* 4 full-time freshmen received athletic scholarships; average amount $19,719.

FINANCIAL AID PROCEDURES

Forms required: FAFSA, state aid form.

Dates and Deadlines: Priority date 2/1; closing date 4/1. Applicants notified on a rolling basis starting 3/1; must reply by 5/1 or within 2 week(s) of notification.

Transfers: Applicants notified on a rolling basis starting 2/1; must reply by 5/1 or within 2 week(s) of notification.

CONTACT

Steve Dwire, Director of Financial Aid
432 Western Avenue, Albany, NY 12203
(518) 458-5464

College of Westchester

White Plains, New York
www.cw.edu   Federal Code: 005208

2-year for-profit business and career college in small city.
Enrollment: 927 undergrads, 13% part-time. 186 full-time freshmen.
Selectivity: Admits over 75% of applicants.

BASIC COSTS (2016-2017)

Tuition and fees: $23,350.
Per-credit charge: $745.
Additional info: Tuition/fee waivers available for unemployed or children of unemployed.

FINANCIAL AID PICTURE

Students with need: Need-based aid available for full-time and part-time students. Work study available nights, weekends, and for part-time students.
Students without need: No-need awards available for academics, alumni affiliation.

FINANCIAL AID PROCEDURES

Forms required: FAFSA, state aid form, institutional form.
Dates and Deadlines: Applicants notified on a rolling basis starting 2/7; must reply within 2 week(s) of notification.

CONTACT

Dianne Pepitone, Director, Student Financial Services
325 Central Avenue, White Plains, NY 10606
(914) 831-0473

Columbia University

New York, New York   Federal Code: 002707
www.columbia.edu   CSS Code: 2116

4-year private university in very large city.
Enrollment: 6,158 undergrads. 1,420 full-time freshmen.
Selectivity: Admits less than 50% of applicants.

BASIC COSTS (2016-2017)

Tuition and fees: $55,161.
Room and board: $13,244.

FINANCIAL AID PICTURE (2016-2017)

Students with need: Need-based aid available for full-time students. Work study available nights, weekends, and for part-time students.
Students without need: This college awards aid only to students with need.
Additional info: Institution has eliminated student loans for those receiving Columbia need-based aid and replaced them with additional University

grants, and significantly reduced the parent contribution for families making less than $100,000 per year.

FINANCIAL AID PROCEDURES

Forms required: FAFSA, CSS PROFILE.
Dates and Deadlines: Priority date 2/15; no closing date. Applicants notified by 4/1; must reply by 5/1 or within 2 week(s) of notification.
Transfers: Closing date 3/1. Applicants notified by 5/15.

CONTACT

1130 Amsterdam Avenue, New York, NY 10027
(212) 854-3711

Columbia University: School of General Studies

New York, New York
www.gs.columbia.edu   Federal Code: E00487

4-year private university and liberal arts college in very large city.
Enrollment: 2,068 undergrads, 27% part-time. 40 full-time freshmen.
Selectivity: Admits less than 50% of applicants.

BASIC COSTS (2016-2017)

Tuition and fees: $53,445.
Per-credit charge: $1,692.
Room and board: $13,586.

FINANCIAL AID PICTURE (2015-2016)

Students with need: Out of 33 full-time freshmen who applied for aid, 26 were judged to have need. Of these, 25 received aid. Average financial aid package met 28% of need; average scholarship/grant was $14,874; average loan was $4,000. For part-time students, average financial aid package was $22,386.
Students without need: 4 full-time freshmen who did not demonstrate need for aid received scholarships/grants; average award was $7,755. No-need awards available for academics.
Scholarships offered: All applicants should submit General Studies Application for Financial Aid.

FINANCIAL AID PROCEDURES

Forms required: FAFSA, institutional form.
Dates and Deadlines: Priority date 6/1; closing date 6/1. Applicants notified on a rolling basis..
Transfers: Applicants notified on a rolling basis starting 4/1.

CONTACT

William Bailey, Director of Educational Financing
408 Lewisohn Hall, Mail Code 4101, New York, NY 10027
(212) 854-5410

Columbia-Greene Community College

Hudson, New York
www.sunycgcc.edu   Federal Code: 006789

2-year public community college in small town.
Enrollment: 1,183 undergrads, 43% part-time. 269 full-time freshmen.

BASIC COSTS (2016-2017)

Tuition and fees: $4,744; out-of-state residents $9,136.
Per-credit charge: $183; out-of-state residents $366.

FINANCIAL AID PICTURE

Students with need: Need-based aid available for full-time and part-time students. Work study available nights, weekends, and for part-time students.

FINANCIAL AID PROCEDURES

Forms required: FAFSA, state aid form, institutional form.

CONTACT
Joel Phelps, Director of Financial Aid
4400 Route 23, Hudson, NY 12534
(518) 828-4181 ext. 3360

Concordia College
Bronxville, New York
www.concordia-ny.edu
Federal Code: 002709

4-year private liberal arts college in small town, affiliated with the Lutheran Church - Missouri Synod.
Enrollment: 886 undergrads.

BASIC COSTS (2016-2017)
Tuition and fees: $30,550.
Room and board: $11,575.

FINANCIAL AID PICTURE
Students with need: Need-based aid available for full-time and part-time students. Work study available nights, weekends, and for part-time students.
Students without need: No-need awards available for academics, athletics, leadership, music/drama, religious affiliation.
Scholarships offered: Fellows Scholarship: $15,000 a year; for 1800 SAT (exclusive of Writing) and 3.5/4.0 GPA. Merit Scholarships: $6,000-$9,000 for 80 average and above. Athletic, Faith Based, and Leadership Scholarships are also available.

FINANCIAL AID PROCEDURES
Forms required: FAFSA, state aid form.
Dates and Deadlines: Priority date 4/1; no closing date. Applicants notified on a rolling basis starting 2/15; must reply by 5/1 or within 3 week(s) of notification.
Transfers: Priority date 6/1; no deadline. Applicants notified on a rolling basis starting 4/1; must reply by 8/1 or within 3 week(s) of notification.

CONTACT
Kenneth Fick, Director of Financial Aid
171 White Plains Road, Bronxville, NY 10708-1923
(914) 337-9300 ext. 2146

Cooper Union for the Advancement of Science and Art
New York, New York
www.cooper.edu
Federal Code: 002710

4-year private visual arts and engineering college in very large city.
Enrollment: 857 undergrads, 1% part-time. 234 full-time freshmen.
Selectivity: Admits less than 50% of applicants.

BASIC COSTS (2017-2018)
Tuition and fees: $45,100.
Per-credit charge: $1,272.
Room and board: $16,270.
Additional info: All admitted students receive a half-tuition scholarship worth $21,625.

FINANCIAL AID PICTURE (2015-2016)
Students with need: Out of 127 full-time freshmen who applied for aid, 122 were judged to have need. Of these, 122 received aid, and 122 had their full need met. Average financial aid package met 100% of need; average scholarship/grant was $19,208; average loan was $2,775. Need-based aid available for part-time students.
Students without need: 234 full-time freshmen who did not demonstrate need for aid received scholarships/grants; average award was $22,170. No-need awards available for academics.

Scholarships offered: All undergraduate students receive at a minimum, half-tuition merit scholarships worth $21,625 annually. In addition, some exceptional students offered smaller merit scholarships typically in the $2,000-4,000 range.
Additional info: All Pell eligible students receive a full tuition scholarship. All undergraduate students receive at a minimum half-tuition merit scholarships. Late financial aid applications processed on rolling basis.

FINANCIAL AID PROCEDURES
Forms required: FAFSA.
Dates and Deadlines: Priority date 3/1; closing date 5/1. Applicants notified on a rolling basis starting 12/20; must reply by 6/30 or within 2 week(s) of notification.
Transfers: Priority date 4/1; no deadline. Applicants notified on a rolling basis; must reply by 6/30 or within 2 week(s) of notification.

CONTACT
Charlie Xu, Senior Director of Student Financial Services
30 Cooper Square, Suite 300, New York, NY 10003-7183
(212) 353-4130

Cornell University
Ithaca, New York
www.cornell.edu
Federal Code: 002711
CSS Code: 2098

4-year private university in large town.
Enrollment: 14,471 undergrads. 3,315 full-time freshmen.
Selectivity: Admits less than 50% of applicants.

BASIC COSTS (2016-2017)
Tuition and fees: $50,953.
Room and board: $13,900.

FINANCIAL AID PICTURE (2016-2017)
Students with need: Out of 1,816 full-time freshmen who applied for aid, 1,513 were judged to have need. Of these, 1,513 received aid, and 1,513 had their full need met. Average financial aid package met 100% of need; average scholarship/grant was $40,333; average loan was $4,775.
Students without need: This college awards aid only to students with need.

FINANCIAL AID PROCEDURES
Forms required: FAFSA, CSS PROFILE.
Dates and Deadlines: Closing date 2/15. Applicants notified by 4/1; must reply by 5/1.
Transfers: Applicants notified on a rolling basis starting 5/1; must reply by 7/1. Submit Cornell aid application forms in addition to regular required forms.

CONTACT
Susan Hitchcock, Director, Financial Aid and Student Employment
410 Thurston Avenue, Ithaca, NY 14850
(607) 255-5145

Corning Community College
Corning, New York
www.corning-cc.edu
Federal Code: 002863
CSS Code: 2106

2-year public community college in large town.
Enrollment: 2,327 undergrads, 30% part-time. 644 full-time freshmen.
Selectivity: Open admission; but selective for some programs.

BASIC COSTS (2016-2017)
Tuition and fees: $4,868; out-of-state residents $9,182.
Per-credit charge: $180; out-of-state residents $360.
Room and board: $9,224.

FINANCIAL AID PICTURE

Students with need: Need-based aid available for full-time and part-time students. Work study available weekends and for part-time students.
Students without need: This college awards aid only to students with need.

FINANCIAL AID PROCEDURES

Forms required: FAFSA, CSS PROFILE, state aid form.
Dates and Deadlines: Applicants notified on a rolling basis starting 4/1; must reply within 4 week(s) of notification.

CONTACT

Nancy Johnson, Director of Financial Aid
One Academic Drive, Corning, NY 14830
(607) 962-9428

Culinary Institute of America

Hyde Park, New York
www.ciachef.edu   Federal Code: 007304

4-year private culinary school in large town.
Enrollment: 2,774 undergrads. 512 full-time freshmen.
Selectivity: Admits over 75% of applicants.

BASIC COSTS (2017-2018)

Tuition and fees: $31,616.
Per-credit charge: $955.
Room and board: $10,870.

FINANCIAL AID PICTURE (2016-2017)

Students with need: Out of 439 full-time freshmen who applied for aid, 393 were judged to have need. Of these, 393 received aid, and 36 had their full need met. Average financial aid package met 79% of need; average scholarship/grant was $13,950; average loan was $3,047.
Students without need: 88 full-time freshmen who did not demonstrate need for aid received scholarships/grants; average award was $5,695. No-need awards available for academics, alumni affiliation, job skills, leadership.

FINANCIAL AID PROCEDURES

Forms required: FAFSA, state aid form.
Dates and Deadlines: Applicants notified on a rolling basis starting 3/5.

CONTACT

Kathleen Gailor, Director of Financial Aid
1946 Campus Drive, Hyde Park, NY 12538-1499
(845) 451-1243

Daemen College

Amherst, New York
www.daemen.edu   Federal Code: 002808

4-year private liberal arts college in small city.
Enrollment: 1,884 undergrads, 14% part-time. 392 full-time freshmen.
Selectivity: Admits 50 to 75% of applicants.

BASIC COSTS (2016-2017)

Tuition and fees: $26,940.
Per-credit charge: $880.
Room and board: $12,425.

FINANCIAL AID PICTURE

Students with need: Need-based aid available for full-time and part-time students. Work study available nights, weekends, and for part-time students.
Students without need: No-need awards available for academics, art, athletics, leadership.
Scholarships offered: President's Scholarship, Dean's Scholarship, Alumni Grant: $2,500-$10,000; renewable awards to freshmen and transfers; based

on high school GPA and SAT scores. Trustee Scholarship: $17,000; 2 awards; and $14,000; 4 awards. Renewable visual arts scholarships: $5,000; 2 awards.

FINANCIAL AID PROCEDURES

Forms required: FAFSA, state aid form.
Dates and Deadlines: Priority date 2/1; no closing date. Applicants notified on a rolling basis starting 2/1; must reply within 2 week(s) of notification.

CONTACT

Jeffrey Pagano, Director of Financial Aid
4380 Main Street, Amherst, NY 14226-3592
(716) 839-8254

Davis College

Johnson City, New York
www.davisny.edu   Federal Code: 015291

4-year private Bible college in large town, affiliated with the nondenominational tradition.
Enrollment: 231 undergrads.

BASIC COSTS (2016-2017)

Tuition and fees: $16,500.
Per-credit charge: $500.
Room and board: $7,700.
Additional info: Tuition at time of enrollment locked for 4 years.

FINANCIAL AID PICTURE

Students with need: Need-based aid available for full-time and part-time students. Work study available nights, weekends, and for part-time students.
Students without need: No-need awards available for academics, alumni affiliation.
Scholarships offered: Heart for Ministry Scholarship: based on personal essay and recommendations about a student's involvement in ministry or the community.

FINANCIAL AID PROCEDURES

Forms required: FAFSA, state aid form, institutional form.
Dates and Deadlines: Applicants notified on a rolling basis.
Transfers: No deadline. Applicants notified on a rolling basis.

CONTACT

Sandra Conklin, Director of Financial Aid
400 Riverside Drive, Johnson City, NY 13790
(607) 729-1581 ext. 331

DeVry College of New York: Midtown Campus

New York, New York
www.devry.edu   Federal Code: 003099

4-year for-profit business and technical college in very large city.
Enrollment: 936 undergrads.

BASIC COSTS (2016-2017)

Tuition and fees: $17,512.
Per-credit charge: $609.
Additional info: Tuition varies by program.

FINANCIAL AID PICTURE

Students with need: Need-based aid available for full-time and part-time students.
Students without need: This college awards aid only to students with need.

CONTACT

180 Madison Avenue, Suite 900, New York, NY 10016

Dominican College of Blauvelt

Orangeburg, New York
www.dc.edu   Federal Code: 002713

4-year private health science and liberal arts college in small town.
Enrollment: 1,461 undergrads, 9% part-time. 253 full-time freshmen.
Selectivity: Admits over 75% of applicants.

BASIC COSTS (2017-2018)
Tuition and fees: $28,448.
Per-credit charge: $834.
Room and board: $12,670.

FINANCIAL AID PICTURE (2016-2017)
Students with need: Out of 248 full-time freshmen who applied for aid, 219 were judged to have need. Of these, 219 received aid, and 31 had their full need met. Average financial aid package met 77% of need; average scholarship/grant was $22,728; average loan was $3,747. For part-time students, average financial aid package was $8,138.
Students without need: 34 full-time freshmen who did not demonstrate need for aid received scholarships/grants; average award was $10,335. No-need awards available for academics, athletics.
Scholarships offered: *Merit:* All applicants considered for non-need based scholarships or grants based on high school GPA and SAT/ACT scores. *Athletic:* 22 full-time freshmen received athletic scholarships; average amount $10,237.
Additional info: Individual financial aid counseling available.

FINANCIAL AID PROCEDURES
Forms required: FAFSA, state aid form.
Dates and Deadlines: Priority date 2/15; no closing date. Applicants notified on a rolling basis starting 2/1; must reply within 2 week(s) of notification.

CONTACT
Stacy Salinas, Director of Financial Aid
470 Western Highway, Orangeburg, NY 10962-1210
(845) 848-7821

Dutchess Community College

Poughkeepsie, New York
www.sunydutchess.edu   Federal Code: 002864

2-year public community college in large town.
Enrollment: 6,503 undergrads, 39% part-time. 1,591 full-time freshmen.
Selectivity: Open admission; but selective for some programs.

BASIC COSTS (2016-2017)
Tuition and fees: $4,068; out-of-state residents $7,596.
Per-credit charge: $147; out-of-state residents $294.
Room and board: $10,478.

FINANCIAL AID PICTURE (2015-2016)
Students with need: 75% of average financial aid package awarded as scholarships/grants, 25% awarded as loans/jobs. Need-based aid available for part-time students.
Students without need: No-need awards available for academics.
Scholarships offered: Dutchess County high school graduates in top 10% of their class; full tuition payment for 4 full-time consecutive semesters.

FINANCIAL AID PROCEDURES
Forms required: FAFSA, state aid form.
Dates and Deadlines: Priority date 5/1; no closing date. Applicants notified on a rolling basis starting 5/15; must reply within 2 week(s) of notification.

CONTACT

Susan Mead, Director of Financial Aid
53 Pendell Road, Poughkeepsie, NY 12601-1595
(845) 431-8030

D'Youville College

Buffalo, New York
www.dyc.edu

4-year private health science and liberal arts college in large city.
Enrollment: 1,652 undergrads, 19% part-time. 239 full-time freshmen.
Selectivity: Admits over 75% of applicants.

BASIC COSTS (2016-2017)
Tuition and fees: $25,210.
Per-credit charge: $770.
Room and board: $11,570.

FINANCIAL AID PICTURE
Students with need: Need-based aid available for full-time and part-time students. Work study available nights, weekends, and for part-time students.
Students without need: No-need awards available for academics, leadership, religious affiliation, ROTC.
Scholarships offered: Presidential Honors Scholarship: for students with 1100 SAT (Math and Verbal) or 24 ACT Composite; covers 50% tuition and 25% of standard double room rate. Academic Initiative Scholarship: For students with 1000-1090 SAT (math & verbal scores only) or 21-23 ACT score and an 85 high school average. The award is for 25% of tuition and 50% of the standard double room rate in Marguerite Hall or 50% of the standard room rate in the apartments for full-time students. Achievement Scholarship: For students with 900-1090 SAT score or 19-23 ACT and an 80-84 high school average, demonstrated leadership and community service. The awards range from $1,000-$4,000. Transfer Achievement Scholarship: For students with a G.P.A. of 2.75-4.0 from previously attended institution(s). The award amounts range from $2,500-$5,000. All awards are renewable for the standard duration of the specific academic program and have GPA and other requirements.

FINANCIAL AID PROCEDURES
Forms required: FAFSA, state aid form.
Dates and Deadlines: Priority date 3/1; no closing date. Applicants notified on a rolling basis starting 4/1; must reply within 2 week(s) of notification.
Transfers: Applicants notified on a rolling basis starting 4/1; must reply within 2 week(s) of notification. .

CONTACT
Matthew Metz, Director of Financial Aid
320 Porter Avenue, Buffalo, NY 14201-1084

Eastman School of Music of the University of Rochester

Rochester, New York   Federal Code: 008124
www.esm.rochester.edu   CSS Code: 2224

4-year private music and performing arts college in small city.
Enrollment: 563 undergrads.
Selectivity: Admits less than 50% of applicants.

BASIC COSTS (2016-2017)
Tuition and fees: $51,106.
Per-credit charge: $1,550.
Room and board: $14,818.

FINANCIAL AID PICTURE (2016-2017)

Students with need: Average financial aid package met 69% of need; average scholarship/grant was $26,704; average loan was $3,543. For part-time students, average financial aid package was $14,540.

Students without need: No-need awards available for academics, alumni affiliation, job skills, leadership, minority status, music/drama, state/district residency.

Scholarships offered: All merit scholarships awarded based on admission criteria and do not require separate application, audition, or interview.

FINANCIAL AID PROCEDURES

Forms required: FAFSA, state aid form, institutional form. CSS Profile required for International students only.

Dates and Deadlines: Closing date 2/28. Applicants notified by 4/15; must reply by 5/1 or within 2 week(s) of notification.

Transfers: No deadline. Applicants notified by 4/15; must reply by 5/1 or within 2 week(s) of notification.

CONTACT

Sheri deNormand, Director of Financial Aid
26 Gibbs Street, Rochester, NY 14604-2599
(585) 274-1070

Elmira Business Institute

Elmira, New York
www.ebi-college.com

2-year for-profit business and career college in large town.
Enrollment: 196 undergrads.
Selectivity: Open admission.

BASIC COSTS (2016-2017)

Additional info: Certificate programs range from $12,700 to $19,600. Associate degree programs range from $25,700 to $28,000. Books and supplies vary depending on program.

FINANCIAL AID PICTURE

Students with need: Need-based aid available for full-time and part-time students.

Students without need: This college awards aid only to students with need.

FINANCIAL AID PROCEDURES

Forms required: FAFSA, state aid form.

Dates and Deadlines: Priority date 5/1; no closing date. Applicants notified on a rolling basis starting 1/1; must reply within 1 week(s) of notification.

CONTACT

Financial Aid Director
303 North Main Street, Elmira, NY 14901
(607) 733-7177

Elmira Business Institute: Vestal

Vestal, New York
www.elmirabusinessinstitute.edu   Federal Code: 009044

2-year for-profit business and career college in small city.
Enrollment: 400 undergrads.
Selectivity: Open admission.

BASIC COSTS (2016-2017)

Additional info: Certificate programs range from $12,700 to $19,600. Associate degree programs range from $25,700 to $28,000. Books and supplies vary depending on program.

FINANCIAL AID PICTURE

Students with need: Need-based aid available for full-time and part-time students.

Students without need: This college awards aid only to students with need.

FINANCIAL AID PROCEDURES

Forms required: FAFSA, state aid form.

Dates and Deadlines: Applicants notified on a rolling basis starting 1/1; must reply within 1 week(s) of notification.

CONTACT

Jeffrey Wood, Director of Finanical Services
4100 Vestal Road, Vestal, NY 13850
(607) 729-8915

Elmira College

Elmira, New York
www.elmira.edu   Federal Code: 002718

4-year private liberal arts and teachers college in large town.
Enrollment: 1,067 undergrads, 9% part-time. 207 full-time freshmen.
Selectivity: Admits over 75% of applicants. GED not accepted.

BASIC COSTS (2017-2018)

Tuition and fees: $41,900.
Per-credit charge: $1,200.
Room and board: $12,000.

FINANCIAL AID PICTURE (2016-2017)

Students with need: Out of 188 full-time freshmen who applied for aid, 170 were judged to have need. Of these, 170 received aid, and 34 had their full need met. Average financial aid package met 73% of need; average scholarship/grant was $27,537; average loan was $3,393. Need-based aid available for part-time students.

Students without need: 37 full-time freshmen who did not demonstrate need for aid received scholarships/grants; average award was $21,312. No-need awards available for academics, leadership, ROTC, state/district residency.

Scholarships offered: Founder Scholarship: $25,000, selection based on GPA, academic curriculum, test scores (if submitted), co-curricular activities; Langdon Award: $20,000, selection based on academic and co-curricular activities, character, and leadership; 1855 Award: $15,000 selection based on leadership through involvement in co-curricular activities.

Additional info: Sibling Scholarship program provides 50% discount on second immediate family member's room and board, regardless of need.

FINANCIAL AID PROCEDURES

Forms required: FAFSA, state aid form.

Dates and Deadlines: Priority date 2/1; no closing date. Applicants notified on a rolling basis starting 12/1; must reply by 5/1 or within 2 week(s) of notification.

Transfers: No deadline. Applicants notified on a rolling basis starting 12/1; must reply by 5/1 or within 2 week(s) of notification.

CONTACT

Kathleen Cohen, Dean of Financial Aid
One Park Place, Elmira, NY 14901
(607) 735-1728

Erie Community College

Buffalo, New York
www.ecc.edu   Federal Code: 010684

2-year public community college in large city.
Enrollment: 9,479 undergrads, 22% part-time. 2,131 full-time freshmen.
Selectivity: Open admission; but selective for some programs.

BASIC COSTS (2016-2017)

Tuition and fees: $5,408; out-of-state residents $10,141.
Per-credit charge: $198; out-of-state residents $396.

FINANCIAL AID PICTURE (2015-2016)

Students with need: 83% of average financial aid package awarded as scholarships/grants, 17% awarded as loans/jobs. Need-based aid available for part-time students. Work study available weekends and for part-time students.
Students without need: This college awards aid only to students with need.

FINANCIAL AID PROCEDURES

Forms required: FAFSA, state aid form.
Dates and Deadlines: Priority date 5/1; no closing date. Applicants notified on a rolling basis starting 4/1; must reply within 2 week(s) of notification.

CONTACT

Scott Weltjen, Director of Financial Aid
6205 Main Street, Williamsville, NY 14221-7095
(716) 851-1677

Eugene Lang College The New School for Liberal Arts

New York, New York
www.newschool.edu   Federal Code: 002780

4-year private liberal arts college in very large city.
Enrollment: 1,658 undergrads, 4% part-time. 490 full-time freshmen.
Selectivity: Admits over 75% of applicants.

BASIC COSTS (2016-2017)

Tuition and fees: $44,540.
Per-credit charge: $1,480.
Room and board: $18,420.

FINANCIAL AID PICTURE

Students with need: Need-based aid available for full-time and part-time students. Work study available nights, weekends, and for part-time students.
Students without need: No-need awards available for academics, art, leadership, minority status, music/drama, state/district residency.

FINANCIAL AID PROCEDURES

Forms required: FAFSA, state aid form.
Dates and Deadlines: Closing date 2/1. Applicants notified on a rolling basis starting 4/1; must reply within 4 week(s) of notification.
Transfers: Must reply within 4 week(s) of notification.

CONTACT

Lisa Shaheen, Director of Student Financial Aid
79 Fifth Avenue, New York, NY 10003
(212) 229-8930

Excelsior College

Albany, New York
www.excelsior.edu   Federal Code: 014251

4-year private virtual liberal arts college in small city.
Enrollment: 35,161 undergrads, 100% part-time.
Selectivity: Open admission; but selective for some programs.

BASIC COSTS (2016-2017)

Per-credit charge: $510.
Additional info: Undergraduate per credit hour charge: $510. For students committed to taking at least 12 Excelsior College credits prior to graduation the enrollment fee is waived. An enrollment fee of up to $1,065 may be charged for evaluation of credits earned elsewhere. Students enrolled via a

partnership (academic, corporate, military) qualify for different fees, tuition, credit requirements and rules based on the individual partnership agreement. Students taking 12 credits annually are not subject to $495 annual student services fee.

FINANCIAL AID PICTURE (2015-2016)

Students with need: 35% of average financial aid package awarded as scholarships/grants, 65% awarded as loans/jobs.
Students without need: This college awards aid only to students with need.
Scholarships offered: Excelsior College has endowed scholarships for a number of student types and various programs.
Additional info: Excelsior College is Title IV eligible for its course-based degree programs; approved for all veterans' education benefit programs.

FINANCIAL AID PROCEDURES

Dates and Deadlines: Applicants notified on a rolling basis; must reply within 2 week(s) of notification.

CONTACT

Thomas Dalton, Assistant Vice President for Enrollment Management, Financial Aid
7 Columbia Circle, Albany, NY 12203
(518) 464-8500

Fashion Institute of Technology

New York, New York
www.fitnyc.edu   Federal Code: 002866

4-year public visual arts and business college in very large city.
Enrollment: 8,168 undergrads, 10% part-time. 1,247 full-time freshmen.
Selectivity: Admits less than 50% of applicants.

BASIC COSTS (2016-2017)

Tuition and fees: $5,335; out-of-state residents $14,515.
Per-credit charge: $191; out-of-state residents $574.
Room and board: $13,386.

FINANCIAL AID PICTURE (2015-2016)

Students with need: Out of 849 full-time freshmen who applied for aid, 632 were judged to have need. Of these, 632 received aid, and 268 had their full need met. Average financial aid package met 71% of need; average scholarship/grant was $6,083; average loan was $2,534. For part-time students, average financial aid package was $6,872.
Students without need: This college awards aid only to students with need.

FINANCIAL AID PROCEDURES

Forms required: FAFSA, state aid form.
Dates and Deadlines: Priority date 2/15; no closing date. Applicants notified on a rolling basis starting 4/1; must reply within 2 week(s) of notification.
Transfers: Applicants notified by 4/15; must reply within 2 week(s) of notification.

CONTACT

Mina Friedmann, Director of Financial Aid
227 West 27th Street, New York, NY 10001-5992
(212) 217-3560

Finger Lakes Community College

Canandaigua, New York
www.flcc.edu   Federal Code: 007532

2-year public community college in small town.
Enrollment: 3,505 undergrads, 28% part-time. 944 full-time freshmen.
Selectivity: Open admission; but selective for some programs.

PART III: FINANCIAL AID COLLEGE BY COLLEGE

BASIC COSTS (2016-2017)

Tuition and fees: $4,952; out-of-state residents $9,320.

Per-credit charge: $183; out-of-state residents $366.

FINANCIAL AID PICTURE (2016-2017)

Students with need: Out of 875 full-time freshmen who applied for aid, 798 were judged to have need. Of these, 715 received aid. Need-based aid available for part-time students.

Students without need: This college awards aid only to students with need.

FINANCIAL AID PROCEDURES

Forms required: FAFSA, state aid form.

Dates and Deadlines: Priority date 3/15; no closing date. Applicants notified on a rolling basis starting 4/1; must reply within 2 week(s) of notification.

CONTACT

Susan Romano, Director, Financial Aid

3325 Marvin Sands Drive, Canandaigua, NY 14424-8395

(585) 785-1275

Five Towns College

Dix Hills, New York

www.ftc.edu   Federal Code: 012561

4-year for-profit business and performing arts college in large town.

Enrollment: 631 undergrads, 10% part-time. 136 full-time freshmen.

Selectivity: Admits 50 to 75% of applicants.

BASIC COSTS (2016-2017)

Tuition and fees: $19,700.

Room and board: $12,270.

FINANCIAL AID PICTURE

Students with need: Need-based aid available for full-time and part-time students. Work study available nights, weekends, and for part-time students.

Students without need: No-need awards available for academics, art, leadership, music/drama.

FINANCIAL AID PROCEDURES

Forms required: FAFSA, state aid form.

Dates and Deadlines: Priority date 4/30; no closing date. Applicants notified on a rolling basis starting 3/1; must reply within 4 week(s) of notification.

Transfers: No deadline. Applicants notified on a rolling basis starting 1/1; must reply within 4 week(s) of notification.

CONTACT

Jason LaBonte, Director of Financial Aid

305 North Service Road, Dix Hills, NY 11746-6055

(631) 656-2164

Fordham University

Bronx, New York   Federal Code: 002722

www.fordham.edu   CSS Code: 2259

4-year private university in very large city, affiliated with the Roman Catholic Church.

Enrollment: 9,096 undergrads, 4% part-time. 2,191 full-time freshmen.

Selectivity: Admits less than 50% of applicants.

BASIC COSTS (2016-2017)

Tuition and fees: $49,073.

Per-credit charge: $1,595.

Room and board: $16,845.

FINANCIAL AID PICTURE (2015-2016)

Students with need: Out of 1,943 full-time freshmen who applied for aid, 1,385 were judged to have need. Of these, 1,385 received aid, and 423 had

their full need met. Average financial aid package met 81% of need; average scholarship/grant was $26,779; average loan was $5,095. For part-time students, average financial aid package was $14,292.

Students without need: 593 full-time freshmen who did not demonstrate need for aid received scholarships/grants; average award was $16,180. No-need awards available for academics, athletics, ROTC.

Scholarships offered: 35 full-time freshmen received athletic scholarships; average amount $28,270.

FINANCIAL AID PROCEDURES

Forms required: FAFSA, CSS PROFILE, state aid form.

Dates and Deadlines: Closing date 2/10. Applicants notified on a rolling basis starting 3/31; must reply by 5/1 or within 2 week(s) of notification.

Transfers: Priority date 2/10; closing date 5/1. Applicants notified on a rolling basis starting 5/1. Transfer students are only eligible for need based aid.

CONTACT

Angela Van Dekker, Associate Vice President of Student Financial Services

Office of Undergraduate Admission, Fordham University, Bronx, NY 10458-9993

(718) 817-3800

Fulton-Montgomery Community College

Johnstown, New York

www.fmcc.edu   Federal Code: 002867

2-year public community college in large town.

Enrollment: 1,728 undergrads.

Selectivity: Open admission; but selective for some programs.

BASIC COSTS (2016-2017)

Tuition and fees: $4,720; out-of-state residents $8,920.

Per-credit charge: $175; out-of-state residents $350.

Room and board: $11,350.

FINANCIAL AID PICTURE

Students with need: Need-based aid available for full-time and part-time students. Work study available nights, weekends, and for part-time students.

Students without need: No-need awards available for academics.

FINANCIAL AID PROCEDURES

Forms required: FAFSA, state aid form.

Dates and Deadlines: Priority date 6/1; no closing date. Applicants notified on a rolling basis starting 6/15; must reply within 2 week(s) of notification.

CONTACT

Rebecca Cozzocrea, Coordinator of Financial Aid

2805 State Highway 67, Johnstown, NY 12095

(518) 736-4651 ext. 8201

Genesee Community College

Batavia, New York

www.genesee.edu   Federal Code: 006782

2-year public community college in large town.

Enrollment: 3,374 undergrads, 31% part-time. 823 full-time freshmen.

Selectivity: Open admission; but selective for some programs.

BASIC COSTS (2016-2017)

Tuition and fees: $4,460; out-of-state residents $5,060.

Room and board: $8,490.

FINANCIAL AID PICTURE (2015-2016)

Students with need: Out of 765 full-time freshmen who applied for aid, 670 were judged to have need. Of these, 655 received aid, and 341 had their full need met. Average financial aid package met 81% of need; average

scholarship/grant was $5,179; average loan was $3,800. For part-time students, average financial aid package was $3,210.

Students without need: 32 full-time freshmen who did not demonstrate need for aid received scholarships/grants; average award was $2,150. No-need awards available for academics, alumni affiliation, athletics, leadership, state/district residency.

Scholarships offered: 25 full-time freshmen received athletic scholarships; average amount $2,150.

FINANCIAL AID PROCEDURES

Forms required: FAFSA, state aid form.

Dates and Deadlines: Priority date 1/1; closing date 5/1. Applicants notified on a rolling basis starting 4/15; must reply within 2 week(s) of notification.

Transfers: No deadline.

CONTACT

Joseph Bailey, Director of Student Financial Services/Assistant Dean for Enrollment Services

One College Road, Batavia, NY 14020-9704

(585) 345-6900

Globe Institute of Technology
New York, New York
www.globe:edu   Federal Code: 025408

4-year for-profit university and business college in very large city.

Enrollment: 447 undergrads.

Selectivity: Open admission; but selective for some programs.

BASIC COSTS (2016-2017)

Additional info: Bachelor's degree programs range from $44,376-$55,470, associate degree programs are $22,188, certificate degree programs are $11,094. Additional fees vary by program. Tuition/fee waivers available for adults, minority students, unemployed or children of unemployed.

FINANCIAL AID PICTURE

Students with need: Need-based aid available for full-time and part-time students. Work study available nights, weekends, and for part-time students.

Students without need: No-need awards available for academics, athletics.

FINANCIAL AID PROCEDURES

Forms required: FAFSA, state aid form, institutional form.

Dates and Deadlines: Applicants notified on a rolling basis.

Transfers: No deadline. Applicants notified on a rolling basis.

CONTACT

Tatyana Nusenbaum, Director of Financial Aid

500 Seventh Avenue, 2nd Floor, New York, NY 10018

(212) 349-4330

Hamilton College
Clinton, New York   Federal Code: 002728
www.hamilton.edu   CSS Code: 2286

4-year private liberal arts college in rural community.

Enrollment: 1,867 undergrads. 472 full-time freshmen.

Selectivity: Admits less than 50% of applicants.

BASIC COSTS (2016-2017)

Tuition and fees: $51,240.

Room and board: $13,010.

FINANCIAL AID PICTURE (2016-2017)

Students with need: Out of 267 full-time freshmen who applied for aid, 247 were judged to have need. Of these, 247 received aid, and 247 had their full need met. Average financial aid package met 100% of need; average scholarship/grant was $43,936; average loan was $3,291.

Students without need: This college awards aid only to students with need.

FINANCIAL AID PROCEDURES

Forms required: FAFSA, CSS PROFILE, state aid form, institutional form.

Dates and Deadlines: Closing date 2/15. Applicants notified by 4/1; must reply by 5/1.

Transfers: Closing date 4/15. Applicants notified by 5/10; must reply by 5/23.

CONTACT

K. Cameron Feist, Director of Financial Aid

198 College Hill Road, Clinton, NY 13323-1293

(315) 859-4413

Hartwick College
Oneonta, New York
www.hartwick.edu   Federal Code: 002729

4-year private liberal arts college in large town.

Enrollment: 1,396 undergrads, 2% part-time. 292 full-time freshmen.

Selectivity: Admits over 75% of applicants.

BASIC COSTS (2016-2017)

Tuition and fees: $42,860.

Per-credit charge: $1,350.

Room and board: $11,510.

FINANCIAL AID PICTURE (2015-2016)

Students with need: Out of 268 full-time freshmen who applied for aid, 254 were judged to have need. Of these, 254 received aid, and 53 had their full need met. Average financial aid package met 82% of need; average scholarship/grant was $27,415; average loan was $4,902. For part-time students, average financial aid package was $12,250.

Students without need: 38 full-time freshmen who did not demonstrate need for aid received scholarships/grants; average award was $22,929. No-need awards available for academics, alumni affiliation, art, athletics, music/drama.

Scholarships offered: 4 full-time freshmen received athletic scholarships; average amount $17,743.

FINANCIAL AID PROCEDURES

Forms required: FAFSA.

Dates and Deadlines: Priority date 2/15; no closing date. Applicants notified on a rolling basis starting 1/15; must reply by 5/1 or within 2 week(s) of notification.

Transfers: Priority date 8/1; no deadline. Applicants notified on a rolling basis starting 3/15; must reply within 2 week(s) of notification.

CONTACT

Melissa Allen, Director of Financial Aid

1 Hartwick Drive, Oneonta, NY 13820-4022

(607) 431-4130

Helene Fuld College of Nursing
New York, New York
www.helenefuld.edu   Federal Code: 015395

2-year private nursing and junior college in very large city.

Enrollment: 486 undergrads.

BASIC COSTS (2016-2017)

Tuition and fees: $19,099.

Per-credit charge: $341.

FINANCIAL AID PICTURE (2016-2017)

Students with need: Need-based aid available for full-time and part-time students.

Students without need: This college awards aid only to students with need.

FINANCIAL AID PROCEDURES

Forms required: FAFSA, state aid form.
Dates and Deadlines: Closing date 6/30. Applicants notified on a rolling basis.

CONTACT

Andrine Thomas, Financial Aid Counselor and Loan Coordinator
24 East 120th Street, New York, NY 10035
(212) 616-7253

Herkimer County Community College

Herkimer, New York
www.herkimer.edu   Federal Code: 004788

2-year public community college in small town.
Enrollment: 1,987 undergrads, 16% part-time. 644 full-time freshmen.
Selectivity: Open admission; but selective for some programs.

BASIC COSTS (2016-2017)

Tuition and fees: $5,050; out-of-state residents $7,780.
Per-credit charge: $159; out-of-state residents $278.
Room and board: $9,620.
Additional info: Tuition/fee waivers available for unemployed or children of unemployed.

FINANCIAL AID PICTURE

Students with need: Need-based aid available for full-time and part-time students. Work study available nights, weekends, and for part-time students.

FINANCIAL AID PROCEDURES

Forms required: FAFSA, state aid form.
Dates and Deadlines: Closing date 4/1. Applicants notified on a rolling basis starting 4/1; must reply within 2 week(s) of notification.

CONTACT

Susan Tripp, Director of Financial Aid
100 Reservoir Road, Herkimer, NY 13350-1598
(315) 866-0300 ext. 8282

Hilbert College

Hamburg, New York
www.hilbert.edu   Federal Code: 002735

4-year private liberal arts college in small city, affiliated with the Roman Catholic Church.
Enrollment: 791 undergrads, 7% part-time. 147 full-time freshmen.
Selectivity: Admits over 75% of applicants.

BASIC COSTS (2016-2017)

Tuition and fees: $20,975.
Per-credit charge: $525.
Room and board: $9,600.
Additional info: Tuition/fee waivers available for adults, minority students.

FINANCIAL AID PICTURE (2016-2017)

Students with need: Out of 85 full-time freshmen who applied for aid, 76 were judged to have need. Of these, 76 received aid, and 12 had their full need met. Average financial aid package met 70% of need; average scholarship/grant was $12,901; average loan was $4,228. For part-time students, average financial aid package was $4,410.
Students without need: 9 full-time freshmen who did not demonstrate need for aid received scholarships/grants; average award was $7,194. No-need awards available for academics, alumni affiliation, leadership, minority status.

FINANCIAL AID PROCEDURES

Forms required: FAFSA, state aid form.
Dates and Deadlines: Priority date 3/1; no closing date. Applicants notified on a rolling basis starting 3/1; must reply within 2 week(s) of notification.
Transfers: No deadline. Applicants notified on a rolling basis; must reply within 2 week(s) of notification.

CONTACT

Beverly Chudy, Director of Student Financial Aid
5200 South Park Avenue, Hamburg, NY 14075-1597
(716) 649-7900 ext. 314

Hobart and William Smith Colleges

Geneva, New York   Federal Code: 002731
www.hws.edu   CSS Code: 2294

4-year private liberal arts college in large town.
Enrollment: 2,241 undergrads. 589 full-time freshmen.
Selectivity: Admits 50 to 75% of applicants.

BASIC COSTS (2016-2017)

Tuition and fees: $51,523.
Room and board: $13,050.

FINANCIAL AID PICTURE (2015-2016)

Students with need: Out of 475 full-time freshmen who applied for aid, 391 were judged to have need. Of these, 381 received aid. Average financial aid package met 82% of need; average scholarship/grant was $32,453; average loan was $3,219. For part-time students, average financial aid package was $18,108.
Students without need: 192 full-time freshmen who did not demonstrate need for aid received scholarships/grants; average award was $13,688. No-need awards available for academics, alumni affiliation, art, leadership, music/drama, religious affiliation.
Scholarships offered: Cornelius and Muriel P. Wood Scholarship: full tuition for 4 years. Richard Hersh Scholarship: full tuition and fees for 4 years. Trustee and Blackwell Scholarships for Academic Excellence: $25,000 annually, for 4 years; based on GPA, test scores, class standing. Faculty Scholarships: $17,000. Presidential Leaders and Service Scholarships: $5,000-$15,000; based on academic excellence, leadership, service, personal qualities. Arts Scholarships: $3,000-$15,000; for special talent in studio art/architecture, creative writing, music, theater, and/or dance.

FINANCIAL AID PROCEDURES

Forms required: FAFSA, CSS PROFILE, state aid form.
Dates and Deadlines: Priority date 2/1; closing date 2/1. Applicants notified by 4/1; must reply by 5/1 or within 2 week(s) of notification.
Transfers: No deadline. Applicants notified on a rolling basis; must reply within 2 week(s) of notification.

CONTACT

Beth Nepa, Director of Financial Aid Services
629 South Main Street, Geneva, NY 14456
(315) 781-3315

Hofstra University

Hempstead, New York
www.hofstra.edu   Federal Code: 002732

4-year private university in large city.
Enrollment: 6,810 undergrads, 5% part-time. 1,648 full-time freshmen.
Selectivity: Admits 50 to 75% of applicants.

BASIC COSTS (2016-2017)

Tuition and fees: $42,160.
Per-credit charge: $1,380.

Room and board: $13,800.
Additional info: Tuition at time of enrollment locked for 4 years.

FINANCIAL AID PICTURE (2015-2016)
Students with need: Out of 1,439 full-time freshmen who applied for aid, 1,175 were judged to have need. Of these, 1,173 received aid, and 303 had their full need met. Average financial aid package met 69% of need; average scholarship/grant was $21,675; average loan was $3,639. For part-time students, average financial aid package was $10,425.
Students without need: 397 full-time freshmen who did not demonstrate need for aid received scholarships/grants; average award was $17,396. No-need awards available for academics, alumni affiliation, art, athletics, leadership, minority status, music/drama, ROTC, state/district residency.
Scholarships offered: *Merit:* Trustee Scholars Program: Full-tuition scholarships for highest achieving admitted students; approximately 30 students awarded annually; candidates had an average SAT (Critical Reading and Math Sections only) /ACT equivalent of 1556 SAT on a 1600 scale (based on the old SAT taken prior to March 2016), weighted GPA of 4.3, and were typically in the top 10% of their high school graduating class. Presidential Scholars Program: candidates had an average SAT (Critical Reading and Math sections only) /ACT equivalent of 1330 SAT on a 1600 scale (based on the old SAT taken prior to March 2016), weighted GPA of 3.9, and were typically in the top 10% of their high school graduating class. University Provost Scholars Program: candidates had an average SAT (Critical Reading and Math sections only) /ACT equivalent of 1184 SAT on a 1600 scale (based on the old SAT taken prior to March 2016) and a weighted GPA of 3.6. University Dean's Scholars Program: candidates had an average SAT (Critical Reading and Math sections only) /ACT equivalent of 1132 SAT on a 1600 scale (based on the old SAT taken prior to March 2016) and a weighted GPA of 3.2. *Athletic:* 21 full-time freshmen received athletic scholarships; average amount $22,919.

FINANCIAL AID PROCEDURES
Forms required: FAFSA, state aid form.
Dates and Deadlines: Priority date 2/1; no closing date. Applicants notified on a rolling basis starting 3/1; must reply by 5/1 or within 2 week(s) of notification.

CONTACT
Sandra Mervius, Director of Financial Aid
Admissions Center, 100 Hofstra University, Hempstead, NY 11549
(516) 463-8000

Houghton College
Houghton, New York
www.houghton.edu   Federal Code: 002734

4-year private liberal arts college in rural community, affiliated with the Wesleyan Church.
Enrollment: 1,037 undergrads, 4% part-time. 264 full-time freshmen.
Selectivity: Admits over 75% of applicants.

BASIC COSTS (2017-2018)
Tuition and fees: $31,240.
Room and board: $8,754.
Additional info: Tuition/fee waivers available for minority students.

FINANCIAL AID PICTURE (2016-2017)
Students with need: Out of 244 full-time freshmen who applied for aid, 216 were judged to have need. Of these, 216 received aid, and 46 had their full need met. Average financial aid package met 80% of need; average scholarship/grant was $19,761; average loan was $4,195. For part-time students, average financial aid package was $5,445.
Students without need: 43 full-time freshmen who did not demonstrate need for aid received scholarships/grants; average award was $18,422. No-need awards available for academics, alumni affiliation, art, minority status, music/drama, religious affiliation, ROTC, state/district residency.

Scholarships offered: Academic Scholarships: $4,000-$10,000. Heritage Scholarships: $12,000. Phi Theta Kappa: $4,000. Art Scholarships: $1,000-$5,000 (based on art portfolio). Music Scholarships: $1,000-$12,500 (based on audition). Excellence Scholarships: $1,000-$4,000. James S. Luckey Scholarship: full tuition.

FINANCIAL AID PROCEDURES
Forms required: FAFSA.
Dates and Deadlines: Priority date 3/1; no closing date. Applicants notified on a rolling basis starting 3/1.
Transfers: No deadline. Applicants notified on a rolling basis starting 3/15; must reply by 5/1 or within 4 week(s) of notification.

CONTACT
Marianne Loper, Director of Student Financial Services
1 Willard Avenue/PO Box 128, Houghton, NY 14744-0128
(585) 567-9328

Iona College
New Rochelle, New York
www.iona.edu   Federal Code: 002737

4-year private business and liberal arts college in small city, affiliated with the Roman Catholic Church.
Enrollment: 3,120 undergrads, 2% part-time. 935 full-time freshmen.
Selectivity: Admits over 75% of applicants.

BASIC COSTS (2016-2017)
Tuition and fees: $36,584.
Per-credit charge: $1,142.
Room and board: $14,400.

FINANCIAL AID PICTURE (2016-2017)
Students with need: Out of 933 full-time freshmen who applied for aid, 833 were judged to have need. Of these, 831 received aid, and 159 had their full need met. Average financial aid package met 14% of need; average scholarship/grant was $5,374; average loan was $3,242. For part-time students, average financial aid package was $7,446.
Students without need: 99 full-time freshmen who did not demonstrate need for aid received scholarships/grants; average award was $19,672. No-need awards available for academics, alumni affiliation, athletics, music/drama, religious affiliation.
Scholarships offered: 52 full-time freshmen received athletic scholarships; average amount $17,882.

FINANCIAL AID PROCEDURES
Forms required: FAFSA, state aid form.
Dates and Deadlines: Priority date 2/15; closing date 4/15. Applicants notified on a rolling basis starting 1/1; must reply by 5/1 or within 2 week(s) of notification.
Transfers: No deadline. Applicants notified on a rolling basis starting 3/1; must reply within 2 week(s) of notification.

CONTACT
Mary Grant, Director of Financial Aid
715 North Avenue, New Rochelle, NY 10801-1890
(914) 633-2497

Island Drafting and Technical Institute
Amityville, New York
www.idti.edu   Federal Code: 007375

2-year for-profit technical and career college in large town.
Enrollment: 106 undergrads. 47 full-time freshmen.
Selectivity: Open admission; but selective for some programs.

BASIC COSTS (2016-2017)
Tuition and fees: $16,200.
Per-credit charge: $525.

FINANCIAL AID PICTURE
Students with need: Need-based aid available for full-time students.
Students without need: This college awards aid only to students with need.

FINANCIAL AID PROCEDURES
Dates and Deadlines: Applicants notified on a rolling basis.

CONTACT
Daniel Greener, Financial Aid Office
128 Broadway, Amityville, NY 11701-2704
(631) 691-8733 ext. 115

Ithaca College
Ithaca, New York   Federal Code: 002739
www.ithaca.edu   CSS Code: 2325

4-year private health science and liberal arts college in large town.
Enrollment: 6,181 undergrads, 1% part-time. 1,632 full-time freshmen.
Selectivity: Admits 50 to 75% of applicants.

BASIC COSTS (2017-2018)
Tuition and fees: $42,884.
Per-credit charge: $1,429.
Room and board: $15,274.
Additional info: Tuition/fee waivers available for minority students.

FINANCIAL AID PICTURE (2016-2017)
Students with need: Out of 1,410 full-time freshmen who applied for aid, 1,138 were judged to have need. Of these, 1,138 received aid, and 632 had their full need met. Average financial aid package met 90% of need; average scholarship/grant was $26,477; average loan was $5,469. For part-time students, average financial aid package was $18,013.
Students without need: 399 full-time freshmen who did not demonstrate need for aid received scholarships/grants; average award was $15,358. No-need awards available for academics, alumni affiliation, leadership, minority status, music/drama, ROTC.
Scholarships offered: President's Scholarship: $20,000; approximately top 10% of applicants. Dean's Scholarship: $13,000-$17,000; approximately top 11% to 35% of applicants. ALANA Scholarship: $2,000-$5,000; representatives of minority groups who show excellent academic achievement. Flora Brown Award: $10,000-$13,000. MLK Scholarship: $25,000 to full tuition; academic excellence; community service involvement; approximately 15. Ithaca Leadership Scholarship: $7,000; record of leadership and above average academic performance; approximately 120. Ithaca Premier Talent Scholarship: maximum $18,000 for music and theater majors; approximately 35. Park Scholar Achievement award: full cost of attendance; outstanding achievement in communications; approximately 20. Ithaca College Merit Scholarship, and Ithaca College National Merit Recognition Award: up to $2,000; for students who designate Ithaca their first-choice institution to National Merit Scholarship Corporation.

FINANCIAL AID PROCEDURES
Forms required: FAFSA, CSS PROFILE.
Dates and Deadlines: Priority date 2/1; no closing date. Applicants notified on a rolling basis starting 2/15; must reply by 5/1.
Transfers: No deadline. Applicants notified on a rolling basis starting 2/15; must reply by 5/1. All institutional need-based and merit awards available for freshmen are also available for transfers.

CONTACT
Lisa Hoskey, Director, Student Financial Services
953 Danby Road, Ithaca, NY 14850-7002
(607) 274-3131

Jamestown Business College
Jamestown, New York
www.jbc.edu   Federal Code: 008495

2-year for-profit business and junior college in large town.
Enrollment: 311 undergrads, 2% part-time. 99 full-time freshmen.
Selectivity: Admits over 75% of applicants.

BASIC COSTS (2016-2017)
Tuition and fees: $12,600.

FINANCIAL AID PICTURE (2015-2016)
Students with need: 81% of average financial aid package awarded as scholarships/grants, 19% awarded as loans/jobs. Need-based aid available for part-time students.
Students without need: No-need awards available for academics.

FINANCIAL AID PROCEDURES
Forms required: FAFSA, state aid form.
Dates and Deadlines: Applicants notified on a rolling basis starting 2/15.
Transfers: Priority date 3/1; no deadline. Applicants notified on a rolling basis starting 5/1.

CONTACT
Diane Sturzenbecker, Financial Aid Officer
7 Fairmount Avenue, Jamestown, NY 14701-0429
(716) 664-5100

Jamestown Community College
Jamestown, New York
www.sunyjcc.edu   Federal Code: 002869

2-year public community college in large town.
Enrollment: 2,657 undergrads, 23% part-time. 768 full-time freshmen.
Selectivity: Open admission; but selective for some programs.

BASIC COSTS (2016-2017)
Tuition and fees: $5,500; out-of-state residents $10,130.
Per-credit charge: $193; out-of-state residents $386.
Room and board: $10,750.

FINANCIAL AID PICTURE (2016-2017)
Students with need: Out of 738 full-time freshmen who applied for aid, 618 were judged to have need. Of these, 618 received aid, and 18 had their full need met. Need-based aid available for part-time students.
Students without need: 32 full-time freshmen who did not demonstrate need for aid received scholarships/grants; average award was $3,920. No-need awards available for academics, alumni affiliation, art, athletics, music/drama, state/district residency.
Scholarships offered: *Merit:* 100% resident tuition scholarship (less federal and state grants) for students who apply for admissions by 3/1 and are in the top 20% of their high school graduating class with Regents diploma if residents of Chautauqua, Cattaraugus, or Allegany counties. Guaranteed in-state tuition rate for students in Warren, Potter, McKean, Forest, Elk and Cameron counties in Pennsylvania, in top 20% of graduating class with an academic diploma. *Athletic:* 3 full-time freshmen received athletic scholarships; average amount $1,167.

FINANCIAL AID PROCEDURES
Forms required: FAFSA, state aid form.
Dates and Deadlines: Priority date 3/1; no closing date. Applicants notified on a rolling basis starting 4/15.

CONTACT
Laurie Vorp, Executive Director of Student Finance and Records
525 Falconer Street, Jamestown, NY 14702-0020
(800) 388-8557

Jefferson Community College

Watertown, New York
www.sunyjefferson.edu   Federal Code: 002870

2-year public community college in large town.
Enrollment: 2,854 undergrads, 28% part-time. 752 full-time freshmen.
Selectivity: Open admission; but selective for some programs.

BASIC COSTS (2016-2017)
Tuition and fees: $5,202; out-of-state residents $7,698.
Per-credit charge: $183; out-of-state residents $287.
Room and board: $10,330.

FINANCIAL AID PICTURE
Students with need: Need-based aid available for full-time and part-time students.
Students without need: This college awards aid only to students with need.

FINANCIAL AID PROCEDURES
Forms required: FAFSA, state aid form, institutional form.
Dates and Deadlines: Priority date 4/1; closing date 8/15. Applicants notified on a rolling basis starting 4/15; must reply within 2 week(s) of notification.
Transfers: No deadline.

CONTACT
James Ambrose, Director of Financial Aid
1220 Coffeen Street, Watertown, NY 13601
(315) 786-2355

Jewish Theological Seminary of America

New York, New York
www.jtsa.edu/list   Federal Code: 002740

4-year private liberal arts college in very large city, affiliated with the Jewish faith.
Enrollment: 157 undergrads. 43 full-time freshmen.
Selectivity: Admits 50 to 75% of applicants.

BASIC COSTS (2016-2017)
Tuition and fees: $20,910.
Per-credit charge: $1,115.
Room only: $11,960.
Additional info: Tuition/fee waivers available for adults.

FINANCIAL AID PICTURE
Students with need: Need-based aid available for full-time and part-time students. Work study available nights, weekends, and for part-time students.
Students without need: No-need awards available for academics, leadership.

FINANCIAL AID PROCEDURES
Forms required: FAFSA, institutional form.
Dates and Deadlines: Closing date 3/1. Applicants notified by 4/1; must reply within 2 week(s) of notification.

CONTACT
Amy Hersh, Registrar/Director of Financial Aid
3080 Broadway, New York, NY 10025
(212) 678-8007

Juilliard School

New York, New York   Federal Code: 002742
www.juilliard.edu   CSS Code: 2340

4-year private music and performing arts college in very large city.
Enrollment: 499 undergrads. 114 full-time freshmen.

Selectivity: Admits less than 50% of applicants.

BASIC COSTS (2016-2017)
Tuition and fees: $41,460.
Room and board: $15,380.

FINANCIAL AID PICTURE (2016-2017)
Students with need: 79% of average financial aid package awarded as scholarships/grants, 21% awarded as loans/jobs. Need-based aid available for part-time students. Work study available nights, weekends, and for part-time students.
Students without need: No-need awards available for music/drama.

FINANCIAL AID PROCEDURES
Forms required: FAFSA, CSS PROFILE, institutional form.
Dates and Deadlines: Closing date 3/1. Applicants notified by 4/1; must reply by 5/1.
Transfers: Applicants notified by 4/1; must reply by 5/1 or within 2 week(s) of notification.

CONTACT
Tina Gonzalez, Director of Financial Aid
60 Lincoln Center Plaza, New York, NY 10023-6588
(212) 799-5000 ext. 211

Keuka College

Keuka Park, New York
www.keuka.edu   Federal Code: 002744

4-year private liberal arts college in rural community, affiliated with the American Baptist Churches in the USA.
Enrollment: 1,722 undergrads, 22% part-time. 319 full-time freshmen.
Selectivity: Admits over 75% of applicants.

BASIC COSTS (2017-2018)
Tuition and fees: $30,846.
Per-credit charge: $999.
Room and board: $11,452.

FINANCIAL AID PICTURE (2015-2016)
Students with need: Out of 312 full-time freshmen who applied for aid, 293 were judged to have need. Of these, 293 received aid, and 26 had their full need met. For part-time students, average financial aid package was $7,401.
Students without need: 22 full-time freshmen who did not demonstrate need for aid received scholarships/grants; average award was $13,303. No-need awards available for academics, alumni affiliation, leadership, minority status.

FINANCIAL AID PROCEDURES
Forms required: FAFSA.
Dates and Deadlines: Priority date 3/17; no closing date. Applicants notified on a rolling basis starting 2/1; must reply by 5/1 or within 2 week(s) of notification.

CONTACT
Jen Bates, Executive Directror of Financial Aid
141 Central Avenue, Keuka Park, NY 14478-0098
(315) 279-5232

The King's College

New York, New York
www.tkc.edu   Federal Code: 040953

4-year private liberal arts college in very large city, affiliated with the nondenominational tradition.
Enrollment: 520 undergrads, 2% part-time. 149 full-time freshmen.

BASIC COSTS (2016-2017)

Tuition and fees: $34,320.
Per-credit charge: $1,410.
Room only: $13,650.

FINANCIAL AID PICTURE (2015-2016)

Students with need: Out of 138 full-time freshmen who applied for aid, 119 were judged to have need. Of these, 119 received aid, and 12 had their full need met. Average financial aid package met 65% of need; average scholarship/grant was $22,725; average loan was $3,375. For part-time students, average financial aid package was $14,018.

Students without need: 30 full-time freshmen who did not demonstrate need for aid received scholarships/grants; average award was $14,626. No-need awards available for academics, leadership.

Scholarships offered: Presidential Scholarships: unlimited number; based on composite SAT/ACT and high school GPA.

FINANCIAL AID PROCEDURES

Forms required: FAFSA.
Dates and Deadlines: Priority date 11/1; no closing date. Applicants notified on a rolling basis starting 11/15.
Transfers: No deadline. Applicants notified on a rolling basis.

CONTACT

Anna Peters, Director of Financial Aid
56 Broadway, New York, NY 10004
(646) 237-8902

Le Moyne College

Syracuse, New York
www.lemoyne.edu
Federal Code: 002748

4-year private liberal arts college in small city, affiliated with the Roman Catholic Church.
Enrollment: 2,793 undergrads, 9% part-time. 634 full-time freshmen.
Selectivity: Admits 50 to 75% of applicants.

BASIC COSTS (2016-2017)

Tuition and fees: $33,030.
Per-credit charge: $672.
Room and board: $12,970.

FINANCIAL AID PICTURE (2015-2016)

Students with need: Out of 602 full-time freshmen who applied for aid, 534 were judged to have need. Of these, 534 received aid, and 132 had their full need met. Average financial aid package met 80% of need; average scholarship/grant was $22,529; average loan was $3,726. For part-time students, average financial aid package was $6,331.

Students without need: 82 full-time freshmen who did not demonstrate need for aid received scholarships/grants; average award was $16,196. No-need awards available for academics, alumni affiliation, athletics, leadership, minority status, ROTC.

Scholarships offered: *Merit:* Presidential Scholarship: $25,000 per year for 4 years; based on 95% GPA, 1300 SAT/29 ACT; must maintain 3.25 GPA. Dean Scholarship: $18,750 per year for 4 years; based on 92% GPA, 1200 SAT/27 ACT; must maintain 3.0 GPA. Ignatian Scholarship: $18,750 per year for 4 years; awarded to students from Jesuit high schools with superior academic records; must maintain 3.0 GPA. Leader Scholarship: $12,500 per year for 4 years; based on 85% GPA, 1050 SAT/22 ACT; must remain in good academic standing. Loyola Scholarship: $18,750 per year for 4 years; for multicultural students with demonstrated academic excellence; must maintain 3.0 GPA. Academic scholarships are based on the student's admission application; to be considered, students must apply by February 1. *Athletic:* 16 full-time freshmen received athletic scholarships; average amount $15,013.

Additional info: Parent loan program at low interest, monthly payment plans and alternative loans for students.

FINANCIAL AID PROCEDURES

Forms required: FAFSA, state aid form.
Dates and Deadlines: Priority date 2/15; no closing date. Applicants notified by 2/15; must reply by 5/1 or within 2 week(s) of notification.
Transfers: Priority date 5/1; no deadline. Applicants notified on a rolling basis starting 3/15; must reply by 5/1 or within 2 week(s) of notification.

CONTACT

Sharon Halpin, Director of Financial Aid
1419 Salt Springs Road, Syracuse, NY 13214-1301
(315) 445-4400

LIM College

New York, New York
www.limcollege.edu
Federal Code: 007466

4-year for-profit business college in very large city.
Enrollment: 1,499 undergrads, 7% part-time. 269 full-time freshmen.
Selectivity: Admits over 75% of applicants.

BASIC COSTS (2017-2018)

Tuition and fees: $26,350.
Per-credit charge: $830.
Room and board: $20,350.

FINANCIAL AID PICTURE (2015-2016)

Students with need: Out of 258 full-time freshmen who applied for aid, 187 were judged to have need. Of these, 184 received aid, and 12 had their full need met. Average financial aid package met 54% of need; average scholarship/grant was $9,697; average loan was $3,309. For part-time students, average financial aid package was $4,452.

Students without need: 43 full-time freshmen who did not demonstrate need for aid received scholarships/grants; average award was $5,446. No-need awards available for academics, leadership, state/district residency.

Scholarships offered: Fashion Scholarship (Honors) Program: Awards of $7,000 are available to incoming freshmen with a minimum 85 average and a SAT score of 1100 or above on the SAT (24 on the ACT). Students will be evaluated on a first come, first served basis. Additional academic criteria will be considered prior to inviting students into the program.

FINANCIAL AID PROCEDURES

Forms required: FAFSA, state aid form.
Dates and Deadlines: Priority date 3/1; closing date 11/15. Applicants notified on a rolling basis; must reply by 7/31 or within 2 week(s) of notification.
Transfers: No deadline. Applicants notified on a rolling basis starting 12/1.

CONTACT

Christopher Barto, Dean of Student Financial Services
12 East 53rd Street, New York, NY 10022
(212) 752-1530

LIU Brooklyn

Brooklyn, New York
http://liu.edu/brooklyn
Federal Code: 002751

4-year private university and liberal arts college in very large city.
Enrollment: 4,177 undergrads, 10% part-time. 709 full-time freshmen.
Selectivity: Admits over 75% of applicants.

BASIC COSTS (2016-2017)

Tuition and fees: $36,256.
Per-credit charge: $1,072.
Room and board: $13,426.

FINANCIAL AID PICTURE (2016-2017)

Students with need: Out of 667 full-time freshmen who applied for aid, 627 were judged to have need. Of these, 615 received aid, and 31 had their

full need met. Average financial aid package met 55% of need; average scholarship/grant was $13,701; average loan was $3,591. For part-time students, average financial aid package was $6,075.

Students without need: 40 full-time freshmen who did not demonstrate need for aid received scholarships/grants; average award was $14,659. No-need awards available for academics, alumni affiliation, art, athletics, music/drama, ROTC.

Scholarships offered: 55 full-time freshmen received athletic scholarships; average amount $28,290.

FINANCIAL AID PROCEDURES

Forms required: FAFSA.

Dates and Deadlines: Priority date 2/15; no closing date. Applicants notified on a rolling basis starting 2/1; must reply within 4 week(s) of notification.

Transfers: No deadline. Applicants notified on a rolling basis; must reply by 5/1 or within 14 week(s) of notification.

CONTACT

Margaret Nelson, Executive Director of Enrollment Services

1 University Plaza, Brooklyn, NY 11201-8423

(718) 488-1037

LIU Post

Brookville, New York

www.liu.edu/post   Federal Code: 002751

4-year private university and liberal arts college in small town.

Enrollment: 3,133 undergrads, 9% part-time. 533 full-time freshmen.

Selectivity: Admits over 75% of applicants.

BASIC COSTS (2016-2017)

Tuition and fees: $36,256.

Per-credit charge: $1,072.

Room and board: $13,426.

FINANCIAL AID PICTURE (2016-2017)

Students with need: Out of 487 full-time freshmen who applied for aid, 408 were judged to have need. Of these, 398 received aid, and 77 had their full need met. Average financial aid package met 58% of need; average scholarship/grant was $9,190; average loan was $3,435. For part-time students, average financial aid package was $5,649.

Students without need: 83 full-time freshmen who did not demonstrate need for aid received scholarships/grants; average award was $14,635. No-need awards available for academics, alumni affiliation, art, athletics, music/drama, ROTC.

Scholarships offered: 97 full-time freshmen received athletic scholarships; average amount $15,501.

FINANCIAL AID PROCEDURES

Forms required: FAFSA.

Dates and Deadlines: Priority date 2/15; closing date 2/15. Applicants notified on a rolling basis starting 2/1; must reply by 5/1 or within 2 week(s) of notification.

Transfers: No deadline. Applicants notified on a rolling basis; must reply by 5/1 or within 14 week(s) of notification.

CONTACT

Joanne Graziano, Executive Director of Enrollment Services

720 Northern Boulevard, Brookville, NY 11548-1300

(516) 299-2553

Long Island Business Institute

Flushing, New York

www.libi.edu   Federal Code: 020937

2-year for-profit business and career college in very large city.

Enrollment: 1,102 undergrads, 11% part-time. 771 full-time freshmen.

Selectivity: Admits over 75% of applicants.

BASIC COSTS (2017-2018)

Tuition and fees: $14,769.

FINANCIAL AID PICTURE (2016-2017)

Students with need: Out of 238 full-time freshmen who applied for aid, 238 were judged to have need. Of these, 238 received aid. For part-time students, average financial aid package was $2,150.

Students without need: 3 full-time freshmen who did not demonstrate need for aid received scholarships/grants; average award was $500. No-need awards available for academics.

FINANCIAL AID PROCEDURES

Forms required: FAFSA, state aid form.

Dates and Deadlines: Closing date 5/1. Applicants notified by 1/1; must reply by 4/30.

CONTACT

Nazaret Kiregian, Director of Financial Aid

136-18 39th Avenue, 5th Floor, Flushing, NY 11354

(631) 499-7100 ext. 13

Manhattan College

Riverdale, New York

www.manhattan.edu   Federal Code: 002758

4-year private engineering and liberal arts college in very large city, affiliated with the Roman Catholic Church.

Enrollment: 3,637 undergrads, 5% part-time. 900 full-time freshmen.

Selectivity: Admits 50 to 75% of applicants.

BASIC COSTS (2016-2017)

Tuition and fees: $40,365.

Room and board: $15,010.

FINANCIAL AID PICTURE (2015-2016)

Students with need: Average financial aid package met 88% of need; average scholarship/grant was $23,453. Need-based aid available for part-time students.

Students without need: This college awards aid only to students with need.

FINANCIAL AID PROCEDURES

Forms required: FAFSA.

Dates and Deadlines: Priority date 3/1; closing date 4/15. Applicants notified on a rolling basis starting 2/15; must reply by 5/1.

Transfers: Priority date 4/1; no deadline.

CONTACT

Denise Scalzo, Director of Student Financial Aid

4513 Manhattan College Parkway, Riverdale, NY 10471

(718) 862-7100

Manhattan School of Music

New York, New York   Federal Code: 002759

www.msmnyc.edu   CSS Code: 2396

4-year private music college in very large city.

Enrollment: 410 undergrads.

BASIC COSTS (2016-2017)

Tuition and fees: $44,700.

Per-credit charge: $1,800.

Room and board: $12,500.

FINANCIAL AID PICTURE

Students with need: Need-based aid available for full-time and part-time students. Work study available nights, weekends, and for part-time students.

Students without need: No-need awards available for academics, alumni affiliation, leadership, music/drama.

FINANCIAL AID PROCEDURES

Forms required: FAFSA, institutional form. Returning International students are required to complete the CSS Profile on a yearly basis.

Dates and Deadlines: Closing date 3/1. Applicants notified by 4/1; must reply by 5/1 or within 2 week(s) of notification.

Transfers: Applicants notified by 4/1; must reply by 5/1 or within 2 week(s) of notification. CSS PROFILE required for transfer students.

CONTACT

Amy Anderson, Dean of Enrollment Management
120 Claremont Avenue, New York, NY 10027-4698
(212) 749-2802 ext. 4463

Manhattanville College

Purchase, New York
www.mville.edu   Federal Code: 002760

4-year private liberal arts and teachers college in small town.
Enrollment: 1,735 undergrads, 2% part-time. 482 full-time freshmen.
Selectivity: Admits 50 to 75% of applicants.

BASIC COSTS (2017-2018)

Tuition and fees: $37,910.
Per-credit charge: $825.
Room and board: $14,520.

FINANCIAL AID PICTURE (2016-2017)

Students with need: Out of 426 full-time freshmen who applied for aid, 378 were judged to have need. Of these, 378 received aid, and 46 had their full need met. Average financial aid package met 77% of need; average scholarship/grant was $6,761; average loan was $3,641. For part-time students, average financial aid package was $22,162.

Students without need: 96 full-time freshmen who did not demonstrate need for aid received scholarships/grants; average award was $20,039. No-need awards available for academics, alumni affiliation, art, music/drama, religious affiliation.

Additional info: Upper level students may earn additional money and academic credit through internship program.

FINANCIAL AID PROCEDURES

Forms required: FAFSA, state aid form.

Dates and Deadlines: Priority date 3/1; no closing date. Applicants notified on a rolling basis starting 1/1; must reply by 5/1 or within 2 week(s) of notification.

Transfers: Closing date 3/1. Must reply by 5/1.

CONTACT

Robert Gilmore, Director of Financial Aid
2900 Purchase Street, Purchase, NY 10577
(914) 323-5357

Maria College

Albany, New York
www.mariacollege.edu   Federal Code: 002763

2-year private health science and liberal arts college in small city.
Enrollment: 770 undergrads, 68% part-time. 22 full-time freshmen.

BASIC COSTS (2016-2017)

Tuition and fees: $14,210.
Per-credit charge: $595.

FINANCIAL AID PICTURE (2016-2017)

Students with need: Average financial aid package met 61% of need; average scholarship/grant was $3,687; average loan was $3,385. For part-time students, average financial aid package was $5,639.

Students without need: This college awards aid only to students with need.

FINANCIAL AID PROCEDURES

Forms required: FAFSA, state aid form.

Dates and Deadlines: Applicants notified on a rolling basis starting 3/1; must reply within 2 week(s) of notification.

Transfers: No deadline. Applicants notified on a rolling basis; must reply within 2 week(s) of notification.

CONTACT

Donna Myers, Financial Aid
700 New Scotland Avenue, Albany, NY 12208
(518) 861-2586

Marist College

Poughkeepsie, New York
www.marist.edu   Federal Code: 002765

4-year private liberal arts college in small city.
Enrollment: 5,308 undergrads, 6% part-time. 1,225 full-time freshmen.
Selectivity: Admits less than 50% of applicants.

BASIC COSTS (2016-2017)

Tuition and fees: $35,210.
Per-credit charge: $650.
Room and board: $14,650.
Additional info: Tuition/fee waivers available for minority students.

FINANCIAL AID PICTURE (2016-2017)

Students with need: Out of 960 full-time freshmen who applied for aid, 695 were judged to have need. Of these, 693 received aid. Average financial aid package met 65% of need; average scholarship/grant was $18,378; average loan was $4,280. For part-time students, average financial aid package was $7,150.

Students without need: No-need awards available for academics, athletics, music/drama, ROTC, state/district residency.

Scholarships offered: Awards vary, as much as $12,000 per recipient.

FINANCIAL AID PROCEDURES

Forms required: FAFSA, institutional form. PROFILE required for early decision and early action applicants.

Dates and Deadlines: Priority date 2/15; closing date 5/1. Applicants notified on a rolling basis starting 4/1; must reply by 5/1 or within 2 week(s) of notification.

Transfers: No deadline. Applicants notified on a rolling basis. FAFSA should be filed as soon as possible after January 1.

CONTACT

Joseph Weglarz, Executive Director, Student Financial Services
3399 North Road, Poughkeepsie, NY 12601-1387
(845) 575-3230

Marymount Manhattan College

New York, New York
www.mmm.edu   Federal Code: 002769

4-year private liberal arts and performing arts college in very large city.
Enrollment: 2,027 undergrads, 10% part-time. 511 full-time freshmen.
Selectivity: Admits over 75% of applicants.

BASIC COSTS (2016-2017)

Tuition and fees: $30,290.

Per-credit charge: $965.

Room and board: $15,990.

Additional info: Tuition/fee waivers available for adults.

FINANCIAL AID PICTURE (2015-2016)

Students with need: Out of 431 full-time freshmen who applied for aid, 348 were judged to have need. Of these, 346 received aid, and 24 had their full need met. Average financial aid package met 51% of need; average scholarship/grant was $14,781; average loan was $3,293. For part-time students, average financial aid package was $6,549.

Students without need: 77 full-time freshmen who did not demonstrate need for aid received scholarships/grants; average award was $9,202. No-need awards available for academics, art, leadership, music/drama, state/district residency.

Scholarships offered: Prospective Freshmen are considered for academic scholarships based on an equal weighting of the SAT (critical reading and math) or ACT Composite score and the academic GPA at time of application. Presidential Scholarship: $12,000 per year. Dean's Scholarship: $10,000 per year. Trustees' Scholarship: $8,000 per year. Recognition Award: $6,000 per year. Talent scholarships: awarded to full-time, degree-seeking entering freshmen in any of the following majors: Acting (BFA), Art (BA), Dance (BA and BFA) and Theatre (BA). Awards range from $1,000 to $6,000 per academic year based on audition or portfolio review.

Additional info: Limited international scholarships for top applicants and diplomats.

FINANCIAL AID PROCEDURES

Forms required: FAFSA, state aid form.

Dates and Deadlines: Priority date 3/15; no closing date. Applicants notified on a rolling basis starting 3/15; must reply by 5/1 or within 2 week(s) of notification.

Transfers: Must submit academic transcripts from previous institutions. Transfer Monitoring is performed in accordance with federal regulations for all transfer students to ensure that students do not exceed their annual federal aid limits.

CONTACT

Maria DeInnocentiis, Asst Vice President - Financial & Registration Services

221 East 71st Street, New York, NY 10021-4597

(212) 517-0556

Medaille College

Buffalo, New York

www.medaille.edu   Federal Code: 002777

4-year private liberal arts college in large city.

Enrollment: 1,635 undergrads.

BASIC COSTS (2016-2017)

Tuition and fees: $27,276.

Per-credit charge: $971.

Room and board: $13,080.

Additional info: Tuition/fee waivers available for adults.

FINANCIAL AID PICTURE

Students with need: Need-based aid available for full-time and part-time students. Work study available nights, weekends, and for part-time students.

Students without need: No-need awards available for academics, leadership.

Scholarships offered: Available from $1,000 to $10,500.

FINANCIAL AID PROCEDURES

Forms required: FAFSA, state aid form.

Dates and Deadlines: Priority date 3/1; no closing date. Applicants notified on a rolling basis starting 3/1; must reply within 2 week(s) of notification.

Transfers: Applicants notified on a rolling basis starting 3/1.

CONTACT

Catherine Buzanski, Director of Financial Aid

18 Agassiz Circle, Buffalo, NY 14214

(716) 880-2256

Mercy College

Dobbs Ferry, New York

www.mercy.edu   Federal Code: 002772

4-year private liberal arts college in large town.

Enrollment: 6,286 undergrads, 18% part-time. 925 full-time freshmen.

Selectivity: Admits over 75% of applicants.

BASIC COSTS (2016-2017)

Tuition and fees: $18,392.

Per-credit charge: $748.

Room and board: $13,700.

FINANCIAL AID PICTURE (2015-2016)

Students with need: Out of 898 full-time freshmen who applied for aid, 838 were judged to have need. Of these, 807 received aid, and 27 had their full need met. Average financial aid package met 56% of need; average scholarship/grant was $11,869; average loan was $3,179. For part-time students, average financial aid package was $4,892.

Students without need: 32 full-time freshmen who did not demonstrate need for aid received scholarships/grants; average award was $4,500. No-need awards available for academics, athletics.

Scholarships offered: 52 full-time freshmen received athletic scholarships; average amount $5,939.

FINANCIAL AID PROCEDURES

Forms required: FAFSA, state aid form.

Dates and Deadlines: Priority date 2/15; no closing date. Applicants notified on a rolling basis starting 2/20; must reply by 5/1 or within 2 week(s) of notification.

Transfers: No deadline. Applicants notified on a rolling basis starting 4/1; must reply within 2 week(s) of notification.

CONTACT

Margaret McGrail, Vice President for Enrollment Services

555 Broadway, Dobbs Ferry, NY 10522

(888) 464-6737

Metropolitan College of New York

New York, New York

www.metropolitan.edu   Federal Code: 009769

4-year private business and liberal arts college in very large city.

Enrollment: 693 undergrads, 10% part-time. 73 full-time freshmen.

Selectivity: Admits less than 50% of applicants.

BASIC COSTS (2017-2018)

Tuition and fees: $19,180.

Per-credit charge: $766.

Additional info: Tuition at time of enrollment locked for 4 years.

FINANCIAL AID PICTURE (2016-2017)

Students with need: Out of 71 full-time freshmen who applied for aid, 69 were judged to have need. Of these, 68 received aid. Average financial aid package met 48% of need; average scholarship/grant was $11,181; average loan was $3,530. For part-time students, average financial aid package was $8,582.

Students without need: 1 full-time freshmen who did not demonstrate need for aid received scholarships/grants; average award was $2,000. No-need awards available for academics.

Additional info: Limited merit scholarships.

FINANCIAL AID PROCEDURES
Forms required: FAFSA.

CONTACT
Douane Campbell, Acting Director of Financial Aid
60 West Street, New York, NY 10006-1735
(212) 343-1234 ext. 3500

Mildred Elley: Albany
Albany, New York
www.mildred-elley.edu   Federal Code: 022195

2-year for-profit junior and career college in small city.
Enrollment: 748 undergrads.
Selectivity: Open admission; but selective for some programs.

BASIC COSTS (2016-2017)
Additional info: Tuition is $450 per credit hour. Additional fees vary depending on program. Tuition at time of enrollment locked for 2 years.

FINANCIAL AID PICTURE
Students with need: Need-based aid available for full-time and part-time students. Work study available nights, weekends, and for part-time students.
Students without need: This college awards aid only to students with need.

FINANCIAL AID PROCEDURES
Forms required: FAFSA, state aid form.
Dates and Deadlines: Applicants notified on a rolling basis starting 7/16; must reply within 2 week(s) of notification.
Transfers: No deadline. Applicants notified on a rolling basis starting 7/16; must reply within 2 week(s) of notification.

CONTACT
Mary Ellen Duffy, Vice President of Financial Aid & Compliance
855 Central Avenue, Albany, NY 12206-1513
(518) 786-0855

Mildred Elley: New York City
New York, New York
www.mildred-elley.edu   Federal Code: 022195

2-year for-profit junior and career college in very large city.
Enrollment: 590 undergrads.
Selectivity: Open admission.

BASIC COSTS (2016-2017)
Additional info: Tuition is $450 per credit hour. Additional fees vary depending on program. Tuition at time of enrollment locked for 2 years.

FINANCIAL AID PICTURE
Students with need: Need-based aid available for full-time and part-time students. Work study available nights, weekends, and for part-time students.
Students without need: This college awards aid only to students with need.

FINANCIAL AID PROCEDURES
Forms required: FAFSA, state aid form.
Transfers: No deadline. Applicants notified on a rolling basis.

CONTACT
Mary Ellen Duffy, Director of Financial Aid
25 Broadway, 16th Floor, New York, NY 10004
(212) 380-9004 ext. 1626

Mohawk Valley Community College
Utica, New York
www.mvcc.edu   Federal Code: 002871

2-year public community college in small city.
Enrollment: 4,298 undergrads, 22% part-time. 1,132 full-time freshmen.
Selectivity: Open admission; but selective for some programs.

BASIC COSTS (2016-2017)
Tuition and fees: $4,822; out-of-state residents $8,906.
Per-credit charge: $165; out-of-state residents $330.
Room and board: $10,100.

FINANCIAL AID PICTURE (2016-2017)
Students with need: Out of 1,054 full-time freshmen who applied for aid, 663 were judged to have need. Of these, 642 received aid, and 529 had their full need met. Average financial aid package met 93% of need; average scholarship/grant was $6,673; average loan was $3,456. For part-time students, average financial aid package was $6,321.
Additional info: First year students must attend an orientation to receive Federal Work Study funds.

FINANCIAL AID PROCEDURES
Forms required: FAFSA, state aid form.
Dates and Deadlines: Priority date 4/15; no closing date. Applicants notified on a rolling basis starting 3/1; must reply within 2 week(s) of notification.
Transfers: No deadline. Applicants notified on a rolling basis; must reply within 2 week(s) of notification.

CONTACT
Michael Pede, Director of Financial Aid
1101 Sherman Drive, Utica, NY 13501-5394
(315) 792-5415

Molloy College
Rockville Centre, New York
www.molloy.edu   Federal Code: 002775

4-year private liberal arts college in large town, affiliated with the Roman Catholic Church.
Enrollment: 3,562 undergrads, 19% part-time. 538 full-time freshmen.
Selectivity: Admits over 75% of applicants.

BASIC COSTS (2016-2017)
Tuition and fees: $29,100.
Per-credit charge: $925.
Room and board: $14,250.
Additional info: Tuition/fee waivers available for unemployed or children of unemployed.

FINANCIAL AID PICTURE (2015-2016)
Students with need: Out of 527 full-time freshmen who applied for aid, 458 were judged to have need. Of these, 456 received aid, and 37 had their full need met. Average financial aid package met 56% of need; average scholarship/grant was $14,182; average loan was $3,142. For part-time students, average financial aid package was $6,146.
Students without need: 58 full-time freshmen who did not demonstrate need for aid received scholarships/grants; average award was $11,780. No-need awards available for academics, alumni affiliation, art, athletics, leadership, music/drama, religious affiliation.
Scholarships offered: *Merit:* Scholar's Program: full tuition for entering full-time freshmen; based on academic achievement and college aptitude test scores; minimum 95 percent high school average and either a minimum 1280 combined SAT score (Critical Reading, math) or a minimum 28 on the ACT; for renewal, must maintain at least a 3.5 cumulative index for a maximum of eight consecutive semesters taking a maximum of 16 credits each semester; recipients must also file required financial aid applications annually

for renewal; application deadline: December 15. **Athletic:** 8 full-time freshmen received athletic scholarships; average amount $6,497.

FINANCIAL AID PROCEDURES
Forms required: FAFSA, state aid form.
Dates and Deadlines: Priority date 4/15; closing date 5/1. Applicants notified on a rolling basis starting 2/1; must reply within 5 week(s) of notification.
Transfers: No deadline. All transfer applicants with a minimum of 30 credits and 3.0 GPA automatically considered for transfer scholarships ranging from $1,500-$3,000.

CONTACT
Ana Lockward, Director of Financial Aid
PO Box 5002, Rockville Centre, NY 11571
(516) 323-4200

Monroe College
Bronx, New York
www.monroecollege.edu   Federal Code: 004799

4-year for-profit business and health science college in very large city.
Enrollment: 5,881 undergrads.
Selectivity: Admits 50 to 75% of applicants.

BASIC COSTS (2016-2017)
Tuition and fees: $14,460.
Per-credit charge: $565.
Room and board: $9,770.

FINANCIAL AID PICTURE
Students with need: Need-based aid available for full-time and part-time students. Work study available nights, weekends, and for part-time students.
Students without need: This college awards aid only to students with need.

FINANCIAL AID PROCEDURES
Forms required: FAFSA.
Dates and Deadlines: Closing date 6/30. Applicants notified on a rolling basis starting 7/1.
Transfers: Applicants notified on a rolling basis.

CONTACT
Daniel Sharon, Financial Aid Director
2501 Jerome Avenue, Bronx, NY 10468
(718) 933-6700

Monroe Community College
Rochester, New York
www.monroecc.edu   Federal Code: 002872

2-year public community college in large city.
Enrollment: 12,425 undergrads, 34% part-time. 2,643 full-time freshmen.
Selectivity: Open admission; but selective for some programs.

BASIC COSTS (2016-2017)
Tuition and fees: $4,591; out-of-state residents $8,691.
Per-credit charge: $171; out-of-state residents $342.
Room only: $6,358.

FINANCIAL AID PICTURE
Students with need: Need-based aid available for full-time and part-time students. Work study available nights, weekends, and for part-time students.
Students without need: This college awards aid only to students with need.

FINANCIAL AID PROCEDURES
Forms required: FAFSA, state aid form.

Dates and Deadlines: Priority date 3/30; no closing date. Applicants notified on a rolling basis starting 3/15; must reply within 2 week(s) of notification.
Transfers: No deadline. Applicants notified on a rolling basis starting 3/15; must reply within 2 week(s) of notification.

CONTACT
Jerome St. Croix, Director of Financial Aid
Office of Admissions-Monroe Community College, Rochester, NY 14692-8908
(585) 292-2050

Mount Saint Mary College
Newburgh, New York
www.msmc.edu   Federal Code: 002778

4-year private liberal arts college in large town, affiliated with the Roman Catholic Church.
Enrollment: 2,106 undergrads, 17% part-time. 384 full-time freshmen.
Selectivity: Admits over 75% of applicants.

BASIC COSTS (2016-2017)
Tuition and fees: $29,048.
Per-credit charge: $935.
Room and board: $14,104.
Additional info: Tuition/fee waivers available for adults.

FINANCIAL AID PICTURE (2016-2017)
Students with need: Out of 375 full-time freshmen who applied for aid, 323 were judged to have need. Of these, 323 received aid, and 54 had their full need met. Average financial aid package met 70% of need; average scholarship/grant was $18,817; average loan was $3,404. For part-time students, average financial aid package was $8,503.
Students without need: 58 full-time freshmen who did not demonstrate need for aid received scholarships/grants; average award was $12,120. No-need awards available for academics, alumni affiliation, leadership, ROTC, state/district residency.
Scholarships offered: Presidential Scholarship: approximately 65% of tuition in the year of enrollment; renewable for three years with minimum 3.0 GPA. Merit Awards: $3,000-$7,500; renewable each year with 2.5 GPA. Based on combined SAT/ACT test scores, GPA, and class rank.

FINANCIAL AID PROCEDURES
Forms required: FAFSA.
Dates and Deadlines: Priority date 2/15; closing date 3/1. Applicants notified on a rolling basis starting 3/1; must reply by 5/1.
Transfers: Applicants notified on a rolling basis starting 3/15; must reply by 5/1.

CONTACT
Jason Franky, Interim Director of Financial Aid
330 Powell Avenue, Newburgh, NY 12550
(845) 569-3194

Nassau Community College
Garden City, New York
www.ncc.edu   Federal Code: 002873

2-year public community college in large town.
Enrollment: 18,204 undergrads, 38% part-time. 3,539 full-time freshmen.
Selectivity: Open admission; but selective for some programs.

BASIC COSTS (2016-2017)
Tuition and fees: $5,248; out-of-state residents $10,116.
Per-credit charge: $203; out-of-state residents $406.

FINANCIAL AID PICTURE

Students with need: Need-based aid available for full-time and part-time students. Work study available nights, weekends, and for part-time students.

Students without need: No-need awards available for academics, minority status.

FINANCIAL AID PROCEDURES

Forms required: FAFSA, state aid form.

Dates and Deadlines: Priority date 6/7; no closing date. Applicants notified on a rolling basis; must reply within 1 week(s) of notification.

CONTACT

Patricia Noren, Director, Financial Aid Office
One Education Drive, Garden City, NY 11530
(516) 572-7259

Nazareth College
Rochester, New York
www.naz.edu   Federal Code: 002779

4-year private liberal arts college in large city, affiliated with the interdenominational tradition.

Enrollment: 2,125 undergrads, 4% part-time. 517 full-time freshmen.

Selectivity: Admits 50 to 75% of applicants.

BASIC COSTS (2016-2017)

Tuition and fees: $32,424.

Per-credit charge: $740.

Room and board: $13,150.

Additional info: Tuition/fee waivers available for minority students.

FINANCIAL AID PICTURE (2016-2017)

Students with need: Out of 498 full-time freshmen who applied for aid, 449 were judged to have need. Of these, 449 received aid, and 188 had their full need met. Average financial aid package met 85% of need; average scholarship/grant was $18,244; average loan was $3,389. For part-time students, average financial aid package was $12,234.

Students without need: 68 full-time freshmen who did not demonstrate need for aid received scholarships/grants; average award was $18,512. No-need awards available for academics, art, leadership, minority status, music/drama, state/district residency.

FINANCIAL AID PROCEDURES

Forms required: FAFSA, state aid form.

Dates and Deadlines: Priority date 2/15; no closing date. Applicants notified on a rolling basis starting 2/1; must reply by 5/1.

Transfers: No deadline. Applicants notified on a rolling basis.

CONTACT

Janice Scheutzow, Director of Financial Aid
4245 East Avenue, Rochester, NY 14618-3790
(585) 389-2310

The New School College of Performing Arts
New York, New York
www.newschool.edu   Federal Code: 002780

4-year private performing arts college in very large city.

Enrollment: 564 undergrads, 3% part-time. 144 full-time freshmen.

Selectivity: Admits less than 50% of applicants.

BASIC COSTS (2016-2017)

Tuition and fees: $44,540.

Per-credit charge: $1,480.

Room and board: $18,420.

FINANCIAL AID PICTURE

Students with need: Need-based aid available for full-time and part-time students. Work study available nights, weekends, and for part-time students.

Students without need: No-need awards available for academics, art, leadership, minority status, music/drama, state/district residency.

FINANCIAL AID PROCEDURES

Forms required: FAFSA, state aid form.

Dates and Deadlines: Closing date 3/1. Applicants notified on a rolling basis starting 4/1; must reply within 4 week(s) of notification.

CONTACT

Lisa Shaheen, Director of Student Financial Aid
79 Fifth Avenue, Floor 5, New York, NY 10003
(212) 229-8930

New York Career Institute
New York, New York
www.nyci.edu   Federal Code: 014576

2-year for-profit career college in very large city.

Enrollment: 204 undergrads.

Selectivity: Open admission.

BASIC COSTS (2016-2017)

Tuition and fees: $13,700.

FINANCIAL AID PICTURE

Students with need: Need-based aid available for full-time and part-time students. Work study available nights.

Students without need: This college awards aid only to students with need.

FINANCIAL AID PROCEDURES

Dates and Deadlines: Applicants notified on a rolling basis.

CONTACT

Brenda Soriano, Director of Student Financial Aid Services
11 Park Place, New York, NY 10007

New York Institute of Technology
Old Westbury, New York
www.nyit.edu   Federal Code: 002782

4-year private engineering and health science college in small town.

Enrollment: 3,577 undergrads, 9% part-time. 699 full-time freshmen.

Selectivity: Admits 50 to 75% of applicants.

BASIC COSTS (2016-2017)

Tuition and fees: $35,160.

Room and board: $13,570.

FINANCIAL AID PICTURE (2015-2016)

Students with need: Out of 639 full-time freshmen who applied for aid, 567 were judged to have need. Of these, 565 received aid. For part-time students, average financial aid package was $9,533.

Students without need: 95 full-time freshmen who did not demonstrate need for aid received scholarships/grants; average award was $12,963. No-need awards available for academics, athletics.

Scholarships offered: 41 full-time freshmen received athletic scholarships; average amount $12,380.

FINANCIAL AID PROCEDURES

Forms required: FAFSA.

Dates and Deadlines: Priority date 3/1; no closing date. Applicants notified on a rolling basis starting 3/1; must reply within 4 week(s) of notification.

CONTACT
Rosemary Ferrucci, Senior Director of Financial Aid
Box 8000, Old Westbury, NY 11568-8000
(516) 686-3835

New York School of Interior Design
New York, New York
www.nysid.edu   Federal Code: 013606

4-year private visual arts college in very large city.
Enrollment: 335 undergrads.

BASIC COSTS (2016-2017)
Tuition and fees: $30,945.
Per-credit charge: $915.
Room and board: $21,000.

FINANCIAL AID PICTURE
Students with need: Need-based aid available for full-time and part-time students. Work study available nights, weekends, and for part-time students.
Students without need: No-need awards available for academics, art.

FINANCIAL AID PROCEDURES
Forms required: FAFSA, state aid form.
Dates and Deadlines: Priority date 8/1; no closing date. Applicants notified on a rolling basis starting 4/15; must reply within 2 week(s) of notification.
Transfers: Applicants notified on a rolling basis starting 4/15; must reply within 2 week(s) of notification.

CONTACT
Audrey Zahor, Financial Aid Coordinator
170 East 70th Street, New York, NY 10021-5110
(212) 472-1500 ext. 204

New York University
New York, New York   Federal Code: 002785
www.nyu.edu   CSS Code: 2562

4-year private university in very large city.
Enrollment: 25,716 undergrads, 4% part-time. 5,886 full-time freshmen.
Selectivity: Admits less than 50% of applicants.

BASIC COSTS (2016-2017)
Tuition and fees: $49,062.
Per-credit charge: $1,373.
Room and board: $17,578.
Additional info: Tuition at time of enrollment locked for 4 years.

FINANCIAL AID PICTURE (2015-2016)
Students with need: Out of 3,880 full-time freshmen who applied for aid, 2,918 were judged to have need. Of these, 2,852 received aid, and 260 had their full need met. Average financial aid package met 67% of need; average scholarship/grant was $34,462; average loan was $3,823. For part-time students, average financial aid package was $13,231.
Students without need: 175 full-time freshmen who did not demonstrate need for aid received scholarships/grants; average award was $4,476.

FINANCIAL AID PROCEDURES
Forms required: FAFSA, CSS PROFILE.
Dates and Deadlines: Closing date 2/15. Applicants notified by 4/1; must reply by 5/1.
Transfers: Priority date 2/15. Applicants notified on a rolling basis; must reply within 3 week(s) of notification. Transfer students must apply for financial aid by November 1st if applicant is a Spring transfer. Spring transfer applicants begin receiving financial aid notification in mid-November. Transfer students must apply for financial aid by April 1st if applicant is a Summer or Fall transfer. Summer and Fall transfer applicants receive financial aid notification

throughout the month of May. Fall transfer applicants for the College of Nursing Second Bachelor's Degree Program begin receiving financial aid notification in April.

CONTACT
M J Knoll-Finn, Vice President for Enrollment Management
665 Broadway, 11th floor, New York, NY 10012-2339
(212) 998-4444

Niagara County Community College
Sanborn, New York
www.niagaracc.suny.edu   Federal Code: 002874

2-year public community college in rural community.
Enrollment: 4,372 undergrads, 23% part-time. 1,068 full-time freshmen.
Selectivity: Open admission; but selective for some programs.

BASIC COSTS (2016-2017)
Tuition and fees: $4,518; out-of-state residents $10,638.
Per-credit charge: $170; out-of-state residents $425.

FINANCIAL AID PICTURE (2015-2016)
Students with need: 60% of average financial aid package awarded as scholarships/grants, 40% awarded as loans/jobs. Need-based aid available for part-time students. Work study available nights.
Students without need: This college awards aid only to students with need.
Additional info: Assistance offered with placing students in part-time employment through the Job Locator office. Students can charge books and food coupons.

FINANCIAL AID PROCEDURES
Forms required: FAFSA, state aid form.
Dates and Deadlines: Priority date 4/1; no closing date. Applicants notified on a rolling basis starting 5/1; must reply within 2 week(s) of notification.
Transfers: Must file appropriate state and federal change forms at least 4 weeks before registration date.

CONTACT
James Trimboli, Director of Financial Aid
3111 Saunders Settlement Road, Sanborn, NY 14132-9460
(716) 614-6266

Niagara University
Niagara University, New York
www.niagara.edu   Federal Code: 002788

4-year private university in small city, affiliated with the Roman Catholic Church.
Enrollment: 3,045 undergrads, 4% part-time. 615 full-time freshmen.
Selectivity: Admits over 75% of applicants.

BASIC COSTS (2016-2017)
Tuition and fees: $30,950.
Per-credit charge: $985.
Room and board: $12,700.
Additional info: Tuition at time of enrollment locked for 4 years.

FINANCIAL AID PICTURE (2016-2017)
Students with need: Out of 533 full-time freshmen who applied for aid, 512 were judged to have need. Of these, 512 received aid, and 268 had their full need met. Average financial aid package met 86% of need; average scholarship/grant was $23,519; average loan was $4,649. For part-time students, average financial aid package was $10,412.
Students without need: 95 full-time freshmen who did not demonstrate need for aid received scholarships/grants; average award was $15,699. No-need awards available for academics, alumni affiliation, athletics, leadership,

minority status, music/drama, religious affiliation, ROTC, state/district residency.

Scholarships offered: *Merit:* Trustee Scholarship: $19,000-$24,000; minimum 94 average; 1220 SAT or 25-26 ACT average; or 91 average, 1280 SAT or 27 ACT; unlimited. Presidential Scholarship: $17,000; 90 average, 1130 SAT or 23 ACT; 85 average; 1190 sat or 24 ACT; unlimited. Achievement Award: $15,000; mid to upper 80 average; 1030-1130 SAT or 20-22 ACT; unlimited. Niagara University Grant: $10,000; mid 80 average; SAT above 1030 or ACT above 20; unlimited. *Athletic:* 40 full-time freshmen received athletic scholarships; average amount $19,483.

Additional info: Opportunity program available for academically and economically disadvantaged students.

FINANCIAL AID PROCEDURES

Forms required: FAFSA, state aid form.

Dates and Deadlines: Priority date 2/15; no closing date. Applicants notified on a rolling basis starting 3/1; must reply within 3 week(s) of notification.

Transfers: Must reply within 3 week(s) of notification. Academic scholarship available: $14,000 per year (3.75 GPA or higher); $13,000 per year (3.50 - 3.749 GPA); $12,000 per year (3.25-3.49 GPA); $11,000 per year (3.0 to 3.249 GPA); $9,000 per year (2.75-2.99 GPA); $8,000 per year (2.5 to 2.749 GPA).

CONTACT

Katie Kocsis, Director of Financial Aid
Gacioch Center, Niagara University, NY 14109
(716) 286-8686

North Country Community College

Saranac Lake, New York
www.nccc.edu   Federal Code: 007111

2-year public community college in small town.

Enrollment: 2,680 undergrads.

Selectivity: Open admission; but selective for some programs.

BASIC COSTS (2016-2017)

Tuition and fees: $5,212; out-of-state residents $11,362.

Per-credit charge: $185; out-of-state residents $441.

Room and board: $9,750.

Additional info: Annual room rate based on single-occupancy bedroom within suite; no double-occupancy rooms available.

FINANCIAL AID PICTURE

Students with need: Need-based aid available for full-time and part-time students. Work study available nights, weekends, and for part-time students.

Students without need: This college awards aid only to students with need.

FINANCIAL AID PROCEDURES

Forms required: FAFSA, state aid form.

Dates and Deadlines: Priority date 4/1; no closing date. Applicants notified on a rolling basis starting 4/1; must reply within 3 week(s) of notification.

CONTACT

Edwin Trathen, Vice President for Enrollment and Student Services
23 Santanoni Avenue, Saranac Lake, NY 12983
(518) 891-2915 ext. 229

Nyack College

Nyack, New York
www.nyack.edu   Federal Code: 002790

4-year private liberal arts and seminary college in large town, affiliated with the Christian and Missionary Alliance.

Enrollment: 1,439 undergrads, 18% part-time. 204 full-time freshmen.

Selectivity: Admits over 75% of applicants.

BASIC COSTS (2017-2018)

Tuition and fees: $25,350.

Per-credit charge: $1,040.

Room and board: $9,450.

FINANCIAL AID PICTURE

Students with need: Need-based aid available for full-time students. Work study available nights, weekends, and for part-time students.

Students without need: No-need awards available for academics, alumni affiliation, athletics, leadership, music/drama, religious affiliation, state/district residency.

FINANCIAL AID PROCEDURES

Forms required: FAFSA.

Dates and Deadlines: Priority date 3/31; no closing date. Applicants notified on a rolling basis starting 3/1; must reply within 4 week(s) of notification.

CONTACT

Steve Phillips, Director of Student Financial Aid
1 South Boulevard, Nyack, NY 10960-3698
(845) 675-4737

Onondaga Community College

Syracuse, New York
www.sunyocc.edu   Federal Code: 002875

2-year public community college in small city.

Enrollment: 7,818 undergrads, 29% part-time. 2,031 full-time freshmen.

Selectivity: Open admission; but selective for some programs.

BASIC COSTS (2016-2017)

Tuition and fees: $5,154; out-of-state residents $9,724.

Per-credit charge: $190; out-of-state residents $380.

Room and board: $9,100.

FINANCIAL AID PICTURE (2015-2016)

Students with need: Out of 1,904 full-time freshmen who applied for aid, 1,671 were judged to have need. Of these, 1,568 received aid, and 58 had their full need met. Average financial aid package met 59% of need; average scholarship/grant was $6,241; average loan was $3,123. For part-time students, average financial aid package was $3,757.

Students without need: This college awards aid only to students with need.

FINANCIAL AID PROCEDURES

Forms required: FAFSA, state aid form.

Dates and Deadlines: Applicants notified on a rolling basis; must reply within 4 week(s) of notification.

CONTACT

Rebecca Rose, Director of Financial Aid
4585 West Seneca Turnpike, Syracuse, NY 13215-4585
(315) 498-2291

Orange County Community College

Middletown, New York
www.sunyorange.edu   Federal Code: 002876

2-year public community college in large town.

Enrollment: 5,271 undergrads, 41% part-time. 1,119 full-time freshmen.

Selectivity: Open admission; but selective for some programs.

BASIC COSTS (2016-2017)

Tuition and fees: $5,260; out-of-state residents $9,896.

Per-credit charge: $193; out-of-state residents $386.

Additional info: Tuition/fee waivers available for unemployed or children of unemployed.

FINANCIAL AID PICTURE (2015-2016)

Students with need: 58% of average financial aid package awarded as scholarships/grants, 42% awarded as loans/jobs. Need-based aid available for part-time students. Work study available nights.

FINANCIAL AID PROCEDURES

Forms required: FAFSA, state aid form.

Dates and Deadlines: Priority date 4/15; closing date 7/1. Applicants notified on a rolling basis starting 4/1; must reply within 4 week(s) of notification.

CONTACT

John Ivankovic, Director of Financial Aid
115 South Street, Middletown, NY 10940-0115
(845) 341-4190

Pace University

New York, New York
www.pace.edu   Federal Code: 002791

4-year private university in very large city.
Enrollment: 5,916 undergrads, 8% part-time. 1,406 full-time freshmen.
Selectivity: Admits over 75% of applicants.

BASIC COSTS (2016-2017)

Tuition and fees: $42,722.
Per-credit charge: $1,180.
Room and board: $18,280.

FINANCIAL AID PICTURE (2016-2017)

Students with need: Out of 1,097 full-time freshmen who applied for aid, 987 were judged to have need. Of these, 986 received aid, and 131 had their full need met. Average financial aid package met 71% of need; average scholarship/grant was $27,583; average loan was $3,985. For part-time students, average financial aid package was $6,426.

Students without need: 325 full-time freshmen who did not demonstrate need for aid received scholarships/grants; average award was $20,954. No-need awards available for academics, alumni affiliation, athletics, music/drama.

FINANCIAL AID PROCEDURES

Forms required: FAFSA.

Dates and Deadlines: Priority date 11/15; no closing date. Applicants notified on a rolling basis starting 12/1; must reply by 5/1 or within 2 week(s) of notification.

Transfers: Applicants notified on a rolling basis starting 3/1; must reply by 5/1 or within 2 week(s) of notification.

CONTACT

Mark Stephens, University Director, Financial Aid
1 Pace Plaza, New York, NY 10038-1598
(877) 672-1830

Pace University: Pleasantville/Briarcliff

Pleasantville, New York
www.pace.edu   Federal Code: 002791

4-year private university in small town.
Enrollment: 2,468 undergrads, 11% part-time. 567 full-time freshmen.
Selectivity: Admits over 75% of applicants.

BASIC COSTS (2016-2017)

Tuition and fees: $42,772.
Per-credit charge: $1,180.
Room and board: $15,476.

FINANCIAL AID PICTURE (2016-2017)

Students with need: Out of 528 full-time freshmen who applied for aid, 477 were judged to have need. Of these, 477 received aid, and 81 had their full need met. Average financial aid package met 81% of need; average scholarship/grant was $32,352; average loan was $4,081. For part-time students, average financial aid package was $7,029.

Students without need: 81 full-time freshmen who did not demonstrate need for aid received scholarships/grants; average award was $23,928. No-need awards available for academics, alumni affiliation, athletics, music/drama.

Scholarships offered: 6 full-time freshmen received athletic scholarships; average amount $11,333.

FINANCIAL AID PROCEDURES

Forms required: FAFSA.

Dates and Deadlines: Priority date 11/15; no closing date. Applicants notified on a rolling basis starting 12/1; must reply by 5/1 or within 2 week(s) of notification.

Transfers: Applicants notified on a rolling basis starting 3/1; must reply by 5/1 or within 2 week(s) of notification.

CONTACT

Mark Stephens, Director of Financial Aid
861 Bedford Road, Pleasantville, NY 10570
(877) 672-1830

Parsons The New School for Design

New York, New York
www.newschool.edu   Federal Code: 002780

4-year private visual arts college in very large city.
Enrollment: 4,299 undergrads, 12% part-time. 924 full-time freshmen.
Selectivity: Admits 50 to 75% of applicants.

BASIC COSTS (2016-2017)

Tuition and fees: $46,036.
Per-credit charge: $1,530.
Room and board: $17,170.

FINANCIAL AID PICTURE

Students with need: Need-based aid available for full-time and part-time students. Work study available nights, weekends, and for part-time students.

Students without need: No-need awards available for academics, art, leadership, minority status, music/drama, state/district residency.

FINANCIAL AID PROCEDURES

Forms required: FAFSA, state aid form.

Dates and Deadlines: Closing date 2/1. Applicants notified on a rolling basis starting 4/1; must reply within 4 week(s) of notification.

CONTACT

Lisa Shaheen, Director of Student Financial Aid
79 Fifth Avenue, Floor 5, New York, NY 10003
(212) 229-8930

Paul Smith's College

Paul Smiths, New York
www.paulsmiths.edu   Federal Code: 002795

4-year private culinary school and liberal arts college in rural community.
Enrollment: 850 undergrads, 1% part-time. 228 full-time freshmen.
Selectivity: Admits over 75% of applicants.

BASIC COSTS (2017-2018)

Tuition and fees: $27,621.
Room and board: $11,870.

FINANCIAL AID PICTURE (2015-2016)

Students with need: Need-based aid available for full-time students. Work study available nights, weekends, and for part-time students.

Students without need: No-need awards available for academics.

Additional info: Merit aid only for international students; no financial aid application required.

FINANCIAL AID PROCEDURES

Forms required: FAFSA.

Dates and Deadlines: Priority date 3/31; no closing date. Applicants notified on a rolling basis starting 3/5; must reply within 4 week(s) of notification.

Transfers: No deadline. Applicants notified by 2/5; must reply within 4 week(s) of notification.

CONTACT

Mary Ellen Chamberlain, Director of Financial Aid

PO Box 265, Routes 30 & 86, Paul Smiths, NY 12970-0265

(518) 327-6220

Phillips School of Nursing at Mount Sinai Beth Israel

New York, New York

www.pson.edu   Federal Code: 006438

2-year private nursing college in very large city.

Enrollment: 202 undergrads, 81% part-time. 1 full-time freshmen.

Selectivity: Admits less than 50% of applicants.

BASIC COSTS (2016-2017)

Tuition and fees: $26,577.

Per-credit charge: $575.

FINANCIAL AID PICTURE

Students with need: Need-based aid available for full-time and part-time students.

Scholarships offered: PVH Scholarship Program: full nursing course tuition; based on academic achievement.

FINANCIAL AID PROCEDURES

Forms required: FAFSA, state aid form, institutional form.

Dates and Deadlines: Closing date 6/30. Applicants notified by 8/1; must reply within 3 week(s) of notification.

Transfers: Priority date 6/1. Applicants notified by 8/1; must reply within 3 week(s) of notification.

CONTACT

Joel Legurre, Financial Aid Manager

776 Sixth Avenue, Fourth Floor, New York, NY 10001

(212) 614-6104

Pratt Institute

Brooklyn, New York

www.pratt.edu   Federal Code: 002798

4-year private university and visual arts college in very large city.

Enrollment: 3,271 undergrads, 3% part-time. 707 full-time freshmen.

Selectivity: Admits 50 to 75% of applicants.

BASIC COSTS (2017-2018)

Tuition and fees: $50,038.

Per-credit charge: $1,548..

Room and board: $12,020.

FINANCIAL AID PICTURE (2016-2017)

Students with need: Need-based aid available for full-time and part-time students.

Students without need: No-need awards available for academics.

FINANCIAL AID PROCEDURES

Forms required: FAFSA, state aid form.

Dates and Deadlines: Priority date 2/1; closing date 3/1. Applicants notified by 3/15; must reply by 4/1.

Transfers: Must reply by 5/1 or within 2 week(s) of notification.

CONTACT

Nedzad Goga, Director of Financial Aid

200 Willoughby Avenue, Brooklyn, NY 11205-3817

(718) 636-3519

Rensselaer Polytechnic Institute

Troy, New York   Federal Code: 002803

www.rpi.edu   CSS Code: 2757

4-year private university in small city.

Enrollment: 6,200 undergrads. 1,691 full-time freshmen.

Selectivity: Admits less than 50% of applicants.

BASIC COSTS (2016-2017)

Tuition and fees: $50,797.

Per-credit charge: $2,060.

Room and board: $14,630.

FINANCIAL AID PICTURE

Students with need: Need-based aid available for full-time students. Work study available nights, weekends, and for part-time students.

Students without need: No-need awards available for academics, alumni affiliation, art, athletics, leadership, minority status, music/drama, ROTC.

Scholarships offered: Rensselaer Medals: $15,000; awarded by participating high schools for excellence in science and mathematics.

FINANCIAL AID PROCEDURES

Forms required: FAFSA, CSS PROFILE.

Dates and Deadlines: Closing date 2/1. Applicants notified by 3/12.

Transfers: No deadline. Applicants notified on a rolling basis starting 3/31. Entering transfer students must complete two applications to apply for institutional and federal need-based aid: FAFSA and Transfer Financial Aid Application/Verification Worksheet (available upon acceptance). A number of special transfer scholarships available each year.

CONTACT

Lynnette Koch, Director of Financial Aid

110 Eighth Street, Troy, NY 12180-3590

(518) 276-6813

Roberts Wesleyan College

Rochester, New York   Federal Code: 002805

www.roberts.edu   CSS Code: 2759

4-year private liberal arts college in large city, affiliated with the Free Methodist Church of North America.

Enrollment: 1,266 undergrads, 5% part-time. 232 full-time freshmen.

Selectivity: Admits 50 to 75% of applicants.

BASIC COSTS (2016-2017)

Tuition and fees: $29,740.

Room and board: $10,212.

FINANCIAL AID PICTURE (2016-2017)

Students with need: Out of 204 full-time freshmen who applied for aid, 187 were judged to have need. Of these, 187 received aid, and 23 had their full need met. Average financial aid package met 79% of need; average scholarship/grant was $21,060; average loan was $4,613. For part-time students, average financial aid package was $5,785.

Students without need: 42 full-time freshmen who did not demonstrate need for aid received scholarships/grants; average award was $13,643.

Scholarships offered: 15 full-time freshmen received athletic scholarships; average amount $8,772.

Additional info: Dollars for Scholars offer matching grants of up to $750.

FINANCIAL AID PROCEDURES

Forms required: FAFSA, CSS PROFILE.

Dates and Deadlines: Applicants notified on a rolling basis starting 11/1; must reply by 5/1 or within 2 week(s) of notification.

Transfers: No deadline. Applicants notified on a rolling basis starting 2/28; must reply within 3 week(s) of notification.

CONTACT

Stephen Field, Director of Student Financial Services

2301 Westside Drive, Rochester, NY 14624-1997

(585) 594-6150

Rochester Institute of Technology

Rochester, New York

www.rit.edu   Federal Code: 002806

4-year private university in large city.

Enrollment: 12,704 undergrads, 4% part-time. 2,903 full-time freshmen.

Selectivity: Admits 50 to 75% of applicants.

BASIC COSTS (2016-2017)

Tuition and fees: $38,568.

Per-credit charge: $1,408.

Room and board: $12,500.

Additional info: Tuition/fee waivers available for unemployed or children of unemployed.

FINANCIAL AID PICTURE (2015-2016)

Students with need: Out of 2,574 full-time freshmen who applied for aid, 2,232 were judged to have need. Of these, 2,231 received aid, and 1,833 had their full need met. Average financial aid package met 87% of need; average scholarship/grant was $22,000; average loan was $4,600. For part-time students, average financial aid package was $9,500.

Students without need: 548 full-time freshmen who did not demonstrate need for aid received scholarships/grants; average award was $11,792. No-need awards available for academics, art, leadership, ROTC.

Scholarships offered: Presidential Scholarships: $10,000-$16,000 per year, Founders Scholarships: $7,000-$10,000 per year.

Additional info: Most juniors and seniors participate in cooperative education program, earning an average $4,500-$6,500 per 3-month employment period through paid employment in jobs related to major.

FINANCIAL AID PROCEDURES

Forms required: FAFSA, state aid form.

Dates and Deadlines: Priority date 3/1; no closing date. Applicants notified on a rolling basis starting 3/15; must reply by 5/1.

Transfers: Priority date 3/15. Applicants notified on a rolling basis starting 4/1; must reply by 5/1. Special merit scholarship programs available specifically for transfers with high GPA.

CONTACT

Larry Chambers, Associate Vice President and Director of Financial Aid

60 Lomb Memorial Drive, Rochester, NY 14623-5604

(585) 475-2186

Rockland Community College

Suffern, New York

www.sunyrockland.edu   Federal Code: 002877

2-year public community college in large town.

Enrollment: 5,821 undergrads.

Selectivity: Open admission.

BASIC COSTS (2016-2017)

Tuition and fees: $4,818; out-of-state residents $9,248.

Per-credit charge: $185; out-of-state residents $370.

FINANCIAL AID PICTURE

Students with need: Need-based aid available for full-time and part-time students. Work study available nights, weekends, and for part-time students.

Scholarships offered: Jack Watson Scholarship: minimum 3.5 high school GPA or 94 average in Regents; 5 awarded; $1,163 per semester; renewable for 2nd year. Alumni Scholarship: for children of alumni; 75 average; varying amounts.

FINANCIAL AID PROCEDURES

Forms required: FAFSA, institutional form.

Dates and Deadlines: Priority date 5/31; no closing date. Applicants notified on a rolling basis starting 6/1.

CONTACT

Debra Bouabidi, Director of Financial Aid

145 College Road, Suffern, NY 10901-3699

(845) 574-4282

The Sage Colleges

Troy, New York

www.sage.edu   Federal Code: 002810

4-year private university in small city.

Enrollment: 1,431 undergrads, 11% part-time. 205 full-time freshmen.

Selectivity: Admits 50 to 75% of applicants.

BASIC COSTS (2016-2017)

Tuition and fees: $28,805.

Per-credit charge: $914.

Room and board: $12,408.

FINANCIAL AID PICTURE (2016-2017)

Students with need: Out of 200 full-time freshmen who applied for aid, 192 were judged to have need. Of these, 192 received aid. Need-based aid available for part-time students.

Students without need: 5 full-time freshmen who did not demonstrate need for aid received scholarships/grants; average award was $13,400. No-need awards available for academics, alumni affiliation, art, leadership, minority status, music/drama, state/district residency.

Scholarships offered: Multiple awards to qualified students: Presidential and Dean's scholarship, first-generation scholarship, valedictorian-salutatorian scholarship, student Sage scholarship, endowed scholarships for minority students and specific majors.

FINANCIAL AID PROCEDURES

Forms required: FAFSA, state aid form.

Dates and Deadlines: Priority date 2/15; no closing date. Applicants notified on a rolling basis starting 1/20; must reply by 5/1 or within 2 week(s) of notification.

Transfers: Applicants notified on a rolling basis starting 3/1.

CONTACT

Kelley Robinson, Director of Financial Aid

65 1st Street, Troy, NY 12180-4115

(518) 244-4525

Saint Bonaventure University

St. Bonaventure, New York

www.sbu.edu   Federal Code: 002817

4-year private university in large town, affiliated with the Roman Catholic Church.

Enrollment: 1,609 undergrads, 1% part-time. 390 full-time freshmen.

Selectivity: Admits 50 to 75% of applicants.

BASIC COSTS (2016-2017)
Tuition and fees: $32,331.
Per-credit charge: $934.
Room and board: $11,463.
Additional info: Tuition/fee waivers available for minority students.

FINANCIAL AID PICTURE (2015-2016)
Students with need: Out of 363 full-time freshmen who applied for aid, 306 were judged to have need. Of these, 306 received aid, and 70 had their full need met. Average financial aid package met 90% of need; average scholarship/grant was $23,396; average loan was $3,963. For part-time students, average financial aid package was $9,126.
Students without need: 82 full-time freshmen who did not demonstrate need for aid received scholarships/grants; average award was $14,942. No-need awards available for academics, athletics, minority status, music/drama, religious affiliation, ROTC, state/district residency.
Scholarships offered: Merit: Buckeye Award: $2,000; for first-time freshmen who graduate from a high school in Ohio (except students receiving athletic awards); renewable. Geographic Diversity Award: $2,000; given to all out-of-state students except those who graduate from high schools in Ohio, who will receive Buckeye Award. **Athletic:** 49 full-time freshmen received athletic scholarships; average amount $14,636.
Additional info: Families experiencing financial difficulties not adequately reflected by the FAFSA should contact the Office of Financial Assistance. Outside scholarships do not reduce other financial aid unless, when added to total aid, the new total exceeds need. If it exceeds need, then loans and work are reduced first.

FINANCIAL AID PROCEDURES
Forms required: FAFSA, state aid form.
Dates and Deadlines: Priority date 2/15; no closing date. Applicants notified on a rolling basis starting 3/1; must reply by 5/1 or within 2 week(s) of notification.
Transfers: Priority date 3/1; no deadline. Applicants notified on a rolling basis starting 3/15; must reply by 5/1 or within 2 week(s) of notification.

CONTACT
Troy Martin, Director of Financial Aid
Box D, St. Bonaventure, NY 14778
(716) 375-2400

St. Elizabeth College of Nursing
Utica, New York
www.secon.edu   Federal Code: 006461

2-year private nursing college in small city, affiliated with the Roman Catholic Church.
Enrollment: 196 undergrads, 69% part-time.
Selectivity: Admits less than 50% of applicants.

BASIC COSTS (2016-2017)
Tuition and fees: $15,570.
Per-credit charge: $425.

FINANCIAL AID PICTURE
Students with need: Need-based aid available for full-time and part-time students.

FINANCIAL AID PROCEDURES
Forms required: FAFSA, state aid form.
Dates and Deadlines: Applicants notified on a rolling basis starting 1/1; must reply within 2 week(s) of notification.

CONTACT
Sherry Wojnas, Director of Finance & Enrollment
2215 Genesee Street, Utica, NY 13501
(315) 801-8206

St. Francis College
Brooklyn Heights, New York
www.sfc.edu   Federal Code: 002820

4-year private liberal arts college in very large city, affiliated with the Roman Catholic Church.
Enrollment: 2,539 undergrads, 8% part-time. 502 full-time freshmen.
Selectivity: Admits 50 to 75% of applicants.

BASIC COSTS (2016-2017)
Tuition and fees: $25,300.
Per-credit charge: $815.
Room only: $14,000.

FINANCIAL AID PICTURE
Students with need: Need-based aid available for full-time and part-time students.
Students without need: No-need awards available for academics, athletics.

FINANCIAL AID PROCEDURES
Forms required: FAFSA, state aid form.
Dates and Deadlines: Priority date 2/15; no closing date. Applicants notified on a rolling basis starting 3/15; must reply within 2 week(s) of notification.
Transfers: No deadline. Applicants notified on a rolling basis.

CONTACT
Hellitz Lopez, Director of Student Financial Services
180 Remsen Street, Brooklyn Heights, NY 11201-9902
(718) 489-5255

St. John Fisher College
Rochester, New York
www.sjfc.edu   Federal Code: 002821

4-year private university and liberal arts college in large town, affiliated with the Roman Catholic Church.
Enrollment: 2,757 undergrads, 5% part-time. 552 full-time freshmen.
Selectivity: Admits 50 to 75% of applicants. GED not accepted.

BASIC COSTS (2016-2017)
Tuition and fees: $31,880.
Per-credit charge: $850.
Room and board: $11,740.

FINANCIAL AID PICTURE (2015-2016)
Students with need: Out of 552 full-time freshmen who applied for aid, 531 were judged to have need. Of these, 440 received aid, and 172 had their full need met. Average financial aid package met 73% of need; average scholarship/grant was $19,284; average loan was $3,668.
Students without need: 112 full-time freshmen who did not demonstrate need for aid received scholarships/grants; average award was $11,756. No-need awards available for academics, leadership.
Scholarships offered: Scholarships range from $10,000 to $14,500. Honors and Science Scholars programs receive additional $3,000 annually. Fisher Service Scholars Program: one-half the total cost of education. First Generation Scholars Program: from $5,000 up to one-half of the total cost of education.

FINANCIAL AID PROCEDURES
Forms required: FAFSA, state aid form.
Dates and Deadlines: Priority date 2/15; no closing date. Applicants notified on a rolling basis starting 3/15; must reply by 5/1 or within 3 week(s) of notification.
Transfers: No deadline. Applicants notified on a rolling basis starting 3/15; must reply within 3 week(s) of notification.

CONTACT

Angela Monnat, Director of Financial Aid
3690 East Avenue, Rochester, NY 14618-3597
(585) 385-8042

St. John's University

Queens, New York
www.stjohns.edu   Federal Code: 002823

4-year private university in very large city, affiliated with the Roman Catholic Church.
Enrollment: 11,768 undergrads, 2% part-time. 3,251 full-time freshmen.
Selectivity: Admits 50 to 75% of applicants.

BASIC COSTS (2016-2017)

Tuition and fees: $39,460.
Per-credit charge: $1,288.
Room and board: $16,760.

FINANCIAL AID PICTURE (2015-2016)

Students with need: Out of 2,971 full-time freshmen who applied for aid, 2,729 were judged to have need. Of these, 2,704 received aid, and 397 had their full need met. Average financial aid package met 70% of need; average scholarship/grant was $9,204; average loan was $3,618. For part-time students, average financial aid package was $10,056.
Students without need: This college awards aid only to students with need.
Scholarships offered: 53 full-time freshmen received athletic scholarships; average amount $25,494.

FINANCIAL AID PROCEDURES

Forms required: FAFSA.
Dates and Deadlines: Priority date 12/15; no closing date. Applicants notified on a rolling basis starting 1/25; must reply within 2 week(s) of notification.
Transfers: No deadline. Applicants notified on a rolling basis starting 1/25; must reply by 5/1. Scholarships available if 12 credits college study completed with a minimum GPA of 3.0.

CONTACT

Jorge Rodriguez, Associate Vice President Student Financial Services
8000 Utopia Parkway, Queens, NY 11439
(718) 990-2000

St. Joseph's College New York: Suffolk Campus

Patchogue, New York
www.sjcny.edu   Federal Code: 002825

4-year private liberal arts and teachers college in large town.
Enrollment: 3,031 undergrads, 15% part-time. 357 full-time freshmen.
Selectivity: Admits 50 to 75% of applicants.

BASIC COSTS (2016-2017)

Tuition and fees: $25,124.
Per-credit charge: $795.

FINANCIAL AID PICTURE (2015-2016)

Students with need: Out of 348 full-time freshmen who applied for aid, 276 were judged to have need. Of these, 276 received aid, and 103 had their full need met. Average financial aid package met 74% of need; average scholarship/grant was $13,006; average loan was $3,032. For part-time students, average financial aid package was $5,781.
Students without need: 65 full-time freshmen who did not demonstrate need for aid received scholarships/grants; average award was $9,903. No-need awards available for academics, alumni affiliation.

FINANCIAL AID PROCEDURES

Forms required: FAFSA, state aid form.
Dates and Deadlines: Priority date 3/15; no closing date. Applicants notified on a rolling basis starting 3/30; must reply by 5/1 or within 2 week(s) of notification.
Transfers: No deadline. Applicants notified on a rolling basis starting 3/30; must reply by 5/1 or within 2 week(s) of notification.

CONTACT

Amy Thompson, Director of Financial Aid
155 West Roe Boulevard, Patchogue, NY 11772-2325
(631) 687-2600

St. Joseph's College of Nursing

Syracuse, New York
www.sjhcon.edu   Federal Code: 006467

2-year private nursing college in small city, affiliated with the Roman Catholic Church.
Enrollment: 287 undergrads, 19% part-time. 2 full-time freshmen.

BASIC COSTS (2017-2018)

Tuition and fees: $21,040.
Per-credit charge: $540.
Room only: $6,000.

FINANCIAL AID PICTURE (2015-2016)

Students with need: 25% of average financial aid package awarded as scholarships/grants, 75% awarded as loans/jobs. Need-based aid available for part-time students.
Students without need: This college awards aid only to students with need.

FINANCIAL AID PROCEDURES

Forms required: FAFSA, state aid form.
Dates and Deadlines: Priority date 3/1; no closing date. Applicants notified on a rolling basis starting 6/15.

CONTACT

Jennifer Prutzman, Coordinator for Financial Aid
206 Prospect Avenue, Syracuse, NY 13203-1892
(315) 448-5040

St. Joseph's College, New York

Brooklyn, New York
www.sjcny.edu   Federal Code: 002825

4-year private liberal arts and teachers college in very large city.
Enrollment: 953 undergrads, 17% part-time. 150 full-time freshmen.
Selectivity: Admits 50 to 75% of applicants.

BASIC COSTS (2016-2017)

Tuition and fees: $25,114.
Per-credit charge: $795.

FINANCIAL AID PICTURE (2015-2016)

Students with need: Out of 149 full-time freshmen who applied for aid, 123 were judged to have need. Of these, 123 received aid, and 24 had their full need met. Average financial aid package met 68% of need; average scholarship/grant was $15,580; average loan was $2,936. For part-time students, average financial aid package was $7,593.
Students without need: 25 full-time freshmen who did not demonstrate need for aid received scholarships/grants; average award was $10,489. No-need awards available for academics, alumni affiliation.

FINANCIAL AID PROCEDURES

Forms required: FAFSA, state aid form.

Dates and Deadlines: Priority date 3/15; no closing date. Applicants notified on a rolling basis starting 3/15; must reply within 2 week(s) of notification.
Transfers: No deadline. Applicants notified on a rolling basis starting 3/30; must reply by 5/1 or within 2 week(s) of notification.

CONTACT
Amy Thompson, Director of Financial Aid
245 Clinton Avenue, Brooklyn, NY 11205-3602
(718) 940-5700

St. Lawrence University
Canton, New York
www.stlawu.edu   Federal Code: 002829

4-year private liberal arts college in small town.
Enrollment: 2,344 undergrads. 565 full-time freshmen.
Selectivity: Admits less than 50% of applicants.

BASIC COSTS (2016-2017)
Tuition and fees: $51,200.
Room and board: $13,190.

FINANCIAL AID PICTURE (2016-2017)
Students with need: Out of 421 full-time freshmen who applied for aid, 373 were judged to have need. Of these, 373 received aid, and 97 had their full need met. Average financial aid package met 85% of need; average scholarship/grant was $35,470; average loan was $3,411.
Students without need: 181 full-time freshmen who did not demonstrate need for aid received scholarships/grants; average award was $17,494. No-need awards available for academics, alumni affiliation, athletics, leadership, minority status, ROTC, state/district residency.
Scholarships offered: Merit: Merit scholarships: $10,000 to $30,000 annually. Augsbury/North Country Scholarship: for students in some schools in northern New York and southern Ontario; nomination by counselor required. Community Service Scholarship: based on past and current service. Presidential Diversity Scholarship: for students of African American, Asian American, Hispanic American and Native American heritage and those who support multiculturalism. Sesquicentennial and University Scholarship: based on academic excellence, character and leadership. Vilas Scholarship: for students interested in business. Leadership Scholarship: based on evidence of leadership in schools and communities. **Athletic:** 12 full-time freshmen received athletic scholarships; average amount $61,390.

FINANCIAL AID PROCEDURES
Forms required: FAFSA.
Dates and Deadlines: Priority date 2/1; closing date 2/1. Applicants notified by 3/30; must reply by 5/1 or within 2 week(s) of notification.
Transfers: Priority date 4/1; closing date 5/1. Applicants notified on a rolling basis starting 6/1; must reply by 5/1 or within 2 week(s) of notification.

CONTACT
Patricia Farmer, Director of Financial Aid
Payson Hall, Canton, NY 13617
(315) 229-5265

St. Thomas Aquinas College
Sparkill, New York
www.stac.edu   Federal Code: 002832

4-year private liberal arts college in large town.
Enrollment: 1,152 undergrads, 5% part-time. 254 full-time freshmen.
Selectivity: Admits over 75% of applicants.

BASIC COSTS (2016-2017)
Tuition and fees: $29,275.
Per-credit charge: $930.

Room and board: $12,390.

FINANCIAL AID PICTURE (2016-2017)
Students with need: Out of 229 full-time freshmen who applied for aid, 207 were judged to have need. Of these, 205 received aid, and 40 had their full need met. Average financial aid package met 34% of need; average scholarship/grant was $10,815; average loan was $3,500. For part-time students, average financial aid package was $9,000.
Students without need: 58 full-time freshmen who did not demonstrate need for aid received scholarships/grants; average award was $13,690. No-need awards available for academics, alumni affiliation, art, athletics, leadership, minority status, music/drama, religious affiliation.
Scholarships offered: 23 full-time freshmen received athletic scholarships; average amount $7,370.

FINANCIAL AID PROCEDURES
Forms required: FAFSA.
Dates and Deadlines: Closing date 6/30. Applicants notified on a rolling basis starting 11/1; must reply within 4 week(s) of notification.
Transfers: Closing date 5/1. Applicants notified on a rolling basis; must reply within 4 week(s) of notification.

CONTACT
Jean-Marie Mohr, Director of Financial Aid
125 Route 340, Sparkill, NY 10976-1050
(845) 398-4097

Sarah Lawrence College
Bronxville, New York   Federal Code: 002813
www.sarahlawrence.edu   CSS Code: 2810

4-year private liberal arts college in small city.
Enrollment: 1,377 undergrads, 1% part-time. 377 full-time freshmen.
Selectivity: Admits less than 50% of applicants.

BASIC COSTS (2016-2017)
Tuition and fees: $52,550.
Room and board: $14,440.

FINANCIAL AID PICTURE (2016-2017)
Students with need: Out of 270 full-time freshmen who applied for aid, 220 were judged to have need. Of these, 219 received aid, and 38 had their full need met. Average financial aid package met 77% of need; average scholarship/grant was $33,546; average loan was $2,244. For part-time students, average financial aid package was $24,169.
Students without need: This college awards aid only to students with need.
Scholarships offered: Presidential and Dean Scholarships: available regardless of need to admitted students demonstrating substantial academic achievement, creativity and potential for leadership; available for up to four years of full-time study contingent on satisfactory academic progress.

FINANCIAL AID PROCEDURES
Forms required: FAFSA, CSS PROFILE, state aid form.
Dates and Deadlines: Priority date 2/1; closing date 2/1. Applicants notified by 4/1; must reply by 5/1.
Transfers: Closing date 3/15. Applicants notified by 5/15. Spring Transfer student must submit financial aid forms by 11/1.

CONTACT
Nicholas Salinas, Director of Financial Aid
1 Mead Way, Bronxville, NY 10708-5999
(914) 395-2570

Schenectady County Community College

Schenectady, New York
www.sunysccc.edu   Federal Code: 006785

2-year public community college in small city.
Enrollment: 4,102 undergrads, 38% part-time. 585 full-time freshmen.
Selectivity: Open admission; but selective for some programs.

BASIC COSTS (2016-2017)
Tuition and fees: $4,368; out-of-state residents $8,088.
Per-credit charge: $155; out-of-state residents $310.

FINANCIAL AID PICTURE (2015-2016)
Students with need: 51% of average financial aid package awarded as scholarships/grants, 49% awarded as loans/jobs. Need-based aid available for part-time students.
Students without need: This college awards aid only to students with need.
Additional info: Federal Work Study for full time students.

FINANCIAL AID PROCEDURES
Forms required: FAFSA.
Dates and Deadlines: Priority date 5/1; no closing date. Applicants notified on a rolling basis starting 3/1; must reply by 8/31.

CONTACT
Mark Bessette, Director of Financial Aid
78 Washington Avenue, Schenectady, NY 12305
(518) 381-1352

School of Visual Arts

New York, New York
www.sva.edu   Federal Code: 007468

4-year for-profit visual arts college in very large city.
Enrollment: 3,602 undergrads, 4% part-time. 742 full-time freshmen.
Selectivity: Admits 50 to 75% of applicants.

BASIC COSTS (2016-2017)
Tuition and fees: $36,500.
Per-credit charge: $1,270.
Room only: $15,400.

FINANCIAL AID PICTURE (2016-2017)
Students with need: Out of 366 full-time freshmen who applied for aid, 330 were judged to have need. Of these, 322 received aid, and 11 had their full need met. For part-time students, average financial aid package was $8,764.
Students without need: 73 full-time freshmen who did not demonstrate need for aid received scholarships/grants; average award was $11,290. No-need awards available for academics, art.
Scholarships offered: SVA matching scholarship available to full- and part-time undergraduate and graduate students. SVA will match 25% of any outside scholarship, up to $2,500, that a student obtains.

FINANCIAL AID PROCEDURES
Forms required: FAFSA, state aid form.
Dates and Deadlines: Priority date 2/1; closing date 3/1. Applicants notified on a rolling basis starting 2/15; must reply within 4 week(s) of notification.
Transfers: No deadline. Applicants notified on a rolling basis; must reply within 4 week(s) of notification.

CONTACT
William Berrios, Director of Financial Aid
209 East 23rd Street, New York, NY 10010-3994
(212) 592-2030

Siena College

Loudonville, New York
www.siena.edu   Federal Code: 002816

4-year private liberal arts college in large town, affiliated with the Roman Catholic Church.
Enrollment: 3,141 undergrads, 3% part-time. 754 full-time freshmen.
Selectivity: Admits 50 to 75% of applicants.

BASIC COSTS (2017-2018)
Tuition and fees: $36,335.
Per-credit charge: $675.
Room and board: $14,550.

FINANCIAL AID PICTURE (2015-2016)
Students with need: Out of 702 full-time freshmen who applied for aid, 605 were judged to have need. Of these, 603 received aid, and 151 had their full need met. Average financial aid package met 82% of need; average scholarship/grant was $23,046; average loan was $3,112. For part-time students, average financial aid package was $18,828.
Students without need: 130 full-time freshmen who did not demonstrate need for aid received scholarships/grants; average award was $13,296. No-need awards available for academics, athletics, leadership, minority status, ROTC, state/district residency.
Scholarships offered: 73 full-time freshmen received athletic scholarships; average amount $18,764.

FINANCIAL AID PROCEDURES
Forms required: FAFSA, state aid form.
Dates and Deadlines: Priority date 10/15; closing date 2/15. Applicants notified by 12/15; must reply by 5/1.

CONTACT
Mary Lawyer, Associate Vice President for Enrollment Management
515 Loudon Road, Loudonville, NY 12211-1462
(518) 783-2427

Skidmore College

Saratoga Springs, New York   Federal Code: 002814
www.skidmore.edu   CSS Code: 2815

4-year private liberal arts college in large town.
Enrollment: 2,661 undergrads, 1% part-time. 714 full-time freshmen.
Selectivity: Admits less than 50% of applicants.

BASIC COSTS (2016-2017)
Tuition and fees: $50,834.
Per-credit charge: $1,657.
Room and board: $13,530.

FINANCIAL AID PICTURE (2016-2017)
Students with need: Out of 340 full-time freshmen who applied for aid, 277 were judged to have need. Of these, 277 received aid, and 277 had their full need met. Average financial aid package met 100% of need; average scholarship/grant was $41,900; average loan was $2,975. Need-based aid available for part-time students.
Students without need: 1 full-time freshmen who did not demonstrate need for aid received scholarships/grants; average award was $12,000. No-need awards available for music/drama.
Scholarships offered: Porter Presidential Scholarships in Science and Mathematics: $15,000 annually; based on outstanding ability and achievement in math, science, or computer science. Filene Undergraduate Music Scholarships: $12,000 annually; based on music ability.

FINANCIAL AID PROCEDURES
Forms required: CSS PROFILE.
Dates and Deadlines: Closing date 2/1. Applicants notified by 4/1; must reply by 5/1.

Transfers: Priority date 4/1. Applicants notified on a rolling basis starting 4/15; must reply within 3 week(s) of notification. Some transfer students eligible for need-based grant assistance.

CONTACT

Beth Post-Lundquist, Director of Financial Aid
815 North Broadway, Saratoga Springs, NY 12866
(518) 580-5750

Suffolk County Community College
Selden, New York
www.sunysuffolk.edu　　　Federal Code: 002878

2-year public community college in large town.
Enrollment: 21,231 undergrads.
Selectivity: Open admission; but selective for some programs.

BASIC COSTS (2016-2017)

Tuition and fees: $5,500; out-of-state residents $10,270.
Per-credit charge: $199; out-of-state residents $398.

FINANCIAL AID PICTURE

Students with need: Need-based aid available for full-time and part-time students. Work study available nights, weekends, and for part-time students.
Students without need: No-need awards available for academics, art, leadership, minority status, music/drama, state/district residency.

FINANCIAL AID PROCEDURES

Forms required: FAFSA, state aid form.
Dates and Deadlines: Priority date 4/15; closing date 6/1. Applicants notified on a rolling basis starting 4/15; must reply within 2 week(s) of notification.
Transfers: No deadline. Applicants notified on a rolling basis starting 4/15.

CONTACT

Rose Bancroft, College Director of Financial Aid
533 College Road, Selden, NY 11784
(631) 451-4110

Sullivan County Community College
Loch Sheldrake, New York
www.sunysullivan.edu　　　Federal Code: 002879

2-year public community college in small town.
Enrollment: 1,074 undergrads, 25% part-time. 325 full-time freshmen.
Selectivity: Open admission; but selective for some programs.

BASIC COSTS (2016-2017)

Tuition and fees: $5,550; out-of-state residents $10,224.
Per-credit charge: $195; out-of-state residents $312.
Room and board: $9,450.

FINANCIAL AID PICTURE (2015-2016)

Students with need: 79% of average financial aid package awarded as scholarships/grants, 21% awarded as loans/jobs. Need-based aid available for part-time students.
Students without need: No-need awards available for academics, leadership, state/district residency.
Additional info: 60% of students hold part-time jobs locally.

FINANCIAL AID PROCEDURES

Forms required: FAFSA.
Dates and Deadlines: Priority date 4/15; no closing date. Applicants notified on a rolling basis starting 5/15; must reply within 2 week(s) of notification.
Transfers: No deadline.

CONTACT

James Winderl, Director of Financial Aid
112 College Road, Loch Sheldrake, NY 12759-5151
(845) 434-5750 ext. 4231

SUNY College at Brockport
Brockport, New York
www.brockport.edu　　　Federal Code: 002841

4-year public liberal arts college in small town.
Enrollment: 7,062 undergrads, 10% part-time. 1,145 full-time freshmen.
Selectivity: Admits 50 to 75% of applicants.

BASIC COSTS (2016-2017)

Tuition and fees: $7,928; out-of-state residents $17,778.
Per-credit charge: $270; out-of-state residents $680.
Room and board: $12,418.

FINANCIAL AID PICTURE (2015-2016)

Students with need: Out of 967 full-time freshmen who applied for aid, 770 were judged to have need. Of these, 758 received aid, and 126 had their full need met. Average financial aid package met 72% of need; average scholarship/grant was $7,010; average loan was $4,827. For part-time students, average financial aid package was $5,285.
Students without need: 53 full-time freshmen who did not demonstrate need for aid received scholarships/grants; average award was $4,662. No-need awards available for academics, alumni affiliation, art, leadership, minority status, music/drama, ROTC.
Scholarships offered: Extraordinary Academic Scholarships: $2,250 to $6,470 per year; minimum qualifications include SAT scores of 1100 (24 ACT), rank in top 50% of class, 90 average or higher.

FINANCIAL AID PROCEDURES

Forms required: FAFSA, state aid form.
Dates and Deadlines: Priority date 1/1; no closing date. Applicants notified on a rolling basis starting 1/1; must reply by 2/1 or within 3 week(s) of notification.

CONTACT

J Atkinson, Director of Enrollment Services/ Director of Financial Aid
350 New Campus Drive, Brockport, NY 14420-2915
(585) 395-2501

SUNY College at Buffalo
Buffalo, New York
www.buffalostate.edu　　　Federal Code: 002842

4-year public liberal arts and teachers college in large city.
Enrollment: 8,360 undergrads, 9% part-time. 1,619 full-time freshmen.
Selectivity: Admits 50 to 75% of applicants.

BASIC COSTS (2016-2017)

Tuition and fees: $7,700; out-of-state residents $17,550.
Room and board: $13,142.
Additional info: Tuition/fee waivers available for minority students.

FINANCIAL AID PICTURE (2015-2016)

Students with need: Need-based aid available for full-time and part-time students.
Students without need: This college awards aid only to students with need.
Scholarships offered: Empire Minority Scholarships: $1,000 annually for 4 years. Honors Program: $2,000 for 2 years and $1,000 for remaining 2 years.

FINANCIAL AID PROCEDURES

Forms required: FAFSA.

Dates and Deadlines: Priority date 3/1; closing date 5/1. Applicants notified on a rolling basis starting 5/1; must reply within 4 week(s) of notification.
Transfers: No deadline.

CONTACT

Connie Cooke, Director of Financial Aid
1300 Elmwood Avenue, Moot Hall, Buffalo, NY 14222-1095
(716) 878-4902

SUNY College at Cortland

Cortland, New York
www2.cortland.edu/home   Federal Code: 002843

4-year public liberal arts and teachers college in large town.
Enrollment: 6,292 undergrads, 2% part-time. 1,016 full-time freshmen.
Selectivity: Admits 50 to 75% of applicants.

BASIC COSTS (2016-2017)

Tuition and fees: $8,106; out-of-state residents $17,956.
Per-credit charge: $270; out-of-state residents $680.
Room and board: $12,200.

FINANCIAL AID PICTURE (2015-2016)

Students with need: Out of 942 full-time freshmen who applied for aid, 680 were judged to have need. Of these, 652 received aid, and 60 had their full need met. Average financial aid package met 67% of need; average scholarship/grant was $5,369; average loan was $3,542. For part-time students, average financial aid package was $7,479.
Students without need: 52 full-time freshmen who did not demonstrate need for aid received scholarships/grants; average award was $3,674. No-need awards available for academics, art, leadership, minority status, music/drama, state/district residency.

FINANCIAL AID PROCEDURES

Forms required: FAFSA, state aid form.
Dates and Deadlines: Priority date 3/1; no closing date. Applicants notified on a rolling basis starting 3/15; must reply by 5/1 or within 4 week(s) of notification.

CONTACT

Karen Gallagher, Director of Financial Aid
PO Box 2000, Cortland, NY 13045-0900
(607) 753-4717

SUNY College at Fredonia

Fredonia, New York
www.fredonia.edu   Federal Code: 002844

4-year public liberal arts college in large town.
Enrollment: 4,359 undergrads, 2% part-time. 918 full-time freshmen.
Selectivity: Admits 50 to 75% of applicants.

BASIC COSTS (2016-2017)

Tuition and fees: $8,089; out-of-state residents $17,939.
Per-credit charge: $270; out-of-state residents $680.
Room and board: $12,730.

FINANCIAL AID PICTURE (2016-2017)

Students with need: Out of 869 full-time freshmen who applied for aid, 707 were judged to have need. Of these, 698 received aid, and 104 had their full need met. Average financial aid package met 65% of need; average scholarship/grant was $6,062; average loan was $5,482. For part-time students, average financial aid package was $5,739.
Students without need: 139 full-time freshmen who did not demonstrate need for aid received scholarships/grants; average award was $3,833. No-need awards available for academics, alumni affiliation, art, minority status, music/drama, state/district residency.

Additional info: More than 80% of students receive financial aid, and over $2 million in merit and need-based scholarships are available to academically qualified, new and returning students each year.

FINANCIAL AID PROCEDURES

Forms required: FAFSA, state aid form.
Dates and Deadlines: Applicants notified on a rolling basis starting 12/1; must reply by 5/1.
Transfers: Priority date 1/31; no deadline. Applicants notified on a rolling basis starting 10/15. Financial aid transcripts required from prior institutions attended.

CONTACT

Daniel Tramuta, Associate Vice President for Enrollment Services & Director of Financial Aid
280 Central Avenue, Fenner House, Fredonia, NY 14063-1136
(716) 673-3253

SUNY College at Geneseo

Geneseo, New York
www.geneseo.edu   Federal Code: 002845

4-year public liberal arts and teachers college in small town.
Enrollment: 5,405 undergrads, 2% part-time. 1,233 full-time freshmen.
Selectivity: Admits 50 to 75% of applicants.

BASIC COSTS (2016-2017)

Tuition and fees: $8,176; out-of-state residents $18,026.
Per-credit charge: $270; out-of-state residents $680.
Room and board: $12,264.

FINANCIAL AID PICTURE (2016-2017)

Students with need: Out of 1,075 full-time freshmen who applied for aid, 603 were judged to have need. Of these, 603 received aid, and 63 had their full need met. Average financial aid package met 40% of need; average scholarship/grant was $2,348; average loan was $2,832. For part-time students, average financial aid package was $5,943.
Students without need: 141 full-time freshmen who did not demonstrate need for aid received scholarships/grants; average award was $3,545. No-need awards available for academics, art, leadership, minority status, music/drama, religious affiliation, state/district residency.

FINANCIAL AID PROCEDURES

Forms required: FAFSA, state aid form.
Dates and Deadlines: Closing date 2/15. Applicants notified on a rolling basis starting 3/15; must reply by 5/1.
Transfers: Priority date 2/15; no deadline. Applicants notified on a rolling basis; must reply by 5/1.

CONTACT

Susan Romano, Director of Financial Aid
1 College Circle, Geneseo, NY 14454-1401
(585) 245-5731

SUNY College at New Paltz

New Paltz, New York
www.newpaltz.edu   Federal Code: 002846

4-year public liberal arts college in large town.
Enrollment: 6,582 undergrads, 6% part-time. 1,089 full-time freshmen.
Selectivity: Admits less than 50% of applicants.

BASIC COSTS (2016-2017)

Tuition and fees: $7,760; out-of-state residents $17,610.
Per-credit charge: $270; out-of-state residents $680.
Room and board: $12,000.

FINANCIAL AID PICTURE (2016-2017)

Students with need: Out of 980 full-time freshmen who applied for aid, 679 were judged to have need. Of these, 669 received aid, and 46 had their full need met. Average financial aid package met 57% of need; average scholarship/grant was $5,256; average loan was $3,348. For part-time students, average financial aid package was $6,186.

Students without need: This college awards aid only to students with need.

FINANCIAL AID PROCEDURES

Forms required: FAFSA, state aid form.

Dates and Deadlines: Priority date 3/15; no closing date. Applicants notified on a rolling basis starting 4/1.

Transfers: No deadline. Applicants notified on a rolling basis starting 4/1; must reply within 4 week(s) of notification.

CONTACT

Maureen Lohan-Bremer, Director of Financial Aid
100 Hawk Drive, New Paltz, NY 12561-2443
(845) 257-3250

SUNY College at Old Westbury

Old Westbury, New York
www.oldwestbury.edu   Federal Code: 007109

4-year public business and liberal arts college in small city.

Enrollment: 4,084 undergrads, 12% part-time. 498 full-time freshmen.

Selectivity: Admits 50 to 75% of applicants.

BASIC COSTS (2016-2017)

Tuition and fees: $7,683; out-of-state residents $17,533.

Per-credit charge: $270; out-of-state residents $680.

Room and board: $11,130.

FINANCIAL AID PICTURE (2016-2017)

Students with need: Out of 339 full-time freshmen who applied for aid, 287 were judged to have need. Of these, 271 received aid, and 271 had their full need met. Average financial aid package met 61% of need; average scholarship/grant was $8,332; average loan was $3,088. For part-time students, average financial aid package was $5,367.

Students without need: 4 full-time freshmen who did not demonstrate need for aid received scholarships/grants; average award was $1,912. No-need awards available for academics, alumni affiliation, state/district residency.

FINANCIAL AID PROCEDURES

Forms required: FAFSA, state aid form, institutional form.

Dates and Deadlines: Closing date 4/1. Applicants notified on a rolling basis starting 4/15; must reply within 2 week(s) of notification.

Transfers: No deadline. Applicants notified on a rolling basis starting 4/15; must reply within 2 week(s) of notification. Financial aid transcript required.

CONTACT

Mildred O'Keefe, Director of Financial Aid
Box 307, Old Westbury, NY 11568-0307
(516) 876-3222

SUNY College at Oswego

Oswego, New York
www.oswego.edu   Federal Code: 002848

4-year public university in large town.

Enrollment: 7,113 undergrads, 3% part-time. 1,440 full-time freshmen.

Selectivity: Admits 50 to 75% of applicants.

BASIC COSTS (2016-2017)

Tuition and fees: $7,957; out-of-state residents $17,807.

Per-credit charge: $270; out-of-state residents $680.

Room and board: $13,390.

FINANCIAL AID PICTURE (2016-2017)

Students with need: Out of 1,305 full-time freshmen who applied for aid, 1,010 were judged to have need. Of these, 1,002 received aid, and 61 had their full need met. Average financial aid package met 83% of need; average scholarship/grant was $8,317; average loan was $4,321. For part-time students, average financial aid package was $8,783.

Students without need: 293 full-time freshmen who did not demonstrate need for aid received scholarships/grants; average award was $2,237. No-need awards available for academics, state/district residency.

Scholarships offered: Annual scholarships: $500 to $4,400; based on class rank in top 15%. Additional residential scholarships for out-of-state students: $4,490 annually; requires on-campus housing.

FINANCIAL AID PROCEDURES

Forms required: FAFSA, state aid form.

Dates and Deadlines: Priority date 2/15; no closing date. Applicants notified on a rolling basis starting 1/15; must reply by 5/1 or within 3 week(s) of notification.

Transfers: No deadline. Applicants notified on a rolling basis starting 3/1; must reply by 5/1 or within 21 week(s) of notification.

CONTACT

Mark Humbert, Director of Financial Aid
229 Sheldon Hall, Oswego, NY 13126-3599
(315) 312-2248

SUNY College at Plattsburgh

Plattsburgh, New York
www.plattsburgh.edu   Federal Code: 002849

4-year public liberal arts and teachers college in large town.

Enrollment: 5,170 undergrads, 7% part-time. 962 full-time freshmen.

Selectivity: Admits 50 to 75% of applicants.

BASIC COSTS (2016-2017)

Tuition and fees: $7,906; out-of-state residents $17,756.

Per-credit charge: $270; out-of-state residents $680.

Room and board: $12,150.

FINANCIAL AID PICTURE (2015-2016)

Students with need: Out of 857 full-time freshmen who applied for aid, 656 were judged to have need. Of these, 647 received aid, and 116 had their full need met. Average financial aid package met 78% of need; average scholarship/grant was $8,751; average loan was $6,688. For part-time students, average financial aid package was $5,871.

Students without need: 176 full-time freshmen who did not demonstrate need for aid received scholarships/grants; average award was $4,613. No-need awards available for academics, alumni affiliation, art, leadership, minority status, music/drama, state/district residency.

FINANCIAL AID PROCEDURES

Forms required: FAFSA, state aid form.

Dates and Deadlines: Priority date 12/15; no closing date. Applicants notified on a rolling basis starting 12/15.

Transfers: No deadline. Applicants notified on a rolling basis.

CONTACT

Todd Moravec, Director of Student Financial Services
Kehoe Administration Building, Plattsburgh, NY 12901
(518) 564-4076

SUNY College at Potsdam
Potsdam, New York
www.potsdam.edu   Federal Code: 002850

4-year public liberal arts and teachers college in large town.
Enrollment: 3,406 undergrads, 3% part-time. 784 full-time freshmen.
Selectivity: Admits 50 to 75% of applicants.

BASIC COSTS (2016-2017)
Tuition and fees: $7,984; out-of-state residents $17,834.
Per-credit charge: $270; out-of-state residents $680.
Room and board: $12,420.

FINANCIAL AID PICTURE (2016-2017)
Students with need: Out of 762 full-time freshmen who applied for aid, 639 were judged to have need. Of these, 638 received aid, and 37 had their full need met. Average financial aid package met 96% of need; average scholarship/grant was $9,812; average loan was $3,904. For part-time students, average financial aid package was $8,434.
Students without need: 59 full-time freshmen who did not demonstrate need for aid received scholarships/grants; average award was $2,905. No-need awards available for academics, art, leadership, music/drama.
Additional info: Apply early to access limited, need-based awards.

FINANCIAL AID PROCEDURES
Forms required: FAFSA, state aid form.
Dates and Deadlines: Priority date 3/1; closing date 5/1. Applicants notified on a rolling basis starting 2/1; must reply by 5/1 or within 4 week(s) of notification.
Transfers: Transfer Scholars Program for incoming transfer students based upon outstanding academic achievement as measured by previous college GPA. $1,000-$3,000 to students with minimum cumulative GPA of 3.25 and higher. Renewable for 1 year with cumulative 3.25 GPA.

CONTACT
Susan Godreau, Director of Financial Aid
44 Pierrepont Avenue, Potsdam, NY 13676
(315) 267-2162

SUNY College at Purchase
Purchase, New York
www.purchase.edu   Federal Code: 006791

4-year public university and liberal arts college in large town.
Enrollment: 3,944 undergrads, 6% part-time. 729 full-time freshmen.
Selectivity: Admits less than 50% of applicants.

BASIC COSTS (2016-2017)
Tuition and fees: $8,267; out-of-state residents $18,117.
Per-credit charge: $270; out-of-state residents $680.
Room and board: $12,952.

FINANCIAL AID PICTURE (2016-2017)
Students with need: Out of 657 full-time freshmen who applied for aid, 471 were judged to have need. Of these, 469 received aid, and 2 had their full need met. Average financial aid package met 44% of need; average scholarship/grant was $8,807; average loan was $3,468. For part-time students, average financial aid package was $8,760.
Students without need: 70 full-time freshmen who did not demonstrate need for aid received scholarships/grants; average award was $2,465. No-need awards available for academics, art, minority status, music/drama.
Additional info: All applicants automatically considered for scholarship upon review of applications, essays, auditions, and/or portfolio.

FINANCIAL AID PROCEDURES
Forms required: FAFSA, state aid form.
Dates and Deadlines: Priority date 2/1; no closing date. Applicants notified on a rolling basis starting 3/1; must reply within 2 week(s) of notification.

Transfers: Financial aid transcripts required from all previously attended institutions.

CONTACT
Corey York, Director of Financial Aid
735 Anderson Hill Road, Purchase, NY 10577-1400
(914) 251-6350

SUNY College of Agriculture and Technology at Cobleskill
Cobleskill, New York
www.cobleskill.edu   Federal Code: 002856

2-year public agricultural and technical college in small town.
Enrollment: 2,288 undergrads, 4% part-time. 755 full-time freshmen.
Selectivity: Admits over 75% of applicants.

BASIC COSTS (2016-2017)
Tuition and fees: $7,931; out-of-state residents $17,781.
Per-credit charge: $269.58; out-of-state residents $680.
Room and board: $13,180.

FINANCIAL AID PICTURE (2015-2016)
Students with need: Out of 711 full-time freshmen who applied for aid, 627 were judged to have need. Of these, 621 received aid, and 5 had their full need met. Average financial aid package met 36% of need; average scholarship/grant was $4,671; average loan was $2,054. For part-time students, average financial aid package was $2,688.
Students without need: 27 full-time freshmen who did not demonstrate need for aid received scholarships/grants; average award was $133. No-need awards available for academics, alumni affiliation, leadership.
Additional info: Application deadline for scholarships March 15. Separate application required, available through admissions office.

FINANCIAL AID PROCEDURES
Forms required: FAFSA, state aid form, institutional form.
Dates and Deadlines: Priority date 2/15; no closing date. Applicants notified on a rolling basis starting 3/1; must reply by 3/1.
Transfers: No deadline. Applicants notified on a rolling basis; must reply within 3 week(s) of notification.

CONTACT
Louise Biron, Director of Financial Aid
Knapp Hall, Cobleskill, NY 12043
(800) 295-8998

SUNY College of Agriculture and Technology at Morrisville
Morrisville, New York
www.morrisville.edu   Federal Code: 002859

4-year public agricultural and technical college in rural community.
Enrollment: 2,765 undergrads, 6% part-time. 811 full-time freshmen.
Selectivity: Admits over 75% of applicants.

BASIC COSTS (2016-2017)
Tuition and fees: $8,023; out-of-state residents $12,553.
Per-credit charge: $270; out-of-state residents $458.
Room and board: $13,838.
Additional info: Tuition/fee waivers available for unemployed or children of unemployed.

FINANCIAL AID PICTURE (2015-2016)
Students with need: Out of 776 full-time freshmen who applied for aid, 691 were judged to have need. Of these, 687 received aid, and 3 had their full need met. Average financial aid package met 48% of need; average

scholarship/grant was $7,325; average loan was $3,363. For part-time students, average financial aid package was $4,691.

Students without need: 119 full-time freshmen who did not demonstrate need for aid received scholarships/grants; average award was $1,711. No-need awards available for academics, alumni affiliation, leadership, minority status, state/district residency.

Scholarships offered: Mustang Merit Awards are offered upon acceptance and are assigned on a first-come, first served basis. Acceptance of any outstanding institutional scholarship offers are due no later than May 1. Failure to accept an offer by May 1 will result in forfeiture of the award, and balance is subject to reassignment. Foundation awards require a separate application due February 1.

FINANCIAL AID PROCEDURES

Forms required: FAFSA, state aid form.

Dates and Deadlines: Priority date 3/1; no closing date. Applicants notified on a rolling basis starting 12/1; must reply by 5/1 or within 4 week(s) of notification.

Transfers: No deadline. Applicants notified on a rolling basis starting 3/15; must reply by 5/1 or within 4 week(s) of notification. Merit scholarships and preferential housing available to qualified transfer students.

CONTACT

Dacia Banks, Director of Financial Aid
PO Box 901, Morrisville, NY 13408-0901

SUNY College of Environmental Science and Forestry

Syracuse, New York
www.esf.edu   Federal Code: 002851

4-year public university and liberal arts college in small city.
Enrollment: 1,751 undergrads, 2% part-time. 318 full-time freshmen.
Selectivity: Admits 50 to 75% of applicants.

BASIC COSTS (2016-2017)

Tuition and fees: $8,103; out-of-state residents $17,953.
Per-credit charge: $270; out-of-state residents $680.
Room and board: $15,750.

FINANCIAL AID PICTURE (2015-2016)

Students with need: Out of 295 full-time freshmen who applied for aid, 262 were judged to have need. Of these, 262 received aid, and 127 had their full need met. Average financial aid package met 82% of need; average scholarship/grant was $6,000; average loan was $4,100. For part-time students, average financial aid package was $4,191.

Students without need: 56 full-time freshmen who did not demonstrate need for aid received scholarships/grants; average award was $3,384. No-need awards available for academics, alumni affiliation, leadership, minority status, ROTC, state/district residency.

Scholarships offered: Merit scholarships: up to 50% of undergraduate tuition; based on high school grades, class rank, and SAT or ACT scores.

FINANCIAL AID PROCEDURES

Forms required: FAFSA, state aid form.

Dates and Deadlines: Priority date 3/1; no closing date. Applicants notified on a rolling basis starting 3/15; must reply by 5/1 or within 2 week(s) of notification.

Transfers: No deadline. Applicants notified on a rolling basis starting 3/15; must reply within 2 week(s) of notification.

CONTACT

Mark Hill, Director of Financial Aid
Gateway Center, Syracuse, NY 13210
(315) 470-6670

SUNY College of Technology at Alfred

Alfred, New York
www.alfredstate.edu   Federal Code: 002854

2-year public liberal arts and technical college in rural community.
Enrollment: 3,712 undergrads, 7% part-time. 1,055 full-time freshmen.
Selectivity: Admits 50 to 75% of applicants.

BASIC COSTS (2016-2017)

Tuition and fees: $8,075; out-of-state residents $17,925.
Per-credit charge: $270; out-of-state residents $406.
Room and board: $11,820.

FINANCIAL AID PICTURE (2015-2016)

Students with need: Out of 1,018 full-time freshmen who applied for aid, 887 were judged to have need. Of these, 869 received aid, and 115 had their full need met. Average financial aid package met 54% of need; average scholarship/grant was $7,217; average loan was $3,333. For part-time students, average financial aid package was $5,599.

Students without need: 56 full-time freshmen who did not demonstrate need for aid received scholarships/grants; average award was $3,417. No-need awards available for academics, alumni affiliation, job skills, music/drama, state/district residency.

FINANCIAL AID PROCEDURES

Forms required: FAFSA, state aid form.

Dates and Deadlines: Applicants notified on a rolling basis starting 11/1; must reply within 4 week(s) of notification.

Transfers: No deadline. Applicants notified on a rolling basis starting 3/15; must reply within 4 week(s) of notification.

CONTACT

Jane Gilliland, Senior Director Student Records and Financial Services
Huntington Administration Building, Alfred, NY 14802-1196
(607) 587-4253

SUNY College of Technology at Canton

Canton, New York
www.canton.edu   Federal Code: 002855

2-year public technical college in small town.
Enrollment: 3,094 undergrads, 14% part-time. 645 full-time freshmen.
Selectivity: Admits over 75% of applicants.

BASIC COSTS (2016-2017)

Tuition and fees: $7,881; out-of-state residents $17,731.
Per-credit charge: $270; out-of-state residents $680.
Room and board: $12,150.

FINANCIAL AID PICTURE (2015-2016)

Students with need: Out of 618 full-time freshmen who applied for aid, 555 were judged to have need. Of these, 550 received aid, and 118 had their full need met. Average financial aid package met 21% of need; average scholarship/grant was $8,722; average loan was $3,511. For part-time students, average financial aid package was $5,166.

Students without need: 6 full-time freshmen who did not demonstrate need for aid received scholarships/grants; average award was $2,667. No-need awards available for academics, alumni affiliation, leadership, minority status, state/district residency.

Additional info: Students can apply after the priority deadline has passed, but not all types of aid will be available.

FINANCIAL AID PROCEDURES

Forms required: FAFSA, state aid form.

Dates and Deadlines: Priority date 3/1; no closing date. Applicants notified on a rolling basis starting 2/15; must reply within 4 week(s) of notification.

Transfers: Financial aid transcripts required from all previously attended schools for mid-year transfers.

CONTACT

Kerrie Cooper, Director of Financial Aid
34 Cornell Drive, Canton, NY 13617-1098
(315) 386-7616

SUNY College of Technology at Delhi

Delhi, New York
www.delhi.edu   Federal Code: 002857

2-year public liberal arts and technical college in rural community.
Enrollment: 3,391 undergrads, 22% part-time. 811 full-time freshmen.
Selectivity: Admits 50 to 75% of applicants.

BASIC COSTS (2016-2017)

Tuition and fees: $8,095; out-of-state residents $17,945.
Per-credit charge: $270; out-of-state residents $452.
Room and board: $11,680.

FINANCIAL AID PICTURE (2015-2016)

Students with need: Out of 688 full-time freshmen who applied for aid,
667 were judged to have need. Of these, 662 received aid, and 21 had their
full need met. Average financial aid package met 57% of need; average
scholarship/grant was $7,908; average loan was $3,285. For part-time students, average financial aid package was $4,472.
Students without need: 8 full-time freshmen who did not demonstrate
need for aid received scholarships/grants; average award was $1,980.

FINANCIAL AID PROCEDURES

Forms required: FAFSA, state aid form.
Dates and Deadlines: Priority date 2/15; no closing date. Applicants notified
on a rolling basis starting 3/1; must reply within 2 week(s) of notification.
Transfers: No deadline. Applicants notified on a rolling basis.

CONTACT

Nancy Hughes, Financial Aid Director
2 Main Street, Delhi, NY 13753-1190
(607) 746-4000

SUNY Downstate Medical Center

Brooklyn, New York
www.downstate.edu   Federal Code: 002839

Upper-division public health science and nursing college in very large city.
Enrollment: 348 undergrads.

BASIC COSTS (2016-2017)

Tuition and fees: $7,074; out-of-state residents $16,924.
Per-credit charge: $270; out-of-state residents $680.
Room only: $4,550.

FINANCIAL AID PICTURE

Students with need: Need-based aid available for full-time and part-time students.

FINANCIAL AID PROCEDURES

Forms required: FAFSA.
Dates and Deadlines: Priority date 3/1; no closing date. Applicants notified
on a rolling basis.

CONTACT

James Newell, Director of Financial Aid
450 Clarkson Avenue, Box 60, Brooklyn, NY 11203-2098
(718) 270-2488

SUNY Empire State College

Saratoga Springs, New York
www.esc.edu   Federal Code: 010286

4-year public liberal arts college in large town.
Enrollment: 9,061 undergrads, 59% part-time. 165 full-time freshmen.
Selectivity: Admits over 75% of applicants.

BASIC COSTS (2016-2017)

Tuition and fees: $6,985; out-of-state residents $16,835.
Per-credit charge: $270; out-of-state residents $680.

FINANCIAL AID PICTURE

Students with need: Need-based aid available for full-time and part-time students.
Students without need: This college awards aid only to students with
need.

FINANCIAL AID PROCEDURES

Forms required: FAFSA, state aid form.
Dates and Deadlines: Priority date 4/1; no closing date. Applicants notified
on a rolling basis; must reply within 3 week(s) of notification.
Transfers: No deadline. Applicants notified on a rolling basis.

CONTACT

Kristina Delbridge, Director of Financial Aid
1 Union Avenue, Saratoga Springs, NY 12866
(518) 587-2100

SUNY Farmingdale State College

Farmingdale, New York
www.farmingdale.edu   Federal Code: 002858

4-year public technical college in large town.
Enrollment: 8,591 undergrads, 21% part-time. 1,248 full-time freshmen.
Selectivity: Admits 50 to 75% of applicants.

BASIC COSTS (2016-2017)

Tuition and fees: $7,860; out-of-state residents $17,710.
Per-credit charge: $270; out-of-state residents $680.
Room and board: $12,764.

FINANCIAL AID PICTURE

Students with need: Need-based aid available for full-time and part-time students.
Students without need: No-need awards available for academics, alumni
affiliation, job skills, state/district residency.

FINANCIAL AID PROCEDURES

Forms required: FAFSA.
Dates and Deadlines: Priority date 4/1; no closing date. Applicants notified
on a rolling basis starting 3/1.

CONTACT

Diane Kazanecki-Kempter, Director of Financial Aid
2350 Broadhollow Road, Farmingdale, NY 11735-1021
(631) 420-2578

SUNY Maritime College

Throggs Neck, New York
www.sunymaritime.edu   Federal Code: 002853

4-year public technical and maritime college in very large city.
Enrollment: 1,626 undergrads, 3% part-time. 334 full-time freshmen.
Selectivity: Admits 50 to 75% of applicants.

BASIC COSTS (2016-2017)

Tuition and fees: $7,834; out-of-state residents $17,684.
Per-credit charge: $270; out-of-state residents $680.
Room and board: $11,948.

FINANCIAL AID PICTURE (2015-2016)

Students with need: Out of 298 full-time freshmen who applied for aid, 193 were judged to have need. Of these, 192 received aid, and 53 had their full need met. Average financial aid package met 41% of need; average scholarship/grant was $4,072; average loan was $1,816. For part-time students, average financial aid package was $3,075.

Students without need: 52 full-time freshmen who did not demonstrate need for aid received scholarships/grants; average award was $1,433. No-need awards available for ROTC.

Scholarships offered: Freshmen New Student Scholarships: $2,500-$10,000 per year, for up to four years; the transfer scholarship award is $1,500 per year, for up to two years. Cadet Appointment Program Scholarship: four-year; full tuition scholarship for undergraduate studies for qualified New York State residents.

Additional info: The Strategic Sealift Officer Program is unique to the maritime schools. The program allows students earning unlimited licenses as Merchant Marine Deck or Engine Officers to be commissioned as an officer in the Navy Reserve upon graduation. Strategic Sealift Officers normally serve on inactive duty in the Individual Ready Reserve allowing them to work as civilians in the maritime industry. Qualified students may apply for the Student Incentive Payments funded by the U.S. Maritime Administration during their freshman year. SIP benefits amount to a maximum of $32,000; $4,000 per semester.

FINANCIAL AID PROCEDURES

Forms required: FAFSA.
Dates and Deadlines: Priority date 3/15; closing date 7/15. Applicants notified on a rolling basis starting 3/15; must reply by 5/1.
Transfers: Must have minimum 2.0 cumulative GPA if degree has not yet been earned.

CONTACT

Andrea Damar, Director of Financial Aid
6 Pennyfield Avenue, Throggs Neck, NY 10465
(718) 409-7268

SUNY Polytechnic Institute

Utica, New York
www.sunypoly.edu   Federal Code: 011678

4-year public business and engineering college in small city.
Enrollment: 1,896 undergrads, 11% part-time. 314 full-time freshmen.
Selectivity: Admits 50 to 75% of applicants.

BASIC COSTS (2016-2017)

Tuition and fees: $7,777; out-of-state residents $17,627.
Per-credit charge: $270; out-of-state residents $680.
Room and board: $12,068.

FINANCIAL AID PICTURE (2016-2017)

Students with need: Out of 288 full-time freshmen who applied for aid, 218 were judged to have need. Of these, 218 received aid, and 218 had their full need met. Average financial aid package met 100% of need; average scholarship/grant was $4,899; average loan was $1,784. For part-time students, average financial aid package was $4,763.

Students without need: 76 full-time freshmen who did not demonstrate need for aid received scholarships/grants; average award was $2,085.

FINANCIAL AID PROCEDURES

Forms required: FAFSA, state aid form.
Dates and Deadlines: Priority date 3/1; no closing date. Applicants notified on a rolling basis starting 3/15; must reply by 5/1 or within 2 week(s) of notification.

Transfers: No deadline. Applicants notified on a rolling basis starting 3/15; must reply within 2 week(s) of notification.

CONTACT

Melissa Rose, Director, Financial Aid
100 Seymour Road, Utica, NY 13502
(315) 792-7210

SUNY University at Albany

Albany, New York
www.albany.edu   Federal Code: 002835

4-year public university in small city.
Enrollment: 12,955 undergrads, 4% part-time. 2,721 full-time freshmen.
Selectivity: Admits 50 to 75% of applicants.

BASIC COSTS (2016-2017)

Tuition and fees: $9,124; out-of-state residents $24,204.
Per-credit charge: $270; out-of-state residents $898.
Room and board: $12,942.

FINANCIAL AID PICTURE

Students with need: Need-based aid available for full-time and part-time students. Work study available nights, weekends, and for part-time students.
Students without need: No-need awards available for academics, athletics, state/district residency.

Scholarships offered: Presidential Scholarship: up to $4,000 per year for NY residents and $6,000 per year for out-of-state students; renewable; requires minimum 90 high school average and combined SAT Critical Reading and Math scores in the upper 1200s or higher.

FINANCIAL AID PROCEDURES

Forms required: FAFSA.
Dates and Deadlines: Priority date 3/15; no closing date. Applicants notified on a rolling basis starting 3/20.

CONTACT

Diane Corbett, Director of Financial Aid
Office of Undergraduate Admissions, University Hall, Albany, NY 12222
(518) 442-3202

SUNY University at Binghamton

Binghamton, New York
www.binghamton.edu   Federal Code: 002836

4-year public university in small city.
Enrollment: 13,578 undergrads, 3% part-time. 2,656 full-time freshmen.
Selectivity: Admits less than 50% of applicants.

BASIC COSTS (2016-2017)

Tuition and fees: $9,271; out-of-state residents $24,351.
Per-credit charge: $270; out-of-state residents $898.
Room and board: $13,590.

FINANCIAL AID PICTURE (2016-2017)

Students with need: Out of 2,181 full-time freshmen who applied for aid, 1,260 were judged to have need. Of these, 1,259 received aid, and 160 had their full need met. Average financial aid package met 63% of need; average scholarship/grant was $9,067; average loan was $3,777. For part-time students, average financial aid package was $6,943.

Students without need: 98 full-time freshmen who did not demonstrate need for aid received scholarships/grants; average award was $6,126. No-need awards available for academics, art, athletics, leadership, minority status, music/drama, state/district residency.

Scholarships offered: 98 full-time freshmen received athletic scholarships; average amount $11,666.

Additional info: Most institutional aid awarded on a first-come first-served basis while considering student's ability to pay (determined by use of the FAFSA application) and the student's academic achievement.

FINANCIAL AID PROCEDURES

Forms required: FAFSA, state aid form.

Dates and Deadlines: Priority date 1/1; closing date 5/1. Applicants notified on a rolling basis starting 1/31; must reply within 2 week(s) of notification.

Transfers: No deadline. Applicants notified on a rolling basis starting 3/1; must reply within 2 week(s) of notification. Awards based on self-reported grade level until an official transfer credit evaluation is completed.

CONTACT

Dennis Chavez, Director, Financial Aid and Student Records
PO Box 6001, Binghamton, NY 13902-6001
(607) 777-2428

SUNY University at Buffalo

Buffalo, New York
www.buffalo.edu   Federal Code: 002837

4-year public university in large city.

Enrollment: 20,102 undergrads, 7% part-time. 4,082 full-time freshmen.

Selectivity: Admits 50 to 75% of applicants.

BASIC COSTS (2016-2017)

Tuition and fees: $9,574; out-of-state residents $26,814.

Per-credit charge: $270; out-of-state residents $988.

Room and board: $13,548.

Additional info: Tuition/fee waivers available for adults, minority students.

FINANCIAL AID PICTURE (2015-2016)

Students with need: Need-based aid available for full-time and part-time students. Work study available nights, weekends, and for part-time students.

Students without need: No-need awards available for academics, art, athletics, minority status, music/drama, state/district residency.

Scholarships offered: Presidential Scholarship: full cost of attendance; minimum 1470 SAT (Critical Reading and Math), or 33 ACT; unweighted high school average of 95 or better; 25 awards. Provost Scholarships: starts at $2,500; minimum high school average of 90; 1200 combined SAT (Critical Reading and Math) or ACT score of 27. Provost Scholarships for outstanding talent in the performing and creative arts: minimum unweighted high school average of 90; minimum 1230 combined SAT (Critical Reading and Math), or minimum 28 ACT. UB Buffalo Partnership Scholars Program: full tuition and fees for up to four consecutive years, a yearly book stipend of $600, and a laptop computer; for students from the Buffalo Public Schools who excel both academically and through civic service to their respective communities.

FINANCIAL AID PROCEDURES

Forms required: FAFSA.

Dates and Deadlines: Priority date 3/1; no closing date. Applicants notified on a rolling basis starting 2/1; must reply by 5/1.

CONTACT

John Gottardy, Director of Financial Aid
12 Capen Hall, Buffalo, NY 14260-1660
(716) 645-2450

SUNY University at Stony Brook

Stony Brook, New York
www.stonybrook.edu   Federal Code: 002838

4-year public university in large town.

Enrollment: 16,863 undergrads, 7% part-time. 2,836 full-time freshmen.

Selectivity: Admits less than 50% of applicants.

BASIC COSTS (2016-2017)

Tuition and fees: $9,000; out-of-state residents $26,240.

Per-credit charge: $270; out-of-state residents $988.

Room and board: $12,882.

FINANCIAL AID PICTURE (2015-2016)

Students with need: Out of 2,139 full-time freshmen who applied for aid, 1,495 were judged to have need. Of these, 1,479 received aid, and 245 had their full need met. Average financial aid package met 71% of need; average scholarship/grant was $10,195; average loan was $3,442. For part-time students, average financial aid package was $5,617.

Students without need: 525 full-time freshmen who did not demonstrate need for aid received scholarships/grants; average award was $5,727. No-need awards available for academics, alumni affiliation, art, athletics, job skills, leadership, music/drama.

Scholarships offered: 54 full-time freshmen received athletic scholarships; average amount $13,675.

FINANCIAL AID PROCEDURES

Forms required: FAFSA, state aid form.

Dates and Deadlines: Priority date 3/1; no closing date. Applicants notified on a rolling basis starting 4/1; must reply by 5/1 or within 2 week(s) of notification.

CONTACT

Jacqueline Pascariello, Director Financial Aid
118 Administration Building, Stony Brook, NY 11794-1901
(631) 632-6840

SUNY Upstate Medical University

Syracuse, New York
www.upstate.edu   Federal Code: 002840

Upper-division public health science and nursing college in small city.

Enrollment: 217 undergrads.

BASIC COSTS (2016-2017)

Tuition and fees: $7,344; out-of-state residents $17,194.

Per-credit charge: $270; out-of-state residents $680.

FINANCIAL AID PICTURE

Students with need: Need-based aid available for full-time and part-time students. Work study available nights, weekends, and for part-time students.

Students without need: This college awards aid only to students with need.

FINANCIAL AID PROCEDURES

Forms required: FAFSA.

Dates and Deadlines: Priority date 3/1; no closing date. Applicants notified on a rolling basis starting 4/1; must reply within 2 week(s) of notification.

Transfers: Applicants notified on a rolling basis starting 4/15; must reply within 2 week(s) of notification.

CONTACT

Mike Pede, Director of Financial Aid
766 Irving Avenue, Syracuse, NY 13210
(315) 464-4329

Swedish Institute

New York, New York
www.swedishinstitute.edu   Federal Code: 021700

2-year for-profit health science college in very large city.

Enrollment: 273 undergrads.

BASIC COSTS (2016-2017)

Additional info: Nursing: $605 per credit; 68 semester credits. Massage Therapy: $520 per credit; 64 semester credits. Advanced Personal Training:

$508 per credit; 62 semester credits. Personal Training: $508 per credit; 37 semester credits. Clinical and Administrative Medical Assistant: $319 per credit; 90 quarter credits. Surgical Technologist: $386 per credit; 94.5 quarter credits. Medical Billing and Coding: $319 per credit; 48 quarter credits. One-time registration fee: $100. Program fees vary per term: ranges from $135 to $705.

FINANCIAL AID PICTURE (2016-2017)
Students with need: Need-based aid available for full-time and part-time students.

Students without need: This college awards aid only to students with need.

FINANCIAL AID PROCEDURES
Forms required: FAFSA, institutional form.

CONTACT
William Bernard, CFO
151 West 26th Street, New York, NY 10001
(212) 924-5900 ext. 223

Syracuse University
Syracuse, New York   Federal Code: 002882
www.syr.edu   CSS Code: 2823

4-year private university in small city.
Enrollment: 14,777 undergrads, 3% part-time. 3,704 full-time freshmen.
Selectivity: Admits 50 to 75% of applicants.

BASIC COSTS (2016-2017)
Tuition and fees: $45,022.
Per-credit charge: $1,891.
Room and board: $15,217.

FINANCIAL AID PICTURE (2016-2017)
Students with need: Need-based aid available for full-time and part-time students.

FINANCIAL AID PROCEDURES
Forms required: FAFSA, CSS PROFILE.
Dates and Deadlines: Closing date 2/1. Applicants notified by 3/15; must reply by 5/1.
Transfers: Closing date 7/1. Applicants notified on a rolling basis starting 3/18; must reply by 5/1 or within 2 week(s) of notification.

CONTACT
Michele Sipley, Director, Financial Aid
900 South Crouse Avenue, Syracuse, NY 13244-5040
(315) 443-1513

Technical Career Institutes
New York, New York
www.tcicollege.edu   Federal Code: 011031

2-year for-profit technical and career college in very large city.
Enrollment: 1,400 undergrads, 17% part-time. 154 full-time freshmen.
Selectivity: Open admission.

BASIC COSTS (2016-2017)
Tuition and fees: $13,800.
Per-credit charge: $548.

FINANCIAL AID PICTURE
Students with need: Need-based aid available for full-time and part-time students.

Students without need: No-need awards available for academics, alumni affiliation.

FINANCIAL AID PROCEDURES
Forms required: FAFSA, institutional form.
Dates and Deadlines: Applicants notified on a rolling basis.

CONTACT
Cynthia Fekaris, Vice President of Financial Aid
320 West 31st Street, New York, NY 10001
(212) 594-4000

Tompkins Cortland Community College
Dryden, New York
www.TC3.edu   Federal Code: 006788

2-year public community college in small town.
Enrollment: 2,493 undergrads, 23% part-time. 707 full-time freshmen.
Selectivity: Open admission; but selective for some programs.

BASIC COSTS (2016-2017)
Tuition and fees: $5,832; out-of-state residents $10,922.
Per-credit charge: $172; out-of-state residents $354.
Room and board: $10,540.

FINANCIAL AID PICTURE
Students with need: Need-based aid available for full-time and part-time students. Work study available nights, weekends, and for part-time students.
Students without need: No-need awards available for academics.

FINANCIAL AID PROCEDURES
Forms required: FAFSA, state aid form, institutional form.
Dates and Deadlines: Priority date 4/15; no closing date. Applicants notified on a rolling basis starting 3/15; must reply within 4 week(s) of notification.

CONTACT
LaSonya Griggs, Director of Financial Aid
170 North Street, Dryden, NY 13053-0139
(607) 844-6580

Touro College
New York, New York
www.touro.edu   Federal Code: 010142

4-year private liberal arts college in very large city.
Enrollment: 5,818 undergrads, 27% part-time. 605 full-time freshmen.
Selectivity: Admits 50 to 75% of applicants.

BASIC COSTS (2016-2017)
Tuition and fees: $16,980.
Per-credit charge: $680.
Room and board: $11,970.

FINANCIAL AID PICTURE (2016-2017)
Students with need: Out of 510 full-time freshmen who applied for aid, 412 were judged to have need. Of these, 412 received aid, and 145 had their full need met. Average financial aid package met 40% of need; average scholarship/grant was $9,264; average loan was $1,702. For part-time students, average financial aid package was $8,305.
Students without need: 74 full-time freshmen who did not demonstrate need for aid received scholarships/grants; average award was $2,017. No-need awards available for academics, alumni affiliation.

FINANCIAL AID PROCEDURES
Forms required: FAFSA, state aid form, institutional form.
Dates and Deadlines: Priority date 5/15; closing date 8/15. Applicants notified on a rolling basis starting 5/1; must reply within 4 week(s) of notification.

CONTACT
Carol Rosenbaum, Director of Financial Aid
27 West 23rd Street, New York, NY 10010
(212) 463-0400

Trocaire College
Buffalo, New York
www.trocaire.edu   Federal Code: 002812

2-year private health science and career college in large city, affiliated with the Roman Catholic Church.
Enrollment: 1,230 undergrads.
Selectivity: Open admission; but selective for some programs.

BASIC COSTS (2016-2017)
Tuition and fees: $16,770.
Per-credit charge: $680.

FINANCIAL AID PICTURE
Students with need: Need-based aid available for full-time and part-time students.
Students without need: No-need awards available for academics, alumni affiliation.

FINANCIAL AID PROCEDURES
Forms required: FAFSA, state aid form.
Dates and Deadlines: Priority date 3/15; no closing date. Applicants notified on a rolling basis starting 3/1; must reply within 2 week(s) of notification.

CONTACT
Jeffrey Lucas, Director of Financial Aid & Scholarships
360 Choate Avenue, Buffalo, NY 14220
(716) 826-1200

Ulster County Community College
Stone Ridge, New York
www.sunyulster.edu   Federal Code: 002880

2-year public community college in small town.
Enrollment: 1,868 undergrads.
Selectivity: Open admission; but selective for some programs.

BASIC COSTS (2016-2017)
Tuition and fees: $5,110; out-of-state residents $9,440.
Per-credit charge: $165; out-of-state residents $330.

FINANCIAL AID PICTURE
Students with need: Need-based aid available for full-time and part-time students.

FINANCIAL AID PROCEDURES
Forms required: FAFSA.
Dates and Deadlines: Priority date 6/1; no closing date. Applicants notified on a rolling basis starting 6/1; must reply within 2 week(s) of notification.

CONTACT
Christopher Chang, Director of Financial Aid
Cottekill Road, Stone Ridge, NY 12484
(845) 687-5058

Union College
Schenectady, New York   Federal Code: 002889
www.union.edu   CSS Code: 2920

4-year private engineering and liberal arts college in small city.
Enrollment: 2,119 undergrads. 560 full-time freshmen.

Selectivity: Admits less than 50% of applicants. GED not accepted.

BASIC COSTS (2016-2017)
Tuition and fees: $51,696.
Room and board: $12,678.

FINANCIAL AID PICTURE (2016-2017)
Students with need: Out of 368 full-time freshmen who applied for aid, 296 were judged to have need. Of these, 295 received aid, and 295 had their full need met. Average financial aid package met 100% of need; average scholarship/grant was $36,393; average loan was $3,573. Need-based aid available for part-time students.
Students without need: 151 full-time freshmen who did not demonstrate need for aid received scholarships/grants; average award was $13,069. No-need awards available for academics, ROTC.

FINANCIAL AID PROCEDURES
Forms required: FAFSA, CSS PROFILE, state aid form.
Dates and Deadlines: Closing date 1/15. Applicants notified by 3/25; must reply by 5/1.
Transfers: No deadline. Applicants notified on a rolling basis; must reply within 2 week(s) of notification. Financial aid applicants must submit the CSS PROFILE form and FAFSA to their respective processing agencies at least two months prior to application deadline.

CONTACT
Linda Parker, Director of Financial Aid
Grant Hall, 807 Union Street, Schenectady, NY 12308-3107
(518) 388-6123

United States Merchant Marine Academy
Kings Point, New York
www.usmma.edu   Federal Code: 002892

4-year public military and maritime college in large town.
Enrollment: 902 undergrads. 260 full-time freshmen.
Selectivity: Admits 50 to 75% of applicants.

BASIC COSTS (2016-2017)
Additional info: All costs for tuition, board, books, and uniforms paid for by Federal Government. Students are required to purchase a compliant laptop computer, academic equipment (as needed), and pay for license fees, transportation costs, laundry and barber services. Students are not paid a monthly salary/stipend, unless they are at sea.

FINANCIAL AID PICTURE (2015-2016)
Students with need: Out of 100 full-time freshmen who applied for aid, 18 were judged to have need. Of these, 18 received aid, and 18 had their full need met. Average financial aid package met 18% of need; average loan was $3,589.
Students without need: This college awards aid only to students with need.
Scholarships offered: Outside award scholarships welcomed and encouraged.
Additional info: Financial Aid awarded on a rolling basis; all students regarded as full time, undergraduates. The academy does not have institutional aid. Only Title IV FSA is awarded. Students will spend a cumulative period of one year at sea, where they will be paid a monthly salary of about $950.

FINANCIAL AID PROCEDURES
Forms required: FAFSA, institutional form.
Dates and Deadlines: Applicants notified on a rolling basis starting 5/1; must reply within 8 week(s) of notification.
Transfers: No deadline. Applicants notified on a rolling basis; must reply within 8 week(s) of notification. Transfer students regarded as freshmen, fall under freshmen aid criteria.

CONTACT
Joseph Becker, Financial Aid Specialist
300 Steamboat Road, Admissions Center, Kings Point, NY 11024-1699
(516) 726-5638

United States Military Academy
West Point, New York
www.westpoint.edu

4-year public liberal arts and military college in small town.
Enrollment: 4,389 undergrads. 1,260 full-time freshmen.
Selectivity: Admits less than 50% of applicants.

BASIC COSTS (2017-2018)
Additional info: There is no tuition to attend the United States Military Academy at West Point. Students (Cadets) that are accepted into West Point become members of the U.S Army, and receive an annual salary, room and board, and medical and dental care. However, there is an initial deposit required from all new incoming Plebe Cadets that is used to cover the initial issue of uniforms, books, supplies, incidentals, and equipment that the New Cadet will need. Upon graduation, cadets are commissioned officers in the U.S. Army and incur a 5-year Active Duty service obligation, and three years of reserve duty.

FINANCIAL AID PICTURE
Additional info: Scholarships can be accepted for a cadet to satisfy the requirement of the initial deposit. However, scholarships from any agency that states the scholarship is to be used for tuition and/or room and board will not be accepted since there is no charge for these items.

CONTACT
646 Swift Road, West Point, NY 10996-1905

University of Rochester
Rochester, New York
www.rochester.edu
Federal Code: 002894
CSS Code: 2928

4-year private university in large city.
Enrollment: 6,223 undergrads, 2% part-time. 1,406 full-time freshmen.
Selectivity: Admits less than 50% of applicants.

BASIC COSTS (2017-2018)
Tuition and fees: $51,898.
Per-credit charge: $1,593.
Room and board: $15,338.

FINANCIAL AID PICTURE (2015-2016)
Students with need: Out of 1,023 full-time freshmen who applied for aid, 794 were judged to have need. Of these, 792 received aid, and 722 had their full need met. Average financial aid package met 97% of need; average scholarship/grant was $40,556; average loan was $3,844. For part-time students, average financial aid package was $12,446.
Students without need: 432 full-time freshmen who did not demonstrate need for aid received scholarships/grants; average award was $13,179. No-need awards available for academics, alumni affiliation, art, leadership, music/drama, ROTC.
Additional info: Alternative loans and financing information available. Need-based aid available for eligible Mexican and Canadian citizens.

FINANCIAL AID PROCEDURES
Forms required: FAFSA, CSS PROFILE, state aid form.
Dates and Deadlines: Closing date 2/15. Applicants notified by 4/1; must reply by 5/1.
Transfers: Priority date 2/15. Applicants notified on a rolling basis starting 4/1; must reply by 8/1.

CONTACT
Samantha Veeder, Associate Dean of College Enrollment/Director of Financial Aid
300 Wilson Boulevard, Rochester, NY 14627-0251
(585) 275-3226

Utica College
Utica, New York
www.utica.edu
Federal Code: 002883

4-year private health science and liberal arts college in small city.
Enrollment: 3,433 undergrads, 20% part-time. 685 full-time freshmen.
Selectivity: Admits over 75% of applicants.

BASIC COSTS (2016-2017)
Tuition and fees: $19,996.
Room and board: $10,434.

FINANCIAL AID PICTURE (2016-2017)
Students with need: Out of 653 full-time freshmen who applied for aid, 583 were judged to have need. Of these, 583 received aid, and 33 had their full need met. Average financial aid package met 59% of need; average scholarship/grant was $5,486; average loan was $3,411. For part-time students, average financial aid package was $6,133.
Students without need: 70 full-time freshmen who did not demonstrate need for aid received scholarships/grants; average award was $4,251. No-need awards available for academics, alumni affiliation.

FINANCIAL AID PROCEDURES
Forms required: FAFSA, state aid form.
Dates and Deadlines: Priority date 3/15; no closing date. Applicants notified on a rolling basis starting 3/1; must reply by 5/1.
Transfers: Applicants notified on a rolling basis.

CONTACT
Laura Bedford, Executive Director of Student Financial Services
1600 Burrstone Road, Utica, NY 13502-4892
(315) 792-3179

Vassar College
Poughkeepsie, New York
www.vassar.edu
Federal Code: 002895
CSS Code: 2956

4-year private liberal arts college in small city.
Enrollment: 2,401 undergrads. 659 full-time freshmen.
Selectivity: Admits less than 50% of applicants.

BASIC COSTS (2016-2017)
Tuition and fees: $53,090.
Room and board: $12,400.

FINANCIAL AID PICTURE (2016-2017)
Students with need: Out of 492 full-time freshmen who applied for aid, 410 were judged to have need. Of these, 410 received aid, and 410 had their full need met. Average financial aid package met 100% of need; average scholarship/grant was $46,243; average loan was $2,631.
Students without need: This college awards aid only to students with need.
Additional info: No loans in the initial financial aid packages for students from families with total income used in need analysis of $60,000 or less.

FINANCIAL AID PROCEDURES
Forms required: FAFSA, CSS PROFILE.
Dates and Deadlines: Closing date 2/1. Applicants notified by 3/30; must reply by 5/1.

Transfers: Closing date 3/15. Applicants notified by 5/1; must reply within 4 week(s) of notification. Limited number of need-based award packages offered to transfers.

CONTACT

Jessica Bernier, Director of Student Financial Services
Box 10, 124 Raymond Avenue, Poughkeepsie, NY 12604-0077
(845) 437-5320

Vaughn College of Aeronautics and Technology

Flushing, New York
www.vaughn.edu   Federal Code: 002665

4-year private engineering college in very large city.
Enrollment: 1,532 undergrads, 17% part-time. 261 full-time freshmen.
Selectivity: Admits over 75% of applicants.

BASIC COSTS (2017-2018)

Tuition and fees: $24,837.
Per-credit charge: $798.
Room and board: $14,185.

FINANCIAL AID PICTURE (2016-2017)

Students with need: Out of 255 full-time freshmen who applied for aid, 225 were judged to have need. Of these, 225 received aid, and 27 had their full need met. Average financial aid package met 89% of need; average scholarship/grant was $5,260; average loan was $1,737. For part-time students, average financial aid package was $7,130.
Students without need: 30 full-time freshmen who did not demonstrate need for aid received scholarships/grants; average award was $7,800. No-need awards available for academics, alumni affiliation.

FINANCIAL AID PROCEDURES

Forms required: FAFSA, state aid form.
Dates and Deadlines: Priority date 3/15; no closing date. Applicants notified on a rolling basis starting 4/15; must reply within 2 week(s) of notification.
Transfers: No deadline. Applicants notified on a rolling basis; must reply within 2 week(s) of notification.

CONTACT

Dorothy Martin, Director of Financial Aid
8601 23rd Avenue, Flushing, NY 11369
(718) 429-6600 ext. 100

Villa Maria College of Buffalo

Buffalo, New York
www.villa.edu   Federal Code: 002896

2-year private visual arts and liberal arts college in large city, affiliated with the Roman Catholic Church.
Enrollment: 584 undergrads, 20% part-time. 145 full-time freshmen.
Selectivity: Admits over 75% of applicants.

BASIC COSTS (2016-2017)

Tuition and fees: $20,770.
Per-credit charge: $670.
Additional info: Tuition/fee waivers available for unemployed or children of unemployed.

FINANCIAL AID PICTURE

Students with need: Need-based aid available for full-time and part-time students.
Students without need: No-need awards available for academics, alumni affiliation, art, leadership.

FINANCIAL AID PROCEDURES

Forms required: FAFSA.
Dates and Deadlines: Applicants notified on a rolling basis starting 2/15; must reply within 2 week(s) of notification.
Transfers: No deadline. Applicants notified on a rolling basis starting 2/15; must reply within 2 week(s) of notification.

CONTACT

Aimee Murch, Director of Financial Aid and Veterans Affairs
240 Pine Ridge Road, Buffalo, NY 14225-3999
(716) 896-0700 ext. 1850

Wagner College

Staten Island, New York
www.wagner.edu   Federal Code: 002899

4-year private liberal arts college in very large city, affiliated with the Lutheran Church in America.
Enrollment: 1,785 undergrads, 2% part-time. 441 full-time freshmen.
Selectivity: Admits 50 to 75% of applicants.

BASIC COSTS (2016-2017)

Tuition and fees: $43,980.
Room and board: $13,260.
Additional info: Tuition/fee waivers available for unemployed or children of unemployed.

FINANCIAL AID PICTURE (2016-2017)

Students with need: Out of 364 full-time freshmen who applied for aid, 324 were judged to have need. Of these, 324 received aid, and 94 had their full need met. Average financial aid package met 76% of need; average scholarship/grant was $17,324; average loan was $2,361.
Students without need: 72 full-time freshmen who did not demonstrate need for aid received scholarships/grants; average award was $22,530. No-need awards available for academics, athletics, music/drama.
Scholarships offered: 34 full-time freshmen received athletic scholarships; average amount $31,875.

FINANCIAL AID PROCEDURES

Forms required: FAFSA, state aid form.
Dates and Deadlines: Priority date 1/15; no closing date. Applicants notified on a rolling basis starting 3/1; must reply by 5/1 or within 3 week(s) of notification.
Transfers: No deadline. Applicants notified on a rolling basis starting 3/1; must reply within 3 week(s) of notification.

CONTACT

Theresa Weimer, Director of Financial Aid
One Campus Road, Staten Island, NY 10301
(718) 390-3183

Webb Institute

Glen Cove, New York
www.webb.edu   Federal Code: 002900

4-year private engineering college in large town.
Enrollment: 92 undergrads. 28 full-time freshmen.
Selectivity: Admits less than 50% of applicants. GED not accepted.

BASIC COSTS (2017-2018)

Tuition and fees: $48,775.
Room and board: $14,750.
Additional info: All enrolled students receive full-tuition scholarships.

FINANCIAL AID PICTURE

Students with need: Need-based aid available for full-time students.

Students without need: This college awards aid only to students with need.

Additional info: Institutionally funded loans available.

FINANCIAL AID PROCEDURES

Forms required: FAFSA, institutional form.

Dates and Deadlines: Priority date 3/1; closing date 7/1. Applicants notified on a rolling basis starting 6/1; must reply within 2 week(s) of notification.

CONTACT

Jocelyn Wilson, Director of Academic Services

298 Crescent Beach Road, Glen Cove, NY 11542-1398

(516) 403-5928

Wells College
Aurora, New York
www.wells.edu
Federal Code: 002901

4-year private liberal arts college in rural community.

Enrollment: 506 undergrads. 170 full-time freshmen.

Selectivity: Admits over 75% of applicants.

BASIC COSTS (2017-2018)

Tuition and fees: $39,600.

Per-credit charge: $1,600.

Room and board: $13,730.

FINANCIAL AID PICTURE (2015-2016)

Students with need: Out of 167 full-time freshmen who applied for aid, 162 were judged to have need. Of these, 162 received aid, and 20 had their full need met. Average financial aid package met 86% of need; average scholarship/grant was $26,670; average loan was $2,940. Need-based aid available for part-time students.

Students without need: 7 full-time freshmen who did not demonstrate need for aid received scholarships/grants; average award was $23,826. No-need awards available for academics, alumni affiliation, leadership.

Scholarships offered: A range of merit-based scholarships are available. During applications review students are also assessed for scholarship awards.

FINANCIAL AID PROCEDURES

Forms required: FAFSA.

Dates and Deadlines: Priority date 12/1; no closing date. Applicants notified on a rolling basis starting 12/15.

Transfers: No deadline. Applicants notified on a rolling basis starting 12/15.

CONTACT

Laura Burns, Director of Financial Aid

170 Main Street, Aurora, NY 13026

(315) 364-3289

Westchester Community College
Valhalla, New York
www.sunywcc.edu
Federal Code: 002881

2-year public community college in large town.

Enrollment: 11,625 undergrads, 42% part-time. 1,807 full-time freshmen.

Selectivity: Open admission; but selective for some programs.

BASIC COSTS (2016-2017)

Tuition and fees: $4,723; out-of-state residents $12,213.

Per-credit charge: $179; out-of-state residents $493.

FINANCIAL AID PICTURE (2015-2016)

Students with need: Out of 1,395 full-time freshmen who applied for aid, 1,154 were judged to have need. Of these, 1,074 received aid. For part-time students, average financial aid package was $1,960.

Students without need: 4 full-time freshmen who did not demonstrate need for aid received scholarships/grants; average award was $1,535. No-need awards available for academics, leadership.

FINANCIAL AID PROCEDURES

Forms required: FAFSA, state aid form.

Dates and Deadlines: Priority date 6/30; no closing date. Applicants notified on a rolling basis starting 4/1; must reply within 4 week(s) of notification.

Transfers: No deadline.

CONTACT

Anita Cook, Director of Financial Aid

75 Grasslands Road, Valhalla, NY 10595

(914) 606-6773

Yeshiva University
New York, New York
www.yu.edu
Federal Code: 002903

4-year private university in very large city.

Enrollment: 2,714 undergrads, 3% part-time. 535 full-time freshmen.

Selectivity: Admits over 75% of applicants.

BASIC COSTS (2016-2017)

Tuition and fees: $40,670.

Per-credit charge: $1,390.

Room and board: $12,135.

FINANCIAL AID PICTURE (2015-2016)

Students with need: Out of 385 full-time freshmen who applied for aid, 306 were judged to have need. Of these, 304 received aid, and 104 had their full need met. Average financial aid package met 91% of need; average scholarship/grant was $13,795; average loan was $2,812. For part-time students, average financial aid package was $14,296.

Students without need: 145 full-time freshmen who did not demonstrate need for aid received scholarships/grants; average award was $9,222. No-need awards available for state/district residency.

Additional info: Essays required of Distinguished Scholarship applicants.

FINANCIAL AID PROCEDURES

Forms required: FAFSA.

Dates and Deadlines: Priority date 2/1; no closing date. Applicants notified on a rolling basis starting 3/15; must reply by 5/1.

CONTACT

Robert Friedman, University Director of Student Finance

500 West 185th Street, New York, NY 10033

(212) 960-5399

Yeshivat Mikdash Melech
Brooklyn, New York
www.mikdashmelech.net
Federal Code: 014615

5-year private rabbinical college for men in very large city, affiliated with the Jewish faith.

Enrollment: 17 undergrads.

Selectivity: Open admission; but selective for some programs.

BASIC COSTS (2016-2017)

Additional info: Tuition/fee waivers available for adults.

FINANCIAL AID PICTURE

Students with need: Need-based aid available for full-time and part-time students. Work study available nights.

Students without need: No-need awards available for academics, leadership, religious affiliation.

FINANCIAL AID PROCEDURES

Forms required: FAFSA, institutional form.

Dates and Deadlines: Applicants notified on a rolling basis starting 5/1.

Transfers: No deadline. Applicants notified on a rolling basis starting 5/1.

CONTACT

Amram Sananes, Financial Aid Administrator

1326 Ocean Parkway, Brooklyn, NY 11230-9963

(718) 339-1090

North Carolina

Alamance Community College

Graham, North Carolina

www.alamancecc.edu   Federal Code: 005463

2-year public community college in large town.

Enrollment: 4,011 undergrads, 39% part-time. 528 full-time freshmen.

Selectivity: Open admission; but selective for some programs.

BASIC COSTS (2016-2017)

Tuition and fees: $2,310; out-of-state residents $8,070.

Per-credit charge: $76; out-of-state residents $268.

FINANCIAL AID PICTURE (2016-2017)

Students with need: 97% of average financial aid package awarded as scholarships/grants, 3% awarded as loans/jobs. Need-based aid available for part-time students. Work study available nights.

Students without need: No-need awards available for academics, state/district residency.

FINANCIAL AID PROCEDURES

Forms required: FAFSA.

Dates and Deadlines: Priority date 5/15; no closing date. Applicants notified on a rolling basis starting 3/15; must reply within 2 week(s) of notification.

Transfers: Supplemental educational opportunity grants limited.

CONTACT

Sabrina Degain, Director of Financial Aid

Box 8000, Graham, NC 27253

(336) 506-4109

Appalachian State University

Boone, North Carolina

www.appstate.edu   Federal Code: 002906

4-year public university in large town.

Enrollment: 16,442 undergrads, 6% part-time. 3,047 full-time freshmen.

Selectivity: Admits 50 to 75% of applicants.

BASIC COSTS (2016-2017)

Tuition and fees: $7,136; out-of-state residents $21,652.

Room and board: $8,100.

Additional info: Tuition at time of enrollment locked for 4 years.

FINANCIAL AID PICTURE (2015-2016)

Students with need: Out of 2,455 full-time freshmen who applied for aid, 1,614 were judged to have need. Of these, 1,492 received aid, and 245 had their full need met. Average financial aid package met 68% of need; average scholarship/grant was $8,447; average loan was $3,291. For part-time students, average financial aid package was $5,624.

Students without need: 103 full-time freshmen who did not demonstrate need for aid received scholarships/grants; average award was $3,648. No-need awards available for academics, alumni affiliation, art, athletics, job

skills, leadership, minority status, music/drama, religious affiliation, ROTC, state/district residency.

Scholarships offered: *Merit:* Wilson Scholars Program: 4 awards available; full institutional cost with a summer stipend; based on academic, leadership, and community service. Chancellor's Scholarship: 10 awards available; full institutional cost; based on academic and leadership. Plemmons Leader Fellow Scholarship: 8-10 awards available; $1500 a year; based on academic and leadership. Diversity Scholarship: 12-15 awards available; $1000 a year; based on academic and leadership. *Athletic:* 35 full-time freshmen received athletic scholarships; average amount $9,984.

FINANCIAL AID PROCEDURES

Forms required: FAFSA.

Dates and Deadlines: Applicants notified on a rolling basis starting 3/15; must reply within 3 week(s) of notification.

Transfers: No deadline. Applicants notified on a rolling basis starting 4/1; must reply within 3 week(s) of notification.

CONTACT

Anthony Jones, Director of Financial Aid

ASU Box 32004, Boone, NC 28608

(828) 262-2190

Barton College

Wilson, North Carolina

www.barton.edu   Federal Code: 002908

4-year private liberal arts college in large town, affiliated with the Christian Church (Disciples of Christ).

Enrollment: 979 undergrads, 8% part-time. 241 full-time freshmen.

Selectivity: Admits less than 50% of applicants.

BASIC COSTS (2016-2017)

Tuition and fees: $29,052.

Per-credit charge: $1,126.

Room and board: $9,634.

Additional info: Tuition/fee waivers available for adults.

FINANCIAL AID PICTURE (2016-2017)

Students with need: Out of 225 full-time freshmen who applied for aid, 215 were judged to have need. Of these, 215 received aid, and 21 had their full need met. Average financial aid package met 65% of need; average scholarship/grant was $20,094; average loan was $3,459. For part-time students, average financial aid package was $7,249.

Students without need: 26 full-time freshmen who did not demonstrate need for aid received scholarships/grants; average award was $11,557. No-need awards available for academics, alumni affiliation, art, athletics, job skills, leadership, minority status, music/drama, religious affiliation, state/district residency.

Scholarships offered: 26 full-time freshmen received athletic scholarships; average amount $11,125.

FINANCIAL AID PROCEDURES

Forms required: FAFSA.

Dates and Deadlines: Closing date 8/19. Applicants notified on a rolling basis starting 12/12; must reply by 8/19.

Transfers: No deadline. Applicants notified on a rolling basis; must reply within 2 week(s) of notification.

CONTACT

Thomas Welch, Director of Financial Aid

Box 5000, Wilson, NC 27893-7000

(252) 399-6323

Beaufort County Community College
Washington, North Carolina
www.beaufortccc.edu   Federal Code: 008558

2-year public community college in small town.
Enrollment: 1,385 undergrads.
Selectivity: Open admission; but selective for some programs.

BASIC COSTS (2016-2017)
Tuition and fees: $2,344; out-of-state residents $8,104.
Per-credit charge: $76; out-of-state residents $268.

FINANCIAL AID PICTURE
Students with need: Need-based aid available for full-time and part-time students.
Students without need: No-need awards available for academics.

FINANCIAL AID PROCEDURES
Forms required: FAFSA, institutional form.
Dates and Deadlines: Closing date 8/1. Applicants notified on a rolling basis starting 5/1; must reply within 2 week(s) of notification.
Transfers: Priority date 6/16; no deadline.

CONTACT
Jo Woolard, Director of Student Financial Aid
Box 1069, Washington, NC 27889
(252) 940-6222

Belmont Abbey College
Belmont, North Carolina
www.belmontabbeycollege.edu   Federal Code: 002910

4-year private liberal arts college in small town, affiliated with the Roman Catholic Church.
Enrollment: 1,523 undergrads.

BASIC COSTS (2016-2017)
Tuition and fees: $18,500.
Per-credit charge: $617.
Room and board: $10,390.

FINANCIAL AID PICTURE (2015-2016)
Students with need: 64% of average financial aid package awarded as scholarships/grants, 36% awarded as loans/jobs. Need-based aid available for part-time students. Work study available nights, weekends, and for part-time students.
Students without need: No-need awards available for academics, athletics.
Scholarships offered: Many merit scholarships offered; ranging from $4,000 to $9,250; based solely on academic achievement.

FINANCIAL AID PROCEDURES
Forms required: FAFSA.
Dates and Deadlines: Priority date 4/1; no closing date. Applicants notified on a rolling basis starting 3/15; must reply within 2 week(s) of notification.
Transfers: Closing date 7/15. Applicants notified on a rolling basis starting 3/15; must reply within 2 week(s) of notification.

CONTACT
Anne Stevens, Director of Financial Aid
100 Belmont - Mt. Holly Road, Belmont, NC 28012-2795
(704) 461-6719

Bennett College for Women
Greensboro, North Carolina
www.bennett.edu   Federal Code: 002911

4-year private liberal arts college for women in large city, affiliated with the United Methodist Church.

Enrollment: 400 undergrads, 3% part-time. 115 full-time freshmen.

BASIC COSTS (2016-2017)
Tuition and fees: $18,513.
Per-credit charge: $633.
Room and board: $8,114.

FINANCIAL AID PICTURE (2016-2017)
Students with need: Out of 112 full-time freshmen who applied for aid, 111 were judged to have need. Of these, 111 received aid. Need-based aid available for part-time students.
Students without need: No-need awards available for academics, religious affiliation, ROTC.

FINANCIAL AID PROCEDURES
Forms required: FAFSA, institutional form.
Dates and Deadlines: Closing date 4/15. Applicants notified by 7/15.

CONTACT
Shawn Guy, Director, Financial Aid
900 East Washington Street, Greensboro, NC 27401-3239
(336) 517-2209

Bladen Community College
Dublin, North Carolina
www.bladencc.edu   Federal Code: 007987

2-year public community college in rural community.
Enrollment: 1,229 undergrads. 139 full-time freshmen.
Selectivity: Open admission; but selective for some programs.

BASIC COSTS (2016-2017)
Tuition and fees: $2,321; out-of-state residents $8,081.
Per-credit charge: $76; out-of-state residents $268.

FINANCIAL AID PICTURE (2015-2016)
Students with need: Out of 127 full-time freshmen who applied for aid, 127 were judged to have need. Of these, 127 received aid, and 124 had their full need met. Average financial aid package met 58% of need; average scholarship/grant was $2,443. For part-time students, average financial aid package was $2,198.
Students without need: 2 full-time freshmen who did not demonstrate need for aid received scholarships/grants; average award was $875.

FINANCIAL AID PROCEDURES
Forms required: FAFSA.
Dates and Deadlines: Priority date 6/1; closing date 7/1. Applicants notified on a rolling basis starting 8/1; must reply within 2 week(s) of notification.

CONTACT
Samantha Benson, Financial Aid Director
Post Office Box 266, Dublin, NC 28332-0266
(910) 879-5562

Blue Ridge Community College
Flat Rock, North Carolina
www.blueridge.edu   Federal Code: 009684

2-year public community and technical college in large town.
Enrollment: 1,327 undergrads.
Selectivity: Open admission; but selective for some programs.

BASIC COSTS (2016-2017)
Tuition and fees: $2,365; out-of-state residents $8,125.
Per-credit charge: $76; out-of-state residents $268.

FINANCIAL AID PICTURE
Students with need: Need-based aid available for full-time and part-time students. Work study available nights.

PART III: FINANCIAL AID COLLEGE BY COLLEGE

Students without need: No-need awards available for academics, athletics, leadership, minority status, state/district residency.

FINANCIAL AID PROCEDURES

Forms required: FAFSA, institutional form.

Dates and Deadlines: Priority date 6/30; no closing date. Applicants notified on a rolling basis starting 2/1; must reply within 4 week(s) of notification.

CONTACT

Lisanne Masterson, Financial Aid Officer

180 West Campus Drive, Flat Rock, NC 28731-9624

(828) 694-1815

Brevard College
Brevard, North Carolina
www.brevard.edu   Federal Code: 002912

4-year private liberal arts college in small town, affiliated with the United Methodist Church.

Enrollment: 697 undergrads, 1% part-time. 246 full-time freshmen.

Selectivity: Admits less than 50% of applicants.

BASIC COSTS (2016-2017)

Tuition and fees: $27,790.

Per-credit charge: $535.

Room and board: $10,500.

FINANCIAL AID PICTURE (2015-2016)

Students with need: Out of 246 full-time freshmen who applied for aid, 198 were judged to have need. Of these, 198 received aid, and 15 had their full need met. Average financial aid package met 61% of need; average scholarship/grant was $16,493; average loan was $3,038. For part-time students, average financial aid package was $10,777.

Students without need: 45 full-time freshmen who did not demonstrate need for aid received scholarships/grants; average award was $8,748. No-need awards available for academics, art, athletics, leadership, music/drama, religious affiliation, state/district residency.

Scholarships offered: 19 full-time freshmen received athletic scholarships; average amount $7,605.

FINANCIAL AID PROCEDURES

Forms required: FAFSA.

Dates and Deadlines: Priority date 2/1; no closing date. Applicants notified on a rolling basis starting 2/1; must reply by 5/1 or within 4 week(s) of notification.

Transfers: No deadline. Applicants notified on a rolling basis; must reply within 4 week(s) of notification. Phi Theta Kappa Scholarship.

CONTACT

Caron Surrett, Director of Financial Aid

One Brevard College Drive, Brevard, NC 28712

(828) 884-8287

Brunswick Community College
Bolivia, North Carolina
www.brunswickcc.edu   Federal Code: 015285

2-year public community college in small town.

Enrollment: 1,468 undergrads.

Selectivity: Open admission; but selective for some programs.

BASIC COSTS (2016-2017)

Tuition and fees: $2,380; out-of-state residents $8,140.

Per-credit charge: $76; out-of-state residents $268.

FINANCIAL AID PICTURE

Students with need: Need-based aid available for full-time and part-time students.

Students without need: No-need awards available for academics, state/district residency.

Additional info: Attendance required at financial aid orientation session for those receiving federal student aid.

FINANCIAL AID PROCEDURES

Forms required: FAFSA, institutional form.

Dates and Deadlines: Priority date 6/1; closing date 6/15. Applicants notified on a rolling basis starting 3/1; must reply by 6/30 or within 2 week(s) of notification.

Transfers: Priority date 6/15; no deadline. Applicants notified on a rolling basis starting 3/1; must reply by 6/30 or within 2 week(s) of notification. Must submit all college transcripts. All transcripts must be evaluated prior to funds being applied to account.

CONTACT

Tracy Somerlad, Director of Student Financial Resources

50 College Road NE, Bolivia, NC 28422

(910) 755-7322

Cabarrus College of Health Sciences
Concord, North Carolina
www.cabarruscollege.edu   Federal Code: 015358

4-year private health science and nursing college in small city.

Enrollment: 431 undergrads, 67% part-time. 19 full-time freshmen.

Selectivity: Admits over 75% of applicants.

BASIC COSTS (2016-2017)

Tuition and fees: $12,950.

Per-credit charge: $384.

FINANCIAL AID PICTURE (2015-2016)

Students with need: Out of 17 full-time freshmen who applied for aid, 17 were judged to have need. Of these, 17 received aid. Need-based aid available for part-time students.

Students without need: 2 full-time freshmen who did not demonstrate need for aid received scholarships/grants; average award was $1,000. No-need awards available for academics, leadership, state/district residency.

Scholarships offered: New Cabarrus College Merit scholarship is offered to first time full time students who meet minimum GPA and Test scores. Information is available on our website and notice of scholarships level awards are sent by the Admissions department in the students acceptance letter.

FINANCIAL AID PROCEDURES

Forms required: FAFSA, state aid form.

Dates and Deadlines: Priority date 4/15; no closing date. Applicants notified on a rolling basis starting 6/15.

Transfers: No deadline. Applicants notified on a rolling basis starting 6/15.

CONTACT

Valerie Richard, Director of Financial Aid

401 Medical Park Drive, Concord, NC 28025-2405

(704) 403-2445

Caldwell Community College and Technical Institute
Hudson, North Carolina
www.cccti.edu   Federal Code: 004835

2-year public community and technical college in small town.

Enrollment: 3,719 undergrads.

Selectivity: Open admission; but selective for some programs.

BASIC COSTS (2016-2017)

Tuition and fees: $2,356; out-of-state residents $8,116.

Per-credit charge: $76; out-of-state residents $268.

FINANCIAL AID PICTURE

Students with need: Need-based aid available for full-time and part-time students.

Students without need: This college awards aid only to students with need.

FINANCIAL AID PROCEDURES

Forms required: FAFSA.

Dates and Deadlines: Closing date 5/1. Applicants notified on a rolling basis starting 6/30.

CONTACT

Julie Ahouse, Director of Financial Aid

2855 Hickory Boulevard, Hudson, NC 28638-2672

(828) 726-2713

Campbell University

Buies Creek, North Carolina

www.campbell.edu   Federal Code: 002913

4-year private university and liberal arts college in rural community, affiliated with the Baptist faith.

Enrollment: 4,490 undergrads, 17% part-time. 884 full-time freshmen.

Selectivity: Admits over 75% of applicants.

BASIC COSTS (2016-2017)

Tuition and fees: $30,050.

Per-credit charge: $575.

Room and board: $10,600.

FINANCIAL AID PICTURE (2016-2017)

Students with need: Out of 813 full-time freshmen who applied for aid, 724 were judged to have need. Of these, 724 received aid, and 143 had their full need met. Average financial aid package met 80% of need; average scholarship/grant was $6,951; average loan was $3,360. For part-time students, average financial aid package was $9,730.

Students without need: 83 full-time freshmen who did not demonstrate need for aid received scholarships/grants; average award was $17,167. No-need awards available for academics, athletics, music/drama, religious affiliation, ROTC, state/district residency.

Scholarships offered: *Merit:* Presidential Scholarship: $13,000-$15,000. Campbell Scholarship: $7,000-$12,000. *Athletic:* 58 full-time freshmen received athletic scholarships; average amount $16,305.

FINANCIAL AID PROCEDURES

Forms required: FAFSA.

Dates and Deadlines: Applicants notified on a rolling basis starting 2/1; must reply within 2 week(s) of notification.

Transfers: Priority date 3/12. Applicants notified on a rolling basis; must reply within 2 week(s) of notification.

CONTACT

Mary Kosin, Director of Financial Aid

PO Box 546, Buies Creek, NC 27506

(800) 334-4111 ext. 1310

Cape Fear Community College

Wilmington, North Carolina

www.cfcc.edu   Federal Code: 005320

2-year public community college in small city.

Enrollment: 7,743 undergrads, 51% part-time. 1,060 full-time freshmen.

Selectivity: Open admission; but selective for some programs.

BASIC COSTS (2016-2017)

Tuition and fees: $2,590; out-of-state residents $8,350.

Per-credit charge: $76; out-of-state residents $268.

FINANCIAL AID PICTURE (2015-2016)

Students with need: 61% of average financial aid package awarded as scholarships/grants, 39% awarded as loans/jobs. Need-based aid available for part-time students. Work study available nights.

Students without need: No-need awards available for academics, athletics, leadership.

FINANCIAL AID PROCEDURES

Forms required: FAFSA.

Dates and Deadlines: Priority date 6/1; no closing date. Applicants notified on a rolling basis starting 4/1; must reply within 2 week(s) of notification.

CONTACT

Rachel Cavenaugh, Interim Director of Financial Aid

411 North Front Street, Wilmington, NC 28401-3910

(910) 362-7055

Carolina Christian College

Winston-Salem, North Carolina

www.carolina.edu

4-year private Bible college in large city, affiliated with the nondenominational tradition.

Enrollment: 19 undergrads.

Selectivity: Open admission.

BASIC COSTS (2016-2017)

Tuition and fees: $4,075.

FINANCIAL AID PICTURE

Students with need: Need-based aid available for full-time and part-time students.

Students without need: This college awards aid only to students with need.

FINANCIAL AID PROCEDURES

Forms required: FAFSA.

Dates and Deadlines: Applicants notified on a rolling basis.

Transfers: No deadline. Applicants notified on a rolling basis.

CONTACT

Bryan Rhoden, Director of Financial Aid

PO Box 777, Winston-Salem, NC 27102

(336) 744-0900 ext. 202

Carolinas College of Health Sciences

Charlotte, North Carolina

www.carolinascollege.edu   Federal Code: 031042

2-year public health science college in very large city.

Enrollment: 443 undergrads, 88% part-time. 1 full-time freshmen.

Selectivity: Open admission; but selective for some programs.

BASIC COSTS (2016-2017)

Tuition and fees: $10,315; out-of-state residents $10,315.

Per-credit charge: $333.

FINANCIAL AID PICTURE (2015-2016)

Students with need: 44% of average financial aid package awarded as scholarships/grants, 56% awarded as loans/jobs. Need-based aid available for part-time students. Work study available nights, weekends, and for part-time students.

Students without need: No-need awards available for academics.

Additional info: The College offers the Carolinas HealthCare System Educational Forgiveness Loan that allows students in a 2-year program to borrow up to $10,000 and up to $5,000 in a 1-year program. The loan may be forgiven if the student obtains an eligible full-time position after graduation.

FINANCIAL AID PROCEDURES

Forms required: FAFSA.

Dates and Deadlines: Priority date 5/1; no closing date. Applicants notified on a rolling basis starting 5/1.

CONTACT

Kim Bradshaw, Dean, Administrative and Financial Services
PO Box 32861, Charlotte, NC 28232-2861
(704) 355-5579

Carteret Community College

Morehead City, North Carolina
www.carteret.edu   Federal Code: 008081

2-year public community and technical college in small town.

Enrollment: 1,382 undergrads.

Selectivity: Open admission; but selective for some programs.

BASIC COSTS (2016-2017)

Tuition and fees: $2,372; out-of-state residents $8,132.

Per-credit charge: $76; out-of-state residents $268.

FINANCIAL AID PICTURE

Students with need: Need-based aid available for full-time and part-time students.

Students without need: No-need awards available for academics, leadership, minority status, state/district residency.

Additional info: Institutional student loan program administered by college. Student may charge up to $600 for books, supplies and tuition per quarter. Repayment due by 11th week of semester.

FINANCIAL AID PROCEDURES

Forms required: FAFSA, institutional form.

Dates and Deadlines: Must reply within 2 week(s) of notification.

CONTACT

Brenda Long, Financial Aid Officer
3505 Arendell Street, Morehead City, NC 28557-2989
(252) 222-6297

Catawba College

Salisbury, North Carolina
www.catawba.edu   Federal Code: 002914

4-year private liberal arts college in large town, affiliated with the United Church of Christ.

Enrollment: 1,276 undergrads, 3% part-time. 311 full-time freshmen.

Selectivity: Admits less than 50% of applicants.

BASIC COSTS (2017-2018)

Tuition and fees: $29,920.

Per-credit charge: $785.

Room and board: $10,488.

Additional info: Tuition/fee waivers available for adults.

FINANCIAL AID PICTURE (2015-2016)

Students with need: Out of 282 full-time freshmen who applied for aid, 252 were judged to have need. Of these, 252 received aid, and 57 had their full need met. Average financial aid package met 78% of need; average scholarship/grant was $7,157; average loan was $3,177. For part-time students, average financial aid package was $5,070.

Students without need: 49 full-time freshmen who did not demonstrate need for aid received scholarships/grants; average award was $17,184. No-need awards available for academics, athletics, leadership, music/drama, religious affiliation, state/district residency.

Scholarships offered: 78 full-time freshmen received athletic scholarships; average amount $8,304.

FINANCIAL AID PROCEDURES

Forms required: FAFSA, state aid form.

Dates and Deadlines: Priority date 3/15; no closing date. Applicants notified on a rolling basis starting 12/15; must reply within 2 week(s) of notification.

CONTACT

Kelli Hand, Director of Financial Aid
2300 West Innes Street, Salisbury, NC 28144-2488
(704) 637-4416

Catawba Valley Community College

Hickory, North Carolina
www.cvcc.edu   Federal Code: 005318

2-year public community college in large town.

Enrollment: 4,165 undergrads.

Selectivity: Open admission; but selective for some programs.

BASIC COSTS (2016-2017)

Tuition and fees: $2,400; out-of-state residents $8,160.

Per-credit charge: $76; out-of-state residents $268.

Additional info: Tuition/fee waivers available for unemployed or children of unemployed.

FINANCIAL AID PICTURE

Students with need: Need-based aid available for full-time and part-time students. Work study available nights.

Students without need: No-need awards available for academics, leadership, music/drama.

FINANCIAL AID PROCEDURES

Forms required: FAFSA.

Dates and Deadlines: Closing date 3/15. Applicants notified on a rolling basis starting 5/15.

CONTACT

Debbie Barger, Director of Scholarships and Financial Aid
2550 Highway 70 SE, Hickory, NC 28602
(828) 327-7000 ext. 4214

Central Carolina Community College

Sanford, North Carolina
www.cccc.edu   Federal Code: 005449

2-year public community college in large town.

Enrollment: 3,511 undergrads, 49% part-time. 506 full-time freshmen.

Selectivity: Open admission; but selective for some programs.

BASIC COSTS (2016-2017)

Tuition and fees: $2,392; out-of-state residents $8,152.

Per-credit charge: $76; out-of-state residents $268.

FINANCIAL AID PICTURE

Students with need: Need-based aid available for full-time and part-time students. Work study available nights.

Students without need: No-need awards available for academics, leadership, state/district residency.

FINANCIAL AID PROCEDURES

Forms required: FAFSA.

Dates and Deadlines: Priority date 6/1; no closing date. Applicants notified on a rolling basis; must reply within 2 week(s) of notification.
Transfers: No deadline.

CONTACT
Heather Willett, Dean Of Student Support Services
1105 Kelly Drive, Sanford, NC 27330
(919) 718-7229

Central Piedmont Community College
Charlotte, North Carolina
www.cpcc.edu   Federal Code: 002915

2-year public community college in very large city.
Enrollment: 17,974 undergrads, 63% part-time. 1,592 full-time freshmen.
Selectivity: Open admission; but selective for some programs.

BASIC COSTS (2016-2017)
Tuition and fees: $2,446; out-of-state residents $8,206.
Per-credit charge: $76; out-of-state residents $268.

FINANCIAL AID PICTURE (2015-2016)
Students with need: 95% of average financial aid package awarded as scholarships/grants, 5% awarded as loans/jobs. Need-based aid available for part-time students.
Students without need: No-need awards available for academics, minority status.

FINANCIAL AID PROCEDURES
Forms required: FAFSA.
Dates and Deadlines: Priority date 4/1; closing date 6/1. Applicants notified on a rolling basis.

CONTACT
Debbie Brooks, Director, Student Financial Aid
PO Box 35009, Charlotte, NC 28235-5009
(704) 330-6942

Chowan University
Murfreesboro, North Carolina
https://www.chowan.edu   Federal Code: 002916

4-year private university and liberal arts college in small town, affiliated with the Southern Baptist Convention.
Enrollment: 1,523 undergrads, 4% part-time. 494 full-time freshmen.
Selectivity: Admits 50 to 75% of applicants.

BASIC COSTS (2017-2018)
Tuition and fees: $24,480.
Per-credit charge: $400.
Room and board: $9,200.

FINANCIAL AID PICTURE (2016-2017)
Students with need: Out of 461 full-time freshmen who applied for aid, 437 were judged to have need. Of these, 437 received aid, and 25 had their full need met. Average financial aid package met 70% of need; average scholarship/grant was $17,810; average loan was $3,323. For part-time students, average financial aid package was $7,348.
Students without need: 7 full-time freshmen who did not demonstrate need for aid received scholarships/grants; average award was $8,929. No-need awards available for academics, athletics, leadership, music/drama, religious affiliation, state/district residency.
Scholarships offered: 2 full-time freshmen received athletic scholarships; average amount $17,800.

FINANCIAL AID PROCEDURES
Forms required: FAFSA.

Dates and Deadlines: Priority date 3/1; no closing date. Applicants notified on a rolling basis starting 3/1; must reply within 2 week(s) of notification.

CONTACT
Sharon Rose, Director of Financial Aid
One University Place, Murfreesboro, NC 27855-9901
(252) 398-1229

Cleveland Community College
Shelby, North Carolina
www.clevelandcc.edu   Federal Code: 008082

2-year public community college in large town.
Enrollment: 2,476 undergrads.
Selectivity: Open admission; but selective for some programs.

BASIC COSTS (2016-2017)
Tuition and fees: $2,372; out-of-state residents $8,132.
Per-credit charge: $76; out-of-state residents $268.

FINANCIAL AID PICTURE
Students with need: Need-based aid available for full-time and part-time students. Work study available nights.
Students without need: No-need awards available for academics.

FINANCIAL AID PROCEDURES
Forms required: FAFSA.
Dates and Deadlines: Priority date 6/27; no closing date. Applicants notified on a rolling basis starting 3/15.

CONTACT
Emily Hurdt, Financial Aid Coordinator
137 South Post Road, Shelby, NC 28152-6224
(704) 669-4204

Coastal Carolina Community College
Jacksonville, North Carolina
www.coastalcarolina.edu   Federal Code: 005316

2-year public community college in small city.
Enrollment: 3,649 undergrads, 46% part-time. 449 full-time freshmen.
Selectivity: Open admission; but selective for some programs.

BASIC COSTS (2016-2017)
Tuition and fees: $2,310; out-of-state residents $8,070.
Per-credit charge: $76; out-of-state residents $268.

FINANCIAL AID PICTURE (2015-2016)
Students with need: 99% of average financial aid package awarded as scholarships/grants, 1% awarded as loans/jobs. Need-based aid available for part-time students. Work study available nights, weekends, and for part-time students.
Students without need: No-need awards available for academics, state/district residency.

FINANCIAL AID PROCEDURES
Forms required: FAFSA, institutional form.
Dates and Deadlines: Priority date 5/15; no closing date. Applicants notified on a rolling basis starting 5/15; must reply within 2 week(s) of notification.

CONTACT
Lyon Tammy, Director for Financial Aid Services
444 Western Boulevard, Jacksonville, NC 28546-6816

College of the Albemarle
Elizabeth City, North Carolina
www.albemarle.edu   Federal Code: 002917

2-year public branch campus and community college in large town.
Enrollment: 1,604 undergrads, 51% part-time.
Selectivity: Open admission; but selective for some programs.

BASIC COSTS (2016-2017)
Tuition and fees: $2,407; out-of-state residents $8,167.
Per-credit charge: $76; out-of-state residents $268.

FINANCIAL AID PICTURE
Students with need: Need-based aid available for full-time and part-time students.
Students without need: No-need awards available for academics, art, leadership, minority status, music/drama, state/district residency.
Additional info: Separate application must be submitted for COA Private Scholarships.

FINANCIAL AID PROCEDURES
Forms required: FAFSA.
Dates and Deadlines: Priority date 3/15; closing date 6/1. Applicants notified on a rolling basis starting 5/1; must reply within 2 week(s) of notification.

CONTACT
Angie Dawson, Director of Admissions and Financial Aid
1208 North Road Street, Elizabeth City, NC 27909
(252) 335-0821 ext. 2355

Craven Community College
New Bern, North Carolina
www.cravencc.edu   Federal Code: 008086

2-year public community college in large town.
Enrollment: 2,665 undergrads, 60% part-time. 164 full-time freshmen.
Selectivity: Open admission; but selective for some programs.

BASIC COSTS (2016-2017)
Tuition and fees: $2,568; out-of-state residents $8,328.
Per-credit charge: $76; out-of-state residents $268.

FINANCIAL AID PICTURE (2015-2016)
Students with need: 96% of average financial aid package awarded as scholarships/grants, 4% awarded as loans/jobs. Need-based aid available for part-time students.

FINANCIAL AID PROCEDURES
Forms required: FAFSA.
Dates and Deadlines: Closing date 6/1. Applicants notified on a rolling basis.

CONTACT
Kathy Banks, Director of Financial Aid
800 College Court, New Bern, NC 28562
(252) 638-7216

Davidson College
Davidson, North Carolina   Federal Code: 002918
www.davidson.edu   CSS Code: 5150

4-year private liberal arts college in small town, affiliated with the Presbyterian Church (USA).
Enrollment: 1,791 undergrads. 514 full-time freshmen.
Selectivity: Admits less than 50% of applicants. GED not accepted.

BASIC COSTS (2016-2017)
Tuition and fees: $47,897.
Room and board: $13,547.

FINANCIAL AID PICTURE (2016-2017)
Students with need: Out of 338 full-time freshmen who applied for aid, 262 were judged to have need. Of these, 262 received aid, and 262 had their full need met. Average financial aid package met 100% of need; average scholarship/grant was $42,011; average loan was $2,719. Need-based aid available for part-time students.
Students without need: 23 full-time freshmen who did not demonstrate need for aid received scholarships/grants; average award was $31,207. No-need awards available for academics, alumni affiliation, art, athletics, leadership, minority status, music/drama, ROTC.
Scholarships offered: *Merit:* Thompson S./Sarah S. Baker Scholarships: comprehensive fees; for first-time students with highest achievements; 3 awarded. John Montgomery Belk Scholarship: comprehensive fees; for Southeast applicants with highest achievements; 6 awarded. Amos Norris Scholarship: full cost; for first-time student athlete; 1 awarded. William Holt Terry Scholarships: full tuition; for first-year students with leadership skills and personal qualities; 2 awarded. John I. Smith Scholars Programs: full tuition; for first-year students with leadership, academic excellence, and commitment to community service; 2 awarded. *Athletic:* 26 full-time freshmen received athletic scholarships; average amount $18,394.
Additional info: The college has increased the money it provides for grants in financial aid packages and eliminated mandatory loans, allowing all students, regardless of socio-economic background, to graduate debt-free.

FINANCIAL AID PROCEDURES
Forms required: FAFSA, CSS PROFILE.
Dates and Deadlines: Closing date 2/15. Applicants notified by 4/1; must reply by 5/1.
Transfers: Applicants notified by 5/15.

CONTACT
David Gelinas, Director of Financial Aid
Box 7156, Davidson, NC 28035-7156
(704) 894-2232

Davidson County Community College
Lexington, North Carolina
www.davidsonccc.edu   Federal Code: 002919

2-year public community college in large town.
Enrollment: 3,487 undergrads.
Selectivity: Open admission; but selective for some programs.

BASIC COSTS (2016-2017)
Tuition and fees: $2,435; out-of-state residents $8,195.
Per-credit charge: $76; out-of-state residents $268.

FINANCIAL AID PICTURE (2015-2016)
Students with need: 54% of average financial aid package awarded as scholarships/grants, 46% awarded as loans/jobs. Need-based aid available for part-time students.
Students without need: No-need awards available for academics, leadership.

FINANCIAL AID PROCEDURES
Forms required: FAFSA.
Dates and Deadlines: Priority date 6/1; no closing date. Applicants notified on a rolling basis starting 5/1; must reply within 2 week(s) of notification.

CONTACT
Lori Blevins, Director, Admissions and Financial Aid
P O Box 1287, Lexington, NC 27293-1287
(336) 249-8186

Duke University

Durham, North Carolina
www.duke.edu

Federal Code: 002920
CSS Code: 5156

4-year private university in large city.
Enrollment: 6,467 undergrads. 1,723 full-time freshmen.
Selectivity: Admits less than 50% of applicants. GED not accepted.

BASIC COSTS (2016-2017)
Tuition and fees: $51,265.
Per-credit charge: $1,489.
Room and board: $14,438.

FINANCIAL AID PICTURE
Students with need: Need-based aid available for full-time students.
Students without need: No-need awards available for academics, alumni affiliation, athletics, leadership, minority status, music/drama, religious affiliation, ROTC, state/district residency.

FINANCIAL AID PROCEDURES
Forms required: FAFSA, CSS PROFILE.
Dates and Deadlines: Closing date 3/15. Applicants notified by 4/1; must reply by 5/1.

CONTACT
Alison Rabil, Director of Financial Aid
2138 Campus Drive, Durham, NC 27708
(919) 684-6225

Durham Technical Community College

Durham, North Carolina
www.durhamtech.edu

Federal Code: 005448

2-year public community and technical college in small city.
Enrollment: 5,120 undergrads.
Selectivity: Open admission; but selective for some programs.

BASIC COSTS (2016-2017)
Tuition and fees: $2,372; out-of-state residents $8,132.
Per-credit charge: $76; out-of-state residents $268.

FINANCIAL AID PICTURE
Students with need: Need-based aid available for full-time and part-time students. Work study available nights.
Students without need: No-need awards available for academics, minority status, state/district residency.
Additional info: Special funds available to single parents for tuition, fees, books, supplies and child care expenses.

FINANCIAL AID PROCEDURES
Forms required: FAFSA.
Dates and Deadlines: Applicants notified on a rolling basis starting 1/31; must reply within 3 week(s) of notification.

CONTACT
Everett Jeter, Director of Financial Aid
1637 Lawson Street, Durham, NC 27703
(919) 536-7209

East Carolina University

Greenville, North Carolina
www.ecu.edu

Federal Code: 002923

4-year public university in small city.
Enrollment: 22,386 undergrads, 12% part-time. 4,308 full-time freshmen.
Selectivity: Admits 50 to 75% of applicants.

BASIC COSTS (2016-2017)
Tuition and fees: $6,916; out-of-state residents $22,874.
Room and board: $9,471.

FINANCIAL AID PICTURE (2016-2017)
Students with need: Out of 3,600 full-time freshmen who applied for aid, 2,647 were judged to have need. Of these, 2,516 received aid, and 262 had their full need met. Average financial aid package met 60% of need; average scholarship/grant was $7,882; average loan was $5,901. For part-time students, average financial aid package was $7,165.
Students without need: No-need awards available for academics, alumni affiliation, art, athletics, music/drama, ROTC.

FINANCIAL AID PROCEDURES
Forms required: FAFSA.
Dates and Deadlines: Priority date 3/1; no closing date. Applicants notified on a rolling basis starting 4/1; must reply within 3 week(s) of notification.

CONTACT
Julie Poorman, Director of Student Financial Aid
Office of Undergraduate Admissions, Greenville, NC 27858-4353
(252) 328-6610

Edgecombe Community College

Tarboro, North Carolina
www.edgecombe.edu

Federal Code: 008855

2-year public community college in large town.
Enrollment: 1,862 undergrads.
Selectivity: Open admission; but selective for some programs.

BASIC COSTS (2016-2017)
Tuition and fees: $2,333; out-of-state residents $8,093.
Per-credit charge: $76; out-of-state residents $268.

FINANCIAL AID PICTURE (2016-2017)
Students with need: Need-based aid available for part-time students. Work study available nights, weekends, and for part-time students.
Students without need: This college awards aid only to students with need.

FINANCIAL AID PROCEDURES
Forms required: FAFSA, institutional form.
Dates and Deadlines: Applicants notified on a rolling basis starting 8/15; must reply within 3 week(s) of notification.
Transfers: No deadline.

CONTACT
Sherlock McDougald, Director of Financial Aid
2009 West Wilson Street, Tarboro, NC 27886
(252) 823-5166 ext. 258

Elizabeth City State University

Elizabeth City, North Carolina
www.ecsu.edu

Federal Code: 002926

4-year public liberal arts college in large town.
Enrollment: 2,276 undergrads.

BASIC COSTS (2016-2017)
Tuition and fees: $4,888; out-of-state residents $17,859.
Room and board: $7,682.

FINANCIAL AID PICTURE
Students with need: Need-based aid available for full-time students. Work study available nights, weekends, and for part-time students.
Students without need: No-need awards available for academics, athletics, minority status, ROTC, state/district residency.

FINANCIAL AID PROCEDURES

Forms required: FAFSA.

Dates and Deadlines: Priority date 3/15; closing date 6/1. Applicants notified on a rolling basis starting 6/1; must reply by 6/30 or within 3 week(s) of notification.

Transfers: Closing date 3/15. Applicants notified on a rolling basis starting 6/30; must reply within 3 week(s) of notification.

CONTACT

Kenneth Wilson, Associate Director of Financial Aid
1704 Weeksville Road, Campus Box 901, Elizabeth City, NC 27909
(252) 335-3283

Elon University

Elon, North Carolina
www.elon.edu

Federal Code: 002927
CSS Code: 5183

4-year private university and liberal arts college in large town.
Enrollment: 6,008 undergrads, 3% part-time. 1,540 full-time freshmen.
Selectivity: Admits 50 to 75% of applicants.

BASIC COSTS (2016-2017)

Tuition and fees: $33,104.
Per-credit charge: $1,041.
Room and board: $11,495.

FINANCIAL AID PICTURE (2016-2017)

Students with need: Out of 849 full-time freshmen who applied for aid, 522 were judged to have need. Of these, 516 received aid, and 74 had their full need met. Average financial aid package met 62% of need; average scholarship/grant was $15,145; average loan was $3,462. Need-based aid available for part-time students.

Students without need: 334 full-time freshmen who did not demonstrate need for aid received scholarships/grants; average award was $7,301. No-need awards available for academics, alumni affiliation, art, athletics, leadership, music/drama, religious affiliation, ROTC.

Scholarships offered: *Merit:* Presidential Scholarships: up to $6,000 annually; based on academic credentials. Fellows Programs (Honors, Business, Communications, Elon College Fellows, Isabella Cannon Leadership, Teaching, International): $5,000-$13,500 annually; based on merit. Elon Teaching Fellows: $5,500 annually. Engineering Scholarships: $8,000 annually. Performing Arts Scholarships: $500-$6,000; talent-based. Music Scholarships: $500-$8,000; talent and need-based. Elon Engagement scholarships: up to $4,500. International Scholar Award range from $2,000 to $4,000 annually. *Athletic:* 68 full-time freshmen received athletic scholarships; average amount $30,510.

FINANCIAL AID PROCEDURES

Forms required: FAFSA, CSS PROFILE.
Dates and Deadlines: Priority date 11/15; no closing date. Applicants notified on a rolling basis starting 3/30.

CONTACT

Patrick Murphy, Director of Financial Planning
2700 Campus Box, Elon, NC 27244-2010
(336) 278-7640

Fayetteville State University

Fayetteville, North Carolina
www.uncfsu.edu

Federal Code: 002928

4-year public university in small city.
Enrollment: 5,518 undergrads, 25% part-time. 669 full-time freshmen.
Selectivity: Admits 50 to 75% of applicants.

BASIC COSTS (2016-2017)

Tuition and fees: $5,060; out-of-state residents $16,668.
Room and board: $7,250.

FINANCIAL AID PICTURE (2016-2017)

Students with need: Out of 654 full-time freshmen who applied for aid, 602 were judged to have need. Of these, 563 received aid, and 58 had their full need met. Average financial aid package met 79% of need; average scholarship/grant was $9,274; average loan was $3,384. For part-time students, average financial aid package was $6,549.

Students without need: No-need awards available for academics, alumni affiliation, athletics, music/drama, ROTC, state/district residency.

FINANCIAL AID PROCEDURES

Forms required: FAFSA.
Dates and Deadlines: Closing date 3/1. Applicants notified on a rolling basis starting 4/15; must reply within 2 week(s) of notification.

CONTACT

Kamesia Ewing, Director of Financial Aid
1200 Murchison Road, Fayetteville, NC 28301-4298
(910) 672-1325

Fayetteville Technical Community College

Fayetteville, North Carolina
www.faytechcc.edu

Federal Code: 007640

2-year public community and technical college in large city.
Enrollment: 9,623 undergrads, 57% part-time. 1,056 full-time freshmen.
Selectivity: Open admission; but selective for some programs.

BASIC COSTS (2016-2017)

Tuition and fees: $2,376; out-of-state residents $8,136.
Per-credit charge: $76; out-of-state residents $268.

FINANCIAL AID PICTURE (2015-2016)

Students with need: Out of 927 full-time freshmen who applied for aid, 747 were judged to have need. Of these, 701 received aid, and 668 had their full need met. Average financial aid package met 95% of need; average scholarship/grant was $5,044; average loan was $5,185. For part-time students, average financial aid package was $3,641.

FINANCIAL AID PROCEDURES

Forms required: FAFSA.
Dates and Deadlines: Applicants notified on a rolling basis starting 4/1.
Transfers: No deadline. Applicants notified on a rolling basis starting 4/1.

CONTACT

Regina Anglin, Assistant Director of Financial Aid
2201 Hull Road, Fayetteville, NC 28303-0236
(910) 678-8448

Forsyth Technical Community College

Winston-Salem, North Carolina
www.forsythtech.edu

Federal Code: 005317

2-year public community and technical college in small city.
Enrollment: 7,434 undergrads, 59% part-time. 601 full-time freshmen.
Selectivity: Open admission; but selective for some programs.

BASIC COSTS (2016-2017)

Tuition and fees: $2,446; out-of-state residents $8,206.
Per-credit charge: $76; out-of-state residents $268.

FINANCIAL AID PICTURE (2016-2017)

Students with need: Out of 460 full-time freshmen who applied for aid, 373 were judged to have need. Of these, 352 received aid, and 248 had

their full need met. Average financial aid package met 70% of need; average scholarship/grant was $5,159; average loan was $2,231. For part-time students, average financial aid package was $8,128.

Students without need: 15 full-time freshmen who did not demonstrate need for aid received scholarships/grants; average award was $5,956. No-need awards available for academics, alumni affiliation, leadership, state/district residency.

Additional info: Apply for aid as close to October 1 as possible for best consideration.

FINANCIAL AID PROCEDURES

Forms required: FAFSA.

Dates and Deadlines: Priority date 6/1; closing date 6/1. Applicants notified on a rolling basis starting 5/1.

Transfers: No deadline. Mid-year transfer students must submit a financial aid transcript from previous college in order for financial aid office to award any Federal Pell Grant funds to eligible students.

CONTACT

Ricky Hodges, Director of Student Financial Services
2100 Silas Creek Parkway, Winston-Salem, NC 27103
(336) 734-7235

Gardner-Webb University

Boiling Springs, North Carolina
www.gardner-webb.edu   Federal Code: 002929

4-year private university and liberal arts college in small town, affiliated with the Southern Baptist Convention.

Enrollment: 2,352 undergrads, 19% part-time. 444 full-time freshmen.

BASIC COSTS (2016-2017)

Tuition and fees: $29,420.
Per-credit charge: $468.
Room and board: $9,700.

FINANCIAL AID PICTURE (2016-2017)

Students with need: Out of 410 full-time freshmen who applied for aid, 359 were judged to have need. Of these, 359 received aid, and 73 had their full need met. Average financial aid package met 76% of need; average scholarship/grant was $8,249; average loan was $3,205. Need-based aid available for part-time students.

Students without need: 85 full-time freshmen who did not demonstrate need for aid received scholarships/grants; average award was $14,101. No-need awards available for academics, athletics, leadership, music/drama, religious affiliation, ROTC, state/district residency.

Scholarships offered: *Merit:* Presidential Fellow: full tuition, room and board for four years; 1 awarded. Academic Fellow: full tuition for four years; 4 awarded. Honors Scholarship $3000; 50 awarded. Selection based on academic accomplishments and interview. *Athletic:* 38 full-time freshmen received athletic scholarships; average amount $17,032.

FINANCIAL AID PROCEDURES

Forms required: FAFSA, state aid form.

Dates and Deadlines: Priority date 3/1; closing date 6/30. Applicants notified on a rolling basis starting 3/1; must reply within 2 week(s) of notification.

Transfers: No deadline. Applicants notified on a rolling basis starting 3/1; must reply within 2 week(s) of notification.

CONTACT

Summer Nance, Assistant Vice President for Financial Planning
PO Box 817, Boiling Springs, NC 28017
(704) 406-4243

Gaston College

Dallas, North Carolina
www.gaston.edu   Federal Code: 002973

2-year public community college in small town.
Enrollment: 5,603 undergrads.
Selectivity: Open admission; but selective for some programs.

BASIC COSTS (2016-2017)

Tuition and fees: $2,386; out-of-state residents $8,146.
Per-credit charge: $76; out-of-state residents $268.

FINANCIAL AID PICTURE (2016-2017)

Students with need: 98% of average financial aid package awarded as scholarships/grants, 2% awarded as loans/jobs.

Students without need: No-need awards available for academics, state/district residency.

Scholarships offered: Academic Scholarship: over 30 available; $1,100; GPA of 3.0 or better. Careers Scholarship: 10 available; $1,100 each, must pursue career in specified engineering technologies or industrial technologies major and have GPA of 3.0 or better.

Additional info: Grants/scholarships available for women pursuing nontraditional roles.

FINANCIAL AID PROCEDURES

Forms required: FAFSA, institutional form.
Dates and Deadlines: Priority date 3/15; closing date 6/30. Applicants notified on a rolling basis.

CONTACT

Everett Jeter, Director of Financial Aid and Veterans Affairs
201 Highway 321 South, Dallas, NC 28034-1499
(704) 922-6227

Greensboro College

Greensboro, North Carolina
www.greensboro.edu   Federal Code: 002930

4-year private liberal arts college in large city, affiliated with the United Methodist Church.
Enrollment: 789 undergrads, 4% part-time. 249 full-time freshmen.
Selectivity: Admits over 75% of applicants.

BASIC COSTS (2016-2017)

Tuition and fees: $28,000.
Room and board: $10,400.

FINANCIAL AID PICTURE (2016-2017)

Students with need: Out of 236 full-time freshmen who applied for aid, 221 were judged to have need. Of these, 221 received aid, and 33 had their full need met. Average financial aid package met 86% of need; average scholarship/grant was $21,358; average loan was $4,036. For part-time students, average financial aid package was $7,431.

Students without need: No-need awards available for academics, alumni affiliation, art, leadership, music/drama, religious affiliation, state/district residency.

Scholarships offered: Barrett Scholarships and Presidential Scholarships: full tuition; fees, room, and board; number of awards vary.

FINANCIAL AID PROCEDURES

Forms required: FAFSA, state aid form, institutional form.
Dates and Deadlines: Priority date 4/15; no closing date. Applicants notified on a rolling basis starting 2/1; must reply within 2 week(s) of notification.
Transfers: Closing date 4/15. Must reply within 4 week(s) of notification.

CONTACT

Lindsay Latham, Director of Financial Aid
815 West Market Street, Greensboro, NC 27401-1875
(336) 272-7102 ext. 217

Guilford College

Greensboro, North Carolina
www.guilford.edu   Federal Code: 002931

4-year private liberal arts college in large city, affiliated with the Society of Friends (Quaker).
Enrollment: 1,682 undergrads, 13% part-time. 421 full-time freshmen.
Selectivity: Admits 50 to 75% of applicants.

BASIC COSTS (2017-2018)
Tuition and fees: $34,215.
Per-credit charge: $1,032.
Room and board: $10,800.

FINANCIAL AID PICTURE (2015-2016)
Students with need: 66% of average financial aid package awarded as scholarships/grants, 34% awarded as loans/jobs. Need-based aid available for part-time students. Work study available nights, weekends, and for part-time students.
Students without need: No-need awards available for academics.
Scholarships offered: Honors Scholarship: $7,500 to full tuition. Presidential Scholarship: $5,000. Incentive grants: $3,000; based on participation or leadership in school or community activities. Quaker Leadership Scholarships: $3,000; candidates must be active members of the Religious Society of Friends.

FINANCIAL AID PROCEDURES
Forms required: FAFSA.
Dates and Deadlines: Priority date 2/15; no closing date. Applicants notified on a rolling basis starting 3/1; must reply within 2 week(s) of notification.

CONTACT
Brian De Young, Director of Student Financial Services
Admissions, New Garden Hall, Greensboro, NC 27410-4108
(336) 316-2354

Guilford Technical Community College

Jamestown, North Carolina
www.gtcc.edu   Federal Code: 004838

2-year public community and technical college in large city.
Enrollment: 10,852 undergrads, 52% part-time. 1,135 full-time freshmen.
Selectivity: Open admission; but selective for some programs.

BASIC COSTS (2016-2017)
Tuition and fees: $2,280; out-of-state residents $8,040.
Per-credit charge: $76; out-of-state residents $268.

FINANCIAL AID PICTURE
Students with need: Need-based aid available for full-time and part-time students.
Students without need: No-need awards available for academics, athletics, leadership, minority status, state/district residency.

FINANCIAL AID PROCEDURES
Forms required: FAFSA.
Dates and Deadlines: Priority date 3/15; closing date 7/25. Applicants notified on a rolling basis starting 7/1; must reply within 2 week(s) of notification.

CONTACT
Lisa Koretoff, Director of Financial Aid
PO Box 309, Jamestown, NC 27282
(336) 334-4822 ext. 50317

Halifax Community College

Weldon, North Carolina
www.halifaxcc.edu   Federal Code: 007986

2-year public community college in small town.
Enrollment: 853 undergrads, 41% part-time. 170 full-time freshmen.
Selectivity: Open admission; but selective for some programs.

BASIC COSTS (2016-2017)
Tuition and fees: $2,412; out-of-state residents $8,172.
Per-credit charge: $76; out-of-state residents $268.

FINANCIAL AID PICTURE (2016-2017)
Students with need: Average financial aid package for all full-time undergraduates was $5,188; for part-time $4,024. 84% awarded as scholarships/grants, 16% awarded as loans/jobs. Work study available nights.
Students without need: No-need awards available for academics.

FINANCIAL AID PROCEDURES
Forms required: FAFSA.
Dates and Deadlines: Priority date 6/1; no closing date. Applicants notified on a rolling basis starting 8/1; must reply within 2 week(s) of notification.
Transfers: No deadline. Applicants notified on a rolling basis; must reply within 2 week(s) of notification.

CONTACT
Tara Keeter, Director, Financial Aid
100 College Drive, Drawer 809, Weldon, NC 27890
(252) 536-7223

Haywood Community College

Clyde, North Carolina
www.haywood.edu   Federal Code: 008083

2-year public community and technical college in rural community.
Enrollment: 1,146 undergrads.
Selectivity: Open admission; but selective for some programs.

BASIC COSTS (2016-2017)
Tuition and fees: $2,383; out-of-state residents $8,143.
Per-credit charge: $76; out-of-state residents $268.

FINANCIAL AID PICTURE
Students with need: Need-based aid available for full-time and part-time students.
Students without need: No-need awards available for academics.
Additional info: Complete FAFSA by priority filing date for consideration for institutional scholarships.

FINANCIAL AID PROCEDURES
Forms required: FAFSA.
Dates and Deadlines: Priority date 6/1; no closing date. Applicants notified on a rolling basis starting 4/15; must reply within 2 week(s) of notification.

CONTACT
Sayward Cabe, Director of Financial Aid
185 Freelander Drive, Clyde, NC 28721-9454
(828) 627-4506

High Point University

High Point, North Carolina
www.highpoint.edu   Federal Code: 002933

4-year private university and liberal arts college in small city, affiliated with the United Methodist Church.
Enrollment: 4,510 undergrads, 1% part-time. 1,362 full-time freshmen.

Selectivity: Admits over 75% of applicants.

BASIC COSTS (2016-2017)
Tuition and fees: $33,405.
Per-credit charge: $927.
Room and board: $12,572.

FINANCIAL AID PICTURE (2015-2016)
Students with need: Out of 834 full-time freshmen who applied for aid, 590 were judged to have need. Of these, 589 received aid, and 106 had their full need met. Average financial aid package met 55% of need; average scholarship/grant was $5,308; average loan was $3,182. For part-time students, average financial aid package was $7,861.
Students without need: 187 full-time freshmen who did not demonstrate need for aid received scholarships/grants; average award was $7,236. No-need awards available for academics, alumni affiliation, art, athletics, leadership, music/drama, religious affiliation, state/district residency.
Scholarships offered: *Merit:* Awarded annually to qualified freshmen: Presidential Fellowship: $9,000-$20,000. High Point Fellowship: $6,000-$9,000. High Point Scholarship: $2,000-$5,000. All scholarships based on merit. Application and interview required. *Athletic:* 67 full-time freshmen received athletic scholarships; average amount $21,030.

FINANCIAL AID PROCEDURES
Forms required: FAFSA, state aid form.
Dates and Deadlines: Priority date 3/1; no closing date. Applicants notified on a rolling basis starting 4/1; must reply within 3 week(s) of notification.
Transfers: No deadline. Applicants notified on a rolling basis starting 5/1; must reply within 3 week(s) of notification.

CONTACT
Ron Elmore, Director of Student Financial Services
One University Parkway, High Point, NC 27268-3598
(336) 841-9128

Isothermal Community College
Spindale, North Carolina
www.isothermal.edu   Federal Code: 002934

2-year public community college in small town.
Enrollment: 2,067 undergrads.
Selectivity: Open admission; but selective for some programs.

BASIC COSTS (2016-2017)
Tuition and fees: $2,334; out-of-state residents $8,094.
Per-credit charge: $76; out-of-state residents $268.

FINANCIAL AID PICTURE
Students with need: Need-based aid available for full-time and part-time students. Work study available nights.
Students without need: No-need awards available for academics, job skills, leadership, minority status, music/drama, state/district residency.

FINANCIAL AID PROCEDURES
Forms required: FAFSA, institutional form.
Dates and Deadlines: Priority date 5/31; closing date 7/1. Applicants notified on a rolling basis starting 4/30; must reply within 4 week(s) of notification.

CONTACT
Jeffery Boyle, Director of Financial Aid
PO Box 804, Spindale, NC 28160-0804
(828) 286-3636 ext. 468

James Sprunt Community College
Kenansville, North Carolina
www.jamessprunt.edu   Federal Code: 007687

2-year public community college in rural community.
Enrollment: 753 undergrads, 45% part-time. 137 full-time freshmen.

Selectivity: Open admission; but selective for some programs.

BASIC COSTS (2016-2017)
Tuition and fees: $2,350; out-of-state residents $8,110.
Per-credit charge: $76; out-of-state residents $268.

FINANCIAL AID PICTURE (2015-2016)
Students with need: Out of 130 full-time freshmen who applied for aid, 125 were judged to have need. Of these, 106 received aid. For part-time students, average financial aid package was $4,463.
Students without need: No-need awards available for academics, state/district residency.

FINANCIAL AID PROCEDURES
Forms required: FAFSA, state aid form, institutional form.
Dates and Deadlines: Priority date 7/15; closing date 7/1. Applicants notified on a rolling basis starting 5/15; must reply within 2 week(s) of notification.

CONTACT
Tracy Ward, Financial Aid Officer
PO Box 398, Kenansville, NC 28349-0398
(910) 296-2503

Johnson C. Smith University
Charlotte, North Carolina
www.jcsu.edu   Federal Code: 002936

4-year private university and liberal arts college in very large city.
Enrollment: 1,324 undergrads, 3% part-time. 301 full-time freshmen.
Selectivity: Admits less than 50% of applicants.

BASIC COSTS (2017-2018)
Tuition and fees: $18,236.
Per-credit charge: $418.
Room and board: $7,100.
Additional info: Tuition/fee waivers available for adults.

FINANCIAL AID PICTURE (2016-2017)
Students with need: Out of 293 full-time freshmen who applied for aid, 278 were judged to have need. Of these, 276 received aid, and 12 had their full need met. Average financial aid package met 57% of need; average scholarship/grant was $13,498; average loan was $3,478. For part-time students, average financial aid package was $3,546.
Students without need: 15 full-time freshmen who did not demonstrate need for aid received scholarships/grants; average award was $13,498. No-need awards available for academics, athletics, music/drama.
Scholarships offered: 7 full-time freshmen received athletic scholarships; average amount $14,223.

FINANCIAL AID PROCEDURES
Forms required: FAFSA, state aid form.
Dates and Deadlines: Priority date 3/1; closing date 4/1. Applicants notified on a rolling basis starting 3/15.
Transfers: No deadline. Applicants notified on a rolling basis starting 4/1.

CONTACT
Shelline Warren, Director of Financial Aid
100 Beatties Ford Road, Charlotte, NC 28216-5398
(704) 378-1035

Johnston Community College
Smithfield, North Carolina
www.johnstoncc.edu   Federal Code: 009336

2-year public community and technical college in large town.
Enrollment: 2,718 undergrads, 49% part-time. 356 full-time freshmen.
Selectivity: Open admission; but selective for some programs.

BASIC COSTS (2016-2017)

Tuition and fees: $2,377; out-of-state residents $8,137.
Per-credit charge: $76; out-of-state residents $268.

FINANCIAL AID PICTURE (2015-2016)

Students with need: 92% of average financial aid package awarded as scholarships/grants, 8% awarded as loans/jobs. Need-based aid available for part-time students.
Students without need: This college awards aid only to students with need.

FINANCIAL AID PROCEDURES

Forms required: FAFSA.
Dates and Deadlines: Priority date 5/1; no closing date. Applicants notified on a rolling basis starting 6/1; must reply within 2 week(s) of notification.

CONTACT

Betty Woodall, Financial Aid Director
PO Box 2350, Smithfield, NC 27577
(919) 209-2036

Laurel University
High Point, North Carolina
www.laureluniversity.edu   Federal Code: 013819

4-year private university and Bible college in small city, affiliated with the interdenominational tradition.
Enrollment: 125 undergrads.

BASIC COSTS (2016-2017)

Tuition and fees: $13,330.
Per-credit charge: $420.
Room only: $3,000.

FINANCIAL AID PICTURE

Students with need: Need-based aid available for full-time and part-time students. Work study available nights.
Scholarships offered: Early Acceptance; $100. Academic Honor; 10% of tuition.
Additional info: Early Acceptance Scholarships, Academic Honor Scholarships, Married Student Credit and Minister/Missionary Dependent Scholarship available.

FINANCIAL AID PROCEDURES

Forms required: FAFSA.
Dates and Deadlines: Priority date 3/15; no closing date. Applicants notified on a rolling basis starting 6/1; must reply within 3 week(s) of notification.
Transfers: Closing date 3/15.

CONTACT

Kady Hill, Director of Financial Aid
1215 Eastchester Drive, High Point, NC 27265-3115
(336) 821-2476

Lees-McRae College
Banner Elk, North Carolina
www.lmc.edu   Federal Code: 002923

4-year private liberal arts college in rural community, affiliated with the Presbyterian Church (USA).
Enrollment: 991 undergrads, 1% part-time. 187 full-time freshmen.
Selectivity: Admits 50 to 75% of applicants.

BASIC COSTS (2017-2018)

Tuition and fees: $24,878.
Per-credit charge: $710.
Room and board: $10,428.

Additional info: Tuition guarantee program available. Tuition at time of enrollment locked for 4 years.

FINANCIAL AID PICTURE (2016-2017)

Students with need: Out of 171 full-time freshmen who applied for aid, 153 were judged to have need. Of these, 153 received aid, and 3 had their full need met. Average financial aid package met 69% of need; average scholarship/grant was $9,539; average loan was $3,500. For part-time students, average financial aid package was $1,071.
Students without need: 15 full-time freshmen who did not demonstrate need for aid received scholarships/grants; average award was $12,723. No-need awards available for academics, athletics, leadership, music/drama, religious affiliation.
Scholarships offered: 73 full-time freshmen received athletic scholarships; average amount $8,382.

FINANCIAL AID PROCEDURES

Forms required: FAFSA, state aid form.
Dates and Deadlines: Priority date 4/15; no closing date. Applicants notified on a rolling basis starting 2/1; must reply within 2 week(s) of notification.

CONTACT

Cathy Shell, Director of Financial Aid
Box 128, Banner Elk, NC 28604
(828) 898-8740

Lenoir Community College
Kinston, North Carolina
www.lenoircc.edu   Federal Code: 002940

2-year public community college in large town.
Enrollment: 1,662 undergrads, 48% part-time. 261 full-time freshmen.
Selectivity: Open admission; but selective for some programs.

BASIC COSTS (2016-2017)

Tuition and fees: $2,399; out-of-state residents $8,159.
Per-credit charge: $76; out-of-state residents $268.

FINANCIAL AID PICTURE (2015-2016)

Students with need: 98% of average financial aid package awarded as scholarships/grants, 2% awarded as loans/jobs. Need-based aid available for part-time students. Work study available nights, weekends, and for part-time students.
Students without need: No-need awards available for academics, athletics, leadership, state/district residency.

FINANCIAL AID PROCEDURES

Forms required: FAFSA.
Dates and Deadlines: Priority date 7/1; closing date 8/15. Applicants notified on a rolling basis starting 8/1; must reply within 2 week(s) of notification.

CONTACT

J Gibbs, Director of Student Financial Aid
PO Box 188, Kinston, NC 28502-0188
(252) 527-6223 ext. 371

Lenoir-Rhyne University
Hickory, North Carolina
www.lr.edu   Federal Code: 002941

4-year private university and liberal arts college in large town, affiliated with the Evangelical Lutheran Church in America.
Enrollment: 1,590 undergrads, 9% part-time. 448 full-time freshmen.
Selectivity: Admits 50 to 75% of applicants.

BASIC COSTS (2016-2017)

Tuition and fees: $33,730.

Per-credit charge: $1,395.

Room and board: $11,060.

Additional info: Tuition/fee waivers available for minority students.

FINANCIAL AID PICTURE (2015-2016)

Students with need: Out of 426 full-time freshmen who applied for aid, 388 were judged to have need. Of these, 388 received aid, and 76 had their full need met. Average financial aid package met 78% of need; average scholarship/grant was $25,436; average loan was $3,296. For part-time students, average financial aid package was $6,290.

Students without need: 59 full-time freshmen who did not demonstrate need for aid received scholarships/grants; average award was $19,466. No-need awards available for academics, alumni affiliation, athletics, leadership, music/drama, religious affiliation.

Scholarships offered: 65 full-time freshmen received athletic scholarships; average amount $10,250.

FINANCIAL AID PROCEDURES

Forms required: FAFSA.

Dates and Deadlines: Applicants notified on a rolling basis; must reply by 5/1 or within 3 week(s) of notification.

CONTACT

Nick Jenkins, Director of Financial Aid
LR Box 7227, Hickory, NC 28603
(800) 277-5721

Livingstone College
Salisbury, North Carolina
www.livingstone.edu   Federal Code: 002942

4-year private liberal arts college in large town, affiliated with the African Methodist Episcopal Zion Church.

Enrollment: 1,204 undergrads.

BASIC COSTS (2016-2017)

Tuition and fees: $17,763.

Room and board: $6,596.

FINANCIAL AID PICTURE

Students with need: Need-based aid available for full-time and part-time students. Work study available nights, weekends, and for part-time students.

Students without need: No-need awards available for academics, alumni affiliation, athletics, leadership, music/drama, religious affiliation, ROTC, state/district residency.

FINANCIAL AID PROCEDURES

Forms required: FAFSA, state aid form.

Dates and Deadlines: Priority date 3/15; closing date 6/30. Applicants notified by 5/1; must reply within 4 week(s) of notification.

CONTACT

Stephanie McNeil, Director of Financial Aid
701 West Monroe Street, Salisbury, NC 28144-5213
(704) 216-6273

Louisburg College
Louisburg, North Carolina
www.louisburg.edu   Federal Code: 002943

2-year private junior college in small town, affiliated with the United Methodist Church.

Enrollment: 685 undergrads, 2% part-time. 337 full-time freshmen.

Selectivity: Admits over 75% of applicants.

BASIC COSTS (2016-2017)

Tuition and fees: $18,007.

Room and board: $10,709.

FINANCIAL AID PICTURE

Students with need: Need-based aid available for full-time students. Work study available nights, weekends, and for part-time students.

Students without need: No-need awards available for academics, art, athletics, leadership, minority status, music/drama, religious affiliation, state/district residency.

Scholarships offered: Academic Merit Scholarships: $2,000-$6,000. Leadership Scholarship: $1,000. Robbins Scholarship: $1,000.

Additional info: Job location and development program helps students obtain work in the community.

FINANCIAL AID PROCEDURES

Forms required: FAFSA, state aid form.

Dates and Deadlines: Priority date 3/1; no closing date.

CONTACT

Tracy Potter, Associate Director of Financial Aid
501 North Main Street, Louisburg, NC 27549
(919) 497-3223

Mars Hill University
Mars Hill, North Carolina
www.mhu.edu   Federal Code: 002944

4-year private liberal arts college in small town, affiliated with the Baptist faith.

Enrollment: 1,332 undergrads, 6% part-time. 394 full-time freshmen.

Selectivity: Admits 50 to 75% of applicants.

BASIC COSTS (2017-2018)

Tuition and fees: $31,804.

Per-credit charge: $1,003.

Room and board: $9,300.

FINANCIAL AID PICTURE

Students with need: Need-based aid available for full-time and part-time students. Work study available nights, weekends, and for part-time students.

Students without need: No-need awards available for academics, athletics, state/district residency.

FINANCIAL AID PROCEDURES

Forms required: FAFSA.

Dates and Deadlines: Priority date 3/15; no closing date. Applicants notified on a rolling basis starting 1/15; must reply within 2 week(s) of notification.

Transfers: No deadline. Applicants notified on a rolling basis; must reply within 2 week(s) of notification.

CONTACT

Nichole Buckner, Director of Financial Aid
Mars Hill University Admissions Office, Mars Hill, NC 28754
(828) 689-1123

Martin Community College
Williamston, North Carolina
www.martincc.edu   Federal Code: 007988

2-year public community and technical college in small town.

Enrollment: 341 undergrads, 42% part-time. 45 full-time freshmen.

Selectivity: Open admission; but selective for some programs.

BASIC COSTS (2016-2017)

Tuition and fees: $2,318; out-of-state residents $8,078.

Per-credit charge: $76; out-of-state residents $268.

FINANCIAL AID PICTURE

Students with need: Need-based aid available for full-time and part-time students. Work study available nights.

Students without need: No-need awards available for academics.

FINANCIAL AID PROCEDURES

Forms required: FAFSA.

Dates and Deadlines: Applicants notified on a rolling basis starting 5/1.

CONTACT

Michelle Cobb, Director of Financial Aid

1161 Kehukee Park Road, Williamston, NC 27892-9988

(252) 789-0244

Mayland Community College

Spruce Pine, North Carolina

www.mayland.edu   Federal Code: 011197

2-year public community college in rural community.

Enrollment: 823 undergrads.

Selectivity: Open admission; but selective for some programs.

BASIC COSTS (2016-2017)

Tuition and fees: $2,399; out-of-state residents $8,159.

Per-credit charge: $76; out-of-state residents $268.

FINANCIAL AID PICTURE (2015-2016)

Students with need: 98% of average financial aid package awarded as scholarships/grants, 2% awarded as loans/jobs. Need-based aid available for part-time students.

FINANCIAL AID PROCEDURES

Forms required: FAFSA, institutional form.

Dates and Deadlines: Priority date 3/15; closing date 6/30. Applicants notified on a rolling basis starting 6/15.

CONTACT

Cassie Forbes, Director, Financial Aid

PO Box 547, Spruce Pine, NC 28777

(828) 766-1234

McDowell Technical Community College

Marion, North Carolina

www.mcdowelltech.edu   Federal Code: 008085

2-year public community and technical college in small town.

Enrollment: 1,323 undergrads.

Selectivity: Open admission; but selective for some programs.

BASIC COSTS (2016-2017)

Tuition and fees: $2,333; out-of-state residents $8,093.

Per-credit charge: $76; out-of-state residents $268.

FINANCIAL AID PICTURE

Students with need: Need-based aid available for full-time and part-time students. Work study available nights.

Students without need: This college awards aid only to students with need.

FINANCIAL AID PROCEDURES

Forms required: FAFSA, institutional form.

Dates and Deadlines: Priority date 3/15; no closing date. Applicants notified on a rolling basis starting 7/1.

CONTACT

Kim Ledbetter, Director of Financial Aid

54 College Drive, Marion, NC 28752

(828) 652-0602

Meredith College

Raleigh, North Carolina

www.meredith.edu   Federal Code: 002945

4-year private liberal arts college for women in large city.

Enrollment: 1,650 undergrads, 2% part-time. 438 full-time freshmen.

Selectivity: Admits 50 to 75% of applicants. GED not accepted.

BASIC COSTS (2016-2017)

Tuition and fees: $34,907.

Per-credit charge: $864.

Room and board: $10,390.

FINANCIAL AID PICTURE (2015-2016)

Students with need: Out of 394 full-time freshmen who applied for aid, 345 were judged to have need. Of these, 345 received aid, and 67 had their full need met. Average financial aid package met 75.55% of need; average scholarship/grant was $22,218; average loan was $3,391. For part-time students, average financial aid package was $7,184.

Students without need: 48 full-time freshmen who did not demonstrate need for aid received scholarships/grants; average award was $14,853. No-need awards available for academics, art, leadership, minority status, music/drama, religious affiliation, state/district residency.

Scholarships offered: Presidential Scholarships: tuition plus a stipend for study abroad; based on superior academic ability and achievement; 3-5 awarded. Talent Scholarships: varying amounts; available for students planning to major in art, music, interior design and computer science/mathematics/pre-engineering; based on on-campus competition. Academic Merit Scholarships: ranging from $14,000-$18,000. Meredith Legacy Scholars: full, four-year scholarship.

FINANCIAL AID PROCEDURES

Forms required: FAFSA.

Dates and Deadlines: Priority date 2/15; no closing date. Applicants notified on a rolling basis starting 3/15; must reply by 5/1 or within 2 week(s) of notification.

Transfers: Priority date 2/15. Applicants notified on a rolling basis.

CONTACT

Kevin Michaelsen, Director of Financial Assistance

3800 Hillsborough Street, Raleigh, NC 27607-5298

(919) 760-8565

Methodist University

Fayetteville, North Carolina

www.methodist.edu   Federal Code: 002946

4-year private liberal arts college in small city, affiliated with the United Methodist Church.

Enrollment: 2,173 undergrads.

BASIC COSTS (2016-2017)

Tuition and fees: $31,980.

Per-credit charge: $1,020.

Room and board: $11,966.

FINANCIAL AID PICTURE

Students with need: Need-based aid available for full-time and part-time students. Work study available nights, weekends, and for part-time students.

Students without need: No-need awards available for academics, alumni affiliation, leadership, music/drama, religious affiliation.

Scholarships offered: Presidential Scholarship: $5,250-$17,000/yr; 3.1+ GPA, 1000+ SAT or 22+ ACT. Merit scholarship: $3,250-$4,250; residential freshmen; 2.9+ GPA, 900+ SAT or 19+ ACT; leadership. SAT scores exclusive of Writing.

FINANCIAL AID PROCEDURES

Forms required: FAFSA, state aid form.

Dates and Deadlines: Priority date 8/1; no closing date. Applicants notified on a rolling basis starting 3/6; must reply within 2 week(s) of notification.
Transfers: No deadline. Applicants notified on a rolling basis; must reply within 2 week(s) of notification.

CONTACT
Bonnie Adamson, Director of Financial Aid
5400 Ramsey Street, Fayetteville, NC 28311-1420
(910) 630-7192

Mid-Atlantic Christian University
Elizabeth City, North Carolina
www.macuniversity.edu   Federal Code: 014101

4-year private university and Bible college in large town, affiliated with the Church of Christ.
Enrollment: 184 undergrads, 14% part-time. 59 full-time freshmen.
Selectivity: Admits 50 to 75% of applicants.

BASIC COSTS (2016-2017)
Tuition and fees: $12,750.
Per-credit charge: $425.
Room and board: $8,400.

FINANCIAL AID PICTURE (2015-2016)
Students with need: Out of 59 full-time freshmen who applied for aid, 52 were judged to have need. Of these, 52 received aid, and 5 had their full need met. Average financial aid package met 66% of need; average scholarship/grant was $6,227; average loan was $3,113. For part-time students, average financial aid package was $5,673.
Students without need: 7 full-time freshmen who did not demonstrate need for aid received scholarships/grants; average award was $3,155. No-need awards available for academics, alumni affiliation, leadership, music/drama, religious affiliation.
Scholarships offered: Full tuition and half tuition available, based on demonstration of exceptional academic ability.

FINANCIAL AID PROCEDURES
Forms required: FAFSA, institutional form.
Dates and Deadlines: Priority date 3/1; no closing date. Applicants notified on a rolling basis starting 5/1; must reply within 2 week(s) of notification.
Transfers: Priority date 3/1; no deadline. Applicants notified on a rolling basis starting 5/1; must reply within 2 week(s) of notification.

CONTACT
Jenny Rowland, Financial Aid Administrator
715 North Poindexter Street, Elizabeth City, NC 27909
(252) 334-2020

Miller-Motte College: Wilmington
Wilmington, North Carolina
www.miller-motte.edu   Federal Code: E00896

4-year for-profit technical college in small city.
Enrollment: 3,463 undergrads.

BASIC COSTS (2016-2017)
Additional info: Certificate programs: $9,540-$20,668, books and supplies $400-$3,900. Associate programs: $25,116-$26,208, books and supplies $4,550-$5,200. Bachelor's programs: $27,600-$56,400, books and supplies $3,900.

FINANCIAL AID PICTURE
Students with need: Need-based aid available for full-time and part-time students. Work study available nights, weekends, and for part-time students.

Students without need: This college awards aid only to students with need.

FINANCIAL AID PROCEDURES
Forms required: FAFSA, institutional form.

CONTACT
Michele Carroll, Financial Services Manager
5000 Market Street, Wilmington, NC 28405
(910) 392-4660

Mitchell Community College
Statesville, North Carolina
www.mitchellcc.edu   Federal Code: 002947

2-year public community college in large town.
Enrollment: 2,672 undergrads.
Selectivity: Open admission; but selective for some programs.

BASIC COSTS (2016-2017)
Tuition and fees: $2,348; out-of-state residents $8,108.
Per-credit charge: $76; out-of-state residents $268.

FINANCIAL AID PICTURE
Students with need: Need-based aid available for full-time and part-time students.

FINANCIAL AID PROCEDURES
Forms required: FAFSA, institutional form.
Dates and Deadlines: Applicants notified on a rolling basis starting 3/1; must reply within 2 week(s) of notification.
Transfers: Students are monitored through NSLDS's Transfer Monitoring List.

CONTACT
Candace Cooper, Director of Financial Aid
500 West Broad Street, Statesville, NC 28677
(704) 878-3256

Montgomery Community College
Troy, North Carolina
www.montgomery.edu   Federal Code: 008087

2-year public community college in small town.
Enrollment: 545 undergrads.
Selectivity: Open admission; but selective for some programs.

BASIC COSTS (2016-2017)
Tuition and fees: $2,385; out-of-state residents $8,145.
Per-credit charge: $76; out-of-state residents $268.

FINANCIAL AID PICTURE (2015-2016)
Students with need: 98% of average financial aid package awarded as scholarships/grants, 2% awarded as loans/jobs. Need-based aid available for part-time students. Work study available nights.
Students without need: No-need awards available for academics, minority status, state/district residency.

FINANCIAL AID PROCEDURES
Forms required: FAFSA, institutional form.
Dates and Deadlines: Closing date 7/1. Applicants notified on a rolling basis starting 3/15; must reply by 7/1.
Transfers: Applicants notified on a rolling basis starting 3/15; must reply by 7/1.

CONTACT
Doni Cody, Director of Financial Aid
1011 Page Street, Troy, NC 27371
(910) 898-9613

Montreat College

Montreat, North Carolina
www.montreat.edu   Federal Code: 002948

4-year private liberal arts college in small town, affiliated with the Reformed Presbyterian Church of North America.
Enrollment: 724 undergrads.

BASIC COSTS (2016-2017)
Tuition and fees: $24,940.
Room and board: $8,637.

FINANCIAL AID PICTURE
Students with need: Need-based aid available for full-time and part-time students. Work study available nights, weekends, and for part-time students.
Students without need: No-need awards available for academics, alumni affiliation, art, athletics, leadership, minority status, music/drama, religious affiliation, state/district residency.

FINANCIAL AID PROCEDURES
Forms required: FAFSA, state aid form.
Dates and Deadlines: Priority date 3/1; no closing date. Applicants notified on a rolling basis starting 3/1; must reply within 2 week(s) of notification.
Transfers: Priority date 4/1; no deadline. Applicants notified on a rolling basis starting 1/15; must reply within 2 week(s) of notification.

CONTACT
Beth Pocock, Director of Financial Aid
P.O. Box 1267, Montreat, NC 28757
(800) 545-4656

Nash Community College

Rocky Mount, North Carolina
www.nashcc.edu   Federal Code: 008557

2-year public community and technical college in small city.
Enrollment: 1,987 undergrads, 46% part-time. 360 full-time freshmen.
Selectivity: Open admission; but selective for some programs.

BASIC COSTS (2016-2017)
Tuition and fees: $2,830; out-of-state residents $9,080.
Per-credit charge: $76; out-of-state residents $268.

FINANCIAL AID PICTURE
Students with need: Need-based aid available for full-time and part-time students. Work study available nights, weekends, and for part-time students.
Students without need: No-need awards available for academics.

FINANCIAL AID PROCEDURES
Forms required: FAFSA, institutional form.
Dates and Deadlines: Priority date 6/30; no closing date. Applicants notified on a rolling basis starting 7/15.

CONTACT
Tammy Lester, Financial Aid Officer
Box 7488, Rocky Mount, NC 27804-0488
(252) 451-8371

North Carolina Agricultural and Technical State University

Greensboro, North Carolina
www.ncat.edu   Federal Code: 002905

4-year public university in small city.
Enrollment: 9,354 undergrads.

BASIC COSTS (2016-2017)
Tuition and fees: $6,265; out-of-state residents $19,025.
Room and board: $7,153.

FINANCIAL AID PICTURE
Students with need: Need-based aid available for full-time and part-time students.
Students without need: No-need awards available for academics.

FINANCIAL AID PROCEDURES
Forms required: FAFSA.
Dates and Deadlines: Priority date 3/1; no closing date. Applicants notified on a rolling basis starting 4/15; must reply within 2 week(s) of notification.

CONTACT
Sherri Avent, Director of Student Financial Aid
Webb Hall, Greensboro, NC 27411-0002
(336) 334-7973

North Carolina Central University

Durham, North Carolina
www.nccu.edu   Federal Code: 002950

4-year public university in small city.
Enrollment: 5,902 undergrads, 11% part-time. 1,128 full-time freshmen.
Selectivity: Admits 50 to 75% of applicants.

BASIC COSTS (2016-2017)
Tuition and fees: $6,051; out-of-state residents $18,509.
Room and board: $8,270.

FINANCIAL AID PICTURE (2015-2016)
Students with need: Need-based aid available for full-time and part-time students.
Students without need: No-need awards available for academics, alumni affiliation, art, athletics, leadership, music/drama, ROTC.
Additional info: Departmental grants based on need plus other available criteria.

FINANCIAL AID PROCEDURES
Forms required: FAFSA.
Dates and Deadlines: Closing date 3/1. Applicants notified by 3/1; must reply within 2 week(s) of notification.

CONTACT
Sharon Oliver, Director of Student Financial Aid
PO Box 19717, Durham, NC 27707
(919) 530-6180

North Carolina State University

Raleigh, North Carolina
www.ncsu.edu   Federal Code: 002972

4-year public university in large city.
Enrollment: 22,346 undergrads, 7% part-time. 4,409 full-time freshmen.
Selectivity: Admits less than 50% of applicants.

BASIC COSTS (2016-2017)
Tuition and fees: $8,880; out-of-state residents $26,399.
Room and board: $10,635.

FINANCIAL AID PICTURE (2016-2017)
Students with need: Out of 3,413 full-time freshmen who applied for aid, 2,057 were judged to have need. Of these, 2,011 received aid, and 531 had their full need met. Average financial aid package met 79.78% of need; average scholarship/grant was $10,579; average loan was $3,164. For part-time students, average financial aid package was $7,581.

Students without need: 200 full-time freshmen who did not demonstrate need for aid received scholarships/grants; average award was $6,113. No-need awards available for academics, alumni affiliation, athletics, leadership, ROTC, state/district residency.

Scholarships offered: *Merit:* Park Scholarships: 4 year scholarship that covers almost all expenses; approximately 50 awarded each year. Goodnight Scholarships: 4 year scholarship that covers more than 75% of all expenses; 50 awarded each year. Caldwell scholarships: awarded at end of freshmen year for 3 years covering most expenses. *Athletic:* 78 full-time freshmen received athletic scholarships; average amount $20,334.

Additional info: Freshman Merit Scholarships; students submitting complete admissions application by the October 15 Early Action deadline automatically considered, additional information may be required after initial review.

FINANCIAL AID PROCEDURES

Forms required: FAFSA.

Dates and Deadlines: Priority date 3/1; no closing date. Applicants notified on a rolling basis starting 4/1.

Transfers: Priority date 3/1; no deadline. Applicants notified by 4/1.

CONTACT

Krista Ringler, Director of Scholarships and Financial Aid
Campus Box 7103, Raleigh, NC 27695-7103
(919) 515-2421

North Carolina Wesleyan College
Rocky Mount, North Carolina
www.ncwc.edu   Federal Code: 002951

4-year private liberal arts college in small city, affiliated with the United Methodist Church.

Enrollment: 2,085 undergrads, 14% part-time. 323 full-time freshmen.

Selectivity: Admits 50 to 75% of applicants.

BASIC COSTS (2016-2017)

Tuition and fees: $29,300.

Per-credit charge: $502.

Room and board: $9,850.

FINANCIAL AID PICTURE

Students with need: Need-based aid available for full-time and part-time students.

Students without need: No-need awards available for academics, religious affiliation.

Additional info: Scholarships based on GPA. Various scholarship and leadership awards available.

FINANCIAL AID PROCEDURES

Forms required: FAFSA.

Dates and Deadlines: Priority date 3/1; no closing date. Applicants notified on a rolling basis starting 1/1; must reply within 2 week(s) of notification.

Transfers: No deadline. Applicants notified on a rolling basis; must reply within 2 week(s) of notification.

CONTACT

Elena Koutouzos, Director of Financial Aid
3400 North Wesleyan Boulevard, Rocky Mount, NC 27804
(252) 985-5295

Pamlico Community College
Grantsboro, North Carolina
www.pamlicocc.edu   Federal Code: 007031

2-year public community college in rural community.

Enrollment: 504 undergrads. 39 full-time freshmen.

Selectivity: Open admission.

BASIC COSTS (2016-2017)

Tuition and fees: $2,323; out-of-state residents $8,083.

Per-credit charge: $76; out-of-state residents $268.

FINANCIAL AID PICTURE (2015-2016)

Students with need: Out of 30 full-time freshmen who applied for aid, 28 were judged to have need. Of these, 28 received aid. For part-time students, average financial aid package was $1,200.

FINANCIAL AID PROCEDURES

Forms required: FAFSA.

Dates and Deadlines: Closing date 6/1. Applicants notified on a rolling basis.

Transfers: No deadline. Applicants notified on a rolling basis.

CONTACT

Melissa Whitman, Financial Aid Officer
PO Box 185, Grantsboro, NC 28529
(252) 249-1851 ext. 3026

Pfeiffer University
Misenheimer, North Carolina
www.pfeiffer.edu   Federal Code: 002955

4-year private university and liberal arts college in rural community, affiliated with the United Methodist Church.

Enrollment: 906 undergrads. 173 full-time freshmen.

BASIC COSTS (2016-2017)

Tuition and fees: $28,995.

Per-credit charge: $640.

Room and board: $10,700.

FINANCIAL AID PICTURE (2015-2016)

Students with need: Out of 160 full-time freshmen who applied for aid, 160 were judged to have need. Of these, 160 received aid, and 21 had their full need met. Average financial aid package met 75% of need; average scholarship/grant was $20,000; average loan was $4,000. For part-time students, average financial aid package was $8,000.

Students without need: 8 full-time freshmen who did not demonstrate need for aid received scholarships/grants; average award was $12,000. No-need awards available for academics, alumni affiliation, leadership, music/drama, religious affiliation, state/district residency.

Scholarships offered: Presidential Scholarship: up to $20,000 University Scholarship: up to $17000 Prudden Scholarship: $9000 to $14,000.

FINANCIAL AID PROCEDURES

Forms required: FAFSA, state aid form.

Dates and Deadlines: Priority date 12/1; no closing date. Applicants notified on a rolling basis; must reply within 2 week(s) of notification.

Transfers: Priority date 1/15.

CONTACT

J. King, Executive Director of Financial Aid
PO Box 960, Misenheimer, NC 28109
(800) 228-1360

Piedmont Community College
Roxboro, North Carolina
www.piedmontcc.edu   Federal Code: 009646

2-year public community college in small town.

Enrollment: 1,005 undergrads.

Selectivity: Open admission; but selective for some programs.

BASIC COSTS (2016-2017)

Tuition and fees: $2,394.5; out-of-state residents $8,154.5.
Per-credit charge: $76; out-of-state residents $268.

FINANCIAL AID PICTURE (2015-2016)

Students with need: 99% of average financial aid package awarded as scholarships/grants, 1% awarded as loans/jobs. Need-based aid available for part-time students.

FINANCIAL AID PROCEDURES

Forms required: FAFSA.
Dates and Deadlines: Priority date 4/1; no closing date. Applicants notified on a rolling basis starting 4/16; must reply within 2 week(s) of notification.

CONTACT

Tasha Williams, Director of Financial Aid/Veterans Affairs
1715 College Drive, Roxboro, NC 27573
(336) 599-1181 ext. 2159

Piedmont International University

Winston-Salem, North Carolina
www.piedmontu.edu   Federal Code: 002956

4-year private university and seminary college in small city, affiliated with the Baptist faith.
Enrollment: 298 undergrads, 41% part-time. 176 full-time freshmen.

BASIC COSTS (2016-2017)

Tuition and fees: $9,650.
Per-credit charge: $295.
Room and board: $6,410.
Additional info: Tuition/fee waivers available for minority students.

FINANCIAL AID PICTURE (2016-2017)

Students with need: Average financial aid package met 41% of need; average scholarship/grant was $5,997; average loan was $3,500. For part-time students, average financial aid package was $5,901.
Students without need: No-need awards available for academics, alumni affiliation, leadership, minority status, religious affiliation.

FINANCIAL AID PROCEDURES

Forms required: FAFSA, institutional form.
Dates and Deadlines: Priority date 3/1; closing date 8/1. Applicants notified on a rolling basis starting 3/1; must reply within 2 week(s) of notification.
Transfers: Applicants notified on a rolling basis starting 3/1.

CONTACT

Chris Ronk, Executive Vice President of Operations
420 South Boad Street, Winston-Salem, NC 27101-5133
(336) 714-7878

Pitt Community College

Greenville, North Carolina
www.pittcc.edu   Federal Code: 004062

2-year public community and technical college in small city.
Enrollment: 8,521 undergrads.
Selectivity: Open admission; but selective for some programs.

BASIC COSTS (2016-2017)

Tuition and fees: $2,354; out-of-state residents $8,114.
Per-credit charge: $76; out-of-state residents $268.

FINANCIAL AID PICTURE

Students with need: Need-based aid available for full-time and part-time students. Work study available nights.
Students without need: No-need awards available for academics, athletics, ROTC.

FINANCIAL AID PROCEDURES

Forms required: FAFSA.
Dates and Deadlines: Priority date 3/15; closing date 5/15. Applicants notified on a rolling basis starting 2/1.

CONTACT

Tamara Glaspie, Financial Aid Director
PO Drawer 7007, Greenville, NC 27835-7007
(252) 483-7326

Queens University of Charlotte

Charlotte, North Carolina
www.queens.edu   Federal Code: 002957

4-year private university in very large city, affiliated with the Presbyterian Church (USA).
Enrollment: 1,504 undergrads, 14% part-time. 274 full-time freshmen.
Selectivity: Admits over 75% of applicants.

BASIC COSTS (2017-2018)

Tuition and fees: $33,532.
Per-credit charge: $464.
Room and board: $11,844.

FINANCIAL AID PICTURE (2016-2017)

Students with need: Out of 226 full-time freshmen who applied for aid, 180 were judged to have need. Of these, 180 received aid, and 46 had their full need met. Average financial aid package met 75% of need; average scholarship/grant was $22,556; average loan was $3,322. For part-time students, average financial aid package was $6,670.
Students without need: 88 full-time freshmen who did not demonstrate need for aid received scholarships/grants; average award was $13,255. No-need awards available for academics, alumni affiliation, art, athletics, leadership, minority status, music/drama, religious affiliation, state/district residency.
Scholarships offered: *Merit:* Presidential Scholarships: full tuition; based on special application/recommendations; deadline 12/13; up to 10 awarded. University Scholarships: range from $7,000-$14,000; based on admitted student's academic profile. *Athletic:* 78 full-time freshmen received athletic scholarships; average amount $14,250.

FINANCIAL AID PROCEDURES

Forms required: FAFSA.
Dates and Deadlines: Applicants notified on a rolling basis starting 2/15; must reply by 5/1 or within 3 week(s) of notification.
Transfers: No deadline. Applicants notified on a rolling basis starting 2/15; must reply by 5/1 or within 3 week(s) of notification.

CONTACT

Christy Majors, Assistant Vice President of Student Financial Services
1900 Selwyn Avenue, Charlotte, NC 28274-0001
(704) 337-2225

Randolph Community College

Asheboro, North Carolina
www.randolph.edu   Federal Code: 005447

2-year public community and technical college in large town.
Enrollment: 2,800 undergrads.
Selectivity: Open admission; but selective for some programs.

BASIC COSTS (2016-2017)

Tuition and fees: $2,348; out-of-state residents $8,108.
Per-credit charge: $76; out-of-state residents $268.

FINANCIAL AID PICTURE

Students with need: Need-based aid available for full-time and part-time students. Work study available nights.

Students without need: No-need awards available for academics, leadership, minority status, state/district residency.

FINANCIAL AID PROCEDURES

Forms required: FAFSA.

Dates and Deadlines: Applicants notified on a rolling basis starting 3/1.

Transfers: No deadline. Applicants notified on a rolling basis starting 3/1.

CONTACT

Chad Williams, Director of Student Support Services
629 Industrial Park Avenue, Asheboro, NC 27205
(336) 633-0200

Richmond Community College
Hamlet, North Carolina
www.richmondcc.edu   Federal Code: 005464

2-year public community college in small town.
Enrollment: 2,321 undergrads.
Selectivity: Open admission; but selective for some programs.

BASIC COSTS (2016-2017)

Tuition and fees: $2,344; out-of-state residents $8,104.
Per-credit charge: $76; out-of-state residents $268.

FINANCIAL AID PICTURE

Students with need: Need-based aid available for full-time and part-time students. Work study available nights.

Students without need: No-need awards available for academics, leadership.

FINANCIAL AID PROCEDURES

Forms required: FAFSA, institutional form.

Dates and Deadlines: Closing date 7/25. Applicants notified on a rolling basis starting 7/8; must reply within 2 week(s) of notification.

CONTACT

Bruce Blackmon, Director of Financial Aid
Box 1189, Hamlet, NC 28345
(910) 410-1726

Roanoke-Chowan Community College
Ahoskie, North Carolina
www.roanokechowan.edu   Federal Code: 008613

2-year public community college in small town.
Enrollment: 903 undergrads.
Selectivity: Open admission; but selective for some programs.

BASIC COSTS (2016-2017)

Tuition and fees: $2,394; out-of-state residents $8,154.
Per-credit charge: $76; out-of-state residents $268.

FINANCIAL AID PICTURE (2015-2016)

Students with need: 98% of average financial aid package awarded as scholarships/grants, 2% awarded as loans/jobs. Need-based aid available for part-time students.

Students without need: No-need awards available for academics.

FINANCIAL AID PROCEDURES

Forms required: FAFSA.

Dates and Deadlines: Priority date 3/15; no closing date. Applicants notified on a rolling basis starting 7/1.

CONTACT

Crystal Harris, Financial Aid Director
109 Community College Road, Ahoskie, NC 27910-9522
(252) 862-1246

Robeson Community College
Lumberton, North Carolina
www.robeson.edu   Federal Code: 008612

2-year public community college in large town.
Enrollment: 1,976 undergrads.
Selectivity: Open admission; but selective for some programs.

BASIC COSTS (2016-2017)

Tuition and fees: $2,393; out-of-state residents $8,153.
Per-credit charge: $76; out-of-state residents $268.

FINANCIAL AID PICTURE

Students with need: Need-based aid available for full-time and part-time students.

FINANCIAL AID PROCEDURES

Forms required: FAFSA.

Dates and Deadlines: Priority date 5/15; no closing date. Applicants notified on a rolling basis starting 7/31.

CONTACT

Teresa Tubbs, Director of Financial Aid
PO Box 1420, Lumberton, NC 28359
(910) 272-3352

Rockingham Community College
Wentworth, North Carolina
www.rockinghamcc.edu   Federal Code: 002958

2-year public community college in rural community.
Enrollment: 1,860 undergrads.
Selectivity: Open admission; but selective for some programs.

BASIC COSTS (2016-2017)

Tuition and fees: $2,376; out-of-state residents $8,136.
Per-credit charge: $76; out-of-state residents $268.

FINANCIAL AID PICTURE

Students with need: Need-based aid available for full-time and part-time students.

Students without need: No-need awards available for academics.

FINANCIAL AID PROCEDURES

Forms required: FAFSA, institutional form.

Dates and Deadlines: Priority date 3/15; no closing date. Must reply within 2 week(s) of notification.

CONTACT

Evans Sarah, Director of Financial Aid
Box 38, Wentworth, NC 27375-0038
(336) 342-4261 ext. 2204

Rowan-Cabarrus Community College
Salisbury, North Carolina
www.rccc.edu   Federal Code: 005754

2-year public community and technical college in large town.
Enrollment: 5,751 undergrads.
Selectivity: Open admission; but selective for some programs.

BASIC COSTS (2016-2017)
Tuition and fees: $2,409; out-of-state residents $8,169.
Per-credit charge: $76; out-of-state residents $268.

FINANCIAL AID PICTURE
Students with need: Need-based aid available for full-time and part-time students. Work study available nights.
Students without need: No-need awards available for academics, job skills, state/district residency.

FINANCIAL AID PROCEDURES
Forms required: FAFSA.
Dates and Deadlines: Priority date 3/15; no closing date. Applicants notified on a rolling basis starting 5/1; must reply within 3 week(s) of notification.
Transfers: No deadline.

CONTACT
Lisa Ledbetter, Director, Financial Aid
Box 1595, Salisbury, NC 28145
(704) 637-0760 ext. 273

St. Andrews University
Laurinburg, North Carolina
www.sa.edu   Federal Code: 002967

4-year private liberal arts college in large town, affiliated with the Presbyterian Church (USA).
Enrollment: 683 undergrads, 10% part-time. 227 full-time freshmen.
Selectivity: Admits 50 to 75% of applicants.

BASIC COSTS (2016-2017)
Tuition and fees: $25,874.
Room and board: $10,396.

FINANCIAL AID PICTURE (2016-2017)
Students with need: Out of 195 full-time freshmen who applied for aid, 190 were judged to have need. Of these, 189 received aid, and 16 had their full need met. Average financial aid package met 70% of need; average scholarship/grant was $17,909; average loan was $3,554. For part-time students, average financial aid package was $3,947.
Students without need: 18 full-time freshmen who did not demonstrate need for aid received scholarships/grants; average award was $10,005. No-need awards available for academics, alumni affiliation, art, athletics, job skills, leadership, music/drama, religious affiliation.
Scholarships offered: 25 full-time freshmen received athletic scholarships; average amount $6,831.

FINANCIAL AID PROCEDURES
Forms required: FAFSA.
Dates and Deadlines: Priority date 5/1; no closing date. Applicants notified on a rolling basis starting 3/1.
Transfers: No deadline. Applicants notified on a rolling basis starting 10/1; must reply within 2 week(s) of notification.

CONTACT
Dawn Young, Director of Student Financial Planning
1700 Dogwood Mile, Laurinburg, NC 28352
(910) 277-5560

Saint Augustine's University
Raleigh, North Carolina
www.st-aug.edu   Federal Code: 002968

4-year private liberal arts college in large city, affiliated with the Episcopal Church.
Enrollment: 944 undergrads, 3% part-time. 347 full-time freshmen.

BASIC COSTS (2017-2018)
Tuition and fees: $17,890.
Per-credit charge: $547.
Room and board: $7,692.

FINANCIAL AID PICTURE
Students with need: Need-based aid available for full-time and part-time students. Work study available nights, weekends, and for part-time students.
Students without need: No-need awards available for academics, art, athletics, leadership, minority status, music/drama, religious affiliation, ROTC, state/district residency.
Scholarships offered: Institutional Merit Scholarships based on high school record, evidence of leadership, and SAT score.

FINANCIAL AID PROCEDURES
Forms required: FAFSA, institutional form.
Dates and Deadlines: Priority date 3/15; no closing date. Applicants notified on a rolling basis starting 3/1; must reply within 2 week(s) of notification.
Transfers: Priority date 3/15; no deadline. Applicants notified on a rolling basis; must reply within 2 week(s) of notification.

CONTACT
Carmela Cohen-Perry, Director of Financial Aid
1315 Oakwood Avenue, Raleigh, NC 27610-2298
(919) 516-4131

Salem College
Winston-Salem, North Carolina
www.salem.edu   Federal Code: 002960

4-year private liberal arts college for women in small city, affiliated with the Moravian Church in America.
Enrollment: 917 undergrads. 184 full-time freshmen.

BASIC COSTS (2016-2017)
Tuition and fees: $27,406.
Room and board: $11,500.
Additional info: Tuition/fee waivers available for adults.

FINANCIAL AID PICTURE (2015-2016)
Students with need: Out of 173 full-time freshmen who applied for aid, 167 were judged to have need. Of these, 167 received aid. Need-based aid available for part-time students.
Students without need: No-need awards available for academics, alumni affiliation, leadership, minority status, music/drama, state/district residency.

FINANCIAL AID PROCEDURES
Forms required: FAFSA.
Dates and Deadlines: Priority date 3/1; no closing date. Applicants notified on a rolling basis starting 3/1; must reply by 5/1 or within 2 week(s) of notification.

CONTACT
Paul Coscia, Director of Financial Aid
601 South Church Street, Winston-Salem, NC 27108
(336) 721-2808

Sampson Community College
Clinton, North Carolina
www.sampsoncc.edu   Federal Code: 007892

2-year public community and technical college in small town.
Enrollment: 1,539 undergrads.
Selectivity: Open admission; but selective for some programs.

BASIC COSTS (2016-2017)
Tuition and fees: $2,357; out-of-state residents $8,117.

Per-credit charge: $76; out-of-state residents $268.

FINANCIAL AID PICTURE
Students with need: Need-based aid available for full-time and part-time students.
Students without need: No-need awards available for academics, state/district residency.

FINANCIAL AID PROCEDURES
Forms required: FAFSA.
Dates and Deadlines: Priority date 5/1; no closing date. Applicants notified on a rolling basis starting 7/15; must reply within 2 week(s) of notification.

CONTACT
Judye Tart, Director of Financial Aid
PO Box 318, Clinton, NC 28329
(910) 592-8084 ext. 2024

Sandhills Community College
Pinehurst, North Carolina
www.sandhills.edu   Federal Code: 002961

2-year public community college in large town.
Enrollment: 2,890 undergrads.
Selectivity: Open admission; but selective for some programs.

BASIC COSTS (2016-2017)
Tuition and fees: $2,446; out-of-state residents $8,206.
Per-credit charge: $76; out-of-state residents $268.

FINANCIAL AID PICTURE (2015-2016)
Students with need: 95% of average financial aid package awarded as scholarships/grants, 5% awarded as loans/jobs. Need-based aid available for part-time students.
Students without need: No-need awards available for academics, state/district residency.

FINANCIAL AID PROCEDURES
Forms required: FAFSA.
Dates and Deadlines: Priority date 7/15; no closing date. Applicants notified on a rolling basis starting 3/1.

CONTACT
Lindsey Farmer, Director of Financial Aid
3395 Airport Road, Pinehurst, NC 28374
(910) 695-3743

Shaw University
Raleigh, North Carolina
www.shawu.edu   Federal Code: 002962

4-year private university and liberal arts college in large city, affiliated with the Baptist faith.
Enrollment: 1,711 undergrads, 6% part-time. 637 full-time freshmen.
Selectivity: Admits less than 50% of applicants.

BASIC COSTS (2017-2018)
Tuition and fees: $16,480.
Per-credit charge: $492.
Room and board: $8,158.

FINANCIAL AID PICTURE
Students with need: Need-based aid available for full-time and part-time students. Work study available nights, weekends, and for part-time students.
Students without need: No-need awards available for academics, athletics, music/drama.
Scholarships offered: Presidential Scholarship: based on GPA and SAT.

FINANCIAL AID PROCEDURES
Forms required: FAFSA.
Dates and Deadlines: Priority date 3/1; closing date 6/30. Applicants notified on a rolling basis starting 3/15.

CONTACT
Gwen Webb, Vice President for Finance and Administration
118 East South Street, Raleigh, NC 27601
(919) 546-8240

South College
Asheville, North Carolina
www.southcollegenc.edu   Federal Code: 010264

2-year for-profit health science and career college in small city.
Enrollment: 263 undergrads.
Selectivity: Open admission; but selective for some programs.

FINANCIAL AID PICTURE
Students with need: Need-based aid available for full-time and part-time students.

FINANCIAL AID PROCEDURES
Forms required: FAFSA, institutional form.
Dates and Deadlines: Applicants notified on a rolling basis; must reply within 4 week(s) of notification.

CONTACT
Ronda Blackman, Financial Aid Director
140 Sweeten Creek Road, Asheville, NC 28803
(828) 398-2500

South Piedmont Community College
Polkton, North Carolina
www.spcc.edu   Federal Code: 007985

2-year public community college in small city.
Enrollment: 2,789 undergrads.
Selectivity: Open admission; but selective for some programs.

BASIC COSTS (2016-2017)
Tuition and fees: $2,515; out-of-state residents $8,275.
Per-credit charge: $76; out-of-state residents $268.

FINANCIAL AID PICTURE
Students with need: Need-based aid available for full-time and part-time students. Work study available nights.
Additional info: Small amount of non-federal scholarship aid available. FAFSA applications received before June 1 will receive first priority.

FINANCIAL AID PROCEDURES
Forms required: FAFSA.
Dates and Deadlines: Priority date 6/1; no closing date. Applicants notified on a rolling basis.

CONTACT
Emily Jarrell, Director of Financial Aid and Veterans Affairs
PO Box 126, Polkton, NC 28135
(704) 272-5326

Southeastern Baptist Theological Seminary
Wake Forest, North Carolina
www.sebts.edu

4-year private Bible and seminary college in large town, affiliated with the Southern Baptist Convention.

Enrollment: 414 undergrads, 43% part-time. 40 full-time freshmen.

Selectivity: Open admission; but selective for some programs.

BASIC COSTS (2016-2017)

Tuition and fees: $10,500; out-of-state residents $10,500.

Per-credit charge: $332.

Room only: $2,580.

FINANCIAL AID PICTURE (2015-2016)

Students with need: Out of 30 full-time freshmen who applied for aid, 22 were judged to have need. Of these, 22 received aid. Average financial aid package met 40% of need; average scholarship/grant was $1,277. For part-time students, average financial aid package was $2,489.

Students without need: This college awards aid only to students with need.

FINANCIAL AID PROCEDURES

Forms required: institutional form.

Dates and Deadlines: Closing date 7/15. Applicants notified on a rolling basis starting 6/1.

Transfers: No deadline. Applicants notified on a rolling basis.

CONTACT

Jesse Parker, Director of Student Resources and Financial Aid

PO Box 1889, Wake Forest, NC 27588

(919) 761-2317

Southeastern Community College

Whiteville, North Carolina

www.sccnc.edu   Federal Code: 002964

2-year public community college in small town.

Enrollment: 968 undergrads, 49% part-time. 177 full-time freshmen.

Selectivity: Open admission; but selective for some programs.

BASIC COSTS (2016-2017)

Tuition and fees: $2,437; out-of-state residents $8,197.

Per-credit charge: $76; out-of-state residents $268.

FINANCIAL AID PICTURE

Students with need: Need-based aid available for full-time and part-time students.

Students without need: No-need awards available for academics, athletics, leadership, music/drama, state/district residency.

FINANCIAL AID PROCEDURES

Forms required: FAFSA.

Dates and Deadlines: Priority date 4/1; no closing date. Applicants notified on a rolling basis starting 6/1; must reply within 2 week(s) of notification.

CONTACT

Justin Cristello, Director of Financial Aid

4564 Chadbourn Highway, Whiteville, NC 28472-0151

(910) 642-7141 ext. 214

Southwestern Community College

Sylva, North Carolina

www.southwesterncc.edu   Federal Code: 008466

2-year public community college in rural community.

Enrollment: 1,703 undergrads, 54% part-time. 200 full-time freshmen.

Selectivity: Open admission; but selective for some programs.

BASIC COSTS (2016-2017)

Tuition and fees: $2,371; out-of-state residents $8,131.

Per-credit charge: $76; out-of-state residents $268.

FINANCIAL AID PICTURE

Students with need: Need-based aid available for full-time and part-time students.

FINANCIAL AID PROCEDURES

Forms required: FAFSA.

Dates and Deadlines: Closing date 6/30. Applicants notified on a rolling basis starting 5/1; must reply within 2 week(s) of notification.

CONTACT

Melody Lawrence, Director of Financial Aid

447 College Drive, Sylva, NC 28779

(800) 447-4091 ext. 4224

Stanly Community College

Albemarle, North Carolina

www.stanly.edu   Federal Code: 011194

2-year public community college in large town.

Enrollment: 2,020 undergrads, 58% part-time. 240 full-time freshmen.

Selectivity: Open admission; but selective for some programs.

BASIC COSTS (2016-2017)

Tuition and fees: $2,456; out-of-state residents $8,216.

Per-credit charge: $76; out-of-state residents $268.

FINANCIAL AID PICTURE (2015-2016)

Students with need: Out of 181 full-time freshmen who applied for aid, 157 were judged to have need. Of these, 157 received aid. Average financial aid package met 40% of need; average scholarship/grant was $4,832. Need-based aid available for part-time students.

Students without need: This college awards aid only to students with need.

FINANCIAL AID PROCEDURES

Forms required: FAFSA, institutional form.

Dates and Deadlines: Applicants notified on a rolling basis starting 6/1; must reply within 2 week(s) of notification.

Transfers: No deadline. Applicants notified on a rolling basis.

CONTACT

Petra Fields, Director of Financial Aid

141 College Drive, Albemarle, NC 28001

(704) 991-0231

Surry Community College

Dobson, North Carolina

www.surry.edu   Federal Code: 002970

2-year public community college in rural community.

Enrollment: 2,075 undergrads, 48% part-time. 350 full-time freshmen.

Selectivity: Open admission; but selective for some programs.

BASIC COSTS (2016-2017)

Tuition and fees: $2,378; out-of-state residents $8,138.

Per-credit charge: $76; out-of-state residents $268.

FINANCIAL AID PICTURE

Students with need: Need-based aid available for full-time and part-time students. Work study available nights.

Students without need: No-need awards available for academics.

FINANCIAL AID PROCEDURES

Forms required: FAFSA, institutional form.

Dates and Deadlines: Closing date 5/1. Applicants notified on a rolling basis starting 6/1; must reply within 2 week(s) of notification.

Transfers: Priority date 6/1.

CONTACT

Andrea Simpson, Director of Financial Aid
ATTN: Admissions Offfice 630 South Main Street, Dobson, NC 27017
(336) 386-3263

Tri-County Community College

Murphy, North Carolina
www.tricountycc.edu   Federal Code: 009430

2-year public community college in small town.
Enrollment: 1,003 undergrads.
Selectivity: Open admission.

BASIC COSTS (2016-2017)

Tuition and fees: $2,339; out-of-state residents $8,099.
Per-credit charge: $76; out-of-state residents $268.

FINANCIAL AID PICTURE (2015-2016)

Students with need: 99% of average financial aid package awarded as scholarships/grants, 1% awarded as loans/jobs. Need-based aid available for part-time students.
Students without need: This college awards aid only to students with need.

FINANCIAL AID PROCEDURES

Forms required: FAFSA.
Dates and Deadlines: Priority date 6/30; no closing date. Applicants notified on a rolling basis starting 6/1; must reply within 4 week(s) of notification.
Transfers: Must reply within 4 week(s) of notification.

CONTACT

Diane Owl, Financial Aid Officer
21 Campus Circle, Murphy, NC 28906
(828) 837-6810

University of Mount Olive

Mount Olive, North Carolina
www.mou.edu   Federal Code: 002949

4-year private university in small town, affiliated with the Free Will Baptists.
Enrollment: 3,152 undergrads.

BASIC COSTS (2016-2017)

Tuition and fees: $19,000.
Per-credit charge: $425.
Room and board: $7,600.

FINANCIAL AID PICTURE

Students with need: Need-based aid available for full-time and part-time students.
Students without need: No-need awards available for academics, art, athletics, leadership, music/drama, religious affiliation.

FINANCIAL AID PROCEDURES

Forms required: FAFSA, state aid form, institutional form.
Dates and Deadlines: Applicants notified on a rolling basis starting 3/1; must reply within 2 week(s) of notification.
Transfers: Special scholarship program available for transfers from North Carolina community colleges.

CONTACT

Katrina Lee, Director of Financial Aid
634 Henderson Street, Mount Olive, NC 28365
(919) 658-7164

University of North Carolina at Asheville

Asheville, North Carolina
www.unca.edu   Federal Code: 002907

4-year public university and liberal arts college in small city.
Enrollment: 3,466 undergrads, 10% part-time. 734 full-time freshmen.
Selectivity: Admits over 75% of applicants. GED not accepted.

BASIC COSTS (2016-2017)

Tuition and fees: $6,842; out-of-state residents $23,237.
Room and board: $8,746.
Additional info: Tuition at time of enrollment locked for 4 years.

FINANCIAL AID PICTURE (2015-2016)

Students with need: Out of 635 full-time freshmen who applied for aid, 416 were judged to have need. Of these, 411 received aid, and 99 had their full need met. Average financial aid package met 77% of need; average scholarship/grant was $7,040; average loan was $3,600. For part-time students, average financial aid package was $7,477.
Students without need: 54 full-time freshmen who did not demonstrate need for aid received scholarships/grants; average award was $2,182. No-need awards available for academics, alumni affiliation, art, athletics, job skills, leadership, music/drama, state/district residency.
Scholarships offered: *Merit:* Limited number of merit based scholarships that range from $1,250 - $4,000 per year. Prospective students must apply by November 15th for consideration. ***Athletic:*** 21 full-time freshmen received athletic scholarships; average amount $11,801.

FINANCIAL AID PROCEDURES

Forms required: FAFSA.
Dates and Deadlines: Priority date 3/1; no closing date. Applicants notified on a rolling basis starting 3/15; must reply within 2 week(s) of notification.
Transfers: Applicants notified on a rolling basis starting 3/15; must reply within 2 week(s) of notification.

CONTACT

Mickey Olin, Assistant Director of Financial Aid
CPO#1320, UNCA, Asheville, NC 28804-8502
(828) 251-6535

University of North Carolina at Chapel Hill

Chapel Hill, North Carolina   Federal Code: 002974
www.unc.edu   CSS Code: 5816

4-year public university in small city.
Enrollment: 18,207 undergrads, 2% part-time. 4,073 full-time freshmen.
Selectivity: Admits less than 50% of applicants. GED not accepted.

BASIC COSTS (2016-2017)

Tuition and fees: $8,566; out-of-state residents $33,648.
Per-credit charge: $286.71; out-of-state residents $1,331.79.
Room and board: $11,218.
Additional info: Fees may be higher for selected programs.

FINANCIAL AID PICTURE (2015-2016)

Students with need: Out of 2,948 full-time freshmen who applied for aid, 1,887 were judged to have need. Of these, 1,887 received aid, and 1,574 had their full need met. Average financial aid package met 100% of need; average scholarship/grant was $17,240; average loan was $4,599. For part-time students, average financial aid package was $9,044.
Students without need: 99 full-time freshmen who did not demonstrate need for aid received scholarships/grants; average award was $10,376. No-need awards available for academics, alumni affiliation, art, athletics, leadership, music/drama, religious affiliation, state/district residency.
Scholarships offered: *Merit:* Morehead-Cain Scholarships: full tuition and expenses; based on academic merit, leadership, athletics, moral character;

approximately 50 awarded. Robertson Scholarships: full tuition and expenses; based on academic merit, leadership, community service; 15-18 awarded. Carolina Scholars: $9,000 for in-state residents; cost of tuition, fees, room and board for non-NC residents; based on academic merit, leadership, residency specifications; 25-30 awarded with majority going to in-state residents. Pogue Scholarships: $9,000 for NC residents; cost of tuition, fees, room and board for non-NC residents; based on academic merit, leadership, involvement and interest in issues of diversity; up to 10 in-state and 3 out-of-state awarded. Colonel Robinson Scholarships: $9,000 for in-state residents; cost of tuition, fees, room and board for non-NC residents; based on academic merit; approximately 15 awarded to NC residents and 10 to non-NC residents. Old Well, College Fellows, and Founders Awards: $2,500-$6,000; based on academic merit, leadership, North Carolina residency; 15-20 awarded. *Athletic:* 78 full-time freshmen received athletic scholarships; average amount $26,007.

Additional info: 100% of all documented need met for both resident and non-resident undergraduates who qualify for need based aid, with a favorable mix of approximately 70% grants and scholarships and 30% loans and work study. A no-loans program available for qualifying low-income students (in-state or out-of-state) whose family's adjusted gross income does not exceed 200% of the federal poverty standard, indexed by family size.

FINANCIAL AID PROCEDURES

Forms required: FAFSA, CSS PROFILE.

Dates and Deadlines: Priority date 3/1; no closing date. Applicants notified on a rolling basis starting 2/5; must reply by 5/1.

CONTACT

Rachelle Feldman, Associate Provost and Director of Scholarships and Student Aid
Jackson Hall, Chapel Hill, NC 27599-2200
(919) 962-8396

University of North Carolina at Charlotte

Charlotte, North Carolina
www.uncc.edu   Federal Code: 002975

4-year public university in very large city.
Enrollment: 23,246 undergrads, 13% part-time. 3,074 full-time freshmen.
Selectivity: Admits 50 to 75% of applicants.

BASIC COSTS (2016-2017)

Tuition and fees: $6,763; out-of-state residents $19,934.
Room and board: $10,470.

FINANCIAL AID PICTURE (2015-2016)

Students with need: Out of 2,548 full-time freshmen who applied for aid, 1,837 were judged to have need. Of these, 1,733 received aid, and 168 had their full need met. Average financial aid package met 61% of need; average scholarship/grant was $7,075; average loan was $3,249. For part-time students, average financial aid package was $7,523.

Students without need: 20 full-time freshmen who did not demonstrate need for aid received scholarships/grants; average award was $2,677. No-need awards available for academics, athletics, leadership, minority status, state/district residency.

Scholarships offered: *Merit:* The Levine Scholars Program awards 15 incoming freshmen students full tuition, room and board, and four summers of experiences to develop leadership skills, social awareness, and international perspective. Students must be nominated by their high school guidance counselor by October 15th of their senior year. The Crown Scholarship program awards scholarships averaging $19,000 annually for tuition and fees, room and board, and other expenses, and $5,000 stipend for University-approved study abroad. The Albert Engineering Leadership Scholarship Program awards annual renewable scholarships for Engineering majors including tuition and fees, room and board, and up to $6,000 professional development allowance for an undergraduate summer research experience

or internship. *Athletic:* 8 full-time freshmen received athletic scholarships; average amount $8,302.

FINANCIAL AID PROCEDURES

Forms required: FAFSA.

Dates and Deadlines: Priority date 3/1; closing date 9/30. Must reply within 3 week(s) of notification.

Transfers: Must reply within 2 week(s) of notification.

CONTACT

Bruce Blackmon, Director of Student Financial Aid
Undergraduate Admissions- Cato Hall, Charlotte, NC 28223-0001
(704) 687-5504

University of North Carolina at Greensboro

Greensboro, North Carolina
www.uncg.edu   Federal Code: 002976

4-year public university in large city.
Enrollment: 15,783 undergrads, 12% part-time. 2,633 full-time freshmen.
Selectivity: Admits 50 to 75% of applicants.

BASIC COSTS (2016-2017)

Tuition and fees: $7,041; out-of-state residents $21,903.
Room and board: $8,580.

FINANCIAL AID PICTURE (2016-2017)

Students with need: Average financial aid package met 80% of need; average scholarship/grant was $6,623; average loan was $3,397. For part-time students, average financial aid package was $5,816.

Students without need: No-need awards available for academics, athletics, music/drama, religious affiliation, ROTC, state/district residency.

FINANCIAL AID PROCEDURES

Forms required: FAFSA.

Dates and Deadlines: Priority date 3/1; no closing date. Applicants notified on a rolling basis starting 3/15; must reply within 3 week(s) of notification.

CONTACT

Deborah Tollefson, Director of Financial Aid
PO Box 26170, Greensboro, NC 27402-6170
(336) 334-5702

University of North Carolina at Pembroke

Pembroke, North Carolina
www.uncp.edu   Federal Code: 002954

4-year public university and liberal arts college in small town.
Enrollment: 5,375 undergrads, 16% part-time. 1,099 full-time freshmen.
Selectivity: Admits 50 to 75% of applicants.

BASIC COSTS (2016-2017)

Tuition and fees: $5,816; out-of-state residents $16,760.
Room and board: $8,573.
Additional info: Health Insurance $2,274.

FINANCIAL AID PICTURE (2016-2017)

Students with need: Out of 1,050 full-time freshmen who applied for aid, 915 were judged to have need. Of these, 889 received aid, and 58 had their full need met. Average financial aid package met 61% of need; average scholarship/grant was $6,924; average loan was $3,388. For part-time students, average financial aid package was $7,938.

Students without need: 10 full-time freshmen who did not demonstrate need for aid received scholarships/grants; average award was $1,644. No-need awards available for academics, alumni affiliation, art, athletics, minority status, music/drama.

Scholarships offered: Academic Scholarships, Endowed Scholarship, University Incentive Scholarship, University Scholarships for Native Americans, Epsilon Sigma Alpha Scholarship.

FINANCIAL AID PROCEDURES

Forms required: FAFSA.

Dates and Deadlines: Priority date 3/1; no closing date. Applicants notified on a rolling basis starting 4/15; must reply by 7/31.

Transfers: No deadline.

CONTACT

Jenelle Handcox, Director of Financial Aid
Box 1510, Pembroke, NC 28372
(910) 521-6255

University of North Carolina at Wilmington

Wilmington, North Carolina
www.uncw.edu   Federal Code: 002984

4-year public university in large city.

Enrollment: 13,609 undergrads, 12% part-time. 2,218 full-time freshmen.

Selectivity: Admits 50 to 75% of applicants.

BASIC COSTS (2016-2017)

Tuition and fees: $6,951; out-of-state residents $20,920.

Room and board: $10,060.

FINANCIAL AID PICTURE

Students with need: Need-based aid available for full-time and part-time students. Work study available nights, weekends, and for part-time students.

Students without need: No-need awards available for academics, alumni affiliation, art, athletics, leadership, minority status, music/drama.

FINANCIAL AID PROCEDURES

Forms required: FAFSA.

Dates and Deadlines: Priority date 3/1; no closing date. Applicants notified on a rolling basis starting 3/15; must reply within 3 week(s) of notification.

Transfers: No deadline. Applicants notified by 3/15; must reply within 3 week(s) of notification.

CONTACT

Frederick Holding, Director of Financial Aid, Scholarships and Veterans Services
601 South College Road, Wilmington, NC 28403-5904
(910) 962-3177

University of North Carolina School of the Arts

Winston-Salem, North Carolina
www.uncsa.edu/   Federal Code: 003981

4-year public visual arts and performing arts college in small city.

Enrollment: 897 undergrads, 2% part-time. 210 full-time freshmen.

Selectivity: Admits less than 50% of applicants.

BASIC COSTS (2017-2018)

Tuition and fees: $9,211; out-of-state residents $25,081.

Room and board: $8,977.

Additional info: Tuition at time of enrollment locked for 4 years.

FINANCIAL AID PICTURE (2016-2017)

Students with need: Out of 183 full-time freshmen who applied for aid, 136 were judged to have need. Of these, 135 received aid, and 11 had their full need met. Average financial aid package met 61% of need; average scholarship/grant was $8,256; average loan was $3,554. For part-time students, average financial aid package was $6,712.

Students without need: 13 full-time freshmen who did not demonstrate need for aid received scholarships/grants; average award was $2,817. No-need awards available for academics, art, leadership, music/drama, state/district residency.

FINANCIAL AID PROCEDURES

Forms required: FAFSA.

Dates and Deadlines: Priority date 3/1; no closing date. Applicants notified on a rolling basis starting 4/1; must reply within 2 week(s) of notification.

CONTACT

Jane Kamiab, Director of Financial Aid
1533 South Main Street, Winston-Salem, NC 27127-2738
(336) 770-3297

Vance-Granville Community College

Henderson, North Carolina
www.vgcc.edu   Federal Code: 009903

2-year public community college in large town.

Enrollment: 2,148 undergrads.

Selectivity: Open admission; but selective for some programs.

BASIC COSTS (2016-2017)

Tuition and fees: $2,409; out-of-state residents $8,169.

Per-credit charge: $76; out-of-state residents $268.

FINANCIAL AID PICTURE (2016-2017)

Students with need: 96% of average financial aid package awarded as scholarships/grants, 4% awarded as loans/jobs. Need-based aid available for part-time students.

Students without need: No-need awards available for academics, leadership, music/drama, state/district residency.

FINANCIAL AID PROCEDURES

Forms required: FAFSA.

Dates and Deadlines: Priority date 3/15; no closing date. Applicants notified on a rolling basis starting 5/1; must reply within 2 week(s) of notification.

CONTACT

Kali Brown, Director of Financial Aid
Box 917, Henderson, NC 27536
(252) 492-2061 ext. 3280

Wake Forest University

Winston-Salem, North Carolina   Federal Code: 002978
www.wfu.edu   CSS Code: 5885

4-year private university in small city.

Enrollment: 4,949 undergrads, 1% part-time. 1,304 full-time freshmen.

Selectivity: Admits less than 50% of applicants.

BASIC COSTS (2016-2017)

Tuition and fees: $49,308.

Per-credit charge: $2,020.

Room and board: $13,404.

FINANCIAL AID PICTURE (2016-2017)

Students with need: Out of 613 full-time freshmen who applied for aid, 407 were judged to have need. Of these, 407 received aid, and 407 had

their full need met. Average financial aid package met 100% of need; average scholarship/grant was $42,637; average loan was $9,264. For part-time students, average financial aid package was $33,032.

Students without need: 29 full-time freshmen who did not demonstrate need for aid received scholarships/grants; average award was $30,453. No-need awards available for academics, alumni affiliation, art, athletics, leadership, music/drama, religious affiliation, ROTC, state/district residency.

Scholarships offered: *Merit:* Reynolds Scholarship: full tuition, room and board, books, fees for 4 years, also provides for summer study; 6 awarded. Joseph G. Gordon Scholarship: full tuition for 4 years; for underrepresented students with exceptional promise and leadership; 7 awarded. Carswell Scholarship: based on intellect and leadership; between 3/4 and full tuition for 4 years, including summer grant for travel and study projects; 10-12 awarded. Presidential Scholarship: for students gifted in areas such as writing, studio art, music theater, debate, leadership, dance, entrepreneurship, and community service; 20 awarded. Poteat Scholarship: $12,100; for North Carolina residents who are active members of a Baptist Church in North Carolina, must make an active contribution to church and society; 18 awarded. *Athletic:* 34 full-time freshmen received athletic scholarships; average amount $59,935.

Additional info: First-year students with an annual family income of less than $40,000 will have their student loans capped at $4,000 per year during their college years. Other financial aid to the students will come from grant and scholarship increases and work-study opportunities.

FINANCIAL AID PROCEDURES

Forms required: FAFSA, CSS PROFILE, state aid form.

Dates and Deadlines: Priority date 1/1; closing date 1/1. Applicants notified on a rolling basis starting 4/1; must reply by 5/1 or within 4 week(s) of notification.

CONTACT

William Wells, Director of Financial Aid
PO Box 7305, Winston-Salem, NC 27109-7305
(336) 758-5154.

Wake Technical Community College

Raleigh, North Carolina
www.waketech.edu   Federal Code: 004844

2-year public community and technical college in large city.
Enrollment: 20,043 undergrads, 62% part-time. 1,817 full-time freshmen.
Selectivity: Open admission; but selective for some programs.

BASIC COSTS (2016-2017)
Tuition and fees: $2,610; out-of-state residents $8,370.
Per-credit charge: $76; out-of-state residents $268.

FINANCIAL AID PICTURE
Students with need: Need-based aid available for full-time and part-time students.
Students without need: No-need awards available for academics, job skills, leadership, ROTC, state/district residency.

FINANCIAL AID PROCEDURES
Forms required: FAFSA, institutional form.
Dates and Deadlines: Priority date 3/15; no closing date. Applicants notified on a rolling basis starting 4/1; must reply within 2 week(s) of notification.
Transfers: Child care grant and NCCCS Grant and Loan Program available.

CONTACT
Regina Huggins, Dean, Financial Aid
9101 Fayetteville Road, Raleigh, NC 27603
(919) 866-5410

Warren Wilson College

Asheville, North Carolina
www.warren-wilson.edu   Federal Code: 002979

4-year private liberal arts college in small city.
Enrollment: 648 undergrads, 1% part-time. 185 full-time freshmen.
Selectivity: Admits over 75% of applicants.

BASIC COSTS (2016-2017)
Tuition and fees: $33,970.
Per-credit charge: $1,386.
Room and board: $10,250.
Additional info: All resident students work between 10-20 hours per week on one of more than 100 work crews. Within the Work Program, students are paid minimum wage (currently $7.25/Hr) and the amount is credited towards the cost of their education each academic year.

FINANCIAL AID PICTURE
Students with need: Need-based aid available for full-time and part-time students.
Students without need: No-need awards available for academics, art, athletics, leadership, religious affiliation, state/district residency.

FINANCIAL AID PROCEDURES
Forms required: FAFSA, state aid form.
Dates and Deadlines: Priority date 3/1; no closing date. Applicants notified on a rolling basis starting 3/1; must reply by 5/1 or within 3 week(s) of notification.
Transfers: No deadline. Applicants notified on a rolling basis starting 3/1; must reply within 3 week(s) of notification.

CONTACT
Lori Lewis, Director of Financial Aid
PO Box 9000, Asheville, NC 28815-9000
(828) 771-2082

Wayne Community College

Goldsboro, North Carolina
www.waynecc.edu   Federal Code: 008216

2-year public community college in large town.
Enrollment: 2,773 undergrads. 277 full-time freshmen.
Selectivity: Open admission; but selective for some programs.

BASIC COSTS (2016-2017)
Tuition and fees: $2,524; out-of-state residents $8,668.
Per-credit charge: $76; out-of-state residents $268.

FINANCIAL AID PICTURE (2015-2016)
Students with need: 96% of average financial aid package awarded as scholarships/grants, 4% awarded as loans/jobs. Need-based aid available for part-time students. Work study available nights, weekends, and for part-time students.
Students without need: No-need awards available for academics.

FINANCIAL AID PROCEDURES
Forms required: FAFSA.
Dates and Deadlines: Priority date 3/15; no closing date. Applicants notified on a rolling basis starting 6/1; must reply within 2 week(s) of notification.
Transfers: Priority date 5/1; no deadline. Applicants notified on a rolling basis starting 4/1; must reply within 2 week(s) of notification.

CONTACT
Brenda Burgess, Financial Aid Director
PO Box 8002, Goldsboro, NC 27533-8002
(919) 739-6735

Western Carolina University

Cullowhee, North Carolina
www.wcu.edu   Federal Code: 002981

4-year public university in small town.
Enrollment: 9,003 undergrads, 13% part-time. 1,646 full-time freshmen.
Selectivity: Admits less than 50% of applicants.

BASIC COSTS (2016-2017)
Tuition and fees: $7,027; out-of-state residents $17,420.
Room and board: $9,516.

FINANCIAL AID PICTURE (2015-2016)
Students with need: Out of 1,493 full-time freshmen who applied for aid, 1,128 were judged to have need. Of these, 1,103 received aid, and 765 had their full need met. Average financial aid package met 87% of need; average scholarship/grant was $11,349; average loan was $6,933. For part-time students, average financial aid package was $8,890.
Students without need: 87 full-time freshmen who did not demonstrate need for aid received scholarships/grants; average award was $5,031. No-need awards available for academics, art, athletics, leadership, music/drama, state/district residency.
Scholarships offered: *Merit:* Institution awards merit-based scholarships each year to students that demonstrate excellent academic, athletic, artistic, professional, cultural and/or civic achievement. The number and amount of awards vary. ***Athletic:*** 27 full-time freshmen received athletic scholarships; average amount $15,195.

FINANCIAL AID PROCEDURES
Forms required: FAFSA, institutional form.
Dates and Deadlines: Priority date 3/15; no closing date. Applicants notified on a rolling basis starting 4/1.

CONTACT
Trina Orr, Director of Student Financial Aid
102 Camp Building, Cullowhee, NC 28723
(828) 227-7290

Western Piedmont Community College

Morganton, North Carolina
www.wpcc.edu   Federal Code: 002982

2-year public community and technical college in large town.
Enrollment: 2,153 undergrads.
Selectivity: Open admission; but selective for some programs.

BASIC COSTS (2016-2017)
Tuition and fees: $2,418; out-of-state residents $8,178.
Per-credit charge: $76; out-of-state residents $268.

FINANCIAL AID PICTURE
Students with need: Need-based aid available for full-time and part-time students.
Students without need: No-need awards available for academics.

FINANCIAL AID PROCEDURES
Forms required: FAFSA.
Dates and Deadlines: Priority date 6/1; no closing date. Applicants notified on a rolling basis starting 6/15; must reply within 2 week(s) of notification.

CONTACT
Dori Barron, Director of Financial Aid
1001 Burkemont Avenue, Morganton, NC 28655-4504
(828) 448-6042

Wilkes Community College

Wilkesboro, North Carolina
www.wilkescc.edu   Federal Code: 002983

2-year public community college in small town.
Enrollment: 2,999 undergrads.
Selectivity: Open admission; but selective for some programs.

BASIC COSTS (2016-2017)
Tuition and fees: $2,420; out-of-state residents $8,180.
Per-credit charge: $76; out-of-state residents $268.

FINANCIAL AID PICTURE
Students with need: Need-based aid available for full-time and part-time students. Work study available nights.
Students without need: No-need awards available for academics, art, job skills, leadership, minority status, music/drama, state/district residency.

FINANCIAL AID PROCEDURES
Forms required: FAFSA.
Dates and Deadlines: Priority date 5/15; closing date 5/15. Applicants notified on a rolling basis starting 5/1; must reply by 8/1.
Transfers: No deadline. Must reply within 6 week(s) of notification.

CONTACT
Vickie Call, Director of Financial Aid
1328 South Collegiate Drive, Wilkesboro, NC 28697-0120
(336) 838-6146

William Peace University

Raleigh, North Carolina
www.peace.edu   Federal Code: 002953

4-year private liberal arts college in large city, affiliated with the Presbyterian Church (USA).
Enrollment: 1,034 undergrads, 15% part-time. 200 full-time freshmen.
Selectivity: Admits 50 to 75% of applicants.

BASIC COSTS (2016-2017)
Tuition and fees: $27,080.
Per-credit charge: $896.
Room and board: $10,350.

FINANCIAL AID PICTURE (2016-2017)
Students with need: Out of 194 full-time freshmen who applied for aid, 182 were judged to have need. Of these, 197 received aid, and 4 had their full need met. Average financial aid package met 60% of need; average scholarship/grant was $9,967; average loan was $2,983. For part-time students, average financial aid package was $9,592.
Students without need: No-need awards available for academics, leadership, music/drama.

FINANCIAL AID PROCEDURES
Forms required: FAFSA.
Dates and Deadlines: Priority date 3/15; no closing date. Applicants notified on a rolling basis starting 1/1.
Transfers: Priority date 2/15; no deadline. Applicants notified on a rolling basis starting 2/3. Transfer merit scholarships available.

CONTACT
Michelle Hemmer, Director of Financial Aid
15 East Peace Street, Raleigh, NC 27604
(919) 508-2349

Wilson Community College
Wilson, North Carolina
www.wilsoncc.edu   Federal Code: 004845

2-year public community college in large town.
Enrollment: 1,786 undergrads.
Selectivity: Open admission; but selective for some programs.

BASIC COSTS (2016-2017)
Tuition and fees: $2,415; out-of-state residents $8,175.
Per-credit charge: $76; out-of-state residents $268.

FINANCIAL AID PICTURE
Students with need: Need-based aid available for full-time and part-time students. Work study available nights.
Students without need: No-need awards available for academics.

FINANCIAL AID PROCEDURES
Forms required: FAFSA, institutional form.
Dates and Deadlines: Priority date 3/15; no closing date. Applicants notified on a rolling basis.
Transfers: No deadline. Applicants notified on a rolling basis.

CONTACT
Lisa Shearin, Director of Financial Aid and Veterans Affairs
Box 4305, Wilson, NC 27893-0305
(252) 246-1274

Wingate University
Wingate, North Carolina
https://www.wingate.edu/   Federal Code: 002985

4-year private university in small town.
Enrollment: 2,076 undergrads, 2% part-time. 640 full-time freshmen.
Selectivity: Admits 50 to 75% of applicants.

BASIC COSTS (2017-2018)
Tuition and fees: $31,120.
Per-credit charge: $1,035.
Room and board: $10,780.

FINANCIAL AID PICTURE (2015-2016)
Students with need: Out of 592 full-time freshmen who applied for aid, 536 were judged to have need. Of these, 507 received aid, and 168 had their full need met. Average financial aid package met 75% of need; average scholarship/grant was $22,223; average loan was $3,055. For part-time students, average financial aid package was $7,468.
Students without need: 108 full-time freshmen who did not demonstrate need for aid received scholarships/grants; average award was $17,350. No-need awards available for academics, alumni affiliation, art, athletics, music/drama.
Scholarships offered: 70 full-time freshmen received athletic scholarships; average amount $10,770.
Additional info: Institutional aid may not be available after June 1.

FINANCIAL AID PROCEDURES
Forms required: FAFSA, state aid form.
Dates and Deadlines: Priority date 5/1; no closing date. Applicants notified on a rolling basis.
Transfers: Priority date 3/1; no deadline. Applicants notified on a rolling basis; must reply within 2 week(s) of notification. Must submit financial aid transcripts from previous colleges attended.

CONTACT
Teresa Williams, Director of Financial Planning
220 N. Camden Drive, Wingate, NC 28174-0157
(704) 233-8209

Winston-Salem State University
Winston-Salem, North Carolina
www.wssu.edu   Federal Code: 002986

4-year public university and health science college in small city.
Enrollment: 4,686 undergrads.

BASIC COSTS (2016-2017)
Tuition and fees: $5,713; out-of-state residents $15,824.
Room and board: $8,846.

FINANCIAL AID PICTURE (2016-2017)
Students with need: Average financial aid package met 64% of need; average scholarship/grant was $9,158; average loan was $3,394. For part-time students, average financial aid package was $6,879.
Students without need: This college awards aid only to students with need.

FINANCIAL AID PROCEDURES
Forms required: FAFSA.
Dates and Deadlines: Priority date 5/1; no closing date. Applicants notified on a rolling basis; must reply within 2 week(s) of notification.
Transfers: Closing date 3/15. Applicants notified on a rolling basis; must reply within 2 week(s) of notification.

CONTACT
Robert Muhammad, Director of Financial Aid
601 Martin Luther King Jr Drive, Winston-Salem, NC 27110
(336) 750-3280

North Dakota

Bismarck State College
Bismarck, North Dakota
https://bismarckstate.edu   Federal Code: 002988

2-year public community and technical college in small city.
Enrollment: 3,060 undergrads, 28% part-time. 789 full-time freshmen.
Selectivity: Open admission; but selective for some programs.

BASIC COSTS (2016-2017)
Tuition and fees: $4,388; out-of-state residents $10,474.
Per-credit charge: $121; out-of-state residents $324.
Room and board: $7,400.
Additional info: Tuition/fee waivers available for minority students.

FINANCIAL AID PICTURE (2015-2016)
Students with need: Out of 613 full-time freshmen who applied for aid, 338 were judged to have need. Of these, 325 received aid, and 118 had their full need met. Average financial aid package met 69% of need; average scholarship/grant was $5,088; average loan was $3,853. For part-time students, average financial aid package was $6,364.
Students without need: 128 full-time freshmen who did not demonstrate need for aid received scholarships/grants; average award was $1,554. No-need awards available for academics, alumni affiliation, art, athletics, minority status, music/drama.
Scholarships offered: 11 full-time freshmen received athletic scholarships; average amount $2,701.

FINANCIAL AID PROCEDURES
Forms required: FAFSA.
Dates and Deadlines: Priority date 4/15; no closing date. Applicants notified on a rolling basis starting 5/1.
Transfers: No deadline. Applicants notified on a rolling basis. Financial aid based on funds available.

CONTACT

Scott Lingen, Director of Financial Aid
PO Box 5587, Bismarck, ND 58506-5587
(701) 224-5494

Cankdeska Cikana Community College

Fort Totten, North Dakota
www.littlehoop.edu   Federal Code: 015793

2-year public community college in rural community.
Enrollment: 126 undergrads.
Selectivity: Open admission.

BASIC COSTS (2016-2017)

Tuition and fees: $3,300; out-of-state residents $3,300.
Room and board: $5,750.

FINANCIAL AID PICTURE

Students with need: Need-based aid available for full-time and part-time students.
Students without need: This college awards aid only to students with need.

FINANCIAL AID PROCEDURES

Forms required: FAFSA, institutional form.
Dates and Deadlines: Priority date 4/15; closing date 8/20. Applicants notified on a rolling basis.

CONTACT

Tina Ploium, Financial Aid Director
Box 269, Fort Totten, ND 58335
(701) 766-2370

Dakota College at Bottineau

Bottineau, North Dakota
www.dakotacollege.edu   Federal Code: 002995

2-year public nursing and junior college in rural community.
Enrollment: 411 undergrads.
Selectivity: Open admission.

BASIC COSTS (2016-2017)

Tuition and fees: $4,281; out-of-state residents $6,015.
Per-credit charge: $144; out-of-state residents $217.
Room and board: $6,780.
Additional info: Tuition/fee waivers available for minority students.

FINANCIAL AID PICTURE

Students with need: Need-based aid available for full-time and part-time students. Work study available nights, weekends, and for part-time students.
Students without need: No-need awards available for academics, alumni affiliation, athletics, minority status, state/district residency.

FINANCIAL AID PROCEDURES

Forms required: FAFSA.
Dates and Deadlines: Priority date 4/15; no closing date. Applicants notified on a rolling basis starting 6/1; must reply within 2 week(s) of notification.

CONTACT

Valerie Heilman, Financial Aid Officer
105 Simrall Boulevard, Bottineau, ND 58318-1198
(701) 228-5437

Dickinson State University

Dickinson, North Dakota
www.dickinsonstate.edu   Federal Code: 002989

4-year public university in large town.
Enrollment: 1,134 undergrads.
Selectivity: Open admission; but selective for some programs.

BASIC COSTS (2016-2017)

Tuition and fees: $6,348; out-of-state residents $8,917.
Per-credit charge: $214; out-of-state residents $321.
Room and board: $6,749.
Additional info: Tuition/fee waivers available for minority students.

FINANCIAL AID PICTURE

Students with need: Need-based aid available for full-time and part-time students. Work study available nights, weekends, and for part-time students.
Students without need: No-need awards available for academics, alumni affiliation, art, athletics, leadership, minority status, music/drama.

FINANCIAL AID PROCEDURES

Forms required: FAFSA.
Dates and Deadlines: Priority date 4/15; no closing date. Applicants notified on a rolling basis starting 5/15; must reply within 4 week(s) of notification.
Transfers: No deadline. Applicants notified on a rolling basis starting 5/15; must reply within 2 week(s) of notification.

CONTACT

Sandy Klein, Director of Financial Aid
291 Campus Drive, Dickinson, ND 58601-4896
(701) 483-2371

Lake Region State College

Devils Lake, North Dakota
www.lrsc.edu   Federal Code: 002991

2-year public community and technical college in small town.
Enrollment: 712 undergrads, 32% part-time. 188 full-time freshmen.
Selectivity: Open admission; but selective for some programs.

BASIC COSTS (2016-2017)

Tuition and fees: $4,203; out-of-state residents $4,203.
Per-credit charge: $139.
Room and board: $6,425.
Additional info: Tuition/fee waivers available for minority students.

FINANCIAL AID PICTURE (2016-2017)

Students with need: Out of 146 full-time freshmen who applied for aid, 103 were judged to have need. Of these, 101 received aid, and 43 had their full need met. Average financial aid package met 82% of need; average scholarship/grant was $5,729; average loan was $4,180. For part-time students, average financial aid package was $9,540.
Students without need: 51 full-time freshmen who did not demonstrate need for aid received scholarships/grants; average award was $993. No-need awards available for academics, athletics, leadership, minority status, music/drama.
Scholarships offered: 19 full-time freshmen received athletic scholarships; average amount $2,630.

FINANCIAL AID PROCEDURES

Forms required: FAFSA.
Dates and Deadlines: Priority date 4/15; no closing date. Applicants notified on a rolling basis starting 5/15; must reply within 4 week(s) of notification.
Transfers: No deadline. Applicants notified on a rolling basis starting 5/15; must reply within 4 week(s) of notification.

CONTACT
Katie Nettell, Director of Financial Aid
1801 College Drive North, Devils Lake, ND 58301-1598
(701) 662-1516

Mayville State University
Mayville, North Dakota
www.mayvillestate.edu   Federal Code: 002993

4-year public business and teachers college in small town.
Enrollment: 819 undergrads.
Selectivity: Open admission; but selective for some programs.

BASIC COSTS (2016-2017)
Tuition and fees: $6,254; out-of-state residents $8,781.
Per-credit charge: $211; out-of-state residents $316.
Room and board: $6,070.
Additional info: Tuition/fee waivers available for minority students.

FINANCIAL AID PICTURE
Students with need: Need-based aid available for full-time and part-time students. Work study available nights, weekends, and for part-time students.
Students without need: No-need awards available for academics, athletics, leadership, minority status, music/drama, state/district residency.

FINANCIAL AID PROCEDURES
Forms required: FAFSA.
Dates and Deadlines: Priority date 2/15; no closing date. Applicants notified on a rolling basis starting 5/1; must reply within 2 week(s) of notification.
Transfers: No deadline. Applicants notified on a rolling basis starting 5/1; must reply within 2 week(s) of notification.

CONTACT
Shirley Hanson, Director of Financial Aid
330 Third Street, NE, Mayville, ND 58257-1299
(701) 788-4767

Minot State University
Minot, North Dakota
www.minotstateu.edu   Federal Code: 002994

4-year public university and liberal arts college in large town.
Enrollment: 2,563 undergrads, 21% part-time. 314 full-time freshmen.
Selectivity: Admits 50 to 75% of applicants.

BASIC COSTS (2016-2017)
Tuition and fees: $6,568; out-of-district residents $6,568; out-of-state residents $6,568.
Per-credit charge: $273.67.
Room and board: $6,249.
Additional info: Tuition/fee waivers available for minority students.

FINANCIAL AID PICTURE (2015-2016)
Students with need: Out of 207 full-time freshmen who applied for aid, 113 were judged to have need. Of these, 110 received aid, and 60 had their full need met. Average financial aid package met 72% of need; average scholarship/grant was $5,572; average loan was $3,830. For part-time students, average financial aid package was $7,514.
Students without need: 80 full-time freshmen who did not demonstrate need for aid received scholarships/grants; average award was $1,178. No-need awards available for academics, alumni affiliation, art, athletics, leadership, minority status, music/drama, state/district residency.
Scholarships offered: 18 full-time freshmen received athletic scholarships; average amount $3,764.
Additional info: Scholarship application deadline is 2/15.

FINANCIAL AID PROCEDURES
Forms required: FAFSA.
Dates and Deadlines: Priority date 2/15; no closing date. Applicants notified on a rolling basis starting 4/1; must reply within 2 week(s) of notification.
Transfers: No deadline. Applicants notified by 5/1; must reply within 2 week(s) of notification.

CONTACT
Laurie Weber, Director of Financial Aid
500 University Avenue West, Minot, ND 58707-5002
(701) 858-3375

North Dakota State College of Science
Wahpeton, North Dakota
www.ndscs.edu   Federal Code: 002996

2-year public junior and technical college in small town.
Enrollment: 2,129 undergrads, 18% part-time. 650 full-time freshmen.
Selectivity: Open admission; but selective for some programs.

BASIC COSTS (2016-2017)
Tuition and fees: $4,446; out-of-state residents $10,748.
Per-credit charge: $126; out-of-state residents $336.
Room and board: $6,720.
Additional info: Tuition/fee waivers available for minority students.

FINANCIAL AID PICTURE (2015-2016)
Students with need: Out of 584 full-time freshmen who applied for aid, 424 were judged to have need. Of these, 403 received aid, and 169 had their full need met. Average financial aid package met 64% of need; average scholarship/grant was $4,999; average loan was $5,476. For part-time students, average financial aid package was $7,838.
Students without need: 37 full-time freshmen who did not demonstrate need for aid received scholarships/grants; average award was $1,010. No-need awards available for academics, alumni affiliation, athletics, leadership, minority status, music/drama, state/district residency.
Scholarships offered: 6 full-time freshmen received athletic scholarships; average amount $1,626.

FINANCIAL AID PROCEDURES
Forms required: FAFSA.
Dates and Deadlines: Priority date 4/15; closing date 4/15. Applicants notified on a rolling basis starting 6/1; must reply within 2 week(s) of notification.
Transfers: No deadline. Must reply within 2 week(s) of notification.

CONTACT
Shelly Blome, Director of Financial Aid
800 North 6th Street, Wahpeton, ND 58076-0001
(701) 671-2207

North Dakota State University
Fargo, North Dakota
www.ndsu.edu   Federal Code: 002997

4-year public university in small city.
Enrollment: 11,682 undergrads, 9% part-time. 2,529 full-time freshmen.
Selectivity: Admits over 75% of applicants.

BASIC COSTS (2016-2017)
Tuition and fees: $8,207; out-of-state residents $19,771.
Per-credit charge: $305; out-of-state residents $814.
Room and board: $7,918.
Additional info: Tuition/fee waivers available for minority students.

FINANCIAL AID PICTURE (2015-2016)

Students with need: Out of 2,137 full-time freshmen who applied for aid, 1,298 were judged to have need. Of these, 1,274 received aid, and 571 had their full need met. Average financial aid package met 75% of need; average scholarship/grant was $5,550; average loan was $6,551. For part-time students, average financial aid package was $8,900.

Students without need: 279 full-time freshmen who did not demonstrate need for aid received scholarships/grants; average award was $2,028.

Scholarships offered: Merit: New Student Scholarships: vary in amount awarded; based on 25 ACT or 1200 SAT (exclusive of writing) and 3.5 GPA. **Athletic:** 32 full-time freshmen received athletic scholarships; average amount $11,579.

FINANCIAL AID PROCEDURES

Forms required: FAFSA.

Dates and Deadlines: Priority date 4/15; no closing date. Applicants notified on a rolling basis starting 4/1.

CONTACT

Jeffrey Jacobs, Director of Financial Aid and Scholarships
Dept. 2832, PO Box 6050, Fargo, ND 58108-6050
(701) 231-6200

Rasmussen College: Bismarck

Bismarck, North Dakota
www.rasmussen.edu

2-year for-profit career college in small city.
Enrollment: 15 undergrads.
Selectivity: Open admission; but selective for some programs.

BASIC COSTS (2016-2017)

Tuition and fees: $13,455.
Per-credit charge: $299.
Additional info: Full-time tuition varies according to program of study. Required course materials fee of $150 per course.

FINANCIAL AID PICTURE

Students with need: Need-based aid available for full-time and part-time students.

FINANCIAL AID PROCEDURES

Forms required: FAFSA, institutional form.
Dates and Deadlines: Applicants notified on a rolling basis.

CONTACT

Debora Murray, Director of Financial Services
1701 East Century Avenue, Bismarck, ND 58503
(701) 530-9600

Rasmussen College: Fargo

Fargo, North Dakota
www.rasmussen.edu   Federal Code: 004846

4-year for-profit career college in small city.
Enrollment: 345 undergrads, 41% part-time. 12 full-time freshmen.
Selectivity: Open admission; but selective for some programs.

BASIC COSTS (2016-2017)

Tuition and fees: $13,455.
Per-credit charge: $299.
Additional info: Full-time tuition varies according to program of study. Required course materials fee of $150 per course.

FINANCIAL AID PICTURE

Students with need: Need-based aid available for full-time and part-time students.

FINANCIAL AID PROCEDURES

Forms required: FAFSA, institutional form.
Dates and Deadlines: Applicants notified on a rolling basis.

CONTACT

Debora Murray, Director of Financial Aid
4012 19th Avenue SW, Fargo, ND 58103
(701) 277-3889

Sitting Bull College

Fort Yates, North Dakota
www.sittingbull.edu   Federal Code: 014993

2-year public community college in small town.
Enrollment: 234 undergrads.
Selectivity: Open admission.

BASIC COSTS (2016-2017)

Tuition and fees: $3,910.

FINANCIAL AID PICTURE

Students with need: Need-based aid available for full-time and part-time students.

FINANCIAL AID PROCEDURES

Forms required: FAFSA, institutional form.
Dates and Deadlines: Priority date 5/1; no closing date. Applicants notified on a rolling basis starting 7/15; must reply within 6 week(s) of notification.
Transfers: No deadline. Applicants notified on a rolling basis.

CONTACT

Donna Seaboy, Financial Aid Director
9299 Highway 24, Fort Yates, ND 58538
(701) 854-8013

Trinity Bible College

Ellendale, North Dakota
www.trinitybiblecollege.edu   Federal Code: 012059

4-year private Bible college in rural community, affiliated with the Assemblies of God.
Enrollment: 190 undergrads, 13% part-time. 63 full-time freshmen.

BASIC COSTS (2016-2017)

Tuition and fees: $15,912.
Room and board: $5,964.

FINANCIAL AID PICTURE

Students with need: Need-based aid available for full-time and part-time students. Work study available nights, weekends, and for part-time students.
Students without need: No-need awards available for academics, alumni affiliation, art, leadership, music/drama, religious affiliation.

FINANCIAL AID PROCEDURES

Forms required: FAFSA.
Dates and Deadlines: Priority date 3/1; closing date 9/1. Applicants notified on a rolling basis starting 3/1; must reply within 3 week(s) of notification.

CONTACT

Lorell Bradley, Financial Aid
50 Sixth Avenue South, Ellendale, ND 58436-7150
(701) 349-5416

Turtle Mountain Community College

Belcourt, North Dakota
www.tm.edu   Federal Code: 009450

2-year private community college in rural community.
Enrollment: 550 undergrads.
Selectivity: Open admission; but selective for some programs.

BASIC COSTS (2016-2017)
Tuition and fees: $2,220.
Per-credit charge: $74.

FINANCIAL AID PICTURE
Students with need: Need-based aid available for full-time and part-time students.
Students without need: No-need awards available for academics, athletics, job skills, leadership, minority status.

FINANCIAL AID PROCEDURES
Forms required: FAFSA, institutional form.
Dates and Deadlines: Priority date 4/15; no closing date.

CONTACT
Alexsis Marcellais, Financial Aid Director
PO Box 340, Belcourt, ND 58316

United Tribes Technical College

Bismarck, North Dakota
www.uttc.edu   Federal Code: 014470

2-year private technical college in small city.
Enrollment: 456 undergrads, 7% part-time. 182 full-time freshmen.
Selectivity: Open admission; but selective for some programs.

BASIC COSTS (2016-2017)
Tuition and fees: $4,482.
Room and board: $3,284.
Additional info: Tuition/fee waivers available for adults, minority students.

FINANCIAL AID PICTURE
Students with need: Need-based aid available for full-time and part-time students. Work study available nights, weekends, and for part-time students.

FINANCIAL AID PROCEDURES
Forms required: FAFSA.
Dates and Deadlines: Priority date 5/29; closing date 6/30. Applicants notified on a rolling basis starting 5/29; must reply within 2 week(s) of notification.

CONTACT
Kathlene Thurman, Financial Aid Director
3315 University Drive, Bismarck, ND 58504
(701) 255-3285 ext. 1211

University of Jamestown

Jamestown, North Dakota
www.uj.edu   Federal Code: 002990

4-year private liberal arts college in large town, affiliated with the Presbyterian Church (USA).
Enrollment: 934 undergrads, 2% part-time. 262 full-time freshmen.
Selectivity: Admits 50 to 75% of applicants.

BASIC COSTS (2017-2018)
Tuition and fees: $21,158.
Per-credit charge: $435.
Room and board: $7,556.

FINANCIAL AID PICTURE (2015-2016)
Students with need: Out of 244 full-time freshmen who applied for aid, 190 were judged to have need. Of these, 190 received aid, and 50 had their full need met. Average financial aid package met 76% of need; average scholarship/grant was $13,361; average loan was $3,512. For part-time students, average financial aid package was $13,589.
Students without need: 96 full-time freshmen who did not demonstrate need for aid received scholarships/grants; average award was $9,167. No-need awards available for academics, alumni affiliation, art, athletics, job skills, leadership, music/drama, religious affiliation.
Scholarships offered: *Merit:* Wilson Scholar: $14,000; Presidential: $10,000, Dean's: $9,000, Honors: $8,000, Trustee: $7,000, Knight: $6,000. *Athletic:* 95 full-time freshmen received athletic scholarships; average amount $3,806.
Additional info: FAFSA must be received by April 15th for residents to be given first consideration for North Dakota state grants.

FINANCIAL AID PROCEDURES
Forms required: FAFSA.
Dates and Deadlines: Applicants notified on a rolling basis starting 2/1.
Transfers: No deadline. Applicants notified on a rolling basis starting 2/1.

CONTACT
Judy Hager, Director of Financial Aid
6081 College Lane, Jamestown, ND 58405
(701) 252-3467 ext. 5556

University of Mary

Bismarck, North Dakota
www.umary.edu   Federal Code: 002992

4-year private university in small city, affiliated with the Roman Catholic Church.
Enrollment: 1,928 undergrads.

BASIC COSTS (2016-2017)
Tuition and fees: $17,130.
Room and board: $6,822.

FINANCIAL AID PICTURE
Students with need: Need-based aid available for full-time and part-time students. Work study available nights, weekends, and for part-time students.
Students without need: No-need awards available for academics, athletics, music/drama, religious affiliation, state/district residency.

FINANCIAL AID PROCEDURES
Forms required: FAFSA.
Dates and Deadlines: Priority date 3/1; no closing date. Applicants notified on a rolling basis starting 2/1; must reply within 2 week(s) of notification.
Transfers: No deadline. Applicants notified on a rolling basis starting 2/1; must reply within 2 week(s) of notification.

CONTACT
Janell Thomas, Director of Student Financial Aid
7500 University Drive, Bismarck, ND 58504-9652
(701) 355-8244

University of North Dakota

Grand Forks, North Dakota
www.und.edu   Federal Code: 003005

4-year public university in small city.
Enrollment: 10,598 undergrads, 17% part-time. 1,903 full-time freshmen.
Selectivity: Admits over 75% of applicants.

BASIC COSTS (2016-2017)
Tuition and fees: $8,137; out-of-state residents $19,291.
Per-credit charge: $278; out-of-state residents $743.

Room and board: $7,630.

FINANCIAL AID PICTURE

Students with need: Need-based aid available for full-time and part-time students.

Scholarships offered: Presidential Scholarship: $2,500-$3,000; based on 29 ACT/1290 SAT (exclusive of Writing) and 3.65 GPA; approximately 180 awarded. Community of Learner's Scholarship: $1,000 per year for 4 years; based on 24 ACT/1090 SAT (exclusive of Writing) and 3.0 GPA; approximately 600 awarded. Presidential Scholarship: $5,000 per year for 4 years; for National Merit Finalists listing UND as their first choice.

FINANCIAL AID PROCEDURES

Forms required: FAFSA.

Dates and Deadlines: Applicants notified on a rolling basis.

CONTACT

Janelle Kilgore, Director of Student Financial Aid

2901 University Avenue Stop 8264, Grand Forks, ND 58202-8264

(701) 777-3121

Valley City State University

Valley City, North Dakota

www.vcsu.edu   Federal Code: 003008

4-year public liberal arts and teachers college in small town.

Enrollment: 958 undergrads, 24% part-time. 158 full-time freshmen.

Selectivity: Admits over 75% of applicants.

BASIC COSTS (2016-2017)

Tuition and fees: $7,195; out-of-state residents $16,016.

Per-credit charge: $176; out-of-state residents $470.

Room and board: $6,072.

Additional info: Tuition/fee waivers available for minority students.

FINANCIAL AID PICTURE (2016-2017)

Students with need: 47% of average financial aid package awarded as scholarships/grants, 53% awarded as loans/jobs. Need-based aid available for part-time students. Work study available nights, weekends, and for part-time students.

Students without need: No-need awards available for academics, athletics, minority status, music/drama.

Scholarships offered: Presidents Scholarship: $2,500 per year for 4 years. Meredith Scholarship: $3,000 per year for 4 years; science or math students only. McCready Scholarship: tuition and books for 4 years.

FINANCIAL AID PROCEDURES

Forms required: FAFSA.

Dates and Deadlines: Priority date 3/15; no closing date. Applicants notified on a rolling basis starting 2/15; must reply within 4 week(s) of notification.

CONTACT

Betty Schumacher, Director of Financial Aid

101 College Street SW, Valley City, ND 58072-4098

(701) 845-7412

Williston State College

Williston, North Dakota

www.willistonstate.edu   Federal Code: 003007

2-year public community and junior college in large town.

Enrollment: 751 undergrads, 18% part-time. 241 full-time freshmen.

Selectivity: Open admission; but selective for some programs.

BASIC COSTS (2016-2017)

Tuition and fees: $5,090; out-of-state residents $5,090.

Per-credit charge: $113.

Room and board: $9,066.

Additional info: Tuition/fee waivers available for minority students.

FINANCIAL AID PICTURE (2015-2016)

Students with need: 85% of average financial aid package awarded as scholarships/grants, 15% awarded as loans/jobs. Need-based aid available for part-time students. Work study available nights, weekends, and for part-time students.

Students without need: No-need awards available for academics, athletics, music/drama.

FINANCIAL AID PROCEDURES

Forms required: FAFSA.

Dates and Deadlines: Priority date 3/15; no closing date. Applicants notified on a rolling basis starting 5/15.

CONTACT

Heather Fink, Financial Aid Director

1410 University Avenue, Williston, ND 58801

(701) 774-4248

Ohio

Allegheny Wesleyan College

Salem, Ohio

www.awc.edu

4-year private Bible college in small town, affiliated with the United Methodist Church.

Enrollment: 69 undergrads.

Selectivity: Open admission.

BASIC COSTS (2016-2017)

Tuition and fees: $6,000.

Per-credit charge: $200.

Room and board: $3,600.

Additional info: Fees range from $5-$110.

FINANCIAL AID PICTURE (2015-2016)

Students with need: 49% of average financial aid package awarded as scholarships/grants, 51% awarded as loans/jobs. Need-based aid available for part-time students.

FINANCIAL AID PROCEDURES

Forms required: FAFSA, state aid form.

Dates and Deadlines: Priority date 8/26; no closing date.

CONTACT

Esther Phelps, Financial Aid Administrator

2161 Woodside Road, Salem, OH 44460-9598

(330) 337-6403

Antioch University Midwest

Yellow Springs, Ohio

www.antiochmidwest.edu   Federal Code: E00553

4-year private university and branch campus college in small town.

Enrollment: 116 undergrads.

BASIC COSTS (2016-2017)

Tuition and fees: $16,210.

Per-credit charge: $527.

FINANCIAL AID PICTURE

Students with need: Need-based aid available for full-time and part-time students. Work study available nights, weekends, and for part-time students.

FINANCIAL AID PROCEDURES

Forms required: FAFSA, institutional form.
Dates and Deadlines: Applicants notified on a rolling basis starting 3/1; must reply within 2 week(s) of notification.
Transfers: No deadline. Applicants notified on a rolling basis starting 4/1; must reply within 2 week(s) of notification.

CONTACT

Kathy John, Director of Financial Aid
900 Dayton Street, Yellow Springs, OH 45387
(937) 769-1840

Art Academy of Cincinnati
Cincinnati, Ohio
www.artacademy.edu   Federal Code: 003011

4-year private visual arts college in large city.
Enrollment: 207 undergrads.

BASIC COSTS (2016-2017)

Tuition and fees: $29,252; out-of-state residents $29,252.
Per-credit charge: $1,177.
Room and board: $6,500.

FINANCIAL AID PICTURE

Students with need: Need-based aid available for full-time and part-time students.
Students without need: No-need awards available for academics, art.
Scholarships offered: Annual scholarships awarded to entering and transfer students and to continuing students based on portfolio competition.

FINANCIAL AID PROCEDURES

Forms required: FAFSA.
Dates and Deadlines: Priority date 4/1; no closing date. Applicants notified on a rolling basis starting 4/1.

CONTACT

Dawn Reck, Financial Aid Director
1212 Jackson Street, Cincinnati, OH 45202
(513) 562-8773

Art Institute of Cincinnati
Cincinnati, Ohio
www.aic-arts.edu   Federal Code: 014804

2-year for-profit visual arts college in large city.
Enrollment: 22 undergrads. 8 full-time freshmen.
Selectivity: Admits 50 to 75% of applicants.

BASIC COSTS (2016-2017)

Tuition and fees: $16,834.
Additional info: Tuition at time of enrollment locked for 2 years.

FINANCIAL AID PICTURE (2015-2016)

Students with need: Out of 8 full-time freshmen who applied for aid, 6 were judged to have need. Of these, 6 received aid. Average financial aid package met 91% of need.
Students without need: No-need awards available for academics, art.

FINANCIAL AID PROCEDURES

Forms required: FAFSA, institutional form.
Dates and Deadlines: Applicants notified on a rolling basis starting 9/1; must reply within 1 week(s) of notification.

Transfers: No deadline. Applicants notified on a rolling basis; must reply within 4 week(s) of notification.

CONTACT

Rita Schrand, Financial Aid Director
1171 East Kemper Road, Cincinnati, OH 45246
(513) 751-1206

Ashland University
Ashland, Ohio
www.ashland.edu   Federal Code: 003012

4-year private university and liberal arts college in large town, affiliated with the Brethren Church.
Enrollment: 3,559 undergrads, 8% part-time. 620 full-time freshmen.
Selectivity: Admits 50 to 75% of applicants.

BASIC COSTS (2016-2017)

Tuition and fees: $20,392.
Room and board: $9,602.
Additional info: Tuition/fee waivers available for minority students, unemployed or children of unemployed.

FINANCIAL AID PICTURE (2016-2017)

Students with need: Out of 564 full-time freshmen who applied for aid, 484 were judged to have need. Of these, 484 received aid. For part-time students, average financial aid package was $6,033.
Students without need: 80 full-time freshmen who did not demonstrate need for aid received scholarships/grants; average award was $9,091. No-need awards available for academics, alumni affiliation, art, athletics, job skills, leadership, minority status, music/drama, religious affiliation, state/district residency.
Scholarships offered: *Merit:* Four-year Freshmen merit awards: range from $26,000 to $46,000; based on high school GPA and highest ACT/SAT score received by March 1 of HS senior year. *Athletic:* 18 full-time freshmen received athletic scholarships; average amount $15,996.

FINANCIAL AID PROCEDURES

Forms required: FAFSA.
Dates and Deadlines: Priority date 3/15; no closing date. Applicants notified on a rolling basis starting 3/1.
Transfers: No deadline. Applicants notified on a rolling basis starting 3/15. Transfer scholarships based on college GPA: $7500 per year based on 3.75 GPA; $5500 per year based on 3.5 - 3.74 GPA; $4500 per year based on 3.25 - 3.49 GPA; $3500 per year based on 3.0 - 3.24 GPA.

CONTACT

Stephen Howell, Director of Financial Aid
401 College Avenue, Ashland, OH 44805-9981
(419) 289-5002

Aultman College of Nursing and Health Sciences
Canton, Ohio
www.aultmancollege.edu   Federal Code: 006487

2-year private health science and nursing college in small city.
Enrollment: 363 undergrads, 72% part-time. 16 full-time freshmen.
Selectivity: Admits 50 to 75% of applicants.

BASIC COSTS (2017-2018)

Tuition and fees: $17,425.
Per-credit charge: $567.

FINANCIAL AID PICTURE (2015-2016)

Students with need: 29% of average financial aid package awarded as scholarships/grants, 71% awarded as loans/jobs. Need-based aid available for part-time students.

Students without need: This college awards aid only to students with need.

Scholarships offered: 1892 Scholarship: two $1,000 awards; for incoming fall or spring freshman based on 3.0 GPA, 25 ACT (or equivalent SAT score); one-page essay and 6 credit hours per semester required. President's scholarship: full tuition paid for first-time, full-time students with 3.8 min GPA and 27 in ACT.

FINANCIAL AID PROCEDURES

Forms required: FAFSA, institutional form.

Dates and Deadlines: Priority date 3/1; closing date 10/1. Applicants notified on a rolling basis starting 6/15; must reply within 2 week(s) of notification.

CONTACT

Briana Williams, Financial Aid Administrator
2600 Sixth Street SW, Canton, OH 44710-1799
(330) 363-6479

Baldwin Wallace University
Berea, Ohio
www.bw.edu
Federal Code: 003014

4-year private university in large town, affiliated with the United Methodist Church.

Enrollment: 3,245 undergrads, 7% part-time. 705 full-time freshmen.

Selectivity: Admits 50 to 75% of applicants.

BASIC COSTS (2017-2018)

Tuition and fees: $31,668.

Per-credit charge: $984.

Room and board: $9,142.

Additional info: Tuition/fee waivers available for minority students.

FINANCIAL AID PICTURE (2016-2017)

Students with need: Out of 674 full-time freshmen who applied for aid, 588 were judged to have need. Of these, 588 received aid, and 113 had their full need met. Average financial aid package met 87% of need; average scholarship/grant was $20,749; average loan was $4,167. For part-time students, average financial aid package was $9,387.

Students without need: 124 full-time freshmen who did not demonstrate need for aid received scholarships/grants; average award was $14,011. No-need awards available for academics, alumni affiliation, art, minority status, music/drama, religious affiliation, state/district residency.

Scholarships offered: Presidential Scholarship: $13,000; ACT 28 or SAT 1260 and above.

FINANCIAL AID PROCEDURES

Forms required: FAFSA.

Dates and Deadlines: Priority date 8/15; no closing date. Applicants notified on a rolling basis starting 1/23.

CONTACT

George Rolleston, Director of Financial Aid
275 Eastland Road, Berea, OH 44017-2005
(440) 826-2108

Belmont College
St Clairsville, Ohio
www.belmontcollege.edu
Federal Code: 009941

2-year public community and technical college in small town.

Enrollment: 1,259 undergrads.

Selectivity: Open admission; but selective for some programs.

BASIC COSTS (2016-2017)

Tuition and fees: $4,389; out-of-state residents $7,488.

Per-credit charge: $105; out-of-state residents $208.

Additional info: Tuition/fee waivers available for unemployed or children of unemployed.

FINANCIAL AID PICTURE

Students with need: Need-based aid available for full-time and part-time students.

Students without need: No-need awards available for state/district residency.

FINANCIAL AID PROCEDURES

Forms required: FAFSA.

Dates and Deadlines: Applicants notified on a rolling basis starting 6/1; must reply within 2 week(s) of notification.

CONTACT

Jody Peeler, Associate Dean of Financial Aid
120 Fox Shannon Place, St. Clairsville, OH 43950
(740) 695-8510

Bluffton University
Bluffton, Ohio
www.bluffton.edu
Federal Code: 003016

4-year private university and liberal arts college in small town, affiliated with the Mennonite Church.

Enrollment: 787 undergrads, 8% part-time. 208 full-time freshmen.

Selectivity: Admits less than 50% of applicants.

BASIC COSTS (2017-2018)

Tuition and fees: $31,672.

Per-credit charge: $1,301.

Room and board: $10,484.

FINANCIAL AID PICTURE (2016-2017)

Students with need: Out of 196 full-time freshmen who applied for aid, 183 were judged to have need. Of these, 183 received aid, and 22 had their full need met. Average financial aid package met 77% of need; average scholarship/grant was $21,909; average loan was $4,775. For part-time students, average financial aid package was $10,620.

Students without need: 24 full-time freshmen who did not demonstrate need for aid received scholarships/grants; average award was $15,631. No-need awards available for academics, alumni affiliation, art, job skills, leadership, minority status, music/drama, religious affiliation, state/district residency.

Additional info: Tuition Equalization Program erases the difference between Bluffton's tuition and academic fees and that of the top state schools.

FINANCIAL AID PROCEDURES

Forms required: FAFSA.

Dates and Deadlines: Priority date 5/1; no closing date. Applicants notified on a rolling basis starting 11/1.

Transfers: No deadline. Applicants notified on a rolling basis starting 11/1.

CONTACT

Christopher Fowler, Director of Financial Aid
1 University Drive, Bluffton, OH 45817-2104
(419) 358-3266

Bowling Green State University
Bowling Green, Ohio
www.bgsu.edu
Federal Code: 003018

4-year public university in large town.

Enrollment: 13,901 undergrads, 6% part-time. 3,375 full-time freshmen.

Selectivity: Admits 50 to 75% of applicants.

BASIC COSTS (2016-2017)

Tuition and fees: $11,057; out-of-district residents $11,057; out-of-state residents $18,593.
Per-credit charge: $379; out-of-state residents $693.
Room and board: $8,690.

FINANCIAL AID PICTURE (2015-2016)

Students with need: Out of 3,088 full-time freshmen who applied for aid, 2,403 were judged to have need. Of these, 2,375 received aid, and 304 had their full need met. Average financial aid package met 80% of need; average scholarship/grant was $6,988; average loan was $3,396. For part-time students, average financial aid package was $9,587.
Students without need: 685 full-time freshmen who did not demonstrate need for aid received scholarships/grants; average award was $4,800. No-need awards available for academics, alumni affiliation, art, athletics, leadership, minority status, music/drama, ROTC, state/district residency.
Scholarships offered: 88 full-time freshmen received athletic scholarships; average amount $17,180.

FINANCIAL AID PROCEDURES

Forms required: FAFSA.
Dates and Deadlines: Priority date 1/15; no closing date. Applicants notified on a rolling basis starting 2/1; must reply within 3 week(s) of notification.
Transfers: Applicants notified on a rolling basis starting 3/15. Transfer students may qualify for the Transfer Opportunity Scholarship or the Thompson Scholarship Program. Transfer students that are Non-Ohio residents may also qualify for the BG Success Scholarship which provides one-half off the nonresident fee.

CONTACT

Betsy Sue Johnson, Director, Student Financial Aid
110 McFall Center, Bowling Green, OH 43403-0085
(419) 372-2651

Bowling Green State University: Firelands College
Huron, Ohio
www.firelands.bgsu.edu   Federal Code: 003018

2-year public branch campus college in small town.
Enrollment: 1,315 undergrads, 35% part-time. 321 full-time freshmen.
Selectivity: Open admission.

BASIC COSTS (2016-2017)

Tuition and fees: $4,946; out-of-state residents $12,254.
Per-credit charge: $196; out-of-state residents $501.

FINANCIAL AID PICTURE

Students with need: Need-based aid available for full-time and part-time students.
Students without need: This college awards aid only to students with need.
Scholarships offered: Firelands Opportunities in College for Underrepresented Students Scholarship: full tuition; for historically underrepresented students in all Firelands majors; 4-6 awards annually.
Additional info: Scholarship application deadline May 1. Technology computer loan program available. Based on need, students may receive computer on semester by semester loan basis.

FINANCIAL AID PROCEDURES

Forms required: FAFSA.
Dates and Deadlines: Priority date 3/1; no closing date. Applicants notified on a rolling basis starting 4/15; must reply within 2 week(s) of notification.

CONTACT

Cheryl Chafee, Assistant Director of Admissions and Financial Aid
One University Drive, Huron, OH 44839-9719
(419) 433-5560

Brown Mackie College: Findlay
Findlay, Ohio
www.brownmackie.edu   Federal Code: 026162

2-year for-profit business and junior college in small city.
Selectivity: Open admission.

BASIC COSTS (2016-2017)

Additional info: Costs vary by program. Certificate programs $14,900-$23,548, books and supplies $650-$950. Diploma programs $15,840-$31,236, books and supplies $650-$900. Associate programs $31,230-$43,848, books and supplies $650-$1,190. Bachelor's programs $62,460-$63,360, books and supplies $650-$1,550.

FINANCIAL AID PICTURE

Students with need: Need-based aid available for full-time and part-time students. Work study available nights, weekends, and for part-time students.
Students without need: No-need awards available for academics, state/district residency.

FINANCIAL AID PROCEDURES

Forms required: FAFSA.
Transfers: No deadline.

CONTACT

Brandy Lanagan, Director of Financial Aid
1700 Fostoria Avenue, Suite 100, Findlay, OH 45840
(419) 423-2211

Brown Mackie College: North Canton
Canton, Ohio
www.brownmackie.edu   Federal Code: 030778

2-year for-profit career college in small city.
Selectivity: Open admission.

BASIC COSTS (2016-2017)

Additional info: Costs vary by program. Diploma programs $16,896-$17,600, books and supplies $650. Associate programs $31,230-$34,960, books and supplies $650-$1,130. Bachelor's program Health Care Management $63,360, books and supplies $650.

FINANCIAL AID PICTURE

Students with need: Work study available nights.

FINANCIAL AID PROCEDURES

Forms required: FAFSA.

CONTACT

Jessica Petitte, Director of Student Financial Services
4300 Munson Street Northwest, Canton, OH 44718-3674

Bryant & Stratton College: Cleveland
Cleveland, Ohio
www.bryantstratton.edu   Federal Code: 022744

2-year for-profit technical and career college in very large city.
Enrollment: 291 undergrads.
Selectivity: Open admission; but selective for some programs.

BASIC COSTS (2016-2017)

Tuition and fees: $17,190.

Per-credit charge: $573.

Additional info: Tuition and fees may vary by program.

FINANCIAL AID PICTURE

Students with need: Need-based aid available for full-time and part-time students. Work study available nights.

Students without need: No-need awards available for academics.

FINANCIAL AID PROCEDURES

Forms required: FAFSA, institutional form.

Dates and Deadlines: Closing date 9/22. Applicants notified on a rolling basis starting 5/1; must reply within 2 week(s) of notification.

Transfers: No deadline. By state regulation, Ohio Institutional Grant can be awarded only 3 times a fiscal year.

CONTACT

DeAuntha Logan, Financial Aid Manager

3121 Euclid Avenue, Cleveland, OH 44115

(216) 771-1700

Bryant & Stratton College: Eastlake

Eastlake, Ohio

www.bryantstratton.edu   Federal Code: 022744

4-year for-profit business college in small town.

Enrollment: 231 undergrads.

Selectivity: Open admission.

BASIC COSTS (2016-2017)

Tuition and fees: $17,190.

Per-credit charge: $573.

Additional info: Tuition and fees may vary by program.

FINANCIAL AID PICTURE

Students with need: Need-based aid available for full-time and part-time students.

Students without need: No-need awards available for academics.

FINANCIAL AID PROCEDURES

Forms required: FAFSA.

Dates and Deadlines: Applicants notified on a rolling basis.

CONTACT

Donna McCullough, Financial Aid Manager

35350 Curtis Boulevard, Eastlake, OH 44095

(440) 510-1112

Bryant & Stratton College: Parma

Parma, Ohio

www.bryantstratton.edu   Federal Code: 015298

4-year for-profit nursing and junior college in small city.

Enrollment: 281 undergrads.

Selectivity: Open admission; but selective for some programs.

BASIC COSTS (2016-2017)

Tuition and fees: $17,190.

Per-credit charge: $573.

FINANCIAL AID PICTURE

Students with need: Need-based aid available for full-time and part-time students. Work study available nights.

Students without need: This college awards aid only to students with need.

FINANCIAL AID PROCEDURES

Forms required: FAFSA.

Dates and Deadlines: Closing date 9/22. Applicants notified on a rolling basis starting 6/1.

Transfers: Transfer form must be completed for state grant.

CONTACT

Laura Shannon, Financial Services Manager

12955 Snow Road, Parma, OH 44130-1013

(216) 265-3151 ext. 231

Capital University

Columbus, Ohio

www.capital.edu   Federal Code: 003023

4-year private university in very large city, affiliated with the Evangelical Lutheran Church in America.

Enrollment: 2,600 undergrads, 6% part-time. 671 full-time freshmen.

Selectivity: Admits 50 to 75% of applicants.

BASIC COSTS (2017-2018)

Tuition and fees: $34,600.

Per-credit charge: $1,144.

Room and board: $10,178.

FINANCIAL AID PICTURE (2015-2016)

Students with need: Out of 637 full-time freshmen who applied for aid, 588 were judged to have need. Of these, 588 received aid, and 179 had their full need met. Average financial aid package met 86% of need; average scholarship/grant was $24,756; average loan was $3,973. For part-time students, average financial aid package was $6,874.

Students without need: 75 full-time freshmen who did not demonstrate need for aid received scholarships/grants; average award was $21,467. No-need awards available for academics, alumni affiliation, minority status, music/drama, religious affiliation, ROTC.

Scholarships offered: Scholarships and grants; $1,000 to full tuition.

FINANCIAL AID PROCEDURES

Forms required: FAFSA.

Dates and Deadlines: Priority date 3/1; no closing date. Applicants notified on a rolling basis starting 12/15; must reply by 3/1.

Transfers: Priority date 7/15.

CONTACT

Susan Kannenwischer, Director of Financial Aid

1 College and Main, Columbus, OH 43209-2394

(614) 236-6511

Case Western Reserve University

Cleveland, Ohio   Federal Code: E00077

www.case.edu   CSS Code: 1105

4-year private university in very large city.

Enrollment: 5,048 undergrads, 1% part-time. 1,264 full-time freshmen.

Selectivity: Admits less than 50% of applicants.

BASIC COSTS (2016-2017)

Tuition and fees: $46,006.

Per-credit charge: $1,900.

Room and board: $14,298.

FINANCIAL AID PICTURE (2016-2017)

Students with need: Out of 841 full-time freshmen who applied for aid, 635 were judged to have need. Of these, 635 received aid, and 386 had their full need met. Average financial aid package met 86% of need; average scholarship/grant was $29,620; average loan was $3,273. For part-time students, average financial aid package was $20,005.

Students without need: 412 full-time freshmen who did not demonstrate need for aid received scholarships/grants; average award was $24,654. No-need awards available for academics, alumni affiliation, art, leadership, music/drama.

FINANCIAL AID PROCEDURES

Forms required: FAFSA, CSS PROFILE, institutional form.

Dates and Deadlines: Priority date 2/15; closing date 5/15. Applicants notified on a rolling basis starting 3/15; must reply by 5/1 or within 2 week(s) of notification.

Transfers: Priority date 2/15.

CONTACT

Venus Puliafico, Director of University Financial Aid

Wolstein Hall, Cleveland, OH 44106-7055

(216) 368-4530

Cedarville University

Cedarville, Ohio

www.cedarville.edu   Federal Code: 003025

4-year private university and liberal arts college in small town, affiliated with the Baptist faith.

Enrollment: 3,065 undergrads, 2% part-time. 819 full-time freshmen.

Selectivity: Admits 50 to 75% of applicants.

BASIC COSTS (2016-2017)

Tuition and fees: $28,110.

Per-credit charge: $1,056.

Room and board: $6,880.

FINANCIAL AID PICTURE (2015-2016)

Students with need: Out of 738 full-time freshmen who applied for aid, 611 were judged to have need. Of these, 611 received aid, and 218 had their full need met. Average financial aid package met 30% of need; average scholarship/grant was $5,541; average loan was $4,508. For part-time students, average financial aid package was $8,015.

Students without need: 180 full-time freshmen who did not demonstrate need for aid received scholarships/grants; average award was $18,639. No-need awards available for academics, athletics, minority status, music/drama, ROTC.

Scholarships offered: 56 full-time freshmen received athletic scholarships; average amount $6,860.

FINANCIAL AID PROCEDURES

Forms required: FAFSA.

Dates and Deadlines: Priority date 3/1; no closing date. Applicants notified on a rolling basis starting 3/1.

Transfers: No deadline. Applicants notified on a rolling basis starting 2/1.

CONTACT

Kim Jenerette, Executive Director of Financial Aid

251 North Main Street, Cedarville, OH 45314-0601

(937) 766-7866

Central Ohio Technical College

Newark, Ohio

www.cotc.edu   Federal Code: 011046

2-year public technical college in large town.

Enrollment: 2,721 undergrads.

Selectivity: Open admission; but selective for some programs.

BASIC COSTS (2016-2017)

Tuition and fees: $4,296; out-of-state residents $7,056.

Per-credit charge: $179; out-of-district residents $294.

FINANCIAL AID PICTURE

Students with need: Need-based aid available for full-time and part-time students. Work study available nights, weekends, and for part-time students.

Students without need: No-need awards available for academics, state/district residency.

Scholarships offered: Presidential Achievement Award: $1,800 annually; based on 3.0 GPA; 5 awarded. Minority Achievement Award: $850 annually; based on 2.5 GPA; 2 awarded.

FINANCIAL AID PROCEDURES

Forms required: FAFSA.

Dates and Deadlines: Priority date 2/15; no closing date. Applicants notified on a rolling basis starting 5/1; must reply within 3 week(s) of notification.

CONTACT

Faith Phillips, Director of Financial Aid

1179 University Drive, Newark, OH 43055

(740) 366-9435

Central State University

Wilberforce, Ohio

www.centralstate.edu   Federal Code: 003026

4-year public university and liberal arts college in rural community.

Enrollment: 1,701 undergrads, 6% part-time. 630 full-time freshmen.

Selectivity: Admits less than 50% of applicants.

BASIC COSTS (2016-2017)

Tuition and fees: $6,246; out-of-state residents $8,096.

Per-credit charge: $275; out-of-state residents $625.

Room and board: $9,934.

FINANCIAL AID PICTURE

Students with need: Need-based aid available for full-time and part-time students. Work study available nights, weekends, and for part-time students.

Students without need: No-need awards available for academics, alumni affiliation, art, athletics, leadership, music/drama, religious affiliation, ROTC.

FINANCIAL AID PROCEDURES

Forms required: FAFSA, institutional form.

Dates and Deadlines: Priority date 2/15; no closing date. Applicants notified by 4/15; must reply by 5/1.

Transfers: No deadline.

CONTACT

Sonia Slomba, Director, Student Financial Aid Office

PO Box 1004, Wilberforce, OH 45384-1004

(937) 376-6519

Chatfield College

Fayetteville, Ohio

www.chatfield.edu   Federal Code: 010880

2-year private liberal arts college in rural community, affiliated with the Roman Catholic Church.

Enrollment: 208 undergrads, 59% part-time. 46 full-time freshmen.

Selectivity: Open admission.

BASIC COSTS (2016-2017)

Tuition and fees: $10,523.

Per-credit charge: $407.

FINANCIAL AID PICTURE

Students with need: Need-based aid available for full-time and part-time students.

Students without need: No-need awards available for academics, leadership.

Additional info: Institutional grants/scholarships given primarily to first-year students to reduce debt load during initial year.

FINANCIAL AID PROCEDURES
Forms required: FAFSA, institutional form.
Dates and Deadlines: Priority date 5/1; closing date 8/3. Applicants notified on a rolling basis starting 4/1; must reply within 2 week(s) of notification.

CONTACT
Dawn Hundley
20918 State Route 251, St. Martin, OH 45118
(513) 875-3344 ext. 146

Cincinnati Christian University
Cincinnati, Ohio
www.ccuniversity.edu   Federal Code: 003029

4-year private university in very large city, affiliated with the Christian Church.
Enrollment: 569 undergrads. 106 full-time freshmen.

BASIC COSTS (2016-2017)
Tuition and fees: $16,664.
Per-credit charge: $650.
Room and board: $7,860.

FINANCIAL AID PICTURE (2015-2016)
Students with need: Out of 104 full-time freshmen who applied for aid, 94 were judged to have need. Of these, 94 received aid, and 12 had their full need met. Average financial aid package met 60% of need; average scholarship/grant was $9,376; average loan was $3,355. For part-time students, average financial aid package was $6,593.
Students without need: 4 full-time freshmen who did not demonstrate need for aid received scholarships/grants; average award was $7,929. No-need awards available for academics, athletics, leadership, minority status, music/drama, religious affiliation, state/district residency.
Scholarships offered: 10 full-time freshmen received athletic scholarships; average amount $6,219.

FINANCIAL AID PROCEDURES
Forms required: FAFSA.
Dates and Deadlines: Priority date 3/1; no closing date. Applicants notified on a rolling basis starting 2/15.
Transfers: No deadline. Applicants notified on a rolling basis starting 2/15.

CONTACT
Marcella Farmer, Financial Aid Director
2700 Glenway Avenue, Cincinnati, OH 45204-3200
(513) 244-8100 ext. 8450

Cincinnati College of Mortuary Science
Cincinnati, Ohio
https://www.ccms.edu   Federal Code: 010906

2-year private school of mortuary science in very large city.
Enrollment: 43 undergrads.

BASIC COSTS (2016-2017)
Tuition and fees: $19,625.
Per-credit charge: $375.

FINANCIAL AID PICTURE
Students with need: Need-based aid available for full-time and part-time students.
Students without need: This college awards aid only to students with need.

FINANCIAL AID PROCEDURES
Forms required: FAFSA.
Transfers: No deadline.

CONTACT
Leslie Boehm, Business Manager/Bursar
645 West North Bend Road, Cincinnati, OH 45224-1428
(513) 761-2020

Cincinnati State Technical and Community College
Cincinnati, Ohio
www.cincinnatistate.edu   Federal Code: 010345

2-year public community and technical college in large city.
Enrollment: 7,229 undergrads, 67% part-time. 1,046 full-time freshmen.
Selectivity: Open admission; but selective for some programs.

BASIC COSTS (2016-2017)
Tuition and fees: $4,717; out-of-state residents $9,177.

FINANCIAL AID PICTURE
Students with need: Need-based aid available for full-time and part-time students. Work study available nights, weekends, and for part-time students.
Students without need: No-need awards available for academics, athletics, state/district residency.

FINANCIAL AID PROCEDURES
Forms required: FAFSA.
Dates and Deadlines: Priority date 2/15; no closing date. Applicants notified on a rolling basis starting 3/15; must reply within 4 week(s) of notification.

CONTACT
LaSaundra Craig, Director of Student Financial Aid/Scholarships
3520 Central Parkway, Cincinnati, OH 45223-2690
(513) 569-1530

Clark State Community College
Springfield, Ohio
www.clarkstate.edu   Federal Code: 004852

2-year public community college in small city.
Enrollment: 4,843 undergrads.
Selectivity: Open admission; but selective for some programs.

BASIC COSTS (2016-2017)
Tuition and fees: $4,180; out-of-state residents $7,820.
Per-credit charge: $121; out-of-state residents $243.

FINANCIAL AID PICTURE
Students with need: Work study available nights, weekends, and for part-time students.

FINANCIAL AID PROCEDURES
Forms required: FAFSA.
Dates and Deadlines: Priority date 6/15; no closing date. Applicants notified on a rolling basis.
Transfers: No deadline. Applicants notified on a rolling basis.

CONTACT
Kathy Klay, Director of Financial Aid
Box 570, Springfield, OH 45501-0570
(937) 328-6034

Cleveland Institute of Art
Cleveland, Ohio
www.cia.edu   Federal Code: 003982

4-year private visual arts college in large city.
Enrollment: 614 undergrads, 1% part-time. 161 full-time freshmen.
Selectivity: Admits 50 to 75% of applicants.

BASIC COSTS (2017-2018)
Tuition and fees: $40,685.
Room and board: $11,880.

FINANCIAL AID PICTURE (2015-2016)
Students with need: Out of 158 full-time freshmen who applied for aid, 154 were judged to have need. Of these, 154 received aid, and 13 had their full need met. Average financial aid package met 62% of need; average scholarship/grant was $24,745; average loan was $3,947. For part-time students, average financial aid package was $5,347.
Students without need: 27 full-time freshmen who did not demonstrate need for aid received scholarships/grants; average award was $15,321. No-need awards available for academics, art.

FINANCIAL AID PROCEDURES
Forms required: FAFSA.
Dates and Deadlines: Closing date 3/15. Must reply by 5/1.
Transfers: Priority date 6/1. Applicants notified on a rolling basis starting 6/15; must reply within 2 week(s) of notification.

CONTACT
Martin Carney, Director of Financial Aid
11610 Euclid Avenue, Cleveland, OH 44106-1710
(216) 421-7425

Cleveland Institute of Music
Cleveland, Ohio
www.cim.edu   Federal Code: 003031

4-year private music college in very large city.
Enrollment: 233 undergrads. 61 full-time freshmen.
Selectivity: Admits less than 50% of applicants.

BASIC COSTS (2016-2017)
Tuition and fees: $49,106.
Per-credit charge: $1,967.
Room and board: $14,382.

FINANCIAL AID PICTURE (2015-2016)
Students with need: Out of 45 full-time freshmen who applied for aid, 31 were judged to have need. Of these, 31 received aid. Need-based aid available for part-time students.
Students without need: 31 full-time freshmen who did not demonstrate need for aid received scholarships/grants; average award was $21,447. No-need awards available for academics, music/drama.

FINANCIAL AID PROCEDURES
Forms required: FAFSA, institutional form.
Dates and Deadlines: Priority date 3/1; closing date 3/1. Applicants notified by 4/1; must reply by 5/1 or within 2 week(s) of notification.
Transfers: Closing date 3/1. Applicants notified by 4/1; must reply by 5/1 or within 2 week(s) of notification.

CONTACT
Kristie Gripp, Director of Financial Aid
11021 East Boulevard, Cleveland, OH 44106
(216) 795-3192

Cleveland State University
Cleveland, Ohio
www.csuohio.edu   Federal Code: 003032

4-year public university in large city.
Enrollment: 11,764 undergrads, 22% part-time. 1,891 full-time freshmen.
Selectivity: Admits over 75% of applicants.

BASIC COSTS (2016-2017)
Tuition and fees: $9,696; out-of-state residents $13,747.
Per-credit charge: $402; out-of-state residents $570.
Room and board: $12,500.

FINANCIAL AID PICTURE (2015-2016)
Students with need: 42% of average financial aid package awarded as scholarships/grants, 58% awarded as loans/jobs. Need-based aid available for part-time students. Work study available nights, weekends, and for part-time students.
Students without need: No-need awards available for academics, alumni affiliation, art, athletics, leadership, music/drama, ROTC.

FINANCIAL AID PROCEDURES
Forms required: FAFSA.
Dates and Deadlines: Priority date 2/15; no closing date. Applicants notified on a rolling basis starting 3/15; must reply within 4 week(s) of notification.

CONTACT
Rachel Schmidt, Director of Financial Aid
2121 Euclid Avenue, Cleveland, OH 44115-2214
(888) 278-6446

College of Wooster
Wooster, Ohio   Federal Code: 003037
www.wooster.edu   CSS Code: 1134

4-year private liberal arts college in large town.
Enrollment: 1,980 undergrads. 545 full-time freshmen.
Selectivity: Admits 50 to 75% of applicants.

BASIC COSTS (2016-2017)
Tuition and fees: $46,860.
Per-credit charge: $1,440.
Room and board: $11,040.

FINANCIAL AID PICTURE (2016-2017)
Students with need: Out of 399 full-time freshmen who applied for aid, 333 were judged to have need. Of these, 333 received aid, and 198 had their full need met. Average financial aid package met 95% of need; average scholarship/grant was $32,506; average loan was $5,948. Need-based aid available for part-time students.
Students without need: 135 full-time freshmen who did not demonstrate need for aid received scholarships/grants; average award was $25,680. No-need awards available for academics, minority status, music/drama, religious affiliation.

FINANCIAL AID PROCEDURES
Forms required: FAFSA, institutional form. Either CSS PROFILE or institution application for prospective students.
Dates and Deadlines: Priority date 2/15; no closing date. Applicants notified on a rolling basis starting 3/15; must reply by 5/1 or within 2 week(s) of notification.
Transfers: Priority date 4/1; no deadline. Applicants notified on a rolling basis.

CONTACT
Dana Kennedy, Director of Financial Aid
Gault Admissions Center, Wooster, OH 44691-2363
(330) 263-2317

Columbus College of Art and Design
Columbus, Ohio
www.ccad.edu   Federal Code: 003039

4-year private visual arts college in very large city.
Enrollment: 1,036 undergrads, 4% part-time. 302 full-time freshmen.
Selectivity: Admits over 75% of applicants.

BASIC COSTS (2017-2018)
Tuition and fees: $33,960.
Per-credit charge: $1,415.
Room and board: $9,370.

FINANCIAL AID PICTURE (2015-2016)
Students with need: Out of 269 full-time freshmen who applied for aid, 242 were judged to have need. Of these, 236 received aid, and 17 had their full need met. Average financial aid package met 57% of need; average scholarship/grant was $17,974; average loan was $5,995. For part-time students, average financial aid package was $12,716.
Students without need: 56 full-time freshmen who did not demonstrate need for aid received scholarships/grants; average award was $12,205. No-need awards available for academics, art, ROTC, state/district residency.

FINANCIAL AID PROCEDURES
Forms required: FAFSA.
Dates and Deadlines: Priority date 12/1; closing date 2/15. Applicants notified on a rolling basis starting 1/15; must reply within 2 week(s) of notification.
Transfers: Closing date 2/15. Applicants notified on a rolling basis.

CONTACT
Anna Marie Schofield, Director of Financial Aid
60 Cleveland Avenue, Columbus, OH 43215-3875
(614) 222-3274

Columbus State Community College
Columbus, Ohio
www.cscc.edu   Federal Code: 006867

2-year public community and technical college in very large city.
Enrollment: 11,561 undergrads, 71% part-time. 909 full-time freshmen.
Selectivity: Open admission; but selective for some programs.

BASIC COSTS (2016-2017)
Tuition and fees: $4,128; out-of-state residents $9,081.
Per-credit charge: $135.93; out-of-state residents $301.03.

FINANCIAL AID PICTURE (2016-2017)
Students with need: Need-based aid available for part-time students.
Students without need: No-need awards available for academics, state/district residency.

FINANCIAL AID PROCEDURES
Forms required: FAFSA.
Dates and Deadlines: Priority date 6/1; no closing date. Applicants notified on a rolling basis starting 4/1.

CONTACT
David Metz, Director of Financial Aid
550 East Spring Street, Columbus, OH 43216-1609
(614) 287-2648

Cuyahoga Community College
Cleveland, Ohio
www.tri-c.edu

2-year public community college in very large city.
Enrollment: 12,772 undergrads, 61% part-time. 1,225 full-time freshmen.

Selectivity: Open admission; but selective for some programs.

BASIC COSTS (2016-2017)
Tuition and fees: $3,172; out-of-district residents $3,953; out-of-state residents $7,468.

FINANCIAL AID PICTURE (2016-2017)
Students with need: 79% of average financial aid package awarded as scholarships/grants, 21% awarded as loans/jobs. Need-based aid available for part-time students. Work study available nights, weekends, and for part-time students.
Students without need: No-need awards available for academics, art, athletics, leadership, minority status, music/drama.

FINANCIAL AID PROCEDURES
Forms required: FAFSA, institutional form.
Dates and Deadlines: Applicants notified on a rolling basis starting 5/15.
Transfers: Priority date 5/13.

CONTACT
Kimberly Nash
2900 Community College Avenue, Cleveland, OH 44115-2878

Davis College
Toledo, Ohio
www.daviscollege.edu   Federal Code: 004855

2-year for-profit junior college in large city.
Enrollment: 190 undergrads.

BASIC COSTS (2016-2017)
Tuition and fees: $16,800.
Per-credit charge: $350.

FINANCIAL AID PICTURE
Students with need: Need-based aid available for full-time and part-time students. Work study available nights, weekends, and for part-time students.
Students without need: This college awards aid only to students with need.

FINANCIAL AID PROCEDURES
Forms required: FAFSA.
Dates and Deadlines: Applicants notified on a rolling basis.
Transfers: No deadline. Applicants notified on a rolling basis. Student completes a clearance withdrawal letter that is completed from the previous school's financial aid office.

CONTACT
Marilyn Bovia, Director of Financial Aid
4747 Monroe Street, Toledo, OH 43623
(419) 473-2700

Daymar College: Chillicothe
Chillicothe, Ohio
www.daymarcollege.edu   Federal Code: 020568

2-year for-profit business college in large town.
Enrollment: 38 undergrads.
Selectivity: Open admission.

BASIC COSTS (2016-2017)
Additional info: Diploma programs: $22,000-$26,500; Associate programs: $33,000. Fees, books supplies range depending on program level and course of study. All costs are subject to change.

FINANCIAL AID PICTURE
Students with need: Need-based aid available for full-time and part-time students.

Students without need: This college awards aid only to students with need.

Scholarships offered: Ohio Legislative Scholarship: administered by the Ohio Council of Private Colleges and Schools, for Ohio-resident high school seniors nominated by their state representative who reviews applications; 2-year tuition for associate degree valued at $11,500.

FINANCIAL AID PROCEDURES
Forms required: FAFSA, institutional form.
Transfers: No deadline.

CONTACT
Connie Pruitt, Financial Aid Coordinator
1410 Industrial Drive, Chillicothe, OH 45601
(740) 774-2063

Defiance College
Defiance, Ohio
www.defiance.edu   Federal Code: 003041

4-year private liberal arts college in large town, affiliated with the United Church of Christ.
Enrollment: 582 undergrads, 13% part-time. 179 full-time freshmen.
Selectivity: Admits 50 to 75% of applicants.

BASIC COSTS (2017-2018)
Tuition and fees: $32,190.
Room and board: $9,950.

FINANCIAL AID PICTURE (2015-2016)
Students with need: Out of 176 full-time freshmen who applied for aid, 167 were judged to have need. Of these, 167 received aid, and 15 had their full need met. Average financial aid package met 67% of need; average scholarship/grant was $19,376; average loan was $3,953. For part-time students, average financial aid package was $5,839.
Students without need: 12 full-time freshmen who did not demonstrate need for aid received scholarships/grants; average award was $10,552. No-need awards available for academics, leadership, minority status, music/drama.
Scholarships offered: Dean's Scholarship: $16,000; High school GPA of 3.5/4.0 scale and ACT composite of 27 or SAT combined score of 1280. Pilgrim Scholarship: $15,000; High school GPA of 3.2/4.0 scale and ACT composite of 24 or SAT combined score of 1160. Trustee Scholarship: $14,000; High school GPA of 2.8/4.0 scale and ACT composite of 21 or SAT combined score of 1060. Achievement Scholarship: $10,000; High school GPA of 2.5 and ACT composite of 18 or SAT combined score of 940. All scholarships awarded upon acceptance.

FINANCIAL AID PROCEDURES
Forms required: FAFSA.
Dates and Deadlines: Priority date 4/1; no closing date. Applicants notified on a rolling basis starting 2/15; must reply by 5/1 or within 2 week(s) of notification.

CONTACT
Amy Francis, Director of Financial Aid
701 North Clinton Street, Defiance, OH 43512-1695
(419) 783-2364

Denison University
Granville, Ohio
www.denison.edu   Federal Code: 003042

4-year private liberal arts college in large town.
Enrollment: 2,261 undergrads. 637 full-time freshmen.
Selectivity: Admits less than 50% of applicants.

BASIC COSTS (2016-2017)
Tuition and fees: $48,960.
Per-credit charge: $1,496.
Room and board: $11,970.
Additional info: Tuition/fee waivers available for adults.

FINANCIAL AID PICTURE (2016-2017)
Students with need: Average financial aid package met 90% of need; average scholarship/grant was $34,624; average loan was $3,758. Need-based aid available for part-time students.
Students without need: 182 full-time freshmen who did not demonstrate need for aid received scholarships/grants; average award was $23,414. No-need awards available for academics, alumni affiliation, art, leadership, minority status, music/drama, state/district residency.

FINANCIAL AID PROCEDURES
Forms required: FAFSA.
Dates and Deadlines: Priority date 3/15; no closing date. Applicants notified on a rolling basis starting 3/28; must reply by 5/1.

CONTACT
Laura Meek, Director of Financial Aid and Student Employment
100 West College, Granville, OH 43023
(740) 587-6279

DeVry University: Columbus
Columbus, Ohio
www.devry.edu   Federal Code: 003099

4-year for-profit university in very large city.
Enrollment: 1,676 undergrads.

BASIC COSTS (2016-2017)
Tuition and fees: $17,512.
Per-credit charge: $609.

FINANCIAL AID PICTURE
Students with need: Need-based aid available for full-time and part-time students.
Students without need: This college awards aid only to students with need.

FINANCIAL AID PROCEDURES
Forms required: FAFSA.
Dates and Deadlines: Applicants notified on a rolling basis.

CONTACT
1350 Alum Creek Drive, Columbus, OH 43209-2705
(614) 253-7291

Eastern Gateway Community College
Steubenville, Ohio
www.egcc.edu   Federal Code: 007275

2-year public community college in large town.
Enrollment: 2,645 undergrads.
Selectivity: Open admission; but selective for some programs.

BASIC COSTS (2016-2017)
Tuition and fees: $3,460; out-of-district residents $3,640; out-of-state residents $4,480.
Per-credit charge: $111; out-of-district residents $117; out-of-state residents $145.

FINANCIAL AID PICTURE
Students with need: Need-based aid available for full-time and part-time students. Work study available nights, weekends, and for part-time students.

Students without need: This college awards aid only to students with need.

Scholarships offered: Horizon Grant: two-year tuition scholarship; awarded to all students graduating from a Jefferson County high school with 2.5 GPA; student must enroll full-time for fall semester immediately following high school graduation.

FINANCIAL AID PROCEDURES

Forms required: FAFSA, institutional form.

Dates and Deadlines: Priority date 4/1; no closing date. Applicants notified on a rolling basis starting 6/15.

CONTACT

Brenda Mallis, Assistant Director of Financial Aid
Eastern Gateway Community College- Jefferson County Campus,
Steubenville, OH 43952
(740) 264-5591 ext. 1633

Edison State Community College
Piqua, Ohio
www.edisonohio.edu   Federal Code: 012750

2-year public community college in large town.

Enrollment: 1,707 undergrads, 67% part-time. 244 full-time freshmen.

Selectivity: Open admission; but selective for some programs.

BASIC COSTS (2016-2017)

Tuition and fees: $4,219; out-of-state residents $7,828.

Per-credit charge: $120; out-of-state residents $241.

FINANCIAL AID PICTURE

Students with need: Need-based aid available for full-time and part-time students. Work study available nights, weekends, and for part-time students.

Students without need: No-need awards available for academics, alumni affiliation, art, athletics, job skills, leadership, minority status, state/district residency.

FINANCIAL AID PROCEDURES

Forms required: FAFSA, institutional form.

Dates and Deadlines: Priority date 5/1; no closing date. Applicants notified on a rolling basis starting 5/15.

CONTACT

Chris Cummings, Director of Student Financial Aid
1973 Edison Drive, Piqua, OH 45356-9253
(937) 778-7910

ETI Technical College of Niles
Niles, Ohio
www.eticollege.edu   Federal Code: 030790

2-year for-profit technical college in large town.

Enrollment: 34 undergrads.

Selectivity: Open admission; but selective for some programs.

BASIC COSTS (2016-2017)

Tuition and fees: $9,808.

Per-credit charge: $362.

Additional info: Each degree program has its own unique tuition charge. The figures shown are an average of all degree programs. Tuition at time of enrollment locked for 2 years.

FINANCIAL AID PICTURE

Students with need: Need-based aid available for full-time and part-time students.

FINANCIAL AID PROCEDURES

Forms required: FAFSA.

Dates and Deadlines: Applicants notified on a rolling basis; must reply within 4 week(s) of notification.

Transfers: No deadline. Applicants notified on a rolling basis; must reply within 4 week(s) of notification.

CONTACT

Kay Madigan, Financial Aid Director
2076 Youngstown Warren Road, Niles, OH 44446-4398
(330) 299-7189

Fortis College: Centerville
Centerville, Ohio
www.fortis.edu   Federal Code: 012267

2-year for-profit junior and technical college in large town.

Enrollment: 887 undergrads.

Selectivity: Open admission.

BASIC COSTS (2016-2017)

Additional info: Bachelor: 20841; associate degree programs: $27,615-44,402; certificates: $16,670-21,902. Books and supplies range $450-3,100 depending on program level and course of study. All costs are subject to change.

FINANCIAL AID PICTURE

Students with need: Need-based aid available for full-time and part-time students.

Students without need: This college awards aid only to students with need.

FINANCIAL AID PROCEDURES

Forms required: FAFSA, institutional form.

Dates and Deadlines: Applicants notified on a rolling basis.

CONTACT

Lynda Linsey, Director of Financial Aid
555 East Alex Bell Road, Centerville, OH 45459-9627

Fortis College: Ravenna
Ravenna, Ohio
www.fortis.edu   Federal Code: 016270

2-year for-profit business college in large town.

Enrollment: 269 undergrads.

BASIC COSTS (2016-2017)

Additional info: Associate degree programs: $26,625-30,720; certificates: $14,147-21,621 depending on program level and course of study. All costs are subject to change.

FINANCIAL AID PICTURE

Students with need: Need-based aid available for full-time and part-time students.

Students without need: This college awards aid only to students with need.

FINANCIAL AID PROCEDURES

Forms required: FAFSA.

Dates and Deadlines: Applicants notified on a rolling basis.

CONTACT

Trudy Young, Financial Aid Director
653 Enterprise Parkway, Ravenna, OH 44266
(330) 297-7319

Franciscan University of Steubenville
Steubenville, Ohio
www.franciscan.edu   Federal Code: 003036

4-year private university in large town, affiliated with the Roman Catholic Church.
Enrollment: 2,038 undergrads, 3% part-time. 453 full-time freshmen.
Selectivity: Admits over 75% of applicants.

BASIC COSTS (2016-2017)
Tuition and fees: $25,680.
Per-credit charge: $840.
Room and board: $8,300.

FINANCIAL AID PICTURE (2016-2017)
Students with need: Out of 376 full-time freshmen who applied for aid, 298 were judged to have need. Of these, 298 received aid, and 50 had their full need met. Average financial aid package met 67% of need; average scholarship/grant was $13,482; average loan was $3,369. For part-time students, average financial aid package was $7,940.
Students without need: 138 full-time freshmen who did not demonstrate need for aid received scholarships/grants; average award was $7,184. No-need awards available for academics, alumni affiliation, leadership, religious affiliation.

FINANCIAL AID PROCEDURES
Forms required: FAFSA.
Dates and Deadlines: Priority date 4/1; no closing date. Applicants notified on a rolling basis starting 2/15.
Transfers: Closing date 8/1. Applicants notified on a rolling basis starting 2/15; must reply within 3 week(s) of notification.

CONTACT
Jody Peeler, Director of Financial Aid
1235 University Boulevard, Steubenville, OH 43952-1763
(740) 283-6226

Franklin University
Columbus, Ohio
www.franklin.edu   Federal Code: 003046

4-year private university and business college in very large city.
Enrollment: 4,049 undergrads.
Selectivity: Open admission; but selective for some programs.

BASIC COSTS (2016-2017)
Tuition and fees: $14,845.
Per-credit charge: $494.

FINANCIAL AID PICTURE
Students with need: Need-based aid available for full-time and part-time students.
Students without need: No-need awards available for academics, leadership, minority status.

FINANCIAL AID PROCEDURES
Forms required: FAFSA.
Dates and Deadlines: Priority date 6/15; no closing date. Applicants notified on a rolling basis; must reply within 2 week(s) of notification.
Transfers: No deadline. Applicants notified on a rolling basis starting 3/15; must reply within 2 week(s) of notification. One scholarship specifically offered for transfer students: Transfer Scholarship.

CONTACT
Goldie Langley, Director of Financial Aid
201 South Grant Avenue, Columbus, OH 43215-5399
(614) 797-4700

Gallipolis Career College
Gallipolis, Ohio
www.gallipoliscareercollege.com   Federal Code: 030079

2-year for-profit business and career college in small town.
Enrollment: 80 undergrads, 25% part-time. 6 full-time freshmen.
Selectivity: Open admission.

BASIC COSTS (2016-2017)
Tuition and fees: $11,370.

FINANCIAL AID PICTURE
Students with need: Need-based aid available for full-time and part-time students.
Students without need: This college awards aid only to students with need.

FINANCIAL AID PROCEDURES
Forms required: FAFSA.

CONTACT
Jeanette Shirey, Financial Aid Administrator
1176 Jackson Pike, Suite 312, Gallipolis, OH 45631
(740) 446-4367

God's Bible School and College
Cincinnati, Ohio
www.gbs.edu   Federal Code: 015691

4-year private Bible college in large city, affiliated with the interdenominational tradition.
Enrollment: 304 undergrads.

BASIC COSTS (2016-2017)
Tuition and fees: $7,040.
Per-credit charge: $225.
Room and board: $4,250.

FINANCIAL AID PICTURE
Students with need: Need-based aid available for full-time and part-time students.
Students without need: No-need awards available for academics, leadership, music/drama, religious affiliation.
Additional info: Institutional work scholarships available.

FINANCIAL AID PROCEDURES
Forms required: FAFSA.
Dates and Deadlines: Priority date 4/30; no closing date. Applicants notified on a rolling basis.

CONTACT
Sharree Pouzar, Financial Aid Coordinator
1810 Young Street, Cincinnati, OH 45202-6838
(513) 721-7944 ext. 1161

Heidelberg University
Tiffin, Ohio
www.heidelberg.edu   Federal Code: 003048

4-year private liberal arts college in large town, affiliated with the United Church of Christ.
Enrollment: 1,116 undergrads, 2% part-time. 371 full-time freshmen.

BASIC COSTS (2016-2017)
Tuition and fees: $29,200.
Room and board: $10,000.

FINANCIAL AID PICTURE (2016-2017)

Students with need: Out of 364 full-time freshmen who applied for aid, 333 were judged to have need. Of these, 333 received aid, and 72 had their full need met. Average financial aid package met 81% of need; average scholarship/grant was $19,650; average loan was $3,950. Need-based aid available for part-time students.

Students without need: 31 full-time freshmen who did not demonstrate need for aid received scholarships/grants; average award was $14,166. No-need awards available for academics, alumni affiliation, music/drama, religious affiliation, state/district residency.

FINANCIAL AID PROCEDURES

Forms required: FAFSA.

Dates and Deadlines: Priority date 3/1; no closing date. Applicants notified on a rolling basis starting 12/15; must reply by 5/1.

Transfers: No deadline. Applicants notified on a rolling basis starting 3/1; must reply by 5/1 or within 2 week(s) of notification.

CONTACT

Juli Weininger, Director of Financial Aid
310 East Market Street, Tiffin, OH 44883-2462
(419) 448-2293

Hiram College

Hiram, Ohio
www.hiram.edu   Federal Code: 003049

4-year private liberal arts college in rural community, affiliated with the Christian Church (Disciples of Christ).

Enrollment: 974 undergrads, 14% part-time. 207 full-time freshmen.

Selectivity: Admits 50 to 75% of applicants.

BASIC COSTS (2016-2017)

Tuition and fees: $33,040.

Room and board: $10,190.

Additional info: Tuition at time of enrollment locked for 4 years.

FINANCIAL AID PICTURE

Students with need: Need-based aid available for full-time and part-time students. Work study available nights, weekends, and for part-time students.

FINANCIAL AID PROCEDURES

Forms required: Not require for domestic applicants.

Transfers: Transfer merit scholarships available. Phi Theta Kappa scholarships available.

CONTACT

Linda Shirey, Director of Student Financial Aid
PO Box 96, Hiram, OH 44234
(330) 569-5107

Hocking College

Nelsonville, Ohio
www.hocking.edu   Federal Code: 007598

2-year public technical college in small town.

Enrollment: 3,130 undergrads.

Selectivity: Open admission; but selective for some programs.

BASIC COSTS (2016-2017)

Tuition and fees: $4,390; out-of-state residents $8,780.

Room and board: $6,310.

FINANCIAL AID PICTURE

Students with need: Need-based aid available for full-time and part-time students. Work study available nights, weekends, and for part-time students.

Students without need: No-need awards available for academics, minority status, state/district residency.

FINANCIAL AID PROCEDURES

Forms required: FAFSA, institutional form.

Dates and Deadlines: Priority date 2/28; no closing date. Applicants notified on a rolling basis starting 4/15.

Transfers: No deadline. Applicants notified on a rolling basis. Non-entitlement aid awarded on first-come, first-served basis.

CONTACT

Muriel Merchant, Director, Financial Aid
3301 Hocking Parkway, Nelsonville, OH 45764-9704
(740) 753-7080

Hondros College

Westerville, Ohio
www.nursing.hondros.edu   Federal Code: 040743

2-year for-profit nursing college in very large city.

Enrollment: 1,520 undergrads.

BASIC COSTS (2016-2017)

Tuition and fees: $18,489.

FINANCIAL AID PICTURE

Students with need: Need-based aid available for full-time and part-time students.

FINANCIAL AID PROCEDURES

Forms required: FAFSA.

Transfers: No deadline. Applicants notified on a rolling basis starting 2/1.

CONTACT

Mary Cannon, Director of Financial Aid
4140 Executive Parkway, Westerville, OH 43081-3855
(614) 508-7200

International College of Broadcasting

Dayton, Ohio
www.icb.edu   Federal Code: 013132

2-year for-profit technical college in small city.

Enrollment: 64 undergrads.

Selectivity: Open admission.

BASIC COSTS (2016-2017)

Tuition and fees: $31,950.

Per-credit charge: $424.67.

FINANCIAL AID PICTURE (2016-2017)

Students with need: Need-based aid available for full-time and part-time students.

FINANCIAL AID PROCEDURES

Forms required: FAFSA.

Dates and Deadlines: Applicants notified on a rolling basis starting 11/1.

CONTACT

Lizzie Miller, Financial Aid Director
6 South Smithville Road, Dayton, OH 45431
(937) 258-8251

James A. Rhodes State College

Lima, Ohio
www.rhodesstate.edu   Federal Code: 010027

2-year public community and technical college in large town.
Enrollment: 3,416 undergrads.
Selectivity: Open admission; but selective for some programs.

BASIC COSTS (2016-2017)
Tuition and fees: $4,810; out-of-state residents $9,611.
Per-credit charge: $160; out-of-state residents $320.

FINANCIAL AID PICTURE
Students with need: Need-based aid available for full-time and part-time students. Work study available nights, weekends, and for part-time students.
Students without need: No-need awards available for academics.

FINANCIAL AID PROCEDURES
Forms required: FAFSA.
Dates and Deadlines: Priority date 2/15; no closing date. Applicants notified on a rolling basis starting 5/1; must reply within 2 week(s) of notification.

CONTACT
Cathy Kohli, Director of Financial Aid
4240 Campus Drive, PS 148, Lima, OH 45804-3597
(419) 995-8800

John Carroll University

University Heights, Ohio
www.jcu.edu   Federal Code: 003050

4-year private university in large town, affiliated with the Roman Catholic Church.
Enrollment: 2,952 undergrads, 1% part-time. 715 full-time freshmen.
Selectivity: Admits over 75% of applicants.

BASIC COSTS (2017-2018)
Tuition and fees: $39,790.
Per-credit charge: $1,275.
Room and board: $11,580.

FINANCIAL AID PICTURE (2016-2017)
Students with need: Out of 649 full-time freshmen who applied for aid, 542 were judged to have need. Of these, 541 received aid, and 157 had their full need met. Average financial aid package met 84% of need; average scholarship/grant was $25,319; average loan was $2,739. For part-time students, average financial aid package was $24,571.
Students without need: No-need awards available for academics, alumni affiliation, leadership, minority status, ROTC, state/district residency.
Additional info: John Carroll grant combined with federal and state grant aid, and the Federal Stafford Loan program to meet the published flat, full-time tuition cost for Pell-eligible Ohio families.

FINANCIAL AID PROCEDURES
Forms required: FAFSA.
Dates and Deadlines: Priority date 2/15; closing date 3/15. Applicants notified on a rolling basis starting 2/15; must reply by 5/1 or within 4 week(s) of notification.
Transfers: Priority date 12/1; closing date 8/1. Applicants notified on a rolling basis starting 3/1; must reply by 8/1 or within 3 week(s) of notification.

CONTACT
Claudia Wenzel, Asst VP for Student Financial Services
Office of Admission, University Heights, OH 44118-4581
(216) 397-4294

Kaplan College: Dayton

Dayton, Ohio
www.dayton.kaplancollege.com   Federal Code: 020520

2-year for-profit technical college in very large city.
Enrollment: 317 undergrads.
Selectivity: Open admission; but selective for some programs.

BASIC COSTS (2016-2017)
Additional info: Associate of Applied Science in Nursing: $41,095. Dental Assistant: $16,814. Electrical Technician: $20,944. Heating, Ventilation, and Air Conditioning/Refrigeration: $20,845. Intravenous (IV) Therapy: $609. Medical Assistant: $15,925. Pharmacy Technician: $15,954. Phlebotomy Technician: $970. Photographic Technology: $46,862. State Tested Nursing Assistant: $1,005.

FINANCIAL AID PICTURE
Students with need: Need-based aid available for full-time and part-time students.

FINANCIAL AID PROCEDURES
Forms required: FAFSA, institutional form.
Dates and Deadlines: Applicants notified on a rolling basis starting 3/1.

CONTACT
Tiphany Pugh, Director of Operations
2800 East River Road, Dayton, OH 45439
(937) 294-6155

Kent State University

Kent, Ohio
www.kent.edu   Federal Code: 003051

4-year public university in large town.
Enrollment: 22,907 undergrads, 11% part-time. 4,335 full-time freshmen.
Selectivity: Admits over 75% of applicants.

BASIC COSTS (2016-2017)
Tuition and fees: $10,012; out-of-state residents $18,376.
Per-credit charge: $456; out-of-state residents $818.
Room and board: $10,720.

FINANCIAL AID PICTURE (2016-2017)
Students with need: Out of 3,911 full-time freshmen who applied for aid, 2,986 were judged to have need. Of these, 2,986 received aid, and 383 had their full need met. Average financial aid package met 62% of need; average scholarship/grant was $6,105; average loan was $4,021. For part-time students, average financial aid package was $6,878.
Students without need: 964 full-time freshmen who did not demonstrate need for aid received scholarships/grants; average award was $5,269. No-need awards available for academics, alumni affiliation, art, athletics, leadership, minority status, music/drama, ROTC, state/district residency.
Scholarships offered: 33 full-time freshmen received athletic scholarships; average amount $18,987.
Additional info: Participant in US Department of Education's Quality Assurance Program and Experimental Sites Program.

FINANCIAL AID PROCEDURES
Forms required: FAFSA.
Dates and Deadlines: Priority date 3/1; no closing date. Applicants notified by 3/15; must reply within 2 week(s) of notification.
Transfers: Applicants notified by 3/15; must reply within 2 week(s) of notification.

CONTACT
Mark Evans, Director of Student Financial Aid
161 Schwartz Center, Kent, OH 44242-0001
(330) 672-2972

Kent State University: Ashtabula

Ashtabula, Ohio
www.kent.edu/ashtabula   Federal Code: 003051

2-year public branch campus college in large town.
Enrollment: 1,909 undergrads, 39% part-time. 148 full-time freshmen.
Selectivity: Open admission; but selective for some programs.

BASIC COSTS (2016-2017)
Tuition and fees: $5,664; out-of-state residents $13,864.
Per-credit charge: $258; out-of-state residents $620.

FINANCIAL AID PICTURE (2016-2017)
Students with need: Out of 139 full-time freshmen who applied for aid, 127 were judged to have need. Of these, 127 received aid, and 4 had their full need met. Average financial aid package met 57% of need; average scholarship/grant was $4,812; average loan was $3,456. For part-time students, average financial aid package was $5,701.
Students without need: 5 full-time freshmen who did not demonstrate need for aid received scholarships/grants; average award was $999. No-need awards available for academics, alumni affiliation, art, athletics, leadership, minority status, music/drama, ROTC, state/district residency.

FINANCIAL AID PROCEDURES
Forms required: FAFSA.
Dates and Deadlines: Priority date 3/1; no closing date. Applicants notified by 3/15; must reply within 2 week(s) of notification.

CONTACT
Kristina Call, Financial Aid Coordinator
3300 Lake Road West, Ashtabula, OH 44004-2299
(440) 964-4213

Kent State University: East Liverpool

East Liverpool, Ohio
www.kent.edu/columbiana   Federal Code: 003056

2-year public branch campus college in large town.
Enrollment: 1,210 undergrads, 42% part-time. 76 full-time freshmen.
Selectivity: Open admission; but selective for some programs.

BASIC COSTS (2016-2017)
Tuition and fees: $5,664; out-of-state residents $13,864.
Per-credit charge: $258; out-of-state residents $620.

FINANCIAL AID PICTURE (2016-2017)
Students with need: Out of 72 full-time freshmen who applied for aid, 54 were judged to have need. Of these, 54 received aid, and 7 had their full need met. Average financial aid package met 63% of need; average scholarship/grant was $4,840; average loan was $3,241. For part-time students, average financial aid package was $6,255.
Students without need: 5 full-time freshmen who did not demonstrate need for aid received scholarships/grants; average award was $2,800. No-need awards available for academics, alumni affiliation, art, athletics, leadership, minority status, music/drama, ROTC, state/district residency.

FINANCIAL AID PROCEDURES
Forms required: FAFSA.
Dates and Deadlines: Priority date 3/1; no closing date. Applicants notified by 3/15; must reply within 2 week(s) of notification.

CONTACT
Chris Winland, Financial Aid Counselor
400 East Fourth Street, East Liverpool, OH 43920
(330) 382-7557

Kent State University: Geauga

Burton, Ohio
www.kent.edu/geauga

2-year public branch campus college in rural community.
Enrollment: 2,124 undergrads, 35% part-time. 284 full-time freshmen.
Selectivity: Open admission; but selective for some programs.

BASIC COSTS (2016-2017)
Tuition and fees: $5,664; out-of-state residents $13,864.
Per-credit charge: $258; out-of-state residents $620.

FINANCIAL AID PICTURE (2016-2017)
Students with need: Out of 230 full-time freshmen who applied for aid, 177 were judged to have need. Of these, 177 received aid, and 9 had their full need met. Average financial aid package met 53% of need; average scholarship/grant was $4,884; average loan was $3,377. For part-time students, average financial aid package was $5,965.
Students without need: 2 full-time freshmen who did not demonstrate need for aid received scholarships/grants; average award was $1,375. No-need awards available for academics, alumni affiliation, art, athletics, leadership, minority status, music/drama, ROTC, state/district residency.

FINANCIAL AID PROCEDURES
Forms required: FAFSA.
Dates and Deadlines: Priority date 3/1; no closing date. Applicants notified by 3/15; must reply within 2 week(s) of notification.

CONTACT
Donna Holcomb, Financial Aid Counselor
Office of Admissions, Burton, OH 44021
(440) 834-3737

Kent State University: Salem

Salem, Ohio
www.kent.edu/columbiana   Federal Code: 003061

2-year public branch campus college in large town.
Enrollment: 1,497 undergrads, 29% part-time. 167 full-time freshmen.
Selectivity: Open admission; but selective for some programs.

BASIC COSTS (2016-2017)
Tuition and fees: $5,664; out-of-state residents $13,664.
Per-credit charge: $258; out-of-state residents $620.

FINANCIAL AID PICTURE (2016-2017)
Students with need: Out of 152 full-time freshmen who applied for aid, 126 were judged to have need. Of these, 126 received aid, and 5 had their full need met. Average financial aid package met 57% of need; average scholarship/grant was $4,867; average loan was $3,486. For part-time students, average financial aid package was $5,642.
Students without need: 5 full-time freshmen who did not demonstrate need for aid received scholarships/grants; average award was $1,158. No-need awards available for academics, alumni affiliation, art, athletics, leadership, minority status, music/drama, ROTC, state/district residency.

FINANCIAL AID PROCEDURES
Forms required: FAFSA.
Dates and Deadlines: Priority date 3/1; no closing date. Applicants notified by 3/15; must reply within 2 week(s) of notification.
Transfers: Priority date 2/15.

CONTACT
Angel Barcey, Financial Aid Counselor
2491 State Route 45 South, Salem, OH 44460
(330) 337-4209

Kent State University: Stark

Canton, Ohio
www.kent.edu/stark   Federal Code: 003054

2-year public branch campus college in large town.
Enrollment: 4,444 undergrads, 30% part-time. 631 full-time freshmen.
Selectivity: Open admission; but selective for some programs.

BASIC COSTS (2016-2017)
Tuition and fees: $5,664; out-of-state residents $13,864.
Per-credit charge: $258; out-of-state residents $620.

FINANCIAL AID PICTURE (2016-2017)
Students with need: Out of 554 full-time freshmen who applied for aid, 434 were judged to have need. Of these, 434 received aid, and 48 had their full need met. Average financial aid package met 63% of need; average scholarship/grant was $4,429; average loan was $3,212. For part-time students, average financial aid package was $5,931.
Students without need: 65 full-time freshmen who did not demonstrate need for aid received scholarships/grants; average award was $1,935. No-need awards available for academics, alumni affiliation, art, athletics, leadership, minority status, music/drama, ROTC, state/district residency.

FINANCIAL AID PROCEDURES
Forms required: FAFSA.
Dates and Deadlines: Priority date 3/1; no closing date. Applicants notified by 3/15; must reply within 2 week(s) of notification.

CONTACT
Amber Wallace, Assistant Director for Financial Aid
6000 Frank Avenue NW, Canton, OH 44720-7599
(330) 244-3251

Kent State University: Trumbull

Warren, Ohio
www.kent.edu/trumbull   Federal Code: 003064

2-year public branch campus college in small city.
Enrollment: 2,231 undergrads, 34% part-time. 229 full-time freshmen.
Selectivity: Open admission; but selective for some programs.

BASIC COSTS (2016-2017)
Tuition and fees: $5,664; out-of-state residents $14,028.
Per-credit charge: $258; out-of-state residents $620.

FINANCIAL AID PICTURE (2016-2017)
Students with need: Out of 211 full-time freshmen who applied for aid, 181 were judged to have need. Of these, 181 received aid, and 15 had their full need met. Average financial aid package met 60% of need; average scholarship/grant was $4,639; average loan was $3,337. For part-time students, average financial aid package was $6,020.
Students without need: 24 full-time freshmen who did not demonstrate need for aid received scholarships/grants; average award was $1,586. No-need awards available for academics, alumni affiliation, art, athletics, leadership, minority status, music/drama, ROTC, state/district residency.

FINANCIAL AID PROCEDURES
Forms required: FAFSA.
Dates and Deadlines: Priority date 3/1; no closing date. Applicants notified by 3/15; must reply within 2 week(s) of notification.

CONTACT
Sarah Helmick, Assistant Director, Enrollment Management and Student Services
4314 Mahoning Avenue, NW, Warren, OH 44483-1998
(330) 675-8970

Kent State University: Tuscarawas

New Philadelphia, Ohio
www.kent.edu/tusc

2-year public branch campus college in large town.
Enrollment: 1,714 undergrads, 34% part-time. 237 full-time freshmen.
Selectivity: Open admission; but selective for some programs and for out-of-state students.

BASIC COSTS (2016-2017)
Tuition and fees: $5,664; out-of-state residents $13,864.
Per-credit charge: $258; out-of-state residents $620.

FINANCIAL AID PICTURE (2016-2017)
Students with need: Out of 201 full-time freshmen who applied for aid, 161 were judged to have need. Of these, 161 received aid, and 15 had their full need met. Average financial aid package met 61% of need; average scholarship/grant was $4,091; average loan was $3,372. For part-time students, average financial aid package was $5,899.
Students without need: 4 full-time freshmen who did not demonstrate need for aid received scholarships/grants; average award was $1,250. No-need awards available for academics, alumni affiliation, art, athletics, leadership, minority status, music/drama, ROTC, state/district residency.

FINANCIAL AID PROCEDURES
Forms required: FAFSA.
Dates and Deadlines: Priority date 3/1; no closing date. Applicants notified by 3/15; must reply within 2 week(s) of notification.
Transfers: Financial aid transcripts from all previous institutions required.

CONTACT
Jason Maurer, Financial Aid Coordinator
330 University Drive NE, New Philadelphia, OH 44663-9403
(330) 339-3391

Kenyon College

Gambier, Ohio
www.kenyon.edu   Federal Code: 003065
                                      CSS Code: 1370

4-year private liberal arts college in rural community, affiliated with the nondenominational tradition.
Enrollment: 1,688 undergrads. 489 full-time freshmen.
Selectivity: Admits less than 50% of applicants.

BASIC COSTS (2016-2017)
Tuition and fees: $51,200.
Room and board: $12,130.

FINANCIAL AID PICTURE (2016-2017)
Students with need: Out of 282 full-time freshmen who applied for aid, 204 were judged to have need. Of these, 204 received aid, and 132 had their full need met. Average financial aid package met 100% of need; average scholarship/grant was $38,978; average loan was $2,501.
Students without need: 66 full-time freshmen who did not demonstrate need for aid received scholarships/grants; average award was $14,585. No-need awards available for academics, art, minority status, music/drama.
Scholarships offered: Honor Scholarships, Science Scholarships, Trustee Opportunity Scholarships: averages around $16,000 a year; competitively based on excellence in academic achievement, extracurricular leadership, and community involvement. Distinguished Academic Scholarships: $2,000-$10,000; based on academic accomplishment, standardized test results, and extracurricular achievement. Scholarships for National Merit finalists available.
Additional info: Financial aid incentive guarantees a loan-free education for 25 students with the greatest need who bring the qualities of creativity, community service, and leadership.

FINANCIAL AID PROCEDURES

Forms required: FAFSA, CSS PROFILE.

Dates and Deadlines: Priority date 2/15; closing date 2/15. Applicants notified by 4/1; must reply by 5/1.

Transfers: Closing date 4/15. Applicants notified by 5/15; must reply by 6/1.

CONTACT

Craig Daugherty, Director of Financial Aid

Kenyon College Admissions Office, Ransom Hall, Gambier, OH 43022-9623

(740) 427-5430

Kettering College

Kettering, Ohio

www.kc.edu   Federal Code: 007035

4-year private health science and nursing college in large city, affiliated with the Seventh-day Adventists.

Enrollment: 584 undergrads, 48% part-time. 50 full-time freshmen.

BASIC COSTS (2016-2017)

Tuition and fees: $14,760.

Per-credit charge: $492.

Room only: $3,900.

FINANCIAL AID PICTURE

Students with need: Need-based aid available for full-time and part-time students.

Students without need: No-need awards available for academics.

FINANCIAL AID PROCEDURES

Forms required: FAFSA, institutional form.

Dates and Deadlines: Priority date 3/31; no closing date. Applicants notified on a rolling basis starting 5/15; must reply within 3 week(s) of notification.

CONTACT

Kim Snell, Director of Student Finance

3737 Southern Boulevard, Kettering, OH 45429-1299

(937) 296-7210

Lake Erie College

Painesville, Ohio

www.lec.edu   Federal Code: 003066

4-year private liberal arts college in large town.

Enrollment: 750 undergrads, 4% part-time. 219 full-time freshmen.

Selectivity: Admits 50 to 75% of applicants.

BASIC COSTS (2017-2018)

Tuition and fees: $30,862.

Per-credit charge: $780.

Room and board: $9,132.

FINANCIAL AID PICTURE (2016-2017)

Students with need: Out of 206 full-time freshmen who applied for aid, 193 were judged to have need. Of these, 192 received aid, and 40 had their full need met. Average financial aid package met 79% of need; average scholarship/grant was $22,391; average loan was $3,452. For part-time students, average financial aid package was $7,500.

Students without need: 16 full-time freshmen who did not demonstrate need for aid received scholarships/grants; average award was $15,649. No-need awards available for academics, art, athletics, leadership, music/drama, state/district residency.

Scholarships offered: 25 full-time freshmen received athletic scholarships; average amount $16,914.

FINANCIAL AID PROCEDURES

Forms required: FAFSA.

Dates and Deadlines: Applicants notified on a rolling basis starting 2/15; must reply by 5/1 or within 4 week(s) of notification.

Transfers: No deadline.

CONTACT

Tricia Pangonis, Director of Financial Aid

391 West Washington Street, Painesville, OH 44077-3389

(440) 375-7100

Lakeland Community College

Kirtland, Ohio

www.lakelandcc.edu   Federal Code: 006804

2-year public community and technical college in large town.

Enrollment: 4,857 undergrads.

Selectivity: Open admission; but selective for some programs.

BASIC COSTS (2016-2017)

Tuition and fees: $3,287; out-of-district residents $4,136; out-of-state residents $9,176.

Per-credit charge: $97.75; out-of-district residents $126.05; out-of-state residents $294.05.

FINANCIAL AID PICTURE

Students with need: Need-based aid available for full-time and part-time students. Work study available nights, weekends, and for part-time students.

Students without need: No-need awards available for academics, art, athletics, job skills, leadership, minority status, music/drama, state/district residency.

Additional info: Loans available for tuition and books.

FINANCIAL AID PROCEDURES

Forms required: FAFSA, institutional form.

Dates and Deadlines: Closing date 3/1. Applicants notified on a rolling basis starting 5/1.

Transfers: Ohio Instructional Grant Transfer Form.

CONTACT

Melissa Amspaugh, Director of Financial Aid

7700 Clocktower Drive, Kirtland, OH 44094-5198

(440) 525-7070

Lorain County Community College

Elyria, Ohio

www.lorainccc.edu   Federal Code: 003068

2-year public community college in small city.

Enrollment: 8,271 undergrads, 66% part-time. 945 full-time freshmen.

Selectivity: Open admission.

BASIC COSTS (2016-2017)

Tuition and fees: $3,077; out-of-district residents $3,679; out-of-state residents $7,302.

Per-credit charge: $118.34; out-of-district residents $141.49; out-of-state residents $280.84.

FINANCIAL AID PICTURE (2015-2016)

Students with need: Out of 849 full-time freshmen who applied for aid, 633 were judged to have need. Of these, 579 received aid, and 30 had their full need met. Average financial aid package met 58% of need; average scholarship/grant was $4,416; average loan was $2,524. For part-time students, average financial aid package was $3,561.

Students without need: 134 full-time freshmen who did not demonstrate need for aid received scholarships/grants; average award was $2,977. No-need awards available for academics, alumni affiliation, art, job skills, leadership, minority status, music/drama, state/district residency.

Scholarships offered: Presidential Scholarship, Trustee Scholarships.

FINANCIAL AID PROCEDURES

Forms required: FAFSA.

Dates and Deadlines: Applicants notified on a rolling basis starting 5/1.

CONTACT

Stephanie Sutton, Manager of Financial Aid

1005 Abbe Road North, Elyria, OH 44035-1691

(490) 366-4034

Lourdes University

Sylvania, Ohio

www.lourdes.edu   Federal Code: 003069

4-year private university in large town, affiliated with the Roman Catholic Church.

Enrollment: 1,108 undergrads, 24% part-time. 212 full-time freshmen.

Selectivity: Admits over 75% of applicants.

BASIC COSTS (2017-2018)

Tuition and fees: $21,640.

Room and board: $9,700.

Additional info: Tuition/fee waivers available for adults.

FINANCIAL AID PICTURE

Students with need: Need-based aid available for full-time and part-time students. Work study available nights, weekends, and for part-time students.

Students without need: No-need awards available for academics, art, athletics, minority status, music/drama, religious affiliation, ROTC, state/district residency.

FINANCIAL AID PROCEDURES

Forms required: FAFSA.

Dates and Deadlines: Priority date 3/1; no closing date. Applicants notified on a rolling basis starting 3/1; must reply within 4 week(s) of notification.

Transfers: Must reply within 4 week(s) of notification.

CONTACT

Deb LaJeunesse, Director of Financial Aid

6832 Convent Boulevard, Sylvania, OH 43560-2898

(419) 824-3732

Malone University

Canton, Ohio

www.malone.edu   Federal Code: 003072

4-year private university in small city, affiliated with the Christian Church.

Enrollment: 1,228 undergrads, 8% part-time. 309 full-time freshmen.

Selectivity: Admits 50 to 75% of applicants.

BASIC COSTS (2017-2018)

Tuition and fees: $29,900.

Per-credit charge: $500.

Room and board: $4,500.

FINANCIAL AID PICTURE (2016-2017)

Students with need: Out of 295 full-time freshmen who applied for aid, 275 were judged to have need. Of these, 275 received aid, and 37 had their full need met. Average financial aid package met 79% of need; average scholarship/grant was $21,480; average loan was $3,380. For part-time students, average financial aid package was $6,979.

Students without need: 31 full-time freshmen who did not demonstrate need for aid received scholarships/grants; average award was $7,766. No-need awards available for academics, alumni affiliation, art, athletics, leadership, music/drama, religious affiliation.

Scholarships offered: 35 full-time freshmen received athletic scholarships; average amount $9,793.

Additional info: Prepayment discounts and employer deferred payments available for students in adult degree-completion programs. Employer deferred payment plan is available for traditional undergraduate students.

FINANCIAL AID PROCEDURES

Forms required: FAFSA.

Dates and Deadlines: Priority date 3/1; closing date 7/31. Applicants notified on a rolling basis starting 10/15; must reply within 2 week(s) of notification.

Transfers: Applicants notified on a rolling basis starting 3/1; must reply within 2 week(s) of notification.

CONTACT

Pamela Pustay, Director of Financial Aid

2600 Cleveland Avenue NW, Canton, OH 44709-3308

(330) 471-8100 ext. 8159

Marietta College

Marietta, Ohio

www.marietta.edu   Federal Code: 003073

4-year private liberal arts college in large town.

Enrollment: 1,077 undergrads, 3% part-time. 243 full-time freshmen.

Selectivity: Admits 50 to 75% of applicants.

BASIC COSTS (2016-2017)

Tuition and fees: $35,330.

Per-credit charge: $1,140.

Room and board: $11,100.

FINANCIAL AID PICTURE (2016-2017)

Students with need: Out of 208 full-time freshmen who applied for aid, 190 were judged to have need. Of these, 190 received aid, and 42 had their full need met. Average financial aid package met 72% of need; average scholarship/grant was $16,588; average loan was $3,335. For part-time students, average financial aid package was $7,822.

Students without need: 18 full-time freshmen who did not demonstrate need for aid received scholarships/grants; average award was $19,903. No-need awards available for academics, alumni affiliation, art, music/drama.

Additional info: Auditions/portfolios for art, creative writing, music and theater required for competitive fine art scholarships.

FINANCIAL AID PROCEDURES

Forms required: FAFSA.

Dates and Deadlines: Priority date 2/15; no closing date. Applicants notified on a rolling basis starting 12/22; must reply by 5/1.

Transfers: Applicants notified on a rolling basis starting 4/1; must reply by 5/1 or within 2 week(s) of notification.

CONTACT

Emily Schuck, Director of Student Financial Services

215 Fifth Street, Marietta, OH 45750-4005

(740) 376-4712

Marion Technical College

Marion, Ohio

www.mtc.edu   Federal Code: 010736

2-year public community and technical college in large town.

Enrollment: 1,636 undergrads.

Selectivity: Open admission; but selective for some programs.

BASIC COSTS (2016-2017)

Tuition and fees: $4,782; out-of-state residents $6,702.

FINANCIAL AID PICTURE

Students with need: Need-based aid available for full-time and part-time students.

Students without need: This college awards aid only to students with need.

Scholarships offered: Foundation Scholarship; first year full tuition; for applicants in top 5% of class. President's Scholarship; $1,500; for applicants in top 50% of class. Tech Prep Scholarship; $1,200; for graduates of Tech Prep program. All scholarships require 2.5 GPA and successful completion of proficiency exams.

FINANCIAL AID PROCEDURES

Forms required: FAFSA, institutional form.

Dates and Deadlines: Closing date 5/1. Applicants notified on a rolling basis.

Transfers: No deadline. Applicants notified on a rolling basis.

CONTACT

Deb Langdon, Coordinator of Financial Aid
1467 Mt. Vernon Avenue, Marion, OH 43302-5694
(740) 389-4636 ext. 334

Mercy College of Ohio
Toledo, Ohio
www.mercycollege.edu   Federal Code: 030970

4-year private health science and nursing college in large city, affiliated with the Roman Catholic Church.

Enrollment: 1,343 undergrads, 63% part-time. 46 full-time freshmen.

Selectivity: Admits 50 to 75% of applicants.

BASIC COSTS (2016-2017)

Tuition and fees: $13,680.
Per-credit charge: $396.
Room only: $5,460.

FINANCIAL AID PICTURE (2016-2017)

Students with need: 45% of average financial aid package awarded as scholarships/grants, 55% awarded as loans/jobs. Need-based aid available for part-time students. Work study available nights, weekends, and for part-time students.

Students without need: No-need awards available for academics, alumni affiliation, leadership, minority status.

FINANCIAL AID PROCEDURES

Forms required: FAFSA.

Dates and Deadlines: Priority date 3/1; no closing date. Applicants notified on a rolling basis starting 3/1; must reply within 2 week(s) of notification.

CONTACT

Julie Leslie, Financial Aid Director
2221 Madison Avenue, Toledo, OH 43604
(419) 251-1219

Miami University: Hamilton
Hamilton, Ohio
www.ham.muohio.edu   Federal Code: 003077

2-year public branch campus college in small city.

Enrollment: 3,386 undergrads.

Selectivity: Open admission; but selective for some programs.

BASIC COSTS (2016-2017)

Tuition and fees: $4,972; out-of-state residents $14,830.

FINANCIAL AID PICTURE

Students with need: Need-based aid available for full-time and part-time students. Work study available nights, weekends, and for part-time students.

Students without need: No-need awards available for academics, athletics, leadership, minority status, state/district residency.

Additional info: Special gift funds for needy, multicultural students who enter with appropriate academic record. Separate application required for scholarships; closing date January 31.

FINANCIAL AID PROCEDURES

Forms required: FAFSA.

Dates and Deadlines: Priority date 2/15; no closing date. Applicants notified on a rolling basis starting 4/1.

Transfers: Transfer students must complete one semester at Miami University to be considered for scholarships.

CONTACT

Archie Nelson
1601 University Boulevard, Hamilton, OH 45011-3399
(513) 785-3123

Miami University: Middletown
Middletown, Ohio
www.mid.muohio.edu   Federal Code: 003077

2-year public branch campus and community college in large town.

Enrollment: 2,034 undergrads.

Selectivity: Open admission; but selective for some programs.

BASIC COSTS (2016-2017)

Tuition and fees: $4,972; out-of-state residents $14,830.

FINANCIAL AID PICTURE

Students with need: Need-based aid available for full-time and part-time students.

Students without need: This college awards aid only to students with need.

FINANCIAL AID PROCEDURES

Forms required: FAFSA.

Dates and Deadlines: Priority date 2/15; no closing date. Applicants notified on a rolling basis.

Transfers: Applicants must file by February 15 to be considered for campus-based aid or alumni scholarships.

CONTACT

Archie Nelson, Director of Admissions and Financial Aid
4200 East University Boulevard, Middletown, OH 45042
(513) 727-3346

Miami University: Oxford
Oxford, Ohio
www.MiamiOH.edu   Federal Code: 003077

4-year public university in large town.

Enrollment: 16,597 undergrads, 3% part-time. 3,806 full-time freshmen.

Selectivity: Admits 50 to 75% of applicants.

BASIC COSTS (2016-2017)

Tuition and fees: $14,288; out-of-state residents $31,592.
Room and board: $12,014.

FINANCIAL AID PICTURE (2015-2016)

Students with need: Out of 2,667 full-time freshmen who applied for aid, 1,486 were judged to have need. Of these, 1,438 received aid, and 388 had their full need met. Average financial aid package met 59% of need; average scholarship/grant was $10,287; average loan was $3,622. For part-time students, average financial aid package was $8,714.

Students without need: 1,285 full-time freshmen who did not demonstrate need for aid received scholarships/grants; average award was $9,337. No-need awards available for academics, art, athletics, leadership, minority status, music/drama, ROTC, state/district residency.

Scholarships offered: 86 full-time freshmen received athletic scholarships; average amount $26,357.

Additional info: The Miami Access Initiative guarantees eligible students with scholarships and/or grants that meet or exceed the cost of tuition and academic fees. Academically competitive Ohio residents entering the Miami University Oxford campus as first-time, full-time freshmen in the fall semester and who have a total family income equal to or less than $35,000 will be considered.

FINANCIAL AID PROCEDURES

Forms required: FAFSA.

Dates and Deadlines: Priority date 2/15; no closing date. Applicants notified on a rolling basis starting 3/20; must reply by 5/1 or within 3 week(s) of notification.

CONTACT

Brent Shock, Director of Student Financial Assistance

301 South Campus Avenue, Oxford, OH 45056

(513) 529-8734

Miami-Jacobs Career College: Columbus

Columbus, Ohio

www.miamijacobs.edu   Federal Code: 021521

2-year for-profit junior college in very large city.

Enrollment: 366 undergrads.

BASIC COSTS (2016-2017)

Additional info: Certificate programs: Dental Assisting $23,092, Massage Therapy $10,600, Medical Billing and Coding $23,495. Books and supplies $1,258-$3,600. Associate programs: Accounting $31,603, Business Administration $31,891, Criminal Justice $31,891, Electronic Health Records $31,699, Medical Assisting $31,891, Paralegal $31,891. Books and supplies $4,800.

FINANCIAL AID PICTURE

Students with need: Work study available nights.

FINANCIAL AID PROCEDURES

Forms required: FAFSA.

CONTACT

Lynn Mizanin, Director of Financial Aid

150 East Gay Street, 15th Floor, Columbus, OH 43215

(330) 867-4030

Miami-Jacobs Career College: Dayton

Dayton, Ohio

www.miamijacobs.edu   Federal Code: 003076

2-year for-profit career college in small city.

Enrollment: 159 undergrads.

BASIC COSTS (2016-2017)

Additional info: Diploma programs: $10,600-$3,300; Associate programs: $28,435-$28,758. Books and supplies $1,900-$4,400. All costs are subject to change.

FINANCIAL AID PICTURE

Students with need: Need-based aid available for full-time and part-time students.

Students without need: This college awards aid only to students with need.

FINANCIAL AID PROCEDURES

Forms required: FAFSA, institutional form.

Dates and Deadlines: Applicants notified on a rolling basis.

CONTACT

Marcia Byrd, Director of Financial Aid

110 North Patterson Boulevard, Dayton, OH 45402

(937) 461-5174

Mount Carmel College of Nursing

Columbus, Ohio

www.mccn.edu   Federal Code: 030719

4-year private nursing college in very large city, affiliated with the Roman Catholic Church.

Enrollment: 926 undergrads, 31% part-time. 99 full-time freshmen.

Selectivity: Admits 50 to 75% of applicants.

BASIC COSTS (2016-2017)

Tuition and fees: $12,673.

Per-credit charge: $403.

FINANCIAL AID PICTURE (2016-2017)

Students with need: Average financial aid package met 35% of need; average scholarship/grant was $4,998; average loan was $3,241. For part-time students, average financial aid package was $8,111.

Students without need: No-need awards available for academics, ROTC.

FINANCIAL AID PROCEDURES

Forms required: FAFSA.

Dates and Deadlines: Priority date 3/1; no closing date. Applicants notified on a rolling basis starting 5/31.

CONTACT

Todd Everett, Financial Aid Director

127 South Davis Avenue, Columbus, OH 43222-1589

(614) 234-1842

Mount St. Joseph University

Cincinnati, Ohio

www.msj.edu   Federal Code: 003033

4-year private liberal arts college in very large city, affiliated with the Roman Catholic Church.

Enrollment: 1,207 undergrads, 17% part-time. 242 full-time freshmen.

Selectivity: Admits over 75% of applicants.

BASIC COSTS (2017-2018)

Tuition and fees: $29,100.

Per-credit charge: $525.

Room and board: $9,266.

Additional info: Transportation for off-campus residents is estimated to be $900, and those who live on-campus is $400.

FINANCIAL AID PICTURE (2015-2016)

Students with need: Need-based aid available for full-time and part-time students. Work study available nights, weekends, and for part-time students.

Students without need: No-need awards available for academics, alumni affiliation, art, leadership, music/drama, ROTC, state/district residency.

Scholarships offered: Elizabeth Seton Scholarship: $13,000; 30-36 ACT 1330 SAT. Presidential Scholarship: $11,500; 26-36 ACT or 1170 SAT. Trustee Scholarship: $10,500; 24-25 ACT or 1090 SAT. Dean's Scholarship: $9,500; 22-23 ACT or 1020 SAT. Merit Award: $8,500; 20-21 ACT or 940 SAT.

FINANCIAL AID PROCEDURES

Forms required: FAFSA.

Dates and Deadlines: Priority date 3/1; no closing date. Applicants notified on a rolling basis starting 1/31; must reply by 5/1 or within 4 week(s) of notification.

Transfers: Applicants notified on a rolling basis starting 2/15; must reply within 4 week(s) of notification. Transfer Scholarship; $5,000; 3.0 college GPA with at least 24 hours earned.

CONTACT

Kathryn Kelly, Director of Student Administrative Services
ATTN: Office of Admission 5701 Delhi Road, Cincinnati, OH 45233-1670
(513) 244-4418

Mount Vernon Nazarene University

Mount Vernon, Ohio
www.mvnu.edu
Federal Code: 007085

4-year private university in large town, affiliated with the Church of the Nazarene.
Enrollment: 1,720 undergrads, 1% part-time. 451 full-time freshmen.
Selectivity: Admits 50 to 75% of applicants.

BASIC COSTS (2017-2018)
Tuition and fees: $28,090.
Per-credit charge: $773.
Room and board: $7,854.
Additional info: Tuition/fee waivers available for minority students.

FINANCIAL AID PICTURE (2016-2017)
Students with need: Out of 346 full-time freshmen who applied for aid, 319 were judged to have need. Of these, 319 received aid, and 112 had their full need met. Average financial aid package met 66% of need; average scholarship/grant was $20,276; average loan was $3,241. For part-time students, average financial aid package was $9,301.
Students without need: 41 full-time freshmen who did not demonstrate need for aid received scholarships/grants; average award was $13,799. No-need awards available for academics, art, athletics, minority status, music/drama, religious affiliation, state/district residency.
Scholarships offered: *Merit:* Academic scholarships: $4,000-$16,000; for first time students based on ACT/SAT and GPA. *Athletic:* 35 full-time freshmen received athletic scholarships; average amount $6,004.
Additional info: Transfer students are not awarded the same amount of academic scholarship.

FINANCIAL AID PROCEDURES
Forms required: FAFSA.
Dates and Deadlines: Priority date 3/1; no closing date. Applicants notified on a rolling basis starting 3/4.
Transfers: No deadline. Applicants notified on a rolling basis starting 3/15; must reply within 2 week(s) of notification. Filing deadline for Ohio financial aid is October 1st.

CONTACT

Jared Sponseller, Director of Student Financial Services
800 Martinsburg Road, Mount Vernon, OH 43050
(740) 392-6868 ext. 4520

Muskingum University

New Concord, Ohio
www.muskingum.edu
Federal Code: 003084

4-year private university and liberal arts college in small town, affiliated with the Presbyterian Church (USA).
Enrollment: 1,498 undergrads, 14% part-time. 319 full-time freshmen.
Selectivity: Admits over 75% of applicants.

BASIC COSTS (2017-2018)
Tuition and fees: $25,062.
Per-credit charge: $595.
Room and board: $11,040.
Additional info: Tuition/fee waivers available for minority students.

FINANCIAL AID PICTURE
Students with need: Need-based aid available for full-time and part-time students.
Students without need: No-need awards available for academics, alumni affiliation, art, leadership, minority status, music/drama, religious affiliation, state/district residency.
Additional info: Scholarship priority date February 1.

FINANCIAL AID PROCEDURES
Forms required: FAFSA.
Dates and Deadlines: Priority date 3/1; no closing date. Applicants notified on a rolling basis starting 3/1; must reply by 5/1 or within 2 week(s) of notification.
Transfers: No deadline. Applicants notified on a rolling basis starting 12/1; must reply by 8/15 or within 2 week(s) of notification.

CONTACT

Jeff Zellers, Vice President of Enrollment
163 Stormont Street, New Concord, OH 43762-1199
(740) 826-8139

North Central State College

Mansfield, Ohio
www.ncstatecollege.edu
Federal Code: 005313

2-year public community and technical college in small city.
Enrollment: 1,902 undergrads, 67% part-time. 301 full-time freshmen.
Selectivity: Open admission; but selective for some programs.

BASIC COSTS (2016-2017)
Tuition and fees: $4,488; out-of-state residents $9,685.
Per-credit charge: $126; out-of-state residents $251.32.

FINANCIAL AID PICTURE
Students with need: Need-based aid available for full-time and part-time students.
Students without need: This college awards aid only to students with need.

FINANCIAL AID PROCEDURES
Forms required: FAFSA.
Dates and Deadlines: Priority date 4/1; no closing date. Applicants notified on a rolling basis starting 5/30; must reply within 1 week(s) of notification.

CONTACT

James Phinney, Assistant Dean of Financial Aid
2441 Kenwood Circle, PO Box 698, Mansfield, OH 44901-0698
(419) 755-4899

Northwest State Community College

Archbold, Ohio
www.northweststate.edu
Federal Code: 008677

2-year public community and technical college in small town.
Enrollment: 1,411 undergrads.
Selectivity: Open admission; but selective for some programs.

BASIC COSTS (2016-2017)
Tuition and fees: $5,061; out-of-state residents $9,601.
Per-credit charge: $157.33; out-of-state residents $308.66.

FINANCIAL AID PICTURE

Students with need: Need-based aid available for full-time and part-time students.

Students without need: No-need awards available for academics.

FINANCIAL AID PROCEDURES

Forms required: FAFSA, institutional form.

Dates and Deadlines: Priority date 6/1; no closing date. Applicants notified on a rolling basis starting 4/1.

Transfers: No deadline. Applicants notified on a rolling basis starting 2/1.

CONTACT

Amber Yocom, Director of Financial Aid

22600 State Route 34, Archbold, OH 43502-9517

(419) 267-1333

Notre Dame College

Cleveland, Ohio

www.notredamecollege.edu   Federal Code: 003085

4-year private nursing and liberal arts college in large town, affiliated with the Roman Catholic Church.

Enrollment: 1,792 undergrads.

BASIC COSTS (2016-2017)

Tuition and fees: $28,300.

Per-credit charge: $545.

Room and board: $9,550.

FINANCIAL AID PICTURE

Students with need: Need-based aid available for full-time students.

Students without need: No-need awards available for academics, athletics, state/district residency.

Scholarships offered: Merit Scholarships; $2,500-$7,500; based on GPA and ACT or SAT scores. Presidential Scholarships; $3,000 awarded in addition to Merit Scholarships; based on 3.9 GPA and 27 ACT or 1210 SAT (exclusive of Writing).

FINANCIAL AID PROCEDURES

Forms required: FAFSA.

Dates and Deadlines: Closing date 5/1. Applicants notified on a rolling basis starting 1/1; must reply within 2 week(s) of notification.

Transfers: No deadline. Applicants notified on a rolling basis.

CONTACT

Mary McCrystal, Director of Student Financial Assistance

4545 College Road, Cleveland, OH 44121-4293

(216) 373-5263

Oberlin College

Oberlin, Ohio   Federal Code: 003086

www.oberlin.edu   CSS Code: 1587

4-year private music and liberal arts college in small town.

Enrollment: 2,895 undergrads, 1% part-time. 762 full-time freshmen.

Selectivity: Admits less than 50% of applicants. GED not accepted.

BASIC COSTS (2016-2017)

Tuition and fees: $52,002.

Per-credit charge: $2,120.

Room and board: $14,010.

FINANCIAL AID PICTURE (2016-2017)

Students with need: Out of 493 full-time freshmen who applied for aid, 408 were judged to have need. Of these, 408 received aid, and 408 had their full need met. Average financial aid package met 100% of need; average scholarship/grant was $38,361; average loan was $4,113. For part-time students, average financial aid package was $43,182.

Students without need: 278 full-time freshmen who did not demonstrate need for aid received scholarships/grants; average award was $13,130. No-need awards available for academics, music/drama.

Scholarships offered: Bonner Scholarship: based on community service. John Frederick Oberlin Scholarship: based on academic merit. Stern Scholarship: based on excellence in sciences. Stamps Leadership Scholarship: based on academic merit and leadership roles. Dean's Scholarship: available to Conservatory of Music students.

FINANCIAL AID PROCEDURES

Forms required: FAFSA, CSS PROFILE, institutional form.

Dates and Deadlines: Closing date 2/1. Applicants notified by 4/1; must reply by 5/1 or within 2 week(s) of notification.

Transfers: Closing date 3/1. Applicants notified by 5/15; must reply within 2 week(s) of notification.

CONTACT

Robert Reddy, Director of Financial Aid

Carnegie Building, 101 North Professor Street, Oberlin, OH 44074-1075

(440) 775-8142

Ohio Business College: Sandusky

Sandusky, Ohio

www.ohiobusinesscollege.edu   Federal Code: 021585

2-year for-profit business college in small city.

Enrollment: 265 undergrads.

Selectivity: Open admission.

BASIC COSTS (2016-2017)

Additional info: Diploma programs: $9,400-$12,375; Associate programs: $21,620-$22,560. Fees, books supplies range depending on program level and course of study. All costs are subject to change.

FINANCIAL AID PICTURE

Students with need: Need-based aid available for full-time and part-time students.

FINANCIAL AID PROCEDURES

Forms required: FAFSA.

CONTACT

Eric Roller, VP Finance

5202 Timber Commons Drive, Sandusky, OH 44870

(419) 627-8345 ext. 14

Ohio Business College: Sheffield

Sheffield Village, Ohio

www.ohiobusinesscollege.edu   Federal Code: 021585

2-year for-profit branch campus and business college in small city.

Enrollment: 410 undergrads.

Selectivity: Open admission.

BASIC COSTS (2016-2017)

Additional info: Diploma programs: $9,400-$12,375; Associate programs: $21,620-$22,560. Fees, books supplies range depending on program level and course of study. All costs are subject to change.

FINANCIAL AID PICTURE

Students with need: Need-based aid available for full-time and part-time students.

FINANCIAL AID PROCEDURES

Forms required: FAFSA.

Dates and Deadlines: Applicants notified on a rolling basis.

CONTACT

Eric Roller, VP Finance

5095 Waterford Drive, Sheffield Village, OH 44055

Ohio Christian University

Circleville, Ohio

www.ohiochristian.edu   Federal Code: 003030

4-year private university and Bible college in large town, affiliated with the Christian Church.

Enrollment: 3,485 undergrads, 30% part-time. 369 full-time freshmen.

Selectivity: Open admission.

BASIC COSTS (2016-2017)

Tuition and fees: $18,940.

Per-credit charge: $565.

Room and board: $7,898.

Additional info: Tuition/fee waivers available for minority students.

FINANCIAL AID PICTURE

Students with need: Need-based aid available for full-time and part-time students.

Students without need: No-need awards available for academics, alumni affiliation, religious affiliation, state/district residency.

Additional info: Religious affiliation tuition discount.

FINANCIAL AID PROCEDURES

Forms required: FAFSA, institutional form.

Dates and Deadlines: Closing date 5/7. Applicants notified on a rolling basis starting 5/1; must reply within 2 week(s) of notification.

Transfers: Closing date 3/1. Applicants notified on a rolling basis; must reply within 2 week(s) of notification.

CONTACT

Wes Brothers, Director of Financial Aid

1476 Lancaster Pike, Circleville, OH 43113

(470) 477-7757

Ohio Dominican University

Columbus, Ohio

www.ohiodominican.edu   Federal Code: 003035

4-year private university and liberal arts college in very large city, affiliated with the Roman Catholic Church.

Enrollment: 1,158 undergrads, 14% part-time. 226 full-time freshmen.

Selectivity: Admits 50 to 75% of applicants.

BASIC COSTS (2016-2017)

Tuition and fees: $31,080.

Per-credit charge: $720.

Room and board: $10,946.

FINANCIAL AID PICTURE

Students with need: Need-based aid available for full-time and part-time students. Work study available nights, weekends, and for part-time students.

Students without need: No-need awards available for academics, athletics, state/district residency.

FINANCIAL AID PROCEDURES

Forms required: FAFSA.

Dates and Deadlines: Priority date 4/1; no closing date. Applicants notified on a rolling basis starting 3/1; must reply within 2 week(s) of notification.

CONTACT

Tara Schneider, Director of Financial Aid

1216 Sunbury Road, Columbus, OH 43219

(614) 251-4778

Ohio Northern University

Ada, Ohio

www.onu.edu   Federal Code: 003089

4-year private university in small town, affiliated with the United Methodist Church.

Enrollment: 1,974 undergrads. 586 full-time freshmen.

BASIC COSTS (2016-2017)

Tuition and fees: $29,820.

Per-credit charge: $1,180.

Room and board: $11,050.

Additional info: Tuition/fee waivers available for minority students.

FINANCIAL AID PICTURE (2015-2016)

Students with need: Out of 560 full-time freshmen who applied for aid, 501 were judged to have need. Of these, 500 received aid, and 111 had their full need met. Average financial aid package met 22% of need; average scholarship/grant was $21,610; average loan was $4,280. For part-time students, average financial aid package was $12,203.

Students without need: 78 full-time freshmen who did not demonstrate need for aid received scholarships/grants; average award was $13,271. No-need awards available for academics, alumni affiliation, art, leadership, minority status, music/drama, ROTC, state/district residency.

Scholarships offered: Presidential Scholarships: $19,000 per year; Trustee Scholarships:$17,000 - $18,000 per year; Deans Scholarships: $14,000 - $16,000 per year; Faculty Scholarships: $10,000 - $12,000 per year.

FINANCIAL AID PROCEDURES

Forms required: FAFSA.

Dates and Deadlines: Applicants notified on a rolling basis starting 12/1.

CONTACT

Melanie Weaver, Director of Financial Aid

525 South Main Street, Ada, OH 45810

(419) 772-2272

Ohio State University Agricultural Technical Institute

Wooster, Ohio

www.ati.osu.edu   Federal Code: 003090

2-year public agricultural and branch campus college in large town.

Enrollment: 704 undergrads, 9% part-time. 306 full-time freshmen.

Selectivity: Open admission; but selective for out-of-state students.

BASIC COSTS (2016-2017)

Tuition and fees: $7,202; out-of-state residents $25,394.

Room and board: $8,420.

FINANCIAL AID PICTURE (2016-2017)

Students with need: Out of 284 full-time freshmen who applied for aid, 202 were judged to have need. Of these, 198 received aid, and 23 had their full need met. Average financial aid package met 65% of need; average scholarship/grant was $4,856; average loan was $4,299. For part-time students, average financial aid package was $7,839.

Students without need: 25 full-time freshmen who did not demonstrate need for aid received scholarships/grants; average award was $2,352. No-need awards available for academics, alumni affiliation, art, athletics, job skills, leadership, minority status, music/drama, ROTC, state/district residency.

FINANCIAL AID PROCEDURES

Forms required: FAFSA.

Dates and Deadlines: Priority date 2/15; no closing date. Must reply by 5/1 or within 4 week(s) of notification.

Transfers: Priority date 2/1. Applicants notified by 4/1; must reply within 4 week(s) of notification.

CONTACT

Barbara LaMoreaux, Coordinator, Financial Aid

1328 Dover Road, Wooster, OH 44691

Ohio State University: Columbus Campus

Columbus, Ohio

www.osu.edu   Federal Code: 003090

4-year public university in very large city.

Enrollment: 44,762 undergrads, 7% part-time. 7,931 full-time freshmen.

Selectivity: Admits 50 to 75% of applicants.

BASIC COSTS (2016-2017)

Tuition and fees: $10,037; out-of-state residents $28,229.

Per-credit charge: $454.7; out-of-state residents $1,212.7.

Room and board: $11,666.

FINANCIAL AID PICTURE (2016-2017)

Students with need: Out of 6,127 full-time freshmen who applied for aid, 3,616 were judged to have need. Of these, 3,570 received aid, and 1,017 had their full need met. Average financial aid package met 75% of need; average scholarship/grant was $10,699; average loan was $3,960. For part-time students, average financial aid package was $8,652.

Students without need: 2,220 full-time freshmen who did not demonstrate need for aid received scholarships/grants; average award was $7,166. No-need awards available for academics, alumni affiliation, art, athletics, job skills, leadership, minority status, music/drama, ROTC, state/district residency.

Scholarships offered: 69 full-time freshmen received athletic scholarships; average amount $25,593.

FINANCIAL AID PROCEDURES

Forms required: FAFSA.

Dates and Deadlines: Priority date 2/1; no closing date. Must reply by 5/1 or within 4 week(s) of notification.

Transfers: Applicants notified on a rolling basis starting 4/1; must reply within 4 week(s) of notification.

CONTACT

Director of Student Financial Aid

Student Academic Services Building, 281 West Lane Avenue, Columbus, OH 43210

(614) 292-0300

Ohio State University: Lima Campus

Lima, Ohio

www.lima.osu.edu   Federal Code: 003090

4-year public university and branch campus college in small city.

Enrollment: 938 undergrads, 11% part-time. 366 full-time freshmen.

Selectivity: Open admission; but selective for out-of-state students.

BASIC COSTS (2016-2017)

Tuition and fees: $7,140; out-of-state residents $25,332.

FINANCIAL AID PICTURE (2016-2017)

Students with need: Out of 333 full-time freshmen who applied for aid, 239 were judged to have need. Of these, 235 received aid, and 30 had their full need met. Average financial aid package met 62% of need; average

scholarship/grant was $4,288; average loan was $3,742. For part-time students, average financial aid package was $7,341.

Students without need: 61 full-time freshmen who did not demonstrate need for aid received scholarships/grants; average award was $1,153. No-need awards available for academics, alumni affiliation, art, athletics, job skills, leadership, minority status, music/drama, ROTC, state/district residency.

FINANCIAL AID PROCEDURES

Forms required: FAFSA.

Dates and Deadlines: Priority date 2/15; no closing date. Applicants notified by 3/15; must reply by 5/1 or within 4 week(s) of notification.

Transfers: Priority date 2/15. Applicants notified on a rolling basis starting 4/1; must reply within 4 week(s) of notification.

CONTACT

4240 Campus Drive, Lima, OH 45804-3596

(614) 292-0300

Ohio State University: Mansfield Campus

Mansfield, Ohio

www.mansfield.ohio-state.edu   Federal Code: 003090

4-year public university and branch campus college in large town.

Enrollment: 1,042 undergrads, 10% part-time. 441 full-time freshmen.

Selectivity: Open admission; but selective for out-of-state students.

BASIC COSTS (2016-2017)

Tuition and fees: $7,140; out-of-state residents $25,332.

Room and board: $3,100; room only: $2,690.

FINANCIAL AID PICTURE (2016-2017)

Students with need: Out of 389 full-time freshmen who applied for aid, 313 were judged to have need. Of these, 309 received aid, and 21 had their full need met. Average financial aid package met 61% of need; average scholarship/grant was $5,103; average loan was $4,388. For part-time students, average financial aid package was $7,198.

Students without need: 44 full-time freshmen who did not demonstrate need for aid received scholarships/grants; average award was $1,600. No-need awards available for academics, alumni affiliation, art, athletics, job skills, leadership, minority status, music/drama, ROTC, state/district residency.

FINANCIAL AID PROCEDURES

Forms required: FAFSA.

Dates and Deadlines: Priority date 2/15; no closing date. Applicants notified by 3/15; must reply by 5/1 or within 4 week(s) of notification.

Transfers: Priority date 2/1. Applicants notified by 4/1; must reply within 4 week(s) of notification.

CONTACT

Ken Sigler, Director of Admissions & Financial Aid

1760 University Drive, Mansfield, OH 44906

(419) 755-4011

Ohio State University: Marion Campus

Marion, Ohio

www.osumarion.osu.edu   Federal Code: 003090

4-year public university and branch campus college in large town.

Enrollment: 1,042 undergrads, 14% part-time. 389 full-time freshmen.

Selectivity: Open admission; but selective for out-of-state students.

BASIC COSTS (2016-2017)

Tuition and fees: $7,140; out-of-state residents $25,332.

FINANCIAL AID PICTURE (2016-2017)

Students with need: Out of 356 full-time freshmen who applied for aid, 249 were judged to have need. Of these, 243 received aid, and 31 had their full need met. Average financial aid package met 65% of need; average scholarship/grant was $5,393; average loan was $3,604. For part-time students, average financial aid package was $7,075.

Students without need: 86 full-time freshmen who did not demonstrate need for aid received scholarships/grants; average award was $2,033. No-need awards available for academics, alumni affiliation, art, athletics, job skills, leadership, minority status, music/drama, ROTC, state/district residency.

FINANCIAL AID PROCEDURES

Forms required: FAFSA.

Dates and Deadlines: Priority date 2/15; no closing date. Applicants notified by 3/15; must reply by 5/1 or within 4 week(s) of notification.

Transfers: Priority date 2/15. Applicants notified by 4/1; must reply within 4 week(s) of notification.

CONTACT

1465 Mount Vernon Avenue, Marion, OH 43302
(740) 389-6786 ext. 6273

Ohio State University: Newark Campus
Newark, Ohio
www.newark.osu.edu   Federal Code: 003090

4-year public branch campus college in large town.
Enrollment: 2,438 undergrads, 12% part-time. 1,235 full-time freshmen.
Selectivity: Open admission; but selective for out-of-state students.

BASIC COSTS (2016-2017)

Tuition and fees: $7,140; out-of-state residents $25,332.

FINANCIAL AID PICTURE (2016-2017)

Students with need: Out of 1,093 full-time freshmen who applied for aid, 845 were judged to have need. Of these, 822 received aid, and 71 had their full need met. Average financial aid package met 60% of need; average scholarship/grant was $4,988; average loan was $4,067. For part-time students, average financial aid package was $7,287.

Students without need: 18 full-time freshmen who did not demonstrate need for aid received scholarships/grants; average award was $1,716. No-need awards available for academics, alumni affiliation, art, athletics, job skills, leadership, minority status, music/drama, ROTC, state/district residency.

FINANCIAL AID PROCEDURES

Forms required: FAFSA.

Dates and Deadlines: Priority date 2/15; no closing date. Applicants notified by 3/15; must reply by 5/1 or within 4 week(s) of notification.

Transfers: Priority date 2/15. Applicants notified on a rolling basis starting 4/1; must reply within 4 week(s) of notification.

CONTACT

1179 University Drive, Newark, OH 43055

Ohio University
Athens, Ohio
www.ohio.edu   Federal Code: 003100

4-year public university in large town.
Enrollment: 23,542 undergrads, 24% part-time. 4,293 full-time freshmen.
Selectivity: Admits 50 to 75% of applicants.

BASIC COSTS (2016-2017)

Tuition and fees: $11,744; out-of-state residents $21,208.
Per-credit charge: $556; out-of-state residents $1,022.

Room and board: $11,176.

FINANCIAL AID PICTURE (2016-2017)

Students with need: Out of 3,623 full-time freshmen who applied for aid, 2,708 were judged to have need. Of these, 2,708 received aid, and 1,142 had their full need met. Average financial aid package met 52% of need; average scholarship/grant was $6,960; average loan was $2,867. For part-time students, average financial aid package was $5,423.

Students without need: 333 full-time freshmen who did not demonstrate need for aid received scholarships/grants; average award was $3,757. No-need awards available for academics, art, athletics, minority status, music/drama, religious affiliation, ROTC.

Scholarships offered: 38 full-time freshmen received athletic scholarships; average amount $21,728.

FINANCIAL AID PROCEDURES

Forms required: FAFSA.

Dates and Deadlines: Closing date 1/15. Applicants notified on a rolling basis starting 2/1; must reply within 3 week(s) of notification.

Transfers: Priority date 5/15; no deadline. Applicants notified on a rolling basis starting 5/15.

CONTACT

Valerie Miller, Director, Student Financial Aid and Scholarships
120 Chubb Hall, Athens, OH 45701-2979
(740) 593-4141

Ohio University: Chillicothe Campus
Chillicothe, Ohio
www.chillicothe.ohiou.edu   Federal Code: 003102

4-year public branch campus college in large town.
Enrollment: 2,236 undergrads.
Selectivity: Open admission; but selective for some programs.

BASIC COSTS (2016-2017)

Tuition and fees: $5,048; out-of-state residents $9,596.
Per-credit charge: $224; out-of-state residents $416.

FINANCIAL AID PICTURE

Students with need: Need-based aid available for full-time and part-time students.

FINANCIAL AID PROCEDURES

Forms required: FAFSA.

Dates and Deadlines: Applicants notified on a rolling basis.

CONTACT

Ashlee Diggs, Coordinator of Student Activities
101 University Drive, Chillicothe, OH 45601
(740) 774-7228

Ohio University: Eastern Campus
St. Clairsville, Ohio
www.eastern.ohiou.edu   Federal Code: 003101

4-year public branch campus college in small town.
Enrollment: 1,010 undergrads.
Selectivity: Open admission; but selective for some programs.

BASIC COSTS (2016-2017)

Tuition and fees: $4,806; out-of-state residents $6,718.
Per-credit charge: $316; out-of-state residents $303.

FINANCIAL AID PICTURE

Students with need: Need-based aid available for full-time and part-time students.

Students without need: No-need awards available for academics, alumni affiliation, minority status.

FINANCIAL AID PROCEDURES
Forms required: FAFSA.
Dates and Deadlines: Priority date 3/15; no closing date.
Transfers: Priority date 3/1; closing date 5/1.

CONTACT
Kevin Chenoweth, Student Services Manager
45425 National Road West, St. Clairsville, OH 43950-9724
(740) 695-1720 ext. 209

Ohio University: Lancaster Campus
Lancaster, Ohio
www.lancaster.ohiou.edu   Federal Code: 003104

4-year public branch campus college in large town.
Enrollment: 2,596 undergrads.
Selectivity: Open admission; but selective for some programs.

BASIC COSTS (2016-2017)
Tuition and fees: $5,050; out-of-state residents $9,596.
Per-credit charge: $227; out-of-state residents $416.

FINANCIAL AID PICTURE
Students with need: Need-based aid available for full-time and part-time students.
Additional info: Scholarship application deadline April 1.

FINANCIAL AID PROCEDURES
Forms required: FAFSA.
Dates and Deadlines: Priority date 2/15; no closing date. Applicants notified on a rolling basis; must reply within 2 week(s) of notification.

CONTACT
Pat Fox, Coordinator of Financial Aid
1570 Granville Pike, Lancaster, OH 43130
(740) 681-3333

Ohio University: Southern Campus at Ironton
Ironton, Ohio
www.ohio.edu/southern   Federal Code: 003103

4-year public branch campus college in large town.
Enrollment: 2,131 undergrads.
Selectivity: Open admission.

BASIC COSTS (2016-2017)
Tuition and fees: $4,806; out-of-state residents $6,718.
Per-credit charge: $216; out-of-state residents $305.

FINANCIAL AID PICTURE
Students with need: Need-based aid available for full-time and part-time students.
Students without need: No-need awards available for academics, state/district residency.

FINANCIAL AID PROCEDURES
Forms required: FAFSA.
Dates and Deadlines: Priority date 3/1; closing date 3/15. Applicants notified on a rolling basis starting 4/1.

CONTACT
Jacki Adkins, Coordinator of Financial Aid and Scholarships
1804 Liberty Avenue, Ironton, OH 45638
(740) 533-4600

Ohio University: Zanesville Campus
Zanesville, Ohio
www.ohio.edu/zanesville   Federal Code: 003108

4-year public branch campus college in large town.
Enrollment: 1,839 undergrads, 23% part-time. 288 full-time freshmen.
Selectivity: Open admission; but selective for some programs.

BASIC COSTS (2016-2017)
Tuition and fees: $4,994; out-of-state residents $9,530.
Per-credit charge: $224; out-of-state residents $416.

FINANCIAL AID PICTURE
Students with need: Need-based aid available for full-time and part-time students.
Students without need: No-need awards available for academics, state/district residency.

FINANCIAL AID PROCEDURES
Forms required: FAFSA.
Dates and Deadlines: Priority date 3/15; no closing date. Applicants notified on a rolling basis starting 4/15; must reply within 2 week(s) of notification.

CONTACT
Vicki DeLucas, Financial Aid Coordinator
1425 Newark Road, Zanesville, OH 43701
(740) 588-1439

Ohio Valley College of Technology
East Liverpool, Ohio
www.ovct.edu   Federal Code: 016261

2-year for-profit junior and technical college in large town.
Enrollment: 146 undergrads.

BASIC COSTS (2016-2017)
Additional info: Diploma programs: $16,820; Associate programs: $22,410. Fees, books supplies range depending on program level and course of study. All costs are subject to change.

FINANCIAL AID PICTURE
Students with need: Need-based aid available for full-time and part-time students.
Students without need: This college awards aid only to students with need.

FINANCIAL AID PROCEDURES
Forms required: FAFSA.
Dates and Deadlines: Applicants notified on a rolling basis; must reply within 6 week(s) of notification.

CONTACT
Rebecca Steckman, Regional Financial Aid Director
15258 State Route 170, East Liverpool, OH 43920-9585
(330) 385-1070

Ohio Wesleyan University
Delaware, Ohio
www.owu.edu   Federal Code: 003109

4-year private liberal arts college in large town, affiliated with the United Methodist Church.
Enrollment: 1,629 undergrads. 464 full-time freshmen.
Selectivity: Admits 50 to 75% of applicants.

BASIC COSTS (2016-2017)
Tuition and fees: $44,090.

Room and board: $11,770.

FINANCIAL AID PICTURE (2015-2016)

Students with need: Out of 396 full-time freshmen who applied for aid, 344 were judged to have need. Of these, 344 received aid, and 58 had their full need met. Average financial aid package met 79% of need; average scholarship/grant was $31,114; average loan was $3,493. For part-time students, average financial aid package was $9,663.

Students without need: 120 full-time freshmen who did not demonstrate need for aid received scholarships/grants; average award was $22,477. No-need awards available for academics, alumni affiliation, art.

FINANCIAL AID PROCEDURES

Forms required: FAFSA.

Dates and Deadlines: Priority date 12/1; no closing date. Applicants notified on a rolling basis starting 2/15; must reply by 5/1 or within 2 week(s) of notification.

Transfers: Priority date 2/15; no deadline. Applicants notified on a rolling basis starting 2/15; must reply by 5/1 or within 2 week(s) of notification.

CONTACT

Kevin Paskvan, Director of Financial Aid
61 South Sandusky Street, Delaware, OH 43015-2398
(740) 368-3050

Otterbein University

Westerville, Ohio
www.otterbein.edu   Federal Code: 003110

4-year private university and liberal arts college in large town, affiliated with the United Methodist Church.

Enrollment: 2,485 undergrads, 8% part-time. 646 full-time freshmen.

Selectivity: Admits 50 to 75% of applicants.

BASIC COSTS (2016-2017)

Tuition and fees: $31,874.

Room and board: $10,408.

Additional info: Tuition/fee waivers available for adults, minority students.

FINANCIAL AID PICTURE (2015-2016)

Students with need: 86% of average financial aid package awarded as scholarships/grants, 14% awarded as loans/jobs. Need-based aid available for part-time students. Work study available nights, weekends, and for part-time students.

Students without need: No-need awards available for academics, alumni affiliation, art, leadership, minority status, music/drama, state/district residency.

FINANCIAL AID PROCEDURES

Forms required: FAFSA.

Dates and Deadlines: Priority date 2/15; no closing date. Applicants notified on a rolling basis starting 2/15.

Transfers: Transfer students must complete appropriate state grant transfer paperwork.

CONTACT

Thomas Yarnell, Director of Financial Aid
One Otterbein College, Westerville, OH 43081
(614) 823-1502

Owens Community College

Toledo, Ohio
www.owens.edu   Federal Code: 005753

2-year public community college in large city.

Enrollment: 8,218 undergrads.

Selectivity: Open admission; but selective for some programs.

BASIC COSTS (2016-2017)

Tuition and fees: $4,414; out-of-state residents $8,698.

Per-credit charge: $153; out-of-state residents $306.

FINANCIAL AID PICTURE

Students with need: Need-based aid available for full-time and part-time students. Work study available nights, weekends, and for part-time students.

Students without need: No-need awards available for academics, athletics, job skills, state/district residency.

Additional info: Other types of financial aid available: federal family education loan program, private foundation loan (SCHELL).

FINANCIAL AID PROCEDURES

Forms required: FAFSA.

Dates and Deadlines: Priority date 3/31; no closing date.

CONTACT

Andrea Morrow, Director, Financial Aid
30335 Oregon Road, Toledo, OH 43699-1947
(567) 661-7343

Pontifical College Josephinum

Columbus, Ohio
www.pcj.edu   Federal Code: 003113

4-year private liberal arts and seminary college for men in very large city, affiliated with the Roman Catholic Church.

Enrollment: 110 undergrads.

BASIC COSTS (2016-2017)

Tuition and fees: $21,992.

Room and board: $9,950.

FINANCIAL AID PICTURE

Students with need: Need-based aid available for full-time and part-time students. Work study available nights, weekends, and for part-time students.

Students without need: This college awards aid only to students with need.

FINANCIAL AID PROCEDURES

Forms required: FAFSA, institutional form.

Dates and Deadlines: Priority date 9/2; no closing date. Applicants notified on a rolling basis starting 8/15; must reply within 2 week(s) of notification.

CONTACT

Marky Leichtnam, Director of Financial Aid
7625 North High Street, Columbus, OH 43235-1499
(614) 985-2212

PowerSport Institute

North Randall, Ohio
www.ohiotech.edu   Federal Code: 011745

2-year for-profit technical college in rural community.

Enrollment: 109 undergrads.

Selectivity: Open admission.

BASIC COSTS (2016-2017)

Tuition and fees: $27,000.

FINANCIAL AID PICTURE

Students with need: Need-based aid available for full-time students.

Students without need: No-need awards available for academics.

FINANCIAL AID PROCEDURES

Forms required: FAFSA, institutional form.

Dates and Deadlines: Applicants notified on a rolling basis starting 1/15.

Transfers: No deadline.

CONTACT
Michael Campbell, Director of Financial Aid
21210 Emery Road, North Randall, OH 44128
(216) 881-1700 ext. 122

Rosedale Bible College
Irwin, Ohio
www.rosedale.edu   Federal Code: 034253

2-year private Bible and junior college in rural community, affiliated with the Mennonite Church.
Enrollment: 58 undergrads.
Selectivity: Open admission.

BASIC COSTS (2017-2018)
Tuition and fees: $8,731.
Per-credit charge: $280.
Room and board: $5,650.

FINANCIAL AID PICTURE
Students with need: Need-based aid available for full-time and part-time students.
Students without need: No-need awards available for academics, leadership, religious affiliation.

FINANCIAL AID PROCEDURES
Forms required: FAFSA, institutional form.
Dates and Deadlines: Applicants notified on a rolling basis.
Transfers: Priority date 5/1. Applicants notified on a rolling basis.

CONTACT
Darnell Brenneman
2270 Rosedale Road, Irwin, OH 43029
(740) 857-1311 ext. 119

School of Advertising Art
Kettering, Ohio
www.saa.edu   Federal Code: 017160

2-year for-profit visual arts college in small city.
Enrollment: 197 undergrads, 2% part-time. 100 full-time freshmen.
Selectivity: Admits 50 to 75% of applicants.

BASIC COSTS (2017-2018)
Tuition and fees: $32,379.
Additional info: Tuition/fee waivers available for minority students.

FINANCIAL AID PICTURE (2015-2016)
Students with need: 34% of average financial aid package awarded as scholarships/grants, 66% awarded as loans/jobs.
Students without need: No-need awards available for academics, art, leadership, minority status.

FINANCIAL AID PROCEDURES
Forms required: FAFSA.
Dates and Deadlines: Priority date 7/1; no closing date. Applicants notified on a rolling basis starting 4/1; must reply by 7/1 or within 1 week(s) of notification.
Transfers: No deadline. Applicants notified on a rolling basis starting 4/1; must reply by 7/1 or within 1 week(s) of notification.

CONTACT
Tracy Gardner, Financial Aid Director
1725 East David Road, Kettering, OH 45440-1612
(937) 294-0592 ext. 106

Shawnee State University
Portsmouth, Ohio
www.shawnee.edu   Federal Code: 009942

4-year public university in large town.
Enrollment: 3,365 undergrads, 12% part-time. 846 full-time freshmen.
Selectivity: Open admission; but selective for some programs.

BASIC COSTS (2016-2017)
Tuition and fees: $7,364; out-of-state residents $13,030.
Room and board: $9,966.

FINANCIAL AID PICTURE (2016-2017)
Students with need: Out of 817 full-time freshmen who applied for aid, 592 were judged to have need. Of these, 592 received aid, and 28 had their full need met. Average financial aid package met 44% of need; average scholarship/grant was $5,954; average loan was $3,360. For part-time students, average financial aid package was $6,419.
Students without need: 116 full-time freshmen who did not demonstrate need for aid received scholarships/grants; average award was $3,522. No-need awards available for academics, athletics, state/district residency.
Scholarships offered: 30 full-time freshmen received athletic scholarships; average amount $2,434.
Additional info: ACT recommended for scholarship applicants.

FINANCIAL AID PROCEDURES
Forms required: FAFSA.
Dates and Deadlines: Applicants notified on a rolling basis starting 12/15.
Transfers: No deadline. Applicants notified on a rolling basis.

CONTACT
Nicole Neal, Director Financial Aid
940 Second Street, Portsmouth, OH 45662
(740) 351-4243

Sinclair Community College
Dayton, Ohio
www.sinclair.edu   Federal Code: 003119

2-year public community college in small city.
Enrollment: 14,642 undergrads, 63% part-time. 1,937 full-time freshmen.
Selectivity: Open admission; but selective for some programs.

BASIC COSTS (2016-2017)
Tuition and fees: $3,070; out-of-district residents $4,480; out-of-state residents $8,560.
Per-credit charge: $99; out-of-district residents $146; out-of-state residents $282.

FINANCIAL AID PICTURE
Students with need: Need-based aid available for full-time and part-time students. Work study available nights, weekends, and for part-time students.
Students without need: No-need awards available for academics, alumni affiliation, art, athletics, leadership, minority status, music/drama, state/district residency.

FINANCIAL AID PROCEDURES
Forms required: FAFSA.
Dates and Deadlines: Priority date 5/1; no closing date. Applicants notified on a rolling basis starting 4/1.
Transfers: No deadline. Applicants notified on a rolling basis starting 4/1.

CONTACT
Matthew Moore, Director, Offfice of Financial Aid and Scholarships
444 West Third Street, Dayton, OH 45402-1460
(937) 512-3000

Southern State Community College
Hillsboro, Ohio
www.sscc.edu   Federal Code: 012870

2-year public community college in small town.
Enrollment: 2,218 undergrads.
Selectivity: Open admission; but selective for some programs.

BASIC COSTS (2016-2017)
Tuition and fees: $4,632; out-of-state residents $8,338.
Per-credit charge: $162; out-of-state residents $306.

FINANCIAL AID PICTURE
Students with need: Need-based aid available for full-time and part-time students. Work study available nights.
Students without need: No-need awards available for academics, art, athletics, music/drama.

FINANCIAL AID PROCEDURES
Forms required: FAFSA, institutional form.
Dates and Deadlines: Priority date 7/1; closing date 9/1. Applicants notified by 4/15; must reply within 2 week(s) of notification.
Transfers: No deadline.

CONTACT
Linda Myers, Financial Aid Director
100 Hobart Drive, Hillsboro, OH 45133
(937) 393-3431 ext. 2610

Stark State College
North Canton, Ohio
www.starkstate.edu   Federal Code: 011141

2-year public community college in small city.
Enrollment: 8,460 undergrads, 63% part-time. 1,018 full-time freshmen.
Selectivity: Open admission; but selective for some programs.

BASIC COSTS (2016-2017)
Tuition and fees: $4,608; out-of-state residents $8,478.
Per-credit charge: $153; out-of-state residents $282.

FINANCIAL AID PICTURE (2015-2016)
Students with need: 56% of average financial aid package awarded as scholarships/grants, 44% awarded as loans/jobs. Need-based aid available for part-time students. Work study available nights, weekends, and for part-time students.
Students without need: This college awards aid only to students with need.

FINANCIAL AID PROCEDURES
Forms required: FAFSA, institutional form.
Dates and Deadlines: Priority date 5/1; no closing date. Applicants notified on a rolling basis starting 4/1; must reply within 4 week(s) of notification.

CONTACT
Amy Welty, Executive Director for Financial Aid, Registration and Enrollment Operations
6200 Frank Avenue NW, North Canton, OH 44720
(330) 494-6170 ext. 4369

Stautzenberger College
Maumee, Ohio
www.sctoday.edu   Federal Code: 004866

2-year for-profit technical and career college in large town.
Enrollment: 708 undergrads.

Selectivity: Open admission; but selective for some programs.

FINANCIAL AID PICTURE
Students with need: Need-based aid available for full-time and part-time students.
Students without need: This college awards aid only to students with need.

FINANCIAL AID PROCEDURES
Forms required: FAFSA.
Dates and Deadlines: Applicants notified on a rolling basis.

CONTACT
Mari Huffman, Financial Aid Director
1796 Indian Wood Circle, Maumee, OH 43537-4007
(419) 866-0261

Stautzenberger College: Brecksville
Brecksville, Ohio
www.sctoday.edu   Federal Code: 004866

2-year for-profit career college in large town.
Enrollment: 335 undergrads.
Selectivity: Open admission.

FINANCIAL AID PICTURE
Students with need: Need-based aid available for full-time and part-time students.
Students without need: This college awards aid only to students with need.

FINANCIAL AID PROCEDURES
Forms required: FAFSA.
Dates and Deadlines: Applicants notified on a rolling basis.
Transfers: No deadline. Applicants notified on a rolling basis.

CONTACT
Mari Huffman, Director of Financial Aid
8001 Katherine Boulevard, Brecksville, OH 44141

Terra State Community College
Fremont, Ohio
www.terra.edu   Federal Code: 008278

2-year public community and technical college in large town.
Enrollment: 2,901 undergrads.
Selectivity: Open admission.

BASIC COSTS (2016-2017)
Tuition and fees: $4,284; out-of-state residents $8,568.

FINANCIAL AID PICTURE
Students with need: Need-based aid available for full-time and part-time students.
Students without need: No-need awards available for academics.

FINANCIAL AID PROCEDURES
Forms required: FAFSA, institutional form.
Dates and Deadlines: Priority date 5/1; no closing date. Applicants notified on a rolling basis starting 5/15.

CONTACT
Christina Bratton, Director of Financial Aid
2830 Napoleon Road, Fremont, OH 43420-9600
(419) 559-2387

Tiffin University

Tiffin, Ohio
www.tiffin.edu   Federal Code: 003121

4-year private university and liberal arts college in large town.
Enrollment: 2,176 undergrads, 20% part-time. 442 full-time freshmen.
Selectivity: Admits 50 to 75% of applicants.

BASIC COSTS (2017-2018)
Tuition and fees: $23,850.
Per-credit charge: $790.
Room and board: $10,900.

FINANCIAL AID PICTURE (2016-2017)
Students with need: Out of 394 full-time freshmen who applied for aid, 366 were judged to have need. Of these, 366 received aid, and 58 had their full need met. Average financial aid package met 68% of need; average scholarship/grant was $15,608; average loan was $3,183. For part-time students, average financial aid package was $6,234.
Students without need: 10 full-time freshmen who did not demonstrate need for aid received scholarships/grants. No-need awards available for academics, alumni affiliation, athletics, leadership, minority status, music/drama, ROTC, state/district residency.
Scholarships offered: 33 full-time freshmen received athletic scholarships; average amount $8,884.

FINANCIAL AID PROCEDURES
Forms required: FAFSA.
Dates and Deadlines: Applicants notified on a rolling basis starting 11/1; must reply within 2 week(s) of notification.
Transfers: No deadline.

CONTACT
Andrea Faber, Director of Financial Aid
155 Miami Street, Tiffin, OH 44883
(800) 968-6446 ext. 3375

Trumbull Business College

Warren, Ohio
www.trumbull.edu   Federal Code: 013585

2-year for-profit business college in large town.
Enrollment: 158 undergrads.
Selectivity: Open admission.

BASIC COSTS (2016-2017)
Tuition and fees: $11,340.
Per-credit charge: $252.

FINANCIAL AID PICTURE
Students with need: Need-based aid available for full-time and part-time students.

FINANCIAL AID PROCEDURES
Forms required: FAFSA.

CONTACT
Justin Cornelius, Financial Assistance Director
3200 Ridge Road, Warren, OH 44484
(330) 369-3200 ext. 12

Union Institute & University

Cincinnati, Ohio
www.myunion.edu   Federal Code: 010923

4-year private university in very large city.
Enrollment: 772 undergrads, 47% part-time. 10 full-time freshmen.

BASIC COSTS (2016-2017)
Tuition and fees: $12,384.
Per-credit charge: $510.

FINANCIAL AID PICTURE (2015-2016)
Students with need: 12% of average financial aid package awarded as scholarships/grants, 88% awarded as loans/jobs. Need-based aid available for part-time students.
Students without need: No-need awards available for academics, state/district residency.

FINANCIAL AID PROCEDURES
Forms required: FAFSA.
Dates and Deadlines: Must reply within 4 week(s) of notification.
Transfers: No deadline. Applicants notified on a rolling basis.

CONTACT
Jean Pohlman, Director, Financial Aid
440 East McMillan Street, Cincinnati, OH 45206
(800) 861-6400 ext. 1115

University of Akron

Akron, Ohio
www.uakron.edu   Federal Code: 003123

4-year public university in small city.
Enrollment: 15,626 undergrads, 14% part-time. 3,803 full-time freshmen.
Selectivity: Admits over 75% of applicants.

BASIC COSTS (2016-2017)
Tuition and fees: $10,662; out-of-state residents $20,496.
Per-credit charge: $359; out-of-state residents $175.
Room and board: $12,395.

FINANCIAL AID PICTURE (2015-2016)
Students with need: Out of 3,602 full-time freshmen who applied for aid, 2,776 were judged to have need. Of these, 2,776 received aid, and 368 had their full need met. Average financial aid package met 55% of need; average scholarship/grant was $5,125; average loan was $3,159. For part-time students, average financial aid package was $3,466.
Students without need: 684 full-time freshmen who did not demonstrate need for aid received scholarships/grants; average award was $5,261. No-need awards available for academics, art, athletics, leadership, music/drama, ROTC, state/district residency.
Scholarships offered: *Merit:* Scholarships for Excellence: $6,000 per year; based on 3.8 GPA, 30 ACT, 1320 SAT (exclusive of Writing); deadline February 1. Presidential Scholarships: $3,000 per year; based on 3.8 GPA, 27 ACT, 1200 SAT. Honors Scholarships: $1,500-$3,000 per year; based on top 10% of class, 3.5 GPA; deadline December 31. Jim and Vanita Oelschlager Leadership Award: $1,000-$17,000 per year; based on leadership and service. Academic Scholarship: $500-$1,500 per year; based on upper 30% of high school class, 21 ACT, 3.0 GPA. Akron Advantage Award: non-resident surcharge reduction of 60% or 100%; for students who meet academic criteria from 49 states outside of Ohio plus U.S. territories. *Athletic:* 13 full-time freshmen received athletic scholarships; average amount $5,140.

FINANCIAL AID PROCEDURES
Forms required: FAFSA, institutional form.
Dates and Deadlines: Priority date 3/1; no closing date. Applicants notified on a rolling basis starting 3/15; must reply within 2 week(s) of notification.
Transfers: Priority date 3/1; no deadline. Applicants notified on a rolling basis starting 6/15; must reply within 2 week(s) of notification.

CONTACT
Jennifer Harpham, Executive Director, Student Financial Aid
Simmons Hall, Akron, OH 44325-2001
(330) 972-7032

PART III: FINANCIAL AID COLLEGE BY COLLEGE

University of Akron: Wayne College
Orrville, Ohio
www.wayne.uakron.edu   Federal Code: 003123

2-year public branch campus and junior college in small town.
Enrollment: 2,461 undergrads, 54% part-time. 265 full-time freshmen.
Selectivity: Open admission.

BASIC COSTS (2016-2017)
Tuition and fees: $6,160; out-of-state residents $14,501.
Per-credit charge: $248; out-of-state residents $526.

FINANCIAL AID PICTURE
Students with need: Need-based aid available for full-time and part-time students. Work study available nights, weekends, and for part-time students.
Students without need: No-need awards available for academics, art, athletics, leadership, minority status, music/drama, state/district residency.
Additional info: All financial aid processed through University of Akron.

FINANCIAL AID PROCEDURES
Forms required: FAFSA, institutional form.
Dates and Deadlines: Closing date 3/15. Applicants notified on a rolling basis starting 4/15.

CONTACT
Theresa Rabbitts, Financial Aid Counselor
1901 Smucker Road, Orrville, OH 44667-9758
(330) 684-8900

University of Cincinnati
Cincinnati, Ohio
www.uc.edu   Federal Code: 003125

4-year public university in large city.
Enrollment: 24,890 undergrads, 14% part-time. 4,976 full-time freshmen.
Selectivity: Admits over 75% of applicants.

BASIC COSTS (2016-2017)
Tuition and fees: $11,000; out-of-state residents $26,334.
Per-credit charge: $389; out-of-state residents $1,028.
Room and board: $10,964.

FINANCIAL AID PICTURE (2016-2017)
Students with need: Out of 4,146 full-time freshmen who applied for aid, 2,926 were judged to have need. Of these, 2,700 received aid, and 178 had their full need met. Average financial aid package met 46% of need; average scholarship/grant was $6,989; average loan was $3,713. For part-time students, average financial aid package was $6,300.
Students without need: 846 full-time freshmen who did not demonstrate need for aid received scholarships/grants; average award was $5,663. No-need awards available for academics, alumni affiliation, art, athletics, leadership, minority status, music/drama, ROTC, state/district residency.
Scholarships offered: 53 full-time freshmen received athletic scholarships; average amount $14,778.

FINANCIAL AID PROCEDURES
Forms required: FAFSA.
Dates and Deadlines: Priority date 12/1; no closing date. Applicants notified on a rolling basis starting 3/15; must reply within 2 week(s) of notification.

CONTACT
Randy Ulses, Director of Financial Aid
PO Box 210091, Cincinnati, OH 45221-0091
(513) 556-1000

University of Cincinnati: Blue Ash College
Blue Ash, Ohio
www.ucblueash.edu   Federal Code: 003125

2-year public branch campus college in large city.
Enrollment: 4,693 undergrads.
Selectivity: Open admission; but selective for some programs.

BASIC COSTS (2017-2018)
Tuition and fees: $6,010; out-of-state residents $14,808.
Per-credit charge: $251; out-of-state residents $617.

FINANCIAL AID PICTURE
Students with need: Need-based aid available for full-time and part-time students.
Students without need: This college awards aid only to students with need.
Scholarships offered: Dean's scholarships: $1,500; based on 2.5 GPA, tech prep program participation, 2-page essay; 10 available. Cincinnatus Scholarship Competition: $1,500 to full tuition, room, board and books; must have 26 ACT or be in top 5% of high school class to qualify.
Additional info: All financial aid applications and awards administered through the UC Clifton campus.

FINANCIAL AID PROCEDURES
Forms required: FAFSA.
Dates and Deadlines: Priority date 3/15; no closing date. Applicants notified on a rolling basis starting 3/15; must reply within 2 week(s) of notification.

CONTACT
9555 Plainfield Road, Blue Ash, OH 45236-1007
(513) 745-5740

University of Cincinnati: Clermont College
Batavia, Ohio
www.ucclermont.edu   Federal Code: 003125

2-year public branch campus college in small town.
Enrollment: 2,339 undergrads, 38% part-time. 521 full-time freshmen.
Selectivity: Open admission; but selective for some programs.

BASIC COSTS (2016-2017)
Tuition and fees: $5,316; out-of-state residents $12,548.
Per-credit charge: $222; out-of-state residents $523.

FINANCIAL AID PICTURE
Students with need: Need-based aid available for full-time and part-time students. Work study available nights, weekends, and for part-time students.
Students without need: No-need awards available for academics, leadership, minority status, state/district residency.
Additional info: All financial aid applications and awards administered through Uptown campus except in-house loans and scholarships.

FINANCIAL AID PROCEDURES
Forms required: FAFSA.
Dates and Deadlines: Applicants notified on a rolling basis.
Transfers: No deadline. Applicants notified on a rolling basis starting 5/1.

CONTACT
Wanda Poling, University Services Associate I
4200 Clermont College Drive, Batavia, OH 45103
(513) 732-5202

University of Dayton

Dayton, Ohio
www.udayton.edu   Federal Code: 003127

4-year private university in small city, affiliated with the Roman Catholic Church.
Enrollment: 8,261 undergrads, 5% part-time. 1,823 full-time freshmen.
Selectivity: Admits 50 to 75% of applicants.

BASIC COSTS (2016-2017)

Tuition and fees: $40,940.
Room and board: $12,680.
Additional info: Tuition/fee waivers available for adults, minority students.

FINANCIAL AID PICTURE (2015-2016)

Students with need: Out of 1,654 full-time freshmen who applied for aid, 1,177 were judged to have need. Of these, 1,177 received aid, and 230 had their full need met. Average financial aid package met 78% of need; average scholarship/grant was $25,334; average loan was $2,784. For part-time students, average financial aid package was $8,599.
Students without need: 631 full-time freshmen who did not demonstrate need for aid received scholarships/grants; average award was $12,811. No-need awards available for academics, alumni affiliation, art, athletics, job skills, leadership, minority status, music/drama, religious affiliation, ROTC, state/district residency.
Scholarships offered: *Merit:* Merit Scholarships: $1,000 to full tuition; based on GPA, ACT/SAT, service and leadership. Visual arts awards: amounts vary; based on student portfolios. Chaminade Scholarships: $2,500; for students accepted to Chaminade Scholars Program. National Merit Scholarships: $1,000 to $2,000; available to all students who are selected by the National Merit Scholarship Corporation and select UD as their first choice. Army ROTC awards: supplements U.S. Army ROTC awards with scholarship incentives. *Athletic:* 42 full-time freshmen received athletic scholarships; average amount $28,025.
Additional info: Guaranteed net-tuition for up to eight semesters of study. Students who visit campus and file the FAFSA prior to March 1st of their senior year in high school are eligible to receive up to $1,000 per year toward their textbooks.

FINANCIAL AID PROCEDURES

Forms required: FAFSA.
Dates and Deadlines: Priority date 2/1; closing date 5/1. Applicants notified on a rolling basis starting 2/15; must reply within 2 week(s) of notification.
Transfers: Priority date 6/1; no deadline. Applicants notified on a rolling basis starting 3/15; must reply within 2 week(s) of notification. Students must submit FAFSA prior to October 1 each year for consideration for state funds.

CONTACT

Catherine Mix, Assistant Vice President and Director of Financial Aid
300 College Park, Dayton, OH 45469-1602
(800) 837-7433

University of Findlay

Findlay, Ohio
www.findlay.edu   Federal Code: 003045

4-year private university and health science college in small city, affiliated with the Church of God.
Enrollment: 2,723 undergrads, 6% part-time. 714 full-time freshmen.
Selectivity: Admits 50 to 75% of applicants.

BASIC COSTS (2016-2017)

Tuition and fees: $32,402.
Per-credit charge: $697.
Room and board: $9,538.

FINANCIAL AID PICTURE (2015-2016)

Students with need: Out of 672 full-time freshmen who applied for aid, 538 were judged to have need. Of these, 538 received aid, and 107 had their full need met. Average financial aid package met 82% of need; average scholarship/grant was $20,654; average loan was $3,248.
Students without need: 176 full-time freshmen who did not demonstrate need for aid received scholarships/grants; average award was $17,874. No-need awards available for academics, alumni affiliation, athletics, music/drama, state/district residency.
Scholarships offered: *Merit:* Full tuition available to select valedictorian/salutatorians. Automatic academic awards available based on GPA, test scores. *Athletic:* 80 full-time freshmen received athletic scholarships; average amount $11,021.

FINANCIAL AID PROCEDURES

Forms required: FAFSA.
Dates and Deadlines: Priority date 8/1; closing date 9/1. Applicants notified on a rolling basis starting 3/1; must reply within 2 week(s) of notification.
Transfers: No deadline.

CONTACT

Edward Recker, Director of Financial Aid
1000 North Main Street, Findlay, OH 45840-3653
(419) 434-4791

University of Mount Union

Alliance, Ohio
www.mountunion.edu   Federal Code: 003083

4-year private university in large town, affiliated with the United Methodist Church.
Enrollment: 2,110 undergrads. 588 full-time freshmen.
Selectivity: Admits over 75% of applicants.

BASIC COSTS (2017-2018)

Tuition and fees: $29,890.
Per-credit charge: $1,260.
Room and board: $10,100.
Additional info: Tuition/fee waivers available for minority students.

FINANCIAL AID PICTURE (2015-2016)

Students with need: Out of 524 full-time freshmen who applied for aid, 455 were judged to have need. Of these, 455 received aid, and 57 had their full need met. Average financial aid package met 80% of need; average scholarship/grant was $18,188; average loan was $5,548. For part-time students, average financial aid package was $8,322.
Students without need: 101 full-time freshmen who did not demonstrate need for aid received scholarships/grants; average award was $13,097. No-need awards available for academics, alumni affiliation, art, job skills, leadership, minority status, music/drama, religious affiliation, ROTC, state/district residency.

FINANCIAL AID PROCEDURES

Forms required: FAFSA.
Dates and Deadlines: Applicants notified on a rolling basis starting 12/1; must reply within 4 week(s) of notification.
Transfers: Closing date 9/1. Applicants notified by 1/1; must reply within 4 week(s) of notification.

CONTACT

Emily Mattison, Director of Student Financial Services
1972 Clark Avenue, Alliance, OH 44601-3929
(330) 823-2674

PART III: FINANCIAL AID COLLEGE BY COLLEGE

University of Northwestern Ohio
Lima, Ohio
www.unoh.edu   Federal Code: 004861

2-year private business and technical college in large town.
Enrollment: 3,600 full-time undergrads.

BASIC COSTS (2016-2017)
Additional info: College of Applied Technologies: $12,000; College of Business, Health Professions, and Occupational Professions: $12,600. Books, supplies, fees range depending on program level and course of study. All costs are subject to change.

FINANCIAL AID PICTURE (2015-2016)
Students with need: Need-based aid available for full-time and part-time students. Work study available nights.
Students without need: No-need awards available for academics, athletics, job skills, minority status, ROTC.

FINANCIAL AID PROCEDURES
Forms required: FAFSA.
Dates and Deadlines: Priority date 4/1; no closing date. Applicants notified on a rolling basis starting 4/30; must reply within 2 week(s) of notification.
Transfers: No deadline. Applicants notified on a rolling basis.

CONTACT
Wendell Schick, Director of Financial Aid
1441 North Cable Road, Lima, OH 45805
(419) 227-3141

University of Rio Grande
Rio Grande, Ohio
www.rio.edu   Federal Code: 003116

4-year private community and liberal arts college in rural community.
Enrollment: 1,165 undergrads.
Selectivity: Open admission; but selective for some programs.

BASIC COSTS (2016-2017)
Tuition and fees: $24,910.
Per-credit charge: $1,014.
Room and board: $10,120.

FINANCIAL AID PICTURE
Students with need: Need-based aid available for full-time and part-time students.
Students without need: No-need awards available for academics, alumni affiliation, athletics, leadership, music/drama, state/district residency.

FINANCIAL AID PROCEDURES
Forms required: FAFSA.

CONTACT
Meghann Fraley, Financial Aid Director
218 North College Avenue, Rio Grande, OH 45674
(740) 245-7218

University of Toledo
Toledo, Ohio
www.utoledo.edu   Federal Code: 003131

4-year public university in large city.
Enrollment: 15,166 undergrads, 15% part-time. 3,345 full-time freshmen.
Selectivity: Open admission; but selective for some programs and for out-of-state students.

BASIC COSTS (2016-2017)
Tuition and fees: $9,975; out-of-state residents $19,313.
Per-credit charge: $335; out-of-state residents $725.
Room and board: $11,724.

FINANCIAL AID PICTURE (2016-2017)
Students with need: Out of 3,092 full-time freshmen who applied for aid, 2,407 were judged to have need. Of these, 2,398 received aid, and 344 had their full need met. Average financial aid package met 64% of need; average scholarship/grant was $9,361; average loan was $3,637. For part-time students, average financial aid package was $7,630.
Students without need: 833 full-time freshmen who did not demonstrate need for aid received scholarships/grants; average award was $6,052. No-need awards available for academics, alumni affiliation, art, athletics, leadership, music/drama, ROTC, state/district residency.
Scholarships offered: 29 full-time freshmen received athletic scholarships; average amount $26,307.
Additional info: March priority date for federal aid. Students encouraged to apply as early as December for priority consideration for institutional aid.

FINANCIAL AID PROCEDURES
Forms required: FAFSA.
Dates and Deadlines: Priority date 3/1; no closing date. Applicants notified on a rolling basis starting 3/1; must reply within 8 week(s) of notification.
Transfers: Priority date 3/1.

CONTACT
Stephen Schissler, AVP Financial Aid & EnrollServ
2801 West Bancroft Street, Toledo, OH 43606-3390
(419) 530-8700

Urbana University
Urbana, Ohio
www.urbana.edu   Federal Code: 003133

4-year private university in large town.
Enrollment: 787 undergrads.

BASIC COSTS (2016-2017)
Tuition and fees: $22,452.
Per-credit charge: $748.
Room and board: $9,182.

FINANCIAL AID PICTURE
Students with need: Need-based aid available for full-time and part-time students. Work study available nights, weekends, and for part-time students.
Students without need: No-need awards available for academics, alumni affiliation, athletics, music/drama.

FINANCIAL AID PROCEDURES
Forms required: FAFSA.
Dates and Deadlines: Priority date 4/1; closing date 8/15. Applicants notified on a rolling basis starting 3/1; must reply within 4 week(s) of notification.
Transfers: No deadline. Applicants notified on a rolling basis starting 3/1; must reply within 4 week(s) of notification.

CONTACT
Samuel Selvage, Director of Financial Aid
579 College Way, Urbana, OH 43078
(937) 772-9251

Ursuline College
Pepper Pike, Ohio
www.ursuline.edu   Federal Code: 003134

4-year private liberal arts college in small town, affiliated with the Roman Catholic Church.

Enrollment: 632 undergrads, 27% part-time. 106 full-time freshmen.
Selectivity: Admits over 75% of applicants.

BASIC COSTS (2016-2017)
Tuition and fees: $30,000.
Per-credit charge: $988.
Room and board: $9,964.

FINANCIAL AID PICTURE (2016-2017)
Students with need: Out of 97 full-time freshmen who applied for aid, 90 were judged to have need. Of these, 90 received aid, and 14 had their full need met. Average financial aid package met 80% of need; average scholarship/grant was $22,189; average loan was $4,191. For part-time students, average financial aid package was $8,530.
Students without need: 15 full-time freshmen who did not demonstrate need for aid received scholarships/grants; average award was $7,963. No-need awards available for academics, alumni affiliation, art, athletics, leadership, ROTC.
Scholarships offered: *Merit:* Ursuline Scholarship: $5,000 to $7,500. Ursuline Award: $1,500 to $4,500. Presidential Scholarship: $11,000. Dean's Scholarship: $9,500. Unlimited number available for each; all renewable. ***Athletic:*** 17 full-time freshmen received athletic scholarships; average amount $14,422.

FINANCIAL AID PROCEDURES
Forms required: FAFSA.
Dates and Deadlines: Priority date 12/1; no closing date. Applicants notified on a rolling basis starting 12/15; must reply within 3 week(s) of notification.
Transfers: No deadline. Applicants notified on a rolling basis; must reply within 4 week(s) of notification.

CONTACT
Mary Lynn Perri, Director of Financial Aid
2550 Lander Road, Pepper Pike, OH 44124-4398
(440) 684-6114

Virginia Marti College of Art and Design
Lakewood, Ohio
www.vmcad.edu   Federal Code: 012896

2-year for-profit visual arts and business college in large city.
Enrollment: 160 undergrads.

BASIC COSTS (2016-2017)
Tuition and fees: $19,350.
Per-credit charge: $390.

FINANCIAL AID PICTURE
Students with need: Need-based aid available for full-time students.
Students without need: This college awards aid only to students with need.

FINANCIAL AID PROCEDURES
Forms required: FAFSA.
Dates and Deadlines: Applicants notified on a rolling basis.

CONTACT
Martha Snodgrass, Financial Aid
11724 Detroit Avenue, Lakewood, OH 44107

Walsh University
North Canton, Ohio
www.walsh.edu   Federal Code: 003135

4-year private university and liberal arts college in small city, affiliated with the Roman Catholic Church.
Enrollment: 2,124 undergrads, 16% part-time. 439 full-time freshmen.

Selectivity: Admits over 75% of applicants.

BASIC COSTS (2016-2017)
Tuition and fees: $28,720.
Per-credit charge: $905.
Room and board: $10,240.

FINANCIAL AID PICTURE (2016-2017)
Students with need: Out of 408 full-time freshmen who applied for aid, 353 were judged to have need. Of these, 353 received aid, and 102 had their full need met. Average financial aid package met 68% of need; average scholarship/grant was $4,672; average loan was $3,380. For part-time students, average financial aid package was $6,680.
Students without need: 55 full-time freshmen who did not demonstrate need for aid received scholarships/grants; average award was $10,550. No-need awards available for academics, alumni affiliation, athletics, music/drama, religious affiliation, state/district residency.
Scholarships offered: 89 full-time freshmen received athletic scholarships; average amount $10,656.

FINANCIAL AID PROCEDURES
Forms required: FAFSA.
Dates and Deadlines: Priority date 5/1; no closing date. Applicants notified on a rolling basis starting 12/16.
Transfers: No deadline. Applicants notified on a rolling basis starting 12/16.

CONTACT
Holly Van Gilder, Financial Aid Director
2020 East Maple Street, North Canton, OH 44720-3396
(330) 490-7146

Washington State Community College
Marietta, Ohio
www.wscc.edu   Federal Code: 010453

2-year public community college in large town.
Enrollment: 971 undergrads, 40% part-time. 201 full-time freshmen.
Selectivity: Open admission; but selective for some programs.

BASIC COSTS (2016-2017)
Tuition and fees: $4,410; out-of-state residents $8,580.
Per-credit charge: $139; out-of-state residents $278.

FINANCIAL AID PICTURE (2015-2016)
Students with need: 58% of average financial aid package awarded as scholarships/grants, 42% awarded as loans/jobs.

FINANCIAL AID PROCEDURES
Forms required: FAFSA, institutional form.
Dates and Deadlines: Applicants notified on a rolling basis starting 5/15; must reply within 2 week(s) of notification.

CONTACT
Reba Bartrug, Interim Director of Financial Aid
710 Colegate Drive, Marietta, OH 45750
(740) 568-1908

Wilberforce University
Wilberforce, Ohio   Federal Code: 003141
www.wilberforce.edu   CSS Code: 1906

4-year private university and liberal arts college in rural community, affiliated with the African Methodist Episcopal Church.
Enrollment: 594 undergrads.

BASIC COSTS (2016-2017)
Tuition and fees: $13,250.
Per-credit charge: $501.

Room and board: $6,650.

Additional info: Tuition/fee waivers available for minority students.

FINANCIAL AID PICTURE

Students with need: Need-based aid available for full-time and part-time students. Work study available nights, weekends, and for part-time students.

Students without need: No-need awards available for academics, alumni affiliation.

Scholarships offered: We encouraged prospective students to fill out their FAFSA as early as possible.

FINANCIAL AID PROCEDURES

Forms required: FAFSA, CSS PROFILE, institutional form.

Dates and Deadlines: Priority date 3/15; closing date 6/30. Applicants notified on a rolling basis starting 3/15; must reply within 2 week(s) of notification.

CONTACT

Terry Jeffries, VP - Enrollment Mgt, Financial Aid

1055 North Bickett Road, Wilberforce, OH 45384-1001

(937) 708-5727

Wilmington College

Wilmington, Ohio

www.wilmington.edu

Federal Code: 003142

4-year private agricultural and liberal arts college in large town, affiliated with the Society of Friends (Quaker).

Enrollment: 1,112 undergrads.

BASIC COSTS (2016-2017)

Tuition and fees: $25,000.

Room and board: $9,600.

FINANCIAL AID PICTURE

Students with need: Need-based aid available for full-time and part-time students.

Students without need: No-need awards available for academics, alumni affiliation, religious affiliation, state/district residency.

FINANCIAL AID PROCEDURES

Forms required: FAFSA.

Dates and Deadlines: Priority date 3/31; closing date 6/1. Applicants notified on a rolling basis starting 3/1; must reply by 5/1 or within 2 week(s) of notification.

CONTACT

Cheryl Louallen, Director of Financial Aid

Box 1325 Pyle Center, Wilmington, OH 45177

(937) 382-6661 ext. 249

Wittenberg University

Springfield, Ohio

www.wittenberg.edu

Federal Code: 003143

4-year private liberal arts college in small city, affiliated with the Evangelical Lutheran Church in America.

Enrollment: 1,903 undergrads, 3% part-time. 553 full-time freshmen.

Selectivity: Admits over 75% of applicants.

BASIC COSTS (2017-2018)

Tuition and fees: $38,790.

Per-credit charge: $1,264.

Room and board: $10,126.

Additional info: Tuition/fee waivers available for adults.

FINANCIAL AID PICTURE (2016-2017)

Students with need: Out of 536 full-time freshmen who applied for aid, 470 were judged to have need. Of these, 467 received aid, and 99 had their full need met. Average financial aid package met 80% of need; average scholarship/grant was $27,073; average loan was $3,427. For part-time students, average financial aid package was $6,793.

Students without need: 83 full-time freshmen who did not demonstrate need for aid received scholarships/grants; average award was $21,589. No-need awards available for academics, alumni affiliation, art, leadership, minority status, music/drama, religious affiliation, state/district residency.

Scholarships offered: University Scholar Award: half tuition; renewable; based on academic achievement and other qualities. Broadwell Chinn Scholarship: half tuition; renewable; based on minority status, academic achievement, and other qualities.

Additional info: Auditions required of applicants for music, theater, and dance scholarships. Portfolio required of applicants for art scholarships.

FINANCIAL AID PROCEDURES

Forms required: FAFSA.

Dates and Deadlines: Priority date 3/1; no closing date. Applicants notified on a rolling basis starting 2/15; must reply by 5/1 or within 2 week(s) of notification.

Transfers: Priority date 5/15; no deadline. Applicants notified on a rolling basis starting 3/15; must reply by 5/15 or within 2 week(s) of notification. No special restrictions for transfer students. Transfer students receive free books.

CONTACT

Jonathan Green, Executive Director of Financial Aid

Ward Street and North Wittenberg, Springfield, OH 45501-0720

(937) 327-7321

Wright State University

Dayton, Ohio

www.wright.edu

Federal Code: 003078

4-year public university in small city.

Enrollment: 11,664 undergrads, 18% part-time. 2,244 full-time freshmen.

Selectivity: Admits over 75% of applicants.

BASIC COSTS (2016-2017)

Tuition and fees: $8,730; out-of-state residents $17,350.

Per-credit charge: $394; out-of-state residents $791.

Room and board: $9,436.

FINANCIAL AID PICTURE (2015-2016)

Students with need: Out of 2,013 full-time freshmen who applied for aid, 1,577 were judged to have need. Of these, 1,555 received aid, and 288 had their full need met. Average financial aid package met 63% of need; average scholarship/grant was $6,695; average loan was $3,522. For part-time students, average financial aid package was $8,059.

Students without need: 387 full-time freshmen who did not demonstrate need for aid received scholarships/grants; average award was $4,069. No-need awards available for academics, alumni affiliation, art, athletics, leadership, minority status, music/drama, ROTC, state/district residency.

Scholarships offered: 42 full-time freshmen received athletic scholarships; average amount $11,154.

FINANCIAL AID PROCEDURES

Forms required: FAFSA.

Dates and Deadlines: Priority date 12/1; no closing date. Applicants notified on a rolling basis starting 12/15.

CONTACT

Amy Barnhart, Assistant Vice President of Enrollment Management and Director of Financial Aid

3640 Colonel Glenn Highway, 108 SU, Dayton, OH 45435

(937) 775-4000

Wright State University: Lake Campus

Celina, Ohio
http://lake.wright.edu/ Federal Code: 003078

2-year public branch campus college in large town.
Enrollment: 1,073 undergrads, 17% part-time. 267 full-time freshmen.
Selectivity: Open admission; but selective for some programs.

BASIC COSTS (2016-2017)

Tuition and fees: $5,842; out-of-state residents $14,462.
Per-credit charge: $265; out-of-state residents $662.

FINANCIAL AID PICTURE (2016-2017)

Students with need: Out of 233 full-time freshmen who applied for aid, 167 were judged to have need. Of these, 164 received aid, and 37 had their full need met. Average financial aid package met 71% of need; average scholarship/grant was $4,269; average loan was $3,423. For part-time students, average financial aid package was $7,217.
Students without need: 38 full-time freshmen who did not demonstrate need for aid received scholarships/grants; average award was $3,336. No-need awards available for academics, alumni affiliation, art, athletics, leadership, minority status, music/drama, ROTC, state/district residency.

FINANCIAL AID PROCEDURES

Forms required: FAFSA.
Dates and Deadlines: Priority date 12/1; no closing date. Applicants notified on a rolling basis starting 12/15; must reply within 2 week(s) of notification.
Transfers: No deadline. Applicants notified on a rolling basis starting 2/15; must reply within 2 week(s) of notification.

CONTACT

Amy Barnhart, Assistant Vice President of Enrollment Management/Director of Financial Aid
7600 Lake Campus Drive, State Route 703, Celina, OH 45822-2952
(937) 775-4000

Xavier University

Cincinnati, Ohio
www.xavier.edu Federal Code: 003144

4-year private university in large city, affiliated with the Roman Catholic Church.
Enrollment: 4,503 undergrads, 5% part-time. 1,149 full-time freshmen.
Selectivity: Admits 50 to 75% of applicants.

BASIC COSTS (2016-2017)

Tuition and fees: $36,150.
Per-credit charge: $674.
Room and board: $11,730.

FINANCIAL AID PICTURE (2015-2016)

Students with need: Out of 996 full-time freshmen who applied for aid, 776 were judged to have need. Of these, 776 received aid, and 75 had their full need met. Average financial aid package met 68% of need; average scholarship/grant was $23,598; average loan was $3,016. For part-time students, average financial aid package was $6,255.
Students without need: 360 full-time freshmen who did not demonstrate need for aid received scholarships/grants; average award was $18,354. No-need awards available for academics, alumni affiliation, art, athletics, leadership, music/drama, religious affiliation.
Scholarships offered: _Merit:_ Saint Francis Xavier Scholarship: full tuition; based on leadership, talent and highest academic achievement; competitive; 10 awarded. Community Engaged Fellowship: $22,000; competitive; 10 awarded. Chancellor Scholarship: $21,000; based on leadership, talent, and highest academic achievement; number of awards varies. Trustee Scholarship: $20,000; based on academic achievement; number of awards varies. Presidential Scholarship: $19,000; based on academic achievement; number

of awards varies. Deans Award: $18,000; based on academic achievement; number of awards varies. Miguel Pro Scholarship: amount varies; awarded annually to students committed to promoting diversity and demonstrate leadership; number varies. Francis X. Weninger Scholarship: amount varies; awarded annually to students who promote diversity in our society and who demonstrate leadership; number varies. **_Athletic:_** 31 full-time freshmen received athletic scholarships; average amount $14,211.

FINANCIAL AID PROCEDURES

Forms required: FAFSA.
Dates and Deadlines: Priority date 2/15; no closing date. Applicants notified on a rolling basis starting 3/1; must reply by 5/1.
Transfers: No deadline. Applicants notified on a rolling basis starting 3/1.

CONTACT

Donna Salak, Director of Financial Aid Operations
3800 Victory Parkway, Cincinnati, OH 45207-5311
(513) 745-3142

Youngstown State University

Youngstown, Ohio
www.ysu.edu Federal Code: 003145

4-year public university in small city.
Enrollment: 10,188 undergrads, 15% part-time. 1,939 full-time freshmen.
Selectivity: Admits 50 to 75% of applicants.

BASIC COSTS (2016-2017)

Tuition and fees: $8,327; out-of-state residents $14,327.
Per-credit charge: $270; out-of-district residents $280; out-of-state residents $520.
Room and board: $8,990.

FINANCIAL AID PICTURE (2015-2016)

Students with need: Out of 1,791 full-time freshmen who applied for aid, 1,517 were judged to have need. Of these, 1,517 received aid, and 158 had their full need met. Average financial aid package met 34% of need; average scholarship/grant was $5,324; average loan was $3,049. For part-time students, average financial aid package was $7,031.
Students without need: 267 full-time freshmen who did not demonstrate need for aid received scholarships/grants; average award was $3,556. No-need awards available for academics, alumni affiliation, athletics, ROTC, state/district residency.
Scholarships offered: 124 full-time freshmen received athletic scholarships; average amount $8,084.

FINANCIAL AID PROCEDURES

Forms required: FAFSA, institutional form.
Dates and Deadlines: Priority date 12/1; no closing date. Applicants notified on a rolling basis starting 12/15; must reply within 2 week(s) of notification.

CONTACT

Elaine Ruse, Director of Financial Aid and Scholarships
One University Plaza, Youngstown, OH 44555-0001
(330) 941-3505

Zane State College

Zanesville, Ohio
www.zanestate.edu Federal Code: 008133

2-year public community and technical college in large town.
Enrollment: 2,607 undergrads.
Selectivity: Open admission; but selective for some programs.

FINANCIAL AID PICTURE

Students with need: Need-based aid available for full-time and part-time students.

FINANCIAL AID PROCEDURES
Forms required: FAFSA.
Dates and Deadlines: Priority date 5/1; closing date 6/30. Must reply by 9/1.

CONTACT
Amanda Reisinger, Financial Aid Director
1555 Newark Road, Zanesville, OH 43701-2626
(740) 454-2501 ext. 1275

Oklahoma

Bacone College
Muskogee, Oklahoma
www.bacone.edu   Federal Code: 003147

4-year private liberal arts college in large town, affiliated with the American Baptist Churches in the USA.
Enrollment: 968 undergrads.

BASIC COSTS (2016-2017)
Tuition and fees: $14,850.
Per-credit charge: $550.
Room and board: $10,100.

FINANCIAL AID PICTURE
Students with need: Need-based aid available for full-time and part-time students. Work study available nights, weekends, and for part-time students.
Students without need: This college awards aid only to students with need.

FINANCIAL AID PROCEDURES
Forms required: FAFSA.
Dates and Deadlines: Priority date 3/31; no closing date. Applicants notified on a rolling basis starting 4/1; must reply within 2 week(s) of notification.
Transfers: No deadline. Applicants notified on a rolling basis.

CONTACT
Misty Oleson, Director of Financial Aid
2299 Old Bacone Road, Muskogee, OK 74403
(918) 781-7340

Cameron University
Lawton, Oklahoma
www.cameron.edu   Federal Code: 003150

4-year public university in small city.
Enrollment: 4,117 undergrads, 26% part-time. 762 full-time freshmen.
Selectivity: Admits over 75% of applicants.

BASIC COSTS (2016-2017)
Tuition and fees: $5,970; out-of-state residents $15,210.
Room and board: $5,102.

FINANCIAL AID PICTURE (2015-2016)
Students with need: Out of 593 full-time freshmen who applied for aid, 472 were judged to have need. Of these, 443 received aid, and 63 had their full need met. Average financial aid package met 64% of need; average scholarship/grant was $6,238; average loan was $3,490. For part-time students, average financial aid package was $6,143.
Students without need: 67 full-time freshmen who did not demonstrate need for aid received scholarships/grants; average award was $1,749. No-need awards available for academics, alumni affiliation, art, athletics, leadership, minority status, music/drama, ROTC, state/district residency.

Scholarships offered: 21 full-time freshmen received athletic scholarships; average amount $4,670.

FINANCIAL AID PROCEDURES
Forms required: FAFSA.
Dates and Deadlines: Priority date 4/1; no closing date. Applicants notified on a rolling basis starting 4/1; must reply within 2 week(s) of notification.
Transfers: Priority date 6/1; no deadline. Applicants notified on a rolling basis starting 6/1. Academic transcripts required.

CONTACT
Gary Garoffolo, Director of Financial Assistance
2800 West Gore Boulevard, Lawton, OK 73505-6377
(580) 581-2293

Carl Albert State College
Poteau, Oklahoma
www.carlalbert.edu   Federal Code: 003176

2-year public community and junior college in large town.
Enrollment: 2,902 undergrads.
Selectivity: Open admission; but selective for some programs.

BASIC COSTS (2016-2017)
Tuition and fees: $3,412; out-of-state residents $4,636.
Per-credit charge: $80.45; out-of-state residents $202.
Room and board: $3,800.
Additional info: Tuition/fee waivers available for minority students.

FINANCIAL AID PICTURE
Students with need: Need-based aid available for full-time and part-time students. Work study available nights.
Students without need: This college awards aid only to students with need.

FINANCIAL AID PROCEDURES
Forms required: FAFSA, institutional form.
Dates and Deadlines: Applicants notified on a rolling basis.

CONTACT
Robin Benson, Director of Financial Aid
1507 South McKenna, Poteau, OK 74953-5208
(918) 647-1343

Connors State College
Warner, Oklahoma
www.connorsstate.edu   Federal Code: 003153

2-year public community and junior college in rural community.
Enrollment: 2,600 undergrads.
Selectivity: Open admission; but selective for some programs.

BASIC COSTS (2016-2017)
Tuition and fees: $3,798; out-of-state residents $8,500.
Per-credit charge: $84; out-of-state residents $241.
Room and board: $5,690.

FINANCIAL AID PICTURE
Students with need: Need-based aid available for full-time and part-time students.
Students without need: No-need awards available for academics, alumni affiliation, athletics, leadership, state/district residency.

FINANCIAL AID PROCEDURES
Forms required: FAFSA, institutional form.
Dates and Deadlines: Closing date 3/1. Applicants notified on a rolling basis starting 4/1; must reply within 2 week(s) of notification.

CONTACT
Jennifer Watkins, Director of Financial Aid
RR 1, Box 1000, Warner, OK 74469-9700
(918) 463-6220 ext. 6220

East Central University

Ada, Oklahoma
www.ecok.edu   Federal Code: 003154

4-year public university in large town.
Enrollment: 3,361 undergrads, 22% part-time. 741 full-time freshmen.

BASIC COSTS (2016-2017)
Tuition and fees: $6,279; out-of-state residents $15,399.
Per-credit charge: $166; out-of-state residents $470.
Room and board: $5,350.

FINANCIAL AID PICTURE (2015-2016)
Students with need: Out of 532 full-time freshmen who applied for aid, 419 were judged to have need. Of these, 419 received aid. For part-time students, average financial aid package was $4,571.
Students without need: 2 full-time freshmen who did not demonstrate need for aid received scholarships/grants; average award was $2,676. No-need awards available for academics, athletics.
Scholarships offered: 46 full-time freshmen received athletic scholarships; average amount $5,626.

FINANCIAL AID PROCEDURES
Forms required: FAFSA.
Dates and Deadlines: Closing date 3/1. Applicants notified on a rolling basis starting 4/15; must reply within 6 week(s) of notification.

CONTACT
Becky Isaacs, Director of Financial Aid
1100 East 14th Street, PMB R-8, Ada, OK 74820
(580) 559-5243

Eastern Oklahoma State College

Wilburton, Oklahoma
www.eosc.edu   Federal Code: 003155

2-year public community college in rural community.
Enrollment: 1,341 undergrads, 32% part-time. 947 full-time freshmen.
Selectivity: Open admission; but selective for some programs.

BASIC COSTS (2016-2017)
Tuition and fees: $4,224; out-of-state residents $7,841.
Per-credit charge: $104.65; out-of-state residents $225.21.
Room and board: $5,697.
Additional info: Tuition/fee waivers available for adults.

FINANCIAL AID PICTURE (2015-2016)
Students with need: Out of 899 full-time freshmen who applied for aid, 660 were judged to have need. Of these, 624 received aid, and 436 had their full need met. Average financial aid package met 55% of need; average scholarship/grant was $2,124; average loan was $3,290. For part-time students, average financial aid package was $3,510.
Students without need: This college awards aid only to students with need.
Scholarships offered: 63 full-time freshmen received athletic scholarships; average amount $2,093.

FINANCIAL AID PROCEDURES
Forms required: FAFSA, institutional form.
Dates and Deadlines: Priority date 3/1; closing date 6/30. Applicants notified on a rolling basis starting 5/1; must reply within 2 week(s) of notification.

Transfers: Priority date 3/1; no deadline. Applicants notified on a rolling basis starting 5/1; must reply within 2 week(s) of notification.

CONTACT
Mimi Kelley, Director of Financial Aid
1301 West Main Street, Wilburton, OK 74578-4999
(918) 465-1771

Langston University

Langston, Oklahoma
www.langston.edu   Federal Code: 003157

4-year public university and liberal arts college in rural community.
Enrollment: 2,040 undergrads, 11% part-time. 604 full-time freshmen.
Selectivity: Admits over 75% of applicants.

BASIC COSTS (2016-2017)
Tuition and fees: $5,108; out-of-state residents $12,850.
Room and board: $9,186.
Additional info: Tuition at time of enrollment locked for 4 years.

FINANCIAL AID PICTURE (2015-2016)
Students with need: Out of 590 full-time freshmen who applied for aid, 560 were judged to have need. Of these, 529 received aid, and 65 had their full need met. Average financial aid package met 48% of need; average scholarship/grant was $5,161. For part-time students, average financial aid package was $1,310.
Students without need: This college awards aid only to students with need.

FINANCIAL AID PROCEDURES
Forms required: FAFSA, state aid form.
Dates and Deadlines: Priority date 3/1; closing date 5/1. Applicants notified on a rolling basis starting 7/15; must reply within 2 week(s) of notification.

CONTACT
Shelia McGill, Financial Aid Director
Box 728, Langston, OK 73050
(405) 466-3282

Mid-America Christian University

Oklahoma City, Oklahoma
www.macu.edu   Federal Code: 006942

4-year private university and liberal arts college in very large city, affiliated with the Church of God.
Enrollment: 2,688 undergrads.
Selectivity: Open admission.

BASIC COSTS (2016-2017)
Tuition and fees: $17,132.
Room and board: $6,721.

FINANCIAL AID PICTURE
Students with need: Need-based aid available for full-time and part-time students.
Students without need: No-need awards available for academics, athletics, leadership, minority status, music/drama, religious affiliation.

FINANCIAL AID PROCEDURES
Forms required: FAFSA.
Dates and Deadlines: Priority date 5/1; no closing date. Applicants notified on a rolling basis starting 5/1.

CONTACT
Christina Padilla, Director of Student Financial Services
3500 SW 119th Street, Oklahoma City, OK 73170
(405) 692-3182

Northeastern Oklahoma Agricultural and Mechanical College

Miami, Oklahoma
www.neo.edu   Federal Code: 316000

2-year public community and junior college in large town.
Enrollment: 2,029 undergrads.
Selectivity: Open admission.

BASIC COSTS (2016-2017)

Tuition and fees: $3,833; out-of-state residents $9,173.
Per-credit charge: $78; out-of-state residents $256.
Room and board: $5,768.

FINANCIAL AID PICTURE

Students with need: Need-based aid available for full-time and part-time students. Work study available nights, weekends, and for part-time students.
Students without need: No-need awards available for academics, athletics, leadership, music/drama, state/district residency.

FINANCIAL AID PROCEDURES

Forms required: FAFSA.
Dates and Deadlines: Priority date 4/1; no closing date. Applicants notified on a rolling basis starting 4/1; must reply by 8/30 or within 2 week(s) of notification.
Transfers: No deadline. Applicants notified on a rolling basis starting 4/1; must reply within 2 week(s) of notification.

CONTACT

David Fisher, Director of Financial Aid
200 I Street Northeast, Miami, OK 74354-6497
(918) 540-6235

Northeastern State University

Tahlequah, Oklahoma
www.nsuok.edu   Federal Code: 003161

4-year public university in large town.
Enrollment: 6,579 undergrads, 27% part-time. 879 full-time freshmen.
Selectivity: Admits over 75% of applicants.

BASIC COSTS (2016-2017)

Tuition and fees: $6,207; out-of-state residents $13,707.
Per-credit charge: $170; out-of-state residents $420.
Room and board: $6,650.
Additional info: Tuition/fee waivers available for adults, minority students.

FINANCIAL AID PICTURE (2016-2017)

Students with need: Out of 828 full-time freshmen who applied for aid, 559 were judged to have need. Of these, 558 received aid, and 479 had their full need met. Average financial aid package met 99% of need; average scholarship/grant was $7,035; average loan was $5,127. For part-time students, average financial aid package was $11,150.
Students without need: 69 full-time freshmen who did not demonstrate need for aid received scholarships/grants; average award was $2,710. No-need awards available for academics, alumni affiliation, art, athletics, leadership, minority status, music/drama, religious affiliation, ROTC, state/district residency.
Scholarships offered: *Merit:* Academic scholarships: up to $10,092 a year for 4 years. Baccalaureate scholarships: up to $11,092. Collegiate scholarships: up to $4,150. Freshmen scholarships: up to $2,350. Green and White scholarships: up to $3,050. Honors scholarship: up to $9,092. Leadership scholarships: up to $9,101. Community Service scholarship: up to $8,092. University scholarships: up to $3,900. Valedictorians scholarship: up to $3,300. *Athletic:* 49 full-time freshmen received athletic scholarships; average amount $4,505.

Additional info: Off-campus job location and development program introduced to assist students with finding off-campus employers to earn money for college expenses.

FINANCIAL AID PROCEDURES

Forms required: FAFSA.
Dates and Deadlines: Priority date 11/1; no closing date. Applicants notified on a rolling basis starting 11/1.
Transfers: Priority date 12/15; no deadline. State grant deadline is April 15.

CONTACT

Teri Cochran, Director of Student Financial Services
600 N Grand Ave, Tahlequah, OK 74464-2399
(918) 444-3456

Northern Oklahoma College

Tonkawa, Oklahoma
www.noc.edu   Federal Code: 003162

2-year public community college in small town.
Enrollment: 5,023 undergrads.
Selectivity: Open admission; but selective for out-of-state students.

BASIC COSTS (2016-2017)

Tuition and fees: $3,249; out-of-state residents $8,409.
Per-credit charge: $78; out-of-state residents $250.
Room and board: $5,770.
Additional info: Tuition/fee waivers available for adults, minority students, unemployed or children of unemployed.

FINANCIAL AID PICTURE

Students with need: Need-based aid available for full-time and part-time students.
Students without need: No-need awards available for academics, art, athletics, music/drama.

FINANCIAL AID PROCEDURES

Forms required: FAFSA, institutional form.
Dates and Deadlines: Priority date 6/1; no closing date. Applicants notified on a rolling basis starting 4/1.

CONTACT

Linda Brown, Director of Financial Aid
Box 310, Tonkawa, OK 74653-0310
(580) 628-6240

Northwestern Oklahoma State University

Alva, Oklahoma
www.nwosu.edu   Federal Code: 003163

4-year public university and teachers college in small town.
Enrollment: 1,858 undergrads, 16% part-time. 425 full-time freshmen.
Selectivity: Admits 50 to 75% of applicants.

BASIC COSTS (2016-2017)

Tuition and fees: $6,391; out-of-state residents $13,238.
Per-credit charge: $191.25; out-of-state residents $419.5.
Room and board: $4,610.

FINANCIAL AID PICTURE

Students with need: Need-based aid available for full-time and part-time students. Work study available nights, weekends, and for part-time students.
Students without need: No-need awards available for academics, alumni affiliation, art, athletics, leadership, music/drama.

FINANCIAL AID PROCEDURES

Forms required: FAFSA.

Dates and Deadlines: Applicants notified on a rolling basis starting 5/1; must reply by 8/15.

CONTACT
Rita Castleberry, Director of Financial Aid
709 Oklahoma Boulevard, Alva, OK 73717-2799
(580) 327-8542

Oklahoma Baptist University
Shawnee, Oklahoma
www.okbu.edu   Federal Code: 003164

4-year private university and liberal arts college in large town, affiliated with the Southern Baptist Convention.
Enrollment: 1,861 undergrads, 3% part-time. 556 full-time freshmen.
Selectivity: Admits 50 to 75% of applicants.

BASIC COSTS (2017-2018)
Tuition and fees: $26,840.
Room and board: $7,150.
Additional info: Tuition/fee waivers available for minority students.

FINANCIAL AID PICTURE (2015-2016)
Students with need: Out of 494 full-time freshmen who applied for aid, 447 were judged to have need. Of these, 447 received aid, and 132 had their full need met. Average financial aid package met 91% of need; average scholarship/grant was $9,131; average loan was $3,282. For part-time students, average financial aid package was $6,648.
Students without need: 105 full-time freshmen who did not demonstrate need for aid received scholarships/grants; average award was $9,320. No-need awards available for academics, art, athletics, leadership, minority status, music/drama, religious affiliation, ROTC.
Scholarships offered: 29 full-time freshmen received athletic scholarships; average amount $11,095.

FINANCIAL AID PROCEDURES
Forms required: FAFSA.
Dates and Deadlines: Priority date 3/1; no closing date. Applicants notified on a rolling basis starting 10/31; must reply within 2 week(s) of notification.
Transfers: Priority date 10/31; no deadline. Applicants notified on a rolling basis starting 10/31. Transfers receive 1 semester of financial aid on probationary basis. During probation semester, must meet SAP requirements in order to receive financial aid in subsequent semesters.

CONTACT
Jonna Raney, Director of Student Financial Services
500 West University, Shawnee, OK 74804
(405) 585-5120

Oklahoma Christian University
Oklahoma City, Oklahoma
www.oc.edu   Federal Code: 003165

4-year private university in very large city, affiliated with the Church of Christ.
Enrollment: 1,887 undergrads, 3% part-time. 452 full-time freshmen.
Selectivity: Admits 50 to 75% of applicants.

BASIC COSTS (2017-2018)
Tuition and fees: $21,670.
Per-credit charge: $900.
Room and board: $7,590.

FINANCIAL AID PICTURE (2015-2016)
Students with need: Out of 376 full-time freshmen who applied for aid, 305 were judged to have need. Of these, 304 received aid, and 131 had

their full need met. Average financial aid package met 68% of need; average scholarship/grant was $3,138; average loan was $2,309. For part-time students, average financial aid package was $10,723.
Students without need: 133 full-time freshmen who did not demonstrate need for aid received scholarships/grants; average award was $6,458. No-need awards available for academics, art, athletics, music/drama, religious affiliation, ROTC.
Scholarships offered: 41 full-time freshmen received athletic scholarships; average amount $5,374.

FINANCIAL AID PROCEDURES
Forms required: FAFSA.
Dates and Deadlines: Priority date 4/1; closing date 8/31. Applicants notified on a rolling basis starting 1/15; must reply within 4 week(s) of notification.
Transfers: Applicants notified on a rolling basis starting 3/1; must reply within 4 week(s) of notification. Will award based on unofficial transcript. Must have all official transcripts before awards will be disbursed.

CONTACT
Judy Cuellar, Director, Student Financial Services
Box 11000, Oklahoma City, OK 73136-1100
(405) 425-5190

Oklahoma City Community College
Oklahoma City, Oklahoma
www.occc.edu   Federal Code: 010391

2-year public community and technical college in very large city.
Enrollment: 13,000 undergrads.
Selectivity: Open admission; but selective for some programs.

BASIC COSTS (2016-2017)
Tuition and fees: $3,391; out-of-state residents $8,425.
Per-credit charge: $88; out-of-state residents $255.
Additional info: Tuition/fee waivers available for adults.

FINANCIAL AID PICTURE
Students with need: Need-based aid available for full-time and part-time students. Work study available nights, weekends, and for part-time students.
Students without need: No-need awards available for academics, alumni affiliation, art, leadership, music/drama, state/district residency.

FINANCIAL AID PROCEDURES
Forms required: FAFSA.
Dates and Deadlines: Priority date 4/15; no closing date. Applicants notified on a rolling basis starting 2/15.
Transfers: Applicants notified on a rolling basis. Those with previous degrees or over 90 credit hours attempted must appeal for eligibility for federally funded financial assistance.

CONTACT
Sonya Gore, Director of Financial Aid
7777 South May Avenue, Oklahoma City, OK 73159
(405) 682-7525

Oklahoma City University
Oklahoma City, Oklahoma
www.okcu.edu   Federal Code: 003166

4-year private university and liberal arts college in very large city, affiliated with the United Methodist Church.
Enrollment: 1,751 undergrads, 9% part-time. 329 full-time freshmen.
Selectivity: Admits 50 to 75% of applicants.

BASIC COSTS (2017-2018)
Tuition and fees: $30,726.

Per-credit charge: $925.

Room and board: $8,624.

Additional info: Tuition/fee waivers available for adults.

FINANCIAL AID PICTURE (2016-2017)

Students with need: Out of 281 full-time freshmen who applied for aid, 215 were judged to have need. Of these, 210 received aid, and 176 had their full need met. Average financial aid package met 65% of need; average scholarship/grant was $18,114; average loan was $3,130. For part-time students, average financial aid package was $8,900.

Students without need: 65 full-time freshmen who did not demonstrate need for aid received scholarships/grants; average award was $15,675. No-need awards available for academics, alumni affiliation, art, athletics, leadership, music/drama, religious affiliation, ROTC, state/district residency.

Scholarships offered: 14 full-time freshmen received athletic scholarships; average amount $8,252.

FINANCIAL AID PROCEDURES

Forms required: FAFSA.

Dates and Deadlines: Priority date 3/1; no closing date. Applicants notified on a rolling basis starting 3/1; must reply within 2 week(s) of notification.

Transfers: Applicants notified on a rolling basis; must reply within 2 week(s) of notification. Financial aid transcripts required from all previously attended institutions whether or not financial aid was received.

CONTACT

Denise Flis, Senior Director, Student Financial Services

2501 North Blackwelder Avenue, Oklahoma City, OK 73106-1493

(405) 208-5211

Oklahoma Panhandle State University

Goodwell, Oklahoma

www.opsu.edu   Federal Code: 003174

4-year public university and liberal arts college in rural community.

Enrollment: 1,261 undergrads.

BASIC COSTS (2016-2017)

Additional info: Tuition at time of enrollment locked for 4 years.

FINANCIAL AID PICTURE

Students with need: Need-based aid available for full-time and part-time students.

Students without need: This college awards aid only to students with need.

FINANCIAL AID PROCEDURES

Forms required: FAFSA, institutional form.

Dates and Deadlines: Priority date 3/15; no closing date.

Transfers: No deadline. Applicants notified on a rolling basis.

CONTACT

Lori Ferguson, Director of Financial Aid

OPSU Admissions, Goodwell, OK 73939-0430

(580) 349-1566

Oklahoma State University

Stillwater, Oklahoma

go.okstate.edu   Federal Code: 003170

4-year public university in large town.

Enrollment: 20,828 undergrads, 12% part-time. 3,936 full-time freshmen.

Selectivity: Admits 50 to 75% of applicants.

BASIC COSTS (2016-2017)

Tuition and fees: $8,321; out-of-state residents $22,443.

Per-credit charge: $164.75; out-of-state residents $635.5.

Room and board: $7,690.

FINANCIAL AID PICTURE (2015-2016)

Students with need: Out of 3,234 full-time freshmen who applied for aid, 2,161 were judged to have need. Of these, 2,109 received aid, and 372 had their full need met. Average financial aid package met 79% of need; average scholarship/grant was $8,337; average loan was $3,181. For part-time students, average financial aid package was $10,162.

Students without need: 1,101 full-time freshmen who did not demonstrate need for aid received scholarships/grants; average award was $6,662. No-need awards available for academics, alumni affiliation, art, athletics, leadership, minority status, music/drama, ROTC, state/district residency.

Scholarships offered: 37 full-time freshmen received athletic scholarships; average amount $10,220.

Additional info: In-state students who file the FAFSA and who have financial need may receive additional funding through the Academic Opportunity Scholarship program.

FINANCIAL AID PROCEDURES

Forms required: FAFSA.

Dates and Deadlines: Priority date 2/1; no closing date. Applicants notified on a rolling basis starting 4/1; must reply by 5/1 or within 2 week(s) of notification.

CONTACT

Chad Blew, Director of Scholarships & Financial Aid

219 Student Union, Stillwater, OK 74078

(405) 744-6604

Oklahoma State University Institute of Technology: Okmulgee

Okmulgee, Oklahoma

www.osuit.edu   Federal Code: 003172

2-year public branch campus and technical college in large town.

Enrollment: 2,293 undergrads, 28% part-time. 588 full-time freshmen.

Selectivity: Open admission; but selective for some programs.

BASIC COSTS (2016-2017)

Tuition and fees: $5,100; out-of-state residents $10,710.

Per-credit charge: $130; out-of-state residents $317.

Room and board: $6,554.

FINANCIAL AID PICTURE

Students with need: Need-based aid available for full-time and part-time students. Work study available nights, weekends, and for part-time students.

Students without need: No-need awards available for academics, alumni affiliation, job skills, leadership, minority status, state/district residency.

Additional info: OSUIT Foundation Scholarship application due March 1.

FINANCIAL AID PROCEDURES

Forms required: FAFSA.

Dates and Deadlines: Priority date 3/1; no closing date. Must reply within 4 week(s) of notification.

Transfers: Priority date 3/1. Applicants notified by 6/1; must reply within 4 week(s) of notification. Requirement of financial aid transcript from any institution(s) attended during transferring academic year.

CONTACT

Matt Short, Financial Aid Director

1801 East Fourth Street, Okmulgee, OK 74447-3901

(918) 293-5290

Oklahoma State University: Oklahoma City

Oklahoma City, Oklahoma
www.osuokc.edu/home   Federal Code: 009647

2-year public branch campus and technical college in very large city.
Enrollment: 5,537 undergrads.
Selectivity: Open admission; but selective for some programs.

BASIC COSTS (2016-2017)
Tuition and fees: $3,634; out-of-state residents $9,922.
Per-credit charge: $95; out-of-state residents $305.
Additional info: Tuition/fee waivers available for adults, minority students.

FINANCIAL AID PICTURE
Students with need: Need-based aid available for full-time and part-time students. Work study available nights, weekends, and for part-time students.
Students without need: This college awards aid only to students with need.

FINANCIAL AID PROCEDURES
Forms required: FAFSA.
Dates and Deadlines: Priority date 7/19; no closing date. Applicants notified on a rolling basis starting 8/1; must reply within 2 week(s) of notification.
Transfers: Applicants notified on a rolling basis.

CONTACT
Bessie Carter, Director of Financial Aid & Scholarships
900 North Portland Avenue, Oklahoma City, OK 73107-6195
(405) 945-8646

Oklahoma Wesleyan University

Bartlesville, Oklahoma
www.okwu.edu   Federal Code: 003151

4-year private university and liberal arts college in large town, affiliated with the Wesleyan Church.
Enrollment: 1,208 undergrads, 48% part-time. 221 full-time freshmen.
Selectivity: Admits 50 to 75% of applicants.

BASIC COSTS (2017-2018)
Tuition and fees: $26,090.
Per-credit charge: $1,030.
Room and board: $8,644.

FINANCIAL AID PICTURE (2016-2017)
Students with need: Out of 204 full-time freshmen who applied for aid, 188 were judged to have need. Of these, 188 received aid, and 25 had their full need met. Average financial aid package met 57% of need; average scholarship/grant was $12,215; average loan was $3,420. For part-time students, average financial aid package was $6,406.
Students without need: 28 full-time freshmen who did not demonstrate need for aid received scholarships/grants; average award was $6,803. No-need awards available for academics, alumni affiliation, athletics, leadership, music/drama, religious affiliation, state/district residency.
Scholarships offered: 37 full-time freshmen received athletic scholarships; average amount $5,348.

FINANCIAL AID PROCEDURES
Forms required: FAFSA.
Dates and Deadlines: Priority date 3/1; no closing date. Applicants notified on a rolling basis starting 3/1.
Transfers: Closing date 8/1. Applicants notified on a rolling basis; must reply within 2 week(s) of notification.

CONTACT
Kandi Molder, Director of Student Financial Services
2201 Silver Lake Road, Bartlesville, OK 74006
(918) 335-6282

Oral Roberts University

Tulsa, Oklahoma
www.oru.edu   Federal Code: 003985

4-year private university and liberal arts college in large city, affiliated with the nondenominational tradition.
Enrollment: 2,979 undergrads, 13% part-time. 474 full-time freshmen.
Selectivity: Admits less than 50% of applicants.

BASIC COSTS (2016-2017)
Tuition and fees: $25,678.
Per-credit charge: $1,031.
Room and board: $10,348.

FINANCIAL AID PICTURE (2016-2017)
Students with need: Average financial aid package met 91% of need; average scholarship/grant was $20,980; average loan was $7,287. For part-time students, average financial aid package was $5,503.
Students without need: No-need awards available for academics, alumni affiliation, art, athletics, job skills, leadership, music/drama.

FINANCIAL AID PROCEDURES
Forms required: FAFSA.
Dates and Deadlines: Applicants notified on a rolling basis starting 12/1; must reply by 5/1.
Transfers: Priority date 3/30. Applicants notified on a rolling basis starting 4/1. Transfer applicants eligible for some scholarships.

CONTACT
William Womack, Director of Financial Aid
7777 South Lewis Avenue, Tulsa, OK 74171
(918) 495-6510

Platt College: Oklahoma City Central

Oklahoma City, Oklahoma
www.plattcolleges.edu   Federal Code: 023068

2-year for-profit branch campus and career college in small city.
Enrollment: 200 undergrads.
Selectivity: Open admission; but selective for some programs.

BASIC COSTS (2016-2017)
Additional info: Certificate programs: Dental Assistant $15,420; Medical Assistant $15,420. Associate programs: Practical Nursing $28,200; Nursing $36,020; Culinary Arts (Morning) $31,720. Bachelor's programs: Nursing $46,120; Hospitality and Restaurant Management $46,020.

FINANCIAL AID PICTURE
Students with need: Need-based aid available for full-time students.

FINANCIAL AID PROCEDURES
Forms required: FAFSA.

CONTACT
Amy Hocker, Financial Aid Director
309 South Ann Arbor, Oklahoma City, OK 73128
(405) 946-7799

Platt College: Tulsa

Tulsa, Oklahoma
www.plattcolleges.edu   Federal Code: 016312

2-year for-profit culinary school and health science college in large city.
Enrollment: 360 undergrads.
Selectivity: Open admission; but selective for some programs.

BASIC COSTS (2016-2017)

Additional info: Certificate programs: Dental Assistant $15,420; Medical Assistant $15,420; Pharmacy Technician $12,500; Pastry Arts (Morning) $22,520. Associate programs: Practical Nursing $28,200; Nursing $36,020; Culinary Arts (Morning) $31,720. Bachelor's programs: Nursing $46,120; Hospitality and Restaurant Management $46,020.

FINANCIAL AID PICTURE

Students with need: Need-based aid available for full-time and part-time students.

Students without need: This college awards aid only to students with need.

FINANCIAL AID PROCEDURES

Forms required: FAFSA.

CONTACT

Linda Bates, Director of Compliance-Financial Services
3801 South Sheridan, Tulsa, OK 74145-1132
(918) 663-9000

Redlands Community College

El Reno, Oklahoma
www.redlandscc.edu   Federal Code: 003156

2-year public community college in large town.
Enrollment: 2,500 undergrads.
Selectivity: Open admission; but selective for some programs.

BASIC COSTS (2016-2017)

Tuition and fees: $3,882; out-of-state residents $6,026.
Per-credit charge: $129; out-of-state residents $201.
Room and board: $7,468.
Additional info: Tuition/fee waivers available for adults.

FINANCIAL AID PICTURE

Students with need: Need-based aid available for full-time and part-time students. Work study available nights, weekends, and for part-time students.
Students without need: No-need awards available for academics, athletics, leadership.

FINANCIAL AID PROCEDURES

Forms required: FAFSA.
Dates and Deadlines: Priority date 8/1; no closing date. Applicants notified on a rolling basis starting 6/1; must reply within 6 week(s) of notification.
Transfers: No deadline. Applicants notified on a rolling basis; must reply within 6 week(s) of notification.

CONTACT

Karen Jeffers, Director of Financial Aid
1300 South Country Club Road, El Reno, OK 73036
(866) 415-6367 ext. 1442

Rogers State University

Claremore, Oklahoma
www.rsu.edu   Federal Code: 003168

4-year public university in large town.
Enrollment: 3,889 undergrads, 39% part-time. 583 full-time freshmen.
Selectivity: Admits over 75% of applicants.

BASIC COSTS (2016-2017)

Tuition and fees: $6,540; out-of-state residents $14,460.
Per-credit charge: $132; out-of-state residents $396.
Room and board: $7,950.

FINANCIAL AID PICTURE (2016-2017)

Students with need: Out of 552 full-time freshmen who applied for aid, 448 were judged to have need. Of these, 442 received aid, and 43 had their full need met. Average financial aid package met 55% of need; average scholarship/grant was $7,177; average loan was $3,254. For part-time students, average financial aid package was $6,730.
Students without need: 22 full-time freshmen who did not demonstrate need for aid received scholarships/grants; average award was $8,898. No-need awards available for academics, alumni affiliation, art, athletics, leadership, music/drama, state/district residency.
Scholarships offered: 18 full-time freshmen received athletic scholarships; average amount $10,005.

FINANCIAL AID PROCEDURES

Forms required: FAFSA.
Dates and Deadlines: Priority date 6/15; no closing date. Applicants notified on a rolling basis starting 4/1; must reply within 1 week(s) of notification.
Transfers: No deadline. Applicants notified on a rolling basis starting 4/1; must reply within 3 week(s) of notification.

CONTACT

Kelly Hicks, Director, Financial Aid
1701 West Will Rogers Boulevard, Claremore, OK 74017-3252
(918) 343-7553

Rose State College

Midwest City, Oklahoma
www.rose.edu   Federal Code: 009185

2-year public community college in small city.
Enrollment: 6,143 undergrads, 55% part-time. 1,061 full-time freshmen.
Selectivity: Open admission; but selective for some programs.

BASIC COSTS (2016-2017)

Tuition and fees: $3,808; out-of-state residents $10,184.
Per-credit charge: $100.65; out-of-state residents $313.2.
Room only: $6,000.

FINANCIAL AID PICTURE (2015-2016)

Students with need: 58% of average financial aid package awarded as scholarships/grants, 42% awarded as loans/jobs. Need-based aid available for part-time students. Work study available nights, weekends, and for part-time students.
Students without need: No-need awards available for academics, athletics, leadership.
Additional info: Ticket to Rose grant available to students from Midwest City/Choctaw high schools to cover unmet need in tuition/fees.

FINANCIAL AID PROCEDURES

Forms required: FAFSA.
Dates and Deadlines: Priority date 6/1; no closing date. Applicants notified on a rolling basis starting 3/1; must reply within 4 week(s) of notification.

CONTACT

Steven Daffer, Director of Financial Aid
6420 SE 15th Street, Midwest City, OK 73110-2799
(405) 733-7424

St. Gregory's University

Shawnee, Oklahoma
www.stgregorys.edu   Federal Code: 003183

4-year private university and liberal arts college in large town, affiliated with the Roman Catholic Church.
Enrollment: 601 undergrads, 23% part-time. 86 full-time freshmen.
Selectivity: Admits less than 50% of applicants.

BASIC COSTS (2016-2017)

Tuition and fees: $21,300.
Per-credit charge: $710.
Room and board: $8,044.
Additional info: Tuition/fee waivers available for adults.

FINANCIAL AID PICTURE (2015-2016)

Students with need: Out of 86 full-time freshmen who applied for aid, 84 were judged to have need. Of these, 84 received aid, and 30 had their full need met. Average financial aid package met 72% of need; average scholarship/grant was $14,540; average loan was $4,500. Need-based aid available for part-time students.

Students without need: 10 full-time freshmen who did not demonstrate need for aid received scholarships/grants; average award was $3,000. No-need awards available for academics, alumni affiliation, art, athletics, job skills, leadership, music/drama, religious affiliation.

Scholarships offered: *Merit:* Leadership Scholarship; $500-$2,000. Academic Scholarship; $500-$5,100. Need-based scholarship; $500-$1,500. *Athletic:* 5 full-time freshmen received athletic scholarships; average amount $2,000.

FINANCIAL AID PROCEDURES

Forms required: FAFSA, institutional form.
Dates and Deadlines: Priority date 3/1; no closing date. Applicants notified on a rolling basis starting 2/15; must reply within 3 week(s) of notification.
Transfers: No deadline. Applicants notified on a rolling basis; must reply within 3 week(s) of notification.

CONTACT

Lori Deardorff, Director of Financial Aid
1900 West MacArthur Drive, Shawnee, OK 74804
(405) 878-5412

Seminole State College

Seminole, Oklahoma
www.sscok.edu   Federal Code: 003178

2-year public community and junior college in small town.
Enrollment: 1,288 undergrads, 33% part-time. 325 full-time freshmen.
Selectivity: Open admission; but selective for some programs.

BASIC COSTS (2016-2017)

Tuition and fees: $4,140; out-of-state residents $9,735.
Per-credit charge: $90.5; out-of-state residents $277.
Room and board: $7,070.

FINANCIAL AID PICTURE (2015-2016)

Students with need: 81% of average financial aid package awarded as scholarships/grants, 19% awarded as loans/jobs. Need-based aid available for part-time students.

Students without need: No-need awards available for academics, art, athletics, leadership, music/drama, state/district residency.

FINANCIAL AID PROCEDURES

Forms required: FAFSA, institutional form.
Dates and Deadlines: Priority date 3/1; no closing date. Applicants notified on a rolling basis starting 1/1; must reply within 4 week(s) of notification.

CONTACT

Melanie Rinehart, Director of Financial Assistance
PO Box 351, Seminole, OK 74818-0351
(405) 382-9247

Southeastern Oklahoma State University

Durant, Oklahoma
www.se.edu   Federal Code: 003179

4-year public liberal arts and teachers college in large town.
Enrollment: 3,130 undergrads, 23% part-time. 386 full-time freshmen.
Selectivity: Admits over 75% of applicants.

BASIC COSTS (2016-2017)

Tuition and fees: $6,450; out-of-state residents $15,720.
Per-credit charge: $198; out-of-state residents $507.
Room and board: $6,535.
Additional info: Tuition/fee waivers available for minority students.

FINANCIAL AID PICTURE (2015-2016)

Students with need: Out of 343 full-time freshmen who applied for aid, 284 were judged to have need. Of these, 278 received aid, and 29 had their full need met. Average financial aid package met 7% of need; average scholarship/grant was $1,899; average loan was $1,369. For part-time students, average financial aid package was $7,204.

Students without need: 14 full-time freshmen who did not demonstrate need for aid received scholarships/grants; average award was $1,008. No-need awards available for academics, alumni affiliation, art, athletics, leadership, minority status, music/drama, state/district residency.

Scholarships offered: 62 full-time freshmen received athletic scholarships; average amount $2,385.

FINANCIAL AID PROCEDURES

Forms required: FAFSA, institutional form.
Dates and Deadlines: Priority date 3/1; no closing date. Applicants notified on a rolling basis starting 4/1.

CONTACT

Tony Lehrling, Director of Student Financial Aid
1405 North Fourth Avenue, PMB 4225, Durant, OK 74701-0607
(580) 745-2186

Southwestern Christian University

Bethany, Oklahoma
www.swcu.edu   Federal Code: 003180

4-year private university and liberal arts college in large town, affiliated with the Pentecostal Holiness Church.
Enrollment: 713 undergrads.

BASIC COSTS (2016-2017)

Tuition and fees: $15,930.
Per-credit charge: $465.
Room and board: $6,300.

FINANCIAL AID PICTURE

Students with need: Need-based aid available for full-time and part-time students. Work study available nights, weekends, and for part-time students.

Students without need: No-need awards available for academics, alumni affiliation, music/drama, religious affiliation, ROTC.

FINANCIAL AID PROCEDURES

Forms required: FAFSA, institutional form.
Dates and Deadlines: Priority date 3/1; no closing date. Applicants notified on a rolling basis starting 4/1; must reply within 2 week(s) of notification.

CONTACT

Kellye Johnson, Director of Financial Aid
Box 340, Bethany, OK 73008
(405) 789-7661 ext. 3456

Southwestern Oklahoma State University

Weatherford, Oklahoma
www.swosu.edu   Federal Code: 003181

4-year public university in large town.
Enrollment: 4,542 undergrads, 19% part-time. 981 full-time freshmen.
Selectivity: Admits over 75% of applicants.

BASIC COSTS (2016-2017)
Tuition and fees: $6,390; out-of-state residents $13,140.
Per-credit charge: $213; out-of-state residents $438.
Room and board: $5,400.

FINANCIAL AID PICTURE
Students with need: Need-based aid available for full-time and part-time students.
Students without need: No-need awards available for academics, alumni affiliation, art, athletics, leadership, music/drama, state/district residency.

FINANCIAL AID PROCEDURES
Forms required: FAFSA, institutional form.
Dates and Deadlines: Closing date 3/1. Applicants notified by 3/15.

CONTACT
Jerome Wichert, Director of Student Financial Services
100 Campus Drive, Weatherford, OK 73096
(508) 774-3786

Spartan College of Aeronautics and Technology

Tulsa, Oklahoma
www.spartan.edu

4-year for-profit technical college in large city.
Enrollment: 849 undergrads.

BASIC COSTS (2016-2017)
Tuition and fees: $16,150.
Additional info: Annual cost shown is for Aviation Maintenance Technology program. Full program costs vary by program ranging from $20,060 to $73,209. Tuition at time of enrollment locked for 4 years.

FINANCIAL AID PICTURE
Students with need: Need-based aid available for full-time and part-time students. Work study available nights, weekends, and for part-time students.

FINANCIAL AID PROCEDURES
Forms required: FAFSA, institutional form.
Dates and Deadlines: Applicants notified on a rolling basis starting 2/1; must reply within 2 week(s) of notification.
Transfers: No deadline. Applicants notified on a rolling basis starting 2/1; must reply within 2 week(s) of notification.

CONTACT
Christina Foster, Financial Aid Director
8820 East Pine Street, Tulsa, OK 74158-2833
(918) 836-6886

Tulsa Community College

Tulsa, Oklahoma
www.tulsacc.edu   Federal Code: 009763

2-year public community college in large city.
Enrollment: 14,224 undergrads, 62% part-time. 2,026 full-time freshmen.
Selectivity: Open admission; but selective for some programs.

BASIC COSTS (2016-2017)
Tuition and fees: $3,803; out-of-state residents $9,803.
Per-credit charge: $97; out-of-state residents $297.
Additional info: Tuition/fee waivers available for minority students.

FINANCIAL AID PICTURE (2016-2017)
Students with need: Out of 1,811 full-time freshmen who applied for aid, 1,225 were judged to have need. Of these, 1,138 received aid, and 115 had their full need met. Average financial aid package met 73% of need; average scholarship/grant was $2,890; average loan was $1,512. For part-time students, average financial aid package was $3,084.
Students without need: 335 full-time freshmen who did not demonstrate need for aid received scholarships/grants; average award was $1,666. No-need awards available for academics, job skills, leadership, music/drama, state/district residency.

FINANCIAL AID PROCEDURES
Forms required: FAFSA.

CONTACT
Karen Jeffers, Director of Financial Aid
6111 East Skelly Drive, Tulsa, OK 74135-6198
(918) 595-7155

Tulsa Welding School

Tulsa, Oklahoma
www.weldingschool.com   Federal Code: 015733

2-year for-profit technical college in very large city.
Enrollment: 1,902 undergrads.
Selectivity: Open admission.

BASIC COSTS (2017-2018)
Additional info: Total program costs vary from $19,880 to $39,432.

FINANCIAL AID PICTURE (2015-2016)
Students with need: 43% of average financial aid package awarded as scholarships/grants, 57% awarded as loans/jobs.
Students without need: This college awards aid only to students with need.

FINANCIAL AID PROCEDURES
Forms required: FAFSA.

CONTACT
Reba Smith, Corporate Compliance Officer
2545 East 11th Street, Tulsa, OK 74104-3909
(918) 587-6789

University of Central Oklahoma

Edmond, Oklahoma
www.uco.edu   Federal Code: 003152

4-year public university in small city.
Enrollment: 14,788 undergrads. 2,265 full-time freshmen.

BASIC COSTS (2016-2017)
Tuition and fees: $6,699; out-of-state residents $16,459.
Room and board: $7,740.
Additional info: Tuition at time of enrollment locked for 4 years.

FINANCIAL AID PICTURE (2015-2016)
Students with need: Out of 1,542 full-time freshmen who applied for aid, 1,170 were judged to have need. Of these, 1,135 received aid, and 185 had their full need met. Average financial aid package met 64% of need; average scholarship/grant was $7,259; average loan was $3,372. Need-based aid available for part-time students.

Students without need: 443 full-time freshmen who did not demonstrate need for aid received scholarships/grants; average award was $2,388. No-need awards available for academics, alumni affiliation, art, athletics, leadership, minority status, music/drama, ROTC, state/district residency.
Scholarships offered: 50 full-time freshmen received athletic scholarships; average amount $8,252.

FINANCIAL AID PROCEDURES

Forms required: FAFSA, institutional form.
Dates and Deadlines: Priority date 5/31; no closing date. Applicants notified on a rolling basis.
Transfers: No deadline. Applicants notified on a rolling basis starting 5/1.

CONTACT

Susan Prater, Director of Student Financial Services
100 North University Drive, Edmond, OK 73034-0151
(405) 974-2727

University of Oklahoma
Norman, Oklahoma
www.ou.edu   Federal Code: 003184

4-year public university in small city.
Enrollment: 21,909 undergrads, 13% part-time. 3,905 full-time freshmen.
Selectivity: Admits 50 to 75% of applicants.

BASIC COSTS (2016-2017)

Tuition and fees: $10,881; out-of-state residents $25,203.
Per-credit charge: $153; out-of-state residents $630.
Room and board: $10,280.
Additional info: Tuition at time of enrollment locked for 4 years; tuition/fee waivers available for adults, minority students.

FINANCIAL AID PICTURE (2015-2016)

Students with need: Out of 2,842 full-time freshmen who applied for aid, 1,833 were judged to have need. Of these, 1,801 received aid, and 1,437 had their full need met. Average financial aid package met 80% of need; average scholarship/grant was $6,608; average loan was $3,620. For part-time students, average financial aid package was $9,318.
Students without need: 616 full-time freshmen who did not demonstrate need for aid received scholarships/grants; average award was $2,984. No-need awards available for academics, alumni affiliation, art, athletics, leadership, music/drama, ROTC.
Scholarships offered: 54 full-time freshmen received athletic scholarships; average amount $18,660.

FINANCIAL AID PROCEDURES

Forms required: FAFSA.
Dates and Deadlines: Priority date 3/1; no closing date. Applicants notified on a rolling basis starting 1/15.
Transfers: No deadline. Applicants notified on a rolling basis starting 1/15; must reply within 6 week(s) of notification.

CONTACT

Caryn Pacheco, Director of Financial Aid
1000 Asp Avenue, Room 127, Norman, OK 73019-4076
(405) 325-5505

University of Science and Arts of Oklahoma
Chickasha, Oklahoma
www.usao.edu   Federal Code: 003167

4-year public university and liberal arts college in large town.
Enrollment: 841 undergrads, 7% part-time. 209 full-time freshmen.

BASIC COSTS (2016-2017)

Tuition and fees: $6,570; out-of-state residents $16,020.
Per-credit charge: $180; out-of-state residents $495.
Room and board: $5,800.
Additional info: Tuition at time of enrollment locked for 4 years.

FINANCIAL AID PICTURE (2016-2017)

Students with need: Out of 163 full-time freshmen who applied for aid, 137 were judged to have need. Of these, 132 received aid, and 32 had their full need met. Average financial aid package met 73% of need; average scholarship/grant was $10,007; average loan was $2,678. For part-time students, average financial aid package was $6,553.
Students without need: 20 full-time freshmen who did not demonstrate need for aid received scholarships/grants; average award was $3,112. No-need awards available for academics, art, athletics, leadership, music/drama, state/district residency.
Scholarships offered: 43 full-time freshmen received athletic scholarships; average amount $10,264.

FINANCIAL AID PROCEDURES

Forms required: FAFSA.
Dates and Deadlines: Priority date 2/1; no closing date. Applicants notified on a rolling basis starting 12/1; must reply within 4 week(s) of notification.
Transfers: No deadline. Applicants notified on a rolling basis starting 2/1; must reply within 4 week(s) of notification.

CONTACT

Laura Coponiti, Director of Financial Aid
1727 West Alabama, Chickasha, OK 73018-5322
(405) 574-1240

University of Tulsa
Tulsa, Oklahoma
utulsa.edu   Federal Code: 003185

4-year private university in large city, affiliated with the Presbyterian Church (USA).
Enrollment: 3,362 undergrads, 3% part-time. 713 full-time freshmen.
Selectivity: Admits less than 50% of applicants.

BASIC COSTS (2017-2018)

Tuition and fees: $41,459.
Per-credit charge: $1,453.
Room and board: $11,116.

FINANCIAL AID PICTURE (2016-2017)

Students with need: Out of 547 full-time freshmen who applied for aid, 439 were judged to have need. Of these, 439 received aid, and 204 had their full need met. Average financial aid package met 87% of need; average scholarship/grant was $6,417; average loan was $5,429. For part-time students, average financial aid package was $16,489.
Students without need: 221 full-time freshmen who did not demonstrate need for aid received scholarships/grants; average award was $23,514. No-need awards available for academics, alumni affiliation, art, athletics, leadership, minority status, music/drama, religious affiliation, ROTC.
Scholarships offered: 85 full-time freshmen received athletic scholarships; average amount $37,901.

FINANCIAL AID PROCEDURES

Forms required: FAFSA.
Dates and Deadlines: Priority date 3/1; no closing date. Applicants notified on a rolling basis starting 3/1; must reply by 5/1 or within 2 week(s) of notification.
Transfers: Priority date 5/1; no deadline. Applicants notified on a rolling basis starting 3/1; must reply by 5/1 or within 2 week(s) of notification.

CONTACT
Vicki Hendrickson, Director of Student Financial Services
Office of Admission, Tulsa, OK 74104-3189
(918) 631-2526

Vatterott College: Oklahoma City
Oklahoma City, Oklahoma
www.vatterott.edu   Federal Code: 020693

2-year for-profit technical and career college in very large city.
Enrollment: 280 undergrads.
Selectivity: Open admission.

BASIC COSTS (2016-2017)
Additional info: Diploma programs: (40 weeks) $14,784; (60 weeks) $24,534. Associate programs: (70 weeks) $25,109-$28,336; (90 weeks) $33,264-$36,072. Costs include fees, books and supplies.

FINANCIAL AID PICTURE
Students with need: Need-based aid available for full-time students.
Students without need: This college awards aid only to students with need.

FINANCIAL AID PROCEDURES
Forms required: FAFSA.

CONTACT
Janice Stepp, Director of Financial Aid
5537 Northwest Expressway, Oklahoma City, OK 73132
(405) 945-0088

Western Oklahoma State College
Altus, Oklahoma
www.wosc.edu   Federal Code: 003146

2-year public community college in large town.
Enrollment: 1,178 undergrads.
Selectivity: Open admission; but selective for some programs.

BASIC COSTS (2017-2018)
Tuition and fees: $3,939; out-of-state residents $8,584.
Per-credit charge: $84; out-of-state residents $268.
Room and board: $4,950.

FINANCIAL AID PICTURE (2016-2017)
Students with need: Need-based aid available for full-time and part-time students. Work study available nights, weekends, and for part-time students.
Students without need: No-need awards available for academics, alumni affiliation, art, athletics, leadership, music/drama, state/district residency.

FINANCIAL AID PROCEDURES
Forms required: FAFSA, institutional form.
Dates and Deadlines: Closing date 3/1. Applicants notified on a rolling basis; must reply within 3 week(s) of notification.

CONTACT
Myrna Cross, Director of Financial Aid/Veterans' Affairs
2801 North Main Street, Altus, OK 73521
(580) 477-7709

Oregon

Art Institute of Portland
Portland, Oregon
https://www.artinstitutes.edu/portland
                                     Federal Code: 007819

4-year for-profit visual arts and liberal arts college in large city.
Enrollment: 1,111 undergrads.

FINANCIAL AID PICTURE
Students with need: Need-based aid available for full-time and part-time students. Work study available nights, weekends, and for part-time students.
Students without need: No-need awards available for art.
Additional info: Applicants encouraged to apply early for financial aid. Scholarship deadlines range from January 1 to March 1.

FINANCIAL AID PROCEDURES
Forms required: FAFSA.
Dates and Deadlines: Priority date 3/1; no closing date. Applicants notified on a rolling basis starting 1/1; must reply within 5 week(s) of notification.
Transfers: No deadline. Applicants notified on a rolling basis starting 1/1.

CONTACT
Lauren Patterson, Director of Student Financial Services
1122 Northwest Davis Street, Portland, OR 97209-2911
(503) 382-4784

Blue Mountain Community College
Pendleton, Oregon
www.bluecc.edu   Federal Code: 003186

2-year public community college in large town.
Enrollment: 591 undergrads.
Selectivity: Open admission; but selective for some programs.

BASIC COSTS (2016-2017)
Tuition and fees: $4,914; out-of-state residents $13,554.
Per-credit charge: $96; out-of-state residents $288.
Additional info: Students in limited entry programs such as dental and nursing and some academic programs such as agriculture, diesel, music and art pay additional program and/or course fees. Washington state, Idaho, Nevada, California and Montana residents all pay in-state rates.

FINANCIAL AID PICTURE
Students with need: Need-based aid available for full-time and part-time students. Work study available nights, weekends, and for part-time students.
Students without need: No-need awards available for athletics, music/drama.

FINANCIAL AID PROCEDURES
Forms required: FAFSA.
Dates and Deadlines: Priority date 3/30; no closing date. Applicants notified on a rolling basis starting 4/1; must reply within 2 week(s) of notification.

CONTACT
Yadira Gonzalez, Director of Student Financial Assistance
2411 NW Carden Avenue, Pendleton, OR 97801
(541) 278-5790

Central Oregon Community College
Bend, Oregon
www.cocc.edu   Federal Code: 003188

2-year public community college in small city.
Enrollment: 5,144 undergrads, 51% part-time. 752 full-time freshmen.
Selectivity: Open admission; but selective for some programs.

BASIC COSTS (2016-2017)
Tuition and fees: $4,534; out-of-district residents $5,974; out-of-state residents $11,869.
Per-credit charge: $93; out-of-district residents $125; out-of-state residents $256.
Room and board: $9,855.

FINANCIAL AID PICTURE (2016-2017)
Students with need: Out of 634 full-time freshmen who applied for aid, 502 were judged to have need. Of these, 499 received aid, and 89 had their full need met. Average financial aid package met 73% of need; average scholarship/grant was $6,212; average loan was $3,103. For part-time students, average financial aid package was $10,677.
Students without need: 12 full-time freshmen who did not demonstrate need for aid received scholarships/grants; average award was $1,267. No-need awards available for academics, state/district residency.
Additional info: Institution-sponsored short-term loans. Extensive part-time student employment.

FINANCIAL AID PROCEDURES
Forms required: FAFSA.
Dates and Deadlines: Applicants notified on a rolling basis starting 4/1; must reply within 4 week(s) of notification.

CONTACT
Kevin Multop, Director of Financial Aid
2600 Northwest College Way, Bend, OR 97703
(541) 383-7260

Chemeketa Community College
Salem, Oregon
www.chemeketa.edu   Federal Code: 003218

2-year public community and junior college in small city.
Enrollment: 9,030 undergrads, 49% part-time. 719 full-time freshmen.
Selectivity: Open admission; but selective for some programs.

BASIC COSTS (2016-2017)
Tuition and fees: $4,320; out-of-state residents $11,610.
Per-credit charge: $80; out-of-state residents $242.

FINANCIAL AID PICTURE (2015-2016)
Students with need: Out of 697 full-time freshmen who applied for aid, 645 were judged to have need. Of these, 625 received aid, and 8 had their full need met. Average financial aid package met 47% of need; average scholarship/grant was $4,735; average loan was $4,822. For part-time students, average financial aid package was $4,961.
Students without need: This college awards aid only to students with need.
Scholarships offered: 18 full-time freshmen received athletic scholarships; average amount $2,204.

FINANCIAL AID PROCEDURES
Forms required: FAFSA.
Dates and Deadlines: Priority date 4/1; no closing date. Applicants notified on a rolling basis starting 6/30; must reply within 2 week(s) of notification.
Transfers: Priority date 6/30; no deadline. Applicants notified on a rolling basis; must reply within 4 week(s) of notification.

CONTACT
Kathy Campbell, Financial Aid Director
Admissions Office, Salem, OR 97309-7070
(503) 399-5018

Clackamas Community College
Oregon City, Oregon
www.clackamas.edu   Federal Code: 004878

2-year public community college in large town.
Enrollment: 5,902 undergrads, 57% part-time. 485 full-time freshmen.
Selectivity: Open admission; but selective for some programs.

BASIC COSTS (2016-2017)
Tuition and fees: $4,412; out-of-state residents $11,927.
Per-credit charge: $90; out-of-state residents $257.

FINANCIAL AID PICTURE
Students with need: Need-based aid available for full-time and part-time students. Work study available nights, weekends, and for part-time students.
Students without need: No-need awards available for academics, art, athletics, leadership, music/drama.
Additional info: Institutional tuition rebate guarantee. Frozen tuition rates for new fall students who graduate within 3 years. Any tuition increase levied by college during those 3 years will be refunded to student upon graduation.

FINANCIAL AID PROCEDURES
Forms required: FAFSA, institutional form.
Dates and Deadlines: Applicants notified on a rolling basis starting 3/15; must reply within 3 week(s) of notification.
Transfers: No deadline. Applicants notified on a rolling basis starting 3/15; must reply within 3 week(s) of notification.

CONTACT
Ryan West, Interim - Financial Aid Director
19600 Molalla Avenue, Oregon City, OR 97045
(503) 594-3099

Clatsop Community College
Astoria, Oregon
www.clatsopcc.edu   Federal Code: 003189

2-year public community and maritime college in large town.
Enrollment: 619 undergrads.
Selectivity: Open admission; but selective for some programs.

BASIC COSTS (2016-2017)
Tuition and fees: $4,995; out-of-state residents $9,450.
Per-credit charge: $99; out-of-state residents $198.

FINANCIAL AID PICTURE
Students with need: Need-based aid available for full-time and part-time students.
Students without need: No-need awards available for academics, art, leadership, minority status, state/district residency.

FINANCIAL AID PROCEDURES
Forms required: FAFSA, institutional form.
Dates and Deadlines: Priority date 5/1; no closing date. Applicants notified on a rolling basis starting 2/1.
Transfers: No deadline. Applicants notified on a rolling basis starting 2/1. Students who apply after July 1 may only be eligible for Pell Grants and loans depending on availability of funds. Reply deadline 1 week before start of classes.

CONTACT

Lloyd Mueller, Director of Financial Aid
1651 Lexington Avenue, Astoria, OR 97103
(503) 338-2412

Concordia University

Portland, Oregon
www.cu-portland.edu   Federal Code: 003191

4-year private liberal arts and teachers college in very large city, affiliated with the Lutheran Church - Missouri Synod.
Enrollment: 1,174 undergrads, 13% part-time. 187 full-time freshmen.
Selectivity: Admits 50 to 75% of applicants.

BASIC COSTS (2016-2017)

Tuition and fees: $29,140.
Per-credit charge: $890.
Room and board: $9,220.
Additional info: Tuition/fee waivers available for adults.

FINANCIAL AID PICTURE (2015-2016)

Students with need: Out of 171 full-time freshmen who applied for aid, 151 were judged to have need. Of these, 151 received aid, and 69 had their full need met. Need-based aid available for part-time students.
Students without need: 33 full-time freshmen who did not demonstrate need for aid received scholarships/grants; average award was $7,080. No-need awards available for academics, alumni affiliation, art, athletics, leadership, minority status, music/drama, religious affiliation.
Scholarships offered: *Merit:* Premier President's Scholarship, $14,000; President's Scholarship; $13,000; Scholar's Scholarship $12,000; Regent's Scholarship; $11,000; Provost's Scholarship $8.000; Dean's Award $6,000; University Award; $7,000; Cavalier's Award; $6,000; Faculty Award $3,500. Merit awarded based on academic index including HS GPA and ACT/SAT test scores. Honors Scholarship 50% tuition discount upon acceptance to Honors Program. *Athletic:* 41 full-time freshmen received athletic scholarships; average amount $13,463.

FINANCIAL AID PROCEDURES

Forms required: FAFSA.
Dates and Deadlines: Applicants notified on a rolling basis starting 12/1.
Transfers: No deadline. Applicants notified on a rolling basis starting 3/1.

CONTACT

Robert Clarke, Financial Aid Director
2811 Northeast Holman Street, Portland, OR 97211-6099
(503) 280-8514

Corban University

Salem, Oregon
www.corban.edu   Federal Code: 001339

4-year private liberal arts college in small city, affiliated with the Baptist faith.
Enrollment: 985 undergrads.

BASIC COSTS (2016-2017)

Tuition and fees: $30,640.
Per-credit charge: $1,250.
Room and board: $9,666.

FINANCIAL AID PICTURE

Students with need: Need-based aid available for full-time and part-time students. Work study available nights, weekends, and for part-time students.
Students without need: No-need awards available for academics, alumni affiliation, athletics, leadership, music/drama, ROTC.

Additional info: The Corban Promise is a policy to retire student debt. After graduation, students who work at least 30 hours a week with incomes below $37,000 will qualify for assistance which increases proportionately as income decreases. Incomes below $20,000 will be eligible for 100% reimbursement.

FINANCIAL AID PROCEDURES

Forms required: FAFSA.
Dates and Deadlines: Priority date 2/1; no closing date. Applicants notified on a rolling basis starting 2/20.

CONTACT

Ellen Zarfas, Director of Financial Aid
5000 Deer Park Drive SE, Salem, OR 97317-9392
(503) 375-7006

Eastern Oregon University

La Grande, Oregon
www.eou.edu   Federal Code: 003193

4-year public university and liberal arts college in large town.
Enrollment: 2,721 undergrads, 38% part-time. 311 full-time freshmen.
Selectivity: Admits over 75% of applicants.

BASIC COSTS (2016-2017)

Tuition and fees: $8,073; out-of-state residents $18,804.
Per-credit charge: $146; out-of-state residents $383.
Room and board: $9,642.

FINANCIAL AID PICTURE (2015-2016)

Students with need: Out of 294 full-time freshmen who applied for aid, 226 were judged to have need. Of these, 226 received aid, and 46 had their full need met. Average financial aid package met 63% of need; average scholarship/grant was $7,574; average loan was $3,223. For part-time students, average financial aid package was $7,195.
Students without need: 53 full-time freshmen who did not demonstrate need for aid received scholarships/grants; average award was $1,583. No-need awards available for academics, art, leadership, minority status, music/drama, state/district residency.
Scholarships offered: *Merit:* University Scholars Scholarships; full-tuition; based on personal essay, recommendations, GPA, activities and awards. *Athletic:* 84 full-time freshmen received athletic scholarships; average amount $2,751.

FINANCIAL AID PROCEDURES

Forms required: FAFSA.
Dates and Deadlines: Applicants notified on a rolling basis; must reply within 4 week(s) of notification.
Transfers: No deadline. Applicants notified on a rolling basis.

CONTACT

Sandy Henry, Director of Financial Aid
One University Boulevard, La Grande, OR 97850
(541) 962-3550

George Fox University

Newberg, Oregon
www.georgefox.edu   Federal Code: 003194

4-year private university and seminary college in large town, affiliated with the Society of Friends (Quaker).
Enrollment: 2,682 undergrads, 8% part-time. 642 full-time freshmen.
Selectivity: Admits over 75% of applicants.

BASIC COSTS (2017-2018)

Tuition and fees: $34,866.

Room and board: $10,886.
Additional info: Tuition/fee waivers available for minority students.

FINANCIAL AID PICTURE (2016-2017)

Students with need: Out of 588 full-time freshmen who applied for aid, 486 were judged to have need. Of these, 486 received aid, and 215 had their full need met. Average financial aid package met 88% of need; average scholarship/grant was $20,148; average loan was $3,093. For part-time students, average financial aid package was $5,719.

Students without need: 152 full-time freshmen who did not demonstrate need for aid received scholarships/grants; average award was $14,413. No-need awards available for academics, alumni affiliation, art, job skills, leadership, minority status, music/drama, religious affiliation.

Scholarships offered: Academic merit awards; $2,500-$15,000 per year; based on GPA, SAT/ACT and rigor of high school curriculum; renewable based on academic performance.

Additional info: Audition required for music and drama scholarships.

FINANCIAL AID PROCEDURES

Forms required: FAFSA, state aid form.
Dates and Deadlines: Priority date 2/1; no closing date. Applicants notified on a rolling basis starting 3/1.
Transfers: Priority date 3/1.

CONTACT

James Oshiro, Director of Financial Aid
414 North Meridian Street #6089, Newberg, OR 97132-2697
(503) 554-2290

Klamath Community College

Klamath Falls, Oregon
www.klamathcc.edu   Federal Code: 034283

2-year public community college in small city.
Enrollment: 1,228 undergrads.
Selectivity: Open admission.

BASIC COSTS (2016-2017)

Tuition and fees: $4,606; out-of-state residents $7,823.
Per-credit charge: $90; out-of-state residents $161.

FINANCIAL AID PICTURE

Students with need: Need-based aid available for full-time and part-time students. Work study available nights.

FINANCIAL AID PROCEDURES

Forms required: FAFSA.
Transfers: No deadline. Applicants notified on a rolling basis.

CONTACT

Robin Sundseth, Financial Aid Director
7390 South 6th Street, Klamath Falls, OR 97603
(541) 882-3521

Lane Community College

Eugene, Oregon
www.lanecc.edu   Federal Code: 003196

2-year public community college in small city.
Enrollment: 8,370 undergrads.
Selectivity: Open admission; but selective for some programs.

BASIC COSTS (2016-2017)

Tuition and fees: $5,123; out-of-state residents $11,783.
Per-credit charge: $103; out-of-state residents $251.

FINANCIAL AID PICTURE

Students with need: Need-based aid available for full-time and part-time students. Work study available nights, weekends, and for part-time students.
Students without need: No-need awards available for art, athletics, minority status, music/drama.

FINANCIAL AID PROCEDURES

Forms required: FAFSA.
Dates and Deadlines: Closing date 2/15. Applicants notified on a rolling basis starting 6/1; must reply within 2 week(s) of notification.

CONTACT

Greg Holmes, Chief Financial Officer
4000 East 30th Avenue, Eugene, OR 97405
(541) 463-3100

Lewis & Clark College

Portland, Oregon   Federal Code: 003197
www.lclark.edu   CSS Code: 4384

4-year private liberal arts college in very large city.
Enrollment: 2,033 undergrads. 506 full-time freshmen.
Selectivity: Admits 50 to 75% of applicants.

BASIC COSTS (2016-2017)

Tuition and fees: $46,894.
Per-credit charge: $2,327.
Room and board: $11,540.

FINANCIAL AID PICTURE (2016-2017)

Students with need: Out of 401 full-time freshmen who applied for aid, 274 were judged to have need. Of these, 274 received aid, and 146 had their full need met. Average financial aid package met 92% of need; average scholarship/grant was $32,589; average loan was $5,443. Need-based aid available for part-time students.

Students without need: 194 full-time freshmen who did not demonstrate need for aid received scholarships/grants; average award was $16,420. No-need awards available for academics, leadership, music/drama.

FINANCIAL AID PROCEDURES

Forms required: FAFSA, CSS PROFILE.
Dates and Deadlines: Priority date 1/15; no closing date. Applicants notified on a rolling basis starting 1/30; must reply by 7/1 or within 2 week(s) of notification.
Transfers: Applicants notified on a rolling basis starting 1/30; must reply by 7/1 or within 2 week(s) of notification. The number of semesters a transfer student may receive institutionally-funded aid is prorated based on the number of transfer credits accepted. Students are notified of the number of semesters of institutional aid they are eligible to receive once the Registrar has completed their final transcript evaluation.

CONTACT

Anastacia Dillon, Director of Financial Aid
0615 SW Palatine Hill Road, Portland, OR 97219-7899
(503) 768-7090

Linfield College

McMinnville, Oregon
www.linfield.edu   Federal Code: 003198

4-year private nursing and liberal arts college in large town, affiliated with the American Baptist Churches in the USA.
Enrollment: 1,603 undergrads, 1% part-time. 393 full-time freshmen.
Selectivity: Admits over 75% of applicants.

BASIC COSTS (2016-2017)

Tuition and fees: $40,105.

Per-credit charge: $1,240.
Room and board: $11,905.

FINANCIAL AID PICTURE (2016-2017)
Students with need: Out of 355 full-time freshmen who applied for aid, 317 were judged to have need. Of these, 317 received aid, and 64 had their full need met. Average financial aid package met 84% of need; average scholarship/grant was $28,872; average loan was $4,590. For part-time students, average financial aid package was $16,140.
Students without need: 72 full-time freshmen who did not demonstrate need for aid received scholarships/grants; average award was $19,324. No-need awards available for academics, leadership, minority status, music/drama.
Scholarships offered: National Merit Award: half to full-tuition for National Merit Finalists who list Linfield as first choice. Other scholarships based on academic record include Trustee Scholarships, Presidential Scholarships, Frances R. Linfield Scholarships, Faculty Scholarships, and Achievement Awards. The Academic Competitive Scholarships are sponsored by departments; separate application required. The Music department offers scholarships available by audition for majors, minors and non-majors. Leadership and Service Scholarship are based on high levels of leadership, initiative, and service to others through student government, school activities, community organizations, and religious or social service agencies.

FINANCIAL AID PROCEDURES
Forms required: FAFSA.
Dates and Deadlines: Priority date 2/1; no closing date. Applicants notified on a rolling basis starting 4/1; must reply by 5/1 or within 2 week(s) of notification.
Transfers: Priority date 4/15. Applicants notified on a rolling basis starting 5/15; must reply by 6/15 or within 2 week(s) of notification. Scholarships available for transfer students include Transfer Scholarships for students who have attended 2- or 4-year accredited colleges full-time and have 3.00 GPA. Honor Society Scholarships for members of Phi Theta Kappa or Alpha Gamma Sigma are available. Chemeketa Scholars at Linfield is a scholarship program for participants in the Chemeketa Scholars program at Chemeketa Community College (Oregon).

CONTACT
Keri Burke, Director of Financial Aid
900 Southeast Baker Street, McMinnville, OR 97128-6894
(503) 883-2225

Linn-Benton Community College
Albany, Oregon
www.linnbenton.edu
Federal Code: 006938

2-year public community college in small city.
Enrollment: 5,727 undergrads, 52% part-time. 1,007 full-time freshmen.
Selectivity: Open admission; but selective for some programs.

BASIC COSTS (2016-2017)
Tuition and fees: $4,832; out-of-state residents $10,758.
Per-credit charge: $99.43; out-of-state residents $231.12.
Additional info: Tuition/fee waivers available for unemployed or children of unemployed.

FINANCIAL AID PICTURE (2015-2016)
Students with need: Out of 495 full-time freshmen who applied for aid, 427 were judged to have need. Of these, 367 received aid, and 40 had their full need met. Average financial aid package met 58% of need; average scholarship/grant was $4,974; average loan was $2,772. For part-time students, average financial aid package was $7,298.
Students without need: 36 full-time freshmen who did not demonstrate need for aid received scholarships/grants; average award was $3,039. No-need awards available for academics, alumni affiliation, art, athletics, leadership, music/drama.

Scholarships offered: 13 full-time freshmen received athletic scholarships; average amount $1,717.

FINANCIAL AID PROCEDURES
Forms required: FAFSA.
Dates and Deadlines: Applicants notified on a rolling basis starting 3/30; must reply within 4 week(s) of notification.

CONTACT
Elaine Robinson, Director of Financial Aid & Veteran's Affairs
6500 Pacific Blvd SW, Albany, OR 97321
(541) 917-4850

Marylhurst University
Marylhurst, Oregon
www.marylhurst.edu
Federal Code: 003199

4-year private university and liberal arts college in large town, affiliated with the Roman Catholic Church.
Enrollment: 398 undergrads, 66% part-time. 4 full-time freshmen.
Selectivity: Admits over 75% of applicants.

BASIC COSTS (2016-2017)
Tuition and fees: $20,835.
Per-credit charge: $463.

FINANCIAL AID PICTURE
Students with need: Out of 4 full-time freshmen who applied for aid, 4 were judged to have need. Of these, 4 received aid. Average financial aid package met 65% of need. Need-based aid available for part-time students.
Students without need: No-need awards available for academics.

FINANCIAL AID PROCEDURES
Forms required: FAFSA, institutional form.
Dates and Deadlines: Priority date 3/1; no closing date. Applicants notified on a rolling basis starting 5/1.
Transfers: No deadline. Applicants notified on a rolling basis starting 5/1.

CONTACT
Tracy Reisinger, Director of Financial Aid
PO Box 261, Marylhurst, OR 97036-0261
(503) 699-6253

Mt. Hood Community College
Gresham, Oregon
www.mhcc.edu
Federal Code: 003204

2-year public community college in small city.
Enrollment: 5,835 undergrads, 61% part-time. 1,120 full-time freshmen.
Selectivity: Open admission; but selective for some programs.

BASIC COSTS (2016-2017)
Tuition and fees: $4,703; out-of-state residents $9,788.
Per-credit charge: $96; out-of-state residents $209.

FINANCIAL AID PICTURE
Students with need: Need-based aid available for full-time and part-time students.
Students without need: No-need awards available for academics.

FINANCIAL AID PROCEDURES
Forms required: FAFSA, institutional form.
Dates and Deadlines: Closing date 4/1. Applicants notified on a rolling basis starting 4/1; must reply within 2 week(s) of notification.

CONTACT
Christi Hart, Financial Aid Director
26000 SE Stark Street, Gresham, OR 97030
(503) 491-7379

Multnomah University
Portland, Oregon
www.multnomah.edu   Federal Code: 003206

4-year private university and seminary college in very large city, affiliated with the interdenominational tradition.
Enrollment: 413 undergrads, 12% part-time. 67 full-time freshmen.
Selectivity: Admits 50 to 75% of applicants.

BASIC COSTS (2017-2018)
Tuition and fees: $24,680.
Room and board: $8,560.

FINANCIAL AID PICTURE (2015-2016)
Students with need: Out of 66 full-time freshmen who applied for aid, 60 were judged to have need. Of these, 60 received aid, and 8 had their full need met. Average financial aid package met 64% of need; average scholarship/grant was $15,044; average loan was $3,134. For part-time students, average financial aid package was $6,827.
Students without need: 7 full-time freshmen who did not demonstrate need for aid received scholarships/grants; average award was $7,228. No-need awards available for academics, alumni affiliation, athletics.
Scholarships offered: 7 full-time freshmen received athletic scholarships; average amount $2,923.

FINANCIAL AID PROCEDURES
Forms required: FAFSA.
Dates and Deadlines: Priority date 4/1; closing date 8/1. Applicants notified on a rolling basis starting 10/1; must reply by 5/1 or within 2 week(s) of notification.
Transfers: Must reply within 2 week(s) of notification.

CONTACT
Mary McGlothlan, Director of Financial Aid
8435 Northeast Glisan Street, Portland, OR 97220
(503) 251-5336

New Hope Christian College
Eugene, Oregon
www.newhope.edu   Federal Code: 015167

4-year private Bible college in small city, affiliated with the nondenominational tradition.
Enrollment: 121 undergrads, 8% part-time. 18 full-time freshmen.

BASIC COSTS (2016-2017)
Tuition and fees: $17,530.
Per-credit charge: $550.
Room and board: $6,100.

FINANCIAL AID PICTURE
Students with need: Need-based aid available for full-time and part-time students. Work study available nights, weekends, and for part-time students.
Students without need: No-need awards available for academics, art, athletics, job skills, leadership, music/drama, religious affiliation, state/district residency.
Scholarships offered: Honors award; $300; 3.7 GPA required.
Additional info: Some early acceptance awards possible for those admitted by May 15. Distance awards to those coming from over 1,000 miles away. Some awards for husbands and wives enrolled at same time.

FINANCIAL AID PROCEDURES
Forms required: FAFSA, institutional form.
Dates and Deadlines: Priority date 4/1; closing date 8/1. Applicants notified on a rolling basis starting 2/1; must reply within 4 week(s) of notification.
Transfers: No deadline.

CONTACT
Brittany Pelton, Director of Financial Aid
2155 Bailey Hill Road, Eugene, OR 97405

Northwest Christian University
Eugene, Oregon
www.nwcu.edu   Federal Code: 003208

4-year private university in small city, affiliated with the Christian Church (Disciples of Christ).
Enrollment: 559 undergrads, 25% part-time. 81 full-time freshmen.
Selectivity: Admits 50 to 75% of applicants.

BASIC COSTS (2016-2017)
Tuition and fees: $27,930.
Per-credit charge: $925.
Room and board: $8,650.

FINANCIAL AID PICTURE (2016-2017)
Students with need: Out of 79 full-time freshmen who applied for aid, 73 were judged to have need. Of these, 73 received aid, and 15 had their full need met. Average financial aid package met 77% of need; average scholarship/grant was $9,094; average loan was $3,089. For part-time students, average financial aid package was $6,421.
Students without need: 8 full-time freshmen who did not demonstrate need for aid received scholarships/grants; average award was $10,587. No-need awards available for academics, alumni affiliation, athletics, leadership, music/drama, religious affiliation.
Scholarships offered: *Merit:* Academic Scholarships; $4,000-$13,000; 2.80-4.00 unweighted GPA; not limited. Leadership Awards; $500-$1,000; school, community, church leadership roles; not limited. *Athletic:* 8 full-time freshmen received athletic scholarships; average amount $3,969.

FINANCIAL AID PROCEDURES
Forms required: FAFSA.
Dates and Deadlines: Priority date 3/1; no closing date. Applicants notified on a rolling basis starting 1/5; must reply within 2 week(s) of notification.
Transfers: No deadline. Applicants notified on a rolling basis starting 1/5; must reply within 2 week(s) of notification.

CONTACT
Jocelyn Hubbs, Director of Financial Aid
828 East 11th Avenue, Eugene, OR 97401-3745
(541) 684-7218

Oregon College of Art & Craft
Portland, Oregon
www.ocac.edu   Federal Code: 030073

4-year private visual arts college in very large city.
Enrollment: 122 undergrads, 12% part-time. 16 full-time freshmen.
Selectivity: Admits 50 to 75% of applicants.

BASIC COSTS (2017-2018)
Tuition and fees: $33,160.
Per-credit charge: $1,315.
Room and board: $9,900.

FINANCIAL AID PICTURE (2015-2016)
Students with need: Out of 14 full-time freshmen who applied for aid, 11 were judged to have need. Of these, 11 received aid, and 3 had their full need met. Average financial aid package met 60% of need; average scholarship/grant was $13,471; average loan was $3,000. For part-time students, average financial aid package was $14,227.

Students without need: 5 full-time freshmen who did not demonstrate need for aid received scholarships/grants; average award was $12,925. No-need awards available for academics, art, job skills, leadership, minority status, music/drama, religious affiliation, ROTC, state/district residency.

FINANCIAL AID PROCEDURES

Forms required: FAFSA.

Dates and Deadlines: Applicants notified on a rolling basis starting 1/15; must reply by 5/1.

CONTACT

Linda Anderson, Financial Aid Director
8245 SW Barnes Road, Portland, OR 97225-6349
(971) 255-4224

Oregon Health & Science University

Portland, Oregon
www.ohsu.edu
Federal Code: 004883

3-year public university and health science college in very large city.
Enrollment: 777 undergrads, 72% part-time.

BASIC COSTS (2016-2017)

Tuition and fees: $17,835; out-of-state residents $31,380.
Per-credit charge: $361; out-of-state residents $662.
Additional info: Tuition shown is for new 2016-2017 undergraduate nursing program in main campus; costs for other programs vary.

FINANCIAL AID PICTURE (2016-2017)

Students with need: Average financial aid package for all full-time undergraduates was $14,409; for part-time $12,028. 22% awarded as scholarships/grants, 78% awarded as loans/jobs. Work study available nights, weekends, and for part-time students.

FINANCIAL AID PROCEDURES

Transfers: Priority date 3/1; no deadline. Applicants notified on a rolling basis starting 4/1; must reply within 4 week(s) of notification.

CONTACT

Rachel Durbin, Director of Financial Aid
3181 SW Sam Jackson Park Road, Portland, OR 97239-3098
(503) 494-7800

Oregon Institute of Technology

Klamath Falls, Oregon
www.oit.edu
Federal Code: 003211

4-year public career college in small city.
Enrollment: 3,446 undergrads.

BASIC COSTS (2016-2017)

Tuition and fees: $9,103; out-of-state residents $25,570.
Room and board: $8,704.
Additional info: Tuition/fee waivers available for minority students.

FINANCIAL AID PICTURE

Students with need: Need-based aid available for full-time and part-time students. Work study available weekends and for part-time students.
Students without need: No-need awards available for academics, athletics, leadership.

FINANCIAL AID PROCEDURES

Forms required: FAFSA.
Dates and Deadlines: Priority date 2/1; no closing date. Applicants notified on a rolling basis starting 4/1.
Transfers: Closing date 2/1.

CONTACT

Tracey Lehman, Director of Financial Aid
3201 Campus Drive, Klamath Falls, OR 97601
(541) 885-1280

Oregon State University

Corvallis, Oregon
www.oregonstate.edu
Federal Code: 003210

4-year public university in small city.
Enrollment: 24,350 undergrads, 24% part-time. 3,340 full-time freshmen.
Selectivity: Admits over 75% of applicants.

BASIC COSTS (2016-2017)

Tuition and fees: $10,366; out-of-state residents $28,846.
Per-credit charge: $187; out-of-state residents $582.
Room and board: $12,153.

FINANCIAL AID PICTURE (2015-2016)

Students with need: Out of 2,872 full-time freshmen who applied for aid, 1,953 were judged to have need. Of these, 1,937 received aid, and 187 had their full need met. Average financial aid package met 65% of need; average scholarship/grant was $7,563; average loan was $3,583. For part-time students, average financial aid package was $11,476.
Students without need: 677 full-time freshmen who did not demonstrate need for aid received scholarships/grants; average award was $4,203. No-need awards available for academics, alumni affiliation, athletics, job skills, leadership, minority status, ROTC, state/district residency.
Scholarships offered: 49 full-time freshmen received athletic scholarships; average amount $24,909.

FINANCIAL AID PROCEDURES

Forms required: FAFSA.
Dates and Deadlines: Priority date 2/28; no closing date. Applicants notified on a rolling basis starting 4/1; must reply within 4 week(s) of notification.

CONTACT

Doug Severs, Director of Financial Aid & Scholarships
104 Kerr Administration Building, Corvallis, OR 97331-2130
(541) 731-2241

Pacific Northwest College of Art

Portland, Oregon
www.pnca.edu
Federal Code: 003207

4-year private visual arts college in very large city.
Enrollment: 399 undergrads, 10% part-time. 79 full-time freshmen.
Selectivity: Admits over 75% of applicants.

BASIC COSTS (2016-2017)

Tuition and fees: $34,550.
Per-credit charge: $1,368.
Room only: $9,504.

FINANCIAL AID PICTURE

Students with need: Need-based aid available for full-time and part-time students. Work study available nights, weekends, and for part-time students.
Students without need: No-need awards available for academics, art.
Scholarships offered: Leta Kennedy Student Scholarships; $10,000; based on artistic merit. Dorothy Lemelson Scholarship; cost of attendance; based on artistic and academic merit; renewable up to 4 years; 1 awarded. Other renewable scholarships available.

FINANCIAL AID PROCEDURES

Forms required: FAFSA.

Dates and Deadlines: Priority date 3/1; no closing date. Applicants notified on a rolling basis starting 4/1; must reply by 5/1 or within 4 week(s) of notification.

Transfers: No deadline. Applicants notified on a rolling basis starting 4/1; must reply by 5/1 or within 4 week(s) of notification.

CONTACT

Heidi Locke, Director of Financial Aid

511 NW Broadway, Portland, OR 97209.

(503) 821-8971

Pacific University

Forest Grove, Oregon

www.pacificu.edu   Federal Code: 003212

4-year private university in large town, affiliated with the United Church of Christ.

Enrollment: 1,848 undergrads, 2% part-time. 431 full-time freshmen.

Selectivity: Admits over 75% of applicants.

BASIC COSTS (2016-2017)

Tuition and fees: $41,054.

Per-credit charge: $1,672.

Room and board: $11,822.

FINANCIAL AID PICTURE (2016-2017)

Students with need: Out of 411 full-time freshmen who applied for aid, 372 were judged to have need. Of these, 372 received aid, and 65 had their full need met. Average financial aid package met 76% of need; average scholarship/grant was $10,695; average loan was $3,748. For part-time students, average financial aid package was $11,298.

Students without need: 56 full-time freshmen who did not demonstrate need for aid received scholarships/grants; average award was $20,244. No-need awards available for academics, alumni affiliation, art, music/drama.

Scholarships offered: Founder's Scholarship; $15,000. Honors Scholarship; $12,000. Presidential Scholarship; $10,000. Trustee Scholarship; $8,500. University Scholarship; $7,500. Pacific Opportunity Award; $5,000. Pacesetters Scholarship; $1,000-$3,000. Music and Forensics Talent Awards; $1,000-$3,000. Number of awards vary.

FINANCIAL AID PROCEDURES

Forms required: FAFSA.

Dates and Deadlines: Priority date 3/1; no closing date. Applicants notified on a rolling basis starting 3/1.

CONTACT

Michael Johnson, Director of Financial Aid

2043 College Way, Forest Grove, OR 97116-1797

(503) 352-2222

Pioneer Pacific College

Wilsonville, Oregon

www.pioneerpacific.edu   Federal Code: 016520

2-year for-profit career college in large town.

Enrollment: 1,195 undergrads.

Selectivity: Open admission; but selective for some programs.

BASIC COSTS (2016-2017)

Additional info: Diploma programs range from $15,925 to $28,860; Associate programs range from $27,150 to $30,150; Bachelor's degrees range from $54,150 to $54,750.

FINANCIAL AID PICTURE

Students with need: Need-based aid available for full-time and part-time students.

Students without need: This college awards aid only to students with need.

Scholarships offered: High school scholarship program and community scholarship program available.

FINANCIAL AID PROCEDURES

Forms required: FAFSA.

Dates and Deadlines: Applicants notified on a rolling basis starting 2/27.

CONTACT

Mark Johnson, Executive Director of Financial Aid

27501 Southwest Parkway Avenue, Wilsonville, OR 97070

(503) 654-8000

Portland Community College

Portland, Oregon

www.pcc.edu   Federal Code: 003213

2-year public community college in very large city.

Enrollment: 27,946 undergrads.

Selectivity: Open admission; but selective for some programs.

BASIC COSTS (2016-2017)

Tuition and fees: $4,737; out-of-state residents $10,542.

Per-credit charge: $97; out-of-state residents $226.

FINANCIAL AID PICTURE

Students with need: Need-based aid available for full-time and part-time students. Work study available nights, weekends, and for part-time students.

Students without need: This college awards aid only to students with need.

FINANCIAL AID PROCEDURES

Forms required: FAFSA.

Dates and Deadlines: Priority date 3/1; no closing date. Applicants notified on a rolling basis starting 6/1; must reply within 3 week(s) of notification.

CONTACT

Bert Logan, Director of Financial Aid

12000 SW 49th Avenue, Portland, OR 97219-7132

(503) 722-4934

Portland State University

Portland, Oregon

www.pdx.edu   Federal Code: 003216

4-year public university in very large city.

Enrollment: 19,119 undergrads, 28% part-time. 1,599 full-time freshmen.

Selectivity: Admits over 75% of applicants.

BASIC COSTS (2016-2017)

Tuition and fees: $8,337; out-of-state residents $24,852.

Per-credit charge: $156; out-of-state residents $523.

Room and board: $10,353.

FINANCIAL AID PICTURE (2015-2016)

Students with need: Out of 1,358 full-time freshmen who applied for aid, 1,054 were judged to have need. Of these, 1,018 received aid, and 85 had their full need met. Average financial aid package met 59% of need; average scholarship/grant was $6,195; average loan was $3,120. For part-time students, average financial aid package was $5,358.

Students without need: 7 full-time freshmen who did not demonstrate need for aid received scholarships/grants; average award was $2,090. No-need awards available for academics, alumni affiliation, art, athletics, leadership, minority status, music/drama, state/district residency.

FINANCIAL AID PROCEDURES

Forms required: FAFSA.

Dates and Deadlines: Priority date 2/28; no closing date. Applicants notified on a rolling basis starting 3/15.
Transfers: No deadline. Applicants notified on a rolling basis.

CONTACT
G Johnson, Director of Financial Aid and Scholarships
PO Box 751-ADM, Portland, OR 97207-0751
(800) 547-8887

Reed College
Portland, Oregon   Federal Code: 003217
www.reed.edu   CSS Code: 4654

4-year private liberal arts college in very large city.
Enrollment: 1,376 undergrads. 354 full-time freshmen.
Selectivity: Admits less than 50% of applicants.

BASIC COSTS (2016-2017)
Tuition and fees: $52,150.
Room and board: $13,150.

FINANCIAL AID PICTURE (2016-2017)
Students with need: Out of 228 full-time freshmen who applied for aid, 184 were judged to have need. Of these, 177 received aid, and 158 had their full need met. Average financial aid package met 100% of need; average scholarship/grant was $37,665; average loan was $2,215.
Students without need: This college awards aid only to students with need.
Additional info: College meets demonstrated need of continuing students who have attended Reed minimum of 2 semesters, who file financial aid applications on time, and who maintain satisfactory academic progress. Institutional aid consideration is for total of 8 semesters.

FINANCIAL AID PROCEDURES
Forms required: FAFSA, CSS PROFILE.
Dates and Deadlines: Priority date 2/1; closing date 2/1. Applicants notified by 4/1; must reply by 5/1.
Transfers: Closing date 3/1. Applicants notified by 5/15; must reply by 6/1 or within 2 week(s) of notification.

CONTACT
Milyon Trulove, Vice President of Admission and Financial Aid
3203 SE Woodstock Boulevard, Portland, OR 97202-8199
(800) 547-4750

Rogue Community College
Grants Pass, Oregon
www.roguecc.edu   Federal Code: 010071

2-year public community college in large town.
Enrollment: 4,097 undergrads, 58% part-time. 406 full-time freshmen.
Selectivity: Open admission; but selective for some programs.

BASIC COSTS (2016-2017)
Tuition and fees: $5,100; out-of-state residents $6,090.
Per-credit charge: $99; out-of-state residents $121.
Additional info: Tuition/fee waivers available for unemployed or children of unemployed.

FINANCIAL AID PICTURE
Students with need: Need-based aid available for full-time and part-time students.
Students without need: No-need awards available for academics.

FINANCIAL AID PROCEDURES
Forms required: FAFSA, institutional form.

Dates and Deadlines: Priority date 5/1; no closing date. Applicants notified on a rolling basis; must reply within 2 week(s) of notification.

CONTACT
Anna Manley, Director of Financial Aid
3345 Redwood Highway, Grants Pass, OR 97527-9291
(541) 956-7501 ext. 1

Southern Oregon University
Ashland, Oregon
www.sou.edu   Federal Code: 003219

4-year public university and liberal arts college in large town.
Enrollment: 4,064 undergrads, 15% part-time. 662 full-time freshmen.
Selectivity: Admits over 75% of applicants.

BASIC COSTS (2016-2017)
Tuition and fees: $8,523; out-of-state residents $23,170.
Per-credit charge: $151; out-of-state residents $477.
Room and board: $12,540.
Additional info: Tuition/fee waivers available for minority students.

FINANCIAL AID PICTURE (2016-2017)
Students with need: 48% of average financial aid package awarded as scholarships/grants, 52% awarded as loans/jobs. Need-based aid available for part-time students. Work study available nights, weekends, and for part-time students.
Students without need: No-need awards available for academics, athletics.

FINANCIAL AID PROCEDURES
Forms required: FAFSA.
Dates and Deadlines: Priority date 3/1; no closing date. Applicants notified on a rolling basis starting 3/2; must reply within 4 week(s) of notification.

CONTACT
Donna Hartmann-Turner, Director of Financial Aid
1250 Siskiyou Boulevard, Ashland, OR 97520-5032
(541) 552-6600

Southwestern Oregon Community College
Coos Bay, Oregon
www.socc.edu   Federal Code: 003220

2-year public culinary school and community college in large town.
Enrollment: 2,239 undergrads.
Selectivity: Open admission; but selective for some programs.

BASIC COSTS (2016-2017)
Tuition and fees: $5,850; out-of-state residents $5,850.
Per-credit charge: $91.
Room and board: $7,769.
Additional info: Tuition/fee waivers available for adults, unemployed or children of unemployed.

FINANCIAL AID PICTURE
Students with need: Need-based aid available for full-time and part-time students.
Students without need: No-need awards available for art, athletics, leadership, music/drama.

FINANCIAL AID PROCEDURES
Forms required: FAFSA.
Dates and Deadlines: Closing date 3/1. Applicants notified on a rolling basis starting 5/1; must reply within 3 week(s) of notification.

CONTACT

Avena Singh, Director of Financial Aid

1988 Newmark Avenue, Coos Bay, OR 97420-2956

(541) 888-7337

Treasure Valley Community College

Ontario, Oregon

www.tvcc.cc   Federal Code: 003221

2-year public community college in large town.

Enrollment: 1,838 undergrads.

Selectivity: Open admission; but selective for some programs.

BASIC COSTS (2016-2017)

Tuition and fees: $5,400; out-of-state residents $5,850.

Room and board: $7,346.

FINANCIAL AID PICTURE

Students with need: Need-based aid available for full-time and part-time students.

Students without need: No-need awards available for academics, athletics, leadership, music/drama.

FINANCIAL AID PROCEDURES

Forms required: FAFSA.

Dates and Deadlines: Applicants notified on a rolling basis starting 5/1.

Transfers: No deadline. Applicants notified on a rolling basis.

CONTACT

Diahann Derrick, Financial Aid Director

650 College Boulevard, Ontario, OR 97914-3423

(541) 881-5833

Umpqua Community College

Roseburg, Oregon

www.umpqua.edu   Federal Code: 003222

2-year public community college in large town.

Enrollment: 1,142 undergrads, 68% part-time. 24 full-time freshmen.

Selectivity: Open admission; but selective for some programs.

BASIC COSTS (2016-2017)

Tuition and fees: $4,748; out-of-state residents $8,013.

Per-credit charge: $105; out-of-state residents $221.

FINANCIAL AID PICTURE (2015-2016)

Students with need: Out of 24 full-time freshmen who applied for aid, 19 were judged to have need. Of these, 19 received aid, and 11 had their full need met. Average financial aid package met 34% of need; average scholarship/grant was $132,494. For part-time students, average financial aid package was $1,829,596.

Students without need: No-need awards available for academics, athletics.

FINANCIAL AID PROCEDURES

Forms required: FAFSA, institutional form.

Dates and Deadlines: Priority date 3/10; no closing date. Applicants notified on a rolling basis starting 2/9; must reply within 2 week(s) of notification.

CONTACT

Michelle Bergmann, Director of Financial Aid

1140 Umpqua College Road, Roseburg, OR 97470-0226

(541) 440-4602

University of Oregon

Eugene, Oregon

www.uoregon.edu   Federal Code: 003223

4-year public university in small city.

Enrollment: 19,773 undergrads, 7% part-time. 4,047 full-time freshmen.

Selectivity: Admits over 75% of applicants.

BASIC COSTS (2016-2017)

Tuition and fees: $10,762; out-of-state residents $33,442.

Per-credit charge: $198; out-of-state residents $702.

Room and board: $12,210.

FINANCIAL AID PICTURE (2015-2016)

Students with need: Out of 3,037 full-time freshmen who applied for aid, 2,059 were judged to have need. Of these, 1,926 received aid, and 140 had their full need met. Average financial aid package met 62% of need; average scholarship/grant was $9,185; average loan was $4,045. For part-time students, average financial aid package was $6,641.

Students without need: 698 full-time freshmen who did not demonstrate need for aid received scholarships/grants; average award was $6,133. No-need awards available for academics, athletics, leadership, minority status, music/drama, ROTC, state/district residency.

Scholarships offered: *Merit:* Stamps Leadership Scholarship: tuition, room, and board for 4 years of undergraduate study and up to $12,000 in enrichment funds to pursue study abroad, unpaid internships, or other experiences; total over four years can add up to approximately $125,000; awarded competitively to outstanding incoming freshmen from Oregon; 5 per year awarded. Summit Scholarships: awards Oregon top scholars $6,000 per year for 4 years; out-of-state top scholars receive $9,000 per year for 4 years. Apex Scholarship: Oregon residents $3,000 per year for 4 years; out-of-state students receive $4,000 per year for 4 years. *Athletic:* 70 full-time freshmen received athletic scholarships; average amount $28,427.

FINANCIAL AID PROCEDURES

Forms required: FAFSA.

Dates and Deadlines: Priority date 3/1; no closing date. Applicants notified on a rolling basis starting 4/15; must reply within 4 week(s) of notification.

CONTACT

Jim Brooks, Asst VP/Director Financial Aid

1217 University of Oregon, Eugene, OR 97403-1217

(541) 346-3221

University of Portland

Portland, Oregon

www.up.edu   Federal Code: 003224

4-year private university in large city, affiliated with the Roman Catholic Church.

Enrollment: 3,762 undergrads, 1% part-time. 961 full-time freshmen.

Selectivity: Admits 50 to 75% of applicants.

BASIC COSTS (2016-2017)

Tuition and fees: $42,014.

Per-credit charge: $1,310.

Room and board: $12,394.

FINANCIAL AID PICTURE (2016-2017)

Students with need: Out of 830 full-time freshmen who applied for aid, 631 were judged to have need. Of these, 630 received aid, and 56 had their full need met. Average financial aid package met 72% of need; average scholarship/grant was $24,717; average loan was $3,640. For part-time students, average financial aid package was $13,899.

Students without need: 302 full-time freshmen who did not demonstrate need for aid received scholarships/grants; average award was $18,662. No-need awards available for academics, athletics, leadership, minority status, music/drama, ROTC.

Scholarships offered: *Merit:* President's Scholarship; up to $10,000; based on academic excellence, school and community involvement, and other factors. Holy Cross Scholarship; up to $6,000; based on academic excellence, school and community involvement, and other factors. Arthur A. Schulte Scholarship; up to $6,000. *Athletic:* 12 full-time freshmen received athletic scholarships; average amount $31,979.

FINANCIAL AID PROCEDURES
Forms required: FAFSA.

Dates and Deadlines: Applicants notified on a rolling basis starting 3/1; must reply by 5/1.

Transfers: No deadline. Applicants notified on a rolling basis; must reply within 4 week(s) of notification.

CONTACT
Janet Turner, Director of Financial Aid
5000 North Willamette Boulevard, Portland, OR 97203-5798
(503) 943-7311

Warner Pacific College
Portland, Oregon
www.warnerpacific.edu   Federal Code: 003225

4-year private liberal arts college in very large city, affiliated with the Church of God.
Enrollment: 478 undergrads, 4% part-time. 91 full-time freshmen.

BASIC COSTS (2016-2017)
Tuition and fees: $22,710.
Room and board: $8,900.

FINANCIAL AID PICTURE (2016-2017)
Students with need: Out of 85 full-time freshmen who applied for aid, 81 were judged to have need. Of these, 81 received aid, and 14 had their full need met. Average financial aid package met 67% of need; average scholarship/grant was $7,239; average loan was $3,449. For part-time students, average financial aid package was $9,210.

Students without need: 16 full-time freshmen who did not demonstrate need for aid received scholarships/grants; average award was $8,594. No-need awards available for academics, athletics, music/drama.

Scholarships offered: 38 full-time freshmen received athletic scholarships; average amount $4,970.

FINANCIAL AID PROCEDURES
Forms required: FAFSA.

Dates and Deadlines: Priority date 3/1; no closing date. Applicants notified on a rolling basis starting 12/1; must reply within 2 week(s) of notification.

Transfers: No deadline. Applicants notified on a rolling basis starting 12/1; must reply within 2 week(s) of notification.

CONTACT
Cindy Pollard, Director of Student Financial Services and Financial Aid
2219 SE 68th Avenue, Portland, OR 97215-4026
(503) 517-1091

Western Oregon University
Monmouth, Oregon
www.wou.edu   Federal Code: 003209

4-year public liberal arts and teachers college in small town.
Enrollment: 4,776 undergrads, 15% part-time. 743 full-time freshmen.
Selectivity: Admits over 75% of applicants.

BASIC COSTS (2016-2017)
Tuition and fees: $8,700; out-of-state residents $23,445.
Per-credit charge: $160; out-of-state residents $483.

Room and board: $9,798.

Additional info: Full participant in the Western Undergraduate Exchange (WUE) WUE Tuition is $10,506. Resident students can also select a Tuition Promise base tuition rate that is not subject to annual adjustments for 4 years. Tuition at time of enrollment locked for 4 years; tuition/fee waivers available for minority students.

FINANCIAL AID PICTURE (2015-2016)
Students with need: Out of 724 full-time freshmen who applied for aid, 569 were judged to have need. Of these, 569 received aid, and 54 had their full need met. Average financial aid package met 57% of need; average scholarship/grant was $7,060; average loan was $3,132. For part-time students, average financial aid package was $7,118.

Students without need: 148 full-time freshmen who did not demonstrate need for aid received scholarships/grants; average award was $505. No-need awards available for academics, alumni affiliation, art, athletics, leadership, minority status, music/drama.

Scholarships offered: 21 full-time freshmen received athletic scholarships; average amount $2,022.

FINANCIAL AID PROCEDURES
Forms required: FAFSA.

Dates and Deadlines: Priority date 2/1; no closing date. Applicants notified on a rolling basis starting 3/25; must reply within 3 week(s) of notification.

CONTACT
Kella Helyer, Director of Financial Aid
345 North Monmouth Avenue, Monmouth, OR 97361
(503) 838-8475

Willamette University
Salem, Oregon
www.willamette.edu   Federal Code: 003227

4-year private university and liberal arts college in small city, affiliated with the United Methodist Church.
Enrollment: 1,867 undergrads, 1% part-time. 473 full-time freshmen.
Selectivity: Admits over 75% of applicants.

BASIC COSTS (2017-2018)
Tuition and fees: $48,164.
Per-credit charge: $1,495.
Room and board: $11,830.

FINANCIAL AID PICTURE (2016-2017)
Students with need: Out of 419 full-time freshmen who applied for aid, 329 were judged to have need. Of these, 329 received aid, and 85 had their full need met. Average financial aid package met 82% of need; average scholarship/grant was $31,229; average loan was $3,497. For part-time students, average financial aid package was $16,653.

Students without need: 137 full-time freshmen who did not demonstrate need for aid received scholarships/grants; average award was $22,438. No-need awards available for academics, alumni affiliation, leadership, minority status, music/drama, religious affiliation.

Scholarships offered: Academic merit awards; $5,000-$15,000; based on superior academic achievement and promise. Music, forensics, theater scholarships; average $3,000-$5,000; based on talent. Mark O. Hatfield Scholarship; full tuition; based on excellent academic record and demonstrated commitment to service leadership.

FINANCIAL AID PROCEDURES
Forms required: FAFSA.

Dates and Deadlines: Priority date 2/1; no closing date. Applicants notified on a rolling basis starting 4/1; must reply by 5/1 or within 2 week(s) of notification.

Transfers: Applicants notified on a rolling basis starting 4/1; must reply by 5/1 or within 2 week(s) of notification.

CONTACT

Patricia Hoban, Director of Financial Aid

900 State Street, Salem, OR 97301-3922

(503) 370-6273

Pennsylvania

Albright College
Reading, Pennsylvania
www.albright.edu   Federal Code: 003229

4-year private liberal arts college in small city, affiliated with the United Methodist Church.

Enrollment: 2,291 undergrads. 596 full-time freshmen.

Selectivity: Admits 50 to 75% of applicants.

BASIC COSTS (2016-2017)
Tuition and fees: $41,544.
Per-credit charge: $1,270.
Room and board: $11,188.

FINANCIAL AID PICTURE (2016-2017)
Students with need: Out of 574 full-time freshmen who applied for aid, 561 were judged to have need. Of these, 560 received aid, and 58 had their full need met. Average financial aid package met 85% of need; average scholarship/grant was $34,162; average loan was $4,955. For part-time students, average financial aid package was $12.

Students without need: 37 full-time freshmen who did not demonstrate need for aid received scholarships/grants; average award was $23,572. No-need awards available for academics, art, religious affiliation.

Scholarships offered: Academic scholarships range from $5,000 to full tuition per year. All scholarships and awards are renewable, typically contingent upon achieving a specified grade point average and/or service commitment.

Additional info: If student's financial aid and admission application is complete by 2/1, college will meet 100% of the family's institutionally determined need.

FINANCIAL AID PROCEDURES
Forms required: FAFSA. The CSS Profile can be optionally completed in the fall prior to the start of student's college experience for early awarding.

Dates and Deadlines: Priority date 2/1; closing date 2/1. Applicants notified on a rolling basis starting 11/1; must reply by 5/1 or within 2 week(s) of notification.

Transfers: Priority date 6/1; no deadline. Applicants notified on a rolling basis starting 2/15.

CONTACT
Chris Hanlon, Director of Financial Aid
North 13th and Bern Streets, Reading, PA 19612-5234
(800) 252-1856

Allegheny College
Meadville, Pennsylvania
www.allegheny.edu   Federal Code: 003230

4-year private liberal arts college in large town, affiliated with the United Methodist Church.

Enrollment: 1,884 undergrads, 1% part-time. 551 full-time freshmen.

Selectivity: Admits 50 to 75% of applicants.

BASIC COSTS (2017-2018)
Tuition and fees: $45,970.
Per-credit charge: $1,895.

Room and board: $11,650.

FINANCIAL AID PICTURE (2016-2017)
Students with need: Out of 496 full-time freshmen who applied for aid, 446 were judged to have need. Of these, 446 received aid, and 122 had their full need met. Average financial aid package met 91% of need; average scholarship/grant was $35,455; average loan was $3,750. For part-time students, average financial aid package was $19,171.

Students without need: 103 full-time freshmen who did not demonstrate need for aid received scholarships/grants; average award was $22,434. No-need awards available for academics, leadership, minority status, state/district residency.

Scholarships offered: Trustee Scholarships: up to $26,000 per year available for entering freshman and $24,000 for entering transfer students.

Additional info: Non need-based financial aid also determined by extra-curricular and co-curricular involvement and special achievement or activities. Daytime work-study programs available.

FINANCIAL AID PROCEDURES
Forms required: FAFSA.

Dates and Deadlines: Priority date 2/15; no closing date. Applicants notified on a rolling basis starting 3/1; must reply by 5/1 or within 4 week(s) of notification.

Transfers: Priority date 6/1; no deadline. Applicants notified on a rolling basis; must reply within 3 week(s) of notification.

CONTACT
Jonathan Boleratz, Director of Financial Aid
Box 5, 520 North Main Street, Meadville, PA 16335
(800) 835-7780

Alvernia University
Reading, Pennsylvania
www.alvernia.edu   Federal Code: 003233

4-year private university and liberal arts college in small city, affiliated with the Roman Catholic Church.

Enrollment: 2,225 undergrads, 23% part-time. 345 full-time freshmen.

Selectivity: Admits 50 to 75% of applicants.

BASIC COSTS (2017-2018)
Tuition and fees: $33,640.
Per-credit charge: $900.
Room and board: $11,690.
Additional info: Tuition/fee waivers available for minority students.

FINANCIAL AID PICTURE (2016-2017)
Students with need: Out of 333 full-time freshmen who applied for aid, 294 were judged to have need. Of these, 294 received aid, and 41 had their full need met. Average financial aid package met 68% of need; average scholarship/grant was $18,943; average loan was $3,211. For part-time students, average financial aid package was $6,496.

Students without need: 53 full-time freshmen who did not demonstrate need for aid received scholarships/grants; average award was $13,488. No-need awards available for academics, ROTC.

Scholarships offered: Presidential Scholarship: $14,000; minimum 1130 SAT (or 25 ACT) and minimum 3.5 GPA. Trustee's Scholarship: $12,000; minimum 1050 SAT (or 23 ACT) and minimum 3.2 GPA. Veronica Founder's Scholarship: $10,000; minimum 980 SAT (or 21 ACT) and 3.0 GPA.

FINANCIAL AID PROCEDURES
Forms required: FAFSA, state aid form.

Dates and Deadlines: Priority date 5/1; no closing date. Applicants notified on a rolling basis starting 11/20; must reply by 5/1.

Transfers: Priority date 5/8; no deadline. Applicants notified on a rolling basis starting 2/20; must reply within 2 week(s) of notification.

CONTACT
Christine Saadi, Associate Director of Financial Aid
400 St. Bernardine Street, Reading, PA 19607-1799
(610) 796-8356

Antonelli Institute of Art and Photography
Erdenheim, Pennsylvania
www.antonelli.edu   Federal Code: 007430

2-year for-profit visual arts and junior college in large town.
Enrollment: 189 undergrads.

BASIC COSTS (2016-2017)
Tuition and fees: $20,920.
Additional info: Tuition quoted is for the photography degree program; annual tuition for the graphic design degree program is $18,820. Estimated kit and supply costs vary depending on degree program. All costs are subject to change.

FINANCIAL AID PICTURE
Students with need: Need-based aid available for full-time and part-time students. Work study available nights.
Students without need: This college awards aid only to students with need.

FINANCIAL AID PROCEDURES
Forms required: FAFSA.
Dates and Deadlines: Applicants notified on a rolling basis; must reply within 2 week(s) of notification.
Transfers: Priority date 3/15; closing date 8/1. Applicants notified on a rolling basis.

CONTACT
Eugene Awot, Director of Financial Aid
300 Montgomery Avenue, Erdenheim, PA 19038-8242
(215) 836-2222

Arcadia University
Glenside, Pennsylvania
www.arcadia.edu   Federal Code: 003235

4-year private university in large town, affiliated with the Presbyterian Church (USA).
Enrollment: 2,367 undergrads, 4% part-time. 598 full-time freshmen.
Selectivity: Admits 50 to 75% of applicants.

BASIC COSTS (2016-2017)
Tuition and fees: $40,920.
Per-credit charge: $660.
Room and board: $13,500.

FINANCIAL AID PICTURE (2015-2016)
Students with need: Out of 589 full-time freshmen who applied for aid, 518 were judged to have need. Of these, 517 received aid, and 50 had their full need met. Average financial aid package met 72% of need; average scholarship/grant was $26,166; average loan was $3,146. For part-time students, average financial aid package was $8,828.
Students without need: 113 full-time freshmen who did not demonstrate need for aid received scholarships/grants; average award was $16,858. No-need awards available for academics, alumni affiliation, art, leadership, music/drama.
Scholarships offered: Distinguished Scholarships: $18,500-$25,000; for full-time, first-year students based on grades, test scores, coursework taken, high school rank and involvement. Achievement Awards: $1,000-$14,500; for

full-time students who have demonstrated outstanding leadership, exceptional community and/or volunteer service or special talents. President's Scholarship: full tuition; based on academic excellence, outstanding leadership, and community and volunteer service. Writing Achievement Awards: offered to those who score among the highest in the applicant pool annually on SAT or ACT writing sections.

FINANCIAL AID PROCEDURES
Forms required: FAFSA, institutional form.
Dates and Deadlines: Priority date 3/1; no closing date. Applicants notified on a rolling basis starting 2/1; must reply by 5/1.
Transfers: No deadline. Applicants notified on a rolling basis starting 11/1.

CONTACT
Holly Kirkpatrick, Director of Enrollment Management and Director of Financial Aid
450 South Easton Road, Glenside, PA 19038-3295
(215) 572-2980

Art Institute of Philadelphia
Philadelphia, Pennsylvania
www.artinstitutes.edu/Philadelphia   Federal Code: 008350

4-year for-profit visual arts college in very large city.
Enrollment: 1,953 undergrads.

FINANCIAL AID PICTURE
Students with need: Need-based aid available for full-time and part-time students. Work study available nights, weekends, and for part-time students.
Additional info: Institute-sponsored scholarships available. May 1st application deadline for Pennsylvania State Grant.

FINANCIAL AID PROCEDURES
Forms required: FAFSA, institutional form.
Dates and Deadlines: Applicants notified on a rolling basis starting 3/1; must reply within 2 week(s) of notification.
Transfers: No deadline. Transfer students applying for financial aid must meet standards for satisfactory academic progress as defined by State Grant Program.

CONTACT
Fatisha Strickland, Director of Student Financial Services
1622 Chestnut Street, Philadelphia, PA 19103-5198
(215) 567-7080 ext. 6392

Art Institute of Pittsburgh
Pittsburgh, Pennsylvania
www.artinstitutes.edu/pittsburgh   Federal Code: 007470

4-year for-profit culinary school and visual arts college in large city.
Enrollment: 900 undergrads.

BASIC COSTS (2016-2017)
Tuition and fees: $23,476.
Room only: $7,956.

FINANCIAL AID PICTURE
Students with need: Need-based aid available for full-time and part-time students.

FINANCIAL AID PROCEDURES
Forms required: FAFSA, institutional form.
Dates and Deadlines: Applicants notified on a rolling basis starting 4/15.

CONTACT
Parker Charlton, Director Student Financial Services
420 Boulevard of the Allies, Pittsburgh, PA 15219-1328
(412) 291-6200

Berks Technical Institute

Wyomissing, Pennsylvania
www.berks.edu   Federal Code: 017149

2-year for-profit business and technical college in small city.
Enrollment: 1,140 undergrads.

FINANCIAL AID PICTURE

Students with need: Need-based aid available for full-time and part-time students.

Students without need: This college awards aid only to students with need.

FINANCIAL AID PROCEDURES

Forms required: FAFSA, state aid form.
Dates and Deadlines: Applicants notified on a rolling basis; must reply within 2 week(s) of notification.
Transfers: Deadline for first-time financial aid applicants is August 1. Deadline for renewal applicants is May 1.

CONTACT

Valerie Wessner, Senior Financial Aid Director
2205 Ridgewood Road, Wyomissing, PA 19610
(610) 372-1722

Bidwell Training Center

Pittsburgh, Pennsylvania
www.bidwell-training.org   Federal Code: 031015

1-year private business and health science college in large city.
Enrollment: 150 undergrads.

FINANCIAL AID PICTURE

Students with need: Need-based aid available for full-time students.
Students without need: This college awards aid only to students with need.

FINANCIAL AID PROCEDURES

Forms required: FAFSA.
Dates and Deadlines: Applicants notified on a rolling basis.

CONTACT

Ken Huselton, Senior Director of Operations
1815 Metropolitan Street, Pittsburgh, PA 15233
(412) 323-4000

Bloomsburg University of Pennsylvania

Bloomsburg, Pennsylvania
www.bloomu.edu   Federal Code: 003315

4-year public university in large town.
Enrollment: 8,734 undergrads, 6% part-time. 1,895 full-time freshmen.
Selectivity: Admits over 75% of applicants.

BASIC COSTS (2016-2017)

Tuition and fees: $10,155; out-of-state residents $21,013.
Room and board: $8,912.
Additional info: Tuition/fee waivers available for minority students.

FINANCIAL AID PICTURE (2016-2017)

Students with need: Out of 1,766 full-time freshmen who applied for aid, 1,272 were judged to have need. Of these, 1,248 received aid, and 108 had their full need met. Average financial aid package met 51% of need; average scholarship/grant was $6,358; average loan was $3,248. For part-time students, average financial aid package was $6,751.

Students without need: 58 full-time freshmen who did not demonstrate need for aid received scholarships/grants; average award was $2,603. No-need awards available for academics, art, athletics, job skills, leadership, minority status, music/drama, ROTC, state/district residency.
Scholarships offered: 62 full-time freshmen received athletic scholarships; average amount $1,958.

FINANCIAL AID PROCEDURES

Forms required: FAFSA.
Dates and Deadlines: Priority date 3/15; no closing date. Applicants notified on a rolling basis starting 4/1.
Transfers: Evaluation of transfer credits must be completed before financial aid can be finalized.

CONTACT

Amanda Kishbaugh, Interim Director of Financial Aid
104 Student Service Center, Bloomsburg, PA 17815
(570) 389-4297

Bradford School: Pittsburgh

Pittsburgh, Pennsylvania
www.bradfordpittsburgh.edu   Federal Code: 009721

2-year for-profit junior college in very large city.
Enrollment: 439 full-time undergrads.

FINANCIAL AID PICTURE

Students with need: Need-based aid available for full-time students.

FINANCIAL AID PROCEDURES

Forms required: FAFSA.

CONTACT

Director of Financial Aid
125 West Station Square Drive, Pittsburgh, PA 15219
(412) 391-6710

Brightwood Career Institute

Broomall, Pennsylvania
https://www.brightwoodcareer.edu/
                                 Federal Code: 007781

2-year for-profit career college in large town.
Enrollment: 560 undergrads.
Selectivity: Open admission.

BASIC COSTS (2016-2017)

Additional info: Tuition varies by program; $14,090-$16,841. Fees, books supplies range depending on program level and course of study. All costs are subject to change.

FINANCIAL AID PICTURE

Students with need: Need-based aid available for full-time and part-time students.

FINANCIAL AID PROCEDURES

Forms required: FAFSA.
Dates and Deadlines: Applicants notified on a rolling basis.

CONTACT

Sheena McGinley, Director of Financial Aid
1991 Sproul Road, Suite 42, Broomall, PA 19008

Bryn Athyn College
Bryn Athyn, Pennsylvania
www.brynathyn.edu

Federal Code: 003228

4-year private liberal arts college in small town, affiliated with the Christian Church.
Enrollment: 293 undergrads, 2% part-time. 71 full-time freshmen.
Selectivity: Admits less than 50% of applicants.

BASIC COSTS (2016-2017)
Tuition and fees: $19,932.
Per-credit charge: $765.
Room and board: $11,538.

FINANCIAL AID PICTURE (2016-2017)
Students with need: Out of 66 full-time freshmen who applied for aid, 60 were judged to have need. Of these, 60 received aid, and 12 had their full need met. Average financial aid package met 72% of need; average scholarship/grant was $11,620; average loan was $3,353. Need-based aid available for part-time students.
Students without need: 5 full-time freshmen who did not demonstrate need for aid received scholarships/grants; average award was $7,960. No-need awards available for academics, religious affiliation.

FINANCIAL AID PROCEDURES
Forms required: FAFSA, state aid form.
Dates and Deadlines: Applicants notified on a rolling basis starting 2/15; must reply within 3 week(s) of notification.
Transfers: No deadline. Applicants notified on a rolling basis starting 7/1; must reply within 6 week(s) of notification.

CONTACT
Brian Keister, Financial Aid Director
PO Box 462, Bryn Athyn, PA 19009-0462
(267) 502-2493

Bryn Mawr College
Bryn Mawr, Pennsylvania
www.brynmawr.edu

Federal Code: 003237
CSS Code: 2049

4-year private liberal arts college for women in very large city.
Enrollment: 1,371 undergrads, 1% part-time. 407 full-time freshmen.
Selectivity: Admits less than 50% of applicants.

BASIC COSTS (2016-2017)
Tuition and fees: $48,790.
Room and board: $15,370.

FINANCIAL AID PICTURE (2016-2017)
Students with need: Out of 288 full-time freshmen who applied for aid, 257 were judged to have need. Of these, 257 received aid, and 257 had their full need met. Average financial aid package met 100% of need; average scholarship/grant was $41,321; average loan was $3,675. For part-time students, average financial aid package was $11,643.
Students without need: This college awards aid only to students with need.

FINANCIAL AID PROCEDURES
Forms required: FAFSA, CSS PROFILE.
Dates and Deadlines: Closing date 1/15. Must reply by 5/1.
Transfers: Closing date 3/1. Must reply by 5/1.

CONTACT
Ethel Desmarais, Director of Financial Aid
101 North Merion Avenue, Bryn Mawr, PA 19010-2899
(610) 526-5245

Bucknell University
Lewisburg, Pennsylvania
www.bucknell.edu

Federal Code: 003238
CSS Code: 2050

4-year private university in small town.
Enrollment: 3,531 undergrads. 950 full-time freshmen.
Selectivity: Admits less than 50% of applicants.

BASIC COSTS (2017-2018)
Tuition and fees: $53,986.
Per-credit charge: $1,473.
Room and board: $13,150.

FINANCIAL AID PICTURE (2016-2017)
Students with need: Out of 496 full-time freshmen who applied for aid, 336 were judged to have need. Of these, 336 received aid, and 336 had their full need met. Average financial aid package met 91% of need; average scholarship/grant was $29,200; average loan was $3,500.
Students without need: 103 full-time freshmen who did not demonstrate need for aid received scholarships/grants; average award was $13,676. No-need awards available for academics, art, athletics, leadership, music/drama, ROTC.
Scholarships offered: *Merit:* Scholarships available to a limited number of students who have demonstrated exceptional achievements in academics, art and performing arts, music, and athletics. *Athletic:* 34 full-time freshmen received athletic scholarships; average amount $37,635.

FINANCIAL AID PROCEDURES
Forms required: FAFSA, CSS PROFILE.
Dates and Deadlines: Closing date 1/15. Must reply by 5/1.
Transfers: Closing date 3/15. Applicants notified by 5/1; must reply by 6/1. Aid restricted to 2-year college graduates.

CONTACT
Andrea Stauffer, Director of Financial Aid
Office of Admissions, Bucknell University, Lewisburg, PA 17837-9988
(570) 577-1331

Bucks County Community College
Newtown, Pennsylvania
www.bucks.edu

Federal Code: 003239

2-year public community college in large town.
Enrollment: 8,076 undergrads, 64% part-time. 1,085 full-time freshmen.
Selectivity: Open admission; but selective for some programs.

BASIC COSTS (2016-2017)
Tuition and fees: $5,360; out-of-district residents $9,560; out-of-state residents $13,760.
Per-credit charge: $140; out-of-district residents $280; out-of-state residents $420.

FINANCIAL AID PICTURE
Students with need: Need-based aid available for full-time and part-time students. Work study available nights, weekends, and for part-time students.
Students without need: No-need awards available for academics, art, music/drama.
Additional info: Files are processed in order of receipt and completion date.

FINANCIAL AID PROCEDURES
Forms required: FAFSA.
Dates and Deadlines: Closing date 5/1. Applicants notified on a rolling basis starting 6/1; must reply within 2 week(s) of notification.
Transfers: Applicants notified on a rolling basis starting 6/1; must reply within 2 week(s) of notification.

CONTACT
Donna Wilkoski, Director of Financial Aid
275 Swamp Road, Newtown, PA 18940
(215) 968-8200

Butler County Community College
Butler, Pennsylvania
www.bc3.edu   Federal Code: 003240

2-year public community college in small city.
Enrollment: 3,686 undergrads.
Selectivity: Open admission; but selective for some programs.

BASIC COSTS (2016-2017)
Tuition and fees: $4,590; out-of-district residents $7,710; out-of-state residents $10,830.
Per-credit charge: $104; out-of-district residents $208; out-of-state residents $312.

FINANCIAL AID PICTURE
Students with need: Need-based aid available for full-time and part-time students.
Students without need: No-need awards available for academics, state/district residency.

FINANCIAL AID PROCEDURES
Forms required: FAFSA.
Dates and Deadlines: Priority date 4/15; no closing date. Applicants notified on a rolling basis starting 5/1; must reply within 2 week(s) of notification.

CONTACT
Julianne Louttit, Director of Financial Aid
PO Box 1203, Butler, PA 16003-1203
(724) 287-8711 ext. 8329

Cabrini University
Radnor, Pennsylvania
www.cabrini.edu   Federal Code: 003241

4-year private liberal arts college in large town, affiliated with the Roman Catholic Church.
Enrollment: 1,475 undergrads, 6% part-time. 399 full-time freshmen.
Selectivity: Admits 50 to 75% of applicants.

BASIC COSTS (2017-2018)
Tuition and fees: $31,350.
Per-credit charge: $550.
Room and board: $12,340.

FINANCIAL AID PICTURE (2015-2016)
Students with need: Out of 383 full-time freshmen who applied for aid, 335 were judged to have need. Of these, 335 received aid, and 70 had their full need met. For part-time students, average financial aid package was $7,056.
Students without need: 59 full-time freshmen who did not demonstrate need for aid received scholarships/grants; average award was $9,892. No-need awards available for academics, alumni affiliation, religious affiliation, ROTC, state/district residency.

FINANCIAL AID PROCEDURES
Forms required: FAFSA.
Dates and Deadlines: Priority date 2/15; no closing date. Applicants notified on a rolling basis starting 3/1; must reply by 5/1.
Transfers: Achievement scholarships available.

CONTACT
Betsy Gingerich, Director of Financial Aid
610 King of Prussia Road, Radnor, PA 19087-3698
(610) 902-8420

Cairn University
Langhorne, Pennsylvania
www.cairn.edu   Federal Code: 003351

4-year private university in small town, affiliated with the Christian Church.
Enrollment: 729 undergrads, 4% part-time. 145 full-time freshmen.
Selectivity: Admits over 75% of applicants.

BASIC COSTS (2017-2018)
Tuition and fees: $26,493.
Per-credit charge: $777.
Room and board: $9,803.

FINANCIAL AID PICTURE (2016-2017)
Students with need: Out of 133 full-time freshmen who applied for aid, 123 were judged to have need. Of these, 123 received aid, and 20 had their full need met. Average financial aid package met 80% of need; average scholarship/grant was $18,778; average loan was $4,092. For part-time students, average financial aid package was $5,630.
Students without need: 22 full-time freshmen who did not demonstrate need for aid received scholarships/grants; average award was $13,011. No-need awards available for academics, leadership, music/drama.
Scholarships offered: Cairn U Merit Scholarship based on high school GPA and SAT scores.

FINANCIAL AID PROCEDURES
Forms required: FAFSA.
Dates and Deadlines: Priority date 3/1; no closing date. Applicants notified on a rolling basis starting 2/1; must reply within 2 week(s) of notification.
Transfers: No deadline. Applicants notified on a rolling basis.

CONTACT
Stephen Cassel, Director of Financial Aid
200 Manor Avenue, Langhorne, PA 19047-2990
(215) 702-4246

California University of Pennsylvania
California, Pennsylvania
www.calu.edu   Federal Code: 003316

4-year public university in small town.
Enrollment: 5,426 undergrads, 15% part-time. 916 full-time freshmen.
Selectivity: Admits over 75% of applicants.

BASIC COSTS (2016-2017)
Tuition and fees: $10,339; out-of-state residents $13,959.
Room and board: $11,038.
Additional info: Tuition/fee waivers available for adults, minority students.

FINANCIAL AID PICTURE (2015-2016)
Students with need: Out of 862 full-time freshmen who applied for aid, 714 were judged to have need. Of these, 714 received aid, and 61 had their full need met. Average financial aid package met 52% of need; average scholarship/grant was $6,565; average loan was $3,186. For part-time students, average financial aid package was $5,924.
Students without need: 26 full-time freshmen who did not demonstrate need for aid received scholarships/grants; average award was $2,923. No-need awards available for academics, athletics, leadership, minority status, music/drama, state/district residency.
Scholarships offered: 15 full-time freshmen received athletic scholarships; average amount $10,385.

FINANCIAL AID PROCEDURES
Forms required: FAFSA.
Dates and Deadlines: Priority date 3/1; no closing date. Applicants notified on a rolling basis starting 4/1.

CONTACT
Jill Fernandes, Director of Financial Aid
250 University Avenue, California, PA 15419-1394
(724) 938-4415

Cambria-Rowe Business College
Johnstown, Pennsylvania
www.crbc.net

2-year for-profit business and career college in small city.
Enrollment: 136 undergrads.
Selectivity: Open admission.

FINANCIAL AID PICTURE
Students with need: Need-based aid available for full-time and part-time students.
Students without need: No-need awards available for academics, leadership.
Scholarships offered: Presidential Grant (3 awarded) 50% tuition; FBLA Scholarship (2 awarded) $3,000.

FINANCIAL AID PROCEDURES
Forms required: FAFSA, state aid form.
Dates and Deadlines: Applicants notified on a rolling basis.
Transfers: Closing date 5/1.

CONTACT
Linda Wess, Director of Financial Aid Services
221 Central Avenue, Johnstown, PA 15902

Cambria-Rowe Business College: Indiana
Indiana, Pennsylvania
www.crbc.net   Federal Code: 004889

2-year for-profit business and career college in small town.
Enrollment: 105 undergrads.

FINANCIAL AID PICTURE
Students with need: Need-based aid available for full-time and part-time students.
Students without need: No-need awards available for academics, leadership.

FINANCIAL AID PROCEDURES
Forms required: FAFSA, state aid form.
Dates and Deadlines: Applicants notified on a rolling basis.
Transfers: Closing date 5/1.

CONTACT
Linda Wess, Director of Financial Aid Services
422 South 13th Street, Indiana, PA 15701
(814) 536-5168

Career Training Academy
New Kensington, Pennsylvania
www.careerta.edu   Federal Code: 026095

2-year for-profit career college in small town.
Enrollment: 171 undergrads.
Selectivity: Open admission; but selective for some programs.

FINANCIAL AID PICTURE
Students with need: Need-based aid available for full-time students.
Students without need: This college awards aid only to students with need.
Additional info: Work study available after class day.

FINANCIAL AID PROCEDURES
Forms required: FAFSA, institutional form.

CONTACT
Amber Tate, Director of Financial Aid
950 Fifth Avenue, New Kensington, PA 15068

Career Training Academy: Monroeville
Monroeville, Pennsylvania
www.careerta.edu   Federal Code: 026095

2-year for-profit branch campus college in small city.
Enrollment: 115 undergrads.
Selectivity: Open admission; but selective for some programs.

FINANCIAL AID PICTURE
Students with need: Need-based aid available for full-time and part-time students.
Students without need: This college awards aid only to students with need.

FINANCIAL AID PROCEDURES
Forms required: FAFSA, state aid form, institutional form.

CONTACT
Amber Tate, Director of Financial Aid
4314 Old William Penn Highway #103, Monroeville, PA 15146
(724) 337-1000

Carlow University
Pittsburgh, Pennsylvania
www.carlow.edu   Federal Code: 003303

4-year private university in large city, affiliated with the Roman Catholic Church.
Enrollment: 1,393 undergrads, 22% part-time. 232 full-time freshmen.
Selectivity: Admits over 75% of applicants.

BASIC COSTS (2016-2017)
Tuition and fees: $27,764.
Per-credit charge: $863.
Room and board: $10,784.

FINANCIAL AID PICTURE (2015-2016)
Students with need: Out of 225 full-time freshmen who applied for aid, 213 were judged to have need. Of these, 213 received aid. For part-time students, average financial aid package was $6,940.
Students without need: No-need awards available for academics, art, athletics, religious affiliation.
Scholarships offered: 40 full-time freshmen received athletic scholarships; average amount $4,875.

FINANCIAL AID PROCEDURES
Forms required: FAFSA, state aid form.
Dates and Deadlines: Priority date 3/15; closing date 5/1. Applicants notified on a rolling basis starting 12/1; must reply within 4 week(s) of notification.
Transfers: No deadline. Applicants notified on a rolling basis; must reply within 4 week(s) of notification.

CONTACT
Natalie Wilson, Director of Financial Aid
3333 Fifth Avenue, Pittsburgh, PA 15213-3165
(412) 578-6058

Carnegie Mellon University

Pittsburgh, Pennsylvania
www.cmu.edu

Federal Code: 003242
CSS Code: 2074

4-year private university in large city.
Enrollment: 6,574 undergrads, 2% part-time. 1,552 full-time freshmen.
Selectivity: Admits less than 50% of applicants.

BASIC COSTS (2017-2018)
Tuition and fees: $53,910.
Per-credit charge: $732.
Room and board: $13,784.

FINANCIAL AID PICTURE (2016-2017)
Students with need: Out of 1,028 full-time freshmen who applied for aid, 758 were judged to have need. Of these, 748 received aid, and 238 had their full need met. Average financial aid package met 86% of need; average scholarship/grant was $39,061; average loan was $2,841. For part-time students, average financial aid package was $22,847.
Students without need: 31 full-time freshmen who did not demonstrate need for aid received scholarships/grants; average award was $12,312. No-need awards available for academics, art, leadership, minority status, music/drama, state/district residency.
Additional info: Early need analysis offered; merit awards available. Financial aid applicants will receive financial aid notification shortly after notification of admission or a spot on the waiting list.

FINANCIAL AID PROCEDURES
Forms required: FAFSA, state aid form, institutional form. Required for institutional financial aid programs only. Not required if applying only for federal financial aid.
Dates and Deadlines: Priority date 2/15; closing date 4/15. Applicants notified by 4/15; must reply by 5/1.
Transfers: Students applying for spring transfer must file FAFSA by 11/1 and are notified of award 12/15 or soon after. College of Fine Arts applicants applying for fall transfer must file FAFSA by 2/15 and are notified of award by 4/15. All other applicants for fall transfer must submit FAFSA by 5/1 and are notified of award during the month of June.

CONTACT
Brian Hill, Director of Student Financial Services
5000 Forbes Avenue, Pittsburgh, PA 15213-3890
(412) 268-8186

Cedar Crest College

Allentown, Pennsylvania
www.cedarcrest.edu

Federal Code: 003243

4-year private liberal arts college for women in small city.
Enrollment: 1,397 undergrads, 37% part-time. 181 full-time freshmen.
Selectivity: Admits 50 to 75% of applicants.

BASIC COSTS (2017-2018)
Tuition and fees: $38,092.
Per-credit charge: $1,250.
Room and board: $11,208.

FINANCIAL AID PICTURE (2016-2017)
Students with need: Out of 175 full-time freshmen who applied for aid, 164 were judged to have need. Of these, 164 received aid, and 24 had their full need met. Average financial aid package met 78% of need; average scholarship/grant was $27,141; average loan was $3,303. For part-time students, average financial aid package was $9,813.
Students without need: 13 full-time freshmen who did not demonstrate need for aid received scholarships/grants; average award was $21,741. No-need awards available for academics, alumni affiliation, art, minority status.

Scholarships offered: Presidential Scholarship; up to half tuition; for freshmen with SAT scores over 1150 and in top 10% of class; renewable for four years with GPA of 3.0. 1867 Award; one-third of tuition; renewable for four years with GPA of 3.0; for freshmen with SAT of 1100 and in top 25% of class. Girl Scout Gold Awards; $1,000 per year; for recipients of the Girl Scout Gold Award. Art, Dance, and Performing Arts Scholarships; $1,500 per year; based on portfolio review, audition, and commitment to the creative process. Governor's School of Excellence Award; $1,000 per year; for graduates of Governor's Schools of Excellence. Hugh O'Brian Youth (HOBY) Awards; $1,000 per year; for freshmen who are HOBY alumnae. SAT scores exclusive of Writing portion.

FINANCIAL AID PROCEDURES
Forms required: FAFSA.
Dates and Deadlines: Priority date 5/1; no closing date. Applicants notified on a rolling basis starting 9/15; must reply within 2 week(s) of notification.
Transfers: Must reply by 5/15. Certain academic scholarships are available for transfers only, such as the Phi Theta Kappa Scholarship, Lifelong Learning Transfer Scholarship and Traditional Transfer Scholarship.

CONTACT
Valerie Kreiser, Director of Student Financial Services
100 College Drive, Allentown, PA 18104-6196
(610) 606-4653

Central Penn College

Summerdale, Pennsylvania
www.centralpenn.edu

Federal Code: 004890

4-year for-profit business and technical college in rural community.
Enrollment: 1,334 undergrads, 76% part-time. 91 full-time freshmen.
Selectivity: Admits less than 50% of applicants.

BASIC COSTS (2017-2018)
Tuition and fees: $18,174.
Per-credit charge: $466.
Room and board: $7,416.

FINANCIAL AID PICTURE (2016-2017)
Students with need: 61% of average financial aid package awarded as scholarships/grants, 39% awarded as loans/jobs. Need-based aid available for part-time students.
Students without need: No-need awards available for academics, alumni affiliation, job skills, leadership, minority status, state/district residency.

FINANCIAL AID PROCEDURES
Forms required: FAFSA, state aid form, institutional form.
Dates and Deadlines: Priority date 3/15; no closing date. Applicants notified on a rolling basis starting 2/1; must reply within 2 week(s) of notification.

CONTACT
Kathy Shepard, Financial Aid Director
600 Valley Road, Summerdale, PA 17093-0309
(717) 728-2261

Chatham University

Pittsburgh, Pennsylvania
www.chatham.edu

Federal Code: 003244

4-year private university and liberal arts college in large city.
Enrollment: 786 undergrads, 10% part-time. 194 full-time freshmen.
Selectivity: Admits 50 to 75% of applicants.

BASIC COSTS (2016-2017)
Tuition and fees: $35,475.
Per-credit charge: $829.

Room and board: $11,042.

FINANCIAL AID PICTURE (2016-2017)

Students with need: Out of 188 full-time freshmen who applied for aid, 160 were judged to have need. Of these, 160 received aid, and 50 had their full need met. Average financial aid package met 74% of need; average scholarship/grant was $8,321; average loan was $3,500. For part-time students, average financial aid package was $4,245.

Students without need: 11 full-time freshmen who did not demonstrate need for aid received scholarships/grants; average award was $15,637. No-need awards available for academics, alumni affiliation, art, music/drama.

Scholarships offered: Presidential Scholarship: up to annual tuition. Trustee Scholarship: $16,000. Dean Scholarship: $14,000. Founders' Scholarship: $12,000. Chatham Scholarship: $10,000. All based on academic excellence and renewable annually based on GPA of 2.8 or higher. The Presidential requires a 3.00 or higher for renewal.

FINANCIAL AID PROCEDURES

Forms required: FAFSA.

Dates and Deadlines: Priority date 3/1; no closing date. Applicants notified on a rolling basis starting 12/1; must reply within 4 week(s) of notification.

Transfers: No deadline. Applicants notified on a rolling basis starting 12/1; must reply within 4 week(s) of notification. Special scholarships are available for transfer students.

CONTACT

Jennifer Burns, Director of Financial Aid
Woodland Road, Pittsburgh, PA 15232
(412) 365-2781

Chestnut Hill College
Philadelphia, Pennsylvania
www.chc.edu
Federal Code: 003245

4-year private liberal arts college in very large city, affiliated with the Roman Catholic Church.

Enrollment: 1,364 undergrads, 19% part-time. 239 full-time freshmen.

Selectivity: Admits over 75% of applicants.

BASIC COSTS (2017-2018)

Tuition and fees: $34,950.

Room and board: $10,400.

FINANCIAL AID PICTURE (2016-2017)

Students with need: Out of 223 full-time freshmen who applied for aid, 209 were judged to have need. Of these, 209 received aid, and 18 had their full need met. Average financial aid package met 67% of need; average scholarship/grant was $25,185; average loan was $3,393. For part-time students, average financial aid package was $7,480.

Students without need: 25 full-time freshmen who did not demonstrate need for aid received scholarships/grants; average award was $16,940. No-need awards available for academics, athletics.

Scholarships offered: *Merit:* Full-tuition and partial-tuition awards based on academics. *Athletic:* 16 full-time freshmen received athletic scholarships; average amount $7,664.

FINANCIAL AID PROCEDURES

Forms required: FAFSA.

Dates and Deadlines: Priority date 1/1; no closing date. Applicants notified on a rolling basis starting 11/1.

Transfers: Priority date 4/15; no deadline. Applicants notified on a rolling basis starting 2/15.

CONTACT

Dawn Snook, Director of Financial Aid
9601 Germantown Avenue, Philadelphia, PA 19118-2693
(215) 248-7182

Cheyney University of Pennsylvania
Cheyney, Pennsylvania
www.cheyney.edu
Federal Code: 003317

4-year public university in small town.

Enrollment: 708 undergrads, 7% part-time. 181 full-time freshmen.

Selectivity: Admits less than 50% of applicants.

BASIC COSTS (2016-2017)

Tuition and fees: $9,534; out-of-state residents $14,240.

Room and board: $11,252.

Additional info: Tuition/fee waivers available for minority students.

FINANCIAL AID PICTURE

Students with need: Need-based aid available for full-time and part-time students.

Students without need: No-need awards available for academics, athletics.

FINANCIAL AID PROCEDURES

Forms required: FAFSA.

Dates and Deadlines: Priority date 3/15; no closing date. Applicants notified on a rolling basis starting 4/1; must reply within 2 week(s) of notification.

CONTACT

Chalene Ervin, Executive Director of Financial Aid
1837 University Circle, Cheyney, PA 19319-0019
(610) 399-2302

Clarion University of Pennsylvania
Clarion, Pennsylvania
www.clarion.edu
Federal Code: 003318

4-year public business and teachers college in small town.

Enrollment: 4,251 undergrads, 16% part-time. 920 full-time freshmen.

Selectivity: Admits over 75% of applicants.

BASIC COSTS (2016-2017)

Tuition and fees: $10,470; out-of-state residents $14,090.

Per-credit charge: $302; out-of-state residents $452.

Room and board: $11,104.

FINANCIAL AID PICTURE (2016-2017)

Students with need: Out of 895 full-time freshmen who applied for aid, 774 were judged to have need. Of these, 763 received aid, and 35 had their full need met. Average financial aid package met 41% of need; average scholarship/grant was $5,655; average loan was $3,320. For part-time students, average financial aid package was $5,722.

Students without need: 66 full-time freshmen who did not demonstrate need for aid received scholarships/grants; average award was $2,197. No-need awards available for academics, alumni affiliation, art, athletics, job skills, leadership, minority status, music/drama, religious affiliation, ROTC, state/district residency.

Scholarships offered: 61 full-time freshmen received athletic scholarships; average amount $3,341.

FINANCIAL AID PROCEDURES

Forms required: FAFSA, state aid form.

Dates and Deadlines: Priority date 5/1; no closing date. Applicants notified on a rolling basis starting 12/23.

CONTACT

Sue Bloom, Director of Student Financial Services
840 Wood Street, Clarion, PA 16214
(814) 393-1071

Clarks Summit University

South Abington Twp, Pennsylvania
https://www.clarkssummitu.edu/   Federal Code: 002670

4-year private university and Bible college in small city, affiliated with the Baptist faith.
Enrollment: 553 undergrads.
Selectivity: Admits less than 50% of applicants.

BASIC COSTS (2017-2018)
Tuition and fees: $23,170.
Per-credit charge: $690.
Room and board: $6,150.

FINANCIAL AID PICTURE (2015-2016)
Students with need: 66% of average financial aid package awarded as scholarships/grants, 34% awarded as loans/jobs. Need-based aid available for part-time students. Work study available nights, weekends, and for part-time students.
Students without need: No-need awards available for academics, leadership, music/drama, religious affiliation.

FINANCIAL AID PROCEDURES
Forms required: FAFSA, institutional form.
Dates and Deadlines: Closing date 5/1. Applicants notified on a rolling basis starting 4/1.

CONTACT
Deborah Cragle, Director of Financial Aid
538 Venard Road, South Abington Twp, PA 18411
(570) 585-9215

Commonwealth Technical Institute

Johnstown, Pennsylvania
www.hgac.org

2-year private technical college in small city.
Enrollment: 77 undergrads.
Selectivity: Open admission.

BASIC COSTS (2016-2017)
Tuition and fees: $11,224.
Room and board: $10,980.

FINANCIAL AID PICTURE
Students with need: Need-based aid available for full-time and part-time students. Work study available nights, weekends, and for part-time students.
Students without need: This college awards aid only to students with need.

FINANCIAL AID PROCEDURES
Forms required: FAFSA.
Dates and Deadlines: Applicants notified on a rolling basis.
Transfers: No deadline. Applicants notified on a rolling basis.

CONTACT
Christopher Zakraysek, Financial Aid Director
727 Goucher Street, Johnstown, PA 15905-3902
(800) 762-4211

Community College of Allegheny County

Pittsburgh, Pennsylvania
www.ccac.edu

2-year public community college in very large city.
Enrollment: 14,710 undergrads, 62% part-time. 1,962 full-time freshmen.

Selectivity: Open admission.

BASIC COSTS (2016-2017)
Tuition and fees: $4,197; out-of-district residents $7,429; out-of-state residents $10,662.
Per-credit charge: $107.75; out-of-district residents $216; out-of-state residents $323.25.

FINANCIAL AID PICTURE
Students with need: Work study available nights, weekends, and for part-time students.
Students without need: No-need awards available for academics, minority status.

FINANCIAL AID PROCEDURES
Forms required: FAFSA.
Dates and Deadlines: Applicants notified on a rolling basis starting 6/1.

CONTACT
Jamie Hightower-Poindexter, Director of Financial Aid
808 Ridge Avenue, Pittsburgh, PA 15212
(412) 323-2323

Community College of Beaver County

Monaca, Pennsylvania
www.ccbc.edu   Federal Code: 006807

2-year public community college in small town.
Enrollment: 2,255 undergrads.
Selectivity: Open admission; but selective for some programs.

BASIC COSTS (2016-2017)
Tuition and fees: $5,790; out-of-district residents $11,130; out-of-state residents $16,470.
Per-credit charge: $153; out-of-district residents $306; out-of-state residents $459.

FINANCIAL AID PICTURE
Students with need: Need-based aid available for full-time and part-time students. Work study available nights, weekends, and for part-time students.
Students without need: No-need awards available for academics, athletics, state/district residency.
Scholarships offered: Academic Excellence Scholarship; full tuition.

FINANCIAL AID PROCEDURES
Forms required: FAFSA, state aid form, institutional form.
Dates and Deadlines: Priority date 5/1; closing date 7/1. Applicants notified on a rolling basis starting 8/5; must reply within 2 week(s) of notification.
Transfers: Priority date 5/6.

CONTACT
Janet Davidson, Director of Financial Aid
One Campus Drive, Monaca, PA 15061-2588
(724) 480-3501

Community College of Philadelphia

Philadelphia, Pennsylvania
www.ccp.edu   Federal Code: 003249

2-year public community college in very large city.
Enrollment: 17,060 undergrads, 72% part-time. 1,617 full-time freshmen.
Selectivity: Open admission; but selective for some programs.

BASIC COSTS (2017-2018)
Tuition and fees: $5,304; out-of-district residents $9,792; out-of-state residents $14,280.
Additional info: Tuition/fee waivers available for unemployed or children of unemployed.

FINANCIAL AID PICTURE
Students with need: Need-based aid available for full-time and part-time students. Work study available nights, weekends, and for part-time students.
Students without need: This college awards aid only to students with need.

FINANCIAL AID PROCEDURES
Forms required: FAFSA, institutional form.
Dates and Deadlines: Closing date 5/1. Applicants notified on a rolling basis.
Transfers: No deadline.

CONTACT
Gim Lim, Director of Financial Aid
1700 Spring Garden Street, Philadelphia, PA 19130-3991
(215) 751-8270

Consolidated School of Business: Lancaster
Lancaster, Pennsylvania
www.csb.edu   Federal Code: 030299

2-year for-profit career college in small city.
Enrollment: 99 undergrads.
Selectivity: Open admission.

BASIC COSTS (2016-2017)
Additional info: Tuition at time of enrollment locked for 2 years; tuition/fee waivers available for unemployed or children of unemployed.

FINANCIAL AID PICTURE
Students with need: Need-based aid available for full-time and part-time students.
Students without need: No-need awards available for academics, leadership.

FINANCIAL AID PROCEDURES
Forms required: FAFSA, state aid form.
Dates and Deadlines: Applicants notified on a rolling basis.

CONTACT
Gail Dougherty, Director of Financial Aid
2124 Ambassador Circle, Lancaster, PA 17603
(717) 394-6211

Consolidated School of Business: York
York, Pennsylvania
www.csb.edu   Federal Code: 022896

2-year for-profit career college in small city.
Enrollment: 107 undergrads.
Selectivity: Open admission.

BASIC COSTS (2016-2017)
Additional info: Tuition at time of enrollment locked for 2 years; tuition/fee waivers available for unemployed or children of unemployed.

FINANCIAL AID PICTURE
Students with need: Need-based aid available for full-time and part-time students.
Students without need: No-need awards available for academics.

FINANCIAL AID PROCEDURES
Forms required: FAFSA, state aid form.
Dates and Deadlines: Applicants notified on a rolling basis.

CONTACT
Gail Dougherty, Director of Financial Aid
York City Business and Industry Park, York, PA 17404
(717) 764-9550

Curtis Institute of Music
Philadelphia, Pennsylvania
www.curtis.edu   Federal Code: 003251

4-year private music college in very large city.

BASIC COSTS (2016-2017)
Room and board: $15,059.
Additional info: Students receive a full-tuition scholarship. All students pay $2,525 in required fees. Students who do not have comprehensive health insurance are required to purchase insurance through the institution; $3,360 for 2016-17.

FINANCIAL AID PICTURE
Students with need: Need-based aid available for full-time and part-time students. Work study available nights, weekends, and for part-time students.
Students without need: This college awards aid only to students with need.
Additional info: All admitted students receive a full tuition scholarship. The estimated value of this scholarship is $37,600.

FINANCIAL AID PROCEDURES
Forms required: FAFSA, institutional form.
Dates and Deadlines: Priority date 3/1; no closing date. Applicants notified on a rolling basis starting 4/1; must reply by 5/1 or within 2 week(s) of notification.
Transfers: Must reply by 5/1 or within 2 week(s) of notification.

CONTACT
Veronica McAuley, Director, Student Financial Assistance
1726 Locust Street, Philadelphia, PA 19103-6187
(215) 717-3188

Dean Institute of Technology
Pittsburgh, Pennsylvania
www.deantech.edu   Federal Code: 009186

2-year for-profit technical college in large city.
Enrollment: 166 undergrads.
Selectivity: Open admission.

FINANCIAL AID PICTURE
Students with need: Need-based aid available for full-time and part-time students.

FINANCIAL AID PROCEDURES
Forms required: FAFSA.
Dates and Deadlines: Closing date 8/1. Applicants notified on a rolling basis; must reply within 8 week(s) of notification.

CONTACT
Nancy Grom, Director of Financial Aid
1501 West Liberty Avenue, Pittsburgh, PA 15226
(412) 531-4433 ext. 121

Delaware County Community College
Media, Pennsylvania
www.dccc.edu

2-year public community college in large town.
Enrollment: 11,742 undergrads. 1,356 full-time freshmen.

Selectivity: Open admission; but selective for some programs.

BASIC COSTS (2016-2017)

Tuition and fees: $5,085; out-of-district residents $10,170; out-of-state residents $15,255.

Per-credit charge: $113; out-of-district residents $226; out-of-state residents $339.

FINANCIAL AID PICTURE (2015-2016)

Students with need: Out of 814 full-time freshmen who applied for aid, 611 were judged to have need. Of these, 611 received aid, and 342 had their full need met. Average financial aid package met 90% of need; average scholarship/grant was $3,048; average loan was $3,500. For part-time students, average financial aid package was $4,724.

Students without need: No-need awards available for academics, job skills, leadership, minority status.

Additional info: DCCC provides federal, college-funded and international work study.

FINANCIAL AID PROCEDURES

Forms required: FAFSA, state aid form.

Dates and Deadlines: Priority date 7/1; no closing date. Applicants notified on a rolling basis starting 11/1.

Transfers: No deadline. Applicants notified on a rolling basis.

CONTACT

Raymond Toole, Director, Financial Aid

901 South Media Line Road, Media, PA 19063

(610) 359-5330

Delaware Valley University

Doylestown, Pennsylvania

www.delval.edu   Federal Code: 003252

4-year private university in large town.

Enrollment: 1,885 undergrads, 7% part-time. 451 full-time freshmen.

Selectivity: Admits 50 to 75% of applicants.

BASIC COSTS (2016-2017)

Tuition and fees: $36,750.

Per-credit charge: $916.

Room and board: $13,254.

Additional info: Full-time equine students pay an additional equine fee of $2,000 per academic year. Tuition/fee waivers available for adults.

FINANCIAL AID PICTURE (2016-2017)

Students with need: Out of 431 full-time freshmen who applied for aid, 381 were judged to have need. Of these, 381 received aid, and 52 had their full need met. Average financial aid package met 66% of need; average scholarship/grant was $22,974; average loan was $4,460. For part-time students, average financial aid package was $7,082.

Students without need: 70 full-time freshmen who did not demonstrate need for aid received scholarships/grants; average award was $18,474. No-need awards available for academics, alumni affiliation, leadership, minority status, music/drama, state/district residency.

FINANCIAL AID PROCEDURES

Forms required: FAFSA, state aid form.

Dates and Deadlines: Priority date 4/15; no closing date. Applicants notified on a rolling basis starting 3/31; must reply by 5/1 or within 2 week(s) of notification.

Transfers: No deadline. Applicants notified on a rolling basis; must reply by 4/1.

CONTACT

Joan Hock, Director of Financial Aid

700 East Butler Avenue, Doylestown, PA 18901-2697

(215) 489-2272

DeSales University

Center Valley, Pennsylvania

www.desales.edu   Federal Code: 003986

4-year private university in large town, affiliated with the Roman Catholic Church.

Enrollment: 2,333 undergrads, 21% part-time. 500 full-time freshmen.

Selectivity: Admits over 75% of applicants.

BASIC COSTS (2016-2017)

Tuition and fees: $34,850.

Per-credit charge: $1,400.

Room and board: $12,400.

FINANCIAL AID PICTURE (2016-2017)

Students with need: Out of 468 full-time freshmen who applied for aid, 397 were judged to have need. Of these, 397 received aid, and 116 had their full need met. Average financial aid package met 73% of need; average scholarship/grant was $20,338; average loan was $3,505. For part-time students, average financial aid package was $7,024.

Students without need: 98 full-time freshmen who did not demonstrate need for aid received scholarships/grants; average award was $17,423. No-need awards available for academics, alumni affiliation, art, leadership, minority status, music/drama, religious affiliation, ROTC.

Scholarships offered: Presidential Scholarships; $18,000 to full tuition; top 5% of class and 1300 SAT. Trustee Scholarships; $6,000 to $10,000; top 15% of class, minimum 1200 SAT. DeSales Scholarships; $4,000; top 25% of class, minimum 1100 SAT. SAT scores exclusive of Writing.

FINANCIAL AID PROCEDURES

Forms required: FAFSA.

Dates and Deadlines: Priority date 2/1; closing date 5/1. Applicants notified on a rolling basis starting 2/15; must reply by 5/1 or within 2 week(s) of notification.

Transfers: No deadline. Applicants notified on a rolling basis. Merit scholarships automatically awarded for transfer students with a qualifying GPA. Award amounts are based on factors such as GPA, courses completed, and credits accumulated. Three levels of transfer scholarships: $3,500, $5,000, and $8,000 per year.

CONTACT

Joyce Farmer, Director of Financial Aid

2755 Station Avenue, Center Valley, PA 18034-9568

(610) 282-1100 ext. 1287

DeVry University: Fort Washington

Fort Washington, Pennsylvania

www.devry.edu

4-year for-profit university in large town.

Enrollment: 436 undergrads.

FINANCIAL AID PICTURE

Students with need: Need-based aid available for full-time and part-time students.

Students without need: This college awards aid only to students with need.

FINANCIAL AID PROCEDURES

Forms required: FAFSA.

Dates and Deadlines: Applicants notified on a rolling basis.

CONTACT

1140 Virginia Drive, Fort Washington, PA 19034-3204

(215) 591-5724

Dickinson College

Carlisle, Pennsylvania
www.dickinson.edu

Federal Code: 003253
CSS Code: 2186

4-year private liberal arts college in large town.
Enrollment: 2,370 undergrads, 1% part-time. 610 full-time freshmen.
Selectivity: Admits less than 50% of applicants.

BASIC COSTS (2016-2017)
Tuition and fees: $51,205.
Per-credit charge: $1,586.
Room and board: $12,794.

FINANCIAL AID PICTURE (2016-2017)
Students with need: Out of 393 full-time freshmen who applied for aid, 367 were judged to have need. Of these, 366 received aid, and 358 had their full need met. Average financial aid package met 100% of need; average scholarship/grant was $40,828; average loan was $3,549.
Students without need: 95 full-time freshmen who did not demonstrate need for aid received scholarships/grants; average award was $9,474. No-need awards available for academics, leadership, music/drama, ROTC.
Scholarships offered: John Dickinson and Benjamin Rush Scholarships: awarded to most academically competitive students. John Montgomery Scholarship: strong grades in a challenging high-school curriculum and demonstrate exceptional talent in any of a variety of areas. Founders Scholarship: strong grades in a challenging high-school curriculum and demonstrate strong leadership, service and commitment in high-school and/or community life.

FINANCIAL AID PROCEDURES
Forms required: FAFSA, CSS PROFILE, state aid form.
Dates and Deadlines: Priority date 11/15; closing date 2/1. Applicants notified by 3/23; must reply by 5/1 or within 2 week(s) of notification.
Transfers: Closing date 4/1. Applicants notified by 5/15; must reply within 2 week(s) of notification.

CONTACT
Richard Heckman, Director of Financial Aid
PO Box 1773, Carlisle, PA 17013-2896
(717) 245-1308

Douglas Education Center

Monessen, Pennsylvania
www.dec.edu

Federal Code: 013957

2-year for-profit visual arts and business college in small town.
Enrollment: 267 undergrads.
Selectivity: Open admission.

BASIC COSTS (2016-2017)
Additional info: Tuition and fees vary depending on program. Examples of Associate's degree programs: Medical Assistant Program, $21,400; The Factory Digital Film-making Program, $33,500. Certificate programs: Cosmetology Program, $16,300; Esthetician and Nail Technologist Program, $5,100. Costs listed include tuition and fees; books, supplies, and additional costs vary by program. All costs are subject to change.

FINANCIAL AID PICTURE
Students with need: Need-based aid available for full-time and part-time students.
Students without need: This college awards aid only to students with need.

FINANCIAL AID PROCEDURES
Forms required: FAFSA.
Dates and Deadlines: Applicants notified on a rolling basis.

CONTACT
Amanda Phillips, Director of Financial Aid
130 Seventh Street, Monessen, PA 15062
(724) 684-3684

Drexel University

Philadelphia, Pennsylvania
www.drexel.edu

Federal Code: 003256
CSS Code: 2194

5-year private university in very large city.
Enrollment: 15,210 undergrads, 13% part-time. 2,324 full-time freshmen.
Selectivity: Admits 50 to 75% of applicants.

BASIC COSTS (2017-2018)
Tuition and fees: $52,002.
Room and board: $13,890.

FINANCIAL AID PICTURE (2016-2017)
Students with need: Out of 1,957 full-time freshmen who applied for aid, 1,610 were judged to have need. Of these, 1,609 received aid, and 496 had their full need met. Average financial aid package met 80% of need; average scholarship/grant was $33,006; average loan was $8,257.
Students without need: 679 full-time freshmen who did not demonstrate need for aid received scholarships/grants; average award was $14,619. No-need awards available for academics, art, athletics, music/drama, ROTC, state/district residency.
Scholarships offered: 38 full-time freshmen received athletic scholarships; average amount $32,568.

FINANCIAL AID PROCEDURES
Forms required: FAFSA, CSS PROFILE.
Dates and Deadlines: Closing date 2/15. Applicants notified by 4/1; must reply by 5/1.
Transfers: Scholarships available in amounts up to $8,000. 3.2 GPA and 30 credit hours at time of application required for eligibility.

CONTACT
3141 Chestnut Street, Philadelphia, PA 19104-2876
(215) 895-2537

DuBois Business College

DuBois, Pennsylvania
www.dbcollege.edu

Federal Code: 004893

2-year for-profit business and technical college in large town.
Enrollment: 90 undergrads.
Selectivity: Open admission.

FINANCIAL AID PICTURE
Students with need: Need-based aid available for full-time students.

FINANCIAL AID PROCEDURES
Forms required: FAFSA.
Dates and Deadlines: Closing date 8/1. Applicants notified on a rolling basis.

CONTACT
Karen Alderton, Financial Aid Director
One Beaver Drive, DuBois, PA 15801
(814) 371-6920

Duquesne University

Pittsburgh, Pennsylvania
www.duq.edu

Federal Code: 003258

4-year private university in large city, affiliated with the Roman Catholic Church.

Enrollment: 6,018 undergrads, 3% part-time. 1,435 full-time freshmen.
Selectivity: Admits 50 to 75% of applicants.

BASIC COSTS (2016-2017)
Tuition and fees: $35,062.
Per-credit charge: $1,162.
Room and board: $11,760.

FINANCIAL AID PICTURE (2015-2016)
Students with need: Out of 1,258 full-time freshmen who applied for aid, 1,019 were judged to have need. Of these, 1,019 received aid, and 214 had their full need met. Average financial aid package met 74% of need; average scholarship/grant was $20,761; average loan was $3,918. For part-time students, average financial aid package was $6,104.
Students without need: 365 full-time freshmen who did not demonstrate need for aid received scholarships/grants; average award was $13,158. No-need awards available for academics, athletics, music/drama, ROTC.
Scholarships offered: *Merit:* Competitive scholarships available for academically and/or artistically talented students. *Athletic:* 80 full-time freshmen received athletic scholarships; average amount $21,710.

FINANCIAL AID PROCEDURES
Forms required: FAFSA, institutional form.
Dates and Deadlines: Closing date 5/1. Applicants notified on a rolling basis starting 2/1; must reply by 5/1 or within 3 week(s) of notification.
Transfers: Applicants notified on a rolling basis starting 2/1; must reply by 5/1 or within 3 week(s) of notification.

CONTACT
Richard Esposito, Director of Financial Aid
600 Forbes Avenue, Administration Building, Pittsburgh, PA 15282-0201
(412) 396-6607

East Stroudsburg University of Pennsylvania
East Stroudsburg, Pennsylvania
www.esu.edu   Federal Code: 003320

4-year public university in large town.
Enrollment: 6,095 undergrads, 8% part-time. 1,285 full-time freshmen.
Selectivity: Admits 50 to 75% of applicants.

BASIC COSTS (2016-2017)
Tuition and fees: $9,952; out-of-state residents $21,044.
Room and board: $8,390.

FINANCIAL AID PICTURE (2015-2016)
Students with need: Out of 1,221 full-time freshmen who applied for aid, 996 were judged to have need. Of these, 955 received aid, and 450 had their full need met. Average financial aid package met 40% of need; average scholarship/grant was $6,277; average loan was $3,147. For part-time students, average financial aid package was $4,787.
Students without need: 2 full-time freshmen who did not demonstrate need for aid received scholarships/grants; average award was $1,065. No-need awards available for academics, alumni affiliation, art, athletics, job skills, leadership, minority status, music/drama, state/district residency.
Scholarships offered: 46 full-time freshmen received athletic scholarships; average amount $3,134.

FINANCIAL AID PROCEDURES
Forms required: FAFSA.
Dates and Deadlines: Priority date 2/16; closing date 2/16. Applicants notified by 3/16; must reply by 5/1.
Transfers: Priority date 5/1; no deadline. Applicants notified on a rolling basis starting 6/1; must reply within 3 week(s) of notification.

CONTACT
Aristalia Benitez, Financial Aid Director
200 Prospect Street, East Stroudsburg, PA 18301-2999
(570) 422-2800

Eastern University
St. Davids, Pennsylvania
www.eastern.edu   Federal Code: 003259

4-year private university in small town, affiliated with the American Baptist Churches in the USA.
Enrollment: 2,045 undergrads, 14% part-time. 374 full-time freshmen.
Selectivity: Admits 50 to 75% of applicants.

BASIC COSTS (2017-2018)
Tuition and fees: $32,315.
Per-credit charge: $695.
Room and board: $10,980.

FINANCIAL AID PICTURE (2015-2016)
Students with need: Out of 350 full-time freshmen who applied for aid, 324 were judged to have need. Of these, 324 received aid, and 48 had their full need met. Average financial aid package met 74% of need; average scholarship/grant was $8,320; average loan was $3,213. For part-time students, average financial aid package was $5,197.
Students without need: 26 full-time freshmen who did not demonstrate need for aid received scholarships/grants; average award was $14,202. No-need awards available for academics, alumni affiliation, leadership, music/drama.
Scholarships offered: Academic scholarships ranging from $5,000-$14,000 per year.

FINANCIAL AID PROCEDURES
Forms required: FAFSA.
Dates and Deadlines: Applicants notified on a rolling basis starting 4/1.
Transfers: No deadline. Applicants notified on a rolling basis starting 3/15. Financial aid transcripts from previous institutions required.

CONTACT
Christal Jennings, Director of Financial Aid
1300 Eagle Road, St. Davids, PA 19087-3696
(610) 341-5842

Edinboro University of Pennsylvania
Edinboro, Pennsylvania
www.edinboro.edu   Federal Code: 003321

4-year public university in small town.
Enrollment: 5,142 undergrads.

BASIC COSTS (2016-2017)
Tuition and fees: $9,985; out-of-state residents $10,640.
Room and board: $9,396.

FINANCIAL AID PICTURE
Students with need: Need-based aid available for full-time and part-time students. Work study available nights, weekends, and for part-time students.
Students without need: No-need awards available for academics, alumni affiliation, art, athletics, leadership, minority status, music/drama, ROTC, state/district residency.

FINANCIAL AID PROCEDURES
Forms required: FAFSA, state aid form.
Dates and Deadlines: Priority date 3/15; no closing date. Applicants notified on a rolling basis starting 2/15; must reply by 8/1.

CONTACT

200 East Normal Street, Edinboro, PA 16444

(888) 611-2680

Elizabethtown College

Elizabethtown, Pennsylvania

www.etown.edu   Federal Code: 003262

4-year private liberal arts college in large town, affiliated with the Brethren Church.

Enrollment: 1,713 undergrads, 1% part-time. 442 full-time freshmen.

Selectivity: Admits 50 to 75% of applicants.

BASIC COSTS (2017-2018)

Tuition and fees: $45,350.

Room and board: $10,990.

FINANCIAL AID PICTURE (2016-2017)

Students with need: Out of 409 full-time freshmen who applied for aid, 354 were judged to have need. Of these, 353 received aid, and 101 had their full need met. Average financial aid package met 83% of need; average scholarship/grant was $29,302; average loan was $3,757. For part-time students, average financial aid package was $23,306.

Students without need: 98 full-time freshmen who did not demonstrate need for aid received scholarships/grants; average award was $23,182. No-need awards available for academics, alumni affiliation, art, leadership, music/drama, religious affiliation.

Scholarships offered: Presidential Scholarship: up to $25,000 annually; top percentages of class and minimum 1300 SAT score. Provost Scholarship: up to $22,500 annually; top 10% of class with minimum 1150 SAT; unlimited number awarded. Dean's Scholarship: up to $20,000 annually; for students with very strong academic achievement who do not qualify for other merit awards; unlimited number awarded. Music scholarships: up to $4,000; based on audition. Stamps Scholarship: full tuition, $4,000 enrichment fund and personal mentor.

FINANCIAL AID PROCEDURES

Forms required: FAFSA.

Dates and Deadlines: Priority date 2/1; no closing date. Applicants notified on a rolling basis starting 11/1; must reply by 5/1 or within 2 week(s) of notification.

Transfers: No deadline. Applicants notified on a rolling basis; must reply within 2 week(s) of notification.

CONTACT

Melodie Jackson, Director of Financial Aid

One Alpha Drive, Elizabethtown, PA 17022-2298

(717) 361-1302

Franklin & Marshall College

Lancaster, Pennsylvania   Federal Code: 003265

www.fandm.edu   CSS Code: 2261

4-year private liberal arts college in small city.

Enrollment: 2,230 undergrads. 639 full-time freshmen.

Selectivity: Admits less than 50% of applicants.

BASIC COSTS (2016-2017)

Tuition and fees: $52,490.

Per-credit charge: $1,631.

Room and board: $13,120.

FINANCIAL AID PICTURE (2016-2017)

Students with need: Out of 417 full-time freshmen who applied for aid, 355 were judged to have need. Of these, 355 received aid, and 355 had

their full need met. Average financial aid package met 100% of need; average scholarship/grant was $44,761; average loan was $3,030.

Students without need: This college awards aid only to students with need.

FINANCIAL AID PROCEDURES

Forms required: FAFSA, CSS PROFILE.

Dates and Deadlines: Priority date 2/15; closing date 2/15. Applicants notified by 4/1; must reply by 5/1.

Transfers: Closing date 5/1. Applicants notified by 6/15.

CONTACT

Clarke Paine, Director of Student Aid

PO Box 3003, Lancaster, PA 17604-3003

(717) 358-3991

Gannon University

Erie, Pennsylvania

www.gannon.edu   Federal Code: 003266

4-year private university in small city, affiliated with the Roman Catholic Church.

Enrollment: 2,597 undergrads, 5% part-time. 626 full-time freshmen.

Selectivity: Admits over 75% of applicants.

BASIC COSTS (2016-2017)

Tuition and fees: $30,042.

Per-credit charge: $710.

Room and board: $11,990.

Additional info: $25 fee per-credit hour for part-time students. Tuition/fee waivers available for adults, unemployed or children of unemployed.

FINANCIAL AID PICTURE (2016-2017)

Students with need: Out of 567 full-time freshmen who applied for aid, 522 were judged to have need. Of these, 520 received aid, and 116 had their full need met. Average financial aid package met 75% of need; average scholarship/grant was $22,430; average loan was $3,404. For part-time students, average financial aid package was $5,127.

Students without need: 89 full-time freshmen who did not demonstrate need for aid received scholarships/grants; average award was $16,558. No-need awards available for academics, athletics, leadership, music/drama, religious affiliation, ROTC.

Scholarships offered: *Merit:* Academic Awards: $1,000 to full tuition; based on high school rank, GPA, and test scores. Diocesan Scholarship: $1,000 Parish Grant; for students that belong to a parish within the Diocese of Erie. Diocesan High School Grant: $1,500; for students who attended a Catholic high school within the Diocese of Erie. Catholic High School Grant: $1,000; for any student who attended a Catholic high school outside of the Diocese of Erie. Athletic scholarships: $1,000 to full tuition, room and board. *Athletic:* 24 full-time freshmen received athletic scholarships; average amount $10,423.

FINANCIAL AID PROCEDURES

Forms required: FAFSA.

Dates and Deadlines: Priority date 3/15; no closing date. Applicants notified on a rolling basis starting 11/1.

Transfers: No deadline. Applicants notified on a rolling basis starting 11/1. Original award package will be re-awarded for transfers who enrolled two semesters or less at another school.

CONTACT

Sharon Krahe, Director of Financial Aid

109 University Square, Erie, PA 16541-0001

(814) 871-7337

Geneva College
Beaver Falls, Pennsylvania
www.geneva.edu   Federal Code: 003267

4-year private liberal arts college in large town, affiliated with the Reformed Presbyterian Church of North America.
Enrollment: 1,458 undergrads, 11% part-time. 289 full-time freshmen.
Selectivity: Admits 50 to 75% of applicants.

BASIC COSTS (2016-2017)
Tuition and fees: $25,680.
Per-credit charge: $870.
Room and board: $9,770.
Additional info: Other programs have different costs per-credit-hour and fees. Tuition/fee waivers available for minority students, unemployed or children of unemployed.

FINANCIAL AID PICTURE (2015-2016)
Students with need: 71% of average financial aid package awarded as scholarships/grants, 29% awarded as loans/jobs. Need-based aid available for part-time students. Work study available nights, weekends, and for part-time students.
Students without need: No-need awards available for academics, alumni affiliation, music/drama, religious affiliation.
Scholarships offered: Academic scholarships, scholarships for National Merit finalists and semifinalists, grants for members of controlling church and other denominations identified by the college.

FINANCIAL AID PROCEDURES
Forms required: FAFSA.
Dates and Deadlines: Priority date 3/15; no closing date. Applicants notified on a rolling basis starting 3/1; must reply by 5/1 or within 4 week(s) of notification.
Transfers: No deadline. Applicants notified on a rolling basis starting 3/1; must reply within 4 week(s) of notification.

CONTACT
Allyson Bentz, Director of Financial Aid
3200 College Avenue, Beaver Falls, PA 15010
(724) 847-6530

Gettysburg College
Gettysburg, Pennsylvania   Federal Code: 003268
www.gettysburg.edu   CSS Code: 2275

4-year private liberal arts college in large town, affiliated with the Evangelical Lutheran Church in America.
Enrollment: 2,379 undergrads. 697 full-time freshmen.
Selectivity: Admits less than 50% of applicants.

BASIC COSTS (2016-2017)
Tuition and fees: $50,860.
Room and board: $12,140.

FINANCIAL AID PICTURE (2016-2017)
Students with need: Out of 451 full-time freshmen who applied for aid, 384 were judged to have need. Of these, 379 received aid, and 341 had their full need met. Average financial aid package met 90% of need; average scholarship/grant was $35,068; average loan was $5,602.
Students without need: 119 full-time freshmen who did not demonstrate need for aid received scholarships/grants; average award was $11,340. No-need awards available for academics, music/drama.
Scholarships offered: Lincoln, Presidential, David Wills, and 1832 Founders Scholarships based on high school GPA, class rank and standardized test scores. The number awarded varies. Wagnild Scholarship and Sunderman Scholarships for music talent; audition required.

FINANCIAL AID PROCEDURES
Forms required: FAFSA, CSS PROFILE.
Dates and Deadlines: Closing date 1/15. Applicants notified by 3/18; must reply by 5/1.
Transfers: Priority date 4/15. Must reply within 2 week(s) of notification.

CONTACT
Christina Gormley, Director of Financial Aid
300 North Washington Street, Gettysburg, PA 17325-1400
(717) 337-6611

Grove City College
Grove City, Pennsylvania
www.gcc.edu   Federal Code: G03269

4-year private liberal arts college in small town, affiliated with the Presbyterian Church (USA).
Enrollment: 2,346 undergrads, 1% part-time. 583 full-time freshmen.
Selectivity: Admits over 75% of applicants.

BASIC COSTS (2016-2017)
Tuition and fees: $16,630.
Per-credit charge: $540.
Room and board: $9,062.

FINANCIAL AID PICTURE (2016-2017)
Students with need: Out of 398 full-time freshmen who applied for aid, 302 were judged to have need. Of these, 301 received aid, and 36 had their full need met. Average financial aid package met 53% of need; average scholarship/grant was $7,804.
Students without need: 42 full-time freshmen who did not demonstrate need for aid received scholarships/grants; average award was $7,203. No-need awards available for academics, leadership, music/drama.
Scholarships offered: Trustee Scholarships; $8,000 to full standard tuition, room, and board awards; issued to a select group of accepted students who meet academic requirements; 24 awarded. Presidential Scholarships; $1,000; awarded to all valedictorians in class of 30 or more and all salutatorians in class of 100 or more. National Merit Scholarships; $2,000; awarded to all National Merit Finalists. Engineering Scholarships; $2,500; 4 awarded. Leadership Scholarships; $2,500; 4 awarded. Alumni Merit Reward Scholarships; $3,000-$6,000 one-year scholarship; 60 awarded.
Additional info: Institutional aid applications required for institutional need-based scholarships. Federal monies are not accepted (Pell Grant, Stafford Loan, Parent Plus Loan, GI Bill, or any other government scholarship or loan program).

FINANCIAL AID PROCEDURES
Forms required: institutional form.
Dates and Deadlines: Closing date 4/15. Applicants notified on a rolling basis starting 3/1; must reply by 5/1.
Transfers: Closing date 8/15. Applicants notified on a rolling basis starting 3/1; must reply within 3 week(s) of notification.

CONTACT
Thomas Ball, Director of Financial Aid
100 Campus Drive, Grove City, PA 16127-2104
(724) 458-3300

Gwynedd Mercy University
Gwynedd Valley, Pennsylvania
www.gmercyu.edu   Federal Code: 003270

4-year private nursing and liberal arts college in large town, affiliated with the Roman Catholic Church.
Enrollment: 1,944 undergrads, 6% part-time. 221 full-time freshmen.

Selectivity: Admits less than 50% of applicants.

BASIC COSTS (2016-2017)
Tuition and fees: $34,380.
Per-credit charge: $700.
Room and board: $11,300.
Additional info: Cost reported is annual tuition for allied health and nursing programs; tuition for other programs, $31,780.

FINANCIAL AID PICTURE (2016-2017)
Students with need: Out of 217 full-time freshmen who applied for aid, 198 were judged to have need. Of these, 198 received aid, and 25 had their full need met. Average financial aid package met 72% of need; average scholarship/grant was $21,708; average loan was $3,417. For part-time students, average financial aid package was $5,707.
Students without need: 21 full-time freshmen who did not demonstrate need for aid received scholarships/grants; average award was $16,095. No-need awards available for academics, alumni affiliation, leadership, minority status, religious affiliation, state/district residency.
Scholarships offered: Presidential scholarship; $10,000; must have 1200 SAT and be in top 30% of class, essay required; 2/15 deadline. Connelly Scholarship; $6,000-$7,000; must have 1100 SAT and be in top 50% of class. Mother Mary Bernard Scholarship; $4,500-$5,000; must have 1000 SAT, be in top 50% of class, and have documented leadership experience. Yearly scholarship for Catholic school graduates; $2,000 (tuition incentive grant). All SAT scores exclusive of Writing.

FINANCIAL AID PROCEDURES
Forms required: FAFSA, institutional form.
Dates and Deadlines: Priority date 3/15; closing date 5/1. Applicants notified on a rolling basis starting 2/15; must reply by 5/1 or within 2 week(s) of notification.

CONTACT
Elizabeth Howard, Director of Student Financial Aid
1325 Sumneytown Pike, Gwynedd Valley, PA 19437-0901
(215) 646-7300 ext. 21483

Harcum College
Bryn Mawr, Pennsylvania
www.harcum.edu   Federal Code: 003272

2-year private junior college in large town.
Enrollment: 1,612 undergrads.

BASIC COSTS (2017-2018)
Tuition and fees: $23,670.
Per-credit charge: $745.
Room and board: $9,600.

FINANCIAL AID PICTURE
Students with need: Need-based aid available for full-time and part-time students. Work study available nights.
Students without need: No-need awards available for academics, alumni affiliation, athletics, leadership.
Scholarships offered: Scholarships available based on academic achievement.

FINANCIAL AID PROCEDURES
Forms required: FAFSA.
Dates and Deadlines: Priority date 4/15; closing date 5/1. Applicants notified on a rolling basis starting 3/1; must reply within 3 week(s) of notification.

CONTACT
Melissa Walsh, Director of Financial Aid
750 Montgomery Avenue, Bryn Mawr, PA 19010-3476
(610) 526-6098

Harrisburg Area Community College
Harrisburg, Pennsylvania
www.hacc.edu   Federal Code: 003273

2-year public community college in small city.
Enrollment: 14,230 undergrads, 69% part-time. 1,242 full-time freshmen.
Selectivity: Open admission; but selective for some programs.

BASIC COSTS (2016-2017)
Tuition and fees: $6,570; out-of-district residents $7,680; out-of-state residents $8,970.
Per-credit charge: $176; out-of-district residents $213; out-of-state residents $256.

FINANCIAL AID PICTURE (2016-2017)
Students with need: Out of 1,069 full-time freshmen who applied for aid, 863 were judged to have need. Of these, 693 received aid. Need-based aid available for part-time students.
Additional info: Federal work study community service positions available.

FINANCIAL AID PROCEDURES
Forms required: FAFSA.
Dates and Deadlines: Priority date 2/15; no closing date. Applicants notified on a rolling basis starting 2/16.
Transfers: PHEAA state grants require separate academic progress review by financial aid staff.

CONTACT
Andrew Marah, Director of Financial Aid
One HACC Drive, Harrisburg, PA 17110-2999
(717) 780-2330

Harrisburg University of Science and Technology
Harrisburg, Pennsylvania
www.harrisburgu.edu   Federal Code: 039483

4-year private university in small city.
Enrollment: 374 undergrads, 9% part-time. 126 full-time freshmen.
Selectivity: Admits over 75% of applicants.

BASIC COSTS (2016-2017)
Tuition and fees: $23,900.
Per-credit charge: $1,000.

FINANCIAL AID PICTURE (2015-2016)
Students with need: Out of 126 full-time freshmen who applied for aid, 119 were judged to have need. Of these, 116 received aid, and 15 had their full need met. Average financial aid package met 64% of need; average scholarship/grant was $17,827; average loan was $3,747. For part-time students, average financial aid package was $6,768.
Students without need: 7 full-time freshmen who did not demonstrate need for aid received scholarships/grants; average award was $15,635. No-need awards available for academics, leadership, state/district residency.
Scholarships offered: Various scholarships; $1,000-$18,000, depending on specific criteria.

FINANCIAL AID PROCEDURES
Forms required: FAFSA.
Dates and Deadlines: Applicants notified on a rolling basis; must reply within 2 week(s) of notification.
Transfers: Priority date 5/1; no deadline. Applicants notified on a rolling basis; must reply within 4 week(s) of notification.

CONTACT
Vincent Frank, Director of Financial Aid
326 Market Street, Harrisburg, PA 17101-2208
(717) 901-5115

Haverford College

Haverford, Pennsylvania
www.haverford.edu

Federal Code: 003274
CSS Code: 2289

4-year private liberal arts college in large town.
Enrollment: 1,261 undergrads. 349 full-time freshmen.
Selectivity: Admits less than 50% of applicants.

BASIC COSTS (2016-2017)
Tuition and fees: $51,024.
Room and board: $15,466.

FINANCIAL AID PICTURE (2016-2017)
Students with need: Out of 197 full-time freshmen who applied for aid, 160 were judged to have need. Of these, 160 received aid, and 160 had their full need met. Average financial aid package met 100% of need; average scholarship/grant was $46,398; average loan was $2,764.
Students without need: This college awards aid only to students with need.
Additional info: Students with a family income below $60,000 per year will not have loans included in their financial aid package. Students with a family income of $60,000 to $99,999 per year will have a loan expectation of $1,500; with a family income of $100,000 to $149,000 the loan expectation is $2,500 each year; with a family income of more than $150,000 the loan expectation is $3,000 each year.

FINANCIAL AID PROCEDURES
Forms required: FAFSA, CSS PROFILE.
Dates and Deadlines: Closing date 2/1. Applicants notified by 4/1; must reply by 5/1.
Transfers: Closing date 3/1.

CONTACT
Michael Colahan, Director of Financial Aid
370 Lancaster Avenue, Haverford, PA 19041-1392
(610) 896-1350

Holy Family University

Philadelphia, Pennsylvania
www.holyfamily.edu

Federal Code: 003275

4-year private university in very large city, affiliated with the Roman Catholic Church.
Enrollment: 1,766 undergrads, 20% part-time. 328 full-time freshmen.
Selectivity: Admits 50 to 75% of applicants.

BASIC COSTS (2017-2018)
Tuition and fees: $30,346.
Per-credit charge: $627.
Room and board: $13,576.

FINANCIAL AID PICTURE (2016-2017)
Students with need: Out of 315 full-time freshmen who applied for aid, 300 were judged to have need. Of these, 300 received aid, and 61 had their full need met. Average financial aid package met 85% of need; average scholarship/grant was $19,313; average loan was $3,665. For part-time students, average financial aid package was $9,954.
Students without need: 28 full-time freshmen who did not demonstrate need for aid received scholarships/grants; average award was $15,929. No-need awards available for academics, athletics, leadership.
Scholarships offered: 47 full-time freshmen received athletic scholarships; average amount $6,781.

FINANCIAL AID PROCEDURES
Forms required: FAFSA.
Dates and Deadlines: Priority date 3/1; closing date 4/1. Applicants notified on a rolling basis starting 3/15; must reply within 4 week(s) of notification.

Transfers: Applicants notified on a rolling basis starting 3/15; must reply within 4 week(s) of notification.

CONTACT
Janice Hetrick, Director of Financial Aid
9801 Frankford Avenue, Philadelphia, PA 19114-2009
(267) 341-3233

Hussian College, School of Art

Philadelphia, Pennsylvania
www.hussianart.edu

Federal Code: 007469

2-year for-profit visual arts college in very large city.
Enrollment: 79 undergrads.

FINANCIAL AID PICTURE
Students with need: Need-based aid available for full-time students.

FINANCIAL AID PROCEDURES
Forms required: FAFSA, state aid form, institutional form.
Dates and Deadlines: Applicants notified on a rolling basis starting 2/15; must reply within 3 week(s) of notification.
Transfers: Priority date 3/15; no deadline. Applicants notified on a rolling basis starting 4/1. August 1 deadline for PHEAA State Grant consideration.

CONTACT
Susan Cohen, Financial Aid Director
The Bourse, Suite 300, Philadelphia, PA 19106
(215) 574-9600 ext. 206

Immaculata University

Immaculata, Pennsylvania
www.immaculata.edu

Federal Code: 003276

4-year private university and liberal arts college in large town, affiliated with the Roman Catholic Church.
Enrollment: 1,459 undergrads, 35% part-time. 216 full-time freshmen.
Selectivity: Admits over 75% of applicants.

BASIC COSTS (2016-2017)
Tuition and fees: $35,210.
Per-credit charge: $530.
Room and board: $12,500.

FINANCIAL AID PICTURE
Students with need: Need-based aid available for full-time and part-time students. Work study available nights, weekends, and for part-time students.
Students without need: No-need awards available for academics, alumni affiliation, art, job skills, leadership, minority status, music/drama, religious affiliation, state/district residency.

FINANCIAL AID PROCEDURES
Forms required: FAFSA.
Dates and Deadlines: Priority date 2/15; closing date 4/15. Applicants notified on a rolling basis starting 2/1; must reply within 2 week(s) of notification.
Transfers: No deadline. Applicants notified on a rolling basis starting 1/1; must reply within 2 week(s) of notification.

CONTACT
Robert Forest, Director of Financial Aid
1145 King Road, Immaculata, PA 19345
(610) 647-4400 ext. 3026

Indiana University of Pennsylvania

Indiana, Pennsylvania
www.iup.edu   Federal Code: 003277

4-year public university in large town.
Enrollment: 10,357 undergrads, 6% part-time. 2,474 full-time freshmen.
Selectivity: Admits over 75% of applicants.

BASIC COSTS (2016-2017)
Tuition and fees: $11,368; out-of-state residents $21,034.
Room and board: $12,402.
Additional info: Tuition is $12,306 for the following: new students who live in Indiana, Maryland, Michigan, New Jersey, New York, Ohio, Virginia and West Virginia; new students from other states who have a high school GPA of at least a 3.0 on a 4.0 grade scale or an 85% on a percentage scale; new transfers students with a cumulative GPA of 3.0 from any and all institutions they attended prior to enrolling at university.

FINANCIAL AID PICTURE (2015-2016)
Students with need: Out of 2,325 full-time freshmen who applied for aid, 1,850 were judged to have need. Of these, 1,837 received aid, and 181 had their full need met. Average financial aid package met 63% of need; average scholarship/grant was $6,693; average loan was $3,635. For part-time students, average financial aid package was $9,823.
Students without need: 122 full-time freshmen who did not demonstrate need for aid received scholarships/grants; average award was $2,021. No-need awards available for academics, alumni affiliation, art, athletics, job skills, leadership, music/drama, ROTC, state/district residency.
Scholarships offered: 67 full-time freshmen received athletic scholarships; average amount $5,614.

FINANCIAL AID PROCEDURES
Forms required: FAFSA, state aid form.
Dates and Deadlines: Priority date 4/15; no closing date. Applicants notified on a rolling basis starting 12/15.
Transfers: Must reply within 2 week(s) of notification.

CONTACT
Ragan Griffin, Director of Financial Aid
120 Sutton Hall, 1011 South Drive, Indiana, PA 15705-1088
(724) 357-2218

JNA Institute of Culinary Arts

Philadelphia, Pennsylvania
www.culinaryarts.edu   Federal Code: 031033

2-year for-profit technical college in very large city.
Enrollment: 65 undergrads.

BASIC COSTS (2016-2017)
Tuition and fees: $12,725.
Additional info: Tuition listed is for the Food Service Diploma Program. Culinary Arts/Restaurant Management Associate Program is $25,300 with a $75 registration fee. All costs are subject to change. Books and Knife Kit are not included in the price of tuition. 2 uniforms are included in tuition.

FINANCIAL AID PICTURE
Students with need: Need-based aid available for full-time students.

FINANCIAL AID PROCEDURES
Forms required: FAFSA.

CONTACT
Nicole Digironimo, Financial Aid Director
1212 South Broad Street, Philadelphia, PA 19146
(215) 468-8800

Johnson College

Scranton, Pennsylvania
www.johnson.edu   Federal Code: 014734

2-year private technical college in small city.
Enrollment: 437 undergrads, 11% part-time. 174 full-time freshmen.

BASIC COSTS (2016-2017)
Tuition and fees: $18,035.
Per-credit charge: $510.
Room and board: $7,100.
Additional info: Required fees for Radiologic, Physical Therapist Assistant and VET are $1,975, Carpentry & HVAC fees are $1,525, Welding fees are $2,075. Other expenses include book, tools and supplies and are estimated at $1,700 per semester.

FINANCIAL AID PICTURE (2015-2016)
Students with need: Out of 166 full-time freshmen who applied for aid, 150 were judged to have need. Of these, 149 received aid, and 7 had their full need met. Average financial aid package met 44% of need; average scholarship/grant was $7,143; average loan was $3,010. For part-time students, average financial aid package was $6,478.
Students without need: 4 full-time freshmen who did not demonstrate need for aid received scholarships/grants; average award was $1,500. No-need awards available for academics.

FINANCIAL AID PROCEDURES
Forms required: FAFSA, state aid form.
Dates and Deadlines: Priority date 5/1; no closing date. Applicants notified on a rolling basis starting 1/15; must reply within 2 week(s) of notification.
Transfers: No deadline. Applicants notified on a rolling basis starting 3/1; must reply within 2 week(s) of notification.

CONTACT
Liz Renda, Senior Director of Finance
3427 North Main Avenue, Scranton, PA 18508
(570) 702-8995

Juniata College

Huntingdon, Pennsylvania
www.juniata.edu   Federal Code: 003279

4-year private liberal arts college in small town.
Enrollment: 1,454 undergrads. 394 full-time freshmen.
Selectivity: Admits 50 to 75% of applicants.

BASIC COSTS (2017-2018)
Tuition and fees: $43,875.
Per-credit charge: $1,765.
Room and board: $12,040.

FINANCIAL AID PICTURE (2016-2017)
Students with need: Out of 350 full-time freshmen who applied for aid, 312 were judged to have need. Of these, 312 received aid, and 80 had their full need met. Average financial aid package met 85% of need; average scholarship/grant was $37,797; average loan was $3,467. Need-based aid available for part-time students.
Students without need: 82 full-time freshmen who did not demonstrate need for aid received scholarships/grants; average award was $23,221. No-need awards available for academics, alumni affiliation, art, minority status, music/drama.
Scholarships offered: Burkholder Scholarship: full tuition and room and board; 1 award; selected from John Stauffer scholarship semi-finalist pool. John Stauffer Scholarship: full tuition; 2 awards; National Merit Finalist or National Achievement Finalist or National Hispanic Recognition status. James Quinter Scholarship: $25,000. Calvert Ellis Scholarship: $16,000-$24,000. Competitive Scholarships: up to $5,000; min GPA 3.5, min SAT 1300.

FINANCIAL AID PROCEDURES

Forms required: FAFSA.

Dates and Deadlines: Closing date 2/15. Applicants notified on a rolling basis starting 3/1; must reply by 5/1.

Transfers: Applicants notified on a rolling basis starting 3/1; must reply by 5/1.

CONTACT

Tracie Patrick, Director of Student Financial Planning

1700 Moore Street, Huntingdon, PA 16652-2196

(814) 641-3142

Kaplan Career Institute: Harrisburg

Harrisburg, Pennsylvania

www.kaplancareerinstitute.com   Federal Code: 004910

2-year for-profit health science and technical college in small city.

Enrollment: 217 undergrads.

Selectivity: Open admission; but selective for some programs.

BASIC COSTS (2016-2017)

Additional info: Associate degree programs: Computer networking technology $36,089; criminal justice $28,985. Diploma programs: Medical assistant $15,365; medical billing and coding $15,315. Fees, books and supplies included. All costs are subject to change.

FINANCIAL AID PICTURE

Students with need: Need-based aid available for full-time and part-time students. Work study available nights.

FINANCIAL AID PROCEDURES

Forms required: FAFSA, institutional form.

CONTACT

Sarah Brooker, Financial Aid Director

5650 Derry Street, Harrisburg, PA 17111-4112

Kaplan Career Institute: Pittsburgh

Pittsburgh, Pennsylvania

www.kaplancareerinstitute.com   Federal Code: 007436

2-year for-profit business and health science college in large city.

Enrollment: 444 undergrads.

BASIC COSTS (2016-2017)

Additional info: Accounting Management: $31,809. Business Administration/Management: $31,837. Computer Numerical Control Machinist: $9,500. Criminal Justice: $31,775. Electrical Technician: $18,064. Federal, State and Local Payroll Tax Workshop: $510. Heating, Ventilation, Air Conditioning and Refrigeration: $17,104. Medical Assistant: $16,471. Medical Assisting: $31,789. Medical Billing and Coding: $13,536. Medical Office Assistant: $13,536. Occupational Therapy Assistant: $34,904. Practical Nursing: $29,806.

FINANCIAL AID PICTURE

Students with need: Need-based aid available for full-time and part-time students. Work study available nights.

Students without need: This college awards aid only to students with need.

FINANCIAL AID PROCEDURES

Forms required: FAFSA, state aid form, institutional form.

Dates and Deadlines: Closing date 4/30. Applicants notified on a rolling basis.

CONTACT

Chrissy Kapusniak, Director of Financial Aid

933 Penn Avenue, Pittsburgh, PA 15222

(412) 261-2647 ext. 265

Keystone College

La Plume, Pennsylvania

www.keystone.edu   Federal Code: 003280

4-year private business and liberal arts college in rural community.

Enrollment: 1,280 undergrads, 16% part-time. 276 full-time freshmen.

Selectivity: Admits over 75% of applicants.

BASIC COSTS (2016-2017)

Tuition and fees: $25,548.

Per-credit charge: $480.

Room and board: $10,352.

Additional info: Textbooks are included in the price of tuition.

FINANCIAL AID PICTURE

Students with need: Need-based aid available for full-time and part-time students. Work study available nights, weekends, and for part-time students.

Students without need: No-need awards available for academics, alumni affiliation, art.

Scholarships offered: Academic Excellence Scholarship: one-half up to full tuition; for full-time, first-time students in the top 5% of their class with SAT scores of 1100 or above (exclusive of Writing). Presidential Scholarship: up to $9,500 each year; based on class rank and SAT/ACT scores. Trustee Scholarship: up to $8,500 each year; based on class rank and SAT/ACT scores. Promise Award: up to $6,500 each year; for students demonstrating non-athletic leadership skills.

FINANCIAL AID PROCEDURES

Forms required: FAFSA, state aid form.

Dates and Deadlines: Priority date 4/1; closing date 5/1. Applicants notified on a rolling basis starting 2/1; must reply within 3 week(s) of notification.

Transfers: Must reply within 2 week(s) of notification.

CONTACT

Delaina Jayne, Director of Financial Assistance and Planning

One College Green, La Plume, PA 18440-0200

(570) 945-8134

Keystone Technical Institute

Harrisburg, Pennsylvania

www.kti.edu   Federal Code: 022342

2-year for-profit culinary school and technical college in small city.

Enrollment: 341 undergrads.

Selectivity: Open admission.

FINANCIAL AID PICTURE

Students with need: Need-based aid available for full-time and part-time students. Work study available nights.

Students without need: This college awards aid only to students with need.

Scholarships offered: Half-tuition scholarships; 13 available to degree-seeking students.

FINANCIAL AID PROCEDURES

Forms required: FAFSA, state aid form.

Dates and Deadlines: Closing date 8/1. Applicants notified on a rolling basis.

Transfers: State grant deadline for first-time recipients August 1. Renewal application deadline May 1.

CONTACT

Tracy Stewart, Financial Aid Coordinator

2301 Academy Drive, Harrisburg, PA 17112-1012

(717) 545-4747

King's College
Wilkes-Barre, Pennsylvania
www.kings.edu

Federal Code: 003282

4-year private business and liberal arts college in small city, affiliated with the Roman Catholic Church.

Enrollment: 1,946 undergrads, 2% part-time. 570 full-time freshmen.

Selectivity: Admits 50 to 75% of applicants.

BASIC COSTS (2016-2017)
Tuition and fees: $34,720.
Per-credit charge: $565.
Room and board: $12,318.

FINANCIAL AID PICTURE (2016-2017)
Students with need: Out of 501 full-time freshmen who applied for aid, 455 were judged to have need. Of these, 455 received aid, and 81 had their full need met. Average financial aid package met 76% of need; average scholarship/grant was $21,094; average loan was $3,733. Need-based aid available for part-time students.

Students without need: 64 full-time freshmen who did not demonstrate need for aid received scholarships/grants; average award was $15,926. No-need awards available for academics, leadership, ROTC.

Additional info: Any minority student with financial need may receive some aid in the form of a diversity scholarship.

FINANCIAL AID PROCEDURES
Forms required: FAFSA.
Dates and Deadlines: Priority date 2/15; no closing date. Applicants notified on a rolling basis starting 3/1; must reply within 2 week(s) of notification.
Transfers: Priority date 2/1; no deadline. Applicants notified on a rolling basis; must reply by 5/1 or within 2 week(s) of notification.

CONTACT
Donna Cerza, Director of Financial Aid
133 North River Street, Wilkes-Barre, PA 18711
(570) 208-5868

Kutztown University of Pennsylvania
Kutztown, Pennsylvania
www.kutztown.edu

Federal Code: 003322

4-year public university in small town.

Enrollment: 7,683 undergrads, 5% part-time. 1,861 full-time freshmen.

Selectivity: Admits over 75% of applicants.

BASIC COSTS (2016-2017)
Tuition and fees: $9,618; out-of-state residents $20,476.
Per-credit charge: $302; out-of-state residents $754.
Room and board: $9,438.

FINANCIAL AID PICTURE (2015-2016)
Students with need: Out of 1,741 full-time freshmen who applied for aid, 1,414 were judged to have need. Of these, 1,385 received aid, and 83 had their full need met. Average financial aid package met 41% of need; average scholarship/grant was $6,118; average loan was $3,364. For part-time students, average financial aid package was $5,847.

Students without need: 211 full-time freshmen who did not demonstrate need for aid received scholarships/grants; average award was $543. No-need awards available for academics, art, athletics, leadership, minority status, music/drama.

Scholarships offered: 86 full-time freshmen received athletic scholarships; average amount $2,175.

FINANCIAL AID PROCEDURES
Forms required: FAFSA.

Dates and Deadlines: Priority date 3/1; no closing date. Applicants notified on a rolling basis starting 3/30; must reply by 5/1 or within 4 week(s) of notification.

CONTACT
Bernard McCree, Director of Financial Aid
Admissions Office, Kutztown, PA 19530-0730
(610) 683-4077

La Roche College
Pittsburgh, Pennsylvania
www.laroche.edu

Federal Code: 003987

4-year private liberal arts college in large city, affiliated with the Roman Catholic Church.

Enrollment: 1,357 undergrads, 15% part-time. 265 full-time freshmen.

Selectivity: Admits over 75% of applicants.

BASIC COSTS (2016-2017)
Tuition and fees: $27,000.
Per-credit charge: $660.
Room and board: $10,924.

FINANCIAL AID PICTURE (2016-2017)
Students with need: Out of 206 full-time freshmen who applied for aid, 188 were judged to have need. Of these, 188 received aid, and 62 had their full need met. Average financial aid package met 94% of need; average scholarship/grant was $9,370; average loan was $3,498. For part-time students, average financial aid package was $3,335.

Students without need: 18 full-time freshmen who did not demonstrate need for aid received scholarships/grants; average award was $21,890. No-need awards available for academics.

FINANCIAL AID PROCEDURES
Forms required: FAFSA.
Dates and Deadlines: Priority date 5/1; no closing date. Applicants notified on a rolling basis starting 11/1; must reply within 2 week(s) of notification.

CONTACT
Sharon Platt, Director of Financial Aid
9000 Babcock Boulevard, Pittsburgh, PA 15237
(412) 536-1125

La Salle University
Philadelphia, Pennsylvania
www.lasalle.edu

Federal Code: 003287

4-year private university and liberal arts college in very large city, affiliated with the Roman Catholic Church.

Enrollment: 3,543 undergrads, 10% part-time. 801 full-time freshmen.

Selectivity: Admits 50 to 75% of applicants.

BASIC COSTS (2016-2017)
Tuition and fees: $41,100.
Room and board: $15,070.

FINANCIAL AID PICTURE (2015-2016)
Students with need: Out of 739 full-time freshmen who applied for aid, 691 were judged to have need. Of these, 691 received aid, and 82 had their full need met. Average financial aid package met 73% of need; average scholarship/grant was $25,952; average loan was $3,656. For part-time students, average financial aid package was $8,074.

Students without need: 95 full-time freshmen who did not demonstrate need for aid received scholarships/grants; average award was $18,091. No-need awards available for academics, athletics, ROTC.

Scholarships offered: *Merit:* Christian Brothers Scholarship; full tuition; based on academics and extracurricular leadership. Community Service Scholarship; half tuition; based on involvement in community service and academics. *Athletic:* 34 full-time freshmen received athletic scholarships; average amount $22,618.

FINANCIAL AID PROCEDURES

Forms required: FAFSA.

Dates and Deadlines: Priority date 2/15; no closing date. Applicants notified on a rolling basis starting 3/15; must reply by 5/1 or within 2 week(s) of notification.

Transfers: Applicants notified on a rolling basis starting 3/15; must reply by 5/1 or within 2 week(s) of notification.

CONTACT

Joseph Alaimo, Financial Aid Director
1900 West Olney Avenue, Philadelphia, PA 19141-1199
(215) 951-1070

Lackawanna College

Scranton, Pennsylvania
www.lackawanna.edu   Federal Code: 003283

2-year private junior college in small city.
Enrollment: 1,418 undergrads. 384 full-time freshmen.
Selectivity: Open admission.

BASIC COSTS (2016-2017)

Tuition and fees: $14,680.
Per-credit charge: $499.
Room and board: $8,800.

FINANCIAL AID PICTURE (2015-2016)

Students with need: Out of 380 full-time freshmen who applied for aid, 360 were judged to have need. Of these, 356 received aid, and 18 had their full need met. Average financial aid package met 49% of need; average scholarship/grant was $7,294; average loan was $3,128. For part-time students, average financial aid package was $5,903.

Students without need: 5 full-time freshmen who did not demonstrate need for aid received scholarships/grants; average award was $4,880. No-need awards available for academics, athletics.

Scholarships offered: 9 full-time freshmen received athletic scholarships; average amount $4,621.

FINANCIAL AID PROCEDURES

Forms required: FAFSA, state aid form, institutional form.

Dates and Deadlines: Priority date 5/1; no closing date. Applicants notified on a rolling basis starting 5/1.

Transfers: No deadline. Applicants notified on a rolling basis starting 5/1; must reply by 5/1.

CONTACT

Matthew Peters, Director of Financial Aid
501 Vine Street, Scranton, PA 18509
(570) 961-7859

Lafayette College

Easton, Pennsylvania   Federal Code: 003284
www.lafayette.edu   CSS Code: 2361

4-year private engineering and liberal arts college in large town.
Enrollment: 2,518 undergrads, 1% part-time. 649 full-time freshmen.
Selectivity: Admits less than 50% of applicants.

BASIC COSTS (2016-2017)

Tuition and fees: $48,885.

Room and board: $14,470.

FINANCIAL AID PICTURE (2016-2017)

Students with need: Out of 411 full-time freshmen who applied for aid, 243 were judged to have need. Of these, 243 received aid, and 243 had their full need met. Average financial aid package met 100% of need; average scholarship/grant was $41,091; average loan was $3,458. Need-based aid available for part-time students.

Students without need: 33 full-time freshmen who did not demonstrate need for aid received scholarships/grants; average award was $27,738. No-need awards available for academics, athletics, leadership, ROTC.

Scholarships offered: *Merit:* Marquis Scholarships; $24,000 per year; based on academic merit, awarded to about 50 entering students. Marquis Fellowships; $40,000 per year, based on academic merit and day-long interview process, awarded to about 10 entering students. Both programs carry a $4,000 one-time stipend to be used for a study abroad program. Creative and Performing Arts Fellowships; based on application; $7,500 toward a studio or performing arts project to be used during four years at Lafayette. *Athletic:* 67 full-time freshmen received athletic scholarships; average amount $37,571.

Additional info: Parent loans, up to $7,500 annually, available with college absorbing interest while student is enrolled. Family has 8 years after graduation to repay. Not limited to those demonstrating need.

FINANCIAL AID PROCEDURES

Forms required: FAFSA, CSS PROFILE.

Dates and Deadlines: Priority date 1/15; closing date 1/15. Applicants notified by 4/1; must reply by 5/1.

Transfers: Closing date 4/1. Applicants notified on a rolling basis starting 5/1; must reply within 2 week(s) of notification.

CONTACT

Ashley Bianchi, Director of Student Financial Aid
118 Markle Hall, Easton, PA 18042
(610) 330-5055

Lancaster Bible College

Lancaster, Pennsylvania
www.lbc.edu   Federal Code: 003285

4-year private Bible college in small city, affiliated with the nondenominational tradition.
Enrollment: 1,409 undergrads.
Selectivity: Admits 50 to 75% of applicants.

BASIC COSTS (2016-2017)

Tuition and fees: $21,800.
Room and board: $8,580.

FINANCIAL AID PICTURE

Students with need: Need-based aid available for full-time and part-time students. Work study available nights, weekends, and for part-time students.

Students without need: No-need awards available for academics, alumni affiliation, leadership, music/drama.

FINANCIAL AID PROCEDURES

Forms required: FAFSA, state aid form.

Dates and Deadlines: Priority date 5/1; no closing date. Applicants notified on a rolling basis starting 3/1; must reply within 3 week(s) of notification.

CONTACT

Karen Fox, Director of Financial Aid
901 Eden Road, Lancaster, PA 17601-5036
(717) 560-8254

Laurel Business Institute
Uniontown, Pennsylvania
www.laurel.edu　　　　　　　Federal Code: 017118

2-year for-profit technical and career college in large town.
Enrollment: 233 undergrads.

FINANCIAL AID PICTURE
Students with need: Need-based aid available for full-time and part-time students.
Students without need: This college awards aid only to students with need.
Scholarships offered: One full tuition, several half tuition (including GED scholarships); based on high school transcripts or GED scores, letters of reference, and personal interview.

FINANCIAL AID PROCEDURES
Forms required: FAFSA, institutional form.
Dates and Deadlines: Applicants notified on a rolling basis; must reply within 4 week(s) of notification.
Transfers: No deadline. Must reply within 4 week(s) of notification.

CONTACT
Stephanie Migyanko, Director of Financial Aid
11 East Penn Street, Uniontown, PA 15401
(724) 439-4900

Lebanon Valley College
Annville, Pennsylvania
www.lvc.edu　　　　　　　Federal Code: 003288

4-year private liberal arts college in small town, affiliated with the United Methodist Church.
Enrollment: 1,649 undergrads, 3% part-time. 428 full-time freshmen.
Selectivity: Admits over 75% of applicants.

BASIC COSTS (2017-2018)
Tuition and fees: $42,180.
Room and board: $11,410.
Additional info: Tuition/fee waivers available for minority students.

FINANCIAL AID PICTURE (2016-2017)
Students with need: Out of 410 full-time freshmen who applied for aid, 367 were judged to have need. Of these, 367 received aid, and 105 had their full need met. Average financial aid package met 83% of need; average scholarship/grant was $26,695; average loan was $3,965. For part-time students, average financial aid package was $7,857.
Students without need: 61 full-time freshmen who did not demonstrate need for aid received scholarships/grants; average award was $21,089. No-need awards available for academics, alumni affiliation, music/drama.
Scholarships offered: Multicultural Fellowship: limited to high school seniors and transfer students who identify most closely as African-American, Asian-American, Hispanic-American, or Native-American. Board of Trustees Scholarship: $23,000 per year. Presidential Scholarship: $21,000 per year. Dean's Scholarship: $19,000 per year. Alfred Tennyson Sumner Scholarship: $17,000 per year. Mary A. Weiss Scholarship: $15,000 per year. Departmental Scholarships: based on major and financial need; ranges from $1,000-$5,000; number awarded varies by department. FAFSA Incentive: $1,000 awarded to incoming students who submit the FAFSA before the deadline; unlimited. Biology Scholarship: $5,000 per year; major in biology, including pre-med/pre-professional health care programs and biology/secondary education certification, and other criteria; three per year. Scholarship in Literature: $5,000 per year; major in English, rank in top 10% of high school class, and other criteria; two per year. Scholarship in Physics: $5,000 per year; major in physics, engineering (the physics track), or physics/secondary education certification, rank in top 10% of class or a strong academic record from a school that does not rank, and other criteria; two per year.

FINANCIAL AID PROCEDURES
Forms required: FAFSA.
Dates and Deadlines: Priority date 2/15; no closing date. Applicants notified on a rolling basis starting 3/1; must reply by 5/1 or within 2 week(s) of notification.
Transfers: No deadline. Applicants notified on a rolling basis starting 3/1; must reply by 5/1 or within 2 week(s) of notification. Students transferring 15 or fewer credits are considered for scholarships on the same basis as high school seniors. Students transferring 16 or more credits are considered for scholarships based on their college academic performance.

CONTACT
Kendra Feigert, Director of Financial Aid
101 North College Avenue, Annville, PA 17003-1400
(717) 867-6181

Lehigh Carbon Community College
Schnecksville, Pennsylvania
www.lccc.edu　　　　　　　Federal Code: 006810

2-year public community college in small town.
Enrollment: 5,485 undergrads, 55% part-time. 956 full-time freshmen.
Selectivity: Open admission; but selective for some programs.

BASIC COSTS (2016-2017)
Tuition and fees: $3,900; out-of-district residents $7,170; out-of-state residents $10,440.
Per-credit charge: $100; out-of-district residents $209; out-of-state residents $318.
Additional info: Tuition/fee waivers available for unemployed or children of unemployed.

FINANCIAL AID PICTURE
Students with need: Need-based aid available for full-time and part-time students. Work study available nights.
Students without need: No-need awards available for academics, job skills.

FINANCIAL AID PROCEDURES
Forms required: FAFSA.
Dates and Deadlines: Priority date 5/1; no closing date. Applicants notified on a rolling basis starting 1/1; must reply within 2 week(s) of notification.
Transfers: No deadline. Applicants notified on a rolling basis.

CONTACT
Marian Snyder, Director of Financial Aid
4525 Education Park Drive, Schnecksville, PA 18078-2502
(610) 799-1133

Lehigh University
Bethlehem, Pennsylvania　　Federal Code: 003289
www.lehigh.edu　　　　　　CSS Code: 2365

4-year private university in small city.
Enrollment: 5,061 undergrads, 1% part-time. 1,249 full-time freshmen.
Selectivity: Admits less than 50% of applicants.

BASIC COSTS (2016-2017)
Tuition and fees: $48,320.
Per-credit charge: $2,000.
Room and board: $12,690.

FINANCIAL AID PICTURE (2016-2017)
Students with need: Out of 791 full-time freshmen who applied for aid, 493 were judged to have need. Of these, 492 received aid, and 392 had their full need met. Average financial aid package met 98% of need; average scholarship/grant was $38,851; average loan was $3,462. For part-time students, average financial aid package was $7,798.

Students without need: 50 full-time freshmen who did not demonstrate need for aid received scholarships/grants; average award was $8,921. No-need awards available for academics, art, athletics, leadership, music/drama, ROTC.

Scholarships offered: *Merit:* Dean's Scholarships; $10,000; for academic excellence and leadership skills. Baker Scholarship; $3,000; for excellence in music or theater and superior academic record. Choral Arts Scholarships; $2,500; for singing talent. Performing Arts Scholarship; $3,000; for those who display exceptional theatrical talent (including performance, design, technical, and playwriting). Snyder Family Marching 97 Scholarships; $1,000-$2,500; for those who demonstrate musical talent and leadership and who fully participate in the marching band. Athletic Awards/Scholarships. *Athletic:* 75 full-time freshmen received athletic scholarships; average amount $35,177.

Additional info: Loans eliminated in financial aid packages for students eligible for financial aid and whose calculated total family income is less than $50,000. Loans limited to $3,000 in financial aid packages for students eligible for financial aid and who have a calculated total family income between $50,000 and $75,000.

FINANCIAL AID PROCEDURES
Forms required: FAFSA, CSS PROFILE.
Dates and Deadlines: Closing date 2/15. Applicants notified by 3/30; must reply by 5/1 or within 3 week(s) of notification.
Transfers: Closing date 3/1. Applicants notified by 5/30; must reply within 3 week(s) of notification.

CONTACT
Jennifer Mertz, Director of Financial Aid
27 Memorial Drive West, Bethlehem, PA 18015
(610) 758-3181

Lincoln University
Lincoln University, Pennsylvania
www.lincoln.edu   Federal Code: 003290

4-year public university and liberal arts college in small town.
Enrollment: 1,824 undergrads, 9% part-time. 453 full-time freshmen.
Selectivity: Admits over 75% of applicants.

BASIC COSTS (2016-2017)
Tuition and fees: $10,694; out-of-state residents $15,582.
Per-credit charge: $315; out-of-state residents $519.
Room and board: $9,268.
Additional info: Tuition at time of enrollment locked for 4 years.

FINANCIAL AID PICTURE (2015-2016)
Students with need: Out of 441 full-time freshmen who applied for aid, 423 were judged to have need. Of these, 421 received aid, and 23 had their full need met. Average financial aid package met 42% of need; average scholarship/grant was $7,026; average loan was $3,433. For part-time students, average financial aid package was $7,150.
Students without need: 10 full-time freshmen who did not demonstrate need for aid received scholarships/grants; average award was $3,466. No-need awards available for academics, alumni affiliation, athletics, music/drama, state/district residency.
Scholarships offered: 16 full-time freshmen received athletic scholarships; average amount $4,718.

FINANCIAL AID PROCEDURES
Forms required: FAFSA.
Dates and Deadlines: Priority date 4/1; no closing date. Applicants notified by 2/1; must reply within 2 week(s) of notification.

CONTACT
Kim Anderson, Director of Financial Aid
1570 Baltimore Pike, Lincoln University, PA 19352-0999
(800) 561-2606

Lock Haven University of Pennsylvania
Lock Haven, Pennsylvania
www.lhup.edu   Federal Code: 003323

4-year public university and liberal arts college in small town.
Enrollment: 3,786 undergrads, 7% part-time. 819 full-time freshmen.
Selectivity: Admits over 75% of applicants.

BASIC COSTS (2016-2017)
Tuition and fees: $10,229; out-of-state residents $19,087.
Room and board: $9,588.

FINANCIAL AID PICTURE (2016-2017)
Students with need: Out of 779 full-time freshmen who applied for aid, 668 were judged to have need. Of these, 661 received aid, and 634 had their full need met. Average financial aid package met 70% of need; average scholarship/grant was $3,027; average loan was $3,332. For part-time students, average financial aid package was $3,736.
Students without need: 14 full-time freshmen who did not demonstrate need for aid received scholarships/grants; average award was $1,852. No-need awards available for academics, art, athletics, leadership, minority status, music/drama, ROTC, state/district residency.
Scholarships offered: 73 full-time freshmen received athletic scholarships; average amount $2,260.

FINANCIAL AID PROCEDURES
Forms required: FAFSA, state aid form.
Dates and Deadlines: Closing date 3/15. Applicants notified on a rolling basis starting 3/15; must reply within 2 week(s) of notification.
Transfers: Priority date 3/15. Applicants notified on a rolling basis starting 3/15; must reply within 2 week(s) of notification.

CONTACT
Robert Fryer, Director Financial Aid
LHU Office of Admissions, Lock Haven, PA 17745
(570) 484-2424

Luzerne County Community College
Nanticoke, Pennsylvania
www.luzerne.edu   Federal Code: 006811

2-year public community college in large town.
Enrollment: 5,063 undergrads, 50% part-time. 900 full-time freshmen.
Selectivity: Open admission; but selective for some programs.

BASIC COSTS (2016-2017)
Tuition and fees: $5,040; out-of-district residents $8,790; out-of-state residents $12,540.
Per-credit charge: $125; out-of-district residents $250; out-of-state residents $375.

FINANCIAL AID PICTURE
Students with need: Need-based aid available for full-time and part-time students.

FINANCIAL AID PROCEDURES
Forms required: FAFSA, state aid form, institutional form.
Dates and Deadlines: Priority date 4/15; no closing date. Applicants notified on a rolling basis starting 7/1.

CONTACT
Mark Carpentier, Director of Financial Aid
1333 South Prospect Street, Nanticoke, PA 18634-3899
(570) 740-0389

Lycoming College
Williamsport, Pennsylvania
www.lycoming.edu   Federal Code: 003293

4-year private liberal arts college in small city, affiliated with the United Methodist Church.
Enrollment: 1,246 undergrads, 1% part-time. 343 full-time freshmen.
Selectivity: Admits 50 to 75% of applicants.

BASIC COSTS (2016-2017)
Tuition and fees: $37,387.
Per-credit charge: $1,139.
Room and board: $11,418.
Additional info: Tuition/fee waivers available for minority students.

FINANCIAL AID PICTURE (2016-2017)
Students with need: Out of 317 full-time freshmen who applied for aid, 304 were judged to have need. Of these, 304 received aid, and 50 had their full need met. Average financial aid package met 85% of need; average scholarship/grant was $31,763; average loan was $3,604. For part-time students, average financial aid package was $7,097.
Students without need: 39 full-time freshmen who did not demonstrate need for aid received scholarships/grants; average award was $25,411. No-need awards available for academics, art, music/drama.

FINANCIAL AID PROCEDURES
Forms required: FAFSA.
Dates and Deadlines: Priority date 5/1; no closing date. Applicants notified on a rolling basis starting 3/1; must reply by 5/1.
Transfers: No deadline.

CONTACT
James Lakis, Director of Financial Aid
700 College Place, Williamsport, PA 17701
(570) 321-4026

Manor College
Jenkintown, Pennsylvania
www.manor.edu   Federal Code: 003294

2-year private junior college in small town, affiliated with the Ukrainian Catholic Church.
Enrollment: 601 undergrads, 33% part-time. 141 full-time freshmen.
Selectivity: Admits over 75% of applicants.

BASIC COSTS (2016-2017)
Tuition and fees: $16,550.
Per-credit charge: $699.
Room and board: $7,500.
Additional info: Tuition/fee waivers available for minority students, unemployed or children of unemployed.

FINANCIAL AID PICTURE (2015-2016)
Students with need: Out of 134 full-time freshmen who applied for aid, 133 were judged to have need. Of these, 133 received aid, and 9 had their full need met. For part-time students, average financial aid package was $3,479.
Students without need: This college awards aid only to students with need.
Scholarships offered: Basilian Scholarship; for every freshman with A or B high school average and minimum 900 SAT (exclusive of Writing).

FINANCIAL AID PROCEDURES
Forms required: FAFSA, state aid form, institutional form.
Dates and Deadlines: Priority date 3/1; no closing date. Applicants notified on a rolling basis; must reply within 1 week(s) of notification.
Transfers: No deadline. Applicants notified on a rolling basis starting 12/1; must reply within 2 week(s) of notification.

CONTACT
Chris Hartman, Director of Financial Aid
700 Fox Chase Road, Jenkintown, PA 19046-3319
(215) 884-2360

Mansfield University of Pennsylvania
Mansfield, Pennsylvania
www.mansfield.edu   Federal Code: 003324

4-year public university in small town.
Enrollment: 2,052 undergrads, 6% part-time. 465 full-time freshmen.
Selectivity: Admits 50 to 75% of applicants.

BASIC COSTS (2016-2017)
Tuition and fees: $11,908; out-of-state residents $21,058.
Room and board: $12,438.

FINANCIAL AID PICTURE (2015-2016)
Students with need: Out of 455 full-time freshmen who applied for aid, 408 were judged to have need. Of these, 408 received aid, and 24 had their full need met. Average financial aid package met 55% of need; average scholarship/grant was $2,868; average loan was $2,404. For part-time students, average financial aid package was $5,466.
Students without need: 15 full-time freshmen who did not demonstrate need for aid received scholarships/grants; average award was $2,436. No-need awards available for academics, alumni affiliation, art, athletics, job skills, leadership, minority status, music/drama, religious affiliation, ROTC, state/district residency.
Scholarships offered: 2 full-time freshmen received athletic scholarships; average amount $5,000.

FINANCIAL AID PROCEDURES
Forms required: FAFSA, state aid form.
Dates and Deadlines: Priority date 2/15; closing date 6/30. Applicants notified on a rolling basis starting 2/17; must reply within 4 week(s) of notification.

CONTACT
Charles Scheetz, Director of Financial Aid
71 Academy Street, Mansfield, PA 16933
(570) 662-4129

Marywood University
Scranton, Pennsylvania
www.marywood.edu   Federal Code: 003296

4-year private university in small city, affiliated with the Roman Catholic Church.
Enrollment: 1,822 undergrads, 6% part-time. 323 full-time freshmen.
Selectivity: Admits 50 to 75% of applicants.

BASIC COSTS (2016-2017)
Tuition and fees: $33,000.
Per-credit charge: $630.
Room and board: $13,900.

FINANCIAL AID PICTURE
Students with need: Need-based aid available for full-time and part-time students. Work study available nights, weekends, and for part-time students.
Students without need: No-need awards available for academics, alumni affiliation, art, leadership, music/drama, ROTC.

FINANCIAL AID PROCEDURES
Forms required: FAFSA, state aid form.
Dates and Deadlines: Priority date 2/15; no closing date. Applicants notified on a rolling basis starting 3/15; must reply by 5/1 or within 3 week(s) of notification.

Transfers: No deadline. Applicants notified on a rolling basis starting 3/1; must reply by 5/1 or within 3 week(s) of notification.

CONTACT
Barbara Schmitt, Director of Financial Aid
2300 Adams Avenue, Scranton, PA 18509-1598
(570) 348-6225

Mercyhurst University
Erie, Pennsylvania
www.mercyhurst.edu   Federal Code: 003297

4-year private university and liberal arts college in small city, affiliated with the Roman Catholic Church.
Enrollment: 2,469 undergrads, 3% part-time. 716 full-time freshmen.
Selectivity: Admits over 75% of applicants.

BASIC COSTS (2016-2017)
Tuition and fees: $34,480.
Per-credit charge: $1,081.
Room and board: $11,624.
Additional info: Tuition/fee waivers available for adults, minority students, unemployed or children of unemployed.

FINANCIAL AID PICTURE
Students with need: Need-based aid available for full-time and part-time students. Work study available nights, weekends, and for part-time students.
Students without need: No-need awards available for academics, alumni affiliation, art, athletics, leadership, minority status, music/drama, religious affiliation, ROTC.

FINANCIAL AID PROCEDURES
Forms required: FAFSA.
Dates and Deadlines: Priority date 3/1; no closing date. Applicants notified on a rolling basis starting 2/15; must reply by 5/1 or within 2 week(s) of notification.
Transfers: No deadline. Applicants notified on a rolling basis; must reply within 2 week(s) of notification.

CONTACT
Carrie Newman, Director of Student Financial Services
501 East 38th Street, Erie, PA 16546-0001
(814) 824-2288

Messiah College
Mechanicsburg, Pennsylvania
www.messiah.edu   Federal Code: 003298

4-year private liberal arts college in small town, affiliated with the interdenominational tradition.
Enrollment: 2,683 undergrads, 1% part-time. 685 full-time freshmen.
Selectivity: Admits over 75% of applicants.

BASIC COSTS (2016-2017)
Tuition and fees: $33,180.
Per-credit charge: $1,350.
Room and board: $9,920.
Additional info: Tuition/fee waivers available for adults, minority students.

FINANCIAL AID PICTURE (2016-2017)
Students with need: Out of 594 full-time freshmen who applied for aid, 519 were judged to have need. Of these, 518 received aid, and 109 had their full need met. Average financial aid package met 74% of need; average scholarship/grant was $18,821; average loan was $3,934. For part-time students, average financial aid package was $8,760.

Students without need: 163 full-time freshmen who did not demonstrate need for aid received scholarships/grants; average award was $15,583. No-need awards available for academics, art, leadership, music/drama, religious affiliation.

FINANCIAL AID PROCEDURES
Forms required: FAFSA.
Dates and Deadlines: Priority date 4/1; no closing date. Applicants notified on a rolling basis starting 12/1; must reply by 5/1 or within 4 week(s) of notification.

CONTACT
Greg Gearhart, Director of Financial Aid
One College Avenue, Suite 3005, Mechanicsburg, PA 17055
(717) 691-6007

Millersville University of Pennsylvania
Millersville, Pennsylvania
www.millersville.edu   Federal Code: 003325

4-year public university and liberal arts college in small town.
Enrollment: 6,879 undergrads, 14% part-time. 1,324 full-time freshmen.
Selectivity: Admits 50 to 75% of applicants.

BASIC COSTS (2016-2017)
Tuition and fees: $11,494; out-of-state residents $20,620.
Per-credit charge: $299; out-of-state residents $754.
Room and board: $12,228.
Additional info: There is a out-of-state tuition reduction program; depending on academic major and qualifications, some students may qualify for a reduced tuition rate of $12,668 or $14,477 for STEM majors.

FINANCIAL AID PICTURE (2015-2016)
Students with need: Out of 1,235 full-time freshmen who applied for aid, 937 were judged to have need. Of these, 895 received aid, and 44 had their full need met. Average financial aid package met 59% of need; average scholarship/grant was $5,438; average loan was $3,207. For part-time students, average financial aid package was $6,161.
Students without need: 51 full-time freshmen who did not demonstrate need for aid received scholarships/grants; average award was $2,598. No-need awards available for academics, athletics, minority status.
Scholarships offered: 18 full-time freshmen received athletic scholarships; average amount $2,849.

FINANCIAL AID PROCEDURES
Forms required: FAFSA.
Dates and Deadlines: Priority date 3/15; no closing date. Applicants notified on a rolling basis starting 3/19; must reply within 2 week(s) of notification.

CONTACT
Dwight Horsey, Director of Financial Aid and Assistant Vice President for Enrollment Management
PO Box 1002, Millersville, PA 17551-0302
(717) 871-5100

Misericordia University
Dallas, Pennsylvania
www.misericordia.edu   Federal Code: 003247

4-year private health science and liberal arts college in large town, affiliated with the Roman Catholic Church.
Enrollment: 2,148 undergrads, 24% part-time. 423 full-time freshmen.
Selectivity: Admits 50 to 75% of applicants.

BASIC COSTS (2017-2018)
Tuition and fees: $31,660.

Per-credit charge: $595.

Room and board: $13,550.

Additional info: Tuition/fee waivers available for adults, minority students.

FINANCIAL AID PICTURE (2016-2017)

Students with need: Out of 411 full-time freshmen who applied for aid, 357 were judged to have need. Of these, 357 received aid, and 76 had their full need met. Average financial aid package met 80% of need; average scholarship/grant was $18,448; average loan was $7,657. For part-time students, average financial aid package was $5,927.

Students without need: 54 full-time freshmen who did not demonstrate need for aid received scholarships/grants; average award was $14,047. No-need awards available for academics, alumni affiliation, leadership, minority status, state/district residency.

Scholarships offered: McAuley Award; $1,000-$5,000 per year; based on out-of-classroom activities. Academic Scholarship; $2,000-$15,000 per year; based on academic abilities.

FINANCIAL AID PROCEDURES

Forms required: FAFSA.

Dates and Deadlines: Priority date 3/1; closing date 5/1. Applicants notified on a rolling basis starting 3/15.

Transfers: No deadline. Applicants notified on a rolling basis starting 3/15.

CONTACT

Joanna Naylor, Assistant Director of Financial Aid

301 Lake Street, Dallas, PA 18612-1098

(570) 674-6280

Montgomery County Community College

Blue Bell, Pennsylvania

www.mc3.edu   Federal Code: 004452

2-year public community college in large town.

Enrollment: 9,791 undergrads, 62% part-time. 1,495 full-time freshmen.

Selectivity: Open admission; but selective for some programs.

BASIC COSTS (2016-2017)

Tuition and fees: $5,610; out-of-district residents $10,230; out-of-state residents $14,850.

Per-credit charge: $144; out-of-district residents $288; out-of-state residents $432.

Additional info: Courses with higher than average operating costs will be assessed additional fees.

FINANCIAL AID PICTURE (2015-2016)

Students with need: Out of 880 full-time freshmen who applied for aid, 862 were judged to have need. Of these, 800 received aid, and 43 had their full need met. Average financial aid package met 23% of need; average scholarship/grant was $3,230; average loan was $1,658. For part-time students, average financial aid package was $3,082.

Students without need: 134 full-time freshmen who did not demonstrate need for aid received scholarships/grants; average award was $2,724. No-need awards available for academics.

FINANCIAL AID PROCEDURES

Forms required: FAFSA.

Dates and Deadlines: Priority date 5/1; no closing date. Applicants notified on a rolling basis starting 2/1.

Transfers: No deadline.

CONTACT

Tracey Richards, Director of Financial Aid

340 DeKalb Pike, Blue Bell, PA 19422

(215) 641-6566

Moore College of Art and Design

Philadelphia, Pennsylvania

www.moore.edu   Federal Code: 003300

4-year private visual arts college for women in very large city.

Enrollment: 368 undergrads.

Selectivity: Admits 50 to 75% of applicants.

BASIC COSTS (2016-2017)

Tuition and fees: $38,480.

Room and board: $14,390.

FINANCIAL AID PICTURE (2015-2016)

Students with need: Need-based aid available for part-time students.

Students without need: No-need awards available for academics, art, leadership.

FINANCIAL AID PROCEDURES

Forms required: FAFSA.

Dates and Deadlines: Priority date 3/1; closing date 5/1. Applicants notified on a rolling basis starting 2/15; must reply within 2 week(s) of notification.

Transfers: Priority date 5/1; no deadline.

CONTACT

Devon Weaver, Director of Financial Aid

The Parkway at 20th Street, Philadelphia, PA 19103-1179

(215) 568-4515

Moravian College

Bethlehem, Pennsylvania

www.moravian.edu   Federal Code: 003301

4-year private liberal arts and seminary college in small city, affiliated with the Moravian Church in America.

Enrollment: 1,928 undergrads, 7% part-time. 485 full-time freshmen.

Selectivity: Admits over 75% of applicants.

BASIC COSTS (2017-2018)

Tuition and fees: $42,024.

Per-credit charge: $1,119.5.

Room and board: $12,694.

FINANCIAL AID PICTURE (2016-2017)

Students with need: Out of 437 full-time freshmen who applied for aid, 407 were judged to have need. Of these, 407 received aid, and 65 had their full need met. Average financial aid package met 80% of need; average scholarship/grant was $27,649; average loan was $3,654. For part-time students, average financial aid package was $11,808.

Students without need: 78 full-time freshmen who did not demonstrate need for aid received scholarships/grants; average award was $17,056. No-need awards available for academics, alumni affiliation, art, leadership, music/drama, religious affiliation, ROTC, state/district residency.

FINANCIAL AID PROCEDURES

Forms required: FAFSA.

Dates and Deadlines: Priority date 3/1; no closing date. Applicants notified on a rolling basis starting 2/16; must reply by 5/1.

CONTACT

Dennis Levy, Director of Financial Aid Services

1200 Main Street, Bethlehem, PA 18018

(610) 861-1330

Mount Aloysius College

Cresson, Pennsylvania
www.mtaloy.edu   Federal Code: 003302

4-year private liberal arts college in small town, affiliated with the Roman Catholic Church.

Enrollment: 1,310 undergrads, 18% part-time. 272 full-time freshmen.
Selectivity: Open admission; but selective for some programs.

BASIC COSTS (2016-2017)
Tuition and fees: $21,850.
Per-credit charge: $770.
Room and board: $9,940.
Additional info: Tuition/fee waivers available for unemployed or children of unemployed.

FINANCIAL AID PICTURE (2016-2017)
Students with need: Out of 272 full-time freshmen who applied for aid, 209 were judged to have need. Of these, 209 received aid. Average financial aid package met 35% of need; average scholarship/grant was $2,880; average loan was $3,800. For part-time students, average financial aid package was $3,210.
Students without need: 63 full-time freshmen who did not demonstrate need for aid received scholarships/grants; average award was $5,000. No-need awards available for academics, art, leadership, music/drama, religious affiliation.

FINANCIAL AID PROCEDURES
Forms required: FAFSA.
Dates and Deadlines: Priority date 4/1; no closing date. Applicants notified on a rolling basis starting 2/15; must reply within 2 week(s) of notification.
Transfers: No deadline.

CONTACT
Stacy Schenk, Director of Financial Aid
7373 Admiral Peary Highway, Cresson, PA 16630
(814) 886-6357

Muhlenberg College

Allentown, Pennsylvania   Federal Code: 003304
www.muhlenberg.edu   CSS Code: 2424

4-year private liberal arts college in small city, affiliated with the Evangelical Lutheran Church in America.
Enrollment: 2,375 undergrads, 3% part-time. 593 full-time freshmen.
Selectivity: Admits less than 50% of applicants.

BASIC COSTS (2016-2017)
Tuition and fees: $48,310.
Per-credit charge: $1,406.25.
Room and board: $11,090.
Additional info: Tuition/fee waivers available for adults, minority students.

FINANCIAL AID PICTURE (2016-2017)
Students with need: Out of 454 full-time freshmen who applied for aid, 349 were judged to have need. Of these, 348 received aid, and 107 had their full need met. Average financial aid package met 85% of need; average scholarship/grant was $31,115; average loan was $3,444. For part-time students, average financial aid package was $7,249.
Students without need: 199 full-time freshmen who did not demonstrate need for aid received scholarships/grants; average award was $12,645. No-need awards available for academics, art, music/drama, religious affiliation.
Scholarships offered: Academic merit awards: $1,000 - $20,000, five additional scholarships in the amount of $40,000. Talent awards: available in the visual or performing art based in audition or portfolio review.

FINANCIAL AID PROCEDURES
Forms required: FAFSA, CSS PROFILE, institutional form.

Dates and Deadlines: Closing date 2/15. Applicants notified by 4/1; must reply by 5/1.
Transfers: Closing date 4/15. Applicants notified by 6/1; must reply by 7/1. Transfers awarded aid on a funds-available basis after returning students and freshmen have been served.

CONTACT
Gregory Mitton, Director of Financial Aid
2400 Chew Street, Allentown, PA 18104
(484) 664-3175

Neumann University

Aston, Pennsylvania
www.neumann.edu   Federal Code: 003988

4-year private university in large town, affiliated with the Roman Catholic Church.
Enrollment: 2,190 undergrads, 27% part-time. 375 full-time freshmen.
Selectivity: Admits over 75% of applicants.

BASIC COSTS (2016-2017)
Tuition and fees: $28,580.
Per-credit charge: $625.
Room and board: $12,158.

FINANCIAL AID PICTURE (2016-2017)
Students with need: Out of 360 full-time freshmen who applied for aid, 328 were judged to have need. Of these, 328 received aid. Average financial aid package met 70% of need; average scholarship/grant was $10,145; average loan was $3,406. For part-time students, average financial aid package was $5,434.
Students without need: This college awards aid only to students with need.

FINANCIAL AID PROCEDURES
Forms required: FAFSA, state aid form.
Dates and Deadlines: Applicants notified on a rolling basis starting 3/1; must reply by 5/1 or within 2 week(s) of notification.
Transfers: No deadline. Applicants notified on a rolling basis; must reply within 2 week(s) of notification.

CONTACT
Andrea Del Vacchio, Director of Financial Assistance
Office of Admissions, Aston, PA 19014-1298
(610) 558-5521

New Castle School of Trades

New Castle, Pennsylvania
www.ncstrades.edu   Federal Code: 007780

2-year for-profit technical college in large town.
Enrollment: 825 undergrads.

FINANCIAL AID PICTURE
Students with need: Need-based aid available for full-time and part-time students.

CONTACT
Trudy Sotter, Financial Aid
4117 Pulaski Road, New Castle, PA 16101
(724) 964-8811

Northampton Community College

Bethlehem, Pennsylvania
www.northampton.edu   Federal Code: 007191

2-year public community college in small city.
Enrollment: 9,450 undergrads, 53% part-time. 1,436 full-time freshmen.
Selectivity: Open admission; but selective for some programs.

BASIC COSTS (2016-2017)
Tuition and fees: $4,170; out-of-district residents $9,030; out-of-state residents $13,290.
Per-credit charge: $97; out-of-district residents $194; out-of-state residents $291.
Room and board: $8,452.
Additional info: Tuition/fee waivers available for unemployed or children of unemployed.

FINANCIAL AID PICTURE (2016-2017)
Students with need: 72% of average financial aid package awarded as scholarships/grants, 28% awarded as loans/jobs. Need-based aid available for part-time students. Work study available nights, weekends, and for part-time students.
Students without need: No-need awards available for academics, alumni affiliation, art, leadership, minority status, music/drama, state/district residency.

FINANCIAL AID PROCEDURES
Forms required: FAFSA, state aid form.
Dates and Deadlines: Priority date 3/31; no closing date. Applicants notified on a rolling basis starting 4/1.

CONTACT
Cindy King, Director of Financial Aid
3835 Green Pond Road, Bethlehem, PA 18020-7599
(610) 861-5510

Orleans Technical Institute

Philadelphia, Pennsylvania
www.orleanstech.edu   Federal Code: 021830

2-year private technical and career college in very large city.
Enrollment: 548 undergrads.

BASIC COSTS (2016-2017)
Additional info: Tuition and required fees vary by program and range from $12,990 to $13,791. Books and supplies vary by program. All costs are subject to change.

FINANCIAL AID PICTURE
Students with need: Need-based aid available for full-time and part-time students. Work study available nights, weekends, and for part-time students.
Students without need: No-need awards available for academics.

FINANCIAL AID PROCEDURES
Forms required: FAFSA, institutional form.
Dates and Deadlines: Applicants notified on a rolling basis.

CONTACT
Latanya Byrd, Director of Student Financial Services
2770 Red Lion Road, Philadelphia, PA 19114
(215) 728-4736 ext. 4736

Peirce College

Philadelphia, Pennsylvania
www.peirce.edu   Federal Code: 003309

4-year private business and technical college in very large city.
Enrollment: 1,484 undergrads, 79% part-time. 18 full-time freshmen.

Selectivity: Open admission; but selective for some programs.

BASIC COSTS (2016-2017)
Tuition and fees: $17,940.
Per-credit charge: $578.

FINANCIAL AID PICTURE (2015-2016)
Students with need: Out of 18 full-time freshmen who applied for aid, 18 were judged to have need. Of these, 18 received aid. Average financial aid package met 56% of need; average scholarship/grant was $10,193; average loan was $2,350. For part-time students, average financial aid package was $6,405.
Students without need: No-need awards available for academics, alumni affiliation, ROTC, state/district residency.
Additional info: Tuition discounts available for US students serving in US military and in protect-and-serve fields.

FINANCIAL AID PROCEDURES
Forms required: FAFSA.
Dates and Deadlines: Applicants notified on a rolling basis starting 5/1.
Transfers: No deadline. Applicants notified on a rolling basis.

CONTACT
Kristina Fripps, Director, Student Financial Aid
1420 Pine Street, Philadelphia, PA 19102-4699
(888) 467-3472 ext. 9370

Penn State Abington

Abington, Pennsylvania
www.abington.psu.edu   Federal Code: 003329

4-year public branch campus college in small city.
Enrollment: 3,950 undergrads, 20% part-time. 863 full-time freshmen.
Selectivity: Admits over 75% of applicants.

BASIC COSTS (2016-2017)
Tuition and fees: $14,172; out-of-state residents $21,742.
Per-credit charge: $543; out-of-state residents $866.

FINANCIAL AID PICTURE (2015-2016)
Students with need: Out of 725 full-time freshmen who applied for aid, 610 were judged to have need. Of these, 596 received aid, and 22 had their full need met. Average financial aid package met 60% of need; average scholarship/grant was $8,148; average loan was $3,259. For part-time students, average financial aid package was $5,676.
Students without need: 59 full-time freshmen who did not demonstrate need for aid received scholarships/grants; average award was $4,288. No-need awards available for academics, alumni affiliation, ROTC.

FINANCIAL AID PROCEDURES
Forms required: FAFSA.
Dates and Deadlines: Priority date 2/15; no closing date. Applicants notified on a rolling basis.
Transfers: No deadline. Applicants notified on a rolling basis. Schools required to obtain student aid information through National Student Loan Data System (NSLDS).

CONTACT
Anna Griswold, Assistant Vice President for Undergraduate Education & Executive Director for Student Aid
1600 Woodland Road, Abington, PA 19001
(814) 865-6301

Penn State Altoona

Altoona, Pennsylvania
www.altoona.psu.edu   Federal Code: 003329

4-year public branch campus college in small city.
Enrollment: 3,491 undergrads, 4% part-time. 1,375 full-time freshmen.

Selectivity: Admits over 75% of applicants.

BASIC COSTS (2016-2017)

Tuition and fees: $14,828; out-of-state residents $22,834.
Per-credit charge: $578; out-of-state residents $911.
Room and board: $11,860.

FINANCIAL AID PICTURE (2015-2016)

Students with need: Out of 1,143 full-time freshmen who applied for aid, 910 were judged to have need. Of these, 883 received aid, and 37 had their full need met. Average financial aid package met 58% of need; average scholarship/grant was $6,906; average loan was $3,403. For part-time students, average financial aid package was $7,114.

Students without need: 98 full-time freshmen who did not demonstrate need for aid received scholarships/grants; average award was $3,251. No-need awards available for academics, alumni affiliation, ROTC.

FINANCIAL AID PROCEDURES

Forms required: FAFSA.
Dates and Deadlines: Priority date 2/15; no closing date. Applicants notified on a rolling basis.
Transfers: No deadline. Applicants notified on a rolling basis. Schools required to obtain student aid information through National Student Loan Data System (NSLDS).

CONTACT

Anna Griswold, Assistant Vice President for Undergraduate Education & Executive Director for Student Aid
3000 Ivyside Park, Altoona, PA 16801
(814) 865-6301

Penn State Beaver

Monaca, Pennsylvania
www.br.psu.edu   Federal Code: 003329

4-year public branch campus college in small town.
Enrollment: 726 undergrads, 13% part-time. 209 full-time freshmen.
Selectivity: Admits over 75% of applicants.

BASIC COSTS (2016-2017)

Tuition and fees: $13,678; out-of-state residents $20,558.
Per-credit charge: $524; out-of-state residents $817.
Room and board: $11,860.

FINANCIAL AID PICTURE (2015-2016)

Students with need: Out of 190 full-time freshmen who applied for aid, 145 were judged to have need. Of these, 143 received aid, and 8 had their full need met. Average financial aid package met 65% of need; average scholarship/grant was $7,497; average loan was $3,483. For part-time students, average financial aid package was $5,291.

Students without need: 37 full-time freshmen who did not demonstrate need for aid received scholarships/grants; average award was $3,476. No-need awards available for academics, alumni affiliation, ROTC.

FINANCIAL AID PROCEDURES

Forms required: FAFSA.
Dates and Deadlines: Priority date 2/15; no closing date. Applicants notified on a rolling basis.
Transfers: No deadline. Applicants notified on a rolling basis. Schools required to obtain student aid information through National Student Loan Data System (NSLDS).

CONTACT

Anna Griswold, Assistant Vice President for Undergraduate Education & Executive Director for Student Aid
100 University Drive, Monaca, PA 15061
(814) 865-6301

Penn State Berks

Reading, Pennsylvania
www.bk.psu.edu   Federal Code: 003329

4-year public branch campus college in small city.
Enrollment: 2,888 undergrads, 12% part-time. 784 full-time freshmen.
Selectivity: Admits over 75% of applicants.

BASIC COSTS (2016-2017)

Tuition and fees: $14,828; out-of-state residents $22,834.
Per-credit charge: $578; out-of-state residents $911.
Room and board: $12,940.

FINANCIAL AID PICTURE (2015-2016)

Students with need: Out of 699 full-time freshmen who applied for aid, 558 were judged to have need. Of these, 545 received aid, and 22 had their full need met. Average financial aid package met 58% of need; average scholarship/grant was $7,280; average loan was $3,390. For part-time students, average financial aid package was $5,604.

Students without need: 48 full-time freshmen who did not demonstrate need for aid received scholarships/grants; average award was $2,826. No-need awards available for academics, alumni affiliation, ROTC.

FINANCIAL AID PROCEDURES

Forms required: FAFSA.
Dates and Deadlines: Priority date 2/15; no closing date. Applicants notified on a rolling basis.
Transfers: No deadline. Applicants notified on a rolling basis. Schools required to obtain student aid information through National Student Loan Data System (NSLDS).

CONTACT

Anna Griswold, Assistant Vice President for Undergraduate Education & Executive Director for Student Aid
Tulpehocken Road, Reading, PA 19610
(814) 865-6301

Penn State Brandywine

Media, Pennsylvania
www.brandywine.psu.edu   Federal Code: 006922

4-year public branch campus college in small town.
Enrollment: 1,379 undergrads, 14% part-time. 369 full-time freshmen.
Selectivity: Admits over 75% of applicants.

BASIC COSTS (2016-2017)

Tuition and fees: $14,134; out-of-state residents $21,568.
Per-credit charge: $542; out-of-state residents $859.

FINANCIAL AID PICTURE (2015-2016)

Students with need: Out of 330 full-time freshmen who applied for aid, 248 were judged to have need. Of these, 240 received aid, and 12 had their full need met. Average financial aid package met 62% of need; average scholarship/grant was $7,384; average loan was $3,104. For part-time students, average financial aid package was $6,985.

Students without need: 56 full-time freshmen who did not demonstrate need for aid received scholarships/grants; average award was $4,095. No-need awards available for academics, alumni affiliation, ROTC.

FINANCIAL AID PROCEDURES

Forms required: FAFSA.
Dates and Deadlines: Priority date 2/15; no closing date. Applicants notified on a rolling basis.
Transfers: No deadline. Applicants notified on a rolling basis. Schools required to obtain student aid information through National Student Loan Data System (NSLDS).

CONTACT

Anna Griswold, Assistant Vice President for Undergraduate Education & Executive Director for Student Aid

25 Yearsley Mill Road, Media, PA 19063

(814) 865-6301

Penn State DuBois

DuBois, Pennsylvania

http://dubois.psu.edu   Federal Code: 003335

4-year public branch campus college in small town.

Enrollment: 608 undergrads, 21% part-time. 162 full-time freshmen.

Selectivity: Admits over 75% of applicants.

BASIC COSTS (2016-2017)

Tuition and fees: $13,616; out-of-state residents $20,496.

Per-credit charge: $524; out-of-state residents $817.

FINANCIAL AID PICTURE (2015-2016)

Students with need: Out of 157 full-time freshmen who applied for aid, 130 were judged to have need. Of these, 130 received aid, and 7 had their full need met. Average financial aid package met 66% of need; average scholarship/grant was $6,405; average loan was $3,171. For part-time students, average financial aid package was $9,687.

Students without need: 8 full-time freshmen who did not demonstrate need for aid received scholarships/grants; average award was $3,888. No-need awards available for academics, alumni affiliation, ROTC.

FINANCIAL AID PROCEDURES

Forms required: FAFSA.

Dates and Deadlines: Priority date 2/15; no closing date. Applicants notified on a rolling basis.

Transfers: No deadline. Applicants notified on a rolling basis. Schools required to obtain student aid information through National Student Loan Data System (NSLDS).

CONTACT

Anna Griswold, Assistant Vice President for Undergraduate Education & Executive Director for Student Aid

1 College Place, DuBois, PA 15801

(814) 865-6301

Penn State Erie, The Behrend College

Erie, Pennsylvania

http://psbehrend.psu.edu   Federal Code: 003329

4-year public branch campus college in small city.

Enrollment: 4,420 undergrads, 5% part-time. 1,170 full-time freshmen.

Selectivity: Admits over 75% of applicants.

BASIC COSTS (2016-2017)

Tuition and fees: $14,828; out-of-state residents $22,834.

Per-credit charge: $578; out-of-state residents $911.

Room and board: $11,860.

FINANCIAL AID PICTURE (2015-2016)

Students with need: Out of 972 full-time freshmen who applied for aid, 799 were judged to have need. Of these, 774 received aid, and 31 had their full need met. Average financial aid package met 62% of need; average scholarship/grant was $7,493; average loan was $3,518. For part-time students, average financial aid package was $6,254.

Students without need: 52 full-time freshmen who did not demonstrate need for aid received scholarships/grants; average award was $3,408. No-need awards available for academics, alumni affiliation, ROTC.

FINANCIAL AID PROCEDURES

Forms required: FAFSA.

Dates and Deadlines: Priority date 2/15; no closing date. Applicants notified on a rolling basis.

Transfers: No deadline. Applicants notified on a rolling basis. Schools required to obtain student aid information through National Student Loan Data System (NSLDS).

CONTACT

Anna Griswold, Assistant Vice President for Undergraduate Education & Executive Director for Student Aid

Metzgar Admissions & Alumni Center, Erie, PA 16563

(814) 865-6301

Penn State Fayette, The Eberly Campus

Lemont Furnace, Pennsylvania

www.fe.psu.edu   Federal Code: 003329

4-year public branch campus college in large town.

Enrollment: 643 undergrads, 13% part-time. 190 full-time freshmen.

Selectivity: Admits over 75% of applicants.

BASIC COSTS (2016-2017)

Tuition and fees: $13,616; out-of-state residents $20,496.

Per-credit charge: $524; out-of-state residents $817.

FINANCIAL AID PICTURE (2015-2016)

Students with need: Out of 180 full-time freshmen who applied for aid, 151 were judged to have need. Of these, 150 received aid, and 7 had their full need met. Average financial aid package met 60% of need; average scholarship/grant was $6,857; average loan was $3,234. For part-time students, average financial aid package was $6,374.

Students without need: 18 full-time freshmen who did not demonstrate need for aid received scholarships/grants; average award was $2,749. No-need awards available for academics, alumni affiliation, ROTC.

FINANCIAL AID PROCEDURES

Forms required: FAFSA.

Dates and Deadlines: Priority date 2/15; no closing date. Applicants notified on a rolling basis.

Transfers: No deadline. Applicants notified on a rolling basis. Schools required to obtain student aid information through National Student Loan Data System (NSLDS).

CONTACT

Anna Griswold, Assistant Vice President for Undergraduate Education & Executive Director for Student Aid

110 Eberly Building, Lemont Furnace, PA 15456

(814) 865-6301

Penn State Greater Allegheny

McKeesport, Pennsylvania

http://ga.psu.edu   Federal Code: 003329

4-year public branch campus college in large town.

Enrollment: 550 undergrads, 10% part-time. 158 full-time freshmen.

Selectivity: Admits over 75% of applicants.

BASIC COSTS (2016-2017)

Tuition and fees: $13,666; out-of-state residents $20,546.

Per-credit charge: $524; out-of-state residents $817.

Room and board: $11,860.

FINANCIAL AID PICTURE (2015-2016)

Students with need: Out of 148 full-time freshmen who applied for aid, 123 were judged to have need. Of these, 123 received aid, and 6 had their full need met. Average financial aid package met 68% of need; average

scholarship/grant was $8,142; average loan was $3,274. For part-time students, average financial aid package was $6,839.

Students without need: 15 full-time freshmen who did not demonstrate need for aid received scholarships/grants; average award was $3,408. No-need awards available for academics, alumni affiliation, ROTC.

FINANCIAL AID PROCEDURES

Forms required: FAFSA.

Dates and Deadlines: Priority date 2/15; no closing date. Applicants notified on a rolling basis.

Transfers: No deadline. Applicants notified on a rolling basis. Schools required to obtain student aid information through National Student Loan Data System (NSLDS).

CONTACT

Anna Griswold, Assistant Vice President for Undergraduate Education & Executive Director for Student Aid

123 Frable Building, McKeesport, PA 15132

(814) 865-6301

Penn State Harrisburg

Middletown, Pennsylvania

www.hbg.psu.edu   Federal Code: 003329

4-year public branch campus college in small town.

Enrollment: 4,200 undergrads, 9% part-time. 853 full-time freshmen.

Selectivity: Admits over 75% of applicants.

BASIC COSTS (2016-2017)

Tuition and fees: $14,828; out-of-state residents $22,834.

Per-credit charge: $578; out-of-state residents $911.

Room and board: $13,460.

FINANCIAL AID PICTURE (2015-2016)

Students with need: Out of 642 full-time freshmen who applied for aid, 533 were judged to have need. Of these, 517 received aid, and 33 had their full need met. Average financial aid package met 59% of need; average scholarship/grant was $7,395; average loan was $3,503. For part-time students, average financial aid package was $7,280.

Students without need: 89 full-time freshmen who did not demonstrate need for aid received scholarships/grants; average award was $2,255. No-need awards available for academics, alumni affiliation, ROTC.

FINANCIAL AID PROCEDURES

Forms required: FAFSA.

Dates and Deadlines: Priority date 2/15; no closing date. Applicants notified on a rolling basis.

Transfers: No deadline. Applicants notified on a rolling basis. Schools required to obtain student aid information through National Student Loan Data System (NSLDS).

CONTACT

Anna Griswold, Assistant Vice President for Undergraduate Education & Executive Director for Student Aid

Swatara Building, Middletown, PA 17057

(814) 865-6301

Penn State Hazleton

Hazleton, Pennsylvania

http://hazleton.psu.edu/   Federal Code: 003338

4-year public branch campus college in large town.

Enrollment: 863 undergrads, 11% part-time. 261 full-time freshmen.

Selectivity: Admits over 75% of applicants.

BASIC COSTS (2016-2017)

Tuition and fees: $14,072; out-of-state residents $21,506.

Per-credit charge: $542; out-of-state residents $859.

Room and board: $11,860.

FINANCIAL AID PICTURE (2015-2016)

Students with need: Out of 247 full-time freshmen who applied for aid, 218 were judged to have need. Of these, 215 received aid, and 7 had their full need met. Average financial aid package met 64% of need; average scholarship/grant was $7,387; average loan was $3,441. For part-time students, average financial aid package was $7,452.

Students without need: 24 full-time freshmen who did not demonstrate need for aid received scholarships/grants; average award was $3,083. No-need awards available for academics, alumni affiliation, ROTC.

FINANCIAL AID PROCEDURES

Forms required: FAFSA.

Dates and Deadlines: Priority date 2/15; no closing date. Applicants notified on a rolling basis.

Transfers: No deadline. Applicants notified on a rolling basis. Schools required to obtain student aid information through National Student Loan Data System (NSLDS).

CONTACT

Anna Griswold, Assistant Vice President for Undergraduate Education & Executive Director for Student Aid

110 Schiavo Hall, University Park, PA 18202

(814) 865-6301

Penn State Lehigh Valley

Center Valley, Pennsylvania

www.lv.psu.edu   Federal Code: 003329

4-year public branch campus college in rural community.

Enrollment: 868 undergrads, 20% part-time. 206 full-time freshmen.

Selectivity: Admits over 75% of applicants.

BASIC COSTS (2016-2017)

Tuition and fees: $14,134; out-of-state residents $21,568.

Per-credit charge: $542; out-of-state residents $859.

FINANCIAL AID PICTURE (2015-2016)

Students with need: Out of 177 full-time freshmen who applied for aid, 131 were judged to have need. Of these, 130 received aid, and 5 had their full need met. Average financial aid package met 63% of need; average scholarship/grant was $8,429; average loan was $3,396. For part-time students, average financial aid package was $7,313.

Students without need: 23 full-time freshmen who did not demonstrate need for aid received scholarships/grants; average award was $1,933. No-need awards available for academics, alumni affiliation, ROTC.

FINANCIAL AID PROCEDURES

Forms required: FAFSA.

Dates and Deadlines: Priority date 2/15; no closing date. Applicants notified on a rolling basis.

Transfers: No deadline. Applicants notified on a rolling basis. Schools required to obtain student aid information through National Student Loan Data System (NSLDS).

CONTACT

Anna Griswold, Assistant Vice President for Undergraduate Education & Executive Director for Student Aid

2809 Saucon Valley Road, Center Vally, PA 18034

(814) 865-6301

Penn State Mont Alto

Mont Alto, Pennsylvania
www.ma.psu.edu   Federal Code: 003329

4-year public branch campus college in rural community.
Enrollment: 902 undergrads, 24% part-time. 238 full-time freshmen.
Selectivity: Admits over 75% of applicants.

BASIC COSTS (2016-2017)
Tuition and fees: $13,678; out-of-state residents $20,558.
Per-credit charge: $524; out-of-state residents $817.
Room and board: $11,860.

FINANCIAL AID PICTURE (2015-2016)
Students with need: Out of 228 full-time freshmen who applied for aid,
189 were judged to have need. Of these, 188 received aid, and 10 had their
full need met. Average financial aid package met 62% of need; average
scholarship/grant was $6,592; average loan was $3,494. For part-time students, average financial aid package was $6,297.
Students without need: 13 full-time freshmen who did not demonstrate
need for aid received scholarships/grants; average award was $3,751. No-
need awards available for academics, alumni affiliation, ROTC.

FINANCIAL AID PROCEDURES
Forms required: FAFSA.
Dates and Deadlines: Priority date 2/15; no closing date. Applicants notified
on a rolling basis.
Transfers: No deadline. Applicants notified on a rolling basis. Schools
required to obtain student aid information through National Student Loan
Data System (NSLDS).

CONTACT
Anna Griswold, Assistant Vice President for Undergraduate Education &
Executive Director for Student Aid
1 Campus Drive, Mont Alto, PA 17237
(814) 865-6301

Penn State New Kensington

New Kensington, Pennsylvania
www.nk.psu.edu   Federal Code: 003329

4-year public branch campus college in large town.
Enrollment: 686 undergrads, 22% part-time. 174 full-time freshmen.
Selectivity: Admits over 75% of applicants.

BASIC COSTS (2016-2017)
Tuition and fees: $13,616; out-of-state residents $20,496.
Per-credit charge: $524; out-of-state residents $817.

FINANCIAL AID PICTURE (2015-2016)
Students with need: Out of 159 full-time freshmen who applied for aid,
124 were judged to have need. Of these, 118 received aid, and 18 had their
full need met. Average financial aid package met 69% of need; average
scholarship/grant was $6,376; average loan was $3,259. For part-time students, average financial aid package was $7,214.
Students without need: 23 full-time freshmen who did not demonstrate
need for aid received scholarships/grants; average award was $3,416. No-
need awards available for academics, alumni affiliation, ROTC.

FINANCIAL AID PROCEDURES
Forms required: FAFSA.
Dates and Deadlines: Priority date 2/15; no closing date. Applicants notified
on a rolling basis.
Transfers: No deadline. Applicants notified on a rolling basis. Schools
required to obtain student aid information through National Student Loan
Data System (NSLDS).

CONTACT
Anna Griswold, Assistant Vice President for Undergraduate Education &
Executive Director for Student Aid
3550 Seventh Street Road, New Kensington, PA 15068
(814) 865-6301

Penn State Schuylkill

Schuylkill Haven, Pennsylvania
www.sl.psu.edu   Federal Code: 003329

4-year public branch campus college in small town.
Enrollment: 759 undergrads, 17% part-time. 214 full-time freshmen.
Selectivity: Admits over 75% of applicants.

BASIC COSTS (2016-2017)
Tuition and fees: $14,072; out-of-state residents $21,506.
Per-credit charge: $542; out-of-state residents $859.
Room and board: $8,240.

FINANCIAL AID PICTURE (2015-2016)
Students with need: Out of 201 full-time freshmen who applied for aid,
185 were judged to have need. Of these, 185 received aid, and 11 had their
full need met. Average financial aid package met 66% of need; average
scholarship/grant was $7,488; average loan was $3,412. For part-time students, average financial aid package was $6,226.
Students without need: 14 full-time freshmen who did not demonstrate
need for aid received scholarships/grants; average award was $3,434. No-
need awards available for academics, alumni affiliation, ROTC.

FINANCIAL AID PROCEDURES
Forms required: FAFSA.
Dates and Deadlines: Priority date 2/15; no closing date. Applicants notified
on a rolling basis.
Transfers: No deadline. Applicants notified on a rolling basis. Schools
required to obtain student aid information through National Student Loan
Data System (NSLDS).

CONTACT
Anna Griswold, Assistant Vice President for Undergraduate Education &
Executive Director for Student Aid
102 Administration Building, Schuylkill Haven, PA 17972
(814) 865-6301

Penn State Shenango

Sharon, Pennsylvania
www.shenango.psu.edu   Federal Code: 003329

4-year public branch campus college in large town.
Enrollment: 462 undergrads, 48% part-time. 51 full-time freshmen.
Selectivity: Admits 50 to 75% of applicants.

BASIC COSTS (2016-2017)
Tuition and fees: $13,296; out-of-state residents $20,042.
Per-credit charge: $504; out-of-state residents $801.

FINANCIAL AID PICTURE (2015-2016)
Students with need: Out of 49 full-time freshmen who applied for aid, 45
were judged to have need. Of these, 45 received aid, and 2 had their full
need met. Average financial aid package met 64% of need; average scholar-
ship/grant was $7,788; average loan was $3,053. For part-time students,
average financial aid package was $7,795.
Students without need: 5 full-time freshmen who did not demonstrate
need for aid received scholarships/grants; average award was $2,182. No-
need awards available for academics, alumni affiliation, ROTC.

FINANCIAL AID PROCEDURES
Forms required: FAFSA.

Dates and Deadlines: Priority date 2/15; no closing date. Applicants notified on a rolling basis.

Transfers: No deadline. Applicants notified on a rolling basis. Schools required to obtain student aid information through National Student Loan Data System (NSLDS).

CONTACT
Anna Griswold, Assistant Vice President for Undergraduate Education & Executive Director for Student Aid
147 Shenango Avenue, Sharon, PA 16146
(814) 865-6301

Penn State University Park
University Park, Pennsylvania
www.psu.edu   Federal Code: 003329

4-year public university in large town.
Enrollment: 41,359 undergrads, 3% part-time. 7,600 full-time freshmen.
Selectivity: Admits 50 to 75% of applicants.

BASIC COSTS (2016-2017)
Tuition and fees: $17,900; out-of-state residents $32,382.
Per-credit charge: $706; out-of-state residents $1,310.
Room and board: $11,860.

FINANCIAL AID PICTURE (2015-2016)
Students with need: Out of 5,468 full-time freshmen who applied for aid, 3,513 were judged to have need. Of these, 3,239 received aid, and 307 had their full need met. Average financial aid package met 58% of need; average scholarship/grant was $7,155; average loan was $3,495. For part-time students, average financial aid package was $8,010.
Students without need: 638 full-time freshmen who did not demonstrate need for aid received scholarships/grants; average award was $4,185. No-need awards available for academics, alumni affiliation, athletics, ROTC.
Scholarships offered: 167 full-time freshmen received athletic scholarships; average amount $27,895.

FINANCIAL AID PROCEDURES
Forms required: FAFSA.
Dates and Deadlines: Priority date 2/15; no closing date. Applicants notified on a rolling basis.
Transfers: No deadline. Applicants notified on a rolling basis. Schools required to obtain student aid information through National Student Loan Data System (NSLDS).

CONTACT
Anna Griswold, Assistant Vice President for Undergraduate Education & Executive Director for Student Aid
201 Shields Building, University Park, PA 16802
(814) 865-6301

Penn State Wilkes-Barre
Lehman, Pennsylvania
www.wb.psu.edu   Federal Code: 003329

4-year public branch campus college in small city.
Enrollment: 477 undergrads, 11% part-time. 141 full-time freshmen.
Selectivity: Admits over 75% of applicants.

BASIC COSTS (2016-2017)
Tuition and fees: $13,540; out-of-state residents $20,420.
Per-credit charge: $524; out-of-state residents $817.

FINANCIAL AID PICTURE (2015-2016)
Students with need: Out of 136 full-time freshmen who applied for aid, 96 were judged to have need. Of these, 93 received aid, and 7 had their full

need met. Average financial aid package met 64% of need; average scholarship/grant was $7,044; average loan was $3,374. For part-time students, average financial aid package was $8,006.
Students without need: 24 full-time freshmen who did not demonstrate need for aid received scholarships/grants; average award was $3,073. No-need awards available for academics, alumni affiliation, ROTC.

FINANCIAL AID PROCEDURES
Forms required: FAFSA.
Dates and Deadlines: Priority date 2/15; no closing date. Applicants notified on a rolling basis.
Transfers: No deadline. Applicants notified on a rolling basis. Schools required to obtain student aid information through National Student Loan Data System (NSLDS).

CONTACT
Anna Griswold, Assistant Vice President for Undergraduate Education & Executive Director for Student Aid
Hayfield House 101, Lehman, PA 18627
(814) 865-6301

Penn State Worthington Scranton
Dunmore, Pennsylvania
www.sn.psu.edu   Federal Code: 003344

4-year public branch campus college in large town.
Enrollment: 1,019 undergrads, 15% part-time. 224 full-time freshmen.
Selectivity: Admits over 75% of applicants.

BASIC COSTS (2016-2017)
Tuition and fees: $14,072; out-of-state residents $21,506.
Per-credit charge: $542; out-of-state residents $859.

FINANCIAL AID PICTURE (2015-2016)
Students with need: Out of 213 full-time freshmen who applied for aid, 177 were judged to have need. Of these, 173 received aid, and 7 had their full need met. Average financial aid package met 62% of need; average scholarship/grant was $7,212; average loan was $3,277. For part-time students, average financial aid package was $7,451.
Students without need: 16 full-time freshmen who did not demonstrate need for aid received scholarships/grants; average award was $3,960. No-need awards available for academics, alumni affiliation, ROTC.

FINANCIAL AID PROCEDURES
Forms required: FAFSA.
Dates and Deadlines: Priority date 2/15; no closing date. Applicants notified on a rolling basis.
Transfers: No deadline. Applicants notified on a rolling basis. Schools required to obtain student aid information through National Student Loan Data System (NSLDS).

CONTACT
Anna Griswold, Assistant Vice President for Undergraduate Education & Executive Director for Student Aid
Dawson Building, Room 5, 120 Ridge View Drive, Dunmore, PA 18512
(814) 865-6301

Penn State York
York, Pennsylvania
www.yk.psu.edu   Federal Code: 003329

4-year public branch campus college in large town.
Enrollment: 1,060 undergrads, 21% part-time. 309 full-time freshmen.
Selectivity: Admits over 75% of applicants.

BASIC COSTS (2016-2017)
Tuition and fees: $14,134; out-of-state residents $21,568.
Per-credit charge: $542; out-of-state residents $859.

FINANCIAL AID PICTURE (2015-2016)
Students with need: Out of 202 full-time freshmen who applied for aid, 148 were judged to have need. Of these, 147 received aid, and 12 had their full need met. Average financial aid package met 63% of need; average scholarship/grant was $6,663; average loan was $3,395. For part-time students, average financial aid package was $6,870.
Students without need: 46 full-time freshmen who did not demonstrate need for aid received scholarships/grants; average award was $3,171. No-need awards available for academics, alumni affiliation, ROTC.

FINANCIAL AID PROCEDURES
Forms required: FAFSA.
Dates and Deadlines: Priority date 2/15; no closing date. Applicants notified on a rolling basis.
Transfers: No deadline. Applicants notified on a rolling basis. Schools required to obtain student aid information through National Student Loan Data System (NSLDS).

CONTACT
Anna Griswold, Assistant Vice President for Undergraduate Education & Executive Director for Student Aid
Room 139, Main Classroom Building, 1031 Edgecomb Avenue, York, PA 17403
(814) 865-6301

Pennsylvania Academy of the Fine Arts
Philadelphia, Pennsylvania
www.pafa.edu
Federal Code: 014653

4-year private visual arts college in very large city.
Enrollment: 195 undergrads.

BASIC COSTS (2016-2017)
Tuition and fees: $36,058.
Per-credit charge: $1,154.

FINANCIAL AID PICTURE
Students with need: Need-based aid available for full-time and part-time students.
Students without need: No-need awards available for academics, alumni affiliation, art.

FINANCIAL AID PROCEDURES
Forms required: FAFSA.
Dates and Deadlines: Closing date 3/1. Applicants notified on a rolling basis; must reply by 5/1 or within 14 week(s) of notification.
Transfers: Applicants notified on a rolling basis starting 1/31; must reply by 5/1 or within 4 week(s) of notification.

CONTACT
Dana Moore, Director of Financial Aid
128 North Broad Street, Philadelphia, PA 19102
(215) 972-2019

Pennsylvania College of Art and Design
Lancaster, Pennsylvania
www.pcad.edu
Federal Code: 016021

4-year private visual arts college in small city.
Enrollment: 231 undergrads, 4% part-time. 71 full-time freshmen.
Selectivity: Admits less than 50% of applicants.

BASIC COSTS (2016-2017)
Tuition and fees: $23,800.
Per-credit charge: $929.
Additional info: Additional fees for required laptop, camera, software purchase: $3,400.

FINANCIAL AID PICTURE (2015-2016)
Students with need: Out of 66 full-time freshmen who applied for aid, 60 were judged to have need. Of these, 60 received aid, and 2 had their full need met. Need-based aid available for part-time students.
Students without need: 5 full-time freshmen who did not demonstrate need for aid received scholarships/grants; average award was $2,519. No-need awards available for academics, art.

FINANCIAL AID PROCEDURES
Forms required: FAFSA, state aid form.
Dates and Deadlines: Priority date 3/1; no closing date. Applicants notified on a rolling basis starting 4/15.

CONTACT
David Hershey, Director of Financial Aid
PO Box 59, Lancaster, PA 17608-0059

Pennsylvania College of Technology
Williamsport, Pennsylvania
www.pct.edu
Federal Code: 003395

4-year public technical college in large town.
Enrollment: 5,395 undergrads, 15% part-time. 1,203 full-time freshmen.
Selectivity: Open admission; but selective for some programs.

BASIC COSTS (2016-2017)
Tuition and fees: $16,080; out-of-state residents $22,890.
Room and board: $11,244.

FINANCIAL AID PICTURE (2015-2016)
Students with need: 38% of average financial aid package awarded as scholarships/grants, 62% awarded as loans/jobs. Need-based aid available for part-time students. Work study available nights, weekends, and for part-time students.
Students without need: No-need awards available for academics, alumni affiliation, leadership, ROTC.

FINANCIAL AID PROCEDURES
Forms required: FAFSA, institutional form.
Dates and Deadlines: Priority date 3/1; no closing date. Applicants notified on a rolling basis starting 12/1; must reply by 7/1 or within 4 week(s) of notification.
Transfers: No deadline. Applicants notified on a rolling basis; must reply by 7/1 or within 4 week(s) of notification.

CONTACT
Dennis Correll, Associate Dean for Financial Aid and Admissions
One College Avenue, Williamsport, PA 17701-5799
(570) 327-4766

Pennsylvania Highlands Community College
Johnstown, Pennsylvania
www.pennhighlands.edu
Federal Code: 031804

2-year public community college in large town.
Enrollment: 1,260 undergrads.
Selectivity: Open admission.

BASIC COSTS (2016-2017)

Tuition and fees: $5,790; out-of-district residents $7,950; out-of-state residents $11,010.

Per-credit charge: $131; out-of-district residents $203; out-of-state residents $305.

Additional info: Lab/Material Fees for specific courses depending on consumable supplies and materials required: $10-$950.

FINANCIAL AID PICTURE (2016-2017)

Students with need: 54% of average financial aid package awarded as scholarships/grants, 46% awarded as loans/jobs. Need-based aid available for part-time students.

Students without need: No-need awards available for academics, state/district residency.

FINANCIAL AID PROCEDURES

Forms required: FAFSA.

Dates and Deadlines: Closing date 4/1. Applicants notified on a rolling basis; must reply by 8/1.

CONTACT

Judith Ebberts, Director of Financial Aid

101 Community College Way, Johnstown, PA 15904

(814) 262-6454

Pennsylvania Institute of Technology

Media, Pennsylvania

www.pit.edu   Federal Code: 010998

2-year private junior and technical college in small town.

Enrollment: 492 undergrads, 72% part-time. 77 full-time freshmen.

Selectivity: Open admission; but selective for some programs.

BASIC COSTS (2016-2017)

Tuition and fees: $13,650.

FINANCIAL AID PICTURE

Students with need: Need-based aid available for full-time and part-time students.

Students without need: No-need awards available for academics, leadership.

Scholarships offered: Presidential Scholarship: half tuition; for current high school graduates; SAT scores required.

Additional info: Application deadline of May 1 for PHEAA and Philadelphia State Grant aid.

FINANCIAL AID PROCEDURES

Forms required: FAFSA, state aid form, institutional form.

Dates and Deadlines: Applicants notified on a rolling basis starting 7/1.

Transfers: No deadline. Applicants notified on a rolling basis starting 7/1.

CONTACT

Laura Blomgren, Director of Financial Aid

800 Manchester Avenue, Media, PA 19063-4098

(610) 892-1536

Philadelphia University

Philadelphia, Pennsylvania

www.PhilaU.edu   Federal Code: 003354

4-year private university in very large city.

Enrollment: 2,733 undergrads, 13% part-time. 484 full-time freshmen.

Selectivity: Admits 50 to 75% of applicants.

BASIC COSTS (2016-2017)

Tuition and fees: $37,800.

Per-credit charge: $605.

Room and board: $12,570.

FINANCIAL AID PICTURE (2016-2017)

Students with need: Out of 456 full-time freshmen who applied for aid, 404 were judged to have need. Of these, 404 received aid, and 38 had their full need met. Average financial aid package met 80% of need; average scholarship/grant was $28,603; average loan was $4,101. Need-based aid available for part-time students.

Students without need: 72 full-time freshmen who did not demonstrate need for aid received scholarships/grants; average award was $13,211. No-need awards available for academics, athletics.

Scholarships offered: 15 full-time freshmen received athletic scholarships; average amount $23,529.

FINANCIAL AID PROCEDURES

Forms required: FAFSA.

Dates and Deadlines: Applicants notified on a rolling basis starting 3/11; must reply by 5/1.

CONTACT

Lisa Cooper, Director of Financial Aid

4201 Henry Avenue, Philadelphia, PA 19144

(215) 951-2940

Pittsburgh Institute of Aeronautics

Pittsburgh, Pennsylvania

www.pia.edu   Federal Code: 005310

2-year private technical college in large city.

Enrollment: 152 undergrads. 52 full-time freshmen.

Selectivity: Open admission.

BASIC COSTS (2016-2017)

Tuition and fees: $15,600.

FINANCIAL AID PICTURE

Students with need: Need-based aid available for full-time students.

FINANCIAL AID PROCEDURES

Forms required: FAFSA.

Dates and Deadlines: Priority date 5/1; no closing date. Applicants notified on a rolling basis.

Transfers: No deadline. Applicants notified on a rolling basis.

CONTACT

Jonathan Vukmanic, Director of Financial Aid

PO Box 10897, Pittsburgh, PA 15236-0897

(412) 346-2100

Pittsburgh Institute of Mortuary Science

Pittsburgh, Pennsylvania

www.pims.edu   Federal Code: 010814

2-year private technical college in large city.

Enrollment: 317 undergrads.

BASIC COSTS (2016-2017)

Tuition and fees: $14,125.

Per-credit charge: $290.

FINANCIAL AID PICTURE

Students with need: Need-based aid available for full-time and part-time students.

FINANCIAL AID PROCEDURES

Forms required: FAFSA.

Dates and Deadlines: Applicants notified on a rolling basis.

Transfers: No deadline. Applicants notified on a rolling basis.

CONTACT

Karen Rocco, Financial Aid Officer
5808 Baum Boulevard, Pittsburgh, PA 15206-3706
(412) 362-8500

Point Park University

Pittsburgh, Pennsylvania
www.pointpark.edu   Federal Code: 003357

4-year private university in large city.
Enrollment: 3,207 undergrads, 15% part-time. 580 full-time freshmen.
Selectivity: Admits 50 to 75% of applicants.

BASIC COSTS (2016-2017)

Tuition and fees: $29,030.
Per-credit charge: $788.
Room and board: $10,840.
Additional info: Students in Conservatory of Performing Arts pay full-time tuition of $35,400 per year ($1004 per-credit hour). Required fees, room and board are the same for COPA and non-COPA students.

FINANCIAL AID PICTURE (2016-2017)

Students with need: Out of 580 full-time freshmen who applied for aid, 526 were judged to have need. Of these, 524 received aid, and 83 had their full need met. Average financial aid package met 75% of need; average scholarship/grant was $21,465; average loan was $4,495. For part-time students, average financial aid package was $7,534.
Students without need: 51 full-time freshmen who did not demonstrate need for aid received scholarships/grants; average award was $13,340. No-need awards available for academics, athletics, music/drama.
Scholarships offered: *Merit:* Institutional Scholarship award amounts may differ for transfer students depending on major. *Athletic:* 18 full-time freshmen received athletic scholarships; average amount $4,830.

FINANCIAL AID PROCEDURES

Forms required: FAFSA.
Dates and Deadlines: Priority date 3/15; closing date 12/1. Applicants notified by 2/15; must reply within 2 week(s) of notification.
Transfers: Priority date 3/15; no deadline. Applicants notified on a rolling basis starting 10/15; must reply by 5/1.

CONTACT

George Santucci, Director of Financial Aid
201 Wood Street, Pittsburgh, PA 15222-1984
(412) 392-3930

Restaurant School at Walnut Hill College

Philadelphia, Pennsylvania
www.walnuthillcollege.edu   Federal Code: 015499

4-year for-profit culinary school and business college in very large city.
Enrollment: 380 undergrads.

FINANCIAL AID PICTURE

Students with need: Need-based aid available for full-time students.
Students without need: No-need awards available for leadership.

FINANCIAL AID PROCEDURES

Forms required: FAFSA, state aid form, institutional form.

CONTACT

Caitlin Snedeker, Director of Financial Aid
4207 Walnut Street, Philadelphia, PA 19104
(267) 295-2311

Robert Morris University

Moon Township, Pennsylvania
www.rmu.edu   Federal Code: 001746

4-year private university in large town.
Enrollment: 4,370 undergrads, 10% part-time. 880 full-time freshmen.
Selectivity: Admits over 75% of applicants.

BASIC COSTS (2016-2017)

Tuition and fees: $28,250.
Per-credit charge: $875.
Room and board: $10,910.

FINANCIAL AID PICTURE (2016-2017)

Students with need: Out of 767 full-time freshmen who applied for aid, 685 were judged to have need. Of these, 685 received aid, and 90 had their full need met. Average financial aid package met 74% of need; average scholarship/grant was $18,623; average loan was $4,989. For part-time students, average financial aid package was $6,596.
Students without need: 153 full-time freshmen who did not demonstrate need for aid received scholarships/grants; average award was $13,372. No-need awards available for academics, athletics, ROTC.
Scholarships offered: 22 full-time freshmen received athletic scholarships; average amount $20,444.

FINANCIAL AID PROCEDURES

Forms required: FAFSA.
Dates and Deadlines: Applicants notified on a rolling basis starting 2/15.

CONTACT

Stephanie Hendershot, Director of Financial Aid
6001 University Boulevard, Moon Township, PA 15108-1189
(412) 397-6250

Rosedale Technical College

Pittsburgh, Pennsylvania
www.rosedaletech.org   Federal Code: 012050

2-year private technical and career college in large city.
Enrollment: 258 undergrads.
Selectivity: Open admission; but selective for some programs.

FINANCIAL AID PICTURE

Students with need: Need-based aid available for full-time students.

FINANCIAL AID PROCEDURES

Forms required: FAFSA.
Dates and Deadlines: Closing date 8/1.

CONTACT

Anna Bartolini, Director of Financial Aid
215 Beecham Drive, Pittsburgh, PA 15205-9791
(412) 521-6200

Rosemont College

Rosemont, Pennsylvania
www.rosemont.edu   Federal Code: 003360

4-year private liberal arts college in small town, affiliated with the Roman Catholic Church.
Enrollment: 614 undergrads, 16% part-time. 1,322 full-time freshmen.
Selectivity: Admits 50 to 75% of applicants.

BASIC COSTS (2016-2017)

Tuition and fees: $19,480.
Per-credit charge: $1,200.

Room and board: $11,500.
Additional info: Tuition/fee waivers available for adults.

FINANCIAL AID PICTURE (2015-2016)
Students with need: Out of 588 full-time freshmen who applied for aid, 179 were judged to have need. Of these, 161 received aid, and 10 had their full need met. Average financial aid package met 70% of need; average scholarship/grant was $29,346; average loan was $3,499. For part-time students, average financial aid package was $7,360.
Students without need: 496 full-time freshmen who did not demonstrate need for aid received scholarships/grants; average award was $22,054. No-need awards available for academics, alumni affiliation.
Scholarships offered: Sister Maria Stella Kelly Art Scholarship; merit award based on artistic excellence for students intending to major in Studio Art. Cornelian Scholarship; full tuition scholarship awarded annually to two outstanding graduates of Catholic high schools.

FINANCIAL AID PROCEDURES
Forms required: FAFSA.
Dates and Deadlines: Priority date 2/15; no closing date. Applicants notified on a rolling basis starting 3/5; must reply by 5/1 or within 4 week(s) of notification.
Transfers: No deadline. Applicants notified on a rolling basis starting 1/1; must reply by 5/1 or within 4 week(s) of notification.

CONTACT
Deborah Cawley, Director of Enrollment Services and Financial Aid Compliance
1400 Montgomery Avenue, Rosemont, PA 19010-1699
(610) 527-0200 ext. 2214

St. Charles Borromeo Seminary - Overbrook
Wynnewood, Pennsylvania
www.scs.edu   Federal Code: 016229

4-year private seminary college for men in large town, affiliated with the Roman Catholic Church.
Enrollment: 66 undergrads. 17 full-time freshmen.
Selectivity: Admits over 75% of applicants.

FINANCIAL AID PICTURE
Students with need: Need-based aid available for full-time students.
Students without need: No-need awards available for religious affiliation.

FINANCIAL AID PROCEDURES
Forms required: FAFSA, institutional form.
Dates and Deadlines: Closing date 4/15. Applicants notified on a rolling basis starting 6/1; must reply by 6/1 or within 4 week(s) of notification.

CONTACT
Nora Downey, Financial Aid Coordinator
100 East Wynnewood Road, Wynnewood, PA 19096
(610) 785-6582

St. Francis University
Loretto, Pennsylvania
www.francis.edu   Federal Code: 003366

4-year private university and liberal arts college in rural community, affiliated with the Roman Catholic Church.
Enrollment: 1,652 undergrads, 7% part-time. 348 full-time freshmen.
Selectivity: Admits 50 to 75% of applicants.

BASIC COSTS (2017-2018)
Tuition and fees: $34,956.

Per-credit charge: $1,057.
Room and board: $11,928.
Additional info: Tuition/fee waivers available for adults.

FINANCIAL AID PICTURE (2016-2017)
Students with need: 69% of average financial aid package awarded as scholarships/grants, 31% awarded as loans/jobs. Need-based aid available for part-time students. Work study available nights, weekends, and for part-time students.
Students without need: No-need awards available for academics, alumni affiliation, athletics, music/drama, religious affiliation.
Scholarships offered: Red Flash Co-Curricular Award: $1,000-$6,000; 2.5 GPA minimum. Assisi Scholarship: $3,000-$7,000; 3.2 GPA,1020 SAT, 22 ACT minimum. Presidential Scholarship: $7,500-$10,000; 3.5 GPA, 1100 SAT, 24 ACT minimum. Founders Award: $10,500-$16,000; 3.7 GPA, 1250 SAT, 28 ACT minimum. Franciscan Scholarship: $2,000 over four years awarded to graduates of a Catholic high school.

FINANCIAL AID PROCEDURES
Forms required: FAFSA.
Dates and Deadlines: Priority date 5/1; no closing date. Applicants notified on a rolling basis starting 3/1.
Transfers: No deadline. Applicants notified on a rolling basis. Associate degree transfer scholarship based on academic achievement. Returning adult student scholarships available to qualifying transfers after one semester.

CONTACT
Shane Himes, Director of Financial Aid
Box 600, Loretto, PA 15940
(814) 472-3010

Saint Joseph's University
Philadelphia, Pennsylvania
www.sju.edu   Federal Code: 003367

4-year private university in very large city, affiliated with the Roman Catholic Church.
Enrollment: 5,238 undergrads, 11% part-time. 1,266 full-time freshmen.
Selectivity: Admits over 75% of applicants.

BASIC COSTS (2016-2017)
Tuition and fees: $43,020.
Room and board: $14,524.
Additional info: Traditional undergraduate day students taking additional credits over 5 courses pay an additional per-credit-hour fee of $1,428. Part-time, adult undergraduate evening division per-credit-hour fee is $573 (non-traditional, adult continuing education). Business and Psychology majors are required to have a laptop but are not required to purchase from the University.

FINANCIAL AID PICTURE (2016-2017)
Students with need: Out of 1,068 full-time freshmen who applied for aid, 832 were judged to have need. Of these, 830 received aid, and 189 had their full need met. Average financial aid package met 79% of need; average scholarship/grant was $24,541; average loan was $7,014. Need-based aid available for part-time students.
Students without need: 356 full-time freshmen who did not demonstrate need for aid received scholarships/grants; average award was $15,393. No-need awards available for academics, alumni affiliation, art, athletics, minority status, music/drama, ROTC.
Scholarships offered: 48 full-time freshmen received athletic scholarships; average amount $19,788.

FINANCIAL AID PROCEDURES
Forms required: FAFSA.
Dates and Deadlines: Priority date 2/15; no closing date. Applicants notified on a rolling basis starting 3/31; must reply by 5/1.
Transfers: Financial aid for transfer students subject to availability of funds.

CONTACT
Susan Wendling, Director of Financial Aid
5600 City Avenue, Philadelphia, PA 19131

St. Vincent College
Latrobe, Pennsylvania
www.stvincent.edu   Federal Code: 003368

4-year private liberal arts college in large town, affiliated with the Roman Catholic Church.
Enrollment: 1,609 undergrads, 2% part-time. 391 full-time freshmen.
Selectivity: Admits 50 to 75% of applicants.

BASIC COSTS (2016-2017)
Tuition and fees: $33,814.
Per-credit charge: $1,018.
Room and board: $11,105.

FINANCIAL AID PICTURE (2016-2017)
Students with need: Out of 361 full-time freshmen who applied for aid, 321 were judged to have need. Of these, 321 received aid, and 98 had their full need met. Average financial aid package met 83% of need; average scholarship/grant was $7,071; average loan was $3,660. For part-time students, average financial aid package was $12,602.
Students without need: 67 full-time freshmen who did not demonstrate need for aid received scholarships/grants; average award was $22,539. No-need awards available for academics, alumni affiliation, leadership, minority status, music/drama, religious affiliation, state/district residency.
Scholarships offered: Academic Scholarship: $5,000 to $20,500, based on high school GPA, class rank, and SAT scores.

FINANCIAL AID PROCEDURES
Forms required: FAFSA.
Dates and Deadlines: Priority date 5/1; no closing date. Applicants notified on a rolling basis starting 10/1.
Transfers: Applicants notified on a rolling basis starting 3/1; must reply within 2 week(s) of notification.

CONTACT
Mary Gazal, Director of Financial Aid
300 Fraser Purchase Road, Latrobe, PA 15650-2690
(800) 782-5549

Seton Hill University
Greensburg, Pennsylvania
www.setonhill.edu   Federal Code: 003362

4-year private university and liberal arts college in large town, affiliated with the Roman Catholic Church.
Enrollment: 1,554 undergrads, 5% part-time. 392 full-time freshmen.
Selectivity: Admits 50 to 75% of applicants.

BASIC COSTS (2016-2017)
Tuition and fees: $33,520.
Per-credit charge: $872.
Room and board: $11,000.
Additional info: Tuition/fee waivers available for adults.

FINANCIAL AID PICTURE (2015-2016)
Students with need: Out of 371 full-time freshmen who applied for aid, 336 were judged to have need. Of these, 336 received aid, and 74 had their full need met. Average financial aid package met 76% of need; average scholarship/grant was $20,878; average loan was $5,534. For part-time students, average financial aid package was $9,418.

Students without need: 65 full-time freshmen who did not demonstrate need for aid received scholarships/grants; average award was $15,028. No-need awards available for academics, alumni affiliation, art, athletics, music/drama.
Scholarships offered: Merit: Presidential and Seton Scholarships; up to full tuition per academic year; given to top students. **Athletic:** 41 full-time freshmen received athletic scholarships; average amount $12,088.

FINANCIAL AID PROCEDURES
Forms required: FAFSA, state aid form, institutional form.
Dates and Deadlines: Priority date 5/1; no closing date. Applicants notified on a rolling basis starting 11/30.
Transfers: Priority date 8/1; closing date 8/15. Applicants notified on a rolling basis starting 1/1; must reply within 2 week(s) of notification. Scholarship available for full-time transfer students with 3.5 GPA.

CONTACT
Tracey Snyder de Baez, Director of Financial Aid
1 Seton Hill Drive, Greensburg, PA 15601
(724) 830-1010

Shippensburg University of Pennsylvania
Shippensburg, Pennsylvania
www.ship.edu   Federal Code: 003326

4-year public university in small town.
Enrollment: 5,853 undergrads, 5% part-time. 1,378 full-time freshmen.
Selectivity: Admits over 75% of applicants.

BASIC COSTS (2016-2017)
Tuition and fees: $11,452; out-of-state residents $19,308.
Per-credit charge: $281; out-of-state residents $679.
Room and board: $11,756.
Additional info: $10,858 for Dual Admit (out-of-state) students and $12,668 for STEM (Science, Technology, Engineering, or Math) and High Achieving (1200 SAT or top 10% of their class) out-of-state students.

FINANCIAL AID PICTURE (2016-2017)
Students with need: Out of 1,292 full-time freshmen who applied for aid, 1,043 were judged to have need. Of these, 1,028 received aid, and 56 had their full need met. Average financial aid package met 48% of need; average scholarship/grant was $6,894; average loan was $3,466. For part-time students, average financial aid package was $6,657.
Students without need: 90 full-time freshmen who did not demonstrate need for aid received scholarships/grants; average award was $4,946. No-need awards available for academics, athletics.
Scholarships offered: 76 full-time freshmen received athletic scholarships; average amount $2,908.

FINANCIAL AID PROCEDURES
Forms required: FAFSA.
Dates and Deadlines: Priority date 3/15; no closing date. Applicants notified on a rolling basis; must reply within 2 week(s) of notification.
Transfers: No deadline. Applicants notified on a rolling basis; must reply within 2 week(s) of notification.

CONTACT
Trina Snyder, Director of Financial Aid
1871 Old Main Drive, Shippensburg, PA 17257-2299
(717) 477-1131

Slippery Rock University of Pennsylvania

Slippery Rock, Pennsylvania
www.sru.edu   Federal Code: 003327

4-year public university in small town.
Enrollment: 7,569 undergrads, 6% part-time. 1,564 full-time freshmen.
Selectivity: Admits 50 to 75% of applicants.

BASIC COSTS (2016-2017)
Tuition and fees: $9,862; out-of-state residents $13,482.
Per-credit charge: $302; out-of-state residents $452.
Room and board: $10,110.

FINANCIAL AID PICTURE (2016-2017)
Students with need: Out of 1,484 full-time freshmen who applied for aid, 1,149 were judged to have need. Of these, 1,144 received aid, and 117 had their full need met. Average financial aid package met 59% of need; average scholarship/grant was $6,389; average loan was $3,708. For part-time students, average financial aid package was $5,737.
Students without need: 208 full-time freshmen who did not demonstrate need for aid received scholarships/grants; average award was $2,635. No-need awards available for academics, alumni affiliation, art, athletics, job skills, leadership, minority status, music/drama, ROTC, state/district residency.
Scholarships offered: 66 full-time freshmen received athletic scholarships; average amount $4,160.
Additional info: May 1 closing date for Pennsylvania state grants.

FINANCIAL AID PROCEDURES
Forms required: FAFSA.
Dates and Deadlines: Priority date 5/1; no closing date. Applicants notified on a rolling basis starting 12/16.
Transfers: No deadline. Applicants notified on a rolling basis starting 12/16.

CONTACT
Alyssa Dobson, Director of Financial Aid
1 Morrow Way, Slippery Rock, PA 16057-1383
(724) 738-2044

South Hills School of Business & Technology

State College, Pennsylvania
www.southhills.edu   Federal Code: 013263

2-year for-profit business and technical college in large town.
Enrollment: 630 undergrads.
Selectivity: Open admission; but selective for some programs.

FINANCIAL AID PICTURE
Students with need: Need-based aid available for full-time and part-time students.
Students without need: This college awards aid only to students with need.

FINANCIAL AID PROCEDURES
Forms required: FAFSA.
Dates and Deadlines: Closing date 6/30. Applicants notified on a rolling basis starting 7/5.
Transfers: No deadline. Must reply by 6/14.

CONTACT
Anne Falk, Financial Aid Director
480 Waupelani Drive, State College, PA 16801-4516
(814) 234-7755

Susquehanna University

Selinsgrove, Pennsylvania   Federal Code: 003369
www.susqu.edu   CSS Code: 2820

4-year private university and liberal arts college in small town, affiliated with the Evangelical Lutheran Church in America.
Enrollment: 2,136 undergrads, 1% part-time. 637 full-time freshmen.
Selectivity: Admits 50 to 75% of applicants.

BASIC COSTS (2016-2017)
Tuition and fees: $43,720.
Per-credit charge: $1,375.
Room and board: $11,620.

FINANCIAL AID PICTURE (2016-2017)
Students with need: Out of 593 full-time freshmen who applied for aid, 511 were judged to have need. Of these, 511 received aid, and 123 had their full need met. Average financial aid package met 83% of need; average scholarship/grant was $31,727; average loan was $3,033. For part-time students, average financial aid package was $6,604.
Students without need: 118 full-time freshmen who did not demonstrate need for aid received scholarships/grants; average award was $24,566. No-need awards available for academics, leadership, minority status, music/drama, ROTC.
Scholarships offered: Academic scholarships; $1,000 to $16,000; renewable annually; based on outstanding academic achievement, personal accomplishment, and/or musical talent. Alumni scholarships; $2,500; for 5 new legacy students with best academic records. Annual scholarships; $2,500; to dependent children of ordained Lutheran clergy. Founder Scholarships; Full tuition; renewable annually; based on outstanding academic achievement and personal accomplishment. University Assistantships; beginning at $5,000 annually, includes professional work experience with a faculty or staff mentor.
Additional info: Graduated pay scale for federal work-study program. $1,000 Visit Grant awarded to enrolling students who make an official campus visit between March 1 of sophomore year and March 1 of senior year of high school.

FINANCIAL AID PROCEDURES
Forms required: FAFSA, CSS PROFILE.
Dates and Deadlines: Priority date 3/1; closing date 5/1. Applicants notified on a rolling basis starting 3/15; must reply by 5/1.
Transfers: Priority date 5/1; closing date 7/1. Applicants notified on a rolling basis; must reply by 5/1. Transfer students eligible for financial aid and scholarship consideration.

CONTACT
Erin Wolfe, Director of Student Financial Services
514 University Avenue, Selinsgrove, PA 17870-1164
(570) 372-4450

Swarthmore College

Swarthmore, Pennsylvania   Federal Code: 003370
www.swarthmore.edu   CSS Code: 2821

4-year private liberal arts college in small town.
Enrollment: 1,617 undergrads. 415 full-time freshmen.
Selectivity: Admits less than 50% of applicants.

BASIC COSTS (2016-2017)
Tuition and fees: $49,104.
Room and board: $14,446.

FINANCIAL AID PICTURE (2016-2017)
Students with need: Out of 290 full-time freshmen who applied for aid, 243 were judged to have need. Of these, 243 received aid, and 243 had

their full need met. Average financial aid package met 100% of need; average scholarship/grant was $46,897.

Students without need: 3 full-time freshmen who did not demonstrate need for aid received scholarships/grants; average award was $48,720. No-need awards available for academics, leadership, state/district residency.

Additional info: All aid is loan-free and packaged to meet full demonstrated need. Financial aid program includes work-study opportunities.

FINANCIAL AID PROCEDURES

Forms required: FAFSA, CSS PROFILE, state aid form.

Dates and Deadlines: Priority date 2/15; closing date 2/15. Applicants notified by 4/1; must reply by 5/1.

Transfers: Closing date 4/1. Applicants notified by 5/15. No aid consideration for foreign national transfer applicants.

CONTACT

Varo Duffins, Director of Financial Aid
500 College Avenue, Swarthmore, PA 19081
(610) 328-8358

Talmudical Yeshiva of Philadelphia
Philadelphia, Pennsylvania   Federal Code: 012523

4-year private rabbinical college for men in very large city, affiliated with the Jewish faith.

Enrollment: 124 undergrads. 37 full-time freshmen.

Selectivity: Admits over 75% of applicants.

BASIC COSTS (2016-2017)

Tuition and fees: $8,500.

Room and board: $7,000.

FINANCIAL AID PICTURE

Students with need: Need-based aid available for full-time students.

Students without need: This college awards aid only to students with need.

FINANCIAL AID PROCEDURES

Forms required: FAFSA, institutional form.

Dates and Deadlines: Priority date 8/1; closing date 5/1. Applicants notified on a rolling basis starting 3/15; must reply within 2 week(s) of notification.

CONTACT

Chaya Hoberman, Financial Aid Officer
6063 Drexel Road, Philadelphia, PA 19131
(215) 477-1000

Temple University
Philadelphia, Pennsylvania
www.temple.edu   Federal Code: 003371

4-year public university in very large city.

Enrollment: 28,709 undergrads, 9% part-time. 4,892 full-time freshmen.

Selectivity: Admits 50 to 75% of applicants.

BASIC COSTS (2016-2017)

Tuition and fees: $15,688; out-of-state residents $25,994.

Per-credit charge: $573; out-of-state residents $899.

Room and board: $11,146.

FINANCIAL AID PICTURE (2015-2016)

Students with need: Out of 4,264 full-time freshmen who applied for aid, 3,482 were judged to have need. Of these, 3,459 received aid, and 976 had their full need met. Average financial aid package met 69% of need; average scholarship/grant was $8,129; average loan was $3,356. For part-time students, average financial aid package was $10,787.

Students without need: 786 full-time freshmen who did not demonstrate need for aid received scholarships/grants; average award was $8,655. No-need awards available for academics, art, athletics, music/drama, ROTC.

Scholarships offered: 81 full-time freshmen received athletic scholarships; average amount $24,293.

FINANCIAL AID PROCEDURES

Forms required: FAFSA.

Dates and Deadlines: Closing date 3/1. Applicants notified on a rolling basis starting 2/15; must reply by 5/1 or within 3 week(s) of notification.

Transfers: Priority date 3/1; no deadline. Must reply within 2 week(s) of notification.

CONTACT

Emilie van Trieste, Associate Director, Student Financial Services
103 Conwell Hall, Philadelphia, PA 19122-6096
(215) 204-2244

Thaddeus Stevens College of Technology
Lancaster, Pennsylvania
www.stevenscollege.edu   Federal Code: 007912

2-year public technical and career college in small city.

Enrollment: 1,056 undergrads. 562 full-time freshmen.

BASIC COSTS (2017-2018)

Tuition and fees: $7,830.

Room and board: $8,140.

Additional info: Tuition/fee waivers available for unemployed or children of unemployed.

FINANCIAL AID PICTURE (2016-2017)

Students with need: 87% of average financial aid package awarded as scholarships/grants, 13% awarded as loans/jobs.

Additional info: Tuition and room and board costs waived for students with adjusted family income of $18,500 or less. Tuition and other costs also waived for orphans.

FINANCIAL AID PROCEDURES

Dates and Deadlines: Priority date 3/15; no closing date. Applicants notified on a rolling basis starting 7/15.

CONTACT

Melissa Wisniewski, Director of Financial Aid & Registrar
750 East King Street, Lancaster, PA 17602
(717) 391-3510

Thiel College
Greenville, Pennsylvania
www.thiel.edu   Federal Code: 003376

4-year private liberal arts college in small town, affiliated with the Evangelical Lutheran Church in America.

Enrollment: 777 undergrads.

Selectivity: Admits over 75% of applicants.

BASIC COSTS (2016-2017)

Tuition and fees: $29,740.

Per-credit charge: $880.

Room and board: $11,700.

FINANCIAL AID PICTURE

Students with need: Need-based aid available for full-time and part-time students. Work study available nights, weekends, and for part-time students.

Students without need: No-need awards available for academics, alumni affiliation, leadership, music/drama, religious affiliation.

FINANCIAL AID PROCEDURES

Forms required: FAFSA, state aid form.
Dates and Deadlines: Priority date 3/15; no closing date. Applicants notified on a rolling basis starting 2/15; must reply within 2 week(s) of notification.
Transfers: Priority date 6/1; no deadline. Applicants notified on a rolling basis starting 2/15; must reply within 2 week(s) of notification.

CONTACT

Cynthia Farrell, Executive Director of Student Financial Services
75 College Avenue, Greenville, PA 16125-2181
(724) 589-2250

Thomas Jefferson University

Philadelphia, Pennsylvania
www.jefferson.edu   Federal Code: 012393

4-year private university and health science college in very large city.
Enrollment: 842 undergrads, 23% part-time.

BASIC COSTS (2016-2017)

Additional info: Costs vary according to program. Examples of full-time (academic year) tuition rates for bachelor's degree programs in radiologic sciences: $30,525; bachelor degree in occupational therapy: $31,648. All full-time students pay an annual technology fee of $510 and a library fee of $360. Academic fees vary by program. On-campus housing ranges from $712 to $2367 per month depending on the facility.

FINANCIAL AID PICTURE

Students with need: Need-based aid available for full-time and part-time students. Work study available nights, weekends, and for part-time students.
Students without need: No-need awards available for academics, leadership, state/district residency.
Scholarships offered: Range of merit-based scholarships available for selected applicants.
Additional info: Applicants must use the IRS DRT process on the FAFSA.

FINANCIAL AID PROCEDURES

Forms required: FAFSA, institutional form.
Dates and Deadlines: Closing date 4/1. Applicants notified on a rolling basis starting 4/1; must reply within 2 week(s) of notification.
Transfers: Applicants notified on a rolling basis starting 11/15; must reply within 2 week(s) of notification.

CONTACT

Susan McFadden, University Director of Financial Aid
130 South Ninth Street, Edison Building, Suite 100, Philadelphia, PA 19107
(215) 955-2867

Triangle Tech: Bethlehem

Bethlehem, Pennsylvania
www.triangle-tech.edu   Federal Code: 014895

2-year for-profit branch campus and technical college in small city.
Enrollment: 120 undergrads.
Selectivity: Open admission.

BASIC COSTS (2016-2017)

Tuition and fees: $16,779.
Additional info: Fees will vary depending on program.

FINANCIAL AID PICTURE

Students with need: Need-based aid available for full-time and part-time students. Work study available nights.
Students without need: No-need awards available for academics.

FINANCIAL AID PROCEDURES

Forms required: FAFSA.

Dates and Deadlines: Applicants notified on a rolling basis.

CONTACT

Catherine Waxter, Director of Financial Aid
3184 Airport Road, Bethlehem, PA 18017
(610) 266-2910

Triangle Tech: DuBois

Falls Creek, Pennsylvania
www.triangle-tech.edu   Federal Code: 021744

2-year for-profit technical college in large town.
Enrollment: 149 undergrads. 71 full-time freshmen.
Selectivity: Open admission.

FINANCIAL AID PICTURE (2015-2016)

Students with need: Out of 67 full-time freshmen who applied for aid, 64 were judged to have need. Of these, 64 received aid, and 11 had their full need met. Average financial aid package met 17% of need; average scholarship/grant was $8,008; average loan was $3,400. Need-based aid available for part-time students.
Students without need: This college awards aid only to students with need.

FINANCIAL AID PROCEDURES

Forms required: FAFSA, state aid form, institutional form.
Dates and Deadlines: Applicants notified on a rolling basis.

CONTACT

Catherine Waxter, Corporate Director of Financial Aid
225 Tannery Row Road, Falls Creek, PA 15840-9544
(724) 832-1050

Triangle Tech: Erie

Erie, Pennsylvania
www.triangle-tech.edu   Federal Code: 014417

2-year for-profit technical and career college in small city.
Enrollment: 30 undergrads. 20 full-time freshmen.
Selectivity: Open admission.

FINANCIAL AID PICTURE (2015-2016)

Students with need: Out of 19 full-time freshmen who applied for aid, 19 were judged to have need. Of these, 19 received aid, and 17 had their full need met. Average financial aid package met 89% of need; average scholarship/grant was $6,747; average loan was $3,099. Need-based aid available for part-time students.
Students without need: This college awards aid only to students with need.

FINANCIAL AID PROCEDURES

Forms required: FAFSA.
Dates and Deadlines: Applicants notified on a rolling basis.

CONTACT

Cathy Waxter, Corporate Director of Financial Aid
2000 Liberty Street, Erie, PA 16502-2594
(724) 832-1050

Triangle Tech: Greensburg

Greensburg, Pennsylvania
www.triangle-tech.edu   Federal Code: 014895

2-year for-profit technical college in large town.
Enrollment: 163 undergrads.

Selectivity: Open admission.

FINANCIAL AID PICTURE

Students with need: Need-based aid available for full-time and part-time students.

FINANCIAL AID PROCEDURES

Forms required: FAFSA, institutional form.
Dates and Deadlines: Applicants notified on a rolling basis starting 1/1.
Transfers: No deadline.

CONTACT

Catherine Waxter, Director of Financial Aid
222 East Pittsburgh Street, Suite A, Greensburg, PA 15601-3304
(724) 832-1050

Triangle Tech: Pittsburgh

Pittsburgh, Pennsylvania
www.triangle-tech.edu   Federal Code: 007839

2-year for-profit technical college in large city.
Enrollment: 169 undergrads.
Selectivity: Open admission; but selective for some programs.

BASIC COSTS (2016-2017)

Tuition and fees: $16,586.
Additional info: Fees will vary depending on program.

FINANCIAL AID PICTURE

Students with need: Need-based aid available for full-time and part-time students. Work study available nights.
Students without need: No-need awards available for academics, state/district residency.

FINANCIAL AID PROCEDURES

Forms required: FAFSA, institutional form.
Dates and Deadlines: Applicants notified on a rolling basis.
Transfers: No deadline.

CONTACT

Cathy Waxter, Corporate Director of Financial Aid
1940 Perrysville Avenue, Pittsburgh, PA 15214-3897
(412) 359-1000

Triangle Tech: Sunbury

Sunbury, Pennsylvania
www.triangle-tech.edu

2-year for-profit technical college in large town.
Enrollment: 96 undergrads. 49 full-time freshmen.
Selectivity: Open admission.

FINANCIAL AID PICTURE

Students with need: Need-based aid available for full-time and part-time students. Work study available nights.

FINANCIAL AID PROCEDURES

Forms required: FAFSA, state aid form, institutional form.
Dates and Deadlines: Applicants notified on a rolling basis.
Transfers: No deadline.

CONTACT

Cathy Waxter, Director of Financial Aid
191 Performance Road, Sunbury, PA 17801

University of Pennsylvania

Philadelphia, Pennsylvania   Federal Code: 003378
www.upenn.edu   CSS Code: 2926

4-year private university in very large city.
Enrollment: 10,019 undergrads, 3% part-time. 2,428 full-time freshmen.
Selectivity: Admits less than 50% of applicants.

BASIC COSTS (2017-2018)

Tuition and fees: $53,534.
Room and board: $15,066.

FINANCIAL AID PICTURE

Students with need: Need-based aid available for full-time and part-time students. Work study available nights, weekends, and for part-time students.
Students without need: This college awards aid only to students with need.
Additional info: All loans have been eliminated from need-based aid packages.

FINANCIAL AID PROCEDURES

Forms required: FAFSA, CSS PROFILE, institutional form.
Dates and Deadlines: Priority date 2/15; no closing date. Applicants notified on a rolling basis starting 4/1; must reply by 5/1.
Transfers: Priority date 3/15. Applicants notified on a rolling basis starting 5/15; must reply within 4 week(s) of notification.

CONTACT

1 College Hall, Philadelphia, PA 19104-6376
(215) 898-1988

University of Pittsburgh

Pittsburgh, Pennsylvania
www.pitt.edu   Federal Code: 008815

4-year public university in large city.
Enrollment: 18,920 undergrads, 4% part-time. 4,010 full-time freshmen.
Selectivity: Admits 50 to 75% of applicants. GED not accepted.

BASIC COSTS (2016-2017)

Tuition and fees: $18,618; out-of-state residents $29,758.
Per-credit charge: $737; out-of-state residents $1,201.
Room and board: $10,950.

FINANCIAL AID PICTURE (2015-2016)

Students with need: Out of 3,308 full-time freshmen who applied for aid, 2,167 were judged to have need. Of these, 2,092 received aid, and 300 had their full need met. Average financial aid package met 54% of need; average scholarship/grant was $9,960; average loan was $4,047. For part-time students, average financial aid package was $6,955.
Students without need: 269 full-time freshmen who did not demonstrate need for aid received scholarships/grants; average award was $10,734. No-need awards available for academics, athletics, minority status.
Scholarships offered: *Merit:* Academic Scholarships; $1,000 to full tuition, room and board; renewable up to 4 years with 3.0 GPA. *Athletic:* 40 full-time freshmen received athletic scholarships; average amount $3,224.

FINANCIAL AID PROCEDURES

Forms required: FAFSA.
Dates and Deadlines: Priority date 3/1; no closing date. Applicants notified on a rolling basis starting 3/15.
Transfers: Priority date 5/1; no deadline. Applicants notified on a rolling basis. Transfer students not eligible for freshman scholarships.

CONTACT

Marc Harding, Chief Enrollment Officer
4227 Fifth Avenue, 1st Floor, Alumni Hall, Pittsburgh, PA 15260
(412) 624-7488

University of Pittsburgh at Bradford

Bradford, Pennsylvania
www.upb.pitt.edu   Federal Code: 003380

4-year public university in large town.
Enrollment: 1,449 undergrads, 6% part-time. 393 full-time freshmen.
Selectivity: Admits 50 to 75% of applicants.

BASIC COSTS (2016-2017)
Tuition and fees: $13,608; out-of-state residents $24,630.
Per-credit charge: $528; out-of-state residents $987.
Room and board: $8,794.

FINANCIAL AID PICTURE (2016-2017)
Students with need: Out of 335 full-time freshmen who applied for aid, 306 were judged to have need. Of these, 303 received aid, and 41 had their full need met. Average financial aid package met 69% of need; average scholarship/grant was $11,048; average loan was $6,891. For part-time students, average financial aid package was $6,456.
Students without need: 25 full-time freshmen who did not demonstrate need for aid received scholarships/grants; average award was $6,423. No-need awards available for academics, alumni affiliation, ROTC, state/district residency.
Scholarships offered: Panther Scholarship; for full-time on-campus residents or students who commute from Cameron, Elk, Forest, McKean, Potter, or Warren counties. Valedictorian/Salutatorian Scholarship; for Pennsylvania students. International Student Scholarship; for international students who plan to enroll full-time and reside on campus.

FINANCIAL AID PROCEDURES
Forms required: FAFSA.
Dates and Deadlines: Priority date 3/1; no closing date. Applicants notified on a rolling basis starting 4/1; must reply within 2 week(s) of notification.
Transfers: No deadline. Applicants notified on a rolling basis starting 4/1; must reply within 2 week(s) of notification. Transfers must meet academic policy guidelines.

CONTACT
Melissa Ibanez, Associate VP for Enrollment Management and Director of Financial Aid
300 Campus Drive, Bradford, PA 16701
(814) 362-7550

University of Pittsburgh at Greensburg

Greensburg, Pennsylvania
www.greensburg.pitt.edu   Federal Code: 003381

4-year public branch campus and liberal arts college in large town.
Enrollment: 1,520 undergrads, 5% part-time. 408 full-time freshmen.
Selectivity: Admits 50 to 75% of applicants.

BASIC COSTS (2016-2017)
Tuition and fees: $13,618; out-of-state residents $24,640.
Per-credit charge: $528; out-of-state residents $987.
Room and board: $9,990.

FINANCIAL AID PICTURE (2015-2016)
Students with need: Out of 375 full-time freshmen who applied for aid, 313 were judged to have need. Of these, 307 received aid, and 28 had their full need met. Average financial aid package met 60% of need; average scholarship/grant was $9,033; average loan was $3,681. For part-time students, average financial aid package was $5,458.
Students without need: 41 full-time freshmen who did not demonstrate need for aid received scholarships/grants; average award was $3,973. No-need awards available for academics, leadership, minority status, state/district residency.

FINANCIAL AID PROCEDURES
Forms required: FAFSA, state aid form.
Dates and Deadlines: Priority date 2/15; no closing date. Applicants notified on a rolling basis starting 3/15; must reply within 3 week(s) of notification.
Transfers: No deadline.

CONTACT
Brandi Darr, Director of Financial Aid
150 Finoli Drive, Greensburg, PA 15601
(724) 836-9881

University of Pittsburgh at Johnstown

Johnstown, Pennsylvania
www.upj.pitt.edu   Federal Code: 008815

4-year public engineering and liberal arts college in small city.
Enrollment: 2,814 undergrads.

BASIC COSTS (2016-2017)
Tuition and fees: $13,624; out-of-state residents $24,646.
Per-credit charge: $528; out-of-state residents $987.
Room and board: $9,390.

FINANCIAL AID PICTURE
Students with need: Need-based aid available for full-time and part-time students.
Students without need: No-need awards available for academics, alumni affiliation, athletics, leadership, ROTC, state/district residency.
Scholarships offered: Achievement, Presidential, and Leadership Scholarships; $2,500 to full tuition yearly; based on high school GPA and SAT/ACT scores.

FINANCIAL AID PROCEDURES
Forms required: FAFSA, state aid form.
Dates and Deadlines: Priority date 4/1; no closing date. Applicants notified on a rolling basis starting 3/1; must reply within 2 week(s) of notification.

CONTACT
Jeanine Lawn, Director of Financial Aid
450 Schoolhouse Road, 157 Blackington Hall, Johnstown, PA 15904-1200
(800) 881-5544

University of Pittsburgh at Titusville

Titusville, Pennsylvania
www.upt.pitt.edu   Federal Code: 008815

2-year public branch campus and liberal arts college in small town.
Enrollment: 327 undergrads.

BASIC COSTS (2016-2017)
Tuition and fees: $11,808; out-of-state residents $21,552.
Per-credit charge: $456; out-of-state residents $862.
Room and board: $10,472.

FINANCIAL AID PICTURE
Students with need: Need-based aid available for full-time and part-time students. Work study available nights, weekends, and for part-time students.
Students without need: No-need awards available for academics.

FINANCIAL AID PROCEDURES
Forms required: FAFSA.
Dates and Deadlines: Priority date 3/1; no closing date. Applicants notified on a rolling basis starting 3/1; must reply within 2 week(s) of notification.
Transfers: No deadline. Applicants notified on a rolling basis starting 4/1; must reply within 2 week(s) of notification. Pennsylvania residents must apply by 5/1 for PHEAA. Transfer students must have completed 24 credits

to renew. Information retrieved from NSLDS is utilized to determine transfer student eligibility for financial aid.

CONTACT
Melissa Ibanez, Director of Financial Aid
UPT Admissions Office, Titusville, PA 16354-0287
(814) 827-4495

University of Scranton
Scranton, Pennsylvania
www.scranton.edu   Federal Code: 003384

4-year private university and liberal arts college in small city, affiliated with the Roman Catholic Church.
Enrollment: 3,757 undergrads, 3% part-time. 1,002 full-time freshmen.
Selectivity: Admits 50 to 75% of applicants.

BASIC COSTS (2016-2017)
Tuition and fees: $42,162.
Per-credit charge: $1,072.
Room and board: $14,264.

FINANCIAL AID PICTURE (2015-2016)
Students with need: Need-based aid available for full-time and part-time students. Work study available nights, weekends, and for part-time students.
Students without need: No-need awards available for academics, ROTC.

FINANCIAL AID PROCEDURES
Forms required: FAFSA.
Dates and Deadlines: Priority date 2/15; no closing date. Applicants notified on a rolling basis starting 3/15; must reply by 5/1 or within 2 week(s) of notification.
Transfers: Institutional grants available based on financial need.

CONTACT
William Burke, Director of Financial Aid
800 Linden Street, Scranton, PA 18510-4699
(570) 941-7700

University of the Arts
Philadelphia, Pennsylvania
www.uarts.edu   Federal Code: 003350

4-year private visual arts and performing arts college in very large city.
Enrollment: 1,693 undergrads, 2% part-time. 413 full-time freshmen.
Selectivity: Admits over 75% of applicants.

BASIC COSTS (2016-2017)
Tuition and fees: $41,464.
Per-credit charge: $1,728.
Room and board: $15,120.

FINANCIAL AID PICTURE
Students with need: Need-based aid available for full-time and part-time students. Work study available nights, weekends, and for part-time students.
Students without need: No-need awards available for academics, art, music/drama.
Scholarships offered: Merit awards; available to students who demonstrate exceptional talent and academic abilities.

FINANCIAL AID PROCEDURES
Forms required: FAFSA, state aid form.
Dates and Deadlines: Priority date 3/1; no closing date. Applicants notified on a rolling basis starting 2/15; must reply by 5/1 or within 2 week(s) of notification.
Transfers: Undergraduate transfers not eligible for federal, state, or university aid if 4-year degree previously conferred.

CONTACT
Michael Light, Director, Student Financial Services
320 South Broad Street, Philadelphia, PA 19102
(215) 717-6170

University of the Sciences
Philadelphia, Pennsylvania
www.usciences.edu   Federal Code: 003353

4-year private health science and pharmacy college in very large city.
Enrollment: 2,090 undergrads, 1% part-time. 314 full-time freshmen.
Selectivity: Admits 50 to 75% of applicants.

BASIC COSTS (2016-2017)
Tuition and fees: $38,850.
Per-credit charge: $1,540.
Room and board: $15,188.
Additional info: A professional-year differential is assessed for students enrolled in the professional phase of the Occupational Therapy, Pharmacy, Physical Therapy, and Physician Assistant Studies programs.

FINANCIAL AID PICTURE (2015-2016)
Students with need: 76% of average financial aid package awarded as scholarships/grants, 24% awarded as loans/jobs. Need-based aid available for part-time students.
Students without need: No-need awards available for academics, athletics.
Scholarships offered: Freshman students are considered for merit scholarships upon time of application. Scholarship notification will be provided with admission decision. No additional essays or applications are required for merit scholarship consideration.

FINANCIAL AID PROCEDURES
Forms required: FAFSA.
Dates and Deadlines: Priority date 3/15; no closing date. Applicants notified on a rolling basis starting 2/15; must reply by 5/1 or within 2 week(s) of notification.

CONTACT
Pamela Ramanathan, Director of Financial Aid
600 South 43rd Street, Philadelphia, PA 19104-4495
(215) 596-8894

University of Valley Forge
Phoenixville, Pennsylvania
www.valleyforge.edu   Federal Code: 003306

4-year private university and liberal arts college in large town, affiliated with the Assemblies of God.
Enrollment: 742 undergrads, 16% part-time. 136 full-time freshmen.
Selectivity: Admits 50 to 75% of applicants.

BASIC COSTS (2017-2018)
Tuition and fees: $21,271.
Room and board: $8,611.
Additional info: Cost for mandatory laptop is included in the required fees.

FINANCIAL AID PICTURE (2016-2017)
Students with need: Average financial aid package met 55% of need; average scholarship/grant was $11,273; average loan was $3,346. For part-time students, average financial aid package was $7,260.
Students without need: 14 full-time freshmen who did not demonstrate need for aid received scholarships/grants; average award was $10,148. No-need awards available for academics, leadership, music/drama, religious affiliation, state/district residency.
Scholarships offered: Trustee's Scholarship, President's Elite Scholarship, President's Plus Scholarship, Dean's Scholarship, Professor's Scholarship;

ranging from full tuition (minimum 3.5 GPA, 1300 SAT or 29 ACT, and upper 10% class rank) to $1,000 (minimum 3.3 GPA and 1030 SAT or 22 ACT); application required for awards; renewable with specified GPA requirement;.

FINANCIAL AID PROCEDURES

Forms required: FAFSA.

Dates and Deadlines: Priority date 5/1; no closing date. Applicants notified on a rolling basis starting 3/1.

Transfers: No deadline. Applicants notified on a rolling basis starting 3/15; must reply within 3 week(s) of notification.

CONTACT

Linda Stein, Director of Financial Aid

1401 Charlestown Road, Phoenixville, PA 19460-2373

(610) 917-1475

Ursinus College

Collegeville, Pennsylvania

www.ursinus.edu   Federal Code: 003385

4-year private liberal arts college in small town.

Enrollment: 1,540 undergrads. 382 full-time freshmen.

Selectivity: Admits over 75% of applicants.

BASIC COSTS (2016-2017)

Tuition and fees: $49,370.

Per-credit charge: $1,543.

Room and board: $12,320.

FINANCIAL AID PICTURE (2016-2017)

Students with need: Out of 336 full-time freshmen who applied for aid, 292 were judged to have need. Of these, 292 received aid, and 91 had their full need met. Average financial aid package met 85% of need; average scholarship/grant was $36,206; average loan was $3,089.

Students without need: 71 full-time freshmen who did not demonstrate need for aid received scholarships/grants; average award was $23,169. No-need awards available for academics, alumni affiliation, leadership, minority status, music/drama, state/district residency.

FINANCIAL AID PROCEDURES

Forms required: FAFSA.

Dates and Deadlines: Closing date 2/1. Applicants notified by 2/1; must reply by 5/1.

Transfers: Closing date 8/1.

CONTACT

Suzanne Sparrow, Director of Student Financial Assistance

PO Box 1000, Collegeville, PA 19426-1000

(610) 409-3600

Valley Forge Military College

Wayne, Pennsylvania

www.vfmac.edu   Federal Code: 003386

2-year private junior and military college in small city.

Enrollment: 204 undergrads. 4 full-time freshmen.

BASIC COSTS (2016-2017)

Tuition and fees: $29,975.

Room and board: $15,400.

FINANCIAL AID PICTURE

Students with need: Need-based aid available for full-time students. Work study available nights, weekends, and for part-time students.

Students without need: This college awards aid only to students with need.

Additional info: Students enrolled in advanced military science program can receive up to $5,000 from the Army. In addition, competitively awarded ROTC scholarships pay average of another $14,100 per school year for direct educational expenses.

FINANCIAL AID PROCEDURES

Forms required: FAFSA.

Transfers: No deadline. Applicants notified on a rolling basis. Must submit transcripts from all previously attended colleges, even if aid was not received.

CONTACT

Elizabeth Sierra, Financial Aid Director

1001 Eagle Road, Wayne, PA 19087

(610) 989-1306

Vet Tech Institute

Pittsburgh, Pennsylvania

www.vettechinstitute.edu   Federal Code: 008568

2-year for-profit health science and technical college in large city.

Enrollment: 385 undergrads.

FINANCIAL AID PICTURE

Students with need: Work study available nights.

Students without need: No-need awards available for academics.

Scholarships offered: $1,000 scholarships; 5 offered to commuters. $2,000 scholarships; 2 offered to students not living at home. Awarded based on results of examination given at school in November and March.

FINANCIAL AID PROCEDURES

Forms required: FAFSA, state aid form.

Dates and Deadlines: Applicants notified on a rolling basis.

CONTACT

Donna Durr, Financial Aid Director

125 Seventh Street, Pittsburgh, PA 15222-3400

(800) 570-0693

Villanova University

Villanova, Pennsylvania   Federal Code: 003388

www.villanova.edu   CSS Code: 2959

4-year private university in large town, affiliated with the Roman Catholic Church.

Enrollment: 6,862 undergrads, 6% part-time. 1,676 full-time freshmen.

Selectivity: Admits less than 50% of applicants.

BASIC COSTS (2016-2017)

Tuition and fees: $49,430.

Per-credit charge: $2,701.

Room and board: $13,093.

FINANCIAL AID PICTURE (2016-2017)

Students with need: Out of 1,168 full-time freshmen who applied for aid, 805 were judged to have need. Of these, 785 received aid, and 149 had their full need met. Average financial aid package met 81% of need; average scholarship/grant was $31,433; average loan was $3,820. For part-time students, average financial aid package was $7,460.

Students without need: 117 full-time freshmen who did not demonstrate need for aid received scholarships/grants; average award was $14,527. No-need awards available for academics, alumni affiliation, athletics, leadership, minority status, religious affiliation, ROTC.

Scholarships offered: 40 full-time freshmen received athletic scholarships; average amount $44,836.

FINANCIAL AID PROCEDURES

Forms required: FAFSA, CSS PROFILE.

Dates and Deadlines: Closing date 1/15. Applicants notified by 4/1; must reply by 5/1 or within 2 week(s) of notification.

Transfers: Closing date 7/15. Applicants notified on a rolling basis starting 5/1; must reply within 2 week(s) of notification.

CONTACT

Bonnie Lee Behm, Director of Financial Assistance
Austin Hall, 800 Lancaster Avenue, Villanova, PA 19085-1672
(610) 519-4010

Washington & Jefferson College

Washington, Pennsylvania
www.washjeff.edu   Federal Code: 003389

4-year private liberal arts college in large town.

Enrollment: 1,371 undergrads. 429 full-time freshmen.

Selectivity: Admits less than 50% of applicants.

BASIC COSTS (2016-2017)

Tuition and fees: $44,900.

Per-credit charge: $1,113.

Room and board: $11,854.

FINANCIAL AID PICTURE (2016-2017)

Students with need: Out of 392 full-time freshmen who applied for aid, 348 were judged to have need. Of these, 348 received aid, and 56 had their full need met. Average financial aid package met 79% of need; average scholarship/grant was $10,406; average loan was $3,622. Need-based aid available for part-time students.

Students without need: 79 full-time freshmen who did not demonstrate need for aid received scholarships/grants; average award was $22,925. No-need awards available for academics, alumni affiliation, leadership.

Scholarships offered: Presidential Scholarship and Scholars Award: based on distinguished academic performance. Joseph Hardy Sr. Scholarship: for students in entrepreneurial studies program. Dean's Award: based on academic performance in high school, distinguished achievement outside the classroom, and good citizenship. Challenge Grant: for students who show academic promise. Alumni Scholarship: for students whose father and/or mother are alumni. Greb Endowed Student International Travel Award Fund and the Swick International Programs Endowed Fund which provide assistance to students who wish to study abroad. The Magellan Project: for students who want to pursue interesting summer projects domestically or abroad.

Additional info: Give It Forward Together is a special fund for students whose economic situations change dramatically while they are enrolled.

FINANCIAL AID PROCEDURES

Forms required: FAFSA.

Dates and Deadlines: Priority date 2/15; no closing date. Applicants notified on a rolling basis starting 12/15; must reply by 5/1.

Transfers: Must reply within 2 week(s) of notification. Students should complete the FAFSA as soon as possible. Financial aid awards will be made when FAFSA has been received and the student has been accepted for admission. For students selected for verification, these awards are estimated until the required tax documentation has been received and reviewed.

CONTACT

Michelle Duffy, Associate VP for Enrollment
60 South Lincoln Street, Washington, PA 15301
(724) 223-6019

Waynesburg University

Waynesburg, Pennsylvania
www.waynesburg.edu   Federal Code: 003391

4-year private liberal arts college in small town, affiliated with the Presbyterian Church (USA).

Enrollment: 1,390 undergrads, 4% part-time. 401 full-time freshmen.

Selectivity: Admits over 75% of applicants.

BASIC COSTS (2016-2017)

Tuition and fees: $22,800.

Per-credit charge: $930.

Room and board: $9,490.

FINANCIAL AID PICTURE (2016-2017)

Students with need: Out of 392 full-time freshmen who applied for aid, 341 were judged to have need. Of these, 340 received aid, and 104 had their full need met. Average financial aid package met 78% of need; average scholarship/grant was $15,203; average loan was $4,455. For part-time students, average financial aid package was $6,291.

Students without need: 59 full-time freshmen who did not demonstrate need for aid received scholarships/grants; average award was $12,275. No-need awards available for academics, alumni affiliation, job skills, state/district residency.

Scholarships offered: A.B. Miller Scholarship: $15,000. Presidential Honor Scholarship: $12,000. Honor Scholarship: $10,000.

FINANCIAL AID PROCEDURES

Forms required: FAFSA.

Dates and Deadlines: Applicants notified on a rolling basis starting 2/15; must reply within 2 week(s) of notification.

Transfers: No deadline. Applicants notified on a rolling basis; must reply within 2 week(s) of notification.

CONTACT

Matthew Stokan, Director of Financial Aid
51 West College Street, Waynesburg, PA 15370-1222
(724) 852-6312

West Chester University of Pennsylvania

West Chester, Pennsylvania
www.wcupa.edu   Federal Code: 003328

4-year public university in large town.

Enrollment: 14,123 undergrads, 9% part-time. 2,381 full-time freshmen.

Selectivity: Admits 50 to 75% of applicants.

BASIC COSTS (2016-2017)

Tuition and fees: $9,720; out-of-state residents $20,578.

Room and board: $12,860.

Additional info: Required fees listed are for in-state students; out-of-state students are charged $2,716.

FINANCIAL AID PICTURE (2015-2016)

Students with need: Out of 2,146 full-time freshmen who applied for aid, 1,494 were judged to have need. Of these, 1,494 received aid, and 125 had their full need met. Average financial aid package met 41% of need; average scholarship/grant was $5,864; average loan was $3,194. For part-time students, average financial aid package was $5,714.

Students without need: 49 full-time freshmen who did not demonstrate need for aid received scholarships/grants; average award was $3,737. No-need awards available for academics, art, athletics, leadership, music/drama, ROTC.

Scholarships offered: 14 full-time freshmen received athletic scholarships; average amount $2,699.

FINANCIAL AID PROCEDURES

Forms required: FAFSA.

Dates and Deadlines: Priority date 2/15; no closing date. Applicants notified on a rolling basis starting 3/15; must reply within 4 week(s) of notification.
Transfers: Applicants notified on a rolling basis starting 2/15; must reply within 4 week(s) of notification.

CONTACT

Dana Parker, Director of Financial Aid
Emil H. Messikomer Hall, West Chester, PA 19383
(610) 436-2627

Westminster College

New Wilmington, Pennsylvania
www.westminster.edu   Federal Code: 003392

4-year private liberal arts college in small town, affiliated with the Presbyterian Church (USA).
Enrollment: 1,158 undergrads, 1% part-time. 297 full-time freshmen.
Selectivity: Admits over 75% of applicants.

BASIC COSTS (2017-2018)

Tuition and fees: $36,230.
Per-credit charge: $1,125.
Room and board: $11,020.

FINANCIAL AID PICTURE (2015-2016)

Students with need: Out of 282 full-time freshmen who applied for aid, 257 were judged to have need. Of these, 257 received aid, and 53 had their full need met. Average financial aid package met 83% of need; average scholarship/grant was $25,451; average loan was $3,490. For part-time students, average financial aid package was $2,670.
Students without need: 40 full-time freshmen who did not demonstrate need for aid received scholarships/grants; average award was $18,586. No-need awards available for academics, alumni affiliation, leadership, minority status, music/drama, religious affiliation, state/district residency.

FINANCIAL AID PROCEDURES

Forms required: FAFSA, institutional form.
Dates and Deadlines: Priority date 5/1; no closing date. Applicants notified on a rolling basis starting 12/15; must reply by 5/1 or within 3 week(s) of notification.

CONTACT

Cheryl Gerber, Director of Financial Aid
Remick Hall, Westminster College, New Wilmington, PA 16172-0001
(724) 946-7102

Westmoreland County Community College

Youngwood, Pennsylvania
www.wccc.edu   Federal Code: 010176

2-year public community college in small town.
Enrollment: 4,316 undergrads, 48% part-time. 756 full-time freshmen.
Selectivity: Open admission; but selective for some programs.

BASIC COSTS (2016-2017)

Tuition and fees: $5,070; out-of-district residents $8,730; out-of-state residents $12,390.
Per-credit charge: $122; out-of-district residents $244; out-of-state residents $366.

FINANCIAL AID PICTURE

Students with need: Need-based aid available for full-time and part-time students. Work study available nights.
Students without need: No-need awards available for academics.

FINANCIAL AID PROCEDURES

Forms required: FAFSA, institutional form.
Dates and Deadlines: Applicants notified on a rolling basis starting 5/1.

CONTACT

Director of Financial Aid
145 Pavilion Lane, Youngwood, PA 15697
(724) 925-4063

Widener University

Chester, Pennsylvania
www.widener.edu   Federal Code: 003313

4-year private university in large town.
Enrollment: 3,331 undergrads, 11% part-time. 728 full-time freshmen.
Selectivity: Admits 50 to 75% of applicants.

BASIC COSTS (2016-2017)

Tuition and fees: $42,870.
Per-credit charge: $1,400.
Room and board: $13,616.

FINANCIAL AID PICTURE (2016-2017)

Students with need: Out of 684 full-time freshmen who applied for aid, 617 were judged to have need. Of these, 616 received aid, and 132 had their full need met. Average financial aid package met 81% of need; average scholarship/grant was $29,160; average loan was $3,850. For part-time students, average financial aid package was $7,600.
Students without need: 61 full-time freshmen who did not demonstrate need for aid received scholarships/grants; average award was $26,500. No-need awards available for academics, leadership, music/drama, ROTC.
Scholarships offered: Academic Scholarships; $4,000 to full tuition; based on SAT and GPA; renewable. Music, leadership, and community service scholarships; based on performance evaluations.

FINANCIAL AID PROCEDURES

Forms required: FAFSA.
Dates and Deadlines: Priority date 12/15; no closing date. Applicants notified on a rolling basis starting 1/30; must reply within 4 week(s) of notification.
Transfers: Transfer scholarships; $2,500 to $10,000; based on GPA and minimum of 24 transferable credits.

CONTACT

Thomas Malloy, Executive Director of Enrollment Services
One University Place, Chester, PA 19013
(610) 499-4174

Wilkes University

Wilkes Barre, Pennsylvania
www.wilkes.edu   Federal Code: 003394

4-year private university in small city.
Enrollment: 2,418 undergrads, 5% part-time. 659 full-time freshmen.
Selectivity: Admits over 75% of applicants.

BASIC COSTS (2016-2017)

Tuition and fees: $33,568.
Per-credit charge: $887.
Room and board: $13,746.

FINANCIAL AID PICTURE (2016-2017)

Students with need: Out of 614 full-time freshmen who applied for aid, 573 were judged to have need. Of these, 573 received aid, and 57 had their full need met. Average financial aid package met 72% of need; average scholarship/grant was $22,754; average loan was $3,461. For part-time students, average financial aid package was $11,402.

Students without need: 38 full-time freshmen who did not demonstrate need for aid received scholarships/grants; average award was $16,263. No-need awards available for academics, leadership, minority status, music/drama.

FINANCIAL AID PROCEDURES

Forms required: FAFSA.

Dates and Deadlines: Priority date 3/1; no closing date. Applicants notified on a rolling basis starting 3/1.

CONTACT

Chanel Greene, Executive Director Financial Aid
84 West South Street, Wilkes-Barre, PA 18766
(570) 408-2000

Williamson College of the Trades
Media, Pennsylvania
www.williamson.edu

2-year private technical college for men in large town, affiliated with the nondenominational tradition.
Enrollment: 265 undergrads.

BASIC COSTS (2016-2017)

Additional info: Entrance fees for freshmen are $255. Annual fees for all students are $225. Shop fees are up to $900 per year. Additional fees may be applicable.

FINANCIAL AID PICTURE

Students with need: Need-based aid available for full-time students.
Students without need: This college awards aid only to students with need.

Additional info: Each enrolled student receives a full scholarship covering tuition, room and board, and textbooks for the three-year program.

FINANCIAL AID PROCEDURES

Dates and Deadlines: Closing date 2/22. Applicants notified by 5/1; must reply by 5/15.

CONTACT

Jay Merillat, Dean of Enrollments
106 South New Middletown Road, Media, PA 19063
(610) 566-1776 ext. 235

Wilson College
Chambersburg, Pennsylvania
www.wilson.edu   Federal Code: 003396

4-year private liberal arts college in large town, affiliated with the Presbyterian Church (USA).
Enrollment: 742 undergrads.
Selectivity: Admits less than 50% of applicants.

BASIC COSTS (2016-2017)

Tuition and fees: $24,430.
Room and board: $11,190.
Additional info: Fees are subject to change.

FINANCIAL AID PICTURE

Students with need: Need-based aid available for full-time and part-time students.
Students without need: No-need awards available for academics, alumni affiliation, leadership, religious affiliation, state/district residency.

Scholarships offered: Presidential Merit Scholarship; $12,000 cumulative GPA 3.75 or higher; Dean's Merit Scholarship; $9,000, 3.40 to 3.74 cumulative GPA; Leadership Merit Scholarship; $3,000 to $6,000, 3.0-3.39 cumulative GPA. Scholarships for full-time students who are members of Presbyterian Church, USA. Curran Scholarships; awarded to incoming students with significant community service.

FINANCIAL AID PROCEDURES

Forms required: FAFSA, state aid form, institutional form.
Dates and Deadlines: Priority date 4/30; no closing date. Applicants notified on a rolling basis starting 2/15.
Transfers: No deadline. Applicants notified on a rolling basis starting 2/15; must reply by 5/1 or within 3 week(s) of notification. Tuition scholarships available to transfer articulation students who hold associate degrees from Harrisburg Area Community College, Hagerstown Community College, Central Penn College, Luzerne County Community College, Lehigh Carbon Community College, Harcum College, Cottey College, Frederick Community College, Howard Community College; transfer merit scholarships for students with 3.0 GPA from 25% to 50% tuition, Phi Theta Kappa scholarship.

CONTACT

Linda Brittain, Dean of Financial Aid
1015 Philadelphia Avenue, Chambersburg, PA 17201-1285
(717) 262-2016

The Workforce Institute's City College
Philadelphia, Pennsylvania
www.citycollege-careers.org/   Federal Code: 031091

2-year private technical and career college in very large city.
Enrollment: 38 undergrads, 37% part-time. 6 full-time freshmen.

BASIC COSTS (2016-2017)

Tuition and fees: $12,147.
Additional info: Full program cost is $23,994; does not include all fees and supplies. There is a required technology fee (lap top) of $540 which occurs during the students' first semester.

FINANCIAL AID PICTURE

Students with need: Need-based aid available for full-time and part-time students. Work study available nights.
Students without need: This college awards aid only to students with need.

FINANCIAL AID PROCEDURES

Forms required: FAFSA, state aid form.
Dates and Deadlines: Applicants notified on a rolling basis starting 1/1; must reply within 2 week(s) of notification.
Transfers: No deadline. Applicants notified on a rolling basis starting 1/1; must reply within 2 week(s) of notification. Because we offer transfer enrollment on a rolling basis, aid is process based on need and remaining eligibility of financial aid at any given start date.

CONTACT

Madeline Sargent, Director of Financial Aid and Operations
1231 North Broad Street, Philadelphia, PA 19122
(215) 568-9215 ext. 2

York College of Pennsylvania
York, Pennsylvania
www.ycp.edu   Federal Code: 003399

4-year private liberal arts college in small city.
Enrollment: 4,154 undergrads, 7% part-time. 890 full-time freshmen.
Selectivity: Admits 50 to 75% of applicants.

BASIC COSTS (2016-2017)
Tuition and fees: $18,780.
Per-credit charge: $525.
Room and board: $10,460.

FINANCIAL AID PICTURE
Students with need: Need-based aid available for full-time and part-time students.
Students without need: No-need awards available for academics, alumni affiliation, minority status, music/drama.
Scholarships offered: All accepted freshman applicants considered for merit scholarships, including Presidential and Dean's Scholarships, based on academic criteria GPA, rank, test scores. Scholarship awards reduce tuition to approximately $7,000-$11,500 annually for many students, not including additional eligibility for need-based financial aid.

FINANCIAL AID PROCEDURES
Forms required: FAFSA.
Dates and Deadlines: Applicants notified on a rolling basis starting 3/1; must reply within 4 week(s) of notification.
Transfers: No deadline. Applicants notified on a rolling basis starting 3/1; must reply within 4 week(s) of notification. Transfer Merit Scholarship: $2,000; $1,000 per semester for entering transfer students with minimum 3.3 GPA.

CONTACT
Calvin Williams, Director of Financial Aid
441 Country Club Road, York, PA 17403-3651
(717) 849-1682

YTI Career Institute: Lancaster
Lancaster, Pennsylvania
www.yti.edu

2-year for-profit technical and career college in small city.
Enrollment: 421 undergrads.
Selectivity: Open admission; but selective for some programs.

BASIC COSTS (2016-2017)
Additional info: Diploma program costs range from $3,000 to $20,100; associate degree programs range from $26,270 to $35,900. Books and supplies range from $450 to $4,500, depending on program. Tuition at time of enrollment locked for 2 years.

FINANCIAL AID PICTURE
Students with need: Need-based aid available for full-time and part-time students.
Students without need: This college awards aid only to students with need.

FINANCIAL AID PROCEDURES
Forms required: FAFSA.
Dates and Deadlines: Applicants notified on a rolling basis; must reply within 4 week(s) of notification.
Transfers: No deadline. Applicants notified on a rolling basis; must reply within 4 week(s) of notification.

CONTACT
Tracey Cole, Director of Financial Aid
3050 Hempland Road, Lancaster, PA 17601
(717) 757-1100

Puerto Rico

American University of Puerto Rico
Bayamon, Puerto Rico
www.aupr.edu   Federal Code: 011941

4-year private university and business college in large city.
Enrollment: 1,343 undergrads, 11% part-time. 958 full-time freshmen.

BASIC COSTS (2016-2017)
Tuition and fees: $6,536.
Additional info: Tuition/fee waivers available for minority students.

FINANCIAL AID PICTURE (2015-2016)
Students with need: 84% of average financial aid package awarded as scholarships/grants, 16% awarded as loans/jobs. Need-based aid available for part-time students.
Students without need: This college awards aid only to students with need.

FINANCIAL AID PROCEDURES
Forms required: FAFSA, institutional form.
Dates and Deadlines: Priority date 4/30; closing date 5/31. Applicants notified by 6/1; must reply within 2 week(s) of notification.

CONTACT
Raquel Torres, Director of Bursar's Office
PO Box 2037, Bayamon, PR 00960-2037
(787) 620-2040 ext. 2031

Atlantic University College
Guaynabo, Puerto Rico
www.atlanticu.edu   Federal Code: 016871

4-year private liberal arts college in small city.
Enrollment: 1,429 undergrads.
Selectivity: Open admission.

BASIC COSTS (2016-2017)
Tuition and fees: $6,870.
Per-credit charge: $140.

FINANCIAL AID PICTURE
Students with need: Need-based aid available for full-time and part-time students. Work study available nights.
Students without need: This college awards aid only to students with need.

FINANCIAL AID PROCEDURES
Forms required: FAFSA, institutional form.
Dates and Deadlines: Closing date 6/30. Applicants notified on a rolling basis starting 4/1; must reply within 2 week(s) of notification.
Transfers: Priority date 1/7; closing date 6/7.

CONTACT
Janice Rivera, Director of Financial Aid
PO Box 3918, Guaynabo, PR 00970
(787) 789-4251

Bayamon Central University
Bayamon, Puerto Rico
www.ucb.edu.pr   Federal Code: 010015

4-year private university and liberal arts college in small city, affiliated with the Roman Catholic Church.

Enrollment: 315 undergrads, 21% part-time. 176 full-time freshmen.

BASIC COSTS (2016-2017)
Tuition and fees: $5,270.
Per-credit charge: $185.
Additional info: Tuition/fee waivers available for unemployed or children of unemployed.

FINANCIAL AID PICTURE (2016-2017)
Students with need: 73% of average financial aid package awarded as scholarships/grants, 27% awarded as loans/jobs. Need-based aid available for part-time students. Work study available nights.
Students without need: This college awards aid only to students with need.

FINANCIAL AID PROCEDURES
Forms required: FAFSA, institutional form.
Dates and Deadlines: Priority date 5/31; closing date 7/2. Applicants notified on a rolling basis starting 5/31; must reply within 6 week(s) of notification.
Transfers: No deadline. Applicants notified on a rolling basis starting 4/30.

CONTACT
Edna Ortiz, Director of Financial Aid Office
PO Box 1725, Bayamon, PR 00960-1725
(787) 786-3030 ext. 2116

Caribbean University
Bayamon, Puerto Rico
www.caribbean.edu   Federal Code: 012525

4-year private university in small city.
Enrollment: 2,920 undergrads, 28% part-time. 249 full-time freshmen.
Selectivity: Open admission; but selective for some programs.

BASIC COSTS (2016-2017)
Tuition and fees: $6,280.
Per-credit charge: $183.

FINANCIAL AID PICTURE (2016-2017)
Students with need: 60% of average financial aid package awarded as scholarships/grants, 40% awarded as loans/jobs. Need-based aid available for part-time students. Work study available nights, weekends, and for part-time students.
Students without need: This college awards aid only to students with need.

FINANCIAL AID PROCEDURES
Forms required: FAFSA.
Dates and Deadlines: Priority date 5/30; no closing date. Applicants notified on a rolling basis starting 7/30; must reply within 2 week(s) of notification.
Transfers: Closing date 5/30. Applicants notified on a rolling basis.

CONTACT
Hector Gracia, Financial Aid Director
PO Box 493, Bayamon, PR 00960-0493
(787) 780-0070 ext. 1128

Columbia Central University: Caguas
Caguas, Puerto Rico
www.columbiacentral.edu   Federal Code: 013517

4-year for-profit university and branch campus college in large city.
Enrollment: 1,383 undergrads, 58% part-time. 199 full-time freshmen.
Selectivity: Open admission; but selective for some programs.

FINANCIAL AID PICTURE (2015-2016)
Students with need: Out of 194 full-time freshmen who applied for aid, 194 were judged to have need. Of these, 194 received aid. For part-time students, average financial aid package was $4,778.
Students without need: This college awards aid only to students with need.

FINANCIAL AID PROCEDURES
Forms required: FAFSA, institutional form.
Transfers: No deadline.

CONTACT
Gloria Mirabal, Financial Aid Director
PO Box 8517, Caguas, PR 00726-8517
(787) 743-4041 ext. 223

Columbia Central University: Yauco
Yauco, Puerto Rico
www.columbiacentral.edu   Federal Code: 008902

2-year for-profit business and health science college in large town.
Enrollment: 361 undergrads, 44% part-time. 58 full-time freshmen.
Selectivity: Open admission; but selective for some programs.

FINANCIAL AID PICTURE (2016-2017)
Students with need: 99% of average financial aid package awarded as scholarships/grants, 1% awarded as loans/jobs. Need-based aid available for part-time students. Work study available nights.
Students without need: This college awards aid only to students with need.

FINANCIAL AID PROCEDURES
Forms required: FAFSA, institutional form.

CONTACT
Gloria Mirabal, Director of Financial Aid
PO Box 3062, Yauco, PR 00698-3062
(787) 856-0845 ext. 112

Conservatory of Music of Puerto Rico
San Juan, Puerto Rico
www.cmpr.edu   Federal Code: 010819

4-year public music college in large city.
Enrollment: 409 undergrads, 32% part-time. 26 full-time freshmen.
Selectivity: Admits over 75% of applicants.

BASIC COSTS (2017-2018)
Tuition and fees: $3,575.
Additional info: Tuition at time of enrollment locked for 4 years.

FINANCIAL AID PICTURE (2015-2016)
Students with need: Average financial aid package met 33% of need; average scholarship/grant was $5,263; average loan was $3,689. For part-time students, average financial aid package was $33.
Students without need: This college awards aid only to students with need.

FINANCIAL AID PROCEDURES
Forms required: FAFSA.
Dates and Deadlines: Applicants notified on a rolling basis starting 4/30.
Transfers: No deadline. Applicants notified on a rolling basis.

CONTACT
Luis Diaz, Director of Financial Aid
951 Ponce de Leon Ave, San Juan, PR 00907-3373
(787) 751-0160 ext. 231

EDIC College

Caguas, Puerto Rico
www.ediccollege.com   Federal Code: 030219

2-year for-profit health science and technical college in large city.
Enrollment: 2,919 undergrads.
Selectivity: Open admission; but selective for some programs.

BASIC COSTS (2017-2018)
Tuition and fees: $6,745.
Per-credit charge: $280.

FINANCIAL AID PICTURE (2016-2017)
Students with need: Need-based aid available for full-time and part-time students. Work study available nights.
Students without need: This college awards aid only to students with need.

FINANCIAL AID PROCEDURES
Forms required: FAFSA, state aid form, institutional form.
Dates and Deadlines: Applicants notified on a rolling basis.
Transfers: No deadline. Applicants notified on a rolling basis.

CONTACT
Julio Melendez, Financial Aid Director
Box 9120, Caguas, PR 00726-9120
(787) 744-8519 ext. 233

EDP University of Puerto Rico: Hato Rey

San Juan, Puerto Rico
www.edpuniversity.edu   Federal Code: 021651

4-year for-profit university in very large city.
Enrollment: 1,560 undergrads, 37% part-time. 81 full-time freshmen.
Selectivity: Admits 50 to 75% of applicants.

BASIC COSTS (2016-2017)
Additional info: Tuition at time of enrollment locked for 4 years.

FINANCIAL AID PICTURE (2015-2016)
Students with need: Out of 79 full-time freshmen who applied for aid, 73 were judged to have need. Of these, 73 received aid. Average financial aid package met 91% of need; average scholarship/grant was $4,752; average loan was $2,988. For part-time students, average financial aid package was $7,229.
Students without need: This college awards aid only to students with need.

FINANCIAL AID PROCEDURES
Forms required: FAFSA.
Dates and Deadlines: Applicants notified on a rolling basis.
Transfers: No deadline. Applicants notified on a rolling basis.

CONTACT
Yaitzaenid Gonzalez Melendez, Financial Aid Administrator
PO Box 192303, Hato Rey, PR 00919-2303
(787) 765-3560 ext. 1278

EDP University of Puerto Rico: San Sebastian

San Sebastian, Puerto Rico
www.edpuniverstiy.edu   Federal Code: 021651

4-year for-profit university in small city.
Enrollment: 1,018 undergrads, 31% part-time. 166 full-time freshmen.
Selectivity: Admits over 75% of applicants.

BASIC COSTS (2017-2018)
Tuition and fees: $5,940.
Additional info: General courses $170.00 per credit, Health courses $174.00 per credit, Addtional fees may apply. Tuition at time of enrollment locked for 4 years.

FINANCIAL AID PICTURE (2015-2016)
Students with need: Out of 164 full-time freshmen who applied for aid, 160 were judged to have need. Of these, 160 received aid. Average financial aid package met 97% of need; average scholarship/grant was $5,035; average loan was $2,908. For part-time students, average financial aid package was $4,366.
Students without need: This college awards aid only to students with need.

FINANCIAL AID PROCEDURES
Forms required: FAFSA.
Dates and Deadlines: Closing date 6/30. Applicants notified on a rolling basis.
Transfers: Closing date 6/30. Applicants notified on a rolling basis.

CONTACT
Yaitzanid Gonzalez, Financial Aid Adininstartor
PO Box 1674, San Sebastian, PR 00685
(787) 896-2252 ext. 3289

Escuela de Artes Plasticas de Puerto Rico

San Juan, Puerto Rico
www.eap.edu   Federal Code: 017345

4-year public visual arts college in large city.
Enrollment: 555 undergrads, 25% part-time. 70 full-time freshmen.
Selectivity: Admits over 75% of applicants.

BASIC COSTS (2017-2018)
Tuition and fees: $4,002; out-of-state residents $6,702.
Per-credit charge: $90; out-of-state residents $180.

FINANCIAL AID PICTURE
Students with need: Need-based aid available for full-time and part-time students.
Students without need: This college awards aid only to students with need.

FINANCIAL AID PROCEDURES
Forms required: FAFSA.
Dates and Deadlines: Priority date 4/11; closing date 5/18. Applicants notified by 7/11.

CONTACT
Alfred Diaz, Financial Aid Officer
PO Box 9021112, San Juan, PR 00902-1112

Huertas College

Caguas, Puerto Rico
www.huertas.edu   Federal Code: 014105

2-year for-profit junior and technical college in large city.
Enrollment: 944 undergrads, 16% part-time. 161 full-time freshmen.
Selectivity: Open admission.

BASIC COSTS (2017-2018)
Tuition and fees: $6,550.
Per-credit charge: $200.

FINANCIAL AID PICTURE (2016-2017)
Students with need: Out of 152 full-time freshmen who applied for aid, 152 were judged to have need. Of these, 152 received aid, and 152 had their full need met. Need-based aid available for part-time students.

Students without need: This college awards aid only to students with need.

FINANCIAL AID PROCEDURES

Forms required: FAFSA, institutional form.
Dates and Deadlines: Applicants notified on a rolling basis.

CONTACT

Wanda Ortiz, Financial Aid Director
PO Box 8429, Caguas, PR 00726
(787) 746-1400

Humacao Community College

Humacao, Puerto Rico
www.hccpr.edu   Federal Code: 014952

2-year private business and community college in small city.
Enrollment: 465 undergrads, 23% part-time. 140 full-time freshmen.
Selectivity: Open admission.

BASIC COSTS (2016-2017)

Tuition and fees: $5,382.

FINANCIAL AID PICTURE (2015-2016)

Students with need: Out of 140 full-time freshmen who applied for aid, 139 were judged to have need. Of these, 139 received aid. Average financial aid package met 99% of need; average scholarship/grant was $5,687. For part-time students, average financial aid package was $5,687.
Students without need: This college awards aid only to students with need.

FINANCIAL AID PROCEDURES

Forms required: FAFSA, state aid form, institutional form.
Dates and Deadlines: Priority date 1/1; closing date 6/30. Applicants notified on a rolling basis starting 3/4; must reply by 1/1 or within 2 week(s) of notification.
Transfers: No deadline. Applicants notified on a rolling basis starting 1/1.

CONTACT

Cheryle Perez, Financial Aid Director
PO Box 9139, Humacao, PR 00792-9139
(787) 852-1430 ext. 234

ICPR Junior College

San Juan, Puerto Rico
www.icprjc.edu   Federal Code: 011940

2-year for-profit junior and career college in large city.
Enrollment: 2,554 undergrads.
Selectivity: Open admission.

BASIC COSTS (2017-2018)

Additional info: Tuition for nursing, medical sonography, culinary arts, pharmacy, dental technology, and commercial pastry and gastronomy is $6,900.00. All other programs $6,540.00.

FINANCIAL AID PICTURE (2016-2017)

Students with need: Need-based aid available for full-time and part-time students. Work study available nights.
Students without need: No-need awards available for academics, state/district residency.

FINANCIAL AID PROCEDURES

Forms required: FAFSA, institutional form.
Dates and Deadlines: Closing date 6/14. Applicants notified on a rolling basis starting 11/15.
Transfers: No deadline.

CONTACT

Palmira Arroyo, Financial Aid Director
PO Box 190304, San Juan, PR 00919-0304
(787) 753-6335 ext. 4201

Inter American University of Puerto Rico: Aguadilla Campus

Aguadilla, Puerto Rico
www.aguadilla.inter.edu   Federal Code: 003939

4-year private university and liberal arts college in small city.
Enrollment: 3,912 undergrads, 14% part-time. 782 full-time freshmen.
Selectivity: Admits less than 50% of applicants.

BASIC COSTS (2016-2017)

Tuition and fees: $6,142.
Per-credit charge: $183.
Additional info: Tuition at time of enrollment locked for 4 years.

FINANCIAL AID PICTURE (2016-2017)

Students with need: 100% of average financial aid package awarded as scholarships/grants, 0% awarded as loans/jobs. Need-based aid available for part-time students. Work study available nights, weekends, and for part-time students.
Students without need: No-need awards available for academics.

FINANCIAL AID PROCEDURES

Forms required: FAFSA.
Dates and Deadlines: Closing date 4/30. Applicants notified by 6/16; must reply by 8/8.
Transfers: No deadline.

CONTACT

Gloria Cortes, Director of Financial Aid
Box 20000, Aguadilla, PR 00605
(787) 891-0925 ext. 2747

Inter American University of Puerto Rico: Arecibo Campus

Arecibo, Puerto Rico
www.arecibo.inter.edu   Federal Code: 005026

4-year private liberal arts college in small city.
Enrollment: 4,303 undergrads.

BASIC COSTS (2016-2017)

Tuition and fees: $6,180.
Per-credit charge: $183.

FINANCIAL AID PICTURE

Students with need: Need-based aid available for full-time and part-time students. Work study available nights, weekends, and for part-time students.
Students without need: No-need awards available for academics, athletics.

FINANCIAL AID PROCEDURES

Forms required: FAFSA, institutional form.
Dates and Deadlines: Closing date 5/15. Applicants notified on a rolling basis.

CONTACT

Ramon de Jesus, Director of Financial Aid
PO Box 4050, Arecibo, PR 00614-4050
(787) 878-5475 ext. 2275

Inter American University of Puerto Rico: Barranquitas Campus

Barranquitas, Puerto Rico
www.br.uipr.edu   Federal Code: 005027

4-year private university in large town.
Enrollment: 1,892 undergrads, 10% part-time. 467 full-time freshmen.
Selectivity: Admits less than 50% of applicants.

BASIC COSTS (2016-2017)
Tuition and fees: $6,142.
Per-credit charge: $183.
Additional info: Tuition/fee waivers available for adults, minority students.

FINANCIAL AID PICTURE (2016-2017)
Students with need: Average financial aid package met 7% of need; average scholarship/grant was $895; average loan was $158. For part-time students, average financial aid package was $193.
Students without need: This college awards aid only to students with need.

FINANCIAL AID PROCEDURES
Forms required: FAFSA.
Dates and Deadlines: Closing date 6/30. Applicants notified on a rolling basis starting 5/10.

CONTACT
Eduardo Fontanez, Financial Aid Director
PO Box 517, Barranquitas, PR 00794
(787) 857-3600 ext. 2050

Inter American University of Puerto Rico: Fajardo Campus

Fajardo, Puerto Rico
www.fajardo.inter.edu   Federal Code: 010763

4-year private university and branch campus college in large town.
Enrollment: 1,984 undergrads, 13% part-time. 474 full-time freshmen.
Selectivity: Admits over 75% of applicants.

BASIC COSTS (2016-2017)
Tuition and fees: $6,180.
Per-credit charge: $183.

FINANCIAL AID PICTURE (2016-2017)
Students with need: 77% of average financial aid package awarded as scholarships/grants, 23% awarded as loans/jobs. Need-based aid available for part-time students. Work study available nights, weekends, and for part-time students.
Students without need: This college awards aid only to students with need.

FINANCIAL AID PROCEDURES
Forms required: FAFSA.
Dates and Deadlines: Closing date 4/30. Applicants notified by 2/1; must reply within 2 week(s) of notification.
Transfers: Priority date 1/1; closing date 4/9. Applicants notified on a rolling basis starting 1/16; must reply within 2 week(s) of notification.

CONTACT
Rafael Marin, Dean of Administration
Call Box 70003, Fajardo, PR 00738-7003
(787) 863-2390 ext. 2309

Inter American University of Puerto Rico: Bayamon Campus

Bayamon, Puerto Rico
www.bayamon.inter.edu   Federal Code: 003938

4-year private university and engineering college in small city.
Enrollment: 4,313 undergrads, 13% part-time. 895 full-time freshmen.
Selectivity: Admits less than 50% of applicants.

BASIC COSTS (2016-2017)
Tuition and fees: $6,180.
Per-credit charge: $183.

FINANCIAL AID PICTURE (2016-2017)
Students with need: Average financial aid package met 5% of need; average scholarship/grant was $718; average loan was $127. For part-time students, average financial aid package was $206.
Students without need: This college awards aid only to students with need.

FINANCIAL AID PROCEDURES
Forms required: FAFSA.
Dates and Deadlines: Priority date 6/30; no closing date. Applicants notified on a rolling basis starting 5/10.

CONTACT
Aurelis Baez, Director of Student Services
500 Dr. John Will Harris Road, Bayamon, PR 00957
(787) 279-1912 ext. 2025

Inter American University of Puerto Rico: Guayama Campus

Guayama, Puerto Rico
www.guayama.inter.edu   Federal Code: 010764

4-year private university in large town.
Enrollment: 1,709 undergrads, 16% part-time. 420 full-time freshmen.
Selectivity: Admits less than 50% of applicants.

BASIC COSTS (2017-2018)
Tuition and fees: $6,482.
Per-credit charge: $187.

FINANCIAL AID PICTURE (2016-2017)
Students with need: Out of 418 full-time freshmen who applied for aid, 416 were judged to have need. Of these, 407 received aid. Average financial aid package met 9% of need; average scholarship/grant was $1,245; average loan was $368. For part-time students, average financial aid package was $524.
Students without need: This college awards aid only to students with need.

FINANCIAL AID PROCEDURES
Forms required: FAFSA.
Dates and Deadlines: Closing date 4/29. Applicants notified by 6/15; must reply by 7/30.
Transfers: No deadline.

CONTACT
Jose Vechini-Rodriguez, Director of Financial Aid
PO Box 10004, Guayama, PR 00785
(787) 864-2222 ext. 2206

Inter American University of Puerto Rico: Metropolitan Campus

San Juan, Puerto Rico
www.metro.inter.edu/index.asp   Federal Code: 003940

4-year private branch campus college in large city.
Enrollment: 6,113 undergrads, 17% part-time. 624 full-time freshmen.
Selectivity: Admits less than 50% of applicants.

BASIC COSTS (2016-2017)
Tuition and fees: $7,302.
Per-credit charge: $183.

FINANCIAL AID PICTURE
Students with need: Need-based aid available for full-time and part-time students. Work study available nights, weekends, and for part-time students.

FINANCIAL AID PROCEDURES
Forms required: FAFSA.
Dates and Deadlines: Closing date 4/30. Applicants notified on a rolling basis.

CONTACT
Lillian Concepcion, Director of Financial Aid
Box 191293, San Juan, PR 00919-1293
(787) 250-1912 ext. 2185

Inter American University of Puerto Rico: Ponce Campus

Mercedita, Puerto Rico
ponce.inter.edu   Federal Code: 005029

4-year private university in large town.
Enrollment: 4,750 undergrads, 13% part-time. 1,190 full-time freshmen.
Selectivity: Admits 50 to 75% of applicants.

BASIC COSTS (2016-2017)
Tuition and fees: $6,180.
Per-credit charge: $183.

FINANCIAL AID PICTURE (2015-2016)
Students with need: Out of 1,184 full-time freshmen who applied for aid, 1,177 were judged to have need. Of these, 1,154 received aid, and 2 had their full need met. Average financial aid package met 10% of need; average scholarship/grant was $1,348; average loan was $238. For part-time students, average financial aid package was $421.
Students without need: This college awards aid only to students with need.
Scholarships offered: Scholarship program for first-time freshmen with a high school academic index of 3.0 or higher.

FINANCIAL AID PROCEDURES
Forms required: FAFSA.

CONTACT
Karen Caquias, Director of Financial Aid
104 Turpo Industrial Park, Mercedita, PR 00715-1602
(787) 284-1912 ext. 2018

Inter American University of Puerto Rico: San German Campus

San German, Puerto Rico
www.sg.inter.edu   Federal Code: 00714

4-year private university in large town.
Enrollment: 3,972 undergrads, 9% part-time. 985 full-time freshmen.

Selectivity: Admits 50 to 75% of applicants.

BASIC COSTS (2016-2017)
Tuition and fees: $6,180.
Per-credit charge: $183.
Room only: $1,200.

FINANCIAL AID PICTURE (2015-2016)
Students with need: Out of 962 full-time freshmen who applied for aid, 948 were judged to have need. Of these, 843 received aid. Average financial aid package met 10% of need; average scholarship/grant was $1,260; average loan was $240. For part-time students, average financial aid package was $296.
Students without need: No-need awards available for academics, athletics.

FINANCIAL AID PROCEDURES
Forms required: FAFSA, institutional form.
Dates and Deadlines: Closing date 5/14. Applicants notified on a rolling basis; must reply by 8/1.

CONTACT
Maria Lugo, Director of Financial Aid
Box 5100, San German, PR 00683-9801
(787) 264-1912 ext. 7250

National University College: Arecibo

Arecibo, Puerto Rico
www.nuc.edu   Federal Code: 015953

3-year for-profit career college in small city.
Enrollment: 1,450 undergrads.

FINANCIAL AID PICTURE
Students with need: Need-based aid available for full-time and part-time students. Work study available nights, weekends, and for part-time students.

FINANCIAL AID PROCEDURES
Forms required: FAFSA.
Dates and Deadlines: Priority date 12/31; closing date 4/30. Applicants notified on a rolling basis starting 5/2; must reply by 5/15 or within 2 week(s) of notification.
Transfers: No deadline.

CONTACT
Evelyn Quinones, Director of Financial Aid
PO Box 4035, MSC 452, Arecibo, PR 00614
(787) 879-5044 ext. 5220

National University College: Bayamon

Bayamon, Puerto Rico
www.nuc.edu   Federal Code: 015953

3-year for-profit career college in large town.
Enrollment: 3,305 undergrads.

FINANCIAL AID PICTURE
Students with need: Need-based aid available for full-time and part-time students. Work study available nights, weekends, and for part-time students.
Students without need: This college awards aid only to students with need.

FINANCIAL AID PROCEDURES
Forms required: FAFSA.
Dates and Deadlines: Priority date 12/31; closing date 4/30. Applicants notified on a rolling basis starting 5/2; must reply by 5/15 or within 2 week(s) of notification.
Transfers: No deadline.

CONTACT

Ivelisse Rios, Director of Financial Aid
PO Box 2036, Bayamon, PR 00960
(787) 780-5134 ext. 4020

National University College: Ponce

Coto Laurel, Puerto Rico
www.nuc.edu

3-year for-profit career college in large city.
Enrollment: 1,229 undergrads.

FINANCIAL AID PICTURE

Students with need: Need-based aid available for full-time and part-time students. Work study available nights, weekends, and for part-time students.
Students without need: This college awards aid only to students with need.

FINANCIAL AID PROCEDURES

Forms required: FAFSA.
Dates and Deadlines: Priority date 12/31; closing date 4/30. Applicants notified on a rolling basis starting 5/2; must reply by 5/15 or within 2 week(s) of notification.
Transfers: No deadline.

CONTACT

Tereangeli Toledo, Director of Financial Aid
PO Box 801243, Coto Laurel, PR 00780-1243

National University College: Rio Grande

Rio Grande, Puerto Rico
www.nuc.edu   Federal Code: E01213

3-year for-profit career college in small town.
Enrollment: 1,816 undergrads.

FINANCIAL AID PICTURE

Students with need: Need-based aid available for full-time and part-time students. Work study available nights, weekends, and for part-time students.
Students without need: This college awards aid only to students with need.

FINANCIAL AID PROCEDURES

Forms required: FAFSA.
Dates and Deadlines: Priority date 12/31; closing date 4/30. Must reply by 5/15 or within 2 week(s) of notification.
Transfers: No deadline.

CONTACT

Nelson Diaz, Director of Financial Aid
PO Box 3064, Rio Grande, PR 00745
(787) 809-5110 ext. 6314

Pontifical Catholic University of Puerto Rico

Ponce, Puerto Rico
www.pucpr.edu   Federal Code: 003936

4-year private university in small city, affiliated with the Roman Catholic Church.
Enrollment: 7,133 undergrads, 10% part-time. 1,272 full-time freshmen.

FINANCIAL AID PICTURE

Students with need: Need-based aid available for full-time and part-time students. Work study available nights, weekends, and for part-time students.

Students without need: No-need awards available for academics, athletics, music/drama.

FINANCIAL AID PROCEDURES

Forms required: FAFSA.
Dates and Deadlines: Closing date 5/15. Applicants notified by 6/15; must reply within 4 week(s) of notification.
Transfers: Priority date 5/11. Applicants notified by 6/15; must reply within 4 week(s) of notification. Distribution of awards based on availability of funds when application received.

CONTACT

Maria Nolasco, Director of Financial Aid
2250 Las Americas Avenue, Suite 284, Ponce, PR 00717-9777
(787) 651-2041

Theological University of the Caribbean

Saint Just, Puerto Rico
www.utcpr.edu

4-year private Bible and seminary college in small city, affiliated with the Church of God.
Enrollment: 262 undergrads, 38% part-time. 35 full-time freshmen.

BASIC COSTS (2016-2017)

Tuition and fees: $4,448.
Per-credit charge: $130.
Room and board: $2,400.

FINANCIAL AID PICTURE (2016-2017)

Students with need: 82% of average financial aid package awarded as scholarships/grants, 18% awarded as loans/jobs. Need-based aid available for part-time students.
Students without need: This college awards aid only to students with need.

FINANCIAL AID PROCEDURES

Forms required: FAFSA.

CONTACT

Frankie Negron, Administration Dean
PO Box 901, Saint Just, PR 00978-0901
(787) 761-0640 ext. 265

Turabo University

Gurabo, Puerto Rico
www.ut.suagm.edu   Federal Code: 011719

4-year private university and engineering college in small city.
Enrollment: 14,170 undergrads, 28% part-time. 2,266 full-time freshmen.
Selectivity: Admits 50 to 75% of applicants.

BASIC COSTS (2016-2017)

Tuition and fees: $5,820.
Per-credit charge: $205.

FINANCIAL AID PICTURE (2015-2016)

Students with need: Need-based aid available for full-time and part-time students.
Students without need: This college awards aid only to students with need.

FINANCIAL AID PROCEDURES

Forms required: FAFSA.
Dates and Deadlines: Priority date 5/30; no closing date.

CONTACT
Carmen Rivera-Lopez, Financial Aid Director
PO Box 3030, Gurabo, PR 00778
(787) 743-7979 ext. 4350

Universal Technology College of Puerto Rico
Aguadilla, Puerto Rico
www.unitecpr.edu   Federal Code: 030297

2-year private health science and career college in small city.
Enrollment: 1,260 undergrads.
Selectivity: Open admission.

FINANCIAL AID PICTURE
Students with need: Need-based aid available for full-time and part-time students. Work study available nights, weekends, and for part-time students.
Students without need: This college awards aid only to students with need.

FINANCIAL AID PROCEDURES
Forms required: FAFSA, state aid form, institutional form.
Dates and Deadlines: Priority date 4/30; closing date 6/30. Applicants notified on a rolling basis starting 2/1; must reply by 6/30.
Transfers: No deadline.

CONTACT
Samuel Hernandez, Financial Aid Administrator
Apartado 1955, Victoria Station, Aguadilla, PR 00605
(787) 882-2065 ext. 313

Universidad Adventista de las Antillas
Mayaguez, Puerto Rico
www.uaa.edu   Federal Code: 005019

4-year private university and liberal arts college in small city, affiliated with the Seventh-day Adventists.
Enrollment: 1,235 undergrads, 8% part-time. 154 full-time freshmen.
Selectivity: Open admission; but selective for some programs.

BASIC COSTS (2016-2017)
Tuition and fees: $6,350.
Per-credit charge: $175.
Room and board: $3,400.

FINANCIAL AID PICTURE (2015-2016)
Students with need: 66% of average financial aid package awarded as scholarships/grants, 34% awarded as loans/jobs. Need-based aid available for part-time students.

FINANCIAL AID PROCEDURES
Forms required: FAFSA, institutional form.
Dates and Deadlines: Applicants notified on a rolling basis starting 8/15; must reply within 3 week(s) of notification.
Transfers: No deadline. Applicants notified on a rolling basis.

CONTACT
Awilda Matos, Director of Financial Aid
PO Box 118, Mayaguez, PR 00681-0118
(787) 834-9595 ext. 2200

Universidad del Este
Carolina, Puerto Rico
www.suagm.edu/une   Federal Code: 011718

4-year private university in small city.
Enrollment: 11,000 undergrads, 30% part-time. 1,601 full-time freshmen.
Selectivity: Open admission; but selective for some programs.

BASIC COSTS (2016-2017)
Tuition and fees: $5,820.
Per-credit charge: $205.

FINANCIAL AID PICTURE
Students with need: Need-based aid available for full-time and part-time students. Work study available nights, weekends, and for part-time students.
Students without need: This college awards aid only to students with need.

FINANCIAL AID PROCEDURES
Forms required: FAFSA, state aid form, institutional form.
Dates and Deadlines: Priority date 5/30; no closing date.

CONTACT
Eigna De Jesús,. Financial Aid Director
PO Box 2010, Carolina, PR 00984-2010
(787) 257-7373 ext. 3304

Universidad Metropolitana
San Juan, Puerto Rico
www.suagm.edu/umet   Federal Code: 025875

4-year private university and liberal arts college in large city.
Enrollment: 11,231 undergrads, 21% part-time. 2,041 full-time freshmen.
Selectivity: Admits 50 to 75% of applicants.

BASIC COSTS (2016-2017)
Tuition and fees: $5,820.
Per-credit charge: $205.

FINANCIAL AID PICTURE
Students with need: Need-based aid available for full-time and part-time students. Work study available nights.
Students without need: This college awards aid only to students with need.

FINANCIAL AID PROCEDURES
Forms required: FAFSA.
Dates and Deadlines: Priority date 5/30; no closing date.

CONTACT
Julio Rodriguez, Financial Aid Director
Apartado 21150, San Juan, PR 00928
(787) 766-1717 ext. 6587

Universidad Pentecostal Mizpa
San Juan, Puerto Rico
www.mizpa.edu   Federal Code: 035313

4-year private university and Bible college in very large city, affiliated with the Pentecostal Holiness Church.
Enrollment: 339 undergrads.
Selectivity: Admits over 75% of applicants.

BASIC COSTS (2017-2018)
Tuition and fees: $5,150.
Per-credit charge: $155.
Room and board: $3,760.

FINANCIAL AID PICTURE (2016-2017)

Students with need: 96% of average financial aid package awarded as scholarships/grants, 4% awarded as loans/jobs. Need-based aid available for part-time students.

Students without need: This college awards aid only to students with need.

FINANCIAL AID PROCEDURES

Forms required: FAFSA.

CONTACT

Ismael Soto, Administrative Dean
RR 16 Box 4800, San Juan, PR 00926
(787) 720-4476 ext. 233

Universidad Politecnica de Puerto Rico

Hato Rey, Puerto Rico
www.pupr.edu   Federal Code: 014255

5-year private university and engineering college in large city.
Enrollment: 3,334 undergrads, 55% part-time. 389 full-time freshmen.
Selectivity: Admits over 75% of applicants.

BASIC COSTS (2016-2017)
Tuition and fees: $8,040.
Per-credit charge: $200.

FINANCIAL AID PICTURE (2016-2017)
Students with need: Average financial aid package met 33% of need; average scholarship/grant was $2,973; average loan was $1,786. For part-time students, average financial aid package was $7,988.
Students without need: No-need awards available for academics, music/drama.

FINANCIAL AID PROCEDURES
Forms required: FAFSA.
Dates and Deadlines: Priority date 5/15; closing date 6/30. Applicants notified by 7/15.

CONTACT
Sergio Villoldo, Director of Financial Aid
PO Box 192017, San Juan, PR 00919-2017
(787) 622-8000 ext. 249

University College of San Juan

San Juan, Puerto Rico
www.cunisanjuan.edu   Federal Code: 010567

4-year public university and community college in large city.
Enrollment: 1,528 undergrads, 16% part-time. 257 full-time freshmen.
Selectivity: Admits over 75% of applicants.

BASIC COSTS (2016-2017)
Tuition and fees: $330.

FINANCIAL AID PICTURE (2015-2016)
Students with need: Out of 240 full-time freshmen who applied for aid, 240 were judged to have need. Of these, 240 received aid, and 240 had their full need met. Average financial aid package met 100% of need; average scholarship/grant was $4,950. For part-time students, average financial aid package was $2,927.
Students without need: This college awards aid only to students with need.

FINANCIAL AID PROCEDURES
Forms required: FAFSA, state aid form, institutional form.
Dates and Deadlines: Applicants notified on a rolling basis starting 8/1.
Transfers: Financial aid transcripts.

CONTACT

Kennia Santos, Director of Financial Aid
180 Jose R. Oliver Avenue, San Juan, PR 00918
(787) 480-2400 ext. 2463

University of Puerto Rico: Aguadilla

Aguadilla, Puerto Rico
www.uprag.edu   Federal Code: 012123

4-year public liberal arts and technical college in small city.
Enrollment: 3,170 undergrads, 7% part-time. 955 full-time freshmen.
Selectivity: Admits less than 50% of applicants.

BASIC COSTS (2016-2017)
Tuition and fees: $2,014.

FINANCIAL AID PICTURE (2015-2016)
Students with need: 98% of average financial aid package awarded as scholarships/grants, 2% awarded as loans/jobs. Need-based aid available for part-time students.
Students without need: This college awards aid only to students with need.

FINANCIAL AID PROCEDURES
Forms required: FAFSA, institutional form.
Dates and Deadlines: Closing date 5/6. Applicants notified on a rolling basis starting 4/1; must reply within 1 week(s) of notification.
Transfers: No deadline.

CONTACT
Marta Soto, Financial Aid Director
Box 6150, Aguadilla, PR 00604-6150
(787) 890-0109

University of Puerto Rico: Arecibo

Arecibo, Puerto Rico
www.upra.edu   Federal Code: 007228

4-year public university and liberal arts college in small city.
Enrollment: 4,062 undergrads, 6% part-time. 933 full-time freshmen.
Selectivity: Admits less than 50% of applicants.

BASIC COSTS (2016-2017)
Tuition and fees: $2,048.
Per-credit charge: $1,904.

FINANCIAL AID PICTURE (2015-2016)
Students with need: 92% of average financial aid package awarded as scholarships/grants, 8% awarded as loans/jobs. Need-based aid available for part-time students. Work study available nights, weekends, and for part-time students.
Students without need: This college awards aid only to students with need.

FINANCIAL AID PROCEDURES
Forms required: FAFSA, institutional form.
Dates and Deadlines: Priority date 5/4; closing date 6/30. Applicants notified on a rolling basis starting 1/1; must reply within 4 week(s) of notification.
Transfers: Closing date 5/30. Must reply within 4 week(s) of notification.

CONTACT
Daliana Fresse, Financial Aid Officer
PO Box 4010, Arecibo, PR 00614-4010
(787) 815-0000 ext. 4500

University of Puerto Rico: Carolina Regional College

Carolina, Puerto Rico
www.uprc.edu   Federal Code: 003942

4-year public university in small city.
Enrollment: 3,819 undergrads, 17% part-time. 927 full-time freshmen.
Selectivity: Admits less than 50% of applicants.

BASIC COSTS (2016-2017)
Tuition and fees: $3,107.

FINANCIAL AID PICTURE (2015-2016)
Students with need: 91% of average financial aid package awarded as scholarships/grants, 9% awarded as loans/jobs. Need-based aid available for part-time students.
Students without need: This college awards aid only to students with need.

FINANCIAL AID PROCEDURES
Forms required: FAFSA, state aid form, institutional form.
Dates and Deadlines: Closing date 4/30. Applicants notified on a rolling basis starting 6/10.

CONTACT
Rafael Ruiz, Financial Aid Director
PO Box 4800, Carolina, PR 00984-4800
(787) 769-0188

University of Puerto Rico: Cayey University College

Cayey, Puerto Rico
www.cayey.upr.edu   Federal Code: 007206

4-year public university and liberal arts college in large town.
Enrollment: 3,741 undergrads, 7% part-time. 807 full-time freshmen.
Selectivity: Admits over 75% of applicants.

BASIC COSTS (2016-2017)
Additional info: Tuition at time of enrollment locked for 4 years.

FINANCIAL AID PICTURE
Students with need: Need-based aid available for full-time and part-time students. Work study available weekends and for part-time students.
Students without need: This college awards aid only to students with need.

FINANCIAL AID PROCEDURES
Forms required: FAFSA.
Dates and Deadlines: Closing date 6/30. Applicants notified by 7/30.
Transfers: Priority date 1/30; closing date 2/28.

CONTACT
Sonia Placeres, Director of Financial Aid
Universidad de Puerto Rico en Cayey Oficina de Admisiones, Cayey, PR 00737-2230
(787) 738-2161 ext. 2061

University of Puerto Rico: Humacao

Humacao, Puerto Rico
www.uprh.edu   Federal Code: 003942

4-year public university and liberal arts college in small city.
Enrollment: 3,931 undergrads.

BASIC COSTS (2016-2017)
Tuition and fees: $1,794.

FINANCIAL AID PICTURE
Students with need: Need-based aid available for full-time and part-time students.
Students without need: No-need awards available for academics, athletics, music/drama.

FINANCIAL AID PROCEDURES
Forms required: FAFSA.
Dates and Deadlines: Priority date 3/1; closing date 6/30. Applicants notified on a rolling basis starting 4/30; must reply by 7/31.

CONTACT
Brunilda Lopez, Director of Financial Aid
Call Box 860, Humacao, PR 00792
(787) 850-9342

University of Puerto Rico: Mayaguez

Mayaguez, Puerto Rico
www.uprm.edu   Federal Code: 003944

5-year public agricultural and engineering college in small city.
Enrollment: 11,989 undergrads, 6% part-time. 2,332 full-time freshmen.
Selectivity: Admits over 75% of applicants.

FINANCIAL AID PICTURE
Students with need: Need-based aid available for full-time and part-time students. Work study available nights, weekends, and for part-time students.
Students without need: This college awards aid only to students with need.

FINANCIAL AID PROCEDURES
Forms required: FAFSA, institutional form.
Dates and Deadlines: Priority date 1/30; closing date 6/30. Applicants notified on a rolling basis starting 6/30.
Transfers: Must reply by 6/30. Deadline according to admission date.

CONTACT
Miriam Barreto, Director of Financial Aid
Admissions Office, Mayaguez, PR 00681-9000
(787) 265-1920

University of Puerto Rico: Medical Sciences

San Juan, Puerto Rico
www.rcm.upr.edu   Federal Code: 003945

4-year public university in large city.
Enrollment: 388 undergrads, 6% part-time.

BASIC COSTS (2016-2017)
Tuition and fees: $2,196.
Per-credit charge: $55; out-of-state residents $120.

FINANCIAL AID PICTURE
Students with need: Need-based aid available for full-time and part-time students. Work study available nights, weekends, and for part-time students.
Students without need: This college awards aid only to students with need.

FINANCIAL AID PROCEDURES
Forms required: FAFSA, institutional form.
Dates and Deadlines: Priority date 4/30; closing date 6/15. Applicants notified on a rolling basis starting 8/1; must reply within 2 week(s) of notification.

CONTACT

Yolanda Rivera, Director of Financial Aid
PO Box 365067, San Juan, PR 00936-5067
(787) 758-2525 ext. 5206

University of Puerto Rico: Ponce

Ponce, Puerto Rico
www.uprp.edu   Federal Code: 009652

4-year public university and branch campus college in small city.
Enrollment: 3,630 undergrads, 6% part-time. 927 full-time freshmen.
Selectivity: Admits less than 50% of applicants.

BASIC COSTS (2016-2017)

Tuition and fees: $2,048.
Additional info: Tuition at time of enrollment locked for 4 years.

FINANCIAL AID PICTURE (2015-2016)

Students with need: Out of 927 full-time freshmen who applied for aid, 806 were judged to have need. Of these, 806 received aid.
Students without need: This college awards aid only to students with need.

FINANCIAL AID PROCEDURES

Forms required: FAFSA, institutional form.
Dates and Deadlines: Closing date 5/30.

CONTACT

Arturo Almodovar, Director
Box 7186, Ponce, PR 00732
(787) 844-8181 ext. 2555

University of Puerto Rico: Rio Piedras

San Juan, Puerto Rico
www.uprrp.edu   Federal Code: 007108

4-year public university in large city.
Enrollment: 13,264 undergrads, 10% part-time. 2,727 full-time freshmen.
Selectivity: Admits less than 50% of applicants.

BASIC COSTS (2016-2017)

Tuition and fees: $2,078.
Per-credit charge: $56.
Room and board: $8,751.

FINANCIAL AID PICTURE (2015-2016)

Students with need: 90% of average financial aid package awarded as scholarships/grants, 10% awarded as loans/jobs. Need-based aid available for part-time students. Work study available nights, weekends, and for part-time students.
Students without need: This college awards aid only to students with need.
Additional info: Tuition waived for honor students, athletes, members of chorus, and others with special talents.

FINANCIAL AID PROCEDURES

Forms required: FAFSA.
Dates and Deadlines: Closing date 4/1.

CONTACT

Aníbal Alvalle, Director of Financial Aid
Box 21907, San Juan, PR 00931-1907
(787) 764-0000 ext. 86125

University of Puerto Rico: Utuado

Utuado, Puerto Rico
uprutuado.edu   Federal Code: 010922

4-year public agricultural college in large town.
Enrollment: 1,429 undergrads, 4% part-time. 651 full-time freshmen.
Selectivity: Admits 50 to 75% of applicants.

BASIC COSTS (2016-2017)

Tuition and fees: $2,053.
Per-credit charge: $55; out-of-state residents $114.

FINANCIAL AID PICTURE (2015-2016)

Students with need: 91% of average financial aid package awarded as scholarships/grants, 9% awarded as loans/jobs. Need-based aid available for part-time students. Work study available nights.
Students without need: This college awards aid only to students with need.

FINANCIAL AID PROCEDURES

Forms required: FAFSA.
Dates and Deadlines: Priority date 5/31; no closing date. Applicants notified on a rolling basis starting 9/30; must reply within 4 week(s) of notification.
Transfers: Priority date 5/30; closing date 6/15. Closing date for Pell Grant applicants March 31.

CONTACT

Edymariel Cortes, Financial Aid Director
PO Box 2500, Utuado, PR 00641
(787) 894-2828 ext. 2601

University of the Sacred Heart

San Juan, Puerto Rico
www.sagrado.edu   Federal Code: 003937

4-year private university and liberal arts college in large city, affiliated with the Roman Catholic Church.
Enrollment: 4,187 undergrads.

BASIC COSTS (2016-2017)

Tuition and fees: $7,200.
Per-credit charge: $200.
Room only: $3,100.

FINANCIAL AID PICTURE

Students with need: Need-based aid available for full-time and part-time students.
Students without need: No-need awards available for academics, athletics.

FINANCIAL AID PROCEDURES

Forms required: FAFSA, institutional form.
Dates and Deadlines: Priority date 4/30; closing date 5/30. Applicants notified on a rolling basis starting 6/15; must reply by 8/30.
Transfers: No deadline.

CONTACT

June Adrade, Director of Financial Aid
Universidad del Sagrado Corazon Oficina de Nuevo Ingreso, San Juan, PR 00914-0383

Rhode Island

Brown University

Providence, Rhode Island
www.brown.edu

Federal Code: 003401
CSS Code: 3094

4-year private university and liberal arts college in small city.
Enrollment: 6,580 undergrads. 1,679 full-time freshmen.
Selectivity: Admits less than 50% of applicants.

BASIC COSTS (2016-2017)
Tuition and fees: $51,366.
Room and board: $13,200.

FINANCIAL AID PICTURE (2016-2017)
Students with need: Out of 955 full-time freshmen who applied for aid, 737 were judged to have need. Of these, 737 received aid, and 737 had their full need met. Average financial aid package met 100% of need; average scholarship/grant was $43,186; average loan was $3,270. For part-time students, average financial aid package was $27,138.
Students without need: This college awards aid only to students with need.

FINANCIAL AID PROCEDURES
Forms required: FAFSA, CSS PROFILE.
Dates and Deadlines: Closing date 2/1. Applicants notified by 4/1; must reply by 5/1.
Transfers: Financial aid for transfer applicants is limited. Transfer admissions are not need-blind. If awarded financial aid, your demonstrated need will be met. In order for an applicant to be considered for available funds, each candidate for financial aid must check "yes" to the Financial Aid question on Form 1 of the admission application and complete the appropriate application forms by the requisite deadlines.

CONTACT
James Tilton, Director of Financial Aid
Box 1876, Providence, RI 02912
(401) 863-2721

Bryant University

Smithfield, Rhode Island
www.bryant.edu

Federal Code: 003402

4-year private business and liberal arts college in large town.
Enrollment: 3,443 undergrads, 1% part-time. 843 full-time freshmen.
Selectivity: Admits 50 to 75% of applicants.

BASIC COSTS (2017-2018)
Tuition and fees: $42,109.
Per-credit charge: $1,033.
Room and board: $15,394.

FINANCIAL AID PICTURE (2016-2017)
Students with need: Need-based aid available for full-time and part-time students. Work study available nights, weekends, and for part-time students.
Students without need: No-need awards available for academics, athletics, minority status, ROTC.

FINANCIAL AID PROCEDURES
Forms required: FAFSA.
Dates and Deadlines: Priority date 2/15; closing date 2/15. Applicants notified by 3/24; must reply by 5/1.
Transfers: Closing date 4/1.

CONTACT
John Canning, Director of Financial Aid
1150 Douglas Pike, Smithfield, RI 02917-1291
(401) 232-6020

Community College of Rhode Island

Warwick, Rhode Island
www.ccri.edu

Federal Code: 004916

2-year public community college in small city.
Enrollment: 14,348 undergrads, 70% part-time. 1,345 full-time freshmen.
Selectivity: Open admission; but selective for some programs.

BASIC COSTS (2016-2017)
Tuition and fees: $4,266; out-of-state residents $11,496.
Per-credit charge: $180; out-of-state residents $534.
Additional info: Tuition/fee waivers available for unemployed or children of unemployed.

FINANCIAL AID PICTURE
Students with need: Need-based aid available for full-time and part-time students. Work study available nights, weekends, and for part-time students.
Students without need: No-need awards available for athletics.

FINANCIAL AID PROCEDURES
Forms required: FAFSA, institutional form.
Dates and Deadlines: Priority date 3/1; closing date 7/1. Applicants notified on a rolling basis starting 5/1; must reply within 2 week(s) of notification.

CONTACT
Andrea LaChapelle, Associate Director of Financial Aid
400 East Avenue, Warwick, RI 02886-1807
(401) 825-2468

Johnson & Wales University: Providence

Providence, Rhode Island
http://admissions.jwu.edu/

Federal Code: 003404

4-year private university in small city.
Enrollment: 8,116 undergrads, 6% part-time. 2,011 full-time freshmen.
Selectivity: Admits over 75% of applicants.

BASIC COSTS (2016-2017)
Tuition and fees: $30,396.
Room and board: $12,672.

FINANCIAL AID PICTURE
Students with need: Need-based aid available for full-time and part-time students.
Students without need: No-need awards available for academics, alumni affiliation, leadership, state/district residency.

FINANCIAL AID PROCEDURES
Forms required: FAFSA.
Dates and Deadlines: Applicants notified on a rolling basis starting 3/1; must reply within 2 week(s) of notification.
Transfers: Transfer scholarships available.

CONTACT
Lynn Robinson, Director of Financial Aid
8 Abbott Park Place, Providence, RI 02903
(800) 342-5598 ext. 4648

New England Institute of Technology

East Greenwich, Rhode Island
www.neit.edu   Federal Code: 007845

4-year private health science and technical college in small city.
Enrollment: 2,853 undergrads, 17% part-time. 444 full-time freshmen.
Selectivity: Open admission; but selective for some programs.

BASIC COSTS (2017-2018)
Tuition and fees: $28,740.
Per-credit charge: $480.
Additional info: Tuition at time of enrollment locked for 4 years.

FINANCIAL AID PICTURE (2015-2016)
Students with need: 30% of average financial aid package awarded as scholarships/grants, 70% awarded as loans/jobs. Need-based aid available for part-time students. Work study available nights, weekends, and for part-time students.
Students without need: No-need awards available for academics.

FINANCIAL AID PROCEDURES
Forms required: FAFSA.
Dates and Deadlines: Applicants notified on a rolling basis.
Transfers: No deadline. Applicants notified on a rolling basis.

CONTACT
Anna Kelly, Director of Financial Aid
One New England Tech Boulevard, East Greenwich, RI 02818
(401) 739-5000 ext. 3354

Providence College

Providence, Rhode Island   Federal Code: 003406
www.providence.edu   CSS Code: 3693

4-year private liberal arts college in small city, affiliated with the Roman Catholic Church.
Enrollment: 4,173 undergrads, 4% part-time. 1,056 full-time freshmen.
Selectivity: Admits 50 to 75% of applicants. GED not accepted.

BASIC COSTS (2016-2017)
Tuition and fees: $46,970.
Per-credit charge: $1,645.
Room and board: $13,790.
Additional info: Tuition/fee waivers available for minority students.

FINANCIAL AID PICTURE (2016-2017)
Students with need: Out of 782 full-time freshmen who applied for aid, 536 were judged to have need. Of these, 536 received aid, and 163 had their full need met. Average financial aid package met 87% of need; average scholarship/grant was $26,741; average loan was $4,821. For part-time students, average financial aid package was $5,460.
Students without need: 143 full-time freshmen who did not demonstrate need for aid received scholarships/grants; average award was $20,837. No-need awards available for academics, athletics, leadership, minority status, music/drama, ROTC.
Scholarships offered: 58 full-time freshmen received athletic scholarships; average amount $34,914.

FINANCIAL AID PROCEDURES
Forms required: FAFSA, CSS PROFILE.
Dates and Deadlines: Priority date 2/1; closing date 2/1. Applicants notified by 3/17; must reply by 5/1.
Transfers: Priority date 4/15; closing date 4/15. Applicants notified on a rolling basis starting 4/15; must reply within 2 week(s) of notification.

CONTACT
Sandra Oliveira, Executive Director of Financial Aid
Harkins Hall 103, 1 Cunningham Square, Providence, RI 02918-0001
(401) 865-2286

Rhode Island College

Providence, Rhode Island   Federal Code: 003407
www.ric.edu

4-year public liberal arts and teachers college in small city.
Enrollment: 7,224 undergrads, 23% part-time. 1,147 full-time freshmen.
Selectivity: Admits 50 to 75% of applicants.

BASIC COSTS (2016-2017)
Tuition and fees: $8,206; out-of-state residents $19,867.
Per-credit charge: $280; out-of-state residents $690.
Room and board: $11,133.
Additional info: Connecticut and Massachusetts students whose permanent address is within a 50-mile radius of the College pay the in-state tuition rate plus 50%. Tuition/fee waivers available for unemployed or children of unemployed.

FINANCIAL AID PICTURE (2016-2017)
Students with need: Out of 1,082 full-time freshmen who applied for aid, 867 were judged to have need. Of these, 821 received aid, and 99 had their full need met. Average financial aid package met 71% of need; average scholarship/grant was $7,802; average loan was $3,343. For part-time students, average financial aid package was $5,678.
Students without need: 36 full-time freshmen who did not demonstrate need for aid received scholarships/grants; average award was $2,406. No-need awards available for academics, alumni affiliation, art, music/drama.
Scholarships offered: Presidential Scholarships: $2,000 per year; for entering freshmen in the top 30% of class; minimum combined SAT score of 1100 (exclusive of Writing); must apply for admission by December 15; approximately 100 awards.

FINANCIAL AID PROCEDURES
Forms required: FAFSA, institutional form.
Dates and Deadlines: Priority date 3/1; no closing date. Applicants notified on a rolling basis starting 3/15; must reply by 5/1 or within 3 week(s) of notification.
Transfers: Priority date 5/15. Applicants notified on a rolling basis starting 3/15; must reply by 5/1 or within 3 week(s) of notification.

CONTACT
Kenneth Ferus, Director of Financial Aid
600 Mount Pleasant Avenue, Providence, RI 02908
(401) 456-8033

Rhode Island School of Design

Providence, Rhode Island   Federal Code: 003409
www.risd.edu   CSS Code: 3726

4-year private visual arts college in small city.
Enrollment: 2,000 undergrads. 464 full-time freshmen.
Selectivity: Admits less than 50% of applicants.

BASIC COSTS (2016-2017)
Tuition and fees: $47,110.
Room and board: $12,850.

FINANCIAL AID PICTURE (2016-2017)
Students with need: Out of 240 full-time freshmen who applied for aid, 175 were judged to have need. Of these, 175 received aid, and 5 had their full need met. Average financial aid package met 67% of need; average scholarship/grant was $23,864; average loan was $3,598.
Students without need: This college awards aid only to students with need.

FINANCIAL AID PROCEDURES
Forms required: FAFSA, CSS PROFILE.
Dates and Deadlines: Closing date 2/15. Applicants notified by 4/1; must reply by 5/1.

Transfers: Closing date 3/15. Applicants notified by 4/1. Transfer students with previous undergraduate degree not eligible for scholarship aid.

CONTACT

Anthony Gallonio, Assistant Vice President of Enrollment Services
2 College Street, Providence, RI 02903-2784
(401) 454-6661

Roger Williams University

Bristol, Rhode Island — Federal Code: 003410
www.rwu.edu — CSS Code: 3729

4-year private university in large town.
Enrollment: 4,586 undergrads, 10% part-time. 1,211 full-time freshmen.
Selectivity: Admits over 75% of applicants.

BASIC COSTS (2016-2017)

Tuition and fees: $31,850.
Per-credit charge: $1,249.
Room and board: $15,412.
Additional info: Tuition at time of enrollment locked for 4 years.

FINANCIAL AID PICTURE (2016-2017)

Students with need: Out of 1,049 full-time freshmen who applied for aid, 844 were judged to have need. Of these, 844 received aid, and 59 had their full need met. Average financial aid package met 81% of need; average scholarship/grant was $13,809; average loan was $3,326. For part-time students, average financial aid package was $4,198.
Students without need: 359 full-time freshmen who did not demonstrate need for aid received scholarships/grants; average award was $11,813. No-need awards available for academics, leadership.

FINANCIAL AID PROCEDURES

Forms required: FAFSA, CSS PROFILE.
Dates and Deadlines: Priority date 1/1; closing date 2/1. Applicants notified on a rolling basis starting 12/15; must reply by 5/1.
Transfers: Priority date 2/1; closing date 1/1. Applicants notified on a rolling basis starting 12/15; must reply by 5/1.

CONTACT

Tracy DaCosta, Assistant Vice President of Enrollment Management
1 Old Ferry Road, Bristol, RI 02809-2921
(401) 254-3100

Salve Regina University

Newport, Rhode Island
www.salve.edu — Federal Code: 003411

4-year private university and liberal arts college in large town, affiliated with the Roman Catholic Church.
Enrollment: 2,090 undergrads, 6% part-time. 548 full-time freshmen.
Selectivity: Admits 50 to 75% of applicants.

BASIC COSTS (2016-2017)

Tuition and fees: $37,820.
Per-credit charge: $1,242.
Room and board: $13,650.

FINANCIAL AID PICTURE (2016-2017)

Students with need: Out of 501 full-time freshmen who applied for aid, 430 were judged to have need. Of these, 430 received aid, and 51 had their full need met. Average financial aid package met 69% of need; average scholarship/grant was $22,871; average loan was $3,357. For part-time students, average financial aid package was $13,906.
Students without need: 101 full-time freshmen who did not demonstrate need for aid received scholarships/grants; average award was $15,628. No-need awards available for academics, alumni affiliation, art, ROTC.

FINANCIAL AID PROCEDURES

Forms required: FAFSA.
Dates and Deadlines: Priority date 3/1; no closing date. Applicants notified on a rolling basis starting 1/3; must reply by 5/1 or within 2 week(s) of notification.
Transfers: No deadline. Applicants notified on a rolling basis starting 3/1; must reply by 5/1 or within 2 week(s) of notification. Must provide financial aid transcripts from previous institutions attended.

CONTACT

Anne McDermott, Director of Financial Aid
100 Ochre Point Avenue, Newport, RI 02840-4192
(401) 341-2901

University of Rhode Island

Kingston, Rhode Island
www.uri.edu — Federal Code: 003414

4-year public university in small town.
Enrollment: 13,777 undergrads, 10% part-time. 3,236 full-time freshmen.
Selectivity: Admits 50 to 75% of applicants.

BASIC COSTS (2016-2017)

Tuition and fees: $12,884; out-of-state residents $28,874.
Per-credit charge: $464; out-of-state residents $1,130.
Room and board: $12,022.
Additional info: Tuition/fee waivers available for unemployed or children of unemployed.

FINANCIAL AID PICTURE (2016-2017)

Students with need: Out of 3,063 full-time freshmen who applied for aid, 2,428 were judged to have need. Of these, 2,347 received aid, and 74 had their full need met. Average financial aid package met 64% of need; average scholarship/grant was $10,594; average loan was $5,786. For part-time students, average financial aid package was $10,041.
Students without need: 350 full-time freshmen who did not demonstrate need for aid received scholarships/grants; average award was $7,094. No-need awards available for academics, alumni affiliation, art, athletics, music/drama, ROTC.
Scholarships offered: *Merit:* Centennial and University Merit Scholarships of varying amounts are awarded by our Admission Office at the time of admission. Criteria are posted on the Admission web site. *Athletic:* 16 full-time freshmen received athletic scholarships; average amount $10,104.

FINANCIAL AID PROCEDURES

Forms required: FAFSA.
Dates and Deadlines: Priority date 3/1; no closing date. Applicants notified on a rolling basis starting 3/15; must reply by 5/1.
Transfers: No deadline. Applicants notified on a rolling basis starting 4/1; must reply within 2 week(s) of notification.

CONTACT

Paul Langhammer, Sr. Associate Director of Enrollment Services
Newman Hall, Kingston, RI 02881-1322
(401) 874-9500

South Carolina

Aiken Technical College

Aiken, South Carolina
www.atc.edu — Federal Code: 010056

2-year public community and technical college in small city.
Enrollment: 2,259 undergrads.

Selectivity: Open admission; but selective for some programs.

BASIC COSTS (2016-2017)
Tuition and fees: $5,350; out-of-district residents $5,800; out-of-state residents $8,192.
Per-credit charge: $167; out-of-district residents $182; out-of-state residents $259.

FINANCIAL AID PICTURE
Students with need: Need-based aid available for full-time and part-time students. Work study available nights, weekends, and for part-time students.
Students without need: No-need awards available for academics, leadership, minority status, state/district residency.
Scholarships offered: Vernon Ford Scholarships; $1,000 annually; based on 3.0 GPA; 8 awarded. Presidential Scholarship; $10,000 annually; 10 awarded.

FINANCIAL AID PROCEDURES
Forms required: FAFSA.
Dates and Deadlines: Priority date 6/1; closing date 7/1. Applicants notified on a rolling basis starting 4/1; must reply within 2 week(s) of notification.
Transfers: Priority date 6/1. Applicants notified on a rolling basis; must reply within 2 week(s) of notification.

CONTACT
Sue Sims, Director of Financial Aid
PO Drawer 696, Aiken, SC 29802
(803) 593-9954 ext. 1261

Allen University
Columbia, South Carolina
www.allenuniversity.edu   Federal Code: 003417

4-year private university and liberal arts college in large city, affiliated with the African Methodist Episcopal Church.
Enrollment: 670 undergrads.

BASIC COSTS (2016-2017)
Tuition and fees: $12,740.
Per-credit charge: $450.
Room and board: $6,560.

FINANCIAL AID PICTURE
Students with need: Need-based aid available for full-time and part-time students.
Students without need: No-need awards available for academics, athletics, music/drama, ROTC.

FINANCIAL AID PROCEDURES
Forms required: FAFSA.
Dates and Deadlines: Priority date 4/15; closing date 7/20. Applicants notified on a rolling basis starting 4/1; must reply within 2 week(s) of notification.
Transfers: No deadline.

CONTACT
Shelline Warren, Financial Aid Director
1530 Harden Street, Columbia, SC 29204
(803) 376-5930

Anderson University
Anderson, South Carolina
www.andersonuniversity.edu   Federal Code: 003418

4-year private university in large town, affiliated with the Southern Baptist Convention.
Enrollment: 2,749 undergrads, 10% part-time. 649 full-time freshmen.
Selectivity: Admits 50 to 75% of applicants.

BASIC COSTS (2016-2017)
Tuition and fees: $25,880.
Per-credit charge: $585.
Room and board: $9,520.
Additional info: Tuition/fee waivers available for adults.

FINANCIAL AID PICTURE (2015-2016)
Students with need: Out of 610 full-time freshmen who applied for aid, 498 were judged to have need. Of these, 498 received aid, and 140 had their full need met. Average financial aid package met 75% of need; average scholarship/grant was $16,925; average loan was $3,916. For part-time students, average financial aid package was $5,935.
Students without need: 150 full-time freshmen who did not demonstrate need for aid received scholarships/grants; average award was $10,598. No-need awards available for academics, art, athletics, leadership, minority status, music/drama, religious affiliation, state/district residency.
Scholarships offered: 43 full-time freshmen received athletic scholarships; average amount $6,407.

FINANCIAL AID PROCEDURES
Forms required: FAFSA, state aid form.
Dates and Deadlines: Priority date 3/1; closing date 6/30. Applicants notified on a rolling basis starting 3/15; must reply by 5/1 or within 2 week(s) of notification.
Transfers: No deadline. Applicants notified on a rolling basis. Transfers are awarded based on college GPA on a different merit scale than Firs-time-freshmen.

CONTACT
Nancy Tate, Director of Financial Aid & Planning
316 Boulevard, Anderson, SC 29621-4002
(864) 231-2070

Benedict College
Columbia, South Carolina
www.benedict.edu   Federal Code: 003420

4-year private liberal arts college in large city, affiliated with the American Baptist Churches in the USA.
Enrollment: 2,464 undergrads.

BASIC COSTS (2016-2017)
Tuition and fees: $19,566.
Per-credit charge: $586.
Room and board: $8,672.

FINANCIAL AID PICTURE
Students with need: Need-based aid available for full-time and part-time students.

FINANCIAL AID PROCEDURES
Forms required: FAFSA.
Dates and Deadlines: Priority date 4/15; no closing date. Applicants notified on a rolling basis starting 4/15.

CONTACT
Sul Black, Vice President of Financial Aid
1600 Harden Street, Columbia, SC 29204
(803) 253-5105

Bob Jones University
Greenville, South Carolina
www.bju.edu   Federal Code: 003421

4-year private liberal arts college in small city, affiliated with the nondenominational tradition.
Enrollment: 2,361 undergrads, 2% part-time. 574 full-time freshmen.

BASIC COSTS (2016-2017)

Tuition and fees: $15,550.

Per-credit charge: $355.

Room and board: $6,470.

FINANCIAL AID PICTURE

Students with need: Need-based aid available for full-time and part-time students. Work study available nights, weekends, and for part-time students.

Students without need: No-need awards available for academics, alumni affiliation, state/district residency.

FINANCIAL AID PROCEDURES

Forms required: FAFSA.

Dates and Deadlines: Priority date 3/1; closing date 7/1. Applicants notified on a rolling basis.

Transfers: Applicants notified on a rolling basis.

CONTACT

Susan Young, Director of Financial Aid

1700 Wade Hampton Boulevard, Greenville, SC 29614

(864) 242-5100 ext. 3040

Central Carolina Technical College

Sumter, South Carolina

www.cctech.edu   Federal Code: 003995

2-year public community and technical college in large town.

Enrollment: 4,300 undergrads.

Selectivity: Open admission; but selective for some programs.

BASIC COSTS (2016-2017)

Tuition and fees: $5,100; out-of-district residents $5,970; out-of-state residents $8,700.

Per-credit charge: $170; out-of-district residents $199; out-of-state residents $290.

FINANCIAL AID PICTURE

Students with need: Need-based aid available for full-time and part-time students. Work study available nights.

FINANCIAL AID PROCEDURES

Forms required: FAFSA.

Dates and Deadlines: Applicants notified on a rolling basis starting 4/11; must reply within 2 week(s) of notification.

CONTACT

Sarah Dowd, Director of Financial Aid

506 North Guignard Drive, Sumter, SC 29150-2499

(803) 778-7831

Charleston Southern University

Charleston, South Carolina

www.csuniv.edu   Federal Code: 003419

4-year private university and liberal arts college in large city, affiliated with the Southern Baptist Convention.

Enrollment: 3,191 undergrads.

Selectivity: Admits 50 to 75% of applicants.

BASIC COSTS (2016-2017)

Tuition and fees: $24,100.

Per-credit charge: $470.

Room and board: $9,600.

FINANCIAL AID PICTURE

Students with need: Need-based aid available for full-time and part-time students. Work study available nights, weekends, and for part-time students.

Students without need: No-need awards available for academics, athletics, religious affiliation, ROTC.

FINANCIAL AID PROCEDURES

Forms required: FAFSA, state aid form.

Dates and Deadlines: Priority date 4/15; no closing date. Applicants notified on a rolling basis starting 3/1; must reply within 2 week(s) of notification.

CONTACT

Jenna Parish, Director of Financial Aid

9200 University Boulevard, Charleston, SC 29406

(843) 863-7050

The Citadel

Charleston, South Carolina

www.citadel.edu   Federal Code: 003423

4-year public military college in large city.

Enrollment: 2,693 undergrads, 7% part-time. 734 full-time freshmen.

Selectivity: Admits over 75% of applicants.

BASIC COSTS (2017-2018)

Tuition and fees: $12,755; out-of-state residents $34,518.

Room and board: $7,924.

FINANCIAL AID PICTURE (2016-2017)

Students with need: Out of 644 full-time freshmen who applied for aid, 495 were judged to have need. Of these, 470 received aid, and 90 had their full need met. Average financial aid package met 52% of need; average scholarship/grant was $13,821; average loan was $3,447. For part-time students, average financial aid package was $9,139.

Students without need: 154 full-time freshmen who did not demonstrate need for aid received scholarships/grants; average award was $7,300. No-need awards available for academics, alumni affiliation, athletics, leadership, minority status, music/drama, religious affiliation, ROTC, state/district residency.

Scholarships offered: 60 full-time freshmen received athletic scholarships; average amount $26,632.

FINANCIAL AID PROCEDURES

Forms required: FAFSA.

Dates and Deadlines: Priority date 3/1; no closing date. Applicants notified on a rolling basis starting 4/1; must reply within 2 week(s) of notification.

Transfers: No deadline. Applicants notified on a rolling basis starting 4/1; must reply within 2 week(s) of notification.

CONTACT

Henry Fuller, Director of Financial Aid

171 Moultrie Street, Charleston, SC 29409

(843) 953-5187

Claflin University

Orangeburg, South Carolina

www.claflin.edu   Federal Code: 003424

4-year private liberal arts college in large town, affiliated with the United Methodist Church.

Enrollment: 1,904 undergrads, 2% part-time. 490 full-time freshmen.

Selectivity: Admits less than 50% of applicants.

BASIC COSTS (2016-2017)

Tuition and fees: $15,982.

Room and board: $8,932.

FINANCIAL AID PICTURE

Students with need: Need-based aid available for full-time and part-time students. Work study available nights.

FINANCIAL AID PROCEDURES

Forms required: FAFSA.

Dates and Deadlines: Closing date 4/15. Applicants notified on a rolling basis starting 5/3; must reply within 2 week(s) of notification.

Transfers: No deadline. Applicants notified on a rolling basis.

CONTACT

Terria Williams, Director of Financial Aid

400 Magnolia Street, Orangeburg, SC 29115

(803) 535-5334

Clemson University

Clemson, South Carolina

www.clemson.edu   Federal Code: 003425

4-year public university and engineering college in large town.

Enrollment: 18,395 undergrads, 3% part-time. 3,681 full-time freshmen.

Selectivity: Admits 50 to 75% of applicants.

BASIC COSTS (2016-2017)

Tuition and fees: $14,318; out-of-state residents $33,300.

Room and board: $9,080.

FINANCIAL AID PICTURE

Students with need: Need-based aid available for full-time and part-time students. Work study available nights, weekends, and for part-time students.

Students without need: No-need awards available for academics, alumni affiliation, art, athletics, leadership, minority status, music/drama, ROTC, state/district residency.

FINANCIAL AID PROCEDURES

Forms required: FAFSA.

Dates and Deadlines: Priority date 3/1; no closing date. Applicants notified by 4/1.

Transfers: Priority date 4/1. Applicants notified on a rolling basis starting 6/1; must reply within 3 week(s) of notification. Transfer students must earn 12 semester hours before being considered for institutional scholarship.

CONTACT

Richard Ritzman, Director of Student Financial Aid

105 Sikes Hall, Clemson, SC 29634-5124

(864) 656-2280

Clinton College

Rock Hill, South Carolina

www.clintoncollege.edu/

2-year private junior and liberal arts college in small city.

Enrollment: 184 undergrads.

Selectivity: Open admission.

BASIC COSTS (2016-2017)

Tuition and fees: $6,994.

Room and board: $9,551.

Additional info: Off-campus residents pay $400 less in fees.

FINANCIAL AID PICTURE

Students with need: Need-based aid available for full-time and part-time students.

Students without need: This college awards aid only to students with need.

FINANCIAL AID PROCEDURES

Forms required: FAFSA.

Transfers: No deadline.

CONTACT

Sadie Jumper, Coordinator of Financial Aid

1029 Crawford Road, Rock Hill, SC 29730

Coastal Carolina University

Conway, South Carolina

www.coastal.edu   Federal Code: 003451

4-year public university in large town.

Enrollment: 9,460 undergrads, 7% part-time. 2,359 full-time freshmen.

Selectivity: Admits 50 to 75% of applicants.

BASIC COSTS (2016-2017)

Tuition and fees: $10,876; out-of-state residents $25,120.

Per-credit charge: $456; out-of-state residents $1,044.

Room and board: $8,890.

FINANCIAL AID PICTURE (2015-2016)

Students with need: Out of 2,112 full-time freshmen who applied for aid, 1,717 were judged to have need. Of these, 1,684 received aid, and 141 had their full need met. Average financial aid package met 44% of need; average scholarship/grant was $4,894; average loan was $8,612. For part-time students, average financial aid package was $4,772.

Students without need: 442 full-time freshmen who did not demonstrate need for aid received scholarships/grants; average award was $12,165. No-need awards available for academics, art, athletics, leadership, ROTC.

Scholarships offered: 101 full-time freshmen received athletic scholarships; average amount $9,727.

FINANCIAL AID PROCEDURES

Forms required: FAFSA.

Dates and Deadlines: Priority date 3/1; no closing date. Applicants notified on a rolling basis starting 3/1; must reply by 5/15.

Transfers: No deadline. Applicants notified on a rolling basis starting 3/1; must reply within 4 week(s) of notification.

CONTACT

Wendy Watts, Director of Financial Aid and Scholarships

PO Box 261954, Conway, SC 29528-6054

(843) 349-2313

Coker College

Hartsville, South Carolina

www.coker.edu   Federal Code: 003427

4-year private liberal arts college in large town.

Enrollment: 1,091 undergrads.

BASIC COSTS (2016-2017)

Tuition and fees: $27,624.

Room and board: $8,568.

Additional info: Tuition/fee waivers available for adults.

FINANCIAL AID PICTURE

Students with need: Need-based aid available for full-time and part-time students. Work study available nights, weekends, and for part-time students.

Students without need: No-need awards available for academics, alumni affiliation, art, athletics, leadership, music/drama.

Scholarships offered: Scholarships for Excellence; up to $17,000 per year; awarded to students showing potential for continued high performance and leadership.

Additional info: Endowed scholarship program for qualified applicants. June 1 deadline for filing South Carolina Tuition Grant forms.

FINANCIAL AID PROCEDURES

Forms required: FAFSA.

Dates and Deadlines: Priority date 4/1; closing date 6/1. Applicants notified on a rolling basis starting 3/1; must reply by 5/1 or within 3 week(s) of notification.

Transfers: No deadline.

CONTACT

Betty Williams, Director of Financial Aid
300 East College Avenue, Hartsville, SC 29550
(843) 383-8055

College of Charleston
Charleston, South Carolina
www.cofc.edu   Federal Code: 003428

4-year public university and liberal arts college in large city.
Enrollment: 10,033 undergrads, 6% part-time. 2,342 full-time freshmen.
Selectivity: Admits over 75% of applicants.

BASIC COSTS (2016-2017)
Tuition and fees: $11,706; out-of-state residents $29,864.
Per-credit charge: $474; out-of-state residents $1,231.
Room and board: $12,048.

FINANCIAL AID PICTURE (2016-2017)
Students with need: Out of 1,840 full-time freshmen who applied for aid, 1,308 were judged to have need. Of these, 1,242 received aid, and 232 had their full need met. Average financial aid package met 53% of need; average scholarship/grant was $2,775; average loan was $3,019. For part-time students, average financial aid package was $8,737.
Students without need: 548 full-time freshmen who did not demonstrate need for aid received scholarships/grants; average award was $10,982. No-need awards available for academics, alumni affiliation, art, athletics, music/drama.
Scholarships offered: 28 full-time freshmen received athletic scholarships; average amount $25,635.

FINANCIAL AID PROCEDURES
Forms required: FAFSA.
Dates and Deadlines: Priority date 3/1; no closing date. Applicants notified on a rolling basis starting 4/1; must reply within 8 week(s) of notification.

CONTACT

Donald Griggs, Director of Financial Assistance and Veterans Affairs
Admissions, Charleston, SC 29424-0001
(843) 953-5540

Columbia College
Columbia, South Carolina
www.columbiasc.edu   Federal Code: 003430

4-year private liberal arts college for women in large city, affiliated with the United Methodist Church.
Enrollment: 1,461 undergrads.
Selectivity: Admits over 75% of applicants.

BASIC COSTS (2016-2017)
Tuition and fees: $28,900.
Per-credit charge: $760.
Room and board: $7,650.

FINANCIAL AID PICTURE
Students with need: Need-based aid available for full-time and part-time students. Work study available nights, weekends, and for part-time students.
Students without need: No-need awards available for academics, alumni affiliation, art, athletics, leadership, music/drama.

Scholarships offered: Founders Scholarship; up to full tuition. Presidential Scholarships; up to $14,000. Trustees Scholarships; up to $12,000. Momentum Scholarships; up to full tuition.

FINANCIAL AID PROCEDURES
Forms required: FAFSA.
Dates and Deadlines: Priority date 4/1; no closing date. Applicants notified on a rolling basis starting 3/15; must reply within 4 week(s) of notification.
Transfers: Priority date 4/15; closing date 8/1. Applicants notified on a rolling basis starting 3/15; must reply within 4 week(s) of notification. Must meet institutional standards of satisfactory academic progress.

CONTACT

Donna Quick, Director of Financial Aid
1301 Columbia College Drive, Columbia, SC 29203
(803) 786-3612

Columbia International University
Columbia, South Carolina
www.ciu.edu   Federal Code: 003429

4-year private university and Bible college in small city, affiliated with the interdenominational tradition.
Enrollment: 488 undergrads, 7% part-time. 99 full-time freshmen.
Selectivity: Admits less than 50% of applicants.

BASIC COSTS (2016-2017)
Tuition and fees: $21,490.
Per-credit charge: $870.
Room and board: $7,760.

FINANCIAL AID PICTURE (2015-2016)
Students with need: Out of 89 full-time freshmen who applied for aid, 77 were judged to have need. Of these, 77 received aid, and 12 had their full need met. Average financial aid package met 68% of need; average scholarship/grant was $14,447; average loan was $3,137. For part-time students, average financial aid package was $9,365.
Students without need: 21 full-time freshmen who did not demonstrate need for aid received scholarships/grants; average award was $8,197. No-need awards available for academics, alumni affiliation, athletics, leadership, minority status, music/drama, state/district residency.
Scholarships offered: *Merit:* Merit Scholarships; $1,000-$7,000. *Athletic:* 2 full-time freshmen received athletic scholarships; average amount $750.
Additional info: Spouse scholarship program.

FINANCIAL AID PROCEDURES
Forms required: FAFSA, state aid form, institutional form.
Dates and Deadlines: Priority date 4/15; no closing date. Applicants notified on a rolling basis starting 3/1; must reply within 2 week(s) of notification.
Transfers: No deadline. Applicants notified on a rolling basis starting 3/15; must reply within 2 week(s) of notification. FAFSA must be processed by June 30 for state need-based aid. State aid requires 1-year residency prior to award in most cases. Non-need-based state aid requires graduation from state high school.

CONTACT

Patty Hix, Director of Financial Aid
PO Box 3122, Columbia, SC 29230-3122
(803) 807-5036

Converse College
Spartanburg, South Carolina
www.converse.edu   Federal Code: 003431

4-year private university and liberal arts college for women in large town.
Enrollment: 864 undergrads, 6% part-time. 243 full-time freshmen.

Selectivity: Admits 50 to 75% of applicants.

BASIC COSTS (2017-2018)
Tuition and fees: $18,030.
Per-credit charge: $875.
Room and board: $10,610.

FINANCIAL AID PICTURE (2016-2017)
Students with need: Out of 231 full-time freshmen who applied for aid, 200 were judged to have need. Of these, 199 received aid, and 34 had their full need met. Average financial aid package met 64% of need; average scholarship/grant was $12,714; average loan was $3,637. For part-time students, average financial aid package was $6,325.
Students without need: 33 full-time freshmen who did not demonstrate need for aid received scholarships/grants; average award was $6,592. No-need awards available for academics, art, athletics, music/drama, ROTC, state/district residency.
Scholarships offered: 18 full-time freshmen received athletic scholarships; average amount $7,178.

FINANCIAL AID PROCEDURES
Forms required: FAFSA.
Dates and Deadlines: Priority date 3/1; no closing date. Applicants notified on a rolling basis starting 3/1; must reply by 5/1 or within 2 week(s) of notification.
Transfers: No deadline. Applicants notified on a rolling basis starting 3/1; must reply by 5/1 or within 2 week(s) of notification.

CONTACT
James Kellam, Director of Financial Planning
580 East Main Street, Spartanburg, SC 29302-0006
(864) 596-9019

Denmark Technical College
Denmark, South Carolina
www.denmarktech.edu   Federal Code: 005363

2-year public technical college in small town.
Enrollment: 579 undergrads, 34% part-time. 130 full-time freshmen.
Selectivity: Open admission.

BASIC COSTS (2016-2017)
Tuition and fees: $3,656; out-of-state residents $6,996.
Room and board: $3,938.

FINANCIAL AID PICTURE
Students with need: Need-based aid available for full-time and part-time students.

FINANCIAL AID PROCEDURES
Forms required: FAFSA.
Dates and Deadlines: Applicants notified on a rolling basis starting 6/1; must reply within 2 week(s) of notification.

CONTACT
Laura Fogel, Director of Financial Aid
1126 Solomon Blatt Boulevard, Denmark, SC 29042
(803) 793-5161

Erskine College
Due West, South Carolina
www.erskine.edu   Federal Code: 003432

4-year private liberal arts and seminary college in rural community, affiliated with the Reformed Presbyterian Church of North America.
Enrollment: 619 undergrads.

BASIC COSTS (2016-2017)
Tuition and fees: $34,560.
Per-credit charge: $1,250.
Room and board: $10,900.

FINANCIAL AID PICTURE
Students with need: Need-based aid available for full-time and part-time students. Work study available nights, weekends, and for part-time students.
Students without need: No-need awards available for academics, alumni affiliation, athletics, leadership, minority status, music/drama, religious affiliation, state/district residency.
Additional info: Filing deadline 5/1 for institutional form, 6/30 for state form.

FINANCIAL AID PROCEDURES
Forms required: FAFSA, state aid form, institutional form.
Dates and Deadlines: Priority date 4/1; no closing date. Applicants notified on a rolling basis starting 12/15; must reply within 2 week(s) of notification.
Transfers: Closing date 5/1. South Carolina residents must have earned 24 hours in previous year to receive tuition grant and 30 hours plus 3.0 GPA to receive the Life Scholarship.

CONTACT
Michelle Lodato, Director of Financial Aid
PO Box 338, Due West, SC 29639-0338
(864) 379-8832

Florence-Darlington Technical College
Florence, South Carolina
www.fdtc.edu   Federal Code: 003990

2-year public community and technical college in small city.
Enrollment: 6,214 undergrads.
Selectivity: Open admission; but selective for some programs.

BASIC COSTS (2016-2017)
Tuition and fees: $5,185; out-of-district residents $5,515; out-of-state residents $7,795.
Per-credit charge: $167; out-of-district residents $178; out-of-state residents $254.

FINANCIAL AID PICTURE
Students with need: Need-based aid available for full-time and part-time students.
Students without need: No-need awards available for academics.

FINANCIAL AID PROCEDURES
Forms required: FAFSA.
Dates and Deadlines: Priority date 5/1; no closing date. Applicants notified on a rolling basis starting 7/1; must reply within 2 week(s) of notification.
Transfers: Priority date 4/1; no deadline.

CONTACT
Tony Otto, Director of Financial Assistance
PO Box 100548, Florence, SC 29501-0548
(843) 661-8085

Forrest Junior College
Anderson, South Carolina
www.forrestcollege.edu   Federal Code: 004924

2-year for-profit junior and career college in large town.
Enrollment: 116 undergrads, 14% part-time. 85 full-time freshmen.
Selectivity: Open admission; but selective for some programs.

BASIC COSTS (2017-2018)
Tuition and fees: $9,195.
Per-credit charge: $245.

FINANCIAL AID PICTURE

Students with need: Need-based aid available for full-time and part-time students. Work study available nights, weekends, and for part-time students.
Students without need: This college awards aid only to students with need.

FINANCIAL AID PROCEDURES

Forms required: FAFSA.
Dates and Deadlines: Applicants notified on a rolling basis starting 4/30; must reply by 5/31 or within 4 week(s) of notification.
Transfers: No deadline. Applicants notified on a rolling basis; must reply within 3 week(s) of notification.

CONTACT

Kathy Childress, Finance Coordinator
601 East River Street, Anderson, SC 29624
(864) 225-7653 ext. 2209

Francis Marion University

Florence, South Carolina
www.fmarion.edu   Federal Code: 009226

4-year public university and liberal arts college in small city.
Enrollment: 3,221 undergrads, 4% part-time. 729 full-time freshmen.
Selectivity: Admits 50 to 75% of applicants.

BASIC COSTS (2016-2017)

Tuition and fees: $10,428; out-of-state residents $20,308.
Per-credit charge: $494; out-of-state residents $988.
Room and board: $7,716.

FINANCIAL AID PICTURE (2016-2017)

Students with need: Out of 563 full-time freshmen who applied for aid, 496 were judged to have need. Of these, 489 received aid, and 136 had their full need met. Average financial aid package met 83% of need; average scholarship/grant was $9,736; average loan was $7,901. For part-time students, average financial aid package was $11,236.
Students without need: 30 full-time freshmen who did not demonstrate need for aid received scholarships/grants; average award was $5,957. No-need awards available for academics, alumni affiliation, art, athletics, leadership, minority status, music/drama, religious affiliation, ROTC, state/district residency.
Scholarships offered: 11 full-time freshmen received athletic scholarships; average amount $13,809.

FINANCIAL AID PROCEDURES

Forms required: FAFSA.
Dates and Deadlines: Priority date 3/1; no closing date. Applicants notified on a rolling basis starting 11/1.
Transfers: No deadline. Applicants notified on a rolling basis starting 11/1.

CONTACT

Kim Ellisor, Director of Financial Assistance
PO Box 100547, Florence, SC 29502-0547
(843) 661-1190

Furman University

Greenville, South Carolina   Federal Code: 003434
www.furman.edu   CSS Code: 5222

4-year private liberal arts college in small city.
Enrollment: 2,780 undergrads, 3% part-time. 748 full-time freshmen.
Selectivity: Admits 50 to 75% of applicants.

BASIC COSTS (2016-2017)

Tuition and fees: $47,164.
Per-credit charge: $1,462.

Room and board: $11,864.

FINANCIAL AID PICTURE (2016-2017)

Students with need: Out of 529 full-time freshmen who applied for aid, 406 were judged to have need. Of these, 406 received aid, and 143 had their full need met. Average financial aid package met 81% of need; average scholarship/grant was $37,293; average loan was $3,344. Need-based aid available for part-time students.
Students without need: 305 full-time freshmen who did not demonstrate need for aid received scholarships/grants; average award was $18,327. No-need awards available for academics, alumni affiliation, art, athletics, leadership, music/drama, religious affiliation, ROTC, state/district residency.
Scholarships offered: 79 full-time freshmen received athletic scholarships; average amount $46,269.
Additional info: 5-point comprehensive education financing plan includes financial aid packaging, money management counseling, debt management counseling, outside scholarship coordination, summer job-match program.

FINANCIAL AID PROCEDURES

Forms required: FAFSA, CSS PROFILE, state aid form, institutional form.
Dates and Deadlines: Closing date 1/15. Applicants notified by 4/1; must reply by 5/1 or within 2 week(s) of notification.
Transfers: Closing date 6/1. For South Carolina Tuition Grant, must have earned 24 credits in previous year. For Life Scholarship, must have 3.0 cumulative GPA and 30 credits earned.

CONTACT

Forrest Stuart, Associate Vice President for Financial Aid
3300 Poinsett Highway, Greenville, SC 29613
(864) 294-2204

Greenville Technical College

Greenville, South Carolina
www.gvltec.edu   Federal Code: 003991

2-year public community and technical college in large city.
Enrollment: 10,353 undergrads, 54% part-time. 1,617 full-time freshmen.
Selectivity: Open admission; but selective for some programs.

BASIC COSTS (2016-2017)

Tuition and fees: $5,070; out-of-district residents $5,520; out-of-state residents $10,350.

FINANCIAL AID PICTURE (2016-2017)

Students with need: 55% of average financial aid package awarded as scholarships/grants, 45% awarded as loans/jobs. Need-based aid available for part-time students. Work study available nights, weekends, and for part-time students.
Students without need: No-need awards available for academics, state/district residency.

FINANCIAL AID PROCEDURES

Forms required: FAFSA.
Dates and Deadlines: Priority date 5/1; no closing date. Applicants notified on a rolling basis starting 5/1; must reply within 2 week(s) of notification.
Transfers: Priority date 10/1; no deadline. Applicants notified on a rolling basis starting 11/15; must reply within 2 week(s) of notification.

CONTACT

Jeff Dennis, Financial Aid Director
PO Box 5616, Greenville, SC 29606-5616
(864) 250-8000

Horry-Georgetown Technical College
Conway, South Carolina
www.hgtc.edu   Federal Code: 004925

2-year public community and technical college in large town.
Enrollment: 6,298 undergrads.
Selectivity: Open admission; but selective for some programs.

BASIC COSTS (2016-2017)
Tuition and fees: $4,978; out-of-district residents $6,148; out-of-state residents $9,868.
Per-credit charge: $157; out-of-district residents $196; out-of-state residents $320.

FINANCIAL AID PICTURE
Students with need: Need-based aid available for full-time and part-time students.
Students without need: No-need awards available for academics, state/district residency.
Additional info: Participates in South Carolina lottery tuition assistance program. Full-time technical college students who are state residents receive assistance for tuition not covered by federal or need-based grants.

FINANCIAL AID PROCEDURES
Forms required: FAFSA.
Dates and Deadlines: Priority date 4/1; closing date 6/30. Applicants notified on a rolling basis starting 4/1.

CONTACT
Susan Thompson, Director of Financial Aid and Veterans Affairs
PO Box 261966, Conway, SC 29528-6066
(843) 349-5251

Lander University
Greenwood, South Carolina
www.lander.edu   Federal Code: 003435

4-year public liberal arts and teachers college in large town.
Enrollment: 2,670 undergrads.

BASIC COSTS (2016-2017)
Tuition and fees: $10,700; out-of-state residents $20,300.
Room and board: $8,583.

FINANCIAL AID PICTURE
Students with need: Need-based aid available for full-time and part-time students. Work study available weekends and for part-time students.
Students without need: No-need awards available for academics, alumni affiliation, art, athletics, job skills, leadership, minority status, music/drama, religious affiliation, ROTC, state/district residency.

FINANCIAL AID PROCEDURES
Forms required: FAFSA.
Dates and Deadlines: Priority date 11/1; closing date 8/1. Applicants notified on a rolling basis starting 12/15.

CONTACT
Fred Hardin, Director of Financial Aid
Stanley Avenue, Greenwood, SC 29649-2099
(864) 388-8340

Limestone College
Gaffney, South Carolina
www.limestone.edu   Federal Code: 003436

4-year private liberal arts college in large town, affiliated with the nondenominational tradition.

Enrollment: 1,195 undergrads, 2% part-time. 363 full-time freshmen.
Selectivity: Admits 50 to 75% of applicants.

BASIC COSTS (2017-2018)
Tuition and fees: $24,900.
Room and board: $9,582.

FINANCIAL AID PICTURE (2016-2017)
Students with need: Out of 349 full-time freshmen who applied for aid, 324 were judged to have need. Of these, 323 received aid, and 41 had their full need met. Average financial aid package met 56% of need; average scholarship/grant was $15,297; average loan was $3,030. For part-time students, average financial aid package was $7,851.
Students without need: 56 full-time freshmen who did not demonstrate need for aid received scholarships/grants; average award was $4,919. No-need awards available for academics, art, athletics, job skills, leadership, music/drama, religious affiliation, ROTC, state/district residency.
Scholarships offered: *Merit:* Presidential Scholarship: full tuition; 1300 SAT, 3.5 GPA. Academic Dean Scholarships: partial tuition; 3.0 GPA. Founders Scholarships: partial tuition. McMillan Scholarships: 3.0 GPA or above. R.S. Campbell Scholarship: SAT above 1100; GPA 3.25 or above; 1 available. Leadership Scholarship: partial tuition. Drada Hoover Scholarship: SAT 1200 or higher exclusive of Writing; GPA 3.5, top 10% of graduating class. Founders scholarship for students with a 2.0 or higher. *Athletic:* 47 full-time freshmen received athletic scholarships; average amount $12,530.

FINANCIAL AID PROCEDURES
Forms required: FAFSA.
Dates and Deadlines: Priority date 2/1; no closing date. Applicants notified on a rolling basis starting 1/15; must reply within 3 week(s) of notification.
Transfers: Priority date 5/1; no deadline. Applicants notified on a rolling basis; must reply within 3 week(s) of notification.

CONTACT
Bobby Greer, Director of Financial Aid
1115 College Drive, Gaffney, SC 29340-3799
(800) 795-7151 ext. 8231

Medical University of South Carolina
Charleston, South Carolina
www.musc.edu   Federal Code: 003438

Upper-division public university in small city.
Enrollment: 205 undergrads.

BASIC COSTS (2016-2017)
Tuition and fees: $15,168; out-of-state residents $23,182.

FINANCIAL AID PICTURE
Students with need: Need-based aid available for full-time and part-time students.

FINANCIAL AID PROCEDURES
Forms required: FAFSA.
Dates and Deadlines: Priority date 10/3; closing date 3/4. Applicants notified on a rolling basis starting 4/30.

CONTACT
Cecile Kamath, Director, Student Financial Aid
41 Bee Street, Charleston, SC 29425-2030
(843) 792-2536

Midlands Technical College
Columbia, South Carolina
www.midlandstech.edu   Federal Code: 003993

2-year public community and technical college in large city.
Enrollment: 10,946 undergrads.

Selectivity: Open admission; but selective for some programs.

BASIC COSTS (2016-2017)

Tuition and fees: $5,024; out-of-district residents $6,224; out-of-state residents $14,624.

FINANCIAL AID PICTURE

Students with need: Need-based aid available for full-time and part-time students.

Students without need: This college awards aid only to students with need.

FINANCIAL AID PROCEDURES

Forms required: FAFSA.

Dates and Deadlines: Priority date 4/15; no closing date. Applicants notified on a rolling basis; must reply within 2 week(s) of notification.

CONTACT

Angela Williams, Director of Student Financial Services
PO Box 2408, Columbia, SC 29202
(803) 738-7792

Morris College

Sumter, South Carolina
www.morris.edu   Federal Code: 003439

4-year private liberal arts college in large town, affiliated with the Baptist faith.

Enrollment: 754 undergrads, 3% part-time. 225 full-time freshmen.

Selectivity: Admits over 75% of applicants.

BASIC COSTS (2016-2017)

Tuition and fees: $13,045.

Per-credit charge: $487.

Room and board: $5,455.

FINANCIAL AID PICTURE (2016-2017)

Students with need: Average financial aid package met 65% of need; average scholarship/grant was $7,855; average loan was $5,354. For part-time students, average financial aid package was $8,012.

Students without need: No-need awards available for academics, athletics, music/drama, state/district residency.

Scholarships offered: *Merit:* Presidential Scholarship; $750-$2,500; rank in the first quarter of graduating class; larger awards available to salutatorians ($2,000) and valedictorians ($2,500); awards renewable up to 4 years if student maintains B average and excellent citizenship record. Luns C. Richardson Endowed Scholarship; $4,500; for full-time students with 3.5 college prep GPA, exceptional letters of recommendation from at least 2 classroom teachers and one guidance counselor, principal, or assistant principal. *Athletic:* 15 full-time freshmen received athletic scholarships; average amount $1,323.

FINANCIAL AID PROCEDURES

Forms required: FAFSA, institutional form.

Dates and Deadlines: Priority date 3/31; closing date 3/31. Applicants notified on a rolling basis starting 4/1; must reply within 2 week(s) of notification.

Transfers: Must reply within 2 week(s) of notification.

CONTACT

Sandra Gibson, Financial Aid Officer
100 West College Street, Sumter, SC 29150-3502
(803) 934-3238

Newberry College

Newberry, South Carolina
www.newberry.edu   Federal Code: 003440

4-year private liberal arts college in large town, affiliated with the Evangelical Lutheran Church in America.

Enrollment: 1,063 undergrads, 1% part-time. 268 full-time freshmen.

Selectivity: Admits 50 to 75% of applicants.

BASIC COSTS (2016-2017)

Tuition and fees: $25,600.

Per-credit charge: $735.

Room and board: $9,790.

FINANCIAL AID PICTURE (2015-2016)

Students with need: Out of 256 full-time freshmen who applied for aid, 240 were judged to have need. Of these, 240 received aid, and 32 had their full need met. Average financial aid package met 67% of need; average scholarship/grant was $19,607; average loan was $3,001. For part-time students, average financial aid package was $8,898.

Students without need: 25 full-time freshmen who did not demonstrate need for aid received scholarships/grants; average award was $10,674. No-need awards available for academics, alumni affiliation, athletics, music/drama, ROTC.

Scholarships offered: 27 full-time freshmen received athletic scholarships; average amount $8,525.

Additional info: The Loan Repayment Promise program assists in the repayment of school debt for eligible graduates who work a minimum of 30 hours per week earning less than $40,000. The reimbursement is based on a graduated scale up to $40,000.

FINANCIAL AID PROCEDURES

Forms required: FAFSA.

Dates and Deadlines: Priority date 3/15; no closing date. Applicants notified on a rolling basis starting 3/15; must reply by 8/20.

Transfers: No deadline. Applicants notified on a rolling basis.

CONTACT

Danielle Bell, Director of Financial Aid
2100 College Street, Newberry, SC 29108
(803) 321-5127

North Greenville University

Tigerville, South Carolina
www.ngu.edu   Federal Code: 003441

4-year private university and liberal arts college in rural community, affiliated with the Southern Baptist Convention.

Enrollment: 2,174 undergrads, 3% part-time. 482 full-time freshmen.

Selectivity: Admits 50 to 75% of applicants.

BASIC COSTS (2016-2017)

Tuition and fees: $17,594.

Room and board: $9,892.

FINANCIAL AID PICTURE

Students with need: Need-based aid available for full-time and part-time students.

Students without need: No-need awards available for academics, athletics, leadership, music/drama, religious affiliation, state/district residency.

FINANCIAL AID PROCEDURES

Forms required: FAFSA.

Dates and Deadlines: Priority date 6/1; closing date 6/30. Applicants notified on a rolling basis starting 8/1; must reply within 2 week(s) of notification.

Transfers: No deadline.

CONTACT
Mike Jordan, Director of Financial Aid
PO Box 1892, Tigerville, SC 29688-1892
(864) 977-7050

Orangeburg-Calhoun Technical College
Orangeburg, South Carolina
www.octech.edu   Federal Code: 006815

2-year public community and technical college in large town.
Enrollment: 2,399 undergrads.
Selectivity: Open admission; but selective for some programs.

BASIC COSTS (2016-2017)
Tuition and fees: $5,240; out-of-district residents $6,470; out-of-state residents $8,690.
Per-credit charge: $165; out-of-district residents $206; out-of-state residents $280.

FINANCIAL AID PICTURE
Students with need: Need-based aid available for full-time and part-time students.
Students without need: This college awards aid only to students with need.
Scholarships offered: College Foundation Scholarship; full academic tuition; for high school valedictorians and salutatorians.

FINANCIAL AID PROCEDURES
Forms required: FAFSA, institutional form.
Dates and Deadlines: Priority date 6/4; no closing date. Applicants notified on a rolling basis starting 5/1; must reply within 2 week(s) of notification.
Transfers: Priority date 6/1. Financial aid transcripts required of mid-year transfers prior to disbursement of aid.

CONTACT
Bobbie Felder, Director of Institutional Research
3250 St. Matthews Road, Orangeburg, SC 29118-8222
(803) 535-1368

Piedmont Technical College
Greenwood, South Carolina
www.ptc.edu   Federal Code: 003992

2-year public community and technical college in small city.
Enrollment: 4,081 undergrads, 60% part-time. 639 full-time freshmen.
Selectivity: Open admission; but selective for some programs.

BASIC COSTS (2016-2017)
Tuition and fees: $4,748; out-of-district residents $4,990; out-of-state residents $6,188.
Per-credit charge: $190; out-of-district residents $200; out-of-state residents $250.

FINANCIAL AID PICTURE (2015-2016)
Students with need: 99% of average financial aid package awarded as scholarships/grants, 1% awarded as loans/jobs. Need-based aid available for part-time students. Work study available nights.
Students without need: This college awards aid only to students with need.

FINANCIAL AID PROCEDURES
Forms required: FAFSA.
Dates and Deadlines: Priority date 5/1; no closing date. Applicants notified on a rolling basis starting 6/1; must reply within 2 week(s) of notification.

CONTACT
Missy Perry, Director of Financial Aid
620 North Emerald Road, Greenwood, SC 29646
(864) 941-8365

Presbyterian College
Clinton, South Carolina
www.presby.edu   Federal Code: 003445

4-year private pharmacy and liberal arts college in small town, affiliated with the Presbyterian Church (USA).
Enrollment: 950 undergrads, 1% part-time. 287 full-time freshmen.
Selectivity: Admits 50 to 75% of applicants.

BASIC COSTS (2017-2018)
Tuition and fees: $37,842.
Room and board: $10,298.

FINANCIAL AID PICTURE
Students with need: Need-based aid available for full-time and part-time students.
Students without need: No-need awards available for academics, alumni affiliation, art, athletics, job skills, leadership, minority status, music/drama, religious affiliation, ROTC, state/district residency.
Scholarships offered: Academic and leadership scholarships: applications by December 5; number and amounts awarded vary; music awards based on audition.

FINANCIAL AID PROCEDURES
Forms required: FAFSA.
Dates and Deadlines: Priority date 3/15; closing date 6/30. Applicants notified on a rolling basis starting 3/15; must reply by 7/1.
Transfers: No deadline. Applicants notified on a rolling basis starting 5/1; must reply within 1 week(s) of notification.

CONTACT
Linda McAnnally, Director of Financial Aid
503 South Broad Street, Clinton, SC 29325-2865
(864) 833-8290

South Carolina State University
Orangeburg, South Carolina
www.scsu.edu   Federal Code: 003446

4-year public university in large town.
Enrollment: 2,499 undergrads, 9% part-time. 614 full-time freshmen.
Selectivity: Admits over 75% of applicants.

BASIC COSTS (2016-2017)
Tuition and fees: $10,420; out-of-state residents $20,500.
Per-credit charge: $434; out-of-state residents $854.
Room and board: $9,890.

FINANCIAL AID PICTURE
Students with need: Need-based aid available for full-time and part-time students.
Students without need: No-need awards available for academics, alumni affiliation, athletics.

FINANCIAL AID PROCEDURES
Forms required: FAFSA, state aid form, institutional form.
Dates and Deadlines: Closing date 5/1. Applicants notified on a rolling basis starting 5/15; must reply by 7/1 or within 4 week(s) of notification.
Transfers: Must reply by 7/1 or within 2 week(s) of notification. Must provide documentation on amount of state aid received, and which semesters it was received, prior to transfer.

CONTACT
Betty Boatwright, Director of Financial Aid
300 College Street NE, Orangeburg, SC 29117
(803) 536-8221

Southern Wesleyan University
Central, South Carolina
www.swu.edu   Federal Code: 003422

4-year private university and liberal arts college in small town, affiliated with the Wesleyan Church.
Enrollment: 1,400 undergrads.

BASIC COSTS (2016-2017)
Tuition and fees: $24,110.
Room and board: $8,020.

FINANCIAL AID PICTURE
Students with need: Need-based aid available for full-time students. Work study available nights, weekends, and for part-time students.
Students without need: No-need awards available for academics, athletics, music/drama.

FINANCIAL AID PROCEDURES
Forms required: FAFSA, institutional form.
Dates and Deadlines: Priority date 3/31; closing date 6/30. Applicants notified on a rolling basis starting 2/1; must reply within 2 week(s) of notification.
Transfers: Priority date 4/1. Applicants notified on a rolling basis starting 2/1; must reply within 2 week(s) of notification.

CONTACT
Kim Jenerette, Financial Aid Director
PO Box 1020, Central, SC 29630-1020
(800) 289-1292

Spartanburg Community College
Spartanburg, South Carolina
www.sccsc.edu   Federal Code: 003994

2-year public community and technical college in small city.
Enrollment: 3,900 undergrads, 46% part-time. 676 full-time freshmen.
Selectivity: Open admission; but selective for some programs.

BASIC COSTS (2016-2017)
Tuition and fees: $4,200; out-of-district residents $5,232; out-of-state residents $8,592.
Per-credit charge: $175; out-of-district residents $218; out-of-state residents $358.

FINANCIAL AID PICTURE
Students with need: Need-based aid available for full-time and part-time students.
Students without need: No-need awards available for academics.
Additional info: Participates in South Carolina lottery tuition assistance program. Full-time technical college students who are state residents receive assistance for tuition not covered by federal or need-based grants.

FINANCIAL AID PROCEDURES
Forms required: FAFSA.
Dates and Deadlines: Priority date 2/28; closing date 5/1. Applicants notified on a rolling basis starting 5/1.
Transfers: No deadline. Applicants notified on a rolling basis starting 8/15.

CONTACT
Jeff Boyle, Director of Financial Aid
Box 4386, Spartanburg, SC 29305-4386
(864) 592-4810

Spartanburg Methodist College
Spartanburg, South Carolina
www.smcsc.edu   Federal Code: 003447

2-year private junior and liberal arts college in small city, affiliated with the United Methodist Church.
Enrollment: 736 undergrads. 425 full-time freshmen.
Selectivity: Admits 50 to 75% of applicants.

BASIC COSTS (2016-2017)
Tuition and fees: $16,860.
Per-credit charge: $425.
Room and board: $8,910.
Additional info: Overload charge (over 18 credit hours), $425/credit hour. Tuition/fee waivers available for adults, unemployed or children of unemployed.

FINANCIAL AID PICTURE
Students with need: Need-based aid available for full-time and part-time students. Work study available weekends and for part-time students.
Students without need: No-need awards available for academics, athletics, religious affiliation.
Scholarships offered: Milliken Scholars; $4,100. Camak Scholars; $3,500. Trustee Scholars; $3,000. Presidential Scholars; $2,400.

FINANCIAL AID PROCEDURES
Forms required: FAFSA, state aid form.
Dates and Deadlines: Priority date 6/30; closing date 8/22. Applicants notified on a rolling basis starting 3/1; must reply within 2 week(s) of notification.
Transfers: No deadline. Applicants notified on a rolling basis starting 3/1; must reply within 2 week(s) of notification. To be eligible for financial aid, full time students must pass the equivalent of 12 hours.

CONTACT
Chris Roberson, Director of Financial Aid
1000 Powell Mill Road, Spartanburg, SC 29301-5899
(864) 587-4382

Technical College of the Lowcountry
Beaufort, South Carolina
www.tcl.edu   Federal Code: 009910

2-year public community and technical college in small city.
Enrollment: 2,231 undergrads.
Selectivity: Open admission; but selective for some programs.

BASIC COSTS (2016-2017)
Tuition and fees: $5,320; out-of-district residents $6,070; out-of-state residents $11,560.
Per-credit charge: $170; out-of-district residents $195; out-of-state residents $378.

FINANCIAL AID PICTURE
Students with need: Need-based aid available for full-time and part-time students.
Students without need: This college awards aid only to students with need.
Additional info: State lottery aid may be available to South Carolina residents who take 6 credit hours or more.

FINANCIAL AID PROCEDURES
Forms required: FAFSA.

CONTACT
Cleo Martin, Director of Financial Aid
921 South Ribaut Road, Beaufort, SC 29901-1288
(843) 525-8337

Tri-County Technical College
Pendleton, South Carolina
www.tctc.edu   Federal Code: 004926

2-year public community and technical college in small town.
Enrollment: 5,894 undergrads.
Selectivity: Open admission; but selective for some programs.

BASIC COSTS (2016-2017)
Tuition and fees: $5,063; out-of-district residents $6,653; out-of-state residents $11,303.

FINANCIAL AID PICTURE
Students with need: Need-based aid available for full-time and part-time students. Work study available nights.
Students without need: No-need awards available for academics, state/district residency.
Scholarships offered: General and departmental scholarships; amounts vary; some have special qualification criteria, such as student's career field or place of residency; more than 125 awarded.
Additional info: Deadline for application to institutional scholarships 4/2.

FINANCIAL AID PROCEDURES
Forms required: FAFSA.
Dates and Deadlines: Priority date 4/1; closing date 7/30. Applicants notified on a rolling basis starting 6/15; must reply within 2 week(s) of notification.
Transfers: No deadline. Applicants notified on a rolling basis starting 6/1.

CONTACT
Adam Ghiloni, Director of Financial Aid
PO Box 587, Pendleton, SC 29670
(864) 646-1650

Trident Technical College
Charleston, South Carolina
www.tridenttech.edu   Federal Code: 004920

2-year public community and technical college in large city.
Enrollment: 11,393 undergrads, 53% part-time. 1,278 full-time freshmen.
Selectivity: Open admission; but selective for some programs.

BASIC COSTS (2016-2017)
Tuition and fees: $4,156; out-of-district residents $4,607; out-of-state residents $7,838.
Per-credit charge: $171.84; out-of-district residents $190.65; out-of-state residents $325.25.

FINANCIAL AID PICTURE (2015-2016)
Students with need: Need-based aid available for full-time and part-time students. Work study available nights, weekends, and for part-time students.
Students without need: No-need awards available for academics, alumni affiliation, state/district residency.

FINANCIAL AID PROCEDURES
Forms required: FAFSA.
Dates and Deadlines: Applicants notified on a rolling basis; must reply within 6 week(s) of notification.
Transfers: No deadline. Applicants notified on a rolling basis; must reply within 6 week(s) of notification.

CONTACT
Charlotte Sorg, Director of Financial Aid/Veterans Assistance
PO.Box 118067, AM-M, Charleston, SC 29423-8067
(843) 574-6147

University of South Carolina: Aiken
Aiken, South Carolina
http://web.usca.edu/   Federal Code: 003449

4-year public university and liberal arts college in large town.
Enrollment: 3,131 undergrads, 15% part-time. 583 full-time freshmen.
Selectivity: Admits 50 to 75% of applicants.

BASIC COSTS (2016-2017)
Tuition and fees: $10,196; out-of-state residents $20,102.
Per-credit charge: $411.75; out-of-state residents $825.
Room and board: $7,466.

FINANCIAL AID PICTURE (2015-2016)
Students with need: Out of 583 full-time freshmen who applied for aid, 424 were judged to have need. Of these, 422 received aid, and 68 had their full need met. Average financial aid package met 63% of need; average scholarship/grant was $7,426; average loan was $3,189. For part-time students, average financial aid package was $7,421.
Students without need: 24 full-time freshmen who did not demonstrate need for aid received scholarships/grants; average award was $1,646. No-need awards available for academics, alumni affiliation, art, athletics, leadership, minority status, music/drama, state/district residency.
Scholarships offered: 24 full-time freshmen received athletic scholarships; average amount $2,860.
Additional info: Students must be enrolled at least half time and be able to present documentation which verifies eligibility to work in the U.S.

FINANCIAL AID PROCEDURES
Forms required: FAFSA.
Dates and Deadlines: Priority date 3/15; no closing date. Applicants notified on a rolling basis starting 4/20; must reply within 2 week(s) of notification.
Transfers: Financial aid transcripts from previous institutions required.

CONTACT
Linda Aubrey-Higgins, Director of Financial Aid
471 University Parkway, Aiken, SC 29801-6399
(803) 641-3476

University of South Carolina: Beaufort
Bluffton, South Carolina
www.uscb.edu   Federal Code: 003450

4-year public university and liberal arts college in large town.
Enrollment: 1,986 undergrads, 18% part-time. 462 full-time freshmen.

BASIC COSTS (2016-2017)
Tuition and fees: $10,341; out-of-state residents $20,805.
Per-credit charge: $408; out-of-state residents $844.
Room and board: $7,800.

FINANCIAL AID PICTURE
Students with need: Need-based aid available for full-time and part-time students. Work study available nights, weekends, and for part-time students.
Students without need: No-need awards available for academics, art, athletics, leadership, religious affiliation, state/district residency.

FINANCIAL AID PROCEDURES
Forms required: FAFSA.
Dates and Deadlines: Priority date 3/1; no closing date. Applicants notified on a rolling basis starting 5/1; must reply within 2 week(s) of notification.
Transfers: No deadline. Applicants notified on a rolling basis starting 5/1.

CONTACT
Patricia Greene, Director and VA Coordinator of Financial Aid
One University Boulevard, Bluffton, SC 29909
(843) 521-3104

University of South Carolina: Columbia
Columbia, South Carolina
www.sc.edu   Federal Code: 003448

4-year public university in small city.
Enrollment: 25,108 undergrads, 6% part-time. 5,128 full-time freshmen.
Selectivity: Admits 50 to 75% of applicants.

BASIC COSTS (2016-2017)
Tuition and fees: $11,854; out-of-state residents $31,282.
Per-credit charge: $477.25; out-of-state residents $1,286.75.
Room and board: $9,700.

FINANCIAL AID PICTURE (2016-2017)
Students with need: Out of 4,125 full-time freshmen who applied for aid, 2,721 were judged to have need. Of these, 2,367 received aid, and 813 had their full need met. Average financial aid package met 40% of need; average scholarship/grant was $5,453; average loan was $3,335. For part-time students, average financial aid package was $6,458.
Students without need: 1,967 full-time freshmen who did not demonstrate need for aid received scholarships/grants; average award was $5,886. No-need awards available for academics, alumni affiliation, art, athletics, job skills, leadership, minority status, music/drama, religious affiliation, ROTC, state/district residency.
Scholarships offered: 95 full-time freshmen received athletic scholarships; average amount $13,670.

FINANCIAL AID PROCEDURES
Forms required: FAFSA.
Dates and Deadlines: Priority date 4/1; no closing date. Applicants notified on a rolling basis starting 4/1.
Transfers: Applicants notified on a rolling basis starting 4/1.

CONTACT
Edgar Miller, Director of Financial Aid and Scholarships
Office of Undergraduate Admissions, Columbia, SC 29208
(803) 777-8134

University of South Carolina: Salkehatchie
Allendale, South Carolina
uscsalkehatchie.sc.edu   Federal Code: 003454

2-year public branch campus college in rural community.
Enrollment: 730 full-time undergrads.

BASIC COSTS (2016-2017)
Tuition and fees: $7,152; out-of-state residents $10,332.
Per-credit charge: $279.25; out-of-state residents $697.25.

FINANCIAL AID PICTURE
Students with need: Need-based aid available for full-time and part-time students. Work study available nights, weekends, and for part-time students.
Students without need: No-need awards available for academics.

FINANCIAL AID PROCEDURES
Forms required: FAFSA.
Dates and Deadlines: Priority date 4/30; no closing date. Applicants notified on a rolling basis starting 6/1.

CONTACT
Julie Hadwin, Director of Financial Aid
PO Box 617, Allendale, SC 29810
(803) 584-3446

University of South Carolina: Sumter
Sumter, South Carolina
www.uscsumter.edu   Federal Code: 003426

2-year public branch campus college in small city.
Enrollment: 650 undergrads.

BASIC COSTS (2016-2017)
Tuition and fees: $7,152; out-of-state residents $17,184.
Per-credit charge: $279.25; out-of-state residents $697.25.

FINANCIAL AID PICTURE
Students with need: Need-based aid available for full-time and part-time students. Work study available nights, weekends, and for part-time students.
Students without need: This college awards aid only to students with need.

FINANCIAL AID PROCEDURES
Forms required: FAFSA.
Dates and Deadlines: Priority date 4/15; no closing date. Applicants notified on a rolling basis starting 4/16; must reply within 2 week(s) of notification.

CONTACT
200 Miller Road, Sumter, SC 29150-2498
(803) 938-3766

University of South Carolina: Union
Union, South Carolina
uscunion.sc.edu   Federal Code: 004927

2-year public branch campus and liberal arts college in small town.
Enrollment: 500 undergrads.

BASIC COSTS (2016-2017)
Tuition and fees: $7,102; out-of-state residents $17,134.
Per-credit charge: $279.25; out-of-state residents $697.25.

FINANCIAL AID PICTURE
Students with need: Work study available nights, weekends, and for part-time students.
Students without need: This college awards aid only to students with need.

FINANCIAL AID PROCEDURES
Forms required: FAFSA.
Dates and Deadlines: Priority date 4/15; no closing date. Applicants notified on a rolling basis starting 7/15; must reply within 2 week(s) of notification.

CONTACT
Bobby Holcombe, Financial Aid Director
PO Drawer 729, Union, SC 29379
(864) 429-8728

University of South Carolina: Upstate
Spartanburg, South Carolina
www.uscupstate.edu   Federal Code: 006951

4-year public university in large city.
Enrollment: 5,495 undergrads, 24% part-time. 693 full-time freshmen.
Selectivity: Admits 50 to 75% of applicants.

BASIC COSTS (2016-2017)
Tuition and fees: $11,065; out-of-state residents $22,063.
Per-credit charge: $446.25; out-of-state residents $904.5.
Room and board: $8,142.

FINANCIAL AID PICTURE (2016-2017)

Students with need: Out of 643 full-time freshmen who applied for aid, 548 were judged to have need. Of these, 543 received aid, and 35 had their full need met. Average financial aid package met 57% of need; average scholarship/grant was $5,521; average loan was $3,253. For part-time students, average financial aid package was $6,637.

Students without need: 21 full-time freshmen who did not demonstrate need for aid received scholarships/grants; average award was $3,449. No-need awards available for academics, athletics, minority status, ROTC, state/district residency.

Scholarships offered: 76 full-time freshmen received athletic scholarships; average amount $6,831.

Additional info: Out-of-state students who are recipients of financial aid may qualify for out-of-state fee waiver. Educational benefits available to veterans and children of deceased/disabled veterans.

FINANCIAL AID PROCEDURES

Forms required: FAFSA, institutional form.

Dates and Deadlines: Priority date 3/1; closing date 7/15. Applicants notified on a rolling basis starting 5/17; must reply within 2 week(s) of notification.

Transfers: Students eligible for financial assistance for total of 5 years or 10 full-time semesters at all post-secondary institutions attended for the bachelor's degree, and 5 full-time semesters of enrollment for associate's degree in nursing.

CONTACT

Bonnie Carson, Director of Financial Aid
800 University Way, Spartanburg, SC 29303
(864) 503-5974

Voorhees College
Denmark, South Carolina
www.voorhees.edu   Federal Code: 003455

4-year private liberal arts college in small town, affiliated with the Episcopal Church.

Enrollment: 415 undergrads, 2% part-time. 150 full-time freshmen.

Selectivity: Admits over 75% of applicants.

BASIC COSTS (2016-2017)

Tuition and fees: $12,630.

Per-credit charge: $484.

Room and board: $7,346.

FINANCIAL AID PICTURE (2015-2016)

Students with need: Need-based aid available for full-time and part-time students. Work study available nights, weekends, and for part-time students.

FINANCIAL AID PROCEDURES

Forms required: FAFSA, institutional form.

Dates and Deadlines: Priority date 4/15; no closing date. Applicants notified on a rolling basis starting 3/1; must reply within 2 week(s) of notification.

CONTACT

Augusta Kitchen, Director of Student Financial Aid
213 Wiggins Road, Denmark, SC 29042
(803) 780-1159

Williamsburg Technical College
Kingstree, South Carolina
www.wiltech.edu   Federal Code: 009322

2-year public community and technical college in small town.

Enrollment: 522 undergrads, 70% part-time. 40 full-time freshmen.

Selectivity: Open admission.

BASIC COSTS (2016-2017)

Tuition and fees: $4,080; out-of-district residents $4,200; out-of-state residents $7,752.

FINANCIAL AID PICTURE (2015-2016)

Students with need: Need-based aid available for part-time students. Work study available nights.

Students without need: No-need awards available for academics, leadership, minority status, state/district residency.

Additional info: Tuition waivers for children of war veterans.

FINANCIAL AID PROCEDURES

Forms required: FAFSA.

Dates and Deadlines: Applicants notified on a rolling basis starting 7/1; must reply within 4 week(s) of notification.

CONTACT

Jean Boos, Director of Financial Aid/Veterans Affairs
601 MLK, Jr. Avenue, Kingstree, SC 29556-4197
(843) 355-4166

Winthrop University
Rock Hill, South Carolina
www.winthrop.edu   Federal Code: 003456

4-year public university in small city.

Enrollment: 4,790 undergrads, 5% part-time. 1,088 full-time freshmen.

Selectivity: Admits 50 to 75% of applicants.

BASIC COSTS (2016-2017)

Tuition and fees: $14,810; out-of-state residents $28,390.

Per-credit charge: $605; out-of-state residents $1,170.

Room and board: $8,572.

FINANCIAL AID PICTURE (2015-2016)

Students with need: Out of 1,006 full-time freshmen who applied for aid, 853 were judged to have need. Of these, 851 received aid, and 133 had their full need met. Average financial aid package met 62% of need; average scholarship/grant was $9,676; average loan was $3,335. For part-time students, average financial aid package was $4,994.

Students without need: 97 full-time freshmen who did not demonstrate need for aid received scholarships/grants; average award was $6,161. No-need awards available for academics, art, athletics, leadership, music/drama.

Scholarships offered: *Merit:* Academic scholarships; $1,500-full tuition and board; awarded to approximately one-third of entering freshman class each year. *Athletic:* 22 full-time freshmen received athletic scholarships; average amount $6,886.

FINANCIAL AID PROCEDURES

Forms required: FAFSA.

Dates and Deadlines: Priority date 3/15; no closing date. Applicants notified on a rolling basis starting 4/1; must reply within 2 week(s) of notification.

Transfers: Transfer students are not eligible for academic scholarship their first year.

CONTACT

Michelle Hare, Director, Office of Financial Aid
701 Oakland Avenue, Rock Hill, SC 29733
(803) 323-2189

Wofford College
Spartanburg, South Carolina
www.wofford.edu   Federal Code: 003457

4-year private liberal arts college in small city, affiliated with the United Methodist Church.

Enrollment: 1,606 undergrads, 1% part-time. 440 full-time freshmen.

Selectivity: Admits 50 to 75% of applicants.

BASIC COSTS (2017-2018)
Tuition and fees: $41,955.
Per-credit charge: $1,605.
Room and board: $12,140.

FINANCIAL AID PICTURE (2016-2017)
Students with need: Out of 380 full-time freshmen who applied for aid, 277 were judged to have need. Of these, 277 received aid, and 128 had their full need met. Average financial aid package met 91% of need; average scholarship/grant was $31,055; average loan was $3,199. For part-time students, average financial aid package was $10,747.
Students without need: 115 full-time freshmen who did not demonstrate need for aid received scholarships/grants; average award was $16,955. No-need awards available for academics, art, athletics, job skills, leadership, minority status, music/drama, religious affiliation, ROTC, state/district residency.
Scholarships offered: 39 full-time freshmen received athletic scholarships; average amount $25,836.

FINANCIAL AID PROCEDURES
Forms required: FAFSA.
Dates and Deadlines: Priority date 3/1; no closing date. Applicants notified on a rolling basis starting 3/15; must reply by 5/1.

CONTACT
Carolyn Sparks, Director of Financial Aid
429 North Church Street, Spartanburg, SC 29303-3663
(864) 597-4160

York Technical College
Rock Hill, South Carolina
www.yorktech.edu   Federal Code: 003996

2-year public community and technical college in large town.
Enrollment: 4,416 undergrads.
Selectivity: Open admission; but selective for some programs.

BASIC COSTS (2016-2017)
Tuition and fees: $5,140; out-of-district residents $5,590; out-of-state residents $11,620.
Per-credit charge: $165; out-of-district residents $180; out-of-state residents $381.

FINANCIAL AID PICTURE
Students with need: Need-based aid available for full-time and part-time students. Work study available nights.
Students without need: No-need awards available for academics, leadership, state/district residency.

FINANCIAL AID PROCEDURES
Forms required: FAFSA.
Dates and Deadlines: Priority date 6/1; no closing date. Applicants notified on a rolling basis starting 4/1; must reply within 2 week(s) of notification.
Transfers: No deadline. Applicants notified on a rolling basis starting 4/1; must reply within 2 week(s) of notification.

CONTACT
Angela Fowler, Director of Financial Aid
452 South Anderson Road, Rock Hill, SC 29730
(803) 327-8005

South Dakota

Augustana University
Sioux Falls, South Dakota
www.augie.edu   Federal Code: 003458

4-year private university in small city, affiliated with the Evangelical Lutheran Church in America.
Enrollment: 1,617 undergrads, 4% part-time. 421 full-time freshmen.
Selectivity: Admits 50 to 75% of applicants.

BASIC COSTS (2016-2017)
Tuition and fees: $30,944.
Per-credit charge: $450.
Room and board: $7,754.
Additional info: Tuition/fee waivers available for minority students.

FINANCIAL AID PICTURE (2016-2017)
Students with need: Out of 337 full-time freshmen who applied for aid, 276 were judged to have need. Of these, 276 received aid, and 78 had their full need met. Average financial aid package met 100% of need; average scholarship/grant was $25,013; average loan was $4,460. For part-time students, average financial aid package was $9,236.
Students without need: 144 full-time freshmen who did not demonstrate need for aid received scholarships/grants; average award was $18,052. No-need awards available for academics, alumni affiliation, art, athletics, leadership, minority status, music/drama, religious affiliation, ROTC, state/district residency.
Scholarships offered: *Merit:* Distinguished Scholars Scholarships: Trustees and Presidential Scholarships for students with a 27 ACT or above and 3.5 GPA and above. ProMusica scholarships, ProDramatis scholarships, ProArtis Scholarships; Fryxell Scholarships for journalism/English majors. *Athletic:* 94 full-time freshmen received athletic scholarships; average amount $10,836.

FINANCIAL AID PROCEDURES
Forms required: FAFSA.
Dates and Deadlines: Priority date 3/1; no closing date. Applicants notified on a rolling basis starting 4/1; must reply within 4 week(s) of notification.
Transfers: No deadline. Applicants notified on a rolling basis starting 4/1; must reply within 4 week(s) of notification.

CONTACT
Tresse Evenson, Director of Financial Aid
2001 South Summit Avenue, Sioux Falls, SD 57197-9990
(605) 274-5216

Black Hills State University
Spearfish, South Dakota
www.bhsu.edu   Federal Code: 003459

4-year public university in large town.
Enrollment: 3,139 undergrads, 31% part-time. 526 full-time freshmen.
Selectivity: Admits less than 50% of applicants.

BASIC COSTS (2016-2017)
Tuition and fees: $8,004; out-of-state residents $10,920.
Per-credit charge: $233; out-of-state residents $330.
Room and board: $6,695.

FINANCIAL AID PICTURE
Students with need: Need-based aid available for full-time and part-time students.
Students without need: This college awards aid only to students with need.

FINANCIAL AID PROCEDURES
Forms required: FAFSA.

Dates and Deadlines: Closing date 2/15. Applicants notified on a rolling basis starting 5/15; must reply within 3 week(s) of notification.

CONTACT
Deb Henriksen, Director of Financial Aid
1200 University Street, Spearfish, SD 57799
(605) 642-6581

Dakota State University
Madison, South Dakota
www.dsu.edu   Federal Code: 003463

4-year public university in small town.
Enrollment: 1,936 undergrads, 34% part-time. 324 full-time freshmen.
Selectivity: Admits over 75% of applicants.

BASIC COSTS (2016-2017)
Tuition and fees: $8,927; out-of-state residents $11,843.
Per-credit charge: $233; out-of-state residents $330.
Room and board: $6,411.

FINANCIAL AID PICTURE (2015-2016)
Students with need: Out of 291 full-time freshmen who applied for aid, 223 were judged to have need. Of these, 223 received aid, and 28 had their full need met. Average financial aid package met 77% of need; average scholarship/grant was $4,187; average loan was $3,235. For part-time students, average financial aid package was $5,645.

Students without need: 53 full-time freshmen who did not demonstrate need for aid received scholarships/grants; average award was $4,379. No-need awards available for academics, alumni affiliation, art, athletics, leadership, minority status, music/drama, state/district residency.

Scholarships offered: 69 full-time freshmen received athletic scholarships; average amount $1,533.

Additional info: Application deadline for grants and scholarships 3/1. No deadline for loan and job applications.

FINANCIAL AID PROCEDURES
Forms required: FAFSA.

Dates and Deadlines: Priority date 3/1; no closing date. Applicants notified on a rolling basis starting 4/1; must reply within 2 week(s) of notification.

Transfers: Priority date 4/1; no deadline. Applicants notified on a rolling basis starting 4/1; must reply within 2 week(s) of notification.

CONTACT
Denise Grayson, Financial Aid Director
820 North Washington Avenue, Madison, SD 57042
(605) 256-5152

Dakota Wesleyan University
Mitchell, South Dakota
www.dwu.edu   Federal Code: 003461

4-year private university and liberal arts college in large town, affiliated with the United Methodist Church.
Enrollment: 782 undergrads, 15% part-time. 172 full-time freshmen.
Selectivity: Admits 50 to 75% of applicants.

BASIC COSTS (2016-2017)
Tuition and fees: $26,050.
Room and board: $7,200.

FINANCIAL AID PICTURE (2016-2017)
Students with need: Need-based aid available for part-time students.

Students without need: No-need awards available for academics, alumni affiliation, art, athletics, leadership, minority status, music/drama, religious affiliation.

FINANCIAL AID PROCEDURES
Forms required: FAFSA.

Dates and Deadlines: Priority date 4/1; no closing date. Applicants notified on a rolling basis starting 3/1; must reply within 2 week(s) of notification.

Transfers: No deadline. Applicants notified on a rolling basis starting 3/1; must reply within 2 week(s) of notification.

CONTACT
Mary Alexander, Director of Financial Aid
1200 West University Avenue, Mitchell, SD 57301-4398
(605) 995-2667

Globe University: Sioux Falls
Sioux Falls, South Dakota
www.globeuniversity.edu   Federal Code: 004642

2-year for-profit career college in small city.
Enrollment: 138 undergrads.
Selectivity: Open admission.

BASIC COSTS (2016-2017)
Additional info: Tuition varies by program. Per-credit-hour charges; $325-$550. Fees vary from $100-$650 per course.

FINANCIAL AID PICTURE
Students with need: Need-based aid available for full-time and part-time students.

FINANCIAL AID PROCEDURES
Forms required: FAFSA, institutional form.

Dates and Deadlines: Applicants notified on a rolling basis starting 7/1; must reply within 2 week(s) of notification.

CONTACT
Elizabeth Augustine, Financial Aid Manager
5101 South Broadband Lane, Sioux Falls, SD 57108
(605) 977-0705

Lake Area Technical Institute
Watertown, South Dakota
www.lakeareatech.edu   Federal Code: 005309

2-year public technical college in large town.
Enrollment: 1,802 undergrads, 12% part-time. 582 full-time freshmen.
Selectivity: Open admission; but selective for some programs.

BASIC COSTS (2016-2017)
Tuition and fees: $6,107; out-of-state residents $6,107.
Per-credit charge: $109.

FINANCIAL AID PICTURE (2015-2016)
Students with need: Out of 553 full-time freshmen who applied for aid, 455 were judged to have need. Of these, 453 received aid, and 49 had their full need met. Average financial aid package met 56% of need; average scholarship/grant was $5,167; average loan was $3,859. For part-time students, average financial aid package was $5,591.

Students without need: This college awards aid only to students with need.

FINANCIAL AID PROCEDURES
Forms required: FAFSA.

Dates and Deadlines: Priority date 4/1; no closing date. Applicants notified on a rolling basis starting 4/1; must reply within 4 week(s) of notification.

Transfers: No deadline. Applicants notified on a rolling basis.

CONTACT
Marlene Seeklander, Financial Aid Director
PO Box 730, Watertown, SD 57201
(605) 882-5284

Mitchell Technical Institute
Mitchell, South Dakota
www.mitchelltech.edu   Federal Code: 008284

2-year public technical college in large town.
Enrollment: 1,093 undergrads, 23% part-time. 344 full-time freshmen.
Selectivity: Admits 50 to 75% of applicants.

BASIC COSTS (2016-2017)
Tuition and fees: $6,030; out-of-state residents $6,030.
Per-credit charge: $109.

FINANCIAL AID PICTURE (2016-2017)
Students with need: 45% of average financial aid package awarded as scholarships/grants, 55% awarded as loans/jobs. Need-based aid available for part-time students. Work study available nights.
Students without need: No-need awards available for academics, alumni affiliation, job skills.
Scholarships offered: Star Student program; $1,000 the first semester (and up to $3,000 total); to students with 24 ACT and 3.0 GPA.

FINANCIAL AID PROCEDURES
Forms required: FAFSA.
Dates and Deadlines: Applicants notified on a rolling basis; must reply within 3 week(s) of notification.
Transfers: No deadline. Applicants notified on a rolling basis.

CONTACT
Morgan Huber, Financial Aid Coordinator
1800 E Spruce Street, Mitchell, SD 57301
(605) 995-3052

Mount Marty College
Yankton, South Dakota
www.mtmc.edu   Federal Code: 003465

4-year private liberal arts college in large town, affiliated with the Roman Catholic Church.
Enrollment: 572 undergrads, 19% part-time. 104 full-time freshmen.
Selectivity: Admits 50 to 75% of applicants.

BASIC COSTS (2016-2017)
Tuition and fees: $25,330.
Room and board: $7,692.

FINANCIAL AID PICTURE (2016-2017)
Students with need: Out of 100 full-time freshmen who applied for aid, 89 were judged to have need. Of these, 89 received aid, and 37 had their full need met. Average financial aid package met 89% of need; average scholarship/grant was $19,650; average loan was $4,258. For part-time students, average financial aid package was $12,728.
Students without need: 9 full-time freshmen who did not demonstrate need for aid received scholarships/grants; average award was $11,944. No-need awards available for academics, athletics, leadership, music/drama, religious affiliation.
Scholarships offered: 8 full-time freshmen received athletic scholarships; average amount $4,605.
Additional info: Prestige scholarships application deadline 2/1.

FINANCIAL AID PROCEDURES
Forms required: FAFSA, institutional form.

Dates and Deadlines: Priority date 3/1; no closing date. Applicants notified on a rolling basis starting 3/15; must reply within 2 week(s) of notification.
Transfers: No deadline. Applicants notified on a rolling basis; must reply within 2 week(s) of notification.

CONTACT
Kenneth Kocer, Director of Financial Assistance
1105 West Eighth Street, Yankton, SD 57078
(605) 668-1589

National American University: Rapid City
Rapid City, South Dakota
www.national.edu   Federal Code: 004057

4-year for-profit business and technical college in small city.
Enrollment: 1,479 undergrads.
Selectivity: Open admission; but selective for some programs.

BASIC COSTS (2016-2017)
Tuition and fees: $17,175.
Per-credit charge: $360.
Additional info: Additional fees may apply.

FINANCIAL AID PICTURE
Students with need: Need-based aid available for full-time and part-time students. Work study available nights, weekends, and for part-time students.
Students without need: This college awards aid only to students with need.
Scholarships offered: Reduced tuition to military students and military dependents with a valid military ID card.

FINANCIAL AID PROCEDURES
Forms required: FAFSA, institutional form.
Dates and Deadlines: Applicants notified on a rolling basis; must reply within 4 week(s) of notification.

CONTACT
Cheryl Bullinger, Director of Financial Aid
5301 South Highway 16, Rapid City, SD 57701

Northern State University
Aberdeen, South Dakota
www.northern.edu   Federal Code: 003466

4-year public university and liberal arts college in large town.
Enrollment: 1,537 undergrads, 14% part-time. 309 full-time freshmen.

BASIC COSTS (2016-2017)
Tuition and fees: $7,887; out-of-state residents $10,803.
Per-credit charge: $233; out-of-state residents $330.
Room and board: $6,984.

FINANCIAL AID PICTURE (2016-2017)
Students with need: Out of 274 full-time freshmen who applied for aid, 185 were judged to have need. Of these, 185 received aid, and 50 had their full need met. Average financial aid package met 77% of need; average scholarship/grant was $5,563; average loan was $4,455. Need-based aid available for part-time students.
Students without need: 65 full-time freshmen who did not demonstrate need for aid received scholarships/grants; average award was $1,246.
Scholarships offered: WolfPACT Scholarship; $5,000-$12,000; based on ACT.

FINANCIAL AID PROCEDURES
Forms required: FAFSA.

Dates and Deadlines: Priority date 3/1; no closing date. Applicants notified on a rolling basis starting 4/15; must reply within 2 week(s) of notification. **Transfers:** Applicants notified by 4/15; must reply within 2 week(s) of notification. Financial aid transcript(s) required from all schools previously attended.

CONTACT

Sharon Kienow, Director of Student Financial Aid
1200 South Jay Street, Aberdeen, SD 57401-7198
(605) 626-2640

Presentation College

Aberdeen, South Dakota
www.presentation.edu
Federal Code: 003467

4-year private business and health science college in large town, affiliated with the Roman Catholic Church.
Enrollment: 750 undergrads.

BASIC COSTS (2016-2017)
Tuition and fees: $18,710.
Room and board: $8,690.

FINANCIAL AID PICTURE
Students with need: Need-based aid available for full-time and part-time students. Work study available nights, weekends, and for part-time students.

FINANCIAL AID PROCEDURES
Forms required: FAFSA.
Dates and Deadlines: Priority date 4/1; no closing date. Applicants notified on a rolling basis starting 5/1; must reply within 2 week(s) of notification.

CONTACT
Janel Wagner, Financial Aid Director
1500 North Main Street, Aberdeen, SD 57401
(605) 229-8429

Sinte Gleska University

Mission, South Dakota
www.sintegleska.edu
Federal Code: 014303

4-year public university and liberal arts college in rural community.
Enrollment: 690 undergrads.
Selectivity: Open admission.

BASIC COSTS (2016-2017)
Tuition and fees: $3,700.
Per-credit charge: $110.

FINANCIAL AID PICTURE
Students with need: Need-based aid available for full-time and part-time students.

FINANCIAL AID PROCEDURES
Forms required: FAFSA.

CONTACT
William Hay, Director of Financial Aid
Box 105, Mission, SD 57555

Sisseton Wahpeton College

Sisseton, South Dakota
www.swc.tc
Federal Code: 016080

2-year public technical college in large town.
Enrollment: 131 undergrads, 37% part-time. 25 full-time freshmen.

Selectivity: Open admission.

BASIC COSTS (2016-2017)
Tuition and fees: $3,984.
Per-credit charge: $115.

FINANCIAL AID PICTURE (2015-2016)
Students with need: 98% of average financial aid package awarded as scholarships/grants, 2% awarded as loans/jobs. Need-based aid available for part-time students.

FINANCIAL AID PROCEDURES
Forms required: FAFSA.
Dates and Deadlines: Priority date 12/15; no closing date. Applicants notified on a rolling basis.

CONTACT
Sylvan Flute, Financial Aid Director
BIA 700, Box 689, Sisseton, SD 57262-0689
(605) 698-3966 ext. 1183

South Dakota School of Mines and Technology

Rapid City, South Dakota
www.sdsmt.edu
Federal Code: 003470

4-year public university in small city.
Enrollment: 2,359 undergrads, 13% part-time. 497 full-time freshmen.
Selectivity: Admits over 75% of applicants.

BASIC COSTS (2016-2017)
Tuition and fees: $9,576; out-of-state residents $13,734.
Per-credit charge: $245; out-of-state residents $383.
Room and board: $6,734.

FINANCIAL AID PICTURE (2015-2016)
Students with need: Out of 481 full-time freshmen who applied for aid, 254 were judged to have need. Of these, 254 received aid, and 100 had their full need met. Average financial aid package met 74% of need; average scholarship/grant was $4,517; average loan was $2,878. For part-time students, average financial aid package was $11,138.
Students without need: 188 full-time freshmen who did not demonstrate need for aid received scholarships/grants; average award was $3,544. No-need awards available for academics, athletics, leadership, minority status, ROTC.
Scholarships offered: *Merit:* Presidential Scholarship; $1,000-$4,000; 5 awarded. Surbeck Scholars; $7,000; 2 awarded. All based on ACT/SAT, GPA, and class rank. Number of awards may vary from year to year depending on availability of funding. *Athletic:* 25 full-time freshmen received athletic scholarships; average amount $4,208.
Additional info: Closing date for scholarship applications 2/1.

FINANCIAL AID PROCEDURES
Forms required: FAFSA.
Dates and Deadlines: Applicants notified on a rolling basis starting 4/15; must reply within 3 week(s) of notification.
Transfers: Must reply by 5/1 or within 6 week(s) of notification.

CONTACT
David Martin, Director of Financial Aid
501 East St. Joseph Street, Rapid City, SD 57701
(605) 394-2274

South Dakota State University

Brookings, South Dakota
www.sdstate.edu
Federal Code: 003471

4-year public university in large town.
Enrollment: 9,778 undergrads, 14% part-time. 2,210 full-time freshmen.

Selectivity: Admits over 75% of applicants.

BASIC COSTS (2016-2017)
Tuition and fees: $8,172; out-of-state residents $11,403.
Per-credit charge: $239; out-of-state residents $346.2.
Room and board: $7,743.

FINANCIAL AID PICTURE
Students with need: Need-based aid available for full-time and part-time students. Work study available nights, weekends, and for part-time students.
Students without need: No-need awards available for academics, alumni affiliation, art, athletics, leadership, minority status, music/drama, state/district residency.

FINANCIAL AID PROCEDURES
Forms required: FAFSA.
Dates and Deadlines: Priority date 3/10; no closing date. Applicants notified on a rolling basis starting 4/1; must reply within 3 week(s) of notification.
Transfers: No deadline. Applicants notified on a rolling basis starting 4/1; must reply within 3 week(s) of notification.

CONTACT
Carolyn Halgerson, Director of Financial Aid
Box 2201 SAD 200, Brookings, SD 57007-0649
(605) 688-4695

Southeast Technical Institute
Sioux Falls, South Dakota
www.southeasttech.edu
Federal Code: 008285

2-year public technical college in small city.
Enrollment: 1,899 undergrads.
Selectivity: Open admission; but selective for some programs.

BASIC COSTS (2016-2017)
Tuition and fees: $6,900; out-of-state residents $6,900.
Per-credit charge: $109.

FINANCIAL AID PICTURE
Students with need: Need-based aid available for full-time and part-time students.
Students without need: This college awards aid only to students with need.

FINANCIAL AID PROCEDURES
Forms required: FAFSA.
Dates and Deadlines: Priority date 5/1; no closing date. Applicants notified on a rolling basis starting 5/1; must reply within 3 week(s) of notification.

CONTACT
Lynette Grabowska, Financial Aid Officer
2320 North Career Avenue, Sioux Falls, SD 57107
(605) 367-7867

University of Sioux Falls
Sioux Falls, South Dakota
www.usiouxfalls.edu
Federal Code: 003469

4-year private university and liberal arts college in small city, affiliated with the American Baptist Churches in the USA.
Enrollment: 1,207 undergrads, 15% part-time. 270 full-time freshmen.
Selectivity: Admits over 75% of applicants.

BASIC COSTS (2017-2018)
Tuition and fees: $27,980.
Room and board: $7,350.
Additional info: Tuition/fee waivers available for adults.

FINANCIAL AID PICTURE (2016-2017)
Students with need: Out of 247 full-time freshmen who applied for aid, 207 were judged to have need. Of these, 207 received aid, and 61 had their full need met. Average financial aid package met 88% of need; average scholarship/grant was $16,403; average loan was $4,926. For part-time students, average financial aid package was $5,244.
Students without need: 57 full-time freshmen who did not demonstrate need for aid received scholarships/grants; average award was $13,527. No-need awards available for academics, art, athletics, leadership, minority status, music/drama, religious affiliation, ROTC, state/district residency.
Scholarships offered: 21 full-time freshmen received athletic scholarships; average amount $12,524.

FINANCIAL AID PROCEDURES
Forms required: FAFSA.
Dates and Deadlines: Priority date 1/1; no closing date. Applicants notified on a rolling basis starting 1/1; must reply within 4 week(s) of notification.
Transfers: Applicants notified on a rolling basis; must reply within 2 week(s) of notification.

CONTACT
Karrie Morgan, Director of Financial Aid
1101 West 22nd Street, Sioux Falls, SD 57105-1699
(605) 331-6623

University of South Dakota
Vermillion, South Dakota
www.usd.edu
Federal Code: 003474

4-year public university in large town.
Enrollment: 6,331 undergrads.

BASIC COSTS (2016-2017)
Tuition and fees: $8,457; out-of-state residents $11,688.
Per-credit charge: $239; out-of-state residents $346.
Room and board: $7,536.

FINANCIAL AID PICTURE
Students with need: Need-based aid available for full-time students.
Students without need: No-need awards available for academics, art, athletics, leadership, minority status, music/drama, ROTC.

FINANCIAL AID PROCEDURES
Forms required: FAFSA.
Dates and Deadlines: Priority date 3/15; no closing date. Applicants notified on a rolling basis starting 5/5.
Transfers: Priority date 5/1.

CONTACT
Julie Pier, Director of Student Financial Aid
414 East Clark Street, Vermillion, SD 57069-2390
(605) 677-5446

Western Dakota Technical Institute
Rapid City, South Dakota
www.wdt.edu
Federal Code: 010170

2-year public technical college in small city.
Enrollment: 824 undergrads, 22% part-time. 166 full-time freshmen.
Selectivity: Open admission; but selective for some programs.

BASIC COSTS (2016-2017)
Tuition and fees: $6,150; out-of-state residents $6,150.

FINANCIAL AID PICTURE (2016-2017)
Students with need: Out of 149 full-time freshmen who applied for aid, 135 were judged to have need. Of these, 135 received aid, and 12 had their

full need met. Average financial aid package met 71% of need; average scholarship/grant was $7,200; average loan was $3,137. For part-time students, average financial aid package was $8,225.

Students without need: 1 full-time freshmen who did not demonstrate need for aid received scholarships/grants; average award was $500.

FINANCIAL AID PROCEDURES

Forms required: FAFSA.

Dates and Deadlines: Priority date 4/20; no closing date. Applicants notified on a rolling basis starting 4/30; must reply within 2 week(s) of notification.

CONTACT

Sharon Martin, Manager of Financial Aid
800 Mickelson Drive, Rapid City, SD 57703
(605) 718-2416

Tennessee

American Baptist College

Nashville, Tennessee
www.abcnash.edu   Federal Code: 010460

4-year private Bible and liberal arts college in large city, affiliated with the Baptist faith.

Enrollment: 160 undergrads.

BASIC COSTS (2016-2017)

Tuition and fees: $11,894.
Room and board: $6,440.

FINANCIAL AID PICTURE

Students with need: Need-based aid available for full-time students.

FINANCIAL AID PROCEDURES

Forms required: FAFSA.

Dates and Deadlines: Priority date 5/1; no closing date. Applicants notified on a rolling basis; must reply within 2 week(s) of notification.

Transfers: Priority date 1/15; closing date 5/1. Applicants notified on a rolling basis starting 6/1; must reply by 7/1.

CONTACT

1800 Baptist World Center Drive, Nashville, TN 37207
(615) 687-6896 ext. 2227

Aquinas College

Nashville, Tennessee
www.aquinascollege.edu   Federal Code: 003477

4-year private liberal arts college in very large city, affiliated with the Roman Catholic Church.

Enrollment: 299 undergrads, 28% part-time. 32 full-time freshmen.

Selectivity: Admits less than 50% of applicants.

BASIC COSTS (2017-2018)

Tuition and fees: $22,850.
Per-credit charge: $830.
Room and board: $9,500.

FINANCIAL AID PICTURE

Students with need: Need-based aid available for full-time and part-time students. Work study available nights, weekends, and for part-time students.

Students without need: No-need awards available for academics, alumni affiliation, leadership, religious affiliation.

FINANCIAL AID PROCEDURES

Forms required: FAFSA.

Dates and Deadlines: Priority date 2/15; no closing date. Applicants notified on a rolling basis starting 2/15; must reply within 2 week(s) of notification.

Transfers: No deadline. Applicants notified on a rolling basis; must reply within 2 week(s) of notification. Transfer students may receive a scholarship based on GPA.

CONTACT

Cynthia Piana, Senior Associate Director of Financial Aid
4210 Harding Pike, Nashville, TN 37205-2086
(615) 297-7545 ext. 442

Austin Peay State University

Clarksville, Tennessee
www.apsu.edu   Federal Code: 003478

4-year public university and liberal arts college in small city.

Enrollment: 9,116 undergrads, 24% part-time. 1,280 full-time freshmen.

Selectivity: Admits over 75% of applicants.

BASIC COSTS (2016-2017)

Tuition and fees: $7,995; out-of-state residents $25,464.
Room and board: $9,711.

FINANCIAL AID PICTURE (2015-2016)

Students with need: Out of 1,247 full-time freshmen who applied for aid, 1,089 were judged to have need. Of these, 1,075 received aid. For part-time students, average financial aid package was $7,731.

Students without need: 143 full-time freshmen who did not demonstrate need for aid received scholarships/grants; average award was $4,869. No-need awards available for academics, art, athletics, leadership, music/drama, ROTC, state/district residency.

Scholarships offered: 22 full-time freshmen received athletic scholarships; average amount $14,002.

FINANCIAL AID PROCEDURES

Forms required: FAFSA.

Dates and Deadlines: Applicants notified on a rolling basis.

CONTACT

Donna Price, Director of Financial Aid
PO Box 4548, Clarksville, TN 37044-4548
(931) 221-7907

Belmont University

Nashville, Tennessee
www.belmont.edu   Federal Code: 003479

4-year private university in very large city, affiliated with the Christian Church.

Enrollment: 6,232 undergrads, 5% part-time. 1,568 full-time freshmen.

Selectivity: Admits over 75% of applicants.

BASIC COSTS (2016-2017)

Tuition and fees: $31,390.
Per-credit charge: $1,140.
Room and board: $11,330.

FINANCIAL AID PICTURE (2016-2017)

Students with need: Out of 1,274 full-time freshmen who applied for aid, 866 were judged to have need. Of these, 866 received aid, and 112 had their full need met. Average financial aid package met 52% of need; average scholarship/grant was $16,826; average loan was $3,671. For part-time students, average financial aid package was $7,890.

Students without need: 499 full-time freshmen who did not demonstrate need for aid received scholarships/grants; average award was $7,515. No-need awards available for academics, art, athletics, leadership, music/drama, religious affiliation, state/district residency.

Scholarships offered: 16 full-time freshmen received athletic scholarships; average amount $26,302.

FINANCIAL AID PROCEDURES

Forms required: FAFSA.

Dates and Deadlines: Priority date 3/1; no closing date. Applicants notified on a rolling basis starting 3/15; must reply by 5/1 or within 2 week(s) of notification.

Transfers: Applicants notified on a rolling basis starting 3/1; must reply by 5/1 or within 2 week(s) of notification. Scholarships available.

CONTACT

Patricia Smedley, Director of Student Financial Services
1900 Belmont Boulevard, Nashville, TN 37212-3757
(615) 460-6403

Bethel University
McKenzie, Tennessee
www.bethelu.edu   Federal Code: 003480

4-year private university and liberal arts college in small town, affiliated with the Cumberland Presbyterian Church.

Enrollment: 4,068 undergrads, 15% part-time. 451 full-time freshmen.

Selectivity: Admits 50 to 75% of applicants.

BASIC COSTS (2017-2018)

Tuition and fees: $16,552.

Per-credit charge: $462.

Room and board: $9,198.

Additional info: .

FINANCIAL AID PICTURE (2015-2016)

Students with need: For part-time students, average financial aid package was $5,697.

Students without need: No-need awards available for academics, athletics, music/drama, religious affiliation, state/district residency.

FINANCIAL AID PROCEDURES

Forms required: FAFSA, institutional form.

Dates and Deadlines: Priority date 3/3; closing date 6/30. Applicants notified on a rolling basis starting 1/1; must reply within 2 week(s) of notification.

Transfers: No deadline. Financial aid transcripts from previously attended institutions required.

CONTACT

David Huss, University Director of Financial Aid
325 Cherry Avenue, McKenzie, TN 38201
(731) 352-4000

Bryan College: Dayton
Dayton, Tennessee
www.bryan.edu   Federal Code: 003536

4-year private liberal arts college in small town, affiliated with the interdenominational tradition.

Enrollment: 987 undergrads, 16% part-time. 204 full-time freshmen.

Selectivity: Admits less than 50% of applicants.

BASIC COSTS (2016-2017)

Tuition and fees: $24,450.

Room and board: $6,990.

Additional info: Tuition/fee waivers available for adults, minority students, unemployed or children of unemployed.

FINANCIAL AID PICTURE (2016-2017)

Students with need: Out of 195 full-time freshmen who applied for aid, 176 were judged to have need. Of these, 176 received aid, and 54 had their full need met. For part-time students, average financial aid package was $21,582.

FINANCIAL AID PROCEDURES

Forms required: FAFSA.

Dates and Deadlines: Priority date 1/31; no closing date. Applicants notified on a rolling basis starting 11/1.

CONTACT

David Haggard, Director of Financial Aid
721 Bryan Drive, Dayton, TN 37321-7000
(423) 775-7339

Carson-Newman University
Jefferson City, Tennessee
www.cn.edu

4-year private liberal arts college in small town, affiliated with the Southern Baptist Convention.

Enrollment: 1,748 undergrads, 2% part-time. 497 full-time freshmen.

Selectivity: Admits 50 to 75% of applicants.

BASIC COSTS (2016-2017)

Tuition and fees: $26,360.

Per-credit charge: $1,050.

Room and board: $8,430.

Additional info: Tuition/fee waivers available for adults, minority students.

FINANCIAL AID PICTURE (2015-2016)

Students with need: Out of 426 full-time freshmen who applied for aid, 426 were judged to have need. Of these, 425 received aid, and 97 had their full need met. Average financial aid package met 81% of need; average scholarship/grant was $18,638; average loan was $2,839. For part-time students, average financial aid package was $6,049.

Students without need: 38 full-time freshmen who did not demonstrate need for aid received scholarships/grants; average award was $11,089. No-need awards available for academics, art, athletics, leadership, music/drama, religious affiliation, ROTC, state/district residency.

Scholarships offered: 31 full-time freshmen received athletic scholarships; average amount $13,290.

FINANCIAL AID PROCEDURES

Forms required: FAFSA.

Dates and Deadlines: Priority date 2/1; no closing date. Applicants notified on a rolling basis starting 2/1; must reply by 5/1.

CONTACT

Danette Seale, Director of Financial Aid
1646 Russell Avenue, Jefferson City, TN 37760
(865) 471-3247

Chattanooga State Community College
Chattanooga, Tennessee
www.chattanoogastate.edu   Federal Code: 003998

2-year public community and technical college in small city.

Enrollment: 8,628 undergrads.

Selectivity: Open admission; but selective for some programs.

BASIC COSTS (2016-2017)

Tuition and fees: $4,249; out-of-state residents $16,814.

FINANCIAL AID PICTURE

Students with need: Need-based aid available for full-time and part-time students. Work study available nights, weekends, and for part-time students.

Students without need: No-need awards available for state/district residency.

FINANCIAL AID PROCEDURES

Forms required: FAFSA.

Dates and Deadlines: Priority date 6/1; no closing date. Applicants notified on a rolling basis starting 4/1; must reply within 2 week(s) of notification.

CONTACT

Reed Allison, Director of Financial Aid
4501 Amnicola Highway, Chattanooga, TN 37406
(423) 697-4402

Christian Brothers University

Memphis, Tennessee
www.cbu.edu   Federal Code: 003482

4-year private university in very large city, affiliated with the Roman Catholic Church.

Enrollment: 1,440 undergrads, 8% part-time. 336 full-time freshmen.

Selectivity: Admits 50 to 75% of applicants.

BASIC COSTS (2016-2017)

Tuition and fees: $30,860.

Per-credit charge: $1,070.

Room and board: $7,000.

Additional info: Tuition/fee waivers available for adults.

FINANCIAL AID PICTURE

Students with need: Need-based aid available for full-time and part-time students.

Students without need: No-need awards available for academics, alumni affiliation, athletics, music/drama, state/district residency.

Additional info: ROTC scholarships available to qualified applicants.

FINANCIAL AID PROCEDURES

Forms required: FAFSA.

Dates and Deadlines: Priority date 2/15; no closing date. Applicants notified on a rolling basis starting 3/1; must reply within 2 week(s) of notification.

Transfers: No deadline. Applicants notified on a rolling basis starting 3/1; must reply within 2 week(s) of notification.

CONTACT

John Lewis, Director of Financial Aid
650 East Parkway South, Memphis, TN 38104-5519
(901) 321-3305

Cleveland State Community College

Cleveland, Tennessee
www.clevelandstatecc.edu   Federal Code: 003999

2-year public community college in small city.

Enrollment: 3,054 undergrads, 49% part-time. 760 full-time freshmen.

Selectivity: Open admission; but selective for some programs.

BASIC COSTS (2016-2017)

Tuition and fees: $4,229; out-of-state residents $16,289.

Per-credit charge: $156; out-of-state residents $642.

FINANCIAL AID PICTURE (2016-2017)

Students with need: Out of 742 full-time freshmen who applied for aid, 493 were judged to have need. Of these, 492 received aid, and 45 had their full need met. Average financial aid package met 60% of need; average

scholarship/grant was $2,194; average loan was $1,388. For part-time students, average financial aid package was $3,386.

Students without need: 250 full-time freshmen who did not demonstrate need for aid received scholarships/grants; average award was $1,969. No-need awards available for athletics, minority status.

FINANCIAL AID PROCEDURES

Forms required: FAFSA, institutional form.

Dates and Deadlines: Priority date 5/15; no closing date. Applicants notified on a rolling basis starting 7/1; must reply within 2 week(s) of notification.

Transfers: Closing date 7/27.

CONTACT

Jamie Hamby, Director of Financial Aid
3535 Adkisson Drive, Cleveland, TN 37320-3570
(423) 472-7141 ext. 215

Columbia State Community College

Columbia, Tennessee
www.columbiastate.edu   Federal Code: 003483

2-year public community college in large town.

Enrollment: 4,271 undergrads.

Selectivity: Open admission; but selective for some programs.

BASIC COSTS (2016-2017)

Tuition and fees: $4,129; out-of-state residents $16,434.

FINANCIAL AID PICTURE

Students with need: Need-based aid available for full-time and part-time students.

Students without need: No-need awards available for academics, athletics, state/district residency.

FINANCIAL AID PROCEDURES

Forms required: FAFSA, institutional form.

Dates and Deadlines: Priority date 3/15; closing date 7/31. Applicants notified on a rolling basis starting 5/15; must reply within 2 week(s) of notification.

CONTACT

Cherry Johnson, Director of Financial Aid
1665 Hampshire Pike, Columbia, TN 38401
(931) 540-8267

Cumberland University

Lebanon, Tennessee
www.cumberland.edu   Federal Code: 003485

4-year private university and liberal arts college in large town.

Enrollment: 1,142 undergrads.

BASIC COSTS (2016-2017)

Tuition and fees: $21,210.

Per-credit charge: $840.

Room and board: $8,400.

FINANCIAL AID PICTURE

Students with need: Need-based aid available for full-time and part-time students.

Students without need: No-need awards available for academics, art, athletics, music/drama.

FINANCIAL AID PROCEDURES

Forms required: FAFSA, institutional form.

Dates and Deadlines: Priority date 2/1; no closing date. Applicants notified on a rolling basis starting 5/1; must reply within 2 week(s) of notification.

Transfers: Priority date 2/15. Applicants notified on a rolling basis starting 5/1.

CONTACT
Beatrice LaChance, Executive Director of Enrollment Services
1 Cumberland Square, Lebanon, TN 37087
(615) 444-2562 ext. 1249

Daymar Institute: Nashville
Nashville, Tennessee
www.daymarinstitute.edu   Federal Code: 004934

2-year for-profit career college in very large city.
Enrollment: 410 undergrads.
Selectivity: Open admission; but selective for some programs.

BASIC COSTS (2016-2017)
Additional info: Diploma programs: $22,000; Associate programs: $33,000-$36,000. Fees, books supplies range depending on program level and course of study. All costs are subject to change.

FINANCIAL AID PICTURE
Students with need: Need-based aid available for full-time and part-time students. Work study available nights.
Students without need: This college awards aid only to students with need.
Additional info: Financial aid form for in-state applicants must be filed before 5/1.

FINANCIAL AID PROCEDURES
Forms required: FAFSA.
Dates and Deadlines: Applicants notified on a rolling basis.
Transfers: Students must notify Tennessee Student Assistance Corporation of institutional change before appropriate deadlines.

CONTACT
Janie Rager, Director of Financial Services
340 & 283 Plus Park at Pavilion Boulevard, Nashville, TN 37217
(615) 361-7555

Dyersburg State Community College
Dyersburg, Tennessee
www.dscc.edu   Federal Code: 006835

2-year public community college in large town.
Enrollment: 1,855 undergrads, 33% part-time. 548 full-time freshmen.
Selectivity: Open admission; but selective for some programs.

BASIC COSTS (2016-2017)
Tuition and fees: $4,229; out-of-state residents $16,475.
Per-credit charge: $156; out-of-state residents $642.

FINANCIAL AID PICTURE (2015-2016)
Students with need: 79% of average financial aid package awarded as scholarships/grants, 21% awarded as loans/jobs. Need-based aid available for part-time students.
Students without need: No-need awards available for academics, alumni affiliation, athletics, job skills, leadership, minority status, music/drama, state/district residency.

FINANCIAL AID PROCEDURES
Forms required: FAFSA.
Dates and Deadlines: Priority date 3/1; no closing date. Applicants notified on a rolling basis starting 3/1; must reply within 2 week(s) of notification.
Transfers: Priority date 3/1.

CONTACT
Kacee Hardy, Director of Financial Aid
1510 Lake Road, Dyersburg, TN 38024
(731) 286-3238

East Tennessee State University
Johnson City, Tennessee
www.etsu.edu   Federal Code: 003487

4-year public university in small city.
Enrollment: 10,709 undergrads, 13% part-time. 1,869 full-time freshmen.
Selectivity: Admits over 75% of applicants.

BASIC COSTS (2016-2017)
Tuition and fees: $8,671; out-of-state residents $26,767.
Per-credit charge: $278; out-of-state residents $996.
Room and board: $7,952.

FINANCIAL AID PICTURE
Students with need: Need-based aid available for full-time and part-time students. Work study available nights, weekends, and for part-time students.
Students without need: No-need awards available for academics, alumni affiliation, art, athletics, leadership, minority status, music/drama, religious affiliation, ROTC, state/district residency.
Additional info: Housing costs payable by installment.

FINANCIAL AID PROCEDURES
Forms required: FAFSA.
Dates and Deadlines: Priority date 4/15; no closing date. Applicants notified on a rolling basis starting 4/15; must reply within 3 week(s) of notification.

CONTACT
Director of Financial Aid
ETSU Box 70731, Johnson City, TN 37614
(423) 439-4300

Fisk University
Nashville, Tennessee
www.fisk.edu   Federal Code: 003490

4-year private liberal arts college in very large city.
Enrollment: 723 undergrads, 2% part-time. 123 full-time freshmen.

BASIC COSTS (2016-2017)
Tuition and fees: $21,480.
Per-credit charge: $817.
Room and board: $10,790.

FINANCIAL AID PICTURE
Students with need: Need-based aid available for full-time and part-time students.
Students without need: This college awards aid only to students with need.

FINANCIAL AID PROCEDURES
Forms required: FAFSA.
Dates and Deadlines: Priority date 3/1; closing date 7/1. Applicants notified on a rolling basis starting 4/1; must reply within 2 week(s) of notification.

CONTACT
Mary Chambliss, Director of Financial Aid
1000 Seventeenth Avenue North, Nashville, TN 37208-3051
(615) 329-8585

Freed-Hardeman University

Henderson, Tennessee
www.fhu.edu   Federal Code: 003492

4-year private university and liberal arts college in small town, affiliated with the Church of Christ.
Enrollment: 1,260 undergrads.

BASIC COSTS (2016-2017)
Tuition and fees: $21,500.
Per-credit charge: $700.
Room and board: $7,950.
Additional info: Tuition/fee waivers available for minority students.

FINANCIAL AID PICTURE
Students with need: Need-based aid available for full-time and part-time students. Work study available nights, weekends, and for part-time students.
Students without need: No-need awards available for academics, art, athletics, leadership, minority status, music/drama.

FINANCIAL AID PROCEDURES
Forms required: FAFSA, institutional form.
Dates and Deadlines: Priority date 2/1; no closing date. Applicants notified on a rolling basis starting 3/10; must reply within 4 week(s) of notification.

CONTACT
Summer Judd, Director of Financial Aid
158 East Main Street, Henderson, TN 38340
(731) 989-6662

Jackson State Community College

Jackson, Tennessee
www.jscc.edu   Federal Code: 004937

2-year public community college in small city.
Enrollment: 3,243 undergrads.
Selectivity: Open admission; but selective for some programs.

BASIC COSTS (2016-2017)
Tuition and fees: $4,500; out-of-state residents $16,746.
Per-credit charge: $156; out-of-state residents $486.
Additional info: Tuition/fee waivers available for adults, minority students.

FINANCIAL AID PICTURE
Students with need: Need-based aid available for full-time and part-time students.
Students without need: No-need awards available for academics, art, athletics, job skills, leadership, minority status, music/drama.

FINANCIAL AID PROCEDURES
Forms required: FAFSA, institutional form.
Dates and Deadlines: Priority date 3/15; no closing date. Applicants notified on a rolling basis starting 5/15; must reply within 2 week(s) of notification.

CONTACT
Dewana Latimer, Director of Financial Aid
2046 North Parkway, Jackson, TN 38301-3797
(731) 425-2605

John A. Gupton College

Nashville, Tennessee
www.guptoncollege.edu   Federal Code: 008859

2-year private school of mortuary science in large city.
Enrollment: 119 undergrads.
Selectivity: Open admission; but selective for some programs.

BASIC COSTS (2016-2017)
Tuition and fees: $10,520.
Per-credit charge: $325.
Room only: $4,000.

FINANCIAL AID PICTURE
Students with need: Need-based aid available for full-time and part-time students.
Students without need: This college awards aid only to students with need.

FINANCIAL AID PROCEDURES
Forms required: FAFSA.
Dates and Deadlines: Applicants notified on a rolling basis; must reply within 2 week(s) of notification.
Transfers: No deadline. Applicants notified on a rolling basis starting 1/1; must reply within 2 week(s) of notification.

CONTACT
Joanna Hayes Dickens, Director of Financial Aid
1616 Church Street, Nashville, TN 37203-2920
(615) 327-3927

Johnson University

Knoxville, Tennessee
www.johnsonu.edu   Federal Code: 003495

4-year private university and Bible college in large city, affiliated with the Christian Church.
Enrollment: 842 undergrads, 18% part-time. 132 full-time freshmen.
Selectivity: Admits 50 to 75% of applicants.

BASIC COSTS (2016-2017)
Tuition and fees: $13,950.
Room and board: $5,820.
Additional info: Tuition/fee waivers available for minority students.

FINANCIAL AID PICTURE
Students with need: Need-based aid available for full-time and part-time students. Work study available nights, weekends, and for part-time students.
Students without need: No-need awards available for academics, leadership, minority status, music/drama, religious affiliation, state/district residency.

FINANCIAL AID PROCEDURES
Forms required: FAFSA, institutional form.
Dates and Deadlines: Closing date 3/1. Applicants notified on a rolling basis starting 4/30; must reply by 8/25 or within 2 week(s) of notification.
Transfers: No deadline.

CONTACT
Kayla Williams, Financial Aid Director
7900 Johnson Drive, Knoxville, TN 37998-0001
(865) 251-2303

King University

Bristol, Tennessee
www.king.edu   Federal Code: 003496

4-year private nursing and liberal arts college in large town, affiliated with the Presbyterian Church (USA).
Enrollment: 2,249 undergrads, 6% part-time. 157 full-time freshmen.
Selectivity: Admits 50 to 75% of applicants.

BASIC COSTS (2016-2017)
Tuition and fees: $27,276.
Room and board: $8,180.

FINANCIAL AID PICTURE (2016-2017)

Students with need: Average financial aid package met 80% of need; average scholarship/grant was $19,422; average loan was $3,901. For part-time students, average financial aid package was $6,432.

Students without need: No-need awards available for academics, art, athletics, music/drama.

FINANCIAL AID PROCEDURES

Forms required: FAFSA.

Dates and Deadlines: Priority date 3/1; no closing date. Applicants notified on a rolling basis starting 12/15; must reply within 4 week(s) of notification.

CONTACT

Chrystal Jefferson, Financial Aid Director
1350 King College Road, Bristol, TN 37620-2699
(423) 652-4725

Lane College

Jackson, Tennessee
www.lanecollege.edu   Federal Code: 003499

4-year private liberal arts college in small city, affiliated with the Christian Methodist Episcopal Church.

Enrollment: 1,427 undergrads, 4% part-time. 397 full-time freshmen.

Selectivity: Admits 50 to 75% of applicants.

BASIC COSTS (2016-2017)

Tuition and fees: $10,280.

Per-credit charge: $375.

Room and board: $6,770.

FINANCIAL AID PICTURE (2016-2017)

Students with need: Out of 397 full-time freshmen who applied for aid, 397 were judged to have need. Of these, 390 received aid. For part-time students, average financial aid package was $9,866.

Students without need: No-need awards available for academics, athletics, religious affiliation.

Scholarships offered: 49 full-time freshmen received athletic scholarships; average amount $4,792.

FINANCIAL AID PROCEDURES

Forms required: FAFSA.

Dates and Deadlines: Priority date 3/1; no closing date. Applicants notified on a rolling basis starting 3/1; must reply within 2 week(s) of notification.

Transfers: No deadline. Applicants notified on a rolling basis; must reply within 2 week(s) of notification.

CONTACT

Shelia Ray, Assistant Director of Financial Aid
545 Lane Avenue, Jackson, TN 38301-4598
(731) 426-7537

Lee University

Cleveland, Tennessee
www.leeuniversity.edu   Federal Code: 003500

4-year private university and liberal arts college in large town, affiliated with the Church of God.

Enrollment: 4,261 undergrads, 10% part-time. 884 full-time freshmen.

Selectivity: Open admission; but selective for some programs.

BASIC COSTS (2016-2017)

Tuition and fees: $15,770.

Per-credit charge: $632.

Room and board: $7,000.

FINANCIAL AID PICTURE (2016-2017)

Students with need: Out of 813 full-time freshmen who applied for aid, 538 were judged to have need. Of these, 538 received aid, and 282 had their full need met. Average financial aid package met 76% of need; average scholarship/grant was $9,738; average loan was $3,031. For part-time students, average financial aid package was $7,173.

Students without need: 239 full-time freshmen who did not demonstrate need for aid received scholarships/grants; average award was $9,345. No-need awards available for academics, alumni affiliation, athletics, leadership, minority status, music/drama, religious affiliation, state/district residency.

Scholarships offered: 41 full-time freshmen received athletic scholarships; average amount $8,862.

FINANCIAL AID PROCEDURES

Forms required: FAFSA.

Dates and Deadlines: Priority date 3/15; no closing date. Applicants notified on a rolling basis starting 2/1.

Transfers: No deadline. Applicants notified on a rolling basis.

CONTACT

Marian Dill, Director of Student Financial Aid
1120 North Ocoee Street, Cleveland, TN 37320-3450
(423) 614-8300

LeMoyne-Owen College

Memphis, Tennessee
www.loc.edu   Federal Code: 003501

4-year private liberal arts college in very large city, affiliated with the Baptist faith.

Enrollment: 959 undergrads, 12% part-time. 189 full-time freshmen.

BASIC COSTS (2016-2017)

Tuition and fees: $10,880.

Per-credit charge: $436.

Room and board: $5,910.

FINANCIAL AID PICTURE

Students with need: Need-based aid available for full-time and part-time students.

Students without need: No-need awards available for academics, athletics, music/drama.

FINANCIAL AID PROCEDURES

Forms required: FAFSA.

Dates and Deadlines: Priority date 4/15; no closing date. Applicants notified on a rolling basis starting 4/1.

Transfers: No deadline. Applicants notified on a rolling basis starting 4/1.

CONTACT

Phyllis Torry, Financial Aid Director
807 Walker Avenue, Memphis, TN 38126
(901) 435-1550

Lincoln College of Technology: Nashville

Nashville, Tennessee
www.nadcedu.com   Federal Code: 007440

1-year for-profit technical college in large city.

Enrollment: 1,782 undergrads.

BASIC COSTS (2016-2017)

Additional info: Certificate programs: $14,754. Diploma programs: $29,867 to $36,344. Associate programs: $35,817. Costs include total tuition, materials, tool fees, and registration fee.

FINANCIAL AID PICTURE

Students with need: Need-based aid available for full-time students. Work study available nights, weekends, and for part-time students.

Students without need: This college awards aid only to students with need.

FINANCIAL AID PROCEDURES

Forms required: FAFSA, state aid form.

Dates and Deadlines: Applicants notified on a rolling basis.

CONTACT

Chris Biddle, Director of Financial Aid
1524 Gallatin Road, Nashville, TN 37206
(615) 650-8202

Lincoln Memorial University

Harrogate, Tennessee
www.lmunet.edu   Federal Code: 003502

4-year private university and liberal arts college in small town.
Enrollment: 1,598 undergrads.

BASIC COSTS (2016-2017)
Tuition and fees: $21,050.
Per-credit charge: $855.
Room and board: $7,550.

FINANCIAL AID PICTURE

Students with need: Need-based aid available for full-time and part-time students.

Students without need: No-need awards available for academics, alumni affiliation, athletics, music/drama, ROTC.

FINANCIAL AID PROCEDURES

Forms required: FAFSA.

Dates and Deadlines: Priority date 2/15; no closing date. Applicants notified on a rolling basis starting 3/15; must reply within 3 week(s) of notification.

CONTACT

Tammy Tomfohrde, Executive Director of Financial Aid
6965 Cumberland Gap Parkway, Harrogate, TN 37752-1901
(423) 869-6336

Lipscomb University

Nashville, Tennessee
www.lipscomb.edu   Federal Code: 003486

4-year private university and liberal arts college in very large city, affiliated with the Church of Christ.
Enrollment: 2,969 undergrads, 11% part-time. 632 full-time freshmen.
Selectivity: Admits 50 to 75% of applicants.

BASIC COSTS (2016-2017)
Tuition and fees: $29,756.
Per-credit charge: $1,150.
Room and board: $11,540.

FINANCIAL AID PICTURE (2016-2017)

Students with need: Out of 632 full-time freshmen who applied for aid, 425 were judged to have need. Of these, 425 received aid, and 105 had their full need met. Average financial aid package met 68% of need; average scholarship/grant was $4,239; average loan was $3,636. For part-time students, average financial aid package was $10,044.

Students without need: 205 full-time freshmen who did not demonstrate need for aid received scholarships/grants; average award was $12,865.

Scholarships offered: 16 full-time freshmen received athletic scholarships; average amount $23,306.

CONTACT

Tiffany Summers, Director of Financial Aid
One University Park Drive, Nashville, TN 37204-3951
(615) 966-1791

Martin Methodist College

Pulaski, Tennessee
www.martinmethodist.edu   Federal Code: 003504

4-year private liberal arts college in small town, affiliated with the United Methodist Church.
Enrollment: 1,050 undergrads.

FINANCIAL AID PICTURE

Students with need: Need-based aid available for full-time and part-time students. Work study available nights, weekends, and for part-time students.

Students without need: No-need awards available for academics, art, athletics, leadership, music/drama, religious affiliation, state/district residency.

Scholarships offered: Two full academic scholarships per year awarded through interview and essay competition.

FINANCIAL AID PROCEDURES

Forms required: FAFSA, institutional form.

Dates and Deadlines: Applicants notified on a rolling basis starting 3/1; must reply within 2 week(s) of notification.

Transfers: Closing date 9/13.

CONTACT

Emma Hlubb, Director of Financial Aid
433 West Madison, Pulaski, TN 38478-2799
(931) 363-9804

Maryville College

Maryville, Tennessee
www.maryvillecollege.edu   Federal Code: 003505

4-year private liberal arts college in large town, affiliated with the Presbyterian Church (USA).
Enrollment: 1,174 undergrads, 1% part-time. 323 full-time freshmen.
Selectivity: Admits 50 to 75% of applicants.

BASIC COSTS (2017-2018)
Tuition and fees: $34,196.
Per-credit charge: $859.
Room and board: $11,144.

FINANCIAL AID PICTURE

Students with need: Need-based aid available for full-time and part-time students. Work study available nights, weekends, and for part-time students.

Students without need: No-need awards available for academics, alumni affiliation, art, leadership, minority status, music/drama, religious affiliation, state/district residency.

FINANCIAL AID PROCEDURES

Forms required: FAFSA.

Dates and Deadlines: Priority date 2/1; no closing date. Applicants notified on a rolling basis starting 3/12; must reply by 5/1 or within 4 week(s) of notification.

CONTACT

Alayne Bowman, Asst. Director of Financial Aid
502 East Lamar Alexander Parkway, Maryville, TN 37804-5907
(865) 981-8100

Memphis College of Art
Memphis, Tennessee
www.mca.edu   Federal Code: 003507

4-year private visual arts college in very large city.
Enrollment: 337 undergrads, 12% part-time. 66 full-time freshmen.
Selectivity: Admits less than 50% of applicants.

BASIC COSTS (2016-2017)
Tuition and fees: $31,700.
Room and board: $8,750.

FINANCIAL AID PICTURE (2016-2017)
Students with need: Out of 63 full-time freshmen who applied for aid, 62 were judged to have need. Of these, 62 received aid, and 9 had their full need met. Average financial aid package met 68% of need; average scholarship/grant was $21,442; average loan was $3,413. For part-time students, average financial aid package was $17,646.
Students without need: 4 full-time freshmen who did not demonstrate need for aid received scholarships/grants; average award was $16,117. No-need awards available for academics, art.
Additional info: Students considered for institutional resources through admissions application process.

FINANCIAL AID PROCEDURES
Forms required: FAFSA.
Dates and Deadlines: Priority date 2/15; no closing date. Applicants notified on a rolling basis starting 3/15; must reply within 3 week(s) of notification.
Transfers: Applicants notified on a rolling basis; must reply within 3 week(s) of notification. Grants of $1,000 awarded to students who attended accredited junior or community college earning at least 60 credit hours.

CONTACT
Aaron White, Director of Financial Aid
1930 Poplar Avenue, Memphis, TN 38104-2764
(901) 272-5136

Middle Tennessee State University
Murfreesboro, Tennessee
www.mtsu.edu   Federal Code: 003510

4-year public university in small city.
Enrollment: 18,998 undergrads, 16% part-time. 2,815 full-time freshmen.
Selectivity: Admits 50 to 75% of applicants.

BASIC COSTS (2016-2017)
Tuition and fees: $8,610; out-of-state residents $26,610.
Per-credit charge: $275; out-of-state residents $989.
Room and board: $8,850.

FINANCIAL AID PICTURE (2015-2016)
Students with need: Out of 2,424 full-time freshmen who applied for aid, 1,908 were judged to have need. Of these, 1,901 received aid, and 232 had their full need met. Average financial aid package met 69% of need; average scholarship/grant was $6,697; average loan was $3,242. For part-time students, average financial aid package was $5,250.
Students without need: 480 full-time freshmen who did not demonstrate need for aid received scholarships/grants; average award was $8,258. No-need awards available for academics, leadership.
Scholarships offered: 54 full-time freshmen received athletic scholarships; average amount $27,184.
Additional info: Deadline for scholarships 2/15.

FINANCIAL AID PROCEDURES
Forms required: FAFSA.
Dates and Deadlines: Priority date 3/1; no closing date. Applicants notified on a rolling basis starting 4/15; must reply within 2 week(s) of notification.

CONTACT
Stephen White, Director of Student Financial Aid
1301 East Main Street, Murfreesboro, TN 37132
(615) 898-2422

Miller-Motte Technical College: Clarksville
Clarksville, Tennessee
www.miller-motte.edu   Federal Code: 026142

2-year for-profit business and health science college in small city.
Enrollment: 404 undergrads.
Selectivity: Open admission; but selective for some programs.

BASIC COSTS (2016-2017)
Additional info: Certificate programs: $10,080-$20,668, books and supplies $400-$1,900. Associate programs: $25,080-$33,180, books and supplies $3,600-$4,800.

FINANCIAL AID PICTURE
Students with need: Need-based aid available for full-time and part-time students. Work study available nights, weekends, and for part-time students.
Students without need: This college awards aid only to students with need.

FINANCIAL AID PROCEDURES
Forms required: FAFSA, institutional form.
Dates and Deadlines: Applicants notified on a rolling basis.
Transfers: No deadline.

CONTACT
Debbie Stratman, Financial Aid Director
1820 Business Park Drive, Clarksville, TN 37040
(931) 553-0071

Milligan College
Milligan College, Tennessee
www.milligan.edu   Federal Code: 003511

4-year private liberal arts college in small city, affiliated with the Christian Church.
Enrollment: 820 undergrads, 7% part-time. 194 full-time freshmen.
Selectivity: Admits 50 to 75% of applicants.

BASIC COSTS (2016-2017)
Tuition and fees: $31,450.
Room and board: $6,700.

FINANCIAL AID PICTURE (2016-2017)
Students with need: Out of 177 full-time freshmen who applied for aid, 155 were judged to have need. Of these, 155 received aid, and 48 had their full need met. Average financial aid package met 78% of need; average scholarship/grant was $21,012; average loan was $3,624. For part-time students, average financial aid package was $6,365.
Students without need: 25 full-time freshmen who did not demonstrate need for aid received scholarships/grants; average award was $11,271. No-need awards available for academics, art, athletics, job skills, leadership, minority status, music/drama, religious affiliation.
Scholarships offered: 35 full-time freshmen received athletic scholarships; average amount $9,203.

FINANCIAL AID PROCEDURES
Forms required: FAFSA.
Dates and Deadlines: Priority date 12/1; no closing date. Applicants notified on a rolling basis starting 12/1; must reply within 2 week(s) of notification.

CONTACT
Diane Keasling, Coordinator of Financial Aid
Box 210, Milligan College, TN 37682
(800) 447-4880

Motlow State Community College
Lynchburg, Tennessee
www.mscc.edu   Federal Code: 006836

2-year public community college in rural community.
Enrollment: 4,803 undergrads, 31% part-time. 1,032 full-time freshmen.
Selectivity: Open admission; but selective for some programs.

BASIC COSTS (2016-2017)
Tuition and fees: $4,051; out-of-state residents $11,971.

FINANCIAL AID PICTURE (2015-2016)
Students with need: Out of 1,030 full-time freshmen who applied for aid, 750 were judged to have need. Of these, 750 received aid, and 129 had their full need met. Average financial aid package met 63% of need; average scholarship/grant was $5,078. For part-time students, average financial aid package was $3,172.
Students without need: 273 full-time freshmen who did not demonstrate need for aid received scholarships/grants; average award was $4,064. No-need awards available for academics, alumni affiliation, art, athletics, leadership, music/drama.
Scholarships offered: 24 full-time freshmen received athletic scholarships; average amount $3,780.

FINANCIAL AID PROCEDURES
Forms required: FAFSA, institutional form.
Dates and Deadlines: Closing date 2/15. Applicants notified on a rolling basis starting 3/15.
Transfers: No deadline. Applicants notified on a rolling basis starting 3/15.

CONTACT
Joe Myers, Director of Financial Aid and Scholarships
Box 8500, Lynchburg, TN 37352-8500
(931) 393-1553

Nashville State Community College
Nashville, Tennessee
www.nscc.edu   Federal Code: 007534

2-year public community and technical college in very large city.
Enrollment: 7,296 undergrads, 49% part-time. 1,491 full-time freshmen.
Selectivity: Open admission; but selective for some programs.

BASIC COSTS (2016-2017)
Tuition and fees: $4,905; out-of-state residents $19,485.

FINANCIAL AID PICTURE (2015-2016)
Students with need: 76% of average financial aid package awarded as scholarships/grants, 24% awarded as loans/jobs. Need-based aid available for part-time students. Work study available nights, weekends, and for part-time students.
Students without need: No-need awards available for academics, minority status.

FINANCIAL AID PROCEDURES
Forms required: FAFSA.
Dates and Deadlines: Priority date 3/1; closing date 7/1. Applicants notified on a rolling basis starting 6/1; must reply within 2 week(s) of notification.

CONTACT
Jennifer Byrd, Director of Financial Aid
120 White Bridge Road, Nashville, TN 37209-4515
(615) 353-3250

National College: Bristol
Bristol, Tennessee
www.national-college.edu   Federal Code: 003726

2-year for-profit business college in large town.
Enrollment: 92 undergrads.
Selectivity: Open admission.

BASIC COSTS (2016-2017)
Tuition and fees: $14,460.
Per-credit charge: $317.

FINANCIAL AID PICTURE
Students with need: Need-based aid available for full-time and part-time students.
Students without need: This college awards aid only to students with need.

FINANCIAL AID PROCEDURES
Forms required: FAFSA.
Dates and Deadlines: Applicants notified on a rolling basis starting 9/1.

CONTACT
Pam Cotton, Director of Financial Aid Compliance and Auditing
1328 Highway 11W, Bristol, TN 37620

National College: Nashville
Nashville, Tennessee
www.ncbt.edu   Federal Code: 003726

2-year for-profit business and technical college in large city.
Enrollment: 102 undergrads.
Selectivity: Open admission.

BASIC COSTS (2016-2017)
Tuition and fees: $14,460.
Per-credit charge: $317.

FINANCIAL AID PICTURE
Students with need: Need-based aid available for full-time and part-time students.
Students without need: This college awards aid only to students with need.

FINANCIAL AID PROCEDURES
Forms required: FAFSA.

CONTACT
Pam Cotton, Director of Financial Aid Compliance and Auditing
1638 Bell Road, Nashville, TN 37211
(615) 333-3344

Northeast State Community College
Blountville, Tennessee
www.NortheastState.edu   Federal Code: 005378

2-year public community and technical college in small city.
Enrollment: 6,124 undergrads.
Selectivity: Open admission; but selective for some programs.

BASIC COSTS (2016-2017)
Tuition and fees: $4,499; out-of-state residents $12,503.

FINANCIAL AID PICTURE
Students with need: Need-based aid available for full-time and part-time students. Work study available nights.

Students without need: No-need awards available for academics, alumni affiliation, art, job skills, leadership, minority status, music/drama, religious affiliation.

FINANCIAL AID PROCEDURES
Forms required: FAFSA.
Dates and Deadlines: Priority date 3/31; no closing date. Applicants notified on a rolling basis starting 3/1; must reply within 3 week(s) of notification.

CONTACT
Cruzita Lucero, Director of Financial Aid
Box 246, Blountville, TN 37617-0246
(423) 323-0252

Nossi College of Art
Nashville, Tennessee
www.nossi.edu   Federal Code: 017347

2-year for-profit visual arts and technical college in large town.
Enrollment: 256 undergrads. 97 full-time freshmen.

BASIC COSTS (2016-2017)
Tuition and fees: $17,700.

FINANCIAL AID PICTURE
Students with need: Need-based aid available for full-time and part-time students.

CONTACT
Mary Kidd, Financial Aid Director
590 Cheron Road, Nashville, TN 37115
(615) 514-2787

O'More College of Design
Franklin, Tennessee
www.omorecollege.edu   Federal Code: 014663

4-year private visual arts college in large town.
Enrollment: 159 undergrads, 6% part-time. 27 full-time freshmen.

BASIC COSTS (2016-2017)
Tuition and fees: $28,176.
Per-credit charge: $1,174.

FINANCIAL AID PICTURE (2015-2016)
Students with need: 72% of average financial aid package awarded as scholarships/grants, 28% awarded as loans/jobs. Need-based aid available for part-time students. Work study available nights, weekends, and for part-time students.
Students without need: This college awards aid only to students with need.

FINANCIAL AID PROCEDURES
Forms required: FAFSA.
Dates and Deadlines: Closing date 4/7.
Transfers: Priority date 4/7; no deadline. Applicants notified by 6/10.

CONTACT
Sara Martin, Financial Aid Director
423 South Margin Street, Franklin, TN 37064-0908
(615) 794-4254 ext. 226

Pellissippi State Community College
Knoxville, Tennessee
www.pstcc.edu   Federal Code: 012693

2-year public community and technical college in small city.
Enrollment: 10,325 undergrads.

Selectivity: Open admission.

BASIC COSTS (2016-2017)
Tuition and fees: $4,270; out-of-state residents $16,516.

FINANCIAL AID PICTURE
Students with need: Need-based aid available for full-time and part-time students. Work study available nights, weekends, and for part-time students.
Students without need: No-need awards available for academics, art, minority status, music/drama.

FINANCIAL AID PROCEDURES
Forms required: FAFSA.
Dates and Deadlines: Priority date 5/1; no closing date. Applicants notified on a rolling basis starting 7/15; must reply within 2 week(s) of notification.

CONTACT
Richard Smelser, Director, Financial Aid
Box 22990, Knoxville, TN 37933-0990
(865) 964-6565

Remington College: Memphis
Memphis, Tennessee
www.memphis.remingtoncollege.edu

2-year private business and technical college in very large city.
Enrollment: 1,361 undergrads.

BASIC COSTS (2016-2017)
Additional info: Diploma programs: ventilation and air conditioning $20,995; medical assisting $19,990; medical billing and coding $15,995; pharmacy technician $20,520. Associate programs: business administration $33,900; business office management $33,900; computer and network administration $33,900; criminal justice $33,900; electronics and computer technology $33,900. Bahelor's program: criminal justice $29,900.

FINANCIAL AID PICTURE
Students with need: Need-based aid available for full-time and part-time students.
Students without need: This college awards aid only to students with need.

FINANCIAL AID PROCEDURES
Forms required: FAFSA, institutional form.
Dates and Deadlines: Applicants notified on a rolling basis; must reply within 2 week(s) of notification.

CONTACT
James Dunn, National Director of Financial Aid
2710 Nonconnah Boulevard, Memphis, TN 38132

Rhodes College
Memphis, Tennessee   Federal Code: 003519
www.rhodes.edu   CSS Code: 1730

4-year private liberal arts college in very large city, affiliated with the Presbyterian Church (USA).
Enrollment: 1,980 undergrads. 507 full-time freshmen.
Selectivity: Admits 50 to 75% of applicants.

BASIC COSTS (2016-2017)
Tuition and fees: $44,942.
Per-credit charge: $1,865.
Room and board: $11,068.

FINANCIAL AID PICTURE (2016-2017)
Students with need: Out of 425 full-time freshmen who applied for aid, 308 were judged to have need. Of these, 308 received aid, and 185 had

their full need met. Average financial aid package met 93% of need; average scholarship/grant was $32,913; average loan was $3,275.

Students without need: 116 full-time freshmen who did not demonstrate need for aid received scholarships/grants; average award was $24,963. No-need awards available for academics, art, minority status, music/drama, religious affiliation.

Additional info: Auditions required for theater and music achievement awards and art achievement awards. Interviews recommended for merit scholarships. Notification of admissions decision for Bellingrath Scholarship applicants by 3/15; must reply by 5/1.

FINANCIAL AID PROCEDURES

Forms required: FAFSA, CSS PROFILE.

Dates and Deadlines: Priority date 3/1; closing date 3/1. Must reply by 5/1.

CONTACT

Michael Morgan, Director of Financial Aid
2000 North Parkway, Memphis, TN 38112
(901) 843-3810

Roane State Community College

Harriman, Tennessee
www.roanestate.edu   Federal Code: 009914

2-year public community and junior college in small town.
Enrollment: 4,421 undergrads.
Selectivity: Open admission; but selective for some programs.

BASIC COSTS (2016-2017)

Tuition and fees: $4,233; out-of-state residents $16,101.

FINANCIAL AID PICTURE

Students with need: Need-based aid available for full-time and part-time students. Work study available nights, weekends, and for part-time students.

Students without need: No-need awards available for academics, art, athletics, leadership, music/drama, state/district residency.

FINANCIAL AID PROCEDURES

Forms required: FAFSA, institutional form.

Dates and Deadlines: Priority date 4/1; no closing date. Applicants notified on a rolling basis starting 5/1.

CONTACT

Robin Townson, Director, Financial Aid
276 Patton Lane, Harriman, TN 37748
(865) 882-4545

Sewanee: The University of the South

Sewanee, Tennessee   Federal Code: 003534
www.sewanee.edu   CSS Code: 1842

4-year private university and liberal arts college in small town, affiliated with the Episcopal Church.
Enrollment: 1,714 undergrads. 514 full-time freshmen.
Selectivity: Admits less than 50% of applicants. GED not accepted.

BASIC COSTS (2017-2018)

Tuition and fees: $45,120.
Per-credit charge: $1,425.
Room and board: $12,880.
Additional info: Tuition, fees, room, and board are guaranteed for four years from the year of entry. Tuition at time of enrollment locked for 4 years.

FINANCIAL AID PICTURE (2016-2017)

Students with need: Out of 351 full-time freshmen who applied for aid, 249 were judged to have need. Of these, 249 received aid, and 72 had their full need met. Average financial aid package met 91% of need; average

scholarship/grant was $28,705; average loan was $3,476. For part-time students, average financial aid package was $5,467.

Students without need: 201 full-time freshmen who did not demonstrate need for aid received scholarships/grants; average award was $13,395. No-need awards available for academics, art, religious affiliation, state/district residency.

Scholarships offered: Benedict Scholarship; full tuition, fees, room and board annually; 2 awarded. Wilkins Scholarship; $15,000 annually; $60,000 total; number awarded determined annually. Quintard Award; $12,000 annually; $48,000 total; number awarded determined annually. Fairbanks Award; $10,000 annually; $40,000 total; number awarded determined annually. Otey Award; $5,000 annually; $20,000 total; number awarded determined annually. Georgia4 Scholarship; $4,000 annually; $16,000 total; all students admitted from Georgia.

FINANCIAL AID PROCEDURES

Forms required: FAFSA, CSS PROFILE.

Dates and Deadlines: Priority date 12/1; closing date 12/1. Applicants notified on a rolling basis starting 2/1; must reply by 5/1 or within 2 week(s) of notification.

CONTACT

Beth Cragar, Associate Dean of Admission for Financial Aid
Office of Admission, Sewanee, TN 37383-1000
(931) 598-1312

South College

Knoxville, Tennessee
www.southcollegetn.edu   Federal Code: 004938

4-year for-profit career college in small city.
Enrollment: 1,139 undergrads.

BASIC COSTS (2016-2017)

Tuition and fees: $21,075.

FINANCIAL AID PICTURE

Students with need: Need-based aid available for full-time and part-time students.

Students without need: This college awards aid only to students with need.

FINANCIAL AID PROCEDURES

Forms required: FAFSA, institutional form.

Dates and Deadlines: Applicants notified on a rolling basis.

Transfers: Priority date 2/1; no deadline. Applicants notified on a rolling basis starting 6/1; must reply within 4 week(s) of notification.

CONTACT

Larry Broadwater, Financial Aid Director
3904 Lonas Drive, Knoxville, TN 37909
(865) 251-1800

Southern Adventist University

Collegedale, Tennessee
www.southern.edu   Federal Code: 003518

4-year private university and liberal arts college in small town, affiliated with the Seventh-day Adventists.
Enrollment: 2,697 undergrads.

BASIC COSTS (2016-2017)

Tuition and fees: $21,150.
Per-credit charge: $850.
Room and board: $6,450.

FINANCIAL AID PICTURE

Students with need: Need-based aid available for full-time and part-time students.

Students without need: No-need awards available for academics, alumni affiliation, art, athletics, leadership, music/drama.

Scholarships offered: Freshman scholarships; based on GPA, ACT/SAT, leadership positions held.

FINANCIAL AID PROCEDURES

Forms required: FAFSA.

Dates and Deadlines: Priority date 3/1; no closing date. Applicants notified on a rolling basis starting 2/15; must reply within 2 week(s) of notification.

Transfers: No deadline. Applicants notified on a rolling basis.

CONTACT

Paula Walter, Associate Vice President for Enrollment Services
PO Box 370, Collegedale, TN 37315-0370
(423) 236-2835

Southwest Tennessee Community College

Memphis, Tennessee
www.southwest.tn.edu
Federal Code: 010439

2-year public community college in very large city.
Enrollment: 8,327 undergrads.
Selectivity: Open admission; but selective for some programs.

BASIC COSTS (2016-2017)

Tuition and fees: $4,059; out-of-state residents $16,038.
Per-credit charge: $156; out-of-state residents $642.
Additional info: Tuition/fee waivers available for minority students.

FINANCIAL AID PICTURE

Students with need: Need-based aid available for full-time and part-time students. Work study available nights, weekends, and for part-time students.

Students without need: No-need awards available for academics, athletics, minority status, music/drama, state/district residency.

FINANCIAL AID PROCEDURES

Forms required: FAFSA.

Dates and Deadlines: Applicants notified on a rolling basis starting 6/1; must reply within 4 week(s) of notification.

CONTACT

Lechelle Davenport, Director Financial Aid
PO Box 780, Memphis, TN 38101-0780
(901) 333-5957

Tennessee State University

Nashville, Tennessee
www.tnstate.edu
Federal Code: 003522

4-year public university in very large city.
Enrollment: 6,871 undergrads, 17% part-time. 1,270 full-time freshmen.
Selectivity: Admits 50 to 75% of applicants.

BASIC COSTS (2016-2017)

Tuition and fees: $7,568; out-of-state residents $20,924.
Per-credit charge: $259; out-of-state residents $789.
Room and board: $7,544.
Additional info: Tuition/fee waivers available for minority students.

FINANCIAL AID PICTURE

Students with need: Need-based aid available for full-time students.
Students without need: No-need awards available for academics.

FINANCIAL AID PROCEDURES

Forms required: FAFSA.

Dates and Deadlines: Priority date 4/1; no closing date. Applicants notified on a rolling basis starting 4/15; must reply within 3 week(s) of notification.

CONTACT

Cynthia Brooks, Vice President of Finance/Accounting
3500 John A. Merritt Boulevard, Nashville, TN 37209-1561
(615) 963-5701

Tennessee Technological University

Cookeville, Tennessee
www.tntech.edu
Federal Code: 003523

4-year public university in large town.
Enrollment: 9,475 undergrads.

BASIC COSTS (2016-2017)

Tuition and fees: $8,551; out-of-state residents $25,586.
Per-credit charge: $293; out-of-state residents $954.
Room and board: $8,956.
Additional info: Tuition/fee waivers available for minority students.

FINANCIAL AID PICTURE

Students with need: Need-based aid available for full-time and part-time students. Work study available nights, weekends, and for part-time students.

Students without need: No-need awards available for academics, alumni affiliation, art, athletics, leadership, minority status, music/drama, ROTC, state/district residency.

Scholarships offered: Presidential Scholarship; $4,000 renewable annually. Awarded to National Merit Finalists.

Additional info: Tuition and/or fee waivers available for children of Tennessee public school teachers.

FINANCIAL AID PROCEDURES

Forms required: FAFSA.

Dates and Deadlines: Priority date 3/15; no closing date. Applicants notified on a rolling basis starting 3/15; must reply within 2 week(s) of notification.

Transfers: No deadline. Applicants notified on a rolling basis starting 6/1; must reply within 2 week(s) of notification.

CONTACT

Lester McKenzie, Director of Student Financial Aid
Office of Admissions, Cookeville, TN 38505-0001
(931) 372-3073

Tennessee Wesleyan College

Athens, Tennessee
www.tnwesleyan.edu
Federal Code: 003525

4-year private liberal arts and teachers college in large town, affiliated with the United Methodist Church.
Enrollment: 999 undergrads, 9% part-time. 246 full-time freshmen.
Selectivity: Admits over 75% of applicants.

BASIC COSTS (2017-2018)

Tuition and fees: $23,800.
Per-credit charge: $580.
Room and board: $7,750.
Additional info: Tuition/fee waivers available for minority students.

FINANCIAL AID PICTURE (2015-2016)

Students with need: Out of 219 full-time freshmen who applied for aid, 197 were judged to have need. Of these, 193 received aid, and 39 had their full need met. Average financial aid package met 71% of need; average scholarship/grant was $17,262; average loan was $3,062. For part-time students, average financial aid package was $9,756.

Students without need: 22 full-time freshmen who did not demonstrate need for aid received scholarships/grants; average award was $9,063. No-need awards available for academics, athletics.
Scholarships offered: 40 full-time freshmen received athletic scholarships; average amount $13,537.

FINANCIAL AID PROCEDURES
Forms required: FAFSA, institutional form.
Dates and Deadlines: Priority date 2/15; no closing date. Applicants notified on a rolling basis starting 2/15; must reply within 2 week(s) of notification.

CONTACT
Lacey Weese, Director of Financial Aid
204 East College Street, Athens, TN 37303
(423) 746-5215

Trevecca Nazarene University
Nashville, Tennessee
www.trevecca.edu   Federal Code: 003526

4-year private university and liberal arts college in very large city, affiliated with the Church of the Nazarene.
Enrollment: 1,990 undergrads, 37% part-time. 395 full-time freshmen.
Selectivity: Admits 50 to 75% of applicants.

BASIC COSTS (2017-2018)
Tuition and fees: $25,100.
Room and board: $8,808.
Additional info: Tuition includes textbook rental cost.

FINANCIAL AID PICTURE (2015-2016)
Students with need: 46% of average financial aid package awarded as scholarships/grants, 54% awarded as loans/jobs.
Students without need: No-need awards available for academics, alumni affiliation, athletics, leadership, minority status, music/drama, religious affiliation.

FINANCIAL AID PROCEDURES
Dates and Deadlines: Priority date 1/1; no closing date. Applicants notified on a rolling basis starting 12/1.

CONTACT
Eddie White, Director of Financial Aid
333 Murfreesboro Road, Nashville, TN 37210
(615) 248-1242

Tusculum College
Greeneville, Tennessee
www.tusculum.edu   Federal Code: 003527

4-year private liberal arts college in large town, affiliated with the Presbyterian Church (USA).
Enrollment: 1,585 undergrads, 11% part-time. 323 full-time freshmen.
Selectivity: Admits 50 to 75% of applicants.

BASIC COSTS (2016-2017)
Tuition and fees: $23,125.
Per-credit charge: $718.
Room and board: $8,500.

FINANCIAL AID PICTURE (2016-2017)
Students with need: Out of 303 full-time freshmen who applied for aid, 278 were judged to have need. Of these, 269 received aid, and 33 had their full need met. Average financial aid package met 83% of need; average scholarship/grant was $10,882; average loan was $3,304. For part-time students, average financial aid package was $5,716.

Students without need: 25 full-time freshmen who did not demonstrate need for aid received scholarships/grants; average award was $10,019. No-need awards available for academics, athletics, leadership, religious affiliation, state/district residency.
Scholarships offered: 103 full-time freshmen received athletic scholarships; average amount $19,069.

FINANCIAL AID PROCEDURES
Forms required: FAFSA.
Dates and Deadlines: Closing date 2/15. Applicants notified on a rolling basis starting 3/15; must reply within 3 week(s) of notification.

CONTACT
Karen Sartain, Director of Financial Aid
60 Shiloh Road, Greeneville, TN 37743
(423) 636-7376

Union University
Jackson, Tennessee
www.uu.edu   Federal Code: 003528

4-year private university and liberal arts college in small city, affiliated with the Southern Baptist Convention.
Enrollment: 2,106 undergrads, 16% part-time. 334 full-time freshmen.
Selectivity: Admits 50 to 75% of applicants.

BASIC COSTS (2016-2017)
Tuition and fees: $30,330.
Per-credit charge: $975.
Room and board: $9,200.
Additional info: Tuition/fee waivers available for minority students.

FINANCIAL AID PICTURE (2016-2017)
Students with need: Out of 315 full-time freshmen who applied for aid, 256 were judged to have need. Of these, 256 received aid, and 91 had their full need met. Average financial aid package met 79% of need; average scholarship/grant was $6,801; average loan was $3,333. For part-time students, average financial aid package was $15,264.
Students without need: 59 full-time freshmen who did not demonstrate need for aid received scholarships/grants; average award was $16,379. No-need awards available for academics, alumni affiliation, art, athletics, job skills, leadership, minority status, music/drama, religious affiliation, state/district residency.
Scholarships offered: 13 full-time freshmen received athletic scholarships; average amount $11,367.

FINANCIAL AID PROCEDURES
Forms required: FAFSA, institutional form.
Dates and Deadlines: Priority date 12/1; no closing date. Applicants notified on a rolling basis starting 3/1; must reply by 5/1 or within 2 week(s) of notification.
Transfers: Priority date 2/1; closing date 2/1. Applicants notified on a rolling basis starting 3/1; must reply by 5/1 or within 2 week(s) of notification.

CONTACT
John Windham, Director of Student Financial Planning
1050 Union University Drive, Jackson, TN 38305-3697
(731) 661-5015

University of Memphis
Memphis, Tennessee
www.memphis.edu   Federal Code: 003509

4-year public university in very large city.
Enrollment: 15,955 undergrads, 22% part-time. 2,647 full-time freshmen.
Selectivity: Admits over 75% of applicants.

BASIC COSTS (2016-2017)

Tuition and fees: $9,497; out-of-state residents $21,209.
Room and board: $9,153.
Additional info: Tuition/fee waivers available for adults, minority students.

FINANCIAL AID PICTURE

Students with need: Need-based aid available for full-time and part-time students. Work study available nights, weekends, and for part-time students.
Students without need: No-need awards available for academics, alumni affiliation, art, athletics, leadership, music/drama, ROTC, state/district residency.
Scholarships offered: Cecil C. Humphreys Presidential Scholarship: $7,500; minimum 30 ACT/1330 SAT (CR+M), 3.5 or higher cumulative high school grade point average. Provost Scholarship: $5,500; minimum 28 ACT/1250 SAT (CR+M), 3.25 or higher cumulative high school grade point average. Valedictorian Scholarship: $4,500; recipient must attend a Tennessee accredited or state approved high school from the following Mississippi counties: DeSoto, Marshall, Tate, Tunica, or Crittenden County in Arkansas. Students must also rank number one in the class and meet the admission requirements. Dean's Scholarship: $3,000; minimum 25 ACT/1130 SAT (CR+M), 3.00 or higher cumulative high school grade point average. Emerging Leaders Scholarship: $5,500; requires a separate application; minimum 21 ACT/ 980 SAT (CR+M) 3.00 or higher cumulative high school grade point average.

FINANCIAL AID PROCEDURES

Dates and Deadlines: Priority date 3/1; closing date 5/1. Applicants notified on a rolling basis starting 3/15; must reply by 8/1.

CONTACT

Karen Smith, Associate Director of Student Financial Aid
101 Wilder Tower, Memphis, TN 38152
(901) 678-4825

University of Tennessee: Chattanooga

Chattanooga, Tennessee
www.utc.edu   Federal Code: 003529

4-year public university in small city.
Enrollment: 10,058 undergrads, 12% part-time. 2,068 full-time freshmen.
Selectivity: Admits over 75% of applicants.

BASIC COSTS (2016-2017)

Tuition and fees: $8,544; out-of-state residents $26,438.
Room and board: $8,960.

FINANCIAL AID PICTURE (2016-2017)

Students with need: Out of 1,963 full-time freshmen who applied for aid, 1,273 were judged to have need. Of these, 1,263 received aid, and 241 had their full need met. Average financial aid package met 72% of need; average scholarship/grant was $8,382; average loan was $3,245. For part-time students, average financial aid package was $5,881.
Students without need: 276 full-time freshmen who did not demonstrate need for aid received scholarships/grants; average award was $3,468. No-need awards available for academics, alumni affiliation, art, athletics, leadership, music/drama, ROTC, state/district residency.
Scholarships offered: 49 full-time freshmen received athletic scholarships; average amount $14,473.

FINANCIAL AID PROCEDURES

Forms required: FAFSA.
Dates and Deadlines: Priority date 5/1; no closing date. Applicants notified on a rolling basis starting 3/1; must reply within 4 week(s) of notification.
Transfers: Applicants notified on a rolling basis starting 3/1; must reply within 6 week(s) of notification.

CONTACT

Jennifer Buckles, Director of Financial Aid
615 McCallie Avenue, Chattanooga, TN 37403
(423) 425-4677

University of Tennessee: Knoxville

Knoxville, Tennessee
www.utk.edu   Federal Code: 003530

4-year public university in large city.
Enrollment: 21,984 undergrads, 6% part-time. 4,840 full-time freshmen.
Selectivity: Admits over 75% of applicants.

BASIC COSTS (2016-2017)

Tuition and fees: $12,724; out-of-state residents $30,914.
Per-credit charge: $362; out-of-state residents $1,121.
Room and board: $10,238.

FINANCIAL AID PICTURE (2016-2017)

Students with need: Out of 4,585 full-time freshmen who applied for aid, 2,880 were judged to have need. Of these, 2,880 received aid, and 607 had their full need met. Average financial aid package met 61% of need; average scholarship/grant was $11,488; average loan was $5,206. For part-time students, average financial aid package was $12,760.
Students without need: This college awards aid only to students with need.
Scholarships offered: 89 full-time freshmen received athletic scholarships; average amount $29,904.
Additional info: Application priority date for scholarships 2/1.

FINANCIAL AID PROCEDURES

Forms required: FAFSA.
Dates and Deadlines: Priority date 2/15; no closing date. Applicants notified on a rolling basis starting 3/15; must reply within 3 week(s) of notification.
Transfers: Priority date 4/1; no deadline. Applicants notified on a rolling basis starting 4/15; must reply within 3 week(s) of notification.

CONTACT

Jeff Gerkin, Director of Financial Aid
320 Student Services Building, Circle Park, Knoxville, TN 37996-0230
(865) 974-1111

University of Tennessee: Martin

Martin, Tennessee
www.utm.edu   Federal Code: 003531

4-year public university in large town.
Enrollment: 5,576 undergrads, 11% part-time. 933 full-time freshmen.
Selectivity: Admits 50 to 75% of applicants.

BASIC COSTS (2016-2017)

Tuition and fees: $9,088; out-of-state residents $14,848.
Per-credit charge: $294; out-of-state residents $534.
Room and board: $5,788.

FINANCIAL AID PICTURE (2016-2017)

Students with need: Out of 902 full-time freshmen who applied for aid, 712 were judged to have need. Of these, 710 received aid, and 152 had their full need met. Average financial aid package met 42% of need; average scholarship/grant was $6,905; average loan was $3,509. For part-time students, average financial aid package was $7,505.
Students without need: This college awards aid only to students with need.
Scholarships offered: 71 full-time freshmen received athletic scholarships; average amount $10,735.

FINANCIAL AID PROCEDURES

Forms required: FAFSA.
Dates and Deadlines: Priority date 2/15; no closing date. Applicants notified on a rolling basis starting 3/15.

CONTACT
Amy Mistric, Assistant Director
201 Administration Building, Martin, TN 38238
(731) 881-7040

Vanderbilt University

Nashville, Tennessee
www.vanderbilt.edu

Federal Code: 003535
CSS Code: 1871

4-year private university in very large city.
Enrollment: 6,844 undergrads, 1% part-time. 1,601 full-time freshmen.
Selectivity: Admits less than 50% of applicants.

BASIC COSTS (2016-2017)
Tuition and fees: $46,110.
Per-credit charge: $1,854.
Room and board: $14,962.

FINANCIAL AID PICTURE (2016-2017)
Students with need: Out of 1,048 full-time freshmen who applied for aid, 854 were judged to have need. Of these, 850 received aid, and 850 had their full need met. Average financial aid package met 100% of need; average scholarship/grant was $42,430; average loan was $3,014.
Students without need: 147 full-time freshmen who did not demonstrate need for aid received scholarships/grants; average award was $21,873. No-need awards available for academics, athletics, leadership, music/drama, ROTC, state/district residency.
Scholarships offered: *Merit:* Scholarship programs; full-tuition plus summer stipends for study abroad, research or service projects; approximately 250 awarded. *Athletic:* 65 full-time freshmen received athletic scholarships; average amount $52,777.
Additional info: Financial aid packages awarded to incoming and returning undergraduate students are need-based loan-free.

FINANCIAL AID PROCEDURES
Forms required: FAFSA, CSS PROFILE.
Dates and Deadlines: Priority date 2/1; no closing date. Applicants notified by 4/1; must reply by 5/1.
Transfers: Priority date 2/1. Applicants notified by 4/1; must reply within 2 week(s) of notification.

CONTACT
Brent Tener, Director of Student Financial Aid
2305 West End Avenue, Nashville, TN 37203-1727
(615) 322-3591

Volunteer State Community College

Gallatin, Tennessee
www.volstate.edu

Federal Code: 009912

2-year public community and junior college in large town.
Enrollment: 6,973 undergrads, 33% part-time. 2,094 full-time freshmen.
Selectivity: Open admission; but selective for some programs.

BASIC COSTS (2016-2017)
Tuition and fees: $4,037; out-of-state residents $15,701.
Additional info: Tuition/fee waivers available for adults, minority students.

FINANCIAL AID PICTURE (2015-2016)
Students with need: Out of 2,045 full-time freshmen who applied for aid, 1,493 were judged to have need. Of these, 1,398 received aid, and 115 had their full need met. Average financial aid package met 58% of need; average scholarship/grant was $4,846; average loan was $2,399. For part-time students, average financial aid package was $3,918.

Students without need: 27 full-time freshmen who did not demonstrate need for aid received scholarships/grants; average award was $1,344. No-need awards available for academics, art, athletics, leadership, minority status, music/drama, state/district residency.
Scholarships offered: 1 full-time freshmen received athletic scholarships; average amount $1,250.

FINANCIAL AID PROCEDURES
Forms required: FAFSA, institutional form.
Dates and Deadlines: Priority date 4/15; no closing date. Applicants notified on a rolling basis; must reply within 2 week(s) of notification.
Transfers: No deadline. Applicants notified on a rolling basis; must reply within 2 week(s) of notification.

CONTACT
Sue Pedigo, Director of Financial Aid
1480 Nashville Pike, Gallatin, TN 37066-3188
(615) 452-8600 ext. 3456

Walters State Community College

Morristown, Tennessee
www.ws.edu

Federal Code: 008863

2-year public culinary school and community college in small city.
Enrollment: 4,553 undergrads.
Selectivity: Open admission; but selective for some programs.

BASIC COSTS (2016-2017)
Tuition and fees: $4,218; out-of-state residents $16,464.
Additional info: Tuition/fee waivers available for minority students.

FINANCIAL AID PICTURE
Students with need: Need-based aid available for full-time and part-time students.
Students without need: No-need awards available for academics, athletics, minority status, music/drama, state/district residency.

FINANCIAL AID PROCEDURES
Forms required: FAFSA.
Dates and Deadlines: Priority date 6/30; no closing date. Applicants notified by 5/10.
Transfers: No deadline. Applicants notified on a rolling basis.

CONTACT
Ashley Edens, Director of Financial Aid
500 South Davy Crockett Parkway, Morristown, TN 37813-6899
(423) 585-6811

Watkins College of Art, Design & Film

Nashville, Tennessee
www.watkins.edu

Federal Code: 031276

4-year private visual arts college in very large city.
Enrollment: 238 undergrads.
Selectivity: Admits over 75% of applicants.

BASIC COSTS (2016-2017)
Tuition and fees: $23,700.
Per-credit charge: $725.
Room only: $6,500.

FINANCIAL AID PICTURE
Students with need: Need-based aid available for full-time and part-time students. Work study available nights, weekends, and for part-time students.
Students without need: No-need awards available for academics, art, minority status.

FINANCIAL AID PROCEDURES
Forms required: FAFSA, institutional form.
Dates and Deadlines: Priority date 4/1; closing date 8/1. Applicants notified on a rolling basis starting 5/1; must reply within 2 week(s) of notification.

CONTACT
Regina Gilbert, Director of Financial Aid
2298 Rosa L. Parks Boulevard, Nashville, TN 37228
(615) 383-4848

Welch College
Nashville, Tennessee
www.welch.edu   Federal Code: 030018

4-year private Bible and teachers college in very large city, affiliated with the Free Will Baptists.
Enrollment: 238 undergrads, 12% part-time. 38 full-time freshmen.
Selectivity: Open admission.

BASIC COSTS (2016-2017)
Tuition and fees: $17,920.
Room and board: $7,260.

FINANCIAL AID PICTURE (2015-2016)
Students with need: Out of 38 full-time freshmen who applied for aid, 35 were judged to have need. Of these, 35 received aid. Average financial aid package met 43% of need; average scholarship/grant was $5,143; average loan was $3,500. For part-time students, average financial aid package was $4,789.
Students without need: 3 full-time freshmen who did not demonstrate need for aid received scholarships/grants; average award was $4,500. No-need awards available for academics, alumni affiliation, art, music/drama.
Scholarships offered: Presidential Honors Scholarship: $1,000 per semester, renewable for 8 semesters; high school GPA 3.5+, and ACT 29+, must maintain college GPA 3.25; awarded to four students yearly.

FINANCIAL AID PROCEDURES
Forms required: FAFSA, institutional form.
Dates and Deadlines: Priority date 4/15; no closing date. Applicants notified on a rolling basis starting 3/15; must reply within 2 week(s) of notification.
Transfers: No deadline.

CONTACT
Angie Edgmon, Financial Aid Coordinator
3606 West End Avenue, Nashville, TN 37205-2403
(615) 844-5214

Williamson College
Franklin, Tennessee
www.williamsoncc.edu   Federal Code: 035315

4-year private liberal arts college in small city, affiliated with the interdenominational tradition.
Enrollment: 69 undergrads.
Selectivity: Open admission; but selective for some programs.

BASIC COSTS (2016-2017)
Tuition and fees: $12,975.
Per-credit charge: $425.

FINANCIAL AID PICTURE
Students with need: Need-based aid available for full-time and part-time students.
Students without need: No-need awards available for academics, state/district residency.
Scholarships offered: Williamson is offering a new College Bound Scholarship for incoming freshman who are Tennessee residents, ACT/SAT scores

of 21/980, who maintain full-time enrollment with a 3.0GPA. Click here, http://www.williamsoncc.edu/scholarships/, for more information on our scholarship program.

FINANCIAL AID PROCEDURES
Forms required: FAFSA.
Dates and Deadlines: Priority date 5/1; no closing date. Applicants notified on a rolling basis starting 5/1; must reply within 2 week(s) of notification.
Transfers: No deadline. Applicants notified on a rolling basis starting 5/1; must reply within 2 week(s) of notification.

CONTACT
Laura Flowers, Director of Financial Aid
274 Mallory Station Road, Franklin, TN 37067
(615) 550-3170

Texas

Abilene Christian University
Abilene, Texas
www.acu.edu   Federal Code: 003537

4-year private university in small city, affiliated with the Church of Christ.
Enrollment: 3,719 undergrads, 5% part-time. 983 full-time freshmen.
Selectivity: Admits 50 to 75% of applicants.

BASIC COSTS (2016-2017)
Tuition and fees: $32,070.
Per-credit charge: $1,334.
Room and board: $9,730.

FINANCIAL AID PICTURE (2016-2017)
Students with need: Out of 911 full-time freshmen who applied for aid, 753 were judged to have need. Of these, 752 received aid, and 183 had their full need met. Average financial aid package met 68% of need; average scholarship/grant was $20,728; average loan was $3,498. For part-time students, average financial aid package was $10,111.
Students without need: 274 full-time freshmen who did not demonstrate need for aid received scholarships/grants; average award was $12,937. No-need awards available for academics, art, athletics, leadership, minority status, music/drama, religious affiliation, state/district residency.
Scholarships offered: *Merit:* Presidential Scholarship: half or full tuition; based on interview, ACT or SAT scores. Academic Scholarship: $3,000-$14,000; based on ACT/SAT, class rank, and performance in high school courses. Transfer Scholarship: $4,000-$8,000; based on GPA. *Athletic:* 38 full-time freshmen received athletic scholarships; average amount $20,987.
Additional info: Early estimate service available.

FINANCIAL AID PROCEDURES
Forms required: FAFSA.
Dates and Deadlines: Priority date 3/1; no closing date. Applicants notified on a rolling basis starting 4/1.

CONTACT
Student Financial Services
ACU Box 29000, Abilene, TX 79699
(325) 674-6850

Alvin Community College
Alvin, Texas
www.alvincollege.edu   Federal Code: 003539

2-year public community and liberal arts college in large town.
Enrollment: 5,658 undergrads.

Selectivity: Open admission; but selective for some programs.

BASIC COSTS (2016-2017)

Tuition and fees: $1,832; out-of-district residents $3,182; out-of-state residents $4,682.

Per-credit charge: $45; out-of-district residents $90; out-of-state residents $140.

FINANCIAL AID PICTURE

Students with need: Need-based aid available for full-time and part-time students. Work study available nights, weekends, and for part-time students.

Students without need: This college awards aid only to students with need.

FINANCIAL AID PROCEDURES

Forms required: FAFSA.

Dates and Deadlines: Applicants notified on a rolling basis; must reply within 2 week(s) of notification.

CONTACT

Dora Sims, Director of Student Financial Aid and Placement
3110 Mustang Road, Alvin, TX 77511-4898
(281) 756-3524

Angelina College

Lufkin, Texas
www.angelina.edu   Federal Code: 006661

2-year public community college in large town.

Enrollment: 5,301 undergrads, 67% part-time. 455 full-time freshmen.

Selectivity: Open admission; but selective for some programs.

BASIC COSTS (2016-2017)

Tuition and fees: $2,370; out-of-district residents $3,660; out-of-state residents $5,040.

Per-credit charge: $66; out-of-district residents $109; out-of-state residents $155.

Room and board: $5,600.

FINANCIAL AID PICTURE

Students with need: Need-based aid available for full-time and part-time students. Work study available nights.

Students without need: No-need awards available for academics, art, athletics, job skills, leadership, music/drama, state/district residency.

Scholarships offered: Angelina Challenge Award: $750 per semester; available to graduating seniors from the six Angelina County high schools; students must receive less than $1,000 in other need-based aid.

FINANCIAL AID PROCEDURES

Forms required: FAFSA.

Dates and Deadlines: Priority date 7/15; no closing date. Applicants notified on a rolling basis starting 3/15.

Transfers: No deadline. Applicants notified on a rolling basis starting 4/1. Transfer students must provide the financial aid office with an official transcript from all colleges previously attended. All transfer credit will be used to calculate maximum time frame for Title IV funds and for completion pace.

CONTACT

Susan Jones, Director of Financial Aid
PO Box 1768, Lufkin, TX 75902-1768
(936) 633-5291

Angelo State University

San Angelo, Texas
www.angelo.edu   Federal Code: 003541

4-year public university in small city.

Enrollment: 5,781 undergrads, 12% part-time. 1,333 full-time freshmen.

Selectivity: Admits 50 to 75% of applicants.

BASIC COSTS (2016-2017)

Tuition and fees: $8,038; out-of-state residents $20,278.

Per-credit charge: $165.2; out-of-state residents $573.2.

Room and board: $7,666.

FINANCIAL AID PICTURE (2015-2016)

Students with need: Out of 1,175 full-time freshmen who applied for aid, 845 were judged to have need. Of these, 842 received aid, and 147 had their full need met. Average financial aid package met 91% of need; average scholarship/grant was $3,601; average loan was $3,231. For part-time students, average financial aid package was $8,324.

Students without need: 251 full-time freshmen who did not demonstrate need for aid received scholarships/grants; average award was $4,177. No-need awards available for academics, art, athletics, leadership, music/drama, ROTC, state/district residency.

Scholarships offered: 70 full-time freshmen received athletic scholarships; average amount $4,592.

FINANCIAL AID PROCEDURES

Forms required: FAFSA.

Dates and Deadlines: Priority date 4/1; no closing date. Applicants notified on a rolling basis starting 4/1; must reply within 4 week(s) of notification.

Transfers: Applicants notified on a rolling basis starting 4/1; must reply within 4 week(s) of notification.

CONTACT

William Bloom, Financial Aid Director
ASU Station #11014, San Angelo, TX 76909-1014
(325) 942-2246

Arlington Baptist College

Arlington, Texas
www.arlingtonbaptistcollege.edu   Federal Code: 014305

4-year private Bible and teachers college in very large city, affiliated with the Baptist faith.

Enrollment: 185 undergrads, 15% part-time. 28 full-time freshmen.

Selectivity: Open admission.

BASIC COSTS (2016-2017)

Tuition and fees: $12,000.

Per-credit charge: $335.

Room and board: $5,800.

FINANCIAL AID PICTURE (2016-2017)

Students with need: Out of 24 full-time freshmen who applied for aid, 24 were judged to have need. Of these, 24 received aid. Average financial aid package met 90% of need. Need-based aid available for part-time students.

Students without need: This college awards aid only to students with need.

FINANCIAL AID PROCEDURES

Forms required: FAFSA, institutional form.

Dates and Deadlines: Priority date 5/17; no closing date. Applicants notified on a rolling basis starting 12/1; must reply by 8/15 or within 2 week(s) of notification.

Transfers: Priority date 4/16; closing date 6/16. Applicants notified by 12/1; must reply by 8/5.

CONTACT

David Ingram, Business Manager
3001 West Division Street, Arlington, TX 76012
(817) 461-8741 ext. 1706

Art Institute of Dallas

Dallas, Texas
www.aid.edu   Federal Code: 017360

4-year for-profit visual arts college in very large city.
Enrollment: 1,155 undergrads.
Selectivity: Open admission; but selective for some programs.

BASIC COSTS (2016-2017)
Tuition and fees: $21,960.
Per-credit charge: $488.

FINANCIAL AID PICTURE
Students with need: Need-based aid available for full-time students.

FINANCIAL AID PROCEDURES
Forms required: FAFSA.
Dates and Deadlines: Applicants notified on a rolling basis.

CONTACT
Jeff Clark, Financial Aid Director
Two North Park, 8080 Park Lane, Dallas, TX 75231
(214) 692-8080

Austin College

Sherman, Texas
www.austincollege.edu   Federal Code: 003543

4-year private liberal arts and teachers college in small city, affiliated with the Presbyterian Church (USA).
Enrollment: 1,274 undergrads. 345 full-time freshmen.
Selectivity: Admits 50 to 75% of applicants.

BASIC COSTS (2016-2017)
Tuition and fees: $37,340.
Room and board: $12,082.

FINANCIAL AID PICTURE (2016-2017)
Students with need: Out of 298 full-time freshmen who applied for aid, 254 were judged to have need. Of these, 254 received aid, and 114 had their full need met. Average financial aid package met 95% of need; average scholarship/grant was $30,923; average loan was $3,528. Need-based aid available for part-time students.
Students without need: 89 full-time freshmen who did not demonstrate need for aid received scholarships/grants; average award was $24,248. No-need awards available for academics, alumni affiliation, art, leadership, music/drama, religious affiliation.

FINANCIAL AID PROCEDURES
Forms required: FAFSA.
Dates and Deadlines: Priority date 3/1; no closing date. Applicants notified on a rolling basis starting 12/1; must reply by 5/1.
Transfers: Applicants notified on a rolling basis starting 3/1; must reply by 5/1.

CONTACT
Laurie Coulter, Executive Director of Financial Aid
900 North Grand Avenue, Suite 6N, Sherman, TX 75090-4400
(903) 813-2900

Austin Community College

Austin, Texas
www.austincc.edu   Federal Code: 012015

2-year public community college in very large city.
Enrollment: 41,543 undergrads. 2,099 full-time freshmen.

Selectivity: Open admission; but selective for some programs.

BASIC COSTS (2016-2017)
Tuition and fees: $2,550; out-of-district residents $10,890; out-of-state residents $13,080.
Per-credit charge: $67; out-of-district residents $345; out-of-state residents $418.
Additional info: In-district and Out-of-district students pay the same tuition, but there is an additional Out-of-district fee that is charged to Out-of-district students.

FINANCIAL AID PICTURE (2015-2016)
Students with need: Out of 1,220 full-time freshmen who applied for aid, 973 were judged to have need. Of these, 876 received aid. Need-based aid available for part-time students.

FINANCIAL AID PROCEDURES
Forms required: FAFSA.
Dates and Deadlines: Priority date 4/1; no closing date. Applicants notified on a rolling basis starting 3/1; must reply within 2 week(s) of notification.

CONTACT
Terry Bazan, Director, Financial Assistance
PO Box 15306, Austin, TX 78761-5306
(512) 223-7550

Austin Graduate School of Theology

Austin, Texas
www.austingrad.edu   Federal Code: 017322

Upper-division private Bible and seminary college in very large city, affiliated with the Church of Christ.
Enrollment: 20 undergrads, 80% part-time.

BASIC COSTS (2016-2017)
Tuition and fees: $10,850.
Per-credit charge: $350.

FINANCIAL AID PICTURE
Students with need: Need-based aid available for full-time and part-time students. Work study available nights.
Students without need: No-need awards available for academics, leadership.
Additional info: Generous scholarships for students taking at least 12 hours. Federal work study program available. Institutional work study program (need-based) available.

FINANCIAL AID PROCEDURES
Forms required: FAFSA, institutional form.
Dates and Deadlines: Priority date 7/1; closing date 8/1.
Transfers: No deadline.

CONTACT
Dave Arthur, Vice President
7640 Guadalupe Street, Austin, TX 78752-1333
(512) 476-2772

Baylor University

Waco, Texas
www.baylor.edu   Federal Code: 003545

4-year private university in small city, affiliated with the Baptist faith.
Enrollment: 14,309 undergrads, 2% part-time. 3,496 full-time freshmen.
Selectivity: Admits less than 50% of applicants.

BASIC COSTS (2017-2018)
Tuition and fees: $43,970.
Per-credit charge: $1,650.

Room and board: $12,163.

FINANCIAL AID PICTURE (2016-2017)

Students with need: Out of 2,687 full-time freshmen who applied for aid, 2,038 were judged to have need. Of these, 2,037 received aid, and 341 had their full need met. Average financial aid package met 69% of need; average scholarship/grant was $24,060; average loan was $2,564. For part-time students, average financial aid package was $16,427.

Students without need: 1,340 full-time freshmen who did not demonstrate need for aid received scholarships/grants; average award was $14,716. No-need awards available for academics, art, athletics, leadership, music/drama, religious affiliation, ROTC.

Scholarships offered: *Merit:* Regent's Scholarship; full tuition; limited to National Merit finalists who list Baylor as first choice; unlimited number. President's Scholarship; Provost's Scholarship; Dean's Scholarship also available. *Athletic:* 73 full-time freshmen received athletic scholarships; average amount $33,569.

FINANCIAL AID PROCEDURES

Forms required: FAFSA. CSS PROFILE accepted but not required for international applicants.

Dates and Deadlines: Priority date 2/1; no closing date. Applicants notified on a rolling basis starting 12/15; must reply by 5/1 or within 2 week(s) of notification.

Transfers: No deadline. Applicants notified on a rolling basis starting 12/15; must reply by 5/1 or within 2 week(s) of notification.

CONTACT

Assistant Vice President
One Bear Place #97056, Waco, TX 76798-7056
(800) 229-5678

Blinn College

Brenham, Texas
www.blinn.edu   Federal Code: 003549

2-year public community college in large town.
Enrollment: 16,851 undergrads, 44% part-time. 4,237 full-time freshmen.
Selectivity: Open admission; but selective for some programs.

BASIC COSTS (2016-2017)

Tuition and fees: $3,030; out-of-district residents $4,740; out-of-state residents $9,330.
Per-credit charge: $50; out-of-district residents $107; out-of-state residents $260.
Room and board: $6,250.

FINANCIAL AID PICTURE

Students with need: Need-based aid available for full-time and part-time students.

FINANCIAL AID PROCEDURES

Forms required: FAFSA, institutional form.
Dates and Deadlines: Priority date 6/1; no closing date. Applicants notified on a rolling basis starting 7/1.
Transfers: Applicants notified on a rolling basis starting 5/15.

CONTACT

Brent Williford, Dean of Financial Aid and Veteran Services
902 College Avenue, Brenham, TX 77833
(979) 830-4149

Brazosport College

Lake Jackson, Texas
www.brazosport.edu   Federal Code: 007287

2-year public community college in large town.
Enrollment: 4,173 undergrads.

Selectivity: Open admission; but selective for some programs.

BASIC COSTS (2016-2017)

Tuition and fees: $2,505; out-of-district residents $3,525; out-of-state residents $5,145.
Per-credit charge: $62; out-of-district residents $96; out-of-state residents $150.

FINANCIAL AID PICTURE

Students with need: Need-based aid available for full-time and part-time students.
Students without need: No-need awards available for academics, art, job skills, leadership, music/drama, state/district residency.

FINANCIAL AID PROCEDURES

Forms required: FAFSA, institutional form.
Dates and Deadlines: Priority date 7/1; no closing date. Applicants notified on a rolling basis starting 5/1.

CONTACT

Kay Wright, Director of Financial Aid
500 College Drive, Lake Jackson, TX 77566
(979) 230-3377

Cedar Valley College

Lancaster, Texas
www.cedarvalleycollege.edu   Federal Code: 014035

2-year public community college in large town.
Enrollment: 3,681 undergrads. 399 full-time freshmen.
Selectivity: Open admission.

BASIC COSTS (2016-2017)

Tuition and fees: $1,770; out-of-district residents $3,330; out-of-state residents $5,220.
Per-credit charge: $59; out-of-district residents $111; out-of-state residents $200.

FINANCIAL AID PICTURE (2015-2016)

Students with need: Out of 399 full-time freshmen who applied for aid, 273 were judged to have need. Of these, 273 received aid.

FINANCIAL AID PROCEDURES

Forms required: FAFSA.
Dates and Deadlines: Priority date 5/1; no closing date. Applicants notified on a rolling basis.

CONTACT

Cathy Adams, Director of Financial Aid
3030 North Dallas Avenue, Lancaster, TX 75134
(972) 587-2599

Central Texas College

Killeen, Texas
www.ctcd.edu   Federal Code: 004003

2-year public community college in small city.
Enrollment: 10,711 undergrads, 81% part-time. 532 full-time freshmen.
Selectivity: Open admission; but selective for some programs.

BASIC COSTS (2016-2017)

Tuition and fees: $2,280; out-of-district residents $2,940; out-of-state residents $6,420.
Per-credit charge: $76; out-of-district residents $98; out-of-state residents $214.
Room and board: $4,800.

FINANCIAL AID PICTURE

Students with need: Need-based aid available for full-time and part-time students. Work study available nights, weekends, and for part-time students.
Students without need: This college awards aid only to students with need.

FINANCIAL AID PROCEDURES

Forms required: FAFSA, institutional form.
Dates and Deadlines: Closing date 6/1. Applicants notified on a rolling basis starting 3/1; must reply within 4 week(s) of notification.

CONTACT

Annabelle Smith, Associate Dean, Financial Aid and Veteran Services
Central Texas College, Killeen, TX 76540-1800
(254) 526-1508

Cisco College
Cisco, Texas
www.cisco.edu   Federal Code: 003553

2-year public community college in small town.
Enrollment: 3,244 undergrads.
Selectivity: Open admission.

BASIC COSTS (2016-2017)

Tuition and fees: $2,940; out-of-district residents $3,840; out-of-state residents $4,920.
Per-credit charge: $98; out-of-district residents $128; out-of-state residents $164.
Room and board: $4,236.

FINANCIAL AID PICTURE (2015-2016)

Students with need: 64% of average financial aid package awarded as scholarships/grants, 36% awarded as loans/jobs.
Students without need: No-need awards available for athletics, music/drama.
Additional info: Financial aid application deadline July 1 for Fall semester, November 1 for Spring semester.

FINANCIAL AID PROCEDURES

Forms required: FAFSA.
Dates and Deadlines: Closing date 7/1. Applicants notified on a rolling basis starting 8/15.
Transfers: Transfer students must submit school code change on the FAFSA to have Student Aid Report sent to Cisco College. Students selected for verification must complete the verification process with college before financial aid can be awarded even if they have award letter from previous institution. Eligibility for financial assistance will be determined once the Student Aid Report is received.

CONTACT

Linda Sellers, Director of Financial Aid
101 College Heights, Cisco, TX 76437
(254) 442-5151

Clarendon College
Clarendon, Texas
www.clarendoncollege.edu   Federal Code: 003554

2-year public community college in rural community.
Enrollment: 1,482 undergrads.
Selectivity: Open admission; but selective for some programs.

BASIC COSTS (2016-2017)

Tuition and fees: $3,030; out-of-district residents $3,720; out-of-state residents $4,650.
Room and board: $4,176.

FINANCIAL AID PICTURE

Students with need: Need-based aid available for full-time and part-time students. Work study available nights, weekends, and for part-time students.
Students without need: No-need awards available for academics, art, athletics, leadership, music/drama, state/district residency.
Scholarships offered: Named and endowed scholarships available based on academic achievement, need, and/or other requirements as stipulated by the scholarship donor.

FINANCIAL AID PROCEDURES

Forms required: FAFSA, institutional form.
Dates and Deadlines: Priority date 8/1; no closing date. Applicants notified on a rolling basis starting 5/15; must reply by 8/15 or within 2 week(s) of notification.
Transfers: No deadline. Applicants notified on a rolling basis starting 11/15; must reply within 4 week(s) of notification.

CONTACT

Susan Russell, Associate Dean of Financial Aid
PO Box 968, Clarendon, TX 79226
(806) 874-3571 ext. 112

Coastal Bend College
Beeville, Texas
www.coastalbend.edu   Federal Code: 003546

2-year public community college in large town.
Enrollment: 5,041 undergrads.
Selectivity: Open admission; but selective for some programs.

BASIC COSTS (2016-2017)

Tuition and fees: $2,646; out-of-district residents $4,506; out-of-state residents $4,956.
Per-credit charge: $70; out-of-district residents $132; out-of-state residents $147.
Room and board: $5,200.

FINANCIAL AID PICTURE

Students with need: Need-based aid available for full-time and part-time students.
Students without need: No-need awards available for academics, leadership.

FINANCIAL AID PROCEDURES

Forms required: FAFSA, institutional form.
Dates and Deadlines: Priority date 5/1; no closing date. Applicants notified on a rolling basis starting 5/1; must reply within 2 week(s) of notification.
Transfers: No deadline. Applicants notified on a rolling basis.

CONTACT

Nora Morales, Director of Financial Aid
3800 Charco Road, Beeville, TX 78102
(361) 354-2238

College of the Mainland
Texas City, Texas
www.com.edu   Federal Code: 007096

2-year public community and technical college in large town.
Enrollment: 2,784 undergrads, 72% part-time. 194 full-time freshmen.
Selectivity: Open admission; but selective for some programs.

BASIC COSTS (2016-2017)

Tuition and fees: $1,773; out-of-district residents $2,973; out-of-state residents $3,873.

FINANCIAL AID PICTURE

Students with need: Need-based aid available for full-time and part-time students. Work study available nights, weekends, and for part-time students.
Students without need: This college awards aid only to students with need.

FINANCIAL AID PROCEDURES

Forms required: FAFSA.

Dates and Deadlines: Priority date 6/1; no closing date. Applicants notified on a rolling basis starting 5/1; must reply within 4 week(s) of notification.

CONTACT

Carl Gordon, Director, Student Financial Services
1200 Amburn Road, Texas City, TX 77591
(409) 933-8274

Collin County Community College District
McKinney, Texas
www.collin.edu   Federal Code: 016792

2-year public community college in large city.
Enrollment: 24,894 undergrads, 62% part-time. 3,398 full-time freshmen.
Selectivity: Open admission; but selective for some programs.

BASIC COSTS (2017-2018)
Tuition and fees: $1,264; out-of-district residents $2,494; out-of-state residents $4,284.
Per-credit charge: $41; out-of-district residents $82; out-of-state residents $142.

FINANCIAL AID PICTURE (2015-2016)
Students with need: Need-based aid available for full-time and part-time students. Work study available nights, weekends, and for part-time students.
Students without need: No-need awards available for academics, art, athletics, job skills, leadership, minority status, music/drama, state/district residency.

FINANCIAL AID PROCEDURES
Forms required: FAFSA, institutional form.
Dates and Deadlines: Priority date 6/1; no closing date. Applicants notified on a rolling basis starting 5/1; must reply within 2 week(s) of notification.
Transfers: Applicants must have cumulative GPA of 2.0 and less than 90 transferable credit hours.

CONTACT
Alan Pixley, Director, Financial Aid & Veterans Affairs
2800 East Spring Creek Parkway, Plano, TX 75074
(972) 881-5760

Commonwealth Institute of Funeral Service
Houston, Texas
www.commonwealthinst.org   Federal Code: 003556

2-year private school of mortuary science in very large city.
Enrollment: 226 undergrads.

BASIC COSTS (2016-2017)
Tuition and fees: $15,620.

FINANCIAL AID PICTURE
Students with need: Need-based aid available for full-time and part-time students.
Students without need: This college awards aid only to students with need.

Scholarships offered: Scholarship awards: $250-$500 based on funds available; recipients selected on academic achievement, leadership and professional promise, as well as any stipulations by the donor, by a committee of Commonwealth Institute graduate employers, alumni, and benefactors.

FINANCIAL AID PROCEDURES
Forms required: FAFSA.
Dates and Deadlines: Priority date 8/31; no closing date. Applicants notified on a rolling basis starting 7/12.

CONTACT
Jessika Jenkins, Director of Financial Aid
415 Barren Springs Drive, Houston, TX 77090-5913
(281) 873-0262

Concordia University Texas
Austin, Texas
www.concordia.edu   Federal Code: 003557

4-year private university and liberal arts college in very large city, affiliated with the Lutheran Church - Missouri Synod.
Enrollment: 1,525 undergrads. 238 full-time freshmen.

BASIC COSTS (2017-2018)
Tuition and fees: $30,600.
Per-credit charge: $970.
Room and board: $10,406.
Additional info: Tuition/fee waivers available for adults.

FINANCIAL AID PICTURE (2016-2017)
Students with need: Out of 164 full-time freshmen who applied for aid, 151 were judged to have need. Of these, 122 received aid, and 21 had their full need met. Average financial aid package met 79% of need; average scholarship/grant was $19,966; average loan was $5,913. For part-time students, average financial aid package was $9,680.
Students without need: 26 full-time freshmen who did not demonstrate need for aid received scholarships/grants; average award was $15,327. No-need awards available for academics, alumni affiliation, leadership, music/drama, religious affiliation.

FINANCIAL AID PROCEDURES
Forms required: FAFSA.
Dates and Deadlines: Priority date 5/1; no closing date. Applicants notified on a rolling basis starting 2/15; must reply within 3 week(s) of notification.
Transfers: Priority date 5/1; no deadline. Applicants notified on a rolling basis starting 2/15; must reply within 3 week(s) of notification. Academic transcripts from all previously attended trade/technical schools and colleges/universities required.

CONTACT
Russell Jeffrey, Director, Student Financial Services
11400 Concordia University Drive, Austin, TX 78726
(512) 313-4681

Criswell College
Dallas, Texas
www.criswell.edu

4-year private Bible and seminary college in very large city, affiliated with the Southern Baptist Convention.
Enrollment: 222 undergrads, 43% part-time. 12 full-time freshmen.

BASIC COSTS (2016-2017)
Tuition and fees: $11,020.
Per-credit charge: $345.

FINANCIAL AID PICTURE
Students with need: Work study available nights.

FINANCIAL AID PROCEDURES
Forms required: FAFSA, institutional form.
Dates and Deadlines: Closing date 4/15. Applicants notified on a rolling basis.

CONTACT
Ta Lisa Pollard, Director of Financial Aid
4010 Gaston Avenue, Dallas, TX 75246-1537
(214) 818-1393

Culinary Institute LeNotre
Houston, Texas
www.culinaryinstitute.edu   Federal Code: 037233

2-year for-profit culinary school and technical college in very large city.
Enrollment: 255 undergrads. 255 full-time freshmen.
Selectivity: Open admission.

BASIC COSTS (2016-2017)
Tuition and fees: $15,828.
Per-credit charge: $11,988.

FINANCIAL AID PICTURE (2015-2016)
Students with need: Out of 211 full-time freshmen who applied for aid, 211 were judged to have need. Of these, 211 received aid.
Students without need: 34 full-time freshmen who did not demonstrate need for aid received scholarships/grants; average award was $2,000.

FINANCIAL AID PROCEDURES
Forms required: FAFSA.
Transfers: No deadline.

CONTACT
Elsa Pina, Financial Aid Manager
7070 Allensby Street, Houston, TX 77022
(713) 692-0077

Dallas Baptist University
Dallas, Texas
www.dbu.edu   Federal Code: 003560

4-year private university in very large city, affiliated with the Baptist faith.
Enrollment: 3,109 undergrads, 24% part-time. 522 full-time freshmen.
Selectivity: Admits less than 50% of applicants.

BASIC COSTS (2016-2017)
Tuition and fees: $26,180.
Per-credit charge: $846.
Room and board: $7,533.

FINANCIAL AID PICTURE (2016-2017)
Students with need: Out of 506 full-time freshmen who applied for aid, 376 were judged to have need. Of these, 373 received aid, and 136 had their full need met. Average financial aid package met 60% of need; average scholarship/grant was $4,008; average loan was $3,321. For part-time students, average financial aid package was $5,860.
Students without need: 119 full-time freshmen who did not demonstrate need for aid received scholarships/grants; average award was $9,994. No-need awards available for academics, athletics, job skills, leadership, music/drama, religious affiliation.
Scholarships offered: 26 full-time freshmen received athletic scholarships; average amount $17,611.

FINANCIAL AID PROCEDURES
Forms required: FAFSA, institutional form.

Dates and Deadlines: Applicants notified on a rolling basis starting 2/1.
Transfers: No deadline. Applicants notified on a rolling basis.

CONTACT
Lee Ferguson, Director of Financial Aid
3000 Mountain Creek Parkway, Dallas, TX 75211-9299
(214) 333-5363

Dallas Christian College
Dallas, Texas
www.dallas.edu   Federal Code: 006941

4-year private Bible college in very large city, affiliated with the nondenominational tradition.
Enrollment: 252 undergrads, 25% part-time. 30 full-time freshmen.

BASIC COSTS (2016-2017)
Tuition and fees: $16,420.
Per-credit charge: $517.
Room and board: $8,420.

FINANCIAL AID PICTURE
Students with need: Need-based aid available for full-time and part-time students.
Students without need: This college awards aid only to students with need.

FINANCIAL AID PROCEDURES
Forms required: FAFSA, institutional form.
Dates and Deadlines: Priority date 5/15; no closing date. Applicants notified on a rolling basis; must reply within 2 week(s) of notification.
Transfers: Priority date 5/1; no deadline. Applicants notified on a rolling basis; must reply within 2 week(s) of notification.

CONTACT
Breanda Gillaspie, Financial Aid Director
2700 Christian Parkway, Dallas, TX 75234-7299
(972) 241-3371 ext. 135

Del Mar College
Corpus Christi, Texas
www.delmar.edu   Federal Code: 003563

2-year public community college in large city.
Enrollment: 7,713 undergrads, 72% part-time. 422 full-time freshmen.
Selectivity: Open admission; but selective for some programs.

BASIC COSTS (2016-2017)
Tuition and fees: $2,914; out-of-district residents $4,414; out-of-state residents $5,524.
Per-credit charge: $56; out-of-district residents $106; out-of-state residents $143.

FINANCIAL AID PICTURE (2015-2016)
Students with need: 81% of average financial aid package awarded as scholarships/grants, 19% awarded as loans/jobs. Need-based aid available for part-time students. Work study available nights, weekends, and for part-time students.

FINANCIAL AID PROCEDURES
Forms required: FAFSA, institutional form.
Dates and Deadlines: Priority date 5/1; no closing date. Applicants notified on a rolling basis starting 7/1; must reply within 2 week(s) of notification.

CONTACT
Nancy Briseno, Director of Financial Aid Services
101 Baldwin Boulevard, Corpus Christi, TX 78404-3897
(361) 698-1293

DeVry University: Irving

Dallas, Texas
www.devry.edu   Federal Code: 010139

4-year for-profit university in small city.
Enrollment: 403 undergrads, 59% part-time. 6 full-time freshmen.

BASIC COSTS (2016-2017)
Tuition and fees: $17,512.
Per-credit charge: $609.

FINANCIAL AID PICTURE
Students with need: Need-based aid available for full-time and part-time students.
Students without need: This college awards aid only to students with need.

CONTACT
Nga Phan, Director, Financial Aid
4800 Regent Boulevard, Suite 200, Dallas, TX 75063-2439
(972) 929-9740

East Texas Baptist University

Marshall, Texas
www.etbu.edu   Federal Code: 003564

4-year private university and liberal arts college in large town, affiliated with the Baptist faith.
Enrollment: 1,218 undergrads, 3% part-time. 340 full-time freshmen.
Selectivity: Admits 50 to 75% of applicants.

BASIC COSTS (2016-2017)
Tuition and fees: $24,700.
Per-credit charge: $790.
Room and board: $8,709.

FINANCIAL AID PICTURE (2015-2016)
Students with need: Out of 324 full-time freshmen who applied for aid, 287 were judged to have need. Of these, 287 received aid, and 28 had their full need met. Average financial aid package met 28% of need; average scholarship/grant was $6,319; average loan was $3,194. For part-time students, average financial aid package was $6,458.
Students without need: 51 full-time freshmen who did not demonstrate need for aid received scholarships/grants; average award was $11,579. No-need awards available for academics, alumni affiliation, leadership, music/drama, religious affiliation, state/district residency.

FINANCIAL AID PROCEDURES
Forms required: FAFSA, institutional form.
Dates and Deadlines: Priority date 6/1; no closing date. Applicants notified on a rolling basis starting 1/1.
Transfers: Applicants notified on a rolling basis starting 1/1.

CONTACT
Tommy Young, Director of Financial Aid
One Tiger Drive, Marshall, TX 75670-1498
(903) 923-2138

Eastfield College

Mesquite, Texas
www.efc.dcccd.edu   Federal Code: 008510

2-year public community and liberal arts college in small city.
Enrollment: 11,369 undergrads, 72% part-time. 510 full-time freshmen.
Selectivity: Open admission.

BASIC COSTS (2016-2017)
Tuition and fees: $1,770; out-of-district residents $3,330; out-of-state residents $5,220.
Per-credit charge: $59; out-of-district residents $111; out-of-state residents $200.

FINANCIAL AID PICTURE
Students with need: Need-based aid available for full-time and part-time students. Work study available nights, weekends, and for part-time students.
Scholarships offered: Lecroy Scholars Program; $600 per semester; based on demonstrated church, community, or academic leadership and 3.0 GPA; requires enrollment in at least 12 credit hours; 5-10 awarded. Erin Tierney Kramp Encouragement Program; $600 per semester; based on demonstrated courage in the face of adversity, moral character, leadership, and high academic standards; requires enrollment in 8 hours for awarding semester, and maintenance of high academic standards; 2 awarded.

FINANCIAL AID PROCEDURES
Forms required: FAFSA, institutional form.
Dates and Deadlines: Priority date 5/1; no closing date. Applicants notified on a rolling basis starting 4/15.

CONTACT
Karen Lazarz, Director of Financial Aid
3737 Motley Drive, Mesquite, TX 75150
(972) 587-7040

El Centro College

Dallas, Texas
www.elcentrocollege.edu   Federal Code: 004453

2-year public community college in very large city.
Enrollment: 8,212 undergrads.
Selectivity: Open admission; but selective for some programs.

BASIC COSTS (2016-2017)
Tuition and fees: $1,770; out-of-district residents $3,330; out-of-state residents $5,220.
Per-credit charge: $59; out-of-district residents $111; out-of-state residents $200.
Additional info: Tuition/fee waivers available for minority students, unemployed or children of unemployed.

FINANCIAL AID PICTURE
Students with need: Need-based aid available for full-time and part-time students.
Additional info: Interview required for financial aid applicants.

FINANCIAL AID PROCEDURES
Forms required: FAFSA.
Dates and Deadlines: Priority date 5/1; no closing date. Applicants notified on a rolling basis; must reply within 2 week(s) of notification.
Transfers: Financial aid transcript may be required from previous institutions attended.

CONTACT
Pamela Lucas, Director
801 Main Street, Dallas, TX 75202
(214) 860-2099

El Paso Community College

El Paso, Texas
www.epcc.edu   Federal Code: 010387

2-year public community college in very large city.
Enrollment: 27,488 undergrads.
Selectivity: Open admission; but selective for some programs.

PART III: FINANCIAL AID COLLEGE BY COLLEGE

BASIC COSTS (2016-2017)

Tuition and fees: $3,420; out-of-state residents $5,640.

Per-credit charge: $94; out-of-state residents $168.

Additional info: Out of state student per credit hour rate is $200 for 1st credit hour, $336 for 2 credit hours, $504 for 3 credit hours. Each additional credit hour is $168.

FINANCIAL AID PICTURE

Students with need: Work study available nights, weekends, and for part-time students.

Students without need: No-need awards available for academics, athletics.

FINANCIAL AID PROCEDURES

Forms required: FAFSA, institutional form.

Dates and Deadlines: Priority date 5/1; no closing date. Applicants notified on a rolling basis starting 7/1; must reply within 2 week(s) of notification.

CONTACT

Linda Gonzalez-Hensgen, Director of Student Financial Services

Box 20500, El Paso, TX 79998

(915) 831-2566

Frank Phillips College

Borger, Texas

www.fpctx.edu   Federal Code: 003568

2-year public community and junior college in large town.

Enrollment: 569 undergrads.

Selectivity: Open admission.

BASIC COSTS (2016-2017)

Tuition and fees: $2,838; out-of-district residents $3,520; out-of-state residents $3,850.

Room and board: $5,040.

FINANCIAL AID PICTURE

Students with need: Need-based aid available for full-time and part-time students. Work study available nights, weekends, and for part-time students.

Students without need: No-need awards available for academics, athletics, music/drama, state/district residency.

Additional info: Some Texas fire department and police department personnel, active duty military personnel, children of military missing in action may qualify for reduced or waived tuition. Out-of-state tuition waived for students living in Oklahoma counties adjacent to Texas.

FINANCIAL AID PROCEDURES

Forms required: FAFSA, institutional form.

Dates and Deadlines: Closing date 7/1. Applicants notified on a rolling basis; must reply within 2 week(s) of notification.

Transfers: No deadline. Applicants notified on a rolling basis.

CONTACT

Beverly Fields, Director of Financial Services

Box 5118, Borger, TX 79008-5118

(806) 457-4200 ext. 796

Galveston College

Galveston, Texas

www.gc.edu   Federal Code: 004972

2-year public community college in small city.

Enrollment: 1,729 undergrads, 69% part-time. 129 full-time freshmen.

Selectivity: Open admission; but selective for some programs.

BASIC COSTS (2016-2017)

Tuition and fees: $1,900; out-of-district residents $2,380; out-of-state residents $4,270.

FINANCIAL AID PICTURE

Students with need: Need-based aid available for full-time and part-time students.

Students without need: This college awards aid only to students with need.

FINANCIAL AID PROCEDURES

Forms required: FAFSA.

Dates and Deadlines: Priority date 6/7; no closing date. Applicants notified on a rolling basis starting 6/1.

CONTACT

Ron Crumedy, V.P. of Student Services/Director of Finanical Aid

4015 Avenue Q, Galveston, TX 77550-7447

(409) 944-1235

Grayson College

Denison, Texas

www.grayson.edu   Federal Code: 003570

2-year public community and technical college in large town.

Enrollment: 4,400 undergrads.

Selectivity: Open admission; but selective for some programs.

BASIC COSTS (2016-2017)

Tuition and fees: $2,310; out-of-district residents $3,450; out-of-state residents $4,830.

Per-credit charge: $49; out-of-district residents $87; out-of-state residents $133.

Room and board: $5,560.

Additional info: Tuition at time of enrollment locked for 2 years.

FINANCIAL AID PICTURE

Students with need: Need-based aid available for full-time and part-time students. Work study available nights.

Students without need: No-need awards available for academics, alumni affiliation, art, athletics, job skills, leadership, minority status, music/drama, state/district residency.

Additional info: Short term loans available.

FINANCIAL AID PROCEDURES

Forms required: FAFSA.

Dates and Deadlines: Priority date 6/1; no closing date. Applicants notified on a rolling basis; must reply within 5 week(s) of notification.

Transfers: No deadline. Applicants notified on a rolling basis; must reply within 5 week(s) of notification.

CONTACT

Donna King, Director of Financial Aid

6101 Grayson Drive, Denison, TX 75020

(903) 463-8642

Hallmark University

San Antonio, Texas

www.hallmarkuniversity.edu   Federal Code: 010509

4-year private university in very large city.

Enrollment: 856 undergrads.

Selectivity: Open admission; but selective for some programs.

BASIC COSTS (2017-2018)

Additional info: Tuition and fees vary by program.

FINANCIAL AID PICTURE

Students with need: Need-based aid available for full-time students.

FINANCIAL AID PROCEDURES

Forms required: FAFSA, institutional form.

Dates and Deadlines: Applicants notified on a rolling basis.
Transfers: No deadline. Applicants notified on a rolling basis.

CONTACT
Grace Calixto, Director of Financial Planning
Hallmark University, San Antonio, TX 78230-1736
(210) 690-9000 ext. 211

Hardin-Simmons University
Abilene, Texas
www.hsutx.edu   Federal Code: 003571

4-year private university in small city, affiliated with the Baptist faith.
Enrollment: 1,621 undergrads, 6% part-time. 393 full-time freshmen.
Selectivity: Admits over 75% of applicants.

BASIC COSTS (2017-2018)
Tuition and fees: $27,440.
Room and board: $8,420.
Additional info: Tuition at time of enrollment locked for 4 years.

FINANCIAL AID PICTURE (2016-2017)
Students with need: Out of 392 full-time freshmen who applied for aid, 301 were judged to have need. Of these, 301 received aid, and 107 had their full need met. Average financial aid package met 92% of need; average scholarship/grant was $8,882; average loan was $2,981. For part-time students, average financial aid package was $11,944.
Students without need: 92 full-time freshmen who did not demonstrate need for aid received scholarships/grants; average award was $14,115. No-need awards available for academics, alumni affiliation, art, leadership, minority status, music/drama, religious affiliation.

FINANCIAL AID PROCEDURES
Forms required: FAFSA.
Dates and Deadlines: Priority date 3/1; no closing date. Applicants notified on a rolling basis starting 2/1; must reply by 6/1.
Transfers: No deadline. Applicants notified on a rolling basis starting 2/1; must reply within 2 week(s) of notification.

CONTACT
Bridget Moore, Director of Financial Aid & Scholarships
PO Box 16050, Abilene, TX 79698-0001
(325) 670-1206

Hill College
Hillsboro, Texas
www.hillcollege.edu   Federal Code: 003573

2-year public community college in small town.
Enrollment: 4,098 undergrads.
Selectivity: Open admission; but selective for some programs.

BASIC COSTS (2016-2017)
Tuition and fees: $2,370; out-of-district residents $3,120; out-of-state residents $3,520.
Room and board: $3,850.

FINANCIAL AID PICTURE
Students with need: Need-based aid available for full-time and part-time students.
Students without need: No-need awards available for academics, athletics, music/drama.

FINANCIAL AID PROCEDURES
Forms required: FAFSA, institutional form.
Dates and Deadlines: Closing date 7/31. Applicants notified on a rolling basis.

CONTACT
Susan Russell, Director of Student Financial Aid
112 Lamar Drive, Hillsboro, TX 76645
(254) 659-7600

Houston Baptist University
Houston, Texas
www.hbu.edu   Federal Code: 003576

4-year private university and liberal arts college in very large city, affiliated with the Baptist faith.
Enrollment: 2,313 undergrads, 7% part-time. 576 full-time freshmen.
Selectivity: Admits less than 50% of applicants.

BASIC COSTS (2016-2017)
Tuition and fees: $30,800.
Per-credit charge: $1,200.
Room and board: $7,858.

FINANCIAL AID PICTURE (2016-2017)
Students with need: Out of 507 full-time freshmen who applied for aid, 466 were judged to have need. Of these, 466 received aid, and 119 had their full need met. Average financial aid package met 78% of need; average scholarship/grant was $20,660; average loan was $5,293. For part-time students, average financial aid package was $15,598.
Students without need: 108 full-time freshmen who did not demonstrate need for aid received scholarships/grants; average award was $14,160. No-need awards available for academics, alumni affiliation, art, athletics, music/drama.
Scholarships offered: *Merit:* Endowed Academic Scholarship; full or three-quarters tuition for four years; limited number available. Founders Academic Scholarship; $15,000 per year, renewable; minimum 1170 SAT or 26 ACT required for freshmen. Presidential Academic Scholarship; $14,000 per year, renewable; minimum 1140 SAT or 25 ACT required for freshmen. Legacy Grant; $13,000 per year, renewable; minimum 1010 SAT or 22 ACT required for freshmen. All SAT scores are exclusive of Writing. Ministerial Dependents Grant; $2,000 per year; for dependent children of ordained/licensed Southern Baptist ministers and missionaries. Grants-In-Aid; awards vary; for students who contribute special abilities or services to the University; awarded in music, art, athletics and nursing. Church Matching Award; awards vary. *Athletic:* 58 full-time freshmen received athletic scholarships; average amount $24,301.

FINANCIAL AID PROCEDURES
Forms required: FAFSA.
Dates and Deadlines: Priority date 3/1; no closing date. Applicants notified on a rolling basis starting 11/15; must reply within 4 week(s) of notification.

CONTACT
Jene Gabbard, Senior Director of Financial Aid and Scholarships
7502 Fondren Road, Houston, TX 77074-3298
(281) 649-3471

Houston Community College System
Houston, Texas
www.hccs.edu   Federal Code: 010422

2-year public community college in very large city.
Enrollment: 56,846 undergrads, 71% part-time. 3,547 full-time freshmen.
Selectivity: Open admission; but selective for some programs.

BASIC COSTS (2016-2017)
Tuition and fees: $2,031; out-of-district residents $4,191; out-of-state residents $4,686.

FINANCIAL AID PICTURE (2015-2016)

Students with need: Out of 2,242 full-time freshmen who applied for aid, 1,893 were judged to have need. Of these, 1,893 received aid, and 1,893 had their full need met. Average financial aid package met 82% of need. Need-based aid available for part-time students.

Students without need: No-need awards available for academics, state/district residency.

Additional info: Although financial aid applications can be submitted at any time during the academic year, FAFSA's received after priority filing date of April 15 will be considered for funding only after all on-time filers have been awarded and then only if funds are available.

FINANCIAL AID PROCEDURES

Forms required: FAFSA.

Dates and Deadlines: Applicants notified on a rolling basis starting 3/15.

CONTACT

Joellen Soucier, Executive Director of Financial Aid
PO Box 667517, MC 1136, Houston, TX 77266-7517
(713) 718-2000 ext. OPT2

Howard College

Big Spring, Texas
www.howardcollege.edu   Federal Code: 003574

2-year public community college in large town.

Enrollment: 4,725 undergrads, 77% part-time. 322 full-time freshmen.

Selectivity: Open admission; but selective for some programs.

BASIC COSTS (2016-2017)

Tuition and fees: $2,560; out-of-district residents $3,970; out-of-state residents $5,420.

Per-credit charge: $67; out-of-district residents $112; out-of-state residents $159.

Room and board: $4,530.

FINANCIAL AID PICTURE

Students with need: Need-based aid available for full-time and part-time students.

Students without need: No-need awards available for academics, art, athletics, leadership, music/drama.

FINANCIAL AID PROCEDURES

Forms required: FAFSA, institutional form.

Dates and Deadlines: Priority date 4/1; no closing date. Applicants notified on a rolling basis starting 7/15; must reply within 2 week(s) of notification.

CONTACT

Candice Draper, Director of Financial Aid
1001 Birdwell Lane, Big Spring, TX 79720
(432) 264-5083

Howard Payne University

Brownwood, Texas
www.hputx.edu   Federal Code: 003575

4-year private university and liberal arts college in large town, affiliated with the Baptist faith.

Enrollment: 1,066 undergrads. 280 full-time freshmen.

Selectivity: Admits over 75% of applicants.

BASIC COSTS (2017-2018)

Tuition and fees: $27,690.

Per-credit charge: $820.

Room and board: $8,304.

FINANCIAL AID PICTURE (2015-2016)

Students with need: Out of 265 full-time freshmen who applied for aid, 238 were judged to have need. Of these, 237 received aid, and 43 had their full need met. Average financial aid package met 74% of need; average scholarship/grant was $16,945; average loan was $2,978. For part-time students, average financial aid package was $7,302.

Students without need: 37 full-time freshmen who did not demonstrate need for aid received scholarships/grants; average award was $11,998. No-need awards available for academics, alumni affiliation, art, leadership, music/drama, religious affiliation, state/district residency.

Scholarships offered: Merit-based scholarship available to all approved home school applicants, $5,000 annually ($20,000 over 4 years).

FINANCIAL AID PROCEDURES

Forms required: FAFSA, institutional form.

Dates and Deadlines: Priority date 3/15; no closing date. Applicants notified on a rolling basis starting 1/16; must reply within 2 week(s) of notification.

CONTACT

Glenda Huff, Director of Student Financial Aid
1000 Fisk Street, Brownwood, TX 76801-2794
(325) 649-8015

Huston-Tillotson University

Austin, Texas
www.htu.edu   Federal Code: 003577

4-year private business and liberal arts college in very large city, affiliated with the United Methodist Church.

Selectivity: Admits less than 50% of applicants.

BASIC COSTS (2016-2017)

Tuition and fees: $14,346.

Per-credit charge: $410.

Room and board: $7,568.

FINANCIAL AID PICTURE

Students with need: Need-based aid available for full-time and part-time students. Work study available nights, weekends, and for part-time students.

Students without need: No-need awards available for academics, athletics, leadership, minority status, music/drama, religious affiliation, state/district residency.

FINANCIAL AID PROCEDURES

Forms required: FAFSA, institutional form.

Dates and Deadlines: Priority date 3/15; no closing date. Applicants notified on a rolling basis starting 4/8; must reply within 2 week(s) of notification.

Transfers: No deadline.

CONTACT

Karen Price-Scott, Assistant Director of Financial Aid
900 Chicon Street, Austin, TX 78702-2795
(512) 505-3031

Jacksonville College

Jacksonville, Texas
www.jacksonville-college.edu   Federal Code: 003579

2-year private junior and liberal arts college in large town, affiliated with the Baptist faith.

Enrollment: 304 undergrads, 9% part-time. 141 full-time freshmen.

Selectivity: Open admission.

BASIC COSTS (2016-2017)

Tuition and fees: $7,900.

Per-credit charge: $210.

Room and board: $6,400.

FINANCIAL AID PICTURE
Students with need: Need-based aid available for full-time and part-time students.

Students without need: No-need awards available for academics, athletics, leadership, music/drama, religious affiliation, state/district residency.

FINANCIAL AID PROCEDURES
Forms required: FAFSA, state aid form, institutional form.

Dates and Deadlines: Priority date 8/1; no closing date. Applicants notified on a rolling basis.

Transfers: No deadline. Applicants notified on a rolling basis.

CONTACT
Paul Galyean, Financial Aid Officer

105 B.J. Albritton Drive, Jacksonville, TX 75766-4759

(903) 586-2518 ext. 7135

Jarvis Christian College
Hawkins, Texas

www.jarvis.edu   Federal Code: 003637

4-year private liberal arts college in rural community, affiliated with the Christian Church (Disciples of Christ).

Enrollment: 863 undergrads.

Selectivity: Open admission; but selective for some programs.

BASIC COSTS (2016-2017)
Tuition and fees: $11,720.

Per-credit charge: $435.

Room and board: $8,190.

FINANCIAL AID PICTURE
Students with need: Need-based aid available for full-time and part-time students. Work study available nights, weekends, and for part-time students.

Students without need: No-need awards available for academics, athletics, religious affiliation.

Additional info: High school transcript required for scholarship consideration.

FINANCIAL AID PROCEDURES
Forms required: FAFSA, state aid form.

Dates and Deadlines: Applicants notified on a rolling basis starting 5/1; must reply by 5/30 or within 2 week(s) of notification.

Transfers: Priority date 4/15; no deadline. Applicants notified on a rolling basis starting 7/1; must reply within 2 week(s) of notification.

CONTACT
Rosamond Gholson, Interim Director of Financial Aid

PO Box 1470, Hawkins, TX 75765-1470

(903) 730-4890 ext. 2410

Kilgore College
Kilgore, Texas

www.kilgore.edu   Federal Code: 003580

2-year public community college in large town.

Enrollment: 5,630 undergrads.

Selectivity: Open admission; but selective for some programs.

BASIC COSTS (2016-2017)
Tuition and fees: $2,040; out-of-district residents $4,200; out-of-state residents $5,700.

Per-credit charge: $38; out-of-district residents $110; out-of-state residents $160.

Room and board: $4,710.

Additional info: Tuition/fee waivers available for unemployed or children of unemployed.

FINANCIAL AID PICTURE
Students with need: Need-based aid available for full-time and part-time students.

Students without need: No-need awards available for academics, alumni affiliation, art, athletics, job skills, leadership, music/drama, state/district residency.

Scholarships offered: Presidential Scholarships: tuition, fees and books for 4 semesters; ACT 25 or top 10% of senior class; 20 available; renewable at 2.5 GPA.

Additional info: State of Texas grants and loans available for honor graduates with unmet needs and for non-traditional students.

FINANCIAL AID PROCEDURES
Forms required: FAFSA, state aid form, institutional form.

Dates and Deadlines: Priority date 6/1; closing date 7/1. Applicants notified on a rolling basis starting 3/1; must reply within 2 week(s) of notification.

Transfers: No deadline. Transfer students must submit financial aid transcript from previous school plus all appropriate internal aid forms and show proof of high school graduation or GED.

CONTACT
Annette Morgan, Director of Financial Aid

1100 Broadway, Kilgore, TX 75662-3299

(903) 983-8183

The King's University
Southlake, Texas

www.tku.edu   Federal Code: 035163

4-year private Bible and seminary college in very large city, affiliated with the nondenominational tradition.

Enrollment: 473 undergrads.

BASIC COSTS (2016-2017)
Tuition and fees: $13,350.

Per-credit charge: $415.

Additional info: Tuition/fee waivers available for adults.

FINANCIAL AID PICTURE
Students with need: Need-based aid available for full-time and part-time students. Work study available nights, weekends, and for part-time students.

Additional info: Specific scholarships may require specific essays.

FINANCIAL AID PROCEDURES
Forms required: FAFSA.

Dates and Deadlines: Applicants notified on a rolling basis; must reply within 4 week(s) of notification.

CONTACT
Jackie Wadleigh, Director of Financial Aid

2121 E Southlake Blvd, Southlake, TX 76092

(817) 722-1731

Lamar Institute of Technology
Beaumont, Texas

www.lit.edu   Federal Code: 036273

2-year public technical college in small city.

Enrollment: 2,739 undergrads, 57% part-time. 435 full-time freshmen.

Selectivity: Open admission; but selective for some programs.

BASIC COSTS (2016-2017)
Tuition and fees: $5,440; out-of-state residents $17,680.

Per-credit charge: $132; out-of-state residents $540.

FINANCIAL AID PICTURE (2015-2016)
Students with need: Out of 331 full-time freshmen who applied for aid, 236 were judged to have need. Of these, 226 received aid, and 38 had their

full need met. For part-time students, average financial aid package was $3,736.

Students without need: 16 full-time freshmen who did not demonstrate need for aid received scholarships/grants; average award was $1,275.

FINANCIAL AID PROCEDURES

Dates and Deadlines: Priority date 4/1; no closing date.

CONTACT

Lisa Schroeder, Director, Student Financial Aid
PO Box 10043, Beaumont, TX 77705
(409) 880-2137

Lamar State College at Orange

Orange, Texas
www.lsco.edu   Federal Code: 016748

2-year public junior and liberal arts college in small city.
Enrollment: 1,901 undergrads.
Selectivity: Open admission; but selective for some programs.

BASIC COSTS (2016-2017)

Tuition and fees: $5,015; out-of-state residents $17,255.
Per-credit charge: $130; out-of-state residents $538.

FINANCIAL AID PICTURE

Students with need: Need-based aid available for full-time and part-time students.

Students without need: This college awards aid only to students with need.

FINANCIAL AID PROCEDURES

Forms required: FAFSA, institutional form.

Dates and Deadlines: Priority date 4/1; no closing date. Applicants notified on a rolling basis starting 5/15; must reply within 2 week(s) of notification.

CONTACT

Kerry Olson, Director of Financial Aid
410 Front Street, Orange, TX 77630
(409) 882-3317

Lamar State College at Port Arthur

Port Arthur, Texas
www.lamarpa.edu   Federal Code: 016666

2-year public community and technical college in small city.
Enrollment: 2,051 undergrads.
Selectivity: Open admission.

BASIC COSTS (2016-2017)

Tuition and fees: $5,659; out-of-state residents $17,938.
Per-credit charge: $132; out-of-state residents $540.
Room and board: $8,370.

FINANCIAL AID PICTURE

Students with need: Need-based aid available for full-time and part-time students. Work study available nights.

Students without need: This college awards aid only to students with need.

FINANCIAL AID PROCEDURES

Forms required: FAFSA, institutional form.

Dates and Deadlines: Priority date 4/1; no closing date. Applicants notified on a rolling basis starting 4/15; must reply within 2 week(s) of notification.

CONTACT

Connie Riley, Director of Financial Aid
Box 310, Port Arthur, TX 77641-0310
(409) 984-6203

Lamar University

Beaumont, Texas
www.lamar.edu   Federal Code: 003581

4-year public university in small city.
Enrollment: 9,079 undergrads, 32% part-time. 1,506 full-time freshmen.
Selectivity: Admits over 75% of applicants.

BASIC COSTS (2016-2017)

Tuition and fees: $9,901; out-of-state residents $22,141.
Per-credit charge: $236; out-of-state residents $644.
Room and board: $8,450.

FINANCIAL AID PICTURE (2015-2016)

Students with need: Out of 1,264 full-time freshmen who applied for aid, 943 were judged to have need. Of these, 915 received aid, and 127 had their full need met. Average financial aid package met 49% of need; average scholarship/grant was $7,618; average loan was $3,176. For part-time students, average financial aid package was $2,976.

Students without need: This college awards aid only to students with need.

FINANCIAL AID PROCEDURES

Forms required: FAFSA, institutional form.

Dates and Deadlines: Applicants notified on a rolling basis; must reply within 2 week(s) of notification.

CONTACT

Jill Rowley, Director of Financial Aid
Box 10009, Beaumont, TX 77710
(409) 880-8450

Lee College

Baytown, Texas
www.lee.edu   Federal Code: 003583

2-year public community college in small city.
Enrollment: 6,817 undergrads.
Selectivity: Open admission; but selective for some programs.

BASIC COSTS (2016-2017)

Tuition and fees: $2,058; out-of-district residents $3,078; out-of-state residents $4,368.
Per-credit charge: $50; out-of-district residents $84; out-of-state residents $127.

FINANCIAL AID PICTURE

Students with need: Need-based aid available for full-time and part-time students.

Students without need: No-need awards available for academics, art, athletics, job skills, leadership, music/drama.

FINANCIAL AID PROCEDURES

Forms required: FAFSA.

Dates and Deadlines: Priority date 4/1; no closing date. Applicants notified on a rolling basis starting 6/1.

Transfers: Priority date 4/15; no deadline. Applicants notified on a rolling basis.

CONTACT

Sharon Steele, Financial Aid Officer
Box 818, Baytown, TX 77522-0818
(281) 425-6388

LeTourneau University

Longview, Texas
www.letu.edu   Federal Code: 003584

4-year private university in small city, affiliated with the nondenominational tradition.
Enrollment: 1,823 undergrads, 32% part-time. 260 full-time freshmen.
Selectivity: Admits less than 50% of applicants.

BASIC COSTS (2016-2017)
Tuition and fees: $28,480.
Room and board: $9,770.

FINANCIAL AID PICTURE (2016-2017)
Students with need: Out of 237 full-time freshmen who applied for aid, 207 were judged to have need. Of these, 207 received aid, and 48 had their full need met. Average financial aid package met 79% of need; average scholarship/grant was $20,002; average loan was $4,663. For part-time students, average financial aid package was $8,408.
Students without need: 52 full-time freshmen who did not demonstrate need for aid received scholarships/grants; average award was $15,640. No-need awards available for academics, religious affiliation.

FINANCIAL AID PROCEDURES
Forms required: FAFSA.
Dates and Deadlines: Priority date 11/1; closing date 8/1. Applicants notified on a rolling basis starting 11/30; must reply within 2 week(s) of notification.

CONTACT
PO Box 7001, Longview, TX 75607-7001
(903) 233-4350

Lone Star College System

The Woodlands, Texas
www.lonestar.edu   Federal Code: 011145

2-year public community college in very large city.
Enrollment: 85,661 undergrads, 69% part-time. 2,701 full-time freshmen.
Selectivity: Open admission; but selective for some programs.

BASIC COSTS (2017-2018)
Tuition and fees: $1,956; out-of-district residents $4,056; out-of-state residents $4,506.

FINANCIAL AID PICTURE (2015-2016)
Students with need: Out of 1,592 full-time freshmen who applied for aid, 1,364 were judged to have need. Of these, 892 received aid, and 27 had their full need met. Average financial aid package met 53% of need; average scholarship/grant was $3,235; average loan was $956. For part-time students, average financial aid package was $5,033.
Students without need: 52 full-time freshmen who did not demonstrate need for aid received scholarships/grants; average award was $1,114. No-need awards available for academics.

FINANCIAL AID PROCEDURES
Forms required: FAFSA.
Dates and Deadlines: Priority date 5/10; no closing date. Applicants notified on a rolling basis starting 4/1.

CONTACT
Tracie Hunter, Executive Director
5000 Research Forest Drive, The Woodlands, TX 77381-4356
(281) 290-2700

Lubbock Christian University

Lubbock, Texas
www.lcu.edu   Federal Code: 003586

4-year private university and liberal arts college in small city, affiliated with the Church of Christ.
Enrollment: 1,471 undergrads, 14% part-time. 320 full-time freshmen.
Selectivity: Admits over 75% of applicants.

BASIC COSTS (2016-2017)
Tuition and fees: $21,166.
Per-credit charge: $685.
Room and board: $6,250.

FINANCIAL AID PICTURE (2016-2017)
Students with need: Out of 256 full-time freshmen who applied for aid, 214 were judged to have need. Of these, 214 received aid, and 22 had their full need met. Average financial aid package met 64% of need; average scholarship/grant was $11,731; average loan was $3,882. For part-time students, average financial aid package was $7,347.
Students without need: 58 full-time freshmen who did not demonstrate need for aid received scholarships/grants; average award was $6,340.
Scholarships offered: 17 full-time freshmen received athletic scholarships; average amount $12,409.

FINANCIAL AID PROCEDURES
Forms required: FAFSA, institutional form.
Dates and Deadlines: Priority date 6/1; no closing date. Applicants notified on a rolling basis starting 3/1.
Transfers: No deadline. Applicants notified on a rolling basis starting 3/1.

CONTACT
Amy Hardesty, Director, Financial Assistance
5601 19th Street, Lubbock, TX 79407-2099
(806) 720-7176

McLennan Community College

Waco, Texas
www.mclennan.edu   Federal Code: 003590

2-year public community and junior college in small city.
Enrollment: 8,609 undergrads, 60% part-time. 988 full-time freshmen.
Selectivity: Open admission; but selective for some programs.

BASIC COSTS (2016-2017)
Tuition and fees: $3,450; out-of-district residents $3,990; out-of-state residents $5,700.
Per-credit charge: $106; out-of-district residents $124; out-of-state residents $181.

FINANCIAL AID PICTURE
Students with need: Need-based aid available for full-time and part-time students.
Students without need: No-need awards available for athletics.
Scholarships offered: Academic scholarship: awarded to individuals selected for Tartan scholar's program.

FINANCIAL AID PROCEDURES
Forms required: FAFSA.
Dates and Deadlines: Closing date 6/1. Applicants notified on a rolling basis starting 5/1.

CONTACT
James Kubacak, Director of Financial Aid
1400 College Drive, Waco, TX 76708
(254) 299-8698

PART III: FINANCIAL AID COLLEGE BY COLLEGE

McMurry University
Abilene, Texas
ww2.mcm.edu   Federal Code: 003591

4-year private university and liberal arts college in small city, affiliated with the United Methodist Church.
Enrollment: 1,016 undergrads, 8% part-time. 297 full-time freshmen.
Selectivity: Admits less than 50% of applicants.

BASIC COSTS (2016-2017)
Tuition and fees: $26,100.
Per-credit charge: $815.
Room and board: $8,244.
Additional info: Students pay a block tuition rate for 12 or more hours per semester for fall and spring semesters. Required fees and the use of a tablet PC and school-related software is also included in tuition cost.

FINANCIAL AID PICTURE (2015-2016)
Students with need: Out of 231 full-time freshmen who applied for aid, 218 were judged to have need. Of these, 218 received aid, and 18 had their full need met. Average financial aid package met 73% of need; average scholarship/grant was $16,297; average loan was $2,991. For part-time students, average financial aid package was $7,081.
Students without need: 20 full-time freshmen who did not demonstrate need for aid received scholarships/grants; average award was $9,741. No-need awards available for academics, art, athletics, job skills, leadership, music/drama, religious affiliation.

FINANCIAL AID PROCEDURES
Forms required: FAFSA, state aid form, institutional form.
Dates and Deadlines: Priority date 3/15; no closing date. Applicants notified on a rolling basis starting 2/1; must reply within 3 week(s) of notification.
Transfers: No deadline. Applicants notified on a rolling basis starting 2/1; must reply by 6/30.

CONTACT
Lori Herrick, Director of Financial Aid
South 14th and Sayles Boulevard, Abilene, TX 79697-0001
(325) 793-4713

Midland College
Midland, Texas
www.midland.edu   Federal Code: 009797

2-year public community college in small city.
Enrollment: 5,644 undergrads.
Selectivity: Open admission; but selective for some programs.

BASIC COSTS (2016-2017)
Tuition and fees: $2,580; out-of-district residents $4,080; out-of-state residents $5,280.
Per-credit charge: $186; out-of-district residents $336; out-of-state residents $456.
Room and board: $4,800.

FINANCIAL AID PICTURE
Students with need: Need-based aid available for full-time and part-time students.
Students without need: No-need awards available for academics, athletics, minority status, music/drama, state/district residency.
Scholarships offered: Legacy Scholarship: varying amounts; renewable; available for full-time or part-time study to graduates of Midland County High Schools.

FINANCIAL AID PROCEDURES
Forms required: FAFSA.
Dates and Deadlines: Priority date 4/2; closing date 6/1. Applicants notified on a rolling basis starting 5/15; must reply within 2 week(s) of notification.

Transfers: No deadline.

CONTACT
Yolanda Ramos, Director of Financial Aid
3600 North Garfield, Midland, TX 79705
(432) 685-4733

Midwestern State University
Wichita Falls, Texas
www.mwsu.edu   Federal Code: 003592

4-year public university and liberal arts college in small city.
Enrollment: 5,307 undergrads, 22% part-time. 734 full-time freshmen.
Selectivity: Admits 50 to 75% of applicants.

BASIC COSTS (2016-2017)
Tuition and fees: $8,294; out-of-state residents $10,244.
Per-credit charge: $175.85; out-of-state residents $238.85.
Room and board: $7,440.
Additional info: Tuition at time of enrollment locked for 4 years.

FINANCIAL AID PICTURE (2016-2017)
Students with need: Out of 666 full-time freshmen who applied for aid, 493 were judged to have need. Of these, 491 received aid, and 258 had their full need met. Average financial aid package met 70% of need; average scholarship/grant was $8,728; average loan was $5,191. For part-time students, average financial aid package was $5,417.
Students without need: 119 full-time freshmen who did not demonstrate need for aid received scholarships/grants; average award was $2,250. No-need awards available for academics, alumni affiliation, art, athletics, leadership, music/drama.
Scholarships offered: 22 full-time freshmen received athletic scholarships; average amount $7,585.

FINANCIAL AID PROCEDURES
Forms required: FAFSA, institutional form.
Dates and Deadlines: Priority date 3/1; no closing date. Applicants notified on a rolling basis starting 4/15; must reply within 4 week(s) of notification.
Transfers: No deadline. Applicants notified on a rolling basis starting 4/15; must reply within 4 week(s) of notification.

CONTACT
Kathy Pennartz, Director of Financial Aid
3410 Taft Boulevard, Wichita Falls, TX 76308-2099
(940) 397-4119

Mountain View College
Dallas, Texas
www.mvc.dcccd.edu   Federal Code: 008503

2-year public community college in very large city.
Enrollment: 7,438 undergrads.
Selectivity: Open admission; but selective for some programs.

BASIC COSTS (2016-2017)
Tuition and fees: $1,770; out-of-district residents $3,330; out-of-state residents $5,220.
Per-credit charge: $59; out-of-district residents $111; out-of-state residents $200.
Additional info: Tuition/fee waivers available for adults.

FINANCIAL AID PICTURE
Students with need: Need-based aid available for full-time and part-time students. Work study available nights, weekends, and for part-time students.

FINANCIAL AID PROCEDURES
Forms required: FAFSA, institutional form.

Dates and Deadlines: Priority date 5/1; no closing date. Applicants notified on a rolling basis starting 6/1.

CONTACT
Pam Shuttlesworth, Director of Financial Aid
Attn: Admissions, Dallas, TX 75211-6599
(214) 860-8688

Navarro College
Corsicana, Texas
www.navarrocollege.edu   Federal Code: 003593

2-year public community and junior college in large town.
Enrollment: 9,230 undergrads, 66% part-time. 1,084 full-time freshmen.
Selectivity: Open admission; but selective for some programs.

BASIC COSTS (2017-2018)
Tuition and fees: $2,400; out-of-district residents $3,870; out-of-state residents $5,400.
Room and board: $5,618.

FINANCIAL AID PICTURE (2015-2016)
Students with need: 66% of average financial aid package awarded as scholarships/grants, 34% awarded as loans/jobs.

FINANCIAL AID PROCEDURES
Forms required: FAFSA.
Dates and Deadlines: Priority date 6/1; no closing date. Applicants notified on a rolling basis starting 7/1; must reply within 2 week(s) of notification.

CONTACT
Krlstal Nicholson, Director of Financial Aid
3200 West Seventh Avenue, Corsicana, TX 75110
(903) 875-7362

North Central Texas College
Gainesville, Texas
www.nctc.edu   Federal Code: 003558

2-year public community college in large city.
Enrollment: 9,427 undergrads.
Selectivity: Open admission; but selective for some programs.

BASIC COSTS (2016-2017)
Tuition and fees: $2,280; out-of-district residents $3,540; out-of-state residents $6,000.
Per-credit charge: $50; out-of-district residents $92; out-of-state residents $174.
Room and board: $3,928.

FINANCIAL AID PICTURE
Students with need: Need-based aid available for full-time and part-time students. Work study available nights.
Students without need: This college awards aid only to students with need.

FINANCIAL AID PROCEDURES
Forms required: FAFSA.
Dates and Deadlines: Priority date 5/1; closing date 6/1. Applicants notified on a rolling basis starting 6/1; must reply within 4 week(s) of notification.

CONTACT
Ashley Tatum, Director of Financial Aid
1525 West California Street, Gainesville, TX 76240
(940) 668-4242

North Lake College
Irving, Texas
www.northlakecollege.edu   Federal Code: 014036

2-year public community and liberal arts college in large city.
Enrollment: 7,793 undergrads.
Selectivity: Open admission.

BASIC COSTS (2016-2017)
Tuition and fees: $1,770; out-of-district residents $3,330; out-of-state residents $5,220.
Per-credit charge: $59; out-of-district residents $111; out-of-state residents $200.

FINANCIAL AID PICTURE
Students with need: Need-based aid available for full-time and part-time students. Work study available nights, weekends, and for part-time students.
Students without need: No-need awards available for academics, minority status, state/district residency.

FINANCIAL AID PROCEDURES
Forms required: FAFSA, state aid form.
Dates and Deadlines: Priority date 3/1; closing date 5/1. Applicants notified on a rolling basis starting 7/1.
Transfers: Priority date 2/1. Applicants notified on a rolling basis starting 8/1.

CONTACT
Paul Felix, Director of Financial Aid
5001 North MacArthur Boulevard, Irving, TX 75038-3899
(972) 273-3321

Northeast Texas Community College
Mount Pleasant, Texas
www.ntcc.edu   Federal Code: 016396

2-year public community college in large town.
Enrollment: 3,037 undergrads.
Selectivity: Open admission; but selective for some programs.

BASIC COSTS (2016-2017)
Tuition and fees: $2,661; out-of-district residents $4,521; out-of-state residents $5,980.
Per-credit charge: $38; out-of-district residents $100; out-of-state residents $148.
Room and board: $6,100.

FINANCIAL AID PICTURE
Students with need: Need-based aid available for full-time and part-time students.

FINANCIAL AID PROCEDURES
Forms required: FAFSA, institutional form.
Dates and Deadlines: Priority date 6/1; no closing date. Applicants notified on a rolling basis starting 6/1.

CONTACT
Kim Lawrence, Dean of Enrollment Management & Director of Financial Aid
2886 FM 1735, Mount Pleasant, TX 75455
(903) 434-8142

Northwest Vista College
San Antonio, Texas
www.alamo.edu/nvc   Federal Code: 033723

2-year public community college in very large city.
Enrollment: 13,221 undergrads, 68% part-time. 1,165 full-time freshmen.

Selectivity: Open admission.

BASIC COSTS (2016-2017)
Tuition and fees: $2,188; out-of-district residents $5,824; out-of-state residents $11,274.

FINANCIAL AID PICTURE
Students with need: Need-based aid available for full-time and part-time students. Work study available nights, weekends, and for part-time students.
Students without need: No-need awards available for academics, leadership.

FINANCIAL AID PROCEDURES
Forms required: FAFSA.
Dates and Deadlines: Priority date 4/1; no closing date. Applicants notified on a rolling basis starting 5/15; must reply within 2 week(s) of notification.

CONTACT
Rosalinda Encina, Associate Director of Student Financial Services
3535 North Ellison Drive, San Antonio, TX 78251-4217
(210) 486-4600

Northwood University: Texas
Cedar Hill, Texas
www.northwood.edu   Federal Code: 013040

4-year private university and business college in large town.
Enrollment: 208 undergrads.

BASIC COSTS (2016-2017)
Tuition and fees: $25,130.
Per-credit charge: $918.
Room and board: $9,880.

FINANCIAL AID PICTURE
Students with need: Need-based aid available for full-time and part-time students. Work study available nights, weekends, and for part-time students.
Students without need: No-need awards available for academics, athletics, leadership.
Scholarships offered: Academic Scholarships: $4,000-$10,000; based on test scores and GPA; unlimited number awarded.

FINANCIAL AID PROCEDURES
Forms required: FAFSA.
Dates and Deadlines: Priority date 3/1; no closing date. Applicants notified on a rolling basis starting 3/1.
Transfers: No deadline. Applicants notified on a rolling basis.

CONTACT
Mark Martin, Director of Financial Aid
1114 West FM 1382, Cedar Hill, TX 75104-1204
(989) 837-4997

Odessa College
Odessa, Texas
www.odessa.edu   Federal Code: 003596

2-year public community college in small city.
Enrollment: 6,186 undergrads, 65% part-time. 603 full-time freshmen.
Selectivity: Open admission; but selective for some programs.

BASIC COSTS (2017-2018)
Tuition and fees: $2,784; out-of-district residents $4,192; out-of-state residents $5,440.
Room and board: $5,377.

FINANCIAL AID PICTURE (2016-2017)
Students with need: Need-based aid available for full-time and part-time students. Work study available nights.

Students without need: No-need awards available for academics, athletics, music/drama.

FINANCIAL AID PROCEDURES
Forms required: FAFSA.
Dates and Deadlines: Priority date 5/1; no closing date. Applicants notified on a rolling basis starting 6/1.

CONTACT
Ashley Warren, Director of Student Financial Aid
201 West University, Odessa, TX 79764-7127
(432) 335-6429

Our Lady of the Lake University of San Antonio
San Antonio, Texas
www.ollusa.edu   Federal Code: 003598

4-year private university in very large city, affiliated with the Roman Catholic Church.
Enrollment: 1,326 undergrads, 11% part-time. 306 full-time freshmen.
Selectivity: Admits 50 to 75% of applicants.

BASIC COSTS (2016-2017)
Tuition and fees: $27,140.
Per-credit charge: $843.
Room and board: $7,872.

FINANCIAL AID PICTURE (2015-2016)
Students with need: Out of 292 full-time freshmen who applied for aid, 271 were judged to have need. Of these, 271 received aid, and 40 had their full need met. Average financial aid package met 75% of need; average scholarship/grant was $17,627; average loan was $3,687. For part-time students, average financial aid package was $6,663.
Students without need: 31 full-time freshmen who did not demonstrate need for aid received scholarships/grants; average award was $8,565. No-need awards available for academics, alumni affiliation, art, athletics, music/drama, religious affiliation.
Scholarships offered: *Merit:* General academic scholarship; $1,205 awarded yearly, renewable. Art/fine arts and music; 4 awarded yearly, renewable. Children of faculty/staff; 60 awarded yearly, renewable. All based on GPA scores and high school record. *Athletic:* 6 full-time freshmen received athletic scholarships; average amount $7,692.

FINANCIAL AID PROCEDURES
Forms required: FAFSA, institutional form.
Dates and Deadlines: Priority date 5/1; no closing date. Applicants notified on a rolling basis starting 3/1; must reply within 2 week(s) of notification.

CONTACT
Esmeralda Flores, Director of Financial Aid
411 Southwest 24th Street, San Antonio, TX 78207-4689
(210) 431-3960

Palo Alto College
San Antonio, Texas
www.alamo.edu/pac   Federal Code: 016615

2-year public community college in very large city.
Enrollment: 9,108 undergrads, 81% part-time. 498 full-time freshmen.
Selectivity: Open admission.

BASIC COSTS (2016-2017)
Tuition and fees: $2,188; out-of-district residents $5,824; out-of-state residents $11,274.

FINANCIAL AID PICTURE

Students with need: Need-based aid available for full-time and part-time students.

Students without need: This college awards aid only to students with need.

Scholarships offered: Alamo Community College District Scholarship: $1,000; 50 awarded.

FINANCIAL AID PROCEDURES

Forms required: FAFSA, state aid form.

Dates and Deadlines: Priority date 4/1; closing date 5/1. Applicants notified on a rolling basis starting 5/31.

CONTACT

Shirley Leija, Director of Financial Aid

1400 West Villaret Boulevard, San Antonio, TX 78224-2499

(210) 486-3600

Panola College

Carthage, Texas

www.panola.edu   Federal Code: 003600

2-year public community and junior college in small town.

Enrollment: 2,667 undergrads, 49% part-time. 374 full-time freshmen.

Selectivity: Open admission; but selective for some programs.

BASIC COSTS (2016-2017)

Tuition and fees: $2,280; out-of-district residents $3,030; out-of-state residents $3,525.

Per-credit charge: $60; out-of-state residents $200.

Room and board: $4,840.

FINANCIAL AID PICTURE (2016-2017)

Students with need: Out of 296 full-time freshmen who applied for aid, 267 were judged to have need. Of these, 263 received aid. For part-time students, average financial aid package was $2,211.

Students without need: 11 full-time freshmen who did not demonstrate need for aid received scholarships/grants; average award was $554. No-need awards available for academics, alumni affiliation, art, athletics, leadership, music/drama.

Scholarships offered: *Merit:* Several departmental and organization-sponsored scholarships, Presidential scholarship, Dean's scholarship. *Athletic:* 31 full-time freshmen received athletic scholarships; average amount $3,552.

FINANCIAL AID PROCEDURES

Forms required: FAFSA, institutional form.

Dates and Deadlines: Priority date 6/1; no closing date. Applicants notified on a rolling basis starting 6/1.

Transfers: No deadline. Applicants notified on a rolling basis.

CONTACT

Denise Welch, Director of Financial Aid

1109 West Panola Street, Carthage, TX 75633

(903) 693-2039

Paris Junior College

Paris, Texas

www.parisjc.edu   Federal Code: 003601

2-year public community and junior college in large town.

Enrollment: 4,806 undergrads.

Selectivity: Open admission; but selective for some programs.

BASIC COSTS (2016-2017)

Tuition and fees: $2,250; out-of-district residents $3,600; out-of-state residents $5,100.

Per-credit charge: $55; out-of-district residents $100; out-of-state residents $150.

Room and board: $5,550.

FINANCIAL AID PICTURE (2015-2016)

Students with need: 98% of average financial aid package awarded as scholarships/grants, 2% awarded as loans/jobs. Need-based aid available for part-time students.

Students without need: No-need awards available for athletics, music/drama.

FINANCIAL AID PROCEDURES

Forms required: FAFSA.

Dates and Deadlines: Applicants notified on a rolling basis starting 6/1.

CONTACT

Linda Slawson, Director of Financial Aid

2400 Clarksville Street, Paris, TX 75460

(903) 782-0429

Paul Quinn College

Dallas, Texas

www.pqc.edu   Federal Code: 003602

4-year private liberal arts college in very large city, affiliated with the African Methodist Episcopal Church.

Enrollment: 420 undergrads.

BASIC COSTS (2016-2017)

Tuition and fees: $8,275.

Per-credit charge: $240.63.

Room and board: $6,000.

FINANCIAL AID PICTURE

Students with need: Need-based aid available for full-time and part-time students.

Students without need: This college awards aid only to students with need.

Scholarships offered: Presidential Scholarship: 100% tuition, fees, room and board; top 15% of class; minimum 3.5 GPA (3.7 for transfer students); at least 23 on the ACT or 1590 on the SAT; essay; renewable. Paul Quinn Scholarship: 50% of tuition, room and board; top 25% of class; minimum 3.25 GPA (3.5 for transfer students); at least 20 on the ACT or 1410 on the SAT; essay; renewable.

FINANCIAL AID PROCEDURES

Forms required: FAFSA, institutional form.

Dates and Deadlines: Priority date 7/1; no closing date. Applicants notified on a rolling basis starting 7/15; must reply within 2 week(s) of notification.

CONTACT

3837 Simpson Stuart Road, Dallas, TX 75241

(214) 379-5497

Prairie View A&M University

Prairie View, Texas

www.pvamu.edu   Federal Code: 003630

4-year public university in small town.

Enrollment: 7,417 undergrads, 8% part-time. 1,608 full-time freshmen.

Selectivity: Admits over 75% of applicants.

BASIC COSTS (2016-2017)

Tuition and fees: $10,059; out-of-state residents $23,378.

Per-credit charge: $240.51; out-of-state residents $684.45.

Room and board: $8,626.

Additional info: Tuition at time of enrollment locked for 4 years.

FINANCIAL AID PICTURE (2015-2016)

Students with need: Out of 1,552 full-time freshmen who applied for aid, 1,448 were judged to have need. Of these, 1,411 received aid, and 93 had their full need met. Average financial aid package met 75% of need; average scholarship/grant was $10,485; average loan was $5,993. For part-time students, average financial aid package was $9,189.

Students without need: 47 full-time freshmen who did not demonstrate need for aid received scholarships/grants; average award was $6,374. No-need awards available for academics, athletics, ROTC.

Scholarships offered: 59 full-time freshmen received athletic scholarships; average amount $11,786.

FINANCIAL AID PROCEDURES

Forms required: FAFSA.

Dates and Deadlines: Closing date 3/15. Applicants notified by 6/1; must reply by 8/1.

Transfers: Closing date 3/1. Applicants notified by 6/1; must reply by 8/1. Minimum 2.0 GPA from all colleges attended required to be considered for financial aid.

CONTACT

Ralph Perri, Director of Financial Aid and Scholarships
PO Box 519, MS 1009, Prairie View, TX 77446-0519
(936) 261-1000

Ranger College

Ranger, Texas
www.rangercollege.edu   Federal Code: 003603

2-year public community and junior college in rural community.
Enrollment: 2,047 undergrads, 53% part-time. 324 full-time freshmen.
Selectivity: Open admission; but selective for some programs.

BASIC COSTS (2016-2017)

Tuition and fees: $2,460; out-of-district residents $3,750; out-of-state residents $4,860.

Per-credit charge: $50; out-of-district residents $93; out-of-state residents $130.

FINANCIAL AID PICTURE (2016-2017)

Students with need: 35% of average financial aid package awarded as scholarships/grants, 65% awarded as loans/jobs. Need-based aid available for part-time students. Work study available nights.

Students without need: This college awards aid only to students with need.

FINANCIAL AID PROCEDURES

Forms required: FAFSA, institutional form.

Dates and Deadlines: Priority date 7/28; no closing date. Applicants notified on a rolling basis; must reply within 3 week(s) of notification.

Transfers: No deadline. Applicants notified on a rolling basis; must reply within 2 week(s) of notification.

CONTACT

Don Hilton, Financial Aid Director
1100 College Circle, Ranger, TX 76470
(254) 647-3234 ext. 117

Remington College: Westchase Campus

Houston, Texas
http://houston.remingtoncollege.edu
Federal Code: E00672

2-year private technical college in very large city.
Enrollment: 609 undergrads.
Selectivity: Open admission.

BASIC COSTS (2016-2017)

Additional info: Cost of diploma programs in Medical Billing and Coding, Pharmacy Technician: $15,995; Electronic Technology, $20,995; Cosmetology, $21,700; Medical Assisting (with or without X-Ray Tech), $20,520; Includes books, equipment, lab fees, and uniforms (if necessary).

FINANCIAL AID PICTURE

Students with need: Need-based aid available for full-time and part-time students. Work study available nights.

Students without need: No-need awards available for state/district residency.

FINANCIAL AID PROCEDURES

Forms required: FAFSA, institutional form.

Dates and Deadlines: Applicants notified on a rolling basis.

CONTACT

James Dunn, National Director of Financial Aid
3110 Hayes Road, Suite 380, Houston, TX 77082

Rice University

Houston, Texas   Federal Code: 003604
www.rice.edu   CSS Code: 6609

4-year private university in very large city.
Enrollment: 3,879 undergrads, 1% part-time. 978 full-time freshmen.
Selectivity: Admits less than 50% of applicants.

BASIC COSTS (2016-2017)

Tuition and fees: $43,918.
Per-credit charge: $1,801.
Room and board: $13,750.

FINANCIAL AID PICTURE (2016-2017)

Students with need: Out of 762 full-time freshmen who applied for aid, 416 were judged to have need. Of these, 415 received aid, and 415 had their full need met. Average financial aid package met 100% of need; average scholarship/grant was $37,253; average loan was $2,892. Need-based aid available for part-time students.

Students without need: 91 full-time freshmen who did not demonstrate need for aid received scholarships/grants; average award was $23,037. No-need awards available for academics, art, athletics, leadership, minority status, music/drama, ROTC, state/district residency.

Scholarships offered: 58 full-time freshmen received athletic scholarships; average amount $39,971.

FINANCIAL AID PROCEDURES

Forms required: FAFSA, CSS PROFILE.

Dates and Deadlines: Closing date 3/1. Applicants notified by 4/1; must reply by 5/1.

Transfers: Priority date 4/1.

CONTACT

Anne Walker, Director of Student Financial Services
6100 Main Street, Houston, TX 77251-1892
(713) 348-4958

Richland College

Dallas, Texas
www.richlandcollege.edu   Federal Code: 008504

2-year public community college in very large city.
Enrollment: 12,762 undergrads.
Selectivity: Open admission.

BASIC COSTS (2016-2017)

Tuition and fees: $1,770; out-of-district residents $3,330; out-of-state residents $5,220.

Per-credit charge: $59; out-of-district residents $111; out-of-state residents $200.

FINANCIAL AID PICTURE
Students with need: Need-based aid available for full-time and part-time students. Work study available nights.
Students without need: No-need awards available for art, leadership, music/drama.

FINANCIAL AID PROCEDURES
Forms required: FAFSA.
Dates and Deadlines: Priority date 5/11; no closing date. Applicants notified on a rolling basis starting 6/1; must reply within 2 week(s) of notification.

CONTACT
Sylvia Holmes, Director of Financial Aid
12800 Abrams Road, Dallas, TX 75243-2199
(972) 238-6188

St. Edward's University
Austin, Texas
https://www.stedwards.edu   Federal Code: 003621

4-year private university in very large city, affiliated with the Roman Catholic Church.
Enrollment: 4,050 undergrads, 11% part-time. 863 full-time freshmen.
Selectivity: Admits 50 to 75% of applicants.

BASIC COSTS (2016-2017)
Tuition and fees: $40,828.
Per-credit charge: $1,348.
Room and board: $12,172.

FINANCIAL AID PICTURE (2016-2017)
Students with need: Out of 760 full-time freshmen who applied for aid, 657 were judged to have need. Of these, 656 received aid, and 84 had their full need met. Average financial aid package met 75% of need; average scholarship/grant was $23,009; average loan was $3,696. For part-time students, average financial aid package was $10,883.
Students without need: 75 full-time freshmen who did not demonstrate need for aid received scholarships/grants; average award was $17,959. No-need awards available for academics, athletics, music/drama.
Scholarships offered: *Merit:* President's Excellence Scholarship: $20,000 per year; minimum 1300 SAT; top 15% of class. Academic Scholar Award: $7,000-$20,000 per year; minimum 1100 SAT; top 25% of class. All SAT scores exclusive of Writing section. *Athletic:* 43 full-time freshmen received athletic scholarships; average amount $21,681.

FINANCIAL AID PROCEDURES
Forms required: FAFSA.
Dates and Deadlines: Priority date 2/1; no closing date. Applicants notified on a rolling basis starting 2/1; must reply by 5/1 or within 2 week(s) of notification.
Transfers: No deadline. Applicants notified on a rolling basis starting 2/1; must reply within 2 week(s) of notification.

CONTACT
Jennifer Beck, Director Financial Services
3001 South Congress Avenue, Austin, TX 78704-6489
(512) 448-8523

St. Mary's University
San Antonio, Texas
www.stmarytx.edu   Federal Code: 003623

4-year private university and liberal arts college in very large city, affiliated with the Roman Catholic Church.

Enrollment: 2,268 undergrads, 4% part-time. 590 full-time freshmen.
Selectivity: Admits over 75% of applicants.

BASIC COSTS (2016-2017)
Tuition and fees: $28,200.
Per-credit charge: $855.
Room and board: $9,300.

FINANCIAL AID PICTURE (2015-2016)
Students with need: Out of 497 full-time freshmen who applied for aid, 458 were judged to have need. Of these, 458 received aid, and 59 had their full need met. Average financial aid package met 75% of need; average scholarship/grant was $20,303; average loan was $3,500. For part-time students, average financial aid package was $8,732.
Students without need: 103 full-time freshmen who did not demonstrate need for aid received scholarships/grants; average award was $19,334. No-need awards available for academics, alumni affiliation, athletics, music/drama, religious affiliation, ROTC, state/district residency.
Scholarships offered: 25 full-time freshmen received athletic scholarships; average amount $14,521.

FINANCIAL AID PROCEDURES
Forms required: FAFSA.
Dates and Deadlines: Priority date 3/31; closing date 6/1. Applicants notified on a rolling basis starting 3/1; must reply by 5/1 or within 2 week(s) of notification.

CONTACT
David Krause, Director of Financial Assistance
One Camino Santa Maria, San Antonio, TX 78228-8504
(210) 436-3141

St. Philip's College
San Antonio, Texas
www.alamo.edu/spc   Federal Code: 003608

2-year public community college in very large city.
Enrollment: 10,201 undergrads.
Selectivity: Open admission; but selective for some programs.

BASIC COSTS (2017-2018)
Tuition and fees: $2,660; out-of-district residents $7,070; out-of-state residents $13,670.

FINANCIAL AID PICTURE (2015-2016)
Students with need: 74% of average financial aid package awarded as scholarships/grants, 26% awarded as loans/jobs. Need-based aid available for part-time students. Work study available nights, weekends, and for part-time students.
Students without need: This college awards aid only to students with need.

FINANCIAL AID PROCEDURES
Forms required: FAFSA.

CONTACT
Harold Whitis, District Director of Student Financial Services
1801 Martin Luther King Drive, San Antonio, TX 78203
(210) 486-2600

Sam Houston State University
Huntsville, Texas
www.shsu.edu   Federal Code: 003606

4-year public university in large town.
Enrollment: 17,902 undergrads, 19% part-time. 2,353 full-time freshmen.
Selectivity: Admits 50 to 75% of applicants.

BASIC COSTS (2016-2017)

Tuition and fees: $9,516; out-of-state residents $21,756.

Per-credit charge: $215.5; out-of-state residents $623.5.

Room and board: $8,986.

FINANCIAL AID PICTURE (2015-2016)

Students with need: Out of 2,095 full-time freshmen who applied for aid, 1,672 were judged to have need. Of these, 1,639 received aid, and 278 had their full need met. Average financial aid package met 82% of need; average scholarship/grant was $9,271; average loan was $5,713. For part-time students, average financial aid package was $7,828.

Students without need: 231 full-time freshmen who did not demonstrate need for aid received scholarships/grants; average award was $2,990. No-need awards available for academics, alumni affiliation, art, athletics, leadership, music/drama, religious affiliation, ROTC, state/district residency.

Scholarships offered: 46 full-time freshmen received athletic scholarships; average amount $10,335.

FINANCIAL AID PROCEDURES

Forms required: FAFSA.

Dates and Deadlines: Priority date 3/15; no closing date. Applicants notified on a rolling basis starting 4/1; must reply within 4 week(s) of notification.

Transfers: No deadline. Applicants notified on a rolling basis starting 3/15; must reply within 4 week(s) of notification.

CONTACT

Lydia Hall, Director of Financial Aid

SHSU Campus Box 2418, Huntsville, TX 77341-2418

(936) 294-1774

San Antonio College

San Antonio, Texas

www.alamo.edu/sac   Federal Code: 009163

2-year public community college in very large city.

Enrollment: 19,523 undergrads.

Selectivity: Open admission; but selective for some programs.

BASIC COSTS (2016-2017)

Tuition and fees: $2,188; out-of-district residents $5,824; out-of-state residents $11,274.

FINANCIAL AID PICTURE

Students with need: Need-based aid available for full-time and part-time students. Work study available nights, weekends, and for part-time students.

Students without need: This college awards aid only to students with need.

Additional info: Leveraging Educational Assistance Partnership, public student incentive grant, towards excellence access and success grants (Texas and Texas II grants) available.

FINANCIAL AID PROCEDURES

Forms required: FAFSA.

Dates and Deadlines: Priority date 3/1; closing date 5/1.

CONTACT

Rose Carreon-Munoz, Associate Director of Student Financial Services

1300 San Pedro Avenue, San Antonio, TX 78212-4299

(210) 486-0600

San Jacinto College

Pasadena, Texas

www.sanjac.edu

2-year public community and technical college in very large city.

Enrollment: 24,153 undergrads, 75% part-time. 2,040 full-time freshmen.

Selectivity: Open admission; but selective for some programs.

BASIC COSTS (2016-2017)

Tuition and fees: $1,800; out-of-district residents $3,150; out-of-state residents $5,100.

Per-credit charge: $50; out-of-district residents $95; out-of-state residents $160.

FINANCIAL AID PICTURE (2015-2016)

Students with need: Out of 1,237 full-time freshmen who applied for aid, 1,099 were judged to have need. Of these, 771 received aid. Average financial aid package met 27% of need; average scholarship/grant was $5,222; average loan was $3,046. For part-time students, average financial aid package was $3,581.

Students without need: This college awards aid only to students with need.

Scholarships offered: 45 full-time freshmen received athletic scholarships; average amount $2,951.

FINANCIAL AID PROCEDURES

Forms required: FAFSA.

Dates and Deadlines: Priority date 6/30; no closing date. Applicants notified on a rolling basis starting 5/1; must reply within 4 week(s) of notification.

Transfers: Priority date 10/31. Applicants notified on a rolling basis starting 4/1; must reply within 4 week(s) of notification. All transfer students must have all transcripts evaluated by the Enrollment Service office.

CONTACT

Robert Merino, Director of Financial Aid

8060 Spencer Highway, Pasadena, TX 77505-5999

(281) 998-6150

Schreiner University

Kerrville, Texas

www.schreiner.edu   Federal Code: 003610

4-year private university and liberal arts college in large town, affiliated with the Presbyterian Church (USA).

Enrollment: 1,181 undergrads, 13% part-time. 294 full-time freshmen.

Selectivity: Admits over 75% of applicants.

BASIC COSTS (2017-2018)

Tuition and fees: $26,750.

Per-credit charge: $1,069.

Room and board: $10,152.

FINANCIAL AID PICTURE (2015-2016)

Students with need: Out of 263 full-time freshmen who applied for aid, 220 were judged to have need. Of these, 220 received aid, and 41 had their full need met. Average financial aid package met 71% of need; average scholarship/grant was $16,171; average loan was $3,051. For part-time students, average financial aid package was $6,055.

Students without need: 74 full-time freshmen who did not demonstrate need for aid received scholarships/grants; average award was $10,014. No-need awards available for academics, art, leadership, music/drama, religious affiliation.

Scholarships offered: Awards for students with exceptional academic achievement and leadership abilities; partial and full tuition; 3.5 GPA and 1100 SAT (exclusive of Writing) or 24 ACT.

FINANCIAL AID PROCEDURES

Forms required: FAFSA.

Dates and Deadlines: Priority date 5/1; no closing date. Applicants notified on a rolling basis starting 2/15; must reply within 2 week(s) of notification.

Transfers: No deadline.

CONTACT

Toni Bryant, Associate Dean of Admissions & Financial Aid

2100 Memorial Boulevard, Kerrville, TX 78028-5697

(830) 896-5411

South Plains College
Levelland, Texas
www.southplainscollege.edu   Federal Code: 003611

2-year public community and junior college in large town.
Enrollment: 7,639 undergrads, 43% part-time. 1,265 full-time freshmen.
Selectivity: Open admission; but selective for some programs.

BASIC COSTS (2016-2017)
Tuition and fees: $2,762; out-of-district residents $4,082; out-of-state residents $4,562.
Room and board: $3,900.

FINANCIAL AID PICTURE (2015-2016)
Students with need: 76% of average financial aid package awarded as scholarships/grants, 24% awarded as loans/jobs. Need-based aid available for part-time students. Work study available nights, weekends, and for part-time students.
Students without need: No-need awards available for academics, athletics, leadership, minority status, state/district residency.

FINANCIAL AID PROCEDURES
Forms required: FAFSA.
Dates and Deadlines: Priority date 6/1; no closing date. Applicants notified on a rolling basis starting 6/30; must reply within 2 week(s) of notification.

CONTACT
Suzan Nazworth, Director of Financial Aid
1401 South College Ave, Levelland, TX 79336
(806) 894-9611

South Texas College
McAllen, Texas
www.southtexascollege.edu   Federal Code: 031034

2-year public community and technical college in very large city.
Enrollment: 33,923 undergrads, 68% part-time. 3,262 full-time freshmen.
Selectivity: Open admission; but selective for some programs.

BASIC COSTS (2016-2017)
Tuition and fees: $3,480; out-of-district residents $3,753; out-of-state residents $7,230.

FINANCIAL AID PICTURE (2015-2016)
Students with need: Need-based aid available for part-time students.
Students without need: No-need awards available for academics.

FINANCIAL AID PROCEDURES
Forms required: FAFSA.
Dates and Deadlines: Priority date 3/15; no closing date. Applicants notified on a rolling basis starting 4/15.
Transfers: No deadline. Applicants notified by 5/15; must reply within 4 week(s) of notification.

CONTACT
Miguel Galvan, Director of Financial Aid
3201 West Pecan Boulevard, McAllen, TX 78502
(956) 872-8375

Southern Methodist University
Dallas, Texas   Federal Code: 003613
www.smu.edu   CSS Code: 6660

4-year private university in very large city, affiliated with the United Methodist Church.
Enrollment: 6,487 undergrads, 3% part-time. 1,522 full-time freshmen.

Selectivity: Admits less than 50% of applicants. GED not accepted.

BASIC COSTS (2016-2017)
Tuition and fees: $50,358.
Per-credit charge: $1,867.
Room and board: $16,125.

FINANCIAL AID PICTURE (2016-2017)
Students with need: Out of 823 full-time freshmen who applied for aid, 592 were judged to have need. Of these, 591 received aid, and 238 had their full need met. Average financial aid package met 90% of need; average scholarship/grant was $21,971; average loan was $3,249. For part-time students, average financial aid package was $18,813.
Students without need: 603 full-time freshmen who did not demonstrate need for aid received scholarships/grants; average award was $23,315. No-need awards available for academics, alumni affiliation, art, athletics, leadership, music/drama.
Scholarships offered: 73 full-time freshmen received athletic scholarships; average amount $57,799.

FINANCIAL AID PROCEDURES
Forms required: FAFSA, CSS PROFILE.
Dates and Deadlines: Priority date 11/1; no closing date. Applicants notified by 1/20; must reply by 5/1.
Transfers: Priority date 4/1. Merit scholarships available for community college and senior institution honor transfers. Students entering without scholarship aid will receive need-based aid up to cost of tuition.

CONTACT
Marc Peterson, Executive Director of Enrollment Services
PO Box 750181, Dallas, TX 75275-0181
(214) 768-3417

Southwest Texas Junior College
Uvalde, Texas
www.swtjc.edu   Federal Code: 003614

2-year public community and junior college in large town.
Enrollment: 6,439 undergrads, 70% part-time. 692 full-time freshmen.
Selectivity: Open admission.

BASIC COSTS (2016-2017)
Tuition and fees: $2,738; out-of-district residents $4,568; out-of-state residents $5,678.
Per-credit charge: $57; out-of-district residents $118; out-of-state residents $155.
Room and board: $4,660.

FINANCIAL AID PICTURE
Students with need: Need-based aid available for full-time and part-time students.

FINANCIAL AID PROCEDURES
Forms required: FAFSA.
Dates and Deadlines: Priority date 6/15; no closing date. Applicants notified on a rolling basis starting 5/1; must reply within 2 week(s) of notification.
Transfers: Financial aid application deadline for specific scholarships 4/1; priority deadline for grants 5/1.

CONTACT
Yvette Hernandez, Director of Financial Aid
2401 Garner Field Road, Uvalde, TX 78801
(830) 591-7368

Southwestern Adventist University

Keene, Texas
www.swau.edu   Federal Code: 003619

4-year private university and liberal arts college in small town, affiliated with the Seventh-day Adventists.
Enrollment: 716 undergrads, 7% part-time. 134 full-time freshmen.
Selectivity: Admits less than 50% of applicants.

BASIC COSTS (2016-2017)
Tuition and fees: $20,276.
Per-credit charge: $819.
Room and board: $7,500.

FINANCIAL AID PICTURE (2016-2017)
Students with need: Out of 123 full-time freshmen who applied for aid, 106 were judged to have need. Of these, 106 received aid, and 17 had their full need met. Average financial aid package met 65% of need; average scholarship/grant was $12,739; average loan was $2,334. For part-time students, average financial aid package was $9,873.
Students without need: 28 full-time freshmen who did not demonstrate need for aid received scholarships/grants; average award was $7,821. No-need awards available for academics, leadership, music/drama.

FINANCIAL AID PROCEDURES
Forms required: FAFSA, institutional form.
Dates and Deadlines: Priority date 3/15; no closing date. Applicants notified on a rolling basis starting 3/15.
Transfers: No deadline. Applicants notified on a rolling basis.

CONTACT
Duane Valencia, Assistant Vice President for Financial Administration, Student Finance
Box 567, Keene, TX 76059
(817) 202-6262

Southwestern Assemblies of God University

Waxahachie, Texas
www.sagu.edu   Federal Code: 003616

4-year private university and Bible college in large town, affiliated with the Assemblies of God.
Enrollment: 1,656 undergrads, 13% part-time. 308 full-time freshmen.

BASIC COSTS (2017-2018)
Tuition and fees: $20,410.
Per-credit charge: $695.
Room and board: $7,060.

FINANCIAL AID PICTURE
Students with need: Need-based aid available for full-time and part-time students.

FINANCIAL AID PROCEDURES
Forms required: FAFSA.
Dates and Deadlines: Priority date 3/1; no closing date. Applicants notified on a rolling basis starting 6/1; must reply within 2 week(s) of notification.

CONTACT
Jeff Francis, Senior Director of Financial Aid
1200 Sycamore Street, Waxahachie, TX 75165
(972) 825-4730

Southwestern Baptist Theological Seminary

Fort Worth, Texas
www.swbts.edu

4-year private Bible and seminary college in very large city, affiliated with the Christian Church.
Enrollment: 543 undergrads.

BASIC COSTS (2017-2018)
Tuition and fees: $15,000.
Per-credit charge: $480.
Room only: $1,890.

FINANCIAL AID PICTURE
Students with need: Need-based aid available for full-time and part-time students.

CONTACT
Adam Mallette, Director of Student Services
PO Box 22000, Fort Worth, TX 76122
(817) 923-1921 ext. 3080

Southwestern Christian College

Terrell, Texas
www.swcc.edu   Federal Code: 003618

4-year private Bible and liberal arts college in large town, affiliated with the Church of Christ.
Enrollment: 143 undergrads, 3% part-time. 59 full-time freshmen.
Selectivity: Open admission.

BASIC COSTS (2016-2017)
Tuition and fees: $8,074.
Per-credit charge: $310.
Room and board: $5,600.

FINANCIAL AID PICTURE (2015-2016)
Students with need: 74% of average financial aid package awarded as scholarships/grants, 26% awarded as loans/jobs. Need-based aid available for part-time students.
Students without need: No-need awards available for academics, athletics, music/drama.

FINANCIAL AID PROCEDURES
Forms required: FAFSA.
Dates and Deadlines: Closing date 6/1. Applicants notified on a rolling basis starting 7/15; must reply within 2 week(s) of notification.

CONTACT
Tonya Dean, Director of Financial Aid
PO Box 10, Terrell, TX 75160
(972) 524-3341 ext. 124

Southwestern University

Georgetown, Texas
www.southwestern.edu   Federal Code: 003620

4-year private liberal arts and performing arts college in large town, affiliated with the United Methodist Church.
Enrollment: 1,477 undergrads, 1% part-time. 381 full-time freshmen.
Selectivity: Admits less than 50% of applicants.

BASIC COSTS (2017-2018)
Tuition and fees: $40,560.
Per-credit charge: $1,690.

Room and board: $11,810.

FINANCIAL AID PICTURE (2016-2017)

Students with need: Out of 314 full-time freshmen who applied for aid, 255 were judged to have need. Of these, 255 received aid, and 92 had their full need met. Average financial aid package met 96% of need; average scholarship/grant was $30,013; average loan was $4,133. For part-time students, average financial aid package was $17,496.

Students without need: 125 full-time freshmen who did not demonstrate need for aid received scholarships/grants; average award was $22,126. No-need awards available for academics, alumni affiliation, art, leadership, minority status, music/drama, religious affiliation.

Scholarships offered: Academic Merit Scholarships; $2,000 to $22,000 per year. Brown Scholarships; full tuition, average room and average board. National Merit Finalist Awards; $2,000 per year. Fine Arts Scholarships; $3,500 to $10,000 per year; for students majoring in art, music or theater; based on talent, auditions or portfolio review. Music Performance Awards; up to $2,500; based on talent and awarded to non-fine arts majors who wish to participate in university ensemble. Dixon Scholarship; $5,000 per year or full tuition; awarded to high-achieving African-American, Hispanic, and Native American students. Beneficiary Grants; $6,000 per year; awarded to dependents of United Methodist clergy. Preministerial Scholarships; $3,000 per year; to students interested in full-time ministry careers.

FINANCIAL AID PROCEDURES

Forms required: FAFSA.

Dates and Deadlines: Priority date 3/1; closing date 3/1. Applicants notified on a rolling basis starting 12/15; must reply by 5/1 or within 2 week(s) of notification.

Transfers: Applicants notified on a rolling basis starting 3/1; must reply by 5/1 or within 2 week(s) of notification.

CONTACT

James Gaeta, Director of Financial Aid
PO Box 770, Georgetown, TX 78627-0770
(512) 863-1259

Stephen F. Austin State University
Nacogdoches, Texas
www.sfasu.edu   Federal Code: 003624

4-year public university in large town.
Enrollment: 10,765 undergrads, 11% part-time. 2,118 full-time freshmen.
Selectivity: Admits 50 to 75% of applicants.

BASIC COSTS (2016-2017)

Tuition and fees: $9,537; out-of-state residents $21,777.
Per-credit charge: $242; out-of-state residents $650.
Room and board: $8,868.

FINANCIAL AID PICTURE (2015-2016)

Students with need: Out of 1,820 full-time freshmen who applied for aid, 1,392 were judged to have need. Of these, 1,391 received aid, and 165 had their full need met. Average financial aid package met 60% of need; average scholarship/grant was $9,758; average loan was $3,644. For part-time students, average financial aid package was $8,999.

Students without need: 317 full-time freshmen who did not demonstrate need for aid received scholarships/grants; average award was $2,332. No-need awards available for academics, alumni affiliation, art, leadership, music/drama, state/district residency.

Scholarships offered: *Merit:* Academic Excellence Scholarship Program; $3,000 per year; rank in top 10% of high school class or top quartile class with 1100 SAT (exclusive of Writing) or 24 ACT; renewable with 3.5 GPA. Dugas Honors Scholarship; $2,500 per semester; active member of School of Honors. University Scholars Program; $2,000 per semester; minimum 1220 SAT, 27 ACT, 3.0 GPA maintenance; up to 11 awarded. Student Foundation Association Leadership Scholarship; amounts vary; demonstrated leadership capabilities and academic achievement throughout high school career; 1

awarded. *Athletic:* 44 full-time freshmen received athletic scholarships; average amount $9,658.

Additional info: For students who qualify, Purple Promise tuition guarantee program covers the remaining balance of any tuition and mandatory fees not covered by other gift aid, for 15 hours per regular semester for up to 4 years.

FINANCIAL AID PROCEDURES

Forms required: FAFSA.

Dates and Deadlines: Priority date 3/15; no closing date. Applicants notified on a rolling basis starting 3/15.

CONTACT

H. Rachele Garrett, Director of Financial Aid
Box 13051, SFA Station, Nacogdoches, TX 75962-3051
(936) 468-2403

Sul Ross State University
Alpine, Texas
www.sulross.edu   Federal Code: 003625

4-year public university in small town.
Enrollment: 1,354 undergrads.

BASIC COSTS (2016-2017)

Tuition and fees: $7,816; out-of-state residents $20,056.
Room and board: $7,988.

FINANCIAL AID PICTURE

Students with need: Need-based aid available for full-time and part-time students.

Students without need: No-need awards available for academics, alumni affiliation, art, leadership, music/drama, state/district residency.

FINANCIAL AID PROCEDURES

Forms required: FAFSA.

Dates and Deadlines: Priority date 3/1; no closing date. Applicants notified by 3/3.

CONTACT

Michael Corbett, Director
PO Box C-2, Alpine, TX 79832
(432) 837-8050

Tarleton State University
Stephenville, Texas
www.tarleton.edu   Federal Code: 003631

4-year public university in large town.
Enrollment: 11,282 undergrads, 29% part-time. 1,917 full-time freshmen.
Selectivity: Admits 50 to 75% of applicants.

BASIC COSTS (2016-2017)

Tuition and fees: $8,466; out-of-state residents $20,706.
Per-credit charge: $154; out-of-state residents $562.
Room and board: $9,970.

FINANCIAL AID PICTURE (2015-2016)

Students with need: Need-based aid available for full-time and part-time students.

Students without need: No-need awards available for academics, alumni affiliation, athletics, leadership, music/drama, ROTC.

Additional info: Tuition guarantee program covers tuition and fees for qualified freshman.

FINANCIAL AID PROCEDURES

Forms required: FAFSA.

Dates and Deadlines: Priority date 3/15; no closing date. Applicants notified on a rolling basis starting 5/1; must reply within 2 week(s) of notification. **Transfers:** No deadline.

CONTACT
Kathy Purvis, Executive Director, Student Financial Aid
Box T-0030, Stephenville, TX 76402
(254) 968-9070

Tarrant County College
Fort Worth, Texas
www.tccd.edu   Federal Code: 003626

2-year public community college in very large city.
Enrollment: 38,363 undergrads.
Selectivity: Open admission; but selective for some programs.

BASIC COSTS (2016-2017)
Tuition and fees: $1,770; out-of-district residents $3,180; out-of-state residents $7,650.
Per-credit charge: $59; out-of-district residents $106; out-of-state residents $255.

FINANCIAL AID PICTURE (2016-2017)
Students with need: 70% of average financial aid package awarded as scholarships/grants, 30% awarded as loans/jobs. Need-based aid available for part-time students.
Students without need: No-need awards available for academics.

FINANCIAL AID PROCEDURES
Forms required: FAFSA, institutional form.
Dates and Deadlines: Priority date 5/1; no closing date. Applicants notified on a rolling basis starting 5/1; must reply within 2 week(s) of notification.
Transfers: No deadline. Applicants notified on a rolling basis.

CONTACT
Samantha Stalnaker, District Director of Financial Aid
300 Trinity Campus Circle, Fort Worth, TX 76102-1964
(817) 515-4243

Temple College
Temple, Texas
www.templejc.edu   Federal Code: 003627

2-year public community college in small city.
Enrollment: 4,874 undergrads.
Selectivity: Open admission; but selective for some programs.

BASIC COSTS (2016-2017)
Tuition and fees: $2,670; out-of-district residents $4,770; out-of-state residents $7,170.
Per-credit charge: $89; out-of-district residents $159; out-of-state residents $239.

FINANCIAL AID PICTURE
Students with need: Need-based aid available for full-time and part-time students. Work study available nights.
Students without need: This college awards aid only to students with need.

FINANCIAL AID PROCEDURES
Forms required: FAFSA.
Dates and Deadlines: Priority date 6/1; no closing date. Applicants notified on a rolling basis starting 5/1; must reply within 4 week(s) of notification.
Transfers: No deadline. Applicants notified on a rolling basis starting 5/1; must reply within 4 week(s) of notification.

CONTACT
Peggy Watts, Director of Financial Aid
2600 South First Street, Temple, TX 76504-7435
(254) 298-8321

Texarkana College
Texarkana, Texas
www.texarkanacollege.edu   Federal Code: 003628

2-year public community college in small city.
Enrollment: 1,443 full-time undergrads.
Selectivity: Open admission.

BASIC COSTS (2017-2018)
Tuition and fees: $2,620; out-of-district residents $4,210; out-of-state residents $5,710.
Per-credit charge: $49; out-of-district residents $102; out-of-state residents $152.

FINANCIAL AID PICTURE (2015-2016)
Students with need: 72% of average financial aid package awarded as scholarships/grants, 28% awarded as loans/jobs. Need-based aid available for part-time students. Work study available nights.
Students without need: No-need awards available for academics, art, music/drama.
Scholarships offered: The Presidential Scholarship will be awarded in the full amount of tuition and fees. This Scholarship is intended for the completion of an Associate degree and will be awarded for two years or until the completion of 60 credit hours. If you are a current-year graduate and have a cumulative, unweighted GPA of 3.25 and are ranked in the top 15% of your class or in the top 10 graduates of your class, you are guaranteed acceptance for this scholarship. If you have a 3.25 GPA but do not meet the other criteria, you may still apply; please write a paragraph with 300 words or less describing your academic and career goals and attach to your application. Priority will be given to students who meet the application deadline of April 1. All recipients must be TSI met in all areas.

FINANCIAL AID PROCEDURES
Forms required: FAFSA, institutional form.
Dates and Deadlines: Priority date 7/24; no closing date. Applicants notified on a rolling basis starting 3/1.
Transfers: Closing date 5/1. Applicants notified on a rolling basis.

CONTACT
Susan Johnston, Director of Financial Aid
2500 North Robison Road, Texarkana, TX 75599
(903) 823-3163

Texas A&M International University
Laredo, Texas
www.tamiu.edu   Federal Code: 009651

4-year public university in small city.
Enrollment: 6,566 undergrads, 26% part-time. 1,010 full-time freshmen.
Selectivity: Admits less than 50% of applicants.

BASIC COSTS (2016-2017)
Tuition and fees: $8,446; out-of-state residents $20,879.
Per-credit charge: $177; out-of-state residents $567.1.
Room and board: $8,936.

FINANCIAL AID PICTURE
Students with need: Need-based aid available for full-time and part-time students. Work study available nights, weekends, and for part-time students.
Students without need: No-need awards available for academics, art, athletics, leadership, music/drama.

FINANCIAL AID PROCEDURES

Forms required: FAFSA, institutional form.

Dates and Deadlines: Priority date 3/15; no closing date. Applicants notified on a rolling basis starting 4/15; must reply within 2 week(s) of notification.

Transfers: No deadline. Applicants notified on a rolling basis starting 11/30; must reply within 2 week(s) of notification.

CONTACT

Laura Elizondo, Director of Financial Aid
5201 University Boulevard, Laredo, TX 78041-1900
(956) 326-2225

Texas A&M University
College Station, Texas
www.tamu.edu   Federal Code: 003632

4-year public university in small city.

Enrollment: 50,392 undergrads, 11% part-time. 8,692 full-time freshmen.

Selectivity: Admits 50 to 75% of applicants.

BASIC COSTS (2017-2018)

Tuition and fees: $10,030; out-of-state residents $30,208.

Per-credit charge: $223; out-of-state residents $895.

Room and board: $10,368.

FINANCIAL AID PICTURE (2016-2017)

Students with need: Out of 6,718 full-time freshmen who applied for aid, 4,254 were judged to have need. Of these, 4,042 received aid, and 1,079 had their full need met. Average financial aid package met 76% of need; average scholarship/grant was $11,549; average loan was $7,685. For part-time students, average financial aid package was $11,369.

Students without need: 1,387 full-time freshmen who did not demonstrate need for aid received scholarships/grants; average award was $4,157. No-need awards available for academics, alumni affiliation, art, athletics, job skills, leadership, music/drama, religious affiliation, ROTC, state/district residency.

Scholarships offered: *Merit:* Texas residents; Regents scholarship, additional $5,000 annually for 4 years, first-generation students incomes <$40,000. Aggie Assurance, minimum scholarships, grants for Pell students, incomes <$30,000; incomes <$60,000 gift aid for tuition only. Students must maintain a 2.5 GPA. *Athletic:* 38 full-time freshmen received athletic scholarships; average amount $8,184.

Additional info: Short-term loans available.

FINANCIAL AID PROCEDURES

Forms required: FAFSA.

Dates and Deadlines: Priority date 3/15; no closing date. Applicants notified on a rolling basis starting 4/1.

CONTACT

Delisa Falks, Executive Director, Scholarships and Financial Aid
750 Agronomy Road, Suite 1601, College Station, TX 77843-0200
(979) 845-3236

Texas A&M University-Commerce
Commerce, Texas
www.tamuc.edu   Federal Code: 003565

4-year public university in small town.

Enrollment: 6,797 undergrads, 25% part-time. 988 full-time freshmen.

Selectivity: Admits less than 50% of applicants.

BASIC COSTS (2016-2017)

Tuition and fees: $8,009; out-of-state residents $20,138.

Per-credit charge: $160; out-of-state residents $550.

Room and board: $8,326.

FINANCIAL AID PICTURE (2015-2016)

Students with need: Out of 890 full-time freshmen who applied for aid, 727 were judged to have need. Of these, 704 received aid, and 54 had their full need met. Average financial aid package met 67% of need; average scholarship/grant was $11,201; average loan was $3,029. For part-time students, average financial aid package was $6,269.

Students without need: 58 full-time freshmen who did not demonstrate need for aid received scholarships/grants; average award was $1,989. No-need awards available for academics, alumni affiliation, art, athletics, job skills, leadership, music/drama, ROTC, state/district residency.

Scholarships offered: 24 full-time freshmen received athletic scholarships; average amount $3,744.

Additional info: Work-study also available for full-time students.

FINANCIAL AID PROCEDURES

Forms required: FAFSA.

Dates and Deadlines: Priority date 4/1; no closing date. Applicants notified on a rolling basis starting 5/1; must reply within 4 week(s) of notification.

CONTACT

Maria Ramos, Director of Financial Aid and Scholarships
Box 3011, Commerce, TX 75429-3011
(903) 886-5091

Texas A&M University-Corpus Christi
Corpus Christi, Texas
www.tamucc.edu   Federal Code: 011161

4-year public university in large city.

Enrollment: 10,205 undergrads, 18% part-time. 2,243 full-time freshmen.

Selectivity: Admits over 75% of applicants.

BASIC COSTS (2016-2017)

Tuition and fees: $9,105; out-of-state residents $21,193.

Per-credit charge: $175.69; out-of-state residents $578.24.

Room and board: $9,874.

FINANCIAL AID PICTURE (2016-2017)

Students with need: Out of 1,890 full-time freshmen who applied for aid, 1,553 were judged to have need. Of these, 1,475 received aid, and 196 had their full need met. Average financial aid package met 55% of need; average loan was $3,223. For part-time students, average financial aid package was $6,597.

Students without need: 137 full-time freshmen who did not demonstrate need for aid received scholarships/grants; average award was $2,533. No-need awards available for academics, art, athletics, leadership, music/drama, ROTC.

Scholarships offered: 61 full-time freshmen received athletic scholarships; average amount $10,995.

FINANCIAL AID PROCEDURES

Forms required: FAFSA.

Dates and Deadlines: Priority date 3/31; no closing date. Applicants notified on a rolling basis starting 4/1; must reply within 2 week(s) of notification.

Transfers: No deadline. Applicants notified on a rolling basis starting 4/1; must reply within 2 week(s) of notification.

CONTACT

Jeannie Gage, Director, Financial Assistance
6300 Ocean Drive, Unit 5774, Corpus Christi, TX 78412-5774
(361) 825-2338

Texas A&M University-Kingsville
Kingsville, Texas
www.tamuk.edu   Federal Code: 003639

4-year public university in large town.

Enrollment: 5,845 undergrads, 13% part-time. 1,263 full-time freshmen.

Selectivity: Admits over 75% of applicants.

BASIC COSTS (2016-2017)
Tuition and fees: $8,050; out-of-state residents $21,356.
Room and board: $8,530.
Additional info: Tuition at time of enrollment locked for 4 years.

FINANCIAL AID PICTURE (2015-2016)
Students with need: Out of 1,109 full-time freshmen who applied for aid, 975 were judged to have need. Of these, 975 received aid, and 916 had their full need met. Average financial aid package met 75% of need; average scholarship/grant was $9,207; average loan was $3,151. For part-time students, average financial aid package was $7,647.
Students without need: 5 full-time freshmen who did not demonstrate need for aid received scholarships/grants; average award was $3,900. No-need awards available for academics, athletics, leadership, minority status, state/district residency.
Scholarships offered: 64 full-time freshmen received athletic scholarships; average amount $5,275.

FINANCIAL AID PROCEDURES
Forms required: FAFSA.
Dates and Deadlines: Priority date 3/15; no closing date. Applicants notified on a rolling basis starting 4/15; must reply within 12 week(s) of notification.

CONTACT
Lisa Seals, Interim Executive Director
MSC 128, Kingsville, TX 78363-8202
(361) 593-3911

Texas A&M University-Texarkana
Texarkana, Texas
www.tamut.edu   Federal Code: 031703

Upper-division public university in small city.
Enrollment: 1,561 undergrads, 35% part-time. 183 full-time freshmen.

BASIC COSTS (2016-2017)
Tuition and fees: $7,257; out-of-state residents $20,616.
Room and board: $8,105.

FINANCIAL AID PICTURE (2015-2016)
Students with need: 61% of average financial aid package awarded as scholarships/grants, 39% awarded as loans/jobs. Need-based aid available for part-time students. Work study available nights, weekends, and for part-time students.
Students without need: No-need awards available for academics, alumni affiliation, art, athletics, job skills, leadership, music/drama, state/district residency.

FINANCIAL AID PROCEDURES
Forms required: FAFSA.
Dates and Deadlines: Priority date 3/15; closing date 9/30. Applicants notified on a rolling basis; must reply within 4 week(s) of notification.
Transfers: Priority date 3/15; closing date 9/30. Applicants notified on a rolling basis; must reply within 10 week(s) of notification. Transfer students must have completed minimum of 54 semester hours of transferable college credit to apply for financial aid and notified applicants must reply within 45 days from date of award letter. Exceptions made on individual basis. April 1 financial aid deadline for scholarships.

CONTACT
Michael Fuller, Director of Financial Aid
7101 University Avenue, Texarkana, TX 75503
(903) 233-3066

Texas Christian University
Fort Worth, Texas   Federal Code: 003636
www.tcu.edu   CSS Code: 6820

4-year private university in very large city, affiliated with the Christian Church (Disciples of Christ).
Enrollment: 8,852 undergrads, 3% part-time. 1,887 full-time freshmen.
Selectivity: Admits less than 50% of applicants. GED not accepted.

BASIC COSTS (2016-2017)
Tuition and fees: $42,670.
Room and board: $12,000.
Additional info: Tuition/fee waivers available for adults, minority students.

FINANCIAL AID PICTURE (2016-2017)
Students with need: Out of 1,066 full-time freshmen who applied for aid, 707 were judged to have need. Of these, 698 received aid, and 282 had their full need met. Average financial aid package met 71% of need; average scholarship/grant was $27,163; average loan was $3,228. For part-time students, average financial aid package was $14,892.
Students without need: 565 full-time freshmen who did not demonstrate need for aid received scholarships/grants; average award was $17,976. No-need awards available for academics, alumni affiliation, art, minority status, music/drama, religious affiliation, ROTC, state/district residency.
Scholarships offered: 71 full-time freshmen received athletic scholarships; average amount $26,691.

FINANCIAL AID PROCEDURES
Forms required: FAFSA, CSS PROFILE.
Dates and Deadlines: Priority date 2/15; closing date 5/1. Applicants notified on a rolling basis starting 12/15.
Transfers: No deadline. Applicants notified on a rolling basis starting 6/15. Transfer students must submit both the FAFSA and the CSS PROFILE to receive financial aid.

CONTACT
Michael Scott, Director of Scholarships and Student Financial Aid
TCU Box 297013, Fort Worth, TX 76129
(817) 257-7858

Texas College
Tyler, Texas
www.texascollege.edu   Federal Code: 003638

4-year private liberal arts college in small city, affiliated with the Christian Methodist Episcopal Church.
Enrollment: 813 undergrads.
Selectivity: Open admission.

BASIC COSTS (2016-2017)
Tuition and fees: $10,008.
Room and board: $8,000.

FINANCIAL AID PICTURE
Students with need: Need-based aid available for full-time and part-time students.
Students without need: No-need awards available for academics, athletics, leadership, music/drama.

FINANCIAL AID PROCEDURES
Forms required: FAFSA, institutional form.
Dates and Deadlines: Priority date 6/1; no closing date. Applicants notified on a rolling basis starting 4/15.

CONTACT
Angela Marshall, Director of Financial Aid
2404 North Grand Avenue, Tyler, TX 75712-4500
(903) 593-8311 ext. 2208

Texas Lutheran University

Seguin, Texas
www.tlu.edu   Federal Code: 003641

4-year private university and liberal arts college in large town, affiliated with the Evangelical Lutheran Church in America.
Enrollment: 1,252 undergrads, 3% part-time. 377 full-time freshmen.
Selectivity: Admits less than 50% of applicants.

BASIC COSTS (2016-2017)
Tuition and fees: $28,910.
Per-credit charge: $945.
Room and board: $9,720.

FINANCIAL AID PICTURE (2016-2017)
Students with need: Out of 350 full-time freshmen who applied for aid, 308 were judged to have need. Of these, 308 received aid. For part-time students, average financial aid package was $8,875.
Students without need: 5 full-time freshmen who did not demonstrate need for aid received scholarships/grants; average award was $500. No-need awards available for academics, alumni affiliation, leadership, music/drama, religious affiliation.
Scholarships offered: National Merit Finalist Scholarship; full tuition. Pacesetter Award for College Excellence; up to $18,000 a year. Locus Aduro Award in Dramatic Media; up to $18,000 a year. Da capo Award in Music; up to $18,000 a year. TLU CHOICE Scholarship; difference between cost at TLU and University of Texas-Austin or Texas AM-College Station. Presidential Scholarship; up to $11,000 a year. Academic Excellence Award; up to $9,000 a year.

FINANCIAL AID PROCEDURES
Forms required: FAFSA.
Dates and Deadlines: Priority date 4/1; no closing date. Applicants notified on a rolling basis starting 3/1; must reply within 4 week(s) of notification.
Transfers: No deadline. Applicants notified on a rolling basis starting 3/1; must reply within 6 week(s) of notification.

CONTACT
Bonnie Trevino, Director Financial Aid
1000 West Court Street, Seguin, TX 78155-5999
(830) 372-8075

Texas Southern University

Houston, Texas
www.tsu.edu   Federal Code: 003642

4-year public university in very large city.
Enrollment: 6,562 undergrads, 12% part-time. 1,219 full-time freshmen.
Selectivity: Admits 50 to 75% of applicants.

BASIC COSTS (2016-2017)
Tuition and fees: $9,001; out-of-state residents $21,241.
Per-credit charge: $100.
Room and board: $10,566.
Additional info: Tuition/fee waivers available for minority students.

FINANCIAL AID PICTURE
Students with need: Need-based aid available for full-time and part-time students. Work study available nights, weekends, and for part-time students.
Students without need: This college awards aid only to students with need.

FINANCIAL AID PROCEDURES
Forms required: FAFSA.
Dates and Deadlines: Priority date 5/15; no closing date. Applicants notified on a rolling basis starting 6/1.
Transfers: Priority date 4/1; closing date 8/30.

CONTACT
Linda Ballard, Director of Financial Aid
3100 Cleburne Street, Houston, TX 77004
(713) 313-7071

Texas State Technical College

Waco, Texas
www.tstc.edu   Federal Code: 003634

2-year public technical college in small city.
Enrollment: 9,184 undergrads, 52% part-time. 1,427 full-time freshmen.
Selectivity: Open admission.

BASIC COSTS (2016-2017)
Tuition and fees: $4,794; out-of-state residents $10,080.
Room and board: $5,420.

FINANCIAL AID PICTURE (2016-2017)
Students with need: 82% of average financial aid package awarded as scholarships/grants, 18% awarded as loans/jobs. Need-based aid available for part-time students.
Students without need: This college awards aid only to students with need.

FINANCIAL AID PROCEDURES
Forms required: FAFSA.
Dates and Deadlines: Priority date 6/1; no closing date. Applicants notified on a rolling basis starting 5/15.
Transfers: No deadline. Applicants notified on a rolling basis.

CONTACT
Jackie Adler, Director, Financial Aid
3801 Campus Drive, Waco, TX 76705
(254) 867-4814

Texas State University

San Marcos, Texas
www.txstate.edu   Federal Code: 003615

4-year public university in large town.
Enrollment: 34,244 undergrads, 18% part-time. 5,513 full-time freshmen.
Selectivity: Admits 50 to 75% of applicants.

BASIC COSTS (2016-2017)
Tuition and fees: $10,218; out-of-state residents $22,458.
Per-credit charge: $258; out-of-state residents $666.
Room and board: $9,132.
Additional info: Tuition at time of enrollment locked for 4 years.

FINANCIAL AID PICTURE (2016-2017)
Students with need: Out of 5,106 full-time freshmen who applied for aid, 3,508 were judged to have need. Of these, 3,340 received aid, and 649 had their full need met. Average financial aid package met 71% of need; average scholarship/grant was $8,169; average loan was $5,067. For part-time students, average financial aid package was $5,601.
Students without need: 225 full-time freshmen who did not demonstrate need for aid received scholarships/grants; average award was $4,568. No-need awards available for academics, art, athletics, leadership, minority status, music/drama, ROTC, state/district residency.
Scholarships offered: *Merit:* Terry Foundation Scholarship; $12,500; 16 awarded. McCoy Scholarship of Excellence; $8,000; number awarded varies. McCoy Scholarship of Distinction; $5,000; number varies. University Scholars; $3,000; 8 awarded. Lone Star Scholarship; $2,500; 10 awarded. *Athletic:* 20 full-time freshmen received athletic scholarships; average amount $10,877.

Additional info: Federal and state work study programs are available for those that qualify. Employment time varies by hiring departments. The Bobcat Promise program guarantees free tuition and mandatory fees for 15 credit hours per semester to Texas residents who are full-time entering freshmen with a family adjusted gross income that does not exceed $35,000.

FINANCIAL AID PROCEDURES

Forms required: FAFSA.

Dates and Deadlines: Priority date 4/1; no closing date. Applicants notified on a rolling basis starting 5/1; must reply within 3 week(s) of notification.

Transfers: Priority date 3/1; no deadline. Applicants notified on a rolling basis starting 5/1; must reply within 3 week(s) of notification.

CONTACT

Christopher Murr, Director of Financial Aid & Scholarship Office
429 North Guadalupe Street, San Marcos, TX 78666-5709
(512) 245-2315

Texas Tech University

Lubbock, Texas
www.ttu.edu   Federal Code: 003644

4-year public university in small city.

Enrollment: 29,587 undergrads, 10% part-time. 5,079 full-time freshmen.

Selectivity: Admits 50 to 75% of applicants.

BASIC COSTS (2016-2017)

Tuition and fees: $9,781; out-of-state residents $21,481.

Per-credit charge: $235; out-of-state residents $625.

Room and board: $8,505.

FINANCIAL AID PICTURE (2015-2016)

Students with need: Out of 3,347 full-time freshmen who applied for aid, 2,454 were judged to have need. Of these, 2,454 received aid, and 419 had their full need met. Average financial aid package met 70% of need; average scholarship/grant was $8,411; average loan was $4,708. For part-time students, average financial aid package was $10,742.

Students without need: 731 full-time freshmen who did not demonstrate need for aid received scholarships/grants; average award was $3,709. No-need awards available for academics, art, athletics, job skills, leadership, music/drama, ROTC.

Scholarships offered: *Merit:* Presidential Scholarships: National Merit finalist, approximately $25,000 per year; $6,000 per year, top 10% of high school graduating class and SAT 1400 or ACT 30; $5,000 per year, top 10% of high school class and SAT 1300 or ACT 27; $4,000 per year, top 25% of high school class and SAT 1200 or ACT 25; all are renewable for up to 4 years. *Athletic:* 46 full-time freshmen received athletic scholarships; average amount $15,489.

Additional info: Red Raider Guarantee program provides free tuition and mandatory fees for up to 15 credit hours per semester to new entering freshman who are Texas residents, enrolled full-time with family adjusted gross incomes that do not exceed $40,000. Eligible students who complete and submit the FAFSA by required deadline are guaranteed to receive funds based on available state and federal allocations. Applications received after the deadline will be awarded based on available funding. Students may qualify for the program for up to eight (8) semesters of full-time enrollment.

FINANCIAL AID PROCEDURES

Forms required: FAFSA.

Dates and Deadlines: Priority date 3/15; no closing date. Applicants notified on a rolling basis; must reply within 2 week(s) of notification.

Transfers: Priority date 3/15; no deadline. Applicants notified on a rolling basis starting 9/16.

CONTACT

Becky Wilson, Director of Financial Aid
Box 45005, Lubbock, TX 79409-5005
(806) 742-3681

Texas Tech University Health Sciences Center

Lubbock, Texas
www.ttuhsc.edu   Federal Code: 010674

Upper-division public university in small city.

Enrollment: 1,221 undergrads.

BASIC COSTS (2016-2017)

Tuition and fees: $9,586; out-of-state residents $21,286.

Room and board: $9,964.

Additional info: Figures shown are for traditional BSN in the School of Nursing.

FINANCIAL AID PICTURE

Students with need: Need-based aid available for full-time and part-time students.

Students without need: No-need awards available for academics.

FINANCIAL AID PROCEDURES

Transfers: No deadline. Applicants notified on a rolling basis.

CONTACT

Marcus Wilson, Director, Financial Aid
3601 Fourth Street, Lubbock, TX 79430

Texas Wesleyan University

Fort Worth, Texas
www.txwes.edu   Federal Code: 003645

4-year private university in very large city, affiliated with the United Methodist Church.

Enrollment: 1,685 undergrads, 12% part-time. 365 full-time freshmen.

Selectivity: Admits less than 50% of applicants.

BASIC COSTS (2016-2017)

Tuition and fees: $26,049.

Per-credit charge: $780.

Room and board: $9,084.

FINANCIAL AID PICTURE (2015-2016)

Students with need: Out of 212 full-time freshmen who applied for aid, 194 were judged to have need. Of these, 194 received aid, and 36 had their full need met. Average financial aid package met 79% of need; average scholarship/grant was $1,964; average loan was $3,098. For part-time students, average financial aid package was $13,570.

Students without need: 166 full-time freshmen who did not demonstrate need for aid received scholarships/grants; average award was $11,232. No-need awards available for academics, alumni affiliation, art, athletics, music/drama, religious affiliation, ROTC, state/district residency.

Scholarships offered: 11 full-time freshmen received athletic scholarships; average amount $11,836.

FINANCIAL AID PROCEDURES

Forms required: FAFSA.

Dates and Deadlines: Priority date 3/1; no closing date. Applicants notified on a rolling basis.

Transfers: No deadline.

CONTACT

Laurie Rosenkrantz, Financial Aid Director
1201 Wesleyan Street, Fort Worth, TX 76105-1536
(817) 531-4420

Texas Woman's University
Denton, Texas
www.twu.edu   Federal Code: 003646

4-year public university in small city.
Enrollment: 9,513 undergrads, 30% part-time. 1,291 full-time freshmen.
Selectivity: Admits over 75% of applicants.

BASIC COSTS (2016-2017)
Tuition and fees: $8,770; out-of-state residents $21,010.
Per-credit charge: $206.26; out-of-state residents $614.26.
Room and board: $7,578.

FINANCIAL AID PICTURE (2016-2017)
Students with need: Out of 1,119 full-time freshmen who applied for aid, 912 were judged to have need. Of these, 909 received aid, and 261 had their full need met. Average financial aid package met 84% of need; average scholarship/grant was $9,318; average loan was $5,703. For part-time students, average financial aid package was $9,879.
Students without need: 131 full-time freshmen who did not demonstrate need for aid received scholarships/grants; average award was $5,341. No-need awards available for academics, art, athletics, leadership, music/drama, state/district residency.
Scholarships offered: *Merit:* Chancellor's Endowed Scholarship; full tuition and fees, room and board; based on high school valedictorian status, extra-curricular activities, SAT score; 2 awarded. Presidential Scholarship; full tuition and fees; awarded to valedictorian or salutatorian. Honors Scholarship; $1,500 annually up to 4 years; based on admission to honors program and SAT score. New Freshman Scholarship; $1,500 annually up to 4 years; based on SAT/ACT score, class rank and GPA. Transfer Student Scholarship; $1,500 annually up to 4 years; based on GPA, must have completed at least 12 credit hours. New Student Scholarship; $1,800 annually up to 4 years; based on high school rank, ACT/SAT score; 150 awarded. *Athletic:* 6 full-time freshmen received athletic scholarships; average amount $5,167.

FINANCIAL AID PROCEDURES
Forms required: FAFSA, state aid form, institutional form.
Dates and Deadlines: Priority date 3/1; no closing date. Must reply by 7/1.

CONTACT
Governor Jackson, Director of Financial Aid
Box 425589, Denton, TX 76204-5589
(940) 898-3064

Trinity University
San Antonio, Texas   Federal Code: 003647
www.trinity.edu   CSS Code: 6831

4-year private university in very large city, affiliated with the Presbyterian Church (USA).
Enrollment: 2,317 undergrads, 2% part-time. 662 full-time freshmen.
Selectivity: Admits less than 50% of applicants.

BASIC COSTS (2016-2017)
Tuition and fees: $39,560.
Per-credit charge: $1,624.
Room and board: $12,754.

FINANCIAL AID PICTURE (2016-2017)
Students with need: Out of 491 full-time freshmen who applied for aid, 332 were judged to have need. Of these, 332 received aid, and 205 had their full need met. Average financial aid package met 97% of need; average scholarship/grant was $30,334; average loan was $3,406. For part-time students, average financial aid package was $6,895.
Students without need: 322 full-time freshmen who did not demonstrate need for aid received scholarships/grants; average award was $20,388. No-need awards available for academics, art, leadership, music/drama.

FINANCIAL AID PROCEDURES
Forms required: FAFSA, CSS PROFILE.
Dates and Deadlines: Priority date 2/15; no closing date. Applicants notified by 3/15; must reply by 5/1.
Transfers: Priority date 5/1; no deadline.

CONTACT
Glendi Gaddis, Director of Financial Aid
One Trinity Place, San Antonio, TX 78212-7200
(210) 999-8315

Trinity Valley Community College
Athens, Texas
www.tvcc.edu   Federal Code: 003572

2-year public community college in large town.
Enrollment: 6,508 undergrads, 68% part-time. 431 full-time freshmen.
Selectivity: Open admission; but selective for some programs.

BASIC COSTS (2016-2017)
Tuition and fees: $2,460; out-of-district residents $4,320; out-of-state residents $4,920.
Per-credit charge: $36; out-of-district residents $98; out-of-state residents $118.
Room and board: $5,650.
Additional info: Tuition/fee waivers available for adults.

FINANCIAL AID PICTURE
Students with need: Need-based aid available for full-time and part-time students. Work study available nights, weekends, and for part-time students.
Students without need: No-need awards available for academics, athletics.

FINANCIAL AID PROCEDURES
Forms required: FAFSA, institutional form.
Dates and Deadlines: Closing date 7/1. Applicants notified on a rolling basis starting 7/1; must reply within 2 week(s) of notification.
Transfers: Students on suspension at previous institution ineligible to receive aid.

CONTACT
Jennifer Evilsizer
100 Cardinal Drive, Athens, TX 75751
(903) 675-6233

Tyler Junior College
Tyler, Texas
www.tjc.edu   Federal Code: 003648

2-year public community and junior college in small city.
Enrollment: 11,475 undergrads, 49% part-time. 2,464 full-time freshmen.
Selectivity: Open admission; but selective for some programs.

BASIC COSTS (2017-2018)
Tuition and fees: $2,784; out-of-district residents $4,524; out-of-state residents $5,244.
Room and board: $8,320.

FINANCIAL AID PICTURE (2015-2016)
Students with need: Out of 1,901 full-time freshmen who applied for aid, 1,604 were judged to have need. Of these, 1,566 received aid, and 25 had their full need met. Average financial aid package met 58% of need; average scholarship/grant was $4,509; average loan was $3,348. For part-time students, average financial aid package was $4,478.
Students without need: 340 full-time freshmen who did not demonstrate need for aid received scholarships/grants; average award was $1,056. No-need awards available for academics, alumni affiliation, art, athletics, music/drama.

Scholarships offered: 439 full-time freshmen received athletic scholarships; average amount $1,759.

FINANCIAL AID PROCEDURES

Forms required: FAFSA, institutional form.

Dates and Deadlines: Priority date 4/1; closing date 6/1. Applicants notified on a rolling basis starting 4/1; must reply within 2 week(s) of notification.

Transfers: Financial aid transcript required if student enrolled same year elsewhere.

CONTACT

Devon Wiggins, Director of Student Financial Aid and Scholarship
Box 9020, Tyler, TX 75711-9020
(903) 510-2385

University of Dallas

Irving, Texas
www.udallas.edu   Federal Code: 003651

4-year private university and liberal arts college in small city, affiliated with the Roman Catholic Church.

Enrollment: 1,393 undergrads, 2% part-time. 371 full-time freshmen.

Selectivity: Admits over 75% of applicants.

BASIC COSTS (2017-2018)

Tuition and fees: $38,716.

Room and board: $11,960.

FINANCIAL AID PICTURE (2016-2017)

Students with need: Out of 314 full-time freshmen who applied for aid, 267 were judged to have need. Of these, 267 received aid, and 73 had their full need met. Average financial aid package met 83% of need; average scholarship/grant was $28,424; average loan was $3,989. For part-time students, average financial aid package was $11,423.

Students without need: 101 full-time freshmen who did not demonstrate need for aid received scholarships/grants; average award was $16,109. No-need awards available for academics, alumni affiliation, art, leadership, minority status, music/drama, religious affiliation, ROTC, state/district residency.

FINANCIAL AID PROCEDURES

Forms required: FAFSA.

Dates and Deadlines: Priority date 3/1; closing date 8/1. Applicants notified on a rolling basis starting 12/1; must reply by 5/1 or within 4 week(s) of notification.

Transfers: No deadline. Applicants notified on a rolling basis starting 3/1; must reply by 5/1 or within 4 week(s) of notification.

CONTACT

Taryn Anderson, Director of Financial Aid
1845 East Northgate Drive, Irving, TX 75062-4736
(972) 721-5266

University of Houston

Houston, Texas
www.uh.edu   Federal Code: 003652

4-year public university in very large city.

Enrollment: 34,688 undergrads, 27% part-time. 4,263 full-time freshmen.

Selectivity: Admits 50 to 75% of applicants.

BASIC COSTS (2016-2017)

Tuition and fees: $10,886; out-of-state residents $26,126.

Per-credit charge: $311; out-of-state residents $819.

FINANCIAL AID PICTURE (2016-2017)

Students with need: Out of 3,329 full-time freshmen who applied for aid, 2,630 were judged to have need. Of these, 2,491 received aid, and 452 had

their full need met. Average financial aid package met 64% of need; average scholarship/grant was $10,308; average loan was $5,475. For part-time students, average financial aid package was $9,222.

Students without need: 377 full-time freshmen who did not demonstrate need for aid received scholarships/grants; average award was $5,924. No-need awards available for academics, alumni affiliation, art, athletics, job skills, leadership, music/drama, ROTC, state/district residency.

Scholarships offered: 49 full-time freshmen received athletic scholarships; average amount $7,232.

Additional info: The Cougar Promise guarantees free tuition and mandatory fees to eligible new in-state freshmen with family incomes at or below $45,000.

FINANCIAL AID PROCEDURES

Forms required: FAFSA.

Dates and Deadlines: Priority date 3/15; no closing date. Applicants notified on a rolling basis starting 2/1.

Transfers: Applicants notified on a rolling basis starting 2/1.

CONTACT

Briget Jans, Executive Director
Office of Admission, Houston, TX 77004
(713) 743-1010

University of Houston-Clear Lake

Houston, Texas
www.uhcl.edu   Federal Code: 011711

4-year public university in very large city.

Enrollment: 5,557 undergrads, 52% part-time. 183 full-time freshmen.

BASIC COSTS (2016-2017)

Tuition and fees: $6,995; out-of-state residents $22,055.

Per-credit charge: $208; out-of-state residents $710.

FINANCIAL AID PICTURE (2015-2016)

Students with need: Out of 168 full-time freshmen who applied for aid, 123 were judged to have need. Of these, 112 received aid, and 13 had their full need met. Average financial aid package met 58% of need; average scholarship/grant was $10,025; average loan was $3,083. For part-time students, average financial aid package was $5,241.

Students without need: 15 full-time freshmen who did not demonstrate need for aid received scholarships/grants; average award was $7,687. No-need awards available for academics, art, minority status, state/district residency.

Scholarships offered: Non-need, merit based scholarships will be available to entering freshmen.

Additional info: UHCL offers the automatic transfer scholarship to any first-time transfer student if their transfer GPA is 2.75 or above upon receiving all transcripts. No application necessary for the scholarship.

FINANCIAL AID PROCEDURES

Forms required: FAFSA.

Dates and Deadlines: Priority date 3/15; no closing date. Applicants notified on a rolling basis starting 4/1; must reply within 2 week(s) of notification.

Transfers: No deadline. Applicants notified on a rolling basis starting 5/15; must reply within 4 week(s) of notification.

CONTACT

Billy Satterfield, Executive Director of Student Financial Aid/Registrar
2700 Bay Area Boulevard, Houston, TX 77058-1098
(281) 283-2480

University of Houston-Downtown
Houston, Texas
www.uhd.edu   Federal Code: 003612

4-year public university in very large city.
Enrollment: 12,758 undergrads, 50% part-time. 829 full-time freshmen.
Selectivity: Admits over 75% of applicants.

BASIC COSTS (2016-2017)
Tuition and fees: $7,181; out-of-state residents $19,421.
Per-credit charge: $201; out-of-state residents $609.

FINANCIAL AID PICTURE (2016-2017)
Students with need: Out of 752 full-time freshmen who applied for aid, 642 were judged to have need. Of these, 587 received aid, and 19 had their full need met. Average financial aid package met 61% of need; average scholarship/grant was $12,002; average loan was $4,277. For part-time students, average financial aid package was $8,826.
Students without need: No-need awards available for academics, leadership.

FINANCIAL AID PROCEDURES
Forms required: FAFSA.
Dates and Deadlines: Applicants notified on a rolling basis starting 4/1; must reply within 4 week(s) of notification.
Transfers: No deadline. Applicants notified on a rolling basis starting 4/15; must reply within 4 week(s) of notification.

CONTACT
LaTasha Goudeau, Director of Scholarships and Financial Aid
One Main Street, Suite S350, Houston, TX 77002
(713) 221-8041

University of Houston-Victoria
Victoria, Texas
www.uhv.edu   Federal Code: 013231

4-year public university in small city.
Enrollment: 2,991 undergrads.

BASIC COSTS (2016-2017)
Tuition and fees: $7,370; out-of-state residents $19,610.
Per-credit charge: $191; out-of-state residents $599.
Room and board: $7,664.

FINANCIAL AID PICTURE
Students with need: Need-based aid available for full-time and part-time students. Work study available weekends and for part-time students.
Students without need: No-need awards available for academics, athletics, leadership, state/district residency.
Additional info: Short-term loans available at registration.

FINANCIAL AID PROCEDURES
Forms required: FAFSA, institutional form.
Dates and Deadlines: Priority date 3/15; no closing date. Applicants notified on a rolling basis starting 3/30; must reply within 3 week(s) of notification.
Transfers: No deadline. Applicants notified on a rolling basis; must reply within 3 week(s) of notification.

CONTACT
Lashon Battles, Financial Aid Director
3007 North Ben Wilson, Victoria, TX 77901-4450
(361) 570-4125

University of Mary Hardin-Baylor
Belton, Texas
www.umhb.edu   Federal Code: 003588

4-year private university in large town, affiliated with the Baptist faith.
Enrollment: 3,217 undergrads, 7% part-time. 746 full-time freshmen.
Selectivity: Admits over 75% of applicants.

BASIC COSTS (2016-2017)
Tuition and fees: $26,650.
Per-credit charge: $810.
Room and board: $7,300.
Additional info: Tuition/fee waivers available for minority students.

FINANCIAL AID PICTURE (2016-2017)
Students with need: Out of 613 full-time freshmen who applied for aid, 515 were judged to have need. Of these, 515 received aid, and 53 had their full need met. Average financial aid package met 65% of need; average scholarship/grant was $15,420; average loan was $3,551. For part-time students, average financial aid package was $8,966.
Students without need: 114 full-time freshmen who did not demonstrate need for aid received scholarships/grants; average award was $7,889. No-need awards available for academics, alumni affiliation, art, leadership, music/drama, religious affiliation.

FINANCIAL AID PROCEDURES
Forms required: FAFSA.
Dates and Deadlines: Priority date 2/15; no closing date. Applicants notified on a rolling basis starting 2/15; must reply within 2 week(s) of notification.
Transfers: No deadline. Applicants notified on a rolling basis starting 11/1; must reply within 2 week(s) of notification.

CONTACT
Ron Brown, Director of Financial Aid
900 College Street, Belton, TX 76513
(254) 295-4517

University of North Texas
Denton, Texas
www.unt.edu   Federal Code: 003594

4-year public university in small city.
Enrollment: 31,209 undergrads, 18% part-time. 4,472 full-time freshmen.
Selectivity: Admits 50 to 75% of applicants.

BASIC COSTS (2016-2017)
Tuition and fees: $10,520; out-of-state residents $22,760.
Per-credit charge: $266; out-of-state residents $674.
Room and board: $8,679.

FINANCIAL AID PICTURE (2016-2017)
Students with need: Out of 3,815 full-time freshmen who applied for aid, 2,952 were judged to have need. Of these, 2,815 received aid, and 310 had their full need met. Average financial aid package met 62% of need; average scholarship/grant was $9,579; average loan was $3,092. For part-time students, average financial aid package was $6,361.
Students without need: 561 full-time freshmen who did not demonstrate need for aid received scholarships/grants; average award was $6,255.
Scholarships offered: 20 full-time freshmen received athletic scholarships; average amount $13,162.

FINANCIAL AID PROCEDURES
Forms required: FAFSA.
Dates and Deadlines: Priority date 3/15; no closing date. Applicants notified on a rolling basis starting 4/1.

CONTACT

Zelma DeLeon, Director of Financial Aid
1401 West Prairie Suite 309, Denton, TX 76203-5017
(940) 565-2302

University of St. Thomas
Houston, Texas
www.stthom.edu   Federal Code: 003654

4-year private university and liberal arts college in very large city, affiliated with the Roman Catholic Church.

Enrollment: 1,750 undergrads, 21% part-time. 272 full-time freshmen.

Selectivity: Admits over 75% of applicants.

BASIC COSTS (2016-2017)

Tuition and fees: $32,100.

Per-credit charge: $1,038.

Room and board: $8,500.

FINANCIAL AID PICTURE (2016-2017)

Students with need: Out of 226 full-time freshmen who applied for aid, 209 were judged to have need. Of these, 208 received aid, and 28 had their full need met. Average financial aid package met 76% of need; average scholarship/grant was $25,468; average loan was $3,388. For part-time students, average financial aid package was $12,341.

Students without need: 55 full-time freshmen who did not demonstrate need for aid received scholarships/grants; average award was $12,426. No-need awards available for academics, athletics, music/drama, religious affiliation, ROTC.

Scholarships offered: 2 full-time freshmen received athletic scholarships; average amount $5,642.

FINANCIAL AID PROCEDURES

Forms required: FAFSA.

Dates and Deadlines: Priority date 4/15; no closing date. Applicants notified on a rolling basis starting 2/15; must reply within 2 week(s) of notification.

CONTACT

Lynda McKendree, Dean of Scholarships and Financial Aid
3800 Montrose Boulevard, Houston, TX 77006-4626
(713) 525-2170

University of Texas at Arlington
Arlington, Texas
www.uta.edu   Federal Code: 003656

4-year public university in large city.

Enrollment: 30,358 undergrads.

BASIC COSTS (2016-2017)

Tuition and fees: $9,202; out-of-state residents $23,046.

Room and board: $8,410.

FINANCIAL AID PICTURE

Students with need: Need-based aid available for full-time and part-time students. Work study available nights, weekends, and for part-time students.

Students without need: No-need awards available for academics, art, athletics, leadership, music/drama, ROTC.

Scholarships offered: Academic Scholarships: $1,000-$4,000 per year; renewable; based on minimum SAT 1050 (exclusive of Writing) or ACT 22, top 25% of high school class.

Additional info: Free tuition to eligible students whose household income is $65,000 or less through the Maverick Promise program.

FINANCIAL AID PROCEDURES

Forms required: FAFSA.

Dates and Deadlines: Priority date 4/15; no closing date. Applicants notified on a rolling basis starting 4/1; must reply within 3 week(s) of notification.

Transfers: Must reply within 3 week(s) of notification. To receive Texas grant or Texas B on Time loan, student must have either received Texas grant or completed associates degree at prior school.

CONTACT

Karen Krause, Director of Financial Aid
UTA Box 19088, Arlington, TX 76019
(817) 272-3561

University of Texas at Austin
Austin, Texas
www.utexas.edu   Federal Code: 003658

4-year public university in very large city.

Enrollment: 39,676 undergrads, 7% part-time. 8,570 full-time freshmen.

Selectivity: Admits less than 50% of applicants.

BASIC COSTS (2016-2017)

Tuition and fees: $10,110; out-of-state residents $35,906.

Room and board: $11,456.

FINANCIAL AID PICTURE (2016-2017)

Students with need: Out of 6,430 full-time freshmen who applied for aid, 3,468 were judged to have need. Of these, 3,466 received aid, and 696 had their full need met. Average financial aid package met 68% of need; average scholarship/grant was $9,642; average loan was $3,406. For part-time students, average financial aid package was $8,252.

Students without need: 24 full-time freshmen who did not demonstrate need for aid received scholarships/grants; average award was $2,208. No-need awards available for academics, art, athletics, leadership, music/drama, ROTC, state/district residency.

Scholarships offered: 193 full-time freshmen received athletic scholarships; average amount $6,836.

FINANCIAL AID PROCEDURES

Forms required: FAFSA, institutional form.

Dates and Deadlines: Priority date 3/15; no closing date. Applicants notified on a rolling basis starting 3/15; must reply by 5/1 or within 3 week(s) of notification.

Transfers: Limited number of scholarship funds available for transfer students.

CONTACT

Diane Sprague, Director of Financial Aid
PO Box 8058, Austin, TX 78713-8058
(512) 475-6282

University of Texas at Dallas
Richardson, Texas
www.utdallas.edu   Federal Code: 009741

4-year public university in very large city.

Enrollment: 17,059 undergrads, 17% part-time. 2,656 full-time freshmen.

Selectivity: Admits 50 to 75% of applicants.

BASIC COSTS (2016-2017)

Tuition and fees: $12,162; out-of-state residents $33,654.

Per-credit charge: $405; out-of-state residents $1,122.

Room and board: $10,668.

Additional info: Tuition at time of enrollment locked for 4 years.

FINANCIAL AID PICTURE (2015-2016)

Students with need: Out of 1,931 full-time freshmen who applied for aid, 1,332 were judged to have need. Of these, 1,296 received aid, and 301 had

their full need met. Average financial aid package met 69% of need; average scholarship/grant was $10,535; average loan was $3,328. For part-time students, average financial aid package was $7,889.

Students without need: 618 full-time freshmen who did not demonstrate need for aid received scholarships/grants; average award was $12,775. No-need awards available for academics.

Scholarships offered: Eugene McDermott Scholars Program Awards; full tuition and fees plus domestic and international travel costs for enhancement of scholar's education; based on being in top 10% of high school class, high scores on entrance exams, evidence of leadership abilities; 20 awarded. Academic Excellence Scholarships; based on SAT/ACT, class rank, high school GPA, AP/Honors work; Achievement level is $3,000/year, Distinction covers tuition/mandatory fees, Honors covers tuition/mandatory fees plus $3,000 stipend.

FINANCIAL AID PROCEDURES

Forms required: FAFSA.

Dates and Deadlines: Priority date 3/31; closing date 4/12. Applicants notified on a rolling basis starting 3/1; must reply within 2 week(s) of notification.

Transfers: Priority date 4/1. Applicants notified on a rolling basis; must reply within 2 week(s) of notification.

CONTACT

Beth Tolan, Director of Financial Aid

Admission and Enrollment Services, Richardson, TX 75080-3021

(972) 883-2941

University of Texas at El Paso

El Paso, Texas

www.utep.edu   Federal Code: 003661

4-year public university in very large city.

Enrollment: 20,376 undergrads, 34% part-time. 3,061 full-time freshmen.

Selectivity: Admits over 75% of applicants.

BASIC COSTS (2016-2017)

Tuition and fees: $7,348; out-of-state residents $20,329.

Per-credit charge: $192.29; out-of-state residents $625.

Room only: $4,815.

FINANCIAL AID PICTURE (2015-2016)

Students with need: Out of 2,915 full-time freshmen who applied for aid, 2,521 were judged to have need. Of these, 2,496 received aid, and 168 had their full need met. Average financial aid package met 66% of need; average scholarship/grant was $9,521; average loan was $5,241. For part-time students, average financial aid package was $10,716.

Students without need: 104 full-time freshmen who did not demonstrate need for aid received scholarships/grants; average award was $5,101. No-need awards available for academics, alumni affiliation, art, athletics, job skills, leadership, minority status, music/drama, religious affiliation, ROTC, state/district residency.

Scholarships offered: 29 full-time freshmen received athletic scholarships; average amount $11,518.

Additional info: Emergency loans available.

FINANCIAL AID PROCEDURES

Forms required: FAFSA, institutional form.

Dates and Deadlines: Priority date 3/15; no closing date. Must reply within 2 week(s) of notification.

Transfers: No deadline. Must reply within 2 week(s) of notification.

CONTACT

Ron Williams, Director of Financial Aid

500 West University Avenue, El Paso, TX 79968

(915) 747-5204

University of Texas at San Antonio

San Antonio, Texas

www.utsa.edu   Federal Code: 010115

4-year public university in very large city.

Enrollment: 24,036 undergrads, 17% part-time. 4,898 full-time freshmen.

Selectivity: Admits over 75% of applicants.

BASIC COSTS (2016-2017)

Tuition and fees: $9,044; out-of-state residents $22,290.

Per-credit charge: $209.95; out-of-state residents $652.

Room and board: $8,074.

FINANCIAL AID PICTURE (2015-2016)

Students with need: Out of 4,186 full-time freshmen who applied for aid, 3,284 were judged to have need. Of these, 3,183 received aid, and 196 had their full need met. Average financial aid package met 57% of need; average scholarship/grant was $8,345; average loan was $3,346. For part-time students, average financial aid package was $5,295.

Students without need: 335 full-time freshmen who did not demonstrate need for aid received scholarships/grants; average award was $2,801. No-need awards available for academics, alumni affiliation, art, athletics, job skills, leadership, music/drama, ROTC, state/district residency.

Scholarships offered: 53 full-time freshmen received athletic scholarships; average amount $13,999.

FINANCIAL AID PROCEDURES

Forms required: FAFSA.

Dates and Deadlines: Priority date 3/15; no closing date. Applicants notified on a rolling basis starting 3/1.

Transfers: No deadline. Applicants notified on a rolling basis starting 4/1; must reply within 4 week(s) of notification.

CONTACT

Lisa Blazer, Assistant Vice President of Financial Aid

One UTSA Circle, San Antonio, TX 78249-0617

(210) 458-7828

University of Texas at Tyler

Tyler, Texas

www.uttyler.edu   Federal Code: 011163

4-year public university in small city.

Enrollment: 6,059 undergrads.

BASIC COSTS (2016-2017)

Tuition and fees: $7,552; out-of-state residents $20,032.

Per-credit charge: $50; out-of-state residents $458.

Room and board: $9,970.

FINANCIAL AID PICTURE

Students with need: Need-based aid available for full-time and part-time students.

Students without need: No-need awards available for academics, art, music/drama.

Additional info: Apply early for all programs.

FINANCIAL AID PROCEDURES

Forms required: FAFSA, state aid form.

Dates and Deadlines: Priority date 4/1; no closing date. Applicants notified on a rolling basis starting 4/15; must reply within 2 week(s) of notification.

CONTACT

Scott Lapinski, Director of Student Financial Aid

3900 University Boulevard, Tyler, TX 75799

(903) 566-7180

University of Texas Health Science Center at Houston

Houston, Texas
www.uth.tmc.edu   Federal Code: 013956

Upper-division public university and health science college in very large city.

Enrollment: 677 undergrads, 18% part-time.

BASIC COSTS (2016-2017)

Tuition and fees: $5,976; out-of-state residents $25,986.

Additional info: Costs are for the school of nursing.

FINANCIAL AID PICTURE (2015-2016)

Students with need: Average financial aid package for all full-time undergraduates was $9,034. 26% awarded as scholarships/grants, 74% awarded as loans/jobs. Need-based aid available for part-time students.

Students without need: This college awards aid only to students with need.

FINANCIAL AID PROCEDURES

Forms required: FAFSA.

Dates and Deadlines: Applicants notified on a rolling basis starting 6/1.

Transfers: No deadline. Applicants notified on a rolling basis.

CONTACT

Araceli Alvarez, Director of Student Financial Aid
Box 20036, Houston, TX 77225
(713) 500-3860

University of Texas Medical Branch at Galveston

Galveston, Texas
www.utmb.edu   Federal Code: 013976

Upper-division public health science and nursing college in large town.

Enrollment: 738 undergrads, 15% part-time. 257 full-time freshmen.

BASIC COSTS (2016-2017)

Tuition and fees: $7,414; out-of-state residents $20,735.

Per-credit charge: $206; out-of-state residents $677.

FINANCIAL AID PICTURE

Students with need: Need-based aid available for full-time and part-time students. Work study available nights, weekends, and for part-time students.

Students without need: No-need awards available for academics, minority status, state/district residency.

FINANCIAL AID PROCEDURES

Forms required: FAFSA.

Dates and Deadlines: Applicants notified on a rolling basis; must reply within 4 week(s) of notification.

CONTACT

Carol Cromie, Assistant Director of Enrollment Services for Financial Aid
301 University Boulevard, Galveston, TX 77555-1305
(409) 772-1215

University of Texas of the Permian Basin

Odessa, Texas
www.utpb.edu   Federal Code: 009930

4-year public university in small city.

Enrollment: 3,642 undergrads, 41% part-time. 386 full-time freshmen.

Selectivity: Admits over 75% of applicants.

BASIC COSTS (2016-2017)

Tuition and fees: $7,060; out-of-district residents $19,540; out-of-state residents $19,540.

Per-credit charge: $186.3; out-of-district residents $602.6; out-of-state residents $602.6.

Room and board: $10,800.

FINANCIAL AID PICTURE (2015-2016)

Students with need: Out of 328 full-time freshmen who applied for aid, 267 were judged to have need. Of these, 253 received aid, and 210 had their full need met. Average financial aid package met 74% of need; average scholarship/grant was $8,650; average loan was $3,225. For part-time students, average financial aid package was $3,194.

Students without need: 251 full-time freshmen who did not demonstrate need for aid received scholarships/grants; average award was $2,862. No-need awards available for academics, art, athletics, leadership, music/drama, state/district residency.

Scholarships offered: 13 full-time freshmen received athletic scholarships; average amount $4,115.

FINANCIAL AID PROCEDURES

Forms required: FAFSA.

Dates and Deadlines: Priority date 7/15; no closing date. Applicants notified on a rolling basis starting 3/15.

CONTACT

Charles Kerestly, Director of Financial Aid
4901 East University, Odessa, TX 79762
(432) 552-2620

University of the Incarnate Word

San Antonio, Texas
www.uiw.edu   Federal Code: 003578

4-year private university in very large city, affiliated with the Roman Catholic Church.

Enrollment: 6,239 undergrads, 28% part-time. 869 full-time freshmen.

Selectivity: Admits over 75% of applicants.

BASIC COSTS (2017-2018)

Tuition and fees: $29,990.

Room and board: $12,436.

FINANCIAL AID PICTURE (2015-2016)

Students with need: Out of 768 full-time freshmen who applied for aid, 700 were judged to have need. Of these, 699 received aid, and 148 had their full need met. Average financial aid package met 59% of need; average scholarship/grant was $19,046; average loan was $3,266. For part-time students, average financial aid package was $5,471.

Students without need: 67 full-time freshmen who did not demonstrate need for aid received scholarships/grants; average award was $5,902. No-need awards available for academics, alumni affiliation, art, athletics, leadership, minority status, music/drama, religious affiliation, ROTC.

Scholarships offered: 91 full-time freshmen received athletic scholarships; average amount $17,086.

Additional info: Students encouraged to pursue outside scholarship programs.

FINANCIAL AID PROCEDURES

Forms required: FAFSA.

Dates and Deadlines: Priority date 4/1; no closing date. Applicants notified on a rolling basis starting 2/15; must reply within 2 week(s) of notification.

Transfers: No deadline. Applicants notified on a rolling basis starting 2/15.

CONTACT

Amy Carcanagues, Director of Financial Assistance
4301 Broadway, San Antonio, TX 78209-6397
(210) 829-6008

Vernon College

Vernon, Texas
www.vernoncollege.edu   Federal Code: 010060

2-year public community and junior college in large town.
Enrollment: 2,367 undergrads.
Selectivity: Open admission; but selective for some programs.

BASIC COSTS (2016-2017)
Tuition and fees: $2,850; out-of-district residents $4,200; out-of-state residents $6,150.
Per-credit charge: $50; out-of-district residents $95; out-of-state residents $200.
Room and board: $3,989.

FINANCIAL AID PICTURE
Students with need: Need-based aid available for full-time and part-time students. Work study available nights, weekends, and for part-time students.
Students without need: This college awards aid only to students with need.

FINANCIAL AID PROCEDURES
Forms required: FAFSA.
Dates and Deadlines: Priority date 7/1; no closing date. Applicants notified on a rolling basis starting 4/1.
Transfers: No deadline. Applicants notified on a rolling basis.

CONTACT
Melissa Elliott, Director of Financial Aid
4400 College Drive, Vernon, TX 76384-4092
(940) 552-6291

Vet Tech Institute of Houston

Houston, Texas
www.bradfordschools.com

2-year for-profit technical college in very large city.
Enrollment: 260 undergrads.

BASIC COSTS (2016-2017)
Additional info: Entire 18 month associate's program is $31,770. Books and supplies: $2,655. On-campus room and board: $13,410.

FINANCIAL AID PICTURE
Students with need: Need-based aid available for full-time students.

CONTACT
4669 Southwest Freeway, Houston, TX 77027

Victoria College

Victoria, Texas
www.victoriacollege.edu   Federal Code: 003662

2-year public community college in small city.
Enrollment: 3,264 undergrads, 68% part-time. 349 full-time freshmen.
Selectivity: Open admission; but selective for some programs.

BASIC COSTS (2016-2017)
Tuition and fees: $2,640; out-of-district residents $4,050; out-of-state residents $4,650.
Per-credit charge: $46; out-of-district residents $93; out-of-state residents $200.

FINANCIAL AID PICTURE (2015-2016)
Students with need: 67% of average financial aid package awarded as scholarships/grants, 33% awarded as loans/jobs.

Students without need: No-need awards available for academics, art, minority status, music/drama.

FINANCIAL AID PROCEDURES
Forms required: FAFSA, institutional form.
Dates and Deadlines: Priority date 4/15; no closing date. Applicants notified on a rolling basis.

CONTACT
Kim Obsta, Director of Financial Aid
2200 East Red River, Victoria, TX 77901
(361) 572-6415

Wade College

Dallas, Texas
www.wadecollege.edu   Federal Code: 010130

2-year for-profit business and career college in very large city.
Enrollment: 250 undergrads.
Selectivity: Open admission; but selective for some programs.

BASIC COSTS (2016-2017)
Tuition and fees: $16,175.
Per-credit charge: $535.
Additional info: Tuition at time of enrollment locked for 2 years.

FINANCIAL AID PICTURE
Students with need: Need-based aid available for full-time and part-time students.
Students without need: This college awards aid only to students with need.

FINANCIAL AID PROCEDURES
Forms required: FAFSA.
Dates and Deadlines: Applicants notified on a rolling basis; must reply within 4 week(s) of notification.

CONTACT
Lisa Hoover, Director of Financial Services
1950 North Stemmons Freeway, Suite 4080, Dallas, TX 75207
(214) 637-3530

Wayland Baptist University

Plainview, Texas
www.wbu.edu   Federal Code: 003663

4-year private university and liberal arts college in large town, affiliated with the Southern Baptist Convention.
Enrollment: 3,567 undergrads, 70% part-time. 316 full-time freshmen.
Selectivity: Admits over 75% of applicants.

BASIC COSTS (2016-2017)
Tuition and fees: $19,110.
Per-credit charge: $595.
Room and board: $7,296.

FINANCIAL AID PICTURE (2016-2017)
Students with need: Out of 272 full-time freshmen who applied for aid, 250 were judged to have need. Of these, 249 received aid, and 23 had their full need met. Average financial aid package met 61% of need; average scholarship/grant was $11,534; average loan was $3,529. For part-time students, average financial aid package was $6,335.
Students without need: 27 full-time freshmen who did not demonstrate need for aid received scholarships/grants; average award was $5,796. No-need awards available for academics, art, athletics, leadership, music/drama, religious affiliation.

Scholarships offered: 39 full-time freshmen received athletic scholarships; average amount $8,542.

FINANCIAL AID PROCEDURES

Forms required: FAFSA, institutional form.

Dates and Deadlines: Applicants notified on a rolling basis starting 2/1; must reply within 3 week(s) of notification.

Transfers: No deadline. Applicants notified on a rolling basis.

CONTACT

Karen LaQuey, Director of Financial Aid

1900 West Seventh Street, CMB #1294, Plainview, TX 79072

(806) 291-3520

Weatherford College

Weatherford, Texas

www.wc.edu   Federal Code: 003664

2-year public community college in large town.

Enrollment: 5,637 undergrads.

Selectivity: Open admission; but selective for some programs.

BASIC COSTS (2016-2017)

Tuition and fees: $2,400; out-of-district residents $3,720; out-of-state residents $5,280.

Room and board: $7,430.

FINANCIAL AID PICTURE

Students with need: Work study available nights, weekends, and for part-time students.

Students without need: This college awards aid only to students with need.

FINANCIAL AID PROCEDURES

Forms required: FAFSA.

Dates and Deadlines: Priority date 7/3; no closing date. Applicants notified on a rolling basis; must reply within 2 week(s) of notification.

CONTACT

Donnie Purvis, Director, Financial Aid

225 College Park Drive, Weatherford, TX 76086

(817) 598-6295

West Coast University: Dallas

Dallas, Texas

www.westcoastuniversity.edu   Federal Code: 036983

4-year for-profit branch campus and nursing college in very large city.

Enrollment: 428 undergrads.

Selectivity: Open admission; but selective for some programs.

BASIC COSTS (2016-2017)

Tuition and fees: $12,930.

FINANCIAL AID PICTURE

Students with need: Need-based aid available for full-time and part-time students. Work study available nights, weekends, and for part-time students.

Students without need: No-need awards available for academics.

FINANCIAL AID PROCEDURES

Forms required: FAFSA, institutional form.

Dates and Deadlines: Closing date 6/30. Applicants notified on a rolling basis.

CONTACT

Monita Saunders, Director of Financial Aid

8435 North Stemmons Freeway, Dallas, TX 75247

(214) 453-4533

West Texas A&M University

Canyon, Texas

www.wtamu.edu   Federal Code: 003665

4-year public university in large town.

Enrollment: 7,384 undergrads, 23% part-time. 1,382 full-time freshmen.

Selectivity: Admits 50 to 75% of applicants.

BASIC COSTS (2016-2017)

Tuition and fees: $7,936; out-of-state residents $8,959.

Per-credit charge: $176.3; out-of-state residents $209.31.

Room and board: $7,196.

FINANCIAL AID PICTURE (2015-2016)

Students with need: Out of 1,178 full-time freshmen who applied for aid, 895 were judged to have need. Of these, 886 received aid, and 182 had their full need met. Average financial aid package met 69% of need; average scholarship/grant was $5,589; average loan was $2,397. For part-time students, average financial aid package was $26,014.

Students without need: 125 full-time freshmen who did not demonstrate need for aid received scholarships/grants; average award was $2,070. No-need awards available for academics, art, athletics, leadership, music/drama.

Scholarships offered: 34 full-time freshmen received athletic scholarships; average amount $6,864.

Additional info: Scholarship deadline February 1.

FINANCIAL AID PROCEDURES

Forms required: FAFSA.

Dates and Deadlines: Priority date 4/15; no closing date. Applicants notified on a rolling basis starting 3/1; must reply within 2 week(s) of notification.

Transfers: No deadline. Applicants notified on a rolling basis; must reply within 2 week(s) of notification. Must provide financial aid transcripts through last semester of attendance. All academic transcripts must be on file.

CONTACT

Marian Giesecke, Director of Financial Aid

WTAMU Box 60907, Canyon, TX 79016-0001

(806) 651-2055

Western Technical College

El Paso, Texas

www.westerntech.edu   Federal Code: 014535

2-year for-profit technical college in very large city.

Enrollment: 862 undergrads.

Selectivity: Open admission; but selective for some programs.

BASIC COSTS (2017-2018)

Additional info: Certificate program range from $10,260 to $27,099. Associate degree programs range from $28,766 to $36,599. Books and supplies, and other program fees vary by program.

FINANCIAL AID PICTURE (2015-2016)

Students with need: Need-based aid available for part-time students. Work study available nights.

Students without need: This college awards aid only to students with need.

FINANCIAL AID PROCEDURES

Forms required: FAFSA.

Dates and Deadlines: Applicants notified on a rolling basis.

CONTACT

Danielle Picchi, Financial Aid Director

9624 Plaza Circle, El Paso, TX 79927

(915) 532-3737 ext. 8105

Western Technical College: Diana Drive
El Paso, Texas
www.westerntech.edu   Federal Code: 014535

2-year for-profit branch campus and technical college in very large city.
Enrollment: 456 undergrads.
Selectivity: Open admission; but selective for some programs.

BASIC COSTS (2016-2017)
Additional info: Certificate programs range from $10,260 to $27,099, associate programs range from $26,982 to $36,599. Fees, books, and tool costs vary depending on program.

FINANCIAL AID PICTURE (2015-2016)
Students with need: 43% of average financial aid package awarded as scholarships/grants, 57% awarded as loans/jobs. Work study available nights.
Students without need: This college awards aid only to students with need.

FINANCIAL AID PROCEDURES
Forms required: FAFSA.
Dates and Deadlines: Applicants notified on a rolling basis.
Transfers: No deadline. Applicants notified on a rolling basis.

CONTACT
Danielle Picchi, Director of Financial Aid
9451 Diana Drive, El Paso, TX 79924
(915) 532-3737 ext. 8105

Western Texas College
Snyder, Texas
www.wtc.edu   Federal Code: 009549

2-year public community and junior college in large town.
Enrollment: 998 undergrads, 72% part-time. 261 full-time freshmen.
Selectivity: Open admission; but selective for some programs.

BASIC COSTS (2016-2017)
Tuition and fees: $3,570; out-of-district residents $4,710; out-of-state residents $5,820.
Room and board: $5,100.

FINANCIAL AID PICTURE
Students with need: Need-based aid available for full-time and part-time students. Work study available nights, weekends, and for part-time students.
Students without need: No-need awards available for academics, art, athletics, leadership, music/drama, state/district residency.

FINANCIAL AID PROCEDURES
Forms required: FAFSA, state aid form, institutional form.
Dates and Deadlines: Priority date 5/1; no closing date. Applicants notified on a rolling basis starting 5/1; must reply within 2 week(s) of notification.
Transfers: No deadline. Applicants notified on a rolling basis.

CONTACT
Greg Torres, Director of Student Financial Aid
6200 College Avenue, Snyder, TX 79549
(866) 270-6184

Wharton County Junior College
Wharton, Texas
www.wcjc.edu   Federal Code: 003668

2-year public community and junior college in small town.
Enrollment: 7,072 undergrads, 60% part-time. 1,190 full-time freshmen.
Selectivity: Open admission; but selective for some programs.

BASIC COSTS (2016-2017)
Tuition and fees: $2,790; out-of-state residents $5,880.
Room and board: $4,100.

FINANCIAL AID PICTURE (2015-2016)
Students with need: 70% of average financial aid package awarded as scholarships/grants, 30% awarded as loans/jobs. Need-based aid available for part-time students.
Students without need: No-need awards available for academics, athletics, music/drama.

FINANCIAL AID PROCEDURES
Forms required: FAFSA, institutional form.
Dates and Deadlines: Closing date 6/1. Applicants notified on a rolling basis starting 3/1; must reply within 8 week(s) of notification.

CONTACT
Richard Hyde, Director of Financial Aid
911 Boling Highway, Wharton, TX 77488-0080
(979) 532-4560 ext. 6345

Wiley College
Marshall, Texas
www.wileyc.edu   Federal Code: 003669

4-year private liberal arts college in large town, affiliated with the United Methodist Church.
Enrollment: 1,172 undergrads.
Selectivity: Open admission; but selective for some programs.

BASIC COSTS (2016-2017)
Tuition and fees: $12,064.
Per-credit charge: $324.
Room and board: $7,194.

FINANCIAL AID PICTURE
Students with need: Need-based aid available for full-time and part-time students.

FINANCIAL AID PROCEDURES
Forms required: FAFSA, institutional form.
Dates and Deadlines: Priority date 4/15; closing date 4/15. Applicants notified on a rolling basis.

CONTACT
Cecelia Jones, Director of Financial Aid
711 Wiley Avenue, Marshall, TX 75670
(903) 927-3217

Utah

Brigham Young University
Provo, Utah
www.byu.edu   Federal Code: 003670

4-year private university in small city, affiliated with the Church of Jesus Christ of Latter-day Saints.
Enrollment: 30,979 undergrads, 10% part-time. 5,036 full-time freshmen.
Selectivity: Admits 50 to 75% of applicants. GED not accepted.

BASIC COSTS (2016-2017)
Tuition and fees: $5,300.
Per-credit charge: $276.
Room and board: $7,448.

FINANCIAL AID PICTURE (2015-2016)

Students with need: Out of 2,539 full-time freshmen who applied for aid, 1,631 were judged to have need. Of these, 1,474 received aid, and 36 had their full need met. Average financial aid package met 26% of need; average scholarship/grant was $4,263; average loan was $3,151. For part-time students, average financial aid package was $4,300.

Students without need: 1,944 full-time freshmen who did not demonstrate need for aid received scholarships/grants; average award was $4,216. No-need awards available for academics, art, athletics, leadership, minority status, music/drama, religious affiliation, ROTC, state/district residency.

Scholarships offered: 134 full-time freshmen received athletic scholarships; average amount $9,964.

Additional info: Students notified of scholarships on or about 4/20.

FINANCIAL AID PROCEDURES

Forms required: FAFSA.

Dates and Deadlines: Priority date 4/15; no closing date. Applicants notified on a rolling basis.

Transfers: Must provide financial aid transcript.

CONTACT

Kirk Strong, Director of Admissions
A-153 ASB, Provo, UT 84602
(801) 422-4104

Broadview Entertainment Arts University

Salt Lake City, Utah
www.broadviewuniversity.edu   Federal Code: 011166

2-year for-profit university and visual arts college in small city.
Enrollment: 151 undergrads.
Selectivity: Open admission.

BASIC COSTS (2016-2017)

Tuition and fees: $14,625.
Additional info: Fees vary from $100-$650 per course.

FINANCIAL AID PICTURE

Students with need: Need-based aid available for full-time and part-time students.

FINANCIAL AID PROCEDURES

Forms required: FAFSA, institutional form.
Dates and Deadlines: Applicants notified on a rolling basis starting 7/1; must reply within 2 week(s) of notification.

CONTACT

Julie Wilbur, Director of Financial Aid
240 East Morris Avenue, Salt Lake City, UT 84115
(801) 300-4300

Broadview University: Layton

Layton, Utah
www.broadviewuniversity.edu   Federal Code: 011166

2-year for-profit university and career college in small city.
Enrollment: 163 undergrads.
Selectivity: Open admission.

BASIC COSTS (2016-2017)

Tuition and fees: $14,625.
Additional info: Fees vary from $100-$650 per course.

FINANCIAL AID PICTURE

Students with need: Need-based aid available for full-time and part-time students.

FINANCIAL AID PROCEDURES

Forms required: FAFSA, institutional form.
Dates and Deadlines: Applicants notified on a rolling basis starting 7/1; must reply within 2 week(s) of notification.

CONTACT

Lina Okazaki, Financial Aid Manager
869 West Hill Field Road, Layton, UT 84041
(801) 660-6000

Broadview University: Orem

Orem, Utah
www.broadviewuniversity.edu   Federal Code: 011166

4-year for-profit university and career college in small city.
Enrollment: 124 undergrads.
Selectivity: Open admission.

BASIC COSTS (2016-2017)

Tuition and fees: $14,625.
Additional info: Fees vary from $100-$650 per course.

FINANCIAL AID PICTURE

Students with need: Need-based aid available for full-time and part-time students.

FINANCIAL AID PROCEDURES

Forms required: FAFSA, institutional form.
Dates and Deadlines: Applicants notified on a rolling basis starting 7/1; must reply within 2 week(s) of notification.

CONTACT

Julie Wilbur, Financial Aid Manager
898 North 1200 West, Orem, UT 84057
(801) 822-5800

Broadview University: West Jordan

West Jordan, Utah
www.broadviewuniversity.edu   Federal Code: 011166

2-year for-profit technical and career college in small city.
Enrollment: 237 undergrads.
Selectivity: Open admission; but selective for some programs.

BASIC COSTS (2016-2017)

Tuition and fees: $14,625.
Additional info: Fees vary from $100-$650 per course.

FINANCIAL AID PICTURE

Students with need: Need-based aid available for full-time and part-time students.

FINANCIAL AID PROCEDURES

Forms required: FAFSA, institutional form.
Dates and Deadlines: Applicants notified on a rolling basis starting 7/1; must reply within 2 week(s) of notification.

CONTACT

Kristi Snow, Financial Aid Manager
1902 West 7800 South, West Jordan, UT 84088
(801) 304-4224

Dixie State University

St George, Utah
www.dixie.edu   Federal Code: 003671

4-year public university in small city.
Enrollment: 7,432 undergrads, 26% part-time. 1,903 full-time freshmen.

Selectivity: Open admission; but selective for some programs.

BASIC COSTS (2016-2017)
Tuition and fees: $4,839; out-of-state residents $13,855.
Per-credit charge: $171; out-of-state residents $547.
Room and board: $6,098.

FINANCIAL AID PICTURE
Students with need: Need-based aid available for full-time and part-time students. Work study available nights, weekends, and for part-time students.
Students without need: No-need awards available for academics, alumni affiliation, art, athletics, job skills, leadership, minority status, music/drama, state/district residency.

FINANCIAL AID PROCEDURES
Forms required: FAFSA.
Dates and Deadlines: Priority date 5/1; closing date 6/30. Applicants notified on a rolling basis starting 3/1.
Transfers: Applicants notified on a rolling basis starting 3/1.

CONTACT
JD Robertson, Director of Financial Aid
225 South 700 East, St. George, UT 84770-3876
(435) 652-7575

Independence University
Murray, Utah
www.independence.edu   Federal Code: 014683

4-year for-profit business and health science college in very large city.
Enrollment: 1,280 undergrads.
Selectivity: Open admission.

BASIC COSTS (2016-2017)
Additional info: Associate programs: $42,387-$49,504. Bachelor's programs: $28,224-$74,753.

FINANCIAL AID PICTURE
Students with need: Need-based aid available for full-time students.
Students without need: This college awards aid only to students with need.
Additional info: Financial aid available for resident students only, not correspondence students.

FINANCIAL AID PROCEDURES
Forms required: FAFSA.
Dates and Deadlines: Closing date 7/23. Applicants notified on a rolling basis.
Transfers: No deadline. Applicants notified on a rolling basis.

CONTACT
Lana Moon, Director of Finance
4021 South 700 East, Suite 400, Murray, UT 84107

LDS Business College
Salt Lake City, Utah
www.ldsbc.edu   Federal Code: 003672

2-year private business and career college in large city, affiliated with the Church of Jesus Christ of Latter-day Saints.
Enrollment: 2,077 undergrads.
Selectivity: Open admission; but selective for some programs.

BASIC COSTS (2016-2017)
Tuition and fees: $3,240.
Room and board: $5,470.

FINANCIAL AID PICTURE
Students with need: Need-based aid available for full-time and part-time students.
Students without need: No-need awards available for academics, leadership.
Scholarships offered: Service scholarships; half-tuition for one semester; for Church of Jesus Christ of Latter-day Saints missionaries who have returned from mission within past year.

FINANCIAL AID PROCEDURES
Forms required: FAFSA.
Dates and Deadlines: Priority date 7/1; no closing date. Applicants notified on a rolling basis starting 3/1; must reply by 7/1 or within 3 week(s) of notification.
Transfers: No deadline. Applicants notified on a rolling basis starting 1/1.

CONTACT
Melanie Conover, Manager of Student Financial Services
95 North 300 West, Salt Lake City, UT 84101-3500
(801) 524-8111

Neumont University
Salt Lake City, Utah
www.neumont.edu   Federal Code: 009948

4-year for-profit engineering and technical college in very large city.
Enrollment: 441 undergrads.

BASIC COSTS (2016-2017)
Tuition and fees: $24,450.
Per-credit charge: $495.
Room only: $5,670.

FINANCIAL AID PICTURE
Students with need: Need-based aid available for full-time and part-time students.
Students without need: No-need awards available for academics, job skills, leadership, state/district residency.

FINANCIAL AID PROCEDURES
Forms required: FAFSA, institutional form.
Dates and Deadlines: Closing date 8/1. Applicants notified on a rolling basis.
Transfers: No deadline. Applicants notified on a rolling basis starting 8/1.

CONTACT
Nate Blanchard, Director of Financial Aid
143 South Main Street, Salt Lake City, UT 84111
(801) 302-2870

Salt Lake Community College
Salt Lake City, Utah
www.slcc.edu   Federal Code: 005220

2-year public community and technical college in very large city.
Enrollment: 21,830 undergrads, 67% part-time. 2,086 full-time freshmen.
Selectivity: Open admission; but selective for some programs.

BASIC COSTS (2016-2017)
Tuition and fees: $3,690; out-of-state residents $11,728.
Additional info: Tuition/fee waivers available for adults, minority students.

FINANCIAL AID PICTURE
Students with need: Need-based aid available for full-time and part-time students. Work study available nights, weekends, and for part-time students.
Students without need: No-need awards available for academics, alumni affiliation, art, athletics, leadership, minority status, music/drama.

FINANCIAL AID PROCEDURES

Forms required: FAFSA, institutional form.

Dates and Deadlines: Priority date 5/1; no closing date. Applicants notified on a rolling basis starting 5/1; must reply within 4 week(s) of notification.

CONTACT

Cristi Millard, Director of Financial Aid
4600 South Redwood Road, Salt Lake City, UT 84130-0808
(801) 957-4410

Snow College

Ephraim, Utah
www.snow.edu   Federal Code: 003679

2-year public junior college in small town.
Enrollment: 3,509 undergrads.
Selectivity: Open admission.

BASIC COSTS (2016-2017)

Tuition and fees: $3,592; out-of-state residents $12,071.
Room only: $1,770.
Additional info: Tuition/fee waivers available for unemployed or children of unemployed.

FINANCIAL AID PICTURE (2016-2017)

Students with need: 70% of average financial aid package awarded as scholarships/grants, 30% awarded as loans/jobs.
Students without need: No-need awards available for academics, alumni affiliation, athletics, leadership, music/drama, state/district residency.

FINANCIAL AID PROCEDURES

Forms required: FAFSA, institutional form.
Dates and Deadlines: Priority date 3/1; closing date 6/1. Applicants notified on a rolling basis starting 8/1; must reply within 1 week(s) of notification.
Transfers: Priority date 3/15; closing date 6/15. Applicants notified on a rolling basis. F.A.T. required for mid-year transfers.

CONTACT

Jack Dalene, Director of Financial Aid
150 East College Avenue, Ephraim, UT 84627
(435) 283-7132

Southern Utah University

Cedar City, Utah
www.suu.edu   Federal Code: 003678

4-year public university in large town.
Enrollment: 6,353 undergrads, 12% part-time. 1,485 full-time freshmen.
Selectivity: Admits 50 to 75% of applicants.

BASIC COSTS (2016-2017)

Tuition and fees: $6,530; out-of-state residents $19,810.
Per-credit charge: $192; out-of-state residents $635.
Room and board: $7,067.

FINANCIAL AID PICTURE (2015-2016)

Students with need: Work study available nights, weekends, and for part-time students.
Students without need: No-need awards available for academics, alumni affiliation, art, athletics, job skills, leadership, minority status, music/drama, ROTC, state/district residency.

FINANCIAL AID PROCEDURES

Forms required: FAFSA.
Dates and Deadlines: Priority date 12/1; no closing date. Applicants notified on a rolling basis starting 11/1; must reply by 5/1.

CONTACT

Jan Carey-McDonald, Director of Financial Aid and Scholarships
351 West University Boulevard, Cedar City, UT 84720
(435) 586-7735

University of Utah

Salt Lake City, Utah
www.utah.edu   Federal Code: 003675

4-year public university in very large city.
Enrollment: 22,748 undergrads, 25% part-time. 3,319 full-time freshmen.
Selectivity: Admits over 75% of applicants.

BASIC COSTS (2016-2017)

Tuition and fees: $8,518; out-of-state residents $27,039.
Room and board: $9,406.

FINANCIAL AID PICTURE (2016-2017)

Students with need: Out of 2,284 full-time freshmen who applied for aid, 1,547 were judged to have need. Of these, 1,511 received aid, and 280 had their full need met. Average financial aid package met 68% of need; average scholarship/grant was $8,212; average loan was $3,240. For part-time students, average financial aid package was $16,155.
Students without need: 1,719 full-time freshmen who did not demonstrate need for aid received scholarships/grants; average award was $7,260. No-need awards available for academics, alumni affiliation, art, athletics, leadership, minority status, music/drama, ROTC, state/district residency.
Scholarships offered: 77 full-time freshmen received athletic scholarships; average amount $26,114.

FINANCIAL AID PROCEDURES

Forms required: FAFSA.
Dates and Deadlines: Priority date 3/1; no closing date. Applicants notified on a rolling basis starting 4/1; must reply by 4/1 or within 6 week(s) of notification.
Transfers: No deadline. Applicants notified on a rolling basis starting 4/15; must reply within 6 week(s) of notification.

CONTACT

Karen Henriquez, Director of Financial Aid
201 South 1460 East, Salt Lake City, UT 84112-9057
(801) 581-6211

Utah State University

Logan, Utah
www.usu.edu   Federal Code: 003677

4-year public university in small city.
Enrollment: 21,833 undergrads, 23% part-time. 4,095 full-time freshmen.

BASIC COSTS (2016-2017)

Tuition and fees: $6,866; out-of-state residents $19,772.
Room and board: $5,870.

FINANCIAL AID PICTURE (2016-2017)

Students with need: Out of 2,591 full-time freshmen who applied for aid, 1,944 were judged to have need. Of these, 1,922 received aid, and 314 had their full need met. Average financial aid package met 64% of need; average scholarship/grant was $4,377; average loan was $3,413. For part-time students, average financial aid package was $5,832.
Students without need: 893 full-time freshmen who did not demonstrate need for aid received scholarships/grants; average award was $2,672. No-need awards available for academics, alumni affiliation, art, athletics, leadership, minority status, music/drama, religious affiliation, ROTC, state/district residency.

Scholarships offered: 94 full-time freshmen received athletic scholarships; average amount $11,824.

FINANCIAL AID PROCEDURES

Forms required: FAFSA.

Dates and Deadlines: Applicants notified on a rolling basis starting 4/1; must reply within 4 week(s) of notification.

Transfers: No deadline. Applicants notified on a rolling basis starting 4/1; must reply within 4 week(s) of notification.

CONTACT

Patti Kohler, Director of Financial Aid

0160 Old Main Hill, Logan, UT 84322-0160

(435) 797-0173

Utah Valley University
Orem, Utah
www.uvu.edu   Federal Code: 004027

4-year public university and technical college in small city.

Enrollment: 26,571 undergrads, 36% part-time. 3,078 full-time freshmen.

Selectivity: Open admission.

BASIC COSTS (2016-2017)

Tuition and fees: $5,530; out-of-state residents $15,690.

FINANCIAL AID PICTURE (2016-2017)

Students with need: Out of 1,894 full-time freshmen who applied for aid, 1,467 were judged to have need. Of these, 1,394 received aid, and 205 had their full need met. Average financial aid package met 67% of need; average scholarship/grant was $4,826; average loan was $2,327. For part-time students, average financial aid package was $6,106.

Students without need: 48 full-time freshmen who did not demonstrate need for aid received scholarships/grants; average award was $1,623. No-need awards available for academics, alumni affiliation, art, athletics, ROTC.

Scholarships offered: 42 full-time freshmen received athletic scholarships; average amount $4,581.

FINANCIAL AID PROCEDURES

Forms required: FAFSA.

Dates and Deadlines: Applicants notified on a rolling basis.

Transfers: No deadline.

CONTACT

Trish Howard, Director of Financial Aid and Scholarship

800 West University Parkway, Orem, UT 84058-5999

(801) 863-8442

Weber State University
Ogden, Utah
https://www.weber.edu   Federal Code: 003680

4-year public university in small city.

Enrollment: 17,795 undergrads.

Selectivity: Open admission; but selective for some programs.

BASIC COSTS (2016-2017)

Tuition and fees: $5,523; out-of-state residents $14,749.

Room and board: $5,907.

FINANCIAL AID PICTURE

Students with need: Need-based aid available for full-time and part-time students. Work study available nights, weekends, and for part-time students.

Students without need: This college awards aid only to students with need.

Additional info: Dream Weber program provides free tuition and general student fees to students whose annual household income is $40,000 or less.

FINANCIAL AID PROCEDURES

Forms required: FAFSA, institutional form.

Dates and Deadlines: Priority date 3/1; no closing date. Applicants notified on a rolling basis starting 3/15; must reply within 2 week(s) of notification.

CONTACT

Jed Spencer, Director of Financial Aid

1137 University Circle, Ogden, UT 84408-1137

(801) 626-7569

Western Governors University
Salt Lake City, Utah
www.wgu.edu   Federal Code: 033394

4-year private virtual university in very large city.

Enrollment: 63,961 undergrads.

Selectivity: Open admission; but selective for some programs.

BASIC COSTS (2016-2017)

Tuition and fees: $6,070.

FINANCIAL AID PICTURE (2015-2016)

Students with need: Average financial aid package for all full-time undergraduates was $4,103. 36% awarded as scholarships/grants, 64% awarded as loans/jobs.

Students without need: This college awards aid only to students with need.

FINANCIAL AID PROCEDURES

Forms required: FAFSA.

Dates and Deadlines: Applicants notified on a rolling basis.

Transfers: No deadline. Applicants notified on a rolling basis.

CONTACT

Robert Collins, VP for Financial Aid

4001 South 700 East, Salt Lake City, UT 84107

(877) 435-7948 ext. 3104

Westminster College
Salt Lake City, Utah
www.westminstercollege.edu   Federal Code: 003681

4-year private liberal arts college in very large city.

Enrollment: 2,095 undergrads, 4% part-time. 430 full-time freshmen.

Selectivity: Admits over 75% of applicants.

BASIC COSTS (2016-2017)

Tuition and fees: $32,104.

Per-credit charge: $1,316.

Room and board: $8,974.

FINANCIAL AID PICTURE (2016-2017)

Students with need: Out of 337 full-time freshmen who applied for aid, 295 were judged to have need. Of these, 295 received aid, and 72 had their full need met. Average financial aid package met 82% of need; average scholarship/grant was $22,738; average loan was $3,696. For part-time students, average financial aid package was $11,484.

Students without need: 108 full-time freshmen who did not demonstrate need for aid received scholarships/grants; average award was $14,729. No-need awards available for academics, alumni affiliation, art, athletics, leadership, minority status, music/drama, ROTC.

Scholarships offered: 15 full-time freshmen received athletic scholarships; average amount $6,133.

FINANCIAL AID PROCEDURES

Forms required: FAFSA.

Dates and Deadlines: Priority date 3/1; no closing date. Applicants notified on a rolling basis starting 2/1; must reply by 5/1 or within 3 week(s) of notification.

Transfers: No deadline. Applicants notified on a rolling basis starting 3/1; must reply within 3 week(s) of notification. Full-time transfer students with 3.0 GPA eligible for work study, loans, scholarships and grants. Merit scholarships based on cumulative transfer GPA range from $7,000-$12,000 per year.

CONTACT

Jenny Ryan, Director of Financial Aid
1840 South 1300 East, Salt Lake City, UT 84105
(801) 832-2500

Vermont

Bennington College

Bennington, Vermont
www.bennington.edu

Federal Code: 003682
CSS Code: 3080

4-year private liberal arts college in large town.
Enrollment: 701 undergrads, 3% part-time. 215 full-time freshmen.
Selectivity: Admits 50 to 75% of applicants.

BASIC COSTS (2017-2018)

Tuition and fees: $52,420.
Per-credit charge: $2,135.
Room and board: $15,040.

FINANCIAL AID PICTURE (2015-2016)

Students with need: Out of 192 full-time freshmen who applied for aid, 142 were judged to have need. Of these, 142 received aid, and 32 had their full need met. Average financial aid package met 84% of need; average scholarship/grant was $36,264; average loan was $2,293. For part-time students, average financial aid package was $14,325.

Students without need: 48 full-time freshmen who did not demonstrate need for aid received scholarships/grants; average award was $11,328. No-need awards available for academics, alumni affiliation, art, leadership, minority status, music/drama.

Additional info: All applicants for undergraduate admission considered for scholarships based on quality of overall application.

FINANCIAL AID PROCEDURES

Forms required: FAFSA, institutional form. CSS PROFILE required of early decision applicants only.
Dates and Deadlines: Closing date 1/3. Applicants notified by 3/25; must reply by 5/1.
Transfers: Priority date 3/15; closing date 8/1. Applicants notified on a rolling basis starting 5/1; must reply by 6/1 or within 2 week(s) of notification.

CONTACT

Heather Clifford, Director of Financial Aid
One College Drive, Bennington, VT 05201-6003
(802) 440-4325

Castleton University

Castleton, Vermont
www.castleton.edu

Federal Code: 003683

4-year public liberal arts college in small town.
Enrollment: 1,890 undergrads.

BASIC COSTS (2016-2017)

Tuition and fees: $11,314; out-of-state residents $26,722.

Per-credit charge: $427; out-of-state residents $1,069.
Room and board: $9,988.
Additional info: Nursing students pay $13,320 in-state, $28,728 out-of-state. Qualified international students and New England Board of Higher Education rate for students from other New England states: 150% of Vermont resident tuition [$15,408]. International rate for qualified nursing students $20,016. International students pay a $100 international fee per semester.

FINANCIAL AID PICTURE

Students with need: Need-based aid available for full-time and part-time students.
Students without need: No-need awards available for academics, alumni affiliation, music/drama, state/district residency.

FINANCIAL AID PROCEDURES

Forms required: FAFSA.
Dates and Deadlines: Priority date 4/1; no closing date. Applicants notified by 2/21; must reply within 2 week(s) of notification.

CONTACT

Kathy O'Meara, Financial Aid Director
Seminary Street, Castleton, VT 05735
(802) 468-1286

Champlain College

Burlington, Vermont
www.champlain.edu

Federal Code: 003684

4-year private liberal arts and career college in large town.
Enrollment: 3,735 undergrads, 31% part-time. 646 full-time freshmen.
Selectivity: Admits 50 to 75% of applicants.

BASIC COSTS (2017-2018)

Tuition and fees: $39,818.
Room and board: $14,906.

FINANCIAL AID PICTURE (2016-2017)

Students with need: Out of 556 full-time freshmen who applied for aid, 481 were judged to have need. Of these, 481 received aid, and 75 had their full need met. Average financial aid package met 71% of need; average scholarship/grant was $21,918; average loan was $3,547. For part-time students, average financial aid package was $6,060.

Students without need: 161 full-time freshmen who did not demonstrate need for aid received scholarships/grants; average award was $10,729. No-need awards available for academics, leadership, minority status.

FINANCIAL AID PROCEDURES

Forms required: FAFSA.
Dates and Deadlines: Priority date 1/15; no closing date. Applicants notified on a rolling basis starting 11/15; must reply by 5/1 or within 2 week(s) of notification.
Transfers: No deadline. Applicants notified on a rolling basis starting 3/1; must reply within 2 week(s) of notification.

CONTACT

Kristi Jovell, Director of Financial Aid
PO Box 670, Burlington, VT 05402-0670
(802) 860-2777

College of St. Joseph in Vermont

Rutland, Vermont
www.csj.edu

Federal Code: 003685

4-year private liberal arts and teachers college in large town, affiliated with the Roman Catholic Church.
Enrollment: 223 undergrads, 9% part-time. 52 full-time freshmen.

Selectivity: Admits 50 to 75% of applicants.

BASIC COSTS (2016-2017)
Tuition and fees: $22,650.
Per-credit charge: $285.
Room and board: $11,250.

FINANCIAL AID PICTURE
Students with need: Need-based aid available for full-time and part-time students. Work study available nights, weekends, and for part-time students.
Students without need: No-need awards available for academics, alumni affiliation.

FINANCIAL AID PROCEDURES
Forms required: FAFSA, institutional form.
Dates and Deadlines: Priority date 3/1; no closing date. Applicants notified on a rolling basis starting 3/1.
Transfers: No deadline. Applicants notified on a rolling basis starting 3/1.

CONTACT
Julie Rosmus, Financial Aid Director
71 Clement Road, Rutland, VT 05701-3899
(802) 773-5900 ext. 3262

Community College of Vermont
Montpelier, Vermont
www.ccv.edu   Federal Code: 011167

2-year public community and liberal arts college in small town.
Enrollment: 3,556 undergrads.
Selectivity: Open admission.

BASIC COSTS (2016-2017)
Tuition and fees: $7,740; out-of-state residents $15,330.
Per-credit charge: $253; out-of-state residents $506.
Additional info: New England Board of Higher Education rate for students from other New England states: 150% of Vermont resident tuition. Available to degree candidates in academic areas not offered by educational institutions in their home states.

FINANCIAL AID PICTURE
Students with need: Need-based aid available for full-time and part-time students. Work study available nights, weekends, and for part-time students.
Students without need: This college awards aid only to students with need.

FINANCIAL AID PROCEDURES
Forms required: FAFSA, state aid form, institutional form.
Dates and Deadlines: Applicants notified on a rolling basis starting 9/1; must reply within 3 week(s) of notification.

CONTACT
Pam Chisholm, Associate Dean of Enrollment
PO Box 489, Montpelier, VT 05601
(802) 828-2800

Goddard College
Plainfield, Vermont
www.goddard.edu   Federal Code: 003686

4-year private liberal arts college in rural community.
Enrollment: 188 undergrads, 6% part-time. 6 full-time freshmen.
Selectivity: Admits 50 to 75% of applicants.

BASIC COSTS (2016-2017)
Tuition and fees: $15,786.
Room and board: $1,598.

FINANCIAL AID PICTURE (2015-2016)
Students with need: Out of 5 full-time freshmen who applied for aid, 5 were judged to have need. Of these, 5 received aid. Average financial aid package met 37% of need; average scholarship/grant was $6,925; average loan was $4,550. For part-time students, average financial aid package was $7,685.
Students without need: No-need awards available for academics, art, job skills, leadership, music/drama, state/district residency.

FINANCIAL AID PROCEDURES
Forms required: FAFSA.
Dates and Deadlines: Applicants notified on a rolling basis starting 3/15; must reply within 4 week(s) of notification.
Transfers: No deadline. Applicants notified on a rolling basis starting 4/15; must reply within 4 week(s) of notification.

CONTACT
Beverly Jene, Director of Financial Aid
123 Pitkin Road, Plainfield, VT 05667
(800) 468-4888

Green Mountain College
Poultney, Vermont
www.greenmtn.edu   Federal Code: 003687

4-year private liberal arts college in small town, affiliated with the United Methodist Church.
Enrollment: 492 undergrads, 4% part-time. 125 full-time freshmen.
Selectivity: Admits over 75% of applicants.

BASIC COSTS (2017-2018)
Tuition and fees: $37,002.
Per-credit charge: $1,185.
Room and board: $11,722.

FINANCIAL AID PICTURE (2016-2017)
Students with need: Out of 125 full-time freshmen who applied for aid, 117 were judged to have need. Of these, 117 received aid, and 17 had their full need met. Average financial aid package met 75% of need; average scholarship/grant was $27,340; average loan was $3,175. For part-time students, average financial aid package was $3,301.
Students without need: 65 full-time freshmen who did not demonstrate need for aid received scholarships/grants; average award was $14,951. No-need awards available for academics, alumni affiliation, religious affiliation, state/district residency.
Additional info: Service/recognition awards available to all students, determined by admission application and supplemental documentation. VT resident grant matching UVM tuition, to help meet on average 90% of a student's demonstrated need.

FINANCIAL AID PROCEDURES
Forms required: FAFSA.
Dates and Deadlines: Priority date 3/1; no closing date. Applicants notified on a rolling basis starting 12/16; must reply by 5/1 or within 3 week(s) of notification.
Transfers: No deadline. Applicants notified on a rolling basis starting 12/16; must reply by 5/1 or within 3 week(s) of notification.

CONTACT
Wendy Ellis, Director of Student Financial Services
One Brennan Circle, Poultney, VT 05764
(802) 287-8210

Johnson State College
Johnson, Vermont
www.jsc.edu
Federal Code: 003688

4-year public liberal arts college in small town.
Enrollment: 1,339 undergrads, 29% part-time. 196 full-time freshmen.

BASIC COSTS (2017-2018)
Tuition and fees: $11,730; out-of-state residents $24,690.
Per-credit charge: $443; out-of-state residents $983.
Room and board: $10,290.

FINANCIAL AID PICTURE
Students with need: Need-based aid available for full-time and part-time students.
Students without need: No-need awards available for academics, alumni affiliation, art, leadership, music/drama, state/district residency.

FINANCIAL AID PROCEDURES
Forms required: FAFSA, state aid form.
Dates and Deadlines: Priority date 3/1; no closing date. Applicants notified on a rolling basis starting 2/15; must reply within 3 week(s) of notification.
Transfers: No deadline. Applicants notified on a rolling basis starting 2/15; must reply within 3 week(s) of notification. Financial aid transcripts from previously attended colleges required.

CONTACT
Lisa Cummings, Director of Financial Aid
337 College Hill, Johnson, VT 05656
(800) 635-1207

Landmark College
Putney, Vermont
www.landmark.edu
Federal Code: 017157

2-year private liberal arts college in small town.
Enrollment: 452 undergrads.

BASIC COSTS (2016-2017)
Tuition and fees: $52,650.
Room and board: $10,970.

FINANCIAL AID PICTURE
Students with need: Need-based aid available for full-time and part-time students. Work study available nights, weekends, and for part-time students.
Students without need: No-need awards available for academics, art, leadership, minority status, music/drama.
Additional info: Students encouraged to apply to state departments of vocational rehabilitation for additional financial assistance.

FINANCIAL AID PROCEDURES
Forms required: FAFSA.
Dates and Deadlines: Priority date 2/15; no closing date. Applicants notified on a rolling basis starting 3/15; must reply within 2 week(s) of notification.
Transfers: Applicants notified on a rolling basis; must reply within 2 week(s) of notification.

CONTACT
Jennifer Desmarais, Director of Financial Aid
19 River Road South, Putney, VT 05346
(802) 387-6718

Lyndon State College
Lyndonville, Vermont
www.lyndonstate.edu
Federal Code: 003689

4-year public liberal arts and performing arts college in small town.
Enrollment: 1,127 undergrads.

Selectivity: Admits over 75% of applicants.

BASIC COSTS (2017-2018)
Tuition and fees: $11,730; out-of-state residents $23,898.
Per-credit charge: $443; out-of-state residents $950.
Room and board: $10,290.
Additional info: Tuition/fee waivers available for unemployed or children of unemployed.

FINANCIAL AID PICTURE
Students with need: Need-based aid available for full-time and part-time students. Work study available nights, weekends, and for part-time students.
Students without need: No-need awards available for academics, leadership.

FINANCIAL AID PROCEDURES
Forms required: FAFSA.
Dates and Deadlines: Priority date 2/1; no closing date. Applicants notified on a rolling basis starting 4/1; must reply within 2 week(s) of notification.

CONTACT
Tanya Bradley, Director of Financial Aid
1001 College Road, Lyndonville, VT 05851
(802) 626-6396

Marlboro College
Marlboro, Vermont
www.marlboro.edu
Federal Code: 003690

4-year private liberal arts college in rural community.
Enrollment: 190 undergrads, 1% part-time. 55 full-time freshmen.
Selectivity: Admits over 75% of applicants.

BASIC COSTS (2017-2018)
Tuition and fees: $40,425.
Per-credit charge: $1,316.
Room and board: $11,930.

FINANCIAL AID PICTURE (2016-2017)
Students with need: Out of 51 full-time freshmen who applied for aid, 46 were judged to have need. Of these, 46 received aid, and 45 had their full need met. Average financial aid package met 77% of need; average scholarship/grant was $36,494; average loan was $3,294. Need-based aid available for part-time students.
Students without need: 3 full-time freshmen who did not demonstrate need for aid received scholarships/grants; average award was $13,000. No-need awards available for academics, leadership.

FINANCIAL AID PROCEDURES
Forms required: FAFSA.
Dates and Deadlines: Closing date 3/1. Applicants notified on a rolling basis starting 3/1; must reply within 2 week(s) of notification.

CONTACT
Cathy Fuller, Director of Financial Aid
PO Box A, Marlboro, VT 05344-0300
(802) 258-9237

Middlebury College
Middlebury, Vermont
www.middlebury.edu
Federal Code: 003691
CSS Code: 3526

4-year private liberal arts college in small town.
Enrollment: 2,513 undergrads, 1% part-time. 606 full-time freshmen.
Selectivity: Admits less than 50% of applicants.

BASIC COSTS (2016-2017)
Tuition and fees: $50,063.

Room and board: $14,269.

FINANCIAL AID PICTURE (2016-2017)

Students with need: Out of 313 full-time freshmen who applied for aid, 256 were judged to have need. Of these, 256 received aid, and 256 had their full need met. Average financial aid package met 100% of need; average scholarship/grant was $44,843; average loan was $3,095. Need-based aid available for part-time students.

Students without need: This college awards aid only to students with need.

Additional info: Need-blind admissions policy; meets full demonstrated financial need of students who qualify for admission, to extent resources permit.

FINANCIAL AID PROCEDURES

Forms required: FAFSA, CSS PROFILE, institutional form.

Dates and Deadlines: Priority date 11/15; closing date 2/1. Applicants notified by 4/1; must reply by 5/1.

Transfers: Closing date 3/1. Applicants notified by 4/10; must reply by 5/1.

CONTACT

Kim Downs-Burns, Associate VP for SFS, Student Financial Services
The Emma Willard House, Middlebury, VT 05753-6002
(802) 443-5158

New England Culinary Institute
Montpelier, Vermont
www.neci.edu   Federal Code: 015904

2-year for-profit culinary school in small town.
Enrollment: 300 undergrads, 14% part-time. 52 full-time freshmen.

BASIC COSTS (2016-2017)

Tuition and fees: $32,050.
Room and board: $8,000.
Additional info: Tuition and fees quoted are for BA in Food and Beverage Business Management. Costs vary by program. Diploma programs $8,300-$8,550, books and supplies $740-$861. Associate programs $40,300-$61,300, books and supplies $740-$1,020. Bachelor's programs $25,200-$88,550, books and supplies $1,160.

FINANCIAL AID PICTURE

Students with need: Need-based aid available for full-time and part-time students. Work study available nights, weekends, and for part-time students.
Students without need: No-need awards available for academics, job skills.

FINANCIAL AID PROCEDURES

Forms required: FAFSA, state aid form.
Dates and Deadlines: Applicants notified on a rolling basis.
Transfers: No deadline. Applicants notified on a rolling basis; must reply within 4 week(s) of notification.

CONTACT

Wendy Soliz, Associate Director of Financial Aid
7 School Street, Montpelier, VT 05602
(802) 225-3242

Norwich University
Northfield, Vermont
www.norwich.edu   Federal Code: 003692

4-year private university and military college in small town.
Enrollment: 3,085 undergrads, 21% part-time. 797 full-time freshmen.
Selectivity: Admits 50 to 75% of applicants.

BASIC COSTS (2017-2018)

Tuition and fees: $38,662.

Per-credit charge: $1,072.
Room and board: $13,372.

FINANCIAL AID PICTURE (2016-2017)

Students with need: Out of 732 full-time freshmen who applied for aid, 675 were judged to have need. Of these, 675 received aid, and 151 had their full need met. Average financial aid package met 86% of need; average scholarship/grant was $32,076; average loan was $4,166. For part-time students, average financial aid package was $7,520.

Students without need: 121 full-time freshmen who did not demonstrate need for aid received scholarships/grants; average award was $24,651. No-need awards available for academics, ROTC, state/district residency.

Additional info: Winners of ROTC scholarships receive full room and board; must maintain 2.75 GPA. Renewable up to 4 years.

FINANCIAL AID PROCEDURES

Forms required: FAFSA.

Dates and Deadlines: Priority date 2/1; no closing date. Applicants notified on a rolling basis starting 12/1; must reply by 8/1.

CONTACT

Martin Daniels, Director of Financial Aid
158 Harmon Drive, Northfield, VT 05663
(802) 485-2015

Saint Michael's College
Colchester, Vermont
www.smcvt.edu   Federal Code: 003694

4-year private liberal arts college in small city, affiliated with the Roman Catholic Church.
Enrollment: 1,863 undergrads, 1% part-time. 458 full-time freshmen.
Selectivity: Admits over 75% of applicants.

BASIC COSTS (2016-2017)

Tuition and fees: $41,975.
Per-credit charge: $1,340.
Room and board: $11,300.

FINANCIAL AID PICTURE (2016-2017)

Students with need: Out of 386 full-time freshmen who applied for aid, 329 were judged to have need. Of these, 329 received aid, and 118 had their full need met. Average financial aid package met 83% of need; average scholarship/grant was $24,168; average loan was $4,965. Need-based aid available for part-time students.

Students without need: 122 full-time freshmen who did not demonstrate need for aid received scholarships/grants; average award was $17,100. No-need awards available for art, athletics, music/drama.

Scholarships offered: 6 full-time freshmen received athletic scholarships; average amount $53,312.

FINANCIAL AID PROCEDURES

Forms required: FAFSA, state aid form.
Dates and Deadlines: Priority date 2/1; no closing date. Applicants notified on a rolling basis starting 12/15.
Transfers: Must reply within 2 week(s) of notification.

CONTACT

Daniel Couture, Director of Student Financial Services
One Winooski Park, Colchester, VT 05439
(802) 654-3244

Southern Vermont College
Bennington, Vermont
www.svc.edu   Federal Code: 003693

4-year private liberal arts college in large town.
Enrollment: 358 undergrads, 2% part-time. 104 full-time freshmen.

Selectivity: Admits 50 to 75% of applicants.

BASIC COSTS (2016-2017)
Tuition and fees: $23,975.
Room and board: $10,800.

FINANCIAL AID PICTURE (2015-2016)
Students with need: Out of 88 full-time freshmen who applied for aid, 88 were judged to have need. Of these, 88 received aid. Average financial aid package met 45% of need; average scholarship/grant was $12,000; average loan was $5,500. Need-based aid available for part-time students.
Students without need: 2 full-time freshmen who did not demonstrate need for aid received scholarships/grants; average award was $12,000. No-need awards available for academics, leadership.
Scholarships offered: Merit scholarships; based on GPA and SAT/ACT.

FINANCIAL AID PROCEDURES
Forms required: FAFSA.
Dates and Deadlines: Priority date 3/1; no closing date. Applicants notified on a rolling basis starting 3/1; must reply by 5/1 or within 2 week(s) of notification.
Transfers: No deadline. Applicants notified on a rolling basis starting 3/15; must reply by 5/1. No limitations on aid for transfer students.

CONTACT
Jennifer Macksey, Vice President for Administration and Finance
982 Mansion Drive, Bennington, VT 05201-6002
(802) 447-6336

Sterling College
Craftsbury Common, Vermont
www.sterlingcollege.edu
Federal Code: 014991

4-year private liberal arts college in rural community.
Enrollment: 119 undergrads.

BASIC COSTS (2016-2017)
Tuition and fees: $36,577.
Room and board: $9,560.

FINANCIAL AID PICTURE
Students with need: Need-based aid available for full-time and part-time students. Work study available nights, weekends, and for part-time students.
Students without need: No-need awards available for academics, leadership, state/district residency.
Scholarships offered: Gladys Brooks: up to $6,000; academic merit, resident of Northeast Kingdom of Vermont, leadership. Presidential Scholarship: up to $5,000; significant academic merit and achievement. Achievement Scholarships: up to $5,000; significant life achievement. Vermont Scholarship: up to $2,000; for Vermont residents. Service Scholarship: up to $5,000; significant service. Bounder Scholarship: $500; applicants who live west of the Mississippi or in the Deep South. SCA Award: $1,000; alumni of Student Conservation Association. Transfer Award: $1,000. Vermont Youth Conservation Corps Award: $1,000; awarded to alumni of VYCC. Work-Learning-Service Credit: $800/semester.

FINANCIAL AID PROCEDURES
Forms required: FAFSA, state aid form, institutional form.
Dates and Deadlines: Priority date 3/15; no closing date. Applicants notified on a rolling basis starting 2/1; must reply by 5/1 or within 3 week(s) of notification.
Transfers: Applicants notified on a rolling basis starting 2/1; must reply within 3 week(s) of notification.

CONTACT
Tim Patterson, Director of Admission and Financial Aid
PO Box 72, Craftsbury Common, VT 05827-0072
(800) 648-3591 ext. 3

University of Vermont
Burlington, Vermont
www.uvm.edu
Federal Code: 003696

4-year public university in large town.
Enrollment: 10,267 undergrads, 3% part-time. 2,388 full-time freshmen.
Selectivity: Admits 50 to 75% of applicants.

BASIC COSTS (2016-2017)
Tuition and fees: $17,300; out-of-state residents $40,364.
Room and board: $11,578.

FINANCIAL AID PICTURE (2015-2016)
Students with need: Out of 1,904 full-time freshmen who applied for aid, 1,448 were judged to have need. Of these, 1,443 received aid, and 240 had their full need met. Average financial aid package met 69% of need; average scholarship/grant was $17,711; average loan was $3,416. For part-time students, average financial aid package was $13,432.
Students without need: 786 full-time freshmen who did not demonstrate need for aid received scholarships/grants; average award was $13,360. No-need awards available for academics, athletics, leadership, minority status, music/drama, ROTC, state/district residency.
Scholarships offered: 54 full-time freshmen received athletic scholarships; average amount $22,359.

FINANCIAL AID PROCEDURES
Forms required: FAFSA.
Dates and Deadlines: Priority date 2/1; no closing date. Applicants notified on a rolling basis starting 3/15; must reply within 3 week(s) of notification.
Transfers: Priority date 3/1; no deadline. Applicants notified on a rolling basis starting 3/15; must reply within 4 week(s) of notification. Merit scholarships are now available to transfer students.

CONTACT
Marie Johnson, Director Student Financial Services
194 South Prospect Street, Burlington, VT 05401-3596
(802) 656-5700

Vermont Technical College
Randolph Center, Vermont
www.vtc.edu
Federal Code: 003698

4-year public nursing and technical college in small town.
Enrollment: 1,437 undergrads, 23% part-time. 213 full-time freshmen.
Selectivity: Admits 50 to 75% of applicants.

BASIC COSTS (2016-2017)
Tuition and fees: $14,026; out-of-state residents $25,858.
Per-credit charge: $540; out-of-state residents $1,033.
Room and board: $9,988.

FINANCIAL AID PICTURE (2016-2017)
Students with need: Out of 205 full-time freshmen who applied for aid, 167 were judged to have need. Of these, 167 received aid, and 13 had their full need met. Average financial aid package met 58% of need; average scholarship/grant was $3,080; average loan was $3,340. For part-time students, average financial aid package was $10,396.
Students without need: 30 full-time freshmen who did not demonstrate need for aid received scholarships/grants; average award was $4,620. No-need awards available for academics.

FINANCIAL AID PROCEDURES
Forms required: FAFSA.
Dates and Deadlines: Priority date 3/1; no closing date. Applicants notified on a rolling basis starting 11/15; must reply within 2 week(s) of notification.

CONTACT
Cathy McCullough, Director of Financial Aid
PO Box 500, Randolph Center, VT 05061-0500
(800) 965-8790

Virginia

American National University: Charlottesville

Charlottesville, Virginia
www.an.edu   Federal Code: 003726

2-year for-profit business college in small city.
Enrollment: 112 undergrads.
Selectivity: Open admission.

BASIC COSTS (2017-2018)
Tuition and fees: $18,735.
Per-credit charge: $412.

FINANCIAL AID PICTURE
Students with need: Need-based aid available for full-time and part-time students.
Students without need: This college awards aid only to students with need.

FINANCIAL AID PROCEDURES
Forms required: FAFSA.
Dates and Deadlines: Applicants notified on a rolling basis.

CONTACT
Pam Cotton, Director of Financial Aid Compliance and Auditing
3926 Seminole Trail, Charlottesville, VA 22903
(540) 986-1800

American National University: Danville

Danville, Virginia
www.an.edu   Federal Code: 003726

2-year for-profit branch campus and business college in small city.
Enrollment: 108 undergrads.
Selectivity: Open admission.

BASIC COSTS (2017-2018)
Tuition and fees: $18,735.
Per-credit charge: $412.

FINANCIAL AID PICTURE
Students with need: Need-based aid available for full-time and part-time students.
Students without need: This college awards aid only to students with need.

FINANCIAL AID PROCEDURES
Forms required: FAFSA.
Dates and Deadlines: Applicants notified on a rolling basis starting 9/1.

CONTACT
Pam Cotton, Director of Financial Aid Compliance and Auditing
336 Old Riverside Drive, Danville, VA 24541
(540) 986-1800

American National University: Harrisonburg

Harrisonburg, Virginia
www.an.edu   Federal Code: 003726

2-year for-profit business college in large town.
Enrollment: 112 undergrads.
Selectivity: Open admission; but selective for some programs.

BASIC COSTS (2017-2018)
Tuition and fees: $18,735.
Per-credit charge: $412.

FINANCIAL AID PICTURE
Students with need: Need-based aid available for full-time and part-time students.
Students without need: This college awards aid only to students with need.

FINANCIAL AID PROCEDURES
Forms required: FAFSA.
Dates and Deadlines: Applicants notified on a rolling basis starting 9/1.

CONTACT
Pam Cotton, Director of Financial Aid Compliance and Auditing
1515 Country Club Road, Harrisonburg, VA 22802
(540) 986-1800

American National University: Lynchburg

Lynchburg, Virginia
www.an.edu   Federal Code: 010489

2-year for-profit business college in small city.
Enrollment: 121 undergrads.
Selectivity: Open admission.

BASIC COSTS (2017-2018)
Tuition and fees: $18,735.
Per-credit charge: $412.

FINANCIAL AID PICTURE
Students with need: Need-based aid available for full-time and part-time students.
Students without need: This college awards aid only to students with need.

FINANCIAL AID PROCEDURES
Forms required: FAFSA.
Dates and Deadlines: Applicants notified on a rolling basis starting 9/1.

CONTACT
Pam Cotton, Director of Financial Aid Compliance and Auditing
104 Candlewood Court, Lynchburg, VA 24502
(540) 986-1000

American National University: Martinsville

Martinsville, Virginia
www.an.edu   Federal Code: 003726

2-year for-profit business and junior college in small city.
Enrollment: 66 undergrads.
Selectivity: Open admission.

BASIC COSTS (2016-2017)
Tuition and fees: $14,460.
Per-credit charge: $317.

FINANCIAL AID PICTURE
Students with need: Need-based aid available for full-time and part-time students.
Students without need: This college awards aid only to students with need.

FINANCIAL AID PROCEDURES
Forms required: FAFSA.
Dates and Deadlines: Applicants notified on a rolling basis.

CONTACT
Pam Cotton, Director of Financial Aid Compliance and Auditing
905 North Memorial Boulevard, Martinsville, VA 24112
(540) 986-1800

American National University: Salem
Roanoke, Virginia
www.an.edu   Federal Code: 003726

4-year for-profit business college in large city.
Enrollment: 160 undergrads.
Selectivity: Open admission.

BASIC COSTS (2016-2017)
Tuition and fees: $14,460.
Per-credit charge: $317.

FINANCIAL AID PICTURE
Students with need: Need-based aid available for full-time and part-time students.
Students without need: This college awards aid only to students with need.

FINANCIAL AID PROCEDURES
Forms required: FAFSA.
Dates and Deadlines: Applicants notified on a rolling basis.

CONTACT
Pam Cotton, Director of Financial Aid Compliance and Auditing
1813 East Main Street, Salem, VA 24153
(540) 986-1800

Art Institute of Washington
Arlington, Virginia
www.aiw.artinstitutes.edu   Federal Code: 009270

4-year for-profit culinary school and visual arts college in small city.
Enrollment: 662 undergrads, 32% part-time. 451 full-time freshmen.

BASIC COSTS (2016-2017)
Tuition and fees: $21,970.
Per-credit charge: $486.
Room only: $10,398.

FINANCIAL AID PICTURE
Students with need: Need-based aid available for part-time students.

FINANCIAL AID PROCEDURES
Forms required: FAFSA, institutional form.

CONTACT
Corey Tyberendt, Director of Student Financial Services
1820 North Fort Myer Drive, Arlington, VA 22209-1802
(703) 358-9550

Averett University
Danville, Virginia
www.averett.edu   Federal Code: 003702

4-year private university and liberal arts college in large town, affiliated with the Baptist faith.
Enrollment: 849 undergrads, 2% part-time. 234 full-time freshmen.
Selectivity: Admits 50 to 75% of applicants.

BASIC COSTS (2016-2017)
Tuition and fees: $31,980.
Per-credit charge: $1,335.
Room and board: $8,990.

FINANCIAL AID PICTURE (2016-2017)
Students with need: Out of 216 full-time freshmen who applied for aid, 207 were judged to have need. Of these, 207 received aid, and 26 had their full need met. Average financial aid package met 71% of need; average scholarship/grant was $22,289; average loan was $3,783. For part-time students, average financial aid package was $8,602.
Students without need: 27 full-time freshmen who did not demonstrate need for aid received scholarships/grants; average award was $17,037. No-need awards available for academics, alumni affiliation, art, job skills, leadership, minority status, music/drama, religious affiliation, state/district residency.
Scholarships offered: Founders Scholarship; $9,000; awarded to students for their quality academic preparation; renewable. Horizon Scholarship; $4,000; based on academic performance; renewable. Phi Theta Kappa Scholarship; $1,000; awarded to community college students who are members of Phi Theta Kappa; must be enrolled in a traditional program; renewable with 3.0 GPA. Ministerial Tuition Discount; $400 (resident students), $200 (commuters); for full-time students who are children of ministers or students preparing for church-related vocations; renewable. Presidential scholarship; $14,000. Deans Scholarship; $12,000.

FINANCIAL AID PROCEDURES
Forms required: FAFSA, state aid form.
Dates and Deadlines: Applicants notified on a rolling basis; must reply within 2 week(s) of notification.
Transfers: No deadline. Applicants notified on a rolling basis starting 2/15; must reply within 2 week(s) of notification.

CONTACT
Carl Bradsher, Director of Student Financial Services
Office of Admissions, Danville, VA 24541
(434) 791-5890

Blue Ridge Community College
Weyers Cave, Virginia
www.brcc.edu   Federal Code: 006819

2-year public community college in large town.
Enrollment: 4,388 undergrads.
Selectivity: Open admission; but selective for some programs.

BASIC COSTS (2016-2017)
Tuition and fees: $5,131; out-of-state residents $10,429.
Per-credit charge: $137; out-of-state residents $314.
Additional info: Out-of-state students pay an additional $600 capital outlay fee.

FINANCIAL AID PICTURE
Students with need: Need-based aid available for full-time and part-time students.
Students without need: No-need awards available for academics, job skills, leadership, minority status.

FINANCIAL AID PROCEDURES

Forms required: FAFSA, institutional form.

Dates and Deadlines: Priority date 5/1; no closing date. Applicants notified on a rolling basis starting 5/30; must reply within 2 week(s) of notification.

CONTACT

Robert Clemmer, Financial Aid Director

Box 80, Weyers Cave, VA 24486-9989

(540) 234-9261 ext. 2223

Bluefield College

Bluefield, Virginia

www.bluefield.edu   Federal Code: 003703

4-year private liberal arts and teachers college in small town, affiliated with the Baptist faith.

Enrollment: 886 undergrads, 10% part-time. 184 full-time freshmen.

Selectivity: Admits over 75% of applicants.

BASIC COSTS (2017-2018)

Tuition and fees: $24,890.

Per-credit charge: $970.

Room and board: $8,843.

FINANCIAL AID PICTURE (2016-2017)

Students with need: Out of 169 full-time freshmen who applied for aid, 163 were judged to have need. Of these, 163 received aid, and 21 had their full need met. Average financial aid package met 66% of need; average scholarship/grant was $16,673; average loan was $3,583. For part-time students, average financial aid package was $5,458.

Students without need: 20 full-time freshmen who did not demonstrate need for aid received scholarships/grants; average award was $5,931. No-need awards available for academics, art, athletics, leadership, music/drama, religious affiliation.

Scholarships offered: 24 full-time freshmen received athletic scholarships; average amount $8,180.

FINANCIAL AID PROCEDURES

Forms required: FAFSA, state aid form.

Dates and Deadlines: Priority date 6/1; no closing date. Applicants notified on a rolling basis starting 3/1; must reply within 3 week(s) of notification.

Transfers: No deadline. Applicants notified on a rolling basis starting 3/1; must reply within 3 week(s) of notification. Transfer students are not eligible to participate in academic essay competition in which students compete for full-tuition and half-tuition scholarships.

CONTACT

Carly Kestner, Director of Financial Aid

3000 College Avenue, Bluefield, VA 24605

(276) 326-4215

Bridgewater College

Bridgewater, Virginia

www.bridgewater.edu   Federal Code: 003704

4-year private liberal arts college in small town, affiliated with the Church of the Brethren.

Enrollment: 1,871 undergrads. 600 full-time freshmen.

Selectivity: Admits 50 to 75% of applicants.

BASIC COSTS (2017-2018)

Tuition and fees: $33,820.

Per-credit charge: $1,150.

Room and board: $12,440.

FINANCIAL AID PICTURE (2016-2017)

Students with need: Out of 569 full-time freshmen who applied for aid, 517 were judged to have need. Of these, 517 received aid, and 155 had their full need met. Average financial aid package met 87% of need; average scholarship/grant was $28,113; average loan was $4,168. Need-based aid available for part-time students.

Students without need: 82 full-time freshmen who did not demonstrate need for aid received scholarships/grants; average award was $21,809. No-need awards available for academics, minority status, music/drama, religious affiliation, state/district residency.

Scholarships offered: Renewable academic scholarships are provided to freshmen based on high school grade point average and other criteria from the applicant's record.

FINANCIAL AID PROCEDURES

Forms required: FAFSA, state aid form.

Dates and Deadlines: Priority date 3/1; no closing date. Applicants notified on a rolling basis starting 12/1; must reply by 5/1 or within 2 week(s) of notification.

Transfers: No deadline. Applicants notified on a rolling basis starting 12/1; must reply by 5/1 or within 2 week(s) of notification.

CONTACT

Scott Morrison, Director of Financial Aid

402 East College Street, Bridgewater, VA 22812-1599

(540) 828-5377

Bryant & Stratton College: Richmond

Richmond, Virginia

www.bryantstratton.edu   Federal Code: 010061

2-year for-profit career college in small city.

Enrollment: 626 undergrads.

Selectivity: Open admission; but selective for some programs.

BASIC COSTS (2016-2017)

Tuition and fees: $17,190.

Per-credit charge: $573.

Additional info: Tuition and fees may vary by program.

FINANCIAL AID PICTURE

Students with need: Need-based aid available for full-time and part-time students. Work study available nights.

Students without need: This college awards aid only to students with need.

FINANCIAL AID PROCEDURES

Forms required: FAFSA.

Dates and Deadlines: Closing date 9/17.

Transfers: No deadline.

CONTACT

Eddie Webster, Financial Aid Manager

8141 Hull Street Road, Richmond, VA 23235

(804) 745-2444

Bryant & Stratton College: Virginia Beach

Virginia Beach, Virginia

www.bryantstratton.edu   Federal Code: 002678

2-year for-profit business and junior college in large city.

Enrollment: 585 undergrads.

Selectivity: Open admission; but selective for some programs.

BASIC COSTS (2016-2017)

Tuition and fees: $17,190.
Per-credit charge: $573.
Additional info: Tuition and fees may vary by program.

FINANCIAL AID PICTURE

Students with need: Need-based aid available for full-time and part-time students. Work study available nights.

FINANCIAL AID PROCEDURES

Forms required: FAFSA.
Dates and Deadlines: Closing date 9/17. Applicants notified on a rolling basis.

CONTACT

Bethann Verbal, Director of Financial Aid
301 Centre Pointe Drive, Virginia Beach, VA 23462-4417
(757) 499-7900

Central Virginia Community College

Lynchburg, Virginia
www.cvcc.vccs.edu   Federal Code: 004988

2-year public community college in small city.
Enrollment: 2,239 undergrads.
Selectivity: Open admission; but selective for some programs.

BASIC COSTS (2016-2017)

Tuition and fees: $4,598; out-of-state residents $10,496.
Per-credit charge: $138; out-of-state residents $315.

FINANCIAL AID PICTURE

Students with need: Need-based aid available for full-time students.
Students without need: No-need awards available for academics, alumni affiliation.
Additional info: Payment plan available.

FINANCIAL AID PROCEDURES

Forms required: FAFSA.
Dates and Deadlines: Priority date 3/15; no closing date. Applicants notified on a rolling basis starting 5/1; must reply within 2 week(s) of notification.

CONTACT

Michael Farris, Dean of Enrollment Management
3506 Wards Road, Lynchburg, VA 24502-2498
(434) 832-7814

Christendom College

Front Royal, Virginia
www.christendom.edu

4-year private liberal arts college in large town, affiliated with the Roman Catholic Church.
Enrollment: 477 undergrads. 119 full-time freshmen.
Selectivity: Admits over 75% of applicants.

BASIC COSTS (2017-2018)

Tuition and fees: $25,580.
Room and board: $9,976.

FINANCIAL AID PICTURE (2016-2017)

Students with need: Out of 88 full-time freshmen who applied for aid, 68 were judged to have need. Of these, 68 received aid. Average financial aid package met 72% of need; average scholarship/grant was $12,292; average loan was $6,752.
Students without need: 29 full-time freshmen who did not demonstrate need for aid received scholarships/grants; average award was $10,527. No-need awards available for academics, alumni affiliation.

Scholarships offered: Padre Pio Full-Tuition Scholarship.
Additional info: Institution does not accept direct federal aid, nor does it participate in indirect programs of federal aid.

FINANCIAL AID PROCEDURES

Forms required: institutional form.
Dates and Deadlines: Priority date 4/1; closing date 6/1. Applicants notified on a rolling basis starting 2/1; must reply within 4 week(s) of notification.

CONTACT

Alisa Polk, Financial Aid Officer
134 Christendom Drive, Front Royal, VA 22630
(800) 877-5456

Christopher Newport University

Newport News, Virginia
www.cnu.edu   Federal Code: 003706

4-year public university and liberal arts college in small city.
Enrollment: 4,921 undergrads, 1% part-time. 1,228 full-time freshmen.
Selectivity: Admits 50 to 75% of applicants. GED not accepted.

BASIC COSTS (2016-2017)

Tuition and fees: $13,054; out-of-state residents $24,680.
Per-credit charge: $327; out-of-state residents $794.
Room and board: $10,914.

FINANCIAL AID PICTURE (2016-2017)

Students with need: Out of 985 full-time freshmen who applied for aid, 580 were judged to have need. Of these, 555 received aid, and 125 had their full need met. Average financial aid package met 72% of need; average scholarship/grant was $6,954; average loan was $3,349. For part-time students, average financial aid package was $4,341.
Students without need: 215 full-time freshmen who did not demonstrate need for aid received scholarships/grants; average award was $3,369. No-need awards available for academics, alumni affiliation, art, leadership, music/drama, ROTC, state/district residency.

FINANCIAL AID PROCEDURES

Forms required: FAFSA.
Dates and Deadlines: Priority date 3/1; no closing date. Applicants notified on a rolling basis starting 3/1; must reply by 5/1.
Transfers: Priority date 3/1; no deadline. Applicants notified on a rolling basis starting 3/1; must reply within 3 week(s) of notification.

CONTACT

Lisa Raines, Vice Provost Enrollment Services and Student Success
1 Avenue of the Arts, Newport News, VA 23606-3072
(757) 594-7170

College of William and Mary

Williamsburg, Virginia   Federal Code: 003705
www.wm.edu   CSS Code: 5115

4-year public university in large town.
Enrollment: 6,245 undergrads, 1% part-time. 1,517 full-time freshmen.
Selectivity: Admits less than 50% of applicants.

BASIC COSTS (2016-2017)

Tuition and fees: $21,234; out-of-state residents $41,718.
Per-credit charge: $400; out-of-state residents $1,150.
Room and board: $11,382.

FINANCIAL AID PICTURE (2015-2016)

Students with need: Out of 1,009 full-time freshmen who applied for aid, 549 were judged to have need. Of these, 516 received aid, and 126 had their full need met. Average financial aid package met 79% of need; average

scholarship/grant was $15,468; average loan was $3,415. For part-time students, average financial aid package was $14,804.

Students without need: 38 full-time freshmen who did not demonstrate need for aid received scholarships/grants; average award was $9,893. No-need awards available for academics, art, athletics, music/drama.

Scholarships offered: 67 full-time freshmen received athletic scholarships; average amount $26,420.

FINANCIAL AID PROCEDURES

Forms required: FAFSA, CSS PROFILE.

Dates and Deadlines: Priority date 3/1; no closing date. Applicants notified on a rolling basis starting 3/15; must reply by 5/1.

Transfers: Applicants notified by 3/15.

CONTACT

Edward Irish, Director of Student Financial Aid
PO Box 8795, Williamsburg, VA 23187-8795
(757) 221-2420

Dabney S. Lancaster Community College

Clifton Forge, Virginia
www.dslcc.edu   Federal Code: 004996

2-year public community and technical college in small town.

Enrollment: 656 undergrads, 46% part-time. 86 full-time freshmen.

Selectivity: Open admission; but selective for some programs.

BASIC COSTS (2016-2017)

Tuition and fees: $4,463; out-of-state residents $10,361.

Per-credit charge: $137; out-of-state residents $314.

FINANCIAL AID PICTURE

Students with need: Need-based aid available for full-time and part-time students. Work study available nights.

Students without need: This college awards aid only to students with need.

FINANCIAL AID PROCEDURES

Forms required: FAFSA.

Dates and Deadlines: Priority date 3/1; closing date 6/30. Applicants notified on a rolling basis starting 4/15; must reply within 2 week(s) of notification.

CONTACT

Angela Graham, Vice President of Financial and Administrative Services
1000 Dabney Drive, Clifton Forge, VA 24422
(540) 863-2861

Danville Community College

Danville, Virginia
www.dcc.vccs.edu   Federal Code: 003758

2-year public community college in small city.

Enrollment: 1,739 undergrads, 42% part-time. 192 full-time freshmen.

Selectivity: Open admission; but selective for some programs.

BASIC COSTS (2016-2017)

Tuition and fees: $4,462; out-of-state residents $9,760.

Per-credit charge: $137; out-of-state residents $314.

Additional info: Out-of-state students pay an additional $600 capital outlay fee.

FINANCIAL AID PICTURE

Students with need: Need-based aid available for full-time and part-time students.

Students without need: This college awards aid only to students with need.

Scholarships offered: Educational Foundation Scholarship: $250 to $1,500; based on separate application; deadline mid-March prior to award year.

FINANCIAL AID PROCEDURES

Forms required: FAFSA.

Dates and Deadlines: Priority date 6/1; no closing date. Applicants notified on a rolling basis starting 5/1; must reply within 2 week(s) of notification.

Transfers: Limited aid available to transfer students admitted in spring semester.

CONTACT

Mary Gore, Assistant Coordinator of Financial Aid
1008 South Main Street, Danville, VA 24541
(434) 797-8439

DeVry University: Arlington

Arlington, Virginia
www.devry.edu

4-year for-profit university in very large city.

Enrollment: 251 undergrads, 51% part-time. 5 full-time freshmen.

BASIC COSTS (2016-2017)

Tuition and fees: $17,512.

Per-credit charge: $609.

FINANCIAL AID PICTURE

Students with need: Need-based aid available for full-time and part-time students.

Students without need: This college awards aid only to students with need.

FINANCIAL AID PROCEDURES

Forms required: FAFSA.

Dates and Deadlines: Applicants notified on a rolling basis.

CONTACT

Director of Student Finance
2450 Crystal Drive, Arlington, VA 22202
(703) 414-4000

Eastern Mennonite University

Harrisonburg, Virginia
www.emu.edu   Federal Code: 003708

4-year private university and liberal arts college in small city, affiliated with the Mennonite Church.

Enrollment: 1,240 undergrads, 13% part-time. 222 full-time freshmen.

Selectivity: Admits 50 to 75% of applicants.

BASIC COSTS (2016-2017)

Tuition and fees: $34,200.

Per-credit charge: $1,350.

Room and board: $10,660.

FINANCIAL AID PICTURE

Students with need: Need-based aid available for full-time and part-time students. Work study available nights, weekends, and for part-time students.

Students without need: No-need awards available for academics, alumni affiliation, art, leadership, religious affiliation, state/district residency.

Scholarships offered: President's Scholarship; minimum 3.9 GPA. Academic Achievement Scholarship; minimum 3.2 GPA. University Grant; minimum 2.5 GPA. 920 SAT (exclusive of Writing) or 20 ACT required for all scholarships. Amounts based on GPA and test scores; no limit on number of awards. Full-tuition scholarships available for 2 honors program applicants with highest test scores and GPA; half tuition scholarships available for next 10 candidates.

FINANCIAL AID PROCEDURES

Forms required: FAFSA, state aid form.

Dates and Deadlines: Priority date 3/1; no closing date. Applicants notified on a rolling basis starting 3/1; must reply within 4 week(s) of notification.

Transfers: No deadline. Applicants notified on a rolling basis starting 3/1; must reply within 4 week(s) of notification.

CONTACT

Michele Hensley, Director of Financial Assistance
1200 Park Road, Harrisonburg, VA 22802-2462
(540) 432-4137

Eastern Shore Community College
Melfa, Virginia
www.es.vccs.edu　　　　　　Federal Code: 003748

2-year public community college in rural community.

Enrollment: 705 undergrads.

Selectivity: Open admission; but selective for some programs.

BASIC COSTS (2016-2017)

Tuition and fees: $4,537; out-of-state residents $9,835.

Per-credit charge: $137; out-of-state residents $314.

Additional info: Out-of-state students pay an additional $600 capital outlay fee.

FINANCIAL AID PICTURE

Students with need: Need-based aid available for full-time and part-time students.

Students without need: This college awards aid only to students with need.

Additional info: ESCC is a member of the Servicemembers Opportunity Colleges program.

FINANCIAL AID PROCEDURES

Forms required: FAFSA.

Dates and Deadlines: Priority date 5/1; no closing date. Applicants notified on a rolling basis starting 6/1; must reply within 2 week(s) of notification.

CONTACT

Carole Read, Financial Aid Officer
29300 Lankford Highway, Melfa, VA 23410-9755
(757) 789-1733

ECPI University
Virginia Beach, Virginia
www.ecpi.edu　　　　　　Federal Code: 010198

4-year for-profit university and health science college in very large city.

Enrollment: 10,242 undergrads.

BASIC COSTS (2016-2017)

Tuition and fees: $15,811.

Additional info: Cost quoted is for Computer & Information Science, Electronics Engineering, Mechanical Engineering, Surgical Technology. Costs very for other programs ranging from $9,792-$19,800.

FINANCIAL AID PICTURE

Students with need: Need-based aid available for full-time and part-time students. Work study available nights.

Students without need: No-need awards available for academics.

FINANCIAL AID PROCEDURES

Forms required: FAFSA.

Dates and Deadlines: Applicants notified on a rolling basis.

Transfers: No deadline. Applicants notified on a rolling basis.

CONTACT

Kathi Turner, Director of Financial Aid
5555 Greenwich Road, Suite 300, Virginia Beach, VA 23462-6542
(757) 671-7171 ext. 55351

Emory & Henry College
Emory, Virginia
www.ehc.edu　　　　　　Federal Code: 003709

4-year private liberal arts college in rural community, affiliated with the United Methodist Church.

Enrollment: 1,004 undergrads, 1% part-time. 284 full-time freshmen.

Selectivity: Admits 50 to 75% of applicants.

BASIC COSTS (2016-2017)

Tuition and fees: $33,700.

Room and board: $11,200.

Additional info: Tuition at time of enrollment locked for 4 years.

FINANCIAL AID PICTURE (2016-2017)

Students with need: Out of 278 full-time freshmen who applied for aid, 254 were judged to have need. Of these, 254 received aid, and 52 had their full need met. Average financial aid package met 85% of need; average scholarship/grant was $27,924; average loan was $2,273. For part-time students, average financial aid package was $11,478.

Students without need: 28 full-time freshmen who did not demonstrate need for aid received scholarships/grants; average award was $17,652. No-need awards available for academics, alumni affiliation, art, music/drama, religious affiliation, state/district residency.

Additional info: Virginia residents eligible for additional in-state tuition grants.

FINANCIAL AID PROCEDURES

Forms required: FAFSA.

Dates and Deadlines: Priority date 3/1; no closing date. Applicants notified on a rolling basis starting 12/1; must reply within 3 week(s) of notification.

Transfers: Closing date 5/15. Applicants notified on a rolling basis starting 2/15; must reply by 6/15 or within 4 week(s) of notification. Financial aid based on academic credits accepted for transfer.

CONTACT

Scarlett Blevins, Director of Student Financial Aid
PO Box 10, Emory, VA 24327
(276) 944-6115

Ferrum College
Ferrum, Virginia
www.ferrum.edu　　　　　　Federal Code: 003711

4-year private liberal arts college in rural community, affiliated with the United Methodist Church.

Enrollment: 1,451 undergrads.

BASIC COSTS (2016-2017)

Tuition and fees: $31,915.

Per-credit charge: $635.

Room and board: $11,090.

FINANCIAL AID PICTURE

Students with need: Need-based aid available for full-time and part-time students.

Students without need: No-need awards available for academics, leadership, religious affiliation, state/district residency.

FINANCIAL AID PROCEDURES

Forms required: FAFSA, state aid form.

Dates and Deadlines: Applicants notified on a rolling basis.

CONTACT

Heather Hollandsworth, Director of Financial Aid

Spilman-Daniel House, 40 Stratton Lane, Ferrum, VA 24088

(540) 365-4282

George Mason University

Fairfax, Virginia

www2.gmu.edu   Federal Code: 003749

4-year public university in large town.

Enrollment: 23,174 undergrads, 18% part-time. 3,154 full-time freshmen.

Selectivity: Admits over 75% of applicants.

BASIC COSTS (2016-2017)

Tuition and fees: $11,300; out-of-state residents $32,582.

Per-credit charge: $342; out-of-state residents $1,229.

Room and board: $10,730.

FINANCIAL AID PICTURE (2015-2016)

Students with need: Out of 2,611 full-time freshmen who applied for aid, 1,893 were judged to have need. Of these, 1,813 received aid, and 119 had their full need met. Average financial aid package met 66% of need; average scholarship/grant was $7,258; average loan was $3,367. For part-time students, average financial aid package was $7,263.

Students without need: 338 full-time freshmen who did not demonstrate need for aid received scholarships/grants; average award was $5,700. No-need awards available for academics, athletics, minority status, music/drama, ROTC.

Scholarships offered: 46 full-time freshmen received athletic scholarships; average amount $25,255.

FINANCIAL AID PROCEDURES

Forms required: FAFSA.

Dates and Deadlines: Priority date 3/1; no closing date. Applicants notified on a rolling basis starting 4/1; must reply within 3 week(s) of notification.

CONTACT

Sandra Tarbox, Director, Student Financial Aid

4400 University Drive, MSN 3A4, Fairfax, VA 22030-4444

(703) 993-2353

Germanna Community College

Locust Grove, Virginia

www.germanna.edu   Federal Code: 008660

2-year public community college in rural community.

Enrollment: 7,379 undergrads.

Selectivity: Open admission; but selective for some programs.

BASIC COSTS (2016-2017)

Tuition and fees: $4,680; out-of-state residents $10,577.

Per-credit charge: $138; out-of-state residents $315.

FINANCIAL AID PICTURE

Students with need: Need-based aid available for full-time and part-time students.

Students without need: No-need awards available for academics.

FINANCIAL AID PROCEDURES

Forms required: FAFSA.

Dates and Deadlines: Priority date 4/1; no closing date. Applicants notified on a rolling basis starting 5/15; must reply within 2 week(s) of notification.

CONTACT

Aaron Whitacre, Director of Financial Aid

2130 Germanna Highway, Locust Grove, VA 22508-2102

(540) 423-9124

Hampden-Sydney College

Hampden-Sydney, Virginia

www.hsc.edu   Federal Code: 003713

4-year private liberal arts college for men in small town, affiliated with the Presbyterian Church (USA).

Enrollment: 1,027 undergrads. 283 full-time freshmen.

Selectivity: Admits 50 to 75% of applicants.

BASIC COSTS (2016-2017)

Tuition and fees: $42,962.

Room and board: $13,286.

FINANCIAL AID PICTURE (2016-2017)

Students with need: Out of 241 full-time freshmen who applied for aid, 198 were judged to have need. Of these, 198 received aid, and 60 had their full need met. Average financial aid package met 81% of need; average scholarship/grant was $28,603; average loan was $3,837. Need-based aid available for part-time students.

Students without need: 82 full-time freshmen who did not demonstrate need for aid received scholarships/grants; average award was $20,519. No-need awards available for academics, leadership, minority status, music/drama, ROTC, state/district residency.

Scholarships offered: Allan Scholarship: $30,000 annually. Venable Scholarship: $25,000 annually. Patrick Henry Scholarship: $20,000 annually. Achievement Awards: range from $5,000-$15,000 annually.

FINANCIAL AID PROCEDURES

Forms required: FAFSA, state aid form.

Dates and Deadlines: Priority date 3/1; closing date 5/1. Applicants notified on a rolling basis starting 12/15; must reply by 5/1 or within 2 week(s) of notification.

Transfers: Priority date 7/1; no deadline. Applicants notified on a rolling basis starting 3/1; must reply within 2 week(s) of notification.

CONTACT

Zita Barree, Director of Financial Aid

PO Box 667, Hampden-Sydney, VA 23943

(434) 223-6119

Hampton University

Hampton, Virginia

www.hamptonu.edu   Federal Code: 003714

4-year private university in small city.

Enrollment: 3,836 undergrads, 5% part-time. 840 full-time freshmen.

Selectivity: Admits 50 to 75% of applicants.

BASIC COSTS (2016-2017)

Tuition and fees: $23,992.

Per-credit charge: $548.

Room and board: $10,684.

FINANCIAL AID PICTURE (2015-2016)

Students with need: Out of 705 full-time freshmen who applied for aid, 580 were judged to have need. Of these, 563 received aid, and 227 had their full need met. Average financial aid package met 40% of need; average scholarship/grant was $5,206; average loan was $5,771. For part-time students, average financial aid package was $4,301.

Students without need: 12 full-time freshmen who did not demonstrate need for aid received scholarships/grants; average award was $2,725. No-need awards available for academics, athletics, job skills, leadership, music/drama, ROTC.

Scholarships offered: 65 full-time freshmen received athletic scholarships; average amount $15,323.

FINANCIAL AID PROCEDURES

Forms required: FAFSA.

Dates and Deadlines: Priority date 2/15; closing date 4/15. Applicants notified on a rolling basis starting 3/1; must reply within 2 week(s) of notification.

CONTACT
Martin Miles, Financial Aid Director
Office of Admission, Hampton, VA 23668
(800) 624-3341

Hollins University
Roanoke, Virginia
www.hollins.edu   Federal Code: 003715

4-year private university and liberal arts college for women in small city.
Enrollment: 647 undergrads, 1% part-time. 224 full-time freshmen.
Selectivity: Admits 50 to 75% of applicants.

BASIC COSTS (2016-2017)
Tuition and fees: $36,835.
Per-credit charge: $1,132.
Room and board: $12,800.

FINANCIAL AID PICTURE (2016-2017)
Students with need: Out of 212 full-time freshmen who applied for aid, 189 were judged to have need. Of these, 189 received aid, and 50 had their full need met. Average financial aid package met 85% of need; average scholarship/grant was $30,186; average loan was $4,128. For part-time students, average financial aid package was $18,360.
Students without need: 35 full-time freshmen who did not demonstrate need for aid received scholarships/grants; average award was $29,647. No-need awards available for academics, alumni affiliation, art, leadership, music/drama, state/district residency.
Scholarships offered: Batten Scholar awards: full tuition; academic merit. Hollins Scholar Awards: $24,000-$28,000; academic merit. Hollins Recognition Awards: at least $20,000/year; academic merit, organizational involvement. Creative Talent Awards: $1,000-$5,000; distinguished achievement in creative writing, music, dance or theater.

FINANCIAL AID PROCEDURES
Forms required: FAFSA, state aid form.
Dates and Deadlines: Priority date 1/1; no closing date. Applicants notified on a rolling basis starting 11/21; must reply by 5/1.
Transfers: Priority date 7/1; closing date 7/31. Applicants notified on a rolling basis starting 12/1. Transfer student merit scholarship amounts range from half of tuition up to $24000 per year. Scholarships also offered for Phi Theta Kappa members.

CONTACT
Mary Jean Sullivan, Director of Scholarships and Financial Assistance
PO Box 9707, Roanoke, VA 24020-1707
(540) 362-6332

J. Sargeant Reynolds Community College
Richmond, Virginia
www.reynolds.edu   Federal Code: 003759

2-year public community college in very large city.
Enrollment: 8,505 undergrads, 69% part-time. 820 full-time freshmen.
Selectivity: Open admission; but selective for some programs.

BASIC COSTS (2016-2017)
Tuition and fees: $4,765; out-of-state residents $10,663.
Per-credit charge: $138; out-of-state residents $315.

FINANCIAL AID PICTURE (2015-2016)
Students with need: Out of 820 full-time freshmen who applied for aid, 443 were judged to have need. Of these, 443 received aid. Need-based aid available for part-time students.
Students without need: No-need awards available for academics.

FINANCIAL AID PROCEDURES
Forms required: FAFSA.
Dates and Deadlines: Closing date 4/15. Applicants notified on a rolling basis starting 7/15; must reply within 2 week(s) of notification.

CONTACT
Kiesha Pope, Director of Financial Aid
PO Box 85622, Richmond, VA 23285-5622
(804) 523-5137

James Madison University
Harrisonburg, Virginia
www.jmu.edu   Federal Code: 003721

4-year public university in large town.
Enrollment: 19,262 undergrads, 4% part-time. 4,432 full-time freshmen.
Selectivity: Admits 50 to 75% of applicants.

BASIC COSTS (2016-2017)
Tuition and fees: $10,342; out-of-state residents $26,116.
Per-credit charge: $196; out-of-state residents $703.
Room and board: $9,334.

FINANCIAL AID PICTURE (2016-2017)
Students with need: Out of 3,183 full-time freshmen who applied for aid, 2,068 were judged to have need. Of these, 1,789 received aid, and 1,582 had their full need met. Average financial aid package met 39% of need; average scholarship/grant was $8,376; average loan was $3,490. For part-time students, average financial aid package was $7,058.
Students without need: 74 full-time freshmen who did not demonstrate need for aid received scholarships/grants; average award was $6,094. No-need awards available for academics, alumni affiliation, art, athletics, leadership, minority status, music/drama, state/district residency.
Scholarships offered: 101 full-time freshmen received athletic scholarships; average amount $18,651.

FINANCIAL AID PROCEDURES
Forms required: FAFSA.
Dates and Deadlines: Priority date 3/1; no closing date. Applicants notified on a rolling basis starting 4/1; must reply within 4 week(s) of notification.
Transfers: Applicants notified on a rolling basis starting 4/1; must reply within 4 week(s) of notification.

CONTACT
Lisa Tumer, Director of Financial Aid and Scholarships
Sonner Hall, MSC 0101, Harrisonburg, VA 22807
(540) 568-7820

Jefferson College of Health Sciences
Roanoke, Virginia
www.jchs.edu   Federal Code: 009893

4-year private health science and nursing college in small city.
Enrollment: 787 undergrads.

BASIC COSTS (2016-2017)
Tuition and fees: $25,150.
Per-credit charge: $715.
Room only: $5,870.

FINANCIAL AID PICTURE

Students with need: Need-based aid available for full-time and part-time students.

Students without need: No-need awards available for academics.

FINANCIAL AID PROCEDURES

Forms required: FAFSA, institutional form.

Dates and Deadlines: Applicants notified on a rolling basis; must reply within 2 week(s) of notification.

CONTACT

Deborah Johnson, Financial Aid Officer

101 Elm Avenue, SE, Roanoke, VA 24013-2222

(540) 985-8483

John Tyler Community College

Chester, Virginia

www.jtcc.edu   Federal Code: 004004

2-year public community college in small city.

Enrollment: 5,946 undergrads, 62% part-time. 752 full-time freshmen.

Selectivity: Open admission; but selective for some programs.

BASIC COSTS (2016-2017)

Tuition and fees: $4,473; out-of-state residents $10,371.

Per-credit charge: $138; out-of-state residents $315.

FINANCIAL AID PICTURE (2015-2016)

Students with need: Need-based aid available for full-time and part-time students. Work study available nights, weekends, and for part-time students.

Students without need: No-need awards available for academics, state/district residency.

FINANCIAL AID PROCEDURES

Forms required: FAFSA.

Dates and Deadlines: Priority date 4/1; no closing date. Applicants notified on a rolling basis starting 5/30.

CONTACT

Tony Jones, Director of Financial Aid

13101 Jefferson Davis Highway, Chester, VA 23831-5316

(855) 874-6684

Liberty University

Lynchburg, Virginia

www.liberty.edu   Federal Code: 010392

4-year private university in small city, affiliated with the Christian Church.

Enrollment: 13,587 undergrads, 3% part-time. 2,914 full-time freshmen.

Selectivity: Admits less than 50% of applicants.

BASIC COSTS (2016-2017)

Tuition and fees: $23,020.

Per-credit charge: $917.

Room and board: $9,306.

FINANCIAL AID PICTURE (2016-2017)

Students with need: Out of 2,760 full-time freshmen who applied for aid, 2,097 were judged to have need. Of these, 2,097 received aid, and 289 had their full need met. Average financial aid package met 58% of need; average scholarship/grant was $10,702; average loan was $3,443. For part-time students, average financial aid package was $7,341.

Students without need: 655 full-time freshmen who did not demonstrate need for aid received scholarships/grants; average award was $8,080. No-need awards available for academics, alumni affiliation, athletics, leadership, music/drama, religious affiliation, ROTC, state/district residency.

Scholarships offered: *Merit:* Liberty Academic Achievement Scholarship: up to $6,000; additional $3,500 could be applied if student is also accepted into the Honors Program; based on high school grades and standardized test scores. *Athletic:* 25 full-time freshmen received athletic scholarships; average amount $15,063.

FINANCIAL AID PROCEDURES

Forms required: FAFSA, state aid form.

Dates and Deadlines: Priority date 3/1; closing date 3/1. Applicants notified on a rolling basis starting 3/15; must reply within 3 week(s) of notification.

Transfers: Applicants notified on a rolling basis starting 3/15; must reply within 3 week(s) of notification.

CONTACT

Robert Ritz, Senior Vice President for University Financial Services

1971 University Boulevard, Lynchburg, VA 24515

(434) 582-2270

Longwood University

Farmville, Virginia

www.longwood.edu   Federal Code: 003719

4-year public university in small town.

Enrollment: 4,194 undergrads, 6% part-time. 901 full-time freshmen.

Selectivity: Admits 50 to 75% of applicants.

BASIC COSTS (2016-2017)

Tuition and fees: $12,240; out-of-state residents $26,670.

Per-credit charge: $245; out-of-state residents $706.

Room and board: $10,685.

FINANCIAL AID PICTURE (2015-2016)

Students with need: 48% of average financial aid package awarded as scholarships/grants, 52% awarded as loans/jobs. Need-based aid available for part-time students. Work study available nights, weekends, and for part-time students.

Students without need: No-need awards available for academics, alumni affiliation, art, athletics, leadership, music/drama, ROTC, state/district residency.

FINANCIAL AID PROCEDURES

Forms required: FAFSA.

Dates and Deadlines: Priority date 3/1; no closing date. Applicants notified on a rolling basis starting 4/1; must reply within 4 week(s) of notification.

Transfers: Closing date 3/1. Applicants notified by 4/1; must reply by 5/1.

CONTACT

Melissa Shepherd, Director of Financial Aid

201 High Street, Farmville, VA 23909-1898

(434) 395-2077

Lord Fairfax Community College

Middletown, Virginia

www.lfcc.edu   Federal Code: 008659

2-year public community college in small town.

Enrollment: 4,262 undergrads.

Selectivity: Open admission; but selective for some programs.

BASIC COSTS (2016-2017)

Tuition and fees: $4,506; out-of-state residents $9,804.

Per-credit charge: $137; out-of-state residents $314.

Additional info: Out-of-state students pay an additional $600 capital outlay fee.

FINANCIAL AID PICTURE

Students with need: Need-based aid available for full-time and part-time students.

Students without need: This college awards aid only to students with need.

FINANCIAL AID PROCEDURES

Forms required: FAFSA.

Dates and Deadlines: Priority date 5/1; no closing date. Applicants notified on a rolling basis starting 6/1.

CONTACT

Aaron Whitacre, Director of Financial Aid
173 Skirmisher Lane, Middletown, VA 22645
(540) 868-7274

Lynchburg College

Lynchburg, Virginia
www.lynchburg.edu   Federal Code: 003720

4-year private university and liberal arts college in small city, affiliated with the Christian Church (Disciples of Christ).

Enrollment: 1,999 undergrads, 3% part-time. 521 full-time freshmen.

Selectivity: Admits 50 to 75% of applicants.

BASIC COSTS (2016-2017)

Tuition and fees: $36,620.

Per-credit charge: $490.

Room and board: $10,120.

Additional info: Tuition/fee waivers available for adults.

FINANCIAL AID PICTURE (2016-2017)

Students with need: Out of 474 full-time freshmen who applied for aid, 418 were judged to have need. Of these, 418 received aid, and 112 had their full need met. Average financial aid package met 81% of need; average scholarship/grant was $25,614; average loan was $2,445. For part-time students, average financial aid package was $8,763.

Students without need: 102 full-time freshmen who did not demonstrate need for aid received scholarships/grants; average award was $19,222. No-need awards available for academics, art, leadership, music/drama, religious affiliation, state/district residency.

FINANCIAL AID PROCEDURES

Forms required: FAFSA, state aid form.

Dates and Deadlines: Priority date 11/1; no closing date. Applicants notified on a rolling basis starting 12/1; must reply by 5/1 or within 2 week(s) of notification.

Transfers: No deadline. Applicants notified on a rolling basis starting 12/1; must reply by 5/1 or within 2 week(s) of notification.

CONTACT

Timothy Saulnier, Director of Financial Aid
1501 Lakeside Drive, Lynchburg, VA 24501-3199
(434) 544-8228

Mary Baldwin University

Staunton, Virginia
www.marybaldwin.edu/   Federal Code: 003723

4-year private liberal arts college for women in large town, affiliated with the Presbyterian Church (USA).

Enrollment: 1,265 undergrads.

BASIC COSTS (2016-2017)

Tuition and fees: $30,635.

Per-credit charge: $455.

Room and board: $9,230.

FINANCIAL AID PICTURE

Students with need: Need-based aid available for full-time and part-time students.

Students without need: No-need awards available for academics, leadership, state/district residency.

FINANCIAL AID PROCEDURES

Forms required: FAFSA, state aid form.

Dates and Deadlines: Priority date 3/1; no closing date. Applicants notified on a rolling basis starting 2/27; must reply by 5/1 or within 2 week(s) of notification.

Transfers: No deadline. Applicants notified on a rolling basis starting 2/1; must reply by 5/1.

CONTACT

Robin Dietrich, Financial Aid Director
Office of Admissions, Staunton, VA 24401
(540) 887-7022

Marymount University

Arlington, Virginia
www.marymount.edu   Federal Code: 003724

4-year private university in small city, affiliated with the Roman Catholic Church.

Enrollment: 2,304 undergrads, 8% part-time. 439 full-time freshmen.

Selectivity: Admits over 75% of applicants.

BASIC COSTS (2017-2018)

Tuition and fees: $30,426.

Per-credit charge: $975.

Room and board: $12,805.

FINANCIAL AID PICTURE (2016-2017)

Students with need: Need-based aid available for full-time and part-time students.

Students without need: No-need awards available for academics, alumni affiliation, leadership, music/drama, ROTC, state/district residency.

Scholarships offered: Freshman Scholarship: guaranteed for full-time freshman with 3.3 GPA and 1050 SAT (exclusive of Writing); renewable for 4 years for students who maintain academic eligibility.

FINANCIAL AID PROCEDURES

Forms required: FAFSA.

Dates and Deadlines: Priority date 3/1; no closing date. Applicants notified by 3/15; must reply within 2 week(s) of notification.

Transfers: No deadline. Applicants notified on a rolling basis starting 3/15; must reply within 2 week(s) of notification. Academic scholarships available; apply by 5/1.

CONTACT

Debbie Raines, Director of Financial Aid
2807 North Glebe Road, Arlington, VA 22207-4224
(703) 284-1530

Miller-Motte Technical College: Lynchburg

Lynchburg, Virginia
www.miller-motte.edu   Federal Code: 004992

2-year for-profit technical college in small city.

Enrollment: 409 undergrads.

Selectivity: Open admission.

BASIC COSTS (2016-2017)

Additional info: Management: $24,768; books and supplies $3,200. Medical Assisting: $24,768; books and supplies $3,200. Surgical Technology: $24,252; books and supplies $2,400. Criminal Justice: $24,768; books and supplies $3,200. Healthcare Technology: $24,768; books and supplies

$3,200. Electronic Health Records: $24,768; books and supplies $3,200. Network Administration and Security: $24,768; books and supplies $3,200. Massage Therapy: $10,480; books and supplies $1,900. Figures are for total program cost.

FINANCIAL AID PICTURE
Students with need: Need-based aid available for full-time and part-time students. Work study available nights.
Students without need: This college awards aid only to students with need.

FINANCIAL AID PROCEDURES
Forms required: FAFSA.
Dates and Deadlines: Applicants notified on a rolling basis.

CONTACT
Kim Hodges, Director of Financial Aid
1011 Creekside Lane, Lynchburg, VA 24502
(434) 239-5222

Mountain Empire Community College
Big Stone Gap, Virginia
www.mecc.edu   Federal Code: 009629

2-year public community college in small town.
Enrollment: 1,600 undergrads.
Selectivity: Open admission; but selective for some programs.

BASIC COSTS (2016-2017)
Tuition and fees: $4,477; out-of-state residents $9,775.
Per-credit charge: $149; out-of-state residents $346.
Additional info: Out-of-state students pay an additional $600 capital outlay fee.

FINANCIAL AID PICTURE (2015-2016)
Students with need: 97% of average financial aid package awarded as scholarships/grants, 3% awarded as loans/jobs. Need-based aid available for part-time students.
Students without need: No-need awards available for academics, state/district residency.
Scholarships offered: Presidential Honor Scholarship; full tuition; for valedictorian or salutatorian.
Additional info: The college does not participate in loan programs. All financial aid is in form of grants, scholarships, or work study. Any loans are obtained privately.

FINANCIAL AID PROCEDURES
Forms required: FAFSA.
Dates and Deadlines: Priority date 5/1; no closing date. Applicants notified on a rolling basis starting 1/1.

CONTACT
Kristy Hall, Director of Enrollment Services
3441 Mountain Empire Road, Big Stone Gap, VA 24219
(276) 523-2400

New River Community College
Dublin, Virginia
www.nr.edu   Federal Code: 005223

2-year public community college in rural community.
Enrollment: 3,900 undergrads.
Selectivity: Open admission.

BASIC COSTS (2016-2017)
Tuition and fees: $4,465; out-of-state residents $10,362.
Per-credit charge: $137.75; out-of-state residents $314.35.

FINANCIAL AID PICTURE
Students with need: Need-based aid available for full-time and part-time students.

FINANCIAL AID PROCEDURES
Forms required: FAFSA, institutional form.
Dates and Deadlines: Closing date 4/16. Applicants notified on a rolling basis.

CONTACT
Lori Nunn, Director of Financial Aid
5251 College Dr, Dublin, VA 24084
(540) 674-3615

Norfolk State University
Norfolk, Virginia
www.nsu.edu   Federal Code: 003765

4-year public university in small city.
Enrollment: 5,284 undergrads.

BASIC COSTS (2016-2017)
Tuition and fees: $8,738; out-of-state residents $21,100.
Per-credit charge: $397; out-of-state residents $796.
Room and board: $9,490.

FINANCIAL AID PICTURE
Students with need: Need-based aid available for full-time and part-time students.
Students without need: No-need awards available for academics, alumni affiliation, athletics, leadership, music/drama, ROTC, state/district residency.

FINANCIAL AID PROCEDURES
Forms required: FAFSA.
Dates and Deadlines: Priority date 5/31; no closing date. Applicants notified on a rolling basis starting 4/1; must reply within 2 week(s) of notification.

CONTACT
Kevin Burns, Director of Student Financial Services
700 Park Avenue, Norfolk, VA 23504
(757) 823-8381

Old Dominion University
Norfolk, Virginia
www.odu.edu   Federal Code: 003728

4-year public university in large city.
Enrollment: 19,606 undergrads, 23% part-time. 2,727 full-time freshmen.
Selectivity: Admits over 75% of applicants.

BASIC COSTS (2016-2017)
Tuition and fees: $10,046; out-of-state residents $27,026.
Per-credit charge: $325; out-of-state residents $891.
Room and board: $10,864.

FINANCIAL AID PICTURE (2016-2017)
Students with need: Out of 2,464 full-time freshmen who applied for aid, 2,039 were judged to have need. Of these, 1,980 received aid, and 360 had their full need met. Average financial aid package met 49% of need; average scholarship/grant was $8,273; average loan was $3,427. For part-time students, average financial aid package was $6,299.
Students without need: 251 full-time freshmen who did not demonstrate need for aid received scholarships/grants; average award was $5,344. No-need awards available for academics, alumni affiliation, art, athletics, leadership, music/drama, ROTC, state/district residency.
Scholarships offered: 80 full-time freshmen received athletic scholarships; average amount $21,607.

FINANCIAL AID PROCEDURES

Forms required: FAFSA.

Dates and Deadlines: Priority date 2/15; closing date 3/15. Applicants notified on a rolling basis starting 3/1; must reply within 2 week(s) of notification.

Transfers: Applicants notified on a rolling basis starting 3/1; must reply within 2 week(s) of notification.

CONTACT

Vera Riddick, Director of Financial Aid
108 Rollins Hall, Norfolk, VA 23529
(757) 683-3683

Patrick Henry College

Purcellville, Virginia
www.phc.edu

Federal Code: 039513
CSS Code: 2804

4-year private liberal arts college in small town, affiliated with the nondenominational tradition.

Enrollment: 263 undergrads, 7% part-time. 51 full-time freshmen.

Selectivity: Admits over 75% of applicants.

BASIC COSTS (2016-2017)

Tuition and fees: $27,922.
Per-credit charge: $1,163.
Room and board: $10,727.

FINANCIAL AID PICTURE (2016-2017)

Students with need: Out of 29 full-time freshmen who applied for aid, 15 were judged to have need. Of these, 15 received aid. Average financial aid package met 35% of need; average scholarship/grant was $7,000. For part-time students, average financial aid package was $3,500.

Students without need: 29 full-time freshmen who did not demonstrate need for aid received scholarships/grants; average award was $9,100. No-need awards available for academics, leadership, music/drama.

FINANCIAL AID PROCEDURES

Forms required: CSS PROFILE.

Dates and Deadlines: Priority date 3/15; closing date 6/15. Applicants notified on a rolling basis starting 3/1; must reply within 4 week(s) of notification.

CONTACT

William Kellaris, Director of Financial Aid
10 Patrick Henry Circle, Purcellville, VA 20132-3197
(540) 441-8140

Patrick Henry Community College

Martinsville, Virginia
www.patrickhenry.edu

Federal Code: 003751

2-year public community college in large town.

Enrollment: 2,524 undergrads.

Selectivity: Open admission.

BASIC COSTS (2016-2017)

Tuition and fees: $4,473; out-of-state residents $10,371.
Per-credit charge: $137.75; out-of-state residents $314.35.

FINANCIAL AID PICTURE

Students with need: Need-based aid available for full-time and part-time students.

FINANCIAL AID PROCEDURES

Forms required: FAFSA.

Dates and Deadlines: Priority date 6/1; no closing date. Applicants notified on a rolling basis starting 6/15.

CONTACT

Cindy Keller, Financial Aid
645 Patriot Avenue, Martinsville, VA 24112
(276) 656-0317

Paul D. Camp Community College

Franklin, Virginia
www.pdc.edu

Federal Code: 009159

2-year public community college in small town.

Enrollment: 727 undergrads.

Selectivity: Open admission; but selective for some programs.

BASIC COSTS (2016-2017)

Tuition and fees: $4,388; out-of-state residents $10,286.
Per-credit charge: $138; out-of-state residents $314.

FINANCIAL AID PICTURE

Students with need: Need-based aid available for full-time and part-time students. Work study available nights, weekends, and for part-time students.

Students without need: This college awards aid only to students with need.

FINANCIAL AID PROCEDURES

Forms required: FAFSA.

Dates and Deadlines: Priority date 5/15; no closing date. Applicants notified on a rolling basis starting 8/1; must reply within 2 week(s) of notification.

CONTACT

Teresa Harrison, Financial Aid Coordinator
100 North College Drive, Franklin, VA 23851-0737
(757) 569-6715

Piedmont Virginia Community College

Charlottesville, Virginia
www.pvcc.edu

Federal Code: 009928

2-year public community college in large town.

Enrollment: 5,438 undergrads. 398 full-time freshmen.

Selectivity: Open admission; but selective for some programs.

BASIC COSTS (2016-2017)

Tuition and fees: $4,557; out-of-state residents $9,855.
Per-credit charge: $138; out-of-state residents $315.
Additional info: Out-of-state students pay an additional $600 capital outlay fee.

FINANCIAL AID PICTURE (2015-2016)

Students with need: 79% of average financial aid package awarded as scholarships/grants, 21% awarded as loans/jobs. Need-based aid available for part-time students. Work study available nights, weekends, and for part-time students.

Students without need: No-need awards available for academics.

FINANCIAL AID PROCEDURES

Forms required: FAFSA.

Dates and Deadlines: Applicants notified on a rolling basis starting 4/1.

Transfers: Must meet Satisfactory Academic Progress standards.

CONTACT

Carol Larson, Director of Financial Aid
501 College Drive, Charlottesville, VA 22902-7589
(434) 961-6545

Radford University
Radford, Virginia
www.radford.edu　　　　　　Federal Code: 003732

4-year public university in large town.
Enrollment: 8,426 undergrads, 4% part-time. 1,747 full-time freshmen.
Selectivity: Admits over 75% of applicants.

BASIC COSTS (2016-2017)
Tuition and fees: $10,081; out-of-state residents $21,716.
Per-credit charge: $291; out-of-state residents $776.
Room and board: $8,946.

FINANCIAL AID PICTURE (2016-2017)
Students with need: Out of 1,504 full-time freshmen who applied for aid, 1,149 were judged to have need. Of these, 1,077 received aid, and 260 had their full need met. Average financial aid package met 80% of need; average scholarship/grant was $8,754; average loan was $3,385. For part-time students, average financial aid package was $5,917.
Students without need: 67 full-time freshmen who did not demonstrate need for aid received scholarships/grants; average award was $5,149. No-need awards available for academics, alumni affiliation, art, athletics, leadership, music/drama, ROTC, state/district residency.
Scholarships offered: *Merit:* Presidential Scholarship: $500 to $16,000; 3.5 GPA or higher; 1180 SAT combined critical reading and math sections or 26 ACT composite; 134 awarded. Academic Excellence Scholarship: $1,000 to $5,000; 3.5 GPA or higher; 1100 SAT combined on critical reading and math sections or 24 ACT composite; 145 awarded. *Athletic:* 15 full-time freshmen received athletic scholarships; average amount $10,025.
Additional info: Student's need and grades considered. Top consideration given to those with greatest need and who apply by deadline.

FINANCIAL AID PROCEDURES
Forms required: FAFSA.
Dates and Deadlines: Priority date 2/15; no closing date. Applicants notified on a rolling basis starting 4/15; must reply within 2 week(s) of notification.

CONTACT
Barbara Porter, Director of Financial Aid
PO Box 6903, Radford, VA 24142
(540) 831-5408

Randolph College
Lynchburg, Virginia
www.randolphcollege.edu　　　Federal Code: 003734

4-year private liberal arts college in small city, affiliated with the United Methodist Church.
Enrollment: 649 undergrads, 1% part-time. 189 full-time freshmen.
Selectivity: Admits over 75% of applicants.

BASIC COSTS (2016-2017)
Tuition and fees: $36,770.
Per-credit charge: $1,500.
Room and board: $12,580.

FINANCIAL AID PICTURE (2016-2017)
Students with need: Out of 163 full-time freshmen who applied for aid, 146 were judged to have need. Of these, 146 received aid, and 30 had their full need met. Average financial aid package met 79% of need; average scholarship/grant was $27,667; average loan was $3,869. For part-time students, average financial aid package was $14,061.
Students without need: 39 full-time freshmen who did not demonstrate need for aid received scholarships/grants; average award was $23,791. No-need awards available for academics, alumni affiliation, art, music/drama, religious affiliation, state/district residency.

Scholarships offered: Gottwald Scholarship: full tuition plus travel stipend; based on academic profile; approximately 3 awarded in each class. Presidential Scholars: $17,500; renewable annually; based on academic profile.

FINANCIAL AID PROCEDURES
Forms required: FAFSA.
Dates and Deadlines: Priority date 4/1; no closing date. Applicants notified on a rolling basis; must reply by 5/1 or within 2 week(s) of notification.
Transfers: Applicants notified on a rolling basis starting 3/1; must reply by 5/1 or within 2 week(s) of notification.

CONTACT
Debi Woodall-Stevens, Director of Student Financial Services
2500 Rivermont Avenue, Lynchburg, VA 24503-1555
(434) 947-8128

Randolph-Macon College
Ashland, Virginia
www.rmc.edu　　　　　　　Federal Code: 003733

4-year private liberal arts college in small town, affiliated with the United Methodist Church.
Enrollment: 1,429 undergrads, 1% part-time. 396 full-time freshmen.
Selectivity: Admits 50 to 75% of applicants.

BASIC COSTS (2017-2018)
Tuition and fees: $40,100.
Room and board: $11,480.

FINANCIAL AID PICTURE (2016-2017)
Students with need: Out of 373 full-time freshmen who applied for aid, 308 were judged to have need. Of these, 308 received aid, and 101 had their full need met. Average financial aid package met 83% of need; average scholarship/grant was $24,778; average loan was $4,659. For part-time students, average financial aid package was $14,627.
Students without need: 88 full-time freshmen who did not demonstrate need for aid received scholarships/grants; average award was $20,207. No-need awards available for academics, alumni affiliation, minority status, religious affiliation, ROTC, state/district residency.
Scholarships offered: Presidential Scholarships: $14,500 up to full-tuition; based solely on the student's academic record and extra-curricular activities; renewable for up to four years. All applicants for admissions considered for academic awards.

FINANCIAL AID PROCEDURES
Forms required: FAFSA, state aid form.
Dates and Deadlines: Priority date 2/15; closing date 3/1. Applicants notified on a rolling basis starting 3/1; must reply by 5/1 or within 2 week(s) of notification.
Transfers: Applicants notified by 3/1; must reply by 5/1 or within 2 week(s) of notification.

CONTACT
Mary Neal, Director of Financial Aid
PO Box 5005, Ashland, VA 23005-5505
(804) 752-7529

Rappahannock Community College
Glenns, Virginia
www.rappahannock.edu　　　　Federal Code: 009160

2-year public community college in rural community.
Enrollment: 1,760 undergrads.
Selectivity: Open admission; but selective for some programs.

PART III: FINANCIAL AID COLLEGE BY COLLEGE

BASIC COSTS (2016-2017)

Tuition and fees: $4,587; out-of-state residents $9,885.

Per-credit charge: $137; out-of-state residents $314.

Additional info: Out-of-state students pay an additional $600 capital outlay fee.

FINANCIAL AID PICTURE

Students with need: Need-based aid available for full-time and part-time students.

FINANCIAL AID PROCEDURES

Forms required: FAFSA, institutional form.

Dates and Deadlines: Priority date 4/15; no closing date. Applicants notified on a rolling basis starting 6/30.

Transfers: No deadline. Applicants notified on a rolling basis.

CONTACT

Sherika Charity, Director of Financial Aid

12745 College Drive, Glenns, VA 23149-2616

(804) 758-6737

Regent University

Virginia Beach, Virginia

www.regent.edu

Federal Code: 030913

4-year private university in large city, affiliated with the interdenominational tradition.

Enrollment: 3,657 undergrads, 40% part-time. 333 full-time freshmen.

Selectivity: Admits 50 to 75% of applicants.

BASIC COSTS (2017-2018)

Tuition and fees: $17,450.

Per-credit charge: $555.

Room and board: $8,480.

FINANCIAL AID PICTURE (2016-2017)

Students with need: Out of 300 full-time freshmen who applied for aid, 246 were judged to have need. Of these, 245 received aid, and 42 had their full need met. Average financial aid package met 55% of need; average scholarship/grant was $9,877; average loan was $3,125. For part-time students, average financial aid package was $7,032.

Students without need: 85 full-time freshmen who did not demonstrate need for aid received scholarships/grants; average award was $7,974. No-need awards available for academics, alumni affiliation, leadership, ROTC.

FINANCIAL AID PROCEDURES

Forms required: FAFSA, state aid form, institutional form.

Dates and Deadlines: Priority date 3/15; no closing date. Applicants notified on a rolling basis starting 12/1; must reply within 2 week(s) of notification.

Transfers: Priority date 7/1; no deadline. Applicants notified on a rolling basis starting 12/1; must reply within 2 week(s) of notification. Must be able to determine number of transfer credits before full award package is offered. Student should submit all academic transcripts in a timely manner to ensure transfer articulation occurs in a timely manner.

CONTACT

Dotti Davidson, Director of Financial Aid Compliance

1000 Regent University Drive, Virginia Beach, VA 23464-9800

(757) 352-4125

Richard Bland College

South Prince George, Virginia

www.rbc.edu

Federal Code: 003707

2-year public junior and liberal arts college in small city.

Enrollment: 1,089 undergrads, 13% part-time. 487 full-time freshmen.

Selectivity: Admits less than 50% of applicants.

BASIC COSTS (2016-2017)

Tuition and fees: $5,712; out-of-state residents $15,792.

Per-credit charge: $238; out-of-state residents $658.

Room and board: $11,540.

FINANCIAL AID PICTURE

Students with need: Need-based aid available for full-time and part-time students.

Students without need: No-need awards available for academics.

Scholarships offered: Presidential Scholarships: average $1,000; for full-time first-time Virginia residents; based on minimum 3.5 GPA.

FINANCIAL AID PROCEDURES

Forms required: FAFSA.

Dates and Deadlines: Priority date 3/1; no closing date. Must reply by 5/1 or within 2 week(s) of notification.

Transfers: No deadline. Applicants notified on a rolling basis; must reply within 2 week(s) of notification.

CONTACT

Director of Financial Aid

11301 Johnson Road, South Prince George, VA 23805

(804) 862-6223

Roanoke College

Salem, Virginia

www.roanoke.edu

Federal Code: 003736

4-year private liberal arts college in large town, affiliated with the Evangelical Lutheran Church in America.

Enrollment: 1,946 undergrads, 1% part-time. 508 full-time freshmen.

Selectivity: Admits 50 to 75% of applicants.

BASIC COSTS (2017-2018)

Tuition and fees: $42,694.

Per-credit charge: $491.

Room and board: $13,258.

Additional info: Commuter students pay a required fee total of $1,334 per year. Tuition/fee waivers available for adults.

FINANCIAL AID PICTURE (2016-2017)

Students with need: Out of 456 full-time freshmen who applied for aid, 389 were judged to have need. Of these, 388 received aid, and 109 had their full need met. Average financial aid package met 82% of need; average scholarship/grant was $29,600; average loan was $4,212. For part-time students, average financial aid package was $6,577.

Students without need: 115 full-time freshmen who did not demonstrate need for aid received scholarships/grants; average award was $21,328. No-need awards available for academics, art, minority status, music/drama, religious affiliation.

Scholarships offered: William Beard Scholarship: up to 2 awarded; full tuition; room and board for four years. David Bittle Scholarship: up to 6 awarded; full tuition for four years. A.M. Bowman Scholarships: up to 50 awarded; $7,000 annually; added to previously awarded college scholarships. Christopher Baughman Scholarship: up to 60 awarded; $4,500 per year; added to previously awarded college scholarships. Julius Dreher Scholarship: up to 75 awarded; $2,500 per year; added to previously awarded college scholarships. John Morehead Scholarship: $1,000 per year; added to previously awarded college scholarships.

FINANCIAL AID PROCEDURES

Forms required: FAFSA, state aid form.

Dates and Deadlines: Priority date 3/1; no closing date. Applicants notified on a rolling basis starting 12/15; must reply by 5/1 or within 2 week(s) of notification.

Transfers: No deadline. Applicants notified on a rolling basis starting 12/15; must reply by 5/1 or within 2 week(s) of notification.

PART III: FINANCIAL AID COLLEGE BY COLLEGE

CONTACT

Thomas Blair, Director of Financial Aid
221 College Lane, Salem, VA 24153-3794
(540) 375-2235

Shenandoah University

Winchester, Virginia
www.su.edu   Federal Code: 003737

4-year private university in large town, affiliated with the United Methodist Church.
Enrollment: 2,087 undergrads, 3% part-time. 458 full-time freshmen.
Selectivity: Admits over 75% of applicants.

BASIC COSTS (2016-2017)

Tuition and fees: $31,322.
Per-credit charge: $877.
Room and board: $9,990.

FINANCIAL AID PICTURE (2016-2017)

Students with need: Out of 413 full-time freshmen who applied for aid, 350 were judged to have need. Of these, 350 received aid, and 27 had their full need met. Average financial aid package met 51% of need; average scholarship/grant was $6,638; average loan was $3,136. For part-time students, average financial aid package was $8,053.
Students without need: 63 full-time freshmen who did not demonstrate need for aid received scholarships/grants; average award was $9,406. No-need awards available for academics, music/drama, religious affiliation.

FINANCIAL AID PROCEDURES

Forms required: FAFSA, state aid form.
Dates and Deadlines: Applicants notified on a rolling basis starting 3/15; must reply within 4 week(s) of notification.
Transfers: No deadline. Applicants notified on a rolling basis starting 11/15; must reply within 4 week(s) of notification.

CONTACT

Karen Bucher, Director of Financial Aid
Office of Admissions, Winchester, VA 22601-5195
(540) 665-4538

Southern Virginia University

Buena Vista, Virginia
www.svu.edu   Federal Code: 003738

4-year private liberal arts college in small town, affiliated with the Church of Jesus Christ of Latter-day Saints.
Enrollment: 703 undergrads.

BASIC COSTS (2016-2017)

Tuition and fees: $15,300.
Per-credit charge: $685.
Room and board: $7,450.

FINANCIAL AID PICTURE

Students with need: Need-based aid available for full-time students.
Students without need: No-need awards available for academics, art, athletics, leadership, music/drama, ROTC.

FINANCIAL AID PROCEDURES

Forms required: FAFSA, state aid form.
Dates and Deadlines: Priority date 5/1; no closing date. Applicants notified on a rolling basis starting 2/15.
Transfers: No deadline. Applicants notified on a rolling basis starting 3/1.

CONTACT

John Brandt, Director of Financial Aid
One University Hill Drive, Buena Vista, VA 24416-3097
(540) 261-4351

Southside Virginia Community College

Alberta, Virginia
www.southside.edu   Federal Code: 008661

2-year public community college in rural community.
Enrollment: 1,786 undergrads, 62% part-time. 249 full-time freshmen.
Selectivity: Open admission; but selective for some programs.

BASIC COSTS (2016-2017)

Tuition and fees: $4,462; out-of-state residents $9,760.
Per-credit charge: $137; out-of-state residents $314.
Additional info: Out-of-state students pay an additional $600 capital outlay fee.

FINANCIAL AID PICTURE (2016-2017)

Students with need: 99% of average financial aid package awarded as scholarships/grants, 1% awarded as loans/jobs. Need-based aid available for part-time students. Work study available nights.
Students without need: No-need awards available for academics.
Scholarships offered: Academic Merit Award: $1,500; for high school graduates within college's service area with 3.0 GPA who do not receive at least $1,500 in need-based aid.

FINANCIAL AID PROCEDURES

Forms required: FAFSA.
Dates and Deadlines: Closing date 6/1. Applicants notified on a rolling basis starting 6/15.
Transfers: State aid limited to in-state residents.

CONTACT

Sally Tharrington, Director of Financial Aid
109 Campus Drive, Alberta, VA 23821
(434) 736-2091

Southwest Virginia Community College

Richlands, Virginia
www.sw.edu   Federal Code: 007260

2-year public community college in small town.
Enrollment: 1,758 undergrads, 38% part-time. 402 full-time freshmen.
Selectivity: Open admission; but selective for some programs.

BASIC COSTS (2016-2017)

Tuition and fees: $4,463; out-of-state residents $10,361.
Per-credit charge: $137.75; out-of-state residents $314.35.
Additional info: 30 Mile Radius Tuition $5,063.

FINANCIAL AID PICTURE (2015-2016)

Students with need: Need-based aid available for part-time students.
Students without need: This college awards aid only to students with need.

FINANCIAL AID PROCEDURES

Forms required: FAFSA, institutional form.
Dates and Deadlines: Priority date 5/30; no closing date. Applicants notified on a rolling basis starting 7/1.

CONTACT

Donna Price, Interim Financial Aid Director
PO Box SVCC, Richlands, VA 24641-1101
(276) 964-7290

Stratford University: Falls Church

Falls Church, Virginia
www.stratford.edu   Federal Code: 017053

4-year for-profit university and career college in large city.
Enrollment: 628 undergrads.
Selectivity: Open admission.

BASIC COSTS (2016-2017)
Tuition and fees: $16,750.
Per-credit charge: $370.

FINANCIAL AID PICTURE
Students with need: Need-based aid available for full-time and part-time students. Work study available nights, weekends, and for part-time students.
Students without need: This college awards aid only to students with need.

FINANCIAL AID PROCEDURES
Forms required: FAFSA.
Dates and Deadlines: Applicants notified on a rolling basis starting 1/1.
Transfers: No deadline. Applicants notified on a rolling basis starting 1/1.

CONTACT
Michael Hargrave, Corporate Financial Aid Director
7777 Leesburg Pike Suite 1LN, Falls Church, VA 22043
(703) 821-8570

Sweet Briar College

Sweet Briar, Virginia
www.sbc.edu   Federal Code: 003742

4-year private liberal arts college for women in rural community.
Enrollment: 320 undergrads, 1% part-time. 134 full-time freshmen.
Selectivity: Admits over 75% of applicants.

BASIC COSTS (2016-2017)
Tuition and fees: $36,425.
Per-credit charge: $1,050.
Room and board: $12,635.
Additional info: Tuition/fee waivers available for adults.

FINANCIAL AID PICTURE (2015-2016)
Students with need: 85% of average financial aid package awarded as scholarships/grants, 15% awarded as loans/jobs. Need-based aid available for part-time students. Work study available nights, weekends, and for part-time students.
Students without need: No-need awards available for academics, art, leadership, music/drama, state/district residency.
Scholarships offered: Founders and Prothro Scholarships; up to $15,000. Commonwealth Scholarships; up to $13,000. Betty Bean Black Scholarships; up to $12,000. Sweet Briar Scholarships; up to $9,000; for students with special talents in specific area. All awards based on academic qualifications; renewable annually with specified GPA.

FINANCIAL AID PROCEDURES
Forms required: FAFSA.
Dates and Deadlines: Priority date 2/15; no closing date. Applicants notified on a rolling basis starting 3/1; must reply by 5/1.

CONTACT
Wanda Spradley, Director of Financial Aid
PO Box 1052, Sweet Briar, VA 24595-1502

Thomas Nelson Community College

Hampton, Virginia
www.tncc.edu   Federal Code: 006871

2-year public community college in small city.
Enrollment: 7,512 undergrads.
Selectivity: Open admission; but selective for some programs.

BASIC COSTS (2016-2017)
Tuition and fees: $4,543; out-of-state residents $10,076.
Per-credit charge: $139; out-of-state residents $316.

FINANCIAL AID PICTURE
Students with need: Need-based aid available for full-time and part-time students. Work study available nights.

FINANCIAL AID PROCEDURES
Forms required: FAFSA, institutional form.
Dates and Deadlines: Priority date 5/1; no closing date. Applicants notified on a rolling basis starting 6/1; must reply within 2 week(s) of notification.
Transfers: No deadline. Applicants notified on a rolling basis; must reply within 2 week(s) of notification.

CONTACT
Kathryn Anderson, Director of Financial Aid, Veterans Affairs, and Scholarships
PO Box 9407, Hampton, VA 23670
(757) 825-2848

Tidewater Community College

Norfolk, Virginia
www.tcc.edu   Federal Code: 003712

2-year public community college in large city.
Enrollment: 20,788 undergrads.
Selectivity: Open admission; but selective for some programs.

BASIC COSTS (2016-2017)
Tuition and fees: $5,298; out-of-state residents $10,596.
Per-credit charge: $139; out-of-state residents $316.
Additional info: Out-of-state students pay an additional $600 capital outlay fee.

FINANCIAL AID PICTURE
Students with need: Need-based aid available for full-time and part-time students.

FINANCIAL AID PROCEDURES
Forms required: FAFSA.
Dates and Deadlines: Priority date 4/1; no closing date. Applicants notified on a rolling basis starting 4/1.

CONTACT
300 Granby Street, Norfolk, VA 23510
(757) 822-1360

University of Management and Technology

Arlington, Virginia
www.umtweb.edu   Federal Code: 041103

4-year for-profit university in very large city.
Enrollment: 871 undergrads.
Selectivity: Open admission; but selective for some programs.

BASIC COSTS (2016-2017)
Tuition and fees: $11,760.

Per-credit charge: $390.

FINANCIAL AID PICTURE (2015-2016)

Students with need: 22% of average financial aid package awarded as scholarships/grants, 78% awarded as loans/jobs.

CONTACT

1901 Fort Myer Drive, Suite 700, Arlington, VA 22209-1609
(703) 516-0035

University of Mary Washington

Fredericksburg, Virginia
www.umw.edu   Federal Code: 003746

4-year public university in small city.
Enrollment: 4,318 undergrads, 11% part-time. 952 full-time freshmen.
Selectivity: Admits 50 to 75% of applicants.

BASIC COSTS (2016-2017)

Tuition and fees: $11,570; out-of-state residents $26,160.
Per-credit charge: $413; out-of-state residents $1,018.
Room and board: $11,118.

FINANCIAL AID PICTURE (2015-2016)

Students with need: Out of 772 full-time freshmen who applied for aid, 465 were judged to have need. Of these, 453 received aid, and 74 had their full need met. Average financial aid package met 46% of need; average scholarship/grant was $3,343; average loan was $3,206. For part-time students, average financial aid package was $5,587.
Students without need: 363 full-time freshmen who did not demonstrate need for aid received scholarships/grants; average award was $2,714. No-need awards available for academics, alumni affiliation, art, leadership, music/drama, state/district residency.
Scholarships offered: Scholarships awarded annually equal to tuition, fees, room and board given to select incoming freshmen with exceptional academic records (Washington scholarships to Virginia residents, Alvey scholarship when available to non-resident). In addition, merit awards up to $4,000 in-state and $8,000 out-of state based on high school GPA and SAT/ACT scores.

FINANCIAL AID PROCEDURES

Forms required: FAFSA.
Dates and Deadlines: Priority date 2/1; closing date 7/1. Applicants notified on a rolling basis starting 3/15; must reply by 5/1 or within 2 week(s) of notification.
Transfers: Applicants notified on a rolling basis starting 3/15; must reply by 5/1 or within 2 week(s) of notification.

CONTACT

Heidi Hunter-Goldsworthy, Director of Financial Aid
1301 College Avenue, Fredericksburg, VA 22401-5300
(540) 654-2468

University of Richmond

University of Richmond, Virginia   Federal Code: 003744
www.richmond.edu   CSS Code: 5569

4-year private university and liberal arts college in small city.
Enrollment: 2,950 undergrads, 1% part-time. 815 full-time freshmen.
Selectivity: Admits less than 50% of applicants.

BASIC COSTS (2016-2017)

Tuition and fees: $49,420.
Per-credit charge: $2,471.
Room and board: $11,460.

FINANCIAL AID PICTURE (2016-2017)

Students with need: Out of 500 full-time freshmen who applied for aid, 349 were judged to have need. Of these, 349 received aid, and 307 had their full need met. Average financial aid package met 100% of need; average scholarship/grant was $40,204; average loan was $2,871. For part-time students, average financial aid package was $45,293.
Students without need: 90 full-time freshmen who did not demonstrate need for aid received scholarships/grants; average award was $33,299. No-need awards available for academics, art, athletics, leadership, music/drama, ROTC.
Scholarships offered: *Merit:* Richmond Scholars: full-tuition; up to 45 awarded to entering freshmen. Presidential Scholarships: one-third tuition. *Athletic:* 66 full-time freshmen received athletic scholarships; average amount $29,777.

FINANCIAL AID PROCEDURES

Forms required: FAFSA, CSS PROFILE.
Dates and Deadlines: Closing date 2/1. Applicants notified by 4/1; must reply within 4 week(s) of notification.
Transfers: Applicants notified by 4/15; must reply within 4 week(s) of notification.

CONTACT

Cynthia Deffenbaugh, Director of Financial Aid
Queally Center for Admissions and Career Services, University of Richmond, VA 23173
(804) 289-8438

University of the Potomac

Herndon, Virginia
www.potomac.edu   Federal Code: 032183

4-year for-profit business college in large town.
Enrollment: 23 undergrads.
Selectivity: Open admission.

BASIC COSTS (2016-2017)

Additional info: Bachelor degree program: $541 per credit; Associate degree programs: $541 per credit; certificates: $250 per credit. Registration fee $100, technology fee $37.50 per credit hour. Books and supplies range depending on program level and course of study. All costs are subject to change.

FINANCIAL AID PICTURE

Students with need: Need-based aid available for full-time and part-time students.

FINANCIAL AID PROCEDURES

Forms required: FAFSA, institutional form.
Dates and Deadlines: Applicants notified on a rolling basis.

CONTACT

Andrea Ford, Director of Financial Aid
2070 Chain Bridge Road, Vienna, VA 22182
(202) 274-2327

University of Virginia

Charlottesville, Virginia   Federal Code: 003745
www.virginia.edu   CSS Code: 5820

4-year public university in small city.
Enrollment: 15,844 undergrads, 3% part-time. 3,682 full-time freshmen.
Selectivity: Admits less than 50% of applicants.

BASIC COSTS (2016-2017)

Tuition and fees: $15,714; out-of-state residents $45,058.
Per-credit charge: $369; out-of-state residents $1,391.

Room and board: $10,726.

FINANCIAL AID PICTURE (2016-2017)

Students with need: Out of 2,646 full-time freshmen who applied for aid, 1,279 were judged to have need. Of these, 1,279 received aid, and 1,279 had their full need met. Average financial aid package met 100% of need; average scholarship/grant was $21,642; average loan was $5,158. For part-time students, average financial aid package was $12,156.

Students without need: 108 full-time freshmen who did not demonstrate need for aid received scholarships/grants; average award was $7,793. No-need awards available for academics, athletics, leadership, minority status, music/drama, state/district residency.

Scholarships offered: 109 full-time freshmen received athletic scholarships; average amount $29,756.

FINANCIAL AID PROCEDURES

Forms required: FAFSA, CSS PROFILE.

Dates and Deadlines: Priority date 3/1; no closing date. Applicants notified by 4/5; must reply by 5/1.

CONTACT

Scott Miller, Director of Financial Aid
Box 433160, Charlottesville, VA 22904-4160
(434) 982-6000

University of Virginia's College at Wise
Wise, Virginia
www.uvawise.edu   Federal Code: 003747

4-year public liberal arts college in small town.
Enrollment: 1,376 undergrads, 7% part-time. 321 full-time freshmen.
Selectivity: Admits over 75% of applicants.

BASIC COSTS (2016-2017)

Tuition and fees: $9,539; out-of-state residents $25,617.
Per-credit charge: $222; out-of-state residents $900.
Room and board: $10,346.

FINANCIAL AID PICTURE (2015-2016)

Students with need: Out of 315 full-time freshmen who applied for aid, 276 were judged to have need. Of these, 276 received aid, and 95 had their full need met. Average financial aid package met 48% of need; average scholarship/grant was $7,606; average loan was $2,278. For part-time students, average financial aid package was $7,953.

Students without need: 17 full-time freshmen who did not demonstrate need for aid received scholarships/grants; average award was $4,495. No-need awards available for academics, alumni affiliation, art, athletics, job skills, leadership, music/drama, religious affiliation, state/district residency.

Scholarships offered: 5 full-time freshmen received athletic scholarships; average amount $2,750.

FINANCIAL AID PROCEDURES

Forms required: FAFSA.

Dates and Deadlines: Closing date 2/15. Applicants notified on a rolling basis starting 2/16; must reply within 4 week(s) of notification.

Transfers: Closing date 2/15. Applicants notified on a rolling basis.

CONTACT

Rebecca Huffman, Director of Financial Aid
1 College Avenue, Wise, VA 24293-4412
(276) 328-0139

Virginia Baptist College
Fredericksburg, Virginia
www.vbc.edu   Federal Code: 038626

4-year private Bible college in large city, affiliated with the Baptist faith.
Enrollment: 75 undergrads, 49% part-time. 7 full-time freshmen.

Selectivity: Open admission.

BASIC COSTS (2016-2017)

Tuition and fees: $5,660.
Per-credit charge: $215.
Room only: $3,500.

FINANCIAL AID PICTURE (2015-2016)

Students with need: 46% of average financial aid package awarded as scholarships/grants, 54% awarded as loans/jobs. Need-based aid available for part-time students. Work study available nights, weekends, and for part-time students.

Students without need: No-need awards available for academics, alumni affiliation, leadership, religious affiliation.

FINANCIAL AID PROCEDURES

Forms required: FAFSA, institutional form.

Dates and Deadlines: Applicants notified on a rolling basis.

Transfers: No deadline. Applicants notified on a rolling basis.

CONTACT

Meg Polivka, Financial Aid Coordinator
4105 Plank Road, Fredericksburg, VA 22407
(540) 785-5440 ext. 318

Virginia Commonwealth University
Richmond, Virginia
www.vcu.edu   Federal Code: 003735

4-year public university in small city.
Enrollment: 22,758 undergrads, 11% part-time. 4,207 full-time freshmen.
Selectivity: Admits 50 to 75% of applicants.

BASIC COSTS (2016-2017)

Tuition and fees: $13,076; out-of-state residents $31,608.
Per-credit charge: $374; out-of-state residents $1,013.
Room and board: $9,919.

FINANCIAL AID PICTURE (2015-2016)

Students with need: Out of 3,260 full-time freshmen who applied for aid, 2,557 were judged to have need. Of these, 2,467 received aid, and 319 had their full need met. Average financial aid package met 53% of need; average scholarship/grant was $7,205; average loan was $3,381. For part-time students, average financial aid package was $5,271.

Students without need: 684 full-time freshmen who did not demonstrate need for aid received scholarships/grants; average award was $10,061. No-need awards available for academics, alumni affiliation, art, athletics, leadership, music/drama.

Scholarships offered: 68 full-time freshmen received athletic scholarships; average amount $25,511.

FINANCIAL AID PROCEDURES

Forms required: FAFSA.

Dates and Deadlines: Priority date 3/1; no closing date. Applicants notified on a rolling basis starting 4/1; must reply within 2 week(s) of notification.

Transfers: Applicants notified by 4/1.

CONTACT

Marc Vernon, Executive Director of Financial Aid
Box 842526, Richmond, VA 23284-2526
(804) 828-6669

Virginia Military Institute
Lexington, Virginia
www.vmi.edu   Federal Code: 003753

4-year public liberal arts and military college in small town.
Enrollment: 1,713 undergrads. 434 full-time freshmen.

Selectivity: Admits 50 to 75% of applicants. GED not accepted.

BASIC COSTS (2016-2017)

Tuition and fees: $17,492; out-of-state residents $41,801.

Per-credit charge: $328; out-of-state residents $1,024.

Room and board: $8,968.

FINANCIAL AID PICTURE (2015-2016)

Students with need: Out of 334 full-time freshmen who applied for aid, 228 were judged to have need. Of these, 225 received aid, and 23 had their full need met. Average financial aid package met 85% of need; average scholarship/grant was $6,632; average loan was $2,848.

Students without need: 32 full-time freshmen who did not demonstrate need for aid received scholarships/grants; average award was $3,880. No-need awards available for academics, alumni affiliation, athletics, leadership, music/drama, ROTC, state/district residency.

Scholarships offered: *Merit:* Institute Scholarship: up to $25,000; 10-12 awarded; based on superior academic performance, demonstrated character and leadership, extracurricular activities, 3.7 GPA, 1250 SAT (exclusive of Writing) or 27 ACT, rank in top 5% of class. *Athletic:* 88 full-time freshmen received athletic scholarships; average amount $8,218.

FINANCIAL AID PROCEDURES

Forms required: FAFSA, institutional form.

Dates and Deadlines: Priority date 3/1; closing date 3/1. Applicants notified on a rolling basis starting 4/1; must reply by 5/1.

CONTACT

Biran Quisenberry, Director of Financial Aid

VMI Office of Admissions, Lexington, VA 24450-9967

(540) 464-7208

Virginia Polytechnic Institute and State University

Blacksburg, Virginia

www.vt.edu   Federal Code: 003754

4-year public university in large town.

Enrollment: 25,725 undergrads, 2% part-time. 6,315 full-time freshmen.

Selectivity: Admits 50 to 75% of applicants.

BASIC COSTS (2016-2017)

Tuition and fees: $12,852; out-of-state residents $29,975.

Per-credit charge: $449.5; out-of-state residents $1,137.75.

Room and board: $8,424.

Additional info: The Out-of-state tuition figure reflects an additional $604 Commonwealth Facility and Equipment Fee. Tuition/fee waivers available for unemployed or children of unemployed.

FINANCIAL AID PICTURE (2015-2016)

Students with need: Out of 4,788 full-time freshmen who applied for aid, 2,651 were judged to have need. Of these, 2,493 received aid, and 528 had their full need met. Average financial aid package met 65% of need; average scholarship/grant was $7,550; average loan was $3,945. Need-based aid available for part-time students.

Students without need: 657 full-time freshmen who did not demonstrate need for aid received scholarships/grants; average award was $3,765. No-need awards available for academics, art, athletics, leadership, minority status, music/drama, ROTC, state/district residency.

Scholarships offered: 93 full-time freshmen received athletic scholarships; average amount $21,395.

FINANCIAL AID PROCEDURES

Forms required: FAFSA.

Dates and Deadlines: Closing date 1/1. Applicants notified by 4/1; must reply by 5/1 or within 4 week(s) of notification.

Transfers: Applicants notified by 4/1. Based on family EFC per FAFSA and available resources. Significant academic scholarships for graduates of Virginia Community College System.

CONTACT

Beth Armstrong, Director of Financial Aid

925 Prices Fork Road, Blacksburg, VA 24061

(540) 231-5179

Virginia State University

Petersburg, Virginia

www.vsu.edu   Federal Code: 003764

4-year public university in large town.

Enrollment: 4,155 undergrads, 3% part-time. 765 full-time freshmen.

Selectivity: Admits over 75% of applicants.

BASIC COSTS (2016-2017)

Tuition and fees: $8,472; out-of-state residents $18,292.

Room and board: $10,562.

FINANCIAL AID PICTURE (2015-2016)

Students with need: Out of 703 full-time freshmen who applied for aid, 703 were judged to have need. Of these, 703 received aid, and 240 had their full need met. Average financial aid package met 60% of need; average scholarship/grant was $5,725; average loan was $3,500. Need-based aid available for part-time students.

Students without need: 160 full-time freshmen who did not demonstrate need for aid received scholarships/grants; average award was $500. No-need awards available for academics, alumni affiliation, art, athletics, leadership, minority status, music/drama, ROTC, state/district residency.

Scholarships offered: *Merit:* Presidential Scholarships: $10,000; based on 3.2 GPA; 1100 SAT/24 ACT. Provost's Scholarships: $6,500; based on 3.0 GPA; 1000 SAT/21 ACT. Fine and Performing Arts Scholarships maybe available based on outstanding talent in music or fine arts; audition or portfolio may be required; recommendation required. Math, Science, and Technology Scholarships maybe available based on 3.0 GPA; above average ability in math, science, or technology; recommendation and essay required. *Athletic:* 17 full-time freshmen received athletic scholarships; average amount $500.

Additional info: Strongly recommend that students apply for scholarship assistance through federal, state, local and private agencies.

FINANCIAL AID PROCEDURES

Forms required: FAFSA, institutional form.

Dates and Deadlines: Priority date 3/31; closing date 5/1. Applicants notified on a rolling basis starting 3/1; must reply within 2 week(s) of notification.

Transfers: No deadline. Applicants notified on a rolling basis starting 3/1; must reply within 2 week(s) of notification.

CONTACT

Myra Phillips, Director, Financial Aid

1 Hayden Drive, Petersburg, VA 23806

(804) 524-5990

Virginia Union University

Richmond, Virginia

www.vuu.edu   Federal Code: 003766

4-year private university and liberal arts college in small city, affiliated with the Baptist faith.

Enrollment: 1,337 undergrads, 2% part-time. 365 full-time freshmen.

Selectivity: Admits less than 50% of applicants.

BASIC COSTS (2016-2017)

Tuition and fees: $16,734.

Per-credit charge: $470.

Room and board: $8,412.

FINANCIAL AID PICTURE (2016-2017)

Students with need: 52% of average financial aid package awarded as scholarships/grants, 48% awarded as loans/jobs. Need-based aid available for part-time students. Work study available nights, weekends, and for part-time students.

Students without need: No-need awards available for academics, athletics, ROTC, state/district residency.

FINANCIAL AID PROCEDURES

Forms required: FAFSA.

Dates and Deadlines: Priority date 4/27; no closing date. Applicants notified on a rolling basis starting 5/1; must reply within 2 week(s) of notification.

Transfers: No deadline. Student must submit financial aid transcript from all prior schools attended before receiving aid.

CONTACT

Karen Gee, Director of Financial Aid

1500 North Lombardy Street, Richmond, VA 23220

(804) 257-5882

Virginia Wesleyan College
Norfolk, Virginia
www.vwc.edu   Federal Code: 003767

4-year private liberal arts college in large city, affiliated with the United Methodist Church.

Enrollment: 1,342 undergrads, 4% part-time. 349 full-time freshmen.

Selectivity: Admits over 75% of applicants.

BASIC COSTS (2017-2018)

Tuition and fees: $36,660.

Per-credit charge: $1,500.

Room and board: $8,943.

Additional info: Tuition/fee waivers available for adults.

FINANCIAL AID PICTURE (2015-2016)

Students with need: Out of 349 full-time freshmen who applied for aid, 304 were judged to have need. Of these, 304 received aid, and 55 had their full need met. Average financial aid package met 89% of need; average scholarship/grant was $21,595; average loan was $6,165. For part-time students, average financial aid package was $7,376.

Students without need: 43 full-time freshmen who did not demonstrate need for aid received scholarships/grants; average award was $21,841. No-need awards available for academics.

Scholarships offered: The Batten Honors College will award 20 four-year Fellowships to selected members of each class. These Batten Fellows will receive academic-leadership scholarships totaling the full amount of tuition each year.

FINANCIAL AID PROCEDURES

Forms required: FAFSA, state aid form.

Dates and Deadlines: Priority date 3/1; no closing date. Applicants notified on a rolling basis starting 10/15; must reply by 5/1 or within 2 week(s) of notification.

Transfers: No deadline. Applicants notified on a rolling basis starting 2/15; must reply by 5/1 or within 2 week(s) of notification.

CONTACT

Teresa Rhyne, Director of Financial Aid

1584 Wesleyan Drive, Norfolk, VA 23502-5599

(757) 455-3345

Virginia Western Community College
Roanoke, Virginia
www.virginiawestern.edu   Federal Code: 003760

2-year public community college in small city.

Enrollment: 5,264 undergrads.

Selectivity: Open admission; but selective for some programs.

BASIC COSTS (2016-2017)

Tuition and fees: $5,092; out-of-state residents $10,990.

Per-credit charge: $139; out-of-state residents $316.

Additional info: Out-of-state students pay an additional $600 capital outlay fee.

FINANCIAL AID PICTURE

Students with need: Need-based aid available for full-time and part-time students.

Students without need: No-need awards available for academics, state/district residency.

Scholarships offered: CCAP scholarships; for qualifying graduates of local high schools.

FINANCIAL AID PROCEDURES

Forms required: FAFSA.

Dates and Deadlines: Applicants notified on a rolling basis starting 4/1.

Transfers: No deadline. Applicants notified on a rolling basis.

CONTACT

Chad Sartini, Financial Aid Officer

3094 Colonial Avenue, Roanoke, VA 24013

(855) 874-6690

Washington and Lee University
Lexington, Virginia   Federal Code: 003768
www.wlu.edu   CSS Code: 5887

4-year private university and liberal arts college in small town.

Enrollment: 1,820 undergrads. 466 full-time freshmen.

Selectivity: Admits less than 50% of applicants.

BASIC COSTS (2016-2017)

Tuition and fees: $48,267.

Per-credit charge: $1,689.

Room and board: $11,380.

FINANCIAL AID PICTURE (2016-2017)

Students with need: Out of 249 full-time freshmen who applied for aid, 211 were judged to have need. Of these, 211 received aid, and 211 had their full need met. Average financial aid package met 100% of need; average scholarship/grant was $40,072; average loan was $528. Need-based aid available for part-time students.

Students without need: 32 full-time freshmen who did not demonstrate need for aid received scholarships/grants; average award was $44,684. No-need awards available for academics.

Additional info: W&L Promise guarantees free tuition to any undergraduate student with family income below $75,000. All students meeting the relevant Early Decision I, Early Decision II, or Regular Decision need-based financial aid deadline will receive aid package that covers their family's institutionally determined need. Loan assistance offered only to offset any additional educational expenses.

FINANCIAL AID PROCEDURES

Forms required: FAFSA, CSS PROFILE.

Dates and Deadlines: Priority date 2/15; closing date 2/15. Applicants notified by 4/1; must reply by 5/1.

Transfers: Transfer students awarded institutional funds only after commitments to enrolled students are met. Notification usually in late summer.

CONTACT

Jim Kaster, Director of Student Financial Aid

204 West Washington Street, Lexington, VA 24450-2116

(540) 458-8720

Wytheville Community College
Wytheville, Virginia
www.wcc.vccs.edu   Federal Code: 003761

2-year public community college in small town.
Enrollment: 1,581 undergrads.
Selectivity: Open admission; but selective for some programs.

BASIC COSTS (2016-2017)
Tuition and fees: $4,493; out-of-state residents $10,391.
Per-credit charge: $138; out-of-state residents $315.

FINANCIAL AID PICTURE
Students with need: Need-based aid available for full-time and part-time students.
Students without need: This college awards aid only to students with need.

FINANCIAL AID PROCEDURES
Forms required: FAFSA, institutional form.
Dates and Deadlines: Priority date 4/1; no closing date. Applicants notified on a rolling basis starting 5/1; must reply within 4 week(s) of notification.

CONTACT
Mary Gallagher, Financial Aid Coordinator
1000 East Main Street, Wytheville, VA 24382
(540) 223-4703

Washington

Antioch University Seattle
Seattle, Washington
www.antiochseattle.edu   Federal Code: 003010

Upper-division private university and liberal arts college in very large city.
Enrollment: 230 undergrads.
Selectivity: Open admission; but selective for some programs.

BASIC COSTS (2016-2017)
Tuition and fees: $27,435.
Per-credit charge: $600.

FINANCIAL AID PICTURE
Students with need: Need-based aid available for full-time and part-time students. Work study available nights, weekends, and for part-time students.

FINANCIAL AID PROCEDURES
Forms required: FAFSA, state aid form.
Dates and Deadlines: Priority date 4/15; no closing date. Applicants notified on a rolling basis starting 3/15; must reply within 2 week(s) of notification.
Transfers: Applicants notified on a rolling basis starting 3/15; must reply within 2 week(s) of notification.

CONTACT
Betsy Raleigh, Vice President for Finance and Administration
2326 Sixth Avenue, Seattle, WA 98121-1814
(206) 268-4010

Art Institute of Seattle
Seattle, Washington
www.ais.edu   Federal Code: 016210

4-year for-profit culinary school and visual arts college in very large city.
Enrollment: 1,703 undergrads.

Selectivity: Open admission; but selective for some programs.

FINANCIAL AID PICTURE
Students with need: Need-based aid available for full-time and part-time students. Work study available nights, weekends, and for part-time students.
Students without need: No-need awards available for academics, art.

FINANCIAL AID PROCEDURES
Forms required: FAFSA, state aid form.
Dates and Deadlines: Applicants notified on a rolling basis.

CONTACT
Angela Hedwall, Director of Student Financial Services
2323 Elliott Avenue, Seattle, WA 98121-1622
(206) 448-2501

Bastyr University
Kenmore, Washington
www.bastyr.edu   Federal Code: 016059

Upper-division private university and health science college in small city.
Enrollment: 227 undergrads, 22% part-time.

BASIC COSTS (2016-2017)
Tuition and fees: $27,834.
Room and board: $15,555.

FINANCIAL AID PICTURE
Students with need: Need-based aid available for full-time and part-time students. Work study available nights, weekends, and for part-time students.
Students without need: No-need awards available for academics, alumni affiliation, job skills, leadership.

FINANCIAL AID PROCEDURES
Forms required: FAFSA, institutional form.
Dates and Deadlines: Priority date 4/15; no closing date. Applicants notified on a rolling basis starting 2/1; must reply within 2 week(s) of notification.
Transfers: No deadline. Applicants notified on a rolling basis; must reply within 3 week(s) of notification.

CONTACT
Danette Wells, Director of Financial Aid
14500 Juanita Drive, NE, Kenmore, WA 98028
(425) 602-3080

Bates Technical College
Tacoma, Washington
www.bates.ctc.edu   Federal Code: 012259

2-year public technical college in small city.
Enrollment: 995 undergrads.
Selectivity: Open admission; but selective for some programs.

BASIC COSTS (2016-2017)
Tuition and fees: $4,602; out-of-state residents $10,011.
Per-credit charge: $81; out-of-state residents $201.

FINANCIAL AID PICTURE
Students with need: Need-based aid available for full-time and part-time students. Work study available nights.
Students without need: This college awards aid only to students with need.

FINANCIAL AID PROCEDURES
Forms required: FAFSA, institutional form.
Dates and Deadlines: Applicants notified on a rolling basis starting 9/7.
Transfers: No deadline. Applicants notified on a rolling basis.

CONTACT
Susan Neese, Financial Aid Officer
1101 South Yakima Avenue, Tacoma, WA 98405
(253) 680-7025

Bellevue College
Bellevue, Washington
www.bellevuecollege.edu   Federal Code: 003769

2-year public community college in small city.
Enrollment: 13,469 undergrads.
Selectivity: Open admission; but selective for some programs.

BASIC COSTS (2016-2017)
Tuition and fees: $4,083; out-of-state residents $9,492.
Per-credit charge: $86; out-of-state residents $206.

FINANCIAL AID PICTURE
Students with need: Need-based aid available for full-time and part-time students. Work study available nights, weekends, and for part-time students.
Students without need: No-need awards available for academics, athletics.

FINANCIAL AID PROCEDURES
Forms required: FAFSA, institutional form.
Dates and Deadlines: Priority date 4/16; no closing date. Applicants notified on a rolling basis starting 8/1.

CONTACT
Sherri Ballantyne, Assistant Dean, Financial Aid
3000 Landerholm Circle SE, Bellevue, WA 98007-6484
(425) 564-2227

Bellingham Technical College
Bellingham, Washington
www.btc.edu   Federal Code: 016227

2-year public technical college in small city.
Enrollment: 2,090 undergrads.
Selectivity: Open admission; but selective for some programs.

BASIC COSTS (2016-2017)
Tuition and fees: $3,886; out-of-state residents $9,295.
Per-credit charge: $81; out-of-state residents $201.

FINANCIAL AID PICTURE
Students with need: Need-based aid available for full-time and part-time students.
Students without need: This college awards aid only to students with need.

FINANCIAL AID PROCEDURES
Forms required: FAFSA, institutional form.
Dates and Deadlines: Priority date 3/1; no closing date. Applicants notified on a rolling basis starting 7/1; must reply within 2 week(s) of notification.

CONTACT
Crystal Bagby, Director of Financial Aid
3028 Lindbergh Avenue, Bellingham, WA 98225-1599
(360) 752-8351

Big Bend Community College
Moses Lake, Washington
www.bigbend.edu   Federal Code: 003770

2-year public community college in large town.
Enrollment: 1,676 undergrads, 22% part-time. 298 full-time freshmen.

Selectivity: Open admission; but selective for some programs.

BASIC COSTS (2016-2017)
Tuition and fees: $4,077; out-of-state residents $9,486.
Per-credit charge: $86; out-of-state residents $206.
Room only: $3,330.

FINANCIAL AID PICTURE (2015-2016)
Students with need: 70% of average financial aid package awarded as scholarships/grants, 30% awarded as loans/jobs. Need-based aid available for part-time students. Work study available nights, weekends, and for part-time students.
Students without need: This college awards aid only to students with need.

FINANCIAL AID PROCEDURES
Forms required: FAFSA, institutional form.
Dates and Deadlines: Priority date 4/15; no closing date. Applicants notified on a rolling basis starting 3/15; must reply within 2 week(s) of notification.

CONTACT
Jeremy Iverson, Director of Financial Aid
7662 Chanute Street NE, Moses Lake, WA 98837-3299
(509) 793-2034

Cascadia College
Bothell, Washington
www.cascadia.edu   Federal Code: 034835

2-year public community college in large town.
Enrollment: 2,310 undergrads, 45% part-time. 358 full-time freshmen.
Selectivity: Open admission.

BASIC COSTS (2016-2017)
Tuition and fees: $3,952; out-of-state residents $9,361.
Per-credit charge: $83; out-of-state residents $203.

FINANCIAL AID PICTURE
Students with need: Work study available nights, weekends, and for part-time students.

FINANCIAL AID PROCEDURES
Forms required: FAFSA, institutional form.
Dates and Deadlines: Priority date 4/15; no closing date.

CONTACT
Deann Holliday, Director of Student Financial Services
18345 Campus Way, NE, Bothell, WA 98011
(425) 352-8564

Central Washington University
Ellensburg, Washington
www.cwu.edu   Federal Code: 003771

4-year public university in large town.
Enrollment: 10,492 undergrads, 10% part-time. 1,473 full-time freshmen.
Selectivity: Admits over 75% of applicants.

BASIC COSTS (2016-2017)
Tuition and fees: $7,653; out-of-state residents $21,501.
Room and board: $10,175.

FINANCIAL AID PICTURE (2015-2016)
Students with need: Out of 1,341 full-time freshmen who applied for aid, 977 were judged to have need. Of these, 965 received aid, and 399 had their full need met. Average financial aid package met 84% of need; average scholarship/grant was $9,959; average loan was $3,137. For part-time students, average financial aid package was $7,363.

Students without need: 2 full-time freshmen who did not demonstrate need for aid received scholarships/grants; average award was $708. No-need awards available for academics, alumni affiliation, art, athletics, job skills, leadership, minority status, music/drama, religious affiliation, ROTC, state/district residency.

Scholarships offered: *Merit:* Merit Tuition Awards are offered to incoming students. Eligibility is based on a prospective student's admissions application. *Athletic:* 49 full-time freshmen received athletic scholarships; average amount $4,431.

FINANCIAL AID PROCEDURES

Forms required: FAFSA.

Dates and Deadlines: Priority date 3/1; closing date 5/1. Applicants notified on a rolling basis starting 5/15; must reply within 4 week(s) of notification.

Transfers: Equal Opportunity Grant available for junior-level transfers from selected Washington counties. May receive up to $2,500/year for three years. Phi Theta Kappa Transfer Honors Program: $1200.

CONTACT

Adrian Naranjo, Director of Financial Aid
400 East University Way, Ellensburg, WA 98926-7463
(509) 963-1611

Centralia College

Centralia, Washington
www.centralia.edu   Federal Code: 003772

2-year public community college in large town.

Enrollment: 2,097 undergrads.

Selectivity: Open admission; but selective for some programs.

BASIC COSTS (2016-2017)

Tuition and fees: $4,188; out-of-state residents $9,597.

Per-credit charge: $86; out-of-state residents $206.

Additional info: Tuition/fee waivers available for unemployed or children of unemployed.

FINANCIAL AID PICTURE

Students with need: Need-based aid available for full-time and part-time students.

Students without need: No-need awards available for academics, alumni affiliation, art, athletics, leadership, minority status, music/drama.

FINANCIAL AID PROCEDURES

Forms required: FAFSA, institutional form.

Dates and Deadlines: Priority date 5/1; closing date 9/1. Applicants notified on a rolling basis starting 7/10; must reply within 2 week(s) of notification.

CONTACT

Tracy Dahl, Director of Financial Aid
600 Centralia College Boulevard, Centralia, WA 98531
(360) 623-8975

City University of Seattle

Seattle, Washington
www.cityu.edu   Federal Code: 013022

4-year private university in very large city.

Enrollment: 905 undergrads.

Selectivity: Open admission; but selective for some programs.

BASIC COSTS (2016-2017)

Additional info: Tuition and fees vary by program and level. Tuition per-credit for undergraduate tuition ranges from $340-$521.

FINANCIAL AID PICTURE

Students with need: Need-based aid available for full-time and part-time students.

Students without need: No-need awards available for academics, alumni affiliation, leadership, minority status, state/district residency.

Additional info: All degree programs approved for veteran's administration education benefits.

FINANCIAL AID PROCEDURES

Forms required: FAFSA.

Dates and Deadlines: Applicants notified on a rolling basis starting 5/1.

CONTACT

Darcy Keller, Director of Financial Aid
521 Wall Street, Seattle, WA 98121
(800) 426-5596

Clark College

Vancouver, Washington
www.clark.edu   Federal Code: 003773

2-year public community college in small city.

Enrollment: 8,339 undergrads, 46% part-time. 723 full-time freshmen.

Selectivity: Open admission; but selective for some programs.

BASIC COSTS (2016-2017)

Tuition and fees: $3,985; out-of-state residents $9,394.

Per-credit charge: $83; out-of-state residents $203.

Additional info: Tuition/fee waivers available for unemployed or children of unemployed.

FINANCIAL AID PICTURE (2015-2016)

Students with need: 97% of average financial aid package awarded as scholarships/grants, 3% awarded as loans/jobs. Need-based aid available for part-time students. Work study available nights, weekends, and for part-time students.

Students without need: No-need awards available for academics, alumni affiliation, art, athletics, leadership, minority status, music/drama, state/district residency.

Scholarships offered: Clark College Foundation Scholarships: $500 to full tuition; recipients selected from those completing Clark's Foundation Standard Scholarship application form.

FINANCIAL AID PROCEDURES

Forms required: FAFSA.

Dates and Deadlines: Priority date 5/15; no closing date. Applicants notified on a rolling basis starting 6/1.

CONTACT

Karen Driscoll, Director of Financial Aid
Welcome Center, MS PUB002, Vancouver, WA 98663
(360) 992-2153

Clover Park Technical College

Lakewood, Washington
www.cptc.edu   Federal Code: 015984

2-year public technical college in small city.

Enrollment: 4,509 undergrads.

Selectivity: Open admission; but selective for some programs.

BASIC COSTS (2016-2017)

Tuition and fees: $3,926; out-of-state residents $9,335.

Per-credit charge: $82; out-of-state residents $203.

FINANCIAL AID PICTURE

Students with need: Need-based aid available for full-time and part-time students. Work study available nights, weekends, and for part-time students.

Students without need: This college awards aid only to students with need.

FINANCIAL AID PROCEDURES

Forms required: FAFSA, institutional form.

Dates and Deadlines: Closing date 4/12. Applicants notified on a rolling basis starting 5/1.

CONTACT

Wendy Joseph, Financial Aid Director
4500 Steilacoom Boulevard, SW, Lakewood, WA 98499-4098
(253) 589-5660

Columbia Basin College
Pasco, Washington
www.columbiabasin.edu　　　　　Federal Code: 003774

2-year public community college in small city.

Enrollment: 1,595 undergrads.

Selectivity: Open admission; but selective for some programs.

BASIC COSTS (2016-2017)

Tuition and fees: $4,419; out-of-state residents $9,828.

Additional info: Tuition/fee waivers available for unemployed or children of unemployed.

FINANCIAL AID PICTURE

Students with need: Need-based aid available for full-time and part-time students. Work study available nights, weekends, and for part-time students.

Students without need: No-need awards available for academics, athletics, state/district residency.

FINANCIAL AID PROCEDURES

Forms required: FAFSA, institutional form.

Dates and Deadlines: Closing date 4/15. Applicants notified on a rolling basis starting 6/15; must reply within 2 week(s) of notification.

CONTACT

Ceci Ratliff, Director of Student Financial Services
2600 North 20th Avenue, Pasco, WA 99301
(509) 542-4715

Cornish College of the Arts
Seattle, Washington
www.cornish.edu　　　　　Federal Code: 012315

4-year private visual arts and performing arts college in very large city.

Enrollment: 649 undergrads, 2% part-time. 167 full-time freshmen.

Selectivity: Admits 50 to 75% of applicants.

BASIC COSTS (2016-2017)

Tuition and fees: $38,370.

Per-credit charge: $1,580.

Room and board: $10,950.

FINANCIAL AID PICTURE (2016-2017)

Students with need: For part-time students, average financial aid package was $19,546.

Students without need: No-need awards available for academics, art, music/drama.

FINANCIAL AID PROCEDURES

Forms required: FAFSA.

Dates and Deadlines: Priority date 2/15; no closing date. Applicants notified on a rolling basis starting 3/15; must reply by 5/1 or within 2 week(s) of notification.

Transfers: No deadline. Applicants notified on a rolling basis; must reply by 2/15.

CONTACT

Monique Theriault, Director for Financial Aid
1000 Lenora Street, Seattle, WA 98121
(206) 726-5014

DigiPen Institute of Technology
Redmond, Washington
www.digipen.edu　　　　　Federal Code: 037243

4-year for-profit visual arts and engineering college in large town.

Enrollment: 976 undergrads. 187 full-time freshmen.

Selectivity: Admits 50 to 75% of applicants.

BASIC COSTS (2017-2018)

Tuition and fees: $29,000.

Per-credit charge: $960.

Additional info: Flat-rate fee structure: students typically take 18-20 credits each semester which equates to 36-40 credits per year. Tuition for this credit amount is $29,800 and $32,800 for nonresident aliens.

FINANCIAL AID PICTURE (2015-2016)

Students with need: Out of 147 full-time freshmen who applied for aid, 118 were judged to have need. Of these, 118 received aid, and 1 had their full need met. Average financial aid package met 67% of need; average scholarship/grant was $7,485; average loan was $9,505. For part-time students, average financial aid package was $6,862.

Students without need: 9 full-time freshmen who did not demonstrate need for aid received scholarships/grants; average award was $8,057. No-need awards available for academics, art, leadership, music/drama.

Scholarships offered: First Scholarship: $5,000; based on essay and academic record; 2 awarded. Art scholarship: up to $10,000; for incoming student who demonstrates considerable artistic talent; 2 awarded. Limited number of scholarships up to $10,000, offered to incoming students who have demonstrated academic achievements and are likely to make a positive impact in the DigiPen community and their chosen field.

Additional info: Federal Work Study available. Many aid programs are on a first-come, first-served basis.

FINANCIAL AID PROCEDURES

Forms required: FAFSA.

Dates and Deadlines: Priority date 2/1; no closing date. Applicants notified on a rolling basis starting 12/1; must reply within 3 week(s) of notification.

Transfers: No deadline. Must reply within 3 week(s) of notification. Transfer students should meet with a financial aid administrator as soon as they are accepted. Must submit prior financial aid history to determine eligibility.

CONTACT

Trinity Huttner, Director of Financial Aid
9931 Willows Road NE, Redmond, WA 98052
(425) 629-5002

Eastern Washington University
Cheney, Washington
www.ewu.edu　　　　　Federal Code: 003775

4-year public university in large town.

Enrollment: 10,546 undergrads, 10% part-time. 1,717 full-time freshmen.

Selectivity: Admits over 75% of applicants.

BASIC COSTS (2016-2017)

Tuition and fees: $6,950; out-of-state residents $23,342.

Per-credit charge: $204; out-of-state residents $750.

Room and board: $10,945.

Additional info: Course fees average approximately $150/year, depending on the courses taken. Students from the WUE states and territories (AK, AZ,

CA, CO, HI, ID, MT, NV, NM, ND, OR, SD, UT, WY, CNMI) are eligible for a tuition discount of approximately $11,230 for 2016-2017.

FINANCIAL AID PICTURE (2015-2016)
Students with need: Out of 1,515 full-time freshmen who applied for aid, 936 were judged to have need. Of these, 936 received aid, and 154 had their full need met. Average financial aid package met 84% of need; average scholarship/grant was $8,734; average loan was $3,251. For part-time students, average financial aid package was $9,145.
Students without need: 145 full-time freshmen who did not demonstrate need for aid received scholarships/grants; average award was $3,435. No-need awards available for academics, alumni affiliation, art, athletics, job skills, music/drama, state/district residency.
Scholarships offered: *Merit:* Killin Scholarship: full tuition; three awards; for academic excellence; must have 3.7 GPA and 1100 SAT score (exclusive of Writing). Honors Scholarship: $4,000; 38 awards; for academic excellence. Presidential Scholarship: $3,000; 75 awards; based on GPA, SAT, early admission. *Athletic:* 45 full-time freshmen received athletic scholarships; average amount $10,965.
Additional info: The High Demand Scholarship program helps low income students pursue "high demand" STEM careers.

FINANCIAL AID PROCEDURES
Forms required: FAFSA.
Dates and Deadlines: Priority date 2/1; no closing date. Applicants notified on a rolling basis starting 2/20; must reply within 4 week(s) of notification.
Transfers: Priority date 2/1; no deadline. Applicants notified on a rolling basis starting 2/20; must reply within 4 week(s) of notification.

CONTACT
Bruce DeFrates, Director of Financial Aid
304 Sutton Hall, Cheney, WA 99004
(509) 359-2314

Edmonds Community College
Lynnwood, Washington
www.edcc.edu   Federal Code: 005001

2-year public community college in small city.
Enrollment: 9,540 undergrads.
Selectivity: Open admission; but selective for some programs.

BASIC COSTS (2016-2017)
Tuition and fees: $4,247; out-of-state residents $9,656.
Per-credit charge: $86; out-of-state residents $206.
Room only: $8,400.

FINANCIAL AID PICTURE
Students with need: Need-based aid available for full-time and part-time students. Work study available nights.
Students without need: No-need awards available for athletics.

FINANCIAL AID PROCEDURES
Forms required: FAFSA, institutional form.
Dates and Deadlines: Priority date 5/1; no closing date. Applicants notified on a rolling basis starting 6/1; must reply within 4 week(s) of notification.

CONTACT
Rae-Ellen Reas, Senior Associate Dean of Enrollment and Financial Services
20000 68th Avenue West, Lynnwood, WA 98036-5912
(425) 640-1457

Everett Community College
Everett, Washington
www.everettcc.edu   Federal Code: 003776

2-year public community college in small city.
Enrollment: 6,990 undergrads.

Selectivity: Open admission; but selective for some programs.

BASIC COSTS (2016-2017)
Tuition and fees: $4,107; out-of-state residents $9,516.
Per-credit charge: $86; out-of-state residents $206.
Room only: $8,055.
Additional info: All rooms are single occupancy.

FINANCIAL AID PICTURE
Students with need: Need-based aid available for full-time and part-time students. Work study available nights, weekends, and for part-time students.
Students without need: No-need awards available for academics, alumni affiliation, art, athletics, job skills, leadership, minority status, music/drama, state/district residency.

FINANCIAL AID PROCEDURES
Forms required: FAFSA, institutional form.
Dates and Deadlines: Priority date 5/5; no closing date. Applicants notified on a rolling basis starting 4/15; must reply within 4 week(s) of notification.
Transfers: No deadline. Applicants notified on a rolling basis starting 6/15; must reply within 4 week(s) of notification.

CONTACT
Andrea Wilson, Director of Student Financial Services
2000 Tower Street, Everett, WA 98201-1352
(425) 388-9280

Evergreen State College
Olympia, Washington
www.evergreen.edu   Federal Code: 008155

4-year public liberal arts college in small city.
Enrollment: 3,732 undergrads, 7% part-time. 577 full-time freshmen.
Selectivity: Admits over 75% of applicants.

BASIC COSTS (2016-2017)
Tuition and fees: $7,414; out-of-state residents $23,887.
Per-credit charge: $218; out-of-state residents $767.
Room and board: $9,360.

FINANCIAL AID PICTURE (2015-2016)
Students with need: Out of 470 full-time freshmen who applied for aid, 378 were judged to have need. Of these, 360 received aid, and 33 had their full need met. Average financial aid package met 55% of need; average scholarship/grant was $9,090; average loan was $3,405. For part-time students, average financial aid package was $7,621.
Students without need: 4 full-time freshmen who did not demonstrate need for aid received scholarships/grants; average award was $6,586. No-need awards available for academics, art, athletics, leadership, state/district residency.
Scholarships offered: 5 full-time freshmen received athletic scholarships; average amount $3,060.
Additional info: Application packets for all scholarships and tuition awards EXCEPT the Merit Award (due by May 2) must be received by February 1. To meet the financial aid priority deadline, the Federal Processor must process the official results of the FAFSA by March 1. FAFSA applications that are rejected or incomplete cannot be considered for priority awarding.

FINANCIAL AID PROCEDURES
Forms required: FAFSA.
Dates and Deadlines: Priority date 2/1; no closing date. Applicants notified on a rolling basis starting 4/1; must reply within 6 week(s) of notification.

CONTACT
Tracy Hall, Director of Financial Aid
2700 Evergreen Parkway NW, Olympia, WA 98505
(360) 867-6205

Gonzaga University
Spokane, Washington
www.gonzaga.edu   Federal Code: 003778

4-year private university and liberal arts college in large city, affiliated with the Roman Catholic Church.
Enrollment: 5,084 undergrads, 1% part-time. 1,338 full-time freshmen.
Selectivity: Admits 50 to 75% of applicants. GED not accepted.

BASIC COSTS (2017-2018)
Tuition and fees: $41,330.
Per-credit charge: $1,110.
Room and board: $11,550.
Additional info: Tuition/fee waivers available for adults.

FINANCIAL AID PICTURE (2015-2016)
Students with need: Out of 1,157 full-time freshmen who applied for aid, 798 were judged to have need. Of these, 798 received aid, and 218 had their full need met. Average financial aid package met 80% of need; average scholarship/grant was $21,166; average loan was $4,816. For part-time students, average financial aid package was $22,761.
Students without need: 502 full-time freshmen who did not demonstrate need for aid received scholarships/grants; average award was $14,749. No-need awards available for academics, alumni affiliation, athletics, leadership, minority status, music/drama, ROTC.
Scholarships offered: _Merit:_ All freshmen are considered for Academic Merit Scholarships: awards range from $3,000 to $10,000. **_Athletic:_** 43 full-time freshmen received athletic scholarships; average amount $22,017.

FINANCIAL AID PROCEDURES
Forms required: FAFSA.
Dates and Deadlines: Priority date 2/1; closing date 6/30. Applicants notified on a rolling basis starting 3/1; must reply by 5/1.
Transfers: No deadline. Applicants notified on a rolling basis; must reply by 4/15 or within 3 week(s) of notification.

CONTACT
Jim White, Director of Financial Aid
502 East Boone Avenue, Spokane, WA 99258-0001
(509) 313-5816

Grays Harbor College
Aberdeen, Washington
www.ghc.edu   Federal Code: 003779

2-year public community college in large town.
Enrollment: 2,302 undergrads.
Selectivity: Open admission; but selective for some programs.

BASIC COSTS (2016-2017)
Tuition and fees: $4,268; out-of-state residents $9,677.
Per-credit charge: $86; out-of-state residents $206.
Additional info: Tuition/fee waivers available for adults, unemployed or children of unemployed.

FINANCIAL AID PICTURE
Students with need: Need-based aid available for full-time and part-time students. Work study available nights.
Students without need: No-need awards available for academics, art, athletics, music/drama.

FINANCIAL AID PROCEDURES
Forms required: FAFSA, institutional form.
Dates and Deadlines: Closing date 5/1. Applicants notified on a rolling basis starting 5/15.

CONTACT
Stacey Savino, Assistant Dean of Financial Aid
1620 Edward P Smith Drive, Aberdeen, WA 98520
(360) 538-4081

Green River College
Auburn, Washington
www.greenriver.edu   Federal Code: 003780

4-year public community college in large town.
Enrollment: 5,878 undergrads.
Selectivity: Open admission; but selective for some programs.

BASIC COSTS (2016-2017)
Tuition and fees: $4,347; out-of-state residents $9,756.
Per-credit charge: $86; out-of-state residents $197.

FINANCIAL AID PICTURE
Students with need: Need-based aid available for full-time and part-time students.
Students without need: This college awards aid only to students with need.

FINANCIAL AID PROCEDURES
Forms required: FAFSA, institutional form.
Dates and Deadlines: Closing date 4/15. Applicants notified on a rolling basis starting 6/30; must reply within 2 week(s) of notification.

CONTACT
Teresa Buchmann, Director of Financial Aid
12401 SE 320th Street, Auburn, WA 98092
(253) 833-9111 ext. 2440

Heritage University
Toppenish, Washington
www.heritage.edu   Federal Code: 003777

4-year private liberal arts and teachers college in small town, affiliated with the interdenominational tradition.
Enrollment: 795 undergrads, 8% part-time. 108 full-time freshmen.
Selectivity: Open admission.

BASIC COSTS (2017-2018)
Tuition and fees: $19,242.
Per-credit charge: $793.

FINANCIAL AID PICTURE
Students with need: Need-based aid available for full-time and part-time students. Work study available nights, weekends, and for part-time students.
Students without need: No-need awards available for academics, leadership, minority status.
Additional info: Undergraduates eligible for and receiving Federal Pell Grant and/or State Need Grant can receive institutional grant aid necessary to reduce their gap with tuition to no more than their eligibility for subsidized Stafford loans.

FINANCIAL AID PROCEDURES
Forms required: FAFSA, institutional form.
Dates and Deadlines: Priority date 2/10; no closing date. Applicants notified on a rolling basis starting 3/1; must reply within 2 week(s) of notification.
Transfers: No deadline. Applicants notified on a rolling basis starting 3/1; must reply within 2 week(s) of notification. A request to the State is made to continue awarding State Need Grant funds to transfer students if they were receiving these funds at their previous institution.

CONTACT
Oscar Verduzco, Director of Financial Aid
3240 Fort Road, Toppenish, WA 98948-9599
(509) 865-8502

Highline College
Des Moines, Washington
www.highline.edu   Federal Code: 003781

2-year public community college in small city.
Enrollment: 6,489 undergrads.
Selectivity: Open admission; but selective for some programs.

BASIC COSTS (2016-2017)
Tuition and fees: $3,927; out-of-state residents $9,336.
Per-credit charge: $86; out-of-state residents $206.

FINANCIAL AID PICTURE
Students with need: Need-based aid available for full-time and part-time students.

FINANCIAL AID PROCEDURES
Forms required: FAFSA.
Dates and Deadlines: Priority date 6/1; no closing date. Applicants notified on a rolling basis starting 6/1.

CONTACT
Lorraine Odom, Director of Financial Aid
2400 South 240th Street, Des Moines, WA 98198-9800
(206) 878-3710

Lake Washington Institute of Technology
Kirkland, Washington
www.lwtech.edu   Federal Code: 005373

2-year public technical college in small city.
Enrollment: 1,770 undergrads, 38% part-time. 282 full-time freshmen.
Selectivity: Open admission; but selective for some programs.

BASIC COSTS (2016-2017)
Tuition and fees: $4,654; out-of-state residents $10,063.
Per-credit charge: $86; out-of-state residents $206.

FINANCIAL AID PICTURE
Students with need: Need-based aid available for full-time and part-time students.

FINANCIAL AID PROCEDURES
Forms required: FAFSA, institutional form.
Dates and Deadlines: Priority date 3/15; closing date 6/16. Applicants notified on a rolling basis.

CONTACT
Bill Chaney, Director of Financial Aid
West Building, W201, Kirkland, WA 98034
(425) 739-8106

Lower Columbia College
Longview, Washington
www.lowercolumbia.edu   Federal Code: 003782

2-year public community college in small city.
Enrollment: 1,263 undergrads, 42% part-time. 205 full-time freshmen.
Selectivity: Open admission; but selective for some programs.

BASIC COSTS (2016-2017)
Tuition and fees: $4,228; out-of-state residents $9,637.
Per-credit charge: $86; out-of-state residents $206.
Additional info: Tuition/fee waivers available for adults, unemployed or children of unemployed.

FINANCIAL AID PICTURE
Students with need: Need-based aid available for full-time and part-time students.

FINANCIAL AID PROCEDURES
Forms required: FAFSA, institutional form.
Dates and Deadlines: Applicants notified on a rolling basis starting 5/1; must reply within 2 week(s) of notification.
Transfers: State-need grant awards transfer with students if previously awarded at another WA institution; SEOG usually not available to transfer students. Student employment, loans, Pell Grant available.

CONTACT
Marisa Geier, Director of Financial Aid
1600 Maple Street, Longview, WA 98632-0310
(360) 442-2390

North Seattle College
Seattle, Washington
www.northseattle.edu   Federal Code: 009704

2-year public community college in very large city.
Enrollment: 2,356 undergrads.
Selectivity: Open admission.

BASIC COSTS (2016-2017)
Tuition and fees: $4,040; out-of-state residents $9,449.
Per-credit charge: $84; out-of-state residents $204.
Additional info: Tuition/fee waivers available for adults, unemployed or children of unemployed.

FINANCIAL AID PICTURE
Students with need: Need-based aid available for full-time and part-time students. Work study available weekends and for part-time students.

FINANCIAL AID PROCEDURES
Forms required: FAFSA.
Dates and Deadlines: Priority date 3/15; closing date 6/30. Applicants notified on a rolling basis starting 6/1; must reply by 9/15.
Transfers: Applicants notified on a rolling basis starting 6/1; must reply by 9/15.

CONTACT
Brianne Sanchez, Director of Financial Aid and Veterans Services
9600 College Way North, Seattle, WA 98103-3599
(206) 934-4706

Northwest College of Art & Design
Poulsbo, Washington
www.ncad.edu   Federal Code: 026021

4-year for-profit visual arts college in small town.
Enrollment: 80 undergrads.
Selectivity: Admits 50 to 75% of applicants.

FINANCIAL AID PICTURE
Students with need: Need-based aid available for full-time and part-time students.
Students without need: No-need awards available for academics, art, state/district residency.

FINANCIAL AID PROCEDURES

Forms required: FAFSA.

Dates and Deadlines: Priority date 3/1; closing date 6/1. Applicants notified on a rolling basis.

CONTACT

Mac Fox, Financial Aid Officer/Title IX Coordinator

16301 Creative Drive NE, Poulsbo, WA 98370-8651

(360) 697-8133

Northwest Indian College

Bellingham, Washington

www.nwic.edu   Federal Code: 021800

2-year public community and liberal arts college in small town.

Enrollment: 542 undergrads, 21% part-time. 63 full-time freshmen.

Selectivity: Open admission.

BASIC COSTS (2016-2017)

Tuition and fees: $4,782; out-of-state residents $11,499.

Per-credit charge: $112; out-of-state residents $309.

Room and board: $4,950.

Additional info: Tuition/fee waivers available for minority students.

FINANCIAL AID PICTURE (2015-2016)

Students with need: 98% of average financial aid package awarded as scholarships/grants, 2% awarded as loans/jobs. Need-based aid available for part-time students.

Students without need: No-need awards available for academics, leadership.

FINANCIAL AID PROCEDURES

Forms required: FAFSA, institutional form.

Dates and Deadlines: Priority date 5/1; no closing date. Applicants notified on a rolling basis.

Transfers: Priority date 5/1; no deadline. Applicants notified on a rolling basis.

CONTACT

Raymond Burns, Director of Admissions and Financial Aid

2522 Kwina Road, Bellingham, WA 98226-9217

(360) 676-2772 ext. 4206

Northwest School of Wooden Boatbuilding

Port Hadlock, Washington

www.nwswb.edu

1-year private technical and maritime college in small town.

Enrollment: 40 undergrads.

Selectivity: Open admission; but selective for some programs.

BASIC COSTS (2017-2018)

Tuition and fees: $19,500.

Per-credit charge: $225.

FINANCIAL AID PICTURE

Students with need: Need-based aid available for full-time students.

Students without need: This college awards aid only to students with need.

FINANCIAL AID PROCEDURES

Forms required: FAFSA, institutional form.

CONTACT

Katie Whalen, Financial Aid Director

42 North Water Street, Port Hadlock, WA 98339

Northwest University

Kirkland, Washington

www.northwestu.edu   Federal Code: 003783

4-year private university and liberal arts college in small city, affiliated with the Assemblies of God.

Enrollment: 1,619 undergrads. 324 full-time freshmen.

Selectivity: Admits over 75% of applicants.

BASIC COSTS (2017-2018)

Tuition and fees: $30,320.

Room and board: $8,400.

FINANCIAL AID PICTURE (2015-2016)

Students with need: Out of 300 full-time freshmen who applied for aid, 254 were judged to have need. Of these, 251 received aid, and 32 had their full need met. Average financial aid package met 71% of need; average scholarship/grant was $14,798; average loan was $3,192. For part-time students, average financial aid package was $5,220.

Students without need: 47 full-time freshmen who did not demonstrate need for aid received scholarships/grants; average award was $7,441. No-need awards available for academics, art, athletics, leadership, music/drama, religious affiliation.

Scholarships offered: 13 full-time freshmen received athletic scholarships; average amount $6,665.

FINANCIAL AID PROCEDURES

Forms required: FAFSA, institutional form.

Dates and Deadlines: Priority date 12/15; closing date 8/1. Applicants notified on a rolling basis starting 3/3; must reply within 4 week(s) of notification.

Transfers: No deadline. Applicants notified on a rolling basis starting 3/30; must reply within 4 week(s) of notification.

CONTACT

Roger Wilson, Director of Financial Aid

5520 108th Avenue, NE, Kirkland, WA 98083-0579

(425) 889-5210

Olympic College

Bremerton, Washington

www.olympic.edu   Federal Code: 003784

2-year public community and liberal arts college in large town.

Enrollment: 7,253 undergrads.

Selectivity: Open admission; but selective for some programs.

BASIC COSTS (2016-2017)

Tuition and fees: $3,957; out-of-state residents $9,366.

Per-credit charge: $86; out-of-state residents $206.

Room only: $4,950.

FINANCIAL AID PICTURE

Students with need: Need-based aid available for full-time and part-time students. Work study available nights.

Students without need: No-need awards available for academics, state/district residency.

Additional info: Waivers available for select groups including Fallen Veterans, Children of Deceased or Disabled Law Enforcement Officers, and others.

FINANCIAL AID PROCEDURES

Forms required: FAFSA, institutional form.

Dates and Deadlines: Priority date 4/17; no closing date. Applicants notified on a rolling basis starting 6/1; must reply within 2 week(s) of notification.

Transfers: No deadline. Applicants notified on a rolling basis starting 6/1.

CONTACT
Heidi Townsend, Director Student Financial Services
1600 Chester Avenue, Bremerton, WA 98337-1699
(360) 475-7160

Pacific Lutheran University
Tacoma, Washington
www.plu.edu   Federal Code: 003785

4-year private university in small city, affiliated with the Evangelical Lutheran Church in America.
Enrollment: 2,743 undergrads, 2% part-time. 677 full-time freshmen.
Selectivity: Admits over 75% of applicants.

BASIC COSTS (2016-2017)
Tuition and fees: $39,450.
Per-credit charge: $1,221.25.
Room and board: $10,330.

FINANCIAL AID PICTURE (2016-2017)
Students with need: Out of 626 full-time freshmen who applied for aid, 544 were judged to have need. Of these, 542 received aid, and 172 had their full need met. Average financial aid package met 90% of need; average scholarship/grant was $27,522; average loan was $7,409. For part-time students, average financial aid package was $20,775.
Students without need: 127 full-time freshmen who did not demonstrate need for aid received scholarships/grants; average award was $21,657. No-need awards available for academics, alumni affiliation, art, leadership, music/drama, religious affiliation, ROTC, state/district residency.

FINANCIAL AID PROCEDURES
Forms required: FAFSA.
Dates and Deadlines: Priority date 12/1; no closing date. Applicants notified on a rolling basis starting 12/15; must reply by 5/1 or within 3 week(s) of notification.
Transfers: No deadline. Applicants notified on a rolling basis; must reply by 5/1. Reply by 05/01 but are able to make accommodations if this is not possible.

CONTACT
Kay Soltis, Director of Financial Aid
12180 Park Ave South, Tacoma, WA 98447-0003
(253) 535-7134

Peninsula College
Port Angeles, Washington
www.pencol.edu   Federal Code: 003786

2-year public community college in large town.
Enrollment: 1,386 undergrads.
Selectivity: Open admission; but selective for some programs.

BASIC COSTS (2016-2017)
Tuition and fees: $4,350; out-of-state residents $9,759.
Per-credit charge: $86; out-of-state residents $206.
Additional info: Tuition/fee waivers available for unemployed or children of unemployed.

FINANCIAL AID PICTURE
Students with need: Need-based aid available for full-time and part-time students.
Students without need: No-need awards available for academics, athletics, job skills.

FINANCIAL AID PROCEDURES
Forms required: FAFSA, institutional form.

Dates and Deadlines: Closing date 4/1. Applicants notified on a rolling basis starting 6/1; must reply within 2 week(s) of notification.

CONTACT
Krista Francis, Director of Financial Aid
1502 East Lauridsen Boulevard, Port Angeles, WA 98362
(360) 417-6390

Pierce College
Lakewood, Washington
www.pierce.ctc.edu   Federal Code: 005000

2-year public community college in small city.
Enrollment: 6,805 undergrads.
Selectivity: Open admission; but selective for some programs.

BASIC COSTS (2016-2017)
Tuition and fees: $4,193; out-of-state residents $9,602.
Per-credit charge: $86; out-of-state residents $206.
Additional info: Tuition/fee waivers available for unemployed or children of unemployed.

FINANCIAL AID PICTURE
Students with need: Need-based aid available for full-time and part-time students.
Students without need: No-need awards available for academics, athletics, music/drama.

FINANCIAL AID PROCEDURES
Forms required: FAFSA, institutional form.
Dates and Deadlines: Closing date 5/1. Applicants notified on a rolling basis starting 4/15.

CONTACT
Mary Richards, Assistant Financial Aid Director
9401 Farwest Drive SW, Lakewood, WA 98498-1999
(253) 964-6544

Renton Technical College
Renton, Washington
www.RTC.edu   Federal Code: 014001

2-year public technical college in large town.
Enrollment: 3,359 undergrads.
Selectivity: Open admission; but selective for some programs.

BASIC COSTS (2016-2017)
Tuition and fees: $4,167; out-of-state residents $9,576.
Per-credit charge: $86; out-of-state residents $206.

FINANCIAL AID PICTURE
Students with need: Need-based aid available for full-time and part-time students.
Students without need: This college awards aid only to students with need.

FINANCIAL AID PROCEDURES
Forms required: FAFSA, institutional form.
Dates and Deadlines: Priority date 5/1; closing date 7/1. Applicants notified on a rolling basis.

CONTACT
Debbie Solomon, Director of Financial Aid
3000 NE Fourth Street, Renton, WA 98056-4195
(425) 235-5841

Saint Martin's University

Lacey, Washington
www.stmartin.edu   Federal Code: 003794

4-year private university in large town, affiliated with the Roman Catholic Church.

Enrollment: 1,178 undergrads, 12% part-time. 149 full-time freshmen.

Selectivity: Admits over 75% of applicants.

BASIC COSTS (2017-2018)

Tuition and fees: $35,656.

Per-credit charge: $1,190.

Room and board: $10,820.

FINANCIAL AID PICTURE (2015-2016)

Students with need: Out of 137 full-time freshmen who applied for aid, 127 were judged to have need. Of these, 127 received aid, and 35 had their full need met. Average financial aid package met 81% of need; average scholarship/grant was $23,613; average loan was $3,126. For part-time students, average financial aid package was $10,725.

Students without need: 19 full-time freshmen who did not demonstrate need for aid received scholarships/grants; average award was $13,526. No-need awards available for academics, alumni affiliation, art, athletics, leadership, minority status, music/drama, religious affiliation, ROTC, state/district residency.

Scholarships offered: 26 full-time freshmen received athletic scholarships; average amount $8,168.

FINANCIAL AID PROCEDURES

Forms required: FAFSA.

Dates and Deadlines: Priority date 1/1; no closing date. Applicants notified on a rolling basis starting 11/21; must reply within 3 week(s) of notification.

CONTACT

Michael Grosso, Director, Office of Financial Aid
5000 Abbey Way SE, Lacey, WA 98503-3200
(360) 438-4397

Seattle Central College

Seattle, Washington
www.seattlecentral.edu   Federal Code: 003787

2-year public community and technical college in very large city.

Enrollment: 8,783 undergrads.

Selectivity: Open admission; but selective for some programs.

BASIC COSTS (2016-2017)

Tuition and fees: $4,105; out-of-state residents $9,514.

Per-credit charge: $85; out-of-state residents $205.

Additional info: Tuition/fee waivers available for unemployed or children of unemployed.

FINANCIAL AID PICTURE

Students with need: Need-based aid available for full-time and part-time students. Work study available nights, weekends, and for part-time students.

Students without need: This college awards aid only to students with need.

Additional info: Currently enrolled international students can apply for institutional scholarship in second year of study.

FINANCIAL AID PROCEDURES

Forms required: FAFSA, institutional form.

Dates and Deadlines: Closing date 7/27. Applicants notified on a rolling basis; must reply within 2 week(s) of notification.

CONTACT

Noel McBride, Assistant Dean, Financial Student Services
1701 Broadway, Seattle, WA 98122
(206) 587-3844

Seattle Pacific University

Seattle, Washington
www.spu.edu   Federal Code: 003788

4-year private university in very large city, affiliated with the Free Methodist Church of North America.

Enrollment: 3,079 undergrads, 3% part-time. 683 full-time freshmen.

Selectivity: Admits over 75% of applicants.

BASIC COSTS (2016-2017)

Tuition and fees: $38,940.

Per-credit charge: $1,070.

Room and board: $10,824.

FINANCIAL AID PICTURE (2016-2017)

Students with need: 71% of average financial aid package awarded as scholarships/grants, 29% awarded as loans/jobs. Work study available nights, weekends, and for part-time students.

Students without need: No-need awards available for academics, alumni affiliation, art, athletics, leadership, minority status, music/drama, religious affiliation, ROTC.

FINANCIAL AID PROCEDURES

Forms required: FAFSA.

Dates and Deadlines: Priority date 2/1; no closing date. Applicants notified on a rolling basis starting 3/15; must reply by 5/1 or within 3 week(s) of notification.

Transfers: No deadline. Applicants notified on a rolling basis starting 3/13; must reply by 5/1 or within 4 week(s) of notification.

CONTACT

Jordan Grant, Director of Financial Aid
3307 Third Avenue West, Suite 115, Seattle, WA 98119-1997
(206) 281-2061

Seattle University

Seattle, Washington
www.seattleu.edu   Federal Code: 003790

4-year private university in very large city, affiliated with the Roman Catholic Church.

Enrollment: 4,748 undergrads, 5% part-time. 982 full-time freshmen.

Selectivity: Admits 50 to 75% of applicants.

BASIC COSTS (2016-2017)

Tuition and fees: $41,265.

Per-credit charge: $900.

Room and board: $11,499.

FINANCIAL AID PICTURE (2016-2017)

Students with need: Out of 829 full-time freshmen who applied for aid, 629 were judged to have need. Of these, 629 received aid, and 77 had their full need met. Average financial aid package met 73% of need; average scholarship/grant was $25,004; average loan was $3,739. For part-time students, average financial aid package was $22,046.

Students without need: 111 full-time freshmen who did not demonstrate need for aid received scholarships/grants; average award was $15,357. No-need awards available for academics, alumni affiliation, athletics, leadership, minority status, music/drama, ROTC, state/district residency.

Scholarships offered: 48 full-time freshmen received athletic scholarships; average amount $25,494.

FINANCIAL AID PROCEDURES

Forms required: FAFSA.

Dates and Deadlines: Priority date 2/1; no closing date. Applicants notified on a rolling basis; must reply by 5/1 or within 2 week(s) of notification.

CONTACT

Jeff Scofield, Director of Student Financial Services
901 12th Avenue, Seattle, WA 98122-4340
(206) 296-2000

Shoreline Community College

Shoreline, Washington
www.shoreline.edu
Federal Code: 003791

2-year public community college in small city.
Enrollment: 3,553 undergrads.
Selectivity: Open admission; but selective for some programs.

BASIC COSTS (2016-2017)

Tuition and fees: $4,152; out-of-state residents $9,561.
Per-credit charge: $84; out-of-state residents $204.

FINANCIAL AID PICTURE

Students with need: Work study available nights, weekends, and for part-time students.
Additional info: Tuition and/or fee waiver for students with need on space-available basis.

FINANCIAL AID PROCEDURES

Forms required: FAFSA, institutional form.
Dates and Deadlines: Closing date 3/31. Applicants notified on a rolling basis starting 8/1; must reply within 3 week(s) of notification.

CONTACT

Chris Melton, Director, Enrollment & Financial Aid Services
16101 Greenwood Avenue North, Seattle, WA 98133
(206) 546-4762

Skagit Valley College

Mount Vernon, Washington
www.skagit.edu
Federal Code: 003792

2-year public community college in large town.
Enrollment: 5,977 undergrads.
Selectivity: Open admission; but selective for some programs.

BASIC COSTS (2016-2017)

Tuition and fees: $4,465; out-of-state residents $9,874.
Per-credit charge: $85; out-of-state residents $205.
Additional info: Tuition/fee waivers available for unemployed or children of unemployed.

FINANCIAL AID PICTURE

Students with need: Need-based aid available for full-time and part-time students. Work study available nights, weekends, and for part-time students.
Students without need: This college awards aid only to students with need.

FINANCIAL AID PROCEDURES

Forms required: FAFSA, institutional form.
Dates and Deadlines: Priority date 5/1; no closing date. Applicants notified on a rolling basis starting 7/1; must reply within 2 week(s) of notification.

CONTACT

Crystal Allison, Associate Dean for Financial Aid
2405 East College Way, Mount Vernon, WA 98273
(360) 416-7666

South Puget Sound Community College

Olympia, Washington
www.spscc.edu
Federal Code: 005372

2-year public community and junior college in small city.
Enrollment: 3,651 undergrads.
Selectivity: Open admission; but selective for some programs.

BASIC COSTS (2016-2017)

Tuition and fees: $4,104; out-of-state residents $9,513.
Per-credit charge: $86; out-of-state residents $206.

FINANCIAL AID PICTURE

Students with need: Need-based aid available for full-time and part-time students.
Students without need: No-need awards available for academics, athletics.

FINANCIAL AID PROCEDURES

Forms required: FAFSA, institutional form.
Dates and Deadlines: Priority date 5/1; closing date 6/27. Applicants notified on a rolling basis starting 7/10; must reply within 2 week(s) of notification.

CONTACT

2011 Mottman Road, SW, Olympia, WA 98512-6218
(360) 596-5232

South Seattle College

Seattle, Washington
www.southseattle.edu
Federal Code: 009706

2-year public community college in very large city.
Enrollment: 3,287 undergrads.
Selectivity: Open admission; but selective for some programs.

BASIC COSTS (2016-2017)

Tuition and fees: $4,257; out-of-state residents $9,666.
Per-credit charge: $86; out-of-state residents $206.
Additional info: Tuition/fee waivers available for unemployed or children of unemployed.

FINANCIAL AID PICTURE

Students with need: Need-based aid available for full-time and part-time students.
Students without need: No-need awards available for academics, state/district residency.

FINANCIAL AID PROCEDURES

Forms required: FAFSA, institutional form.
Dates and Deadlines: Priority date 3/15; closing date 5/9. Applicants notified on a rolling basis starting 7/1.

CONTACT

Maria Rebecchi, Financial Aid Manager
6000 16th Avenue, SW, Seattle, WA 98106-1499
(206) 934-5317

Spokane Falls Community College

Spokane, Washington
www.spokanefalls.edu
Federal Code: 009544

2-year public community college in small city.
Enrollment: 8,530 undergrads.
Selectivity: Open admission; but selective for some programs.

BASIC COSTS (2016-2017)

Tuition and fees: $4,607; out-of-state residents $10,016.
Per-credit charge: $86; out-of-state residents $206.

Additional info: Tuition/fee waivers available for unemployed or children of unemployed.

FINANCIAL AID PICTURE

Students with need: Need-based aid available for full-time and part-time students.

Students without need: This college awards aid only to students with need..

FINANCIAL AID PROCEDURES

Forms required: FAFSA, institutional form.

Dates and Deadlines: Priority date 5/13; no closing date. Applicants notified on a rolling basis starting 5/15; must reply within 2 week(s) of notification.

CONTACT

Jille Shankar, Associate Dean of Financial Aid and Student Employment
3410 West Fort George Wright Drive, Spokane, WA 99224
(509) 533-3550

Tacoma Community College

Tacoma, Washington
www.tacomacc.edu   Federal Code: 003796

2-year public community college in small city.
Enrollment: 7,384 undergrads.
Selectivity: Open admission; but selective for some programs.

BASIC COSTS (2016-2017)
Tuition and fees: $4,339; out-of-state residents $9,748.
Per-credit charge: $105.66; out-of-state residents $282.37.
Additional info: Tuition/fee waivers available for unemployed or children of unemployed.

FINANCIAL AID PICTURE

Students with need: Need-based aid available for full-time and part-time students. Work study available nights, weekends, and for part-time students.
Students without need: This college awards aid only to students with need.

FINANCIAL AID PROCEDURES

Forms required: FAFSA, institutional form.

Dates and Deadlines: Priority date 3/26; no closing date. Applicants notified on a rolling basis starting 7/20; must reply within 4 week(s) of notification.

CONTACT

Kim Matison, Director, Financial Aid Services
6501 South 19th Street, Tacoma, WA 98466-9971
(253) 566-5080

University of Puget Sound

Tacoma, Washington
www.pugetsound.edu   Federal Code: 003797

4-year private university and liberal arts college in small city.
Enrollment: 2,506 undergrads, 1% part-time. 674 full-time freshmen.
Selectivity: Admits over 75% of applicants.

BASIC COSTS (2016-2017)
Tuition and fees: $46,552.
Per-credit charge: $1,461.
Room and board: $11,800.

FINANCIAL AID PICTURE (2016-2017)

Students with need: Out of 525 full-time freshmen who applied for aid, 386 were judged to have need. Of these, 386 received aid, and 63 had their full need met. Average financial aid package met 77% of need; average scholarship/grant was $26,770; average loan was $4,805. Need-based aid available for part-time students.

Students without need: 286 full-time freshmen who did not demonstrate need for aid received scholarships/grants; average award was $16,832. No-need awards available for academics, alumni affiliation, art, leadership, music/drama, religious affiliation.

Scholarships offered: Alumni, Faculty, Dean's, President's, Trustee Scholarships: all incoming freshman considered; $15,000-$19,000; based on the student's overall admission application, including academic performance in high school and standardized test scores; no separate scholarship application required.

FINANCIAL AID PROCEDURES

Forms required: FAFSA. Students applying for Early Decision must complete the CSS PROFILE for notification of need-based financial aid eligibility.

Dates and Deadlines: Priority date 1/15; no closing date. Applicants notified by 3/15; must reply by 5/1 or within 2 week(s) of notification.

Transfers: Priority date 3/1; no deadline. Applicants notified on a rolling basis starting 3/15.

CONTACT

Maggie Mittuch, Associate Vice President of Student Financial Services
1500 North Warner Street, Tacoma, WA 98416-1062
(253) 879-3214

University of Washington

Seattle, Washington
www.washington.edu   Federal Code: 003798

4-year public university in very large city.
Enrollment: 29,990 undergrads, 6% part-time. 6,716 full-time freshmen.
Selectivity: Admits less than 50% of applicants.

BASIC COSTS (2016-2017)
Tuition and fees: $10,753; out-of-state residents $34,791.
Per-credit charge: $323; out-of-state residents $1,124.
Room and board: $11,691.

FINANCIAL AID PICTURE (2016-2017)

Students with need: Out of 4,664 full-time freshmen who applied for aid, 2,743 were judged to have need. Of these, 2,275 received aid, and 1,100 had their full need met. Average financial aid package met 82% of need; average scholarship/grant was $14,000; average loan was $5,500. For part-time students, average financial aid package was $12,000.

Students without need: 350 full-time freshmen who did not demonstrate need for aid received scholarships/grants; average award was $6,000. No-need awards available for academics, alumni affiliation, art, athletics, job skills, leadership, music/drama, ROTC, state/district residency.

Scholarships offered: *Merit:* Husky Promise: guaranteed full tuition and standard fees for eligible Washington state students. *Athletic:* 50 full-time freshmen received athletic scholarships; average amount $10,500.

FINANCIAL AID PROCEDURES

Forms required: FAFSA.

Dates and Deadlines: Priority date 1/15; no closing date. Applicants notified by 4/1; must reply by 5/1.

Transfers: Closing date 1/15.

CONTACT

Kay Lewis, Director of Student Financial Aid
1410 Northeast Campus Parkway, Box 355852, Seattle, WA 98195-5852
(206) 543-6101

University of Washington Bothell

Bothell, Washington
www.uwb.edu   Federal Code: 003798

4-year public branch campus college in large town.
Enrollment: 5,078 undergrads, 13% part-time. 786 full-time freshmen.

Selectivity: Admits over 75% of applicants.

BASIC COSTS (2016-2017)
Tuition and fees: $10,690; out-of-state residents $34,728.
Per-credit charge: $323; out-of-state residents $1,124.
Room and board: $10,833.

FINANCIAL AID PICTURE (2016-2017)
Students with need: Out of 632 full-time freshmen who applied for aid, 484 were judged to have need. Of these, 451 received aid, and 110 had their full need met. Average financial aid package met 82% of need; average scholarship/grant was $15,000; average loan was $5,500. For part-time students, average financial aid package was $9,000.
Students without need: 45 full-time freshmen who did not demonstrate need for aid received scholarships/grants; average award was $7,300. No-need awards available for academics, state/district residency.

FINANCIAL AID PROCEDURES
Forms required: FAFSA.
Dates and Deadlines: Priority date 1/15; no closing date. Applicants notified by 4/1; must reply by 5/1.

CONTACT
Danette Iyall, Assistant Director, Financial Aid
Box 358500, Enrollment Management, Bothell, WA 98011
(425) 352-5240

University of Washington Tacoma
Tacoma, Washington
www.tacoma.uw.edu   Federal Code: 003798

4-year public university in small city.
Enrollment: 4,252 undergrads, 12% part-time. 498 full-time freshmen.
Selectivity: Admits over 75% of applicants.

BASIC COSTS (2016-2017)
Tuition and fees: $10,831; out-of-state residents $34,869.
Per-credit charge: $323; out-of-state residents $1,124.
Room and board: $10,230.

FINANCIAL AID PICTURE (2016-2017)
Students with need: Out of 460 full-time freshmen who applied for aid, 361 were judged to have need. Of these, 329 received aid, and 110 had their full need met. Average financial aid package met 82% of need; average scholarship/grant was $15,000; average loan was $5,500. For part-time students, average financial aid package was $9,000.
Students without need: 30 full-time freshmen who did not demonstrate need for aid received scholarships/grants; average award was $3,000. No-need awards available for academics, state/district residency.

FINANCIAL AID PROCEDURES
Forms required: FAFSA.
Dates and Deadlines: Priority date 1/15; no closing date. Applicants notified by 4/1; must reply by 5/1.
Transfers: Applicants notified on a rolling basis starting 11/15.

CONTACT
Kimberly Fee, Director for Financial Aid and Scholarships
Campus Box 358430, Tacoma, WA 98402-3100
(253) 692-4374

Walla Walla Community College
Walla Walla, Washington
www.wwcc.edu   Federal Code: 005006

2-year public community and technical college in large town.
Enrollment: 6,572 undergrads.

Selectivity: Open admission; but selective for some programs.

BASIC COSTS (2016-2017)
Tuition and fees: $4,359; out-of-state residents $9,768.
Per-credit charge: $86; out-of-state residents $206.
Additional info: Tuition/fee waivers available for unemployed or children of unemployed.

FINANCIAL AID PICTURE
Students with need: Need-based aid available for full-time and part-time students. Work study available nights.
Students without need: No-need awards available for academics, athletics, leadership, music/drama.

FINANCIAL AID PROCEDURES
Forms required: FAFSA, institutional form.
Dates and Deadlines: Priority date 3/1; no closing date. Applicants notified on a rolling basis starting 6/1; must reply within 2 week(s) of notification.

CONTACT
Danielle Hodgen, Director of Financial Aid
500 Tausick Way, Walla Walla, WA 99362-9972
(509) 527-4301

Walla Walla University
College Place, Washington
www.wallawalla.edu   Federal Code: 003799

4-year private university and liberal arts college in large town, affiliated with the Seventh-day Adventists.
Enrollment: 1,650 undergrads, 4% part-time. 372 full-time freshmen.
Selectivity: Open admission; but selective for some programs.

BASIC COSTS (2017-2018)
Tuition and fees: $27,495.
Per-credit charge: $738.
Room and board: $7,485.

FINANCIAL AID PICTURE (2015-2016)
Students with need: Out of 311 full-time freshmen who applied for aid, 253 were judged to have need. Of these, 252 received aid, and 99 had their full need met. Average financial aid package met 96% of need; average scholarship/grant was $5,605; average loan was $3,421. For part-time students, average financial aid package was $23,281.
Students without need: 115 full-time freshmen who did not demonstrate need for aid received scholarships/grants; average award was $10,457. No-need awards available for academics, leadership, music/drama, state/district residency.

FINANCIAL AID PROCEDURES
Forms required: FAFSA, institutional form.
Dates and Deadlines: Priority date 4/30; no closing date. Applicants notified on a rolling basis starting 2/15.

CONTACT
Cassie Ragenovich, Director of Student Financial Services
204 South College Avenue, College Place, WA 99324-3000
(509) 527-2815

Washington State University
Pullman, Washington
www.wsu.edu   Federal Code: 003800

4-year public university in large town.
Enrollment: 24,362 undergrads, 12% part-time. 4,625 full-time freshmen.
Selectivity: Admits 50 to 75% of applicants.

BASIC COSTS (2016-2017)

Tuition and fees: $9,884; out-of-state residents $24,516.

Per-credit charge: $494; out-of-state residents $1,226.

Room and board: $11,356.

Additional info: Note that fees vary by campus.

FINANCIAL AID PICTURE (2015-2016)

Students with need: Out of 3,873 full-time freshmen who applied for aid, 2,833 were judged to have need. Of these, 2,763 received aid, and 405 had their full need met. Average financial aid package met 65% of need; average scholarship/grant was $11,490; average loan was $3,740. For part-time students, average financial aid package was $7,297.

Students without need: 1,188 full-time freshmen who did not demonstrate need for aid received scholarships/grants; average award was $3,921. No-need awards available for academics, alumni affiliation, art, athletics, job skills, leadership, minority status, music/drama, religious affiliation, ROTC, state/district residency.

Scholarships offered: *Merit:* Distinguished Regents Scholars receive tuition and fees; Regents Scholars receive $4,000 per year; renewable; based on high school GPA, standardized test scores, community, civic, and co-curricular involvement; educator or tribal council recommendations; residency; 10 Distinguished Regents Scholar awards, number of Regents Scholar awards varies. University Achievement Award: $2,000 to $4,000; granted to Washington high school students who meet GPA and SAT/ACT requirements and apply for freshman admission to Pullman campus by January 31 priority date; renewable for one year. Cougar Academic Award: $4,000 or $9,000 per year; renewable for three years; out-of-state students; based on high school grades, standardized test scores. Lighty Leadership Award: full tuition for out-of-state students; based on academic achievement and community involvement; number varies. National Merit Scholarships: full tuition for up to four years for National Merit semifinalists who list Washington State University as their first choice and enroll fall semester after high school graduation; number varies. *Athletic:* 87 full-time freshmen received athletic scholarships; average amount $26,857.

FINANCIAL AID PROCEDURES

Forms required: FAFSA, state aid form.

Dates and Deadlines: Closing date 1/31. Applicants notified on a rolling basis starting 2/1; must reply within 2 week(s) of notification.

Transfers: Applicants notified on a rolling basis starting 4/15. Transfer Achievement Award offered to entering transfer students who have already earned their associate degree and are transferring to the Pullman campus. Must be residents of Washington, have a minimum grade point average of 3.0, and demonstrate financial need through the FAFSA. Award is valued at $2,500 and renewable for a second year.

CONTACT

Brian Dixon, Director of Financial Aid and Scholarships

370 Lighty Student Services Bldg, Pullman, WA 99164-1067

(509) 335-9711

Wenatchee Valley College

Wenatchee, Washington

www.wvc.edu   Federal Code: 003801

2-year public community college in large town.

Enrollment: 2,465 undergrads.

Selectivity: Open admission; but selective for some programs.

BASIC COSTS (2016-2017)

Tuition and fees: $3,957; out-of-state residents $9,366.

Room only: $4,005.

Additional info: Tuition/fee waivers available for adults, unemployed or children of unemployed.

FINANCIAL AID PICTURE

Students with need: Need-based aid available for full-time and part-time students.

Students without need: No-need awards available for academics, athletics.

FINANCIAL AID PROCEDURES

Forms required: FAFSA.

Dates and Deadlines: Closing date 3/1. Applicants notified by 7/2; must reply within 3 week(s) of notification.

Transfers: Priority date 3/1. Applicants notified on a rolling basis.

CONTACT

Kevin Berg, Financial Aid Director

1300 Fifth Street, Wenatchee, WA 98801-1799

(509) 682-6845

Western Washington University

Bellingham, Washington

www.wwu.edu   Federal Code: 003802

4-year public university in small city.

Enrollment: 14,483 undergrads, 8% part-time. 2,859 full-time freshmen.

Selectivity: Admits over 75% of applicants.

BASIC COSTS (2016-2017)

Tuition and fees: $7,652; out-of-state residents $21,596.

Room and board: $10,350.

Additional info: Tuition/fee waivers available for adults, minority students.

FINANCIAL AID PICTURE (2016-2017)

Students with need: Out of 2,353 full-time freshmen who applied for aid, 1,414 were judged to have need. Of these, 1,371 received aid, and 279 had their full need met. Average financial aid package met 86% of need; average scholarship/grant was $8,614; average loan was $3,952. For part-time students, average financial aid package was $10,926.

Students without need: 88 full-time freshmen who did not demonstrate need for aid received scholarships/grants; average award was $2,009. No-need awards available for academics, alumni affiliation, art, athletics, job skills, leadership, minority status, music/drama, state/district residency.

Scholarships offered: 12 full-time freshmen received athletic scholarships; average amount $5,019.

Additional info: Short-term student loans ranging from $100 to $1,000 available on a quarterly basis.

FINANCIAL AID PROCEDURES

Forms required: FAFSA.

Dates and Deadlines: Priority date 2/15; no closing date. Applicants notified on a rolling basis starting 3/20; must reply by 5/1 or within 3 week(s) of notification.

Transfers: No deadline. Applicants notified on a rolling basis starting 3/20; must reply within 3 week(s) of notification. Some state aid not available for out-of-state transfer students.

CONTACT

Jim DeWilde, Associate Director of Financial Aid

516 High Street, Bellingham, WA 98225-9009

(360) 650-3470

Whatcom Community College

Bellingham, Washington

www.whatcom.ctc.edu   Federal Code: 010364

2-year public community college in small city.

Enrollment: 4,020 full-time undergrads.

Selectivity: Open admission; but selective for some programs.

BASIC COSTS (2016-2017)

Tuition and fees: $4,306; out-of-state residents $9,715.

Per-credit charge: $85; out-of-state residents $206.

FINANCIAL AID PICTURE

Students with need: Need-based aid available for full-time and part-time students. Work study available nights.

Students without need: No-need awards available for academics, athletics, state/district residency.

FINANCIAL AID PROCEDURES

Forms required: FAFSA, institutional form.

Dates and Deadlines: Closing date 4/1. Applicants notified on a rolling basis starting 7/1; must reply within 3 week(s) of notification.

CONTACT

David Klaffke, Director of Financial Aid

237 West Kellogg Road, Bellingham, WA 98226

(360) 383-3010

Whitman College

Walla Walla, Washington
www.whitman.edu

Federal Code: 003803
CSS Code: 4951

4-year private liberal arts college in large town.

Enrollment: 1,463 undergrads, 1% part-time. 405 full-time freshmen.

Selectivity: Admits 50 to 75% of applicants.

BASIC COSTS (2016-2017)

Tuition and fees: $47,862.

Per-credit charge: $1,978.

Room and board: $11,910.

FINANCIAL AID PICTURE (2016-2017)

Students with need: Out of 311 full-time freshmen who applied for aid, 168 were judged to have need. Of these, 168 received aid, and 34 had their full need met. Average financial aid package met 90% of need; average scholarship/grant was $32,417; average loan was $2,443. For part-time students, average financial aid package was $15,653.

Students without need: 119 full-time freshmen who did not demonstrate need for aid received scholarships/grants; average award was $11,561. No-need awards available for academics, art, minority status, music/drama.

FINANCIAL AID PROCEDURES

Forms required: FAFSA, CSS PROFILE.

Dates and Deadlines: Priority date 11/15; closing date 2/1. Applicants notified by 4/1; must reply by 5/1.

Transfers: Closing date 3/1. Applicants notified by 4/22; must reply by 5/15.

CONTACT

Tony Cabasco, Dean of Admission and Financial Aid

345 Boyer Avenue, Walla Walla, WA 99362-2046

(509) 527-5178

Whitworth University

Spokane, Washington
www.whitworth.edu

Federal Code: 003804

4-year private university and liberal arts college in large city, affiliated with the Presbyterian Church (USA).

Enrollment: 2,280 undergrads, 1% part-time. 592 full-time freshmen.

Selectivity: Admits over 75% of applicants.

BASIC COSTS (2016-2017)

Tuition and fees: $40,562.

Per-credit charge: $1,650.

Room and board: $11,170.

Additional info: Tuition/fee waivers available for minority students.

FINANCIAL AID PICTURE (2016-2017)

Students with need: Out of 511 full-time freshmen who applied for aid, 429 were judged to have need. Of these, 428 received aid, and 69 had their full need met. Average financial aid package met 80% of need; average scholarship/grant was $28,026; average loan was $3,987. For part-time students, average financial aid package was $17,695.

Students without need: 155 full-time freshmen who did not demonstrate need for aid received scholarships/grants; average award was $21,396. No-need awards available for academics, alumni affiliation, art, minority status, music/drama, ROTC.

Scholarships offered: Mind & Heart Scholarship: $22,000 per year for four years; 3.75 GPA and 1400 SAT or 30 ACT. Presidential Scholarship: $20,000 per year for four years; 4.0 GPA regardless of test scores or 3.75 GPA and 1320 SAT or 28 ACT. Trustee Scholarship: $18,000 per year for four years; 3.9 GPA regardless of test scores or 3.6 GPA and 1290 SAT or 27 ACT. Whitworth Scholarship: $16,000 per year for four years; 3.5 GPA regardless of test scores or 1220 SAT or 25 ACT. Founder's Scholarship: $14,000 per year for four years; 3.4-3.49 GPA regardless of test scores or 1180 SAT or 24 ACT.

FINANCIAL AID PROCEDURES

Forms required: FAFSA.

Dates and Deadlines: Priority date 12/1; no closing date. Applicants notified on a rolling basis starting 1/17.

Transfers: Priority date 4/1; no deadline. Applicants notified on a rolling basis starting 3/15.

CONTACT

Traci Stensland, Director of Financial Aid

300 West Hawthorne Road, Spokane, WA 99251-2515

(509) 777-3215

Yakima Valley Community College

Yakima, Washington
www.yvcc.edu

Federal Code: 003805

2-year public community college in small city.

Enrollment: 4,105 undergrads.

Selectivity: Open admission; but selective for some programs.

BASIC COSTS (2016-2017)

Tuition and fees: $4,325; out-of-state residents $9,734.

Per-credit charge: $86; out-of-state residents $206.

Additional info: Tuition/fee waivers available for unemployed or children of unemployed.

FINANCIAL AID PICTURE

Students with need: Need-based aid available for full-time and part-time students. Work study available nights, weekends, and for part-time students.

Students without need: No-need awards available for athletics.

FINANCIAL AID PROCEDURES

Forms required: FAFSA.

Dates and Deadlines: Closing date 4/15. Applicants notified on a rolling basis starting 8/1; must reply within 2 week(s) of notification.

Transfers: Priority date 4/15; no deadline. Applicants notified on a rolling basis starting 8/1; must reply within 2 week(s) of notification.

CONTACT

Janet Cantelon, Director, Office of Student Financial Aid

PO Box 22520, Yakima, WA 98907-2520

(509) 574-6855

West Virginia

Alderson-Broaddus University
Philippi, West Virginia
www.ab.edu   Federal Code: 003806

4-year private liberal arts college in small town, affiliated with the American Baptist Churches in the USA.
Enrollment: 972 undergrads, 4% part-time. 261 full-time freshmen.
Selectivity: Admits less than 50% of applicants.

BASIC COSTS (2016-2017)
Tuition and fees: $25,350.
Room and board: $7,990.

FINANCIAL AID PICTURE (2016-2017)
Students with need: Out of 250 full-time freshmen who applied for aid, 228 were judged to have need. Of these, 228 received aid, and 61 had their full need met. Average financial aid package met 91% of need; average scholarship/grant was $22,405; average loan was $3,393. For part-time students, average financial aid package was $5,937.
Students without need: 30 full-time freshmen who did not demonstrate need for aid received scholarships/grants; average award was $8,761. No-need awards available for academics, athletics, music/drama, state/district residency.
Scholarships offered: *Merit:* IMPACT Scholarship: $15,000; 25 ACT or 1150 SAT and 3.5 GPA required for consideration; 5 awards. *Athletic:* 21 full-time freshmen received athletic scholarships; average amount $15,420.

FINANCIAL AID PROCEDURES
Forms required: FAFSA, state aid form.
Dates and Deadlines: Priority date 3/1; no closing date. Applicants notified on a rolling basis starting 3/1; must reply within 2 week(s) of notification.

CONTACT
Amy King, Director of Financial Aid
101 College Hill Drive, Philippi, WV 26416
(304) 457-6354

American National University: Princeton
Princeton, West Virginia
www.an.edu   Federal Code: 003726

2-year for-profit business college in small city.
Enrollment: 104 undergrads.
Selectivity: Open admission.

BASIC COSTS (2016-2017)
Tuition and fees: $14,460.
Per-credit charge: $317.

FINANCIAL AID PICTURE
Students with need: Need-based aid available for full-time and part-time students.
Students without need: This college awards aid only to students with need.

FINANCIAL AID PROCEDURES
Forms required: FAFSA.
Dates and Deadlines: Applicants notified on a rolling basis starting 9/1.

CONTACT
Pam Cotton, Director of Financial Aid Compliance and Auditing
421 Hilltop Drive, Princeton, WV 24739

American Public University System
Charles Town, West Virginia
www.apus.edu   Federal Code: 038193

4-year for-profit virtual university in small town.
Enrollment: 37,826 undergrads, 94% part-time. 137 full-time freshmen.
Selectivity: Open admission.

BASIC COSTS (2016-2017)
Tuition and fees: $8,150.
Per-credit charge: $270.

FINANCIAL AID PICTURE (2015-2016)
Students with need: Out of 122 full-time freshmen who applied for aid, 120 were judged to have need. Of these, 120 received aid, and 1 had their full need met. Average financial aid package met 39% of need; average scholarship/grant was $4,238; average loan was $3,929. For part-time students, average financial aid package was $5,888.
Students without need: 9 full-time freshmen who did not demonstrate need for aid received scholarships/grants; average award was $244.
Additional info: Students should complete a Federal Student Aid Intent Form and register for classes at least 37 days prior to start to allow sufficient time for financial aid process.

FINANCIAL AID PROCEDURES
Forms required: FAFSA, institutional form.
Dates and Deadlines: Applicants notified on a rolling basis starting 3/1.
Transfers: Must reply within 2 week(s) of notification. Students should ensure that financial aid is processed and confirmed at least 10-14 days prior to beginning a semester.

CONTACT
Keith Wellings, Vice President, Financial Aid and Compliance
111 West Congress Street, Charles Town, WV 25414
(877) 777-9081

Appalachian Bible College
Mount Hope, West Virginia
https://abc.edu   Federal Code: 007544

4-year private Bible college in large town, affiliated with the nondenominational tradition.
Enrollment: 160 undergrads, 2% part-time. 41 full-time freshmen.
Selectivity: Admits 50 to 75% of applicants.

BASIC COSTS (2016-2017)
Tuition and fees: $14,000.
Per-credit charge: $375.
Room and board: $7,570.

FINANCIAL AID PICTURE
Students with need: Need-based aid available for full-time and part-time students.
Students without need: No-need awards available for leadership.
Scholarships offered: Christian Workers' Children Scholarship: $4,000 per year; maintain 2.75 GPA for renewal. Church Matching Scholarship: Totals up to $5,000 per year; based on church endorsement. Scholastic Achievement Scholarship: $1,000 per year; based on 24 ACT or 1650 SAT.

FINANCIAL AID PROCEDURES
Forms required: FAFSA, state aid form, institutional form.
Dates and Deadlines: Priority date 6/15; closing date 9/15. Applicants notified on a rolling basis starting 1/15.
Transfers: Applicants notified on a rolling basis starting 1/15.

CONTACT
Laura Martin, Director of Financial Aid
Director of Admissions, Mount Hope, WV 25880
(304) 877-6428 ext. 321

Bethany College

Bethany, West Virginia
www.bethanywv.edu   Federal Code: 003808

4-year private liberal arts college in rural community, affiliated with the Christian Church (Disciples of Christ).
Enrollment: 622 undergrads. 208 full-time freshmen.
Selectivity: Admits 50 to 75% of applicants.

BASIC COSTS (2016-2017)
Tuition and fees: $27,438.
Per-credit charge: $1,104.
Room and board: $9,924.

FINANCIAL AID PICTURE (2015-2016)
Students with need: Out of 208 full-time freshmen who applied for aid, 191 were judged to have need. Of these, 191 received aid, and 34 had their full need met. Average financial aid package met 81% of need; average scholarship/grant was $9,532; average loan was $4,753. For part-time students, average financial aid package was $16,841.
Students without need: 10 full-time freshmen who did not demonstrate need for aid received scholarships/grants; average award was $15,941. No-need awards available for academics, alumni affiliation, leadership, music/drama, religious affiliation, state/district residency.
Additional info: Scholarships available for travel program.

FINANCIAL AID PROCEDURES
Forms required: FAFSA.
Dates and Deadlines: Priority date 10/1; no closing date. Applicants notified on a rolling basis starting 2/15; must reply by 5/1 or within 2 week(s) of notification.
Transfers: No deadline.

CONTACT
Jason McClain, Director of Financial Aid
Office of Enrollment, Bethany, WV 26032-0428
(304) 829-7611

Blue Ridge Community and Technical College

Martinsburg, West Virginia
www.blueridgectc.edu   Federal Code: 039573

2-year public community and technical college in small city.
Enrollment: 2,001 undergrads, 49% part-time. 282 full-time freshmen.
Selectivity: Open admission.

BASIC COSTS (2016-2017)
Tuition and fees: $3,864; out-of-state residents $6,984.
Per-credit charge: $161; out-of-state residents $291.

FINANCIAL AID PICTURE
Students with need: Need-based aid available for full-time and part-time students.

FINANCIAL AID PROCEDURES
Forms required: FAFSA.
Dates and Deadlines: Applicants notified on a rolling basis; must reply within 2 week(s) of notification.

CONTACT
Anna Crawford, Director of Financial Aid
13650 Apple Harvest Drive, Martinsburg, WV 25403
(304) 260-4380 ext. 2105

Bluefield State College

Bluefield, West Virginia
www.bluefieldstate.edu   Federal Code: 003809

4-year public liberal arts and technical college in large town.
Enrollment: 1,362 undergrads, 18% part-time. 213 full-time freshmen.
Selectivity: Admits over 75% of applicants.

BASIC COSTS (2016-2017)
Tuition and fees: $6,408; out-of-state residents $12,876.

FINANCIAL AID PICTURE (2016-2017)
Students with need: Out of 208 full-time freshmen who applied for aid, 174 were judged to have need. Of these, 169 received aid, and 12 had their full need met. Average financial aid package met 65% of need; average scholarship/grant was $2,521; average loan was $4,372. For part-time students, average financial aid package was $3,453.
Students without need: 16 full-time freshmen who did not demonstrate need for aid received scholarships/grants; average award was $808. No-need awards available for academics, athletics.
Scholarships offered: 16 full-time freshmen received athletic scholarships; average amount $586.

FINANCIAL AID PROCEDURES
Forms required: FAFSA, institutional form.
Dates and Deadlines: Priority date 3/1; no closing date. Applicants notified on a rolling basis starting 6/1.
Transfers: No deadline.

CONTACT
Tom Ilse, Director of Financial Aid
219 Rock Street, Bluefield, WV 24701
(304) 327-4020

Catholic Distance University

Charles Town, West Virginia
www.cdu.edu   Federal Code: 041242

Upper-division private virtual university in small town, affiliated with the Roman Catholic Church.
Enrollment: 103 undergrads.
Selectivity: Open admission; but selective for some programs.

BASIC COSTS (2016-2017)
Tuition and fees: $9,150.
Per-credit charge: $305.

FINANCIAL AID PICTURE
Students with need: Need-based aid available for full-time students.

FINANCIAL AID PROCEDURES
Forms required: FAFSA.

CONTACT
Amy Shouse, Financial Aid Officer
115 West Congress Street, Charles Town, WV 25414
(304) 724-5000 ext. 702

Concord University

Athens, West Virginia
www.concord.edu   Federal Code: 003810

4-year public university and liberal arts college in small town.
Enrollment: 1,996 undergrads, 6% part-time. 469 full-time freshmen.

BASIC COSTS (2016-2017)
Tuition and fees: $7,080; out-of-state residents $15,564.

Per-credit charge: $194; out-of-state residents $648.
Room and board: $8,400.

FINANCIAL AID PICTURE (2016-2017)

Students with need: Out of 447 full-time freshmen who applied for aid, 365 were judged to have need. Of these, 302 received aid, and 131 had their full need met. Average financial aid package met 83% of need; average scholarship/grant was $5,113; average loan was $2,948. For part-time students, average financial aid package was $5,608.

Students without need: 64 full-time freshmen who did not demonstrate need for aid received scholarships/grants; average award was $3,473. No-need awards available for academics, alumni affiliation, leadership.

Scholarships offered: 24 full-time freshmen received athletic scholarships; average amount $6,362.

Additional info: March 1 priority deadline for state forms. April 15 priority deadline for FAFSA.

FINANCIAL AID PROCEDURES

Forms required: FAFSA.

Dates and Deadlines: Priority date 3/1; no closing date. Applicants notified on a rolling basis starting 5/1; must reply within 2 week(s) of notification.

CONTACT

Debra Turner, Director of Financial Aid
PO Box 1000, Athens, WV 24712-1000
(304) 384-6069

Davis and Elkins College

Elkins, West Virginia
www.dewv.edu   Federal Code: 003811

4-year private liberal arts college in small town, affiliated with the Presbyterian Church (USA).
Enrollment: 874 undergrads.

BASIC COSTS (2016-2017)

Tuition and fees: $28,842.
Room and board: $9,250.

FINANCIAL AID PICTURE

Students with need: Need-based aid available for full-time and part-time students. Work study available nights, weekends, and for part-time students.
Students without need: No-need awards available for academics, alumni affiliation, art, athletics, leadership, music/drama, religious affiliation, state/district residency.
Scholarships offered: Highlands Scholarship Program: $14,000 for residential students; $11,000 for commuter students; for freshmen students from surrounding seven counties with at least 2.5 GPA.

FINANCIAL AID PROCEDURES

Forms required: FAFSA.

Dates and Deadlines: Priority date 3/1; closing date 8/1. Applicants notified on a rolling basis; must reply by 8/30.

Transfers: Applicants notified on a rolling basis; must reply by 8/30.

CONTACT

Matthew Summers, Director of Financial Planning
100 Campus Drive, Elkins, WV 26241-3996
(304) 637-1990

Eastern West Virginia Community and Technical College

Moorefield, West Virginia
www.easternwv.edu

2-year public community and technical college in rural community.
Enrollment: 526 undergrads.

Selectivity: Open admission.

FINANCIAL AID PICTURE

Students with need: Need-based aid available for full-time and part-time students.

FINANCIAL AID PROCEDURES

Forms required: FAFSA, institutional form.

Dates and Deadlines: Priority date 6/1; no closing date. Applicants notified on a rolling basis; must reply within 2 week(s) of notification.

CONTACT

Amanda Sites, Director of Financial Aid
316 Eastern Drive, Moorefield, WV 26836
(304) 434-8000

Fairmont State University

Fairmont, West Virginia
www.fairmontstate.edu   Federal Code: 003812

4-year public university in large town.
Enrollment: 3,687 undergrads, 11% part-time. 808 full-time freshmen.
Selectivity: Admits 50 to 75% of applicants.

BASIC COSTS (2016-2017)

Tuition and fees: $6,950; out-of-state residents $14,666.
Per-credit charge: $281; out-of-state residents $603.
Room and board: $9,100.
Additional info: Tuition/fee waivers available for adults, minority students.

FINANCIAL AID PICTURE (2015-2016)

Students with need: Out of 780 full-time freshmen who applied for aid, 586 were judged to have need. Of these, 580 received aid, and 75 had their full need met. Average financial aid package met 72% of need; average scholarship/grant was $6,883; average loan was $2,920. For part-time students, average financial aid package was $4,736.

Students without need: This college awards aid only to students with need.

Scholarships offered: 21 full-time freshmen received athletic scholarships; average amount $6,868.

FINANCIAL AID PROCEDURES

Forms required: FAFSA.

Dates and Deadlines: Priority date 3/1; no closing date. Applicants notified on a rolling basis starting 4/1; must reply within 2 week(s) of notification.

Transfers: Academic transcripts required.

CONTACT

Patricia Weimer, Director of Financial Aid and Scholarships
Office of Admissions, Fairmont, WV 26554-2470
(304) 367-4213

Glenville State College

Glenville, West Virginia
www.glenville.edu   Federal Code: 003813

4-year public liberal arts and teachers college in rural community.
Enrollment: 1,347 undergrads, 22% part-time. 320 full-time freshmen.
Selectivity: Admits 50 to 75% of applicants.

BASIC COSTS (2016-2017)

Tuition and fees: $7,344; out-of-state residents $16,600.
Per-credit charge: $306; out-of-state residents $692.

FINANCIAL AID PICTURE

Students with need: Need-based aid available for full-time and part-time students. Work study available nights, weekends, and for part-time students.

Students without need: No-need awards available for academics, athletics, music/drama, state/district residency.

FINANCIAL AID PROCEDURES

Forms required: FAFSA.

Dates and Deadlines: Priority date 2/1; no closing date. Applicants notified on a rolling basis starting 3/1; must reply within 3 week(s) of notification.

CONTACT

Karen Lay, Director of Financial Aid
200 High Street, Glenville, WV 26351-1292
(304) 462-4103

Kanawha Valley Community and Technical College

South Charleston, West Virginia
www.kvctc.edu   Federal Code: 040386

2-year public community and technical college in small town.
Selectivity: Open admission; but selective for some programs.

FINANCIAL AID PICTURE

Students with need: Work study available nights, weekends, and for part-time students.

Students without need: No-need awards available for academics, state/district residency.

Additional info: All students may apply for tuition waivers. Financial aid deadline enforced only if Federal financial aid is the only source of payment.

FINANCIAL AID PROCEDURES

Dates and Deadlines: Closing date 6/30.

CONTACT

Mary Blizzard, Director of Financial Aid
2001 Union Carbide Drive, South Charleston, WV 25303
(304) 205-6600

Marshall University

Huntington, West Virginia
www.marshall.edu   Federal Code: 003815

4-year public university in small city.
Enrollment: 8,699 undergrads, 9% part-time. 1,882 full-time freshmen.
Selectivity: Admits over 75% of applicants.

BASIC COSTS (2016-2017)

Tuition and fees: $7,154; out-of-state residents $16,382.
Per-credit charge: $251.5; out-of-state residents $636.
Room and board: $10,126.

FINANCIAL AID PICTURE (2016-2017)

Students with need: Out of 1,824 full-time freshmen who applied for aid, 1,409 were judged to have need. Of these, 1,398 received aid, and 459 had their full need met. Average financial aid package met 50% of need; average scholarship/grant was $7,050; average loan was $5,335. For part-time students, average financial aid package was $5,066.

Students without need: 310 full-time freshmen who did not demonstrate need for aid received scholarships/grants; average award was $2,523. No-need awards available for academics, alumni affiliation, art, athletics, minority status, music/drama, ROTC, state/district residency.

Scholarships offered: *Merit:* Michael Perry Scholarship: $500 based on 3.2 GPA and 20 ACT; $750 based on 3.5 GPA and 23 ACT, or 3.2 GPA and 25 ACT; one-year only. Presidential Scholarship: $1,250; 3.5 GPA and 25 ACT; renewable with 3.5 GPA. John Marshall Scholarship: tuition waiver plus $1,250 stipend; 3.5 GPA and 30 ACT; renewable yearly with 3.5 GPA. Yeager

scholarship: full tuition and fees; full room and board; book allowance; stipend; personal computer for use during program; $4,000 toward study abroad; 28 ACT/1260 SAT (exclusive of Writing). *Athletic:* 87 full-time freshmen received athletic scholarships; average amount $13,769.

FINANCIAL AID PROCEDURES

Forms required: FAFSA, state aid form.

Dates and Deadlines: Priority date 3/1; no closing date. Applicants notified on a rolling basis starting 4/1.

Transfers: Priority date 1/1.

CONTACT

Kathy Bialk, Director of Financial Aid
One John Marshall Drive, Huntington, WV 25755
(304) 696-3162

Mountain State College

Parkersburg, West Virginia
www.msc.edu   Federal Code: 005008

2-year for-profit junior and career college in large town.
Enrollment: 189 undergrads.
Selectivity: Open admission.

BASIC COSTS (2016-2017)

Tuition and fees: $8,215.

FINANCIAL AID PICTURE

Students with need: Work study available nights, weekends, and for part-time students.

FINANCIAL AID PROCEDURES

Forms required: FAFSA.

Dates and Deadlines: Applicants notified on a rolling basis.

CONTACT

Faye Wagoner, Director of Student Financial Services
1508 Spring Street, Parkersburg, WV 26101-3993
(304) 485-5487

Ohio Valley University

Vienna, West Virginia
www.ovu.edu   Federal Code: 003819

4-year private university and liberal arts college in small city, affiliated with the Church of Christ.
Enrollment: 157 undergrads, 1% part-time. 146 full-time freshmen.
Selectivity: Admits 50 to 75% of applicants.

BASIC COSTS (2017-2018)

Tuition and fees: $21,100.
Per-credit charge: $700.
Room and board: $7,700.

FINANCIAL AID PICTURE (2015-2016)

Students with need: Out of 122 full-time freshmen who applied for aid, 108 were judged to have need. Of these, 102 received aid, and 14 had their full need met. Average financial aid package met 64% of need; average scholarship/grant was $13,468; average loan was $2,832. Need-based aid available for part-time students.

Students without need: 15 full-time freshmen who did not demonstrate need for aid received scholarships/grants; average award was $4,543. No-need awards available for academics, alumni affiliation, art, athletics, job skills, leadership, minority status, music/drama, religious affiliation, ROTC, state/district residency.

Scholarships offered: 20 full-time freshmen received athletic scholarships; average amount $12,775.

FINANCIAL AID PROCEDURES

Forms required: FAFSA.

Dates and Deadlines: Priority date 5/1; no closing date. Applicants notified on a rolling basis starting 3/1.

Transfers: No deadline. Applicants notified on a rolling basis starting 3/15; must reply within 4 week(s) of notification.

CONTACT

Lindsay Cole, Director of Financial Aid
One Campus View Drive, Vienna, WV 26105
(304) 865-6077

Potomac State College of West Virginia University

Keyser, West Virginia
www.potomacstatecollege.edu   Federal Code: 003829

2-year public branch campus and junior college in small town.

Enrollment: 1,204 undergrads, 7% part-time. 630 full-time freshmen.

Selectivity: Open admission; but selective for out-of-state students.

BASIC COSTS (2016-2017)

Tuition and fees: $4,056; out-of-state residents $10,416.

Room and board: $8,752.

FINANCIAL AID PICTURE

Students with need: Need-based aid available for full-time and part-time students.

Students without need: No-need awards available for academics, athletics.

FINANCIAL AID PROCEDURES

Forms required: FAFSA.

Dates and Deadlines: Priority date 3/1; no closing date. Applicants notified on a rolling basis starting 3/15; must reply within 2 week(s) of notification.

Transfers: Applicants notified on a rolling basis starting 3/1; must reply within 3 week(s) of notification.

CONTACT

Harlan Shreve, Chief Business Officer
75 Arnold Street, Keyser, WV 26726
(304) 788-6820

Salem International University

Salem, West Virginia
www.salemu.edu   Federal Code: 003820

4-year for-profit university and liberal arts college in rural community.

Enrollment: 402 undergrads.

BASIC COSTS (2016-2017)

Tuition and fees: $12,920.

Per-credit charge: $530.

Room and board: $7,480.

FINANCIAL AID PICTURE

Students with need: Need-based aid available for full-time and part-time students. Work study available nights, weekends, and for part-time students.

Students without need: No-need awards available for academics.

Scholarships offered: Scholarships; extensive amount awarded; based on high school GPA, standardized test scores. Breed-related awards; for students in equine career and industry management program. Awards for GED diploma recipients; based on academic excellence.

FINANCIAL AID PROCEDURES

Forms required: FAFSA.

Dates and Deadlines: Priority date 4/15; no closing date. Applicants notified on a rolling basis starting 2/15; must reply within 4 week(s) of notification.

Transfers: Priority date 3/1; closing date 4/15. Applicants notified on a rolling basis starting 3/1.

CONTACT

Daniel Ronan, Director of Financial Aid and Compliance
223 West Main Street, Salem, WV 26426
(317) 805-1793

Shepherd University

Shepherdstown, West Virginia
www.shepherd.edu   Federal Code: 003822

4-year public university in small town.

Enrollment: 3,094 undergrads, 13% part-time. 560 full-time freshmen.

Selectivity: Admits over 75% of applicants.

BASIC COSTS (2016-2017)

Tuition and fees: $7,170; out-of-state residents $17,482.

Per-credit charge: $293; out-of-state residents $687.

Room and board: $10,054.

Additional info: Tuition/fee waivers available for minority students.

FINANCIAL AID PICTURE (2016-2017)

Students with need: Out of 541 full-time freshmen who applied for aid, 372 were judged to have need. Of these, 365 received aid, and 122 had their full need met. Average financial aid package met 83% of need; average scholarship/grant was $5,381; average loan was $3,114. For part-time students, average financial aid package was $11,540.

Students without need: 139 full-time freshmen who did not demonstrate need for aid received scholarships/grants; average award was $10,039. No-need awards available for academics, art, athletics, job skills, leadership, minority status, music/drama, state/district residency.

Scholarships offered: 47 full-time freshmen received athletic scholarships; average amount $6,339.

FINANCIAL AID PROCEDURES

Forms required: FAFSA, state aid form.

Dates and Deadlines: Priority date 3/1; no closing date. Applicants notified on a rolling basis starting 12/16; must reply within 3 week(s) of notification.

Transfers: No deadline. Applicants notified on a rolling basis starting 11/1; must reply within 3 week(s) of notification.

CONTACT

Joyce Cabral, Director of Financial Aid
PO Box 5000, Shepherdstown, WV 25443-5000
(304) 876-5470

Southern West Virginia Community and Technical College

Mount Gay, West Virginia
www.southernwv.edu   Federal Code: 003816

2-year public community and technical college in small town.

Enrollment: 2,002 undergrads.

Selectivity: Open admission; but selective for some programs.

BASIC COSTS (2016-2017)

Tuition and fees: $4,120; out-of-state residents $9,812.

Room and board: $6,377.

FINANCIAL AID PICTURE

Students with need: Need-based aid available for full-time and part-time students.

FINANCIAL AID PROCEDURES

Forms required: FAFSA.

Dates and Deadlines: Applicants notified on a rolling basis.

CONTACT
August Kafer, Financial Aid Director
PO Box 2900, Mount Gay, WV 25637
(304) 896-7382

University of Charleston
Charleston, West Virginia
www.ucwv.edu   Federal Code: 003818

4-year private university in small city.
Enrollment: 1,733 undergrads, 30% part-time. 297 full-time freshmen.
Selectivity: Admits 50 to 75% of applicants.

BASIC COSTS (2016-2017)
Tuition and fees: $29,900.
Per-credit charge: $380.
Room and board: $9,100.

FINANCIAL AID PICTURE
Students with need: Need-based aid available for full-time and part-time students. Work study available nights, weekends, and for part-time students.
Students without need: No-need awards available for academics, alumni affiliation, art, athletics, leadership, music/drama, ROTC.
Additional info: All university tuition discounts (scholarships) based on family or student need and talent. Higher need awards given to middle and lower income students.

FINANCIAL AID PROCEDURES
Forms required: FAFSA, state aid form, institutional form.
Dates and Deadlines: Priority date 3/1; closing date 8/15. Applicants notified on a rolling basis starting 3/1; must reply by 5/1 or within 4 week(s) of notification.
Transfers: Applicants notified on a rolling basis starting 4/1; must reply by 5/1 or within 4 week(s) of notification.

CONTACT
Nina Morton, Director of Financial Aid
2300 MacCorkle Avenue, SE, Charleston, WV 25304
(304) 357-4947

Valley College
Martinsburg, West Virginia
www.valley.edu   Federal Code: G26094

2-year for-profit career college in large town.
Enrollment: 140 undergrads.
Selectivity: Open admission.

BASIC COSTS (2016-2017)
Additional info: Annual costs vary by program ranging from $13,065 to $14,925.

FINANCIAL AID PICTURE
Students with need: Need-based aid available for full-time and part-time students.

FINANCIAL AID PROCEDURES
Forms required: FAFSA, institutional form.
Dates and Deadlines: Applicants notified on a rolling basis.
Transfers: No deadline. Applicants notified on a rolling basis.

CONTACT
Kellie Thayer, Director of Financial Aid
287 Aikens Center, Martinsburg, WV 25404
(304) 263-0979

West Liberty University
West Liberty, West Virginia
www.westliberty.edu   Federal Code: 003823

4-year public university in rural community.
Enrollment: 1,919 undergrads, 6% part-time. 434 full-time freshmen.
Selectivity: Admits 50 to 75% of applicants.

FINANCIAL AID PICTURE
Students with need: Need-based aid available for full-time and part-time students. Work study available nights, weekends, and for part-time students.
Students without need: No-need awards available for academics, alumni affiliation, art, athletics, music/drama, state/district residency.
Additional info: Non-need based student employment available at food service, college union, bookstore, and tutoring office. Resident assistant and campus security jobs also available.

FINANCIAL AID PROCEDURES
Forms required: FAFSA.
Dates and Deadlines: Priority date 3/1; no closing date. Applicants notified on a rolling basis starting 3/1; must reply within 2 week(s) of notification.
Transfers: Financial aid transcript required from all previous colleges attended regardless of whether aid was received.

CONTACT
Katie Cooper, Director of Financial Aid
208 University Drive, West Liberty, WV 26074
(304) 336-8016

West Virginia Business College: Nutter Fort
Benwood, West Virginia
www.wvbc.edu   Federal Code: 010861

2-year for-profit business college in small city.
Selectivity: Open admission; but selective for some programs.

FINANCIAL AID PICTURE
Students with need: Need-based aid available for full-time and part-time students.
Students without need: This college awards aid only to students with need.

FINANCIAL AID PROCEDURES
Forms required: FAFSA, institutional form.

CONTACT
James Weir, Financial Aid Manager
1052 Main Street, Wheeling, WV 26003
(304) 232-0361

West Virginia Junior College
Morgantown, West Virginia
www.wvjc.edu   Federal Code: 005007

2-year for-profit junior college in large town.
Enrollment: 291 undergrads.
Selectivity: Open admission.

FINANCIAL AID PICTURE
Students with need: Need-based aid available for full-time and part-time students.

FINANCIAL AID PROCEDURES
Forms required: FAFSA.
Dates and Deadlines: Applicants notified on a rolling basis.

CONTACT
Patricia Callen, Executive Director
148 Willey Street, Morgantown, WV 26505

West Virginia Junior College: Bridgeport
Bridgeport, West Virginia
www.wvjc.edu   Federal Code: 010573

2-year for-profit health science and junior college in large town.
Enrollment: 188 undergrads.
Selectivity: Open admission; but selective for some programs.

FINANCIAL AID PICTURE
Students with need: Need-based aid available for full-time and part-time students.

FINANCIAL AID PROCEDURES
Forms required: FAFSA, state aid form.

CONTACT
Frances Jenkins, Financial Aid Director
176 Thompson Drive, Bridgeport, WV 26330
(304) 842-4007 ext. 105

West Virginia Junior College: Charleston
Charleston, West Virginia
www.wvjc.edu   Federal Code: 010573

2-year for-profit junior and career college in small city.
Enrollment: 213 undergrads.
Selectivity: Open admission.

FINANCIAL AID PICTURE
Students with need: Need-based aid available for full-time and part-time students.

FINANCIAL AID PROCEDURES
Forms required: FAFSA.
Dates and Deadlines: Applicants notified on a rolling basis.

CONTACT
Katherine Barnes, Financial Aid Director
1000 Virginia Street East, Charleston, WV 25301

West Virginia Northern Community College
Wheeling, West Virginia
www.wvncc.edu   Federal Code: 010920

2-year public community and technical college in large town.
Enrollment: 1,429 undergrads.
Selectivity: Open admission; but selective for some programs.

BASIC COSTS (2016-2017)
Tuition and fees: $3,419; out-of-state residents $10,355.
Additional info: Tuition/fee waivers available for adults.

FINANCIAL AID PICTURE
Students with need: Need-based aid available for full-time and part-time students.

FINANCIAL AID PROCEDURES
Forms required: FAFSA, institutional form.
Dates and Deadlines: Priority date 3/15; no closing date. Applicants notified on a rolling basis starting 3/10.

CONTACT
Janet Fike, Vice President of Student Services/Director of Financial Aid
1704 Market Street, Wheeling, WV 26003
(304) 214-8844

West Virginia State University
Institute, West Virginia
www.wvstateu.edu   Federal Code: 003826

4-year public liberal arts and teachers college in small town.
Enrollment: 2,011 undergrads, 12% part-time. 413 full-time freshmen.
Selectivity: Admits less than 50% of applicants.

BASIC COSTS (2016-2017)
Tuition and fees: $6,996; out-of-state residents $15,572.
Per-credit charge: $287; out-of-state residents $644.
Room and board: $11,388.

FINANCIAL AID PICTURE
Students with need: Need-based aid available for full-time and part-time students. Work study available nights, weekends, and for part-time students.
Students without need: No-need awards available for academics, athletics, ROTC, state/district residency.

FINANCIAL AID PROCEDURES
Dates and Deadlines: Applicants notified on a rolling basis.
Transfers: Closing date 6/30. Applicants notified on a rolling basis starting 3/1; must reply within 2 week(s) of notification.

CONTACT
JoAnn Ross, Director of Financial Aid
124 Ferrell Hall, Institute, WV 25112-1000
(304) 204-4369

West Virginia University
Morgantown, West Virginia
www.wvu.edu   Federal Code: 003827

4-year public university in small city.
Enrollment: 21,428 undergrads, 4% part-time. 4,948 full-time freshmen.
Selectivity: Admits over 75% of applicants.

BASIC COSTS (2016-2017)
Tuition and fees: $7,992; out-of-district residents $7,992; out-of-state residents $22,488.
Per-credit charge: $333; out-of-state residents $937.
Room and board: $10,218.

FINANCIAL AID PICTURE (2015-2016)
Students with need: Out of 4,305 full-time freshmen who applied for aid, 2,939 were judged to have need. Of these, 2,883 received aid, and 617 had their full need met. Average financial aid package met 72% of need; average scholarship/grant was $4,814; average loan was $2,826. For part-time students, average financial aid package was $4,969.
Students without need: 910 full-time freshmen who did not demonstrate need for aid received scholarships/grants; average award was $2,382. No-need awards available for academics, alumni affiliation, art, athletics, job skills, leadership, minority status, music/drama, religious affiliation, ROTC, state/district residency.
Scholarships offered: 64 full-time freshmen received athletic scholarships; average amount $20,863.

FINANCIAL AID PROCEDURES
Forms required: FAFSA.
Dates and Deadlines: Priority date 3/1; no closing date. Applicants notified on a rolling basis starting 3/15; must reply within 2 week(s) of notification.

Transfers: Applicants notified on a rolling basis starting 4/1; must reply within 4 week(s) of notification. Transfer scholarship available to those students who apply by 7/1 and transfer minimum of 15 hours with 3.0 GPA.

CONTACT
Sandra Oerly-Bennett, Executive Director of Financial Aid
Office of Admissions, Morgantown, WV 26506-6009
(800) 344-9881

West Virginia University at Parkersburg
Parkersburg, West Virginia
www.wvup.edu   Federal Code: 003828

2-year public community college in large town.
Enrollment: 3,800 undergrads.
Selectivity: Open admission; but selective for some programs.

BASIC COSTS (2016-2017)
Tuition and fees: $3,384; out-of-state residents $7,920.

FINANCIAL AID PICTURE
Students with need: Need-based aid available for full-time and part-time students. Work study available nights, weekends, and for part-time students.
Students without need: No-need awards available for academics, leadership, state/district residency.

FINANCIAL AID PROCEDURES
Forms required: FAFSA.
Dates and Deadlines: Priority date 3/1; no closing date. Applicants notified on a rolling basis; must reply within 2 week(s) of notification.

CONTACT
Heather Skidmore, Director of Financial Aid
300 Campus Drive, Parkersburg, WV 26104-8647
(304) 424-8310

West Virginia University Institute of Technology
Montgomery, West Virginia
www.wvutech.edu   Federal Code: 003825

4-year public engineering and liberal arts college in small town.
Enrollment: 1,109 undergrads, 12% part-time. 268 full-time freshmen.
Selectivity: Admits 50 to 75% of applicants.

BASIC COSTS (2016-2017)
Tuition and fees: $6,648; out-of-state residents $16,728.
Per-credit charge: $277; out-of-state residents $697.
Room and board: $9,814.

FINANCIAL AID PICTURE (2015-2016)
Students with need: Out of 231 full-time freshmen who applied for aid, 181 were judged to have need. Of these, 181 received aid, and 30 had their full need met. Average financial aid package met 72% of need; average scholarship/grant was $5,331; average loan was $2,284. For part-time students, average financial aid package was $4,222.
Students without need: 26 full-time freshmen who did not demonstrate need for aid received scholarships/grants; average award was $2,619. No-need awards available for academics, alumni affiliation, art, athletics, job skills, leadership, minority status, music/drama, ROTC, state/district residency.
Scholarships offered: *Merit:* Academic scholarships; students meeting academic criteria will receive scholarship/tuition waiver offer; renewable each year upon meeting the stated requirements. *Athletic:* 108 full-time freshmen received athletic scholarships; average amount $5,558.

FINANCIAL AID PROCEDURES
Forms required: FAFSA.
Dates and Deadlines: Priority date 3/1; no closing date. Applicants notified on a rolling basis starting 3/15; must reply within 2 week(s) of notification.
Transfers: No deadline. Applicants notified on a rolling basis starting 3/21; must reply within 4 week(s) of notification.

CONTACT
Michael White, Director of Financial Aid Services
405 Fayette Pike, Montgomery, WV 25136-2436
(304) 442-3140

West Virginia Wesleyan College
Buckhannon, West Virginia
www.wvwc.edu   Federal Code: 003830

4-year private liberal arts college in small town, affiliated with the United Methodist Church.
Enrollment: 1,382 undergrads, 1% part-time. 387 full-time freshmen.
Selectivity: Admits over 75% of applicants.

BASIC COSTS (2016-2017)
Tuition and fees: $29,952.
Room and board: $8,248.

FINANCIAL AID PICTURE (2016-2017)
Students with need: Out of 350 full-time freshmen who applied for aid, 307 were judged to have need. Of these, 307 received aid, and 88 had their full need met. Average financial aid package met 84% of need; average scholarship/grant was $25,954; average loan was $3,286. For part-time students, average financial aid package was $1.
Students without need: 45 full-time freshmen who did not demonstrate need for aid received scholarships/grants; average award was $17,278. No-need awards available for academics, alumni affiliation, art, athletics, leadership, music/drama, religious affiliation.
Scholarships offered: 35 full-time freshmen received athletic scholarships; average amount $11,533.

FINANCIAL AID PROCEDURES
Forms required: FAFSA.
Dates and Deadlines: Priority date 2/15; no closing date. Applicants notified on a rolling basis starting 3/1; must reply within 4 week(s) of notification.
Transfers: No deadline. Applicants notified on a rolling basis starting 3/15; must reply within 4 week(s) of notification. Financial aid transcripts required from all institutions previously attended.

CONTACT
Susan George, Director of Financial Aid
59 College Avenue, Buckhannon, WV 26201-2998
(304) 473-8080

Wheeling Jesuit University
Wheeling, West Virginia
www.wju.edu   Federal Code: 003831

4-year private university and liberal arts college in small city, affiliated with the Roman Catholic Church.
Enrollment: 1,131 undergrads.

BASIC COSTS (2016-2017)
Tuition and fees: $28,110.
Room and board: $7,796.

FINANCIAL AID PICTURE
Students with need: Need-based aid available for full-time and part-time students. Work study available nights, weekends, and for part-time students.

Students without need: No-need awards available for academics, alumni affiliation, athletics, music/drama, religious affiliation.

FINANCIAL AID PROCEDURES

Forms required: FAFSA.

Dates and Deadlines: Priority date 3/1; closing date 8/1. Applicants notified on a rolling basis starting 3/10; must reply within 2 week(s) of notification.

Transfers: No deadline. Applicants notified on a rolling basis starting 3/10; must reply within 2 week(s) of notification. Academic scholarships available to qualified transfer students.

CONTACT

Christie Tomczyk, Director of Financial Aid
316 Washington Avenue, Wheeling, WV 26003-6295
(304) 243-2304

Wisconsin

Alverno College
Milwaukee, Wisconsin
www.alverno.edu   Federal Code: 003832

4-year private liberal arts college for women in very large city, affiliated with the Roman Catholic Church.
Enrollment: 1,380 undergrads, 23% part-time. 163 full-time freshmen.
Selectivity: Admits 50 to 75% of applicants.

BASIC COSTS (2016-2017)
Tuition and fees: $26,932.
Per-credit charge: $1,093.
Room and board: $7,884.

FINANCIAL AID PICTURE (2016-2017)
Students with need: For part-time students, average financial aid package was $15.

Students without need: No-need awards available for academics, alumni affiliation.

Scholarships offered: Four-year academic scholarships: range from $20,000 to $66,000. Clare Scholarships: $12,000 for four years or $48,000. Must be from a high school that is part of the Archdiocese of Milwaukee, GPA of 2.8 or higher, replaces four-year academic scholarship.

FINANCIAL AID PROCEDURES
Forms required: FAFSA.

Dates and Deadlines: Priority date 3/1; no closing date. Applicants notified on a rolling basis starting 11/1; must reply within 2 week(s) of notification.

Transfers: No deadline. Applicants notified on a rolling basis; must reply within 2 week(s) of notification. Transfer students are eligible for academic scholarships.

CONTACT
Amy Christen, Director of Financial Aid
3400 South 43rd Street, Milwaukee, WI 53234-3922
(414) 382-6046

Bellin College
Green Bay, Wisconsin
www.bellincollege.edu   Federal Code: 006639

4-year private health science college in small city.
Enrollment: 360 undergrads, 36% part-time. 37 full-time freshmen.
Selectivity: Admits over 75% of applicants.

BASIC COSTS (2017-2018)
Tuition and fees: $21,513.

FINANCIAL AID PICTURE (2015-2016)
Students with need: Need-based aid available for full-time and part-time students. Work study available nights, weekends, and for part-time students.
Students without need: No-need awards available for academics.
Scholarships offered: Academic Scholarship: $10,000-40,000 renewable conditionally. Spread over length of enrollment; based on high school GPA, ACT scores or transfer GPA.
Additional info: Freshmen and sophomores receive aid through University of Wisconsin-Green Bay while juniors and seniors receive aid through Bellin College. Admissions Scholarship program for new undergrad students. Possible awards ranging from $8,000-$1,200.

FINANCIAL AID PROCEDURES
Forms required: FAFSA.

Dates and Deadlines: Priority date 3/1; no closing date. Applicants notified on a rolling basis starting 4/1; must reply within 2 week(s) of notification.

Transfers: Priority date 3/1; no deadline. Applicants notified on a rolling basis starting 4/1; must reply within 2 week(s) of notification.

CONTACT
Lena Goodman, Director of Financial Aid
3201 Eaton Road, Green Bay, WI 54311
(920) 433-6638

Beloit College
Beloit, Wisconsin
www.beloit.edu   Federal Code: 003835

4-year private liberal arts college in large town.
Enrollment: 1,315 undergrads. 382 full-time freshmen.
Selectivity: Admits 50 to 75% of applicants.

BASIC COSTS (2016-2017)
Tuition and fees: $47,060.
Per-credit charge: $1,394.
Room and board: $8,146.

FINANCIAL AID PICTURE (2016-2017)
Students with need: 80% of average financial aid package awarded as scholarships/grants, 20% awarded as loans/jobs. Work study available nights, weekends, and for part-time students.
Students without need: No-need awards available for academics, leadership, minority status, music/drama.
Scholarships offered: Presidential Scholarships: $18,000-$25,000 per year; Eaton Scholarships: $10,000-$18,000 per year; The American Field Service/Rotary Overseas/Youth for Understanding/U.S Citizens Living Overseas: $5,000 per year; The Charles Winter Wood Scholarship for underrepresented students: Up to $40,000 per year; The Founders Scholarship for National Merit Finalists: $5,000 per year; Music scholarships: $5,000 per year.

FINANCIAL AID PROCEDURES
Forms required: FAFSA. PROFILE required for early decision/early action applicants only.
Dates and Deadlines: Priority date 3/1; closing date 3/1. Applicants notified on a rolling basis starting 3/1; must reply by 5/1.
Transfers: No deadline. Applicants notified on a rolling basis starting 4/1; must reply by 5/1 or within 2 week(s) of notification.

CONTACT
Victoria Gack, Assistant Director of Student Financial Services
700 College Street, Beloit, WI 53511-5595
(608) 363-2663

Blackhawk Technical College

Janesville, Wisconsin
www.blackhawk.edu   Federal Code: 005390

2-year public technical college in small city.
Enrollment: 2,034 undergrads, 60% part-time. 173 full-time freshmen.
Selectivity: Open admission; but selective for some programs.

BASIC COSTS (2016-2017)
Tuition and fees: $4,104; out-of-state residents $6,059.
Per-credit charge: $130; out-of-state residents $196.
Additional info: Material fees vary by program; minimum $4.50 per course.
$10 per credit fee for online courses.

FINANCIAL AID PICTURE
Students with need: Need-based aid available for full-time and part-time students. Work study available nights.

FINANCIAL AID PROCEDURES
Forms required: FAFSA.
Dates and Deadlines: Closing date 4/30. Applicants notified on a rolling basis starting 3/15.

CONTACT
Deena Wettstein, Director of Financial Aid
PO Box 5009, Janesville, WI 53547-5009
(608) 757-7664

Bryant & Stratton College: Milwaukee

Milwaukee, Wisconsin
www.bryantstratton.edu   Federal Code: 005009

2-year for-profit business and junior college in very large city.
Enrollment: 1,266 undergrads.

BASIC COSTS (2016-2017)
Tuition and fees: $17,190.
Per-credit charge: $573.
Additional info: Tuition and fees may vary by program.

FINANCIAL AID PICTURE
Students with need: Work study available nights.
Students without need: This college awards aid only to students with need.

FINANCIAL AID PROCEDURES
Forms required: FAFSA.
Dates and Deadlines: Closing date 9/22. Applicants notified on a rolling basis; must reply within 2 week(s) of notification.

CONTACT
Robert Hoffman, Financial Aid Manager
310 West Wisconsin Avenue, Suite 500, Milwaukee, WI 53203
(414) 276-5200

Cardinal Stritch University

Milwaukee, Wisconsin
www.stritch.edu   Federal Code: 003837

4-year private university in very large city, affiliated with the Roman Catholic Church.
Enrollment: 1,503 undergrads, 20% part-time. 154 full-time freshmen.
Selectivity: Admits over 75% of applicants.

BASIC COSTS (2016-2017)
Tuition and fees: $28,212.
Per-credit charge: $880.

Room and board: $7,940.

FINANCIAL AID PICTURE (2016-2017)
Students with need: Average financial aid package met 81% of need; average scholarship/grant was $22,013; average loan was $3,317. For part-time students, average financial aid package was $8,016.
Students without need: No-need awards available for academics, alumni affiliation, art, athletics, music/drama, religious affiliation.

FINANCIAL AID PROCEDURES
Forms required: FAFSA.
Dates and Deadlines: Priority date 3/15; no closing date. Applicants notified on a rolling basis starting 2/24; must reply within 2 week(s) of notification.

CONTACT
Mark Quistorf, Director of Financial Aid
6801 North Yates Road, Box 516, Milwaukee, WI 53217-7516
(414) 410-4048

Carroll University

Waukesha, Wisconsin
www.carrollu.edu   Federal Code: 003838

4-year private university and liberal arts college in small city, affiliated with the Presbyterian Church (USA).
Enrollment: 2,911 undergrads, 7% part-time. 667 full-time freshmen.
Selectivity: Admits 50 to 75% of applicants.

BASIC COSTS (2017-2018)
Tuition and fees: $31,144.
Per-credit charge: $390.
Room and board: $9,494.

FINANCIAL AID PICTURE (2016-2017)
Students with need: Out of 606 full-time freshmen who applied for aid, 539 were judged to have need. Of these, 539 received aid, and 180 had their full need met. Average financial aid package met 88% of need; average scholarship/grant was $20,001; average loan was $3,625. Need-based aid available for part-time students.
Students without need: 133 full-time freshmen who did not demonstrate need for aid received scholarships/grants; average award was $16,349. No-need awards available for academics, alumni affiliation, art, leadership, music/drama, ROTC.

FINANCIAL AID PROCEDURES
Forms required: FAFSA.
Dates and Deadlines: Applicants notified on a rolling basis starting 2/15; must reply by 5/1 or within 2 week(s) of notification.
Transfers: No deadline. Applicants notified on a rolling basis starting 2/15.

CONTACT
Dawn Scott, Director of Student Financial Services
100 North East Avenue, Waukesha, WI 53186-9988
(262) 524-7296

Carthage College

Kenosha, Wisconsin
www.carthage.edu   Federal Code: 003839

4-year private liberal arts college in small city, affiliated with the Evangelical Lutheran Church in America.
Enrollment: 2,818 undergrads, 6% part-time. 722 full-time freshmen.
Selectivity: Admits 50 to 75% of applicants.

BASIC COSTS (2017-2018)
Tuition and fees: $41,950.
Per-credit charge: $575.

Room and board: $11,600.
Additional info: Tuition/fee waivers available for minority students.

FINANCIAL AID PICTURE

Students with need: Need-based aid available for full-time and part-time students.

Students without need: No-need awards available for academics, alumni affiliation, art, leadership, minority status, music/drama, religious affiliation.

Scholarships offered: Presidential Scholarship Program: range from 75% tuition to full tuition; room and board; renewable; separate scholarship application; 35 awarded. Business Scholarship: three awarded; range from $27,000/year to full tuition; renewable; requires separate scholarship application; restricted to accounting, finance, management and marketing majors. Multicultural Scholarship: four awarded; full tuition; renewable; requires separate scholarship application. Math/Science Scholarship: three awarded; range from $27,000/year to full tuition; renewable; requires separate scholarship application; restricted to math and natural science majors. Modern Language Scholarship: eight awarded; $27,000/year; renewable; requires separate scholarship application; restricted to Chinese, French, German and Japanese majors. Fine Arts Scholarships: $500-$10,000/year; renewable; requires separate audition/portfolio; open to majors and non majors in music and theater and majors in studio art or graphic design. Tarble Scholarships: number awarded variable; up to $25,000 year; renewable; requires separate scholarship application; restricted to California residents.

FINANCIAL AID PROCEDURES

Forms required: FAFSA.
Dates and Deadlines: Priority date 2/15; no closing date. Applicants notified on a rolling basis starting 3/1.
Transfers: Priority date 2/15; no deadline. Applicants notified on a rolling basis starting 3/1.

CONTACT

Vatistas Vatistas, Director of Financial Aid
2001 Alford Park Drive, Kenosha, WI 53140-1994
(262) 551-6001

Chippewa Valley Technical College

Eau Claire, Wisconsin
www.cvtc.edu   Federal Code: 005304

2-year public technical college in small city.
Enrollment: 3,283 undergrads, 39% part-time. 611 full-time freshmen.
Selectivity: Open admission; but selective for some programs.

BASIC COSTS (2016-2017)

Tuition and fees: $4,172; out-of-state residents $6,127.
Per-credit charge: $130; out-of-state residents $196.
Additional info: Material fees vary by program; minimum $4.50 per course. $10 per credit fee for online courses.

FINANCIAL AID PICTURE

Students with need: Need-based aid available for full-time and part-time students. Work study available nights, weekends, and for part-time students.

FINANCIAL AID PROCEDURES

Forms required: FAFSA.
Dates and Deadlines: Priority date 3/15; no closing date. Applicants notified on a rolling basis starting 4/30; must reply within 2 week(s) of notification.

CONTACT

Barbara Cloutier, Financial Aid Manager
620 West Clairemont Avenue, Eau Claire, WI 54701-6162
(715) 833-6252

College of Menominee Nation

Keshena, Wisconsin
www.menominee.edu   Federal Code: 031251

2-year private community college in rural community.
Enrollment: 661 undergrads.
Selectivity: Open admission; but selective for some programs.

BASIC COSTS (2016-2017)

Tuition and fees: $7,600.

FINANCIAL AID PICTURE

Students with need: Need-based aid available for full-time and part-time students. Work study available nights.
Students without need: This college awards aid only to students with need.

FINANCIAL AID PROCEDURES

Forms required: FAFSA.
Dates and Deadlines: Priority date 4/15; no closing date. Applicants notified on a rolling basis.
Transfers: No deadline. Applicants notified on a rolling basis.

CONTACT

Nicole Fish, Financial Aid Director
N 172 State Highway 47/55, Keshena, WI 54135-1179
(715) 799-5600 ext. 3039

Columbia College of Nursing

Glendale, Wisconsin
www.ccon.edu   Federal Code: 041594

4-year private nursing college in very large city.
Enrollment: 142 undergrads, 20% part-time.

BASIC COSTS (2016-2017)

Tuition and fees: $28,116.
Per-credit charge: $1,126.

FINANCIAL AID PICTURE (2016-2017)

Students with need: Average financial aid package for all full-time undergraduates was $11,574; for part-time $10,841. 39% awarded as scholarships/grants, 61% awarded as loans/jobs.
Students without need: No-need awards available for academics.

FINANCIAL AID PROCEDURES

Forms required: FAFSA. CCON is an upper division school and all students are junior or senior level students and 100% of student body transfers in.
Dates and Deadlines: Priority date 3/15; no closing date. Applicants notified on a rolling basis starting 3/15; must reply by 6/1.
Transfers: No deadline. Applicants notified on a rolling basis starting 3/1; must reply by 6/1.

CONTACT

Wendy Hilvo, Financial Aid Director
4425 North Port Washington Road, Glendale, WI 53212-1099
(414) 326-2337

Concordia University Wisconsin

Mequon, Wisconsin
www.cuw.edu   Federal Code: 003842

4-year private university and liberal arts college in large town, affiliated with the Lutheran Church - Missouri Synod.
Enrollment: 3,551 undergrads, 25% part-time. 477 full-time freshmen.
Selectivity: Admits 50 to 75% of applicants.

BASIC COSTS (2016-2017)

Tuition and fees: $27,910.

Per-credit charge: $1,152.

Room and board: $10,280.

FINANCIAL AID PICTURE (2016-2017)

Students with need: Out of 454 full-time freshmen who applied for aid, 390 were judged to have need. Of these, 390 received aid, and 128 had their full need met. Average financial aid package met 80% of need; average scholarship/grant was $16,404; average loan was $7,197. For part-time students, average financial aid package was $6,127.

Students without need: 79 full-time freshmen who did not demonstrate need for aid received scholarships/grants; average award was $12,481. No-need awards available for academics, art, minority status, music/drama.

FINANCIAL AID PROCEDURES

Forms required: FAFSA.

Dates and Deadlines: Priority date 3/15; closing date 4/15. Applicants notified on a rolling basis starting 2/15; must reply within 3 week(s) of notification.

CONTACT

Steve Taylor, Director of Financial Aid

12800 North Lake Shore Drive, Mequon, WI 53097

(262) 243-4392

Edgewood College

Madison, Wisconsin

www.edgewood.edu   Federal Code: 003848

4-year private liberal arts college in small city, affiliated with the Roman Catholic Church.

Enrollment: 1,615 undergrads, 10% part-time. 303 full-time freshmen.

Selectivity: Admits over 75% of applicants.

BASIC COSTS (2016-2017)

Tuition and fees: $27,530.

Per-credit charge: $866.

Room and board: $9,870.

FINANCIAL AID PICTURE (2015-2016)

Students with need: Out of 274 full-time freshmen who applied for aid, 243 were judged to have need. Of these, 243 received aid, and 24 had their full need met. Average financial aid package met 79% of need; average scholarship/grant was $17,036; average loan was $3,993. For part-time students, average financial aid package was $7,292.

Students without need: 48 full-time freshmen who did not demonstrate need for aid received scholarships/grants; average award was $6,737. No-need awards available for academics, alumni affiliation, art, leadership, music/drama, religious affiliation.

Scholarships offered: Academic/Merit Scholarships range from $6,000-$13,000 per year and are based upon cumulative high school grade point average and ACT or SAT score. We also offer competitive scholarships for freshmen students which range from $500-full tuition per year.

FINANCIAL AID PROCEDURES

Forms required: FAFSA.

Dates and Deadlines: Priority date 3/1; no closing date. Applicants notified on a rolling basis starting 3/15; must reply by 5/1.

Transfers: No deadline. Applicants notified on a rolling basis starting 3/15; must reply by 5/1 or within 2 week(s) of notification. Our Academic/Merit Scholarships range from $2,000-$6,500 per year and are based upon a student's cumulative transfer grade point average. We also offer competitive scholarships for transfer students which range from $500-1/2 tuition per year.

CONTACT

Kari Gribble, Director of Edgewood Central and Financial Aid

1000 Edgewood College Drive, Madison, WI 53711-1997

(608) 663-4300

Fox Valley Technical College

Appleton, Wisconsin

www.fvtc.edu   Federal Code: 009744

2-year public technical college in small city.

Enrollment: 5,972 undergrads, 62% part-time. 350 full-time freshmen.

Selectivity: Open admission; but selective for some programs.

BASIC COSTS (2016-2017)

Tuition and fees: $3,911; out-of-state residents $5,866.

Per-credit charge: $130; out-of-state residents $196.

Additional info: Material fees vary by program; minimum $4.50 per course. $10 per credit fee for online courses.

FINANCIAL AID PICTURE (2015-2016)

Students with need: 45% of average financial aid package awarded as scholarships/grants, 55% awarded as loans/jobs. Need-based aid available for part-time students. Work study available weekends and for part-time students.

Students without need: This college awards aid only to students with need.

FINANCIAL AID PROCEDURES

Forms required: FAFSA.

Dates and Deadlines: Priority date 4/15; no closing date. Applicants notified on a rolling basis.

CONTACT

Stacy Doran, Director Student Financial Services

1825 North Bluemound Drive, Appleton, WI 54912-2277

(920) 735-5650

Gateway Technical College

Kenosha, Wisconsin

www.gtc.edu   Federal Code: 005389

2-year public technical college in small city.

Enrollment: 6,180 undergrads, 79% part-time. 369 full-time freshmen.

Selectivity: Open admission; but selective for some programs.

BASIC COSTS (2017-2018)

Tuition and fees: $3,989; out-of-state residents $5,983.

FINANCIAL AID PICTURE (2015-2016)

Students with need: Need-based aid available for full-time and part-time students.

Students without need: No-need awards available for state/district residency.

FINANCIAL AID PROCEDURES

Forms required: FAFSA, institutional form.

Dates and Deadlines: Priority date 7/1; no closing date. Applicants notified on a rolling basis starting 5/1; must reply within 2 week(s) of notification.

CONTACT

Justin Kehring, Director of Student Financial Aid

400 County Road H, Elkhorn, WI 53121

(262) 564-3072

Globe University: Appleton

Grand Chute, Wisconsin
www.globeuniversity.edu   Federal Code: 004642

2-year for-profit career college in small city.
Enrollment: 203 undergrads.
Selectivity: Open admission.

BASIC COSTS (2016-2017)
Additional info: Tuition varies by program. Per-credit-hour charges; $325-$550. Fees, books supplies range depending on program level and course of study. All costs are subject to change.

FINANCIAL AID PICTURE
Students with need: Need-based aid available for full-time and part-time students.

FINANCIAL AID PROCEDURES
Forms required: FAFSA, institutional form.
Dates and Deadlines: Applicants notified on a rolling basis starting 7/1; must reply within 2 week(s) of notification.

CONTACT
Jonathan Allen, Financial Aid Manager
5045 West Grande Market Drive, Grand Chute, WI 54913
(920) 364-1100

Globe University: Eau Claire

Eau Claire, Wisconsin
www.globeuniversity.edu   Federal Code: 004642

2-year for-profit career college in small city.
Enrollment: 153 undergrads.
Selectivity: Open admission.

BASIC COSTS (2016-2017)
Additional info: Tuition varies by program. Per-credit-hour charges; $325-$550. Fees, books supplies range depending on program level and course of study. All costs are subject to change.

FINANCIAL AID PICTURE
Students with need: Need-based aid available for full-time and part-time students.

FINANCIAL AID PROCEDURES
Forms required: FAFSA, institutional form.
Dates and Deadlines: Applicants notified on a rolling basis starting 7/1; must reply within 2 week(s) of notification.

CONTACT
Kenton Davis, Financial Aid Manager
4955 Bullis Farm Road, Eau Claire, WI 54701
(715) 855-6600

Globe University: Green Bay

Green Bay, Wisconsin
www.globeuniversity.edu   Federal Code: 004642

4-year for-profit university and career college in small city.
Enrollment: 185 undergrads.
Selectivity: Open admission.

BASIC COSTS (2016-2017)
Additional info: Tuition varies by program. Per-credit-hour charges; $325-$550. Fees, books supplies range depending on program level and course of study. All costs are subject to change.

FINANCIAL AID PICTURE
Students with need: Need-based aid available for full-time and part-time students.

FINANCIAL AID PROCEDURES
Forms required: FAFSA, institutional form.
Dates and Deadlines: Applicants notified on a rolling basis starting 7/1; must reply within 2 week(s) of notification.

CONTACT
Kristin Thyrion, Financial Aid Manager
2620 Development Drive, Green Bay, WI 54311
(920) 264-1600

Globe University: La Crosse

Onalaska, Wisconsin
www.globeuniversity.edu   Federal Code: 004642

2-year for-profit career college in large town.
Enrollment: 178 undergrads.
Selectivity: Open admission.

BASIC COSTS (2016-2017)
Additional info: Tuition varies by program. Per-credit-hour charges; $325-$550. Fees, books supplies range depending on program level and course of study. All costs are subject to change.

FINANCIAL AID PICTURE
Students with need: Need-based aid available for full-time and part-time students.

FINANCIAL AID PROCEDURES
Forms required: FAFSA, institutional form.
Dates and Deadlines: Applicants notified on a rolling basis starting 7/1; must reply within 2 week(s) of notification.

CONTACT
Michael Waters, Financial Aid Manager
2651 Midwest Drive, Onalaska, WI 54650
(608) 779-8600

Globe University: Madison East

Madison, Wisconsin
www.globeuniversity.edu   Federal Code: 004642

2-year for-profit career college in small city.
Enrollment: 217 undergrads.
Selectivity: Open admission.

BASIC COSTS (2016-2017)
Additional info: Tuition varies by program. Per-credit-hour charges; $325-$550. Fees, books supplies range depending on program level and course of study. All costs are subject to change.

FINANCIAL AID PICTURE
Students with need: Need-based aid available for full-time and part-time students.

FINANCIAL AID PROCEDURES
Forms required: FAFSA, institutional form.
Dates and Deadlines: Applicants notified on a rolling basis starting 7/1; must reply within 2 week(s) of notification.

CONTACT
Bill Vache, Director of Financial Aid
4901 Eastpark Boulevard, Madison, WI 53718
(608) 216-9400

Globe University: Middleton
Middleton, Wisconsin
www.globeuniversity.edu   Federal Code: 004642

2-year for-profit career college in large town.
Enrollment: 182 undergrads.
Selectivity: Open admission.

BASIC COSTS (2016-2017)
Additional info: Tuition varies by program. Per-credit-hour charges; $325-$550. Fees, books supplies range depending on program level and course of study. All costs are subject to change.

FINANCIAL AID PICTURE
Students with need: Need-based aid available for full-time and part-time students.

FINANCIAL AID PROCEDURES
Forms required: FAFSA, institutional form.
Dates and Deadlines: Applicants notified on a rolling basis starting 7/1; must reply within 2 week(s) of notification.

CONTACT
Brittanie Dempsey, Financial Aid Manager
1345 Deming Way, Middleton, WI 53562
(608) 830-6900

Globe University: Wausau
Rothschild, Wisconsin
www.globeuniversity.edu   Federal Code: 004642

2-year for-profit career college in small town.
Enrollment: 122 undergrads.
Selectivity: Open admission.

BASIC COSTS (2016-2017)
Additional info: Tuition varies by program. Per-credit-hour charges; $325-$550. Fees, books supplies range depending on program level and course of study. All costs are subject to change.

FINANCIAL AID PICTURE
Students with need: Need-based aid available for full-time and part-time students.

FINANCIAL AID PROCEDURES
Forms required: FAFSA, institutional form.
Dates and Deadlines: Applicants notified on a rolling basis starting 7/1; must reply within 2 week(s) of notification.

CONTACT
Cheng Heu, Financial Aid Manager
1480 Country Road XX, Rothschild, WI 54474
(715) 301-1300

Herzing University: Madison
Madison, Wisconsin
www.herzing.edu/madison   Federal Code: 009621

3-year for-profit business and career college in small city.
Enrollment: 1,045 undergrads.
Selectivity: Open admission; but selective for some programs.

BASIC COSTS (2016-2017)
Additional info: Diploma programs: $12,560. Associate programs: $12,560-$17,500. Bachelor's programs: $12,560-$13,000. All costs are subject to change.

FINANCIAL AID PICTURE
Students with need: Need-based aid available for full-time and part-time students.

FINANCIAL AID PROCEDURES
Forms required: FAFSA, institutional form.
Dates and Deadlines: Applicants notified on a rolling basis.

CONTACT
Beverly Faga, Director of Financial Services
5218 East Terrace Drive, Madison, WI 53718
(608) 249-6611

Lac Courte Oreilles Ojibwa Community College
Hayward, Wisconsin
www.lco.edu   Federal Code: 017199

2-year public community college in small town.
Enrollment: 245 undergrads, 58% part-time. 27 full-time freshmen.
Selectivity: Open admission.

BASIC COSTS (2016-2017)
Tuition and fees: $5,700.
Per-credit charge: $190.

FINANCIAL AID PICTURE
Students with need: Need-based aid available for full-time students.
Students without need: This college awards aid only to students with need.

FINANCIAL AID PROCEDURES
Forms required: FAFSA.
Dates and Deadlines: Applicants notified on a rolling basis.

CONTACT
Kelly Quaderer, Financial Aid Director
13466 West Trepania Road, Hayward, WI 54843

Lakeland University
Sheboygan, Wisconsin
www.lakeland.edu   Federal Code: 003854

4-year private liberal arts college in small city, affiliated with the United Church of Christ.
Enrollment: 1,977 undergrads.
Selectivity: Admits 50 to 75% of applicants.

BASIC COSTS (2016-2017)
Tuition and fees: $26,560.
Room and board: $8,620.

FINANCIAL AID PICTURE
Students with need: Need-based aid available for full-time and part-time students. Work study available nights, weekends, and for part-time students.
Students without need: No-need awards available for academics, alumni affiliation, art, religious affiliation.
Scholarships offered: Trustees' Scholarship: $11,000; minimum GPA of 3.5 and minimum ACT of 24. Presidential Scholarship: $8,000; 3.25-3.49 GPA and 21 or greater ACT. Dean's Scholarship: $7,000; 3.0-3.24 GPA and 21 or greater ACT. Faculty Scholarship: $6,000; 2.75-2.99 GPA and 19 or greater ACT.

FINANCIAL AID PROCEDURES
Forms required: FAFSA, institutional form.
Dates and Deadlines: Priority date 3/15; no closing date. Applicants notified on a rolling basis starting 2/15; must reply within 2 week(s) of notification.

CONTACT
Patty Taylor, Director of Financial Aid
Box 359, Sheboygan, WI 53082-0359
(920) 565-1032 ext. 2371

Lakeshore Technical College
Cleveland, Wisconsin
www.gotoltc.edu   Federal Code: 009194

2-year public technical college in rural community.
Enrollment: 2,138 undergrads.
Selectivity: Open admission; but selective for some programs.

BASIC COSTS (2016-2017)
Tuition and fees: $3,911; out-of-state residents $5,866.
Per-credit charge: $130; out-of-state residents $196.
Additional info: Material fees vary by program; minimum $4.50 per course.
$10 per credit fee for online courses.

FINANCIAL AID PICTURE
Students with need: Need-based aid available for full-time and part-time students. Work study available nights.
Students without need: This college awards aid only to students with need.

FINANCIAL AID PROCEDURES
Forms required: FAFSA, institutional form.
Dates and Deadlines: Priority date 6/1; no closing date. Applicants notified on a rolling basis starting 6/1; must reply within 3 week(s) of notification.

CONTACT
Jessica Hemenway, Financial Aid Manager
1290 North Avenue, Cleveland, WI 53015-9761
(920) 693-1118

Lawrence University
Appleton, Wisconsin
www.lawrence.edu   Federal Code: 003856
                                   CSS Code: 1398

4-year private music and liberal arts college in small city.
Enrollment: 1,507 undergrads, 1% part-time. 374 full-time freshmen.
Selectivity: Admits 50 to 75% of applicants.

BASIC COSTS (2016-2017)
Tuition and fees: $44,844.
Room and board: $9,654.
Additional info: Tuition/fee waivers available for minority students.

FINANCIAL AID PICTURE (2016-2017)
Students with need: Out of 301 full-time freshmen who applied for aid, 244 were judged to have need. Of these, 244 received aid, and 135 had their full need met. Average financial aid package met 95% of need; average scholarship/grant was $33,637; average loan was $5,023. For part-time students, average financial aid package was $31,584.
Students without need: 124 full-time freshmen who did not demonstrate need for aid received scholarships/grants; average award was $22,716. No-need awards available for academics, alumni affiliation, minority status, music/drama.
Scholarships offered: Scholarships range from $5,000 to $23,000 per year.

FINANCIAL AID PROCEDURES
Forms required: FAFSA. CSS PROFILE required for applicants seeking institutionally-funded need-based aid.
Dates and Deadlines: Priority date 2/1; no closing date. Applicants notified on a rolling basis starting 2/5; must reply by 5/1.
Transfers: Priority date 4/1; no deadline. Applicants notified on a rolling basis starting 5/1.

CONTACT
Ken Anselment, Dean of Admissions and Financial Aid
711 East Boldt Way SPC 29, Appleton, WI 54911-5699
(920) 832-6583

Maranatha Baptist University
Watertown, Wisconsin
www.mbu.edu   Federal Code: 016394

4-year private Bible and liberal arts college in large town, affiliated with the Baptist faith.
Enrollment: 764 undergrads, 12% part-time. 132 full-time freshmen.
Selectivity: Admits 50 to 75% of applicants.

BASIC COSTS (2016-2017)
Tuition and fees: $14,260.
Per-credit charge: $546.
Room and board: $6,720.

FINANCIAL AID PICTURE (2015-2016)
Students with need: Out of 125 full-time freshmen who applied for aid, 118 were judged to have need. Of these, 118 received aid, and 13 had their full need met. Average financial aid package met 51% of need; average scholarship/grant was $7,232; average loan was $3,205. For part-time students, average financial aid package was $6,411.
Students without need: 13 full-time freshmen who did not demonstrate need for aid received scholarships/grants; average award was $3,961. No-need awards available for academics, alumni affiliation, religious affiliation.

FINANCIAL AID PROCEDURES
Forms required: FAFSA.
Dates and Deadlines: Applicants notified on a rolling basis starting 1/1.
Transfers: Financial aid transcript or equivalent required.

CONTACT
Randy Hibbs, Financial Aid Director
745 West Main Street, Watertown, WI 53094
(920) 206-2318

Marian University
Fond du Lac, Wisconsin
www.marianuniversity.edu   Federal Code: 003861

4-year private university and liberal arts college in large town, affiliated with the Roman Catholic Church.
Enrollment: 1,475 undergrads, 20% part-time. 282 full-time freshmen.
Selectivity: Admits over 75% of applicants.

BASIC COSTS (2016-2017)
Tuition and fees: $28,380.
Per-credit charge: $450.
Room and board: $7,000.

FINANCIAL AID PICTURE (2015-2016)
Students with need: Out of 280 full-time freshmen who applied for aid, 260 were judged to have need. Of these, 260 received aid, and 21 had their full need met. Average financial aid package met 64% of need; average scholarship/grant was $15,501; average loan was $2,712. For part-time students, average financial aid package was $4,624.
Students without need: 20 full-time freshmen who did not demonstrate need for aid received scholarships/grants; average award was $11,837. No-need awards available for academics, state/district residency.
Scholarships offered: Academic Achievement Award: $7,500; based on 3.5 GPA, 25 ACT, top 15% of class; 7 awarded. Presidential Scholarship: $5,000; based on 3.1 GPA, top 20% of class. Naber Leadership Scholarship: $3,000; based on 2.5 GPA, top 50% of class.

FINANCIAL AID PROCEDURES

Forms required: FAFSA, institutional form.

Dates and Deadlines: Priority date 3/1; no closing date. Applicants notified on a rolling basis starting 3/1; must reply within 4 week(s) of notification.

Transfers: No deadline. Applicants notified on a rolling basis; must reply within 4 week(s) of notification.

CONTACT

John Smith, Interim Director of Financial Aid

45 South National Avenue, Fond du Lac, WI 54935-4699

(920) 923-7614

Marquette University
Milwaukee, Wisconsin
www.marquette.edu   Federal Code: 003863

4-year private university in very large city, affiliated with the Roman Catholic Church.

Enrollment: 8,053 undergrads, 2% part-time. 2,002 full-time freshmen.

Selectivity: Admits over 75% of applicants.

BASIC COSTS (2016-2017)

Tuition and fees: $38,470.

Per-credit charge: $995.

Room and board: $11,440.

FINANCIAL AID PICTURE (2016-2017)

Students with need: Out of 1,647 full-time freshmen who applied for aid, 1,241 were judged to have need. Of these, 1,241 received aid, and 332 had their full need met. Average financial aid package met 82% of need; average scholarship/grant was $23,771; average loan was $5,249. For part-time students, average financial aid package was $10,123.

Students without need: 735 full-time freshmen who did not demonstrate need for aid received scholarships/grants; average award was $14,756. No-need awards available for academics, athletics, leadership, music/drama, ROTC.

Scholarships offered: 40 full-time freshmen received athletic scholarships; average amount $27,234.

FINANCIAL AID PROCEDURES

Forms required: FAFSA.

Dates and Deadlines: Applicants notified on a rolling basis starting 3/3.

Transfers: No deadline. Applicants notified on a rolling basis starting 3/15; must reply by 5/1 or within 3 week(s) of notification. Transfer scholarships available.

CONTACT

Susan Teerink, Director of Student Financial Aid

PO Box 1881, Milwaukee, WI 53201-1881

(414) 288-0200

Mid-State Technical College
Wisconsin Rapids, Wisconsin
www.mstc.edu   Federal Code: 005380

2-year public technical college in large town.

Enrollment: 3,100 undergrads.

Selectivity: Open admission; but selective for some programs.

BASIC COSTS (2016-2017)

Tuition and fees: $3,911; out-of-state residents $5,866.

Per-credit charge: $130; out-of-state residents $196.

Additional info: Material fees vary by program; minimum $4.50 per course. $10 per credit fee for online courses.

FINANCIAL AID PICTURE

Students with need: Need-based aid available for full-time and part-time students. Work study available nights, weekends, and for part-time students.

Students without need: No-need awards available for academics, leadership.

FINANCIAL AID PROCEDURES

Forms required: FAFSA.

Dates and Deadlines: Priority date 4/15; no closing date. Applicants notified on a rolling basis starting 5/30; must reply within 2 week(s) of notification.

Transfers: No deadline.

CONTACT

Mary Jo Green, Financial Aid Supervisor

500 32nd Street North, Wisconsin Rapids, WI 54494

(715) 422-5501

Milwaukee Area Technical College
Milwaukee, Wisconsin
www.matc.edu   Federal Code: 003866

2-year public junior and technical college in very large city.

Enrollment: 13,403 undergrads, 66% part-time. 1,030 full-time freshmen.

Selectivity: Open admission; but selective for some programs.

BASIC COSTS (2016-2017)

Tuition and fees: $4,418; out-of-state residents $6,373.

Per-credit charge: $130; out-of-state residents $196.

Additional info: Material fees vary by program; minimum $4.50 per course. $10 per credit fee for online courses. Tuition/fee waivers available for minority students.

FINANCIAL AID PICTURE

Students with need: Need-based aid available for full-time and part-time students.

Students without need: No-need awards available for academics.

FINANCIAL AID PROCEDURES

Forms required: FAFSA.

Dates and Deadlines: Priority date 3/15; no closing date. Applicants notified on a rolling basis starting 4/15.

Transfers: No deadline. Applicants notified on a rolling basis starting 4/15.

CONTACT

Camille Nicolai, Director of Financial Aid

700 West State Street, Milwaukee, WI 53233-1443

(414) 297-8875

Milwaukee Institute of Art & Design
Milwaukee, Wisconsin
www.miad.edu   Federal Code: 014203

4-year private visual arts college in very large city.

Enrollment: 628 undergrads, 2% part-time. 182 full-time freshmen.

Selectivity: Admits 50 to 75% of applicants.

BASIC COSTS (2016-2017)

Tuition and fees: $34,920.

Per-credit charge: $1,122.

Room and board: $9,100.

FINANCIAL AID PICTURE (2015-2016)

Students with need: Out of 173 full-time freshmen who applied for aid, 160 were judged to have need. Of these, 160 received aid, and 17 had their full need met. Average financial aid package met 66% of need; average loan was $4,793. For part-time students, average financial aid package was $10,717.

Students without need: 22 full-time freshmen who did not demonstrate need for aid received scholarships/grants; average award was $12,068. No-need awards available for academics, art.

Scholarships offered: Merit scholarships are awarded to students based on submitted portfolio of work.

FINANCIAL AID PROCEDURES

Forms required: FAFSA.

Dates and Deadlines: Priority date 2/15; no closing date. Applicants notified on a rolling basis starting 3/1; must reply by 5/1 or within 2 week(s) of notification.

Transfers: No deadline. Applicants notified on a rolling basis starting 4/1; must reply by 5/1 or within 2 week(s) of notification.

CONTACT

Carol Masse, Executive Director of Financial Aid
273 East Erie Street, Milwaukee, WI 53202
(414) 847-3270

Milwaukee School of Engineering
Milwaukee, Wisconsin
www.msoe.edu   Federal Code: 003868

4-year private university in very large city.
Enrollment: 2,675 undergrads, 4% part-time. 494 full-time freshmen.
Selectivity: Admits 50 to 75% of applicants.

BASIC COSTS (2017-2018)

Tuition and fees: $39,429.
Per-credit charge: $655.
Room and board: $9,102.
Additional info: Tuition/fee waivers available for minority students.

FINANCIAL AID PICTURE (2015-2016)

Students with need: Out of 475 full-time freshmen who applied for aid, 422 were judged to have need. Of these, 422 received aid, and 105 had their full need met. Average financial aid package met 82% of need; average scholarship/grant was $25,627; average loan was $3,129. For part-time students, average financial aid package was $7,345.

Students without need: 90 full-time freshmen who did not demonstrate need for aid received scholarships/grants; average award was $12,435. No-need awards available for academics, alumni affiliation, ROTC, state/district residency.

Scholarships offered: Presidential Scholarship: full tuition; awarded to students with high academic standing; 8 awarded.

FINANCIAL AID PROCEDURES

Forms required: FAFSA.

Dates and Deadlines: Priority date 3/15; no closing date. Applicants notified on a rolling basis starting 3/1; must reply within 2 week(s) of notification.

Transfers: Applicants notified on a rolling basis.

CONTACT

Steven Midthun, Director, Financial Aid
1025 North Broadway, Milwaukee, WI 53202-3109
(414) 277-7223

Moraine Park Technical College
Fond du Lac, Wisconsin
www.morainepark.edu   Federal Code: 005303

2-year public technical college in large town.
Enrollment: 3,143 undergrads.
Selectivity: Open admission; but selective for some programs.

BASIC COSTS (2016-2017)

Tuition and fees: $3,911; out-of-state residents $5,866.
Per-credit charge: $130; out-of-state residents $196.
Additional info: Material fees vary by program; minimum $4.50 per course. $10 per credit fee for online courses.

FINANCIAL AID PICTURE

Students with need: Need-based aid available for full-time and part-time students. Work study available nights.

Students without need: No-need awards available for academics, job skills, leadership, minority status, state/district residency.

FINANCIAL AID PROCEDURES

Forms required: FAFSA, institutional form.

Dates and Deadlines: Priority date 5/1; no closing date. Applicants notified on a rolling basis starting 5/15; must reply within 2 week(s) of notification.

Transfers: Priority date 4/15; no deadline. Applicants notified on a rolling basis starting 5/15.

CONTACT

Julie Waldvogel, Financial Aid Associate
235 North National Avenue, Fond du Lac, WI 54935-1940

Mount Mary University
Milwaukee, Wisconsin
www.mtmary.edu   Federal Code: 003869

4-year private university and liberal arts college for women in very large city, affiliated with the Roman Catholic Church.
Enrollment: 789 undergrads, 10% part-time. 147 full-time freshmen.
Selectivity: Admits 50 to 75% of applicants.

BASIC COSTS (2017-2018)

Tuition and fees: $29,510.
Per-credit charge: $860.
Room and board: $8,530.

FINANCIAL AID PICTURE (2015-2016)

Students with need: Out of 141 full-time freshmen who applied for aid, 133 were judged to have need. Of these, 133 received aid, and 10 had their full need met. Average financial aid package met 79% of need; average scholarship/grant was $24,145; average loan was $3,373. For part-time students, average financial aid package was $8,200.

Students without need: 14 full-time freshmen who did not demonstrate need for aid received scholarships/grants; average award was $13,973. No-need awards available for academics, alumni affiliation, art, leadership, music/drama.

FINANCIAL AID PROCEDURES

Forms required: FAFSA.

Dates and Deadlines: Priority date 12/1; no closing date. Applicants notified on a rolling basis starting 12/1; must reply within 2 week(s) of notification.

Transfers: Must reply within 2 week(s) of notification.

CONTACT

Debra Duff, Director of Financial Aid
2900 North Menomonee River Parkway, Milwaukee, WI 53222-4597
(414) 930-3044

Nicolet Area Technical College
Rhinelander, Wisconsin
www.nicoletcollege.edu   Federal Code: 008919

2-year public community and technical college in small town.
Enrollment: 921 undergrads, 64% part-time. 163 full-time freshmen.
Selectivity: Open admission; but selective for some programs.

BASIC COSTS (2016-2017)

Tuition and fees: $3,911; out-of-state residents $5,866.

Per-credit charge: $130; out-of-state residents $196.

Additional info: Material fees vary by program; minimum $4.50 per course. $10 per credit fee for online courses.

FINANCIAL AID PICTURE (2015-2016)

Students with need: Out of 142 full-time freshmen who applied for aid, 118 were judged to have need. Of these, 117 received aid, and 13 had their full need met. Average financial aid package met 93% of need; average scholarship/grant was $485; average loan was $3,565. For part-time students, average financial aid package was $4,729.

Students without need: 3 full-time freshmen who did not demonstrate need for aid received scholarships/grants; average award was $1,125. No-need awards available for academics, state/district residency.

FINANCIAL AID PROCEDURES

Forms required: FAFSA.

Dates and Deadlines: Priority date 4/15; no closing date. Applicants notified on a rolling basis starting 5/1; must reply within 2 week(s) of notification.

Transfers: No deadline. Applicants notified on a rolling basis starting 5/1; must reply within 2 week(s) of notification.

CONTACT

Jill Price, Director of Financial Aid

Box 518, Rhinelander, WI 54501

(715) 365-4423

Northcentral Technical College

Wausau, Wisconsin

www.ntc.edu   Federal Code: 005387

2-year public community and technical college in small city.

Enrollment: 3,449 undergrads, 60% part-time. 373 full-time freshmen.

Selectivity: Open admission; but selective for some programs.

BASIC COSTS (2016-2017)

Tuition and fees: $3,911; out-of-state residents $5,866.

Per-credit charge: $130; out-of-state residents $196.

Additional info: Material fees vary by program; minimum $4.50 per course. $10 per credit fee for online courses.

FINANCIAL AID PICTURE (2015-2016)

Students with need: Out of 370 full-time freshmen who applied for aid, 264 were judged to have need. Of these, 264 received aid, and 264 had their full need met. Average financial aid package met 100% of need; average scholarship/grant was $4,559; average loan was $2,774. Need-based aid available for part-time students.

Students without need: 67 full-time freshmen who did not demonstrate need for aid received scholarships/grants; average award was $840.

FINANCIAL AID PROCEDURES

Forms required: FAFSA.

Dates and Deadlines: Applicants notified on a rolling basis.

Transfers: No deadline.

CONTACT

Jeff Cichon, Director of Financial Aid

1000 West Campus Drive, Wausau, WI 54401

(715) 675-3331 ext. 5862

Northeast Wisconsin Technical College

Green Bay, Wisconsin

www.nwtc.edu   Federal Code: 005301

2-year public community and technical college in small city.

Enrollment: 8,526 undergrads.

Selectivity: Open admission; but selective for some programs.

BASIC COSTS (2016-2017)

Tuition and fees: $3,911; out-of-state residents $5,866.

Per-credit charge: $130; out-of-state residents $196.

Additional info: Material fees vary by program; minimum $4.50 per course. $10 per credit fee for online courses.

FINANCIAL AID PICTURE

Students with need: Need-based aid available for full-time and part-time students. Work study available nights, weekends, and for part-time students.

FINANCIAL AID PROCEDURES

Forms required: FAFSA.

Dates and Deadlines: Priority date 4/15; no closing date. Applicants notified on a rolling basis starting 6/1; must reply within 2 week(s) of notification.

Transfers: No deadline. Applicants notified on a rolling basis starting 6/1; must reply within 2 week(s) of notification.

CONTACT

Emily Ysebaert, Financial Aid Director

2740 West Mason Street, Green Bay, WI 54307-9042

(920) 498-5444

Northland College

Ashland, Wisconsin

www.northland.edu   Federal Code: 003875

4-year private liberal arts college in small town, affiliated with the United Church of Christ.

Enrollment: 562 undergrads, 1% part-time. 168 full-time freshmen.

Selectivity: Admits 50 to 75% of applicants.

BASIC COSTS (2017-2018)

Tuition and fees: $35,157.

Per-credit charge: $650.

Room and board: $8,886.

FINANCIAL AID PICTURE (2016-2017)

Students with need: Out of 164 full-time freshmen who applied for aid, 147 were judged to have need. Of these, 147 received aid, and 28 had their full need met. Average financial aid package met 85% of need; average scholarship/grant was $24,697; average loan was $3,831. For part-time students, average financial aid package was $11,952.

Students without need: 21 full-time freshmen who did not demonstrate need for aid received scholarships/grants; average award was $19,541. No-need awards available for academics, alumni affiliation, art, job skills, leadership, minority status, music/drama, religious affiliation, state/district residency.

FINANCIAL AID PROCEDURES

Forms required: FAFSA.

Dates and Deadlines: Priority date 3/15; no closing date. Applicants notified on a rolling basis starting 3/1; must reply by 5/1 or within 4 week(s) of notification.

Transfers: No deadline.

CONTACT

Kelly Dunn, Director of Financial Aid

1411 Ellis Avenue, Ashland, WI 54806-3999

(715) 682-1255

Rasmussen College: Appleton

Appleton, Wisconsin

www.rasmussen.edu

4-year for-profit branch campus and career college in small city.

Enrollment: 149 undergrads, 87% part-time. 19 full-time freshmen.

Selectivity: Open admission; but selective for some programs.

BASIC COSTS (2016-2017)
Tuition and fees: $13,455.
Per-credit charge: $299.
Additional info: Full-time tuition varies according to program of study. Required course materials fee of $150 per course.

FINANCIAL AID PICTURE
Students with need: Need-based aid available for full-time and part-time students.

FINANCIAL AID PROCEDURES
Forms required: FAFSA, institutional form.
Dates and Deadlines: Applicants notified on a rolling basis.

CONTACT
Debora Murray, Director of Financial Aid
3500 East Destination Drive, Appleton, WI 54915

Rasmussen College: Green Bay
Green Bay, Wisconsin
www.rasmussen.edu

2-year for-profit career college in small city.
Enrollment: 447 undergrads, 47% part-time. 16 full-time freshmen.
Selectivity: Open admission; but selective for some programs.

BASIC COSTS (2016-2017)
Tuition and fees: $13,455.
Per-credit charge: $299.
Additional info: Full-time tuition varies according to program of study. Required course materials fee of $150 per course.

FINANCIAL AID PICTURE
Students with need: Need-based aid available for full-time and part-time students.

FINANCIAL AID PROCEDURES
Forms required: FAFSA, institutional form.
Dates and Deadlines: Applicants notified on a rolling basis.

CONTACT
Debora Murray, Financial Aid Director
904 South Taylor Street, Suite 100, Green Bay, WI 54303-2349

Rasmussen College: Wausau
Wausau, Wisconsin
www.rasmussen.edu

2-year for-profit career college in large town.
Enrollment: 252 undergrads, 37% part-time. 13 full-time freshmen.
Selectivity: Open admission; but selective for some programs.

BASIC COSTS (2016-2017)
Tuition and fees: $13,455.
Per-credit charge: $299.
Additional info: Full-time tuition varies according to program of study. Required course materials fee of $150 per course.

FINANCIAL AID PICTURE
Students with need: Need-based aid available for full-time and part-time students.

FINANCIAL AID PROCEDURES
Forms required: FAFSA, institutional form.
Dates and Deadlines: Applicants notified on a rolling basis.

CONTACT
Debora Murray, Director of Financial Aid
1101 Westwood Drive, Wausau, WI 54401

Ripon College
Ripon, Wisconsin
www.ripon.edu   Federal Code: 003884

4-year private liberal arts college in small town.
Enrollment: 778 undergrads. 209 full-time freshmen.
Selectivity: Admits 50 to 75% of applicants.

BASIC COSTS (2017-2018)
Tuition and fees: $41,835.
Per-credit charge: $1,300.
Room and board: $8,156.

FINANCIAL AID PICTURE (2016-2017)
Students with need: Out of 195 full-time freshmen who applied for aid, 179 were judged to have need. Of these, 179 received aid, and 58 had their full need met. Average financial aid package met 88% of need; average scholarship/grant was $28,884; average loan was $4,699. Need-based aid available for part-time students.
Students without need: 27 full-time freshmen who did not demonstrate need for aid received scholarships/grants; average award was $20,832. No-need awards available for academics, alumni affiliation, art, leadership, minority status, music/drama, religious affiliation, ROTC, state/district residency.
Scholarships offered: Pickard Scholarship Competition: $22,000-$30,000 per year; based on 3.8 GPA, 28 ACT/1260 SAT; invitation only. Knop Scholars Program: full-tuition; for natural science or math major; based on 3.8 GPA, top 5% of class, interview; invitation only; one awarded. Rolling Academic Scholarships: $14,000 to $18,000 per year; consideration given to students who have academic and/or leadership achievements in their schools and communities. Army ROTC Scholarships: up to $5,000 per year. Diversity Scholarships: $20,000. Communication Consortium Scholarships: $20,000; interview required. Art Scholarships: $20,000 maximum award; portfolio required. Theater Scholarships: up to $20,000; interview required. Music Scholarships: $20,000; audition required. Evans Achievement Awards: $10,000 per year; not available to academic scholarship recipients. Boy/Girl State Scholarships: up to $16,000. Legacy Awards: $8,000. United Church of Christ Scholarships: $8,000; application required. Alumni Award; $8,000; recommendation letter from alumnus required.

FINANCIAL AID PROCEDURES
Forms required: FAFSA.
Dates and Deadlines: Priority date 3/1; closing date 6/15. Applicants notified on a rolling basis starting 3/1; must reply within 2 week(s) of notification.
Transfers: Priority date 3/1; no deadline. Applicants notified on a rolling basis starting 3/1; must reply within 2 week(s) of notification.

CONTACT
David Woodward, Director of Financial Aid
300 West Seward Street, Ripon, WI 54971-0248
(920) 748-8301

St. Norbert College
De Pere, Wisconsin
www.snc.edu   Federal Code: 003892

4-year private liberal arts college in large town, affiliated with the Roman Catholic Church.
Enrollment: 2,064 undergrads, 1% part-time. 601 full-time freshmen.
Selectivity: Admits over 75% of applicants.

BASIC COSTS (2017-2018)

Tuition and fees: $36,593.

Per-credit charge: $1,121.

Room and board: $9,467.

FINANCIAL AID PICTURE (2015-2016)

Students with need: Out of 537 full-time freshmen who applied for aid, 463 were judged to have need. Of these, 463 received aid, and 101 had their full need met. Average financial aid package met 82% of need; average scholarship/grant was $20,925; average loan was $4,005. For part-time students, average financial aid package was $7,414.

Students without need: 108 full-time freshmen who did not demonstrate need for aid received scholarships/grants; average award was $14,163. No-need awards available for academics, art, leadership, minority status, music/drama, ROTC, state/district residency.

FINANCIAL AID PROCEDURES

Forms required: FAFSA.

Dates and Deadlines: Priority date 1/1; no closing date. Applicants notified on a rolling basis starting 1/1; must reply within 2 week(s) of notification.

CONTACT

Jessica Rafeld, Director of Financial Aid

100 Grant Street, De Pere, WI 54115-2099

(888) 786-6721

Silver Lake College of the Holy Family

Manitowoc, Wisconsin

www.sl.edu   Federal Code: 003850

4-year private liberal arts college in large town, affiliated with the Roman Catholic Church.

Enrollment: 262 undergrads. 61 full-time freshmen.

Selectivity: Admits 50 to 75% of applicants.

BASIC COSTS (2016-2017)

Tuition and fees: $14,650.

Room and board: $12,760.

FINANCIAL AID PICTURE (2015-2016)

Students with need: Out of 53 full-time freshmen who applied for aid, 53 were judged to have need. Of these, 53 received aid, and 5 had their full need met. Need-based aid available for part-time students.

Students without need: 1 full-time freshmen who did not demonstrate need for aid received scholarships/grants; average award was $9,000. No-need awards available for academics, athletics, music/drama, state/district residency.

FINANCIAL AID PROCEDURES

Forms required: FAFSA.

Dates and Deadlines: Priority date 5/1; no closing date. Applicants notified on a rolling basis starting 12/1.

Transfers: No deadline. Applicants notified on a rolling basis starting 12/1. Institutional scholarship and grant assistance available to transfer students.

CONTACT

Erica Ploeckelman, Director of Student Financial Aid

2406 South Alverno Road, Manitowoc, WI 54220

(920) 686-6175

Southwest Wisconsin Technical College

Fennimore, Wisconsin

www.swtc.edu   Federal Code: 007699

2-year public technical college in rural community.

Enrollment: 1,430 undergrads, 47% part-time.

Selectivity: Open admission; but selective for some programs.

BASIC COSTS (2016-2017)

Tuition and fees: $3,911; out-of-state residents $5,866.

Per-credit charge: $130; out-of-state residents $196.

Additional info: Material fees vary by program; minimum $4.50 per course. $10 per credit fee for online courses.

FINANCIAL AID PICTURE

Students with need: Work study available nights.

FINANCIAL AID PROCEDURES

Forms required: FAFSA, institutional form.

Dates and Deadlines: Priority date 4/15; no closing date. Applicants notified on a rolling basis starting 5/15; must reply within 4 week(s) of notification.

CONTACT

Joy Kite, Director of Financial Aid

1800 Bronson Boulevard, Fennimore, WI 53809

(608) 822-2319

University of Wisconsin-Baraboo/Sauk County

Baraboo, Wisconsin

www.baraboo.uwc.edu   Federal Code: 003897

2-year public branch campus and liberal arts college in large town.

Enrollment: 600 undergrads.

BASIC COSTS (2016-2017)

Tuition and fees: $5,282; out-of-state residents $12,266.

Per-credit charge: $197.93; out-of-state residents $488.92.

FINANCIAL AID PICTURE

Students with need: Need-based aid available for full-time and part-time students. Work study available nights.

Students without need: This college awards aid only to students with need.

Scholarships offered: Campus scholarships: $250 to full tuition.

FINANCIAL AID PROCEDURES

Forms required: FAFSA, institutional form.

Dates and Deadlines: Priority date 4/15; no closing date. Applicants notified on a rolling basis starting 4/15; must reply within 3 week(s) of notification.

Transfers: Must reply within 3 week(s) of notification.

CONTACT

Marilyn Krump, Director of Student Financial Aid

1006 Connie Road, Baraboo, WI 53913-1098

(608) 263-7727

University of Wisconsin-Barron County

Rice Lake, Wisconsin

www.barron.uwc.edu   Federal Code: 003897

2-year public branch campus and junior college in small town.

Enrollment: 422 undergrads.

BASIC COSTS (2016-2017)

Tuition and fees: $5,264; out-of-state residents $12,248.

Per-credit charge: $197.11; out-of-state residents $488.92.

FINANCIAL AID PICTURE

Students with need: Need-based aid available for full-time and part-time students.

FINANCIAL AID PROCEDURES

Forms required: FAFSA.

Dates and Deadlines: Priority date 4/15; no closing date. Applicants notified on a rolling basis starting 6/1.

CONTACT
William Trippett, Director of Student Financial Aid
1800 College Drive, Rice Lake, WI 54868

University of Wisconsin-Eau Claire
Eau Claire, Wisconsin
www.uwec.edu   Federal Code: 003917

4-year public university in small city.
Enrollment: 9,798 undergrads, 6% part-time. 2,226 full-time freshmen.
Selectivity: Admits over 75% of applicants.

BASIC COSTS (2016-2017)
Tuition and fees: $8,813; out-of-state residents $16,386.
Per-credit charge: $307; out-of-state residents $622.
Room and board: $6,984.

FINANCIAL AID PICTURE (2015-2016)
Students with need: Out of 1,909 full-time freshmen who applied for aid, 1,214 were judged to have need. Of these, 1,197 received aid, and 249 had their full need met. Average financial aid package met 85% of need; average scholarship/grant was $5,786; average loan was $3,942. For part-time students, average financial aid package was $6,201.
Students without need: 158 full-time freshmen who did not demonstrate need for aid received scholarships/grants; average award was $1,804. No-need awards available for academics, art, leadership, minority status, music/drama, state/district residency.
Scholarships offered: Wisconsin Academic Excellence Scholars: $2,250; selected H.S. valedictorians; renewable; selected by high school National Merit Scholarship finalists; to $5,000. To be eligible for most of the following awards, an incoming freshmen needs to have at least a 25 ACT and be in the top 25% of class: Centennial Scholarship: $5,000; 25 awards. Mark of Excellence Award: $2,000. Diversity Scholar: up to $6,000 a year for 4 years; 4 awards. Diversity Achievement: up to $2,000; 15 awards. Blugold Fellowship: $1,500 scholarship and $1,2000 research stipend; renewable; 20 awards. Freshman Honor Scholarship: invited to the University Honors Program; $1,000; approximately 160 awards. Variety of other merit based scholarships range from $500 to full in-state tuition; awards vary. Out of-state student scholarship (not including MN Residence) $1,000; awards vary.

FINANCIAL AID PROCEDURES
Forms required: FAFSA.
Dates and Deadlines: Priority date 4/15; no closing date. Applicants notified on a rolling basis starting 4/15.

CONTACT
Kathleen Sahlhoff, Director of Financial Aid
111 Schofield Hall, Eau Claire, WI 54701
(715) 836-3000

University of Wisconsin-Fond du Lac
Fond du Lac, Wisconsin
www.fdl.uwc.edu   Federal Code: 003897

2-year public liberal arts college in large town.
Enrollment: 626 undergrads.

BASIC COSTS (2016-2017)
Tuition and fees: $5,258; out-of-state residents $12,243.
Per-credit charge: $197.93; out-of-state residents $488.92.

FINANCIAL AID PICTURE
Students with need: Need-based aid available for full-time and part-time students.
Students without need: No-need awards available for academics, leadership, music/drama.

FINANCIAL AID PROCEDURES
Forms required: FAFSA.
Dates and Deadlines: Priority date 4/15; no closing date. Applicants notified on a rolling basis starting 6/1; must reply within 2 week(s) of notification.

CONTACT
William Trippett, Director of Student Financial Aid
400 University Drive, Fond du Lac, WI 54935-2950
(608) 262-5928

University of Wisconsin-Fox Valley
Menasha, Wisconsin
www.uwfox.uwc.edu   Federal Code: 011459

2-year public liberal arts college in small city.
Enrollment: 1,393 undergrads.
Selectivity: Admits over 75% of applicants.

BASIC COSTS (2016-2017)
Tuition and fees: $5,134; out-of-state residents $12,118.

FINANCIAL AID PICTURE
Students with need: Need-based aid available for full-time and part-time students. Work study available nights, weekends, and for part-time students.
Students without need: No-need awards available for academics, leadership.

FINANCIAL AID PROCEDURES
Forms required: FAFSA.
Dates and Deadlines: Priority date 4/15; no closing date. Applicants notified on a rolling basis starting 6/1; must reply within 3 week(s) of notification.

CONTACT
William Trippett, Director of Student Financial Aid
1478 Midway Road, Menasha, WI 54952-2850
(608) 262-5928

University of Wisconsin-Green Bay
Green Bay, Wisconsin
www.uwgb.edu   Federal Code: 003899

4-year public university and liberal arts college in small city.
Enrollment: 5,502 undergrads, 28% part-time. 824 full-time freshmen.
Selectivity: Admits over 75% of applicants.

BASIC COSTS (2016-2017)
Tuition and fees: $7,878; out-of-state residents $15,451.
Per-credit charge: $262; out-of-state residents $578.
Room and board: $7,186.

FINANCIAL AID PICTURE (2016-2017)
Students with need: Out of 723 full-time freshmen who applied for aid, 555 were judged to have need. Of these, 555 received aid, and 149 had their full need met. Average financial aid package met 74% of need; average scholarship/grant was $6,023; average loan was $5,915. For part-time students, average financial aid package was $8,792.
Students without need: 83 full-time freshmen who did not demonstrate need for aid received scholarships/grants; average award was $1,457. No-need awards available for academics, art, athletics, leadership, minority status, music/drama.
Scholarships offered: 11 full-time freshmen received athletic scholarships; average amount $7,391.
Additional info: Auditions required for music and theater scholarships. Tuition is waived for eligible Wisconsin veterans and their family members under the Wisconsin GI Bill. Veterans from outside of Wisconsin are charged the in-state tuition rate regardless of residency. Waivers for children of Wisconsin police/firemen who were slain in the line of duty.

FINANCIAL AID PROCEDURES

Forms required: FAFSA.

Dates and Deadlines: Priority date 4/1; no closing date. Applicants notified on a rolling basis starting 1/1; must reply within 3 week(s) of notification.

Transfers: Must reply within 3 week(s) of notification.

CONTACT

James Rohan, Director of Financial Aid and Student Employment

2420 Nicolet Drive, Green Bay, WI 54311-7001

(920) 465-2075

University of Wisconsin-La Crosse
La Crosse, Wisconsin
www.uwlax.edu   Federal Code: 003919

4-year public university in small city.

Enrollment: 9,486 undergrads, 4% part-time. 2,060 full-time freshmen.

Selectivity: Admits over 75% of applicants.

BASIC COSTS (2016-2017)

Tuition and fees: $8,917; out-of-state residents $17,438.

Per-credit charge: $316.03; out-of-state residents $671.1.

Room and board: $6,025.

FINANCIAL AID PICTURE (2015-2016)

Students with need: Out of 1,791 full-time freshmen who applied for aid, 1,066 were judged to have need. Of these, 1,018 received aid, and 227 had their full need met. Average financial aid package met 70% of need; average scholarship/grant was $4,476; average loan was $3,388. For part-time students, average financial aid package was $5,108.

Students without need: 174 full-time freshmen who did not demonstrate need for aid received scholarships/grants; average award was $2,187. No-need awards available for academics, alumni affiliation, art.

FINANCIAL AID PROCEDURES

Forms required: FAFSA.

Dates and Deadlines: Priority date 3/15; no closing date. Applicants notified on a rolling basis starting 4/1.

CONTACT

Louise Janke, Director of Financial Aid

1725 State Street, Cleary Center, La Crosse, WI 54601

(608) 785-8604

University of Wisconsin-Madison
Madison, Wisconsin
www.wisc.edu   Federal Code: 003895

4-year public university in small city.

Enrollment: 29,536 undergrads, 5% part-time. 6,414 full-time freshmen.

Selectivity: Admits 50 to 75% of applicants.

BASIC COSTS (2016-2017)

Tuition and fees: $10,488; out-of-state residents $32,738.

Per-credit charge: $386; out-of-state residents $1,313.

Room and board: $10,446.

Additional info: Minnesota Resident Reciprocity Tuition Rate: $12,546.

FINANCIAL AID PICTURE (2016-2017)

Students with need: Out of 4,249 full-time freshmen who applied for aid, 2,468 were judged to have need. Of these, 2,307 received aid, and 906 had their full need met. Average financial aid package met 77% of need; average scholarship/grant was $10,922; average loan was $5,651. For part-time students, average financial aid package was $11,612.

Students without need: 422 full-time freshmen who did not demonstrate need for aid received scholarships/grants; average award was $4,365. No-need awards available for academics, alumni affiliation, art, athletics, job

skills, leadership, minority status, music/drama, ROTC, state/district residency.

Scholarships offered: 75 full-time freshmen received athletic scholarships; average amount $26,303.

FINANCIAL AID PROCEDURES

Forms required: FAFSA.

Dates and Deadlines: Priority date 12/1; no closing date. Applicants notified on a rolling basis starting 3/1; must reply within 3 week(s) of notification.

CONTACT

Derek Kindle, Director of Student Financial Aid

702 West Johnson Street, Suite 1101, Madison, WI 53715-1007

(608) 262-3060

University of Wisconsin-Manitowoc
Manitowoc, Wisconsin
www.manitowoc.uwc.edu   Federal Code: 003897

2-year public branch campus and liberal arts college in large town.

Enrollment: 508 undergrads.

BASIC COSTS (2016-2017)

Tuition and fees: $5,172; out-of-state residents $12,156.

Per-credit charge: $197.93; out-of-state residents $488.92.

FINANCIAL AID PICTURE

Students with need: Need-based aid available for full-time and part-time students. Work study available nights.

Students without need: This college awards aid only to students with need.

FINANCIAL AID PROCEDURES

Forms required: FAFSA.

Dates and Deadlines: Priority date 3/1; no closing date. Applicants notified on a rolling basis starting 5/1; must reply within 2 week(s) of notification.

Transfers: Priority date 5/1; no deadline.

CONTACT

Bill Trippett, Director of Student Financial Aid

705 Viebahn Street, Manitowoc, WI 54220-6699

(920) 683-4707

University of Wisconsin-Marathon County
Wausau, Wisconsin
www.uwmc.uwc.edu   Federal Code: 003903

2-year public liberal arts college in small city.

Enrollment: 1,138 undergrads.

BASIC COSTS (2016-2017)

Tuition and fees: $5,212; out-of-state residents $12,196.

Per-credit charge: $197.93; out-of-state residents $488.92.

FINANCIAL AID PICTURE

Students with need: Need-based aid available for full-time and part-time students. Work study available nights.

Students without need: This college awards aid only to students with need.

FINANCIAL AID PROCEDURES

Forms required: FAFSA, institutional form.

Dates and Deadlines: Priority date 4/15; no closing date. Applicants notified on a rolling basis starting 6/1; must reply within 3 week(s) of notification.

CONTACT

Bill Trippett, Director of Student Financial Aid
518 South Seventh Avenue, Wausau, WI 54401-5396
(715) 261-6235

University of Wisconsin-Marinette

Marinette, Wisconsin
www.marinette.uwc.edu   Federal Code: 003897

2-year public branch campus and liberal arts college in large town.
Enrollment: 350 undergrads.

BASIC COSTS (2016-2017)

Tuition and fees: $5,155; out-of-state residents $12,139.
Per-credit charge: $197.93; out-of-state residents $488.92.

FINANCIAL AID PICTURE

Students with need: Need-based aid available for full-time and part-time students. Work study available nights.
Students without need: This college awards aid only to students with need.

FINANCIAL AID PROCEDURES

Forms required: FAFSA.
Dates and Deadlines: Priority date 4/15; no closing date. Applicants notified on a rolling basis.

CONTACT

Bill Trippett, Director of Student Financial Aid
750 West Bay Shore Street, Marinette, WI 54143
(715) 735-4301

University of Wisconsin-Marshfield/Wood County

Marshfield, Wisconsin
www.marshfield.uwc.edu   Federal Code: 003897

2-year public branch campus college in small city.
Enrollment: 650 undergrads.

BASIC COSTS (2016-2017)

Tuition and fees: $5,207; out-of-state residents $12,191.
Per-credit charge: $197.93; out-of-state residents $488.92.

FINANCIAL AID PICTURE

Students with need: Need-based aid available for full-time and part-time students. Work study available nights, weekends, and for part-time students.
Students without need: No-need awards available for academics.
Scholarships offered: Special Entering Scholarships: $1,000; based on academic excellence; 2 awarded. Ken and Ardyce Helting Scholarship: $1,000; priority given to physically challenged or learning disabled; 1 awarded. Valedictorian, Salutatorian and National Merit Finalist and Semi-Finalists: $1,000; ACT of 25 or better. Greenhouse Scholarship: priority to students in Environmental Studies; 1 awarded. Patrice Ptacek Memorial Scholarship: 2 letters of recommendation; 1 awarded. Woman of the Future Scholarship: $1,000; must be full-time female freshman entering sophomore year, well-defined career goals other than nursing; 1 awarded.

FINANCIAL AID PROCEDURES

Forms required: FAFSA.
Dates and Deadlines: Closing date 4/15. Applicants notified on a rolling basis starting 4/1.
Transfers: Priority date 4/15; no deadline. Applicants notified on a rolling basis starting 4/1.

CONTACT

William Trippett, Director of Student Financial Aid
2000 West Fifth Street, Marshfield, WI 54449
(715) 389-6500

University of Wisconsin-Milwaukee

Milwaukee, Wisconsin
www.uwm.edu   Federal Code: 003896

4-year public university in very large city.
Enrollment: 20,000 undergrads, 13% part-time. 3,122 full-time freshmen.
Selectivity: Admits 50 to 75% of applicants.

BASIC COSTS (2016-2017)

Tuition and fees: $9,543; out-of-state residents $19,901.
Room and board: $10,350.

FINANCIAL AID PICTURE (2016-2017)

Students with need: Out of 2,803 full-time freshmen who applied for aid, 2,173 were judged to have need. Of these, 2,094 received aid, and 623 had their full need met. Average financial aid package met 40% of need; average scholarship/grant was $5,995; average loan was $3,447. For part-time students, average financial aid package was $6,505.
Students without need: 23 full-time freshmen who did not demonstrate need for aid received scholarships/grants; average award was $2,874. No-need awards available for academics, art, athletics, leadership, music/drama.
Scholarships offered: 32 full-time freshmen received athletic scholarships; average amount $7,184.

FINANCIAL AID PROCEDURES

Forms required: FAFSA.
Dates and Deadlines: Priority date 3/1; no closing date. Applicants notified on a rolling basis starting 3/15.
Transfers: Priority date 3/1; no deadline. Applicants notified on a rolling basis.

CONTACT

Timothy Opgenorth, Director of Financial Aid
P.O. Box 413, Milwaukee, WI 53201
(414) 229-4541

University of Wisconsin-Oshkosh

Oshkosh, Wisconsin
www.uwosh.edu   Federal Code: 003920

4-year public university in small city.
Enrollment: 9,502 undergrads, 13% part-time. 1,489 full-time freshmen.
Selectivity: Admits 50 to 75% of applicants.

BASIC COSTS (2016-2017)

Tuition and fees: $7,594; out-of-state residents $15,167.
Per-credit charge: $267.59; out-of-state residents $583.13.

FINANCIAL AID PICTURE

Students with need: Need-based aid available for full-time and part-time students.
Students without need: No-need awards available for academics, art, job skills, leadership, minority status, music/drama, ROTC, state/district residency.

FINANCIAL AID PROCEDURES

Forms required: FAFSA.
Dates and Deadlines: Priority date 3/15; no closing date. Applicants notified on a rolling basis starting 4/15; must reply within 2 week(s) of notification.
Transfers: Must send financial aid transcript to university.

CONTACT

Kim Donat, Director of Financial Aid

800 Algoma Boulevard, Oshkosh, WI 54901-8602

(920) 424-3377

University of Wisconsin-Parkside

Kenosha, Wisconsin

www.uwp.edu   Federal Code: 005015

4-year public university in small city.

Enrollment: 4,154 undergrads, 22% part-time. 634 full-time freshmen.

Selectivity: Admits over 75% of applicants.

BASIC COSTS (2016-2017)

Tuition and fees: $7,507; out-of-state residents $15,496.

Per-credit charge: $262; out-of-state residents $595.

Room and board: $7,824.

Additional info: Minnesota reciprocity tuition: $7,036; Midwest Student Exchange Program tuition: $9,448.

FINANCIAL AID PICTURE

Students with need: Need-based aid available for full-time and part-time students. Work study available nights, weekends, and for part-time students.

Students without need: No-need awards available for academics, art, athletics, leadership, music/drama, state/district residency.

FINANCIAL AID PROCEDURES

Forms required: FAFSA.

Dates and Deadlines: Priority date 3/15; no closing date. Applicants notified on a rolling basis starting 4/1; must reply within 2 week(s) of notification.

CONTACT

Kristina Klemens, Director of Financial Aid

PO Box 2000, Kenosha, WI 53141-2000

(262) 595-2574

University of Wisconsin-Platteville

Platteville, Wisconsin

www.uwplatt.edu   Federal Code: 003921

4-year public university in large town.

Enrollment: 7,676 undergrads, 9% part-time. 1,533 full-time freshmen.

Selectivity: Admits over 75% of applicants.

BASIC COSTS (2016-2017)

Tuition and fees: $7,604; out-of-state residents $15,454.

Room and board: $7,160.

FINANCIAL AID PICTURE (2016-2017)

Students with need: 42% of average financial aid package awarded as scholarships/grants, 58% awarded as loans/jobs. Need-based aid available for part-time students. Work study available nights, weekends, and for part-time students.

Students without need: This college awards aid only to students with need.

FINANCIAL AID PROCEDURES

Forms required: FAFSA.

Dates and Deadlines: Priority date 3/15; no closing date. Applicants notified on a rolling basis starting 6/1; must reply within 2 week(s) of notification.

CONTACT

Brian Bird, Interim Director of Financial Aid

One University Plaza, Platteville, WI 53818

(608) 342-1836

University of Wisconsin-Richland

Richland Center, Wisconsin

www.richland.uwc.edu   Federal Code: 003897

2-year public liberal arts college in small town.

Enrollment: 320 undergrads.

Selectivity: Open admission; but selective for some programs.

BASIC COSTS (2016-2017)

Tuition and fees: $5,368; out-of-state residents $12,352.

Per-credit charge: $197.93; out-of-state residents $488.92.

FINANCIAL AID PICTURE

Students with need: Need-based aid available for full-time and part-time students. Work study available nights, weekends, and for part-time students.

Students without need: This college awards aid only to students with need.

FINANCIAL AID PROCEDURES

Forms required: FAFSA.

Dates and Deadlines: Priority date 4/1; no closing date. Applicants notified on a rolling basis starting 5/15; must reply within 3 week(s) of notification.

CONTACT

William Trippett, Director of Student Financial Aid

1200 Highway 14 West, Richland Center, WI 53581

(608) 647-6186 ext. 3

University of Wisconsin-River Falls

River Falls, Wisconsin

www.uwrf.edu   Federal Code: 003923

4-year public university and liberal arts college in large town.

Enrollment: 5,346 undergrads, 9% part-time. 886 full-time freshmen.

Selectivity: Admits 50 to 75% of applicants.

BASIC COSTS (2016-2017)

Tuition and fees: $7,981; out-of-state residents $15,554.

Room and board: $6,545.

FINANCIAL AID PICTURE (2015-2016)

Students with need: Out of 824 full-time freshmen who applied for aid, 590 were judged to have need. Of these, 539 received aid, and 5 had their full need met. Average financial aid package met 52% of need; average scholarship/grant was $4,771; average loan was $3,716. For part-time students, average financial aid package was $6,020.

Students without need: This college awards aid only to students with need.

FINANCIAL AID PROCEDURES

Forms required: FAFSA.

Dates and Deadlines: Priority date 3/15; no closing date. Applicants notified on a rolling basis starting 4/15.

Transfers: No deadline. Applicants notified on a rolling basis starting 4/1.

CONTACT

Robert Bode, Director of Financial Aid

410 South 3rd Street, River Falls, WI 54022-5001

(715) 425-3141

University of Wisconsin-Rock County

Janesville, Wisconsin

www.rock.uwc.edu   Federal Code: 003897

2-year public branch campus and liberal arts college in small city.

Enrollment: 1,220 undergrads.

BASIC COSTS (2016-2017)

Tuition and fees: $5,187; out-of-state residents $12,171.
Per-credit charge: $197.93; out-of-state residents $488.92.

FINANCIAL AID PICTURE

Students with need: Need-based aid available for full-time and part-time students. Work study available nights, weekends, and for part-time students.
Students without need: This college awards aid only to students with need.

FINANCIAL AID PROCEDURES

Forms required: FAFSA, institutional form.
Dates and Deadlines: Closing date 3/15. Applicants notified on a rolling basis starting 6/1; must reply within 3 week(s) of notification.

CONTACT

William Trippet, Director of Student Financial Aid
2909 Kellogg Avenue, Janesville, WI 53546-5699
(608) 758-6565 ext. 200

University of Wisconsin-Sheboygan
Sheboygan, Wisconsin
www.sheboygan.uwc.edu   Federal Code: 003897

2-year public community and liberal arts college in small city.
Enrollment: 769 undergrads.
Selectivity: Open admission.

BASIC COSTS (2016-2017)

Tuition and fees: $5,186; out-of-state residents $12,170.
Per-credit charge: $197.93; out-of-state residents $488.92.

FINANCIAL AID PICTURE

Students with need: Need-based aid available for full-time and part-time students.
Students without need: No-need awards available for academics, art, leadership, music/drama.

FINANCIAL AID PROCEDURES

Forms required: FAFSA, institutional form.
Dates and Deadlines: Priority date 4/15; no closing date. Applicants notified on a rolling basis starting 6/1; must reply within 2 week(s) of notification.
Transfers: No deadline. Applicants notified on a rolling basis.

CONTACT

Mary Balde, Student Financial Aid Officer
One University Drive, Sheboygan, WI 53081
(920) 459-6633

University of Wisconsin-Stevens Point
Stevens Point, Wisconsin
www.uwsp.edu   Federal Code: 003924

4-year public university in large town.
Enrollment: 8,169 undergrads, 6% part-time. 1,782 full-time freshmen.
Selectivity: Admits over 75% of applicants.

BASIC COSTS (2016-2017)

Tuition and fees: $8,030; out-of-state residents $16,297.
Per-credit charge: $279.09; out-of-state residents $623.53.
Room and board: $6,714.

FINANCIAL AID PICTURE (2015-2016)

Students with need: Out of 1,585 full-time freshmen who applied for aid, 1,045 were judged to have need. Of these, 1,045 received aid, and 62 had their full need met. Average financial aid package met 67% of need; average scholarship/grant was $5,122; average loan was $4,414. For part-time students, average financial aid package was $6,239.

Students without need: 142 full-time freshmen who did not demonstrate need for aid received scholarships/grants; average award was $1,411. No-need awards available for academics, alumni affiliation, art, music/drama, ROTC.
Additional info: Tuition discounts offered to qualified residents from other states. Tuition waiver for state veterans.

FINANCIAL AID PROCEDURES

Forms required: FAFSA.
Dates and Deadlines: Priority date 3/15; closing date 5/1. Applicants notified on a rolling basis starting 3/1; must reply within 4 week(s) of notification.
Transfers: No deadline.

CONTACT

Paul Watson, Director of Financial Aid
Student Services Center, Stevens Point, WI 54481
(715) 346-4771

University of Wisconsin-Stout
Menomonie, Wisconsin
www.uwstout.edu   Federal Code: 003915

4-year public university in large town.
Enrollment: 8,178 undergrads, 17% part-time. 1,588 full-time freshmen.
Selectivity: Admits over 75% of applicants.

BASIC COSTS (2016-2017)

Tuition and fees: $9,394; out-of-state residents $17,140.
Per-credit charge: $234; out-of-state residents $492.
Room and board: $6,624.
Additional info: Laptop computer is included with payment of fees.

FINANCIAL AID PICTURE (2016-2017)

Students with need: Out of 1,378 full-time freshmen who applied for aid, 940 were judged to have need. Of these, 901 received aid, and 114 had their full need met. Average financial aid package met 81% of need; average scholarship/grant was $4,480; average loan was $4,053. For part-time students, average financial aid package was $8,360.
Students without need: 52 full-time freshmen who did not demonstrate need for aid received scholarships/grants; average award was $1,852. No-need awards available for academics.
Scholarships offered: Wisconsin Academic Excellence Scholarship: $2,250; selected by high school. National Merit Finalist Scholarship: $2,000; automatically awarded to NMSQT finalist. National Merit Semifinalist Scholarship: $1,000; automatically awarded to NMSQT semifinalist. Chancellor's Academic Honor Scholarship: $1,000; automatically awarded to top 5% of high school class with ACT of 25 who enroll by July 15.

FINANCIAL AID PROCEDURES

Forms required: FAFSA.
Dates and Deadlines: Priority date 3/15; no closing date. Applicants notified on a rolling basis starting 3/31; must reply within 4 week(s) of notification.

CONTACT

Beth Boisen, Director of Financial Aid
1 Clocktower Plaza, Menomonie, WI 54751
(715) 232-1363

University of Wisconsin-Superior
Superior, Wisconsin
www.uwsuper.edu   Federal Code: 003925

4-year public university and liberal arts college in small city.
Enrollment: 2,257 undergrads, 20% part-time. 371 full-time freshmen.
Selectivity: Admits 50 to 75% of applicants.

BASIC COSTS (2016-2017)

Tuition and fees: $8,087; out-of-state residents $15,660.
Per-credit charge: $272; out-of-state residents $588.
Room and board: $6,520.

FINANCIAL AID PICTURE (2016-2017)

Students with need: Out of 293 full-time freshmen who applied for aid, 217 were judged to have need. Of these, 214 received aid, and 40 had their full need met. Average financial aid package met 85% of need; average scholarship/grant was $5,033; average loan was $3,704. For part-time students, average financial aid package was $9,289.
Students without need: 18 full-time freshmen who did not demonstrate need for aid received scholarships/grants; average award was $1,533. No-need awards available for academics, alumni affiliation, art, leadership, minority status, music/drama, state/district residency.
Additional info: Non resident Tuition Waiver (NTW) available to non-resident students on limited basis.

FINANCIAL AID PROCEDURES

Forms required: FAFSA.
Dates and Deadlines: Priority date 3/15; no closing date. Applicants notified on a rolling basis starting 4/1; must reply by 5/1 or within 4 week(s) of notification.
Transfers: No deadline. Applicants notified on a rolling basis starting 3/15; must reply by 5/1 or within 4 week(s) of notification.

CONTACT

Donna Dahlvang, Director of Financial Aid
Belknap and Catlin, Superior, WI 54880
(715) 394-8200

University of Wisconsin-Washington County

West Bend, Wisconsin
www.washington.uwc.edu   Federal Code: 003897

2-year public branch campus and liberal arts college in large town.
Enrollment: 810 undergrads.

BASIC COSTS (2016-2017)

Tuition and fees: $5,150; out-of-state residents $12,134.
Per-credit charge: $197.93; out-of-state residents $488.92.

FINANCIAL AID PICTURE

Students with need: Need-based aid available for full-time and part-time students. Work study available weekends and for part-time students.
Students without need: No-need awards available for academics.

FINANCIAL AID PROCEDURES

Forms required: FAFSA.
Dates and Deadlines: Priority date 4/15; no closing date. Applicants notified on a rolling basis starting 4/30; must reply within 3 week(s) of notification.
Transfers: No deadline.

CONTACT

Maria Graciano, Director of Student Financial Aid
400 University Drive, West Bend, WI 53095
(262) 335-5207

University of Wisconsin-Waukesha

Waukesha, Wisconsin
www.waukesha.uwc.edu   Federal Code: 003897

2-year public branch campus and junior college in small city.
Enrollment: 1,929 undergrads.

BASIC COSTS (2016-2017)

Tuition and fees: $5,195; out-of-state residents $12,179.
Per-credit charge: $197.93; out-of-state residents $488.92.

FINANCIAL AID PICTURE

Students with need: Need-based aid available for full-time and part-time students. Work study available nights, weekends, and for part-time students.
Students without need: No-need awards available for academics, alumni affiliation, art, leadership, minority status, music/drama, state/district residency.
Scholarships offered: University of Wisconsin-Waukesha Scholarship Program: numerous scholarships; amounts vary.

FINANCIAL AID PROCEDURES

Forms required: FAFSA.
Dates and Deadlines: Priority date 4/1; no closing date. Applicants notified on a rolling basis starting 4/1; must reply within 3 week(s) of notification.

CONTACT

Bill Trippett, Director of Student Financial Aid
1500 North University Drive, Waukesha, WI 53188
(262) 521-5210

University of Wisconsin-Whitewater

Whitewater, Wisconsin
www.uww.edu   Federal Code: 003926

4-year public university in large town.
Enrollment: 10,775 undergrads, 7% part-time. 2,220 full-time freshmen.
Selectivity: Admits over 75% of applicants.

BASIC COSTS (2016-2017)

Tuition and fees: $7,650; out-of-state residents $16,223.
Per-credit charge: $272; out-of-state residents $629.
Room and board: $6,376.

FINANCIAL AID PICTURE (2016-2017)

Students with need: Out of 2,002 full-time freshmen who applied for aid, 1,367 were judged to have need. Of these, 1,290 received aid, and 534 had their full need met. Average financial aid package met 56% of need; average scholarship/grant was $5,354; average loan was $3,445. Need-based aid available for part-time students.
Students without need: 124 full-time freshmen who did not demonstrate need for aid received scholarships/grants; average award was $2,357. No-need awards available for academics, art, minority status, music/drama, state/district residency.

FINANCIAL AID PROCEDURES

Forms required: FAFSA.
Dates and Deadlines: Priority date 3/1; no closing date. Applicants notified on a rolling basis starting 4/1; must reply within 3 week(s) of notification.
Transfers: No deadline. Applicants notified on a rolling basis starting 4/1; must reply within 3 week(s) of notification.

CONTACT

Carol Miller, Director of Financial Aid
800 West Main Street, Whitewater, WI 53190-1790
(262) 472-1130

Viterbo University

La Crosse, Wisconsin
www.viterbo.edu   Federal Code: 003911

4-year private university in small city, affiliated with the Roman Catholic Church.
Enrollment: 1,861 undergrads, 20% part-time. 311 full-time freshmen.
Selectivity: Admits 50 to 75% of applicants.

BASIC COSTS (2016-2017)

Tuition and fees: $26,150.

Room and board: $8,930.

Additional info: Tuition/fee waivers available for minority students.

FINANCIAL AID PICTURE

Students with need: Need-based aid available for full-time and part-time students. Work study available nights, weekends, and for part-time students.

Students without need: No-need awards available for academics, alumni affiliation, art, athletics, leadership, minority status, music/drama, ROTC.

Scholarships offered: Fine arts scholarships: up to $10,000 per year; for incoming full-time freshmen and transfer students talented in areas of art, music or theater. Dr. Scholl Scholarship: full, 4-year tuition; must enroll full-time and maintain 3.5 GPA, 1 awarded. Viterbo University Scholarship: $1,000-$8,000 per year; based on academic history; incoming freshmen and transfers automatically considered; renewable.

FINANCIAL AID PROCEDURES

Forms required: FAFSA, institutional form.

Dates and Deadlines: Priority date 3/15; no closing date. Applicants notified on a rolling basis starting 4/1; must reply within 3 week(s) of notification.

CONTACT

900 Viterbo Drive, La Crosse, WI 54601-8804

(608) 796-3900

Waukesha County Technical College

Pewaukee, Wisconsin

www.wctc.edu   Federal Code: 005294

2-year public technical college in large town.

Enrollment: 5,044 undergrads, 68% part-time. 304 full-time freshmen.

Selectivity: Open admission; but selective for some programs.

BASIC COSTS (2016-2017)

Tuition and fees: $4,145; out-of-state residents $6,100.

Per-credit charge: $130; out-of-state residents $196.

Additional info: Material fees vary by program; minimum $4.50 per course. $10 per credit fee for online courses.

FINANCIAL AID PICTURE (2015-2016)

Students with need: 34% of average financial aid package awarded as scholarships/grants, 66% awarded as loans/jobs. Work study available nights.

Students without need: No-need awards available for academics.

FINANCIAL AID PROCEDURES

Forms required: FAFSA.

Dates and Deadlines: Priority date 4/1; no closing date. Applicants notified on a rolling basis starting 4/30.

CONTACT

Tim Jacobson, Financial Aid Manager

Office of Admissions, C-019, Pewaukee, WI 53072

(262) 691-5436

Western Technical College

La Crosse, Wisconsin

www.westerntc.edu   Federal Code: 003840

2-year public community and technical college in small city.

Enrollment: 4,000 undergrads.

Selectivity: Open admission; but selective for some programs.

BASIC COSTS (2016-2017)

Tuition and fees: $3,911; out-of-state residents $5,866.

Per-credit charge: $130; out-of-state residents $196.

Room and board: $6,250.

Additional info: Tuition/fee waivers available for unemployed or children of unemployed.

FINANCIAL AID PICTURE

Students with need: Need-based aid available for full-time and part-time students. Work study available nights, weekends, and for part-time students.

FINANCIAL AID PROCEDURES

Forms required: FAFSA, institutional form.

Dates and Deadlines: Priority date 3/1; no closing date. Applicants notified on a rolling basis starting 4/1.

CONTACT

Jerolyn Grandall, Student Financial Services Manager

400 Seventh Street North, La Crosse, WI 54601

(608) 785-9302

Wisconsin Indianhead Technical College

Shell Lake, Wisconsin

www.witc.edu   Federal Code: 011824

2-year public technical college in small town.

Enrollment: 2,667 undergrads, 60% part-time. 164 full-time freshmen.

Selectivity: Open admission; but selective for some programs.

BASIC COSTS (2016-2017)

Tuition and fees: $3,911; out-of-state residents $5,866.

Per-credit charge: $130; out-of-state residents $196.

Additional info: Material fees vary by program; minimum $4.50 per course. $10 per credit fee for online courses.

FINANCIAL AID PICTURE (2015-2016)

Students with need: 52% of average financial aid package awarded as scholarships/grants, 48% awarded as loans/jobs. Need-based aid available for part-time students. Work study available nights, weekends, and for part-time students.

Students without need: This college awards aid only to students with need.

FINANCIAL AID PROCEDURES

Forms required: FAFSA.

Dates and Deadlines: Priority date 4/15; no closing date. Applicants notified on a rolling basis starting 4/15; must reply by 9/1 or within 4 week(s) of notification.

CONTACT

Terry Klein, Director of Financial Aid

505 Pine Ridge Drive, Shell Lake, WI 54871

(715) 468-2815 ext. 2243

Wisconsin Lutheran College

Milwaukee, Wisconsin

www.wlc.edu   Federal Code: 014658

4-year private liberal arts college in very large city, affiliated with the Wisconsin Evangelical Lutheran Synod.

Enrollment: 1,060 undergrads.

BASIC COSTS (2016-2017)

Tuition and fees: $27,984.

Per-credit charge: $720.

Room and board: $9,620.

FINANCIAL AID PICTURE

Students with need: Need-based aid available for full-time and part-time students.

Students without need: No-need awards available for academics, art, leadership, music/drama, ROTC.

FINANCIAL AID PROCEDURES

Forms required: FAFSA, institutional form.

Dates and Deadlines: Priority date 3/1; no closing date. Applicants notified on a rolling basis starting 3/15; must reply within 2 week(s) of notification.

Transfers: No deadline. Applicants notified on a rolling basis; must reply within 2 week(s) of notification. Transfer scholarship and transfer grant available for qualifying students.

CONTACT

Linda Loeffel, Financial Aid Director
8800 West Bluemound Road, Milwaukee, WI 53226-4699
(414) 443-8856

Wyoming

Casper College

Casper, Wyoming
www.caspercollege.edu   Federal Code: 003928

2-year public community college in small city.

Enrollment: 2,536 undergrads, 36% part-time. 508 full-time freshmen.

Selectivity: Open admission; but selective for some programs and for out-of-state students.

BASIC COSTS (2016-2017)

Tuition and fees: $2,832; out-of-state residents $7,104.

Per-credit charge: $89; out-of-state residents $267.

Room and board: $6,520.

Additional info: Western Undergraduate Exchange students qualify for reduced rates.

FINANCIAL AID PICTURE

Students with need: Need-based aid available for full-time and part-time students. Work study available nights, weekends, and for part-time students.

Students without need: No-need awards available for academics, art, athletics, leadership, music/drama, state/district residency.

FINANCIAL AID PROCEDURES

Forms required: FAFSA.

Dates and Deadlines: Priority date 3/15; no closing date. Applicants notified on a rolling basis starting 4/1.

Transfers: No deadline. Applicants notified on a rolling basis starting 4/1.

CONTACT

Shannon Eskam, Director of Student Financial Assistance
125 College Drive, Casper, WY 82601
(307) 268-2510

Central Wyoming College

Riverton, Wyoming
www.cwc.edu   Federal Code: 005018

2-year public community college in large town.

Enrollment: 1,058 undergrads, 42% part-time. 215 full-time freshmen.

Selectivity: Open admission; but selective for some programs.

BASIC COSTS (2016-2017)

Tuition and fees: $3,036; out-of-state residents $7,308.

Per-credit charge: $89; out-of-state residents $267.

Room and board: $5,374.

Additional info: Western Undergraduate Exchange (WUE) students qualify for reduced rates.

FINANCIAL AID PICTURE (2015-2016)

Students with need: Out of 153 full-time freshmen who applied for aid, 110 were judged to have need. Of these, 110 received aid. Need-based aid available for part-time students.

Students without need: No-need awards available for academics, alumni affiliation, art, athletics, leadership, minority status, music/drama, state/district residency.

Scholarships offered: Honors Scholarships: in-state tuition and general fees plus $300 book stipend; for graduating high school seniors with 3.5 GPA or 25 ACT. Seniors Scholarships: in-state tuition; for graduating high school seniors with 3.0-3.49 GPA or 22 ACT. Full academic scholarships: in-state tuition, general fees, room and board, books and supplies; for Wyoming National Merit finalists.

FINANCIAL AID PROCEDURES

Forms required: FAFSA, institutional form.

Dates and Deadlines: Priority date 4/15; no closing date. Applicants notified on a rolling basis starting 5/1; must reply within 2 week(s) of notification.

CONTACT

Scott McFarland, Director of Financial Aid
2660 Peck Avenue, Riverton, WY 82501
(307) 855-2150

Eastern Wyoming College

Torrington, Wyoming
www.ewc.wy.edu   Federal Code: 003929

2-year public community college in small town.

Enrollment: 611 undergrads.

Selectivity: Open admission.

BASIC COSTS (2016-2017)

Tuition and fees: $2,976; out-of-state residents $7,248.

Per-credit charge: $89; out-of-state residents $267.

Room and board: $6,136.

Additional info: Western Undergraduate Exchange (WUE) students qualify for reduced rates.

FINANCIAL AID PICTURE

Students with need: Need-based aid available for full-time and part-time students. Work study available nights, weekends, and for part-time students.

Students without need: No-need awards available for academics, alumni affiliation, art, athletics, leadership, music/drama.

Additional info: Installment payment plan on room and board contracts offered.

FINANCIAL AID PROCEDURES

Forms required: FAFSA, institutional form.

Dates and Deadlines: Priority date 3/15; no closing date. Applicants notified on a rolling basis starting 1/1.

CONTACT

Susan Stephenson, Financial Aid DIrector
3200 West C Street, Torrington, WY 82240
(800) 658-3195 ext. 8325

Laramie County Community College

Cheyenne, Wyoming
www.lccc.wy.edu   Federal Code: 009259

2-year public community college in small city.

Enrollment: 3,008 undergrads, 46% part-time. 445 full-time freshmen.

Selectivity: Open admission; but selective for some programs.

BASIC COSTS (2016-2017)

Tuition and fees: $3,306; out-of-state residents $7,578.

Per-credit charge: $89; out-of-state residents $267.

Room and board: $7,988.

Additional info: Western Undergraduate Exchange (WUE) students qualify for reduced tuition and fees of $4,362.

FINANCIAL AID PICTURE (2015-2016)

Students with need: Out of 373 full-time freshmen who applied for aid, 237 were judged to have need. Of these, 232 received aid, and 37 had their full need met. Average financial aid package met 71% of need; average loan was $2,902. For part-time students, average financial aid package was $4,227.

Students without need: 157 full-time freshmen who did not demonstrate need for aid received scholarships/grants; average award was $1,464. No-need awards available for academics, alumni affiliation, art, athletics, job skills, leadership, minority status, music/drama, religious affiliation, state/district residency.

Scholarships offered: 46 full-time freshmen received athletic scholarships; average amount $6,283.

FINANCIAL AID PROCEDURES

Forms required: FAFSA, institutional form.

Dates and Deadlines: Priority date 4/1; no closing date. Applicants notified on a rolling basis starting 4/1; must reply within 2 week(s) of notification.

Transfers: No deadline. Applicants notified on a rolling basis starting 4/1; must reply within 2 week(s) of notification.

CONTACT

Jennifer Almli, Director of Financial Aid

1400 East College Drive, Cheyenne, WY 82007-3299

(307) 778-1281

Northwest College

Powell, Wyoming

www.nwc.edu   Federal Code: 003931

2-year public community and junior college in small town.

Enrollment: 1,337 undergrads, 29% part-time. 389 full-time freshmen.

Selectivity: Open admission; but selective for some programs and for out-of-state students.

BASIC COSTS (2016-2017)

Tuition and fees: $3,191; out-of-state residents $7,463.

Per-credit charge: $89; out-of-state residents $267.

Room and board: $5,512.

Additional info: Western Undergraduate Exchange students qualify for reduced rates.

FINANCIAL AID PICTURE (2015-2016)

Students with need: Need-based aid available for full-time and part-time students. Work study available nights, weekends, and for part-time students.

Students without need: No-need awards available for academics, alumni affiliation, art, athletics, leadership, minority status, music/drama, religious affiliation, state/district residency.

FINANCIAL AID PROCEDURES

Forms required: FAFSA, institutional form.

Dates and Deadlines: Priority date 2/15; no closing date. Applicants notified on a rolling basis; must reply within 2 week(s) of notification.

Transfers: Priority date 2/15. Applicants notified on a rolling basis.

CONTACT

Shaman Quinn, Financial Aid and Scholarships Director

Orendorff Bldg, Powell, WY 82435-1898

(307) 754-6158

Sheridan College

Sheridan, Wyoming

www.sheridan.edu   Federal Code: 003930

2-year public community college in large town.

Enrollment: 2,002 undergrads, 34% part-time. 534 full-time freshmen.

Selectivity: Open admission; but selective for some programs.

BASIC COSTS (2016-2017)

Tuition and fees: $3,156; out-of-state residents $7,428.

Per-credit charge: $89; out-of-state residents $267.

Room and board: $6,907.

Additional info: Western Undergraduate Exchange (WUE) students qualify for reduced rates.

FINANCIAL AID PICTURE

Students with need: Need-based aid available for full-time and part-time students. Work study available nights, weekends, and for part-time students.

Students without need: No-need awards available for academics, art, athletics, leadership, music/drama, state/district residency.

Scholarships offered: Academic scholarships; in-state tuition and fees; based on 25 ACT/1120 SAT (exclusive of Writing); renewable.

FINANCIAL AID PROCEDURES

Forms required: FAFSA, institutional form.

Dates and Deadlines: Priority date 3/1; no closing date. Applicants notified on a rolling basis; must reply within 3 week(s) of notification.

CONTACT

Heidi Balster, Interim Director of Financial Aid

PO Box 1500, Sheridan, WY 82801-1500

(307) 674-6446 ext. 2100

University of Wyoming

Laramie, Wyoming

www.uwyo.edu   Federal Code: 003932

4-year public university in large town.

Enrollment: 9,622 undergrads, 16% part-time. 1,675 full-time freshmen.

Selectivity: Admits over 75% of applicants.

BASIC COSTS (2016-2017)

Tuition and fees: $5,055; out-of-state residents $16,215.

Per-credit charge: $124; out-of-state residents $496.

Room and board: $10,320.

FINANCIAL AID PICTURE (2015-2016)

Students with need: Out of 1,342 full-time freshmen who applied for aid, 862 were judged to have need. Of these, 842 received aid, and 202 had their full need met. Average financial aid package met 66% of need; average scholarship/grant was $5,261; average loan was $3,290. For part-time students, average financial aid package was $5,630.

Students without need: 439 full-time freshmen who did not demonstrate need for aid received scholarships/grants; average award was $4,316. No-need awards available for academics, alumni affiliation, art, athletics, leadership, minority status, music/drama, ROTC, state/district residency.

Scholarships offered: *Merit:* Western Heritage Scholarship: number awarded and packages vary. President's High School Honor Scholarship: covers undergraduate fees and tuition; number awarded varies. *Athletic:* 108 full-time freshmen received athletic scholarships; average amount $2,267.

FINANCIAL AID PROCEDURES

Forms required: FAFSA.

Dates and Deadlines: Priority date 3/1; no closing date. Applicants notified on a rolling basis starting 3/9.

CONTACT

Kathy Bobbitt, Director of Student Financial Aid
Dept 3435, Laramie, WY 82071
(307) 766-2116

Western Wyoming Community College

Rock Springs, Wyoming
www.westernwyoming.edu   Federal Code: 003933

2-year public community college in large town.

Enrollment: 2,553 undergrads, 64% part-time. 195 full-time freshmen.

Selectivity: Open admission; but selective for some programs.

BASIC COSTS (2016-2017)

Tuition and fees: $2,356; out-of-state residents $6,628.

Per-credit charge: $89; out-of-state residents $267.

Room and board: $5,065.

Additional info: Western Undergraduate Exchange (WUE) students qualify for reduced rates.

FINANCIAL AID PICTURE (2015-2016)

Students with need: Need-based aid available for part-time students.

Students without need: No-need awards available for academics, art, athletics, music/drama, state/district residency.

FINANCIAL AID PROCEDURES

Forms required: FAFSA.

Dates and Deadlines: Priority date 4/1; no closing date. Applicants notified on a rolling basis starting 2/15; must reply within 2 week(s) of notification.

CONTACT

Nicole Castillon, Financial Aid Officer
Box 428, Rock Springs, WY 82902-0428
(307) 382-1643

Part IV

Scholarship Lists

Academic scholarships

Alabama
Alabama State University
Amridge University
Athens State University
Bevill State Community College
Birmingham-Southern College
Bishop State Community College
Calhoun Community College
Central Alabama Community College
Chattahoochee Valley Community College
Enterprise State Community College
Faulkner State Community College
Faulkner University
Gadsden State Community College
George C. Wallace Community College at Dothan
George C. Wallace State Community College at Selma
Huntingdon College
Jacksonville State University
Jefferson Davis Community College
Jefferson State Community College
Judson College
Lurleen B. Wallace Community College
Northeast Alabama Community College
Northwest-Shoals Community College
Oakwood University
Samford University
Selma University
Shelton State Community College
Snead State Community College
Southeastern Bible College
Spring Hill College
Stillman College
Talladega College
Troy University
Tuskegee University
United States Sports Academy
University of Alabama
University of Alabama
      Birmingham
      Huntsville
University of Mobile
University of Montevallo
University of North Alabama
University of South Alabama
University of West Alabama
Wallace State Community College at Hanceville

Alaska
Alaska Bible College
Alaska Pacific University
University of Alaska
      Anchorage
      Fairbanks
      Southeast

Arizona
Arizona Christian University
Arizona State University
Arizona Western College
DeVry University
      Phoenix
Dine College
Eastern Arizona College
Grand Canyon University
Mesa Community College
Northern Arizona University
Northland Pioneer College
Prescott College
Scottsdale Community College
South Mountain Community College
Southwest University of Visual Arts

Tohono O'odham Community College
University of Advancing Technology
University of Arizona
Yavapai College

Arkansas
Arkansas Northeastern College
Arkansas State University
Arkansas State University
      Beebe
      Mid-South
      Mountain Home
Arkansas Tech University
Black River Technical College
Central Baptist College
College of the Ouachitas
Crowley's Ridge College
Ecclesia College
Harding University
Henderson State University
Hendrix College
John Brown University
Lyon College
National Park College
North Arkansas College
Northwest Arkansas Community College
Ouachita Baptist University
Philander Smith College
Phillips Community College of the University of Arkansas
Rich Mountain Community College
Southeast Arkansas College
Southern Arkansas University
Southern Arkansas University Tech
University of Arkansas
University of Arkansas
      Community College at Batesville
      Community College at Hope
      Community College at Morrilton
      for Medical Sciences
      Fort Smith
      Little Rock
      Monticello
      Pine Bluff
University of Central Arkansas
University of the Ozarks
Williams Baptist College

California
Academy of Art University
Alliant International University
American Academy of Dramatic Arts: West
Art Institute of California
      Los Angeles
      Orange County
Azusa Pacific University
Bethesda University of California
Biola University
Brandman University
California Baptist University
California College of the Arts
California Institute of Integral Studies
California Institute of the Arts
California Lutheran University
California Maritime Academy
California Polytechnic State University: San Luis Obispo
California State Polytechnic University: Pomona
California State University
      Bakersfield
      Channel Islands
      Chico
      Dominguez Hills
      East Bay

Fresno
Fullerton
Long Beach
Northridge
San Marcos
Stanislaus
Chaffey College
Chapman University
Charles Drew University of Medicine and Science
Claremont McKenna College
Cogswell Polytechnical College
College of the Canyons
College of the Desert
Columbia College
Concordia University Irvine
Deep Springs College
DeVry University
      Pomona
Dominican University of California
East Los Angeles College
El Camino College
Empire College
Fashion Institute of Design and Merchandising
      Los Angeles
      San Diego
      San Francisco
Glendale Community College
Golden Gate University
Golden West College
Harvey Mudd College
Holy Names University
Hope International University
Hult International Business School
Humboldt State University
Humphreys College
Imperial Valley College
John F. Kennedy University
John Paul the Great Catholic University
La Sierra University
Life Pacific College
Loyola Marymount University
Marymount California University
The Master's University
Mendocino College
Menlo College
Merced College
Mills College
Mount Saint Mary's University
Mount San Jacinto College
Napa Valley College
Notre Dame de Namur University
Occidental College
Otis College of Art and Design
Pacific States University
Pacific Union College
Pepperdine University
Pitzer College
Point Loma Nazarene University
Providence Christian College
Riverside City College
St. Mary's College of California
Samuel Merritt University
San Deigo Miramar College
      San Diego Miramar College
San Diego Christian College
San Diego State University
San Francisco Art Institute
San Francisco State University
San Joaquin Delta College
San Jose State University
Santa Clara University
Santa Rosa Junior College
Scripps College
Simpson University
Soka University of America
Sonoma State University
Southern California Institute of Architecture
SUM Bible College & Theological Seminary
Taft College
Touro University Worldwide
University of California
      Berkeley

Davis
Los Angeles
Merced
Riverside
San Diego
Santa Barbara
Santa Cruz
University of La Verne
University of Redlands
University of San Diego
University of San Francisco
University of Southern California
University of the Pacific
University of the West
Vanguard University of Southern California
West Coast University
      Los Angeles
West Coast University: Ontario
West Coast University: Orange County
Westmont College
Whittier College
William Jessup University
Woodbury University
Yuba College

Colorado
Adams State University
Arapahoe Community College
Colorado Christian University
Colorado College
Colorado Mesa University
Colorado Northwestern Community College
Colorado School of Mines
Colorado State University
Colorado State University
      Pueblo
Colorado Technical University
Community College of Aurora
Community College of Denver
DeVry University
      Westminster
Fort Lewis College
Front Range Community College
Johnson & Wales University
      Denver
Lamar Community College
Metropolitan State University of Denver
Naropa University
Nazarene Bible College
Northeastern Junior College
Otero Junior College
Pueblo Community College
Red Rocks Community College
Regis University
Rocky Mountain College of Art & Design
Trinidad State Junior College
University of Colorado
      Boulder
      Colorado Springs
      Denver
University of Denver
University of Northern Colorado
Western State Colorado University
Westwood College
      Denver North

Connecticut
Albertus Magnus College
Central Connecticut State University
Fairfield University
Goodwin College
Housatonic Community College
Lincoln College of New England
Lyme Academy College of Fine Arts
Mitchell College
Norwalk Community College
Quinnipiac University
Sacred Heart University
St. Vincent's College
Southern Connecticut State University
Trinity College
Tunxis Community College
University of Bridgeport

University of Connecticut
University of Hartford
University of New Haven
University of Saint Joseph
Western Connecticut State University

Delaware
Delaware College of Art and Design
Delaware State University
Delaware Technical Community College
    Jack F. Owens Campus
    Stanton/Wilmington Campus
    Terry Campus
Goldey-Beacom College
University of Delaware
Wesley College
Wilmington University

District of Columbia
American University
Catholic University of America
George Washington University
Howard University
Trinity Washington University

Florida
Art Institute of Fort Lauderdale
Ave Maria University
Baptist College of Florida
Barry University
Beacon College
Bethune-Cookman University
Broward College
Brown Mackie College
    Miami
Carlos Albizu University
Chipola College
College of Central Florida
Daytona State College
DeVry University
    Miramar
    Orlando
Eastern Florida State College
Eckerd College
Flagler College
Florida Agricultural and Mechanical University
Florida Atlantic University
Florida College
Florida Gateway College
Florida Gulf Coast University
Florida Institute of Technology
Florida International University
Florida Keys Community College
Florida National University
Florida Southern College
Florida SouthWestern State College
Florida State College at Jacksonville
Florida State University
Gulf Coast State College
Hillsborough Community College
Hobe Sound Bible College
Hodges University
Indian River State College
Jacksonville University
Johnson & Wales University
    North Miami
Johnson University: Florida
Jones College
Jose Maria Vargas University
Keiser University
Lake-Sumter State College
Lynn University
Miami Dade College
New College of Florida
North Florida Community College
Northwest Florida State College
Nova Southeastern University
Palm Beach Atlantic University
Palm Beach State College
Pasco-Hernando State College
Pensacola State College
Polk State College
Ringling College of Art and Design

Rollins College
Saint Leo University
St. Petersburg College
Saint Thomas University
Santa Fe College
Schiller International University
Seminole State College of Florida
South Florida State College
Southeastern University
State College of Florida, Manatee-Sarasota
Stetson University
Tallahassee Community College
Trinity Baptist College
Trinity College of Florida
University of Central Florida
University of Florida
University of Miami
University of North Florida
University of South Florida
University of South Florida
    Saint Petersburg
    Sarasota-Manatee
University of Tampa
University of West Florida
Warner University
Webber International University

Georgia
Abraham Baldwin Agricultural College
Agnes Scott College
Albany State University
Albany Technical College
Andrew College
Armstrong State University
Art Institute of Atlanta
Athens Technical College
Berry College
Brenau University
Brewton-Parker College
Central Georgia Technical College
Clark Atlanta University
Clayton State University
College of Coastal Georgia
Columbus State University
Covenant College
Dalton State College
Darton State College
DeVry University
    Decatur
East Georgia State College
Emmanuel College
Emory University
Fort Valley State University
Georgia College and State University
Georgia Gwinnett College
Georgia Highlands College
Georgia Institute of Technology
Georgia Perimeter College
Georgia Piedmont Technical College
Georgia Southern University
Georgia Southwestern State University
Georgia State University
Gordon State College
Herzing University
    Atlanta
Kennesaw State University
LaGrange College
Life University
Luther Rice University
Mercer University
Middle Georgia State University
Morehouse College
Oglethorpe University
Oxford College of Emory University
Paine College
Piedmont College
Point University
Reinhardt University
Savannah State University
Savannah Technical College
Shorter University
South Georgia State College
Spelman College

Thomas University
Toccoa Falls College
Truett McConnell University
University of Georgia
University of North Georgia
University of West Georgia
Valdosta State University
Wesleyan College
Wiregrass Georgia Technical College
Young Harris College

Hawaii
Brigham Young University-Hawaii
Chaminade University of Honolulu
Hawaii Pacific University
Hawaii Tokai International College
University of Hawaii
    Hilo
    Honolulu Community College
    Kapiolani Community College
    Manoa
    West Oahu
    Windward Community College

Idaho
Boise Bible College
Boise State University
Brigham Young University-Idaho
College of Idaho
College of Western Idaho
Eastern Idaho Technical College
Idaho State University
Lewis-Clark State College
New Saint Andrews College
North Idaho College
Northwest Nazarene University
University of Idaho

Illinois
Augustana College
Aurora University
Benedictine University
Benedictine University at Springfield
Black Hawk College
Blackburn College
Blessing-Rieman College of Nursing & Health
    Sciences
Bradley University
Carl Sandburg College
Chicago State University
College of DuPage
College of Lake County
Concordia University Chicago
Danville Area Community College
DePaul University
DeVry University
    Chicago
    Online
Dominican University
East-West University
Eastern Illinois University
Elgin Community College
Elmhurst College
Eureka College
Governors State University
Greenville College
Heartland Community College
Highland Community College
Illinois Central College
Illinois College
Illinois Eastern Community Colleges
    Frontier Community College
    Lincoln Trail College
    Olney Central College
    Wabash Valley College
Illinois Institute of Art
    Schaumburg
Illinois Institute of Technology
Illinois State University
Illinois Valley Community College
Illinois Wesleyan University
International Academy of Design and
    Technology
    Chicago

Joliet Junior College
Judson University
Kaskaskia College
Kendall College
Kishwaukee College
Knox College
Lake Forest College
Lake Land College
Lakeview College of Nursing
Lewis University
Lincoln Christian University
Lincoln College
Lincoln Land Community College
Loyola University Chicago
MacCormac College
MacMurray College
McHenry County College
McKendree University
Midstate College
Millikin University
Monmouth College
Moody Bible Institute
Moraine Valley Community College
Morrison Institute of Technology
National-Louis University
North Central College
North Park University
Northeastern Illinois University
Northern Illinois University
Northwestern College
Oakton Community College
Olivet Nazarene University
Parkland College
Principia College
Quincy University
Resurrection University
Richland Community College
Robert Morris College
    Robert Morris University: Chicago
Rockford University
Roosevelt University
Rush University
Saint Anthony College of Nursing
St. Francis Medical Center College of Nursing
Saint Xavier University
Sauk Valley Community College
School of the Art Institute of Chicago
Shawnee Community College
Shimer College
South Suburban College of Cook County
Southeastern Illinois College
Southern Illinois University Carbondale
Southern Illinois University Edwardsville
Southwestern Illinois College
Spoon River College
Trinity Christian College
Trinity College of Nursing & Health Sciences
Trinity International University
Triton College
University of Chicago
University of Illinois
    Chicago
    Springfield
    Urbana-Champaign
University of St. Francis
VanderCook College of Music
Waubonsee Community College
Western Illinois University
Wheaton College

Indiana
Ancilla College
Anderson University
Ball State University
Bethel College
Butler University
Calumet College of St. Joseph
DePauw University
Earlham College
Franklin College
Goshen College
Grace College
Hanover College

Holy Cross College
Huntington University
Indiana Institute of Technology
Indiana State University
Indiana University
 Bloomington
 East
 Kokomo
 Northwest
 Purdue University Fort Wayne
 Purdue University Indianapolis
 South Bend
 Southeast
Indiana Wesleyan University
Manchester University
Marian University
Oakland City University
Purdue University
Purdue University
 North Central
 Northwest
Rose-Hulman Institute of Technology
Saint Joseph's College
St. Mary-of-the-Woods College
Saint Mary's College
Taylor University
Trine University
University of Evansville
University of Indianapolis
University of Notre Dame
University of Saint Francis
University of Southern Indiana
Valparaiso University
Vincennes University
Wabash College

Iowa
Allen College
Briar Cliff University
Buena Vista University
Central College
Clarke University
Coe College
Cornell College
Des Moines Area Community College
Dordt College
Drake University
Ellsworth Community College
Emmaus Bible College
Faith Baptist Bible College and Theological
 Seminary
Graceland University
Grand View University
Grinnell College
Hawkeye Community College
Iowa Central Community College
Iowa State University
Iowa Wesleyan College
Kaplan University
 Cedar Falls
 Cedar Rapids
 Davenport
 Mason City
Loras College
Luther College
Mercy College of Health Sciences
Morningside College
Mount Mercy University
North Iowa Area Community College
Northeast Iowa Community College
Northwestern College
St. Ambrose University
St. Luke's College
Shiloh University
Simpson College
Southeastern Community College
Southwestern Community College
University of Dubuque
University of Iowa
University of Northern Iowa
Upper Iowa University
Vatterott College
 Des Moines

Waldorf University
Wartburg College
Western Iowa Tech Community College
William Penn University

Kansas
Allen County Community College
Baker University
Barclay College
Barton County Community College
Benedictine College
Bethany College
Bethel College
Butler Community College
Central Christian College of Kansas
Coffeyville Community College
Colby Community College
Cowley County Community College
Dodge City Community College
Donnelly College
Emporia State University
Fort Hays State University
Friends University
Garden City Community College
Hesston College
Highland Community College
Hutchinson Community College
Independence Community College
Johnson County Community College
Kansas City Kansas Community College
Kansas State University
Kansas Wesleyan University
Labette Community College
Manhattan Area Technical College
Manhattan Christian College
McPherson College
MidAmerica Nazarene University
Neosho County Community College
Newman University
North Central Kansas Technical College
Ottawa University
Pittsburg State University
Pratt Community College
Seward County Community College
Southwestern College
Sterling College
Tabor College
University of Kansas
University of Kansas Medical Center
University of St. Mary
Washburn University
Wichita Area Technical College
Wichita State University

Kentucky
Alice Lloyd College
Asbury University
Ashland Community and Technical College
Beckfield College
Bellarmine University
Big Sandy Community and Technical College
Bluegrass Community and Technical College
Brescia University
Campbellsville University
Centre College
Clear Creek Baptist Bible College
Daymar College
 Bowling Green
 Owensboro
Eastern Kentucky University
Georgetown College
Hopkinsville Community College
Jefferson Community and Technical College
Kentucky Christian University
Kentucky Mountain Bible College
Kentucky State University
Kentucky Wesleyan College
Maysville Community and Technical College
Midway College
Morehead State University
Murray State University
National College
 Danville

Florence
Lexington
Louisville
Pikeville
Richmond
Northern Kentucky University
Owensboro Community and Technical College
St. Catharine College
Somerset Community College
Southeast Kentucky Community and Technical
 College
Spalding University
Spencerian College
Spencerian College: Lexington
Sullivan College of Technology and Design
Thomas More College
Transylvania University
Union College
University of Kentucky
University of Louisville
University of the Cumberlands
West Kentucky Community and Technical
 College
Western Kentucky University

Louisiana
Baton Rouge Community College
Bossier Parish Community College
Centenary College of Louisiana
Delgado Community College
Dillard University
Grambling State University
Louisiana College
Louisiana State University
 Alexandria
 Eunice
 Health Sciences Center
 Shreveport
Louisiana State University and Agricultural and
 Mechanical College
Louisiana Tech University
Loyola University New Orleans
McNeese State University
Nicholls State University
Northwestern State University
Our Lady of the Lake College
Remington College
 Baton Rouge
St. Joseph Seminary College
South Louisiana Community College
Southeastern Louisiana University
Southern University and Agricultural and
 Mechanical College
Tulane University
University of Holy Cross
University of Louisiana
 Monroe
University of New Orleans
Xavier University of Louisiana

Maine
Bowdoin College
College of the Atlantic
Eastern Maine Community College
Husson University
Maine College of Art
Maine Maritime Academy
Saint Joseph's College of Maine
Thomas College
Unity College
University of Maine
University of Maine
 Augusta
 Farmington
 Fort Kent
 Machias
 Presque Isle
University of New England
University of Southern Maine
Washington County Community College
York County Community College

Maryland
Allegany College of Maryland
Bowie State University
Capitol Technology University
Carroll Community College
Cecil College
Chesapeake College
College of Southern Maryland
Community College of Baltimore County
Coppin State University
Frederick Community College
Frostburg State University
Garrett College
Goucher College
Hood College
Johns Hopkins University
Johns Hopkins University: Peabody
 Conservatory of Music
Loyola University Maryland
Maryland Institute College of Art
McDaniel College
Montgomery College
Morgan State University
Mount St. Mary's University
Notre Dame of Maryland University
Prince George's Community College
St. John's College
St. Mary's College of Maryland
Salisbury University
Stevenson University
Towson University
University of Maryland
 Baltimore County
 College Park
 Eastern Shore
 University College
Washington Adventist University
Washington College
Wor-Wic Community College

Massachusetts
American International College
Anna Maria College
Assumption College
Babson College
Bard College at Simon's Rock
Bay Path University
Bay State College
Becker College
Benjamin Franklin Institute of Technology
Bentley University
Berklee College of Music
Berkshire Community College
Boston Architectural College
Boston Baptist College
Boston College
Boston University
Brandeis University
Bridgewater State University
Bristol Community College
Bunker Hill Community College
Cape Cod Community College
Clark University
College of the Holy Cross
Curry College
Dean College
Eastern Nazarene College
Elms College
Emerson College
Emmanuel College
Endicott College
Fisher College
Fitchburg State University
Framingham State University
Franklin W. Olin College of Engineering
Gordon College
Hampshire College
Hellenic College/Holy Cross
Holyoke Community College
Laboure College
Lasell College
Lesley University
Massachusetts College of Art and Design

Massachusetts College of Liberal Arts
Massachusetts Maritime Academy
MCPHS University
Merrimack College
Montserrat College of Art
Mount Holyoke College
Mount Wachusett Community College
New England Conservatory of Music
Newbury College
Nichols College
North Shore Community College
Northeastern University
Northern Essex Community College
Northpoint Bible College
Pine Manor College
Quinsigamond Community College
Regis College
Salem State University
School of the Museum of Fine Arts
Simmons College
Smith College
Springfield College
Stonehill College
Suffolk University
Tufts University
University of Massachusetts
    Amherst
    Boston
    Dartmouth
    Lowell
Wentworth Institute of Technology
Western New England University
Westfield State University
Wheaton College
Wheelock College
Worcester Polytechnic Institute
Worcester State University

Michigan
Adrian College
Albion College
Alma College
Alpena Community College
Andrews University
Aquinas College
Baker College
    Auburn Hills
    Cadillac
    Clinton Township
    Flint
    Jackson
    Muskegon
    Owosso
    Port Huron
Bay College
Calvin College
Central Michigan University
Cleary University
College for Creative Studies
Concordia University
Cornerstone University
Davenport University
Delta College
Eastern Michigan University
Ferris State University
Finlandia University
Glen Oaks Community College
Gogebic Community College
Grace Bible College
Grand Rapids Community College
Grand Valley State University
Great Lakes Christian College
Henry Ford College
Hillsdale College
Hope College
Jackson College
Kalamazoo College
Kalamazoo Valley Community College
Kellogg Community College
Kettering University
Kirtland Community College
Kuyper College
Lake Superior State University

Lansing Community College
Lawrence Technological University
Macomb Community College
Madonna University
Marygrove College
Michigan State University
Michigan Technological University
Mid Michigan Community College
Monroe County Community College
Montcalm Community College
Mott Community College
Northern Michigan University
Northwestern Michigan College
Northwood University
    Michigan
Oakland Community College
Oakland University
Olivet College
Robert B Miller College
    Robert B. Miller College
Rochester College
Sacred Heart Major Seminary
Saginaw Valley State University
Schoolcraft College
Southwestern Michigan College
Spring Arbor University
University of Detroit Mercy
University of Michigan
University of Michigan
    Flint
Walsh College of Accountancy and Business
    Administration
Washtenaw Community College
Wayne State University
Western Michigan University

Minnesota
Art Institute International Minnesota
    Art Institutes International Minnesota
Augsburg College
Bemidji State University
Bethany Lutheran College
Bethel University
Carleton College
College of St. Benedict
College of St. Scholastica
Concordia College: Moorhead
Concordia University St. Paul
Crossroads College
Crown College
Dakota County Technical College
Fond du Lac Tribal and Community College
Gustavus Adolphus College
Hamline University
Itasca Community College
Lake Superior College
Le Cordon Bleu College of Culinary Arts
    Minneapolis-St. Paul
Macalester College
Martin Luther College
McNally Smith College of Music
Metropolitan State University
Minneapolis College of Art and Design
Minnesota State College - Southeast Technical
Minnesota State Community and Technical
    College
Minnesota State University
    Mankato
    Moorhead
National American University
    Bloomington
Normandale Community College
North Central University
North Hennepin Community College
Northland Community & Technical College
Northwest Technical College
Northwestern Health Sciences University
Oak Hills Christian College
Pine Technical & Community College
Rainy River Community College
St. Catherine University
Saint Cloud State University
St. Cloud Technical and Community College

St. John's University
St. Mary's University of Minnesota
St. Olaf College
Southwest Minnesota State University
University of Minnesota
    Crookston
    Duluth
    Morris
    Rochester
    Twin Cities
University of Northwestern - St. Paul
University of St. Thomas
Winona State University

Mississippi
Alcorn State University
Belhaven University
Blue Mountain College
Coahoma Community College
Copiah-Lincoln Community College
Delta State University
East Central Community College
East Mississippi Community College
Hinds Community College
Holmes Community College
Itawamba Community College
Jackson State University
Jones County Junior College
Meridian Community College
Millsaps College
Mississippi College
Mississippi Delta Community College
Mississippi Gulf Coast Community College
Mississippi State University
Mississippi University for Women
Mississippi Valley State University
Northeast Mississippi Community College
Pearl River Community College
Rust College
Tougaloo College
University of Mississippi
University of Mississippi
    University of Southern Mississippi
University of Mississippi Medical Center
William Carey University

Missouri
Avila University
Calvary Bible College and Theological
    Seminary
Central Methodist University
Chamberlain College of Nursing
    St. Louis
College of the Ozarks
Columbia College
Conception Seminary College
Cottey College
Crowder College
Culver-Stockton College
DeVry University
    Kansas City
Drury University
East Central College
Evangel University
Fontbonne University
Goldfarb School of Nursing at Barnes-Jewish
    College
Hannibal-LaGrange University
Harris-Stowe State University
Jefferson College
Kansas City Art Institute
Lincoln University
Lindenwood University
Maryville University of Saint Louis
Metropolitan Community College - Kansas City
Mineral Area College
Missouri Baptist University
Missouri Southern State University
Missouri State University
Missouri State University
    West Plains
Missouri University of Science and Technology
Missouri Valley College

Missouri Western State University
Moberly Area Community College
North Central Missouri College
Northwest Missouri State University
Ozark Christian College
Park University
Research College of Nursing
Rockhurst University
St. Charles Community College
St. Louis Community College
Saint Louis University
St. Luke's College
Southeast Missouri State University
Southwest Baptist University
State Fair Community College
State Technical College of Missouri
Stephens College
Three Rivers Community College
Truman State University
University of Central Missouri
University of Missouri
    Columbia
    Kansas City
    St. Louis
Washington University in St. Louis
Webster University
Westminster College
William Jewell College
William Woods University

Montana
Blackfeet Community College
Carroll College
Chief Dull Knife College
Dawson Community College
Flathead Valley Community College
Fort Peck Community College
Little Big Horn College
Miles Community College
Montana State University
Montana State University
    Billings
    Great Falls College
    Northern
Montana Tech of the University of Montana
Rocky Mountain College
University of Great Falls
University of Montana
University of Montana: Western

Nebraska
Bellevue University
BryanLGH College of Health Sciences
Central Community College
Chadron State College
Clarkson College
College of Saint Mary
Concordia University
Creative Center
Creighton University
Doane University
Grace University
Hastings College
Metropolitan Community College
Mid-Plains Community College
Midland University
Nebraska Christian College
Nebraska College of Technical Agriculture
Nebraska Methodist College of Nursing and
    Allied Health
Nebraska Wesleyan University
Northeast Community College
Peru State College
Southeast Community College
Union College
University of Nebraska
    Kearney
    Lincoln
    Omaha
Wayne State College
Western Nebraska Community College
York College

Nevada
Art Institute of Las Vegas
Roseman University of Health Sciences
Sierra Nevada College
Truckee Meadows Community College
University of Nevada
    Las Vegas
    Reno
Western Nevada College

New Hampshire
Colby-Sawyer College
Franklin Pierce University
Keene State College
New England College
New Hampshire Institute of Art
Plymouth State University
Rivier University
Saint Anselm College
Southern New Hampshire University
Thomas More College of Liberal Arts
University of New Hampshire
University of New Hampshire at Manchester

New Jersey
Berkeley College
Bloomfield College
Brookdale Community College
Caldwell University
Camden County College
Centenary University
The College of New Jersey
College of St. Elizabeth
Cumberland County College
DeVry University
    North Brunswick
Drew University
Eastern International College
Felician University
Georgian Court University
Kean University
Mercer County Community College
Monmouth University
Montclair State University
New Jersey Institute of Technology
Ocean County College
Passaic County Community College
Pillar College
Ramapo College of New Jersey
Raritan Valley Community College
Rider University
Rowan College at Burlington County
Rowan University
Rutgers, The State University of New Jersey
    Camden Campus
    New Brunswick/Piscataway Campus
    Newark Campus
Saint Peter's University
Salem Community College
Seton Hall University
Stevens Institute of Technology
Stockton University
Sussex County Community College
Union County College
Warren County Community College
William Paterson University of New Jersey

New Mexico
Clovis Community College
Eastern New Mexico University
Eastern New Mexico University: Roswell
Luna Community College
Mesalands Community College
Navajo Technical University
New Mexico Highlands University
New Mexico Institute of Mining and
    Technology
New Mexico Junior College
New Mexico Military Institute
New Mexico State University
New Mexico State University
    Alamogordo
    Carlsbad

Northern New Mexico College
St. John's College
San Juan College
Santa Fe Community College
Santa Fe University of Art and Design
Southwest University of Visual Arts
Southwestern Indian Polytechnic Institute
University of New Mexico
University of the Southwest
Western New Mexico University

New York
Adelphi University
Adirondack Community College
Albany College of Pharmacy and Health
    Sciences
Alfred University
ASA College
Bard College
Berkeley College
Berkeley College of New York City
Briarcliffe College
Bryant & Stratton College
    Albany
    Syracuse
Canisius College
Cayuga Community College
Cazenovia College
City University of New York
    Baruch College
    Brooklyn College
    City College
    College of Staten Island
    Hunter College
    Medgar Evers College
    Queens College
    York College
Clarkson University
College of Mount St. Vincent
College of New Rochelle
College of Saint Rose
College of Westchester
Columbia University
    School of General Studies
Concordia College
Cooper Union for the Advancement of Science
    and Art
Corning Community College
Culinary Institute of America
Daemen College
Davis College
Dominican College of Blauvelt
Dutchess Community College
D'Youville College
Eastman School of Music of the University of
    Rochester
Elmira Business Institute
Elmira Business Institute: Vestal
Elmira College
Eugene Lang College The New School for
    Liberal Arts
Finger Lakes Community College
Five Towns College
Fordham University
Fulton-Montgomery Community College
Genesee Community College
Globe Institute of Technology
Hartwick College
Hilbert College
Hobart and William Smith Colleges
Hofstra University
Houghton College
Iona College
Ithaca College
Jamestown Business College
Jamestown Community College
Jefferson Community College
Jewish Theological Seminary of America
Keuka College
The King's College
Le Moyne College
LIM College
Long Island Business Institute

Long Island University
    LIU Brooklyn
    LIU Post
Manhattan College
Manhattan School of Music
Manhattanville College
Marist College
Marymount Manhattan College
Medaille College
Mercy College
Metropolitan College of New York
Mildred Elley
    Albany
    New York City
Molloy College
Monroe College
Monroe Community College
Mount Saint Mary College
Nassau Community College
Nazareth College
The New School College of Performing Arts
New York Institute of Technology
New York School of Interior Design
Niagara County Community College
Niagara University
Nyack College
Onondaga Community College
Pace University
Pace University: Pleasantville/Briarcliff
Parsons the New School for Design
    Parsons The New School for Design
Paul Smith's College
Pratt Institute
Rensselaer Polytechnic Institute
Rochester Institute of Technology
The Sage Colleges
Saint Bonaventure University
St. Francis College
St. John Fisher College
St. John's University
St. Joseph's College New York: Suffolk
    Campus
St. Joseph's College, New York
St. Lawrence University
St. Thomas Aquinas College
Sarah Lawrence College
Schenectady County Community College
School of Visual Arts
Siena College
Suffolk County Community College
Sullivan County Community College
SUNY
    College at Brockport
    College at Buffalo
    College at Cortland
    College at Fredonia
    College at Geneseo
    College at New Paltz
    College at Old Westbury
    College at Oneonta
    College at Oswego
    College at Plattsburgh
    College at Potsdam
    College at Purchase
    College of Agriculture and Technology at
        Cobleskill
    College of Agriculture and Technology at
        Morrisville
    College of Environmental Science and
        Forestry
    College of Technology at Alfred
    College of Technology at Canton
    Farmingdale State College
    University at Albany
    University at Binghamton
    University at Buffalo
    University at Stony Brook
Technical Career Institutes
Tompkins Cortland Community College
Touro College
Trocaire College
Union College
University of Rochester

Utica College
Vaughn College of Aeronautics and Technology
Villa Maria College of Buffalo
Wagner College
Webb Institute
Wells College
Westchester Community College
Yeshivat Mikdash Melech

North Carolina
Alamance Community College
Appalachian State University
Asheville-Buncombe Technical Community
    College
Barton College
Beaufort County Community College
Belmont Abbey College
Bennett College for Women
Blue Ridge Community College
Brevard College
Brunswick Community College
Cabarrus College of Health Sciences
Campbell University
Cape Fear Community College
Carolinas College of Health Sciences
Carteret Community College
Catawba College
Catawba Valley Community College
Central Carolina Community College
Central Piedmont Community College
Chowan University
Cleveland Community College
Coastal Carolina Community College
College of the Albemarle
Davidson College
Davidson County Community College
Duke University
Durham Technical Community College
East Carolina University
Elizabeth City State University
Elon University
Fayetteville State University
Forsyth Technical Community College
Gardner-Webb University
Gaston College
Greensboro College
Guilford College
Guilford Technical Community College
Halifax Community College
Haywood Community College
High Point University
Isothermal Community College
James Sprunt Community College
Johnson & Wales University
    Charlotte
Johnson C. Smith University
Johnston Community College
Lees-McRae College
Lenoir Community College
Lenoir-Rhyne University
Livingstone College
Louisburg College
Mars Hill University
Martin Community College
McDowell Technical Community College
Meredith College
Methodist University
Mid-Atlantic Christian University
Montgomery Community College
Montreat College
Nash Community College
North Carolina Agricultural and Technical State
    University
North Carolina Central University
North Carolina State University
North Carolina Wesleyan College
Pfeiffer University
Piedmont International University
Pitt Community College
Queens University of Charlotte
Randolph Community College
Richmond Community College
Roanoke-Chowan Community College

Rockingham Community College
Rowan-Cabarrus Community College
St. Andrews University
Saint Augustine's University
Salem College
Sampson Community College
Sandhills Community College
Shaw University
Southeastern Community College
Stanley Community College
    Stanly Community College
Surry Community College
University of Mount Olive
University of North Carolina
    Asheville
    Chapel Hill
    Charlotte
    Greensboro
    Pembroke
    School of the Arts
    Wilmington
Vance-Granville Community College
Wake Forest University
Wake Technical Community College
Warren Wilson College
Wayne Community College
Western Carolina University
Western Piedmont Community College
Wilkes Community College
William Peace University
Wilson Community College
Wingate University
Winston-Salem State University

North Dakota
Bismarck State College
Dakota College at Bottineau
Dickinson State University
Lake Region State College
Mayville State University
Minot State University
North Dakota State College of Science
Trinity Bible College
Turtle Mountain Community College
University of Jamestown
University of Mary
Valley City State University
Williston State College

Ohio
Art Academy of Cincinnati
Art Institute of Cincinnati
Ashland University
Aultman College of Nursing and Health
    Sciences
Baldwin Wallace University
Bluffton University
Bowling Green State University
Bowling Green State University: Firelands
    College
Brown Mackie College
    Findlay
Bryant & Stratton College
    Cleveland
    Eastlake
    Parma
Capital University
Case Western Reserve University
Cedarville University
Central Ohio Technical College
Central State University
Chatfield College
Cincinnati Christian University
Cincinnati State Technical and Community
    College
Cleveland Institute of Art
Cleveland Institute of Music
Cleveland State University
College of Wooster
Columbus College of Art and Design
Columbus State Community College
Cuyahoga Community College
Defiance College

Denison University
DeVry University
    Columbus
Eastern Gateway Community College
Edison State Community College
Franciscan University of Steubenville
Franklin University
God's Bible School and College
Heidelberg University
Hocking College
James A. Rhodes State College
John Carroll University
Kent State University
Kent State University
    Ashtabula
    East Liverpool
    Geauga
    Salem
    Stark
    Trumbull
    Tuscarawas
Kenyon College
Kettering College
Lake Erie College
Lakeland Community College
Lorain County Community College
Lourdes University
Malone University
Marietta College
Marion Technical College
Mercy College of Ohio
Miami University
    Hamilton
    Oxford
Mount Carmel College of Nursing
Mount St. Joseph University
Mount Vernon Nazarene University
Muskingum University
Northwest State Community College
Notre Dame College
Oberlin College
Ohio Christian University
Ohio Dominican University
Ohio Northern University
Ohio State University
    Agricultural Technical Institute
    Columbus Campus
    Lima Campus
    Mansfield Campus
    Marion Campus
    Newark Campus
Ohio University
Ohio University
    Eastern Campus
    Southern Campus at Ironton
    Zanesville Campus
Ohio Wesleyan University
Otterbein University
Owens Community College
Pontifical College Josephinum
PowerSport Institute
Rosedale Bible College
School of Advertising Art
Shawnee State University
Sinclair Community College
Southern State Community College
Stark State College
Terra State Community College
Tiffin University
Union Institute & University
University of Akron
University of Akron: Wayne College
University of Cincinnati
University of Cincinnati
    Blue Ash College
    Clermont College
University of Dayton
University of Findlay
University of Mount Union
University of Northwestern Ohio
University of Rio Grande
University of Toledo
Urbana University

Ursuline College
Walsh University
Wilberforce University
Wilmington College
Wittenberg University
Wright State University
Wright State University: Lake Campus
Xavier University
Youngstown State University

Oklahoma
Cameron University
Carl Albert State College
Connors State College
East Central University
Eastern Oklahoma State College
Langston University
Mid-America Christian University
Northeastern Oklahoma Agricultural and
    Mechanical College
Northeastern State University
Northern Oklahoma College
Northwestern Oklahoma State University
Oklahoma Baptist University
Oklahoma Christian University
Oklahoma City Community College
Oklahoma City University
Oklahoma Panhandle State University
Oklahoma State University
Oklahoma State University
    Institute of Technology: Okmulgee
    Oklahoma City
Oklahoma Wesleyan University
Oral Roberts University
Redlands Community College
Rogers State University
Rose State College
St. Gregory's University
Seminole State College
Southeastern Oklahoma State University
Southern Nazarene University
Southwestern Christian University
Southwestern Oklahoma State University
Tulsa Community College
University of Central Oklahoma
University of Oklahoma
University of Science and Arts of Oklahoma
University of Tulsa
Western Oklahoma State College

Oregon
Central Oregon Community College
Chemeketa Community College
Clackamas Community College
Clatsop Community College
Concordia University
Corban University
Eastern Oregon University
George Fox University
Lewis & Clark College
Linfield College
Linn-Benton Community College
Marylhurst University
Mt. Hood Community College
Multnomah University
New Hope Christian College
Northwest Christian University
Oregon College of Art & Craft
Oregon Institute of Technology
Oregon State University
Pacific Northwest College of Art
Pacific University
Portland State University
Rogue Community College
Southern Oregon University
Treasure Valley Community College
Umpqua Community College
University of Oregon
University of Portland
Warner Pacific College
Western Oregon University
Willamette University

Pennsylvania
Albright College
Allegheny College
Alvernia University
Arcadia University
Berks Technical Institute
Bloomsburg University of Pennsylvania
Bryn Athyn College
Bryn Mawr College
Bucknell University
Bucks County Community College
Butler County Community College
Cabrini University
Cairn University
California University of Pennsylvania
Cambria-Rowe Business College
Cambria-Rowe Business College: Indiana
Carlow University
Carnegie Mellon University
Cedar Crest College
Central Penn College
Chatham University
Chestnut Hill College
Cheyney University of Pennsylvania
Clarion University of Pennsylvania
Clarks Summit University
Community College of Allegheny County
Community College of Beaver County
Consolidated School of Business
    Lancaster
    York
Delaware County Community College
Delaware Valley University
DeSales University
DeVry University
    Fort Washington
Dickinson College
Drexel University
Duquesne University
East Stroudsburg University of Pennsylvania
Eastern University
Edinboro University
    Pennsylvania
Elizabethtown College
Gannon University
Geneva College
Gettysburg College
Grove City College
Gwynedd Mercy University
Harcum College
Harrisburg University of Science and
    Technology
Holy Family University
Immaculata University
Indiana University of Pennsylvania
Johnson College
Juniata College
Keystone College
King's College
Kutztown University of Pennsylvania
La Roche College
La Salle University
Lackawanna College
Lafayette College
Lancaster Bible College
Laurel Technical Institute
Lebanon Valley College
Lehigh Carbon Community College
Lehigh University
Lincoln University
Lock Haven University of Pennsylvania
Lycoming College
Manor College
Mansfield University of Pennsylvania
Marywood University
Mercyhurst University
Messiah College
Millersville University of Pennsylvania
Misericordia University
Montgomery County Community College
Moore College of Art and Design
Moravian College

Mount Aloysius College
Muhlenberg College
Neumann University
Northampton Community College
Orleans Technical Institute
Peirce College
Penn State
  Abington
  Altoona
  Beaver
  Berks
  Brandywine
  DuBois
  Erie, The Behrend College
  Fayette, The Eberly Campus
  Greater Allegheny
  Harrisburg
  Hazleton
  Lehigh Valley
  Mont Alto
  New Kensington
  Schuylkill
  Shenango
  University Park
  Wilkes-Barre
  Worthington Scranton
  York
Pennsylvania Academy of the Fine Arts
Pennsylvania Colleg of Art and Design
  Pennsylvania College of Art and Design
Pennsylvania College of Health Sciences
Pennsylvania College of Technology
Pennsylvania Highlands Community College
Pennsylvania Institute of Technology
Philadelphia University
Point Park University
Robert Morris University
Rosemont College
St. Francis University
Saint Joseph's University
St. Vincent College
Seton Hill University
Shippensburg University of Pennsylvania
Slippery Rock University of Pennsylvania
Susquehanna University
Swarthmore College
Temple University
Thiel College
Thomas Jefferson University
Triangle Tech
  Bethlehem
  DuBois
  Pittsburgh
University of Pittsburgh
University of Pittsburgh
  Bradford
  Greensburg
  Johnstown
  Titusville
University of Scranton
University of the Arts
University of the Sciences
University of Valley Forge
Ursinus College
Valley Forge Military College
Vet Tech Institute
Villanova University
Washington & Jefferson College
Waynesburg University
West Chester University of Pennsylvania
Westminster College
Westmoreland County Community College
Widener University
Wilkes University
Wilson College
York College of Pennsylvania
YTI Career Institute
  Lancaster

Puerto Rico
ICPR Junior College
Inter American University of Puerto Rico
  Aguadilla Campus
  Arecibo Campus
  Barranquitas Campus
  Bayamon Campus
  Ponce Campus
  San German Campus
Pontifical Catholic University of Puerto Rico
Turabo University
Universidad del Este
Universidad Metropolitana
Universidad Pentecostal Mizpa
Universidad Politecnica de Puerto Rico
University of Puerto Rico
  Bayamon University College
  Cayey University College
  Humacao
  Mayaguez
  Utuado
University of the Sacred Heart

Rhode Island
Bryant University
Johnson & Wales University
  Providence
New England Institute of Technology
Providence College
Rhode Island College
Rhode Island School of Design
Roger Williams University
Salve Regina University
University of Rhode Island

South Carolina
Aiken Technical College
Allen University
Anderson University
Bob Jones University
Charleston Southern University
The Citadel
Clemson University
Coastal Carolina University
Coker College
College of Charleston
Columbia College
Columbia International University
Converse College
Erskine College
Florence-Darlington Technical College
Francis Marion University
Furman University
Greenville Technical College
Horry-Georgetown Technical College
Lander University
Limestone College
Morris College
Newberry College
North Greenville University
Piedmont Technical College
Presbyterian College
South Carolina State University
Southern Wesleyan University
Spartanburg Community College
Spartanburg Methodist College
Tri-County Technical College
Trident Technical College
University of South Carolina
  Aiken
  Beaufort
  Columbia
  Salkehatchie
  Sumter
  Union
  Upstate
Williamsburg Technical College
Winthrop University
Wofford College
York Technical College

South Dakota
Augusta University
  Augustana University
Black Hills State University
Dakota State University
Dakota Wesleyan University
Mitchell Technical Institute
Mount Marty College
South Dakota School of Mines and Technology
South Dakota State University
Southeast Technical Institute
University of Sioux Falls
University of South Dakota

Tennessee
Aquinas College
Austin Peay State University
Belmont University
Bethel University
Carson-Newman University
Christian Brothers University
Columbia State Community College
Cumberland University
Dyersburg State Community College
East Tennessee State University
Fisk University
Freed-Hardeman University
Jackson State Community College
Johnson University
King University
Lane College
Lee University
LeMoyne-Owen College
Lincoln Memorial University
Martin Methodist College
Maryville College
Memphis College of Art
Middle Tennessee State University
Milligan College
Motlow State Community College
Nashville State Community College
National College
  Bristol
  Nashville
Northeast State Community College
O'More College of Design
Pellissippi State Community College
Rhodes College
Roane State Community College
Sewanee: The University of the South
Southern Adventist University
Southwest Tennessee Community College
Tennessee State University
Tennessee Technological University
Tennessee Wesleyan College
Trevecca Nazarene University
Tusculum College
Union University
University of Memphis
University of Tennessee
  Chattanooga
  Knoxville
  Martin
Vanderbilt University
Volunteer State Community College
Walters State Community College
Watkins College of Art, Design & Film
Welch College
Williamson College

Texas
Abilene Christian University
Alvin Community College
Amarillo College
Angelina College
Angelo State University
Arlington Baptist College
Austin College
Austin Graduate School of Theology
Baptist Missionary Association Theological
  Seminary
Baylor University
Brazosport College
Brookhaven College
Central Texas College
Clarendon College
Coastal Bend College
College of the Mainland
Collin County Community College District
Commonwealth Institute of Funeral Service
Concordia University Texas
Dallas Baptist University
East Texas Baptist University
El Paso Community College
Frank Phillips College
Galveston College
Grayson College
Hardin-Simmons University
Hill College
Houston Baptist University
Houston Community College System
Howard College
Howard Payne University
Huston-Tillotson University
Jacksonville College
Jarvis Christian College
Kilgore College
Lamar University
Lee College
LeTourneau University
Lone Star College System
McMurry University
Midland College
Midwestern State University
North Central Texas College
North Lake College
Northwest Vista College
Northwood University
  Texas
Odessa College
Our Lady of the Lake University of San
  Antonio
Palo Alto College
Panola College
Paul Quinn College
Prairie View A&M University
Ranger College
Rice University
St. Edward's University
St. Mary's University
Sam Houston State University
San Jacinto College
Schreiner University
South Plains College
South Texas College
Southern Methodist University
Southwestern Adventist University
Southwestern Christian College
Southwestern University
Stephen F. Austin State University
Sul Ross State University
Tarleton State University
Tarrant County College
Texarkana College
Texas A&M International University
Texas A&M University
Texas A&M University
  Commerce
  Corpus Christi
  Kingsville
  Texarkana
Texas Christian University
Texas College
Texas Lutheran University
Texas Southern University
Texas State Technical College
Texas State University
Texas Tech University
Texas Tech University Health Sciences Center
Texas Wesleyan University
Texas Woman's University
Trinity University
Trinity Valley Community College
Tyler Junior College
University of Dallas
University of Houston
University of Houston
  Clear Lake
  Downtown
  Victoria
University of Mary Hardin-Baylor
University of St. Thomas

University of Texas
    Arlington
    Austin
    Dallas
    El Paso
    Medical Branch at Galveston
    the Permian Basin
    San Antonio
    Tyler
University Of Texas Rio Grande Valley
University of the Incarnate Word
Vernon College
Victoria College
Wayland Baptist University
West Coast University: Dallas
West Texas A&M University
Western Texas College
Wharton County Junior College

Utah

Brigham Young University
Dixie State University
LDS Business College
Neumont University
Salt Lake Community College
Snow College
Southern Utah University
University of Utah
Utah State University
Utah Valley University
Weber State University
Western Governors University
Westminster College

Vermont

Bennington College
Castleton University
Champlain College
College of St. Joseph in Vermont
Goddard College
Green Mountain College
Johnson State College
Landmark College
Lyndon State College
Marlboro College
New England Culinary Institute
Norwich University
Southern Vermont College
Sterling College
University of Vermont
Vermont Technical College

Virginia

American National University
    Charlottesville
    Danville
    Harrisonburg
    Lynchburg
    Martinsville
Averett University
Blue Ridge Community College
Bluefield College
Bridgewater College
Bryant & Stratton College
    Richmond
Central Virginia Community College
Christendom College
Christopher Newport University
College of William and Mary
DeVry University
    Arlington
Eastern Mennonite University
ECPI University
Emory & Henry College
Ferrum College
George Mason University
Germanna Community College
Hampden-Sydney College
Hampton University
Hollins University
J. Sargeant Reynolds Community College
James Madison University
Jefferson College of Health Sciences

John Tyler Community College
Liberty University
Longwood University
Lynchburg College
Mary Baldwin University
Marymount University
Mountain Empire Community College
Norfolk State University
Northern Virginia Community College
Old Dominion University
Patrick Henry College
Paul D. Camp Community College
Piedmont Virginia Community College
Radford University
Randolph College
Randolph-Macon College
Regent University
Richard Bland College
Roanoke College
Shenandoah University
Southern Virginia University
Southside Virginia Community College
Southwest Virginia Community College
Stratford University: Falls Church
Sweet Briar College
University of Mary Washington
University of Richmond
University of Virginia
University of Virginia's College at Wise
Virginia Baptist College
Virginia Commonwealth University
Virginia Military Institute
Virginia Polytechnic Institute and State
    University
Virginia State University
Virginia Union University
Virginia Wesleyan College
Virginia Western Community College
Washington and Lee University
Wytheville Community College

Washington

Art Institute of Seattle
Bastyr University
Bellevue College
Big Bend Community College
Central Washington University
Centralia College
City University of Seattle
Clark College
Clover Park Technical College
Columbia Basin College
Cornish College of the Arts
DigiPen Institute of Technology
Eastern Washington University
Everett Community College
Evergreen State College
Gonzaga University
Grays Harbor College
Heritage University
Northwest College of Art & Design
Northwest Indian College
Northwest University
Olympic College
Pacific Lutheran University
Peninsula College
Pierce College
Saint Martin's University
Seattle Pacific University
Seattle University
Skagit Valley College
South Puget Sound Community College
South Seattle College
Tacoma Community College
University of Puget Sound
University of Washington
University of Washington Bothell
University of Washington Tacoma
Walla Walla Community College
Walla Walla University
Washington State University
Wenatchee Valley College
Western Washington University

Whatcom Community College
Whitman College
Whitworth University

West Virginia

Alderson-Broaddus University
American National University
    Princeton
Bethany College
Bluefield State College
Concord University
Davis and Elkins College
Fairmont State University
Glenville State College
Kanawha Valley Community and Technical
    College
Marshall University
Ohio Valley University
Potomac State College of West Virginia
    University
Salem International University
Shepherd University
University of Charleston
West Liberty University
West Virginia Business College
    Nutter Fort
West Virginia State University
West Virginia University
West Virginia University at Parkersburg
West Virginia University Institute of
    Technology
West Virginia Wesleyan College
Wheeling Jesuit University

Wisconsin

Alverno College
Bellin College
Beloit College
Cardinal Stritch University
Carroll University
Carthage College
College of Menominee Nation
Columbia College of Nursing
Concordia University Wisconsin
Edgewood College
Lakeland University
Lakeshore Technical College
Lawrence University
Maranathan Baptist University
    Maranatha Baptist University
Marian University
Marquette University
Mid-State Technical College
Milwaukee Area Technical College
Milwaukee Institute of Art & Design
Milwaukee School of Engineering
Moraine Park Technical College
Mount Mary University
Nicolet Area Technical College
Northland College
Ripon College
St. Norbert College
Silver Lake College of the Holy Family
University of Wisconsin
    Baraboo/Sauk County
    Eau Claire
    Fond du Lac
    Fox Valley
    Green Bay
    La Crosse
    Madison
    Marshfield/Wood County
    Milwaukee
    Oshkosh
    Parkside
    Richland
    River Falls
    Rock County
    Sheboygan
    Stevens Point
    Stout
    Superior
    Washington County

    Waukesha
    Whitewater
Viterbo University
Waukesha County Technical College
Wisconsin Lutheran College

Wyoming

Casper College
Central Wyoming College
Eastern Wyoming College
Laramie County Community College
Northwest College
Sheridan College
University of Wyoming
Western Wyoming Community College

Art scholarships

Alabama
Alabama State University
Athens State University
Birmingham-Southern College
Chattahoochee Valley Community College
Enterprise State Community College
Faulkner State Community College
Gadsden State Community College
Jacksonville State University
Jefferson State Community College
Judson College
Lurleen B. Wallace Community College
Northeast Alabama Community College
Northwest-Shoals Community College
Samford University
Selma University
Shelton State Community College
Snead State Community College
Southern Union State Community College
Spring Hill College
Talladega College
Troy University
University of Alabama
University of Alabama
    Birmingham
    Huntsville
University of Montevallo
University of North Alabama
University of South Alabama
University of West Alabama

Alaska
Alaska Pacific University
University of Alaska
    Anchorage
    Fairbanks

Arizona
Arizona State University
Arizona Western College
Eastern Arizona College
Glendale Community College
Grand Canyon University
Northern Arizona University
Northland Pioneer College
University of Advancing Technology
University of Arizona

Arkansas
Arkansas Northeastern College
Arkansas State University
Harding University
Henderson State University
Hendrix College
John Brown University
Lyon College
Ouachita Baptist University
Southern Arkansas University
University of Arkansas
University of Arkansas
    Little Rock
    Pine Bluff
University of Central Arkansas
University of the Ozarks
Williams Baptist College

California
Academy of Art University
Art Institute of California
    Orange County
California Baptist University
California College of the Arts
California Institute of Integral Studies
California Institute of the Arts
California Lutheran University
California Polytechnic State University: San
    Luis Obispo
California State University
    Bakersfield
    Chico
    Dominguez Hills
    Fresno
    Fullerton
    Long Beach
    Stanislaus
Chapman University
College of the Canyons
College of the Desert
Columbia College
    Hollywood
El Camino College
Irvine Valley College
La Sierra University
Laguna College of Art and Design
Loyola Marymount University
Marymount California University
Notre Dame de Namur University
Otis College of Art and Design
Pacific Union College
Pepperdine University
Point Loma Nazarene University
Riverside City College
San Diego State University
San Francisco Art Institute
San Jose State University
Santa Rosa Junior College
Sonoma State University
University of California
    Riverside
    San Diego
    Santa Cruz
University of La Verne
University of Redlands
University of Southern California
University of the Pacific
Westmont College
Whittier College
William Jessup University

Colorado
Adams State University
Arapahoe Community College
Colorado Mesa University
Colorado State University
Colorado State University
    Pueblo
Fort Lewis College
Naropa University
Northeastern Junior College
Pueblo Community College
Rocky Mountain College of Art & Design
University of Colorado
    Boulder
    Denver
University of Denver
Western State Colorado University

Connecticut
Fairfield University
Lyme Academy College of Fine Arts
Mitchell College
Sacred Heart University
University of Bridgeport
University of Connecticut
University of Hartford
University of New Haven
Western Connecticut State University

Delaware
Delaware College of Art and Design
Delaware State University
University of Delaware

District of Columbia
George Washington University
Howard University

Florida
Barry University
Chipola College
Digital Media Arts College
Eckerd College
Flagler College
Florida Agricultural and Mechanical University
Florida International University
Florida Keys Community College
Florida Southern College
Florida SouthWestern State College
Florida State College at Jacksonville
Florida State University
Hillsborough Community College
Jacksonville University
Lake-Sumter State College
Miami Dade College
North Florida Community College
Nova Southeastern University
Palm Beach Atlantic University
Ringling College of Art and Design
Rollins College
Santa Fe College
Seminole State College of Florida
State College of Florida, Manatee-Sarasota
Stetson University
Tallahassee Community College
University of Florida
University of South Florida
University of South Florida
    Saint Petersburg
    Sarasota-Manatee
University of Tampa
University of West Florida
Warner University

Georgia
Andrew College
Armstrong State University
Art Institute of Atlanta
Berry College
Brenau University
Clark Atlanta University
Columbus State University
Covenant College
Darton State College
Emmanuel College
Emory University
Georgia College and State University
Georgia Highlands College
Georgia Perimeter College
Georgia Southern University
Georgia Southwestern State University
Georgia State University
Kennesaw State University
LaGrange College
Mercer University
Middle Georgia State University
Morehouse College
Oglethorpe University
Piedmont College
Reinhardt University
Shorter University
University of North Georgia
University of West Georgia
Valdosta State University
Wesleyan College
Young Harris College

Hawaii
Brigham Young University-Hawaii
University of Hawaii
    Hilo
    Manoa

Idaho
Boise State University
Brigham Young University-Idaho
Idaho State University
Lewis-Clark State College
North Idaho College
University of Idaho

Illinois
American Academy of Art
Augustana College
Aurora University
Benedictine University at Springfield
Black Hawk College
Bradley University
Carl Sandburg College
College of DuPage
College of Lake County
Danville Area Community College
DePaul University
Dominican University
Eastern Illinois University
Elgin Community College
Elmhurst College
Eureka College
Greenville College
Illinois College
Illinois Institute of Art
    Schaumburg
Illinois Institute of Technology
Illinois State University
Illinois Valley Community College
Illinois Wesleyan University
Judson University
Knox College
Lake Forest College
Lewis University
Lincoln College
Loyola University Chicago
McKendree University
Millikin University
Monmouth College
North Central College
North Park University
Northeastern Illinois University
Northern Illinois University
Oakton Community College
Olivet Nazarene University
Quincy University
Richland Community College
Robert Morris College
    Robert Morris University: Chicago
Roosevelt University
School of the Art Institute of Chicago
Shawnee Community College
South Suburban College of Cook County
Southeastern Illinois College
Southern Illinois University Carbondale
Southern Illinois University Edwardsville
Southwestern Illinois College
Spoon River College
Trinity Christian College
University of Illinois
    Chicago
    Springfield
    Urbana-Champaign
University of St. Francis
Waubonsee Community College
Western Illinois University
Wheaton College

Indiana
Anderson University
Calumet College of St. Joseph
Franklin College
Goshen College
Grace College
Huntington University
Indiana State University
Indiana University
    Bloomington
    Purdue University Fort Wayne
    Purdue University Indianapolis
    Southeast
Indiana Wesleyan University
Marian University
Saint Joseph's College
St. Mary-of-the-Woods College
Saint Mary's College
Taylor University
University of Evansville

University of Indianapolis
University of Saint Francis
University of Southern Indiana
Valparaiso University
Vincennes University
Wabash College

Iowa
Briar Cliff University
Buena Vista University
Central College
Clarke University
Coe College
Cornell College
Dordt College
Drake University
Ellsworth Community College
Graceland University
Grand View University
Iowa Central Community College
Iowa State University
Iowa Wesleyan College
Kirkwood Community College
Loras College
Luther College
Morningside College
Mount Mercy University
North Iowa Area Community College
Northwestern College
St. Ambrose University
Simpson College
Southeastern Community College
University of Iowa
University of Northern Iowa
Western Iowa Tech Community College

Kansas
Allen County Community College
Baker University
Benedictine College
Bethany College
Bethel College
Butler Community College
Coffeyville Community College
Cowley County Community College
Emporia State University
Fort Hays State University
Friends University
Garden City Community College
Hesston College
Highland Community College
Hutchinson Community College
Independence Community College
Kansas City Kansas Community College
Kansas State University
Kansas Wesleyan University
McPherson College
Neosho County Community College
Newman University
Pittsburg State University
Pratt Community College
Sterling College
Tabor College
University of Kansas
University of St. Mary
Washburn University
Wichita State University

Kentucky
Asbury University
Bellarmine University
Brescia University
Campbellsville University
Centre College
Eastern Kentucky University
Georgetown College
Jefferson Community and Technical College
Kentucky State University
Kentucky Wesleyan College
Midway College
Morehead State University
Murray State University
Northern Kentucky University

Owensboro Community and Technical College
Spalding University
Sullivan College of Technology and Design
Thomas More College
Transylvania University
University of Kentucky
University of Louisville
Western Kentucky University

Louisiana
Centenary College of Louisiana
Dillard University
Grambling State University
Louisiana College
Louisiana Tech University
Loyola University New Orleans
McNeese State University
Northwestern State University
Xavier University of Louisiana

Maine
Maine College of Art
University of Maine
York County Community College

Maryland
Bowie State University
Carroll Community College
Chesapeake College
Goucher College
Maryland Institute College of Art
Montgomery College
Notre Dame of Maryland University
Salisbury University
Stevenson University
Towson University
University of Maryland
    Baltimore County
    College Park
    Eastern Shore
Washington College

Massachusetts
Boston Architectural College
Boston University
Bristol Community College
Cape Cod Community College
Endicott College
Gordon College
Hampshire College
Holyoke Community College
Lesley University
Massachusetts College of Art and Design
Massachusetts College of Liberal Arts
Montserrat College of Art
Mount Wachusett Community College
School of the Museum of Fine Arts
Springfield College
University of Massachusetts
    Amherst
    Lowell

Michigan
Adrian College
Albion College
Alma College
Alpena Community College
Aquinas College
Calvin College
Central Michigan University
College for Creative Studies
Concordia University
Eastern Michigan University
Ferris State University
Glen Oaks Community College
Gogebic Community College
Grand Valley State University
Hillsdale College
Hope College
Jackson College
Kalamazoo College
Kellogg Community College
Madonna University
Marygrove College

Michigan State University
Mid Michigan Community College
Monroe County Community College
Mott Community College
Northern Michigan University
Oakland University
Olivet College
Saginaw Valley State University
Southwestern Michigan College
Spring Arbor University
University of Michigan
University of Michigan
    Flint
Wayne State University
Western Michigan University

Minnesota
Augsburg College
Bemidji State University
Bethany Lutheran College
Bethel University
College of St. Benedict
Concordia College: Moorhead
Concordia University St. Paul
Gustavus Adolphus College
Hamline University
Minneapolis College of Art and Design
Minnesota State Community and Technical
    College
Minnesota State University
    Mankato
    Moorhead
Normandale Community College
North Hennepin Community College
Saint Cloud State University
St. John's University
St. Mary's University of Minnesota
St. Olaf College
Southwest Minnesota State University
University of Minnesota
    Duluth
    Twin Cities
Winona State University

Mississippi
Belhaven University
Blue Mountain College
Copiah-Lincoln Community College
Delta State University
East Central Community College
East Mississippi Community College
Hinds Community College
Itawamba Community College
Jones County Junior College
Meridian Community College
Millsaps College
Mississippi College
Mississippi State University
Tougaloo College
University of Mississippi
University of Mississippi
    University of Southern Mississippi
William Carey University

Missouri
Avila University
College of the Ozarks
Columbia College
Cottey College
Crowder College
Culver-Stockton College
Drury University
East Central College
Evangel University
Fontbonne University
Hannibal-LaGrange University
Harris-Stowe State University
Jefferson College
Kansas City Art Institute
Lincoln University
Lindenwood University
Maryville University of Saint Louis
Mineral Area College

Missouri Southern State University
Missouri State University
Missouri Western State University
Moberly Area Community College
Northwest Missouri State University
Park University
St. Charles Community College
St. Louis Community College
Saint Louis University
Southeast Missouri State University
Southwest Baptist University
State Fair Community College
Truman State University
University of Central Missouri
University of Missouri
    Columbia
    Kansas City
    St. Louis
Washington University in St. Louis
Webster University
William Woods University

Montana
Carroll College
Dawson Community College
Montana State University
Montana State University
    Billings
University of Great Falls
University of Montana: Western

Nebraska
Central Community College
Chadron State College
Concordia University
Creative Center
Creighton University
Doane University
Hastings College
Mid-Plains Community College
Midland University
Nebraska Wesleyan University
Peru State College
University of Nebraska
    Kearney
    Lincoln
    Omaha
Wayne State College
Western Nebraska Community College

Nevada
Truckee Meadows Community College
University of Nevada
    Reno

New Hampshire
Franklin Pierce University
Keene State College
New England College
New Hampshire Institute of Art
Plymouth State University
Southern New Hampshire University
University of New Hampshire

New Jersey
Caldwell University
The College of New Jersey
College of St. Elizabeth
Drew University
Georgian Court University
Kean University
Monmouth University
Montclair State University
New Jersey Institute of Technology
Rowan University
Rutgers, The State University of New Jersey
    Camden Campus
    New Brunswick/Piscataway Campus
    Newark Campus
Stockton University
Union County College
William Paterson University of New Jersey

New Mexico
Eastern New Mexico University
New Mexico Highlands University
New Mexico Junior College
New Mexico State University
Santa Fe University of Art and Design
University of New Mexico
Western New Mexico University

New York
Adelphi University
Alfred University
Canisius College
City University of New York
    Baruch College
    City College
    College of Staten Island
College of New Rochelle
College of Saint Rose
Daemen College
Eugene Lang College The New School for
    Liberal Arts
Five Towns College
Hartwick College
Hobart and William Smith Colleges
Hofstra University
Houghton College
Jamestown Community College
Long Island University
    LIU Brooklyn
    LIU Post
Manhattanville College
Marymount Manhattan College
Molloy College
Nazareth College
The New School College of Performing Arts
New York School of Interior Design
Parsons the New School for Design
    Parsons The New School for Design
Rensselaer Polytechnic Institute
Rochester Institute of Technology
The Sage Colleges
St. John's University
St. Thomas Aquinas College
School of Visual Arts
Suffolk County Community College
SUNY
    College at Brockport
    College at Cortland
    College at Fredonia
    College at Geneseo
    College at New Paltz
    College at Plattsburgh
    College at Potsdam
    College at Purchase
    University at Binghamton
    University at Buffalo
    University at Stony Brook
University of Rochester
Villa Maria College of Buffalo

North Carolina
Appalachian State University
Barton College
Brevard College
College of the Albemarle
Davidson College
East Carolina University
Elon University
Greensboro College
High Point University
Louisburg College
Meredith College
Montreat College
North Carolina Central University
Queens University of Charlotte
St. Andrews University
Saint Augustine's University
University of Mount Olive
University of North Carolina
    Asheville
    Chapel Hill
    Pembroke

School of the Arts
    Wilmington
Wake Forest University
Warren Wilson College
Western Carolina University
Wilkes Community College
Wingate University

North Dakota
Bismarck State College
Dickinson State University
Minot State University
Trinity Bible College
University of Jamestown

Ohio
Art Academy of Cincinnati
Art Institute of Cincinnati
Ashland University
Baldwin Wallace University
Bluffton University
Bowling Green State University
Bowling Green State University: Firelands
    College
Case Western Reserve University
Central State University
Cleveland Institute of Art
Cleveland State University
Columbus College of Art and Design
Cuyahoga Community College
Denison University
Edison State Community College
Kent State University
Kent State University
    Ashtabula
    East Liverpool
    Geauga
    Salem
    Stark
    Trumbull
    Tuscarawas
Kenyon College
Lake Erie College
Lakeland Community College
Lorain County Community College
Lourdes University
Malone University
Marietta College
Miami University
    Oxford
Mount St. Joseph University
Mount Vernon Nazarene University
Muskingum University
Ohio Northern University
Ohio State University
    Agricultural Technical Institute
    Columbus Campus
    Lima Campus
    Mansfield Campus
    Marion Campus
    Newark Campus
Ohio University
Ohio Wesleyan University
Otterbein University
Pontifical College Josephinum
School of Advertising Art
Sinclair Community College
Southern State Community College
University of Akron
University of Akron: Wayne College
University of Cincinnati
University of Dayton
University of Mount Union
University of Toledo
Ursuline College
Wittenberg University
Wright State University
Wright State University: Lake Campus
Xavier University

Oklahoma
Cameron University
Carl Albert State College

Northeastern State University
Northern Oklahoma College
Northwestern Oklahoma State University
Oklahoma Baptist University
Oklahoma Christian University
Oklahoma City Community College
Oklahoma City University
Oklahoma Panhandle State University
Oklahoma State University
Oral Roberts University
Rogers State University
St. Gregory's University
Seminole State College
Southeastern Oklahoma State University
Southwestern Oklahoma State University
University of Central Oklahoma
University of Oklahoma
University of Science and Arts of Oklahoma
University of Tulsa
Western Oklahoma State College

Oregon
Art Institute of Portland
Clackamas Community College
Clatsop Community College
Concordia University
Eastern Oregon University
George Fox University
Lane Community College
Linn-Benton Community College
New Hope Christian College
Oregon College of Art & Craft
Pacific Northwest College of Art
Pacific University
Portland State University
Southwestern Oregon Community College
Western Oregon University

Pennsylvania
Albright College
Arcadia University
Berks Technical Institute
Bloomsburg University of Pennsylvania
Bucknell University
Bucks County Community College
Carlow University
Carnegie Mellon University
Cedar Crest College
Chatham University
Clarion University of Pennsylvania
DeSales University
Drexel University
East Stroudsburg University of Pennsylvania
Edinboro University
    Pennsylvania
Elizabethtown College
Immaculata University
Indiana University of Pennsylvania
Juniata College
Keystone College
Kutztown University of Pennsylvania
Lehigh University
Lock Haven University of Pennsylvania
Lycoming College
Mansfield University of Pennsylvania
Marywood University
Mercyhurst University
Messiah College
Moore College of Art and Design
Moravian College
Mount Aloysius College
Muhlenberg College
Northampton Community College
Pennsylvania Academy of the Fine Arts
Pennsylvania Colleg of Art and Design
    Pennsylvania College of Art and Design
Saint Joseph's University
Seton Hill University
Slippery Rock University of Pennsylvania
Temple University
University of the Arts
West Chester University of Pennsylvania

Puerto Rico
Colegio de Cinematografia Artes y Television
Humacao Community College
University of Puerto Rico
    Mayaguez

Rhode Island
Rhode Island College
Rhode Island School of Design
Salve Regina University
University of Rhode Island

South Carolina
Anderson University
Clemson University
Coastal Carolina University
Coker College
College of Charleston
Columbia College
Converse College
Francis Marion University
Furman University
Lander University
Limestone College
Presbyterian College
University of South Carolina
    Aiken
    Beaufort
    Columbia
Winthrop University
Wofford College

South Dakota
Augusta University
    Augustana University
Dakota State University
Dakota Wesleyan University
South Dakota State University
University of Sioux Falls
University of South Dakota

Tennessee
Austin Peay State University
Belmont University
Carson-Newman University
Cumberland University
East Tennessee State University
Freed-Hardeman University
Jackson State Community College
King University
Martin Methodist College
Maryville College
Memphis College of Art
Milligan College
Motlow State Community College
Northeast State Community College
O'More College of Design
Pellissippi State Community College
Rhodes College
Roane State Community College
Sewanee: The University of the South
Southern Adventist University
Tennessee Technological University
Union University
University of Memphis
University of Tennessee
    Chattanooga
    Knoxville
    Martin
Volunteer State Community College
Watkins College of Art, Design & Film
Welch College

Texas
Abilene Christian University
Angelina College
Angelo State University
Austin College
Baylor University
Brazosport College
Clarendon College
College of the Mainland
Collin County Community College District
Galveston College

Grayson College
Hardin-Simmons University
Houston Baptist University
Howard College
Howard Payne University
Kilgore College
Lee College
McMurry University
Midwestern State University
Our Lady of the Lake University of San
    Antonio
Panola College
Rice University
Richland College
Sam Houston State University
San Jacinto College
Schreiner University
Southern Methodist University
Southwestern University
Stephen F. Austin State University
Sul Ross State University
Temple College
Texarkana College
Texas A&M International University
Texas A&M University
Texas A&M University
    Commerce
    Corpus Christi
    Texarkana
Texas Christian University
Texas State University
Texas Tech University
Texas Wesleyan University
Texas Woman's University
Trinity University
Tyler Junior College
University of Dallas
University of Houston
University of Houston
    Clear Lake
University of Mary Hardin-Baylor
University of Texas
    Arlington
    Austin
    El Paso
    the Permian Basin
    San Antonio
    Tyler
University Of Texas Rio Grande Valley
University of the Incarnate Word
Victoria College
Wayland Baptist University
West Texas A&M University
Western Texas College

Utah
Brigham Young University
Dixie State University
Salt Lake Community College
Southern Utah University
University of Utah
Utah State University
Utah Valley University
Weber State University
Westminster College

Vermont
Bennington College
Goddard College
Johnson State College
Landmark College
Saint Michael's College

Virginia
Averett University
Bluefield College
Christopher Newport University
College of William and Mary
Eastern Mennonite University
Emory & Henry College
Hollins University
James Madison University
Longwood University

Lynchburg College
Old Dominion University
Radford University
Randolph College
Roanoke College
Southern Virginia University
Sweet Briar College
University of Mary Washington
University of Richmond
University of Virginia's College at Wise
Virginia Commonwealth University
Virginia Polytechnic Institute and State
    University
Virginia State University

Washington
Art Institute of Seattle
Central Washington University
Centralia College
Clark College
Cornish College of the Arts
DigiPen Institute of Technology
Eastern Washington University
Everett Community College
Evergreen State College
Grays Harbor College
Northwest College of Art & Design
Northwest University
Pacific Lutheran University
Saint Martin's University
Seattle Pacific University
University of Puget Sound
University of Washington
Washington State University
Western Washington University
Whitman College
Whitworth University

West Virginia
Davis and Elkins College
Fairmont State University
Marshall University
Ohio Valley University
Shepherd University
University of Charleston
West Liberty University
West Virginia University
West Virginia University Institute of
    Technology
West Virginia Wesleyan College

Wisconsin
Cardinal Stritch University
Carroll University
Carthage College
Concordia University Wisconsin
Edgewood College
Lakeland University
Milwaukee Institute of Art & Design
Mount Mary University
Northland College
Ripon College
St. Norbert College
University of Wisconsin
    Baraboo/Sauk County
    Eau Claire
    Green Bay
    La Crosse
    Madison
    Manitowoc
    Milwaukee
    Oshkosh
    Parkside
    Richland
    River Falls
    Sheboygan
    Stevens Point
    Superior
    Waukesha
    Whitewater
Viterbo University
Wisconsin Lutheran College

Wyoming
Casper College
Central Wyoming College
Eastern Wyoming College
Laramie County Community College
Northwest College
Sheridan College
University of Wyoming
Western Wyoming Community College

Athletic scholarships

Archery

Arizona
Dine College M,W

California
College of the Redwoods M

Georgia
Emmanuel College M,W

Kentucky
Midway College W
University of the Cumberlands M,W

Mississippi
Blue Mountain College M,W

Badminton

California
Fresno City College M,W

New Jersey
New Jersey Institute of Technology M

Baseball

Alabama
Alabama Agricultural and Mechanical University M
Alabama Southern Community College M
Alabama State University M
Auburn University M
Auburn University at Montgomery M
Central Alabama Community College M
Chattahoochee Valley Community College M
Concordia College M
Enterprise State Community College M
Faulkner State Community College M
George C. Wallace Community College at Dothan M
George C. Wallace State Community College at Selma M
Jacksonville State University M
Jefferson Davis Community College M
Lawson State Community College M
Lurleen B. Wallace Community College M
Marion Military Institute M
Miles College M
Samford University M
Selma University M
Shelton State Community College M
Snead State Community College M
Southern Union State Community College M
Spring Hill College M
Troy University M
Tuskegee University M
University of Alabama M
University of Alabama
　Birmingham M
　Huntsville M
University of Mobile M
University of Montevallo M
University of North Alabama M
University of South Alabama M
University of West Alabama M
Wallace State Community College at Hanceville M

Arizona
Arizona Christian University M
Arizona State University M
Arizona Western College M
Central Arizona College M
Chandler-Gilbert Community College M
Cochise College M
Eastern Arizona College M
GateWay Community College M
Glendale Community College M
Grand Canyon University M
Mesa Community College M
Paradise Valley Community College M
Scottsdale Community College M
South Mountain Community College M
University of Arizona M
Yavapai College M

Arkansas
Arkansas State University M
Arkansas Tech University M
Crowley's Ridge College M
Ecclesia College M
Harding University M
Henderson State University M
Lyon College M
North Arkansas College M
Ouachita Baptist University M
Southern Arkansas University M
University of Arkansas M
University of Arkansas
　Fort Smith M
　Little Rock M
　Pine Bluff M
University of Central Arkansas M
Williams Baptist College M

California
Academy of Art University M
Azusa Pacific University M
Biola University M
California Baptist University M
California Polytechnic State University: San Luis Obispo M
California State Polytechnic University: Pomona M
California State University
　Chico M
　Dominguez Hills M
　Fresno M
　Fullerton M
　Long Beach M
　Los Angeles M
　Monterey Bay M
　Northridge M
　Sacramento M
　San Bernardino M
　Stanislaus M
Concordia University Irvine M
Fresno City College M
Fresno Pacific University M
Grossmont College M
Holy Names University M
Hope International University M
La Sierra University M
Loyola Marymount University M
The Master's University M
Menlo College M
Pepperdine University M
Point Loma Nazarene University M
St. Mary's College of California M
San Diego Christian College M
San Diego State University M
San Jose State University M

Santa Clara University M
Simpson University M
Sonoma State University M
Stanford University M
University of Antelope Valley M
University of California
　Berkeley M
　Davis M
　Irvine M
　Los Angeles M
　Riverside M
　Santa Barbara M
University of San Diego M
University of San Francisco M
University of Southern California M
University of the Pacific M
Vanguard University of Southern California M
Westmont College M
William Jessup University M
Yuba College M

Colorado
Colorado Christian University M
Colorado Mesa University M
Colorado Northwestern Community College M
Colorado School of Mines M
Colorado State University
　Pueblo M
Lamar Community College M
Metropolitan State University of Denver M
Northeastern Junior College M
Otero Junior College M
Regis University M
Trinidad State Junior College M
University of Colorado
　Colorado Springs M
University of Northern Colorado M

Connecticut
Central Connecticut State University M
Fairfield University M
Post University M
Quinnipiac University M
Sacred Heart University M
Southern Connecticut State University M
University of Bridgeport M
University of Connecticut M
University of Hartford M
University of New Haven M

Delaware
Delaware State University M
Delaware Technical Community College
　Jack F. Owens Campus M
University of Delaware M
Wilmington University M

District of Columbia
George Washington University M
Georgetown University M

Florida
Ave Maria University M
Barry University M
Bethune-Cookman University M
Chipola College M
College of Central Florida M
Daytona State College M
Eastern Florida State College M
Eckerd College M
Edward Waters College M
Embry-Riddle Aeronautical University M
Flagler College M
Florida Atlantic University M
Florida Gulf Coast University M
Florida Institute of Technology M
Florida Memorial University M
Florida Southern College M
Florida State College at Jacksonville M
Florida State University M
Gulf Coast State College M
Hillsborough Community College M
Indian River State College M
Jacksonville University M

Lake-Sumter State College M
Lynn University M
Miami Dade College M
Northwest Florida State College M
Nova Southeastern University M
Palm Beach Atlantic University M
Palm Beach State College M
Pasco-Hernando State College M
Pensacola State College M
Polk State College M
Rollins College M
Saint Johns River State College M
Saint Leo University M
St. Petersburg College M
Saint Thomas University M
Santa Fe College M
South Florida State College M
Southeastern University M
State College of Florida, Manatee-Sarasota M
Stetson University M
Tallahassee Community College M
University of Central Florida M
University of Florida M
University of Miami M
University of North Florida M
University of South Florida M
University of Tampa M
University of West Florida M
Warner University M
Webber International University M

Georgia
Abraham Baldwin Agricultural College M
Albany State University M
Andrew College M
Armstrong State University M
Augusta University M
Brewton-Parker College M
Clark Atlanta University M
Columbus State University M
Darton State College M
East Georgia State College M
Emmanuel College M
Georgia College and State University M
Georgia Gwinnett College M
Georgia Highlands College M,W
Georgia Institute of Technology M
Georgia Perimeter College M
Georgia Southern University M
Georgia Southwestern State University M
Georgia State University M
Gordon State College M
Kennesaw State University M
Mercer University M
Middle Georgia State University M
Morehouse College M
Paine College M
Point University M
Reinhardt University M
Savannah State University M
Shorter University M
Thomas University M
Truett McConnell University M
University of Georgia M
University of North Georgia M
University of West Georgia M
Valdosta State University M
Young Harris College M

Hawaii
Hawaii Pacific University M
University of Hawaii
　Manoa M

Idaho
College of Idaho M
College of Southern Idaho M
Lewis-Clark State College M
Northwest Nazarene University M

Illinois
Benedictine University at Springfield M
Black Hawk College M
Bradley University M

Carl Sandburg College M
Chicago State University M
College of Lake County M
Danville Area Community College M
Eastern Illinois University M
Elgin Community College M
Highland Community College M
Illinois Central College M
Illinois Eastern Community Colleges
    Lincoln Trail College M
    Olney Central College M
    Wabash Valley College M
Illinois Institute of Technology M
Illinois State University M
John A. Logan College M
John Wood Community College M
Judson University M
Kankakee Community College M
Kaskaskia College M
Kishwaukee College M
Lake Land College M
Lewis and Clark Community College M
Lewis University M
Lincoln Christian University M
Lincoln College M
Lincoln Land Community College M
McHenry County College M
McKendree University M
Moraine Valley Community College M
Morton College M
Northern Illinois University M
Northwestern University M
Olivet Nazarene University M
Parkland College M
Quincy University M
Rend Lake College M
Robert Morris College
    Robert Morris University: Chicago M
Saint Xavier University M
Sauk Valley Community College M
South Suburban College of Cook County M
Southeastern Illinois College M
Southern Illinois University Carbondale M
Southern Illinois University Edwardsville M
Southwestern Illinois College M
Spoon River College M
Trinity Christian College M
Trinity International University M
University of Illinois
    Chicago M
    Springfield M
    Urbana-Champaign M
University of St. Francis M
Western Illinois University M

Indiana
Ancilla College M
Ball State University M
Bethel College M
Butler University M
Calumet College of St. Joseph M
Goshen College M
Grace College M
Holy Cross College M
Huntington University M
Indiana Institute of Technology M
Indiana State University M
Indiana University
    Bloomington M
    Purdue University Fort Wayne M
    Southeast M
Indiana Wesleyan University M
Marian University M
Oakland City University M
Purdue University M
Purdue University
    North Central M
    Northwest M
Saint Joseph's College M
Taylor University M
University of Evansville M
University of Indianapolis M
University of Notre Dame M

University of Saint Francis M
University of Southern Indiana M
Valparaiso University M
Vincennes University M

Iowa
Briar Cliff University M
Clarke University M
Des Moines Area Community College M
Dordt College M
Ellsworth Community College M
Graceland University M
Grand View University M
Iowa Central Community College M
Iowa Lakes Community College M
Iowa Western Community College M
Kirkwood Community College M
Morningside College M
Mount Mercy University M
Muscatine Community College M
North Iowa Area Community College M
Northwestern College M
St. Ambrose University M
Southeastern Community College M
Southwestern Community College M
University of Iowa M
Upper Iowa University M
Waldorf University M
William Penn University M

Kansas
Allen County Community College M
Baker University M
Barton County Community College M
Benedictine College M
Bethany College M
Brown Mackie College
    Salina M
Butler Community College M
Central Christian College of Kansas M
Cloud County Community College M
Coffeyville Community College M
Colby Community College M
Cowley County Community College M
Dodge City Community College M
Emporia State University M
Fort Scott Community College M
Friends University M
Garden City Community College M
Hesston College M
Highland Community College M
Hutchinson Community College M
Independence Community College M
Johnson County Community College M
Kansas City Kansas Community College M
Kansas State University M
Kansas Wesleyan University M
Labette Community College M
McPherson College M
MidAmerica Nazarene University M
Neosho County Community College M
Newman University M
Ottawa University M
Pittsburg State University M
Pratt Community College M
Seward County Community College M
Southwestern College M
Sterling College M
Tabor College M
University of Kansas M
University of St. Mary M
Washburn University M
Wichita State University M

Kentucky
Alice Lloyd College M
Asbury University M
Bellarmine University M
Brescia University M
Campbellsville University M
Eastern Kentucky University M
Georgetown College M
Kentucky State University M

Kentucky Wesleyan College M
Lindsey Wilson College M
Morehead State University M
Murray State University M
Northern Kentucky University M
St. Catharine College M
Union College M
University of Kentucky M
University of Louisville M
University of Pikeville M
University of the Cumberlands M
Western Kentucky University M

Louisiana
Bossier Parish Community College M
Delgado Community College M
Grambling State University M
Louisiana State University
    Eunice M
    Shreveport M
Louisiana State University and Agricultural and
    Mechanical College M
Louisiana Tech University M
Loyola University New Orleans M
McNeese State University M
Nicholls State University M
Northwestern State University M
Southeastern Louisiana University M
Southern University and Agricultural and
    Mechanical College M
Tulane University M
University of Louisiana
    Monroe M
University of Louisiana at Lafayette M
University of New Orleans M

Maine
University of Maine M

Maryland
Anne Arundel Community College M
Chesapeake College M
College of Southern Maryland M
Community College of Baltimore County M
Coppin State University M
Garrett College M
Hagerstown Community College M
Harford Community College M
Mount St. Mary's University M
Towson University M
University of Maryland
    Baltimore County M
    College Park M
    Eastern Shore M

Massachusetts
American International College M
Boston College M
Merrimack College M
Northeastern University M
Stonehill College M
University of Massachusetts
    Amherst M
    Lowell M

Michigan
Aquinas College M
Central Michigan University M
Cleary University M
Concordia University M
Davenport University M
Eastern Michigan University M
Glen Oaks Community College M
Hillsdale College M
Kalamazoo Valley Community College M
Kellogg Community College M
Lake Michigan College M
Lansing Community College M
Macomb Community College M
Madonna University M
Marygrove College M
Michigan State University M
Mott Community College M
Muskegon Community College M

Northwood University
    Michigan M
Oakland University M
Rochester College M
Saginaw Valley State University M
St. Clair County Community College M
Siena Heights University M
Spring Arbor University M
University of Michigan M
Wayne State University M
Western Michigan University M

Minnesota
Concordia University St. Paul M
Minnesota State University
    Mankato M
Saint Cloud State University M
Southwest Minnesota State University M
University of Minnesota
    Crookston M
    Duluth M
    Twin Cities M
Winona State University M

Mississippi
Alcorn State University M
Belhaven University M
Blue Mountain College M
Copiah-Lincoln Community College M
Delta State University M
East Central Community College M
East Mississippi Community College M
Hinds Community College M
Holmes Community College M
Itawamba Community College M
Jackson State University M
Jones County Junior College M
Meridian Community College M
Mississippi Gulf Coast Community College M
Mississippi Valley State University M
Northwest Mississippi Community College M
Southwest Mississippi Community College M
University of Mississippi M
University of Mississippi
    University of Southern Mississippi M
William Carey University M

Missouri
Avila University M
Central Methodist University M
College of the Ozarks M
Columbia College M
Crowder College M
Culver-Stockton College M
Drury University M
Evangel University M
Hannibal-LaGrange University M
Harris-Stowe State University M
Jefferson College M
Lindenwood University M
Maryville University of Saint Louis M
Metropolitan Community College - Kansas City
    M
Mineral Area College M
Missouri Baptist University M
Missouri Southern State University M
Missouri State University M
Missouri University of Science and Technology
    M
Missouri Valley College M
Missouri Western State University M
North Central Missouri College M
Northwest Missouri State University M
Park University M
Research College of Nursing M
Rockhurst University M
St. Louis Community College M
Saint Louis University M
Southeast Missouri State University M
Southwest Baptist University M
Three Rivers Community College M
Truman State University M
University of Central Missouri M

University of Missouri
Columbia M
St. Louis M
William Jewell College M
William Woods University M

Montana
Dawson Community College M
Miles Community College M
Montana State University
Billings M

Nebraska
Bellevue University M
Concordia University M
Creighton University M
Doane University M
Grace University M
Hastings College M
Mid-Plains Community College M
Midland University M
Northeast Community College M
Peru State College M
University of Nebraska
Kearney M
Lincoln M
Omaha M
Wayne State College M
Western Nebraska Community College M
York College M

Nevada
University of Nevada
Las Vegas M
Reno M

New Hampshire
Franklin Pierce University M
Southern New Hampshire University M

New Jersey
Bloomfield College M
Brookdale Community College M
Caldwell University M
County College of Morris M
Fairleigh Dickinson University
Metropolitan Campus M
Mercer County Community College M
Monmouth University M
New Jersey Institute of Technology M
Raritan Valley Community College M
Rider University M
Rowan College at Burlington County M
Rutgers, The State University of New Jersey
New Brunswick/Piscataway Campus M
Saint Peter's University M
Salem Community College M
Seton Hall University M
Sussex County Community College M

New Mexico
Eastern New Mexico University M
New Mexico Highlands University M
New Mexico Junior College M
New Mexico Military Institute M
New Mexico State University M
University of New Mexico M
University of the Southwest M

New York
Adelphi University M
ASA College M
Canisius College M
City University of New York
Queens College M
College of Saint Rose M
Concordia College M
Dominican College of Blauvelt M
Fordham University M
Globe Institute of Technology M
Hofstra University M
Iona College M
Le Moyne College M

Long Island University
LIU Brooklyn M
LIU Post M
Manhattan College M
Marist College M
Mercy College M
Molloy College M
Monroe College M
Monroe Community College M
New York Institute of Technology M
Niagara University M
Nyack College M
Orange County Community College M
Pace University M
Pace University: Pleasantville/Briarcliff M
Saint Bonaventure University M
St. John's University M
St. Thomas Aquinas College M
Siena College M
SUNY
University at Albany M
University at Binghamton M
University at Buffalo M
University at Stony Brook M
Wagner College M

North Carolina
Appalachian State University M
Barton College M
Belmont Abbey College M
Brevard College M
Campbell University M
Catawba College M
Chowan University M
Davidson College M
Duke University M
East Carolina University M
Elizabeth City State University M
Elon University M
Gardner-Webb University M
Guilford Technical Community College M
High Point University M
Lenoir Community College M
Lenoir-Rhyne University M
Louisburg College M
Mars Hill University M
Montreat College M
North Carolina Agricultural and Technical State
University M
North Carolina State University M
Pitt Community College M
Saint Augustine's University M
Southeastern Community College M
University of Mount Olive M
University of North Carolina
Asheville M
Chapel Hill M
Charlotte M
Greensboro M
Wilmington M
Wake Forest University M
Western Carolina University M
Wingate University M

North Dakota
Bismarck State College M
Dakota College at Bottineau M
Dickinson State University M
Lake Region State College M
Mayville State University M
Minot State University M
North Dakota State University M
University of Jamestown M
University of Mary M
Valley City State University M
Williston State College M

Ohio
Ashland University M
Bowling Green State University M
Cedarville University M
Clark State Community College M
Edison State Community College M

Kent State University M
Lake Erie College M
Lakeland Community College M
Lourdes University M
Malone University M
Miami University
Oxford M
Mount Vernon Nazarene University M
Notre Dame College M
Ohio Dominican University M
Ohio State University
Columbus Campus M
Ohio University M
Owens Community College M
Shawnee State University M
Sinclair Community College M
Tiffin University M
University of Cincinnati M
University of Dayton M
University of Findlay M
University of Northwestern Ohio M
University of Rio Grande M
University of Toledo M
Urbana University M
Walsh University M
Wright State University M
Xavier University M
Youngstown State University M

Oklahoma
Bacone College M
Cameron University M
Carl Albert State College M
Connors State College M
East Central University M
Eastern Oklahoma State College M
Mid-America Christian University M
Northeastern Oklahoma Agricultural and
Mechanical College M
Northeastern State University M
Northern Oklahoma College M
Northwestern Oklahoma State University M
Oklahoma Baptist University M
Oklahoma Christian University M
Oklahoma City University M
Oklahoma Panhandle State University M
Oklahoma State University M
Oklahoma Wesleyan University M
Oral Roberts University M
Redlands Community College M
Rogers State University M
Rose State College M
St. Gregory's University M
Seminole State College M
Southeastern Oklahoma State University M
Southern Nazarene University M
Southwestern Oklahoma State University M
University of Central Oklahoma M
University of Oklahoma M
University of Science and Arts of Oklahoma M
Western Oklahoma State College M

Oregon
Blue Mountain Community College M
Chemeketa Community College M
Clackamas Community College M
Concordia University M
Corban University M
Lane Community College M
Linn-Benton Community College M
Mt. Hood Community College M
Oregon Institute of Technology M
Oregon State University M
Portland State University M
Southwestern Oregon Community College M
Treasure Valley Community College M
University of Oregon M
University of Portland M
Western Oregon University M

Pennsylvania
Bloomsburg University of Pennsylvania M
California University of Pennsylvania M

Chestnut Hill College M
Clarion University of Pennsylvania M
East Stroudsburg University of Pennsylvania M
Gannon University M
Indiana University of Pennsylvania M
Kutztown University of Pennsylvania M
La Salle University M
Lackawanna College M
Lock Haven University of Pennsylvania M
Mansfield University of Pennsylvania M
Mercyhurst University M
Millersville University of Pennsylvania M
Penn State
University Park M
Philadelphia University M
Point Park University M
Saint Joseph's University M
Seton Hill University M
Shippensburg University of Pennsylvania M
Slippery Rock University of Pennsylvania M
University of Pittsburgh M
University of the Sciences M
Villanova University M
West Chester University of Pennsylvania M

Puerto Rico
Inter American University of Puerto Rico
Aguadilla Campus M
Barranquitas Campus M
Bayamon Campus M
Metropolitan Campus M
Ponce Campus M
San German Campus M
Turabo University M
Universidad del Este M
Universidad Metropolitana M
University of Puerto Rico
Arecibo M
Carolina Regional College M
Humacao M
Mayaguez M
Utuado M

Rhode Island
Bryant University M
Community College of Rhode Island M
University of Rhode Island M

South Carolina
Anderson University M
Charleston Southern University M
The Citadel M
Claflin University M
Clemson University M
Coastal Carolina University M
Coker College M
College of Charleston M
Erskine College M
Francis Marion University M
Furman University M
Lander University M
Limestone College M
Morris College M
Newberry College M
North Greenville University M
Presbyterian College M
Southern Wesleyan University M
Spartanburg Methodist College M
University of South Carolina
Aiken M
Columbia M
Sumter M
Upstate M
Voorhees College M
Winthrop University M
Wofford College M

South Dakota
Augusta University
Augustana University M
Dakota State University M
Dakota Wesleyan University M
Mount Marty College M

Northern State University M
University of Sioux Falls M

Tennessee
Austin Peay State University M
Belmont University M
Bethel University M
Bryan College
 Dayton M
Carson-Newman University M
Chattanooga State Community College M
Christian Brothers University M
Cleveland State Community College M
Columbia State Community College M
Cumberland University M
Dyersburg State Community College M
East Tennessee State University M
Freed-Hardeman University M
Hiwassee College M
Jackson State Community College M
King University M
Lee University M
LeMoyne-Owen College M
Lincoln Memorial University M
Lipscomb University M
Martin Methodist College M
Middle Tennessee State University M
Milligan College M
Motlow State Community College M
Roane State Community College M
Southwest Tennessee Community College M
Tennessee Technological University M
Tennessee Wesleyan College M
Trevecca Nazarene University M
Tusculum College M
Union University M
University of Memphis M
University of Tennessee
 Knoxville M
 Martin M
Vanderbilt University M
Walters State Community College M

Texas
Abilene Christian University M
Alvin Community College M
Angelina College M
Angelo State University M
Baylor University M
Blinn College M
Brookhaven College M
Clarendon College M
Dallas Baptist University M
El Paso Community College M
Frank Phillips College M
Galveston College M
Grayson College M
Hill College M
Houston Baptist University M
Howard College M
Jarvis Christian College M
Lamar University M
Laredo Community College M
Lubbock Christian University M
McLennan Community College M
Midland College M
North Central Texas College M
Northeast Texas Community College M
Odessa College M
Panola College M
Paris Junior College M
Prairie View A&M University M
Ranger College M
Rice University M
St. Edward's University M
St. Mary's University M
Sam Houston State University M
San Jacinto College M
Southwestern Assemblies of God University M
Stephen F. Austin State University M
Tarleton State University M
Texas A&M University M

Texas A&M University
 Corpus Christi M
 Texarkana M
Texas Christian University M
Texas Southern University M
Texas State University M
Texas Tech University M
Texas Wesleyan University M
Trinity Valley Community College M
University of Houston M
University of Texas
 Arlington M
 Austin M
 of the Permian Basin M
 San Antonio M
University of the Incarnate Word M
Vernon College M
Wayland Baptist University M
Weatherford College M
West Texas A&M University M
Western Texas College M
Wharton County Junior College M
Wiley College M

Utah
Brigham Young University M
Dixie State University M
Salt Lake Community College M
University of Utah M
Utah Valley University M

Virginia
Bluefield College M
College of William and Mary M
George Mason University M
James Madison University M
Liberty University M
Longwood University M
Norfolk State University M
Old Dominion University M
Radford University M
University of Richmond M
University of Virginia M
University of Virginia's College at Wise M
Virginia Commonwealth University M
Virginia Military Institute M
Virginia Polytechnic Institute and State
 University M
Virginia State University M

Washington
Big Bend Community College M
Central Washington University M
Centralia College M
Columbia Basin College M
Edmonds Community College M
Everett Community College M
Gonzaga University M
Grays Harbor College M
Green River College M
Lower Columbia College M
Olympic College M
Pierce College M
Saint Martin's University M
Shoreline Community College M
Skagit Valley College M
Spokane Community College M
Tacoma Community College M
University of Washington M
Walla Walla Community College M
Washington State University M
Yakima Valley Community College M

West Virginia
Alderson-Broaddus University M
Bluefield State College M
Concord University M
Davis and Elkins College M
Fairmont State University M
Marshall University M
Ohio Valley University M
Potomac State College of West Virginia
 University M
Salem International University M

Shepherd University M
University of Charleston M
West Liberty University M
West Virginia State University M
West Virginia University M
West Virginia University Institute of
 Technology M
West Virginia Wesleyan College M
Wheeling Jesuit University M

Wisconsin
University of Wisconsin
 Milwaukee M
 Parkside M
Viterbo University M

Basketball

Alabama
Alabama Agricultural and Mechanical
 University M,W
Alabama Southern Community College M,W
Alabama State University M,W
Auburn University M,W
Auburn University at Montgomery M,W
Chattahoochee Valley Community College M,W
Concordia College M,W
Enterprise State Community College M,W
Faulkner State Community College M,W
Faulkner University M,W
Gadsden State Community College M,W
George C. Wallace State Community College
 at Selma M,W
Jacksonville State University M,W
Jefferson Davis Community College M
Judson College W
Lawson State Community College M,W
Lurleen B. Wallace Community College M,W
Marion Military Institute M
Miles College M,W
Samford University M,W
Shelton State Community College M,W
Snead State Community College M,W
Southern Union State Community College M,W
Spring Hill College M,W
Troy University M,W
Tuskegee University M,W
University of Alabama M,W
University of Alabama
 Birmingham M,W
 Huntsville M,W
University of Mobile M,W
University of Montevallo M,W
University of North Alabama M,W
University of South Alabama M,W
University of West Alabama M,W
Wallace State Community College at
 Hanceville M,W

Alaska
University of Alaska
 Anchorage M,W
 Fairbanks M,W

Arizona
Arizona Christian University M,W
Arizona State University M,W
Arizona Western College M,W
Central Arizona College M,W
Chandler-Gilbert Community College M,W
Cochise College M,W
Eastern Arizona College M,W
Embry-Riddle Aeronautical University
 Prescott Campus M,W
Glendale Community College M,W
Grand Canyon University M,W
Mesa Community College M,W
Northern Arizona University M,W
Scottsdale Community College M,W
South Mountain Community College M,W

University of Arizona M,W
Yavapai College M,W

Arkansas
Arkansas State University M,W
Arkansas State University
 Mid-South M,W
Arkansas Tech University M,W
Crowley's Ridge College M,W
Ecclesia College M,W
Harding University M,W
Henderson State University M,W
John Brown University M,W
Lyon College M,W
North Arkansas College M,W
Ouachita Baptist University M,W
Philander Smith College M,W
Southern Arkansas University M,W
University of Arkansas M,W
University of Arkansas
 Fort Smith M,W
 Little Rock M,W
 Monticello M,W
 Pine Bluff M,W
University of Central Arkansas M,W
Williams Baptist College M,W

California
Academy of Art University M,W
Azusa Pacific University M,W
Biola University M,W
California Baptist University M,W
California Polytechnic State University: San
 Luis Obispo M,W
California State Polytechnic University:
 Pomona M,W
California State University
 Bakersfield M
 Chico M,W
 Dominguez Hills M,W
 Fresno M,W
 Fullerton M,W
 Long Beach M,W
 Los Angeles M,W
 Monterey Bay M,W
 Northridge M,W
 Sacramento M,W
 San Bernardino M,W
 Stanislaus M,W
Concordia University Irvine M,W
Dominican University of California M,W
Fresno City College M,W
Fresno Pacific University M,W
Grossmont College M,W
Holy Names University M,W
Hope International University M,W
Humboldt State University M,W
La Sierra University M,W
Loyola Marymount University M,W
The Master's University M,W
Menlo College M,W
Notre Dame de Namur University M,W
Pepperdine University M,W
Point Loma Nazarene University M,W
St. Mary's College of California M,W
San Diego Christian College M,W
San Diego State University M,W
San Jose State University M,W
Santa Clara University M,W
Simpson University M,W
Sonoma State University M,W
Stanford University M,W
University of Antelope Valley M,W
University of California
 Berkeley M,W
 Davis M,W
 Irvine M,W
 Los Angeles M,W
 Merced M,W
 Riverside M,W
 Santa Barbara M,W
University of San Diego M,W
University of San Francisco M,W

University of Southern California M,W
University of the Pacific M,W
Vanguard University of Southern California M,W
Westmont College M,W
William Jessup University M,W
Yuba College M,W

Colorado
Adams State University M,W
Colorado Christian University M,W
Colorado Mesa University M,W
Colorado Northwestern Community College M,W
Colorado School of Mines M,W
Colorado State University M,W
Colorado State University
    Pueblo M,W
Fort Lewis College M,W
Lamar Community College M,W
Metropolitan State University of Denver M,W
Northeastern Junior College M,W
Otero Junior College M,W
Regis University M,W
Trinidad State Junior College M,W
University of Colorado
    Boulder M,W
    Colorado Springs M,W
University of Denver M,W
University of Northern Colorado M,W
Western State Colorado University M,W

Connecticut
Central Connecticut State University M,W
Fairfield University M,W
Post University M,W
Quinnipiac University M,W
Sacred Heart University M,W
Southern Connecticut State University M,W
University of Bridgeport M,W
University of Connecticut M,W
University of Hartford M,W
University of New Haven M,W

Delaware
Delaware State University M,W
Delaware Technical Community College
    Stanton/Wilmington Campus M,W
Goldey-Beacom College M,W
University of Delaware M,W
Wilmington University M,W

District of Columbia
American University M,W
George Washington University M,W
Georgetown University M,W
Howard University M,W
University of the District of Columbia M,W

Florida
Ave Maria University M,W
Barry University M,W
Bethune-Cookman University M,W
Chipola College M,W
College of Central Florida M,W
Daytona State College M,W
Eastern Florida State College M,W
Eckerd College M,W
Edward Waters College M,W
Embry-Riddle Aeronautical University M,W
Flagler College M,W
Florida Agricultural and Mechanical University M
Florida Atlantic University M,W
Florida College M
Florida Gulf Coast University M,W
Florida Institute of Technology M,W
Florida Memorial University M,W
Florida National University M
Florida Southern College M,W
Florida State College at Jacksonville M,W
Florida State University M,W
Gulf Coast State College M,W
Hillsborough Community College M,W

Indian River State College M,W
Jacksonville University M,W
Lynn University M,W
Miami Dade College M,W
Northwest Florida State College M,W
Nova Southeastern University M,W
Palm Beach Atlantic University M,W
Palm Beach State College M,W
Pasco-Hernando State College M
Pensacola State College M,W
Polk State College M
Rollins College M,W
Saint Leo University M,W
St. Petersburg College M,W
Saint Thomas University M,W
Santa Fe College M,W
Southeastern University M,W
State College of Florida, Manatee-Sarasota M
Stetson University M,W
Tallahassee Community College M,W
University of Central Florida M,W
University of Florida M,W
University of Miami M,W
University of North Florida M,W
University of South Florida M,W
University of Tampa M,W
University of West Florida M,W
Warner University M,W
Webber International University M,W

Georgia
Albany State University M,W
Andrew College W
Armstrong State University M,W
Augusta University M,W
Brenau University W
Brewton-Parker College M,W
Clark Atlanta University M,W
Clayton State University M,W
College of Coastal Georgia M,W
Columbus State University M,W
Darton State College W
East Georgia State College M,W
Emmanuel College M,W
Fort Valley State University M,W
Georgia College and State University M,W
Georgia Highlands College M,W
Georgia Institute of Technology M,W
Georgia Perimeter College M,W
Georgia Southern University M,W
Georgia Southwestern State University M,W
Georgia State University M,W
Gordon State College M
Kennesaw State University M,W
Life University M,W
Mercer University M,W
Middle Georgia State University M,W
Morehouse College M
Paine College M,W
Point University M,W
Reinhardt University M,W
Savannah State University M,W
Shorter University M,W
Truett McConnell University M,W
University of Georgia M,W
University of North Georgia M,W
University of West Georgia M,W
Valdosta State University M,W
Young Harris College M,W

Hawaii
Brigham Young University-Hawaii M,W
Chaminade University of Honolulu M,W
Hawaii Pacific University M,W
University of Hawaii
    Hilo M
    Manoa M,W

Idaho
Boise State University M,W
College of Idaho M,W
College of Southern Idaho M,W
Idaho State University M,W

Lewis-Clark State College M,W
North Idaho College M,W
Northwest Nazarene University M,W
University of Idaho M,W

Illinois
Benedictine University at Springfield M,W
Black Hawk College M,W
Bradley University M,W
Carl Sandburg College M,W
Chicago State University M,W
College of Lake County M,W
Danville Area Community College M,W
DePaul University M,W
Eastern Illinois University M,W
Elgin Community College M,W
Governors State University M,W
Highland Community College M,W
Illinois Central College M,W
Illinois Eastern Community Colleges
    Lincoln Trail College M,W
    Olney Central College M,W
    Wabash Valley College M,W
Illinois State University M,W
John A. Logan College M,W
John Wood Community College M,W
Judson University M,W
Kankakee Community College M,W
Kaskaskia College M,W
Kishwaukee College M,W
Lake Land College M,W
Lewis and Clark Community College M,W
Lewis University M,W
Lincoln Christian University M,W
Lincoln College M,W
Lincoln Land Community College M,W
Loyola University Chicago M,W
McHenry County College M,W
McKendree University M,W
Moraine Valley Community College M,W
Morton College M,W
Northern Illinois University M,W
Northwestern University M,W
Olivet Nazarene University M,W
Parkland College M,W
Quincy University M,W
Rend Lake College M,W
Robert Morris College
    Robert Morris University: Chicago M,W
Saint Xavier University M
Sauk Valley Community College M,W
Shawnee Community College M,W
South Suburban College of Cook County M,W
Southeastern Illinois College M,W
Southern Illinois University Carbondale M,W
Southern Illinois University Edwardsville M,W
Southwestern Illinois College M,W
Trinity Christian College M,W
Trinity International University M,W
University of Illinois
    Chicago M,W
    Springfield M,W
    Urbana-Champaign M,W
University of St. Francis M,W
Waubonsee Community College M,W
Western Illinois University M,W

Indiana
Ancilla College M,W
Ball State University M,W
Bethel College M,W
Butler University M,W
Calumet College of St. Joseph M,W
Goshen College M,W
Grace College M,W
Holy Cross College M,W
Huntington University M,W
Indiana Institute of Technology M,W
Indiana State University M,W
Indiana University
    Bloomington M,W
    Northwest M,W
    Purdue University Fort Wayne M,W

Purdue University Indianapolis M,W
    South Bend M,W
    Southeast M,W
Indiana Wesleyan University M,W
Marian University M,W
Oakland City University M,W
Purdue University M,W
Purdue University
    North Central M
    Northwest M
Saint Joseph's College M,W
St. Mary-of-the-Woods College W
Taylor University M,W
University of Evansville M,W
University of Indianapolis M,W
University of Notre Dame M,W
University of Saint Francis M,W
University of Southern Indiana M,W
Valparaiso University M,W
Vincennes University M,W

Iowa
Briar Cliff University M,W
Clarke University M,W
Des Moines Area Community College M,W
Dordt College M,W
Drake University M,W
Ellsworth Community College M,W
Graceland University M,W
Grand View University M,W
Iowa Central Community College M,W
Iowa Lakes Community College M,W
Iowa State University M,W
Iowa Western Community College M,W
Kirkwood Community College M,W
Marshalltown Community College M,W
Morningside College M,W
Mount Mercy University M,W
North Iowa Area Community College M,W
Northwestern College M,W
St. Ambrose University M,W
Southeastern Community College M,W
Southwestern Community College M,W
University of Iowa M,W
University of Northern Iowa M,W
Upper Iowa University M,W
Waldorf University M,W
William Penn University M,W

Kansas
Allen County Community College M,W
Baker University M,W
Barton County Community College M,W
Benedictine College M,W
Bethany College M,W
Bethel College M,W
Brown Mackie College
    Salina M,W
Butler Community College M,W
Central Christian College of Kansas M,W
Cloud County Community College M,W
Coffeyville Community College M,W
Colby Community College M,W
Cowley County Community College M,W
Dodge City Community College M,W
Emporia State University M,W
Fort Hays State University M,W
Fort Scott Community College M,W
Friends University M,W
Garden City Community College M,W
Hesston College M,W
Highland Community College M,W
Hutchinson Community College M,W
Independence Community College M,W
Johnson County Community College M,W
Kansas City Kansas Community College M,W
Kansas State University M,W
Kansas Wesleyan University M,W
Labette Community College M,W
McPherson College M,W
MidAmerica Nazarene University M,W
Neosho County Community College M,W
Newman University M,W

Northwest Kansas Technical College M,W
Ottawa University M,W
Pittsburg State University M,W
Pratt Community College M,W
Seward County Community College M,W
Southwestern College M,W
Sterling College M,W
Tabor College M,W
University of Kansas M,W
University of St. Mary M,W
Washburn University M,W
Wichita State University M,W

Kentucky
Alice Lloyd College M,W
Asbury University M,W
Bellarmine University M,W
Brescia University M,W
Campbellsville University M,W
Eastern Kentucky University M,W
Georgetown College M,W
Kentucky State University M,W
Kentucky Wesleyan College M,W
Lindsey Wilson College M,W
Midway College W
Morehead State University M,W
Murray State University M,W
Northern Kentucky University M,W
St. Catharine College M,W
Union College M,W
University of Kentucky M,W
University of Louisville M,W
University of Pikeville M,W
University of the Cumberlands M,W
Western Kentucky University M,W

Louisiana
Bossier Parish Community College M,W
Dillard University M,W
Grambling State University M,W
Louisiana State University
    Eunice W
    Shreveport M,W
Louisiana State University and Agricultural and
    Mechanical College M,W
Louisiana Tech University M,W
Loyola University New Orleans M,W
McNeese State University M,W
Nicholls State University M,W
Northwestern State University M,W
Southeastern Louisiana University M,W
Southern University
    New Orleans M,W
Southern University and Agricultural and
    Mechanical College M,W
Tulane University M,W
University of Louisiana
    Monroe M,W
University of Louisiana at Lafayette M,W
University of New Orleans M,W
Xavier University of Louisiana M,W

Maine
University of Maine M,W
University of Maine
    Augusta M,W

Maryland
Allegany College of Maryland M,W
Anne Arundel Community College M,W
Bowie State University M,W
Chesapeake College M,W
College of Southern Maryland M,W
Community College of Baltimore County M,W
Coppin State University M,W
Garrett College M,W
Hagerstown Community College M,W
Harford Community College M,W
Howard Community College M,W
Loyola University Maryland M,W
Morgan State University M,W
Mount St. Mary's University M,W
Towson University M,W
University of Maryland

Baltimore County M,W
College Park M,W
Eastern Shore M,W
Washington Adventist University M,W

Massachusetts
American International College M,W
Assumption College M,W
Bentley University M,W
Boston College M,W
Boston University M,W
College of the Holy Cross M,W
Merrimack College M,W
Northeastern University M,W
Roxbury Community College M
Stonehill College M,W
University of Massachusetts
    Amherst M,W
    Lowell M,W

Michigan
Alpena Community College M,W
Aquinas College M,W
Central Michigan University M,W
Concordia University M,W
Cornerstone University M,W
Davenport University M,W
Delta College M,W
Eastern Michigan University M,W
Ferris State University M,W
Glen Oaks Community College M,W
Gogebic Community College M,W
Grand Valley State University M,W
Hillsdale College M,W
Kalamazoo Valley Community College M,W
Kellogg Community College M,W
Lake Michigan College M,W
Lake Superior State University M,W
Lansing Community College M,W
Lawrence Technological University M,W
Macomb Community College M,W
Madonna University M,W
Marygrove College M,W
Michigan State University M,W
Michigan Technological University M,W
Mott Community College M,W
Muskegon Community College M,W
Northern Michigan University M,W
Northwood University
    Michigan M,W
Oakland Community College M,W
Oakland University M,W
Rochester College M,W
Saginaw Valley State University M,W
St. Clair County Community College M,W
Schoolcraft College M,W
Siena Heights University M,W
Spring Arbor University M,W
University of Detroit Mercy M,W
University of Michigan M,W
University of Michigan
    Dearborn M,W
Wayne State University M,W
Western Michigan University M,W

Minnesota
Bemidji State University M,W
Concordia University St. Paul M,W
Minnesota State University
    Mankato M,W
    Moorhead M,W
Saint Cloud State University M,W
Southwest Minnesota State University M,W
University of Minnesota
    Crookston M,W
    Duluth M,W
    Twin Cities M,W
Winona State University M,W

Mississippi
Alcorn State University M,W
Belhaven University M,W
Blue Mountain College M,W
Coahoma Community College M,W

Copiah-Lincoln Community College M,W
Delta State University M,W
East Central Community College M,W
East Mississippi Community College M,W
Hinds Community College M,W
Holmes Community College M,W
Itawamba Community College M,W
Jackson State University M,W
Jones County Junior College M,W
Meridian Community College M,W
Mississippi Gulf Coast Community College
    M,W
Mississippi Valley State University M,W
Northwest Mississippi Community College
    M,W
Southwest Mississippi Community College
    M,W
Tougaloo College M,W
University of Mississippi M,W
University of Mississippi
    University of Southern Mississippi M,W
William Carey University M,W

Missouri
Avila University M,W
Central Methodist University M,W
College of the Ozarks M,W
Columbia College M,W
Cottey College W
Crowder College W
Culver-Stockton College M,W
Drury University M,W
Evangel University M,W
Hannibal-LaGrange University M,W
Harris-Stowe State University M,W
Jefferson College W
Lincoln University M,W
Lindenwood University M,W
Maryville University of Saint Louis M,W
Metropolitan Community College - Kansas City
    M,W
Mineral Area College M,W
Missouri Baptist University M,W
Missouri Southern State University M,W
Missouri State University M,W
Missouri State University
    West Plains M
Missouri University of Science and Technology
    M,W
Missouri Valley College M,W
Missouri Western State University M,W
Moberly Area Community College M,W
North Central Missouri College M,W
Northwest Missouri State University M,W
Park University M,W
Research College of Nursing M,W
Rockhurst University M,W
St. Louis Community College M,W
Saint Louis University M,W
Southeast Missouri State University M,W
Southwest Baptist University M,W
State Fair Community College M,W
Stephens College W
Three Rivers Community College M,W
Truman State University M,W
University of Central Missouri M,W
University of Missouri
    Columbia M,W
    Kansas City M,W
    St. Louis M,W
William Jewell College M,W
William Woods University M,W

Montana
Carroll College M,W
Dawson Community College M,W
Miles Community College M,W
Montana State University M,W
Montana State University
    Billings M,W
    Northern M,W
Montana Tech of the University of Montana
    M,W

Rocky Mountain College M,W
University of Great Falls M,W
University of Montana M,W
University of Montana: Western M,W

Nebraska
Bellevue University M
Central Community College M
Chadron State College M,W
College of Saint Mary W
Concordia University M,W
Creighton University M,W
Doane University M,W
Grace University M,W
Hastings College M,W
Mid-Plains Community College M,W
Midland University M,W
Northeast Community College M,W
Peru State College M,W
University of Nebraska
    Kearney M,W
    Lincoln M,W
    Omaha M,W
Wayne State College M,W
Western Nebraska Community College M,W
York College M,W

Nevada
University of Nevada
    Las Vegas M,W
    Reno M,W

New Hampshire
Franklin Pierce University M,W
Saint Anselm College M,W
Southern New Hampshire University M,W
University of New Hampshire M,W

New Jersey
Bloomfield College M,W
Brookdale Community College M,W
Caldwell University M,W
County College of Morris M,W
Essex County College M,W
Fairleigh Dickinson University
    Metropolitan Campus M,W
Felician University M,W
Georgian Court University M,W
Mercer County Community College M,W
Monmouth University M,W
New Jersey Institute of Technology M,W
Raritan Valley Community College M,W
Rider University M,W
Rowan College at Burlington County M,W
Rutgers, The State University of New Jersey
    New Brunswick/Piscataway Campus
    M,W
Saint Peter's University M,W
Salem Community College M,W
Seton Hall University M,W
Union County College W

New Mexico
Eastern New Mexico University M,W
New Mexico Highlands University M,W
New Mexico Junior College M,W
New Mexico Military Institute M
New Mexico State University M,W
University of New Mexico M,W
University of the Southwest M,W
Western New Mexico University M,W

New York
Adelphi University M,W
ASA College M,W
Canisius College M,W
City University of New York
    Queens College M,W
Colgate University M,W
College of Saint Rose M,W
Concordia College M,W
Daemen College M,W
Dominican College of Blauvelt M,W
Fordham University M,W

Genesee Community College M,W
Globe Institute of Technology M,W
Hofstra University M,W
Iona College M,W
Le Moyne College M,W
Long Island University
    LIU Brooklyn M,W
    LIU Post M,W
Manhattan College M,W
Marist College M,W
Mercy College M,W
Molloy College M,W
Monroe College M
Monroe Community College M
New York Institute of Technology M,W
Niagara County Community College M,W
Niagara University M,W
Nyack College M,W
Orange County Community College M,W
Pace University M,W
Pace University: Pleasantville/Briarcliff M,W
Roberts Wesleyan College M,W
Saint Bonaventure University M,W
St. Francis College M,W
St. John's University M,W
St. Thomas Aquinas College M,W
Siena College M,W
SUNY
    University at Albany M,W
    University at Binghamton M,W
    University at Buffalo M,W
    University at Stony Brook M,W
Syracuse University M,W
Wagner College M,W

North Carolina
Appalachian State University M,W
Barton College M,W
Belmont Abbey College M,W
Brevard College M,W
Campbell University M,W
Catawba College M,W
Chowan University M,W
Davidson College M,W
Duke University M,W
East Carolina University M,W
Elizabeth City State University M,W
Elon University M,W
Fayetteville State University M,W
Gardner-Webb University M,W
Guilford Technical Community College M,W
High Point University M,W
Johnson C. Smith University M,W
Johnston Community College M,W
Lees-McRae College M,W
Lenoir Community College M,W
Lenoir-Rhyne University M,W
Livingstone College M,W
Louisburg College M,W
Mars Hill University M,W
Montreat College M,W
North Carolina Agricultural and Technical State
    University M,W
North Carolina Central University M,W
North Carolina State University M,W
Queens University of Charlotte M,W
St. Andrews University M,W
Saint Augustine's University M,W
Shaw University M,W
University of Mount Olive M,W
University of North Carolina
    Asheville M,W
    Chapel Hill M,W
    Charlotte M,W
    Greensboro M,W
    Wilmington M,W
Wake Forest University M,W
Western Carolina University M,W
Wingate University M,W
Winston-Salem State University M,W

North Dakota
Bismarck State College M,W
Dakota College at Bottineau M,W

Dickinson State University M,W
Lake Region State College M,W
Mayville State University M,W
Minot State University M,W
North Dakota State College of Science M,W
North Dakota State University M,W
University of Jamestown M,W
University of Mary M,W
University of North Dakota M,W
Valley City State University M,W
Williston State College M,W

Ohio
Ashland University M,W
Bowling Green State University M,W
Cedarville University M,W
Central State University M,W
Cincinnati State Technical and Community
    College M,W
Clark State Community College M,W
Cleveland State University M,W
Edison State Community College M,W
Kent State University M,W
Lake Erie College M,W
Lakeland Community College M,W
Lourdes University M,W
Malone University M,W
Miami University
    Oxford M,W
Mount Vernon Nazarene University M,W
Notre Dame College M,W
Ohio Dominican University M,W
Ohio State University
    Columbus Campus M,W
Ohio University M,W
Owens Community College M,W
Shawnee State University M,W
Sinclair Community College M,W
Southern State Community College M,W
Tiffin University M,W
University of Akron M,W
University of Cincinnati M,W
University of Dayton M,W
University of Findlay M,W
University of Northwestern Ohio M,W
University of Rio Grande M,W
University of Toledo M,W
Urbana University M,W
Ursuline College W
Walsh University M,W
Wright State University M,W
Xavier University M,W
Youngstown State University M,W

Oklahoma
Bacone College M,W
Cameron University M,W
Connors State College M,W
East Central University M,W
Eastern Oklahoma State College M,W
Langston University M,W
Mid-America Christian University M,W
Northeastern Oklahoma Agricultural and
    Mechanical College M,W
Northeastern State University M,W
Northern Oklahoma College M,W
Northwestern Oklahoma State University M,W
Oklahoma Baptist University M,W
Oklahoma Christian University M,W
Oklahoma City University M,W
Oklahoma Panhandle State University M,W
Oklahoma State University M,W
Oklahoma Wesleyan University M,W
Oral Roberts University M,W
Redlands Community College M,W
Rogers State University M,W
St. Gregory's University M,W
Seminole State College M,W
Southeastern Oklahoma State University M,W
Southern Nazarene University M,W
Southwestern Oklahoma State University M,W
University of Central Oklahoma M,W
University of Oklahoma M,W

University of Science and Arts of Oklahoma
    M,W
University of Tulsa M,W
Western Oklahoma State College M,W

Oregon
Blue Mountain Community College M,W
Chemeketa Community College M,W
Clackamas Community College M,W
Concordia University M,W
Corban University M,W
Eastern Oregon University M,W
Lane Community College M,W
Linn-Benton Community College M,W
Mt. Hood Community College M,W
Multnomah University M,W
New Hope Christian College M
Northwest Christian University M,W
Oregon Institute of Technology M,W
Oregon State University M,W
Portland Community College M,W
Portland State University M,W
Southern Oregon University M,W
Southwestern Oregon Community College
    M,W
Treasure Valley Community College M,W
University of Oregon M,W
University of Portland M,W
Warner Pacific College M,W
Western Oregon University M,W

Pennsylvania
Bloomsburg University of Pennsylvania M,W
Bucknell University M,W
California University of Pennsylvania M,W
Carlow University M,W
Chestnut Hill College M,W
Cheyney University of Pennsylvania M,W
Clarion University of Pennsylvania M,W
Drexel University M,W
Duquesne University M,W
East Stroudsburg University of Pennsylvania
    M,W
Edinboro University
    of Pennsylvania M,W
Gannon University M,W
Harcum College M,W
Holy Family University M,W
Indiana University of Pennsylvania M,W
Kutztown University of Pennsylvania M,W
La Salle University M,W
Lackawanna College M,W
Lafayette College M,W
Lehigh University M,W
Lock Haven University of Pennsylvania M,W
Mansfield University of Pennsylvania M,W
Mercyhurst University M,W
Millersville University of Pennsylvania M,W
Penn State
    University Park M,W
Philadelphia University M,W
Point Park University M,W
Robert Morris University M,W
St. Francis University M,W
Saint Joseph's University M,W
Seton Hill University M,W
Shippensburg University of Pennsylvania M,W
Slippery Rock University of Pennsylvania M,W
Temple University M,W
University of Pittsburgh M,W
University of Pittsburgh
    Johnstown M,W
University of the Sciences M,W
Valley Forge Military College M,W
Villanova University M,W
West Chester University of Pennsylvania M,W

Puerto Rico
Bayamon Central University M,W
Inter American University of Puerto Rico
    Aguadilla Campus M,W
    Arecibo Campus M
    Barranquitas Campus M

Bayamon Campus M,W
Fajardo Campus M
Guayama Campus M,W
Metropolitan Campus M,W
Ponce Campus M,W
San German Campus M,W
Turabo University M,W
Universidad del Este M,W
Universidad Metropolitana M,W
Universidad Politecnica de Puerto Rico M
University of Puerto Rico
    Arecibo M,W
    Bayamon University College M,W
    Carolina Regional College M,W
    Cayey University College M,W
    Humacao M,W
    Mayaguez M,W
    Ponce M,W
    Utuado M
University of the Sacred Heart M

Rhode Island
Bryant University M,W
Community College of Rhode Island M,W
Providence College M,W
University of Rhode Island M,W

South Carolina
Allen University M,W
Anderson University M,W
Charleston Southern University M,W
The Citadel M
Claflin University M,W
Clemson University M,W
Coastal Carolina University M,W
Coker College M,W
College of Charleston M,W
Columbia College W
Columbia International University M,W
Converse College W
Erskine College M,W
Francis Marion University M,W
Furman University M,W
Lander University M,W
Limestone College M,W
Morris College M,W
Newberry College M,W
North Greenville University M,W
Presbyterian College M,W
South Carolina State University M,W
Southern Wesleyan University M,W
Spartanburg Methodist College M,W
University of South Carolina
    Aiken M,W
    Columbia M,W
    Upstate M,W
Voorhees College M,W
Winthrop University M,W
Wofford College M,W

South Dakota
Augusta University
    Augustana University M,W
Black Hills State University M,W
Dakota State University M,W
Dakota Wesleyan University M,W
Mount Marty College M,W
Northern State University M,W
South Dakota School of Mines and Technology
    M,W
South Dakota State University M,W
University of Sioux Falls M,W
University of South Dakota M,W

Tennessee
Austin Peay State University M,W
Belmont University M,W
Bethel University M,W
Bryan College
    Dayton M,W
Carson-Newman University M,W
Chattanooga State Community College M,W
Christian Brothers University M,W
Cleveland State Community College M,W

Columbia State Community College M,W
Cumberland University M,W
Dyersburg State Community College M,W
East Tennessee State University M,W
Freed-Hardeman University M,W
Hiwassee College M,W
Jackson State Community College M,W
King University M,W
Lane College M,W
Lee University M,W
LeMoyne-Owen College M,W
Lincoln Memorial University M,W
Lipscomb University M,W
Martin Methodist College M,W
Middle Tennessee State University M,W
Milligan College M,W
Motlow State Community College M,W
Roane State Community College M,W
Southwest Tennessee Community College M,W
Tennessee State University M,W
Tennessee Technological University M,W
Tennessee Wesleyan College M,W
Trevecca Nazarene University M,W
Tusculum College M,W
Union University M,W
University of Memphis M,W
University of Tennessee
    Chattanooga M,W
    Knoxville M,W
    Martin M,W
Vanderbilt University M,W
Volunteer State Community College M,W
Walters State Community College M,W

Texas
Abilene Christian University M,W
Angelina College M,W
Angelo State University M,W
Baylor University M,W
Blinn College M,W
Brookhaven College M
Clarendon College M,W
Collin County Community College District M,W
Dallas Baptist University M
Frank Phillips College M,W
Hill College M,W
Houston Baptist University M,W
Howard College M,W
Jacksonville College M,W
Jarvis Christian College M,W
Kilgore College M,W
Lamar University M,W
Lee College M
Lubbock Christian University M,W
McLennan Community College M,W
Midland College M,W
Midwestern State University M,W
Odessa College M,W
Panola College M,W
Paris Junior College M,W
Prairie View A&M University M,W
Ranger College M,W
Rice University M,W
St. Edward's University M,W
St. Mary's University M,W
Sam Houston State University M,W
San Jacinto College M,W
South Plains College M,W
Southern Methodist University M,W
Southwestern Assemblies of God University M,W
Stephen F. Austin State University M,W
Tarleton State University M,W
Temple College M,W
Texas A&M University M,W
Texas A&M University
    Commerce M,W
    Corpus Christi M,W
Texas Christian University M,W
Texas Southern University M,W
Texas State University M,W
Texas Tech University M,W

Texas Wesleyan University M,W
Texas Woman's University W
Trinity Valley Community College M,W
Tyler Junior College M,W
University of Houston M,W
University of North Texas M,W
University of St. Thomas M,W
University of Texas
    Arlington M,W
    Austin M,W
    of the Permian Basin M,W
    San Antonio M,W
University of the Incarnate Word M,W
Wayland Baptist University M,W
Weatherford College M,W
West Texas A&M University M,W
Western Texas College M,W
Wiley College M,W

Utah
Brigham Young University M,W
Dixie State University M,W
Salt Lake Community College M,W
Snow College M,W
Southern Utah University M,W
University of Utah M,W
Utah State University M,W
Utah Valley University M,W
Weber State University M,W
Westminster College M,W

Vermont
Saint Michael's College M,W
University of Vermont M,W

Virginia
Bluefield College M,W
College of William and Mary M,W
George Mason University M,W
Hampton University M,W
James Madison University M,W
Liberty University M,W
Longwood University M,W
Norfolk State University M,W
Old Dominion University M,W
Radford University M,W
University of Richmond M,W
University of Virginia M,W
University of Virginia's College at Wise M,W
Virginia Commonwealth University M,W
Virginia Military Institute M
Virginia Polytechnic Institute and State University M,W
Virginia State University M,W
Virginia Union University M,W

Washington
Big Bend Community College M,W
Central Washington University M,W
Centralia College M,W
Clark College M,W
Columbia Basin College M,W
Eastern Washington University M,W
Edmonds Community College M,W
Everett Community College M,W
Evergreen State College M,W
Gonzaga University M,W
Grays Harbor College M,W
Green River College M,W
Highline College M,W
Lower Columbia College M,W
Northwest Indian College M,W
Northwest University M,W
Olympic College M,W
Peninsula College M,W
Pierce College M,W
Saint Martin's University M,W
Seattle Pacific University M,W
Seattle University M,W
Shoreline Community College M,W
Skagit Valley College M,W
Spokane Community College M,W
Tacoma Community College M,W
University of Washington M,W

Walla Walla Community College M,W
Washington State University M,W
Western Washington University M,W
Whatcom Community College M,W
Yakima Valley Community College M,W

West Virginia
Alderson-Broaddus University M,W
Bluefield State College M,W
Concord University M,W
Davis and Elkins College M,W
Fairmont State University M,W
Glenville State College M,W
Marshall University M,W
Ohio Valley University M,W
Potomac State College of West Virginia University M,W
Salem International University M,W
Shepherd University M,W
University of Charleston M,W
West Liberty University M,W
West Virginia State University M,W
West Virginia University M,W
West Virginia University Institute of Technology M,W
West Virginia Wesleyan College M,W
Wheeling Jesuit University M,W

Wisconsin
Cardinal Stritch University M,W
Marquette University M,W
Silver Lake College of the Holy Family M,W
University of Wisconsin
    Green Bay M,W
    Madison M,W
    Milwaukee M,W
    Parkside M,W
Viterbo University M,W

Wyoming
Casper College M,W
Central Wyoming College M,W
Eastern Wyoming College M,W
Laramie County Community College M
Northwest College M,W
Sheridan College M,W
University of Wyoming M,W
Western Wyoming Community College M,W

Bowling

Arizona
Arizona Christian University M,W

Arkansas
Arkansas State University W
University of Arkansas
    Pine Bluff W

Connecticut
Post University W
Sacred Heart University W

Delaware
Delaware State University W
Wilmington University W

District of Columbia
Howard University W

Florida
Bethune-Cookman University W
Webber International University M,W

Georgia
Emmanuel College M,W
Life University M,W
Savannah College of Art and Design M,W

Illinois
Judson University M,W
McKendree University M,W

Robert Morris College
    Robert Morris University: Chicago M,W
University of St. Francis M,W

Indiana
Ancilla College M,W
Calumet College of St. Joseph M,W
Huntington University M,W
Indiana Institute of Technology M,W
Marian University M,W
Valparaiso University W
Vincennes University M

Iowa
Clarke University M,W
Graceland University M,W
Grand View University M,W
Iowa Central Community College M,W
Mount Mercy University M,W
St. Ambrose University M,W
Waldorf University M,W

Kansas
Baker University W
Kansas Wesleyan University M,W
Newman University M,W
Wichita State University M,W

Kentucky
Campbellsville University M,W
St. Catharine College M,W
University of Pikeville M,W
University of the Cumberlands M,W

Louisiana
Southern University and Agricultural and Mechanical College W

Maryland
Bowie State University W
Coppin State University W
Morgan State University W
University of Maryland
    Eastern Shore W

Michigan
Aquinas College M,W
Cleary University M,W
Concordia University M,W
Davenport University M,W
Kirtland Community College M,W
Lawrence Technological University M,W
Madonna University M,W
Saginaw Valley State University M
Schoolcraft College M,W

Mississippi
Blue Mountain College M,W
Jackson State University W
Mississippi Valley State University M,W

Missouri
Columbia College W
Culver-Stockton College M,W
Drury University W
Lincoln University W
Missouri Baptist University M,W

Nebraska
Hastings College M,W
Midland University M,W
University of Nebraska
    Lincoln W

New Jersey
Caldwell University W
Fairleigh Dickinson University
    Metropolitan Campus W
Monmouth University W

New York
Adelphi University W
Daemen College W

Long Island University
  LIU Brooklyn W
  LIU Post W
Molloy College W

North Carolina
Blue Ridge Community College M
Chowan University W
Elizabeth City State University W
Johnson C. Smith University W
Livingstone College M,W
North Carolina Central University M,W
Saint Augustine's University W
Shaw University W

Ohio
Notre Dame College M,W
University of Northwestern Ohio M,W
Urbana University M,W
Ursuline College W

Pennsylvania
Chestnut Hill College W
Cheyney University of Pennsylvania W
Duquesne University W
Kutztown University of Pennsylvania W
Lackawanna College W

Tennessee
Bethel University M,W
Martin Methodist College M,W
Tennessee Wesleyan College M,W

Texas
Jarvis Christian College M,W
Prairie View A&M University W
Sam Houston State University W
Stephen F. Austin State University W
Texas Southern University W

Virginia
Norfolk State University W

Wisconsin
Viterbo University M,W

Cheerleading

Alabama
Alabama Southern Community College M,W
Auburn University at Montgomery M,W
Faulkner State Community College M,W
Shelton State Community College M,W
Southern Union State Community College M,W
Troy University M,W
Tuskegee University M,W
University of Alabama M,W
University of Alabama
  Huntsville M,W
University of Mobile M,W
University of North Alabama M,W
University of South Alabama M,W
University of West Alabama M,W
Wallace State Community College at
  Hanceville M,W

Arizona
Arizona Christian University W
Arizona Western College M,W
Glendale Community College M,W

Arkansas
Arkansas Tech University M,W
John Brown University W
Lyon College M,W
North Arkansas College W
University of Arkansas
  Fort Smith M,W
  Little Rock W
  Monticello M,W
University of Central Arkansas M,W
Williams Baptist College M,W

California
California Baptist University W
Concordia University Irvine M,W
San Jose State University M,W

Delaware
Delaware State University M,W
University of Delaware M,W

Florida
University of Central Florida M,W
University of Florida M,W
Warner University M,W
Webber International University M,W

Georgia
Brenau University W
Brewton-Parker College M,W
Columbus State University M,W
Emmanuel College M,W
Gordon State College W
Point University M,W
Reinhardt University M,W
Shorter University M,W
Young Harris College M,W

Hawaii
Hawaii Pacific University M,W
University of Hawaii
  Manoa M,W

Idaho
Boise State University M,W
College of Southern Idaho M,W
North Idaho College M,W

Illinois
Benedictine University at Springfield M,W
Judson University M,W
Kaskaskia College M,W
Lewis University W
McKendree University M,W
Northwestern University M,W
Olivet Nazarene University M,W
Robert Morris College
  Robert Morris University: Chicago M,W
University of St. Francis M,W

Indiana
Ancilla College M,W
Bethel College M,W
Grace College M,W
Indiana Institute of Technology M,W
Indiana Wesleyan University M,W
Marian University M,W
Oakland City University W
University of Saint Francis M,W
Vincennes University M,W

Iowa
Briar Cliff University W
Graceland University M,W
Grand View University W
Iowa Western Community College M,W
Kirkwood Community College W
Mount Mercy University M,W
Northwestern College M,W
St. Ambrose University M,W
Waldorf University M,W
William Penn University M,W

Kansas
Allen County Community College M,W
Baker University M,W
Barton County Community College M,W
Benedictine College M,W
Bethany College M,W
Central Christian College of Kansas M,W
Cloud County Community College M,W
Coffeyville Community College M,W
Colby Community College M,W
Cowley County Community College M,W
Dodge City Community College M,W
Emporia State University M,W
Fort Scott Community College W

Friends University M,W
Garden City Community College M,W
Highland Community College M,W
Hutchinson Community College M,W
Independence Community College M,W
Kansas Wesleyan University M,W
Labette Community College M,W
McPherson College M,W
MidAmerica Nazarene University M,W
Neosho County Community College M,W
Newman University M,W
Ottawa University M,W
Pratt Community College M,W
Seward County Community College M,W
Southwestern College M,W
Tabor College M,W
University of St. Mary M,W
Washburn University M,W
Wichita State University M,W

Kentucky
Bellarmine University M,W
Campbellsville University M,W
Georgetown College W
Kentucky State University W
Northern Kentucky University M,W
St. Catharine College M,W
Union College M,W
University of Pikeville M,W
University of the Cumberlands M,W

Louisiana
Bossier Parish Community College M,W
Loyola University New Orleans M,W
McNeese State University M,W
University of Louisiana
  Monroe M,W
University of Louisiana at Lafayette M,W

Maryland
Morgan State University W

Massachusetts
American International College M,W

Michigan
Concordia University M,W
Cornerstone University M,W
Davenport University W
Northwood University
  Michigan M,W
Siena Heights University M,W
University of Detroit Mercy M,W
Wayne State University M,W

Mississippi
Blue Mountain College M,W
Copiah-Lincoln Community College M,W
East Central Community College M,W
East Mississippi Community College M,W
Hinds Community College M,W
Itawamba Community College M,W
Mississippi Gulf Coast Community College
  M,W
Mississippi State University M,W
Northwest Mississippi Community College W
Southwest Mississippi Community College
  M,W
University of Mississippi M,W
William Carey University M,W

Missouri
Avila University W
Central Methodist University W
Culver-Stockton College M,W
Drury University M,W
Evangel University M,W
Hannibal-LaGrange University M,W
Harris-Stowe State University M,W
Maryville University of Saint Louis M,W
Missouri Baptist University M,W
Missouri Valley College M,W
Moberly Area Community College M,W
Northwest Missouri State University M,W

Southeast Missouri State University M,W
University of Missouri
  Kansas City M,W
William Jewell College M,W
William Woods University W

Montana
Rocky Mountain College M,W
University of Montana M,W
University of Montana: Western M,W

Nebraska
Concordia University W
Doane University W
Hastings College W
Midland University M,W
Peru State College W
York College M,W

Nevada
University of Nevada
  Las Vegas M,W
  Reno M,W

New Mexico
New Mexico Junior College M,W

New York
ASA College W
Hofstra University M,W
Nyack College M,W

North Carolina
Brevard College W
Elon University M,W
Gardner-Webb University M,W
Lenoir-Rhyne University M,W
Mars Hill University M,W
Methodist University M,W
Queens University of Charlotte M,W
University of North Carolina
  Wilmington M,W

Ohio
Ashland University W
Lourdes University M,W
Notre Dame College W
Tiffin University M,W
University of Northwestern Ohio W
University of Rio Grande M,W
Urbana University M,W
Wright State University M,W

Oklahoma
Bacone College M,W
Cameron University M,W
Connors State College M,W
Eastern Oklahoma State College M,W
Langston University M,W
Mid-America Christian University M,W
Northeastern Oklahoma Agricultural and
  Mechanical College M,W
Northern Oklahoma College M,W
Northwestern Oklahoma State University M,W
Oklahoma Christian University M,W
Oklahoma City University M,W
Oklahoma Panhandle State University M,W
Oklahoma State University M,W
Oral Roberts University M,W
Rogers State University M,W
St. Gregory's University M,W
Southeastern Oklahoma State University M,W
Southern Nazarene University M,W
Southwestern Oklahoma State University M,W
University of Oklahoma M,W
University of Science and Arts of Oklahoma
  M,W
University of Tulsa M,W
Western Oklahoma State College M,W

Oregon
Southwestern Oregon Community College
  M,W

Pennsylvania
Gannon University W
Millersville University of Pennsylvania M,W
St. Francis University M,W
Seton Hill University M,W

Puerto Rico
Inter American University of Puerto Rico
Aguadilla Campus M,W
University of Puerto Rico
Carolina Regional College M,W
Cayey University College M,W
Humacao M,W

South Carolina
Anderson University W
Clemson University M,W
Limestone College M,W
Morris College M,W
Newberry College M,W
North Greenville University M,W
Presbyterian College M,W
Spartanburg Methodist College M,W
University of South Carolina
Columbia M,W

South Dakota
Dakota Wesleyan University M,W
University of Sioux Falls M,W

Tennessee
Bethel University M,W
Bryan College
Dayton M,W
Cumberland University M,W
Dyersburg State Community College M,W
Freed-Hardeman University W
Hiwassee College M,W
King University M,W
Lee University M,W
Martin Methodist College W
Milligan College M,W
Tennessee Technological University M,W
Tennessee Wesleyan College M,W
Tusculum College W
University of Memphis M,W
University of Tennessee
Martin W

Texas
Angelina College M,W
Baylor University W
Clarendon College M,W
East Texas Baptist University M,W
Houston Baptist University M,W
Howard College M,W
Paris Junior College M,W
Ranger College M,W
Sam Houston State University M,W
San Jacinto College M,W
South Plains College M,W
Southern Methodist University M,W
Southwestern Assemblies of God University W
Tarleton State University M,W
Temple College M,W
Texas Southern University M,W
Texas Wesleyan University M,W
Trinity Valley Community College M,W
Tyler Junior College M,W
University of Texas
of the Permian Basin M,W
Wayland Baptist University M,W

Utah
Brigham Young University W
Snow College M,W
Southern Utah University M,W
Weber State University M,W

Virginia
Bluefield College M,W
Liberty University M,W
Old Dominion University M,W

West Virginia
Alderson-Broaddus University M,W
University of Charleston M,W

Wyoming
University of Wyoming M,W
Western Wyoming Community College M,W

Cricket

California
College of the Redwoods M

Cross-country

Alabama
Alabama Agricultural and Mechanical
University M,W
Alabama State University M,W
Auburn University M,W
Auburn University at Montgomery M,W
Jacksonville State University M,W
Marion Military Institute M,W
Miles College M,W
Samford University M,W
Spring Hill College M,W
Troy University M,W
University of Alabama M,W
University of Alabama
Birmingham W
Huntsville M,W
University of Mobile M,W
University of North Alabama M,W
University of South Alabama M,W
University of West Alabama M,W

Alaska
University of Alaska
Anchorage M,W
Fairbanks M,W

Arizona
Arizona Christian University M,W
Arizona State University M,W
Central Arizona College M,W
Dine College M,W
Embry-Riddle Aeronautical University
Prescott Campus M,W
Glendale Community College M,W
Grand Canyon University M,W
Mesa Community College M,W
Northern Arizona University M,W
Paradise Valley Community College M,W
University of Arizona M,W
Yavapai College W

Arkansas
Arkansas State University M,W
Arkansas Tech University W
Ecclesia College M,W
Harding University M,W
Henderson State University W
John Brown University M,W
Lyon College M,W
Ouachita Baptist University W
Southern Arkansas University M,W
University of Arkansas M,W
University of Arkansas
Fort Smith M,W
Little Rock M,W
Monticello W
Pine Bluff M,W
University of Central Arkansas M,W

California
Academy of Art University M,W
Azusa Pacific University M,W
Biola University M,W
California Baptist University M,W

California Polytechnic State University: San
Luis Obispo M,W
California State Polytechnic University:
Pomona M,W
California State University
Chico M,W
Dominguez Hills W
Fresno M,W
Fullerton M,W
Long Beach M,W
Los Angeles M,W
Monterey Bay M,W
Northridge M,W
Sacramento M,W
Stanislaus M,W
Concordia University Irvine M,W
Fresno City College M,W
Fresno Pacific University M,W
Holy Names University M,W
Hope International University M,W
Humboldt State University M,W
Loyola Marymount University M,W
The Master's University M,W
Menlo College M,W
Notre Dame de Namur University M,W
Pepperdine University M,W
Point Loma Nazarene University W
St. Mary's College of California M,W
San Diego Christian College M,W
San Diego State University W
San Jose State University M,W
Santa Clara University M,W
Santiago Canyon College M,W
Simpson University M,W
Soka University of America M,W
Stanford University M,W
University of Antelope Valley M,W
University of California
Berkeley M,W
Davis M,W
Irvine M,W
Los Angeles M,W
Merced M,W
Riverside M,W
Santa Barbara M,W
University of San Diego M,W
University of San Francisco M,W
University of Southern California W
University of the Pacific W
Vanguard University of Southern California
M,W
Westmont College M,W
William Jessup University M,W

Colorado
Adams State University M,W
Colorado Christian University M,W
Colorado Mesa University M,W
Colorado School of Mines M,W
Colorado State University M,W
Colorado State University
Pueblo M,W
Fort Lewis College M,W
Regis University M,W
University of Colorado
Boulder M,W
Colorado Springs M,W
University of Northern Colorado M,W
Western State Colorado University M,W

Connecticut
Central Connecticut State University M,W
Fairfield University M,W
Post University M,W
Quinnipiac University M,W
Sacred Heart University M,W
Southern Connecticut State University M,W
University of Bridgeport M,W
University of Connecticut M,W
University of Hartford M,W
University of New Haven M,W

Delaware
Delaware State University M,W
Goldey-Beacom College M,W
Wilmington University M,W

District of Columbia
American University M,W
George Washington University M,W
Georgetown University M,W
Howard University M,W

Florida
Ave Maria University M,W
Bethune-Cookman University M,W
Chipola College W
Embry-Riddle Aeronautical University M,W
Flagler College M,W
Florida Atlantic University M,W
Florida Institute of Technology M,W
Florida Southern College M,W
Florida State University M,W
Jacksonville University W
Lynn University W
Nova Southeastern University M,W
Palm Beach Atlantic University M,W
Pasco-Hernando State College W
Saint Leo University M,W
Saint Thomas University M,W
South Florida State College W
Southeastern University M,W
Stetson University M,W
University of Central Florida W
University of Florida M,W
University of Miami M,W
University of North Florida M,W
University of South Florida M,W
University of Tampa M,W
University of West Florida M,W
Warner University M,W
Webber International University M,W

Georgia
Albany State University M,W
Augusta University M,W
Brenau University W
Brewton-Parker College M,W
Clark Atlanta University M,W
Clayton State University M,W
Columbus State University M,W
Darton State College M,W
Emmanuel College M,W
Georgia College and State University M,W
Georgia Institute of Technology M,W
Georgia Southern University W
Georgia Southwestern State University W
Georgia State University M,W
Gordon State College M,W
Kennesaw State University M,W
Life University M,W
Mercer University M,W
Morehouse College M
Paine College M,W
Point University M,W
Reinhardt University M,W
Savannah College of Art and Design M,W
Savannah State University M,W
Shorter University M,W
Truett McConnell University M,W
University of Georgia M,W
University of West Georgia M,W
Valdosta State University M,W
Young Harris College M,W

Hawaii
Brigham Young University-Hawaii M,W
Chaminade University of Honolulu M,W
Hawaii Pacific University M,W
University of Hawaii
Hilo M,W
Manoa W

Idaho
Boise State University M,W
College of Idaho M,W

College of Southern Idaho M,W
Idaho State University M,W
Lewis-Clark State College M,W
Northwest Nazarene University M,W
University of Idaho M,W

Illinois

Benedictine University at Springfield M,W
Bradley University M,W
Chicago State University M,W
College of Lake County M,W
Danville Area Community College M,W
DePaul University M,W
Eastern Illinois University M,W
Governors State University M,W
Illinois Central College M,W
Illinois Institute of Technology M,W
Illinois State University M,W
Judson University M,W
Kaskaskia College M,W
Lewis University M,W
Lincoln Christian University M,W
Lincoln College M,W
Loyola University Chicago M,W
McKendree University M,W
Moraine Valley Community College M,W
Morton College M,W
Northern Illinois University W
Northwestern University W
Olivet Nazarene University M,W
Quincy University M,W
Robert Morris College
    Robert Morris University: Chicago M,W
Saint Xavier University M,W
Sauk Valley Community College M,W
Southern Illinois University Carbondale M,W
Southern Illinois University Edwardsville M,W
Spoon River College M,W
Trinity Christian College M,W
University of Illinois
    Chicago M,W
    Springfield M,W
    Urbana-Champaign M,W
University of St. Francis M,W
Waubonsee Community College M,W
Western Illinois University M,W

Indiana

Ancilla College M,W
Ball State University W
Bethel College M,W
Butler University M,W
Calumet College of St. Joseph M,W
Goshen College M,W
Grace College M,W
Huntington University M,W
Indiana Institute of Technology M,W
Indiana State University M,W
Indiana University
    Bloomington M,W
    Purdue University Fort Wayne M,W
    Purdue University Indianapolis M,W
Indiana Wesleyan University M,W
Marian University M,W
Oakland City University M,W
Purdue University M,W
Purdue University
    Northwest M,W
Saint Joseph's College M,W
St. Mary-of-the-Woods College W
Taylor University M,W
University of Evansville M,W
University of Indianapolis M,W
University of Notre Dame M,W
University of Saint Francis M,W
University of Southern Indiana M,W
Valparaiso University M,W
Vincennes University M,W

Iowa

Briar Cliff University M,W
Clarke University M,W
Dordt College M,W

Drake University M,W
Ellsworth Community College M,W
Graceland University M,W
Grand View University M,W
Iowa Central Community College M,W
Iowa State University M,W
Iowa Western Community College M,W
Morningside College M,W
Mount Mercy University M,W
North Iowa Area Community College M,W
Northwestern College M,W
St. Ambrose University M,W
Scott Community College M,W
University of Iowa M,W
University of Northern Iowa M,W
Upper Iowa University M
Waldorf University M,W
William Penn University M,W

Kansas

Allen County Community College M,W
Baker University M,W
Barton County Community College M,W
Benedictine College M,W
Bethany College M,W
Bethel College M,W
Butler Community College M,W
Central Christian College of Kansas M,W
Cloud County Community College M,W
Coffeyville Community College M,W
Colby Community College M,W
Cowley County Community College M,W
Dodge City Community College M,W
Emporia State University M,W
Fort Hays State University M,W
Friends University M,W
Garden City Community College M,W
Hesston College M,W
Highland Community College M,W
Hutchinson Community College M,W
Johnson County Community College M,W
Kansas City Kansas Community College M,W
Kansas State University M,W
Kansas Wesleyan University M,W
McPherson College M,W
MidAmerica Nazarene University M,W
Neosho County Community College M,W
Newman University M,W
Northwest Kansas Technical College M,W
Ottawa University M,W
Pittsburg State University M,W
Pratt Community College M,W
Southwestern College M,W
Sterling College M,W
Tabor College M,W
University of Kansas M,W
University of St. Mary M,W
Washburn University M,W
Wichita State University M,W

Kentucky

Asbury University M,W
Bellarmine University M,W
Brescia University M,W
Campbellsville University M,W
Eastern Kentucky University M,W
Georgetown College M,W
Kentucky State University M,W
Kentucky Wesleyan College M,W
Lindsey Wilson College M,W
Midway College W
Morehead State University M,W
Murray State University W
Northern Kentucky University M,W
St. Catharine College M,W
Union College M,W
University of Kentucky M,W
University of Louisville M,W
University of Pikeville M,W
University of the Cumberlands M,W
Western Kentucky University M,W

Louisiana

Dillard University M,W
Grambling State University M,W
Louisiana State University and Agricultural and
    Mechanical College M,W
Louisiana Tech University M,W
Loyola University New Orleans M,W
McNeese State University M,W
Nicholls State University M,W
Northwestern State University M,W
Southeastern Louisiana University M,W
Southern University
    New Orleans M,W
Southern University and Agricultural and
    Mechanical College M,W
Tulane University M,W
University of Louisiana
    Monroe M,W
University of Louisiana at Lafayette M,W
University of New Orleans M,W
Xavier University of Louisiana M,W

Maine

University of Maine M,W

Maryland

Bowie State University M,W
Community College of Baltimore County M,W
Coppin State University M,W
Hagerstown Community College M,W
Harford Community College M,W
Loyola University Maryland M,W
Morgan State University M,W
Mount St. Mary's University M,W
Towson University W
University of Maryland
    Baltimore County M,W
    College Park W
    Eastern Shore M,W
Washington Adventist University M,W

Massachusetts

American International College M,W
Boston College M,W
Boston University M,W
College of the Holy Cross W
Merrimack College M,W
Northeastern University M,W
Stonehill College M,W
University of Massachusetts
    Amherst M,W
    Lowell M,W

Michigan

Alpena Community College M
Aquinas College M,W
Central Michigan University M,W
Cleary University M,W
Concordia University M,W
Cornerstone University M,W
Davenport University M,W
Eastern Michigan University M,W
Ferris State University M,W
Gogebic Community College M,W
Grand Valley State University M,W
Hillsdale College M,W
Kirtland Community College M,W
Lake Superior State University M,W
Lansing Community College M,W
Lawrence Technological University M,W
Macomb Community College M,W
Madonna University M,W
Michigan State University M,W
Michigan Technological University M,W
Mott Community College M,W
Muskegon Community College M,W
Northern Michigan University W
Northwood University
    Michigan M,W
Oakland Community College M,W
Oakland University M,W
Saginaw Valley State University M,W
Siena Heights University M,W

Spring Arbor University M,W
University of Detroit Mercy M,W
University of Michigan M,W
University of Michigan
    Dearborn M,W
Wayne State University M,W
Western Michigan University W

Minnesota

Concordia University St. Paul M,W
Minnesota State University
    Mankato M,W
    Moorhead M,W
Saint Cloud State University M,W
University of Minnesota
    Duluth M,W
    Twin Cities M,W
Winona State University M,W

Mississippi

Alcorn State University M,W
Belhaven University M,W
Blue Mountain College M,W
Delta State University W
Jackson State University M,W
Mississippi State University W
Mississippi Valley State University M,W
Tougaloo College M,W
University of Mississippi M,W
University of Mississippi
    University of Southern Mississippi M,W

Missouri

Avila University M,W
Central Methodist University M,W
Columbia College M,W
Cottey College W
Culver-Stockton College M,W
Drury University M,W
Evangel University M,W
Hannibal-LaGrange University M,W
Lincoln University W
Lindenwood University M,W
Maryville University of Saint Louis M,W
Metropolitan Community College - Kansas City
    W
Missouri Baptist University M,W
Missouri Southern State University M,W
Missouri State University M,W
Missouri University of Science and Technology
    M,W
Missouri Valley College M,W
Northwest Missouri State University M,W
Park University M,W
Rockhurst University W
Saint Louis University M,W
Southeast Missouri State University M,W
Southwest Baptist University M,W
Stephens College W
Truman State University M,W
University of Central Missouri M,W
University of Missouri
    Columbia M,W
    Kansas City M,W
William Jewell College M,W
William Woods University M,W

Montana

Carroll College M,W
Flathead Valley Community College M,W
Montana State University M,W
Montana State University
    Billings M,W
Rocky Mountain College M,W
University of Great Falls M,W
University of Montana M,W

Nebraska

College of Saint Mary W
Concordia University M,W
Creighton University M,W
Doane University M,W
Hastings College M,W
Midland University M,W

Peru State College W
University of Nebraska
    Kearney M,W
    Lincoln M,W
Wayne State College M,W
York College M,W

Nevada
Sierra Nevada College M,W
University of Nevada
    Las Vegas W
    Reno W

New Hampshire
Franklin Pierce University M,W
Saint Anselm College M,W
Southern New Hampshire University M,W
University of New Hampshire M,W

New Jersey
Bloomfield College M,W
Caldwell University M,W
Fairleigh Dickinson University
    Metropolitan Campus M,W
Felician University M,W
Georgian Court University M,W
Monmouth University M,W
Rider University M,W
Rutgers, The State University of New Jersey
    New Brunswick/Piscataway Campus
    M,W
Saint Peter's University M,W
Seton Hall University M,W

New Mexico
Eastern New Mexico University M,W
Navajo Technical University M,W
New Mexico Highlands University M,W
New Mexico Junior College M,W
New Mexico State University M,W
University of New Mexico M,W
University of the Southwest M,W

New York
Adelphi University M,W
Canisius College M,W
City University of New York
    Queens College M,W
College of Saint Rose M,W
Concordia College M,W
Daemen College M,W
Dominican College of Blauvelt M,W
Fordham University M,W
Hofstra University M,W
Iona College M,W
Le Moyne College M,W
Long Island University
    LIU Brooklyn W
    LIU Post M,W
Manhattan College M,W
Marist College M,W
Molloy College M,W
New York Institute of Technology M,W
Niagara University M,W
Nyack College M,W
Pace University M,W
Pace University: Pleasantville/Briarcliff M,W
Roberts Wesleyan College M,W
Saint Bonaventure University M,W
St. Francis College M,W
St. John's University W
St. Thomas Aquinas College M,W
Siena College M,W
SUNY
    University at Albany M,W
    University at Binghamton M,W
    University at Buffalo M,W
    University at Stony Brook M,W
Syracuse University M,W
Wagner College M,W

North Carolina
Appalachian State University M,W
Barton College M,W

Belmont Abbey College M,W
Brevard College M,W
Campbell University M,W
Catawba College M,W
Chowan University M,W
Davidson College M,W
East Carolina University M,W
Elon University M,W
Fayetteville State University M,W
Gardner-Webb University M,W
High Point University M,W
Johnson C. Smith University M,W
Lees-McRae College M,W
Lenoir-Rhyne University M,W
Livingstone College M,W
Mars Hill University M,W
Montreat College M,W
North Carolina Agricultural and Technical State
    University M,W
North Carolina Central University M,W
North Carolina State University M,W
Queens University of Charlotte M,W
St. Andrews University M,W
Saint Augustine's University M,W
Shaw University M,W
University of Mount Olive M,W
University of North Carolina
    Asheville M,W
    Chapel Hill M,W
    Charlotte M,W
    Greensboro M,W
    Wilmington M,W
Wake Forest University M,W
Wingate University M,W
Winston-Salem State University M,W

North Dakota
Dickinson State University M,W
Minot State University M,W
North Dakota State University M,W
University of Jamestown M,W
University of Mary M,W
University of North Dakota M,W
Valley City State University M,W

Ohio
Ashland University M,W
Bowling Green State University M,W
Cedarville University M,W
Central State University M,W
Cleveland State University W
Kent State University M,W
Lake Erie College M,W
Lourdes University M,W
Malone University M,W
Miami University
    Oxford M,W
Mount Vernon Nazarene University M,W
Notre Dame College M,W
Ohio Dominican University M,W
Ohio State University
    Columbus Campus M,W
Ohio University M,W
Shawnee State University M,W
Tiffin University M,W
University of Akron M,W
University of Cincinnati M,W
University of Dayton M,W
University of Findlay M,W
University of Rio Grande M,W
University of Toledo M,W
Urbana University M,W
Ursuline College W
Walsh University M,W
Wright State University M,W
Xavier University M,W
Youngstown State University M,W

Oklahoma
Cameron University M
East Central University M,W
Langston University M,W
Northwestern Oklahoma State University M,W

Oklahoma Baptist University M,W
Oklahoma Christian University M,W
Oklahoma City University M,W
Oklahoma Panhandle State University M,W
Oklahoma State University M,W
Oklahoma Wesleyan University M,W
Oral Roberts University M,W
Rogers State University M,W
St. Gregory's University M,W
Southeastern Oklahoma State University W
Southern Nazarene University M,W
Southwestern Oklahoma State University W
University of Central Oklahoma W
University of Oklahoma M,W
University of Science and Arts of Oklahoma
    M,W
University of Tulsa M,W

Oregon
Clackamas Community College M,W
Concordia University M,W
Corban University M,W
Eastern Oregon University M,W
Lane Community College M,W
Mt. Hood Community College M,W
Multnomah University M,W
Northwest Christian University M,W
Oregon Institute of Technology M,W
Portland State University M,W
Southern Oregon University M,W
Southwestern Oregon Community College
    M,W
Treasure Valley Community College M,W
University of Oregon M,W
University of Portland M,W
Warner Pacific College M,W
Western Oregon University M,W

Pennsylvania
Bloomsburg University of Pennsylvania M,W
Bucknell University W
California University of Pennsylvania M,W
Carlow University M,W
Chestnut Hill College M,W
Cheyney University of Pennsylvania M,W
Clarion University of Pennsylvania W
Duquesne University M,W
East Stroudsburg University of Pennsylvania
    M,W
Edinboro University
    of Pennsylvania M,W
Gannon University M,W
Holy Family University M,W
Indiana University of Pennsylvania M,W
Kutztown University of Pennsylvania M,W
La Salle University M,W
Lackawanna College M,W
Lehigh University M,W
Lock Haven University of Pennsylvania M,W
Mansfield University of Pennsylvania W
Mercyhurst University M,W
Millersville University of Pennsylvania W
Penn State
    University Park M,W
Philadelphia University M,W
Point Park University M,W
St. Francis University M,W
Saint Joseph's University M,W
Seton Hill University M,W
Shippensburg University of Pennsylvania M,W
Slippery Rock University of Pennsylvania M,W
Temple University M,W
University of Pittsburgh M,W
University of the Sciences M,W
Valley Forge Military College M,W
Villanova University M,W
West Chester University of Pennsylvania M,W

Puerto Rico
Bayamon Central University M,W
Inter American University of Puerto Rico
    Aguadilla Campus M,W
    Barranquitas Campus M,W

Bayamon Campus M,W
Guayama Campus M,W
Ponce Campus M,W
San German Campus M,W
Turabo University M,W
Universidad del Este M,W
Universidad Metropolitana M,W
University of Puerto Rico
    Arecibo W
    Cayey University College M,W
    Humacao M,W
    Mayaguez M,W
    Ponce M,W
    Utuado M,W
University of the Sacred Heart M,W

Rhode Island
Bryant University M,W
Providence College M,W
University of Rhode Island M,W

South Carolina
Anderson University M,W
Charleston Southern University M,W
The Citadel M,W
Claflin University M,W
Clemson University M,W
Coastal Carolina University M,W
Coker College M,W
College of Charleston M,W
Columbia College W
Columbia International University M,W
Converse College W
Erskine College M,W
Francis Marion University M,W
Furman University M,W
Limestone College M,W
Morris College M,W
Newberry College M,W
North Greenville University M,W
Presbyterian College M,W
South Carolina State University M,W
Southern Wesleyan University M,W
Spartanburg Methodist College M,W
University of South Carolina
    Aiken W
    Columbia W
    Upstate M,W
Voorhees College M,W
Winthrop University M,W
Wofford College M,W

South Dakota
Augusta University
    Augustana University M,W
Black Hills State University M,W
Dakota State University M,W
Dakota Wesleyan University M,W
Mount Marty College M,W
Northern State University M,W
South Dakota School of Mines and Technology
    M,W
South Dakota State University M,W
University of Sioux Falls M,W
University of South Dakota M,W

Tennessee
Austin Peay State University M,W
Belmont University M,W
Bethel University M,W
Bryan College
    Dayton M,W
Carson-Newman University M,W
Christian Brothers University M,W
Cumberland University M,W
East Tennessee State University M,W
Hiwassee College M,W
King University M,W
Lee University M,W
LeMoyne-Owen College M
Lincoln Memorial University M,W
Lipscomb University M,W
Middle Tennessee State University M,W
Milligan College M,W

Tennessee Technological University M,W
Tennessee Wesleyan College M,W
Trevecca Nazarene University M,W
Tusculum College M,W
Union University M,W
University of Memphis M,W
University of Tennessee
   Chattanooga M,W
   Martin M,W
Vanderbilt University M,W

Texas
Abilene Christian University M,W
Angelo State University M,W
Baylor University M,W
Clarendon College M,W
Dallas Baptist University W
Houston Baptist University M,W
Jacksonville College M,W
Lamar University M,W
Lubbock Christian University M,W
Midwestern State University W
Odessa College M,W
Prairie View A&M University M,W
Rice University M,W
St. Edward's University M,W
Sam Houston State University M,W
South Plains College M,W
Southern Methodist University W
Southwestern Assemblies of God University
   M,W
Stephen F. Austin State University M,W
Tarleton State University M,W
Texas A&M University
   Commerce M,W
Texas Christian University M,W
Texas Southern University M,W
Texas State University M,W
Texas Tech University M,W
Texas Wesleyan University M,W
University of Houston M,W
University of North Texas M,W
University of Texas
   Austin M,W
   of the Permian Basin M,W
   San Antonio M,W
University of the Incarnate Word M,W
Wayland Baptist University M,W
West Texas A&M University M,W
Western Texas College M,W

Utah
Brigham Young University M,W
Dixie State University M,W
Southern Utah University M,W
University of Utah W
Utah State University M,W
Utah Valley University M,W
Westminster College M,W

Vermont
University of Vermont M,W

Virginia
Bluefield College M,W
College of William and Mary M,W
George Mason University M,W
Hampton University M,W
James Madison University W
Liberty University M,W
Longwood University M,W
Norfolk State University M,W
Radford University M,W
University of Richmond W
University of Virginia M,W
University of Virginia's College at Wise M,W
Virginia Commonwealth University M,W
Virginia Military Institute M,W
Virginia Polytechnic Institute and State
   University M,W
Virginia State University M,W
Virginia Union University M,W

Washington
Central Washington University M,W
Clark College M,W
Eastern Washington University M,W
Everett Community College M,W
Gonzaga University M,W
Highline College M,W
Northwest University M,W
Olympic College M,W
Saint Martin's University M,W
Seattle Pacific University M,W
Seattle University M,W
Spokane Community College M,W
Washington State University M,W
Western Washington University M,W

West Virginia
Alderson-Broaddus University M,W
Bluefield State College M,W
Concord University M,W
Davis and Elkins College M,W
Fairmont State University M,W
Glenville State College M,W
Marshall University M,W
Ohio Valley University M,W
Potomac State College of West Virginia
   University M,W
University of Charleston M,W
West Liberty University M,W
West Virginia State University W
West Virginia University W
West Virginia Wesleyan College M,W
Wheeling Jesuit University M,W

Wisconsin
Cardinal Stritch University M,W
Marquette University M,W
Silver Lake College of the Holy Family M,W
University of Wisconsin
   Green Bay M,W
   Madison M,W
   Milwaukee M,W
   Parkside M,W
Viterbo University M,W

Wyoming
Central Wyoming College M,W
Sheridan College M,W
University of Wyoming M,W

Diving

Alabama
Auburn University M,W
University of Alabama M,W

Arizona
Arizona State University M,W
Northern Arizona University W
University of Arizona M,W

Arkansas
Ouachita Baptist University M,W
University of Arkansas W

California
California Baptist University M,W
California State University
   Fresno W
   Northridge M,W
College of the Redwoods M
Pepperdine University W
San Diego State University W
Soka University of America M,W
Stanford University M,W
University of California
   Berkeley M,W
   Davis W
   Los Angeles M,W
University of San Diego W
University of Southern California M,W

Colorado
Colorado State University W
Colorado State University
   Pueblo W
University of Denver M,W
University of Northern Colorado W

Connecticut
Central Connecticut State University W
Fairfield University W
University of Connecticut M,W

District of Columbia
George Washington University M,W
Georgetown University M,W
Howard University M,W

Florida
Florida State University M,W
Indian River State College M,W
Nova Southeastern University M,W
University of Florida M,W
University of Miami M,W

Georgia
Georgia Institute of Technology M,W
Georgia Southern University W
University of Georgia M,W

Hawaii
University of Hawaii
   Manoa M,W

Idaho
University of Idaho W

Illinois
Illinois Institute of Technology M,W
Illinois State University W
Lincoln College M,W
McKendree University M,W
Northwestern University M,W
Southern Illinois University Carbondale M,W
University of Illinois
   Chicago M,W
   Urbana-Champaign W
Western Illinois University M,W

Indiana
Ball State University M,W
Indiana State University W
Indiana University
   Bloomington M,W
   Purdue University Indianapolis M,W
Purdue University M,W
University of Evansville M,W
University of Notre Dame M,W
Valparaiso University M,W

Iowa
University of Iowa M,W

Kentucky
Asbury University M,W
University of Kentucky M,W
University of Louisville M,W

Louisiana
Louisiana State University and Agricultural and
   Mechanical College M,W

Maine
University of Maine W

Maryland
Loyola University Maryland M,W
Towson University M,W

Massachusetts
Boston College M,W
Boston University M,W
Northeastern University W
University of Massachusetts
   Amherst M,W

Michigan
Eastern Michigan University M,W
Grand Valley State University M,W
Michigan State University M,W
Northern Michigan University W
Oakland University M,W
University of Michigan M,W
Wayne State University M,W

Minnesota
Minnesota State University
   Mankato M,W
   Moorhead W
Saint Cloud State University M,W
University of Minnesota
   Twin Cities M,W

Mississippi
Delta State University M,W

Missouri
Drury University M,W
Lindenwood University M,W
Maryville University of Saint Louis W
Saint Louis University M,W
University of Missouri
   Columbia M,W

Nebraska
University of Nebraska
   Kearney W
   Lincoln W

Nevada
University of Nevada
   Las Vegas M,W
   Reno W

New Hampshire
University of New Hampshire W

New Jersey
Rider University M,W
Rutgers, The State University of New Jersey
   New Brunswick/Piscataway Campus
   M,W
Saint Peter's University M,W

New Mexico
New Mexico State University W
University of New Mexico W

New York
College of Saint Rose M,W
Fordham University M,W
Iona College M,W
Le Moyne College M,W
Marist College M,W
Niagara University M,W
Pace University M,W
Pace University: Pleasantville/Briarcliff M
Saint Bonaventure University M,W
St. Francis College M,W
Siena College W
SUNY
   University at Binghamton M,W
   University at Buffalo M,W
   University at Stony Brook W

North Carolina
Davidson College M,W
East Carolina University M,W
University of North Carolina
   Chapel Hill M,W
   Wilmington M,W

North Dakota
University of North Dakota M,W

Ohio
Ashland University M,W
Cleveland State University M,W
Malone University M,W
Miami University
   Oxford M,W

Notre Dame College M,W
Ohio University W
University of Akron W
University of Cincinnati M,W
University of Findlay M,W
University of Toledo W
Wright State University M,W

Oklahoma
Oklahoma Baptist University M,W

Pennsylvania
Clarion University of Pennsylvania M,W
Drexel University M,W
La Salle University M,W
Lehigh University M,W
Penn State
   University Park M,W
St. Francis University W
University of Pittsburgh M,W
Villanova University W
West Chester University of Pennsylvania M,W

Rhode Island
Bryant University M,W
University of Rhode Island W

South Carolina
Clemson University M,W
University of South Carolina
   Columbia M,W

South Dakota
South Dakota State University M,W
University of South Dakota M,W

Texas
Southern Methodist University M,W
Texas A&M University M,W
Texas Christian University M,W
University of Houston W
University of North Texas W
University of Texas
   Austin M,W

Utah
Brigham Young University M,W
University of Utah M,W

Vermont
University of Vermont W

Virginia
George Mason University M,W
James Madison University W
Liberty University W
Old Dominion University M,W
University of Richmond W
University of Virginia M,W
Virginia Military Institute M
Virginia Polytechnic Institute and State
   University M,W

West Virginia
West Virginia University M,W

Wisconsin
University of Wisconsin
   Green Bay M,W
   Milwaukee M,W

Wyoming
University of Wyoming M,W

Equestrian

Alabama
Auburn University W

California
California State University
   Fresno W

Delaware
Delaware State University W

Georgia
Savannah College of Art and Design M,W
University of Georgia W

Indiana
St. Mary-of-the-Woods College W

Kentucky
Midway College W

Minnesota
University of Minnesota
   Crookston W

Nebraska
Nebraska College of Technical Agriculture
   M,W

New Mexico
New Mexico State University W

New York
Long Island University
   LIU Post W

North Carolina
St. Andrews University M,W

Ohio
Tiffin University M,W

Oklahoma
Northeastern Oklahoma Agricultural and
   Mechanical College M,W
Oklahoma Panhandle State University M,W
Oklahoma State University W

Pennsylvania
Seton Hill University W

South Carolina
University of South Carolina
   Columbia W

South Dakota
South Dakota State University W

Tennessee
University of Tennessee
   Martin W

Texas
Baylor University W
Southern Methodist University W
Texas A&M University W
Texas Christian University W
West Texas A&M University W

Wyoming
Laramie County Community College M,W

Fencing

California
Stanford University M,W

Illinois
Northwestern University W

Indiana
University of Notre Dame M,W

Michigan
University of Detroit Mercy M,W
Wayne State University M,W

New Jersey
Fairleigh Dickinson University
   Metropolitan Campus W
New Jersey Institute of Technology M,W

Rutgers, The State University of New Jersey
   New Brunswick/Piscataway Campus
   M,W

New York
City University of New York
   Queens College W
Long Island University
   LIU Post W
St. John's University M,W

North Carolina
University of North Carolina
   Chapel Hill M,W

Ohio
Cleveland State University M,W
Ohio State University
   Columbus Campus M,W

Pennsylvania
Bucknell University M,W
Penn State
   University Park M,W
Temple University W

Field Hockey

California
Stanford University W
University of California
   Berkeley W
   Davis W
University of the Pacific W

Connecticut
Fairfield University W
Quinnipiac University W
Sacred Heart University W
Southern Connecticut State University W
University of Connecticut W

Delaware
University of Delaware W

District of Columbia
American University W
Georgetown University W

Illinois
Northwestern University W

Indiana
Ball State University W

Iowa
University of Iowa W

Kentucky
Bellarmine University W
University of Louisville W

Maine
University of Maine W

Maryland
Towson University W
University of Maryland
   College Park W

Massachusetts
American International College W
Boston College W
Boston University W
College of the Holy Cross W
Merrimack College W
Northeastern University W
Stonehill College W
University of Massachusetts
   Lowell W

Michigan
Central Michigan University W
Michigan State University W
University of Michigan W

Missouri
Lindenwood University W
Missouri State University W
Saint Louis University W

New Hampshire
Franklin Pierce University W
Saint Anselm College W
University of New Hampshire W

New Jersey
Monmouth University W
Rider University W
Rutgers, The State University of New Jersey
   New Brunswick/Piscataway Campus W

New York
Adelphi University W
Colgate University W
Hofstra University W
Long Island University
   LIU Brooklyn W
   LIU Post W
Mercy College W
Molloy College W
Pace University W
Pace University: Pleasantville/Briarcliff W
Siena College W
SUNY
   University at Albany W
Syracuse University W

North Carolina
Appalachian State University W
Davidson College W
Duke University W
Queens University of Charlotte W
University of North Carolina
   Chapel Hill W
Wake Forest University W

Ohio
Kent State University W
Miami University
   Oxford W
Ohio State University
   Columbus Campus W
Ohio University W

Pennsylvania
Bloomsburg University of Pennsylvania W
Bucknell University W
Drexel University W
East Stroudsburg University of Pennsylvania W
Indiana University of Pennsylvania W
Kutztown University of Pennsylvania W
La Salle University W
Lafayette College W
Lehigh University W
Lock Haven University of Pennsylvania W
Mansfield University of Pennsylvania W
Mercyhurst University W
Millersville University of Pennsylvania W
Penn State
   University Park W
Robert Morris University W
St. Francis University W
Saint Joseph's University W
Seton Hill University W
Shippensburg University of Pennsylvania W
Slippery Rock University of Pennsylvania W
Temple University W
Villanova University W
West Chester University of Pennsylvania W

Rhode Island
Bryant University W
Providence College W

South Carolina
Limestone College W
Newberry College W

Vermont
University of Vermont W

Virginia
College of William and Mary W
James Madison University W
Liberty University W
Longwood University W
Old Dominion University W
University of Richmond W
University of Virginia W
Virginia Commonwealth University W

Football (non-tackle)

Georgia
Life University M,W

Illinois
Olivet Nazarene University M

Football (tackle)

Alabama
Alabama Agricultural and Mechanical
    University M
Alabama State University M
Auburn University M
Faulkner University M
Jacksonville State University M
Miles College M
Samford University M
Troy University M
Tuskegee University M
University of Alabama M
University of Alabama
    Birmingham M
University of North Alabama M
University of West Alabama M

Arizona
Arizona Christian University M
Arizona State University M
Arizona Western College M
Eastern Arizona College M
Glendale Community College M
Mesa Community College M
Northern Arizona University M
Scottsdale Community College M
University of Arizona M

Arkansas
Arkansas State University M
Arkansas Tech University M
Harding University M
Henderson State University M
Ouachita Baptist University M
Southern Arkansas University M
University of Arkansas M
University of Arkansas
    Monticello M
    Pine Bluff M
University of Central Arkansas M

California
Azusa Pacific University M
California Polytechnic State University: San
    Luis Obispo M
California State University
    Fresno M
    Sacramento M
Fresno City College M
Grossmont College M
Humboldt State University M
San Diego State University M
San Jose State University M
Stanford University M

University of California
    Berkeley M
    Davis M
    Los Angeles M
University of Southern California M
Yuba College M

Colorado
Adams State University M
Colorado Mesa University M
Colorado School of Mines M
Colorado State University M
Colorado State University
    Pueblo M
Fort Lewis College M
University of Colorado
    Boulder M
University of Northern Colorado M
Western State Colorado University M

Connecticut
Central Connecticut State University M
Sacred Heart University M
Southern Connecticut State University M
University of Connecticut M
University of New Haven M

Delaware
Delaware State University M
University of Delaware M

District of Columbia
Georgetown University M
Howard University M

Florida
Ave Maria University M
Bethune-Cookman University M
Florida Agricultural and Mechanical University
    M
Florida Atlantic University M
Florida State University M
Southeastern University M
University of Central Florida M
University of Florida M
University of Miami M
University of South Florida M
University of West Florida M
Webber International University M

Georgia
Albany State University M
Clark Atlanta University M
Fort Valley State University M
Georgia Institute of Technology M
Georgia Military College M
Georgia Southern University M
Georgia State University M
Kennesaw State University M
Mercer University M
Morehouse College M
Point University M
Reinhardt University M
Savannah State University M
Shorter University M
University of Georgia M
University of West Georgia M
Valdosta State University M

Hawaii
University of Hawaii
    Manoa M

Idaho
Boise State University M
Idaho State University M
University of Idaho M

Illinois
Eastern Illinois University M
Illinois State University M
McKendree University M
Northwestern University M
Olivet Nazarene University M
Quincy University M

Robert Morris College
    Robert Morris University: Chicago M
Saint Xavier University M
Southern Illinois University Carbondale M
Trinity International University M
University of Illinois
    Urbana-Champaign M
University of St. Francis M
Western Illinois University M

Indiana
Ball State University M
Indiana State University M
Indiana University
    Bloomington M
Marian University M
Purdue University M
Saint Joseph's College M
Taylor University M
University of Indianapolis M
University of Notre Dame M
University of Saint Francis M

Iowa
Briar Cliff University M
Dordt College M
Ellsworth Community College M
Graceland University M
Grand View University M
Iowa Central Community College M
Iowa State University M
Iowa Western Community College M
Morningside College M
Northwestern College M
St. Ambrose University M
University of Iowa M
University of Northern Iowa M
Upper Iowa University M
Waldorf University M
William Penn University M

Kansas
Baker University M
Benedictine College M
Bethany College M
Bethel College M
Butler Community College M
Coffeyville Community College M
Dodge City Community College M
Emporia State University M
Fort Hays State University M
Fort Scott Community College M
Friends University M
Garden City Community College M
Highland Community College M
Hutchinson Community College M
Independence Community College M
Kansas State University M
Kansas Wesleyan University M
McPherson College M
MidAmerica Nazarene University M
Ottawa University M
Pittsburg State University M
Southwestern College M
Sterling College M
Tabor College M
University of Kansas M
University of St. Mary M
Washburn University M

Kentucky
Campbellsville University M
Eastern Kentucky University M
Georgetown College M
Kentucky Christian University M
Kentucky State University M
Kentucky Wesleyan College M
Lindsey Wilson College M
Murray State University M
Union College M
University of Kentucky M
University of Louisville M
University of Pikeville M

University of the Cumberlands M
Western Kentucky University M

Louisiana
Grambling State University M
Louisiana State University and Agricultural and
    Mechanical College M
Louisiana Tech University M
McNeese State University M
Nicholls State University M
Northwestern State University M
Southeastern Louisiana University M
Southern University and Agricultural and
    Mechanical College M
Tulane University M
University of Louisiana
    Monroe M
University of Louisiana at Lafayette M

Maine
University of Maine M

Maryland
Bowie State University M
Morgan State University M
Towson University M
University of Maryland
    College Park M

Massachusetts
American International College M
Boston College M
College of the Holy Cross M
Merrimack College M
Stonehill College M
University of Massachusetts
    Amherst M

Michigan
Central Michigan University M
Concordia University M
Davenport University M
Eastern Michigan University M
Ferris State University M
Grand Valley State University M
Hillsdale College M
Michigan State University M
Michigan Technological University M
Northern Michigan University M
Northwood University
    Michigan M
Saginaw Valley State University M
Siena Heights University M
University of Michigan M
Wayne State University M
Western Michigan University M

Minnesota
Bemidji State University M
Concordia University St. Paul M
Minnesota State University
    Mankato M
    Moorhead M
Saint Cloud State University M
Southwest Minnesota State University M
University of Minnesota
    Crookston M
    Duluth M
    Twin Cities M
Winona State University M

Mississippi
Alcorn State University M
Belhaven University M
Coahoma Community College M
Copiah-Lincoln Community College M
Delta State University M
East Central Community College M
East Mississippi Community College M
Hinds Community College M
Holmes Community College M
Itawamba Community College M
Jackson State University M
Jones County Junior College M

Mississippi Gulf Coast Community College M
Mississippi Valley State University M
Northwest Mississippi Community College M
Southwest Mississippi Community College M
University of Mississippi M
University of Mississippi
    University of Southern Mississippi M

Missouri
Avila University M
Central Methodist University M
Culver-Stockton College M
Evangel University M
Lincoln University M
Lindenwood University M
Missouri Baptist University M
Missouri Southern State University M
Missouri State University M
Missouri University of Science and Technology
   M
Missouri Valley College M
Missouri Western State University M
Northwest Missouri State University M
Southeast Missouri State University M
Southwest Baptist University M
Truman State University M
University of Central Missouri M
University of Missouri
    Columbia M
William Jewell College M

Montana
Carroll College M
Montana State University M
Montana State University
    Northern M
Montana Tech of the University of Montana M
Rocky Mountain College M
University of Montana M
University of Montana: Western M

Nebraska
Chadron State College M
Concordia University M
Doane University M
Hastings College M
Midland University M
Peru State College M
University of Nebraska
    Kearney M
    Lincoln M
Wayne State College M

Nevada
University of Nevada
    Las Vegas M
    Reno M

New Hampshire
Saint Anselm College M
University of New Hampshire M

New Jersey
Monmouth University M
Rutgers, The State University of New Jersey
    New Brunswick/Piscataway Campus M

New Mexico
Eastern New Mexico University M
New Mexico Highlands University M
New Mexico Military Institute M
New Mexico State University M
University of New Mexico M
Western New Mexico University M

New York
ASA College M
Fordham University M
Long Island University
    LIU Post M
Pace University M
Pace University: Pleasantville/Briarcliff M
SUNY
    University at Albany M
    University at Buffalo M

University at Stony Brook M
Syracuse University M
Wagner College M

North Carolina
Appalachian State University M
Brevard College M
Catawba College M
Chowan University M
Duke University M
East Carolina University M
Elizabeth City State University M
Elon University M
Fayetteville State University M
Gardner-Webb University M
Johnson C. Smith University M
Lenoir-Rhyne University M
Livingstone College M
Mars Hill University M
North Carolina Agricultural and Technical State
    University M
North Carolina Central University M
North Carolina State University M
St. Andrews University M
Saint Augustine's University M
Shaw University M
University of North Carolina
    Chapel Hill M
    Charlotte M
Wake Forest University M
Western Carolina University M
Wingate University M
Winston-Salem State University M

North Dakota
Dickinson State University M
Mayville State University M
Minot State University M
North Dakota State College of Science M
North Dakota State University M
University of Jamestown M
University of Mary M
University of North Dakota M
Valley City State University M

Ohio
Ashland University M
Bowling Green State University M
Kent State University M
Lake Erie College M
Malone University M
Miami University
    Oxford M
Notre Dame College M
Ohio Dominican University M
Ohio State University
    Columbus Campus M
Ohio University M
Tiffin University M
University of Akron M
University of Cincinnati M
University of Findlay M
University of Toledo M
Urbana University M
Walsh University M
Youngstown State University M

Oklahoma
Bacone College M
East Central University M
Langston University M
Northeastern Oklahoma Agricultural and
   Mechanical College M
Northeastern State University M
Northwestern Oklahoma State University M
Oklahoma Baptist University M
Oklahoma Panhandle State University M
Oklahoma State University M
Southeastern Oklahoma State University M
Southern Nazarene University M
Southwestern Oklahoma State University M
University of Central Oklahoma M
University of Oklahoma M
University of Tulsa M

Oregon
Eastern Oregon University M
Oregon State University M
Portland State University M
Southern Oregon University M
University of Oregon M
Western Oregon University M

Pennsylvania
Bloomsburg University of Pennsylvania M
Bucknell University M
California University of Pennsylvania M
Chestnut Hill College M
Cheyney University of Pennsylvania M
Clarion University of Pennsylvania M
Duquesne University M
East Stroudsburg University of Pennsylvania M
Edinboro University
    of Pennsylvania M
Gannon University M
Indiana University of Pennsylvania M
Kutztown University of Pennsylvania M
Lackawanna College M
Lehigh University M
Lock Haven University of Pennsylvania M
Mansfield University of Pennsylvania M
Mercyhurst University M
Millersville University of Pennsylvania M
Penn State
    University Park M
Robert Morris University M
St. Francis University M
Seton Hill University M
Shippensburg University of Pennsylvania M
Slippery Rock University of Pennsylvania M
Temple University M
University of Pittsburgh M
Valley Forge Military College M
Villanova University M
West Chester University of Pennsylvania M

Rhode Island
Bryant University M
University of Rhode Island M

South Carolina
Charleston Southern University M
The Citadel M
Clemson University M
Coastal Carolina University M
Furman University M
Limestone College M
Newberry College M
North Greenville University M
Presbyterian College M
South Carolina State University M
University of South Carolina
    Columbia M
Wofford College M

South Dakota
Augusta University
    Augustana University M
Black Hills State University M
Dakota State University M
Dakota Wesleyan University M
Northern State University M
South Dakota School of Mines and Technology
   M
South Dakota State University M
University of Sioux Falls M
University of South Dakota M

Tennessee
Austin Peay State University M
Bethel University M
Carson-Newman University M
Cumberland University M
Lane College M
Middle Tennessee State University M
Tennessee State University M
Tennessee Technological University M
Tusculum College M
University of Memphis M

University of Tennessee
    Chattanooga M
    Knoxville M
    Martin M
Vanderbilt University M

Texas
Abilene Christian University M
Angelo State University M
Baylor University M
Blinn College M
Houston Baptist University M
Kilgore College M
Midwestern State University M
Prairie View A&M University M
Rice University M
Sam Houston State University M
Southern Methodist University M
Southwestern Assemblies of God University M
Stephen F. Austin State University M
Tarleton State University M
Texas A&M University M
Texas A&M University
    Commerce M
Texas Christian University M
Texas Southern University M
Texas State University M
Texas Tech University M
Texas Wesleyan University M
Trinity Valley Community College M
Tyler Junior College M
University of Houston M
University of North Texas M
University of Texas
    Austin M
    of the Permian Basin M
    San Antonio M
University of the Incarnate Word M
Wayland Baptist University M
West Texas A&M University M

Utah
Brigham Young University M
Dixie State University M
Snow College M
Southern Utah University M
University of Utah M
Utah State University M
Weber State University M

Virginia
Bluefield College M
College of William and Mary M
Hampton University M
James Madison University M
Liberty University M
Norfolk State University M
Old Dominion University M
University of Richmond M
University of Virginia M
University of Virginia's College at Wise M
Virginia Military Institute M
Virginia Polytechnic Institute and State
    University M
Virginia State University M
Virginia Union University M

Washington
Central Washington University M
Eastern Washington University M
University of Washington M
Washington State University M

West Virginia
Alderson-Broaddus University M
Concord University M
Fairmont State University M
Glenville State College M
Marshall University M
Shepherd University M
University of Charleston M
West Liberty University M
West Virginia State University M

West Virginia University M
West Virginia Wesleyan College M

Wisconsin
University of Wisconsin
    Madison M

Wyoming
University of Wyoming M

Golf

Alabama
Alabama State University M,W
Auburn University M,W
Central Alabama Community College M
Faulkner State Community College M,W
Faulkner University M,W
Jacksonville State University M,W
Jefferson State Community College M,W
Marion Military Institute M,W
Samford University M,W
Spring Hill College M,W
Troy University M,W
University of Alabama M,W
University of Alabama
    Birmingham M,W
University of Mobile M,W
University of Montevallo M,W
University of North Alabama M
University of South Alabama M,W
University of West Alabama M,W
Wallace State Community College at
    Hanceville M,W

Arizona
Arizona Christian University M,W
Arizona State University M,W
Chandler-Gilbert Community College M,W
Eastern Arizona College M
Embry-Riddle Aeronautical University
    Prescott Campus M,W
Glendale Community College M
Grand Canyon University M,W
Mesa Community College M,W
Northern Arizona University W
Paradise Valley Community College M,W
Scottsdale Community College M
University of Arizona M,W

Arkansas
Arkansas State University M,W
Arkansas Tech University M,W
Ecclesia College M,W
Harding University M,W
Henderson State University M,W
Lyon College M,W
University of Arkansas M,W
University of Arkansas
    Fort Smith M,W
    Little Rock M,W
    Monticello M,W
    Pine Bluff M,W
University of Central Arkansas M,W

California
Academy of Art University M,W
Biola University M,W
California Baptist University M,W
California Polytechnic State University: San
    Luis Obispo M,W
California State University
    Bakersfield M
    Chico M
    Dominguez Hills M
    Fresno M,W
    Fullerton M,W
    Long Beach M,W
    Monterey Bay M,W
    Northridge M
    Sacramento M,W

San Bernardino M
    Stanislaus M
Dominican University of California M,W
Fresno City College M,W
Holy Names University M,W
Hope International University M,W
Loyola Marymount University M
The Master's University M
Menlo College M,W
Notre Dame de Namur University M
Pepperdine University M,W
Point Loma Nazarene University W
St. Mary's College of California M
San Diego State University M,W
San Jose State University M,W
Santa Clara University M,W
Santiago Canyon College M,W
Simpson University M,W
Sonoma State University M
Stanford University M,W
University of California
    Berkeley M,W
    Davis M,W
    Irvine M,W
    Los Angeles M,W
    Riverside M
    Santa Barbara M
University of San Diego M
University of San Francisco M,W
University of Southern California M,W
University of the Pacific M
William Jessup University M

Colorado
Adams State University M,W
Colorado Christian University M,W
Colorado Mesa University M,W
Colorado State University M,W
Colorado State University
    Pueblo M,W
Fort Lewis College M
Lamar Community College M
Northeastern Junior College M,W
Otero Junior College M,W
Regis University M,W
University of Colorado
    Boulder M,W
    Colorado Springs M,W
University of Denver M,W
University of Northern Colorado M,W

Connecticut
Central Connecticut State University M,W
Fairfield University M
Post University M,W
Quinnipiac University W
Sacred Heart University M,W
University of Connecticut M
University of Hartford M,W

Delaware
Goldey-Beacom College M
Wilmington University M

District of Columbia
George Washington University M
Georgetown University M,W

Florida
Ave Maria University M,W
Barry University M,W
Bethune-Cookman University M,W
Daytona State College W
Eastern Florida State College M
Eckerd College M,W
Embry-Riddle Aeronautical University M,W
Flagler College M,W
Florida Atlantic University M,W
Florida Gulf Coast University M,W
Florida Institute of Technology M,W
Florida Southern College M,W
Florida State University M,W
Jacksonville University M,W
Lynn University M,W

Nova Southeastern University M,W
Palm Beach Atlantic University M,W
Rollins College M,W
Saint Leo University M,W
Saint Thomas University M
Southeastern University M
Stetson University M,W
University of Central Florida M,W
University of Florida M,W
University of Miami W
University of North Florida M,W
University of South Florida M,W
University of Tampa M,W
University of West Florida M,W
Warner University M,W
Webber International University M,W

Georgia
Abraham Baldwin Agricultural College M
Andrew College M
Armstrong State University M,W
Augusta University M,W
Brenau University W
Brewton-Parker College M
Clayton State University M
College of Coastal Georgia M,W
Columbus State University M,W
Darton State College M
Emmanuel College M
Georgia College and State University M
Georgia Institute of Technology M
Georgia Southern University M
Georgia Southwestern State University M
Georgia State University M,W
Kennesaw State University M,W
Mercer University M,W
Paine College M
Point University M,W
Reinhardt University M
Savannah College of Art and Design M,W
Shorter University M,W
Thomas University M,W
Truett McConnell University M,W
University of Georgia M,W
University of North Georgia M,W
University of West Georgia M,W
Valdosta State University M
Young Harris College M,W

Hawaii
Chaminade University of Honolulu M
Hawaii Pacific University M
University of Hawaii
    Hilo M
    Manoa M,W

Idaho
Boise State University M,W
College of Idaho M,W
Idaho State University W
Lewis-Clark State College M,W
Northwest Nazarene University M
University of Idaho M,W

Illinois
Benedictine University at Springfield M,W
Black Hawk College M
Bradley University M,W
Chicago State University M,W
College of Lake County M,W
DePaul University M
Eastern Illinois University M,W
Elgin Community College M,W
Governors State University M,W
Highland Community College M
Illinois Central College M
Illinois Eastern Community Colleges
    Frontier Community College M,W
Illinois State University M,W
John A. Logan College M,W
Judson University M,W
Kaskaskia College M,W
Kishwaukee College M,W
Lewis and Clark Community College M

Lewis University M,W
Lincoln College M,W
Loyola University Chicago M,W
McKendree University M,W
Moraine Valley Community College M
Northern Illinois University M,W
Northwestern University M,W
Olivet Nazarene University M
Parkland College M
Quincy University M,W
Rend Lake College M,W
Robert Morris College
    Robert Morris University: Chicago M,W
Sauk Valley Community College M
Southern Illinois University Carbondale M,W
Southern Illinois University Edwardsville M,W
University of Illinois
    Springfield M,W
    Urbana-Champaign M,W
University of St. Francis M,W
Waubonsee Community College M
Western Illinois University M,W

Indiana
Ancilla College M,W
Ball State University M,W
Bethel College M,W
Butler University M,W
Calumet College of St. Joseph M,W
Grace College M,W
Holy Cross College M,W
Huntington University M,W
Indiana Institute of Technology M,W
Indiana State University W
Indiana University
    Bloomington M,W
    Purdue University Fort Wayne M,W
    Purdue University Indianapolis M,W
Indiana Wesleyan University M,W
Marian University M,W
Oakland City University M,W
Purdue University M,W
Purdue University
    North Central M
    Northwest M
Saint Joseph's College M,W
St. Mary-of-the-Woods College W
Taylor University M
University of Evansville M,W
University of Indianapolis M,W
University of Notre Dame M,W
University of Saint Francis M,W
University of Southern Indiana M,W
Valparaiso University M,W
Vincennes University M

Iowa
Briar Cliff University M,W
Clarke University M,W
Dordt College M,W
Drake University M,W
Ellsworth Community College M,W
Graceland University M,W
Grand View University M,W
Iowa Central Community College M,W
Iowa Lakes Community College M,W
Iowa State University M,W
Iowa Western Community College M,W
Kirkwood Community College M
Marshalltown Community College M,W
Morningside College M,W
Mount Mercy University M,W
North Iowa Area Community College M,W
Northwestern College M,W
St. Ambrose University M,W
Southeastern Community College M,W
Southwestern Community College M
University of Iowa M,W
University of Northern Iowa M,W
Upper Iowa University M,W
Waldorf University M,W
William Penn University M,W

Kansas

Allen County Community College M
Baker University M,W
Barton County Community College M,W
Bethany College M,W
Bethel College M,W
Central Christian College of Kansas M,W
Coffeyville Community College M,W
Colby Community College M,W
Dodge City Community College M,W
Friends University M,W
Garden City Community College M
Hesston College M
Hutchinson Community College M
Independence Community College M
Johnson County Community College M
Kansas City Kansas Community College M
Kansas State University M,W
Kansas Wesleyan University M,W
Newman University M,W
Northwest Kansas Technical College M,W
Ottawa University M
Southwestern College M,W
Sterling College M,W
University of Kansas M,W
Washburn University M
Wichita State University M,W

Kentucky

Asbury University M,W
Bellarmine University M,W
Brescia University M,W
Campbellsville University M,W
Eastern Kentucky University M,W
Georgetown College M,W
Kentucky State University M
Kentucky Wesleyan College M,W
Lindsey Wilson College M,W
Midway College W
Morehead State University M
Murray State University M,W
Northern Kentucky University M,W
St. Catharine College M,W
Union College M,W
University of Kentucky M,W
University of Louisville M,W
University of Pikeville M,W
University of the Cumberlands M,W
Western Kentucky University M,W

Louisiana

Grambling State University M
Louisiana State University and Agricultural and
    Mechanical College M,W
Louisiana Tech University M
Loyola University New Orleans M,W
McNeese State University M,W
Nicholls State University M
Southeastern Louisiana University M
Southern University and Agricultural and
    Mechanical College M
University of Louisiana
    Monroe M
University of Louisiana at Lafayette M
University of New Orleans M

Maryland

College of Southern Maryland M,W
Coppin State University W
Harford Community College M
Loyola University Maryland M
Towson University M,W
University of Maryland
    College Park M,W

Massachusetts

American International College M,W
Boston College M,W
Boston University W
Merrimack College W

Michigan

Aquinas College M,W
Cleary University M,W

Concordia University M,W
Cornerstone University M,W
Davenport University M,W
Eastern Michigan University M,W
Ferris State University M,W
Grand Valley State University M,W
Hillsdale College M
Kirtland Community College M,W
Lake Superior State University M,W
Lawrence Technological University M,W
Madonna University M,W
Michigan State University M,W
Mott Community College M
Muskegon Community College M
Northern Michigan University M
Northwood University
    Michigan M,W
Oakland Community College M
Oakland University M,W
Saginaw Valley State University M
Siena Heights University M,W
Spring Arbor University M,W
University of Detroit Mercy M,W
University of Michigan M,W
Wayne State University M,W
Western Michigan University W

Minnesota

Concordia University St. Paul M,W
Minnesota State University
    Mankato M,W
    Moorhead W
Saint Cloud State University M,W
Southwest Minnesota State University W
University of Minnesota
    Crookston M,W
    Twin Cities M,W
Winona State University M,W

Mississippi

Alcorn State University M,W
Belhaven University M,W
Blue Mountain College M,W
Copiah-Lincoln Community College M
Delta State University M
East Central Community College M
East Mississippi Community College M,W
Hinds Community College M
Itawamba Community College M
Jackson State University M,W
Meridian Community College M
Mississippi Gulf Coast Community College M
Mississippi Valley State University M,W
Northwest Mississippi Community College M
University of Mississippi M,W
University of Mississippi
    University of Southern Mississippi M,W
William Carey University M,W

Missouri

Avila University M,W
Central Methodist University M,W
Columbia College M,W
Cottey College W
Culver-Stockton College M,W
Drury University M,W
Evangel University M,W
Hannibal-LaGrange University M,W
Lincoln University M,W
Lindenwood University M,W
Maryville University of Saint Louis M,W
Missouri Baptist University M,W
Missouri Southern State University M
Missouri State University M,W
Missouri Valley College M,W
Missouri Western State University M
North Central Missouri College M
Northwest Missouri State University W
Park University W
Research College of Nursing M,W
Rockhurst University M,W
Southwest Baptist University M
Stephens College W

Truman State University W
University of Central Missouri M
University of Missouri
    Columbia M,W
    Kansas City M,W
    St. Louis M,W
William Jewell College M,W
William Woods University M,W

Montana

Carroll College M,W
Miles Community College M,W
Montana State University W
Montana State University
    Billings M,W
    Northern W
Montana Tech of the University of Montana
    M,W
Rocky Mountain College M,W
University of Great Falls M,W
University of Montana W

Nebraska

Bellevue University M,W
Chadron State College W
College of Saint Mary W
Concordia University M,W
Creighton University M,W
Doane University M,W
Hastings College M,W
Mid-Plains Community College M
Midland University M,W
Northeast Community College M
Peru State College W
University of Nebraska
    Kearney M,W
    Lincoln M,W
    Omaha M,W
York College M,W

Nevada

Sierra Nevada College M,W
University of Nevada
    Las Vegas M,W
    Reno M,W

New Hampshire

Franklin Pierce University M
Saint Anselm College M

New Jersey

Brookdale Community College M
Fairleigh Dickinson University
    Metropolitan Campus M,W
Monmouth University M,W
Rider University M
Rowan College at Burlington County M,W
Rutgers, The State University of New Jersey
    New Brunswick/Piscataway Campus
    M,W
Saint Peter's University M
Salem Community College M
Seton Hall University M,W

New Mexico

New Mexico Junior College M
New Mexico Military Institute M
New Mexico State University M,W
University of New Mexico M,W
University of the Southwest M,W
Western New Mexico University M,W

New York

Adelphi University M,W
Canisius College M
College of Saint Rose M,W
Concordia College M
Daemen College M
Dominican College of Blauvelt M
Hofstra University M,W
Iona College M
Le Moyne College M,W
Long Island University
    LIU Brooklyn M,W
    LIU Post W

Manhattan College M
Niagara University M,W
Nyack College M
Pace University: Pleasantville/Briarcliff W
Roberts Wesleyan College M
Saint Bonaventure University M
St. John's University M,W
Siena College M,W
SUNY
    University at Albany W
    University at Binghamton M
Wagner College M,W

North Carolina

Appalachian State University M,W
Barton College M
Belmont Abbey College M,W
Brevard College M
Campbell University M,W
Catawba College M,W
Chowan University M
Davidson College M
Duke University M,W
East Carolina University M,W
Elizabeth City State University M
Elon University M,W
Fayetteville State University M
Gardner-Webb University M,W
High Point University M,W
Johnson C. Smith University M
Johnston Community College M,W
Lenoir-Rhyne University M,W
Mars Hill University M
Montreat College M,W
North Carolina Central University M,W
North Carolina State University M,W
Pitt Community College M
Queens University of Charlotte M,W
St. Andrews University M
Saint Augustine's University M
University of Mount Olive M
University of North Carolina
    Asheville M
    Chapel Hill M,W
    Charlotte M
    Greensboro M,W
    Wilmington M,W
Wake Forest University M,W
Western Carolina University M,W
Wingate University M,W

North Dakota

Dickinson State University M,W
Minot State University M,W
North Dakota State University W
University of Jamestown M,W
University of Mary W
University of North Dakota M,W
Valley City State University M,W

Ohio

Ashland University M,W
Bowling Green State University M,W
Cedarville University M
Central State University M,W
Cleveland State University M,W
Kent State University M,W
Lakeland Community College M
Lourdes University M,W
Malone University M,W
Miami University
    Oxford M
Mount Vernon Nazarene University M,W
Notre Dame College M,W
Ohio Dominican University M,W
Ohio State University
    Columbus Campus M,W
Ohio University M,W
Owens Community College M
Shawnee State University M,W
Tiffin University M,W
University of Akron M
University of Cincinnati M,W

University of Dayton M
University of Findlay M,W
University of Northwestern Ohio M,W
University of Toledo M,W
Urbana University M,W
Ursuline College W
Walsh University M,W
Wright State University M
Xavier University M,W
Youngstown State University M,W

Oklahoma
Bacone College M,W
Cameron University M,W
East Central University M,W
Mid-America Christian University M
Northeastern State University M,W
Northwestern Oklahoma State University M,W
Oklahoma Baptist University M,W
Oklahoma Christian University M
Oklahoma City University M,W
Oklahoma Panhandle State University M,W
Oklahoma State University M,W
Oklahoma Wesleyan University M,W
Oral Roberts University M,W
Redlands Community College W
Rogers State University M,W
St. Gregory's University W
Seminole State College M,W
Southeastern Oklahoma State University M
Southern Nazarene University M,W
Southwestern Oklahoma State University M,W
University of Central Oklahoma M,W
University of Oklahoma M,W
University of Tulsa W

Oregon
Concordia University M,W
Corban University M,W
Multnomah University M,W
New Hope Christian College M,W
Northwest Christian University M,W
Oregon State University M,W
Portland State University W
Southwestern Oregon Community College
    M,W
University of Oregon M,W
Warner Pacific College M,W

Pennsylvania
California University of Pennsylvania M,W
Carlow University M,W
Chestnut Hill College M,W
Clarion University of Pennsylvania M,W
Drexel University M
Gannon University M,W
Indiana University of Pennsylvania M
Kutztown University of Pennsylvania W
La Salle University M,W
Lackawanna College M
Lehigh University M,W
Mercyhurst University M,W
Millersville University of Pennsylvania M,W
Penn State
    University Park M,W
Philadelphia University M
St. Francis University M,W
Saint Joseph's University M
Seton Hill University W
Temple University M
University of the Sciences M,W
West Chester University of Pennsylvania M,W

Rhode Island
Bryant University M
University of Rhode Island M

South Carolina
Anderson University M,W
Charleston Southern University M,W
The Citadel W
Clemson University M
Coastal Carolina University M,W
Coker College M,W

College of Charleston M,W
Columbia College W
Converse College W
Erskine College M,W
Francis Marion University M
Furman University M,W
Lander University M,W
Limestone College M,W
Newberry College M,W
North Greenville University M,W
Presbyterian College M,W
Southern Wesleyan University M
Spartanburg Methodist College M,W
University of South Carolina
    Aiken M
    Columbia M,W
Winthrop University M,W
Wofford College M,W

South Dakota
Augusta University
    Augustana University M,W
Dakota Wesleyan University M,W
Mount Marty College M,W
South Dakota School of Mines and Technology
    M,W
South Dakota State University M,W
University of Sioux Falls M,W

Tennessee
Austin Peay State University M,W
Belmont University M,W
Bethel University M,W
Bryan College
    Dayton M,W
Carson-Newman University M
Christian Brothers University M,W
Cumberland University M,W
East Tennessee State University M,W
Hiwassee College M,W
King University M,W
Lee University M,W
LeMoyne-Owen College M,W
Lincoln Memorial University M,W
Lipscomb University M,W
Martin Methodist College M,W
Middle Tennessee State University M,W
Milligan College M
Tennessee State University M,W
Tennessee Technological University M,W
Tennessee Wesleyan College M,W
Trevecca Nazarene University M,W
Tusculum College M,W
Union University M,W
University of Memphis M,W
University of Tennessee
    Chattanooga M,W
    Knoxville M,W
    Martin M
Vanderbilt University M,W
Walters State Community College M,W

Texas
Abilene Christian University M
Baylor University M,W
Dallas Baptist University W
Houston Baptist University M,W
Jacksonville College M,W
Jarvis Christian College M
Lamar University M,W
Lubbock Christian University M,W
McLennan Community College M
Midland College M
Midwestern State University M,W
Odessa College M
Prairie View A&M University M,W
Ranger College M,W
Rice University M
St. Edward's University M,W
St. Mary's University M,W
Sam Houston State University M,W
Southern Methodist University M,W
Stephen F. Austin State University M,W

Tarleton State University W
Texas A&M University M,W
Texas A&M University
    Commerce M
    Corpus Christi W
Texas Christian University M,W
Texas Southern University M,W
Texas State University M,W
Texas Tech University M,W
Texas Wesleyan University M,W
Tyler Junior College M,W
University of Houston M,W
University of North Texas M,W
University of St. Thomas M,W
University of Texas
    Austin M,W
    San Antonio M,W
University of the Incarnate Word M,W
Wayland Baptist University M,W
West Texas A&M University M,W
Western Texas College M,W

Utah
Brigham Young University M,W
Dixie State University M,W
Southern Utah University M,W
University of Utah M
Utah State University M
Utah Valley University M,W
Weber State University M,W
Westminster College M,W

Virginia
Bluefield College M
College of William and Mary M,W
George Mason University M
Hampton University M,W
James Madison University M,W
Liberty University M
Longwood University M,W
Old Dominion University M,W
Radford University M,W
University of Richmond M,W
University of Virginia M,W
Virginia Commonwealth University M
Virginia Polytechnic Institute and State
    University M,W
Virginia State University M,W
Virginia Union University M,W

Washington
Centralia College W
Columbia Basin College M,W
Eastern Washington University W
Edmonds Community College M,W
Gonzaga University M,W
Grays Harbor College M,W
Green River College M
Olympic College M,W
Saint Martin's University M,W
Seattle University M,W
Skagit Valley College M,W
Spokane Community College M,W
University of Washington M,W
Walla Walla Community College M,W
Washington State University M,W
Western Washington University M,W

West Virginia
Alderson-Broaddus University M,W
Bluefield State College M
Concord University M
Davis and Elkins College M
Fairmont State University M,W
Glenville State College M,W
Marshall University M,W
Ohio Valley University M,W
Salem International University M,W
Shepherd University M
University of Charleston M
West Liberty University M,W
West Virginia State University M
West Virginia University Institute of
    Technology M

West Virginia Wesleyan College M,W
Wheeling Jesuit University M,W

Wisconsin
Cardinal Stritch University M,W
Silver Lake College of the Holy Family M,W
University of Wisconsin
    Green Bay M,W
    Madison M,W
    Parkside M
Viterbo University M,W

Wyoming
Central Wyoming College M,W
Eastern Wyoming College M
University of Wyoming M,W

Gymnastics

Alabama
Auburn University W
University of Alabama W

Alaska
University of Alaska
    Anchorage W

Arizona
Arizona State University W
University of Arizona W

Arkansas
University of Arkansas W

California
California State University
    Sacramento W
San Jose State University W
Stanford University M,W
University of California
    Berkeley M,W
    Davis W
    Los Angeles W
    Santa Barbara W

Colorado
University of Denver W

Connecticut
Southern Connecticut State University W
University of Bridgeport W

District of Columbia
George Washington University W

Florida
University of Florida W

Georgia
University of Georgia W

Idaho
Boise State University W

Illinois
Illinois State University W
Northern Illinois University W
University of Illinois
    Chicago M,W
    Urbana-Champaign M,W

Indiana
Ball State University W

Iowa
Iowa State University W
University of Iowa M,W

Kansas
Fort Hays State University M

Kentucky
University of Kentucky W

Louisiana
Louisiana State University and Agricultural and Mechanical College W

Maryland
Towson University W
University of Maryland
  College Park W
Washington Adventist University M,W

Michigan
Central Michigan University W
Eastern Michigan University W
Michigan State University W
University of Michigan M,W
Western Michigan University W

Minnesota
University of Minnesota
  Twin Cities M,W

Missouri
Lindenwood University W
Southeast Missouri State University W
University of Missouri
  Columbia W

Nebraska
University of Nebraska
  Lincoln M,W

New Hampshire
University of New Hampshire W

New Jersey
Rutgers, The State University of New Jersey
  New Brunswick/Piscataway Campus W

North Carolina
North Carolina State University W
University of North Carolina
  Chapel Hill W

Ohio
Bowling Green State University W
Kent State University W
Ohio State University
  Columbus Campus M,W

Oklahoma
University of Oklahoma M,W

Oregon
Oregon State University W

Pennsylvania
Penn State
  University Park M,W
Temple University W
University of Pittsburgh W
West Chester University of Pennsylvania W

Tennessee
Southern Adventist University M,W

Texas
Texas Woman's University W

Utah
Brigham Young University W
Southern Utah University W
University of Utah W
Utah State University W

Virginia
College of William and Mary M,W

Washington
Seattle Pacific University W
University of Washington W

West Virginia
Alderson-Broaddus University W
West Virginia University W

Ice hockey

Alabama
University of Alabama
  Huntsville M

Alaska
University of Alaska
  Anchorage M
  Fairbanks M

Arizona
Arizona State University M

Colorado
Colorado College M
University of Denver M

Connecticut
Quinnipiac University M,W
Sacred Heart University M,W
University of Connecticut M,W

Georgia
Life University M

Indiana
University of Notre Dame M

Iowa
Waldorf University M

Maine
University of Maine M,W

Massachusetts
American International College M
Bentley University M
Boston College M,W
Boston University M,W
College of the Holy Cross M
Merrimack College M,W
Northeastern University M,W
University of Massachusetts
  Amherst M
  Lowell M

Michigan
Davenport University M,W
Ferris State University M
Lake Superior State University M
Michigan State University M
Michigan Technological University M
Northern Michigan University M
University of Michigan M
Western Michigan University M

Minnesota
Bemidji State University M,W
Minnesota State University
  Mankato M,W
Saint Cloud State University M,W
University of Minnesota
  Duluth M,W
  Twin Cities M,W

Missouri
Lindenwood University W

Nebraska
Midland University M,W
University of Nebraska
  Omaha M

New Hampshire
Franklin Pierce University M,W
University of New Hampshire M,W

New York
Canisius College M
Clarkson University M,W
Colgate University M,W
Monroe Community College M
Niagara University M
Rensselaer Polytechnic Institute M,W
St. Lawrence University M,W
Syracuse University W

North Dakota
Dakota College at Bottineau M
University of North Dakota M,W
Williston State College M

Ohio
Bowling Green State University M
Miami University
  Oxford M
Ohio State University
  Columbus Campus M,W

Pennsylvania
Mercyhurst University M,W
Penn State
  University Park M,W
Robert Morris University M,W

Rhode Island
Providence College M,W

Vermont
University of Vermont M,W

Wisconsin
University of Wisconsin
  Madison M,W

Judo

Puerto Rico
Bayamon Central University M,W
Inter American University of Puerto Rico
  Aguadilla Campus M,W
  Ponce Campus M,W
Turabo University W
Universidad Metropolitana M,W
University of Puerto Rico
  Arecibo M,W
  Humacao M,W

Lacrosse

Arizona
Arizona State University W

California
California State University
  Fresno W
Concordia University Irvine M,W
Dominican University of California M
Notre Dame de Namur University M
St. Mary's College of California W
San Diego State University W
Stanford University W
University of California
  Davis W

Colorado
Adams State University M,W
Colorado Mesa University M,W
Colorado State University
  Pueblo M,W
Fort Lewis College W
Regis University W
University of Colorado
  Boulder W
  Colorado Springs W
University of Denver M,W

Connecticut
Central Connecticut State University W
Fairfield University M,W
Post University M,W
Quinnipiac University M,W
Sacred Heart University M,W
Southern Connecticut State University W
University of Bridgeport W
University of Connecticut W
University of Hartford M
University of New Haven W

Delaware
Delaware Technical Community College
  Terry Campus M
University of Delaware M,W
Wilmington University W

District of Columbia
American University W
Georgetown University M,W
Howard University W

Florida
Embry-Riddle Aeronautical University M,W
Florida Institute of Technology M
Florida Southern College M,W
Jacksonville University M,W
Lynn University M
Saint Leo University M,W
Stetson University W
University of Florida W
University of Tampa M,W

Georgia
Emmanuel College M,W
Kennesaw State University W
Mercer University M,W
Point University M,W
Savannah College of Art and Design M,W
Shorter University M,W
Truett McConnell University W
Young Harris College M,W

Illinois
Judson University M
McKendree University W
Northwestern University W
Robert Morris College
  Robert Morris University: Chicago M,W

Indiana
Ancilla College M,W
Bethel College W
Indiana Institute of Technology M,W
University of Indianapolis M,W
University of Notre Dame M,W

Iowa
Clarke University M,W
St. Ambrose University M

Kansas
Central Christian College of Kansas M
University of St. Mary M,W

Kentucky
Asbury University M,W
Bellarmine University M
Georgetown College W
Union College M
University of Louisville W
University of the Cumberlands M,W

Maryland
Anne Arundel Community College M,W
Community College of Baltimore County M,W
Harford Community College M,W
Howard Community College M,W
Johns Hopkins University M,W
Loyola University Maryland M,W
Mount St. Mary's University M,W
Towson University M,W
University of Maryland
  College Park M,W

Massachusetts
American International College M,W
Boston College W
Boston University M,W
College of the Holy Cross M,W
Merrimack College M,W
Stonehill College W
University of Massachusetts
Amherst M,W
Lowell M,W

Michigan
Cleary University M,W
Davenport University M
Lawrence Technological University M,W
Madonna University M,W
Siena Heights University M,W
University of Detroit Mercy M,W
University of Michigan M,W
University of Michigan
Dearborn M

Minnesota
Concordia University St. Paul W
University of Minnesota
Duluth M,W

Missouri
Columbia College M
Lindenwood University M,W
Missouri Baptist University M,W
Missouri Valley College M,W
Rockhurst University M,W

Nebraska
Midland University W

Nevada
Sierra Nevada College M,W

New Hampshire
Franklin Pierce University M,W
Saint Anselm College M,W
Southern New Hampshire University M,W
University of New Hampshire W

New Jersey
Caldwell University W
Georgian Court University M,W
Monmouth University M,W
Rutgers, The State University of New Jersey
New Brunswick/Piscataway Campus
M,W
Union County College M

New York
Adelphi University M,W
Canisius College M,W
City University of New York
Queens College W
Colgate University M,W
College of Saint Rose M
Dominican College of Blauvelt M,W
Hofstra University M,W
Iona College W
Le Moyne College M,W
Long Island University
LIU Brooklyn M,W
LIU Post M,W
Manhattan College M,W
Marist College M,W
Mercy College M,W
Molloy College M,W
Monroe Community College M
New York Institute of Technology M,W
Niagara University W
Nyack College W
Pace University M,W
Pace University: Pleasantville/Briarcliff M,W
Roberts Wesleyan College M,W
Saint Bonaventure University W
St. John's University M
Siena College M,W
SUNY

University at Albany M,W
University at Binghamton M,W
University at Stony Brook M,W
Syracuse University M,W
Wagner College M,W

North Carolina
Barton College W
Belmont Abbey College M,W
Brevard College M,W
Campbell University W
Catawba College M,W
Chowan University M,W
Davidson College W
Duke University M
Elon University W
High Point University M,W
Laurel University M
Lees-McRae College M,W
Lenoir-Rhyne University M,W
Mars Hill University M
Queens University of Charlotte M,W
St. Andrews University M
University of North Carolina
Chapel Hill M,W
Wingate University M,W

Ohio
Lake Erie College M,W
Lourdes University M,W
Notre Dame College W
Ohio State University
Columbus Campus M,W
Tiffin University M
University of Cincinnati W
University of Findlay M,W
Urbana University W
Ursuline College W
Walsh University M,W

Oklahoma
Oklahoma Baptist University W

Oregon
University of Oregon W

Pennsylvania
Bloomsburg University of Pennsylvania W
Bucknell University M,W
Chestnut Hill College M,W
Drexel University M,W
Duquesne University M,W
Gannon University W
Holy Family University W
Indiana University of Pennsylvania W
Kutztown University of Pennsylvania W
La Salle University W
Lehigh University M,W
Lock Haven University of Pennsylvania W
Mercyhurst University M,W
Millersville University of Pennsylvania W
Penn State
University Park M,W
Philadelphia University W
Robert Morris University M,W
St. Francis University W
Saint Joseph's University M,W
Seton Hill University M,W
Shippensburg University of Pennsylvania W
Slippery Rock University of Pennsylvania W
Temple University W
West Chester University of Pennsylvania W

Rhode Island
Bryant University M,W
Providence College M

South Carolina
Coastal Carolina University W
Coker College M,W
Columbia College W
Converse College W
Erskine College W
Furman University M,W

Limestone College M,W
Newberry College W
North Greenville University M,W
Presbyterian College W
Wofford College W

Tennessee
Lee University W
Tennessee Wesleyan College M,W
Tusculum College M,W
Vanderbilt University W

Utah
Westminster College M,W

Vermont
University of Vermont M,W

Virginia
College of William and Mary W
George Mason University W
James Madison University W
Liberty University W
Longwood University W
Old Dominion University W
Radford University W
University of Richmond M,W
University of Virginia M,W
Virginia Commonwealth University W
Virginia Military Institute M
Virginia Polytechnic Institute and State
University W

West Virginia
Alderson-Broaddus University M,W
Potomac State College of West Virginia
University M,W
Shepherd University W
West Virginia Wesleyan College W
Wheeling Jesuit University M,W

Wisconsin
Marquette University M,W

Rifle

Alabama
Jacksonville State University M,W

Alaska
University of Alaska
Fairbanks M,W

Georgia
Columbus State University M,W
Emmanuel College M,W
Georgia Southern University W
University of North Georgia M,W

Iowa
Grand View University M,W
Iowa Central Community College M,W

Kentucky
Morehead State University M,W
Murray State University M,W
University of Kentucky M,W

Mississippi
University of Mississippi W

Missouri
Hannibal-LaGrange University M,W

Nebraska
Concordia University M,W
Midland University M,W
University of Nebraska
Lincoln W

Nevada
University of Nevada
Reno M,W

Ohio
Ohio State University
Columbus Campus M
University of Akron W

Pennsylvania
University of the Sciences M,W

South Carolina
The Citadel M,W
Wofford College M,W

Tennessee
Bethel University M,W
University of Memphis M,W
University of Tennessee
Martin M,W

Texas
Texas Christian University W

Virginia
Virginia Military Institute M,W

West Virginia
West Virginia University M,W

Rodeo

Alabama
Troy University M,W
University of West Alabama M,W

Arizona
Central Arizona College M,W
Cochise College M,W
Dine College M,W

Arkansas
Southern Arkansas University M,W
University of Arkansas
Monticello M,W

Colorado
Colorado Northwestern Community College
M,W
Northeastern Junior College M,W
Otero Junior College M,W

Idaho
Boise State University M,W
College of Southern Idaho M,W

Iowa
Iowa Central Community College M,W

Kansas
Coffeyville Community College M,W
Colby Community College M
Dodge City Community College M,W
Fort Hays State University M
Fort Scott Community College M,W
Garden City Community College M,W
Northwest Kansas Technical College M,W
Pratt Community College M,W

Louisiana
McNeese State University M,W

Mississippi
East Mississippi Community College M,W

Missouri
Missouri Valley College M,W
Northwest Missouri State University M,W

Montana
Dawson Community College M,W
Miles Community College M,W
Montana State University M,W
Montana State University
Northern M,W
University of Montana: Western M,W

Nebraska
Chadron State College M,W
Mid-Plains Community College M,W
Nebraska College of Technical Agriculture
    M,W

New Mexico
Eastern New Mexico University M,W
Navajo Technical University M,W
New Mexico Junior College M,W

North Dakota
Dickinson State University M

Oklahoma
Bacone College M,W
Connors State College M,W
Northeastern Oklahoma Agricultural and
    Mechanical College M,W
Northwestern Oklahoma State University M,W
Oklahoma Panhandle State University M,W
Southeastern Oklahoma State University M,W
Southwestern Oklahoma State University M,W
Western Oklahoma State College M,W

Oregon
Blue Mountain Community College M,W
Eastern Oregon University M,W
Treasure Valley Community College M,W

South Dakota
Mitchell Technical Institute M,W

Tennessee
University of Tennessee
    Martin M,W

Texas
Clarendon College M,W
East Texas Baptist University M,W
Hill College M,W
Howard College M,W
North Central Texas College M
Northeast Texas Community College M,W
Odessa College M,W
Panola College M,W
Ranger College M,W
Sam Houston State University M,W
South Plains College M,W
Tarleton State University M,W
Trinity Valley Community College M,W
Vernon College M,W
Weatherford College M,W
Western Texas College M,W
Wharton County Junior College M,W

Utah
Snow College M,W

Washington
Central Washington University M,W
Walla Walla Community College M,W

Wyoming
Casper College M,W
Central Wyoming College M,W
Eastern Wyoming College M,W
Laramie County Community College M,W
Northwest College M,W
Sheridan College M,W
University of Wyoming M,W

Rowing (crew)

Alabama
University of Alabama W

California
California State University
    Sacramento W
Humboldt State University W
Loyola Marymount University W
St. Mary's College of California W

San Diego State University W
Stanford University M,W
University of California
    Berkeley M,W
    Los Angeles M,W
University of San Diego W
University of Southern California W

Connecticut
Fairfield University M,W
University of Connecticut W

Delaware
University of Delaware W

District of Columbia
George Washington University M,W
Georgetown University M,W

Florida
Ave Maria University W
Barry University W
Embry-Riddle Aeronautical University M,W
Florida Institute of Technology M,W
Jacksonville University M,W
Nova Southeastern University W
Stetson University W
University of Central Florida W
University of Miami W
University of Tampa W

Indiana
Indiana University
    Bloomington W
University of Notre Dame W

Iowa
University of Iowa W

Kansas
Kansas State University W
University of Kansas W

Kentucky
University of Louisville W

Massachusetts
Boston College W
Boston University M,W
College of the Holy Cross W
Merrimack College W
Northeastern University M,W
University of Massachusetts
    Amherst W

Michigan
Eastern Michigan University W
Michigan State University W
University of Michigan W

Nebraska
Creighton University W

New Jersey
Rutgers, The State University of New Jersey
    New Brunswick/Piscataway Campus
    M,W

New York
Fordham University W
Manhattan College W
Marist College W
SUNY
    University at Buffalo W
Syracuse University M,W

North Carolina
Duke University W
University of North Carolina
    Chapel Hill W

Oklahoma
Oklahoma City University M,W
University of Central Oklahoma W
University of Oklahoma W
University of Tulsa W

Pennsylvania
Drexel University M,W
Duquesne University W
La Salle University M,W
Lehigh University W
Mercyhurst University M,W
Philadelphia University M,W
Robert Morris University W
Saint Joseph's University M,W
Temple University M,W

Rhode Island
University of Rhode Island W

South Carolina
Clemson University W

Tennessee
University of Tennessee
    Knoxville W

Texas
Southern Methodist University W
University of Texas
    Austin W

Virginia
George Mason University W
Old Dominion University W
University of Virginia W

Washington
Gonzaga University W
Seattle Pacific University W
University of Washington M,W
Washington State University W
Western Washington University M,W

West Virginia
University of Charleston W
West Virginia University W

Wisconsin
University of Wisconsin
    Madison M,W

Rugby

California
University of California
    Berkeley M

Colorado
Colorado School of Mines M,W

Connecticut
Quinnipiac University W

Georgia
Life University M,W

Indiana
Bethel College M

Massachusetts
American International College M,W

Michigan
Davenport University M,W

New York
Molloy College W

Pennsylvania
West Chester University of Pennsylvania W

Texas
East Texas Baptist University M,W

Washington
Central Washington University M,W

Skiing

Alaska
University of Alaska
    Anchorage M,W
    Fairbanks M,W

Colorado
Colorado Mountain College M,W
University of Colorado
    Boulder M,W
University of Denver M,W
Western State Colorado University M,W

Idaho
College of Idaho M,W

Michigan
Michigan Technological University M,W
Northern Michigan University M,W

Minnesota
Saint Cloud State University W
University of Minnesota
    Twin Cities M,W

Montana
Montana State University W
Rocky Mountain College M,W

Nevada
Sierra Nevada College M,W

New Hampshire
Saint Anselm College M,W
University of New Hampshire M,W

New Mexico
University of New Mexico M,W

North Carolina
Lees-McRae College M,W

Tennessee
Carson-Newman University M,W

Utah
University of Utah M,W
Westminster College M,W

Vermont
University of Vermont M,W

Wisconsin
University of Wisconsin
    Green Bay M,W

Soccer

Alabama
Auburn University W
Auburn University at Montgomery M,W
Judson College W
Samford University W
Spring Hill College M,W
Troy University W
University of Alabama W
University of Alabama
    Birmingham M,W
    Huntsville M,W
University of Mobile M,W
University of Montevallo M,W
University of North Alabama W
University of South Alabama W
University of West Alabama M,W

Arizona
Arizona Christian University M,W
Arizona State University W
Arizona Western College M,W
Chandler-Gilbert Community College M,W
Cochise College W
Embry-Riddle Aeronautical University
    Prescott Campus M,W
GateWay Community College M,W
Glendale Community College M,W
Grand Canyon University M,W
Mesa Community College M,W
Northern Arizona University W
Paradise Valley Community College M,W
Scottsdale Community College M,W
South Mountain Community College M
University of Arizona W
Yavapai College M

Arkansas
Arkansas State University W
Ecclesia College M,W
Harding University M,W
John Brown University M,W
Lyon College M,W
Ouachita Baptist University M,W
University of Arkansas W
University of Arkansas
    Little Rock M,W
    Pine Bluff W
University of Central Arkansas M,W
Williams Baptist College M

California
Academy of Art University M,W
Azusa Pacific University M,W
Bethesda University of California M
Biola University M,W
California Baptist University M,W
California Polytechnic State University: San
    Luis Obispo M,W
California State Polytechnic University:
    Pomona M,W
California State University
    Bakersfield M,W
    Chico M,W
    Dominguez Hills M,W
    Fresno W
    Fullerton M,W
    Los Angeles M,W
    Monterey Bay M,W
    Northridge M
    Sacramento M,W
    San Bernardino M,W
    Stanislaus M,W
Concordia University Irvine M,W
Dominican University of California M,W
Fresno City College M,W
Fresno Pacific University M,W
Grossmont College W
Holy Names University M,W
Hope International University M,W
Humboldt State University M,W
Loyola Marymount University M,W

The Master's University M,W
Menlo College M,W
Notre Dame de Namur University M,W
Pepperdine University W
Point Loma Nazarene University M,W
St. Mary's College of California M,W
San Diego Christian College M,W
San Diego State University M,W
San Jose State University M,W
Santa Clara University M,W
Santiago Canyon College M,W
Simpson University M,W
Soka University of America M,W
Sonoma State University M,W
Stanford University M,W
University of Antelope Valley M,W
University of California
    Berkeley M,W
    Davis M,W
    Irvine M,W
    Los Angeles M,W
    Merced M,W
    Riverside M,W
    Santa Barbara M,W
University of San Diego M,W
University of San Francisco M,W
University of Southern California W
University of the Pacific W
Vanguard University of Southern California
    M,W
Westmont College M,W
William Jessup University M,W
Yuba College M,W

Colorado
Adams State University M,W
Colorado Christian University M,W
Colorado College W
Colorado Mesa University M,W
Colorado Northwestern Community College
    M,W
Colorado School of Mines M,W
Colorado State University M,W
Colorado State University
    Pueblo M,W
Fort Lewis College M,W
Metropolitan State University of Denver M,W
Northeastern Junior College M,W
Otero Junior College M,W
Regis University M,W
Trinidad State Junior College M,W
University of Colorado
    Boulder W
    Colorado Springs M,W
University of Denver M,W
University of Northern Colorado W

Connecticut
Central Connecticut State University M,W
Fairfield University M,W
Post University M,W
Quinnipiac University M,W
Sacred Heart University M,W
Southern Connecticut State University M,W
University of Bridgeport M,W
University of Connecticut M,W
University of Hartford M,W
University of New Haven M,W

Delaware
Delaware State University W
Delaware Technical Community College
    Stanton/Wilmington Campus M
    Terry Campus M
Goldey-Beacom College M,W
University of Delaware M,W
Wilmington University M,W

District of Columbia
American University M,W
George Washington University M,W
Georgetown University M,W
Howard University M,W

Florida
Ave Maria University M,W
Barry University M,W
Eastern Florida State College M,W
Eckerd College M,W
Embry-Riddle Aeronautical University M,W
Flagler College M,W
Florida Atlantic University M,W
Florida College M,W
Florida Institute of Technology M,W
Florida National University M
Florida Southern College M,W
Florida State University W
Jacksonville University M,W
Lynn University M,W
Nova Southeastern University M,W
Palm Beach Atlantic University M,W
Polk State College W
Rollins College M,W
Saint Leo University M,W
Saint Thomas University M,W
Southeastern University M,W
Stetson University M,W
University of Central Florida M,W
University of Florida W
University of Miami W
University of North Florida M,W
University of South Florida M,W
University of Tampa M,W
University of West Florida M,W
Warner University M,W
Webber International University M,W

Georgia
Abraham Baldwin Agricultural College W
Andrew College M,W
Brenau University W
Brewton-Parker College M,W
Clayton State University M,W
Columbus State University W
Darton State College M,W
Emmanuel College M,W
Georgia College and State University W
Georgia Gwinnett College M,W
Georgia Military College M,W
Georgia Perimeter College M,W
Georgia Southern University W
Georgia Southwestern State University M,W
Georgia State University M,W
Gordon State College W
Kennesaw State University W
Life University M,W
Mercer University M,W
Middle Georgia State University M,W
Point University M,W
Reinhardt University M,W
Savannah College of Art and Design M,W
Shorter University M,W
Thomas University M,W
Truett McConnell University M,W
University of Georgia W
University of North Georgia M,W
University of West Georgia W
Valdosta State University W
Young Harris College M,W

Hawaii
Brigham Young University-Hawaii M,W
Chaminade University of Honolulu M,W
Hawaii Pacific University M,W
University of Hawaii
    Manoa W

Idaho
Boise State University W
College of Idaho M,W
Idaho State University W
Northwest Nazarene University W
University of Idaho W

Illinois
Benedictine University at Springfield M,W
Bradley University M

Chicago State University W
College of Lake County M,W
DePaul University M,W
Eastern Illinois University M,W
Elgin Community College M,W
Illinois Central College M,W
Illinois Institute of Technology M,W
Illinois State University W
Judson University M,W
Kankakee Community College M
Kaskaskia College M,W
Kishwaukee College M
Lewis and Clark Community College M,W
Lewis University M,W
Lincoln Christian University M,W
Lincoln College M,W
Lincoln Land Community College M
Loyola University Chicago M,W
McHenry County College M
McKendree University M,W
Moraine Valley Community College M,W
Morton College M
Northern Illinois University M,W
Northwestern University M,W
Olivet Nazarene University M,W
Parkland College M,W
Quincy University M,W
Robert Morris College
    Robert Morris University: Chicago M,W
Saint Xavier University M,W
South Suburban College of Cook County M
Southern Illinois University Edwardsville M,W
Southwestern Illinois College M
Trinity Christian College M,W
Trinity International University M,W
University of Illinois
    Chicago M
    Springfield M,W
    Urbana-Champaign W
University of St. Francis M,W
Waubonsee Community College M,W
Western Illinois University M,W

Indiana
Ancilla College M,W
Ball State University W
Bethel College M,W
Butler University M,W
Calumet College of St. Joseph M,W
Goshen College M,W
Grace College M,W
Holy Cross College M,W
Huntington University M,W
Indiana Institute of Technology M,W
Indiana State University W
Indiana University
    Bloomington M,W
    Purdue University Fort Wayne M,W
    Purdue University Indianapolis M,W
Indiana Wesleyan University M,W
Marian University M,W
Oakland City University M,W
Purdue University W
Purdue University
    Northwest M,W
Saint Joseph's College M,W
St. Mary-of-the-Woods College W
Taylor University M,W
University of Evansville M,W
University of Indianapolis M,W
University of Notre Dame M,W
University of Saint Francis M,W
University of Southern Indiana M,W
Valparaiso University M,W

Iowa
Briar Cliff University M,W
Clarke University M,W
Dordt College M,W
Drake University M,W
Graceland University M,W
Grand View University M,W
Iowa Central Community College M,W

Iowa State University W
Iowa Western Community College M,W
Kirkwood Community College M
Morningside College M,W
Mount Mercy University M,W
North Iowa Area Community College M
Northwestern College M,W
St. Ambrose University M,W
Scott Community College M,W
University of Iowa W
University of Northern Iowa W
Upper Iowa University M,W
Waldorf University M,W
William Penn University M,W

Kansas
Allen County Community College M,W
Baker University M,W
Barton County Community College M,W
Benedictine College M,W
Bethany College M,W
Bethel College M,W
Butler Community College W
Central Christian College of Kansas M,W
Cloud County Community College M,W
Coffeyville Community College M,W
Dodge City Community College M,W
Emporia State University W
Friends University M,W
Garden City Community College M,W
Hesston College M,W
Hutchinson Community College W
Johnson County Community College M
Kansas City Kansas Community College M
Kansas State University W
Kansas Wesleyan University M,W
MidAmerica Nazarene University M,W
Neosho County Community College M,W
Newman University M,W
Northwest Kansas Technical College M,W
Ottawa University M,W
Southwestern College M,W
Sterling College M,W
Tabor College M,W
University of Kansas W
University of St. Mary M,W
Washburn University W

Kentucky
Asbury University M,W
Bellarmine University M,W
Brescia University M,W
Campbellsville University M,W
Georgetown College M,W
Kentucky Wesleyan College M,W
Lindsey Wilson College M,W
Midway College W
Morehead State University W
Murray State University W
Northern Kentucky University M,W
St. Catharine College M,W
Union College M,W
University of Kentucky M,W
University of Louisville M,W
University of Pikeville M,W
University of the Cumberlands M,W

Louisiana
Louisiana State University and Agricultural and
    Mechanical College W
McNeese State University W
Nicholls State University W
Northwestern State University W
Southeastern Louisiana University W
Southern University and Agricultural and
    Mechanical College W
University of Louisiana
    Monroe W
University of Louisiana at Lafayette W

Maine
University of Maine M,W
University of Maine
    Augusta M,W

Maryland
Anne Arundel Community College W
Chesapeake College M
College of Southern Maryland M,W
Community College of Baltimore County M,W
Hagerstown Community College M,W
Harford Community College M,W
Loyola University Maryland M,W
Mount St. Mary's University W
Towson University W
University of Maryland
    College Park M,W
Washington Adventist University M,W

Massachusetts
American International College M,W
Boston College M,W
Boston University M,W
College of the Holy Cross M,W
Merrimack College M,W
Northeastern University M,W
Stonehill College M,W
University of Massachusetts
    Amherst M,W
    Lowell M,W

Michigan
Aquinas College M,W
Central Michigan University W
Cleary University M,W
Concordia University M,W
Cornerstone University M,W
Davenport University M,W
Delta College W
Eastern Michigan University W
Ferris State University W
Grand Valley State University W
Lake Michigan College M,W
Lawrence Technological University M,W
Madonna University M,W
Marygrove College M,W
Michigan State University M,W
Michigan Technological University W
Northern Michigan University W
Northwood University
    Michigan M,W
Oakland University M,W
Rochester College M,W
Saginaw Valley State University M,W
Schoolcraft College M,W
Siena Heights University M,W
Spring Arbor University M,W
University of Detroit Mercy M,W
University of Michigan M,W
University of Michigan
    Dearborn M
Western Michigan University M,W

Minnesota
Bemidji State University W
Concordia University St. Paul W
Minnesota State University
    Mankato W
    Moorhead W
Saint Cloud State University W
Southwest Minnesota State University W
University of Minnesota
    Crookston W
    Duluth W
    Twin Cities W
Winona State University W

Mississippi
Alcorn State University W
Belhaven University M,W
Delta State University M,W
East Central Community College M,W
Hinds Community College M,W
Holmes Community College M
Jackson State University W
Jones County Junior College M,W
Meridian Community College M,W

Mississippi Gulf Coast Community College
    M,W
Northwest Mississippi Community College
    M,W
Southwest Mississippi Community College
    M,W
University of Mississippi W
University of Mississippi
    University of Southern Mississippi W
William Carey University M,W

Missouri
Avila University M,W
Central Methodist University M,W
Columbia College M,W
Culver-Stockton College M,W
Drury University M,W
East Central College M
Hannibal-LaGrange University M,W
Harris-Stowe State University M,W
Jefferson College M
Lindenwood University M,W
Maryville University of Saint Louis M,W
Metropolitan Community College - Kansas City
    M,W
Missouri Baptist University M,W
Missouri Southern State University M,W
Missouri State University M,W
Missouri University of Science and Technology
    M,W
Missouri Valley College M,W
Northwest Missouri State University W
Park University M,W
Research College of Nursing M,W
Rockhurst University M,W
St. Louis Community College M
Saint Louis University M,W
Southeast Missouri State University W
Southwest Baptist University M,W
Stephens College W
Truman State University M,W
University of Central Missouri W
University of Missouri
    Columbia W
    Kansas City M,W
    St. Louis M,W
William Jewell College M,W
William Woods University M,W

Montana
Carroll College M,W
Montana State University
    Billings M,W
Rocky Mountain College M,W
University of Great Falls W
University of Montana W

Nebraska
Bellevue University M,W
College of Saint Mary W
Concordia University M,W
Creighton University M,W
Doane University M,W
Grace University M,W
Hastings College M,W
Midland University M,W
Northeast Community College M,W
University of Nebraska
    Lincoln W
    Omaha M,W
Wayne State College W
Western Nebraska Community College M,W
York College M,W

Nevada
Sierra Nevada College M,W
University of Nevada
    Las Vegas M,W
    Reno W

New Hampshire
Franklin Pierce University M,W
Saint Anselm College M,W

Southern New Hampshire University M,W
University of New Hampshire M,W

New Jersey
Bloomfield College M,W
Caldwell University M,W
County College of Morris W
Essex County College M
Fairleigh Dickinson University
    Metropolitan Campus M,W
Felician University M,W
Georgian Court University M,W
Mercer County Community College M,W
Monmouth University M,W
New Jersey Institute of Technology M,W
Rider University M,W
Rowan College at Burlington County M,W
Rutgers, The State University of New Jersey
    New Brunswick/Piscataway Campus
    M,W
Saint Peter's University M,W
Salem Community College W
Seton Hall University M,W
Sussex County Community College W

New Mexico
Eastern New Mexico University M,W
New Mexico Highlands University W
New Mexico State University W
University of New Mexico M,W
University of the Southwest M,W

New York
Adelphi University M,W
ASA College M
Bryant & Stratton College
    Syracuse M,W
Canisius College M,W
City University of New York
    Queens College M
Colgate University M,W
College of Saint Rose M,W
Concordia College M,W
Daemen College M,W
Dominican College of Blauvelt M,W
Fordham University M,W
Globe Institute of Technology M
Hartwick College M
Hofstra University M,W
Iona College M,W
Le Moyne College M,W
Long Island University
    LIU Brooklyn M,W
    LIU Post M,W
Manhattan College M,W
Marist College M,W
Mercy College M,W
Molloy College M,W
Monroe Community College M,W
New York Institute of Technology M,W
Niagara University M,W
Nyack College M,W
Pace University W
Pace University: Pleasantville/Briarcliff W
Roberts Wesleyan College M,W
Saint Bonaventure University M,W
St. Francis College M
St. John's University M,W
St. Thomas Aquinas College M,W
Siena College M,W
SUNY
    University at Albany M,W
    University at Binghamton M,W
    University at Buffalo M,W
    University at Stony Brook M,W
Syracuse University M,W
Wagner College W

North Carolina
Appalachian State University M,W
Barton College M,W
Belmont Abbey College M,W
Brevard College M,W
Campbell University M,W

Catawba College M,W
Chowan University M,W
Davidson College M,W
Duke University M,W
East Carolina University W
Elon University M,W
Gardner-Webb University M,W
High Point University M,W
Laurel University M,W
Lees-McRae College M,W
Lenoir-Rhyne University M,W
Louisburg College M,W
Mars Hill University M,W
Montreat College M,W
North Carolina State University M,W
Queens University of Charlotte M,W
St. Andrews University M,W
University of Mount Olive M,W
University of North Carolina
 Asheville M,W
 Chapel Hill M,W
 Charlotte M,W
 Greensboro M,W
 Pembroke W
 Wilmington M,W
Wake Forest University M,W
Western Carolina University W
Wingate University M,W

North Dakota
North Dakota State University W
University of Jamestown M,W
University of Mary M,W
University of North Dakota W

Ohio
Ashland University M,W
Bowling Green State University M,W
Bryant & Stratton College
 Eastlake M
Cedarville University M,W
Cincinnati State Technical and Community
 College M,W
Cleveland State University M,W
Kent State University W
Lake Erie College M,W
Lakeland Community College M
Lourdes University M,W
Malone University M,W
Miami University
 Oxford W
Mount Vernon Nazarene University M,W
Notre Dame College M,W
Ohio Dominican University M,W
Ohio State University
 Columbus Campus M,W
Ohio University W
Owens Community College M,W
Shawnee State University M,W
Southern State Community College M
Tiffin University M,W
University of Akron M,W
University of Cincinnati M,W
University of Dayton M,W
University of Findlay M,W
University of Northwestern Ohio M,W
University of Rio Grande M,W
University of Toledo M,W
Urbana University M,W
Ursuline College W
Walsh University M,W
Wright State University M,W
Xavier University M,W
Youngstown State University W

Oklahoma
Bacone College M,W
East Central University W
Eastern Oklahoma State College M,W
Mid-America Christian University M,W
Northeastern Oklahoma Agricultural and
 Mechanical College M,W
Northeastern State University M,W

Northern Oklahoma College M,W
Northwestern Oklahoma State University W
Oklahoma Baptist University M,W
Oklahoma Christian University M,W
Oklahoma City University M,W
Oklahoma State University W
Oklahoma Wesleyan University M,W
Oral Roberts University M,W
Rogers State University M,W
Rose State College M,W
St. Gregory's University M,W
Seminole State College W
Southern Nazarene University M,W
Southwestern Oklahoma State University W
University of Central Oklahoma W
University of Oklahoma W
University of Science and Arts of Oklahoma
 M,W
University of Tulsa M,W

Oregon
Concordia University M,W
Corban University M,W
Eastern Oregon University M,W
Lane Community College M,W
Multnomah University M
Northwest Christian University M,W
Oregon Institute of Technology W
Oregon State University M,W
Portland State University W
Southern Oregon University W
Southwestern Oregon Community College
 M,W
Treasure Valley Community College M,W
University of Oregon W
University of Portland M,W
Warner Pacific College M,W
Western Oregon University W

Pennsylvania
Bloomsburg University of Pennsylvania M,W
Bucknell University M,W
California University of Pennsylvania M,W
Carlow University M,W
Chestnut Hill College M,W
Clarion University of Pennsylvania W
Drexel University M,W
Duquesne University M,W
East Stroudsburg University of Pennsylvania
 M,W
Edinboro University
 of Pennsylvania W
Gannon University M,W
Harcum College M,W
Holy Family University M,W
Indiana University of Pennsylvania W
Kutztown University of Pennsylvania W
La Salle University M,W
Lackawanna College W
Lafayette College M
Lehigh University M,W
Lock Haven University of Pennsylvania M,W
Mercyhurst University M,W
Millersville University of Pennsylvania M,W
Penn State
 University Park M,W
Philadelphia University M,W
Point Park University M,W
Robert Morris University M,W
St. Francis University M,W
Saint Joseph's University M,W
Seton Hill University M,W
Shippensburg University of Pennsylvania M,W
Slippery Rock University of Pennsylvania M,W
Temple University M,W
University of Pittsburgh M,W
Valley Forge Military College M,W
Villanova University M,W
West Chester University of Pennsylvania M,W

Puerto Rico
Inter American University of Puerto Rico
 Aguadilla Campus M,W

Bayamon Campus M
 Guayama Campus M
 Ponce Campus M,W
 San German Campus M
Turabo University M
Universidad Metropolitana W
University of Puerto Rico
 Arecibo M,W
 Carolina Regional College M
 Cayey University College M,W
 Mayaguez M
 Utuado M,W

Rhode Island
Bryant University M,W
Community College of Rhode Island M,W
Providence College M,W
University of Rhode Island M,W

South Carolina
Anderson University M,W
Charleston Southern University M,W
The Citadel W
Clemson University M,W
Coastal Carolina University M,W
Coker College M,W
College of Charleston M,W
Columbia College W
Columbia International University M
Converse College W
Erskine College M,W
Francis Marion University M,W
Furman University M,W
Lander University M,W
Limestone College M,W
Newberry College M,W
North Greenville University M,W
Presbyterian College M,W
South Carolina State University W
Southern Wesleyan University M,W
Spartanburg Methodist College M,W
University of South Carolina
 Aiken M,W
 Columbia M,W
 Upstate M,W
Winthrop University M
Wofford College M,W

South Dakota
Augusta University
 Augustana University W
Dakota Wesleyan University M,W
Mount Marty College M,W
Northern State University W
South Dakota State University W
University of Sioux Falls W
University of South Dakota W

Tennessee
Austin Peay State University W
Belmont University M,W
Bethel University M,W
Bryan College
 Dayton M,W
Carson-Newman University M,W
Christian Brothers University M,W
Cumberland University M,W
East Tennessee State University M,W
Freed-Hardeman University M,W
Hiwassee College M,W
King University M,W
Lee University M,W
Lincoln Memorial University M,W
Lipscomb University M,W
Martin Methodist College M,W
Middle Tennessee State University W
Milligan College M,W
Motlow State Community College W
Tennessee Technological University W
Tennessee Wesleyan College M,W
Trevecca Nazarene University M,W
Tusculum College M,W
Union University M,W
University of Memphis M,W

University of Tennessee
 Chattanooga W
 Knoxville W
 Martin W
Vanderbilt University W

Texas
Abilene Christian University W
Angelo State University W
Baylor University W
Brookhaven College W
Dallas Baptist University W
Hill College M,W
Houston Baptist University M,W
Jacksonville College M,W
Jarvis Christian College M,W
Lubbock Christian University M,W
Midwestern State University M,W
Northeast Texas Community College M,W
Paris Junior College M,W
Prairie View A&M University W
Ranger College M,W
Rice University W
St. Edward's University M,W
St. Mary's University M,W
Sam Houston State University W
San Jacinto College M
Southern Methodist University M,W
Southwestern Assemblies of God University
 M,W
Stephen F. Austin State University W
Texas A&M University W
Texas A&M University
 Commerce W
 Corpus Christi W
 Texarkana M,W
Texas Christian University W
Texas Southern University W
Texas State University W
Texas Tech University W
Texas Wesleyan University M,W
Texas Woman's University M
Tyler Junior College M
University of Houston W
University of North Texas W
University of St. Thomas M,W
University of Texas
 Austin W
 of the Permian Basin M,W
 San Antonio W
University of the Incarnate Word M,W
Wayland Baptist University M,W
West Texas A&M University M,W
Western Texas College M,W

Utah
Brigham Young University W
Dixie State University M,W
Snow College M,W
Southern Utah University W
University of Utah W
Utah State University W
Utah Valley University W
Weber State University W
Westminster College M,W

Vermont
University of Vermont M,W

Virginia
Bluefield College M,W
College of William and Mary M,W
George Mason University M,W
James Madison University M,W
Liberty University M,W
Longwood University M,W
Old Dominion University M,W
Radford University M,W
University of Richmond W
University of Virginia M,W
Virginia Commonwealth University M,W
Virginia Military Institute M,W
Virginia Polytechnic Institute and State
 University M,W

Washington

Central Washington University W
Clark College M,W
Columbia Basin College M,W
Eastern Washington University W
Edmonds Community College M,W
Everett Community College M,W
Evergreen State College M,W
Gonzaga University M,W
Green River College M
Highline College M,W
Lower Columbia College W
Northwest University M,W
Peninsula College M,W
Pierce College M
Saint Martin's University M,W
Seattle Pacific University M,W
Seattle University M,W
Shoreline Community College M,W
Skagit Valley College M,W
Spokane Community College W
Tacoma Community College M,W
University of Washington M,W
Walla Walla Community College M,W
Washington State University W
Western Washington University M,W
Whatcom Community College M,W
Yakima Valley Community College W

West Virginia

Alderson-Broaddus University M,W
Concord University W
Davis and Elkins College M,W
Marshall University M,W
Ohio Valley University M,W
Salem International University M,W
Shepherd University M,W
University of Charleston M,W
West Virginia University M,W
West Virginia Wesleyan College M,W
Wheeling Jesuit University M,W

Wisconsin

Cardinal Stritch University M,W
Marquette University M,W
Silver Lake College of the Holy Family M,W
University of Wisconsin
    Green Bay M,W
    Madison M,W
    Milwaukee M,W
    Parkside M,W
Viterbo University M,W

Wyoming

Central Wyoming College M,W
Laramie County Community College M,W
Northwest College M,W
Sheridan College M,W
University of Wyoming W
Western Wyoming Community College M,W

Softball

Alabama

Alabama Southern Community College W
Alabama State University W
Auburn University W
Central Alabama Community College W
Chattahoochee Valley Community College W
Concordia College W
Enterprise State Community College W
Faulkner State Community College W
Faulkner University W
Gadsden State Community College W
George C. Wallace Community College at Dothan W
Jacksonville State University W
Jefferson Davis Community College W
Judson College W
Lurleen B. Wallace Community College W
Marion Military Institute W

Miles College W
Samford University W
Shelton State Community College W
Snead State Community College W
Southern Union State Community College W
Spring Hill College W
Troy University W
Tuskegee University W
University of Alabama W
University of Alabama
    Birmingham W
    Huntsville W
University of Mobile W
University of Montevallo W
University of North Alabama W
University of West Alabama W
Wallace State Community College at Hanceville W

Arizona

Arizona Christian University W
Arizona State University W
Arizona Western College W
Central Arizona College W
Chandler-Gilbert Community College W
Eastern Arizona College W
Embry-Riddle Aeronautical University Prescott Campus W
GateWay Community College W
Glendale Community College W
Grand Canyon University W
Mesa Community College W
Paradise Valley Community College W
Scottsdale Community College W
South Mountain Community College W
University of Arizona W

Arkansas

Arkansas Tech University W
Crowley's Ridge College W
Ecclesia College W
Henderson State University W
Lyon College W
North Arkansas College W
Ouachita Baptist University W
Southern Arkansas University W
University of Arkansas W
University of Arkansas
    Monticello W
    Pine Bluff W
University of Central Arkansas W
Williams Baptist College W

California

Academy of Art University W
Azusa Pacific University W
Biola University W
California Baptist University W
California Polytechnic State University: San Luis Obispo W
California State University
    Bakersfield W
    Chico W
    Dominguez Hills W
    Fresno W
    Fullerton W
    Long Beach W
    Monterey Bay W
    Northridge W
    Sacramento W
    San Bernardino W
    Stanislaus W
Concordia University Irvine W
Dominican University of California W
Fresno City College W
Grossmont College W
Holy Names University W
Hope International University W
Humboldt State University W
La Sierra University W
Loyola Marymount University W
Menlo College W
Notre Dame de Namur University W

St. Mary's College of California W
San Diego Christian College W
San Diego State University W
San Jose State University W
Santa Clara University W
Sonoma State University W
Stanford University W
University of Antelope Valley W
University of California
    Berkeley W
    Davis W
    Los Angeles W
    Riverside W
    Santa Barbara W
University of San Diego W
University of the Pacific W
Vanguard University of Southern California W
William Jessup University W
Yuba College W

Colorado

Adams State University W
Colorado Mesa University W
Colorado Northwestern Community College W
Colorado School of Mines W
Colorado State University W
Colorado State University
    Pueblo W
Fort Lewis College W
Lamar Community College W
Northeastern Junior College W
Otero Junior College W
Regis University W
Trinidad State Junior College W
University of Northern Colorado W

Connecticut

Central Connecticut State University W
Fairfield University W
Post University W
Quinnipiac University W
Sacred Heart University W
Southern Connecticut State University W
University of Bridgeport W
University of Connecticut W
University of New Haven W

Delaware

Delaware State University W
Delaware Technical Community College
    Jack F. Owens Campus W
    Stanton/Wilmington Campus W
    Terry Campus W
Goldey-Beacom College W
University of Delaware W
Wilmington University W

District of Columbia

Georgetown University W

Florida

Ave Maria University W
Barry University W
Bethune-Cookman University W
Chipola College W
College of Central Florida W
Daytona State College W
Eastern Florida State College W
Eckerd College W
Edward Waters College W
Embry-Riddle Aeronautical University W
Flagler College W
Florida Atlantic University W
Florida Gulf Coast University W
Florida Institute of Technology W
Florida Southern College W
Florida State College at Jacksonville W
Florida State University W
Gulf Coast State College W
Hillsborough Community College W
Indian River State College W
Jacksonville University W
Lake-Sumter State College W
Lynn University W

Miami Dade College W
North Florida Community College W
Northwest Florida State College W
Nova Southeastern University W
Palm Beach Atlantic University W
Palm Beach State College W
Pasco-Hernando State College W
Pensacola State College W
Polk State College W
Rollins College W
Saint Johns River State College W
Saint Leo University W
St. Petersburg College W
Saint Thomas University W
Santa Fe College W
South Florida State College W
Southeastern University W
State College of Florida, Manatee-Sarasota W
Stetson University W
Tallahassee Community College W
University of Central Florida W
University of Florida W
University of North Florida W
University of South Florida W
University of Tampa W
University of West Florida W
Warner University W
Webber International University W

Georgia

Abraham Baldwin Agricultural College W
Albany State University W
Andrew College W
Armstrong State University W
Augusta University W
Brenau University W
Brewton-Parker College W
Clark Atlanta University W
College of Coastal Georgia W
Columbus State University W
Darton State College W
East Georgia State College W
Emmanuel College W
Georgia College and State University W
Georgia Gwinnett College W
Georgia Highlands College M,W
Georgia Institute of Technology W
Georgia Military College W
Georgia Perimeter College W
Georgia Southern University W
Georgia Southwestern State University W
Georgia State University W
Gordon State College W
Kennesaw State University W
Mercer University W
Middle Georgia State University W
Paine College W
Point University W
Reinhardt University W
Shorter University W
South Georgia State College W
Thomas University W
Truett McConnell University W
University of Georgia W
University of North Georgia W
University of West Georgia W
Valdosta State University W
Young Harris College W

Hawaii

Brigham Young University-Hawaii W
Chaminade University of Honolulu W
Hawaii Pacific University W
University of Hawaii
    Hilo W
    Manoa W

Idaho

Boise State University W
College of Idaho W
College of Southern Idaho M,W
Idaho State University W

North Idaho College W
Northwest Nazarene University W

Illinois
Benedictine University at Springfield W
Black Hawk College W
Bradley University W
Carl Sandburg College W
College of Lake County W
Danville Area Community College W
DePaul University W
Eastern Illinois University W
Elgin Community College W
Highland Community College W
Illinois Central College W
Illinois Eastern Community Colleges
    Lincoln Trail College W
    Olney Central College W
    Wabash Valley College W
Illinois State University W
John A. Logan College W
John Wood Community College W
Judson University W
Kankakee Community College W
Kaskaskia College W
Kishwaukee College W
Lake Land College W
Lewis University W
Lincoln College W
Lincoln Land Community College W
Loyola University Chicago W
McHenry County College W
McKendree University W
Moraine Valley Community College W
Morton College W
Northern Illinois University W
Northwestern University W
Olivet Nazarene University W
Parkland College W
Quincy University W
Rend Lake College W
Robert Morris College
    Robert Morris University: Chicago W
Saint Xavier University W
Sauk Valley Community College W
Shawnee Community College W
South Suburban College of Cook County W
Southeastern Illinois College W
Southern Illinois University Carbondale W
Southern Illinois University Edwardsville W
Southwestern Illinois College W
Spoon River College W
Trinity Christian College W
Trinity International University W
University of Illinois
    Chicago W
    Springfield W
    Urbana-Champaign W
University of St. Francis W
Waubonsee Community College W
Western Illinois University W

Indiana
Ancilla College W
Ball State University W
Bethel College W
Butler University W
Calumet College of St. Joseph W
Goshen College W
Grace College W
Huntington University W
Indiana Institute of Technology W
Indiana State University W
Indiana University
    Bloomington W
    Purdue University Fort Wayne W
    Purdue University Indianapolis W
Indiana Wesleyan University W
Marian University W
Oakland City University W
Purdue University W
Purdue University
    North Central W
    Northwest W

Saint Joseph's College W
St. Mary-of-the-Woods College W
Taylor University W
University of Evansville W
University of Indianapolis W
University of Notre Dame W
University of Saint Francis W
University of Southern Indiana W
Valparaiso University W

Iowa
Briar Cliff University W
Clarke University W
Dordt College W
Drake University W
Ellsworth Community College W
Graceland University W
Grand View University W
Iowa Central Community College W
Iowa Lakes Community College W
Iowa State University W
Iowa Western Community College W
Kirkwood Community College W
Marshalltown Community College W
Morningside College W
Mount Mercy University W
Muscatine Community College W
North Iowa Area Community College W
Northwestern College W
St. Ambrose University W
Southeastern Community College W
Southwestern Community College W
University of Iowa W
University of Northern Iowa W
Upper Iowa University W
Waldorf University W
William Penn University W

Kansas
Allen County Community College W
Baker University W
Barton County Community College W
Benedictine College W
Bethany College W
Brown Mackie College
    Salina W
Butler Community College W
Central Christian College of Kansas W
Cloud County Community College W
Coffeyville Community College W
Colby Community College W
Cowley County Community College W
Dodge City Community College W
Emporia State University W
Fort Hays State University W
Fort Scott Community College W
Friends University W
Garden City Community College W
Hesston College W
Highland Community College W
Hutchinson Community College W
Independence Community College W
Johnson County Community College W
Kansas City Kansas Community College W
Kansas Wesleyan University W
Labette Community College W
McPherson College W
MidAmerica Nazarene University W
Neosho County Community College W
Newman University W
Ottawa University W
Pittsburg State University W
Pratt Community College W
Seward County Community College W
Southwestern College W
Sterling College W
Tabor College W
University of Kansas W
University of St. Mary W
Washburn University W
Wichita State University W

Kentucky
Asbury University W
Bellarmine University W
Brescia University W
Campbellsville University W
Eastern Kentucky University W
Georgetown College W
Kentucky State University W
Kentucky Wesleyan College W
Lindsey Wilson College W
Midway College W
Morehead State University W
Murray State University W
Northern Kentucky University W
St. Catharine College W
Union College W
University of Kentucky W
University of Louisville M
University of Pikeville W
University of the Cumberlands W
Western Kentucky University W

Louisiana
Bossier Parish Community College W
Louisiana State University
    Eunice W
Louisiana State University and Agricultural and
    Mechanical College W
Louisiana Tech University W
McNeese State University W
Nicholls State University W
Northwestern State University W
Southeastern Louisiana University W
Southern University and Agricultural and
    Mechanical College W
University of Louisiana
    Monroe W
University of Louisiana at Lafayette W

Maine
University of Maine W

Maryland
Bowie State University W
Chesapeake College W
College of Southern Maryland W
Community College of Baltimore County W
Coppin State University W
Garrett College W
Hagerstown Community College W
Harford Community College W
Morgan State University W
Mount St. Mary's University W
Towson University W
University of Maryland
    College Park W
    Eastern Shore W

Massachusetts
American International College W
Boston College W
Boston University W
College of the Holy Cross W
Merrimack College W
Stonehill College W
University of Massachusetts
    Amherst W
    Lowell W

Michigan
Alpena Community College W
Aquinas College W
Central Michigan University W
Cleary University W
Concordia University W
Cornerstone University W
Davenport University M,W
Delta College W
Eastern Michigan University W
Ferris State University W
Glen Oaks Community College W
Grand Valley State University W
Henry Ford College W
Hillsdale College W

Kalamazoo Valley Community College W
Kellogg Community College W
Lake Michigan College W
Lake Superior State University W
Lansing Community College W
Madonna University W
Michigan State University W
Mott Community College W
Muskegon Community College W
Northwood University
    Michigan W
Oakland Community College W
Oakland University W
Rochester College W
Saginaw Valley State University W
St. Clair County Community College W
Siena Heights University W
Spring Arbor University W
University of Detroit Mercy W
University of Michigan W
University of Michigan
    Dearborn W
Wayne State University W
Western Michigan University W

Minnesota
Bemidji State University W
Concordia University St. Paul W
Minnesota State University
    Mankato W
    Moorhead W
Saint Cloud State University W
Southwest Minnesota State University W
University of Minnesota
    Crookston W
    Duluth W
    Twin Cities W
Winona State University W

Mississippi
Alcorn State University W
Belhaven University W
Blue Mountain College W
Copiah-Lincoln Community College W
Delta State University W
East Central Community College W
East Mississippi Community College W
Hinds Community College W
Holmes Community College W
Itawamba Community College W
Jackson State University W
Jones County Junior College W
Meridian Community College W
Mississippi Gulf Coast Community College W
Mississippi Valley State University W
Northwest Mississippi Community College W
Southwest Mississippi Community College W
University of Mississippi W
University of Mississippi
    University of Southern Mississippi W
William Carey University W

Missouri
Avila University W
Central Methodist University W
Columbia College W
Cottey College W
Culver-Stockton College W
Drury University W
East Central College W
Evangel University W
Hannibal-LaGrange University W
Harris-Stowe State University W
Jefferson College W
Lincoln University W
Lindenwood University W
Maryville University of Saint Louis W
Metropolitan Community College - Kansas City
    W
Missouri Baptist University W
Missouri Southern State University W
Missouri State University W

Missouri University of Science and Technology W
Missouri Valley College W
Missouri Western State University W
North Central Missouri College W
Northwest Missouri State University W
Park University W
Research College of Nursing W
Rockhurst University W
St. Louis Community College W
Saint Louis University W
Southeast Missouri State University W
Southwest Baptist University W
Stephens College W
Three Rivers Community College W
Truman State University W
University of Central Missouri W
University of Missouri
    Columbia W
    Kansas City W
    St. Louis W
William Jewell College W
William Woods University W

Montana
Carroll College W
Montana State University
    Billings W
University of Great Falls W
University of Montana W

Nebraska
Bellevue University W
College of Saint Mary W
Concordia University W
Creighton University W
Doane University W
Grace University W
Hastings College W
Mid-Plains Community College W
Midland University W
Northeast Community College W
Peru State College W
University of Nebraska
    Kearney W
    Lincoln W
    Omaha W
Wayne State College W
Western Nebraska Community College W
York College W

Nevada
University of Nevada
    Las Vegas W
    Reno W

New Hampshire
Franklin Pierce University W
Saint Anselm College W
Southern New Hampshire University M,W

New Jersey
Bloomfield College W
Brookdale Community College W
Caldwell University W
County College of Morris W
Fairleigh Dickinson University
    Metropolitan Campus W
Felician University W
Georgian Court University W
Mercer County Community College W
Monmouth University W
Raritan Valley Community College W
Rider University W
Rowan College at Burlington County W
Rutgers, The State University of New Jersey
    New Brunswick/Piscataway Campus W
Saint Peter's University W
Salem Community College W
Seton Hall University W

New Mexico
Eastern New Mexico University W
New Mexico Highlands University W

New Mexico State University W
University of New Mexico W
University of the Southwest W
Western New Mexico University W

New York
Adelphi University W
Canisius College W
City University of New York
    Queens College W
Colgate University W
College of Saint Rose W
Concordia College W
Dominican College of Blauvelt W
Fordham University W
Hofstra University W
Iona College W
Le Moyne College W
Long Island University
    LIU Brooklyn W
    LIU Post W
Manhattan College W
Marist College W
Mercy College W
Molloy College W
New York Institute of Technology W
Niagara University W
Nyack College W
Orange County Community College W
Pace University: Pleasantville/Briarcliff W
Saint Bonaventure University W
St. John's University W
St. Thomas Aquinas College W
Siena College W
SUNY
    University at Albany W
    University at Binghamton W
    University at Buffalo W
    University at Stony Brook W
Syracuse University W
Wagner College W

North Carolina
Appalachian State University W
Barton College W
Belmont Abbey College W
Brevard College W
Campbell University W
Catawba College W
Chowan University W
East Carolina University W
Elizabeth City State University W
Elon University W
Fayetteville State University W
Gardner-Webb University W
Johnson C. Smith University W
Lees-McRae College W
Lenoir-Rhyne University W
Louisburg College W
Mars Hill University W
Montreat College W
North Carolina Central University W
North Carolina State University W
Pitt Community College W
Queens University of Charlotte W
St. Andrews University W
Saint Augustine's University W
Shaw University W
University of Mount Olive W
University of North Carolina
    Chapel Hill W
    Charlotte W
    Greensboro W
    Wilmington W
Western Carolina University W
Wingate University W
Winston-Salem State University W

North Dakota
Dakota College at Bottineau W
Dickinson State University W
Lake Region State College W
Mayville State University W

Minot State University W
North Dakota State University W
University of Jamestown W
University of Mary W
University of North Dakota W
Valley City State University W
Williston State College W

Ohio
Ashland University W
Bowling Green State University W
Cedarville University W
Cleveland State University W
Kent State University W
Lake Erie College W
Lakeland Community College W
Lourdes University W
Malone University W
Miami University
    Oxford W
Mount Vernon Nazarene University W
Notre Dame College W
Ohio Dominican University W
Ohio University W
Owens Community College W
Shawnee State University W
Sinclair Community College W
Southern State Community College W
Tiffin University W
University of Akron W
University of Dayton W
University of Findlay W
University of Northwestern Ohio W
University of Rio Grande W
University of Toledo W
Urbana University W
Ursuline College W
Walsh University W
Wright State University W
Youngstown State University W

Oklahoma
Bacone College W
Cameron University W
Carl Albert State College W
Connors State College W
East Central University W
Eastern Oklahoma State College W
Mid-America Christian University W
Northeastern Oklahoma Agricultural and
    Mechanical College W
Northeastern State University W
Northern Oklahoma College W
Northwestern Oklahoma State University W
Oklahoma Baptist University W
Oklahoma Christian University W
Oklahoma City University W
Oklahoma Panhandle State University M,W
Oklahoma State University W
Oklahoma Wesleyan University W
Rogers State University W
Rose State College W
St. Gregory's University W
Seminole State College W
Southeastern Oklahoma State University W
Southern Nazarene University W
Southwestern Oklahoma State University W
University of Central Oklahoma W
University of Oklahoma W
University of Science and Arts of Oklahoma W
University of Tulsa W
Western Oklahoma State College W

Oregon
Blue Mountain Community College W
Clackamas Community College W
Concordia University W
Corban University W
Eastern Oregon University W
Mt. Hood Community College W
Northwest Christian University W
Oregon Institute of Technology W
Oregon State University W

Portland State University W
Southern Oregon University W
Southwestern Oregon Community College W
Treasure Valley Community College W
University of Oregon W

Pennsylvania
Bloomsburg University of Pennsylvania W
Bucknell University W
California University of Pennsylvania W
Carlow University W
Chestnut Hill College W
Clarion University of Pennsylvania W
Drexel University W
East Stroudsburg University of Pennsylvania W
Edinboro University
    of Pennsylvania W
Gannon University W
Holy Family University W
Indiana University of Pennsylvania W
Kutztown University of Pennsylvania W
La Salle University W
Lackawanna College W
Lehigh University W
Lock Haven University of Pennsylvania W
Mansfield University of Pennsylvania W
Mercyhurst University W
Millersville University of Pennsylvania W
Penn State
    University Park W
Philadelphia University W
Point Park University W
Robert Morris University W
St. Francis University W
Saint Joseph's University W
Seton Hill University W
Shippensburg University of Pennsylvania W
Slippery Rock University of Pennsylvania W
University of Pittsburgh W
University of the Sciences W
Villanova University W
West Chester University of Pennsylvania W

Puerto Rico
Inter American University of Puerto Rico
    Aguadilla Campus M,W
    Barranquitas Campus M,W
    Bayamon Campus M,W
    Guayama Campus M,W
    Ponce Campus M,W
Universidad del Este W
Universidad Metropolitana W
University of Puerto Rico
    Arecibo W
    Carolina Regional College W
    Cayey University College W
    Humacao W
    Mayaguez W
    Ponce M,W
    Utuado M

Rhode Island
Bryant University W
Community College of Rhode Island W
Providence College W
University of Rhode Island W

South Carolina
Anderson University W
Charleston Southern University W
Claflin University W
Coastal Carolina University W
Coker College W
College of Charleston W
Columbia College W
Erskine College W
Francis Marion University W
Furman University W
Lander University W
Limestone College W
Morris College W
Newberry College W
North Greenville University W
Presbyterian College W

South Carolina State University W
Southern Wesleyan University W
Spartanburg Methodist College W
University of South Carolina
 Aiken W
 Columbia W
 Upstate W
Voorhees College W
Winthrop University W

South Dakota
Augusta University
 Augustana University W
Dakota State University W
Dakota Wesleyan University W
Mount Marty College W
Northern State University W
South Dakota State University M,W
University of Sioux Falls W
University of South Dakota W

Tennessee
Austin Peay State University W
Belmont University W
Bethel University W
Bryan College
 Dayton W
Carson-Newman University W
Christian Brothers University W
Cleveland State Community College W
Columbia State Community College W
Cumberland University W
Dyersburg State Community College W
East Tennessee State University W
Freed-Hardeman University W
Hiwassee College W
Jackson State Community College W
King University W
Lee University W
LeMoyne-Owen College W
Lincoln Memorial University W
Lipscomb University W
Martin Methodist College W
Middle Tennessee State University W
Milligan College W
Motlow State Community College W
Roane State Community College W
Southwest Tennessee Community College W
Tennessee State University W
Tennessee Technological University W
Tennessee Wesleyan College W
Trevecca Nazarene University W
Tusculum College W
Union University W
University of Tennessee
 Chattanooga W
 Knoxville W
 Martin W
Walters State Community College W

Texas
Abilene Christian University W
Alvin Community College W
Angelina College W
Angelo State University W
Baylor University W
Blinn College M
Clarendon College W
Frank Phillips College W
Galveston College W
Grayson College W
Hill College W
Houston Baptist University W
Howard College W
Kilgore College W
Lubbock Christian University W
McLennan Community College W
Midland College W
Midwestern State University W
Northeast Texas Community College W
Odessa College W
Paris Junior College W
Prairie View A&M University W

Ranger College W
St. Edward's University W
St. Mary's University W
Sam Houston State University W
San Jacinto College W
Southwestern Assemblies of God University W
Stephen F. Austin State University W
Tarleton State University W
Temple College W
Texas A&M University W
Texas A&M University
 Texarkana W
Texas Southern University W
Texas State University W
Texas Tech University W
Texas Wesleyan University W
Texas Woman's University W
Trinity Valley Community College W
University of Houston W
University of North Texas W
University of Texas
 Arlington W
 Austin W
 of the Permian Basin W
 San Antonio W
University of the Incarnate Word W
Vernon College W
Weatherford College W
Western Texas College W
Wiley College W

Utah
Brigham Young University W
Dixie State University W
Salt Lake Community College W
Snow College W
Southern Utah University W
University of Utah W
Utah State University W
Utah Valley University W
Weber State University W

Virginia
Bluefield College W
George Mason University W
Hampton University W
James Madison University W
Liberty University W
Longwood University W
Norfolk State University W
Radford University W
University of Virginia W
University of Virginia's College at Wise W
Virginia Polytechnic Institute and State
 University W
Virginia State University W
Virginia Union University W

Washington
Big Bend Community College W
Central Washington University W
Centralia College W
Columbia Basin College W
Edmonds Community College W
Everett Community College W
Grays Harbor College W
Green River College W
Highline College W
Lower Columbia College W
Northwest University W
Olympic College W
Pierce College W
Saint Martin's University W
Seattle University W
Shoreline Community College W
Skagit Valley College W
Spokane Community College W
University of Washington W
Walla Walla Community College W
Western Washington University W
Yakima Valley Community College W

West Virginia
Alderson-Broaddus University W
Bluefield State College W

Concord University W
Davis and Elkins College W
Fairmont State University W
Glenville State College W
Marshall University W
Ohio Valley University W
Potomac State College of West Virginia
 University W
Salem International University W
Shepherd University W
University of Charleston W
West Liberty University W
West Virginia State University W
West Virginia University Institute of
 Technology W
West Virginia Wesleyan College W
Wheeling Jesuit University W

Wisconsin
Cardinal Stritch University W
Silver Lake College of the Holy Family W
University of Wisconsin
 Green Bay W
 Madison W
 Parkside W
Viterbo University W

Squash

Pennsylvania
Drexel University M,W

Swimming

Alabama
Auburn University M,W
University of Alabama M,W

Alaska
University of Alaska
 Fairbanks W

Arizona
Arizona State University M,W
Grand Canyon University M,W
Northern Arizona University W
University of Arizona M,W

Arkansas
Henderson State University M,W
Ouachita Baptist University M,W
University of Arkansas W
University of Arkansas
 Little Rock M,W

California
Biola University M,W
California Baptist University M,W
California Polytechnic State University: San
 Luis Obispo M,W
California State University
 Bakersfield M,W
 Fresno W
 Northridge M,W
 San Bernardino M,W
Concordia University Irvine M,W
Fresno Pacific University M,W
Grossmont College M,W
Loyola Marymount University W
Pepperdine University W
San Diego State University W
San Jose State University W
Soka University of America M,W
Stanford University M,W
University of California
 Berkeley M,W
 Davis W
 Los Angeles M,W
 Santa Barbara M,W

University of San Diego W
University of Southern California M,W
University of the Pacific M,W
Vanguard University of Southern California
 M,W

Colorado
Adams State University W
Colorado Mesa University M,W
Colorado School of Mines M,W
Colorado State University W
Colorado State University
 Pueblo W
University of Denver M,W
University of Northern Colorado W

Connecticut
Central Connecticut State University W
Fairfield University M,W
Sacred Heart University W
Southern Connecticut State University M,W
University of Bridgeport M,W
University of Connecticut M,W

Delaware
University of Delaware W

District of Columbia
George Washington University M,W
Georgetown University M,W
Howard University M,W

Florida
Florida Atlantic University M,W
Florida Institute of Technology M,W
Florida Southern College M,W
Florida State University M,W
Indian River State College M,W
Lynn University W
Nova Southeastern University M,W
Saint Leo University M,W
University of Florida M,W
University of Miami W
University of North Florida W
University of Tampa M,W

Georgia
Brenau University W
Darton State College M,W
Emmanuel College M,W
Georgia Institute of Technology M,W
Georgia Southern University W
Life University M,W
Point University M,W
Savannah College of Art and Design M,W
University of Georgia M,W

Hawaii
University of Hawaii
 Manoa M,W

Idaho
Boise State University W
College of Idaho M,W
University of Idaho W

Illinois
Eastern Illinois University M,W
Illinois Institute of Technology M,W
Illinois State University W
Lewis University M,W
Lincoln College M,W
McKendree University M,W
Northwestern University M,W
Olivet Nazarene University M,W
Quincy University W
Southern Illinois University Carbondale M,W
University of Illinois
 Chicago M,W
 Urbana-Champaign W
Western Illinois University M,W

Indiana
Ball State University M,W
Indiana State University W

Indiana University
Bloomington M,W
Purdue University Indianapolis M,W
Purdue University M,W
University of Evansville M,W
University of Indianapolis M,W
University of Notre Dame M,W
Valparaiso University M,W

Iowa
Iowa Central Community College M,W
Iowa State University W
Morningside College M,W
University of Iowa M,W
University of Northern Iowa W

Kansas
Tabor College M,W
University of Kansas W

Kentucky
Asbury University M,W
Bellarmine University M,W
Campbellsville University M,W
Lindsey Wilson College M,W
St. Catharine College M
University of Kentucky M,W
University of Louisville M,W
University of the Cumberlands M,W

Louisiana
Louisiana State University and Agricultural and
Mechanical College M,W
Tulane University W
University of Louisiana
Monroe M,W

Maine
University of Maine W

Maryland
Loyola University Maryland M,W
Mount St. Mary's University W
Towson University M,W

Massachusetts
Boston College M,W
Boston University M,W
College of the Holy Cross W
Merrimack College W
Northeastern University W
University of Massachusetts
Amherst M,W

Michigan
Eastern Michigan University M,W
Grand Valley State University M,W
Hillsdale College W
Michigan State University M,W
Northern Michigan University W
Oakland University M,W
University of Michigan M,W
Wayne State University M,W

Minnesota
Minnesota State University
Mankato M,W
Saint Cloud State University M,W
University of Minnesota
Twin Cities M,W

Mississippi
Delta State University M,W

Missouri
Drury University M,W
Lindenwood University M,W
Maryville University of Saint Louis W
Missouri State University M,W
Missouri University of Science and Technology
M
Saint Louis University M,W
Truman State University W

University of Missouri
Columbia M,W
William Jewell College M,W

Nebraska
College of Saint Mary W
University of Nebraska
Kearney W
Lincoln W
Omaha W

Nevada
University of Nevada
Las Vegas M,W
Reno W

New Hampshire
Franklin Pierce University W
University of New Hampshire W

New Jersey
Monmouth University M,W
New Jersey Institute of Technology M,W
Rider University M,W
Rutgers, The State University of New Jersey
New Brunswick/Piscataway Campus
M,W
Saint Peter's University M,W
Seton Hall University M,W

New Mexico
New Mexico State University W
University of New Mexico W

New York
Adelphi University M,W
Canisius College M,W
City University of New York
Queens College M,W
College of Saint Rose M,W
Fordham University M,W
Iona College M,W
Le Moyne College M,W
Long Island University
LIU Brooklyn W
LIU Post W
Manhattan College M,W
Marist College M,W
Monroe Community College W
Niagara University M,W
Pace University M,W
Pace University: Pleasantville/Briarcliff M,W
Saint Bonaventure University M,W
St. Francis College M,W
Siena College W
SUNY
University at Binghamton M,W
University at Buffalo M,W
Wagner College W

North Carolina
Barton College M,W
Campbell University W
Catawba College M,W
Chowan University W
Davidson College M,W
East Carolina University M,W
Gardner-Webb University M,W
Lenoir-Rhyne University M,W
Mars Hill University M,W
North Carolina Agricultural and Technical State
University W
North Carolina State University M,W
Queens University of Charlotte M,W
University of North Carolina
Chapel Hill M,W
Wilmington M,W
Wingate University M,W

North Dakota
University of North Dakota M,W

Ohio
Ashland University M,W
Bowling Green State University W

Cleveland State University M,W
Malone University M,W
Miami University
Oxford M,W
Notre Dame College M,W
Ohio State University
Columbus Campus M,W
Ohio University W
University of Akron W
University of Cincinnati M,W
University of Findlay M,W
University of Toledo M,W
Urbana University M,W
Ursuline College W
Wright State University M,W
Xavier University M,W
Youngstown State University W

Oklahoma
Oklahoma Baptist University M,W
Oklahoma Christian University M,W

Oregon
Oregon State University W

Pennsylvania
Bloomsburg University of Pennsylvania M,W
Bucknell University M,W
California University of Pennsylvania W
Clarion University of Pennsylvania M,W
Drexel University M,W
Duquesne University W
East Stroudsburg University of Pennsylvania W
Edinboro University
of Pennsylvania W
Gannon University M,W
Indiana University of Pennsylvania M,W
Kutztown University of Pennsylvania W
La Salle University M,W
Lehigh University M,W
Lock Haven University of Pennsylvania W
Mansfield University of Pennsylvania W
Millersville University of Pennsylvania W
Penn State
University Park M,W
St. Francis University W
Shippensburg University of Pennsylvania M,W
University of Pittsburgh M,W
Villanova University W
West Chester University of Pennsylvania M,W

Puerto Rico
Bayamon Central University M,W
Inter American University of Puerto Rico
Aguadilla Campus M,W
Bayamon Campus M,W
Ponce Campus M,W
Turabo University M,W
University of Puerto Rico
Cayey University College M
Humacao M,W
Mayaguez M,W
University of the Sacred Heart M,W

Rhode Island
Bryant University M,W
University of Rhode Island W

South Carolina
Columbia College W
Converse College W
Limestone College M,W
University of South Carolina
Columbia M,W

South Dakota
Northern State University W
South Dakota State University M,W
University of South Dakota M,W

Tennessee
King University M,W
University of Tennessee
Knoxville M,W
Vanderbilt University W

Texas
Rice University W
Southern Methodist University M,W
Texas A&M University M,W
Texas Christian University M,W
University of Houston W
University of North Texas W
University of Texas
Austin M,W
of the Permian Basin M,W
University of the Incarnate Word M,W
Wayland Baptist University M,W

Utah
Brigham Young University M,W
University of Utah M,W

Vermont
University of Vermont W

Virginia
George Mason University M,W
James Madison University W
Liberty University M,W
University of Richmond W
University of Virginia M,W
Virginia Military Institute M
Virginia Polytechnic Institute and State
University M,W

Washington
Seattle University M,W
Washington State University W

West Virginia
Alderson-Broaddus University M,W
Davis and Elkins College M,W
Fairmont State University M,W
Marshall University W
West Virginia University M,W
West Virginia Wesleyan College M,W
Wheeling Jesuit University M,W

Wisconsin
University of Wisconsin
Green Bay M,W
Madison M,W
Milwaukee M,W

Wyoming
University of Wyoming M,W

Synchronized swimming

Alabama
University of Alabama
Birmingham W

California
Stanford University W

New York
Canisius College W

Texas
University of the Incarnate Word W

Table tennis

Arizona
South Mountain Community College M,W

Puerto Rico
Inter American University of Puerto Rico
Aguadilla Campus M,W
Barranquitas Campus M,W
Bayamon Campus M,W
Metropolitan Campus M,W
Ponce Campus M,W

Universidad Metropolitana M,W
Universidad Politecnica de Puerto Rico W
University of Puerto Rico
    Arecibo M,W
    Cayey University College M,W
    Mayaguez M,W
    Ponce M,W
    Utuado M,W

Texas
Texas Wesleyan University M,W

Tennis

Alabama
Alabama Agricultural and Mechanical
    University M,W
Alabama State University M,W
Auburn University M,W
Auburn University at Montgomery M,W
Central Alabama Community College W
Faulkner State Community College M,W
Gadsden State Community College M
Jacksonville State University M,W
Judson College W
Marion Military Institute M,W
Samford University M,W
Snead State Community College W
Spring Hill College M,W
Troy University M,W
Tuskegee University M,W
University of Alabama M,W
University of Alabama
    Birmingham M,W
    Huntsville M,W
University of Mobile M,W
University of Montevallo W
University of North Alabama M,W
University of South Alabama M,W
University of West Alabama M,W

Arizona
Arizona Christian University M,W
Arizona State University M,W
Eastern Arizona College W
Glendale Community College M,W
Grand Canyon University M,W
Northern Arizona University M,W
Paradise Valley Community College M,W
South Mountain Community College M,W
University of Arizona M,W

Arkansas
Arkansas State University W
Arkansas Tech University W
Harding University M,W
Henderson State University W
John Brown University M,W
Ouachita Baptist University M,W
Southern Arkansas University W
University of Arkansas M,W
University of Arkansas
    Fort Smith M,W
    Little Rock M,W
    Pine Bluff M,W
University of Central Arkansas W

California
Academy of Art University W
Azusa Pacific University M
Biola University M,W
California Polytechnic State University: San
    Luis Obispo M,W
California State University
    Bakersfield W
    Fresno M,W
    Fullerton W
    Long Beach W
    Los Angeles M,W
    Northridge W
    Sacramento M,W

Concordia University Irvine M,W
Dominican University of California W
Fresno City College M,W
Fresno Pacific University M,W
Grossmont College M,W
Holy Names University M,W
Hope International University M,W
Loyola Marymount University M,W
Notre Dame de Namur University W
Pepperdine University M,W
Point Loma Nazarene University M,W
St. Mary's College of California W
San Diego Christian College M,W
San Diego State University M,W
San Jose State University W
Santa Clara University M,W
Sonoma State University M,W
Stanford University M,W
University of California
    Berkeley W
    Davis M,W
    Irvine M,W
    Los Angeles M,W
    Santa Barbara M,W
University of San Diego M,W
University of San Francisco M,W
University of Southern California M,W
University of the Pacific M,W
Westmont College M,W

Colorado
Colorado Christian University M,W
Colorado Mesa University M,W
Colorado State University W
Colorado State University
    Pueblo M,W
Metropolitan State University of Denver M,W
University of Colorado
    Boulder W
University of Denver M,W
University of Northern Colorado M,W

Connecticut
Fairfield University M,W
Post University M,W
Quinnipiac University M,W
Sacred Heart University M,W
University of Connecticut M,W
University of Hartford M,W
University of New Haven W

Delaware
Delaware State University W
Goldey-Beacom College W

District of Columbia
George Washington University M,W
Georgetown University M,W
Howard University M,W

Florida
Ave Maria University M,W
Barry University M,W
Bethune-Cookman University M,W
Eastern Florida State College W
Eckerd College M,W
Embry-Riddle Aeronautical University M,W
Flagler College M,W
Florida Atlantic University M,W
Florida Gulf Coast University M,W
Florida Institute of Technology M,W
Florida Southern College M,W
Florida State College at Jacksonville W
Florida State University M,W
Hillsborough Community College W
Lynn University M,W
Palm Beach Atlantic University M,W
Rollins College M,W
Saint Leo University M,W
Saint Thomas University M,W
Southeastern University M,W
Stetson University M,W
University of Central Florida M,W
University of Florida M,W

University of Miami M,W
University of North Florida M,W
University of South Florida M,W
University of Tampa W
University of West Florida M,W
Warner University M,W
Webber International University M,W

Georgia
Abraham Baldwin Agricultural College M,W
Albany State University W
Armstrong State University M,W
Augusta University M,W
Brenau University W
Clark Atlanta University W
Clayton State University W
College of Coastal Georgia M,W
Columbus State University M,W
Emmanuel College M,W
Fort Valley State University M,W
Georgia College and State University M,W
Georgia Gwinnett College M,W
Georgia Institute of Technology M,W
Georgia Perimeter College M,W
Georgia Southern University M,W
Georgia Southwestern State University M,W
Georgia State University M,W
Kennesaw State University M,W
Mercer University M,W
Morehouse College M
Point University M,W
Reinhardt University M,W
Savannah College of Art and Design M,W
Savannah State University W
Shorter University M,W
South Georgia State College W
University of Georgia M,W
University of North Georgia M,W
University of West Georgia W
Valdosta State University M,W
Young Harris College M,W

Hawaii
Brigham Young University-Hawaii M,W
Chaminade University of Honolulu W
Hawaii Pacific University M,W
University of Hawaii
    Hilo M,W
    Manoa M,W

Idaho
Boise State University M,W
College of Idaho W
Idaho State University M,W
Lewis-Clark State College M,W
University of Idaho M,W

Illinois
Bradley University W
Chicago State University M,W
College of Lake County M,W
DePaul University M,W
Eastern Illinois University M,W
Elgin Community College M,W
Judson University M,W
Kaskaskia College M,W
Lewis and Clark Community College M,W
Lewis University M,W
McHenry County College M,W
McKendree University M,W
Moraine Valley Community College M,W
Northern Illinois University M,W
Northwestern University M,W
Olivet Nazarene University M,W
Quincy University M,W
Rend Lake College W
Sauk Valley Community College M,W
Southern Illinois University Carbondale M,W
Southern Illinois University Edwardsville M,W
University of Illinois
    Chicago M,W
    Springfield M,W
    Urbana-Champaign M,W
University of St. Francis M,W

Waubonsee Community College M,W
Western Illinois University W

Indiana
Ancilla College M,W
Ball State University M,W
Bethel College M,W
Butler University M,W
Calumet College of St. Joseph M,W
Goshen College M,W
Grace College M,W
Huntington University M,W
Indiana Institute of Technology M,W
Indiana University
    Bloomington M,W
    Purdue University Fort Wayne M,W
    Purdue University Indianapolis M,W
Indiana Wesleyan University M,W
Marian University M,W
Oakland City University M,W
Purdue University M,W
Purdue University
    Northwest M,W
Saint Joseph's College M,W
Taylor University M,W
University of Evansville W
University of Indianapolis M,W
University of Notre Dame M,W
University of Saint Francis M,W
University of Southern Indiana M,W
Valparaiso University M,W

Iowa
Briar Cliff University M,W
Drake University M,W
Graceland University M,W
Grand View University M,W
Iowa Central Community College M,W
Iowa State University W
Morningside College M,W
Northwestern College W
St. Ambrose University M,W
University of Iowa M,W
University of Northern Iowa W
Upper Iowa University W

Kansas
Baker University M,W
Barton County Community College M,W
Bethany College M,W
Bethel College M,W
Central Christian College of Kansas M,W
Cowley County Community College M,W
Emporia State University M,W
Fort Hays State University W
Friends University M,W
Hesston College M,W
Johnson County Community College M,W
Kansas State University W
Kansas Wesleyan University M,W
Labette Community College W
McPherson College M,W
Newman University M,W
Seward County Community College M,W
Southwestern College M,W
Tabor College M,W
University of Kansas W
Washburn University M,W
Wichita State University M,W

Kentucky
Asbury University M,W
Bellarmine University M,W
Brescia University M,W
Campbellsville University M,W
Eastern Kentucky University M,W
Georgetown College M,W
Kentucky Wesleyan College W
Lindsey Wilson College M,W
Midway College W
Morehead State University M,W
Murray State University M,W
Northern Kentucky University M,W
St. Catharine College M

Union College M,W
University of Kentucky M,W
University of Louisville M,W
University of Pikeville M,W
University of the Cumberlands M,W
Western Kentucky University M,W

Louisiana
Dillard University M,W
Grambling State University M,W
Louisiana State University
    Shreveport W
Louisiana State University and Agricultural and
    Mechanical College M,W
Louisiana Tech University W
Loyola University New Orleans M,W
McNeese State University W
Nicholls State University M,W
Northwestern State University W
Southeastern Louisiana University W
Southern University and Agricultural and
    Mechanical College W
Tulane University M,W
University of Louisiana at Lafayette M,W
University of New Orleans M,W
Xavier University of Louisiana M,W

Maryland
College of Southern Maryland M,W
Coppin State University M,W
Harford Community College M,W
Loyola University Maryland M,W
Morgan State University M,W
Mount St. Mary's University M,W
Towson University W
University of Maryland
    College Park W
    Eastern Shore W

Massachusetts
American International College M,W
Boston College M,W
Boston University W
Merrimack College M,W
Stonehill College M,W
University of Massachusetts
    Amherst W

Michigan
Aquinas College M,W
Cleary University M,W
Davenport University M,W
Eastern Michigan University W
Ferris State University M,W
Grand Valley State University M,W
Hillsdale College M,W
Lake Superior State University M,W
Lawrence Technological University M,W
Michigan State University M,W
Michigan Technological University M,W
Northwood University.
    Michigan M,W
Oakland Community College W
Oakland University W
Saginaw Valley State University W
Spring Arbor University M,W
University of Detroit Mercy M,W
University of Michigan M,W
Wayne State University M,W
Western Michigan University M,W

Minnesota
Bemidji State University W
Minnesota State University
    Mankato M,W
    Moorhead W
Saint Cloud State University M,W
Southwest Minnesota State University W
University of Minnesota
    Crookston W
    Duluth W
    Twin Cities M,W
Winona State University W

Mississippi
Alcorn State University M,W
Belhaven University M,W
Blue Mountain College M,W
Copiah-Lincoln Community College M,W
Delta State University M,W
East Central Community College M
Hinds Community College M,W
Holmes Community College M,W
Jackson State University M,W
Jones County Junior College M,W
Meridian Community College M,W
Mississippi Gulf Coast Community College
    M,W
Mississippi Valley State University M,W
Northwest Mississippi Community College
    M,W
Tougaloo College M,W
University of Mississippi M,W
University of Mississippi
    University of Southern Mississippi M,W

Missouri
Drury University M,W
Evangel University M,W
Lindenwood University M,W
Maryville University of Saint Louis W
Missouri Baptist University M,W
Missouri Valley College M,W
Missouri Western State University W
Northwest Missouri State University M,W
Research College of Nursing M,W
Rockhurst University M,W
Saint Louis University M,W
Southeast Missouri State University W
Southwest Baptist University M,W
Stephens College W
University of Missouri
    Columbia W
    Kansas City M,W
    St. Louis M,W
William Jewell College M,W
William Woods University M,W

Montana
Montana State University M,W
Montana State University
    Billings M,W
University of Montana M,W

Nebraska
College of Saint Mary W
Concordia University M,W
Creighton University M,W
Hastings College M,W
Midland University M,W
University of Nebraska
    Kearney M,W
    Lincoln M,W
    Omaha M,W

Nevada
University of Nevada
    Las Vegas M,W
    Reno M,W

New Hampshire
Franklin Pierce University M,W
Saint Anselm College M,W
Southern New Hampshire University M,W

New Jersey
Bloomfield College M
Caldwell University M,W
Fairleigh Dickinson University
    Metropolitan Campus M,W
Monmouth University M,W
New Jersey Institute of Technology M,W
Rider University M,W
Rutgers, The State University of New Jersey
    New Brunswick/Piscataway Campus
    M,W
Saint Peter's University M,W
Seton Hall University W

New Mexico
New Mexico Military Institute M
New Mexico State University M,W
University of New Mexico M,W
University of the Southwest M,W
Western New Mexico University M,W

New York
Adelphi University M,W
ASA College M,W
City University of New York
    Queens College M,W
College of Saint Rose W
Concordia College M,W
Daemen College M,W
Fordham University W
Hofstra University M,W
Le Moyne College M,W
Long Island University
    LIU Brooklyn W
    LIU Post W
Marist College M,W
Molloy College W
New York Institute of Technology M,W
Niagara University M,W
Roberts Wesleyan College M,W
Saint Bonaventure University M,W
St. Francis College M,W
St. John's University M,W
Siena College M,W
SUNY
    University at Albany W
    University at Binghamton M,W
    University at Buffalo M,W
    University at Stony Brook M,W
Syracuse University W
Wagner College M,W

North Carolina
Appalachian State University M,W
Barton College M,W
Belmont Abbey College M,W
Brevard College M,W
Campbell University M,W
Catawba College M,W
Chowan University M,W
Davidson College M,W
Duke University M,W
East Carolina University M,W
Elizabeth City State University W
Elon University M,W
Fayetteville State University W
Gardner-Webb University M,W
Johnson C. Smith University M,W
Lees-McRae College M,W
Lenoir-Rhyne University M,W
Mars Hill University M,W
North Carolina Agricultural and Technical State
    University W
North Carolina Central University M,W
North Carolina State University M,W
Queens University of Charlotte M,W
St. Andrews University W
Saint Augustine's University M,W
Shaw University M,W
University of Mount Olive M,W
University of North Carolina
    Asheville M,W
    Chapel Hill M,W
    Charlotte M,W
    Greensboro M,W
    Wilmington M,W
Wake Forest University M,W
Western Carolina University M
Wingate University M,W
Winston-Salem State University M,W

North Dakota
University of Mary W
University of North Dakota W

Ohio
Ashland University W
Bowling Green State University W

Cedarville University M,W
Central State University M,W
Cleveland State University M,W
Miami University
    Oxford W
Ohio State University
    Columbus Campus M,W
Shawnee State University M,W
Tiffin University M,W
University of Akron W
University of Cincinnati W
University of Dayton M,W
University of Findlay M,W
University of Northwestern Ohio M,W
University of Toledo M,W
Ursuline College W
Walsh University M,W
Wright State University M,W
Xavier University M,W
Youngstown State University M,W

Oklahoma
Bacone College M,W
Cameron University M,W
East Central University M,W
Northeastern State University W
Oklahoma Baptist University M,W
Oklahoma State University M,W
Oklahoma Wesleyan University M,W
Oral Roberts University M,W
Seminole State College M,W
Southeastern Oklahoma State University M,W
Southern Nazarene University M,W
University of Central Oklahoma W
University of Oklahoma M,W
University of Tulsa M,W

Oregon
Portland State University W
Southern Oregon University W
Treasure Valley Community College M,W
University of Oregon M,W
University of Portland M,W

Pennsylvania
Bloomsburg University of Pennsylvania M,W
California University of Pennsylvania W
Carlow University W
Chestnut Hill College M,W
Clarion University of Pennsylvania W
Drexel University M,W
Duquesne University M,W
East Stroudsburg University of Pennsylvania W
Edinboro University
    of Pennsylvania M,W
Holy Family University W
Indiana University of Pennsylvania W
Kutztown University of Pennsylvania M,W
La Salle University M,W
Lackawanna College W
Lehigh University M,W
Mercyhurst University M,W
Millersville University of Pennsylvania M,W
Penn State
    University Park M,W
Philadelphia University M,W
St. Francis University M,W
Saint Joseph's University M,W
Seton Hill University W
Shippensburg University of Pennsylvania W
Slippery Rock University of Pennsylvania W
Temple University M,W
University of Pittsburgh W
University of the Sciences M,W
West Chester University of Pennsylvania M,W

Puerto Rico
Inter American University of Puerto Rico
    Aguadilla Campus M,W
    Barranquitas Campus M,W
    Bayamon Campus M,W
    Ponce Campus M,W
    San German Campus M,W
Turabo University M,W

Universidad Metropolitana M,W
University of Puerto Rico
   Bayamon University College M,W
   Carolina Regional College M,W
   Cayey University College M,W
   Mayaguez M,W
   Ponce M,W
University of the Sacred Heart M

Rhode Island
Bryant University M,W
University of Rhode Island W

South Carolina
Anderson University M,W
Charleston Southern University M,W
The Citadel M
Clemson University M,W
Coastal Carolina University M,W
Coker College M,W
College of Charleston M,W
Columbia College W
Converse College W
Erskine College M,W
Francis Marion University M,W
Furman University M,W
Lander University M,W
Limestone College M,W
Newberry College M,W
North Greenville University M,W
Presbyterian College M,W
South Carolina State University M,W
Spartanburg Methodist College M,W
University of South Carolina
   Aiken M,W
   Columbia M,W
   Upstate M,W
Winthrop University M,W
Wofford College M,W

South Dakota
Augusta University
   Augustana University M,W
Mount Marty College W
South Dakota State University M,W
University of Sioux Falls W

Tennessee
Austin Peay State University M,W
Belmont University M,W
Bethel University M,W
Carson-Newman University M,W
Christian Brothers University M,W
Cumberland University M,W
East Tennessee State University M,W
King University M,W
Lee University M,W
LeMoyne-Owen College M,W
Lincoln Memorial University M,W
Lipscomb University M,W
Martin Methodist College M,W
Middle Tennessee State University M,W
Milligan College M,W
Tennessee State University M,W
Tennessee Technological University M
Tennessee Wesleyan College M,W
Tusculum College M,W
Union University M,W
University of Memphis M,W
University of Tennessee
   Chattanooga M,W
   Knoxville M,W
   Martin W
Vanderbilt University M,W

Texas
Abilene Christian University M,W
Baylor University M,W
Collin County Community College District M,W
Dallas Baptist University W
Jacksonville College M,W
Lamar University M,W
Laredo Community College M,W
Midwestern State University M,W

North Central Texas College W
Prairie View A&M University M,W
Rice University M,W
St. Edward's University M,W
St. Mary's University M,W
Sam Houston State University W
Southern Methodist University M,W
Stephen F. Austin State University W
Tarleton State University W
Temple College M,W
Texas A&M University M,W
Texas A&M University
   Corpus Christi M,W
   Texarkana M,W
Texas Christian University M,W
Texas Southern University M,W
Texas State University W
Texas Tech University M,W
Texas Wesleyan University W
Tyler Junior College M,W
University of Houston W
University of North Texas W
University of Texas
   Arlington M,W
   Austin M,W
   of the Permian Basin M,W
   San Antonio M,W
University of the Incarnate Word M,W

Utah
Brigham Young University M,W
Dixie State University W
Southern Utah University M,W
University of Utah M,W
Utah State University M,W
Weber State University M,W

Virginia
Bluefield College M,W
College of William and Mary M,W
George Mason University M,W
Hampton University M,W
James Madison University M,W
Liberty University M,W
Longwood University M,W
Norfolk State University M,W
Old Dominion University M,W
Radford University M,W
University of Richmond M,W
University of Virginia M,W
University of Virginia's College at Wise M,W
Virginia Commonwealth University M,W
Virginia Military Institute M
Virginia Polytechnic Institute and State
   University M,W
Virginia State University M,W
Virginia Union University M,W

Washington
Eastern Washington University M,W
Gonzaga University M,W
Green River College M,W
Seattle University M,W
Shoreline Community College M,W
Skagit Valley College M,W
Spokane Community College M,W
University of Washington M,W
Washington State University W

West Virginia
Alderson-Broaddus University W
Bluefield State College M,W
Concord University M,W
Davis and Elkins College M,W
Fairmont State University M,W
Marshall University W
Salem International University M
Shepherd University M,W
University of Charleston M,W
West Liberty University M,W
West Virginia State University M,W
West Virginia University W
West Virginia Wesleyan College M,W

Wisconsin
Cardinal Stritch University M,W
Marquette University M,W
University of Wisconsin
   Green Bay M,W
   Madison M,W
   Milwaukee W

Wyoming
University of Wyoming W

Track and field

Alabama
Alabama Agricultural and Mechanical
   University M,W
Alabama State University M,W
Auburn University M,W
Miles College M,W
Samford University M,W
Spring Hill College M,W
Troy University M,W
Tuskegee University M,W
University of Alabama M,W
University of Alabama
   Birmingham W
   Huntsville M,W
University of Mobile M,W
University of South Alabama M,W
University of West Alabama M,W

Arizona
Arizona Christian University M,W
Arizona State University M,W
Central Arizona College M,W
Embry-Riddle Aeronautical University
   Prescott Campus M,W
Glendale Community College M,W
Grand Canyon University M,W
Mesa Community College M,W
Northern Arizona University M,W
Paradise Valley Community College M,W
University of Arizona M,W

Arkansas
Arkansas State University M,W
Harding University M,W
Southern Arkansas University M,W
University of Arkansas M,W
University of Arkansas
   Little Rock M,W
   Pine Bluff M,W
University of Central Arkansas M,W

California
Academy of Art University M,W
Azusa Pacific University M,W
Biola University M,W
California Baptist University M,W
California Polytechnic State University: San
   Luis Obispo M,W
California State Polytechnic University:
   Pomona M,W
California State University
   Bakersfield M,W
   Chico M,W
   Dominguez Hills W
   Fresno M,W
   Fullerton M,W
   Long Beach M,W
   Los Angeles M,W
   Northridge M,W
   Sacramento M,W
   Stanislaus M,W
Concordia University Irvine M,W
Fresno City College M,W
Fresno Pacific University M,W
Hope International University M,W
Humboldt State University M,W
The Master's University M,W
Menlo College M,W

Pepperdine University M,W
Point Loma Nazarene University W
St. Mary's College of California M,W
San Diego State University W
San Jose State University W
Santa Clara University M,W
Santiago Canyon College M,W
Soka University of America M,W
Sonoma State University M,W
Stanford University M,W
University of California
   Berkeley M,W
   Davis M,W
   Irvine M,W
   Los Angeles M,W
   Santa Barbara M,W
University of San Diego W
University of San Francisco M,W
University of Southern California M,W
Vanguard University of Southern California
   M,W
Westmont College M,W
William Jessup University M,W
Yuba College M,W

Colorado
Adams State University M,W
Colorado Mesa University M,W
Colorado School of Mines M,W
Colorado State University M,W
Colorado State University
   Pueblo M,W
University of Colorado
   Boulder M,W
   Colorado Springs M,W
University of Northern Colorado M,W
Western State Colorado University M,W

Connecticut
Central Connecticut State University M,W
Post University M,W
Quinnipiac University W
Sacred Heart University M,W
Southern Connecticut State University W
University of Connecticut M,W
University of New Haven M,W

Delaware
Delaware State University M,W
University of Delaware W

District of Columbia
American University M,W
Georgetown University M,W
Howard University M,W

Florida
Bethune-Cookman University M,W
Edward Waters College M
Embry-Riddle Aeronautical University M,W
Flagler College M,W
Florida Agricultural and Mechanical University
   M,W
Florida Atlantic University W
Florida Institute of Technology M,W
Florida Memorial University M
Florida State University M,W
Jacksonville University W
Nova Southeastern University M,W
Saint Thomas University M,W
University of Central Florida W
University of Florida M,W
University of Miami M,W
University of North Florida M,W
University of South Florida M,W
University of Tampa M,W
University of West Florida M,W
Warner University M,W
Webber International University M,W

Georgia
Albany State University M,W
Brenau University W
Clark Atlanta University M,W

Columbus State University M,W
Emmanuel College M,W
Fort Valley State University M,W
Georgia Institute of Technology M,W
Georgia Southern University W
Georgia State University W
Kennesaw State University M,W
Life University M,W
Mercer University W
Morehouse College M
Paine College M,W
Savannah State University M,W
Shorter University M,W
University of Georgia M,W
University of West Georgia W

Hawaii
University of Hawaii
        Manoa W

Idaho
Boise State University M,W
College of Idaho M,W
Idaho State University M,W
Lewis-Clark State College M,W
Northwest Nazarene University M,W
University of Idaho M,W

Illinois
Bradley University M,W
Chicago State University M,W
DePaul University M,W
Eastern Illinois University M,W
Illinois State University M,W
Judson University M,W
Lewis University M,W
Lincoln College M,W
Loyola University Chicago M,W
McKendree University M,W
Northern Illinois University W
Olivet Nazarene University M,W
Robert Morris College
        Robert Morris University: Chicago M,W
Southern Illinois University Carbondale M,W
Southern Illinois University Edwardsville M,W
Trinity Christian College M,W
University of Illinois
        Chicago M,W
        Springfield M,W
        Urbana-Champaign M,W
University of St. Francis M,W
Western Illinois University M,W

Indiana
Ancilla College M,W
Ball State University W
Bethel College M,W
Butler University M,W
Goshen College M,W
Grace College M,W
Huntington University M,W
Indiana Institute of Technology M,W
Indiana State University M,W
Indiana University
        Bloomington M,W
        Purdue University Fort Wayne W
Indiana Wesleyan University M,W
Marian University M,W
Purdue University M,W
Saint Joseph's College M,W
Taylor University M,W
University of Indianapolis M,W
University of Notre Dame M,W
University of Saint Francis M,W
Valparaiso University M,W
Vincennes University M,W

Iowa
Briar Cliff University M,W
Clarke University M,W
Dordt College M,W
Drake University M,W
Graceland University M,W
Iowa Central Community College M,W

Iowa State University M,W
Iowa Western Community College M,W
Morningside College M,W
Mount Mercy University M,W
North Iowa Area Community College M,W
Northwestern College M,W
St. Ambrose University M,W
University of Iowa M,W
University of Northern Iowa M,W
Waldorf University M,W
William Penn University M,W

Kansas
Allen County Community College M,W
Baker University M,W
Barton County Community College M,W
Benedictine College M,W
Bethany College M,W
Bethel College M,W
Butler Community College M,W
Cloud County Community College M,W
Coffeyville Community College M,W
Colby Community College M,W
Cowley County Community College M,W
Dodge City Community College M,W
Emporia State University M,W
Fort Hays State University M,W
Friends University M,W
Garden City Community College M,W
Hesston College M,W
Highland Community College M,W
Hutchinson Community College M,W
Johnson County Community College M,W
Kansas City Kansas Community College M,W
Kansas State University M,W
Kansas Wesleyan University M,W
McPherson College M,W
MidAmerica Nazarene University M,W
Neosho County Community College M,W
Northwest Kansas Technical College M,W
Ottawa University M,W
Pittsburg State University M,W
Pratt Community College M,W
Southwestern College M,W
Sterling College M,W
Tabor College M,W
University of Kansas M,W
University of St. Mary M,W
Washburn University M,W
Wichita State University M,W

Kentucky
Asbury University M,W
Bellarmine University M,W
Brescia University M,W
Campbellsville University M,W
Eastern Kentucky University M,W
Georgetown College M,W
Kentucky State University M,W
Lindsey Wilson College M,W
Midway College W
Morehead State University M,W
Murray State University W
Northern Kentucky University M,W
St. Catharine College M,W
University of Kentucky M,W
University of Louisville M,W
University of Pikeville M,W
University of the Cumberlands M,W
Western Kentucky University M,W

Louisiana
Dillard University M,W
Grambling State University M,W
Louisiana State University and Agricultural and
        Mechanical College M,W
Louisiana Tech University M,W
Loyola University New Orleans M,W
McNeese State University M,W
Nicholls State University W
Northwestern State University M,W
Southeastern Louisiana University M,W

Southern University and Agricultural and
        Mechanical College M,W
Tulane University M,W
University of Louisiana
        Monroe M,W
University of Louisiana at Lafayette M,W
University of New Orleans M,W

Maine
University of Maine M,W

Maryland
Bowie State University M,W
Coppin State University M,W
Hagerstown Community College M,W
Morgan State University M,W
Mount St. Mary's University M,W
Towson University W
University of Maryland
        College Park M,W
        Eastern Shore M,W
Washington Adventist University M,W

Massachusetts
American International College M,W
Boston College M,W
Boston University M,W
College of the Holy Cross W
Merrimack College M,W
Northeastern University M,W
Stonehill College M,W
University of Massachusetts
        Amherst M,W
        Lowell M,W

Michigan
Aquinas College M,W
Central Michigan University M,W
Concordia University M,W
Cornerstone University M,W
Davenport University M,W
Eastern Michigan University M,W
Ferris State University M,W
Grand Valley State University M,W
Hillsdale College M,W
Lake Superior State University M,W
Macomb Community College M,W
Madonna University M,W
Michigan State University M,W
Michigan Technological University M,W
Northern Michigan University W
Northwood University
        Michigan M,W
Saginaw Valley State University M,W
Siena Heights University M,W
University of Detroit Mercy M,W
University of Michigan M,W
Wayne State University W
Western Michigan University W

Minnesota
Bemidji State University M,W
Concordia University St. Paul M,W
Minnesota State University
        Mankato M,W
        Moorhead M,W
Saint Cloud State University M,W
University of Minnesota
        Duluth M,W
        Twin Cities M,W
Winona State University W

Mississippi
Alcorn State University M,W
Hinds Community College M,W
Holmes Community College M
Jackson State University M,W
Mississippi Valley State University M,W
University of Mississippi M,W
University of Mississippi
        University of Southern Mississippi M,W

Missouri
Central Methodist University M,W
Cottey College W

Culver-Stockton College M,W
Drury University M,W
Evangel University M,W
Hannibal-LaGrange University M,W
Lincoln University M,W
Lindenwood University M,W
Maryville University of Saint Louis M,W
Missouri Baptist University M,W
Missouri Southern State University M,W
Missouri State University M,W
Missouri University of Science and Technology
        M,W
Missouri Valley College M,W
Northwest Missouri State University M,W
Park University M,W
Saint Louis University M,W
Southeast Missouri State University M,W
Southwest Baptist University M,W
Truman State University M,W
University of Central Missouri M,W
University of Missouri
        Columbia M,W
        Kansas City M,W
William Jewell College M,W
William Woods University M,W

Montana
Montana State University M,W
Montana State University
        Billings M,W
Rocky Mountain College M,W
University of Montana M,W
University of Montana: Western M,W

Nebraska
Chadron State College M,W
Concordia University M,W
Doane University M,W
Hastings College M,W
Midland University M,W
University of Nebraska
        Kearney M,W
        Lincoln M,W
        Omaha W
Wayne State College M,W
York College M,W

Nevada
University of Nevada
        Las Vegas W
        Reno W

New Hampshire
Franklin Pierce University M,W
University of New Hampshire M,W

New Jersey
Caldwell University M,W
Essex County College M,W
Fairleigh Dickinson University
        Metropolitan Campus M,W
Felician University M,W
Georgian Court University M,W
Monmouth University M,W
Rider University M,W
Rutgers, The State University of New Jersey
        New Brunswick/Piscataway Campus
        M,W
Saint Peter's University M,W

New Mexico
Eastern New Mexico University M,W
New Mexico Highlands University W
New Mexico Military Institute M
New Mexico State University W
University of New Mexico M,W
University of the Southwest M,W

New York
Adelphi University M,W
City University of New York
        Queens College W
College of Saint Rose M,W
Daemen College M,W

Dominican College of Blauvelt M,W
Fordham University M,W
Iona College M,W
Le Moyne College M,W
Long Island University
    LIU Brooklyn M,W
    LIU Post M,W
Manhattan College M,W
Marist College M,W
Molloy College M,W
Niagara University W
Roberts Wesleyan College M,W
St. Francis College M,W
St. John's University W
St. Thomas Aquinas College M,W
SUNY
    University at Albany M,W
    University at Binghamton M,W
    University at Buffalo M,W
    University at Stony Brook M,W
Syracuse University M,W
Wagner College M,W

North Carolina
Appalachian State University M,W
Barton College M,W
Belmont Abbey College M,W
Brevard College M,W
Campbell University M,W
Davidson College M,W
East Carolina University M,W
Elon University W
Fayetteville State University W
Gardner-Webb University M,W
High Point University M,W
Johnson C. Smith University M,W
Lees-McRae College M,W
Lenoir-Rhyne University M,W
Livingstone College M,W
Mars Hill University M,W
Montreat College M,W
North Carolina Agricultural and Technical State
    University M,W
North Carolina Central University M,W
North Carolina State University M,W
Queens University of Charlotte M,W
Saint Augustine's University M,W
Shaw University M,W
University of Mount Olive M,W
University of North Carolina
    Asheville M,W
    Chapel Hill M,W
    Charlotte M,W
    Greensboro M,W
    Wilmington M,W
Wake Forest University M,W
Wingate University M,W
Winston-Salem State University M,W

North Dakota
Dickinson State University M,W
Minot State University M,W
North Dakota State University M,W
University of Jamestown M,W
University of Mary M,W
University of North Dakota M,W
Valley City State University M,W

Ohio
Ashland University M,W
Bowling Green State University W
Cedarville University M,W
Central State University M,W
Kent State University M,W
Lake Erie College M,W
Lourdes University M,W
Malone University M,W
Miami University
    Oxford M,W
Mount Vernon Nazarene University M,W
Notre Dame College M,W
Ohio Dominican University M,W

Ohio State University
    Columbus Campus M,W
Ohio University W
Shawnee State University M,W
Tiffin University M,W
University of Akron M,W
University of Cincinnati M,W
University of Dayton W
University of Findlay M,W
University of Rio Grande M,W
University of Toledo W
Ursuline College W
Walsh University M,W
Wright State University W
Xavier University M,W
Youngstown State University M,W

Oklahoma
Bacone College M,W
Langston University W
Oklahoma Baptist University M,W
Oklahoma Christian University M,W
Oklahoma City University M,W
Oklahoma State University M,W
Oklahoma Wesleyan University M,W
Oral Roberts University M,W
Rogers State University M,W
St. Gregory's University M,W
Southern Nazarene University M,W
University of Central Oklahoma W
University of Oklahoma M,W
University of Tulsa M,W

Oregon
Clackamas Community College M,W
Concordia University M,W
Corban University M,W
Eastern Oregon University M,W
Lane Community College M,W
Mt. Hood Community College M,W
Northwest Christian University M,W
Oregon Institute of Technology M,W
Portland State University M,W
Southern Oregon University M,W
Southwestern Oregon Community College
    M,W
Treasure Valley Community College M,W
University of Oregon M,W
University of Portland M,W
Warner Pacific College M,W
Western Oregon University M,W

Pennsylvania
Bloomsburg University of Pennsylvania M,W
Bucknell University M,W
California University of Pennsylvania M,W
Chestnut Hill College M,W
Cheyney University of Pennsylvania M,W
Clarion University of Pennsylvania W
Duquesne University M,W
East Stroudsburg University of Pennsylvania
    M,W
Edinboro University
    of Pennsylvania M,W
Harcum College M,W
Holy Family University M,W
Indiana University of Pennsylvania M,W
Kutztown University of Pennsylvania M,W
La Salle University M,W
Lehigh University M,W
Lock Haven University of Pennsylvania M,W
Millersville University of Pennsylvania W
Penn State
    University Park M,W
Robert Morris University W
St. Francis University M,W
Saint Joseph's University M,W
Seton Hill University M,W
Shippensburg University of Pennsylvania M,W
Slippery Rock University of Pennsylvania M,W
Temple University W
University of Pittsburgh M,W

Villanova University M,W
West Chester University of Pennsylvania M,W

Puerto Rico
Bayamon Central University M,W
Inter American University of Puerto Rico
    Aguadilla Campus M,W
    Barranquitas Campus M,W
    Bayamon Campus M,W
    Fajardo Campus M,W
    Guayama Campus M,W
    Metropolitan Campus M,W
    Ponce Campus M,W
    San German Campus M,W
Turabo University M,W
Universidad del Este M,W
Universidad Metropolitana M,W
Universidad Politecnica de Puerto Rico M,W
University of Puerto Rico
    Arecibo M,W
    Bayamon University College M,W
    Carolina Regional College M,W
    Humacao M,W
    Mayaguez M,W
    Ponce M,W
    Utuado M,W
University of the Sacred Heart M,W

Rhode Island
Bryant University M,W
Providence College M,W
University of Rhode Island M,W

South Carolina
Anderson University M,W
Charleston Southern University M,W
The Citadel M,W
Claflin University M,W
Clemson University M,W
Coastal Carolina University M,W
Converse College W
Furman University M,W
Limestone College M,W
Morris College M,W
North Greenville University M,W
South Carolina State University M,W
University of South Carolina
    Columbia M,W
    Upstate M,W
Voorhees College M,W
Winthrop University M,W
Wofford College M,W

South Dakota
Augusta University
    Augustana University M,W
Black Hills State University M,W
Dakota State University M,W
Dakota Wesleyan University M,W
Mount Marty College M,W
Northern State University M,W
South Dakota School of Mines and Technology
    M,W
South Dakota State University M,W
University of Sioux Falls M,W
University of South Dakota M,W

Tennessee
Austin Peay State University W
Belmont University M,W
Bethel University M,W
Bryan College
    Dayton M,W
Christian Brothers University M,W
East Tennessee State University M,W
King University M,W
Lee University M,W
Lipscomb University M,W
Middle Tennessee State University M,W
Milligan College M,W
Tennessee State University M,W
Tennessee Technological University W
Trevecca Nazarene University M,W
Tusculum College M,W

University of Memphis M,W
University of Tennessee
    Chattanooga M,W
    Knoxville M,W
Vanderbilt University W

Texas
Abilene Christian University M,W
Angelo State University M,W
Baylor University M,W
Dallas Baptist University W
Houston Baptist University M,W
Jarvis Christian College M,W
Lamar University M,W
Prairie View A&M University M,W
Rice University M,W
Sam Houston State University M,W
South Plains College M,W
Stephen F. Austin State University M,W
Tarleton State University M,W
Texas A&M University M,W
Texas A&M University
    Commerce M,W
    Corpus Christi M,W
Texas Christian University M,W
Texas Southern University M,W
Texas State University M,W
Texas Tech University M,W
Texas Wesleyan University M,W
University of Houston M,W
University of North Texas M,W
University of Texas
    Austin M,W
    San Antonio M,W
University of the Incarnate Word M,W
Wayland Baptist University M,W
Western Texas College M,W
Wiley College M,W

Utah
Brigham Young University M,W
Southern Utah University M,W
University of Utah W
Utah State University M,W
Utah Valley University M,W
Weber State University M,W
Westminster College M,W

Vermont
University of Vermont M,W

Virginia
College of William and Mary M,W
George Mason University M,W
Hampton University M,W
James Madison University W
Liberty University M,W
Norfolk State University M,W
Radford University W
University of Richmond W
University of Virginia M,W
Virginia Commonwealth University M,W
Virginia Military Institute M,W
Virginia Polytechnic Institute and State
    University M,W
Virginia State University M,W
Virginia Union University M,W

Washington
Central Washington University M,W
Clark College M,W
Eastern Washington University M,W
Evergreen State College M,W
Highline College M,W
Northwest University M,W
Olympic College M
Saint Martin's University M,W
Seattle Pacific University M,W
Seattle University M,W
Spokane Community College M,W
University of Washington M,W
Washington State University M,W
Western Washington University M,W

West Virginia
Alderson-Broaddus University M,W
Glenville State College M,W
Marshall University W
University of Charleston W
West Liberty University M,W
West Virginia University W
West Virginia Wesleyan College M,W
Wheeling Jesuit University M,W

Wisconsin
Cardinal Stritch University M,W
Marquette University M,W
University of Wisconsin
 Madison M,W
 Milwaukee M,W
 Parkside M,W
Viterbo University M,W

Wyoming
University of Wyoming M,W

Triathlon

Alabama
University of West Alabama W

Arizona
Arizona State University W

New York
Daemen College W

North Carolina
Queens University of Charlotte M,W

Volleyball

Alabama
Alabama Agricultural and Mechanical
 University W
Alabama State University W
Auburn University W
Faulkner State Community College M,W
Faulkner University W
Gadsden State Community College W
George C. Wallace State Community College
 at Selma W
Jacksonville State University W
Jefferson Davis Community College W
Judson College W
Lawson State Community College W
Miles College M,W
Samford University W
Southern Union State Community College W
Spring Hill College W
Troy University W
Tuskegee University W
University of Alabama W
University of Alabama
 Birmingham W
 Huntsville W
University of Mobile W
University of Montevallo W
University of North Alabama W
University of South Alabama W
University of West Alabama W
Wallace State Community College at
 Hanceville W

Alaska
University of Alaska
 Anchorage W
 Fairbanks W

Arizona
Arizona Christian University W
Arizona State University W
Arizona Western College W

Chandler-Gilbert Community College W
Eastern Arizona College W
Embry-Riddle Aeronautical University
 Prescott Campus W
Glendale Community College W
Grand Canyon University M,W
Northern Arizona University W
Scottsdale Community College W
University of Arizona W
Yavapai College W

Arkansas
Arkansas State University W
Arkansas Tech University W
Crowley's Ridge College W
Harding University W
Henderson State University W
John Brown University W
Lyon College W
Ouachita Baptist University W
Philander Smith College W
Southern Arkansas University W
University of Arkansas W
University of Arkansas
 Fort Smith W
 Little Rock W
 Pine Bluff W
University of Central Arkansas W
Williams Baptist College W

California
Academy of Art University W
Azusa Pacific University W
Biola University W
California Baptist University M,W
California Polytechnic State University: San
 Luis Obispo W
California State Polytechnic University:
 Pomona W
California State University
 Bakersfield W
 Chico W
 Dominguez Hills W
 Fresno W
 Fullerton W
 Long Beach M,W
 Los Angeles W
 Monterey Bay W
 Northridge M,W
 Sacramento W
 San Bernardino W
 Stanislaus W
Concordia University Irvine M,W
Dominican University of California W
Fresno City College W
Fresno Pacific University W
Grossmont College M,W
Holy Names University M,W
Hope International University M,W
Humboldt State University W
Loyola Marymount University W
The Master's University W
Menlo College M,W
Notre Dame de Namur University W
Pepperdine University M,W
Point Loma Nazarene University W
St. Mary's College of California W
San Diego Christian College W
San Diego State University W
San Jose State University W
Santa Clara University W
Simpson University W
Sonoma State University W
Stanford University M,W
University of Antelope Valley W
University of California
 Berkeley W
 Davis W
 Irvine M,W
 Los Angeles W
 Merced M,W
 Riverside W
 Santa Barbara M,W

University of San Diego W
University of San Francisco W
University of Southern California M,W
University of the Pacific M,W
Vanguard University of Southern California W
Westmont College W
William Jessup University W
Yuba College W

Colorado
Adams State University W
Colorado Christian University W
Colorado Mesa University W
Colorado Northwestern Community College W
Colorado School of Mines W
Colorado State University W
Colorado State University
 Pueblo W
Fort Lewis College W
Lamar Community College W
Metropolitan State University of Denver W
Northeastern Junior College W
Otero Junior College W
Regis University W
Trinidad State Junior College W
University of Colorado
 Boulder W
 Colorado Springs W
University of Denver W
University of Northern Colorado W
Western State Colorado University W

Connecticut
Central Connecticut State University W
Fairfield University W
Post University W
Quinnipiac University W
Sacred Heart University M,W
Southern Connecticut State University W
University of Bridgeport W
University of Connecticut W
University of Hartford W
University of New Haven W

Delaware
Delaware State University W
Goldey-Beacom College W
University of Delaware W
Wilmington University W

District of Columbia
American University W
George Washington University W
Georgetown University W
Howard University W

Florida
Ave Maria University W
Barry University W
Bethune-Cookman University W
College of Central Florida W
Daytona State College W
Eastern Florida State College W
Eckerd College W
Embry-Riddle Aeronautical University W
Flagler College W
Florida Agricultural and Mechanical University
 W
Florida Atlantic University W
Florida College W
Florida Gulf Coast University W
Florida Institute of Technology W
Florida Memorial University W
Florida National University W
Florida Southern College W
Florida State College at Jacksonville W
Florida State University W
Gulf Coast State College W
Hillsborough Community College W
Indian River State College W
Jacksonville University W
Lake-Sumter State College W
Lynn University W
Miami Dade College W

Nova Southeastern University W
Palm Beach Atlantic University W
Palm Beach State College W
Pasco-Hernando State College W
Pensacola State College W
Polk State College W
Rollins College W
Saint Johns River State College W
Saint Leo University W
St. Petersburg College W
Saint Thomas University W
South Florida State College W
Southeastern University W
State College of Florida, Manatee-Sarasota W
Stetson University W
University of Central Florida W
University of Florida W
University of Miami W
University of North Florida W
University of South Florida W
University of Tampa W
University of West Florida W
Warner University M,W
Webber International University W

Georgia
Abraham Baldwin Agricultural College W
Albany State University W
Andrew College W
Armstrong State University W
Augusta University W
Brenau University W
Brewton-Parker College W
Clark Atlanta University W
College of Coastal Georgia W
Emmanuel College M,W
Fort Valley State University W
Georgia College and State University M,W
Georgia Institute of Technology W
Georgia Southern University W
Georgia State University W
Kennesaw State University W
Life University M
Mercer University W
Paine College W
Point University W
Savannah State University W
Shorter University W
Truett McConnell University W
University of Georgia W
University of West Georgia W
Valdosta State University W

Hawaii
Brigham Young University-Hawaii W
Chaminade University of Honolulu W
Hawaii Pacific University W
University of Hawaii
 Hilo W
 Manoa M,W

Idaho
Boise State University W
College of Idaho W
College of Southern Idaho W
Idaho State University W
Lewis-Clark State College W
North Idaho College W
Northwest Nazarene University W
University of Idaho W

Illinois
Benedictine University at Springfield W
Black Hawk College W
Bradley University W
Carl Sandburg College W
Chicago State University W
College of Lake County W
DePaul University W
Eastern Illinois University W
Elgin Community College W
Governors State University M,W
Highland Community College W
Illinois Central College W

Illinois Institute of Technology W
Illinois State University W
John A. Logan College W
Judson University M,W
Kankakee Community College W
Kaskaskia College W
Kishwaukee College W
Lake Land College W
Lewis and Clark Community College W
Lewis University M,W
Lincoln Christian University W
Lincoln College W
Loyola University Chicago M,W
McHenry County College W
McKendree University M,W
Moraine Valley Community College W
Morton College W
Northern Illinois University W
Northwestern University W
Olivet Nazarene University W
Parkland College W
Quincy University M,W
Rend Lake College W
Robert Morris College
    Robert Morris University: Chicago M,W
Saint Xavier University W
Sauk Valley Community College W
South Suburban College of Cook County W
Southern Illinois University Carbondale W
Southern Illinois University Edwardsville W
Southwestern Illinois College W
Trinity Christian College W
Trinity International University W
University of Illinois
    Chicago W
    Springfield W
    Urbana-Champaign W
University of St. Francis W
Waubonsee Community College W
Western Illinois University W

Indiana
Ancilla College W
Ball State University M,W
Bethel College W
Butler University W
Calumet College of St. Joseph M,W
Goshen College W
Grace College W
Huntington University W
Indiana Institute of Technology W
Indiana State University W
Indiana University
    Bloomington W
    Purdue University Fort Wayne M,W
    Purdue University Indianapolis W
    Southeast W
Indiana Wesleyan University W
Marian University W
Oakland City University W
Purdue University W
Purdue University
    North Central W
    Northwest W
Saint Joseph's College W
Taylor University W
University of Evansville W
University of Indianapolis W
University of Notre Dame W
University of Saint Francis W
University of Southern Indiana W
Valparaiso University W
Vincennes University W

Iowa
Briar Cliff University W
Clarke University M,W
Des Moines Area Community College W
Dordt University W
Drake University W
Ellsworth Community College W
Graceland University M,W
Grand View University M,W

Iowa Central Community College W
Iowa Lakes Community College W
Iowa State University W
Iowa Western Community College W
Kirkwood Community College W
Morningside College W
Mount Mercy University M,W
North Iowa Area Community College W
Northwestern College W
St. Ambrose University M,W
Southeastern Community College W
Southwestern Community College W
University of Iowa W
University of Northern Iowa W
Upper Iowa University W
Waldorf University W
William Penn University W

Kansas
Allen County Community College W
Baker University W
Barton County Community College W
Benedictine College W
Bethany College W
Bethel College W
Butler Community College W
Central Christian College of Kansas W
Cloud County Community College W
Coffeyville Community College W
Colby Community College W
Cowley County Community College W
Dodge City Community College W
Emporia State University W
Fort Hays State University W
Fort Scott Community College W
Friends University W
Garden City Community College W
Hesston College W
Highland Community College W
Hutchinson Community College W
Independence Community College W
Johnson County Community College W
Kansas City Kansas Community College W
Kansas State University W
Kansas Wesleyan University W
Labette Community College W
McPherson College W
MidAmerica Nazarene University W
Neosho County Community College W
Newman University W
Ottawa University W
Pittsburg State University W
Pratt Community College W
Seward County Community College W
Southwestern College W
Sterling College W
Tabor College W
University of Kansas W
University of St. Mary W
Washburn University W
Wichita State University W

Kentucky
Asbury University W
Bellarmine University W
Brescia University W
Campbellsville University W
Eastern Kentucky University W
Georgetown College W
Kentucky State University W
Kentucky Wesleyan College W
Lindsey Wilson College W
Midway College W
Morehead State University W
Murray State University W
Northern Kentucky University W
St. Catharine College W
Union College W
University of Kentucky W
University of Louisville W
University of Pikeville W
University of the Cumberlands W
Western Kentucky University W

Louisiana
Dillard University W
Louisiana State University and Agricultural and
    Mechanical College W
Louisiana Tech University W
Loyola University New Orleans W
McNeese State University W
Nicholls State University W
Northwestern State University W
Southeastern Louisiana University W
Southern University and Agricultural and
    Mechanical College W
Tulane University W
University of Louisiana
    Monroe W
University of Louisiana at Lafayette W
University of New Orleans W
Xavier University of Louisiana W

Maine
University of Maine W

Maryland
Bowie State University W
Chesapeake College W
College of Southern Maryland W
Community College of Baltimore County W
Coppin State University W
Garrett College W
Hagerstown Community College W
Harford Community College W
Loyola University Maryland W
Morgan State University W
Towson University W
University of Maryland
    College Park W
    Eastern Shore W

Massachusetts
American International College W
Boston College W
College of the Holy Cross W
Merrimack College W
Northeastern University W
Stonehill College W
University of Massachusetts
    Lowell W

Michigan
Alpena Community College W
Aquinas College W
Central Michigan University W
Concordia University W
Cornerstone University W
Davenport University W
Eastern Michigan University W
Ferris State University W
Gogebic Community College W
Grand Valley State University W
Hillsdale College W
Kalamazoo Valley Community College W
Kellogg Community College W
Lake Michigan College W
Lake Superior State University W
Lansing Community College W
Lawrence Technological University W
Macomb Community College W
Madonna University W
Marygrove College W
Michigan State University W
Michigan Technological University W
Mott Community College W
Muskegon Community College W
Northern Michigan University W
Northwood University
    Michigan W
Oakland Community College W
Oakland University W
Rochester College W
Saginaw Valley State University W
St. Clair County Community College W
Schoolcraft College W
Siena Heights University M,W

Spring Arbor University W
University of Michigan W
University of Michigan
    Dearborn W
Wayne State University W
Western Michigan University W

Minnesota
Bemidji State University W
Concordia University St. Paul W
Minnesota State University
    Mankato W
    Moorhead W
Saint Cloud State University W
Southwest Minnesota State University W
University of Minnesota
    Crookston W
    Duluth W
    Twin Cities W
Winona State University W

Mississippi
Alcorn State University W
Belhaven University W
Jackson State University W
Mississippi Valley State University W
University of Mississippi W
University of Mississippi
    University of Southern Mississippi W

Missouri
Avila University W
Central Methodist University W
College of the Ozarks W
Columbia College W
Cottey College W
Culver-Stockton College M,W
Drury University W
East Central College W
Evangel University W
Hannibal-LaGrange University W
Harris-Stowe State University W
Jefferson College W
Lindenwood University M,W
Maryville University of Saint Louis W
Metropolitan Community College - Kansas City
    W
Mineral Area College W
Missouri Baptist University M,W
Missouri Southern State University W
Missouri State University W
Missouri State University
    West Plains W
Missouri Valley College M,W
Missouri Western State University W
Northwest Missouri State University W
Park University M,W
Research College of Nursing W
Rockhurst University W
Saint Louis University W
Southeast Missouri State University W
Southwest Baptist University W
Stephens College W
Truman State University W
University of Central Missouri W
University of Missouri
    Columbia W
    Kansas City W
    St. Louis W
William Jewell College W
William Woods University W

Montana
Carroll College W
Montana State University W
Montana State University
    Billings W
    Northern W
Montana Tech of the University of Montana W
Rocky Mountain College W
University of Great Falls W
University of Montana W
University of Montana: Western W

Nebraska
Bellevue University W
Central Community College W
Chadron State College W
College of Saint Mary W
Concordia University W
Creighton University W
Doane University W
Grace University W
Hastings College W
Mid-Plains Community College W
Midland University W
Northeast Community College W
Peru State College W
University of Nebraska
    Kearney W
    Lincoln W
    Omaha W
Wayne State College W
Western Nebraska Community College W
York College W

Nevada
University of Nevada
    Las Vegas W
    Reno W

New Hampshire
Franklin Pierce University W
Saint Anselm College W
University of New Hampshire W

New Jersey
Bloomfield College W
Caldwell University W
County College of Morris W
Fairleigh Dickinson University
    Metropolitan Campus W
Georgian Court University W
New Jersey Institute of Technology M,W
Rider University W
Rutgers, The State University of New Jersey
    New Brunswick/Piscataway Campus W
    Newark Campus M
Saint Peter's University W
Seton Hall University W

New Mexico
Eastern New Mexico University W
New Mexico Highlands University W
New Mexico State University W
University of New Mexico W
University of the Southwest W
Western New Mexico University W

New York
Adelphi University W
Canisius College W
City University of New York
    Queens College W
Colgate University W
College of Saint Rose W
Concordia College W
Daemen College W
Dominican College of Blauvelt W
Fordham University W
Globe Institute of Technology W
Hofstra University W
Iona College W
Le Moyne College W
Long Island University
    LIU Brooklyn W
    LIU Post W
Manhattan College W
Marist College W
Mercy College W
Molloy College W
New York Institute of Technology W
Niagara University W
Nyack College W
Pace University W
Pace University: Pleasantville/Briarcliff W
Roberts Wesleyan College W
St. Francis College W

St. John's University W
Siena College W
SUNY
    University at Albany W
    University at Binghamton W
    University at Buffalo W
    University at Stony Brook M,W
Syracuse University W

North Carolina
Appalachian State University W
Barton College M,W
Belmont Abbey College M,W
Brevard College W
Campbell University W
Catawba College W
Chowan University W
Davidson College W
Duke University W
East Carolina University M,W
Elizabeth City State University W
Elon University W
Fayetteville State University W
Gardner-Webb University W
Guilford Technical Community College W
High Point University W
Johnson C. Smith University W
Laurel University W
Lees-McRae College M,W
Lenoir Community College W
Lenoir-Rhyne University W
Livingstone College W
Louisburg College W
Mars Hill University W
Montreat College W
North Carolina Agricultural and Technical State
    University W
North Carolina Central University W
North Carolina State University W
Pitt Community College W
Queens University of Charlotte M,W
St. Andrews University W
Saint Augustine's University W
Shaw University W
Southeastern Community College W
University of Mount Olive W
University of North Carolina
    Asheville W
    Chapel Hill W
    Charlotte W
    Greensboro W
    Wilmington W
Wake Forest University W
Western Carolina University W
Wingate University W
Winston-Salem State University W

North Dakota
Bismarck State College W
Dakota College at Bottineau W
Dickinson State University W
Lake Region State College W
Mayville State University W
Minot State University W
North Dakota State College of Science W
North Dakota State University W
University of Jamestown W
University of Mary W
University of North Dakota W
Valley City State University W
Williston State College W

Ohio
Ashland University W
Bowling Green State University W
Cedarville University W
Central State University W
Clark State Community College W
Cleveland State University W
Edison State Community College W
Kent State University W
Lake Erie College W
Lakeland Community College W

Lourdes University M,W
Malone University W
Miami University
    Oxford W
Mount Vernon Nazarene University W
Notre Dame College W
Ohio Dominican University W
Ohio State University
    Columbus Campus M,W
Ohio University W
Owens Community College W
Shawnee State University W
Sinclair Community College W
Southern State Community College W
Tiffin University W
University of Akron W
University of Cincinnati W
University of Dayton W
University of Findlay W
University of Northwestern Ohio W
University of Rio Grande W
University of Toledo W
Urbana University W
Ursuline College W
Walsh University W
Wright State University W
Xavier University W
Youngstown State University W

Oklahoma
Bacone College W
Cameron University W
East Central University W
Langston University W
Mid-America Christian University W
Northeastern Oklahoma Agricultural and
    Mechanical College W
Northwestern Oklahoma State University M,W
Oklahoma Baptist University W
Oklahoma City University W
Oklahoma Panhandle State University W
Oklahoma Wesleyan University W
Oral Roberts University W
Redlands Community College W
St. Gregory's University W
Seminole State College W
Southeastern Oklahoma State University W
Southern Nazarene University W
Southwestern Oklahoma State University W
University of Central Oklahoma W
University of Oklahoma W
University of Tulsa W

Oregon
Blue Mountain Community College W
Chemeketa Community College W
Clackamas Community College W
Concordia University W
Corban University W
Eastern Oregon University W
Linn-Benton Community College W
Mt. Hood Community College W
Multnomah University W
New Hope Christian College W
Northwest Christian University W
Oregon Institute of Technology W
Oregon State University W
Portland State University W
Southern Oregon University W
Southwestern Oregon Community College W
Treasure Valley Community College W
University of Oregon W
University of Portland W
Warner Pacific College W
Western Oregon University W

Pennsylvania
Bucknell University W
California University of Pennsylvania W
Carlow University W
Chestnut Hill College W
Cheyney University of Pennsylvania W
Duquesne University W

East Stroudsburg University of Pennsylvania W
Edinboro University
    of Pennsylvania W
Gannon University W
Harcum College W
Holy Family University W
Indiana University of Pennsylvania W
Kutztown University of Pennsylvania W
La Salle University W
Lackawanna College W
Lehigh University W
Lock Haven University of Pennsylvania W
Mercyhurst University W
Millersville University of Pennsylvania W
Penn State
    Lehigh Valley M
    University Park M,W
Philadelphia University W
Point Park University W
Robert Morris University W
St. Francis University M,W
Seton Hill University W
Shippensburg University of Pennsylvania W
Slippery Rock University of Pennsylvania W
Temple University W
University of Pittsburgh W
University of the Sciences W
Villanova University W
West Chester University of Pennsylvania W

Puerto Rico
Bayamon Central University M,W
Inter American University of Puerto Rico
    Aguadilla Campus M,W
    Barranquitas Campus M,W
    Bayamon Campus M,W
    Metropolitan Campus M,W
    Ponce Campus M,W
    San German Campus M,W
Turabo University M,W
Universidad del Este M,W
Universidad Metropolitana M,W
Universidad Politecnica de Puerto Rico M,W
University of Puerto Rico
    Arecibo M,W
    Bayamon University College M,W
    Carolina Regional College M,W
    Cayey University College M,W
    Humacao M,W
    Mayaguez M,W
    Ponce M,W
    Utuado M,W
University of the Sacred Heart M,W

Rhode Island
Bryant University W
Community College of Rhode Island W
University of Rhode Island W

South Carolina
Anderson University W
Charleston Southern University W
The Citadel W
Claflin University W
Clemson University W
Coastal Carolina University W
Coker College M,W
College of Charleston W
Columbia College W
Converse College W
Erskine College W
Francis Marion University W
Furman University W
Lander University W
Limestone College M,W
Morris College W
Newberry College W
North Greenville University M,W
Presbyterian College W
South Carolina State University W
Southern Wesleyan University W
Spartanburg Methodist College W
University of South Carolina

Aiken W
Columbia W
Upstate W
Winthrop University W
Wofford College W

South Dakota
Augusta University
    Augustana University W
Black Hills State University W
Dakota State University W
Dakota Wesleyan University W
Mount Marty College W
Northern State University W
South Dakota School of Mines and Technology W
South Dakota State University W
University of Sioux Falls W

Tennessee
Austin Peay State University W
Belmont University W
Bethel University W
Bryan College
    Dayton W
Carson-Newman University W
Christian Brothers University W
Cumberland University W
East Tennessee State University W
Freed-Hardeman University W
Hiwassee College W
King University M,W
Lane College W
Lee University W
LeMoyne-Owen College W
Lincoln Memorial University W
Lipscomb University W
Martin Methodist College W
Middle Tennessee State University W
Milligan College W
Tennessee State University W
Tennessee Technological University W
Tennessee Wesleyan College W
Trevecca Nazarene University W
Tusculum College W
Union University W
University of Memphis W
University of Tennessee
    Chattanooga W
    Knoxville W
    Martin W

Texas
Abilene Christian University W
Angelo State University W
Baylor University W
Blinn College W
Brookhaven College W
Clarendon College W
Dallas Baptist University W
Frank Phillips College W
Hill College W
Houston Baptist University W
Jarvis Christian College M,W
Lamar University W
Laredo Community College W
Lee College W
Lubbock Christian University W
Midland College W
Midwestern State University W
North Central Texas College W
Panola College W
Prairie View A&M University M,W
Ranger College W
Rice University W
St. Edward's University W
St. Mary's University W
Sam Houston State University W
San Jacinto College W
Southern Methodist University W
Southwestern Assemblies of God University W
Stephen F. Austin State University W
Tarleton State University W

Temple College W
Texas A&M University W
Texas A&M University
    Commerce W
    Corpus Christi W
Texas Christian University W
Texas Southern University W
Texas State University W
Texas Tech University W
Texas Wesleyan University W
Texas Woman's University W
Trinity Valley Community College W
Tyler Junior College W
University of Houston W
University of North Texas W
University of St. Thomas W
University of Texas
    Arlington W
    Austin W
    of the Permian Basin W
    San Antonio W
University of the Incarnate Word W
Vernon College W
Wayland Baptist University W
West Texas A&M University W
Western Texas College W
Wharton County Junior College W
Wiley College W

Utah
Brigham Young University M,W
Dixie State University W
Salt Lake Community College W
Snow College W
Southern Utah University W
University of Utah W
Utah State University W
Utah Valley University W
Weber State University W
Westminster College W

Virginia
Bluefield College M,W
College of William and Mary W
George Mason University M,W
Hampton University W
James Madison University W
Liberty University W
Norfolk State University W
Radford University W
University of Virginia W
University of Virginia's College at Wise W
Virginia Commonwealth University W
Virginia Polytechnic Institute and State University W
Virginia State University W
Virginia Union University W

Washington
Big Bend Community College W
Central Washington University W
Centralia College W
Clark College W
Columbia Basin College W
Eastern Washington University W
Edmonds Community College W
Everett Community College W
Evergreen State College W
Gonzaga University W
Grays Harbor College W
Green River College W
Highline College W
Lower Columbia College W
Northwest University W
Olympic College W
Pierce College W
Saint Martin's University W
Seattle University W
Shoreline Community College W
Skagit Valley College W
Spokane Community College W
Tacoma Community College W
University of Washington W

Walla Walla Community College W
Washington State University W
Western Washington University W
Whatcom Community College W
Yakima Valley Community College W

West Virginia
Alderson-Broaddus University M,W
Bluefield State College W
Concord University W
Davis and Elkins College W
Fairmont State University W
Glenville State College W
Marshall University W
Ohio Valley University W
Salem International University W
Shepherd University W
University of Charleston W
West Liberty University W
West Virginia State University W
West Virginia University W
West Virginia University Institute of Technology W
West Virginia Wesleyan College W
Wheeling Jesuit University W

Wisconsin
Cardinal Stritch University M,W
Marquette University W
Silver Lake College of the Holy Family W
University of Wisconsin
    Green Bay W
    Madison W
    Milwaukee M,W
    Parkside W
Viterbo University W

Wyoming
Casper College W
Central Wyoming College W
Eastern Wyoming College W
Laramie County Community College W
Northwest College W
Sheridan College W
University of Wyoming W
Western Wyoming Community College W

Water polo

Arizona
Arizona State University W

California
California Baptist University M,W
California State University
    Bakersfield W
    Long Beach M,W
    Monterey Bay W
Concordia University Irvine M,W
Fresno Pacific University M,W
Grossmont College M,W
Loyola Marymount University M,W
Pepperdine University M
San Diego State University W
San Jose State University M,W
Santa Clara University M,W
Sonoma State University W
Stanford University M,W
University of California
    Berkeley M,W
    Davis M,W
    Irvine M,W
University of Southern California M,W
University of the Pacific M,W

District of Columbia
George Washington University M

Florida
Florida Atlantic University W

Hawaii
University of Hawaii
    Manoa W

Illinois
McKendree University M,W

Indiana
Indiana University
    Bloomington W

Michigan
University of Michigan W

New York
City University of New York
    Queens College M
Fordham University M
Hartwick College W
Iona College M,W
Marist College W
St. Francis College M,W
Siena College W
Wagner College W

Pennsylvania
Gannon University M,W
La Salle University M,W
Mercyhurst University M,W

Puerto Rico
University of Puerto Rico
    Mayaguez M

Virginia
Virginia Military Institute M,W

Weight lifting

New York
United States Merchant Marine Academy M,W

Puerto Rico
Inter American University of Puerto Rico
    Aguadilla Campus M,W
    Ponce Campus M,W
    San German Campus M,W
Turabo University M,W
Universidad del Este M
Universidad Metropolitana M,W
Universidad Politecnica de Puerto Rico M,W
University of Puerto Rico
    Arecibo M,W
    Carolina Regional College M,W
    Cayey University College M,W
    Humacao M,W
    Utuado M,W

Wrestling

Arizona
Arizona State University M
Embry-Riddle Aeronautical University
    Prescott Campus M

Arkansas
Ouachita Baptist University M

California
California Baptist University M
California Polytechnic State University: San Luis Obispo M
California State University
    Bakersfield M
Fresno City College M
Menlo College M,W
Stanford University M
University of California
    Los Angeles M,W

Colorado
Adams State University M
Colorado Mesa University M

Colorado School of Mines M
Colorado State University
    Pueblo M
Otero Junior College M
University of Northern Colorado M
Western State Colorado University M

Connecticut
Sacred Heart University M

District of Columbia
American University M

Georgia
Brewton-Parker College M
Darton State College M
Emmanuel College M,W
Life University M,W
Shorter University M
Truett McConnell University M

Idaho
Boise State University M
North Idaho College M

Illinois
City Colleges of Chicago
    Wilbur Wright College M,W
Judson University M
Lincoln College M
McKendree University M,W
Northern Illinois University M
Northwestern University M
Southern Illinois University Edwardsville M
University of Illinois
    Urbana-Champaign M

Indiana
Ancilla College M
Calumet College of St. Joseph M
Indiana Institute of Technology M
Indiana University
    Bloomington M
Purdue University M
University of Indianapolis M

Iowa
Briar Cliff University M
Ellsworth Community College M
Graceland University M
Grand View University M
Iowa Central Community College M
Iowa State University M
Iowa Western Community College M
North Iowa Area Community College M
Northwestern College M
University of Iowa M
University of Northern Iowa M
Upper Iowa University M
Waldorf University M,W
William Penn University M

Kansas
Baker University M
Benedictine College M
Bethany College M
Central Christian College of Kansas M
Cloud County Community College M
Colby Community College M
Fort Hays State University M
Kansas Wesleyan University M
Labette Community College M
Neosho County Community College M
Newman University M
Northwest Kansas Technical College M,W
Pratt Community College M
University of St. Mary M,W

Kentucky
Campbellsville University M,W
Lindsey Wilson College M
St. Catharine College M
University of the Cumberlands M,W

Maryland
University of Maryland
    College Park M

Massachusetts
American International College M

Michigan
Central Michigan University M
Davenport University M
Eastern Michigan University M
Michigan State University M
Muskegon Community College M
University of Michigan M

Minnesota
Minnesota State University
    Mankato M
    Moorhead M
Saint Cloud State University M
Southwest Minnesota State University M
University of Minnesota
    Twin Cities M

Missouri
Drury University M
Hannibal-LaGrange University M
Lindenwood University M
Maryville University of Saint Louis M
Missouri Baptist University M,W
Missouri Valley College M,W
University of Central Missouri M
University of Missouri
    Columbia M

Montana
Montana State University
    Northern M
University of Great Falls M

Nebraska
Chadron State College M
Concordia University M
Hastings College M
Midland University M,W
University of Nebraska
    Kearney M
    Lincoln M
York College M

New Jersey
Rider University M
Rutgers, The State University of New Jersey
    New Brunswick/Piscataway Campus M

New York
Hofstra University M
Long Island University
    LIU Post M
Niagara County Community College M
SUNY
    University at Binghamton M
    University at Buffalo M

North Carolina
Appalachian State University M
Belmont Abbey College M
Campbell University M
Davidson College M
Duke University M
Gardner-Webb University M
North Carolina State University M
University of North Carolina
    Chapel Hill M

North Dakota
Dickinson State University M
North Dakota State University M
University of Jamestown M,W
University of Mary M

Ohio
Ashland University M
Cleveland State University M
Kent State University M

Lake Erie College M
Lourdes University M
Notre Dame College M
Ohio State University
    Columbus Campus M
Ohio University M
Tiffin University M
University of Findlay M

Oklahoma
Bacone College M
Northeastern Oklahoma Agricultural and
    Mechanical College M
Oklahoma City University M,W
Oklahoma State University M
University of Central Oklahoma M
University of Oklahoma M

Oregon
Clackamas Community College M
Oregon State University M
Southern Oregon University M
Southwestern Oregon Community College M

Pennsylvania
Bloomsburg University of Pennsylvania M
Bucknell University M
Clarion University of Pennsylvania M
Drexel University M
East Stroudsburg University of Pennsylvania M
Edinboro University
    of Pennsylvania M
Gannon University M
Kutztown University of Pennsylvania M
Lehigh University M
Lock Haven University of Pennsylvania M
Mercyhurst University M
Millersville University of Pennsylvania M
Penn State
    University Park M
Seton Hill University M
Shippensburg University of Pennsylvania M
University of Pittsburgh M
University of Pittsburgh
    Johnstown M

Puerto Rico
Inter American University of Puerto Rico
    Aguadilla Campus M
    Bayamon Campus M
    Ponce Campus M,W
University of Puerto Rico
    Arecibo M
    Bayamon University College M
    Humacao M
    Mayaguez M
University of the Sacred Heart M

South Carolina
Anderson University M
The Citadel M
Coker College M
Limestone College M
Newberry College M
Spartanburg Methodist College M

South Dakota
Augusta University
    Augustana University M
Dakota Wesleyan University M
Northern State University M
South Dakota State University M

Tennessee
Carson-Newman University M
Cumberland University M
King University M,W
University of Tennessee
    Chattanooga M

Texas
Wayland Baptist University M,W

Utah
Utah Valley University M

Virginia
George Mason University M
Old Dominion University M
University of Virginia M
Virginia Military Institute M
Virginia Polytechnic Institute and State
    University M

Washington
Highline College M

West Virginia
Alderson-Broaddus University M
West Liberty University M
West Virginia University M

Wisconsin
University of Wisconsin
    Madison M
    Parkside M

Wyoming
Northwest College M
University of Wyoming M
Western Wyoming Community College M

Music/drama scholarships

Alabama
Alabama State University
Bevill State Community College
Birmingham-Southern College
Central Alabama Community College
Chattahoochee Valley Community College
Enterprise State Community College
Faulkner State Community College
Faulkner University
Gadsden State Community College
Huntingdon College
Jacksonville State University
Jefferson State Community College
Judson College
Lurleen B. Wallace Community College
Northeast Alabama Community College
Northwest-Shoals Community College
Samford University
Selma University
Shelton State Community College
Snead State Community College
Talladega College
Troy University
University of Alabama
University of Alabama
    Birmingham
    Huntsville
University of Mobile
University of Montevallo
University of North Alabama
University of South Alabama
University of West Alabama
Wallace State Community College at
    Hanceville

Alaska
Alaska Pacific University
University of Alaska
    Anchorage
    Fairbanks
    Southeast

Arizona
Arizona Christian University
Arizona State University
Arizona Western College
Eastern Arizona College
Glendale Community College
Grand Canyon University
Northern Arizona University
Northland Pioneer College
South Mountain Community College
University of Arizona

Arkansas
Arkansas Northeastern College
Arkansas State University
Arkansas State University
    Beebe
Arkansas Tech University
Black River Technical College
Central Baptist College
Crowley's Ridge College
Ecclesia College
Harding University
Henderson State University
Hendrix College
John Brown University
Lyon College
National Park College
Northwest Arkansas Community College
Ouachita Baptist University
Philander Smith College
Phillips Community College of the University
    of Arkansas

Southern Arkansas University
University of Arkansas
University of Arkansas
    Fort Smith
    Little Rock
    Monticello
    Pine Bluff
University of Central Arkansas
University of the Ozarks
Williams Baptist College

California
American Academy of Dramatic Arts: West
American Jewish University
Azusa Pacific University
Bethesda University of California
Biola University
California Baptist University
California Institute of Integral Studies
California Institute of the Arts
California Lutheran University
California Polytechnic State University: San
    Luis Obispo
California State University
    Bakersfield
    Chico
    Dominguez Hills
    East Bay
    Fresno
    Fullerton
    Long Beach
    Stanislaus
Chapman University
College of the Canyons
College of the Desert
Concordia University Irvine
Dominican University of California
El Camino College
Holy Names University
Hope International University
Irvine Valley College
La Sierra University
Loyola Marymount University
The Master's University
Mendocino College
Mills College
Mount Saint Mary's University
Mount San Jacinto College
Notre Dame de Namur University
Occidental College
Pacific Union College
Pepperdine University
Point Loma Nazarene University
Providence Christian College
Riverside City College
St. Mary's College of California
San Diego Christian College
San Diego State University
San Francisco Conservatory of Music
San Jose State University
Santa Clara University
Santa Rosa Junior College
Shasta Bible College and Graduate School
Simpson University
Sonoma State University
University of California
    Riverside
    San Diego
    Santa Cruz
University of La Verne
University of Redlands
University of San Diego
University of Southern California
University of the Pacific

Vanguard University of Southern California
Westmont College
Whittier College
William Jessup University
Yuba College

Colorado
Adams State University
Arapahoe Community College
Colorado Christian University
Colorado Mesa University
Colorado School of Mines
Colorado State University
Colorado State University
    Pueblo
Community College of Aurora
Fort Lewis College
Naropa University
Northeastern Junior College
Pueblo Community College
Regis University
University of Colorado
    Boulder
    Denver
University of Denver
University of Northern Colorado
Western State Colorado University

Connecticut
Fairfield University
Sacred Heart University
University of Bridgeport
University of Connecticut
University of Hartford
Western Connecticut State University

Delaware
University of Delaware

District of Columbia
American University
Catholic University of America
George Washington University
Howard University

Florida
Ave Maria University
Baptist College of Florida
Barry University
Bethune-Cookman University
Chipola College
College of Central Florida
Daytona State College
Eckerd College
Flagler College
Florida Agricultural and Mechanical University
Florida Atlantic University
Florida College
Florida Gateway College
Florida Gulf Coast University
Florida Institute of Technology
Florida International University
Florida Southern College
Florida SouthWestern State College
Florida State College at Jacksonville
Florida State University
Gulf Coast State College
Hillsborough Community College
Indian River State College
Jacksonville University
Johnson University: Florida
Lynn University
Miami Dade College
North Florida Community College
Palm Beach Atlantic University
Pensacola State College
Rollins College
Santa Fe College
Seminole State College of Florida
South Florida State College
Southeastern University
State College of Florida, Manatee-Sarasota
Stetson University
Tallahassee Community College

University of Florida
University of Miami
University of North Florida
University of South Florida
University of South Florida
    Sarasota-Manatee
University of Tampa
University of West Florida
Warner University

Georgia
Agnes Scott College
Albany State University
Andrew College
Armstrong State University
Berry College
Brenau University
Clark Atlanta University
Clayton State University
Columbus State University
Covenant College
Darton State College
Emmanuel College
Emory University
Fort Valley State University
Georgia College and State University
Georgia Institute of Technology
Georgia Perimeter College
Georgia Southern University
Georgia Southwestern State University
Georgia State University
Gordon State College
Kennesaw State University
LaGrange College
Mercer University
Middle Georgia State University
Morehouse College
Oglethorpe University
Paine College
Piedmont College
Point University
Reinhardt University
Savannah State University
Shorter University
Spelman College
Truett McConnell University
University of North Georgia
University of West Georgia
Valdosta State University
Wesleyan College
Young Harris College

Hawaii
Brigham Young University-Hawaii
Hawaii Pacific University
University of Hawaii
    Hilo
    Manoa

Idaho
Boise Bible College
Boise State University
Brigham Young University-Idaho
Idaho State University
Lewis-Clark State College
North Idaho College
Northwest Nazarene University
University of Idaho

Illinois
Augustana College
Aurora University
Benedictine University
Black Hawk College
Bradley University
Carl Sandburg College
College of DuPage
College of Lake County
Concordia University Chicago
Danville Area Community College
DePaul University
Eastern Illinois University
Elgin Community College
Elmhurst College

Eureka College
Illinois Central College
Illinois College
Illinois State University
Illinois Valley Community College
Illinois Wesleyan University
Judson University
Kishwaukee College
Knox College
Lake Forest College
Lewis University
Lincoln College
Loyola University Chicago
McHenry County College
McKendree University
Millikin University
Monmouth College
Moody Bible Institute
North Central College
North Park University
Northeastern Illinois University
Northern Illinois University
Northwestern University
Oakton Community College
Olivet Nazarene University
Parkland College
Quincy University
Richland Community College
Robert Morris College
    Robert Morris University: Chicago
Rockford University
Saint Xavier University
Shawnee Community College
South Suburban College of Cook County
Southeastern Illinois College
Southern Illinois University Carbondale
Southern Illinois University Edwardsville
Southwestern Illinois College
Spoon River College
Trinity Christian College
Trinity International University
University of Illinois
    Chicago
    Springfield
    Urbana-Champaign
University of St. Francis
VanderCook College of Music
Waubonsee Community College
Western Illinois University
Wheaton College

Indiana
Anderson University
Ball State University
Bethel College
Butler University
Calumet College of St. Joseph
DePauw University
Franklin College
Goshen College
Grace College
Huntington University
Indiana State University
Indiana University
    Bloomington
    Purdue University Fort Wayne
    Southeast
Indiana Wesleyan University
Manchester University
Marian University
Purdue University
Saint Mary's College
Taylor University
Trine University
University of Evansville
University of Indianapolis
University of Saint Francis
University of Southern Indiana
Valparaiso University
Vincennes University
Wabash College

Iowa
Briar Cliff University
Buena Vista University
Central College
Clarke University
Coe College
Cornell College
Dordt College
Drake University
Ellsworth Community College
Faith Baptist Bible College and Theological
    Seminary
Graceland University
Grand View University
Iowa Central Community College
Iowa State University
Iowa Wesleyan College
Iowa Western Community College
Kirkwood Community College
Luther College
Morningside College
Mount Mercy University
North Iowa Area Community College
Northwestern College
St. Ambrose University
Simpson College
Southwestern Community College
University of Dubuque
University of Iowa
University of Northern Iowa
Waldorf University
Wartburg College
Western Iowa Tech Community College
William Penn University

Kansas
Allen County Community College
Baker University
Barclay College
Benedictine College
Bethany College
Bethel College
Butler Community College
Central Christian College of Kansas
Coffeyville Community College
Colby Community College
Cowley County Community College
Dodge City Community College
Emporia State University
Fort Hays State University
Friends University
Garden City Community College
Hesston College
Highland Community College
Hutchinson Community College
Independence Community College
Kansas City Kansas Community College
Kansas State University
Kansas Wesleyan University
Manhattan Christian College
McPherson College
MidAmerica Nazarene University
Neosho County Community College
Newman University
Ottawa University
Pittsburg State University
Pratt Community College
Southwestern College
Sterling College
Tabor College
University of Kansas
University of St. Mary
Washburn University
Wichita State University

Kentucky
Asbury University
Ashland Community and Technical College
Bellarmine University
Brescia University
Campbellsville University
Centre College
Eastern Kentucky University

Georgetown College
Kentucky Christian University
Kentucky Mountain Bible College
Kentucky State University
Kentucky Wesleyan College
Morehead State University
Murray State University
Northern Kentucky University
Owensboro Community and Technical College
Thomas More College
Transylvania University
Union College
University of Kentucky
University of Louisville
University of the Cumberlands
Western Kentucky University

Louisiana
Bossier Parish Community College
Centenary College of Louisiana
Delgado Community College
Dillard University
Grambling State University
Louisiana College
Louisiana State University and Agricultural and
    Mechanical College
Louisiana Tech University
Loyola University New Orleans
McNeese State University
Nicholls State University
Northwestern State University
Southeastern Louisiana University
Tulane University
University of New Orleans
Xavier University of Louisiana

Maine
University of Maine
University of Maine
    Augusta
    Farmington
University of Southern Maine

Maryland
Bowie State University
Goucher College
Hood College
Johns Hopkins University: Peabody
    Conservatory of Music
Montgomery College
Notre Dame of Maryland University
Salisbury University
Towson University
University of Maryland
    Baltimore County
    College Park
    Eastern Shore
Washington College

Massachusetts
Anna Maria College
Assumption College
Berklee College of Music
Boston Conservatory
Boston University
Bristol Community College
Cape Cod Community College
Dean College
Emerson College
Endicott College
Gordon College
Hampshire College
Holyoke Community College
Massachusetts College of Liberal Arts
Merrimack College
Mount Wachusett Community College
New England Conservatory of Music
North Shore Community College
Northpoint Bible College
Springfield College
University of Massachusetts
    Amherst
    Lowell
Western New England University

Michigan
Adrian College
Albion College
Alma College
Alpena Community College
Andrews University
Aquinas College
Calvin College
Central Michigan University
Concordia University
Cornerstone University
Eastern Michigan University
Ferris State University
Gogebic Community College
Grace Bible College
Grand Valley State University
Great Lakes Christian College
Hillsdale College
Hope College
Kalamazoo College
Kellogg Community College
Kuyper College
Macomb Community College
Madonna University
Marygrove College
Michigan State University
Monroe County Community College
Mott Community College
Northern Michigan University
Oakland University
Olivet College
Rochester College
Saginaw Valley State University
Schoolcraft College
Southwestern Michigan College
Spring Arbor University
University of Michigan
University of Michigan
    Flint
Wayne State University
Western Michigan University

Minnesota
Augsburg College
Bemidji State University
Bethany Lutheran College
Bethel University
College of St. Benedict
College of St. Scholastica
Concordia College: Moorhead
Concordia University St. Paul
Crossroads College
Crown College
Gustavus Adolphus College
Hamline University
McNally Smith College of Music
Minnesota State Community and Technical
    College
Minnesota State University
    Mankato
    Moorhead
Normandale Community College
North Central University
Saint Cloud State University
St. John's University
St. Mary's University of Minnesota
St. Olaf College
Southwest Minnesota State University
University of Minnesota
    Crookston
    Duluth
    Twin Cities
University of Northwestern - St. Paul
University of St. Thomas
Winona State University

Mississippi
Belhaven University
Blue Mountain College
Copiah-Lincoln Community College
Delta State University
East Central Community College
East Mississippi Community College

Hinds Community College
Itawamba Community College
Jackson State University
Jones County Junior College
Meridian Community College
Millsaps College
Mississippi College
Mississippi Gulf Coast Community College
Mississippi State University
Mississippi University for Women
Northeast Mississippi Community College
Pearl River Community College
Rust College
Tougaloo College
University of Mississippi
University of Mississippi
    University of Southern Mississippi
William Carey University

Missouri
Avila University
Calvary Bible College and Theological
   Seminary
Central Methodist University
College of the Ozarks
Columbia College
Cottey College
Crowder College
Culver-Stockton College
Drury University
East Central College
Evangel University
Fontbonne University
Hannibal-LaGrange University
Harris-Stowe State University
Jefferson College
Lincoln University
Lindenwood University
Maryville University of Saint Louis
Mineral Area College
Missouri Baptist University
Missouri Southern State University
Missouri State University
Missouri University of Science and Technology
Missouri Western State University
Moberly Area Community College
Northwest Missouri State University
Park University
Rockhurst University
St. Charles Community College
St. Louis Community College
Saint Louis University
Southeast Missouri State University
Southwest Baptist University
State Fair Community College
Stephens College
Truman State University
University of Central Missouri
University of Missouri
   Columbia
   Kansas City
   St. Louis
Webster University
Westminster College
William Jewell College
William Woods University

Montana
Carroll College
Dawson Community College
Montana State University
Montana State University
   Billings
   Great Falls College
Montana Tech of the University of Montana
Rocky Mountain College
University of Great Falls
University of Montana

Nebraska
Central Community College
Chadron State College
College of Saint Mary

Concordia University
Creighton University
Doane University
Grace University
Hastings College
Mid-Plains Community College
Midland University
Nebraska Wesleyan University
Northeast Community College
Peru State College
University of Nebraska
   Kearney
   Lincoln
   Omaha
Wayne State College
Western Nebraska Community College
York College

Nevada
Truckee Meadows Community College
University of Nevada
   Las Vegas

New Hampshire
Keene State College
New England College
Plymouth State University
Saint Anselm College
Southern New Hampshire University
University of New Hampshire

New Jersey
Caldwell University
The College of New Jersey
Drew University
Kean University
New Jersey Institute of Technology
Rowan University
Rutgers, The State University of New Jersey
   Camden Campus
   New Brunswick/Piscataway Campus
   Newark Campus
Seton Hall University
Stevens Institute of Technology
William Paterson University of New Jersey

New Mexico
Eastern New Mexico University
New Mexico Highlands University
New Mexico Junior College
New Mexico Military Institute
New Mexico State University
Santa Fe University of Art and Design
University of New Mexico
Western New Mexico University

New York
Adelphi University
Alfred University
Canisius College
City University of New York
   City College
   College of Staten Island
College of New Rochelle
College of Saint Rose
Concordia College
Corning Community College
Eastman School of Music of the University of
   Rochester
Eugene Lang College The New School for
   Liberal Arts
Five Towns College
Hartwick College
Hobart and William Smith Colleges
Hofstra University
Houghton College
Iona College
Ithaca College
Jamestown Community College
Juilliard School
Long Island University
   LIU Brooklyn
   LIU Post
Manhattan School of Music

Manhattanville College
Marist College
Marymount Manhattan College
Molloy College
Monroe Community College
Nazareth College
The New School College of Performing Arts
Niagara University
Nyack College
Pace University
Pace University: Pleasantville/Briarcliff
Parsons the New School for Design
   Parsons The New School for Design
Rensselaer Polytechnic Institute
The Sage Colleges
Saint Bonaventure University
St. John's University
St. Thomas Aquinas College
Skidmore College
Suffolk County Community College
SUNY
   College at Brockport
   College at Cortland
   College at Fredonia
   College at Geneseo
   College at New Paltz
   College at Oneonta
   College at Plattsburgh
   College at Potsdam
   College at Purchase
   College of Technology at Alfred
   University at Binghamton
   University at Buffalo
   University at Stony Brook
University of Rochester
Wagner College

North Carolina
Appalachian State University
Barton College
Brevard College
Campbell University
Catawba College
Catawba Valley Community College
Chowan University
College of the Albemarle
Davidson College
Duke University
East Carolina University
Elon University
Fayetteville State University
Gardner-Webb University
Greensboro College
High Point University
Isothermal Community College
Johnson C. Smith University
Lees-McRae College
Lenoir-Rhyne University
Livingstone College
Louisburg College
Meredith College
Methodist University
Mid-Atlantic Christian University
Montreat College
North Carolina Central University
Pfeiffer University
Queens University of Charlotte
St. Andrews University
Saint Augustine's University
Salem College
Shaw University
Southeastern Community College
University of Mount Olive
University of North Carolina
   Asheville
   Chapel Hill
   Greensboro
   Pembroke
   School of the Arts
   Wilmington
Vance-Granville Community College
Wake Forest University
Western Carolina University

Wilkes Community College
William Peace University
Wingate University

North Dakota
Bismarck State College
Dickinson State University
Lake Region State College
Mayville State University
Minot State University
North Dakota State College of Science
Trinity Bible College
University of Jamestown
University of Mary
Valley City State University
Williston State College

Ohio
Ashland University
Baldwin Wallace University
Bluffton University
Bowling Green State University
Bowling Green State University: Firelands
   College
Capital University
Case Western Reserve University
Cedarville University
Central State University
Cincinnati Christian University
Cleveland Institute of Music
Cleveland State University
College of Wooster
Cuyahoga Community College
Defiance College
Denison University
God's Bible School and College
Heidelberg University
Kent State University
Kent State University
   Ashtabula
   East Liverpool
   Geauga
   Salem
   Stark
   Trumbull
   Tuscarawas
Kenyon College
Lake Erie College
Lakeland Community College
Lorain County Community College
Lourdes University
Malone University
Marietta College
Miami University
   Oxford
Mount St. Joseph University
Mount Vernon Nazarene University
Muskingum University
Oberlin College
Ohio Northern University
Ohio State University
   Agricultural Technical Institute
   Columbus Campus
   Lima Campus
   Mansfield Campus
   Marion Campus
   Newark Campus
Ohio University
Otterbein University
Pontifical College Josephinum
Sinclair Community College
Southern State Community College
Tiffin University
University of Akron
University of Akron: Wayne College
University of Cincinnati
University of Dayton
University of Findlay
University of Mount Union
University of Rio Grande
University of Toledo
Urbana University
Walsh University

Wittenberg University
Wright State University
Wright State University: Lake Campus
Xavier University

Oklahoma

Cameron University
Carl Albert State College
Eastern Oklahoma State College
Langston University
Mid-America Christian University
Northeastern Oklahoma Agricultural and
   Mechanical College
Northeastern State University
Northern Oklahoma College
Northwestern Oklahoma State University
Oklahoma Baptist University
Oklahoma Christian University
Oklahoma City Community College
Oklahoma City University
Oklahoma Panhandle State University
Oklahoma State University
Oklahoma Wesleyan University
Oral Roberts University
Rogers State University
St. Gregory's University
Seminole State College
Southeastern Oklahoma State University
Southwestern Christian University
Southwestern Oklahoma State University
Tulsa Community College
University of Central Oklahoma
University of Oklahoma
University of Science and Arts of Oklahoma
University of Tulsa
Western Oklahoma State College

Oregon

Blue Mountain Community College
Clackamas Community College
Concordia University
Corban University
Eastern Oregon University
George Fox University
Lane Community College
Lewis & Clark College
Linfield College
Linn-Benton Community College
New Hope Christian College
Northwest Christian University
Oregon College of Art & Craft
Pacific University
Portland State University
Southwestern Oregon Community College
Treasure Valley Community College
University of Oregon
University of Portland
Warner Pacific College
Western Oregon University
Willamette University

Pennsylvania

Arcadia University
Berks Technical Institute
Bloomsburg University of Pennsylvania
Bucknell University
Bucks County Community College
Cairn University
California University of Pennsylvania
Carnegie Mellon University
Chatham University
Clarion University of Pennsylvania
Clarks Summit University
Delaware Valley University
DeSales University
Dickinson College
Drexel University
Duquesne University
East Stroudsburg University of Pennsylvania
Eastern University
Edinboro University
   Pennsylvania
Elizabethtown College

Gannon University
Geneva College
Gettysburg College
Grove City College
Immaculata University
Indiana University of Pennsylvania
Juniata College
Kutztown University of Pennsylvania
Lancaster Bible College
Lebanon Valley College
Lehigh University
Lincoln University
Lock Haven University of Pennsylvania
Lycoming College
Mansfield University of Pennsylvania
Marywood University
Mercyhurst University
Messiah College
Moravian College
Mount Aloysius College
Muhlenberg College
Northampton Community College
Point Park University
St. Francis University
Saint Joseph's University
St. Vincent College
Seton Hill University
Slippery Rock University of Pennsylvania
Susquehanna University
Temple University
Thiel College
University of the Arts
University of Valley Forge
Ursinus College
Valley Forge Military College
West Chester University of Pennsylvania
Westminster College
Widener University
Wilkes University
York College of Pennsylvania

Puerto Rico

Colegio de Cinematografia Artes y Television
Humacao Community College
Inter American University of Puerto Rico
   Ponce Campus
Pontifical Catholic University of Puerto Rico
Universidad Politecnica de Puerto Rico
University of Puerto Rico
   Aguadilla
   Humacao
   Mayaguez

Rhode Island

Providence College
Rhode Island College
University of Rhode Island

South Carolina

Allen University
Anderson University
The Citadel
Clemson University
Coker College
College of Charleston
Columbia College
Columbia International University
Converse College
Erskine College
Francis Marion University
Furman University
Lander University
Limestone College
Morris College
Newberry College
North Greenville University
Presbyterian College
Southern Wesleyan University
University of South Carolina
   Aiken
   Columbia
Winthrop University
Wofford College

South Dakota

Augusta University
   Augustana University
Dakota State University
Dakota Wesleyan University
Mount Marty College
South Dakota State University
University of Sioux Falls
University of South Dakota

Tennessee

Austin Peay State University
Belmont University
Bethel University
Carson-Newman University
Christian Brothers University
Cumberland University
Dyersburg State Community College
East Tennessee State University
Fisk University
Freed-Hardeman University
Jackson State Community College
Johnson University
King University
Lee University
LeMoyne-Owen College
Lincoln Memorial University
Martin Methodist College
Maryville College
Milligan College
Motlow State Community College
Northeast State Community College
Pellissippi State Community College
Rhodes College
Roane State Community College
Southern Adventist University
Southwest Tennessee Community College
Tennessee Technological University
Trevecca Nazarene University
Union University
University of Memphis
University of Tennessee
   Chattanooga
   Knoxville
   Martin
Vanderbilt University
Volunteer State Community College
Walters State Community College
Welch College

Texas

Abilene Christian University
Angelina College
Angelo State University
Austin College
Baylor University
Brazosport College
Brookhaven College
Cisco College
Clarendon College
College of the Mainland
Collin County Community College District
Concordia University Texas
Dallas Baptist University
East Texas Baptist University
Frank Phillips College
Galveston College
Grayson College
Hardin-Simmons University
Hill College
Houston Baptist University
Howard College
Howard Payne University
Huston-Tillotson University
Jacksonville College
Kilgore College
Lee College
McMurry University
Midland College
Midwestern State University
Odessa College
Our Lady of the Lake University of San
   Antonio

Panola College
Paris Junior College
Rice University
Richland College
St. Edward's University
St. Mary's University
Sam Houston State University
San Jacinto College
Schreiner University
Southern Methodist University
Southwestern Adventist University
Southwestern Christian College
Stephen F. Austin State University
Sul Ross State University
Tarleton State University
Temple College
Texarkana College
Texas A&M International University
Texas A&M University
Texas A&M University
   Commerce
   Corpus Christi
   Texarkana
Texas Christian University
Texas College
Texas Lutheran University
Texas State University
Texas Tech University
Texas Wesleyan University
Texas Woman's University
Trinity University
Tyler Junior College
University of Dallas
University of Houston
University of Mary Hardin-Baylor
University of St. Thomas
University of Texas
   Arlington
   Austin
   El Paso
   the Permian Basin
   San Antonio
   Tyler
University Of Texas Rio Grande Valley
University of the Incarnate Word
Vernon College
Victoria College
Wayland Baptist University
West Texas A&M University
Western Texas College
Wharton County Junior College

Utah

Brigham Young University
Dixie State University
Salt Lake Community College
Snow College
Southern Utah University
University of Utah
Utah State University
Weber State University
Westminster College

Vermont

Bennington College
Castleton University
Goddard College
Johnson State College
Landmark College
Saint Michael's College
University of Vermont

Virginia

Averett University
Bluefield College
Bridgewater College
Christopher Newport University
College of William and Mary
Emory & Henry College
George Mason University
Hampden-Sydney College
Hampton University

Hollins University
James Madison University
Liberty University
Longwood University
Lynchburg College
Marymount University
Norfolk State University
Old Dominion University
Patrick Henry College
Radford University
Randolph College
Roanoke College
Shenandoah University
Southern Virginia University
Sweet Briar College
University of Mary Washington
University of Richmond
University of Virginia
University of Virginia's College at Wise
Virginia Commonwealth University
Virginia Military Institute
Virginia Polytechnic Institute and State
    University
Virginia State University

Washington

Central Washington University
Centralia College
Clark College
Cornish College of the Arts
DigiPen Institute of Technology
Eastern Washington University
Everett Community College
Gonzaga University
Grays Harbor College
Northwest University
Pacific Lutheran University
Pierce College
Saint Martin's University
Seattle Pacific University
Seattle University
University of Puget Sound
University of Washington
Walla Walla Community College
Walla Walla University
Washington State University
Western Washington University
Whitman College
Whitworth University

West Virginia

Alderson-Broaddus University
Bethany College
Davis and Elkins College
Fairmont State University
Glenville State College
Marshall University
Ohio Valley University
Shepherd University
University of Charleston
West Liberty University
West Virginia University
West Virginia University Institute of
    Technology
West Virginia Wesleyan College
Wheeling Jesuit University

Wisconsin

Beloit College
Cardinal Stritch University
Carroll University
Carthage College
Concordia University Wisconsin
Edgewood College
Lawrence University
Marquette University
Mount Mary University
Northland College
Ripon College
St. Norbert College
Silver Lake College of the Holy Family
University of Wisconsin
    Baraboo/Sauk County

Eau Claire
Fond du Lac
Green Bay
Madison
Manitowoc
Milwaukee
Oshkosh
Parkside
Richland
River Falls
Rock County
Sheboygan
Stevens Point
Superior
Waukesha
Whitewater
Viterbo University
Wisconsin Lutheran College

Wyoming

Casper College
Central Wyoming College
Eastern Wyoming College
Laramie County Community College
Northwest College
Sheridan College
University of Wyoming
Western Wyoming Community College

ROTC scholarships

Air Force ROTC

Alabama
Alabama State University
Auburn University
Auburn University at Montgomery
Birmingham-Southern College
Bishop State Community College
Faulkner University
Huntingdon College
Jefferson State Community College
Marion Military Institute
Miles College
Samford University
Shelton State Community College
Spring Hill College
Stillman College
Troy University
Tuskegee University
University of Alabama
University of Alabama
    Birmingham
University of Mobile
University of Montevallo
University of South Alabama
University of West Alabama

Alaska
Alaska Pacific University
University of Alaska
    Anchorage

Arizona
Arizona Christian University
Arizona State University
Coconino County Community College
DeVry University
    Phoenix
Embry-Riddle Aeronautical University
    Prescott Campus
Estrella Mountain Community College
GateWay Community College
Mesa Community College
Northern Arizona University
Phoenix College
University of Arizona
Yavapai College

Arkansas
John Brown University
Northwest Arkansas Community College
University of Arkansas
University of Arkansas
    Fort Smith

California
Azusa Pacific University
Biola University
California Baptist University
California Institute of Technology
California Lutheran University
California Maritime Academy
California State University
    Dominguez Hills
    Fresno
    Los Angeles
    Northridge
    Sacramento
    San Bernardino
    San Marcos
Canada College
Chabot College
Chapman University
Claremont McKenna College

College of the Sequoias
Cuyamaca College
De Anza College
Foothill College
Fresno City College
Harvey Mudd College
Holy Names University
Irvine Valley College
Los Angeles Mission College
Loyola Marymount University
The Master's University
Menlo College
Mission College
Mount San Antonio College
National University
Notre Dame de Namur University
Occidental College
Ohlone College
Pepperdine University
Pitzer College
Point Loma Nazarene University
Pomona College
Riverside City College
Sacramento City College
St. Mary's College of California
Samuel Merritt University
San Diego Christian College
San Diego City College
San Diego State University
San Francisco State University
San Jose State University
Santa Clara University
Scripps College
Solano Community College
Sonoma State University
Stanford University
University of California
    Berkeley
    Davis
    Irvine
    Los Angeles
    Riverside
    Santa Barbara
    Santa Cruz
University of Redlands
University of San Diego
University of San Francisco
University of Southern California
University of the Pacific
Vanguard University of Southern California
West Coast University: Orange County
West Valley College
Westmont College
William Jessup University

Colorado
Arapahoe Community College
Colorado Christian University
Colorado School of Mines
Colorado State University
Front Range Community College
Metropolitan State University of Denver
Red Rocks Community College
Regis University
University of Colorado
    Boulder
    Denver
University of Denver
University of Northern Colorado

Connecticut
Capital Community College
Central Connecticut State University
Eastern Connecticut State University
Fairfield University

Quinnipiac University
Sacred Heart University
Southern Connecticut State University
Tunxis Community College
University of Connecticut
University of Hartford
University of New Haven
Wesleyan University
Western Connecticut State University
Yale University

Delaware
Delaware State University
University of Delaware
Wilmington University

District of Columbia
American University
Catholic University of America
George Washington University
Georgetown University
Howard University
Trinity Washington University
University of the District of Columbia

Florida
Barry University
Bethune-Cookman University
Broward College
Daytona State College
Eastern Florida State College
Eckerd College
Embry-Riddle Aeronautical University
Florida Agricultural and Mechanical University
Florida Atlantic University
Florida College
Florida International University
Florida Southern College
Florida State University
Hillsborough Community College
Lynn University
Miami Dade College
Polk State College
Saint Leo University
Santa Fe College
Tallahassee Community College
University of Central Florida
University of Florida
University of Miami
University of South Florida
University of Tampa
University of West Florida
Valencia College

Georgia
Agnes Scott College
Clayton State University
Emory University
Georgia Institute of Technology
Georgia State University
Kennesaw State University
Morehouse College
Oglethorpe University
Oxford College of Emory University
Spelman College
University of Georgia
University of West Georgia
Valdosta State University

Hawaii
Brigham Young University-Hawaii
Chaminade University of Honolulu
Hawaii Pacific University
University of Hawaii
    Honolulu Community College
    Manoa
    West Oahu

Idaho
Lewis-Clark State College
University of Idaho

Illinois
Elmhurst College
Illinois Institute of Technology

John A. Logan College
Lewis University
Lincoln Land Community College
Loyola University Chicago
McKendree University
North Central College
North Park University
Northeastern Illinois University
Northwestern University
Parkland College
Saint Xavier University
Shawnee Community College
Shimer College
Southern Illinois University Carbondale
Southern Illinois University Edwardsville
Southwestern Illinois College
University of Chicago
University of Illinois
    Chicago
    Urbana-Champaign
Wheaton College

Indiana
Bethel College
Butler University
DePauw University
Holy Cross College
Indiana State University
Indiana University
    Bloomington
    Purdue University Indianapolis
    South Bend
    Southeast
Purdue University
Rose-Hulman Institute of Technology
Saint Mary's College
Trine University
University of Notre Dame
Valparaiso University
Vincennes University

Iowa
Coe College
Drake University
Grand View University
Hawkeye Community College
Iowa State University
Iowa Western Community College
University of Iowa

Kansas
Baker University
Kansas State University
Manhattan Christian College
MidAmerica Nazarene University
University of Kansas
University of St. Mary
Washburn University

Kentucky
Asbury University
Bellarmine University
Centre College
Georgetown College
Kentucky State University
Midway College
Northern Kentucky University
Spalding University
Thomas More College
Transylvania University
University of Kentucky
University of Louisville
Western Kentucky University

Louisiana
Dillard University
Grambling State University
Louisiana State University and Agricultural and
    Mechanical College
Louisiana Tech University
Loyola University New Orleans
Our Lady of the Lake College
Southern University
    New Orleans

Southern University and Agricultural and
    Mechanical College
Tulane University
University of Holy Cross
University of New Orleans
Xavier University of Louisiana

Maine
University of Maine
    Augusta
University of Southern Maine

Maryland
Anne Arundel Community College
Bowie State University
Goucher College
Johns Hopkins University
Loyola University Maryland
Prince George's Community College
Salisbury University
Stevenson University
Towson University
University of Maryland
    Baltimore County
    College Park

Massachusetts
American International College
Amherst College
Anna Maria College
Assumption College
Bay Path University
Becker College
Bentley University
Boston College
Boston University
Brandeis University
Bridgewater State University
Clark University
College of the Holy Cross
Elms College
Harvard College
Holyoke Community College
Massachusetts Institute of Technology
MCPHS University
Merrimack College
Middlesex Community College
Mount Holyoke College
Nichols College
Northeastern University
Pine Manor College
Quinsigamond Community College
Salem State University
Smith College
Springfield College
Tufts University
University of Massachusetts
    Amherst
    Boston
    Lowell
Wellesley College
Wentworth Institute of Technology
Western New England University
Westfield State University
Williams College
Worcester Polytechnic Institute
Worcester State University

Michigan
Central Michigan University
Concordia University
Eastern Michigan University
Finlandia University
Lansing Community College
Lawrence Technological University
Michigan State University
Michigan Technological University
Oakland University
Olivet College
Spring Arbor University
University of Michigan
University of Michigan
    Dearborn
    Flint
Wayne State University

Minnesota
Anoka-Ramsey Community College
Augsburg College
Bethel University
Century College
College of St. Scholastica
Concordia College: Moorhead
Concordia University St. Paul
Hamline University
Inver Hills Community College
Macalester College
Minnesota State University
    Moorhead
North Central University
North Hennepin Community College
St. Catherine University
University of Minnesota
    Crookston
    Duluth
    Twin Cities
University of Northwestern - St. Paul
University of St. Thomas

Mississippi
Belhaven University
East Mississippi Community College
Jackson State University
Millsaps College
Mississippi College
Mississippi State University
Mississippi University for Women
Northwest Mississippi Community College
Pearl River Community College
University of Mississippi
University of Mississippi
    University of Southern Mississippi
William Carey University

Missouri
Central Methodist University
Columbia College
Fontbonne University
Lindenwood University
Missouri University of Science and Technology
Saint Louis University
Southeast Missouri State University
Stephens College
University of Central Missouri
University of Missouri
    Columbia
    St. Louis
Washington University in St. Louis
Webster University
Westminster College

Montana
Montana State University

Nebraska
Bellevue University
Clarkson College
College of Saint Mary
Concordia University
Creighton University
Doane University
Grace University
Nebraska Methodist College of Nursing and
    Allied Health
Nebraska Wesleyan University
University of Nebraska
    Lincoln
    Medical Center
    Omaha
York College

Nevada
Nevada State College
University of Nevada
    Las Vegas

New Hampshire
Colby-Sawyer College
Franklin Pierce University
Keene State College

New England College
Plymouth State University
Rivier University
University of New Hampshire

New Jersey
Brookdale Community College
The College of New Jersey
Fairleigh Dickinson University
    College at Florham
    Metropolitan Campus
Felician University
Kean University
Monmouth University
New Jersey Institute of Technology
Princeton University
Ramapo College of New Jersey
Raritan Valley Community College
Rutgers, The State University of New Jersey
    Camden Campus
    New Brunswick/Piscataway Campus
    Newark Campus
Stevens Institute of Technology
Union County College
William Paterson University of New Jersey

New Mexico
Central New Mexico Community College
Dona Ana Community College of New Mexico
    State University
National American University
    Albuquerque
New Mexico State University
New Mexico State University
    Alamogordo
University of New Mexico

New York
Adelphi University
Barnard College
Cazenovia College
City University of New York
    Queens College
Clarkson University
College of Mount St. Vincent
College of Saint Rose
Columbia University
Columbia University
    School of General Studies
Cornell University
Elmira College
Fordham University
Hamilton College
Hobart and William Smith Colleges
Hudson Valley Community College
Iona College
Ithaca College
Le Moyne College
Manhattan College
Maria College
Mercy College
Mesivta Torah Vodaath Seminary
Monroe Community College
Nazareth College
New York Institute of Technology
New York University
Onondaga Community College
Pace University
Pace University: Pleasantville/Briarcliff
Rensselaer Polytechnic Institute
Rochester Institute of Technology
The Sage Colleges
St. Francis College
St. John Fisher College
St. Lawrence University
St. Thomas Aquinas College
Sarah Lawrence College
Schenectady County Community College
Siena College
Skidmore College
SUNY
    College at Brockport
    College at Cortland

    College at Geneseo
    College at Old Westbury
    College at Oswego
    College at Potsdam
    College of Agriculture and Technology at
        Morrisville
    College of Environmental Science and
        Forestry
    College of Technology at Canton
    Farmingdale State College
    University at Albany
    University at Binghamton
    University at Stony Brook
SUNY Polytechnic Institute
Syracuse University
Union College
United States Merchant Marine Academy
University of Rochester
Utica College
Vaughn College of Aeronautics and Technology

North Carolina
Bennett College for Women
Catawba College
Catawba Valley Community College
Davidson College
Duke University
East Carolina University
Elon University
Fayetteville State University
Gardner-Webb University
Greensboro College
High Point University
Meredith College
Methodist University
North Carolina Agricultural and Technical State
    University
North Carolina Central University
North Carolina State University
Randolph Community College
University of Mount Olive
University of North Carolina
    Chapel Hill
    Charlotte
    Greensboro
    Pembroke
William Peace University
Wingate University

North Dakota
Mayville State University
North Dakota State University
University of North Dakota

Ohio
Ashland University
Baldwin Wallace University
Bowling Green State University
Capital University
Case Western Reserve University
Cedarville University
Central State University
Cleveland Institute of Art
Cleveland State University
Columbus State Community College
Cuyahoga Community College
Franciscan University of Steubenville
Heidelberg University
Hiram College
Hocking College
John Carroll University
Kent State University
Kent State University
    East Liverpool
    Salem
    Stark
    Trumbull
    Tuscarawas
Lourdes University
Miami University
    Hamilton
    Middletown
    Oxford

Mount St. Joseph University
Ohio Christian University
Ohio Dominican University
Ohio Northern University
Ohio State University
   Agricultural Technical Institute
   Columbus Campus
   Lima Campus
   Mansfield Campus
   Marion Campus
   Newark Campus
Ohio University
Ohio University
   Lancaster Campus
Ohio Wesleyan University
Otterbein University
Sinclair Community College
Tiffin University
University of Akron
University of Akron: Wayne College
University of Cincinnati
University of Cincinnati
   Blue Ash College
University of Dayton
University of Findlay
University of Mount Union
University of Toledo
Wilberforce University
Wittenberg University
Wright State University
Xavier University
Youngstown State University

Oklahoma
Northeastern Oklahoma Agricultural and
   Mechanical College
Oklahoma Baptist University
Oklahoma Christian University
Oklahoma City University
Oklahoma State University
Oral Roberts University
Rose State College
St. Gregory's University
Southern Nazarene University
University of Oklahoma
University of Tulsa

Oregon
Concordia University
Corban University
George Fox University
Linfield College
Linn-Benton Community College
Oregon State University
Pacific University
Portland State University
University of Oregon
University of Portland
Warner Pacific College
Western Oregon University
Willamette University

Pennsylvania
Bloomsburg University of Pennsylvania
Bryn Athyn College
Bryn Mawr College
Cabrini University
Cairn University
Carlow University
Carnegie Mellon University
Chatham University
Clarks Summit University
Drexel University
Duquesne University
Eastern University
Keystone College
King's College
La Roche College
La Salle University
Lincoln University
Marywood University
Misericordia University
Neumann University

Penn State
   Abington
   Altoona
   Brandywine
   Hazleton
   New Kensington
   University Park
   Wilkes-Barre
   Worthington Scranton
Point Park University
Robert Morris University
Rosemont College
Saint Joseph's University
St. Vincent College
Swarthmore College
Temple University
Thomas Jefferson University
University of Pennsylvania
University of Pittsburgh
University of Pittsburgh
   Greensburg
University of Scranton
University of the Sciences
Valley Forge Military College
Villanova University
Washington & Jefferson College
West Chester University of Pennsylvania
Widener University
Wilkes University

Puerto Rico
Bayamon Central University
Inter American University of Puerto Rico
   Aguadilla Campus
   Fajardo Campus
   Metropolitan Campus
   San German Campus
Pontifical Catholic University of Puerto Rico
Turabo University
Universidad Metropolitana
Universidad Politecnica de Puerto Rico
University of Puerto Rico
   Mayaguez
   Rio Piedras

Rhode Island
Brown University

South Carolina
Anderson University
Benedict College
Charleston Southern University
The Citadel
Claflin University
Clemson University
College of Charleston
Southern Wesleyan University
Tri-County Technical College
University of South Carolina
   Columbia
   Salkehatchie
Winthrop University

South Dakota
Augusta University
   Augustana University
Dakota State University
South Dakota State University
University of Sioux Falls

Tennessee
Austin Peay State University
Belmont University
Christian Brothers University
LeMoyne-Owen College
Lipscomb University
Middle Tennessee State University
Rhodes College
Southwest Tennessee Community College
Tennessee State University
Tennessee Technological University
Tennessee Wesleyan College
University of Memphis

University of Tennessee
   Knoxville
Vanderbilt University
Welch College

Texas
Alvin Community College
Angelo State University
Austin Community College
Baylor University
College of the Mainland
Collin County Community College District
Concordia University Texas
Dallas Baptist University
Houston Baptist University
Houston Community College System
Lamar University
Lone Star College System
Lubbock Christian University
McLennan Community College
Midwestern State University
North Central Texas College
Prairie View A&M University
Rice University
St. Edward's University
St. Mary's University
San Antonio College
San Jacinto College
Southern Methodist University
Southwestern University
Tarrant County College
Texas A&M University
Texas A&M University
   Commerce
Texas Christian University
Texas Lutheran University
Texas State University
Texas Tech University
Texas Wesleyan University
Texas Woman's University
Trinity University
University of Dallas
University of Houston
University of Houston
   Downtown
   Victoria
University of Mary Hardin-Baylor
University of North Texas
University of St. Thomas
University of Texas
   Arlington
   Austin
   Dallas
   San Antonio
University of the Incarnate Word
Wayland Baptist University
Weatherford College

Utah
Brigham Young University
LDS Business College
Salt Lake Community College
University of Utah
Utah State University
Utah Valley University
Weber State University
Westminster College

Vermont
Lyndon State College
Norwich University
Saint Michael's College

Virginia
George Mason University
James Madison University
Liberty University
Mary Baldwin University
Marymount University
Piedmont Virginia Community College
University of Virginia
Virginia Military Institute
Virginia Polytechnic Institute and State
   University

Washington
Central Washington University
Clark College
Highline College
Saint Martin's University
Seattle Pacific University
Seattle University
South Puget Sound Community College
Spokane Community College
University of Washington
University of Washington Bothell
University of Washington Tacoma
Washington State University

West Virginia
Fairmont State University
Shepherd University
West Virginia University

Wisconsin
Alverno College
Carroll University
Carthage College
Edgewood College
Maranathan Baptist University
   Maranatha Baptist University
Marquette University
Milwaukee School of Engineering
University of Wisconsin
   Madison
   Milwaukee
   Parkside
   Stout
   Superior
   Whitewater
Wisconsin Lutheran College

Wyoming
Laramie County Community College
University of Wyoming

Army ROTC

Alabama
Alabama Agricultural and Mechanical
   University
Alabama State University
Auburn University
Auburn University at Montgomery
Birmingham-Southern College
Bishop State Community College
Faulkner University
Gadsden State Community College
Huntingdon College
Jacksonville State University
Jefferson State Community College
Judson College
Marion Military Institute
Miles College
Samford University
Shelton State Community College
Southern Union State Community College
Spring Hill College
Stillman College
Talladega College
Troy University
Tuskegee University
University of Alabama
University of Alabama
   Birmingham
   Huntsville
University of Mobile
University of Montevallo
University of North Alabama
University of South Alabama

Alaska
University of Alaska
   Anchorage
   Fairbanks

Arizona
Arizona State University
Embry-Riddle Aeronautical University
    Prescott Campus
GateWay Community College
Grand Canyon University
Mesa Community College
Northern Arizona University
Paradise Valley Community College
Phoenix College
Southwest University of Visual Arts
University of Arizona
Yavapai College

Arkansas
Arkansas State University
Arkansas State University
    Beebe
Arkansas Tech University
Central Baptist College
College of the Ouachitas
Harding University
Henderson State University
Hendrix College
John Brown University
Northwest Arkansas Community College
Ouachita Baptist University
University of Arkansas
University of Arkansas
    Fort Smith
    Little Rock
    Monticello
    Pine Bluff
University of Central Arkansas
Williams Baptist College

California
Azusa Pacific University
Biola University
California Baptist University
California Institute of Technology
California Lutheran University
California Polytechnic State University: San
    Luis Obispo
California State Polytechnic University:
    Pomona
California State University
    Dominguez Hills
    Fresno
    Fullerton
    Long Beach
    Los Angeles
    Northridge
    Sacramento
    San Bernardino
    San Marcos
Canada College
Chabot College
Chapman University
City College of San Francisco
Claremont McKenna College
De Anza College
Diablo Valley College
Foothill College
Fresno City College
Harvey Mudd College
Holy Names University
Hope International University
Los Angeles Mission College
Loyola Marymount University
The Master's University
Mills College
National University
Occidental College
Pepperdine University
Pitzer College
Point Loma Nazarene University
Pomona College
Riverside City College
Sacramento City College
St. Mary's College of California
Samuel Merritt University
San Diego Christian College

San Diego City College
San Diego State University
San Francisco State University
San Jose State University
Santa Clara University
Scripps College
Sonoma State University
Stanford University
University of California
    Berkeley
    Davis
    Irvine
    Los Angeles
    Riverside
    Santa Barbara
    Santa Cruz
University of La Verne
University of Redlands
University of San Diego
University of San Francisco
University of Southern California
Vanguard University of Southern California
West Valley College
Westmont College
Whittier College

Colorado
Arapahoe Community College
Colorado Christian University
Colorado College
Colorado School of Mines
Colorado State University
Colorado State University
    Pueblo
Colorado Technical University
Community College of Denver
Front Range Community College
Johnson & Wales University
    Denver
Metropolitan State University of Denver
Red Rocks Community College
Regis University
University of Colorado
    Boulder
    Colorado Springs
    Denver
University of Denver
University of Northern Colorado

Connecticut
Capital Community College
Central Connecticut State University
Eastern Connecticut State University
Fairfield University
Quinnipiac University
Southern Connecticut State University
Trinity College
Tunxis Community College
University of Bridgeport
University of Connecticut
University of Hartford
University of New Haven
Western Connecticut State University
Yale University

Delaware
Delaware State University
University of Delaware
Wesley College
Wilmington University

District of Columbia
American University
Catholic University of America
George Washington University
Georgetown University
Howard University
Trinity Washington University
University of the District of Columbia

Florida
Barry University
Bethune-Cookman University
Broward College

Daytona State College
Eastern Florida State College
Eckerd College
Embry-Riddle Aeronautical University
Florida Agricultural and Mechanical University
Florida Atlantic University
Florida College
Florida Institute of Technology
Florida International University
Florida Memorial University
Florida Southern College
Florida State College at Jacksonville
Florida State University
Hillsborough Community College
Jacksonville University
Northwest Florida State College
Palm Beach Atlantic University
Pasco-Hernando State College
Pensacola State College
Polk State College
Saint Leo University
St. Petersburg College
Santa Fe College
Seminole State College of Florida
Southeastern University
Stetson University
Tallahassee Community College
University of Central Florida
University of Florida
University of Miami
University of North Florida
University of South Florida
University of South Florida
    Saint Petersburg
University of Tampa
University of West Florida
Valencia College

Georgia
Agnes Scott College
Albany State University
Armstrong State University
Augusta University
Clark Atlanta University
Clayton State University
Columbus State University
Covenant College
East Georgia State College
Emory University
Fort Valley State University
Georgia College and State University
Georgia Gwinnett College
Georgia Institute of Technology
Georgia Military College
Georgia Southern University
Georgia State University
Kennesaw State University
Mercer University
Middle Georgia State University
Morehouse College
Oglethorpe University
Oxford College of Emory University
Paine College
Savannah State University
Spelman College
University of Georgia
University of North Georgia
Wesleyan College

Hawaii
Brigham Young University-Hawaii
Chaminade University of Honolulu
Hawaii Pacific University
University of Hawaii
    Hilo
    Honolulu Community College
    Manoa
    West Oahu
    Windward Community College

Idaho
Boise State University
Brigham Young University-Idaho

College of Idaho
Idaho State University
Lewis-Clark State College
North Idaho College
Northwest Nazarene University
University of Idaho

Illinois
Aurora University
Benedictine University
Bradley University
Carl Sandburg College
Chicago State University
DePaul University
Eastern Illinois University
Elmhurst College
Illinois Institute of Technology
Illinois State University
Illinois Wesleyan University
John A. Logan College
Judson University
Kankakee Community College
Kaskaskia College
Kishwaukee College
Lewis and Clark Community College
Lewis University
Lincoln Land Community College
Loyola University Chicago
McKendree University
Monmouth College
North Central College
North Park University
Northeastern Illinois University
Northern Illinois University
Northwestern University
Olivet Nazarene University
Parkland College
Robert Morris College
    Robert Morris University: Chicago
Shawnee Community College
Shimer College
Southern Illinois University Carbondale
Southern Illinois University Edwardsville
Southwestern Illinois College
Spoon River College
University of Chicago
University of Illinois
    Chicago
    Urbana-Champaign
University of St. Francis
Waubonsee Community College
Western Illinois University
Wheaton College

Indiana
Ball State University
Bethel College
Butler University
DePauw University
Franklin College
Holy Cross College
Indiana Institute of Technology
Indiana State University
Indiana University
    Bloomington
    Kokomo
    Northwest
    Purdue University Fort Wayne
    Purdue University Indianapolis
    South Bend
    Southeast
Indiana Wesleyan University
Marian University
Purdue University
Purdue University
    North Central
    Northwest
Rose-Hulman Institute of Technology
Saint Mary's College
University of Evansville
University of Indianapolis
University of Notre Dame
University of Saint Francis

University of Southern Indiana
Valparaiso University
Vincennes University

Iowa
Allen College
Briar Cliff University
Buena Vista University
Clarke University
Coe College
Drake University
Grand View University
Hawkeye Community College
Iowa State University
Iowa Western Community College
Loras College
Morningside College
University of Dubuque
University of Iowa
University of Northern Iowa

Kansas
Baker University
Benedictine College
Haskell Indian Nations University
Kansas State University
Manhattan Christian College
MidAmerica Nazarene University
Pittsburg State University
University of Kansas
University of St. Mary
Washburn University

Kentucky
Asbury University
Bellarmine University
Campbellsville University
Centre College
Eastern Kentucky University
Elizabethtown Community and Technical
    College
Georgetown College
Jefferson Community and Technical College
Kentucky State University
Kentucky Wesleyan College
Midway College
Morehead State University
Murray State University
Northern Kentucky University
Owensboro Community and Technical College
Spalding University
Thomas More College
Transylvania University
University of Kentucky
University of Louisville
University of Pikeville
Western Kentucky University

Louisiana
Dillard University
Grambling State University
Louisiana State University
    Alexandria
    Shreveport
Louisiana State University and Agricultural and
    Mechanical College
Louisiana Tech University
Loyola University New Orleans
Northwestern State University
Our Lady of the Lake College
Southeastern Louisiana University
Southern University
    New Orleans
Southern University and Agricultural and
    Mechanical College
Tulane University
University of Holy Cross
University of Louisiana
    Monroe
University of Louisiana at Lafayette
University of New Orleans
Xavier University of Louisiana

Maine
Colby College
Eastern Maine Community College
Husson University
Maine Maritime Academy
Saint Joseph's College of Maine
University of Maine
University of Maine
    Augusta
University of New England
University of Southern Maine

Maryland
Allegany College of Maryland
Anne Arundel Community College
Bowie State University
Capitol Technology University
Coppin State University
Goucher College
Hood College
Johns Hopkins University
Loyola University Maryland
Maryland Institute College of Art
McDaniel College
Morgan State University
Mount St. Mary's University
Notre Dame of Maryland University
Prince George's Community College
Salisbury University
Stevenson University
Towson University
University of Baltimore
University of Maryland
    Baltimore County
    College Park

Massachusetts
American International College
Amherst College
Assumption College
Babson College
Bay Path University
Becker College
Bentley University
Berklee College of Music
Boston College
Boston University
Brandeis University
Bridgewater State University
Clark University
College of the Holy Cross
Curry College
Elms College
Emmanuel College
Endicott College
Fisher College
Fitchburg State University
Gordon College
Harvard College
Holyoke Community College
Massachusetts Institute of Technology
Massachusetts Maritime Academy
MCPHS University
Middlesex Community College
Mount Holyoke College
Mount Wachusett Community College
Nichols College
Northeastern University
Pine Manor College
Quinsigamond Community College
Regis College
Roxbury Community College
Salem State University
Simmons College
Smith College
Springfield College
Stonehill College
Suffolk University
Tufts University
University of Massachusetts
    Amherst
    Boston
    Dartmouth

Lowell
Wellesley College
Wentworth Institute of Technology
Western New England University
Westfield State University
Wheaton College
Worcester Polytechnic Institute
Worcester State University

Michigan
Adrian College
Alma College
Aquinas College
Baker College
    Jackson
Calvin College
Central Michigan University
Concordia University
Cornerstone University
Davenport University
Eastern Michigan University
Ferris State University
Finlandia University
Grace Bible College
Hope College
Kalamazoo College
Kuyper College
Lansing Community College
Madonna University
Michigan State University
Michigan Technological University
Northern Michigan University
Olivet College
Spring Arbor University
University of Michigan
University of Michigan
    Dearborn
    Flint
Washtenaw Community College
Wayne State University
Western Michigan University

Minnesota
Anoka-Ramsey Community College
Augsburg College
Bethany Lutheran College
Bethel University
College of St. Benedict
Concordia College: Moorhead
Concordia University St. Paul
Crown College
Gustavus Adolphus College
Hamline University
Inver Hills Community College
Macalester College
Minnesota State University
    Mankato
    Moorhead
North Central University
North Hennepin Community College
St. Catherine University
Saint Cloud State University
St. John's University
St. Mary's University of Minnesota
University of Minnesota
    Twin Cities
University of Northwestern - St. Paul
University of St. Thomas
Winona State University

Mississippi
Alcorn State University
Belhaven University
Delta State University
East Mississippi Community College
Hinds Community College
Jackson State University
Jones County Junior College
Millsaps College
Mississippi College
Mississippi State University
Mississippi University for Women
Mississippi Valley State University

Northeast Mississippi Community College
Pearl River Community College
Tougaloo College
University of Mississippi
University of Mississippi
    University of Southern Mississippi
William Carey University

Missouri
Avila University
Calvary Bible College and Theological
    Seminary
Central Methodist University
College of the Ozarks
Columbia College
Evangel University
Fontbonne University
Harris-Stowe State University
Lincoln University
Lindenwood University
Maryville University of Saint Louis
Metropolitan Community College - Kansas City
Missouri Baptist University
Missouri Southern State University
Missouri State University
Missouri University of Science and Technology
Missouri Valley College
Missouri Western State University
Park University
Research College of Nursing
Rockhurst University
St. Louis Community College
    Florissant Valley
Saint Louis University
Southwest Baptist University
State Fair Community College
Stephens College
Truman State University
University of Central Missouri
University of Missouri
    Columbia
    Kansas City
    St. Louis
Washington University in St. Louis
Webster University
Wentworth Military Junior College
Westminster College
William Jewell College
William Woods University

Montana
Carroll College
Montana State University
Montana State University
    Billings
Rocky Mountain College
University of Montana

Nebraska
Bellevue University
BryanLGH College of Health Sciences
Chadron State College
Clarkson College
College of Saint Mary
Concordia University
Creighton University
Doane University
Nebraska Wesleyan University
University of Nebraska
    Kearney
    Lincoln
    Medical Center
    Omaha
Wayne State College
York College

Nevada
College of Southern Nevada
Truckee Meadows Community College
University of Nevada
    Las Vegas
    Reno

New Hampshire
Colby-Sawyer College
Dartmouth College
Franklin Pierce University
Granite State College
Keene State College
New England College
Plymouth State University
Rivier University
Saint Anselm College
Southern New Hampshire University
University of New Hampshire

New Jersey
Berkeley College
Bloomfield College
Brookdale Community College
Caldwell University
The College of New Jersey
Drew University
Fairleigh Dickinson University
    College at Florham
    Metropolitan Campus
Felician University
Kean University
Middlesex County College
Monmouth University
New Jersey Institute of Technology
Princeton University
Ramapo College of New Jersey
Raritan Valley Community College
Rider University
Rowan University
Rutgers, The State University of New Jersey
    Camden Campus
    New Brunswick/Piscataway Campus
    Newark Campus
Saint Peter's University
Seton Hall University
Stevens Institute of Technology

New Mexico
Central New Mexico Community College
Dona Ana Community College of New Mexico
    State University
New Mexico Military Institute
New Mexico State University
Southwest University of Visual Arts
University of New Mexico

New York
Adelphi University
Alfred University
Barnard College
Canisius College
Cazenovia College
City University of New York
    Baruch College
    City College
    Lehman College
    Queens College
    Queensborough Community College
    York College
Clarkson University
Colgate University
College of Mount St. Vincent
College of New Rochelle
College of Saint Rose
Columbia University
Columbia University
    School of General Studies
Cooper Union for the Advancement of Science
    and Art
Cornell University
Daemen College
D'Youville College
Elmira College
Erie Community College
Fordham University
Genesee Community College
Hamilton College
Herkimer County Community College
Hilbert College

Hobart and William Smith Colleges
Hofstra University
Houghton College
Hudson Valley Community College
Iona College
Ithaca College
The King's College
Le Moyne College
Long Island University
    LIU Brooklyn
    LIU Post
Manhattan College
Maria College
Marist College
Medaille College
Mercy College
Molloy College
Monroe College
Monroe Community College
Mount Saint Mary College
Nazareth College
New York Institute of Technology
New York University
Niagara County Community College
Niagara University
Onondaga Community College
Pace University
Pace University: Pleasantville/Briarcliff
Pratt Institute
Rensselaer Polytechnic Institute
Rochester Institute of Technology
The Sage Colleges
Saint Bonaventure University
St. Francis College
St. John Fisher College
St. John's University
St. Lawrence University
Siena College
Skidmore College
SUNY
    College at Brockport
    College at Buffalo
    College at Cortland
    College at Fredonia
    College at Geneseo
    College at Old Westbury
    College at Oswego
    College at Potsdam
    College of Agriculture and Technology at
        Morrisville
    College of Environmental Science and
        Forestry
    College of Technology at Alfred
    College of Technology at Canton
    Farmingdale State College
    Maritime College
    University at Albany
    University at Binghamton
    University at Buffalo
    University at Stony Brook
    Upstate Medical University
SUNY Polytechnic Institute
Syracuse University
Talmudical Seminary Oholei Torah
Union College
United States Merchant Marine Academy
University of Rochester
Utica College
Vaughn College of Aeronautics and Technology
Wagner College

North Carolina
Appalachian State University
Bennett College for Women
Campbell University
Catawba College
Davidson College
Duke University
East Carolina University
Elizabeth City State University
Elon University
Fayetteville State University
Gardner-Webb University

Greensboro College
High Point University
Johnson & Wales University
    Charlotte
Livingstone College
Meredith College
Methodist University
Mid-Atlantic Christian University
North Carolina Agricultural and Technical State
    University
North Carolina Central University
North Carolina State University
North Carolina Wesleyan College
Pfeiffer University
Pitt Community College
Queens University of Charlotte
Saint Augustine's University
Salem College
Shaw University
University of North Carolina
    Chapel Hill
    Charlotte
    Greensboro
    Pembroke
Wake Forest University
Wake Technical Community College
William Peace University
Wingate University
Winston-Salem State University

North Dakota
Mayville State University
North Dakota State University
University of North Dakota

Ohio
Ashland University
Baldwin Wallace University
Bowling Green State University
Capital University
Case Western Reserve University
Cedarville University
Central State University
Cincinnati State Technical and Community
    College
Cleveland Institute of Art
Cleveland State University
Columbus State Community College
Denison University
DeVry University
    Columbus
Franciscan University of Steubenville
Franklin University
Heidelberg University
Hiram College
Hocking College
John Carroll University
Kent State University
Kent State University
    East Liverpool
    Salem
    Stark
    Trumbull
    Tuscarawas
Lourdes University
Miami University
    Oxford
Mount St. Joseph University
Notre Dame College
Ohio Dominican University
Ohio Northern University
Ohio State University
    Agricultural Technical Institute
    Columbus Campus
    Lima Campus
    Mansfield Campus
    Marion Campus
    Newark Campus
Ohio University
Ohio University
    Lancaster Campus
Ohio Wesleyan University
Otterbein University

Sinclair Community College
Tiffin University
University of Akron
University of Akron: Wayne College
University of Cincinnati
University of Cincinnati
    Blue Ash College
    Clermont College
University of Dayton
University of Findlay
University of Mount Union
University of Northwestern Ohio
University of Toledo
Urbana University
Ursuline College
Wilberforce University
Wittenberg University
Wright State University
Xavier University
Youngstown State University

Oklahoma
Cameron University
Langston University
Northeastern State University
Oklahoma Christian University
Oklahoma City University
Oklahoma State University
Southern Nazarene University
University of Central Oklahoma
University of Oklahoma

Oregon
Central Oregon Community College
Corban University
Eastern Oregon University
Lewis & Clark College
Linn-Benton Community College
Oregon State University
Pacific University
Portland State University
Southern Oregon University
University of Oregon
University of Portland
Western Oregon University
Willamette University

Pennsylvania
Albright College
Alvernia University
Bloomsburg University of Pennsylvania
Bryn Athyn College
Bucknell University
Cabrini University
California University of Pennsylvania
Carlow University
Carnegie Mellon University
Chatham University
Cheyney University of Pennsylvania
Clarion University of Pennsylvania
Clarks Summit University
Community College of Philadelphia
DeSales University
Dickinson College
Drexel University
Duquesne University
East Stroudsburg University of Pennsylvania
Eastern University
Edinboro University
    Pennsylvania
Gannon University
Geneva College
Gettysburg College
Harrisburg Area Community College
Holy Family University
Immaculata University
Indiana University of Pennsylvania
Keystone College
King's College
Kutztown University of Pennsylvania
La Roche College
La Salle University
Lackawanna College

Lafayette College
Lehigh Carbon Community College
Lehigh University
Lincoln University
Lock Haven University of Pennsylvania
Lycoming College
Mansfield University of Pennsylvania
Marywood University
Mercyhurst University
Millersville University of Pennsylvania
Misericordia University
Moravian College
Muhlenberg College
Neumann University
Penn State
   Abington
   Altoona
   Berks
   Brandywine
   DuBois
   Erie, The Behrend College
   Fayette, The Eberly Campus
   Harrisburg
   Lehigh Valley
   Mont Alto
   University Park
   Wilkes-Barre
   Worthington Scranton
Pennsylvania College of Technology
Point Park University
Robert Morris University
Rosemont College
St. Francis University
Saint Joseph's University
St. Vincent College
Shippensburg University of Pennsylvania
Slippery Rock University of Pennsylvania
Susquehanna University
Swarthmore College
Temple University
University of Pennsylvania
University of Pittsburgh
University of Pittsburgh
   Bradford
   Greensburg
   Johnstown
University of Scranton
University of the Sciences
Valley Forge Military College
Villanova University
Washington & Jefferson College
Waynesburg University
West Chester University of Pennsylvania
Westminster College
Widener University
Wilkes University
Wilson College

Puerto Rico
American University of Puerto Rico
Bayamon Central University
Caribbean University
EDP University of Puerto Rico: Hato Rey
Inter American University of Puerto Rico
   Aguadilla Campus
   Arecibo Campus
   Barranquitas Campus
   Bayamon Campus
   Guayama Campus
   Metropolitan Campus
   San German Campus
Pontifical Catholic University of Puerto Rico
Turabo University
Universidad del Este
Universidad Metropolitana
Universidad Politecnica de Puerto Rico
University of Puerto Rico
   Aguadilla
   Arecibo
   Bayamon University College
   Cayey University College
   Mayaguez
   Ponce

   Rio Piedras
   Utuado

Rhode Island
Brown University
Bryant University
Community College of Rhode Island
Johnson & Wales University
   Providence
Providence College
Rhode Island College
Roger Williams University
Salve Regina University
University of Rhode Island

South Carolina
Allen University
Benedict College
Charleston Southern University
The Citadel
Claflin University
Clemson University
Coastal Carolina University
Columbia College
Converse College
Francis Marion University
Furman University
Greenville Technical College
Lander University
Limestone College
Morris College
Newberry College
North Greenville University
Orangeburg-Calhoun Technical College
Presbyterian College
South Carolina State University
Southern Wesleyan University
Spartanburg Methodist College
Tri-County Technical College
University of South Carolina
   Columbia
   Lancaster
   Salkehatchie
   Sumter
   Upstate
Voorhees College
Winthrop University
Wofford College

South Dakota
Augusta University
   Augustana University
Black Hills State University
Dakota State University
Dakota Wesleyan University
Mount Marty College
National American University
   Rapid City
South Dakota School of Mines and Technology
South Dakota State University
University of South Dakota

Tennessee
Austin Peay State University
Belmont University
Carson-Newman University
Christian Brothers University
Cumberland University
East Tennessee State University
Fisk University
Jackson State Community College
Lane College
LeMoyne-Owen College
Lincoln Memorial University
Lipscomb University
Middle Tennessee State University
Pellissippi State Community College
Rhodes College
Southwest Tennessee Community College
Tennessee Technological University
Tennessee Wesleyan University
Trevecca Nazarene University
Union University
University of Memphis

University of Tennessee
   Chattanooga
   Knoxville
   Martin
Vanderbilt University
Walters State Community College
Welch College

Texas
Angelina College
Austin Community College
Baylor University
Central Texas College
Concordia University Texas
Dallas Baptist University
Del Mar College
El Centro College
El Paso Community College
Houston Baptist University
Houston Community College System
Laredo Community College
Lone Star College System
Lubbock Christian University
Northwest Vista College
Our Lady of the Lake University of San
   Antonio
Palo Alto College
Prairie View A&M University
Rice University
St. Edward's University
St. Mary's University
St. Philip's College
Sam Houston State University
San Antonio College
San Jacinto College
Southern Methodist University
Southwestern Assemblies of God University
Stephen F. Austin State University
Tarleton State University
Tarrant County College
Texas A&M International University
Texas A&M University
Texas A&M University
   Corpus Christi
   Kingsville
Texas Christian University
Texas Lutheran University
Texas Southern University
Texas State University
Texas Tech University
Texas Wesleyan University
Texas Woman's University
Trinity University
University of Dallas
University of Houston
University of Houston
   Downtown
University of Mary Hardin-Baylor
University of North Texas
University of St. Thomas
University of Texas
   Arlington
   Austin
   Dallas
   El Paso
   San Antonio
University Of Texas Rio Grande Valley
University of the Incarnate Word
Wayland Baptist University

Utah
Brigham Young University
Dixie State University
LDS Business College
Salt Lake Community College
Southern Utah University
University of Utah
Utah State University
Utah Valley University
Weber State University
Westminster College

Vermont
Castleton University
Champlain College
Johnson State College
Lyndon State College
Middlebury College
Norwich University
Saint Michael's College
University of Vermont
Vermont Technical College

Virginia
Christopher Newport University
College of William and Mary
George Mason University
Hampden-Sydney College
Hampton University
James Madison University
John Tyler Community College
Liberty University
Longwood University
Mary Baldwin University
Marymount University
Norfolk State University
Old Dominion University
Piedmont Virginia Community College
Radford University
Randolph-Macon College
Regent University
Richard Bland College
Southern Virginia University
Southside Virginia Community College
Tidewater Community College
University of Mary Washington
University of Richmond
University of Virginia
University of Virginia's College at Wise
Virginia Commonwealth University
Virginia Military Institute
Virginia Polytechnic Institute and State
   University
Virginia State University
Virginia Union University
Virginia Wesleyan College
Washington and Lee University

Washington
Central Washington University
Clark College
Eastern Washington University
Gonzaga University
Highline College
Northwest University
Pacific Lutheran University
Pierce College
Saint Martin's University
Seattle Pacific University
Seattle University
Spokane Community College
Spokane Falls Community College
University of Puget Sound
University of Washington
University of Washington Bothell
University of Washington Tacoma
Walla Walla University
Washington State University
Whitworth University

West Virginia
Fairmont State University
Glenville State College
Marshall University
University of Charleston
West Virginia State University
West Virginia University
West Virginia University Institute of
   Technology

Wisconsin
Alverno College
Bellin College
Edgewood College

Maranathan Baptist University
     Maranatha Baptist University
Marian University
Marquette University
Milwaukee School of Engineering
Ripon College
St. Norbert College
University of Wisconsin
     Eau Claire
     Green Bay
     La Crosse
     Madison
     Milwaukee
     Oshkosh
     Parkside
     Platteville
     River Falls
     Stevens Point
     Stout
     Whitewater
Viterbo University

Wyoming
Laramie County Community College
University of Wyoming

Naval ROTC

Alabama
Auburn University
Stillman College
Tuskegee University

Arizona
Arizona State University
GateWay Community College
Mesa Community College
University of Arizona

California
California Maritime Academy
California State University
     San Marcos
Contra Costa College
Diablo Valley College
Foothill College
Mission College
National University
Point Loma Nazarene University
Riverside City College
Sacramento City College
Samuel Merritt University
San Diego State University
Sonoma State University
Stanford University
University of California
     Berkeley
     Davis
     Los Angeles
     Santa Cruz
University of Redlands
University of San Diego
University of Southern California

Colorado
Regis University
University of Colorado
     Boulder

Connecticut
Capital Community College
Tunxis Community College
Yale University

District of Columbia
Catholic University of America
George Washington University
Georgetown University
University of the District of Columbia

Florida
Embry-Riddle Aeronautical University
Florida Agricultural and Mechanical University
Florida State College at Jacksonville
Florida State University
Jacksonville University
Pasco-Hernando State College
Tallahassee Community College
University of Florida
University of North Florida
University of South Florida
University of Tampa

Georgia
Armstrong State University
Clark Atlanta University
Clayton State University
Emory University
Georgia Institute of Technology
Georgia State University
Morehouse College
Oglethorpe University
Oxford College of Emory University
Savannah State University
Spelman College

Hawaii
Brigham Young University-Hawaii

Idaho
Lewis-Clark State College
University of Idaho

Illinois
Illinois Institute of Technology
Lincoln Land Community College
Loyola University Chicago
Northwestern University
Parkland College
Shawnee Community College
Shimer College
University of Illinois
     Chicago
     Urbana-Champaign

Indiana
Indiana University
     South Bend
Purdue University
Saint Mary's College
University of Notre Dame

Iowa
Hawkeye Community College
Iowa State University

Kansas
University of Kansas
Washburn University

Louisiana
Dillard University
Louisiana State University and Agricultural and
     Mechanical College
Loyola University New Orleans
Southern University
     New Orleans
Southern University and Agricultural and
     Mechanical College
Tulane University
University of Holy Cross
University of New Orleans
Xavier University of Louisiana

Maine
Husson University
Maine Maritime Academy
University of Maine
University of Maine
     Augusta

Maryland
University of Maryland
     Baltimore County
     College Park

Massachusetts
Boston College
Boston University
College of the Holy Cross
Harvard University
Massachusetts Institute of Technology
Massachusetts Maritime Academy
MCPHS University
Northeastern University
Tufts University
University of Massachusetts
     Boston
Worcester Polytechnic Institute
Worcester State University

Michigan
Eastern Michigan University
Finlandia University
University of Michigan
University of Michigan
     Dearborn
     Flint

Minnesota
Anoka-Ramsey Community College
Augsburg College
Macalester College
North Hennepin Community College
University of Minnesota
     Twin Cities
University of St. Thomas

Mississippi
Tougaloo College
University of Mississippi

Missouri
Columbia College
Stephens College
University of Missouri
     Columbia

Nebraska
BryanLGH College of Health Sciences
Nebraska Wesleyan University
University of Nebraska
     Lincoln
York College

New Hampshire
Rivier University

New Jersey
Princeton University
Rutgers, The State University of New Jersey
     New Brunswick/Piscataway Campus
     Newark Campus

New Mexico
Central New Mexico Community College
National American University
     Albuquerque
University of New Mexico

New York
Barnard College
College of New Rochelle
College of Saint Rose
Columbia University
Columbia University
     School of General Studies
Cornell University
Eastman School of Music of the University of
     Rochester
Fordham University
Maria College
Mesivta Torah Vodaath Seminary
Molloy College
Monroe Community College
Rensselaer Polytechnic Institute
Rochester Institute of Technology
The Sage Colleges
St. John Fisher College
SUNY
     College at Brockport

Farmingdale State College
     Maritime College
Talmudical Seminary Oholei Torah
Union College
United States Merchant Marine Academy
University of Rochester

North Carolina
Duke University
North Carolina State University
University of North Carolina
     Chapel Hill

Ohio
Cleveland Institute of Art
Cuyahoga Community College
Miami University
     Hamilton
     Middletown
     Oxford
Ohio State University
     Agricultural Technical Institute
     Columbus Campus
     Lima Campus
     Mansfield Campus
     Marion Campus
     Newark Campus
Ohio University
     Lancaster Campus
Sinclair Community College
University of Cincinnati
     Blue Ash College

Oklahoma
University of Oklahoma

Oregon
Linn-Benton Community College
Oregon State University
Western Oregon University

Pennsylvania
Cabrini University
Carlow University
Carnegie Mellon University
Chatham University
Drexel University
Duquesne University
Penn State
     University Park
Robert Morris University
Saint Joseph's University
Swarthmore College
Temple University
Thomas Jefferson University
University of Pennsylvania
University of Pittsburgh
Villanova University
Widener University

Puerto Rico
Universidad Metropolitana

Rhode Island
Brown University

South Carolina
Allen University
The Citadel
University of South Carolina
     Columbia
     Salkehatchie

Tennessee
Belmont University
Christian Brothers University
Fisk University
Rhodes College
Tennessee Wesleyan College
University of Memphis
Vanderbilt University

Texas
Houston Baptist University
Prairie View A&M University

Rice University
Texas A&M University
Texas Woman's University
University of Houston
University of Texas
    Arlington
    Austin

Utah
University of Utah
Weber State University
Westminster College

Vermont
Norwich University

Virginia
Hampton University
Mary Baldwin University
Norfolk State University
Old Dominion University
Regent University
Tidewater Community College
University of Virginia
Virginia Military Institute
Virginia Polytechnic Institute and State
    University

Washington
Seattle University
Spokane Community College
University of Washington
University of Washington Bothell
University of Washington Tacoma
Washington State University

Wisconsin
Edgewood College
Marquette University
Milwaukee School of Engineering
University of Wisconsin
    Madison
    Milwaukee

Glossary

Accelerated program. A college program of study completed in less time than is usually required, most often by attending classes in summer or by taking extra courses during the regular academic terms.

Accreditation. A process that ensures that a college meets acceptable standards in its programs, facilities, and services. Only colleges that are accredited by an agency recognized by the U.S. Department of Education may distribute federal financial aid to their students.

ACT. A college admission examination given at test centers on specified dates. Please visit the organization's website for further information.

Advanced placement. Admission or assignment of a first-year college student to an advanced course in a certain subject on the basis of evidence that the student has successfuly completed the equivalent of the college's course in that subject. See *AP (Advanced Placement Program).*

Agricultural college. A college or university that primarily trains students in the agricultural sciences and agribusiness operations.

American Opportunity Tax Credit. A federal income tax credit of as much as $2,500 per year, available for the first four years of college for each eligible student in a family. The amount of the credit is determined by income eligibility guidelines. See also *Lifetime Learning Tax Credit.*

AmeriCorps. A national network of community service programs for which people volunteer and from which they earn an education award that can used to pay for college or pay back student loans.

AP (Advanced Placement Program). An academic program of the College Board that provides high school students with the opportunity to study and learn at the college level. AP offers courses in 38 subjects, each culminating in an AP Exam. High schools offer the courses and administer the exams to interested students. Most colleges and universities accept qualifying AP Exam scores for credit, advanced placement or both.

Articulation agreement. A formal agreement between two colleges to facilitate the successful transfer of students from one college to the other without duplication of course work.

Associate degree. A degree granted by a college or university upon completion of a two-year, full-time program of study or its part-time equivalent.

Award letter. A means of notifying admitted students of the financial aid being offered by the college or university. The award letter provides information on the types and amounts of aid offered, as well as the students' responsibilities, and the conditions governing the awards.

Bachelor's degree. A degree received upon completion of a four- or five-year full-time program of study (or its part-time equivalent) at a college or university. The bachelor of arts (B.A.), bachelor of science (B.S.) and bachelor of fine arts (B.F.A.) are the most common such degrees.

Bible college. An undergraduate institution whose program includes a significant element of Bible study. Most Bible colleges seek to prepare their students for vocational or lay Christian ministry.

Branch campus. A part of a college, university or community college that is geographically separate from the main campus, has its own faculty and administration, and may have separate admissions requirements and degree programs.

Bursar. The college official responsible for handling billing and payments for tuition, fees, housing, etc.

Business college. A college that primarily prepares students to work in an office or entrepreneurial setting. The curriculum may focus on management, clerical positions, or both.

Campus. The physical location of a college or university. Includes classroom buildings, libraries, research facilities, dormitories, dining halls and administration buildings.

Campus-based programs. Federal financial aid programs that are administered directly by the college's financial aid office, which awards the aid in accordance with federal guidelines. Includes the Federal Supplemental Educational Opportunity Grant Program, Federal Perkins Loan Program and the Federal Work-Study Program.

Candidates' reply date. The date by which admitted students must accept or decline an offer of admission and (if any) financial aid. Most colleges and universities follow the College Board-sponsored Candidates' Reply Date Agreement (CRDA), under which they agree to not require a decision from applicants before May 1. The purpose is to give applicants time to hear from all the colleges to which they have applied before having to make a commitment to any of them.

Career college. Usually a for-profit two-year college that trains students for specific occupations. Also known as a vocational/technical school.

CB code. A four-digit College Board code number that students use to designate colleges or scholarship programs to receive their SAT score reports.

Certificate. An award for completing a particular program or course of study, sometimes given by two-year colleges or vocational/technical schools.

CLEP (College-Level Examination Program). A College Board program in which students receive college credit by earning a qualifying score in any of 33 examinations in business, composition and literature, world languages, history and social sciences, and science and mathematics. Exams are administered at over 1,800 test centers. Over 2,900 colleges and universities grant credit for passing a CLEP exam.

College. The generic term for an institution of higher education. Also a term used to designate divisions within a university.

Community/junior college. A two-year college. Community colleges are public, whereas junior colleges are private. Both usually offer vocational programs as well as the first two years of a four-year program.

Comprehensive fee. If the college combines tuition, fees, room, and board expenses, that single figure is called a comprehensive fee.

Consortium. A group of colleges and universities that share a common geographic location, and often allow students to take classes and use facilities at any of the member colleges. Larger consortiums, at the state or regional level, may offer in-state tuition to out-of-state students.

Cooperative education (co-op). A career-oriented program in which students alternate class attendance and employment in business, industry, or government. Co-op students usually receive both academic credit and payment for their work. Five years are normally required for completion of a bachelor's degree, but that includes about a year's practical work experience.

Core curriculum. A group of courses, usually in the liberal arts, designated by a college as one of the requirements for a degree. Some colleges have both core-curriculum requirements and general-education requirements.

Cost of attendance. A total of expenses, among them tuition and fees (including loan fees), books and supplies, and the student's living expenses while attending school. The cost of attendance is compared with the student's expected family contribution to determine the student's need for financial aid.

Coverdell Education Savings Account. A federal income-tax provision (formerly referred to as the Education IRA) that enables taxpayers to establish a college savings plan. The amount contributed earns interest and/or dividends on a tax-free basis.

Credit/placement by examination. Academic credit or placement out of introductory courses granted by a college to entering students who have demonstrated proficiency in college-level studies through examinations such as those administered by the College Board's AP and CLEP programs.

Credit Hour. The standard unit of measurement for a college course. Each credit hour requires one classroom hour per week. For financial aid purposes, students taking at least 12 credit hours of classes in a semester are considered to be attending the college full-time, and students taking at least six credit hours are considered half-time.

CSS code. A four-digit College Board number that students use to designate colleges or scholarship programs to receive their CSS Profile information. If a college requires financial aid applicants to submit the CSS Profile form, its CSS code will appear in its description in Part III of this book. A complete list of all CSS codes can also be viewed on the CSS Profile website.

CSS/Financial Aid PROFILE (CSS Profile). A web-based application service offered by the College Board and used by some colleges, universities, and private scholarship programs to award their private financial aid funds. Students complete the application online. The College Board processes and reports the application data to the institutions. The CSS Profile is not a federal form and may not be used to apply for federal student aid.

Culinary school. A vocational college that primarily prepares students to work as chefs or caterers.

Deferred admission. Postponing enrollment, usually for one year, after being accepted for admission by a college.

Degree. An award given by a college or university certifying that a student has completed a course of study. See also *bachelor's degree, associate degree, graduate degree.*

Dependent student. For federal financial aid purposes, such students are either under the age of 24, attend an undergraduate program, are not married, do not have children of their own, are not orphans or wards of the court, or veterans of the active-duty armed services. The term is used to define eligibility for certain financial aid programs, regardless of whether or not the student lives with a parent, receives financial support from a parent, or is claimed on a parent's tax return. If a student is defined as dependent, parental financial information must be supplied on the FAFSA and on institutional aid applications.

Direct Loan Program. See *Federal Direct Loan Program.*

Dual enrollment. The practice of allowing students to enroll in college courses while still in high school.

Early Action. A nonbinding early decision program in which a student can receive an admission decision from one or more colleges and universities earlier than the standard response date but is not required to accept the admission offer or to make a deposit before May 1. Compare to *Early Decision*, which is a binding program.

Early action single choice. An early action program in which the student may only apply early action to one college or university.

Early Decision. A binding program where students commit to enroll at a college if admitted and offered a satisfactory financial aid package.

EFC (Expected family contribution). The total amount students and their families are expected to pay toward college costs out-of-pocket for one academic year. The amount is derived from a need analysis of the family's overall financial circumstances.

Elective. A course that is not required for a chosen major or the college's core curriculum, but that can be used to fulfill credit hours required for graduation.

Employer tuition assistance. Money that employers offer to employees or their dependents for use in paying education costs.

Engineering college/institute/school. An institution of higher education that primarily prepares students for careers as licensed professional engineers or engineering technologists.

FAFSA (Free Application for Federal Student Aid). A form completed by all applicants for federal student aid. In many states, completion of the FAFSA is also sufficient to establish eligibility for state-sponsored aid programs. There is no charge for completing the FAFSA, and you can file it any time after October 1 of the year before the academic year for which you are seeking aid (e.g., after October 1, 2017, for the academic year 2018–19).

Federal code number. A six-digit number that identifies a specific college to which students want their FAFSA information submitted. Each college's federal code appears in its profile in Part III of this book. Formerly known as the Title IV code.

Federal Direct Loan Program. A program whereby participating schools administer federal loans that students and parents borrow directly from the U.S. Department of Education. Direct loans include the subsidized and unsubsidized Federal Stafford Loan, PLUS Loan, and Loan Consolidation programs.

Federal methodology. A need-analysis formula used by colleges and universities to determine students' financial need for the purpose of awarding federal financial aid. The federal methodology uses information submitted by students on the FAFSA to assess their ability to pay for college and calculate their expected family contribution. See also *institutional methodology.*

Federal student aid. A number of programs sponsored by the federal government that award students loans, grants or work-study jobs for the purpose of meeting their financial need.

Federal Work-Study Program. A campus-based financial aid program that allows students to meet some of their financial need by working on- or off-campus while attending school.

Fee waiver. A waiver that significantly reduces the amount a student must pay for an application for admission or financial aid, standardized tests, or other college-related expenses. Fee waivers are most commonly awarded to low-income students, but are sometimes also awarded to students who are senior citizens or in the military.

FERPA (Family Educational Rights and Privacy Act). A federal law that protects the privacy of student education records.

Financial aid. Money awarded to students to help them pay for college. Financial aid comes in the form of scholarships, grants, loans, and work-study opportunities.

Financial aid application form. A form that collects information on the student, his or her income and assets, and (for dependent students) his or her parents' income and assets.

Financial aid award letter. See *Award letter*.

Financial aid package. The total financial aid offered to a student by a college, including all loans, grants, scholarships and work-study opportunities.

Financial need. The difference between the total cost of attending a college and a student's expected family contribution (EFC).

529 Plan. See *Section 529 Plan*.

Fixed interest rate. An interest rate on a loan that is fixed for the lifetime of the loan. Compare to *Variable interest rate*.

For-profit college/university. A private institution operated by its owners as a profit-making enterprise. Sometimes referred to as a "proprietary" college.

Free Application for Federal Student Aid. See *FAFSA*.

FSA ID. A username and password combination that serves as a student's or parent's identifier to allow access to personal information in various U.S. Department of Education systems and acts as a digital signature on the FAFSA.

Full need. A student's entire financial need at a college. A college that offers a financial aid package covering the complete difference between the cost of attendance and the expected family contribution is "meeting full need." See also *Gapping*.

Full-time status. Enrollment at a college or university for 12 or more credit hours per semester. Students must be enrolled full time to qualify for the maximum award available to them from federal grant programs.

Gapping. A practice by which a college does not meet the full financial need of an admitted student, leaving a gap that must be filled by the student's own financial resources, in addition to the student's expected family contribution. See also *Unmet need*.

General education requirements. Courses that give undergraduates a background in the natural sciences, social sciences, mathematics, literature, language and fine arts. Some colleges refer to general education courses as the *core curriculum*; at others, a few courses within the general education requirements are core courses that all students must take.

Gift aid. Financial aid in the form of scholarships or grants that do not have to be repaid.

Grade point average (GPA) or ratio. A system used by many schools for evaluating the overall scholastic performance of students. Grade points are determined by first multiplying the number of hours given for a course by the numerical value of the grade and then dividing the sum of all grade points by the total number of hours carried. The most common system of numerical values for grades is A = 4, B = 3, C = 2, D = 1, and E or F = 0. Also called quality point average or ratio.

Graduate degree. A degree (master's, doctoral, or professional) pursued after a student has earned a bachelor's degree.

Grant. A financial aid award given to a student that does not have to be paid back. The terms "grant" and "scholarship" are often used interchangeably, but grants tend to be awarded solely on the basis of financial need, while scholarships may require the student to demonstrate merit.

Half-time status. Enrollment at a college or university for at least 6 credit hours per semester, but fewer than the 12 credit hours required to qualify as full time. Students must be enrolled at least half time to qualify for federal student aid loan programs.

Health sciences college. An institution of higher education that primarily prepares students to enter work in a clinic, hospital or private medical practice.

Independent student. For financial aid purposes, a student who is either age 24 or older, married, a veteran, an orphan, or has legal dependents. Independent students do not need to provide parental information to be considered for federal financial aid programs. However, private institutions may require independent students to provide parental information on their institutional forms in order to be considered for nonfederal sources of funding.

In-district tuition. The tuition charged by a community college or state university to residents of the district from which it draws tax support. Districts are usually individual counties or cities, but sometimes are larger.

In-state tuition. The tuition that a public institution charges residents of its state. Some community colleges and state universities charge this rate to students who are not residents of their district, but who are residents of their state.

Institutional form. A college's own financial aid application form. Some institutional forms are designed to collect additional information on a family's finances beyond what is collected on the FAFSA, and are required of all applicants. Others serve specific purposes and are only required from certain students, for example early decision applicants or student athletes.

Institutional Methodology. A need-analysis formula used by some colleges and universities to determine students' financial need and award their own institutional funds. Compared to the *federal methodology*, the IM takes into account a broader and deeper picture of family assets to determine a student's expected family contribution.

International Baccalaureate (IB). A high school curriculum offered by some schools in the United States and other countries. Please visit the organization's website for further information.

Internship. Any short-term, supervised work, usually related to a student's major, for which academic credit is earned. The work can be full time or part time, on or off campus, paid or unpaid.

IRS Data Retrieval Tool. Accessible from FAFSA on the Web, this tool allows you or your parents to access the IRS tax return information needed to complete the FAFSA and to transfer the data directly onto your FAFSA online. For many colleges, the IRS Data Retrieval process is the preferred means of completing your FAFSA.

Junior college. See *Community/junior college.*

Liberal arts. The study of the humanities (literature, the arts and philosophy), history, foreign languages, social sciences, mathematics and natural sciences. Liberal arts study guides students in developing general knowledge and reasoning ability rather than specific skills.

Liberal arts college. A college that emphasizes the liberal arts in its core curriculum and academic offerings and does not offer vocation or professional programs.

Lifetime Learning Tax Credit. A federal income tax credit of as much as $2,000 per household annually; available to eligible taxpayers based on "out-of-pocket" tuition and fee expenditures, according to income eligibility guidelines. See also *American Opportunity Tax Credit.*

Major. The subject area in which students concentrate, or specialize, during their undergraduate study. At most colleges, students take one-third to one-half of their courses in their chosen major; the rest is devoted to core requirements and electives.

Maritime college/institute/academy. An institution of higher education that prepares students to operate commercial shipping or fishing vessels. Upon graduation, students of most maritime academies are commissioned as officers in the United States Merchant Marine, and simultaneously commissioned as officers in the U.S. Navy Reserve.

Master Promissory Note (MPN). A special type of promissory note used to obtain a Federal Stafford loan.

Merit aid. Financial aid awarded on the basis of academic qualifications, artistic or athletic talent, leadership qualities, or similar traits. Financial need may or may not be an additional requirement.

Military college/institute/academy. An institution of higher education that prepares students (who are called "cadets" while enrolled) to become active-duty officers in the armed services. Cadets usually participate in military training assignments during the summer term in addition to attending the college in the fall and spring semesters.

Minor. Course work that is not as extensive as that in a major but gives students some specialized knowledge of a second field.

NCAA. The National Collegiate Athletic Association. The NCAA is the largest collegiate athletic association, governing league play in 23 championship sports.

Need analysis. The process of analyzing the student's household and financial information to calculate an EFC and financial need. See also *Federal Methodology, Institutional Methodology*.

Need-analysis form. See *Financial aid application form*.

Need-based aid. Financial aid given to students who have demonstrated financial need, calculated by subtracting the student's expected family contribution from a college's total cost of attendance.

Need-blind admission. The policy of determining whether a student should be admitted to a college without regard to his or her financial need.

Non-need-based aid. Financial aid awarded without regard to the student's demonstrated ability to pay for college.

Nursing college. An institution of higher education that primarily prepares students to become registered nurses (RNs) or licensed practical nurses (LPNs).

Open admission. The college admissions policy of admitting any student with a high school diploma or its equivalent (e.g. GED), space permitting, without regard to conventional academic qualifications, such as high school subjects, grades, or admission test scores.

Origination fee. A fee charged to a borrower to cover the costs of processing a loan.

Out-of-state tuition. The tuition a public college or university charges residents of other states.

Outside resources. Student financial aid granted by a source other than the college. Examples include scholarships from private foundations, employer tuition assistance and veterans' educational benefits.

Parents' contribution. The amount a student's parents are expected to pay toward college costs from their own income and assets. The parents' contribution and the student's contribution together constitute the total expected family contribution (EFC).

Part-time status. Enrollment at a college or university for 11 or fewer credit hours per semester.

Pell Grant. A federally funded and administered need-based grant to undergraduate students. Congress annually sets the dollar range; for 2017-18 the maximum award is $5,920. Eligibility for Pell Grants is based on a student's expected family contribution, the total cost of attendance at the college, and whether the student is attending the college full time or part time.

Perkins Loan. A federally funded, need-based, low-interest student loan. Repayment does not begin until after graduation, and payments may be deferred for periods of service in the military, Peace Corps or other approved organizations. The loan may be totally forgiven if the student enters a career of service as a public health nurse, law enforcement officer, public school teacher or social worker.

PLUS (Federal Parents' Loan for Undergraduate Students). A federal direct loan program that permits parents of undergraduate students to borrow up to the full cost of education, less any other financial aid the student may have received.

Prepaid tuition plan. See *Section 529 Plans*.

Portfolio. A collection of a student's work that demonstrates skills and accomplishments. Portfolios may be physical or digital. Academic portfolios can include student written papers and projects, and art portfolios can include created objects, such as paintings, photography, fashion illustrations, and more. Some scholarship programs request a portfolio.

Priority date. The date by which applications for financial aid must be received to be given the strongest possible consideration. After that date, applicants are considered on a first-come, first-served basis.

Private college/university. An educational institution of higher education not supported by public taxes and operated on a not-for-profit basis. May be independent or affiliated with a religious denomination.

Promissory note. A binding legal document that a borrower signs to get a loan. By signing this note, a borrower promises to repay the loan, with interest, in specified installments. The promissory note also includes any information about origination fees, grace periods, deferment or cancellation provisions, and the borrower's rights and responsibilities with respect to that loan.

Proprietary college/university. See *For-profit college/university.*

PSAT/NMSQT® (Preliminary SAT/National Merit Scholarship Qualifying Test). A comprehensive program that helps schools put students on the path to college. The PSAT/NMSQT is administered by high schools to sophomores and juniors each year in October and serves as the qualifying test for scholarships awarded by the National Merit Scholarship Corporation.

Public college/university. An institution of higher education supported by public taxes.

Quarter. An academic calendar period of about 12 weeks. Four quarters make up an academic year, but at colleges using the quarter system, students make normal academic progress by attending three quarters each year.

Reciprocity agreement: An agreement between neighboring states that allows residents to attend a public college in either state at the in-state tuition rate.

Regular admission. Admission during the college's normal calendar for admission, as opposed to Early Decision or Early Action admission.

Renewal FAFSA. A simplified reapplication form for federal student aid. The Renewal FAFSA allows continuing students to update the prior year's FAFSA, rather than completing the entire FAFSA for each award year.

Residency requirements. The minimum number of terms that a student must spend taking courses on campus (as opposed to independent study, transfer credits from other colleges or credit-by-examination) to be eligible for graduation. Can also refer to the minimum amount of time a student is required to have lived in-state in order to qualify for the in-state tuition rate at a public college or university.

Rolling admission. An admission procedure by which the college considers each student's application as soon as all the required credentials, such as school record and test scores, have been received. The college usually notifies an applicant of its decision without delay.

Room and board. The cost of housing and meals for students who reside on campus and/or dine in college-operated meal halls.

ROTC (Reserve Officers' Training Corps). Programs conducted by certain colleges that prepare students to become military officers while they attend college. There are both scholarship and nonscholarship programs available for each branch: Army, Navy, Air Force, and Marines (the Coast Guard and Merchant Marine do not sponsor ROTC programs). While in college, students take some military courses each year for credit and attend training sessions. After college they must complete a period of service in the military.

Safety school. A college you'd like to attend that's also sure to accept you. Usually a public college in your state that is not selective in its admission criteria or practices open admissions.

SAR (Student Aid Report). A report sent to students in response to their having filed the FAFSA. The SAR contains information the student provided on the FAFSA as well as the federally calculated expected family contribution.

SAT. A college admission exam that tests reading, writing and language, and mathematics skills. It is given on specified dates throughout the year at test centers in the United States and other countries. The SAT is used by most colleges and sponsors of financial aid programs.

Satisfactory academic progress. Standards set by a college or university to determine whether a student is meeting sufficient academic standards. The student must achieve these standards to continue to receive financial aid.

SAT Subject Tests. Admission tests in specific subjects given at test centers in the United States and other countries on specified dates throughout the year. The tests are used by colleges for help in both evaluating applicants for admission and determining course placement, and exemption of enrolled first-year students.

Scholarship. A type of financial aid that doesn't have to be repaid. Scholarships may be based on need, on need combined with merit, or solely on the basis of merit or some other qualification, such as minority status. See also *Grant*.

School. In this book, used generically to refer interchangeably to colleges, universities and other institutions of higher education. At some universities, a "school" is a subdivision of the university — for example, the administrative unit that offers nursing courses may be called the "college of nursing" at one institution, and the "school of nursing" at another.

Section 529 Plans. State-sponsored college savings programs commonly referred to as "529 Plans" after the section of the Internal Revenue Code that provides the plan's tax breaks. There are two kinds: college savings plans; and prepaid tuition plans, in which parents can pay in advance for tuition at public institutions in their state of residence.

Self-help aid. Student financial aid, such as loans and work-study jobs, that requires repayment or employment.

Semester. A period of about 16 weeks. Colleges on a semester system offer two semesters of instruction a year; there may also be an additional summer session.

SEOG (Federal Supplemental Educational Opportunity Grant Program). A federal program that provides need-based grants of up to $4,000 a year for undergraduate study. Each college is given a certain total amount of SEOG money each year to distribute among their financial aid applicants and determines the amount to which the student is entitled.

Simplified needs test. A need analysis used by the federal government that excludes a family's assets when calculating the expected family contribution for low- to moderate-income families who file simplified tax returns (1040A, 1040EZ).

Stafford Loan. A federal direct loan program that allows students to borrow money for educational expenses. *Subsidized* Stafford loans are based on need; the federal government pays the interest while the student is in college, and repayment does not begin until after graduation. *Unsubsidized* Stafford loans are not based on need; anyone may apply for one regardless of their ability to pay for college. For both programs, the amounts that may be borrowed depend on the student's year in school.

Student expense budget. A calculation of the annual cost of attending college that is used to determine your financial need. Student expense budgets usually include tuition and fees, books and supplies, room and board, personal expenses, and transportation. Sometimes additional expenses are included for students with special education needs, students who have a disability, or students who are married or have children.

Student's contribution. The amount you are expected to pay toward college costs from your own income and assets, as opposed to your parents'.

Study abroad. Any arrangement by which a student completes part of the college program — typically the junior year but sometimes only a semester or a summer — by studying in another country.

Subsidized loan. A need-based student loan for which the federal or state government pays the interest on the loan while the student is in college. See also *Unsubsidized loan*.

Supplemental Educational Opportunity Grant. See *SEOG*.

Taxable income. Income earned from wages, salaries and tips, as well as from interest income, dividends, alimony, estates or trust income, business or farm profits, and rental or property income. Some scholarship awards must be reported as taxable income.

TEACH (Teacher Education Assistance for College and Higher Education) Grant. A federal grant program that provides up to $4,000 per year to students who intend to teach in a public or private elementary or secondary school serving students from low-income families. Recipients must teach in such a school for at least four academic years within eight years of completing the program of study for which they received the grant.

Teacher's college. A college that specializes in preparing students to teach in elementary or secondary schools. Most teacher's colleges offer a curriculum that combines a study of the liberal arts with the study of pedagogy.

Technical college/school. A college that offers a wide variety of vocational programs to students.

Terminal program. An education program designed to prepare students for immediate employment. These programs usually can be completed in fewer than four years beyond high school and are available in most community colleges and trade schools.

Title IV code. See *Federal code number.*

Transcript. A copy of a student's official academic record listing all courses taken and grades received.

Transfer program. An academic program in a community or junior college primarily for students who plan to continue their studies in a four-year college or university.

Transfer student. A student who has attended another college for any period, which may be defined by various colleges as any time from a single term up to three years. A transfer student may receive credit for all or some of the courses successfully completed before the transfer.

Trimester. An academic calendar period of about 15 weeks. Three trimesters make up one year. Students normally take classes for two trimesters each year but in some colleges can accelerate their progress by taking classes in all three trimesters.

Tuition. The price of instruction at a college. Tuition may be charged per term or per credit hour.

Undergraduate. A college student in the first, second, third, or fourth year of an academic program leading to an associate or bachelor's degree.

University. An institution of higher education that is divided into several colleges, schools or institutes. Students typically have to apply for admission to a specific college, which may have its own requirements. Generally, university students take classes in the college to which they were accepted, but have access to shared facilities such as libraries and laboratories.

Unmet need. The difference between a student's total available resources (financial aid plus the student's expected family contribution) and the total cost of attendance at a specific institution. See also *Gapping.*

Unsubsidized loan. An education loan that is not based on need, and therefore not subsidized by the government; the borrower is responsible for accrued interest throughout the life of the loan. See also *Subsidized loan.*

Upper-division college. A college that offers only the junior and senior years of study towards a bachelor's degree.

Variable interest rate. An interest rate that changes on an annual basis to better reflect market rates.

Virtual college/university. A degree-granting, accredited institution wherein all courses are delivered online or by other means of distance learning, with no physical campus.

Work-study. An arrangement by which a student combines employment and college study. The employment may be an integral part of the academic program (as in cooperative education and internships) or simply a means of paying for college. See also *Federal Work-Study Program.*

Alphabetical Index of Colleges

Take learning to new heights.

With 38 courses in everything from Computer Science to Art History, AP® gives high school students the opportunity to earn college credit and stand out on college applications.

collegeboard.org/ap

© 2017 The College Board.

AP® ◊ CollegeBoard

Show up ready on test day.

Now, the best way to get ready for the SAT is free for everyone. The College Board partnered with Khan Academy® to create Official SAT® Practice. It's free, personalized, and the only online practice tool from the makers of the test. It's simply the best way to prepare. Sign up today.

satpractice.org

◊ CollegeBoard **SAT** | KHANACADEMY

Register
and read

students are already learning

it is easier than ever with

ctice on Khan Academy®.

ents to register today.

AT®   CollegeBoard